JANUARY – DECEMBER 2009

Published by CQ Press, A Division of SAGE
2300 N Street, N.W., Suite 800, Washington, D.C. 20037

Photo credits, clockwise from top left: Getty Images/Ron Sachs-Pool; Getty Images/Bill Pugliano; AP Photo/ Eric Jamison; Getty Images/Joshua Gates-Weisberg-Pool; AFP/Getty Images/Emmanuel Dunand; Getty Images/ William Thomas Cain

ISBN 978-1-60871-249-6
ISSN 1056-2036

CQ Researcher

CQ Researcher is the choice of researchers seeking information on issues in the news. Investigated and written by an experienced journalist, each *CQ Researcher* offers an in-depth, balanced look at a controversial issue. Now in its 81st year, *CQ Researcher* received the prestigious Sigma Delta Chi Award for Journalism Excellence in 1999 for a ten-part series on health care and the American Bar Association's 2002 Silver Gavel Award for a nine-part series on liberty and justice issues.

Each *CQ Researcher* report opens with an overview of that issue's topic, followed by a discussion of three key questions that drive the debate surrounding the topic. The answers provided are not conclusive but serve to highlight the range of opinions among different parties. The overview and issue questions are followed by a background section that places the issue in historical context.

"Current Situation" examines the activities of legislators, citizen groups and others influencing the debate. "Outlook" offers insights by experts on what may happen in the future. Each report also features illuminating images, tables and maps, as well as a presentation of views from representatives on opposing sides of the debate. A chronology identifying milestones in the debate and bibliographies of key sources for further research round out the report.

CITING *CQ RESEARCHER*

Sample formats for citing these reports in a bibliography include the ones listed below. Preferred styles and formats vary, so please check with your instructor or professor.

MLA STYLE

Weeks, Jennifer. "Factory Farms." <u>CQ Researcher,</u> 12 Jan. 2007: 25–48.

APA STYLE

Weeks. J. (2007, January 12). Factory farms. *CQ Researcher, 17,* 25–48.

CHICAGO STYLE

Weeks, Jennifer. "Factory Farms." *CQ Researcher,* January 12, 2007, 25–48.

ACCESSING *CQ RESEARCHER*

CQ Researcher is available in print and online. For access, visit your library or http://library.cqpress.com/cqresearcher.

For subscription pricing and a free trial, call 1-800-834-9020, or e-mail librarymarketing@cqpress.com.

CONTENTS   JANUARY — DECEMBER 2009

Published by CQ Press, a division of SAGE Publications

www.cqresearcher.com

Confronting Warming

Can states and localities prevent climate change?

G rowing concern about climate change has led
states and cities to adopt new policies to try to
conserve energy and reduce emissions of carbon dioxide and other greenhouse gases. Cali-
fornia recently adopted new rules that aim to reduce such gases
by 30 percent by 2020, while a cap on carbon emissions in the
Northeast took effect Jan. 1. But critics say the efforts are more
symbolic than substantive, pushing real sacrifices far off into the
future. Many business groups, meanwhile, complain that the new
rules will increase the cost of energy and hurt the economy —
despite current promises that a "Green New Deal" can create jobs.
The Obama administration promises to be far more aggressive in
addressing global warming than the skeptical Bush White House.
Even though the issue is coming to the fore in Washington, states
and cities that have filled the policy vacuum in recent years
pledge to stay vigilant in addressing the issue.

*Biking down Broadway is a breeze thanks to a new
lane just for bicycles and pedestrians. New York and
other cities are reducing carbon emissions by
promoting car and bike sharing and purchasing
environmentally friendly vehicle fleets.*

CQ Researcher • Jan. 9, 2009 • www.cqresearcher.com
Volume 19, Number 1 • Pages 1-24

CQ Researcher

Jan. 9, 2008
Volume 19, Number 1

MANAGING EDITOR: Thomas J. Colin
tcolin@cqpress.com

ASSISTANT MANAGING EDITOR: Kathy Koch
kkoch@cqpress.com

ASSOCIATE EDITOR: Kenneth Jost

STAFF WRITERS: Thomas J. Billitteri,
Marcia Clemmitt, Peter Katel

CONTRIBUTING WRITERS: Rachel S. Cox,
Sarah Glazer, Alan Greenblatt,
Barbara Mantel, Patrick Marshall,
Tom Price, Jennifer Weeks

DESIGN/PRODUCTION EDITOR: Olu B. Davis

ASSISTANT EDITOR: Darrell Dela Rosa

FACT-CHECKER/PROOFREADER: Eugene J. Gabler

EDITORIAL INTERNS: Alexis Irvin, Vyomika Jairam

CQ PRESS

A Division of
SAGE Publications

PRESIDENT AND PUBLISHER:
John A. Jenkins

**EXECUTIVE DIRECTOR,
REFERENCE INFORMATION GROUP:**
Alix B. Vance

DIRECTOR, ONLINE PRODUCT DEVELOPMENT:
Jennifer Q. Ryan

CQ Press is a registered trademark of Congressional Quarterly Inc.

CQ Researcher (ISSN 1056-2036) is printed on acid-free paper. Published weekly, except; (Jan. wk. 1) (April wk. 2) (May wk. 4) (July wks. 1, 2) (Aug. wks. 3, 4) (Nov. wk. 4) and (Dec. wk. 4), by CQ Press, a division of SAGE Publications. Annual full-service subscriptions start at $803. For pricing, call 1-800-834-9020, ext. 1906. To purchase a CQ Researcher report in print or electronic format (PDF), visit www. cqpress.com or call 866-427-7737. Single reports start at $15. Bulk purchase discounts and electronic-rights licensing are also available. Periodicals postage paid at Washington, D.C., and additional mailing offices. POSTMASTER: Send address changes to CQ Researcher, 2300 N St., N.W., Suite 800, Washington, DC 20037.

Cover: Getty Images/Mario Tama

Confronting Warming

BY ALAN GREENBLATT

THE ISSUES

John Coleman concentrates on cutting energy use for the city of Fayetteville, Ark., as if his job depended on it. In fact, it does.

"I got the City Council to let me hire this person based on the promise that we would reduce our energy consumption to more than cover his or her salary," recalls Fayetteville Mayor Dan Coody.

Coleman has found easy pickings all over town — even at City Hall: inefficient thermostats, wasteful light-bulbs, computers that are left on all night. In 2007, Fayetteville budgeted $1.9 million for utility costs, but thanks to Coleman ended up spending about $180,000 less than that. "You just barely covered my salary," Coleman joked at an end-of-year meeting. "I get to stick around for another year." [1]

Actually, they more than covered his salary of $57,000. Coleman is one of dozens of so-called sustainability directors now employed by cities around the country. (Coody got the idea from a similar program in Seattle.) By switching police departments from paper tickets to electronic ones, or looking for dramatic savings by putting municipal utilities on an energy diet, these environmental specialists are helping city officials like Coody make good on their promise to cut down on emissions that cause global warming.

Scientists say a buildup of six types of heat-trapping gases in the Earth's atmosphere are beginning to cause potentially dramatic climate changes,

Solar panels cover the Staples Center arena in Los Angeles. As a national leader in anti-pollution and energy-saving efforts, California adopted the first statewide "green" building code and vehicle fuel-efficiency standards.

Getty Images/David McNew

such as planetary warming, melting ice caps, rising sea levels and intensified droughts, floods and hurricanes. The gases — called "greenhouse" gases (GHG) because they act as a greenhouse by retaining the sun's heat in Earth's atmosphere — are emitted when carbon-based fossil fuels like oil, coal and natural gas are burned. Under the 1997 Kyoto Protocol, industrialized countries were asked to reduce their GHG emissions — often referred to as "carbon" emissions because carbon dioxide (CO_2) is the most abundant greenhouse gas — by 5.2 percent below 1990 levels by 2012. The U.S. reduction target was set at 7 percent. *

Although the U.S. government is not bound by the treaty, hundreds of mayors, including Coody, have pledged to abide by the protocol, even though it was never ratified by the Senate and has been explicitly rejected by President George W. Bush. But local officials believe it still provides a good guidepost for their own efforts in the fight against climate change. [2]

During the Bush years, global warming became an increasingly pressing topic — yet growing public concern never translated into serious policy breakthroughs in Washington. While Congress and the White House slept, however, state and local governments throughout the country have come up with their own methods for limiting pollutants that scientists believe are contributing to climate change.

"I was one of many Americans who were outraged when my country would not sign the Kyoto Protocol," says Minneapolis Mayor R. T. Rybak. "The federal government dropped the ball on a critical environmental issue."

Cities are not only tightening their own energy belts but increasingly issuing new rules, such as stricter building codes, to make sure that residents and businesses cut back as well.

Among states, California has been leading the way. A 2006 law imposed the first statewide cap on carbon emissions. California also adopted the first statewide green-building code last

---

* The six types of greenhouse gases are carbon dioxide, methane, nitrous oxide, hydrofluorocarbons, perfluorocarbons and sulfur hexafluoride.

Many States Set Energy-Efficiency Standards

Energy efficiency standards are in place in 21 states, including all the Northeast states except New Hampshire and Rhode Island. Some standards encourage greater efficiency in generation, transmission and use of electricity and natural gas. Others require utilities to generate a fixed percentage of their power from renewable sources such as wind and solar.

States With Energy-Efficiency Standards
(As of August 2008)

Have standards
No standards

Sources: World Resources Institute; Environmental Protection Agency

summer, and the state has long been the leader in setting fuel-efficiency standards for vehicles. [3]

Numerous states — but not all — have engaged in other serious efforts to address climate change. About half the states, for instance, require utilities to generate a significant share of their power from renewable, non-carbon-based sources such as wind and solar. And many states are encouraging greater use of biofuels, such as ethanol. Groups of states in the Northeast, Upper Midwest and interior West have formed regional compacts to create "cap-and-trade" systems.

Under cap and trade, large polluters such as power plants are issued permits for each ton of carbon they emit. Companies that reduce the amount of

pollution they spew are able to sell, or "trade," permits they don't need.

"States have been tripping all over themselves to show national leadership on this issue," says Barry G. Rabe, a professor of environmental policy at the University of Michigan. "California, I would argue, has made as heavy an investment in time and treasury into climate change as any government on Earth, including the European Union."

President-elect Barack Obama has said he will approve a waiver for California and 19 other states to regulate greenhouse gas emissions from vehicles. California passed a law in 2002 to do just that, and it has been widely imitated by other states. But states have not been able to enforce the policy absent a waiver from the

Environmental Protection Agency (EPA), which the Bush White House has blocked. [4]

Obama has promised to do more than just sign off on state actions, though. "When I am president, any governor who's willing to promote clean energy will have a partner in the White House," Obama said in a videotaped address to state leaders gathered at a climate change summit in California in November. "Any company that's willing to invest in clean energy will have an ally in Washington. And any nation that's willing to join the cause of combating climate change will have an ally in the United States of America." [5]

As a candidate, Obama pledged to pursue a national cap-and-trade system to limit carbon emissions. Prominent supporters of cap and trade now hold key committee posts in Congress, including Henry A. Waxman, the new chair of the House Energy and Commerce Committee, and Barbara Boxer, chair of the Senate Environment and Public Works Committee. Both are California Democrats.

But attempts to pass cap-and-trade legislation have failed four times over the last five years, and it's not clear the outcome will be different this year or next. Even if federal lawmakers do act, so much momentum has built up in this area among state and local leaders that it's unlikely they'll suddenly concede the issue to Washington.

At the November climate change summit, California Republican Gov. Arnold Schwarzenegger and leaders of more than a dozen other states and provinces from other countries pledged to work together to slash greenhouse gas emissions. Fighting global warming, Schwarzenegger declared, couldn't be just a matter of national policy but must go "province by province." [6]

Not everyone has climbed on board the limited-carbon bandwagon, however. In November, Gov. Rick Perry, R-Texas, argued strongly against a national cap-and-trade policy, warning that it would "cripple the Texas energy sector, irreparably damaging both the state and national economies and severely impacting national oil and gas supplies." [7]

And not everyone who supports limiting greenhouse gases believes state and local efforts are effective. "Carbon dioxide is a naturally occurring gas that is fairly well blended in the atmosphere around the world," says Myron Ebell, director of energy and global warming policy at the Competitive Enterprise Institute, a free-enterprise advocacy group. "If California does something and China and India don't, then what we do is virtually useless."

Ebell and other critics also argue that the efforts undertaken thus far may have been good public relations but are not effective at reducing carbon emissions. Often, public officials have done little more than pledge to reduce emissions or increase use of alternative fuels at some distant date in the future. In a way, Ebell suggests, their actions have been reminiscent of a famous prayer of Saint Augustine: "Give me chastity and continence, but not yet."

But the policies pursued by state and local leaders have been evolving rapidly. A decade ago, few people thought they even had a role in addressing an issue that was global in scope. State and local laws, however, have quickly changed from being mainly symbolic to having real teeth, with penalties for noncompliance for entities ranging from utilities to developers, all in the span of a few short years.

As state and local leaders continue to contemplate ways of addressing climate change, here are some of the issues they are debating:

Should states regulate carbon emissions?

In the absence of federal action, states are making ambitious efforts to

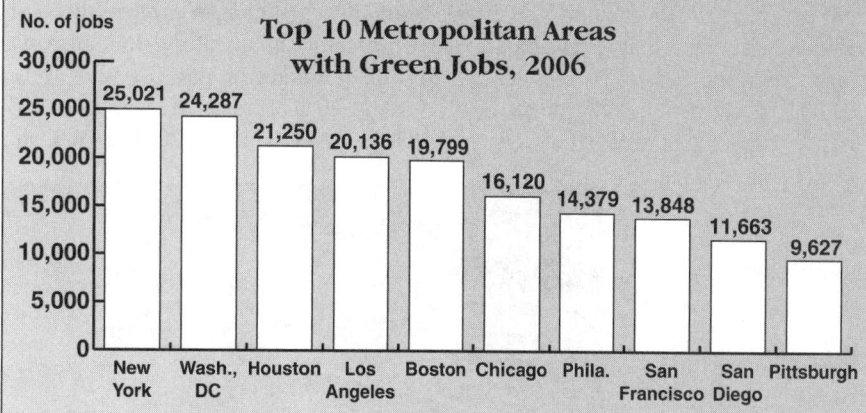

New York Offers Most 'Green' Jobs

More than 25,000 "green" jobs were available in the New York metropolitan area in 2006, the most of any metropolitan area in the country. Three of the top 10 cities were in California — totaling more than 45,000 jobs.

Top 10 Metropolitan Areas with Green Jobs, 2006

No. of jobs

Metropolitan Area	No. of jobs
New York	25,021
Wash., DC	24,287
Houston	21,250
Los Angeles	20,136
Boston	19,799
Chicago	16,120
Phila.	14,379
San Francisco	13,848
San Diego	11,663
Pittsburgh	9,627

Source: "Current and Potential Green Jobs in the U.S. Economy," Global Insight, October 2008

cut down on carbon usage. In the last few years, they have sought to regulate auto tailpipe emissions, required utilities to generate significant shares of their power from renewable energy sources and denied permits to coal-fired power plants. (*See sidebar, p. 14.*)

Several states in the Northeast, West and Midwest have formed regional compacts to create cap-and-trade systems, setting limits on emissions from major polluters. A few have even set overall limits on carbon emissions on a statewide basis. California led the way in 2006 with a law that would reduce the state's total carbon emissions to 1990 levels by 2020.

"The political will to do something about climate change has grown substantially," says Patrick Hogan, a regional policy coordinator at the Pew Center on Global Climate Change. "An important thing to bear in mind is that several actions that states are taking, like renewable energy portfolio standards, will deliver economic and environmental benefits beyond anything related to climate change."

But not everyone applauds the state action. There was considerable internal debate within the Bush administration about granting California a waiver to regulate tailpipe emissions — a regulatory course more than a dozen other states stand ready to follow. California's tailpipe law has also been the subject of several lawsuits.

Despite a Supreme Court decision that appeared to bolster California's argument and advice from some Environmental Protection Agency officials to grant the waiver, the White House was concerned that a waiver could lead states to impose varying fuel-economy standards that would create a burden for the automobile industry. [8]

The incoming Obama administration is expected to approve the waiver for California and the other states. But even if that argument is about to be settled, there are endless debates about whether state actions will help or hurt their economies.

Margo Thorning, senior vice president of the American Council for Capital Formation, a Washington think tank, argues that the various state actions necessarily will increase energy costs. "Over the past 15 years, I've participated in or seen many of the analyses of the economic impact of reducing greenhouse gases," she says. "In every case there is a slower economy and less overall employment, even though new green jobs are created. The reason that happens is that renewables are more expensive."

Ebell, at the Competitive Enterprise Institute, agrees that state efforts on climate change will lead to higher energy costs and that various industries will look to Washington to create a single standard rather than having to satisfy a patchwork quilt of competing regulations.

Some of the state requirements are not realistic anyway, argues Rabe, the University of Michigan professor. He notes that California set a renewable-energy standard for utilities of 20 percent by 2010, which the state clearly won't meet. (It's at 11 percent now.) Legislators this year debated raising the standard to 33 percent by 2020. Rabe calls it "hubris" to create ever-tougher but elusive standards for the future.

"State regulators and state legislatures are putting a lot of pressure onto utilities to invest in alternative energy like windmills that are very expensive but are not viable power, by which I mean they're not available at times of peak demand," Ebell says.

But John Cahill, an attorney who helped design the Regional Greenhouse Gas Initiative, the Northeast's cap-and-trade program, as an aide to former Republican New York Gov. George E. Pataki, says complaints that such programs could hurt the economy are missing the point.

"The fact is that carbon is having a long-term impact on our country's and the world's natural resources," Cahill says. "What we're trying to do with cap and trade is capture the cost of our emissions, rather than making future generations pay for it."

And Ron Burke, Midwest climate change director at the Union of Concerned Scientists, says states and localities are trying to "get ahead of trends" that point to lower usage of carbon in the future, whether due to declining oil supplies or environmental concerns.

"Every city and state that does a greenhouse gas inventory gets a step ahead," Burke says. "They'll be better prepared to deal with a low-carbon economy in the future."

Burke also argues that state efforts to require utilities to turn to renewable energy sources is part of a long tradition of environmental activism. He notes that California's law seeking to regulate tailpipe emissions is in keeping with the state's historic role in promoting more efficient cars.

Due to its smog problems, the state was granted special status under the Clean Air Act of 1970 to set air-quality standards that are stricter than federal limits. California's subsequent standards have often been adopted by other states, and thus by carmakers.

"If not for California's leadership, I think it's fair to say that cars wouldn't be as clean today as they are," Burke says. "We would have suffered through more bad air days over the last 30 years."

Can local governments prevent global warming?

Seattle Mayor Greg Nickels still recalls his concern as he looked out over the Cascade Mountains during the winter of 2005. The snowpack his city relies on for both drinking water and hydroelectric power had just about failed to materialize.

"At that point, it was sort of an 'Aha' moment," he says. "Climate change went from being an esoteric issue affecting someone else in the near future to hitting us here, now."

Nickels has since spearheaded an effort among local officials to abide by the Kyoto Protocol, even though it hasn't been ratified by the U.S. Senate. More than 900 mayors have signed on from cities that are home to a total of more than 81 million Americans, according to the U.S. Conference of Mayors. "We as mayors recognize the threat of hurricanes, drought and the lack of snowpacks" that have been linked to global warming, Nickels says. "It's our obligation to take action."

Minneapolis Mayor R. T. Rybak says people thought he was "flaky" when he replaced the city's gas-guzzling Ford Crown Victoria with a Prius like the one above. "I was not considered as flaky by the time I switched from a Prius to a plug-in," he adds. Many cities are not only tightening their own energy belts but increasingly issuing new rules to force residents and businesses to cut back as well.

Getty Images/David Paul Morris

But there are limits on what local officials can do. They lack the authority to regulate the dominant sources of greenhouse gas emissions — power plants and vehicles. The mayors' efforts, as a result, have mostly been small-bore affairs. Many local officials lack the ability even to measure their cities' total emission levels, let alone reduce them.

In many instances, their actions appear more symbolic than substantive. Critics say it's going to take more than door-to-door promotion of new lightbulbs, to cite one Minneapolis initiative, or replacing inefficient streetlights, to prevent global warming.

"Virtually all of the actions that have been taken at the local level are symbolic," says Ebell, of the Competitive Enterprise Institute. "They are meant to gain immediate public approval for the current incumbent and put all the responsibility for achieving those future goals on some future officeholder."

Even some environmentalists concede that the mayors' efforts, while obviously well-intentioned, won't put a serious dent in carbon emissions as yet.

"It's a mixed bag," says Teri Shore, a campaign director with Friends of the Earth in San Francisco. "You've got a lot of cities and counties that have signed up and set goals, but the harder part comes with actually implementing those goals."

The University of Michigan's Rabe notes that because of the lack of standardized emissions reporting, it's hard to know whose efforts have been successful and which haven't. For example, it was only in September that Chicago put forward models of the first city-specific climate-change projections.

At that time, Chicago Mayor Richard M. Daley announced a plan to reduce the city's greenhouse gas emissions by 25 percent in 2020, compared with 1990 levels, through tougher building codes, improved transportation, re-

Midwest Has Most Wind Potential

North Dakota has the potential to produce more than 1.2 trillion kilowatt hours of wind energy annually— more than any other state. Most of the 20 states with the greatest potential are in the West and Midwest.

States With the Most Wind Energy Potential
(in billions of kilowatt hours annually)

North Dakota	1,210
Texas	1,190
Kansas	1,070
South Dakota	1,030
Montana	1,020
Nebraska	868
Wyoming	747
Oklahoma	725
Minnesota	657
Iowa	551
Colorado	481
New Mexico	435
Idaho	73
Michigan	65
New York	62
Illinois	61
California	59
Wisconsin	58
Maine	56
Missouri	52

Source: "Current and Potential Green Jobs in the U.S. Economy," Global Insight, *October 2008*

duced industrial pollution and use of clean and renewable energy sources.

"We can't solve the world's climate change problem in Chicago," Daley said, "but we can do our part." [9]

Chicago had already drawn praise for its green rooftops program, which boasts plantings on more than 200 buildings, including City Hall and the Target and Apple stores. But not even the cities that have been most ambitious about trying to meet their reduction targets have succeeded. Promises by big-city mayors to plant a million trees each have run into obstacles such as cost and lack of usable land. And New York City Mayor Michael Bloomberg's plan to charge cars a "congestion pricing" fee for driving into parts of Manhattan was rejected by the state legislature in April.

"Every locality is really good about talking about the virtues of their programs, but I don't think we've seen careful analysis and scrutiny about what works and doesn't," Rabe says. "What you have is a lot of self-celebration and claiming of success."

But Rabe notes that the municipal experiments are just getting under way. And Shore says that cities are trying to remake themselves into "green incubators" and engaging in a friendly competition to find the best ways of limiting their local carbon "footprints."

"Having hundreds of cities across the country doing a test-run of innovations is a good thing," says Kathleen Casey Ridihalgh, a Sierra Club regional representative in Seattle. "It kind of gives us a huge pilot test of what we need to do at the federal level."

Toward this end, mayors are reducing municipal electricity use, planting thousands if not millions of trees, promoting car and bike sharing and purchasing more environmentally friendly vehicle fleets themselves — and, in New York, requiring cabbies to do the same. [10]

"People thought I was flaky when I took office and got rid of the city's Crown Victoria that was getting 10 miles per gallon and replaced it with a Prius," says Minneapolis Mayor Rybak. "I was not considered as flaky by the time I switched from a Prius to a plug-in."

New Jobs Accompany 'Green' Strategies

Many new jobs are expected to be created if certain "green" economic initiatives — such as retrofitting buildings and harnessing wind and solar power — are launched. Many of the jobs are engineering-related, but blue-collar jobs would be created as well.

Potential 'Green' Investments and Jobs

Building Retrofitting — *Electricians, heating/air conditioning installers, carpenters, construction equipment operators, roofers, insulation workers, carpenter helpers, industrial truck drivers, construction managers, building inspectors*

Mass Transit/Freight Rail — *Civil engineers, rail track layers, electricians, welders, metal fabricators, engine assemblers, bus drivers, dispatchers, locomotive engineers, railroad conductors*

Smart Grid — *Computer software engineers, electrical engineers, electrical equipment assemblers, electrical equipment technicians, machinists, team assemblers, construction laborers, operating engineers, electrical power line installers and repairers*

Wind Power — *Environmental engineers, iron and steel workers, millwrights, sheet metal workers, machinists, electrical equipment assemblers, construction equipment operators, industrial truck drivers, industrial production managers, first-line production supervisors*

Solar Power — *Electrical engineers, electricians, industrial machinery mechanics, welders, metal fabricators, electrical equipment assemblers, construction equipment operators, installation helpers, laborers, construction managers*

Advanced Biofuels — *Chemical engineers, chemists, chemical equipment operators, chemical technicians, mixing and blending machine operators, agricultural workers, industrial truck drivers, farm product purchasers, agricultural and forestry supervisors, agricultural inspectors*

Source: Robert Pollin, et al., "Green Recovery: A Program to Create Good Jobs and Start Building a Low-Carbon Economy," Center for American Progress, Sept. 2008

James Brainard, the mayor of Carmel, Ind., and co-chair of a climate change task force for the U.S. Conference of Mayors, says that local officials can have an enormous impact due to their influence over building codes and transportation planning. He points out that metropolitan areas since World War II have been designed around automobile driving.

Cutting down on vehicle miles traveled, or VMT, has become a top goal of environmental activists and land-use planners. "Mayors are the ones who decide how planning and zoning are going to take place," Brainard says. "We have to train our planning commissioners and others to insist on good city design where one is not forced to drive from place to place."

Even a prominent advocate of local action such as Seattle's Nickels concedes federal action will be necessary not only to meet the Kyoto standards but also to surpass them. But cities can still have considerable influence over transportation and land-use planning.

Perhaps as important, cities have helped spark and keep alive a dialogue about translating concerns about climate change into tangible action. "Mayor Nickels getting various mayors to sign off on climate change predates what we did at the state level," says Terry Tamminen, who served as an energy and environment adviser to California Gov. Schwarzenegger. "It's a great way to stimulate action at the next level of government."

Should state and local governments do more to prepare for the consequences of climate change?

While she was still running for vice president, Gov. Sarah Palin, R-Alaska, said during a September interview with Katie Couric of CBS News that she wasn't "going to solely blame all of man's activities" for climate change, arguing that "the world's weather patterns are cyclical."

"But," she added, "[it] kind of doesn't matter at this point, as we debate what caused it. The point is, it's real, we need to do something about it." [11]

Palin received some criticism during the campaign for these remarks and others that suggested she denied a link between human activity and global warming. How could she address the problem, critics asked, if she wouldn't examine the underlying cause?

That argument aside, Palin's stance — skepticism about global warming's roots but acceptance of it as real — reflects an increasingly important part of the larger debate: If climate change is already having real impacts — and will continue to do so, even if efforts to reduce greenhouse gas emissions succeed — how should governments begin to adapt to the resulting problems, such as flooding, coastal erosion and species loss? Should they, for example, build higher seawalls to offset rising sea levels?

"Alaska has been thinking about adaptation certainly more than it has been thinking about reducing emissions, and that's because it's on the front lines of climate change," says Hogan of the Pew climate change center.

Up until the last year or two, most environmentalists dismissed talk about adaptation. Their concern seemed to be that shifting the policy debate away from efforts to prevent climate change by cutting down on carbon emissions amounted to Palin-style denials that human activity causes global warming.

They also felt that planning for the effects brought about by climate change was defeatist. "It was seen as a potential smokescreen behind which high-emission countries could hide so they wouldn't have to make binding agreements to reduce," said Nathan Hultman, a professor of science, technology and international affairs at Georgetown University. [12]

The notion that adaptation is just a smokescreen seems to be changing. The Intergovernmental Panel on Climate Change, which shared the 2007 Nobel Peace Prize with former Vice President Al Gore, has been

California state Sen. Fran Pavley sponsored legislation in 2002 to regulate tailpipe emissions. In 2006, another law she authored called for reductions in industrial carbon dioxide emissions from power plants, oil refineries and other plants by 25 percent by 2020. The law includes penalties for noncompliance.

Getty Images/Mark Mainz

stressing the importance of adaptation in recent reports, while a group of scientists published an article in *Nature* in 2007 called "Lifting the Taboo on Adaptation." [13]

There are still advocates who argue that discussion about how to adapt to climate shifts amounts to a distraction from the larger project of reducing emissions. "There are people out there working on adaptation, but I have to say the overwhelming effort is to try to reduce our emissions," says Tom Adams, president of the California League of Conservation Voters. "At this point, some fairly significant climate impacts are inevitable, but a lot of us feel that this is a genuine planetary emergency, and it's imperative that we cut emissions."

Cahill, the former aide to New York Gov. Pataki, makes a similar point. "My concern is about using adaptation as a diversion program from a national cap-and-trade program," he says. "I would just be wary of something talking about adaptation without national cap and trade."

Still, Cahill and other environmentalists recognize that, even if all carbon emissions ceased tomorrow, changes are already occurring, and there is already enough carbon dioxide in the air to guarantee more changes to come. For that reason, policy makers are increasingly concerned about how to plan for the changes.

Not surprisingly, the issue has drawn the most attention in areas along coastlines, such as Maryland and Oregon. But because climate change will manifest itself differently in different locales, adaptation questions are drawing attention all over. For instance, Republican Gov. James Douglas of Vermont has been working with the state university to begin crafting plans to help the forestry and farming industries cope with climate change's local effects.

And Seattle Mayor Nickels' concerns about diminishing snowpack are increasingly shared in the Puget Sound area. In parts of the nearby Cascade Range, snowpack has declined by as much as 60 percent. In response, King County, which includes Seattle, has begun planning backwards from 2050, formulating plans to adapt to climate change effects seen as likely to occur even if carbon emissions are significantly cut between now and then.

Officials expect coastal-erosion problems associated with rising sea levels, health effects such as new infectious diseases and heat stroke, increasing numbers of forest fires and ecological issues affecting salmon. In 2007, the county council agreed to a tax inspired by such looming dangers, part of County Executive Ron Sims' $335 million plan to bolster river levees and reduce flood risks.

The county is now building climate-change risks into all of its long-term planning and policy development. "We're learning to define ourselves not in 2009 terms but in 2050 terms," Sims said. "We're making decisions based on something that has not occurred yet." [14]

Like most environmentalists, Burke of the Union of Concerned Scientists says that both responses to climate change — reduction of carbon emissions, or "mitigation," and adaptation — are important.

Still, he says, "If you had to argue one versus the other, which I don't think is really helpful, I think mitigation is a higher priority given the urgency with which we need to create these reductions.

"You see that reflected in how most cities and states are going about their planning," Burke continues. "They're definitely doing the mitigation piece first and then moving onto adaptation."

Relatively few jurisdictions have turned full-scale attention to adaptation and planning questions. Even normally proactive California has barely paid attention to adaptation issues, according to a recent study, and is unprepared for flooding, coastal erosion and loss of wildlife habitat predicted to occur in coming decades due to higher temperatures. [15] Last Nov. 14, Gov. Schwarzenegger issued an executive order to identify the state's biggest vulnerabilities to rising sea levels and draft an "adaptation strategy." [16]

States and local governments face a practical challenge when it comes to crafting adaptation plans. Much of the science in this area has been, not surprisingly, global in scope. Thus, planning for climate change's local impacts will require experts to "downscale" large-scale data to make them applicable and useful for communities.

But Sims argues that it's imperative for states, cities and counties to accept the need to make decisions based on scientific modeling rather than historical experience.

"With all the discussion we've had on global warming, I am stunned that people haven't realized that it's actually going to occur," he says. "The ice caps are melting now. They're not going to refreeze next year because we reduce our emissions. We're going to live in that world. So plan for it." ∎

BACKGROUND

States Take Charge

Climate change has become such a hot issue among state and local officials that it's worth remembering they have taken it seriously only for a few years. "We're still very much at the embryonic stage of dealing with climate change in this country," says Cahill, the former aide to Gov. Pataki. "But at the same time, the train has left the station."

Although environmentalists deride President Bush for not squarely addressing global warming, the Clinton administration's record was not notably better. Congress rejected President Bill Clinton's 1993 proposal to impose a tax on energy, and the Senate passed a unanimous resolution in 1997 that it

would reject the Kyoto Protocol if it harmed the U.S. economy.

At first, states expressed skepticism about Kyoto, with 16 passing legislation opposing its ratification in 1998 and 1999. Most were resolutions simply stating an opinion, but some states forbade their agencies from any unilateral steps to reduce greenhouse gases. [17]

But it soon became clear that many states were eager to address the problem of global warming, particularly after Bush's formal rejection of Kyoto in 2001. "Ironically . . . American states may be emerging as international leaders at the very time the national government continues to be portrayed as an international laggard on global climate change," the University of Michigan's Rabe wrote in 2004. [18]

Most initial state-level efforts were largely symbolic, lacking specific mandates or resources. As early as 1989, New Jersey Gov. Thomas Kean, a Republican, signed an executive order instructing all state agencies to take the lead in reducing greenhouse gases.

But New Jersey and other states soon put real teeth into their efforts. In 2001, Massachusetts Gov. Jane Swift, also a Republican, issued a rule limiting a variety of pollutants from six major power plants, including the nation's first carbon dioxide standards. "The new, tough standards will help ensure older power plants in Massachusetts do not contribute to regional air pollution, acid rain and global warming," Swift said. [19] Her action was soon copied in New Hampshire.

But California quickly emerged as the leader among states in addressing the issue. As the only state allowed to set air pollution controls stricter than those mandated by federal law (thanks to a provision in the Clean Air Act), California is an almost constant environmental battlefield. There was strong pressure from environmental forces to move on the issue of greenhouse gases at the start of this decade, with both

Continued on p. 12

Chronology

1980s-1990s
Despite growing scientific concern, U.S. officials make mostly symbolic efforts to address global warming.

1988
The United Nations and the World Meteorological Organization create the International Panel on Climate Change (IPCC) to assess scientific information related to global warming.

1989
New Jersey Gov. Thomas Kean directs state agencies to start cutting greenhouse gas emissions (GHG).

1990
Amendments to the Clean Air Act introduce states to emissions trading.

1992
Delegates to World Environmental Summit in Rio de Janeiro adopt U.N. Framework Convention on Climate Change, calling on industrialized nations to voluntarily reduce emissions to 1990 levels by 2000.

1997
The Kyoto Protocol is adopted in Kyoto, Japan, on Dec. 11, committing industrialized countries to cut GHG emissions by an average of 5 percent below 1990 levels by 2012. The treaty goes into effect in 2005; 183 countries have ratified it so far, but not the United States. The Clinton administration signed it in 1997, but the Senate had voted unanimously in July to oppose any treaty that would harm the U.S. economy and exempt developing countries.

1998-1999
Sixteen states pass legislation and resolutions critical of the Kyoto treaty and GHG reduction efforts.

1999
A law deregulating electricity in Texas includes a provision promoting renewable energy, sparking large-scale efforts to harvest wind energy in the state.

2000s *Federal inaction spurs local action to cut GHGs.*

2002
California regulates GHG emissions from vehicles.

2005
Governors from seven Northeastern states form Regional Greenhouse Gas Initiative to create a cap-and-trade system limiting emissions. . . . U.S. Conference of Mayors encourages cities to abide by Kyoto Protocol emission limits.

2006
California enacts first statewide cap on carbon emissions as part of a landmark global warming law. . . . Washington is first major U.S. city to mandate green construction for all large private buildings.

2007
In response to a case brought by Massachusetts and other states, Supreme Court rules Environmental Protection Agency can regulate carbon dioxide as a pollutant. . . . Regulator in Kansas denies permits for two 700-megawatt power plants due to GHG pollution concerns.

2008
April 7: New York State Assembly kills a plan by Mayor Michael Bloomberg to charge drivers an $8 "congestion pricing" fee for entering parts of Manhattan. . . . April 22: Los Angeles City Council approves ordinance requiring developers to meet tougher environmental building standards. . . . June 6: Senate rejects a vote to consider federal greenhouse gas legislation that includes a national cap-and-trade system. . . . July 18: California Building Standards Commission approves first statewide "green building codes," requiring greater energy efficiency in both commercial and residential properties. . . . Sept. 18: Chicago Mayor Richard M. Daley announces a plan to reduce GHG emissions by 25 percent by 2020, compared with 1990 levels, through tougher building codes and improved transportation. . . . Sept. 30: California Gov. Arnold Schwarzenegger signs bill that will award increased state and federal transportation funds to regions that encourage dense development. . . . Nov. 19: Governors of Illinois, Wisconsin and California sign agreement with counterparts in Indonesia and Brazil to address forestry issues pertaining to global warming. . . . Canada reverses course and expresses support for a North American cap-and-trade system. . . . Dec. 8: Local government groups urge Congress and the incoming Obama administration to devote $10 billion to their efforts to create green jobs and promote energy efficiency as part of an economic stimulus plan. . . . Dec. 11: California Air Resources Board moves to implement the state's 2006 global warming law, approving a plan to cut emissions 25 percent by 2020.

2009
Jan. 1: Northeast's multistate limits on carbon emissions take effect. . . . March 3: Los Angeles voters will decide whether to require Department of Water and Power to install solar collectors on roofs of government, commercial and industrial buildings by 2014.

'Green' Jobs Counted on to Revive Economy

But critic says stimulus program won't help.

In October, Progressive Insurance announced the winner of its $10 million Automotive X Prize, a competition to encourage students to develop designs for safe, low-emission, "production capable" cars. Among the finalists were engineering students from West Philadelphia High School.

"Our team has built four cars, including a hybrid Jeep that gets double the mileage it's supposed to get," said Lawrence Jones-Mahoney, 18. "If we can do it as high school students, why can't the major auto companies?" [1]

Amid the nation's current economic doldrums, many people see green manufacturing projects as a hopeful sign. Investment in alternative energy and more efficient automobiles and buildings was high and growing rapidly over the past year, at least until the price of oil began to drop.

Many still are counting on "green collar" jobs to revive the economy, restoring the manufacturing sector in places where it's long been in decline. "American cities have suffered more than anyone from the loss of manufacturing jobs," says Minneapolis Mayor R. T. Rybak. "Cities have become the green incubators for America."

Every month seems to see another study released suggesting that there will be an explosion of investment and job creation in the green sector. The Center for American Progress estimates that a government-funded $100 billion green stimulus package would create 2 million jobs in the next two years for engineers, machinists, construction workers and others. [2]

The Apollo Alliance, a coalition of business, labor and environmental groups, estimates that a $300 billion investment over 10 years will create 3.3 million jobs in renewable energy, hybrid cars and infrastructure replacement. [3] The U.S. Conference of Mayors forecasts 4.2 million green jobs by 2038 and suggests that cities and towns prepare to compete for them. [4]

"Everything that is good for global warming is good for jobs," says Van Jones, author of the 2008 book *The Green Collar Economy.* "Buildings do not weatherize themselves, wind turbines do not construct themselves, solar panels do not install themselves. Real people are going to have to get up in the morning and do these things."

This is one of the central premises of *New York Times* columnist Thomas Friedman's 2008 bestselling book, *Hot, Flat and Crowded* — that energy-technology jobs will serve as a cornerstone of economic revival in this country, in large part because they mostly cannot be done by workers overseas.

President-elect Barack Obama has pledged to make green jobs and manufacturing a centerpiece of any economic-stimulus package. "President-elect Obama did a great job on the campaign trail [communicating] that this is an opportunity, an economic opportunity for America, and that if we miss it, other countries in the world will be way ahead of us," Kansas Gov. Kathleen Sebelius, a Democrat, said at a November climate-change summit in California. "Jobs are clearly part of this." [5]

For all the apparent promise, however, the interest in green technology has not yet translated either into mass employment or a huge economic windfall. "People are talking about this in the future, but it's not happening today," says Eric Crawford, president of Greenman Alliance, a Milwaukee-based recruiting firm. "Everyone wants a green job," but the demand for such jobs totally outstrips the supply.

And government investment in clean technology has not always reaped large dividends. Under New Jersey's energy master plan, solar power should account for more than 2 percent of the Garden State's electricity by 2020. But solar systems now generate only 0.07 percent of current energy needs.

Continued from p. 10

the legislature and governor's mansion in Democratic hands for the first time in two decades.

California lawmakers responded in 2002, enacting a measure to regulate tailpipe emissions — greenhouse gases released from vehicles — which in 1999 accounted for 37 percent of carbon dioxide emissions in the state. [20]

The idea came from Bluewater Network, a San Francisco environmental group that has since become part of Friends of the Earth, a global organization. They found their sponsor in then-state Rep. Fran Pavley, a Democratic freshman willing to take on the fight when more prominent legislators were avoiding it. "We were happy at that point to find any progressive author, because we knew it would be a difficult bill," said Bluewater Executive Director Russell Long.

The legislation survived a committee challenge and was ready to reach the floor by the middle of 2001, but Pavley held off on a vote until 2002 so she could broaden her backing. Car makers and oil companies spent an estimated $5 million attempting to sink it, and she was ardently attacked by talk-radio hosts for impinging on the freedom of Californians to drive SUVs and other large vehicles.

Pavley responded with polls demonstrating overwhelming popular support for the bill, even among SUV owners. She also got help from water-quality districts, religious leaders, technology executives from Silicon Valley and celebrities such as Paul Newman, Tom Hanks and former President Clinton, who called wavering lawmakers. Her bill's progress was helped immeasurably, however, by legislative

That's despite the fact that the state has already handed out more than $170 million in rebates to encourage their installation. To meet its 2020 goal, the state would have to spend $11 billion more. "We need to do things differently because ratepayers can't keep paying for rebates indefinitely," says Jeanne M. Fox, president of New Jersey's Board of Public Utilities. [6]

"This idea that we're going to have a massive environmental WPA — it's not going to help the economy, it's going to hurt the economy," says Myron Ebell, director of energy and global warming policy at the Competitive Enterprise Institute, referring to the Depression-era jobs program, the Works Progress Administration.

Putting government money into green energy would not create great economic returns, Ebell suggests, because — at least so far — renewable energy is more expensive than dirty fuels such as coal. It also means directing dollars away from other fields entirely, he says.

"I believe just on a very simple analysis that there is no question it will take net jobs out of the economy and it will be a net economic harm," Ebell says.

Even if Ebell's right, however, the goal of green investment is not only to stimulate the economy but also to help clean up the environment. In a column published in *The New York*

About half the states require utilities to generate a portion of their power from renewable sources, such as wind and solar. Above, wind turbines near Palm Springs, Calif.

Times just after the November election, former Vice President Al Gore called for large governmental investments in clean energy as the optimum way to address climate change — a shift from his traditional focus on increased regulation of carbon pollution. [7]

"With his op-ed, Gore has reversed the longstanding green-lobby prioritization of regulation first and investment second," wrote Michael Shellenberger and Ted Nordhaus for *The New Republic Online*. [8]

[1] Jim Motavalli, "Upstart Team Eyes the X Prize," *The New York Times*, Sept. 7, 2008, p. AU6.

[2] Robert Pollin, *et al.*, "Green Recovery: A Program to Create Good Jobs and Start Building a Low-Carbon Economy," Center for American Progress, September 2008.

[3] "The New Apollo Program: Clean Energy, Good Jobs," The Apollo Alliance, September 2008.

[4] "Current and Potential Green Jobs in the U.S. Economy," *Global Insight*, October 2008.

[5] "Governors Say Climate Change Programs Can Aid Economic Recovery," *Carbon Control News*, Nov. 24, 2008.

[6] Anthony DePalma, "New Jersey Dealing With Solar Policy's Success," *The New York Times*, June 25, 2008, p. B1.

[7] Al Gore, "The Climate for Change," *The New York Times*, Nov. 9, 2008, p. WK10.

[8] Michael Shellenberger and Ted Nordhaus, "A New Inconvenient Truth," *The New Republic Online*, Nov. 17, 2008, www.tnr.com/politics/story.html?id=971eed4b-1dc8-4afd-a8fe-193c373286ac.

leaders who showed the former civics teacher some parliamentary tricks to ensure its passage.

Her law required the state's Air Resources Board to adopt "cost-effective" and "reasonable" restrictions on carbon dioxide emissions from cars and light trucks by 2005, with automakers having until 2009 to comply. Not surprisingly, carmakers have fought the law through numerous court challenges.

A total of 19 other states have since enacted laws saying they will abide by California's rules once they are approved, but the Bush administration has refused to grant California the necessary waiver.

"All we asked for was permission to enforce, because the rules were all in place," California Air Resources Board spokesman Stanley Young said in a recent interview. "We've been ready for two years on Pavley. The rules were fully fleshed out. They were formally adopted back in 2005, and we're ready to move on them as soon as we get the green light."

Pavley was back in 2006 with another piece of legislation designed to address global warming. The measure

to address stationary sources of pollution aims to reduce industrial carbon dioxide emissions by 25 percent by 2020. It affects not only power plants but also other polluters such as oil refineries and cement plants.

The legislation was the first in the nation to require a cap-and-trade system. It also served to codify limits on future greenhouse gas emissions that Schwarzenegger had outlined in 2005. The 2006 law represented the first imposition of statewide, enforceable limits on GHG emissions that include penalties for noncompliance.

Kansas Regulator Blocks Coal-Fired Plants

Project is among 60 canceled in 2008 to protect environment.

Many people would be surprised to find Kansas at the epicenter of a nationwide environmental debate. Yet the decision by Rod Bremby, secretary of the Kansas Department of Health and Environment (KDHE), to block a pair of massive coal-fired power plants has set off one of the nation's fiercest political and legal environmental battles.

Several other states have blocked coal-fired plants over the past year, but Bremby is the only regulator to have done so strictly out of concern for climate change and without getting specific statutory cover from the legislature. "To approve the permit didn't seem a reasonable option, given that carbon dioxide is a pollutant," he said in an interview, "and we're talking about 11 million tons of carbon."

Bremby delayed making his coal-plant decision until after the U.S. Supreme Court's ruling in a case (*Massachusetts v. EPA*) brought in 2007 by Massachusetts and other states seeking to force the federal Environmental Protection Agency to regulate greenhouse gases.

The states' victory — along with an opinion from the Kansas attorney general that Bremby had the authority to block the permit — allowed him to overrule his own staff and refuse Sunflower Electric Power Corp.'s application to build its $3.6 billion power-plant project outside Holcomb.

The project is one of roughly 60 coal-fired plants canceled over the past year due to environmental concerns. Florida Gov. Charlie Crist asked a utility to cancel two projects in his state. The Texas energy giant TXU Corp. has shelved eight out of 11 planned coal plants, investing heavily in wind energy instead. Only three out of 10 plants once planned for southern Illinois remain active. [1] Nowadays, wherever a coal-fired plant is proposed, the Sierra Club or an allied group steps forward with a lawsuit to block it. [2]

"There have been other decisions in which state public utility commissions or environmental regulators have blocked construction or operation of coal-fired plants on the basis of climate change," says Robert Glicksman, a University of Kansas law professor, "but those have been based on legislation designed to minimize pollution or used climate change coupled with other factors."

In Washington state, for instance, the legislature in 2007 limited the amount of greenhouse gases coal plants could emit. To obtain construction permits, energy companies must show they can capture or sequester any carbon dioxide above strict limits.

Because Kansas lacks such legislation, and despite the attorney general's opinion, many critics say Bremby overstepped his authority. Kansas law gives the secretary authority to block emissions found to endanger health or the environment. But that power, according to the health department's own testimony, applies only to emergencies, says Jay Emler, who chairs the state Senate Utilities Committee.

Legislators — their attention focused by a million-dollar lobbying campaign by Sunflower and its allies — voted three times to ban Bremby's department from regulating greenhouse gases.

States Challenge the EPA

States have been exploring numerous other avenues toward curbing emissions in recent years. In 2007, first Western and then Midwestern states joined together in regional compacts meant to mirror and build on the Northeast's Regional Greenhouse Gas Initiative, which aims to set up cap-and-trade systems to limit emissions. Various states have taken steps to encourage use of high-efficiency vehicles, either through purchases for their own fleets or tax incentives for individuals to purchase them. States such as New Mexico, New Jersey and Minnesota have recently crafted and adopted plans for reducing their overall greenhouse gas emissions.

But environmentalists and state officials alike have been hoping the federal government would take action. In the face of its reluctance to regulate greenhouse gas emissions, several environmental groups as early as 1999 had petitioned the EPA to use its authority under the Clean Air Act to regulate the gases. The agency denied it had such authority and also argued that the link between greenhouse gases and climate change was not firmly established.

Massachusetts and 11 other states appealed the EPA's denial. In April 2007, the Supreme Court ruled, 5-4, in the states' favor, noting that they had standing to bring such a case due to the "risk of catastrophic harm" they faced as sovereign entities. Justice John Paul Stevens wrote that the EPA had provided "no reasonable explanation for its refusal to decide whether greenhouse gases cause or contribute to climate change." In his dissent, Chief Justice John G. Roberts Jr. argued that it was an issue better decided by Congress and the executive branch. [21]

But the court's majority determined that carbon dioxide was indeed an air pollutant under the federal Clean Air Act, and that law gives California the authority to regulate any such pollutant, as long as the state can get a waiver from the EPA. Other states are then allowed to follow California's rules.

The Supreme Court decision set the political stage for Congress to set

Each time, Democratic Gov. Kathleen Sebelius sided with Bremby and vetoed their efforts. The legislature came close to overriding her, but fell short.

The battle is now left to the state and federal courts, which are weighing a half-dozen lawsuits. Environmentalists, needless to say, are delighted by the outcome so far, believing that delays, and their concomitant costs, can only serve to move power generation away from coal. "Each time you step back and reassess the politics and economics of coal," says Bob Eye, a Sierra Club attorney and former KDHE counsel, "things are more difficult for the coal-plant proponents."

Plant advocates, of course, make exactly the opposite argument, saying the protracted fighting will simply cause Sunflower to look to friendlier states. Uncertainty about permitting — as well as the state's general regulatory climate — has caused problems for the business community, which put energy costs at the top of its list of concerns in a Kansas Chamber of Commerce survey last fall. "We've heard people saying that because of what happened last session they feel that the state has hung a big 'We're not open for business' sign out," said Kent Eckles, the chamber's vice president for government affairs. [3]

Action by Rod Bremby ignited fierce battle in Kansas.

U.S. House Select Committee on Energy Independence and Global Warming

"His decision, which I say is nothing but a political decision, has had a disastrous effect on the economy of Kansas," says Sen. Emler, "and will until it's rectified."

Bremby and his allies have pointed out that Sunflower was the only applicant not to receive a clean-air permit, out of more than 3,100 applications received during the six years Sebelius has been governor. But the issue is expected to be front and center again during the upcoming legislative session.

"I anticipate a full-blown debate until we get this fixed," says Senate President Steve Morris, who strongly supports Sunflower's project.

Then again, Bremby always suspected he couldn't win many friends with his decision. "We knew going in that we were in a no-win situation," he says, "There would be litigation either way we went."

[1] Michael Hawthorne, "How Coal Got a Dirty Name," *Chicago Tribune*, July 9, 2008, p. 1.

[2] Judy Pasternak, "Coal at Heart of Climate Battle," *Los Angeles Times*, April 14, 2008, p. A1.

[3] Jeannine Koranda, "Climate Cleanup Costs Could Trickle Down," *The Wichita Eagle*, Nov. 10, 2008, p. A1.

a new mileage standard for cars and light trucks. In December 2007 President Bush signed into law requirements that a car manufacturer's entire fleet average 35 miles per gallon by 2020.

But just hours after that bill was signed, EPA Administrator Stephen L. Johnson dashed hopes that the *Massachusetts v. EPA* decision would lead the agency to approve California's waiver application for enforcement of the Pavley bill. "The Bush administration is moving forward with a clear national solution, not a confusing patchwork of state rules, to reduce America's climate footprint from vehicles," Johnson said in a statement. Congress has since investigated the circumstances surrounding Johnson's decision. [22] ∎

CURRENT SITUATION

Limiting Land Use

American governors are now working with partners from around the world, as well as with each other, to combat environmental threats. On Nov. 19, governors from 13 states and regional leaders from four other nations signed a declaration to work together to combat global warming. The statement was the capstone of a climate summit organized by California's Schwarzenegger.

Under a separate agreement, Illinois, California and Wisconsin pledged to work with the governors of six provinces within Indonesia and Brazil to help slow tropical deforestation and land degradation through joint projects and incentive programs.

"When California passed its global warming law two years ago, we were out there on an island, so we started forming partnerships everywhere we could," Schwarzenegger said. [23]

On Dec. 11, the California Air Resources Board approved a set of regulations designed to implement the state's 2006 greenhouse gas law. It aims to reduce carbon emissions to 1990 levels by 2020, which would amount to a 25 percent cut. The plan will allow businesses to buy and sell emission credits, impose fees on water use and require utilities to generate a full third of their power from renewable sources — about three times as much as they do currently.

California estimates that about 30 percent of its greenhouse gas emissions come from cars. The new vehicle regulations would account for 18 percent of the state's overall reduction goal, according to the new state plan. The air board's plan also includes a "feebate" proposal, which would give rebates to people buying fuel-efficient cars, while adding fees to the purchase of gas-guzzlers. [24]

The Air Resources Board will almost certainly have to revisit some of these issues in response to a major land-use bill Schwarzenegger signed last September, known as SB 375, which directed the board to come up with regional greenhouse gas reduction targets by September 2010. The next step under the law calls for regional planning boards to rewrite their master plans in ways that seek to meet those targets. The ones that come closest will be rewarded with extra federal and state transportation dollars.

The best way to meet the standards, argues Adams at the California League of Conservation Voters, is to cut down on sprawl. He points out that the number of miles traveled per vehicle is still growing at one-and-a-half times the rate of population growth. It's only by creating more compact and energy-efficient communities, Adams believes, that the state's long-term environmental goals can be achieved.

It's no surprise that environmentalists backed SB 375, but it also had the support of home builders, who liked the prospect of more predictability in the zoning process. One of the bill's main goals is inducing localities to coordinate their major planning tasks — transportation, land use and housing. Few have been able to do that up to now.

In addition, SB 375 provides relief from certain air-quality standards that had, perversely, discouraged developers from undertaking "infill" projects that use small plots of undeveloped land within existing communities. "Builders thrive on certainty, knowing what the rules are," says Tim Coyle, a senior vice president at the California Building Industry Association. Local

The rooftop garden atop Chicago's City Hall is one of about 200 such green roofs in the city. Mayor Richard M. Daley announced in 2008 the first city-specific climate-change projections in the nation along with plans to reduce greenhouse gas emissions by 25 percent in 2020, compared with 1990 levels.

governments also supported the law. Although it provides incentives and creates a policy-making framework, it doesn't create specific mandates for any individual regions.

SB 375 will take years to implement, but it already has received lots of attention from other states. "It's really a very important piece of legislation," says Peter Kasabach, executive direc-

tor of New Jersey Future, a smart-growth group. "How we develop our land is going to impact our greenhouse-gas targets.

"A lot of folks think that if we drive hybrids or change our lightbulbs, we'd be OK," he says. "But a significant amount of our greenhouse gas targets will be met by how we get around and reduce vehicle miles traveled."

Green Building

The number of local governments attempting to shrink their carbon footprints continues to grow, with more than 900 mayors having signed a pledge to bring their cities in line with the Kyoto Protocol's carbon reduction targets.

In 2007, Congress authorized up to $2 billion a year in block grants for state and local programs designed to save energy. "If we reflect back on the mayors' initiative, it was such a powerful vehicle to establish the voice of local action," says Michelle Wyman, executive director of the American affiliate of the international group ICLEI-Local Governments for Sustainability. "There's increasing sentiment that local climate action is where the real work is being done in the United States."

In September, Chicago Mayor Daley unveiled what *The New York Times* described as "perhaps the most aggressive plan of any major American city to reduce heat-trapping gases." [25] The plan, which aims to cut Chicago's carbon output by 25 percent by 2020, focuses on tougher building codes.

Green building codes have drawn the most attention among local govern-

Continued on p. 18

At Issue:

Can "green" jobs revive the U.S. economy?

BRACKEN HENDRICKS
SENIOR FELLOW, AND
BENJAMIN GOLDSTEIN
RESEARCH ASSOCIATE, CENTER FOR AMERICAN PROGRESS

FROM "A STRATEGY FOR GREEN RECOVERY," NOV. 10, 2008

*t*here is a growing consensus in Washington and on Main Streets across the country that the economy needs a jump-start. There are compelling reasons why the infrastructure and workforce components of the economic stimulus and re-covery package should be "green."

Confronting the mounting energy and global warming crises represents an extraordinary opportunity to reinvigorate the economy through investment in clean, sustainable, low-carbon energy sources. Investment in new, clean technologies and im-proving energy efficiency can drive immediate spending into some of the hardest-hit sectors of the economy, such as con-struction and manufacturing, and can ensure that this infusion flows directly into job creation and domestic investment. Fur-ther, smart policies for energy efficiency can reduce household utility bills and free up income for consumer spending.

There are many ways that government spending can boost the economy and create jobs as part of a stimulus and recovery pro-gram. Yet dollars directed toward renewable energy and energy efficiency would result in more jobs than spending in most other areas, including, for example, rebates for increasing household consumption, which was the primary aim of the $168 billion stimulus program last April. "Green" investments, on average, cre-ate more than twice as many jobs per dollar invested as tradition-al, fossil fuel-based generating technologies by redirecting money previously spent on wasted energy and imported fuel toward ad-vanced technology, modern infrastructure and skilled labor.

Green investments also pave the road for sustained economic recovery. Larger, capital-intensive, green infrastructure projects such as renewable-energy generating facilities may take two years to get fully up and running but will be good job creators with a dependable economic-multiplier effect. About 22 percent of total household expenditures go to imports. But only about 9 percent of a green infrastructure investment program purchases imports. This is another critical advantage of a green economic-recovery program: Investments are focused primarily on increasing domes-tic productive capacity, improving national infrastructure and mak-ing the entire economy more efficient over the long term.

Confronting energy and climate challenges will require a sus-tained commitment and long-term policy framework. But near-term green investments can immediately stimulate the economy, create millions of good jobs and put a solid down payment on the low-carbon future vital for our economic growth.

MARGO THORNING
SENIOR VICE PRESIDENT AND CHIEF ECONOMIST, AMERICAN COUNCIL FOR CAPITAL FORMATION

WRITTEN FOR CQ RESEARCHER, JANUARY 2009

*t*he U.S. economy has slowed markedly in recent months, prompting some to suggest putting even more taxpayer dollars into subsidized renewable energy in the United States. Advocates claim lots of new "green collar" jobs would be created, and the threat of global warming would be lessened. Both claims are unlikely to be realized.

Despite many years of tax credits and taxpayer-funded re-search and development, most forms of renewable energy are still not competitive with electricity generated by coal, natural gas or nuclear power. Wind-powered electricity is estimated to cost as much as 50 percent more than coal-fired generation, and solar generation up to 700 percent more.

Both wind and solar must be backed up by conventional generation capacity, which adds greatly to their cost, because the wind does not always blow, and the sun is available only 12 hours a day. Furthermore, renewable resources are often geographically remote, and building transmission lines to large metropolitan areas is expensive.

Proposals like that of the Center for American Progress to invest $100 billion-$200 billion of taxpayer money in green in-frastructure are based on the flawed premise that raising the price of conventional energy through a tax on carbon emis-sions and using the money to pay for more expensive renew-able energy will promote economic recovery. In fact, substi-tuting higher-cost energy for lower-cost conventional energy will slow U.S. economic and job growth.

A study by the American Council for Capital Formation and the National Association of Manufacturers shows that if the U.S. had adopted the Senate's Lieberman-Warner global warming bill last year, overall U.S. employment would have been reduced by 850,000 to 1,860,000 jobs in 2014. This figure includes gains from new green jobs. The high energy prices required to curb greenhouse gas emissions cause net job loss even after taking into account increased employment in renewable energy.

What's more, a recent EPA report concluded that even if the United States achieved the emission-reduction targets in the Lieberman-Warner bill, it would make virtually no difference in global greenhouse gas concentrations unless developing coun-tries also adopt stringent reduction targets.

Although renewable energy has a role to play in the U.S. economy, the Obama administration should consider policies to promote U.S. energy supplies of all types and avoid unrealistic climate change policies.

Continued from p. 16

ments seeking to cut back on carbon. Buildings account for 40 to 50 percent of a city's energy demands. They use a fourth of the drinking water and produce 35 percent of the solid waste, mostly in the form of construction materials. And buildings make up anywhere from 30 to 70 percent of municipal carbon emissions, according to the American Institute of Architects (AIA).

Many cities have received grants from former President Clinton's foundation to rewrite their codes, but far more are pursuing such strategies on their own. In November, more than 25,000 local officials attended the "Greenbuild" conference in Boston sponsored by the U.S. Green Building Council. [26]

The trend has exploded in recent years. From 2003 to 2007, the number of cities with green building programs grew by 418 percent, from 22 to 92, according to the AIA. By mid-2008, 14 percent of municipalities with populations of more than 50,000 had adopted such programs, with many more cities planning programs soon.

By and large, cities' green building programs are based on the standards of the council's rating system, known as LEED (Leader in Energy and Environmental Design). To encourage developers to build green, cities are offering tax incentives, reductions in permit fees and access to grants for projects that meet certain environmental benchmarks. Some cities offer bonus density allowances — a green building project might be

exempt from height restrictions, for example. But the most popular incentive by far is expedited permitting for green projects. Cities can implement such a policy at virtually no cost to themselves, which has proven extremely attractive.

Some cities are going further and actually requiring energy-efficient construction through their building codes. Washington, D.C., in 2006 became the

A motorist in San Rafael, Calif., checks his tailpipe exhaust level. California passed a law in 2002 to regulate tailpipe emissions, and 19 other states followed suit. The Bush White House has blocked the other states from enforcing their laws, but President-elect Barack Obama has said he will approve a waiver allowing enforcement.

Getty Images/Justin Sullivan

first major U.S. city to mandate green construction for all private buildings of at least 50,000 square feet, beginning in 2012. But in 2007, Boston became the first city actually to implement a green requirement for private construction and renovation projects.

Since then, a handful of other cities have adopted similar mandates. San Francisco last August adopted the strictest codes of any U.S. city so far, requiring green standards for any residential buildings taller than 75 feet and commercial buildings of more than 5,000 square feet.

Last July, California became the first state to require certain environmental standards in its statewide building code.

Cap-and-Trade

In September, 10 Northeastern states concluded their first auction selling the right to emit carbon dioxide from power plants. The idea, as explained by the plan's architect, former Pataki aide Cahill, is to translate everyone's awareness that carbon emissions have a price into an actual cost.

Cap-and-trade auctions have taken place for years as a means of reducing acid-rain-causing sulfur dioxide, and the European Union runs a cap-and-trade program for carbon. But the Northeastern effort — known as the Regional Greenhouse Gas Initiative, or RGGI (pronounced "Reggie") — was the first CO_2 auction in the United States.

RGGI, which went into force on Jan. 1, places an overall regional limit on the amount of carbon that power plants can emit. The cap-and-trade plan is the central mechanism for regulating and limiting carbon emissions. Each utility has a permit for each ton of carbon it is allowed to emit — and the number of permits will steadily shrink over time. Utilities that emit less than their quota can sell their excess permits. (That's the "trade" part of cap and trade.)

The Northeastern states aren't the only ones interested in such an approach. In the West, seven states and four Canadian provinces are developing a similar regime, with negotiators having drawn up a blueprint for their governors in September. In the Midwest, six other states are working on a regional carbon-trading program. Florida is developing its own program, although it may join forces either with the Western effort or RGGI.

The history of RGGI, in particular, includes many touch-and-go moments when states dropped out of or rejoined the program. But the effort has stayed afloat based on the hope that once carbon emissions carry a price, utilities will burn less coal, oil and natural gas because it's in their economic interest, while carbon-free alternatives will become comparatively more attractive.

Not everyone agrees that such a scenario will play out. Wind power, for instance, is already heavily subsidized yet still can't compete on price with coal. And the region-by-region approach that's now in place leaves plenty of opportunities open for undermining the system.

In the Northeast, for example, it would be easy enough for a big industrial customer in New York, which is part of RGGI, to look for cheaper power generated by coal plants in Pennsylvania or Ohio, which are not part of the initiative. If that occurs, said Kenneth Pokalsky, a regulatory analyst for the Business Council of New York State, "We'll have the worst of both worlds: higher energy costs in New York to implement a program that has no discernible impact on worldwide greenhouse gas emissions." [27]

Nevertheless, hoping to build on the RGGI model and benefit from lessons learned there and from the troubled European model, the system being developed in the West is even bolder. The Western Climate Initiative is targeting not just carbon dioxide but five other greenhouse gases as well. And the WCI isn't limiting its scope to power plants. Instead, it's trying to bring all major industries, transportation fuels and residential furnaces, stoves and hot-water heaters into its system.

Such an ambitious approach may represent the logical evolution of cap and trade, but it nonetheless has made business groups, local governments and unions nervous about the potential impact on their costs and the economy.

Officials involved in WCI are tweaking their plans, looking at giving away a good share of emission allowances rather than auctioning them off. They're also seeking other ways to protect entities that would be affected if the system takes effect.

Focus on Renewables

Even as the regional cap-and-trade systems get under way, more than half the states are trying to cut down on coal as a share of their power sources individually. Twenty-seven states now require utilities to rely on renewable sources such as wind and solar to generate a significant share of electricity — up to 25 percent in future years. That's nearly twice as many states as had renewable portfolio standards in place just five years ago.

"It's an important step in the process of weaning ourselves from foreign oil," said Rhode Island state Sen. David E. Bates, who helped push through legislation in 2004 that requires a 20 percent renewable energy portfolio in his state by 2020. "We provided incentives for companies to produce renewable energy. We also took great pains to make it a workable formula. You can't tell a national grid to produce green energy in 20 years without making sure the energy is available." [28]

Meeting the required targets remains quite a challenge, however, especially in coal-dependent regions such as the South and Midwest. Coal generates about half the nation's electricity.

Joe Manchin, the governor of West Virginia, has touted wind energy but noted in a recent interview that his state's coal production is key for the entire Eastern Seaboard. "Economists and scientists . . . will tell you that coal is going to be the primary factor that's going to power this nation and most of the world for the next 30 to 50 years." [29]

According to the American Wind Energy Association, wind energy capacity has been growing rapidly, with wind turbines installed in 2008 capable of generating 7,500 megawatts of additional electricity. That's up from 5,249 megawatts installed in 2007. But 7,500 megawatts is still only enough electricity to power about 2 million homes. [30] ■

OUTLOOK

Will Washington Help?

If California has been a leader in state-level efforts to prevent climate change, two Californians are likely to have a profound effect on the national response to the issue. Sen. Barbara Boxer, who chairs the Senate Environment and Public Works Committee, has pledged to introduce legislation to create a national cap-and-trade program in this Congress. Henry A. Waxman, another California Democrat, will be Boxer's counterpart in the House, having ousted legendary Rep. John D. Dingell, D-Mich., as chairman of the Energy and Commerce Committee in November.

Dingell, who has been in Congress for a half-century and had been the panel's top Democrat since 1981, represents the Detroit area and has been a leading champion of the auto industry in Congress. His replacement by Waxman was widely seen as a signal that House Democrats will favor a more aggressive approach on climate change.

President-elect Obama, for his part, has also promised to make climate change a priority — a switch from the outgoing Bush administration. Obama is expected to approve the EPA waiver to allow California and 19 other states to regulate greenhouse gas emissions from vehicles.

But even if new leadership in Washington appears ready to tackle an issue long left to states and localities, does that mean national policy will trump the efforts of lower levels of government?

A lot will depend, of course, on what form congressional action will take. Plenty of people are skeptical, despite the changed circumstances in Washington, that Congress will actually act on cap and trade or any equally ambitious responses to global warming. There has been a lot of talk that caution will remain a watchword, given the fragile state of the economy. Further regulation may be seen as more than the economy — and the tottering auto sector in particular — can bear.

"Yes, there will be concerns about the current economic climate," says former Pataki aide Cahill, who helped design the Regional Greenhouse Gas Initiative (RGGI). "But it will take several years to develop the regulatory framework to go ahead and implement a national cap and trade. We all have enough confidence in the economy that it won't still be where it is now."

But the Competitive Enterprise Institute's Ebell points out that a Senate vote to consider last year's major climate-change legislation received only 48 votes — far short of the 60 needed under Senate rules to formally consider the bill. Although Democrats picked up seven seats in the November elections, some of them replaced Republicans who had voted in favor of the bill.

"I think there will be somewhat more enthusiasm for cap and trade in the 111th Congress than in the 110th," Ebell says, "but I don't know that it will translate into actual legislation."

If Congress does manage to overcome its own procedural hurdles and economic concerns to move major greenhouse gas legislation, one of the biggest challenges for lawmakers will be how to balance competing desires among states. Some, such as California, Massachusetts and New Jersey, will want to be rewarded for their pioneering efforts. Others in the South and Midwest, though, will not want to be penalized for not having acted sooner. It will be tough to create a national system that balances those different interests.

Rabe, the University of Michigan policy professor, says Congress has only recently taken into account the role that states and localities are playing. He says states will lobby to ensure that any federal system allows them maximum flexibility to set their own courses, while demanding that any money generated by a cap-and-trade system be shared generously with them. "States and localities are going to want it both ways," Rabe says.

But the fact that states and localities will be very much part of the national debate demonstrates how well-established their role in addressing climate change has already become. They may have gotten into the game due mainly to federal inaction. Still, many observers predict that states, cities

and counties will continue to address this challenge even if Congress and the White House agree on climate change legislation.

"Even if we get federal climate change legislation — or when we get it — that doesn't eliminate the need for states and cities to have their own strategies, their own plans," says the Union of Concerned Scientists' Burke.

Given the growing understanding that global warming is misnamed — that climate change will play out very differently around the world, with some regions heating up and others cooling down and some getting drier while others get wetter — states and localities should continue their work, suggests Hogan at the Pew Center on Global Climate Change.

"There should be a substantial role for the states," Hogan says. "The history of environmental regulation teaches us that the states do some things well, and the feds do some things well.

"Environmental goals are typically best achieved when all levels of government are doing their part." ∎

Notes

[1] Ellen Perlman, "Mister Sustainability," *Governing*, April 2008, p. 36.

[2] For background, see the following *CQ Researcher* reports: Marcia Clemmitt, "Climate Change," Jan. 27, 2006, pp. 73-96; Mary H. Cooper, "Global Warming Treaty," Jan. 26, 2001, pp. 41-64; Mary H. Cooper, "Alternative Fuels," Feb. 25, 2005, pp. 173-196, and Thomas J. Billitteri, "Reducing Your Carbon Footprint," Dec. 5, 2008, pp. 985-1008; and the following *CQ Global Researcher* reports: Colin Woodard, "Curbing Climate Change," February 2007, pp. 27-50, and Jennifer Weeks, "Carbon Trading," November 2008, pp. 295-320.

[3] Michael Grunwald, "Arnold Schwarzenegger," *Time*, Oct. 6, 2008, p. 60.

[4] For background, see Mary H. Cooper, "Bush and the Environment," *CQ Researcher*, Oct. 25, 2002, pp. 865-896.

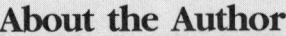

About the Author

Alan Greenblatt is a staff writer at *Governing* magazine. He previously covered elections, agriculture and military spending for *CQ Weekly*, where he won the National Press Club's Sandy Hume Award for political journalism. He graduated from San Francisco State University in 1986 and received a master's degree in English literature from the University of Virginia in 1988. His recent *CQ Researcher* reports include "Sex Offenders" and "Pension Crisis."

[5] Samantha Young, "Schwarzenegger Opens Climate Summit With Obama," The Associated Press, Nov. 19, 2008.

[6] Margot Roosevelt, "California Offers to Lead on Climate Change Fight," *Los Angeles Times*, Nov. 20, 2008, p. A22.

[7] Kate Galbraith, "Texas Worries About a Carbon Cap," *The New York Times Green Inc. Blog*, http://greeninc.blogs.nytimes.com/2008/12/04/texas-worries-about-a-carbon-cap/, Dec. 4, 2008.

[8] Juliet Eilperin, "Ex-EPA Official Says White House Pulled Rank," *The Washington Post*, July 23, 2008, p. A4. The case is *Massachusetts v. EPA*.

[9] Dirk Johnson, "Chicago Unveils Multifaceted Plan to Curb Emissions of Heat-Trapping Gases," *The New York Times*, Sept. 19, 2008, p. A13.

[10] Alan Greenblatt, "Cities vs. Carbon," *CQ Weekly*, Nov. 19, 2007, p. 3474.

[11] Alec MacGillis, "Palin Gives Beliefs, Demurs on Policies," *The Washington Post*, Oct. 1, 2008, p. A7.

[12] Alan Zarembo and Thomas H. Maugh II, "U.N. Says It's time to Adapt to Warming," *Los Angeles Times*, Nov. 17, 2007, p. A1.

[13] Roger Pielke Jr., *et al.*, "Lifting the Taboo on Adaptation," *Nature*, Feb. 8, 2007, p. 445.

[14] Christopher Swope, "Local Warming," *Governing*, December 2007, p. 25.

[15] Louise Bedsworth and Ellen Hanak, "Preparing California for a Changing Climate," Public Policy Institute of California, November 2008.

[16] Chris Bowman, "California Bulks Up Defenses Against Tide of Global Warming," *The Sacramento Bee*, Nov. 24, 2008, p. A1.

[17] Barry G. Rabe, *Statehouse and Greenhouse* (2004), p. 20.

[18] *Ibid.*, p. xiv.

[19] *Ibid.*, p. 77.

[20] Alan Greenblatt, "Fran Pavley: Legislative Prodigy," *Governing*, September 2002, p. 80.

[21] Linda Greenhouse, "Justices Say EPA Has Power to Act on Harmful Gases," *The New York Times*, April 8, 2007, p. A1.

[22] John M. Broder and Felicity Barringer, "EPA Says 17 States Can't Set Greenhouse Gas Rules for Cars," *The New York Times*, Dec. 20, 2007, p. A1.

[23] John M. Broder, "Obama Affirms Climate Change Goals," *The New York Times*, Nov. 19, 2008, p. A4, www.nytimes.com/2008/11/19/us/politics/19climate.html.

[24] Michael Gardner, "Emissions Plan Calls for Tougher Rules, Fees," *The San Diego Union-Tribune*, Nov. 21, 2008, p. A1.

[25] Dirk Johnson, "Chicago Unveils Multifaceted Plan to Curb Emissions of Heat-Trapping Gases," *The New York Times*, Sept. 19, 2008, p. A13.

[26] David Beard, "At Least 25,000 at Greenbuild Conference in Boston," *The Boston Globe Greenblog*, Nov. 19, 2008, www.boston.com/lifestyle/green/greenblog/2008/11/at_least_25000_at_greenbuild_c.html.

[27] Tom Arrandale, "Carbon Goes to Market," *Governing*, September 2008, p. 26.

[28] Chelsea Waugaman, "Voltage Charge," *Governing*, November 2005, p. 76.

[29] Mannix Porterfield, "Manchin Wants Aggressive Renewable Energy Policy," Beckley [West Virginia] *Register-Herald*, Oct. 20, 2008.

[30] Dirk Lammers, "US Wind Energy Adds 1,400 MW of Capacity," The Associated Press, Oct. 22, 2008.

FOR MORE INFORMATION

American Council for Capital Formation, 1750 K St., N.W., Suite 400, Washington, DC 20006; (202) 293-5811; www.aacf.org. A business research group that promotes economic growth and "cost effective environmental policies."

Climate Change Division, U.S. Environmental Protection Agency, 1200 Pennsylvania Ave., N.W., Washington, DC 20460; (202) 343-9990; www.epa.gov/climatechange. Provides comprehensive information about science, health effects, regulations and policies concerning global warming.

Climate Communities, 1130 Connecticut Ave., N.W., Suite 300, Washington, DC 20036; (202) 261-6011; www.climatecommunities.us. A national coalition of cities and counties that lobbies and educates federal policy makers in support of local efforts to address climate change.

Competitive Enterprise Institute, 1899 L St., N.W., 12th Floor, Washington, DC 20036; (202) 340-4034; www.cei.org. A think tank and advocacy organization that promotes free enterprise and limited government.

Environmental Council of the States, 444 N. Capitol St., N.W., Suite 445, Washington, DC 20001; (202) 624-3660; www.ecos.org. The association of state environmental agencies, provides a clearinghouse of information for members and lobbies federal authorities.

Heartland Institute, 19 S. LaSalle St., Suite 903, Chicago, IL 60603; (312) 377-4000; www.globalwarmingheartland.org. A conservative think tank that presents conferences and issues publications skeptical about the role of humans in causing climate change.

ICLEI-Local Governments for Sustainability, 436 14th St., Suite 1520, Oakland, CA 94612; (510) 844-0699; www.iclei.org/us. An international organization that provides grants and technical assistance to local governments seeking to increase energy efficiency.

Mayors Climate Protection Center, U.S. Conference of Mayors, 1620 I St., N.W., Washington, DC 20006; (202) 861-6700; http://usmayors.org/climateprotection. Provides assistance to mayors attempting to reduce greenhouse gas emissions.

Pew Center on Global Climate Change, 2010 Wilson Blvd., Suite 1550, Arlington, VA 22201; (703) 516-4146; www.pewclimate.org. Supports and disseminates research related to climate change.

U.S. Climate Change Science Program, 1717 Pennsylvania Ave., N.W., Washington, DC 20006; (202) 223-6262; www.climatescience.gov. Integrates research on climate change performed by 13 federal agencies.

Bibliography

Selected Sources

Books

Linstroth, Tommy, and Ryan Bell, *Local Action: The New Paradigm in Climate Change Policy*, University of Vermont Press, 2007.
An environmental consultant and a planner use case studies to illustrate how local governments are fighting global warming.

Rabe, Barry G., *Statehouse and Greenhouse: The Emerging Politics of American Climate Change Policy*, Brookings Institution Press, 2004.
A political scientist explains how states came to be lead actors in the fight against climate change and what their initial strategies were.

Articles

Arrandale, Tom, "Carbon Goes to Market," *Governing*, September 2008, p. 26.
Many states, especially those in the Northeast, are moving ahead with regional cap-and-trade systems to cut down on carbon emissions.

Davidson, Paul, "Utilities Shrink the Role of Coal," *USA Today*, Sept. 22, 2008, p. 4B.
Power companies are shifting away from coal-fired electricity amid increased regulatory hurdles due to global warming concerns.

Gerstenzang, James, and Janet Wilson, "White House Puts Warming Threats on Back Burner," *Los Angeles Times*, July 12, 2008, p. A1.
The Bush administration rejects the Environmental Protection Agency's conclusions about global warming threats.

Gore, Al, "The Climate for Change," *The New York Times*, Nov. 9, 2008, p. WK10.
The former vice president emphasizes the need for direct government investments in clean energy technology.

Johnson, Dirk, "Chicago Unveils Multifaceted Plan to Curb Emissions of Heat-Trapping Gases," *The New York Times*, Sept. 19, 2008, p. A13.
Following 18 months of research, Chicago Mayor Richard M. Daley releases a plan to reduce greenhouse gas emissions by 25 percent by 2020.

McGreevey, Patrick, and Margot Roosevelt, "Sprawl Measure OKd, Smog Bill Dies," *Los Angeles Times*, Oct. 1, 2008, p. B1.
The California legislature has approved a bill that rewards communities that take urban sprawl and global warming into account in their development planning.

Perlman, Ellen, "Mr. Sustainability," *Governing*, April 2008, p. 36.
The new sustainability coordinator in Fayetteville, Ark., is succeeding in his efforts to get city departments to cut down on energy usage.

Roosevelt, Margot, "California Offers to Lead on Climate Change Fight," *Los Angeles Times*, Nov. 20, 2008, p. A22.
Led by California, a dozen U.S. states have agreed with counterparts in five countries overseas to reduce greenhouse gas emissions.

Swope, Christopher, "Local Warming," *Governing*, December 2007, p. 25.
Many communities throughout the country, particularly those in the Seattle area, are starting to plan for the consequences of climate change.

Reports and Studies

"Analysis of the Lieberman-Warner Climate Security Act (S. 2191)," American Council for Capital Formation, National Association of Manufacturers, March 2008, www.accf.org/pdf/NAM/fullstudy031208.pdf.
Examining a congressional cap-and-trade proposal, a study underwritten by two business groups finds that it would severely undermine economic growth.

Aulisi, Andrew, *et al.*, "Climate Policy in the State Laboratory: How States Influence Federal Regulation and the Implications for Climate Change Policy in the United States," World Resources Institute, August 2007, pdf.wri.org/climate_policy_in_the_state_laboratory.pdf.
An environmental organization provides a report on states' aggressive climate change policies, with particular attention to those in California and the Northeast's Regional Greenhouse Gas Initiative.

Bedsworth, Louise, and Ellen Hanak, "Preparing California for a Changing Climate," Public Policy Institute of California, November 2008, www.ppic.org/content/pubs/report/R_1108LBR.pdf.
A leading think tank finds that California is not prepared to cope with global warming.

Pollin, Robert, *et al.*, "Green Recovery: A Program to Create Good Jobs and Start Building a Low-Carbon Economy," Center for American Progress, September 2008, www.americanprogress.org/issues/2008/09/pdf/green_recovery.pdf.
Economists at the University of Massachusetts find that a $100 billion initiative would both lower greenhouse gas emissions and provide an economic stimulus for the country.

The Next Step:

Additional Articles from Current Periodicals

Green Jobs

Dorschner, John, "Green Means Growth for Some Kinds of Jobs," *The Miami Herald*, June 4, 2008, p. C1.

A push to be environmentally conscious may provide employment for workers in several industries, according to a University of Massachusetts study.

Greenhouse, Steven, "Millions of Jobs of a Different Collar," *The New York Times*, March 26, 2008, p. SPG1.

Labor unions view green jobs as a replacement for positions lost to overseas outsourcing and manufacturing.

Lazar, Kay, "Firms Creating 'Green-Collar' Jobs," *Boston Globe*, Feb. 21, 2008, p. Reg1.

Lawmakers and educators are finding ways to transform traditional white- and blue-collar jobs into so-called "green-collar" jobs.

Local Governments

Faiola, Anthony, and Robin Shulman, "Cities Take Lead on Environment as Debate Drags at Federal Level," *The Washington Post*, June 9, 2007, p. A1.

Increasingly, city governments are working to reduce carbon emissions while similar federal measures are stalled.

Mishra, Raja, "Mayor Aims to Cut City's Greenhouse Emissions," *The Boston Globe*, April 13, 2007, p. A1.

Boston Mayor Thomas Menino has proposed reducing greenhouse gas emissions for city vehicles and buildings.

Stiffler, Lisa, "It Takes a City to Limit Greenhouse Gases," *Seattle Post-Intelligencer*, Sept. 22, 2007, p. B3.

Seattle's Climate Action Now campaign — funded by the city government — serves as a clearinghouse for local climate change information.

Wynn, Will, "Austinites Need to Think Globally and Act Locally," *Austin American-Statesman* (Texas), Feb. 18, 2007, p. G3.

The mayor of Austin, Texas, is trying to make his city the leading U.S. city in the fight against global warming.

Renewable Energy

Brunswick, Mark, "Renewable Energy Gets a Big Boost," *Star Tribune* (Minnesota), Feb. 20, 2007, p. 1A.

The Minnesota legislature has approved a bill that would require more wind, solar and hydrogen power in the state.

Langton, Elizabeth, "North Texas Cities Investing in Renewable Energy Sources," *Dallas Morning News*, Sept. 10, 2007, p. 1B.

Three North Texas cities are among the first in the state to purchase renewable energy credits to help offset the use of traditional power.

Shafer, J. M., "Rural Colorado and Renewable Energy," *Denver Post*, Feb. 1, 2007, p. B7.

Colorado rural communities can use their own renewable resources to pursue energy economies that are uniquely their own.

State Regulation

"State Aims to Calculate Carbon Cleanup Costs," The Associated Press, June 20, 2007.

New Mexico regulators have ordered the state's largest utility company to figure out the cost of reducing carbon emissions from coal-fired plants.

Baker, David R., "Emission Plan From UC Team," *The San Francisco Chronicle*, Aug. 4, 2007, p. C1.

University of California researchers have detailed a plan for the state to reduce greenhouse gases and carbon in its fuels.

Koranda, Jeannine, "More States Step in to Limit Carbon Emissions," *Wichita Eagle* (Kansas), March 22, 2008, p. A1.

Gov. Kathleen Sebelius, D-Kan., has stripped the state's environmental regulator of the power to block future plants based on carbon emissions.

Trowbridge, Gordon, and J. J. McCorvey, "McCain Backs States' Rules on Emissions," *Detroit News*, July 19, 2008, p. 1A.

Sen. John McCain said he supports state efforts to limit automobile emissions, a stance strongly at odds with Detroit carmakers.

In-depth Reports on Issues in the News

Are you writing a paper?

Need backup for a debate?

Want to become an expert on an issue?

For 80 years, students have turned to *CQ Researcher* for in-depth reporting on issues in the news. Reports on a full range of political and social issues are now available. Following is a selection of recent reports:

Civil Liberties
Limiting Lawsuits, 12/08
Affirmative Action, 10/08
Gay Marriage Showdowns, 9/08
America's Border Fence, 9/08
Immigration Debate, 2/08
Prison Reform, 4/07

Crime/Law
Mexico's Drug War, 12/08
Prostitution Debate, 5/08
Public Defenders, 4/08
Gun Violence, 5/07

Education
Reading Crisis? 2/08
Discipline in Schools, 2/08
Student Aid, 1/08
Racial Diversity in Public Schools, 9/07
Stress on Students, 7/07

Environment
Reducing Carbon Footprint, 12/08
Protecting Wetlands, 10/08
Buying Green, 2/08
Future of Recycling, 12/07

Health/Safety
Heart Health, 9/08
Global Food Crisis, 6/08
Preventing Memory Loss, 4/08

International Affairs/Politics
The National Debt, 11/08
Financial Bailout, 10/08
Political Conventions, 8/08
Human Rights in China, 7/08
Race and Politics, 7/08
Campaign Finance Reform, 6/08

Social Trends
Falling Birthrates, 11/08
Regulating Credit Cards, 10/08
Internet Accuracy, 8/08
Financial Crisis, 5/08
Cyberbullying, 5/08

Terrorism/Defense
Rise in Counterinsurgency, 9/08
Cost of the Iraq War, 4/08

Youth
Debating Hip-Hop, 6/07

Upcoming Reports

Preventing Cancer, 1/16/09   Future of the Auto Industry, 1/23/09   Obama Presidency, 1/30/09

ACCESS

CQ Researcher is available in print and online. For access, visit your library or www.cqresearcher.com.

STAY CURRENT

To receive notice of upcoming *CQ Researcher* reports, or learn more about *CQ Researcher* products, subscribe to the free e-mail newsletters, *CQ Researcher Alert!* and *CQ Researcher News*: http://cqpress.com/newsletters.

PURCHASE

To purchase a *CQ Researcher* report in print or electronic format (PDF), visit www.cqpress.com or call 866-427-7737. Single reports start at $15. Bulk purchase discounts and electronic-rights licensing are also available.

SUBSCRIBE

Annual full-service *CQ Researcher* subscriptions—including 44 reports a year, monthly index updates, and a bound volume—start at $803. Add $25 for domestic postage.

CQ Researcher Online offers a backfile from 1991 and a number of tools to simplify research. For pricing information, call 800-834-9020, ext. 1906, or e-mail librarysales@cqpress.com.

CQResearcher

Published by CQ Press, a division of SAGE Publications

www.cqresearcher.com

Preventing Cancer

Are too few resources devoted to prevention?

D eaths from cancer and new cancer cases have decreased slightly in the past few years. It's the first time the statistics have declined over an extended period and the best piece of news yet to come out of the nation's 38-year-old "war on cancer." Despite scientists' early optimism that the discovery of an actual cancer cure was imminent, most recent gains have come instead from earlier detection and cancer-prevention achievements, especially lower smoking rates. Those gains have prompted calls for a shift in federal cancer programs toward prevention and detection and away from research, which has been funded much more generously. Prevention proponents say focusing more on prevention and detection makes sense because cancer biology now demonstrates that individuals' cancers vary so widely and contain so many cell mutations that new, widely effective treatments will be even harder to come by than previously expected.

Smoking is the nation's single, greatest cause of cancer. Public health experts say cancer will kill around half of current smokers if they continue to smoke, with up to 40 percent of the deaths occurring in middle age.

CQ Researcher • Jan. 16, 2009 • www.cqresearcher.com
Volume 19, Number 2 • Pages 25-48

RECIPIENT OF SOCIETY OF PROFESSIONAL JOURNALISTS AWARD FOR
EXCELLENCE ◆ AMERICAN BAR ASSOCIATION SILVER GAVEL AWARD

CQ PRESS

Cover: Getty Images/Mike Simons

CQ Researcher

Jan. 16, 2009
Volume 19, Number 2

MANAGING EDITOR: Thomas J. Colin
tcolin@cqpress.com

ASSISTANT MANAGING EDITOR: Kathy Koch
kkoch@cqpress.com

ASSOCIATE EDITOR: Kenneth Jost

STAFF WRITERS: Thomas J. Billitteri, Marcia Clemmitt, Peter Katel

CONTRIBUTING WRITERS: Rachel S. Cox, Sarah Glazer, Alan Greenblatt, Barbara Mantel, Patrick Marshall, Tom Price, Jennifer Weeks

DESIGN/PRODUCTION EDITOR: Olu B. Davis

ASSISTANT EDITOR: Darrell Dela Rosa

FACT-CHECKER/PROOFREADER: Eugene J. Gabler

EDITORIAL INTERNS: Alexis Irvin, Vyomika Jairam

CQ PRESS

A Division of SAGE Publications

PRESIDENT AND PUBLISHER:
John A. Jenkins

EXECUTIVE DIRECTOR, REFERENCE INFORMATION GROUP:
Alix B. Vance

DIRECTOR, ONLINE PRODUCT DEVELOPMENT:
Jennifer Q. Ryan

CQ Researcher (ISSN 1056-2036) is printed on acid-free paper. Published weekly, except; (Jan. wk. 1) (May wk. 4) (July wks. 1, 2) (Aug. wks. 3, 4) (Nov. wk. 4) and (Dec. wk. 4), by CQ Press, a division of SAGE Publications. Annual full-service subscriptions start at $803. For pricing, call 1-800-834-9020, ext. 1906. To purchase a CQ Researcher report in print or electronic format (PDF), visit www. cqpress.com or call 866-427-7737. Single reports start at $15. Bulk purchase discounts and electronic-rights licensing are also available. Periodicals postage paid at Washington, D.C., and additional mailing offices. POSTMASTER: Send address changes to CQ Researcher, 2300 N St., N.W., Suite 800, Washington, DC 20037.

Preventing Cancer

BY MARCIA CLEMMITT

THE ISSUES

When Sen. Edward M. Kennedy, D-Mass., was diagnosed with brain cancer in May 2008, it wasn't the first time a Kennedy had confronted the deadly disease. Two of Kennedy's three children have been diagnosed with cancer.

An above-the-knee leg amputation followed by then-experimental chemotherapy cured his 12-year-old son Edward of bone cancer in 1973. In 2002, Kennedy's daughter, Kara, then 42, was diagnosed with lung cancer, which was also halted by surgery. In 1988, Kennedy's other son, Rep. Patrick Kennedy, D-R.I., then 20, was diagnosed with a benign spinal tumor, which was surgically removed. [1]

In each case, Sen. Kennedy was an aggressive advocate, seeking out a range of medical opinions before choosing a course, and observers have no doubt that he's taking the same approach with his own cancer. "This family has had cancer laid in front of it, and each time they have beaten it," said David J. Sugarbaker, chief of thoracic surgery at Boston's Brigham and Women's Hospital, who operated on Kara Kennedy. "They have an insatiable appetite for information and answers." [2]

Sen. Kennedy's tumor was surgically removed last summer, but brain cancer is harder to beat than many other cancers, partly because it's more difficult to remove the entire tumor.

Now back in the Senate, Kennedy hopes to shepherd to passage a comprehensive cancer bill — conceived of before his diagnosis — to improve

Sen. Edward M. Kennedy, D-Mass., is back in the Senate after having a cancerous brain tumor surgically removed last summer. Both Kennedy and President-elect Barack Obama plan to push for more aggressive action on cancer research this year. But many experts say the most effective strategy would be to focus more on detection and prevention.

Getty Images/Mark Wilson

the process of turning lab science into effective drugs to treat cancer. With President-elect Barack Obama, whose mother died of ovarian and uterine cancer, also hoping to overhaul the federal cancer program's clinical initiatives, 2009 could be a banner year for cancer patient advocates. However, many experts say effective cancer treatments are, and will remain, elusive and that the most effective strategy in the future would be to focus more on detection and prevention.

Cancer drugs are "particularly likely to fail in development compared to other therapies," according to an expert panel at a September 2008 conference at the Brookings Institution think tank in Washington. "One estimate shows that 60 percent of cancer-drug development programs fail in the late clinical phase." [3]

Eventually, scientists are likely to uncover key cell molecules that can be targeted with drugs that will keep some cancers in check, but gene science is in its infancy, says Kenneth W. Kinzler, a professor of oncology at the Johns Hopkins School of Medicine. Thus, he says, "from a practical point of view, prevention, early diagnosis and behavioral modification" — to squelch cancer-causing habits like smoking — "are really important."

Furthermore, individuals' cancers mutate in such a way that they eventually become resistant to even drugs that were initially effective, says Kinzler, whose lab has produced the first genetic profiles of colon, breast, pancreatic and brain tumors. Thus, no single drug treatment is likely to outrun cancer over the long haul.

In short, cancer remains such a formidable force that prevention is a far more potent anti-cancer strategy than previously imagined, said Kinzler's colleague Bert Vogelstein, co-director of Hopkins' Kimmel Cancer Center. "It's accurate to say that 99 percent of applied cancer research now goes toward developing new therapeutics," Vogelstein said, but "it is . . . apparent from [gene] studies like ours that it is going to be even more difficult . . . than previously expected to derive real cures from such therapies. The proportion of effort and funding devoted to other ways of managing cancer, such as prevention and early detection, should be greatly increased." [4]

Pancreatic Cancer Is Most Lethal Form

Only 5 percent of Americans with pancreatic cancer survive for five years, compared with 15 percent of lung cancer victims and 89 percent of those with breast cancer. Lung and colorectal cancer cause the most deaths each year in the United States.

Most Common Forms of Cancer in the U.S.
(Listed in order of lethality)

Type of Cancer	5-Year Survival Rate	No. of Deaths	Risk Factors
Pancreatic Cancer	5%	34,300	Smoking, chewing tobacco and being heavily exposed to chemicals, dyes and pesticides increase risk. Mainly strikes people over age 55.
Lung Cancer	15%	161,840	Most deaths are related to tobacco smoke. Lung cancer is also the largest cause of cancer deaths worldwide.
Stomach Cancer	24%	10,900	Though rare in the U.S., it's the second-biggest cancer killer worldwide, with 900,000 deaths. Infection with *Helicobacter pylori*, a common bacterium also associated with ulcers, may be a major cause, but most who carry it don't get the disease. Smoking doubles risk.
Brain/Nervous-System Tumors	29%	Over 13,000	Even "benign" brain tumors can fatally damage the brain. Risk factors largely unknown.
Multiple Myeloma	34%	10,700	African-Americans are twice as likely as whites to get the immune system disease.
Ovarian Cancer	45%	Over 15,500 women	Family history, obesity, childlessness, use of estrogen as hormone replacement therapy and use of talcum powder in the genital area are risk factors.
Leukemia	50%	21,700	Exposure to high levels of radiation and to certain chemicals, such as benzene and some chemotherapy drugs, increase risk.
Colorectal Cancer	64%	50,000	Nine of 10 cases occur in people over age 50. Mortality higher among long-term smokers than nonsmokers.
Non-Hodgkin's Lymphoma	79%	Over 19,000	Can occur at any age. Risk factors largely unknown.
Breast Cancer	89%	40,500 women	Five to 10 percent of breast cancers are inherited. Having more than two alcoholic drinks daily, being overweight and having extra fat at the waist increase risk.
Prostate Cancer	99%	28,600	Two out of three cancers occur in men over age 65. Eating large amounts of red meat or high-fat dairy products increases risk.

Source: National Cancer Institute

Cancer prevention can make a huge difference, experts insist. For example, ending smoking "could cut the cancer burden by 30 percent," says Gerald N. Wogan, a professor emeritus of chemistry at the Massachusetts Institute of Technology.

In fact, U.S. smoking rates have been declining for about two decades, but the rate of decline has slowed recently. In 2007, the percentage of people over 18 who smoke dropped below 20 percent — to 19.8 percent, amounting to about 43 million smokers — for the first time since at least the 1960s. But the percentage of high school students who smoked remained constant, at 20 percent, between 2003 to 2007. [5]

But prevention continues to receive fewer funds and less attention than treatment, say many experts. Prevention-related findings routinely are ignored for years after evidence emerges, says Samuel Epstein, professor emeritus of environmental and occupational medicine at the University of Illinois School of Public Health.

For example, the National Cancer Institute (NCI) waited until 2002 to declare that hormone-replacement therapy raised women's cancer risks, although at least a decade's worth of earlier studies strongly suggested the connection, he says. And as early as 1994, research strongly linked talcum powder use to lethal ovarian cancer, especially in black women, but the Food and Drug Administration (FDA) "ignored it," he says. "Today the evidence of the connection is overwhelming," but in the United States, "the idea is, if you get cancer, it's your own fault" for smoking or eating fatty foods, and manufactured products aren't to blame.

Meanwhile, recent drug-development research has swallowed up billions of dollars and years of scientists' time while producing relatively few results, says Guy B. Faguet, author of the 2008 book *The War on Cancer* and a professor emeritus of medicine at the Medical College of Georgia. The World

Health Organization lists 17 cancer drugs that really make a difference, "and they were all developed before 1970," he says.

In addition, science has "fads and fashions, mostly driven by technology," says Wogan. And thanks to new, lightning-fast gene-sequencing technology, "genetics is everything" is the fashion today, while research on prevention-related questions — such as how cancer-promoting substances or processes (carcinogens) interact with cells to cause cancer — is being "left by the wayside."

Tobacco has been the subject of the highest-profile debate over carcinogens. But some environmental-health experts say cancerous changes in our cells result from a lifetime of mostly low-level exposure to a variety of substances, including many industrial chemicals, and that U.S. law takes this too lightly.

"A growing body of evidence from both human and animal models indicates that exposure of fetuses, young children and adolescents to radiation and environmental chemicals puts them at considerably higher risk for later-life breast cancer diagnosis," according to the Breast Cancer Fund. Furthermore, the rising incidence of breast cancer after World War II "paralleled the proliferation of synthetic chemicals," says the group. [6]

Many other countries take a more cautious approach to potential carcinogens, says Richard Clapp, a professor of environmental health at the Boston University School of Public Health. The World Health Organization's International Agency for Research on Cancer (IARC) issues a consensus listing of more than 100 substances that cause cancer in humans. "A third of the substances are industrial in origin," and many European governments limit the use of all items on the list, "since we now understand that long-term low-dose exposure" — generally construed as harmless by U.S. regulatory agen-

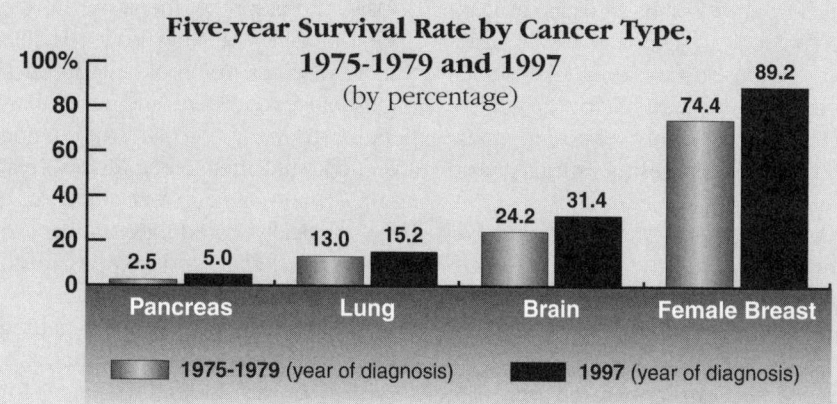

Cancer Survival Rates Steadily Increasing

The five-year survival rates for many types of cancer have increased from three decades ago. Breast cancer had one of the largest increases: jumping 14.8 points, from 74.4 percent to 89.2 percent.

Five-year Survival Rate by Cancer Type, 1975-1979 and 1997
(by percentage)

	Pancreas	Lung	Brain	Female Breast
1975-1979 (year of diagnosis)	2.5	13.0	24.2	74.4
1997 (year of diagnosis)	5.0	15.2	31.4	89.2

Source: Surveillance, Epidemiology and End Results Program, National Cancer Institute

cies — can actually have a cumulative carcinogenic effect, he says.

"In the workplace, we have [Occupational Safety and Health Administration] lists of carcinogens, but we aren't enforcing them," Clapp says. The new science of "green chemistry" — which seeks to develop less toxic compounds and processes — can develop non-carcinogenic substitutes for toxic chemicals, he says. "It's not like life will fall apart if we don't use trichloroethylene to clean oily parts."

But others argue that lifestyle causes — like cigarette smoking — remain the real cancer threat and that most of the to-do over potential industrial carcinogens is misplaced.

"Some environmental pollutants, like pesticides, have been shown to induce cancer in laboratory animals at high doses, but they pose little risk to most people because of very low concentrations in air, land or water," said the American Institute for Cancer Research (AICR). And while "some workers come into regular contact with known carcinogens, such as asbestos, nickel, cadmium, uranium, radon, vinyl chloride, and benzene . . . it is important to re-

member that the vast majority of Americans are not exposed" to these risks. [7]

Besides preventive efforts, finding cancers early, when they can be cut out surgically or killed by drugs and radiation more easily than later-stage cancers, is crucial for future progress, many scientists say. Like prevention, however, screening has been less of a focus than treatment.

It's now known that every cancer contains a multitude of mutated genes, which means the war on cancer will be "more of a guerrilla war" than previously thought, said Kinzler. "The best long-term strategy may be early detection of tumors, when the number of guerrilla warriors is still small and more easily handled." [8]

At present, Americans don't do a very good job of detecting cancers early, says University of Chicago professor of medicine Richard L. Schilsky, chairman of the country's oldest National Cancer Institute-sponsored clinical-trials group, the Cancer and Leukemia Group. For example, only about half of the Americans who should be screened for colon cancer are screened, even though early detection is known to decrease mortality for colon cancer, says Schilsky, president of the American Society of Clinical Oncology (ASCO).

But others warn that much screening is imperfect and carries its own risks. Mammography screening "finds too many cancers," for example, said H. Gilbert Welch, a professor of medicine at Dartmouth Medical School in New Hampshire. "Because doctors don't know which cancers will be harmful, we treat all of them," unnecessarily exposing some women to disfiguring surgery and chemotherapy side effects. [9]

As lawmakers, physicians and patient groups mull the future of cancer control, here are some of the questions being asked:

Are we screening enough people for cancer?

Many experts insist that screening more patients for cancer would save lives and money. But there's reason to believe that some widespread screening is picking up conditions that aren't dangerous.

Early detection is vital for two reasons: Surgery can cure some early-stage cancers, unlike drug treatment and radiation, which only delay cancer's progress. Moreover, in later stages cancers have accumulated genetic mutations that increase their ability to evade both drug treatments and the body's own defenses, says Johns Hopkins' Kinzler.

Although current screening methods cannot catch all or most cancers, screening is still "a conceptually viable" way to control cancer, because improved screening methods likely will emerge from the human genome database, according to Faguet at the Medical College of Georgia. [10]

Responsibility falls on primary-care doctors to screen for cancer and all other diseases, but sparse communication among medical specialties makes that difficult, says the University of Chicago's Schilsky. "It's not as easy as you'd like" to get up-to-date screening recommendations, since there is no one-stop shop that covers cancer

and all the other diseases primary-care physicians should screen for, he says.

Nationwide screening for colon cancer beginning at age 55 would save at least two dollars for every dollar it costs, according to Scott Tenner, an associate professor of medicine at the State University of New York's Health Sciences Center in Brooklyn. But lack of insurance coverage and other barriers keep many people from being screened until they enter Medicare at age 65, when cancers that could have been surgically cured have advanced to become lethal and expensive to treat, he said. [11]

But Medicare patients aren't getting recommended screenings either, according to the federal Agency for Healthcare Research and Quality. For example, from 1998-2004, only 25 percent received colorectal cancer screenings, the agency said. [12]

And screening tests are desperately needed for other big killers, some of which are considerably more deadly and rarer — such as pancreatic cancer — than cancers that we have screening tests for, says A. William Blackstock, Jr., an associate professor of radiation oncology at the Wake Forest University School of Medicine. "If you catch a disease late, there's not much you can ever do about it," and lack of screening methods mean lethal diseases like pancreatic cancer are virtually always caught late, he says.

Nevertheless, the rate of cancer screening has increased enormously over the past few decades. For example, mortality from cervical cancer declined long ago in the United States, largely because of widespread screening with Pap tests, which began in the 1950s, says John Bailar, a former chief of the NCI's demography section.

But some physicians warn that aggressive screening is not a panacea, because screening methods can't fully distinguish between deadly and benign tumors. For every 1,000 women who have regular mammography screening

over a 10-year period, one woman will live longer because a cancer was detected at a treatable state, but five others will receive unnecessary cancer treatment, according to an analysis of international data. [13]

"Whether this is too high a price to pay is open to debate," but women and policy makers should consider it as they make decisions, the authors wrote. [14]

Prostate-cancer screening based on finding PSA — prostate specific antigen — in men's blood has a similar statistical picture, according to Thomas A. Stamey, a professor emeritus of urology at the Stanford University School of Medicine. "It's immoral for surgeons not to tell patients that we [men] all get prostate cancer as we age," said Stamey, who, at age 76, said he hadn't been screened for several years. "Do we really want to screen 100,000 men to save 226 from dying of prostate cancer?" he asked. "It's about the same chance of my not driving home safely tonight." [15]

"The media have taken it on ourselves to promote everybody getting screened for everything," believing that's the right public-health message, says medical journalist Shannon Brownlee, author of *Overtreated: Why Too Much Medicine Is Making Us Sicker and Poorer.* In international comparisons, U.S. survival rates for some cancers — such as a 99 percent five-year survival rate for prostate cancer — "make us look like geniuses," says Brownlee. But "if you're treating a lot of things that didn't need to be treated [in the first place], of course people are going to survive."

And screening doesn't always lengthen lives. In a 2007 study of computed tomography (CT) scanning of current and former smokers, researchers from New York's Memorial Sloan-Kettering Cancer Center found nearly three times as many lung cancers as predicted but also found that the early detection and treatment "did not lead to a corresponding decrease in advanced lung cancers or a reduction in deaths." [16]

In fact, too much screening for all kinds of ills actually is raising our cancer risk, says Brownlee. Increasingly, physicians order CT scans for many medical complaints and even to pick up hidden ills in healthy people. Within the next few years, "Americans will be getting 100 million scans a year, and each is one hell of a dose of radiation" — at least 100 times a chest X-ray, says Brownlee. "It's very clear that we are causing cancer."

Are too few resources devoted to cancer prevention?

Critics say prevention has long been downplayed by the cancer establishment, even though organizations like the American Cancer Society and the NCI insist they are just as serious about preventing cancer as they are in treating it, citing efforts to stamp out cigarette smoking as an example of prevention programs.

"We very firmly believe in prevention," says Christy Schmidt, senior director for policy of the society's Cancer Action Network.

In fact, interest in cancer prevention research appears to be increasing as health-care costs continue to rise, said a 2007 report from the President's Cancer Panel, a group of experts that monitors the cancer landscape. For example, larger employers and some state and local governments are devising and implementing "wellness programs," including such cancer-prevention activities as smoking cessation and exercise classes. [17]

Moreover, 21st-century research that highlights cancer's complexities has intensified the focus on prevention — including environmental factors — say some cancer researchers. [18] In the past, "everybody was convinced cancer was genetic and assumed it came from what you were born with," says H. Kim Lyerly, director of Duke University's Comprehensive Cancer Center. Scientists assumed that identical twins, for instance, would be susceptible to

> ### Smoking Is the Biggest Cause of Cancer
>
> *Scientists agree that smoking is the single, biggest cause of cancer. In addition to lung cancer, smoking significantly increases the risk for pancreas, stomach, kidney and bladder cancer.*
>
> ### *Smoking. . . .*
>
> Causes more than a quarter of cancer deaths in developed countries.
>
> Will kill around half of current smokers if they continue to smoke, including up to 40 percent of them in middle age.
>
> Causes 9 in 10 cases of lung cancer.
>
> Causes two out of three cases of bladder cancer in men and one in three in women.
>
> Doubles the risk of kidney cancer.
>
> Is the only preventable cause of pancreatic cancer.
>
> Causes about one in five cases of stomach cancer.
>
> *Source: Cancer Research UK*

cancer in exactly the same way, he says. "Then it turned out that it was only a 10-15 percent chance," he says.

Thus, the environment — ranging from chemicals in the air and water to differing hormone levels in the body — accounts for the other 85-90 percent of cancer risk, Lyerly says. And since many environmental factors are avoidable, this new knowledge has led scientists to focus heavily on prevention, he says.

"We already have enough data to be able to say that a third of cancers could be prevented with healthy eating, weight management and exercise and another third with stopping tobacco use," says AICR nutrition education consultant Karen Collins.

Yet, prevention efforts can take a long time to pay off. Recent improved cancer mortality and incidence numbers are the fruit of prevention efforts long in the pipeline, physicians point out. For example, smoking-cessation efforts launched in the 1970s have finally paid off with fewer cancer cases in 2008, according to the latest numbers, says Black-

stock at Wake Forest. But many analysts say that if significant new strides are to be made, prevention efforts must be greatly enhanced.

Bailar, the former head of the NCI's demography section, says an unbiased review of new cancer mortality statistics reveals a pattern: The improvement in cancer death rates is more related to prevention and early detection than to cancer treatment, even though research funding has traditionally run about four to one the other way.

Prevention and detection have long been "the poor stepsisters" of cancer medicine, says Bailar. When he started out in cancer research in the mid-1950s, he says, "the interest was moving to treatment, and it's been there ever since."

Prevention research funding "is still quite limited" compared with support for research on detection and treatment, the President's Cancer Panel said in 2007. Especially lacking is research on how to help people change unhealthy behaviors and how policy changes — such as city planning —

Funding for Cancer Outpaces Other Diseases

Cancer researchers at the National Cancer Institute will receive nearly twice as much in 2009 as researchers for infectious diseases, such as tuberculosis and HIV-AIDS.

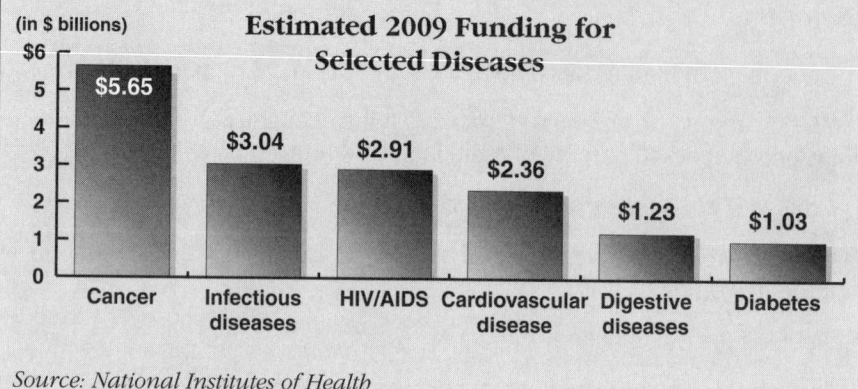

Estimated 2009 Funding for Selected Diseases

(in $ billions)

- Cancer: $5.65
- Infectious diseases: $3.04
- HIV/AIDS: $2.91
- Cardiovascular disease: $2.36
- Digestive diseases: $1.23
- Diabetes: $1.03

Source: National Institutes of Health

could get people to exercise more, the group said. [19]

In addition, many millions of Americans — especially low-paid and part-time workers, the uninsured and minorities — continue to lack access to wellness services like smoking-cessation programs, said the panel. [20]

And as for exposure to workplace carcinogens, the federal Occupational Safety and Health Administration (OSHA) specifies what substances are carcinogenic and at what levels and can legally limit workers' exposure, "but we haven't been using those tools," says Boston University's Clapp.

Anti-tobacco efforts also could go much further, says Ross Brownson, co-director of the Prevention Research Center at the Saint Louis University School of Public Health. States such as California and Massachusetts have seen smoking rates plummet in response to strong anti-smoking programs, he says. "But we haven't had a national strategy."

In the late 1990s, when the tobacco industry settled two landmark lawsuits brought by the states, the $246 billion settlement was intended to fund model anti-smoking initiatives nationwide, he says. "But the money ultimately didn't go where it was sup-posed to go," funding roads and other priorities instead, Brownson says. [21]

The AICR would like to see indus-tries finance more research on cancer risk. For example, "the meat industry has a lot at stake" in knowing exactly what it is about red meat that causes its consumption to increase the con-sumer's risk of developing cancer, says Collins. For instance, it may be the form of iron, called heme iron, that reddens the meat, she says. And do less-studied meats, such as bison, pose the same risks as beef? she asks. "This is an area where we've thought that private orga-nizations might step forward and rec-ommend cooking meats in a certain way" to cut carcinogens, she says.

Chemoprevention, a more contro-versial form of prevention, may forestall development of cancer in high-risk peo-ple. Some chemoprevention drugs have been discovered — such as tamoxifen and raloxifene for women at high risk for breast cancer — but "are not wide-ly used," says the University of Chica-go's Schilsky. More research is needed to profile the highest-risk people, he says, since "it's probably not cost ef-fective" to use the drugs for a broad population because they must be taken for many years.

But critics say chemoprevention is oversold. Breast cancer takes 12 to 15 years to develop, and research estab-lishing chemoprevention as a successful therapy lasted no more than five years, making it unclear whether the drugs actually prevent breast cancer "or mere-ly delay its onset," said Maryann Napoli, associate director of the New York City-based Center for Medical Con-sumers, which disseminates evaluations of medical treatments.

Trials involving women believed to be at high risk for breast cancer showed that 1.7 percent developed breast can-cer during the five-year trial of the chemoprevention drug if they took a drug while 3.4 percent of those who didn't take the drug developed can-cer. With such low numbers of sup-posedly high-risk women developing cancer even without the preventive therapy, more research is needed to determine who is at high risk, partic-ularly since the drugs can raise the risk of uterine cancer, blood clots and strokes, said Napoli. [22]

Have we paid too little attention to carcinogens in the environment?

Exposure to carcinogens likely con-tributes to many if not all cancers. Car-cinogens range from those outside the body — such as chemicals or radia-tion — to those inside, such as hor-mones or physical changes that occur when organs suffer inflammation.

But debate has long raged over how heavily to focus on possible triggers such as industrial chemicals, largely because tracing environmental causes is an un-certain business, leaving regulators to make decisions based on inconclusive data.

"There are a lot of people who have a vested interest in not looking at the environment issue" because chemical use by industries permeates modern life, says Alice Shabecoff, co-author with her husband, former *New York Times* environment reporter Philip Shabecoff, of *Poisoned Profits: The Toxic Assault on Our Children.*

"It is not a coincidence that the decrease in carcinogen-control regulations, studies and government publications corresponds to the rapid shrinkage of the United States' industrial workforce and . . . trade unions" because industry advocacy, not science, has convinced the government to back off, said Jeanne Mager Stellman, professor of environmental and occupational health sciences at the State University of New York's Downstate Medical Center in Brooklyn. [23]

But fears that regulating carcinogenic substances will drive companies out of business are overblown, Shabecoff says. "When toxics are found, why can't you just make a different kind of product?" she asks. For every product with toxic ingredients, "we found another comparable product that doesn't have them," proving that it can be done, she says.

For example, while many deodorants have been found to contain potentially toxic chemicals called phthalates, a few commercial products, such as Dove Powder Anti-Perspirant Deodorant and Lady Speed Stick Soft Anti-Perspirant, do not, according to the University of Illinois' Epstein. [24]

Currently, many U.S. companies are reformulating products to meet tough, new European Union standards for chemical toxicity (see p. 39).

In the United States, when concerns are raised that a product or process contributes to cancer, many industries routinely respond by funding research to raise doubts about the finding, says David Michaels, a research professor of environmental and occupational health at The George Washington University School of Public Health. "How ridiculous can it get? There is widespread agreement in the scientific community that broad-spectrum ultraviolet radiation, whether from sunlight or from tanning lamps, causes skin cancer," he wrote. "Yet trade associations representing the indoor tanning industry have attempted to derail the 'cancer-causing' designation by questioning the scientific evidence." [25]

Industry-sponsored research is "strongly associated with pro-industry conclusions," according to Michaels. For example, in studies of lung-cancer risk for workers exposed to beryllium — a lightweight metal often combined with other metals to strengthen them — "three government-funded analyses find an elevated risk while the one industry-funded analysis . . . does not." [26]

Moreover, recent research has shown that cancer-causing agents combine their effects in unknown ways, says Boston University's Clapp, undercutting the argument that the carcinogenic effect of one chemical can be ignored because its individual cancer-causing effect appears small. For example, someone exposed to tobacco smoke or asbestos may have a 10-times greater risk of developing cancer than someone exposed to neither, he says, but someone exposed to both has a 55-times greater risk. Thus, even agents that don't increase cancer risk significantly on their own may interact with other exposures to greatly increase risk and should be considered carcinogenic, Clapp says.

Industry advocates say if a chemical is found to cause cancer only in large doses, it shouldn't be banned if most people are exposed only to small amounts at a time. But that argument doesn't hold water, said French virologist Luc Montagnier, winner of the 2008 Nobel Prize for medicine, since over time people develop an "accumulation of these doses — they all add up. A little dose of radiation here, and exposure to some chemical there, a little bit of something in your food and so on. . . . All of this adds up to create an oxidant field, and it's the totality of this field which does all the damage and may bring about a cancer." [27]

Testing chemicals for their carcinogenic effects lags woefully behind industrial developments, according to James Huff, associate director for chemical carcinogenesis at the National Institute of Environmental Health Sciences. The U.S. National Toxicology Program (NTP), established in 1978, has tested about 600 chemicals — 0.6 percent of chemicals on the market — for carcinogenesis and found nearly half to have some carcinogenic properties, he wrote. Likewise, the International Agency for Research on Cancer has tested about 950 chemicals and found about 100 to be carcinogenic and more than 300 probably or possibly carcinogenic. [28]

"The number of chemicals that have not yet been tested is staggering," and thousands enter the marketplace every year, Huff said. "We live in a chemical soup," he pointed out, while the NTP initiates, at most, only about five new bioassays per year. "We must test more chemicals for carcinogenicity than are currently being evaluated." [29]

But others aren't convinced that industry-related carcinogens are something to worry about. Bailar, the former chief of the NCI's demography section, is skeptical about apparent increases in childhood cancers, which some advocates blame on industrial products. He cites a "cautionary tale" from Japan, where concern rose in the 1980s about apparent increases in neuroblastoma in infants. But a government program that apparently found and treated "a lot of cancers" ended up having "no detectable effect on mortality rates," raising serious questions about whether the cancer epidemic actually existed in the first place, he says.

The NCI says it already pays adequate attention to the issue. The National Institutes of Health (NIH) will spend $705 million on breast-cancer research in fiscal 2008, including nearly $100 million on the role of the environment in breast-cancer development, according to the testimony of

Deborah Winn, associate director of NCI's epidemiology and genetics research program, before the House Energy and Commerce Health Subcommittee last May. [30]

Industries deny that they deliberately try to raise doubts about whether their substances cause cancer. Cleveland-based beryllium manufacturer Brush Wellman denies it's ever sought to downplay the health risks associated with its product. The company "first put warning labels on its products and sent letters to all of its customers warning them of . . . potential health hazards . . . in 1949" and continues to evaluate the potential exposure risks, wrote Marc Kolanz, a certified industrial hygienist employed by the company. [31]

Others say lifestyle-related behaviors, such as smoking and lack of exercise, are so significant that any potential carcinogenic effects of environmental chemicals are trivial by comparison. "Chemicals in our food and the environment do not have a significant impact on overall cancer risk in the United States," said Elizabeth M. Whelan, president of the American Council on Science and Health, a nonprofit science-information group that has frequently taken pro-industry stances. "Most cancers are related to lifestyle factors." [32]

The American Institute for Cancer Research, which studies the effect of diet and lifestyle on cancer, agrees that Americans greatly overestimate the health threats of industrial factors such as pesticides and electric power lines. "Scientists do have a good idea about which factors increase cancer risk," says the institute. "Yet they aren't the factors many people associate with cancer."

For example, an AICR survey found that 71 percent of Americans believed pesticide residues are a factor in cancer incidence, even though "there is no proven link between pesticide residues on produce and cancer occurrence." [33]

BACKGROUND

'War on Cancer'

Hope that science could defeat cancer surged in the 1960s, when the United States vowed to put humans on the moon by decade's end.

Leading the campaign ever since her husband Albert died of colon cancer in 1952 was New York philanthropist Mary Lasker. Her coalition of cancer activists persistently urged federal officials to launch an all-out government effort to find a cure. Lasker was able to finance her medical advocacy using the fortune her husband had amassed in advertising. Considered the father of modern advertising, Lasker, ironically, was the brains behind the Lucky Strike cigarette ad campaign "Reach for a Lucky instead of a sweet" — possibly the first ad to specifically target women to buy cigarettes, a major carcinogen. [34]

Mrs. Lasker's persistent advocacy efforts culminated in December 1969 — five months after U.S. astronaut Neil Armstrong became the first human to walk on the moon — when her Citizens Committee for the Conquest of Cancer ran a full-page *New York Times* ad imploring President Richard M. Nixon with the boldface headline: "Mr. Nixon: You Can Cure Cancer."

At the time, little was known about cancer's cellular and genetic bases. But faith in what science could accomplish was running high, and the ad boasted, "America can do this." It continued: "Dr. Sidney Farber, past president of the American Cancer Society, believes: 'We are so close to a cure for cancer. We lack only the will and the kind of money and comprehensive planning that went into putting a man on the moon.' 'Why don't we try to conquer cancer by America's 200th birthday?" [35]

The advocates got their way. Just two years later, on Dec. 23, 1971, Nixon signed the National Cancer Act, saying it could be "the most significant action taken during this administration." Nixon and the U.S. Congress declared a "war on cancer," and ever since then heroic rhetoric has all but promised a pharmaceutical cure for cancer was just around the corner.

But while federal funding for cancer research has consistently outstripped spending on other diseases — $5.65 billion for cancer research at the NIH in 2009, for example, compared to $2.9 billion for HIV/AIDS and $2.4 billion for cardiovascular disease — cancer mortality statistics have barely budged. [36]

Losing the War

Declaring "recent advances in the knowledge of this dread disease" offered great opportunity, the National Cancer Act authorized large funding increases for the NCI. Patient advocates recommended breaking the institute out of NIH entirely — to free researchers from what some considered a stifling bureaucracy. While lawmakers rejected that radical notion, they gave the NCI's director unprecedented authority to submit annual budget requests directly to the president, rather than to the NIH.

Advocates and lawmakers who had backed the legislation were thrilled. But most of the scientists in the audience at the bill-signing ceremony "did not smile," said one observer. "The hoopla . . . implied the conquest of cancer in the near future because a couple of hundred million dollars a year more were to be channeled into cancer research. Those of us who knew the 'state of the art' had cause to worry." [37]

The worriers had it right, but they were drowned out by the misplaced enthusiasm and "self delusion," says the Medical College of Georgia's Faguet.

Continued on p. 36

Chronology

1930s-1960s
Research intensifies on using drugs to treat cancer along with radiation and surgery; chemotherapy helps reduce mortality from so-called liquid cancers like leukemia.

1937
Congress establishes National Cancer Institute (NCI) as an independent agency to research the causes and treatment of cancer.

1938
Science publishes an article showing non-smokers live a decade longer than smokers.

1939
Hormones are found to spur the growth of certain cancers.

1943
The "Pap" test is introduced for screening for cervical cancer, leading to an eventual 75 percent drop in U.S. deaths from cervical cancer.

1944
NCI is incorporated into the National Institutes of Health.

1946
A cousin of the chemical-warfare agent mustard gas becomes the first effective chemotherapy.

1948
As smoking continues to rise in popularity, lung cancer is found to have increased five times faster than other cancers.

1959
NCI environmental cancer chief Wilhelm Hueper submits a 20-page chronicle of political efforts to quash his research.

1964
Surgeon general releases first report linking lung cancer and smoking.

1970s-1990s
Scientists find cancer is caused by gene mutations, some inherited but most due to interactions between human cells and their environment.

1971
President Richard M. Nixon declares a "war on cancer." . . . National Cancer Act of 1971 gives NCI $1.6 billion over three years. . . . Cigarette ads on the radio are banned.

1979
American Medical Association states for the first time that cigarette smoking harms the lungs but stops short of saying it causes cancer.

1980
National Toxicology Program publishes list of 25 chemicals that cause cancer or gene mutations.

1992
Environmental Protection Agency declares secondhand tobacco smoke a Class A carcinogen — the most dangerous type.

1994
The BRCA1 and BRCA2 "breast cancer" genes are identified.

1998
Clinton administration allows Medicare to pay for some experimental cancer treatments. . . . States get windfall after settling a lawsuit against tobacco companies, but little of the money funds smoking-cessation programs.

2000s
Researchers seek new drugs that only target cancerous cell molecules, eschewing chemotherapy's cell-killing approach. Individual patients' cancers differ far more than expected.

2001
Food and Drug Administration approves Novartis' Gleevec, one of the first drugs to target a cellular molecule — an enzyme that runs amok in chronic myeloid leukemia — rather than simply killing cancer cells.

2002
NCI Director Andrew von Eschenbach is accused of politicizing the institute after he deletes from an online fact sheet a statement that abortion does not increase the risk of breast cancer.

2003
The human genome is deciphered.

2004
A 50-year British study finds long-time smokers die 10 years earlier than non-smokers, but quitting at age 50 halves the extra risk.

2006
NIH launches project to map the DNA of all cancers.

2008
Researchers discover the gene profile of glioblastoma, the deadliest brain cancer. . . . African-Americans continue to fall behind whites in cancer mortality rates, due to poorer screening and treatment. . . . Long-term incense use is found to raise the risk of respiratory-tract cancers. . . . President-elect Barack Obama promises to increase the number of patients in clinical trials. . . . Vitamin D deficiency is found to contribute to many cancers.

How Treatment Hype Hurts Cancer Care

When hope trumps science, it can be painful and costly.

Exaggerated hopes for new cancer treatment can sometimes prove painful and costly to patients. Take the use of bone-marrow transplants, coupled with high-dose chemotherapy, for advanced breast cancer. Beginning in the late 1980s, some oncologists began prescribing the controversial treatment, which had worked with some other cancers, even though only one small study seemed to show an effect with breast cancer, while other evidence suggested the treatments might make patients sicker. But with few other therapies available, hope soon displaced caution. [1]

The expensive, painful treatment quickly became the rage among oncologists, the media, litigators and lawmakers, all of whom pushed insurers to cover the procedure as women's last, best hope. "Hope trumped science" and "politics trumped policy," wrote George C. Halvorson, CEO of Kaiser Permanente, the big managed-care organization, and George J. Isham, medical director of HealthPartners, an HMO based in Bloomington, Minn. "[G]ood-hearted lawmakers" and courts around the country required insurers to cover the procedure, they explained, despite warnings that clinical trials were needed to determine its effectiveness. [2]

As often happens, media coverage fueled enthusiasm, according to health writer Shannon Brownlee, a senior fellow at the nonpartisan New America Foundation think tank. "I looked at 1,000 stories," she says, and 90 percent portrayed the transplants as "women's last chance," framing the treatment as a Homeric epic with villains — the cancer and, eventually, insurance companies who refused to pay — a physician hero and a patient, suffering victim.

Entrepreneurship also played a role. Physicians and others set up local clinics to perform the therapy, further pressuring insurers to pay, says Richard A. Rettig, a co-author of the 2007 book *False Hope: Bone Marrow Transplantation for Breast Cancer.*

It was not the first time financial incentives trumped clinical judgment, said Guy B. Faguet, a professor emeritus of medicine at the Medical College of Georgia. For example, he said, when doctors own radiation facilities, radiotherapy use jumps 53 percent, charges rise 42 percent and consultation time between doctors and patients drops 18 percent, compared to the national average. [3]

Ironically, when clinical trials were launched to test the bone-marrow transplant idea, the existence of the trials themselves signaled clinicians that the treatment was worthwhile, says Rettig, encouraging even more doctors to offer it. And the rush to treat made it harder to recruit trial subjects: Women who knew they could get the treatment outside of the trials were reluctant to participate because they feared they might be placed in the no-treatment "control" section of the experiments, Rettig says.

By the mid-1990s the transplant frenzy led at least eight states to legally require insurers to cover the procedure. [4] In 1993, a California jury ordered the insurer HealthNet to pay cancer patient Nelene Fox $89 million for refusing coverage of the treatment. But in 1999, a large, definitive clinical trial found that the transplant/chemo combination treatment did not improve survival rates for breast cancer. And many women had suffered serious side effects, including heart failure, bone-marrow disease and even death.

Continued from p. 34

The cancer-research money pipeline opened up by the law has produced theory after theory that proponents hoped would quickly lead to highly effective treatments, if not cures. But none of these hypotheses led to significantly "more efficacious cancer management, and today the outcome of most cancer patients remains grim." [38]

For example, over the 30 years from 1973 to the early 1990s, the overall median survival rate for advanced lung cancer — the nation's biggest cancer killer — only edged up from 6.9 months to 7.3 months and the three-year survival rate after diagnosis rose from 2 percent to only 4 percent, said Faguet. "Since that time, no break-throughs occurred," he said. "The No. 1 cancer killer in the U.S. remains essentially unaffected" after more than 50 years of clinical drug trials and 35 years of the cancer war. [39]

Moreover, says Faguet, the media collude with scientists to oversell the idea that there's been progress. "Ninety-nine percent of the treatment ideas scientists try fall through, but the media don't want to report stories that say, 'You remember that big discovery we told you about five years ago? Well, in practice it doesn't work,' " he says.

The belief that effective cancer treatments are just around the corner has helped foster the notion that it's OK to stint on prevention, says Bailar, the former NCI demography chief.

"When I came out of medical school in 1955, a friend advised, 'Don't go to NCI. The problems they deal with are just about solved,' " Bailar recalls. In the intervening half-century, however, heart disease mortality has been "dropping like a rock" while cancer mortality has decreased only marginally. "Even where we have drugs that work, they don't work as well as you'd expect."

"A number of years ago, there was a great excitement over Gleevec" (chemical name, imatinib) — one of the first of the new breed of drugs that target specific molecules that help cancer cells proliferate rather than simply killing dividing cells, he says. But while Gleevec has been successful with some cancers, such as a form of

By then at least 42,000 women had received the treatment, not including those in the clinical trials, at a total cost — at $80,000 per patient — of more than $3 billion.

Despite the costly bone-marrow transplant debacle, some cancer researchers and oncologists are optimistic that 21st-century cancer science — including understanding of genetic changes and molecular mechanisms — has advanced to the point where optimistic predictions about successful cancer treatments are no longer hype but reality. Food and Drug Administration chief Andrew von Eschenbach, who served as director of the National Cancer Institute (NCI) for four years, said in 2005 the institute had "committed itself [to] eliminate the suffering and death" caused by cancer by 2015. [5]

But other analysts caution that such grand visions can be more of a danger than a help in cancer medicine. "Some people with visions are hallucinating," says Paul Goldberg, editor of *The Cancer Letter*, a medical newsletter. When it comes to cancer science, "sometimes the worst thing you can have is somebody with a vision."

In fact, points out Goldberg's wife Kirsten — publisher of the newsletter — von Eschenbach's "grandiose vision" actually crippled the NCI by shifting the focus to "far-out things like nanotechnology" while shortchanging approaches that might have borne more fruit.

"A visit to the annual [American Society of Clinical Oncology] meeting will convince one how desperate we are for any sign, no matter how minor, that a treatment might work," said Joseph V. Simone, a professor emeritus of pediatrics and medicine at the University of Utah, referring to how oncologists grasp at even the slimmest hint that a new treatment might work. "We share our patients' desperation, but we do them no favor by adopting unproven therapies as the standard of care." [6]

Rettig favors a new partnership between the NCI, patient-advocacy groups and insurers that would issue formal public statements about which experimental treatments need clinical-trial evaluation. Insurers would then fund the clinical trials, promising to cover whatever procedures are proved safe and effective. Such a move, Rettig says, would protect insurers from the kinds of lawsuits they faced over bone-marrow transplants.

[1] For background, see Michelle M. Mello and Troyen A. Brennan, "The Controversy Over High-Dose Chemotherapy With Autologous Bone Marrow Transplant for Breast Cancer," *Health Affairs*, September/October 2001, pp. 101-117.

[2] George C. Halvorson and George J. Isham, *Epidemic of Care; A Call for Safer, Better, and More Accountable Health Care* (2003), p. 58.

[3] Guy B. Faguet, *The War on Cancer: An Anatomy of Hope, A Blueprint for Failure* (2008), p. 122.

[4] Kristianna Pettibone, Lisa Lineberger and Regina el Arculli, "State Legislative Mandates for Insurance Coverage of Breast Cancer Treatment Services," paper presented at the annual research meeting of the Academy for Health Services Research and Policy, June 23, 2002, www.scld-nci.net/presentations/breastcancer020623.pdf.

[5] Andrew von Eschenbach, "Eliminating the Suffering and Death Due to Cancer by 2015," *Medical Progress Bulletin*, Manhattan Institute, September 2005, www.manhattan-institute.org/pdf/mpb_01.pdf.

[6] Joseph V. Simone, "A Cautionary Tale," "Simone's OncOpinion" column, *Oncology Times*, July 10, 2007, p. 11.

leukemia and some stomach tumors, it hasn't turned out to be as broadly applicable as many observers initially expected, he says.

Furthermore, cancer is now understood to be not one but hundreds, perhaps thousands, of different diseases. "You'd need 150 Gleevecs just for breast cancer," says Paul Goldberg, editor of the Washington, D.C.-based *Cancer Letter*. "And there aren't going to be a hundred Gleevecs."

"That's the story of cancer," says Bailar. "We've spent 50 years with the best scientific talent working hard to find cures, and we're still floundering around. At a certain point, don't you need to say there's probably nothing magic out there waiting to be discovered?"

Environmental Consciousness

Even among cancer researchers who favor prevention, sparring has persisted for decades over whether environmental factors unique to the industrial age — such as radiation and synthetic chemicals — have received enough attention as potential causes.

Some of the earliest cancer research targeted environmental exposures. In the 18th century, Italian physician Bernardino Ramazzini noted the low incidence of cervical cancer and the relatively high incidence of breast cancer among nuns. The observation eventually led to the discovery that a sexually transmitted virus — human papillomavirus — caused most cervical cancer and that breast cancer was related to levels of a woman's own hormones. [40] In the same century, British physician Percival Potts described a cancer that afflicted London's chimney sweeps after soot collected under their scrotums, while his countryman, John Hill, linked tobacco smoking to cancer.

But while research on cancer treatments stirs up outsized hype and hopes — including researchers' dreams of fortune and fame — prevention studies have long been dogged by industry and government concerns that important substances or activities would be deemed carcinogenic.

Continued on p. 39

New Findings Raise New Questions

Genetics and therapeutic vaccines reveal new complexities.

New findings in genetics and the inner workings of cells may hold promise for major advances in cancer therapy, but the new findings also point to previously unimagined complexities in one of humanity's most feared diseases.

"We are the first generation who has read our genetic code, and it's been known for only four years," says Kenneth W. Kinzler, a professor of oncology at the Johns Hopkins University School of Medicine who researches the genetic basis of cancer. That means "we now have the road map of the enemy," he says. "So though we've been waging the war on cancer since 1972, this is a unique time" for cancer science, Kinzler says.

Not all the hot science is genetic, though.

For example, some scientists are pursuing so-called therapeutic vaccines — aimed at boosting a patient's immune system to fight cancer — based on a long-proposed but still highly controversial theory that cancers arise in our bodies repeatedly but are mostly rejected before they grow. The theory is bolstered by the fact that people with AIDS and other immunosuppressive conditions develop more cancers.

To date, however, "no therapeutic vaccines have been approved by the Food and Drug Administration," says Jeffrey Schlom, head of the National Cancer Institute (NCI) immunotherapeutics group.

Nevertheless, therapeutic vaccines are working in at least some patients, Schlom says.

Vaccinations against infectious diseases like the flu inject minute amounts of disease proteins into the body, triggering an immune system response to destroy the invaders. Some scientists think the same thing could be done with cancer. Earlier experiments, however, in which highly concentrated tumor proteins were injected into a cancer patient did not work, says Schlom. But more recent studies have found that if the immune system is revved up by injecting, for instance, a touch of smallpox virus (which a previously inoculated patient's body will already recognize) along with the tumor protein, the immune system *does* act against the cancer, Schlom says.

"It's the difference between just jumping and jumping on a trampoline" — keeping the immune system highly active to enhance its natural anti-tumor activity, he says.

Therapeutic vaccines will not work with advanced tumors or fast-moving cancers because the immune system's anti-tumor response is too subdued, even when enhanced, Schlom says. "But we can pick out those patients who have more indolent disease, and they'll benefit more from vaccines than from chemotherapy" and also avoid chemotherapy's painful side effects, he says. Recent vaccine trials in prostate cancer, for example, show increased survival for patients who get the vaccine, he says.

In the realm of cancer genetics, scientists discovered about a decade ago that women who inherited certain mutated forms of two genes — dubbed BRCA1 and BRCA2 — had greatly increased risk of developing breast or ovarian cancer.

Today, thousands of women undergo genetic screening to find out whether they have inherited mutated genes. Some women learn that they have mutations known to be harmful — and can then decide whether to take drugs or have surgery to ward off potential cancers. But many find themselves in a more perplexing category. They have mutations — sometimes ones that haven't even been seen before — but no one knows whether the gene variants they carry raise cancer risks or not.

"It's a matter of life or death," but the information gained through genetic screening often doesn't bring a doctor nearer to knowing whether the patient has increased cancer risk, says Shyam Sharan, head of the NCI's Genetics of Cancer Susceptibility Section.

That's where Sharan's mouse genetics laboratory comes in handy.

"In humans you look at the tumor and see hundreds of thousands of changes" in the DNA, but "you don't know what was the initial thing" in the chain of cancer causation, says Sharan. But thanks to advances in gene technology, biologists can place a mutated human gene into mice and see the result. In the mouse, "you can change things one at a time" and see what happens. Does the particular gene mutation "affect the normal development? Does it help the mouse survive a little longer?"

But cancer is not just a disease of genes but a disease of genes that have mutated through their interactions with the environment, says Gerald N. Wogan, a professor emeritus of chemistry at the Massachusetts Institute of Technology. Even identical twins — with identical gene profiles — don't develop the same cancers in most cases, for example.

For that reason, genetic studies "still will only leave us a catalog of what the changes are" in a cell that's turned cancerous but won't enlighten us on how and why those changes happen, says Wogan.

That's the realm of cancer-prevention research, at least in part, and it's changing, says Karen Collins, a nutrition education consultant to the American Institute for Cancer Research, which funds research on links between cancer and diet, physical activity and weight management.

For example, "There's a gene we all have, the tumor-suppression gene, and dietary changes can turn it on or off," says Collins. "That's leading prevention scientists to ask a startling question: What if the way you eat could change your genes? Ten years ago, that would have been so wild a thought that the question never would have been asked, but today it's a hot area."

Continued from p. 37

William Hueper, director of the NCI's environmental section from 1948 to 1964, was an early proponent of studying environmental links to cancer but was ultimately barred from pursuing some such studies because of concern his work would compromise advances in nuclear energy. [41]

Hueper launched a study of European uranium miners, who suffered high rates of lung cancer, but he was prevented from presenting his results about the uranium-cancer link to a medical-society meeting in 1952 after the federal Atomic Energy Commission objected. The NCI subsequently prevented him from conducting any further investigations into "the causation of cancer in man related to environmental exposure to carcinogenic chemical, physical, and parasitic agents," said Robert N. Proctor, a professor of the history of science at Stanford University. [42]

Many battles over government regulation of potential environmental carcinogens — which could cost industry or society significant amounts of money and inconvenience — turn on the question of what constitutes adequate scientific evidence to act.

"A 'known-to-be-a-human-carcinogen' determination should only be made if there is sufficient evidence of carcinogenicity from epidemiological studies that indicates a causal relationship between exposure to the . . . substance . . . and human cancer," said the American Chemistry Council, an industry group. "Mechanistic or other scientific informa-

Tour de France champion American Lance Armstrong is dramatic proof that cancer is no longer a death sentence for everyone. He was diagnosed in 1996 with testicular cancer that had spread to his lungs, abdomen and brain. After surgery and chemotherapy, he was declared cancer-free and returned to racing.

AFP/Getty Images/Jaime Reina

tion should not be used to bolster insufficient epidemiological evidence." [43]

Many environmental scientists disagree. Human epidemiological studies that definitively show a cause-effect link between environmental exposures and cancer are extremely difficult to carry out, they argue, so other types of evidence, such as animal studies, should also be considered.

In every case where epidemiological studies have followed up on rodent studies, the epidemiological research "has confirmed the mouse results," says the University of Illinois' Epstein. "I'm unaware of any mouse study in which there's contrary epidemiological data," he says. Furthermore, for reasons of funding and practicality, most rodent studies include relatively small numbers of animals. As a result, they are not very "sensitive" — they pick up only cancerous effects that are very large, affecting a large proportion of the population, Epstein says.

Industries' influence on epidemiological research to protect their financial interests has hurt the public, argues Devra Davis, director of the University of Pittsburgh Cancer Institute's Center for Environmental Oncology. In 1988, for example, Davis said Sir Richard Doll, a celebrated epidemiologist from Britain's Oxford University, showed that the industrial chemical vinyl chloride caused only fatal angiosarcoma of the liver, not several other cancers, as the World Health Organization's International Agency for Research on Cancer had believed.

"As a result of this analysis by an eminent authority, workers who developed the more common tumors of the brain, liver and lung after exposures to vinyl chloride . . . were not able to get compensation for them," Davis said. But 12 years later it was revealed that Doll may not have been "a disinterested expert," as he had claimed, but since 1979 had been paid $1,500 a day as a consultant to the giant chemical manufacturer Monsanto. [44]

Many European environmental regulators, unlike those in the United States, hew to the "precautionary principle" — that it's better to act against a potential cause of serious public or environmental harm rather than wait for scientific certainty. That's the principle behind the European Union's 2006 REACH (Registration, Evaluation, Authorization and Restriction of Chemicals) initiative, which requires manufacturers and importers to report to a central database detailed information about industrial substances used in their products and

Getting Drugs from the Lab to the Bedside

Rare forms of cancer face unique obstacles.

With a slew of technical and scientific issues confronting biomedical researchers, analysts say the focus of federal cancer programs should shift to clinical research in an effort to move effective treatments quickly from the laboratory to the bedside.

Both Congress and President-elect Barack Obama say they'll propose legislation this year to bolster clinical research — studies that explore whether a proposed treatment is safe and effective in human patients — a move most analysts say should be a top priority.

But other obstacles remain. For instance, clinical studies are especially difficult to arrange for rarer cancers, leading some patient-advocacy groups to create clinical-trial infrastructures of their own. For instance, the Multiple Myeloma Research Foundation was started in 1998 by Kathy Giusti, then an executive for the drug company G. D. Searle, who had just been diagnosed with multiple myeloma, a relatively rare cancer of the immune system. When Giusti, of New Canaan, Conn., learned no drugs for her condition were in the development pipeline, she used her knowledge of the drug industry to change that.

The foundation raises funds to support laboratories worldwide conducting multiple myeloma research and has established a consortium of 14 research institutions pursuing research cooperatively — a rarity in the biomedical research world, where competition for academic prestige and lucrative patents keeps most research proprietary.

The foundation's streamlined administrative setup — bolstered by a joint tissue bank and signed agreements by participants to operate transparently — has sped up early-stage clinical trials on priority therapies, says Anne Quinn Young, the foundation's program director for communication, education and outreach.

The foundation provides "an incredible brain trust" for mutual assistance and avoids duplication of effort, which is a special boon to smaller biotech companies, where therapies often originate but "who need whatever help they can get" to further the work, says Young. "We went from no therapies to four approvals by the Food and Drug Administration [FDA] in four years," and last year alone "we opened seven trials."

Once a drug appears to be effective, getting it developed also proves tricky. Normally, cancer drugs are approved to treat one cancer and then are used "off label" in quasi experimentation by physicians to treat other cancers, says Paul Goldberg, editor of *The Cancer Letter* newsletter. "But you can't do that any more because drugs cost too darn much" — $10,000 a month or more for some recently approved treatments. As a re-

sult, public and private insurers now demand specific FDA approval for a drug for any kind of cancer, he says.

Moreover, today's experimental treatments don't kill cancer cells as with older chemotherapy drugs but are designed to impede cells' ability to proliferate by targeting particular molecules or processes.

Thus, cancer researchers and the FDA are looking for quicker ways to show that a drug works rather than waiting to see whether patients who take it survive longer. But so far that quest has led mostly to confusion, according to an expert panel at a September conference at the Brookings Institution think tank in Washington, D.C.

"Measures of disease progression, health-related quality of life, patient-reported symptoms and biomarkers" — such as a protein in the blood that indicates a cancer has progressed to a certain stage — "have been proposed and tested in clinical studies, but consensus has not been reached on the role of these endpoints in determining the overall benefit of a therapy," the group said. [1]

Measuring whether a drug lengthens a patient's "time to progression" — the amount of time between when a patient enters a study and when his or her disease progresses to a more advanced stage — has become popular for measuring drug effectiveness. But, in fact, nobody understands how to gauge time to progression accurately and without bias, Goldberg says.

Two recent drug approvals — of the kidney-cancer drug sorafenib (brand-name Nexavar) and the breast-cancer drug bevacizumab (brand-name Avastin) — were based solely on evidence of lengthened time to progression, with no statistical evidence the drugs helped patients survive longer. That underscores the critical need to agree on how the endpoint is defined and interpreted, said the Brookings panel. [2]

Further complicating matters, scientists now know that cancer is many diseases and that cancers vary from one patient to another. So drug therapy will need to become a "personalized" treatment in which drugs are prescribed only for patients whose cancers match certain criteria. That would require the FDA to figure out how to approve both a drug and a test to determine whether the drug suits the patient.

So far, "Nobody understands how to do that," Goldberg says.

---

[1] Raymond DuBois, *et al.*, "Issue Brief," Conference on Clinical Cancer Research, September 2008.

[2] *Ibid.*

to progressively phase out those the European Chemicals Agency deems too dangerous.

Some cancer experts say Europe's "precautionary" model has merit. Ronald

B. Herberman, director of the University of Pittsburgh's Cancer Institute, cautioned university staff to use speakerphones or wireless headsets instead of cell phones and to limit children's

cell phone use to emergencies. While researchers haven't found a clear link between cell phone use and cancer, "at the heart of my concern is that we

Continued on p. 42

At Issue:

Should phthalates and bisphenol in plastics be restricted?

TED SCHETTLER
*SCIENCE DIRECTOR, SCIENCE AND
ENVIRONMENTAL HEALTH NETWORK*

FROM TESTIMONY BEFORE HOUSE SUBCOMMITTEE ON
COMMERCE, TRADE AND CONSUMER PROTECTION,
JUNE 10, 2008

*t*he chemicals being discussed today are in the bodies of virtually every American. They are in fetuses, infants and children. Phthalates are produced in large amounts and used in many consumer products, including construction materials, insect repellants, paints, cosmetics, personal-care products, air fresheners and others. In general, phthalates are not tightly bound in these products, and people are exposed when they use them or from general environmental contamination.

People are not exposed to single phthalates but rather to mixtures of these chemicals. It is essential to consider these exposures collectively when drawing conclusions about the risks associated with exposures to any particular phthalate. . . .

Studies from the Centers for Disease Control and Prevention show that exposure to bisphenol A is widespread in the general population. Ninety-three percent of people in the representative study population had detectable levels of bisphenol A in their urine. Fetuses and infants have markedly reduced capacity to transform the active form of bisphenol A into the inactive form excreted in the urine and so are at particular risk.

Health effects . . . include neurobehavioral changes, impacts on reproductive-system development and function, abnormal numbers of chromosomes in dividing cells, predisposition to cancer and insulin resistance as it is seen in diabetes.

Animal testing shows that low-level bisphenol A exposures during fetal development or infancy modify the development of the prostate gland and breast, permanently altering their tissue architecture in ways that predispose them to later disease, including cancer. In some cases, these changes are themselves precancerous. These abnormalities occur in animal studies at levels of exposure similar to those to which people in the general public are now exposed.

I urge you to think about this from a public health perspective and ask what amount or strength of evidence we should require before taking action to reduce or eliminate exposures to these chemicals, particularly in vulnerable populations. That is a public policy decision, which should be informed by good science, and also by values and common sense. Do we wait for irrefutable proof of harm in people before taking action?

The limits of epidemiological research will always make it difficult to tease out some cause-and-effect relationships, even when they exist. It is particularly difficult when the entire population is already exposed to chemicals of concern. But policy makers need to decide when evidence is sufficient to act, even in the face of scientific uncertainty.

MARIAN K. STANLEY
*SENIOR DIRECTOR, AMERICAN CHEMISTRY
COUNCIL*

FROM TESTIMONY BEFORE HOUSE SUBCOMMITTEE ON
COMMERCE, TRADE AND CONSUMER PROTECTION,
JUNE 10, 2008.

*p*hthalates are primarily used to make vinyl soft and flexible. Flexible vinyl products are used in our cars, home and workplaces. Both the U.S. National Toxicology Program and the European Union have performed risk assessments on phthalates and have generally found no significant risk to children from exposure.

The U.S. Centers for Disease Control and Prevention (CDC) has also tested thousands of Americans for evidence of exposure to phthalates. The CDC data show that average human exposure is far below levels set by the U.S. Environmental Protection Agency as protective of human health and that exposure levels are actually declining.

It is unfortunate that some media reports referred to a handful of studies that attempt to link phthalate exposure to adverse health effects. Many of the studies are biased in their design, test only a small sample size or have uncontrollable variables. Other studies ignore or exaggerate real-world human exposure. Some studies are based on findings in rodents at extremely high exposure levels. Similar studies in primates do not show these same effects.

In today's world, zero exposure to anything is impossible, and with today's advances in analytical techniques, incredibly tiny amounts can be measured. These levels do not necessarily constitute a health risk.

Bisphenol A (BPA) is a chemical building block used primarily to make polycarbonate plastic — a lightweight, highly shatter-resistant plastic with optical clarity comparable to glass — and epoxy resins. Both are used in a wide array of products, many of which improve health and safety. . . .

The Food and Drug Administration regulates the use of bisphenol A in food-contact materials, such as baby bottles, water bottles and coatings on food cans. . . . The agency said in July 2007 that "FDA is unaware of any specific study in which humans exposed to BPA through any food containers experienced miscarriages, birth defects or cancer. Human exposure levels to BPA from its use in food-contact materials is in fact many orders of magnitude lower than the levels of BPA that showed no adverse effects in animal studies."

From a toxicological perspective, BPA and phthalates are among the most well-defined chemicals on Earth. They have been the subject of hundreds of studies in lab animals and numerous government-sponsored assessments. Accordingly, based on the science and the use patterns for these compounds, no restriction on their uses is warranted at this time.

How to Lower Your Risk of Cancer

- **Don't smoke, or, if you do smoke, quit.** Smoking is linked to at least 15 different types of cancer and accounts for at least 30 percent of all cancer deaths. People who quit, even after decades as smokers, almost immediately begin reducing their risk.

- **Limit your sun exposure.** Sun damage throughout your lifetime can eventually cause cancer, as can tanning beds and sunlamps. And while generous use of sunscreen — at least a whole handful in each application — limits exposure to so-called UVB rays, it doesn't block all of them and frequently offers little or no protection against UVA rays, which also are dangerous. Avoid the midday sun, stay in the shade when you can and wear lightweight clothing and hats with brims to cut your exposure.

- **Keep your weight down and eat a wide variety of plant-based foods, including whole grains, beans and at least five servings of fruits and vegetables daily.** Variety is important because many "micronutrients" found in different foods play cancer-fighting roles in the body.

- **Be physically active.** Children and adolescents should aim for 60 minutes daily of moderately vigorous exercise, at least five days a week, and adults should aim for at least 30 to 45 minutes. Anything that makes you breathe harder, such as brisk walking or stair climbing, counts. Exercise can be spaced throughout the day.

- **Drink alcohol only in moderation.** Men who consume more than two drinks per day on average and women who consume more than one drink per day have a higher risk of developing several forms of cancer.

Source: American Cancer Society

CURRENT SITUATION

Action In Congress

Both Congress' Democratic majority and President-elect Obama plan to address cancer research and treatment with legislation.

This year "will be one of the most active legislative years in a long time," says Dick Woodruff, chief lobbyist for the American Cancer Society's Cancer Action Network.

Sens. Edward M. Kennedy, D-Mass., and Kay Bailey Hutchison, R-Texas, are developing a comprehensive bill, expected to be introduced early this year, to increase research funding, spur research on early detection and provide better access to screening and treatment for uninsured people.

"We need an entirely new model" to coordinate a "fragmented and piecemeal system of addressing cancer" by linking research, prevention and treatment into a "continuum of comprehensive cancer care," said Kennedy, then-chairman of the Health, Education, Labor and Pensions Committee, at a hearing in May, less than two weeks before he was diagnosed with a malignant brain tumor. [49]

The cancer-advocacy community also wants the FDA to regulate tobacco, says Woodruff. The House passed such a bill in July 2008, but the legislation languished in the Senate, so lawmakers will start again in the new year.

Woodruff expects the bill to become law this time. The legislation has at least 60 Senate cosponsors and will probably garner votes from 10 more senators, he says. "We will work with the Senate leadership so Republicans can offer the amendments

Continued from p. 40

shouldn't wait for a definite study . . . but err on the side of being safe rather than sorry later," he said. [45]

In fact, in the early 2000s congressional Democrats, including Sen. Frank Lautenberg, D-N.J., drafted legislation "to overhaul U.S. regulations to resemble" the EU's then-proposed REACH reforms, said the University of Illinois' Epstein. [46]

But REACH is not a good model for the United States to follow and is opposed by both private industries and the Bush administration, said Joseph G. Acker, president of the Synthetic Organic Chemical Manufacturers Association. "Despite interest from far left-wing corners of Congress, which have a great interest in adopting a REACH-type system here in the U.S., REACH is losing steam as the new model." [47]

In recent meetings with government officials from several Asian-Pacific nations, "we described for them major trade challenges that U.S.-based chemical companies now have because of REACH," said Acker, and "it became clear . . . that these governments see more disadvantages to adopting REACH than advantages." [48]

they want on the floor, but there's only one senator who's said he wants to filibuster" the bill, and "that's not enough" to stop passage, Woodruff says.

Under the legislation, the FDA could require testing tobacco products to stop companies from making false health and safety claims, Woodruff says. By the time this is done, the health-warning label "will take up half the package," he predicts.

Also on the prevention front, Sens. Christopher J. Dodd, D-Conn., and Jack Reed, D-R.I., have introduced legislation to require the FDA to require labels warning that sunscreen products currently protect only against the sun's UVB rays, which cause sunburn and increase the risk of skin cancer, but not against UVA rays, which also cause skin cancer. [50]

Since Democrats took over control of Congress in 2007, committees also have been mulling tighter regulation of several potentially carcinogenic chemicals, such as bisphenol A, used in plastics manufacture. (*See "At Issue," p. 41.*)

Obama's Plan

President-elect Obama's cancer plan would double federal research funding over five years, increase the numbers of patients in clinical trials, eliminate Medicare and Medicaid patient copays for screening, expand funding for smoking cessation and provide guidance for patients navigating the treatment system. [51]

"Obama's goal to put 10 percent of patients in clinical trials is terrific," says *Cancer Letter* Editor Goldberg.

NCI funding for clinical research has "taken a big hit" in recent years as the agency has struggled to prop up basic-research initiatives amid slowed congressional funding, says his

wife, *Cancer Letter* Publisher Kirsten Boyd Goldberg. Furthermore, even between 1998 and 2003, when Congress doubled NIH funding, money for NCI's cooperative groups — researchers, cancer centers and community doctors around the United States who do clinical research — only went up by 50 percent, she says.

"Physicians out there are subsidizing" NCI's clinical research — receiving $2,000 to support a patient's clinical-trial participation when a drug company would offer $6,000 or $8,000 — "and though the doctors do it because they truly believe in it, that can't go on forever," publisher Goldberg says.

It's important that the groups get support to continue their work because their research asks different questions than drug-company-sponsored researchers, who aim solely at getting a drug approved, says Paul Goldberg. By contrast, cooperative groups may even come out with conclusions like "Hey, don't use that drug," he says. "The more you squeeze the groups, the more you may lose" such valuable insights into what actually constitutes the best cancer care, he says.

Not everyone is so pleased with Obama's plan. The president-elect "is putting all the emphasis on oncology — there seems to be no emphasis on prevention in the plan at all," the University of Illinois' Epstein says.

There's also room to wonder whether the government can come up with cash for cancer in the midst of an economic meltdown.

"Money is the elephant in the room, the main stumbling block for all these things," says David Bernstein, senior science policy analyst for the American Association for Cancer Research. Nevertheless, "we're still optimistic about money because research is an economic stimulus," he says. ∎

Prevention Ahead?

Shifting cancer science toward prevention won't be easy, but a growing worldwide cancer burden makes prevention efforts vital.

"We probably could get rid of 90 percent of lung cancer by ending smoking, but we don't know how to accomplish that, so we need research on how to help people quit who want to quit," as well as much more prevention research, says Bailar, the former head of the NCI's demography section.

Even so, "it's going to be a long, slow process to get that research program reoriented" because a prevention focus is a "totally different world" from a treatment focus, says Bailar. "You can't just turn a treatment person into a detection, screening and prevention researcher. It's sometimes hard even to persuade them that there's another path to be investigated."

The war on cancer launched a multibillion-dollar, multifaceted enterprise that is now set in its ways, and the scientists, physicians and companies involved have no incentive to change, according to *War on Cancer* author Faguet at the Medical College of Georgia.

"The information pipeline, generated by clinical researchers and supported by their sponsors and publishers, fosters standards of care that are reinforced by financial incentives and the extraordinary capacity of physicians for self-delusion and by unrealistic expectations of consumers, nurtured by the media," Faguet wrote. [52]

As developing countries make headway against some infectious diseases, and heart disease in industrialized countries recedes as a killer, cancer is taking a larger toll.

However, even though the approximately 4 million annual cancer deaths in low- and middle-income countries outnumber the 3 million annual deaths from AIDS, cancer remains low on those nations' health-care priority lists, according to a 2007 National Academy of Sciences report. Furthermore, in low-income countries, most people with cancer have no access to potentially curative treatments, and in middle-income countries treatment is "generally limited," said the report. [53]

Those facts strengthen the case for prevention, and some very successful approaches for addressing cancer in developing countries have been proposed, says MIT's Wogan. For example, the combined effects of hepatitis B infection and exposure to aflatoxins — fungi that contaminate stored crops — cause many developing-world cancers, "and an obvious approach is vaccination" against hepatitis B, he says.

Indoor air pollution from unventilated cooking fires also is "a huge problem globally," he says. "Just putting a chimney on the stove" constitutes effective prevention.

Implementing preventive measures "will only continue to grow more important as cancer rapidly overtakes heart disease as the No. 1 killer," Wogan says. ∎

Notes

[1] For background, see Sally Jacobs, "Kennedy, His Children, and Cancer," *The Boston Globe*, May 25, 2008.

[2] Quoted in *ibid.*

[3] Richard Schilsky, Jeffrey Abrams, Janet Woodcock, Gwen Fyfe and Robert Irwin, "Issue Brief," Conference on Clinical Cancer Research, September 2008.

[4] Quoted in John Russell, "Cancer Studies Suggest Pathways Are Best Targets," *Bio-IT World*, Sept. 25, 2008, www.bio-itworld.com.

[5] Bill Hendrick, "Smoking Rate Is Declining in the U.S.," *WebMD*, Nov. 13, 2008, www.webmd.com/smoking-cessation/news/20081113/smoking-rate-is-declining-in-us.

[6] Janet Gray, ed., *State of the Evidence: The Connection Between Breast Cancer and the Environment*, Breast Cancer Fund (2008), p. 15.

[7] *Ibid.*

[8] "Comprehensive Genetic Blueprints Revealed for Lethal Pancreatic, Brain Cancers," press release, Johns Hopkins Medical Institutions, Sept. 4, 2008, www.hopkinskimmelcancercenter.org.

[9] H. Gilbert Welch, "Seek, and You'll Find," *Minneapolis Star Tribune*, Nov. 6, 2008, www.startribune.com.

[10] Guy B. Faguet, *The War on Cancer: Anatomy of Failure, A Blueprint for the Future* (2008), p. 156.

[11] "Colon Cancer Screening Before Medicare Age Could Save Millions in Federal Health Care Dollars," *Science Daily*, Oct. 6, 2008, www.sciencedaily.com.

[12] Quoted in "Recent Studies Confirm Significant Underuse of Colorectal Cancer Screening," *Science Daily*, Jan. 3, 2008, www.sciencedaily.com.

[13] Quoted in Maryann Napoli, "Mammography Screening — Both Good and Bad News,"

Center for Medical Consumers Web site, September 2005, www.medicalconsumers.org. The analysis is by Karsten Juhl Jorgensen and Peter C. Gotzsche of the Danish branch of the Cochrane Collaboration, an international nonprofit group that publishes evidence-based information on health-care procedures based on systematic review of the research.

[14] Quoted in *ibid.*

[15] Quoted in Maryann Napoli, "Early Promoters of PSA Screening for Prostate Cancer Do a Turnabout," Center for Medical Consumers Web site, February 2005, www.Medicalconsumers.org.

[16] 'Study Shows No Benefit for CT Screening for Lung Cancer," press release, Memorial Sloan-Kettering Cancer Center, March 6, 2007, www.mskcc.org; Peter B. Bach, *et al.*, "Computed Tomography Screening and Lung Cancer Outcomes," *Journal of the American Medical Association*, March 7, 2007, pp. 953-961.

[17] "Promoting Healthy Lifestyles: Policy, Program, and Personal Recommendations for Reducing Cancer Risk, 2006-2007 Annual Report," President's Cancer Panel, National Cancer Institute, August 2007, http://deainfo.nci.nih.gov/advisory/pcp/pcp07rpt/pcp07rpt.pdf, p. i.

[18] For background, see Nellie Bristol, "HPV Vaccine," *CQ Researcher*, May 11, 2007, pp. 409-432.

[19] "Promoting Healthy Lifestyles," *op. cit.*

[20] *Ibid.*, p. ii.

[21] For background, see Kenneth Jost, "Closing in on Tobacco," *CQ Researcher*, Nov. 12, 1999, pp. 977-1000.

[22] Maryann Napoli, "Drugs to Reduce Breast Cancer Risk: Is It Worth It?" Center for Medical Consumers Web site, May 2006, www.medicalconsumers.org.

[23] Jeanne Mager Stellman, "Delusions, Illusions and Ongoing Neglect of Hazard Recognition, Regulation and Control of Industrial Carcinogens," Presentation to the President's Cancer Panel, Sept. 16, 2008, www.firstscience.com/home/news/breaking-news-all-topics/immediate-action-needed-to-prevent-industrial-manslaughter-says-expert_52622.html.

[24] Samuel S. Epstein and Randall Fitzgerald, *Toxic Beauty* (forthcoming, 2009), p. 142.

[25] David Michaels, "Manufactured Uncertainty: Protecting Public Health in the Age of Contested Science and Product Defense," *Annals of the New York Academy of Sciences*, September 2006, pp. 149-162.

[26] *Ibid.*, p. 156.

[27] Quoted in Richard Clapp, *Industrial Carcinogens: A Need for Action*, The Collaborative

About the Author

Staff writer **Marcia Clemmitt** is a veteran social-policy reporter who previously served as editor in chief of *Medicine & Health* and staff writer for *The Scientist*. She has also been a high-school math and physics teacher. She holds a liberal arts and sciences degree from St. John's College, Annapolis, and a master's degree in English from Georgetown University. Her recent reports include "Mortgage Crisis," "Climate Change," "Health Care Costs" and "Preventing Memory Loss."

on Health and the Environment Web site, Sept. 16, 2008, www.healthandenvironment.org/?module=uploads&func=download&fileId=558.

[28] James Huff, "More Toxin Tests Needed," letter to the editor, *Science*, Feb. 8, 2008, p. 725.

[29] *Ibid.*

[30] Deborah Winn, testimony before House Energy and Commerce Health Subcommittee, May 21, 2008.

[31] Marc Kolanz, "Beryllium History and Public Policy," *Public Health Reports*, July-August 2008, p. 426.

[32] Elizabeth M. Whelan, "Quackery Promoters Are Wrong. With Some Exceptions, Cancer Death Rates Are Declining," Quackwatch Web site, www.quackwatch.org.

[33] "Everything Doesn't Cause Cancer," American Institute for Cancer Research, November 2007, www.aicr.com.

[34] Faguet, *op. cit.*, p. 96.

[35] Quoted in Richard A. Rettig, *Cancer Crusade: The Story of The National Cancer Act of 1971* (2005), p. 79.

[36] "Estimates of Funding for Various Disease, Conditions, Research Areas," National Institutes of Health, Feb. 5, 2008, www.nih.gov/news/fundingresearchareas.htm. For background, see Rettig, *op. cit.*, and Faguet, *op. cit.* For additional background, see Adriel Bettelheim, "Cancer Treatments," *CQ Researcher*, Sept. 11, 1998, pp. 785-808, and Sarah Glazer, "Breast Cancer," *CQ Researcher*, June 27, 1997, pp. 553-576.

[37] Rettig, *op. cit.*, p. 277.

[38] Faguet, *op. cit.*, p. 78.

[39] *Ibid.*, p. 79.

[40] For background, see Bristol, *op. cit.*

[41] For background, see Robert N. Proctor, *Cancer Wars: How Politics Shape What We Know and Don't Know About Cancer* (1995).

[42] *Ibid.*, p. 42.

[43] American Chemistry Council, letter to National Toxicology Program Associate Director, Jan. 30, 2004, www.americanchemistry.com.

[44] Devra Davis, *The Secret History of the War on Cancer* (2007), p. 378.

[45] Quoted in Tara Parker-Pope, "Prominent Cancer Doctor Warns About Cellphones," "Well blog," *The New York Times* Web site, July 24, 2008, http://well.blogs.nytimes.com.

[46] Quoted in "Reaching for Control of Carcinogenic Chemicals," Environmental News Service, May 5, 2004, www.ens-newswire.com/ens/may2004/2004-05-05-02.asp.

[47] Joseph G. Acker, "Joe's Blog," Synthetic Organic Chemical Manufacturers Association Web site, Oct. 9, 2008, http://joesblog.socma.org.

[48] *Ibid.*

[49] Sen. Edward M. Kennedy, statement before Senate Health, Education, Labor, and Pensions Committee, May 8, 2008, http://kennedy.senate/gov.

[50] "Senators Dodd, Reed Seek to Improve Sunscreen Safety Standards," press release from office of Sen. Christopher Dodd, Aug. 1, 2008, http://dodd.senate/gov/index.php?q=node/4527.

[51] The Obama-Biden Plan to Combat Cancer, www.barackobama.com.

[52] Faguet, *op. cit.*, p. 182.

[53] Frank A. Sloan and Hellen Gelband, eds., *Cancer Control Opportunities in Low- and Middle-Income Countries*, Committee on Cancer Control in Low- and Middle-Income Countries (2007), National Academy of Sciences, p. 9.

FOR MORE INFORMATION

American Association for Cancer Research, 615 Chestnut St., 17th Floor, Philadelphia, PA 19106-4404; (215) 440-9300; www.aacr.org. Promotes and disseminates research on cancer.

American Cancer Society, 901 E St., N.W., #500, Washington, DC 20004; (202) 661-5700; www.cancer.org. Promotes elimination of cancer.

American Chemistry Council, 1300 Wilson Blvd., Arlington, VA 22209; (703) 741-5000; www.americanchemistry.com. Represents leading chemical companies, including significant business groups such as the Plastics Division and Chlorine Chemistry Division.

American Council on Science and Health, 1995 Broadway, 2nd Floor, New York, NY 10023-5860; (212) 362-7044; www.acsh.org. Disseminates information on environmental-health questions, supporting a cautious approach to regulation.

American Institute for Cancer Research, 1759 R St., N.W., Washington, DC 20009; (202) 328-7744; www.aicr.org. Supports and disseminates research into the roles of diet, physical activity and weight management in cancer prevention.

American Society of Clinical Oncology, 1900 Duke St., #200, Alexandria, VA 22314; (703) 299-0150; www.asco.org. Advocates research and improved cancer care.

Cancer Prevention Coalition, c/o University of Illinois at Chicago School of Public Health, MC 922, 2121 West Taylor St., Chicago, IL 60612; (312) 996-2297; www.preventcancer.org. Seeks more attention to cancer prevention and tighter regulation of potential environmental carcinogens.

Collaborative on Health and the Environment, c/o Commonweal, P.O. Box 316, Bolinas, CA 94924; www.healthandenvironment.org. A coalition concerned with potential health effects of toxins and chemicals in the environment.

National Cancer Institute, 31 Center Dr., Bldg. 31, #11A48, MSC-2590, Bethesda, MD 20892-2590; (301) 496-5615; www.cancer.gov. Federal agency that conducts and funds research on cancer.

Science Daily, www.sciencedaily.com/news/health_medicine/cancer. An advertising-supported online publication that carries dozens of reports on cancer research.

Science and Environmental Health Network, 217 Welch Ave., Suite 101, Ames, IA 50014; (515) 268-0600; www.sehn.org. Advocates use of the "precautionary principle" as a new basis for environmental and public health policy.

Skin Deep, www.cosmeticsdatabase.com. Web site maintained by the activist nonprofit Environmental Working Group, which rates the safety of cosmetics and personal-care products.

Bibliography

Selected Sources

Books

Davis, Devra, *The Secret History of the War on Cancer*, Basic Books, 2007.

An epidemiology professor at the University of Pittsburgh's Graduate School of Public Health says prevention and the role of environmental risks — especially industrial products like chemicals and radiation — have been deliberately ignored for economic reasons throughout the war on cancer.

Faguet, Guy B., *The War on Cancer: An Anatomy of Failure, A Blueprint for the Future*, Springer, 2008.

A hematologist, oncologist and professor emeritus at the Medical College of Georgia delves into the history of cancer research and treatment — particularly how financial incentives affect treatment strategies — and argues that the war on cancer demands a significant overhaul.

Rettig, Richard A., *et al.*, *False Hope: Bone Marrow Transplantation for Breast Cancer*, Oxford University Press, 2007.

A group of health-care analysts chronicle how over-enthusiastic oncologists, the media and lawsuits against insurers helped to fuel the popularity of an unapproved, risky therapy for breast cancer, which was eventually proved useless and unsafe.

Welch, H. Gilbert, *Should I Be Tested for Cancer? Maybe Not and Here's Why*, University of California Press, 2006.

A professor of medicine at Dartmouth Medical School examines how screening apparently healthy people for cancer can result in some cancers being missed and some patients being exposed to invasive, unnecessary procedures for conditions that would never progress to cancer.

Articles

Abelson, Reed, "Quickly Vetted, Treatment Is Offered to Patients," *The New York Times*, Oct. 26, 2008, p. A1.

The Food and Drug Administration's process for approving some cancer treatments, such as radiation, is much less rigorous than the agency's scrutiny of experimental drugs.

Begley, Sharon, "Where Are the Cures?" *Newsweek*, Nov. 10, 2008, p. 56.

Few biomedical discoveries about cancer ever turn into effective treatments or prevention strategies, partly because scientific insights rarely suggest practical application and because turning bench-science findings into drugs or devices that can be tested on humans gets little support.

Parker-Pope, Tara, "Early Test for Cancer Isn't Always Best Course," *The New York Times*, Aug. 12, 2008, p. F5.

The United States Preventive Services Task Force recommends that prostate-cancer screening be stopped at age 75 and that doctors advise men of all ages of both the risks and benefits of screening, which can lead to false positives and treatments that can cause incontinence and impotence.

Saporito, Bill, "He Won His Battle With Cancer. So Why Are Millions of Americans Still Losing Theirs?" *Time*, Sept. 15, 2008, p. 36.

Private groups are trying to ensure that cancer funding is strategically used to produce cures.

Reports and Studies

"Cancer and the Environment: What You Need to Know, What You Can Do," National Cancer Institute/National Institute of Environmental Health Sciences, August 2003, www.niehs.nih.gov/health/docs/cancer-enviro.pdf.

As many as two-thirds of all cancers are linked to environmental factors ranging from cigarette smoking and lack of exercise to air pollutants and pesticides, and many if not most such cancers are probably preventable.

"Food, Nutrition, Physical Activity and the Prevention of Cancer: A Global Perspective," American Institute for Cancer Research/World Cancer Research Fund, 2007, www.dietandcancerreport.org.

An expert panel dissects the evidence on the carcinogenic or cancer-fighting effects of various diets and exercise patterns around the world and recommends prevention strategies.

"Promoting Healthy Lifestyles: Policy, Program, and Personal Recommendations for Reducing Cancer Risk," President's Cancer Panel, National Cancer Institute, 2006-2007 Annual Report, Aug. 2007, http://deainfo.nci.nih.gov/advisory/pcp/pcp07rpt/pcp07rpt.pdf.

A presidentially appointed panel of cancer experts and advocates find that federal state, and local government policies promote unhealthy eating and lack of exercise and that government officials haven't done enough to end tobacco use.

Gray, Janet, ed., "State of the Evidence: The Connection Between Breast Cancer and the Environment," Breast Cancer Fund, 2008, www.breastcancerfund.org.

A nonprofit concerned with environmental health argues that high levels of radiation and synthetic-chemical use connected with industrial society have increased the incidence of breast cancer over the past half century.

The Next Step:

Additional Articles from Current Periodicals

Cancer Drugs

Grace, Kerry E., "Expanded Gardasil Use on Hold," *The Wall Street Journal*, Jan. 9, 2009, www.wsj.com.

The Food and Drug Administration is waiting for more data from Merck before approving a drug that prevents cervical cancer in women ages 27 to 45.

Hitti, Miranda, "Patrick Swayze Opens Up About Pancreatic Cancer," *WebMD.com*, Jan. 7, 2009.

Actor Patrick Swayze is trying an experimental drug as part of his pancreatic cancer treatment.

Carcinogens

Bakalar, Nicholas, "Smokeless Tobacco on Par With Cigarettes," *The New York Times*, Aug. 21, 2007, p. F6.

A new study finds that smokeless tobacco may be as potent as cigarettes in delivering nicotine and carcinogens.

Chandler, Kim, "State Proposes Stricter Rule for Carcinogens in Waterways," *Birmingham News* (Alabama), Dec. 15, 2007, p. 1D.

The Alabama Environmental Management Commission has voted to reduce the amount of cancer-causing carcinogens in state waterways.

Cone, Marla, "Common Chemicals Linked to Breast Cancer," *Los Angeles Times*, May 14, 2007, p. A1.

Some chemicals identified as breast carcinogens are regulated to protect public health, but many of those in consumer products are not.

Eilperin, Juliet, "EPA Rejects Carcinogenic Wood Preservative for Home Use," *The Washington Post*, Jan. 9, 2007, p. A3.

Federal officials have rejected an industry bid to use a known carcinogen as a preservative in lumber amid fears of increased cancer risk for plant workers.

Prevention

Ackerman, Todd, "$35 Million Gift Boosts Cancer Fight," *Houston Chronicle*, May 15, 2008, p. B1.

A Houston energy magnate has given the University of Texas $35 million to boost efforts to prevent cancer.

Breen, Kim, "Perry Ready for Texas to Be Major Player in Cancer Fight," *Dallas Morning News*, June 14, 2007, p. 1B.

Texas Gov. Rick Perry has signed legislation for a $3 billion plan to establish the Cancer Prevention and Research Institute of Texas.

Moreno, Sylvia, "Thinking Prevention," *The Washington Post*, May 13, 2008, p. HE1.

The Cancer Preventorium at the Washington Hospital Center is aimed at drawing in low-income Latino women for prevention.

Wangsness, Lisa, "Patrick Seeks $72M Hike in Health Aid," *The Boston Globe*, Feb. 26, 2007, p. A1.

Massachusetts Gov. Deval Patrick has announced an increase in the budget for public health spending, largely to expand cancer prevention services.

Screening

Alonso-Zaldivar, Ricardo, "FDA Scientists Complain to Obama of 'Corruption,' " The Associated Press, Jan. 8, 2009.

A group of federal scientists says corrupt practices at the Food and Drug Administration are leading to inefficient cancer-detection devices being approved.

Johnson, David A., "Colonoscopies Save Lives," *Chicago Sun Times*, May 7, 2007, p. A40.

About 90 percent of the colon cancer deaths could have been prevented by proper screening.

Parker-Pope, Tara, "Panel Urges End to Screening for Prostate Cancer at Age 75," *The New York Times*, Aug. 5, 2008, p. A1.

The U.S. Preventive Services Task Force says screening men 75 and older for prostate cancer causes more harm than good.

Rubin, Rita, "Screening Tests May Miss Prostate Cancer in Obese Patients," *USA Today*, Nov. 21, 2007, p. 11D.

High blood volumes may cause some popular screening tests to miss certain cancers in overweight men.

CITING CQ RESEARCHER

Sample formats for citing these reports in a bibliography include the ones listed below. Preferred styles and formats vary, so please check with your instructor or professor.

<u>MLA STYLE</u>

Jost, Kenneth. "Rethinking the Death Penalty." <u>CQ Researcher</u> 16 Nov. 2001: 945-68.

<u>APA STYLE</u>

Jost, K. (2001, November 16). Rethinking the death penalty. *CQ Researcher, 11*, 945-968.

<u>CHICAGO STYLE</u>

Jost, Kenneth. "Rethinking the Death Penalty." *CQ Researcher*, November 16, 2001, 945-968.

In-depth Reports on Issues in the News

Are you writing a paper?

Need backup for a debate?

Want to become an expert on an issue?

For 80 years, students have turned to *CQ Researcher* for in-depth reporting on issues in the news. Reports on a full range of political and social issues are now available. Following is a selection of recent reports:

Civil Liberties
Limiting Lawsuits, 12/08
Affirmative Action, 10/08
Gay Marriage Showdowns, 9/08
America's Border Fence, 9/08
Immigration Debate, 2/08
Prison Reform, 4/07

Crime/Law
Mexico's Drug War, 12/08
Prostitution Debate, 5/08
Public Defenders, 4/08
Gun Violence, 5/07

Education
Reading Crisis? 2/08
Discipline in Schools, 2/08
Student Aid, 1/08
Racial Diversity in Public Schools, 9/07
Stress on Students, 7/07

Environment
Reducing Carbon Footprint, 12/08
Protecting Wetlands, 10/08
Buying Green, 2/08
Future of Recycling, 12/07

Health/Safety
Heart Health, 9/08
Global Food Crisis, 6/08
Preventing Memory Loss, 4/08

International Affairs/Politics
The National Debt, 11/08
Financial Bailout, 10/08
Political Conventions, 8/08
Human Rights in China, 7/08
Race and Politics, 7/08
Campaign Finance Reform, 6/08

Social Trends
Falling Birthrates, 11/08
Regulating Credit Cards, 10/08
Internet Accuracy, 8/08
Financial Crisis, 5/08
Cyberbullying, 5/08

Terrorism/Defense
Rise in Counterinsurgency, 9/08
Cost of the Iraq War, 4/08

Youth
Debating Hip-Hop, 6/07

Upcoming Reports

Toxic Chemicals, 1/23/09   Obama Presidency, 1/30/09   Future of the Auto Industry, 2/6/09

ACCESS

CQ Researcher is available in print and online. For access, visit your library or www.cqresearcher.com.

STAY CURRENT

To receive notice of upcoming *CQ Researcher* reports, or learn more about *CQ Researcher* products, subscribe to the free e-mail newsletters, *CQ Researcher Alert!* and *CQ Researcher News*: http://cqpress.com/newsletters.

PURCHASE

To purchase a *CQ Researcher* report in print or electronic format (PDF), visit www.cqpress.com or call 866-427-7737. Single reports start at $15. Bulk purchase discounts and electronic-rights licensing are also available.

SUBSCRIBE

Annual full-service *CQ Researcher* subscriptions—including 44 reports a year, monthly index updates, and a bound volume—start at $803. Add $25 for domestic postage.

CQ Researcher Online offers a backfile from 1991 and a number of tools to simplify research. For pricing information, call 800-834-9020, ext. 1906, or e-mail librarysales@cqpress.com.

Published by CQ Press, a division of SAGE Publications

www.cqresearcher.com

Regulating Toxic Chemicals

Do we know enough about chemical risks?

C hemicals are integral to many everyday products, from electronics and toys to building materials and household goods. But environmental, health and consumer advocates say the agencies responsible for protecting Americans from exposure to harmful chemicals are allowing too many dangerous substances into the market without testing them for toxicity. Some goods, such as medicines, are tested for safety before they can be sold, but many common products do not go through premarket safety screening. Many concerns focus on infants and young children, who are especially sensitive to toxic hazards. Chemical manufacturers say the existing regulatory system works effectively and can be tightened to address new concerns, but critics argue that a precautionary approach — which would require producers to show that materials are safe before they can be marketed — would protect consumers more fully.

Children may be more vulnerable than adults to toxic substances because their bodies are still developing, they absorb more contaminants in proportion to their body size and activities like crawling and mouthing objects expose them to more risks.

CQ Researcher • Jan. 23, 2009 • www.cqresearcher.com
Volume 19, Number 3 • Pages 49-72

I N S I D E ThIS Report

REGULATING TOXIC CHEMICALS

CQ Researcher

Jan. 23, 2009
Volume 19, Number 3

MANAGING EDITOR: Thomas J. Colin
tcolin@cqpress.com

ASSISTANT MANAGING EDITOR: Kathy Koch
kkoch@cqpress.com

ASSOCIATE EDITOR: Kenneth Jost

STAFF WRITERS: Thomas J. Billitteri,
Marcia Clemmitt, Peter Katel

CONTRIBUTING WRITERS: Rachel S. Cox,
Sarah Glazer, Alan Greenblatt,
Barbara Mantel, Patrick Marshall,
Tom Price, Jennifer Weeks

DESIGN/PRODUCTION EDITOR: Olu B. Davis

ASSISTANT EDITOR: Darrell Dela Rosa

FACT-CHECKER/PROOFREADER: Eugene J. Gabler

EDITORIAL INTERNS: Vyomika Jairam

CQ PRESS

**A Division of
SAGE Publications**

PRESIDENT AND PUBLISHER:
John A. Jenkins

EXECUTIVE DIRECTOR,
REFERENCE INFORMATION GROUP:
Alix B. Vance

DIRECTOR, ONLINE PRODUCT DEVELOPMENT:
Jennifer Q. Ryan

CQ Press is a registered trademark of Congressional Quarterly Inc.

CQ Researcher (ISSN 1056-2036) is printed on acid-free paper. Published weekly, except; (Jan. wk. 1) (May wk. 4) (July wks. 1, 2) (Aug. wks. 3, 4) (Nov. wk. 4) and (Dec. wk. 4), by CQ Press, a division of SAGE Publications. Annual full-service subscriptions start at $803. For pricing, call 1-800-834-9020, ext. 1906. To purchase a CQ Researcher report in print or electronic format (PDF), visit www. cqpress.com or call 866-427-7737. Single reports start at $15. Bulk purchase discounts and electronic-rights licensing are also available. Periodicals postage paid at Washington, D.C., and additional mailing offices. POSTMASTER: Send address changes to CQ Researcher, 2300 N St., N.W., Suite 800, Washington, DC 20037.

Regulating Toxic Chemicals

BY JENNIFER WEEKS

THE ISSUES

In October 2007, the Eastman Chemical Co. of Kingsport, Tenn., introduced Tritan, a new plastic boasting "faster molding cycles compared to many other types of transparent polymers," plus enhanced durability and high gloss. [1]

But Tritan had another feature that made the plastics market take special notice: The new resin did not contain bisphenol A (BPA), a chemical widely found in rigid plastic products like food containers and baby bottles.

BPA has been used in consumer products for decades, although researchers have known since the 1930s that in mammals the chemical mimics estrogen, the natural hormone that regulates female sexual development and reproductive cycles. Endocrine disruption, as the effect is known, has been linked to developmental, reproductive and other problems in wildlife and laboratory animals, and some researchers believe it has a similar impact in humans. [2]

Until the late 1990s scientists thought BPA was only harmful at high doses, but then some studies showed that quantities as low as a few parts per billion could have toxic effects. They also demonstrated that BPA could leach from bottles and can linings into infant formula and food. [3] Then in 2008 the federally funded National Toxicology Program warned that current exposure levels to BPA posed some concern for "effects on the brain, behavior and prostate gland in fetuses, infants and children." [4] In contrast, the Food and Drug Administration (FDA), which

Concern about exposure to the chemical bisphenol A (BPA), widely used in hundreds of products, is prompting consumers and retailers to switch to BPA-free products. The National Toxicology Program warned recently that BPA poses some concern for "effects on the brain, behavior and prostate gland in fetuses, infants and children." Wal-Mart, Target, and other large companies have stopped selling products containing BPA.

Getty Images/David McNew

regulates exposure to BPA from food packaging, maintained it was safe.

Consumers and retailers opted to be safe rather than sorry, especially after Canada banned BPA from baby bottles in April. Wal-Mart, Target, REI, Costco and other large companies pulled products containing BPA from their shelves or found substitutes. Many of these stores now sell hard plastic water bottles made with Tritan copolyester, prominently marked as BPA-free.

"They're selling fantastically," says Carolyn Beem, public affairs manager for L.L. Bean, the Maine outdoor retailer. "We're not experts in science,

but we are experts in listening and responding to our customers. With all of the reports out there, it seemed like a good time to start again." In March 2008 Eastman expanded Tritan production to keep up with demand. [5]

In addition to BPA, environmentalists and consumer advocates warn that many other materials in commercial products may be harmful to human health, including:

• polyvinyl chloride (PVC) plastic, used in items such as shower curtains and water pipes;

• phthalates, a group of chemicals used to make plastics soft and pliable; and

• polybrominated diphenylethers (PBDEs), chemicals added to foams and fabrics as flame retardants.

In addition, some consumer goods contain materials widely known to be toxic, such as lead in popular brands of lipstick. [6]

"Consumers assume when they buy a product that someone has vetted it to make sure it's safe, but that doesn't always happen," says Sarah Janssen, a physician and environmental health expert at the Natural Resources Defense Council (NRDC), an advocacy group. "They're at a disadvantage because most of the important information isn't even on the label."

Humans are exposed to many potentially harmful substances in their daily lives, from air and water pollutants to household contaminants like mold and dust. Over time some of these exposures may cause cancer or other serious problems, such as birth defects or organ damage. Some of these illnesses result from lifestyle choices: for example, smoking, inactivity and obesity are major causes of cancer in the United States. [7] But workers and consumers also can be exposed unknowingly to risky materials that are legally used in commercial products.

Human exposure to toxic chemicals is controlled by several different agencies, depending on how the chemical is used and where people come in contact with it. The Environmental Protection Agency (EPA) regulates industrial chemicals and pesticides, while the FDA controls food additives, drugs and cosmetics and the Consumer Product Safety Commission (CPSC) oversees thousands of other consumer goods, from personal care products to toys. Workplace exposure to chemicals is regulated by the Occupational Safety and Health Administration (OSHA). Some materials must be tested for toxicity before marketing, but in other cases manufacturers merely have to notify regulators that they are going to start producing them.

Many experts think federal policy should be more consistent. "The agencies have very different approaches because they are covered by laws that find wildly varying levels of risk acceptable," says David Michaels, a professor of environmental and occupational health at George Washington University and a former assistant secretary of Energy. "We should be thinking about ways to harmonize standards across these agencies, because their actions affect each other. They allow

A sign warns that dangerous industrial chemicals were dumped in a lake near Gary, Ind. In 1979 the Environmental Protection Agency banned production of polychlorinated biphenyls (PCBs), which cause cancer and birth defects in laboratory animals, and set timetables for phasing out their use in various industries.

different levels of exposure for many of the same chemicals."

Chemical manufacturers say the Toxic Substances Control Act (TSCA) — the core law that regulates industrial chemicals — is working. "TSCA has protected human health and the environment," says Michael Walls, managing director for regulatory and technical affairs at the American Chemistry Council (ACC), a chemical industry trade group. "There are areas where we can reform it, and we're encouraged that proposals have been offered to amend the law, not to replace it." The chemical industry is working with EPA to make more data available on

hazards from widely used chemicals and assess how chemical exposures affect children's health.

Many critics worry that it is too easy for new materials to enter commerce before their effects have been well studied. They are especially concerned about the growing field of nanotechnology, which uses microscopic particles to enhance products ranging from sunscreen to medications. Reducing materials to the nano scale makes it easier to apply them precisely: for example, chemotherapy drugs can be targeted directly at tumors. But materials acquire new properties at this scale, and scientists are still analyzing the toxicity of many nanomaterials.

"Nanotechnology is taking our understanding of what makes something harmful and how we deal with that, and turning it upside down," said Andrew Maynard, chief science advisor to the Project on Emerging Nanotechnologies, in April 2008 congressional testimony. "New, engineered nanomaterials are prized for their unconventional properties. But these same properties may also lead to new ways of causing harm to people and the environment." [8]

In 2007 the European Union (EU) launched a new system for regulating chemicals that differs markedly from the U.S. approach. Under the REACH (Registration, Evaluation, Authorization and Restriction of Chemicals) policy, companies that produce or import chemicals in large volumes have to register their products with the EU and provide data on their properties and uses. Chemicals must be shown to be

Getty Images/Scott Olson

safe before they can enter commerce. U.S. companies doing business in Europe have to comply with the directive. [9] (*See sidebar, p. 62.*)

REACH is based on the so-called precautionary principle, which can be traced back through history but was articulated as a basis for environmental regulation at an international conference in 1998: "When an activity raises threats of harm to the environment or human health, precautionary measures should be taken even if some cause-and-effect relationships are not fully established scientifically." [10]

In contrast, many U.S. laws require regulators to produce scientific evidence that a substance is harmful before it can be removed from the market. Environmental and health advocates want the United States to adopt a more precautionary approach to regulation. But critics say the precautionary principle is too vague to be a viable basis for regulation and fails to balance risks and benefits. (*See "At Issue," p. 65.*)

For example, EPA banned use of the insecticide DDT in the U.S. in 1972 because it harmed the environment, but in 2006 the World Health Organization endorsed DDT for controlling mosquito-borne malaria in developing countries. [11] Some environmental groups want DDT banned worldwide, along with other persistent organic pollutants, but other advocates — including health experts — say it should remain in use until safer alternatives are developed. [12]

As Congress, regulators, businesses and advocates debate how to protect consumers from harmful exposures, here are some issues they are considering:

Do we know enough about chemical risks?

Chemicals are central to the economy and to many products that Americans associate with modern living. They underpin a $637 billion indus-

Concerns Linger Over Exposure to Bisphenol A

Scientists say they have "negligible concern" to "some concern" about the health effects of exposure to bisphenol A, a chemical commonly used in the production of plastics.

The National Toxicology Program uses the following five-level scale of concern for adverse effects from exposure to BPA:

Serious concern

Concern

Developmental toxicity for fetuses, infants and children (effects on the brain, behavior and prostate gland) — **Some concern**

Developmental toxicity for fetuses, infants and children (effects on the mammary gland and early puberty in females, and reproductive toxicity in workers) — **Minimal concern**

Reproductive toxicity in adult men and women and malformations in newborns — **Negligible concern**

How to Reduce Your Exposure to Bisphenol A:

Don't microwave polycarbonate plastic food containers. Bisphenol A may break down from repeated use at high temperatures.

Avoid plastic containers with the number 7 on the bottom. (www.recyclenow.org/r_plastics.html)

Don't wash polycarbonate plastic containers in the dishwasher with harsh detergents.

Reduce your use of canned foods.

When possible, opt for glass, porcelain or stainless steel containers, especially for hot foods or liquids.

Use infant formula bottles and toys that are bisphenol A-free.

Source: National Toxicology Program

try in the United States and generated over $135 billion in export revenues as of 2006. [13] Innovations in chemistry have contributed to technical advances such as composite materials for vehicles, stronger adhesives, faster microprocessors for computers and recyclable plastics.

Jan. 23, 2009 53

Core responsibility for regulating the massive chemical industry falls to the EPA, which is authorized under the Toxic Substances Control Act of 1976 (TSCA) to collect information about industrial chemicals from manufacturers and to limit or ban those that pose unreasonable risks. [14] Today EPA has some 82,000 chemicals in its TSCA inventory, of which about 62,000 were already in use when the law was passed. On average, more than 700 new chemicals are introduced each year. [15]

Although TSCA gives EPA the power to review chemicals already in commerce, the testing burden falls mainly on the agency rather than on manufacturers. As a result, EPA has required testing for fewer than 200 of the 62,000 chemicals that were in commerce in the 1970s. TSCA also requires the agency to show substantial evidence that a substance already in use poses an unreasonable risk in order to limit its use. EPA has banned only five chemicals or classes of chemicals under TSCA, and one of these efforts was overruled by a federal court in 1991. [16]

For new chemicals, manufacturers have to notify EPA before they start production and provide information on production volumes, expected uses and any test data that they have. However, most companies do not voluntarily test their products. Instead of testing new chemicals directly, EPA uses scientific models to compare their properties to similar existing chemicals and identify potential hazards. According to the Government Accountability Office (GAO), these reviews have led to actions that reduced risks from over 3,600 new chemicals. [17]

Critics say that the U.S. needs a broader and more proactive policy for regulating chemicals. "Our approach is barbaric and out of date. We used to be the leader decades ago, but now we're behind," says Lois Gibbs, founder and director of the Center for Health, Environment & Justice. In the late 1970s

Gibbs organized homeowners in Niagara Falls, N.Y., after learning that their neighborhood had been built on top of a leaking toxic waste dump called Love Canal; after two years, the federal government relocated the families.

"The U.S. is much more science-bound than other countries. There's a presumption that we understand all of the harmful interactions from exposure to toxics, but we don't," Gibbs argues. "Industry doesn't want anything changed until there's proof beyond the shadow of a doubt that it will cause harm, but we're just not that smart."

Manufacturers say that the U.S. regulatory system is fundamentally sound. "TSCA gives EPA broad authority to collect information, order testing, prohibit new uses of a substance and label or ban substances," says Walls at the American Chemistry Council. "We can enhance it to promote more systematic review and give the public more information about what chemicals are being produced." Under a program called the High Production Volume (HPV) Challenge, launched in 1998, chemical companies are voluntarily testing about 2,800 chemicals that are produced or imported in quantities of at least 1 million pounds per year and providing the information to EPA. About 1,400 data sets have been completed to date.

But GAO, while calling the HPV Challenge "laudable," has concluded that TSCA makes it too expensive and time-consuming for EPA to review chemical hazards. [18] In order to force companies to do testing EPA has to issue a regulation, a process that can take several years. "Given the difficulties involved in requiring testing, EPA officials do not believe that TSCA provides an effective means for testing a large number of existing chemicals," GAO reported in 2006. As a solution, it recommended empowering EPA to require companies to do chemical testing and provide the data to regulators.

Both EPA and FDA also need better testing methods in order to regulate toxic substances effectively. Scientists agree that current approaches, which rely heavily on animal testing, are too slow and expensive to cover hundreds of new chemicals each year and are not well-suited to predict harm from very low doses. "We need to bring our methodologies into the 21st century by making them less animal-intensive and getting higher throughputs," or testing many substances quickly, says John Bucher, associate director of the federally funded National Toxicology Program (NTP), which studies the impact of chemicals on human health.

Current test methods typically give rats or mice large doses of chemicals, look for end points like cancer or organ damage and then extrapolate those responses from animals to humans — a complex and often controversial process. A 2007 report by the National Research Council called for a new approach focused on "toxicity pathways" — changes that occur in networks of cells due to chemical exposure and which eventually may lead to adverse health effects. For example, exposure might initially cause hormone levels to change or tissues to become inflamed. The study recommended developing rapid systems for testing chemicals in cell cultures to identify toxicity pathways — a shift that it predicted would greatly reduce the need for animal testing and focus more attention on human biology and exposures. [19]

The NTP shares this vision, says Bucher. "These would be short-term assays [tests] with very simple readouts that could be run 24/7 just by punching buttons and would give a signature of biological interactions that a particular chemical would have," he says. "We hope that certain structures will be related to particular chemical classes and that that will let us make judgments about which chemicals should go through more sophisticated studies or should not be authorized for significant human exposures."

Are we commercializing nanotechnologies too quickly?

Many nanoscale materials (particles as small as 1/100,000th of the width of a human hair) have unique chemical, physical or biological characteristics that are different from larger particles of the same materials. Because they have distinctive properties such as high electrical conductivity, nanomaterials have special uses and are showing up in hundreds of consumer products, from kitchenware with antibacterial silver coatings to paints impregnated with silica particles that repel graffiti.

Consumer advocates worry that some of these applications could pose health risks, and that government agencies do not know enough about nanomaterials to regulate them effectively. An EPA fact sheet states the challenge bluntly: "At this early stage of the development of nanotechnology, there are few detailed studies on the effects of nanoscale materials in the body or the environment . . . it is not yet possible to make broad conclusions about which nanoscale substances may pose risks." [20]

Twenty-six federal agencies, including EPA, FDA and the CPSC, participate in the National Nanotechnology Initiative, a federal program that supports research on promising applications of nanotechnology and on environmental health and safety (EHS) issues. From fiscal 2005 through 2008, these agencies spent an estimated $180 million on research to address EHS questions. [21]

Scientists agree that animal testing is generally too slow and expensive to cover hundreds of new chemicals each year and is not well-suited to predict harm from very low doses. The National Research Council has called for testing chemicals in cell cultures, a shift it predicted would greatly reduce the need for animal testing.

Getty Images/China Photos

But keeping up with this fast-growing field is challenging for regulators. "I do not pretend to understand nanotechnology, and our agency does not pretend to have a grasp on this complicated subject either," CPSC Commissioner Thomas H. Moore told a Senate subcommittee in March 2007. "For fiscal year 2007, we were only able to devote $20,000 in funds to do a literature review on nanotechnology. Other agencies are asking for, and getting, millions of dollars for research in this area." [22]

Four months later an FDA task force report on regulating nanomaterials pointed out that because of their unique properties, the agency might need new testing equipment and methods to predict how they will react in body tissues. [23] Other agencies studying nanotechnologies confirm they often behave in surprising ways. "It is a daily occurrence in our labs that one of our standard assays doesn't work because of the unusual properties of these nanomaterials," said Scott E. McNeil, director of the National Cancer Institute's Nanotechnology Characterization Laboratory, at a conference last March. [24]

Some watchdog groups want to stop the marketing of nanoproducts until they are proven safe. Last May a coalition of health, environmental, and consumer groups petitioned EPA to control products containing nano-silver, which is highly effective at killing bacteria, fungi and other microorganisms. Because of this property, nano-silver has been added to garments (to kill odor), food storage containers, soaps, air purifiers and dozens of other products.

The petitioners argued that nano-silver in the environment could kill plants, benign microbes, fish and other aquatic species and might also threaten human health. They called on EPA to regulate the material as a pesticide and require comprehensive safety testing before any products containing it could be marketed. [25]

At a minimum, critics say, manufacturers should be required to label products containing nanoparticles so that consumers can choose whether or not to buy them. A study by Consumers Union found that four out of five sunscreens that claimed to be nano-free actually contained nanoparticles

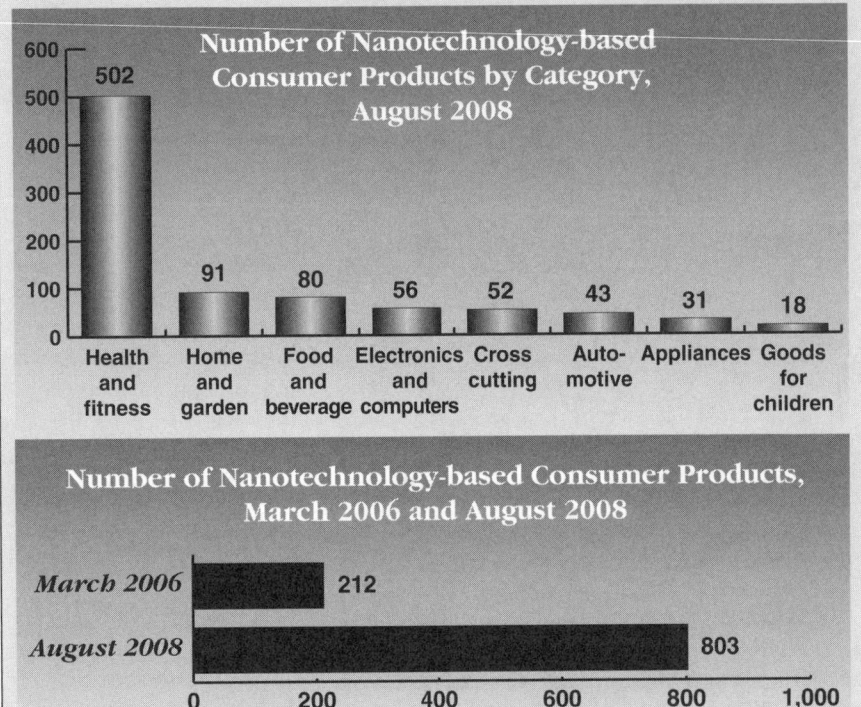

Use of Nanotechnology Is Increasing

More than 800 consumer products containing nanomaterials were in the marketplace as of August 2008 — nearly quadruple the amount from just two years earlier. Some 60 percent of the products were related to health and fitness.

Number of Nanotechnology-based Consumer Products by Category, August 2008

- Health and fitness: 502
- Home and garden: 91
- Food and beverage: 80
- Electronics and computers: 56
- Cross cutting: 52
- Automotive: 43
- Appliances: 31
- Goods for children: 18

Number of Nanotechnology-based Consumer Products, March 2006 and August 2008

- March 2006: 212
- August 2008: 803

Source: The Project on Emerging Nanotechnologies, Woodrow Wilson International Center for Scholars

of titanium dioxide and/or zinc oxide, two compounds that help protect against ultraviolet radiation. [26]

"Size matters. Materials at the nanoscale should be considered new particles and have to go through new safety assessments," says Michael Hansen, senior staff scientist at Consumers Union. "Right now, it's assumed that if a material has been tested for bulk applications, it's safe. But when you reduce things to such small sizes, their behavior and surface area can change drastically. You can't assume that something safe at the macro scale is safe at the nano scale."

Some experts say that health concerns may be exaggerated. "When we started looking at them, we found that the properties of nanomaterials in products, such as particle size, often were different from what manufacturers said they were. People didn't always know what they were studying," says the NTP's Bucher. "We completely characterized the materials we were working with and then administered them to animals in ways that might mimic human exposures. Our studies suggest that some risks are lower than reports in the literature have suggested."

For example, according to Bucher, many reports predicted that titanium dioxide in sunscreen would penetrate skin readily, but the NTP concluded that won't happen unless the skin is cut or scraped. However, he cautions,

this does not prove that all nanomaterials are harmless. "Every product is going to be different," he says.

Even if many nanomaterials are harmless, weak and underfunded regulatory agencies may have trouble distinguishing benign products from risky ones. Marla Felcher, an expert on marketing and consumer issues at Harvard University's Kennedy School of Government, says the Consumer Product Safety Commission is unprepared for the challenge. "CPSC is playing catch-up," she says. "More than half of the nanotechnology goods on the market come under its jurisdiction, and the funding it has to work with is a drop in the bucket."

But Felcher says the CPSC needs more than additional staffing and funding to ensure that nanomaterials in consumer products are safe. It also needs new authority to make manufacturers identify products that contain these substances and to impose mandatory safety standards for products based on new technologies, she says. (Today the agency relies on industry to develop and comply with voluntary safety standards). [27]

Hansen is hopeful the EPA will regulate nano-silver as a pesticide, but he says the FDA has so far refused to agree that nanomaterials are categorically different from their conventional counterparts. "The biggest exposures come from items that you put on or in your body and that contain free [non-bound] nanoparticles, like food ingredients and personal care products," says Hansen. "Scientific studies are saying that these materials need to be regulated."

Would stricter regulations hurt manufacturers and consumers?

Regulating chemicals in consumer products more stringently would affect chemical companies and manufacturers that use those chemicals to make retail goods. Chemical toxicity testing is expensive, and many business leaders say that substitutes for widely used materials like BPA will be more expensive and could produce inferior products. Health, environmental and consumer groups respond that safer products don't always cost much more, and in any case are worth a cost premium.

Even if a chemical poses risks, only some uses may require substitutes. "Health and safety concerns about a chemical like BPA are dictated as much by how it's used as by its chemistry. I'm more concerned about using it in baby bottles than in auto parts or compact discs," says Terry Collins, a professor of chemistry and director of the Institute for Green Science at Carnegie Mellon University.

Industry representatives say the risks of BPA have been widely studied and that removing it from food containers, as many critics urge, will be difficult. "BPA has been part of epoxy resin can linings for more than 50 years, and that's why we have canned goods with long shelf lives," says Steven Hentges, executive director of the American Chemistry Council's Polycarbonate/BPA Global Group. These linings prevent metallic flavors from migrating into food and keep acidic foods like tomatoes from corroding the cans.

"Substitutes have to be safer than what's being replaced, and no alternatives have been as thoroughly tested as BPA" says Hentges. The European Food Safety Authority concluded last July that BPA was safe in food packages. Canada banned BPA in baby bottles as a precautionary measure and declared it a toxic substance, but has not removed the material from food packaging for adults. Canadian regulators are funding studies to see whether further steps are needed to limit how much BPA is released into the environment. [28]

But other options exist. Many Americans buy juices, soups, sauces and chopped tomatoes in brick-shaped cartons, which were originally introduced in Europe. These containers, which are about 75 percent paper, 20 percent polyethylene plastic and 5 percent aluminum, typically cost more than canned goods, but foods packaged this way retain more color and flavor than canned foods because the food and the container are sterilized separately. The boxes can be recycled with milk and juice cartons. [29]

"There also are ways to can food so that it doesn't contain such high levels of BPA," says Janssen at the Natural Resources Defense Council. "Japan set voluntary standards for reducing BPA use in canned food, and now a lot of Japanese canned goods have a polyethylene layer inside that seals the epoxy resin lining so that BPA doesn't migrate into food. Industry should be thinking about more sustainable techniques instead of fighting to maintain the status quo."

Chemical companies and consumer advocates are also debating risks associated with phthalates, especially in children's toys. In 1998 a coalition of environmental and consumer groups petitioned the CPSC to ban toys that contained phthalates and were designed for children under age 6, citing studies suggesting that these materials could be toxic and the fact that young children commonly chewed on soft plastic toys. An expert panel convened by the commission found some risk from the phthalate DINP and asked toy makers to remove phthalates from toys voluntarily. According to the American Chemistry Council most companies removed phthalates from teethers, rattlers and pacifiers. [30]

The European Union also studied phthalates and imposed a temporary ban on six forms of the chemicals in toys and teething items in 1999. In 2005 it made the ban permanent, requiring manufacturers to eliminate three phthalates (DEHP, DBP and BBP) from all toys and to remove three others (DINP, DIDP and DNOP) from toys and child-care items that could be mouthed by children. [31]

EU regulators acted in response to studies that suggested, but did not prove, that exposure to phthalates could have toxic effects or cause abnormal reproductive development, especially in boys. A 2005 study in the United States reached a similar conclusion, but a U.S. government review panel found that animal studies that showed a connection were not necessarily applicable to people. [32] However, California, Washington and Vermont passed state-level bans. In 2008 Congress permanently banned DEHP, DBP and BBP from toys and set an interim ban on the other three types pending a safety review by the CPSC. [33]

Many businesses opposed the measure. "[M]anufacturers would be forced to use more expensive alternatives that may subject them to additional safety and legal liability concerns, and consumers would be exposed to products containing alternatives that have not been approved for use in children's products by any federal agency," the U.S. Chamber of Commerce wrote to Senate members early in 2008. [34]

Chemical industry representatives maintain that scientific evidence shows phthalates to be safe. "The pro-regulatory side considers phthalates guilty until proven innocent. They want to act even though the data is not conclusive," says Allen Blakey, vice president of the Vinyl Institute, a trade group for companies that manufacture vinyl and vinyl products (many of which contain phthalates to make them soft and flexible).

But toy manufacturers seem to be adapting to phthalate restrictions. Observers predicted the U.S. ban could drive some of China's small and uncompetitive toy manufacturers out of business, but other Chinese companies already make toys with phthalates for U.S. markets and without them for sale in the EU. [35] BASF, a major German chemical company, still produces DEHP in the United States but developed a new plasticized version called Hexamoll DINCH, which it markets to toy makers as a product "whose health safety is beyond all question" and "an ideal solution to adapting their products to the requirements of the new EU regulation." [36] ∎

BACKGROUND

Reactive Regulation

Through the 19th century, as the United States grew from a nation of small-scale farmers into an industrial powerhouse, few standards protected people from hazardous materials. And even when government began to regulate dangerous products and substances in the early 20th century, controls were almost always put in place belatedly after scandals or disasters.

Muckraking journalist Upton Sinclair spurred passage of early consumer-protection laws with his 1906 novel *The Jungle*, which described filthy conditions in Chicago's meatpacking industry. Simultaneously, a series of articles in *Collier's* magazine spotlighted false claims and unsafe ingredients in so-called patent (non-prescription) medicines. Many of these concoctions were sold as cure-alls for numerous diseases but contained addictive substances like cocaine, heroin or alcohol. "[F]raud, exploited by the skillfulest [sic] of advertising bunco men, is the basis of the trade," author Samuel Hopkins Adams charged. [37]

In response Congress passed the Meatpacking Act and the first Food and Drug Act, which authorized government regulators to inspect meat processing plants and to seize products that were mislabeled or contained harmful or spoiled ingredients. However, manufacturers were not required to list all of the ingredients in foods or medicines or submit any information to the government before marketing them.

In 1933 the Food and Drug Administration proposed a complete revision of the Food and Drug Act, but Congress failed to act until 107 people in 15 states died in 1937 after taking elixir of sulfanilamide for strep infections. A chemist had created a liquid form of sulfanilamide, a new and effective prescription medicine, by dissolving the powdered medication in diethylene glycol, a chemical normally used as antifreeze, which he failed to realize was poisonous. [38] This tragedy spurred passage of the Federal Food, Drug, and Cosmetic Act, which required new drugs to be tested for safety before marketing.

As Congress debated safety standards, the fast-growing chemical industry was inventing myriad new materials. Important chemical products developed in the 1920s and '30s included polychlorinated biphenyls (PCBs), used as coolants and lubricants; synthetic estrogens (female hormones); and organic pesticides like the mosquito-killer DDT. Nineteenth-century inventors had already discovered many basic types of plastic, and by World War II these materials were widely used in applications including cellophane, vinyl, nylon and Teflon coatings.

During this period the labor movement gained strength as workers formed unions and won the right to collective bargaining. One of their priorities was making workplaces safer. Government agencies started to regulate safety, initially focusing on industries like mining and manufacturing, where workers were frequently injured by machinery, fires and explosions. Toxic exposure was also emerging as a serious hazard. For example, by the 1930s manufacturers knew that workers who inhaled silica dust or asbestos had high rates of lung disease, and medical researchers were starting to connect asbestos inhalation with cancer.

Under President Franklin D. Roosevelt (1933-1945), the Labor Department worked with industry and unions to improve workplace safety, mainly through voluntary safety codes and better training programs. During the economic boom of the 1950s occupational safety became a more established professional field, but it focused on traumatic injuries such as falls or machine accidents rather than exposure to dangerous materials. In one industrial hygienist's words, it was hard to draw attention to safety issues "unless people saw the blood drip." [39]

New Guardians

As corporations shifted from wartime manufacturing to civilian products, new materials streamed into commercial use, including vaccines, food additives, pesticides and herbicides and an avalanche of consumer goods. Most Americans welcomed these products, but research soon showed that some were unsafe.

By the late 1950s government regulators had banned more than a dozen food additives because they caused cancer, organ damage or other toxic effects in animals. [40] In 1958 Congress adopted the Delaney Clause, which barred all food additives that had been shown to cause cancer in laboratory animals. Six years later Surgeon General Luther Terry released a report stating that smoking caused cancer, and Congress passed a law requiring cigarette packs to carry health warning labels. [41] However, the tobacco industry — which had created its own scientific arm, the Tobacco Industry Research Committee, to refute incriminating studies — argued that smoking was a personal choice, and successfully lobbied against any limits on cigarette advertising or marketing.

By this time other toxic exposures were in the news. Rachel Carson's 1962 bestseller *Silent Spring* warned that persistent organic pesticides like DDT were accumulating in the environment, harming fish and birds and contaminating food supplies. In the same year it was disclosed that thousands of babies in Asia, Africa and Europe had been born with deformed or missing limbs after their mothers took thalidomide, a new sedative that the FDA was then close to approving for sale in the United States.

Continued on p. 61

Chronology

1900-1960
Government begins regulating consumer goods to protect buyers; fast-growing chemical industry produces thousands of materials that are quickly put to use.

1906
Congress authorizes federal inspections of meatpacking plants and outlaws adulterated or mislabeled foods and drugs.

1929
Chemical companies start making polychlorinated biphenyls (PCBs).

1930
Food and Drug Administration (FDA) is established. . . . Studies show asbestos can cause cancer.

1938
After tainted medicine kills 105 people, Congress passes Food, Drug and Cosmetic Act, requirng food additives and drugs to be proven safe. . . . British scientists produce diethylstilbestrol (DES), a synthetic estrogen, which is approved to treat gynecological ailments.

1939
Swiss chemist Paul Müller discovers that the synthetic chemical DDT is an effective insect killer. Müller later wins Nobel Prize after DDT-B is widely used to protect troops from typhus and malaria during World War II.

1954
Cigarette manufacturers create Tobacco Industry Research Council in response to scientific findings of health threats from smoking.

1958
Delaney Clause to Food, Drug and Cosmetic Act bans food additives that cause cancer in animals.

1960-1980
New agencies protect consumers and workers from hazardous substances. Studies find popular chemicals can harm health.

1962
Rachel Carson's bestseller *Silent Spring* warns of environmental and health threats from DDT.

1964
Surgeon general declares smoking hazardous to health; warning labels are required on cigarettes.

1970
Environmental Protection Agency (EPA) is created.

1971
Occupational Safety and Health Administration (OSHA) is established. . . . DES is linked to vaginal cancer.

1972
Consumer Product Safety Commission (CPSC) is established. . . . EPA bans DDT.

1976
Toxic Substances Control Act (TSCA) authorizes EPA to regulate chemicals but exempts 62,000 substances.

1977
CPSC bans nearly all uses of lead paint, including on toys.

1980-2000
Anti-regulatory forces challenge new, protective standards.

1980
Supreme Court's "benzene decision" says OSHA must show significant risks before limiting a chemical's use.

1983
OSHA requires employers to show workers how to use toxic chemicals.

1986
California mandates warning labels for products with chemicals that cause cancer or birth defects.

1990
Congress requires leaded gasoline to be phased out by 1996.

1996
Food Quality Protection Act tightens standard for pesticide residues in food and requires special protection for infants and children.

1997
Study finds bisphenol A (BPA) alters reproductive development in mice.

2000-Present
Support grows for natural and organic products.

2000
National Nanotechnology Initiative is launched.

2003
Congress approves $3.7 billion over four years for nanotech research, but only a small amount is earmarked for studying health impacts.

2007
European Union's REACH chemical regulation enters into force.

2008
Congress strengthens CPSC and bans lead and six phthalates from children's toys. . . . Canada bans BPA from baby bottles. . . . FDA committee concludes BPA is not harmful in food packaging, but the agency's review panel faults the study's methods.

Americans' Bodies Contain Over 100 Chemicals

Some cause cancer and other health problems.

Studies indicate that all human beings alive today carry traces of many industrial chemicals in their bodies. Some of these substances enter during fetal development or infanthood, carried by maternal blood and breast milk. In addition, we inhale airborne pollutants, ingest pesticide residues and chemical additives with our food and drinking water and absorb others through our skin. Exposure can happen in the workplace, outdoors or inside homes and schools.

Some so-called "chemical body burdens" in humans are harmless, but others can cause cancer, birth defects, developmental problems and other serious health impacts. Many are still being studied. The presence of a chemical in the body does not necessarily mean it will cause harm, but scientists say chemical exposure is pervasive in modern society, and they underscore the importance of testing widely used chemicals for toxic effects.

"I find it remarkable that in this day and age one of the primary ways by which the toxic effects of chemicals are discovered is still the 'body in the morgue' method," writes epidemiologist and former assistant secretary of Energy David Michaels. "An industrial worker dies from some very unusual condition, and we ask why. Well, some of us ask."

For example, Michaels notes, chemical companies that make diacetyl (the main ingredient in artificial butter flavor) did not know that breathing the compound could cause lung damage until workers in popcorn factories became ill. Manufacturers had been required to test diacetyl as a food ingredient, but not as an airborne contaminant in the workplace. [1]

According to a 2005 report from the Centers for Disease Control and Prevention (CDC), well over 100 chemicals are present in Americans at detectable levels, including heavy metals like cadmium and mercury, phthalates and many pesticides. Levels of some chemicals have fallen in recent years, notably lead (which has been banned from gasoline and house paint) and substances found in secondhand cigarette smoke. [2]

Others are more worrisome. For example, the CDC found that almost 6 percent of women of childbearing age had blood levels of mercury that were borderline dangerous. Mercury is a potent neurotoxin that can cause birth defects, nervous system damage and other harmful effects. It is emitted into the air from sources including coal-burning power plants and incinerators, then falls back to the surface and concentrates in the food chain. Humans are exposed mainly by eating fish that contain high amounts of mercury.

Another 2005 study commissioned by two advocacy organizations, Commonweal and the Environmental Working Group, tested umbilical cord blood from 10 babies born in U.S. hospitals during the previous year. Researchers found an average of 200 industrial chemicals and pollutants in the samples, including mercury, environmental pollutants known as dioxins and pesticides. This study showed that pollutants cross the placenta from mother to fetus as infants grow in utero, exposing the gestating infants to a complex mixture of chemicals during critical months of development. [3]

Living far from industrial sources does not necessarily make people safer from exposures. Indigenous peoples in the Arctic have some of the highest body concentrations of mercury, PCBs and other pollutants of any region on the planet, thanks to global wind patterns and ocean currents that carry pollutants to the poles. Inuit, Aleut, and other native people in Greenland, Alaska and Canada eat large quantities of locally caught meat and fish, which contain high concentrations of chemicals. [4]

Recent studies show that concentrations of some toxins in Arctic food animals are stabilizing, thanks to international agreements limiting use of some of the most hazardous chemicals. [5] However, toxic chemicals remain a major threat to Arctic indigenous peoples' traditional way of life — an ironic fate for people who neither produce nor use most of these products.

An Inuit woman in Iqaluit, Nunavut, Canada, dries a caribou skin. Toxic chemicals remain a major threat to traditional ways of life in the Arctic.

AFP/Getty Images/Andre Forget

[1] David Michaels, *Doubt Is Their Product: How Industry's Assault on Science Threatens Your Health* (Oxford University Press, 2008), p. 247.

[2] "Third National Report on Human Exposure to Environmental Chemicals," 2005, www.cdc.gov/exposurereport/report.htm, and "Spotlight on Mercury," both Centers for Disease Control and Prevention, www.cdc.gov/Exposure Report/pdf/factsheet_mercury.pdf.

[3] "Body Burden — The Pollution in Newborns," *Environmental Working Group*, July 14, 2005, http://archive.ewg.org/reports/bodyburden2/contentindex.php.

[4] Marla Cone, *Silent Snow: The Slow Poisoning of the Arctic* (2006).

[5] "Toxic Chemical Levels Finally Dropping in Arctic Food Animals, New Study Shows," The Canadian Press news agency, July 14, 2008.

Continued from p. 58

In 1965 consumer activist Ralph Nader amplified pressure on the government to regulate dangerous products with his book *Unsafe at Any Speed*, which attacked U.S. automakers for refusing to include safety devices like seat belts and filling cars with confusing and distracting features. [42] The book and subsequent congressional hearings generated new safety requirements and oversight agencies for passenger cars.

The Nixon administration created other agencies to regulate industry more tightly and protect consumers, including the Environmental Protection Agency (EPA) in 1970, the Occupational Safety and Health Administration (OSHA) in 1971 and the Consumer Product Safety Commission (CPSC) in 1972. Along with the FDA, each of the new agencies had some responsibility for protecting workers and the public from toxic threats, although the scope of their powers varied.

During the 1970s federal regulators passed some important protective measures. EPA banned DDT use in 1972 because of its harmful environmental impacts. In 1979 the agency banned production of PCBs, which had been shown to cause cancer and birth defects in laboratory animals, and set timetables for phasing out their use in various industries. In 1977 the CPSC banned lead paint and its use on toys and furniture. OSHA set occupational exposure standards for many hazardous substances and developed requirements (finalized in the early 1980s) for businesses to identify and label hazardous chemicals in the workplace and tell employees how to use them safely.

Business Pushes Back

Many controls adopted in the 1970s made the environment cleaner and improved public health. But industry

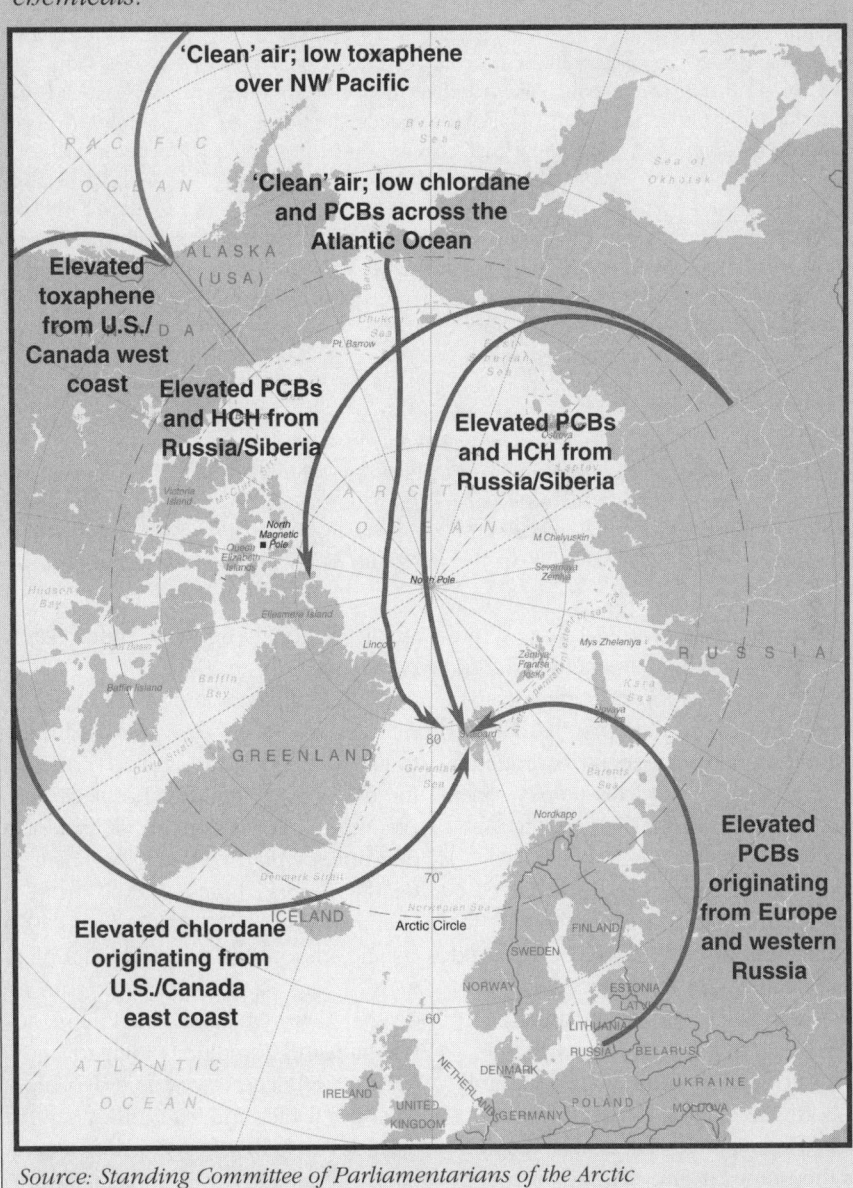

The Polluted Arctic

Atmospheric and ocean currents carry persistent organic pollutants around the world far from their sources and concentrate them in some regions, notably the Arctic, where they are a threat to indigenous peoples and wildlife. Even relatively "clean" air from non-industrial areas contains low levels of pesticides and other chemicals.

Source: Standing Committee of Parliamentarians of the Arctic

and conservative politicians argued that government regulators were becoming high-handed and that excessive regulations slowed economic growth. President Ronald Reagan (1981-1989) made reducing government's power a centerpiece of his administration, cutting budgets at EPA, OSHA and CPSC and appointing officials who were hostile to regulation.

European Regulators Take 'Precautionary' Approach

Chemical companies must show products are safe.

Chemicals are big business in Europe as well as in the United States, but the European Union (EU) has taken a sharply different approach to regulating chemical risks. In 2007 the EU's new REACH policy (Registration, Evaluation, Authorization, and Restriction of Chemicals) went into effect. In the United States, regulators must show that chemicals pose risks to human health or the environment before they can limit their production or use. But REACH takes essentially the opposite approach: Companies must show that chemicals will not harm human health or the environment before they can be marketed.

During an 11-year phase-in period, businesses that produce or import any chemical into the EU in quantities greater than one metric ton per year will have to register it with the new European Chemicals Agency and submit information about its physical and chemical properties, how it will be made, how to use it safely and how it affects human health and the environment. More detailed information is required for chemicals that are produced in larger volumes. EU officials estimate that about 30,000 chemicals now in use will be subject to REACH. [1]

Manufacturers of chemicals deemed to pose especially high risks — such as those that cause cancer, birth defects or endocrine disruption or that persist and are toxic in the environment — will have to apply to the European Commission

for authorization. They will have to show that it is not technically or economically feasible to use safer substitutes, and that the risks from using the chemical can be controlled. REACH allows regulators to ban or restrict the use of chemicals that pose unacceptable risks to human health or the environment and limits the amount of health-related data that manufacturers can shield as proprietary information.

Many U.S. health and environmental advocates say REACH is a better model for regulating hazardous substances than the Toxic Substances Control Act (TSCA), and that the U.S. should emulate Europe by moving in a more precautionary direction. "TSCA is really ineffective and needs to be updated," says Sarah Janssen, a scientist at the Natural Resources Defense Council. "It limits EPA's ability to request toxicity information from manufacturers; there are thousands of chemicals on the market now without toxicity information; and there's no requirement for companies to notify EPA if they increase production or start using chemicals in new ways. REACH isn't perfect, but it's definitely a lot better than what we have, which is basically a free-for-all."

U.S. chemical companies and the Bush administration lobbied hard against REACH, arguing that it was too complex and expensive, posed a barrier to foreign exporters outside of Europe and could cause American workers to lose their jobs. C. Boyden

---

Reagan also required the White House Office of Management and Budget to review proposed new rules — a policy that his successors continued — and signed an executive order directing agencies not to issue new ones unless their potential benefits to society were greater than their costs. [43] Many policy experts agreed that cost-benefit analysis was a useful tool for setting priorities, but others worried that health and environmental benefits were hard to quantify and would be undervalued.

Critics charged the Reagan administration with leading a "retreat from safety." "The agencies no longer respond to the needs of unorganized victims of technological hazards. Instead, they service the business executives and stockholders who are responsible for the hazards," wrote Joan Claybrook, president of the Nader-founded activist group Public Citizen and former head

of the National Highway Traffic Safety Administration, in 1984. [44]

In this climate some of the most significant new steps were so-called right-to-know policies, which did not limit the use of risky materials but gave people more information about potential exposures. After methyl isocyanate, a deadly industrial gas, leaked from a chemical plant in Bhopal, India, in 1984 (killing some 4,000 people) and a plant in West Virginia the next year (with no deaths), Congress passed the Emergency Planning and Community Right to Know Act in 1986. The law required companies to tell EPA and state officials what hazardous chemicals were used in significant quantities at their plants and to notify emergency responders about any chemical releases.

Another major step in 1986 was the passage in California of Proposition 65, a ballot initiative that directed the state to publish an annual list of chemicals

used in California that were known to cause cancer, birth defects or other reproductive harms. Businesses had to warn people before exposing them to significant risks from listed chemicals — for example, by putting warning labels on processed food or signs in workplaces where listed substances were used. [45]

The Clinton administration (1993-2001) was more receptive to new health and safety regulations than its predecessors. FDA Commissioner David Kessler declared cigarettes to be "drug delivery devices," an acknowledgment that nicotine was addictive, and called for limiting marketing and sales to young people. In 1996 Clinton signed the Food Quality Protection Act, which tightened standards for pesticide residues in foods and required EPA to consider children's higher sensitivity to these chemicals when it set tolerance levels.

In 1998 the administration called for chemical companies to perform

Gray, the U.S. ambassador to the EU, said REACH would "be hell for American multinationals. . . . Our position is if we don't stop it, it will multiply like kudzu." [2] Now, however, U.S. manufacturers are reformulating their products for sale in Europe and preparing to register them.

Michael Walls, managing director at the American Chemistry Council, the main U.S. chemical industry trade group, acknowledges that REACH breaks some valuable ground. "It's raised the issue of how we assure safe use, and it's promoted dialogue about how certain chemicals are used in sectors like electronics, automobiles and aerospace," he says. But, Walls argues, REACH does not pay enough attention to how chemicals are used, which is one determinant of how risky they are. "There are some opportunities to consider specific uses, but chemicals are identified for regulation specifically based on hazardous characteristics, and we don't think that's the way to prioritize," he says.

No regulatory decisions have been made under REACH yet. A preregistration phase for existing chemicals ended last November, and regulators now are considering which substances should require authorization before they can be used. By December 2010 companies must submit data on high-volume chemicals (those produced in quantities over 1,000 metric tons per year) and highly toxic chemicals produced in smaller quantities. "REACH is still untested and unproven, and we have concerns about whether some of its provisions are workable," says Walls.

But some activists already would like to make REACH even more stringent. For example, Janssen argues the system does not pay enough attention to endocrine-disrupting chemicals. "Some chemicals aren't produced in very big volumes, but they have serious impacts at very low volumes," she says. "Hormones work in the parts-per-billion to parts-per-trillion range in your body — very small doses have really big impacts." And REACH does not explicitly cover nanomaterials, although manufacturers who want to use an existing chemical substance at the nano level will have to supply additional information on the nanoform's specific properties and describe measures to minimize risks from them. [3]

[1] "Chemical Regulation: Comparison of U.S. and Recently Enacted European Union Approaches to Protect Against the Risks of Toxic Chemicals," U.S. Government Accountability Office, August 2007.

[2] Mark Schapiro, *Exposed: The Toxic Chemistry of Everyday Products and What's at Stake for American Power* (2007), p. 253.

[3] "REACH and Nanomaterials," European Commission, http://ec.europa.eu/enterprise/reach/reach/more_info/nanomaterials/index_en.htm.

voluntary toxicity testing on chemicals in use that had not been tested — and threatened to require it if industry did not comply. Subsequently the EPA, the chemical industry and the advocacy group Environmental Defense announced the High Production Volume (HPV) Challenge, which aimed to complete toxicity testing by 2004 on about 2,800 industrial chemicals made or imported into the U.S. in large quantities.

Along with cancer and birth defects, Americans started to hear in the 1990s about so-called endocrine disruptors — chemicals that interfered with hormones responsible for regulating biological processes throughout the body, such as brain growth and sexual development. Scientists were finding evidence that endocrine disruptors were causing reproductive abnormalities, population declines and other negative impacts in wildlife. Some studies linked pesticides that mimicked estrogen, the female sex hormone, with increased risk of breast cancer.

Other researchers were alarmed by falling human sperm counts. "Every man sitting in this room today is half the man his grandfather was," University of Florida zoologist Louis Guillette told a Senate committee in 1993. "Are our children going to be half the men we are?" Three years later, the best-selling book *Our Stolen Future* argued that endocrine disruptors posed pervasive health risks but that federal controls on toxic chemicals were overly focused on detecting and controlling cancer risks. "The assumptions about toxicity and disease that have framed our thinking for the past three decades are inappropriate and act as obstacles to understanding a different kind of damage," the authors contended. [46]

New Worries

Under President George W. Bush (2001-2009), momentum once again swung from strong regulation to voluntary compliance strategies in which companies agreed to police themselves. With pro-business officials in charge at many regulatory agencies and limited budgets, the pace of federal regulation dropped sharply. Rulemaking fell by more than 50 percent at FDA and 57 percent at EPA between 2001 and 2008 compared with those agencies' records during the Clinton administration. OSHA withdrew more than a dozen regulations that had been proposed under Clinton and delayed taking action on silica dust after identifying it as a workplace health threat. [47]

Conservative advocates generally supported the shift to deregulation, arguing that excessive health and safety regulations were burdens on the economy and often were not the most effective way to protect public health or the environment. "Regulations unquestionably force the issue, but usually at a very high cost to the economy and to property rights," wrote American Enterprise Institute analyst Steven Hayward in 2008. "This kind of bureaucratic environmentalism has about played itself out, and is decreasingly relevant to the local environmental problems that remain to be tackled." [48]

At the same time, however, consumers and even some large industries were asking federal agencies for more regulation. From 2007 through mid-2008 a string of product scares made headlines, including U.S.-grown spinach carrying hazardous bacteria, imported pet food and seafood adulterated with chemicals, and recalls of toys found to contain lead paint. [49] Many of these products, including the tainted pet food and toys, came from China, while contaminated fish was shipped from China and other countries in Asia and from Latin America. In May 2008 FDA Commissioner Andrew von Eschenbach asked Congress for $275 million in immediate funding to improve oversight of drugs, medical products and imported food. [50]

Two months later Congress passed the Consumer Product Safety Act of 2008, which overhauled the CPSC and increased its staffing, required toys and other children's products to be tested for safety before they entered the market and banned lead and several types of phthalates from children's products. "This reform is much needed, long overdue and necessary to ensure that CPSC can successfully ensure the safety of consumer products," said Rachel Weintraub, director of product safety and senior counsel at the Consumer Federation of America. ■

CURRENT SITUATION

FDA and BPA

As debate continues over potential health risks from BPA, the FDA is at the center of controversy. Last August the agency released a draft assessment concluding that BPA in food packaging did not pose a health risk. But an advisory panel that reviewed the draft report found a number of flaws, such as omitting studies suggesting BPA could have harmful effects, using too few infant formula samples and not considering cumulative exposures. The reviewers concluded that "the Margins of Safety defined by the FDA as 'adequate' are, in fact, inadequate." [51] (A margin of safety is the gap between the lowest dose of BPA expected to cause harm and the actual exposure that scientists expect to occur.)

The FDA is reviewing these arguments and has pledged to provide a response by this February. "FDA agrees that, due to the uncertainties raised in some studies relating to the Potential effects of low-dose exposure to bisphenol A, additional research would be valuable," says agency spokesperson Michael Herndon. "[The agency] is already moving forward with planned research to address the potential low-dose effects of bisphenol A, and we will carefully evaluate the findings of these studies."

Critics argue the FDA has deliberately downplayed low-dose exposures to avoid having to issue new regulations. "We're replaying what happened with lead regulation," says Carnegie Mellon chemistry Professor Terry Collins. "Trade associations fought against banning lead from house paint and gasoline for 70 years by beating up doctors who said lead was bad for children and funding studies that only looked at high doses.

EPA chose for years not to look at risks from ultra-low doses, and FDA is doing the same thing now. It's very confusing to the public, and these impacts are showing up across the population."

The National Toxicology Program's Bucher agrees that the FDA needs new methods to evaluate BPA. "The academic studies that found effects at low doses assessed exposures to very fine degrees," he says. "FDA's guidelines for industry studies don't require such detail, and they're just not adequate to pick up subtle changes that can occur from low-dose exposures, such as behavior differences between male and female mouse pups."

The NTP is still trying to answer important questions about BPA, says Bucher: "We know what doses animals receive in studies, but we don't know much about where it goes and how much of it reaches different tissues, or how quickly it's eliminated from the body. It's not eliminated as quickly in young animals as in older ones, and we think that's true in humans as well." He expects that the NTP will soon initiate a study to see whether prenatal exposure to BPA can lead to cancer. "Earlier studies started dosing in young adults, but clearly the most sensitive periods are earlier than that," Bucher adds.

Activist Congress

Although research is ongoing, some members of Congress have already called for new limits on chemicals in consumer products, starting with a ban on BPA in food and beverage containers. Several legislators cited a November 2008 study by the *Milwaukee Journal Sentinel* that found plastic products labeled as "microwave safe" leached potentially harmful doses of BPA when they were heated. "Parents always err on the side of caution when it comes to their kids' health. We think the law should do the same," said Sen. Charles E. Schumer, D-NY. [52] He introduced legislation in

Continued on p. 66

At Issue:

Does the precautionary principle make us safer?

WENDY E. WAGNER
PROFESSOR OF LAW
UNIVERSITY OF TEXAS

WRITTEN FOR *CQ RESEARCHER*, JANUARY 2009

*t*he regulation of chemicals in the United States epitomizes what can go wrong when a legal system adopts a non-precautionary approach. Under the Toxic Substances Control Act (TSCA), manufacturers are not required to do any pre- or post-market testing on their chemicals unless mandated by the Environmental Protection Agency. At the same time, there are few to no rewards under the act for producing safer or better-tested chemicals, at least with regard to latent hazards.

In fact, chemical manufacturers that do voluntarily test their chemicals may put themselves at a competitive disadvantage: They not only produce evidence that can be used against them by regulators and plaintiffs' attorneys but also dedicate resources to testing that are unlikely to be recouped in sales — either because the testing reveals unwelcome risks or because the positive results cannot be validated readily by consumers or investors.

The TSCA's non-precautionary approach is partly to blame for the resulting ignorance about the long-term safety of most chemicals and for the lack of incentives to develop safer, "greener" chemicals. Over the 30-year-plus history of the legislation, EPA has required testing for fewer than 200 chemicals. Most of the remaining 75,000 chemicals produced during that period are essentially unrestricted and unreviewed with regard to their health and environmental impacts. While such a counter-productive regulatory scheme would seem at first blush a perfect candidate for public-spirited reform, the highest-stakes participants in toxics policy are the chemical manufacturers, who not surprisingly have become well-organized and steadfast in their opposition to reform.

Fortunately, the European Union's REACH directive will produce valuable toxicity information on chemicals, whether U.S. manufacturers want it or not. Through its mandatory testing requirements, REACH (registration, evaluation, authorization and restriction of chemicals) may also generate incentives for safer chemical substitutes.

In the United States, the precautionary features of REACH could be supplemented by creating additional rewards for producing safer chemicals. For example, EPA could preside over petitions filed by manufacturers seeking regulatory certification of a chemical's superiority relative to its competitors. Pitting manufacturers against one another through such adjudication will help draw out information on the toxicity of chemicals and reward greener chemical companies, while at the same time undermining the unified resistance of chemical manufacturers to modifications in TSCA's non-precautionary approach.

GARY MARCHANT
PROFESSOR OF LAW
ARIZONA STATE
UNIVERSITY

WRITTEN FOR *CQ RESEARCHER*, JANUARY 2009

*t*he precautionary principle (PP) attempts to address a serious problem: How should we deal with uncertain risks?

Bisphenol A, Teflon, thimerosal in vaccines, melamine in baby formula and phthalates in fire retardants are just some of the uncertain risks on the front pages of newspapers today. Which ones should we restrict now, and which should we just study more before taking action?

Unfortunately, the PP fails to provide a coherent or useful answer to this critical question. The problem, as H. L. Mencken once noted: "[t]here is always an easy solution to every human problem — neat, plausible, and wrong."

Since originating in Europe approximately 40 years ago, the PP is now binding law in Europe, Canada, Australia and several Asian nations, has been incorporated in over 60 international treaties and has been adopted by several U.S. cities. Yet, the PP is problematic, especially when enacted as a binding legal rule. First, there is no standard or official definition of "the" precautionary principle, and dozens of unofficial versions exist. Which version applies will make a huge difference in many decisions.

Second, available interpretations of the PP offer no clear guidance on key questions, such as what manufacturers must do to satisfy the PP and how costs are factored in. Without answering these fundamental questions, the PP opens the door to arbitrary decisions motivated by political bias, protectionism and other inappropriate motives, rather than objective scientific evidence of risk.

Thus, relying on the PP, Norway banned Kellogg's Corn Flakes because the added vitamins could theoretically harm some ultra-susceptible person. France banned Red Bull energy drinks because the caffeine might harm pregnant women (but did not ban coffee or wine) and Denmark banned cranberry fruit drinks because vitamin C might harm some people.

More tragically, Zambia cited the PP to deny U.S. food aid to its starving population because of the possible presence of genetically modified corn (which Americans routinely eat with no apparent consequences). The European Union even used the PP to justify governmental subsidization of the coal industry, even though coal is not generally perceived as the most environmentally friendly energy source. With the PP, however, no further explanation is needed.

Finally, the PP fails to consider that many new technologies, such as biotechnology and nanotechnology, offer the promise of enormous benefits, including health and environmental gains. By failing to consider these effects, the PP fails its own test for seeking to prohibit dangerous innovations.

Continued from p. 64

2008 that would have banned BPA from products designed for children ages 7 and under, while Rep. Edward J. Markey, D-Mass., introduced a House bill that would have eliminated BPA from all food and beverage packaging. [53]

At least 13 states are also considering BPA bans. However, one such proposal failed in California in August 2008. Food processors, chemical manufacturers and packaging companies opposed the bill, which would have banned use of BPA in products for children ages 3 and under. "California's legislators made the right decision for consumers," said the American Chemistry Council's Hentges.

Another 2008 congressional bill that is likely to be reintroduced, the Kid-Safe Chemicals Act, would require more sweeping reforms to the Toxic Substances Control Act and the chemical-testing process. [54] The measure seeks to "eliminate the exposure of all children, workers, consumers and sensitive subgroups to harmful chemicals distributed in commerce by calendar year 2020." The measure would:

- require industry to demonstrate that chemicals in use are safe;
- authorize EPA to require additional testing for health effects at low doses and for nanomaterials;
- expand analysis by the Centers for Disease Control and Prevention (CDC) of chemical residues in humans; and
- provide new funds to promote safer alternatives.

"It is critical that we modernize our nation's chemical safety laws," said Rep. Henry A. Waxman, D-Calif., a sponsor of the House bill and the new chair of the Energy and Commerce Committee. "The Kid-Safe Chemicals Act will deliver what its name implies — a non-toxic environment for our children."

Another chemical issue on Congress's agenda is reauthorization of the National Nanotechnology Initiative (NNI), which coordinates nanotechnology research by federal agencies. The House passed a reauthorization bill with little controversy in 2008, but nanotechnology may face a bumpier ride in the Senate. In December 2008 the National Research Council released a review of NNI's research plan for studying potential health and environmental risks of nanotechnologies. While the study did not address whether current uses of nanomaterials posed risks to the public, it found that NNI did not have an adequate strategy for answering that question.

NNI's plan "does not describe a clear strategy for nano-risk research. It lacks input from a diverse stakeholder group, and it lacks essential elements, such as a vision and a clear set of objectives, a comprehensive assessment of the state of the science, a plan or road map that describes how research progress will be measured, and the estimated resources required to conduct such research," the NRC review stated. [55]

Making Exceptions

Banning products does not always end debate over them. Bans on phthalates in children's products under the 2008 Consumer Product Safety Improvement Act were scheduled to start on Feb. 10, 2009, but lawyers representing toy wholesalers and retailers wrote to the CPSC in late 2008 that the ban would impose "significant financial hardship" on their clients — especially if they were left with useless products after the deadline passed.

In response CPSC General Counsel Cheryl Falvey held that the law did not contain a "clear statement of unambiguous intent" to apply the ban to existing toys, so manufacturers could keep selling items in their inventories that contained the proscribed materials. [56] Two advocacy groups, the Natural Resources Defense Council and Public Citizen, filed suit against the agency, arguing that all items containing the phthalates in question should be re-

moved from shelves by the February 2009 deadline. "The CPSC decision will generate and prolong exposure to known hormone-disrupting chemicals. . . . There is no way for [consumers] to know whether products on store shelves after the ban date contain phthalates or not," the groups argued. [57]

Many toy vendors and manufacturers also say the law's Feb. 10 deadline for applying tough, new lead levels could cost them heavily. By that date toys may contain no more than 600 parts per million by weight of lead, a trace amount that will ratchet further down over time. Falvey ruled in November that unlike the phthalate ban, the new lead ban (which was worded differently in the law) did apply to existing toys. But some toy company owners said that testing their entire inventories for lead would be extremely expensive, and that retailers might send entire shipments back if there were worries about whether some items met the standard. [58] According to the CDC, only certified laboratories can test toys accurately for lead. [59]

Another proposed ban, on polyvinyl chloride (PVC) plastics, passed through the California Assembly and two Senate committees last year but then stalled in the Senate Appropriations Committee. PVC is used for many applications, including water pipes, medical tubing and numerous types of packaging. But critics like the Center for Health, Environment, and Justice (CHEJ) call PVC "poison plastic" because it can release chemicals such as phthalates and dioxins (a family of persistent, toxic, chlorinated hydrocarbon chemicals) during its life cycle, and its production exposes workers to other hazardous materials.

Debate over the California bill showed the difficulty of making up-or-down decisions about substances that have many uses but also pose risks. As the bill moved through various committees, legislators exempted a number of products from the ban, including medical devices, packaging for medications and containers for petroleum products. "It's easy for attackers to dismiss PVC, but not so easy for the marketplace," says the Vinyl Institute's Blakey.

Many large manufacturers and retailers have adopted policies to phase out PVC in products or packaging, including Mattel, Nike, Sony, Target, Wal-Mart, K-Mart and Sears. But Blakey calls these steps responses to political pressure and argues that PVC products are safe. Retailers, he says, "are misinformed and pressured. They don't have a lot of staff to verify critiques, and they want the issue to go away."

Activists don't deny that they're pushing companies to drop PVC, but they say safer alternatives are available. "There are some substances that don't have substitutes, so we have to use them carefully. But there are all kinds of substitutes for PVC," says CHEJ President Lois Gibbs. The center published a guide in 2008 that lists dozens of sources for toys, clothing, mattresses and other goods made without PVC. (However, as the guide notes, the center does not endorse any of the listed substitute products, manufacturers, or retailers.) [60]

The Obama Administration

M any environmentalists are optimistic about what the newly inaugurated President Barack Obama will do about toxic chemicals. Obama has embraced green issues during his campaign and since his election. Although the economic meltdown undoubtedly will force Obama to pare down his campaign wish list, his transition team has been examining new environmental policies that could be adopted quickly, including some Clinton-era initiatives that could be resurrected.

During his inaugural speech on Jan. 20, Obama said he would "restore science to its rightful place" and has vowed to listen more closely to scientific advisers and environmental experts, whose advice the Bush administration often ignored or overruled. "I think we are in store for something new," said William Reilly, who led the

Environmental Protection Agency under President George H. W. Bush. "His pledge to follow the science will be reassuring to a lot of people, including those who fear the regulators are going to run amok." [61]

Within hours after Obama's inauguration, his Chief of Staff Rahm Emmanuel ordered a halt on all work on unfinished Bush administration regulations until they can be reviewed by the new team. Bush issued 100 new rules after Obama was elected in November, including one that President Obama strenuously opposes, which would make it much harder for the government to regulate toxic substances and hazardous chemicals in the workplace. [62]

Earlier, Obama and four other senators had proposed a measure to block the new rule and wrote a letter urging the department to scrap it, saying it would "create serious obstacles to protecting workers from health hazards on the job." [63]

The administration probably will also reconsider a Jan. 15 EPA health advisory urging Americans not to drink water with more than 0.4 parts per billion (ppb) of perfluorooctanoic acid (PFOA) — a toxic chemical linked to cancer, liver damage and birth defects that is used to make Teflon and other non-stick coatings. [64]

Some scientists have urged limits as low as 0.02 parts per billion of PFOA, and, in fact, his pick to lead the EPA, New Jersey Environmental Protection Commissioner Lisa Jackson, recommended a level of 0.04 parts per billion in her state — 10 times stricter than the new federal limit.

Richard Wiles, executive director of the Environmental Working Group — a nonprofit organization that has pushed for stricter regulation of PFOA — said the EPA's new advisory was "essentially legalizing unsafe exposure levels. Nobody should have to drink a cancer-causing Teflon chemical in their water." [65]

OUTLOOK

Green Chemistry

T he task of regulating the chemical industry's constant stream of new products for health and safety risks can seem hopelessly daunting. But some experts see a way: green chemistry, which seeks to design chemicals and chemical processes with reduced environmental impacts. [66]

Since the mid-1990s, green chemistry has developed into an active research field. The EPA provides grants, awards and fellowships for green chemistry achievements, and the American Chemical Society's Green Chemistry Institute works to advance green principles across all fields of chemical research. About a dozen U.S. universities offer green chemistry programs, and major corporations like GE and BASF are investing billions of dollars in green applications, such as alternative energy systems.

Winners of the EPA's green chemistry awards for 2008 included Battelle, which developed bio-based resins and toners for office copiers and printers. Made from soy and corn feedstocks instead of petroleum products, the inks are easier to remove from paper than conventional toner, which reduces the amount of energy needed to recycle waste paper. Another winner, Nalco, designed technology to monitor the water that circulates through many building cooling systems. The Nalco system adds chemicals to keep cooling water clean only when needed, saving water and energy and reducing the quantity of chemicals in discharged cooling water. [67]

Although the field is growing rapidly, Carnegie Mellon Professor Collins says government leadership is needed. "Federal investment in green chemistry is almost nonexistent, and we desperately need it," he says. "We need to prioritize hazards and figure out how to design against them." Collins recently invented an environmentally friendly catalyst that can break down harmful pollutants into less-toxic substances. [68]

The Green Chemistry Research and Development Act, which was passed by the House in 2007 and introduced in the Senate, would provide $188 million over three years for agencies to support research, development, education and training in green chemistry.

"Modern science keeps giving us new warnings about many of the chemicals we use every day, from home cleaning products to the food we put on our family's table," said Sen. John Kerry, D-Mass., a cosponsor of the Senate bill. "It's time for Washington to respond by helping to build a whole, new chemistry industry that's on a mission to make America greener."

Reducing serious risks is key, says Collins. "Green chemistry could exist without focusing on hazardous products, and it would probably do all kinds of nice little things. But to be authentic, it has to deal with hazards." ∎

Notes

[1] "All About Eastman Tritan Copolyester," www.eastman.com/company/news_center/News_archive/2007.

[2] "Endocrine Disruptors," National Institute of Environmental Health Sciences, February 2007.

[3] "Timeline: BPA from Invention to Phase-Out," Environmental Working Group, April 22, 2008, www.ewg.org/node/26291/print.

[4] "Bisphenol A (BPA)," National Toxicology Program, September 2008, www.niehs.nih.gov/health/docs/bpa-factsheet.pdf.

[5] "Eastman Expanding Tritan Copolyester Capacity," Reuters, March 13, 2008. For background, see Jennifer Weeks, "Buying Green," *CQ Researcher*, Feb. 29, 2008, pp. 193-216.

[6] "A Poison Kiss: The Problem of Lead in Lipstick," Campaign for Safe Cosmetics, October 2007, www.safecosmetics.org/docUploads/A%20Poison%20Kiss.pdf.

[7] For background, see Marcia Clemmitt, "Preventing Cancer," *CQ Researcher*, Jan. 9, 2009, pp. 25-48.

[8] Testimony of Andrew D. Maynard before Committee on Science and Technology, U.S. House of Representatives, April 16, 2008, p. 5.

[9] For background, see Brian Beary, "The New Europe," *CQ Global Researcher*, August 2007, pp. 181-210, and Kenneth Jost, "Future of the European Union," *CQ Researcher*, Oct. 28, 2005, pp. 909-932.

[10] "Wingspread Statement on the Precautionary Principle," www.sehn.org/ppfaqs.html.

[11] "WHO gives indoor use of DDT a clean bill of health for controlling malaria," World Health Organization, Sept. 15, 2006.

[12] "Alternatives to DDT on International Radar," United Nations Environment Programme, November 2008.

[13] "The Business of Chemistry," American Chemistry Council, August 2007.

[14] Exceptions include pesticides, which EPA regulates under a separate law, and food additives, drugs, and cosmetics, which are controlled by the Food and Drug Administration.

[15] "Chemical Regulation: Actions Are Needed to Improve the Effectiveness of EPA's Chemical Review Program," U.S. Government Accountability Office, Aug. 2, 2006, p. 1.

[16] The five chemicals are PCBs, chlorofluorocarbons, dioxin, asbestos, and hexavalent chromium for use as a water treatment chemical. EPA's decision banning asbestos was reversed in *Corrosion Proof Fittings v. EPA*, 947 F. 2d 1201 (1991).

[17] GAO, *op. cit.*, p. 3.

[18] "Toxic Substances Control Act: Legislative Changes Could Make the Act More Effective, Sept. 26, 1994; "Chemical Regulation: Options Exist to Improve EPA's Ability to Assess Health Risks and Manage Its Chemical Review Program," June 1, 2005; and "Chemical Regulation: Actions Are Needed to Improve the Effectiveness of EPA's Chemical Review Program," Aug. 2, 2006, all U.S. Government Accountability Office.

[19] "Toxicity Testing in the 21st Century: A Vision and a Strategy," National Research Council (2007), pp. 48-52.

[20] "Fact Sheet for Nanotechnology Under the Toxic Substances Control Act," U.S. Environmental Protection Agency, www.epa.gov/oppt/nano/nano-facts.htm.

[21] E. Clayton Teague, Director, National Nanotechnology Coordination Office, testimony before House Subcommittee on Research and Science Education, Oct. 31, 2007, pp. 1-4.

[22] Thomas H. Moore, Commissioner, Consumer Product Safety Commission, testimony before Senate Commerce Subcommittee on Consumer Affairs, Insurance, and Automotive Safety, March 21, 2007, p. 7.

[23] "Nanotechnology: A Report of the U.S. Food and Drug Administration Nanotechnology Task Force," July 25, 2007, pp. 12-15.

[24] David J. Hanson, "FDA Confronts Nanotechnology," *Chemical & Engineering News*, March 17, 2008.

[25] Online at www.nanoaction.org/nanoaction/doc/CTA_nano-silver%20petition__final_5_1_08.pdf.

[26] "No-Nano Sunscreens?" *Consumer Reports*, December 2008.

[27] E. Marla Felcher, "The Consumer Product Safety Commission and Nanotechnology," *PEN 14*, Project on Emerging Nanotechnologies, August 2008.

[28] "Baby Bottle Chemical Levels Safe, EU Agency Says," Reuters, July 23, 2008; "Health Canada Responds to Concerns Raised About Bisphenol A in Canned Food," Health Canada, May 29, 2008; "Canada Declares BPA a Health Hazard," *USA Today*, Oct. 18, 2008.

[29] Kate Murphy, "Business: Thinking Outside the Can," *The New York Times*, March 14, 2004; "Frequently Asked Questions," Hain Celestial Canada, www.hain-celestial.ca/index.php/faq/.

[30] For a chronology see "Phthalates and Children's Toys," American Chemistry Council, Phthalate Information Center, www.phthalates.org/yourhealth/childrens_toys.asp.

[31] "New EU Phthalates Directive Finalised," *Intertek Labtest*, July 2005.

About the Author

Jennifer Weeks is a *CQ Researcher* contributing writer in Watertown, Mass., who specializes in energy and environmental issues. She has written for *The Washington Post*, *The Boston Globe Magazine* and other publications, and has 15 years' experience as a public-policy analyst, lobbyist and congressional staffer. She has an A.B. degree from Williams College and master's degrees from the University of North Carolina and Harvard.

[32] Jocelyn Kaiser, "Panel Finds No Proof That Phthalates Harm Infant Reproductive Systems," *Science*, Oct. 21, 2005.

[33] "Congress Passes Consumer Product Safety Improvement Act," *Beveridge & Diamond*, July 31, 2008.

[34] Letter online at www.uschamber.com/issues/letters/2008/080304_phthalate_ban.htm.

[35] Bohan Loh and Judith Wang, "U.S. Ban To Shake up China Toy Sector," *ICIS News*, July 31, 2008; Mark Schapiro, *Exposed: The Toxic Chemistry of Everyday Products and What's at Stake for American Power* (2007), pp. 56-57.

[36] "A Plasticizer for Sensitive Applications," *Science Around Us*, BASF, June 2007.

[37] Samuel Hopkins Adams, "The Great American Fraud: Articles on the Nostrum Evil and Quacks," Reprinted from *Collier's Weekly* (Collier, 1905), p. 3.

[38] "Taste of Raspberries, Taste of Death: The 1937 Elixir Sulfanilamide Incident," *FDA Consumer Magazine*, U.S. Food and Drug Administration, June 1981.

[39] Gregg LaBar, "Seven Decades of Safety: Good Times Take Their Toll," *EHS Today*, Oct. 1, 2008.

[40] "Food Additives," Center for Science in the Public Interest, www.cspinet.org/reports/chemcuisine.htm#Food%20additive.

[41] "The Reports of the Surgeon General," National Library of Medicine, http://profiles.nlm.nih.gov/NN/Views/Exhibit/narrative/smoking.html.

[42] Ralph Nader, *Unsafe at Any Speed: The Designed-In Dangers of the American Automobile* (1965).

[43] Philip Shabecoff, "Reagan Order on Cost-Benefit Analysis Stirs Economic and Political Debate," *The New York Times*, Nov. 7, 1981.

[44] Joan Claybrook *et al.*, *Retreat From Safety: Reagan's Attack on America's Health* (1984), p. xi.

[45] "Proposition 65 in Plain Language," California Office of Environmental Health Hazard Assessment, www.oehha.org/prop65/background/p65plain.html.

[46] Theo Colborn, Dianne Dumanoski and John Peterson Myers, *Our Stolen Future: Are We Threatening Our Fertility, Intelligence, and Survival?* (1996).

[47] Stephen Labaton, "OSHA Leaves Worker Safety in Hands of Industry," *The New York Times*, April 25, 2007.

[48] Steven Hayward, "Happy Earth Day," *Human Events Online*, April 22, 2008.

[49] For background see Jennifer Weeks, "Fish Farming," *CQ Researcher*, July 27, 2007, pp. 625-648, and Peter Katel, "Consumer Safety," *CQ Researcher*, Oct. 12, 2007, pp. 841-864.

[50] Gardiner Harris, "F.D.A. Chief Writes Congress for Money," *New York*, May 14, 2008.

[51] "Scientific Peer-Review of the Draft Assessment of Bisphenol A for Use in Food Contact Applications," U.S. Food and Drug Administration Science Board Subcommittee on Bisphenol A, Oct. 31, 2008, p. 4.

[52] Meg Kissinger, "Lawmakers to Seek Ban on BPA," *Milwaukee Journal Sentinel*, Nov. 17, 2008.

[53] S. 2928, introduced April 29, 2008, and H.R. 6228, introduced June 10, 2008.

[54] S. 3040 and H.R. 6100, both introduced May 20, 2008.

[55] National Research Council, *Review of Federal Strategy for Nanotechnology-Related Environmental, Health, and Safety Research* (2008), prepublication version, p. 6.

[56] The letter and CPSC advisory opinion are online at www.cpsc.gov/LIBRARY/FOIA/advisory/320.pdf.

[57] The complaint is online at http://docs.nrdc.org/health/files/hea_08120401a.pdf.

[58] Melanie Trottman, "Vendors Urge Relaxed Lead-Safety Rule," *The Wall Street Journal*, Nov. 18, 2008.

[59] "Toys and Childhood Lead Exposure," Centers for Disease Control and Prevention, www.cdc.gov/nceh/lead/faq/toys.htm.

[60] "Pass Up the Poison Plastic," Center for Health, Environment and Justice, November 2008, www.besafenet.com/pvc/documents/PVC-Guide-1.pdf.

[61] Michael Hawthorne, "Change gets green light; His plans for environmental legislation may have big impact," *Chicago Tribune*, Nov. 19, 2008, p. C4.

[62] Robert Pear, "Bush Aides Rush to Enact a Rule Obama Opposes," *The New York Times*, Nov. 29, 2008, www.nytimes.com/2008/11/30/washington/30labor.html?ref=us.

[63] Quoted in *ibid*.

[64] See Michael Hawthorne, "U.S. warns of Teflon chemical in water," *Chicago Tribune*, Jan. 16, 2009, p. C18.

[65] *Ibid*.

[66] "Introduction to the Concept of Green Chemistry," U.S. Environmental Protection Agency, www.epa.gov/greenchemistry/pubs/about_gc.html.

[67] "Award Winners," U.S. Environmental Protection Agency, www.epa.gov/greenchemistry/pubs/pgcc/past.html.

[68] "Green Catalysts Provide Promise for Cleaning Toxins and Pollutants," *Science Daily*, Aug. 20, 2008.

FOR MORE INFORMATION

American Chemistry Council, 1300 Wilson Blvd., Arlington, VA 22209; (703) 741-5000; www.americanchemistry.com. The main trade organization for the U.S. chemical industry.

Center for Health, Environment and Justice, P.O. Box 6806, Falls Church, VA 22040; (703) 237-2249; www.chej.org. A grassroots advocacy group that works to protect communities from exposure to dangerous environmental chemicals.

Consumer Product Safety Commission, 4330 East West Highway, Bethesda, MD 20814; (301) 504-7921; www.cpsc.gov. The federal agency charged with protecting the public from unreasonable risks from products.

Consumers Union, 101 Truman Ave., Yonkers, NY 10703; (914) 378-2000; www.consumersunion.org. A nonprofit group that tests products.

National Nanotechnology Coordination Office, 4201 Wilson Blvd., Stafford II Room 405, Arlington, VA 22230; (703) 292-8626; www.nano.gov. Provides information about federal research and development of nanotechnologies.

National Toxicology Program, 111 T.W. Alexander Dr., Research Triangle Park, NC 27709; (919) 541-3665; http://ntp.niehs.nih.gov. A Department of Health and Human Services agency that studies the impact of chemicals on human health.

Project on Emerging Nanotechnologies, One Woodrow Wilson Plaza, 1300 Pennsylvania Ave., N.W., Washington, DC 20004; (202) 691-4282; www.nanotechproject.org. Provides independent, objective analysis of nanotechnology.

Project on Scientific Knowledge and Public Policy, 2100 M St., N.W., Suite 203, Washington, DC 20052; (202) 994-0774; www.defendingscience.org. Examines how science is used and misused in government decision-making.

Bibliography

Selected Sources

Books

Hilts, Philip J., *Protecting America's Health: The FDA, Business, and One Hundred Years of Regulation*, Knopf, 2003.
A health and science reporter traces the history of the Food and Drug Administration and business resistance to regulation.

Michaels, David, *Doubt Is Their Product: How Industry's Assault on Science Threatens Your Health*, Oxford University Press, 2008.
An epidemiologist and former assistant secretary of Energy criticizes what he calls the "product defense industry" for promoting doubt and uncertainty about whether unsafe products should be regulated.

Schapiro, Mark, *Exposed: The Toxic Chemistry of Everyday Products and What's at Stake for American Power*, Chelsea Green, 2007.
An investigative journalist argues that Europe is replacing the United States as a commercial leader by setting high standards that require manufacturers to develop safer products.

Shabecoff, Philip, and Alice Shabecoff, *Poisoned Profits: The Toxic Assault on Our Children*, Random House, 2008.
Two journalists link rising levels of childhood illness and death to toxic exposures in children's homes, schools and neighborhoods.

Articles

Cone, Marla, "A Greener Future," *Los Angeles Times*, Sept. 14 and 19, 2008.
Once an obscure subfield, green chemistry is slowly changing the chemical industry, but more funding and training are needed before it becomes the mainstream approach.

Henig, Robin Marantz, "Our Silver-Coated Future," *On Earth*, fall 2007.
Nano-silver, the most widely used nanomaterial, illustrates the need for safety testing and new regulations for nanotechnologies.

Hogue, Cheryl, "The Future of U.S. Chemical Regulation," *Chemical & Engineering News*, Jan. 8, 2007.
American Chemistry Council Managing Director Michael Walls and University of Massachusetts-Lowell Professor Joel Ticknor debate whether U.S. law regulating commercial chemicals is stringent enough.

Pereira, Joseph, "Protests Spur Stores to Seek Substitute for Vinyl in Toys," *The Wall Street Journal*, Feb. 12, 2008.
Under pressure from consumers and advocacy groups, toy makers are exploring substitute materials without vinyl or phthalates.

Rosenberg, Tina, "What the World Needs Now is DDT," *The New York Times Magazine*, April 11, 2004.
DDT is a cheap way to kill mosquitoes that carry malaria, but the pesticide's toxic reputation and the challenging logistics of effective spraying campaigns have made it hard for the countries that most need help to use it.

Spivak, Cary, Susanne Rust and Meg Kissinger, "Are Your Products Safe? You Can't Tell," *Milwaukee Journal Sentinel*, Nov. 25, 2007.
Shampoo, carpets, skin lotions, clothing and many other consumer products contain endocrine-disrupting chemicals that cause cancer and other health problems in laboratory animals. Critics call U.S. government efforts to regulate these substances "an abject failure."

Reports and Studies

"Chemical Regulation: Comparison of U.S. and Recently Enacted European Union Approaches to Protect Against the Risks of Toxic Chemicals," U.S. Government Accountability Office, Aug. 17, 2007.
The report compares U.S. chemical regulation under the Toxic Substances Control Act (TSCA) and the European Union's REACH directive.

"Third National Report on Human Exposure to Environmental Chemicals," Centers for Disease Control and Prevention, 2005, www.cdc.gov/exposurereport/report.htm.
This ongoing assessment of human exposure to environmental chemicals, based on human specimens such as blood and urine, finds that levels of some substances such as blood lead and secondhand cigarette smoke have fallen, but that many other chemicals are widely present throughout the U.S. population, including known hazardous substances.

"Toxicity Testing in the 21st Century: A Vision and a Strategy," National Research Council, 2008.
The council charts a course for making chemical toxicity testing faster, more affordable and more accurate while reducing reliance on animal studies.

Felcher, E. Marla, "The Consumer Product Safety Commission and Nanotechnology," Project on Emerging Nanotechnologies, August 2008, www.nanotechproject.org/process/assets/filed/7033/pen14.pdf.
An expert on business and consumer protection argues that the commission is ill-prepared to regulate nanomaterials in consumer products.

The Next Step:

Additional Articles from Current Periodicals

Body Chemicals

"Study: Oregonians Full of Toxic Chemicals," *Confederated Umatilla Journal* **(Oregon), December 2007, p. 9.**

A study concludes that Oregonians have at least nine and as many as 16 out of 29 toxic chemicals tested for in their bodies.

Rabb, Sara, "Air Pollution: Toxic Hot Spots," *Pensacola News Journal* **(Florida), March 9, 2008, p. 1A.**

A two-county area in Florida is trying to determine whether there's a connection between air pollution and elevated rates of health problems.

VanderHart, Dirk, "Monitoring Turns Up Toxins in Air Around School," *Springfield News-Leader* **(Missouri), Dec. 11, 2008, p. 1A.**

Long-term exposure to toxic air at a Missouri elementary school could produce increased instances of cancer.

Nanotechnologies

Fernholm, Ann, "Consumers Not Always Aware of Presence of Nanotechnology," *The San Francisco Chronicle*, **May 12, 2008, p. D3.**

Three or four nanotechnology-based products enter the market annually, but it isn't easy to know if products contain nanoparticles.

Ruckelshaus, William, and J. Clarence Davies, "An EPA for the 21st Century," *The Boston Globe*, **July 7, 2007, p. A9.**

Meeting the oversight challenges of nanotechnology — estimated to represent $2.6 trillion in manufactured goods by 2014 — requires the Environmental Protection Agency (EPA) to adapt more modern research methods.

Van, Jon, "Nanotechnology Could Be Basis of Future Cures," *Chicago Tribune*, **April 23, 2007, p. C5.**

Nanotechnology has the potential to grow new tissue in order to treat conditions such as Alzheimer's or Parkinson's disease.

Products

Chambers, Jennifer, "Some Toys Have Toxic Chemicals," *Detroit News*, **Nov. 26, 2008, p. 1B.**

Excessive amounts of toxic chemicals are present in many toys intended for children under age 3, according to the U.S. Public Research Group.

Dugan, John, "Students Find Toxic Chemicals," *Marin Independent Journal* **(California), May 10, 2008.**

Students at a California high school have discovered that toxic chemicals are present in many of the products used at their school.

Gathright, Alan, "Saying Yuck to Toxins in Toys, Protesters Chuck Rubber Ducks," *Rocky Mountain News* **(Colorado), May 21, 2008, p. 24.**

Phthalates are a class of toxic chemicals used to make plastic in baby teethers and are also present in industrial solvents, insecticides and paints.

Regulations

"State Panel Urges Cutting Chemicals in Products," **The Associated Press, Dec. 16, 2008.**

Gov. Arnold Schwarzenegger, R-Calif., wants California to force companies to disclose the chemicals they put in products and analyze their effects on the environment.

Coile, Zachary, "EPA Was Stymied By White House," *The San Francisco Chronicle*, **April 30, 2008, p. A1.**

A congressional watchdog agency has concluded that the Bush administration has repeatedly intervened in the governmental scientific process for assessing the risks associated with toxic chemicals.

DePalma, Anthony, "E.P.A. Is Sued by 12 States Over Reports on Chemicals," *The New York Times*, **Nov. 29, 2007, p. A25.**

Twelve states are suing the EPA for weakening regulations that for two decades have required businesses to report the toxic chemicals that they use, store and release.

Richardson, John, "Maine to Consider Tracking Toxins in Toys, Products," *Portland Press Herald*, **Feb. 27, 2008, p. A1.**

Two bills in the Maine legislature would create lists of chemicals deemed to pose great threats to public health.

CITING CQ RESEARCHER

Sample formats for citing these reports in a bibliography include the ones listed below. Preferred styles and formats vary, so please check with your instructor or professor.

MLA STYLE

Jost, Kenneth. "Rethinking the Death Penalty." CQ Researcher 16 Nov. 2001: 945-68.

APA STYLE

Jost, K. (2001, November 16). Rethinking the death penalty. *CQ Researcher, 11*, 945-968.

CHICAGO STYLE

Jost, Kenneth. "Rethinking the Death Penalty." *CQ Researcher*, November 16, 2001, 945-968.

In-depth Reports on Issues in the News

Are you writing a paper?

Need backup for a debate?

Want to become an expert on an issue?

For 80 years, students have turned to *CQ Researcher* for in-depth reporting on issues in the news. Reports on a full range of political and social issues are now available. Following is a selection of recent reports:

Civil Liberties
Limiting Lawsuits, 12/08
Affirmative Action, 10/08
Gay Marriage Showdowns, 9/08
America's Border Fence, 9/08
Immigration Debate, 2/08
Prison Reform, 4/07

Crime/Law
Mexico's Drug War, 12/08
Prostitution Debate, 5/08
Public Defenders, 4/08
Gun Violence, 5/07

Education
Reading Crisis? 2/08
Discipline in Schools, 2/08
Student Aid, 1/08
Racial Diversity in Public Schools, 9/07
Stress on Students, 7/07

Environment
Reducing Carbon Footprint, 12/08
Protecting Wetlands, 10/08
Buying Green, 2/08
Future of Recycling, 12/07

Health/Safety
Preventing Cancer, 1/09
Heart Health, 9/08
Global Food Crisis, 6/08
Preventing Memory Loss, 4/08

International Affairs/Politics
The National Debt, 11/08
Financial Bailout, 10/08
Political Conventions, 8/08
Human Rights in China, 7/08
Race and Politics, 7/08

Social Trends
Falling Birthrates, 11/08
Regulating Credit Cards, 10/08
Internet Accuracy, 8/08
Financial Crisis, 5/08
Cyberbullying, 5/08

Terrorism/Defense
Rise in Counterinsurgency, 9/08
Cost of the Iraq War, 4/08

Youth
Debating Hip-Hop, 6/07

Upcoming Reports

Obama Presidency, 1/30/09   Future of the Auto Industry, 2/6/09   Homeland Security, 2/13/09

ACCESS

CQ Researcher is available in print and online. For access, visit your library or www.cqresearcher.com.

STAY CURRENT

To receive notice of upcoming *CQ Researcher* reports, or learn more about *CQ Researcher* products, subscribe to the free e-mail newsletters, *CQ Researcher Alert!* and *CQ Researcher News*: http://cqpress.com/newsletters.

PURCHASE

To purchase a *CQ Researcher* report in print or electronic format (PDF), visit www.cqpress.com or call 866-427-7737. Single reports start at $15. Bulk purchase discounts and electronic-rights licensing are also available.

SUBSCRIBE

Annual full-service *CQ Researcher* subscriptions—including 44 reports a year, monthly index updates, and a bound volume—start at $803. Add $25 for domestic postage.

CQ Researcher Online offers a backfile from 1991 and a number of tools to simplify research. For pricing information, call 800-834-9020, ext. 1906, or e-mail librarysales@cqpress.com.

Published by CQ Press, a division of SAGE Publications

www.cqresearcher.com

The Obama Presidency

Can Barack Obama deliver the change he promises?

A s the 44th president of the United States, Barack Hussein Obama confronts a set of challenges more daunting perhaps than any chief executive has faced since the Great Depression and World War II. At home, the nation is in the second year of a recession that Obama warns may get worse before the economy starts to improve. Abroad, he faces the task of withdrawing U.S. forces from Iraq, reversing the deteriorating conditions in Afghanistan and trying to ease the Israeli-Palestinian conflict. Still, Obama begins his four years in office with the biggest winning percentage of any president in 20 years and a strong Democratic majority in both houses of Congress. In addition, as the first African-American president, Obama starts with a reservoir of goodwill from Americans and people and governments around the world. But he began encountering criticism and opposition from Republicans in his first days in office as he filled in the details of his campaign theme: "Change We Can Believe In."

Making history: President Barack Obama, the first African-American president of the United States, and first lady Michelle Obama walk in the Inaugural Parade in Washington after his swearing in on Jan. 20, 2009.

CQ Researcher • Jan. 30, 2009 • www.cqresearcher.com
Volume 19, Number 4 • Pages 73-104

RECIPIENT OF SOCIETY OF PROFESSIONAL JOURNALISTS AWARD FOR
EXCELLENCE ◆ AMERICAN BAR ASSOCIATION SILVER GAVEL AWARD

THE OBAMA PRESIDENCY

CQ Researcher

Jan. 30, 2009
Volume 19, Number 4

MANAGING EDITOR: Thomas J. Colin
tcolin@cqpress.com

ASSISTANT MANAGING EDITOR: Kathy Koch
kkoch@cqpress.com

ASSOCIATE EDITOR: Kenneth Jost

STAFF WRITERS: Thomas J. Billitteri, Marcia Clemmitt, Peter Katel

CONTRIBUTING WRITERS: Sarah Glazer, Alan Greenblatt, Barbara Mantel, Patrick Marshall, Tom Price, Jennifer Weeks

DESIGN/PRODUCTION EDITOR: Olu B. Davis

ASSISTANT EDITOR: Darrell Dela Rosa

FACT-CHECKING: Eugene J. Gabler, Michelle Harris

EDITORIAL INTERN: Vyomika Jairam

CQ PRESS

A Division of SAGE Publications

PRESIDENT AND PUBLISHER:
John A. Jenkins

EXECUTIVE DIRECTOR, REFERENCE INFORMATION GROUP:
Alix B. Vance

DIRECTOR, ONLINE PRODUCT DEVELOPMENT:
Jennifer Q. Ryan

CQ Press is a registered trademark of Congressional Quarterly Inc.

CQ Researcher (ISSN 1056-2036) is printed on acid-free paper. Published weekly, except; (Jan. wk. 1) (May wk. 4) (July wks. 1, 2) (Aug. wks. 3, 4) (Nov. wk. 4) and (Dec. wk. 4), by CQ Press, a division of SAGE Publications. Annual full-service subscriptions start at $803. For pricing, call 1-800-834-9020, ext. 1906. To purchase a CQ Researcher report in print or electronic format (PDF), visit www. cqpress.com or call 866-427-7737. Single reports start at $15. Bulk purchase discounts and electronic-rights licensing are also available. Periodicals postage paid at Washington, D.C., and additional mailing offices. POSTMASTER: Send address changes to CQ Researcher, 2300 N St., N.W., Suite 800, Washington, DC 20037.

The Obama Presidency

BY KENNETH JOST AND THE *CQ RESEARCHER* STAFF

THE ISSUES

They came to Washington in numbers unprecedented and with enthusiasm unbounded to bear witness and be a part of history: the inauguration of Barack Hussein Obama on Jan. 20, 2009, as the 44th president of the United States and the first African-American ever to serve as the nation's chief executive.

After taking the oath of office from Chief Justice John G. Roberts Jr., Obama looked out at the estimated 1.8 million people massed at the Capitol and National Mall and delivered an inaugural address nearly as bracing as the sub-freezing temperatures.

With hardly the hint of a smile, Obama, 47, outlined the challenges confronting him as the fifth-youngest president in U.S. history. The nation is at war, he noted, the economy "badly weakened" and the public beset with "a sapping of confidence."

"Today I say to you that the challenges we face are real," Obama continued in his 18-minute speech. "They are serious and they are many. They will not be met easily or in a short span of time. But know this, America — they will be met." [1] (*See economy sidebar, p. 82; foreign policy sidebar, p. 88.*)

The crowd received Obama's sobering message with flag-waving exuberance and a unity of spirit unseen in Washington for decades. Despite Democrat Obama's less-than-landslide 7 percentage-point victory over John McCain on Nov. 4, hardly any sign of political dissent or partisan opposition surfaced on Inauguration Day or during the weekend of celebration that preceded it. (*See maps, p. 76; poll, p. 77.*)

The largest crowd in Washington history cheers President Barack Obama after his swearing in on Jan. 20, 2009. An estimated 1.8 million high-spirited, flag-waving people gathered at the Capitol and National Mall, but thousands more were turned away by police due to overcrowding.

AP Photo/Evan Vucci

"It's life-changing for everyone," said Rhonda Gittens, a University of Florida journalism student, "because of who he is, because of how he represents everyone." Gittens traveled to Washington with some 50 other members of the school's black student union.

The inaugural crowd included tens of thousands clustered on side streets after the U.S. Park Police determined the mall had reached capacity. The crowd was bigger than for any previous inauguration — at least three times larger than when the outgoing president, George W. Bush, had first taken the oath of office eight years earlier. The total number also exceeded independent estimates cited for any of Wash-

ington's protest marches or state occasions in the past. *

The spectators came from all over the country and from many foreign lands. "He's bringing change here," said Clayton Preira, a young Brazilian accompanying three fellow students on a two-month visit to the United States. "He's bringing change all over the world." The spectators were of all ages, but overall the crowd seemed disproportionately young. "He really speaks to young people," said Christian McLaren, a white University of Florida student.

Most obviously and most significantly, the crowd was racially and ethnically diverse — just like the new first family. Obama himself is the son of a black Kenyan father and a white Kansan mother. His wife Michelle, he often remarks, carries in her the blood of slaves and of slave owners. Among those behind the first lady on the dais were Obama's half-sister, Maya Soetoro-Ng, whose father was Indonesian, and her husband, Konrad Ng, a Chinese-American. Some of Obama's relatives from Kenya came as well, wearing colorful African garb.

The vast numbers of black Americans often gave the event the air of an old-time church revival. In quieter

---

* Crowd estimates for President Obama's inauguration ranged from 1.2 million to 1.8 million. Commonly cited estimates for other Washington events include: March on Washington for Jobs and Freedom, 1963, 250,000; President John F. Kennedy's funeral, 1963, 800,000; inauguration of President Lyndon B. Johnson, 1965, 1.2 million; Peace Moratorium, 1969, 250,000; Million Man March, 1995, 400,000-800,000; March for Life, 1998, 225,000; March for Women's Lives, 2004, 500,000-800,000.

Obama Victory Changed Electoral Map

Barack Obama won nine traditionally Republican states in the November 2008 election that George W. Bush had won easily in 2004, and his electoral and popular vote totals were significantly higher than Bush's. In 2004, Bush won with 50.7 percent of the vote to John Kerry's 48.3 percent. By comparison Obama garnered 52.9 percent to Sen. John McCain's 45.7. In the nation's new political map, the Democrats dominate the landscape, with the Republicans clustered in the South, the Plains and the Mountain states.

Presidential Election, 2004

Democrat: John Kerry

Republican: George W. Bush

Total electoral vote:		Total popular vote:	
Republican	*286*	Republican	*62,040,610*
Democrat	*251*	Democrat	*59,028,444*

* One "unfaithful" elector voted for John Edwards.

Presidential Election, 2008

Democrat: Barack Obama

Republican: John McCain

Total electoral vote:		Total popular vote:	
Democrat	*365*	Democrat	*69,456,897*
Republican	*173*	Republican	*59,934,814*

* Due to the Nebraska's proportional allocation system, McCain received four electoral votes and Obama one.

Source: Federal Election Commission

moments, many struggled to find the words to convey the significance, both historic and personal. "It hasn't sunk in yet," Marcus Collier, a photographer from New York City, remarked several hours later.

David Moses, a health-care supervisor in New York City, carried with him a picture of his late father, who had encouraged him and his brother to join the anti-segregation sit-ins of the early 1960s in their native South Carolina. "It's the culmination of a long struggle," Moses said, "that still has a long way to go."

Shannon Simmons, who had not yet been born when Congress passed major civil rights legislation in the 1960s, brought her 12-year-old daughter from their home in New Orleans. "It's historic," said Simmons, who made monthly contributions to the Obama campaign. "It's about race, but it's more than that. I believe he can bring about change." (*See sidebar, p. 78.*)

For black Americans, old and young alike, the inauguration embodied the lesson that Obama himself had often articulated — that no door need be viewed as closed to any American, regardless of race. For Obama himself, the inauguration climaxed a quest that took him from the Illinois legislature to the White House in only 12 years.

To win the presidency, Obama had to defy political oddsmakers by defeating then-Sen. Hillary Rodham Clinton, the former first lady, for the Democratic nomination and then beating McCain, the veteran Arizona senator and Vietnam War hero. Obama campaigned hard against the Bush administration's record, blaming Bush, among other things, for mismanaging the U.S. economy as well as the wars in Iraq and Afghanistan.

After a nod to Bush's record of service and help during the transition, Obama hinted at some of those criticisms in his address. "The nation cannot prosper long when it favors only the prosperous," he declared, referencing tax cuts enacted in Bush's first year in office that Obama had called for repealing.

On national defense, "we reject the false choice between our safety and our ideals," Obama continued. The Bush administration had come under fierce attack from civil liberties and human rights advocates for aggressive detention and interrogation policies adopted after the Sept. 11, 2001, terrorist attacks on the United States. (*See "At Issue," p. 96.*)

Despite the attacks, Obama also sounded conservative notes throughout the speech, blaming economic woes in part on a "collective failure to make hard choices" and calling for "a new era of responsibility." Republicans in the audience were pleased. "He wasn't pointing fingers just toward Bush," said Rhonda Hamlin, a social worker from Alexandria, Va. "He was pointing fingers toward all of us."

With the inauguration behind him, Obama went quickly to work. Within hours, the administration moved to institute a 120-day moratorium on legal proceedings against the approximately 245 detainees still being held at the Guantánamo Bay Naval Base in Cuba. Obama had repeatedly pledged during the campaign to close the prison; two days later he signed a second decree, ordering that the camp be closed within one year.

Then on his first full day as president, Obama on Jan. 21 issued stringent ethics rules for administration officials and conferred separately with his top economic and military advisers to begin mapping plans to try to lift the U.S. economy out of its yearlong recession and bring successful conclusions to the conflicts in Iraq and Afghanistan.

By then, the Inauguration Day truce in partisan conflict was beginning to break down. House Republicans pointed to a Congressional Budget Office study questioning the likely impact of the Democrats' $825-billion economic stimulus package, weighted toward spending instead of tax cuts. "The money that they're going to throw out the door, at the end of the day, is not going to work," said Rep. Devin Nunes, R-Calif., a member of the tax-writing

Public Gives Obama Highest Rating

Barack Obama began his presidency with 79 percent of Americans having a favorable impression of him — higher than the five preceding presidents. George W. Bush entered office with a 62 percent favorability rating; he left with a 33 percent approval rating, lowest of post-World War II presidents except Harry S. Truman and Richard M. Nixon.

Do you have a favorable impression of . . . ?

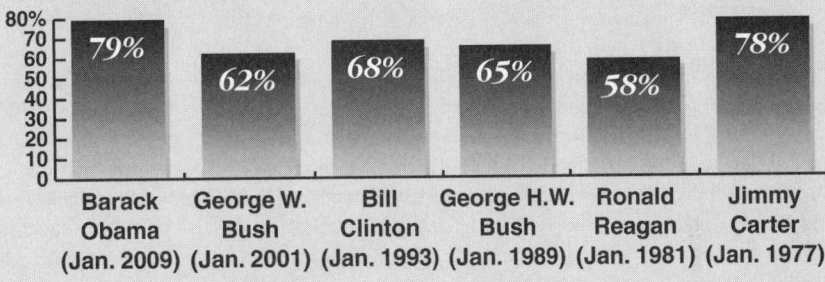

Source: The Washington Post, *Jan. 18, 2009*

House Ways and Means Committee. (*See "At Issue," p. 97.*)

The partisan division raised questions whether Democratic leaders could stick to the promised schedule of getting a stimulus plan to Obama's desk for his signature by the time of the Presidents' Day congressional recess in mid-February. More broadly, the Republicans' stance presaged continuing difficulties for Obama as he turned to other ambitious agenda items, including his repeated pledge to overhaul the nation's health-care system. (*See sidebar, p. 92.*)

Obama included health care in his inaugural litany of challenges, along with education, climate change and technology. For now, those initiatives lie in the future. In the immediate days after his euphoric inauguration, here are some of the major questions being debated:

Is President Obama on the right track in fixing the U.S. economy?

As president-elect, Obama spent his first full week in Washington in early January first warning of trillion-dollar federal budget deficits for years to come and then making urgent appeals for pub-

lic support for a close to trillion-dollar stimulus to get the economy moving.

Members of Congress from both parties and advocates and economic experts of all persuasions agree on the need for a good-sized federal recovery program for the seriously ailing U.S. economy. And most agree on a prescription that combines spending increases and tax cuts. But there is sharp disagreement as to the particulars between tax-cutting conservatives and pump-priming liberals, with deficit hawks worried that both of the prescribed remedies could get out of hand.

With the plan's price tag then being estimated somewhere around $800 billion, Obama made his first sustained appeal for public support in a somber, half-hour address on Jan. 8 at George Mason University in Fairfax, Va., outside Washington. Any delay, he warned, could risk double-digit unemployment. He outlined plans to "rebuild America" ranging from alternative energy facilities and new school classrooms to computerized medical records, but he insisted the plan would not entail "a slew of new government programs." He reiterated his

First Black President Made Race a Non-Issue

Obama's personal attributes swept voters' doubts aside.

Barack Obama took the oath of office the day after this year's Martin Luther King holiday, and he accepted the Democratic presidential nomination last August on the 45th anniversary of King's celebrated "I Have a Dream" speech.

For millions of Americans, Obama's election as the nation's first African-American president seemed to fulfill the promise of King's "dream" of a nation in which citizens "will not be judged by the color of their skin, but by the content of their character."

"Obviously, for an African-American to win the presidency, given the history of this country . . . is a remarkable thing," Obama said after the election. "If you think about grandparents who are alive today who grew up under Jim Crow, that's a big leap." [1]

While Obama clearly benefited from the sacrifices of the civil rights generation — to which he has paid homage — his politics are different from the veterans of that movement. Older black politicians such as the Rev. Jesse Jackson seemed to base their candidacies mainly on issues of particular concern to African-Americans. But black politicians of Obama's generation, such as Massachusetts Gov. Deval Patrick and Newark Mayor Cory Booker (both Democrats), have run on issues of broader concern — in Obama's case, first on the war in Iraq and later on the economic meltdown.

"The successful ones start from the outside by appealing to white voters first, and work back toward their base of black voters," said broadcast journalist Gwen Ifill, author of the new book *The Breakthrough: Politics and Race in the Age of Obama.* [2]

Black voters initially were reluctant to support Obama — polls throughout 2007 showed Sen. Hillary Rodham Clinton with a big lead among African-Americans — but he picked up their support as it became clear he was the first black candidate with a realistic hope of winning the White House. Clinton's support among blacks dropped markedly in the wake of remarks by former President Bill Clinton that many found demeaning.

But many white Democratic voters remained reluctant to support Obama, particularly in Appalachia. Exit polling during the Pennsylvania primary, for example, showed that 16 percent of whites had considered race in making their pick, with half of those saying they would not support Obama in the fall. [3]

Obama also was bedeviled by videotaped remarks of his pas-

tor, the Rev. Jeremiah Wright, which were incendiary and deemed unpatriotic. But Obama responded with a widely hailed speech on race in March 2008 in which he acknowledged both the grievances of working-class whites and the continuing legacy of economic disadvantages among blacks. Obama said his own life story "has seared into my genetic makeup the idea that this nation is more than the sum of its parts — that out of many, we are truly one." [4]

As the general election campaign got under way, it was clear that race would continue to be a factor. One June poll showed that 30 percent of Americans admit prejudice. [5] And, despite Obama's lead, there was debate throughout the campaign about the so-called Bradley effect — the suggestion that people will lie to pollsters about their true intentions when it comes to black candidates. *

But neither Obama nor Arizona Sen. John McCain, his Republican rival, made explicit pleas based on race, with McCain refusing to air ads featuring Wright. As the campaign wore on, no one forgot that Obama is black — but most doubters put that fact aside in favor of more pressing concerns.

"For a long time, I couldn't ignore the fact that he was black. I'm not proud of that," Joe Sinitski, a 48-year-old Pennsylvania voter, told *The New York Times.* "I was raised to think that there aren't good black people out there." [6] But Sinitski ended up voting for Obama, along with many other whites won over by Obama's personal attributes or convinced that issues such as the economy trumped race.

Exit polls showed that Obama prevailed among those who considered race a significant factor, 53 to 46 percent. [7] "In difficult economic times, people find the price of prejudice is just a little too high," said outgoing North Carolina Gov. Mike Easley, a Democrat. [8]

"The Bradley effect really was not a significant factor, despite much concern, fear and hyperventilation about it leading up to the election," says Scott Keeter, a pollster with the Pew Research

---

* The Bradley effect refers to Tom Bradley, an African-American who lost the 1982 race for governor in California despite being ahead in voter polls going into the election.

---

campaign promise of a "$1,000 tax cut for 95 percent of working-class families" but made no mention of business tax cuts being included as sweeteners for Republican lawmakers.

Within days, Obama's plan was taking flack from left and right in the blogosphere. Writing on the liberal HuffingtonPost.com, Robert Kuttner, co-

editor of *American Prospect* magazine, denounced the spending plan as too small and the business tax cuts as "huge concessions" in a misguided effort at "post-partisanship." From the right, columnist Neal Boortz accused Obama on the conservative TownHall.com of using the economic crisis as "cover for increased government spending that he's

been promising since the day he announced his candidacy."

Allen Schick, a professor of economics at the University of Maryland in College Park and formerly an economics specialist with the Congressional Research Service, sees weaknesses with both components of the Obama plan. "We really have no model to deal with

Center. "Race was a consideration to people, but what it wasn't, invariably, was a negative consideration for white voters. It was a positive consideration for many white voters who saw Obama as a candidate who could help the country toward racial reconciliation."

Obama carried more white voters than former Vice President Al Gore or Sen. John Kerry of Massachusetts, the two previous Democratic nominees. Still, he could not have prevailed without black and Hispanic voters, particularly in the three Southern states he carried. In Virginia — a state that had voted Republican since 1964 — Obama lost by 21 points among white voters, according to exit polls.

His victory clearly did not bring racial enmity to its end. In December, Chip Saltsman, a candidate for the Republican Party chairmanship, sent potential supporters a CD containing the song "Barack the Magic Negro," a parody popularized by right-wing talk show host Rush Limbaugh during the campaign. And, when Senate Democrats initially balked in January at seating Roland Burris as Obama's replacement, Rep. Bobby Rush, D-Ill, played the race card, warning them not to "hang or lynch the appointee," comparing the move to Southern governors who sought to block desegregation. [9]

But still polls suggest that most Americans believe Obama's presidency will be a boon for race relations. A *USA Today*/Gallup Poll taken the day after the November election showed that two-thirds predicted black-white relations "will eventually be worked out" — by far the highest total in the poll's history. [10]

In the future, white males may no longer be the default inhabitants of America's most powerful position. The present generation and those in the future are likely to grow up thinking it's a normal state of affairs for the country to be led by a black president. "For a lot of African-Americans, it already has made them feel better and more positive about the coun-

Michelle Obama holds the Bible used to swear in President Abraham Lincoln as Barack Obama takes the oath of office from Supreme Court Chief Justice John G. Roberts Jr.

try and American society," says David Bositis, an expert on black voting at the Joint Center for Political and Economic Studies.

"When you ask my kids what they want to be when they grow up, they always say they want to work at McDonald's or Wal-Mart," said Joslyn Reddick, principal at a predominantly black school in Selma, Ala., a city from which King led an historic march for voting rights in 1965.

"Now they will see that an African-American has achieved the highest station in the United States," Reddick said. "They can see for themselves that dreams can come true." [11]

— Alan Greenblatt,
staff writer, Governing magazine

[1] Bryan Monroe, "The Audacity of Victory," *Ebony*, January 2009, p. 16.

[2] Sam Fulwood III, "The New Face of America," *Politico.com*, Jan. 13, 2009.

[3] Alan Greenblatt, "Changing U.S. Electorate," *CQ Researcher*, May 30, 2008, p. 459.

[4] The Obama speech, "A More Perfect Union," is at www.youtube.com/watch?v=pWe7wTVbLUU. The text of the March 18, 2008, speech, "A More Perfect Union," is found in *Change We Can Believe In: Barack Obama's Plan to Renew America's Promise* (2008), pp. 215-232.

[5] Jon Cohen and Jennifer Agiesta, "3 in 10 Americans Admit to Race Bias," *The Washington Post*, June 22, 2008, p. A1.

[6] Michael Sokolove," The Transformation," *The New York Times*, Nov. 9, 2008, p. WK1.

[7] John B. Judis, "Did Race Really Matter?" *Los Angeles Times*, Nov. 9, 2008, p. 34.

[8] Rachel L. Swarns, "Vaulting the Racial Divide, Obama Persuaded Americans to Follow," *The New York Times*, Nov. 5, 2008, p. 7.

[9] Clarence Page, "Hiding Behind Black Voters," *Chicago Tribune*, Jan. 4, 2009, p. 24.

[10] Susan Page, "Hopes Are High for Race Relations," *USA Today*, Nov. 7, 2008, p. 1A.

[11] Dahleen Glanton and Howard Witte, "Many Marvel at a Black President," *Chicago Tribune*, Nov. 5, 2008, p. 6.

the question of what's the right number" for the stimulus, he says. "And we're not even sure that the stimulus will do the job, especially if a lot of the spending is wasteful."

As for the tax cuts, Schick calls them "harebrained, more intended to look good and buy support than to actually get the economy moving." In

particular, he criticized a proposed $3,000 jobs credit for employers. "We know from the past that employers don't hire people for just a few shekels," he says. Eventually, the jobs credit was dropped, but the package still includes business tax breaks such as a $16 billion provision to allow businesses to use 2008 and 2009 loss-

es to offset profits for the previous five years instead of two.

Conservatives favor tax cuts, but not the middle-class tax cut that Obama is proposing. "A well-designed tax cut is the only effective short-term stimulus," says J. D. Foster, a senior fellow at the Heritage Foundation. But Foster, who worked in the Office of Management

Cabinet Includes Stars, Superstars and Surprises

President Obama made his Cabinet selections in record time, and his appointees run the gamut of race, ethnic origin, gender, age and even party affiliation. Those in top posts include Sen. Hillary Rodham Clinton at State and Robert Gates continuing at Defense. Besides Gates, one other Republican was chosen: Transportation's Ray LaHood. New Mexico Gov. Bill Richardson's withdrawal left the Commerce post unfilled along with the director of Drug Control Policy. Cabinet-level appointees include four women, two Asian-Americans, two Hispanics and two African-Americans.

Name, Age Department	Date of Nomination	Date of Confirmation	Previous Positions
Hillary Rodham Clinton, 61, State	Dec. 1	Jan. 21	New York U.S. senator (2001-09); first lady (1993-2001); Arkansas first lady (1979-81, 1983-92)
Timothy Geithner, 47, Treasury	Nov. 24	Jan. 26	President, Federal Reserve Bank of New York (2003-09); under secretary, Treasury (1998-2001)
Robert Gates, 65, Defense*	Dec. 1	Dec. 6, 2006 *	Defense secretary (2006-present); director, CIA (1991-93); deputy national security adviser (1989-91)
Eric Holder, 57, Attorney General	Dec. 1		Deputy attorney general (1997-2001); U.S. attorney (1993-97); judge, D.C. Superior Court (1988-93)
Ken Salazar, 53, Interior	Dec. 17	Jan. 20	Colorado U.S. senator (2005-09); Colorado attorney general (1999-2005)
Tom Vilsack, 58, Agriculture	Dec. 17	Jan. 20	Iowa governor (1999-2007); Iowa state senator (1992-99)
Hilda Solis, 51, Labor	Dec. 19		California U.S. representative (2001-09); California state senator (1995-2001)
Tom Daschle, 61, Health & Human Services	Dec. 11		South Dakota U.S. senator (1987-2005); Senate majority leader (2001, 2001-03); South Dakota U.S. representative (1979-87)
Shaun Donovan, 42, Housing and Urban Development	Dec. 13	Jan. 22	Commissioner, New York City Dept. of Housing Preservation and Development (2004-08); deputy assistant secretary, HUD (2000-01)

and Budget in the Bush administration, calls either for extending or making permanent Bush's across-the-board rate cuts, which primarily benefited upper-income taxpayers.

From the opposite side, Chad Stone, chief economist with the liberal Center on Budget Policy and Priorities, endorses Obama's approach. "Tax cuts should be focused on people of low and moderate means, who are much more likely to spend the extra money they get," he says.

Academic economists, however, caution that tax cuts may not deliver a lot of bang for the buck in terms of short-term stimulus. Studies indicate that taxpayers pocketed at least one-third of the $500 tax rebate the government disbursed to counteract the 2001 recession.

Advocates and observers on both sides warn that the spending side of the package may also be less effective than hoped if political forces play too large a role in shaping it. "If it goes to pork, if it goes to green jobs that may sound good in the short term but may not have a market response or a market for them, then it's a waste," Paul Gigot, editorial page editor of *The Wall Street Journal*, said on NBC's "Meet the Press" on Jan. 11.

"If the stuff that gets added is not very effective as stimulus or the things that are good get pulled out, that would not be good," says Stone.

For its part, the budget-restraint advocacy group Concord Coalition sees political forces as driving up the total cost of the package — in spending and tax cuts alike — with no regard for the long-term impact. "Nothing is ever taken off the table," says Diane Lim Rogers, the coalition's chief economist.

Rogers complains of "political pressure to come up with tax cuts even though economists are having trouble figuring out whether they're going to do any good." At the same time, she says spending has to be designed "as thoughtfully as possible, not in a way that the federal government ends up literally just throwing money out the door."

A range of experts also call for renewed efforts to solve the mortgage and foreclosure crisis, saying that homeowners are not going to start spending again without confidence-restoring steps. Indeed, Federal Reserve Chairman Ben Bernanke pointedly told a conference in December that steps to reduce foreclosures "should be high on the agenda" in any economic recovery plan. [2]

Despite questions and concerns about the details, however, support for strong action is all but universal. "We have no choice," said Mark Zandi, chief economist of Moody's Economy.com and a former adviser to the McCain campaign, also on "Meet the Press." "If we don't do something like this — a stimulus package, a foreclosure mitigation plan — the economy is going to slide away."

Is President Obama on the right track in Iraq and Afghanistan?

At the start of his presidential campaign in February 2007, candidate Obama was unflinchingly calling for withdrawing all U.S. combat forces from Iraq within 16 months after taking office. But his tone began changing as he neared the Democratic nomination in summer 2008. And in his first extended broadcast interview after the election, President-elect Obama said on NBC's "Meet the Press" on Dec. 7 only that he would summon military advisers on his first day in office and direct them to prepare a plan for "a responsible drawdown."

Obama also did nothing to knock down host Tom Brokaw's forecast of a "residual force" of 35,000 to 50,000 U.S. troops in Iraq through the end of his term. "I'm not going to speculate on the numbers," Obama said, but he went on to promise "a large enough force in the region" to protect U.S. personnel and to "ferret out any terrorist activity." In addition, Obama voiced disappointment with developments in Afghanistan and said

Name, Age, Department	Date of Nomination	Date of Confirmation	Previous Positions
Ray LaHood, 63, Transportation	Dec. 19	Jan. 22	Illinois U.S. representative (1995-2009); state representative (1982-83)
Steven Chu, 60, Energy	Dec. 15	Jan. 20	Director, Lawrence Berkeley National Laboratory, Dept. of Energy (2004-09); professor, UC-Berkeley (2004-present); Nobel Prize winner, physics (1997)
Arne Duncan, 44, Education	Dec. 16	Jan. 20	C.E.O, Chicago Public Schools (2001-09)
Eric Shinseki, 66, Veterans Affairs	Dec. 7	Jan. 20	Chief of staff, Army (1999-2003)
Janet Napolitano, 51, Homeland Security	Dec. 1	Jan. 20	Arizona governor (2003-09); attorney general (1999-2002)
Rahm Emmanuel, 49, Chief of Staff	Nov. 6	NA	Illinois U.S. representative (2003-09); senior adviser to the president (1993-98)
Lisa Jackson, 46, Environmental Protection Agency	Dec. 15	Jan. 22	Chief of staff, governor of New Jersey (2008-09); commissioner, New Jersey Dept. of Environmental Protection (2006-2008)
Peter Orszag, 40, Office of Management and Budget	Nov. 25	Jan. 20	Director, Congressional Budget Office (2007-08); adviser, National Economic Council (1997-98)
Susan Rice, 44, Ambassador to the United Nations	Dec. 1	Jan. 22	Assistant secretary, State (1997-2001); National Security Council (1993-97)
Ron Kirk, 54, Trade Representative	Dec. 19		Mayor of Dallas (1995-2002)

Department heads are listed in order of succession under Presidential Succession Act; nondepartment heads were given Cabinet-level status.

* Gates was confirmed when first nominated by President George W. Bush and did not have to be re-confirmed.

Compiled by Vyomika Jairam; all photos by Getty Images

that "additional troops" and "more effective diplomacy" would be needed to achieve U.S. goals there.

Many foreign policy observers are viewing Obama's late campaign and post-election stances as a salutary shift from

Bleak Economy Getting Bleaker

Economists widely agree a stimulus plan is needed.

When Barack Obama took office on Jan. 20, he inherited the most battered U.S. economy since World War II — and one of the shakiest to confront a new president in American history.

And the view from the Oval Office is likely to get bleaker before the gloom begins to lift.

"There are very serious questions on the financial side and apprehension among many parties that there may be more bad news to come," says Kent Hughes, director of the Program on Science, Technology, America and the Global Economy at the Woodrow Wilson Center for Scholars.

Already, Obama has stepped into the worst unemployment picture in 16 years, with the jobless rate at 7.2 percent and 11.1 million people out of work. The economy lost 1.9 million jobs during the last four months of 2008 — 524,000 in December alone. [1]

Economists worry that rising unemployment in manufacturing, construction, retailing and other sectors foreshadows an even more dismal future, at the very least in the short term. Dean Baker, co-director for the Center for Economic and Policy Research, a liberal think tank in Washington, says he expects another million or so jobs to disappear through February, then the pace of job loss to slow if Congress acts to stimulate the economy.

Obama must figure out not only how to get people back to work but also how to restore their confidence in the economy. A punishing credit crisis and cascade of grim news from Wall Street has led consumers to stop spending on everything from restaurant meals to houses and autos. [2]

Home sales have plunged in recent months, foreclosures are hitting record levels and a study by PMI Mortgage Insurance Co. estimates that half of the nation's 50-largest Metropolitan Statistical Areas have an "elevated or high probability" of experiencing lower home prices by the end of the third quarter of 2010 compared to the same quarter of 2008. [3]

Retail sales, a key indicator of consumer confidence, fell in December 2008 for the sixth month in a row, according to the Commerce Department. [4] The International Council of Shopping Centers said chain-store sales in December posted their biggest year-to-year decline since researchers began tracking figures in 1970. [5]

Rebecca Blank, a senior fellow at the Brookings Institution and former member of President Bill Clinton's Council of Economic Advisers, says the unemployment numbers "suggest the economy is still on the way down," and the decline in holiday sales is "surely going to lead to some bankruptcies and belt tightening in the retail sector."

Indeed, such trouble is already occurring. The shopping centers group estimated that 148,000 retail stores closed last year and that more than 73,000 will be shuttered in the first half of 2009. [6] Among the latest examples: Bankrupt electronics chain Circuit City said in January that it was closing its remaining 567 stores, putting some 30,000 employees out of work.

To revive the economy, the new administration — most visibly Obama himself — is urging Congress to quickly approve a stimulus package that could approach $900 billion. Much of the money would likely go toward tax cuts and public infrastructure projects, though how, exactly, the government would allocate it remains a matter of intense political debate.

One thing seems certain, though: The cost of a stimulus package, added to the hundreds of billions of dollars already spent to shore up the nation's flagging financial system, will add to the bulging federal deficit.

"The thing you know for sure is that a stimulus is going to add to the debt, which is [now] quite frightening, and it's going to make it worse," says June O'Neill, an economics professor at the City University of New York's Baruch College and a former director of the Congressional Budget Office (CBO) during the Clinton administration.

---

ideology to pragmatism. "It seems very clear that he will not fulfill his initial pledge to withdraw all U.S. forces from Iraq in 16 months — which is only wise," says Thomas Donnelly, a resident fellow on defense and national security issues at the American Enterprise Institute (AEI).

"I personally have been very impressed with [Obama's] thinking and his way of assembling a national security team," says Kenneth Pollack, director of the Brookings Institution's Saban Center for Middle East Policy. "This is not

a man who plays by the traditional American political rules."

Obama invited speculation about a shift toward the center by selecting Clinton and Robert Gates as the two Cabinet members on his national security team along with a retired Marine general, James Jones, as national security adviser. (*See chart, p. 80.*) Clinton had voted for the Iraq War in late 2002, though she echoed Obama during the campaign in calling for troop withdrawals. As Bush's secretary of Defense, Gates had overseen the "surge" in U.S. forces during 2007.

"This is a group of people who are very sober, very intelligent, fully aware of the importance of Iraq to America's security interests and of the fragility of the situation there," says Pollack.

Some anti-war activists were voicing concern about Obama's seeming shift within days of his election. "Obama has very successfully branded himself as anti-war, but the fact remains that he's willing to keep a residual force in Iraq indefinitely, [and] he wants to escalate in Afghanistan," said Matthis Chiroux of Iraq Veterans Against the

In January the CBO projected a $1.2 trillion deficit for the fiscal year. A stimulus plan would add even more pressure on Obama to get federal spending under control. "My own economic and budget team projects that, unless we take decisive action, even after our economy pulls out of its slide, trillion-dollar deficits will be a reality for years to come," Obama said. [7]

Still, a wide spectrum of economists — including conservatives who typically look askance at government spending — agree that a stimulus plan is necessary.

Martin Feldstein, a Harvard University economist and former chair of the Council of Economic Advisers in the Reagan administration, told a House committee in January that stopping the economic slide and restoring "sustainable growth" requires fixing the housing crisis and adopting a "fiscal stimulus of reduced taxes and increased government spending." [8]

Feldstein pointed out that past recessions started after the Federal Reserve raised short-term interest rates to fight inflation. Once inflation was under control, the Fed cut rates, which spurred a recovery. But the current recession is different, Feldstein said: It wasn't caused by the Fed tightening up on fiscal policy, and thus rate cuts haven't succeeded in reviving the economy.

"Because of the dysfunctional credit markets and the collapse of housing demand, monetary policy has had no traction in its attempt to lift the economy," he said.

That poses an especially daunting challenge for Obama. Baker of the Center for Economic and Policy Research says

The battered economy that confronts President Obama includes record foreclosure rates and plummeting home values. Above, a foreclosed home in Nevada, the state with the nation's highest foreclosure rate.

Getty Images/Ethan Miller

that the current crisis, occurring amid a broad collapse of the financial markets, more closely resembles the Great Depression than any other recession since then.

Most postwar recessions "were the result of the Fed raising rates," says Baker. "That meant we knew how to reverse it. This one, there's not an easy answer to. We're not going to see [another] Great Depression — not double-digit unemployment for a decade." But in terms of the severity of the problem, Baker adds, the Great Depression is the "closest match" to what confronts the new administration.

— *Thomas J. Billitteri*

[1] Bureau of Labor Statistics, "Employment Situation Summary," Jan. 9, 2009, www.bls.gov/news.release/empsit.nr0.htm.

[2] For coverage of the economic crisis, see the following *CQ Researcher* reports: Thomas J. Billitteri, "Financial Bailout," Oct. 24, 2008, pp. 865-888; Kenneth Jost, "Financial Crisis," May 9, 2008, pp. 409-432; Marcia Clemmitt, "Regulating Credit Cards," Oct. 10, 2008, pp. 817-840; and Marcia Clemmitt, "The National Debt," Nov. 14, 2008, pp. 937-960.

[3] News release, "PMI Winter 2009 Risk Index Indicates Broader Risk Spreading Across Nation's Housing Markets," PMI Mortgage Insurance Co., Jan. 14, 2009.

[4] Bob Willis, "U.S. Economy: Retail Sales Decline for a Sixth Month," Bloomberg, Jan. 14, 2009, www.bloomberg.com.

[5] V. Dion Haynes and Howard Schneider, "A Brutal December for Retailers," *The Washington Post*, Jan. 9, 2009, p. 2D.

[6] *Ibid.*

[7] Quoted in David Stout and Edmund L. Andrews, "$1.2 Trillion Deficit Forecast as Obama Weighs Options," *The New York Times*, Jan. 8, 2009, www.nytimes.com/2009/01/08/business/economy/08deficit.html?scp=2&sq=deficit&st=cse.

[8] Martin Feldstein, "The Economic Stimulus and Sustained Economic Growth," statement to the House Democratic Steering and Policy Committee, Jan. 7, 2009, www.nber.org/feldstein/EconomicStimulusandEconomicGrowthStatement.pdf.

War. "My hope is that he starts bringing home the troops from Iraq immediately, but I think those of us in the anti-war movement could find ourselves disappointed." [3]

Since then, however, criticism of Obama's emerging policies has been virtually non-existent from the anti-war and Democratic Party left. "He seems to be accelerating the withdrawal, which is terrific," says Robert Borosage, co-director of the Campaign for America's Future. Borosage is "concerned" about the residual force in Iraq because of

the risk that U.S. troops will become involved in "internecine battles." But he adds, "That's what he's promised, and I think he'll fulfill his promise."

Donnelly and Pollack, however, both view a continuing U.S. role in Iraq as vital. "There's good progress, but a long way to go," says Donnelly. "A huge American role is going to be needed through the four years of the Obama administration." Pollack agrees. "Iraq is far from solved. Whether we like it or not, Iraq is a vital interest for the United States of America."

In his campaign and since, Obama has treated Afghanistan as more important to U.S. interests and harshly criticized the Bush administration for — in his view — ignoring the conflict there. Afghanistan "had had a huge rhetorical place in the Obama campaign," says Donnelly. "The idea being that Afghanistan was the good war, the more important war, and that Iraq was a dead end strategically."

P. J. Crowley, a senior fellow at the liberal think tank Center for American Progress, calls Obama's focus on

Afghanistan "correct" but emphasizes the need for a multipronged effort to stabilize and reform the country's U.S.-backed government. "Returning our weight of effort [to Afghanistan] is a right approach," says Crowley, who was spokesman for the National Security Council under President Bill Clinton.

"More troops may help in a narrow sense," Crowley continues, "but I don't think anyone suggests that more troops are the long-term solution in Afghanistan. The insertion of U.S. forces is logical in the short- to mid-term, but it has to be part of a broader strategy."

But Pollack questions the value of any additional U.S. troops at all. "The problems of Afghanistan are not principally military; they are principally political and diplomatic," he says. "Unless this new national security team can create a military mission that is of value to what is ultimately a diplomatic problem, it's going to be tough to justify to the country the commitment of those additional troops."

Borosage also worries about an increased U.S. military presence in Afghanistan. "A permanent occupation of Afghanistan is a recipe for defeat," he says.

All of the experts stress that U.S. policy in Afghanistan now plays a secondary part in the fight with the al Qaeda terrorist group, which carried out the 9/11 attacks in the United States. "There is no al Qaeda in Afghanistan," says Donnelly. "Al Qaeda has now reconstituted itself in the tribal areas of northwest Pakistan."

Donnelly questions Afghanistan's importance to U.S. interests altogether but ultimately supports continued U.S. involvement. "The only thing worse

than being engaged in Afghanistan," he says, "is turning our backs on it."

Is President Obama on the right track in winning support for his programs in Congress?

As president of Harvard University, Lawrence Summers clashed so often and so sharply with faculty and others that he was forced out after only

State Department staffers greet new Secretary of State Hillary Rodham Clinton on her first day of work, Jan. 22, 2009.

five years in office. But when Summers went to Capitol Hill as President-elect Obama's designee to be top White House economic adviser, the normally self-assured economist told lawmakers that he and other administration officials plan to be all ears.

"All of us have been instructed that when it comes to Congress, to listen and not just talk," Summers told House Democrats in a Jan. 9 meeting to discuss Obama's economic recovery plan. [4]

Within days after the new Congress was sworn in on Jan. 6, however, lawmakers on both sides of the political aisle were, in fact, taking pot shots at Obama's plan. Republicans were calling for hearings after the plan was unveiled — a move seen as jeopardizing Obama's goal of signing a stimulus bill into law before Congress' mid-February recess. Meanwhile,

some Democratic lawmakers were questioning the business tax cuts being considered for the package, calling them examples of what they considered the discredited philosophy of "trickle-down economics."

Despite the criticisms, Obama was upbeat about his relations with Congress in an interview broadcast on ABC's "This Weekend" on Jan. 11. "One of the things that we're trying to set a tone of is that, you know, Congress is a co-equal branch of government," Obama told host George Stephanopoulos. "We're not trying to jam anything down people's throats."

Veteran Congress-watchers in Washington are giving Obama high marks in his dealings with Capitol Hill so far, while also praising Congress for asserting its own constitutional prerogatives.

"Obama is off to a very good start with Congress, and, just as importantly, Congress is off to a good start with him," says Thomas Mann, a senior fellow at the Brookings Institution. "No more [status as a] potted plant for the first branch or an inflated sense of presidential authority by the second, but instead a serious engagement between the players at the opposite ends of Pennsylvania Avenue."

Obama is "in good shape," says Stephen Hess, a senior fellow emeritus at Brookings who began his Washington career as a White House staffer under President Dwight D. Eisenhower in the 1950s. Hess credits Obama in particular with seeking to consult with Republican as well as Democratic lawmakers.

"He was very shrewd after talking with Democrats to talk with Republicans," says Hess, who also teaches at George Washington University. "He has given the opposition the sense that he's open, he's listening. He's reached out

AFP/Getty Images/Mark Ralston

Big-Name Policy 'Czars' Head for West Wing

Appointments may signal decline in Cabinet's influence.

President Barack Obama has tapped several high-profile Washington insiders to fill new and existing senior White House positions, indicating the new administration is shifting policy making from the Cabinet to the influential White House West Wing.

The new so-called policy "czars" include former Sen. Tom Daschle, D-S.D., at the Office of Health Reform (he is also Health and Human Services secretary); former assistant Treasury secretary Nancy Killefer, leading efforts to cut government waste as the nation's first chief performance officer; former Environmental Protection Agency Administrator Carol Browner as the new coordinator of energy and climate policy; and former New York City Council member Adolfo Carrion Jr., who is expected to head the Office of Urban Affairs.

"We're going to have so many czars," said Thomas J. Donohue, president of the U.S. Chamber of Commerce. "It's going to be a lot of fun, seeing the czars and the regulators and the czars and the Cabinet secretaries debate." [1]

In another major West Wing appointment, former Treasury secretary and Harvard President Lawrence Summers becomes director of the existing National Economic Council. In the weeks leading up to the inauguration, analysts noted that Summers, and not then-Treasury secretary-designate Timothy Geithner, was leading then-President-elect Obama's efforts to draft a new financial stimulus package.

But Paul Light, an expert on governance at New York University, questions the role the new "czars" will play. "It's a symbolic gesture of the priority assigned to an issue, and I emphasize the word symbolic," he said. "There've been so many czars over the last 50 years, and they've all been failures. Nobody takes them seriously anymore." [2]

— *Vyomika Jairam*

[1] Michael D. Shear and Ceci Connolly, "Obama Assembles Powerful West Wing; Influential Advisers May Compete With Cabinet," *The Washington Post*, Jan. 14, 2009, p. A1.

[2] Laura Meckler " 'Czars' Ascend at White House," *The Wall Street Journal*, Dec. 15, 2005, p. A6.

to them when he doesn't need them — which of course is the right time to reach out to them."

Norman Ornstein, a resident scholar at the American Enterprise Institute, similarly credits Obama with having gone "further in consulting members of the opposition party than any president I can remember." Writing in the Capitol Hill newspaper *Roll Call*, Ornstein also said Obama is well aware of lawmakers' "issues and sensitivities." For example, Ornstein noted the president-elect's personal apology to Senate Intelligence Committee Chair Dianne Feinstein, D-Calif., for failing to give her advance word in early January of the planned nomination of Leon Panetta to head the Central Intelligence Agency. [5]

The lapse of protocol on the Panetta nomination — which Feinstein later promised to support — may well have been the only avoidable misstep by the Obama team in its dealings with Congress. Criticisms of the economic recovery program as it took shape could hardly have been avoided. And Republican senators naturally looked for ways to find fault with some of Obama's Cabinet nominees — such as their criticism of Attorney General-designate Eric Holder for his role in President Clinton's pardon of fugitive financier Marc Rich and Treasury Secretary-designate Timothy Geithner for his late payment of tens of thousands of dollars in federal income taxes.

A prominent, retired GOP congressman, however, says Obama is doing well so far and predicts the economic crisis may give him a longer than usual pass with lawmakers from both parties. "He has the advantage of a honeymoon, and perhaps the second advantage of the economic conditions of the country, which I think will help the Congress to gather around his program," says Bill Frenzel, a guest scholar at the Brookings Institution and a Minnesota congressman for two decades before his retirement in 1991.

"We're talking about both Republicans and Democrats," Frenzel continues. "Democrats are going to want to be independent, and Republicans are going to want to take whacks at him when they can. But I think there is a mood of wanting to help the president when they can for a while."

Ornstein and Hess caution, however, that new presidents cannot expect the honeymoon to last very long. Ornstein writes that Obama's hoped-for supermajority support in Congress "may be doable on stimulus" and "perhaps even on health care." But he says an era of "post-partisan politics" will require "some serious steps" by party leaders and rank-and-file members.

For his part, Hess says Obama may eventually begin to disappoint some within his own party — but not yet. "Democrats will for a while cut him a great deal of slack," Hess explains. "Reason No. 1, he's not George W. Bush. Reason No. 2, they're going to get some of what they want. And reason No. 3, some of those folks have become wiser about the way politics is played in this town." ∎

Chronology: 1961-2006

1960s-1970s

Obama born to biracial, binational couple; begins education in Indonesia after mother's remarriage, then returns to Hawaii.

1961
Barack Hussein Obama born on Aug. 4, 1961, in Honolulu; parents Stanley Ann Dunham and Barack Obama Sr. meet as students at University of Hawaii; father leaves family behind two years later for graduate studies at Harvard, return to native Kenya.

1967-1971
Obama's mother remarries, family moves to Indonesia; Obama attends a secular public elementary school with a predominantly Muslim student body until mother decides he should return to Hawaii for schooling.

1971-1979
"Barry" Obama lives with grandparents Stanley and Madelyn Dunham; graduates with honors from Punahou School, one of three black students at the elite private school; enrolls in Occidental College in Los Angeles but transfers later to Columbia University in New York City.

1980s-1990s

Works as community organizer in Chicago, gets law degree, enters politics.

1983
Obama graduates with degree in political science from Columbia University; floods civil rights organizations with job applications.

1985-1988
Works on housing, employment issues as community organizer in Far South Side neighborhood in Chicago.

Summer 1988
Visits Kenya for first time.

1988-1991
Enrolls in Harvard Law School in fall 1988; graduates in 1991 after serving as president of *Harvard Law Review* — the first African-American to hold that position.

1992-1995
Returns to Chicago; marries Michelle Robinson in 1992; runs voter registration project; works as lawyer, lecturer at University of Chicago Law School.

1995
Dreams from My Father is published; mother dies just after publication (Nov. 7, 1995).

1996
Elected to Illinois legislature as senator representing Chicago's Hyde Park area; serves for eight years.

———— • ————

2000-2006

Enters national political stage as U.S. senator, Democratic keynoter.

2000
Loses badly in Democratic primary for U.S. House seat held by Rep. Bobby Rush.

2002
Opposes then-imminent war in Iraq.

2004
Gains Democratic nomination for U.S. Senate from Illinois. . . . Wins wide praise for keynote address to Democratic National Convention. . . . Elected U.S. senator from Illinois: third African-American to serve in Senate since Reconstruction.

2005-2006
Earns reputation as hard worker in Senate; compiles liberal voting record; manages Democrats' initiative on ethics reform. . . . *Audacity of Hope* is published (October 2006). . . . Deflects intense speculation about possible presidential bid.

BACKGROUND

'A Mutt, Like Me'

Barack Obama's inauguration as president represents a 21st-century version of the American dream: the election of a native-born citizen, both black and white, with roots in Kansas and Kenya. Abandoned by his father and later living apart from his mother, Obama was nurtured in his formative years by doting white grandparents and educated in elite schools before turning to community organizing in inner-city Chicago and then to a political career that moved from the Illinois statehouse to the White House in barely 12 years. [6]

Barack Hussein Obama was born in Honolulu on Aug. 4, 1961, to parents he later described in his memoir *Dreams from My Father* as a "white as vanilla" American mother and a "black as pitch" Kenyan father. Barack Obama Sr. and Stanley Ann Dunham married, more or less secretly, after having met as students at the University of Hawaii. Stanley Ann's "moderately liberal" parents accepted the union. In Kenya —

Chronology: 2007-2009

2007 *Obama enters presidential race as underdog to New York Sen. Hillary Rodham Clinton; nearly matches Clinton in "money primary" in advance of Iowa caucuses.*

Feb. 10, 2007
Obama announces candidacy for Democratic nomination for president at rally in Springfield, Ill., three weeks after Clinton, former first lady, joined race; Democratic field eventually includes eight candidates.

March-December 2007
Democratic candidates engage in 17 debates, with no knockout punches; Obama closes gap with Clinton in polls, fundraising.

2008 *Obama gains Democratic nomination after drawn-out contest with Clinton; beats Republican Sen. John McCain as economic issues take center stage.*

January-February
Obama scores upset in Iowa caucuses (Jan. 3); Clinton wins New Hampshire primary (Jan. 9); field narrows to two candidates by end of January.

March-April
Clinton wins big-state primaries, including Ohio (March 4) and Pennsylvania (April 22); Obama edges ahead in delegates.

May-June
Obama gains irreversible lead after Indiana, North Carolina primaries (May 6); clinches nomination after final primaries (June 2).

July
Obama goes to Iraq, reaffirms 16-month pullout timetable; speaks at big rally in Berlin, Germany.

August
Obama picks Delaware Sen. Joseph R. Biden as running mate; accepts nomination with speech promising Iraq withdrawal, domestic initiatives; McCain chooses Alaska Gov. Sarah Palin as running mate.

September-October
Obama holds his own in three debates with McCain (Sept. 26, Oct. 7, Oct. 15); McCain challenge to go to Washington to push financial bailout plan ends with advantage to Obama.

Nov. 4
Obama victory is signaled with victories in "red states" in East, Midwest; networks declare him winner as polls close in West (11 p.m., Eastern time).

November-December
Obama completes Cabinet selections; works on economic recovery plan; vacations in Hawaii.

2009 *Obama inaugurated before largest crowd in Washington history.*

Jan. 5-19
Obama, in Washington, starts public campaign for economic recovery plan. . . . Congress reconvenes with Democrats holding 256-178 majority in House with one vacancy, 57-41 majority in Senate with two seats vacant. . . . More high-level nominations; Commerce post in limbo after Bill Richardson withdraws because of ethics investigation in New Mexico.

Jan. 20
Obama is inaugurated as 44th president; uses inaugural address to detail "serious" challenges at home, abroad; promises that challenges "will be met." . . . President moves quickly over next week to reverse some Bush administration policies; lobbies Congress on economic stimulus package, but Republicans continue to push for less spending, more tax cuts.

---

where Barack Sr. already had a wife and child — the family did not. The marriage lasted only two years; Barack left his wife and child behind to go to graduate school at Harvard. Stanley Ann filed for divorce, citing standard legal grounds.

His mother's second marriage, to an Indonesian student, Lolo Soetoro, took young Barry, as he was then called, to his Muslim stepfather's native country

at the age of 6. Lolo worked as a geologist in post-colonial Indonesia; his mother taught English. They had a child, Obama's half-sister, Maya. (Maya Soetoro-Ng now teaches high school history in Honolulu.) Barry attended a predominantly Muslim school that would be falsely depicted as an Islamist madrassa during the 2008 campaign. His mother, meanwhile, taught her son

about the civil rights struggles in America and eventually sent him back to Hawaii for schooling. The marriage ended later, a victim of cultural and personality differences.

Barry returned to live with grandparents Stanley and Madelyn Dunham — "Gramps" and "Toot" (her nickname came from the Hawaiian word for grandmother). They provided him

Myriad Global Problems Confront Obama

Two wars, the Middle East and terrorism top the list.

President Barack Obama faces immense foreign-policy challenges — two wars and a turbulent global scene that includes continuing conflict in the Middle East — all against the backdrop of a global economic crisis.

Tens of thousands of U.S. troops are at war in Iraq and Afghanistan. Israel, America's closest Mideast ally, has just suspended a devastating military offensive in the Gaza Strip that could restart at any time. And Islamist terrorism remains a constant threat, with al Qaeda leader Osama bin Laden still at large. [1]

Obama divided his early days in office between wartime matters, the latest Mideast crisis and the economic meltdown. By all indications, he will be walking a tightrope between domestic and international affairs for the forseeable future.

"A president in these circumstances is going to want to do everything possible to ensure that the transformative and ambitious and very difficult projects of domestic policy that have been designated as the priority for this new administration are not inhibited or disrupted by early failures, in counterterrorism or foreign policy," Steve Coll, president and CEO of the New America Foundation, a nonpartisan think tank, told a pre-inauguration conference on security issues.

Obama's inaugural address restated his commitment to withdraw U.S. forces from Iraq, which is more peaceful after more than five years of war but still violent and torn by political intrigue. [2]

In Afghanistan, however, escalating warfare is tied to another source of U.S. worries: Pakistan. Concern escalated in late November following coordinated terrorist attacks on hotels and other sites in Mumbai — India's financial and cultural capital — which were traced to a jihadist group in Pakistan with deep ties to that country's intelligence agency. [3] Some 175 people were killed and 200 wounded.

The group, Lashkar-e-Taiba, also has at least some operational link to al Qaeda and bin Laden, who is believed to be hiding in Pakistan's northern tribal region, bordering Afghanistan. Another al Qaeda ally, the Taliban guerrillas who are fighting the Afghan government and U.S. and NATO troops in Afghanistan, use Pakistan as a headquarters. [4]

"Moreover," a government commission on weapons of mass destruction and terrorism said in December, "given Pakistan's tense relationship with India, its buildup of nuclear weapons is exacerbating the prospect of a dangerous nuclear arms race in South Asia that could lead to a nuclear conflict." [5]

The other daunting foreign-policy issue facing the new Obama administration — conflict between Israel and the Palestinians — offers slender prospects for peace. "Two states living side by side in peace and security — right now that stands about as much chance as Bozo the Clown becoming president of the United States," says Aaron David Miller, a former Mideast peace adviser to six secretaries of State.

The biggest obstacle, Miller says, is the "broken and dysfunctional" state of the Palestinian national movement. Fatah, the secular party that runs the West Bank, has a negotiating relationship with Israel. Hamas, the elected Islamist party and militia that initially seized power in an anti-Fatah coup in Gaza in 2007, deems Israel illegitimate. Hamas sponsored or tolerated rocket fire into Israel from Gaza but halted rocketing at the beginning of a cease-fire that began in June 2008. But Israel accused Hamas of building up its arsenal and retaliated by limiting the flow of goods into the region. In December, Hamas announced it wouldn't renew the already shaky truce, blaming the Israeli embargo and military moves. From then on, Hamas stepped up rocketing.

Israel's recent 22-day anti-Hamas offensive in Gaza cost some 1,300 Palestinian lives. The Palestinians estimated the civilian death toll at 40 percent to 70 percent of the fatalities; Israel put the toll at about 25 percent of the total. Israeli fatalities totaled 13, including three civilians. [6]

The scale of Israel's Gaza offensive is renewing calls for the U.S. government to change its relationship to Israel. "The days of America's exclusive ties to Israel may be coming to an end," Miller wrote in *Newsweek* in January. Obama, however, reaffirmed his support for Israel in his Jan. 26 interview with the Arabic-language network Al Arabiya. [7]

Those interests also would require devising a response to what the United States believes is a nuclear arms development project by Iran, which supports Hamas politically and finan-

the stable, supportive home life that he had somewhat lacked so far. He gained admission to the prestigious Punahou School as one of only three black students. His father visited once — Barack's only time spent with him after the divorce — and spoke to one of his son's classes about life in Africa. Obama's mother came back to Hawaii for studies in anthropology, but when

she returned to Indonesia for field work Barack chose to stay in Hawaii.

At Punahou, Obama excelled as a student and played with the state championship basketball team his senior year. He graduated in 1979 and enrolled at Occidental College in Los Angeles. Two years later, he transferred to Columbia University in New York. By now, Obama was well aware of racial issues in the

United States — and his ambiguous place in the story. "I learned to slip back and forth between my black and white worlds," he wrote in *Dreams from My Father.* More recently, as president-elect, Obama referred self-deprecatingly to his background. In describing the kind of puppy he would have preferred to get for his two young daughters, but for Malia's allergies, Obama said, "A mutt, like me."

cially — a sign, for some, of how all Middle Eastern issues are interconnected.

"One of the great mistakes we have made has been to believe we can compartmentalize these different policies, that we can somehow separate what is happening between Israel and the Palestinians from what's happening in Iraq and what's happening in Iran and what's happening in Egypt and Saudi Arabia and everywhere else in the Middle East," said Kenneth M. Pollack, a senior fellow at the Brookings Institution and former CIA analyst of the region. "Linkage is a reality." [8]

Another set of connections ties past U.S. support for NATO membership by Ukraine and Georgia to chilled U.S. relations with Russia, which views the potential presence of Western military allies — and U.S. missiles — on its borders as hostile.

Despite the Cold War echoes of that dispute, some foreign-affairs experts argue that Obama actually confronts a less perilous international panorama than some of his recent predecessors. "We don't have the Cold War and World War II," says Michael Mandelbaum, director of the foreign policy program at Johns Hopkins University's School of Advanced International Studies. "Those were existential threats. What the incoming president faces are annoying and troublesome, but not existential threats."

That picture could change if jihadist radicals took over nuclear-armed Pakistan. For now, Mandelbaum argues the biggest international and domestic dangers are one and the same — the economic meltdown.

But success for the huge spending package that Obama wants will require participation by China, America's major creditor. "China has been lending us money by buying our bonds," Mandelbaum says. "That huge stimulus package is not going to work unless we get some cooperation from the Chinese."

Palestinians in Gaza search the rubble of their homes for usable items after an Israeli air strike on Jan. 5, 2009.

Getty Images

In short, the American way of life very much depends on China, Mandelbaum says: "For what Americans care about, for what matters in the world, the issue of where and how we borrow money for the stimulus and where and how we rebalance the economy dwarfs Gaza in importance, and is more important than Iraq and Afghanistan."

— Peter Katel

[1] For coverage of the Iraq and Afghanistan wars, the Middle East and Islamic fundamentalism, see the following *CQ Researcher* reports: Peter Katel, "Cost of the Iraq War," April 25, 2008, pp. 361-384; Peter Katel, "New Strategy in Iraq," Feb. 23, 2007, pp. 169-192; and Peter Katel, "Middle East Tension," Oct. 27, 2006, pp. 889-912. Also see the following *CQ Global Researcher* reports: Roland Flamini, "Afghanistan on the Brink," June 2007, pp. 125-150; Robert Kiener, "Crisis in Pakistan," December 2008, pp. 321-348; and Sarah Glazer, "Radical Islam in Europe," November 2007, pp. 265-294.

[2] Alissa J. Rubin, "Iraq Unsettled by Political Power Plays," *The New York Times*, Dec. 25, 2008, www.nytimes.com/2008/12/26/world/middleeast/26baghdad.html; and Alissa J. Rubin, "Bombs Kill 5 in Baghdad, but Officials Avoid Harm," *The New York Times*, Jan. 20, 2009, www.nytimes.com/2009/01/21/world/middleeast/21iraq.html.

[3] Jane Perlez and Somini Sengupta, "Mumbai Attack is Test for Pakistan on Curbing Militants," *The New York Times*, Dec. 3, 2008, www.nytimes.com/2008/12/04/world/asia/04pstan.html?scp=5&sq=Mumbai Lashkar ISI&st=cse.

[4] For a summary and analysis, see K. Alan Kronstadt and Kenneth Katzman, "Islamist Militancy in the Pakistan-Afghanistan Border Region and U.S. Policy," Congressional Research Service, Nov. 21, 2008, http://fpc.state.gov/documents/organization/113202.pdf.

[5] See "World at Risk," Commission on the Prevention of Weapons of Mass Destruction Proliferation and Terrorism, December 2008, p. xxiii.

[6] See Steven Erlanger, "Weighing Crimes and Ethics in the Fog of Urban Warfare," *The New York Times*, Jan. 16, 2009, www.nytimes.com/2009/01/17/world/middleeast/17israel.html?scp=1&sq=Gaza civilian death percent&st=cse; Amy Teibel, "Last Israeli troops leave Gaza, completing pullout," The Associated Press, Jan. 21, 2009, http://news.yahoo.com/s/ap/ml_israel_palestinians.

[7] Aaron David Miller, "If Obama Is Serious, He should get tough with Israel," *Newsweek*, Jan. 3, 2009, www.newsweek.com/id/177716.

[8] Quoted in Adam Graham-Silverman, "Conflict in Gaza Strip Presents Immediate Challenge for New President," *CQ Today*, Jan. 20, 2009.

Graduating from Columbia in 1983 with a degree in political science, Obama decided to take on the so-called Reagan revolution by becoming a community organizer — aiming, as he wrote, to bring about "change . . . from a mobilized grass roots." Obama flooded civil rights organizations to no avail until he was hired in 1985 by Gerald Kellman, a white organizer looking for an African-

American to help with community development and mobilization in a Far South Side section of Chicago. Obama's three years in Chicago brought him face to face with the gritty realities of urban life and the disillusionment of the disadvantaged. He later described the time as "the best education I ever had." [7]

Obama enrolled in Harvard Law School in 1988. [8] He wrote nothing

about the decision in his memoir and has said little about it elsewhere. Before going, he visited Kenya, where his father had died in an automobile accident six years earlier. Obama described enjoying the meeting with his extended family while acutely conscious of the cultural gap. At Harvard, he excelled as a student, played pick-up basketball and had only a limited social life after meeting his future wife, Michelle Robinson, a lawyer he had met while working for a Chicago law firm as a summer associate. His election in 1990 as president of the *Harvard Law Review* — as a compromise between conservative and liberal factions — marked the first time an African-American had held the prestigious position.

His barrier-breaking gained enough attention to get Obama an invitation from a literary agent, Jane Dystel, to write a book. [9] Obama planned to write about race relations, but in the three years of writing it turned into more of a personal memoir. Obama has said he was unmindful of political consequences in the writing and that he rejected a suggestion from one of his editors to delete references to drug use while in college. The book garnered respectable reviews — and the audio version won a Grammy — but no more than middling sales. Obama's mother read page proofs and lived just long enough to see it published. She died of ovarian cancer in November 1995. [10]

Red, Blue and Purple

O bama needed only 10 years to rise from the back benches of the Illinois legislature to a front seat on the national political stage. His political ambition misled him only once: in a failed run for the U.S. House. But he succeeded in other endeavors on the strength of hard work, personal intelligence, political acumen and earnest efforts to bridge the differences of race, class and partisan affiliation.

Obama entered politics in 1995 as the chosen successor of a one-term state senator, Alice Palmer. But he turned on his mentor when she sought re-election after all, following a losing bid in a special election for a U.S. House seat. Obama successfully challenged signatures on Palmer's nominating petitions and had her disqualified (and the other candidates too) to win the Democratic nomination unopposed and eventual election.

As a Democrat in a Republican-controlled legislature and a liberal with no connection to his party's organization, Obama worked to develop personal ties — some formed in a weekly poker game. Among his accomplishments: ethics legislation, a state earned-income tax credit and a measure, backed by law enforcement, to require videotaped interrogations in all capital cases. [11]

After four years in office, Obama decided in 2000 to mount a primary challenge to the popular and much better known Democratic congressman, Bobby Rush. The race was foolhardy from the outset. But — as Obama recounts in his second book, *The Audacity of Hope* — he suffered a grave embarrassment when he failed to return from a family vacation in Hawaii in time to vote

on a major gun control bill in a specially called legislative session. Rush won handily. [12] In the 2008 presidential campaign, Obama's absence on the gun control vote was cited along with many other instances when he voted "present" as evidence of risk-averse gamesmanship on his part — a depiction vigorously disputed by the campaign.

His ambition unquenched, Obama began deciding by fall 2002 to run for the U.S. Senate seat then held by Republican Peter Fitzgerald, a vulnerable incumbent who eventually decided not to seek re-election. In October, at the invitation of a peace activist group, he delivered to an anti-war rally in Chicago his now famous speech opposing the then-imminent U.S. war in Iraq. Obama formally entered the Senate race in 2003 as the underdog to multimillionaire Blair Hull and state Comptroller Dan Hynes. But Hull's candidacy collapsed after allegations of abuse against his ex-wife. Hynes ran a lackluster campaign, while Obama waged a determined, disciplined drive that netted him nearly 53 percent of the vote in a seven-way race. [13]

Obama's debut on the national stage came in July 2004 after the presumptive Democratic presidential nominee, Massachusetts Sen. John Kerry, picked him to deliver the keynote address at the party's convention. Obama drafted the speech himself, according to biographer David Mendell. The night before, he told a friend, "My speech is pretty good." It was better than that. Obama wove his personal story together with verbal images of working-class America to lead up to the passage — rebroadcast thousands of times since — envisioning a unified

Barack Obama's riveting, highly personal keynote address at the 2004 Democratic National Convention made him an overnight star and presidential contender.

AFP/Getty Images/Timothy A. Clary

nation instead of the "pundits' " image of monochromatic "Red States" and "Blue States." The speech "electrified the convention hall," *The Washington Post* reported the next day, and made Obama a rising star to be watched. [14]

By the time of the speech, political fortune had already shone on Obama back in Illinois. Divorce files of his Republican opponent in the Senate race, Jack Ryan, made public in June, showed that Ryan had pressured his wife to go with him to sex clubs and have sex in front of others. Ryan, a multimillionaire businessman, resisted pressure to withdraw for more than a month. Once Ryan bowed out — three days after Obama's speech — GOP leaders had to scramble for an opponent. They eventually lured Alan Keyes, a conservative African-American from Maryland, to be the sacrificial lamb in the race. Obama won with a record-setting 70 percent of the vote to take his seat in January 2005 as only the third African-American to serve in the U.S. Senate since Reconstruction.

Obama entered the Senate with the presidency on his mind but also the recognition that he must succeed first in a club with low tolerance for celebrity without substance. A profile in Congressional Quarterly's *Politics in America* published with his presidential campaign under way in 2007 credited Obama with "a reputation as a hard worker, a good listener and a quick study." [15]

With Democrats in the majority, Obama was designated in 2007 to spearhead the party's work on ethics reform — a role that prompted an icy exchange with his future opponent, Sen. McCain, who had expected to work with Democrats on a bipartisan approach. The eventual package included a ban on senators' discounted trips on corporate jets, but not — as Obama had pushed for — outside enforcement of ethics rules.

Obama had more success working with other Republicans, including Oklahoma's Tom Coburn (Internet access to government databases) and Indiana's Richard Lugar (international destruction of conventional weapons). Overall, however, his voting record was solidly liberal and reliably party-line. In the 2008 race, the McCain campaign repeatedly tried to debunk Obama's image of post-partisanship by challenging him to cite a significant example of departing from Democratic Party positions.

'Yes, We Can'

Obama won the Democratic nomination for president in a come-from-behind victory over frontrunner Hillary Clinton on the strength of fundraising prowess, message control and a pre-convention strategy focused on amassing delegates in caucus as well as primary states. He took an even bigger financial advantage into the general election but pulled away from McCain only after the nation's dire economic news in October drove the undecideds decisively toward the candidate promising "change we can believe in." [16]

Despite intense speculation and Obama's evident interest, he decided to run only after heart-to-heart talks with Michelle while vacationing in Hawaii in December 2006. Michelle's reluctance stemmed from the effects on the family and fear for Obama's personal safety. In the end, she agreed — with one stipulation: Obama had to give up smoking. That promise remains a work in progress. In his post-election appearance on NBC's "Meet the Press" on Dec. 7, Obama promised only that, "you will not see any violations" of the White House's no-smoking rule while he is president.

Obama entered the race with a speech to an outdoor rally on a cold Feb. 10, 2007, in Springfield, Ill. After acknowledging the "audacity" of his campaign, Obama laid out a platform of reshaping the economy, tackling the health-care crisis and ending the war in Iraq. He started well behind Clinton in the polls and in organization. In the early debates — with eight candidates in all

— Obama himself rated his performance as "uneven," according to *Newsweek*'s post-election account. [17] By December, however, Obama had pulled ahead of Clinton in some New Hampshire polling and was in a virtual dead-heat in the all-important "money primary."

The Iowa caucuses on Jan. 3, 2007, gave Obama an unexpected win with about 38 percent of the vote and left only two other viable candidates standing: former North Carolina Sen. John Edwards, who came in second; and Clinton, who finished a disappointing third. Five days later, however, Clinton regained her stride with a 3-percentage-point victory over Obama in the first-in-the-nation New Hampshire primary. Edwards' third-place finish kept him in the race, but he dropped out on Jan. 30 after finishing third in primaries in Florida and his birth state of South Carolina.

The one-on-one between Obama and Clinton continued through May. Clinton bested Obama in a series of supposedly "critical" late-season primaries — notably, Ohio and Pennsylvania — even as Obama pulled ahead in delegates thanks to caucus state victories and also-ran proportional-representation winnings from the primaries. He turned the most serious threat to his campaign — his relationship with the sometimes fiery black minister, Jeremiah Wright — into a plus of sorts with a stirring speech on racial justice delivered in Philadelphia on March 18. With Clinton's "electability" arguments unavailing, Obama mathematically clinched the nomination on June 3 as the two split final primaries in Montana and South Dakota. Clinton withdrew four days later, promising to work hard for Obama's election.

With nearly three months before the convention, Obama went to Iraq and Europe to burnish his national security and foreign policy credentials. His 16-month timetable for withdrawal now essentially matched the Iraqi government's own position — weakening a Republican line of attack. An address to a

Daschle Appointment Shows Commitment to Health-Care Reforms

But a vote on a specific plan may be delayed until next year.

"The flaws in our health system are pervasive and corrosive. They threaten our health and economic security," said former Sen. Tom Daschle, D-S.D., President Obama's nominee for secretary of Health and Human Services (HHS), at his initial confirmation hearing before the Senate Health, Education, Labor, and Pensions (HELP) Committee on Jan. 8. [1]

Throughout his campaign, Obama promised to make good-quality health care accessible to all Americans. Many observers see his choice of Daschle — who recently coauthored a book laying out a plan for universal insurance coverage — to lead both HHS and a new White House Office of Health Policy as a sign of the new president's commitment to health-care reform, which he has called the key to economic security. [2] "I talk to hardworking Americans every day who worry about paying their medical bills and getting and keeping health insurance for their families," Obama said. [3]

In the final presidential debate on Oct. 15, 2008, Obama laid out the essence of his health overhaul. "If you've got health insurance through your employer, you can keep your health insurance," he said. "If you don't have health insurance, then what we're going to do is to provide you the option of buying into the same kind of federal pool [of private insurance plans] that [Republican presidential nominee] Sen. McCain and I enjoy as federal employees, which will give you high-quality care, choice of doctors at lower costs, because so many people are part of this insured group," Obama said. [4]

In addition, Obama's plan would:

- require insurance companies to accept all applicants, including those with already diagnosed illnesses — or "pre-existing conditions" — that insurers often decline to cover;

- create a federally regulated national "health insurance exchange" where people could buy coverage from a range of approved private insurers and possibly from a public insurance program as well;
- provide subsidies to help lower-income people buy coverage;
- require all children to have health insurance; and
- require employers except small businesses to either provide "meaningful" coverage to workers or pay a percentage of payroll toward the costs of a public plan. [5]

Points of potential controversy include whether all Americans should be required to buy health coverage.

During the presidential primary campaign, Obama sparred with fellow Democratic candidate Sen. Hillary Rodham Clinton, D-N.Y., who called for a mandate on individuals to buy insurance. Obama disagreed, saying, "my belief is that if we make it affordable, if we provide subsidies to those who can't afford it, they will buy it," and that only children's coverage should be required. [6]

But many analysts, including Daschle, point out that unless coverage is required many people will buy it only after they become sick, making it impossible for health insurance to perform its main task — spreading the costs of care among as many people as possible, not just among those who happen to be sick at a given time.

"The only way we can achieve universal coverage is to require everybody to either purchase private insurance or enroll in a public program," Daschle wrote. [7]

If Obama ends up authorizing a new government-run insurance plan to compete with private insurers for enrollees, as most Democrats favor, the plan could face tough opposition from Republicans.

huge and adoring crowd in Berlin underscored Obama's promise to raise U.S. standing in the world. The McCain campaign countered with an ad mocking Obama's celebrity status. On the eve of the convention, Obama picked Biden as his running mate. The selection won praise as sound, if safe. The four-day convention in Denver (Aug. 25-28) went off without a hitch. Obama's acceptance speech drew generally high marks, but some criticism for its length and predictable domestic-policy prescriptions.

McCain countered the next day by picking Alaska Gov. Sarah Palin as his running mate. The surprise selection

energized the GOP base but raised questions among observers and voters about his judgment. For the rest of the campaign, the McCain camp tried but failed to find an Obama weak spot. Obama had already survived personal attacks about ties to Rev. Wright, indicted Chicago developer Tony Rezko and one-time radical William Ayers. He had also fended off attacks for breaking his pledge to limit campaign spending by taking public funds. Improved ground conditions in Iraq shifted the contest from national security — McCain's strength — to the economy: Democratic turf. Obama held his own in three debates and used

his financial advantage — he raised a record $742 million in all — to engage McCain not only in battleground states but also in supposedly safe GOP states.

By Election Day, the outcome was hardly in doubt. Any remaining uncertainty vanished when Virginia, Republican since 1968, went to Obama early in the evening. By 9:30, one blog had declared Obama the winner. The networks waited until the polls closed on the West Coast — 11 p.m. in the East — to declare Obama to be the 44th president of the United States. In Chicago's Grant Park, tens of thousands of supporters chanted "Yes, we can," as Obama strode on stage.

"Forcing private plans to compete with federal programs, with their price controls and ability to shift costs to taxpayers, will inevitably doom true competition and could ultimately lead to a single-payer, government-run health-care program," said Sen. Michael Enzi, R-Wyo., the top Republican on the HELP Committee. "Any new insurance coverage must be delivered through private health-insurance plans." [8]

Congressional Democrats stand ready to work with the Obama administration to move health-care reform quickly. Two very influential senators, HELP Committee Chairman Sen. Edward Kennedy, D-Mass., and Finance Committee Chairman Sen. Max Baucus, D-Mont., were already crafting health-reform legislation last year and are expected to begin a strong push for legislation soon. But the press of other business and the time-consuming process of gathering support for a specific plan will put off a vote until the end of this year or the beginning of 2010, predicted Rep. Pete Stark, D-Calif., chairman of the House Ways and Means Health Subcommittee. "I don't think we'll do it in the first 100 days," said Stark. [9]

Ironically, the struggling economy, which leaves many more Americans worried about their jobs and therefore their health coverage, may have opened the door for reform by giving business owners, doctors and others a greater stake in getting more people covered, said Henry Aaron, a senior fellow in economic studies at the centrist Brookings Institution. "Before the economic collapse . . . the odds of national reform were nil," but the nation's economic stress makes it somewhat more likely, especially since Congress has been spending large amounts of money on other industries, Aaron said. [10]

Nevertheless, Aaron and some other analysts say the climate for health-care reform may not be much different from that in 1993 when the tide quickly turned against the Clinton administration's attempt at providing universal health care.

The times are "similar," and despite the desire of many for reform, the details will be painful and will spark push-back, Stuart Butler, vice president of the conservative Heritage Foundation, told PBS' "NewsHour." "When you say, 'We've got to make the system efficient by reducing unnecessary costs' . . . that means people's jobs and . . . doctors are going to rebel against that." [11]

— *Marcia Clemmitt*

[1] Quoted in "Daschle: Health Care Flaws Threaten Economic Security," CNNPolitics.com, Jan. 8, 2009, www.cnn.com/2009/POLITICS/01/08/daschle.confirmation.

[2] For background see the following *CQ Researcher* reports by Marcia Clemmitt: "Universal Coverage," March 30, 2007, pp. 265-288, and "Rising Health Costs," April 7, 2006, pp. 289-312.

[3] Barack Obama, "Modern Health Care for All Americans," *The New England Journal of Medicine*, Oct. 9, 2008, p. 1537.

[4] Quoted in "In Weak Economy, Obama May Face Obstacles to Health Care Reform," PBS "NewsHour," Nov. 20, 2008, www.pbs.org.

[5] "2008 Presidential Candidate Health Care Proposals: Side-by-Side Summary," health08.org, Kaiser Family Foundation, www.health08.org.

[6] Quoted in Jacob Goldstein, "Clinton and Obama Spar Over Insurance Mandates," *The Wall Street Journal* Health Blog, Feb. 1, 2008, http://blogs.wsj.com.

[7] Quoted in Teddy Davis, "Obama and Daschle at Odds on Individual Mandates," ABC News blogs, Dec. 11, 2008, http://blogs.abcnews.com.

[8] "Enzi Asks Obama Health Cabinet Nominee Daschle Not to Doom Health-Care Competition," press statement, office of Sen. Mike Enzi, Jan. 8, 2009, http://enzi.senate.gov.

[9] Quoted in Jeffrey Young, "Rep. Stark: No Health Reform Vote in Early '09," *The Hill*, Dec. 17, 2008, http://thehill.com.

[10] Quoted in Ben Weyl, "Experts Predict a Health Overhaul Despite Troubled Economy," *CQ Healthbeat*, Dec. 9, 2008.

[11] "In Weak Economy, Obama May Face Obstacles to Health Care Reform," *op. cit.*

"If there is anyone out there," Obama began, "who still doubts that America is a place where all things are possible; who still wonders if the dream of our founders is alive in our time; who still questions the power of our democracy, tonight is your answer." [18]

A Team of Centrists?

President-elect Obama began the 76 days between election and inauguration by hitting nearly pitch-perfect notes in his dealings with official Washington — including President Bush and members of Congress — and with the public at large. Beginning with his first post-election session with reporters, Obama sounded both somber but hopeful in confronting what he continually referred to as the worst economic crisis in generations. He completed his selection of Cabinet appointees in record time before taking an end-of-December vacation with his family in Hawaii. Some discordant notes were sounded as Inauguration Day neared in January. But on the eve of the inauguration, polls showed Obama entering the Oval Office with unprecedented levels of personal popularity and hopeful support. (*See graph, p. 77.*)

Acknowledging the severity of the economic crisis, Obama started the announcement of Cabinet-level appointments on Nov. 24 by introducing an economic team that included New York Federal Reserve Bank President Timothy Geithner to be secretary of the Treasury. Geithner had been deeply involved in the Fed's moves in the financial bailout. Obama also named Summers, who had served as deputy undersecretary of the Treasury in the Clinton administration, as special White House assistant for economic policy.

A week later, Obama introduced a national security team that included Hillary

Clinton as secretary of State and Gates as holdover Pentagon chief. Clinton accepted the post only after weighing the offer against continuing in the Senate with possibly enhanced visibility and influence. In addition, the appointment required former President Clinton to disclose donors to his post-presidential foundation to try to reduce potential conflicts of interest with his wife's new role.

Along with Gates, Obama also introduced Gen. Jones, a retired Marine commandant and former North Atlantic Treaty Organization supreme commander, as his national security adviser. He also said that he would nominate Holder, a former deputy attorney general, for attorney general; Gov. Janet Napolitano of Arizona for secretary of Homeland Security; and Susan E. Rice, a former assistant secretary of State, for ambassador to the United Nations with Cabinet rank. Holder was in line to be the first African-American to head the Justice Department.

Other Cabinet nominations followed in rapid succession: New Mexico Gov. Bill Richardson, like Clinton one of the contenders for the Democratic nomination, for Commerce; Gen. Eric Shinseki, a critic of Iraq War policies, for Veterans Affairs; and former Senate Democratic Leader Tom Daschle of South Dakota, for Health and Human Services and a new White House office as health reform czar.

Obama picked Shaun Donovan, commissioner of New York City's housing department, for Housing and Urban Development; outgoing Illinois Rep. Ray LaHood, a Republican, for Transportation; and Chicago public schools Commissioner Arne Duncan, a reformer with good relations with Chicago teacher unions, for Education. Steven Chu, a Nobel Prize-winning scientist and an advocate of measures to reduce global warming, was picked for Energy. Sen. Kenneth Salazar, a Colorado Democrat with a moderate record on environmental and land use issues, was tapped for Interior. Former Iowa Gov. Tom

Vilsack, who had supported Clinton for the nomination, was chosen for Agriculture. And Rep. Hilda Solis, a California Democrat and daughter of a union family, was designated for Labor.

As Obama prepared to leave for Hawaii, some supporters were griping about the moderate cast of his selections. "We just hoped the political diversity would have been stronger," Tim Carpenter, executive director of Progressive Democrats of America, told Politico.com. But official Washington appeared to be giving him top marks. *The Washington Post* described the future Cabinet as dominated by "practical-minded centrists who have straddled big policy debates rather than staking out the strongest pro-reform positions." [19]

Obama arrived in Washington on Jan. 4 to enroll daughters Malia, 10, and Natasha ("Sasha"), 7, in the private Sidwell Friends School and begin two hectic work weeks before a long weekend of pre-inaugural events. By then, problems had begun to arise, including a corruption scandal over the selection of Obama's successor in the Senate; the withdrawal of one of his Cabinet nominees; and questions about several of his nominees for top posts.

The Senate seat controversy stemmed from a federal investigation of Illinois Gov. Rod Blagojevich that included tape-recorded comments by the Democratic chief executive that were widely depicted as attempting to sell the appointment for political contributions or other favors. In charging Blagojevich with corruption, U.S. Attorney Patrick Fitzgerald specifically cleared Obama of any involvement. But Obama had been forced to answer questions on the issue from Hawaii and had lined up with Senate Democratic Leader Harry Reid in promising not to seat any Blagojevich appointee. When Blagojevich went ahead and appointed former state Comptroller Roland Burris, an African-American, Reid initially resisted but eventually bowed to the fait accompli and welcomed Burris to the Senate.

Richardson had withdrawn from the Commerce post on Jan. 3 after citing a federal probe into a possible "pay for play" scandal in New Mexico.

Two other Cabinet nominees faced critical questions as Senate confirmation hearings got under way. Treasury Secretary-designate Geithner was disclosed to have failed to pay Social Security and Medicare taxes for several years and to have paid back taxes and interest only after being audited. Attorney General-designate Holder faced questions about his role in recommending that President Clinton pardon fugitive financier Marc Rich and in submitting a pardon application for members of the radical Puerto Rican independence movement FALN. Both seemed headed toward confirmation, however. ∎

CURRENT SITUATION

Moving Quickly

Beginning with his first hours in office, President Obama is moving quickly to put his stamp on government policies by fulfilling campaign promises on such issues as government ethics, secrecy and counterterrorism. Along with the flurry of domestic actions, Obama opened initiatives on the diplomatic front by promising an active U.S. role to promote peace in the Middle East and naming high-level special envoys for the Israeli-Palestinian dispute and the strategically important region of South Asia, including Afghanistan and Pakistan.

In the biggest news of his first days in office, Obama on Jan. 22 signed executive orders to close the Guantánamo prison camp within one year and to prohibit the use of "enhanced"

Continued on p. 98

Vice President Biden Brings Foreign-Policy Savvy

"I want to be the last guy in the room on every important decision."

The inauguration of Joseph R. Biden Jr. as the 47th vice president of the United States caps a journey almost as improbable as Barack Obama's. During seven terms as a U.S. senator from Delaware, Biden has never lived in Washington, instead commuting daily by train from Wilmington. In 1972, at age 29, he became the sixth-youngest senator ever elected, leading many to believe the White House was in his future.

But after two failed presidential campaigns — in 1988 and in the last election — Biden seemed fated to remain a Senate lifer.

Along the way he rose to become chairman of the Judiciary Committee and gained national prominence while leading the confirmation hearings of Supreme Court nominees Robert Bork and Clarence Thomas. He had also served twice as chairman of the Foreign Relations Committee.

Obama's limited time in the Senate and lack of international experience led to increased speculation that he would select Biden as his running mate to bridge the gap. "[Joe Biden is] a leader who sees clearly the challenges facing America in a changing world, with our security and standing set back by eight years of failed foreign policy," Obama said in introducing Biden as his selection on Aug. 23, 2008.

But the new president has yet to clarify the specific role Biden will play in the new administration. The appointment of Hillary Rodham Clinton as secretary of State all but ensures that Biden, despite his impressive résumé, will not be the point man on foreign policy as initially expected.

Nor does anyone expect him to emulate former Vice President Dick Cheney's muscular role. Upon taking office in 2001, Cheney demanded — and President George W. Bush approved — a mandate to give him access to "every table and every meeting," expressing his voice in "whatever area the vice president feels he wants to be active in," recalls former White House Chief of Staff Joshua B. Bolten. [1]

Cheney's push to expand presidential war-making authority is arguably his most lasting legacy, but he also served as a gatekeeper for Supreme Court nominees, editor of tax proposals and arbiter of budget appeals.

While most vice presidents arrive eager to expand the influence of their position, Biden faces the unusual conundrum of figuring out how to scale it back. "The only value of power is the effect, the efficacy of its use," he told *The New York Times*. "And all the power Cheney had did not result in effective outcomes." But without any direct constitutional authority in the executive branch, Biden does not want to return to the days when vice presidents were neither seen nor heard. "I don't think the measure is whether or not I accrete the vestiges of power; it matters whether or not the president listens to me." [2]

And although he says he doesn't seek to wield as much influence as Cheney, many don't expect the loquacious Biden to follow Al Gore either, who in 1992 was assigned a defined portfolio by President Bill Clinton to work on environmental and technology matters. "I think his fundamental role is as a trusted counselor," said Obama senior adviser David Axelrod. "I think that when Obama selected him, he selected him to be a counselor and an adviser on a broad range of issues." [3]

And that's exactly how Biden — who at first balked at accepting the position — wants it. "I don't want to have a portfolio," Biden says. "I don't want to be the guy who handles U.S.-Russian relations or the guy who reinvents government."

"I want to be the last guy in the room on every important decision."

"It's irrelevant what the outside world perceives. What is relevant is whether or not I'm value-added," Biden contends. And very few debate his credentials for the position.

"I'm the most experienced vice president since anybody. Anybody ever serve 36 years as a United States senator?" he asks. [4]

Newly sworn in Vice President Joseph R. Biden, his wife, Jill, and son Beau greet crowds during the Inaugural Parade.

Getty Images/Ron Sachs-Pool

But in all likelihood Biden's first move to Washington will surely be his last.

At age 66, he says he has no plans to pursue the presidency, or return to the Senate for that matter, in 2016 — the last full year of a possible second term for Obama. That suggests he'll truly serve Obama's ambitions rather than his own.

"This is in all probability, and hopefully, a worthy capstone in my career," he said.

— Darrell Dela Rosa

[1] Barton Gellman and Jo Becker, " 'A Different Understanding With the President,' " *The Washington Post*, June 24, 2007, blog.washingtonpost.com/cheney/chapters/chapter_1.

[2] Peter Baker, "Biden Outlines Plans to Do More With Less Power," *The New York Times*, Jan. 14, 2009, www.nytimes.com/2009/01/15/us/politics/15biden.html?_r=1.

[3] Helene Cooper, "For Biden, No Portfolio but the Role of a Counselor," *The New York Times*, Nov. 25, 2008, www.nytimes.com/2008/11/26/us/politics/26biden.html.

[4] Baker, *op. cit.*

At Issue:

Should Congress and the president create a commission to investigate the Bush administration's counterterrorism policies?

FREDERICK A. O. SCHWARZ JR.
CHIEF COUNSEL, BRENNAN CENTER FOR JUSTICE, NEW YORK UNIVERSITY SCHOOL OF LAW; CO-AUTHOR, UNCHECKED AND UNBALANCED: PRESIDENTIAL POWER IN A TIME OF TERROR (NEW PRESS, 2008)

WRITTEN FOR *CQ RESEARCHER*, JANUARY 2009

*i*n his inaugural address, President Obama rejected "as false the choice between our safety and our ideals." Throughout our history, seeking safety in times of crisis has often made it tempting to ignore the wise restraints that make us free and to rush into actions that do not serve the nation's long-term interests. (The Alien and Sedition Acts at the dawn of the republic and the herding of Japanese citizens into concentration camps early in World War II are among many historic examples.) After 9/11 we again overreacted to crisis, this time by descending into practices including torture, extraordinary rendition, warrantless wiretapping and indefinite detention. Each breached American values and thus made America *less* safe.

Our new president is taking steps to reject these actions. And some say this is all that is needed because we need to look forward. Others clamor for criminal prosecutions because to hold our heads high wrongdoers should be held to account.

But, to me, neither of these positions is right. Prosecution is not likely to be productive, and could well be unfair. At the same time, failure to learn more about how we went wrong poses two dangers: First, if we blind our eyes to the truth, we increase the risk of repetition when the next crisis comes.

Second, clearly and fairly assessing and reporting what went wrong — and right — in our reactions to 9/11 will honor America's commitment to openness and the rule of law. Committing ourselves to a full exploration is consistent with the ethos the new president articulated on his first day in office: "The way to make government responsible is to hold it accountable. And the way to make government accountable is to make it transparent."

For these two reasons, I have recommended that the president and Congress appoint an independent, nonpartisan commission to investigate national counterterrorism policies. This is the best way to achieve accountability and an understanding of how to design an effective counterterrorism policy that comports with fundamental values.

Shortly after his reelection in 1864, President Abraham Lincoln nicely articulated the necessity of learning from the past without seeking punishment: "Let us study the incidents of [recent history], as philosophy to learn wisdom from, and none of them as wrongs to be revenged."

DAVID B. RIVKIN JR. AND LEE A. CASEY
WASHINGTON ATTORNEYS WHO SERVED IN THE JUSTICE DEPARTMENT UNDER PRESIDENTS REAGAN AND GEORGE H. W. BUSH

WRITTEN FOR *CQ RESEARCHER*, JANUARY 2009

a special commission would be both unnecessary and harmful. First, multiple congressional inquiries have already aired and analyzed all of the Bush administration's key legal and policy decisions. Indeed, whether through disclosures, leaks, media and/or congressional investigations, both the process and substance of the administration's war-related decisions have been publicized to an unprecedented extent. If any further inquiry into these policies is necessary, the normal congressional and executive branch investigatory tools are always available, including additional hearings.

Second, a special commission would be fundamentally unfair, beginning — as it would — with the proposition that the Bush policies represent systematic wrongdoing. The Bush policies were based upon well-established case law and reasonable legal extrapolation from the available authorities. Simply because the Supreme Court ultimately decided to change the legal landscape does not mean the Bush administration ignored the law; it did not. Moreover, although there have been many problems and certainly some abuses over the past seven years — Abu Ghraib being a case in point — these have been remarkably rare when compared with past armed conflicts and/or counterterrorism campaigns like the one Britain conducted in Northern Ireland.

A commission would also inevitably involve attacks on career officials in the intelligence community and the departments of Justice and Defense, not merely Bush political appointees. When combined with past investigations, the commission's work would inevitably burden, distract and demoralize the nation's intelligence capabilities. The end result would be the extension of a bureaucratic culture that already favors excessive caution and inaction among our key intelligence and law enforcement officials — the very developments, acknowledged by the 9/11 Commission, as contributing mightily to the analytical, legal and policy failures of 9/11.

Finally, a commission would warp our constitutional fabric and harm civil liberties. While many commissions have operated throughout American history, they have not focused on potential prosecutions. Such a private or quasi-governmental commission would not be constrained by the legal and constitutional limits on Congress and the executive branch, thus raising a host of important constitutional questions.

That the commission's supporters — so determined to vindicate the rights of enemy combatant detainees — seem untroubled by these issues is both ironic and terribly sad.

At Issue:

Will Obama's economic stimulus revive the U.S. economy?

DEAN BAKER
*CO-DIRECTOR, CENTER FOR ECONOMIC
AND POLICY RESEARCH*

WRITTEN FOR *CQ RESEARCHER*, JANUARY 2009

*p*resident Obama's stimulus proposal is a very good start toward rescuing the economy. In assessing the plan, it is vitally important to recognize the seriousness of the downturn. The economy lost an average of more than 500,000 jobs a month in the last three months of 2008. In fact, the actual job loss could have been over 600,000 a month due to the way in which the Labor Department counts jobs in new firms that are not in its survey.

The recent announcements of job loss suggest that the rate of job loss may have accelerated even further. It is possible that we are now losing jobs at the rate of 700,000 a month. This is important, because people must understand the urgency of acting as quickly as possible.

With this in mind, the package being debated does a good job of getting money into the economy quickly. According to the projections of the Congressional Budget Office (CBO), 62 percent of the spending in the package will reach the economy before the end of 2010, with most of the rest coming in 2011. This money will be giving the economy a boost when we need it most.

At this point, there is considerable research on the impact of tax cuts, and the evidence suggests that they do not have nearly as much impact on the economy, primarily because a large portion of any tax cut is saved. According to Martin Feldstein, President Reagan's chief economist, just 10 percent of the tax cuts sent out last spring were spent. The rest was saved. Increased savings can be beneficial to household balance sheets, but savings will not boost the economy right now.

There will also be long-term benefits from President Obama's package. For example, the CBO projected we would save more than $90 billion on medical expenses over the next decade by computerizing medical records, which will be financed through the stimulus. In addition, weatherizing homes and offices and modernizing the electrical grid will substantially reduce our future energy use.

The Obama administration projects that this package will generate close to 4 million jobs, and several independent analysts have arrived at similar numbers. This will not bring the economy back to full employment, but it is still a huge improvement over doing nothing.

The cost of this bill sounds large, but it is important to remember that the need is large. If we were to just do nothing, the economy would continue to spiral downward, with the unemployment rate reaching double-digit levels in the near future.

J. D. FOSTER
*NORMAN B. TURE SENIOR FELLOW IN THE
ECONOMICS OF FISCAL POLICY,
THE HERITAGE FOUNDATION*

WRITTEN FOR *CQ RESEARCHER*, JANUARY 2009

*p*resident Barack Obama promises to create 3.5 million new jobs by the end of 2010, and that vow provides a clear measure by which to judge whether his policies work.

U.S. employment stood at about 113 million people in December 2008, so the Obama jobs pledge will be met if 116.5 million people are working by the end of 2010. Reaching this goal will require effective stimulus policies — and the only fiscal policy that can come close to reaching the goal is to cut marginal tax rates.

Obama's target for jobs creation was chosen carefully. Employment peaked at about 115.8 million jobs in November 2007. Obama's jobs pledge at that time was to create 2.5 million jobs, for a total of 116.5 million private sector jobs.

The November 2008 jobs report showed a half-million jobs lost, so his job-creating target rose by a half-million, affirming the 116.5 million target. Then last month's jobs report showed another half-million jobs lost, and the president raised the target again to its current 3.5 million total.

To stimulate the economy, Obama and congressional Democrats have focused on massive new spending programs. However, the federal budget deficit is likely to exceed $2.5 trillion over the next two years even before any stimulus is added. If deficit spending were truly stimulative, the economy would be at risk of overheating by now, not sliding deeper into recession.

Additional deficit spending won't be any more effective than the first $2 trillion, because government spending doesn't create additional demand in the economy. Deficit spending must be financed by borrowing, so while government spending increases demand, government borrowing reduces demand. Worse, since the government's likely to borrow between $3 trillion and $4 trillion over the next two years, the enormous waves of government debt will likely drive interest rates up. That would only prolong the recession and weaken the recovery.

An effective fiscal stimulus would defer the massive 2011 tax hike (higher tax rates on dividends and capital gains are scheduled to kick in), and also cut individual and corporate tax rates further to reduce the impediments to starting new businesses, hiring, working and investing.

To meet his goal, President Obama should junk his ideology and the wasteful spending that goes with it and focus on cutting marginal tax rates. That's the only way to hit his jobs creation target.

Continued from p. 94

interrogation techniques such as waterboarding by CIA agents or any other U.S. personnel. Human rights groups hailed the actions. "Today is the beginning of the end of that sorry chapter in our nation's history," said Elisa Massimino, executive director and CEO of Human Rights First.

Some Republican lawmakers, however, questioned the moves. "How does it make sense," House GOP Whip Eric Cantor asked, "to close down the Guantánamo facility before there is a clear plan to deal with the terrorists inside its walls?"

An earlier directive, signed late in the day on Jan. 20, ordered Defense Secretary Gates to halt for 120 days any of the military commission proceedings against the remaining 245 detainees at Guantánamo. Separately, Obama directed a review of the case against Ali Saleh Kahlah al-Marri, a U.S. resident and the only person designated as an enemy combatant being held in the U.S.

The ethics and information directives signed on Jan. 21 followed Obama's campaign pledges to limit the "revolving door" between government jobs and lobbyist work and to make government more transparent and accountable.

The new ethics rules bar any executive branch appointees from seeking lobbying jobs during Obama's administration. They also ban gifts from lobbyists to anyone in the administration. Good-government groups praised the new policies as the strictest ethics rules ever adopted. Fred Wertheimer, president of the open-government group Democracy 21, called them "a major step in setting a new tone and attitude for Washington."

On information policy, Obama superseded a Bush administration directive promising legal support for agencies seeking to resist disclosure of government records under the Freedom of Information Act. Instead, Obama called on all agencies to release information whenever possible. "For a long time now, there's been too much secrecy in this city," Obama said at a swearing-in ceremony for senior White House staff.

Obama also signed an executive order aimed at greater openness for presidential records following the congressionally established five-year waiting period after any president leaves office. The order supersedes a Bush administration directive in 2001 by giving the incumbent president, not a former president, decision-making authority on whether to invoke executive privilege to prevent release of the former president's records.

On foreign policy, Obama on his first full day in office turned to the fragile cease-fire in Gaza by placing calls to four Mideast leaders: Egyptian President Hosni Mubarak, Israeli Prime Minister Ehud Olmert, Jordanian King Abdullah and Palestinian Authority President Mahmoud Abbas. Obama offered U.S. assistance to try to solidify the cease-fire that had been adopted over the Jan. 17-18 weekend by Israel and Hamas, the ruling party in Gaza.

Israel had begun an offensive against Hamas on Dec. 27 in an effort to halt cross-border rocket attacks into Israel by Hamas supporters. During the transition, Obama had limited himself to a brief statement regretting the loss of life on both sides. White House press secretary Robert Gibbs said Obama used the calls from the Oval Office to pledge U.S. support for consolidating the cease-fire by preventing the smuggling of arms into Hamas from neighboring Egypt. He also promised U.S. support for "a major reconstruction effort for Palestinians in Gaza," Gibbs said.

The next day, Obama took a 10-block ride to the State Department for Hillary Clinton's welcome ceremony as secretary following her 94-2 Senate confirmation on Jan. 21. As part of the event, Clinton announced the appointment of special envoys George Mitchell for the Middle East and Richard Holbrooke for Afghanistan and Pakistan.

In his remarks, Obama renewed support for a two-state solution: Israel and a Palestinian state "living side by side in peace and security." He also promised to refocus U.S. attention on what he called the "perilous" situation in Afghanistan, where he said violence had increased dramatically and a "deadly insurgency" had taken root.

Returning to domestic issues, Obama on Jan. 23 signed — as expected — an order to lift the so-called Mexico City policy prohibiting U.S. aid to any non-governmental organizations abroad that provide abortion counseling or services. The memorandum instructed Secretary of State Clinton to lift what Obama called the "unwarranted" restrictions. The policy was first put in place by President Ronald Reagan in 1984, rescinded by President Clinton in 1993 and then reinstituted by President Bush in 2001.

After the weekend, Obama reversed another of Bush's policies on Jan. 26 by directing Environmental Protection Agency Administrator Lisa Jackson to reconsider the request by the state of California to adopt automobile emission standards stricter than those set under federal law. In a reversal of past practice, the Bush administration EPA had denied California's waiver request in December 2007. On the same day, Obama instructed Transportation Secretary Ray LaHood to tighten fuel efficiency standards for cars and light trucks beginning with 2011 model cars.

Working With Congress

President Obama is pressing Congress for quick action on an economic stimulus plan even as bipartisan support for a proposal remains elusive. Meanwhile, the new administration is struggling to find ways to make the financial bailout approved before Obama took office more effective in aiding distressed homeowners and unfreezing credit markets.

House Democrats moved ahead with an $825-billion stimulus package after the tax and spending elements won approval in separate, party-line votes by the House

Ways and Means Committee on Jan. 22 and the House Appropriations Committee the day before. The full House was scheduled to vote on the package on Jan. 28 after deadline for this issue, but approval was assured given the Democrats' 256-178 majority in the chamber.

Obama used his first weekly address as president on Jan. 24 — now not only broadcast on radio but also posted online as video on YouTube and the White House Web site — to depict his American Recovery and Reinvestment Plan as critical to get the country out of an "unprecedented" economic crisis. The plan, he said, would "jump-start job creation as well as long-term economic growth." Without it, he warned, unemployment could reach double digits, economic output could fall $1 trillion short of capacity and many young Americans could be forced to forgo college or job training.

Without mentioning the tax and spending plan's minimum total cost, Obama detailed a long list of infrastructure improvements to be accomplished in energy, health care, education and transportation. He mentioned a $2,500 college tax credit but did not note other items in the $225 billion in tax breaks included in the plan — either his long-advocated $1,000 tax break for working families or the various business tax cuts added as sweeteners for Republicans.

Republicans, however, remained unconvinced. Replying to Obama's address, House Minority Leader John Boehner called the plan "chock-full of government programs and projects, most of which won't provide immediate relief to our ailing economy." On "Meet the Press" the next day, the Ohio lawmaker again called for more by way of tax cuts, criticized the job-creating potential of Obama's plan and warned of opposition from most House Republicans.

Appearing on another of the Sunday talk shows, McCain told "Fox News Sunday" host Chris Wallace, "I am opposed to most of the provisions in the bill. As it stands now, I would not support it."

On a second front, the principal members of Obama's economic team are assuring Congress of major changes to come in the second stage of the $700-billion financial rescue plan approved last fall. During confirmation hearings, Treasury Secretary-designate Geithner promised the Senate Finance Committee on Jan. 21 to expect "much more substantial action" to address the problem of troubled banks that has chilled both consumer and corporate credit markets since fall 2008.

Geithner's comments on the financial bailout were overshadowed by sharp questions from Republican senators about the nominee's tax problems while working for the International Monetary Fund. For several years, Geithner failed to pay Social Security and Medicare taxes, which the IMF — as an international institution — does not withhold from employees' pay as domestic employers do. Geithner repeatedly apologized for the mistake and pointed to his payment of back taxes plus interest totaling more than $40,000. In the end, the committee voted 18-5 to recommend confirmation; the full Senate followed suit on Jan. 26 in a 60-34 vote. *

On the bailout, Geithner said he would increase the transparency and accountability of the program once he assumed the virtually unfettered responsibility for dispensing the remaining $350 billion. He acknowledged criticisms that so far the program has benefited large financial institutions but done little for small businesses. He also promised to restrict dividends by companies that receive government help.

With many banks still holding billions in troubled assets on their balance sheets, speculation is increasing in Washington and in financial circles

---

* Attorney General-designate Holder, Obama's other controversial Cabinet nominee, was expected to be confirmed by the full Senate on Jan. 29 or 30, after deadline for this issue, following the Senate Judiciary Committee's 17-2 vote on Jan. 28 to recommend confirmation.

about dramatic action by the government. Possible moves include the creation of a government-run "bad bank" to buy distressed assets from financial institutions or even outright nationalization of one or more banks.

"People continue to be surprised by the poor condition of the banks," says Dean Baker, co-director of the Center for Economic and Policy Research, a liberal think tank in Washington. "Whatever plans they may have made a month ago might be seen as inadequate given the severity of the problem of the banking system."

With the stimulus package on the front burner, however, Obama went to Capitol Hill on Jan. 27 for separate meetings to lobby House and Senate Republicans to support the measure. The closed-door session with the full House GOP conference lasted an hour — slightly longer than scheduled, causing the president to be late for the start of the meeting on the other side of the Capitol with Republican senators.

In between meetings, Obama challenged GOP lawmakers to try to minimize partisan differences. "I don't expect 100 percent agreement from my Republican colleagues, but I do hope we can put politics aside," he said.

For their part, House Republican leaders expressed appreciation for the president's visit and his expressed willingness to compromise. But some renewed their opposition to the proposal in its current form. Rep. Tom Price of Georgia, chairman of the conservative House Republican Study Committee, said the proposal "remains rooted in a liberal, big-government ideology."

Obama's meeting with GOP senators came on the same day that the Senate Finance and Appropriations committees were marking up their versions of the stimulus package. The Senate was expected to vote on the proposal over the weekend, giving the two chambers two weeks to iron out their differences if the bill was to reach Obama's desk before the Presidents' Day recess. ∎

OUTLOOK

Peril and Promise

One week after taking office, President Obama is getting high marks from experts on the presidency for carefully stage-managing his first policy initiatives while discreetly moving to set realistic expectations for the months ahead.

"He's started out quite impressively," says Fred Greenstein, professor of politics emeritus at Princeton University in New Jersey and the dean of American scholars on the U.S. presidency. "So far, it's been a striking rollout week."

Other experts agree. "The Obama administration has met expectations for the first week," says Meena Bose, chair of the Peter S. Kalikow Center for the Study of the American Presidency at Hofstra University in Hempstead, N.Y. "There's been virtually no drama, which is an indication of how he intends to run his administration."

"The indications are all positive," says Bruce Buchanan, a professor of political science at the University of Texas in Austin and author of several books on the presidency. Like the others, Buchanan says Obama is holding on to popular support while striving either to win over or to neutralize Republicans on Capitol Hill.

The wider world outside Washington, however, is giving Obama no honeymoon in office. The U.S. economy is continuing to lag, while violence and unrest continue to simmer in three global hot spots: Gaza, Iraq and Afghanistan.

On the economy, Obama has initiated a daily briefing from senior adviser Summers in addition to the daily briefing on foreign policy and national security issues. "Frankly," Obama told congressional leaders on Jan. 23, "the news has not been good." The day before, the Commerce Department had reported that new-home construction fell to its slowest pace since reporting on monthly rates began in 1959. On the same day, new claims for unemployment benefits matched the highest level seen in a quarter-century. [20]

Meanwhile, leading U.S. policy makers were giving downbeat assessments of events in Afghanistan and Iraq. In testimony to the Senate Armed Services Committee, Defense chief Gates warned on Jan. 27 to expect "a long and difficult fight" in Afghanistan A few days earlier, the outgoing U.S. ambassador to Iraq, Ryan Crocker, warned that what he called "a precipitous withdrawal" could jeopardize the country's stability and revive al Qaeda in Iraq. And special envoy Mitchell left Washington for the Mideast on Jan. 26, just as the fragile cease-fire between Hamas and Israel was jeopardized by the death of an Israeli soldier from a roadside bomb and an Israeli air strike in retaliation.

Obama continues to work at the problems with the same kind of message control that served him well in the election. After reaping a full day's worth of mostly favorable news coverage on the Guantánamo issue, the administration began directing laser-like attention to the economy from Jan. 22 on. For example, the repeal of the Bush administration's ban on funding international groups that perform abortions was announced late on Friday, Jan. 23 — a dead zone for news coverage.

On foreign policy, Obama emphasized the Mitchell and Holbrooke appointments by personally going to the State Department for the announcements. And he underscored the inaugural's outreach to Muslims by granting his first formal television interview as president to the Arabic satellite television network Al Arabiya. Obama called for a new partnership with the Muslim world "based on mutual respect and mutual interest." One of his main tasks, he told the Dubai-based network in an interview aired on Jan. 27, is to communicate that "the Americans are not your enemy." [21]

Obama and his senior aides are also signaling to supporters that some of their agenda items will have to wait. In a pre-inauguration interview with *The Washington Post*, for example, he reiterated his support for a labor-backed bill to make it easier to unionize workers but downgraded it to a post-stimulus agenda item. Similarly, press secretary-designate Gibbs repeated Obama's support for repealing the military's "don't ask, don't tell" policy on homosexuals on the transition's Web site on Jan. 13, but the next day expanded on the answer: "Not everything will get done in the beginning," Gibbs said. [22]

Greenstein and Bose view Obama's inaugural address — which many observers faulted for rhetorical flatness — as a conscious, initial step to lower expectations about the pace of the promised "change we can believe in." Greenstein calls it a "get-down-to-work" address. Obama himself again evoked the inaugural's theme of determination in the face of adversity when he spoke to congressional leaders immediately following the address.

About This Report

This special expanded issue of *CQ Researcher* was written by Associate Editor Kenneth Jost, with contributions by writers Marcia Clemmitt, Peter Katel, Thomas J. Billitteri, Alan Greenblatt, Darrell Dela Rosa and Vyomika Jairam. Jost is a graduate of Harvard College and Georgetown University Law Center. He is the author of the *Supreme Court Yearbook* and editor of *The Supreme Court from A to Z* (both CQ Press). His previous reports include "Electing the President," "Presidential Power" and "The Bush Presidency."

"What's happening today is not about me," Obama said at the joint congressional luncheon on Inauguration Day. "It is about the American people. They understand that we have arrived at a moment of great challenge for our nation, a time of peril, but also extraordinary promise."

"President Obama has done everything he can to tamp down this sense that he somehow walks on water," says Bose. "He has done everything he can to show that he is a man of substance."

"We have to recognize that these challenges aren't going to be met overnight and that we have to have confidence that we're going to meet them," she continues. "Now the question is, 'Can he govern? Can he show results?' " ∎

Notes

[1] The text and video of the inaugural address are available on the redesigned White House Web site: www.whitehouse.gov. Some crowd reaction from Christopher O'Brien of CQ Press' College Division.

[2] Quoted in Clea Benson, "An Economy in Foreclosure," CQ Weekly, Jan. 12, 2009.

[3] Quoted in Aamer Madhani, "Will Obama Stick to Timetable?" Chicago Tribune, Nov. 6, 2008, p. 11.

[4] Quoted in Shailagh Murray and Paul Kane, "Democratic Congress Shows It Will Not Bow to Obama," The Washington Post, Jan. 11, 2009, p. A5.

[5] Norman Ornstein, "First Steps Toward 'Post-Partisanship' Show Promise," Roll Call, Jan. 14, 2009.

[6] For a compact, continuously updated biography, see Barack Obama, www.biography.com. Background also drawn from Barack Obama, Dreams from My Father: A Story of Race and Inheritance (2004 ed.; originally published 1995). See also David Mendell, Obama: From Promise to Power (2007).

[7] Quoted in Serge Kovaleski, "Obama's Organizing Years: Guiding Others and Finding Himself," The New York Times, July 7, 2008, p. A1.

[8] Background drawn from Jody Kantor, "In Law School, Obama Found Political Voice," The New York Times, Jan. 28, 2007, sec. 1, p. 1.

[9] Background drawn from Janny Scott, "The Story of Obama, Written by Obama," The New York Times, May 18, 2008, p. A1.

[10] For a story on his mother's influence on Obama, see Amanda Ripley, "A Mother's Story," Time, April 21, 2008, p. 36.

[11] See David Jackson and Ray Long, "Showing his bare knuckles: In first campaign, Obama revealed hard-edged, uncompromising side in eliminating party rivals," Chicago Tribune, April 4, 2007, p. 1; Rick Pearson and Ray Long, "Careful steps, looking ahead: After arriving in Springfield, Barack Obama proved cautious, but it was clear to many he had ambitions beyond the state Senate," ibid., May 3, 2007, p. 1.

[12] See Barack Obama, The Audacity of Hope: Thoughts on Reclaiming the American Dream (2006), pp. 105-107.

[13] See David Mendell, "Obama routs Democratic foes; Ryan tops crowded GOP field," Chicago Tribune, March 17, 2004, p. 1.

[14] For the full text of the 2,165-word speech, see http://obamaspeeches.com/002-Keynote-Address-at-the-2004-Democratic-National-Convention-Obama-Speech.htm. For Mendell's account, see Obama, op. cit., pp. 272-285. Obama's conversation with Martin Nesbitt may have been reported first in David Bernstein, "The Speech," Chicago Magazine, July 2007; the anecdote is briefly repeated in Evan Thomas, "A Long Time Coming": The Inspiring, Combative 2008 Campaign and the His-toric Election of Barack Obama (2009), p. 6. For the Post's account, see David S. Broder, "Democrats Focus on Healing Divisions," July 28, 2004, p. A1.

[15] CQ's Politics in America 2008 (110th Congress), www.cnn.com/video/#/video/world/2007/01/22/vause.obama.school.cnn.

[16] Some background from Thomas, op. cit.

[17] Ibid., p. 9.

[18] Many versions of the speech are posted on YouTube, including a posting of CNN's coverage.

[19] Carpenter was quoted in Carrie Budoff Brown and Nia-Milaka Henderson, "Cabinet: Middle-of-the-roaders' dream?" Politico, Dec. 19, 2008; Alec MacGillis, "For Obama Cabinet, a Team of Moderates," The Washington Post, Dec. 20, 2008, p. A1.

[20] See Kelly Evans, "Home Construction at Record Slow Pace," The Wall Street Journal, Jan. 23, 2009, p. A3.

[21] See Paul Schemm, "Obama tells Arabic network US 'is not your enemy,' " The Associated Press, Jan. 27, 2009.

[22] Obama quoted in Dan Eggen and Michael D. Shear, "The Effort to Roll Back Bush Policies Continues," The Washington Post, Jan. 27, 2009, p. A4; Gibbs quoted in, "Obama aide: Ending 'don't ask, don't tell' must wait," CNN.com, Jan. 15, 2009.

FOR MORE INFORMATION

American Enterprise Institute for Public Policy Research, 1150 17th St., N.W., Washington, DC 20036; (202) 862-5800; www.aei.org. Conservative think tank researching issues on government, economics, politics and social welfare.

Campaign for America's Future, 1825 K St., N.W., Suite 400, Washington, DC 20006; (202) 955-5665; www.ourfuture.org. Advocates progressive policies.

Center for American Progress, 1333 H St., N.W., 10th Floor, Washington, DC 20005; (202) 682-1611; www.americanprogress.org. Left-leaning think tank promoting a government that ensures opportunity for all Americans.

Center for Economic and Policy Research, 1611 Connecticut Ave., N.W., Suite 400, Washington, DC 20009; (202) 293-5380; www.cepr.net. Promotes open debate on key economic and social issues.

Center on Budget and Policy Priorities, 820 First St., N.E., Suite 510, Washington, DC 20002; (202) 408-1080; www.cbpp.org. Policy organization working on issues that affect low- and moderate-income families and individuals.

Concord Coalition, 1011 Arlington Blvd., Suite 300, Arlington, VA 22209; (703) 894-6222; www.concordcoalition.org. Nonpartisan, grassroots organization promoting responsible fiscal policy and spending.

Heritage Foundation, 214 Massachusetts Ave., N.E., Washington, DC 20002; (202) 546-4400; www.heritage.org. Conservative think tank promoting policies based on free enterprise, limited government and individual freedom.

Bibliography

Selected Sources

Books by Barack Obama

Dreams from My Father: A Story of Race and Inheritance (Three Rivers Press, 2004; originally published by Times Books, 1995) is a literate, insightful memoir written in the three years after Obama's graduation from Harvard Law School. The three parts chronicle his "origins" from his birth through college, his three years as a community organizer in Chicago and his two-month pre-law school visit to his father's homeland, Kenya.

The Audacity of Hope: Thoughts on Reclaiming the American Dream (Crown, 2006) is a political manifesto written as Obama considered but had not definitively decided on a presidential campaign. The book opens with a critique of the "bitter partisanship" of current politics and an examination of "common values" that could underline "a new political consensus." Later chapters specifically focus on issues of faith and of race. Includes index.

Change We Can Believe In: Barack Obama's Plan to Renew America's Promise (Three Rivers Press, 2008), which includes a foreword by Obama, outlines steps for "reviving our economy," "investing in our prosperity," "rebuilding America's leadership" and "perfecting our union." Also includes texts of seven speeches from his declaration of candidacy on Feb. 7, 2007, to his July 24, 2008, address in Berlin.

Books About Barack Obama

The only objective, full-length biography is *Obama: From Promise to Power* (Amistad/Harper Collins, 2007) by David Mendell, the *Chicago Tribune* political reporter who began covering Obama in his first race for the U.S. Senate. An updated version was published in 2008 under the title *Obama: The Promise of Change*.

Two critical biographies appeared during the 2008 campaign: David Freddoso, *The Case Against Barack Obama: The Unlikely Rise and Unexamined Agenda of the Media's Favorite Candidate* (Regnery, 2008); and Jerome Corsi, *The Obama Nation: Leftist Politics and the Cult of Personality* (Threshold, 2008). Freddoso, a writer with National Review Online, wrote what one reviewer called a "fact-based critique" depicting Obama as "a fake reformer and a real liberal." Corsi, a conservative author and columnist best known for his book *Unfit for Command* attacking Democratic presidential nominee John Kerry in 2004, came under fierce criticism from the Obama campaign and independent observers for undocumented allegations about Obama's background.

Two post-election books chronicle the 2008 campaign. Evan Thomas, *"A Long Time Coming": The Inspiring, Combative*

2008 Campaign and the Historic Election of Barack Obama (Public Affairs, 2009) is the seventh in *Newsweek's* quadrennial titles documenting presidential campaigns on the basis of reporting by a team of correspondents, with some reporting specifically not for publication until after the election. Chuck Todd and Sheldon Gawiser, *How Barack Obama Won: A State-by-State Guide to the Historic 2008 Presidential Election* (Vintage, 2009) gives an analytical overview of the campaign and election with detailed voting analyses of every state. A third title, *Obama: The Historic Journey*, is due for publication Feb. 16 by *The New York Times* and Callaway; the author is Jill Abramson, the *Times'* managing editor, in collaboration with the newspaper's reporters and editors.

Other books include John K. Wilson, *Barack Obama: The Improbable Ques*t (Paradigm, 2008), an admiring analysis of Obama's political views and philosophy by a lawyer who recalls having been a student in Obama's class on racism and the law at the University of Chicago Law School; Paul Street, *Barack Obama and the Future of American Politics* (Paradigm, 2009), a critical depiction of Obama as a "power-conciliating centrist"; and Jabiri Asim, *What Obama Means: For Our Culture, Our Politics, Our Future* (Morrow, 2009) a depiction of Obama as creating a new style of racial politics — less confrontational than in the past but equally committed to social justice and more productive of results.

Articles

Purdum, Todd, "Raising Obama," *Vanity Fair*, March 2008.
The magazine's national editor, formerly a *New York Times* reporter, provided an insightful portrait of Obama midway through the 2008 primary season.

Von Drehle, David, "Person of the Year: Barack Obama: Why History Can't Wait," *Time*, Dec. 29, 2008.
Time's selection of Obama as person of the year includes an in-depth interview of the president-elect by Managing Editor Richard Stengel, Editor-at-large von Drehle and Time Inc. Editor-in-chief John Huey. The full text is at time.com/obamainterview.

On the Web

The Obama administration unveiled a redesigned White House Web site (www.whitehouse.gov) at 12:01 p.m. on Jan. 20, 2009 — even before President-elect Obama took the oath of office. The "Briefing Room" includes presidential announcements as well as a "Blog" sometimes being updated several times a day. "The Agenda" incorporates Obama's campaign positions, subject by subject. The site includes video of the president's speeches, including the inaugural address as well as the weekly presidential address — previously broadcast only on radio.

The Next Step:

Additional Articles from Current Periodicals

Congressional Support

Montgomery, Lori, "Congress Urges Spending Restraint," *The Washington Post*, Jan. 8, 2009, p. A2.

Pleas from Congress to curb government spending may dampen enthusiasm for some of Obama's most ambitious priorities.

Parsons, Christi, and Peter Nicholas, " 'Change' Crashes Into the Washington Way," *Chicago Tribune*, Jan. 12, 2009, p. A5.

Differences between the Obama administration's viewpoint on government and what has been labeled the "Washington way" has created tension between Obama and some former congressional colleagues.

Zeleny, Jeff, "Initial Steps by Obama Suggest a Bipartisan Flair," *The New York Times*, Nov. 24, 2008, p. A15.

President-elect Obama has turned to Republican lawmakers for advice on policy proposals and Cabinet appointments.

Economy

Bacon Jr., Perry, "Obama Stresses Plan's Job Potential," *The Washington Post*, Jan. 11, 2009, p. A1.

Obama advisers say the administration's economic stimulus proposal would save or create nearly 4 million jobs.

Calmes, Jackie, and Jeff Zeleny, "Obama Vows Swift Action on Vast Stimulus Package," *The New York Times*, Nov. 23, 2008, p. A1.

President-elect Obama says he will outline a far more ambitious plan of spending and tax cuts than what he projected during his campaign.

Helman, Scott, "Transit Funds Present Quandary for Obama," *The Boston Globe*, Dec. 19, 2008, p. A24.

The Obama administration is facing great debate over how to spend an expected $50 billion from his economic stimulus plan for transportation projects across the country.

Tankersley, Jim, "Obama Energy Plan May Be Losing Steam," *Los Angeles Times*, Jan. 16, 2009, p. A16.

Obama's economic stimulus plan is unlikely to include major investments in green infrastructure, largely because blueprints for high-speed rail systems and a sprawling web of power lines don't yet exist.

International Crises

LaFranchi, Howard, "With Obama, What Change for Mideast?" *The Christian Science Monitor*, Jan. 23, 2009, p. 25.

The Obama administration is searching for key partners in the Middle East to address daunting challenges such as Arab-Israeli peace.

Smith, R. Jeffrey, "2 U.S. Airstrikes Offer a Concrete Sign of Obama's Pakistan Policy," *The Washington Post*, Jan. 24, 2009, p. A1.

Two U.S. missile strikes in northwestern Pakistan suggest the Obama administration is committed to maintaining military pressure on terrorist groups in the region.

Iraq and Afghanistan

Bumiller, Elisabeth, and Thom Shanker, "Military Planners, in Nod to Obama, Are Preparing for a Faster Iraq Withdrawal," *The New York Times*, Jan. 15, 2009, p. A12.

Military commanders are drawing up plans for a faster withdrawal of troops in Iraq in anticipation that Obama will reject current proposals as too slow.

DeYoung, Karen, "Afghan Conflict Will Be Reviewed," *The Washington Post*, Jan. 13, 2009, p. A1.

The Obama administration intends to approve Pentagon plans to send 30,000 additional troops to Afghanistan but does not anticipate the increase to significantly change the direction of the conflict.

Levinson, Charles, "Obama's Plan for Iraq About to Meet Reality," *USA Today*, Nov. 12, 2008, p. 1A.

Stability in Iraq could be disrupted, and renewed chaos could ensue if Obama withdraws U.S. troops too quickly.

Wallsten, Peter, "Afghanistan Warning Sounded," *Los Angeles Times*, Jan. 26, 2009, p. A1.

Vice President Joseph R. Biden says troop casualties will climb in Afghanistan as the Obama administration shifts priorities in the war on terror.

In-depth Reports on Issues in the News

Are you writing a paper?

Need backup for a debate?

Want to become an expert on an issue?

For 80 years, students have turned to *CQ Researcher* for in-depth reporting on issues in the news. Reports on a full range of political and social issues are now available. Following is a selection of recent reports:

Civil Liberties
Limiting Lawsuits, 12/08
Affirmative Action, 10/08
Gay Marriage Showdowns, 9/08
America's Border Fence, 9/08
Immigration Debate, 2/08
Prison Reform, 4/07

Crime/Law
Mexico's Drug War, 12/08
Prostitution Debate, 5/08
Public Defenders, 4/08
Gun Violence, 5/07

Education
Reading Crisis? 2/08
Discipline in Schools, 2/08
Student Aid, 1/08
Racial Diversity in Public Schools, 9/07
Stress on Students, 7/07

Environment
Reducing Carbon Footprint, 12/08
Protecting Wetlands, 10/08
Buying Green, 2/08
Future of Recycling, 12/07

Health/Safety
Regulating Toxic Chemicals, 1/09
Preventing Cancer, 1/09
Heart Health, 9/08
Global Food Crisis, 6/08

International Affairs/Politics
The National Debt, 11/08
Financial Bailout, 10/08
Political Conventions, 8/08
Human Rights in China, 7/08
Race and Politics, 7/08

Social Trends
Falling Birthrates, 11/08
Regulating Credit Cards, 10/08
Internet Accuracy, 8/08
Financial Crisis, 5/08
Cyberbullying, 5/08

Terrorism/Defense
Rise in Counterinsurgency, 9/08
Cost of the Iraq War, 4/08

Youth
Debating Hip-Hop, 6/07

Upcoming Reports

Future of the Auto Industry, 2/6/09   Homeland Security, 2/13/09   Public Works, 2/20/09

ACCESS

CQ Researcher is available in print and online. For access, visit your library or www.cqresearcher.com.

STAY CURRENT

To receive notice of upcoming *CQ Researcher* reports, or learn more about *CQ Researcher* products, subscribe to the free e-mail newsletters, *CQ Researcher Alert!* and *CQ Researcher News*: http://cqpress.com/newsletters.

PURCHASE

To purchase a *CQ Researcher* report in print or electronic format (PDF), visit www.cqpress.com or call 866-427-7737. Single reports start at $15. Bulk purchase discounts and electronic-rights licensing are also available.

SUBSCRIBE

Annual full-service *CQ Researcher* subscriptions—including 44 reports a year, monthly index updates, and a bound volume—start at $803. Add $25 for domestic postage.

CQ Researcher Online offers a backfile from 1991 and a number of tools to simplify research. For pricing information, call 800-834-9020, ext. 1906, or e-mail librarysales@cqpress.com.

Auto Industry's Future

Can energy-efficient vehicles revive the Big Three?

Bad news is battering Detroit-based General Motors as well as the other Big Three U.S. automakers. GM reported that its January 2009 sales fell 49 percent, and Chrysler's dropped 55 percent. Toyota now outranks GM as the world's biggest carmaker.

A s U.S. automakers post steep declines in profits amid a global credit crisis and a worldwide slowdown in vehicle sales, policy experts are debating their long-term prospects. General Motors and Chrysler received billions of dollars in emergency federal loans and are under intense government pressure to find a path toward profitability. Ford lost a record amount last year but insists it can survive without federal help. Management and the United Auto Workers union argue that letting even one automobile giant fail would have catastrophic consequences for the U.S. economy. Skeptics say, however, that automakers have had years to reform themselves and that without steep cost reductions, more union concessions and major sacrifices by dealers and suppliers, the industry's future is dim. Both domestic and foreign automakers are pouring resources into a new generation of electric and hybrid vehicles they hope will revive the industry.

Published by CQ Press, a division of SAGE Publications

www.cqresearcher.com

CQ Researcher • Feb. 6, 2009 • www.cqresearcher.com
Volume 19, Number 5 • Pages 105-128

Cover: AFP/Getty Images/Jeff Haynes

CQ Researcher

Feb. 6, 2009
Volume 19, Number 5

MANAGING EDITOR: Thomas J. Colin
tcolin@cqpress.com

ASSISTANT MANAGING EDITOR: Kathy Koch
kkoch@cqpress.com

ASSOCIATE EDITOR: Kenneth Jost

STAFF WRITERS: Thomas J. Billitteri,
Marcia Clemmitt, Peter Katel

CONTRIBUTING WRITERS: Sarah Glazer,
Alan Greenblatt, Barbara Mantel,
Patrick Marshall, Tom Price, Jennifer Weeks

DESIGN/PRODUCTION EDITOR: Olu B. Davis

ASSISTANT EDITOR: Darrell Dela Rosa

FACT-CHECKING: Eugene J. Gabler,
Michelle Harris

EDITORIAL INTERN: Vyomika Jairam

CQ PRESS

**A Division of
SAGE Publications**

PRESIDENT AND PUBLISHER:
John A. Jenkins

**EXECUTIVE DIRECTOR,
REFERENCE INFORMATION GROUP:**
Alix B. Vance

DIRECTOR, ONLINE PRODUCT DEVELOPMENT:
Jennifer Q. Ryan

CQ Press is a registered trademark of Congressional Quarterly Inc.

CQ Researcher (ISSN 1056-2036) is printed on acid-free paper. Published weekly, except; (Jan. wk. 1) (May wk. 4) (July wks. 1, 2) (Aug. wks. 3, 4) (Nov. wk. 4) and (Dec. wk. 4), by CQ Press, a division of SAGE Publications. Annual full-service subscriptions start at $803. For pricing, call 1-800-834-9020, ext. 1906. To purchase a *CQ Researcher* report in print or electronic format (PDF), visit www. cqpress.com or call 866-427-7737. Single reports start at $15. Bulk purchase discounts and electronic-rights licensing are also available. Periodicals postage paid at Washington, D.C., and additional mailing offices. POSTMASTER: Send address changes to *CQ Researcher*, 2300 N St., N.W., Suite 800, Washington, DC 20037.

Auto Industry's Future

By Thomas J. Billitteri

THE ISSUES

U.S. automakers, by their own admission, have made a lot of mistakes over the years. Too much emphasis on trucks and SUVs; poor quality; and failure to respond to the growing consumer demand for fuel efficiency.

But their biggest blunder of all — at least in the public relations realm — may have been the three private jets. Amid the most serious economic crisis to face the nation since the Great Depression, the chief executives of Ford, General Motors and Chrysler each took his own corporate jet to Washington to ask Congress for billions in aid.

Predictably, lawmakers (and late-night comedians) had a field day. "There's a delicious irony in seeing private luxury jets flying into Washington, D.C., and people coming off of them with tin cups in their hands," said Rep. Gary L. Ackerman (D-N.Y.). Afterwards, with billions in loans in hand, GM Chairman Richard Wagoner predicted brighter days ahead.

"When we get done and get through this, we will have an industry . . . positioned for real long-term success," the embattled executive told a Detroit radio audience. "There is going to be some point when it's morning, and the sun is going to come up." [1]

But Wagoner's forecast may have been overly optimistic. The global economic crisis has darkened the sky over the entire auto industry, and the outlook for Detroit's Big Three — GM, Ford and Chrysler — appears especially gloomy.

Beleaguered union and auto industry officials prepare to ask the Senate Banking, Housing and Urban Affairs Committee for some $30 billion in aid on Dec. 4, 2008. From left: GM Chairman Richard Wagoner; United Auto Workers President Ron Gettelfinger; Ford CEO Alan Mulally and Chrysler Chairman Robert L. Nardelli.

Getty Images/Chip Somodevilla

Car and light-truck sales at GM and Chrysler — both of which received low-interest bridge loans — were down 23 and 30 percent, respectively, last year. [2] Both companies, under pressure to show they are cutting costs as part of the bailout agreement, reportedly were offering new buyouts this month to hourly workers that included cash payments and vouchers for vehicle purchases.

Sales were down 21 percent at Ford, which declined a federal loan. The company, which reported a record $14.6 billion loss for 2008, believes it can survive without federal aid.

Sales results for the Big Three in

January, including declines of 49 percent at Ford and 55 percent at Chrysler, showed that the storm over Detroit is growing even more ominous. In fact, in January, Toyota usurped GM's 78-year reign as the world's biggest carmaker.

The bad economy and plunging sales figures are only part of the gloom hanging over Detroit. Experts say the domestic auto industry is mired axle deep in challenges that include massive benefits for retirees, labyrinthine dealer franchise laws that hinder automakers' ability to downsize and reorganize and growing foreign competition on U.S. soil.

Under the $17.4 billion loan agreement, GM and Chrysler have until March 31 to show they are on the road to financial viability. But key terms — or "targets" — remain negotiable, meaning the Obama administration and Congress will bear the burden of oversight in coming months. [3]

To thrive — or at least survive — Detroit must move at a race-car pace to remake itself into a more cost-efficient, nimble and innovative business, experts say. That will require new concessions on wages and work rules from the United Auto Workers (UAW) union, compromises from suppliers, creditors and dealers and an uncharacteristic degree of flexibility by management, they say.

The UAW has pledged cooperation but also said it will resist targets in the loan agreement that, it argues, single out workers. The targets aim, in part, to make work rules and wages competitive with those at foreign-owned U.S. plants by the end of 2009. "We will work with the Obama administration and the new Congress to

Feb. 6, 2009   107

Light-Vehicle Sales Plummeted in 2008

About 13 million passenger cars and lights trucks were sold in the United States in 2008, a decline of 18 percent from a year ago. Sales of Hondas and Toyotas dropped 8 and 15 percent, respectively, compared to a decline of about 21 percent for Ford and General Motors.

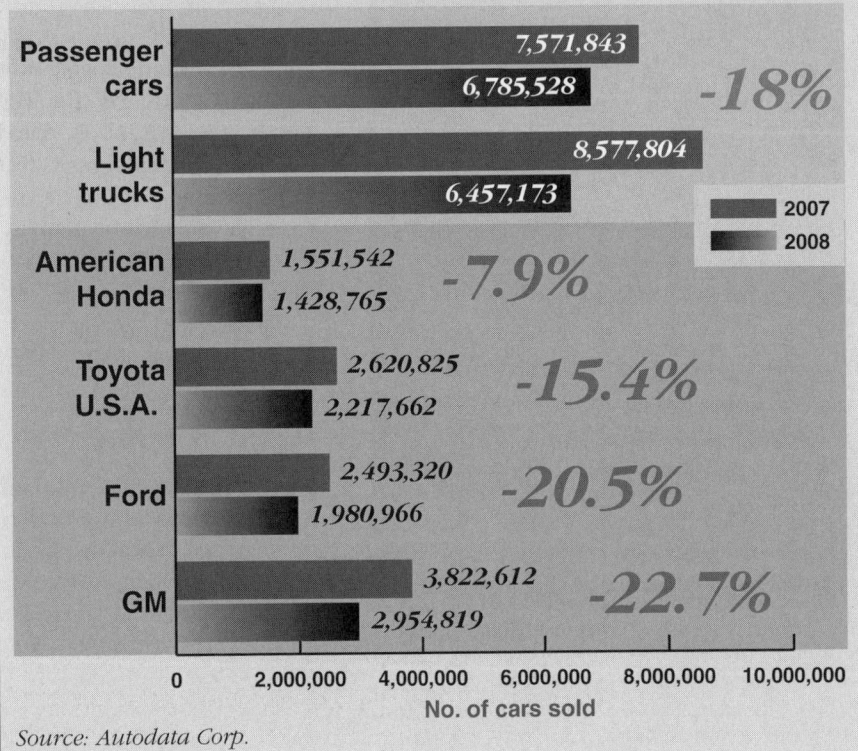

U.S. Passenger Car and Light-Truck Sales, 2007 and 2008

	2007	2008	Change
Passenger cars	7,571,843	6,785,528	-18%
Light trucks	8,577,804	6,457,173	
American Honda	1,551,542	1,428,765	-7.9%
Toyota U.S.A.	2,620,825	2,217,662	-15.4%
Ford	2,493,320	1,980,966	-20.5%
GM	3,822,612	2,954,819	-22.7%

No. of cars sold

Source: Autodata Corp.

The auto industry's woes are likely to add pressure on President Barack Obama and the Democrat-controlled Congress to reshape the nation's health-care and energy policies, which are closely tied to Detroit's fortunes. Experts say a national health-care plan could reduce the costly benefits the Big Three shoulder for workers and retirees. And a policy that deemphasizes oil could induce more consumers to embrace hybrid vehicles and make automakers' product planning less unpredictable and more environmentally friendly.

But for now, far-reaching policy changes may be difficult to pull off because of the worldwide recession, and no car manufacturer — domestic or foreign — has escaped the wreckage. Last year Toyota's U.S. car and light-truck sales fell 15 percent and Honda's 8 percent, and their December sales results were worse than those of either GM or Ford, according to Autodata.

"The tough times are hitting us far faster, wider and deeper than expected," said Katsuaki Watanabe, the outgoing president of Toyota Motor Corp., which projected its first operating loss in 70 years. [8]

Still, experts say Detroit's problems are far deeper than those facing foreign-based makers, in part because of past decisions the domestic manufacturers have made. The car companies themselves acknowledged missteps in December as they sought to wrest some $34 billion in federal aid from Congress — a gambit blocked by conservative Republicans.

"We made mistakes," GM's Wagoner told the Senate Banking Committee, citing a failure to make the company's operations more flexible and move faster into the U.S. market for smaller, more fuel-efficient vehicles. [9] In a trade journal ad, GM apologized for violating Americans' trust by, among other things, letting quality lag behind industry standards and designs to become "lackluster," skewing its product mix toward trucks and

ensure that these unfair conditions are removed," said UAW President Ron Gettelfinger. [4]

The recession, which has choked off credit and slowed car sales to a crawl, is making Detroit's job all the harder. In recent weeks, many experts said they expected the economic slowdown to force Chrysler — generally viewed as the weakest of the Big Three — to file for bankruptcy or merge with another company.

In January, the Italian car company Fiat agreed to acquire a 35 percent stake in Chrysler, which Chrysler Chairman Robert L. Nardelli said would enable the automaker to offer a broader lineup of vehicles while adhering to conditions of the federal bailout. [5] But the deal reportedly depends on Chrysler getting $3 billion in additional government loans. [6]

"It would be difficult for Chrysler to be sustainable by itself," David E. Cole, chairman of the Center for Automotive Research in Ann Arbor, Mich., said before the Fiat deal became public. As for GM and Ford, "We just don't know," he said. "Once the economy begins to have a little life, it could make a huge difference." But, he added, "It's a race against time."

In mid-January, Wagoner said that while GM wanted to avoid a Chapter 11 bankruptcy reorganization, its viability was "not 100 percent" certain. [7]

SUVs and agreeing to "unsustainable" employee-compensation plans.

The stakes in achieving long-term viability of the auto industry could not be higher, economists and policy makers say.

From plastics and electronics to glass and steel, the auto industry is among the nation's biggest consumers of U.S.-manufactured goods. Economists say a failure of even one auto company — especially GM or Ford — could set off a cascade of devastating job losses, send parts suppliers into bankruptcy and further destabilize auto production. The fallout would also hit businesses that rely indirectly on the auto industry, such as retailers in manufacturing towns.

The Economic Policy Institute, a liberal think tank in Washington, says the collapse of the domestic auto industry could eliminate up to 3.3 million American jobs, with much of the damage in Rust Belt states like Michigan and Indiana, which already are reeling from this year's economic travails.

Similarly, the Center for Automotive Research estimated that a shutdown of the Big Three would eliminate nearly 3 million jobs in the first year, with a slow recovery in employment afterwards. A shutdown would cost government $60 billion the first year alone, the group said. [10]

It was fear of a domino-like economic tumble that led former President George W. Bush in December to throw automakers a lifeline. "In the midst of a financial crisis and a recession, allowing the U.S. auto industry to collapse is not a responsible course of action," he said in announcing that the Treasury Department would use money from the Troubled Asset Relief Program (TARP) — the $700 billion financial-industry rescue plan passed in early October — to prop up Detroit. [11]

But support for a rescue has been far from overwhelming, both in Congress and on Main Street. "I believe it is wrong to make the American taxpayers an un-

How Auto Industry Shutdown Could Affect Jobs

More than 3.3 million jobs would be lost if the U.S. automobile industry shut down, with more than 400,000 occurring in Michigan and more than 300,000 in California. About one-quarter of the losses would be affected by General Motors alone. There would also be significant job losses in the West, East and South.

States With Biggest Job Losses If Auto Industry Shuts Down

State	GM only	Total industry shutdown
Michigan	112,500	407,300
California	84,500	305,900
Ohio	60,500	219,100
Texas	55,200	200,000
Illinois	42,800	154,900
Indiana	40,700	147,300
New York	39,900	144,600
Florida	34,900	126,300
Pennsylvania	33,200	120,100
Tennessee	29,400	106,400

Source: Robert E. Scott, "When Giants Fall: Shutdown of one or more U.S. automakers could eliminate up to 3.3 million U.S. jobs," Economic Policy Institute, December 2008

secured creditor to the automakers," Sen. Johnny Isakson, R-Ga., said after Bush announced his rescue plan. [12]

Obama backed the bailout, saying a collapse of the auto industry would have had "devastating" economic consequences. But he tempered his support with a tough message. "The auto companies must not squander this chance to reform bad management practices and begin the long-term restructuring that is absolutely required to save this critical industry and the millions of American jobs that depend on it," he said. [13]

As policy makers, industry executives and union leaders seek to salvage the domestic auto industry, here are some of the key questions they are facing:

Was the bailout the right move?

In announcing the loans, President Bush said carmakers were so finan-

cially fragile that "if we were to allow the free market to take its course now, it would almost certainly lead to disorderly bankruptcy and liquidation for the automakers. Under ordinary economic circumstances, I would say this is the price that failed companies must pay. . . . But these are not ordinary circumstances." [14]

Bush extended $9.4 billion to GM and $4 billion to Chrysler. Congress could decide to authorize another $4 billion for GM this month, when it is supposed to submit a plan for long-term viability. Chrysler is hoping for another $3 billion.

But critics have strenuously objected to the bailout and the use of TARP money to carry it out. Using TARP money "would be legally wrong, economically wrong and counterproductive to turning around these troubled businesses," wrote Andrew M. Grossman, a policy analyst at the Heritage Foundation, and James L. Gattuso, a research fellow at the conservative think tank, a week before the funding was approved. [15]

Earlier, as industry executives unsuccessfully sought financial help from Congress, Grossman argued that a bailout promised "continued stagnation and decline" and that reorganization under the bankruptcy process offered "the only chance that automakers have to rebound and survive in the global marketplace." [16]

Outside of the bankruptcy process, Grossman argued, automakers would have "neither the legal ability nor the incentives or wherewithal to reform their labor agreements, consolidate their brands, eliminate massive redundancies, find new leadership and rethink, from top to bottom, how they produce and market automobiles."

The critics also included some key congressional Republicans from Southern states where foreign auto plants are located. Without "sufficient reforms" by the UAW and auto companies, "We do not believe any amount of money will succeed in saving these companies," seven senators declared shortly before Bush approved the bailout. They were: South Carolina's Jim DeMint, Alabama's Jeff Sessions, Texas' John Cornyn and Georgia's Saxby Chambliss, plus Tom Coburn of Oklahoma, Michael Enzi of Wyoming and John Ensign of Nevada. [17]

A letter signed by 26 House members, including Texas Republican Jeb Hensarling, said a federal rescue would "shield the companies" from making necessary reforms "and set a costly precedent that the federal government will bail out other failing companies and industries." [18]

But withholding federal aid ultimately might have been the costliest option, some contend. "We couldn't bear to take that risk, given where the economy is now," says Gilbert Frisbie, clinical associate professor of marketing at Indiana University and a longtime auto-industry consultant.

As carmakers unsuccessfully pleaded with Congress for more than $30 billion in loans in early December, Anderson Economic Group, based in East Lansing, Mich., and BBK, an international business advisory firm, said the bankruptcy of two of the three companies could result in a nationwide financial impact four times worse than if the aid was granted. Under such a scenario, more than 1.8 million jobs would disappear within a year, and federal and state tax revenue would decline nearly $70 billion over a two-year period, the firms said. [19]

Still, some experts have argued that a government-structured bankruptcy would give the troubled carmakers the best chance of succeeding in the long term. Prominent among them is Paul Ingrassia, a former Dow Jones executive and *Wall Street Journal* reporter who won a Pulitzer Prize for his coverage of GM.

"I've advocated a federal restructuring trustee, with the same powers as a bankruptcy trustee, as an integral part of any bailout plan," he wrote in the *Journal* in mid-December, before the bailout. "The trustee wouldn't tell car companies that accept federal loans what cars they should build. But he or she would have the power to cut through contractual obligations to workers, dealers, parts suppliers and others so that the automakers can emerge with viable business models. That means fewer brands and dealers, as well as a streamlined labor contract. Without these changes, the loan dollars will go down the drain." [20]

But supporters of the loans say bankruptcy would have drastically undermined the auto industry's chances of eventual recovery. Consumers would be reluctant to buy cars from a manufacturer going through bankruptcy for fear warranties wouldn't be honored and parts wouldn't be available, a point that Bush and auto company executives stressed.

Moreover, loan supporters say that if even a single carmaker went bust, particularly in a "disorderly" bankruptcy — one executed in haste in the face of a critical cash shortage — the supply chain for the entire domestic auto industry would have been disrupted.

Michael Smitka, an economics professor at Washington and Lee University who follows the auto industry closely, notes, for example, that only a handful of companies supply headlamps to all domestic and foreign auto plants in the United States. An abrupt shutdown of a big manufacturer like GM could choke off so much headlamp business that the suppliers would have difficulty sustaining their operations, he says. That could lead to production slowdowns and layoffs at other auto manufacturers, which in turn could cause losses at companies that make windshields or engines, and the fallout would continue rippling throughout the economy.

Smitka also says that a company undergoing an abrupt bankruptcy proceeding likely would have to trim engineering and other skilled positions needed to enhance innovation — "the capacity to make components for more fuel-efficient cars," for example. "If you cut back, you in effect declare that you intend to go out of business" down the road, he says.

Experts also note that the auto industry is an engine of national innovation, providing a market for everything from cutting-edge electronics to advanced materials and pushing suppliers to innovate as well.

Still, Smitka says, by March 31 the auto companies should be able to present a "coherent strategic plan" to deal with the recession and return to profitability. And, he says, management should show it is sacrificing alongside the rank and file, suppliers and others with a stake in the industry's future.

"I have little sympathy for the bonus rank of the Detroit Three," he said in November as Detroit executives began to appeal for federal aid. "There are plenty of hungry managers around. If someone thinks life is impossible without all the perks, then let them hunt for an employer in some other industry who will provide them." [21]

Is the UAW primarily to blame for Detroit's woes?

As Washington deliberated over whether to extend aid to Detroit, pundits and policy makers engaged in a politically charged debate over whether and how much the UAW is responsible for the domestic industry's travails.

Gary Burtless, a senior fellow at the Brookings Institution and former Carter administration economist, argues that while the automakers were wrong to negotiate contracts locking Detroit into huge benefit costs, he says the union "is not the decisive source" of the domestic automakers' trouble. "The main problem is they are not building cars consumers want to buy." Detroit put too much faith in profit-generating SUVs, he says, and failed to anticipate a shift toward demand for smaller, fuel-efficient vehicles.

But others argue that much of the domestic industry's troubles stem from Byzantine work rules and collective-bargaining agreements that hobble management's ability to cut costs and remain flexible.

"[H]ow can we explain that whenever GM, Ford and Chrysler leave our shores, they compete well in foreign markets as varied as Europe, South America and China?" wrote Logan Robinson, a law professor at the University of Detroit Mercy and former auto-industry lawyer. He added: "The most striking difference appears to be that the Detroit Three are unionized, and the foreign [automakers operating in the United States] are, overwhelmingly, not." The UAW's "very strength has allowed it to permeate into every aspect of manufacturing in the Detroit Three." [22]

Part of the debate over the UAW's role in Detroit's troubles revolves around compensation and benefits for unionized workers. Critics of the union often cite a U.S. labor cost of around $73 per hour for the Big Three. But the UAW calls that figure "outdated and inaccurate." [23] And some in Congress agree.

The Plug-in Future for GM

GM rolls out the Chevy Volt electric car at the North American International Auto Show on Jan. 11, 2009. Sales of the heavily promoted Volt begin in fall 2010, at an estimated $30,000-$40,000. GM Vice Chairman Bob Lutz unveils the Cadillac Converj, a more luxurious version of the Volt.

"We've heard this garbage about 73 bucks an hour," Sen. Bob Casey, D-Pa., said during a hearing in December to consider federal aid for Detroit. "It's a total lie. I think some people have perpetrated that deliberately, in a calculated way, to mislead the American people about what we're doing here." [24]

The UAW says the figure includes not only health care, pension and other compensation for current workers but also benefits for retirees that are spread across the active work force. "Active workers never receive any of this compensation in any form, so it is not accurate to

Auto Industry Employs More Than 2 Million

Approximately 2.2 million Americans are employed in the automobile industry, with a high concentration of the jobs located in Rust Belt states such as Michigan, Ohio, Indiana and Pennsylvania. New-car dealerships account for half of the jobs in the industry, while parts manufacturing accounts for about a third.

Automobile Industry Jobs by State

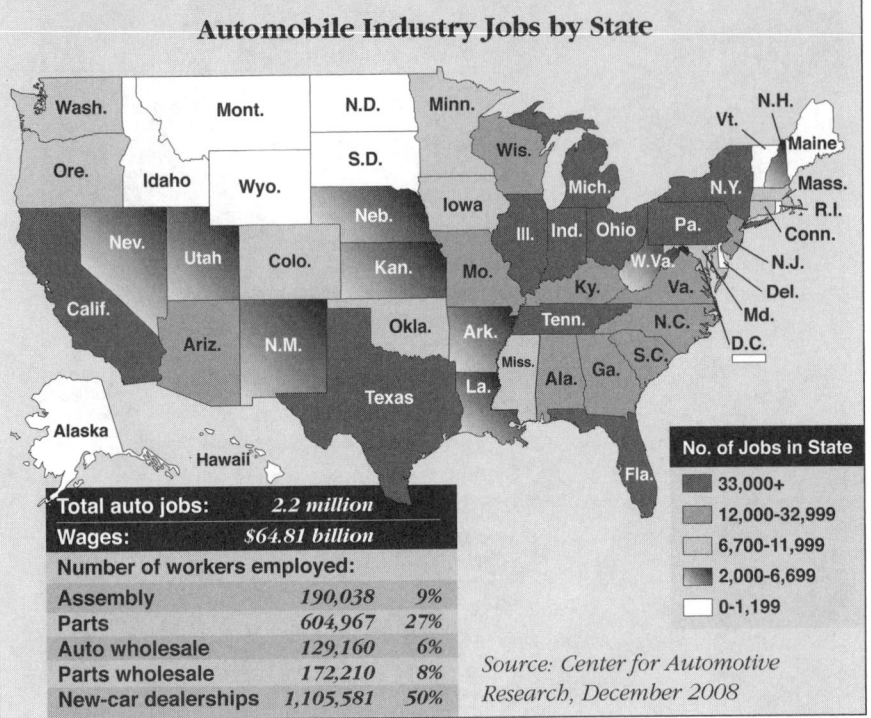

No. of Jobs in State	
▓	33,000+
▓	12,000-32,999
░	6,700-11,999
▒	2,000-6,699
□	0-1,199

Total auto jobs:	2.2 million	
Wages:	$64.81 billion	
Number of workers employed:		
Assembly	190,038	9%
Parts	604,967	27%
Auto wholesale	129,160	6%
Parts wholesale	172,210	8%
New-car dealerships	1,105,581	50%

Source: Center for Automotive Research, December 2008

describe it as part of their 'earnings,' " the union argues. [25]

Wages at the Big Three are about $33 an hour for skilled-trades workers, $28 for assemblers and about $14 for newly hired workers, the UAW said. According to a report in the *Toledo Blade*, Toyota said its workers make about $30 an hour, Nissan pays about $25, and Honda $28.87. [26]

New York Times economics correspondent David Leonhardt dissected the $73 figure this way:

• Cash payments, including wages, overtime and vacation pay, which add up to around $40 an hour, though the figure varies slightly by company and year.

• Benefits such as medical insurance and pensions, which add up to about $15 an hour.

Together, Leonhardt wrote, those two add to about $55 an hour, compared to roughly $45 an hour for non-union workers at Honda or Toyota, with most of the gap stemming from lower benefits at the Japanese-owned automakers.

• Retiree benefits that equate to about $15 an hour and are fixed costs unrelated to the number of vehicles a company makes.

"[T]his $15 isn't mainly a reflection of how generous the retiree benefits are," Leonhardt wrote, but rather "of how many retirees there are. The Big Three built up a huge pool of retirees long before Honda and Toyota opened plants in this country." [27]

GM has 96,000 active U.S. employees and 497,000 retired workers, compared with only 300 retired workers in

the United States for Toyota, according to *The Wall Street Journal*, which called GM "one of the largest providers of health-care coverage in the world." It added, "Including the dependents of retired workers who are covered by GM, the automaker provides health care for almost one million people." [28]

Comparing the cost of fringe benefits of Big Three workers and those at foreign-owned U.S. plants is difficult because foreign makers don't report all their labor costs in a form that makes it possible to do a straightforward comparison. But the available data are revealing.

GM spent $4.8 billion on health care last year, which added about $1,500 to the cost of each vehicle, while analysts estimate that Toyota's health-care costs add about $200 to each of its cars and trucks, the *Journal* reported. [29]

In 2007 the UAW ratified a groundbreaking four-year contract that lifted some burdens from the automakers. Not only did the contract usher in lower wages for new hires but it also excluded them from the automakers' traditional retiree health and pension plans. [30]

In addition, it shifted billions of dollars in retiree health-care costs, starting next year, to an independent UAW-run trust called the Voluntary Employee Beneficiary Association (VEBA). The trust is funded by company and employee contributions, but among the controversial targets in the bridge-loan agreement is one requiring the UAW to accept at least half of future company contributions in the form of stock — a move that could eat away at retirement benefits if the carmakers' shares continue to lose value.

Both GM and Chrysler have ended a controversial "Jobs Bank" program under which laid-off workers continued to draw pay. Suspension of the program was among the concessions the union leadership made as Detroit appealed for help from Congress in December. The UAW also said it would allow the companies to delay payments to the VEBA trust. [31] As negotiations between the UAW and auto industry began early this year over terms of the Bush administration's bridge-loan agreement, it was unclear how much more the union would bend.

The debate over the union's role in Detroit's plight hasn't just been about wages and benefits but also about work rules and union power. The UAW denies that its work rules make the domestic automakers less efficient than foreign-owned non-union ones. But critics argue that the union has hobbled management at a time when nimbleness is needed to survive.

On a recent radio broadcast, Ingrassia, the auto journalist, read a lengthy and arcane paragraph from what he called the "inch-plus-thick" UAW master contract with GM, adding, "I mean, honestly, it is just impossible to run a business with this kind of a — you know, governance, primarily." [32]

Can the domestic automakers survive?

In the short term, the entire auto industry's prospects depend significantly on how quickly the economic crisis abates. "Until demand recovers, nobody's going to be building that many cars in America, regardless of the name of the company," says James Rubenstein, a professor of geography at Miami University in Ohio who has written widely on the American auto industry.

The availability of credit, which has been squeezed dry by the global economic crisis, will have a major impact on demand, economists say.

A pre-Christmas decision by the Treasury Department to inject $6 billion into GMAC, a lender co-owned by GM and Chrysler's majority shareholder, Cerberus Capital Management, was expected to help spur sales, and possibly keep GM out of bankruptcy court.

"While an eventual GM Chapter 11 [bankruptcy reorganization] cannot be entirely dismissed . . . federal aid to GMAC suggests the government is probably now so financially entangled in the GM complex that a Chapter 7 liquidation of [GM's operations] seems

highly unlikely," said Himanshu Patel, an analyst with JP Morgan Chase. [33]

Likewise, the Treasury Department gave Chrysler's financing arm a $1.5 billion loan in mid-January in a move designed to ease credit and boost sales.

Some in Congress want to go further than cash infusions and bridge loans, though. Sen. Barbara A. Mikulski, D-Md., for example, introduced legislation in November that would give tax breaks to new-car buyers, a proposal backed by the National Automobile Dealers Association, but Senate Republicans blocked it. [34] She reintroduced the idea on Feb. 3. (*See "At Issue," p. 121.*)

Even if stimulus measures boost sales in the short term, however, the domestic automakers face the Herculean task of cost-cutting, downsizing and reorganizing that experts say is needed to make them fit for the long haul.

"It has to involve substantial restructuring," says Frisbie of Indiana University. "They need to rethink their size, how many brands they can support, their direction, product lineup and their role in consumers' life and lifestyle and as an economic force."

The economic stakes in the industry's survival are extremely high. More than 700,000 people worked for motor vehicle and parts manufacturers at the end of November, according to Bureau of Labor Statistics data cited by *The Wall Street Journal*, down by more than 116,000 jobs from the same month in 2007. Another 1.1 million people worked for auto dealers. [35] About 200,000 people work for the Detroit Big Three, according to Center for Automotive Research data cited in the *Journal*, compared with 113,000 who work in the United States for foreign-based producers. [36]

Under the terms of the bridge loans, GM and Chrysler must show that they can achieve a "positive net present value" — in other words, they have to show they can become profitable and pay back the loans at some point. Skepticism is

widespread about that prospect, though.

"Financial viability requires projecting a positive net present value, taking into account all current and future costs," wrote Peter Morici, a professor at the University of Maryland School of Business and former chief economist at the U.S. International Trade Commission. [37]

"Given the depressed auto market, a positive cash flow cannot be accomplished soon, and GM and Chrysler will be asking for more federal loans when they table their plans by March 31. If the auto market stays depressed into 2010, Ford will likely seek assistance. Given the likely duration of the recession, loans of well over $100 billion will be needed. Much of those could prove gifts, with the loans never truly repaid."

Morici went on to say that unless Detroit can slash debt, rid itself of liabilities for retired autoworkers and line up labor costs and work rules with those of Japanese companies operating in the United States, "they simply cannot hope to be consistently profitable. Yet, the [loan] agreement permits the automakers to vary from those conditions if they can still demonstrate a net positive present value. Enter the accounting magicians."

Some experts suggest that the prognosis is most favorable for Ford and dimmest for Chrysler.

"I don't see GM going out of business," says John Revitte, a professor in the School of Labor and Industrial Relations at Michigan State University. "The worst case would be a structured government-sponsored bankruptcy." More and more of GM's business comes from overseas markets, he says.

Ford, like the other Big Three automakers, has faced big losses and declining sales, but it also has had a hefty cushion of cash and a line of bank credit. [38] Ford had nearly $19 billion in cash at the end of last year's third quarter, more than GM, and a nearly $11 billion bank line of credit negotiated in 2006. [39]

"Whether it was lucky or planned, the decision to borrow the money has turned out to be a huge positive for Ford," said auto consultant John Casesa of Casesa Shapiro Group. [40]

Still, "They don't have an endless supply of cash," analyst Pete Hastings of Morgan Keegan, an investment banking firm, said in December. "If GM and Chrysler are in the emergency room, Ford is in the waiting area next to go in." [41]

Alan Mulally, Ford's CEO, said in early January that his company did not need federal help. "We're clearly in a different place, and we do not need the money," he said on the Fox Business Network. [42] ∎

BACKGROUND

Bumps in the Road

Shortly before William C. Durant founded General Motors in September 1908, he sought financing from the fabled banker J. Pierpont Morgan, who dismissed the budding auto executive as "an unstable visionary." Wrote Durant: "[M]oney is hard to get owing to a somewhat unaccountable feeling of uneasiness and a general distrust of the automobile proposition." [43]

Durant soon got his company off the ground, and its stock soared. But the "feeling of uneasiness" about the auto industry that Durant lamented returned — with a vengeance.

"[W]hen the overcrowded automobile industry failed to deliver on inflated expectations in the early 1920s, auto stocks plunged," *The Wall Street Journal* noted in a 2001 article on market bubbles. "GM lost two-thirds of its stock value in six months. A panicked Mr. Durant borrowed money and feverishly bought the shares in a futile attempt to prop them up." But although GM recovered, it was "too late for its founder, who lost his entire fortune and wound up running a bowling alley." [44]

The tumultuous '20s weren't the last time that trouble stalked the auto industry. Over the last century, a parade of automobile nameplates, from Hudson and Packard to Auburn and Studebaker, disappeared from the scene. Assembly lines ground to a halt over labor disputes, including a pivotal 44-day sit-down strike at a GM plant in Flint, Mich., in the 1930s that led to recognition of the United Auto Workers as the sole bargaining agent for GM employees.

And global events, highlighted by the transplant of foreign manufacturers into the American heartland, shook Detroit like potholes on a racetrack.

The bumps began in the 1970s. At the start of the decade, GM, Ford and Chrysler sold more than 80 percent of cars and light trucks in the United States. [45] But their dominance soon slipped. The Arab oil embargo pushed gas prices to historic levels in the mid-1970s, creating demand for fuel-efficient foreign-made cars and hurting ill-prepared domestic automakers. Soon, American streets were crowded with foreign brands.

Toyota, which began marketing cars in the United States in 1957, sold its millionth vehicle to an American customer in the 1970s and surpassed Volkswagen to become the top import brand in 1975. [46] Honda introduced its iconic Civic subcompact in the United States in 1972 and its midsize Accord four years later. By 1980, GM, Ford and Chrysler's share of U.S. sales had skidded to 74 percent. [47]

Mileage Mandate

Ratcheting up the pressure on the Big Three was a move by Congress in 1975 to mandate corporate average fuel economy (CAFE) standards for automakers. Critics have long argued that they forced automakers to turn out money-losing small cars to bring average mileage into line with federal limits. Meanwhile, they say, be-

cause the law allowed higher mileage limits for light trucks, it had the unintended consequence of encouraging automakers to produce gas-guzzling SUVs, which are more profitable for Detroit than small cars. [48]

Many blame the auto industry for flooding the market with gas-guzzlers, but experts point out that Detroit was also satisfying consumer demands. Detroit "pushed trucks, but of course the reason was, that's what people wanted to buy," says Cole at the Center for Automotive Research.

Smitka of Washington and Lee University says the CAFE standards "turned out to be a golden opportunity that the Detroit Three were proactive with."

Still, at first the mileage mandate threw the domestic auto industry into turmoil. "It meant that the companies would have to redesign their cars under terrible deadline pressure and suffer greatly inflated new costs," the late journalist David Halberstam wrote in *The Reckoning*, his seminal mid-1980s book on the auto industry. "This placed an ominous burden on the industry, and, even more ominous, the burden fell on the companies in inverse proportion to their strength." [49]

Among the casualties was Chrysler. Reeling from the effects of foreign competition and the energy crisis, it sought a bailout from Washington, a move that presaged the desperate struggles — and bitter debates over federal aid — swirling around Detroit now.

"In 1979, when Chrysler teetered perilously close to bankruptcy, the nation gasped at the idea that one of America's industrial giants might shut its doors," *New York Times* auto writer Micheline Maynard wrote in *The End of Detroit*, a 2003 book about the industry's troubles. "While there were cynics who argued that Chrysler should be allowed to go out of business — the victim of its own mismanagement — its supporters rallied to convince Congress to pass $1.5 billion in loan guarantees, giving the company time to find its way back." [50]

Continued on p. 116

Chronology

1900s-1930s
Early days of U.S. auto industry marked by explosive growth, tensions with workers.

1903
Henry Ford and investor group form Ford Motor Co.

1908
William C. Durant forms General Motors. . . . Ford introduces Model T.

1925
Chrysler Corp. is founded.

1937
Strike forces GM to recognize United Auto Workers unions.

1950s-1970s
Big Three dominate U.S. auto market with big cars; Toyota begins import revolution.

1956
Ford sells common stock to public.

1957
Toyota begins selling in U.S.

1968
Toyota introduces compact Corolla.

1970s-1980s
Arab oil embargo helps drive consumers toward fuel-efficient foreign cars; Congress passes fuel-economy rules.

1970
Big Three account for over 85 percent of U.S. car sales.

1972
GM opens plant in South Korea. . . . Honda introduces compact Civic; midsize Accord arrives later.

1975
Congress passes corporate average fuel economy (CAFE) regulations but allows weaker standards for light trucks. . . . Toyota surpasses Volkswagen to become top U.S. import.

1980
GM announces plans for European plants. . . . CEO Lee Iacocca wins federal bailout of Chrysler. . . . Big Three share of U.S. car sales at 74 percent.

1982
Honda begins production in Ohio.

1984
GM and Toyota open joint car-production venture in Fremont, Calif.

1990s-2000
Automakers profit from mushrooming SUV sales; environmental concerns spur hybrid technology.

1990
Robert C. Stempel becomes GM CEO, agrees to expand Jobs Bank that guarantees pay to laid-off autoworkers. . . . First GM Saturn produced. . . . Ford introduces Explorer, nation's top-selling SUV.

1992
John F. Smith Jr. replaces Stempel.

1998
Chrysler and Daimler-Benz merge.

2000
Richard Wagoner takes over at GM, which announces phaseout of Oldsmobile. . . . Toyota introduces hybrid Prius.

2001-2009
UAW makes major labor concessions, but high gas prices and recession batter foreign and domestic automakers.

2001
Zero-percent financing by domestic automakers helps restore economic confidence after terrorist attacks.

2006
Boeing executive Alan Mulally replaces William Ford Jr. as CEO, steers Ford toward fuel-efficient products.

2007
Cerberus Capital Management acquires majority interest in Chrysler from Daimler for $7.4 billion. . . . Big Three sign new contract with UAW that creates private trust for financing future health obligations.

2008
Global auto sales plunge. . . . Big Three CEOs pummeled after arriving in Washington on corporate jets to plead for federal aid from Congress. . . . Congress rejects plea, asks CEOs to return with detailed turnaround plans, but political squabbling nixes relief in Senate. On Dec. 19 White House announces $17.4 billion in bridge loans for GM, Chrysler. Lender GMAC, co-owned by GM and Cerberus, gets $6 billion. . . . U.S. automakers' sales plunge more than 18 percent in 2008. . . . Toyota sales fell 15 percent and Honda's 8 percent in 2008.

2009
Domestic and foreign carmakers showcase plug-in and hybrid-powered vehicles at North American International Auto Show in Detroit. . . . GM loses status to Toyota as world's biggest car company, announces 2,000 layoffs in Michigan, Ohio.

Even Chinese Automakers Are Going Green

Consumers will soon have wide choice of hybrid and electric cars.

Green is the new gold in the auto-making world. From Detroit to Tokyo to Schenzhen, domestic and foreign carmakers are beginning to showcase a new generation of vehicles that run on electricity or hybrid power. While the recent plunge in gasoline prices has made it far cheaper to drive a conventionally fueled vehicle than just a few months ago — when pump prices exceeded $4 a gallon — experts say fuel efficiency remains a top priority for drivers.

"Consumers are completely reconsidering everything about buying a car, in terms of what attributes they're looking for," said Stephen Berkov, executive director of client strategy at Edmunds.com, an automotive Web site. "Now, the No. 1 factor would be fuel efficiency — that's a paradigm shift. Automotive marketing has always been about performance, and now it's about fuel efficiency." [1]

Such sentiment explains automakers' zeal for new vehicle technology that not only preserves natural resources and the environment but also draws drivers to new-car showrooms. President Barack Obama's pledge to promote clean energy and green jobs could boost interest in hybrid and electric vehicles, as could a resurgence in gas prices that is likely to occur with a revival of the world economy.

Along with established car companies, high-profile niche players are racing to develop green cars. They include Tesla Motors Inc., a small California company building high-performance, all-electric cars selling for more than $100,000.

But developing green cars is expensive and time-consuming, the technology behind them continues to evolve and the consumer market is subject to swings in oil prices and buyer whims. In December, Toyota said it was putting on hold in-definitely the opening of a new Mississippi plant built to produce the gasoline-electric Prius hatchback. [2]

On the other hand, the cost of green cars could fall as production volumes increase and technology advances. Green cars are getting support from government officials and others seeking to reduce dependence on oil. In Hawaii, the state government and Hawaiian Electric Co. endorsed a plan in December to create a system featuring a network of recharging stations and battery-swap sites for use by electric cars. [3] The plan calls for a partnership with Better Place, an alternative energy company founded by former software executive Shai Agassi. [4]

William C. Ford Jr., executive chairman of the Ford Motor Co., which is aiming to sell an all-electric, battery-powered vehicle by 2011, told *The New York Times* that his company felt compelled by competitive pressure to offer electric cars. "Frankly, I think it's a gamble not to do it. It's clear that society is headed down this road." [5]

Ford's electric vehicle, which the company says will be able to travel 100 miles on a single charge, is part of a plan to market four new hybrid or electric Fords in the next four years. [6] Ford has been selling hybrids — which combine gasoline and battery power — since 2004, when it introduced the hybrid model of its Escape SUV. Ford is expected to begin selling a 2010 hybrid model of its Fusion midsize sedan this spring. Its 41-miles-per-gallon in-city driving and 36 on the highway beats Toyota's Camry hybrid (33 and 34 miles per gallon, respectively). [7]

Ford's effort is just one example of the race to embrace green cars. Here are some other efforts revving up:

Continued from p. 114

Chrysler recovered under the leadership of CEO Lee Iacocca, whom the automaker wooed from the presidency of Ford. In 1983 Iacocca introduced the minivan, a hot-selling innovation that presaged the SUV. But it didn't stop the slide in Detroit's dominance.

Foreign Automakers Arrive

Honda began producing cars in Marysville, Ohio, in 1982. The next year, Nissan opened a plant in Smyrna, Tenn., leading what would become a flood of foreign manufacturers into the South, where land and labor were relatively cheap, local governments offered tantalizing incentives to woo foreign companies and the United Auto Workers did not hold sway, as in Detroit.

The South has seen a "staggering" amount of foreign auto production, the conservative *Weekly Standard* noted recently, in an article subtitled, "Plenty of car makers make a go of it in this country — they're just non-union and not headquartered in Detroit." Mercedes, Honda and Hyundai plants in Alabama turn out 750,000 vehicles annually, Volkswagen is constructing a plant near Chattanooga, Tenn., and Kia is building in West Point, Ga., the magazine noted. [51]

Efforts by congressional Republicans from the South to block federal aid for Detroit late last year led some critics to see the move as a gambit to shift economic growth to the low-wage South at the expense of the North.

"If the major U.S. automobile companies go under," Michael Lind wrote in the left-leaning online publication *Salon.com*, "it will be partly because timely federal aid for them was blocked by members of Congress like Tennessee Sen. Bob Corker, whose states have created their own counter-Detroit in the form of Japanese, Korean and German transplant factories." Added Lind, a senior fellow at the New

- General Motors plans to begin selling its heavily promoted Chevrolet Volt electric car in fall 2010. Expected to cost from $30,000 to $40,000, the Volt is propelled by an electric motor that runs on lithium-ion batteries that can be recharged from a home electric outlet.

  The batteries are designed to last for the first 40 miles, after which a gasoline generator can keep the batteries charged and the car going for up to 400 miles at the equivalent of 50 miles per gallon, according to GM. Recharging the battery takes between three and six-and-a-half hours, depending on whether a 110-volt or 220-volt supply is used. [8]

  GM showed off an electric Cadillac Converj concept car at the North American International Auto Show in Detroit in January.

- Chrysler introduced three electric prototypes last year — the Dodge EV, Jeep EV and Chrysler EV. The company intends to introduce an electric vehicle for the North American market in 2010. [9]

Japanese carmakers — and even the Chinese — also are moving aggressively into the electric-car market:

- Toyota, a leader in hybrid gasoline-battery technology, plans to sell a small all-electric car in 2012 and to test a plug-in version of its hybrid Prius using lithium-ion batteries late this year. [10] It also reportedly is developing a solar-powered vehicle, though marketing is thought to be years away. [11]

- Honda plans a new version of its Honda Insight hybrid in April that is expected to sell for no more than $20,000, or about 10-20 percent below the price of a Prius. [12]

- Mitsubishi and Fuji Heavy Industries, Subaru's parent companies, are testing electric cars, and Nissan's CEO has said it will have an electric car for U.S. and Japanese consumers as soon as 2010. [13]

- Chinese company BYD Auto Co. set a target date of 2011 to begin selling an electric crossover vehicle and a plug-in hybrid sedan.

[1] Quoted in Sharon Silke Carty, "Ford scores marketing coup with thrifty fusion hybrid," *USA Today*, Dec. 22, 2008, www.usatoday.com/money/autos/2008- 12-22-ford-fusion-fuel-efficient_N.htm.

[2] Alan Ohnsman, "Toyota to Delay Mississippi Prius Plant Construction," Bloomberg, Dec. 15, 2008.

[3] John Markoff, "Hawaii Endorses Plan for Electric Cars," *The New York Times*, Dec. 3, 2008.

[4] Rebecca Smith, "Hawaii Makes Big Bet on Electric Cars," *The Wall Street Journal*, Dec. 3, 2008.

[5] Bill Vlasic, "Detroit Goes for Electric Cars, but Will Drivers?" *The New York Times*, Jan. 11, 2009.

[6] Brent Snavely, "Electric car is just the beginning, Ford says," *Detroit Free Press*, Jan. 12, 2009. See Richard L. Worsnop, "Electric Cars," *CQ Researcher*, July 9, 1993, pp. 577-600.

[7] Bill Vlasic, "Ford Hybrid Emphasizes High Mileage," *The New York Times*, Dec. 31, 2008.

[8] General Motors Corp., "Chevy Volt FAQs," http://gm-volt.com/chevy-volt-faqs/.

[9] "Announcement of the Fiat-Chrysler Alliance," online.wsj.com, Jan. 20, 2009.

[10] Martin LaMonica, "Toyota to build electric town car, plug-in hybrids," CNET News, Jan. 11, 2009.

[11] Yuri Kageyama, "Report: Toyota developing solar powered green car," The Associated Press, Jan. 1, 200p, http://apnews.myway.com/article/20090101/D95EDCU80.html. The article cites reporting in the *Nikkei*, a Japanese business daily.

[12] Keith Buglewicz, "New Honda Hybrid Contender Challenges Champ Prius," *Wired*, Jan. 11, 2009.

[13] Vlasic, "Detroit Goes for Electric Cars, but Will Drivers?" *op. cit.*

America Foundation, a think tank in Washington: "The South will have risen by bringing down the North. [Confederate President] Jefferson Davis will have had his revenge." [52]

In tracing ways in which Detroit lost its way in recent years, Maynard wrote that for a long time after entering the American market, the Japanese manufacturers "consistently delivered on their basic task, the small-car market. Detroit seemed willing to cede that market, because GM, Ford and Chrysler hadn't found a way to build cars to compete with these 'rice burners' at a profit, and they really didn't want to be bothered figuring out how to do so. . . .

"Detroit's executives argued that the success of foreign vehicles was limited. Subcompacts and compacts might be desired by ecology-minded individuals or small families, but once consumers needed more space or comfort, buyers, Detroit assumed, would automatically come home to American automobiles." [53]

But once the Japanese companies understood the kind of cars consumers needed and wanted, they started producing them — in U.S. plants led by American executives, many of whom were schooled by the Detroit companies, Maynard wrote. "What unites [the] foreign-based companies is that they have developed a better sense of what their American customers want than Detroit has. They have shown a willingness to change and go beyond the status quo that has made them leaders in the increasingly fast-paced car marketplace." [54]

The pedal-to-the-metal rise of the Japanese companies strikes many as ironic, given the Big Three's storied legacy. "When I was a kid, the government talked about breaking [GM] up because it was too powerful," recalls Revitte of Michigan State.

What caused foreign-based "transplants" to leave Detroit in the dust is a complex question, and the theories are passionate.

When GM Closed the Janesville Plant

"The trickle-down is staggering. It's like watching something melt."

Two days before Christmas, the last big Chevrolet Tahoe SUV rolled off the historic assembly line at the General Motors plant in Janesville, Wis., severing a link between the city and the automaker that stretched back 90 years.

The factory, GM's oldest, was built in 1918 to make tractors and became a Chevrolet plant five years later. [1] Over the decades the plant produced cars, trucks and SUVs, most recently the popular Tahoe. But last summer's spike in gasoline prices, coupled with the economic crisis and financial pressures weighing heavily on the auto industry, led GM to halt production. After a small crew completes an order of trucks this spring for Isuzu under a joint venture with GM, the plant will cease operations, a GM spokesman said.

About 2,400 GM jobs have disappeared at the Janesville plant in the past year, and roughly 1,200 jobs have gone away at other companies in town that supplied parts and logistical support to the plant, says Doug Venable, director of economic development in Janesville, a south-central Wisconsin city with a population of about 60,000. As recently as 2000 or 2001, GM employed 5,000 in Janesville, he said.

Among the casualties is former GM electrician Harry Larson, a 25-year veteran of the plant. "It hurts," says Larson, 57, who adds that he has been drawing unemployment benefits. "It's not an easy thing to lose your job."

"It's unfortunate this happened at the same time that the national economy is in such dire straits," says economic-development

director Venable." Still, he says, while GM has been a "big part of our economy," other industries have grown in recent years. Health care recently exceeded the GM plant — once the city's biggest employer — in number of jobs, he says.

In 1990, GM had 5,100 employees and a payroll of $240 million in Rock County — about 7 percent of the work force and 10 percent of payroll. In 2007, GM's share of employment had shrunk to about 3.3 percent of the county's labor force of 83,000, and wage and salary income accounted for less than 5 percent of the county's payroll.

"Over the last 15 years, GM was more efficient, more highly automated" and could "produce the same number of vehicles with fewer dollars of input," Venable says.

The plant closing "is not the end of Janesville as a community," he says. "Certainly it's going to be felt, but is the town ready to close up and turn out the lights? No."

Still, the closing of an auto plant can have a profound impact on a metropolitan area like Janesville. Howard Wial, a fellow in the Metropolitan Policy Program at the Brookings Institution think tank, estimated that a single job at a Big Three auto company or supplier in a metro area may support up to two jobs in other fields, ranging from supermarkets to doctors' offices. [2]

Janesville isn't alone in feeling the fallout from the auto industry's woes. In December alone, GM shut its SUV plant in Moraine, Ohio, and Chrysler closed its SUV plant in Newark,

"To put it concisely, the transplants operate under conditions imposed by the free market," the conservative editorial page of *The Wall Street Journal* opined, whereas "Detroit lives on Fantasy Island." [55] The *Journal* argued, in part, that the gap in labor costs stemming from Detroit's benefit obligations "reflects the way Big Three management and unions have conspired to make themselves uncompetitive."

Also dogging the Big Three, some argue, is a perception that domestic vehicles are inferior in quality to those produced by foreign makers, a view that took hold in the 1970s and '80s. Today, says Rubenstein of Miami University in Ohio, "there's no statistically significant difference in quality among any of the cars, but unfortunately for the Big Three that's not good enough,

because once people gave up on them and switched over to a Honda or Toyota, there's no reason to go back if you're satisfied with what you've got."

Outdated Dealer System

In addition, critics say Detroit is hobbled by an antiquated dealer system that hurts Detroit's ability to shape itself to 21st-century market realities.

The bad economy already has put dealers under pressure. GM's goal is to close 1,750 showrooms — 27 percent of the total — over four years. Chrysler plans to thin its 3,300 U.S. dealerships but hasn't set a target. [56] Ford, in a business plan submitted to Congress in early December, said it "clearly [has] too many dealers" and pledged to contin-

ue an effort to downsize and restructure its network in its largest 130 metro markets. [57] The consulting firm Grant Thornton LLP said 3,800 dealers — about a fifth of the national total — would need to close by the end of this year because of poor sales, rising operating costs and credit shortages. [58]

Yet culling dealerships won't be easy because of a thicket of state franchise laws. "In a number of states there [are] these very elaborate procedures that you have to go through to shut dealerships," said University of Chicago law Professor Douglas Baird. "In some states you just can't do it at all." [59]

State laws also bar automakers from owning dealerships or selling cars directly to the public — including online. "They can't take an order over the Internet for a made-to-order car

Del., each idling more than 1,000 workers. [3] In Kokomo, Ind., roughly a fifth of the city's employment is tied to the precarious fortunes of the auto and auto-parts industry. [4]

In Janesville and the surrounding area, the impact of the plant closing, coupled with the deep national recession, is taking a toll, says Gail Graham, president of the United Way of North Rock County, which allocates money to charitable groups in the region.

"You want to know what's going to happen to the United States if we don't help the auto industry?" she declares. "Come to Janesville."

Graham says that "largely due to GM closing" and job loss among auto-industry suppliers in the area, the United Way lopped $400,000 from its 2008 fund-raising goal, cutting it from $1.75 million last year to $1.35 million this year. Referring to autoworkers who have traditionally donated to the local United Way, she says, "When they don't work, we don't get paid. This is an employee campaign that runs year-round. The dollars come out of their paycheck."

Smiles hide the tears for Janesville assembly plant manager Gary Malkus and 28-year employee Lauria Bell after the last car rolled off the assembly line on Dec. 23, 2008.

Getty Images/Bill Olmsted-Pool

Meanwhile, Graham says, the rough economy is pushing up demand for social services in the Janesville region. "Numbers are skyrocketing" at a clinic that serves people without medical insurance, and "food banks are stretched to the limit," she says.

"The trickle-down is staggering. It's like watching something melt."

Graham says the plant closing did produce a small consolation for the United Way's fund-raising efforts. "We got the last vehicle off the line. All the employees signed it on the inside. We're raffling it off."

[1] The Associated Press, "Hugs, tears as GM workers leave Janesville plant for last time," Dec. 23, 2008.

[2] See Howard Wial, "How a Metro Nation Would Feel the Loss of the Detroit Three Automakers," Metropolitan Policy Program, Brookings Institution, December 2008, www.brookings.edu/~/media/Files/rc/papers/2008/1212_automakers_wial/automakers_wial.pdf.

[3] See Nick Bunkley and Bill Vlasic, "Nearly the End of the Line for S.U.V.'s," The New York Times, Dec. 24, 2008, and Jane M. Von Bergen, "What About the Safety Net? A Lot of People Are Falling Through," Philadelphia Inquirer, Dec. 21, 2008.

[4] Wial, op. cit.

like Dell [does with computers] because the states have made it illegal," said Morici of the University of Maryland. If automakers could sell online, they could likely cut inventory expenses and "lop something like $1,000 off the cost of making one of their cars," he said. [60]

The National Automobile Dealers Association says the nation's 20,000 new-car and truck dealers are "the economic engine of Main Street," employing 1.1 million people, more than the Big Three combined. [61] "Car dealerships are massively credit-intensive enterprises, and they are seen by lenders as more of a risk without state laws to protect them from being closed down," Bailey Wood, an NADA spokesman, said in defense of the dealer system. He said the average

dealership invests $11 million into its enterprise over the years and that "if you suspended state franchise laws in general it would threaten the nation's economic stability." [62]

Global Trade

As experts look both backward at the roots of the auto industry's woes and forward to potential solutions, they focus not only on such issues as vehicle quality, consumer whims, union work rules and credit shortages but also on the nuances of trade and oil policy and trends in global consumer demand.

Kent Hughes, director of the Program on Science, Technology, America and the Global Economy at the

Woodrow Wilson International Center for Scholars, says that while Detroit has made its share of mistakes, three public policies have also helped shape the fate of the Big Three.

For one thing, he says, in the postwar free-trade model that rose to prominence in the mid-1970s, "you had a situation in which the established companies in the U.S. were carrying a private-sector, welfare-system burden while they were competing with companies [in Japan and Europe] where that responsibility was shared across the whole community. And as productivity accelerated and competition increased, you developed this enormous imbalance" with legacy costs for pensions, medical and job-loss benefits incurred by private American industry.

In addition, Hughes says, the U.S. policy of keeping gasoline prices extraordinarily low compared to prices overseas has led American auto companies to be caught short when pump prices have suddenly shot up, as they did last summer.

"It's kind of the Pogo moment," Hughes says of gas-price policy. "We have met the enemy and he is us. Every time you have had one of these oil shocks, the companies were caught producing the wrong kind of car" — that is, they were meeting demand for "low-gas-price" cars at times when the oil market suddenly became more expensive. The Japanese car companies, on the other hand, "started in a national environment where gas was extremely expensive."

Hughes also says that "for very good geopolitical reasons," Japan was allowed to keep its currency undervalued, which gave Japanese companies a significant price advantage over domestic manufacturers.

Detroit has long argued that currency manipulation by Japan and others, along with other trade barriers, has given foreign manufacturers an edge. "America cannot continue to lead a free-trade agenda while other nations strategically subsidize, support and protect their industries at our expense," Darin Gilley, president of UAW Local 1760, wrote in the St. Louis Post-Dispatch. [63] And Gettelfinger, the UAW president, told Congress, "Our free-trade agreements should be fairer-trade agreements." [64]

But others are skeptical. "The troubles of the Big Three are all made in the USA, and they can't blame competition from South Korea or Japan," says Daniel T. Griswold, director of the Center for Trade Policy Studies at the Cato Institute. "Americans just prefer, on average, to buy foreign-nameplate cars to [those made by] the Big Three."

Detroit's "biggest competitors are not overseas but in other U.S. states," Griswold adds. "You can't blame currency manipulation for the relative success of foreign-owned plants" in places like Texas, Mississippi and South Carolina. ■

CURRENT SITUATION

Government Rescue

As 2009 moves into full swing, many continue to view the car market as a wreck. GM lost its status as the world's biggest carmaker, reporting that it sold about 8.4 million cars and trucks last year, compared with more than 8.9 million for Toyota. [65]

For the entire industry, Autodata reported that U.S. sales of cars and light trucks made by both domestic and foreign producers fell 36 percent in December, the fourth consecutive month that sales failed to crack a million. For all of 2008, sales were off 18 percent to 13.24 million vehicles, the lowest since 1992. [66]

And the bad news continued into this year. GM's U.S. sales in January plunged 49 percent and Chrysler's 55 percent, while Ford and Toyota reported declines of about 40 percent and 32 percent, respectively.

The coming weeks may tell whether GM, Chrysler and the UAW are willing and able to make significant progress toward the long-term financial viability that was a condition of the Bush administration's bailout agreement, and whether Ford can continue to make it on its own.

Wagoner, the GM chief executive, said in mid-January that the automaker had sufficient funding to last through March but could seek more government loans beyond the $13.4 billion allocated in the Bush bailout agreement, Reuters reported. [67]

"The $13.4 billion is consistent with what we asked for through the first quarter under our downside market scenario,

which is the way the market is running," Wagoner said. "We will obviously review the whole plan and at that point we'll see what requirements are." [68]

The agreement includes "binding" conditions, such as requirements that GM and Chrysler limit executive pay, sell their corporate jets and refrain from issuing shareholder dividends until the loans are repaid. But it also includes non-binding "targets," aimed significantly at the UAW, that leave room for negotiation with the new Obama administration. [69]

Those targets include slashing unsecured debt by two-thirds by swapping it for shareholder equity, eliminating the controversial UAW Jobs Bank, making half of the auto companies' contributions to the UAW's retiree health trust in the form of stock rather than cash, and making wages and work rules competitive with those of foreign car companies operating in the United States by the end of this year.

Obama's Approach

Gettelfinger, the UAW president, has charged that the agreement puts too much of an onus on unionized workers and isn't spread evenly enough among all players in the industry. "Other stakeholders have to step in here," he told a broadcast audience shortly after the Bush bailout. "The management, the suppliers, the dealers, the creditors, everybody's going to have to step up. You can't wring it all out of the working men and women." [70]

In a newspaper column in early January, Gettelfinger pledged that the domestic auto industry will "do the hard work necessary to rebuild," but he criticized the loan terms, saying they were "not right" to demand "steeper and faster concessions from the UAW than from any other part of the industry. . . .

"We'll work with the Obama administration and the new Congress to implement a more balanced approach." [71]

Continued on p. 122

At Issue:

Should new-car loans be tax deductible?

SEN. BARBARA A. MIKULSKI, D-MD.

WRITTEN FOR *CQ RESEARCHER*, FEBRUARY 2009

DANIEL IKENSON
ASSOCIATE DIRECTOR, CENTER FOR TRADE
POLICY STUDIES, CATO INSTITUTE

WRITTEN FOR *CQ RESEARCHER*, JANUARY 2009

*w*e are confronting the most severe economic crisis in generations, and we must act quickly and boldly to confront it and create and save jobs.

That is why I introduced an amendment to the American Recovery and Reinvestment Act (ARRA) that creates a tax incentive to encourage people to go into auto showroom.

Why is this a good idea? If someone buys a car, someone's got to make it, someone's got to service it and someone has to provide administrative support. Stimulating Americans' demand for new cars will save jobs up and down the automotive supply chain.

Before I introduced this proposal in the Senate, I visited an automobile dealership in Maryland. A receptionist told me, "Barb, I've worked here on and off for 43 years. I've been able to raise my kids, I've earned a good living, I did the back-office work, and I want to keep on doing it. I'm not ready for Social Security, and for God's sake, don't put the money in Wall Street. I want to keep working."

Right now, our automobile industry is languishing. Last month U.S. auto companies posted their lowest sales totals in more than two decades. The Big Three are at risk of going under, which could cost the government around $156 billion over three years in lost taxes and unemployment benefits. Even worse, the auto industry's collapse would also cost around 3 million Americans their jobs, their health care and their hope for a secure retirement.

Unlike other tax and spending provisions in the ARRA, my provision doesn't spend taxpayer dollars in ways that may not even help the economy. It only costs the Treasury money when someone buys a car.

My amendment also helps states struggling with their bleakest budget outlook in decades. States rely on tax revenues from new car sales to finance infrastructure projects and other big-ticket spending items. In many states, the sales tax is around 6 percent, meaning that when a resident purchases a $25,000 car, the state gets $1,500 in revenue.

I was overjoyed when in a bipartisan vote 70 of my colleagues joined me in support of my amendment. I will continue to fight to keep it in the final economic-recovery package that is signed by President Obama. We've helped the sharks and the whales. Isn't it about time we started helping the minnows?

*b*y allowing car and truck buyers to deduct auto loan interest expenses and sales taxes from their income tax bills, the Mikulski amendment is intended to spur automobile purchases. And that, according to Sen. Mikulski, would "save jobs in the American automobile industry, help consumers and get our economy back on track."

But the amendment is unlikely to spark that chain of events. Although an allowance to write off interest payments and sales tax theoretically could boost sales, the evidence strongly suggests that the impact would be negligible. After all, most auto producers have been offering better incentives than that — like zero percent financing. And dealerships have slashed prices — in some cases well below cost — to induce purchases. Yet, sales continue to decline. It's hard to imagine how tax-deductible interest payments would spur auto purchases when forgoing interest payments altogether hasn't.

Even if Mikulski's plan did spur sales, the impact on jobs would be indiscernible. Producers would attribute new revenues to the temporary demand stimulus, not to a structural demand shift. Accordingly, they would have no incentive to invest and hire more workers — or to slow plant closures or the dismissal of workers. Just look at what happened to business investment and employment after the Bush rebate checks were issued last spring. They both continued their declines, paying no heed to the $150 billion stimulus package.

General Motors and Chrysler have already received taxpayer funds, which are being used to subsidize demand in the form of price cuts and interest-free loans. Further subsidizing price cuts through tax deductions will only increase the industry's reliance on government gimmicks and defer the necessary reforms.

If Congress really wants to help the auto industry recover, it should take a look at the supply side of the equation. Carmakers have been burdened with costly, inefficient rules both imposed by Congress and agreed through labor negotiations. Fuel-efficiency mandates, for example, compel automakers to produce vehicles with low or no profit margins. That hurts the bottom line and discourages investment and hiring. Inflexible, inefficient union work rules and near-full compensation for idled workers have also contributed to the industry's red ink. A bankruptcy judge could help sort that out.

Reducing costs and getting the incentives right on the supply side are keys to industry revitalization. But that process is only hampered by policy makers who claim their snake oil can insulate us all from every economic ache and pain.

Continued from p. 120

U.S. Rep. Barney Frank, D-Mass., chairman of the powerful House Financial Services Committee, has pledged to fight provisions in the loan agreement imposing labor concessions, particularly those seeking to equalize wages and work rules with those of foreign transplants by the end of the year. The union strictures are "an unfair assault on working men and women" inserted into the auto-bailout agreement unilaterally by the Bush administration, he charged. [72]

Obama, who was elected with the UAW's backing, is expected to come under union pressure to back away from some of the targets in the loan agreement. It remains to be seen how far he will be willing to go, though. He has said he wants "to make sure that it's not just workers who are bearing the brunt" of the auto industry's restructuring and that "all shareholders are going to have to play a part in the process." [73]

But the depth of the economic recession, the auto industry's progress this winter toward restructuring itself, and the capacity of the federal government to extend more bailout money all could influence the administration's moves.

In an interview on NBC's "Meet the Press" in early December, before the Bush administration approved the bridge loans, Obama said the Big Three "made repeated strategic mistakes. They have not managed that industry the way they should have, and I've been a strong critic of the auto industry's failure to adapt to changing times — building small cars and energy-efficient cars," Obama said.

But he also called the industry "the backbone of American manufacturing" and added, "I don't think it's an option to simply allow it to collapse." [74]

Among the Obama administration's options in coming months is simply to give Detroit more time — and perhaps more loans — to weather the recession and get its house in order. Another is to steer the auto companies toward a government-structured bankruptcy reorganization, or something close to it.

"On paper, Mr. Obama will inherit a club to wield against the automakers and the unions: he can threaten to 'call' the loans and require repayment in 30 days" if loan conditions aren't met, *The New York Times* noted. "Yet as a practical matter, demanding immediate repayment would be enormously difficult to do, unless Mr. Obama chose to drive the two icons of American industrial strength into bankruptcy court during the first 70 days of his administration." [75]

Global Crisis

The requirements of the loan agreement are not the only hurdles facing Detroit. The auto companies, UAW, suppliers, dealers and others with a stake in the outcome of the industry have a long and twisting road ahead of them — a road made all the more perilous by the global economic crisis.

In documents they submitted to the Senate Banking Committee in early November, the Big Three spelled out ambitious plans to restructure themselves to achieve long-term financial viability. Among the highlights:

• GM said it planned to reduce its nameplate count from 48 last year to 40 in 2012, shift its product lineup so that 22 of 24 new vehicles in 2009-2012 are more fuel-efficient cars and car-based "crossovers," invest some $2.9 billion in "alternative-fuel and advanced-propulsion technologies" by 2012 and introduce its Volt electric vehicle next year. (*See sidebar, p. 116.*) [76]

• Ford said that based on its current business-planning assumptions it expected pre-tax results for its overall and North American automotive business operations to break even or be profitable in 2011. Ford also said it planned to invest some $14 billion in the United States on advanced fuel-efficiency technologies and products over the next seven years. [77]

• Chrysler said it planned 24 major vehicle introductions from this year through 2012 and that 73 percent of its vehicles in the 2009 model year would be more fuel-efficient than 2008 models. Chrysler said its first electric-drive vehicle was slated for introduction in 2010. [78]

Of course, the prospects for the auto industry depend on many things, including the economic outlook and the climate for competition. That climate remains hot even as consumer demand cools.

For example, Volkswagen is investing $1 billion in its new factory in Chattanooga and expects to begin producing 250,000 vehicles there annually in 2012. Audi, VW's upscale brand, plans to boost its U.S. marketing budget 15 percent this year. And BMW, which introduced its One Series small car in the U.S. market last year, plans to introduce new models of the Mini Cooper this year. [79]

Last fall, Hans Dieter Pötsch, VW's chief financial officer, acknowledged the inroads that companies such as Toyota have made in the United States. But he said VW had succeeded in competing with the Japanese car companies elsewhere. "We are the leader in China, not Toyota," he said. "We are already competing successfully against them in other parts of the world. Why not in the U.S.?" [80]

The future of the domestic auto industry will depend in no small part on how the Obama administration handles not only the auto-industry bailout in the months ahead, but also an overall stimulus package and legislative initiatives on such issues as energy, health-care, tax and trade policy.

"If hypothetically over the course of the next year we went to a universal health insurance," it could help to ease the financial burden on domestic carmakers posed by retired autoworkers, says Hughes, the Woodrow Wilson scholar.

On the energy front, Obama issued orders to federal regulators that are expected to toughen fuel-economy and auto-pollution standards — and add new pressures on the U.S. auto industry.

Obama instructed the Environmental Protection Agency to reconsider an application by California and 13 other states to impose tight tailpipe-emission and mileage standards. The Bush administration had opposed the state effort. Obama also told the Transportation Department to issue guidelines related to a 2007 law calling for an industry-wide average fuel-efficiency standard of 35 miles per gallon by 2020, compared with the current 27.5. The Bush administration had not issued such guidelines. [81]

Some argue that a gas tax would be more effective than the traditional approach of using Corporate Average Fuel Economy standards to push automakers and consumers to take energy efficiency and pollution concerns more seriously. "We need to shift away from CAFE with an energy tax," says Smitka of Washington and Lee University. "The U.S. is really unique among many markets in lacking a sensible energy policy."

But with the economy in a deep recession, a gas-tax hike may well be a non-starter. Responding on "Meet the Press" to a question about a gasoline tax, Obama said, "Putting additional burdens on American families right now, I think, is a mistake." [82] ■

OUTLOOK

Too Many Cars?

In the near term, the auto industry's prospects depend in significant ways on the future of the American economy. With unemployment above 7 per-

The battered global economy claims another victim: a Jeep dealership in San Francisco. The nation's new-car dealers employ about 1.1 million people — about half the auto industry's job force.

cent and climbing, and the global recession deepening, demand for new cars is likely to remain seriously depressed.

"We expect the first half of 2009 to feel a lot like the last months of 2008," said Emily Kolinski Morris, an economist at Ford. [83]

Many industry experts worry that Detroit is cranking out more cars than consumers can reasonably be expected to buy. And demand is likely to slow further before it picks up again. AutoNation Inc., the country's largest auto-dealer chain, said it cut its vehicle orders 60 percent during the next three months. [84] "We have three to four months of inventory to work through," Mike Jackson, AutoNation's CEO, told the *Detroit Free Press*. [85]

Late last month, GM said that because of lagging sales, it planned to lay off 2,000 workers at plants in Michigan and Ohio and stop production for several weeks at nine U.S. factories over the next six months. [86]

A slowdown in auto production could hit minorities especially hard. The Economic Policy Institute reported that by last November, almost 20,000 African-American autoworkers had lost jobs since the recession began in December 2007, a 13.9 percent employment decline. That compared with a decline of

4.4 percent for all manufacturing workers. [87]

"African-Americans earn much higher wages in the auto industry than in other parts of the economy, and the loss of these solid, middle-class jobs would be devastating," the institute said. "The motor vehicle and parts industry, a sector of the economy that has been particularly welcoming to African-Americans, is becoming a shrinking island of prosperity."

On the more distant horizon, U.S. automakers are likely to find themselves locked in new competitive battles with foreign car producers. Already, Chinese manufacturers are eyeing the American market, though the poor economy is likely to keep them at bay for a while.

At the North American International Auto Show in Detroit in January, Chinese companies BYD Auto Co., based in Shenzhen, and Brilliance Auto, based in Shenyang, put their vehicles on display between those of GM and Ford. [88]

BYD set a target date of 2011 to begin selling an electric crossover vehicle and a plug-in hybrid sedan. Wang Chua-Fu, chairman and president of BYD Co., said the company planned to develop sales and distribution networks in North America.

Still, said auto-industry analyst Rebecca Lindland, "We have to see some recovery in this market before you can build a business case for starting a business in this market." [89] ■

Notes

[1] Dow Jones, "GM CEO Defends UAW, Hopeful for a Deal," Dec. 22, 2008, http://money.cnn.com/news/newsfeeds/articles/djf500/200812221009DOWJONESDJONLINE000298_FORTUNE5.htm.

[2] "U.S. Light Vehicle Retail Sales-December 2008," Autodata, www.motorintelligence.com/m_frameset.html.

[3] See "Fact Sheet: Financing Assistance to Facilitate the Restructuring of Auto Manufacturers to Attain Financial Viability," Dec. 19, 2008, www.whitehouse.gov/news/releases/2008/12/20081219-6.html.

[4] "UAW applauds auto loans but says workers must not be singled out for unfair conditions," United Auto Workers, Dec. 19, 2008, www.uaw.org/auto/12_19_08auto1.cfm.

[5] Nick Bunkley, "Fiat Acquires 35% Stake in Chrysler," *The New York Times*, Jan. 20, 2009, www.nytimes.com/2009/01/21/business/21chrysler.html?hp.

[6] John D. Stoll and Stacy Meichtry, "Chrysler-Fiat Deal Needs U.S. Loans," *The Wall Street Journal*, Jan. 21, 2009, p. 1B.

[7] John D. Stoll and Sharon Terlep, "UAW, Bondholder Talks Slow GM's Revamp," *The Wall Street Journal*, Jan. 13, 2009.

[8] Yuri Kageyama, "Toyota projects first loss in 70 years, bowing to global slowdown," The Associated Press, Dec. 22, 2008, http://biz.yahoo.com/ap/081222/as_japan_toyota.html.

[9] Testimony before Senate Committee on Banking, Housing and Urban Affairs, Dec. 4, 2008, http://clipsandcomment.com/wp-content/uploads/2008/12/wagonergmtestimony12408.pdf.

[10] David Cole, *et al.*, "The Impact on the U.S. Economy of a Major Contraction of the Detroit Three Automakers," Nov. 4, 2008, www.cargroup.org.

[11] White House press release, "President Bush Discusses Administration's Plan to Assist Automakers," Dec. 19, 2008, www.whitehouse.gov/news/releases/2008/12/20081219.html.

[12] Herman Wang, "GOP lawmakers pan Bush's auto bailout," *Chattanooga Times Free Press*, www.msnbc, Dec. 20, 2008, www.msnbc.msn.com/id/28321668/.

[13] "Obama on auto bailout," *Politico*, Dec. 19, 2008, www.politico.com/news/stories/1208/16749.html.

[14] White House press release, *op. cit.*

[15] Andrew M. Grossman and James L. Gattuso, "TARP: Now a Slush Fund for Detroit," Heritage Foundation, No. 2170, Dec. 12, 2008.

[16] Andrew M. Grossman, "Automakers Need Bankruptcy, Not Bailout," Heritage Foundation, No. 33, Nov. 14, 2008.

[17] Scott Conroy, "GOP Senators Write Bush To Oppose Using TARP Funds for Auto Bailout," Dec. 16, 2008, CBS News.

[18] See http://images.newsmax.com/pdfs/auto_bailout_dec08.pdf.

[19] Press release, "Anderson Economic Group, Automaker Bankruptcy Would Cost Taxpayers Four Times More Than Amount of Federal Bridge Loans," Dec. 8, 2008.

[20] Paul Ingrassia, "Bush Blinks on the Auto Bailout," *The Wall Street Journal*, Dec. 15, 2008, p. A19.

[21] Quoted in "BandAid Will Not Help U.S. Auto Industry, Says Washington and Lee Economist," Washington and Lee University, Nov. 19, 2008, www.wlu.edu/x27644.xml.

[22] Logan Robinson, "Why Detroit Has an Especially Bad Union Problem," *The Wall Street Journal*, Dec. 30, 2008, p. A11.

[23] UAW, "The truth about UAW members and the U.S. auto industry," Dec. 2, 2008, www.uaw.org/auto/12_02_08auto1.cfm.

[24] Quoted in David Leonhardt, "$73 an Hour: Adding It Up," *The New York Times*, Dec. 10, 2008.

[25] UAW, *op. cit.*

[26] Steve Eder, "UAW workers' pay on par with Japanese competitors in U.S.," *Toledo Blade*, Dec. 13, 2008, www.toledoblade.com/apps/pbcs.dll/article?AID=/20081213/BUSINESS02/812130362.

[27] Leonhardt, *op. cit.*

[28] Neal Boudette, in "Ten Hard Questions Facing the 'Car Czar,' " *The Wall Street Journal*, Jan. 22, 2009, p. 12A.

[29] *Ibid.*

[30] UAW, *op. cit.*

[31] Sharon Silke Carty, "UAW suspends jobs bank, delays retiree fund payments," *USA Today*, Dec. 4, 2008.

[32] Quoted on National Public Radio's "The Diane Rehm Show," "The Fate of the Auto Industry," WAMU, Nov. 17, 2008.

[33] Patel's statement came in a research note quoted in John D. Stoll, "With U.S. Help, GMAC Revs Up Car Loans," *The Wall Street Journal*, Dec. 31, 2008, p. B1.

[34] Press release, "Mikulski Angered by Senate Inaction," Nov. 20, 2008.

[35] Kate Linebaugh, in "Ten Hard questions Facing the 'Car Czar,' " *op. cit.*

[36] *Ibid.*

[37] Peter Morici, "Bush's auto plan will test Obama's union loyalties," Reuters, Dec. 22, 2008, http://blogs.reuters.com/great-debate/2008/12/22/bushs-auto-plan-will-test-obamas-union-loyalties/.

[38] Bill Vlasic, "A Risk for Ford in Shunning Bailout, and Possibly a Reward," *The New York Times*, Dec. 20, 2008.

[39] *Ibid.*

[40] Quoted in *ibid.*

[41] Quoted in Sholnn Freeman, "Ford, Others Still Must Negotiate Rough Road," *The Washington Post*, Dec. 20, 2008, p. D1.

[42] Megan Whalen, "Mulally: Ford in different place than rest," *The Detroit Free Press*, Jan. 9, 2009.

[43] Axel Madsen, *The Deal Maker* (1999), pp. 115-116.

[44] Stephen E. Frank and E.S. Browning, "Bursting of the Tech Bubble Has a Familiar 'Pop' to It," *The Wall Street Journal*, March 2, 2001.

[45] Kenneth E. Train and Clifford Winston, "Vehicle Choice Behavior and the Declining Market Share of U.S. Automakers," AEI-Brookings Joint Center for Regulatory Studies, May 2006.

[46] Terry Box, "Toyota Marks 50 years in U.S.," *Dallas Morning News*, Oct. 28, 2007.

[47] Train and Winston, *op. cit.*

[48] For background, see Barbara Mantel, "Energy Efficiency," *CQ Researcher*, May 19, 2006, pp. 433-456, and Mary H. Cooper, "SUV Debate," *CQ Researcher*, May 16, 2003, pp. 449-472.

[49] David Halberstam, *The Reckoning* (1986), p. 529.

[50] Micheline Maynard, *The End of Detroit* (2003), p. 10.

[51] Fred Barnes, "The Other American Auto Industry," *The Weekly Standard*, Dec. 22, 2008, www.weeklystandard.com/Content/Public/Articles/000/000/015/918gvijq.asp.

About the Author

Thomas J. Billitteri is a *CQ Researcher* staff writer based in Fairfield, Pa., who has more than 30 years' experience covering business, nonprofit institutions and public policy for newspapers and other publications. His recent *CQ Researcher* reports include "Campaign Finance," "Human Rights in China" and "Financial Bailout." He holds a BA in English and an MA in journalism from Indiana University.

[52] Michael Lind, "The Economic Civil War," *Salon.com*, Dec. 18, 2008, www.salon.com/opinion/feature/2008/12/18/third_reconstruction/.

[53] Maynard, *op. cit.*, p. 21.

[54] *Ibid.*, pp. 21, 23.

[55] "America's Other Auto Industry," *The Wall Street Journal*, Dec. 1, 2008.

[56] Greg Bensinger, "GM, Chrysler to Thin Dealer Ranks as U.S. Gives Aid," Bloomberg, Dec. 29, 2008, www.bloomberg.com/apps/news?pid=20601103&sid=aOzFpIwgR0a4&refer=news.

[57] "Ford Motor Company Business Plan" submitted to Senate Banking Committee, Dec. 2, 2008, p. 11.

[58] Roland Jones, "Auto dealers face days of reckoning," MSNBC, Dec. 17, 2008, www.msnbc.msn.com/id/28142528/.

[59] Quoted in Bensinger, *op. cit.*

[60] Quoted in Jones, *op. cit.*

[61] Open letter, National Automobile Dealers Association, "Auto Dealers: The Economic Engine of Main Street," Nov. 17, 2008, www.nada.org/Advocacy+Outreach/Auto+Financing+Resources/USATodayAd.htm.

[62] Quoted in Jones, *op. cit.*

[63] Darin Gilley, "What has crippled America's auto industry? Mistakes in tax, trade, health care and energy policies," *St. Louis Post-Dispatch*, Dec. 24, 2008, p. 9B.

[64] Kendra Marr, "For Auto Industry, Bailout Considered Just a First Step," *The Washington Post*, Dec. 11, 2008, p. 1D.

[65] The Associated Press, "GM Falls Behind Toyota in Annual Global Sales," Jan. 21, 2009, www.nytimes.com/aponline/2009/01/21/business/AP-GM-Global-Sales.html.

[66] Figures are from Autodata Corp., a research firm in Woodcliff Lake, N.J., and are cited in Sharon Terlep and Matthew Dolan, "Auto Makers Close Books on Awful Year, Face More Ills," *The Wall Street Journal*, Jan. 6, 2009.

[67] Kevin Krolicki, "GM says could seek further loans," Reuters, Jan. 12, 2009.

[68] Quoted in *ibid.*

[69] See "Fact Sheet: Financing Assistance to Facilitate the Restructuring of Auto Manufacturers to Attain financial Viability," The White House, Dec. 19, 2008.

[70] Quoted in "Gettelfinger: UAW not included in negotiations with Bush," *The Detroit Free Press*, Dec. 22, 2008, www.freep.com/article/20081222/BUSINESS01/81222022/1014. The newspaper said Gettelfinger's comments came on Fox Business Network's "Money for Breakfast" program.

[71] Ron Gettelfinger, "Gettelfinger: Change policies to aid auto industry," *Detroit News*, Jan. 2, 2009, www.detnews.com/apps/pbcs.dll/article?AID=2009901020310.

[72] "Frank Statement on White House Auto Rescue Plan," Dec. 19, 2008, www.house.gov/frank/autobailrobo.html.

[73] Jonathan Weisman, "Rescue to Give Obama Enormous Influence Over Industry," *The Wall Street Journal*, Dec. 20-21, 2008, p. A6.

[74] Quoted on "Meet the Press," Dec. 7, 2008, www.msnbc.msn.com/id/28097635/.

[75] David E. Sanger, David M. Herszenhorn and Bill Vlasic, "Bush Aids Detroit, but Hard Choices Wait for Obama," *The New York Times*, Dec. 20, 2008.

[76] "General Motors Corporation Restructuring Plan for Long-Term Viability Submitted to Senate Banking Committee & House of Representatives Financial Services Committee," Dec. 2, 2008, http://financialservices.house.gov/GMPlan.pdf.

[77] Press release, "Ford Motor Company Submits Business Plan to Congress," www.ford.com/about-ford/news-announcements/press-releases/press-releases-detail/pr-ford-motor-company-submits-29508. See also "Ford Motor Company Business Plan Submitted to the Senate Banking Committee," Dec. 2, 2008, http://media.ford.com/images/10031/Ford_Motor_Company_Business_Plan.pdf.

[78] Press release, "Highlights of Chrysler LLC Plan Submitted Today to the Senate Committee on Banking, Housing and Urban Affairs and the House Committee on Financial Services," Dec. 2, 2008, www.media.chrysler.com/newsrelease.do?id=8390&mid=1. See also "Chrysler's Plan for Short-Term and Long-Term Viability," Senate Committee on Banking, Housing and Urban Affairs, Dec. 4, 2008.

[79] Kate Linebaugh, "Europeans Raise Pressure on Detroit," *The Wall Street Journal*, Jan. 5, 2009.

[80] Quoted in *ibid.*

[81] See John M. Broder and Peter Baker, "Obama's Order Is Likely to Tighten Auto Standards," *The New York Times*, Jan. 26, 2009, and William Branigin, Juliet Eilperin and Steven Mufson, "Obama Plans to Overhaul Environmental Policies," *The Washington Post*, Jan. 26, 2009.

[82] Quoted on "Meet the Press," *op. cit.*, Dec. 7, 2008, www.msnbc.msn.com/id/28097635/.

[83] Terlep and Dolan, *op. cit.*

[84] Sarah A. Webster, "Growing inventory tops industry concerns," *The Detroit Free Press*, Jan. 12, 2009.

[85] Quoted in *ibid.*

[86] Kimberly S. Johnson, "GM to lay off 2,000 workers, cut production," The Associated Press, Jan. 26, 2009, www.breitbart.com/article.php?id=D95UVNJ81&show_article=1.

[87] Mary M. Chapman, "Black Workers Hurt by Detroit's Ills," *The New York Times*, Dec. 30, 2008.

[88] The Associated Press, "Chinese Automakers Face Headwinds to U.S. Sales," Jan. 12, 2009, www.nytimes.com/aponline/2009/01/12/business/AP-Auto-Show-China.html.

[89] Quoted in *ibid.*

FOR MORE INFORMATION

Center for Automotive Research, 1000 Victors Way, Suite 200, Ann Arbor, MI 48108; (734) 662-1287; www.cargroup.org. Studies trends in the automotive industry.

Center for Trade Policy Studies, Cato Institute, 1000 Massachusetts Ave., N.W., Washington, DC 20001; (202) 842-0200; www.freetrade.org. Think tank advocating open markets for wider choices and lower prices for businesses and consumers.

Edmunds.com, 1620 26th St., Suite 400S, Santa Monica, CA 90404; (310) 309-6300; www.edmunds.com. Online source for automotive information.

National Automobile Dealers Association, 8400 Westpark Dr., McLean VA 22101; (703) 821-7000 or (800) 252-6232; www.nada.org. Trade association for more than 19,700 new-car and truck dealers with more than 43,000 franchises.

Program on Science, Technology, America and the Global Economy, Woodrow Wilson International Center for Scholars, 1300 Pennsylvania Ave., N.W., Washington, DC 20004; (202) 691-4000; www.wilsoncenter.org/index.cfm?fuseaction=topics.home&topic_id=1408. Explores key developments and innovative systems that influence the economic growth of the United States.

United Autoworkers, Solidarity House, 8000 East Jefferson Ave., Detroit, MI 48214; (313) 926-5000; www.uaw.org. Labor union representing about 513,000 active members and more than 575,000 retired members in the United States, Canada and Puerto Rico.

Bibliography

Selected Sources

Books

Halberstam, David, *The Reckoning*, William Morrow and Co., 1986.
A celebrated journalist provides an in-depth look at Japan's early challenge to American industrial might largely through the stories of two automakers, Ford and Nissan.

Madsen, Axel, *The Deal Maker*, John Wiley & Sons, 1999.
The biography of William C. Durant, who founded General Motors a century ago, illuminates the rough-and-tumble early years of American auto production.

Maxton, Graeme P., and John Wormald, *Time for a Model Change*, Cambridge University Press, 2004.
Directors of a strategic-consulting firm focusing on the global auto industry argue in this data-filled book that car companies must redefine their business and "re-cut them along new and much more economically attractive lines."

Maynard, Micheline, *The End of Detroit*, Doubleday, 2003.
A *New York Times* auto-industry reporter argues that the Big Three car companies stumbled in the 1990s in part by putting too much emphasis on trucks and sport-utility vehicles.

Shnayerson, Michael, *The Car That Could*, Random House, 1996.
A journalist presents an early inside look at the business, technological and political developments behind General Motors' creation of a revolutionary electric vehicle in the 1990s — a project GM ultimately abandoned.

Articles

Barnes, Fred, "The Other American Auto Industry," *The Weekly Standard*, Dec. 22, 2008, www.weeklystandard.com/Content/Public/Articles/000/000/015/918gvijq.asp.
The South has attracted a "staggering" amount of auto production from foreign manufacturers, and the companies have succeeded with the help of government inducements, inexpensive land and labor and the absence of the United Auto Workers.

Bartiromo, Maria, "Carlos Ghosn on Detroit and the Future of the Auto Business," *Business Week*, Dec. 1, 2008, www.businessweek.com/magazine/content/08_48/b4110 000510031.htm?campaign_id=rss_topStories.
The chief executive of both Renault of France and Nissan of Japan says in this Q&A that "everything is lined up to push toward consolidation of the [auto] industry."

French, Ron, "How General Motors and the nation are losing an epic battle to tame the health care beast," *Detroit News*, Sept. 26, 2006, www.detnews.com/apps/pbcs.dll/article?AID=/20060926/LIFESTYLE03/609260338.
Worker and retiree medical bills are driving the world's largest automaker "deep into financial trouble," concludes this examination of GM's health-care liabilities.

Ingrassia, Paul, "The Case for Chapter 11," *Condé Nast Portfolio*, December 2008/January 2009.
Rather than being a "death sentence," a bankruptcy filing by General Motors could provide the company a chance to streamline its operations, argues a veteran auto-industry journalist.

Muller, Joann, "Time Is Up," *Forbes*, Dec. 22, 2008, www.forbes.com/forbes/2008/1222/032.html.
Assuming General Motors survives its financial crisis, it will look far leaner than it has been, with far fewer nameplates, models, factories and dealers, and its troubles will be painful for taxpayers as well as workers, says a business journalist.

Reports and Studies

Anderson, Patrick L., and Kriss Andrews, "Taxpayer Cost of Federal Financing of Auto Manufacturers Compared with Likely Costs of Bankruptcies in Industries," Anderson Economic Group and BBK, Dec. 8, 2008, www.andersoneconomicgroup.com/Portals/0/upload/CostComp-Bankrutpcy-AEGBBK.pdf.
Bankruptcy in the auto industry would be far costlier to taxpayers than federal bridge loans, the study concludes.

Cole, David, *et al.*, "The Impact on the U.S. Economy of a Major Contraction of the Detroit Three Automakers," Center for Automotive Research, Nov. 4, 2008, www.cargroup.org/documents/FINALDetroitThreeContractionImpact_3_000.pdf.
The research group says nearly 3 million jobs would disappear in the first year if the Big Three automakers shut their U.S. operations.

Scott, Robert E., "When Giants Fall," Economic Policy Institute, Dec. 3, 2008, Briefing Paper #227, http://epi.3cdn.net/2bd165784352680c37_i7m6b9eqf.pdf.
The think tank concludes that the shutdown of one or more of the domestic automakers could wipe out up to 3.3 million American jobs.

Wial, Howard, "How a Metro Nation Would Feel the Loss of the Detroit Three Automakers," Metropolitan Policy Program, Brookings Institution, December 2008, www.brookings.edu/~/media/Files/rc/papers/2008/1212_automakers_wial/automakers_wial.pdf.
The loss of auto or auto-parts jobs amounting to 1 percent of a metro area's employment could mean the loss of up to 3 percent of the area's jobs overall, concludes a Brookings scholar.

The Next Step:

Additional Articles from Current Periodicals

Bailout

Bookman, Jay, "Putting Politicians in Charge of Detroit?" *Atlanta Journal-Constitution*, **Dec. 8, 2008.**

A bailout plan for automakers could include a Cabinet-level oversight board and a provision to withdraw any money if overseers don't see an attempt by automakers to reform themselves.

Chaddock, Gail Russell, "Tough Line on Auto Bailout May Extend to Other Industries," *The Christian Science Monitor*, **Dec. 15, 2008, p. 2.**

A $14 billion auto bailout opens up arguments in Congress over which struggling industries should receive bailouts.

Dorning, Mike, "Obama Advisors: Carmakers Need a Recovery Plan," *Los Angeles Times*, **Nov. 24, 2008, p. C5.**

President Obama's advisors have suggested that automakers should present viable proposals for restructuring prior to receiving any federal bailout funds.

Ramirez, Charles E., and Mark Hicks, "Mayors Want Part of Auto Bailout," *Detroit News*, **Nov. 11, 2008, p. 1B.**

Mayors of four Detroit suburbs want a share of the federal bailout sought by the Big Three automakers to help redevelop shuttered facilities and factories.

Employment

Bentayou, Frank, and Robert Schoenberger, "Auto Industry Not Alone in Its Downward Spiral," *Plain Dealer* **(Ohio), Nov. 14, 2008, p. A1.**

About 71,000 jobs in Cleveland and northeastern Ohio depend on a healthy automotive industry.

Copeland, Larry, "African Americans Feel Auto Industry's Pain," *USA Today*, **Jan. 21, 2009, p. 9B.**

The crisis of the auto industry threatens to undermine a half-century's employment and economic gain by the black middle class.

McCurdy, Dave, "Keeping Auto Industry Healthy Remains Critical," *Detroit News*, **Nov. 19, 2008, p. 11A.**

Every automotive plant job generates another five jobs among suppliers and the surrounding community, compared to just two additional jobs for every Wall Street position.

Hybrid Cars

Healey, James R., "Ford Plans Plug-In Hybrids for 2012," *USA Today*, **Feb. 3, 2009, p. 8A.**

Ford plans to showcase plug-in hybrid vehicles by 2012, promising 30 miles on battery power before using any gasoline.

Mufson, Steven, "The Car of the Future — But at What

Cost?" *The Washington Post*, **Nov. 25, 2008, p. A1.**

Hybrid vehicles are becoming more popular, but making them profitable is a challenge facing many automakers.

Sherman, Don, "Cranking the Volt to 100 M.P.G.," *The New York Times*, **Nov. 16, 2008, p. AU1.**

The Chevrolet Volt should easily double the fuel efficiency of most other hybrid vehicles, such as the Toyota Prius.

Unions

Aguilar, Louis, "United Auto Workers Will Suspend Jobs Bank, Make Other Concession to Aid Automakers and Win Bailout," *Detroit News*, **Dec. 4, 2008.**

The United Auto Workers is willing to suspend its controversial jobs bank and consider modifications to its contracts if it helps the Big Three secure bailout funds.

Puzzanghera, Jim, "Senate GOP Took a Swipe at Unions," *Los Angeles Times*, **Dec. 13, 2008, p. A1.**

Many Republican congressmen are refusing to help the United Auto Workers in any bailout deals.

Stoll, John D., "UAW, Bondholder Talks Slow GM's Revamp," *The Wall Street Journal*, **Jan. 13, 2009, p. B1.**

General Motors is struggling to meet mandates of its federal bailout agreement amid unproductive negotiations with the United Auto Workers.

Whoriskey, Peter, "Views on Auto Aid Fall on North-South Divide," *The Washington Post*, **Dec. 14, 2008, p. A1.**

Non-union auto employees — who aren't expected to receive a share of any bailout funds — are opposed to a bailout for Detroit's Big Three.

CITING CQ RESEARCHER

Sample formats for citing these reports in a bibliography include the ones listed below. Preferred styles and formats vary, so please check with your instructor or professor.

MLA STYLE

Jost, Kenneth. "Rethinking the Death Penalty." CQ Researcher 16 Nov. 2001: 945-68.

APA STYLE

Jost, K. (2001, November 16). Rethinking the death penalty. *CQ Researcher, 11,* 945-968.

CHICAGO STYLE

Jost, Kenneth. "Rethinking the Death Penalty." *CQ Researcher,* November 16, 2001, 945-968.

In-depth Reports on Issues in the News

Are you writing a paper?

Need backup for a debate?

Want to become an expert on an issue?

For 80 years, students have turned to *CQ Researcher* for in-depth reporting on issues in the news. Reports on a full range of political and social issues are now available. Following is a selection of recent reports:

Civil Liberties
Limiting Lawsuits, 12/08
Affirmative Action, 10/08
Gay Marriage Showdowns, 9/08
America's Border Fence, 9/08
Immigration Debate, 2/08
Prison Reform, 4/07

Crime/Law
Mexico's Drug War, 12/08
Prostitution Debate, 5/08
Public Defenders, 4/08
Gun Violence, 5/07

Education
Reading Crisis? 2/08
Discipline in Schools, 2/08
Student Aid, 1/08
Racial Diversity in Public Schools, 9/07
Stress on Students, 7/07

Environment
Reducing Carbon Footprint, 12/08
Protecting Wetlands, 10/08
Buying Green, 2/08
Future of Recycling, 12/07

Health/Safety
Preventing Cancer, 1/09
Heart Health, 9/08
Global Food Crisis, 6/08
Preventing Memory Loss, 4/08

International Affairs/Politics
The Obama Presidency, 1/09
The National Debt, 11/08
Financial Bailout, 10/08
Political Conventions, 8/08
Race and Politics, 7/08

Social Trends
Falling Birthrates, 11/08
Regulating Credit Cards, 10/08
Internet Accuracy, 8/08
Financial Crisis, 5/08
Cyberbullying, 5/08

Terrorism/Defense
Rise in Counterinsurgency, 9/08
Cost of the Iraq War, 4/08

Youth
Debating Hip-Hop, 6/07

Upcoming Reports

Homeland Security, 2/13/09   Public Works, 2/20/09   Closing Guantánamo, 2/27/09

ACCESS

CQ Researcher is available in print and online. For access, visit your library or www.cqresearcher.com.

STAY CURRENT

To receive notice of upcoming *CQ Researcher* reports, or learn more about *CQ Researcher* products, subscribe to the free e-mail newsletters, *CQ Researcher Alert!* and *CQ Researcher News*: http://cqpress.com/newsletters.

PURCHASE

To purchase a *CQ Researcher* report in print or electronic format (PDF), visit www.cqpress.com or call 866-427-7737. Single reports start at $15. Bulk purchase discounts and electronic-rights licensing are also available.

SUBSCRIBE

Annual full-service *CQ Researcher* subscriptions—including 44 reports a year, monthly index updates, and a bound volume—start at $803. Add $25 for domestic postage.

CQ Researcher Online offers a backfile from 1991 and a number of tools to simplify research. For pricing information, call 800-834-9020, ext. 1906, or e-mail librarysales@cqpress.com.

Published by CQ Press, a division of SAGE Publications

www.cqresearcher.com

Homeland Security

Is America safe from terrorism today?

F ollowing the Sept. 11, 2001, terrorist attacks, the U.S. government created the Department of Homeland Security, giving it stepped-up power to shadow and detain terrorism suspects. Then-President George W. Bush credited these measures — and intelligence and military operations abroad — with preventing new attacks on U.S. soil in the nearly eight years since 9/11. But some intelligence experts argue that the new department failed to coordinate the nation's many turf-conscious intelligence agencies, and that continued U.S. military pressure has rendered Osama bin Laden's al Qaeda terrorist network incapable of mounting new attacks within the United States. Moreover, jihadist cells that have wreaked havoc in Europe lack counterparts in the U.S., where Muslims are far less alienated, experts say. Still, the danger of a new attack remains. According to an emerging school of thought, Americans should learn to live with the possibility of an eventual attack, rather than expecting government to eliminate all danger.

Al Qaeda terrorists crash United Airlines Flight 175 into the World Trade Center's south tower at 9:03 a.m. on Sept. 11, 2001, about 17 minutes after other hijackers flew American Airlines Flight 11 into the north tower.

CQ Researcher • Feb. 13, 2009 • www.cqresearcher.com
Volume 19, Number 6 • Pages 129-152

CQ Researcher

Feb. 13, 2009
Volume 19, Number 6

MANAGING EDITOR: Thomas J. Colin
tcolin@cqpress.com

ASSISTANT MANAGING EDITOR: Kathy Koch
kkoch@cqpress.com

ASSOCIATE EDITOR: Kenneth Jost

STAFF WRITERS: Thomas J. Billitteri, Marcia Clemmitt, Peter Katel

CONTRIBUTING WRITERS: Sarah Glazer, Alan Greenblatt, Barbara Mantel, Patrick Marshall, Tom Price, Jennifer Weeks

DESIGN/PRODUCTION EDITOR: Olu B. Davis

ASSISTANT EDITOR: Darrell Dela Rosa

FACT-CHECKING: Eugene J. Gabler, Michelle Harris

EDITORIAL INTERN: Vyomika Jairam

CQ PRESS

A Division of SAGE Publications

PRESIDENT AND PUBLISHER:
John A. Jenkins

EXECUTIVE DIRECTOR, REFERENCE INFORMATION GROUP:
Alix B. Vance

CQ Press is a registered trademark of Congressional Quarterly Inc.

CQ Researcher (ISSN 1056-2036) is printed on acid-free paper. Published weekly, except; (Jan. wk. 1) (May wk. 4) (July wks. 1, 2) (Aug. wks. 3, 4) (Nov. wk. 4) and (Dec. wk. 4), by CQ Press, a division of SAGE Publications. Annual full-service subscriptions start at $803. For pricing, call 1-800-834-9020, ext. 1906. To purchase a CQ Researcher report in print or electronic format (PDF), visit www. cqpress.com or call 866-427-7737. Single reports start at $15. Bulk purchase discounts and electronic-rights licensing are also available. Periodicals postage paid at Washington, D.C., and additional mailing offices. POSTMASTER: Send address changes to CQ Researcher, 2300 N St., N.W., Suite 800, Washington, DC 20037.

Cover: Getty Images/Spencer Platt

Homeland Security

BY PETER KATEL

THE ISSUES

The attackers struck in the last days of November 2008. With terrifying precision, shooters in five two-man teams moved from target to target, unleashing lethal bursts of automatic weapons fire in the train station, an upscale restaurant, two luxury hotels and a Jewish cultural center.

By the time the terrorists had been killed or captured three days later, 173 people had been slain. [1]

The massacre occurred in Mumbai, India, but 7,800 miles away, New York City Police Commissioner Raymond W. Kelly couldn't help but notice some troubling parallels. Mumbai, he told the Senate Homeland Security Committee in January, is "the country's financial capital, a densely populated, multi-cultural metropolis and a hub for the media and entertainment industries. Obviously, these are also descriptions of New York City."

In the post-9/11 world, Kelly's job is to make such connections. But among Americans in general, beset by foreclosures, job layoffs and other manifestations of the global economic meltdown, terrorism fears have diminished in the years since the Sept. 11, 2001, attacks on the World Trade Center and Pentagon.

"There may be a false sense of security in the United States because we haven't been attacked in seven years," says Bruce Hoffman, a professor at Georgetown University's School of Foreign Service and former scholar-in-residence for counterterrorism at the Central Intelligence Agency (CIA).

The Taj Mahal Hotel in Mumbai burns last November during attacks by Islamic militants throughout the city — India's financial capital — that killed 173 people. Afterwards, New York City's police commissioner noted chilling parallels between the two huge metropolises.

AFP/Getty Images/Indranil Mukherjee

Indeed, while the Mumbai attacks seem as distant from the United States as South Asia itself, Hoffman and others view Mumbai as a wake-up call for the United States.

The attacks have been linked to Lashkar-e-Taiba (LeT), or the "Army of the Pure," a Pakistani group with deep connections to Pakistan's intelligence service. LeT seeks to force India to cede Kashmir to Pakistan, which, like Kashmir is majority Muslim. The group shares longstanding ties with Osama bin Laden's jihadist group al Qaeda, which carried out the 9/11 attacks. [2]

While the daily fear that gripped Americans after Sept. 11 may have faded, the nation nonetheless has remained on high alert ever since, its security infrastructure extensively strengthened.

Creation of the Department of Homeland Security (DHS) the year after the attacks reflected officials' certainty that further terrorist strikes were imminent. Since then, increasingly intense airport screenings provide constant reminders of danger, along with warnings by terrorism experts that the United States' 361 ports and long borders leave the nation vulnerable.

"America's margin of safety against a WMD (weapon of mass destruction) attack is shrinking," a blue-ribbon congressional commission reported in December, pointing specifically at Pakistan and the jihadist groups flourishing there. "Were one to map terrorism and weapons of mass destruction today, all roads would intersect in Pakistan. . . . Trends in South Asia, if left unchecked, will increase the odds that al Qaeda will successfully develop and use a nuclear device or biological weapon against the United States or its allies." [3]

Bin Laden is doing his best to keep fears alive. Five days before Barack Obama's Jan. 20 inauguration, a recording released by bin Laden said the new president was "inheriting two wars, in which he is not able to continue, and we are on our way to open other fronts, God willing." [4]

Thought to be holed up in the mountainous tribal-ruled belt of northwestern Pakistan, bin Laden and his top commanders — notably Ayman al-Zawahiri, an Egyptian doctor who is considered al Qaeda's second-in-command — remain America's No. 1

Inside the Department of Homeland Security

After the Sept. 11, 2001, terrorist attacks, Congress created the Department of Homeland Security in an effort to reassure the American public and improve intelligence gathering and processing. The DHS employs some 200,000 people in two-dozen separate agencies, most culled from other departments. But many major intelligence agencies remain outside the new department, leading to criticism the DHS left untouched the biggest problem revealed by 9/11: The inability of U.S. intelligence services, notably the CIA and FBI, to share and digest collected intelligence.

Agencies That Moved to the Department of Homeland Security
(Departments where agencies were previously located are in parentheses.)

Border and Transportation Security
U.S. Customs Service (Treasury)
Bureau of Citizenship and Immigration Services (Justice)
Federal Protective Service (General Services Administration)
Transportation Security Administration (Transportation)
Federal Law Enforcement Training Center (Treasury)
Animal and Plant Health Inspection Service (Agriculture, part transferred)
Office for Domestic Preparedness (Justice)

Emergency Preparedness and Response
Federal Emergency Management Agency (formerly independent)
Strategic National Stockpile and the National Disaster Medical System (Health and Human Services)
Nuclear Incident Response Team (Energy)
Domestic Emergency Support Teams (Justice)
National Domestic Preparedness Office (FBI)

Information Analysis and Infrastructure Protection
Critical Infrastructures Office (Commerce)
Federal Computer Incident Response Center (General Services Administration)
National Communications System (Defense)
National Infrastructure Protection Center (FBI)
Energy Security and Assurance Program (Energy)

Science and Technology
Chemical, Biological, and Radiological Countermeasures Program (Energy)
Environmental Measures Laboratory (Energy)
National Biological Warfare Defense Analysis Center (Defense)
Plum Island Animal Disease Center (Agriculture)

Citizenship and Immigration Services

Bureau of Citizenship and Immigration Services (Justice)

Coast Guard (Transportation)

Secret Service (Treasury)

Source: Department of Homeland Security

counterterrorism targets. As Defense Secretary Robert Gates told the Senate Armed Services Committee in January: "We will go after al Qaeda wherever al Qaeda is." [5]

Still, some veteran terrorism analysts say bin Laden's network no longer commands the funds, communications facilities nor technical expertise necessary to plan and carry out a major attack in the United States.

Marc Sageman, a former CIA officer in Pakistan, notes that the London subway and bus attacks in 2005 mark the last effective al Qaeda action outside Asia or Africa. [6] "There has not been a single fatality from al Qaeda or an al Qaeda-linked group in the West since July 7, 2005," Sageman, now a consultant to the NYPD's counterterrorism division, told a Washington conference sponsored by the Cato Institute think tank in January.

Another longtime expert on al Qaeda, Peter Bergen, noted recently that intensive investigations since 9/11 failed to uncover a single al Qaeda "sleeper cell" in the United States or any operatives on immediate missions. "While a small-bore attack may be organized by a Qaeda wannabe at some point, a catastrophic, mass-casualty assault along the lines of 9/11 is no longer plausible," said Bergen, a journalist and a fellow at the nonpartisan New America Foundation, who interviewed bin Laden in 1997. [7]

John Mueller, an Ohio State University political scientist, has been arguing for several years that U.S. officials have vastly exaggerated the extent of terrorism danger to the United States. "It's looking more and more that 9/11 was an outlier," says Mueller, author of a 2006 book on terrorism. "Even if you assume that U.S. protection measures are 90 percent effective, that would mean that some al Qaeda agents would have been caught entering the United States. The fact that the government can't find any means that al Qaeda isn't trying." [8]

Even experts who question the need for some security procedures call Mueller's position extreme. Al Qaeda and its allies "would kill you if they could," says James Jay Carafano, director of the conservative Heritage Foundation's Kathryn and Shelby Cullom Davis Institute for International Studies. Minimizing terrorism threats would be risky, he argues. "If you get a cold and just ignore it, then you get pneumonia and die."

However, experiments conducted last year by journalist Jeffrey Goldberg suggest that domestic aviation security, at least, wouldn't stop terrorists. Goldberg got on a flight from Minneapolis-St. Paul to Washington with a forged boarding pass, no driver's license and a coat (in summertime) over an Osama bin Laden t-shirt. A security supervisor let Goldberg through. " 'All right, you can go,' " he said, pointing me to the X-ray line. " 'But let this be a lesson for you.' " [9]

Transportation Security Administration (TSA) Director Kip Hawley previously told one of Goldberg's key sources, security guru Bruce Schneier, that the agency's intelligence service effectively spots potentially dangerous passengers before they reach airports. "Our intel operation works closely with other international and domestic agencies," Hawley told Schneier. [10]

Other intelligence experts argue for paying close attention to the shared jihadist roots and operational ties between al Qaeda and LeT, the apparent Mumbai attack mastermind. "Bin Laden was an early supporter of the group and provided some of the initial funding," writes Bruce Riedel, a former CIA expert on Pakistan now at the Brookings Institution think tank. He has noted that the first major al Qaeda operative arrested after 9/11, Abu Zubayda, was nabbed in an LeT safe house in Islamabad. [11]

Riedel, author of a recent book on al Qaeda, predicts that Mumbai sets a pattern for future attacks. [12] "I think this will become a role model for ter-

Security-Related Agencies Not Included in the Department of Homeland Security
Central Intelligence Agency
National Security Agency
Department of Defense   Defense Intelligence Agency   Northern Command
Department of Health and Human Services   National Institutes of Health   Centers for Disease Control and Prevention
Department of the Interior   National Park Service Police   Bureau of Land Management Police
Department of Justice   Federal Bureau of Investigation
Department of State   Bureau of Consular Affairs
Department of Transportation   Federal Aviation Administration
Department of Treasury   Bureau of Alcohol, Tobacco, Firearms, and Explosives

Source: Donald F. Kettl, System Under Stress: Homeland Security and American Politics, *2nd ed., CQ Press, 2007*

rorists around the world," he told the German news magazine *Der Spiegel.* "You will see the copycat phenomenon where others will try to imitate what has just happened in Mumbai." [13]

Some say it's an easy model to adapt. "In Mumbai, the terrorists demonstrated that with simple tactics and low-tech weapons they can produce vastly disproportionate results," Brian M. Jenkins, a terrorism analyst at the RAND Corporation think tank, told the Senate Homeland Security Committee. Their weapons, he noted, amounted essentially to a 1940s-era arsenal — rifles, pistols and grenades. [14]

By attacking a non-aviation transportation hub, the attackers reinforced another warning by many terrorism analysts — jihadists' adaptability. "I think what Homeland Security has done well up to this point is to prepare defenses to respond to the last attack," says Roger Cressey, transnational threat director for the National Security Council during the Clinton administration. "If you look at TSA, it's more focused on aviation than on any other element of transportation."

Many other terrorism experts point to al Qaeda's apparent obsessiveness about aviation and highly symbolic targets. Sept. 11 provided the clearest example. In addition to the hijackers aiming at the World Trade Center and Pentagon a fourth plane apparently had targeted the Capitol or White House. It crashed in Shanksville, Pa., after passengers rushed the cockpit. [15]

In fact, jihadists had tried toppling the towers once before, exploding a bomb in the garage in 1993. After fast police work rolled up nearly the entire network of conspirators, counterterrorism expert Hoffman warned that the danger hadn't passed.

"The fact there haven't been any more attacks doesn't mean we're out of the woods," he said. "Terrorism doesn't work in a predictable fashion." He was speaking in 1994, seven years before 9/11.

As counterterrorism experts and lawmakers seek to keep America safe, here are some of the questions they are debating:

Does al Qaeda remain a danger within the United States?

Even before the Sept. 11 attacks, the small group of al Qaeda leaders around Osama bin Laden had become the prime target of U.S. counterterrorism efforts. They remain so today, with many in the national-security community convinced that as long as al Qaeda exists, it's plotting attacks on U.S. soil.

Along with many in the military and intelligence communities, Defense Secretary Gates sees current U.S military efforts in Afghanistan as countering another 9/11. "My own personal view is that our primary goal is to prevent Afghanistan from being used as a base for terrorists and extremists to attack the United States and our allies," Gates told the Senate Armed Services Committee in late January. [16]

In this view, Qaeda's track record — going back to the U.S.-supported war against the Soviet occupation of Afghanistan during the 1980s — reveals a battle-hardened, highly trained and imaginative leadership that should never be underestimated.

A clear indication that al Qaeda may be down but not out came with the arrests of 24 Britons in 2006 for plotting to blow up transatlantic airliners in midflight to the United States, using small bombs filled with explosive liquid. In the end, only eight were put on trial and three convicted — of conspiracy to commit murder, not of more serious charges of trying to mount a massive suicide attack. Still, authorities in both countries maintained they had foiled a serious plot, which included preparation of "martyrdom videos" by some defendants. [17]

All of the defendants were Muslims, six of them Pakistani, and counterterrorism officials said some had gotten training in Pakistan from an al Qaeda explosives expert. [18]

The bin Laden group's ability to keep operating in its Pakistani sanctuary is the key to the continuing danger it poses, intelligence professionals say. In November, then-CIA Director Michael Hayden told foreign-policy specialists that al Qaeda was still the intelligence agency's main target. "Al Qaeda, operating from its safe haven in Pakistan's tribal areas, remains the most clear and present danger to the safety of the United States," Hayden said. "If there is a major strike against this country, it will bear the fingerprints of al Qaeda." [19]

Hayden and others who share his view acknowledge that bin Laden's organization now has far less freedom in its presumed location in Pakistan than it did before late 2001, when it enjoyed the hospitality of Afghanistan's Taliban government.

The constant targeting of the group by the United States — which has a $25 million bounty on bin Laden — combined with help from European, Asian and some Middle Eastern allies, is limiting action by al Qaeda, some counterterrorism experts say. "It's more difficult to travel, more difficult to cross borders," says P. J. Crowley, a former National Security Council staffer who is homeland security director at the Center for American Progress, a think tank with close ties to the Obama administration. "In the late 1990s they had training capability in Afghanistan, and they've lost that."

Despite the apparent difficulty of operating outside the Pakistani tribal area, Crowley says enough legal traffic exists between Pakistan and Pakistani immigrants in Europe to give cover to al Qaeda operatives. "When you compare the United States to Europe, the ongoing risk of an attack is even higher in Europe."

But a member of two congressional commissions on terrorism and WMD argues that Europe is a bridge to the United States on which holders

A U.S. Customs and Border Protection officer at the Port of Newark, N.J., uses a hand-held radiation detector to check a shipping container that was stopped for further inspection after it passed through a radiation detector. Some terrorism experts say poor security at U.S. ports leaves the nation vulnerable to terrorism.

AP Photo/Mel Evans

of Western European passports can travel easily. "If it's in Europe's living room, then it's on our doorstep," says former Rep. Timothy J. Roemer, D-Ind., who served on the 9/11 Commission convened after the attacks and on the recent Commission on the Prevention of Weapons of Mass Destruction Proliferation and Terrorism. He is now president of the Center for National Policy think tank.

At the WMD commission, Roemer recalls, "When we talked to our intelligence people in the United States, they continued to say al Qaeda has become stronger since 9/11 and that the threat to the homeland radiates from the Pakistani border area."

The Heritage Foundation's Carafano argues that al Qaeda is suffering the effects of unrelenting targeting by the United States. "Are they directing operations in the methodical way that they did before 9/11?" he asks. "There's zero evidence of that."

A former career U.S. Army officer, Carafano acknowledges al Qaeda may be capable of inspiring or encouraging terrorist acts in the United States. But al Qaeda made its reputation with spectacular, coordinated operations in different locations — such as the bombings of two U.S. embassies in Africa and the 9/11 attacks, which involved the hijacking of four airliners. "The question is, can they do a terrorist attack in a systematic way? That is real terror," Carafano says. "They don't have the capacity to do that. A little splinter cell will do something, and five seconds later they're going to get rolled up."

Nevertheless, an old spy-world dictum holds that there's no way to know what you don't know. "From my point of view, the lesson of 9/11 is the price of complacency," says Georgetown's Hoffman. "We knew there was a threat from al Qaeda before 9/11. We deluded ourselves into thinking it was an overseas threat and couldn't possibly come here."

On Feb. 10, in a sign that worries about terrorism continue, the government of Saudi Arabia asked Interpol, the international police force based in Lyon, France, to issue an unprecedented global alert to apprehend 85 fugitives suspected of ties to al Qaeda.

Is the Department of Homeland Security set up effectively to spot potential threats?

The huge and diverse department wins little praise for organization. Its constituent elements range from the entire Customs, Border Patrol and immigration-control forces to the Coast Guard, Secret Service and Federal Emergency Management Agency (FEMA).

"I voted against it," says Roemer. "I believed that we were cobbling together a 20th-century Frankenstein for 21st-century threats."

Roemer's criticism reflects a widely shared view among security professionals. But forcing the department to reverse course would waste time and energy better spent improving the department's operations, they say. "We really don't have the choice to go backwards — reorganizing, rearranging and dismantling," Roemer says.

Security experts readily volunteer suggestions for improvements, such as the need for more sharing of intelligence between DHS and other counterterrorism agencies. "We need . . . the new secretary to really push hard on that," RAND terrorism expert Jenkins told lawmakers, arguing that restrictions on access to information within the government remain stuck in the Cold War era. "We are now dealing with nebulous networks, fast-moving developments, and we have to come up with a lot more streamlined processing for moving intelligence and information around in the system." [20]

In simple bureaucratic terms, structure is an issue for new Homeland Security Secretary Janet Napolitano, not only because of the large number of agencies pulled into the new department but also because of those that were left out. (*See charts, pp. 132-133.*) Agencies outside DHS include the CIA, FBI and National Security Agency — the three biggest counterterrorism agencies and the ones that were at the center of the debate that gave rise to the department's creation. [21]

Following Sept. 11, officials learned that intelligence and law-enforcement agencies had picked up indications of a terrorist plot but hadn't fully compared notes. As a result, intelligence experts hadn't "connected the dots" pointing to 9/11. "The importance of integrated, all-source analysis cannot be overstated," the 9/11 Commission said in its landmark 2004 report. "Without it, it is not possible to 'connect the dots.' " [22]

By 2004, the DHS had already been created. The move followed a policy reversal by the Bush administration, which had resisted early pressure to create a new Cabinet department for domestic security.

The few federal terrorism charges the government did file, however, were brought by the Justice Department. Homeland Security became known largely for airport security and for the disastrous FEMA response to Hurricane Katrina in 2005. [23]

"The sheer complexity of creating and unifying such a wide-ranging operation remains an enormous problem," says Donald F. Kettl, a University of Pennsylvania political scientist and the author of a book on homeland security.

Indeed, he says, although the department's range of responsibilities vastly increased, the "dot-collecting" agencies remained unconnected. "There are important pieces of the apparatus that are not included," he says. "The main problem that the department was set up to cure is left unanswered."

Although many experts share Kettl's concern, some think the new Obama administration can offset the department's built-in shortcomings.

Cressey, the former White House counterterrorism official, expects

Secretary Napolitano and her staff to zero in on DHS structural problems. Presently, he says, at least 22 senior officials report directly to her. "That's insane, it's unworkable," he says, pointing to the Pentagon as a model of how to set up a massive department.

Cressey adds that any reorganization would have to be precise and detailed, so as to do no harm. "The Secret Service and Customs are working reasonably well, as is the Coast Guard," he says. "You don't want to screw up any agency within the department that is successfully executing its mission."

But Crowley at the Center for American Progress argues that, while modest reforms are possible, the department suffers from deep structural and managerial flaws.

He cites a New Year's Day episode in which a group of American Muslim travelers were forced off a Washington-to-Orlando flight because a passenger became alarmed. [24] "TSA says there are 20 layers of security," he says. "There should have been points within the system where someone could say, 'Hey there's no real threat here. The layer that alarmed was the 20th, and least reliable. The way the system reacted, it didn't seem to trust the other 19 layers; it just defaulted to the maximum response."

Is the United States focusing anti-terrorism resources in the right places?

Former President George W. Bush and his senior officials have credited the security measures they put into ef-

fect after 9/11 with preventing further attacks on the United States. "We'll leave behind a vastly upgraded network of homeland defenses," Bush said at the Army War College in Carlisle, Pa., shortly before leaving office. "Federal, state and local law enforcement officers are working together more closely than ever before. The number of border patrol agents has doubled since 2001. Our airports and seaports have bolstered screening procedures." [25]

A Port Authority policeman guards the Holland Tunnel linking New York City and New Jersey following reports in July 2006 that jihadists had planned to bomb the tunnel and other New York landmarks, including the United Nations.

Getty Images/Chris Hondros

Bush made oblique mention of missile strikes launched from unmanned aircraft onto reported al Qaeda and Taliban targets in Pakistan. "With weapons like the Predator drone in our arsenal, our troops can conduct precision strikes on terrorists in hard-to-reach areas while sparing innocent life," he said. (Obama has ordered the strikes continued, and government officials say they are crippling al Qaeda and its fellow jihadists.) [26]

For his part, former Vice President Dick Cheney put special emphasis on warrantless monitoring of phone calls and e-mail. "I think what the National

Security Agency did . . . working with the CIA at the direction of the president, was masterfully done," Cheney told CBS' "Face the Nation" about two weeks before leaving office. "I think it provided crucial intelligence for us. It's one of the main reasons we've been successful in defending the country against further attacks." [27]

Critics of the monitoring program say the government would have been able to obtain warrants quickly if the eavesdropping had been important. Others insist that the absence — so far — of a sequel to 9/11 reflects terrorists' weakness more than it does tougher security measures.

The intelligence effort does get a back-handed compliment from the leading skeptic on counterterrorism programs. "If there's nothing to find, then intelligence-gathering is a waste," says Mueller of Ohio State University. "But it probably makes more sense than trying to protect everything, because there's an infinite number of targets."

As for tighter port and border controls, security skeptics say tougher inspections at official crossings, higher fences and more patrolling to keep out illegal crossers may simply deter foreigners from entering the United States to find jobs. But, these experts add, U.S. borders remain open to savvy and determined operators. "If you have any doubt about terrorists' ability to bring a bomb to an American city, remember, they could always hide it in a bale of marijuana, which we know comes to [every] American city," Graham Allison, director of the Belfer Center for Science and International Affairs at Harvard's Kennedy School of Government, told the House Armed Services Committee in January. [28]

Less than two weeks later, *The New York Times* reported that Mexican marijuana exporters have "routinely transported industrial-sized loads of marijuana" over the border — and under it, using tunnels. [29]

The security weakness Allison pointed to stems from a lack of strategic focus, argues Center for National Policy President Roemer, who served with Allison on the WMD Commission. "If you focus on everything, you focus on nothing," Roemer says. Specifically, he questions whether the drive to assemble "watch lists" of terrorism suspects has produced valid results.

Meanwhile, other problem areas have been neglected, Roemer says. "What about nuclear security, biosecurity, cybersecurity? These are things we should have looked at two years ago, on which we've done precious little."

Even so, other experts argue, the continuing emphasis on airline security reflects attention to jihadists' targeting preferences. "If you were advising a terrorist group, you'd tell them, 'The one area the government pays attention to is aviation.' Yet they keep going for it," says Daniel Byman, director of the Security Studies Program at Georgetown.

Byman, a former 9/11 Commission staffer, says jihadists have focused on airliners for good reason, at least from their point of view. "It's a highly symbolic target, and an attack on one is seen as having a huge psychological effect."

While many experts agree, some analysts argue that airport procedures may look more imposing and rigorous than they are. "Somebody smart and determined is going to be able to defeat the process, I have a feeling," says Kettl of

the University of Pennsylvania. "Can someone get a bomb on a plane? Probably." He acknowledges, however, that breaking into a cockpit has become far more difficult.

"The underlying and more important issue" about airport security, he says, "is that it gives citizens a feeling they have a free pass — that at bottom the government is in control, and we don't have to worry." ∎

Former Gov. Janet Napolitano, D-Ariz., the new secretary of Homeland Security, is expected to focus on structural problems at the huge agency, including developing better information-sharing with the CIA, FBI and National Security Agency.

Getty Images/Scott Olson

BACKGROUND

Mideast Conflict

Conflict between Israel and Palestinians emerged as a U.S. security

issue in the 1960s, but only in retrospect. Sirhan Sirhan, the gunman who assassinated New York Sen. Robert F. Kennedy, D-N.Y., in 1968, was a Jerusalem-born Arab angered at Kennedy's support for Israel during the Six-Day War of 1967.

"My only connection with Robert Kennedy was his sole support of Israel and his deliberate attempt to send . . . 50 bombers to Israel to obviously do harm to the Palestinians," Sirhan told British journalist David Frost 20 years later. [30]

At the time of the assassination in a Los Angeles hotel kitchen, however, Sirhan was generally described as mentally ill rather than politically motivated. His legal defense, in fact, was that he was incapable of premeditated killing. Only in recent years has his act come to be seen as a harbinger of political violence in the Middle East.

A year after Kennedy's death, terrorists indisputably targeting Israel hijacked a Tel Aviv-bound TWA airliner from Los Angeles. A man and a woman from the Che Guevara Commando Unit of the Popular Front for the Liberation of Palestine boarded in Rome. Apparently believing Israeli Ambassador to the United States Yitzhak Rabin was aboard, the hijackers eventually forced the plane to land in Syria. No passengers were killed. [31]

Further hijackings, as well as bombings and other attacks, mostly in Western Europe, in the 1970s and '80s, were rooted in the Middle East. The most notorious was the seizure of Israeli athletes at the 1972 Olympic Games in Munich by Palestinian gunmen. All 11 hostages and five of eight gunmen were killed, most of them in a failed rescue attempt. [32]

The next year, Palestine Liberation Organization (PLO) gunmen kidnapped two U.S. diplomats and a Belgian envoy in Khartoum, Sudan. The attackers demanded the release of Sirhan and hundreds of other Palestinians imprisoned elsewhere. The U.S. refused to negotiate, and the three were executed. [33]

Subsequently, PLO leader Yasser Arafat secretly pledged to the United States to refrain from violence outside of Israel. But other Middle East groups adopted similar tactics.

In April 1983, a suicide bomber from an organization named Islamic Jihad killed 63 people at the U.S. Embassy in Beirut, Lebanon, where President Ronald Reagan had deployed 1,200 Marines to help enforce a cease-fire in a civil war. No retaliation was attempted. Then, in October, a suicide truck-bomber blew up the U.S. peacekeepers' barracks in Beirut, killing 241 Marines. U.S. intelligence blamed Hezbollah, a Lebanese militia organized largely by Iran. [34]

The backdrop was the 1982 Israeli invasion of Lebanon. Iran's radical religious rulers — newly in power after the 1979 overthrow of the shah (king), a close U.S. ally who was friendly to Israel — saw Hezbollah as a force to challenge both those foes.

A deadly event in the region's biggest country had its own connection to Israel and the United States. In 1981, Islamist members of the Egyptian army assassinated President Anwar Sadat in retaliation for his signing of a peace treaty with Israel — a move the United States had supported. A young Islamist doctor played a minor role in the assassination conspiracy — Ayman al-Zawahiri, who would later become bin Laden's chief strategist. [35]

On U.S. Soil

The violence spawned by the Mideast conflict hit U.S. soil with full force in 1993. On Feb. 26 of that year, a powerful truck bomb detonated in the base-ment parking lot beneath the World Trade Center in New York, killing six people. Police quickly discovered a terrorist cell of recent immigrants, mostly Palestinians, who had come to the United States from Egypt, Jordan and other Middle Eastern countries.

The bombers turned out to be more zealous than competent. The operative who rented the Ryder van that carried the fertilizer bomb reported the vehicle stolen so he could claim his deposit. The FBI — which had traced the van to the rental agency — arrested him and then nabbed most of his comrades. [36]

But the mastermind, Ramzi Yousef, a Kuwaiti national of Pakistani descent, had fled. Schooled in explosives at a training camp in Afghanistan — during the Taliban's rule — Yousef was the key link between the 1993 bombing and the 9/11 attack eight years later.

He was captured in Pakistan in 1995, tried and convicted in the United States and sentenced to life plus 240 years in prison; his co-conspirators received 240-year sentences. [37]

The trade center bombing investigation revealed another jihadist plot — to bomb New York landmarks including the United Nations and the Holland and Lincoln tunnels. The nine so-called "landmarks" defendants were all convicted and sentenced to terms ranging from 11 years (for a cooperating witness) to life. In a third related case, a man convicted of conspiracy to murder Meir Kahane, a violently anti-Arab Israeli-American rabbi who was assassinated in a New York hotel in 1990, received a life sentence. [38]

Except for two U.S.-born, non-Arab converts to Islam, all of those convicted in the 1993 trade center bombing and the related conspiracies were immigrants from Egypt and other Middle Eastern countries.

But even as prosecutors prepared the cases against these conspirators, a white American ex-GI triggered the explosion that was — until Sept. 11, 2001 — the most destructive act of terrorism on U.S. soil.

Timothy McVeigh, a veteran of the 1991 Persian Gulf War devoted to neo-Nazi ideology, blew up the Alfred P. Murrah Federal Building in Oklahoma City on April 19, 1995. McVeigh was arrested in a traffic stop shortly after his ammonia-fertilizer bomb, packed into a van, exploded in front of the building, killing 168 people, including 19 children. Convicted of murder and conspiracy, he was executed on June 11, 2001. [39]

The bombing sparked a wave of concern about homegrown extremists. Law enforcement agencies and journalists zeroed in on the "militia" movement — loosely coordinated bands of white men inclined to survivalism, gun rights and, typically, far-right politics. They constituted "a secretive, paranoid and profoundly alienated political subculture that may now constitute a threat to law and order," *Newsweek* said. [40]

But the movement dwindled after the Oklahoma bombing, though right-wing extremists were involved in a later, smaller-scale bombing and several murders. One of the most notorious was the 1999 shooting of three children and two adults at the North Valley Jewish Community Center near Los Angeles (all survived), followed by the murder of a Filipino-American postman. The lone shooter, Buford O. Furrow Jr., a member of the neo-Nazi Aryan Nation, pleaded guilty to murder and other charges and was sentenced to life in prison. [41]

Al Qaeda

As the threat posed by domestic far-right extremists waned, bin Laden turned to U.S. targets in Africa and the Mideast.

Continued on p. 140

Chronology

1960s-1980s
Anti-American terrorism spawned by Arab-Israeli conflict spreads through the Mideast and Europe, barely touching U.S.

1968
Palestinian immigrant Sirhan Sirhan assassinates Sen. Robert F. Kennedy, D-N.Y., for supporting Israel.

1973
Palestine Liberation Organization gunmen in Sudan kill two U.S. diplomats and a Belgian after U.S. refuses to free Sirhan.

1979
Soviet Union invades Afghanistan, prompting millionaire Saudi exile Osama bin Laden to join anti-Soviet jihad.

1981
Jihadists arrested after assassination of Egyptian President Anwar Sadat include Ayman al-Zawahiri, who heads for Afghanistan after he is freed.

1983
Islamic Jihad organization blows up U.S. Embassy in Beirut, Lebanon, in retaliation for U.S. intervention in civil war, killing 63. . . . Six months later, another bomb, apparently planted by Hezbollah, destroys U.S. Marine barracks and kills 241.

1990s
Mideast terrorism hits U.S. soil, while far-right extremists escalate their violence.

1990
Anti-Arab Rabbi Meir Kahane is assassinated in New York by a Palestinian immigrant.

1993
A mostly Mideast immigrant cell detonates a truck bomb under New York's World Trade Center, killing six. . . . Investigation leads to discovery of related conspiracy to blow up New York landmarks.

1995
Far-right extremist Timothy McVeigh bombs Oklahoma City federal building, killing 168 and prompting worries about domestic terrorism.

1998
Al Qaeda operatives bomb two U.S. embassies in Africa, killing 220.

1999
Library of Congress report warns that al Qaeda could crash an airplane into the Pentagon.

2000s
Al Qaeda becomes primary target of U.S. counterterrorism operations even before 9/11.

2000
Al Qaeda suicide bombers hit *USS Cole* in Yemen, killing 17 and prompting retaliatory U.S. missile strikes, which miss Osama bin Laden.

2001
Nearly 3,000 die in Sept. 11 attacks on World Trade Center and the Pentagon and the crash of a fourth hijacked plane in Shanksville, Pa. . . . Anthrax-filled envelopes are sent to media organizations and political figures, killing five. . . . President George W. Bush forms homeland security office. . . . Richard Reid tries detonating a shoe bomb on a Paris-Miami flight.

2002
Administration warn that new al Qaeda attacks are imminent. . . . Congress creates new Cabinet-level Department of Homeland Security.

. . . Jose Padilla is arrested as "enemy combatant," accused of plotting to detonate a "dirty bomb."

2003
Homeland Security Secretary Tom Ridge advises Americans to stock up on protective equipment including duct tape, provoking widespread ridicule.

2004
9/11 Commission documents government's failure to "connect the dots" and respond to intelligence warnings before the attacks. . . . Spain-based jihadists bomb Madrid commuter trains, killing 191.

2005
British-based jihadists bomb London subway and bus system, killing 52.

2006
FBI charge seven men in Miami's Liberty City neighborhood, with conspiracy to destroy Chicago's Sears Tower and other targets. . . . British charge alleged jihadists with plotting to detonate liquid bombs on airliners.

2007
First trial of Miami terrorism defendants ends in mistrial; one defendant is acquitted.

2008
Padilla is sentenced to 17 years. . . . Five Muslim immigrants convicted of plot to kill U.S. soldiers at Fort Dix, N.J. . . . Terrorist assault in Mumbai, India, kills 173, alarms U.S. officials.

2009
Osama bin Laden predicts continuing economic meltdown in U.S. . . . President Barack Obama orders continued rocket and missile attacks on al Qaeda sites in Pakistan. . . . Obama weighs merging homeland security and national security councils.

Commission Warns of Bioterrorism Threat

But skeptic says terrorist groups don't have the know-how.

Immediately after the Sept. 11, 2001, attacks, U.S. intelligence operatives and officials who'd been tracking the al Qaeda terrorist group for years didn't doubt for a second. "I knew immediately this was [Osama] bin Laden," former CIA Director George J. Tenet told CBS News six years later. "There was no doubt what had happened." But no such certainty accompanied a deadly anthrax attack that was launched soon after 9/11. [1]

Arguably, it posed an even scarier future than the 9/11 attacks. Finding unknown enemies is far tougher than tracking down foes who, ultimately, announce themselves, as bin Laden eventually did.

And stopping the spread of a disease or infection poses a bigger challenge than looking for survivors of a bombing. For one thing, no cures exist yet for some disease agents, including the Ebola virus. Nevertheless, the extent to which terrorists are capable of deploying bioweapons is a subject of sharp debate. [2]

Controversy also surrounds the 2001 anthrax case. The government's only suspect killed himself last year without leaving a confession, but FBI officials say they're confident that Bruce E. Ivins, a career microbiologist at the U.S. Army's biodefense laboratory at Fort Detrick, Md., mailed the envelopes filled with powdered anthrax spores that killed five people and sickened 17 others in September and October of 2001.

But before announcing that conclusion, the FBI had spent years building a case against Mark Hatfill, another Fort Detrick scientist. And officials concede that the evidence concerning Ivins isn't absolutely conclusive.

Far from it, some independent scientists say. Microbiologist Richard O. Spertzel told *The New York Times* last year he's unpersuaded that Ivins had transformed anthrax spores into a weapon by drying them. But if he did, Spertzel said, and "an individual can make that kind of product, just by drying it, we are in deep trouble as a nation and a world." [3]

Independently, a congressional panel announced in late 2008 that trouble looms. "Unless the world community acts decisively and with great urgency, it is more likely than not that a weapon of mass destruction will be used in a terrorist attack somewhere in the world by the end of 2013," said the Commission on the Prevention of Weapons of Mass Destruction Proliferation and Terrorism. "The Commission further believes that terrorists are more likely to be able to obtain and use a biological weapon than a nuclear weapon." [4]

While the commission conceded that highly specialized knowledge and equipment would be indispensable to mount a bioattack, it noted that trained biologists are relatively numerous. "Terrorists are trying to upgrade their capabilities and could do so by recruiting skilled scientists," the commission said. [5]

Meanwhile, the Government Accountability Office (GAO) reported in late 2008 that security is sub-par at two of the five U.S. laboratories authorized to handle deadly pathogens, the WMD commission said. The two insecure facilities were at Georgia State University in Atlanta and the Southwest Foundation for Biomedical Research in San Antonio, Texas. [6]

No one questions that advanced science can provide lethal weapons to people who want to wreak death and destruction.

Continued from p. 138

In 1998, al Qaeda operatives simultaneously bombed the U.S. embassies in Nairobi, Kenya, and Dar es Salaam, Tanzania, killing at least 220 people and wounding more than 4,000 others, the vast majority of them local nationals. [42]

Then, in 2000, an al Qaeda suicide team in a small, inflatable boat filled with explosives pulled up beside the *USS Cole*, an American warship, in the port of Aden, in Yemen and blew a hole in the ship's side, killing 17 crew members.

In retaliation, the Clinton administration, which had been tracking bin Laden's moves, launched cruise missiles against al Qaeda training camps in Afghanistan, from Navy war-ships in the Arabian Sea. But bin Laden had left one of the camps. [43]

Even before the attack on the *Cole*, some counterterrorism officials — as well as government researchers relying on open-source materials — had been trying to draw more high-level attention to bin Laden. By September 1999, the Library of Congress warned in a non-classified report commissioned by an unnamed government agency (apparently the CIA): "Al-Qaida poses the most serious terrorist threat to U.S. security interests." [44]

Citing Washington as a likely prime target for a "spectacular" attack, the report said: "Suicide bomber(s) belonging to al-Qaida's Martyrdom Battalion could crash-land an aircraft packed with high explosives (C-4 and semtex) into the Pentagon, the Headquarters of the Central Intelligence Agency, or the White House." [45]

The authors of the dead-on analysis couldn't have known it at the time, but only months earlier, bin Laden had approved a new attack on the World Trade Center planned by Khalid Shaikh Muhammed, the uncle of Ramzi Yousef. The attackers would use hijacked airliners as flying bombs.

In the aftermath of the attack on the *Cole*, U.S. officials and non-governmental terrorism experts repeatedly warned Americans to prepare for more. In May 2002, for instance, administration officials told reporters that al Qaeda operatives had stepped

But it's not as clear that a biological assault on the United States looms in the near future.

Milton Leitenberg, senior research scholar at the University of Maryland's Center for International and Security Studies, cites evidence that terrorist groups lag far behind the scientific curve. Pointing to the 2001 anthrax attack, Leitenberg asked a recent conference held by the Cato Institute think tank, "What does this have to do with what a terrorist group could do, and how soon they could do that?" Answering his own question, he replied, "Next to nothing. What we've found so far is that those people have been abysmally ignorant of how to read the technical, professional literature. What is on jihadi Web sites comes from American poisoners' handbooks sold here at gun shows, which can't make anything. What it would make is just garbage."

He reached that conclusion following an exhaustive study of the evidence left by al Qaeda operatives in Afghanistan — the same evidence that some experts have cited as a sign of the growing danger of a biological weapon attack. In a study published by the U.S. Army War College, Leitenberg said the evidence shows, in fact, that U.S. officials' public voicing of alarm at terrorists armed with bioweapons prompted al Qaeda's interest in the first place.

Computer disks with writings by Ayman al-Zawahiri, al Qaeda's second-in-command, show him remarking that "the enemy drew our attention to" the possibility of deploying bioweapons. Leitenberg traces the source to a 1997 press conference by then-Defense Secretary William S. Cohen, who held up a five-pound bag of sugar to show how small a quantity of anthrax spores it would take to cause mass fatalities.

"An edifice of institutes, programs, conferences and publicists has grown up which continue the exaggeration and scaremongering," Leitenberg wrote. "This persistent exaggeration is not benign: It is almost certainly the single greatest factor in provoking interest in BW [biological warfare] among terrorist groups." [7]

Bioweapons could become a menace in the future, Leitenberg told the conference. But for the foreseeable future, naturally occurring epidemics pose a far bigger danger. HIV, tuberculosis and malaria kill 5 million people a year, he said. And bioterrorism? "Zero."

[1] Quoted in Daniel Schorn, "George Tenet: At the Center of the Storm," CBS News, April 27, 2007, www.cbsnews.com/stories/2007/04/25/60minutes/main2728375_page2.shtml.

[2] See "World at Risk: The Report of the Commission on the Prevention of WMD Proliferation and Terrorism," December 2006, p. 3, www.preventwmd.gov/report/.

[3] Quoted in Eric Lichtblau and Nicholas Wade, "F.B.I. Details Anthrax Case, But Doubts Remain," The New York Times, Aug. 18, 2008, www.nytimes.com/2008/08/19/us/19anthrax.html?pagewanted=all.

[4] See "World at Risk," op. cit., pp. xv, 74-75.

[5] Ibid., p. 11.

[6] Ibid., pp. 3-4. For the GAO report, see "Biosafety Laboratories: Perimeter Security Assessment of the Nation's Five BSL-4 Laboratories," Government Accountability Office, September 2008, www.gao.gov/new.items/d081092.pdf.

[7] See Milton Leitenberg, "Assessing the Biological Weapons and Bioterrorism Threat: U.S. Army War College, December 2005, pp. 35, 89, www.cissm.umd.edu/papers/files/assessing_bw_threat.pdf.

up the pace of their communications, in a probable prelude to an attack. [46]

Days later, Vice President Cheney, appearing on NBC's "Meet the Press," said future attacks were "not a matter of if, but when." And over the next two days, FBI Director Robert S. Mueller said that suicide bomber attacks in the United States were "inevitable," while Defense Secretary Donald H. Rumsfeld spoke of terrorists acquiring weapons of mass destruction. [47]

Instead, the years following the Sept. 11 strike would see jihadist terrorists strike at Westerners (or Jews) in non-U.S. locations, including Madrid, London, Bali and Casablanca, as well as the recent assault in Mumbai.

With one exception, no attacks by Is-lamist militants were launched within the United States. Richard C. Reid, a British citizen, tried to light the fuse of a small but powerful bomb concealed in his shoe, while aboard a Paris to Miami flight in December 2001. Passengers and crew managed to extinguish the fuse. Reid, a convert to Islam, pleaded guilty while declaring his allegiance to bin Laden and was sentenced to life in prison. [48]

In early 2009, a half-dozen Miami men went on trial for the third time, after two mistrials, on charges of plotting religiously inspired terrorism. Their trial follows a half-dozen similar trials around the country that produced mixed outcomes. None of those accused carried out a successful attack.

The one terrifying attack that did occur following Sept. 11 had no Qaeda connection. Three weeks after Sept. 11, envelopes containing spores of the deadly lung disease anthrax were mailed to political and media figures. The anthrax — accompanied by threatening notes in the name of Islam — killed five people and sickened 17. Al Qaeda or a similar organization was widely presumed to be the sender, though none claimed responsibility.

The FBI soon pointed, instead, to a scientist at the military's main biodefense laboratory in Fort Detrick, Md. No charges were ever filed against the scientist, Steven J. Hatfill, whom FBI officials had called a "person of interest." Then, in July 2008 — after agreeing to pay Hatfill $4.6 million to

Critics Question Constant Terrorism Warnings

Security expert dismisses airport screening as "security theater."

When Americans go to the airport, they might as well be going to a Broadway show, says security expert and skeptic Bruce Schneier. To describe the protective measures Americans encounter all too often, he coined the term "security theater" — "security primarily designed to make us feel safer, but not actually safer."

His prime example: airport security searches.

"Banning box cutters since 9/11, or taking off our shoes since ["shoe bomber"] Richard Reid, has not made us any safer," he wrote two years ago on his influential blog. "And a long-term prohibition against liquid carry-ons won't make us safer, either. It's not just that there are ways around the rules, it's that focusing on tactics is a losing proposition. It's easy to defend against what the terrorists planned last time, but it's shortsighted. If we spend billions fielding liquid-analysis machines in airports, and the terrorists use solid explosives, we've wasted our money." [1]

The founder of a computer-security company and now chief technology security officer of BT (British Telecom), Schneier writes and speaks in bolder tones than most others in the field. But some of his arguments are gaining ground.

Donald F. Kettl, a University of Pennsylvania political scientist and homeland security specialist, notes that widespread ridicule of airport screening — he calls it "screening theater" — reflects its low level of credibility.

Kettl acknowledges, however, that insiders have told him the security system did prevent some terrorist incidents — a point suggested by Transportation Security Administration Director Kip Hawley.

Nonetheless, what the public sees of security measures has done little to inspire confidence — even when confidence might be warranted — critics say.

The ridicule ended a Homeland Security Department effort to extend security beyond airports and elsewhere, Kettl notes. Gov. Tom Ridge, R-Pa., the first Homeland Security secretary, had suggested in 2003 that citizens stock up on duct tape and other supplies in case of disaster. "It created enormous amounts of laughter, but it was basic advice about how to prepare," Kettl says. "In some ways, it was not bad advice."

Still, in a climate dominated by warnings of imminent terrorist strikes, Ridge's small-scale advice to everyday citizens seemed mostly to inspire late-night TV comedians.

Paradoxically, critics say, government warnings may exaggerate terrorists' power. The vast size of the United States makes a tiny enemy such as al Qaeda incapable of inflicting death and destruction on a national scale, many experts note. But trying to stop attacks nationwide can wind up causing more damage than the strike itself, says John Mueller, an Ohio State University political scientist who argues that the government has exaggerated the extent of danger from terrorism. "Fear is costly in terms of overreaction expenditures like the war in Iraq," he says.

Other critics say the stoking of fear has left citizens feeling there is little they can do if disaster does strike. "Washington has been sounding the alarm about apocalyptic terrorist groups while providing the American people with no meaningful guidance on how to deal with the threats they pose or the consequences of a successful attack," wrote Stephen E. Flynn, a senior counterterrorism fellow at the Council on Foreign Relations think tank and former Coast Guard officer. [2]

Given the impossibility of guaranteeing there will be no attacks in a nation as big as the United States, Flynn says, citizen

settle a lawsuit he filed alleging violations of the Privacy Act — the FBI reported that it had been closing in on another Fort Detrick scientist, Bruce E. Ivins. Aware that arrest was imminent, Ivins committed suicide. [49]

FBI officials say circumstantial and scientific evidence make Ivins' guilt clear. Some of his colleagues and other scientists dispute that conclusion. And officials concede the absence of definitive proof. [50]

Homeland Security

With expectations of new attacks running high after 9/11, President Bush created a presidential office of homeland security nine days after the attacks. Some Democratic lawmakers, and even some of his own Cabinet members, argued for a new agency dedicated to ensuring domestic security. But Bush, who portrayed himself as a small-government conservative, resisted the idea. A crisis, however severe, shouldn't automatically prompt major government expansion, he held. [51]

Bush chose Pennsylvania Gov. Tom Ridge, a Republican, to coordinate the work of 40 government agencies with counter-terrorism responsibilities. They included the FBI, Central Intelligence Agency and Centers for Disease Control and Prevention as well as the Federal Aviation Administration (FAA).

But nine months later, events forced a new, more radical approach. Minnesota FBI agent Colleen Rowley told the Senate Judiciary Committee that her bosses had responded lackadaisically to her urgent requests — shortly before Sept. 11 — for a warrant to search the computer of Zacarias Moussaoui, whom she suspected of training to fly a hijacked plane.

Bush concluded that the explosive testimony would renew calls to create a new department that wouldn't fail to connect the dots next time. The administration's Homeland Security helplessness is especially troubling in a society that has grown dependent on instantly available goods and services.

"The United States is becoming a brittle nation," Flynn wrote. "An increasingly urbanized and suburbanized population has embraced just-in-time lifestyles tethered to ATM machines and 24-hour stores that provide instant access to cash, food and gas. When the power goes out and these modern conveniences fail, Americans are incapacitated. Meanwhile, two decades of taxpayer rebellion have stripped away the means necessary for government workers to provide help during emergencies." [3]

In addition, Flynn told a recent security conference, the federal government's capabilities have also eroded. He cited a program to issue machine-readable credentials, after background investigations, to 1.5 million workers at U.S. ports. The card is being issued, but scanning machines aren't available yet, Flynn said. The Transportation Security Administration is scheduling card-reader tests for early 2009. [4]

A program involving truck drivers, who are among the port workers required to carry the cards, won rare praise from Schneier. Highway Watch was a 2005 Homeland Secu-

A traveler at Chicago's O'Hare Airport dons disposable booties after taking off her shoes for a security check.

Getty Images/Tim Boyle

rity project to train truckers to look for dangerous or suspicious activities or conditions. "This program has a lot of features I like in security systems: It's dynamic . . . it relies on trained people paying attention and it's not focused on a specific threat," Schneier wrote. [5]

But the program didn't survive. "The U.S. Department of Homeland Security has elected to fund another trucking security program," says an undated announcement on the program's Web site. "We will continuously provide updates on this site as to the future of the program as developments occur." [6]

---

[1] See Bruce Schneier, "Last Week's Terrorism Arrests," "Schneier on Security" blog, Aug. 13, 2006, www.schneier.com/blog/archives/2006/08/terrorism_secur.html.

[2] See Stephen E. Flynn, "America the Resilient: Defying Terrorism and Mitigating Natural Disasters," *Foreign Affairs*, March-April, 2008, www.foreignaffairs.org/20080301faessay87201-p0/stephen-e-flynn/america-the-resilient.html.

[3] *Ibid.*

[4] "TWIC Pilot Test," Transportation Security Administration, undated, www.tsa.dhs.gov/what_we_do/layers/twic/pilot_test.shtm.

[5] "Truckers Watching the Highway," Schneier blog, *op. cit.*, Dec. 8, 2005, www.schneier.com/blog/archives/2005/12/truckers_watchi.html.

[6] "Highway Watch," Homeland Security Department, undated, www.highwaywatch.com.

Department bill proposed unifying 22 government agencies, but not including the two of the most critical counterterrorism organizations — the FBI and CIA (nor the National Security Agency, which monitors communications). Administration officials argued that their front-line work shouldn't be slowed by reorganization tasks.

If the criteria for inclusion in the new department seemed unclear, so did its very mission. Ridge, who was quickly confirmed as the department's first director, contributed to the confusion when he announced in 2003 that the department's duties would include hunting down sexual predators who operated through the Web.

The connection to counterterrorism seemed distant, at best. But the episode reflected senior officials' belief that the post-Sept. 11 sense of emergency that gave rise to the department wouldn't last.

Indeed, other non-terrorism-related missions were built into the new agency. The inclusion of the Border Patrol and the Immigration and Naturalization Service (now Immigration and Customs Enforcement) meant considerable focus on illegal immigration. And with FEMA now included in the new department, Homeland Security was also responsible for natural disaster response — a responsibility that became a handicap, as the botched response to Hurricane Katrina demonstrated in 2005.

The Katrina disaster validated a 2003 Congressional Research Service report. Homeland Security's color-coded "threat level" indicator was one of eight separate disaster warning systems, the CRS noted, for catastrophes including severe weather, chemical and biological contamination from government stockpiles and presidential alerts. All of the systems operated independently.

And the department's notifications to state and local officials about threat-level changes followed a mid-20th-century tempo. The police chief in Portland, Maine, for example, told congressional researchers he'd learn of changes from CNN eight hours before hearing from the agency.

The exclusion of the FBI and CIA aroused considerable criticism when the Bush administration and lawmakers were hammering out the legislation creating the department. "I am concerned that this is a damage-control document that was more designed to divert the nation's focus from the problems at the CIA and FBI than intelligently reorganize our security bureaus," Rep. John Conyers Jr., D-Mich., said in June 2002. [52]

But many security professionals argued that integrating foreign intelligence and domestic counterterrorism into one agency would be a mistake — as would separating counterterrorism from law enforcement. "There is a real benefit to keeping the counterterrorism and domestic spying aspects housed in an agency that understands what it means to operate within the rule of law," an anonymous official told *The Washington Post*. [53] ■

CURRENT SITUATION

Testing Time

President Obama is spending his early days in office under the shadow of expectations that terrorists will test him in the near future. "Presidents Bill Clinton and George W. Bush and U.K. Prime Minister Gordon Brown share at least one sobering experience: Each saw a major domestic terrorist attack by al Qaeda and its allies during his first year in office," two think tanks closely tied to the new administration reported last year in drawing up domestic security advice. [54]

The Center for American Progress Action Fund and Third Way, a new think tank, issued that reminder in the course of advising the new pres-

ident to streamline the domestic security decision-making process.

The 1993 World Trade Center bombing occurred about a month after Clinton took office. Bush had been president only nine months when the 9/11 attackers struck. And Brown had been prime minister for four weeks when a small group of immigrant doctors from the Middle East and an engineer from India tried to detonate homemade car bombs in London and Glasgow in June 2007. [55]

Once terrorists strike, no one in the White House would have time to refine organizational structure, the think tanks said, arguing that Obama should fold his domestic counterterrorism staff into the National Security Council (NSC), which traditionally deals with foreign policy matters. "Homeland security should not be viewed as distinct from national security," they said. "In today's globalized world . . . it is difficult to envision where homeland security ends and national security begins."

Some caution that the focus on the jihadist threat may lead to neglect of danger close to home — far-right extremists enraged by an African-American in the White House. Mark Potok, an expert on hate groups at the Southern Poverty Law Center, says that Obama's election electrified the white-supremacist movement. "Two of the larger groups had their servers crash as a result of all the traffic they got," says Potok, director of the group's Intelligence Project. "Will that translate into actual new members? It certainly could."

New membership wouldn't guarantee violence, though the possibility would increase. Fred Burton, a former State Department counterterrorism director, questions whether the FBI and other law-enforcement agencies have kept up their monitoring of the far right. "I see that as a challenge," he says. "Historically, the FBI has not been very nimble in shifts of emphasis." Burton is vice president for

counterterrorism and corporate security at Stratfor, a consulting and analysis firm in Austin, Texas.

Still, the overwhelming focus for terrorism experts remains the jihadist movement. The creation of a separate Homeland Security Council may reflect the fears that prevailed at that time of al Qaeda "sleeper cells" that could spring into action at any time.

Obama shows signs of heeding the calls for a new approach. As his top counterterrorism adviser, he appointed an ex-career CIA official with extensive experience abroad. John O. Brennan was chief of staff to then-CIA Director George J. Tenet in 1999-2001 and head of the National Counterterrorism Center in 2004-2005, having served previously as the agency's station chief in Saudi Arabia.

White House staffers told reporters that Obama hadn't yet decided whether to merge the president's domestic security and national security staffs, which would be a departure from the setup under the Bush administration. But during the administration's first weeks, all indications were that the merger would be ordered. Even some Bush administration veterans endorsed the plan.

C. Stewart Verdery, a former deputy Homeland Security secretary under Bush, said his department had found getting attention from NSC difficult. "You want your issues considered," he told *The New York Times*. "You don't want to be off in some second bucket." [56]

Bush's last Homeland Security director, Kenneth Wainstein, conceded shortly before Bush left office that the logic behind the operation he had supervised was open to question. "When you look at the organization chart, you see it's not the cleanest org chart around," he told a Washington think tank recently. [57]

Not all Bush officials approve of the merger idea, however. His national security adviser, Stephen J. Hadley, reportedly has advised his successors against the plan, on the grounds that

Continued on p. 146

At Issue:

Is the chance of a nuclear terrorist attack virtually nonexistent?

JOHN MUELLER
POLITICAL SCIENCE PROFESSOR,
OHIO STATE UNIVERSITY

EXCERPTED FROM CATO INSTITUTE CONFERENCE
PRESENTATION, JAN. 12, 2009

*t*he chances of a terrorist group getting nuclear weapons are almost vanishingly small. You're a terrorist, OK, and you have to find highly enriched uranium. The scientist working for you may be incompetent. You're going to have to use criminals to get it out of the country. You're probably going to have to kill them once they've done what they've done. They may think of that and decide not to cooperate.

Building the bomb is difficult; you have to get the precise blueprints and a lot of expensive equipment. And you have to get scientists and engineers who are willing to give up their lives for the project, because there's going to be an international effort to try to find them after the bomb is discovered or blown up.

Then you have to get it across an international border and get it to Times Square. You have to find somebody in the country who is technologically capable of getting it to the goal and then setting it off.

People say it would be difficult but not impossible. I agree. Leaning very heavily in favor of the terrorists, difficult but not impossible means one chance in three of being successful [or] about one chance in three-and-a-half billion. I'm willing to say I'm off by factor of 1,000 — so, one chance in three-and-a-half million. You're putting everything, including your life, at stake for a gamble of one-in-three-and-a-half million.

An atomic bomb going off in [Washington, D.C.] would be a horrific disaster. Therefore, even if the probability is very low you still have to worry about it. The question is, how low does a probability have to get before you stop worrying about it?

We don't get along all that well with the Russians. They could easily kill 40 million to 50 million Americans if they worked at it, and we don't worry about that. It must be that the probability even of that horrific catastrophe has gotten so low that it has passed out of our consideration.

Al Qaeda is the only terrorist group that seems to want to attack the United States. It's about 150 people running around Afghanistan and Pakistan. Then there's the leaderless jihadis who are connecting on the Internet. The idea that these guys could make a nuclear weapon — come on. They can't even figure out each others' chatroom codes half the time.

Video and podcasts of the conference accessible at:
http://cato.org/events/counterterrorism/index.html.

JIM WALSH
SENIOR RESEARCH ASSOCIATE, SECURITY
STUDIES PROGRAM, MASSACHUSETTS
INSTITUTE OF TECHNOLOGY

EXCERPTED FROM CATO INSTITUTE CONFERENCE
PRESENTATION, JAN. 12, 2009

i think it's somewhere between nearly impossible and inevitable that there will be a nuclear terrorist attack. We're working in a world of uncertainty. This is a classic, low-probability, high-consequence event.

How much risk can we tolerate? I find John's statistical estimate of the likelihood of a nuclear attack unpersuasive. If I got up before 9/11 and said, there are 20 obstacles to carrying out [an attack] — what happens if they went and said they wanted to learn how to fly a plane but not land it, certainly they would be caught, and so on. I could have made it sound highly improbable. Is it one chance in a hundred?

What if I went to the Environmental Protection Agency or the Food and Drug Administration and said there's a one-in-one-hundred chance that this chemical is going to kill you. You think they'd allow it? I don't think so.

John thinks that we'll notice when uranium is missing. I doubt that if we don't have a baseline inventory that tells us how much uranium there is. He says non-state actors can't get detailed blueprints needed for bomb construction. The International Atomic Energy Agency says those blueprints are still floating around. I do worry about countries that have nuclear weapons today. And I think we should worry about them as much as we worry about those that might get them in the future.

The other question to be addressed is, what action should we take? John's argument is, the probability is low so we don't have to worry about it. I think it's odd to say we should wait until the terrorists have more capability before we do something. Better to do something now, when the risk is low and we have the time to be successful. The paradox is that for all the alarmism, we haven't done much about the problem. We have moved ever so modestly to lock down nuclear materials.

I think most terrorists are not interested in nuclear weapons. I'm underwhelmed by al Qaeda's technical capability. John's implicit notion is that al Qaeda is the only possible candidate for nuclear terrorism. I worry about al Qaeda 4.0 — kids in Europe who go to good schools 20 years from now or types of terrorists we don't even imagine. In the 1970s we thought it was all ideological — we did not see the terrorists that we have today.

Video and podcasts of the conference accessible at:
http://cato.org/events/counterterrorism/index.html.

Continued from p. 144
it would lessen attention to some important matters. [58]

For Hadley, in particular, the issue cuts deep, especially in the context of a brand-new administration. As deputy national security adviser before 9/11, he and his then-boss, National Security Adviser Condoleezza Rice, had failed to take effective action on a drumbeat of intelligence reports that a spectacular attack appeared imminent. "Hadley told us that before 9/11, he and Rice did not feel they had the job of coordinating domestic agencies," the 9/11 commission reported in 2004. "There was a clear disparity in the levels of response to foreign versus domestic threats. . . . Far less was done domestically." [59]

Back to Court

As the Obama administration was getting under way, federal prosecutors in Miami were starting up the third trial of a group of Miami men whom the government has depicted as terrorists in training. Jury selection began in late January.

The "Liberty City Six," named for the impoverished African-American district where the defendants lived, had seen two previous attempts to send them to prison end in mistrials. One of their codefendants was acquitted in 2007, at the group's first trial.

Jurors and defense lawyers have belittled the government's determination to win convictions on charges of con-

spiring to provide material support to a foreign terrorist organization — al Qaeda — and to destroy Chicago's Sears Tower and other buildings. The group of penniless construction workers did

A canine officer patrols San Francisco International Airport on July 3, 2007, the start of the Independence Day holiday. Creation of the Department of Homeland Security after the 9/11 attacks, along with stepped up airport security, reflected officials' near-certainty that further terrorist strikes were imminent.

have a leader who had talked of jihad to a government informant who was wired for recording. But they had no explosives, no connection to al Qaeda and no weapons beyond a samurai sword. "There was really nothing that indicated that this was a real threat," Jeffrey Agron, jury foreman at the first trial, told *The New York Times.* [60]

The Miami trial is the last of a series of terrorism-related cases brought by the Justice Department under the Bush administration, with mixed results. As with the Liberty City group, initial charges tended to be announced in the gravest terms. Attorney General Alberto Gonzales said in announcing indictments against the men in 2006 that they were "homegrown terrorists." He also conceded that they "posed no immediate threat." [61]

Gonzales' predecessor, John Ashcroft, set the standard for such announce-

ments. In the middle of a 2002 trip to Russia, the then-attorney general said that authorities had arrested Brooklyn-born Jose Padilla, designating him an "enemy combatant," on charges that he was plotting with al Qaeda to detonate a radiological "dirty bomb" in the United States. [62]

After nearly five years of litigation concerning the limits of presidential power to order an American citizen indefinitely detained, the Justice Department backed down from its position before the case reached the Supreme Court. Prosecutors then charged him in civilian court, dropping the "dirty bomb" allegation because it was based on interrogation evidence that wouldn't have been admissible in court. He was convicted of conspiracy and support for terrorism and sentenced in 2008 to 17 years in prison — though prosecutors had argued for a life sentence. [63]

Sentencing is scheduled later this year for five Muslim immigrants who were convicted in December 2008 of planning to kill soldiers at Fort Dix, N.J. The convicted men, all longtime residents of the United States with no military training, had tried to buy assault weapons and had spoken about jihad to a government informant. Their lawyers said the men, mostly in their 20s, hadn't been serious, though they had practiced at a firing range. [64]

"The word should go out to any other would-be terrorists of the homegrown variety that the United States will find you, infiltrate your group, prosecute you and send you to prison for a very long time," Ralph J. Marra Jr., the acting U.S. attorney for New Jersey, said after the men were convicted. [65]

As Marra suggested, and as Miami's Liberty City case also shows, the Justice Department aggressively deployed informants to gather evidence against young men who spoke of mounting attacks.

A trial outcome elsewhere in the country may also have encouraged Miami prosecutors to pursue a third trial in the Liberty City case. In November 2008, federal prosecutors in Dallas won convictions in a second trial against five directors of a Muslim charity, the Holy Land Foundation for Relief and Development. The men were found guilty of channeling millions of dollars to Hamas, the Palestinian organization that governs the Gaza Strip and that the United States classifies as a terrorist group. Sentencing is pending. [66]

For supporters of the Bush administration approach, the overall results will discourage would-be jihadists in the United States. "It is a very aggressive counterterrorism effort, and it seems to be working," James Lewis, a senior fellow at the Center for Strategic and International Studies, told the *Los Angeles Times*. [67]

Critics charge, though, that the administration hyped small-fry braggarts into deadly jihadists. In the Liberty City trials, said Bruce Winick, a University of Miami law professor who has been following the case, "A government informant got a bunch of guys together to swear a loyalty oath to al Qaeda. It's B-movie, really, more than a criminal case." [68] ∎

OUTLOOK

The Next Generation

Whatever else Osama bin Laden did to the United States, he altered the perspective of the political and governing class. The number of books, reports and conferences on ter-

rorism and America's vulnerabilities seems to remain on the increase.

To some extent, of course, the rate of publication and of conference-holding has been accelerated in 2008 and early 2009 by the coming to power of a new president, and the possibility that al Qaeda would want to greet him with a major attack of some kind.

But during the first weeks, at least, of the Obama administration, no terrorist strike had occurred.

For some terrorism experts, the absence of attacks following 9/11 — despite nearly universal predictions — served as a lesson. "I was clearly wrong," says Byman at Georgetown University's Security Studies Program. Heavy pressure on al Qaeda in its Pakistani redoubt is the main force working against its undoubted desire to mount a sequel to the 2001 attacks.

"It's difficult for them to do sophisticated long-term attacks," Byman says. "So local resources are important. In Europe, where they have local resources, they hit." Small groups of al Qaeda wannabes might conceivably make attempts in the United States, he acknowledges. "They can certainly kill, but I would be surprised if they could pull off anything on the scale of al Qaeda."

Whatever bin Laden's organization may have gained in global notoriety, and — in some circles — prestige, as a result of 9/11, that recognition also brought the continuing U.S. counterattack that lately has taken the form of deadly airstrikes in Pakistan. And the battle-hardened, lifelong jihadists who formed the core of the group are no longer as numerous, leaving a new wave of young, European Muslims from immigrant families who can be more easily dealt with, says ex-CIA officer Sageman, a psychiatrist by training.

"Our main goal should be the prevention of radicalization of the next generation — to take the glory out of terrorism," he told the Cato conference in January. "That's the main reason people want to become terrorists. It's to be-

come like the Terminator. If you look at the transcripts of what they talk about when we bug their apartments, they talk about the Terminator, about Rambo" — the movie action heroes.

Ways to lessen the alienation that puts young Muslims in a Terminator frame of mind would be a smaller U.S. presence in the Middle East, Sageman said. That reasoning is consistent with Obama's vow to pull out of Iraq, to promote Israel-Palestinian peace and to build friendlier relations with the Muslim world in general.

Some others in the counterterrorism world speak in similar terms. Cressey, the Clinton-era National Security Council veteran, says, "After you've eliminated the core that has the terrorist capability, how do you ensure over the long term that fewer people are interested in choosing terrorism to express their grievances? That's the challenge for the Obama administration, one that he understands."

Even so, some who've examined U.S. vulnerabilities observe that bin Laden's recent threat amounted to more than violence, however terrifying that violence was. In the pre-inauguration message, bin Laden gloried in the U.S. economic meltdown. "This talk about weakness and recession of the American ascendancy as well as the collapse of its economy, is not a talk of hopes, but testimonies given by leaders themselves which they couldn't conceal any longer," bin Laden said in his Jan. 15 recording. [69]

Roemer, the former member of the 9/11 and WMD commissions, implicitly acknowledges that bin Laden's analysis was grounded in reality. "A decade from now, will our greatest threat be something that al Qaeda has done to us, or something that we've done to ourselves?" Roemer asks. "Will it be an al Qaeda attack on one of our cities, or our failure to have addressed a 51 percent dropout rate in inner-city schools or investing in and protecting the energy grid?"

Bin Laden, Roemer says, knows how to exploit his enemy's responses. "He has an economic strategy — bleed America, make us spend money on wars. He can win by bleeding us to death economically, in effect having us do to ourselves what he couldn't do. We can't allow that. Our economic security priority has to be elevated, and the fear card cannot be played." ∎

Notes

[1] Extensive media coverage of the attacks includes Eric Schmitt, Somini Sengupta and Jane Perlez, "U.S. and India See Link to Militants in Pakistan," *The New York Times*, Dec. 2, 2008, www.nytimes.com/2008/12/03/world/asia/03 mumbai.html?scp=105&sq=mumbaiattack&st=cse. Also see K. Alan Kronstadt, "Terrorist Attacks in Mumbai, India, and Implications for U.S. Interests," Congressional Research Service, Dec. 19, 2008, www.fas.org/sgp/crs/terror/R40087.pdf.

[2] *Ibid.* Also see "Lashkar-e-Taiba denies role in Mumbai attacks," Reuters, Nov. 27, 2008, http://in.reuters.com/article/topNews/idININdia-36740420081127.

[3] See "World at Risk: The Report of the Commission on the Prevention of WMD Proliferation and Terrorism," December 2006, pp. xv-xxii, 74-75, www.preventwmd.gov/report/.

[4] See "English Translation of Osama bin Laden's 'Call for Jihad to Stop Aggression Against Gaza,' " Worldanalysis.net, Jan. 15, 2009, http://worldanalysis.net/modules/article/view.article.php?129/c40.

[5] See "Senate Armed Services Committee Holds Hearing on Challenges Facing the Defense Department," *CQ Congressional Transcripts*, Jan. 27, 2009.

[6] For background, see Peter Katel, "Global Jihad," *CQ Researcher*, Oct. 14, 2005, pp. 857-880.

[7] See Peter Bergen, "Safe at Home," *The New York Times*, Dec. 14, 2008, p. W10.

[8] Mueller's book is *Overblown: How Politicians and the Terrorism Industry Inflate National Security Threats and Why We Believe Them* (2006).

[9] Jeffrey Goldberg, "The Things He Carried," *The Atlantic*, November 2008, www.theatlantic.com/doc/200811/airport-security.

[10] Bruce Schneier, "Interview with Kip Hawley," blog, July 30, 2007, www.schneier.com/interview-hawley.html.

[11] Bruce Riedel, "Terrorism in India and the Global Jihad," Brookings Institution, Nov. 30, 2008, www.brookings.edu/articles/2008/1130_india_terrorism_riedel.aspx.

[12] Bruce Riedel, *The Search for Al Qaeda: Its Leadership, Ideology, and Future* (2008).

[13] Quoted in " 'A Nightmare We Cannot Afford in the 21st Century,' " *Spiegel Online International*, Dec. 8, 2008, www.spiegel.de/international/world/0,1518,595148,00.html.

[14] "Senate Homeland Security and Governmental Affairs Committee Holds Hearing on 'Lessons From the Mumbai Terrorist Attacks,' " *CQ Transcripts*, Jan. 28, 2009.

[15] Passengers on the fourth hijacked plane thwarted the attack on Washington when they learned via cell phones about the other attacks and forced the plane down in Shanksville, Pa.

[16] "Senate Armed Services Committee. . . .," *op. cit.*

[17] Janet Stobart and Sebastian Rotella, "3 in Britain convicted of conspiracy," *Los Angeles Times*, Sept. 9, 2008, p. A3; John F. Burns and Elaine Sciolino, "No One Convicted of Terror Plot to Bomb Planes," *The New York Times*, Sept. 9, 2008, p. A1.

[18] *Ibid.*

[19] "CIA Director Hayden — State of al Qaeda Today," Atlantic Council of the United States,

Nov. 13, 2008, www.acus.org/event_blog/cia-director-event.

[20] "Senate Homeland Security . . . Mumbai Attacks," *op. cit.*

[21] Donald F. Kettl, *System Under Stress: Homeland Security and American Politics* (2007).

[22] The 9/11 Commission Report," National Commission on Terrorist Attacks Upon the United States (2004), p. 408, www.9-11commission.gov/report/911Report.pdf.

[23] *Ibid.* For background see Pamela M. Prah, "Disaster Preparedness," *CQ Researcher*, Nov. 18, 2005, pp. 981-1004.

[24] Amy Gardner, "9 Muslim Passengers Removed From Jet," *The Washington Post*, Jan. 2, 2009, p. B1, and Cynthia Dizikes, "Muslim families are taken off flight," *Los Angeles Times*, Jan. 3, 2009, p. A10.

[25] "Bush Remarks on Security at U.S. Army War College," America.gov, Dec. 17, 2008, www.america.gov/st/texttrans-english/2008/December/20081217171510xjsnommis0.0446741.html.

[26] *Ibid.* Also see Tom Gjelten, "U.S. Officials: Al-Qaida Leadership Cadre 'Decimated,' " National Public Radio, Feb. 3, 2009, www.npr.org/templates/story/story.php?storyId=100195353.

[27] "Face the Nation," CBS News, Jan. 4, 2009, www.cbsnews.com/htdocs/pdf/FTN_010409.pdf.

[28] "House Armed Services Committee Holds Hearing on Preventing Weapons of Mass Destruction and Terrorism," *CQ Transcripts*, Jan. 22, 2009. For background, see Pamela M. Prah, "Port Security," *CQ Researcher*, April 21, 2006, pp. 385-408.

[29] Solomon Moore, "Border Proves No Obstacle for Mexican Cartels," *The New York Times*, Feb. 2, 2009, p. A1.

[30] Quoted in Sasha Issenberg, "Slaying gave US a first taste of Mideast terror," *The Boston Globe*, June 5, 2008, www.boston.com/news/nation/washington/articles/2008/06/05/slaying_gave_us_a_first_taste_of_mideast_terror/?page=full.

[31] Unless otherwise indicated, material in this subsection is drawn from Timothy Naftali, *Blind Spot: The Secret History of American Counterterrorism* (2005), pp. 35-41.

[32] Matthew Davis, "Athens 2004 remembers Munich 1972," BBC News, Aug. 20, 2004, http://news.bbc.co.uk/2/hi/europe/3581866.stm.

[33] Naftali, *op. cit.*, pp. 68-73.

[34] *Ibid.*, pp. 130-135. For background, see Peter Katel, "Middle East Tensions," *CQ Researcher*, Oct. 27, 2006, pp. 889-912. Riedel, *The Search for Al Qaeda, op. cit.*, pp. 16-21.

[35] Naftali, *op. cit.*, pp. 231-234.

[36] Benjamin Weiser, "Mastermind Gets Life for Bombing of Trade Center," *The New York Times*,

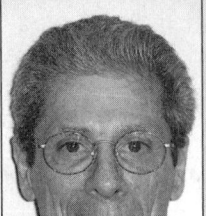

About the Author

Peter Katel is a *CQ Researcher* staff writer who previously reported on Haiti and Latin America for *Time* and *Newsweek* and covered the Southwest for newspapers in New Mexico. He has received several journalism awards, including the Bartolomé Mitre Award for coverage of drug trafficking, from the Inter-American Press Association. He holds an A.B. in university studies from the University of New Mexico. His recent reports include "Mexico's Drug War" and "Future of the Military."

Jan. 9, 1998, p. A1; John J. Goldman, "2 Found Guilty in Bombing of Trade Center," *Los Angeles Times*, Nov. 13, 1997, p. A1.

[38] Joseph P. Fried, "Sheik Sentenced to Life in Prison in Bombing Plot," *The New York Times*, Jan. 18, 1996, p. A1.

[39] "Defiant McVeigh dies in silence," BBC News, June 11, 2001, http://news.bbc.co.uk/1/hi/world/americas/1382602.stm.

[40] Tom Morganthau, "The View From the Far Right," *Newsweek*, May 1, 1995, www.newsweek.com/id/103757/page/1.

[41] James Sterngold, "Supremacist Who Killed Postal Worker Avoids Death Sentence," *The New York Times*, Jan. 24, 2001, http://query.nytimes.com/gst/fullpage.html?res=9F0CEED61E3CF937A15752C0A9679C8B63.

[42] "Report of the Accountability Review Boards on the Embassy Bombings in Nairobi and Dar es Salaam on Aug. 7, 1998," www.state.gov/www/regions/africa/accountability_report.html.

[43] Unless otherwise indicated, material in this subsection is drawn from the 9/11 Commission report, *op. cit.*, p. 134, www.9-11commission.gov/report/911Report.pdf.

[44] Quoted in Bruce Maxwell, *Homeland Security: A Documentary History* (2004), p. 182. For full report, see Rex A. Hudson, *The Sociology and Psychology of Terrorism: Who Becomes a Terrorist and Why?* (September 1999), Library of Congress, www.loc.gov/rr/frd/pdf-files/Soc_Psych_of_Terrorism.pdf.

[45] *Ibid.*

[46] Ronald Brownstein, "Terror Warnings Offer Cautionary Tale," *Los Angeles Times*, May 23, 2002, p. A10.

[47] Quoted in *ibid.*

[48] Pam Belluck, "Unrepentant Shoe Bomber Is Given a Life Sentence For Trying to Blow Up Jet," *The New York Times*, Jan. 31, 2003.

[49] Scott Shane and Eric Lichtblau, "Scientist's Suicide Linked to Anthrax Inquiry," *The New York Times*, Aug. 2, 2008, www.nytimes.com/2008/08/02/washington/02anthrax.html?scp=1&sq="BruceIvins"anthrax&st=cse.

[50] Scott Shane, "Portrait Emerges of Anthrax Suspect's Troubled Life," *The New York Times*, Jan. 3, 2009, www.nytimes.com/2009/01/04/us/04anthrax.html?scp=3&sq="BruceIvins"anthrax&st=cse.

[51] Unless otherwise indicated, this subsection is drawn from Kettl, *op. cit.*

[52] Quoted in Elisabeth Bumiller with Alison Mitchell, "Bush Predicts Turf War in Creation of New Department," *The New York Times*, June 8, 2002, p. A11.

[53] Quoted in Jim VandeHei and Dan Eggen, "Hill Eyes Shifting Parts of FBI, CIA," *The Washington Post*, June 13, 2002, p. A1.

[54] "Homeland Security Presidential Transition Initiative," Center for American Progress Action Fund, and Third Way, November 2008, p. 1, www.americanprogressaction.org/issues/2008/pdf/homeland_security_transition.pdf.

[55] For background on the London-Glasgow bombing attempts, see Sebastian Rotella, "Unusual duo at center of British case," *Los Angeles Times*, July 7, 2007, p. A5. Also see Sarah Glazer, "Radical Islam in Europe," *CQ Global Researcher*, November 2007.

[56] Peter Baker, "Obama is Reported Set to Revise Counterterrorism Efforts," *The New York Times*, Jan. 8, 2009, p. A22.

[57] Quoted in Eileen Sullivan and Pamela Hess, "Obama plans to overhaul counterterrorism apparatus," The Associated Press, Jan. 8, 2009, www.google.com/hostednews/ap/article/ALeqM5iOLjTMSexoKymgOZO2ed0Q-4PicQD95J469O0.

[58] *Ibid.*

[59] The 9/11 Commission report, *op. cit.*, p. 263.

[60] Damien Cave, "After 2 Mistrials, Prosecutors Try Again to Prove Jihad Plot," *The New York Times*, Jan. 27, 2009, p. A22.

[61] Quoted in Scott Shane and Andrea Zarate, "F.B.I. Killed Plot in Talking Stage, A Top Aide Says," *The New York Times*, June 24, 2006, p. A1.

[62] Quoted in Dan Eggen and Susan Schmidt, "'Dirty Bomb' Plot Uncovered, U.S. Says," *The Washington Post*, June 11, 2002, p. A1.

[63] Peter Woriskey and Dan Eggen, "Judge Sentences Padilla to 17 Years, Cites His Detention," *The Washington Post*, Jan. 23, 2008, p. A1; Carol J. Williams, "Arrested in '02, 'dirty bomb' suspect Padilla to be tried," *Los Angeles Times*, April 16, 2007, p. A8.

[64] Julian E. Barnes, "Five in N.J. convicted of plot to kill soldiers," *Los Angeles Times*, Dec. 23, 2008, p. A8.

[65] Quoted in *ibid.*

[66] Gretel C. Kovach, "Five Convicted in Terrorism Financing Trial," *The New York Times*, Nov. 24, 2008, www.nytimes.com/2008/11/25/us/25charity.html?ref=us.

[67] Barnes, *op. cit.*

[68] Quoted in Cave, *op. cit.*

[69] "English Translation of Osama bin Laden's Call for Jihad. . . .," *op. cit.*

FOR MORE INFORMATION

America's War Against Terrorism, World Trade Center/Pentagon Terrorism and the Aftermath, 203 Hatcher Graduate Library, University of Michigan Library; www.lib.umich.edu/govdocs/usterror.html. Administers a massive archive on major terrorism-related issues.

Counterterrorism Blog; http://counterterrorismblog.org. A content-rich site with plentiful links to documents and news reports.

Homeland Security Watch; www.hlswatch.com. A Washington-based blog that follows daily events at the Homeland Security Department.

In Case of Emergency, Read Blog; http://incaseofemergencyblog.com. A blog by an author writing a book on citizen preparedness for disasters, with links to documents and reports on related events.

Jihadica, www.jihadica.com. International blog by military intellectuals tracking developments in the Sunni jihadist world via blog posts, with links to primary sources, many in Arabic.

National Consortium for the Study of Terrorism and Responses to Terrorism (START), 3300 Symons Hall, University of Maryland, College Park, MD 20742; (301) 405-6600; www.start.umd.edu. A Homeland Security Department-funded think tank that runs an enormous database of terrorist incidents since 1970.

Senate Committee on Homeland Security and Governmental Affairs, 340 Dirksen Senate Office Building, Washington, DC 20510; (202) 224-2627; http://hsgac.senate.gov/public/index.cfm?Fuseaction=Home.Home. A valuable source of information on hearings and reports.

Bibliography

Selected Sources

Books

Ervin, Clark Kent, *Open Target: Where America is Vulnerable to Attack*, Palgrave MacMillan, 2006.

An ex-inspector general of the Department of Homeland Security exposes what he argues are grave deficiencies in the department, as well as their consequences for the country.

Kettl, Donald F., *System Under Stress: Homeland Security and American Politics*, CQ Press, 2007.

The electoral and bureaucratic politics involved in the creation of the Department of Homeland Security are analyzed by a University of Pennsylvania political scientist.

Mueller, John, *Overblown: How Politicians and the Terrorism Industry Inflate National Security Threats, and Why We Believe Them*, Free Press, 2006.

An Ohio State University political scientist issues a stinging indictment of what he deems to be a chronic exaggeration of terrorism dangers.

Naftali, Timothy, *Blind Spot: The Secret History of American Counterterrorism*, Basic Books, 2005.

Decades of U.S. anti-terrorism work predating 9/11 are examined by a historian who now directs the National Archives' Richard Nixon Presidential Library and Museum.

Riedel, Bruce, *The Search for Al Qaeda: Its Leadership, Ideology, and Future*, Brookings Institution, 2008.

A former CIA expert examines al Qaeda's capacity to strike.

Sageman, Marc, *Leaderless Jihad: Terror Networks in the 21st Century*, University of Pennsylvania, 2008.

A former CIA officer examines the spread of jihadist doctrine beyond the original al Qaeda organization.

Articles

Burton, Fred, and Ben West, "From the New York Landmarks to the Mumbai Attack," *Stratfor*, Dec. 3, 2008, www.stratfor.com/weekly/20081203_new_york_landmarks_plot_mumbai_attack.

Intelligence analysts trace the Mumbai attacks to a thwarted 1993 plot to attack sites in New York.

Gorman, Siobhan, and Susan Schmidt, "Officials Worry Attacks in Mumbai Could Spur Copycats in the West," *The Wall Street Journal*, Dec. 11, 2008, online.wsj.com/article/SB122895354114996367.html.

Experts worry that the low-tech but deadly assault on Mumbai could appeal to would-be jihadists outside Asia.

Hoffman, Bruce, "The Myth of Grass-Roots Terrorism: Why

Osama bin Laden Still Matters," *Foreign Affairs*, May-June, 2008; and Sageman, Marc, and Bruce Hoffman, "Does Osama Still Call the Shots?" *Foreign Affairs*, July-August, 2008.

Experts debate the future of jihadist terrorism.

Johnson, Carrie, "Bad Economy May Fuel Hate Groups, Experts Warn," *The Washington Post*, Jan. 11, 2009, p. A4.

An economic meltdown is a classic stimulus to right-wing extremism — a historical precedent that has terrorism experts on guard.

Johnson, Carrie, and Walter Pincus, "Few Clear Wins in U.S. Anti-Terror Cases," *The Washington Post*, April 21, 2008, p. A1.

Correspondents chronicle the mixed results of post-9/11 terrorism trials.

Weiner, Tim, "The Kashmir Connection: A Puzzle," *The New York Times*, Dec. 6, 2008, query.nytimes.com/gst/fullpage.html?res=9D05E6D91438F934A35751C1A96E9C8B63.

A *New York Times* correspondent and author of a history of the CIA reports on evidence of possible ties between al Qaeda and the Pakistani group Lashkar-e-Taiba.

Reports and Studies

"Biosafety Laboratories: Perimeter Security Assessment of the Nation's Five BSL-4 Laboratories," Government Accountability Office, September 2008, www.gao.gov/new.items/d081092.pdf.

Congressional staffers have discovered lax security in two laboratories authorized to work with deadly pathogens.

"Planning Guidance for Response to a Nuclear Detonation," Homeland Security Council, Jan. 16, 2009, www.afrri.usuhs.mil/outreach/pdf/planning-guidance.pdf.

A White House agency advises city and county officials as well as emergency responders on how to prepare for the first three days following a nuclear explosion.

Benjamin, Daniel, "Strategic Counterterrorism," Brookings Institution, October, 2008, www.brookings.edu/papers/2008/10_terrorism_benjamin.aspx.

A former Clinton-era counterterrorism specialist critiques the Bush administration's military approach to fighting terrorists.

Randol, Mark A., "Homeland Security Intelligence: Perceptions, Statutory Definitions, and Approaches," Congressional Research Service, Jan. 14, 2009, fas.org/sgp/crs/intel/RL33616.pdf.

A writer for Congress' analytical arm examines options for restructuring domestic intelligence on terrorism.

The Next Step:

Additional Articles from Current Periodicals

Al Qaeda

Carter, Sara A., "Al Qaeda Seen Planning Another Attack on U.S.," *The Washington Times*, Feb. 6, 2008, p. A1.

Senior intelligence officials have told the Senate Select Committee on Intelligence the al Qaeda terrorist group is using operatives in Iraq to help prepare another strike on the United States.

DeYoung, Karen, and Walter Pincus, "Al-Qaeda's Gains Keep U.S. at Risk, Report Says," *The Washington Post*, July 18, 2007, p. A1.

Al Qaeda has reestablished its central organization and training infrastructure over the past two years, putting the United States at high risk, according to a new intelligence estimate.

Lake, Eli, "Al Qaeda Cell May Be Loose in U.S., British Plot Hints," *New York Sun*, Aug. 6, 2007, p. 1.

Intelligence gleaned from car bombers in Britain suggests that an al Qaeda cell may be in the United States.

Shane, Scott, "Same People, Same Threat," *The New York Times*, July 18, 2007, p. A1.

After years of war in Afghanistan and Iraq, as well as targeted killings in Pakistan and Yemen, al Qaeda remains a major threat to the United States.

Biological Weapons

Chong, Jia-Rui, "Research Into Potent Bioagents Increases the Risk," *Los Angeles Times*, Oct. 3, 2007, p. A1.

American universities and research laboratories are not well-equipped to handle the increasing number of programs centering on biodefense.

Hall, Mimi, "Changes Made to Bioterror Warning Program," *USA Today*, Feb. 8, 2007, p. 3A.

The Homeland Security inspector general contends that sensors designed to give early warnings of a bioterrorist attack are being handled and stored sloppily.

Kellman, Barry, "Flier With Tuberculosis Raises Red Flags About Bioterrorism," *Chicago Tribune*, May 31, 2007, p. A23.

An air passenger with tuberculosis suggests that groups lacking technological sophistication are very capable of executing a bioterrorist attack.

Cyber-Security

Caterinicchia, Dan, "Federal Energy Regulatory Commission Approves Cyber Security Standards for Power Providers," The Associated Press, Jan. 17, 2008.

Federal regulators have approved the first cyber-security standards for the electric industry amid concerns over vulnerabilities of the nation's power grid.

Matthews, William, "Security Experts Predict Cyber Attacks Will Increase," *Air Force Times*, Nov. 10, 2008, p. 26.

Cyber attacks are expected to play a larger role among hostile nations seeking to subvert the U.S. economy and its infrastructure.

Nakashima, Ellen, "Cyber Attack Data-Sharing Is Lacking, Congress Told," *The Washington Post*, Sept. 19, 2008, p. D2.

U.S. intelligence agencies are refusing to share information regarding foreign cyber attacks against companies for fear of exposing intelligence-gathering methods.

Department of Homeland Security

Mercer, Marsha, "Creating Real Homeland Security," *Seattle Post-Intelligencer*, Dec. 9, 2008, p. A14.

It seems unrealistic to expect Homeland Security Secretary Janet Napolitano to reform the department's bureaucracy and protect the U.S. from the growing threat of terrorism at the same time.

Ransom, Lou, "Homeland Security Brings No Security to Our Homes," *Chicago Defender*, Feb. 20, 2008, p. 14.

The Department of Homeland Security doesn't provide much security to the United States because it looks for threats outside the country's borders without much attention to those within.

Savage, Charlie, "US Doles Out Millions for Street Cameras," *The Boston Globe*, Aug. 12, 2007, p. A1.

The Department of Homeland Security has given millions of dollars to local governments to purchase high-tech video-camera networks in an effort to combat terrorism.

CITING *CQ RESEARCHER*

Sample formats for citing these reports in a bibliography include the ones listed below. Preferred styles and formats vary, so please check with your instructor or professor.

MLA STYLE

Jost, Kenneth. "Rethinking the Death Penalty." CQ Researcher 16 Nov. 2001: 945-68.

APA STYLE

Jost, K. (2001, November 16). Rethinking the death penalty. *CQ Researcher, 11*, 945-968.

CHICAGO STYLE

Jost, Kenneth. "Rethinking the Death Penalty." *CQ Researcher*, November 16, 2001, 945-968.

In-depth Reports on Issues in the News

Are you writing a paper?

Need backup for a debate?

Want to become an expert on an issue?

For 80 years, students have turned to *CQ Researcher* for in-depth reporting on issues in the news. Reports on a full range of political and social issues are now available. Following is a selection of recent reports:

Civil Liberties
Limiting Lawsuits, 12/08
Affirmative Action, 10/08
Gay Marriage Showdowns, 9/08
America's Border Fence, 9/08
Immigration Debate, 2/08
Prison Reform, 4/07

Crime/Law
Mexico's Drug War, 12/08
Prostitution Debate, 5/08
Public Defenders, 4/08
Gun Violence, 5/07

Education
Reading Crisis? 2/08
Discipline in Schools, 2/08
Student Aid, 1/08
Racial Diversity in Public Schools, 9/07
Stress on Students, 7/07

Environment
Reducing Carbon Footprint, 12/08
Protecting Wetlands, 10/08
Buying Green, 2/08
Future of Recycling, 12/07

Health/Safety
Preventing Cancer, 1/09
Heart Health, 9/08
Global Food Crisis, 6/08
Preventing Memory Loss, 4/08

International Affairs/Politics
The Obama Presidency, 1/09
The National Debt, 11/08
Financial Bailout, 10/08
Political Conventions, 8/08
Race and Politics, 7/08

Social Trends
Falling Birthrates, 11/08
Regulating Credit Cards, 10/08
Internet Accuracy, 8/08
Financial Crisis, 5/08
Cyberbullying, 5/08

Terrorism/Defense
Rise in Counterinsurgency, 9/08
Cost of the Iraq War, 4/08

Youth
Debating Hip-Hop, 6/07

Upcoming Reports

Public Works Jobs, 2/20/09   Closing Guantánamo, 2/27/09   Future of Middle Class, 3/6/09

ACCESS

CQ Researcher is available in print and online. For access, visit your library or www.cqresearcher.com.

STAY CURRENT

To receive notice of upcoming *CQ Researcher* reports, or learn more about *CQ Researcher* products, subscribe to the free e-mail newsletters, *CQ Researcher Alert!* and *CQ Researcher News*: http://cqpress.com/newsletters.

PURCHASE

To purchase a *CQ Researcher* report in print or electronic format (PDF), visit www.cqpress.com or call 866-427-7737. Single reports start at $15. Bulk purchase discounts and electronic-rights licensing are also available.

SUBSCRIBE

Annual full-service *CQ Researcher* subscriptions—including 44 reports a year, monthly index updates, and a bound volume—start at $803. Add $25 for domestic postage.

CQ Researcher Online offers a backfile from 1991 and a number of tools to simplify research. For pricing information, call 800-834-9020, ext. 1906, or e-mail librarysales@cqpress.com.

Published by CQ Press, a division of SAGE Publications

www.cqresearcher.com

Public-Works Projects

Do they stimulate the economy more than tax cuts?

To battle the Great Depression, President Franklin D. Roosevelt put millions of unemployed Americans to work on New Deal projects such as repairing roads and building cabins in national parks. To stimulate today's ailing economy, Congress has enacted a $787 billion package that includes tax cuts and spending on infrastructure, including expanding highway and rail systems and weatherizing buildings. But many conservatives argue that government spending does not create jobs and merely diverts money from the private sector, which they call the only true engine of job creation. Meanwhile, infrastructure experts worry that if federal public-works dollars are spent too quickly, the money will go to eco-unfriendly projects, such as additional highway lanes that encourage fossil-fuel use and suburban sprawl, rather than to more future-oriented "green" initiatives like expanding rail and public transit and upgrading the electrical grid to accommodate alternative power sources.

Workers install a generator at a Tennessee Valley Authority power plant in 1953. Launched in 1933 as one of the first New Deal programs, the TVA brought electricity to the impoverished region while putting tens of thousands of people to work.

CQ Researcher • Feb. 20, 2009 • www.cqresearcher.com
Volume 19, Number 7 • Pages 153-176

CQ PRESS

RECIPIENT OF SOCIETY OF PROFESSIONAL JOURNALISTS AWARD FOR EXCELLENCE ◆ AMERICAN BAR ASSOCIATION SILVER GAVEL AWARD

CQ Researcher

Feb. 20, 2009
Volume 19, Number 7

MANAGING EDITOR: Thomas J. Colin
tcolin@cqpress.com

ASSISTANT MANAGING EDITOR: Kathy Koch
kkoch@cqpress.com

ASSOCIATE EDITOR: Kenneth Jost

STAFF WRITERS: Thomas J. Billitteri,
Marcia Clemmitt, Peter Katel

CONTRIBUTING WRITERS: Rachel Cox,
Sarah Glazer, Alan Greenblatt,
Barbara Mantel, Patrick Marshall, Tom Price,
Jennifer Weeks

DESIGN/PRODUCTION EDITOR: Olu B. Davis

ASSISTANT EDITOR: Darrell Dela Rosa

FACT-CHECKING: Eugene J. Gabler,
Michelle Harris

EDITORIAL INTERN: Vyomika Jairam

CQ PRESS

A Division of
SAGE Publications

PRESIDENT AND PUBLISHER:
John A. Jenkins

EXECUTIVE DIRECTOR,
REFERENCE INFORMATION GROUP:
Alix B. Vance

CQ Press is a registered trademark of Congressional Quarterly Inc.

CQ Researcher (ISSN 1056-2036) is printed on acid-free paper. Published weekly, except; (Jan. wk. 1) (May wk. 4) (July wks. 1, 2) (Aug. wks. 3, 4) (Nov. wk. 4) and (Dec. wk. 4), by CQ Press, a division of SAGE Publications. Annual full-service subscriptions start at $803. For pricing, call 1-800-834-9020, ext. 1906. To purchase a CQ Researcher report in print or electronic format (PDF), visit www. cqpress.com or call 866-427-7737. Single reports start at $15. Bulk purchase discounts and electronic-rights licensing are also available. Periodicals postage paid at Washington, D.C., and additional mailing offices. POSTMASTER: Send address changes to CQ Researcher, 2300 N St., N.W., Suite 800, Washington, DC 20037.

Cover: Getty Images/*Time Life* Pictures/Margaret Bourke-White

Public-Works Projects

BY MARCIA CLEMMITT

THE ISSUES

Matthew Sinkovec, a truck driver for an excavation company in northeastern Ohio, used to have plenty of work hauling materials to home-construction sites. But as the economic crisis battered the Cleveland area, work dried up.

"Instead of four jobs lined up, I'd get one and then wait for another," he said. Eventually, "the bottom just fell out," and he was laid off last November. Now, he mostly stays home, trying to conserve money, and hopes to find another construction job before his unemployment checks end. "I try not to think about this lasting too long," he said. "That is a real scary thought." [1]

The construction business was among the first to slow drastically as the United States entered a recession in December 2007, but most other industries now also have slowed — with accompanying layoffs. In January 2009 alone, 598,000 people nationwide lost their jobs, the biggest monthly total since 1974. [2] And in some places, net job loss has been a long-term phenomenon. Hard-hit Ohio, for example, has lost nearly a quarter of its manufacturing jobs since 2000 and 5 percent of its jobs overall. [3]

In response, President Barack Obama and congressional Democrats developed the American Recovery and Reinvestment Act and declared the so-called stimulus package their first major legislative priority of 2009. Enacted by Congress on Feb. 13 and signed into law by Obama on Feb. 17, the act is designed to pump

Thirteen motorists died when Minneapolis' I-35 W Bridge over the Mississippi River collapsed in 2007, dramatizing the poor condition of the nation's highways, dams and other infrastructure. President Obama's stimulus plan is designed to pump additional demand for goods and services into the economy, largely by creating jobs and repairing and retooling American infrastructure for the future. Obama signed the measure into law on Feb. 17, calling it "the most sweeping economic recovery package in our history.

additional demand for goods and services into the economy, partly by creating jobs and retooling infrastructure for the future. It is "the most sweeping economic recovery package in our history . . . putting Americans to work . . . in critical areas . . . that will bring real and lasting change for generations to come," Obama said. [4]

Parts of the bill's economic-stimulus provisions are familiar — tax cuts and boosts in aid programs such as unemployment benefits and Medicaid. But it's the first major economic-recovery plan to include federal spending for public works like highways and energy-efficiency upgrades for buildings since President Bill Clinton proposed, but ultimately dropped, such a proposal in 1993. [5]

Conservative analysts and most congressional Republicans were quick to denounce the public-works spending provisions as a waste of taxpayer dollars that won't help the economy.

"We have no evidence from recent or distant history" that public-works spending creates jobs or spurs the economy, says Ronald D. Utt, a senior research fellow at the conservative Heritage Foundation. The Obama plan is partly modeled on the Depression-era job-creation initiatives of President Franklin D. Roosevelt's New Deal. "I don't know that that many people were ultimately employed" by those 1930s programs, Utt says.

Obama says the programs will benefit the economy both in the current recession and long term. For example, grants to weatherize homes — modifying them to reduce energy consumption — will "immediately put people back to work," he told CBS News. "And we're going to train people who are out of work, including young people, to do the weatherization. "Not only are you immediately putting people back to work, but you're also [helping] families on energy bills and . . . laying the groundwork for long-term energy independence." [6] Other projects would repair highways, create high-speed rail systems and make public buildings energy-efficient.

Spending Provides More Stimulus Than Tax Cuts

Stimulus items that increase spending provide more return — or "bang for the buck" — than tax cuts, according to Moody's economist Mark Zandi. Increasing spending on infrastructure, for example, is expected to yield $1.59 in revenue for every dollar spent by the federal government, compared with $1.22 for a lump-sum tax rebate.

"Bang for the Buck" for Select Stimulus Programs

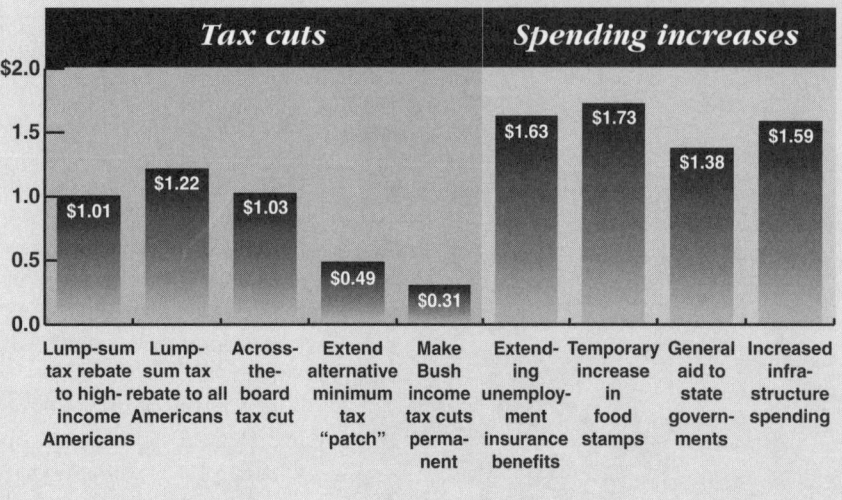

Tax cuts					Spending increases			
$1.01	$1.22	$1.03	$0.49	$0.31	$1.63	$1.73	$1.38	$1.59
Lump-sum tax rebate to high-income Americans	Lump-sum tax rebate to all Americans	Across-the-board tax cut	Extend alternative minimum tax "patch"	Make Bush income tax cuts permanent	Extending unemployment insurance benefits	Temporary increase in food stamps	General aid to state governments	Increased infrastructure spending

Source: Mark Zandi, testimony before House Committee on the Budget, January 2009

A stimulus package similar to the one Congress approved should create between 3.3 million and 4.1 million jobs over the next two years — around 1.3 million of them from public-works programs — according to Christina Romer, chair of the White House Council of Economic Advisers, and Jared Bernstein, chief economist for Vice President Joseph Biden. More than 90 percent of the jobs created will be in the private sector, about a third of them in construction and manufacturing. [7]

Nevertheless, the plan can't possibly create enough jobs to offset the losses the economy is suffering, Romer and Bernstein caution.

About 11.6 million people were unemployed in January — 4.1 million more than a year earlier — and job losses are expected to continue into 2010, according to the U.S. Bureau of Labor Statistics. [8]

Our $15-trillion-per-year economy has taken at least a 5 percent hit —

$750 billion — in the demand for goods and services that keeps business humming, says James K. Galbraith, an economist and a professor of government at the Lyndon B. Johnson School of Public Affairs at the University of Texas, Austin. "Infrastructure is not going to make up a $750 billion to $1 trillion hole in economic activity," he says.

Infrastructure experts also caution that the country's longtime neglect and underfunding of infrastructure maintenance and planning means that some public-works projects will suffer some delay before they're up and running.

"Up to a point, public works are a good way" to stimulate job creation, says Richard G. Little, director of the Keston Institute for Public Finance and Infrastructure Policy at the University of Southern California. However, in the present workforce we don't have the welders, the heavy equipment operators and other skilled workers we need, he says.

"A stimulus package with real sticking power should support training in the construction trades for the vast number of young and underemployed people for whom college is not the career solution," Little said. [9]

The key question for many is whether infrastructure spending that creates jobs quickly can also be visionary enough to strengthen the nation and economy long term.

Public-works spending can contribute toward stabilizing the economy in the short term, depending on how quickly the money can be spent, "but, much more important, the public works of today will redefine how we live in the future," says Galbraith, noting that the Interstate Highway System launched by President Dwight D. Eisenhower in the 1950s created America's suburbs.

When it comes to federal infrastructure spending, "forget about stimulating the economy over the next year," says Robert P. Inman, a professor of finance and economics at the University of Pennsylvania's Wharton School of Finance. "The rewards should be found in the project itself," and, ideally, the benefits should be national, he says.

For example, "if you give money to Pennsylvania to invest in education, their kids will be more productive, and they'll end up living everywhere in the country," benefiting the whole nation, he says. In the best-case scenario, the dollars would go to inner-city and other poor schools, he says, thus aiding a cause "that we value but that wouldn't have received help otherwise" — a good test for the worth of government spending, he adds.

There's tension between projects that will give local economies a quick boost and those that would best serve future needs, says Anthony Shorris, a fellow at the liberal Century Foundation think tank and former executive director of the Port Authority of New York and New Jersey. "The fastest thing to build is a new road, but it's the opposite of everything we want" in the long run, producing more sprawling development and more carbon-emitting automobiles, he says.

"If the wrong things are done, they may do damage with this [stimulus] bill," says John Norquist, president of the Congress for the New Urbanism, a Chicago-based nonprofit that promotes walkable environments and sustainable development.

"It's crucial to think beyond the current crisis," says Guian A. McKee, an associate professor of history at the University of Virginia. "What do we want the structure of this economy to be 10 to 15 years from now? Do we want mass transit, alternative energy?" If so, then it's time to focus on such projects, he says. "While we need the shovel-ready stuff for the crisis, we shouldn't neglect the long-term things," he says.

At present, though, "we haven't really developed a vision of the 21st-century U.S. economy, so we don't know what infrastructure we need to support it," says Armando Carbonell, a senior fellow at the Lincoln Institute of Land Policy, a think tank in Cambridge, Mass. To create a vision for the transportation system, for example, "we need to know where the current system breaks down" and stymies important travels, he says. For example, highways and air travel are congested and frustrating in the Northeast Corridor, so we know that providing a rail alternative is a good possibility, he says.

"You need the target, and you need the vision, because tomorrow is going to be different from today," Carbonell says.

"If we're going to have an infrastructure feeding frenzy, make sure government builds public works that will make us more productive as a nation," such as roads, bridges, mass transit, integrated information technology in public industries like health care, and military recapitalization, said New Hampshire Sen. Judd Gregg, top-ranking Republican on the Senate Budget Committee. "This is about bringing the nation out of this recession in a manner that makes us more competitive in the international market." [10]

Job Loss Likely to Exceed Job Creation

Economists predict the stimulus plan will create 1.3 million new public-works jobs and possibly two or three times as many jobs overall (right graph). U.S. employment has declined by 3.6 million since the start of the recession in December 2007. Nearly 600,000 jobs were lost in January — eight times the number lost in the same month a year earlier (left graph).

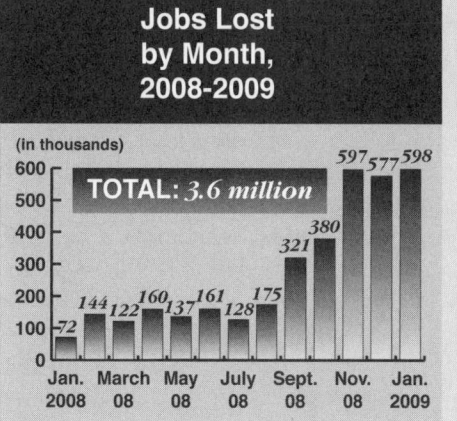

Jobs Lost by Month, 2008-2009

(in thousands)

TOTAL: *3.6 million*

72, 144, 122, 160, 137, 161, 128, 175, 321, 380, 597, 577, 598

Jan. 2008, March 08, May 08, July 08, Sept. 08, Nov. 08, Jan. 2009

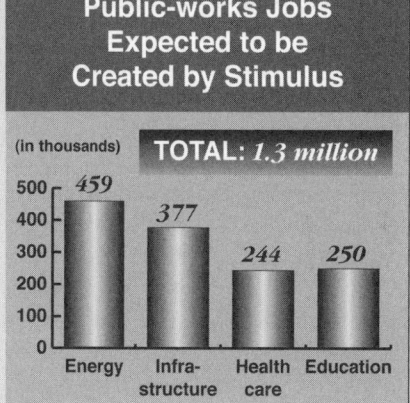

Public-works Jobs Expected to be Created by Stimulus

(in thousands)

TOTAL: *1.3 million*

459, 377, 244, 250

Energy, Infrastructure, Health care, Education

Sources: Bureau of Labor Statistics; Christina Romer and Jared Bernstein, "The Job Impact of the American Recovery and Reinvestment Plan," Offices of the President and Vice President, January 2009

As lawmakers, economists and infrastructure experts debate how to put Americans back to work, here are some of the questions being asked:

Will federal spending on public works create jobs?

The final stimulus plan banks heavily on projects such as expanding and repairing highway and rail systems and modernizing schools. But many conservative lawmakers and analysts argue that government spending cannot create jobs but only diverts money from the private sector, which they call the only true engine of job creation.

"Despite the rhetoric of 'government job creation,' economic logic denies the possibility that jobs can, on net, be created by government," Thomas J. DiLorenzo, a professor of economics at Baltimore-based Loyola College, wrote in an analysis for the libertarian Cato Institute think tank. That's because "gov-

ernment jobs programs . . . are usually financed by taxation or borrowing," diverting resources from private-sector business investment. [11]

Some infrastructure spending proposed by Democrats, especially so-called green projects, would not create jobs at all, Tyler Cowen, a professor of economics at George Mason University in Fairfax, Va., told National Public Radio. "Take solar energy," Cowen said. "The whole point of solar energy is that the sun does more of the work." [12]

New Deal government spending was not a great job creator, demonstrating that the Obama plan won't be either, argued Amity Shlaes, a columnist for Bloomberg News and senior fellow at the Council on Foreign Relations think tank. When FDR took office in 1933, unemployment was around 25 percent and remained above 14 percent between 1931 and 1940, not counting the jobs in federal public-works programs that Shlaes contends were temporary "make-work" jobs created only to provide paychecks, not for any real purpose. [13]

Most economists do count New Deal jobs as real employment, Shlaes acknowledged. Even then, she said, depression unemployment rates never get below 9 percent, but that's "hardly a jobless target to which the Obama administration would aspire."

For one thing, says the Heritage Foundation's Utt, federal jobs created won't necessarily match the skills of those who need work. "Will a roofer easily make the transition to laying concrete on highways?" he asks. "And finance people aren't going to get involved in working for the National Park Service."

Furthermore, a typical highway project spends only about 27 percent of its funding in the first year, according to the Federal Highway Administration, "so an infrastructure project will only make a little difference" in fighting the current recession, Utt says.

Even so-called shovel-ready projects take time to produce paychecks, acknowledges Alan Rubin, director of government relations for Buchanan Ingersoll, a national law and lobbying firm in Pittsburgh. For substantial projects — those creating 400 jobs or more — it takes about 90 days to hire a general contractor, says Rubin, then another month for the contractor to find a banking partner and meet bonding and insurance requirements and then two more weeks before workers get the first paycheck, he says.

"Infrastructure money won't have an impact until late 2009 or early 2010," so it likely won't shorten the recession, "although it may give some help" once the economy starts to rebound on its own, says Wharton's Inman.

But supporters of public-works initiatives reject the criticisms. For one thing, public spending doesn't divert resources from private business investment during a serious recession, said John D. Porcari, Maryland's secretary of transportation. "I hear from

contractors all the time they don't have any private-sector work. . . . To be blunt about it, it's so bad out there that additional work right now would be the difference between holding onto employees and letting people go," Porcari said. [14]

And public-works jobs will offset some job losses even if the projects take time to get off the ground because in the last two recessions weaknesses in the labor market persisted well after the economy began its turnaround, John S. Irons, research and policy director at the liberal Economic Policy Institute, told the House Committee on Transportation and Infrastructure in October. [15]

Furthermore, economists now generally acknowledge that "this is going to be a long recession" that will continue to need stimulus months from now, says Roger Hickey, co-director of the progressive advocacy group Campaign for America's Future. "I think the public knows these layoffs they're experiencing now are just the beginning and that [earlier] tax cuts" — such as the tax rebates of 2008 and various other tax cuts before that — did not stop the downturn in the early 2000s, he says.

Economists estimate that $1 billion in construction spending creates between 14,000 and 47,000 jobs, so a $75 billion increase for infrastructure would support more than 1 million jobs in areas such as manufacturing, retail sales, scientific and technical jobs, administration and waste management, Irons said. [16]

In addition, the public needs to believe in something in order to spur businesses to take initiative again, and public-works spending that provides work and strengthens infrastructure can help build that belief, says McKee at the University of Virginia.

"This is the most perfect time . . . to lay out a plan to rebuild America, just like Roosevelt has done because it would stimulate the economy and it would create a tremendous amount of jobs," Gov. Arnold Schwarzeneg-

ger, R-Calif., told CNN. "It's not spending. It's an investment" in a stronger economy, he said. [17]

Some construction managers say they're counting on public-works funds to keep hiring. "I told my managers that based on the expectation of a stimulus plan, we should continue interviewing people at colleges, hoping to have work for them by the time they graduate in the spring," said Brian Burgett, president of a construction firm in Frederickton, Ohio. [18]

Contrary to what some conservative analysts argue, the New Deal did create jobs, says Jason Scott Smith, an assistant professor of history at the University of New Mexico and author of *Building New Deal Liberalism: The Political Economy of Public Works, 1933-1956*. Smith rejects Bloomberg columnist Shlaes' argument that public-works jobs are of limited value because they are mostly temporary. Temporary workers get and spend paychecks, helping boost business, he says.

"Except in the 1937-38 recession, unemployment fell every year of the New Deal," wrote Eric Rauchway, a professor of history at the University of California, Davis. Private, non-farm, non-governmental employment was "markedly lower under Roosevelt" than under Herbert Hoover, his predecessor. "The New Deal wasn't just offering make-work, it was stimulating the economy." [19]

Infrastructure must not only be built but maintained, and those jobs will be permanent and local, says the Century Foundation's Shorris. "You can outsource a new train, but not maintenance," he says.

With the right management strategies, it's even possible for infrastructure projects to defy the odds and become operational quickly, says William Eggers, global director for Deloitte Research — Public Services, a Washington branch of the international Deloitte consultancy. After the 1994 Northridge earthquake toppled a Los Angeles freeway, the road was rebuilt in two months — instead of a year or more as expected — "by putting in performance standards and changing procurement rules," Eggers says.

Does infrastructure construction strengthen the economy?

Proponents argue that well-targeted federal infrastructure spending can bolster the economy quickly as well as over the long term, but many critics say tax cuts are always a better economic booster.

"Americans might well rue the day when they trusted the federal government to spend the nation into prosperity," wrote Jacob G. Hornberger, president of the Future of Freedom Foundation, a conservative and libertarian advocacy group in Fairfax, Va. "It just isn't going to happen." [20]

The United States already spends substantial amounts annually on infrastructure — $102 billion in 2007 and $114 billion in 2008, for example, writes Lawrence Kudlow, a conservative economist and *National Review* columnist. "Didn't do much for growth, did it?" [21]

School modernization, touted by Democrats as a way to prepare future U.S. workers to meet economic challenges, won't accomplish its goal, said Lisa Snell, director of education research at the libertarian Reason Foundation. Stimulus funds could "more than double the current, total federal education budget" to more than $200 billion, but "unfortunately, this huge expansion is unlikely to spur improvements," she said. U.S. average per-pupil expenditure is already high, compared to other nations, yet student achievement lags behind many countries, and she notes that the plan would not require schools and teachers to adopt better practices. [22]

Japan has repeatedly tried infrastructure spending to end a nearly two-decade-long recession but failed, conservative commentators say.

An infrastructure-focused stimulus "may be intuitively attractive," but historical evidence suggests that its im-

House and Senate Differ on Spending

Wide differences in funding separated many items in the House and Senate versions of the stimulus plan. Construction funds for schools and colleges took a big hit between the early and final versions of the measure. Federal-building construction and modernization was also cut, although defense-related spending, including construction, increased. Development of high-speed rail was boosted in the final bill, but greener investments in public transit received much less.

Public-Works Projects in Stimulus Plan
(in $ billions)

Item	House version	Senate version	Final version
Highway grants	$30 billion	$27.1 billion	$29 billion
Grants for public transit investment	$7.5	$8.4	$8.4
State and local government energy grants	$6.9	$4.7	$6.3
Defense environmental cleanup	$0.5	$5.5	$6
Advanced broadband program	$2.3	$6.6	$4.3
Modernization of defense facilities	$4.5	$2.5	$4.2
Energy efficiency for public housing	$2.5	$2.2	$2.2
Community health centers infrastructure	$1	$1.9	$2
K-12 school construction	$14	$0	$0
Public transit modernizations	$2	$0	$0
FEMA critical infrastructure construction	$0	$0.5	$0
State grants for high-speed and inter-city rail	0	$2	$8

Source: House Committee on Rules

pact "is very modest and unlikely to enhance recovery or deter recession," said Utt at the Heritage Foundation. "The Japanese government implemented such a program during the 1990s, and the consequence was two decades of economic stagnation." [23]

Japan's infrastructure-building boom "yielded painfully little," said Bloomberg's Shlaes. "The Nikkei [stock average] stayed down. The country's standards of living failed to keep pace with the rest of the world's." [24]

But other analysts say massive government-funded infrastructure spending in Japan failed to restart the economy because the country didn't address its deeply flawed banking system, which crippled private lending and investment.

Japan's "banking sector was broken," says lobbyist Rubin, undercutting the ability of public-works spending to stimulate the economy. Similarly, he says, restoring the U.S. banking sector to good health will be vital to effective public-works spending. [25]

Transportation Spending to Focus on Roads

More than 75 percent of the stimulus funds that 19 states plan to spend on transportation target new highways while only 17 percent would go for "green" options such as public transit. Massachusetts, however, is targeting more than half its funding to transit and bike or pedestrian paths.

Anticipated Stimulus Spending on Transportation by 19 Select States

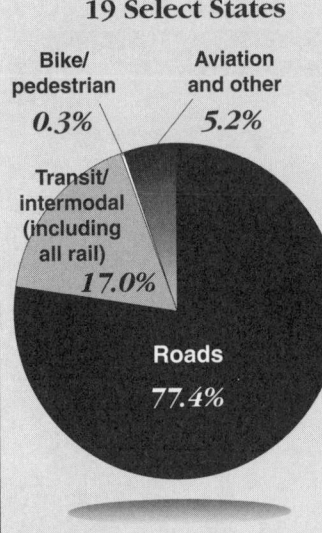

Bike/ pedestrian
0.3%

Aviation and other
5.2%

Transit/ intermodal (including all rail)
17.0%

Roads
77.4%

Examples of State Spending Plans

State	Roads	Transit/ intermodal (including all rail)	Bike/ pedestrian	Aviation and other
Ala.	100%	0%	0%	0%
Calif.	60.6%	37.1%	0%	2.3%
Florida	98.9%	1.0%	0%	0%
Mass.	29.7%	47.1%	2.2%	21.0%
N.C.	83.3%	10.2%	0%	6.1%
Texas	97.3%	2.3%	0%	0%

* Figures may not total 100 due to rounding.

Note: Only 19 states have released their transportation spending plans thus far.

Source: Phineas Baxandall, "Economic Stimulus or Simply More Misguided Spending?" U.S. PIRG Education Fund, January 2009

"Even when the government says it'll give you $50 million" for an infrastructure project, "they're not going to give you your payroll" in the form of upfront cash on day one, Rubin explains. Instead, "you get a government-backed guarantee" that the money will arrive in increments down the line. "So you need construction loans from banks to tide you over from one government check to the next," as well as to pay the architects and engineers who have to be on the payroll before building begins. Thus, credit availability is crucial, even if the government is funding projects, he says.

In addition to a continuing banking crisis that crippled lending, Japan's small size — "smaller than Illinois" with a population nearly half that of the United States — led the government to invest in redundant projects,

such as airports too close to each other, that didn't actually improve things, says the University of New Mexico's Smith. Unlike the United States, Japan also had not neglected its infrastructure in good economic times, so it had much less need for maintenance and updating projects, he says.

Increased infrastructure spending is "a particularly effective way to stimulate the economy," Mark Zandi, chief economist of Moody's Economy.com, told the House Committee on the Budget in January. "The boost to GDP from every dollar spent on public infrastructure is large — an estimated $1.59 — and there is little doubt that the nation has underinvested in infrastructure for some time, to the increasing detriment of the nation's long-term growth prospects." [26]

Nevertheless, virtually all analysts caution that a thoughtful vision of future needs must guide infrastructure spending if it's to benefit the economy long term. [27]

It's fine for the initial $50 billion to $100 billion disbursed for infrastructure to focus on projects that can be done quickly, but the next group "needs to be better thought out," says the University of Southern California's Little. Infrastructure built during Roosevelt's New Deal and the Eisenhower administration's federal highway initiatives helped bolster the U.S. economy for years, but all the projects "were guided by preexisting visions" of what future needs would be, he says.

"The middle of the 21st century won't look the same as the middle of the 20th, but so far I haven't seen a vision" articulated by the Obama administration, Little says. "We're not seeing somebody saying, 'Wow, we're going to retool this system,' but just, 'This is the quickest way to spend a couple of hundred billion dollars.'" Assessment is critical to build only what will be truly useful, he says. For example, Pittsburgh, population 350,000, has a water system that could serve a million people, based on erroneous estimates that the city would keep growing, Little says. "Those sunk costs last forever, and we don't want to repeat that too many times."

"There has to be some process for reviewing these projects," says Dean Baker, co-director of the liberal Center for Economic and Policy Research. Road-building projects of the past three decades "have promoted sprawl," for example, an outcome it's important to avoid this time around.

"We're not very good at making trade-offs across disciplines," says the Century Foundation's Shorris. For example, "a lot of the capacity of New York airports is taken up by people going to D.C. and Boston," he explains. When Germany's Frankfurt airport faced a similar situation, "they took the money and used it for trains." "But where in America do we get to have the conversation" that leads to such a cross-sector solution? Shorris asks. The fragmented U.S. system, including 50 state governments that seldom think regionally, makes big-picture planning difficult, he says.

Funding infrastructure construction but ignoring future upkeep — which costs 4-6 percent of gross domestic product annually ($500-$700 billion) just for current infrastructure — also would diminish the success of public works, says Little. [28]

His suggestion: Trillions of dollars that sit in public-sector pension funds and in the federal Social Security Trust Fund awaiting workers' retirement could be lent to the states for revenue-producing projects such as highways, then repaid with interest. "Motorists using the facilities would also benefit because a portion of the tolls paid would support the long-term solvency" of the U.S. retirement system, says Little. [29]

Recession or no, federal "infrastructure spending makes a lot of sense on its own terms," provided it will provide benefits down the line to the nation in excess of what's paid for it, says Wharton's Inman. In the best-case scenario, when state governors submit lists of potentially fundable projects, "you would evaluate these things on their own terms, and if a project promises significant interstate value," then the federal government would consider funding it, he says. "Lacking that, the state government should do the project on its own."

In a recession, however, the question is a bit different, Inman continues. Economic theory holds that by stimulating "aggregate demand" for goods and services anywhere in the nation during a recession, the economy of the whole country can be revived, he says. If that's true, federal funding for a Pennsylvania infrastructure project that would benefit only Pennsylvanians could still be a good idea, since the spending itself would increase the nation's aggre-

gate demand. However, "economists, in fact, know very little about this" or about the role of states in affecting the national economy and can't argue it conclusively, he says.

Is the Democratic public-works spending plan too big?

Many economists say the present recession is so dire that only massive government spending has a chance to jump-start the economy. However, many conservatives argue that public-works spending at the levels proposed by Democrats will run up the national debt to disastrous proportions. [30]

The Democrats' stimulus plan will cause a dangerous expansion of the national debt, according to the House Republican Study Committee. The federal debt may grow by an unprecedented $2 trillion in 2009, an unsustainable burden given that it already grew by more than $2 trillion during the last two years, the panel argues. [31]

"In principle, every dollar spent by the government could cause national income to increase by more than a dollar it if leads to a more vibrant economy," noted Harvard University Professor of Economics N. Gregory Mankiw. But "the fly in the ointment . . . is the long-run fiscal picture. Increased government spending may be a good short-run fix, but it would add to the budget deficit," making it harder to fulfill other responsibilities like paying Social Security and Medicare benefits to the baby boomers now beginning to retire. So he thinks Democratic spending plans are too big. [32]

The federal government may not currently be equipped to manage spending of the scale contemplated, said Rudolph G. Penner, a senior fellow at the centrist Urban Institute and former director of the Congressional Budget Office. "It looks like the federal budget for highways would increase more than one-third," but "I do not hear of plans to increase the size of the federal bureaucracy temporarily by comparable

amounts, and one wonders whether the existing civil service can provide adequate oversight." [33]

Big infrastructure requires both public and private players, and "it won't work unless everybody buys in and says, 'I'm going to do it straight,' " says lobbyist Rubin. To convince the public that "government needs to be part of the solution, government has to be responsible" and "be an honest broker so it doesn't turn people off," a necessity that has already been somewhat compromised by tax problems among some White House nominees, he says. [34]

But other analysts argue that, given the nearly unprecedented magnitude of the economic downturn, the proposed public-works spending may actually be too small.

The economy is on the way to losing between $1.1 trillion and $1.2 trillion in demand for goods and services this year, due to the decline in home and non-home construction and the loss of large chunks of many Americans' home equity and investments, said liberal economist Baker. Meanwhile, the two-year stimulus package as a whole — including all spending and tax cuts — would add back just under $400 billion per year, said Baker. "I don't think it's large enough." [35]

"Maybe private credit will recover faster than I think likely," so that some government spending will end up destructively competing with private spending, said University of Texas economist Galbraith. "But even allowing for this possibility, action now should be on a grand scale. It is far easier to trim back" provisions as the economy expands "than it will be to repeat the political effort of passing a large expansion package if the first one is too small." [36]

A sizable infrastructure-spending plan is warranted because of stingy U.S. spending on infrastructure for decades — 2.5 percent of gross domestic product annually — compared to the international average of 4 percent, says

Carbonell at the Lincoln Institute of Land Policy. "Places that are growing tend to invest more" in public works, and, unlike some of our international competitors, "we haven't maintained our infrastructure or adapted it to changing conditions," he says.

Infrastructure spending in the House-proposed stimulus legislation is "almost minuscule," complained Rep. John L. Mica, R-Fla., top-ranking Republican on the House Transportation and Infrastructure Committee.

"They keep comparing this to Eisenhower, but he proposed a $500 billion highway system, and they're going to put $30 billion" into roads and bridges, said Mica. "How farcical can you be? Give me a break."

Instead of spreading funding thinly over many federal programs, Mica would have liked to see the administration focus efforts on some large goal, such as building high-speed rail in important travel corridors around the country. [37]

Only about $300 billion of the stimulus "goes to job creation — that's about 3.5 million jobs" or "only 2 percentage points on the unemployment rate," said Richard C. Levin, president of Yale University and a professor of economics. "That's not enough. There are lots of great public-works projects that would be well worth supporting. . . . What about . . . activities that put people to work right away, cleaning up public parks, weather-stripping homes, offices, schools, government buildings?" [38] ∎

BACKGROUND

The Great Depression

Governments have long taken responsibility for building and maintaining society's infrastructure, from parks and libraries to highways and airports. Traditionally, however, governments generally did little or nothing to counteract economic downturns, relying on market forces to bring back prosperity, no matter how painful the consequences.

Confronting the Great Depression of the 1930s, President Franklin D. Roosevelt (FDR) made the first large-scale attempt to link infrastructure building with "economic stimulus" — putting money into people's pockets through tax cuts or government spending to pump up demand for goods and services. [39] But economists and politicians had already formulated a role for public-works spending in tough times.

In the first three decades of the 20th century, England, Germany and several other countries — along with Pennsylvania and California — enacted plans to use infrastructure building to stabilize faltering economies. So-called public-works "reserves" would list important infrastructure-building projects to be undertaken only in times of rising unemployment.

"The aggregate volume of public works . . . is so great that if . . . 20 percent . . . were deferred each year and the accumulation executed in a year of depression . . . the lifting power of public works would be at least one-third of the deadweight of . . . a depression" and would "almost iron out the fluctuations in unemployment," said the U.S. President's Conference on Unemployment in 1921. [40]

Columbia University economist Leo Wolman, who opposed the creation of an actual reserve, nevertheless said that if governments funded public-works projects of real economic importance during a recession, they could "constitute a stimulus to business and would lead, if done on a large scale, to the progressive diffusion of employment," although they would not provide jobs for the majority of the jobless. [41]

After the economy turned sour following the stock market crash in 1929, Republican President Hoover initially tried public-works spending. Between 1928 and 1932, private construction dropped off by 86.4 percent. In 1931, 1932, and 1933, Congress authorized boosts in federal highway-building grants from $75 million to $125 million per year, and in 1930 Hoover requested still more public-works funding, in the form of an emergency appropriation of $150 million to keep the previously authorized infrastructure projects going longer.

Beginning in 1931, however, Hoover opposed additional public-works appropriations except to build revenue-producing projects. "The vice in . . . the proposals . . . is that they include public works of remote usefulness; they impose unbearable burdens upon the taxpayer; they unbalance the budget and demoralize government credit," he wrote in a 1932 letter to the American Society of Civil Engineers. "A larger and far more effective relief to unemployment at this stage can be secured by increased aid to 'income-producing works,' " such as "waterworks, toll-bridges, toll-tunnels, docks and any other such activities which charge for their service and whose earning capacity provides a return upon the investment." [42]

When Roosevelt took office in March 1933, the Depression had deepened and spread to Europe, partly because U.S. investment had played such a large part in sustaining European nations devastated by World War I. When U.S. prosperity and investment dipped, Europe's war-damaged economy fell still further. In response, FDR not only launched public-works projects in the United States but also joined with other international leaders in urging Europe to follow suit.

"In the period immediately before us, governments must employ such means as are at their disposal to relieve the unemployment by public works, and

Continued on p. 164

Chronology

1920s-1930s
Economic boom, partly fueled by heavy borrowing by stock-market investors, is followed by the Crash of 1929. President Franklin D. Roosevelt's New Deal launches the first major government programs aimed at stimulating the economy.

October 1929
Stock market crashes. . . . Banks begin to fail as debtors default on their loans, and panicking depositors try to withdraw their money.

1932
Industrial production falls 45 percent from 1929 levels as the Great Depression begins and spreads worldwide. . . . Roosevelt is elected to his first term.

1933
Twenty-five percent of all U.S. workers are unemployed. . . . Roosevelt and Congress establish Works Progress Administration, Civilian Conservation Corps and Tennessee Valley Authority to employ laid-off workers and create new public infrastructure.

1934
Heavy government spending enables Sweden to become the first nation to recover from the Depression.

1935
U.S. unemployment rate declines to 20 percent.

1936
Roosevelt is reelected in a landslide. . . . U.S. unemployment rate is just under 17 percent. . . . Military spending pulls Germany out of the Depression.

1937
Unemployment rate falls to 14 percent. . . . Rising federal deficits prompt Roosevelt to cut back on federal public-works spending.

1938
Economic growth slows again as unemployment rises to 19 percent.

1939
Economic growth revives, and unemployment falls to 17 percent as U.S. defense spending rises in anticipation of war.

1940s-1950s
Federal spending on World War II and Interstate Highway System helps keep unemployment low.

1941
U.S. manufacturing output is up 50 percent over 1939.

1956
President Dwight D. Eisenhower commits $25 billion to building the new highway system, raising the federal funding share from 50 percent to 90 percent.

1960s-1980s
Amid rising prosperity, government job creation loses ground to tax cuts as the preferred way to stimulate the economy when business slows.

1977
Congress approves $6 billion (around $21 billion in today's currency) in public-works spending proposed by President Jimmy Carter as an economic stimulus, but the proposals aren't enough to offset soaring unemployment.

1990s-2000s
Economists warn that rapid economic growth propelled by speculative "bubbles" like high housing prices isn't sustainable. Transportation engineers warn about infrastructure neglect.

1993
President Bill Clinton proposes to spend $69 billion on infrastructure, housing and environmental retooling but withdraws the plan after criticism.

2002
Lawmakers mull infrastructure spending as economic stimulus but cut taxes instead.

2008
Recession that began in December 2007 deepens. . . . Tax rebates offered as economic stimulus don't reverse nation's economic slump, and Congress mulls public-works spending, asking governors to suggest "shovel-ready" projects. . . . China and European Union countries include infrastructure investment in economic-stimulus plans for the recession that's now spread worldwide. . . . American job losses hit 3.6 million.

2009
Newly inaugurated President Barack Obama and congressional Democrats propose public-works spending as economic stimulus; congressional Republicans fight to reduce such spending and add more tax cuts but mostly vote against it anyway. . . . Economists warn that unless the banking crisis is solved, neither spending nor tax cuts will reinvigorate the economy. . . . January job losses total 598,000. . . . Congress passes $787 billion stimulus bill on Feb. 13 and Obama signs it into law on Feb. 17.

'Transformational' Projects Focus on the Future

Goal is energy efficiency, not maintaining the status quo.

When public money is being spent on infrastructure improvements, it's vital to select "transformational" projects, or those that pave the way for a better future, says Michael A. Bernstein, a professor of history and senior vice president for academic affairs at Tulane University. In the 1930s and '40s, for example, transformational infrastructure spending supported the development of economy-transforming tools such as antibiotics, radio and television and air travel, he says.

Today, however, a transformational vision of infrastructure might mean "backing off from air travel and investing more in rail," Bernstein says.

One transformation crucial to developing infrastructure for the future is to seek energy efficiency, he says. But that vision runs headlong into the status quo when it comes to government funding for public-works projects, many analysts say. Last fall, for example, Congress asked state transportation departments to submit lists of "shovel-ready" infrastructure projects that could be funded in a stimulus package.

The 19 states that released their lists to the public mostly focused on projects that would ignore smart energy use, according to the consumer group U.S.PIRG (Public Interest Research Group). The states "prioritize new highways while paying relatively little attention to repairing crumbling bridges and roads and even less emphasis on forward-looking transportation options, such as public transit and intercity rail," says a January U.S.PIRG analysis. [1]

On average, the 19 states would spend more than 75 percent of the funds on highways and only 17 percent on public transit or intercity rail. "This would be a step backward from even the grossly inadequate 20 percent share received by transit in federal transportation laws since the 1970s," says U.S. PIRG. [2]

In search of shovel-ready projects, the federal government is opting to send funds to states with a long history of favoring limited-access highways such as freeways that bypass towns or neighborhoods, warns John Norquist, president of the Chicago-based Congress for the New Urbanism, which promotes walkable environments and sustainable development.

"Road builders could make money paving streets" rather than by building new highways, and, in fact, such projects are every bit as "shovel ready," Norquist says. Cities and villages should be getting a third of the money, at least, to improve their road networks, rather than funneling the money to new highways that encourage the building of ever-more-distant suburbs, he says. Rather than putting stimulus funds to work creating more energy-inefficient sprawl, planners should look to the European and Canadian examples, where highways link population centers but aren't used to bypass small towns or neighborhoods. "They haven't built a new freeway in Toronto since 1968," he says.

Beyond transportation, at least some states also are seeing the "jobs potential and the economic-development potential" in "green" energy projects, making them a good target for economic-recovery funding, says Lew Milford, president of the Clean Energy States Alliance, which supports green projects.

A growing number of states have set up dedicated funding

Continued from p. 162

these efforts of individual governments will achieve their fullest effect if they can be made a part of a synchronized international program," Roosevelt and Italian Finance Minister Guido Jung declared at the 1933 World Monetary and Economic Conference. [43]

The pitch was less successful with Europe's cash-strapped governments than Roosevelt hoped, however, with Britain declining to participate at all. Britain had already tried to jump-start its economy with public-works expenditures and found it "unduly expensive" and therefore "an experiment we are not going to repeat," said British Board of Trade President Walter Runciman. [44]

Stimulus at Cooperstown

In the United States, Roosevelt launched several federal agencies to create jobs while producing public works for the nation. Winning public support for the initiatives was not always easy, however. In a way, baseball saved the day.

When Major League Baseball celebrated its 100th anniversary with a June 12, 1939, All-Star game between the American and National leagues and the opening of the National Baseball Hall of Fame and Museum, the event showcased not just the national pastime but brand-new Doubleday Field

in Cooperstown, N.Y. Like thousands of other ball fields, stadiums and parks built during the 1930s, the field was a project of a New Deal agency, the Works Progress Administration (WPA), created in 1935 to generate public jobs for the unemployed. [45]

The popularity of baseball and other sports helped win public support for the WPA, which provided jobs for about 8.5 million people during its eight-year existence. The WPA created more than 125,000 public buildings, including hundreds of sports facilities, 8,000 parks, 75,000 bridges and some 650,000 miles of roads, at a total cost of about $11 billion. [46]

At the dedication of a Detroit stadium, Roosevelt noted that "some people

streams — from sources such as small charges on utility bills — to subsidize development of wind, biomass and other alternative energy sources, and a federal grants program in alternative energy could easily direct its grants to those funds, Milford explains. States realize that green energy "is no longer just an environmental thing" but a job maker, he says. "If you're putting up solar panels all the time, you generate skilled jobs for installers, and these jobs are local and non-exportable," he says.

Giving more Americans an equitable shot at economic advancement can and should also be accomplished by transformative public-works projects, says Judith Bell, president of PolicyLink, an Oakland, Calif., advocacy group that promotes social-equity projects, such as public-transit investments. It is especially helpful to low-income people trying to get and stay on their feet because low-income communities have the least access to cars, she says. Transit spending also produces 19 percent more jobs than highway spending, she says.

"The [Bush] administration turned its back on housing," and that's another area that the public-works spending should target, especially now, Bell says. "Giving cities and localities the ability to use resources to renovate the foreclosed homes helps cities," she says. School repair, especially in low-income communities, and broadband-Internet expansion in rural areas also would reap benefits across the socioeconomic spectrum, she says.

Many infrastructure analysts caution, however, that technology-related projects, like broadband expansion, require thoughtful planning, which may be tough to achieve through economic-stimulus legislation.

"The first rule of technology investment is you spend time understanding the end user," said Craig Settles, an Oakland technology consultant. "If you don't do this well, you end up throwing . . . potentially billions down a rat hole for things that people don't need or can't use." [3]

Updating the nation's electricity-transmission grid, for example, won't necessarily promote clean energy as many expect, said Patrick Mazza, research director for Climate Solutions, an anti-global warming advocacy group. "Better transmission can empower new coal plants as well as new wind farms, so we better make sure there is a green priority on any new lines," he said. [4]

For any public-works funding to succeed, America needs to change its attitude toward infrastructure, which has been "build it, then forget about maintaining it," says Michael A. Pagano, dean of the College of Urban Planning and Public Affairs at the University of Illinois, Chicago.

"If this new [stimulus] funding is going to add more capacity [without providing for maintenance], then we are in trouble because we have a long history of ignoring what we've got," Pagano says.

---

[1] Phineas Baxandall, "Economic Stimulus or Simply More Misguided Spending?" U.S. PIRG, Jan. 5, 2009, www.uspirg.org/uploads/75/pU/75pUUIAl1Eteahknhlx-OA/State-Stimulus-paper-FINAL2.pdf.

[2] Ibid.

[3] Quoted in David M. Herszenhorn, "Internet Money in Fiscal Plan: Wise or Waste?" The New York Times, Feb. 3, 2009, p. A1.

[4] Peter Mazza, comment posted in response to Mark Clayton, "For a Spiffier Electric Grid: $11 Billion," The New Economy Blog, The Christian Science Monitor, Jan. 28, 2009, http://features.csmonitor.com/economyrebuild/2009/01/27/for-a-spiffier-electric-grid-11-billion.

---

in this country have called it 'boon-doggling' for us to build stadiums and parks and forests to improve the recreation facilities of the nation. My friends, if this stadium can be called boon-doggling, then I am for boondoggling, and so are you." [47]

Recreation projects aside, however, the WPA enjoyed less public support than some other infrastructure initiatives, such as the massive Tennessee Valley Authority (TVA), according to Jennifer Long, an associate professor of economics at the University of Science and Arts of Oklahoma. Many mistrusted "government involvement in the economy" and gave their wholehearted support mainly to programs whose results they saw as

potentially significant for their future, she wrote. [48]

One of the earliest New Deal agencies, the TVA was created shortly after Roosevelt's 1933 inauguration. Rather than jobs, its primary purpose was to promote economic development in the poverty-plagued Tennessee Valley by damming flood-prone rivers to protect farms and generate electricity. Nevertheless, the unprecedented construction effort — building seven dams between 1933 and 1941 — employed some 50,000 people, mostly unskilled local workers doing manual labor. [49]

By rights, TVA's goal of electrifying the region "should have been subject to the same doubts about inappropriate involvement [in the economy] that

haunted the WPA," since power production is often a private-sector enterprise, noted Long. However, the TVA was hailed by the public in Tennessee as a success "before ground was broken for the first dam, partly because so many people stood to be helped," Long wrote. "People celebrated [it] as the beginning of a new era of economic prosperity" even as they viewed WPA's much smaller projects skeptically, as "necessary evils" to tide the region "over until normal times returned." [50] By 1939, the TVA brought electricity to some 288,000 homes [51] and today provides electricity to around 8.5 million customers in seven states. [52]

Continued on p. 167

Solving the Infrastructure-Maintenance Dilemma

European governments turn to public-private partnerships.

With public coffers low in recent years, some states and localities have turned to public-private partnerships (PPP) to build and maintain infrastructure, such as offering 90-year leases to build and operate toll highways. The company usually pays an upfront, lump sum for the right to operate a road or other facility, then keeps the tolls collected.

But some PPP experts say the U.S. projects aren't really "partnerships" at all because they offer too few benefits to taxpayers, unlike PPPs in countries with more experience in public-private collaboration, especially the United Kingdom (U.K.).

The cash-strapped U.K. turned to PPPs in the 1980s to undertake infrastructure projects and has continued with the partnerships, says Irene Walsh, leader of the U.S. infrastructure and project-finance practice at Deloitte Financial Advisory Services.

Britain uses PPPs to build and operate schools, hospitals, rail lines, drinking-water systems and much more, says Stephen Harris, international development officer at the Tribal Group, a London firm that consults on private participation in delivering public services. Currently, about 15 percent of British capital projects are PPPs, which are limited to projects costing over 20 million pounds sterling (around $30 million U.S.), Harris says.

And, contrary to popular conception in the United States, PPP-run public services and facilities operate more efficiently and are "more consumer focused" than before the PPP conversion, Harris argues.

That success didn't come easily, however, Harris acknowledges. In the early years "we made every possible kind of mistake you could make" in structuring projects that could earn steady income for a company while serving the public good, he says.

Because PPP contracts are completely different from traditional government contracts, they pose the biggest problem for unwary governments, he says.

Mainly, a private company that wins a contract from a British town to build, operate and maintain a school for 25 years "has to raise all the money to build the thing," says Harris. "They don't get a single penny from the government until the children and teachers are ready to move in." Once the facility opens, the government pays the company set fees to operate it according to strict government standards, he says. If a light goes out in a classroom, the company has a limited amount of time to fix it, or their pay is docked.

A traditional government contract for a school, for example, might specify that it should be a building with 14 classrooms and two offices "and the doors should be this wide," he says. But Britain's PPP contracts use what he calls "output specifications" — a precise description of what the facility must accomplish for citizens, Harris explains. The contract might say

something like, "Please provide educational facilities for a population of 5,500 for 25 years," says Harris. This kind of contract "brings in the innovation of the private sector," allowing a contractor to construct a smaller school building and accomplish some of the education via the Internet, for example, he says.

Furthermore, contracts "allow no deterioration whatsoever for 25 years" and penalize companies by cutting off government payments if standards aren't met, Harris says.

This solves an age-old infrastructure dilemma, says Harris. "If you just throw in money to build something and don't provide any money to maintain it, in 15 years you'll be right back where you started," with a decrepit building or water system, he says. "But once you've got a contract, it's the private sector's job to maintain it to a standard" that the government explicitly sets, he says.

The private sector benefits by getting "a guaranteed income for 25 years, which helps a company's share values," says Harris.

But unwary governments will face serious pitfalls. And there are "hardly any" governments currently PPP-savvy enough to write the contracts without getting the short end of the stick, Harris says. In America "there aren't any PPP experts," for example, he says. "In the U.S., people confuse privatization" — simply transferring facilities or services to private-sector operation — "with public-private partnerships," but "the issue with that is lack of control over quality," Harris says.

Privatized projects or PPPs with bad contracts can go horribly wrong, says Harris. For instance, a company running a PPP highway project in Toronto quickly jacked up tolls from $5 to $14, but when the government tried to sue it lost the case in court because the contract allowed the increase, he says. A water system in Australia became contaminated with cryptosporidium — a microorganism that causes severe gastrointestinal symptoms — but the locality couldn't hold the contractor responsible because cryptosporidium wasn't on a list of banned microorganisms in the contract, says Harris. "What the contract should have said was, 'At all times the water must be drinkable,' " Harris says.

With money tight and infrastructure deficiencies widespread, there's growing interest in pursuing PPPs, but Congress should create an expert PPP group to offer advice and assistance "before governors get screwed," says Frank M. Rapoport, chairman of the global infrastructure and PPP team at the national law and lobbying firm McKenna Long and Aldridge.

"Five years ago, if you asked [U.S. builders], 'Are you interested in sharing the risk?' " on a public-works project in the British fashion, most would have said, "No, I want to build it and walk away," as they've done under traditional government contract work, Rapoport says. But today a growing number of companies are open to new kinds of PPPs, he says.

Continued from p. 165

New Deal Economics

T he New Deal convinced many doubters that the government could and should act to prevent the worst consequences of private-sector slumps. Opinions split, however, between supporters of British economist John Maynard Keynes, who embraced government spending on public-works programs — and those who favored tax cuts to encourage individuals and businesses to buy and invest.

In the 1930s, backers of government action to ease recession focused on employment as the key to stabilizing the economy.

"I believe in the inherent right of every citizen to employment at a living wage and pledge my support to . . . public works, such as . . . flood control and land reclamation, to provide employment for all surplus labor at all times," Roosevelt said in a 1932 campaign statement. [53]

Critics point out that, despite Roosevelt's interventions, U.S. unemployment remained high until the 1940s, when the nation began manufacturing war materiel, and the remaining vast numbers of jobless were drafted into the military. Still, most analysts over the years have concluded that Roosevelt's infrastructure spending helped boost the Depression economy and provided lasting societal benefits as well.

Between 1933 and 1937, for example, the U.S. economy grew by around 9 percent each year, up from zero annual growth in the immediately preceding years, says the University of New Mexico's Smith.

It's unfair to criticize New Deal projects for failing to bring employment all the way back to pre-Depression levels since the employment drop-off from the boom years of the late 20s was so extreme, says the University of Virginia's McKee.

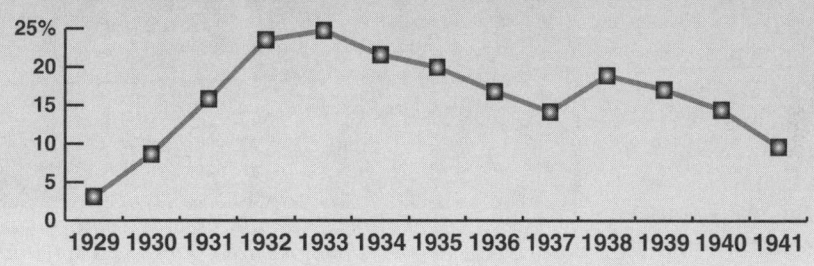

Unemployment Hit 25 Percent in Depression

Unemployment shot up after the stock market crash in 1929. At the height of the Great Depression, nearly 25 percent of American workers were jobless — or about 13 million out of a labor force of 52 million. The jobless rate began dropping with President Franklin D. Roosevelt's New Deal public-works program, begun in 1933, then spiked again in the late 1930s when he scaled back the jobs program in an effort to balance the budget. Jobs created as the nation prepared for World War II finally brought unemployment under control.

Percentage of U.S. Labor Force Unemployed, 1929-1941

Source: U.S. Bureau of the Census

Moreover, the infrastructure programs were a boon to the private sector, not a bane, Smith says. The federal government worked with private contractors like the big construction firms Bechtel and Brown & Root (now part of KBR), which "stayed afloat through the Depression" thanks to public works, he says.

By the mid-1930s, the economy was growing again, with manufacturing output and productivity increasing at pre-Depression rates, although unemployment remained high compared to the 1920s. In 1937, however, the economy took a new, shocking downturn, as manufacturing dropped off and unemployment shot up.

Economic historians don't agree about the cause of the slump.

"The conservative literature says that the 1936 recession came from government intervening too much in the market," says Michael A. Bernstein, a professor of history and senior vice president for academic affairs at Tulane University. "But I would say that it

happened because FDR didn't do enough" spending to give the economy the full boost it needed.

Growth resumed in 1938, but boom times only returned beginning in late 1940, when the war already raging in Europe increased demand for American armaments and other materiel.

World War and Beyond

"W orld War II ultimately succeeded in ending the Depression because we spent so much," Bernstein says. "Nobody worried about the federal budget on Dec. 8, 1941," the day after the Japanese attacked Pearl Harbor, the big U.S. Navy base in Hawaii.

Construction of military bases and other infrastructure across the country fed the economic boom in the 1940s, thus "testing and proving" the proposition that infrastructure spending is stimulative, Smith says.

But the long-term economy-building effects of the New Deal are perhaps its most important — though overlooked — legacy, says McKee. Innumerable infrastructure projects provided a foundation for economic growth over decades, says Smith. For example, the New Deal built around 480 airports and constructed new schools in half of the nation's 3,000-plus counties, all of which "contributed greatly to the economic growth we saw after World War II," he says.

But many conservative analysts, then as now, viewed federal public-works spending as much inferior to tax cuts for building the economy. This view has gradually become the mainstream position in the past half-century, largely because it seems to many like a much more direct way to spur the increased demand for goods and services that prompt businesses to begin investing again.

A "defining moment" came when Congress failed to pass the Democrat-sponsored Full Employment Act of 1945, says McKee. [54] The bill was inspired by economist Keynes' idea that government action can boost demand for goods and services at times when fluctuating business investment creates unemployment and the belief — based on observation of historical business cycles — that a private-market economy will always have periods of high unemployment.

Based on the proposition that "all Americans able to work and desiring to work are entitled to an opportunity for useful, remunerative, regular, and full-time employment," the bill would have required the government to

Electricity-generating windmills rise 300 feet in Spanish Fork, Utah. The economic-stimulus package directs some funding to the alternative-energy sector — including wind power — which several state governments are banking on for long-term job creation.

Getty Images/George Frey

boost its own spending to increase employment during all business-cycle downturns. In 1946, Congress passed a watered-down version of the legislation, setting full employment as a national goal but not requiring any government action to produce it. [55]

"Had they passed the [original] bill — and it looked for a while as if they would — we would have had the government committed to a more activist employment policy," McKee says.

After World War II, the federal government continued substantial public-works spending, although, as Keynesian economics gradually fell out of favor, opponents increasingly blasted it as wasteful and worthless. In the 1950s, conservative Sen. Barry Goldwater, R-Ariz., branded President Eisenhower, a fellow Republican, a "dime-store New Dealer" when he used federal money to build the massive Interstate Highway System, says Smith. Still, most Americans backed the project.

Despite the success of the highway project, increasing worries about

wasteful, ineffective "pork-barrel" spending by Congress created skepticism about whether federal infrastructure dollars could ever be spent appropriately. [56] Beginning in the late 1960s, the idea that the economy is best managed through tax cuts gradually became the standard approach, supported even by most liberals, says McKee.

Common wisdom doesn't necessarily survive hard times, however. Last year, as the economy faltered, then-candidate Obama and others began to propose infrastructure spending rather than tax cuts as a major component of an economic-stimulus and renewal plan. Their approach was bolstered by repeated warnings over the last several years that the United States had dangerously neglected upkeep on its roads and bridges. ∎

CURRENT SITUATION

Republicans Balk

A $787 billion stimulus bill — the American Reinvestment and Recovery Act — is now law. Congress passed the legislation on Feb. 13 and President Obama signed it into law four days later.

"What makes this recovery plan so important is not just that it will create or save three-and-a-half million jobs over

Continued on p. 170

At Issue:

Can government infrastructure spending boost the economy?

DEAN BAKER
CO-DIRECTOR, CENTER FOR ECONOMIC AND POLICY RESEARCH

WRITTEN FOR *CQ RESEARCHER*, FEBRUARY 2009

*t*he Obama administration has wisely chosen to make re-building public infrastructure the centerpiece of its stimulus package. The proposal includes funding not only for traditional infrastructure, like repairing roads and bridges, but also for green infrastructure such as weatherizing and retrofitting buildings to reduce energy consumption and modernization of the nation's electric grid.

Infrastructure is extremely effective as a stimulus since shovel-ready projects can start to create jobs soon after they are authorized. These projects put money in workers' pockets that they will spend. As a result, infrastructure spending has a substantial multiplier effect.

Moodys.com estimated the multiplier for infrastructure projects at 1.59, meaning that we will get $1.59 of additional economic output for each dollar spent on infrastructure. By comparison, the multiplier for payroll tax cuts is less than 1.0 and for business tax cuts just 0.3. This gap is likely to be even larger now, since many families will use tax cuts to rebuild their savings after losing most of their wealth in the housing crash.

Ideally, the spending will go to projects that would have been undertaken in any case, even if not immediately. For example, thousands of schools across the country desperately need repairs, such as new roofs or plumbing. And a considerable backlog of repairs to roads and bridges can be drawn down through this stimulus package.

There are also a large number of energy-conserving improvements that can pay for themselves in three or four years. For example, standard home retrofits cost around $3,000, and typically produce annual savings in the range of $750 to $1,000. If the federal government can provide incentives to encourage individuals, businesses and governments to carry through retrofits, there will be enduring benefits in reduced energy costs and greenhouse gas emissions.

But two notable pitfalls endanger this path. First, there will be some waste and corruption. That happens when you spend hundreds of billions of dollars. President Obama is establishing mechanisms to minimize this problem by ensuring that the process of disbursing funds is as open as possible.

The other risk is that we will spend money on environmentally harmful projects, such as highways that encourage suburban sprawl. This can and must be prevented. We can tolerate some waste, since it is important that money be spent quickly. But it makes no sense to spend billions of dollars in ways that will worsen our environmental problems.

RONALD D. UTT
SENIOR RESEARCH FELLOW THE HERITAGE FOUNDATION

WRITTEN FOR *CQ RESEARCHER*, FEBRUARY 2009

*t*here is good news and bad news in the American Recovery and Investment Act, proposed by the Democrats. The good news is the authors heed the skepticism of many fiscal conservatives and resist pressure for a massive commitment to transportation infrastructure. Conservatives argued that an infrastructure spending plan would have only a limited impact on the recovery because such projects take months to get off the ground and years to complete, offering little immediate relief in this most difficult time for the economy.

This bit of good news, unfortunately, is overwhelmed by the other 93 percent of the spending plans included in the proposal, making the plan little more than a massive bailout of ineffective federal programs and state governments. It also extends the federal government deep into new areas of responsibility like public-school construction and broadband investment, from which it may never extract itself. From public housing to the Economic Development Administration to the Rural Utility Service to Community Development Block Grants — and to a host of other petitioners — the authors of the bill appear to have been on a search for every questionable program they could find, and then threw billions at them.

The recovery act represents a massive and unprecedented peacetime transfer of wealth and income from the beleaguered taxpayers to government. And by its focus on the mediocre and the unnecessary, it also represents an unprecedented peacetime destruction of wealth our economy can't afford.

Moreover, at a time of economic peril, this plan will make things worse by absorbing massive volumes of scarce resources and credit that might better be deployed in the nation's already badly deprived, and federally mismanaged, credit markets.

A year from now we will be looking at a weaker economy, and Congress will be contemplating an even larger bailout of government. And soon we will find ourselves living in the kind of desultory economy more common to continental Europe than the vibrant economy that has made us the most prosperous and dynamic nation on earth.

With this at stake, Congress has offered a history-changing challenge to the new president, and in his first few weeks in office he must decide whether the voters put him there for a purpose no better than validating a massive congressional fraud on the nation's workers. Destiny beckons, Mr. President.

Continued from p. 168

the next two years, including nearly 60,000 in Colorado," Obama said from Denver after signing the measure. "It's that we are putting Americans to work doing the work that America needs done in critical areas that have been neglected for too long, work that will bring real and lasting change for generations to come."

Debates over infrastructure and other spending in the act have been intense and follow old patterns, for the most part.

The legislation includes $281 billion in tax cuts and $506 billion in spending — of which well under $300 billion is infrastructure-related — spread out over a two-year period, and passage did not come easily. [57]

Republicans in Washington balked when Obama and congressional Democrats first proposed a bill with substantial public-works components ranging from highways to mass transit to schools.

The bill "may create some government jobs, but actually . . . what it does is take money out of the economy," said Rep. Paul Broun, R-Ga., on Jan. 28. "It takes money away from those who are producing and gives it to government. . . . This is a huge leap towards socialism." [58]

"Let's get this notion out of our heads that the government creates jobs," newly elected Republican National Committee Chairman Michael Steele told CNN. "Not in the history of mankind has the government ever created a job. Small-business owners do, small enterprises do, not the government. When the government contract runs out, that job goes away." [59]

Not all conservatives oppose government spending to spur renewed business activity in a recession, however.

"The only way to prevent a deepening recession will be a temporary program of increased government spending," said Martin Feldstein, a Harvard University professor of economics who was an adviser to Republi-

can presidential candidate Sen. John McCain, R-Ariz. The lag time for getting infrastructure projects off the ground has meant they didn't provide much stimulus in previous recessions, but "this downturn is likely to last much longer" than the average 12 months, so public-works spending can help, Feldstein said. [60]

The spending "should include not only money for infrastructure such as bridges and roads but also for a wide range of equipment," such as "rebuilding some of the military capacity . . . depleted by the wars in Iraq and Afghanistan," said Feldstein. Shoring up federal research agencies such as the National Institutes of Health and the National Science Foundation also would help, Feldstein told PBS. That "wouldn't create a lot" of immediate jobs but "wouldn't cost a lot of money" either and would build the economy for the long term. [61]

Nevertheless, public-works provisions were among those that many congressional Republicans singled out as wasteful and ineffective, along with money for preventive-health programs such as smoking cessation and prevention of sexually transmitted disease, and extra funding for the 2010 census. As the bill began making its way through Congress, Republican lawmakers criticized a number of infrastructure-related items, including:

- $448 million to construct new headquarters for the Department of Homeland Security;
- $200 million to create public computer centers at community colleges;
- $500 million for flood-reduction projects on the Mississippi River;
- $6 billion to make federal buildings "green" and energy efficient;
- $500 million for state and local fire stations, and
- $850 million for Amtrak. [62]

As a result of the GOP opposition, the bill passed, 244-188, in the House

on Jan. 28 without a single Republican vote; 11 Democrats also opposed it. [63]

Action on the legislation then moved to the Senate, where Republicans also battled infrastructure spending provisions and threatened to filibuster — stall a vote on the legislation with endless debate — until the spending items were reduced or removed. The 100-member Senate, where Democrats and two Democratic-leaning Independents hold 58 seats, requires 60 votes to pass legislation over a filibuster. The Senate's bill contained more tax cuts than the House version, including a $15,000 tax credit for buying a home.

In early February, in order to win the handful of Republican votes needed for a 60-vote majority, a group of centrist Republicans and Democrats, led by Sens. Susan Collins, R-Maine, and Ben Nelson, D-Neb., proposed partially or totally cutting many of the bill's spending provisions, including:

- watershed rehabilitation;
- distance-learning and telemedicine projects;
- broadband Internet;
- energy-efficiency modernization of federal buildings;
- new Coast Guard facilities;
- construction of K-12 schools and, higher-education facilities, and
- modernization and energy-efficiency renovations to public housing. [64]

Passing the Stimulus

Republicans say even the final centrists' bill still contains too much spending. "We are going to amass the largest debt in the history of this country, and we are going to ask our kids and grandkids to pay for it," McCain told CBS News on Feb. 8. [65]

Many economists, however, say the centrists' infrastructure and other spending cuts have made the bill too small to either create enough jobs now or strengthen the economy long term.

The cuts in school construction spending, along with cuts in aid for states, "will ensure that we have at least 600,000 fewer Americans employed over the next two years," Princeton University Professor of Economics Paul Krugman, winner of the 2008 Nobel Prize for economics, wrote on Feb. 7. [66]

Analysts on the left argue that projects like energy-efficiency improvements and railroads would create a sounder foundation for economic growth than the "bubbles" that have driven economic growth in recent years — such as the unreasonably high share values awarded by Wall Street to so-called "dot.coms" during the 1990s and the now burst "housing bubble" of the 2000s.

History demonstrates a strong link between infrastructure investment and economic growth, according to an analysis prepared by University of Massachusetts Professor of Economics Robert Pollin and Associate Research Professor James Heintz for the Alliance for American Manufacturing. Between 1950 and 1979, U.S. public investment in infrastructure like transportation and electricity transmission grew by an annual average 4 percent, while annual growth in the gross domestic product (GDP) averaged around 4.1 percent, Pollin and Heintz said. By contrast, between 1980 and 2007 growth in infrastructure investment slowed to 2.3 percent annually while GDP growth slowed to an annual average of 2.9 percent. [67]

Federal spending on "green" projects, in particular, "will create about 17 jobs for every $1 million" spent, and the resulting jobs will be more sustainable in an energy-strapped future, Pollin said. [68]

Obama, infrastructure experts and many congressional Democrats argue that U.S. infrastructure badly needs upgrading if the country is to remain economically competitive as the world changes, and only public-works spending can make this happen.

"I never saw a tax cut fix a bridge," Rep. Barney Frank, D-Mass., chairman of the House Banking Committee, told ABC News. [69]

Meanwhile, as recession shakes economies worldwide, other countries also have turned to stimulus legislation that's heavy on public-works spending for a temporary boost. China recently proposed a $586 billion stimulus package, including railway, road and airport construction, and the European Union (EU) has adopted a $256 billion package with significant infrastructure investment by most EU countries. [70] A $27.7 billion Australian stimulus package includes $19 billion in infrastructure spending. [71] ■

OUTLOOK

Recovery Time

The fate of future attempts to link federal public-works spending with economic recovery may hinge on what happens over the next couple of years.

If the Congressional Budget Office (CBO) is correct in predicting recovery beginning late this year, "it is best to think of the stimulus not as something that will much limit the rise in unemployment but rather as something that will hasten the recovery," the Urban Institute's Penner told the Senate Budget Committee. Only time will tell whether CBO's forecast is correct or overly optimistic, however, he said. [72]

Many, but not all, economists expect the economy to experience an unusually long recession, with a turnaround not beginning until at least 2010.

"I'm on the optimistic side of the scale. I do think we have a pretty good shot at a reasonable form of recovery by the end of this calendar year," says Tara M. Sinclair, assistant professor of economics and international affairs at

George Washington University in Washington, D.C. Americans will tighten their purse strings this year, but extra government spending on public works and other things will offset some of that current consumer caution, she says. Longer term, "we're Americans, and we love stuff," and aren't likely to fall into the long-term recessionary pattern of Japan, where the public has helped slow economic recovery for decades because of their unwillingness to spend money, Sinclair predicts.

A prolonged recession might make infrastructure spending more crucial to a stimulus, since it would be needed to boost employment during the darkest times, said Krugman. And that looks likely to happen, he said. Economic forecasters surveyed by *The Wall Street Journal* "predict, on average, that unemployment will reach 8.1 percent by [the] end [of] 2009 and peak at 8.4 percent" in 2010, Krugman said. "That's a forecast of what will happen with the stimulus plan, not of what would happen absent stimulus, which would presumably be considerably worse."

Ironically, however, that scenario might also put an end to any more attempts by Democrats to propose public investments in infrastructure, no matter how worthy, since it "could easily be spun by conservatives as a failure of Obama's policies," he said. [73] ■

Notes

[1] For background, see Janet H. Cho and Tom Breckenridge, "Ohio Has Lost 263,383 Jobs — 5% of its Work Force — Since 2000, Data Shows," *The* [Cleveland] *Plain Dealer*, Feb. 4, 2009, http://blog.cleveland.com.

[2] Shobhana Chandra, "U.S. Economy: Jobless Rate Soars and Payrolls Plunge by 598,000." Bloomberg.com, Feb. 6, 2009, www.bloomberg.com.

[3] Cho and Breckenridge, *op. cit.*

[4] Quoted in David Young, "Economic Recovery Starts in Denver," *Loveland Connection*, Feb. 18, 2009, www.coloradoan.com/article/20090218/LOVELAND01/90218004.

[5] For background, see Richard Rubin, Benton Ives and Clea Benson, "Congress' Role: Help or Hinder," *CQ Weekly*, Jan. 21, 2008, p. 192.

[6] Obama on Daschle: "I Messed Up," transcript, CBS News, Feb. 3, 2009, www.cbsnews.com.

[7] Christina Romer and Jared Bernstein, "The Job Impact of the American Recovery and Reinvestment Plan," Transition Office of Barack Obama, Jan. 9, 2009, http://otrans.3cdn.net/45593e8ecbd339d074_l3m6bt1te.pdf.

[8] "The Employment Situation: January 2009," Bureau of Labor Statistics, Feb. 5, 2009, www.bls.gov/news.release/empsit.nr0.htm.

[9] Richard G. Little, "Stimulus Has to Include More than Money for Building," *San Jose Mercury News*, Nov. 24, 2008, www.mercurynews.com/opinion/ci_11064540.

[10] Judd Gregg, "How to Make Sure the Stimulus Works," *The Wall Street Journal*, Jan. 4, 2009, http://online.wsj.com.

[11] Thomas J. DiLorenzo, "The Myth of Job Creation," Policy Analysis No. 48, Cato Institute, Feb. 19, 1984, www.cato.org.

[12] Quoted in "The Problems with a Fiscal Stimulus," "Marketplace," National Public Radio, http://marketplace.publicradio.org, Jan. 5, 2009.

[13] Amity Shlaes, "The Krugman Recipe for Depression," *The Wall Street Journal*, Nov. 29, 2008, http://online.wsj.com.

[14] Quoted in Lori Montgomery, "Critics Say Roads Projects Won't Jump-Start Economy," *The Washington Post*, Oct. 30, 2008, p. D1.

[15] Testimony before House Committee on Transportation and Infrastructure, Oct. 29. 2008, http://transportation.house.gov/Media/File/Full%20Committee/20081029/Irons.pdf.

[16] *Ibid*.

[17] Transcript, "Late Edition with Wolf Blitzer," CNN, Nov. 9, 2008, http://transcripts.cnn.com/TRANSCRIPTS/0811/09/le.01.html.

[18] Quoted in Jonathan Karp, "Construction Industry Counts on Obama," *The Wall Street Journal*, Jan. 14, 2009, p. C10.

[19] Eric Rauchway, "FDR's Latest Critics: Was the New Deal UnAmerican?" *Slate*, July 5, 2007, www.slate.com.

[20] Jacob G. Hornberger, "Obama's Public-Works Folly," "Hornberger's Blog," The Future of Freedom Foundation, Jan. 5, 2009, www.fff.org.

[21] Lawrence Kudlow, "Infrastructure Spending Is No Cure-All," The Corner blog, *National Review* online, Dec. 9, 2008, http://cprmer.nationalreview.com.

[22] Lisa Snell, "Huge Stimulus Plan Won't Change the Education System's Status Quo," Reason Foundation, Jan. 27, 2009, http://reason.org.

[23] Ronald D. Utt, "Learning from Japan: Infrastructure Won't Boost the Economy," *Backgrounder No. 2222*, Heritage Foundation, Dec. 16, 2008, www.heritage.org.

[24] Amity Shlaes, "The Perils of a Cement Tsunami," *The Washington Post*, Dec. 10, 2008, p. A25.

[25] For background, see Thomas J. Billitteri, "Financial Bailout," *CQ Researcher*, Oct. 24, 2008, pp. 865-888, and Kenneth Jost, "Financial Crisis," *CQ Researcher*, May 9, 2008, pp. 409-432.

[26] Testimony before House Committee on the Budget, Jan. 27, 2009.

[27] For background, see Marcia Clemmitt, "Aging Infrastructure," *CQ Researcher*, Sept. 28, 2007, pp. 793-816.

[28] Richard G. Little, "Not the Macquarie Model: Using U.S. Sovereign Wealth to Renew America's Civil Infrastructure," paper prepared for America 2050, Jan. 9. 2009, www.america2050.org/upload/2009/01/Paper_Richard_Little.pdf.

[29] *Ibid*.

[30] For background, see Marcia Clemmitt, "The National Debt," *CQ Researcher*, Nov. 14, 2008, pp. 937-960.

[31] H.R. 1 — The American Recovery and Investment Act, Legislative Bulletin, Republican Study Committee, Jan. 27, 2009, http://rsc.price.house.gov/News/DocumentSingle.aspx?DocumentID=109553.

[32] N. Gregory Mankiw, "What Would Keynes Have Done?" *The New York Times*, Nov. 30, 3008, p. BU4.

[33] Rudolph G. Penner, "Addressing Short- and Long-Term Fiscal Challenges," testimony before Senate Budget Committee, Jan. 21, 2009, http://budget.senate.gov/democratic/testimony/2009/Penner-1-21-testimony.pdf.

[34] See Anne E. Kornblut and Michael D. Shear, "Obama Says He erred in Nominations," *The Washington Post*, Feb. 4, 2009, p. A1.

[35] Quoted in " Some of the Math Is Simple," "Talking Points Memo," Feb. 4, 2009, www.talkingpointsmemo.com.

[36] Quoted in Mark Thoma, "Is the Deficit a Threat to a Future Recovery?" *Global Macro EconoMonitor*, RGE Monitor, Dec. 4, 2008, www.rgemonitor.com.

[37] Quoted in Alec MacGillis, "Democrats Among Stimulus Skeptics," *The Washington Post*, Jan. 28, 2009, p. A1.

[38] Quoted in Arianna Huffington, "Stimulus Package: If You Jump Halfway Across a Chasm You Fall Into the Abyss," *Huffington Post* blog, Feb. 2, 2009, www.huffingtonpost.com.

[39] For background, see P. Webbink, "Federal Relief of Economic Distress," *Editorial Research Reports*, Dec. 8, 1930; B. W. Patch, "Public Works and National Recovery," *Editorial Research Reports*, July 18, 1933; M. Packman, "New Highways," *Editorial Research Reports*, Dec. 13, 1954; Kenneth Jost, "Stimulating the Economy," *CQ Researcher*, Jan. 10, 2003, pp. 1-24.

[40] Quoted in Patch, *op. cit.*

[41] *Ibid*.

[42] Herbert Hoover, letter to Herbert S. Crocker of the American Society of Civil Engineers, May 21, 1932, "The Depression Papers of Herbert Hoover," www.geocities.com/mb_williams/hooverpapers/1932/paper19320521.html.

[43] Quoted in Patch, *op. cit.*

[44] *Ibid*.

[45] Robert Kossuth, "Boondoggling, Baseball, and the WPA," *Nine: A Journal of Baseball History and Culture* (fall 2000), p. 56.

[46] "Public Works Administration," *Encyclopedia Britannica Online*, 2008, www.britannica.com.

[47] Quoted in Kossuth, *op. cit.*

About the Author

Staff writer **Marcia Clemmitt** is a veteran social-policy reporter who previously served as editor in chief of *Medicine & Health* and staff writer for *The Scientist*. She has also been a high-school math and physics teacher. She holds a liberal arts and sciences degree from St. John's College, Annapolis, and a master's degree in English from Georgetown University. Her recent reports include "Mortgage Crisis," "The National Debt" and "Regulating Credit Cards."

[48] Jennifer Long, "Government Job Creation Programs — Lessons from the 1930s and 1940s," *Journal of Economic Issues*, December 1999, p. 903.

[49] *Ibid.*

[50] *Ibid.*

[51] "Early History of the Tennessee Valley Authority," Bruderheim Rural Electrification Association, www.bruderheim-rea.ca/ TVA.htm.

[52] "TVA Board Approves Rate Adjustment," press release, Tennessee Valley Authority, July 22, 2005, www.tva.gov/news/releases/jul sep05/budget.htm.

[53] Quoted in B. W. Patch, "Roosevelt Policies in Practice," *Editorial Research Reports*, Sept. 25, 1936.

[54] For background, see B. W. Patch, "Full Employment," in *Editorial Research Reports*, July 30, 1945, available at *CQ Researcher Plus Archive*, http://library.cqpress.com.

[55] Quoted in G. J. Santoni, "The Employment Act of 1946: Some History Notes," *Federal Reserve Bank of St. Louis Review*, November 1986, p. 5, http://research.stlouisfed.org/publications/review/86/11/Employment_Nov1986.pdf.

[56] For background, see Marcia Clemmitt, "Pork Barrel Politics," *CQ Researcher*, June 6, 2006, pp. 529-552.

[57] Andrew Taylor, "Congress Readies Final Vote on $787 Billion Stimulus Bill," The Associated Press, Feb. 13, 2009, www.google.com/hostednews/ap/article/ALeqM5gdDrWnoMueqVFI-Uo1ClxVZur22AD96ARQGO3.

[58] *Congressional Record*, Jan. 28, 2009, p. H769.

[59] Wolf Blitzer, "The Situation Room," transcript, CNN.com, Feb. 2, 2009, http://transcripts.cnn.com/TRANSCRIPTS/0902/02/sitroom.02.html.

[60] Martin Feldstein, "The Stimulus Plan We Need Now," *The Washington Post*, Oct. 30, 2008, p. A23.

[61] "A Conversation About Obama's Economic Stimulus Package," "Charlie Rose Show," PBS, Jan. 6, 2009, www.charlierose.com/view/interview/9899.

[62] "What GOP Leaders Deem Wasteful in Senate Stimulus Bill," "CNN Politics," Feb. 3, 2009, www.cnn.com.

[63] For background, see Jonathan Weisman, Greg Hitt and Naftali Bendavid, "House Passes Stimulus Package," *The Wall Street Journal*, Jan. 29, 2009, http://online.wsj.com/article/SB 123315486943524321.html.

[64] "FY 2009 Economic Recovery and Reinvestment Supplemental," Feb. 7, 2009, http://senateconservatives.files.wordpress.com/2009/02/nelson-collins-stimulus-final2.pdf.

FOR MORE INFORMATION

America 2050, 4 Irving Place, Suite 711-S, New York, NY 10003; (212) 253-5795; www.America2050.org. A policy-analysis and advocacy group interested in overhauling U.S. infrastructure to meet future economic and environmental needs.

Blueprint America, www.pbs.org/wnet/blueprintamerica. The Web site of a series of PBS television documentaries on infrastructure, with interviews, links and reports on infrastructure and related economic issues, including stimulus proposals.

Center for American Progress, 1333 H St., N.W., 10th Floor, Washington, DC 20005; (202) 682-1611; www.americanprogress.org. Progressive think tank that analyzes economic issues and proposals on stimulus legislation and infrastructure.

The Century Foundation, 41 East 70th St., New York, NY 10021; (212) 535-4441; www.tcf.org. Liberal think tank that analyzes economic and infrastructure issues.

The Heritage Foundation, 214 Massachusetts Ave., N.E., Washington, DC 20002-4999; (202) 546-4400; www.heritage.org. Conservative think tank that analyzes economic issues, including infrastructure spending and the economic stimulus.

Lincoln Institute of Land Policy, 113 Brattle St., Cambridge, MA 02138-3400; (617) 661-3016; www.lincolninst.edu. Analyzes land-use issues, including infrastructure planning and economic development.

Manhattan Institute, 2 Vanderbilt Ave., New York, NY 10017; (212) 599-7000; www.manhattan-institute.org. Conservative think tank that analyzes economic issues, including proposals on infrastructure funding and stimulus.

Metropolitan Policy Program, The Brookings Institution, 1775 Massachusetts Ave., N.W., Washington, DC 20036; (202) 797-6000; www.brookings.edu. Research group at a centrist think tank that analyzes policy proposals affecting cities and metropolitan areas.

Political Economy Research Institute, University of Massachusetts, Gordon Hall, 418 N. Pleasant St., Suite A, Amherst, MA 01002; (413) 545-6355; www.peri.umass.edu. Analyzes policy ideas related to globalization, unemployment, economic development and the environment.

[65] Michelle Levi, "McCain: Stimulus Bill Is Generational Theft," "Political Hotsheet," CBS News, Feb. 8, 2009, www.cbsnews.com/blogs/2009/02/08/politics/politicalhotsheet/entry4783514.shtml.

[66] Paul Krugman, "What the Centrists Have Wrought," The Conscience of a Liberal Blogs, *The New York Times* blogs, Feb. 7, 2009, http://krugman.blogs.nytimes.com/2009/02/07/what-the-centrists-have-wrought.

[67] James Heintz, Robert Pollin and Heidi Garrett-Peltier, "How Infrastructure Investments Support the U.S. Economy: Employment, Productivity and Growth," University of Massachusetts Political Economy Research Institute, January 2009.

[68] For background, see Marcia Clemmitt, "Mortgage Crisis," *CQ Researcher*, Nov. 2, 2007, pp. 913-936.

[69] Quoted in James Gordon Meek, "President Obama to GOP: You Can Help Me Spend the Billions," *New York Daily News*, Feb. 1, 2009, www.nydailynews.com.

[70] Eric Lotke, "Falling Apart, Falling Behind," "Blog for Our Future," Campaign for America's Future, Dec. 4, 2008, www.ourfuture.org.

[71] "Factbox: Key Planks of Australia's Stimulus Packages," Reuters, Feb. 13, 2009, http://in.reuters.com/article/asiaCompanyAndMarkets/idINSYD36217320090213.

[72] Penner, *op. cit.*

[73] Paul Krugman, "Forecasts," The Conscience of a Liberal blog, *The New York Times* blogs, Jan. 6, 2009, http://krugman.blogs.nytimes.com.

Bibliography

Selected Sources

Books

Krugman, Paul, *The Return of Depression Economics and the Crisis of 2008*, W.W. Norton, 2008.
A Princeton economics professor and Nobel Prize winner argues that some of the same problems that led to the Great Depression have returned in our globalized world.

Leighninger, Robert D., Jr., *Long-Range Public Investment: The Forgotten Legacy of the New Deal*, University of South Carolina Press, 2007.
An Arizona State University sociologist catalogs the range of public works created in the New Deal and examines their impact on the U.S economy and infrastructure.

Smith, Jason Scott, *Building New Deal Liberalism: The Political Economy of Public Works, 1933-1956*, Cambridge University Press, 2005.
A University of New Mexico assistant professor of history argues that New Deal infrastructure investment paved the way for the economic growth that followed World War II.

Articles

Feldstein, Martin, "Defense Spending Would Be Great Stimulus," *The Wall Street Journal* online, Dec. 24, 2008, http://online.wsg.com.
The former chairman of President Ronald Reagan's Council of Economic Advisers argues that spending for military and research infrastructure would be an effective economic stimulus.

MacGillis, Alec, and Michael D. Shear, "Stimulus Package to First Pay for Routine Repairs," *The Washington Post*, Dec. 14, 2008, p. A1.
The need to create economy-stimulating jobs quickly may be at odds with hopes of creating public works that will benefit the economy long term.

Reports and Studies

Baxandall, Phineas, "Economic Stimulus or Simply More Misguided Spending?" U.S. PIRG, December 2008, www.calpirg.org/uploads/8B/eI/8BeIuP6wmZ1AR24UZUp6SQ/State-Stim-Report_CALPIRG_Final.pdf.
States' proposals for shovel-ready infrastructure funding put too much emphasis on highways, according to an analyst for a consumer group.

Edwards, Chris, "10 Reasons to Oppose a Stimulus Package for the States," *Tax & Budget Bulletin No. 51*, The Cato Institute, December 2008, www.cato.org/pubs/tbb/tbb_1208-51.pdf.
An analyst for a libertarian think tank argues that infra-structure investments would dangerously raise the federal debt and aren't needed because states have generously funded public works in recent years.

Heintz, James, Robert Pollin and Heidi Garrett-Peltier, "How Infrastructure Investments Support the U.S. Economy: Employment, Productivity and Growth," Political Economy Research Institute, University of Massachusetts, January 2009, www.americanmanufacturing.org/wordpress/wp-content/uploads/2009/01/peri_aam_finaljan16_new.pdf.
Economists argue that neglect of the nation's infrastructure, beginning in the 1970s, endangers future economic growth.

Pollin, Robert, and Jeannette Wicks-Lim, "Job Opportunities for a Green Economy," Political Economy Research Institute, University of Massachusetts, June 2008, www.peri.umass.edu/fileadmin/pdf/other_publication_types/Green_Jobs_PERI.pdf.
Economists argue that millions of manufacturing and construction workers would find permanent work in an economy focused on green energy.

Romer, Christina, and Jared Bernstein, "The Job Impact of the American Recovery and Reinvestment Plan," White House, Jan. 9, 2009, http://otrans.3cdn.net/45593e8ecbd339d074_l3m6bt1te.pdf.
Economic advisers to President Barack Obama and Vice President Joseph Biden estimate a stimulus package emphasizing infrastructure, energy projects and school repair would add or save three-and-a-half-million jobs through 2010.

Shorris, Anthony E., "Breaking Down Walls: Overcoming Institutional Barriers to Infrastructure Investment," The Century Foundation, 2008, www.tcf.org/publications/economicsinequality/shorris.pdf.
U.S. infrastructure has long been underfunded, from an economic-policy standpoint, but refocusing attention on public works would require overhauling antiquated government systems, writes a fellow at the liberal think tank.

Utt, Ronald D., "Learning from Japan: Infrastructure Spending Won't Boost the Economy," *Backgrounder No. 2222*, The Heritage Foundation, Dec. 16, 2008, www.heritage.org/research/economy/bg2222.cfm.
Japan's repeated attempts to boost its economy through public-works spending were a lengthy, expensive failure.

Utt, Ronald D., "More Transportation Spending: False Promises of Prosperity and Job Creation," *Backgrounder No. 2121*, The Heritage Foundation, April 2, 2008, www.heritage.org/Research/Budget/bg2121.cfm.
An economist at a conservative think tank argues that infra-structure spending occurs too slowly to stem a recession.

The Next Step:

Additional Articles from Current Periodicals

Government Structures

"It Will Take More Than Money to Solve the Nation's Infrastructure Crisis," *Ascribe Newswire*, **Nov. 20, 2008.**

Vast sets of agencies and political entities spread across all levels of government make it difficult to organize smart trade-offs for potential public-works investments.

Gottesman, Jan, "Study Examines New Public Works Set Up," *Telegram & Gazette* **(Worcester, Mass.), Jan. 16, 2009, p. 3.**

Two officials in Massachusetts are examining ways to make the state's Department of Public Works operate more efficiently.

Infrastructure

Cooper, Michael, "U.S. Infrastructure Is in Dire Straits, Report Says," *The New York Times*, **Jan. 28, 2009, p. A16.**

More than 25 percent of the nation's bridges are structurally deficient and need to be propped up by the stimulus package, according to the American Society of Civil Engineers.

Glaeser, Edward L., "Infrastructure Needs a Bill of Its Own," *The Boston Globe*, **Feb. 6, 2009, p. A15.**

Non-repair-related infrastructure spending should be taken out of Obama's stimulus package because major infrastructure projects cannot be done quickly.

Schmid, John, "Stimulus Money Sought to Support Water Projects," *Milwaukee Journal Sentinel*, **Feb. 5, 2009.**

A group of Milwaukee-area civic leaders is urging Washington lawmakers to include water infrastructure spending as part of the national economic stimulus package.

Job Creation

Nicholas, Peter, and Janet Hook, "Jobs, Energy Key to Obama Stimulus Plan," *The New York Times*, **Dec. 6, 2008, p. C1.**

A stimulus package that focuses on clean energy has the potential to create "jobs of the future."

Nussbaum, Paul, "Region Ready for a Quick Economic Fix," *The Philadelphia Inquirer*, **Dec. 12, 2008, p. A1.**

South New Jersey is anticipating the restoration of lost jobs if it receives money from the economic stimulus package for the upgrading of its public works.

Oliphant, James, "For Florida Town, Stimulus Fight Hits Home," *Chicago Tribune*, **Feb. 8, 2009, p. A7.**

The stimulus package could create thousands of jobs in Florida if money is provided to upgrade water and sewage systems.

Rampell, Catherine, "Layoffs Spread to More Sectors of the Economy," *The New York Times*, **Jan. 27, 2009, p. A1.**

Stimulus spending on public works may take some time to get going, but some companies could bring back displaced workers if the initiative generates new orders.

Public-Private Partnerships

Curtin, Daniel M., "Private Money Could Save Public Projects," *Sacramento Bee*, **Feb. 3, 2009, p. A15.**

At least $500 billion — with much coming from private funds — will be needed over the next 20 years to build an environmentally cleaner infrastructure for California.

Guardino, Carl, and Jim Wunderman, "To Stretch Our Tax Dollars, We Must Embrace Public-Private Partnerships," *San Jose Mercury News*, **Jan. 12, 2009.**

Public-private partnerships use the resources of business and government to effectively finance, design and build public-works projects.

Lockyer, Bill, "Public-Private Infrastructure Fight Ruinous," *Sacramento Bee*, **Jan. 26, 2009, p. A13.**

The single-minded focus to increase private companies' share of the public-works market has brought California closer to fiscal calamity.

Rothfeld, Michael, and Jordan Rau, "Governor's Aide Has Ties to Former Firm," *Los Angeles Times*, **Jan. 2, 2009, p. B1.**

A company with close ties to California Gov. Arnold Schwarzenegger is positioned to benefit from his plans to include private interests in public works.

CITING CQ RESEARCHER

Sample formats for citing these reports in a bibliography include the ones listed below. Preferred styles and formats vary, so please check with your instructor or professor.

MLA STYLE

Jost, Kenneth. "Rethinking the Death Penalty." CQ Researcher 16 Nov. 2001: 945-68.

APA STYLE

Jost, K. (2001, November 16). Rethinking the death penalty. *CQ Researcher, 11*, 945-968.

CHICAGO STYLE

Jost, Kenneth. "Rethinking the Death Penalty." *CQ Researcher*, November 16, 2001, 945-968.

In-depth Reports on Issues in the News

Are you writing a paper?

Need backup for a debate?

Want to become an expert on an issue?

For 80 years, students have turned to *CQ Researcher* for in-depth reporting on issues in the news. Reports on a full range of political and social issues are now available. Following is a selection of recent reports:

Civil Liberties
Limiting Lawsuits, 12/08
Affirmative Action, 10/08
Gay Marriage Showdowns, 9/08
America's Border Fence, 9/08
Immigration Debate, 2/08
Prison Reform, 4/07

Crime/Law
Mexico's Drug War, 12/08
Prostitution Debate, 5/08
Public Defenders, 4/08
Gun Violence, 5/07

Education
Reading Crisis? 2/08
Discipline in Schools, 2/08
Student Aid, 1/08
Racial Diversity in Public Schools, 9/07
Stress on Students, 7/07

Environment
Reducing Carbon Footprint, 12/08
Protecting Wetlands, 10/08
Buying Green, 2/08
Future of Recycling, 12/07

Health/Safety
Preventing Cancer, 1/09
Heart Health, 9/08
Global Food Crisis, 6/08
Preventing Memory Loss, 4/08

International Affairs/Politics
The Obama Presidency, 1/09
The National Debt, 11/08
Financial Bailout, 10/08
Political Conventions, 8/08
Race and Politics, 7/08

Social Trends
Falling Birthrates, 11/08
Regulating Credit Cards, 10/08
Internet Accuracy, 8/08
Financial Crisis, 5/08

Terrorism/Defense
Homeland Security, 2/09
Rise in Counterinsurgency, 9/08
Cost of the Iraq War, 4/08

Youth
Debating Hip-Hop, 6/07

Upcoming Reports

Closing Guantánamo, 2/27/09
Future of Middle Class, 3/6/09

Vanishing Jobs, 3/13/09
GOP Future, 3/20/09

Extreme Sports, 3/27/09
Bankruptcy, 4/3/09

ACCESS

CQ Researcher is available in print and online. For access, visit your library or www.cqresearcher.com.

STAY CURRENT

To receive notice of upcoming *CQ Researcher* reports, or learn more about *CQ Researcher* products, subscribe to the free e-mail newsletters, *CQ Researcher Alert!* and *CQ Researcher News*: http://cqpress.com/newsletters.

PURCHASE

To purchase a *CQ Researcher* report in print or electronic format (PDF), visit www.cqpress.com or call 866-427-7737. Single reports start at $15. Bulk purchase discounts and electronic-rights licensing are also available.

SUBSCRIBE

Annual full-service *CQ Researcher* subscriptions—including 44 reports a year, monthly index updates, and a bound volume—start at $803. Add $25 for domestic postage.

CQ Researcher Online offers a backfile from 1991 and a number of tools to simplify research. For pricing information, call 800-834-9020, ext. 1906, or e-mail librarysales@cqpress.com.

CQ Researcher

Published by CQ Press, a division of SAGE Publications

www.cqresearcher.com

Closing Guantánamo

Can Obama close the detention camp within one year?

P resident Obama on his second full day in office ordered the closing of the Guantánamo detention camp within a year. The facility at the U.S. Naval Station in Cuba has been controversial ever since President George W. Bush decided in late 2001 to use it to hold suspected enemy combatants captured in Afghanistan and elsewhere. Both Obama and Republican candidate John McCain promised during the presidential campaign to close the facility if elected. But that poses many difficult issues about the camp's remaining 241 prisoners. The government wants to send many to other countries — with few takers so far — but worries that some may resume hostile activities against the United States. Some may be brought to the U.S. for trial, but those prosecutions would raise a host of uncharted legal issues. Meanwhile, opposition already has surfaced to any plans for housing detainees in the United States. And human-rights advocates worry the Obama administration may continue to back some form of preventive detention for suspected terrorists.

A shackled detainee is taken to an interrogation session at the U.S. Naval Station at Guantánamo Bay, Cuba, soon after President George W. Bush ordered the controversial facility opened in January 2002 to house suspected enemy combatants captured in the Afghanistan war and elsewhere.

CQ Researcher • Feb. 27, 2009 • www.cqresearcher.com
Volume 19, Number 8 • Pages 177-200

Cover: AP Photo/Andres Leighton

CQ Researcher

Feb. 27, 2009
Volume 19, Number 8

MANAGING EDITOR: Thomas J. Colin
tcolin@cqpress.com

ASSISTANT MANAGING EDITOR: Kathy Koch
kkoch@cqpress.com

ASSOCIATE EDITOR: Kenneth Jost

STAFF WRITERS: Thomas J. Billitteri, Marcia Clemmitt, Peter Katel

CONTRIBUTING WRITERS: Rachel Cox, Sarah Glazer, Alan Greenblatt, Barbara Mantel, Patrick Marshall, Tom Price, Jennifer Weeks

DESIGN/PRODUCTION EDITOR: Olu B. Davis

ASSISTANT EDITOR: Darrell Dela Rosa

FACT-CHECKING: Eugene J. Gabler, Michelle Harris

EDITORIAL INTERN: Vyomika Jairam

CQ PRESS

A Division of SAGE Publications

PRESIDENT AND PUBLISHER:
John A. Jenkins

EXECUTIVE DIRECTOR,
REFERENCE INFORMATION GROUP:
Alix B. Vance

CQ Press is a registered trademark of Congressional Quarterly Inc.

CQ Researcher (ISSN 1056-2036) is printed on acid-free paper. Published weekly, except; (Jan. wk. 1) (May wk. 4) (July wks. 1, 2) (Aug. wks. 3, 4) (Nov. wk. 4) and (Dec. wk. 4), by CQ Press, a division of SAGE Publications. Annual full-service subscriptions start at $803. For pricing, call 1-800-834-9020, ext. 1906. To purchase a CQ Researcher report in print or electronic format (PDF), visit www.cqpress.com or call 866-427-7737. Single reports start at $15. Bulk purchase discounts and electronic-rights licensing are also available. Periodicals postage paid at Washington, D.C., and additional mailing offices. POSTMASTER: Send address changes to CQ Researcher, 2300 N St., N.W., Suite 800, Washington, DC 20037.

Closing Guantánamo

BY KENNETH JOST

THE ISSUES

Mohammed Jawad has spent more than a quarter of his young life in the prison at Guantánamo Bay, Cuba, for an offense he says he didn't commit.

The government says the Afghani teenager threw a grenade at a U.S. military jeep in Kabul in 2002, wounding two American soldiers and their Afghan interpreter.

Jawad, who was 16 or 17 at the time, claims he was working to clear land mines when the attack occurred and that another youth was responsible. Jawad says he confessed under coercion while in custody in Afghanistan and again at the U.S. detention camp at Guantánamo Bay, Cuba, only after more than a year of abusive interrogation.

Then, in a pair of rulings in October and November, an Army judge threw out the confessions that the prosecution had said were central to the case. Col. Stephen Henley ruled that Jawad had confessed the first time only after Afghan soldiers threatened to kill him and his family. The statements made in Guantánamo, Henley said, were also coerced. [1]

With a case so badly handled, Jawad would seem to be an obvious candidate for release from the controversial prison camp that President George W. Bush ordered to be established in 2002 for "enemy combatants" captured in the Afghanistan war or elsewhere. In its final week in office, however, the Bush administration on Jan. 13 urged the review panel that acts as an appeals court for the military commission system at Guantánamo to reverse the rulings in Jawad's case and allow the prosecution to go forward.

President Barack Obama signs an executive order on Jan. 22 — his second full day in office — to close the U.S. prison at Guantánamo Bay within a year. Human-rights advocates and lawmakers on both sides of the political aisle agree the controversial facility should be closed. But finding countries willing to take the 241 detainees remains a problem, and Republicans are warning they will oppose efforts to house prisoners in the United States.

After taking office only a week later, President Obama signed an executive order for a review of all pending Guantánamo cases and the closure of the facility — which now houses 241 prisoners — within one year. In Jawad's case, however, the new administration returned to the military review panel to ask for a 120-day delay before it rules on Jawad's case. The panel granted the request, over the objections of Jawad's lawyers.

Obama's action — on his second full day in office — moved toward fulfilling his repeated campaign pledge to close Guantánamo, known as "Gitmo." Human rights advocates, who have strongly criticized Guantánamo and the legal rules the Bush administration established for enemy combatant cases,

are applauding Obama's move.

"Today is the beginning of the end of this sorry chapter in our nation's history," Elisa Massimino, executive director and CEO of Human Rights First, said after Obama signed the order. "The message this sends to the world could not be clearer: The United States is ready to reclaim its role as a nation committed to human rights and the rule of law."

Even some former Bush administration officials agree the time has come to close the facility. John Bellinger, who was legal adviser at the State Department and National Security Council during the Bush administration, says he has "very strongly" supported closing this "albatross around our necks."

"The benefits of Guantánamo have been outweighed by the legacy costs of Guantánamo, and that has been true for some time," says Charles "Cully" Stimson, former assistant secretary of Defense for detainee affairs and now a senior legal fellow at the conservative Heritage Foundation. The facility has taken "a moral toll" on the U.S. image at home and abroad, he says.

Robert Chesney, a respected national security expert now a visiting professor at the University of Texas Law School in Austin, says Guantánamo reflects a broader failure of policy on how to deal with suspected terrorists captured both within and outside the United States since the Sept. 11, 2001, attacks on the World Trade Center and Pentagon by the Islamic terrorist group al Qaeda.

"For more than seven years, we've struggled to define a counterterrorism policy that is effective, that is politically sustainable and simultaneously reflects our core values as Americans," Chesney

America's Controversial Prison in the Caribbean

The U.S. Naval Station at Guantánamo Bay has come a long way since its days as a coaling station. The U.S. acquired the 45-mile-square base on Cuba's southeastern tip in 1903 after helping the island, a former Spanish colony, gain its independence during the Spanish-American war. Today the base houses about 8,400 U.S. personnel — including about 2,200 military and civilian personnel at the detention facilities — and 241 prisoners.

remarked as he opened a panel discussion at the school on Feb. 3. "We have not yet succeeded in doing this." [2]

Despite indications of editorial and public support for Obama's action, Republicans are raising questions and apparently setting the stage to criticize the closure if suspected terrorists are transferred to facilities within the United States. ""Most families neither want nor need hundreds of terrorists seeking to kill Americans in their communities," House GOP Whip Eric Cantor of Virginia said in a statement issued the same day.

Another critic, however, notes that Obama's executive order did nothing other than promise a review of case files

and set a goal of closing the facility. "He hasn't really done much," says Andrew McCarthy, legal editor of *National Review* and chairman of the Center for Law and Counterterrorism at the Foundation for the Defense of Democracies.

McCarthy has backhanded praise for the interim nature of Obama's move, which he says contrasts with candidate Obama's "demagogic, overheated rhetoric" during the campaign. "What he has obviously found is that there are very difficult issues, very complex issues that have to be worked through with respect to the detainees," McCarthy says.

"It was unfortunate that he and people who are like-minded were crit-

ical of Guantánamo," McCarthy adds, "when in point of fact if you didn't have Guantánamo, you would need to have something like it, whether it was inside the United States or outside." (*See sidebar, p. 188.*)

In establishing Guantánamo, President Bush said the camp would be used to house "the worst of the worst" suspected terrorists. But the national security and human-rights camps diverge on how to regard the 779 prisoners who have been held at Guantánamo over its seven-year history, some 540 of whom have been released. Among the detainees still being held, Bellinger predicts the Obama administration will find "a lot of bad people left, or at least many in the gray area."

"We've known all along that not everyone held at Guantánamo had any business being held there at all," counters Sharon Bradford Franklin, senior counsel with the Constitution Project, an advocacy group that seeks to find consensus on constitutional issues.

Outside government, the most extensive study of the Guantánamo detainees appears to have been conducted by Benjamin Wittes, a senior fellow at the Brookings Institution think tank and author of a highly regarded new book on counterterrorism policies, *Law and the Long War.* Wittes writes that his examination of the information publicly available on the detainees indicated many of them had incriminating ties to al Qaeda. An updated compilation by Wittes available on the Brookings Web site, however, shows that only a small fraction of the prisoners still being held are considered major al Qaeda leaders. [3] (*See chart, p. 184.*)

Paradoxically, Obama's pledge to close Guantánamo appears to be contributing to an increase in tensions in the prison camp. A special Defense Department review team that spent almost two weeks at Guantánamo concluded in February that detainees are being treated humanely in compliance with the provisions of the Geneva Conventions regarding wartime captives. But the report noted a nearly sixfold increase in disciplinary incidents by detainees since September 2008 and tied the increase in part to detainees' "uncertainty and anxiety about the future." [4]

Along with Guantánamo, the Obama administration inherits an array of legal proceedings. Obama's order froze proceedings in the military tribunal system, which thus far has secured three convictions: Ali Hamza Ahmad Suliman al-Bahlul, Osama bin Laden's alleged media secretary, was found guilty of 35 counts relating to support of terrorism and sentenced to life in prison; Salim Ahmed Hamdan, bin Laden's former driver, was convicted on reduced charges; and David Hicks, the so-called Australian Taliban, pleaded guilty to one count of providing material support of terrorism. He and Hamdan were essentially sentenced to time served and have since been released. But pending cases in federal courts up to and including the Supreme Court are continuing.

The high court is scheduled to hear a case on April 22 testing whether the government can hold without trial a Qatari native — Ali Saleh Kahlah al-Marri — as an enemy combatant after he was arrested while lawfully residing in the United States on a student visa. In a closely divided ruling, the federal appeals court in Richmond, Va., said yes — but with more judicial scrutiny than proposed by the Bush administration. In one of its first moves, the Obama administration asked for and was granted an extension of time to file the government's brief with the high court.

In a separate case, the federal appeals court for the District of Colum-

bia is reconsidering whether former Guantánamo detainees can sue government officials for alleged torture and religious discrimination. The Supreme Court sent the case back to the appeals court in December to consider the impact of the justices' decision in June that Guantánamo detainees can use federal habeas corpus to challenge their confinement. [5]

Former detainee Said Ali al-Shihri's return to terrorist activity in Yemen underscores the complications in carrying out Obama's decision to close down Guantánamo, The New York Times said.

The pending cases are forcing the Obama administration to make policy decisions sooner than the one-year timetable outlined for closing Guantánamo, according to Chesney. "There will not be as much new time as the administration would like," Chesney said at the panel discussion. "The litigation calendar will force them to take positions much faster than that."

As the administration's review continues, here are some of the major questions being debated:

Should the government continue repatriating Guantánamo detainees to other countries?

The day after President Obama signed the executive order on closing Guantánamo, a front-page New York Times story stated that one of the detainees already released from the camp, Said

Ali al-Shihri, had returned to terrorist activity as the head of al Qaeda's Yemeni branch. The newspaper said that Al Shihri's role — allegedly announced in an Internet statement and confirmed by U.S. counterintelligence officials — "underscores the complications" in carrying out Obama's decision. [6]

In the seven years it has taken to complete legal proceedings against three Guantánamo detainees, the Bush administration released nearly 540 other prisoners, most of them to their home countries after what former State Department legal adviser Bellinger describes as "arduous negotiations." In the administration's last week in office, the Defense Department claimed that 18 of those released have been confirmed as "returning to the fight," and another 43 are suspected of having done so. [7]

The Defense Intelligence Agency report has no specifics and — like earlier DIA compilations on the subject — widely questioned. "I don't want to deride that as an urban myth, but I don't have a very high level of confidence in the claims," says Eugene Fidell, president of the National Institute of Military Justice, who teaches military law at Yale Law School. Nevertheless, the total figure of 61 — representing 11 percent of those released — is cited by national security hawks as evidence that the emphasis on reducing the Guantánamo population has been and still is mistaken.

"Thus far, it's shown itself to be a terrible idea," says McCarthy, a former federal prosecutor. "To the extent that we're trying to shovel people into other countries, all that does is to empty out Gitmo, but it doesn't make the problem any better. It makes the problem in many ways worse."

Sending Guantánamo detainees to third countries, however, is the first — and principal — step in the blueprint for closing the facility that human-rights advocates issued while the presidential campaign was under way. Under the plans outlined by Human Rights First and the Center for Strategic and International Studies (CSIS), detainees who could not be tried in the United States might be transferred to their home countries or third countries for prosecution. Those not suspected of criminal activity should be repatriated or — if they faced the likelihood of torture — sent to third countries. [8]

The report by a CSIS working group, questions the claimed number of detainees who have returned to terrorist activities, but acknowledges the "security risks" in the policies. "There are risks associated with keeping Guantánamo open and there are risks with closing Guantánamo," says report author Sarah Mendelson, director of the center's human-rights and security initiative. "We came to the conclusion that the cost of keeping Guantánamo open is far greater than the cost of closing it."

The blueprint for closing the camp may rest, in part, on unrealistic premises, however. Prosecution, repatriation and resettlement have all proved to be elusive goals. "Virtually no country has been able to detain or prosecute the people we've returned to them," Bellinger says. As one example, he says there are no domestic laws making it a crime to travel to Afghanistan, where many of the detainees were taken into custody.

As for repatriation, the Saudi government is credited with operating a model rehabilitation program, but in early February it listed as terrorism suspects 11 former Guantánamo prisoners who went through the program. Yemen, the home country of the largest number of remaining detainees, has no rehabilitation program whatsoever. [9]

In any event, McCarthy mocks the whole concept of rehabilitation. "You can't really seriously think that you're going to send these people to Saudi Arabia, which is the cradle of Wahhabism, and through re-education camp and then they're not going to be a jihadist any more," he says. "It's just a silly idea."

Resettlement presents its own difficulties, Bellinger says. "Most of these countries don't want these people back," he says. "They view them as troublemakers." And third countries — notably, in Europe — are reluctant to admit detainees that the U.S. government has publicly labeled as dangerous terrorists. Matthew Waxman, a Columbia Law School professor who served in the Bush administration in the then new position of assistant secretary of Defense for detainee affairs, says the Obama administration will face "a very difficult road" in persuading third countries to admit released detainees unless the United States itself is willing to resettle some of them.

Mendelson predicts that European governments will be more willing to work with the Obama administration — given its commitment to closing Guantánamo — than they were while Bush was in office. The CSIS report also outlines steps to strengthen law enforcement, detention facilities and reintegration programs in other countries where detainees are sent after release. Still, Mendelson writes, "We cannot guarantee nor will we pretend that the risk of releasing or transferring detainees is zero."

Waxman agrees. "All options to close Guantánamo carry some risks," he says.

Should Guantánamo detainees be prosecuted in civilian courts?

FBI agents arrested Jose Padilla as he arrived at Chicago's O'Hare International Airport on May 8, 2002, on suspicion of planning to plant so-called dirty bombs at sites in the United States. The Bush administration held the Brooklyn-born Padilla as an enemy combatant for more than three years. But because of his U.S. citizenship, Padilla was held not in Guantánamo but at the U.S. Naval Brig in Charleston, S.C.

Fearing an adverse ruling in Padilla's habeas corpus challenge to his confinement, the government decided early in 2006 to indict Padilla and try him in a civilian criminal court. The strategy paid off on Aug. 16, 2007, when a federal jury in Miami convicted Padilla of conspiracy and material support of terrorism — charges that led to the 17-year prison sentence he is now serving. [10]

Critics of Guantánamo — and its military tribunals — point to the Padilla trial and scores of others since 2001 as evidence that civilian courts are up to the task of prosecuting suspected terrorists. The U.S. criminal justice system "has proven an effective venue for prosecuting terrorist suspects," Mendelson writes in the CSIS report, "especially when compared with the military commissions." The report counts 107 jihadist terrorist cases — some with multiple defendants — tried in civilian courts since 2001 with 145 convictions. [11]

"We recommend very firmly that prosecutions should be handled by Article III courts," says the Constitution Project's Franklin, referring to the constitutional provisions establishing the federal judiciary. Military law may be applicable for "actual combatants captured on the battlefield," she acknowledges, but all others "can be and should be prosecuted in civilian courts."

National security hawks like McCarthy and a range of other experts, including some Guantánamo critics, counter by pointing to a host of practical difficulties in prosecuting enemy combatants in civilian courts. Speaking at the Texas law school panel, Wittes, a former editorial writer on legal issues for *The Washington Post*, outlined several reasons why such prosecutions "might not be viable" for many Guantánamo detainees. Evidence against some may be tainted by coercion or torture, unavailable because classified as secret or inadmissible because of mundane courtroom issues, such as proving chain of custody or the like. And in many cases the quantity and quality of the evidence may simply be insufficient, Wittes says, to meet the beyond-a-reasonable-doubt standard applicable in criminal trials.

McCarthy, one of the prosecutors in the 1995 conspiracy conviction of Omar Abdel-Rahman, the so-called blind sheik implicated in the 1993 World Trade Center bombing, says terrorism defendants' rights to discover prosecution evidence present a problem even in a successful case. "The discovery rules and the trial process itself [are] an intelligence gold mine for the terrorist organization at large," he says. "And there is no real way to prevent that from happening if you're going to have a trial that deserves the name of a trial."

McCarthy and Wittes both favor creation of what is being called a national security court to handle terrorism cases. In general, proponents of such courts envision a specialized federal civilian court applying the substantive and procedural law of military tribunals. A national security court would be "a better fit," McCarthy says, than either the regular civilian justice system or the military commissions operating at Guantánamo. (See "At Issue," p. 193.)

The military tribunals, in fact, appear not to have performed to anyone's satisfaction. CSIS's Mendelson calls them "ineffective and inefficient." From a somewhat different perspective, ex-Pentagon official Stimson says he pronounced the system "dead" more than a year ago. Despite his service in the Defense Department, Stimson favors federal court trials for the more complex Guantánamo cases because federal prosecutors are likely to be more experienced than most military lawyers.

Human-rights advocates generally minimize the difficulties claimed by the critics of civilian trials. The CSIS report notes, for example, that the federal statute against material support of terrorism does not require "heavy evi-

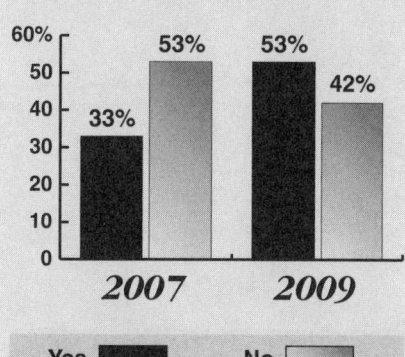

Most Americans Now Favor Closing Base

More than half of all Americans said in January they favor closing the U.S. military prison at Guantánamo Bay, Cuba, up from one-third two years earlier.

Do you think the United States should close the prison at Guantánamo Bay?

Note: Percentages not shown of those with no opinion.

Sources: Gallup Poll; Washington Post/ABC News Poll

dentiary burdens" and permits long prison sentences. In any event, the report adds, the use of civilian trials "denies terrorist suspects the symbolic value of special, extrajudicial treatment."

Columbia Law School's Waxman expects the Obama administration to look at criminal prosecutions as "the preferred option" for detainees who are not released to other countries, and he supports that stance. "One of the lessons of the Bush years is that legitimacy is not only important from a rule of law perspective but also from a strategic perspective," he says. "The United States has a strategic interest in promoting certain rule-of-law principles and in demonstrating the legal durability and legitimacy of its counterterrorism policies to garner additional international cooperation."

Should some Guantánamo detainees be held indefinitely without military or civilian trial?

Four times, the Bush administration went before the Supreme Court to claim the power to hold suspected enemy combatants for indefinite periods with no more than a limited right to challenge their detentions and no more than the most limited judicial review. And four times the Supreme Court said no.

In the first of the rulings, the court in 2004 said U.S. citizens held as enemy combatants were entitled to some hearing before "a neutral decisionmaker." On the same day, the court issued the first of a series of three decisions on the foreigners held at Guantánamo. The series culminated in the 2008 ruling that guaranteed the detainees the right to challenge their incarceration through federal habeas corpus proceedings. [12]

The expansive claim to hold wartime captives indefinitely was one of the primary criticisms that human-rights advocates made against the Bush administration's Guantánamo policies. "The sheer fact of using the geographic location of Guantánamo is not . . . the source of the problem," explains Franklin of the Constitution Project. "The source of the problem was the notion of the prior administration that this created a law-free zone, a legal black hole, and that they could be exempt from any of the principles of the U.S. Constitution, international law or the Geneva Conventions" dealing with wartime captives.

Now, two of President Obama's principal appointees on detention and interrogation policies are signaling that this administration, too, will claim some power to hold suspected terrorists captured in war-like circumstances for indefinite periods. "There's going to be a group of prisoners that, very frankly, are going to have to be held in detainment for a long time," CIA Director-designate Leon Panetta told the Senate Intelligence Committee during his confirmation hearing on Feb. 5.

Few Leaders Among Guantánamo Detainees

The 241 prisoners being held at the U.S. Naval Station at Guantána-mo Bay include 36 alleged al Qaeda or Taliban leaders and 199 fighters or operatives, according to an independent examination of the records (top). Among the detainees who have responded to the military's allegations against them, nearly two-thirds have admitted some affiliation with terrorist organizations; the remainder deny any association with al Qaeda or the Taliban (bottom)

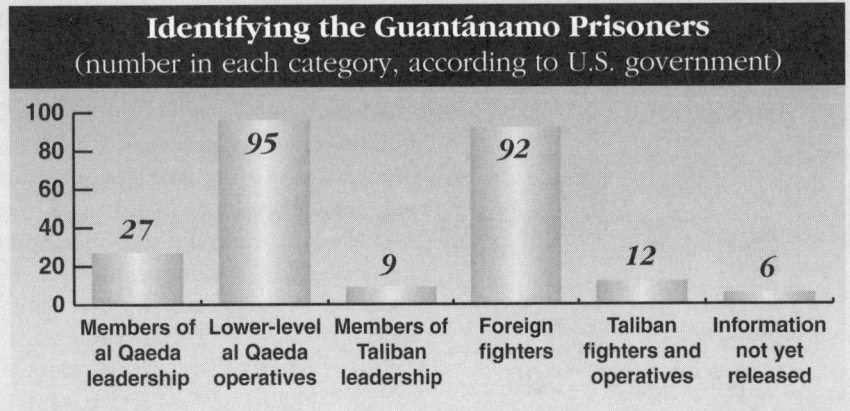

Identifying the Guantánamo Prisoners
(number in each category, according to U.S. government)

27 — Members of al Qaeda leadership
95 — Lower-level al Qaeda operatives
9 — Members of Taliban leadership
92 — Foreign fighters
12 — Taliban fighters and operatives
6 — Information not yet released

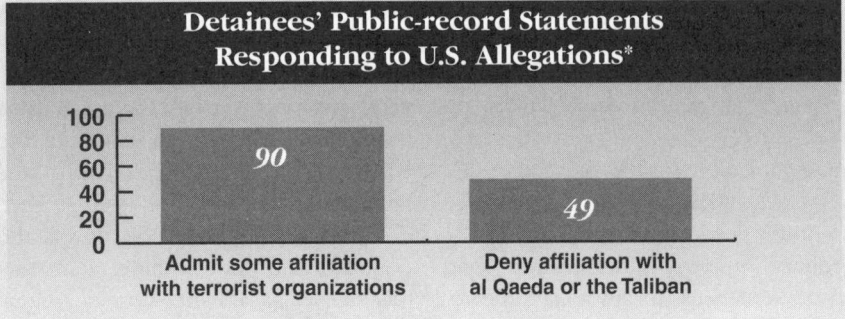

Detainees' Public-record Statements Responding to U.S. Allegations*

90 — Admit some affiliation with terrorist organizations
49 — Deny affiliation with al Qaeda or the Taliban

* In addition to the relevant statements from 139 detainees, 80 detainees made no statements or made statements that do not materially bear on the military's allegations against them.

Source: Benjamin Wittes and Zaahira Wyne, The Current Detainee Population of Guantánamo: An Empirical Study, *Brookings Institution, January 2009, www.brookings.edu/reports/2008/1216_detainees_wittes.aspx*

In his confirmation hearing earlier, Attorney General-designate Eric Holder had endorsed the power to hold an enemy combatant "for the duration of the conflict," but only with judicial review at least once a year to determine whether the prisoner is dangerous. "That kind of review has to be a part of what we do," Holder told the Senate Judiciary Committee on Jan. 16.

Human-rights advocates are concerned. "If we go down the road of a detention-without-charge regime, we will ultimately be moving Guantánamo to the United States rather than closing it," says Mendelson at CSIS.

"The Obama administration made great gains when it announced the plan to close Guantánamo," Jennifer Daskal, senior counterterrorism counsel for

Human Rights Watch, told the *Los Angeles Times.* "Many of those gains will be undercut if the administration is perceived as merely transferring the system of indefinite detention to U.S. soil." [13]

Security-minded experts, however, say the power to hold enemy combatants without trial is both well established and essential. "In our wars, we have held millions of prisoners of war, and they've never had legal proceedings," says McCarthy. He labels as "preposterous" the human-rights groups' stance that the government cannot hold enemy combatants indefinitely.

Unlike the Bush administration, however, defenders of the detention power are calling for Congress and the courts to be involved in establishing rules for holding enemy combatants and reviewing their confinement. "There are some number of people that we're going to have to continue to detain outside the criminal justice system," the Brookings Institution's Wittes said during the Texas law school panel. He calls for Congress to authorize detention and for any detentions to be reviewed by federal courts.

Former Bush administration officials Bellinger and Stimson also say the other branches of government need to be involved. Bellinger wants Congress to authorize detentions for specified periods of time after a given date. Stimson says detentions should be "subjected to periodic review — a very robust review — with heavy lawyer and court involvement."

Military-law expert Fidell, however, opposes any legislation authorizing preventive detention. "I don't think it can be done consistent with our legal system," he says. The Constitution Project's Franklin agrees. "We should be taking people into custody only if we can make a probable-cause showing that they have committed a terrorism offense," she says.

Stimson believes only a "very few" detainees may be too dangerous to release but impossible to try. Over time, he says, there will be a growing presumption against continued detention.

He even predicts that the Obama administration might decide that it is not worthwhile to continue to hold this small category of detainees and will find a way to transfer them.

University of Texas law Professor Chesney, however, is not surprised the administration is defending the detention power for now. "The Obama administration is not going to completely forswear the power to hold clandestine, non-state actors," he says. Like others, however, he calls for judicial review to ensure proper treatment and adequate basis for continued detention.

"The executive order leaves open a range of options of how [the administration] is going to detain terrorism suspects in the future, and that's a good thing," says Columbia law Professor Waxman. "It would be an error to close off options." ■

BACKGROUND

'The Least Worst Place'

With the nation still reeling from the 9/11 terrorist attacks, President Bush made the fateful decision in fall 2001 that suspected enemy combatants captured in Afghanistan and suspected terrorists apprehended elsewhere would be held at the U.S. Naval Station at Guantánamo Bay, Cuba. The decision came to be criticized on two related grounds. The detainees were held out of sight and largely incommunicado, and the administration argued against any judicial review over the detainees. More than two years after the first detainees arrived at Gitmo, the Supreme Court dealt the administration's legal strategy a setback by ruling in June 2004 that federal courts had jurisdiction to hear habeas corpus challenges by the detainees.

Congress set the stage for the detentions by passing, at Bush's request, a resolution authorizing the use of force against "those nations, organizations and persons" responsible for the 9/11 attacks. Bush used the resolution to launch a war against Afghanistan's Taliban government, which he said had harbored the al Qaeda terrorist organization. He then signed an executive order on Nov. 13 authorizing the Defense Department to detain al Qaeda members or anyone else responsible for terrorist activity against the United States and to try the detainees, if at all, before military tribunals.

After consulting with the Justice Department, Defense Secretary Donald Rumsfeld decided to hold the detainees at Guantánamo, which he described on Dec. 27 as "the least worst place" for confinement. The Justice Department's Office of Legal Counsel supported the decision, predicting that federal courts likely would rule detainees at Guantánamo had no access to federal courts to challenge their confinement.

Initially, the decision appeared to be drawing tentative acceptance, with Guantánamo viewed as a logical place to hold suspected terrorists — a secure facility removed from areas of conflict. Military authorities welcomed reporters to the base to tout the speed in constructing the jail cells of the so-called Camp X-Ray.

Criticism began, however, within days of the first prisoners' arrival on Jan. 11, 2002. The International Red Cross faulted the administration for permitting release of pictures of the detainees as they arrived. Amnesty International criticized holding the detainees incommunicado. Criticism increased as Bush announced — and reconfirmed over opposition from Secretary of State Colin Powell — that the detainees would not be regarded as covered by the provisions of the Geneva Conventions. Several European governments said the detainees should be granted prisoner-of-war status.

The controversy moved into the courts on Feb. 19, when lawyers from the Center for Constitutional Rights filed a habeas corpus petition challenging the detentions on behalf of two Britons, Shafiq

Rasul and Javaid Iqbal, and David Hicks, an Australian. The petition claimed the prisoners were being held in "indefinite" and "unreviewable" detention in violation of international law and the U.S. Constitution. "The government has just gone too far here," said the center's president, Michael Ratner.

Legal experts questioned that day cast doubt on the prisoners' chances. "The case has a gut appeal," George Washington University law professor Mary Cheh remarked. "But not everything that is deeply troubling is unconstitutional." [14] The experts' doubts appeared to be well-founded when U.S. District Judge Colleen Kollar-Kotelly rejected the challenge in July, ruling that the detainees had no constitutional rights because Guantánamo was not formally part of the United States.

Meanwhile, the administration was making the momentous decision behind the scenes to authorize "enhanced interrogation" techniques against some of the Guantánamo detainees as well as some of the suspected terrorists being held at then-secret CIA prisons in Europe. In a critical step, the Justice Department's Office of Legal Counsel issued an advisory memorandum on Aug. 1, 2002, advising the CIA that a specific list of interrogation techniques would not constitute torture because they were not "specifically intended to inflict severe pain and physical suffering."

Armed with that opinion, military intelligence agents sought and obtained permission to use techniques such as sleep deprivation against some Guantánamo detainees. FBI agents disagreed on the legality and the effectiveness of the techniques, but Rumsfeld signed off on some of the methods in a memo dated Dec. 2. He rescinded the approval for some of the techniques in April 2003. Rasul and Iqbal contend in pending lawsuits that they continued to be mistreated up until their eventual release in March 2004.

In the habeas corpus case, the Guantánamo detainees lost a second round with a ruling in March 2003 by the U.S. Court of Appeals for the District of Columbia Circuit. The appellate judges upheld the lower court's ruling that the Guantánamo detainees could not use habeas corpus to challenge their confinement. In November the Supreme Court agreed to rule on the issue in a pair of consolidated cases — *Rasul v. Bush* and a second case on behalf of a dozen Kuwaitis.

The move set up the first definitive test of the administration's legal strategy and ended seven months later with a limited but decisive setback. By a 6-3 vote, the court ruled on June 28, 2004, that federal courts had jurisdiction to hear the habeas corpus cases. The ruling left all other issues for future cases. Dissenting justices said the ruling was bad law and bad policy. But Ratner hailed the decision. "This is a major victory for the rule of law," he said.

'A Law-Free Zone?'

The Bush administration dug in its heels after the Supreme Court's habeas corpus decision by twice persuading Congress to approve legislation to keep the Guantánamo detainees out of federal court. Instead, the administration planned to try the detainees before specially created military "commissions" with limited substantive and procedural rights. Legal challenges slowed the commissions, however, and eventually led to two additional Supreme Court rulings rejecting the administration's strategy. At the same time, the administration worked to transfer Guantánamo detainees to their home countries but encountered reluctance and resistance as other countries came to view the facility as emblematic of a policy of lawless mistreatment of wartime captives.

The administration fashioned its Guantánamo policies against the backdrop of a worldwide controversy over mistreatment of enemy combatants symbolized by the documented abuse of Iraqi pris-

oners at the U.S.-run jail at Abu Ghraib, outside Baghdad. Images broadcast around the world beginning in May 2004 touched off demands at home and abroad for stronger rules to require humane treatment of all U.S.-held prisoners, including the Guantánamo detainees. But the administration also wanted to cut off habeas corpus petitions.

The result was the Detainee Treatment Act, passed in December 2005, which prohibited inhumane treatment of prisoners and limited interrogation techniques used by military intelligence agents to those approved in the *U.S. Army Field Manual.* But the act also sought to bar federal courts from hearing habeas corpus petitions by Guantánamo detainees, including cases already pending.

Meanwhile, the military commission proceedings were being challenged by one of the Guantánamo prisoners, Salim Ahmed Hamdan, a Yemeni-born Muslim accused of being the driver for the al Qaeda leader, Osama bin Laden. Hamdan had been captured in Afghanistan, brought to Guantánamo in January 2002 and designated as eligible for trial in July 2003. He then filed a habeas corpus petition challenging the military commissions as inconsistent with the Uniform Code of Military Justice (UCMJ) and the procedural provisions of the Geneva Conventions.

After conflicting rulings from lower courts, the Supreme Court ruled, 5-3, in Hamdan's favor in June 2006. Preliminarily, the court held that the Detainee Treatment Act did not eliminate habeas corpus cases filed before the law was enacted. The court went on to hold that President Bush had failed to show any need to depart from the UCMJ's regular procedures for military trial. The majority also said the military commissions did not comply with the Geneva Conventions.

The administration pushed Congress to respond quickly by passing a new law, the Military Commissions Act, which revised procedures for the military tribunals and explicitly barred all habeas

corpus petitions from Guantánamo. To help move the bill, Bush announced on Sept. 6, 2006, that he was transferring 14 "high-value" terror suspects to Guantánamo from the secret CIA prisons. The transferred prisoners included Khalid Shaikh Mohammed, accused of masterminding the 9/11 attacks and eventually identified as one of three prisoners subjected to waterboarding during interrogation. With midterm congressional election campaigns under way, Bush's decision to move high-profile al Qaeda suspects to Guantánamo spurred Congress to act on a supposed Guantánamo fix before the elections. Congress completed action on the bill at the end of the month; Bush signed it into law on Oct. 17.

The revamped military commissions finally produced the system's first conviction in March 2007, when the Australian Hicks pleaded guilty to a newly codified charge of providing material support to terrorism. Hicks, a convert to Islam, had been turned over to U.S. forces by the U.S.-backed Northern Alliance in Afghanistan in November 2001. A military panel sentenced Hicks to seven years' imprisonment on the charge, but under the plea deal he was returned to Australia to serve only an additional nine months. After his release, Hicks acknowledged that he trained at al Qaeda camps and fought for the Taliban, but he denied any hostile actions against the United States.

Hicks' guilty plea came not long after the D.C. Circuit in February had given the Bush administration a legal victory by upholding the Military Commissions Act, including its bar to habeas corpus petitions by the Guantánamo prisoners. In June, however, the Supreme Court agreed to hear the appeals by the detainees. The lead case, *Boumediene v. Bush*, was brought on behalf of six Algerians arrested in Bosnia on suspicion of plotting to bomb the U.S. Embassy in Sarajevo. In dramatic arguments in December, Solicitor General Paul Clement

Continued on p. 188

Chronology

2001-Present

U.S. Naval Station at Guantánamo Bay, Cuba, is used to hold enemy combatants after 9/11; Bush administration loses effort to block federal court challenges; Obama administration promises to close prison camp by Jan. 22, 2010.

2001
Terrorists attack the United States (Sept. 11). . . . Congress authorizes use of military force against countries, organizations or individuals responsible for attacks (Sept. 18). . . . U.S. forces capture hundreds of suspected "enemy combatants" in Afghanistan war; President George W. Bush signs executive order authorizing military detention (Nov. 13). . . . Guantánamo Bay is chosen for detention facility; Justice Department predicts detainees cannot use habeas corpus to challenge their confinement (Dec. 28).

2002
First detainees brought to Guantánamo (Jan. 11); detentions prompt immediate controversy and legal challenges (January-February); challenges rejected in several courts. . . . Justice Department memo narrows definition of "torture," approves some "enhanced" interrogation techniques (Aug. 1). . . . Pentagon officials sign off on enhanced interrogation (November/December).

2003
Federal appeals court bars habeas corpus by Guantánamo detainees (March 11). . . . Defense Secretary Donald Rumsfeld approves new interrogation rules, including 24 of 35 recommended enhanced techniques (April 16). . . . Supreme Court agrees to rule on habeas corpus issue (Nov. 10).

2004
Four Britons released to United Kingdom, with no charges; later file civil suits for damages (March 9). . . . Images of inmate-abuse at Abu Ghraib prison in Iraq broadcast worldwide (May). . . . Supreme Court upholds federal court jurisdiction over detainees' habeas corpus petitions (June 28).

2005
Detainee Treatment Act (DTA) limits interrogation techniques, bars habeas corpus for detainees (December).

2006
Supreme Court allows pending habeas corpus cases despite DTA; rules military commissions violate U.S. military law, Geneva Conventions (June 29). . . . President Bush announces transfer of 14 "high-value" prisoners to Guantánamo (Sept. 6). . . . Congress passes, Bush signs Military Commissions Act; law prohibits all pending, future habeas corpus actions by detainees, allows limited review of military commissions by appeals court (October).

2007
Military Commissions Act upheld by D.C. Circuit court in *Boumediene* case (Feb. 20) . . . Australian David Hicks pleads guilty to supporting terrorism; sent to Australia to finish serving sentence (March). . . . Supreme Court decides to review *Boumediene* decision; hears arguments (Dec. 5).

2008
Democrat Barack Obama, Republican John McCain cinch nominations for president, promise to close Guantánamo (spring). . . . Supreme Court rules, 5-4, Military Commissions Act unconstitutional; ruling guarantees habeas corpus rights for detainees (June 12). . . . Salim Ahmed Hamdan, driver for al Qaeda leader Osama bin Laden, convicted on reduced charges, given 5-1/2-year sentence (Aug. 6-7); released to Yemen (Nov. 25). . . . Federal judge orders 17 Chinese Muslims held at Guantánamo brought to U.S. for release (Oct. 7). . . . Obama elected, begins transition (November-December). . . . Five of six detainees in *Boumediene* case ordered released by federal judge for lack of evidence (Nov. 21).

2009
Military judge says would-be hijacker Mohammed al Qahtani was "tortured" while at Guantánamo (Jan. 14). . . . Obama sworn in; denies "false choice" between liberty, security (Jan. 20). . . . Obama signs executive order to close Guantánamo within one year; orders review of detainee cases; limits use of enhanced interrogation techniques (Jan. 22). . . . Military judge says would-be hijacker Mohammed al Qahtani was "tortured" while at Guantánamo (Jan. 14). . . . Obama sworn in; denies "false choice" between liberty, security (Jan. 20). . . . Obama signs executive order to close Guantánamo within one year; orders review of detainee cases; limits use of "enhanced interrogation" techniques (Jan. 22). . . . Administration reaffirms opposition to habeas corpus for prisoners held at Bagram Air Force Base in Afghanistan (Feb. 20). . . . First Guantánamo detainee released under Obama administration; upon arrival in Britain, Binyam Mohamed describes "medieval" torture during detention in Morocco (Feb. 22-23). . . . Pentagon review team says Guantánamo meets Geneva Conventions standards; human rights groups disagree (Feb. 23). . . . Defense Department review team says Guantánamo conditions comply with Geneva Conventions; rights groups disagree (Feb. 23).

From Imperial Outpost to Post-9/11 'Gulag'

Inside the prison at Guantánamo Bay.

The prison camp that became a reviled symbol of the Bush administration's "war on terror" welcomes visitors — in person or online — to witness what is officially described as "safe, humane, legal and transparent care and custody of detained enemy combatants."

The online tour of the detention camp at the U.S. Naval Station, Guantánamo Bay, Cuba (www.jtfgtmo.southcom.mil) depicts a state-of-the-art correctional facility with a 12,000-volume library, exercise equipment and recreational areas.

The pictures contrast sharply with the indelible images first shown to the world after suspected terrorists from Afghanistan and elsewhere began arriving in January 2002: prisoners in orange jumpsuits forced to crouch near chain-link fences or being led around in shackles by burly guards.

The 320 open-air, steel-mesh cages of Camp X-Ray were in use only until April 2002, but a federal judge has ordered them preserved as evidence in litigation challenging the conditions of confinement. Today, most of the 241 detainees are housed in three facilities built later as Guantánamo — widely known as "Gitmo" — was transformed from short-term expedient to long-term policy.

There are three main camps, according to an online primer provided by *The Miami Herald* (www.miamiherald.com/Guantánamo). Camp 4 resembles a traditional prisoner-of-war camp with 10-cot bunkhouses and common eating area, communal showers and athletic facilities. Camp 5 is a maximum-security facility with single-prisoner cells controlled by a centralized locking system and closed-circuit surveillance. Camp 6 was converted from minimum to maximum security after a fight between guards and detainees in Camp 4 in May 2006. The facility has single-occupancy cells where prisoners are locked up 22 hours a day.

In addition, about 15 men are believed to be housed in supersecret Camp 7, which was built for the "high-level" former CIA captives that Bush ordered transferred to Guantánamo in September 2006. The existence of the camp was not confirmed until December 2007, and its exact location remains shrouded. Among the prisoners believed to be there is Khalid Sheikh Mohammed, charged along with four others with masterminding the Sept. 11, 2001, terrorist attacks on the United States.

A separate facility, dubbed Camp Justice, was built during the Bush administration to hold trials of detainees before the specially created military commissions. President Obama suspended those proceedings for 120 days pending an interagency review of detainees' case files by Attorney General Eric Holder. [1]

The naval base itself houses about 8,400 U.S. military and civilian personnel — including 2,200 at the detention facilities. It occupies a 45-square-mile tract — about three-fourths of the size of the District of Columbia — near the southeastern tip of Cuba. The United States acquired the base under a lease with Cuba in 1903 after helping the former Spanish colony gain its independence as part of the Spanish-American War. [2]

U.S. rights to the base — then used as a coaling station — were reaffirmed in a 1934 treaty that calls for the United States to pay Cuba about $4,000 per year. Termination of the lease requires consent of both governments. The United States has continued to pay the lease amount, but since the Cuban Revolution of the late 1950s the government of Fidel Castro has refused to cash the checks.

The base made news in 1958, when 29 sailors and Marines were kidnapped by Cuban rebels and held for 22 days. During the Cuban Missile Crisis four years later, civilian and military personnel and families were evacuated. Two years later, Castro's government cut off water and supply routes to the base. Since then, the base has had its own power and water sources.

Guantánamo faded from the news and receded in strategic significance until the 1980s and '90s, when it became a holding facility for Cuban and Haitian refugees fleeing to the United States. Under Presidents George H. W. Bush and Bill Clinton, the Coast Guard picked up the refugees on rafts on the high seas and held them in ramshackle facilities on the base to avoid bringing them to U.S. soil.

The Clinton administration lost a legal battle over the refugee issue in June 1993, when a federal judge ordered that 150 HIV-positive Haitian refugees who qualified for political asylum could not be excluded from the United States because of their health status. Later that month, however, the Supreme Court ruled the government could return Haitian refugees captured at sea to their home country without giving them the chance to apply for asylum.

Guantánamo receded from the news for the rest of the decade but emerged in fall 2001 when the Defense and Justice departments decided it was the best place to bring enemy combatants captured in the Afghanistan war and suspected terrorists rounded

Continued from p. 186

contended that the act gave the detainees sufficient judicial review to substitute for habeas corpus.

Representing the detainees, former Solicitor General Seth Waxman insisted the government's argument amounted to treating Guantánamo as a "law-free zone." In June 2008, the court sided narrowly but decisively with the detainees against the government. Writing for a five-vote majority, Justice Anthony M. Kennedy said the detainees were entitled to habeas corpus because the United States exercised "de facto sovereignty" over Guantánamo.

'An Enormous Failure'

Political and legal events combined in 2008 to create broader support for closing Guantánamo. The Bush administration resisted the conclusion, however, even as both major-party

up elsewhere. A legal opinion by John Yoo, then a deputy in the Justice Department's Office of Legal Counsel and now a law professor in California, forecast — wrongly — that the Supreme Court would not allow Guantánamo prisoners to challenge their detention in court because the base was not on U.S. soil.

In a new book detailing the initial history of the detention camp, Karen Greenberg, executive director of the Center on Law and Security at New York University School of Law, says the first commander, Marine Brig. Gen. Michael Lehnert, welcomed visits by the International Committee of the Red Cross (ICRC) and sought to comply with the Geneva Conventions even though President Bush had said they did not apply. Lehnert was eased out within a few months, however, after Defense Secretary Donald Rumsfeld ordered more stringent treatment of the prisoners to aid interrogation. [3]

For more than a year, official policy approved by Rumsfeld sanctioned "enhanced interrogation" techniques at the camp such as sleep deprivation, "stress positions" and forced nakedness. Rumsfeld withdrew approval for many of the challenged techniques in a memorandum signed in April 2003. Criticism of the camp continued, however. In November 2004 a leaked ICRC report described some discipline for prisoners as "tantamount to torture." In May 2005, the human-rights group Amnesty International labeled Guantánamo "the gulag of our time."

Through the years, some international visitors have dissented from this image of the camp. After visiting in 2007, Brookings scholar Wittes described the camp as "coolly professional." [4] Charles "Cully" Stimson, an assistant secretary of Defense who helped oversee the facility from January 2006 to February 2007, says interrogation complied with the *U.S. Army Field Manual.* "During my tenure and going forward, we were not engaged in any practices that would be considered cruel, inhuman or degrading at all," he says.

A guard talks to a Guantánamo detainee inside the open yard at Camp 4, the medium-security detention center that resembles a military prisoner of war camp.

AFP/Getty Images/Brennan Linsley

Stimson and others note the many stresses for the young guards at the camp, ranging from periodic hunger strikes to urine- and feces-filled baggies thrown in a guard's face. The Guantánamo Web site notes without comment the different conditions of confinement for "compliant" and "noncompliant" prisoners. But the site also says that all prisoners "regardless of compliancy" are furnished a Koran, prayer mat, prayer beads and cap. The Muslim prisoners are aided in their religious observances by arrows in each cell pointing to Mecca and by prison schedules that take account of the observance of daily prayers.

As part of the Obama administration's decision to close Guantánamo within one year, Defense Secretary Robert Gates ordered a review to determine whether the camp complies with all provisions of the Geneva Conventions on humane treatment of wartime captives. The report, released on Feb. 23, found no violations but recommended some changes to improve conditions. Human-rights groups faulted the report and called for broader changes.

Meanwhile, White House Counsel Gregory Craig and Attorney General Holder visited the prison in separate day visits on Feb. 19 and 23, respectively. No reporters accompanied either official, and neither had immediate comments after returning to Washington.

[1] For a description, see Jeffrey Toobin, "Camp Justice," *The New Yorker,* April 14, 2008, pp. 32-38.

[2] Some background drawn from U.S. Navy, "History of Guantánamo Bay," undated (www.cnic.navy.mil/Guantánamo/index.htm). For a detailed history, the site recommends M.E. Murphy, *The History of Guantánamo Bay 1494-1964,* published in two volumes in 1953 and 1964.

[3] Karen Greenberg, *The Least Worst Place: Guantánamo's First 100 Days* (2009). For a summary, see Karen Greenberg, "When Gitmo Was (Relatively) Good," *The Washington Post,* Jan. 25, 2009, p. B1.

[4] Benjamin Wittes, *Law and the Long War: The Future of Justice in the Age of Terror* (2008), p. 73.

presidential candidates endorsed the step, and the government's stance in Guantánamo cases met a host of legal difficulties in court. Obama's election — after he had strongly criticized Bush policies in a range of areas — seemed to portend quick action on Guantánamo. But the executive order that

Obama signed on his second full day in the White House only started a process and gave the administration a full year to complete the closure of the camp.

By the time of the Supreme Court decision recognizing habeas corpus rights for Guantánamo prisoners,

Obama and McCain had cinched their respective nominations. Both had already endorsed closing Guantánamo, but they differed on the court ruling. Obama hailed the decision as a victory for the rule of law, while McCain called it "one of the worst decisions" in the country's history. President Bush said he agreed with the dissenters in the case, but promised to comply. Behind the scenes, Bush's advisers considered closing the camp but rejected the idea — despite Bush's professed desire to do so — because of what the advisers concluded were unacceptable political and legal risks. [15]

Meanwhile, the administration was heading toward a serious embarrassment in the first-ever military commission trial: the prosecution of Salim Hamdan, the detainee most closely identified with challenging the Guantánamo regime. When Hamdan's trial opened on July 22, the prosecution depicted his role as bin Laden's former driver as vital to al Qaeda's war against the United States. Defense lawyers instead painted him as a poor Muslim in need of a job. After a two-week trial, the military jury sided mostly with the defense. The panel acquitted Hamdan of the most serious charges and convicted him on Aug. 6 only of material support of terrorism. The next day, the jury sentenced Hamdan to an unexpectedly short 5-1/2 years; the judge said he would credit Hamdan with the 61 months he had already served.

With economic issues dominating the presidential campaign, Obama and McCain devoted scant attention to Guantánamo during their parties' national conventions in late August and early September, respectively. Obama had laid out his position earlier, on June 18, where he called Guantánamo "an enormous failure" and "legal black hole" that had weakened support abroad for U.S. anti-terrorism policies. In his acceptance speech, Obama made only a less specific promise to "restore our moral standing." Accepting the GOP nomination a week later, McCain thanked Bush for keeping the country safe after 9/11 and left any criticism of Bush policies unspoken.

In the fall, the administration sustained two more blows to its Guantánamo policies when two federal judges in Washington — for the first time — ordered the release of detainees. On Oct. 7, Judge

Ricardo Urbina directed the government to free 17 Chinese Muslims, known as Uighurs, who had been held at Guantánamo since they were rounded up in Afghanistan in fall 2001. The Uighurs, ethnic Turkic Muslim separatists from western China, contended they had been seeking refuge from the Chinese government. The administration initially described them as terrorists, but by 2008 acknowledged they were not enemy combatants. The dissident Uighurs remained at Guantánamo, however, because they could not be sent back to China, which classifies Uighurs as terrorists, and no other country would take them. The government won an appeals court stay of Urbina's ruling quickly, and later — after Obama took office — a reversal of the decision. (*See sidebar, p. 191.*)

The next month, Judge Richard Leon ruled the government had no legal basis for holding five of the six detainees from the *Boumediene* case. Speaking from the bench — with the prisoners listening by teleconference from Guantánamo — Leon noted that the government had dropped charges relating to the alleged bombing plot but still contended the group planned to go to Afghanistan to fight against U.S. forces. Leon said the government's case relied "exclusively" on classified evidence from one unnamed source whose reliability and credibility could not be adequately evaluated. He called the evidence "too thin a reed" to justify continued imprisonment and ordered five of the six released "forthwith." Leon found sufficient evidence, however, to justify the charge that Bensayah Belkacem had aided transportation logistics for al Qaeda members.

With Obama preparing to take office, the government suffered one more setback: On Jan. 14 Leon ordered the release of a Chadian-born detainee, Mohammed al Gharani, who had been captured at age 14 and accused by other detainees of having lived in al Qaeda guest houses. The evidence was inconsistent and unverified, Leon said.

Eight days later, Obama signed the executive order promising a new review of all the Guantánamo case files and closure of the facility within a year. McCain was among those who endorsed the president's decision. [16] ■

CURRENT SITUATION

Detainee Cases Reviewed

A Justice Department task force is beginning close review of case files on the 241 remaining Guantánamo detainees following visits to the prison camp by two top Obama administration officials and the first release of a detainee since Obama took office.

White House Counsel Gregory Craig and Attorney General Holder made separate day trips to Guantánamo in late February, the first visits to the facility for each. No reporters accompanied Craig or Holder on the trips. Craig was accompanied on his Feb. 18 trip by Jeh C. Johnson, the Defense Department's general counsel. Holder took half a dozen close aides with him for a similar trip on Feb. 23. A Justice Department spokesman told reporters in Washington that Holder was to discuss case histories of specific detainees and tour detention facilities and Camp Justice, the courtroom complex built for the military commissions.

Among those accompanying Holder was Matthew Olsen, a veteran Justice Department official whom Holder named on Feb. 20 to head an interagency task force charged with assembling information on each of the remaining detainees and recommending proper dispositions of their cases. Olsen had been a Justice Department prosecutor for nearly 10 years before being named in September 2006

Continued on p. 192

What Can Be Done With the Uighurs?

Even the U.S. wants to release 17 Chinese Muslims.

Seventeen Chinese Muslims held at the Guantánamo prison camp since 2002 deny that they are "enemy combatants" against the United States. The government agrees and wants to release the men, members of the Uighur Muslim community in western China.

When a federal judge last fall ordered that the Uighurs be brought to the United States to be released, however, the Bush administration appealed the decision. And last week the federal appeals court for the District of Columbia Circuit agreed that federal courts cannot order a foreigner admitted into the United States — a ruling that leaves the puzzle for the Obama administration to try to solve. [1]

The Uighurs are members of a Turkic ethnic group considered by the Chinese government to be separatist terrorists. Before the Sept. 11, 2001, terrorist attacks on the United States, the dissident Uighurs had been receiving firearms training at a camp run by the Eastern Turkistan Islamic Group near Tora Bora, Afghanistan — the same area where al Qaeda training camps are found. They fled to Pakistan after U.S. air strikes destroyed their camp but were captured, turned over to U.S. forces and brought to Guantánamo.

Initially, the government depicted the Uighurs as enemy combatants because of alleged connections between the Turkistan group and al Qaeda or Afghanistan's Taliban government. But the U.S. Court of Appeals for the District of Columbia, ruling on a habeas corpus case brought by one of the Uighurs, said the government had not produced enough evidence to support the accusation. [2]

The Bush administration bowed to the ruling and stepped up efforts to release the men to third countries. The Uighurs cannot be returned to their home country because they contend — and the U.S. government does not dispute — that they could face arrest, torture or execution in China. But the government's six-year-long depiction of the Uighurs as dangerous terrorists has left other countries reluctant to accept them.

In October, U.S. District Judge Ricardo Urbina moved to resolve the dilemma by ordering the Uighurs to be released into the United States. After questioning the government's claim that the Uighurs could be dangerous if admitted into the country, Urbina ruled on Oct. 7 that their continued detention was unlawful. "Separation of powers concerns do not trump . . . the unalienable right of liberty," he said. [3]

The government immediately asked for and obtained a stay to Urbina's ruling pending an appeal. The three-judge panel's Feb. 18 ruling on the appeal backed the government's position that Urbina had exceeded his authority.

"It is not within the province of any court, unless expressly authorized by law, to review the determination of the political branch of the government to exclude a given alien," Senior Circuit Judge A. Raymond Randolph wrote for a two-judge majority. The third judge, Judith Rogers, disagreed with the legal ruling but said Urbina had acted prematurely because the Uighurs had never sought admission to the United States.

The case was argued before the appellate panel on Nov. 24, while the Bush administration was still in office. With the case pending, lawyers for the Uighurs wrote to Obama administration officials on Jan. 23 — the day after President Obama signed an executive order promising to close Guantánamo within one year — urging that the men be immediately released.

A Washington, D.C.-based association of Uighurs offered to help the prisoners establish residences in the United States. "We have people offering them places to stay, English training, employment," said Nury Turkel, a past president of the Uyghur American Association. "We don't want anyone to think they will be a burden on society." [4]

Lawyers for the Uighurs said they would continue their efforts to free the men, but one said the appeals court decision limits the impact of the Supreme Court's decision in June 2008 guaranteeing Guantánamo detainees the right to habeas corpus. "You win and still can't get out," Susan Baker Manning told *The Washington Post*. The administration had no immediate comment on the decision. [5]

Seventeen Chinese Muslims, or Uighurs, held since 2002 have been ordered released from Guantánamo. Five other Uighurs, including the four above, were recently released to Albania.

Center for Human Rights in the Americas

[1] The decision is *Kiyemba v. Obama*, 08-5424, U.S. Court of Appeals for the District of Columbia Circuit, Feb. 18, 2009, http://pacer.cadc.uscourts.gov/common/opinions/200902/08-5424-1165428.pdf. For coverage, see Lyle Denniston, "Uighurs Barred From U.S.," SCOTUSBlog, Feb. 18, 2009, www.scotusblog.com/wp/uighurs-barred-from-us/#more-8725. Background drawn from court opinion and ongoing coverage on SCOTUSBlog.

[2] The case is *Parhat v. Gates*, 532 F.3d 834 (D.C. Cir. 2008). For coverage, see William Glaberson, "Evidence Faulted in Detainee Case," *The New York Times*, July 1, 2008, p. A1.

[3] For coverage, see Ben Winograd, "Judge Orders Uighurs to U.S.; Government Appeals," SCOTUSBlog, Oct. 7, 2008. The story links to a transcript of the Oct. 7 hearing before Urbina.

[4] Quoted in Steve Hendrix, "D.C. Area Families Are Ready to Receive Uighur Detainees," *The Washington Post*, Oct. 8, 2008, p. A8. The association uses a different spelling of Uighur.

[5] Quoted in Del Quentin Wilber and Carrie Johnson, "Court Blocks Release of 17 Uighurs Into U.S.," *The Washington Post*, Feb. 19, 2009, p. A4.

Continued from p. 190

as deputy assistant attorney general for the then newly established National Security Division.

Olsen's task force will be dealing with case files that one former military prosecutor has described as being in "a state of disarray." Darrel Vandeveld, a former lieutenant colonel in the Army Reserve, made the critical statement in January, four months after he had resigned as a prosecutor in Guantánamo for what he said were reasons of conscience. [17]

Vandeveld, a senior deputy attorney general in Pennsylvania in civilian life, told *The Washington Post* that case files were disorganized, information scattered between different databases and physical evidence stored in unknown locations or in some instances missing. Military officials denied Vandeveld's accusations, *The Post* said. The newspaper quoted Col. Lawrence Morris, chief military prosecutor, as saying that Vandeveld had not raised concerns with him and also suggesting that Vandeveld had resigned after being passed over for a promotion.

In a second story, however, *The Post* quoted ex-Defense official Stimson as saying that while at the Pentagon he had persistent problems compiling information on individual detainees. The newspaper also noted references in Justice Department filings in habeas corpus cases to the unexpected difficulties the government faced in assembling case files on individual detainees.

The officials' trips came as the administration was completing preparations for the release of one of the highest-profile Guantánamo detainees: Binyam Mohamed, an Ethiopian-born British citizen who had been accused of planning to detonate "dirty bombs" in the United States. Mohamed claimed that after being held in Afghanistan and Pakistan, he was transferred to Morocco for 18 months and tortured there before being brought to Guantánamo.

Mohamed was flown from Guantánamo on Feb. 22 and arrived in Eng-

land the next day. As part of the release, Mohamed reportedly agreed to a lifetime prohibition against travel to the United States. *The New York Times* reported that the British government told U.S. officials that, under British and European human-rights laws, it could not impose other travel or surveillance restrictions on Mohamed. [18]

The Justice Department announced Mohamed's departure in a press release instead of the Defense Department, as had been the practice under the Bush administration. The Justice Department has said that an additional 57 detainees have been approved for transfer or release, but are awaiting agreements with third countries. That number includes the 17 Chinese Muslims and three others who have won habeas corpus cases but are not yet released.

Obama administration officials are counting on increased cooperation between other countries, including U.S. allies in Europe, to help empty Guantánamo before Obama's one-year deadline for closing the facility. At least three countries — Spain, Estonia and Latvia — have signaled a willingness to accept released detainees, but Italy says it won't because no Italians are being held there. "I can absolutely rule out that the closing of Guantánamo will have any consequences for Italy," Gianfranco Fini, the speaker of Italy's Chamber of Deputies and a close ally of Prime Minister Silvo Berlusconi, was quoted as telling House Speaker Nancy Pelosi, D-Calif., on Feb. 16 during a visit by the U.S. lawmaker. [19]

The Guantánamo developments come against a backdrop of concern among some human-rights and civil liberties advocates about the direction of Obama administration policies on national security issues. The American Civil Liberties Union, for example, criticized the administration after Justice Department lawyers in February reaffirmed before a federal appeals court the invocation of the state secrets privilege to try to block the trial of a suit by former prisoners

attacking the practice of "rendition" of detainees to other countries. [20]

Meanwhile, the administration is giving no encouragement to proposals on Capitol Hill for an in-depth investigation of Bush administration detention and interrogation policies. Senate Judiciary Committee Chairman Patrick J. Leahy, D-Vt., is proposing a "truth commission" to look at interrogation and detention, among other topics. But Obama gave the proposal no support when questioned at his first prime-time news conference. "Generally speaking, I'm more interested in looking forward than I am in looking back," Obama said on Feb. 9.

Torture Suits Stymied

A civil suit by four Britons released from Guantánamo in 2004 after two years' confinement could result in the first detailed courtroom airing of allegations of torture and abusive treatment of detainees at the U.S. prison camp. But — barring an unlikely shift by the Obama administration — the case will come to trial only if a federal appeals court decision dismissing the suit is reversed either by that court or by the Supreme Court.

The suit is one of several cases seeking to air former detainees' allegations of torture that have been stymied because of legal or diplomatic hurdles. The roadblocks are persisting even after the Pentagon's top judge in the Guantánamo detainee cases in January confirmed allegations of torture used against a Saudi national identified as a would-be 9/11 hijacker. And so far the Obama administration has shown no signs of easing barriers to former detainees seeking compensation in civil courts for mistreatment while prisoners at Guantánamo or elsewhere during the Bush administration.

The four British Muslims all claim they were rounded up by mistake during the Afghanistan war in fall 2001 and subjected to abusive interrogation

Continued on p. 194

At Issue:

Should Congress create a national security court for enemy combatant cases?

ANDREW C. MCCARTHY
LEGAL-AFFAIRS EDITOR,
NATIONAL REVIEW

WRITTEN FOR *CQ RESEARCHER*, FEB. 20, 2009

*i*t has been a relief to see President Obama retreat from the irresponsible rhetoric of his campaign regarding various security measures that have protected the nation from a reprise of the Sept. 11 attacks. The president now explicitly recognizes that there are numerous terrorists who threaten the United States but cannot be tried in the civilian courts — his preferred forum. The answer is a special national security court.

As we learned in the 1990s, the federal courts are more than adequate in providing due process for jihadists hell-bent on killing Americans. All of the terrorists indicted were convicted. Nevertheless, due process for our enemies, while not unimportant, can never be our primary aim, not if government is to tend to its first responsibility — the security of the governed.

Between the 1993 bombing of the World Trade Center and its destruction on 9/11, radical Islam became bigger and bolder. American targets were repeatedly attacked — including Khobar Towers (19 U.S. Air Force members killed), the U.S. embassies in eastern Africa (over 200 killed) and the *USS Cole* (17 U.S. sailors killed). Yet, because of the high burdens and elaborate protections of the criminal justice system — a system designed to protect Americans — only 29 terrorists were successfully prosecuted in the eight-year period when prosecution in federal court was our nation's principal counterterrorism strategy.

The effect of this weak response was to encourage more attacks. Indeed, Osama bin Laden himself has been under charges by the Justice Department since June 1998 but has killed thousands of Americans in the ensuing decade — adding counts to the indictment does not seem to deter him much. Ditto Khalid Shaikh Mohammed, who had also been under indictment for years while he planned the 9/11 atrocities. It told our enemies that we could be attacked with virtual impunity.

We have not suffered another attack since 9/11 primarily because we moved in late 2001 to a law-of-war paradigm, which permits terrorists — enemies in war, not just defendants in a case — to be detained without trial, until the conclusion of hostilities. That philosophy, coupled with a comprehensive counterterrorism strategy that does not unduly rely on criminal prosecutions, has helped us prevent terrorist attacks from happening, rather than contenting ourselves with prosecuting a handful of jihadists after innocents have been slaughtered.

If we don't want 9/11 results, we can't go back to a 9/10 mentality.

EDWARD L. DOWD JR. (left)
FORMER U.S. ATTORNEY, EASTERN DISTRICT OF MISSOURI;
EARL SILBERT, *FORMER U.S. ATTORNEY, DISTRICT OF COLUMBIA*

WRITTEN FOR *CQ RESEARCHER*, FEB. 20, 2009

*a*s former federal prosecutors, we have a deep understanding and appreciation for the enormity of the crimes that terrorists commit. We strongly support the severe punishment of convicted terrorists. However, we should not create national security courts to handle these prosecutions.

For over 230 years, federal courts have protected our fundamental constitutional rights while overseeing the prosecution and punishment of criminals, including terrorists. Indeed, over the past 20 years, more than 120 terrorism-related cases were prosecuted without jeopardizing our national security. This well-tested system is responsible for the convictions of Timothy McVeigh and Terry Nichols (Oklahoma City bombers), Ramzi Yousef and Sheikh Abdel Rahman (1993 World Trade Center bombers), Zacarias Moussaoui (member of al Qaeda who was involved in 9/11), and many others.

National security court proposals, by lessening due-process standards, threaten to undermine the constitutional rights safeguarded by our existing criminal justice system. Moreover, by depriving suspects of basic constitutional rights, any convictions by national security courts would be subject to challenge.

The argument that terrorist suspects require a special "terrorist court" with fewer rights undermines the presumption of innocence at the heart of the American judicial system. We do not yet know who among the detainees are guilty of acts of terrorism and who might be innocent. While we share the goal of convicting those who commit terrorist crimes, we cannot support a separate and unequal criminal justice system that does not protect basic constitutional rights. Nor should we adopt national security courts to oversee a legalized system of indefinite preventive detention without trial for terrorist suspects. Detaining individuals indefinitely without charge simply because we "believe" they are dangerous would violate both our Constitution and fundamental American values.

We join with the Constitution Project's bipartisan Liberty and Security committee in urging that our traditional federal courts continue to be the venue for prosecutions for terrorism offenses.

To do otherwise would allow our ideals and rights to be destroyed by the very terrorists we are seeking to convict. As we undertake the critical task of closing detention facilities and prosecuting detainees for crimes of international terrorism, we should reject this dangerous proposal.

Administration Backs Bagram Detentions

Conditions called more severe than at Guantánamo

As the detainee population at Guantánamo Bay, Cuba, has fallen, the number of alleged enemy combatants being held at Bagram Air Force base in Afghanistan, outside the capital city of Kabul, has soared to more than 600 prisoners. Conditions at their makeshift prison are described as more severe than those at Guantánamo.

Under President George W. Bush, the government claimed the power to hold the Bagram prisoners indefinitely without charge — the same legal position that the Supreme Court ultimately rejected in regard to the Guantánamo detainees. Now a federal judge in Washington is considering habeas corpus petitions challenging their detentions filed by four prisoners who were captured outside Afghanistan and brought to Bagram. [1]

The four prisoners — two Yemenis, an Afghan and a Tunisian — deny any affiliation with al Qaeda or the Taliban or hostile conduct or activities directed against the United States. The government is claiming that the prisoners have no right to challenge their detentions because they are being held outside U.S. territory.

Lawyers from the Stanford International Human Rights Clinic, the International Justice Network and the Yale International Human Rights Clinic represent the four men. In a Jan. 7 hearing, Barbara Olshansky, a visiting professor at Stanford University, told Judge John Bates that the case showed that the government "has not learned the lessons of Guantánamo."

Bates, who was appointed to the bench by Bush in 2001, signaled doubts about the government's position in the hearing, according to The Associated Press. [2] "These individuals are no different than those detained at Guantánamo except where they're housed," Bates said during the three-hour hearing.

Bates also challenged arguments by Justice Department lawyer John O'Quinn that the prisoners could not be released because they might return to the battlefield. "They were not on the battlefield to begin with," Bates said. O'Quinn disagreed. "Post-9/11, the battle is not limited to the traditional battlefield," he said.

In the hearing, Bates questioned whether the government's stance would change once President Obama took office. O'Quinn said he could not answer. Two weeks later, Bates on Jan. 22 issued an order asking the new administration whether it wanted to "refine its views" in the case. In a two-sentence reply filed on Feb. 20, the administration said, "the Government adheres to its previously articulated position."

---

[1] The case is *Makaleh v. Gates*, U.S. District Court for the District of Columbia Circuit, 06-1669. Background drawn from Eric Schmitt, "Two Prisons, Similar Issues for President," *The New York Times*, Jan. 27, 2009, p. A1; Lyle Denniston, "Obama asked for views on Bagram detainees," SCOTUS-Blog, Jan. 23, 2009, www.scotusblog.com/wp/obama-asked-for-views-on-bagram-detainees.

[2] Lara Jakes, "Detainees in Afghanistan seeking right for release," The Associated Press, Jan. 7, 2009.

Continued from p. 192

amounting to torture at Guantánamo before essentially being cleared and released after diplomatic pressure from the British government. Three of the men — Shafiq Rasul, Asif Iqbal and Rhuhel Ahmed — say they were aiding humanitarian relief efforts in Afghanistan when they were captured by forces aligned with the notorious Uzbek warlord Rashim Dotsum and turned over to U.S. forces for a bounty. The fourth, Jamal al-Harith, was taken into custody when U.S. forces took over a Taliban jail where he was being held on suspicion of being a British spy.

In their civil suit filed in federal court in Washington in 2004 after their release, the men claim that they were subjected at Guantánamo to beatings, solitary confinement, exposure to extreme heat and cold, threats of attack from unmuzzled dogs, nudity and sleep deprivation. In addition to those claimed constitutional violations, the suit claims that alleged interference with their religious beliefs violated the federal Religious Freedom Restoration Act.

Without addressing the allegations, the government won a ruling from the U.S. Court of Appeals for the District of Columbia Circuit in January 2008 dismissing the suit on legal grounds. The three-judge panel rejected the constitutional claims because the plaintiffs were held outside U.S. territory. As an alternative basis for dismissal, the court said the military officials named as defendants were entitled to qualified immunity from suit. [21]

The Supreme Court in December ordered the appeals court to reconsider the decision in light of its June 12 ruling permitting Guantánamo detainees to bring habeas corpus actions. The appeals court has ordered a new round of briefs to be filed in March, but Eric Lewis, the private lawyer representing the men, is pessimistic about getting a ruling from a panel that he describes as "not sympathetic." He says he will appeal an unfavorable ruling to the Supreme Court.

"Civil accountability is the one mechanism of accountability that's out there," says Lewis, a Washington attorney handling the case on a pro bono basis. "There's been a fair amount of confirmation [of mistreatment] that's come in, essentially through statements made, books written, but no judicial accountability."

In another high-profile Guantánamo-related case, the Obama administration in February followed the Bush administration's stance in invoking a "state secrets" privilege to block a civil suit by five current or former detainees over the Bush administration's practice of "extraordinary rendition," or sending suspected terrorists to other countries, where they allege they were tortured. The plaintiffs are seeking civil damages from a private airline for its alleged role in transporting them in cooperation with the CIA.

The Bush administration won a lower court ruling to dismiss the case on the ground that a trial would inevitably disclose state secrets. When the case was argued on Feb. 9 before the federal appeals court in San Francisco, Justice Department lawyers reaffirmed that position and said under questioning the stance had been "thoroughly vetted with appropriate officials" in the new administration.

Two of the five plaintiffs were eventually taken to Guantánamo. One was released in 2008; the other — Binyham Mohamed — was released on Feb. 22. The British government says it has evidence Mohamed was tortured while in Moroccan custody, but blocked its release after the Bush administration threatened to review intelligence sharing arrangements with Britain if the material was disclosed. After a British court reluctantly bowed to that decision, the White House issued a statement thanking the British government "for its continued commitment to protect sensitive national security information." [22]

Allegations of torture at Guantánamo gained new currency after the Defense Department judge overseeing the military commissions system confirmed that she blocked the prosecution of Mohammed al-Qahtani in May 2008 because she was convinced he had been tortured. Susan Crawford, who has the title of convening authority of the military commissions, made the statement in an interview with *The Washington Post's* Bob Woodward published in January. [23]

Qahtani is alleged to have planned to join the 9/11 hijackings but was denied entry into the United States. He was captured in Afghanistan, transported to Guantánamo and interrogated over 50 days from November 2002 to January 2003.

In the interview, Crawford details "abusive" techniques that included prolonged interrogation and forced nudity that had "a medical impact" on him. "His treatment met the legal definition of torture," Crawford is quoted as saying. Military prosecutors attempted to file new charges without using statements made during the interrogation, but Crawford said in the interview that she would not allow the case to proceed. ■

OUTLOOK

Looking for Closure

With the Guantánamo prison camp now slated to be closed, the Pentagon is making available on its Web site the most complete picture of conditions at the facility the government has ever published. The 85-page report by the review team appointed by Defense Secretary Gates in January details everything from the detainees' bedding, clothing and food and water to religious practices, health care and access to lawyers and others.

Despite finding the facility in compliance with humane-treatment requirements of the Geneva Conventions, the report recommends a number of steps "consistent with the approach of Chain of Command to continually enhance conditions of detainment." As examples, the team — headed by Adm. Patrick Walsh, vice chief of naval operations — recommends increasing detainees' opportunities for socialization, improving trust between health providers and detainees and video recording all interrogations.

At some length, the report describes the procedures for force-feeding hunger strikers and concludes the practices comply with international law standards. But the report fails to note — except in a letter from the American Civil Liberties

Union attached as an appendix — that some 30 detainees, more than 10 percent of the population, are now on hunger strikes to protest conditions at the camp. Two prisoners, the ACLU says, have been force-fed through their noses since August 2005.

Human-rights groups and lawyers for the detainees rejected the report's conclusions. Susan Havens, a New York City lawyer who has been visiting Guantánamo since 2004, told *The New York Times* that conditions "are worse than they have ever been." The ACLU pronounced the conditions in violation of domestic and international law, and along with Amnesty International and Human Rights First called for a host of specific changes plus monitoring by independent human-rights groups. [24]

As the dispute illustrates, the Obama administration is not yet satisfying the groups that waged seven years of legal and political warfare against the Bush administration's policies on detention and interrogation. Whether or not President Obama succeeds in closing the Guantánamo prison camp by Jan. 22, 2010, the Guantánamo story — in all its ramifications — seems likely to continue, perhaps for years to come.

The administration's increased transparency regarding Guantánamo is apt to result in increased news coverage as detainees are transferred or released to other countries or brought to the United States for trial or detention. Many of the detainees will themselves seek out coverage. When he arrived in Britain this week, ex-detainee Binyam Mohamed issued a statement through the human-rights group Reprieve: "I am not asking for vengeance, only that the truth should be made known, so that nobody in the future should have to endure what I have endured." [25]

Other detainees are less likely to seek attention, but critics of the administration probably will scrutinize the background and biographies of prisoners as they are released and watch for any evidence that any of them turn to anti-U.S. activities. "The Republican Party or at least parts of it are ready, willing and able to jump if some person who is released creates some havoc," says military-law expert Fidell.

Court cases are certain to drag on, repeatedly giving the administration hard choices to adopt or repudiate legal stances the government took under President Bush. The administration may be able to skirt one high-profile case: the habeas corpus appeal by Ali Saleh Kahlah al-Marri, the Qatari arrested as an al Qaeda sleeper agent while in the United States on a student visa. Chesney, the Texas law professor, and other observers speculate that the government could avert the April 27 arguments at the Supreme Court by indicting him and prosecuting him in a civilian criminal court. Civil cases seeking damages for past conduct, however, are less susceptible to being sidestepped.

The possible transfer of any of the prisoners to U.S. facilities is already stirring opposition from lawmakers or other officials in communities that might be affected. Possible detention facilities in the United States include the U.S. Disciplinary Barracks at Fort Leavenworth, Kansas, the military's only maximum-security prison; Camp Pendleton in California; the Charleston Naval Brig in South Carolina, and the federal Supermax prison in Florence, Colo.

Lawmakers from all four states are raising objections. Both Kansas senators — Republicans Sam Brownback and Pat Roberts — have introduced legislation along with Missouri Republican. Sen. Christopher "Kit" Bond to require a 90-day study before any transfer. Rep. Henry Brown, R-S.C., has a similar bill for his state. Rep. Duncan Hunter, R-Calif., wants to prohibit use of federal funds to transfer detainees to Camp Pendleton, which is near his San Diego-area district. And members of Colorado's congressional delegation had earlier argued that a civilian prison is unsuitable for military purposes. [26]

Meanwhile, the war in Afghanistan could further increase the number of prisoners at Bagram Air Base — and the number of legal challenges. "Afghanistan is still a physical location of actual counterinsurgency where the war is heating up not cooling down," Chesney says.

Any congressional moves to investigate Bush administration policies will also serve to prolong the story and help spotlight Obama policies as well. In addition, legislative proposals to regulate terrorism-related detention, interrogation and surveillance — including preventive detention — could force the administration's hands on some policy areas. But, says Brookings scholar Wittes, "Congress since the war on terror has never been the lead actor and it will not be."

In a somewhat surprising comment, White House counsel Craig left open the possibility of administration support for preventive detention. "It's possible but hard to imagine Barack Obama as the first president of the United States to introduce a preventive-detention law," Craig told the *New Yorker's* Jane Mayer. [27]

Facing innumerable economic issues, Congress is showing no interest so far in revisiting the detention and interro-gation issues that sharply divided Democrats and Republicans over the past seven years. But Craig is making clear that the White House understands the administration's actions will be closely watched.

"We don't own the problem — it was created by the previous administration," Craig said in the interview. "But we'll be held accountable for how we handle this." ∎

Notes

[1] For coverage, see Lyle Denniston, "Jawad Torture Case Put on Hold," SCOTUSBlog, Feb. 4, 2009, www.scotusblog.com/wp/?s=jawad.

[2] A Webcast of the panel discussion, "The Post-Guantánamo Era: A Dialogue on the Law and Policy of Detention and Counterterrorism," is available at www.utexas.edu/law/news/2009/020309_webcast_post_Guantánamo.html. Other speakers included Bellinger; Stephen Vladeck, a professor at American University College of Law in Washington; and Benjamin Wittes of the Brookings Institution. Quotes in this report from Bellinger and Wittes are from the panel discussion. For background on counterterrorism policies since 9/11, see these *CQ Researcher* reports: Peter Katel, "Homeland Security," Feb. 13, 2009, pp. 129-152; Peter Katel and Kenneth Jost, "Treatment of Detainees," Aug. 25, 2006, pp. 673-696; Peter Katel, "Global Jihad," Oct. 14, 2005, pp. 857-880; Kenneth Jost, "Re-examining 9/11," June 4, 2004, pp. 493-516; Mary H. Cooper, "Hating America," Nov. 23, 2001, pp. 969-992; and David Masci and Kenneth Jost, "War on Terrorism," Oct. 12, 2001, pp. 817-848. See also these *CQ Global Researcher* reports: Robert Kiener, "Crisis in Pakistan," December 2008, pp. 321-348; Sarah Glazer, "Radical Islam in Europe," November 2007, pp. 265-294, and Seth Stern, "Torture Debate," September 2007, pp. 211-236.

[3] Benjamin Wittes, *Law and the Long War: The Future of Justice in the Age of Terror* (2008), pp. 72-102; Benjamin Wittes and Zaahira Wyne, "The Current Detainee Population of Guantánamo," Brookings Institution, Dec. 16, 2008 (periodically updated), www.brookings.edu/reports/2008/1216_detainees_wittes.aspx.

[4] Department of Defense, "Review Of Department Compliance With President's Executive

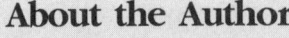
About the Author

Associate Editor **Kenneth Jost** graduated from Harvard College and Georgetown University Law Center. He is the author of the *Supreme Court Yearbook* and editor of *The Supreme Court from A to Z* (both *CQ Press*). He was a member of the *CQ Researcher* team that won the American Bar Association's 2002 Silver Gavel Award. His previous reports include "Treatment of Detainees" and "War on Terrorism."

Order On Detainee Conditions Of Confinement," February 2009, p. 5, App. 18, www.defenselink.mil/pubs/pdfs/REVIEW_OF_DEPARTMENT_COMPLIANCE_WITH_PRESIDENTS_EXECUTIVE_ORDER_ON_DETAINEE_CONDITIONS_OF_CONFINEMENTa.pdf.

[5] The case is *Boumediene v. Bush*, 553 U.S. — (June 12, 2008). For an account, see Kenneth Jost, "Guantánamo Detainees Entitled to Habeas Corpus," *Supreme Court Yearbook 2007-2008*.

[6] Robert F. Worth, "Freed by U.S., Saudi Becomes a Qaeda Chief," *The New York Times*, Jan. 23, 2009, p. A1.

[7] For coverage, see David Morgan, "Pentagon: 61 ex-Guantánamo detainees return to terrorism," Reuters, Jan. 13, 2009.

[8] Human Rights First, "How to Close Guantánamo: Blueprint for the Next Administration," August 2008 (updated November 2008), www.humanrightsfirst.org/pdf/080818-USLS-gitmo-blueprint.pdf; Center for Strategic and International Studies, "Closing Guantánamo: From Bumper Sticker to Blueprint," September 2008, www.csis.org/hrs/gtmoreport. See also Human Rights Watch, "Fighting Terrorism Fairly and Effectively," Nov. 16, 2008, www.hrw.org/en/reports/2008/11/16/fighting-terrorism-fairly-and-effectively.

[9] Robert F. Worth, "Saudis Issue List of 85 Terrorism Suspects," *The New York Times*, Feb. 4, 2009, p. A5.

[10] For coverage, see Abby Goodnough and Scott Shane, "Padilla Is Guilty on All Charges in Terror Trial," *The New York Times*, Aug. 17, 2007, p. A1; Adam Liptak, "A New Model of Terror Trial," *The New York Times*, Aug. 18, 2007, p. A1.

[11] CSIS Report, *op. cit.*, pp. 15-16.

[12] The cases are *Hamdi v. Rumsfeld*, 542 U.S. 507 (2004); *Rasul v. Bush*, 542 U.S. 466 (2004); *Hamdan v. Rumsfeld*, 548 U.S. 557 (2006); and Boumediene, *op. cit*. For accounts, see respective editions of Kenneth Jost, *Supreme Court Yearbook*, CQ Press.

[13] Quoted in Julian E. Barnes, "Review of Guantánamo Detainees Begins," *Los Angeles Times*, Feb. 14, 2009, p. A11.

[14] Ratner quoted in Philip Shenon, "Suit to Be Filed on Behalf of 3 Captives," *The New York Times*, Feb. 19, 2002, p. A5; Cheh quoted in Naftali Bendavid, "U.S. illegally holding 3 detainees in Cuba, suit claims; Legal experts say families' lawyers face uphill battles," *Chicago Tribune*, Feb. 20, 2002, p. 3.

[15] See Steven Lee Myers, "Bush Decides to Keep Guantánamo Open," *The New York Times*, Oct. 21, 2008, p. A16.

[16] Executive Order: Review and Disposition of Individuals Detained at the Guantánamo Bay Naval Base and Closure of Detention Facilities, www.whitehouse.gov/the_press_office/Closure_Of_Guantanamo_Detention_Facilities/, Jan. 22, 2009.

[17] See Peter Finn, "Evidence in Terror Cases Said to Be in Chaos," *The Washington Post*, Jan. 14, 2009, p. A8. Additional quotes and background from a follow-up story by Karen De Young and Peter Finn, "Guantánamo Case Files in Disarray," *ibid.*, Jan. 25, 2009, p. A5.

[18] See Raymond Bonner, "Detainee to Return to Britain, as Efforts to Prove Torture Claims Continue," *The New York Times*, Feb. 23, 2009, p. A5.

[19] "Officials says Italy will not take Gitmo inmates," The Associated Press, Feb. 16, 2009.

[20] The U.S. case pending before the Ninth Circuit is *Mohamed v. Jeppesen Dataplan*, Inc., 08-5693. For coverage, see Maura Dolan and Carol J. Williams, "Court urged to deny rendition trial," *Los Angeles Times*, Feb. 10, 2009, p. A10. See also Glenn Greenwald, "Binyam Mohamed, war crimes investigations, and American exceptionalism," *Salon.com*, Feb. 19, 2009.

[21] The decision is *Rasul v. Myers*, 06-5209, D.C. Circuit, Jan. 11, 2008, http://pacer.cadc.uscourts.gov/docs/common/opinions/200801/06-5209a.pdf.

[22] For a critical account before Mohamed's release, see Glenn Greenwald, "Binyam Mohamed, war crimes investigations, and American exceptionalism," *Salon.com*, Feb. 19, 2009.

[23] Bob Woodward, "Detainee Tortured, Says U.S. Official," *The Washington Post*, Jan. 14, 2009, p. A1.

[24] Havens quoted in William Glaberson, "Administration Draws Fire for Report on Guantánamo," *The New York Times*, Feb. 24, 2009, p. A13. The ACLU, Amnesty International and Human Rights First letters are included as appendices to the Pentagon report, *op. cit*.

[25] Reprieve-UK represents about 30 Guantánamo detainees; Mohamed's statement is available on its Web site: www.reprieve.org.uk/Press_Statement_of_Binyam_Mohamed.htm.

[26] Suzanne Gamboa, "Lawmakers: Guantánamo detainees should 'Keep Out,' " The Associated Press, Feb. 2, 2009.

[27] Jane Mayer, "The Hard Cases," *The New Yorker*, Feb. 23, 2009, p. 41.

Bibliography

Selected Sources

Books

Cole, David, *Justice at War: The Men and Ideas That Shaped America's War on Terror*, New York Review Books, 2008.

A professor at Georgetown University Law Center critically examines the roles played by, among others, Vice President Dick Cheney, attorneys general John Ashcroft and Alberto Gonzales and Justice Department lawyer John Yoo in the formation of the Bush administration's legal policies in the war on terror. Includes chapter notes.

Greenberg, Karen, *The Least Worst Place: Guantánamo's First 100 Days*, Oxford University Press, 2009.

This early history of the prison camp at Guantánamo Bay depicts the supplanting of a military commander's liberal policies by more stringent conditions and treatment as ordered by Defense Secretary Donald Rumsfeld. Greenberg is executive director of the Center on Law and Security, New York University School of Law. Includes notes, six-page bibliography.

Marguiles, Joseph, *Guantánamo and the Abuse of Presidential Power*, Simon & Schuster, 2006.

This critical account is by one of the lawyers in the Supreme Court case that opened the door to habeas corpus challenges by Guantánamo detainees. Includes notes.

Mayer, Jane, *The Dark Side: The Inside Story of How the War on Terror Turned into a War on American Ideals*, Doubleday, 2008.

A writer for *The New Yorker* provides a detailed, critical account of the Bush administration's policies on detention, interrogation and surveillance. Includes notes, nine-page bibliography.

Wittes, Benjamin, *Law and the Long War: The Future of Justice in the Age of Terror*, Penguin, 2008.

A legal scholar at the Brookings Institution argues in this influential, ideology-crossing book for new bodies of law — to be crafted by Congress and the executive — dealing with detention, interrogation, trial and surveillance in the new national security environment in "the age of terror."

Worthington, Andy, *The Guantánamo Files: The Stories of the 774 Detainees in America's Illegal Prison*, Pluto Press, 2007, www.andyworthington.co.uk/.

An avowedly leftist British journalist gives detailed accounts of the experiences of prisoners held at Guantánamo and at Bagram Air Base in Afghanistan, relating disturbing allegations of mistreatment and intimidation. Includes detailed notes. Worthington updates his coverage on his Web site: www.andyworthington.co.uk/. For first-person accounts by former detainees, see Moazzam Begg with Victoria Brittain, *Enemy Combatant: My Imprisonment at Guantánamo, Bagram, and Kandahar* (New Press, 2006) and Murat Kurnaz with Helmut Kuhn, *Five Years of My Life: An Innocent Man at Guantánamo* (Palgrave/Macmillan, 2008).

Articles

Chandrasekaran, Rajiv, "From Captive to Suicide Bomber," *The Washington Post*, Feb. 22, 2009, p. A1; "A 'Ticking Time Bomb' Goes Off," *ibid.*, Feb. 23, 2009, p. A1.

The two-part story traces the story of Abdallah al-Ajmi from his capture in Afghanistan and nearly four-year imprisonment at Guantánamo through his release to his native Kuwait and his death as a "suicide bomber" in Iraq in an attack on an Iraqi outpost that killed 13 Iraqi soldiers.

Toobin, Jeffrey, "Camp Justice," *The New Yorker*, April 14, 2008, p. 32.

The CNN legal affairs correspondent provides a close look at the court facilities at Guantánamo — built for military commission proceedings that President Obama suspended as part of his review of detainees' cases and his plan to close the prison camp by 2010.

Reports and Studies

Garcia, Michael John, *et al.*, "Closing the Guantánamo Detention Center: Legal Issues," Congressional Research Service, Jan. 22, 2009, http://assets.opencrs.com/rpts/R40139_20090122.pdf.

The 37-page, carefully annotated report thoroughly covers the legal background and current legal issues relating to the closing of the Guantánamo detention center.

Prieto, Daniel B., "War About Terror: Civil Liberties and National Security After 9/11," Council on Foreign Relations, February 2009, www.cfr.org/publication/18373/.

The 116-page "working paper" by an adjunct fellow at the Council on Foreign Relations comprehensively examines civil liberties issues in regard to post-9/11 national security policies. The working paper is based on work by a task force composed of more than two dozen members that — according to the council's president — "was unable to agree on a set of meaningful conclusions" on the issues discussed.

Wittes, Benjamin, and Zaahira Wyne, "The Current Detainee Population of Guantánamo," Brookings Institute, Dec. 16, 2008 (periodically updated), www.brookings.edu/reports/2008/1216_detainees_wittes.aspx.

The site provides the most up-to-date information on the Guantánamo detainees.

On the Web

The Miami Herald has provided comprehensive coverage of Guantánamo and compiled much of that coverage on a continuously updated section of its Web site: www.miami-herald.com/Guantánamo/.

The Next Step:

Additional Articles from Current Periodicals

Bagram Air Base Prisoners

Lasseter, Tom, "Abuse Plagued Afghan Camps, Too," *Seattle Times*, June 16, 2008, p. A3.

Former guards and detainees say Bagram Air Base was a center of systematic brutality for nearly two years.

Schmitt, Eric, "Two Prisons, Similar Issues for President," *The New York Times*, Jan. 27, 2009, p. A1.

The fate of hundreds of prisoners at Bagram Air Base — with few privileges and virtually no access to lawyers — presents an early challenge to the Obama administration.

Wilber, Del Quentin, "In Courts, Afghanistan Air Base May Become Next Guantánamo," *The Washington Post*, June 29, 2008, p. A14.

The Justice Department says Bagram prisoners shouldn't have the same rights as those in Guantánamo.

Civilian Trials

Conery, Ben, "Rules for Trials Seen As Lacking," *The Washington Times*, July 22, 2008, p. A3.

The Supreme Court has given Guantánamo detainees the right to use civilian courts to challenge detention but offers little guidance on how such hearings should be conducted.

Issenberg, Sasha, and Farah Stockman, "McCain Blasts Ruling on Guantánamo," *The Boston Globe*, June 14, 2008, p. A6.

Sen. John McCain, R-Ariz., has criticized a Supreme Court ruling giving Guantánamo prisoners the right to challenge their detention in civilian courts.

Rosenberg, Carol, "Senator: Give Detainees Rights," *The Miami Herald*, March 24, 2007, p. A3.

Sen. Arlen Specter, R-Pa., favors restoring civilian court review of Guantánamo detention cases to ensure the availability of habeas corpus rights for detainees.

White, Josh, "Guantánamo Detainee Rejects Court Procedure," *The Washington Post*, April 30, 2008, p. A4.

Military hearings for Guantánamo detainees have been criticized for their departures from established procedures.

Releasing Detainees

Barnes, Julian E., "Justice Begins Review of Guantánamo Detainees," *Los Angeles Times*, Feb. 14, 2009, p. A11.

The Obama administration has begun reviewing which detainees at Guantánamo can be prosecuted and which can be transferred to other countries.

Clancy, Paddy, "Ireland Wants Gitmo Prisoners," *Irish Voice*, Jan. 28, 2009, p. 6.

Ireland is prepared to resettle detainees from the U.S. military facility in Guantánamo Bay, Cuba, so long as there is a common European Union approach.

Mazzetti, Mark, and Scott Shane, "Where Will Guantánamo Detainees Go?" *The New York Times*, Jan. 24, 2009, p. A13.

Republican lawmakers argue that closing Guantánamo could allow terrorists to get off on legal technicalities and be released across the United States.

Sell, Julie, "Europe Weighs Helping U.S. Close Guantánamo," *Myrtle Beach Sun-News* (South Carolina), Jan. 20, 2009, p. A11.

European politicians are debating whether to help President Obama closed Guantánamo by accepting some of the detainees.

Uighurs

Gillies, Rob, "3 Uighurs at Guantánamo Ask Canada for Asylum," The Associated Press, Feb. 4, 2009.

Three Uighurs cleared for release from Guantánamo have applied for political asylum in Canada amid fears of prosecution if they were turned over to China.

Spiegel, Peter, and Barbara Demick, "Poised for Release — But to Where?" *Los Angeles Times*, Feb. 18, 2009, p. A5.

China is insisting that Uighurs held at Guantánamo by the United States be sent back to China to face trial for separatist activities.

Yen, Hope, "Conservatives Call on Bush to Free Muslim Uighurs," *The Miami Herald*, Nov. 20, 2008.

A group of Republicans has called on President Bush to release 17 Uighurs at Guantánamo, claiming their continued detention undermines U.S. standing in the world.

CITING CQ RESEARCHER

Sample formats for citing these reports in a bibliography include the ones listed below. Preferred styles and formats vary, so please check with your instructor or professor.

<u>MLA STYLE</u>

Jost, Kenneth. "Rethinking the Death Penalty." <u>CQ Researcher</u> 16 Nov. 2001: 945-68.

<u>APA STYLE</u>

Jost, K. (2001, November 16). Rethinking the death penalty. *CQ Researcher, 11*, 945-968.

<u>CHICAGO STYLE</u>

Jost, Kenneth. "Rethinking the Death Penalty." *CQ Researcher*, November 16, 2001, 945-968.

In-depth Reports on Issues in the News

Are you writing a paper?

Need backup for a debate?

Want to become an expert on an issue?

For 80 years, students have turned to *CQ Researcher* for in-depth reporting on issues in the news. Reports on a full range of political and social issues are now available. Following is a selection of recent reports:

Civil Liberties
Limiting Lawsuits, 12/08
Affirmative Action, 10/08
Gay Marriage Showdowns, 9/08
America's Border Fence, 9/08
Immigration Debate, 2/08
Prison Reform, 4/07

Crime/Law
Mexico's Drug War, 12/08
Prostitution Debate, 5/08
Public Defenders, 4/08
Gun Violence, 5/07

Education
Reading Crisis? 2/08
Discipline in Schools, 2/08
Student Aid, 1/08
Racial Diversity in Public Schools, 9/07
Stress on Students, 7/07

Environment
Reducing Carbon Footprint, 12/08
Protecting Wetlands, 10/08
Buying Green, 2/08
Future of Recycling, 12/07

Health/Safety
Preventing Cancer, 1/09
Heart Health, 9/08
Global Food Crisis, 6/08
Preventing Memory Loss, 4/08

International Affairs/Politics
The Obama Presidency, 1/09
The National Debt, 11/08
Financial Bailout, 10/08
Political Conventions, 8/08
Race and Politics, 7/08

Social Trends
Public-Works Projects, 2/09
Falling Birthrates, 11/08
Regulating Credit Cards, 10/08
Internet Accuracy, 8/08

Terrorism/Defense
Homeland Security, 2/09
Rise in Counterinsurgency, 9/08
Cost of the Iraq War, 4/08

Youth
Debating Hip-Hop, 6/07

Upcoming Reports

Future of Middle Class, 3/6/09
Vanishing Jobs, 3/13/09

GOP's Future, 3/20/09
Extreme Sports, 3/27/09

Bankruptcy, 4/3/09
Wrongful Convictions, 4/10/09

ACCESS

CQ Researcher is available in print and online. For access, visit your library or www.cqresearcher.com.

STAY CURRENT

To receive notice of upcoming *CQ Researcher* reports, or learn more about *CQ Researcher* products, subscribe to the free e-mail newsletters, *CQ Researcher Alert!* and *CQ Researcher News*: http://cqpress.com/newsletters.

PURCHASE

To purchase a *CQ Researcher* report in print or electronic format (PDF), visit www.cqpress.com or call 866-427-7737. Single reports start at $15. Bulk purchase discounts and electronic-rights licensing are also available.

SUBSCRIBE

Annual full-service *CQ Researcher* subscriptions—including 44 reports a year, monthly index updates, and a bound volume—start at $803. Add $25 for domestic postage.

CQ Researcher Online offers a backfile from 1991 and a number of tools to simplify research. For pricing information, call 800-834-9020, ext. 1906, or e-mail librarysales@cqpress.com.

CQ Researcher

Published by CQ Press, a division of SAGE Publications

www.cqresearcher.com

Middle-Class Squeeze

Is more government aid needed?

M illions of families who once enjoyed the American dream of home ownership and upward financial mobility are sliding down the economic ladder — some into poverty. Many have been forced to seek government help for the first time. The plunging fortunes of working families are pushing the U.S. economy deeper into recession as plummeting demand for goods and services creates a downward economic spiral. A consumption binge and growing consumer debt beginning in the 1990s contributed to the middle-class squeeze, but the bigger culprits were exploding prices for necessities such as housing, medical care and college tuition, cuts in employer-funded benefits and, some say, government policies that favored the wealthy. President Barack Obama has promised major aid for the middle class, and some economists are calling for new programs — most notably national health coverage — to assist working Americans.

Stacks of medical bills confront Dan and Debra Daskus of Minersville, Pa., following his treatments for cancer. After he could no longer work, he lost his job and health benefits at a small prefabrication factory.

CQ Researcher • March 6, 2009 • www.cqresearcher.com
Volume 19, Number 9 • Pages 201-224

RECIPIENT OF SOCIETY OF PROFESSIONAL JOURNALISTS AWARD FOR EXCELLENCE ◆ AMERICAN BAR ASSOCIATION SILVER GAVEL AWARD

CQ Researcher

March 6, 2009
Volume 19, Number 9

MANAGING EDITOR: Thomas J. Colin
tcolin@cqpress.com

ASSISTANT MANAGING EDITOR: Kathy Koch
kkoch@cqpress.com

ASSOCIATE EDITOR: Kenneth Jost

STAFF WRITERS: Thomas J. Billitteri, Marcia Clemmitt, Peter Katel

CONTRIBUTING WRITERS: Rachel Cox, Sarah Glazer, Alan Greenblatt, Barbara Mantel, Patrick Marshall, Tom Price, Jennifer Weeks

DESIGN/PRODUCTION EDITOR: Olu B. Davis

ASSISTANT EDITOR: Darrell Dela Rosa

FACT-CHECKING: Eugene J. Gabler, Michelle Harris

EDITORIAL INTERN: Vyomika Jairam

CQ PRESS

A Division of
SAGE Publications

PRESIDENT AND PUBLISHER:
John A. Jenkins

EXECUTIVE DIRECTOR,
REFERENCE INFORMATION GROUP:
Alix B. Vance

CQ Press is a registered trademark of Congressional Quarterly Inc.

CQ Researcher (ISSN 1056-2036) is printed on acid-free paper. Published weekly, except; (Jan. wk. 1) (May wk. 4) (July wks. 1, 2) (Aug. wks. 3, 4) (Nov. wk. 4) and (Dec. wk. 4), by CQ Press, a division of SAGE Publications. Annual full-service subscriptions start at $803. For pricing, call 1-800-834-9020, ext. 1906. To purchase a CQ Researcher report in print or electronic format (PDF), visit www.cqpress.com or call 866-427-7737. Single reports start at $15. Bulk purchase discounts and electronic-rights licensing are also available. Periodicals postage paid at Washington, D.C., and additional mailing offices. POSTMASTER: Send address changes to CQ Researcher, 2300 N St., N.W., Suite 800, Washington, DC 20037.

Cover: *Philadelphia Inquirer*/Rapport Press/Tom Gralish

Middle-Class Squeeze

BY THOMAS J. BILLITTERI

THE ISSUES

Cindy Dreeszen, 41, and her husband may have seemed like unlikely visitors to the Interfaith food pantry last month in affluent Morris County, N.J., 25 miles from New York City. Both have steady jobs and a combined income of about $55,000 a year. But with "the cost of everything going up and up" and a second baby due, the couple was looking for free groceries.

"I didn't think we'd even be allowed to come here," Ms. Dreeszen told *The New York Times*. "This is totally something that I never expected to happen, to have to resort to this." [1]

Countless middle-class Americans are thinking similar thoughts these days as they ponder their suddenly fragile futures.

Millions of families who once enjoyed the American dream of upward mobility and financial security are sliding rapidly down the economic ladder — some into poverty. Many are losing their homes along with their jobs, and telling their children to rethink college. [2] And while today's economic crisis has made life for middle-class households worse, the problems aren't new. Pressure on the middle-class has been building for years and is likely to persist long after the current recession — now 14 months old — is over.

The middle class "is in crisis and decline," says sociologist Kevin Leicht, director of the Institute for Inequality Studies at the University of Iowa.

"Between wages that have been stagnant [in inflation-adjusted terms]

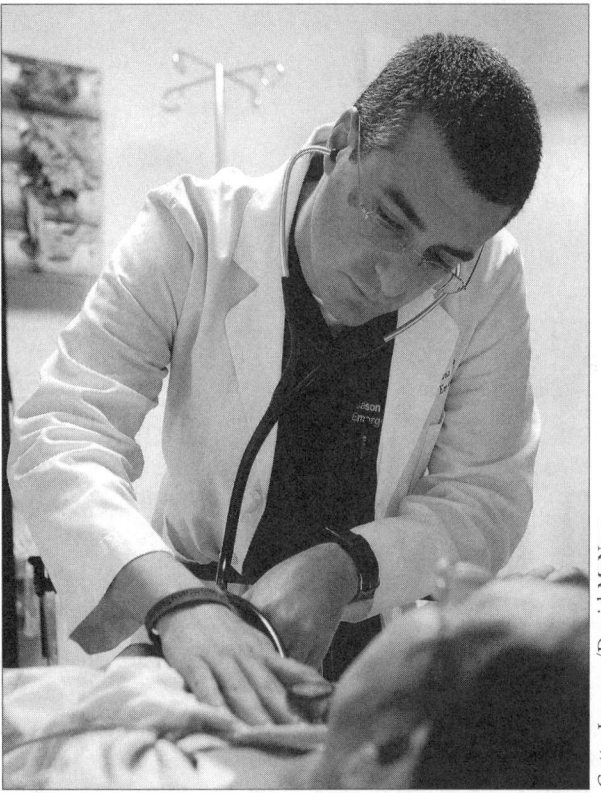

Affordable health care for all Americans is a key element of the budget recently announced by President Barack Obama, along with other policies aimed squarely at helping the middle class. Nearly half of home foreclosures in 2006 were caused, at least partly, by financial issues stemming from a medical problem, according to the advocacy group Families USA. Above, emergency room physician Jason Greenspan cares for a patient in Panorama City, Calif.

since the middle of the 1970s and government policies that are weighted exclusively in the direction of the wealthy, the only thing that has been holding up most of the American middle class is access to cheap and easy credit."

No official definition of the "middle class" exists. (*See sidebar, p. 212.*) But most Americans — except perhaps the very richest and poorest — consider themselves in that broad category, a fact not lost on Washington policy makers.

Indeed, President Barack Obama announced a 10-year budget on Feb. 28 that takes direct aim at the challenges facing America's middle class and the growing concentration of wealth at the top of the income scale. [3] Key ele-

ments of the plan include shifting more costs to the wealthiest Americans and overhauling health care to make it more affordable. [4]

In further recognition of the importance of the middle-class, Obama has named Vice President Joseph R. Biden to chair a new White House Task Force on Middle Class Working Families. It will examine everything from access to college and child- and eldercare issues to business development and the role of labor unions in the economy. [5]

"Talking about the middle class is the closest that American politicians and maybe Americans are willing to go to emphasize the fact that we have growing inequality in this country," says Jacob Hacker, a political scientist at the University of California, Berkeley, and a leading social-policy expert. "A very small proportion of the population is getting fabulously rich, and the rest of Americans are getting modestly richer or not much richer at all."

What's at stake goes far beyond economics and family finances, though, experts say. "A large middle class, especially one that is politically active, tends to be a kind of anchor that keeps your country from swinging back and forth," says sociologist Teresa Sullivan, provost and executive vice president for academic affairs at the University of Michigan and co-author of *The Fragile Middle Class: Americans in Debt*. What's more, she says, "there are typical values that middle-class families acquire and pass on to their children," and those values "tend to be very good for democracy."

Right now, though, the middle class is under threat.

www.cqresearcher.com   **March 6, 2009**   **203**

Belt-Tightening Is in Middle Class' Future

A quarter of middle-class Americans expect to have trouble paying their bills this year, and half expect to reduce household spending and have trouble saving for the future.

In the following year, will you have . . .

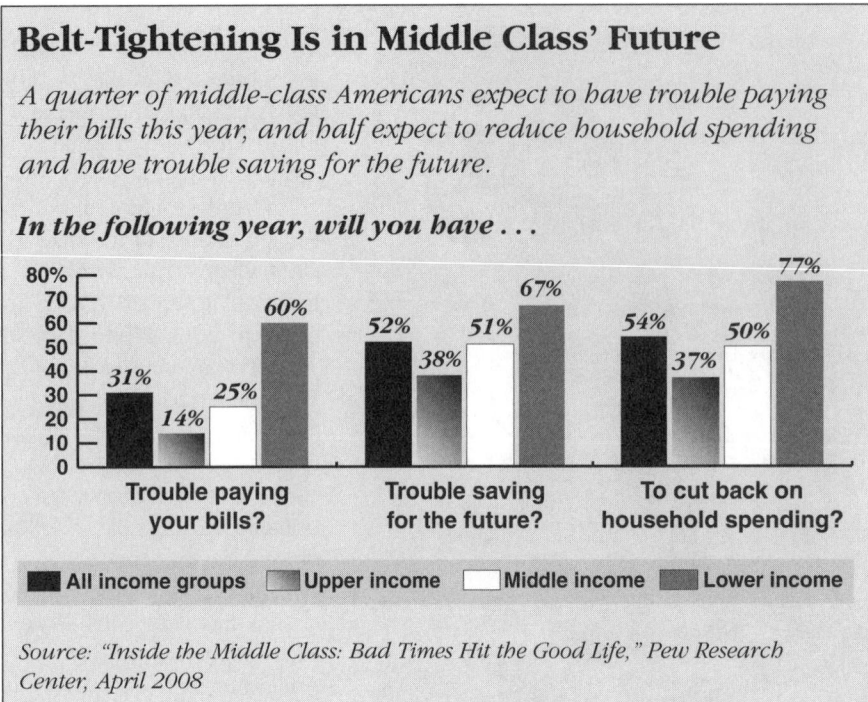

Source: "Inside the Middle Class: Bad Times Hit the Good Life," Pew Research Center, April 2008

In a study of middle-class households, Dēmos, a liberal think tank in New York, estimated that 4 million families lost their financial security between 2000 and 2006, raising the total to 23 million. Driving the increase, Dēmos said, were declines in financial assets, then-rising housing costs and a growing lack of health insurance. [6]

"In America the middle class has been a lifestyle, a certain way of life," says Jennifer Wheary, a co-author of the study. "It's been about being able to have a very moderate existence where you could do things like save for your retirement, put your kids through school, get sick and not worry about getting basic care. And those kinds of things are really imperiled right now."

In another study, the Pew Research Center found this year that "fewer Americans now than at any time in the past half-century believe they're moving forward in life." [7]

Among the findings:

• Nearly two-thirds of Americans said their standard of living was higher than that of their parents at the same age, but more than half said they'd ei-ther made no progress in life over the past five years or had fallen backward.

• Median household income rose 41 percent since 1970, but upper-income households outperformed those in the middle tier in both income gains and wealth accumulation. The median net worth of upper-income families rose 123 percent from 1983 to 2004, compared with 29 percent for middle-income families.

• Almost eight in 10 respondents said it was more difficult now for those in the middle class to maintain their standard of living compared with five years ago. In 1986, 65 percent felt that way.

Lane Kenworthy, a sociology and political science professor at the University of Arizona who studies income inequality and poverty, says "the key thing that's happened" to the middle class over the past three decades "is slow income growth compared to general economic growth." Moreover, Kenworthy says a bigger and bigger portion of economic growth has accrued to the wealthiest 1 percent, whether the measure is basic wages or total compensation, which includes the value

of employee-sponsored and government benefits.

Even the economic boom leading up to today's recession has proved illusory, new Federal Reserve data show. While median household net worth — assets minus debt — rose nearly 18 percent in the three years ending in late 2007, the increase vanished amid last year's drastic declines in home and stock prices, according to the Fed's triennial "Survey of Consumer Finances." "Adjusting for those declines, Fed officials estimated that the median family was 3.2 percent poorer as of October 2008 than it was at the end of 2004," *The New York Times* noted. [8]

A hallmark of middle-class insecurity reflects what Hacker calls "the great risk shift" — the notion that government and business have transferred the burden of providing affordable health care, income security and retirement saving onto the shoulders of working Americans, leaving them financially stretched and vulnerable to economic catastrophe.

"Over the last generation, we have witnessed a massive transfer of economic risk from broad structures of insurance, including those sponsored by the corporate sector as well as by government, onto the fragile balance sheets of American families," Hacker wrote. "This transformation . . . is the defining feature of the contemporary American economy — as important as the shift from agriculture to industry a century ago." [9]

The challenge of solving the problems facing the American middle class will confront policy makers for years to come. Some experts say the key is growth in good jobs — those with good pay, good benefits and good, secure futures. Others argue that solving the nation's health-care crisis is the paramount issue.

One thing is certain, experts say: Leaving the fate of the American middle class to chance is not an option.

"We're believers in hard work, and we're increasingly in a situation where the difference between whether or not a middle-class family prospers comes down to luck, says Amelia Warren Tyagi, co-author of *The Two-Income Trap: Why Middle-Class Mothers and Fathers Are Going Broke*. "And that's an idea that makes us really uncomfortable."

Here are some of the questions that policy makers and average Americans are asking about the middle class:

Is a stable middle class a thing of the past?

First lady Michelle Obama remembers what some call the good old days of middle-class security.

"I am always amazed," she told a gathering, "at how different things are now for working women and families than when I was growing up. . . . When I was growing up, my father — as you know, a blue-collar worker — was able to go to work and earn enough money to support a family of four, while my mom stayed home with me and my brother. But today, living with one income, like we did, just doesn't cut it. People can't do it — particularly if it's a shift-worker's salary like my father's." [10]

Brookings Institution researchers noted in 2007 that two-thirds of American adults had higher family incomes than their parents did in the late 1960s and early '70s, but a third were worse off. Moreover, they pointed out, the intergenerational gains largely stemmed from dual paychecks in families. [11]

"Men's earnings have grown little, if at all," while those of women "have risen along with their greater involvement in the work world," they said. "So, yes, today's families are better off than their own parents were. . . . But they are also working more and struggling with the greater time pressures of juggling work and family responsibilities." [12]

At the same time, many economists say the earnings of middle-class working families have not kept pace with gains by the wealthy. They point to Congressional Budget Office data showing that from 1979 through 2005, the average after-tax income of the top

Income Gap Getting Wider

The gap between the wealthiest Americans and everybody else grew to its widest point since at least 1979.* The top 1 percent of households received 70 times as much in average after-tax income as the bottom one-fifth and 21 times as much as the middle one-fifth — in both cases the widest gaps on record. From 1979-2005, the top 1 percent saw its income rise 228 percent compared to a rise of only 21 percent for the middle one-fifth of Americans.

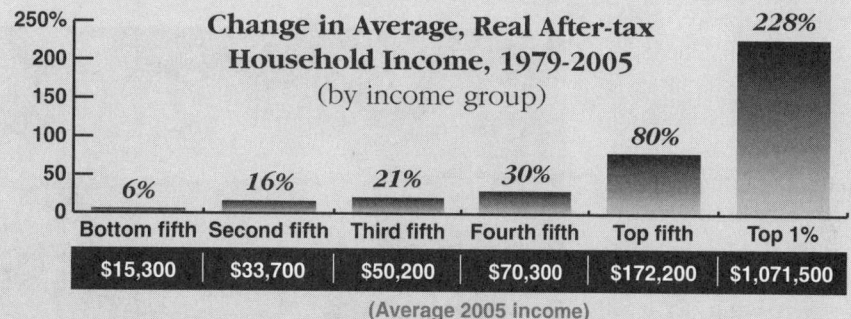

Change in Average, Real After-tax Household Income, 1979-2005
(by income group)

Bottom fifth	Second fifth	Third fifth	Fourth fifth	Top fifth	Top 1%
6%	16%	21%	30%	80%	228%
$15,300	$33,700	$50,200	$70,300	$172,200	$1,071,500

(Average 2005 income)

* *Data go back only to 1979.*

Source: Arloc Sherman, "Income Inequality Hits Record Levels, New CBO Data Show," Center on Budget and Policy Priorities, December 2007

1 percent rose 228 percent, compared with 21 percent for the middle fifth of the population. For the poorest fifth, the increase during the 25-year period was just 6 percent. [13]

Emmanuel Saez, an economist at the University of California, Berkeley, concluded last year that those in the top 1 percent of income distribution captured roughly half of the overall economic growth from 1993 to 2006, and almost three-fourths of income growth in the 2002-2006 period. [14]

"It's the very top of the economic ladder that's pulled away from the rest," Berkeley political scientist Hacker says. "Depending on which source you look at, it's the top 1 percent, or the top one-half of 1 percent, or the top one-tenth of 1 percent that's really received the lion's share of the gain in our economy overall. . . . It would be one thing if we saw middle-class Americans hold onto or even expand their wealth and economic security. But they're more in debt and less secure than they were 20 years ago."

The reasons the middle class is running in place or falling behind can be elusive, though. Kenworthy of the University of Arizona cites a litany of factors — technological changes in the workplace, globalization of trade and the outsourcing of jobs overseas, declining influence of labor unions, slow growth in the proportion of workers with at least a high-school diploma and a stagnant minimum wage — that have helped dampen the economic progress of the middle class. But, he says, social scientists and economists don't have a "good handle on which matter most." [15]

John Schmitt, senior economist at the Center for Economic and Policy Research, a liberal think tank, disputes the notion that technology and globalization are immutable forces that have, in themselves, hurt the middle class. "We've had technological growth at a rapid pace in the United States from the early 1800s," he says, and after World War II the country saw "massive technological innovation," including the introduction of computers.

Those "were huge, potentially disruptive innovations, but we had a social structure that had a lot of protections and guarantees for workers," including "a decent minimum wage, significant union representation" and a strong regulatory framework.

"The real story is that we've made a lot of decisions about economic policy that have had the effect of shifting the playing field toward employers and away from workers at a whole lot of levels," Schmitt says.

As that shift occurred, job security has suffered, many economists say.

In a recent study, Schmitt found that the share of "good jobs" — those paying at least $17 per hour and offering health insurance and a pension — declined 2.3 percentage points in the 2000-2006 business cycle, far more than in comparable periods in the 1980s and '90s. A "sharp deterioration" in employer-provided health plans was a "driving force" in the decline of good jobs, which was most pronounced among male workers, he found. [16]

Meanwhile, career employment — employment with a single employer from middle age to retirement — is no longer the norm, according to researchers at Boston College. Only half of full-time workers ages 58 to 62 are still with the same employer for whom they worked at age 50, they found. [17]

And manufacturing — long a bedrock of middle-class lifestyles — has shrunk from about a third of non-farm employment to only 10 percent since 1950. [18]

Still, interpretations of income and other economic data can vary widely among economists, depending on their political viewpoint. While not diminishing the severe pressures many in the middle class are feeling right now, some conservative economists have a more optimistic view of the jobs issue and long-term middle-class gains in general.

In a study last year, James Sherk, Bradley Fellow in Labor Policy at the

Vice President Joseph Biden, chair of the new White House Task Force on Middle Class Working Families, listens to a presentation on creating "green" jobs at the University of Pennsylvania on Feb. 27, 2009. President Obama directed the panel to examine issues such as access to college, business development and the role of labor unions in the economy.

Heritage Foundation, challenged the notions "that the era of good jobs is slipping away" and that workers' benefits are disappearing. [19]

"Throughout the economy, jobs paying high wages in fields requiring more education are more available today than they were a generation

ago, while low-wage, low-skill jobs are decreasing," he wrote. And, he added, "employer-provided health insurance and pensions are as available now as they were in the mid-1990s. Worker pension plans have improved significantly, with most employers shifting to defined-contribution pensions that provide workers with more money for retirement and do not penalize them for switching jobs."

In an interview, Sherk said that while many middle-class families are struggling today, over the long term they have not, on average, fallen behind overall growth in the economy. Average earnings have risen in step with productivity, he said.

But others are not sanguine about the status of the middle class, long-term or otherwise.

"For quite some time, we've had a sizable minority of the middle class under enormous strain and on the verge of crisis, and since the recent meltdown the proportion of middle-class families in crisis increased exponentially," says Tyagi, who co-authored *The Two-Income Trap* with her mother, Harvard law Professor Elizabeth Warren, chair of a congressional panel overseeing last fall's $700 billion financial bailout. "Many families teetering on the uncomfortable edge have been pushed over."

Is overconsumption at the root of the middle class' problems?

In a recent article about the collapse of the Florida real estate market, *New Yorker* writer George Packer quotes a woman in Cape Coral who, with her husband, had built a home on modest incomes, borrowed against its value, spent some of the money on vacations and cruises, and then faced foreclosure after her husband was laid off.

"I'm not saying what we did was perfect," the woman said. "We spent our money and didn't save it. But we had it, and we didn't see that this was going to happen." [20]

Such vignettes are commonplace these days as the economy plummets and home foreclosures soar. So, too, is the view that many middle-class consumers brought trouble to their own doorsteps by overconsuming and failing to save.

Thomas H. Naylor, a professor emeritus of economics at Duke University and co-author of *Affluenza: The All-Consuming Epidemic*, says the vulnerability of the middle class has been "enhanced by [its] behavior." He blames both consumer excess and the influence of advertising and media.

"On the one hand, consumers have done it to themselves. They've made choices to spend the money," Naylor says. "On the other hand, they've had lots of encouragement and stimulation from corporate America. The big guns are aimed at them, and it's very difficult to resist the temptation."

Pointing to the Federal Reserve's recent "Survey of Consumer Finances," Nobel laureate and *New York Times* economic columnist Paul Krugman wrote that the fact that "the net worth of the average American household, adjusted for inflation, is lower now than it was in 2001" should, at one level, "come as no surprise.

"For most of the last decade America was a nation of borrowers and spenders, not savers. The personal savings rate dropped from 9 percent in the 1980s to 5 percent in the 1990s, to just 0.6 percent from 2005 to 2007, and household debt grew much faster than personal income. Why should we have expected net worth to go up?"

But, Krugman went on to say, until recently Americans thought they were getting wealthier, basing their belief

Being Middle Class Takes More Income

The minimum income needed for a three-person household to be considered in the middle class was about 40 percent higher in 2006 than in 1969.

Economic Definition of Middle-class Household of Three

(in constant January 2008 dollars)

Year	Income
1969	$31,755 to $63,509
1979	$37,356 to $74,712
1989	$41,386 to $82,771
1999	$45,920 to $91,841
2006	$44,620 to $89,241

Source: "Inside the Middle Class: Bad Times Hit the Good Life," Pew Research Center, April 2008

on statements saying their homes and stock portfolios were appreciating faster than the growth of their debts. [21]

In fact, many economists say the picture of consumer behavior and household savings is far more complex than simple theories of overconsumption suggest.

President Obama weighed in at a press conference in early February, saying, "I don't think it's accurate to say that consumer spending got us into this mess." But he added that "our savings rate has declined, and this economy has been driven by consumer spending for a very long time. And that's not going to be sustainable."

Schmitt, of the Center for Economic and Policy Research, contends that what has hurt the middle class the most are steep cost increases of necessities, not spending on luxuries. "There's a lot of argument about overconsumption, but my argument is that consumption of basic necessities is not subject to big price savings," he says.

"Housing, education, health care — those are much more expensive than they used to be. That's where people are feeling the pinch."

Housing prices doubled between the mid-1990's and 2007. [22] Average tuition, fees and room-and-board charges at private four-year institutions have more than doubled since 1978-79, to $34,132. [23] And growth in national health expenditures has outpaced gross national product (GNP) growth every year at least since the late 1990s. [24]

One study found that among adults earning $40,000 to $60,000, the proportion of adults spending 10 percent or more of their income on health care doubled between 2001 and 2007, from 18 percent to 36 percent. [25]

"Health care is the epicenter of economic security in the United States today," says Hacker, the University of California political scientist. "It's not the only thing impinging on families finances, but it's one of the areas where the need is greatest."

Economist Robert H. Frank, author of *Falling Behind: How Rising Inequality Harms the Middle Class*, argues that as the wealthiest Americans have acquired bigger and more expensive houses and luxury possessions, their behavior has raised the bar for middle-class consumers, leading them to spend more and more of their incomes on bigger houses and upscale goods.

While some of the spending may be frivolous, he says, many consumers have felt compelled to keep up with rising economic and cultural standards — and often for practical reasons: Bigger, more expensive homes typically are in neighborhoods with the best schools, and upscale clothing has become the norm for those who want to dress for success.

"There are people you could say have brought this on themselves," Frank says of the troubles middle-class families are now facing. "If you've charged a bunch of credit cards to the max [for things] that aren't really essential, is that your fault? You bet. But most of it I

Fewer Americans Say They Are Better Off

The percentage of Americans who said they were better off in 2008 than they were five years earlier dropped to 41 percent in 2008, the lowest confidence level since 1964.

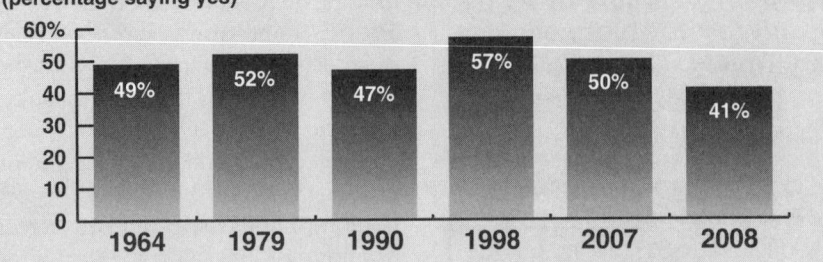

Are you better off now than you were five years ago?

(percentage saying yes)

Source: "Inside the Middle Class: Bad Times Hit the Good Life," Pew Research Center, April 2008

don't think is. You need a decent suit to go for a job interview. You can buy the cheap suit, but you won't get the call-back. You can break the rules at any turn, but there's a price for that."

In their book on two-income middle-class families, Tyagi and Warren attacked the "rock-solid" myth that "middle-class families are rushing headlong into financial ruin because they are squandering too much money on Red Lobster, Gucci and trips to the Bahamas." [26]

In fact, they wrote, after studying consumer bankruptcy data and other sources, "Today, after an average two-income family makes its house payments, car payments, insurance payments and child-care payments, they have less money left over, even though they have a second, full-time earner in the workplace," than an average single-earner family did in the early 1970s. [27]

One-paycheck households headed by women are among the most vulnerable. In an analysis of 2004 Federal Reserve Board data, the Consumer Federation of America found that the 31 million women who head households had median household income of $22,592, compared with $43,130 for all households. And women on their own had a median net worth of less

than $33,000 compared with about $93,000 for all households. [28]

Are aggressive new government programs needed to bolster the middle class?

Last year, former Republican Rep. Ernest Istook of Oklahoma criticized then-presidential candidates Hillary Clinton and Obama for arguing that "America is a place where the middle class is repressed" by rising income inequality, stagnating wages, soaring medical and college costs and other woes.

"For both candidates," wrote Istook, a Heritage Foundation fellow, "the answer to all these problems is a rush of new government programs." He pointed to Heritage Foundation studies arguing that wage-growth data have been understated and that the poor are doing better than they were 14 years earlier.

"Convincing Americans that they need government to do all these things," he wrote, "hinges on convincing them that they are victims in need of rescue. . . . It's not enough for America's left to show sympathy for victims of real tragedies like 9/11 or Katrina. Now they must elevate every challenge into a crisis, provoking a sense of desperation that more and bigger government is the answer." [29]

Yet that is not how many policy advocates view the question of government help for the middle class. The pressures weighing on working families — heightened by the current economic crisis — are so great, they argue, that bold government action is needed to keep working Americans from further economic harm.

"We talk about the big financial institutions as too big to fail," says University of California political scientist Hacker. "But most Americans have until recently been apparently viewed as too small to save."

Without policy changes, including ones that make education and health care more affordable and help people build assets, "instability is going to stay," argues Wheary of Dēmos.

Yet, while the needs of the middle class are a favorite rhetorical device for politicians, they often disagree about the best way to advance those interests. This year's $787 billion stimulus package, which emerged from a cauldron of partisan bickering, is a case in point.

President Obama, speaking to employees of Caterpillar Inc. in February, said the stimulus plan is "about giving people a way to make a living, support their families and live out their dreams. Americans aren't looking for a handout. They just want to work." [30] But Rep. John A. Boehner of Ohio, a key Republican opponent of the president's recovery plan, said it "will do little to create jobs, and will do more harm than good to middle-class families and our economy." [31]

An overhaul of health-care policy is a key priority for many policy experts. Families USA, an advocacy group supporting affordable health care, pointed to research showing that nearly half of home foreclosures in 2006 were caused, at least partly, by financial issues growing out of a medical problem. [32]

Also key, many liberal policy analysts say, is solving what they see as a growing pension crisis, made more perilous for middle-class workers by the Wall Street crash. (*See sidebar, p. 214.*) Rep. George Miller, D-Calif., chairman of the House Education and Labor Committee, says private retirement-savings vehicles like 401(k) plans "have become little more than a high-stakes crap shoot. If you didn't take your retirement savings out of the market before the crash, you are likely to take years to recoup your losses, if at all." [33]

And crucial to the future of the middle class, many experts say, are sound policies for job creation and retention.

"The major policy change we need is to decide that good steady jobs with good wages are a family value," says Leicht of the University of Iowa. "It's good jobs at good wages that last — that's the Rosetta Stone."

Leicht says "our entire system of consumption is built around the idea that you accumulate a lot of debts when you're young, then you get a steady job and your income steadily rises and you gradually pay off your debt as you age." But nowadays, he says, the average job lasts only four to five years. "If you're constantly starting over, you never get out of the hole."

Leicht wants to see a 25 percent break on corporate taxes for businesses that create "high-quality jobs" — ones lasting at least five years and paying at least 30 percent above the median income of a family of four, which in 2007 was $75,675, according to the U.S. Census Bureau.

Kenworthy, the University of Arizona sociologist, advocates temporary "wage insurance" that would "prop up your earnings for a little while if you lost your job and took a new one that paid considerably less."

Not counting the current economic crisis, Kenworthy says, "there really isn't a problem in the United States with long-term unemployment. Most people are able to get a job within six months." Even so, he adds, such jobs often come "at a lower salary." ■

Getty Images/Spencer Platt

Getty Images/Justin Sullivan

Consumerism at its Finest

Some economists say the higher cost of necessities like health care, rather than spending on luxury items like big-screen TVs or new cars, has hit consumers hardest. Moreover, Americans' personal savings rate from 2005 to 2007 was just 0.6 percent — down from 9 percent in the 1980s — with household debt growing faster than personal income.

BACKGROUND

Evolving Concept

During the 2008 presidential campaign, the Rev. Rick Warren, pastor of giant Saddleback Church in Lake Forest, Calif., asked Democrat Obama and Republican John McCain to define "rich."

Obama said that "if you are making $150,000 a year or less as a family, then you're middle class, or you may be poor. But $150 [thousand] down you're basically middle class." He added, though, that "obviously, it depends on [the] region and where you're living." McCain answered the question another way, saying — perhaps with tongue in cheek — that as a definition of rich, "if you're just talking about income, how about $5 million?" [34]

Besides helping to open a window on the candidates' views and personalities, the exchange underscored how highly subjective social and economic class can be.

That's nothing new. For centuries, the concept of a "middle class" has been evolving.

"The middle class first came into existence in early modern Europe as a new social class for which the economic basis was financial rather than feudal — the system in which the nobility owned land and others (serfs, peons) worked it," according to Andrew Hoberek, an associate professor of English at the University of Missouri, Columbia, and author of *The Twilight of the Middle Class: Post World War II American Fiction and White-Collar Work*. [35]

In the United States, the term "middle class" didn't start showing up until the 1830s or 1840s, says Jennifer L. Goloboy, an independent scholar. [36] But years earlier, she says, a segment of the population began to embrace values that would come to define the American middle class, including diligence, frugality, self-restraint and optimism.

"The early republic was such an aspirational time, and it was disproportionately young," Goloboy says. "These young people came to the cities hoping for the best, and they clung to ideas of how they would make it. That's sort of the root of middle-class values. They believed that if they held to these values they were middle class, even if they were not necessarily successful yet."

As the American economy matured in the 20th century, industrialization both nurtured and threatened the nation's budding middle class. Pioneering automaker Henry Ford helped nurture it by paying high wages and encouraging mass consumption of his cars. But the gap between rich and poor remained wide, and industrialization made life precarious for the working class when jobs disappeared.

"The paramount evil in the working-man's life is irregularity of employment," Supreme Court Justice Louis D. Brandeis wrote in 1911. [37] Historian David Kennedy noted that Brandeis' view "was echoed in Robert and Helen Merrell Lynd's classic study *Middletown* a decade later, when they cited 'irregularity of employment' as the major factor that defined the difference between the life trajectories of the working class and the middle class." [38]

During the Great Depression of the 1930s, unemployment soared to 25 percent, and many Americans fell from middle-class stability into destitution. But from the ashes of the Depression came President Franklin D. Roosevelt's New Deal program, which *New York Times* columnist Krugman says created the modern middle class. [39]

"Income inequality declined drastically from the late 1930s to the mid-1940s, with the rich losing ground while working Americans saw unprecedented gains," he wrote. [40]

The New Deal "made America a middle-class society," Krugman wrote this year in *Rolling Stone* magazine. "Under FDR, America went through what labor historians call the Great Compression, a dramatic rise in wages for ordinary workers that greatly reduced income inequality. Before the Great Compression, America was a society of rich and poor; afterward it was a society in which most people, rightly, considered themselves middle class." [41]

After World War II, the U.S. economy blossomed, aided by the GI Bill, which helped millions of former service members buy homes and get college educations. In 1946, construction began on Levittown, one of a series of massive housing developments that became national models of middle-class suburbia.

The postwar boom helped spawn the contemporary notion of the American Dream — a home, a car or two (or three), a good job, paid vacation and a comfortable suburban lifestyle. By 1960, median family income was 30 percent higher in purchasing power than a decade earlier, and more than 60 percent of homes were owner-occupied, compared with 44 percent just before World War II. [42]

Downward Slide

But many economists say the good times began to wane in the 1970s, and for a variety of reasons that can be difficult to untangle. The shift away from manufacturing toward a service economy helped erode middle-class security, as did the increasingly competitive nature of globalization, many economists say. Some also cite the declining power of unions. In 1979, 27 percent of employed wage-and-salary workers in the United States were covered by a collective bargaining agreement, but that figure has steadily declined over the years. It stood at less than 14 percent in 2008. [43]

Continued on p. 212

Chronology

1800-1929
Industrial age shifts employment from farm to factory, setting stage for rise of middle class.

October 1929
Stock market crash marks end of a speculative bubble on Wall Street.

1930-1970
Great Depression sends unemployment soaring, President Roosevelt crafts New Deal social and economic legislation and postwar boom spurs growth of middle class.

1933
Unemployment rate reaches 25 percent; Congress passes flood of New Deal legislation.

1935
President Franklin D. Roosevelt signs Social Security Act into law.

1939
Food Stamp program starts.

1944
Roosevelt signs Servicemen's Readjustment Act, or GI Bill, into law; by 1952, the law backed nearly 2.4 million home loans for World War II veterans, and by 1956 nearly 8 million vets had participated in education or training programs.

1946
Construction starts on New York's Levittown, one of three low-cost post-World War II residential communities that would come to define middle-class suburbia.

1960
Median family income is 30 percent higher in purchasing power than a decade earlier, and more than 60 percent of homes are owner-occupied, compared with 44 percent just before World War II.

1970-1995
Oil shocks, inflation, foreign competition, and other changes mark tougher era for middle-class Americans.

1979
U.S. manufacturing employment peaks at 21.4 million workers.

1981
President Ronald Reagan fires 11,000 striking members of the Professional Air Traffic Controllers Organization, helping to weaken the power of organized labor; Reagan persuades Congress to pass largest tax cuts in U.S. history.

1981-82
Severe recession rocks U.S. economy, sending the unemployment rate to 10.8 percent, the highest since the Great Depression.

Oct. 19, 1987
Dow Jones Industrial Average loses 23 percent of its value.

1996-Present
Home ownership peaks, and consumer spending soars, but good times end as home values plummet, financial institutions collapse and nation sinks into recession.

1996
Congress ends 60-year welfare entitlement program, imposing work requirements and putting time limits on cash benefits.

1997
Federal minimum wage raised to $5.15 an hour.

2000
Federal poverty rate falls to 11.3 percent, lowest since 1974.

2001-2006
Housing prices in many cities double, and home-equity loans help lead to soaring consumer spending.

2004
Home-ownership rate peaks at 69 percent.

2008
Federal minimum wage rises to $6.55 an hour; it is set to increase to $7.25 effective July 24, 2009. . . . U.S. seizes Fannie Mae and Freddie Mac, Lehman Brothers files for bankruptcy and Washington Mutual collapses in biggest bank failure in history. . . . President George W. Bush signs $700 billion financial rescue bill but recession deepens.

2009
President Barack Obama announces budget seeking to aid middle class and forms Middle Class Task Force headed by Vice President Joseph Biden; first meeting focuses on "green jobs." . . . Federal unemployment rate rises to 7.6 percent in January (12.6 percent for African-Americans and 9.7 for Hispanics). . . . Labor Department says employers took 2,227 "mass layoff actions" in January, resulting in nearly 238,000 job cuts; from December 2007 through January 2009, mass layoff events totaled more than 25,700. . . . Claims for unemployment benefits exceed 5 million for first time in history. . . . Home foreclosures are reported on 274,399 U.S. properties in January, up 18 percent from January 2008.

What Does 'Middle Class' Really Mean?

Does the definition include income? Number of cars in the garage?

At his first White House press conference, President Barack Obama promised tax relief for "working and middle-class families." But what, exactly, does it mean to be in the "middle class"?

No official definition exists. Politicians, journalists and pundits freely use the term, often without attaching a precise meaning to it. And in opinion polls, most Americans — uncomfortable defining themselves as "rich" or "poor" — place themselves in the category of the middle class, even if their incomes reflect the outer limits of wealth or poverty.

In a report last year, the Pew Research Center noted that the term "middle class" is both "universally familiar" and "devilishly difficult to pin down."

"It is both a social and economic construct, and because these domains don't always align, its borders are fuzzy," Pew said. "Is a $30,000-a-year resident in brain surgery lower class? Is a $100,000-a-year plumber upper middle class?"

In a national survey of more than 2,400 American adults, Pew asked people to define themselves. It found that 53 percent said they were middle class. But, Pew said, "behind the reassuring simplicity of this number lies a nest of anomalies."

For example, it said, 41 percent of adults with annual household incomes of $100,000 or more said they were middle class, as did 46 percent of those with household incomes below $40,000. And of those in between, roughly a third said they were not middle class.

"If being middle income isn't the sole determinant of being middle class, what else is?" Pew added. "Wealth? Debt? Homeownership? Consumption? Marital status? Age? Race and ethnicity? Education? Occupation? Values?"[1]

Christian Weller, an associate professor of public policy at the University of Massachusetts, Boston, and a fellow at the liberal Center for American Progress, says that often, people count the number of cars in a garage or the square footage of a house to judge another person's economic standing. But, he says, "that's not really how people perceive and define middle class. . . . One part of middle class is an aspirational definition: 'I'll be able to send my kids to college, I'll be able to create a better future for my children, and do I have a secure lifestyle right now?'

"That goes beyond just simply having a good job," he says. "That means, do you have health insurance coverage, do you

have enough savings, do you own your own home, do you have retirement savings?" And, Weller adds, "By all those measures middle-class security has been eroding substantially."

Many economists look at the concept of a middle class through the lens of household-income data gathered by the federal government. Median household income was $50,233 in 2007, the latest year for which data are available.[2] That was the midpoint in the distribution, with half of households having more income and half less.[3]

The government also separates household income into five "quintiles," from lowest to highest. Some might consider "middle class" to mean only the third quintile — the one in the very middle — with incomes between $39,101 and $62,000. But many economists consider that view to be too cramped. Some count the third and fourth quintiles, with an upper limit of $100,000 in household income in 2007. Among the broadest definitions of middle class is one encompassing the three income quintiles in the middle, from $20,292 to $100,000.

Of course, using household income to measure the middle class has its own problems. For example, a family might seem solidly middle class based on its income, but parents may be toiling at two jobs each to raise their income level into the middle tier of the distribution tables. They might make good incomes but lack health insurance, putting them and their children at risk of a catastrophic financial collapse. Or they may live in a high-cost region of the country, where a supposed middle-class income of around $50,000 or $60,000 a year simply can't cover the bills.

One thing is certain, say those who have studied the American middle class: Its survival is crucial to the nation's future.

"It is the heart of the country, it's the heart of our democracy, it's the heart of our economy, it's the heart of our population," says Amelia Warren Tyagi, co-author of *The Two-Income Trap: Why Middle-Class Mothers and Fathers Are Going Broke*. "So while it may not be easy to define with precision, it's extremely important."

---

[1] Paul Taylor, *et al.*, "Inside the Middle Class: Bad Times Hit the Good Life," Pew Research Center, April 9, 2008, p. 3, http://pewsocialtrends.org/assets/pdf/MC-Middle-class-report.pdf.

[2] U.S. Department of Commerce, Bureau of the Census, "Historical Income Tables — Households," www.census.gov/hhes/www/income/histinc/h05.html.

[3] In 2007, the United States had about 116,783,000 households.

Continued from p. 210

In remarks tied to formation of his middle-class task force, Obama said, "I do not view the labor movement as part of the problem; to me it's part of the solution. We need to level the playing field for workers and the unions that repre-

sent their interest, because we know that you cannot have a strong middle class without a strong labor movement."[44]

Hacker, the University of California political scientist, says that "employers at one time were encouraged by unions, the federal tax code and their own

competitive instincts to provide very strong guaranteed benefits to many of their workers in the form of defined-benefit pension plans [and] good health insurance coverage."

But, he says, "over the last generation the work force has changed, and the competitive environment in which employers have operated changed in ways that have made it much less attractive for many employers to provide such benefits. There used to be a kind of implicit long-term contract in many workplaces, enforced in part by unions, that is no longer there. So it's much more of a free-agent economic culture, which means that it's good for some workers but imposes a lot more risk on all of them."

Many conservatives disagree, though, on the role of unions in helping the middle class. "Numerous studies have shown that unions are not the answer to increasing prosperity for American workers or the economy," the U.S. Chamber of Commerce stated in a paper on the issue. It added: "Organized labor's claims that unionization is a ticket to the middle class cannot be squared with data showing that increased unionization decreases competitiveness and leads to slower job growth." [45]

Besides the issue of union influence, critics often cite Reagan-era economic policies, which included cuts in tax rates for those in upper-income brackets, as contributing to inequality and hurting the middle class.

The criticism is not universal. George Viksnins, a professor emeritus of economics at Georgetown University, argues that so-called Reaganomics was a plus for the middle class. "Perhaps the most significant positive aspect of the Reaganomics program of lower taxes and regulatory reforms is the tremendous increase in employment," he wrote. [46] In an interview, he said that "lowering marginal tax rates held out a lot of hope for young members of the middle class that they might get to keep some of the income" they earned "and didn't need to work quite as hard in sheltering it."

But others see the Reagan years differently. "Yes, there was a boom in the mid-1980s, as the economy recovered from a severe recession," Krugman, the Nobel economist and *Times* columnist,

wrote. "But while the rich got much richer, there was little sustained economic improvement for most Americans. By the late 1980s, middle-class incomes were barely higher than they had been a decade before — and the poverty rate had actually risen." [47]

The University of Iowa's Leicht is highly critical of another legacy of the 1980s: deregulation of the banking industry, which he says set the stage for a massive increase in easy credit. The explosion in consumer lending that began in the 1980s helped millions of working Americans buy homes and cars, Leicht acknowledges, but he says the credit binge has come back to haunt the middle class now as home-foreclosure rates and personal bankruptcies soar.

"Starting in about the mid-1980s, we decided as a nation, through a number of mechanisms, that being loaned money was a perfect substitute for being paid it as long as you could buy things that represented middle-class status like houses and cars," Leicht says.

Middle Class Enjoys Some of 'Life's Goodies'

More than two-thirds of middle-class Americans enjoy at least three of "life's goodies," such as high-speed Internet and more than one vehicle, according to the Pew Research Center. But half as many middle class as wealthy Americans have vacation homes, household help and children in private school.

Percentage of Americans who have. . .

Item	All incomes	Upper income	Middle income	Lower income
Cable or satellite service	70%	80%	71%	62%
Two or more cars	70	83	72	57
High-speed Internet	66	80	67	50
High-definition or flat screen TV	42	59	42	28
Young child in private school	15	31	14	6
Paid household help	16	36	13	7
A vacation home	10	19	9	4

Source: "Inside the Middle Class: Bad Times Hit the Good Life," Pew Research Center, April 2008

Impact of Globalization

Like the impact of so-called supply-side Reaganomics, the effects of globalization and trade policy are often hotly debated. While some argue they have, on balance, helped the U.S. economy, others say they have undermined middle-class security. (*See "At Issue," p. 217.*)

In his 2006 book *War on the Middle Class*, CNN anchor Lou Dobbs wrote "[i]n their free-trade fervor, Republicans and Democrats alike, most economists, certainly corporate leaders, and business columnists assure us that the loss of millions of jobs to other countries is the inevitable result of a modern global economy. The result, they promise us, will be a higher standard of living for everyone in America — and especially for the rest of the planet."

But Dobbs went on to say that millions of U.S. manufacturing jobs already had vanished and that many more jobs — including millions of white-collar

Economic Meltdown Batters Retirement Plans

Reform proposals call for limiting risk to workers.

The economy may look bleak for millions of middle-class Americans, but for those in or near retirement, it's downright scary.

Experts say the steep downturns in stock and real estate values, along with soaring layoffs among older workers, have left millions worrying that they won't have enough income to see them through their golden years. And the crash has underscored what critics see as the weaknesses of 401(k) accounts — tax-advantaged plans that require employees to assume the primary responsibility for building and managing their retirement nest eggs.

"The collapse of the housing bubble, coupled with the plunge in the stock market, has exposed the gross inadequacy of our system of retirement income," Dean Baker, co-director of the Center for Economic and Policy Research, a liberal think tank in Washington, told a House committee in February. [1]

At the same hearing, Alicia H. Munnell, director of the Center for Retirement Research at Boston College, said the center's National Retirement Risk Index, which projects the share of households that will not be able to maintain their living standard in retirement, jumped from 31 percent in 1983 to 44 percent in 2006 and rises to 61 percent when health-care expenses are factored in.

Munnell said that in the two years following the stock market's peak on Oct. 9, 2007, the market value of assets in 401(k) retirement plans and Individual Retirement Accounts fell roughly 30 percent. For people ages 55 to 64, she said, median holdings in 401(k) plans went from a modest $60,000 or so in 2007 to $42,000 at the end of 2008. [2]

Critics have long warned of serious faults in the nation's private system of retirement savings. The number of so-called defined-benefit plans, which provide for guaranteed pensions, has been shrinking, while defined-contribution plans like

401(k)s have risen from supplemental savings vehicles in the early 1980s to what they are now: the main or sole retirement plan for most American workers covered by an employer-sponsored retirement plan. [3]

Jacob S. Hacker, a political scientist at the University of California in Berkeley, said the historical "three-legged stool" of retirement security — Social Security, private pensions and personal savings — is now precarious.

"The central issue for retirement security is . . . the risk," he told a congressional hearing last fall. "Retirement wealth has not only failed to rise for millions of families; it has also grown more risky, as the nation has shifted more of the responsibility for retirement planning from employers and government onto workers and their families. [4]

Several proposals have surfaced for revamping the retirement system, some bolder than others.

Teresa Ghilarducci, a professor at the New School for Social Research in New York, wants Congress to establish "Guaranteed Retirement Accounts," in which all workers not enrolled in an equivalent or better defined-benefit pension plan would participate. A contribution equal to 5 percent of each worker's earnings would go into an account each year, with the cost shared equally between worker and employer. A $600 federal tax credit would offset employees' contributions.

Money in the accounts would be managed by the federal government and earn a guaranteed 3 percent rate of return, adjusted for inflation. When a worker retired, the account would convert to an annuity that provides income until death, though a small portion could be taken in a lump sum at retirement. Those who died before retirement could leave only half their accounts to heirs; those who died after retiring could leave half the final balance minus benefits received. [5]

service positions — were expected to do so in coming years, with the information-technology industry leading the way. "The free-trade-at-any-price enthusiasts once promised us that all those millions of people who lost their positions in manufacturing would find even better ones in the tech industry. But today no one is saying which industry will be the source of replacement for those jobs lost to outsourcing." [48]

C. Fred Bergsten, director of the Peterson Institute for International Economics, appearing on the PBS show "The NewsHour with Jim Lehrer," said

studies by his organization have shown that the U.S. economy is $1 trillion a year richer as a result of globalization during the past 50 years.

Nonetheless, Bergsten said "there are losers . . . , costs . . . [and] downsides" to globalization and that the United States "has done a very poor job" in dealing with those problems. "You lose your health care when you lose your job. Unemployment insurance is miserably inadequate. Trade-adjustment assistance works, but it doesn't even cover [service] workers who get outsourced, and it's inadequate."

But Thea Lee, policy director and chief international economist at the AFL-CIO, who also appeared on the PBS program, was more critical of globalization than Bergsten. "We've had the wrong kind of globalization," she said. "It's been a corporate-dominated globalization, which has not really served working people here or our trading partners very well. . . . We've seen this long-term, decades-long stagnation of wages and growth of wage inequality in the United States even as we've been in a period of tremendous economic growth, productivity

The plan has drawn criticism. Paul Schott Stevens, president and CEO of the Investment Company Institute, which represents the mutual-fund industry, called it "a non-starter." [6] Jan Jacobson, senior counsel for retirement policy at the American Benefits Council, said, "We believe the current employer-sponsored system is a good one that should be built on." [7]

But Ghilarducci told the *AARP Bulletin Today* that "people just want a guaranteed return for their retirement. The essential feature of my proposal is that people and employers would be relieved of being tied to the financial market." [8]

Hacker advocates an approach called "universal 401(k)" plans. The plans would be available to all workers, regardless of whether their employer offered a traditional retirement plan. All benefits would remain in the same account throughout a worker's life, and money could be withdrawn before retirement only at a steep penalty, as is the case with today's 401(k) plans. The plans would be shielded against excessive investments in company stock, and the default investment option would be a low-cost index fund that has a mix of stocks and bonds. Over time, the mix would change automatically to limit risk as a worker aged.

At age 65, government would turn a worker's account into a lifetime annuity that guarantees a flow of retirement income, unless the worker explicitly requested otherwise and showed he or she had enough assets to withstand market turmoil.

Teresa Ghilarducci, a professor at the New School for Social Research, says Congress should establish "Guaranteed Retirement Accounts" for workers not enrolled in similar pension plans.

Employers would be encouraged to match workers' contributions to the plans, and government could give special tax breaks to companies offering better matches for lower-paid workers. [9]

Says Hacker, "We have to move toward a system in which there is a second tier of pension plans that is private but which provides key protections that were once provided by defined-benefit pension plans."

[1] "Strengthening Worker Retirement Security," testimony before House Committee on Education and Labor, Feb. 24, 2009, http://edlabor.house.gov/documents/111/pdf/testimony/20090224DeanBakertestimony.pdf.

[2] "The Financial Crisis and Restoring Retirement Security," testimony before House Committee on Education and Labor, Feb. 24, 2009, http://edlabor.house.gov/documents/111/pdf/testimony/20090224AliciaMunnellTestimony.pdf.

[3] *Ibid.* For background, see Alan Greenblatt, "Pension Crisis," *CQ Researcher*, Feb. 17, 2006, pp. 145-168, and Alan Greenblatt, "Aging Baby Boomers," *CQ Researcher*, Oct. 19, 2007, pp. 865-888.

[4] "The Impact of the Financial Crisis on Workers' Retirement Security," testimony before House Committee on Education and Labor field hearing, San Francisco, Oct. 22, 2008.

[5] For a detailed explanation, see, Teresa Ghilarducci, "Guaranteed Retirement Accounts: Toward retirement income security," Economic Policy Institute, *Briefing Paper No. 204*, Nov. 20, 2007, www.sharedprosperity.org/bp204/bp204.pdf.

[6] Stevens and Jacobson are quoted in Doug Halonen, "401(k) plans could be facing total revamp," *Financial Week*, Oct. 29, 2008.

[7] *Ibid.*

[8] Quoted in Carole Fleck, "401(k) Plans: Too Risky for Retirement Security?" *AARP Bulletin Today*, Dec. 17, 2008, http://bulletin.aarp.org/yourmoney/retirement/articles/401_k_plans_too_risky_for_retirement_security_.html.

[9] See Jacob S. Hacker, *The Great Risk Shift* (2006), pp. 185-187. See also Testimony before House Committee on Education and Labor, Oct. 22, 2008, *op. cit.*

growth, technological improvements and increase in globalization." [49]

However one may interpret the economic history of recent decades, few observers would disagree that the middle class is now caught in the greatest economic downdraft in generations.

"We've really had an erosion of economic security and economic opportunity," and it occurred "very rapidly" after 2001, says Christian Weller, an associate professor of public policy at the University of Massachusetts, Boston, and a fellow at the liberal Center for American Progress.

After a "five-year window" of employment and wage growth during the late 1990s, Weller says, pressure on the middle class began accelerating in 2001. "There are different explanations, but one is . . . that after the 2001 recession [corporate] profits recovered much faster than in previous recessions, to much higher levels, and corporations were unchecked. They could engage in outsourcing and all these other techniques to boost their short-term profits, but obviously to the detriment of employees. I think what we ended up with was very slow em-

ployment growth, flat or declining wages and declining benefit coverage."

And overlaid on all of that, Weller says, was the unprecedented boom in housing.

Even before the housing bubble burst, though, the middle class was on shaky ground, as Weller noted in an article early last year. In 2004, fewer than a third of families had accumulated enough wealth to equal three months of income, he found. And that was counting all financial assets, including retirement savings, minus debt. [50]

"For quite some time," says *Two-Income Trap* co-author Tyagi, "we've had a sizable minority of the middle class under enormous strain and on the verge of crisis, and since the recent meltdown the proportion of middle-class families in crisis increased exponentially.

"Many families teetering on the uncomfortable edge have been pushed over. I really see the [home] foreclosure crisis as front and center in this. We can't overestimate how important home ownership is to the middle class is, and what a crisis losing a home is." ■

CURRENT SITUATION

Narrowing the Gap

Joel Kotkin, a presidential fellow at Chapman University in Orange, Calif., and author of *The City: A Global History*, wrote recently that "over the coming decades, class will likely constitute the major dividing line in our society — and the greatest threat to America's historic aspirations." [51]

With the gap between rich and poor growing and even a college degree no assurance of upward mobility, Kotkin wrote, President Obama's "greatest challenge . . . will be to change this trajectory for Americans under 30, who supported him by two to one. The promise that 'anyone' can reach the highest levels of society is the basis of both our historic optimism and the stability of our political system. Yet even before the recession, growing income inequality was undermining Americans' optimism about the future."

Obama's legislative agenda, along with his middle-class task force, aims to narrow the class gap. But the deep recession, along with a partisan divide on Capitol Hill, could make some of his key goals difficult and costly to reach.

In announcing his budget, Obama did not hesitate to draw class distinctions between "the wealthiest few" and the "middle class" made up of "responsible men and women who are working harder than ever, worrying about their jobs and struggling to raise their families." He acknowledged that his political opponents are "gearing up for a fight" against his budget plan, which includes tax cuts for all but the richest Americans, universally available health-care coverage and other policies aimed squarely at the middle class. Yet, he said, "The system we have now might work for the powerful and well-connected interests that have run Washington for far too long, but I don't. I work for the American people." [52]

Republicans also are invoking middle-class concerns in expressing their opposition to Obama's budget. Delivering the GOP response to Obama's weekly address, Sen. Richard Burr, R-N.C., said the budget would require the typical American family to pay $52,000 in interest alone over the next decade. [53]

"Like a family that finds itself choking under the weight of credit-card balances and finance charges," said Burr, "the federal government is quickly obligating the American people to a similar fate.

The stimulus package signed by the president in February includes payroll-tax breaks for low- and moderate-income households and an expanded tax credit for higher-education expenses. But costly overhauls of health and retirement policies remain on the table.

Douglas W. Elmendorf, director of the Congressional Budget Office, told a Senate budget panel in February that without changes in health-insurance policy, an estimated 54 million people under age 65 will lack medical insurance by 2019, compared with 45 million this year. The projection "largely reflects the expectation that health-care costs and health-insurance premiums will continue to rise faster than people's income." [54]

Meanwhile, the abrupt collapse of the global financial markets has decimated middle-class retirement accounts. Between June 30 and September 30 of 2008, retirement assets fell 5.9 percent, from $16.9 trillion to $15.9 trillion, according to the latest tally by the Investment Company Institute, which represents the mutual-fund industry. [55]

In announcing his middle-class task force, Obama said his administration would be "absolutely committed to the future of America's middle class and working families. They will be front and center every day in our work in the White House." [56]

The group includes the secretaries of Labor, Health and Human Services, Education and Commerce, plus the heads of the National Economic Council, Office of Management and Budget, Domestic Policy Council and Council of Economic Advisors. [57]

According to the White House, the task force will aim to:

- Expand opportunities for education and lifelong training;
- Improve work and family balance;
- Restore labor standards, including workplace safety;
- Help to protect middle-class and working-family incomes, and
- Protect retirement security.

The group's first meeting, on Feb. 27, focused on so-called green jobs.

Jared Bernstein, Vice President Biden's chief economist and a task force member, told *The Christian Science Monitor* that the group "has a different target" than the recently enacted $787 billion economic-stimulus plan, which includes huge government outlays with a goal of creating millions of jobs. "It's less about job quantity than job quality," Bernstein told the *Monitor* in an e-mail. "Its goal is to make sure that once the economy begins to expand again, middle-class families will reap their fair share of the growth, something that hasn't happened in recent years." [58]

Continued on p. 218

At Issue:

Has U.S. trade and globalization policy hurt the middle class?

THEA LEE
POLICY DIRECTOR, AFL-CIO

WRITTEN FOR *CQ RESEARCHER*, MARCH 2, 2009

*t*he middle class is not a single entity — nor is trade and globalization policy. The clothes we wear, the food we eat, the air we breathe, the jobs we have, the places we choose to live — all are affected by trade and globalization policy, but in many different ways.

I would argue, nonetheless, that U.S. trade and globalization policy has failed the middle class in numerous ways. It has eroded living standards for a large majority of American workers, undermined our social, environmental, consumer safety and public health protections, exacerbated our unsustainable international indebtedness, weakened our national security and compromised our ability to innovate and prosper in the future.

Most significant, especially during this global downturn, the negative impact of globalization on American wages should be a top concern — both for policy makers and for business. Economists may disagree about the magnitude of the effect, but few would dispute that globalization has contributed to the decades-long stagnation of real wages for American workers.

The Economic Policy Institute's L. Josh Bivens finds that the costs of globalization to a full-time median-wage earner in 2006 totaled approximately $1,400, and about $2,500 for a two-earner household. It only makes intuitive sense that if the point of globalization is to increase U.S. access to vast pools of less-skilled, less-protected labor, wages at home will be reduced — particularly for those workers without a college degree. And this impact will only grow in future years, as trade in services expands. We won't be able to rebuild our real economy and the middle class if we can't figure out how to use trade, tax, currency and national investment policies to reward efficient production at home — not send it offshore.

That is not to say, however, that trade and globalization in themselves are inherently pernicious. U.S. globalization policies in recent decades prioritized the interests of mobile, multinational corporations over domestic manufacturers, workers, farmers and communities. At the same time, they undermined prospects for equitable, sustainable and democratic development in our trading partners.

If we are going to move forward together in the future, we need to acknowledge that our current policies have not always delivered on their potential or their promise — particularly for middle-class workers. If new trade and globalization initiatives are to gain any political momentum, we will need deep reform in current policies.

C. FRED BERGSTEN
DIRECTOR, PETERSON INSTITUTE FOR INTERNATIONAL ECONOMICS

WRITTEN FOR *CQ RESEARCHER*, MARCH 2, 2009

*t*he backlash in the United States against globalization is understandable but misplaced. Despite widespread and legitimate concerns about worsening income distribution, wage stagnation and job insecurity, all serious economics studies show that globalization is only a modest cause of these problems. In the aggregate, globalization is a major plus for the U.S. economy and especially for the middle class.

An in-depth study by our nonpartisan institute demonstrates that the U.S. economy is $1 trillion per year richer as a result of global trade integration over the last half-century, or almost $10,000 per household. These gains accrue from cheaper imports, more high-paying export jobs and faster productivity growth. The American economy could gain another $500 billion annually if we could lift the remaining barriers to the international flow of goods and services.

Of course, any dynamic economic change, like technology advances and better corporate management, affects some people adversely. The negative impact of globalization totals about $50 billion a year due to job displacement and long-term income reductions. This is not an insignificant number, but the benefit-to-cost ratio from globalization is still a healthy 20-to-1.

The United States could not stop globalization even if it wanted to. But it must expand the social safety net for those displaced while making sure that our workers and firms can compete in a globalized world.

The Obama administration and the new Congress have already begun to shore up these safety nets through the fiscal stimulus package. Unemployment insurance has been substantially liberalized. Sweeping reform of the health care system has begun. Most important, Trade Adjustment Assistance has been dramatically expanded to cover all trade-impacted workers and communities.

We must also remember that globalization has lifted billions of the poorest citizens out of poverty. No country has ever achieved sustained modernization without integrating into the world economy, with China and India only the latest examples. The flip side is that products and services from these countries greatly improve the purchasing power and an array of consumer choices for the American middle class.

Fears of globalization have expanded during the current worldwide downturn. But strong export performance kept our economy growing through most of last year, and global cooperation is now necessary to ignite the needed recovery.

Continued from p. 216

Biden expressed a similar sentiment in an op-ed piece in *USA Today*. "Once this economy starts growing again, we need to make sure the benefits of that growth reach the people responsible for it. We can't stand by and watch as that narrow sliver of the top of the income scale wins a bigger piece of the pie — while everyone else gets a smaller and smaller slice," he wrote. [59]

In late January, as he pushed Congress to pass the stimulus plan, Obama said that not only would the task force focus on the middle class but that "we're not forgetting the poor. They are going to be front and center because they, too, share our American Dream."

Cash-Strapped States

Cash-strapped state governments are on the front lines of dealing with the swelling ranks of the nation's poor. States are struggling to handle a rising number of Americans in need of welfare assistance as the economy weakens — some of them middle-class households pushed over the financial edge by job losses and home foreclosures.

Despite the economic collapse, 18 states reduced their welfare rolls last year, and the number of people nationally receiving cash assistance was at or near the lowest point in more than four decades, a *New York Times* analysis of state data found. [60]

Michigan, with one of the nation's highest unemployment rates, reduced its welfare rolls 13 percent, and Rhode Island cut its by 17 percent, the *Times* said.

"Of the 12 states where joblessness grew most rapidly," the *Times* said, "eight reduced or kept constant the number of people receiving Temporary Assistance for Needy Families, the main cash welfare program for families with children. Nationally, for the 12 months

Soaring home foreclosures and job losses are battering middle class families. Home prices doubled between the mid-1990s and 2007, prompting many families to borrow against the higher values and take out cash for vacations and other expenditures. When values began plummeting, families with job losses and limited or no savings found themselves underwater.

ending October 2008, the rolls inched up a fraction of 1 percent."

While the recession has devastated households across the demographic spectrum, it has been especially hard on minorities. The overall unemployment rate in January stood at 7.6 percent, but it was 12.6 percent for African-Americans and 9.7 percent for Hispanics. The rate for whites was 6.9 percent. What's more, unemployment among minorities has been rising faster than for whites. [61]

The crash of the auto industry, among the most spectacular aspects of the past year's economic crisis, has devastated African-Americans.

About 118,000 African-Americans worked in the auto industry in November 2008, down from 137,000 in December 2007, the start of the recession, according to researchers at the Economic Policy Institute, a liberal think tank. [62]

"One of the engines of the black middle class has been the auto sector," Schmitt, told *USA Today* in January. In the late 1970s, "one of every 50 African-Americans in the U.S. was working in the auto sector. These jobs were the best jobs. Particularly for African-Americans who had migrated from the South, these were the culmination of a long, upward trajectory of economic mobility." [63]

For those living in high-cost urban areas — whether black, Hispanic or white — the strain of maintaining a middle-class standard of living is especially acute. According to 2008 survey data by the Pew research organization, more than a fourth of those who defined themselves as middle class who lived in high-cost areas said they had just enough money for basic expenses, or not even that much, compared with 16 percent living in low-cost metropolitan areas. [64]

In New York City, the nation's biggest urban area, people earning the median area income in the third quarter of 2008 could afford only about 11 percent of the homes in the metro area — the lowest proportion in the country — according to the Center for an Urban Future, a Manhattan think tank. To be in the middle class in Manhattan, according to the center's analysis, a person would need to make $123,322 a year, compared with $72,772 in Boston, $63,421 in Chicago and $50,000 in Houston. [65]

"New York has long been a city that has groomed a middle class, but that's a more arduous job today," said Jonathan Bowles, the center's director and a co-author of the report. "There's a tremendous amount of positives about the city, yet so many middle-class families seem to be stretched to their limits." [66] ∎

Getty Images/Ethan Miller

OUTLOOK

Silver Lining?

No cloud is darker over the middle class than the deepening recession. "Everything points to this being at least three years of a weak economy," Nobel economist Krugman told a conference in February sponsored by several liberal groups. [67]

The economic crisis, he said, is "out of control," and "there's no reason to think there's any spontaneous mechanism for recovery. . . . My deep concern is not simply that it will be a very deep slide but that it will become entrenched."

Still, Krugman said, "If there's any silver lining to [the crisis], it's reopening the debate about the role of public policy in the economy."

Many liberals argue that policy changes in such areas as health-care coverage and higher-education benefits offer avenues for lifting middle-class families out of the economic mire and that getting medical costs under control is a key to the nation's long-term fiscal health. But many conservatives oppose more government spending. Advancing major reforms amid partisan bickering and a budget deficit inflated by bailouts, recession and war will be difficult.

University of Arizona political scientist Kenworthy says focusing policy changes on people living below the poverty level could be "easier to sell politically" and would still benefit those in higher income brackets.

"For example, think about the minimum wage," he says. Raising it "has an effect further up the wage distribution. The same with the earned-income tax credit," a refundable credit for low and moderate working people and families. "If it's made more generous, it has effects a bit further up. The same with health care."

As Washington grapples with potential policy changes, the plunging economy is forcing many middle-class consumers to live within their means. Many see that as a good thing.

"I certainly think some of the entitlements we have come to expect, like two homes, a brand-new car every couple of years, college education for all the kids, a yacht or two, expensive vacations — some of this will need to be reoriented," says Georgetown University's Viksnins. "Some reallocation of people's priorities is really necessary."

Yet, long-term optimism hasn't vanished amid the current economic gloom. "We will rebuild, we will recover and the United States of America will emerge stronger than before," Obama declared in an address on Feb. 24 to a joint session of Congress.

Viksnins says he is "utterly hopeful" about the future of the middle class.

And Sherk, the Heritage Foundation labor-policy fellow, says that "as long as your skills are valuable, you're going to find a job that pays you roughly at your productivity."

"For people in jobs disappearing from the economy, it's going to mean a substantial downward adjustment in standard of living," Sherk says. But "those in the middle class who have some college education, or have gone to a community college or have skills, broadly speaking, most will wind up on their feet again." ∎

Notes

[1] Julie Bosman, "Newly Poor Swell Lines at Food Banks," *The New York Times*, Feb. 20, 2009, www.nytimes.com/2009/02/20/nyregion/20food.html?scp=1&sq=newly%20poor&st=cse.

[2] For background, see the following *CQ Researcher* reports: Marcia Clemmitt, "Public Works Projects," Feb. 20, 2009, pp. 153-176; Kenneth Jost, "Financial Crisis," May 9, 2008, pp. 409-432; Thomas J. Billitteri, "Financial Bailout," Oct. 24, 2008, pp. 865-888; Marcia Clemmitt, "Mortgage Crisis," Nov. 2, 2007, pp. 913-936, and Barbara Mantel, "Consumer

Debt," March 2, 2007, pp. 193-216.

[3] For background see Kenneth Jost, "The Obama Presidency," *CQ Researcher*, Jan. 30, 2009, pp. 73-104.

[4] Jackie Calmes, "Obama, Breaking 'From a Troubled Past,' Seeks a Budget to Reshape U.S. Priorities," *The New York Times*, Feb. 27, 2009, p. A1. For background, see the following *CQ Researcher* reports: Marcia Clemmitt, "Rising Health Costs," April 7, 2006, pp. 289-312, and Marcia Clemmitt, "Universal Coverage," March 30, 2007, pp. 265-288.

[5] For background, see the following *CQ Researcher* reports: Thomas J. Billitteri, "Domestic Poverty," Sept. 7, 2007, pp. 721-744; Alan Greenblatt, "Upward Mobility," April 29, 2005, pp. 369-392; and Mary H. Cooper, "Income Equality," April 17, 1998, pp. 337-360.

[6] Demos and Institute on Assets & Social Policy at Brandeis University, *From Middle to Shaky Ground: The Economic Decline of America's Middle Class, 2000-2006* (2008).

[7] Paul Taylor, *et al.*, "Inside the Middle Class: Bad Times Hit the Good Life," Pew Research Center, April 9, 2008, http://pewsocialtrends.org/assets/pdf/MC-Middle-class-report.pdf, p. 5.

[8] Edmund L. Andrews, "Fed Calls Gain in Family Wealth a Mirage," Feb. 13, 2009, www.nytimes.com/2009/02/13/business/economy/13fed.html?ref=business. The study is by Brian K. Bucks, *et al.*, "Changes in U.S. Family Finances from 2004 to 2007: Evidence from the Survey of Consumer Finances," *Federal Reserve Bulletin*, Vol. 95, February 2009, www.federalreserve.gov/pubs/bulletin/2009/pdf/scf09.pdf.

[9] Jacob S. Hacker, *The Great Risk Shift* (2006), pp. 5-6.

[10] Quoted in Ta-Nehisi Coates, "American Girl," *The Atlantic*, January/February 2009.

[11] Julia B. Isaacs and Isabel V. Sawhill, "The Frayed American Dream," Brookings Institution, Nov. 28, 2007, www.brookings.edu/opinions/2007/1128_econgap_isaacs.aspx.

[12] *Ibid.*

[13] Arloc Sherman, "Income Inequality Hits Record Levels, New CBO Data Show," Center on Budget and Policy Priorities, Dec. 14, 2007, www.cbpp.org/12-14-07inc.htm. The CBO report is "Historical Effective Federal Tax Rates: 1979 to 2005," www.cbo.gov/doc.cfm?index=8885. Figures are inflation adjusted and are in 2005 dollars.

[14] Emmanuel Saez, "Striking it Richer: The Evolution of Top Incomes in the United States," University of California, Berkeley, March 15,

2008, http://elsa.berkeley.edu/~saez-UStopincomes-2006prel.pdf.

[15] For background, see the following *CQ Researcher* reports: "Pamela M. Prah, "Labor Unions' Future," Sept. 2, 2005, pp. 709-732; Brian Hansen, "Global Backlash," Sept. 28, 2001, pp. 761-784; Mary H. Cooper, "World Trade," June 9, 2000, pp. 497-520; Mary H. Cooper, "Exporting Jobs," Feb. 20, 2004, pp. 149-172; and the following *CQ Global Researcher* reports: Samuel Loewenberg, "Anti-Americanism," March 2007, pp. 51-74, and Ken Moritsugu, "India Rising," May 2007, pp. 101-124.

[16] John Schmitt, "The Good, the Bad, and the Ugly: Job Quality in the United States over the Three Most Recent Business Cycles," Center for Economic and Policy Research, November 2007, www.cepr.net/documents/publications/goodjobscycles.pdf.

[17] Alicia H. Munnell and Steven A. Sass, "The Decline of Career Employment," Center for Retirement Research, Boston College, September 2008, http://crr.bc.edu/images/stories/ib_8-14.pdf.

[18] Richard Florida, "How the Crash Will Reshape America," *The Atlantic*, March 2009, www.theatlantic.com/doc/200903/meltdown-geography.

[19] James Sherk, "A Good Job Is Not So Hard to Find," Heritage Foundation, June 17, 2008 and revised and updated Sept. 2, 2008, www.heritage.org/research/labor/cda08-04.cfm.

[20] George Packer, "The Ponzi State," *The New Yorker*, Feb. 9 and 16, 2009.

[21] Paul Krugman, "Decade at Bernie's," *The New York Times*, Feb. 16, 2009, www.nytimes.com/2009/02/16/opinion/16krugman.html?scp=1&sq=decade%20at%20bernie's&st=cse.

[22] Federal Housing Finance Agency, "U.S. Housing Price Index Estimates 1.8 Percent Price Decline From October to November," Jan. 22, 2009, www.ofheo.gov/media/hpi/MonthlyHPI12209F.pdf.

[23] College Board, "Trends in College Pricing 2008," http://professionals.collegeboard.com/profdownload/trends-in-college-pricing-2008.pdf.

[24] Department of Health and Human Services, Centers for Medicare and Medicaid Services, www.cms.hhs.gov/NationalHealthExpendData/downloads/tables.pdf.

[25] Sara R. Collins, *et al.*, "Losing Ground: How the Loss of Adequate Health Insurance Is Burdening Working Families: Findings from the Commonwealth Fund Biennial Health Insurance Surveys, 2001-2007," Commonwealth Fund, Aug. 20, 2008, www.commonwealthfund.org/Content/Publications/Fund-Reports/2008/Aug/Losing-Ground-How-the-Loss-of-Adequate-Health-Insurance-Is-Burdening-Working-Families-8212-Finding.aspx.

[26] Elizabeth Warren and Amelia Warren Tyagi, *The Two-Income Trap* (2003), p. 19.

[27] *Ibid*, pp. 51-52.

[28] Press release, "'Women on Their Own' in Much Worse Financial Condition Than Other Americans," Consumer Federation of America, Dec. 2, 2008, www.consumerfed.org/pdfs/Women_America_Saves_Tele_PR_12-2-08.pdf.

[29] Ernest Istook, "Land of the free and home of the victims," Heritage Foundation, Feb. 29, 2008, www.heritage.org/Press/Commentary/ed022908b.cfm.

[30] "Remarks by the President to Caterpillar Employees," Feb. 12, 2009, www.whitehouse.gov.

[31] Foon Rhee, "Partisan spat continues on stimulus," Political Intelligence blog, *The Boston Globe*, Feb. 17, 2009, www.boston.com/news/politics/politicalintelligence/2009/02/partisan_spat_c.html.

[32] Fact Sheet, "The Hidden Link: Health Costs and Family Economic Insecurity," Families USA, January 2009, www.familiesusa.org/assets/pdfs/the-hidden-link.pdf. The research cited by Families USA is by Christopher Tarver Robertson, *et al.*, "Get Sick Get Out: The Medical Causes of Home Mortgage Foreclosures," *Health Matrix Vol. 18*, 2008, pp. 65-105.

[33] Reuters, "U.S. may need new retirement savings plans: lawmaker," Feb. 24, 2009, www.reuters.com/article/domesticNews/idUSTRE51N5UM20090224.

[34] Lynn Sweeton, "Transcript of Obama, McCain at Saddleback Civil Forum with Pastor Rick Warren," *Chicago Sun Times*, Aug. 18, 2008, http://blogs.suntimes.com/sweet/2008/08/transcript_of_obama_mccain_at.html.

[35] Quoted in Jeanna Bryner, "American Dream and Middle Class in Jeopardy," www.livescience.com, October 9, 2008, www.livescience.com/culture/081009-middle-class.html.

[36] See Jennifer L. Goloboy, "The Early American Middle Class," *Journal of the Early Republic*, Vol. 25, No. 4, winter 2005.

[37] Quoted in David Kennedy, *Freedom From Fear* (1999), p. 264.

[38] *Ibid*.

[39] For historical background, see *CQ Researcher Plus Archive* for a large body of contemporary coverage during the 1930s and 1940s in *Editorial Research Reports*, the precursor to the *CQ Researcher*.

[40] Paul Krugman, "The Conscience of a Liberal: Introducing This Blog" *The New York Times*, Sept. 18, 2007, http://krugman.blogs.nytimes.com/2007/09/18/introducing-this-blog/.

[41] Paul Krugman, "What Obama Must Do: A Letter to the New President," *Rolling Stone*, Jan. 14, 2009, www.rollingstone.com/politics/story/25456948/what_obama_must_do.

[42] James T. Patterson, *Grand Expectations* (1996), p. 312.

[43] Barry Hirsch, Georgia State University, and David Macpherson, Florida State University, "Union Membership, Coverage, Density, and Employment Among All Wage and Salary Workers, 1973-2008," www.unionstats.com.

[44] "Remarks by the President and the Vice President in Announcement of Labor Executive Orders and Middle-Class Working Families Task Force," Jan. 30, 2009, www.whitehouse.gov/blog_post/Todaysevent/.

[45] U.S. Chamber of Commerce, "Is Unionization the Ticket to the Middle Class? The Real Economic Effects of Labor Unions," 2008, www.uschamber.com/assets/labor/unionrhetoric_econeffects.pdf.

[46] George J. Viksnins, "Reaganomics after Twenty Years," www9.georgetown.edu/faculty/viksning/papers/Reaganomics.html.

[47] Paul Krugman, "Debunking the Reagan Myth," *The New York Times*, Jan. 21, 2008, www.nytimes.com/2008/01/21/opinion/21krugman.html?scp=1&sq=%22Debunking%20the%20Reagan%20Myth%22&st=cse.

About the Author

Thomas J. Billitteri is a *CQ Researcher* staff writer based in Fairfield, Pa., who has more than 30 years' experience covering business, nonprofit institutions and public policy for newspapers and other publications. His recent *CQ Researcher* reports include "Campaign Finance," "Human Rights in China" and "Financial Bailout." He holds a BA in English and an MA in journalism from Indiana University.

[48] Lou Dobbs, *War on the Middle Class* (2006), p. 112.

[49] Transcript, "In Bad Economy, Countries Contemplate Protectionist Measures," "The NewsHour with Jim Lehrer," Feb. 19, 2009, www.pbs.org/newshour/bb/business/jan-june09/trade_02-19.html.

[50] Christian Weller, "The Erosion of Middle-Class Economic Security After 2001," *Challenge*, Vol. 51, No. 1, January/February 2008, pp. 45-68.

[51] Joel Kotkin, "The End of Upward Mobility?" *Newsweek*, Jan. 26, 2009, p. 64.

[52] "Remarks of President Barack Obama, Weekly Address," Feb. 28, 2009, www.whitehouse.gov/blog/09/02/28/Keeping-Promises/.

[53] "Burr delivers GOP challenge to Obama's budget," www.wral.com, Feb. 28, 2009, www.wral.com/news/local/story/4635676/.

[54] Statement before the Committee on the Budget, U.S. Senate, "Expanding Health Insurance Coverage and Controlling Costs for Health Care," Feb. 10, 2009, www.cbo.gov/ftpdocs/99xx/doc9982/02-10-HealthVolumes_Testimony.pdf.

[55] Investment Company Institute, "Retirement Assets Total $15.9 Trillion in Third Quarter," Feb. 19, 2009, www.ici.org/home/09_news_q3_retmrkt_update.html#TopOfPage.

[56] Quoted in Jeff Zeleny, "Obama Announces Task Force to Assist Middle-Class Families," *The New York Times*, Dec. 22, 2008.

[57] Cited at www.whitehouse.gov/blog_post/about_the_task_force_1/.

[58] Mark Trumbull, "Will Obama's plans help the middle class?" *The Christian Science Monitor*, Dec. 24, 2008.

[59] Joe Biden, "Time to put middle class front and center," *USA Today*, Jan. 30, 2009.

[60] Jason DeParle, "Welfare Aid Isn't Growing as Economy Drops Off," *The New York Times*, Feb. 2, 2009.

[61] See Bureau of Labor Statistics, "The Employment Situation: January 2009," www.bls.gov/news.release/empsit.nr0.htm.

[62] Robert E. Scott and Christian Dorsey, "African Americans are especially at risk in the auto crisis," Economic Policy Institute, Snapshot, Dec. 5, 2008, www.epi.org/economic_snapshots/entry/webfeatures_snapshots_20081205/.

[63] Quoted in Larry Copeland, "Auto industry's slide cuts a main route to the middle class," *USA Today*, Jan. 20, 2009, www.usatoday.com/money/autos/2009-01-20-blacks-auto-industry-dealers_N.htm.

[64] D'Vera Cohn, "Pricey Neighbors, High Stress," Pew Social and Demographic Trends, May 29, 2008, www.pewsocialtrends.org/pubs/711/middle-class-blues.

[65] Jonathan Bowles, *et al.*, "Reviving the City of Aspiration: A study of the challenges facing New York City's middle class," Center for an Urban Future, Feb. 2009, www.nycfuture.org/images_pdfs/pdfs/CityOfAspiration.pdf.

[66] Quoted in Daniel Massey, "City faces middle-class exodus," *Crain's New York Business*, Feb. 5, 2009, www.crainsnewyork.com/article/20090205/FREE/902059930.

[67] Krugman spoke at the "Thinking Big, Thinking Forward" conference in Washington on Feb. 11 sponsored by *The American Prospect*, the Institute for America's Future, Dēmos and the Economic Policy Institute.

FOR MORE INFORMATION

Brookings Institution, 1775 Massachusetts Ave., N.W., Washington, DC 20036; (202) 797-6000; www.brookings.edu. Independent research and policy institute conducting research in economics, governance, foreign policy and development.

Center on Budget and Policy Priorities, 820 First St., N.E., Suite 510, Washington, DC 20002; (202) 408-1080; www.cbpp.org. Studies fiscal policies and public programs affecting low- and moderate-income families and individuals.

Center for Economic and Policy Research, 1611 Connecticut Ave., N.W., Suite 400, Washington, DC 20009; (202) 293-5380; www.cepr.net. Works to better inform citizens on the economic and social choices they make.

Center for Retirement Research, Boston College, 140 Commonwealth Ave., Chestnut Hill, MA 02467; (617) 552-1762; www.crr.bc.edu. Researches and provides the public and private sectors with information to better understand the issues facing an aging population.

Center for an Urban Future, 120 Wall St., 20th Floor, New York, NY, 10005; (212) 479-3341; www.nycfuture.org. Dedicated to improving New York City by targeting problems facing low-income and working-class neighborhoods.

Consumer Federation of America, 1620 I St., N.W., Suite 200, Washington, DC 20006; (202) 387-6121; www.consumerfed.org. Advocacy and research organization promoting pro-consumer policies before Congress and other levels of government.

Dēmos, 220 Fifth Ave., 5th Floor, New York, NY 10001; (212) 633-1405; www.demos.org. Liberal think tank pursuing an equitable economy with shared prosperity and opportunity.

Heritage Foundation, 214 Massachusetts Ave., N.E., Washington, DC 20002; (202) 546-4400; www.heritage.org. Formulates and promotes public policies based on a conservative agenda.

Middle Class Task Force, 1600 Pennsylvania Ave., N.W., Washington, DC 20500; (202) 456-1414; www.whitehouse.gov/strongmiddleclass. Presidential task force headed by Vice President Joseph R. Biden working to raise the living standards of middle-class families.

Pew Research Center, 1615 L St., N.W., Suite 700, Washington, DC 20036; (202) 419-4300; www.pewresearch.org. Provides nonpartisan research and information on issues, attitudes and trends shaping the United States.

U.S. Chamber of Commerce, 1615 H St., N.W., Washington, DC 20062; (202) 659-6000; www.uschamber.com. Business federation lobbying for free enterprise before all branches of government.

Bibliography

Selected Sources

Books

Dobbs, Lou, *War on the Middle Class*, Viking, 2006.

The CNN broadcaster argues that the American government and economy are dominated by a wealthy and politically powerful elite who have exploited working Americans.

Frank, Robert H., *Falling Behind: How Rising Inequality Harms the Middle Class*, University of California Press, 2007.

The Cornell University economist argues that most income gains in recent decades have gone to people at the top, leading them to build bigger houses, which in turn has led middle-income families to spend a bigger share of their incomes on housing and curtail spending in other important areas.

Hacker, Jacob S., *The Great Risk Shift*, Oxford University Press, 2006.

A professor of political science argues that economic risk has shifted from "broad structures of insurance," including those sponsored by corporations and government, "onto the fragile balance sheets of American families."

Uchitelle, Louis, *The Disposable American*, Alfred A. Knopf, 2006.

A *New York Times* business journalist, writing before the current economic crises threw millions of workers out of their jobs, calls the layoff trend "a festering national crisis."

Articles

Copeland, Larry, "Auto industry's slide cuts a main route to the middle class," *USA Today*, Jan. 20, 2009, www.usatoday.com/money/autos/2009-01-20-blacks-auto-industry-dealers_N.htm?loc=interstitialskip.

The financial crisis in the auto industry "has been more devastating for African-Americans than any other community," Copeland writes.

Gallagher, John, "Slipping standard of living squeezes middle class," *Detroit Free Press*, Oct. 12, 2008, www.freep.com/article/20081012/BUSINESS07/810120483.

America's middle-class living standard "carried generations from dirt-floor cabins to manicured suburban subdivisions," Gallagher writes, but it "has sputtered and stalled."

Kotkin, Joel, "The End of Upward Mobility?" *Newsweek*, Jan. 26, 2009, www.newsweek.com/id/180041.

A presidential fellow at Chapman University writes that class, not race, "will likely constitute the major dividing line in our society."

Samuelson, Robert J., "A Darker Future For Us," *Newsweek*, Nov. 10, 2008, www.newsweek.com/id/166821/output/print.

An economic journalist argues that the central question confronting the new administration is whether the economy is at an historic inflection point, "when its past behavior is no longer a reliable guide to its future."

Weller, Christian, "The Erosion of Middle-Class Economic Security After 2001," *Challenge*, Vol. 51, No. 1, January/February 2008, pp. 45-68.

An associate professor of public policy at the University of Massachusetts, Boston, and senior fellow at the liberal Center for American Progress concludes that the gains in middle-class security of the late 1990s have been entirely eroded.

Reports and Studies

Bowles, Jonathan, Joel Kotkin and David Giles, "Reviving the City of Aspiration: A study of the challenges facing New York City's middle class," Center for an Urban Future, February 2009, www.nycfuture.org/images_pdfs/pdfs/CityOfAspiration.pdf.

Major changes to the nation's largest city have greatly diminished its ability to both create and retain a sizeable middle class, argues this report.

Schmitt, John, "The Good, the Bad, and the Ugly: Job Quality in the United States over the Three Most Recent Business Cycles," Center for Economic and Policy Research, November 2007, www.cepr.net/documents/publications/goodjobscycles.pdf.

The share of "good jobs," defined as ones paying at least $17 an hour and offering employer-provided medical insurance and a pension, deteriorated in the 2000-2006 business cycle.

Sherk, James, "A Good Job Is Not So Hard to Find," Heritage Foundation, June 17, 2008, www.heritage.org/research/labor/cda08-04.cfm.

Job opportunities have expanded the most in occupations with the highest wages, the conservative think tank states.

Taylor, Paul, *et al.*, "Inside the Middle Class: Bad Times Hit the Good Life," Pew Research Center, April 2008, http://pewsocialtrends.org/assets/pdf/MC-Middle-class-report.pdf.

The report aims to present a "comprehensive portrait of the middle class" based on a national opinion survey and demographic and economic data.

Wheary, Jennifer, Thomas M. Shapiro and Tamara Draut, "By A Thread: The New Experience of America's Middle Class," Dēmos and the Institute on Assets and Social Policy at Brandeis University, 2007, www.demos.org/pubs/BaT112807.pdf.

The report includes a "Middle Class Security Index" that portrays how well middle-class families are faring in the categories of financial assets, education, income and health care.

The Next Step:

Additional Articles from Current Periodicals

Consumer Behavior

Albright, Mark, "For Buyers, Restraint Replaces Indulgence," *St. Petersburg Times*, Sept. 30, 2008, p. 4B.

Consumer attitudes toward spending have been changing since 2005 largely due to tighter credit markets and higher product prices.

Leonhardt, David, "Buying Binge Slams to Halt," *The New York Times*, Nov. 12, 2008, p. A1.

Consumer spending appears likely to fall in 2009 for the first time since 1980, and by the largest amount since 1942.

Simon, Ellen, "Meltdown 101: Should Consumers Drive the Economy?" The Associated Press, Nov. 28, 2008.

Consumer spending comprises 70 percent of the total U.S. economy, making conditions difficult when consumers refuse to spend.

Spriggs, William E., " 'Our Economy Is Drowning in Debt,'" *The Miami Herald*, Oct. 31, 2008, p. A19.

Consumers who have bought beyond their means are largely to blame for the nation's economic crisis.

Government Programs

Blumner, Robyn, "Bail Out America? Employ Americans," *St. Petersburg Times*, Dec. 14, 2008, p. 5P.

Middle-class job protection should be incorporated into all of the massive bailouts that taxpayers are funding.

Buffenbarger, R. Thomas, "U.S. Jobs Worth Fighting For," *Chicago Tribune*, Feb. 8, 2009, p. A31.

Manufacturing jobs — which are key to a middle-class life for millions of Americans — must be protected and created under any stimulus package.

Rucker, Philip, "Obama Tax Cuts Likely Soon," *The Washington Post*, Dec. 29, 2008, p. A4.

Obama's economic stimulus plan includes immediate tax cuts for middle-class families, with the hope of enacting permanent tax cuts soon thereafter.

Middle Class Task Force

Kornblut, Anne E., and Anthony Faiola, "Biden to Lead Task Force on Issues of the Middle Class," *The Washington Post*, Jan. 31, 2009, p. A3.

Vice President Joe Biden will be leading a presidential task force working to raise the living standards of middle-class, working families in the country.

Stout, David, "With a Swipe at Bush, Obama Acts to Bolster Labor," *The New York Times*, Jan. 31, 2009, p. A14.

The Obama administration's Middle Class Task Force seeks to reverse many of the policies toward organized labor enacted during George W. Bush's years in office.

Von Bergen, Jane M., "Biden to Promote Green Jobs in Philadelphia," *The Philadelphia Inquirer*, Feb. 26, 2009, p. C1.

Increasing green jobs is a top priority for Vice President Joe Biden and the administration's Middle Class Task Force.

Retirement Plans

"Fidelity Sees Rise in 401(k) Deposits," *The Wall Street Journal*, Jan. 29, 2009, p. C6.

Fidelity Investments says contributions to its 401(k) plans increased in 2008, but that balances fell an average of 27 percent largely due to hardship withdrawals.

Aguilera, Elizabeth, "No More Retirement," *Denver Post*, Feb. 11, 2009, p. B7.

Battered retirement accounts are causing many senior citizens to forgo retirement and re-enter the work force.

Boselovic, Len, "401(k) Matches Surviving Downturn," *Pittsburgh Post-Gazette*, Jan. 7, 2009.

Matching 401(k) contributions have not been a major casualty as Western Pennsylvania companies cut costs amid a recession.

Mui, Ylan Q., "Senate Weighing New Rules for Retirement Funds," *The Washington Post*, Feb. 22, 2009, p. F1.

Target-date retirement funds are coming under increased scrutiny as investors try to contain losses from the current economic downturn.

CITING CQ RESEARCHER

Sample formats for citing these reports in a bibliography include the ones listed below. Preferred styles and formats vary, so please check with your instructor or professor.

<u>MLA STYLE</u>

Jost, Kenneth. "Rethinking the Death Penalty." <u>CQ Researcher</u> 16 Nov. 2001: 945-68.

<u>APA STYLE</u>

Jost, K. (2001, November 16). Rethinking the death penalty. *CQ Researcher, 11*, 945-968.

<u>CHICAGO STYLE</u>

Jost, Kenneth. "Rethinking the Death Penalty." *CQ Researcher*, November 16, 2001, 945-968.

In-depth Reports on Issues in the News

Are you writing a paper?

Need backup for a debate?

Want to become an expert on an issue?

For 80 years, students have turned to *CQ Researcher* for in-depth reporting on issues in the news. Reports on a full range of political and social issues are now available. Following is a selection of recent reports:

Civil Liberties
Limiting Lawsuits, 12/08
Affirmative Action, 10/08
Gay Marriage Showdowns, 9/08
America's Border Fence, 9/08
Immigration Debate, 2/08
Prison Reform, 4/07

Crime/Law
Mexico's Drug War, 12/08
Prostitution Debate, 5/08
Public Defenders, 4/08
Gun Violence, 5/07

Education
Reading Crisis? 2/08
Discipline in Schools, 2/08
Student Aid, 1/08
Racial Diversity in Public Schools, 9/07
Stress on Students, 7/07

Environment
Reducing Carbon Footprint, 12/08
Protecting Wetlands, 10/08
Buying Green, 2/08
Future of Recycling, 12/07

Health/Safety
Preventing Cancer, 1/09
Heart Health, 9/08
Global Food Crisis, 6/08
Preventing Memory Loss, 4/08

International Affairs/Politics
The Obama Presidency, 1/09
The National Debt, 11/08
Financial Bailout, 10/08
Political Conventions, 8/08
Race and Politics, 7/08

Social Trends
Public-Works Projects, 2/09
Falling Birthrates, 11/08
Regulating Credit Cards, 10/08
Internet Accuracy, 8/08

Terrorism/Defense
Homeland Security, 2/09
Rise in Counterinsurgency, 9/08
Cost of the Iraq War, 4/08

Youth
Debating Hip-Hop, 6/07

Upcoming Reports

Vanishing Jobs, 3/13/09
GOP's Future, 3/20/09

Extreme Sports, 3/27/09
Bankruptcy, 4/3/09

Wrongful Convictions, 4/10/09

ACCESS

CQ Researcher is available in print and online. For access, visit your library or www.cqresearcher.com.

STAY CURRENT

To receive notice of upcoming *CQ Researcher* reports, or learn more about *CQ Researcher* products, subscribe to the free e-mail newsletters, *CQ Researcher Alert!* and *CQ Researcher News*: http://cqpress.com/newsletters.

PURCHASE

To purchase a *CQ Researcher* report in print or electronic format (PDF), visit www.cqpress.com or call 866-427-7737. Single reports start at $15. Bulk purchase discounts and electronic-rights licensing are also available.

SUBSCRIBE

Annual full-service *CQ Researcher* subscriptions—including 44 reports a year, monthly index updates, and a bound volume—start at $803. Add $25 for domestic postage.

CQ Researcher Online offers a backfile from 1991 and a number of tools to simplify research. For pricing information, call 800-834-9020, ext. 1906, or e-mail librarysales@cqpress.com.

CQ Researcher

Published by CQ Press, a division of SAGE Publications

www.cqresearcher.com

Vanishing Jobs

Will the president's plan reduce unemployment?

T he news is grim and getting grimmer. The jobless rate recently hit 8.1 percent — the highest level in a quarter-century. American workers lost 651,000 jobs in February alone. All told, more than 12.5 million Americans are jobless — including 2.9 million who have been unemployed for at least 27 weeks. The nation is banking on the Obama administration's newly enacted, $787 billion "economic stimulus" bill to spark job growth through government spending on infrastructure projects and other programs. Conservatives argue that the spending won't help, and some liberals say the magnitude of the crisis calls for still more stimulus money. The huge spending measure also includes funds to encourage states to expand eligibility for unemployment insurance, though some governors are resisting on the grounds that their states will wind up footing future bills. With no quick turnaround predicted, creating or saving jobs will remain the top priority for President Barack Obama and the millions of citizens counting on his administration's rescue plan.

Laid-off Yahoo! employees remove their personal belongings from the Sunnyvale, Calif., offices on Dec. 10, 2008. The firm's 1,500 job cuts are among 4.4 million layoffs that have occurred so far in the current recession.

CQ Researcher • March 13, 2009 • www.cqresearcher.com
Volume 19, Number 10 • Pages 225-248

Cover: AP Photo/Paul Sakuma

CQ Researcher

March 13, 2009
Volume 19, Number 10

MANAGING EDITOR: Thomas J. Colin
tcolin@cqpress.com

ASSISTANT MANAGING EDITOR: Kathy Koch
kkoch@cqpress.com

ASSOCIATE EDITOR: Kenneth Jost

STAFF WRITERS: Thomas J. Billitteri, Marcia Clemmitt, Peter Katel

CONTRIBUTING WRITERS: Rachel Cox, Sarah Glazer, Alan Greenblatt, Barbara Mantel, Patrick Marshall, Tom Price, Jennifer Weeks

DESIGN/PRODUCTION EDITOR: Olu B. Davis

ASSISTANT EDITOR: Darrell Dela Rosa

FACT-CHECKING: Eugene J. Gabler, Michelle Harris

EDITORIAL INTERN: Vyomika Jairam

CQ PRESS

A Division of SAGE Publications

PRESIDENT AND PUBLISHER:
John A. Jenkins

**EXECUTIVE DIRECTOR,
REFERENCE INFORMATION GROUP:**
Alix B. Vance

CQ Press is a registered trademark of Congressional Quarterly Inc.

CQ Researcher (ISSN 1056-2036) is printed on acid-free paper. Published weekly, except; (Jan. wk. 1) (May wk. 4) (July wks. 1, 2) (Aug. wks. 3, 4) (Nov. wk. 4) and (Dec. wk. 4), by CQ Press, a division of SAGE Publications. Annual full-service subscriptions start at $803. For pricing, call 1-800-834-9020, ext. 1906. To purchase a CQ Researcher report in print or electronic format (PDF), visit www. cqpress.com or call 866-427-7737. Single reports start at $15. Bulk purchase discounts and electronic-rights licensing are also available. Periodicals postage paid at Washington, D.C., and additional mailing offices. POSTMASTER: Send address changes to CQ Researcher, 2300 N St., N.W., Suite 800, Washington, DC 20037.

Vanishing Jobs

BY PETER KATEL

THE ISSUES

A layoff last year knocked Duane Simmons' life off its foundation. "I don't hold it against nobody," the 62-year-old machinist says, without apparent bitterness, "because the same thing is happening everywhere."

Indeed, in February alone, a record 651,000 Americans lost their jobs, pushing the unemployment rate to 8.1 percent — the highest in 25 years — and the number of unemployed workers to 12.5 million. A whopping 4.4 million jobs have been lost just since the December 2007 start of The Great Recession — as *The New York Times* calls the current economic crisis. [1]

Simmons' troubles began when Kennametal, a global metalworking, mining and tool company, bought Manchester Tool Co. of New Franklin, Ohio, where Simmons had labored for 33 years — virtually his entire working life. Kennametal quickly closed the plant where Simmons worked.

He moved his family to Newton, N.C., but his hopes for a new job have failed to materialize. Back home in Ohio, Simmons' $900-a-month home mortgage proved too heavy a burden, and soon the house was in foreclosure. The pressure of other debts forced Simmons and his wife into bankruptcy. And once his 26 weeks of unemployment insurance were exhausted, the couple began dipping into savings to pay rent and other expenses, with a little help from their son.

As the financial crisis last year expanded into all sectors of the economy, jobs and joblessness became the No. 1

The line of job-seekers stretches around the block and back again at a Feb. 11 federal jobs fair in Atlanta. As the nation's financial/housing crisis has expanded into all economic sectors, employment has become the No. 1 issue for millions of Americans. President Barack Obama says the economic stimulus package Congress passed in February will "create or save" 3.6 million jobs, but skeptics doubt it will work.

AP Photo/*Atlanta Journal-Constitution*/Rich Addicks

issue for millions of Americans. A poll conducted for The Associated Press in mid-February showed that 47 percent of respondents were worried about losing their jobs, and 65 percent knew someone who had been laid off. [2]

The pace and scale of layoffs accelerated in early 2009, with Jan. 27 an especially bleak day: Companies announcing big layoffs that day included Home Depot (7,000), Caterpillar (20,000), Texas Instruments (1,800) and Sprint Nextel (8,000). All in all, the first month of the year saw 598,000 jobs evaporate. [3] Then in February General Motors eliminated 10,000 more jobs, even though struggling carmakers had already cut their workforce in 2006-2008 by

80,000, using buyouts and early retirements. [4]

Each layoff announcement accelerates the economic decline that President Barack Obama and his team of economic advisers is struggling to reverse. "Without jobs, people can't earn," he said in mid-February at the signing ceremony in Denver for the $787 billion American Recovery and Reinvestment Act — the so-called economic stimulus bill — designed to "create or save" 3.6 million jobs. "And when people can't earn, they can't spend. And if they don't spend, it means more jobs get lost. It's a vicious cycle." [5]

Critics — even some liberals — say more needs to be done. "The Obama administration is . . . trying to mitigate the slump, not end it," wrote Princeton University economist Paul Krugman, winner of the 2008 Nobel Prize in economics and an influential *New York Times* columnist. "The stimulus bill, on the administration's own estimates, will limit the rise in unemployment but fall far short of restoring full employment." [6]

But White House Chief of Staff Rahm Emanuel dismissed the idea that a bill sized to Krugman's satisfaction could have gotten through Congress. "How many bills has he passed?" Emanuel carped in *The New Yorker*. [7]

In fact, despite Obama's call for bipartisanship, every single Republican in Congress — save for three senators — voted against the stimulus legislation, which includes billions of dollars to finance public-works spending. Many GOP leaders are denouncing the sweeping measure on the grounds that increased government spending alone won't end the job losses.

Michigan Had Highest Unemployment Rate

Michigan had the nation's highest unemployment rate — 11.6 percent — in January, largely due to the faltering auto industry. The South was among the hardest-hit regions, with many states at or above the nation's 7.6 percent jobless rate in January.

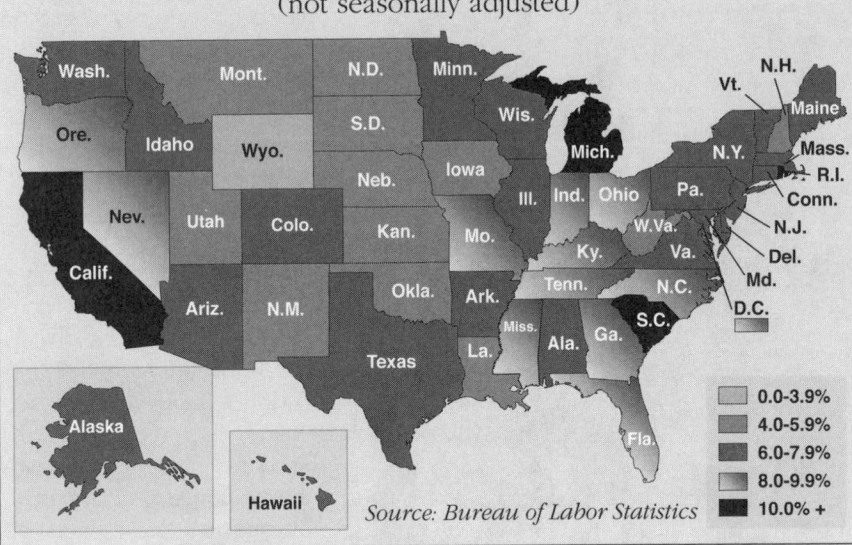

Unemployment Rate by State, January 2009
(not seasonally adjusted)

0.0-3.9%
4.0-5.9%
6.0-7.9%
8.0-9.9%
10.0% +

Source: Bureau of Labor Statistics

"It's filled with social policy and costs too much," said Mississippi Gov. Haley Barbour. "You could create just as many jobs for about half as much money." [8]

But other Republican governors, especially those in hard-hit states, backed the president. "I think he's on the right track," said Gov. Charlie Crist of Florida, which lost more than a quarter-million jobs last year. [9]

Nationally, layoffs are eliminating jobs far beyond blue-collar workers like Simmons in the ever-shrinking manufacturing sector. The financial-services industry is shedding so many workers that in New York City — the nation's financial capital — Mayor Michael Bloomberg has announced a $45 billion retraining program for pink-slipped investment bankers. [10]

"I have competitors closing up shop and going to live with their parents," says a financial software specialist in the New York area whose own contracts with banks and hedge funds have vaporized.

Newspapers and magazines, already reeling because millions of readers are going to the Web for free news, are laying off thousands of reporters and editors as advertising, the lifeblood of the news business, slows to a trickle. Newspapers have cut more than 3,000 jobs already this year, after slashing more than 15,000 in 2008, according to "Paper Cuts," a layoff monitor. [11]

"I'd like to stay in journalism," says journalist William Triplett, who recently lost his job as Washington correspondent for *Variety*, the entertainment-news daily. "But I don't know if I can make a sustainable living at it."

Major law firms have laid off 6,598 lawyers and staff members since Jan. 1, 2008 — more than half of them since the beginning of this year. [12]

Health care is one of the only sectors of the economy adding jobs, according to the U.S. Bureau of Labor Statistics: It showed a 30 percent in-

crease in employment between February 2008 and February 2009. [13]

With few exceptions, the impact of the stimulus legislation has yet to be felt. In early March, state officials and politicians across the country were still drawing up lists of projects they planned to start with the new funds.

Meanwhile, Americans who have been laid off or who fear layoffs have cut back on shopping — forcing more layoffs in retail and manufacturing. Consumer spending fell 4 percent in the second half of 2008 after rising steadily for more than 20 years, the Commerce Department reported in March, and savings rose to 5 percent of disposable income in January — a 14-year high. [14]

"People who lose their jobs are going to be spending less," says Heidi Shierholz, a labor economist at the Economic Policy Institute, a liberal think tank. "For people hanging onto jobs in this climate, there is enormous economic insecurity. If you have the opportunity to build yourself a little cushion, putting off big-ticket purchases, now is the time you're going to do it — which further pushes out the recovery, until we get people feeling confident again."

But economists say the vicious cycle of layoffs, reduced spending and business retrenchment or outright failure won't wind down for some time. The Federal Reserve's influential Open Market Committee, which sets interest rates, concluded in late January that unemployment will "remain substantially above its longer-run sustainable rate at the end of 2011, even absent further economic shocks." [15]

As the economic meltdown continues — worldwide as well as within the United States — references to the Great Depression of the 1930s are increasing. In late February, Mark Zandi, chief economist of Moody's Economy.com, told *The New York Times* it was becoming more likely that the recession could turn into a "mild depression." [16]

His "mild" qualifier is rooted in historical reality. Americans haven't reached anywhere near an early-1930s level of misery. By 1932, the year Franklin D. Roosevelt was elected president, the unemployed "lived in the primitive conditions of a preindustrial society stricken by famine," a leading historian of the era wrote. [17]

In fact, conservatives cite statistics showing that today's 8.1 percent unemployment rate has not even reached the level of the 1981-1982 recession, when the jobless rate reached 10.1 percent. [18] "We've had worse recessions," says James Sherk, a labor policy fellow at the Heritage Foundation. "This is not the most painful, so far."

But Heather Boushey — a senior economist at the liberal Center for American Progress, which has close ties to the Obama administration — points out that there are 5 million more people unemployed compared to a year ago. "This is the largest annual jump in the number of unemployed since the U.S. Bureau of Labor Statistics began tabulating this data just after World War II," she writes. [19]

Roosevelt's New Deal — a set of programs designed to stimulate the economy, create publicly financed jobs and regulate business and financial practices — dented unemployment but hardly ended it. By 1940, the year before the United States entered World War II, 14.6 percent of workers were unemployed — well below 1933's catastrophic level of 25 percent but above the annual rates since then. [20]

Economists and historians are still arguing about the New Deal's effectiveness in countering the Depression. (*See "Background," p. 234.*) But not in dispute is the social safety net created by the Roosevelt administration, including unemployment insurance (UI).

In 2008, laid-off workers received more than $43 billion in UI payments, including $34 million in "extended benefits" designed to counteract the effects of unusually high unemployment. [21] But only 37 percent of laid-off

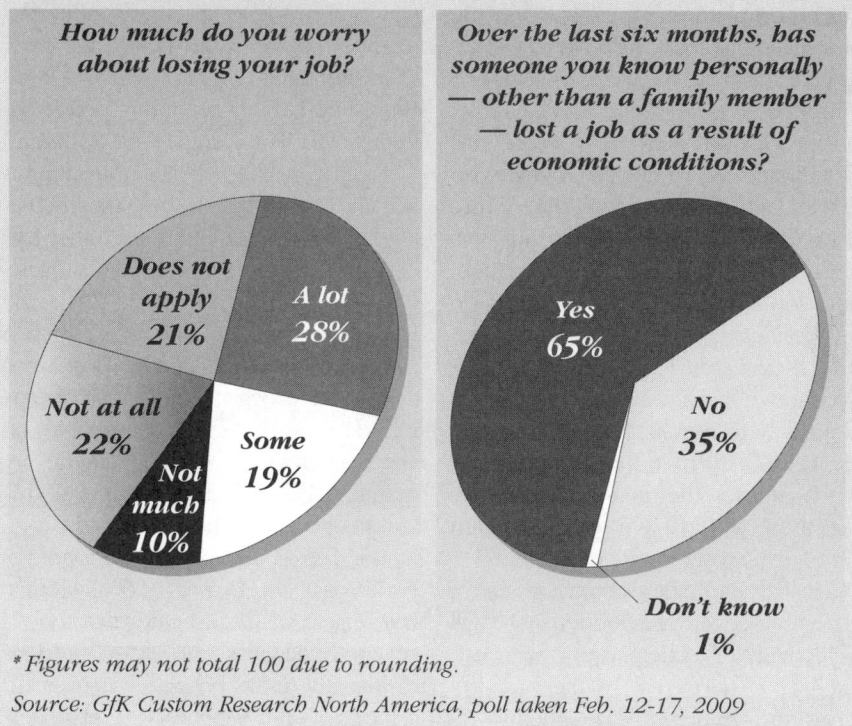

Almost Half of Americans Worry About Job Loss

Forty-seven percent of Americans currently have some concern over losing their job due to economic conditions. Nearly one-third say they worry a lot. Sixty-five percent say they know somebody — other than a family member — who has lost a job due to the recession.

How much do you worry about losing your job?

- Does not apply 21%
- A lot 28%
- Not at all 22%
- Not much 10%
- Some 19%

Over the last six months, has someone you know personally — other than a family member — lost a job as a result of economic conditions?

- Yes 65%
- No 35%
- Don't know 1%

* Figures may not total 100 due to rounding.

Source: GfK Custom Research North America, poll taken Feb. 12-17, 2009

workers receive benefits, in part because some states exclude part-time and temporary workers. [22] And some Republican Southern governors — including Bobby Jindal of Louisiana — say they'll refuse stimulus money tied to expanding UI eligibility, which they claim will unfairly burden states in later years. (*See "Current Situation," p. 240.*)

Even some former full-time workers are excluded from extra benefits. In his new home state of North Carolina, machinist Simmons says he couldn't get coverage past the standard 26 weeks because he had started withdrawing money from his 401(k) retirement fund. "I found afterward that I can't get unemployment and the 401(k) at once," he says. "It's my fault."

Will the economic stimulus bill create or save 3.6 million jobs, as promised?

Reversing the worsening unemployment trend is among the Obama administration's top goals — and biggest challenges — and the president's careful language shows his keen awareness of the strength of the current he's trying to reverse.

"We passed the most sweeping economic recovery package in history, to create or save 3.5 million new jobs," Obama told a "fiscal responsibility summit" at the White House on Feb. 23, apparently a slip of the tongue, since the earlier-stated goal has been 3.6 million jobs. [23]

The oft-used "create or save" phrase makes clear that the president is not promising to create 3.6 million new jobs.

But if companies start hiring again in big enough numbers to move the jobless rate in a healthy direction, Obama will be able to take credit for saving jobs, even if the unemployment rate doesn't reach an ideal level. "We've already lost 3.6 million jobs," says economist Boushey at the Center for American Progress. "So saving or creating that many jobs would just get us back to where we were. It seems like a reasonable goal."

But Harvard University economist and blogger N. Gregory Mankiw, who served as chairman of the White House Council of Economic Advisers under President George W. Bush, ridiculed Obama's careful expression as "political genius." "You can measure how many jobs are created between two points in time. But there is no way to measure how many jobs are saved. Even if things get much, much worse, the president can say that there would have been 4 million fewer jobs without the stimulus." [24]

However adroitly Obama finesses his goal, the deeper question remains: Will his economic rescue package turn back the tide of job cuts? In the broadest terms, the "stimulus" is designed to revive the economy by pumping federal dollars into public-works projects, funding "green" energy projects such as manufacturing and installing solar panels, repairing the transportation infrastructure and extending broadband Internet access to rural areas. [25]

Also included are $400 tax credits for those earning less than $75,000 a year — calculated to put an extra $8 in the weekly paychecks of people still working. A household living on one minimum-wage salary would get additional tax credits amounting to $1,200 for a family of four. "Cutting taxes for working families helps to create jobs because these families are the most likely to spend the money," the White House said. [26]

Obama's approach reflects criticism of the effectiveness of a 2008 Bush administration $600 cash rebate to taxpayers earning less than $75,000. Recipients tended to save the money rather than spend it on goods and services.

The Economic Policy Institute's Shierholz, calls the Obama plan well-conceived. "There is no way you can spend $800 billion in a well-targeted way and not have it make a huge difference. This is a big help," she says. (The institute's former director, Jared Bernstein, is now economic policy adviser to Vice President Joseph R. Biden.)

Shierholz acknowledges the stimulus will take a long time to help most working families. In fact, like some other left-of-center policy experts, she suggests Obama is aiming too low. While the goal of creating or saving 3.6 million jobs may equal the number lost since the recession began, she says, it doesn't include jobs for the 127,000 people, on average, who enter the job market every month. "The working-age population is always growing," she points out.

But Lee E. Ohanian, an economics professor at the University of California, Los Angeles (UCLA), argues that the recovery package is unlikely to produce meaningful results because it isn't aimed at the banks' unwillingness to lend money. "The key impediments to recovery lie in the financial system," he says. Nothing in the recovery bill makes banks more likely to lend money, he argues.

Moreover, he says, the largely unspent Bush tax rebates bode ill for the Obama tax cuts. "It's not a bad idea to put money back into people's hands," he says, "but advertising it as a way of increasing consumer spending flies in the face of the evidence."

But some in grass-roots America say the Obama plan meets the common-sense test. In Atlanta, activist Cindia Cameron cited plans by her city's mayor to spend public-works money on projects at Atlanta's Hartsfield-Jackson International Airport and other infrastructure and to hire 200 police officers. "I am expecting that to happen," said Cameron. "People will be doing work that I'll be able to see." [27]

Cameron, national organizing director of 9to5, which campaigns for better conditions for low-wage female workers, said she's hearing some optimism — though tempered — from job-seekers. "People we know who are looking for jobs are looking for light on the horizon and are counting on the fact that this money will be coming through. There's now four applicants for every job, maybe soon there'll be only three."

Still, skeptical economists cite the magnitude of the crisis and the fact that hiring usually doesn't pick up until the end of a recovery. "All the evidence we have is that the economy is going down," says Rebecca M. Blank, a specialist in poverty and unemployment at the Brookings Institution. "The stimulus plan may pause things for a while. But the economy is rocky enough that I wouldn't want to say with any degree of certainty that we'll see job growth soon."

Is retraining for new skills the best option for laid-off workers?

The new recovery act includes nearly $4 billion for job training, including retraining "dislocated" workers who need new skills demanded in the modern workplace. In funding that program, Congress and the administration are relying on a strategy politicians often turn to in hard times.

In 1962, the John F. Kennedy administration had Congress enact a $435 million retraining program for workers whose jobs were endangered by a wave of imports flooding the country due to lower tariffs. But Arnold R. Weber, a University of Chicago economist who studied the programs, found that retraining was more complicated than politicians made it sound.

Writing in the wake of a recession that had cost 900,000 jobs, Weber warned: "Retraining programs are not likely to increase the total number of job opportunities in the economy. Large-scale, persistent unemployment ultimately can only be dissipated by maintaining the appropriate levels of aggregate demand and production." In fact, he concluded, "training activities are most effective in an economic climate of full employment." [28]

But Weber also acknowledged that on an individual level, retraining could indeed help workers upgrade their skills to become more employable. Over the decades that followed, the technological changes that rolled through the American workplace made the idea of retraining appealing to politicians and workers.

Industrial employees, especially, are keenly aware of the effects of technological modernization. "I didn't go on machines with computer-operated controls," says Mitchell Rice, 62, a former coworker of Duane Simmons at Manchester Tool Co. "I thought it was better for younger people to get on those machines; I didn't have much time left to work."

Essentially, Rice skipped his chance at retraining. He hadn't figured on being laid off at age 61, while still capable of working and still dependent on his pay and benefits.

Retraining advocates do not claim that new skills will benefit every laid-off worker or that employees nearing retirement age are all good retraining prospects. But retraining offers possibilities for those with the aptitude to re-learn jobs currently in high demand, or likely to be.

"The average age of apprentices in this country has risen to the late 20s," says Robert I. Lerman, an economics professor at American University in Washington who specializes in apprenticeship and other skill-building programs. "Even somebody in their 40s, if they want to get into 'green' jobs, can take a carpentry apprenticeship."

That approach can let apprentices learn a wide variety of skills, Lerman says. For example, someone who apprenticed on retrofitting homes with energy-saving insulation can also work on commercial buildings.

The realization that learning new skills isn't a panacea makes skeptics

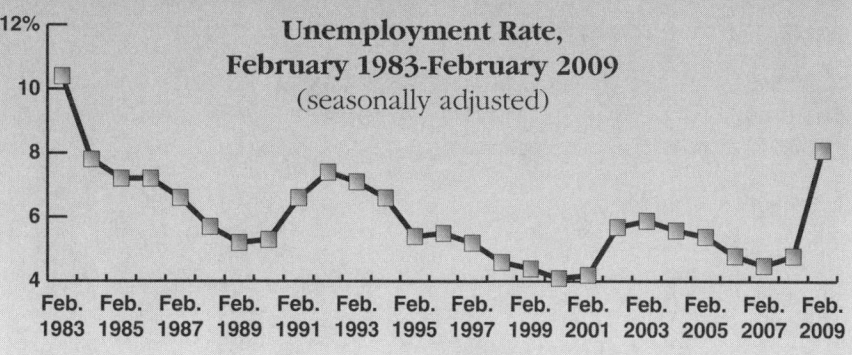

Jobless Rate Hits 25-Year Record

The unemployment rate surpassed 8 percent in February 2009 — the highest level since February 1983, when it hit 10.4 percent. More than 12 million Americans were unemployed in February, according to the Bureau of Labor Statistics.

Unemployment Rate, February 1983-February 2009
(seasonally adjusted)

Source: Bureau of Labor Statistics, March 6, 2009

view retraining as merely an individual option. Some note that an unemployed person might as well learn new skills, because he or she has more to gain than to lose by doing so.

"Outside of the health sector, there isn't a sector that isn't shrinking right now," says Blank of Brookings. "The only reason to think about retraining . . . is to think in the long run. The opportunity cost to do some additional skills-building is very low."

But for many people, the practical obstacles may be too great, she adds. For example, "Very few people who are unemployed can afford to pay college tuition," she says.

Boushey of the Center for American Progress says the recovery act, with its green-jobs emphasis, will allow entire communities to push for retraining that would provide a big enough labor pool to attract new employers. In rust-belt areas where housing prices fell even before they did elsewhere, she says, "Many people can't afford to move, so they need jobs to come to them. This is one of the least-discussed, most challenging problems in the labor market right now."

In effect, retraining gives communities a chance to bet on what new industry will come into their region.

The notion of retraining as a purely individual possibility "doesn't do a lot for a person living in a community where a GM plant just shut down and they can't sell their home," she says. "You need solutions that recognize this is a community problem."

But the University of California's Ohanian says trying to predict what industries will take off, and where, is a huge challenge. Instead, he advocates tax credits and other incentives for individuals wanting to retrain. "In the last 25 years we've seen a world of haves and have-nots develop," he says. "Receiving an education above and beyond high school is essential to succeeding in today's economy."

As to what skills laid-off workers should try to acquire or expand, Ohanian says he would leave it up to the individuals. "We know that people, for the most part, make pretty good decisions in terms of the educational opportunities they want to pursue."

Should unemployment insurance be extended beyond what the recovery act allows?

Unemployment insurance, which strings a safety net under some laid-off Americans, was created in 1935 as

Layoffs Accelerated in 2008

In the fourth quarter of 2008, more than half a million workers lost their jobs in "mass" layoffs — involving at least 50 people at one company — nearly 75 percent more than in the same period in 2007. In 2008 overall, nearly 1.4 million people lost their jobs in mass layoffs.

Jobs Lost in Mass Layoffs, 2007 and 2008

(No. of workers)

Fourth Quarter Layoffs*

- Oct.-Dec. 2007: 301,592
- Oct.-Dec. 2008: 508,859

Total Layoffs*

- 2007: 965,935
- 2008: 1,383,553

* Lasting at least 31 days

Source: "Extended Mass Layoffs in the Fourth Quarter of 2008 and Annual Totals for 2008," Bureau of Labor Statistics, February 2009

part of the Roosevelt administration's New Deal. The economic stimulus bill signed by Obama on Feb. 17 authorizes state governments to extend the time limits and eligibility standards for UI payments, which are limited in some states. UI standards are set by state governments, which pay the full cost of the basic program, financed primarily through taxes on employers.

The basic UI program provides 26 weeks of payments to those who lose their jobs through no fault of their own. Payments — calculated at 50 percent of an individual worker's past salary — average $293 a week, or about 35 percent of the average nationwide weekly wage. [29]

The federal government imposes its own employer UI tax, which funds some unemployment extensions enacted during recessions. For instance, in 1970, Congress authorized states to extend UI benefits an additional 13

weeks when unemployment is high — such as now. Last year, Congress added 20 more weeks, plus an extra 13 weeks for states with exceptionally high unemployment. [30]

The stimulus bill expands the program yet again, by shifting the entire cost of the 2009-2010 "extended benefits" program to the federal government and by covering more unemployed workers. It also adds $25 to each unemployment check in 2009-2010. [31]

Because states' eligibility standards and payments vary widely, the number of laid-off workers receiving the benefit — and how much they get — differs enormously from state to state. For example, 69 percent of jobless workers in Idaho in June, 2008, were receiving unemployment insurance but only 18 percent in South Dakota. [32]

The Government Accountability Office (GAO) reported in 2007 that low-wage and part-time workers are more

than twice as likely to lose their jobs, but only half as likely to receive unemployment benefits. In 1995-2003 (the most recent year for which full data is available), the GAO found that 55 percent of higher-wage workers who lost their jobs collected UI, compared to only 30 percent of low-wage workers employed the same length of time. [33]

The GAO hypothesized that the discrepancy in UI participation was due to declining union strength (because union members are well-informed about benefits) and the migration of manufacturing to states with stricter UI eligibility.

Given the current economic climate, demands for further UI extensions are certain to arise. "That's why it's called a safety net," says the Economic Policy Institute's Shierholz. "We have these programs to help maintain living standards, because for most people there is nothing to rely on but the labor market."

Moral or humanitarian reasons aside, Shierholz echoes a widely held belief that UI stimulates the economy in bad times because recipients immediately spend the money. "You get money into the hands of the long-term unemployed," she says. "Their savings have been depleted; they're most likely to spend UI on necessities in their local economies."

Conservative economists like the Heritage Foundation's Sherk argue that extending UI helps keep unemployment rates high by giving unemployed workers an incentive not to move to higher-employment states. "Workers spend less time looking for jobs and are less willing to make adjustments," Sherk says. "It's human nature, it's understandable. I'm not blaming them for it." (*See "At Issue," p. 241.*)

Sherk concedes that there are humanitarian reasons for extending UI, but he rejects the thesis that helping unemployed workers pay their bills benefits the economy as a whole. "You can't simply assume that every UI dollar goes into new spending," he says, citing a Heritage study he helped conduct.

It concluded that any spending is offset by the effects of higher unemployment and by the taxes paid to support the UI payments. [34]

But University of California economist Ohanian — who questions both the likely impact of the Obama stimulus and the New Deal itself — argues that UI provides far more bang for the buck than other stimulus measures. "It's a more direct approach than expanding various federal expenditures in areas with high unemployment," he says.

Moreover, the classic economic argument that extending UI gives people an incentive not to look hard for work becomes less relevant in recessions as severe as the present one, Ohanian says. "It is really hard to find a job right now," he says.

Nevertheless, others warn, UI shouldn't be extended indefinitely. "You've got to mix the carrot and the stick," says Tim Duy, director of the Oregon Economic Forum at the University of Oregon and a former Treasury Department economist. "You don't want to starve people back into the labor force, but you want to give them some support."

Duy says 26 weeks of unemployment insurance isn't enough in the present circumstances. "Fifty-two weeks is certainly better, and should it be another 26 weeks on top of that, I probably wouldn't lose any sleep," he says. "But you can certainly slip from being too stingy to too generous." ∎

BACKGROUND

Fighting the Depression

Massive unemployment was the hallmark of the world's most profound economic crisis. In the years after the U.S. stock market crashed in 1929, millions of jobs vanished as the entire global manufacturing and trading system

nearly ground to a halt. Officially, the U.S. unemployment rate reached 25 percent by 1933, but estimates of the actual rate ranged as high as 50 percent. [35]

Even at the more conservative level, about 12 million working-age Americans lacked jobs (the country's population then was about 126 million). With federal unemployment insurance still two years away, hundreds of thousands of destitute jobless Americans relied on soup kitchens set up by charities.

Starving Chicago teachers who hadn't been paid for months were fainting in their classrooms; 5,000 banks had collapsed, wiping out 9 million savings accounts; crops rotted in fields as farmers lost their land or their customers. "Many believed that the long era of economic growth in the Western world had come to an end," wrote historian William E. Leuchtenburg in a classic study of the New Deal. [36]

President Herbert Hoover's response to the crisis was widely considered inadequate given the scale of the disaster. A federal construction program in 1931, for example, was designed to employ just 100,000 men. But Hoover rebuffed calls for more muscular measures, including a massive expansion in public-works projects.

"The problem of unemployment cannot be solved by any magic of appropriations from the public treasury," the President's Organization on Unemployment Relief declared on Dec. 22, 1931. The federal government's role was simple, the panel said: "Stop borrowing except to meet unavoidable deficits, balance our budgets and live within our income." [37]

Not surprisingly, the armies of homeless people living in makeshift settlements mockingly called them "Hoovervilles." [38]

Given Hoover's weak efforts, the tide of joblessness swamped local efforts. In 174 cities, donations to "community chest" federations — the precursors to the United Way — increased 15 percent from 1930 to 1931. In Philadelphia alone, charitable "relief"

spending soared 404 percent between September 1930 and September 1931. In Chicago, the increase was 267 percent, and in New York, 125 percent.

Roosevelt took office on March 4, 1933, embarking immediately on an accelerated campaign to launch programs — known collectively as the New Deal — to put people back to work. [39]

Along the way, the New Deal reshaped the relationship between citizens and the government, and between the government and the economy. "Who can now imagine," wrote the late Arthur Schlesinger Jr., a leading historian of the New Deal, "a day when America offered no Social Security, no unemployment compensation, no food stamps, no Federal guarantee of bank deposits, no Federal supervision of the stock market, no Federal protection for collective bargaining, no Federal standards for wages and hours, no Federal support for farm prices or rural electrification, no Federal refinancing for farm and home mortgages, no Federal commitment to high employment or to equal opportunity — in short, no Federal responsibility for Americans who found themselves, through no fault of their own, in economic or social distress?" [40]

However, the New Deal was controversial at the time, and the economic debate surrounding its effectiveness has gotten a second wind in the present crisis. UCLA's Ohanian and Harold L. Cole of the University of Pennsylvania contend the New Deal prolonged the Great Depression. Writing in *The Wall Street Journal* recently, they blame the Roosevelt administration's promotion of "fair competition" codes in all industries — which encouraged trade associations to set industry-wide wages — with suppressing competition, forcing prices and wages up. "We have calculated that manufacturing wages were as much as 25 percent above the level that would have prevailed without the New Deal," they write, which "prevented the normal forces of supply and demand from restoring full employment." [41]

Advocates of massive government intervention say FDR's later retreat from aggressive spending prevented the New Deal from further improving the employment picture. "After winning a smashing election victory in 1936," writes Nobel Prize-winning economist Krugman, "the Roosevelt administration cut spending and raised taxes, precipitating an economic relapse that drove the unemployment rate back into double digits." [42]

The real engine of recovery, economists of all political stripes agree, was World War II, with its massive government-directed industrial production.

Boom and Gloom

The economic growth that started during the war continued for about three decades after combat ended in 1945. The prolonged expansion included rising education levels, as returning veterans used the new G.I. Bill to continue their educations; pent-up demand for consumer products, such as cars, kitchen appliances and clothing; and major public-works projects.

The signature public works undertaking was the massive Interstate Highway System, launched in 1956 and conceived by President Dwight D. Eisenhower. The system speeded up deliveries between manufacturers and markets while making it easier for ordinary Americans to strike out for new jobs in new territories. [43]

All the construction, production and consumption made jobs plentiful and easy to retain. In fact, writes Louis Uchitelle, an economic correspondent for *The New York Times*, there was a widespread belief that business had a duty to avoid layoffs. He points to what happened in 1948 in Nashua, N.H., when the community's biggest employer, a textile manufacturer, announced it would close two mills, laying off 3,500 workers.

The Textile Workers of America union fought back. A Senate subcommittee investigated the company, effectively forcing it to keep one mill open. City and state officials then attracted other employers to the city, and all the laid-off employees eventually found other work. [44]

Uchitelle cites a 1954 study that paints an employment picture nationwide that's scarcely recognizable today. Among employees changing jobs, he writes, "quitting was the norm; layoffs were an infrequent occurrence." And even laid-off employees found satisfactory new jobs. [45]

Nevertheless, even in relatively stable times, the fortunes of individual companies and industries rose and fell, sometimes affecting the economy as a whole. The country experienced six recessions from 1948-1975, lasting from eight to 16 months, according to the National Bureau of Economic Research. [46]

But even during these downturns, unemployment generally remained below worrisome levels. During the quarter-century from 1945 to 1970, unemployment climbed above 5 percent during only eight years. [47] However, the conditions that were conducive to decades of relatively high job security began changing in the early 1970s.

In 1971, the global system of currency exchange rates that initially promoted U.S. exports collapsed. Then the 1973 oil embargo against the United States by the Organization of Petroleum Exporting Countries marked the end of the era of cheap oil and relatively cheap foreign-made products — especially from Japan.

But Japanese exports began improving in quality, providing major competition to U.S. companies. In many cases, the U.S. companies surrendered. The steel industry led the way in 1977, when the big Youngstown Sheet & Tube steelmaker announced it would close a mill in Youngstown, Ohio, putting 5,000 workers on the street — considered a major

layoff at the time. President Jimmy Carter arranged loan guarantees to workers who wanted to modernize the plant and run it themselves, but that plan failed. More steel plants closed in 1979, at a cost of 13,000 jobs.

Reagan and Reaganism

Characterized by his admirers as a visionary who guided the United States to new economic heights, and by his detractors as a promoter of winner-take-all capitalism that ultimately damaged the economy, President Ronald Reagan took office in 1981 vowing to create a new relationship between government and the economy.

Regulatory supervision of business declined (continuing a trend begun by Reagan's Democratic predecessor, Carter), unions lost clout, and "marginal" income tax rates — the rate imposed on a taxpayer's highest earnings — were cut from 70 percent to 28 percent. [48]

In one of his first moves, Reagan took on organized labor — a major player in national politics at the time. In 1981, when the nation's air traffic controllers went on strike for higher pay and shorter hours, Reagan fired all 11,500 members of the controllers union — who had defied a legal ban on work stoppages by federal employees — and hired permanent replacements. [49]

Steven Greenhouse, labor reporter for *The New York Times*, concludes in a recent book that Reagan's groundbreaking move was crucial to further weakening the already-challenged unions. "Companies now warned workers," Greenhouse writes, "that if they went on strike they might permanently lose their jobs." Unions now represent 12.4 percent of the U.S. workforce — and only 7.6 percent of the nongovernmental workforce — down from 20 percent in 1983. [50]

Reagan pushed his agenda at a time of rising fear and anxiety over foreign

Continued on p. 236

Chronology

1929-1945
Great Depression brings record unemployment; New Deal programs offer some relief.

1931
As unemployment grows, President Herbert Hoover refuses to expand public-works programs.

1933
Unemployment hits 25 to 50 percent, and Franklin D. Roosevelt launches New Deal to restart economy and create jobs.

1935
Unemployment insurance is created to protect laid-off workers.

1937
Unemployment falls to 14.3 percent as New Deal programs kick in.

1938
Unemployment rebounds to 19 percent after Roosevelt retreats from some New Deal policies.

1941
Massive war buildup begins.

1942
Jobless rate falls to 4.7 percent.

1948-1962
Postwar boom sees expanding economy and stable employment.

1948
Congress supports Textile Workers Union effort to force a textile company to partly rescind a layoff.

1956
Federal government begins building Interstate Highway System.

1962
Congress passes $435 million worker-retraining program as foreign products appear in U.S. marketplace.

1970s-1990s
U.S. economy begins changing in response to massive foreign imports, outsourcing by U.S. firms, decline of unions and wave of mergers and acquisitions.

1970
Congress extends unemployment insurance for high-unemployment periods.

1973
Oil producers' embargo ends era of cheap, plentiful petroleum — further weakening many U.S. employers.

1977
Youngstown Sheet & Tube shuts down a plant, laying off 5,000 steel workers — underscoring the weakening of U.S. manufacturing.

1981
Newly inaugurated President Ronald Reagan fires 11,500 air traffic controllers' union members — and dissolves the union — for violating federal anti-strike law.

1982
Worst post-war recession sends unemployment rate to 10.8 percent.

1984
Jack Welch becomes chairman of General Electric, lays off 25 percent of payroll over three years.

1988
New owner of RJR Nabisco lays off 50,000 employees — more than half the workforce.

1992
Unemployment reaches 7.4 percent during 1991-1992 recession.

1997
New technology spurs rapid growth, jobless rate falls to 4.6 percent.

2000s
Economy resumes growth after brief recession, but continuing employment lag prompts concern; "Great Recession" ends recovery.

2002
Unemployment rate climbs back to 6 percent.

2003
Concern grows over "jobless" recoveries.

2005
Unemployment drops to 4.8 percent, but number of "discouraged" ex-workers remains high.

December 2007
Current recession begins.

2008
Plummeting real estate prices trigger economic meltdown, resulting in 3.6 million layoffs.

2009
President Barack Obama signs $787 billion "stimulus" bill, claiming it will "save or create" 3.6 million jobs. . . . States begin deciding which projects to fund with stimulus money, but some Southern GOP governors vow to forego money that would force them to pay higher long-term unemployment benefits. Jobless rate hits 8.1 percent at end of February; recession has cost 4.4 million jobs.

Behind the Grim Statistics, Grim Stories, Real People

"I can't imagine how I'd do it if I didn't live at home."

Behind the depressing unemployment statistics lie grim stories of people dealing — some better than others — with sudden, equally grim changes in their lives.

For Elaine Moore Kane, 47, losing her $15-an-hour data-entry job at the Fulton County Courthouse in Atlanta has left her getting by on what she can "rake, scrape and borrow — and God's grace." Her condo is in foreclosure, and she expects her car to be repossessed any day.

Kane readily acknowledges that, technically speaking, she quit her job to care for her 72-year-old mother, who has dementia, diabetes and asthma. Although the recently passed economic stimulus bill includes an unemployment insurance "modernization" program that would cover her situation, she's ineligible.

Kane has been in the workforce for a long time, having worked as a hotel clerk and a home health-care aide, among other jobs. But she's never faced such a drought of openings. "I frequent the Department of Labor for job searches. I try to create opportunities," she says, in a hopeful tone.

For now, Kane at least has a roof over her head. As a caregiver, she's authorized to live in her mother's government-subsidized apartment. But Kane's resources extend virtually no further.

Mitchell Rice — a 62-year-old machinist laid off last year after nearly a lifetime's work at Manchester Tool Co. of Akron, Ohio — would seem to have far more in the way of specialized experience. But, he says, "There doesn't seem to be anything out there."

Rice does receive unemployment insurance, but he and his wife are paying the full $630 monthly cost of health insurance under COBRA — the program that allows laid-off workers to keep their coverage if they pay for it. Under the stimulus bill,

the federal government will pay 65 percent of COBRA participants' costs, but Rice says he was told he was ineligible. "I'm going to contact a congressman or someone," he says.

"You go through a period where you're real upset," Rice says of the layoff. "Then you realize you're not going to have a job anymore."

At age 36, Savoie Lockhart of Atlanta is not in a position to quit trying. But she's not having much luck. "I haven't been able to find anything," says Lockhart, who worked for more than eight years as a human resources officer for Wayne Farms, a poultry-processing company. The firm closed the plant where Lockhart had worked.

Now, the 401(k) account that represented Lockhart's savings is nearly tapped out. Getting by — barely — on $300 a week in unemployment insurance, Lockhart was planning to move out of her $855-a-month apartment into one renting for $500.

On the positive side, Lockhart has a son in college, on a full football scholarship at the University of Louisiana at Monroe. Another son, though, is still in high school. "I'm going to have to apply for financial aid and see how things go," she says.

Lockhart had worked her way up into human resources even though she lacked professional certification in the field. Now her job search is hindered by both the dismal economy and the missing credential.

"The Internal Revenue Service was going to be doing some hiring," Lockhart says. "I had an interview, and went a second time and they took [identification] pictures and signed us up for a training class. A week before training was supposed to start, they sent me an e-mail that because of budget constraints, they weren't going to hire my group."

Continued from p. 234

competition. Concern among businessmen and workers about cheap foreign imports forced Reagan — in actions rarely recalled today — to sign the Worker Adjustment and Retraining Notification Act. The 1988 law required companies with 100 or more workers to give 60 days' warning of any layoff of more than 500 employees. Today, Uchitelle reports, the law technically remains in force but has been so weakened with exemptions as to become irrelevant. [51]

Also often forgotten, Reagan's two terms were marked by import quotas on steel, textiles and other products,

designed to buy time for U.S. manufacturers to build up their competitive edge. The outcome was greater efficiency with fewer workers in some companies and industries — and complete retreat in others.

For example, late-20th-century America's major contribution to the world economy, the personal computer, was in nearly all cases manufactured abroad. From 1973 to 2007, the nation's manufacturing workforce shrank from 24 percent to 10 percent of all non-agricultural employees. [52]

As the transformation of U.S. industry escalated, corporations began reaping profits less from manufacturing and

more from buying or merging with other companies. In the process, they downsized or shuttered insufficiently profitable operations and reaped the benefits in the form of higher stock prices. The symbol of the new business model was General Electric Chairman Jack Welch. He took the top job in 1981 and within three years had laid off 118,000 employees — 25 percent of the workforce. [53]

Meanwhile, buyers of companies — known as "corporate raiders" — were financing acquisitions with "junk" bonds, so called because they were rated too risky for regular investors. They also carried high interest rates, which left the raiders so loaded with debt that their first

As for medical insurance, "Thank God, I haven't been sick," Lockhart says.

Many laid-off workers may be thinking about going back to school for more credentials, but that doesn't guarantee job stability either. In Bedminster, N.J., Patrick McCloskey, whose Ph.D in genetics and molecular biology enabled him to work for universities and biotech companies, has been jobless for a year. And he's learning that a lot of Ph.Ds, JDs and MBAs are unemployed as well.

"As I network I certainly run into more people than I expected who find themselves on the wrong end of a pink slip," he says, "more than I expected in the sense that my network tends to be fairly highly credentialed."

Still, McCloskey, 45, is upbeat. "I know it's going to be a hard search," he says. "But . . . at the end of the day, I'll find a job." For now, though, he lacks health insurance. "I considered getting catastrophic coverage. It's prudent for me to do so. But it's also prudent for me to pay my mortgage."

Another doctorate-holder in the same field, Roger Barthelson, 54, expects to lose his job in June as an assistant research scientist at the University of Arizona, Tucson, a state institution where he went to work after years in academia and the biotech industry. Both industry and academia, he says, hire Ph.Ds from abroad — who are generally lower-paid than Amer-

Despite a Ph.D in genetics and molecular biology, Patrick McCloskey, of Bedminster, N.J. — is still unemployed after losing his $125,000-a-year job in the pharmaceutical industry a year ago.

AP Photo/Mel Evans

icans — which keeps salaries low. But he has nothing against foreign scientists, he adds.

If a funding shortfall eliminates his $42,000-a-year job, Barthelson says he and his wife could cope on her salary from a medical instruments firm. "We would have to cut back on expenditures," he says, "and we would not be putting away for retirement."

He shares the frustration of other scientists. "Why aren't we using our capabilities instead of having us sit around without resources to do what we're trained to do?" he asks.

Young people with fewer responsibilities are naturally better equipped to cope with the bleak job climate. In New York, Brian Pitre, 23, lost his first post-college job, at a two-person marketing agency. But as he looks for another position, his living circumstances are easing the hardship. "I can't imagine how I'd do it if I didn't live at home."

Thanks to his parents, Pitre can live comfortably on the UI checks he expects to receive soon. He certainly doesn't feel singled out by misfortune.

"I could count on more than two feet and hands the number of people I know who are laid off," he says. "Every day it seems like someone is getting the ax. We're all in the same boat."

---

moves invariably involved layoffs to cut expenses. RJR Nabisco, for example, was bought by Wall Street financier Henry R. Kravis in 1988. To pay down the borrowed portion of the $25 billion purchase price, he sold parts of the company and laid off some 50,000 employees — more than half the payroll. [54]

Critics decried the lavish rewards for speculators, contrasted with what they saw as shabby treatment of employees. The new business model, they said, was an ultimately self-defeating style of capitalism in which big profits created by paper transactions were favored over the production of goods and services and the reliable, good-

paying — usually unionized — jobs it provided.

"While the rich got much richer, there was little sustained economic improvement for most Americans," Nobel Prize-winner Krugman wrote. [55]

From the other side of the political fence, the view couldn't differ more. "Reagan's record includes sweeping economic reforms and deep across-the-board tax cuts, market deregulation and sound monetary policies to contain inflation," Peter B. Sperry, then of the Heritage Foundation, wrote in 2001. "His policies resulted in the largest peacetime economic boom in American history and nearly 35 million more jobs." [56]

Jobless Recoveries

Months after taking office, Reagan was greeted by the start of one of the two longest recessions in the postwar U.S. economy, both lasting 16 months. The "Reagan recession" began in July 1981 and ran until November 1982.

Judged the most serious, until then, of all post-war recessions, the early-'80s recession pushed unemployment to a rate yet to be reached during the present crisis: 10.8 percent. Employment began picking up in 1984, but the unemployment rate didn't hit bottom until Reagan was almost out of office —

What Will Happen to the American Workplace?

Three books offer early insights into the future of jobs.

Some of the leading indicators of hard times in the U.S. workforce came in the form of a trio of books by newspaper reporters — themselves members of a hard-hit sector of the economy.

In 2006, *The Disposable American: Layoffs and Their Consequences*, by Louis Uchitelle, an economics reporter for *The New York Times*, chronicled the decline of the dependable job and reliable employer. Two years later, labor reporter Steven Greenhouse, another Timesman, followed with *The Big Squeeze: Tough Times for the American Worker*, and Peter Gosselin, then the national economics correspondent of the *Los Angeles Times*, published *High Wire: The Precarious Financial Lives of American Families*.

The books focus on different dimensions of the labor market. But the writers — who all started out in a pre-Web world when newspapers and magazines thrived — draw parallel conclusions: American workers, whether blue- or white-collar, are getting less for the investment of their labor — including job security — than employees received during the flush quarter-century after World War II.

Disparities in income — documented by Greenhouse from government statistics — accompanied a growing disregard for employees, the books argue. [1] In the three accounts, workers are increasingly treated as interchangeable commodities to be overworked, outsourced or laid off virtually at will.

"No one is going to outlaw layoffs . . . from long-lived jobs by legislative fiat," Gosselin writes. Thus, "we need to decouple employment from many of the safety-net programs that employers have provided." [2]

Health-care coverage, for example, shouldn't end with a layoff, he argued. That position reflects, at least in principle, Obama's stance. Gosselin now has joined the administration as a speechwriter for Treasury Secretary Timothy F. Geithner. [3]

Uchitelle and Greenhouse remain at *The Times*. Their books compiled dozens of tales of life in workplaces where pressures on employees, by the authors' accounts, are rising at the same time that protection against job loss is disappearing.

Much like Gosselin, Uchitelle says workers need better cushioning against job loss than today's unemployment insurance offers. He also favors government discouragement of layoffs. "If we do manage to diminish layoffs, we will have taken a big step toward repairing a larger framework," he wrote. "Stable jobs and sufficient incomes in stable communities are powerful equalizers." [4]

The reporters' conclusions fall broadly within the Democratic policy universe. Conservatives, though, have largely refrained from confronting the authors directly. The two leading conservative magazines, *National Review* and the *Weekly Standard*, didn't review any of them.

In fact, the only mention came in a mocking squib in *National Review* in 2006, when unemployment was running at 4.6 percent.

---

in late 1988 — when it declined to 5.3 percent. [57]

Still, as Sperry notes, steady job growth marked Reagan's tenure, and the recovery stands as one of the pillars of the Reagan legend — evidence that his political-economic doctrine yielded positive results. But behind the falling unemployment rate, a trend emerged that later would prove problematic.

Two Bureau of Labor Statistics economists noted in analyzing employment trends in 1985 that the manufacturing sector continued shrinking, shedding about 200,000 jobs from 1984 to 1985. Meanwhile, the so-called service sector was expanding, especially non-bank credit agencies. "This growth is tied to recent banking deregulation, which has lowered barriers to entry and encouraged growth and compe-

tition in the savings and lending industry," they concluded. [58]

Another trend emerged in the 1990s and continued into the 2000s. After eight-month recessions that opened each decade, recoveries were marked by a far slower return to low unemployment than had been the case in earlier business cycles. By 2003, the "jobless recovery" began to worry at least one top government economist: Federal Reserve Chairman Ben S. Bernanke, then a member of the Fed's Board of Governors. His conclusion: Businesses needed fewer workers.

At the time, the unemployment rate stood at 5.8 percent. But by rough calculation, he said, that left about 3.5 million fewer people working than was necessary for a healthy economy. He concluded that as companies learned to use new technology, they could do

more with fewer workers. And American goods production continued to decline as imports accounted for more than one-quarter of manufactured products consumed by Americans — about double the foreign share in the 1980s, Bernanke said during a 2003 speech in Pittsburgh. [59]

"If (as some have argued) the jobless recovery is in part the result of an unusually high pace of structural change, then the degree of longer-term mismatch between workers' skills and the available jobs may have increased," Bernanke said. Ultimately, he drew a more optimistic conclusion, forecasting strong employment growth in 2004 and beyond. [60]

In fact, employment rose only slowly. It wasn't until January 2005 that the share of Americans with jobs reached its early-2001 level. But the

"He [Uchitelle] tries to debunk the idea that the economy has been creating about 200,000 new jobs each month," the unsigned entry said. "After his debunking, it turns out that the claim is, well, true. But the numbers allegedly conceal a problem. The pace of new hiring has not been very fast; the reason . . . is that fewer people are being fired or quitting their jobs. This might not look like bad news to most people." [5]

Since then, the news changed. In today's climate, conservatives are campaigning against broadening social protections and heavier regulation of business, both advocated by the three reporters. For conservatives, these measures amount to European-style socialism, hence contrary to American political tradition.

Writing in *The Wall Street Journal*, two leading conservative policy experts argued that Obama's push for universal health coverage bodes ill. "It will . . . put America on a glide path toward European-style socialism," wrote Peter Wehner, a former deputy assistant to President George W. Bush, and Rep. Paul Ryan, R-Wis. "We need only look to Great Britain and elsewhere to see the effects of socialized health care on the broader economy. Once a large number of citizens get their health care from the state, it dramatically alters their attachment to government. Every time a tax cut is proposed, the guardians of the new medical-welfare state will argue that tax cuts would come at the expense of health care — an argument that would resonate with middle-class families entirely dependent on the government for access to doctors and hospitals." [6]

Making a broader argument, Canadian conservative Mark Steyn wrote in *National Review* that the dangers of the European-style socialism — including "job-for-life security that he sees in Obama's policies — run even deeper. "When the state 'gives' you plenty," he warned, "when it takes care of your health, takes cares of your kids, takes care of your elderly parents, takes care of every primary responsibility of adulthood — it's not surprising that the citizenry cease to function as adults: Life becomes a kind of extended adolescence." [7]

Whether that vision or the three journalists' views predominate may determine what happens to the American workplace.

[1] Steven Greenhouse, *The Big Squeeze: Tough Times for the American Worker* (2009 edition), p. 40.

[2] Peter Gosselin, *High Wire: The Precarious Financial Lives of American Families* (2008), p. 318.

[3] Michael Calderone, "Dem exclusive? Reporters jump ship," *Politico*, Feb. 18, 2009, http://news.yahoo.com/s/politico/20090218/pl_politico/18971.

[4] Louis Uchitelle, *The Disposable American: Layoffs and Their Consequences* (2007 edition), p. 207.

[5] "The Week," *National Review*, April 10, 2006.

[6] Peter Wehner and Paul Ryan, "Beware of the Big-Government Tipping Point," *The Wall Street Journal*, Jan. 16, 2009, http://online.wsj.com/article/SB123207075026188601.html.

[7] Mark Steyn, "Prime Minister Obama: Will European statism supplant the American Way?" *National Review*, March 23, 2009.

number of discouraged job-seekers who had stopped looking for work — 416,000 — remained higher than before the 2001 recession, according to the Bureau of Labor Statistics. [61]

Meanwhile, some companies were prospering. And many cash-rich companies were using their money to buy other firms, often leading to layoffs. For example, Oracle Corp. bought PeopleSoft Inc. for $11 billion in late 2004, laying off 5,000 employees. [62]

Economists and businesspeople saw no mystery in the seeming paradox of booming business and slow employment. Drew Brousseau, managing director S. G. Cowen, an investment firm, told *The Los Angeles Times*: "A lot of the information industries that are drivers of growth these days are not as person-intensive as manufacturing." [63]

CURRENT SITUATION

Spending the Money

Lawmakers and bureaucrats throughout the country are meeting to decide where to spend the billions of dollars in stimulus funds heading to state capitols.

According to administration estimates, the American Recovery and Reinvestment Act of 2009 will "create or save" anywhere from 8,000 jobs in Wyoming to 396,000 in California. [64] In New York, officials representing nearly two-dozen agencies are hunkered down in Albany combing through hundreds of proposals from cities and counties vying for a chunk of the $24.6 billion the state will receive (estimated jobs impact: 215,000). By the first week in March, the proposals added up to $41.8 billion worth of projects — almost twice as much as the state will get. [65]

"Things have been so bleak for so long, where there was no money for any kind of project," said lobbyist Steven B. Weingarten, who represents several transportation agencies. "Once they saw there was money on the table, they said, 'We need to take a shot, any way we can.' " [66]

To abide by Obama's promise to keep the spending "transparent," a government Web site lists approved transportation-related projects certified by governors as meeting federal standards. By early March, 21 states and Puerto Rico had posted certifications for projects that would spend their portion of the $27 billion being made available for road and bridge work. [67]

A separate pot of $8.4 billion is destined for public transit projects, with New York taking the lion's share at $1.2 billion, and California $1 billion. [68]

Inevitably, the reality that many projects won't be funded is colliding with the ambitions of the politicians involved. Obama's hometown mayor, Richard Daley of Chicago, has been criticized because, by early March, he hadn't announced plans for spending his city's share of Illinois' $9 billion in stimulus funds (estimated jobs impact: 148,000).

"We did not put that out publicly," Daley said in early February, "because once you start putting it out publicly, you know, the newspapers, the media is going to be ripping it apart." [69]

Not surprisingly, Daley's critics had a field day contrasting that policy with the Obama promise of transparency. "In a normal city, such wish lists would be transparent, and the public would have a chance to comment, and if it chooses, to rip it apart," wrote Dennis Byrne, a Chicago commentator. He added that, apart from Obama himself, top aides including Chief of Staff Emanuel are Chicagoans. [70]

Of course, Chicago isn't the only place where public interest in job creation is intense. In Georgia (estimated jobs impact: 106,000), the director of Georgia State University's Economic Forecasting Center warned that tough times are likely to get tougher. The state would lose 143,000 jobs this year, said Rajeev Dhawan, who expects the stimulus bill to hasten recovery by only a few months. "After the last recession, we made up [jobs] we lost in about three years," he said. "This time, it is going to be a while." [71]

Governors' Resistance

After nearly unanimous Republican opposition to the stimulus legislation, GOP governors are split on whether to take all the money destined for their states.

One Southern faction doesn't object to building roads and infrastructure, but they do oppose taking funds contingent on expanding eligibility for unemployment insurance. Nationwide, states are being offered $7 billion for the first-year costs of expanding state unemployment insurance programs.

"You're talking about temporary federal spending triggering a permanent change in state law," Louisiana Gov. Jindal said in explaining why he wouldn't accept some $99 million in UI money. [72]

Barbour of Mississippi, Mark Sanford of South Carolina and Rick Perry of Texas agreed. "I remain opposed to . . . burdening the state with ongoing expenditures long after the funding has dried up," Perry told Obama in a letter. [73]

Their objections reflect longstanding conservative opinion that extending unemployment insurance discourages the jobless from seeking work. But another Southern Republican governor, Crist of Florida, favors taking the UI expansion funds along with the rest. [74] And Western and Midwestern GOP governors, including Arnold Schwarzenegger of California, also plan to take all the stimulus money.

At least one Southern GOP governor has changed his mind about accepting the UI money. "The changes we believe will be required in state law are feasible and relatively minimal," said Georgia Gov. Sonny Perdue. [75]

One of the changes Jindal and his colleagues don't like would make laid-off employees who've worked less than a year eligible for UI. Another would enlarge the pool of UI-eligible jobless workers by including unemployed part-time employees and those who quit work for major family reasons, including domestic violence; workers who qualify for benefits but need more money to cover dependent family members' needs; and laid-off workers who re-

quire extra benefits in order to get training in new skills. [76]

The recovery act adopted the new catagories wholesale from a separate bill, the Unemployment Insurance Modernization Act (UIMA), introduced in 2009 by Rep. James McDermott, D-Wash. Conservative lawmakers objected to expanding UI to cover all of the unemployed, not simply those who are laid off.

In early January, Senate Minority Leader Mitch McConnell, R-Ky., had said he "might" support expanding UI to part-time workers. But he went on to anticipate objections by Jindal and other GOP governors. "Do we, in the name of stimulus, want to make long-term, systemic changes?" McConnell asked. [77]

An advocate of UI expansion, Rick McHugh, Midwest coordinator of the New York-based National Employment Law Project, calls the objections groundless. States whose governors are resisting the changes and the money that comes with them — Texas, Mississippi and Louisiana — "run stingy programs," he says, by paying minimum benefits and charging companies low unemployment insurance taxes. "They can keep taxes low because they're shifting the burden so that unemployed workers, their families, communities and charities bear the burden of unemployment instead of the taxpayers."

The average weekly unemployment benefit in Louisiana is $209.12, and it's $182.74 in Mississippi. In Texas, where the UI average is somewhat higher at $302.94, only 25 percent of the unemployed qualify for benefits. [78]

Layoff Alternatives

As the economy keeps shrinking — taking jobs with it — some employers are trying to stave off layoffs by cutting pay or cutting hours. Furloughs, or involuntary unpaid leaves — a traditional cost-cutting move in

Continued on p. 242

At Issue:

Does extending unemployment benefits boost joblessness?

JAMES SHERK
BRADLEY FELLOW IN LABOR POLICY
HERITAGE FOUNDATION

WRITTEN FOR *CQ RESEARCHER*, MARCH 2009

ongress has increased the time laid-off workers can collect unemployment insurance (UI) payments to almost a year. Unfortunately these extended benefits have unintended consequences: They keep unemployed workers out of work longer and increase the unemployment rate.

Economic research conclusively demonstrates that extending the time unemployed workers can collect UI payments extends the time those workers stay unemployed. Dozens and dozens of studies reach the same conclusion.

It's not that unemployed workers enjoy being on the dole. Yes, some abuse the system, but most unemployed workers want to work. UI makes the need to find a new job less pressing. A recent study found that workers spend three times more time looking for work when their UI benefits expire than they do when they can rely on benefits. So while most UI recipients want a job, they do not look as intently as they would without government benefits.

This is a problem because workers are not replaceable cogs in the corporate machine. Employers need workers with unique skills: A laid-off Wall Street financier's talents do little for a software engineering firm. One worker or job is not just as good as another. It takes time and effort for employees to find jobs that put their unique skills to good use. Without that effort workers stay unemployed longer, regardless of economic circumstances.

Studies show that UI increases the time workers stay jobless by about the same amount in both recessions and booms. In both good times and bad, workers need to take the time to search for jobs that match their unique abilities. Twenty weeks of added payments — what Congress passed — causes the typical UI recipient to stay unemployed between three and four weeks longer.

This reduces the competition for jobs for everyone else, but not by much. The reduced competition for jobs from workers on UI will enable workers without benefits to find jobs five days faster than they otherwise would.

As a result, extended UI benefits increase the total unemployment rate. Heritage Foundation calculations show that the current extended benefits have increased the unemployment rate by more than 0.2 percentage points.

Good intentions aside, extended UI benefits do not help the economy.

HEATHER BOUSHEY
SENIOR ECONOMIST
CENTER FOR AMERICAN PROGRESS

WRITTEN FOR *CQ RESEARCHER*, MARCH 2009

altering job creation and lower consumption are keeping the unemployment rate high. Providing extended unemployment insurance (UI) benefits is boosting consumption — and thus helping to create jobs.

Employers have shed nearly 3.6 million jobs since December 2007, and about 11.1 million workers were unemployed by the end of 2008, yet there were only 2.7 million job openings — more than four unemployed workers for every available job.

The argument that unemployment insurance increases the unemployment rate hinges on two hypotheses: If the unemployed did not have benefits to rely on everyone would find a job, and unemployment benefits do not effectively stimulate the economy. On both counts, the evidence undermines these hypotheses.

Even if every worker with unemployment benefits took an extra week to job search, jobs will not go unfilled. Workers are lining up — even in 20-degree weather — to apply for jobs. In New York City, a job fair that had never attracted more than 2,000 people saw 5,103 show up last week. In Columbus, Ga., nearly 800 people lined up to fill about 150 positions for a new restaurant opening at the National Infantry Museum and Soldier Center at Patriot Park.

Around the nation, these stories are disturbingly common. Quite simply, there are not enough jobs to go around. Further, fewer than half of the unemployed workers nationwide receive UI benefits. For every worker receiving benefits, there's one without benefits who is ever more desperate to find a job. Consequently, no job goes unfilled for very long.

Unemployment benefits are a well-targeted economic stimulus. The 5.1 million workers who receive unemployment benefits can maintain their spending, which boosts their local economies. And, in general, research shows that without unemployment benefits recessions are longer and deeper.

Benefits flow to communities with the highest unemployment rates. To receive benefits, a worker must have been steadily employed during the previous year, been laid off through no fault of their own, be able and available for work and actively searching for work. In communities where many unemployed workers fit these criteria, the local economy is certainly in trouble.

Eliminating or reducing unemployment benefits will not create jobs and will reduce consumption. In these hard economic times, unemployment benefits are providing an important bulwark against poverty for millions of families while helping to keep local economies afloat.

Continued from p. 240

heavy industry, such as automobile manufacturing — have spread to universities, state governments and high-tech companies.

"Had we not done this, we would have had to lay off about 1,000 administrative personnel," Matt McElrath, human-resources chief for Arizona State University, told *The Wall Street Journal* after the college ordered staff to take furloughs of nine to 15 days by the end of June. The unpaid leaves responded to an $88 million budget cut by the Arizona legislature. [79]

California and Maryland state governments also ordered furloughs, as did Clemson University, Gulfstream Aerospace and the newspaper companies Media General and Gannett.

Some management experts say furloughs are better than layoffs in some ways. "Companies are . . . much more wary of the damage layoffs can cause, and the risks to their ability to rebound when the economy turns around if they cut too deeply," said John Challenger, chief executive of the outplacement consulting firm Challenger, Gray & Christmas. [80]

But when it comes to cutting pay instead of hours, other experts report mixed emotions in the executive suite. "Usually, companies say they prefer layoffs to pay cuts," Yale economics Professor Truman Bewley said. "It gets the misery out the door." [81]

Clearly, the United States isn't South Korea, where layoffs are nearly taboo. In late February, officials of

Korean industry groups, unions, civic organizations and government ministries committed to a "grand bargain for social unity" — meaning that companies won't lay off workers, unions will accept lower or frozen wages and the government will grant tax breaks to companies that hold to the bargain. "We have to go through this together," Shim Hoyong, a factory worker for Shinchang Electrics Co., said. "If one disappears, it's awkward and uncomfortable." [82]

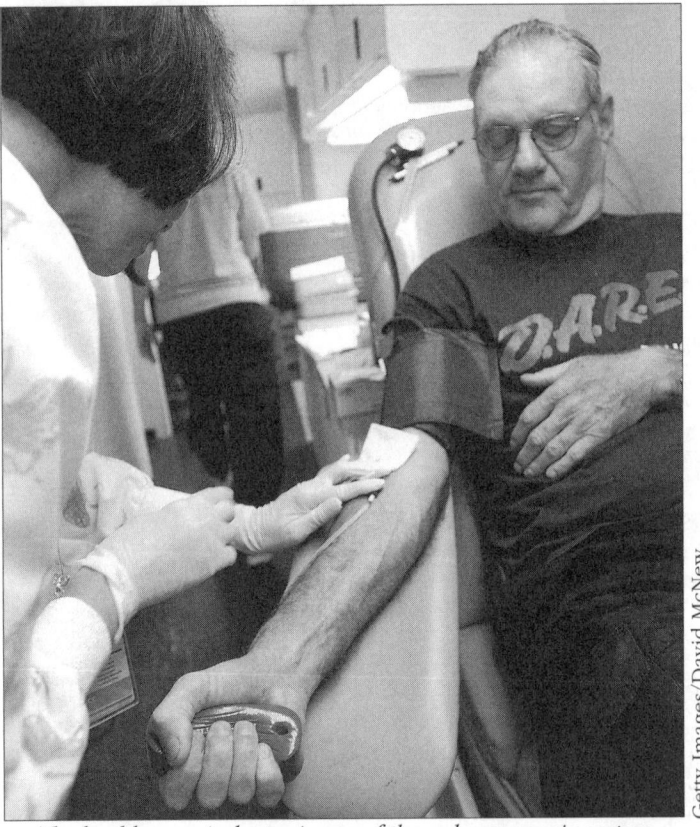

The health-care industry is one of the only economic sectors adding jobs, according to the U.S. Bureau of Labor Statistics. Employment in health-care jobs jumped 30 percent within the last year, largely because of the growing number of aging Americans.

Furloughed Americans speak in much the same way, even in the absence of grand bargains. "I've gone through several rounds of layoffs, and those were much worse," a Gannett journalist told Reuters. "Once you've seen your friend laid off, you'd much rather do the furlough." [83] ∎

OUTLOOK

The 'Great Recession'

The global sweep and intensity of the "Great Recession" is prompting economists and policy experts to ponder further structural changes to the economy and the workplace that until now have been considered unimaginable. In fact, conditions are deteriorating so quickly and with such force that old certainties are eroding.

For instance, there is renewed interest in "outsider" theorists such as Nikolai Kondratieff, a Russian economist of the early Soviet period who was executed in 1938, at the height of the Stalinist purges. Kondratieff held that capitalist economies run in 50-year cycles ending in depressions. The theory gets little notice in prosperous times. But an economic historian, David Colander of Middlebury College in Vermont, told *The New York Times*: "A good profession should take its outsiders more seriously. The worst thing for policy makers is to think they are right." [84]

For the moment, the economists that policy makers traditionally consult are scratching their heads. "If consumer demand is going to lag, what's that going to mean and how long will that go on?" asks Harry Holzer, an economist and professor of public policy at Georgetown University's Public Policy Institute. "And there are two other trends —

baby boomers retiring, which in one sense is good, but if assets remain depressed they won't be able to retire; and the growing job outsourcing to India and China, which will tend to slacken the labor market."

'Slackening' is economist jargon for declining demand for workers — a development that bodes ill for job-seekers.

President Obama has said repeatedly that making the U.S. health-care industry more efficient could help American companies deal with international competitors in countries that provide subsidized universal health care and thus do not have the same high health insurance costs that saddle U.S. companies.

Boushey, the senior economist at the Obama-friendly Center for American Progress, says the health care industry — the only sector of the U.S. economy not shedding jobs — could remain strong even if its costs come down. "We spend almost twice as much of GDP on health care as other advanced economies," she says. "That extra money . . . could be spent on something else."

Echoing administration strategy, Boushey also suggests that development of environmentally friendly — "green" — energy industries could attract workers from the hard-hit manufacturing sector. But how soon wind, solar and other energy alternatives can compete with fossil fuel suppliers remains an open question.

Consequently, over the next several years, industrial workers are likely to continue to suffer the effects of global competition. "People may have to get used to job opportunities that, at least for awhile, aren't as lucrative as the ones we're losing," says Ohanian of UCLA. "Either they'll be unemployed, or they will make as much as 40 percent to 50 percent less than they've been making."

They may also find themselves settling for jobs they might never have considered before. In Perry Township, near Canton, Ohio, Edison Junior High

School recently announced an opening for a janitor's job, paying $15 to $16 an hour, plus benefits. By the March 9 deadline, the school system had received 835 applications. [85]

Industries hit by forces other than global competition — such as the news media — are likely to feel the same effects, Ohanian says. "I feel for you guys," he adds.

If many elements of the future remain uncertain, opinion is unanimous that real estate-fueled credit binges are over. "We're not going to have people using their homes as ATMs because we thought the value of homes was going up," says economist Shierholz of the Economic Policy Institute. "We have this big gap in the economy that was being fueled by something that is not coming back."

The shrinking consumer credit sector won't affect all segments of society equally, says Duy of the Oregon Economic Forum. "The housing and credit boom were supportive of persons with lower educational levels and skill sets," he says. "We're not going to have an easy time transitioning those people into jobs."

Ripple effects will negatively affect small businesses, he predicts. At one time, Duy says, "Lots of people could start a small boutique and sell $600 pairs of shoes to people making $30,000 a year. Those days are in the past, most likely. What do those people do?"

The answer would interest millions of Americans. But, like much else about the future of jobs in the United States, it's not an answer that anyone has at the moment. ∎

Notes

[1] "Employment Situation Summary," U.S. Bureau of Labor Statistics, March 6, 2009, www.bls.gov/news.release/empsit.nr0.htm. Also, Jack Healy, "651,000 Jobs Reported Lost in February," The New York Times, March 6, 2009, www.nytimes.com/2009/03/07/business/econo-

my/07jobs.html?_r=1&hp.

[2] "The AP-GfK Poll," GfK Roper Public Affairs and Media, Feb. 12-17, 2009 (interview dates), http://surveys.ap.org/data%5CGfK%5CAP-GfK%20Poll%20Topline%2002 1809.pdf.

[3] Jack Healy, "62,000 Jobs Are Cut by U.S. and Foreign Companies," The New York Times, Jan. 27, 2009, www.nytimes.com/2009/01/27/business/economy/27jobcuts.html?partner=rss. "Employment Situation Summary," op. cit.

[4] Kendra Marr, "GM Slashing 10,000 jobs," The Washington Post, Feb. 11, 2009, p. D2; Bill Vlasic, "Ford is Pushing Buyout Offers to Its Workers," The New York Times, Feb. 26, 2008, p. A1.

[5] "Remarks by the President and Vice President at Signing of the American Recovery and Reinvestment Act," White House, Feb. 17, 2009, www.whitehouse.gov/the_press_office/Remarks-by-the-President-and-Vice-President-at-Signing-of-the-American-Recovery-and-Reinvestment-Act/.

[6] Paul Krugman, "Who'll Stop the Pain?" The New York Times, Feb. 19, 2009, www.nytimes.com/2009/02/20/opinion/20krugman.html.

[7] Ryan Lizza, "The Gatekeeper," The New Yorker, March 2, 2009, www.newyorker.com/reporting/2009/03/02/090302fa_fact_lizza?currentPage=all.

[8] Robert Pear and J. David Goodman, "Governors' Fight Over Stimulus May Define G.O.P.," The New York Times, Feb. 23, 2009, www.nytimes.com/2009/02/23/us/politics/23governors.html?scp=1&sq=Governors'FightOverStimulus&st=cse.

[9] "Regional State Employment and Unemployment Summary," Bureau of Labor Statistics, Jan. 27, 2009, www.bls.gov/news.release/laus.nr0.htm.

[10] Patrick McGeehan, "City Plans to Retrain, and Retain, Laid-Off Wall Streeters," The New York Times, Feb. 18, 2009, www.nytimes.com/2009/02/19/nyregion/19bankers.html.

[11] See "paper cuts" (blog), updated frequently, http://graphicdesignr.net/papercuts/?page_id=1088.

[12] "Layoff Tracker," updated March 4, 2009, http://lawshucks.com/layoff-tracker.

[13] "Employees on nonfarm payrolls by industry sector and selected industry detail," U.S. Bureau of Labor Statistics, March 6, 2009, www.bls.gov/news.release/empsit.t14.htm.

[14] Kelly Evans, "Shoppers' New Frugality Hurts Business," The Wall Street Journal, March 3, 2009, http://online.wsj.com/article/SB123600014821809081.html.

[15] "Minutes of the Federal Open Market Committee," Jan. 27-28, 2009, www.federalreserve.gov/monetarypolicy/files/fomcminutes20090128.pdf.

[16] Peter S. Goodman, "Sharper Downturn Clouds Obama Spending Plans," *The New York Times*, Feb. 27, 2009, www.nytimes.com/2009/02/28/business/economy/28recession.html?scp=3&sq=depression&st=cse.

[17] William E. Leuchtenburg, *Franklin D. Roosevelt and the New Deal, 1932-1940* (1963), pp. 1-29.

[18] "Labor Force Statistics from the Current Population Survey," U.S. Bureau of Labor Statistics (updated regularly), http://data.bls.gov/PDQ/servlet/SurveyOutputServle.

[19] Heather Boushey, "For Workers, The Grim News Just Keeps Coming," Center for American Progress, March 6, 2009, www.americanprogress.org/issues/2009/03/grim_news.html/print.html.

[20] "Employment status of the civilian noninstitutional population, 1940 to date," Bureau of Labor Statistics, updated annually, ftp://ftp.bls.gov/pub/special.requests/lf/aat1.txt.

[21] "UI Data Summary for United States," Department of Labor, updated quarterly, http://workforcesecurity.doleta.gov/unemploy/content/data_stats/datasum08/DataSum_2008_4.pdf.

[22] Maurice Emsellem, *et al.*, "Helping the Jobless Helps Us All: The Central Role of Unemployment Insurance in America's Economic Recovery," Center for American Progress Action Fund, November 2008, www.americanprogressaction.org/issues/2008/pdf/unemployment_insurance.pdf.

[23] "Opening Remarks at Fiscal Responsibility Summit," transcript, *The New York Times*, Feb. 23, 2009, www.nytimes.com/2009/02/23/us/politics/23text-summit.html?scp=5&sq="createorsave"&st=cse.

[24] Greg Mankiw, "Create or Save," Greg Mankiw's Blog, Feb. 19, 2009, http://gregmankiw.blogspot.com/2009/02/create-or-save.html.

[25] For background, see Marcia Clemmitt, "Public-Works Projects," *CQ Researcher*, Feb. 20, 2009, pp. 153-176.

[26] "American Recovery and Reinvestment Act: A Progressive Plan to Create Jobs and Help Families," The White House, Feb. 17, 2009, www.whitehouse.gov/assets/documents/Recovery_Act_Working_Families_2-17.pdf. Also see, James Oliphant, "Stimulus package tax credit should mean $8 to $10 a week," *Los Angeles Times*, Feb. 18, 2009, p. A8.

[27] For Atlanta Mayor Shirley Franklin's plans see Eric Stirgus, "Franklin wants Perdue to take stimulus money," *Atlanta Journal-Constitution*, Feb. 26, 2009, www.ajc.com/metro/content/metro/stories/2009/02/26/franlin_perdue_stimulus.html.

[28] Arnold R. Weber, "Retraining the Unemployed," University of Chicago, Graduate School of Business, undated (early 1960s), p. 16, www.chicagogsb.edu/faculty/selectedpapers/sp4.pdf.

[29] Emsellem, *et al.*, *op. cit.*

[30] "Emergency Unemployment Compensation (EUC) Extended," Department of Labor, Feb. 17, 2009, http://workforcesecurity.doleta.gov/unemploy/supp_ac.asp. Also, "Question & Answer: The Economic Recovery Bill's New "Extended Benefits: State Option," National Employment Law Project, Feb. 16, 2009, www.nelp.org/page/-/UI/eb.report.feb.09.pdf?nocdn=1.

[31] *Ibid.*

[32] Emsellem, *et al.*, *op. cit.*, p. 17.

[33] "Unemployment Insurance: Low-Wage and Part-Time Workers Continue to Experience Low Rates of Receipt," Government Accountability Office, September 2007, www.gao.gov/new.items/d071147.pdf.

[34] James Sherk and Karen A. Campbell, "Extended Unemployment Insurance — No Economic Stimulus," Heritage Foundation, Nov. 18, 2008, pp. 5-6, www.heritage.org/research/economy/cda08-13.cfm.

[35] For background, see Jane Tanner, "Unemployment Benefits," *CQ Researcher*, April 25, 2003, pp. 369-392. Also, "Report on the American Workforce," Bureau of Labor Statistics, 2001, pp. 4-5, www.bls.gov/opub/rtaw/rtawhome.htm#introduction.

[36] Leuchtenburg, *op. cit.*, pp. 1-29.

[37] G. B. Galloway, "Relief of Unemployment," *Editorial Research Reports*, Dec. 28, 1931, available in *CQ Researcher Plus Archives*.

[38] Photos of some Hoovervilles can be seen at Hoovervilles, Photograph Collage, The Library of Congress, Sept. 26, 2002, http://memory.loc.gov/learn/features/timeline/depwwii/depress/hoovers.html.

[39] Leuchtenberg, *op. cit.*

[40] Arthur Schlesinger Jr., "The 'Hundred Days' of FDR," *The New York Times*, April 10, 1983, Sect. 3, p. 1.

[41] Harold L. Cole and Lee E. Ohanian, "How Government Prolonged the Depression," *The Wall Street Journal*, Feb. 2, 2009, http://online.wsj.com/article/SB123353276749137485.html.

[42] Paul Krugman, "Franklin Delano Obama?" *The New York Times*, Nov. 10, 2008, p. A29.

[43] "Welcome to the Eisenhower Interstate Highway Web Site," undated, www.fhwa.dot.gov/interstate/homepage.cfm.

[44] Louis Uchitelle, *The Disposable American: Layoffs and Their Consequences* (2007), pp. 43-45. Unless otherwise indicated, the remainder of this subsection is drawn from this book.

[45] *Ibid.*

[46] "U.S. Business Cycle Expansions and Contractions," National Bureau of Economic Research, updated Dec. 1, 2008, www.nber.org/cycles. The private, nonprofit, nonpartisan NBER is the national authority on when recessions begin and end.

[47] Uchitelle, *op. cit.*; and "Employment status of the civilian noninstitutional population, 1940 to date," Bureau of Labor Statistics, undated, www.bls.gov/cps/cpsaat1.pdf.

[48] "The Great Expansion — How It Was Achieved and How It Can Be Sustained," Joint Economic Committee, April, 2000, staff report, p.11, http://chuckskipton.com/uploads/growth_v4_-_no_cover.PDF.

[49] Steven Greenhouse, *The Big Squeeze: Tough Times for the American Worker* (2009), pp. 81-82.

[50] *Ibid.* Union membership numbers come from "Union Members Summary," U.S. Bureau of Labor Statistics, Jan. 28, 2009, www.bls.gov/news.release/union2.nr0.htm.

[51] Uchitelle, *op. cit.*, p. 138.

[52] Marlene A. Lee and Mark Mather, "U.S. Labor Force Trends," *Population Bulletin*, June 2008, Population Reference Bureau, pp. 7-8,

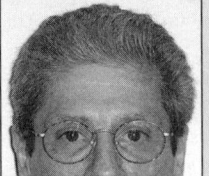

About the Author

Peter Katel is a *CQ Researcher* staff writer who previously reported on Haiti and Latin America for *Time* and *Newsweek* and covered the Southwest for newspapers in New Mexico. He has received several journalism awards, including the Bartolomé Mitre Award for coverage of drug trafficking, from the Inter-American Press Association. He holds an A.B. in university studies from the University of New Mexico. His recent reports include "Mexico's Drug War" and "Future of the Military."

www.prb.org/pdf08/63.2uslabor.pdf.

[53] Uchitelle, *op. cit.*, pp. 132-134.

[54] *Ibid.*, pp. 140-141.

[55] Paul Krugman, "Debunking the Reagan Myth," *The New York Times*, Jan. 21, 2008, www.nytimes.com/2008/01/21/opinion/21krugman.html.

[56] Peter B. Sperry, "The Real Reagan Economic Record: Responsible and Successful Fiscal Policy," Heritage Foundation, March 1, 2001, www.heritage.org/Research/taxes/bg1414.cfm.

[57] "Labor Force Statistics from the Current Population Survey," Bureau of Labor Statistics, http://data.bls.gov/ PDQ/servlet/SurveyOutputServlet?data_tool=latest_numbers&series_id=LNS14000000; also see Richard M. Devens Jr., "Employment and unemployment in the first half of 1988," Bureau of Labor Statistics, www.bls.gov/opub/mlr/1988/08/art3full.pdf.

[58] Susan E. Shank and Patricia M. Getz, "Employment and unemployment: developments in 1985," Bureau of Labor Statistics, February 1986, pp. 6-8, www.bls.gov/opub/mlr/1986/02/art1full.pdf.

[59] "Remarks by Governor Ben S. Bernanke, Global Economic and Investment Outlook Conference," Nov. 6, 2003, www.federalreserve.gov/boarddocs/speeches/2003/200311062/default.htm.

[60] *Ibid.*

[61] Emy Sok, "Lower unemployment in 2005," Bureau of Labor Statistics, March 2006, p. 10, www.bls.gov/opub/mlr/2006/03/art1full.pdf.

[62] *Ibid.*

[63] Nicholas Riccardi, "Economy's Growing, but Where Are the New Jobs?" *Los Angeles Times*, Feb. 15, 2005, p. A1.

[64] "American Recovery and Reinvestment Act: State-by-State Jobs Impact," The White House, Feb. 13, 2009, www.whitehouse.gov/assets/documents/Recovery_Act_state-by-state_jobs_2-131.pdf.

[65] Nicholas Confessore, "Amid Albany's Budget Crisis, A Rush to Spend U.S. Billions," *The New York Times*, March 5, 2009, p. A1. Also, "New York's Guide to the American Recovery and Reinvestment Act," undated, www.economicrecovery.ny.gov/index.htm.

[66] Confessore, *ibid.*

[67] "Certifications Required by Sections 1201, 1511 and 1607 of the American Recovery and Reinvestment Act of 2009," http://testimony.ost.dot.gov/ARRAcerts.

[68] "$8.4 billion for Public Transit," recovery.gov, March 5, 2009, www.recovery.gov/?q=node/202.

FOR MORE INFORMATION

Economic Policy Institute, 1333 H St., N.W., Suite 300, East Tower, Washington, DC 20005; (202) 775-8810; www.epi.org. Think tank with ties to organized labor and the Obama administration that places a heavy emphasis on job-related issues.

The Heritage Foundation, 214 Massachusetts Ave., N.E., Washington, DC 20002; (202) 546-4400; www.heritage.org. Conservative think tank issuing regular analyses and commentaries on the economy and unemployment.

National Employment Law Project, 75 Maiden Lane, Suite 601, New York, NY 10038; (212) 285-3025; www.nelp.org. Advocacy organization for workers and the unemployed providing information on unemployment insurance and other issues.

NewMajority.com; www.newmajority.com. Organization for dissident Republicans formed by former George W. Bush speechwriter David Frum that urges the party to rethink its positions on the economy.

U.S. Bureau of Labor Statistics, 2 Massachusetts Ave., N.E., Washington, DC 20212; (202) 691-5200; www.bls.gov. Statistical arm of the Department of Labor providing data about all aspects of employment and unemployment.

W. E. Upjohn Institute for Employment Research, 300 S. Westnedge Ave., Kalamazoo, MI 49007; (269) 343-5541; www.upjohninst.org. Nonpartisan think tank specializing in various aspects of employment and labor, including unemployment insurance.

[69] Dan Mihalopoulos, "Daley refuses to release stimulus project list," "Clout Street" (*Chicago Tribune* political blog), Feb. 4, 2009, http://newsblogs.chicagotribune.com/clout_st/2009/02/daley-refuses-to-release-stimulus-project-list.html.

[70] Dennis Byrne, "Daley's great, big hush-hush," *Chicago Tribune*, March 3, 2009, p. A25.

[71] Michael E. Kanell, "2011 turnaround seen for Georgia," *Atlanta Journal-Constitution*, Feb. 26, 2009, p. B1.

[72] Jan Moller, "Jindal rejects federal aid for jobless," *Times-Picayune* (New Orleans), Feb. 21, 2009, p. A1.

[73] Michael Luo, "Jobless Angry at Possibility of No Benefits," *The New York Times*, Feb. 26, 2009, www.nytimes.com/2009/02/27/us/27govs.html.

[74] Robert Pear and J. David Goodman, "Governors' Fight Over Stimulus May Define G.O.P.," *The New York Times*, Feb. 22, 2009, www.nytimes.com/2009/02/23/us/politics/23governors.html?partner=rss&emc=rss.

[75] James Salzer, "Perdue cuts deep, won't refuse funds," *Atlanta Journal-Constitution*, March 4, 2009, p. A1.

[76] "The Unemployment Insurance Modernization Act: Filling the Gaps in the Unemployment Safety Net While Stimulating the Economy," National Employment Law Project, Jan. 30, 3009, http://nelp.3cdn.net/c763952a5b73e8852c_3iim6sj65.pdf.

[77] "This Week," transcript, ABC News, Jan. 4, 2009, http://abcnews.go.com/ThisWeek/story?id=6573506&page=1.

[78] "Unemployment Insurance Data Summary," Department of Labor, http://workforcesecurity.doleta.gov/unemploy/content/data_stats/datasum08/DataSum_2008_4.pdf.

[79] Dana Mattioli and Sara Murray, "Employers Hit Salaried Staff With Furloughs," *The Wall Street Journal*, Feb. 24, 2009, http://online.wsj.com/article/SB123542559566852689.html.

[80] Andrea Hopkins, "Unpaid furloughs a trend for U.S. white-collar jobs," Reuters, Feb. 25, 2009, www.reuters.com/.

[81] Mary Ann Podmolik, "More companies, such as Acco Brands, turning to pay cuts to avoid more layoffs," *Chicago Tribune*, Feb. 17, 2009, www.chicagotribune.com/business/chi-tues_pay_cuts0217feb17,0,3374713.story.

[82] Evan Ramstad, "Koreans Take Pay Cuts to Stop Layoffs," *The Wall Street Journal*, March 3, 2009, p. A1.

[83] Hopkins, *op. cit.*

[84] Kyle Crichton, "Economic Lessons From Lenin's Seer," *The New York Times*, Feb. 14, 2009, www.nytimes.com/2009/02/15/weekinreview/15crichton.html.

[85] Benjamin Duer, "More than 800 apply for school janitor's job," CantonRep.com, March 9, 2009, www.cantonrep.com/archive/x1593365705/More-than-800-apply-for-school-janitor-s-job.

Bibliography
Selected Sources

Books

Epstein, Lita, *Surviving a Layoff: A Week-to-Week Guide to Getting Your Life Back Together*, Adams Media, 2009.

A professional retirement planner advises the newly laid-off on how to deal with their circumstances and bounce back.

Krugman, Paul, *The Return of Depression Economics and the Crisis of 2008*, W. W. Norton, 2008.

One of the Bush administration's toughest critics — now chiding Obama from the left — the Nobel Prize-winning economist and *New York Times* columnist analyzes the financial meltdown, its causes and possible solutions.

Woods, Thomas E., *Meltdown: A Free-Market Look at Why the Stock Market Collapsed, the Economy Tanked, and Government Bailouts Will Make Things Worse*, Regnery, 2009.

A conservative libertarian argues that government bailouts will delay economic recovery.

Articles

Aeppel, Timothy, and Justin Lahart, "Lean Factories Find It Hard to Cut Jobs Even in a Slump," *The Wall Street Journal*, March 9, 2009, p. A1.

U.S. manufacturing is so automated and efficient, laying off highly trained workers is difficult.

The Associated Press, "Buffett Says Nation Will Face Higher Unemployment," *The New York Times*, March 9, 2009, www.nytimes.com/aponline/2009/03/09/business/AP-Buffett-Economy.html.

Respected businessman Warren Buffett says the short-term future looks grim.

Baum, Geraldine, "It's Web 101 for this experienced intern," *Los Angeles Times*, March 6, 2009, www.latimes.com/news/printedition/front/la-na-senior-intern6-2009mar06,0,3173555.story.

As the media industry implodes, a former six-figure-salaried editor becomes an unpaid Web site intern to learn new skills.

Frayter, Karina, "IBM to laid-off: Want a job in India?" CNN, Feb. 5, 2009, http://money.cnn.com/2009/02/05/news/companies/ibm_jobs/.

In a reflection of how many operations IBM has moved abroad, the company is offering laid-off workers a chance to keep working — in another country.

Gerencher, Kristen, "Helping us through tough times," MarketWatch, Oct. 23, 2008, www.marketwatch.com.

A financial journalist discusses the growing psychological toll as the pace of layoffs continues unabated.

Leonhardt, David, "Job Losses Show Breadth of Recession," *The New York Times*, March 4, 2009, www.nytimes.com/2009/03/04/business/04leonhardt.html.

An economics correspondent reports that the pain of layoffs has spread wide, both geographically and demographically, though non-college graduates are especially affected.

Luo, Michael, "Months After Plant Closed, Many Still Struggling," *The New York Times*, Feb. 9, 2009, www.nytimes.com/2009/02/10/us/10factory.html.

Laid-off workers attempt to rebuild their lives.

Neil, Martha, "February Free Fall: Major Law Firms Lay Off Another 2,000-Plus Attorneys and Staff," *ABA Journal*, Feb. 26, 2009, http://abajournal.com/news/february_freefall_firms_ax_attorneys_freeze_pay.

The American Bar Association continues its coverage of major layoffs at big law firms, a new development in the upper reaches of the profession.

Reports and Studies

Dubay, Curtis, *et al.*, "Economic Stimulus Pushed by Flawed Jobs Analysis," Heritage Foundation, Jan. 28, 2009, www.heritage.org/research/economy/wm2252.cfm.

Three conservative analysts say tax cuts will create more jobs than government spending.

Jacobson, Louis, *et al.*, "Estimating the Returns to Community College for the Study of Labor (IZA)," February, 2004, Federal Reserve Bank of Chicago, December 2002, www.chicagofed.org/publications/workingpapers/papers/wp2002-31.pdf.

Three economists say taking math and science in community colleges improves potential earnings of laid-off workers.

Lerman, Robert I., "Are Skills the Problem? Reforming the Education and Training System in the United States," Upjohn Institute for Employment Research, 2008, www.american.edu/cas/econ/faculty/lerman/Ch2Lerman.pdf.

An advocate of expanding apprenticeship programs examines the consequences of education and job-training systems that don't reflect the varied ways in which people learn.

Vroman, Wayne, "Unemployment Insurance: Current Situation and Potential Reforms," Urban Institute, Feb. 3, 2009, www.urban.org/UploadedPDF/411835_unemployment_insurance.pdf.

An economist for a liberal think tank recommends steps to keep states' unemployment trust funds — the source of most benefits — healthy.

The Next Step:

Additional Articles from Current Periodicals

Job Forecasts

Magin, Janis L., "Forecast Finds Construction Still Strong," *Pacific Business News* **(Hawaii), Sept. 8, 2008.**

Although Hawaii's construction industry has slowed significantly, the number of construction jobs in the state is expected to gently decline in 2009.

Pierson, David, "UCLA Economists Expect Dismal 2009," *Los Angeles Times*, **Dec. 11, 2008, p. C6.**

The nation's unemployment rate will rise to 8.5 percent by late 2009 or early 2010, and 2 million jobs could be lost nationwide this year, according to a UCLA forecast.

Recovery and Reinvestment Act

Koff, Stephen, "Stimulus Bill Has Billions for Ohio Projects," *Cleveland Plain Dealer*, **Feb. 15, 2009, p. A1.**

The American Recovery and Reinvestment Act will create or save about 133,000 jobs in Ohio, 90 percent of them in the private sector.

Montgomery, Lori, "Trim to Stimulus Carves Into Goals for Job Creation," *The Washington Post*, **Feb. 13, 2009, p. A6.**

Congressional negotiations to trim billions of dollars from the stimulus package to satisfy Senate Republicans have diminished the plan's potential for job creation.

Pender, Kathleen, "Hard to Find the Jobs in This Stimulus Plan," *The San Francisco Chronicle*, **Feb. 15, 2009, p. K1.**

An unemployed person would have trouble reading the Recovery and Reinvestment Act and finding out where to look for work, at least in the near future.

Schoof, Renee, "Focus on Energy May Create Jobs," *The Miami Herald*, **Feb. 17, 2009, p. A4.**

Many of the jobs potentially created by the economic stimulus package are rooted in plans to combat global warming and reduce the nation's dependence on fossil fuels.

Retraining

Abate, Tom, "Next Task: Retraining Workers," *The San Francisco Chronicle*, **Feb. 17, 2009, p. C1.**

New "green" jobs may help Silicon Valley pull out of the recession, but the area faces the challenge of retraining its current workforce.

Bouchard, Kelley, "Recession Sparks Run on Retraining," *Portland Press Herald* **(Maine), Jan. 12, 2009, p. A1.**

Layoffs and the exportation of jobs overseas have led to an increase in the enrollment in retraining programs across the country.

Cronin, Brenda, "Retraining Services Could Clear Hurdle for Jobless," The Associated Press, Dec. 29, 2008.

Laid-off workers must retrain for new occupations in order to reach their previous wage levels.

Miller, Matthew, "Job Training Bill Opens New Doors," *Lansing State Journal* **(Michigan), Dec. 23, 2008, p. 1A.**

The Michigan state legislature has passed a bill allowing community colleges to create training programs for companies adding new jobs and new businesses entering the state.

Unemployment Insurance

"Missouri Unemployment Council Opposes Federal Money for Unemployment Compensation," *Kansas City Business Journal*, **March 3, 2009.**

The Missouri State Unemployment Council says the state should not accept $133.2 million from the federal government for the Missouri Unemployment Trust Fund because it would cost the state millions of dollars annually in the long run.

Downing, Neil, "R.I. Jobless to Get Boost in Benefits," *Providence Journal-Bulletin* **(Rhode Island), Feb. 13, 2009, p. 1.**

The economic stimulus package could give Rhode Island's 35,000 out-of-work residents an extra $25 in their weekly unemployment benefits.

Keefe, Bob, "Perdue May Turn Down Some Funds," *Atlanta Journal-Constitution*, **Feb. 23, 2009, p. 1A.**

Georgia is slated to receive $220 million in federal aid to bolster its unemployment-insurance program, but Gov. Sonny Perdue is worried the money could force the state to change its unemployment laws.

Citing CQ Researcher

Sample formats for citing these reports in a bibliography include the ones listed below. Preferred styles and formats vary, so please check with your instructor or professor.

MLA STYLE

Jost, Kenneth. "Rethinking the Death Penalty." CQ Researcher 16 Nov. 2001: 945-68.

APA STYLE

Jost, K. (2001, November 16). Rethinking the death penalty. CQ Researcher, 11, 945-968.

CHICAGO STYLE

Jost, Kenneth. "Rethinking the Death Penalty." CQ Researcher, November 16, 2001, 945-968.

In-depth Reports on Issues in the News

Are you writing a paper?

Need backup for a debate?

Want to become an expert on an issue?

For 80 years, students have turned to *CQ Researcher* for in-depth reporting on issues in the news. Reports on a full range of political and social issues are now available. Following is a selection of recent reports:

Civil Liberties
Limiting Lawsuits, 12/08
Affirmative Action, 10/08
Gay Marriage Showdowns, 9/08
America's Border Fence, 9/08
Immigration Debate, 2/08
Prison Reform, 4/07

Crime/Law
Mexico's Drug War, 12/08
Prostitution Debate, 5/08
Public Defenders, 4/08
Gun Violence, 5/07

Education
Reading Crisis? 2/08
Discipline in Schools, 2/08
Student Aid, 1/08
Racial Diversity in Public Schools, 9/07
Stress on Students, 7/07

Environment
Reducing Carbon Footprint, 12/08
Protecting Wetlands, 10/08
Buying Green, 2/08
Future of Recycling, 12/07

Health/Safety
Preventing Cancer, 1/09
Heart Health, 9/08
Global Food Crisis, 6/08
Preventing Memory Loss, 4/08

International Affairs/Politics
The Obama Presidency, 1/09
The National Debt, 11/08
Financial Bailout, 10/08
Political Conventions, 8/08
Race and Politics, 7/08

Social Trends
Public-Works Projects, 2/09
Falling Birthrates, 11/08
Regulating Credit Cards, 10/08
Internet Accuracy, 8/08

Terrorism/Defense
Homeland Security, 2/09
Rise in Counterinsurgency, 9/08
Cost of the Iraq War, 4/08

Youth
Debating Hip-Hop, 6/07

Upcoming Reports

GOP's Future, 3/20/09

Future of Newspapers, 3/27/09

Extreme Sports, 4/3/09

Wrongful Convictions, 4/10/09

High-Speed Trains, 4/17/09

Judicial Elections, 4/24/09

ACCESS

CQ Researcher is available in print and online. For access, visit your library or www.cqresearcher.com.

STAY CURRENT

To receive notice of upcoming *CQ Researcher* reports, or learn more about *CQ Researcher* products, subscribe to the free e-mail newsletters, *CQ Researcher Alert!* and *CQ Researcher News*: http://cqpress.com/newsletters.

PURCHASE

To purchase a *CQ Researcher* report in print or electronic format (PDF), visit www.cqpress.com or call 866-427-7737. Single reports start at $15. Bulk purchase discounts and electronic-rights licensing are also available.

SUBSCRIBE

Annual full-service *CQ Researcher* subscriptions—including 44 reports a year, monthly index updates, and a bound volume—start at $803. Add $25 for domestic postage.

CQ Researcher Online offers a backfile from 1991 and a number of tools to simplify research. For pricing information, call 800-834-9020, ext. 1906, or e-mail librarysales@cqpress.com.

Published by CQ Press, a division of SAGE Publications

www.cqresearcher.com

Future of the GOP

Can Republicans stage a comeback?

Former Lt. Gov. Michael Steele of Maryland is the first African-American to head the Republican Party, reflecting the GOP's nascent efforts to broaden its appeal, especially to minorities and young voters.

L ast November's sweeping election of Barack Obama and further losses in Congress presented Republicans with their worst defeat in more than a decade. Republicans recognize that they are at a low ebb but believe they still have a firm foundation for success. Congressional Republicans have decided to oppose Obama's spending proposals, rather than trying to collaborate in a bipartisan fashion. They believe a clear statement of core party principles — lower taxes and limited government — will still be popular. Others aren't convinced, arguing that the party must adapt to challenges it faces among minorities, the young and voters outside the South. Other parties have snapped back quickly from similar losses, but some predict that Republicans face a long period in the political wilderness. Meanwhile, it's not clear who speaks for the party — the congressional leadership, potential presidential aspirants such as Alaska Gov. Sarah Palin and Louisiana Gov. Bobby Jindal, or even radio talk-show host Rush Limbaugh.

CQ Researcher • March 20, 2009 • www.cqresearcher.com
Volume 19, Number 11 • Pages 249-272

Cover: Getty Images/Meet the Press/Alex Wong

CQ Researcher

March 20, 2009
Volume 19, Number 11

MANAGING EDITOR: Thomas J. Colin
tcolin@cqpress.com

ASSISTANT MANAGING EDITOR: Kathy Koch
kkoch@cqpress.com

ASSOCIATE EDITOR: Kenneth Jost

STAFF WRITERS: Thomas J. Billitteri, Marcia Clemmitt, Peter Katel

CONTRIBUTING WRITERS: Rachel Cox, Sarah Glazer, Alan Greenblatt, Barbara Mantel, Patrick Marshall, Tom Price, Jennifer Weeks

DESIGN/PRODUCTION EDITOR: Olu B. Davis

ASSISTANT EDITOR: Darrell Dela Rosa

FACT-CHECKING: Eugene J. Gabler, Michelle Harris

EDITORIAL INTERN: Vyomika Jairam

CQ PRESS

A Division of SAGE

PRESIDENT AND PUBLISHER:
John A. Jenkins

EXECUTIVE DIRECTOR,
REFERENCE INFORMATION GROUP:
Alix B. Vance

CQ Press is a registered trademark of Congressional Quarterly Inc.

CQ Researcher (ISSN 1056-2036) is printed on acid-free paper. Published weekly, except; (Jan. wk. 1) (May wk. 4) (July wks. 1, 2) (Aug. wks. 3, 4) (Nov. wk. 4) and (Dec. wk. 4), by CQ Press, a division of SAGE Publications. Annual full-service subscriptions start at $803. For pricing, call 1-800-834-9020, ext. 1906. To purchase a *CQ Researcher* report in print or electronic format (PDF), visit www. cqpress.com or call 866-427-7737. Single reports start at $15. Bulk purchase discounts and electronic-rights licensing are also available. Periodicals postage paid at Washington, D.C., and additional mailing offices. POSTMASTER: Send address changes to *CQ Researcher*, 2300 N St., N.W., Suite 800, Washington, DC 20037.

Future of the GOP

BY ALAN GREENBLATT

THE ISSUES

As Senate minority leader, Mitch McConnell is arguably the nation's most powerful Republican. When he addressed the Republican National Committee (RNC) on Jan. 29, the Kentucky senator spoke of grim news for his party.

"Over the past two elections, we've lost 13 Senate seats and 51 House seats," McConnell said. "Our most reliable voters are in decline as a percentage of the overall vote, and Democratic voter registration is on the rise."

After Democratic Sen. Barack Obama's historic victory last November, Republicans are now the clear minority party, and some say they could be in danger of staying in the political wilderness for a long time.

It's tempting for Republicans to blame their problems on President George W. Bush, who left office with a 22 percent approval rating — the lowest since Gallup began polling more than 70 years ago. [1] The litany of Bush failures is familiar: The Iraq War, now in its seventh year; the administration's abysmal response to New Orleans' needs during Hurricane Katrina; corruption scandals that cost the GOP support even among the party faithful.

Finally, Republicans were blamed for the fiscal crisis that erupted last September. "The economic meltdown had a profound effect on this election," veteran Republican consultant Tony Fabrizio said in a radio interview two days after Election Day. [2]

The result was a Democratic sweep, with Obama carrying states that had

As a social conservative who touts her tax-cutting prowess, Alaska Gov. Sarah Palin appeals to the Republican Party base. Her selection as Sen. John McCain's running mate initially boosted his chances, but in her early interviews with the media Palin appeared ill-prepared, leading some prominent Republicans to question McCain's judgment in selecting her.

Getty Images/William Thomas Cain

been solidly Republican for decades and racking up the largest popular vote of any Democrat since Lyndon B. Johnson in 1964. Having lost their congressional majorities in 2006, Republicans saw their numbers slip further in 2008.

William Frey, a demographer at the Brookings Institution, says, "Republicans were certainly hurt by the economy, but if the economy had stayed normal, they would have been hurt terrifically by the changes in geography of President Bush and his brand of Republicanism." Frey's point: The GOP has become largely identified with conservative social issues popular in the South and risks becoming a regional party appealing primarily to the

South, parts of the Mountain West and the Great Plains.

Republicans last fall were shut out on the coasts and lost the suburbs for the first time since 1996. "As Republicans, we know that commonsense, conservative principles aren't regional," McConnell told the RNC. "But I think we have to admit that our sales job has been."

But the party faces other demographic challenges: It is losing ground among minorities and the most educated voters. "The Republican Party is increasingly white, rural and old, in a country that is increasingly less of all those things," says Jonathan Martin, who covers the party for *Politico*. "This is now emphatically a minority party in this country."

Many Republicans would disagree, despite the party's recent losses. After all, they point out, after Bush's re-election in 2004 Republicans were talking confidently of building a "permanent majority." "It was only a few years ago Republicans were thinking they were the natural majority in the country," says William F. Connelly Jr., a political scientist at Washington and Lee University. "Democrats might not want to operate on that assumption too quickly."

But Ruy Teixeira, a Democratic analyst and senior fellow at both the left-leaning Century Foundation and the liberal Center for American Progress, says things are different today. "Democrats in 2002 and 2004 still had the demographic wind at their back. Republicans don't have that. Not only did they get clobbered, not only did they make some mistakes, but the demographic wind is in their face."

Majority of States Favored Democrats in 2008

Twenty-nine states and the District of Columbia had Democratic Party affiliation advantages of 10 points or greater in 2008, including all states in the Northeast and far West and all but Indiana in the Great Lakes region. An additional six states had Democratic advantages ranging between 5 and 9 points. In contrast, only five states were either solidly or leaning Republican in 2008. Ten states were deemed competitive.

Political Orientation of the States

States are considered "solidly" Democratic or Republican if they have a party identification of 10 percentage points or more; "leaning" if the advantage is 5 to 9 points and "competitive" if the partisan advantage is less than 5 points.

Solidly Democrat
Leaning Democrat
Competitive
Leaning Republican
Solidly Republican

Source: Gallup Poll

And House Republicans in particular face big disadvantages, says John J. Pitney Jr., a political scientist at California's Claremont McKenna College. Democrats hold 32 of the 33 House districts in which African-Americans make up 40 percent or more of the population — the only exception being a Louisiana seat where an indicted Democrat was ousted last fall. They also control 31 of the 35 mostly Hispanic seats — all but the four Florida districts dominated by Cuban-Americans, who have long favored Republicans. In addition, Democrats hold all 22 House seats in New England, and all but three of the 29 districts in New York — much of which used to be fertile GOP territory.

While there's some overlap among those seats, they give Democrats a 103-seat head start toward the 218 needed for a majority. "If Republicans concede these districts, they have to get two-thirds of the rest, which is tough to do," Pitney says.

Besides problems appealing to minorities and voters in the most populous parts of the country, Republicans have a hard time attracting voters under 30, two-thirds of whom voted for Obama. "People who have come of age during the last decade are the most Democratic population of any cohort," says Gary Jabobson, a political scientist at the University of California, San Diego. "That might be the

most striking legacy of the Bush years in terms of the national, partisan political system."

Then-Republican National Committee Chairman Mike Duncan in December launched an in-house think tank, the Center for Republican Renewal. "Republicans have grown accustomed to having our party recognized as the 'Party of Ideas,' but we must acknowledge that many Americans today believe the party is stale and does not deserve that label," Duncan wrote in a memo to the RNC. [3]

But he was replaced in January by Michael Steele, a former Maryland lieutenant governor, who quickly canned the think tank. "I'm trying to avoid the use of words that start with 're,' words like renewal, rebuild, recharge, re-this and re-that," Steele wrote in a memo to RNC members. "I'm convinced we should not re-anything. Instead, we must stand proudly for the timeless principles our party has always stood for." [4]

So far, Steele's argument has carried the day within the party. Republicans say the party lost its way during the Bush years by running up deficits and overspending. They say it needs to return to arguing for lower taxes and limited government.

"Liberalism's preferred solution to working-class insecurity — making America more like Europe through a vast expansion of the tax-and-transfer state — is still unpopular with most voters," write conservative authors Ross Douthat and Reihan Salam in their book *Grand New Party.* [5]

All but three congressional Republicans opposed the $787 billion stimulus package enacted in February. The GOP's congressional leadership has resisted Obama's entreaties for bipartisan cooperation to help solve the economic crisis and has actively discouraged members from collaborating with Democrats.

"We will lose on legislation, but we will win the message war every day, and every week, until November 2010," said Rep. Patrick McHenry, R-N.C. "Our goal is to bring down approval numbers for [Speaker Nancy] Pelosi and for House Democrats. That will take repetition. This is a marathon, not a sprint." [6]

But so far, public opinion polls suggest Republicans are losing the message war. Obama's approval ratings are much higher than the GOP's, and Americans give him higher marks for dealing with the economy.

While Republicans believe they have regained their footing with a back-to-basics message on taxes and the size of government, some people say they are not reading the mood of the moment, when many Americans are looking to Washington for action in response to the economic crisis.

And while the party's base seems content with that message, it's not clear who speaks for the party — the congressional leadership, potential presidential aspirants such as Alaska Gov. Sarah Palin, or even radio talk-show host Rush Limbaugh. A recent Rasmussen survey found that 68 percent of Republicans say their party lacks a clear leader. [7]

Gov. Bobby Jindal of Louisiana was considered the party's leading new star but stumbled in his first big national appearance. Although Jindal's performance giving the Republican Party's official response to President Obama's Feb. 24 address to Congress was widely panned — both by liberals angered by its message and conservatives unhappy with his style — Jindal is still considered a comer in GOP circles. The former Rhodes scholar is known to be highly intelligent and has won praise through his efforts to reform Medicaid. Also, Jindal is just 37 — giving him plenty of time to make a comeback on the national stage after a weak initial outing.

Steele has sought to fill the party's void, making near-constant media appearances. But even some RNC mem-

Democrats Widening Gap Between Parties

The number of Americans who self-identify as "Democrats" has increased in the last three years while the number of those identifying as Republicans has dropped a similar amount. In 2008, 8% more Americans identified themselves as Democrats than Republicans, the largest difference in the last 20 years.

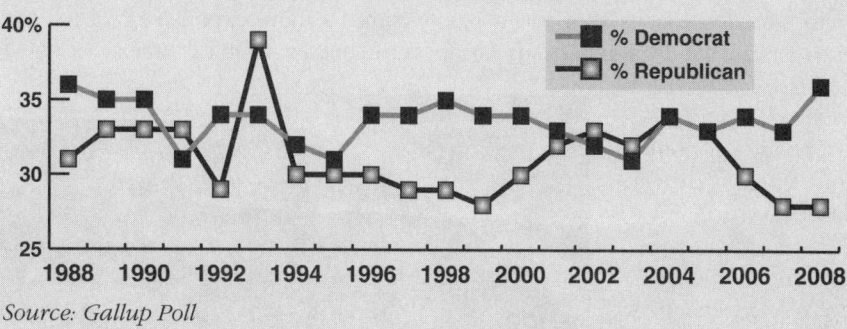

Source: Gallup Poll

bers have complained that he has stumbled repeatedly in his early days as titular head of the party. Two months into his tenure, however, Steele began to cut back on his media appearances in the wake of an interview with *GQ* in which he expressed support for abortion rights. Steele denied that that was his position. But his need to clarify a number of his public statements led party activists to say he should concentrate on the nuts-and-bolts work of rebuilding the party, such as fundraising and appointing key staff.

Asked about Steele's performance on CNN's "The Situation Room" on March 4, Nicolle Wallace, a former top adviser to Bush and Arizona Sen. John McCain's 2008 presidential campaign, said, "At the beginning of 'American Idol,' there are a lot of singers and a lot of them are pretty terrible and that's where the Republican Party is right now.

"We're at the beginning of our season," Wallace continued. "By the time the Republican Party has to stand before voters again, we'll have our act together."

As the GOP seeks a new strategy, here are some questions political observers are asking:

Is America a center-right nation?

Republicans insist that America remains hungry for conservative ideas. A week before last November's election, *Newsweek's* cover story declared America a center-right nation — "a fact that a President Obama would forget at his peril."

"Americans . . . [tend] to be more conservative than liberal," wrote Editor Jon Meacham, noting that twice as many people consider themselves conservative, compared with liberals (40 percent to 20 percent in *Newsweek's* poll). He also pointed out that Democrats had won only three of the previous 10 presidential elections, "and in those years they were led by Southern Baptist nominees who ran away from the liberal label." [8]

Obama, of course, went on to win the election handily, while the Democrats expanded their majorities in the House and Senate. But some analysts say Democrats didn't so much win the election as the Republicans lost it.

The question about whether Americans have gotten more liberal — as opposed to just more Democratic — is central to Republican hopes for a comeback. Voters clearly disapproved of the Bush White House. But if they disapprove of the GOP's broader foundations — such as lower taxes and limited government — it would make a return to power much more difficult.

Peter Wehner, a former Bush White House official now at the Ethics and Public Policy Center, argues the election was not so much an ideological victory for Democrats as it was a partisan one. That is, Republicans were blamed for myriad mistakes and the crumbling economy, but voters didn't suddenly turn liberal in reaction against conservative ideas.

"Political and personal scandals have tarnished the GOP's image," Wehner wrote in *The Washington Post.* "The early years of the Iraq War were badly mismanaged. The financial crisis, fairly or not, is laid at the feet of Republicans. Around 90 percent of the nation believes America is on the wrong track, and the GOP is perceived as the responsible party." 9

Grover Norquist, president of Americans for Tax Reform and a prominent Republican strategist, says the Obama campaign ran away from the liberal label, knowing progressive policies remain a tough sell. "You can't say people are sick of tax cuts," he says. "He promised more than anything else that he wouldn't raise taxes on anyone with incomes over $250,000."

But Obama is clearly not governing as a conservative. He's already expanded government health insurance for children, and his budget includes a $634 billion "down payment" toward further coverage. He also proposed a cap-and-trade program that will seek to cut carbon dioxide emissions by imposing fees on large polluters.

It's become a Republican talking point to call this expansion of government effort "socialist." The question is whether the public views things that negatively, or whether it welcomes a more expansive role for government in troubled times.

Then-President George W. Bush relaxes at his ranch in Crawford, Texas. He left office in January with a 22-percent approval rating — the lowest since Gallup began polling more than 70 years ago. Many Republicans blame the Democrats' sweep in the 2008 elections on perceived failures during Bush's two terms, including the Iraq War, the administration's poor response to Hurricane Katrina and the economic crisis.

AFP/Getty Images/Jim Watson

Karlyn Bowman, a polling expert at the conservative American Enterprise Institute (AEI), says "ideological identification" hasn't changed. "Most people consider themselves moderate, with about 35 percent conservative and about 18 percent liberal," she says.

"I'm not at all convinced we're seeing a bigger appetite for government," Bowman says. "We're clearly seeing an appetite for government to do something."

But Teixeira, the Democratic analyst, says it would be easy for Republicans to fool themselves into thinking voter attitudes haven't changed much. "If you ask people if they find government wasteful, you get a very high level of agreement," he says. But the same people "are saying now's the time for universal health care and greater energy efficiency and college affordability."

The debate is complicated by the fact that Republicans have succeeded in turning "liberal" into a dirty word. President George H. W. Bush referred to it as "the L-word" during his 1988 campaign. Since then, many Democrats have rejected the label in favor of "progressive." So even if liberalism is making a comeback, you might not know it.

Michael Franc, vice president of government relations at the conservative Heritage Foundation, says exit polls show there are still many more conservatives than liberals, with "a slight advantage even on the West Coast." But, he concedes, "A lot of people who have positions that are liberal may identify themselves as moderate."

Some scholars believe Americans are more pragmatic than ideological, willing to bend their ideas about what government should or should not do, based on the challenges of the day. "The country is basically centrist and will be moved by which party and leaders are proposing what [seem like] sensible solutions, given the context of the moment," says Sean Wilentz, a Princeton University historian. "When they loved [President] Franklin D. Roosevelt, they weren't necessarily all left-wing liberals."

Conversely, suggests Jacobson, the University of California political scientist, the country shifted to the right under President Ronald Reagan after the inflation and high tax rates of the 1970s. "People were willing to accept Republican policies, as long as they didn't dismantle New Deal entitlements," he says.

While Americans are basically pragmatists, political scientist Jacobson suggests the pendulum is swinging left again. "Right now, you're having people willing to accept a vast increase of government activity in the economy because the economy is so bad," he says.

And that, concludes Teixeira, indicates the country's mood is less conservative than it was at the start of the decade. "For several years, attitudes toward government and its role have been changing, toward a more optimistic view of what government should be doing and what areas it should be engaged in."

While Obama is clearly convinced that Teixeira's line of thinking is right — and Republicans argue against his expansionist policies — *Newsweek* seems to have changed its mind. Meacham and Assistant Managing Editor Evan Thomas wrote a cover story in February declaring, "We are all socialists now." [10]

Can Republicans appeal to minorities and the young?

In 2001, former Republican Party Chairman Rich Bond told *The Washington Post*, "We've taken white guys about as far as that group can go. We are in need of diversity, women, Latino, African-American, Asian. . . . That is where the future of the Republican Party is." [11]

Since then, however, GOP support has only grown whiter. In last year's presidential election, Sen. McCain drew 55 percent of the white vote, compared with 43 percent for Obama, according to exit polls. But Obama took two-thirds of the Hispanic vote and 95 percent of the African-American vote. [12]

Obama also took 66 percent of the under-30 vote. That may be in part because the minority share of the younger electorate is growing rapidly. Only 62 percent of voters between the ages of 18 and 29 were white in 2008 — down from 74 percent in 2000, according to Scott Keeter, survey research director for the Pew Research Center.

"Young people were stronger for

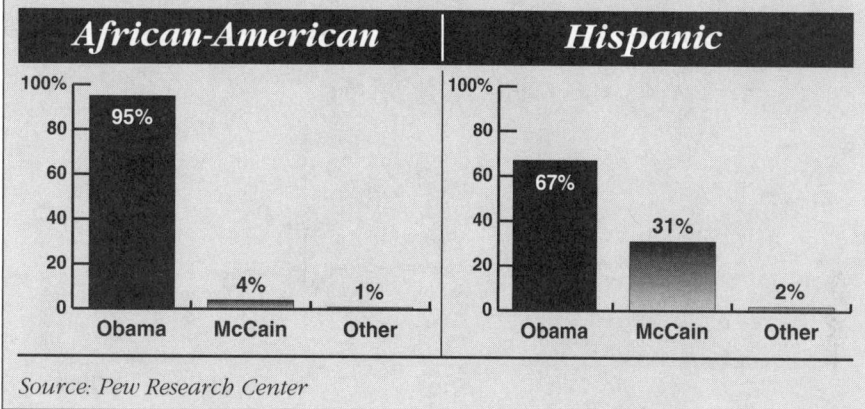

Blacks, Hispanics Heavily Favored Obama

Virtually all African-Americans chose Barack Obama over John McCain in the recent election. Among Hispanics, less than one-third chose McCain.

2008 Presidential Election Voting by Minority Group

African-American — Obama 95%, McCain 4%, Other 1%

Hispanic — Obama 67%, McCain 31%, Other 2%

Source: Pew Research Center

Obama than Democrats in general," he says. "Sixty-one percent of voters under 30 identify or lean Democratic. There's an almost 30-point gap among this age group. If these young people keep this tendency, this is going to be a real problem for the Republicans."

But Keeter says young people tend not to be as anchored in their voting habits and may switch allegiances if they find that Obama does not deliver.

"Young people are fickle," agrees AEI's Bowman. "Clearly, Obama has made an extraordinary start with young people, but I'm not convinced they're wedded to the Democratic Party at this point."

Some political scientists point out that people usually grow more conservative as they age and take on greater responsibilities, such as parenting and home ownership.

But others disagree. Some generational cohorts start out voting one way and stay that way. Aside from young people, the most Democratic portion of the electorate last year was the over-75 crowd — those who grew up during President Roosevelt's New Deal program aimed at rescuing the country from the Great Depression. And people who

came of age during Reagan's presidency in the 1980s are still more Republican than Democratic.

The GOP — short for Grand Old Party — will have a tough time winning back today's young people, suggests Democratic analyst Teixeira, even with Bush gone from the scene.

Younger voters tend to be more tolerant than the electorate as a whole when it comes to issues such as immigrants and gay marriage. "This is the most socially liberal part of the electorate," he says, "Republicans are totally out of step culturally with them."

Teixeira also believes Democrats may benefit from "generational lock-in. Once you're identified with one party, you tend to keep it as you age."

Some in GOP circles say the party needs to learn to use Twitter, Facebook and other relatively new social-networking and communication tools — as the Obama campaign has done — in order to reach younger voters. "The conservative spirit is very much alive in young voters," says Jessica Colon, chair of the Young Republican National Federation. "They need to know the party will speak their language through technology."

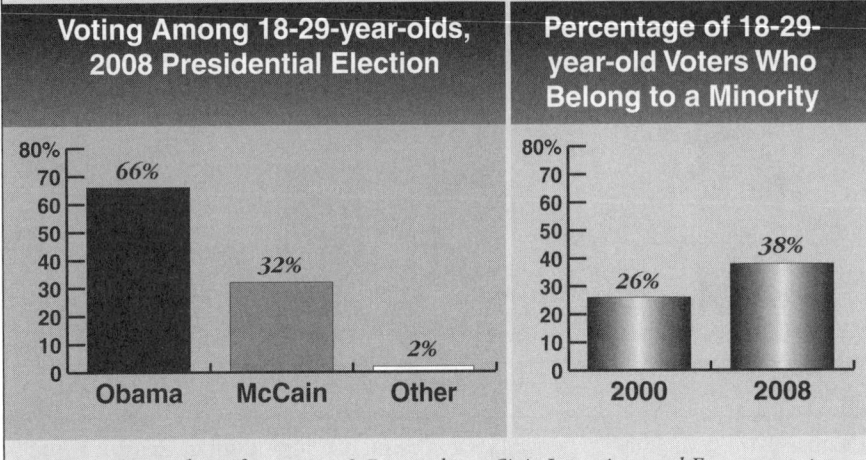

Minorities and Youths Favor Democrats

Young Americans voted overwhelmingly for Democratic candidate Barack Obama in 2008 (graph at left). Minorities now represent nearly 40 percent of the youth demographic, which generally votes Democratic (graph at right).

Voting Among 18-29-year-olds, 2008 Presidential Election

- Obama: 66%
- McCain: 32%
- Other: 2%

Percentage of 18-29-year-old Voters Who Belong to a Minority

- 2000: 26%
- 2008: 38%

Sources: Center for Information & Research on Civic Learning and Engagement, Tufts University

Republicans' standing among minority voters, particularly Hispanics, is also worrisome. Forty percent of Latinos voted for Bush in 2004, but Hispanic support for the GOP dropped in 2008 due to the poor economy and the party's general hard line on immigration — particularly a bill passed by the House in 2005 that would have deemed illegal immigrants as felons.

"They cannot afford the Hispanic vote to become like the African-American vote," says Connelly, the political scientist at Washington and Lee University. "If it does, they will become something like a permanent minority."

Norquist, the president of Americans for Tax Reform, concedes the GOP has a lot of work to do in winning back Hispanic support but says it can be done. He compares it with the Catholic vote, which had been heavily Democratic but now favors the GOP.

"People like Tom Tancredo were insulting," Norquist says, referring to a former Colorado House Republican and 2008 presidential aspirant whose campaign was predominately anti-immigrant. But, he adds, "Tancredo's not in office any more, and we nominated the most pro-immigrant candidate."

Republicans say minority voters, like the population as a whole, can be won over with a convincing economic message. In addition, Republicans point out that Hispanics tend to be fairly conservative on social issues. Roger Hedgecock, a former San Diego mayor who now hosts a radio talk show, notes that both African-Americans and Hispanics supported Proposition 8, the California initiative that banned gay marriage last fall.

"There's no intrinsic reason why basic conservative principles of limited but energetic and effective government, individual freedom and economic opportunity can't be made appealing to blacks, to Hispanics and others," says Peter Berkowitz, a senior fellow at the Hoover Institution at Stanford University.

"We need messengers . . . young, Hispanic, black, a cross section," Steele, the GOP's first African-American chairman, told *The Washington Times.* "We want them to convey that the modern-day GOP looks like the conservative party that stands on principles, but we want to apply them to urban-suburban hip-hop settings." [13]

Steele's comments were much mocked, however, especially after he added, "We need to uptick our image with everyone, including one-armed midgets."

Is the GOP a national party?

At his RNC speech in January, Minority Leader McConnell noted that in 1984 — the year he was first elected to the Senate — Republicans "were everywhere," with governors and senators and presidential electoral votes coming from all around the country. But "a lot has changed since then," he noted.

"You can walk from Canada to Mexico and from Maine to Arizona without ever leaving a state with a Democratic governor," he said. Democratic Arizona Gov. Janet Napolitano has since been sworn in as secretary of Homeland Security, leaving Republican Jan Brewer in charge back home.

"Not a single Republican senator represents the tens of millions of Americans on the West Coast," McConnell said. "And on the East Coast, you can drive from North Carolina to New Hampshire without touching a single state that has a Republican in the U.S. Senate."

McConnell warned the GOP is in danger of becoming a regional party. "In politics," he said, "there's a name for a regional party: It's called a minority party."

McConnell is not the only Republican wondering if the GOP is in danger of becoming a solely regional force. The defeat of Connecticut Republican Rep. Christopher Shays last fall left the GOP without a single House member in the six New England states. And Democrats had control of every legislative chamber east of Ohio and north of Virginia except the Pennsylvania Senate. [14]

Perhaps most troubling for the GOP is the fact that Obama not only preserved his party's recent lock on the West Coast and the Northeast but also carried the entire Upper Midwest, including Ohio — which had supported President Bush in both 2000 and 2004 — and Indiana, which hadn't voted Democratic since 1964. He also won Virginia (Republican since 1964) and North Carolina (Republican since 1976).

"What we thought was our electoral map no longer is our map," said Republican consultant Fabrizio on National Public Radio's "On Point."

With Republican strength clearly rooted in the South and parts of the Interior West, the party must win in areas that have grown accustomed to voting Democratic in order to win a national election.

Jacobson, the University of California political scientist, points out that during the relatively close elections between 1988 and 2008, both parties were somewhat regional in strength — with Democrats strongest on the coasts and Republicans dominating the Interior West, the Plains States and the South. The Upper Midwest was the most competitive area.

But Republicans have lost strength in the Upper Midwest and in Mountain West states like Colorado and New Mexico, "and, of course, New England," he says. "Republicans are increasingly a party of the South and the Plains States. To the extent they play to their conservative Southern base, they can't do very well in lots of other places. There also now aren't enough socially conservative Republicans to create a majority out of."

Thus, the central question is: Have Republicans, by playing to the concerns of more conservative Southern voters, alienated voters in the more moderate Northeast and in suburban precincts nationwide?

"There is a danger for the Republicans [to be] seen as not just regional but regional in a way that seems unfriendly toward large parts of the country or large swaths of the elec-

"In Need of Diversity"

Crowds at the 2008 Republican National Convention (top) reflect the party's tendency toward white, older Americans. The narrow demographic profile once prompted former Republican Party Chairman Rich Bond to note, "We are in need of diversity, women, Latino, African-American, Asian. . . . That is where the future of the Republican Party is." By contrast, young and minority voters are a major presence at the Democratic National Convention (bottom).

torate," says Michael Barone, a columnist and fellow at the conservative American Enterprise Institute.

Not everyone is convinced the GOP message only plays well in the South and the Plains. Voting patterns within states, say some analysts, are more complex than the simplistic Republican "red" and Democratic "blue" labels displayed on news broadcasts on election nights.

For instance, GOP governors preside over states that vote "blue" presidentially, such as California and Minnesota and even half the New England states. "Republicans still have strongholds around the country in terms of both legislatures and governors," says Tim Storey, an elections expert with the National Conference of State Legislatures.

"In Washington state and Pennsylvania, our attorney general candidates both won huge in blue states," says Carrie Cantrell, spokeswoman for the Republican State Leadership Committee. "We can win in areas when our candidates focus on state and local issues."

But what about the party's national message? Is there a danger that Republicans nationally will sound too much like the party of one or two regions?

The GOP's congressional leadership has been disproportionately Southern for more than a decade. Now, due to defeats in more moderate areas such as New England, the GOP congressional caucuses are dominated by districts that are more conservative than the nation as a whole. The Northern Mountain West and the South now supply nearly half the nation's House Republicans and fully three-fifths of the Republicans in the Senate.

"When it comes to the House of Representatives, a map of the Republican Party looks like a Dalmatian," says Claremont McKenna College's Pitney. "The party is viable in some places and nonexistent in others."

Many Republicans insist the party's core message of lower taxes and limited government can still attract voters anywhere. "It will play well regionally," says Solomon Yue, a member of the Republican National Committee from "blue" Oregon. "All love freedom. All love a good economy creating jobs, and lower taxes to create jobs."

For now, though, the party's problem is that, given the increasingly regional nature of the GOP membership, there may be a tendency to legislate in parochial ways that don't reflect the desires of the entire nation. After Congress defeated an auto industry bailout package last December, *National Journal* Political Editor Ronald

Brownstein noted that the GOP vote broke along regional lines: The Northeastern and Midwestern Republicans were closely divided, but Republicans from the South, Mountain West and Plains voted strongly against the plan, which predominantly benefited companies in Michigan — and union workers. Those who did support it "had a General Motors plant in or near his district," Brownstein noted.

"Republican legislators in the most competitive states face the risk of being defined by an agenda that reflects only the priorities of bedrock conservative places," Brownstein wrote. "In congressional caucuses so skewed toward the right, it's not clear who will have an instinct for what might rebuild the GOP in Connecticut or California." [15] ∎

BACKGROUND

GOP's 'Southern Strategy'

The New Deal coalition cobbled together by Franklin D. Roosevelt in response to the Great Depression propelled Democrats to victory in all but two of the nine presidential elections from 1932 to 1964.

"The Republicans were the party of the Northeast, of business, of the middle classes and of white Protestants, while the Democrats enjoyed a clear majority among the working classes, organized labor, Catholics and the South" at all political levels, wrote pollster Everett Carll Ladd Jr. [16]

The high-water mark for Democrats came in 1964, when Johnson won the largest share of the popular presidential vote in modern times, and the party took two-thirds of the House and Senate seats. But hidden by that victory were the seeds of GOP growth and the birth of the modern conservative movement.

The GOP standard-bearer, Arizona Sen. Barry M. Goldwater, opposed the 1964 Civil Rights Act, helping to bring five Southern states into the GOP column. The South had been solidly Democratic since the Civil War, but Goldwater's conservatism — and his regional appeal — began to shift the Republican centers of gravity from the party's traditional homes in the Midwest and Northeast to the South and West.

"The civil rights movement was bound to destroy the New Deal coalition, because it depended on the South," says Princeton historian Wilentz.

About a third of the South's House districts broke with tradition and elected Republicans in 1966, in part due to a backlash against Johnson's liberal Great Society agenda, which included a major rewrite of immigration law, the creation of Medicare and passage of both the Civil Rights and the Voting Rights acts. All told, Republicans picked up 47 House seats, three Senate seats and eight governorships — including the election of Reagan as governor of California.

"If Goldwater had only brought Southern whites into the Republican coalition, he would not have proved to be a transformative figure," write two authors associated with *The Economist*. "But he also linked conservatism to a very different region — the booming West." [17]

In 1968 — a tumultuous year punctuated by street rioting following the assassination of the Rev. Martin Luther King Jr. — Richard M. Nixon, built on Goldwater's inroads by pursuing his "Southern strategy" — exploiting white voters' fears of the growing political power and demands of African-Americans.

The Democratic share of the presidential vote plummeted from a record 61 percent in 1964 to 43 percent in 1968, with third-party candidate George Wallace appealing even more directly to voter anxiety than Nixon. In his

Continued on p. 260

Chronology

1960s-1980s

Republicans make inroads into traditional Democratic bastions, such as the South.

1964
President Lyndon B. Johnson wins by a landslide, but five Deep South states oppose him, weakening Democratic control of the region.

1966
In response to Johnson's Great Society and civil rights laws, GOP gains 47 House seats, three Senate seats, eight governorships.

1968
Richard M. Nixon wins presidency — the first of five Republicans to win the White House in six elections. An era of divided federal government begins that lasts, with few interruptions, until 2002.

1973
Supreme Court's *Roe v. Wade* decision legalizes abortion, spurring evangelicals to greater political involvement.

1974
Nixon resigns amid Watergate scandal; 75 new Democrats, "Watergate babies," are elected to House versus 17 Republicans.

1980
Ronald Reagan addresses 20,000 evangelicals at so-called "wedding ceremony of evangelicals and the Republican Party"; he is elected president by attracting white working-class voters and the South by touting low taxes, strong defense and conservative cultural stances.

1984
Reagan is reelected in a 49-state landslide, sapping Democratic strength among union members.

1990s

GOP asserts control of Congress for the first time in decades.

1992
Democrat Bill Clinton wins the White House by appealing on economic issues to working-class voters who "play by the rules." Democrats win popular vote in this and three of next four presidential elections.

1994
Republicans take the House for first time in 40 years, along with the Senate, in reaction to Clinton policies on taxes, health coverage, gun control.

1998
For first time since 1934, the president's party gains seats in a midterm election, largely in backlash to the GOP investigation into Clinton's sex life.

---•---

2000s

Second Bush presidency ushers in complete Republican domination of U.S. politics, but GOP's monopoly on power quickly runs its course.

2000
Gov. George W. Bush loses the popular vote but wins the presidency by taking a majority of electoral votes after Supreme Court ends a 36-day recount standoff in Florida. GOP gains control of White House and Congress for first time since 1954.

2001
Sen. James Jeffords, R-Vt., abandons Republican Party, giving Democrats control of previously tied Senate.

2002
Bush's active campaigning helps build up House GOP majority and assists party in winning back Senate.

2004
Record 40 percent of Latinos vote for Bush's reelection.

2005
GOP Party Chairman Ken Mehlman apologizes to African-Americans for seeking "to benefit politically from racial polarization." . . . Bush is criticized for his handling of Hurricane Katrina. . . . House Republicans pass immigration bill that would reclassify illegal immigrants as felons, angering Hispanics.

2006
Democrats regain control of Congress; whites give marginal support to Republicans, but blacks, Hispanics and Asians vote for Democrats.

2008
Democrat Barack Obama wins largest percentage of votes of any Democrat since Johnson to become nation's first African-American president. Democrats also gain in House, Senate, governorships and state legislatures. Obama carries traditional GOP states such as Indiana, North Carolina and Virginia and trounces Arizona Sen. John McCain among African-Americans, Hispanics and young voters.

2009
Republicans elect Michael Steele as their first African-American party chairman (Jan. 30). . . . Steele apologizes to radio talk-show host Rush Limbaugh for calling him "ugly" and "incendiary" (March 2). . . . Alaska Gov. Sarah Palin is scheduled to deliver the keynote address at the Senate-House Dinner, the GOP's major fundraising event (June 8).

Does Rush Limbaugh Speak for the GOP?

One thing is certain: He puts Republicans in a bind.

Rush Limbaugh did more than just engender controversy with his comment that he hopes President Barack Obama will fail. The conservative radio talk-show host — arguably the nation's most popular radio personality — also helped trigger a debate about whether he is the de facto leader of the Republican Party.

Four days before Obama's inauguration, Limbaugh said on his show, "I would be honored if the drive-by media headlined me all day long: 'Limbaugh: I Hope Obama Fails.' Somebody's gotta say it."

Democrats didn't get angry. Instead, they sensed an opportunity. Party strategists James Carville and Stanley Greenberg had conducted polling last fall that found Limbaugh drew mostly negative responses, particularly among those under age 40. "Democrats realized they could roll out a new GOP bogeyman for the post-Bush era by turning to an old one in Limbaugh, a polarizing figure since he rose to prominence in the 1990s," reports Jonathan Martin of *Politico*. [1]

Democratic groups such as the Democratic Congressional Campaign Committee (DCCC) and Americans United for Change used Limbaugh's comments to raise money and featured them in ads seeking to pressure Republican senators to support Obama's economic stimulus plan.

But Limbaugh's profile took off after he repeated his wish that the president fail at a highly publicized speech on Feb. 27

Radio talk-show host Rush Limbaugh raised hackles when he said he hopes President Obama fails.

at the Conservative Political Action Conference. Asked who speaks for the Republican Party on CBS' "Face the Nation" on March 1, White House Chief of Staff Rahm Emmanuel cited Limbaugh.

"He has laid out his vision, in my view, and he said it clearly, and I compliment him for that," Emmanuel said. "He's asked for President Obama, and called for President Obama, to fail."

Republican House members who took over Congress in 1994 — providing their party with its first House majority in 40 years — made Limbaugh an honorary member of their freshman class. "Rush is as responsible for what happened here as much as anyone," Vin Weber, a former Republican representative from Minnesota, said at the class' orientation. [2]

Limbaugh retained his influence — and an audience estimated as high as 20 million listeners per week for his daily radio show — through the Bush presidency, with Vice President Dick Cheney appearing frequently as a guest. Last year, Limbaugh signed an eight-year, $400 million contract with his syndicator. [3]

But what lent credence to more current claims from Democrats that Limbaugh has an outsized influence within GOP circles was a series of apologies from Republicans who had slighted him. Most prominently, after Republican Party Chairman Michael Steele criticized Limbaugh on CNN on Feb. 28 as an "entertainer" who is "ugly" and "incendiary," he quickly called Limbaugh to apologize, praising him as a "strong conservative voice." [4]

Continued from p. 258

1969 book *The Emerging Republican Majority*, Nixon aide Kevin Phillips wrote, "This repudiation visited upon the Democratic Party for its ambitious social programming and inability to handle the urban and Negro revolutions was comparable to that given conservative Republicanism in 1932 for its failures to cope with the economic crisis of the Depression." [18]

The newfound Republican strength in the South — combined with rising support in the Mountain West

and Plains States — gave the GOP what for a long time looked like a "lock" on the Electoral College. Republicans won five of the six next presidential elections from 1968 to 1988, losing only the post-Watergate contest of 1976.

The Rise of Reagan

The Watergate scandal, which led to Nixon's resignation in 1974, helped usher in 75 House Democrats

— the so-called Watergate Babies — compared to just 17 Republican freshmen. That big advantage helped Democrats maintain a 20-year-old lock on the House for 20 additional years.

But Reagan's landslide 1980 win helped end the GOP's 26-year drought in the Senate, creating a Republican majority that lasted for six years. In addition, it marked the rise of a new, more conservative Republican Party: Reagan stressed lower taxes, smaller government and a robust defense. Social conservatives also favored

Rep. Phil Gingrey, R-Ga., also recently apologized for making comments that upset Limbaugh's fans. The self-criticisms have led to the DCCC putting up an "I'm Sorry, Rush," Web page that automatically generates apologies to the talk-show host. [5]

"Whenever a Republican criticizes him, they have to run back and apologize to him and say they were misunderstood," Emmanuel said. "He is the voice and the intellectual force and the energy behind the Republican Party."

Other prominent Republicans, including Rep. Mike Pence of Indiana and Louisiana Gov. Bobby Jindal, defended Limbaugh and his place in the conservative firmament. They said he clearly hoped Obama's liberal policies would fail, not that he hoped the Obama presidency — and the country — would fail.

House Minority Leader John Boehner, R-Ohio, and other Republicans said the whole flap, which dominated Washington discussion for a few days earlier this month, was a "distraction" dreamed up by Democrats. But the fact that the new GOP chairman felt obligated quickly to retract his criticisms of Limbaugh worried some on the right.

Ross Douthat, a columnist for *The New York Times*, wrote on his blog that Limbaugh's demands for fealty are part of a "long-running campaign to isolate would-be conservative reformers." He also argues that Limbaugh, with an entertainer's need to provoke, is "a poor candidate to fill the role of spokesman (and

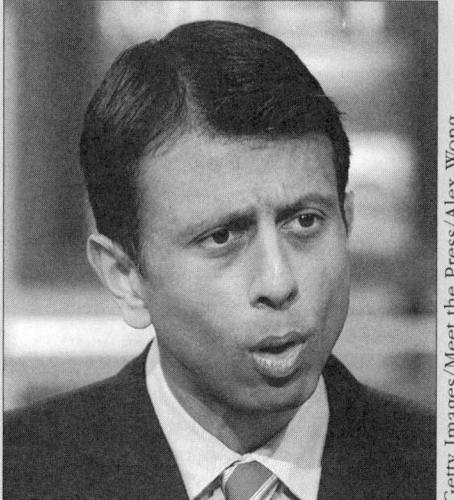

Gov. Bobby Jindal of Louisiana is among the prominent Republicans who defended Limbaugh and his role as a party leader.

ideological enforcer) for the conservative opposition." [6]

Limbaugh, who has a long history of making controversial and even offensive statements, is certain to provide Democratic critics with more fodder. On his show March 6, Limbaugh derided Obama's health-care policies, saying, "Before it's all over, it'll be called the Ted Kennedy memorial health-care bill," a reference to the ailing Democratic senator from Massachusetts.

Regardless of whether Democrats successfully manufactured a controversy or whether Limbaugh is guilty of self-promotion, the radio personality has put Republicans in a tough spot.

"Republican political leaders face a dilemma," says John J. Pitney Jr., a political scientist at Claremont McKenna College in California. "Embrace Rush, and they also embrace his radioactive record. Criticize Rush and risk incurring the wrath of the Dittoheads" — Limbaugh's large band of ardent listeners.

[1] Jonathan Martin, "Rush Job: Inside Dems' Limbaugh Plan," *Politico.com*, March 4, 2009, www.politico.com/news/stories/0309/19596.html.

[2] Katherine Q. Seelye, "Republicans Get a Pep Talk From Rush Limbaugh," *The New York Times*, Dec. 12, 1994, p. A16.

[3] Paul Farhi, "Limbaugh's Audience Size? It's Largely Up in the Air," *The Washington Post*, March 7, 2009, p. C1.

[4] Perry Bacon Jr., "GOP Seeks Balance With Conservative Icon Limbaugh," *The Washington Post*, March 4, 2009, p. A1.

[5] The apology spoof is at www.dccc.org/content/sorry.

[6] Ross Douthat, "Rush and Olbermann," *TheAtlantic.com*, March 3, 2009, http://rossdouthat.theatlantic.com/archives/2009/03/rush_and_olbermann.php.

Reagan, who promoted their agenda rhetorically, if not all that actively once in office.

The Democrats' New Deal coalition, meanwhile, continued to fracture as the GOP began tapping into white working-class support. Despite his open hostility toward unions, Reagan's hard line on foreign policy appealed to working-class voters, as did his economic optimism — which was borne out by a lengthy period of economic expansion after an early recession. So strong was his appeal that this group

of disaffected voters became known as Reagan Democrats.

Reagan also helped bring Christian conservatives firmly into the Republican camp. A year after the founding of the Moral Majority, an organization started in 1979 to mobilize fundamentalists for political causes, Reagan appealed for their support directly, addressing a gathering of 20,000 evangelicals, praising their efforts and questioning evolution. Ralph Reed, later the executive director of the Christian Coalition, which would supersede the Moral Majority as

the leading force among Christian-right groups during the 1990s, called the meeting "the wedding ceremony of evangelicals and the Republican Party." [19] Evangelicals in recent election cycles have generally been estimated to represent 40 percent of the GOP primary vote.

In 1992, Bill Clinton managed to break the Republican "lock" on the White House, in large part by moving his party toward the ideological center. But Republicans soon staged a coup at the congressional level. In 1994,

Adoring Republicans Forget Reagan's Pragmatism

"There's a lot of mythology built around him."

During the 2008 GOP presidential primary campaign, Arizona Sen. John McCain and former Massachusetts Gov. Mitt Romney found plenty of issues to disagree about. Things really got heated, however, when they began trading barbs about which of them former President Ronald Reagan might favor.

"If we can't trust Mitt Romney on Ronald Reagan, how can we trust him to lead America?" a McCain campaign ad asked.

Twenty years after his presidency ended and five years after his death, Reagan remains an iconic figure in Republican circles. At a forum in January, all six candidates for the post of party chairman cited him as their favorite president.

"He's the new Lincoln," says Grover Norquist, an anti-tax activist. "He defines the modern Republican Party."

Reagan fashioned a winning coalition of defense hawks and social and fiscal conservatives, bringing millions of evangelicals and Democrats troubled by the liberal direction of their party into the GOP tent. He is often credited with restoring an economy hobbled by inflation and for winning the Cold War with the Soviet Union.

"He had a successful presidency at a challenging time," says Scott Keeter, director of survey research at the Pew Research Center. "He was associated with a clear enunciation of some core Republican values."

But, as Keeter notes, Reagan was also more of a pragmatist than is sometimes remembered. Every political party celebrates the great leaders of its past, with the portrait often becoming more glowing over time. That's been especially true with Reagan.

Norquist runs the Reagan Legacy Project, which aims to put Reagan's image on U.S. currency and have "significant public landmarks" named for the 40th president in every state and county in the country. Norquist concedes that the effort to burnish Reagan's historical credentials is deliberate, suggesting that history is as open to public-relations persuasion as contemporary news accounts. "One thing I noticed the left doing was the tremendous effort to control the past, such as the deifying of John F. Kennedy, naming every building after him," he said. "I wanted to make sure that the left didn't do to Reagan's legacy what they did to Coolidge and Harding. You fight for the control of the present, the past and the future." [1]

As a result, Reagan is remembered as more of a purist than he actually was — someone who might not be able to pass the ideological tests now administered in his name. Today's Reagan acolytes not only ignore the failures of his administration, such as the Iran-Contra scandal, but also overlook the compromises he made on core issues like taxes and defense policy.

"Republicans have mythologized him as their hero, as one who stuck to his principles and also had broad appeal," says Gary Jacobson, a political scientist at the University of California, San Diego. "They forget that one of the reasons he had broad popular appeal is that he compromised. In government, he was willing to adapt and make deals if he had to."

Although Reagan enacted large income tax cuts during his first year in office, he raised taxes by record amounts the following year and raised taxes nearly every year he remained in office. [2] Reagan also broke ranks with the conservative commentariat and much of the nation's military and diplomatic establishment in deciding that Soviet Premier Mikhail Gorbachev was a leader he could negotiate with on arms control. [3]

Rep. Newt Gingrich of Georgia, by then the de facto leader of the GOP's congressional wing, had recruited a nationwide farm team of Republicans indoctrinated with his message of hope, opportunity and sharp partisanship. Virtually all GOP House candidates in 1994 signed onto Gingrich's 10-point "Contract With America," which promised floor votes within 100 days on issues including tax cuts, welfare overhaul, increased defense spending and balancing the budget and congressional term limits.

Although polls showed most voters had not heard of the contract, they embraced the party's general anti-government message after Clinton's massive health-care overhaul plan went down in flames. In the midterm elections of 1994 Republicans captured the Senate after an eight-year interim and broke the Democratic Party's 40-year hold on the House. The contract lent the new majority a clear governing agenda in 1995, and the House passed all of its agenda items except term limits. By April 1995, Gingrich was the dominant figure on the political landscape, trumpeting the contract's success in a nationally televised address, while Clinton feebly reminded a news conference of his constitutional "relevance."

But Clinton soon regained his political footing and shocked the GOP by vetoing a budget package that contained much of their policy agenda. The public appeared to blame Republicans — and Gingrich in particular — for the resulting government shutdown. Gingrich became a lightning rod, featured in countless Democratic campaign commercials in the 1996 elections. Clinton was reelected easily, and Democrats made a net gain of nine House seats in 1996. Ten Republicans refused to vote for Gingrich's 1997 reelection as speaker.

"All of this has been airbrushed from the new literature of Reagan," concluded *The Washington Monthly* in 2003, which also noted Reagan's softer-than-remembered record on issues such as abortion and Social Security. "A sober review of Reagan's presidency doesn't yield the seamlessly conservative record being peddled today."[4]

Michael Franc, a lobbyist for the conservative Heritage Foundation, says Regan deserves credit for redefining the relationship between the individual and the state and making it clear that the Cold War could be won. But he concedes, "There is a school of Reagan adulation that puts on rose-colored glasses and ignores certain things, such as him raising taxes."

Most Republicans argue that Reagan was the greatest modern proponent of core party principles, so asking, "What would Reagan do?" is a worthwhile question to keep asking. "The issues of the '80s are different from where we are now, but the motivating ideas and principles that President Reagan embraced inspire people today," says Carrie Cantrell, spokeswoman for the Republican State Leadership Committee.

Sean Wilentz, a liberal historian and author of *The Age of Reagan*, argues that Republicans would do better to learn from Reagan's record as a pragmatist than to continue hoisting him up as a conservative standard-bearer. "Going back to Reagan

President Ronald Reagan is remembered as more of a purist than he actually was.

AFP/Getty Images/Carlos Schiebeck

would be a mistake," he says. "If they think Ronald Reagan had a policy blueprint for moving the country forward, it's almost 30 years out of date."

Some observers — including a few Republicans — agree that continuing to cast the party so strongly in Reagan's mythical image is a mistake, if only because times and the list of issues that are most pressing have changed. "The problem with [congressional Republicans] in terms of intellectual philosophy is they are stuck with Reagan," conservative *New York Times* columnist David Brooks said on ABC's "This Week" on March 8. "They are stuck with the idea that government is always the problem."

But for Republican leaders — and most of the party rank and file — Reagan remains above all the person who turned things around, and they remain content to stand in his shadow.

"There's a lot of mythology built around him," Jacobson says. "It's so central to the Republican message right now, there's not going to be any revision on that front in our lifetimes."

[1] From an interview with the author around the time of Reagan's death.
[2] Ross Douthat and Reihan Salam, *Grand New Party* (2008), p. 81.
[3] "A Friendship That Frightened America's Cold Warriors," *The Economist*, Feb. 28, 2009, p. 88.
[4] Joshua Green, "Reagan's Liberal Legacy," *The Washington Monthly*, January 2003, p. 28.

Bush Takes Charge

Although he lost the popular vote in 2000, George W. Bush benefited from the demographic trends that had been moving voters into the Republican column. He carried every Southern state and 74 percent of the evangelical vote. [20] The most certain predictor of support for Bush in both his elections was regular church attendance.

Bush sought to portray himself as an inclusive candidate, featuring many black and Hispanic speakers at his nominating convention. He also was careful not to take a hard line against immigrants.

He had run as a "compassionate conservative" and worked well with Democrats during his first years in office in crafting the No Child Left Behind education reform act, which mandates regular achievement tests. He also initiated a streak of massive annual tax cuts.

Following the terrorist attacks of Sept. 11, 2001, Congress gave the administration the tools it asked for, including authorization to go to the war against Afghanistan and the USA Patriot Act, which dramatically expanded law enforcement authority. [21] But as Bush turned his attention to the war against Iraq, the brief bipartisan glow lifted from Washington.

The administration pushed for a vote authorizing the war just before the 2002 elections, to put doubters on record. Republicans used that fight and the one over creation of the Department of Homeland Security (DHS) to partisan advantage that fall, unseating some Democrats on charges they were not patriotic. "A spirit more akin to that of Joseph McCarthy and Richard Nixon than of Ronald Reagan — flatly equating partisan loyalty with patriotism — dominated the administration's rhetoric," Princeton University historian Wilentz writes. [22]

Bush made a record 90 campaign appearances, visiting 15 states in the last five days before the election. [23] Republicans regained control of the Senate and added to their narrow six-seat House majority, and Bush got much of the credit.

In 2004, against a weak opponent in Massachusetts Democratic Sen. John F. Kerry, Bush handily won reelection after courting the GOP base, including millions of evangelicals who had not voted in 2000. Bush had appealed to them by taking a hard line on abortion, stem-cell research and gay marriage — an issue that got millions of evangelical voters to the polls to defeat anti-gay-marriage referenda in 2004, a year after courts in Kerry's home state legalized same-sex unions. The electoral map remained nearly unchanged since 2000, when it was famously divided into Republican red and Democratic blue states. Only three states switched their votes. But Bush managed to carry the first presidential popular-vote majority since his father's 1988 election.

Bush's chief political adviser, Karl Rove, boasted about creating a "permanent Republican majority" comprised of social conservatives and anti-tax voters. The plan was to use governmental programs to reward party supporters, while sapping Democratic strength, such as trial lawyers and labor unions. But it was not to be.

Republican Implosion

Bush's occasional attempts to reach beyond his base proved futile during his second term, when the GOP-controlled House in 2006 refused to vote on a moderate Senate-passed immigration bill negotiated by his administration. A tougher immigration bill passed by the House drove down GOP support among Hispanics from 40 percent in 2004 to 30 percent or less in 2006. [24]

The administration's widely criticized handling of the devastation in New Orleans wrought by Hurricane Katrina erased any small gains his party had made among African-Americans. Meanwhile, many suburban and highly educated voters had begun to turn against the GOP, concerned about the party's opposition to stem-cell research, the teaching of evolution in schools and political interference with the decision about whether to keep a brain-dead Florida woman, Terri Schiavo, alive.

Congressional Republicans sought to protect their majority through aggressive fundraising and, in part, an explosion in earmarks, which became major tools for protecting incumbents and soliciting members' votes on key issues. [25] A series of scandals led to disaffection among fiscal conservatives and legal problems for several prominent Republicans, including House Majority Leader Tom DeLay, R-Texas.

In 2006, 42 freshman Democrats were elected to the House, compared with just 13 Republicans, giving the party its first majority since 1994. Democrats also "ran the table" in the Senate, winning seven of the eight competitive contests to take a narrow 51-49 majority. Although political corruption and congressional overspending played their part, most observers agreed that dissatisfaction with the war in Iraq was the predominant factor in the Democratic sweep. [26]

In 2008, with neither Bush nor Vice President Dick Cheney running — or at all popular — Republicans were left without an obvious champion. During the primary season the party's affections appeared to drift from one candidate to the next.

Eventually, the party's primary rules gave the advantage to the initial front-runner, Sen. McCain. Although generally conservative, McCain was considered an apostate by many Republicans for authoring a campaign-finance limitation law and for promoting an immigration bill that included a path to amnesty for illegal immigrants.

Primary exit polls indicated McCain often trailed among conservatives, but since most Republican primaries are "winner-take-all" affairs, McCain took 100 percent of the delegates from states like Florida, for example, where he won only 36 percent of the vote.

His underwhelming victory margins and his shaky standing with the party faithful left him in an unusual position. Most presidential candidates seek to appease their party's bases during the primary season and then tack toward the center to appeal to general-election voters. But McCain had to keep placating the conservative GOP base.

That included his choice of a running mate. McCain chose Palin, the previously little-known freshman governor of Alaska. As a social conservative who bragged about her ability to cut taxes, Palin appealed strongly to the Republican base. The selection and the attention the ticket received during the party's national convention led to McCain's first polling lead against Democratic Sen. Obama.

But that lead quickly evaporated. In her initial interviews with the media, Palin appeared ill-prepared, leading some voters — including some prominent Republicans such as former Secretary of State Colin L. Powell — to question McCain's judgment in selecting her.

By mid-September, Obama had recaptured the lead when the financial markets began to collapse. Obama eventually won with 52.9 percent of the popular vote — the largest margin of any Democrat since Johnson's 61.1 percent in 1964. [27] Obama also reshaped the Electoral College map, carrying traditionally Republican strongholds such as Indiana, Virginia, North Carolina, Florida and Colorado.

Continued on p. 266

At Issue:

Should Republicans work with President Obama on a bipartisan basis?

CHRISTINE TODD WHITMAN
*FORMER GOVERNOR OF NEW JERSEY
CO-CHAIR, REPUBLICAN LEADERSHIP
COUNCIL*

WRITTEN FOR *CQ RESEARCHER*, MARCH 16, 2009

*a*t this crucial time in our nation's history Republicans have an opportunity to lend their hand to addressing the challenges our country faces. It is time to set aside political power struggles and work together with the Democrats to find solutions for the recession, the ongoing wars in Iraq and Afghanistan and the rapidly expanding federal deficit. We cannot afford to wait until the next election cycle to highlight these issues and then attempt to solve them — both parties need to cooperate now to address these looming concerns.

While Republicans should not provide blanket support for President Obama's policies, they can fulfill the much-needed role of the "loyal opposition." What's needed right now is a constructive debate and proactive proposals that ensure a fiscally conservative voice is heard in Washington. It is not enough to simply be the party of "no" — the Republican Party can and must offer its own solutions to the challenges in order to prove that Republicans are an active part of the solution.

We have already seen the consequences of not having a true bipartisan approach to problem-solving, and that is a blame that can be laid at the door of both parties. Despite the fact that the Democrats enjoy almost total control of the legislative and executive branches of our federal government, the GOP missed a tremendous opportunity to put forth a clean, pork-free alternative bill with tax relief that would stimulate spending immediately. A bill that directly addressed the current economic crisis — and nothing more — would have been an improvement over the enormous stimulus package President Obama signed into law, and it would have emphasized the relevance and creative thinking of the Republicans in Congress.

Given the recent Democratic proposals to tax everything above a certain income, even health-insurance plans, Republicans should not be afraid to draw a line in the sand when our basic principles are directly challenged. However, we must also be willing to support the president when it is in the country's best interest. For the sake of our country's prosperity, I want the Obama administration to succeed in addressing the crises we face. It is my hope that Republicans in Congress will put aside partisanship enough to help. If we take the lead on this cooperation, it will be hard for the Democrats not to follow and, if they don't, then the country needs to know.

RUSH LIMBAUGH
SYNDICATED RADIO TALK-SHOW HOST

FROM REMARKS TO THE CONSERVATIVE POLITICAL ACTION CONFERENCE, FEB. 28, 2009

*o*ne thing that we can all do is stop assuming that the way to beat them is with better policy ideas right now. When I talk to people about the Obama budget or the Obama Porkulus bill or whatever else, and they start talking to me in the terms of process and policy, I say stop it. Who is setting the process or policy? They are. You want to tweak it? No.

From the standpoint of what we have to do, folks, this is not about taking a policy or a process that the Democrats have put forward and fighting around the edges. If we're going to convince the minds and hearts of the American people that what's about to happen to them is as disastrous as anything in their lives in peacetime, we're going to have to talk about principles, because our principles are not present in what's happening here.

So where the hell do we go to compromise what we believe in when our principles are not their principles, they're just the opposite of what's happening?

This notion that I want the president to fail, folks, this shows you a sign of the problem we've got. That's nothing more than common sense and to not be able to say it, why in the world do I want rampant government growth, indebtedness, wealth that's not even being created yet that is being spent? What possibly is in this that anybody of us wants to succeed?

Did the Democrats want the war on Iraq to fail? They certainly did. They not only wanted the war in Iraq to fail, they proclaimed it a failure. The last thing they wanted was to win. They hoped George Bush failed. So what is so strange about being honest to say that I want Barack Obama to fail if his mission is to restructure and reform this country so that capitalism and individual liberty are not its foundation? Why would I want that to succeed?

We're in for a real battle. We are talking about the United States of America — and there will always be an America, don't misunderstand me — we're talking about it remaining the country we were all born into and reared and grown into. And it's under assault. It's always under assault. But it's never been under assault like this from within before. And it's a serious, serious battle.

Continued from p. 264

Democrats also picked up 21 more House seats, giving them a 79-vote majority, and seven Senate seats for a total of 58, pending the outcome of a still-contested recount in Minnesota.

After such a sweeping loss, many expected the GOP to engage in a "circular firing squad," with various factions warring over who was most to blame. As happened after the 2006 elections, conservatives said Republicans failed because their message hadn't been conservative enough and that the party had lost its "brand definition" as the party of limited government. Bush had raised federal spending faster than any president since LBJ and turned a surplus into record deficits.

"Republicans in Congress began to act like the Democrats they'd gotten rid of in the '90s. The president began to spend money like he was Lyndon Johnson, and the result was that voters began to get very upset," David A. Keene, chairman of the American Conservative Union, told CNN. "So, yes, you have to go back to your basics." [28]

Both House Minority Leader John A. Boehner, R-Ohio, and House GOP Whip Eric Cantor of Virginia say the GOP doesn't want to be the "party of no," reflexively opposing Obama's initiatives.

"We have to be a party of principles," says Yue, the Republican National Committeeman from Oregon, "articulating what we stand for and applying it consistently."

Florida Gov. Charlie Crist, a Republican who has worked with Democrats on some issues in his state, was widely criticized by the party for supporting President Obama's economic stimulus package. Several GOP governors, including Louisiana's Bobby Jindal, say they will reject some of the stimulus funds.

Getty Images/Meet the Press/Alex Wong

CURRENT SITUATION

Party Enforcers

Boehner has been candid about the GOP's need to play defense. "I have been trying to get my Republican colleagues to understand that we are not in the legislative business," he said recently. "We will spend more time communicating [with the public via media appearances] because that is what we can do." [29]

So far, the strategy doesn't seem to be working. Although some polls initially indicated the congressional GOP's oppositional approach was shoring up support among GOP stalwarts, Republicans trail far behind Obama in terms of approval ratings and the public's sense of who is working best to address the nation's economic woes.

There are no signs that Republican congressional leaders are benefiting from the public's concern about major economic policies, according to a new poll by the Pew Research Center. In fact, approval of Republican congressional leaders has fallen from 34 percent in February to 28 percent currently, the lowest rating for GOP leaders in nearly 14 years of Pew Research surveys. [30]

Meanwhile, a bipartisan poll commissioned by National Public Radio found that fewer voters think the country is on the wrong track — 63 percent compared to 80 percent last May — and that Democrats enjoy about a 10- to 12-point advantage on virtually every major policy issue, including health care, energy, the deficit, taxes, the stimulus package and the president's budget. [31]

"As we're going into these big debates about the direction of the country, we have the Democrats with a consistent advantage on ideas," said Democratic pollster Stan Greenberg, who conducted the telephone poll with Republican Glen Bolger in mid-March.

Bolger did find bright spots in the poll. Despite Obama's overall approval rating of 59 percent, when asked whether they'd vote for the Republican or Democratic congressional candidate if the 2010 elections were held today, the result was a tie: 42-42. While Obama still has intense support from his base, Bolger noted, "That doesn't mean that people want one side to have a blank check."

He also found it encouraging that Obama's approval ratings have dropped to less than 50 percent among independents. "He's not up on the pedestal among independents like he had been right after the election and right around the inauguration," Bolger said.

Every party that finds itself suddenly out of power must decide whether to be part of the governing process or merely the party of opposition. Congressional GOP leaders have discouraged rank-and-file House members from working collaboratively with Democrats. In the Senate, the story is slightly more complicated.

Senators tend to be more independent, and their individual votes matter more. In today's Senate, any legislation of importance needs 60 votes in order to break a filibuster and move to a final vote. Democrats currently number just 58, so they must wrangle a handful of Republican votes in order to pass major bills.

That's what happened with the stimulus package. Democrats restructured the bill to appeal to three moderate Republican senators — Arlen Specter of Pennsylvania and Olympia J. Snowe and Susan Collins of Maine. Together with a group of conservative Democrats, led by Ben Nelson of Nebraska, they cut the package's overall price tag by $100 billion.

Collins said she received some pressure from fellow Republicans not to negotiate. But she pointed out that she was the only Republican elected to federal office from all of New England last fall. "I see it as an affirmation of the approach I take to governing," she said. [32]

Pat Toomey, president of the Club for Growth, an organization that promotes lower taxes and limited government, called the stimulus votes of the three GOP moderates "a shocking betrayal" and said he was considering a primary campaign against Specter next year. In 2004, Toomey, then a Republican congressman, narrowly lost a primary challenge against Specter, 51 percent to 49 percent.

As an incumbent, Specter enjoyed the support of President Bush and other party leaders — something he won't get in 2010. On March 4, Republican Party Chairman Steele told radio host Laura Ingraham that withholding party funds from Republicans who voted for the stimulus is "absolutely on the table for me."

The likely challenge to Specter mirrors other intraparty fights within the GOP. Republicans who support tax increases can count on facing primary challengers backed by groups such as Club for Growth and Americans for Tax Reform. "If you are going to be a team, "then there are going to be some team rules and team expectations," Republican Gov. Tim Pawlenty said of six Minnesota legislators who were challenged by party members in their primaries after voting to override Pawlenty's veto of a tax-raising transportation package last year. [33]

Norquist of Americans for Tax Reform concedes that such retributive acts don't always work. Most of the incumbent legislators his group targeted for defeat in Oregon and Virginia following state tax increases, for example, were reelected. "Not everyone who strays gets defeated, but your chances go way up," he says.

A Bigger Tent?

The stimulus debate extended into the states, with several Republican governors said to harbor national ambitions — Mark Sanford of South Carolina, Haley Barbour of Mississippi and Bobby Jindal of Louisiana — vowing to reject portions of the money. [34] Florida Gov. Charlie Crist, a Republican who has worked with Democrats on some issues in his state, drew party heat for supporting the package.

"I don't think he's helped any national Republican ambitions he may have by stepping up to the plate and batting for the other team," veteran GOP strategist Alex Castellanos told *The Miami Herald*. "At the moment when we've finally found our voice and remember who we are as Republicans, Charlie Crist forgets. It's stunning." [35]

A few conservative voices say the GOP should stop insisting on orthodoxy regarding such issues as abortion and taxes in order to expand the party's appeal. Alienating RINOs — Republicans in Name Only — can only hurt the GOP's chances of returning to majority status, they say.

"As the party gets smaller in Congress, it gets purer. That's why it seems to get more ideologically strident," says Connelly of Washington and Lee University. "Democrats became the majority because they did a remarkable job of recruiting Democrats who could win in red states."

But Franc of the Heritage Foundation says by returning to their roots Republicans are reacting quickly to Obama's ascension and his unwelcome ideas. "There's a natural period for a party to go through grievance after a loss," he says. "But Obama and the Democrats came out charging, and they didn't give the Republicans time to go through those stages. In some ways, the Democrats, by moving so expeditiously, denied Republicans that process, which would have led to the circular firing squad."

Others suggest that, rather than finding a winning message by returning to "core principles," Republicans are experiencing the problem that dogged Democrats throughout the 1970s and '80s: Believing the public still adheres to their ideas, despite ample evidence to the contrary.

"It takes parties some time to recognize that they're pursuing a losing strategy," says Democratic analyst Teixeira. ■

OUTLOOK

Republican Prospects

In a sense, Republicans have nowhere to go but up. Their share of the House, Senate, state legislatures and governorships are all lower than they were before the Republican tide swept the party to power in 1994.

History suggests the party out of power will gain seats in midterm elections. That has happened in every election since 1934, except in 1998 and 2002. "Losing the White House actually provides an advantage in midterms," suggests Connelly.

Republicans appear unlikely to win back the House or Senate next year, so party hopes in 2010 will largely turn on census data, which shows the U.S. population shifting to the South and West. After next year's census, Republican-leaning states such as Georgia, Nevada, Utah and Texas appear likely to gain congressional seats, while Democratic strongholds like Illinois, Massachusetts, New York and Michigan are expected to lose seats. "We're going to be moving 13 congressional districts to red states in the next redistricting," Norquist says.

Republicans also have cause for optimism in the two gubernatorial contests this year. Virginia Democrats are having a contentious primary season, while in New Jersey Republican former U.S. Attorney Christopher J. Christie is expected to do well against Democratic Gov. Jon Corzine, whose approval ratings are down because he is seen as well-meaning but often ineffectual.

Still, Corzine has spent tens of millions in his previous races for the Senate and governorship, and New Jersey Republicans have consistently squandered statewide opportunities. The party controlling the White House has lost the Virginia governor's race ever since 1977, but Democrats there feel they are on a roll, having won the governorship twice and captured both U.S. Senate seats and the state Senate, as well as carrying the state in the presidential contest for the first time since 1964.

Three-dozen governorships will be in play next year, almost half of them open due to term limits. Democrats are hoping to recapture generally friendly states like California, Hawaii and Rhode Island but will have to defend more seats across the country — 20 — than the GOP, 16.

"We know it's going to be a challenging year for us," says Nathan Daschle, executive director of the Democratic Governors Association. "We're going to have a number of seats we need to protect in states where we've had successful two-term governors but which we consider red states."

These races aside, the future of the Republican Party will likely be determined by the 2012 presidential race. But it's anyone's guess, at this point, who will be the party's nominee, let alone his or her chances against Obama.

Despite Obama's famous win and early popularity, Republicans aren't giving up. They recall their 1966 and 1968 comebacks after President Johnson's landslide reelection in 1964 and their success in capturing Congress in 1994, just two years after Clinton won the White House.

But the Clinton election represented the culmination of a long process in which moderate Democrats seized control of a party dominated by its most liberal extreme. Some observers draw comparisons to the Conservative Party in England, which lost power in 1997 and only now appears poised to take it back under the moderating influence of David Cameron.

"I would liken it to the transformation of the Tory Party in the U.K," says Republican Gov. Jon Huntsman Jr. of Utah. "They went through two or three election cycles without recognizing the issues that the younger citizens in the U.K. really felt strongly about. . . . They started branching out through, maybe, taking a second look at the issues of the day, much like we're going to have to do for the Republican Party." [36]

But Republicans have not even begun to rethink their platform or public image. Princeton's Wilentz notes that "a lot of Democratic energy and support came from disdain for Bush, who is no longer on the scene. That may be fueling Republican hope."

That might be a mistake, he argues, comparing today's Republicans to the Democrats of the early 1980s, who "were always believing the country was basically on their side" even as they were losing. Republicans, he says, are "going to be in trouble for a long time, and they're going to be in denial for a long time."

Larry J. Sabato, director of the University of Virginia's Center for Politics, says Republicans are right to believe their fortunes rest in opposing Obama. They need for him and other Democrats to falter in order to return to power. But they also need a positive platform ready to sell to Americans when they're ready to turn their attention back to the GOP.

"Republicans will regain power when Democrats mess up," he says. "That's the cycle of American political-party history." ∎

About the Author

Alan Greenblatt is a staff writer at *Governing* magazine. He previously covered elections, agriculture and military spending for *CQ Weekly*, where he won the National Press Club's Sandy Hume Award for political journalism. He graduated from San Francisco State University in 1986 and received a master's degree in English literature from the University of Virginia in 1988. His recent *CQ Researcher* reports include "Changing U.S. Electorate" and "Democrats in Congress."

Notes

[1] "Bush's Final Approval Rating: 22 Percent,"

CBSNews.com, Jan. 16, 2009, www.cbs news.com/stories/2009/01/16/opinion/polls/main4728399.shtml.

[2] "On Point With Tom Ashbrook," National Public Radio, Nov. 6, 2008.

[3] Greg Sargent, "In Private Memo, RNC Chief Concedes that GOP is Bereft of Ideas, Vows Change of Direction," TPM-ElectionCentral, Dec. 19, 2008, http://tpm-electioncentral.talkingpointsmemo.com/2008/12/in_internal_memo_rnc_chief_con.php.

[4] Perry Bacon Jr., "Six Vying to Become the Next RNC Chair," The Washington Post, Jan. 3, 2009, p. A1.

[5] Ross Douthat and Reihan Salam, Grand New Party (2008), p. 125.

[6] Richard E. Cohen, "GOP's Dilemma: Substance Versus Spin," National Journal, March 7, 2009.

[7] "Republicans See Their Party As Leaderless," Rasmussen Reports, March 9, 2009, www.rasmussenreports.com/public_content/politics/general_politics/republicans_see_their_party_as_leaderless.

[8] Jon Meacham, "It's Not Easy Bein' Blue," Newsweek, Oct. 27, 2008, p. 32.

[9] Peter Wehner, "The GOP's Road Back," The Washington Post, Oct. 27, 2008, p. A13.

[10] Jon Meacham and Evan Thomas, "We Are All Socialists Now," Newsweek, Feb. 16, 2009, p. 23.

[11] Thomas B. Edsall, "Census a Clarion Call for Democrats, GOP," The Washington Post, July 8, 2001, p. A5.

[12] "Inside Obama's Sweeping Victory," Pew Research Center, Nov. 5, 2008, http://pewresearch.org/pubs/1023/exit-poll-analysis-2008.

[13] Ralph Z. Hallow, "Steele: GOP Needs 'Hip-Hop' Makeover," The Washington Times, Feb. 19, 2009.

[14] Alan Greenblatt, "Slow and Steady Wins in State Races," CQ Weekly, Nov. 10, 2008, p. 3019.

[15] Ronald Brownstein, "A Dangerous Imbalance for the GOP," National Journal, Dec. 20, 2008.

[16] Everett Carll Ladd Jr., "The Shifting Party Coalitions, 1932 to 1976," in Seymour Martin Lipset, ed., Emerging Coalitions in American Politics (1978), p. 83.

[17] John Micklethwait and Adrian Wooldridge, The Right Nation (2004), p. 57.

[18] Kevin Phillips, The Emerging Republican Majority (1969), p. 25.

[19] Barbara Sinclair, Party Wars (2006), p. 49.

[20] Ibid., p. 51.

[21] For background, see David Masci and Patrick Marshall, "Civil Liberties in Wartime," CQ Researcher, Dec. 14, 2001, pp. 1017-1040; Kenneth Jost, "Rebuilding Afghanistan," CQ Researcher, Dec. 21, 2001, pp. 1041-1064;

and Adriel Bettelheim, "Presidential Power," CQ Researcher, Nov. 15, 2002, pp. 945-968.

[22] Sean Wilentz, The Age of Reagan (2008), p. 441.

[23] Thomas E. Mann and Norman J. Ornstein, The Broken Branch: How Congress is Failing America and How to Get it Back on Track (2006), p. 133.

[24] "Latinos and the 2006 Midterm Election," Pew Hispanic Center, Nov. 27, 2006.

[25] Mann and Ornstein, op. cit., p. 178.

[26] For background, see Ronald Brownstein, "Election 2006: States Change Colors," Los Angeles Times, Nov. 9, 2006, p. A18.

[27] For Johnson vote, see "Historical Election Results, Electoral College Box Scores 1789-1996," www.archives.gov/federal-register/electoral-college/scores.html#1964; for Obama vote, see "2008 President Election, Popular Vote Totals," both from U.S. National Archives and Records Administration, www.archives.gov/federal-register/electoral-college/2008/popular-vote.html.

[28] Scott J. Anderson, "Moderates to Blame for GOP Losses, Conservative Leader Says," CNN.com, Nov. 7, 2008, www.cnn.com/2008/POLITICS/11/07/conservatives.election/index.html.

[29] Cohen, op. cit.

[30] "Obama's Approval Rating Slips Amid Division Over Economic Proposals; GOP Congressional Leaders' Ratings Hit New Low — 28%," The Pew Research Center for the People & the Press, March 16, 2009.

[31] Mara Liasson, "NPR Poll: More Voters Think U.S. Is On Right Track," "Morning Edition," National Public Radio, March 17, 2009, www.npr.org/templates/story/story.php?storyId=101974694. The poll results are at http://media.npr.org/documents/2009/mar/npr poll/nprpoll_presentation.pdf.

[32] Paul Kane, "Key GOP Senator in Stimulus Deal Is Known for Centrist Approach," The Washington Post, Feb. 12, 2009, p. A8.

[33] Alan Greenblatt, "Renegade Retribution," Governing, May 2008, p. 22.

[34] For background, see Peter Katel, "Vanishing Jobs," CQ Researcher, March 13, 2009, pp. 225-248.

[35] Adam C. Smith, "GOP Seethes Over Crist's Stimulus-Plan Support," The Miami Herald, Feb. 13, 2009, p. A3.

[36] Jonathan Martin, "Huntsman Takes Aim at GOP," Politico, March 1, 2009, www.politico.com/news/stories/0309/19455.html.

FOR MORE INFORMATION

American Conservative Union, 1007 Cameron St., Alexandria, VA 22314; (703) 836-8602; www.conservative.org. Communicates and lobbies for the goals and principles of conservatism.

American Enterprise Institute, 1150 17th St., N.W., Washington, DC 20036; (202) 862-5800; www.aei.org. Conservative think tank dedicated to research and education on issues of government, politics, economics and social welfare.

Cato Institute, 1000 Massachusetts Ave., N.W., Washington, DC 20001; (202) 842-0200; www.cato.org. Policy research foundation promoting ideas based on principles of limited government and free markets.

Heritage Foundation, 214 Massachusetts Ave., N.E., Washington, DC 20002; (202) 546-4400; www.heritage.org. Works to formulate and promote public policies based on free enterprise, limited government and a strong national defense.

Pew Research Center, 1615 L St., N.W., Suite 700, Washington, DC 20036; (202) 419-4300; www.pewresearch.org. Nonpartisan "fact tank" providing information on issues, attitudes and trends shaping the United States.

Republican Governors Association, 1747 Pennsylvania Ave., N.W., Suite 250, Washington, DC 20006; (202) 662-4140; www.rga.org. Association of governors of the Republican Party that works to get GOP gubernatorial candidates elected and reelected.

Republican National Committee, 310 First St., S.E., Washington, DC 20003; (202) 863-8500; www.rnc.org. Committee responsible for developing and promoting the Republican platform as well as coordinating fundraising and election strategies.

Republican State Leadership Committee, 1800 Diagonal Rd., Suite 230, Alexandria, VA 22314; (571) 480-4860; www.rslc.com. National caucus of Republican state leaders working to elect Republican state attorneys general, lieutenant governors, secretaries of state and legislators.

Bibliography
Selected Sources

Books

Douthat, Ross, and Reihan Salam, *Grand New Party: How Republicans Can Win the Working Class and Save the American Dream*, Doubleday, 2008.

Two conservative writers associated with *The Atlantic* suggest that cultural liberalism doesn't appeal to working-class voters but that the GOP needs to hone its economic message to get their support.

Gould, Lewis, *Grand Old Party: A History of the Republicans*, Random House, 2003.

A University of Texas historian concludes that contemporary Republicans have rejected the ideas of Lincoln, Theodore Roosevelt and Eisenhower in the embrace of conservatism.

Micklethwait, John, and Adrian Wooldridge, *The Right Nation*, Penguin Press, 2004.

Two *Economist* editors trace the history of the modern conservative movement from the vantage of what seems in retrospect to have been its high point.

Perlstein, Rick, *Nixonland: The Rise of a President and the Fracturing of a Nation*, Scribner, 2008.

A liberal historian associated with the Campaign for America's Future argues that Richard M. Nixon perfected a politics of division and polarization that remains influential to this day.

Thomas, Evan, and *Newsweek* staff, *A Long Time Coming: The Inspiring, Combative 2008 Campaign and the Historic Election of Barack Obama*, PublicAffairs, 2009.

An expansion of the magazine's behind-the-scenes reporting on the two presidential campaigns.

Wilentz, Sean, *The Age of Reagan: A History, 1974-2008*, Harper, 2008.

The Princeton historian examines the last 35 years as a period dominated by conservatism, with Ronald Reagan and his supporters offering voters a better guide to navigating changing societal trends than Democrats.

Articles

Allen, Mike, and Andy Barr, "Steele Trap? GOP Fears Grow," *Politico.com*, March 4, 2009, www.politico.com/news/stories/0309/19588.html.

Some Republicans worry that GOP Chairman Michael Steele is turning out to be a bad pick.

Bacon, Perry Jr., "GOP Looks to Escalate Attacks on Obama," *The Washington Post*, March 7, 2009, p. A4.

After initially attacking congressional Democrats instead of the more popular President Obama, Republicans decide to criticize the president directly regarding spending.

Brownstein, Ronald, "A Dangerous Imbalance for the GOP," *National Journal*, Dec. 20, 2008.

A vote on an auto bailout package shows a regional schism, which the political writer warns points to problems for a congressional GOP dominated by the South and Mountain West.

Cantor, Eric, "The GOP's Path Back," *Politico.com*, Jan. 29, 2005, www.politico.com/news/stories/0109/18111.html.

The House minority whip contends that despite its losses the GOP still has a good foundation for the future based on empowering individuals in free markets.

Cohen, Richard E., "GOP's Dilemma: Substance Versus Spin," *National Journal*, March 7, 2009.

Republican congressional leaders are discouraging members from working with Democrats, favoring a strategy of outright confrontation.

Green, Joshua, "Reagan's Liberal Legacy," *The Washington Monthly*, January 2003, p. 28.

President Reagan was more open to compromise than today's conservatives are willing to admit.

Martin, Jonathan, "Rush Job: Inside Dems' Limbaugh Plan," *Politico.com*, March 4, 2009, www.politico.com/news/stories/0309/19596.html.

Democrats sought to emphasize the influence within GOP ranks of conservative talk-show host Rush Limbaugh because they knew him to be unpopular.

Smith, Ben, "For GOP: All Pain, No Gain," *Politico.com*, March 5, 2009, www.politico.com/news/stories/0309/19636.html.

Longtime GOP strategists express confidence their party will come back but admit that it's still in freefall at the moment.

Tanenhaus, Sam, "Conservatism Is Dead," *TNR.com*, Feb. 18, 2009, www.tnr.com/politics/story.html?id=9dfd540a-3d44-4684-a333-415ef34efa5b.

The New York Times editor argues that the brand of conservative thought that has been a mainstay of American politics for four decades has run out of ideas.

Weigel, David, "Right Nation No More," *Guardian.co.uk*, Jan. 5, 2009, www.guardian.co.uk/commentisfree/cifamerica/2009/jan/05/republicans-us-politics-weigel.

The article contends that Micklethwait and Wooldridge's book (*see above*) needs updating, given how too many congressional districts now favor Democrats.

The Next Step:

Additional Articles from Current Periodicals

GOP Governors

Fouhy, Beth, "GOP Governors Press Congress to Pass Stimulus Bill," The Associated Press, Jan. 31, 2009.

Most Republican governors have broken with their party colleagues in Congress over the economic stimulus.

Issenberg, Sasha, "Governor Jindal: Restore GOP Ideals," *The Boston Globe*, Feb. 25, 2009, p. A11.

A focus on applying Republican ideals to the economy suggests Louisiana Gov. Bobby Jindal may be a party savior.

Salisbury, Bill, "Pawlenty Not Among the Top Choices of Conservatives for 2012," *St. Paul Pioneer Press* (Minnesota), Feb. 27, 2009.

A poll taken by the Conservative Political Action Committee suggests Minnesota Gov. Tim Pawlenty is not a leading candidate for the 2012 Republican presidential nomination.

Smith, Adam C., "GOP Seethes Over Charlie Crist's Stimulus-Plan Support," *The Miami Herald*, Feb. 13, 2009, p. A3.

Despite Gov. Charlie Crist's popularity in Florida, his support for the Democrats' stimulus package has angered many Republicans.

Minorities

Bacon Jr., Perry, "Steele Is RNC's First Black Chairman," *The Washington Post*, Jan. 31, 2009, p. A1.

The Republican National Committee has elected former Maryland Lt. Gov. Michael Steele to lead the party, making him the GOP's first black chairman.

Carroll, Susan, "Latinos Flipped Red States to Blue," *Houston Chronicle*, Nov. 7, 2008, p. A1.

A record turnout of Latinos in the 2008 election swung several traditionally Republican states to the Democrats.

Greer, Jim, "GOP Must Reject Racially Divisive Rhetoric," *Orlando Sentinel*, Jan. 8, 2009, p. A9.

A growing minority population in Florida suggests that Florida Republicans must continue building coalitions and reaching out to minorities to remain relevant.

Harmon, Steven, "Minority Vote on Prop. 8 Key to GOP Future?" *Contra Costa Times* (California), Nov. 23, 2008.

A large minority vote for California's Proposition 8 — which bans same-sex marriage — suggests Republicans share common interests with blacks and Latinos.

Sarah Palin

Bumiller, Elisabeth, "How Internal Battles Divided the McCain and Palin Camps," *The New York Times*, Nov. 6, 2008, p. P9.

Sarah Palin's upstaging of John McCain was largely blamed for the Republican loss in the presidential election.

Olson, Laura, "For Palin Fans, a Team of Their Own," *Los Angeles Times*, Dec. 21, 2008, p. A20.

Sarah Palin's emergence into national politics has drawn many women into the Republican Party.

Simon, Roger, "Win or Lose, Palin Will Be Back in 2012," *Chicago Sun Times*, Oct. 30, 2008, p. 23.

Many Republican pundits are suggesting that Sarah Palin has given the party hope and has earned the right to pursue the presidency in 2012.

Youth

Bettencourt, D. J., "Republicans Ignore Youth Voters at Their Peril," *Union Leader* (New Hampshire), Dec. 30, 2008, p. 9.

New-voter registration, especially among college students, allowed Democrats for the first time in recent history to surpass Republicans in the number of registered New Hampshire voters.

Jonsson, Patrik, "Young Republicans Seek a New Kind of Party," *The Christian Science Monitor*, Dec. 18, 2008, p. 25.

College Republicans are working to develop a more pragmatic type of conservatism to appeal to more young voters.

Rowland, Kara, "For Conservative Youths, a Zeal to Convert Peers," *The Washington Times*, March 3, 2009, p. B1.

The Young Conservatives Coalition is seeking new leaders after Sen. John McCain lost the youth vote to President Barack Obama by a margin of 2 to 1.

Citing CQ Researcher

Sample formats for citing these reports in a bibliography include the ones listed below. Preferred styles and formats vary, so please check with your instructor or professor.

MLA STYLE

Jost, Kenneth. "Rethinking the Death Penalty." CQ Researcher 16 Nov. 2001: 945-68.

APA STYLE

Jost, K. (2001, November 16). Rethinking the death penalty. *CQ Researcher, 11,* 945-968.

CHICAGO STYLE

Jost, Kenneth. "Rethinking the Death Penalty." *CQ Researcher,* November 16, 2001, 945-968.

In-depth Reports on Issues in the News

Are you writing a paper?

Need backup for a debate?

Want to become an expert on an issue?

For 80 years, students have turned to *CQ Researcher* for in-depth reporting on issues in the news. Reports on a full range of political and social issues are now available. Following is a selection of recent reports:

Civil Liberties
Closing Guantánamo, 2/09
Limiting Lawsuits, 12/08
Affirmative Action, 10/08
Gay Marriage Showdowns, 9/08
America's Border Fence, 9/08
Immigration Debate, 2/08

Crime/Law
Mexico's Drug War, 12/08
Prostitution Debate, 5/08
Public Defenders, 4/08
Gun Violence, 5/07

Education
Reading Crisis? 2/08
Discipline in Schools, 2/08
Student Aid, 1/08
Racial Diversity in Public Schools, 9/07
Stress on Students, 7/07

Environment
Confronting Warming, 1/09
Reducing Carbon Footprint, 12/08
Protecting Wetlands, 10/08
Buying Green, 2/08

Health/Safety
Regulating Toxic Chemicals, 1/09
Preventing Cancer, 1/09
Heart Health, 9/08
Global Food Crisis, 6/08

International Affairs/Economy
Middle-Class Squeeze, 3/09
Public-Works Projects, 2/09
The Obama Presidency, 1/09
The National Debt, 11/08
Financial Bailout, 10/08

Social Trends
Public-Works Projects, 2/09
Falling Birthrates, 11/08
Regulating Credit Cards, 10/08
Internet Accuracy, 8/08

Terrorism/Defense
Homeland Security, 2/09
Rise in Counterinsurgency, 9/08
Cost of the Iraq War, 4/08

Youth
Debating Hip-Hop, 6/07

Upcoming Reports

Future of Newspapers, 3/27/09
Extreme Sports, 4/3/09

Wrongful Convictions, 4/10/09
High-Speed Trains, 4/17/09

Judicial Elections, 4/24/09
Hate Groups, 5/1/09

ACCESS

CQ Researcher is available in print and online. For access, visit your library or www.cqresearcher.com.

STAY CURRENT

To receive notice of upcoming *CQ Researcher* reports, or learn more about *CQ Researcher* products, subscribe to the free e-mail newsletters, *CQ Researcher Alert!* and *CQ Researcher News*: http://cqpress.com/newsletters.

PURCHASE

To purchase a *CQ Researcher* report in print or electronic format (PDF), visit www.cqpress.com or call 866-427-7737. Single reports start at $15. Bulk purchase discounts and electronic-rights licensing are also available.

SUBSCRIBE

Annual full-service *CQ Researcher* subscriptions—including 44 reports a year, monthly index updates, and a bound volume—start at $803. Add $25 for domestic postage.

CQ Researcher Online offers a backfile from 1991 and a number of tools to simplify research. For pricing information, call 800-834-9020, ext. 1906, or e-mail librarysales@cqpress.com.

CQ Researcher

Published by CQ Press, a division of SAGE Publications

www.cqresearcher.com

Future of Journalism

Will newspapers' decline weaken democracy?

T homas Jefferson once famously remarked that if he had to choose between government without newspapers or newspapers without government, he wouldn't hesitate to preserve newspapers. Today, however, newspapers across the country are declining in circulation, advertising and profitability. Some are ceasing to publish. Others are reducing or closing Washington and state-capital bureaus, laying off staff and cutting back the news coverage they provide. Many journalists, scholars, political activists and government officials worry that government without newspapers could be on the horizon, and that citizens then would be unable to obtain sufficient information for effective self-government. As more Americans turn to the Internet and cable television for news, however, others are hopeful that new forms of journalism will fill the gaps. Meanwhile, newspapers are attempting to give themselves new birth online.

After publishing for 150 years, Denver's Rocky Mountain News *shut down on Feb. 27, ending daily newspaper competition in the city. Scores of other papers are cutting staffs, closing bureaus or facing bankruptcy.*

CQ Researcher • March 27, 2009 • www.cqresearcher.com
Volume 19, Number 12 • Pages 273-296

Cover: Getty Images/John Moore

CQ Researcher

March 27, 2009
Volume 19, Number 12

MANAGING EDITOR: Thomas J. Colin
tcolin@cqpress.com

ASSISTANT MANAGING EDITOR: Kathy Koch
kkoch@cqpress.com

ASSOCIATE EDITOR: Kenneth Jost

STAFF WRITERS: Thomas J. Billitteri, Marcia Clemmitt, Peter Katel

CONTRIBUTING WRITERS: Rachel Cox, Sarah Glazer, Alan Greenblatt, Barbara Mantel, Patrick Marshall, Tom Price, Jennifer Weeks

DESIGN/PRODUCTION EDITOR: Olu B. Davis

ASSISTANT EDITOR: Darrell Dela Rosa

FACT-CHECKING: Eugene J. Gabler, Michelle Harris

EDITORIAL INTERN: Vyomika Jairam

CQ PRESS

A Division of SAGE

PRESIDENT AND PUBLISHER:
John A. Jenkins

EXECUTIVE DIRECTOR,
REFERENCE INFORMATION GROUP:
Alix B. Vance

CQ Press is a registered trademark of Congressional Quarterly Inc.

CQ Researcher (ISSN 1056-2036) is printed on acid-free paper. Published weekly, except; (Jan. wk. 1) (May wk. 4) (July wks. 1, 2) (Aug. wks. 3, 4) (Nov. wk. 4) and (Dec. wk. 4), by CQ Press, a division of SAGE Publications. Annual full-service subscriptions start at $803. For pricing, call 1-800-834-9020, ext. 1906. To purchase a *CQ Researcher* report in print or electronic format (PDF), visit www. cqpress.com or call 866-427-7737. Single reports start at $15. Bulk purchase discounts and electronic-rights licensing are also available. Periodicals postage paid at Washington, D.C., and additional mailing offices. POSTMASTER: Send address changes to *CQ Researcher*, 2300 N St., N.W., Suite 800, Washington, DC 20037.

Future of Journalism

BY TOM PRICE

THE ISSUES

Forty-three years ago, *Time* magazine posed a provocative question on its cover: "Is God Dead?" The answer turned out to be: "not so much."

This February, the magazine's cover pondered ways to stave off the death of newspapers. With the industry copiously bleeding red ink, reporters and editors losing jobs by the thousands and online news becoming increasingly popular — and controversial — *Time*'s editors aren't the only people wondering about journalism's future. Certainly the recent news has been grim:

• The *Rocky Mountain News* shut down on Feb. 27 after reporting about the Denver region for 150 years. [1]

• The 146-year-old *Seattle Post-Intelligencer* turned off its presses on March 17, becoming a Web-only publication. [2]

• *The Christian Science Monitor*, a highly regarded national daily newspaper since 1908, plans in April to become a Web and e-mail publication, offering only a weekly, magazine-like, printed edition. [3]

• Thirty-three newspapers — including the *Los Angeles Times*, *Chicago Tribune* and *Philadelphia Inquirer* — sought Chapter 11 bankruptcy protection from December through February. [4]

• Even the mighty *New York Times*, heavily in debt, in early 2009 borrowed an additional $250 million at 14 percent interest from Mexican billionaire Carlos Slim Helu, once described by *The Times* itself as having a "robber baron reputation." [5]

Newspapers across the country are declining in circulation, advertising

The last copies of the Seattle Post-Intelligencer *roll off the press on March 17. After 146 years, the PI is becoming an online-only news operation. More than 450 daily newspapers have disappeared in the United States since 1940. While many Americans worry that democracy will suffer if citizens cannot obtain sufficient information for effective self-government, others are hopeful that online journalism — perhaps supported by philanthropy or even government itself — will fill the gaps.*

Getty Images/Robert Giroux

and profitability. In 2008 alone, publicly traded newspaper stock prices fell 83 percent. [6] The Fitch credit-rating service forecasts more newspaper closures this year and next, which could leave a growing number of cities with no newspaper at all. [7]

The collapse of newspapers threatens to leave "a dramatically diminished version of democracy in its wake," John Nichols and Robert McChesney warned.

"Journalism is collapsing, and with it comes the most serious threat in our lifetimes to self-government," wrote Nichols, *The Nation*'s Washington correspondent, and McChesney, a University of Illinois communications pro-

fessor. "As journalists are laid off and newspapers cut back or shut down, whole sectors of our civic life go dark. [8]

Thomas Jefferson once famously remarked that, if he had to choose between government without newspapers or newspapers without government, he wouldn't hesitate to preserve newspapers. [9] In the subsequent 222 years, Americans have had both, and newspapers have been citizens' primary source of information about government at all levels.

Many journalists, scholars, lobbyists and government officials worry that the decline of newspapers will leave citizens without sufficient information for effective self-government. They also worry that the fragmented nature of Internet and cable television audiences could turn the clock back to the late-18th and early-19th centuries, when a large number of partisan newspapers printed more opinion than news, and many readers read only publications with which they agreed.

As more Americans turn to the Internet and cable television for news, however, others are hopeful that new forms of journalism will fill the gaps. They envision cable news channels, bloggers, other online content providers and newspapers' own Web sites picking up the slack. [10]

Ironically, newspapers' readership appears to be higher now than ever before as more and more readers access their papers online. U.S. daily newspapers sell about 51 million copies a day, [11] while hosting nearly 75 million unique visitors on their Web sites each month. [12] *The New York Times* sells about a million newspapers daily

Newspaper Industry Numbers Falling

The number of daily newspapers in the United States declined by more than 450 from 1940 to 2007 (top graph). During the same period, circulation increased to its highest point in 1984, then declined by nearly 20 percent (bottom graph).

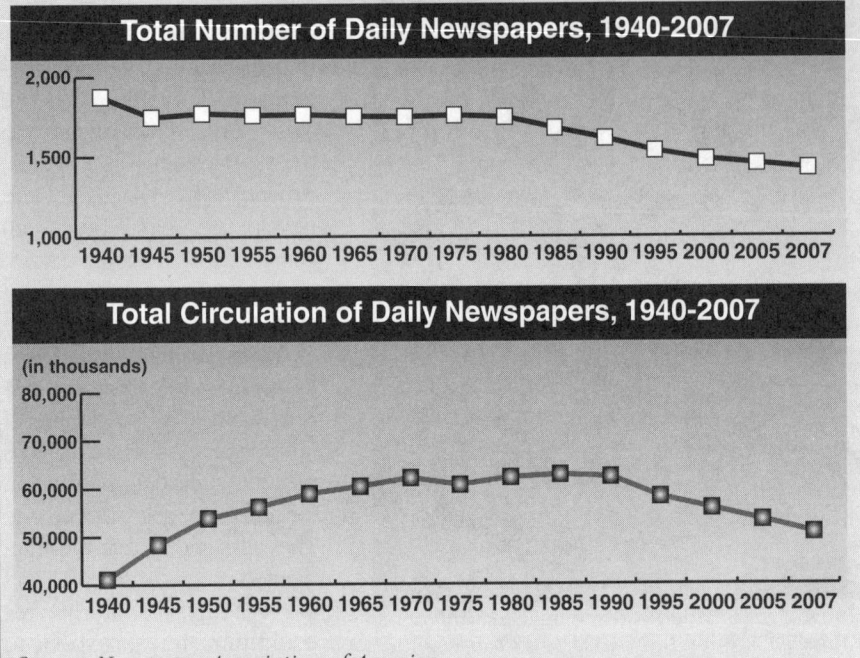

Source: Newspaper Association of America

and about 1.4 million on Sunday, while its Web site attracts 20 million unique visitors monthly. [13]

Circulation and advertising revenues have been in a steady decline, however, and newspapers have not figured out how to profit from their Web sites. Only about 10 percent of newspaper advertising revenues are earned on the Internet. [14]

Journalists, scholars, entrepreneurs and philanthropists are looking for ways to finance high-quality, comprehensive reporting online. In addition to the traditional for-profit model, they are experimenting with nonprofit news organizations and philanthropic support of journalistic enterprises. Some are discussing government funding.

No less an Internet luminary than Google CEO Eric Schmidt views the loss of newspapers as "a real tragedy."

"Journalism is a central part of democracy," he said. "I don't think bloggers make up the difference." [15]

In fact, most news online is produced by newspapers or by organizations that are funded substantially by newspapers, such as The Associated Press. Many television organizations field significant newsgathering operations. But most lag far behind their newspaper counterparts — particularly at the local, regional and state levels — and they often follow newspapers' reporting leads.

"The decline of newspapers has a big ripple effect," says Peter Shane, executive director of the Knight Commission on the Information Needs of Communities in a Democracy, "because to a substantial extent television and radio news always has been based on local newspapers' reporting."

Yet, nearly across the board, news-

papers are shrinking the government coverage that's most important to informing citizens in a democracy. Papers that remain in business are cutting staff, closing bureaus and reducing the number of reporters who cover public affairs full time.

Even as the United States is involved in an ever more globalized world — fighting wars in Iraq and Afghanistan, guarding against far-flung terrorist organizations, competing in a globalized economy — U.S. news organizations are bringing their foreign correspondents home.

And with a new administration shaking up Washington and the troubled global economy looking to Washington for leadership, newspapers are shrinking or closing their Washington bureaus. [16] More than 40 regional correspondents — those who cover a particular community's interests in the nation's capital — lost their jobs over the last three years. [17] Even major papers — including the *Los Angeles Times*, *Chicago Tribune* and *Baltimore Sun* — have cut the size of their Washington bureaus. [18] Other publications have eliminated their Washington staffs entirely — notably *The San Diego Union* whose D.C. reporters won a 2006 Pulitzer Prize for exposing corrupt U.S. Rep. Randy "Duke" Cunningham, who now sits in jail. [19] Newspapers in half the states now have no congressional correspondent. [20]

Associated Press Senior Vice President Sue Cross lamented declining coverage of city, county and state governments as well — not just the number of reporters but their expertise. "Seasoned beat reporters are, in many cases, leaving the industry," she said. [21]

Virginia's capital press corps shrank by half during the last decade, according to AP Richmond Correspondent Bob Lewis. [22] Maryland media are sending half as many correspondents to Annapolis to cover state government as they did just two years ago, former AP reporter Tom Stukey said. [23] In Broward County, Fla. (Fort Lauderdale), Commissioner John Rodstrom said, local newspapers have cut their county government coverage in half in a year. [24]

"So who's watching out for the interests of the public?" former *Boston Globe* investigative reporter Walter Robinson asks. "The answer is darn fewer people than used to be."

The reduction in regional correspondents has generated particular concern in Washington. Regional reporters' importance goes beyond uncovering wrongdoing, according to Michael Gessel, a longtime congressional aide who now works as a Washington lobbyist for the Dayton Development Corp. in Ohio. "At least equally important is the day-to-day — and sometimes mundane — coverage of what our elected officials do that isn't scandalous," Gessel says.

Members of Congress often work hardest on matters that get the most coverage by news media in their districts, Gessel explains. Without a hometown reporter tracking the districts' interests in Washington, he says, those interests are likely to get less congressional attention.

Citizens also need to know when government does things well, he adds. "All democracies require consent of the governed. If people only hear about scandals, then that consent is withdrawn. Practically speaking, that means less willingness to have their tax dollars support government."

Political Science Professor Gary Jacobson, of the University of California, San Diego, is among those who discount the loss of local newspapers' Washington-based reporting. "You don't have to be in D.C. to find out what [members of Congress] are doing," Jacobson said. Reporters can interview lawmakers on their frequent visits home, he said, and citizens can track legislators' activity by accessing government documents online. [25]

Journalists, lobbyists and government officials said Jacobson's comments reflect a misunderstanding of how governments really work. "When you're

---

Newspapers Getting More Online Traffic

Nearly 75 million people visited a newspaper Web site in January 2009, an increase of more than 80 percent from the same month five years earlier.

Unique Visitors to Newspaper Web Sites

Source: Newspaper Association of America

---

walking the halls of Congress and you are going into members' offices every day and you're developing sources, over time those people tell you things the public needs to know but lawmakers want to keep away from the public," says Andrew Alexander, chief of the recently closed Cox Newspapers Washington Bureau and now ombudsman for *The Washington Post*. "That's what's being lost."

A Washington correspondent must know the actors and understand the processes of the federal government, Gessel says. "You can't get that by phone, by Internet or by e-mail."

As journalists, scholars and politicians try to navigate the new media environment, here are some of the questions they are asking about the future of democracy:

Can the Internet fill the reporting gaps caused by the decline of newspapers?

News-reporting sites are popping up on the Internet even faster than newspapers are losing circulation.

On Jan. 12, for instance, *GlobalPost* went online in an ambitious effort to do the kind of international journalism that newspapers and television networks have scaled back. Led by news veterans, the site promises comprehensive, frontline reporting by more than 60 freelance correspondents in more than 40 countries. [26] The new operation hopes to turn a profit by selling advertising, syndicating its reporting to other news organizations and selling $199-a-year subscriptions to a premium service. [27]

Two years earlier, other news veterans launched *Politico*, which quickly became a popular source of political news during the long campaign that carried Barack Obama to the White House. *Politico* — a Web site and a newspaper distributed free in Washington — is performing ahead of its business plan and expects to turn a profit this year, says Editor-in-Chief John Harris, a 21-year veteran of *The Washington Post*.

Across the country, countless sites have been created to cover local and regional communities. They range from highly professional organizations covering major metropolitan areas to primarily volunteer operations serving small communities to professional-amateur collaborations of all sizes.

MinnPost in Minnesota and *Voice of San Diego* have won widespread praise for practicing high-quality, professional journalism, for instance. Smaller, mostly amateur, sites contain little more than announcements from community organizations. *The New York Times* and the *Chicago Tribune* have assigned professionals to oversee networks of volunteers who report for Web sites operated by those papers, focusing on news about specific neighborhoods.

The Internet surpassed newspapers as Americans' favorite source of national and international news in late 2008. Both trailed television by a substantial margin among the population at large. But Americans younger than 30 turned

---

to the Internet as often as to television — and twice as often as to newspapers. [28] Readers still turn to newspapers more than to the Internet for local news. [29]

Most of the news Americans obtain on the Web is not produced by online news organizations, however. On Election Day 2008, for instance, seven of the 10 most-popular Internet news sites belonged to CNN, MSNBC, Fox News, *The New York Times*, Tribune Newspapers, *The Washington Post* and *USA Today*. The others — Yahoo! News, AOL News and Google News — simply aggregate content produced by newsgathering organizations such as newspapers and television networks. [30] Many other Web sites also link to reports produced by traditional news organizations.

"Very interesting and hopeful things are happening on the Web," says Geneva Overholser, director of the University of Southern California's journalism school. However, she adds, "many people think the only thing that will work online will be niche publications," not replacements for comprehensive newspapers.

Politico and *GlobalPost* are promising examples of niche sites that might succeed by attracting national or international audiences that advertisers want to reach. *Politico*, for instance, sells most of its ads to organizations that want to influence the federal government, and many of those ads appear in the printed edition, which targets an elite Washington audience.

Another is Joshua Micah Marshall's "Talking Points Memo," which won the prestigious George Polk Award for Legal Reporting in 2007 for "tenacious investigative reporting" of the Bush administration's questionable firings of U.S. attorneys. TPM "connected the dots and found a pattern of federal prosecutors being forced from office for failing to do the Bush administration's bidding," which "sparked interest by the traditional news media

and led to the resignation of Attorney General Alberto Gonzales," the Polk judges said. [31]

Started by Marshall as a one-man blog in 2000, TPM now has a staff of 17.

National niche sites can succeed because of economies of scale, says Henry Heilbrunn, a new-media management consultant and former Associated Press executive. Such sites might need smaller staffs than those providing comprehensive coverage to a metropolitan area, but they could still sell to a large national advertising base, he contends.

"There's no sign anywhere of anything replacing the comprehensive metropolitan newspaper, replacing the kind of watchfulness that even a mediocre city newspaper might offer," says Tom Rosenstiel, director of the Project for Excellence in Journalism.

Journalists should stop wringing their hands about the Internet's shortcomings and focus on what creative things they can do online, says New York University journalism Professor Jay Rosen.

"I think the kind of check that newspapers can provide — if they're run well and if they are big and strong — is very hard to get any other way, so I do not look forward to newspapers' decline," Rosen says. "But what I think about it is irrelevant to the market mechanisms and technological changes that are hollowing out the newspapers' business model."

Others worry that online news sites can't serve Americans who don't have Internet access, a group that tends to be older and poorer than the general public. While nearly all young Americans go online, nearly three-quarters of Americans older than 75 do not. That also is true for a majority between 70 and 75, more than a third between 60 and 69, a quarter between 50 and 59 and a fifth between 45 and 49. [32]

Business consultant James Moore — who advises newspapers to shut down their presses and become online-only operations — argues that publi-

cations can't afford to worry about those lost readers. "They are not the people advertisers reach out to," Moore says. "The people they're going after are people in the 35-to-45 category. You have to look to the future, and the future is the young."

Are the new media bad for democracy?

On Oct. 3, 2008, CNN's *iReport* Internet site reported, incorrectly, that Apple CEO Steve Jobs had been rushed to the hospital after a heart attack. The account quickly was repeated on other Web sites, and Apple stock fell more than 9 percent in 12 minutes — a total loss of $9 billion in the company's value. [33]

A month earlier, the Bloomberg financial Web site mistakenly posted a six-year-old report about United Airlines' 2002 bankruptcy filing. Thinking the airline was going bankrupt again, investors dumped the stock, which lost three-quarters of its value before the NASDAQ stock exchange halted trading. A financial newsletter had found the old newspaper story while doing a Google search and passed it on to Bloomberg believing it was current. [34]

The credibility of the erroneous reports was enhanced by CNN's and Bloomberg's reputations as legitimate news organizations. But in both cases the reports appeared on the organizations' Web sites without being vetted.

The incidents illustrate some criticisms of Internet-based news operations.

Many bloggers — and even some traditional media — are cavalier about accuracy on the Web, critics complain. Moreover, they say, Internet public-affairs sites tend to publish more opinion than fact, much of it vicious, mean-spirited and profane. And they worry that fragmentation of the online audience can lead many Web surfers to experience a narrow, distorted view of the world in what some call the Internet "echo chamber."

Indeed, the Jobs story was repeated by blogger Henry Blodget on the widely read *Silicon Alley Insider* Web site. Blodget later unapologetically proclaimed he would do it again, noting he had warned readers he didn't know if the report was true.

"You, our readers, are smart enough to know the difference between rumors and facts, and you are smart enough to evaluate what we tell you," Blodget said. Posting unverified information "flushes out the truth," he argued. "We wouldn't want you to not tell us what everyone was talking about because you couldn't verify it." [35]

That's an example of what Rosenstiel and Bill Kovach — former Washington bureau chief of *The New York Times* and former editor of *The Atlanta Journal-Constitution* — have termed "the journalism of assertion." Traditional journalistic ethics require that facts be confirmed before they're published, Rosenstiel and Kovach said. Many figures on talk radio, cable news and the Internet are "less interested in substantiating whether something is true and more interested in getting it into the public discussion." [36] While they coined the phrase a decade ago, Rosenstiel says, it's even more true today.

CNN also defended its unverified *iReports* by noting the Web site carries a disclaimer that "the stories submitted by users are not edited, fact-checked or screened before they post." [37]

CNN says it created *iReports* to extend CNN's newsgathering reach and to increase viewers' personal attachment to the cable network. It checks the accuracy of *iReporters*' contributions only before using them in its telecasts.

A growing number of news organizations are recruiting volunteer, "citizen" journalists, especially online, as a way to compensate for cutbacks in their professional reporting staffs.

"News organizations are really getting squeezed, and so it's incumbent on them to be looking for ways to engage citizens in the process," William Grueskin, academic-affairs dean at the Columbia University journalism school, noted. Citizen involvement "can be a very powerful influence when harnessed the right way," he added, "but sometimes it goes awry." [38]

At the *Chicago Tribune*'s *Triblocal* Web site, for example, which recruits amateurs to contribute community news, most stories about the 2008 Third Congressional District Democratic primary turned out to have been written by one candidate's publicist. [39]

Journalism historian Anthony Fellow at California State University, Fullerton, is among those who worry about the fragmentation of the Internet audience among ideologically oriented sites. "We're back to the party press era" after the Revolutionary War, he says, "the viciousness that went on between the two camps, the name-calling."

Matthew Hindman, an assistant professor of political science at Arizona State University, sees such partisanship as a natural outcome of the decline of monopoly newspapers.

"The local newspapers, as monopolies, have been inclined to neutrality, to alienating as few of their potential readers as they can," he says. "The more news outlets there are, the greater need to differentiate outlets from each other. Ideology is an effective way to do that. Conservative sites share very little traffic with liberal sites."

Fully 80 percent of talk-radio host Rush Limbaugh's listeners describe themselves as conservative, for instance. [40] During the 2008 campaign, Fox News Channel viewers were most likely to be Republicans while MSNBC viewers tended to be Democrats. [41]

City University of New York journalism Professor Jeff Jarvis rejects the echo-chamber charge. "We have more arguments than ever," he says. "The echo chamber was when there was one newspaper in town."

Similarly, the Knight commission's Shane says, "It would be surprising, in the most networked environment in human history, if people actually come across fewer things that are new to them than they did in the last half of the 20th century."

Most Americans aren't limiting themselves to partisan sites. Just 5 percent of the general public and 10 percent of conservatives say they listen to Limbaugh regularly, for instance. [42] According to the Project for Excellence in Journalism's 2007 report on the "State of the News Media," two-thirds of Americans prefer to get their news from neutral sources, while just a quarter want sources that share their point of view. [43]

Can philanthropy save journalism?

David Swensen, who manages Yale University's $17 billion endowment, thinks he knows how to save America's newspapers: Turn them into non-profit institutions supported by charitable endowments just like Yale's.

"Endowments would enhance newspapers' autonomy while shielding them from the economic forces that are now tearing them down," he wrote with Yale financial analyst Michael Schmidt. "Endowments would transform newspapers into unshakable fixtures of American life, with greater stability and enhanced independence that would allow them to serve the public good more effectively." [44]

A $5 billion endowment, for example, would support *The New York Times*' newsgathering operation, which is the largest in the newspaper business, they wrote. The paper could continue to earn income from advertising and subscriptions to pay other expenses.

The proposal quickly was endorsed by Steve Coll, a *New Yorker* writer and former *Washington Post* managing editor, who estimated a $2 billion endowment could support *The Post*. [45]

Those are huge numbers, but not unheard of in the endowment world. Yale's endowment is nearly five times what *The Times* would need, according to Swensen and Schmidt's calculations.

Audience Grew for Cable and Online News

Cable TV and online news were the only two forms of media exhibiting significant audience growth from 2007 to 2008. Audiences for more traditional forms of media had noticeable declines, with newspapers and magazines declining the most.

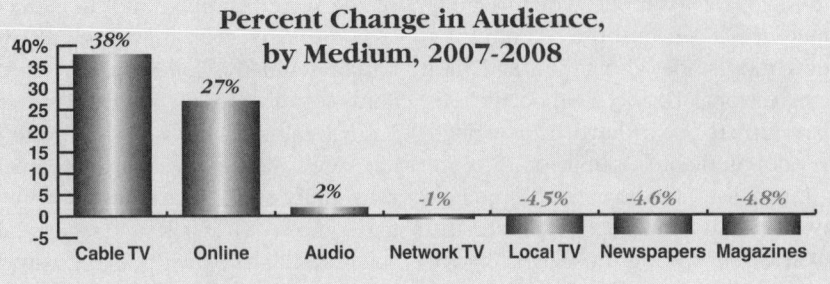

Percent Change in Audience, by Medium, 2007-2008

Source: Pew Project for Excellence in Journalism

Harvard's is more than seven times larger. Eighteen universities' endowments exceed $5 billion. [46] Multibillionaire Warren Buffet could fund *The Post*'s endowment with about 5 percent of his fortune, Coll said. [47]

The idea has attracted critics as well as supporters.

Media analyst Alan Mutter and Zachary Seward, an assistant editor at Harvard University's Nieman Journalism Lab, calculated it would cost $114 billion to endow every newspaper in America. Their number skews high, however, because they used the highest newspaper employment in U.S. history — 56,900 journalists in 1990 — and assumed it would cost an average $100,000 to support each employee's wage, fringe benefits and business expenses. The Bureau of Labor Statistics says the average newspaper reporter earns less than $40,000 a year. [48]

Others attacked the very concept of nonprofit newspapers. "They declare surrender, that there's not a market demand for journalism," complains Jarvis at the City University of New York. "I believe there is market demand, and the hard work now is to find the new business model that will work."

Market discipline produces better journalism, according to Jonathan Weber, whose for-profit *New West*

Web site covers the Rocky Mountain region from Missoula, Mont. "The core problem that nonprofit journalism will never be able to solve properly is deciding what is worthy," Weber argued. "In a business, the customers ultimately decide what is worthy, for better and for worse."

New West earns income from running conferences as well as from online advertising, he said, "and we have some more new business angles up our sleeve." [49]

Philanthropy-supported and nonprofit journalism are growing phenomena, however. *MinnPost* and *Voice of San Diego* raise funds from foundations, wealthy individuals and businesses. They also recruit dues-paying members, following the model of public broadcasting.

The Knight Foundation, built on the wealth of the now-defunct Knight Newspapers chain, awards millions of dollars in grants to scores of journalism projects every year and encourages other philanthropies to do the same. "We're trying to convince foundations that a core need is not just health, education and welfare but also information," Gary Kebbel, the foundation's journalism program director, explained. [50] The Kaiser Family Foundation, known for its support of health

care, has created a news service to cover health policy. The foundation hired two veteran journalists to run the organization, and they plan to hire a half-dozen reporters and several editors and to contract for projects by freelance journalists. Their work will appear on the Kaiser Health News Web site, and other media will be encouraged to republish it. The organization also will conduct projects in partnership with other news media, something the foundation has done on a selective basis since the mid 1990s.

The foundation started the news service because "news organizations are every year becoming less capable of producing coverage of these complex issues as their budgets are being slashed," foundation President Drew Altman said.

Other philanthropies are bankrolling health news organizations in California, Florida and Kansas. [51]

Charlotte Hall, president of the American Society of Newspaper Editors, said she could envision philanthropies supporting specific newspaper projects — "investigative reporting or an important local beat, for example. But a new kind of firewall would be needed to assure independent reporting and unencumbered editing." [52]

Richard Tofel, general manager of *ProPublica*, says his nonprofit investigative reporting organization has established the same protections for its newsroom that good newspapers traditionally do. *ProPublica*'s funders and directors "never know what we're going to publish before we publish it," Tofel says. "They don't see stories before they're printed. Post-publication, their contact is limited to top editors."

The New York Times reported in December the Justice Department is investigating possible improper conduct by a bank owned until 2006 by *ProPublica*'s major funder and board chairman, San Francisco billionaire Herbert Sandler. [53]

Continued on p. 282

In Hard Times, Papers Turn to Cooperation

Broader coverage offsets loss of journalistic competition.

Hard-driving newsmen Ben Hecht and Charles MacArthur have to be spinning in their graves. Their celebrated 1928 play, *The Front Page*, depicted the cutthroat competition they experienced as Chicago newspaper reporters, when numerous dailies fought to break the news first.

Today Chicago has just two dailies, both facing severe financial challenges. Most cities have one, and many could lose that newspaper as well. And a growing number of surviving papers are looking to cooperate rather than compete in order to cut costs.

The eight largest newspapers in Ohio have agreed to share their staffs' work. So have Florida's *Miami Herald, St. Petersburg Times, Palm Beach Post* and (Fort Lauderdale) *Sun Sentinel*. Even *The Washington Post*, one of America's very best — and most competitive — papers, has begun to cooperate with the neighboring *Baltimore Sun*.

The Ohio papers share each other's stories and coordinate their state government coverage. During the 2008 political campaign, the papers conducted a joint polling project. The papers are scattered around the state and don't have a great deal of overlapping readership, their editors say.

The arrangement enables each newspaper to provide more information to its readers than it could on its own, *Dayton Daily News* Editor Kevin Riley says.

"We could have sat around and complained that none of us could afford to have any polling," he explains. "Instead, we got a statewide poll that cost us more than any one paper would have been able to pay."

The Daily News no longer covers Ohio State football, using *Columbus Dispatch* reporting instead. *The Dispatch* carries *Daily News* coverage of the Cincinnati Reds.

In Florida, *The Herald* and *Times* have created a joint, six-reporter state capital bureau. *The Herald, Post* and *Sun Sentinel* have entered an agreement to share routine coverage in order to free reporters for more enterprise reporting. With Florida International University, they created the South Florida News Service, through which journalism students will produce video and audio content for the three newspapers as well as stories. [1]

The Washington-Baltimore agreement covers routine reporting about Maryland, but not state government or University of Maryland sports, where *The Post* and *Sun* continue to compete. [2]

The agreements have raised concerns about loss of journalistic competition.

"It could be a good thing," Florida state Sen. Dan Gelber said about the arrangements in his state. "But I do worry. I'm a big believer that there needs to be plenty of competition. A vibrant press corps in our state's capital is crucial." [3]

"If you have fewer people covering things," Ohio University journalism Professor Patrick Washburn says, "you have fewer viewpoints, and fewer viewpoints is not good." A politician can "spin" one reporter to get his views across easier than he can spin several, Washburn adds.

"I think competition makes us better, because it creates more diversity of viewpoints and makes us work harder" says Andrew Alexander, *The Washington Post*'s ombudsman. He worries that quality may decline "when there's no urgency to beat the other guy or to go deeper than someone else."

On the other hand, he adds, "I sympathize with the editors. If you don't have enough staff to cover the local school board meeting, you have to make a choice."

Riley acknowledges that editors and reporters need to be aware of the pitfalls of diminished competition and have to "challenge ourselves to make sure we're doing our job and serving the public good." But, he adds, competition is not necessarily valuable when it leads eight reporters to do the same routine story.

"When that could be done with one and the others could be working on enterprise stories with more importance, you're not being smart," he says. "We could have that group of reporters covering more ground."

Similarly, *Miami Herald* Editor Anders Gyllenhaal said the Florida cooperation "helps us focus on 100 percent more enterprise." [4] In announcing the agreements, *The Herald* promised readers "more deep and probing stories on the important issues across Florida." The arrangements "increase our ability to look beyond the news, to take on investigative projects and to do the kind of explanatory work that is particularly important at the state government level." [5]

Journalism consultant Michele McLellan endorsed the cooperation and predicted more will come.

"Sure, it's important to have more than one watchdog on duty at the statehouse," she said. "But too often the watchdogs became the herd, covering the same hearings, writing up the same turn-of-screw procedural votes, and capturing the same political skirmishes that never quite enlighten real motivations or inform about policy." [6]

---

[1] "New Tallahassee Bureau Expands Our Coverage," *The Miami Herald*, Dec. 7, 2008, p. L1.

[2] Michael S. Rosenwald, "Washington Post, Baltimore Sun to Share Content," *The Washington Post*, Dec. 23, 2008, p. D3.

[3] "New Tallahassee Bureau Expands Our Coverage," *op. cit.*

[4] Michele McLellan, "Turning Rivalries into Partnerships," Knight Digital Media Center, Jan. 13, 2009, www.knightdigitalmediacenter.org/leadership_blog/comments/turning_rivalries_into_partnerships.

[5] "New Tallahassee Bureau Expands Our Coverage," *op. cit.*

[6] McLellan, *op. cit.*

Continued from p. 280

Some newspaper advocates even have suggested government funding.

Sweden subsidizes newspapers in weak market positions. [54] France is increasing its newspaper subsidies from $362 million to about $620 million annually. [55] The national government is obligated to "make sure an independent, free and pluralistic press exists," French President Nicolas Sarkozy said. [56]

In the United States, owners of *The Inquirer* and *Daily News* in Philadelphia discussed possible state aid with Pennsylvania Gov. Ed Rendell. [57]

On March 24, U.S. Sen. Ben Cardin, D-Md., introduced legislation to exempt newspaper advertising and circulation revenue from taxation, Bloomberg News reported.

U.S. newspapers are in such dire straits, Nichols and McChesney argued in *The Nation*, that only government can save them. "Just as there came a moment when policy makers recognized the necessity of investing tax dollars to create a public education system to teach our children, so a moment has arrived at which we must recognize the need to invest tax dollars to create and maintain newsgathering, reporting and writing with the purpose of informing all our citizens," they wrote. [58]

The Knight commission's Shane argues that "we don't have a strong tradition of government-run media, and we have a lot of distrust of government media being an adequate watchdog on government. I'm not sure *The Executive Branch Daily* would be a good substitute for *The Washington Post*."

For a news organization "to truly do its job as a watchdog," new-media consultant Heilbrunn agrees, "the people who are paying can't be the people being watched."

Nichols and McChesney point out, however, that the government has subsidized news media since the birth of the republic.

"The government implemented extraordinary postal subsidies for the dis-

tribution of newspapers," they wrote. "It also instituted massive newspaper subsidies through printing contracts and the paid publication of government notices." [59]

Moreover, they argued, broadcast and cable licenses represent subsidies to newer media. ■

BACKGROUND

Early Newspapers

Before the first American newspaper was published — in 1690 — a system of private reporting informed 16th-century European businessmen. Scattered about European cities, these journalists prepared handwritten letters that reported on prices, trade, transportation, politics, war and anything else their subscribers might be interested in.

Each letter was sent to just one businessman or company. New York University's Rosen likened them to today's specialty newsletters "that only big firms and rich people can afford." Like today's traditional media, Rosen said, the newsletters needed to be accurate, interpretive and entertaining. [60]

That was not true for the early American newspapers, which were partisan, opinionated and often owned by the political parties they wrote about. [61] Colonial authorities shut down the first American newspaper, *Publick Occurrences Both Forreign and Domestick*, after one issue in 1690 because the publisher had not obtained a government license.

Before American newspapers began to proliferate in the 18th century, historian Fellow says, news was disseminated orally at coffeehouses. "People would come in and say their news and they'd discuss the news." The Internet, on which "everybody can be a journalist," harkens to those days, Fellow observes.

What Harvard historian Jill Lepore termed "the real birth of the American newspaper" occurred in 1721, when James Franklin began publishing the *New-England Courant*. [62]

Without a license, he published political essays, opinion, satire and some news. "I hereby invite all Men, who have Leisure, Inclination and Ability, to speak their Minds with Freedom, Sense and Moderation, and their Pieces shall be welcome to a Place in my Paper," he proclaimed. [63]

Franklin's contrarian publication scandalized Puritan minister Cotton Mather of Boston, angered government officials and got Franklin jailed twice. Ordered to submit his publications to government review or cease printing, he turned the paper over to his younger brother Benjamin, who continued as an irritant to the establishment.

"The Business of Printing has chiefly to do with Men's Opinions," Benjamin Franklin acknowledged. Another early newspaperman declared: "Professions of impartiality I shall make none. They are always useless, and are besides perfect nonsense." [64]

These early papers tended to read like "one long and uninterrupted invective," Lepore said. [65] But their inflammatory protestations helped touch off the American Revolution. And they took important strides toward the press freedom that the Constitution and Supreme Court rulings guarantee today.

Partisan attack and character assassination became so common in the early days of the republic that journalism historian Frank Luther Mott labeled the first third of the 19th century "the dark ages of partisan journalism." [66]

"Right after the revolution, parties paid newspapers to support them, and you had no ethical codes," explains Ohio University journalism Professor Patrick Washburn, editor of the *Journalism History* journal.

According to Fellow, "Journalists were basically stenographers for politicians.

Continued on p. 284

Chronology

1900s-1920s
Newspapers experiment with financing, launch crusades to improve society.

1906
Referring to newspaper and magazine exposés, President Theodore Roosevelt complains of "muckrakers" who can't lift their eyes above "the filth of the floor."

1908
Church-supported *Christian Science Monitor* begins publishing.

1911
Chicago Day Book tries to publish without advertising.

1912
New York Independent Editor Hamilton Holt prepares model for an endowment-supported newspaper.

1914
Los Angeles government begins publishing the *Municipal News*.

1930s-1970s
Industry consolidation is followed by "Golden Age" of newspapers.

1930
Consolidation leaves just one newspaper in eight cities with more than 100,000 residents.

1937-1939
Ninety-eight papers close or disappear in mergers.

1948
Television networks cover the 1948 political conventions, pose tough competition for newspapers.

1950
Newspapers sell more than 35 percent of U.S. advertising, but begin steady decline.

1966
Mid-size dailies earn average profit of 23 percent. . . . Gannett chain sells stock to the public, opening itself to shareholder pressure.

1967
New York Times goes public with two classes of stock, leaving Ochs-Sulzberger family in control.

1968
Newspapers sell $5.2 billion in ads versus $3.1 billion for television.

1970
Chains own half of daily newspapers with two-thirds of circulation.

1971
New York Times publishes secret "Pentagon Papers" history of Vietnam War; Supreme Court says newspapers can publish without "prior restraint" from government.

1974
The Washington Post's Watergate reporting leads to President Richard M. Nixon's resignation.

1980s-Present
Free content from electronic media threaten newspapers.

1980
Number of daily newspapers drops below 1,750, beginning steady decline.

1982
Gannett launches *USA Today*; other papers copy its style.

1984
Daily newspaper circulation peaks at 63.3 million.

1991
World Wide Web invented.

1993
New York Times goes online.

1998
Cyber-gossip Matt Drudge reveals *Newsweek* investigation of Clinton-Lewinsky affair.

1999
All but two of 100 largest newspapers publish online.

2005
All but two of 20 largest papers lose circulation. Papers cut 2,200 jobs.

2007
Classified advertising plummets; newspapers eliminate nearly 1,500 jobs. . . . *Politico* Web site becomes popular source of political news.

2008
Internet surpasses newspapers as Americans' favorite source of national and international news, but newspapers top Internet as local news source.

2009
Circulation for 1,400 dailies drops to 51 million; newspaper Web sites draw 75 million. . . . *Rocky Mountain News* shuts down (Feb. 27), *Seattle Post-Intelligencer* shifts to Web-only publication (March 17) and *New York Times* borrows $250 million from Mexican billionaire. . . . *Ann Arbor News* announces it will stop publishing and become a Web-based community-news operation (March 23). . . . U.S. Sen. Ben Cardin, D-Md., introduces Newspaper Revitalization Act to exempt newspaper ad and circulation revenue from taxation.

Frustrated Newspaper Executives Fight Back

Industry is "a long way from dead."

Randy Siegel is president of Parade Publications, publisher of the colorful, quick-reading tabloid that is delivered with nearly 450 newspapers each Sunday. Although he plays a very different role from Jay Smith, Brian Tierney and Donna Barrett, head of the primarily small-town Community Newspaper Holdings, all share one thing in common: Frustration over continual obituaries for the newspaper industry.

So late last year they launched the Newspaper Project to counter all the doomsayers. Thus far they've produced three pro-newspaper advertisements, which have appeared in more than 400 papers. The first proclaimed that more Americans read newspapers on Super Bowl Sunday than watched the football game. The others carried the themes "Defending Freedom Daily Since 1776" and "America's First Portable Information Device."

Smith, who retired last year as president of Cox Newspapers, says the new organization wants to "bring balance and perspective to the discussion of where newspapers are headed in these times. It's really important that we quit hanging the crepe and talking about newspapers in the past tense, because they're a long way from dead."

Smith and Tierney, the CEO of the company that owns *The Philadelphia Inquirer* and *Daily News*, know from personal experience about the challenges the industry faces. The Philadelphia papers recently sought Chapter 11 bankruptcy protection. A few months after Smith retired, Cox decided to sell most of its newspapers, even though most are profitable. Still, the industry's problems aren't as unsolvable as many people seem to think, Smith and Tierney argue.

Some newspapers are much healthier than others, he points out, and all are suffering from the current recession. Some of the most prominent newspapers — including in Philadelphia — are in trouble because their owners took on too much debt,

Tierney says. Without the debt service, he says, the Philadelphia papers would be profitable.

Even in their current state, newspapers provide much more thorough coverage than any other medium, Smith argues.

"The hometown newspaper is the source of the most complete and the most credible information that people in that community have," Smith says. "If you're in the public sector in that community, you don't make a move without thinking, 'What if this ends up on the front page of the paper.' "

No other Philadelphia medium "does what we do," Tierney says, ticking off several recent investigative projects that required "months of reporting and tons of editing, fact-checking and lawyering" — plus several hundred thousand dollars of staff time and expenses, he adds.

Despite circulation and revenue declines, he says, the two newspapers have an unduplicated daily readership of 1.2 million, and another 500,000 to 1 million people visit the publications' Web sites.

While the percentage of 18-to-34-year-olds who read a newspaper has declined from 62 percent in 1978 to 34 percent now, that's still a hefty number, Tierney says. The maker of Red Bull energy drink "wishes one-third of that group bought a can of Red Bull today. If McDonald's had one of three people visiting McDonald's today, they'd be happy."

"What newspapers are facing right now," Smith says, "is the double whammy of dealing with structural change that has been ongoing for more than a decade and continues to accelerate and that is compounded by the historic economic turmoil. Economic cycles have a way of changing, and one of my concerns is that we don't do structural damage while we're in the throes of a bad economic cycle. When that cycle begins to change and begins to improve the economy, I want to make sure we have something left that's worth talking about in the way of newspapers."

Continued from p. 282

Their job was to take what a politician said and improve it."

Early newspapers also experienced something that plagues a growing number of 21st-century publishers — failure. Between 1690 and 1820 more than 2,100 went out of business after two years or less. Nevertheless, the number of newspapers soared from 37 at the end of the Revolution to 1,258 in 1835.

As late as 1850, only 5 percent of American newspapers were considered "neutral and independent." At

about that time, however, newspapers began to place more emphasis on reporting facts. Partisan papers became increasingly willing to criticize political and government leaders even of their own party.

The decade leading up to the Civil War was a time of great political activism and a great time to be in the newspaper business. Nearly three-quarters of eligible voters participated in the 1852 and 1856 presidential elections. Newspaper editors and publishers often wielded great political power. Some Northern newspapers became important

instruments in the crusade against slavery. Writers commented on newspapers' wide readership and high influence.

Author and political leader Charles Ingersoll termed newspapers "the daily fare of nearly every meal in almost every family." Philosopher Ralph Waldo Emerson described businessmen on a commuter train eagerly purchasing the "magical sheets — twopence a head his bread of knowledge costs — and instantly the entire rectangular assembly, fresh from their breakfast, are bending as one man over their second breakfast." [67]

The *Times* Model

In 1860, *The New York Times* set out an operating plan that eventually would become the underlying principle for most American newspapers: A paper's "proper business is to publish facts, in such a form and temper as to lead men of all parties to rely upon its statements of facts." [68] By 1880, a quarter of American newspapers declared themselves independent, neutral or local, rather than partisan — a proportion that increased to a third by 1890. As newspapers became less partisan, party loyalty among the people declined.

The number of newspapers grew phenomenally during the late 1800s, from 3,000 in 1860 to 4,500 in 1870 to 7,000 in 1880. Many of those were published weekly or less frequently, but the number of dailies also jumped from 574 in 1870 to 2,226 in 1900, when their circulation reached 15 million. Large cities counted their competing papers in double digits.

Investigations and "crusades" grew in importance for newspapers and magazines in the early 20th century. Publications attacked government corruption, political bosses, business monopolies and child labor. They inspired fundraising efforts after disasters and campaigned for better schools, roads and parks. Investigative reporters — derisively dubbed "muckrakers" by Theodore Roosevelt, after the character in John Bunyan's *Pilgrim's Progress* who never lifted his eyes from the muck — exposed wrongdoing by business executives and government officials.

Publishers experimented with various forms of financing their newspapers in the early 20th century. [69] In 1908, the First Church of Christ, Scientist, in Boston began to publish *The Christian Science Monitor*, which printed just one religious article in each issue and became a widely respected publication over the following century. (In 1850, the Mormon church begun publishing the *Deseret*

News, which remains one of Salt Lake City's two newspapers.)

New York Independent Editor Hamilton Holt drew up a model for an endowment-supported newspaper, but it wasn't implemented.

The Los Angeles city government published the *Municipal News* for several years after 1914. The mayor, City Council and any political party that won more than 3 percent of the city vote were given newspaper space to use as they wished.

In 1911, the *Chicago Day Book* began publishing without ads, trying to support itself through subscriptions alone. It died during World War I, a victim of readers' preference for having advertising in their newspapers.

The advent of radio in the 1920s increased competition for reader/viewer attention, advertising revenues and political influence. But newspapers continued to thrive, nearly doubling their circulation and more than tripling ad revenue between 1910 and 1930.

Radio networks broadcast the 1924 national political conventions live, and parties and candidates began to cater to the new medium's needs. [70]

'Golden Age'

The 20th century also was marked by newspaper consolidation, which led editors to seek to please a wider range of readers, not just supporters of a particular party or ideology. While earlier years had been marked by fierce competition throughout the country, eight cities with more than 100,000 residents became one-publisher towns by 1930. During the Great Depression, 98 newspapers were closed or disappeared in mergers in the brief period between 1937 and 1939. [71]

Television became newspapers' biggest threat in the 1950s. Networks televised the 1948 political conventions and launched ambitious political reporting efforts thereafter. The parties and candidates began to cater to the new

medium, just as they had to radio. [72] On the business side, newspapers' share of advertising revenue began a long, steady decline. [73]

"Radio and television gave you an immediacy that you didn't have before," Ohio University's Washburn points out. "Suddenly you could sit anywhere in the country where you could see television, and you could watch the candidates up close."

The visual immediacy of television reporting also propelled the Civil Rights Movement in the 1950s and '60s and helped turn public opinion against the Vietnam War in the late '60s and early '70s.

Newspaper consolidation continued throughout the second half of the 20th century, creating monopolies or near monopolies in most American cities. "The newspaper became a tollgate between the local retailer and local consumers," Hindman at Arizona State University explains. "If you wanted somebody to go to J.C. Penney or if you wanted to sell your old guitar, you had to take out an ad in the local newspaper."

As a result, publications were able to charge high advertising rates, earn healthy profits, build large newsgathering teams, employ knowledgeable reporters to cover specialized beats and send correspondents around the world. Some publishers wielded their economic and political power selfishly. More often, they emphasized professionalism and civic responsibility. Journalists' educational level rose. Professional organizations and educational institutions emphasized the importance of ethics.

Former *Washington Post* Managing Editor Coll described the period as a Golden Age of journalism, during which metropolitan newspapers were defined by "professional, civil-service-style, relentless, independent-thinking reporting and observation." The newspapers' economic strength enabled "high-quality family owners" to protect journalists from political and commercial pressure — "not perfectly, but largely," Coll said. "Yes, the big papers [sometimes] failed, as in the run-up to the Iraq War, but they succeeded much more often. They practiced a kind of journalism that, on the whole, was better for a democratic constitutional system than any journalism ever practiced before, anywhere." [74]

The era was epitomized by young *Washington Post* reporters Bob Woodward and Carl Bernstein's dogged digging into the Watergate scandal that led to President Richard M. Nixon's resignation in 1974.

Chain Reaction

Journalists' sense of propriety and responsibility before cable television and the Internet stands in stark contrast to the no-holds-barred style of reporting today.

In 1964, FBI Director J. Edgar Hoover invited Washington reporters to his office to listen to tapes that proved conclusively that the Rev. Dr. Martin Luther King Jr. was cheating on his wife. No one wrote a story, and the existence of the tapes was not publicized for nearly 20 years. Journalists generally considered public figures' private lives to be off-limits.

"Imagine Hoover sharing his tapes with professional Internet gossip Matt Drudge," Rosenstiel and Kovach wrote. "How would CNN handle the leaked tapes if the network knew MSNBC was about to be given the same information?

"Harris Wofford, the former Pennsylvania senator who had known King since the early 1950s, believes that in the media culture of the 1990s, one of the most important Americans of the 20th century would have been destroyed, and American history would have been quite different." [75]

In 1982 the Gannett newspaper chain made a profound impact on American newspapers by launching *USA Today* — the first nationwide general-audience paper. Newspapers across the country soon mimicked *USA Today*'s

emphasis on colorful graphics and short articles.

In the latter 20th century, newspapers also became consolidated into large chains whose shares traded on public stock markets. Investors with little interest in quality journalism pressured publishers to increase profits. While some founding families maintained control through special classes of stock, they also were pressed to ramp up earnings. A 2001 study by three journalism professors concluded that investors in publicly traded companies were "concerned with . . . continuously improved profitability" and "indifferent to news or, more disturbingly, its quality." [76]

The number of daily newspapers remained above 1,750 until 1980, when a steady decline began, leaving just more than 1,400 publishing now. Total daily circulation peaked at 63.3 million in 1984 and dropped to about 51 million today. [77]

Dean Singleton, CEO of MediaNews Group, which owns more than 55 daily newspapers, said last June the industry was done in by "the proliferation of cable news channels, the inexorable trend toward two-wage earners per household working outside the home, time-pressed lifestyles, the emergence of the Internet, the explosion and fragmentation of all forms of media . . . consolidation in our industry, combined with public ownership and subsequent pressure from institutional and large shareholders." [78]

Consolidation in other industries hurt, too. "The merger of Macy's and the May Co. resulted in substantial consolidation of department store print spending," Singleton continued. "The merger of Sears and K-Mart had the same effect." Craig's List and other online services cut deeply into classified advertising, which comprised 40 percent of newspaper ad revenues in 2000. [79] Classified revenue dropped by more than half between then and 2007. [80]

In retrospect, newspapers have been criticized for letting others seize opportunity on the Internet. They didn't

ignore the Web entirely, however. By 1999, 98 of the 100 largest newspapers were publishing online and several — notably *The Washington Post*, *The Wall Street Journal* and *USA Today* — had established staffs dedicated to Internet journalism. ∎

CURRENT SITUATION

Cutting Back

After conducting a nationwide survey of news executives, the Project for Excellence in Journalism described the typical American newspaper of 2008:

"It has fewer pages than three years ago. Its stories are shorter. It publishes less news about foreign and national affairs, science and the arts. It has shrunk the crossword puzzle and may have dropped television listings and stock tables.

"Buyouts of veteran reporters have left the staff smaller and younger, with less institutional memory, less knowledge of the community, less understanding of individual beats and less experience gathering news. The staff also is under greater pressure, and there are fewer editors to catch mistakes."

The survey did find some bright spots: Today's newspaper journalists are "more tech-savvy and more oriented to serving the demands of both print and the Web." Their newspaper has strengthened some local coverage, and "investigative reporting remains highly valued." [81]

Hall at the American Society of Newspaper Editors calls this "the most exciting — and most scary — time imaginable for media." Newspapers are shrinking — and dying — left and right. They are trying desperately to figure out how they can make money with their widely read Internet sites. And they are

A Growing Lineup of Online Sources

Many Internet sites in recent years have begun offering news and opinion — from the left to the right — including the following:

DailyKos.com — News, commentary and debate for readers and activists on the left-liberal side.

Drudge Report, drudgereport.com — Demonstrated power of Internet by reporting *Newsweek*'s investigation of Clinton-Lewinsky affair before magazine was ready to publish. Consists almost entirely of links to news reports, columnists.

FreeRepublic.com — A popular site for political conservatives, featuring news and discussion.

GlobalPost, www.globalpost.com — Experienced editors coordinate more than 60 freelance correspondents in more than 40 countries.

The Huffington Post, www.huffingtonpost.com — Perhaps the most prominent public-affairs site, now calls itself "The Internet Newspaper." Contains many left-leaning blogs, links to mainstream news reports and creative use of volunteer "citizen journalists."

Kaiser Health News, www.kaiserhealthnews.org — Financed by the Kaiser Family Foundation, two veteran journalists supervise staff and freelancers who cover health.

Knight Citizen News Network, www.kcnn.org/citmedia_sites — Provides links to nearly 800 community news sites of varied quality.

MinnPost, www.minnpost.com — Former editor and publisher of the *Minneapolis Star Tribune* leads professional staff providing news and analysis about Minnesota.

Politico, www.politico.com — A professional staff, led by *Washington Post* veterans, quickly made *Politico* a popular site for news of the 2008 campaign. Now focuses on the federal government. (Also publishes free paper in Washington.)

ProPublica, www.propublica.org — Philanthropy-supported organization, led by veteran journalists, does investigative reporting that can be reproduced by other media.

Seattle Post-Intelligencer, www.seattlepi.com — Internet-only survivor of the daily newspaper that shut down its presses on March 17.

SFGate.com — One of the earliest and most popular major-market newspaper Web sites, launched in 1993 by *San Francisco Chronicle*.

Slashdot.com — Daily aggregation of news reports of interest to techies.

Philanthropy-supported ProPublica *is among scores of online news and opinion sites launched in the past 15 years in response to the decline in newspaper publishing and the increasing popularity of blogs and other new media.*

Screenshot/CQ Researcher Staff

Talking Points Memo, www.talkingpointsmemo.com — One-man blog has grown to a staff of 17 who report, analyze and comment on public affairs.

Technorati.com — Content-rich site offers news, blogs, commentary involving the technology universe.

Voice of San Diego, www.voiceofsandiego.org — Staff of young professionals, supported by philanthropy, covers local public affairs, with emphasis on investigative reporting.

---

witnessing an uncountable number of competitors pop up online.

"We need to experiment boldly and guard our values," Hall said. "I think we can do both." [82]

On the one hand, newspapers — especially larger ones — are cutting back to save money. Over the last three years, 85 percent of dailies with more than 100,000 circulation reduced staff, and 52 percent of smaller papers did. [83] All together, U.S. newspapers eliminated nearly 1,500 jobs in 2007 alone and another 5,000 in 2008. [84] *The Chicago Tribune* sliced its news staff

by a third over the last year. [85]

Editorial cartoonists, once a staple of nearly every metropolitan newspaper, have not escaped the cuts. Cartoonists have been laid off or not replaced at such major papers as *The Baltimore Sun, Chicago Tribune, Los Angeles Times, Akron Beacon Journal, Cincinnati Enquirer* and *St. Paul Pioneer Press*. Papers that use syndicated cartoons will feel the pinch, too, because most syndicated cartoonists earn the bulk of their income from their newspaper employers and wouldn't be able to survive on syndication alone. [86]

"Syndication is really just beer money for most cartoonists," said Stuart Carlson, who accepted a buyout from his cartooning job at the *Milwaukee Journal Sentinel* last year. [87]

Beyond direct staff cuts, *The Detroit News* and *The Detroit Free Press*, once among the largest newspapers in America, cut home delivery to three days a week, telling readers they can buy the papers at newsstands at other times or use the publications' Web sites. The decision will save newsprint and delivery costs. [88] McClatchy Newspapers — publisher of 30 dailies and more weeklies

— froze its pension plans, suspended contributions to employees' 401(k) retirement accounts and imposed a companywide pay freeze. [89] For only the second time in its 86-year history, the American Society of Newspaper Editors canceled its annual convention because many members decided they couldn't justify the expense of attending. (The previous cancellation was during World War II.) [90]

MediaNews has shipped some production functions overseas. [91] Journalists in India are writing news stories, such as about corporate earnings reports, for the Thomson Reuters wire service. [92]

New Partnerships

To continue covering public affairs with shrinking staffs, a growing number of publications are entering into partnerships — both with other professional media and with volunteers.

The *News-Press* in Fort Myers, Fla., has created a three-reporter investigative reporting team that will be assisted by 15 volunteers from the community, including retired attorneys, accountants, police officers, educators and even an FBI agent. [93] Use of amateurs reminds Ohio University's Washburn of small-town papers publishing students' reports of high-school activities and news about clubs submitted by club members.

Meanwhile, newly created organizations are attempting to fill the gaps left by newspaper cutbacks, and often they make their work available to the traditional media.

Since 2006, journalism students at five universities have been producing in-depth reports on major public issues that they post on the Web and let other media republish. Called News21, the project is funded by the Knight Foundation and the Carnegie Corp. Their reports have been carried by *The Miami Herald, The National Journal,* United Press International and other professional news organizations. [94]

And journalism students at Northeastern University in Boston have produced a dozen investigative reporting projects since 2007 that have appeared on the front page of *The Boston Globe.* The students are taught by Walter Robinson, who retired in 2006 as head of *The Globe's* investigative reporting team.

Robinson calls the arrangement "win, win, win. The kids love it — you can't imagine how much fun it is for them to go out to find a story nobody else can find and then see their names on the front page of a major paper. It's great for the newspaper, because the newspaper can use all the extra horsepower it can find at a time when every newspaper has fewer resources. And it's great for the university."

One of the most ambitious uses of amateurs was *The Huffington Post's* "Off the Bus" project during the 2008 presidential campaign.

In 2007, Arianna Huffington's blog invited readers to become volunteer reporters. By the end of 2008, 12,000 had participated. [95] They were coordinated by a handful of professional staff. [96]

Volunteer Mayhill Fowler attracted the most attention with reports that embarrassed Obama and former President Bill Clinton. She recorded Obama at a San Francisco fundraiser when he gave his analysis of why "bitter" small-town residents "cling to guns and religion" — a comment used against him throughout the campaign. She recorded Clinton calling *New York Times* reporter Todd Purdum "sleazy" and a "scumbag" — a rant for which Clinton later apologized.

The reports created controversy not only for the politicians' comments but because Fowler failed in both cases to identify herself as a journalist. [97] That led *The Huffington Post* to instruct correspondents to make their affiliation clear. [98]

Less controversially, "Off the Bus" assigned a large number of volunteers to compile the biographies of super delegates to the Democratic National Convention and sent 18 to observe

Obama canvassers in the fall. The canvassing project produced a report that the Iraq War was not as big an issue as many thought it would be. [99]

The Pulitzer Center on Crisis Reporting supports international coverage, both by freelancers and news organizations. The center focuses on "independent international journalism that U.S. media organizations are increasingly less willing to undertake." Center-supported reports have appeared in *The New York Times, Los Angeles Times, The Washington Post, The Christian Science Monitor* and other publications, as well as on television and radio. [100]

A new organization in San Francisco is trying to drum up reader-financed reporting of local stories. Freelancers pitch story ideas, with budgets, on the *Spot.us* Web site, and readers can contribute. *Spot.us* contributors have funded reports about aging, wastewater, the health of San Francisco Bay beaches, political advertisements and other topics. The stories appear on the *Spot.us* Web site and have been picked up by other media. [101]

Some newly created news organizations have pulled off major scoops. *The Voice of San Diego,* for instance, uncovered conflicts of interest and hidden pay raises in city government, dissemination of misleading crime statistics and other misdeeds. The Web site "is doing really significant work, putting local politicians and businesses on the hot seat," according to Dean Nelson, director of the journalism program at San Diego's Point Loma Nazarene University. [102]

Impact of the Web

In the midst of circulation declines and financial stress, newspapers' readership may be higher than ever because of the popularity of their Web sites and the larger number of other sites that link to newspaper-produced content. Unique visitors to *The New York Times* site grew from 14.6 million in September 2007 to 20 million just a year later. [103]

Continued on p. 290

At Issue:

Should newspapers shut down their presses?

JAMES MOORE
*MEDIA CONSULTANT AND CO-AUTHOR,
BUSH'S BRAIN*

WRITTEN FOR *CQ RESEARCHER*, MARCH 2009

Stop the presses. They're wasting paper. Newspapers have lost their place in our culture. A few are clinging to life, but they are only dinosaurs too blind and dumb to find a tar pit to stumble into and die.

It is argued that papers still make money and that many people still don't have computers. There was once a time when a lot of people didn't have telephones or televisions either. Those devices are now ubiquitous, and computers can also be publicly accessed just as easily.

Businesses don't make money by marketing to customer segments at the margins. People clinging to inky newsprint tend to be older and more attached to tradition. Their demographic, however, is not the source of the money. Advertisers want to reach that gold-encrusted and acquisition-hungry 25-48 demographic. Print ads aren't going to dip into those wallets and purses.

Publishers are also desperately hugging their printed copies because they still make money. The car dealers in local communities love to see their Thursday morning full-page ads. But my guess is most people buying cars today go to Cars.com or one of the other automotive Web sites and price shop. They may even begin by shopping on the Web. Eventually, the buyer links back to the local dealer's Web site. Tell me again how that print ad fits into this? It wastes paper, ink, time and money.

Drop the printed version, and paper pushers have nowhere to go but onto the Web. Traffic on the paper's news site goes up and, consequently, so does ad revenue.

Publishers complain that there isn't enough space on a Web page to sell the most lucrative ads. Web technology, though, now allows specific ads to pop up that target viewers logging on from particular ZIP codes. This is productive and meaningful advertising that small businesses like a family-owned restaurant can afford, and it will drive their foot traffic. Otherwise, they are stuck with the 4-inch x 4-inch ad on a big page and nobody notices.

New eyeballs viewing that Web page might also buy single articles of special interest or enter archives placed behind a pay wall. Big-money operations can purchase the top-dollar banner ads and drop-downs, and the money will flow like a righteous stockholder river.

Newspapers are for wrapping fish. The Internet is for providing information.

JOHN F. STURM
*PRESIDENT AND CEO, NEWSPAPER
ASSOCIATION OF AMERICA*

WRITTEN FOR *CQ RESEARCHER*, MARCH 2009

at the heart of the debate over the future business model of newspapers — print versus online — some might see a logical question: Why are we having this conversation? Online is growing audience, while print circulation is on the decline. Print is expensive to produce, while online is fantastically cost-efficient. What's to discuss?

When you take a closer look at print, the answer is, "quite a bit." The future is not print or online. It is both, creating a combined digital and print platform that makes newspapers the most efficient medium — and media buy — in any given market.

Those who point to a recent string of bankruptcies and a few shifts to Web-only publication as the end for print are rushing to some shaky conclusions.

One mistake is to focus on the decline while ignoring the base audience. Every day, 105 million adults read the print product. We must not ignore the steep downtrend in circulation, or that print faces challenges as audiences get younger, but if a new medium had more than 100 million loyal, daily users we would be calling it the face of a new age of communication.

Perspective is also important in understanding the decline in print advertising. Declining classified ads are a problem — in part self-created because newspapers were slow to protect the franchise. But despite 2008's economic turmoil, print does not have an audience problem. It has a recession problem — the same recession that incinerated trillions of dollars in global equity and shut the doors of a growing list of well-known companies.

There is also the matter of relative revenues. Newspaper Web sites continue to attract advertisers, and digital — in all its forms — is clearly a big part of our future. The shift in the balance, however, is going to be gradual. It will take time, experience and confidence before online spending reaches parity with print — and pricing for online reflects its value.

Most important to the communities we serve: Print is the home of the talented reporters and editors who have the skill and responsibility to find the facts and present them fairly and in depth.

Recessions end. By the time the economy heals and ad spending improves, the media landscape may be forever changed. But the newspaper industry — and its print component — will remain a strong source of high-quality, credible reporting for years to come.

Continued from p. 288

"Newspapers and their Web sites generally have the largest audience among local news sources," Hall said. [104] But papers still generate 90 percent of their shrinking income from their printed products. [105]

As they struggle to increase their Internet earnings, newspapers are beefing up their Web sites and expanding into other new media.

Thirty-two newspapers can be read on the wireless Kindle reading device for from $5.99 to $14.99 a month. Subscriptions are available to national publications such as *The New York Times* and *The Wall Street Journal*, regional papers such as the *San Francisco Chronicle* and the *Seattle Times,* and foreign papers such as *Shanghai Daily* and *Frankfurter Allgemeine.* [106]

Almost alone among American newspapers, the *Arkansas Democrat-Gazette* restricts its Web site to its paper subscribers or others who pay $4.95 a month for electronic access. [107]

Newspapers and their staffs also are jumping onto Twitter, Facebook, YouTube and other social-networking sites, some of which are popular on cell phones and other wireless devices as well as through computer Internet connections. [108]

Nearly 800 newspapers have entered a consortium with Yahoo! in an effort to increase advertising on their Web sites. An effort to sell print ads through Google failed. [109] ∎

OUTLOOK

Newspapers Doomed?

A consensus is growing among journalists and scholars that newspapers as we've known them are doomed, but journalism always will be in demand.

What they don't know is when the last newspaper will dismantle its presses — or if a few will survive — and what kind of journalism will be preserved. Could anyone have imagined the enormous changes that have occurred in just the last three years? asks former *Boston Globe* investigative reporter Robinson.

"I think there's an information franchise at the local level that is up for grabs," New York University's Rosen says. "I cannot say newspapers will grab it. I don't see them as the one and only watchdog, as the institution that produces an informed public. When you widen the lens, it's not how many reporters but how do government officials get held accountable."

Jay Smith, who retired last year as president of the Cox Newspapers chain, agrees that "far more important than the future of newspapers is the future of journalism." Smith expects printed newspapers to continue to shrink in size and circulation, while their online presence grows.

The City University of New York's Jarvis says successful newspapers will identify their "core" value to readers, which probably includes "investigative journalism, watchdog journalism, throwing sunlight on government, maybe consumer journalism. I believe the market will demand that core, and journalists will respond."

Except for a rare national publication, a newspaper's core also will be local news, he says. To provide national, international and specialized news, a newspaper's Web site can link to other publications' work, he says.

The Web will enable newspapers to serve neighborhoods better than the printed page, which is limited by how much information it can carry, Rosen says. The Internet also allows newspapers to sell advertising to small businesses that couldn't afford printed papers' rates, he says.

Jarvis and Rosen argue that newspapers will have to recruit amateur volunteers to provide comprehensive coverage, particularly at the local level. "Journalists need to become educa-tors" to train volunteers to be effective reporters, Jarvis says.

Others are less comfortable with that model. "So many public-policy stories today require not just going to meetings and listening to what people say but accessing records, acquiring data and analyzing that data," says Shane at the Knight Commission on the Information Needs of Communities. "Amateurs are better than nothing, but they're not better than having trained people with experience and a deep knowledge of the community."

Similarly, Brian Tierney, CEO and publisher of *The Philadelphia Inquirer* and *Daily News,* scoffs: "The idea that citizen journalists are going to replace traditionally trained and paid journalists is like saying citizen surgeons are going to replace people who actually have a degree in medicine."

Niche Web sites with national audiences enjoy the best prospects, many say. So do sites with valuable information that some audiences will pay premium prices for.

"I think we're going to see an increase in very dense but narrow sites of information for which people will pay something online," Smith says. "If it's a business or a special-interest group that wants that information, they may pay handsomely for it."

But that prospect worries former *Atlanta Journal-Constitution* Editor Kovach and others. If general-circulation newspapers decline and important information is available only from expensive vendors, "the people get less information while the people in power get more information." he said. "If we talk about a government as Abraham Lincoln did — 'of the people, by the people, for the people' — then that democracy is in trouble." [110]

Online journalism will be supported by advertising, just as it has been in print, Jarvis says. Others believe online news organizations must charge for their content.

"The excellence of what we have

down the pike will be entirely determined by the quality of the demand," the University of Southern California's Overholser says. "If the public demands news and is willing to pay for it, they'll get it." A "micropayments" system — by which readers would pay a few cents for each story they read or for other content they access — could provide the solution, she says.

New York Times business columnist David Carr said journalists should draw hope from Apple CEO Jobs' success with iTunes. "When iTunes began, the music industry was being decimated by file sharing," he wrote. "By coming up with an easy user interface and obtaining the cooperation of a broad swath of music companies, Mr. Jobs helped pull the business off the brink." [111]

Newspaper executives also are looking to the cable TV model and asking if a fee for news could be built into Internet access fees. And they are exploring the possibility of earning commissions by linking their sites to retailers. [112]

For his part, Tierney says the Philadelphia newspapers are exploring how to charge for online content. "We're going to have to find a way to encourage people to pay for quality journalism," he says. "To create great content, we've got to pay people. We just can't give it away." ∎

Notes

[1] "Rocky Mountain News Closing after Friday Edition," *Carlsbad* (New Mexico) *Current-Argus*, Feb. 26, 2009.

[2] Dan Richman and Andrea James, "Seattle P-I to Publish Last Edition Tuesday," *Seattle Post-Intelligencer*, March 16, 2009, www.seattlepi.com/business/403793_piclosure17.html.

[3] David Cook, "Monitor Shifts from Print to Web-Based Strategy," *The Christian Science Monitor*, Oct. 28, 2008, www.csmonitor.com/2008/1029/p25s01-usgn.htm.

[4] "Rocky Mountain News Closing," *op. cit.*

[5] Michael Hirschorn ,"End Times," *The Atlantic*, January/February 2009, www.theatlantic.com/doc/200901/new-york-times (re debt),

and Howard Kurtz, "How Low Will Newspapers' Ad Revenues Go?" *The Washington Post*, Feb. 19, 2009, p. C1 (re reputation).

[6] "The State of the News Media 2009," Project for Excellence in Journalism 2009, www.stateofthenewsmedia.com/2009/index.htm.

[7] Hirschorn, *op. cit.* For background, see Kenneth Jost, "Future of Newspapers," *CQ Researcher*, Jan. 20, 2006, pp. 49-72, and Kathy Koch, "Journalism Under Fire," *CQ Researcher*, Dec. 25, 1998, pp. 1121-1144.

[8] John Nichols and Robert W. McChesney, "The Death and Life of Great American Newspapers," *The Nation*, March 18, 2009, pp. 11-20, www.thenation.com/doc/20090406/nichols_mcchesney. Their book, *Saving Journalism: The Soul of Democracy*, will be published by New Press in the fall.

[9] David Swensen and Michael Schmidt, "News You Can Endow," *The New York Times*, Jan. 28, 2009, www.nytimes.com/2009/01/28/opinion/28swensen.html?_r=2.

[10] For background see Marcia Clemmitt, "Internet Accuracy," *CQ Researcher*, Aug. 1, 2008, pp. 625-648, and Kenneth Jost and Melissa Hipolit, "Blog Explosion," *CQ Researcher*, June 9, 2006, pp. 505-528.

[11] *Editor and Publisher International Yearbook*, www.naa.org/TrendsandNumbers/Total-Paid-Circulation.aspx.

[12] "Newspaper Web Site Audience Rises Twelve Percent in 2008," Newspaper Association of America, www.naa.org/PressCenter/SearchPressReleases/2009/NEWSPAPER-WEB-SITE-AUDIENCE-RISES.aspx.

[13] Hirschorn, *op. cit.*

[14] Alan Mutter, "Monitor Move Doesn't Spell End of Print," *Reflections of a Newsosaur*, Oct. 28, 2008, newsosaur.blogspot.com/2008/10/monitor-move-doesnt-spell-end-of-print.html.

[15] Adam Lashinsky, "CEO Eric Schmidt Wishes He Could Rescue Newspapers," *Fortune*, Jan. 7, 2009.

[16] For background on the economy, see Kenneth Jost, *et al.*, "The Obama Presidency," *CQ Researcher*, Jan. 30, 2009; Peter Katel, "Vanishing Jobs," *CQ Researcher*, March 13, 2009, pp. 225-248, and Thomas J. Billitteri, "Financial Bailout," *CQ Researcher*, Oct. 24, 2008, pp. 865-888.

[17] Jennifer Dorroh, "Endangered Species," *American Journalism Review*, December/January 2009, www.ajr.org/Article.asp?id=4645.

[18] Richard Perez-Peña, "Big News in Washington, but Far Fewer Cover It," *The New York Times*, Dec. 18, 2008, p. 1.

[19] Perez-Peña, *op. cit.*

[20] "The State of the News Media 2009," *op. cit.*

[21] Jim Wayne, "Sue Cross on the News Industry's Bleak State, Bright Future," *Online Journalism Review*, www.ojr.org/ojr/stories/080410wayne-associated-press, April 10, 2008.

[22] Marc Fisher, "Bloggers Can't Fill the Gap Left by Shrinking Press Corps," *The Washington Post*, March 1, 2009, p. C1.

[23] *Ibid.*

[24] Bob Norman, "The Fourth Estate Sale," *New Times Broward Palm Beach*, Jan. 15, 2009, www.browardpalmbeach.com/2009-01-15/news/the-fourth-estate-sale.

[25] Dorroh, *op. cit.*

[26] "International News Web Site Globalpost.Com To Go Live January 12," *Global Post*, www.globalpost.com/sites/default/files/globalpost/infopages/gpreleases/FWIS-Final-LaunchPR.pdf.

[27] "Business Model," *Global Post*, www.globalpost.com/businessmodel.

[28] "Internet Overtakes Newspapers as News Source," Pew Research Center for the People & the Press, Dec. 23, 2008, pewresearch.org/pubs/1066/internet-overtakes-newspapers-as-news-source.

[29] "Stop the Presses?" Pew Research Center for the People & the Press, March 12, 2009, pewresearch.org/pubs/1147/newspapers-struggle-public-not-concerned.

[30] Nielsen Online, www.nielsen-online.com/pr/pr_081105.pdf.

[31] "Long Island University Announces Winners of 2007 George Polk Awards," The George Polk Awards in Journalism, www.brooklyn.liu.edu/polk/press/2007.html.

[32] Sydney Jones and Susannah Fox, "Generations Online in 2009," Pew Internet & American Life Project, Jan. 28, 2009, pewresearch.org/pubs/1093/generations-online.

[33] Reyhan Harmanci, "CNN Discovers Downside of 'Citizen Journalism,' " *San Francisco Chronicle*, Oct. 5, 2008, p. A7.

[34] Justin Baer, "United Shares Plunge on Old News Story," *Financial Times*, Sept. 8, 2008, www.ft.com/cms/s/0/b843a240-7ddd-11dd-bdbd-000077b07658.html?nclick_check=1; "Old Bankruptcy Story Causes United Stock To Plunge," CBS, Sept. 9, 2008, cbs2.com/business/united.airlines.stock.2.813391.html?detectflash=false.

[35] Henry Blodget, "Post Hate Mail about Our Link to Steve Jobs Heart Attack Report Here," *Silicon Alley Insider*, Oct. 4, 2008, www.alleyinsider.com/2008/10/why-we-published-that-steve-jobs-heart-attack-report.

[36] Bill Kovach and Tom Rosenstiel, *Warp Speed: America in the Age of the Mixed Media Culture* (1999).

[37] www.ireport.com/index.jspa.

[38] James Callan, "CNN's Citizen Journalism Goes 'Awry' With False Report on Jobs," Bloomberg, Oct. 4, 2008, www.bloomberg.com/apps/news?pid=newsarchive&sid=atekONWyM7As.

[39] Michael Miner, "Citizen Journalism: A Field Day for the Flacks?" Chicago Reader, Jan. 24, 2008, www.chicagoreader.com/features/stories/hottype/08124/.

[40] "Limbaugh Holds onto His Niche — Conservative Men," Pew Research Center for the People & the Press, Feb. 3, 2009, pewresearch.org/pubs/1102/limbaugh-audience-conservative-men.

[41] "Continuing Partisan Divide in Cable TV News Audience," Pew Research Center for the People & the Press, people-press.org/report/467/internet-campaign-news.

[42] "Limbaugh Holds onto His Niche — Conservative Men," op. cit.

[43] "State of the News Media 2007, Project for Excellence in Journalism, www.stateofthenewsmedia.org/2007/narrative_overview_publicattitudes.asp?cat=8&media=1.

[44] Swensen and Schmidt, op. cit.

[45] Steve Coll, "Nonprofit Newspapers," The New Yorker, Jan. 28, 2009, www.newyorker.com/online/blogs/stevecoll/2009/01/nonprofit-newsp.html.

[46] Jack Stripling, "Fortunes Falling," Inside Higher Ed, Jan. 27, 2009, www.insidehighered.com/news/2009/01/27/endowments.

[47] Coll, op. cit.

[48] Zachary M. Seward, "Endowing Every U.S. Newspaper: $114 Billion. Innovation: Priceless," Nieman Journalism Lab, www.niemanlab.org/2009/01/endowing-every-american-newspaper-114-billion-innovation-priceles;

"May 2007 National Industry-Specific Occupational Employment and Wage Estimates," Bureau of Labor Statistics, May 12, 2008, www.bls.gov/oes/2007/may/naics5_511110.htm.

[49] Jonathan Weber, "The Trouble with Non-Profit Journalism," New West, Jan. 30, 2009, www.newwest.net/topic/article/the_problem_with_non_profit_journalism/C559/L559.

[50] David Westphal, "The State of Independent Local Online News Part 6: Start-ups Look for Foundation Support," Online Journalism Review, Nov. 11, 2008, www.ojr.org/ojr/people/davidwestphal/200811/1568.

[51] Kevin Sack, "Filling the Gap in Health Journalism," International Herald Tribune, Nov. 23, 2008, www.iht.com/articles/2008/11/23/technology/health.php; "Kaiser Family Foundation to Launch Non-Profit Health Policy News Service," Kaiser Family Foundation, Oct., 2008, www.kff.org/newsroom/khn102908nr.cfm.

[52] David Westphal, "Newspapers May Seek Philanthropy to Support News-Gathering," Online Journalism Review, Jan. 22, 2009, www.ojr.org/ojr/people/davidwestphal/200901/1627.

[53] Michael Moss and Geraldine Fabrikant, "Once Trusted Mortgage Pioneers, Now Scrutinized," The New York Times, Dec. 24. 2008, www.nytimes.com/2008/12/25/business/25sandler.html.

[54] "Global News Professionals Offer Open-minded Alternatives for American Journalism," Missouri School of Journalism, April 4, 2008, journalism.missouri.edu/news/2008/04-08-npc-centennial.html.

[55] Eric Pfanner, "France to Aid Newspapers," International Herald Tribune, Jan. 23, 2009, www.iht.com/articles/2009/01/23/business/ads.4-414765.php.

[56] Laurent Pirot, "Sarkozy Offers New Help for French Print Media," The Associated Press,

Jan. 23, 2009, www.sfgate.com/cgi-bin/article.cgi?f=/n/a/2009/01/23/financial/f090344S36.DTL.

[57] Howard Kurtz, "How Low Will Newspapers' Ad Revenues Go?" The Washington Post, Feb. 19, 2009, p. C1.

[58] Nichols and McChesney, op. cit.

[59] Nichols and McChesney, op. cit.

[60] Jay Rosen, "Where's the Business Model for News, People?" Press Think, April 22, 2008, journalism.nyu.edu/pubzone/weblogs/pressthink/2008/04/22/business_model.html.

[61] Unless otherwise noted, this historical section draws from the following sources: Frank Luther Mott, American Journalism: A History (1962); Mitchell Stephens, "History of Newspapers," written for Collier's Encyclopedia, www.nyu.edu/classes/stephens/Collier%27s%20page.htm; Jost, "Future of Newspapers," op. cit.; Roger Stretimatter, Mightier Then the Sword: How the News Media Have Shaped American History (1997); Jean Folkerts, Dwight L. Teeter Jr. and Edward Caudill, Voices of a Nation: A History of Mass Media in the United States (2009).

[62] Jill Lepore, "The Day the Newspaper Died," The New Yorker, Jan. 26, 2009, www.newyorker.com/arts/critics/atlarge/2009/01/26/090126crat_atlarge_lepore?currentPage=all.

[63] Ibid.

[64] Ibid.

[65] Ibid.

[66] Mott, op. cit., p. 167.

[67] Doris Kearns Goodwin, Team of Rivals: The Political Genius of Abraham Lincoln (2006), pp. 140-141.

[68] William H. Rentschler, "The Most Illustrious Journalist No One Ever Heard of," USA Today Magazine, Society for the Advancement of Education, July 1998, findarticles.com/p/articles/mi_m1272/is_n2638_v127/ai_20954323.

[69] Nikki Usher, "New Business Models for News Are Not That New," Knight Digital Media Center, Dec. 17, 2008, www.ojr.org/ojr/people/nikkiusher/200812/1604.

[70] Tom Price, "Political Conventions: Have They Outlived Their Usefulness?" CQ Researcher, Aug. 8, 2008, p. 663.

[71] Jay Smith, "Time To Stand up for Newspapers," The Philadelphia Inquirer, Feb. 2, 2009, www.philly.com/inquirer/opinion/38791802.html.

[72] Price, op. cit., pp. 660-661.

[73] "Making the Leap Beyond 'Newspaper Companies,'" American Press Institute, February 2008, www.newspapernext.org/Making_the_Leap.pdf.

[74] Steve Coll, "Nonprofit Newspapers," The New Yorker, Jan. 28, 2009, www.newyorker.com/online/blogs/stevecoll/2009/01/nonprofit-newsp.html.

About the Author

Tom Price, a Washington-based freelancer and contributing writer for *CQ Researcher*, has worked for six newspapers, two of which still publish. Before going freelance, he was a correspondent in the Cox Newspapers Washington Bureau and chief politics writer for the *Dayton Daily News* and *The Journal Herald*. He is co-author of *Changing The Face of Hunger: One Man's Story of How Liberals, Conservatives, Democrats, Republicans and People of Faith Are Joining Forces to Help the Hungry, the Poor, and the Oppressed*. His work has appeared in *The New York Times*, *Time*, *Rolling Stone* and other periodicals. He earned a bachelor of science in journalism at Ohio University.

[75] Kovach and Rosenstiel, *op. cit.*

[76] Jost, *op. cit.*, Jan. 20, 2006.

[77] National Newspaper Association, www.naa.org/TrendsandNumbers/Total-Paid-Circulation.aspx.

[78] "Dean Singleton's Speech in Sweden: 19 of the Top 50 US Newspapers Are Losing Money," *Business Week*, June 9, 2008, www.businessweek.com/innovate/FineOnMedia/archives/2008/06/dean_singletons.html.

[79] Philip Meyer, "The Elite Newspaper of the Future," *American Journalism Review*, October/November 2008, www.ajr.org/article_printable.asp?id=4605.

[80] Alan Mutter, "$7.5B sales plunge forecast for newspapers," *Reflections of a Newsosaur*, Oct. 12, 2008, newsosaur.blogspot.com/2008/10/75b-sales-plunge-forecast-for.html.

[81] "The Changing Newsroom," Project for Excellence in Journalism, Aug. 7, 2008, journalism.org/print/11961.

[82] Westphal, *op. cit.*, Jan. 22, 2009.

[83] "The Changing Newsroom," *op. cit.*

[84] "The State of the News Media 2009," *op. cit.*

[85] Ann Saphir, "Chicago Tribune Trims Newsroom Staff," *Crain's Chicago Business*, Feb. 12, 2009, www.chicagobusiness.com/cgi-bin/news.pl?id=32995,www.chicagobusiness.com/cgi-bin/news.pl?id=32995.

[86] Lindsay Kalter, "As Newspapers Dispense with Their Editorial Cartoonists, Vibrant Local Commentary Is Diminished," *American Journalism Review*, December/January 2009, www.ajr.org/Article.asp?id=4648.

[87] *Ibid.*

[88] Ed White, "Detroit Papers Drop Home Delivery to 3 Days a Week," The Associated Press, Dec. 17, 2008, www.washingtonpost.com/wp-dyn/content/article/2008/12/16/AR2008121602699.html?hpid=sec-business.

[89] Melanie Turner, "McClatchy to Freeze Pensions, Suspend 401(k) Match," *Sacramento Business Journal*, Feb. 5, 2009, triangle.bizjournals.com/triad/stories/2009/02/02/daily59.html.

[90] "ASNE Cancels 2009 Convention," American Society of Newspaper Editors, Feb. 27, 2009, www.asne.org/index.cfm?id=7268.

[91] "Dean Singleton's Speech in Sweden," *op. cit.*

[92] Matt Sedensky, "MediaNews CEO: Outsourcing Could Help Save Money," The Associated Press, Oct. 20, 2008.

[93] Terry Eberle, "Watchdog Journalism Page Launches Monday," *The News-Press* (Fort Myers, Fla.), Feb. 8, 2009, p. 10-B; "The News-Press presents Team Watchdog," May 27, 2007, www.news-press.com/apps/pbcs.dll/article?AID=/20070527/NEWS01/705270387/1075.

[94] "Latest News," News21, newsinitiative.org; John Mecklin, "The New New Media," Miller-McCune Center for Research, Media and Public Policy, Oct. 2, 2008, www.miller-mccune.com/article/the-new-new-media.

[95] Arianna Huffington and Jay Rosen, "Thanks to the People Who Worked on OffTheBus; Here's What Comes Next," *The Huffington Post*, Nov. 17, 2008, www.huffingtonpost.com/arianna-huffington-and-jay-rosen/thanks-to-the-people-who-_b_144476.html.

[96] Mark Glaser, "Semi-Pro Journalism Teams Give Alternative View of U.S. Elections," Public Broadcasting System, March 13, 2008, www.pbs.org/mediashift/2008/03/semi-pro-journalism-teams-give-alternative-view-of-us-elections073.html.

[97] Paul Farhi, "Off the Bus," *American Journalism Review*, December/January 2009, www.ajr.org/Article.asp?id=4644.

[98] Katharine Q. Seelye, "Off the Bus, but Growing Thousands Strong," *The New York Times*, July 23, 2008, www.nytimes.com/2008/07/23/us/politics/23web-seelye.html?ei=5124&en=a86c8467fe83154e&ex=1374552000&partner=permalink&exprod=permalink&pagewanted=print.

[99] Farhi, *op. cit.*

[100] "Our Mission," Pulitzer Center on Crisis Reporting, pulitzercenter.org/openmenu.cfm?id=1.

[101] David Cohn, "Creating a New Platform to Support Reporting," *Neiman Reports*, winter 2008, www.nieman.harvard.edu/reports.aspx; spot.us.

[102] Richard Pérez-Peña, "Web Sites That Dig for News Rise as Watchdogs," *The New York Times*, Nov. 18, 2008, www.nytimes.com/2008/11/18/business/media/18voice.html?_r=2&hp=&pagewanted=print.

[103] Arielle Emmett, "Traditional News Outlets Turn to Social Networking Web Sites in an Effort to Build Their Online Audiences," *American Journalism Review*, December/January 2009, www.ajr.org/Article.asp?id=4646.

[104] Westphal, *op. cit.*, Jan. 22, 2009.

[105] Mutter, *op. cit.*, Oct. 28, 2008.

[106] www.amazon.com/s/qid=1237150180/ref=sr_pg_1?ie=UTF8&rs=165389011&rh=n%3A165389011&page=1.

[107] Jonathan Rauch, "How to Save Newspapers — and Why," *National Journal*, Jan. 14, 2008, www.nationaljournal.com/njmagazine/st_20080614_5036.php.

[108] Emmett, *op. cit.*

[109] Alana Semuels, "Google Gives up on Newspaper Advertising Partnership," *Los Angeles Times*, Jan. 21, 2009, www.latimes.com/technology/la-fi-google21-2009jan21,0,6566191.story.

[110] Dorroh, *op. cit.*

[111] David Carr, "Let's Invent an iTunes for News," *The New York Times*, Jan. 12, 2009, www.nytimes.com/2009/01/12/business/media/12carr.html?_r=2.

[112] "The State of the News Media 2009," *op. cit.*

FOR MORE INFORMATION

John S. and James L. Knight Foundation, 200 South Biscayne Blvd., Miami, FL 33131-2349; (305) 908-2600; www.knightfoundation.org. Supports research organizations and news media, with recent emphasis on the Internet.

Newspaper Association of America, 4401 Wilson Blvd., Suite 900, Arlington, VA 22203-1867; (571) 366-1000; www.naa.org. Advocates for newspaper interests, publishes information about newspaper performance, such as print circulation, Web site visits.

The Newspaper Project, news.newspaperproject.org. Organized by newspaper executives to promote notion that newspapers are important and not yet dead.

Pew Research Center for the People & the Press, 1615 L St., N.W., Suite 700, Washington, DC 20036; (202) 419-4350; people-press.org. Conducts polls about attitudes toward the news media and public policy issues; publishes reports about the media and public affairs.

The Poynter Institute, 801 Third St. South, St. Petersburg, FL 33701; (888) 769-6837; www.poynter.org. Journalism education organization posts wide-ranging information about the news business.

Project for Excellence in Journalism, 1615 L St., N.W., Suite 700, Washington, DC 20036; (202) 419-3650; www.journalism.org. Conducts extensive research on journalism; publishes annual report on "The State of the News Media."

Bibliography

Selected Sources

Books

Fellow, Anthony, *American Media History*, Wadsworth Publishing, 2009.
The director of California State University at Fullerton's journalism program traces the development of American media.

Folkerts, Jean, Dwight L. Teeter Jr. and Edward Caudill, *Voices of a Nation: A History of Mass Media in the United States*, Allyn & Bacon, 2009.
Three journalism professors put the history of American media in a cultural context.

Hindman, Matthew, *The Myth of Digital Democracy*, Princeton University Press, 2008.
An assistant political science professor at Arizona State University argues the Internet has not been such a revolutionary force in American politics after all.

Stretimatter, Roger, *Mightier then the Sword: How the News Media Have Shaped American History*, Westview Press, 2007.
An American University journalism professor analyzes the impact of journalists from Tom Paine to Rush Limbaugh.

Articles

Blodget, Henry, "Post Hate Mail about Our Link to Steve Jobs Heart Attack Report Here," *Silicon Alley Insider*, Oct. 4, 2008, www.alleyinsider.com/2008/10/why-we-published-that-steve-jobs-heart-attack-report.
A well-read blogger argues that it's OK to post unverified news online.

Carr, David, "Let's Invent an iTunes for News," *The New York Times*, Jan. 12, 2009, www.nytimes.com/2009/01/12/business/media/12carr.html?_r=2.
The Times' business columnist suggests newspapers learn from the music business, which defeated free Internet file-sharing and now sells billions of tracks online.

Dorroh, Jennifer, "Endangered Species," *American Journalism Review*, December/January 2009, www.ajr.org/Article.asp?id=4645.
Dorroh explores the damage done to democracy when newspapers stop covering their communities' interests in Washington.

Emmett, Arielle, "Traditional News Outlets Turn to Social Networking Web Sites in an Effort to Build Their Online Audiences," *American Journalism Review*, December/January 2009, www.ajr.org/Article.asp?id=4646.
Emmett looks at how news organizations are recruiting audiences through Facebook and other social-networking media.

Nichols, John, and Robert W. McChesney, "The Death and Life of Great American Newspapers," *The Nation*, March 18, 2009, pp. 11-20, www.thenation.com/doc/20090406/nichols_mcchesney.
Journalist Nichols and communications Professor McChesney passionately argue that government subsidy is the only way to halt the decline of American journalism.

Swensen, David, and Michael Schmidt, "News You Can Endow," *The New York Times*, Jan. 28, 2009, www.nytimes.com/2009/01/28/opinion/28swensen.html?_r=2.
Swensen, who manages Yale University's endowment, and Yale analyst Schmidt argue that philanthropists can save newspapers.

Weber, Jonathan, "The Trouble with Non-Profit Journalism," *New West*, Jan. 30, 2009, www.newwest.net/topic/article/the_problem_with_non_profit_journalism/C559/L559.
The founder of a for-profit online-journalism organization explains his opposition to philanthropic support for news media.

Reports and Studies

"News In the Public Interest: A Free and Subsidized Press," Manship School of Mass Communication, Reilly Center for Media & Public Affairs, Louisiana State University, 2004.
Media executives and scholars discuss the pros and cons of alternative ways to finance journalism.

"The State of the News Media," Project for Excellence in Journalism, 2009, www.stateofthenewsmedia.com/2009/index.htm.
This annual report looks at American journalism from traditional newspapers to the newest online sites.

Adler, Richard P., "Next-Generation Media: The Global Shift: A Report of the Forum on Communications and Society," Aspen Institute Communications and Society Program, 2007, http://staging.aspeninstitute.org/sites/default/files/content/docs/communications%20and%20society%20program/NEXTGENERATION.PDF.
Media's impact on society is discussed by leaders of old and new media, other businesses, government, academe and nonprofit organizations.

Miel, Persephone, and Robert Faris, "News and Information as Digital Media Come of Age," Berkman Center for Internet and Society, Harvard University, 2008, http://cyber.law.harvard.edu/sites/cyber.law.harvard.edu/files/Overview_MR.pdf.
The authors explore the benefits and dangers to society posed by the migration of news reporters and consumers from print to the Internet.

The Next Step:

Additional Articles from Current Periodicals

Democracy

Kriel, Lomi, "Good Reporting Said Vital to Democracy," San Antonio Express-News, Oct. 7, 2008, p. 2B.

Readers are turning to Web sites that reflect their viewpoints rather than to more reliable mainstream news outlets.

Maradiaga, Francisco, "Media Group: Journalism Should Inform, Not Entertain," The Miami Herald, Oct. 2, 2008.

Traditional values of journalism and its role in democracy should not be forgotten amid rising technology, according to the Inter American Press Association.

Pimentel, O. Ricardo, "Journalism That Matters: It's More Vital Than Ever," Milwaukee Journal Sentinel, Dec. 7, 2008, p. J3.

Public-service reporting will always be central to a democracy, whether by newspapers or another medium.

Internet Journalism

Kershaw, Sarah, "A Different Way to Pay for the News You Want," The New York Times, Aug. 24, 2008, p. WK4.

"Community-funded journalism" uses the Internet to solicit ideas and funding for investigative articles.

Rosenthal, Phil, "Can HuffPo Be Papers' Best Friend?" Chicago Tribune, June 22, 2008, p. C3.

The Huffington Post is attempting to localize its Web site in all major news markets within the United States.

Wharton, David, "Matter of Substance," Los Angeles Times, June 22, 2008, p. D1.

As sports blogs have grown in popularity they have exercised more caution and set more boundaries concerning content.

Newspaper Operations

"Potential Buyer Emerges for Maine Newspapers," The Associated Press, July 31, 2008.

An investor group has emerged as a potential buyer for Blethen Maine Newspapers.

Dickerson, Marla, "Mexican Billionaire Makes Bet on the New York Times," Los Angeles Times, Sept. 12, 2008, p. C2.

Mexican financier Carlos Slim Helu has given a $250 million loan to The New York Times Co. to help make debt payments amid declining advertising revenue.

Perez-Peña, Richard, "Rocky Mountain News Fails to Find Buyer and Will Close," The New York Times, Feb. 27, 2009, p. B6.

Unable to find a buyer, Colorado's oldest newspaper — The Rocky Mountain News — will stop publishing.

Pryne, Eric, "The Last Deadline," Seattle Times, March 17, 2009, p. A1.

The Seattle Post-Intelligencer has ceased print production and will become the largest U.S. daily newspaper to shift to an online-only format.

Philanthropy

"Ex-WSJ Chief Will Lead Investigative Journalism Venture," The Associated Press, Oct. 15, 2007.

ProPublica is an investigative journalism outlet funded by philanthropists and headed by a former managing editor at The Wall Street Journal.

Clifford, Stephanie, "Philanthropist Giving Millions to Two Schools of Journalism," The New York Times, June 23, 2008, p. C4.

The Tow Foundation has given $8 million to Columbia and New York universities to study how the newspaper business can succeed online.

Foer, Franklin, et al., "How a Philanthropic Network Can Save Journalism," The Chronicle of Philanthropy, Feb. 26, 2009, p. 37.

Partnerships between news organizations and philanthropies would provide much-needed funding for journalism while bringing attention to social problems that philanthropists seek to address.

Scharfenberg, David, "Aiding Tomorrow's Journalists Today," The Boston Globe, Feb. 2, 2009, p. A13.

News advocates have suggested making tax laws favorable so that philanthropies can buy news outlets, while others have suggested the creation of a national journalism fund.

Citing CQ Researcher

Sample formats for citing these reports in a bibliography include the ones listed below. Preferred styles and formats vary, so please check with your instructor or professor.

MLA Style

Jost, Kenneth. "Rethinking the Death Penalty." CQ Researcher 16 Nov. 2001: 945-68.

APA Style

Jost, K. (2001, November 16). Rethinking the death penalty. CQ Researcher, 11, 945-968.

Chicago Style

Jost, Kenneth. "Rethinking the Death Penalty." CQ Researcher, November 16, 2001, 945-968.

In-depth Reports on Issues in the News

Are you writing a paper?

Need backup for a debate?

Want to become an expert on an issue?

For 80 years, students have turned to *CQ Researcher* for in-depth reporting on issues in the news. Reports on a full range of political and social issues are now available. Following is a selection of recent reports:

Civil Liberties
Closing Guantánamo, 2/09
Limiting Lawsuits, 12/08
Affirmative Action, 10/08
Gay Marriage Showdowns, 9/08
America's Border Fence, 9/08
Immigration Debate, 2/08

Crime/Law
Mexico's Drug War, 12/08
Prostitution Debate, 5/08
Public Defenders, 4/08
Gun Violence, 5/07

Education
Reading Crisis? 2/08
Discipline in Schools, 2/08
Student Aid, 1/08
Racial Diversity in Public Schools, 9/07
Stress on Students, 7/07

Environment
Confronting Warming, 1/09
Reducing Carbon Footprint, 12/08
Protecting Wetlands, 10/08
Buying Green, 2/08

Health/Safety
Regulating Toxic Chemicals, 1/09
Preventing Cancer, 1/09
Heart Health, 9/08
Global Food Crisis, 6/08

Politics/Economy
Future of the GOP, 3/09
Middle-Class Squeeze, 3/09
Public-Works Projects, 2/09
The Obama Presidency, 1/09
The National Debt, 11/08
Financial Bailout, 10/08

Social Trends
Public-Works Projects, 2/09
Falling Birthrates, 11/08
Regulating Credit Cards, 10/08
Internet Accuracy, 8/08

Terrorism/Defense
Homeland Security, 2/09
Rise in Counterinsurgency, 9/08
Cost of the Iraq War, 4/08

Youth
Debating Hip-Hop, 6/07

Upcoming Reports

Extreme Sports, 4/3/09

Wrongful Convictions, 4/10/09

High-Speed Trains, 4/17/09

Judicial Elections, 4/24/09

Hate Groups, 5/1/09

ACCESS

CQ Researcher is available in print and online. For access, visit your library or www.cqresearcher.com.

STAY CURRENT

To receive notice of upcoming *CQ Researcher* reports, or learn more about *CQ Researcher* products, subscribe to the free e-mail newsletters, *CQ Researcher Alert!* and *CQ Researcher News*: http://cqpress.com/newsletters.

PURCHASE

To purchase a *CQ Researcher* report in print or electronic format (PDF), visit www.cqpress.com or call 866-427-7737. Single reports start at $15. Bulk purchase discounts and electronic-rights licensing are also available.

SUBSCRIBE

Annual full-service *CQ Researcher* subscriptions—including 44 reports a year, monthly index updates, and a bound volume—start at $803. Add $25 for domestic postage.

CQ Researcher Online offers a backfile from 1991 and a number of tools to simplify research. For pricing information, call 800-834-9020, ext. 1906, or e-mail librarysales@cqpress.com.

Published by CQ Press, a division of SAGE Publications

www.cqresearcher.com

Extreme Sports

Are they too dangerous?

The wild world of so-called extreme sports ranges from motorcyclists executing double back flips to kayakers navigating deadly Class 5 rapids to mixed martial arts (MMA) — also known as "ultimate fighting" — where combatants use kicks, punches and stress holds. But many "extreme" athletes reject the label, arguing that the term marginalizes their sports as the sole province of adrenaline and violence junkies, when they actually require high degrees of skill. Now legislatures in New York and other states are considering bans on MMA. Proponents say the matches, legal at the pro level in 37 states, are safer than boxing and emphasize fighters' broad-based martial-arts training. But opponents argue that allowing such a wide variety of aggressive moves in a single fight is barbaric. However, skateboarders and other extreme athletes cite statistics showing that traditional sports such as boxing and football cause injuries and deaths at a higher rate than any of the extreme sports.

Georges St. Pierre pummels BJ Penn during their mixed martial arts title match last Jan. 31 in Las Vegas. St. Pierre won when the fight was stopped after four rounds.

CQ Researcher • April 3, 2009 • www.cqresearcher.com
Volume 19, Number 13 • Pages 297-320

Cover: AP Photo/Eric Jamison

CQ Researcher

April 3, 2009
Volume 19, Number 13

MANAGING EDITOR: Thomas J. Colin
tcolin@cqpress.com

ASSISTANT MANAGING EDITOR: Kathy Koch
kkoch@cqpress.com

ASSOCIATE EDITOR: Kenneth Jost

STAFF WRITERS: Thomas J. Billitteri, Marcia Clemmitt, Peter Katel

CONTRIBUTING WRITERS: Rachel Cox, Sarah Glazer, Alan Greenblatt, Barbara Mantel, Patrick Marshall, Tom Price, Jennifer Weeks

DESIGN/PRODUCTION EDITOR: Olu B. Davis

ASSISTANT EDITOR: Darrell Dela Rosa

FACT-CHECKING: Eugene J. Gabler, Michelle Harris

EDITORIAL INTERN: Vyomika Jairam

CQ PRESS

A Division of SAGE

PRESIDENT AND PUBLISHER:
John A. Jenkins

EXECUTIVE DIRECTOR,
REFERENCE INFORMATION GROUP:
Alix B. Vance

CQ Researcher (ISSN 1056-2036) is printed on acid-free paper. Published weekly, except; (Jan. wk. 1) (May wk. 4) (July wks. 1, 2) (Aug. wks. 3, 4) (Nov. wk. 4) and (Dec. wk. 4), by CQ Press, a division of SAGE Publications. Annual full-service subscriptions start at $803. For pricing, call 1-800-834-9020, ext. 1906. To purchase a CQ Researcher report in print or electronic format (PDF), visit www. cqpress.com or call 866-427-7737. Single reports start at $15. Bulk purchase discounts and electronic-rights licensing are also available. Periodicals postage paid at Washington, D.C., and additional mailing offices. POSTMASTER: Send address changes to CQ Researcher, 2300 N St., N.W., Suite 800, Washington, DC 20037.

Extreme Sports

BY MARCIA CLEMMITT

THE ISSUES

Canadian teenager Dean Lewis' biggest mistake may have been getting into the ring in Winnipeg with a more experienced fighter. Just 18, he had a lot to learn about the "extreme" sport of mixed martial arts (MMA), which allows combatants to use potentially deadly moves from kickboxing, jujitsu, sumo and other combat techniques. After a series of blows to his head and body, the young man collapsed in the ring with brain swelling and a severe concussion. As his lungs filled with blood, ringside doctors put a breathing tube down his throat; Lewis suffered several seizures on the way to the hospital. [1]

It was "the bloodiest fight I have ever seen live," said Keith Grienke, who blogs about MMA at cageplay.com. An "illegal upkick to the nose" was the blow that ultimately felled Lewis, Grienke said. [2]

After recovering, Lewis said he wanted to start training again as soon as possible, but that isn't going to happen. According to one of his trainers, Winnipeg MMA fighter Rodrigo Monduruca, Lewis "will never be able to fight again — ever."

MMA is the most controversial of the many so-called extreme sports that have vaulted onto the national stage in recent decades.* While it is un-

A BASE jumper free falls from a 3,000-foot cliff in Lysebotn, Norway, as other jumpers watch and record the action. "BASE" stands for the four categories of fixed objects jumpers use: building, antenna, span, Earth. After jumping, they deploy a parachute, "wingsuit," or both.

AFP/Getty Images/Thomas Bjoernflaten

_____

* Extreme sports are generally defined as individual rather than team-oriented activities that athletes essentially invent by coloring outside the lines of the traditional sport world, often by attempting extreme feats or performing in unusual venues.

questionably the bloodiest, it is far from alone. Controversy also has dogged other extreme sports such as snowboarding, skateboarding, kayaking down waterfalls and BASE jumping — or parachuting from buildings, bridges and cliffs.

Critics argue that the sports are overly risky; that some, like skateboarding, damage property; and that many, like snowboarding, promote reckless, even thuggish, behavior. Moreover, they say spectators are attracted by the potential for severe injury and violence, and they scoff at the claim that the craving to watch "the bloodiest fight" is healthy But many athletes say their events are mislabeled as "ex-

treme," preferring the term "action sports" for pursuits that they say are more about skills than thrills.

"I . . . have a problem with it being a 'sport' just because someone defines it as a sport," said Terri Mills, a planning commission member in West Valley City, Utah, where tighter MMA regulations are being considered out of concern that bouts may encourage brawls or other violence among spectators. [3]

MMA's skyrocketing popularity means that if states don't regulate it, illegal — and potentially far more dangerous — bouts will proliferate, says Bernie Profato, executive director of the Ohio Athletic Commission, which regulates MMA in the state. The public is drawn to many sports, including NASCAR, because of a craving to witness risk and violence, and unregulated fights are the dangerous ones, says Profato. Before Ohio regulated MMA, unregulated fights occurred all over the state, but since 2005, when MMA became legalized and regulated in Ohio, the state hasn't had a single unregulated event, he says. Regulated events require certified ring doctors, ban certain tactics and take other precautions.

Once considered a niche market, action sports are attracting growing interest from the biggest media names. The CBS television network raised eyebrows in 2008 when it announced plans to periodically broadcast MMA matches in prime time on Saturday nights. [4] Also last year, NBC television expanded its action-sports broadcasts beyond competitions to include "lifestyle" coverage of top athletes, and ESPN launched a cluster of online sites to offer up-to-

Extreme Fighting Permitted in Most States

At least 32 states and the District of Columbia permit both amateur and professional mixed martial arts (MMA), also known as extreme or ultimate fighting. MMA is banned at the pro level in seven states and permitted as a pro-only sport in six other states.

Regulation of Mixed Martial Arts

Amateur and Pro bouts both allowed
Amateur Yes/Pro No
Amateur No/Pro Yes
Amateur and Pro both banned
Bouts legal but no regulating body
No data available

Source: International Sport Combat Federation, Feb. 16, 2009

the-minute coverage of online sports from BMX to "freeskiing." [5]

The public's rising interest in action sports comes from advertisers and TV sports channels that choose the most "extreme" images to sell products ranging from athletic shoes to soda.

They focus on "the adrenaline rush because that's what sells to the couch potato," says Dale Stuart, a clinical psychologist in Torrance, Calif., who is a seven-time world champion in freestyle skydiving, in which gymnastics tricks are performed during free fall.

"People are basically afraid of the unknown, and when they think about skydiving, for example, they think, 'I'm going to be up there with no idea what to do,' " she says. They don't realize that before jumping "divers spend a whole day with a coach," learning what to do.

While risk is certainly an element in sports like skydiving, practitioners are "usually success-oriented people, aware of the risks and making conscious, thoughtful decisions about what they do," Stuart says.

Action athletes generally do have "thrill-seeking" personalities, says Frank Farley, a professor of psychology at Philadelphia's Temple University, who coined the term Type T to describe such people. But many Type Ts are the opposite of reckless, Farley says. "Those who live prepare" for their sports, he says. "They don't want to die. They want the challenges, the creativity, the risky experiences. So they prepare."

Type Ts do push the envelope, not just in sports but in science and the arts, Farley says. And while some Type Ts push it in negative ways, such as by taking drugs or committing crimes, many

others are society's creators and innovators. "If we didn't have these people, we'd be back in the cave," Farley says.

Snowboarding has furnished many an extreme image to marketers, but that's far from the full picture, according to Holly Thorpe, a snowboarder and lecturer in sport and leisure studies at the University of Waikato in New Zealand. There are more than 18.5 million snowboarders worldwide, ranging in age from 5 to 75, making "the notion of snowboarding as extreme [seem] obtuse," she wrote.

Nevertheless, "with more than 75 percent of American snowboarders under the age of 24 and males constituting approximately 70 percent of all boarders, it is no wonder that stereotypes continue to abound," Thorpe acknowledged. [6]

Action sports like freestyle motocross — in which motorcycle riders do jumps and acrobatics — and whitewater kayaking do pose dangers, participants acknowledge.

While preparation is vital to most action sports, the situation will always throw unforeseen risk into the mix, such as a slippery surface, says Farley. Motorcycle stunt riders like Robbie Knievel — son of the legendary Evil Knievel — "practice over and over again, but at the moment of takeoff it's always risky," he says. "Very competent people die all the time doing things like climbing Mt. Everest."

Freestyle skiing — skiing off an icy ramp in order to perform airborne acrobats — was banned as a competitive sport in the 1960s and '70s because athletes falling from a five-story height while twisting and turning risked serious injury. But "this did not deter . . . athletes from training and competing unofficially" or prevent media coverage, said Kenneth P. Burres, a back surgeon in Montclair, Calif. Today, it's an Olympic event, and standardized venues and equipment have reduced the injury rate, though high risk remains, he wrote. [7]

"The fact that they're called 'extreme' sports means, if you make a mistake, you die," says Ron Watters, an adjunct professor of outdoor education at Idaho State University. In extreme climbing, for example, "the edge that you walk between life and death is a knife edge," he says. Casual spectators can be tempted into danger if they fail to realize the people that make these highly entertaining DVDs of high-risk activities "did not just start doing the sport yesterday. They started out with teachers," he says.

While media images of many action sports depict rugged individualism, teamwork is actually the order of the day and helps make sports safer, says Jay Young, a West Virginia-based writer and rock climber who runs the Web site rockclimbing.com. "It's very common for a person to fall off a rock but very uncommon for them to hit the ground" because most people climb in groups, literally tied together, he says.

Progressing from marathon running to the even more extreme Ironman triathlon — a 2.4-mile swim, followed by a 112-mile bike ride and a 26.2-mile marathon — "I actually find myself healthier," says Taneen L. Carvell, president of a Washington, D.C., marketing firm, who completed her first Ironman nine days after turning 40. The multiple skills required of an Ironman athlete demand that "you know your body" and cross-train in a more balanced way than runners often do, she says. "You're out there for 12 or 13 hours, not three," as in a marathon, so you must be thoroughly healthy, she says.

"One of the nice things" about action sports like skateboarding "is that each kid can express himself at his own level," without needing top skills just to stay in the game as a teenager, as is the case with many traditional sports like baseball, says John R. Ricciardi, Jr., president and founder of the New Jersey-based Action Sports Association, a nonprofit that aims to expand corporate, government and parental support for action sports. Most action sports "are

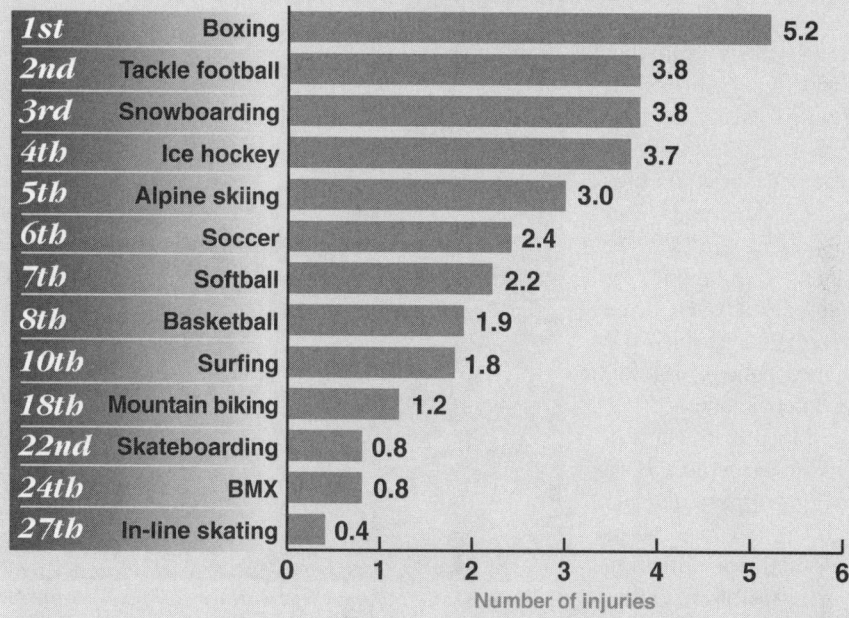

Traditional Sports Have Higher Injury Rates

Snowboarders have the third-highest injury rate among traditional and extreme sports. Among other extreme sports, surfing ranks 10th, mountain biking 18th and in-line skating 27th.

Injury Rates for Selected Traditional and Extreme Sports
(Injuries per 1,000 athlete exposures*)

Rank	Sport	Number of injuries
1st	Boxing	5.2
2nd	Tackle football	3.8
3rd	Snowboarding	3.8
4th	Ice hockey	3.7
5th	Alpine skiing	3.0
6th	Soccer	2.4
7th	Softball	2.2
8th	Basketball	1.9
10th	Surfing	1.8
18th	Mountain biking	1.2
22nd	Skateboarding	0.8
24th	BMX	0.8
27th	In-line skating	0.4

* Athlete exposures represents the number of times a participant engages in the activity in a year.

Source: American Sports Data Inc., May 15, 2003. According to several sources, including medical associations, these are the most up-to-date and comprehensive data available on sports injuries.

healthy lifestyle habits" that one can pursue for decades, he says. Furthermore, "a lot of kids have problems at home, and these sports can be their salvation; my kids used the skateboard to work through their problems," like their parents' divorce, says Ricciardi.

Skateboarding "does cause minor property damage," but that's far from its essence, says Ocean Howell, a former professional skateboarder who is a writer and a graduate student in architectural history at the University of California, Berkeley. "If you see a kid going down the street, you may think he's a thuggy jerk, but if he's jumping on and off the curbs on a skateboard, making it look smooth, then

that kid has a tremendous work ethic," Howell says. "That kid is practicing an art form, and has an interest in doing something right."

As states debate legalizing MMA and cities mull opening public parks to skateboarders, here are some of the questions being asked about extreme sports:

Should "ultimate fighting" be banned?

Now called mixed martial arts (MMA) by practitioners, the combat sport once mainly known as ultimate fighting or cage fighting — after the mesh enclosures bouts are sometimes conducted in — has grown fast as a spectator sport in recent years. New televised and live events pop up regularly in the United States and elsewhere, including Canada and Great Britain, and TV networks that shunned the sport in the '90s are embracing it in the new millennium. [8] Now legal as a pro and amateur sport in 32 states and Washington, D.C., the contests mix techniques from jujitsu, kickboxing and other combat disciplines. Critics argue that allowing fighters to choose so many alternate ways to attack opponents makes the sport too brutal and dangerous. But proponents say a wide variety of techniques rewards skill over brute force and lessens the chance fighters will suffer brain injuries.

Both the British and American medical associations oppose ultimate fighting because of its potential for inflicting permanent physical harm to participants, and the AMA "encourages states that have not banned these events to pass a law doing so," says Robert Reilly, a New York State Assemblyman who is leading a ban effort in his state.

"Cage-fighting events do nothing more than promote violence and drunken depravity in our city," said Teresa A. Larson, chairman of the Family Violence Response Team in Webster County, Iowa. "It's basic street fighting with a few 'rules' thrown in for appearances." [9]

Some question whether regulators are capable of holding the bouts in check, as in Lewis' near-tragic bout in Winnipeg. Mayor Sam Katz blamed Lewis' injury in February on the referee, a ringside doctor and the Manitoba Boxing Commission, which regulates MMA in the province. [10]

Winnipeg City Council member Grant Nordman doesn't want MMA fights in the city, partly because he's worried about liability. "I was disappointed that a young man was beaten as badly as [Lewis] was," he said. "Is the city culpable in any regard when there is a mishap or . . . a fatality from a regulated fight?" [11]

Kyle Bennett of the United States competes in the Men's BMX semifinals at the 2008 Olympic Games in Beijing. In the United States, a growing number of municipalities are creating parks for skateboarding and other action sports like BMX, or bike racing across tough terrain and obstacles. The U.S. boasts well over 2,100 such parks today.

Nordman instructed the city's Community Services Department to explore options for Winnipeg to ban MMA events. [12]

The fight preferences of North American audiences — who are used to boxing rather than leverage- and balance-based martial arts like jujitsu — may add some danger to American MMA matches, acknowledges Jeffrey Vigil, an MMA coach and trainer in Albuquerque, N.M. "In American bouts, you hear booing" any time an MMA fighter is on the ground, for example, he says. "But in Japan, as soon as fighters are on the ground, you can hear a pin drop in a 20,000-person arena. They know the technique, and they see the technique of what the

guy on the bottom can do to get on top," and they respect it, while North American fans often just want to see more hits.

Unlike in boxing, it's not considered a disgrace to lose an MMA bout, and even the world champion doesn't have an undefeated record, says the Ohio Athletic Commission's Profato. That makes MMA much safer than boxing, since a fighter doesn't lose respect in the sport if he "taps out" and says, "I've had enough," and the referee ends the match.

MMA is based on skill, not brute force, which makes for a safer activity, says Vigil, who eight years ago became involved in MMA and Brazilian jujitsu, in which many top MMA fighters specialize.

"People go into a jujitsu gym with the state of mind that because they fought in the streets" they can master the art quickly, Vigil says. But trainers "will put the weakest person" from the training program up against street-fight-hardened neophytes, "and they'll beat those beginners. When I started, they put me up against one of the girls, and I thought, 'I'll go light on her,' but she beat me pretty badly.

"A lot of times guys don't come back" after that experience, he continues. Vigil did return and finally beat his first, much smaller, opponent, "but it took me several months."

Athletes in several traditional, well-accepted sports take much more injurious pounding than MMA fighters generally do, says Vigil. "Football is dangerous! You have a 300-pound man and a 180-pound man going after each other," with repeated hits, "but it's the sport that everybody loves," he says. "A boxer gets hit [repeatedly] for three 12-minute rounds."

Even in the early days when MMA was billed as "no-holds-barred," it was less dangerous than boxing, said David Plotz, editor of the online magazine *Slate*. MMA's U.S. reputation "fell victim to cultural determinism about what a fight is" — i.e., a punching match, period, Plotz wrote. But "in countries such as Brazil and Japan, where no-holds-barred fighting has a long history, it is popular and uncontroversial." [13]

Some may overestimate the dangers of MMA because they don't understand the skills it involves, suggests Vigil. For instance, some critics consider the knee and elbow strikes as particularly dangerous. Those techniques come from a Thai martial art called Muay Thai boxing, in which the knee and elbow "are used like a knife," he says. "You learn to do it fast and hard but not really full contact," resulting in cuts to the skin. Bleeding from such cuts can often stop a fight, he says.

Some worry about MMA's essentially unpadded gloves, which don't cover the whole hand, unlike boxing gloves, arguing that the lack of padding makes the sport more dangerous to those who are punched. "But it's just the reverse," said Plotz. "The purpose of boxing gloves is not to cushion the head but to shield the knuckles. Without gloves, a boxer would break his hands after a couple of punches to the skull. That's why ultimate fighters won't throw multiple skull punches," unlike boxers. [14]

MMA training inculcates discipline and mental exercise and doesn't make fighters punch drunk, so it is healthier than training for what boxers do, says Vigil. "One day you train in boxing, and the next day it's jujitsu," which requires leverage and balance, he says. In the process, "you're training your brain to make it smarter," sizing up situations to figure out which martial discipline would work best and then switching quickly from using the fists to using the feet or putting a wrestling hold on an opponent.

Women Participate in Many Extreme Sports

More than half of all in-line skaters and nearly half of the Alpine skiers are women. Several other extreme sports attract smaller but still sizable proportions of females. By contrast, only 15 percent of skydivers are women, and they are a negligible presence in sports such as motocross, BMX and drag racing.

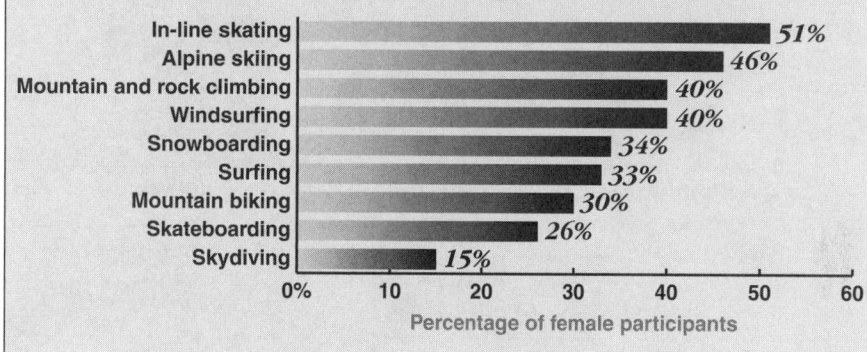

Female Participation in Selected Extreme Sports

Source: Berkshire Encyclopedia of Extreme Sports, 2007

"I grew up rough," in a gang-heavy area of Phoenix, Vigil continues. "My brother got shot in the head. I wish I'd had a sport like this when I was growing up" to channel aggressions and develop self-esteem from mastering techniques. Vigil offers classes in Brazilian jujitsu and MMA to men in a local halfway house who've recently been released from prison. Five of the men now train at his gym, and he regularly meets their parole officers, who praise the training, he says.

Are extreme sports more dangerous than other sports?

On Feb. 9, 24-year-old freestyle motocross rider and X Games gold medalist Jeremy Lusk died after he crashed attempting a back flip while holding onto his motorcycle's seat at an X sports event in Costa Rica. Lusk's death was reported by newspapers and Web sites around the world and raised new questions about whether action sports may be growing too dangerous. Nevertheless, many analysts say that, with a few exceptions, injury rates for action sports are com-

parable to or lower than those in many popular traditional sports. [15]

Mountain climbing and extreme "air" sports such as BASE jumping and skydiving have higher death rates than most other sports, according to the University of Waikato's Thorpe and Douglas Booth, a professor in the School of Physical Education at New Zealand's University of Otago. In those pursuits, about 800 participants will die for every 100 million days of participation, they report. That's compared to about 70 deaths per 100 million days of activity in water sports like surfing and water skiing, 30 for horse riding, 16 for rugby and five for boxing. [16]

Motorized extreme sports such as freestyle motocross also are quite dangerous, studies conclude. For example, a Japanese study of elite motorcycle competitors deemed injury rates "high," with the 117 athletes surveyed reporting they'd suffered 60 major injuries, at a rate of 22.4 serious injuries for every 1,000 hours of biking. [17]

The Brain Injury Association of Canada campaigns for safety measures in action sports — as well as in some

Skateboarding Outdraws Football, Rivals Baseball

The number of skateboarders in the United States nearly tripled from 1995 to 2005, to 12 million. By contrast, the popularity of baseball dropped 7 percent during the same period, to 14.6 million players.

U.S. Participation in Skateboarding, Football and Baseball; 1995 and 2005

(in millions)

Source: Ocean Howell, "Skatepark as Neoliberal Playground: Urban Governance, Recreation Space, and the Cultivation of Personal Responsibility," Space and Culture, SAGE Publications, August 2008

traditional sports such as ice hockey — because the dominance of ice sports in Canada exposes many young athletes to high-speed impacts. Brain injuries are the biggest cause of death and long-term disability for children and young adults, with many of the accidents sports-related, the association says. [18]

Inexperienced participants are at highest risk. Between 1951 and 2000, 2,350 fatalities were reported among North American mountain climbers, and more than 50 percent of the deaths were among climbers with less than three years' experience. Rookie errors included lack of detailed planning, late starts that stranded climbers in low-temperature nights and failure to turn back when weather conditions worsened. [19]

In rock climbing lingo, relative beginners "who know enough to be dangerous" are called "gumbies," and their numbers may be on the rise, partly because of the proliferation of indoor climbing gyms, says Young of rockclimbing.com. "The prevailing view among climbers is that the gyms have made the sport so much more accessible that it may be too easy for

people to take a couple of lessons" and assume they have the know-how to climb unknown rocks. "There's nothing to stop them from buying a rope" and tackling a rock they're not ready for, Young says.

Many action sports involve high speed and heights, factors that pose special risks to young brains, says Gregory J. O'Shanick, a Richmond, Va.-based psychiatrist who is national medical director of the Brain Injury Association of America. Fast, sharp head movements can injure the brain even without an impact, and "the younger the brain the more chance for devastation," whether brain tissue bumps against ridges in the skull or different layers of brain tissue simply shift position relative to one another, he says. The brain's important frontal lobes, which house the decision-making faculties, among other important functions, don't develop fully until about age 20, and studies show that even small injuries can prevent the brain from developing normally.

Based on injury rates, snowboarding is the third-riskiest sport, behind two traditional sports — boxing and tackle football, according to the University of Waikato's Thorpe. (*See graph,*

p. 301.) At least one study also shows that snowboarders are more than twice as likely as skiers to suffer serious fractures and concussions. About a quarter of all snowboard injuries — mostly caused by falls — occur during a person's first experience with the sport, and nearly half occur during the first season, Thorpe says. [20]

However, while generally considered extreme athletes, snowboarders actually face a lower fatality risk than traditional skiers, Thorpe says. [21]

Aside from snowboarding, none of the other non-motorized extreme sports has a particularly high injury rate, according to a 2003 survey by American Sports Data, a market research firm in Fort Mill, S.C. Surfing is 10th in risk potential, with 1.8 injuries for every 1,000 times athletes participate. [22]

"I have 6,000 jumps and never a serious problem," says freestyle skydiver Stuart. "People who pay attention and are aware of their decision processes can do high-risk sports very safely," she says. Skydiving is among only a handful of sports that require safety training and credentials, however, she notes.

The public may believe action sports are more dangerous partly because their main experience with the sports is through watching professionals on television, says Scott Kip, a longtime amateur street skateboarder and a Philadelphia-based furniture designer and cabinetmaker. "Skateboarding is actually very safe, but people don't believe that," he says. "It's only pros who go down stairs," for example, "and it takes a tremendous amount of practice and focus" to do those stunts.

Outdoor sports have boomed over the past few decades, "but generally the accident rates are still pretty low," says Steven Guthrie, an assistant professor of outdoor education at Pennsylvania's Lock Haven University. "Adventure sports" — such as kayaking — "are generally safer than ordinary sports. And the leader-led stuff like rock climbing is generally quite safe. You have this image that this isn't true," because "every time there is a dramatic rescue of climbers, it's played up." But such incidents are rare, he says.

"There's always a chance to die, but you don't go out and try to kill yourself," says Tom Burt, one of a small group of "big-mountain" snowboarders, who specialize in riding very high peaks, including Mt. Everest. "To say that what I do is the most dangerous aspect of snowboarding . . . well, it's a relative thing because of ability, training and experience." [23]

"One of my pet peeves is hearing people refer to climbing as an adrenaline sport. Anybody who does it knows it's the opposite," says Young of rockclimbing.com. "Yes, adrenaline is pumping when you're 70 feet above the ground and 40 feet out from the wall, but to climb at a high level you need to be able to function well in spite of adrenaline. These are the situations we plop ourselves into," but the goal is less the adrenaline rush than the challenge of using one's skills to master both the rush and the situation.

In fact, action sports can improve mental health, some analysts say. Skateboarding may get a bad rap, since schools don't generally sponsor it, many public places ban it and "not a lot of adults participate in it," according to a 2005 study by researchers at the University of North Carolina at Chapel Hill. "But we found that adolescents who skateboard

Nineteen-year-old Shaun White of the United States competes in the Men's Snowboard Half-pipe Final at the 2006 Torino Winter Olympic Games in Italy. He went on to win the gold medal.

actually fared well in terms of self-esteem and were less likely to engage in risky behaviors compared to teens who watch a lot of TV," said co-author Penny Gordon-Larsen, an assistant professor of nutrition. [24]

Have media portrayals boosted action sports?

Over the past two decades, sports television and commercial advertisers have ramped up their use of action-sports images, the more extreme the better. YouTube and other Web sites have become home to thousands, if not millions, of individually and commercially made videos, from "wingsuit" flying to acrobatic maneuvers performed on snowmobiles. There's no question that media images have piqued public interest, but critics say the media often portrays the sports inaccurately and may entice novices into trying dangerous stunts.

The ESPN network and other sponsors of extreme sports have assisted action athletes tremendously, despite the fact that many "feel a moral obligation to trash" extreme-sports media like the X Games merely "because ESPN is a large corporation," potentially at odds with the individualistic, rebel spirit of action sports, said Ron Semiao, creator of ESPN's X Games. "When I see more kids buying skateboards and more skaters doing ads for Pepsi and AT&T, I think" the media coverage "is a good thing for the skateboard industry," he said. [25]

Individual and small-company media are a means of building communities of athletes to share friendship and techniques, action athletes say.

"Skydivers love to show off what they've done," and video is the only way to accomplish that, says psychologist and skydiver Stuart. Freestyle skydiving, she says, was actually created by shared videos. After several years of skydivers passing around videos of acrobatic tricks they were performing, a group formed to create competitions and standards to make freestyle a full-fledged sport. Through videos, "people feed off of and learn from what others are doing," she says.

Shared video also has helped create an international community of skateboarders, says former professional skateboarder Howell. Beginning in the 1980s, small-scale video technology allowed skaters to share techniques worldwide. "I could go to Tel Aviv tomorrow and see the same moves" as skateboarders perform in the U.S. or Brazil, for example, Howell says. The result is a kind of "global youth culture; you can have instant friends" abroad, bonding over skating moves.

While some action athletes complain that negative or sensational media coverage harms action sports' image, others relish it. "The wilder I get, the better [boarders] like it," said professional snowboarder Damian Sanders of his bad-boy media image, which he cultivated by sporting a black Mohawk and filing his teeth into the shape of fangs. [26]

But exposure to violent sports can be harmful to audiences, says Temple University psychologist Farley. "Some psychologists say that it gives you an outlet, but while I'd love that to be true, I don't think it is," he says. "I would speculate — because we don't know for sure — that seeing [violence] creates an acceptance of violence and might stimulate you" to commit violent acts that you otherwise would not have.

Media may bear some responsibility for bad decision-making in action sports, says Watters at Idaho State University. "Young men, especially, they're watching the videos and these guys are doing crazy things, they want to go out and try it without putting in the apprenticeship," he says. Even *National Geographic* advertisements can have a bad effect on some people, he says. "They attract people to things before they're ready," such as solo climbing and snowboarding on extremely steep slopes.

Videos and televised events often feature athletes without helmets or other protective gear, says psychiatrist O'Shanick at the American Brain Injury Association. "It's a matter of role modeling," with kids following what their idols do, he says.

"More than half of students who reported engaging in risky behavior"

such as extreme sports stunts, "said they exaggerated it if they were being videotaped," according to the Brain Injury Association of Canada. [27]

Some argue that media coverage both creates a more-extreme-than-reality public image and pushes athletes to perform more dangerous stunts than they otherwise would. For example, in 2004, professional snowboarder Tara Dakides was seriously injured attempting a 360-degree-rotation stunt live on "The Late Show with David Letterman." Warmer weather than expected and "the pressure of a big-time production diminished Dakides' chances of successfully completing the stunt," said the University of Waikato's Thorpe. Ensuing news coverage of the crash reinforced snowboarding's extreme-sport status, she said. [28]

"The media stigmatize and stereotype the people who do these sports as inconsiderate of their loved ones," says Stuart, whose pairing of gymnastic moves with skydiving led newscasters to feature her as an athlete who "went completely contrary to the image of the sport, which is of reckless, impulsive people." One couple told Stuart she saved their marriage when she appeared on television showing the "sophisticated, elegant, controlled" aspect of skydiving, she says. Previously, the wife had perceived her husband as "indulgent and self-interested" by participating in a sport that most media coverage and advertising images portray as involving reckless flirting with death.

In the late 1990s, "television and corporate sponsors recognized the huge potential in these activities to tap into the young, male market," said Thorpe. To snare that highly desirable, hard-to-reach demographic, advertisers "went to great lengths to portray action sports participants as extreme in their perilous approach." [29]

"Some of the commercialization that's happened has really grabbed hold of the negative aspects of being a teenager," driving public hostility to sports like

skateboarding, says Kip, the Philadelphia furniture maker and skateboarder. Linking products to "cool" images, such as the most extreme action-sports stunts, is "the easiest way to market products in the mall to teenagers desperately groping for a sense of identity," he says.

But extreme marketing, while serving advertisers' interests, has not done well by action athletes themselves, Kip says. "There are 13 to 15 million people in the United States who identify themselves as skateboarders," he says. The sport "is more popular than baseball." But largely because of bad-boy media and marketing images, "some people believe that "all of these people have no sense of right and wrong."

"The worst — God help me, but it's Bam Margera, who I have skateboarded with many times in the 14 years I've lived in Philadelphia," he continues. "Jackass," the MTV television show and movie and video series that first launched Margera as an enormously wealthy media icon, "is partly funny and creative, but it also has created a horrible image of skateboarding. It's hard to calculate the damage he's done" to the sport "by taking hold of the negative things" like super-dangerous stunts, extreme practical jokes and property damage." ■

BACKGROUND

Ancient Extremists

From the dawn of human history, thrill-seekers have pushed to the limit in risky encounters, much like today's action athletes. [30]

In wrestling, for example, the ancient Greeks "had no hesitation about using all kinds of neck holds, including . . . strangleholds," according to classical-history scholar Michael B.

Continued on p. 309

Chronology

1960s-1970s
Skateboarding begins when surfers use wheeled boards on sidewalks to stay in shape during the off-season.

1965
Michigan chemical engineer Sherman Poppen makes the first snowboard.

1978
California skydivers Michael Pelky and Brian Schubert are injured performing the first BASE jump, parachuting off El Capitan Mountain in Yosemite National Park. . . . First Ironman triathlon held in Hawaii.

1979
First modern bungee jumps are made from the 250-foot Clifton Suspension Bridge in Bristol, England. The jumpers are quickly arrested.

1980s-1990s
TV coverage and product marketing using extreme-sports images proliferate.

1981
U.S. BASE Association is created.

1988
First commercial bungee-jumping site opens at New Zealand's 129-foot Karawau Bridge.

1993
Martial arts bouts in Denver launch "ultimate fighting" — later known as "mixed martial arts" (MMA) — as a spectator sport.

1995
ESPN holds the first Summer Extreme Games. The next year the event is rebranded as the X Games to appeal to international audiences.

1997
The first Winter X Games are televised to 198 countries

1998
New Yorker Jessica Ann Kluetmeier, 29, is injured during the first legal BASE jump from Seattle's 520-foot Space Needle. . . . Snowboarding debuts at the Nagano Olympic Games. . . . Jari Kuosma of Finland and Robert Pecnik of Croatia develop a "wingsuit" enabling BASE jumpers to glide at 100 miles per hour.

2000s
MMA becomes one of the fastest-growing spectator sports. More women participate in action sports.

2000
While campaigning for president, Sen. John McCain, R-Ariz., calls for a ban on ultimate fighting and persuades major cable companies to temporarily drop coverage of the pay-per-view matches. . . . Davo Karnicar of Slovenia becomes first person to ski nonstop down Mt. Everest.

2001
In a bid to get state and local authorities to sanction ultimate fighting, the sport's leaders agree to ban some risky moves, including head-butting and "fish-hooking." Nevada pioneers the matches.

2002
Frenchman Marco Siffredi vanishes during a snowboard descent of Mt. Everest, a feat he completed successfully in 2001.

2004
Chinese government launches Chinese Extreme Sports Association.

2005
World's largest skate park opens in Shanghai, China.

2006
Rally Car Racing and BMX Big Air are added to the X Games. . . . African-American hip-hop artist Lupe Fiasco records the song "Kick, Push," reflecting skateboarding's growing popularity in minority neighborhoods. . . . American extreme-skiing pioneer Doug Coombs, 48, dies in fall over a cliff in the French Alps. . . . Pay-per-view TV revenues for MMA top $220 million, higher than boxing's record PPV revenues of $200 million, set in 1999.

2007
Sam Vasquez, a 35-year-old father from Texas, dies from head injuries suffered in an MMA bout. He is believed to be the third MMA athlete to die from fight injuries.

2008
Frenchman Alexandre Caizergues sets a kite-surfing speed record of 58.2 miles per hour.

2009
Levi LaVallee of Minnesota completes the first snowmobile double backflip during the Winter X Games. . . . California freestyle motocross racer Jeremy Lusk, 24, dies from a head injury after crashing during a backflip. . . . On Feb. 21, more than 1.2 million male viewers ages 18-49 watch the Saturday night MMA show "UFC 95," making it the day's most-watched TV show by men. . . . Shane McConkey, a 39-year-old American skier, BASE jumper and father of one, dies during filming for a video while attempting to perform a double backflip on skis after jumping off a cliff in Italy's Dolomite mountains.

Young, White Men Dominate Extreme Sports

Skateboarding is beginning to attract non-white athletes.

The typical action athlete is young, white and male, and most tend to have gregarious, sensation-hungry personalities. Indeed, young men in their late teens and early 20s are "a dominant force" in most extreme sports, with the average age of male skateboarders, snowboarders, artificial-wall climbers and in-line skaters being 14, 19, 20 and 20.5 years, respectively. [1]

A full 89 percent of snowboarders are white, and many are upper-middle-class. Indeed, some minority athletes say that money is a serious bar to participating, said Holly Thorpe, a snowboarder and lecturer in sport and leisure studies at the University of Waikato in New Zealand. [2]

Marc Frank Montoya, the first and only Mexican-American professional snowboarder, says that expensive ski-lift tickets are the upper class' way to keep poor people out of the sport, according to Thorpe. "They charge like 50 or 60 bucks" for a ticket, said Montoya. "That's how they keep city kids from going up and snowboarding," he said. [3]

The rise of the action sports culture and its commercialization on TV sports networks and in advertising, may reflect young, white men's search for an identity separate from the "establishment" image attached to older, white men, says Kyle W. Kusz, associate professor of cultural studies of sport and physical culture at the University of Rhode Island.

Marc Frank Montoya is the first and only Mexican-American pro snowboarder.

Courtesy www.nzsnowboard.com

In the mid-1990s, when action sports exploded on the national scene, "we were having many conversations about multiculturalism and diversity," and most top traditional sports like basketball and football were dominated by black athletes, says Kusz. In response, many snowboarders, for example, adopted a "hip-hop aesthetic" and began "tagging" — painting graffiti — he says. The sports were "a way of making white guys seems authentic and edgy."

To a much greater degree than for traditional sports, women were involved in today's action sports from the earliest days, in the 1960s and '70s, Thorpe said. Nevertheless, action sports were and to some extent remain "a social institution created by men for men," she said. [4]

Some women found their action-sports accomplishments met with hostility, Thorpe said. For example, in 1995, Alison Hargreaves of the United Kingdom became only the second person ever to climb Mt. Everest solo and without using oxygen, a feat that would likely would have enshrined her permanently among sports' great achievers, had she been male. But in 1998, when she died descending after her second successful Everest climb, media accounts instead blasted Hargreaves as an "errant, unthinking mother" who had "effectively abandoned her children," Thorpe said. [5]

Of all action sports, skateboarding has been the most open to lower-income and non-white athletes.

In the 1980s, "we lower-middle-class suburbanites began busing long hours into urban centers, where we would skateboard the sculptural wastelands of old redevelopment projects with the inner-city kids," said former professional skateboarder Ocean Howell of his teenage skateboarding years. [6]

Compared to the gear required by other extreme sports — perhaps $2,000 to outfit a kayaker, for example, — skateboards can be had for $70 or $80, Howell notes.

In recent years, ethnic-minority neighborhoods have added skateboarding to the traditional roster of sidewalk games. "You had basketball, you had strikeouts, you had street football, which you played manhole-to-manhole," said Bahr Brown, owner of Harlem's first skate shop, opened in 2006. Now a kid comes in my shop and he's like, 'Yo, Mom, can I get a skateboard?' " [7]

But some key personality traits bind extreme athletes together, class, race and gender aside, many athletes say.

"Sensation seekers tend to be extroverts," and extreme-sports enthusiasts tend to form "very close communities" both in person and online, says Alisha Blakeney, a kayaker and graduate student at Auburn University, in Montgomery, Ala. Action athletes tend to be consumed with their sports. "It's just ridiculous how much of my life revolves around kayaking," says Blakeney, who's held kayaking-related jobs and also researches her sport as a graduate student.

[1] Holly Thorpe, "Gender," *Berkshire Encyclopedia of Extreme Sports*, 2007.

[2] Holly Thorpe, "Boarders, Babes and Bad-Asses: Theories of a Female Physical Youth Culture," doctoral thesis, 2007.

[3] Quoted in *ibid.*.

[4] Thorpe, "Gender," *op. cit.*

[5] *Ibid.*

[6] Ocean Howell, "Extreme Market Research," *Topic* magazine, spring 2003, www.webdelsol.com.

[7] Quoted in Ben Detrick, "Skateboarding Rolls Out of the Suburbs," *The New York Times*, Nov. 11, 2007, Sec. 9, p. 8.

Continued from p. 306

Poliakoff. In the mid-fifth century, B.C., the wrestler Leontiskos was awarded Olympic prizes for matches he won after breaking opponents' fingers, he writes. [31]

The Greeks even had their own version of MMA — pankration, in which contestants were allowed to use a wide variety of unarmed fighting techniques, including punches and kicks to the head. Incredibly, an Olympic pankration crown was awarded posthumously to the fighter Arrichion. Just before his death from a stranglehold, Arrichion had forced his opponent to surrender, overcome by the pain Arrichion had inflicted when he dislocated a bone in the man's ankle. [32]

Non-combat sports have long pushed the envelope as well. For centuries, Hawaiian islanders hurtled headfirst down steep, snowless mountains on narrow, toboggan-like sleds, called *papa holua*, at 50 miles an hour. Western missionaries banned the sport in 1825, complaining about its dangers. If . . . "the sled flipped over during its running, it would mean the death of the rider by the edge of the sled," noted an 1865 article in a Hawaiian newspaper. "Much pleasure was brought by this sport, though injury and death were sometimes the ending." [33]

The most avid thrill-seekers were often explorers, whose exploits expanded human knowledge and wealth, says Idaho State University's Watters. Turn-of-the-century Anglo-Irish Antarctic explorer Ernest Shackleton, for example, is said to have placed the following newspaper ad seeking companions for one of his trips: "Men wanted for Hazardous Journey. Small wages, bitter cold, long months of complete darkness, constant danger, safe return doubtful." [34]

Beginning around the mid-19th century, "we began to have more adventure for adventure's sake" in in-

More than 7,000 women participated in an in-line skating marathon in Berlin, Germany, in 2007. Women constitute more than half of all in-line skaters but make up much smaller percentages of other extreme sports.

dustrializing countries, with intense, outdoor sports gradually gaining popularity among a population who once might have found life risky enough just traveling west in a covered wagon, Watters says.

In modern times, adventurous sports morphed from rare, solitary pursuits into common activities, says Lori Holyfield, an associate professor of sociology at the University of Arkansas. Some sociologists dub such activities "edgework" — intentional experiences that bring together risk and uncertainty with one's own skills, Holyfield says.

"As our jobs have become more routine and predictable, a thirst for edgework" has grown among many, especially white-collar workers, Holyfield says. Many desk workers crave not only edgework but the physical activity involved in sports like kayaking and climbing, she says. In contrast, "blue-collar working folk don't often use their non-work time on this kind of stuff. They use leisure time to rest their bodies."

Action-sports participation skyrocketed as the baby boom generation (born between 1946 and 1964) reached young adulthood. The 1960s and '70s saw an extraordinary increase in outdoor activities, said Watters. "So many members of this generation flocked to the rivers and mountains that land management agencies had to impose restrictions on use" for the first time, he said. [35]

Action sports took on a more extreme character as Generation X (born between 1965 and 1980) came of age, he continued. Generation Xers "embraced competition and particularly risk, pushing back the limits of every outdoor sport — and inventing some new ones of their own." [36]

Marketers' Dream

Beginning in the 1980s, marketers seized on the most extreme images of whitewater rafting, wakeboarding and other sports to sell products from beer to antihistamine.

Most action athletes have a personality type known as "sensation seeker" or "thrill-seeker," says Donald R. Self, a professor of marketing at Alabama's Auburn University, at Montgomery. This group includes around one-seventh of the population, about half of whom are under age 25, he says.

Marketers use sensation seekers "to spot a new trend in music, in sports, whatever," says Self, who considers himself such a person. Studying thrill-seekers' preferences identifies what the rest of society will soon perceive as cool, because "others wait until they see us having fun" in an activity, "and then it becomes safe enough for them to try," he says.

Action Sports Versus the Environment

Clashes have changed cityscapes worldwide.

Traditional sports like baseball and gymnastics are played in gyms and on fields set aside for the purpose, and strict rules determine who scores and who doesn't. But most action sports take a nearly opposite approach. Snowboarders, climbers and BASE jumpers pursue their sports in public, multi-use spaces, using their skills to overcome obstacles in the environment in brand-new ways, such as when a kayaker descends a waterfall or a skateboarder kick-flips a board onto, then off of, a park bench.

The use of real-world venues provides the element of uncertainty and risk that allows athletes to stretch themselves, says Lori Holyfield, an associate professor of sociology at the University of Arkansas.

Skateboarding, for example, "is a lot like golf except for one thing" — the use of the real world as its playground, says Scott Kip, a longtime amateur street skateboarder and a Philadelphia-based furniture designer and cabinetmaker. In both sports, "you develop your personal set of skills and then apply them to a terrain that challenges you and gives you a yardstick" to measure progress, he says. "But skateboarding has an extra, creative component, since you're always looking for something you can do a skateboard trick on."

In the early days of the action-sports boom, at least, the creative, open-space dimension "had a nice environmental benefit," says Ronald Watters, an adjunct professor of outdoor education at Idaho State University. People pursuing outdoor sports "want to have parks and open areas," and they push for public policies to create and preserve such spaces, he says.

Over the years, however, action athletes' use of public spaces has often pitted them against public officials and the general public. Even though a "back-to-nature movement" fueled the outdoor-recreation boom of the 1960s and '70s, some lands suffered a "love-it-to-death" syndrome, says Steven Guthrie, an assistant professor of outdoor education at Penn-

sylvania's Lock Haven University. And in recent years, action sports have attracted "very competitive people" who "are not very environmentally attuned," Guthrie says. Growing numbers of athletes see the land as an obstacle to be conquered rather than a natural treasure to be protected, he says. That makes things even tougher for federal land managers, for example, who are charged with protecting public lands but have had their resources cut in recent years, Guthrie says.

"The old backpackers' credo, 'Leave only footprints, take only pictures,' is even more true in BASE" jumping — super-risky, generally illegal, very low-altitude parachute jumping from buildings, broadcast antennas, bridges and geological features like cliffs, said Tom Aiello, a veteran jumper in Twin Falls, Idaho, who works on the Web site basejumper.com. Fatality risks in the sport make even hospitable landowners leery of liability, and failing to respect sites quickly leads to having those sites closed to jumpers, Aiello said. [1]

Another clash occurred when snowboarding's popularity took off in the 1970s and '80s, and its young, brash culture conflicted with the more staid world of skiing. In the beginning, when snowboarders were few, "we were undercover, on our best behavior, and we dressed like skiers to seem legitimate," said Bev Sanders, cofounder with her husband of Lake Tahoe, Calif.-based Avalanche Snowboards. But "as soon as there were new kids who didn't realize how tenuous our position was, there was attitude," exacerbated by snowboarders' tendency to cut across ski trails, she said. [2]

Most skiers "visualize[d] snowboarders as a bunch of skate rats who [were] going to terrorize the mountain," said David Schmidt, national sales manager for Burton Snowboards. [3]

Skateboarders have long been in intense conflict with city officials, property owners and office workers looking for a teenager-free spot for an outdoor lunch.

In the past 25 years, whole industries have grown up to capitalize on people's desire to follow action athletes' lead, says the University of Arkansas' Holyfield. "Wilderness" clothing sells to millions who never kayak or snowboard. Travel and leisure companies offer packaged activities that Holyfield dubs "pseudo edgework," like climbing gyms and guided whitewater raft trips that offer the taste of edgy activities with much of the risk removed, she says.

Advertisers have latched onto the idea of "extreme" — often illustrated with action-sports images — to sell all kinds of products, said former pro skateboarder Howell. "There is now an 'extreme pizza' in my neighborhood. . . . Nissan sells an SUV called the 'X-Terra.' . . . There are firms that offer 'extreme consulting,' " he observed. [37]

PepsiCo's action-sports ad campaigns in the 1990s for Mountain Dew — pairing daredevil action with jaded commentary by teenage boys, who intoned,

"Done that. Did that. Been there. Tried that" in response to various extreme stunts — made the beverage one of the world's fastest-growing soft drinks and a nearly $5-billion per-year business, according to New Zealand-based sports historians Booth and Thorpe. [38]

Television's X Games have been a big moneymaker for sponsors and ESPN, generating $40 million in revenues by only their third season, in 1997, says Ricciardi of the Action Sports Association.

One such conflict took place a few years ago at Love Park in downtown Philadelphia, where a "national skateboarding scene had developed" over the previous decade, says Kip. The park's layout was so skateboard-friendly that some pros actually moved to town to practice and shoot videos there, he says.

Love Park was "the skateboarder's equivalent of a neighborhood playground

Sandro Dias of Brazil competes in the Skateboard Vert Men's Final during the 2006 ESPN X Games at the Staples Center in Los Angeles. He won the gold in the event, which uses a vertical ramp that is a larger version of a half-pipe ramp.

Getty Images/Jeff Gross

Bacon didn't get his hoped-for arrest. "We didn't want to cause more trouble than it was worth," said a sergeant at the scene. [5] City officials remained unmoved, however, and skateboarding continues to be illegal in the park.

Indeed, municipalities' and property owners' battle against skateboarders has literally changed landscapes worldwide.

Street spaces increasingly sport rounded, unskatable ledges, and companies have

where you could play a game of pick-up with [basketball super-star] Alan Iverson," Kip says. By the early 2000s, however, then-Mayor John Street was doing everything he could to eliminate skateboarding in the park, including frequent arrests of skateboarders, he says.

Several groups, including the nonprofit Skateboard Advocacy Network (SAN) founded by Kip, struggled for years to convince Street to relent. SAN won endorsements from the major news media for its efforts, and Vista, Calif.-based action-sport shoe-maker DC Shoes anted up a million dollars to pay for 10 years of park upkeep, a "more than adequate" amount to pay for skateboarders' wear and tear, according to Kip.

In 2002, Edmund Bacon, the then-92-year-old retired city planner who'd first envisioned the park in his 1932 senior thesis as an undergraduate architecture student at Cornell University, showed up to protest the city's actions. "I want to ride a skateboard across Love Park and get arrested . . . to protest what the mayor has done," said Bacon, a Philadelphia icon and the father of actor Kevin Bacon. [4]

designed several types of brackets — one popular kind is dubbed a "pig ear" — to put on potentially skatable surfaces of all kinds, says Kip. "It looks terrible, but it does deter skateboarders." Kip says the sale of deterrents is over-enthusiastic. On the University of Pennsylvania's Philadelphia campus, for example, "every horizontal surface will have these things on it, including a ledge as high as your neck" that "in a million years you couldn't get your skateboard up on," he says.

---

[1] Tom Aiello, "Tom Aiello on Ethics," *basejumper.com*, June 27, 2007, www.basejumper.com.

[2] Quoted in Susanna Howe, *(Sick) A Cultural History of Snowboarding* (1998), p. 40.

[3] Quoted in Holly Thorpe, "Snowboarding," *Berkshire Encyclopedia of Extreme Sports* (2007), pp. 286-294.

[4] Quoted in Howard Altman, "Love Burns Bacon," *Philadelphia City Paper*, Oct. 31, 2002, www.citypaper.net.

[5] Quoted in *ibid*.

Action sports have become popular worldwide "far faster than established sports" did, said Booth and Thorpe, thanks to factors including "an historically unique conjuncture of mass communications, corporate sponsors, entertainment industries" and a burgeoning and relatively wealthy young-adult population, they wrote. [39]

"As snowboarding became popularized and incorporated into the mainstream, it adopted many of the trappings of traditional modern sports: corporate

sponsorship, large prize monies, rationalized systems of rules, hierarchical and individualistic star systems, win-at-all costs values and the creation of heroes and heroines," some of whom earn seven-figure incomes, said Thorpe. [40]

Ironies and ambivalence abound, however. For example, the heavy marketing of action sports — viewed by many athletes as individualistic, even countercultural pursuits — has created walking contradictions: "rebel athletes who look like . . . corporate billboards,"

said Michael Messner, a professor of sociology and gender studies at the University of Southern California. [41]

In 1990, for example, world champion snowboarder Craig Kelly retired "at the peak of his career from the competitive circuit that he likened to prostitution," said Thorpe. "Society is full of rules," said Kelly, "and I use the time I spend in the mountains as an opportunity to free myself of all constraints. . . . The [rule-bound, corporate-driven] World Tour restricted the freedom that I found." [42]

Olympics Woo Youths With Extreme Sports

In: snowboarding and BMX; out: baseball and softball.

For the first time in the Summer Olympics, the 2008 Beijing Games awarded medals in bicycle motocross — more commonly known as BMX — an extreme form of bicycle racing and trick riding.

The addition was widely seen as an attempt to capitalize on the success of extreme sports in the Winter Games. "We believe that this introduction will definitely enhance the Olympic program," International Olympic Committee (IOC) President Jacques Rogge said. [1]

Extreme sports initially were introduced to the Winter Games in an effort to make them relevant to suburban youths with no interest in bobsledding or Alpine skiing. Two snowboarding events — giant slalom and half-pipe — led the way for Olympic extreme sports debuting during the 1998 Nagano Games. Snowboard cross was introduced in 2006 in Torino, Italy.

"The Olympics need snowboarding more than snowboarding needs the Olympics," said Dave Schriber, vice president of marketing for Burton, a leading snowboard manufacturer and pioneer. [2]

Indeed, as ESPN's X Games (formerly known as the Extreme Games) has risen in popularity among youths, the Olympics has struggled to keep up.

"The Winter Olympics are about speed," said NBC Sports President Dick Ebersol during his network's coverage of the Winter Olympics in Salt Lake City. "The Winter Games also include sports like freestyle skiing and snowboarding, which resonate with young viewers who have grown up with extreme sports." [3]

But skeptics question the presence of extreme sports among more traditional events. Aside from having its own highly desirable youth demographic, snowboarding also has its own lifestyle and culture. Riders flaunt "attitude," using their own slang and copious tattoos. And the extreme insouciance of many snowboarders makes many critics wonder if they actually take the Olympics seriously.

For example, American snowboarder Shaun White told NBC's Bob Costas during the 2006 Torino Games that the gold medal he won "should help me score more babes." [4]

Even some within the sport question how a culture that has branded itself as anti-establishment can be mainstream at the same time. "The lifestyle that snowboarding is, people want to preserve that," says Jeremy Forster, snowboard director for the U.S. Ski Association. "It's something that these kids do every day. The Olympics come once every four years. They don't want to change for the Olympics." [5]

Nonetheless, extreme sports seem to be integral to the future of the Olympics. Ski cross will makes its debut next year in Vancouver. In-line skating is currently under consideration by the IOC for the 2016 Summer Olympics. Meanwhile, the inclusion of BMX has led to the phasing out of baseball and softball as medal events in 2012.

Even communist China, the host of the 2008 Games, is preparing its future Olympians for this trend by creating its own Extreme Sports Association.

"It's a pretty natural fit, if you look at what kids are interested in," says USA BMX Freestyle President Steve Swope. "I'm not taking away from traditional sports, but if you look at youth culture, it's a natural progression to see action sports in the Olympics." [6]

— *Darrell Dela Rosa*

[1] Liz Clarke, "In the Spotlight: BMX," *The Washington Post,* Aug. 6, 2008, p. H12.
[2] Allen St. John, "I'm on the Olympic Team? Bummer!" *The New York Times Magazine,* Jan. 27, 2002, p. 32.
[3] Dennis Tuttle, "Games Feature Youthful Daring," *The Washington Post,* Feb. 3, 2002, p. Y7.
[4] Lisa Fabrizio, "Olympic Distress," *American Spectator,* Feb. 15, 2006, spectator.org/archives/2006/02/15/olympic-distress.
[5] Pete Iorizzo, "Winter Games Getting Cooler," *The Times Union* (New York), Feb. 5, 2006, p. B1.
[6] Matt Higgins, "Global Reach, and Olympic Goals," *The New York Times,* Aug. 6, 2006, p. B7.

CURRENT SITUATION

Into the Mainstream

Efforts to make some action sports like skateboarding more accessible to the public by adding them to school physical-education classes are gaining adherents. But attempts to gain even wider acceptance for "ultimate fighting" remain controversial, with legislative battles heating up in several states.

Skateboarding is alive and well and evolving, says former pro skateboarder Howell. In fact, the current economic crisis is contributing to that evolution, providing skaters with new obstacles to tackle in cities "with heavy foreclosure rates," he says. Especially in warmer climates like California, even street skateboarders are developing a new taste for skating vertical rather than horizontal surfaces, such as emptied pools in the backyards of foreclosed houses.

With many parks and sidewalks now bristling with skater-hostile features like strategically placed metal brackets, a new generation of specially built skate parks is springing up, many designed based on input from skateboarders, Howell says. The ancestors of this new wave of parks were actually built by skateboarders themselves, beginning in the 1990s.

Continued on p. 314

At Issue:

Should states legalize mixed martial arts bouts?

BERNIE PROFATO
EXECUTIVE DIRECTOR,
OHIO ATHLETIC COMMISSION

WRITTEN FOR *CQ RESEARCHER*, APRIL 2009

*i*ntroduced in the early 1990s, mixed martial arts (MMA) is at times mistakenly called ultimate fighting, because the sport's top promoter is the company Ultimate Fighting Championships (UFC), which is also an advocate for safety standards.

Soon after its introduction, Sen. John McCain, R-Ariz., tried to have MMA banned. He called it "human cockfighting," and, at the time, he was right. It was a no-holds-barred competition. Today, though, all that's changed in states where the sport is legal.

Ohio legalized MMA in 2005 and sets standards for professional and amateur fights. MMA fighters strongly back the regulations because they know the regulations support and protect them. Among other things, there's a 35-and-over class of fighters to keep older contestants from being overmatched by younger, quicker fighters. And in Ohio you must be 18 or older to participate.

Although the public doesn't realize it, some other combat and contact sports are much riskier. MMA has fewer fatalities than football, and MMA referees call more fouls than in boxing.

MMA fighters generally don't spar daily like boxers but only once a week, spending much of their training time on other martial arts like jujitsu. Because of that, they take many fewer blows to the head than boxers and are at less risk for long-term brain injury.

If a boxer is knocked down, the fight usually starts again after a referee issues a mandatory eight count, and referees may permit fights to continue with the boxer not having full capacity. That's dangerous because the brain hasn't rebounded from the last big hit it took. When an MMA fighter is down, the other fighter can go on hitting him, which looks more dangerous to the audience. But, in fact, as soon as the referee sees a fighter is not able to protect himself, the whole fight is over.

Many people are irresistibly attracted to combat sports, and MMA is becoming more and more popular. If states don't legalize it, then unregulated fights will occur in gyms and the back rooms of bars, with no doctors or referees on hand. Fights like that really can be "no holds barred" and can leave fighters badly injured, or even dead.

With regulation, everybody has a fair chance to be protected. But if state legislatures don't legalize and regulate MMA, what will they do when a mother calls crying because her son has been critically injured or killed in an unregulated fight?

ROBERT REILLY
MEMBER, NEW YORK STATE ASSEMBLY,
D-COLONIE

WRITTEN FOR *CQ RESEARCHER*, APRIL 2009

*t*rying to define violence in ultimate fighting mirrors Supreme Court Justice Potter Stewart's comment about the difficulty in defining pornography: "I know it when I see it." The judge was distinguishing between true art and the pornography that some would justify by calling it a form of art. So with ultimate fighting: Although some would justify it as a form of athletic art, most "know violence when they see it" and are appalled by it.

Examples of the permitted violence in recent televised fights include a fighter being knocked apparently unconscious and while falling being kneed in the temple. Another fighter was punched in the head and fell apparently unconscious while the opponent slammed his forearm into his head from a standing position. All of these "moves" are permitted by the rules. Indeed, most people find it offensive when they see a person grabbing another person by the hair and kneeing them in the stomach. Simply stated, you know violence when you see it.

A recent study, "Incidence of Injury in Professional Mixed Martial Arts Competitions," reports that 46.2 percent of mixed martial arts (MMA) fights ended in either knockouts or technical knockouts. In 171 matches, 40.3 percent ended with at least one injured fighter. Interestingly, a knockout was not considered an injury. These statistics are indisputable evidence of the danger of ultimate fighting. The American Medical Association has opposed ultimate fighting and "encourages states that have not banned these events to pass a law doing so." The British Medical Association also calls for a ban based on medical evidence of acute injury and chronic brain damage.

The Minnesota group Advocates for Human Rights summarizes the effects on society of exposure to violence: "To the extent that a society values violence, attaches prestige to violent conduct or defines violence as normal or legitimate or functional behavior, the values of individuals within that society will develop accordingly."

The data make clear that legalizing and promoting ultimate fighting in New York state would be injurious to our people and society as a whole. The physical harm to the contestants has been documented. Legislators simply must make a decision on the effect of ultimate fighting on their society and whether they believe it is detrimental.

A society is defined in part by its art. If ultimate fighting is an art form, we must ask ourselves if this is how we wish to be defined.

Continued from p. 312

In an unused area under Burnside Bridge in Portland, Ore., for example, a group of older skaters with construction-industry experience "just started pouring concrete" to fashion ramps and obstacles like simulated swimming pools, Howell says. Soon the new park was attracting skaters from all over the area, but when the city government found out about the squatters' creation, "they were going to bulldoze it," he says.

The bulldozing plan stopped dead, however, after neighbors protested, telling officials that the busy skate park had stabilized their neighborhood, cutting down on thefts and other street crime, Howell says. Portland experienced a municipal change of heart and now enthusiastically supports the park.

Similar parks modeled on Burnside — where skateboarders themselves "go under an overpass and start pouring concrete" — have sprung up in cities including Oakland, Seattle and Philadelphia, says Howell. Some "eventually get sanctioned by cities, and some don't," but acceptance appears to be increasing, he says. Sen. Barbara Boxer, D-Calif., "even showed up at the one in Oakland, saying, 'I don't want this torn down,' " Howell says.

A growing number of municipalities also have taken the lead in creating parks for skateboarding and other action sports like BMX biking — bike racing across tough terrain and obstacles. The U.S. boasts well over 2,100 such parks today — at least one in every state — a greater than tenfold increase since 1997, when there were only about 165 parks nationwide. [43]

Some parks are far from ideal, says Philadelphia skater and furniture maker Kip. "You often see parks with only one obstacle in the middle and people spending most of their time lined up waiting to use it," he says.

With the local government's blessings, famed daredevil Alain "French Spiderman" Robert climbs 4,980-foot Tianmen Mountain in 2007 in Zhangjiajie, Hunan Province, China.

Getty Images/Emmanuel Aguirre

In at least one municipal park, skaters have "had trouble with non-skating drug users and delinquents," according to the Vista, Calif.-based Tony Hawk Foundation, founded by skateboard superstar Hawk to help non-affluent communities develop action-sports facilities. That can easily happen if a city makes "the mistake of placing the park in a secluded spot," sheltered by trees or hills, "that the delinquents used before the park was built," the foundation notes. In such cases, skateboarding functions as a spectator sport for local drug users. [44]

But many towns are designing parks that echo skaters' preferred habitat — city streets — and are more centrally located and accessible, according to Howell. "With significant input from the skateboard industry and from local skateboarders themselves, cities have hired skate park design firms to provide facilities containing a jumble of design elements simulating the urban spaces that skateboarders have inhabited, often illegally," he wrote. [45]

Some cities around the world are actually designing multi-use spaces intended to invite skateboarding, reversing the trend of driving skateboarders away from multiple-use parks. The movement is at least partly spawned by architects fascinated by the way skilled skateboarders navigate city terrain, says Howell.

The grounds of a new opera house in Oslo, Norway, for example, were specifically designed to be skatable. Architects consulted skateboarders about their favorite surface textures and put unpleasant-to-roll-on rough marble over ramps surrounding the auditorium, where quiet is needed, and smooth, wheel-friendly stone on benches and ledges to invite skating elsewhere. [46]

Little Skaters' League?

In the United States, action sports like skateboarding and rock climbing are finding their way into physical education classes, as schools encourage sedentary kids to exercise.

"We're trying to focus on lifetime activities that are non-competitive and individualized so kids can learn at their own pace," said Jake Gerig, a P.E. teacher at Oak Elementary School, in Albany, Ore., where skateboarding has joined the curriculum. [47]

Skatepass, a Colorado-based company founded by a former professional snowboarder, sells the only in-school skateboarding program. It's currently used in at least 20 school districts in 11 states, according to the company. [48] However-er, in tough economic times, it's not clear how many schools can afford to build rock-climbing walls or buy the Skatepass curriculum, whose kit prices start at $3,000 for 20 sets of helmets, protective pads and boards. [49]

The Action Sports Association's Ricciardi founded his New Jersey-based organization to encourage sports-oriented companies, groups like the Boy Scouts, government agencies and parents to support making action sports mainstream activities that operate like soccer and baseball, with youth recreational leagues, school teams and dedicated facilities in parks and playgrounds. He even envisioned funding for athletes, including college scholarships that could provide a career path to the X Games for the top athletes.

"I'm a skateboard dad, and lots of times I was the only dad in the park watching," Ricciardi says.

"These kids were doing phenomenal things that nobody knew about. But if I went to the baseball field, all the parents were there," he said. Baseball parents "buy kids a new bat when they break one," but if a skateboard causes some damage, "the parents yell." That's because up to now "everything society has provided for youth is old school." It's time to change the vision of sports to highlight the action sports that younger generations love, he says.

"The model is to assimilate it across the country, like the spread of soccer," he continues, noting that the effort already has started with skateboard leagues and clubs in California.

Action sports can help boost businesses and the economy, Ricciardi says. Building parks for skateboarding and BMX biking, for example, could be part of an economic stimulus package, similar to President Franklin D. Roosevelt's programs to boost employment during the Great Depression, he suggests. [50]

Currently, the hundreds of companies involved in action-sports-related marketing haven't really connected with the idea of putting together Little League-type systems to support their sports on a wide basis, says Ricciardi. But he likens the current era to the early days of NASCAR — before stock cars were covered in commercial logos. An equivalent change in action sports like skateboarding is on the horizon, he says.

Not everyone is sure that individualistic action sports ought to be corralled into organized leagues, however. "Even my kids sometimes say, 'Dad, don't mess this up!' " Ricciardi acknowledges.

Fights Break Out

Mixed martial arts may be today's fastest-growing spectator sport, with amateur or pro bouts legal in 40 states and many countries. But MMA advocates are fighting to gain even wider acceptance of the sport, despite criticism of extreme fighting as excessively violent.

MMA matches televised on cable and pay-per-view by the Spike network in the United States have seen audiences swell by double-digit percentages in recent years, with young men the primary viewers. In February, Tampa hosted its first live fight, drawing 7,596 fans, and in April 2008, the first legal live fight in Canada sold out Montreal's 21,000-seat Bell Centre. [51]

The top MMA fight promoter — Las Vegas-based Ultimate Fighting Championship (UFC) — is lobbying Congress to head off federal regulation. Sen. John McCain, R-Ariz., and Rep. Peter T. King, R-N.Y., are sponsoring legislation to create a new federal commission to oversee boxing, and UFC hopes to dissuade lawmakers from including MMA under its jurisdiction. However, King has said that he has no intention of adding MMA to the bill because he fears that doing so might endanger its enactment. [52]

Meanwhile, disputes over efforts to expand or curb MMA's growth are occurring in several states, including Maine, Massachusetts, New Mexico and New York.

MMA's popularity is expanding in Utah, where it is legal, but some local groups worry that the fights could incite brawls. In West Valley City, members of the Planning Commission and City Council are debating a rule that would allow bouts only in 2,000-plus-seat facilities with bolted, immovable seating to discourage chair-throwing fights among spectators. [53]

South Carolina banned live matches in 2003, but now some state senators want to repeal the ban. "As long as we're making sure the sport is not just a barroom brawl, I don't think there will be any serious opposition" to legalizing MMA, said Republican state Sen. Paul Campbell. He argues that "we'd need to outlaw boxing and professional wrestling, too," if the MMA ban were to continue, since it's inconsistent and unfair to ban only one form of combat sport. [54]

But in Webster County, Iowa, Larson, the chairman of the Family Violence Response Team, sees another side to MMA bouts. "As if the violence in the ring isn't enough, drunken spectators brawl during and after the event," she wrote in the local newspaper. "Our already short-staffed police force gets called to break up these fights. David Neil, the Iowa athletic commissioner, reported that at one event he attended, children present had to be placed in the ring for their own protection as fights took place in the audience." [55] ∎

OUTLOOK

Extreme Future?

Action athletes will certainly keep pushing the boundaries, inspired by advancing technology and humans' insatiable curiosity. But analysts aren't sure that the recent boom in extreme sports will continue.

Over the past few decades, as action sports have boomed, the pursuits "have become more and more intense," a trend that looks likely to continue as athletes seek untried challenges, says Guthrie of Pennsylvania's Lock Haven University. Where federal public-land managers once saw kayakers navigating rapids, today they see them plummeting down waterfalls, and BASE jumpers don wingsuits to fly at 100 miles per hour within a few feet of cliff walls, he says.

Increasingly, action athletes are migrating "to the edges of places," away from tightly regulated National Park lands to areas that are more loosely supervised by the Forest Service, for example, Guthrie says. Public lands in the Southwest deserts are especially fragile and prone to environmental damage from the extreme motor sports increasingly practiced there, he says.

Meanwhile, as gender roles continue to change, few doubt that women will continue to be attracted to action sports in greater numbers. Snowboarding, kayaking and paintball were the three fastest-growing sports for women heading into the new millennium, and skateboarding was sixth, while the number of women who surfed every day swelled by 280 percent between 1999 and 2003. [56]

The once-enormous barriers to women's participation in edgy activities "are melting away," says Temple University psychologist Farley, who believes

the barriers were "social and traditional," not related to women's interests or capabilities. [57] He points out that the youngest person ever to climb Mt. Everest is a Nepali woman who was 15 at the time of her first ascent as a guide.

Increases in women's participation aside, however, some analysts predict that action athletes' numbers may soon fall.

While finding that Americans overall participated in more outdoor activities in 2007 than in 2006, the Outdoor Industry Foundation's 2008 survey discovered a falloff among those ages 6 to 17. Among the young, participation in outdoor activities of all kinds (including but not limited to action sports) dropped by 11.6 percent over the year. That may signal a long-term trend, since young people who don't play outdoors "are far less likely to be active participants" in outdoor activities as adults, says the group. [58]

With a major recession and other upheavals such as climate change in the offing, "our society is becoming risky again, and that may cause consumers to seek out security" rather than flirt with danger, says the University of Arkansas' Holyfield.

Idaho State University's Watters concurs. If typical patterns hold for how activities change from generation to generation, "we're going to see less of an interest" in action sports over the next few decades, he says. "Each generation sort of reinvents itself, and wants to be a little different," so the boomers' and generation Xers' love of action sports will likely wane among their children. ∎

About the Author

Staff writer **Marcia Clemmitt** is a veteran social-policy reporter who previously served as editor in chief of *Medicine & Health* and staff writer for *The Scientist*. She has also been a high-school math and physics teacher. She holds a liberal arts and sciences degree from St. John's College, Annapolis, and a master's degree in English from Georgetown University. Her recent reports include "Preventing Cancer" and "Public-Works Projects."

Notes

[1] For background, see Kirk Penton, "Fighter's Career Over," *Winnipeg* [Alberta] *Sun* Web site, Feb. 8, 2009, www.winnipegsun.com/news/winnipeg/2009/02/08/8307306-sun.html.

[2] Keith Grienke, "CFC 1 Prelim Play-by-Play: Perez and Lewis Bring the House Down," *Cageplay.com* blog, Feb. 8, 2009, www.cageplay.com/blog/2009/02/08/cfc-1-prelim-play-by-play-perez-and-lewis-bring-the-house-down.

[3] Quoted in Maria Villaseñor, "WVC Looks to Regulate Ultimate Fighting," *The Salt Lake Tribune*, Feb. 11, 2009, www.sltrib.com.

[4] Michael Hiestand, "Foray Into Mixed Martial Arts Gives CBS Optimism," *USA Today* online, June 1, 2008, www.usatoday.com.

[5] Dawn C. Chmielewski, "ESPN Plans to Launch Online Network Dedicated to 'Action Sports,' " *Los Angeles Times*, July 30, 2008, http://articles.latimes.com/2008/jul/30/business/fi-espn30.

[6] Holly Thorpe, "Snowboarding," *Berkshire Encyclopedia of Extreme Sports* (2007), pp. 286-294.

[7] Kenneth P. Burres, *The Spine in Extreme Sports*, www.fitcentric.com/download/Spine%20in%20Extrm%20Sports_10_03.pd.

[8] Dave Doyle, "MMA Myths Debunked Again," Yahoo! Sports Canada, May 30, 2008, http://ca.sports.yahoo.com/mma/news?slug=dd-mmamyths052908&prov=yhoo&type=lgns.

[9] Teresa A. Larson, letter to the editor, *The* [Fort Dodge, Iowa] *Messenger*, Dec. 16, 2007, www.messengernews.net.

[10] Joe Paraskevas, "Mixed Martial Arts: Mayor Blames Officials for Injury," *Winnipeg Free Press*, Feb. 19, 2009, www.winnipegfreepress.com/local/mixed_martial_arts_mayor_blames_officials_for_injury-39836592.html.

[11] "Mixed Martial Arts Ban Urged After Teen Suffers Brain Injury, Seizures," Canadian Broadcasting News, Feb. 9, 2009, www.cbc.ca.

[12] Luke Thomas, "Lift the Ban Watch: South Carolina Makes Progress, Problems Arise in Canada," *Bloody Elbow* Web site, Feb. 10, 2009, www.bloodyelbow.com.

[13] David Plotz, "Fight Clubbed," *Slate*, Nov. 17, 1999, www.slate.com.

[14] *Ibid.*

[15] For background, see W.B. Dickinson, Jr., "Deaths and Injuries in Sports," *Editorial Research Reports 1963*, Vol. II, June 12, 1963.

[16] Douglas Booth and Holly Thorpe, "The Meaning of Extreme," *Berkshire Encyclopedia*

of *Extreme Sports* (2007), pp. 181-197.

[17] Y. Tomida, *et al.*, "Injuries in Elite Motorcycle Racing in Japan," *British Journal of Sports Medicine*, August 2005, pp. 508-511.

[18] "The Teenage Brain: Extreme Genes + Exploitation," *Wipe Out* Web site, Knowledge Network/Brain Injury Association of Canada, http://wipeout.knowledgenetwork.ca/wipeout.html.

[19] "Avocations and Occupations," *Risk Insights*, November 2004, p. 11.

[20] Thorpe, "Snowboarding," *op. cit.*

[21] *Ibid.*

[22] "New National Study Is First Since 1970s to Document Full Range of Sports Injuries," press release, American Sports Data, May 15, 2003, www.americansportsdata.com.

[23] Thorpe, "Snowboarding," *op. cit.*

[24] "Wide Variety of Physical Activities May Protect Teens Against Risky Behavior," press release, University of North Carolina, Gillings School of Global Public Health, April 5, 2006, www.sph.unc.edu.

[25] Quoted in Kathryn Jay, *More Than Just a Game: Sports In American Life Since 1945* (2004), p. 233.

[26] Quoted in Thorpe, "Snowboarding," *op. cit.* See also Austin Murphy, "What a Ride," *Sports Illustrated Vault*, Feb. 27, 2006, http://vault.sportsillustrated.cnn.com/vault/article/magazine/MAG1105807/index.htm.

[27] "The Teenage Brain: Extreme Genes + Exploitation," *op. cit.*

[28] Thorpe, "Snowboarding," *op. cit.*

[29] Holly Thorpe, "The Psychology of Extreme Sports," in Tatian Ryba and Robert Shinke, eds., *The Cultural Turn in Sport and Exercise Psychology*, forthcoming.

[30] Booth and Thorpe, *op. cit.*

[31] Michael B. Poliakoff, *Combat Sports in the Ancient World: Competition, Violence, and Culture* (1995), p. 28.

[32] George M. Hollenback, "Arrichion's Last Fight: What Really Happened?" *Journal of Combative Sport*, September 2003, http://ejmas.com/jcs/jcsart_hollenback_0903.htm.

[33] "Lonoikamakahiki," *Hawaii Alive* Web site, www.hawaiialive.org and Daniel Brock, "Archaeologist Works to Preserve Hawaiian Sledding," *West Hawaii Today*, April 20, 2008, www.westhawaiitoday.com/articles/2008/04/20/local/local05.txt.

[34] Quoted in Roland Huntford, *Shackleton* (1985), p. 365.

[35] Ron Watters, "Generational Analysis: A New Method of Examining the History of Outdoor Adventure Activities and a Possible Predictor of Long Range Trends," 2006, www.isu.edu/outdoor/Generations.html.

[36] *Ibid.*

[37] Ocean Howell, "Extreme Market Research: Tales from the Underbelly of Skater-Cool," *Topic* magazine, spring 2003, www.webdelsol.com/Topic/articles,04/howell.html.

[38] Booth and Thorpe, *op. cit.*

[39] *Ibid.*

[40] Thorpe, "Snowboarding," *op. cit.*

[41] Quoted in Thorpe, "Snowboarding," *op. cit.*

[42] Quoted in *ibid.*

[43] Ocean Howell, "Skatepark as Neoliberal Playground: Urban Governance, Recreation Space, and the Cultivation of Personal Responsibility," *Space and Culture*, Aug. 1, 2008.

[44] "Frequently Asked Questions," Tony Hawk Foundation Web site, www.tonyhawkfoundation.org/faq.asp.

[45] Howell, "Skatepark as Neoliberal Playground," *op. cit.*

[46] Andrew Blum, "New Oslo Opera House Is Really a Stealth Skate Park," *Wired*, Nov. 24, 2008, www.wired.com.

[47] Quoted in Tracy Loew, "Skateboarding Kickflips Into P.E.," *USA Today*, June 18, 2008.

[48] "Company Q & A, Skatepass," *Malakye.com* Web site, March 1, 2008, www.malakye.com/asp/front/CMSPage.asp?TYP_ID=2&ID=1252.

[49] Loew, *op. cit.*

[50] For background, see Marcia Clemmitt, "Public-Works Projects," *CQ Researcher*, Feb. 20, 2009, pp. 153-176.

[51] Jeannie Naujeck, "UFC Ready to Strike," *Nashville Business Journal*, Feb. 13, 2009, http://nashville.bizjournals.com.

[52] Frederic J. Frommer, "The Influence Game: Mixed Martial Arts Lobbyists Seek Escape From Federal Regulation's Hold," The Associated Press, [Minneapolis-St. Paul] *Star Tribune.com*, Feb. 3, 2009, www.startribune.com.

[53] Villaseñor, *op. cit.*

[54] Josh Eboch, "Bill Would Legalize 'Ultimate Fighting' Bouts," *Charleston* [South Carolina] *City Paper*, March 26, 2008, www.charlestoncitypaper.com.

[55] Larson, *op. cit.*

[56] Thorpe, "Gender and Extreme Sports," *op. cit.*

[57] For background, see Richard L. Worsnop, "Gender Equity in Sports," *CQ Researcher*, April 18, 1997, pp. 337-360.

[58] "Outdoor Recreation Participation Report 2008," Outdoor Foundation/Outdoor Industry Association, 2008, www.outdoorfoundation.org, p. 8.

FOR MORE INFORMATION

BASEjumper.com, 277 Mountain View Dr., Brentwood, CA 94513; www.basejumper.com. Web site provides information and discussion about issues of concern to low-altitude parachutists known as BASE jumpers.

ESPN Action Sports, ESPN Plaza, Bristol, CT 06010; http://espn.go.com/action. Web site of the TV network that broadcasts the X Games provides news about action sports.

Gravity Sports International, 571 Cheshire St., Berlin, NH 03570; (603) 783-9692; www.gravitysportsinternational.com. Organization promotes sports like street luge and gravity biking.

MMA Fighting.com, www.mmafighting.com. Online magazine provides news from around the world on mixed martial arts.

National Parks Traveler, www.nationalparkstraveler.com. Independent webzine reports on issues involving national parks, including action-sports activities in the parks.

Tony Hawk Foundation, 1611-A S. Melrose Dr. #360, Vista, CA 92081; (760) 477-2479; www.tonyhawkfoundation.org/contact_us.asp. Nonprofit supports public skateboard parks in low-income communities.

United States of America Snowboard Association, P.O. Box 3927, Truckee, CA 96160; www.usasa.org. Promotes and regulates snowboarding competitions.

Wipe Out Web site, Knowledge Network television, Canada; http://wipeout.knowledgenetwork.ca/wipeout.html. Dramatic videos show the dangers of sports-related brain injuries, a leading cause of death and disability among children.

Bibliography

Selected Sources

Books

Booth, Douglas, and Holly Thorpe, eds., *Berkshire Encyclopedia of Extreme Sports*, Berkshire Publishing Group, 2007.
Sports historians from two New Zealand universities assemble essays analyzing the history, demographics and philosophy of action sports. The collection includes commentary on media coverage, rules and governing bodies and controversial issues such as women's participation.

Howe, Susanna, *(Sick): A Cultural History of Snowboarding*, St. Martin's Press, 1998.
A writer and amateur snowboarder chronicles the sport's development from the invention of the first wooden boards through its debut as an Olympic event.

Jay, Kathryn, *More Than Just a Game: Sports in American Life Since 1945*, Columbia University Press, 2004.
A historian and writer chronicles the development of modern sports, including action sports and the X Games.

Soden, Garrett, *Defying Gravity: Land Divers, Roller Coasters, Gravity Bums, and the Human Obsession With Falling*, W.W. Norton, 2003.
The history of gravity sports extends back centuries to the ancient "land divers" of the Vanuatu Islands in the South Pacific.

Articles

Adams, Glenn, "Bill Seeks Maine's Recognition, Regulation of Mixed Martial Arts," The Associated Press, *The Seattle Times*, March 18, 2009, http://seattletimes.nwsource.com/html/politics/2008880278_apxgrmixedmartialarts.html.
Maine joins the list of states debating regulation of mixed martial arts (MMA) competition. A cosponsor of legislation to regulate MMA said "there's an opportunity, there's an interest, there's a fan base" for the sport, but no "guiding structure to let this happen." But an opponent urged lawmakers to shun "the type of vicious events that are contemplated in the bill."

Appleton, Josie, "What's So Extreme About Extreme Sports," *Spiked*, Aug. 30, 2005, www.spiked-online.com/Articles/0000000CAD26.htm.
A British online magazine distinguishes between action sports that are true sports and others that "are little more than PR products," whose participants "will only perform for the camera." Free running, for example — in which participants use street features and urban architecture as a venue for performing acrobatics — "became a media phenomenon before it built up a decent base of participants; now it can be more for show than self-development," remarks the author.

Borden, Mark, "Shaun White's Business Is Red Hot," *Fast Company.com*, Jan. 14, 2009, www.fastcompany.com.
Olympic snowboarding gold medalist Shaun White parlays his athletic career and business savvy into a marketing behemoth, complete with his own line of action sportswear.

Detrick, Ben, "Skateboarding Rolls Out of the Suburbs," *The New York Times*, Nov. 11, 2007, Sec. 9, p. 8.
Interest in skateboarding grows in low-income and minority urban communities.

Loew, Tracy, "Skateboarding Kickflips Into PE," *USA Today*, June 18, 2008, p. 7D.
Some students who might not make the team in traditional sports find their inner athletes when schools offer skateboarding lessons.

Mickle, Tripp, "China: Action's Next Frontier," *Sports Business Journal*, April 14, 2008, p. 1, www.sportsbusinessjournal.com/article/58658.
In 2004, the Chinese government created the Chinese Extreme Sports Foundation to push competition and commercialization of action sports, but it can be a tough sell in a culture that's long emphasized community, not individual, effort.

Naujeck, Jeannie, "UFC Ready to Strike: Growing Sports Promotion Makes Entry Into Nashville," *Nashville Business Journal*, Feb. 13, 2009, http://nashville.bizjournals.com.
Advocates of "ultimate fighting" say cities that open their venues to the live bouts can boost local economies by tens of millions of dollars.

Reports and Studies

"Outdoor Recreation Participation Report 2008," Outdoor Foundation/Outdoor Industry Association, 2008, www.outdoorfoundation.org/pdf/ResearchParticipation2008.pdf.
While overall outdoor-recreation participation ticked up between 2006 and 2007, a steep 11.6 percent drop in participation by children and teens ages 6 through 17 suggests the craze for action and adventure sports may be dying out.

Howell, Ocean, "The Poetics of Security: Skateboarding, Urban Design, and the New Public Space," Urban Action 2001 Web site, Urban Studies Program, San Francisco State University, http://skateboarding.transworld.net/2003/01/09/the-poetics-of-security/.
A former professional skateboarder chronicles the history of media depictions of skateboarding and the long-running battles between skateboarders and property owners over the use of public space.

The Next Step:

Additional Articles from Current Periodicals

Media Influence

Chmielewski, Dawn C., "ESPN Courts Fans of 'Action Sports,' " *Los Angeles Times*, July 30, 2008, p. C1.

ESPN is establishing its Action Sports Network to give extreme sports extended coverage, hoping to cultivate a network audience beyond the middle-aged male sports fan.

Rodriguez, Rick, "What's a Sport?" *Sacramento Bee*, July 14, 2007, p. A18.

Pop culture, new trends and what's covered on sports-oriented television channels are changing viewer perceptions about extreme sports and other competitions.

Warren, Allan, "Media Image of Injured Skier Is Wrong," *Anchorage Daily News*, April 23, 2008, p. B6.

A participant was injured in an extreme skiing competition benefiting charity, but the media criticize his participation as a "stupid decision" brought on by a competition.

Olympics

Glock, Allison, "Shaun White, Snowboarding's Hottest Star, Is Set to Blow Up in Skateboarding, Too," *ESPN The Magazine*, July 2006, sports.espn.go.com/espnmag/story?id=3246499.

Olympic snowboarding gold medalist Shaun White is attempting to find similar success in skateboarding at the X Games.

Gomez, Brian, "Rolling Toward Ratification," *The* (Colorado Springs) *Gazette*, June 18, 2008, p. SP1.

Roller sports are seeking to become a medal event during the Summer Games of 2016.

Ruibal, Sal, "BMX Racing Gets Bump From Beijing," *USA Today*, Sept. 3, 2008, p. 9C.

BMX's successful Olympic debut in Beijing has spawned interest in the racing aspect of the sport.

Safety

Hachat, Josh, "Fallen Hero: NHRA Need to Look Into Safety Issues," *Newark Advocate* (Ohio), June 25, 2008, p. 1.

An increasing number of fatalities indicates just how dangerous — perhaps too dangerous — Funny Car racing can be.

Hooker, Sara, "Skateboarding Accident a Lesson to All, Doctors Say," *Chicago Daily Herald*, Aug. 16, 2007, p. 1.

A fatal skateboarding accident has led trauma experts and neurosurgeons at an Illinois hospital to push helmet use as one of the hospital's top safety initiatives.

Naito, Jon, "For Freeskiers, Risk Is a Part of the Culture," *Seattle Post-Intelligencer*, Feb. 23, 2008, p. A1.

Extreme skiers are disciplined and prepared during their outings, but many acknowledge that there is a heightened risk for serious injury in what they do.

Norcross, Don, "Top Skateboarders Say Danger Part of Business," *San Diego Union-Tribune*, July 31, 2008, p. D6.

Skateboarders say there is a certain level of danger in any sport, but that participants should make their own decisions over whether or not to partake.

Ultimate Fighting

Jenkins, Nate, "Violent Sport Regulations Are Often Lax," The Associated Press, Feb. 23, 2008.

Tragedy and injury will inevitably force states to increase regulation for sanctioned mixed martial arts matches.

Porretto, John, "Mixed Martial Arts Fighter Dies After Injuries in Bout," The Associated Press, Dec. 3, 2007.

A mixed martial arts fighter has died in a hospice six weeks after suffering injuries and a stroke during a sanctioned bout in Houston.

Schneiderman, R.M., "Companies Warm to Sponsoring Mixed Martial Arts," *The New York Times*, Jan. 21, 2009, p. B3.

Mixed martial arts has long been considered too risky for corporate America, but recent success has led to mainstream advertisers dabbling in sponsorship deals.

Sievert, Steve, "Sport Has Survived and Is Here to Stay," *Houston Chronicle*, Dec. 10, 2007, p. D2.

Lawmakers and regulators have tried to keep ultimate fighting relegated to underground status, but increasing popularity has led it to the mainstream.

CITING *CQ RESEARCHER*

Sample formats for citing these reports in a bibliography include the ones listed below. Preferred styles and formats vary, so please check with your instructor or professor.

<u>MLA STYLE</u>

Jost, Kenneth. "Rethinking the Death Penalty." <u>CQ Researcher</u> 16 Nov. 2001: 945-68.

<u>APA STYLE</u>

Jost, K. (2001, November 16). Rethinking the death penalty. *CQ Researcher, 11,* 945-968.

<u>CHICAGO STYLE</u>

Jost, Kenneth. "Rethinking the Death Penalty." *CQ Researcher,* November 16, 2001, 945-968.

In-depth Reports on Issues in the News

Are you writing a paper?

Need backup for a debate?

Want to become an expert on an issue?

For 80 years, students have turned to *CQ Researcher* for in-depth reporting on issues in the news. Reports on a full range of political and social issues are now available. Following is a selection of recent reports:

Civil Liberties
Closing Guantánamo, 2/09
Limiting Lawsuits, 12/08
Affirmative Action, 10/08
Gay Marriage Showdowns, 9/08
America's Border Fence, 9/08
Immigration Debate, 2/08

Crime/Law
Mexico's Drug War, 12/08
Prostitution Debate, 5/08
Public Defenders, 4/08
Gun Violence, 5/07

Education
Reading Crisis? 2/08
Discipline in Schools, 2/08
Student Aid, 1/08
Racial Diversity in Public Schools, 9/07
Stress on Students, 7/07

Environment/Society
Future of Journalism, 3/09
Confronting Warming, 1/09
Reducing Carbon Footprint, 12/08
Protecting Wetlands, 10/08
Buying Green, 2/08

Health/Safety
Regulating Toxic Chemicals, 1/09
Preventing Cancer, 1/09
Heart Health, 9/08
Global Food Crisis, 6/08

Politics/Economy
Future of the GOP, 3/09
Middle-Class Squeeze, 3/09
Public-Works Projects, 2/09
The Obama Presidency, 1/09
The National Debt, 11/08
Financial Bailout, 10/08

Upcoming Reports

Wrongful Convictions, 4/10/09   High-Speed Trains, 4/17/09   Judicial Elections, 4/24/09

ACCESS

CQ Researcher is available in print and online. For access, visit your library or www.cqresearcher.com.

STAY CURRENT

To receive notice of upcoming *CQ Researcher* reports, or learn more about *CQ Researcher* products, subscribe to the free e-mail newsletters, *CQ Researcher Alert!* and *CQ Researcher News*: http://cqpress.com/newsletters.

PURCHASE

To purchase a *CQ Researcher* report in print or electronic format (PDF), visit www.cqpress.com or call 866-427-7737. Single reports start at $15. Bulk purchase discounts and electronic-rights licensing are also available.

SUBSCRIBE

Annual full-service *CQ Researcher* subscriptions—including 44 reports a year, monthly index updates, and a bound volume—start at $803. Add $25 for domestic postage.

CQ Researcher Online offers a backfile from 1991 and a number of tools to simplify research. For pricing information, call 800-834-9020, ext. 1906, or e-mail librarysales@cqpress.com.

CQResearcher

Published by CQ Press, a division of SAGE Publications

www.cqresearcher.com

Business Bankruptcy

Are U.S. bankruptcy laws effective?

Some of the largest bankruptcies in U.S. history have occurred in the past seven months, led by Lehman Brothers investment bank and Washington Mutual savings and loan. The Obama administration is now threatening General Motors and Chrysler with a government-managed bankruptcy if they don't come up with an aggressive restructuring plan in short order. While the two automakers' woes have captured the headlines, thousands of other firms — many in retail and real estate — are quietly trying to avoid bankruptcy court. Last year the number of bankruptcies rose more than 50 percent over the previous year — to more than 43,000. Some experts say the government needs to step in and lend money to bankrupt companies while other critics say Congress made emerging from bankruptcy almost impossible for some companies when it amended the Bankruptcy Code in 2005.

Circuit City, the nation's second-largest electronics retailer, announced in January it was going out of business after an unsuccessful effort to reorganize under Chapter 11 of the Bankruptcy Code. It had 34,000 employees and more than 700 stores.

CQ Researcher • April 10, 2009 • www.cqresearcher.com
Volume 19, Number 14 • Pages 321-344

Cover: Getty Images/Mark Ralston

CQ Researcher

April 10, 2009
Volume 19, Number 14

MANAGING EDITOR: Thomas J. Colin
tcolin@cqpress.com

ASSISTANT MANAGING EDITOR: Kathy Koch
kkoch@cqpress.com

ASSOCIATE EDITOR: Kenneth Jost

STAFF WRITERS: Thomas J. Billitteri, Marcia Clemmitt, Peter Katel

CONTRIBUTING WRITERS: Rachel Cox, Sarah Glazer, Alan Greenblatt, Barbara Mantel, Patrick Marshall, Tom Price, Jennifer Weeks

DESIGN/PRODUCTION EDITOR: Olu B. Davis

ASSISTANT EDITOR: Darrell Dela Rosa

FACT-CHECKING: Eugene J. Gabler, Michelle Harris

EDITORIAL INTERN: Vyomika Jairam

CQ PRESS

A Division of SAGE

PRESIDENT AND PUBLISHER:
John A. Jenkins

EXECUTIVE DIRECTOR,
REFERENCE INFORMATION GROUP:
Alix B. Vance

CQ Press is a registered trademark of Congressional Quarterly Inc.

CQ Researcher (ISSN 1056-2036) is printed on acid-free paper. Published weekly, except; (Jan. wk. 1) (May wk. 4) (July wks. 1, 2) (Aug. wks. 3, 4) (Nov. wk. 4) and (Dec. wk. 4), by CQ Press, a division of SAGE Publications. Annual full-service subscriptions start at $803. For pricing, call 1-800-834-9020, ext. 1906. To purchase a CQ Researcher report in print or electronic format (PDF), visit www. cqpress.com or call 866-427-7737. Single reports start at $15. Bulk purchase discounts and electronic-rights licensing are also available. Periodicals postage paid at Washington, D.C., and additional mailing offices. POSTMASTER: Send address changes to CQ Researcher, 2300 N St., N.W., Suite 800, Washington, DC 20037.

Business Bankruptcy

BY BARBARA MANTEL

THE ISSUES

"I f you dare, climb aboard Terminator Salvation: The Ride," Six Flags challenges on its Web page for the state-of-the-art roller coaster opening this spring at its Los Angeles theme park. But Six Flags, which operates theme, water and animal parks across the country, is in desperate need of its own salvation. While executives say the company has plenty of cash to finance its operations, it does not make enough to service its enormous debt. Talks with bondholders to restructure nearly $900 million in debt have hit a snag, and the company may have to file for bankruptcy. President Mark Shapiro said the company's parks would remain open no matter what happens in its debt negotiations, which he called "a back-of-the-house issue exclusively." [1]

But executives have to be wondering how many patrons would feel comfortable taking the "five belly-flopping hills" of a bankrupt company's newest roller coaster or any other high-speed attraction, perhaps worrying it was cutting back on safety measures.

While the potential bankruptcy of General Motors or Chrysler is front page news, thousands of other companies, like Six Flags, are less noisily trying to avoid that same fate. [2] Tens of thousands have already succumbed. According to the federal government, 43,546 businesses filed for bankruptcy in 2008, a 54 percent increase from the year before. That number also exceeds the wave of bankruptcies in 2002 that followed the last recession,

Thrill-seekers take the plunge on "Superman: Ride of Steel" at the Six Flags Amusement Park in Agawam, Mass. Along with major corporations like General Motors and Chrysler, the company is one of thousands of U.S. firms trying to avoid bankruptcy. More than 43,000 businesses filed for bankruptcy last year, a 54 percent increase over the year before.

AFP/Getty Images/Thomas Bjoernflaten

when 38,540 businesses filed for protection. [3] (*See chart, p. 327.*)

Those earlier bankruptcies were heavily concentrated in the telecommunications, media and technology industries of the dot.com bust. But this time around, bankruptcies are hitting everything from financial institutions and retailers to newspapers and energy companies. Some of the biggest names to file for bankruptcy in 2008 include the investment bank Lehman Brothers Holdings — the largest bankruptcy in U.S. history — the media firm Tribune Company, Washington Mutual, a savings and loan, and IndyMac Bancorp, according to data compiled by BankruptcyData.com. The list in 2009 includes, so far, the global

Lyondell Chemical Co., gaming giant Trump Entertainment Resorts, door manufacturer Masonite Corp. and the Journal Register Co., a publisher of regional newspapers. (*See box, p. 325.*)

"Nothing is looking good right now," says Jack Williams, resident scholar at the American Bankruptcy Institute and a professor at Georgia State University College of Law. The economy contracted at a 6.2 percent rate in the fourth quarter of 2008, the largest decline since 1982, and many economists are predicting the worst recession since World War II. "Real estate hasn't hit bottom yet," says Williams, "retail is in a state of oversupply and under-demand, and the auto industry is failing." [4]

Williams expects the bankruptcy news to only worsen as the year progresses. Most small businesses facing bankruptcy can't survive no matter what help they receive, so they liquidate under Chapter 7 of the Bankruptcy Code, but larger companies often seek protection under Chapter 11, which allows them to try and reorganize. (*See chapter definitions, p. 328.*) Williams is predicting a 50 percent increase in Chapter 11 filings compared to last year, primarily in retail, real estate and food establishments. "It will mean that in all likelihood everyone in the U.S. will be dealing with a company in bankruptcy, either as a creditor, a customer or we will know an employee."

Many experts agree that the single biggest factor behind the run-up in bankruptcies is the recent era of easy money. "Even more important than the economy, at least for public companies, is how much debt companies have taken on," says George Putnam,

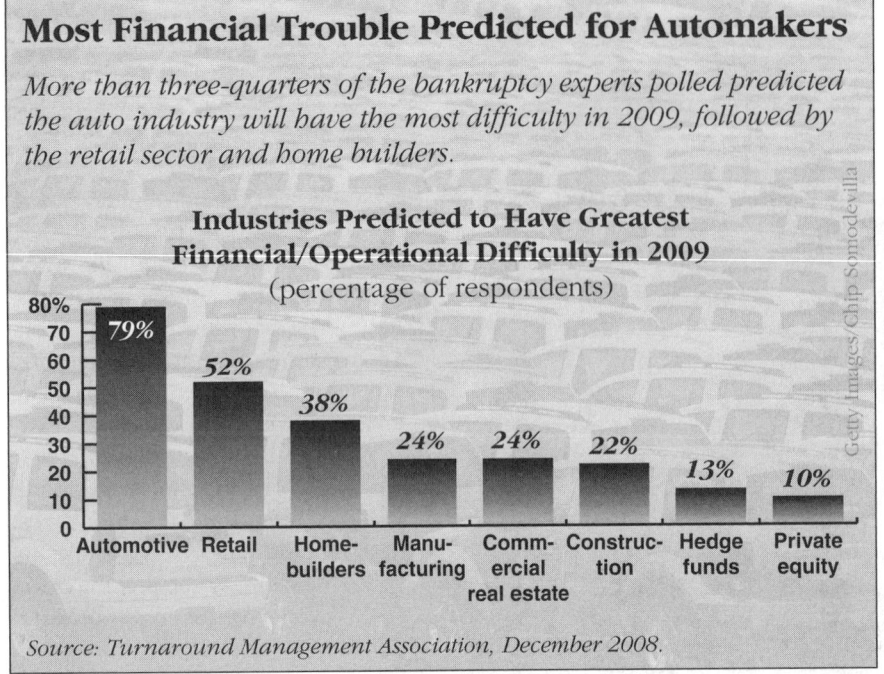

Most Financial Trouble Predicted for Automakers

More than three-quarters of the bankruptcy experts polled predicted the auto industry will have the most difficulty in 2009, followed by the retail sector and home builders.

Industries Predicted to Have Greatest Financial/Operational Difficulty in 2009
(percentage of respondents)

- Automotive: 79%
- Retail: 52%
- Home-builders: 38%
- Manu-facturing: 24%
- Comm-ercial real estate: 24%
- Construc-tion: 22%
- Hedge funds: 13%
- Private equity: 10%

Source: Turnaround Management Association, December 2008.

founder of New Generation Research in Boston. "The more debt you have out there, the more likely there are to be bankruptcies." Like consumers and the government, businesses have been on something of a borrowing binge, to finance acquisitions, expand, increase dividends to shareholders and cover a myriad of other expenditures. The most recent wave began in 2003, as companies issued an increasing number of high-yield bonds — bonds rated "speculative grade" or below "investment grade," meaning the chance of default is higher than for other bonds. In addition, private equity firms contributed to the borrowing binge by using leverage to buy the stock of public companies and convert them to private ownership and pay themselves dividends.

When the recession hit in December 2007, many companies couldn't make debt payments as their revenues fell. With credit markets frozen and lenders reluctant to refinance that debt, many companies responded by seeking bankruptcy protection under Chapter 11.

Not all companies are able to reorganize; some end up liquidating. "For large companies, the success rate of emerging from Chapter 11 as a going concern is probably 60-65 percent," says Edward Altman, a corporate finance expert at New York University's Stern School of Business. But this year and next, Altman expects "the ability to emerge will be considerably lower." For example, Linen 'n Things, jewelry and furniture retailer Fortunoff and department store chain Mervyns all ended up shutting their doors after filing for Chapter 11.

Experts blame the rise in Chapter 11 liquidations on several factors, including the dramatic decline in the number of firms that typically loan to companies in bankruptcy so they can continue to operate and eventually emerge. In addition, the type of creditor holding a company's pre-bankruptcy debt has expanded beyond traditional lenders to include private equity firms and hedge funds. "They don't care whether the company can be rehabilitated," says Williams. "For them, it's a way through a debt position to control assets out of bankruptcy for cents on the dollar," and to perhaps arrange the sale of those assets to purchasers in which they may also have a stake.

Moreover, over the past nine years there has been a dramatic shift in control of the bankruptcy process from a company's managers to its creditors. According to Barry Adler, a professor at New York University School of Law, it started in about 2000 as lenders began to routinely write provisions into loan agreements that, when triggered by the debtor's financial distress, shifted control of the debtor's financial decisions from management to creditors. [5]

Then in 2005, Congress amended the Bankruptcy Code in ways that further limited a debtor's control over the bankruptcy process.

This striking change in bankruptcy has generated widespread controversy. Some, like Adler, think it may be for the best. "This is just my theoretical speculation, but there is good reason to think that the change from equity and management control to creditor control has sped the inevitable liquidation of firms, and for the better," says Adler. "If a firm is not going to survive because it is economically unviable, then it isn't clear that society is served by delaying the inevitable."

But others say firms that should survive are no longer being given the chance. "Today, Chapter 11 is not a process in which a debtor and creditors work together to rehabilitate a debtor," said Harvey Miller, lead bankruptcy lawyer for Lehman Brothers, in recent congressional testimony. Debtor protections have been stripped away, he explained. "Virtually every group with an effective lobbyist came forward and was able to obtain special-interest legislation," including creditors like shopping center and commercial-property owners who hold a debtor's leases, and financial institutions that loan a company money. [6]

In this era of record-breaking bankruptcies, here are some of the questions companies, suppliers, bankers, stockholders, bondholders, legal experts and members of Congress are asking:

Should the federal government provide financing to bankrupt companies?

Seven weeks after Lyondell Chemical filed for Chapter 11 in early January, the judge in the case approved an $8 billion "debtor-in-possession," or DIP, loan to the Houston-based company, one of the largest bankruptcy loans in U.S. history. Such loans are "the fuel that keeps companies going through bankruptcy, allowing them to continue paying their suppliers and their employees as they try to become profitable again," according to Thompson Financial News. [7] Exit financing, another class of bankruptcy loans, is needed at the end of the process when the company is ready to emerge from Chapter 11.

But despite the record-setting size of Lyondell's loan, most companies are struggling to find bankruptcy financing, and the consequence is, essentially, death. "Without bankruptcy financing, you can neither keep the company alive long enough to fix it or to sell it," says Jeffrey Wurst, a bankruptcy lawyer in Uniondale, N.Y. Experts estimate that as recently as a year and a half ago as many as 30 companies were vying to provide bankruptcy financing, and today there are fewer than five.

Historically, financial institutions have been eager to provide the cash necessary for firms to survive the bankruptcy process because these loans are the first to be paid back, command high interest rates and fees and rarely default. "I get e-mails every day from lenders saying they are looking to make DIP loans," says Wurst. But they can no longer find borrowers that look like a good risk, he says.

Companies entering bankruptcy these days already have pledged so many of their assets as collateral for earlier loans that there's nothing left to pledge to a new lender. Not only have companies put up their inventories, accounts receivable, equipment and plants as collateral, oftentimes they have put up intangibles like intellectual property as well, long before bankruptcy was even contemplated.

Lehman's $700 Billion Bankruptcy Is Largest

The $700 billion bankruptcy filing by Lehman Brothers in September 2008 was the largest such filing in 20 years and twice as large as the second-largest bankruptcy — Washington Mutual — which failed 11 days after Lehman.

The 20-Largest Public Company Bankruptcy Filings Since 1980
(in $ millions)

Company	Bankruptcy date	Company type	Assets
Lehman Brothers Holdings Inc.	Sept. 15, 2008	Investment bank	$691,063
Washington Mutual Inc.	Sept. 26, 2008	Savings and loan holding co.	$327,913
WorldCom, Inc.	July 21, 2002	Telecommunications	$103,914
Enron Corp.	Dec. 2, 2001	Energy trading, natural gas	$65,503
Conseco, Inc.	Dec. 17, 2002	Financial services holding co.	$61,392
Pacific Gas and Electric Co.	April 6, 2001	Electricity and natural gas	$36,152
Texaco, Inc.	April 12, 1987	Petroleum and petrochemicals	$34,940
Financial Corp. of America	Sept. 9, 1988	Financial services and savings and loans	$33,864
Refco Inc.	Oct. 17, 2005	Brokerage services	$33,333
IndyMac Bancorp, Inc.	July 31, 2008	Bank holding company	$32,734
Global Crossing Ltd.	Jan. 28, 2002	Global communications carrier	$30,185
Bank of New England Corp.	Jan. 7, 1991	Interstate bank holding company	$29,773
Lyondell Chemical Co.	Jan. 6, 2009	Global manufacturer of chemicals	$27,392
Calpine Corp.	Dec. 20, 2005	Integrated power company	$27,216
New Century Financial Corp.	April 2, 2007	Real estate investment trust	$26,147
UAL Corp.	Dec. 9, 2002	Passenger air carrier	$25,197
Delta Air Lines Inc.	Sept. 14, 2005	Passenger airline	$21,801
Adelphia Communications Corp.	June 25, 2002	Telecommunications	$21,499
Mcorp	March 31, 1989	Banking and financial services	$20,228
Mirant Corp.	July 14, 2003	Electric services	$19,415

Source: BankruptcyData.com

Even when unencumbered assets can be found that could be pledged for a DIP loan, their value keeps dropping and is difficult to determine in this economic climate. "It's comparatively easy to value an asset if the business is going to be running a year from now, but it's hard to know that will be the case now," says David Skeel, a professor of corporate law at the University of Pennsylvania Law School. "And it's comparatively easy to value an asset if you know there is an active market for the assets of companies," he adds, "but there aren't liquid markets for much of anything right now."

With traditional providers of bankruptcy financing stepping back, companies in Chapter 11 have had to turn to their existing lenders. And the interest rates, fees and conditions those lenders are imposing are often onerous. "The interest rates for DIP financing are astronomical now," says William Lenhart, national director of business restructuring services for BDO Consulting. "In addition, the post-petition financing may only be for 60, 90 or 120 days," he adds, which often leaves no time to reorganize and forces the debtor into a sale or liquidation.

Many times the DIP loan doesn't actually include much fresh money. Lenders roll their pre-bankruptcy loans into the DIP financing, garnering higher interest rates and fees in the process. In addition, as the value of a debtor's assets continues to decline, lenders will often restrict the amount it can borrow even further. After Circuit City's bankruptcy filing last November, it arranged DIP financing with a face value of $1.1 billion from its existing bank group. But Circuit City's

lawyers told the bankruptcy judge that when all was said and done, there would only be $50 million of fresh money available to the retailer, at a cost of $30 million in fees and expenses. [8] A little more than three months after filing, Circuit City shut down, selling its assets and letting its 34,000 employees go.

Some bankruptcy experts argue the credit markets are simply broken and that the federal government may need

Gerald Grinstein, CEO of Delta Air Lines, leaves bankruptcy court in New York on April 25, 2007, after Delta's plan to exit bankruptcy was approved. During a 19-month reorganization, the nation's third-largest airline cut 6,000 jobs and added flights to foreign destinations.

to step in. "My bottom line is that I would much rather have the government provide DIP financing in a bankruptcy than bail out an industry," says Skeel. Providing DIP financing would be cheaper, he says, because "all a bankrupt company needs is enough cash to fund its operations; it doesn't have to pay its general creditors."

Choosing which industries to help would be tricky. "The government would have to prioritize industries," says Skeel, "based on which would have the most devastating consequences if companies filed for bankruptcy and could not find financing." Altman of New York University says

that if General Motors ends up in Chapter 11, the federal government should step in and provide the necessary DIP financing, which he estimates could amount to as much as $50 billion.

But Altman is not prescribing the same medicine for other companies. "There are not too many companies like GM," he says. Rather than provide bankruptcy financing directly to other companies in Chapter 11, he recommends government arm-twisting of traditional lenders of DIP and exit loans — many of whom received bailout money themselves — to get back in the game.

Or the government, he says, could set up a DIP fund and arm-twist the country's largest banks and corporations, like General Electric, which have financial subsidiaries, to contribute a total of $40-$50 billion.

On second thought, he says, the government could be a contributor as well. "Why not," he asks, "if that would get it going, since DIP financing is usually a pretty good investment?"

But other bankruptcy experts say this multibillion-dollar corner of the credit markets is not broken and needs no government intervention. "Bankruptcy financing is a way in which the market imposes discipline on businesses," says Williams of the American Bankruptcy Institute. "If the market itself will not provide financing because it's not confident that the business will generate enough revenue to cover the cost and return on that investment, then if the government provides that financing instead, it's doing so for reasons that have nothing to do with economic reality."

Did amendments to the Bankruptcy Code in 2005 destroy the ability of some firms to reorganize?

A growing number of U.S. companies are finding it increasingly difficult to emerge from Chapter 11 and instead have had to liquidate. Retailers have been particularly hard hit, drowning in the perfect storm created by the deep recession and the credit squeeze. But some business-turnaround experts hold the changes Congress made to the Bankruptcy Code in 2005 partially to blame. In fact, since that time, almost every retailer that has filed for Chapter 11 has had to shut its doors. The casualty list ranges from Linens 'n Things to the Sharper Image.

"Some of us fear . . . that Chapter 11 is no longer working as Congress intended it," said Rep. Steve Cohen, D-Tenn., chairman of the House Judiciary Subcommittee on Commercial and Administrative Law, at a hearing his panel held on March 11 entitled, "Circuit City Unplugged: Why Did Chapter 11 Fail to Save 34,000 Jobs?" [9] It may be time, Cohen says, to roll back some of the amendments Congress made to the Bankruptcy Code more than three years ago.

Before the amendments, companies in Chapter 11 had 60 days to assume or terminate their leases of non-residential real estate, and the bankruptcy courts would often extend that deadline for months, even years. Now companies have a maximum of 210 days, unless landlords agree to more. Critics say the change has been devastating for retailers, whose business is often seasonal.

"Most retailers need at least 12 to 18 months to see if they have a viable business plan to emerge from bankruptcy, testing that plan through at least one holiday season," says Lenhart of BDO Consulting. "They close underperforming stores, they cut merchandise, and it all takes time." Now they don't have so much time, and, some

Bankruptcy Filings on the Rise Again

The number of business bankruptcy filings in federal courts rose more than 50 percent from 2007 to 2008 after declining for several years. The decline began in 2002, as the economy recovered from the dot-com bust.

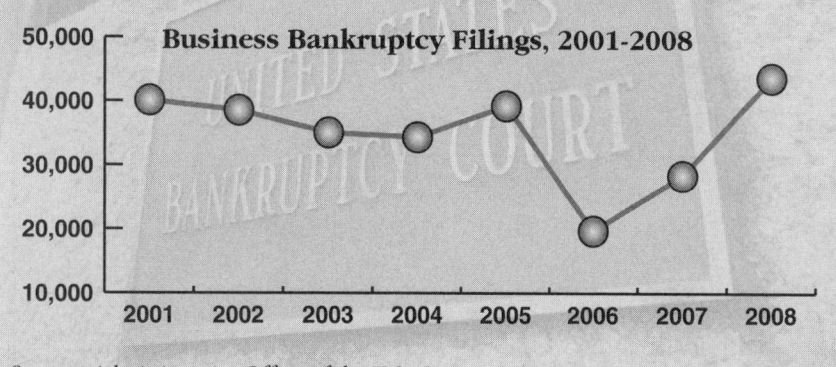

Business Bankruptcy Filings, 2001-2008

Source: Administrative Office of the U.S. Courts

say, retailers are forced to make premature decisions to close stores that ultimately might have been profitable.

Even worse is the spillover effect the 2005 changes have had on bankruptcy financing. "The last thing the lender wants is the store to go dark while the inventory — the collateral for the loan — is still in there," says Lenhart. "So lenders are giving debtors very little time to decide whether to restructure or liquidate."

That spillover effect "is a major precipitating factor in the Chapter 11 liquidation of retailer debtors," said Isaac Pachulski, a member of the National Bankruptcy Conference, a nonprofit organization of lawyers, professors and bankruptcy judges, at the March hearing. "The conference believes that the inflexibility of the 210-day time limit is unwarranted," said Pachulski, "and that this fixed time limit for the assumption or rejection of non-residential real property leases should be eliminated." [10]

"No, it should not," says Malachy Kavanagh, a spokesman for the International Council of Shopping Centers. "First of all, it took seven years to get that done in 2005." He says 210 days is plenty of time for a retailer to re-

ject or accept a lease because retailers "know what stores are performing well and which ones are underperforming when they go into bankruptcy." The real cause of all the liquidations among retailers, he says, is "the huge amount of debt they piled up" in the days of easy credit that they now cannot service in this deep recession. Besides, he says, it is harmful to all the other tenants in a shopping mall if the anchor store is failing and not generating much foot traffic.

In any case, Kavanagh says landlords are sometimes willing to allow a retailer to extend a lease beyond the 210 days. That's true, says Lenhart, "but it is still very difficult."

In 2005, Congress also pushed certain vendors to the front of the line of those waiting for payment in a bankruptcy case, a move that critics say can suck the cash out of companies trying to reorganize. Previously, if a vendor had delivered supplies to a company within 20 days of the company filing for bankruptcy, that vendor had to wait in line with all other unsecured creditors to receive payment. Now that vendor must be paid in full, in cash, on the date that a debtor's reorganization plan takes effect.

The Paths to Bankruptcy

Federal bankruptcy law provides several ways individuals, businesses, cities and organizations can file for bankruptcy, or seek relief from an inability to pay creditors. Two of the most widely used are Chapter 7, which liquidates all available assets, essentially wiping out all debts and, if a business, ceasing operation, and Chapter 11, which provides for the reorganization of a business in order to maintain operations and pay creditors over time. Here are the main bankruptcy chapters:

Chapter 7 — Provides for "liquidation." (i.e., the sale of a debtor's non-exempt property and the distribution of the proceeds to creditors.)

Chapter 9 — Provides for reorganization of municipalities, including cities and towns, as well as villages, counties, taxing districts, municipal utilities and school districts.

Chapter 11 — Provides, in general, for reorganization, usually involving a corporation or partnership. A debtor usually proposes a plan for the reorganization to keep its operations afloat and pay creditors over time. Individuals can also seek relief under this chapter.

Chapter 12 — Provides for adjustment of debts for a "family farmer" or a "family fisherman," as defined in the Bankruptcy Code.

Chapter 13 — Provides for adjustment of debts for an individual with regular income. Allows a debtor to keep property and pay debts over time, usually for three to five years.

Source: Administrative Office of U.S. Courts

"Given the nature of Circuit City's business and the value of its deliveries, it should come as no surprise that the amount of goods received by it in the 20 days prior to the [date it filed for bankruptcy] amounted to a staggering sum," testified Richard Pachulski, lead counsel to Circuit City's creditors' committee. The total value of such claims by vendors delivering TVs, computers, camcorders, furniture and other equipment to Circuit City during that timeframe came to nearly $350 million. [11]

If a debtor cannot pay these claims, the bankruptcy case is considered "administratively insolvent," and the company cannot reorganize and emerge from Chapter 11. This amendment, said Richard Pachulski, "changed the face of bankruptcies and put into question whether companies in certain industries, particularly the auto and retail industries, can be successfully reorganized under Chapter 11." [12]

"The impact of this change in the law may be overstated," said Todd Zywicki, a professor at George Mason University School of Law who also testified at the March hearing.

On a practical level, Zywicki said, bankruptcy judges already had the discretion to grant "critical vendor" status to suppliers considered essential to the bankrupt company's ability to function, allowing the company to pay those vendors' pre-bankruptcy claims. [13]

The recession, the credit squeeze and the drop in consumer spending, he said, likely would have driven many of the retailers filing for Chapter 11 out of business regardless of the 2005 amendments to the Bankruptcy Code. "Bankruptcy cannot and should not be used to save economically failed enterprises," testified Zywicki. "Chapter 11 cannot reverse the creative destruction of the competitive marketplace or force consumers to buy goods and services that they don't want."

"I don't think Professor Zywicki was thinking at all about the workers who lost their jobs," says Rep. Cohen. "Chapter 11 is supposed to be a hospital and instead it has become a morgue." Cohen is convinced that the 2005 amendments to the Bankruptcy Code have made it impossible for some companies that could have successfully reorganized to do so, and he favors repeal. So does Rep. Jerrold Nadler, D-N.Y., chairman of the House Judiciary Subcommittee on the Constitution, Civil Rights and Civil Liberties. On April 2, Nadler introduced the Business Reorganization and Job Preservation Act of 2009, which would repeal some of the more contentious 2005 amendments.

Should a bankrupt company's ability to terminate its union contract be restricted?

Like many other newspaper owners across the country, the Star Tribune Co., publisher of Minnesota's largest newspaper, is losing money. But the paper is also burdened by hundreds of millions of dollars of debt it took on when the private equity firm Avista Capital Partners LP borrowed heavily to buy the paper from The McClatchy Company in 2007.

By mid-January of this year, Star Tribune found it could not survive without the protection of bankruptcy and filed for Chapter 11. Just one month later, it filed a motion with the court seeking to reject its collective-bargaining agreement with its printer's union, the Graphic Communications Conference of the International Brotherhood of Teamsters, in order to save $3.5 million in labor costs. The agreement wasn't due to expire until November 2010. On March 13, just hours before the judge was to make his decision, the union and the company reached a settlement.

The teamsters are being buffeted from all sides. Last October, a bankruptcy judge ruled that Frontier Airlines could break its contract with the union, which represents the airline's mechanics, aircraft cleaners and related workers. Within days the union announced it would appeal.

"Today, a bankruptcy, or even a threatened bankruptcy, can break these promises and undermine private-sector unions in ways perhaps not anticipated by the [Bankruptcy] Code's architects," said Samuel Gerdano, executive director of the American Bankruptcy Institute. "The result is that the near-term future for benefits won at the bargaining table is as bleak as it's been in the history of the American labor movement." [14]

Back in 1984, Congress created Section 1113 of the Bankruptcy Code to protect employees in a bankruptcy case. The requirements that a com-

The Tribune Co., publisher of the Chicago Tribune and the Los Angeles Times, filed for bankruptcy protection in December 2008, joining the ranks of thousands of other troubled U.S. firms, including many media companies.

pany in Chapter 11 must meet before it can ask a judge to allow it to reject a collective-bargaining agreement are stringent:

- A company must make a proposal to the union to modify the existing agreement that includes changes necessary to permit reorganization;
- The proposal must be based on complete and reliable information;
- It must provide the union with the information necessary for it to evaluate the proposal; and
- It must meet at reasonable times with the union, and it must negotiate in good faith.

The sides have 51 days to agree on concessions. If they can't, the judge then rules whether the company can reject the existing union contract. If he is to rule in the company's favor, he must find that the above conditions have been met and that the union refused to accept the company's proposal without good cause. [15]

Unions argue, however, that in practice Section 1113 is not protecting workers as designed. "The standards have been subverted by corporations," says Marcus Migliore,

managing attorney for the Air Line Pilots Association, International (ALPA). "And bankruptcy judges are overly sympathetic to debtor corporations and not focused enough on the employees and their families."

Not so, says Washington lawyer Michael Bernstein, a specialist in bankruptcy and restructuring. "I think the balance is good right now," says Bernstein, "and the best evidence of that fact is that the overwhelming majority of situations where the company believes it needs relief from a collective-bargaining agreement are resolved by negotiation." And when negotiations fail, Bernstein says, sometimes judges allow a debtor to terminate a union contract and sometimes they don't.

But union lawyers say companies are not negotiating in good faith. Aided by the tight deadline and the threat of a pro-company ruling from a sympathetic judge, companies, they say, are able to wring draconian concessions from unions that are far more than necessary. "The relief debtors are seeking is both stunningly broad and long-term," said New York lawyer Babette Ceccotti, testifying before Congress on behalf of the AFL-CIO last year. Ceccotti pointed to United Airlines, which paid a special, $250 million dividend to its shareholders in 2008 "but has resisted the unions' requests to begin their contract talks early before the 2009 amendable date of the agreements reached with its labor groups while in bankruptcy." [16]

Part of the problem is that bankruptcy courts don't always agree on how to interpret the 1113 standards. "The U.S. Court of Appeals for the

Third Circuit has determined that a debtor firm only could obtain relief that is necessary to avoid liquidation, while other circuits have ruled that companies are entitled to relief that will make them a viable competitor in the industry." [17]

Unions also complain that labor is asked to sacrifice far more than management. "Management is taking pensions, they're taking 40 percent pay raises and million-dollar bonuses all in the name of retaining the same people who drove the company into the ditch in the fist place," says Migliore.

But Bernstein says trying to create some kind of precise equivalence between the treatment of hourly employees and management would be counterproductive. "I don't think it is fair to restructure a company solely by cutting union wages and benefits," says Bernstein, "but in determining the nature of the sacrifice and the amount of the sacrifice, it is important to look at the market wage for different jobs."

Unions would like to see Congress tighten the 1113 standards even further and restrict judicial discretion. For instance they would like to see the language changed so that concessions are not just "necessary to permit the reorganization of the debtor," as 1113 puts it, but are the minimal savings necessary to permit the debtor to exit bankruptcy and avoid liquidation, and they would like to see restrictions on management pay and benefits. House Judiciary Chairman John Conyers, D-Mich., introduced the Protecting Employees and Retirees in Business Bankruptcies Act of 2007 last session, and unions are hoping that a revised bill is introduced this year.

"But even new laws cannot change the economic reality of unsparing global competition," said Gerdano of the American Bankruptcy Institute, who adds that many are calling for "greater imagination on the part of both management and union leaders, to think

beyond the duration of a short-term labor contract." [18]

BACKGROUND

The Chaotic 1800s

"Whether a society forgives its debtors and how it bestows or withholds forgiveness are matters of economic and legal consequence," writes Bruce H. Mann in his book *Republic of Debtors*. "They also go to the heart of what a society values." [19]

In colonial America, forgiveness was not the order of the day, and insolvency was considered a moral failure. There was no such thing as voluntary bankruptcy, where a debtor could seek protection from creditors and get a fresh start. Bankruptcy was involuntary and often involved prison "until debts were paid or until property was liquidated or creditors agreed to the release of the debtor." [20]

Each colony crafted its own bankruptcy law, and some "became known as debtor's havens because of their unwillingness to enforce commercial obligations." [21] In response, the Founding Fathers included in the Constitution a clause that gave Congress the right to pass "uniform laws on the subject of bankruptcy." [22] But for more than a century, Congress used that authority to pass only temporary laws that it quickly repealed after public protests.

"Agitation for bankruptcy legislation rose to a fever pitch at roughly 20-year intervals throughout the 19th century," writes the University of Pennsylvania's Skeel in his book *Debt's Dominion*. [23] After an economic depression in 1793, Congress passed the first federal bankruptcy law in 1800, which was purely a remedy for creditors, who could petition a federal district court to place a merchant with

unpaid debts into involuntary bankruptcy. But complaints of high costs and the difficulty of traveling to distant federal courts led to its repeal three years later.

In 1841, in response to the Panic of 1837, Congress passed a second bankruptcy law, which permitted voluntary bankruptcy and included relief for non-merchants. "The 1841 Act . . . was a watershed event in bankruptcy history" writes Charles J. Tabb, a professor of law at the University of Illinois, in the *American Bankruptcy Law Review*. "For the first time, a financially troubled debtor could file for bankruptcy and receive a discharge." [24] But as the economic crisis passed, it was quickly repealed. After the Civil War ravaged the economy, Congress passed a third law in 1867, which, for the first time, included protections for corporations. But, again, Congress repealed it, this time after 11 years.

The controversy over these short-lived laws tended to divide along geographical lines. "Because Southerners feared that Northern creditors would use bankruptcy law as a collection device to displace Southern farmers from their homesteads," writes Skeel, "the strongest opposition to federal bankruptcy legislation came from the South." Commercial Northeastern states, on the other hand, "were much more likely to view federal bankruptcy legislation as essential to the promotion of commercial enterprise." [25]

New Bankruptcy Laws

"With the development and opening of the West and the beginning of large-scale industrialization as America approached the 20th century, commerce in America began to expand greatly," write David Kennedy and R. Spencer Clift III in the *Journal of Bankruptcy Law and Practice*, and agricultural interests lost influence. [26]

Continued on p. 333

Chronology

1700s-1870s
Congress passes three temporary bankruptcy laws.

Colonial Era
Each colony has its own bankruptcy law; inconsistencies lead to some colonies becoming known as "debtors' havens."

1787
Constitution gives Congress power to "pass uniform laws on the subject of bankruptcies."

1800
Congress passes first bankruptcy law after Panic of 1797 leads to imprisonment of thousands of debtors. Bankruptcy is involuntary; repealed after three years.

1833
Federal imprisonment for debt is abolished.

1841
Second bankruptcy law permits voluntary bankruptcy and covers non-merchants; repealed after one year.

1867
After the Civil War a third bankruptcy law makes it easier for Northern businessmen to collect from Southern debtors; repealed after 11 years.

1880s-1930s
After century of instability, Congress passes long-term bankruptcy law.

1884
Over-investing in railroad construction leads to economic panic.

1893
Depression causes factory shutdowns, job losses and bank failures.

1898
Nelson act allows individuals to declare bankruptcy.

1938
Chandler act amends Nelson act, allows bankruptcy for individuals who can repay their debts.

1950s-1970
Consumer credit expands, bankruptcies rise.

1950
Diners Club becomes first general-purpose credit card.

1967
Personal bankruptcy filings rise dramatically.

1970
Congress establishes Commission on the Bankruptcy Laws of the United States to recommend changes to the amended 1898 Act. . . . Penn Central declares bankruptcy.

1978-2005
Congress substantially changes Bankruptcy Code.

1978
Bankruptcy Reform Act replaces Nelson Act, streamlining business bankruptcy, encouraging individuals with regular incomes to restructure debts and establishing bankruptcy courts.

1984
Supreme Court holds in *NLRB v.*
Bildisco & Bildisco that debtors who file for bankruptcy under Chapter 11 can reject a collective-bargaining agreement. . . . Bankruptcy Amendments and Federal Judgeship Act creates requirements a corporate debtor must meet before rejecting a collective-bargaining agreement and tightens reins on personal debtors.

1994
Congress amends Bankruptcy Code again and creates second National Bankruptcy Review Commission.

2005
Bankruptcy Abuse Prevention and Consumer Protection Act makes filing for personal bankruptcy more expensive, time-consuming and restrictive and shifts power over business bankruptcy process away from debtors and toward creditors.

2007-Present
Financial crisis leads to big bankruptcies.

2008
Lehman Brothers becomes largest bankruptcy in U.S. history (September); 11 days later Washington Mutual becomes the second-largest. . . . Circuit City files for Chapter 11 bankruptcy (November), shuts down three months later. . . . Tribune Co. files for bankruptcy (December).

2009
Lyondell Chemical Co. becomes 13th-largest public company to file for bankruptcy (January). . . . Rep. Jerrold Nadler, D-N.Y., introduces Business Reorganization and Job Preservation Act, calling for repeal of some 2005 amendments to Bankruptcy Code (April 2).

Protecting Suppliers of 'Too Big to Fail' Companies

Should the Bankruptcy Code shield vendors of automakers and other big firms?

The failure of General Motors and the Chrysler Corp. could cause a cascade of business failures among auto suppliers, many industry experts worry. In the March issue of the American Bankruptcy Institute Journal, *George Kuney, a professor at the University of Tennessee College of Law, and San Francisco lawyer Michael St. James propose changing the Bankruptcy Code to create a new Chapter 10 for "too big to fail" companies like the automakers, which would protect suppliers. Contributing writer Barbara Mantel discussed their proposal with St. James in March.*

CQ: What happens to the money a company owes its suppliers under Chapter 11 of the Bankruptcy Code?

MSJ: While post-bankruptcy goods and services are supposed to be paid in full, everything that is owed pre-bankruptcy is frozen until the end of the case so that everybody gets the same 7 cents, or 10 cents or 72 cents on the dollar. It's a perfectly good system if you want to make sure everyone gets the same distribution at the end.

CQ: So what is the problem?

MSJ: The problem with "too big to fail" companies is that you expect cascading insolvencies, where the companies that are dependent on them — their suppliers — fail because their current accounts receivable are going to be frozen for months and even years, and these suppliers don't have enough excess cash flow to roll with it.

CQ: Doesn't Chapter11 have a provision for this, the "critical vendor" provision?

MSJ: The premise of the critical vendor motion is extortion. The company in bankruptcy comes into court and says, "I need this kind of widget supplied to me, and there is only one vendor who can supply it, and that vendor won't sell to me because I'm freezing the accounts payable to them." So the company says to the bankruptcy judge, "Judge, grant me an exception and let me pay this vendor his pre-bankruptcy debt so I can stay in business."

CQ: Why won't that prevent cascading bankruptcies among suppliers?

MSJ: It's not a solution for a couple of reasons. The first

is that the whole concept is very controversial; there are a couple of courts in the country that will routinely grant critical vendor motions — Delaware and the Southern District of New York, for instance — and a large number of courts that won't.

CQ: What is the other reason?

MSJ: The critical vendor order doesn't give suppliers any sense of comfort that they will, in fact, be protected. If I am a supplier to Chrysler, I don't know if Chrysler will get a critical vendor order, and if they do, I don't know if they'll think that I'm a critical vendor. So if Chrysler files for bankruptcy, I have to consider laying off employees and shutting down because I don't know if I'm going to get paid.

CQ: How would your Chapter 10 work?

MSJ: What is behind our Chapter 10 approach is an effort to provide a sense of stability and certainty to the vendors of a "too big to fail" business so that they have a reasonable expectation that they will continue to operate unaffected by the bankruptcy filing. What we've proposed is that, unlike the current situation, ordinary course vendors and employees get treated essentially as if there were no bankruptcy filing, and all of their bills get paid as they used to get paid.

CQ: Doesn't that defeat the purpose of bankruptcy, to protect a debtor from creditors?

MSJ: Well, no. It's really an effort to focus the bankruptcy process on the fundamentals, which for "too big to fail" companies would be reworking the operating business — perhaps shutting plants, perhaps changing suppliers, perhaps eliminating some long-term contracts, perhaps adjusting labor contracts — and adjusting the financial structure.

CQ: What is a "too big to fail" company?

MSJ: We're studying that. What we're aiming for is something that looks at the magnitude of everyone a company pays every month — all of the parts suppliers, all of the people who provide services, all of the employees — and how broadly it is spread through the economy. And by enacting a new Chapter 10 for these "too big to fail" companies, we could avoid imposing cascading business failures on society.

San Francisco lawyer Michael St. James.

Courtesy Michael St. James

Continued from p. 330

As a result, Congress was able to pass the nation's first permanent bankruptcy legislation, the landmark Nelson Act, which remained in effect for 80 years. Yet "the road to the passage of the 1898 Act was anything but smooth," according to Tabb. Southern and Western agricultural interests continued to oppose a bankruptcy law, but, once again, economic panics — this time in 1884 and in 1893 — provided the catalyst for federal legislation.

"The 1898 Act ushered in the modern era of liberal debtor treatment in United States bankruptcy laws," writes Tabb. While the earlier, temporary laws had allowed a debtor to discharge his debts, there were many restrictions, including the need for consent from a certain percentage of creditors. According to Tabb, the 1898 Act abolished those restrictions. [27]

Kennedy and Clift write that the 1898 Act:

- "gave birth to the fresh financial start principle;
- allowed for both voluntary and involuntary proceedings;
- afforded relief to individuals and most corporations and partnerships;
- established a uniform system of bankruptcy administration;
- delegated more functions and duties to 'bankruptcy referees.' " [28]

In response to the Great Depression and after years of debate, Congress passed the Chandler Act in 1938, which amended the Nelson Act to provide for reorganization of a debtor as an alternative to liquidation of a debtor's assets. Together they are known as the Bankruptcy Act, and ever since, according to Kennedy and Clift, "there has existed in America a congressional policy favoring reorganization over liquidation, where possible." [29]

"With the 1960s came increasingly vocal calls for Congress to undertake its first global reconsideration of the bankruptcy laws since the Chandler

Auto Industry Showdown

President Obama ordered General Motors and Chrysler in March to radically restructure or face bankruptcy, rejecting the restructuring plans the automakers had submitted for government approval because "neither goes far enough." The administration gave GM 60 days to come up with a fresh plan to slash its debt and retiree costs and reshape its operations; Chrysler was given 30 days to revise and complete a previously announced merger with the Italian automaker Fiat. Auto workers demonstrate at the North American Auto Show in Washington, D.C., in January, adding to the pressure on General Motors and Chrysler (bottom). In addition to coming up with more radical plans to close plants, eliminate brands and reposition themselves in the marketplace, the two firms must convince the United Automobile Workers union to make large concessions on wages, benefits and retiree health-care costs.

Congress Expands Scope of Exempt Financial Contracts

Experts debate merits of "safe harbor" provision.

When Congress amended the Bankruptcy Code in 2005, most of the headlines focused on filing for personal bankruptcy, which lawmakers made more time-consuming and expensive.

But Congress also made several, little-noticed changes to business-bankruptcy law that are now generating significant debate as more and more struggling businesses consider bankruptcy protection.

In seeking bankruptcy protection under Chapter 11, a debtor can ask the court to reject a contract it considers burdensome. However, a so-called "automatic stay" prevents parties on the other side of the contract from doing the same. But there are exceptions to the automatic stay, known as "safe harbors," and in 2005 Congress created more of them.

Congress greatly expanded the kinds of financial contracts that are outside the control of bankruptcy law. According to *The Wall Street Journal*, "credit default swaps, repurchase agreements, mortgage-backed securities and other derivatives were added to the list of financial contracts exempted from the Bankruptcy Code's automatic stay." In other words, parties on the other side of these contracts can break them and seize any underlying collateral. [1]

Suppose General Motors has entered into currency contracts to hedge against the risks of currency fluctuations in its global markets, suggests Columbia University law Professor Edward Morrison. If GM enters bankruptcy, creditors would not be able to seize its plants, and vendors would have to honor their contracts to supply auto parts. "But the counterparty to those currency hedges would be free to terminate the hedge," explains Morrison, "and to seize collateral that GM has posted to support its obligations under that currency hedge, assuming that GM is on the losing side of that contract."

Congress expanded the safe harbors exemption in 2005 because lawmakers wanted to protect the financial markets from systemic failure if financial players were unable to collect on contracts when a large company went bankrupt. There is much debate, however, as to whether that has been the result.

For instance, when Lehman Brothers filed for bankruptcy in September 2008, traders settled, or "unwound," billions of dollars' worth of financial contracts as the investment bank turned to the bankruptcy court for protection. Financial markets, though, were not spared, and credit markets froze. "If you have a massive market player like Lehman," says Morrison, "the safe harbors are not going to prevent a market meltdown."

But it could have been worse, says Harold Novikoff, a bankruptcy lawyer in New York. "Clearly, everyone closing out at the same time on hundreds of thousands of Lehman's swap claims hurt the market," he says. "But by letting people exercise their rights, it saved other people from failing themselves."

The 2005 safe harbor provision also allowed Lehman to quickly clear the accounts of its broker-dealer subsidiary and sell it to Barclays Bank, he says. The weekend before its parent company

Act," writes Skeel. The reason was simple. Personal bankruptcy filings "had risen to previously unheard-of levels, and each year seemed to bring a new record." After averaging about 10,000 a year, the number of personal bankruptcies steadily climbed in the 1950s and '60s, peaking in 1967 at 191,729. [30] Many experts blamed the increase in consumer debt and the advent of the general-purpose credit card as well as a decline in the stigma of bankruptcy. In 1970, Congress responded by creating the Commission on the Bankruptcy Laws of the United States to study and suggest changes to existing law.

While individual bankruptcies were climbing only two notable business failures occurred during this period, according to BankruptcyData.com. In 1970 the Penn Central railroad became the largest bankruptcy up to that point, and five years later the W. T. Grant Co., a general merchandise retailer, became the second-largest. [31]

After several studies and much debate, Congress finally passed the Bankruptcy Reform Act of 1978, which replaced the amended Nelson Act. This law, together with its amendments, is known as the Bankruptcy Code and governs bankruptcy practice today.

"The Bankruptcy Code retained much of the substance of the Bankruptcy Act," writes J. Michael Deasy, U.S. Bankruptcy Judge for the District of New Hampshire, "but it modified its provisions to provide a single, uniform procedure for business reorganizations." [32]

In addition to streamlining business bankruptcy, the Code encouraged individuals with regular income to use Chapter 13, in which a debtor keeps his property and pays his debts over time, rather than Chapter 7, in which much of a debtor's property is sold and the proceeds distributed to creditors. The Code also established a separate system of bankruptcy courts and removed the cap on fees for bankruptcy lawyers.

Amending the Code

Congress has amended the Bankruptcy Reform Act of 1978 several

filed for bankruptcy, the subsidiary had entered repurchase agreements, a type of derivative, with major mutual and money-market funds. JP Morgan Chase bank lent the subsidiary more than $87 billion to help it unwind those agreements. JP Morgan did so, says Novikoff, because the loan was structured so that it qualified as a financial contract exempt from an automatic stay, and thus was protected in case the subsidiary also went bankrupt.

"If JP Morgan had not made the advance, the major mutual and money-market funds would have received securities instead of cash," says Novikoff, "and they would have then been in the position of trying to dump those securities into what was already a chaotic market."

While experts debate the benefits of the 2005 safe harbors measure, many agree that there are costs.

"Gaming the system is one of my major concerns," says Jay Westbrook, a law professor at the University of Texas at Austin. "You can take virtually any contract and write it to look like a swap agreement, even if it is for goods and services," he says, "and therefore exempt it from bankruptcy." In addition,

Lehman Brothers Holdings became the largest bankruptcy in U.S. history when it filed for bankruptcy last year. The storied Wall Street investment bank had assets of nearly $700 billion and more than 25,000 employees. The federal government declined to bail out the firm.

(Photo credit, vertical text: Getty Images/Mario Tama)

since so many contracts in the business world revolve around buying and selling items that could be considered commodities, those contracts could be considered exempt from an automatic stay, he says.

"Suppose I'm in business making electronics, and I need copper," says Westbrook. "I'm not a financial player, I make stuff, but because copper is a commodity that is traded on a commodity exchange, my copper contracts could be considered exempt from bankruptcy." That means the supplier could cancel the contract, and if the bankrupt electronics maker cannot find another supplier, it may have to shut down.

To reduce the risk of abuse, Morrison and others suggest narrowing the scope of safe harbors. "Perhaps make them available only in cases where the debtor is a significant financial-market participant," he says, "or limit the kind of collateral that can be seized to only financial collateral." That way, if a creditor dresses up a loan as one of these exempt financial contracts, it couldn't seize a factory.

[1] Kristina Doss, "A Kinder Bankruptcy Law is Sought as Filings Soar," *The Wall Street Journal*, Jan. 21, 2009. p. C3.

times in response to both lobbying from special interests and various Supreme Court decisions. For instance, in 1984, the court held in *NLRB v. Bildisco & Bildisco* that a Chapter 11 debtor could reject a collective-bargaining agreement and unilaterally modify that agreement. "The resulting furor pushed Congress into speedy action," writes the University of Illinois' Tabb, and "the consumer credit industry and other special-interest groups . . . seized the opportunity to obtain desired changes in the Bankruptcy Code." [33]

Among other things, the Bankruptcy Amendments and Federal Judgeship Act of 1984 added bankruptcy judgeships, created a list of requirements before a corporate debtor could reject a collective-bargaining agree-

ment and tightened the reins on personal debtors in response to "the hotly debated allegation that many consumer debtors were abusing the bankruptcy laws." [34] In 1994, Congress again amended the Bankruptcy Code and concurrently created a second National Bankruptcy Review Commission, just 24 years after the first one.

By 2005, the consumer credit industry had convinced Congress that consumers continued to abuse the bankruptcy laws, and Congress passed the Bankruptcy Abuse Prevention and Consumer Protection Act. The legislation made filing for personal bankruptcy more expensive, time consuming and restrictive. Filings reached record levels before the bill took effect, and then plunged the following

year. While the highly contentious debate focused on the personal bankruptcy provisions of the act, Congress also made significant changes to business bankruptcy law as well, shifting more of the power over the bankruptcy process away from debtors to their creditors. Debtors were required to pay more creditors up front, given less time to make key decisions about leases and allowed less time to exclusively fashion a plan of reorganization.

Since the current recession began in December 2007 and the financial crisis took hold in 2008, both personal and business bankruptcies have begun to climb. Lehman Brothers filed for bankruptcy in September, 2008, the largest bankruptcy in U.S. history.

A Bankruptcy Glossary

Automatic stay — *An injunction that automatically stops lawsuits, foreclosures, garnishments and all collection activity against the debtor the moment a bankruptcy petition is filed.*

Creditor — *One to whom a debtor owes money or who claims to be owed money by a debtor.*

Debtor — *A person who has filed a petition for relief under the Bankruptcy Code.*

Executory contract or lease — *Generally includes contracts or leases under which both parties to an agreement have duties remaining to be performed. If a contract or lease is executory, a debtor may assume or reject it.*

Lien — *The right to take and hold, or sell, the property of a debtor as security or payment for a debt or duty.*

Liquidation — *Sale of a debtor's property with the proceeds to be used for the benefit of creditors.*

Motion to lift the automatic stay — *A request by a creditor to allow him to take action against a debtor or a debtor's property that would otherwise be prohibited by the automatic stay.*

Plan — *A debtor's detailed description of how the debtor proposes to pay creditors' claims over a fixed period of time.*

Priority claim — *An unsecured claim that is entitled to be paid ahead of other unsecured claims that are not entitled to priority status. Priority refers to the order in which these unsecured claims are to be paid.*

Secured creditor — *A creditor holding a claim against a debtor who has the right to take and hold, or sell, certain property of the debtor in satisfaction of some or all of the claim.*

Secured debt — *Debt backed by a mortgage, pledge of collateral or other lien; debt for which the creditor has the right to pursue specific pledged property upon default.*

Undersecured claim — *A debt secured by property that is worth less than the full amount of the debt.*

Unsecured claim — *A claim or debt for which a creditor holds no special assurance of payment, such as a mortgage or lien; a debt for which credit is extended based solely upon the creditor's assessment of the debtor's future ability to pay.*

Source: "Bankruptcy Basics," Administrative Office of U.S. Courts

And a series of retailers have closed shop, including household names like Circuit City, unable to reorganize out of Chapter 11. Members of Congress are once again holding hearings on the Bankruptcy Code and talking of amending it, this time in favor of debtors. ■

CURRENT SITUATION

The Auto Industry

Chapter 11 reorganization is looking increasingly likely for the U.S. auto industry.

At the end of March, President Barack Obama issued General Motors and Chrysler tight deadlines to radically restructure or face bankruptcy. As part of the ultimatum, Obama rejected the restructuring plans that the automakers had submitted for government approval, determining that "neither goes far enough." [35] The president also forced GM's chairman and chief executive, Rick Wagoner, to resign.

The administration gave GM 60 days to come up with a fresh, more aggressive plan to slash its debt and retiree costs and reshape its operations; Chrysler was given 30 days to revise and complete a previously announced merger with the Italian automaker Fiat. The administration's Auto Task Force has concluded that Chrysler is no longer a viable company on its own. In the meantime, the government is providing both companies with an unspecified amount of working capital with the promise of more aid if their new restructuring plans meet government approval.

Any additional aid would be on top of a combined $17.4 billion in government loans that GM and Chrysler already received in December, which the companies are close to burning through despite having embarked on an overhaul of their operations. Ford, which also lost billions of dollars last year, has, so far, not asked for government bailout money.

GM and Chrysler have a tough road ahead. In addition to coming up with more radical plans to close plants, eliminate brands and reposition themselves

Continued on p. 338

At Issue:

Should companies lose the freedom to choose where to file for bankruptcy?

LYNN LOPUCKI
SECURITY PACIFIC BANK PROFESSOR OF LAW, UCLA SCHOOL OF LAW

WRITTEN FOR *CQ RESEARCHER*, APRIL 2009

*l*arge, public companies such as Enron, Worldcom and Lehman Brothers can choose their bankruptcy courts. They should lose that freedom for three reasons:
- They were never intended to have it.
- It harms the companies and their investors.
- It is corrupting the bankruptcy courts.

This "freedom" comes from a law that allows a debtor to file at its "domicile" or "where the case of an affiliate is pending." The drafters didn't anticipate that a company such as the Tribune Company — whose headquarters and principal operations are in Chicago — could use the law to file in Delaware, its state of incorporation, where its only connection is the filing of a piece of paper and the payment of a small fee once each year.

Nor did the drafters anticipate that a company such as Winn-Dixie — which operates in the Southeast — could form a shell New York corporate subsidiary, assign some debt to it, put it in bankruptcy in New York, and then, 12 days after the farce began, put Winn-Dixie in bankruptcy in New York on the ground that "the case of an affiliate is pending" there.

Empirical studies show this "freedom" harms, rather than benefits, the companies. Managers choose courts that let them take big bonuses or shield them from personal liability. Bankruptcy lawyers recommend courts that will award them higher fees. Bank lenders insist on courts that will let them charge outrageously high fees for financing the bankruptcy and have "drop dead" control over the companies. One study showed that companies choosing Delaware — the court most often chosen — were seven times more likely to be back in bankruptcy within five years.

Reorganizing big, bankrupt companies is a glamorous, multibillion-dollar industry. Some courts compete for that industry by favoring the positions of parties who can bring the court more cases — corrupt or failed executives, bankruptcy advisers and bankruptcy financiers. The losers are all the other parties to the bankruptcy case — creditors, shareholders, employees, landlords, suppliers and customers.

The Delaware bankruptcy court has six judges even though the state doesn't generate enough bankruptcy cases internally to keep one judge busy. To protect their own jobs, those judges must rule in ways that keep the cases coming. That is not fair to other parties. The lesson to draw is that one side in litigation should not be choosing the court. Companies should be limited to filing at their headquarters or the location of their principal assets.

ROBERT RASMUSSEN
DEAN, UNIVERSITY OF SOUTHERN CALIFORNIA GOULD SCHOOL OF LAW

WRITTEN FOR *CQ RESEARCHER*, APRIL 2009

*t*he next great wave of corporate bankruptcies is upon us. Current law provides companies with extraordinary flexibility in choosing which court to handle their Chapter 11. That flexibility should be maintained. It ensures that experienced courts confront the challenges that the next few years will bring.

No one disputes that companies use the freedom they have under the Bankruptcy Code to select where to file their cases. Roughly 60 percent of large, publicly held companies filing for Chapter 11 in the last five years have selected either the Delaware or Southern District of New York bankruptcy courts.

Many benign reasons explain this preference. Companies choose courts with experience. Overseeing the reorganization of a large corporation is no ministerial task. Judges have to create an environment where the parties can decide on the proper course for the company. They need to know when to intervene and when to let the parties craft a solution. Delaware and the Southern District of New York have been handling a predominant share of large cases for over 15 years.

Today's large corporations have complex capital structures. New financing instruments such as second-lien loans and credit-default swaps complicate the restructuring efforts. A *Fortune* 500 company does not want to be a learning experience.

All agree that companies pick courts strategically. The crucial question is the extent to which decision-makers' interests align with maximizing the value of the company. Gone are the days when Chapter 11 could provide a refuge for those who had steered the company into distress. Turnaround experts have often been put in place before a company files for bankruptcy. The company often must consult with its lenders over venue. These lenders, who often will end up with a large share of any reorganized company, will be slow to endorse a venue that consumes value.

In bankruptcy as in life, it is often better to make the pie bigger than to fight over the size of the slices. Claims that the data show that current practice is corrupt miss the mark. These assertions rest on debatable assumptions, and one needs to attend to the limits of available evidence.

Each wave of corporate restructurings since the time of the railroads has brought new sets of challenges. We cannot predict the nature of what bankruptcy judges will confront in the coming years, but we are best served by allowing companies to take the most difficult cases to courts that have gained the confidence of those with money on the table.

Continued from p. 336

in the marketplace, they must convince the United Automobile Workers union (UAW) to make large and unpalatable concessions on wages, benefits and retiree health-care costs. The automakers must also strike tough bargains with bondholders and creditors. Months of negotiations on both fronts have been unsuccessful.

Acknowledging that negotiations may fail, President Obama said Chapter 11 is a distinct option for either company. "What I'm talking about is using our existing legal structure as a tool that, with the backing of the U.S. government, can make it easier for General Motors and Chrysler to quickly clear away old debts that are weighing them down so that they can get back on their feet and onto a path to success," he said. [36] Obama may also be hoping that just the threat of bankruptcy will accelerate negotiations between the automakers and its stakeholders.

"Our strong preference is to complete this restructuring out of court," GM said in a press statement that same day. "However, GM will take whatever steps are necessary to successfully restructure the company, which could include a court-supervised process." [37] Chrysler did not acknowledge the threat of bankruptcy in its statement. "While we recognize that we still have substantial hurdles to resolve, Chrysler is committed to working closely with Fiat, the administration, U.S. Treasury and the Task Force to secure the support of necessary stakeholders," said Chairman and CEO Bob Nardelli. [38] The UAW did not issue a statement.

The prospect of bankruptcy has been shadowing General Motors and Chrysler for months, with experts divided on whether bankruptcy is just the medicine the companies need to cut debt and reduce retiree costs or whether bankruptcy would be a poison that scares away customers and forces the eventual liquidation of the

The Sharper Image is among a growing number of troubled U.S. companies finding it increasingly difficult to reorganize under Chapter 11 of the Bankruptcy Code and instead having to liquidate. Retailers have been particularly hard hit, drowning in the perfect storm created by the deep recession and the credit squeeze. But some bankruptcy experts hold the changes Congress made to the Bankruptcy Code in 2005 partially to blame.

shrinking auto giants. Customers are already scarce; GM and Chrysler lost a combined $38 billion in 2008 as car sales fell to their lowest levels in 25 years. [39] This year is looking even worse, with car sales in January and February 38 percent lower than the same period the year before, according to *WardsAuto.com.* [40]

The Obama administration is anxious to avoid the sudden and chaotic bankruptcy of GM and Chrysler, which many fear could trigger a wave of failures among auto suppliers, who comprise the nation's largest manufacturing sector. More than 40 major suppliers filed for Chapter 11 restructuring in 2008, and the Motor & Equipment Manufacturers Association has said that another third of the industry is in "imminent financial dis-

tress" with another third heading in that direction. [41] In response to the association's plea for help, the administration unveiled in early March the Auto Supplier Support Program, which sets aside up to $5 billion for suppliers to give them "the confidence they need to continue shipping parts, pay their employees and continue their operations." [42]

In place of the usual bankruptcy filing, the administration is considering a government-managed Chapter 11 process that would allow GM and Chrysler to wring concessions from the UAW and creditors quickly. "What I'm not talking about is a process where a company is simply broken up, sold off and no longer exists. We're not talking about that," said the president. "And what I'm not talking about is a company that's stuck in court for years, unable to get out." [43] Acknowledging that customers are worried that a bankrupt automaker would not honor warranties for service and repairs, President Obama announced that the federal government would fully back those warranties starting March 30.

Both GM and Chrysler have bankruptcy experts working on Chapter 11 contingency plans to separate the "good" assets from the "bad" and have been in constant consultations with officials from the Auto Task Force and Treasury Department. In the event of a bankruptcy filing by either company, it is almost certain the government would provide tens of billions of dollars of debtor-in-possession (DIP) financing, a form of bankruptcy loan that is increasingly difficult for bankrupt companies to arrange in the current credit squeeze.

Cities in Trouble

Municipalities, just like businesses and individuals, can file for bankruptcy. And Jefferson County, Ala., may be headed for the biggest municipal bankruptcy in U.S. history. The county — home to Birmingham, the state's largest city — is carrying $3.9 billion in sewer debt that it can't pay. While its creditors are willing to make some concessions, any deal to restructure the debt depends on state lawmakers allowing the county to divert local sales tax revenues from servicing school debt to servicing sewer debt. So far state lawmakers have taken no action.

"It is a financial disaster that was to a large degree invented, packaged and sold by Wall Street," according to *Fortune* magazine." [44] In a nutshell, the county refinanced its sewer debt in the early 2000s with variable-rate securities and complicated hedging strategies, and when the credit markets froze, its interest payments shot up far beyond what sewer revenues could cover. Bribery and kickbacks also played a part. Three former members of the County Commission have been found guilty of federal corruption charges related to sewer construction or debt restructuring; the latest to be indicted is Birmingham Mayor Larry Langford, who was commission president from 2002 to 2006. He has pleaded not guilty.

Municipalities — counties, cities, towns, school districts and other public improvement districts — rarely go bankrupt; it's too much of a stigma and can seriously jeopardize their ability to borrow in the future. They'll lay off workers, raise taxes and fees, negotiate with creditors and do just about anything to avoid it. Since Congress gave municipalities the right to file for bankruptcy in 1937 — called Chapter 9 — just 564 have done so. Only two filed last year. [45] When municipalities do declare bankruptcy, it is often because of some unique event, perhaps a large legal judgment, a poor financial investment, an infrastructure project whose revenues fell far below expectations or fraud.

But one of the municipalities that filed in 2008, Vallejo, Calif., faced conditions that were not so unique, namely slumping real estate values and rising pension and health-care costs. Dean Gloster, an attorney representing Vallejo's unions, called the town "the canary in the coal mine" and predicted that even better-run cities would be facing similar issues soon. [46]

In fact, several municipal bankruptcy experts predict many more municipalities will declare bankruptcy this year and next. "I'm looking for about a dozen in 2009 and maybe double or triple that in 2010, depending on levels of government stimulus," says Richard Ciccarone, chief research officer at McDonnell Investment Management in Oak Brook, Ill. Ciccarone says the 2009 number is not particularly alarming and that most of those bankruptcies will be redevelopment districts, so-called special-purpose entities that a city or county sets up to fund infrastructure. But if he's correct about 2010, the number of failures would be the largest in decades, far surpassing the 18 municipal bankruptcies filed in 1987, the year the stock market crashed.

The pressures are building. For the past 20 or 30 years, state and local governments have not been fully funding their employee pension plans. In addition, many of their pension managers, says Ciccarone, have assumed an unrealistic return on their investments when planning for the future. Given the past year's slide in the stock market, when those actuarial assumptions are eventually adjusted, the degree to which pension plans are underfunded could expand to crisis proportions. "They're going to have to increase the contributions to their pension funds enormously; they could triple," says Ciccarone.

Add to that the trillions of dollars needed to repair and maintain the nation's bridges, roads, sewer lines and other critical infrastructure, plus the reduction in sales tax, property tax and income tax revenue that's normally seen during a recession, and the mismatch between revenues and costs widens dramatically. [47]

At the same time, cities must continue to provide essential services. "If you don't people will move out, you'll lose your tax base and you'll have a death spiral," says Chicago lawyer James Spiotto, a bankruptcy expert. "That's what happened to Bridgeport, Conn., in 1991."

Spiotto says the country is at a crossroads. "It's in the hands of every municipality and every state to see whether we are going to have a significant increase in Chapter 9 filings or very little," he says. States may have to set up oversight commissions for emergency financial relief or make bridge loans to municipalities to help them balance their budgets, says Spiotto, and municipalities will have to seriously rein in spending.

Ironically, simply threatening to follow Vallejo into bankruptcy may help cities cut costs and avoid bankruptcy. In mid-March, the bankruptcy judge in the Vallejo case ruled in the city's favor when he indicated that he has the power to void the city's union contracts. That decision increased pressure on the two unions that had resisted renegotiating their contracts and the generous salaries and benefits they contain. Gloster said he has heard that other cities are already pointing to Vallejo as they bargain with their own unions. [48] ■

OUTLOOK

'Cleaning Up the Mess'

"I think we're going to see at least five quarters of serious economic problems," says New York bankruptcy lawyer Wurst, "and insolvency counsel are going to be busy for the next five to eight years cleaning up the mess." Wurst says he is interviewing new hires and borrowing lawyers from his firm's other departments to keep up with the work.

At the end of 2008, the Turnaround Management Association polled its members — corporate managers specializing in troubled companies, bankers, attorneys, investors, judges, academics and liquidators — for their 2009 forecasts. By an overwhelming margin, they predicted the auto industry would have the greatest difficulties with its finances and operations, followed by retail, homebuilding, manufacturing, commercial real estate, construction and hedge funds. (*See chart p. 324.*)

If members were polled again, says James Shein, a professor at Northwestern University's Kellogg School of Management who supervised the survey, there would be at least one addition to the list. "I would put in media," he says. "It is much clearer now that media companies, in particular newspapers, are in a lot more trouble now than people realized."

Shein classifies troubled companies according to where they are on a "crisis curve," and the earlier problems are caught along that curve, the easier they are to fix, he says.

He calls the first stop on the curve "the blinded phase." "Management is overly optimistic about the future and thinks any weak conditions are temporary," says Shein. The next stop is the "inaction phase," where management wakes up but studies problems to death. Then comes the "faulty action phase" where management does something, but it's the wrong something. "They downsize, for instance, without really figuring where they want to go and how to get there. Downsizing becomes the goal rather than a tool." The next phase is the "crisis phase," where the company is bleeding cash, losing employees and scaring away both suppliers and customers. And last is dissolution, often achieved through bankruptcy.

Avoiding the crisis curve or getting off early requires foresight. "The biggest mistake corporate leaders make," says Sydney Finkelstein, a professor at Dartmouth College's Tuck School of Business, "is not developing an early-warning system in the first place."

Finkelstein, the co-author of a new book on corporate decision making — *Think Again* — says corporate boards usually do a good job of tracking financials like the amount of product shipped, market share and return on assets, but by the time these financial indicators go south, it's often too late. What really makes a difference in a company's future, he says, is the so-called "soft stuff," things like leadership, teamwork, critical thinking. "It is things like this rather than the hard numbers that are the key warning signs of trouble," says Finkelstein, "and corporate boards don't do a good job of tracking the soft stuff." To help, Finkelstein has put together a complex survey that assesses what employees think of how well management encourages debate, copes with competitive threats, promotes teamwork and thinks strategically.

So far, says Finkelstein, it's been used in 100 companies. ∎

Notes

[1] William Pack, "Six Flags debt weighs on company," *San Antonio Express-News*, March 12, 2009, p. 2C.

[2] For background on the economic crisis, see the following *CQ Researcher* reports: Thomas J. Billitteri, "Financial Bailout," Oct. 24, 2008, pp. 865-888, and Kenneth Jost, "Financial Crisis," May 9, 2008, pp. 409-432.

[3] U.S. Courts Bankruptcy Statistics, www.uscourts.gov/bnkrpctystats/statistics.htm#calendar.

[4] For background, see the following *CQ Researcher* reports: Thomas J. Billitteri, "Auto Industry's Future," Feb. 6, 2009, pp. 105-128, Thomas J. Billitteri, "Middle-Class Squeeze," March 6, 2009, pp. 201-224, and Marcia Clemmitt, "Mortgage Crisis," Nov. 2, 2007, pp. 913-936.

[5] Barry E. Adler, Vedran Capkun and Lawrence A. Weiss, "Destruction of Value in the New Era of Chapter 11," *Working Paper*, Oct. 12, 2008, p. 2, http://ssrn.com/abstract=795987.

[6] Testimony of Harvey R. Miller, before House Judiciary Subcommittee on Commercial and Administrative Law, "Circuit City Unplugged: Why Did Chapter 11 Fail to Save 34,000 Jobs?" March 11, 2009. pp. 4, 7.

[7] "Bankruptcy financing gets pricier and more elusive," Thomson Financial News Super Focus, Oct. 12, 2008.

[8] Testimony of Richard M. Pachulski before House Judiciary Subcommittee on Commercial and Administrative Law, "Circuit City Unplugged: Why Did Chapter 11 Fail to Save 34,000 Jobs?" March 11, 2009, p. 7.

[9] Video Webcast of hearing, http://judiciary.house.gov/hearings/hear_090311_1.html.

[10] Testimony of Isaac Pachulski before House Judiciary Subcommittee on Commercial and Administrative Law, "Circuit City Unplugged: Why Did Chapter 11 Fail to Save 34,000 Jobs?" March 11, 2009, p. 20.

[11] Testimony of Richard Pachulski, *op. cit.*

About the Author

Barbara Mantel is a freelance writer in New York City whose work has appeared in *The New York Times*, the *Journal of Child and Adolescent Psychopharmacology* and *Mamm Magazine*. She is a former correspondent and senior producer for National Public Radio and has won several journalism awards, including the National Press Club's Best Consumer Journalism Award and Lincoln University's Unity Award. She holds a B.A. in history and economics from the University of Virginia and an M.A. in economics from Northwestern University.

¹² *Ibid.*

¹³ Testimony of Todd Zywicki before House Judiciary Subcommittee on Commercial and Administrative Law, March 11, 2009.

¹⁴ Samuel Gerdano, "The Future of Collective Bargaining Under Bankruptcy," The American Bankruptcy Institute, undated, www.abiworld.org/AM/Template.cfm?Section=Home&TEMPLATE=/CM/ContentDisplay.cfm&CONTENTID=41342.

¹⁵ Jeremy Johnson, "The Rejection of Collective Bargaining Agreements — New Cases and Developments," *DLA Piper*, September 2006, www.dlapiper.com/rejection_of_collective_bargaining/.

¹⁶ Testimony of Babette Ceccotti before House Judiciary Subcommittee on Commercial and Administrative Law, "Protecting Employees and Retirees in Business Bankruptcies Act of 2007," June 5, 2008, p. 9.

¹⁷ "Pro-Corporate Bankruptcy Courts," *Labor Blog*, Oct. 26, 2004, www.nathannewman.org/laborblog/archive/001915.shtml.

¹⁸ Gerdano, *op. cit.*

¹⁹ Bruce H. Mann, *Republic of Debtors: Bankruptcy in the Age of American Independence* (2002), p. 2.

²⁰ J. Michael Deasy, United States Bankruptcy Judge, District of New Hampshire, "History of Bankruptcy Law in the United States," May 2004, www.rarolc.net/programs/download.php?fcid=2&fid=136.

²¹ *Ibid.*

²² U.S. Constitution, Article I, Section 8, Clause 4, www.archives.gov/exhibits/charters/constitution_transcript.html.

²³ David A. Skeel, *Debt's Dominion: A History of Bankruptcy Law in America* (2001), p. 25.

²⁴ Charles Jordan Tabb, "The History of the Bankruptcy Laws in the United States," *American Bankruptcy Institute Law Review*, spring 1995. p. 8.

²⁵ Skeel, *op. cit.*, p. 26.

²⁶ David S. Kennedy and R. Spencer Clift, III, "An Historical Analysis of Insolvency Laws and Their Impact on the Role, Power, and Jurisdiction of Today's United States Bankruptcy Court and Its Judicial Officers," *Journal of Bankruptcy Law and Practice*, January/February 2000, p. 7.

²⁷ Tabb, *op. cit.*, p. 13.

²⁸ Kennedy and Clift, *op. cit.*, p. 7.

²⁹ *Ibid.*, p. 8.

³⁰ Skeel, *op. cit.*, pp. 136-137.

³¹ "A Brief History of Bankruptcy," BankruptcyData.com, pp. 2-3, undated.

³² Deasy, *op. cit.*, p. 2.

³³ Tabb, *op. cit.*, p. 21.

FOR MORE INFORMATION

Administrative Office of the United States Courts, 1 Columbus Circle, N.W., Washington, DC 20544; (202) 502-2600; www.uscourts.gov. Government office that serves the federal judiciary in carrying out its constitutional mission to provide equal justice under law; posts bankruptcy statistics and basic bankruptcy information on its Web site.

American Bankruptcy Institute, 44 Canal Center Plaza, Suite 400, Alexandria, VA 22314; (703) 739-0800; www.abiworld.org. Multidisciplinary, nonpartisan organization dedicated to research and education on matters related to insolvency.

Association of Insolvency & Restructuring Advisors, 221 Stewart Ave., Suite 207, Medford, OR 97501; (541) 858-1665; www.aira.org. National not-for-profit organization serving the needs of business-turnaround, restructuring and bankruptcy practitioners.

BankruptcyData.com, New Generation Research, Inc., 225 Friend St., Suite 801, Boston, MA 02114; (617) 573-9550; www.bankruptcydata.com. Leading provider of information on companies in bankruptcy and financial distress.

Bankruptcy Research Database, UCLA Law School, 405 Hilgard Ave., Los Angeles, CA 90095; (310) 794-5722; www.webbrd.com. Web-based business bankruptcy research tool enabling visitors to design and execute an empirical study of large, public company bankruptcy cases.

National Bankruptcy Conference, 10332 Main St., Fairfax, VA 22030; (703) 273-4918; www.nationalbankruptcyconference.org. Leading bankruptcy scholars and practitioners studying bankruptcy laws.

New York Institute of Credit, 380 Lexington Ave., New York, NY 10168; (212) 551-7920; wwwnyic.org. Nonprofit educational organization offering courses in credit granting and bank lending and whose faculty consists primarily of credit executives, accountants and lawyers.

Turnaround Management Association, 150 South Wacker Dr., Suite 900, Chicago, IL 60606; (312) 578-6900; www.turnaround.org. International nonprofit association dedicated to corporate renewal and turnaround management.

³⁴ *Ibid.*, p.22.

³⁵ "Remarks by the President on the American Automotive Industry," March 30, 2009, www.whitehouse.gov/the_press_office/Remarks-by-the-President-on-the-American-Automotive-Industry-3/30/09/.

³⁶ *Ibid.*

³⁷ GM Statement on Auto Industry Restructuring, March 30, 2009, http://media.gm.com/servlet/GatewayServlet?target=http://image.emerald.gm.com/gmnews/viewmonthlyreleasedetail.do?domain=74&docid=53307.

³⁸ Chrysler LLC Chairman and CEO, Bob Nardelli, "Chrysler Statement in Response to the Announcement by the Administration, U.S. Treasury and President's Auto Task Force, March 30, 2009, www.chryslerllc.com/en/news/.

³⁹ Bill Vlasic and Sheryl Gay Stolberg, "U.S. Expected to Give More Financing to Automakers," *The New York Times*, March 28, 2009, p. B4.

⁴⁰ WardsAuto.com, http://wardsauto.com/keydata/USSalesSummary0902/.

⁴¹ "Parts Suppliers Submit Formal Assistance Request to Treasury," press release, Motor & Equipment Manufacturers Association, Feb. 13, 2009.

⁴² "Treasury Announces Auto Supplier Support Program," U.S. Department of Treasury, March 19, 2009, www.treas.gov/press/releases/tg64.htm.

⁴³ "Remarks by the President on the American Automotive Industry," *op. cit.*

⁴⁴ David Whitford, "Birmingham on the Brink," *Fortune*, Oct. 27, 2008, p. 114.

⁴⁵ James Spiotto, "The Storm Grows In Intensity," Chapman and Cutler, LLP, January 2009, pp. 38, 39.

⁴⁶ Anya Sostek, "Vallejo's Fiscal Freefall," *Governing*, November 2008, p. 52.

⁴⁷ For background, see Marcia Clemmitt, "Public-Works Projects," *CQ Researcher*, Feb. 20, 2009, pp. 153-176, and Marcia Clemmitt, "Aging Infrastructure," *CQ Researcher*, Sept. 28, 2007, pp. 793-816.

⁴⁸ Sostek, *op. cit.*

Bibliography

Selected Sources

Books

Finkelstein, Sydney, Jo Whitehead and Andrew Campbell, *Think Again: Why Good Leaders Make Bad Decisions and How to Keep it From Happening to You*, Harvard Business School Press, 2009.

Using examples from business, politics, and history, the authors offer a model for making better decisions, describing the key red flags to watch for and detailing decision-making safeguards.

Mann, Bruce H., *Republic of Debtors: Bankruptcy in the Age of American Independence*, Harvard University Press, 2002.

A professor at Harvard Law School explores the subject of debt and insolvency in early-American history.

Skeel, David A., *Debt's Dominion: A History of Bankruptcy Law in America*, Princeton University Press, 2001.

A law professor at the University of Pennsylvania traces the evolution of American bankruptcy law from its beginnings in 1800.

Articles

Humer, Caroline, "Bankruptcy financing gets pricier and more elusive," *Thomson Financial News Super Focus*, Oct. 12, 2008, www.reuters.com/article/ousiv/idUS TRE49B22Z20081012?sp=true.

Companies filing for bankruptcy are having trouble getting debtor-in-possession financing, which allows them to pay their suppliers and employees as they try to reorganize.

Pack, William, "Six Flags debt weighs on company," *San Antonio Express-News*, March 12, 2009, p. 2C, www.mysan antonio.com/business/Six_Flags_filing_highlights_viability _concerns.html.

Six Flags struggles to refinance its debt and might have to pursue bankruptcy.

Sostek, Anya, "Vallejo's Fiscal Freefall," *Governing*, November 2008, p. 52, www.governing.com/articles/0811vallejo.htm.

Other cities may consider following Vallejo, Calif., which declared bankruptcy in spring 2008.

Vlasic, Bill, and Sheryl Gay Stolberg, "U.S. Expected to Give More Financing to Automakers," *The New York Times*, March 28, 2009, p. B4, www.nytimes.com/2009/03/ 28/business/economy/28auto.html?hp.

The Obama administration will extend short-term aid to GM and Chrysler and impose deadlines for the companies to get concessions from union workers and bondholders.

Whitford, David, "Birmingham on the Brink (of Bankruptcy)," *Fortune*, Oct. 27, 2008, p. 114, money.cnn.com/ 2008/10/13/news/economy/Birmingham_brink_Whitford. fortune/.

Jefferson County (Birmingham), Ala., tries to avoid bankruptcy as it struggles to make payments on more than $3 billion in sewer debt.

Reports and Testimony

Adler, Barry E., Vedran Capkun and Lawrence A. Weiss, "Destruction of Value in the New Era of Chapter 11," *Working Paper*, Oct. 12, 2008, http://ssm.com/abstract/795987.

The financial conditions of firms filing for bankruptcy after 2001 show a significant and prolonged deterioration compared to firms filing before 2000.

Johnson, Jeremy R., "The Rejection of Collective Bargaining Agreements — New Cases and Developments," *DLA Piper News & Insights*, September 2006.

A Chapter 11 debtor's ability to reject its collective-bargaining agreements is often a pivotal issue.

Kennedy, David S., and R. Spencer Clift, III, "An Historical Analysis of Insolvency Laws and Their Impact on the Role, Power, and Jurisdiction of Today's United States Bankruptcy Court and Its Judicial Officers," *Journal of Bankruptcy Law and Practice*, January/February 2000.

The authors discuss the historical development of the U.S. bankruptcy court.

Tabb, Charles Jordan, "The History of the Bankruptcy Laws in the United States," *American Bankruptcy Institute Law Review*, spring 1995.

The author reviews the history of U.S. bankruptcy laws, dating back to the English antecedents.

Testimony of Harvey R. Miller, House Subcommittee on Commercial and Administrative Law, "Circuit City Unplugged: Why Did Chapter 11 Fail to Save 34,000 Jobs?" March 11, 2009.

A prominent bankruptcy lawyer says some of the 2005 amendments to the Bankruptcy Code have made it more difficult for debtors to reorganize in Chapter 11 and recommends their revision or repeal.

Testimony of Todd J. Zywicki, House Judiciary Subcommittee on Commercial and Administrative Law, "Circuit City Unplugged: Why Did Chapter 11 Fail to Save 34,000 Jobs?" March 11, 2009.

The George Mason University law professor says the 2005 amendments to the Bankruptcy Code may have contributed to the liquidations of retailers in Chapter 11 but that the recession and poor management were the main factors.

The Next Step:

Additional Articles from Current Periodicals

Auto Industry

Gray, Kathleen, and Brent Snavely, "Automakers Seem to Get Bumpier Ride Than Banks," *Detroit Free Press*, April 5, 2009, p. A6.

Auto manufacturers aren't getting the same treatment from the government for bankruptcy protection as banking institutions.

Marr, Kendra, "Struggling Auto Parts Suppliers Prepare to Seek Federal Aid," *The Washington Post*, Jan. 27, 2009, p. A6.

Auto-industry woes extend beyond just manufacturers.

Rising, Malin, "Sweden's Saab in Contact With 20 Potential Buyers," The Associated Press, April 6, 2009.

General Motors is trying to sell its struggling Swedish line in an attempt to stave off further financial woes.

Snyder, Jesse, and Bradford Wernle, "Outside Events Deal Crippling Blow to Cerberus' Plan to Rescue Chrysler," *Automotive News*, Feb. 16, 2009, p. 24.

The authors look at the years since the venture capitalist firm Cerberus bought Chrysler, and the lead up to its current financial situation.

Bankruptcy Law

Hamburger, Tom, "No Bankruptcy Aid for Homeowners," *Los Angeles Times*, Sept. 29, 2008, p. A10.

Changes made to the bankruptcy law mean that homeowners cannot seek revisions on loans for their primary residences.

Johnson, Andrew, "Selective Bankruptcy," *The Arizona Republic*, Oct. 22, 2008, p. B1.

Changes in the bankruptcy code have allowed real-estate developers to claim losses on specific properties, as opposed to overall company losses.

Kearsley, Kelly, "Congress Urged to Enact Looser Bankruptcy Laws," *News Tribune* (Washington), Jan. 8, 2009, p. D1.

Twenty-two state attorneys general are encouraging Congress to loosen bankruptcy laws in order to reduce home foreclosures.

Sidoti, Liz, "Obama News, Most Recent 60 Days: Proposes Bankruptcy Changes," The Associated Press, July 8, 2008.

Barack Obama advocated for making changes to the bankruptcy code during his presidential campaign.

Government

Irwin, Neil, and Kendra Marr, "White House Won't Appoint a 'Car Czar,' " *The Washington Post*, Feb. 16, 2009, p. A6.

The White House has decided not to appoint a single individual to oversee the restructuring of the auto industry, but rather to make it a coordinated effort between multiple federal offices.

Jacobs, Stevenson, and Tom Krisher, "What if the Government Bailed Out of Bailouts?" The Associated Press, March 18, 2009.

Experts analyze how markets would react if the government were to stop providing bailouts.

LoBianco, Tom, "Geithner Hints at Banker Ousters," *The Washington Times*, April 6, 2009, p. A6.

Treasury Secretary Timothy Geithner says the government would make changes to the banking industry if necessary.

Rising Bankruptcies

Carey, Pete, "Bankruptcies on the Rise," *San Jose Mercury News*, Oct. 24, 2008.

The San Francisco Bay Area has seen a rise in individuals and small businesses declaring bankruptcy.

Sisk, Chas, "Bankruptcies Snuff Out Tenn. Small Businesses," *The Tennessean*, Nov. 17, 2008.

Changes in the economy have adversely affected small businesses in the Tennessee Valley.

Strom, Stephanie, "Bankruptcy Now Touching Nonprofits," *The New York Times*, Feb. 20, 2009, p. A17.

The rise in bankruptcies is now affecting non-profits, as many such organizations struggle to maintain operations.

Citing CQ Researcher

Sample formats for citing these reports in a bibliography include the ones listed below. Preferred styles and formats vary, so please check with your instructor or professor.

__MLA STYLE__

Jost, Kenneth. "Rethinking the Death Penalty." CQ Researcher 16 Nov. 2001: 945-68.

__APA STYLE__

Jost, K. (2001, November 16). Rethinking the death penalty. *CQ Researcher, 11*, 945-968.

__CHICAGO STYLE__

Jost, Kenneth. "Rethinking the Death Penalty." *CQ Researcher*, November 16, 2001, 945-968.

In-depth Reports on Issues in the News

Are you writing a paper?

Need backup for a debate?

Want to become an expert on an issue?

For 80 years, students have turned to *CQ Researcher* for in-depth reporting on issues in the news. Reports on a full range of political and social issues are now available. Following is a selection of recent reports:

Civil Liberties
Closing Guantánamo, 2/09
Limiting Lawsuits, 12/08
Affirmative Action, 10/08
Gay Marriage Showdowns, 9/08
America's Border Fence, 9/08
Immigration Debate, 2/08

Crime/Law
Mexico's Drug War, 12/08
Prostitution Debate, 5/08
Public Defenders, 4/08
Gun Violence, 5/07

Education
Reading Crisis? 2/08
Discipline in Schools, 2/08
Student Aid, 1/08
Racial Diversity in Public Schools, 9/07
Stress on Students, 7/07

Environment/Society
Future of Journalism, 3/09
Confronting Warming, 1/09
Reducing Carbon Footprint, 12/08
Protecting Wetlands, 10/08
Buying Green, 2/08

Health/Safety
Extreme Sports, 4/09
Regulating Toxic Chemicals, 1/09
Preventing Cancer, 1/09
Heart Health, 9/08
Global Food Crisis, 6/08

Politics/Economy
Future of the GOP, 3/09
Middle-Class Squeeze, 3/09
Public-Works Projects, 2/09
The Obama Presidency, 1/09
The National Debt, 11/08

Upcoming Reports

Wrongful Convictions, 4/17/09	High-Speed Trains, 4/24/09	Judicial Elections, 5/1/09

ACCESS

CQ Researcher is available in print and online. For access, visit your library or www.cqresearcher.com.

STAY CURRENT

To receive notice of upcoming *CQ Researcher* reports, or learn more about *CQ Researcher* products, subscribe to the free e-mail newsletters, *CQ Researcher Alert!* and *CQ Researcher News*: http://cqpress.com/newsletters.

PURCHASE

To purchase a *CQ Researcher* report in print or electronic format (PDF), visit www.cqpress.com or call 866-427-7737. Single reports start at $15. Bulk purchase discounts and electronic-rights licensing are also available.

SUBSCRIBE

Annual full-service *CQ Researcher* subscriptions—including 44 reports a year, monthly index updates, and a bound volume—start at $803. Add $25 for domestic postage.

CQ Researcher Online offers a backfile from 1991 and a number of tools to simplify research. For pricing information, call 800-834-9020, ext. 1906, or e-mail librarysales@cqpress.com.

CQ Researcher

Published by CQ Press, a division of SAGE Publications

www.cqresearcher.com

Wrongful Convictions

Is overhaul of the criminal justice system needed?

U ntil March 2009, few Americans had heard of Ronald Cotton, who was convicted in North Carolina of raping a college student and served 11 years in prison before being exonerated by DNA testing. Now Cotton is a household name because of a book about his case and appearances on "60 Minutes" and NBC's "Today" show. As recently as 10 years ago, the proposition that innocent men and women regularly end up in prison failed to find traction. Today, thanks to the power of DNA evidence, media coverage and the establishment of innocence projects, there is general acceptance that wrongful convictions indeed occur. Dozens of states have passed laws to prevent wrongful convictions and compensate those wrongly imprisoned. Defense attorneys and many academics say wrongful convictions are a recurrent problem requiring substantial changes in the criminal justice system, but prosecutors, police and other academics say mistaken convictions are such a small percentage of all cases that the system should mostly be left alone.

Joshua Kezer, 34, is among 235 men and women who are free today after DNA testing showed they were wrongfully convicted. Kezer was released in February after 14 years in prison in Missouri for a murder the judge said he did not commit.

CQ Researcher • April 17, 2009 • www.cqresearcher.com
Volume 19, Number 15 • Pages 345-372

RECIPIENT OF SOCIETY OF PROFESSIONAL JOURNALISTS AWARD FOR EXCELLENCE ◆ AMERICAN BAR ASSOCIATION SILVER GAVEL AWARD

April 17, 2009
Volume 19, Number 15

MANAGING EDITOR: Thomas J. Colin
tcolin@cqpress.com

ASSISTANT MANAGING EDITOR: Kathy Koch
kkoch@cqpress.com

ASSOCIATE EDITOR: Kenneth Jost

STAFF WRITERS: Thomas J. Billitteri,
Marcia Clemmitt, Peter Katel

CONTRIBUTING WRITERS: Rachel Cox,
Sarah Glazer, Alan Greenblatt,
Barbara Mantel, Patrick Marshall,
Tom Price, Jennifer Weeks

DESIGN/PRODUCTION EDITOR: Olu B. Davis

ASSISTANT EDITOR: Darrell Dela Rosa

FACT-CHECKING: Eugene J. Gabler,
Michelle Harris

EDITORIAL INTERN: Vyomika Jairam

CQ PRESS

A Division of SAGE

PRESIDENT AND PUBLISHER:
John A. Jenkins

EXECUTIVE DIRECTOR,
REFERENCE INFORMATION GROUP:
Alix B. Vance

CQ Press is a registered trademark of Congressional Quarterly Inc.

CQ Researcher (ISSN 1056-2036) is printed on acid-free paper. Published weekly, except; (Jan. wk. 1) (May wk. 4) (July wks. 1, 2) (Aug. wks. 3, 4) (Nov. wk. 4) and (Dec. wk. 4), by CQ Press, a division of SAGE Publications. Annual full-service subscriptions start at $803. For pricing, call 1-800-834-9020, ext. 1906. To purchase a *CQ Researcher* report in print or electronic format (PDF), visit www. cqpress.com or call 866-427-7737. Single reports start at $15. Bulk purchase discounts and electronic-rights licensing are also available. Periodicals postage paid at Washington, D.C., and additional mailing offices. POSTMASTER: Send address changes to *CQ Researcher*, 2300 N St., N.W., Suite 800, Washington, DC 20037.

Cover: AP Photo/Kelley McCall

Wrongful Convictions

BY STEVE WEINBERG

THE ISSUES

Darryl Burton walked out of a Missouri prison in 2008 after serving 24 years for a murder he did not commit. He had proclaimed his innocence from the day of his arrest in St. Louis. Sixteen years into his prison sentence, Burton's hope for release took an upward tick when Centurion Ministries agreed to look into his case.

The nonprofit organization in Princeton, N.J., was founded by James McCloskey, an ordained minister and former business executive who has spent the last 29 years investigating alleged wrongful convictions. Working with a paid staff of five and a dozen volunteers, McCloskey reviews thousands of inmates' requests for assistance every year and selects the few his organization can afford to investigate. Entirely dependent on donations from private individuals, Centurion has played a major role in more than 40 exonerations. [1]

Nobody knows how many innocent men and women are serving prison terms for crimes they did not commit. There is no doubt, however, that since DNA testing became accepted as accurate some 15 years ago, 235 inmates have been freed because of the forensic technique, according to the Innocence Project, a national organization based in New York City. [2]

But testable DNA material shows up in only about 10 percent of crimes — mainly murder and rape — that lead to arrests. Moreover, in most jurisdictions, fewer than 10 percent of all crimes charged proceed all the way to trial. In cases with trial records, it is

Former inmate Alan Crotzer, left, applauds on Oct. 21, 2008, as Florida Gov. Charlie Crist signs legislation compensating Crotzer for the 24 years he spent in prison after being wrongly convicted of rape and robbery. Half the states allow compensation for victims of wrongful convictions.

AP Photo/*Tampa Tribune*/Colin Hackley

sometimes possible to determine later the innocence of a convicted defendant. But most inmates end up in prison by pleading guilty before trial, leaving a scant public record. [3]

In the 2006 decision by the U.S. Supreme Court in *Kansas v. Marsh*, Justice Antonin Scalia, writing a concurring opinion to the majority ruling, said the wrongful-conviction rate across the nation is minuscule. [4] (*See "At Issue," p. 365.*) Scalia quoted approvingly from a *New York Times* op-ed by Joshua Marquis, the district attorney in Clatsop County (Astoria), Ore., and a director of the National District Attorneys Association. Marquis, citing what he considered a misguided study by a law professor, wrote, "Let's give the professor the benefit of the doubt

— let's assume that he understated the number of innocents by roughly a factor of ten, that instead of 340 there were 4,000 people in prison who weren't involved in the crime in any way. During that same 15 years, there were more than 15 million felony convictions across the country. That would make the error rate .027 percent, or, to put it another way, a success rate of 99.973 percent." [5]

In fact, Scalia asserted, numerous cases labeled "exonerations" are nothing of the sort. Instead, they are primarily violations of defendants' due-process rights. "Most are based on legal errors that have little or nothing to do with guilt. The studies cited by the dissent demonstrate nothing more."

One of the scholars mentioned critically by Scalia is Samuel R. Gross, a University of Michigan law professor. After studying Scalia's opinion, Gross called the .027 percent error rate Scalia cited "absurd." Gross noted that "almost everything we know about false convictions is based on exonerations in rape and murder cases, which account for only 2 percent of felony convictions. Within that important but limited sphere, we have learned a lot in the past 30 years; outside it, our ignorance is nearly complete."

Gross argues that cases involving a plea agreement — and thus no trial — frequently lead to undocumented wrongful convictions. Innocent individuals plead guilty, Gross says, because they worry an adverse jury verdict will result in a longer prison sentence than the deal offered by the prosecutor — or even the death penalty. [6]

Half the States Compensate for Mistakes

Twenty-seven states plus the District of Columbia and the federal government allow compensation for those wrongly convicted of a crime, but many of the laws have shortcomings, according to the Innocence Project.

Compensation for the Wrongly Convicted

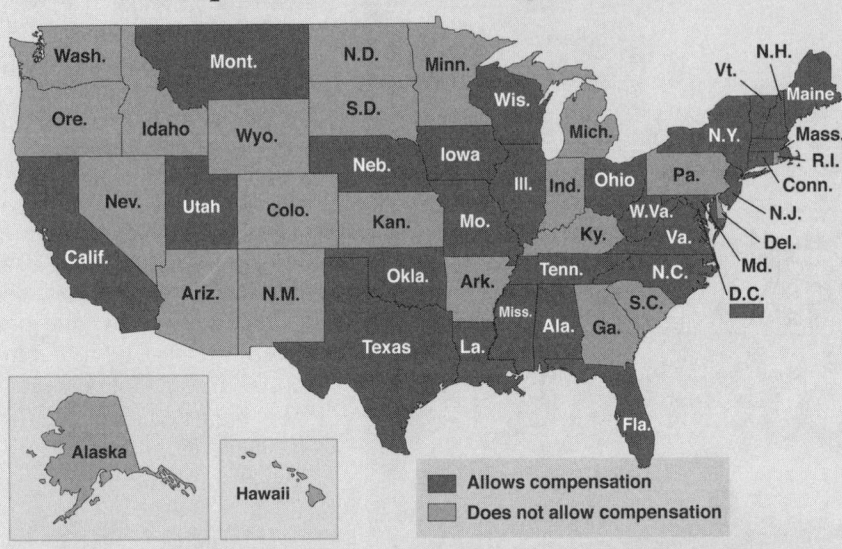

Allows compensation
Does not allow compensation

The nonprofit Innocence Project says state wrongful-conviction compensation laws have several common shortcomings, including:

- Compensation may take years to receive and is often insufficient to rebuild a life.

- Failing to provide immediate services like re-entry funds, access to job training, educational, health and legal services.

- Failing to provide uniform, statutory access to compensation. For example, some states require "private compensation bills" to be passed in order to compensate an exoneree, which means he must mount a costly political campaign to get lawmakers to pass a bill on his behalf.

- Prohibiting compensation to those who "contributed" to their wrongful convictions, effectively excluding those who falsely confessed or pled guilty.

- Denying additional remedy for those who can prove their wrongful convictions resulted from evident and intentional civil rights violations as opposed to simple, but unintentional, error.

- Preventing compensation for individuals with felony convictions in unrelated cases.

Source: Innocence Project, April 14, 2009

A great deal more is at stake with wrongful convictions beyond simply the welfare of innocent individuals in prison. There is also the sobering reality that every time an innocent defendant is incarcerated, the actual murderer or rapist or armed robber might be at large, committing more crimes. Also at stake is public trust in the criminal justice system. Mistrust due to repeated wrongful convictions leads to decreased citizen cooperation with police and jurors who disbelieve prosecutors.

Generalizations about the criminal justice system are difficult to make, because it is not really a unified system. Instead, arrests, pretrial negotiations and trials are decentralized. The United States is divided into more than 2,300 local criminal jurisdictions, each served by an elected or appointed prosecutor (most commonly known as a district attorney), judges and police agencies. Superimposed onto the local jurisdictions is the federal system, with at least one federal prosecutor (called a U.S. attorney) and federal judges in each state. Some jurisdictions have no documented wrongful convictions. Others have spawned multiple wrongful convictions. [7]

The National District Attorneys Association argues that wrongful convictions are episodic, not epidemic, and almost always arise from well-intentioned law enforcement work, not from incompetence or dishonesty. If pressed to place a number on wrongful convictions, district attorneys tend to say it's less than 1 percent of all cases charged. Conversely, members of the National Association of Criminal Defense Lawyers say wrongful convictions are epidemic in multiple jurisdictions and frequently arise from incompetent or dishonest law enforcement personnel. If pressed, defense lawyers say the percentage of wrongful convictions is between 5 and 10 percent. [8]

For its part, the American Bar Association (ABA) acknowledges the reality of wrongful convictions. A report by the ABA's Ad Hoc Innocence Committee to Ensure the Integrity of the Criminal Process offers numerous recommendations aimed at reducing wrongful convictions. The frequency of wrongful convictions "undermines the assumption that the criminal justice system sufficiently protects the innocent," according to the report. [9]

Increased public awareness of wrongful convictions, like that of so many other social problems, has been generated by the news and entertainment media. The public has been bombarded by exoneree stories in recent years, including best-selling author Scott Turow's novel *Reversible Errors*; the stage play "The Exonerated"; the celebrated documentary movie "The Thin Blue Line"; the Hollywood drama "Just Cause," starring Sean Connery and Laurence Fishburne, plus, of course, "CSI" and numerous other television police procedurals.

Indeed, some prosecutors and judges refer to the "CSI effect," in which real-life juries acquit defendants because the forensic evidence police present fails to match the quality of the fictional evidence that TV police evidence technicians working in sophisticated labs uncover — all within an hour. [10]

The new awareness of wrongful convictions has led to numerous in-depth studies of the problem and a wide range of enacted and pending legislation in many states, from new funding for crime labs to compensation for wrongly convicted men and women.

Since his release from prison in Missouri last year, Burton, like many exonerees, has attended occasional gatherings of other exonerees. Invariably, they exhibit forgiveness remarkable to behold. When they speak in anger, it is almost always because they say they have never received apologies from the police officers and prosecutors who wrongly sent them to prison, or they have trouble finding decent jobs, often be-

cause they lack job skills or potential employers wonder if they are truly innocent. [11]

Ronald Cotton was found innocent and released after nearly a dozen years in prison in North Carolina for a rape he didn't commit. (*See sidebar, p. 358.*) He forgives Jennifer Thompson-Cannino, the woman whose mistaken testimony convicted him, but still feels angry about the aftermath. In a book about his conviction and redemption, co-authored with her, Cotton explains: "All those years with bars and razor wire around me — you're no better than a dog in a cage. After being locked up for so long, they just toss you out and expect you to deal with it. I had no money, and how could I explain on job applications where I had been for the last 11 years?" [12]

As legal experts and prisoner advocates study ways to improve the criminal justice system, here are some of the questions being asked:

Are wrongful convictions a serious problem?

Defense lawyers, law professors and other academic researchers and a growing number of journalists believe wrongful convictions are frequent. Police personnel, prosecutors and an apparently small number of law professors and academic researchers believe wrongful convictions occur in such a small percentage of cases that systemic reforms are unnecessary.

Although the debate over the size of the problem goes back to the beginning of the 20th century, it did not become high profile until the late 1980s, when the use of DNA to determine actual innocence or confirm guilt became available. [13] Suddenly, those who believed wrongful convictions had been undercounted began to accumulate indisputable proof, while those who saw it as a minuscule problem decided they needed to make a case for their point of view. The

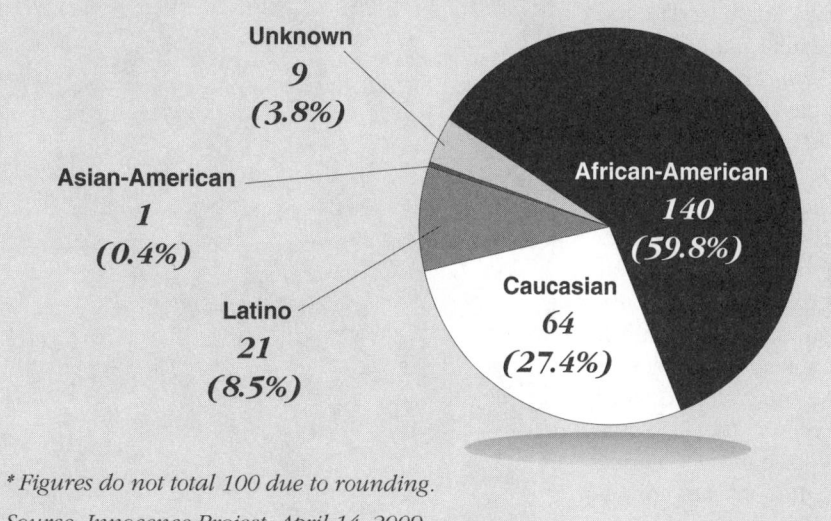

Most DNA Exonerees Are Black

Nearly 60 percent of the 235 convicted prisoners who have been exonerated by DNA evidence since 1989 — when the first exoneration occurred — have been black. That's more than any other race and more than twice the number of Caucasians.

Race of Prisoners Exonerated by DNA Since 1989

Unknown
9
(3.8%)

Asian-American
1
(0.4%)

Latino
21
(8.5%)

African-American
140
(59.8%)

Caucasian
64
(27.4%)

* Figures do not total 100 due to rounding.

Source: Innocence Project, April 14, 2009

debate became entangled in the larger controversy about the morality and effectiveness of the death penalty, placing an emotional fog over the numbers discussion.

In 1987, Professors Hugo Adam Bedau and Michael L. Radelet wrote a *Stanford Law Review* article in which they cited 350 cases of apparent wrongful convictions, some of which had placed defendants on death row. A year later, in the same publication, lawyers Paul G. Cassell and Stephen J. Markman, who had served in the U.S. Justice Department during the Republican administration of Ronald Reagan, questioned Bedau and Radelet's data, saying many of the 350 did not qualify as wrongful convictions. Reversing a conviction on narrow procedural grounds is not the same as freeing a prisoner because of actual innocence, Cassell and Markman said. [14]

Within academia, the debate about the accuracy of wrongful conviction statistics has not abated and eventually spilled over into the Supreme Court and the mass media.

Debates about wrongful convictions often focus on the role of local prosecutors. Researchers from the nonpartisan Center for Public Integrity, in Washington, D.C., identified nearly 11,500 court rulings from around the nation dealing with allegations of district attorney misconduct over 30 years. In about 2,000 of the rulings, judges cited prosecutorial misconduct when dismissing charges at trial, reducing

Dallas County District Attorney Craig Watkins, the first elected African-American district attorney in Texas, is taking unusual action for a prosecutor: He is reviewing seemingly closed cases that might have resulted in wrongful convictions, and so far reviews ordered by Watkins have led to the exonerations of multiple inmates.

AP Photo/Tony Gutierrez

prison sentences or reversing findings of guilt. [15]

Some prosecutors stood out over and over as the targets of those rulings, according to the center's report. For example: "When Larry Johnson walked out of a Missouri prison during the summer of 2002, exonerated by DNA testing from a wrongful rape conviction after avowing his innocence for 18 years, St. Louis legal community insiders nodded knowingly as word trickled out who had led the prosecution back in 1984 — Nels C. Moss Jr.," said the report. "Moss, an assistant circuit attorney for the city of St. Louis and later a trial prosecutor in neighboring St. Charles County,

earned a well-deserved reputation as an aggressive, effective trial prosecutor. During his 33 years of trying cases for the people, however, he simultaneously was a recidivist breaker of the rules by which prosecutors are supposed to operate."

According to the center, Moss' conduct was formally challenged in at least 24 cases after he joined the city prosecutor's office in 1968. In seven of those, judges reversed the conviction, declared a mistrial or issued some other ruling adverse to the prosecution. The judges ruled that Moss had reneged during trial on a pre-trial stipulation with the defense; called the jury's attention to the defendant's failure to testify, thereby compromising the Fifth Amendment rights of the accused; alluded to the defendant's prior criminal conduct, a violation of the rules of evidence; introduced inadmissible material from the separate trial of an accomplice; promised during jury selection or opening statements to present testimony never offered; attacked the truthfulness of defense counsel; cast aspersions on the integrity of an insanity defense; and inflamed jurors' emotions during closing argument.

Moss said he performed his job aggressively but legally and expressed pride in his ability to win convictions on behalf of the citizens who paid his salary. Johnson's exoneration surprised him, Moss said, especially given what he believed had been the credibility of the testimony by the rape victim. [16]

Do aggressive prosecutors such as Moss contribute to a "large" wrongful-conviction problem? Prosecutors and police say no, using the ratio of documented exonerations to arrests as their starting point. Defense lawyers and law professors conducting long-term studies see the problem as "large," or at least significant, because every wrongful conviction shakes faith in the criminal justice system and allows the actual perpetrators to go unpunished.

Critics of the system have compared the situation to airplane crashes. While most flights take off and land safely, the critics say that crashes often result in numerous deaths and should not be tolerated. The critics note that the National Transportation Safety Board issues an in-depth report on each airplane crash, its findings enhanced by subpoena power and independence from the political process. Why not require an in-depth, publicly available report on every wrongful conviction by an agency with similar authority? the critics ask. [17]

Marquis, the Clatsop County district attorney, described prosecutorial misconduct as at worst "episodic, those few cases being rare enough to merit considerable attention by both the courts and the media." Furthermore, Marquis said, when prosecutors do err, "the overwhelming majority of prosecutorial errors are harmless, not harmful, meaning that there was no malice on the part of the district attorney, and that there was no unjust result." [18]

AP Photo/Harry Cabluck

Judge Barbara Hervey of the Texas Court of Criminal Appeals in Austin, which handles death penalty appeals, created a Criminal Justice Integrity Unit last year to examine and correct problems in the criminal justice system, including mistaken eyewitness evidence, crime lab unreliability, inadequate defense counsel and coerced or false confessions.

Do errors by forensic laboratories contribute to wrongful convictions?

The major causes of wrongful convictions — mistaken eyewitness identification, false confessions and false informant testimony — are no longer in doubt. (*See sidebar, p. 362.*) But concern has grown over the role played by crime laboratories, which test evidence gathered by crime scene investigators. The vast majority of the nation's 359 accredited crime laboratories are located within police agencies. [19]

Critics say corrupt or inadequately trained crime lab personnel wreak untold havoc in the criminal justice system, but police and crime lab officials say the damage is limited to only a few renegade employees.

Crime laboratories are now in the reform spotlight for several reasons, including the popularity of television police dramas like "CSI: Miami"; studies of crime laboratories, including a massive, congressionally mandated examination released in February by the National Academy of Sciences; criticism by advocacy groups; and attentive journalism. [20]

Close examinations of crime-laboratory procedures "have revealed that, in some cases, substantive information and testimony based on faulty forensic science analyses may have contributed to wrongful convictions of innocent people," according to the National Academy report. "This fact has demonstrated the potential danger of giving undue weight to evidence and testimony derived from imperfect testing and analysis. Moreover, imprecise or exaggerated expert testimony has sometimes contributed to the admission of erroneous or misleading evidence." [21]

The 2006 report by the American Bar Association's Ad Hoc Innocence Committee recommended that crime lab and medical examiner offices be accredited, examiners certified and procedures standardized and published to ensure "the validity, reliability and timely analysis of forensic evidence."

Yet following those recommendations might do little to avoid wrongful convictions due to laboratory incompetence and fraud as long as the analysts are employees of law enforcement agencies, the ABA said. "Cops in lab coats"

Continued on p. 353

DNA Exonerations Spark Reforms

Over the last 20 years DNA exonerations have led to a variety of reforms in the nation's criminal justice system, including the following measures that have been enacted or are under consideration in the various states:

- **Access to Post-Conviction DNA Evidence Testing** — Without specific laws ensuring "statutory access" to DNA testing to prove their innocence, prisoners can face a protracted legal battle to get access to that evidence and may be denied testing. Forty-six states — except Alabama, Alaska, Massachusetts and Oklahoma — now provide statutory access to post-conviction DNA testing. Three of the four remaining states — Alabama, Alaska and Massachusetts — have introduced legislation to provide access, and Nevada, New York, Ohio and Texas have introduced additional measures to further increase access.

- **Forensic Standards and Oversight** — The National Academy of Sciences recommended in February 2009 that oversight, research and support for forensic sciences be strengthened and that a National Institute of Forensic Science be created to direct research, establish scientifically validated standards and make sure the standards are consistently applied nationwide. Furthermore, a 2004 federal law required that states seeking federal funds for state crime labs be able to investigate allegations of forensic misconduct, negligence or error. California, Maryland, Minnesota, New York, Texas and Virginia have created forensic science commissions to help ensure the quality and reliability of forensic evidence. Minnesota, Texas and Virginia have introduced legislation to strengthen their commissions.

- **Eyewitness Identification Reform** — Several states have adopted a range of procedural reforms to decrease inaccurate eyewitness identifications, including:
  1. *Statewide training* — Georgia
  2. *Requiring certain reforms shown to increase the accuracy of eyewitness identifications* — West Virginia, New Jersey and North Carolina
  3. *Requiring written policies regarding the use of eyewitness identification procedures* — Maryland, Wisconsin
  4. *Establishing a task force to recommend enhanced eyewitness identification protocols* — Vermont
  5. *Promulgating "double-blind sequential" guidelines and incorporating them into law enforcement training* — Georgia, New Jersey, North Carolina and Wisconsin. The following local jurisdictions already use sequential double-blind as standard procedure: Denver, Colo.; Northampton, Mass.; Madison, Wis.; Milwaukee, Wis.; Hennepin County, Minn.; Ramsey County, Minn.; Santa Clara County, Calif.

These states have legislation pending that would address eyewitness misidentification: Connecticut, District of Columbia, Hawaii, Kentucky, Massachusetts, Missouri, New Mexico, New York, Ohio, Oregon, Pennsylvania, Rhode Island and Texas.

- **Criminal Justice Reform Commissions** — The following states have created some form of commission to study the causes and remedies of wrongful convictions — California, Connecticut, Illinois, North Carolina, New York, Pennsylvania, Texas and Wisconsin. Efforts to form commissions have been begun in South Carolina and Tennessee. Texas has legislation pending that would strengthen its commission.

- **Preservation of Evidence** — Twenty-six states have implemented reforms on preserving DNA evidence through the proper retention, cataloging and handling of biological evidence from crime scenes. For a list of the states, go to www.innocenceproject.org/Content/253.php. Legislative reforms on preservation of evidence are pending in Alaska, Colorado, Illinois, Montana, Nevada, New Jersey, New York, Ohio, Oregon, Texas and West Virginia.

- **Mandated Recording of Interrogations** — Legislation requiring the recording of interrogations has been enacted in Illinois, Maine, Maryland, Nebraska, New Mexico, North Carolina, Wisconsin and the District of Columbia, and state supreme courts have taken action on the issue in Alaska, Iowa, Massachusetts, Minnesota, New Hampshire and New Jersey. Some 500 local jurisdictions nationwide have voluntarily adopted policies to record interrogations. Reforms are pending to mandate the recording of interrogations in Arizona, Arkansas, Connecticut, Indiana, Kansas, Missouri, Montana, New Jersey, New York, North Carolina, Oregon, Pennsylvania, Rhode Island, South Carolina, Tennessee, Texas and Ohio.

Source: Innocence Project, April 14, 2009

Continued from p. 351

have demonstrated actual and alleged pro-prosecution bias in laboratories in state after state, the ABA report said, noting studies that have found perhaps a third of exonerations involve "tainted or fraudulent science." [22]

What happened in West Virginia demonstrates at the extreme how even one corrupt worker can shake the foundation of justice. Starting in the 1970s, Fred Zain, a West Virginia State Police officer, was assigned to the crime laboratory as a serologist after telling his supervisors he had a college degree in biology with a minor in chemistry. In fact, he had not minored in chemistry and had received a failing grade in organic chemistry, bringing it up to only a D after retaking the course.

With his minimal training as well as a corner-cutting attitude and a pro-prosecution bias, Zain began acting not only as a supposed blood expert but also as prosecutor, jury and judge. If the evidence appeared weak against a defendant whom Zain considered sleazy, he made the evidence look stronger by falsifying test results.

Zain's dishonesty escaped meaningful scrutiny until 1992. By then he had moved to Texas, where in 1989 he began reprising his role, this time in the Bexar County (San Antonio) crime laboratory, where he remained until 1993, when signs of misconduct in cases there led to his dismissal.

The key to unlocking Zain's misconduct showed up in the case of Glen Dale Woodall, who had been convicted in West Virginia in 1987 of two sexual-assault charges. At the trial, Zain testified falsely that the blood match between a victim and Woodall would occur in only six of 10,000 men — especially vital testimony, because the remaining evidence against Woodall added up to nothing convincing. Maintaining his innocence from the start, Woodall petitioned for his freedom, and an appellate court ordered a new DNA-

DNA Exonerations at a Glance

- Since 1989, 235 prisoners have been exonerated due to DNA evidence.
- Those exonerated served 2,920 years in prison.
- Seventeen exonerees served time on death row.
- Exonerations have been won in 34 states.
- The average exoneree served 12 years.
- The average exoneree was 26 when convicted.

Source: Innocence Project, April 14, 2009

testing technique to be applied to the evidence. As a result, Woodall was exonerated.

The extent of the damage done by Zain had become so evident by 1993 that William C. Forbes, the prosecuting attorney in Kanawha County, asked the Supreme Court of West Virginia to approve an investigation. The resulting report by former Judge James O. Holliday revealed a shockingly corrupted justice system.

In determining which cases to re-examine, Holliday said evidence offered by Zain "at any time in any criminal prosecution should be deemed invalid, unreliable and inadmissible." Supreme Court justices called Zain's conduct "shocking," representing "egregious violations of the right of a defendant to a fair trial. They stain our judicial system and mock the ideal of justice under law." At least 134 cases relying in significant part on Zain's findings needed re-examination. In the end, Zain's misconduct led directly to the release of five West Virginia inmates and one in Texas. [23]

In Houston, numerous workers at the police department crime laboratory compromised hundreds of cases until television station KHOU began airing an exposé in November 2002. Within a month, Houston's police chief commissioned an outside review of the laboratory's DNA and serology units. The chief eventually shuttered the DNA

unit while figuring out how to re-test 407 criminal cases that might have been compromised. Further review revealed compromised cases in the toxicology unit, so the police chief suspended testing there, too.

The failures at the Houston laboratory carry "implications both for ensuring that the guilty are convicted and the innocent are exonerated," said an outside audit report paid for by the city government. "From the perspective of making sure the innocent are exonerated, the crime lab failed to perform genetic-marker analyses that, in some cases, might have excluded an individual suspect as a potential donor of evidence, such as semen stains related to a sexual assault." [24]

Crime laboratory administrators have tended to resist accusations of widespread responsibility for wrongful convictions. John Collins, editor of the independent periodical *Crime Lab Report*, and Jay Jarvis, associate editor, describe themselves as "experienced accreditation inspectors" with "extensive management and casework experiences in the forensic sciences." In a rebuttal to the critics, they say statistics alleging frequent crime lab involvement in wrongful convictions are highly inflated. [25]

The experts studying wrongful convictions for the National Academy left no doubt that police crime laboratories across the nation need more funding to hire qualified staff, train them better, purchase equipment and eliminate backlogs that allow crimes to go unsolved. [26]

The study raised the possibility of separating crime laboratories from police agencies. Ralph Keaton, executive director of the American Society of Crime Laboratory Directors/Laboratory Accreditation Board, opposed such a change. "The recommendation suggests that law enforcement agencies tend to be biased and seek to prove guilt rather than seek the truth," Keaton wrote. "In actuality, the vast majority of forensic laboratories that operate within law enforcement agencies exonerate suspects as routinely as they implicate suspects [and] the cost, both financially and in lost productivity, to make such a transition is too great to make this the best way to achieve the desired outcome." [27]

Would systemic reform reduce the number of wrongful convictions?

Critics of the criminal justice system sometimes note that in the final analysis human nature causes many wrongful convictions and that, as the adage goes, "You can't change human nature." Others, including the American Bar Association, counter that it might be possible, however, to offset the influence of human behavior through improved training, legislation prescribing specific protocols during the investigative and pretrial stages and effective discipline for law enforcement agents who misbehave.

Human nature often plays a role in wrongful convictions when police and prosecutors settle too soon on the identity of the person they think is the perpetrator. That tilt, whether conscious or unconscious, skews their interpretations of a suspect's words and actions, leading them to assign guilt while paying too little attention to alternate suspects.

The Center for Public Integrity report on the behavior of prosecutors — who often use police reports to guide their impressions of suspects — provides an in-depth study on the wrongful murder conviction of Ellen Reasonover, a 24-year-old single mother in St. Louis County, Mo. Police and prosecutors lacked leads regarding the murder of a service-station attendant, and the crime scene yielded nothing — no forensic evidence, murder weapon, eyewitness testimony or obvious motive. Stymied police asked neighborhood residents to provide any information they had, however sketchy.

Reasonover was among those who tried to help. She lived near the service station and had stopped in around the time of the murder to get change to use at a nearby self-service laundry. But police and prosecutors, under pressure to close the case, quickly labeled Reasonover a suspect for reasons that never became clear before, during or after the trial. While in jail, she allegedly confessed to two cellmates whom she didn't know. At trial, the conviction before an all-Caucasian jury rested entirely on the testimony of the cellmates, who had been offered reduced sentences for their help.

Reasonover, an African-American, served 16 years for murder before a federal judge released her after evidence of police and prosecutor misconduct emerged at an evidentiary hearing. The judge decided if the jury had known about the deals between prosecutors and the jailhouse informants, Reasonover would have been acquitted at trial. The actual murderer has never been caught. [28]

Part of the systemic reform suggested by the American Bar Association includes the use of jailhouse informants. The ABA report suggests that all law enforcement jurisdictions "ensure that no prosecution occur based solely upon uncorroborated jailhouse informant testimony." [29] The ABA report also recommends changes designed to:

- Reduce false confessions;
- Improve eyewitness identification procedures;
- Better equip crime laboratories;

- Educate police investigators and prosecutors in new ways to minimize problems before suspects are arrested, after suspects are in custody and at trial; and
- Ensure defense attorneys are educated well enough to provide adequate representation in all cases, especially felonies carrying long prison sentences. [30]

In a foreword to the ABA report, Barry C. Scheck, co-founder and co-director of the Innocence Project, notes that positive changes "in states red and blue, coastal and interior, large and small, prove that these reforms and the issues they address transcend party lines, geographic location and population size. Indeed, with each passing day more people recognize the systemic flaws that have lain dormant in our criminal-justice system, and to our collective credit jurisdictions are increasingly responding by enacting the necessary reforms." [31]

Many lawmakers and legal experts say legislation also could reduce wrongful convictions at the federal level, including amending the Antiterrorism and Effective Death Penalty Act. Congress approved the law in 1996 to bring greater finality to the criminal justice process by limiting inmates' habeas corpus petitions, which seek to give prisoners another day in court to appeal their convictions. In addition to setting time limits for habeas filings, the law required federal courts to defer to state court rulings, unless the rulings are shown to be clearly unreasonable. [32]

A law more conducive to repairing wrongful convictions might have helped Burton after his 1984 murder conviction in St. Louis. Long after his conviction, compelling new evidence of his innocence surfaced. A panel of three judges from the Eighth U.S. Circuit Court of Appeals said it tended to believe Burton's innocence claim but could do nothing about it because the law restricting habeas corpus reviews left no avenue to grant freedom.

The Burton ruling noted "a confounding array of procedural impediments that prevent consideration of the merits of claims, as well as substantive barriers that establish modes of review utterly inhospitable to prisoners." The judges said they understood that many of the barriers and impediments "represent sound efforts to curb the groundswell of frivolous and duplicative habeas petitions." But, they added, "the writ of habeas corpus is not a one-way path designed to defeat prisoners' claims. Rather, our habeas jurisprudence is a balancing act requiring careful attention to each of the important, yet often opposing, principles at stake. Even as we screen meritless petitions, therefore, we must take care not to shut the door to prisoners whose claims cause us to doubt the fairness of their convictions."

Unfortunately, the three judges said, "Burton's habeas petition depicts a troubling scenario. One cannot read the record in this case without developing a nagging suspicion that the wrong man may have been convicted of capital murder and armed criminal action in a Missouri courtroom. Since his trial and imprisonment, new evidence has come to light that shakes the limbs on the prosecution's case. . . . A layperson would have little trouble concluding Burton should be permitted to present his evidence of innocence in some forum. Unfortunately, Burton's claims and evidence run headlong into the thicket of impediments erected by courts and by Congress. Burton's legal claims permit him no relief, even as the facts suggest he may well be innocent."

The judges hoped that Missouri would provide a forum, either judicial or executive, for considering the mounting evidence that Burton's conviction had been procured "by perjured or flawed eyewitness testimony." [33]

But several years passed, with Burton still imprisoned, until digging by Centurion Ministries investigators and skillful maneuvering by the group's

Finally Free

Charles Chatman (top, middle) leaves court in Dallas on Jan. 3, 2008, after a judge released him and recommended that his rape conviction be overturned as a result of DNA testing that lawyers say proves his innocence. Chatman, flanked by his attorney Jeff Blackburn and his aunt Ethel Bradley, spent 26 years in prison. After spending 23 years in prison for a murder he didn't commit, Robert Lee Stinson celebrates his freedom last Jan. 30 with two plates of fried shrimp in Wisconsin Dells, Wis. His sister Charlene is at his side (bottom).

lawyers resulted in a new hearing at the state level. After the hearing, a state court judge ordered Burton released from prison. [34]

Scheck and Peter Neufeld, co-directors of the Innocence Project, are among many of the defense lawyers and legal scholars who criticized Congress for approving the Antiterrorism and Effective Death Penalty Act and President Bill Clinton for signing it. "In its zeal to achieve finality in death-penalty litigation, Congress eviscerated the great writ of habeas corpus, the mechanism used for almost 200 years by state prisoners who wanted a federal court to review the justice of their state convictions," Scheck and Neufeld wrote. "This 'reform' legislation requires federal courts to presume state courts are right about many things that state courts often are wrong about. Everyone agrees that it is a terrible thing for an innocent person to be imprisoned. Far worse, though, would be for a politician to take a moderate line on crime." [35] ∎

BACKGROUND

New Awareness

Although wrongful convictions have occurred, undoubtedly, since the beginning of the U.S. criminal justice system, it wasn't until the early 1930s that awareness of their persistent occurrence in jurisdictions across

the nation seemed to take root. The clarion call came from Edwin M. Borchard, a Yale University law professor, in his book *Convicting the Innocent: Sixty-Five Actual Errors of Criminal Justice.*

The popularity of television police dramas like "CSI: Miami" has helped put crime laboratories in the reform spotlight. According to a recent National Academy of Sciences report on crime-lab procedures, "faulty forensic-science analyses may have contributed to wrongful convictions of innocent people."

www.sidereel.com

Borchard knew many readers would find his case studies unbelievable, given the overwhelming faith Americans had in the court system. As a Massachusetts prosecutor said, according to Borchard, "Innocent men are never convicted. Don't worry about it; it never happens in the world. It is a physical impossibility." But, Borchard responded flatly, "The present collection of 65 cases, which have been collected from a much larger number, is a refutation of this supposition." [36]

Lawyer and writer Erle Stanley Gardner understood the wrongful-conviction phenomenon. Best known as the author of Perry Mason mystery novels, Gardner devoted a significant portion of his earnings in the late 1940s to creating the Court of Last Resort, a private tribunal that

investigated suspected wrongful convictions. In 1952, Gardner published a book about the effort, presenting the story behind exonerations he, his staff and a network of volunteers engineered.

Among his reform proposals, the idealistic Gardner suggested placement of "power in the hands of the courts to see that the defense of each person accused of a crime is adequately and competently conducted. This includes the power — in fact, the duty — of courts to appoint impartial, competent experts to furnish the court and counsel for both sides with pertinent technical information both before and during trial." Not even a lawyer with Gardner's determination and reach, however, could erase the systemic problems leading to wrongful convictions. [37]

Throughout the 1960s, '70s and '80s, journalists and academic researchers followed the path trod by Borchard and Gardner, publishing case studies of suspected and documented wrongful convictions. The most mammoth effort — covering several hundred defendants — came in a 1992 book by Professors Bedau and Radelet and Constance E. Putnam, a writer married to Bedau, *In Spite of Innocence: Erroneous Convictions in Capital Cases.* [38]

The Chicago Connection

In the 1970s Chicago journalists began compiling information that would, eventually, help trigger reform

Continued on p. 360

Chronology

1930s–1950s
Academic researchers and reformers say wrongful convictions are more numerous than generally acknowledged by those running the criminal justice system.

1932
Yale University law Professor Edwin M. Borchard publishes *Convicting the Innocent: Sixty-five Actual Errors of Criminal Justice*, a seminal work that raises awareness of wrongful convictions.

1952
Lawyer and author Erle Stanley Gardner, creator of the Perry Mason detective series, establishes the Court of Last Resort, hiring skilled investigators to examine claims of wrongful convictions.

1960s
Supreme Court expands the reasons convictions can be reviewed to include prosecutorial misconduct.

1963
Supreme Court's *Brady v. Maryland* decision requires prosecutors to share exculpatory evidence with defense counsel.

1964
Publication of *The Innocents* by journalist Edward D. Radin renews awareness of the prevalence of wrongful convictions.

1970s–1980s
Journalists investigate wrongful conviction cases, begin tapping wrongful conviction clinics for stories.

1975
Reporting by *The Miami Herald*'s Gene Miller frees Florida death-row inmates Freddie Pitts and Wilbert Lee. Journalists around the nation take note of Miller's stories when he wins the Pulitzer Prize.

1982
Hysteria over alleged ritual child abuse at day-care centers spawns numerous wrongful conviction cases. In California's Kern County, prosecutors target at least a dozen purported child sex rings allegedly involving multiple adults abusing numerous children. Eventually, journalist Edward Humes' 1999 book *Mean Justice* provides detailed accounts of the prosecutorial overzealousness and wrongful convictions.

1983
Jorge De Los Santos is freed from a New Jersey prison after being convicted of a murder eight years earlier. Prison chaplain James McCloskey spearheads the exoneration after hearing his innocence claim. McCloskey starts Centurion Ministries to help overturn wrongful convictions. Organizations investigating wrongful convictions are a fledgling and evolving concept, none serving inmates nationwide.

1990s
As innocence projects and journalism investigations expand, lawmakers narrow legal gateways to post-conviction litigation.

1992
Barry Scheck and Peter Neufeld found the Innocence Project, focusing on DNA-based exonerations.

1996
President Bill Clinton signs the Antiterrorism and Effective Death Penalty Act narrowing inmates' right to file habeas corpus petitions.

1999
Chicago Tribune begins series on flaws in the criminal justice system that lead to wrongful convictions.

2000–Present
Tolerance of wrongful convictions erodes as the number rises.

2000
The debut of the CBS-TV crime show "CSI" heightens awareness of DNA and other forensic evidence but raises unrealistic expectations of prosecutors among potential and actual jurors.

2003
Gov. George Ryan, R-Ill., a former death penalty supporter, declares a state moratorium on executions after learning that more innocent inmates had been on death row than guilty ones. The week before leaving the governorship, he commutes the death sentences of 167 inmates and pardons four.

2009
New innocence projects arise and established ones expand amidst a variety of new studies — exemplified by the New York State Bar Association's comprehensive report highlighting the pervasiveness of criminal justice shortcomings. . . . In June the U.S. Supreme Court is expected to rule on an appeal by an Alaska man, William G. Osborne, who wants to be able to analyze DNA evidence used in his 1995 conviction for kidnapping and sexual assault.

The Case of the Look-Alike Rapist

North Carolina case shows the unreliability of eyewitnesses.

Ronald Cotton did not rape Jennifer Thompson on a sultry, summer night in July 1984 in Burlington, N.C. Bobby Leon Poole, a dead-ringer for Cotton, actually committed the rape.

But when detective Mike Gauldin showed six photographs to Thompson and later summoned her to a lineup including seven black males, she picked Cotton both times.

At first, Thompson felt unsure about two men in the lineup, one of them holding number four, the other holding number five. She asked the police officer running the lineup to order each of the men to speak the words he had spoken while assaulting her: "Shut up or I'll cut you." After hearing number five speak a second time, Thompson just knew: "I looked at his face. He had a light mustache; his eyes looked cold. His body was long and lean. He knew to wear brown, I thought, because he knew he had been wearing dark blue the night of my assault. And he knew to wear his hair differently. It was him. There was no doubt in my mind." [1]

Thompson, a senior at Elon College, had intentionally stayed alert during the sexual assault, seeking identifying characteristics of her rapist. She provided a detailed verbal description. She sat with a police artist until she was satisfied with the composite sketch.

At the hospital, a rape kit examination was conducted to collect forensic evidence, and police collected additional forensic evidence from her apartment, which Thompson kept tidy. She seemed like the perfect witness from the prosecution's standpoint.

During the photo identification and the lineup, police told Thompson the rapist might not show up as part of the mix, and that she did not have to choose anyone. As far as can be determined so many years later, the only impropriety involved Gauldin telling Thompson, "We thought that might be the guy. It's the same person you picked from the photos." By uttering those words, Gauldin unintentionally increased Thompson's level of certainty before Cotton's trial.

Another detective told Thompson that Cotton worked at a restaurant near the rape scene. A restaurant manager had called police about Cotton after seeing the composite sketch. The same detective told Thompson about Cotton's criminal record, including a prior crime involving intended sexual assault aimed at a white female. Again, Thompson felt validated in her identification of Cotton.

Cotton unintentionally hurt his own defense when he mixed up his dates during voluntary discussions with police, thereby giving an alibi that the prosecutor could disprove. When Cotton later tried to set the alibi dates straight, police and prosecutors — not surprisingly — scoffed.

At trial, the judge refused to allow Cotton's attorney to put a memory expert on the witness stand who would have explained to jurors that rape victims and other eyewitnesses sometimes make mistakes, no matter how certain they sound. The jurors paid little attention to the fact that no forensic evidence linked Cotton to the rape, and that Thompson never mentioned Cotton's scars while providing a detailed identification.

The jurors also had no idea another woman who was raped on the same night, by the same perpetrator, had failed to identify Cotton but instead pointed to a different man in the lineup — a man who could not have committed the crime. Because the second rape victim had failed to identify Cotton, prosecutors did not immediately file charges against him for that assault.

Despite the rulings against Cotton, he refused to seek a plea bargain and plead guilty to a crime he never committed. "Despite the bars all around me, I was an innocent man. God knew it, and I knew it, and I would rather die incarcerated than admit to being the rapist they claimed I was."

On Jan. 18, 1985, after jurors found him guilty, Cotton was sentenced to life plus 50 years.

Cotton and Poole eventually ended up in the same prison, where Poole was serving time for an unconnected Burlington rape. The first time he saw Poole, Cotton thought he looked a lot like the composite drawing that led to his own arrest. "I looked at the short hair, the thin mustache and the mouth that wasn't too wide but was full. He was light-skinned, lighter than me. And it flashed in my mind: the composite picture of the suspect in the rapes they pegged me for. . . . The guy standing in front of me looked just like him."

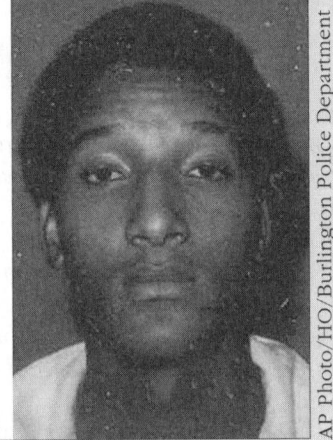

Ronald Cotton, right, pictured in 1984, was released from prison 11 years after DNA testing showed that Bobby Poole, left, pictured in 1985, actually raped a college student.

AP Photo/HO/Burlington Police Department

Others in the prison sometimes confused Poole and Cotton, even though Cotton was five inches taller. Cotton asked Poole if he had committed the Thompson rape and the rape of another woman the same night. Poole said no, but with a look that caused Cotton to suspect otherwise.

Using a standard appellate strategy, Cotton's lawyer won a new trial on a procedural issue — the judge should have allowed the jury to hear that a second woman raped the same night by a man with the same *modus operandi* had failed to identify Cotton. The second trial occurred in November 1987. By then, the prosecutor had persuaded the second victim, Mary Reynolds, to accuse Cotton, on the grounds that she had been too fearful during the lineup to identify her actual rapist. Suddenly, a new trial looked to Cotton more like a hazard than a blessing.

But at the new trial, with the jury out of sight, the judge heard testimony from another prison inmate that Poole had confessed to the Thompson and Reynolds rapes. The judge also heard lawyers for both sides question Poole, who maintained he had never committed those two rapes. The judge decided the jury would not hear the confession testimony nor see Poole.

However, both Thompson and Reynolds, sitting in the courtroom, did see Poole, their actual rapist. They did not recognize him, so never wavered from their testimony that Cotton had assaulted them. After the guilty verdict, Cotton returned to prison — now sentenced to two life terms.

Then in 1992, Richard Rosen, a University of North Carolina law professor, became interested in the case. He asked to examine the evidence and obtained a court order allowing evidence to be tested using newly available DNA technology. Thompson was asked to give a blood sample, because biological material from the rape had degraded. Upset, she complied, and tried not to worry. She knew in her heart that Cotton was guilty and that the DNA test would confirm her identification.

She was wrong. In mid-1995, nearly three years after Rosen began his re-examination, DNA results cleared Cotton and implicated Poole.

Ronald Cotton and Jennifer Thompson, shown in 2000, co-authored a book about Cotton and Thompson's mistaken testimony. They now give talks together on wrongful convictions. Cotton has been profiled on "60 Minutes" and appeared on NBC's "Today" show.

Incredulous, Thompson felt extreme guilt that she had taken away more than a decade of Cotton's freedom. Two years later, working through Gauldin, she asked to meet Cotton to apologize. Both her husband and Cotton's wife expressed reservations about a meeting, but Thompson felt compelled to apologize in person, and Cotton wanted to hear the apology face to face.

After that initial meeting, during which Cotton bestowed forgiveness, he and Thompson talked long distance, then met again. Eventually, they accepted requests to speak about the wrongful conviction and the reconciliation. They also co-authored a book about their intertwined lives and today sometimes travel together to speak to audiences about the frequent role of eyewitness misidentification in wrongful convictions.

"Although Ron had helped me overcome so much, I still had a hard time forgiving myself for being less than perfect, Thompson says. "This was not like screwing up a recipe. The mistake I made had impacted people's lives for years, and I felt it was my burden to carry."

Only after hearing Gary Wells, an Iowa State University researcher, explain the common nature of mistaken eyewitness identification did Thompson's feelings of inadequacy and guilt begin to fade.

Gauldin, who became chief of police in Burlington, also took to heart the lesson about mistaken eyewitnesses. Under his leadership the police department became the first in North Carolina to require sequential proceedings — which allow witnesses to see suspects in person or through photographs one at a time, instead of simultaneously — and double-blind procedures — which prevent police officers dealing with witnesses from knowing the identity of the alleged perpetrator, so they cannot provide unintentional or intentional clues. [2]

---

[1] Jennifer Thompson-Cannino, Ronald Cotton and Erin Torneo, *Picking Cotton: Our Memoir of Injustice and Redemption* (2009), p. 37. Court rulings on the Cotton case before his exoneration are located at 318 NC 663 and 394 SE 2d 456. Other information is from the book unless otherwise noted. See also Jim Morrill, "Rage, Finally Set Free," *Raleigh News & Observer*, March 29, 2009, and "What Jennifer Saw," "Frontline," February 1997.

[2] *Picking Cotton, op. cit.*, p. 284.

Continued from p. 356

efforts, such as videotaping of police interrogations. In 1978, Rob Warden founded the magazine *Chicago Lawyer*, which year after year exposed misconduct by police and prosecutors that had led to unfair trials and sometimes to wrongful convictions. Warden began to achieve recognition outside Chicago after collaborating with David Protess, a freelance reporter and Northwestern University journalism professor.

During the 1990s, Warden and Protess collaborated on two books about instances of actual innocence. In one of the cases, Protess and his journalism students played a vital role in exonerating four men convicted for the kidnapping, rape and double murder of a young couple. The students not only won freedom for Dennis Williams, Verneal Jimerson, Kenny Adams and Willie Rainge — the so-called Ford Heights Four — but also helped identify the actual perpetrators. In doing so, they helped demonstrate the potential of DNA testing in actual innocence proceedings. At a forensics laboratory in Boston, a scientist compared DNA from all four defendants with DNA from the crime scene and found no matches.

"It was an historic result — the first time in the annals of forensic science that multiple defendants had been excluded as sources of semen in a rape case," Protess and Warden noted. [39]

DNA quickly came to dominate the wrongful convictions discussion. One of the enlightened prosecutors present at the creation was then-San Diego Deputy District Attorney

Innocence Project Co-Directors Peter Neufeld (left) and Barry Scheck testify early this year at a New York State Bar Association hearing on criminal justice system reforms that can prevent future wrongful convictions.

www.joshuakristal.com

George "Woody" Clarke. "Few dramatic changes have taken place in the world of solving crime," wrote Clarke, now a Superior Court judge. "Fingerprints were universally hailed as one of the most significant new weapons placed at the disposal of law enforcement. But their utility is limited to the relatively few cases in which fingerprints are left at crime scenes and can be discovered. Tests to determine whether guns have been fired by a suspect, hypnosis and even voiceprints have been used in investigations with mixed and controversial results. But when [the] science [of DNA] joined with law enforcement and the legal system in 1986, the justice system began a transformation like no other it had ever experienced." [40]

With DNA exonerations becoming almost commonplace, the *Chicago Tribune* started a remarkable, decade-long run of investigative reporting that made a measurable impact in persuading more and more citizens about the reality of wrongful convictions. In January 1999 the newspaper published a five-part series of articles that found nearly 400 cases where prosecutors

had won homicide convictions through deception — hiding evidence favorable to defendants, allowing witnesses to lie, and more. The series documented cases going back to 1963 in which courts reversed murder convictions because of prosecutors bending or breaking the law. [41]

Ten months later, the *Tribune* published another in-depth series that examined hundreds of murder cases in which Illinois prosecutors, mostly in Cook County (Chicago), had charged defendants with a capital crime and asked for the death penalty. The journalists identified 326 reversals by appeals courts attributed in whole or in part to the conduct of prosecutors. Both series named names, holding incompetent and venal police and prosecutors accountable. Later, *Tribune* reporters and editors delved into wrongful convictions caused by defense lawyer incompetence, out-of-control police, forensic analysts in law enforcement crime laboratories, and more. The investigative pieces continued into 2008. [42]

Illinois Gov. George Ryan credited the *Tribune* stories with his January 2003 decision to suspend the death penalty and commute sentences of numerous inmates, including all those on death row. "Our system in Illinois is rotten to the core, arbitrary, capricious, unjust, racist and unfair to the poor, and also to the families of the victims," Ryan said. Illinois has not executed an inmate since Ryan imposed the moratorium. [43]

Other newspapers, magazines, broadcasters and Web sites staffed by trained journalists — often inspired by the *Tribune* investigations — added to the accounts of wrongful convictions elsewhere. [44]

CURRENT SITUATION

New Studies

Blue-ribbon commissions in states around the country are conducting in-depth inquiries into wrongful convictions and producing massive reports frequently containing detailed suggestions for reform. Reports issued by commissions in Illinois, Virginia and New York state have received especially widespread attention.

The New York State Bar Association Task Force on Wrongful Convictions in January 2009 looked at 53 wrongful convictions. The 22-member panel included private-practice lawyers, judges, prosecutors, law professors and a law enforcement officer.

The commission identified six root causes of wrongful convictions and found that almost every exoneration involved more than one of the following causes:

- Mistaken identification by the victim or other eyewitnesses;
- Mishandling of forensic evidence, combined with the failure to use DNA testing when available;
- Extraction and use of false confessions;
- Reliance on false testimony by jailhouse informants;
- Incompetent defense counsel; and
- General errors by police officers, prosecutors or judges.

The commission report included numerous, detailed recommendations for change. For example, to halt prosecutors from illegally withholding evidence that might be favorable to the defendant (called a "Brady violation"), the report suggests the following steps: "If Brady information relevant to the defense has not been given to the de-

fense or has been delivered in a late turnover, or if false testimony is used at trial, relief on appeal or collateral challenge should be granted unless the state shows there was no possibility the information would have affected the decision." [45]

Another study was undertaken by the Innocence Commission for Virginia (ICVA), a three-way collaboration including a regional innocence project, the Washington-based Constitution Project, a research and reform organization, and the Administration of Justice Program at George Mason University in Fairfax, Va. Eleven law firms contributed $500,000 to launch the Virginia study in 2003. Two years later, the commission published its report, "A Vision for Justice." [46]

Commission Chairman Jon B. Gould, a lawyer who teaches at George Mason, said the statewide study "offers insights into the sources of wrongful convictions and recommendations for reforms in order to prevent future tragic errors."

The long list of reform recommendations included three meant to minimize premature focusing on a specific suspect. The first of the three warned, "Tunnel vision, in which officers jump too quickly to the conclusion that a particular suspect is guilty or focus solely on one person to the exclusion of other viable suspects, is a special danger in law enforcement. Law enforcement agencies should train their officers to document all exculpatory, as well as inculpatory, evidence about a particular individual that they discover and to include this information in their official reports to ensure that all exculpatory evidence information comes to the attention of prosecutors and subsequently to defense attorneys." [47]

In Illinois, the Governor's Commission on Capital Punishment included novelist Turow. It made 85 recommendations aimed at lowering the number of wrongful convictions. Turow, a

still-practicing lawyer, found the experience surprisingly revealing.

"Many of our findings flew in the face of what I had taken for granted during my years as a prosecutor, and even as a defense lawyer," Turow said. "For instance, one of the fixed stars of the universe of criminal justice is the idea that nobody voluntarily confesses to a crime she or he didn't commit. For this reason, a confession is regarded as the best possible evidence, and cops work hard in their interrogations of suspects to get admissions to the crime. . . . Thus, the persistence of purported confessions by innocent people in Illinois' exonerated cases was a wakeup call to me." [48]

Legislative Initiatives

Reforms recommended by blue-ribbon commissions are sparking proposals for changes in the criminal justice system from legislators and governors around the nation. Achieving change is rarely effortless, however. Even when influential forces align to promote reform, resistance arises — often from within law enforcement — stalling or blocking legislative initiatives.

After the exonerations of two Ohio inmates, for example, the *Innocence Project Blog* noted earlier this year, "A bill pending before the Ohio legislature would grant wider access to post-conviction DNA testing, require changes to lineup procedures and [mandate] the electronic recording of interrogations. Some police and prosecutorial organizations resisted the changes, saying they would be costly for police departments to implement and generally prevent police from doing their jobs."

Gene Rowe, chief of the Richmond Heights, Ohio, Police Department, had protested that the bill, if approved, would lead to higher city taxes and cause police officers to deal with additional paperwork.

Systemic Defects Blamed for Wrongful Convictions

Mistaken eyewitnesses and false confessions top the list.

DNA exoneration cases provide "irrefutable proof" that wrongful convictions are not isolated or rare events but arise from systemic defects in the U.S. justice system, according to the Innocence Project. [1] During 15-plus years of study, the nonprofit legal clinic has identified what it considers three major flaws in the system:

Eyewitness misidentification — Police, prosecutors, jurors and judges often depend heavily on confident-sounding eyewitnesses. But decades of research show such confidence can be misplaced. Led by Iowa State University psychology Professor Gary Wells, the research suggests simple reforms that law enforcement agencies could implement to minimize eyewitness mistakes, including:

- Using double-blind identification procedures in which no one involved in administering the lineup or photo-spread knows which lineup member is the suspect;
- Carefully instructing eyewitnesses not to assume that the actual perpetrator is in the lineup or photo-spread;
- Ensuring that all lineup members match the eyewitness description of the perpetrator;
- Having the witness recite how confident he/she was in the selection immediately upon making the identification, and;
- When possible, videotaping or recording a lineup.

Judges should also make wider use of "special jury instructions and expert testimony on eyewitness identification problems to assist fact-finders in fairly evaluating the evidence in appropriate cases," according to Wells. [2]

Unvalidated/Improper Forensic Science — While DNA testing was developed through extensive scientific research at top academic centers, many other forensic techniques — such as hair microscopy, bite-mark comparisons, firearm toolmark analysis and shoe-print comparisons — have never been subjected to rigorous scientific evaluation. Meanwhile, forensics techniques that have been properly validated — such as serology, commonly known as blood typing — are sometimes improperly conducted or inaccurately conveyed in trial testimony. In some cases, forensic analysts have fabricated results or engaged in other misconduct. In February 2009, the National Academy of Sciences (NAS) released an unprecedented report finding that many forensic disciplines are unvalidated or misused. The NAS called for the creation of an independent, science-based federal agency to stimulate research, set national standards for forensic science and oversee enforcement of those standards.

False Confessions — Studies of wrongful convictions show that suspects frequently confess to crimes they did not commit. Some of the confessors are mentally challenged and thus extremely suggestible to police allegations during questioning. Others naïvely believe interrogators will allow them to return home if they admit to guilt. Still other confessors break down under psychological or physical coercion.

The American Bar Association (ABA) recommends that law enforcement agencies completely videotape or audiotape custodial interrogations, which has received widespread support. Even University of Utah law Professor Paul G. Cassell, a former federal prosecutor and judge who doubts the extent of wrongful convictions — says "virtual unanimity [exists] . . . that videotaping interrogations is an effective solution to the false confession problem." [3]

In the face of such opposition, compromise legislation would be better than nothing, said Republican state Sen. Bill Seitz of Cincinnati. Reducing wrongful convictions across Ohio "is too important" to wait for the legislature to approve a perfect bill, Seitz said. "We've got real problems with real-life people. All I would say to anybody who doesn't like this bill is: What if it was you in jail for 18 years for a crime you didn't commit?" [49]

Reform proposals that seem noncontroversial and affordable gain traction in some locales and languish in others. Universal acceptance in a nation with more than 2,300 local prosecutor jurisdictions and far more police agencies seems hopeless.

Calls for recording interrogations of suspects often meet with resistance, although audio recordings would seem to be within the budget of every police agency, given the revolution in electronics. Audiovisual recording equipment is more expensive, but not by much. Yet the overwhelming majority of state legislatures and local law enforcement agencies have not initiated recording of interrogations, despite the documented potential for reducing wrongful convictions. [50]

Legislation requiring recordings has been enacted in Illinois, Maine, Maryland, Nebraska, New Mexico, North Carolina, Wisconsin and the District of Columbia, and state supreme courts have taken action on the issue in Alaska, Iowa, Massachusetts, Minnesota and New Hampshire. In New Jersey action was taken by the attorney general's office. Some local police departments, such as Phoenix, Los Angeles, Denver and Houston, have instituted recording procedures internally. [51]

The *Innocence Project Blog* keeps pace with reform proposals, as do organizations with a stake in the outcomes, including the National District Attorneys Association and the National Association of Criminal Defense Lawyers.

False Informant Testimony — The ABA recommends that no prosecution proceed "based solely upon uncorroborated jailhouse informant testimony." Prosecutors often make deals with unreliable, self-interested jailhouse snitches, as in the Ellen Reasonover case, in which a St. Louis County woman served 16 years in prison for a murder she did not commit. The prosecutor convicted Reasonover based entirely on the testimony of two women she interacted with briefly in jail shortly after her arrest. Both were recidivists with reputations for lying. The prosecutor illegally failed to disclose the deals he made with the informants, and an all-white jury convicted Reasonover, an African-American, coming within one vote (11-1) of a death sentence. [4]

Los Angeles Times reporters Ted Rohrlich and Robert W. Stewart exposed the dangers of relying on jailhouse snitches in a 1989 series focusing on Leslie Vernon White, a longtime police informant who agreed to show law enforcement officials how easily he could concoct believable lies about other inmates.

"Equipped with only a telephone and the last name of the inmate he did not know, White impersonated police officers and prosecutors and squeezed enough information from law enforcement officials to fabricate a plausible confession," the journalists wrote. "Then he created a phony record showing that he and the accused had been together in jail." The reporters also found credible evidence that some district attorneys knew their jailhouse informants were lying but called them as witnesses anyway. [5]

White was thus able to circumvent the two-pronged test normally used by prosecutors to safeguard against false informant testimony: Did the informant reveal details known only to the criminal? And did the informant and defendant actually spend time together in jail?

In 2004, Illinois began requiring extensive disclosure by the prosecution if a jailhouse informant is used as a witness. Disclosure must include the informant's complete criminal history, all deals already offered or expected to be offered by the prosecution, the time and place of statements made by the informant against the defendant, who heard the statements, the details of how the statements were conveyed to law enforcement officers; details about any recantations by the informant; previous cases in which the informant testified for the prosecution and the nature of promises, inducements or benefits offered by the prosecution in those cases.

---

[1] Affiliated with the Benjamin N. Cardozo School of Law at Yeshiva University in New York, the Innocence Project is dedicated to exonerating wrongfully convicted people through DNA testing and reforming the criminal justice system to prevent future injustice. At a clinic, law students handle case work while supervised by a team of attorneys and clinic staff.

[2] See Gary Wells, "Eyewitness Identification: Systemic Reforms," *Wisconsin Law Review*, 2006/2, p. 615. Also see "Achieving Justice: Freeing the Innocent, Convicting the Guilty," American Bar Association, Criminal Justice Section, 2006, p. 29.

[3] Paul G. Cassell, "Balanced Approaches to the False Confession Problem: A Brief Comment on Ofshe, Leo and Alschuler," *Denver University Law Review*, 1997, p. 1123. Among the best research on false confessions is Richard A. Leo and Richard J. Ofshe, "The Consequences of False Confessions: Deprivations of Liberty and Miscarriages of Justice in the Age of Psychological Interrogation," *Journal of Criminal Law and Criminology*, 1998, p. 429.

[4] "Achieving Justice: Freeing the Innocent, Convicting the Guilty," *op. cit.*, p. 63. Also see Steve Weinberg, "Railroaded," *The American Lawyer*, August 2000. Centurion Ministries includes information about each of its exonerations at www.centurionministries.org.

[5] Ted Rohrlich and Robert W. Stewart, "Jailhouse Snitches: Trading Lies for Freedom," *Los Angeles Times*, April 16, 1989, p. A1. Also see Rob Warden, "The Snitch System: How Incentivized Witnesses Put 37 Innocent Americans on Death Row," Center on Wrongful Convictions, Bluhm Legal Clinic, Northwestern University School of Law, 2002.

Outside the criminal justice system, several organizations track proposed and completed legislative efforts. For example, the National Conference of State Legislatures Web site lists state legislation enacted. In Illinois, for example, the legislation:

- "Provides that a defendant may request Integrated Ballistic Identification System testing or forensic DNA testing on evidence not previously requested because the technology was not available.

- Requires any new fingerprint evidence that does not match the defendant or victim to be submitted to the Federal Bureau of Investigation's Integrated Automated Fingerprint Identification System.

- Requires the creation of guidelines for all mandated recordings of custodial interrogations in homicide investigations." [52]

The Innocence Project Web site offers model legislation on issues such as post-conviction DNA testing; preservation of evidence (so that it is available to test after the case is otherwise closed); systemwide oversight of forensic evidence; improved eyewitness identification procedures; videotaping interrogations in their entirety; and the creation of innocence commissions to examine the causes of specific wrongful convictions after they become public knowledge.

While suggesting changes within the states, the Innocence Network (an association of nonprofit legal clinics and criminal justice resource centers of which the Innocence Project is a founding member) also relies on the Federal Justice for All Act, approved by Congress in 2004. The law granted federal prisoners claiming innocence the right to petition for post-conviction DNA testing; established mechanisms to improve the quality of defense lawyer representation in death penalty cases; and required independent investigations of serious crime-laboratory problems if the laboratories wanted to obtain federal financial assistance.

Publication of the National Academy of Sciences' massive report about crime-laboratory reform may spawn legislation that would spur the scientific research and quality controls necessary to enhance the accuracy of forensic evidence.

Some calls for reform seem to gain traction throughout the states, including giving inmates the right to seek post-conviction DNA testing based on claims of actual innocence. In 2009, South Dakota and Mississippi became the 45th and 46th states to approve such legislation. Alaska, on the other hand, has resisted the change, leading advocates of reform to argue earlier this year in the United States Supreme Court that the resistance is unconstitutional. [53]

The issue reached the court in an appeal by an Alaska man, William G. Osborne, who wants to be able to analyze DNA evidence used in his 1995 conviction for kidnapping and sexual assault. Alaska is one of six states with no law providing defendants or inmates access to DNA evidence. A ruling in the case, argued on March 2, is expected by the end of June.

Obviously, new legislation cannot result in a post-conviction DNA test if the DNA material has been misplaced by law enforcement agencies or degraded due to passage of time or inadequate storage methods. Thus, comprehensive legislation is sometimes the goal of reformers, who see it as vital to link

Former inmate Alan Newton embraces Cardozo law student Ben Zviti, who helped the Innocence Project bring about his release, on the day of his exoneration at the Bronx Criminal Court in New York City in 2006.

Innocence Project

the right to post-conviction DNA testing with improvements in evidence storage. Reformers have also learned that after passage of the desired legislation, state agencies frequently lack the money or understanding to implement the changes.

In an era of state budget deficits, the push by innocence projects and similar groups to provide innocent inmates with post-conviction compensation might face increased obstacles. Earlier this year, Nebraska became the 27th state to provide compensation without requiring an exonerated inmate to sue in court. Like most existing compensation laws, however, the Nebraska legislation contains limitations that some advocates consider inappropriate, such as a low, $500,000 cap on compensation for what might have been decades of wrongful imprisonment. Furthermore, many of the compensation laws deny or scrimp on social services to help exonerees readjust to the world outside prison. In Georgia, without a compensation law, legislators have been debating whether to grant an individual award to a man freed after 28 years in prison for a rape he did not commit. [54]

While reformers will continue to push for new legislation in Congress and in state legislatures, those who seek to reduce wrongful convictions are quite likely to seek change from the courts as often as practical. That is especially true when the crafting of a remedy through legislation seems impractical.

A representative example can be found in the U.S. Supreme Court case of *Luis E. Melendez-Diaz v. Massachusetts.* The Innocence Network filed a joint brief supporting the argument of Melendez-Diaz that he has a right to cross-examine a state forensics witness who played a role in his drug-related conviction. Massachusetts courts have ruled that prosecutors are allowed to submit the forensics report into evidence without further scrutiny at trial. The rulings rest "entirely on a myth of infallibility — a myth that finds no basis in the reality of state forensics practices throughout the country," according to the brief from the innocence projects. [55] ∎

OUTLOOK

New Hope

Traditionally, police and prosecutors have been reluctant to acknowledge wrongful convictions. But as the evidence mounts of persistent flaws in the criminal justice system, prosecutors, especially, are taking a more realistic view of the flaws and even sounding contrite more frequently.

Continued on p. 366

At Issue:

Can the number of wrongful convictions be calculated?

SAMUEL R. GROSS
*PROFESSOR, SCHOOL OF LAW
UNIVERSITY OF MICHIGAN*

FROM "CONVICTING THE INNOCENT," *ANNUAL REVIEW
OF LAW AND SOCIAL SCIENCE*, DECEMBER 2008

*a*lmost everything we know about false convictions is based on exonerations in rape and murder cases, which together account for only 2 percent of felony convictions. Within that important but limited sphere we have learned a lot in the past 30 years; outside it, our ignorance is nearly complete. . . .

In 1923, Judge Learned Hand wrote in a federal district court opinion that "our [criminal] procedure has always been haunted by the ghost of the innocent man convicted. It is an unreal dream." At the time, with no systematic data one way or the other, this could be taken as a statement of faith, an expression of red-blooded self-confidence and optimism.

Eighty-three years later, Justice Antonin Scalia was more specific in a concurring opinion in the Supreme Court, if less eloquent. He claimed that American criminal convictions have an "error rate of 0.027 percent — or, to put it another way, a success rate of 99.973 percent." Given what we knew by 2006, the charitable explanation for such an assertion is self-deception. . . . If false convictions really were vanishingly rare — 0.027 percent or some other absurd figure — they would not be much of a problem.

That estimate, and similar ones, are based on some version of dividing the number of known false convictions — exonerations — by the total of all convictions, ignoring the fact that almost all of these exonerations occurred in a few narrow categories of crime (primarily murder and rape) and that even within those categories many false convictions remain unknown, perhaps the great majority.

By this logic we could estimate the proportion of baseball players who have used steroids by dividing the number of major league players who have been caught by the total number of baseball players at all levels — major league, minor leagues, semipro, college and Little League, and maybe throwing in football and basketball players as well. . . . There are more prisoners behind bars in the United States for robbery than for any other crime — about 20 percent more than for murder and nearly three times as many as for rape. And yet there have been only a handful of robbery exonerations in the past 25 years. However little we may know about the frequency of false convictions for rape and murder, we know far less about robbery.

Reprinted, with permission from Annual Review of Law and Social Science, *Vol. 4, (c)2008 by Annual Reviews,* www.annualreviews.org

JUSTICE ANTONIN SCALIA
U.S. SUPREME COURT

CONCURRING OPINION, *KANSAS V. MICHAEL LEE
MARSH*, 548 U.S. 163, JUNE 26, 2006

*i*n identifying exonerees, the dissent [by Justices Stevens and Souter] is willing to accept anybody's say-so. It engages in no critical review, but merely parrots articles or reports that support its attack on the American criminal justice system. The dissent places significant weight, for instance, on the . . . report compiled by the appointees of an Illinois governor who had declared a moratorium upon the death penalty and who eventually commuted all death sentences in the state. . . .

The dissent claims that this report identifies 13 inmates released from death row after they were determined to be innocent. To take one of these cases, discussed by the dissent as an example of a judgment "as close to innocence as any judgments courts normally render," the defendant was twice convicted of murder. After his first trial, the Supreme Court of Illinois reversed his conviction based upon certain evidentiary errors and remanded his case for a new trial. The second jury convicted Smith again. The Supreme Court of Illinois again reversed the conviction because it found that the evidence was insufficient to establish guilt beyond a reasonable doubt. . . .

In its inflation of the word "exoneration," the [Samuel R.] Gross article hardly stands alone; mischaracterization of reversible error as actual innocence is endemic in abolitionist rhetoric, and other prominent catalogues of "innocence" in the death-penalty context suffer from the same defect. . . . Since 1976 there have been approximately a half million murders in the United States. In that time, 7,000 murderers have been sentenced to death; about 950 of them have been executed; and about 3,700 are currently on death row. As a consequence of the sensitivity of the criminal justice system to the due-process rights of defendants sentenced to death, almost two-thirds of those death sentences are overturned.

Virtually none of those reversals, however, are attributable to a defendant's actual innocence. Most are based on legal errors that have little or nothing to do with guilt. The studies cited by the dissent demonstrate nothing more. Like other human institutions, courts and juries are not perfect. One cannot have a system of criminal punishment without accepting the possibility that someone will be punished mistakenly. That is a truism, not a revelation. But with regard to the punishment of death in the current American system, that possibility has been reduced to an insignificant minimum.

This explains why those ideologically driven to ferret out and proclaim a mistaken modern execution have not a single verifiable case to point to, whereas it is easy as pie to identify plainly guilty murderers who have been set free.

Continued from p. 364

In March, Patricia R. Lykos, district attorney for Harris County (Houston), issued a report explaining the mistaken 2002 arrest of Ricardo Rachell and his wrongful conviction for assaulting a child in 2003. Rachell spent five years in prison. Lykos blamed law enforcement personnel involved in every step of the case. She and Houston Police Chief Harold L. Hurtt apologized to Rachell, those who know him personally and to the citizenry of Harris County. The nine-page report might have seemed like no big deal to the casual observer. But to those who study wrongful convictions in Harris County and across the nation, it felt like fresh air, and maybe the start of something momentous. Prosecutors in the past rarely admitted mistakes publicly — or only privately to those whose lives they have marked forever.

Naming names of just about everybody responsible, Lykos and Hurtt mentioned "a series of unfortunate events, blunders and omissions. There was a cascading, system-wide breakdown."[56]

Elsewhere in Texas, Dallas County District Attorney Craig Watkins has taken an unusual step for a prosecutor: He and his staff are reviewing seemingly closed cases that might have resulted in wrongful convictions.

Indeed, prosecutors increasingly are willing to collaborate with innocence projects to reopen cases — even those that might make the district attorney's office appear foolish, inept or venal. So far, the reviews ordered by Watkins, the first elected African-American district attorney in Texas, have led to the exonerations of multiple inmates, bringing the total to 19 in Dallas County alone during the current century. Millions of Americans learned about the initiative when "60 Minutes," the CBS television news magazine, featured Watkins in its May 4, 2008, broadcast. The cases were reviewed in cooperation with the Innocence Project of Texas.[57]

The demonstrated success of statewide innocence projects, coupled with the new atmosphere of hope, is encouraging the creation of new efforts in states poorly served by their criminal justice systems. Start-ups can look to the low-budget but extremely effective Centurion Ministries and to the largest of the organizations — the Innocence Project — for inspiration and procedural guidance.

Montana has recently joined the roster of states served by innocence projects. Montana had to deal with alleged and actual wrongful convictions due to incompetence and dishonesty within the state police crime laboratory. In Missouri, the Midwestern Innocence Project has expanded across the state and is now working on its first Oklahoma case and eventually hopes to accept cases in four other states.

Innocence projects focusing on wrongful convictions close to home have banded together without much fanfare to form what they term The Innocence Network, now boasting 52 members. Investigations of alleged wrongful convictions rarely stop at state lines, because witnesses and documents often must be retrieved across the nation. Members of The Innocence Network assist each other when travel costs and knowledge of faraway criminal justice systems become factors in the investigations.[58]

On Sept. 27, 2008, Darryl Burton, freed from prison in Missouri just a month earlier, sat in a leafy backyard in Princeton, N.J., under a white tent with about 125 other partygoers, many of them other exonerated men and women. The party was organized by Centurion Ministries, which had helped Burton establish his innocence after 24 years in prison.

"The Centurion Ministries tradition is to mark every freedom obtained with a celebration," said McCloskey, the organization's founder.

As for Burton, he commented, "This seems surreal. I'm still pinching myself. This is unbelievable." ■

Notes

[1] For an account of Darryl Burton's exoneration, see the Centurion Ministries newsletter, Nov. 19, 2008, www.centurionministries.org. Judge Richard G. Callahan issued the opinion freeing Burton on Aug. 18, 2008.

[2] The number of wrongful convictions in the United States varies depending on the source and methodology. Some compilers define "exonerations" as cases in which the wrongly convicted individual played absolutely no role in the crime. Others define "exonerations" more loosely, such as when a defendant was present at a crime scene, did nothing but watch, yet ended up in prison because a prosecutor mistakenly charged him with firing a gun. The 235 in the count by the Innocence Project, a national organization based in New York City, represent inmates

---

About the Author

Steve Weinberg is a freelance magazine writer and book author in Columbia, Mo., who has been writing about wrongful convictions for nearly two decades. After turns as a newspaper staff reporter and a magazine staff writer, Weinberg began freelancing full time in 1978. He is the author of eight nonfiction books. Amidst his reporting and writing, he served as executive director of Investigative Reporters and Editors, an international membership organization, from 1983-1990. Weinberg also teaches a course about the criminal justice system at the University of Missouri Journalism School, where he earned BJ and MJ degrees.

freed from prison after a specific forensic technique used after conviction showed biological material found at a crime scene did not belong to them.

[3] In most, if not all, of the thousands of prosecutorial jurisdictions across the United States DNA cases constitute only a small percentage of all cases, and the vast majority of cases never reach trial. See Samuel R. Gross, "Convicting the Innocent," *Annual Review of Law and Social Science*, December 2008, pp. 173-192.

[4] The decision is *Kansas v. Marsh*, 548 U.S. 163 (2006).

[5] Joshua Marquis, "The Innocent and the Shammed," *The New York Times*, Jan. 26, 2006, p. A23.

[6] Gross, *op. cit.*

[7] Steven W. Perry, "National Survey of Prosecutors," Bureau of Justice Statistics, Office of Justice Programs, U.S. Department of Justice, July 2006.

[8] In the past decade, the author has interviewed staff and dozens of lawyer members from both the National District Attorneys Association and the National Association of Criminal Defense Lawyers.

[9] "Achieving Justice: Freeing the Innocent, Convicting the Guilty," American Bar Association, Criminal Justice Section, 2006, p. xv.

[10] For a recent reference to the "CSI Effect," see Max M. Houck, "CSI: Reality," *Scientific American*, July 2006, p. 85.

[11] The author has interviewed and also spoken informally to at least a dozen exonerees, including Darryl Burton, Ellen Reasonover and Joshua Kezer, and has attended gatherings of exonerees.

[12] Jennifer Thompson-Cannino, Ronald Cotton and Erin Torneo, *Picking Cotton: Our Memoir of Injustice and Redemption* (2009), p. 220.

[13] For background, see Kenneth Jost, "DNA Databases," *CQ Researcher*, May 28, 1999, pp. 449-472.

[14] Hugo Adam Bedau and Michael L. Radelet, "Miscarriages of Justice in Potentially Capital Cases," *Stanford Law Review*, November 1987, pp. 21-179. See also Stephen J. Markman and Paul G. Cassell, "Protecting the Innocent: A Response to the Bedau-Radelet Study," *Stanford Law Review*, November 1988, pp. 121-160. The same issue contains a nine-page rejoinder by Bedau and Radelet, "The Myth of Infallibility: A Reply to Markman and Cassell."

[15] "Harmful Error: Investigating America's Local Prosecutors," The Center for Public Integrity, 2003. For background, see Kenneth Jost,

"Prosecutors and the Law," *CQ Researcher*, Nov. 9, 2007, pp. 937-960.

[16] The author developed the idea for the study, then served as chief reporter and writer, with research assistance from team members Neil Gordon and Brooke Williams. Bennett L. Gershman, a Pace University law professor, is almost certainly the leading academic expert regarding prosecutorial misconduct. His textbook, *Prosecutorial Misconduct*, is updated annually for the publisher Thomson-West.

[17] "Investigating Forensic Problems in the United States: How the Federal Government Can Strengthen Oversight Through the Coverdell Grant Program," Innocence Project, Benjamin N. Cardozo School of Law, Yeshiva University, March 2009, p. 68.

[18] Center for Public Integrity, *op. cit.*, p. 110; letter from Joshua Marquis dated July 7, 2003.

[19] The number is accurate as of April 2009, according to the self-regulatory organization that accredits crime laboratories, www.ascld-lab.org.

[20] See Tom Price, "The Future of Journalism," *CQ Researcher*, March 27, 2009, pp. 273-296.

[21] *Strengthening Forensic Science in the United States: A Path Forward*, National Research Council of the National Academies (2009). Several committees share authorship of the book: Committee on Identifying the Needs of the Forensic Science Community; Committee on Science, Technology, and Law; Policy and Global Affairs; Committee on Applied and Theoretical Statistics; Division on Engineering and Physical Sciences. See also Solomon Moore, "Science Found Wanting in Nation's Crime Labs," *The New York Times*, Feb. 4, 2009.

[22] American Bar Association, *op. cit.*, p. 48.

[23] The *Zain* case has spawned extensive documentation in court rulings and journalistic accounts. The most enlightening of all those resources is found at 438 S.E. 2d 501 (1993). Also see "Discredited Chemist Fred Zain, 52, Dies," *Charleston Gazette*, Dec. 4, 2002, and Janet Elliott, "Lawyers Seek Access to Bexar County Lab; New District Attorney Reviews Zain's Work," *Texas Lawyer*, Aug. 2, 1999.

[24] Michael R. Bromwich, "Final Report of the Independent Investigator for the Houston Police Department Crime Laboratory and Property Room," June 13, 2007, www.hpdlabinvestigation.org.

[25] John Collins and Jay Jarvis, "The Wrongful Conviction of Forensic Science," *Crime Lab Report: Media and Public Policy Analysis for the Forensic Science Community*, July 16, 2008.

[26] *Strengthening Forensic Science in the Unit-

ed States: A Path Forward*, *op. cit.*, February 2009.

[27] Ralph M. Keaton, "Don't Relocate Crime Labs," *USA Today*, April 6, 2009, p. 14A.

[28] Center for Public Integrity, *op. cit.*, p. 14. For background on the Reasonover case, also see Steve Weinberg, "Railroaded," *The American Lawyer*, August 2000.

[29] American Bar Association, *op. cit.*, p. 63.

[30] The primary drafters consisted of ABA staff member Kristie Kennedy and law professors Paul Giannelli and Myrna Raeder. The rest of the committee included two prosecutors, two judges, a police crime laboratory director, a police department administrator, a defense attorney and three additional law professors.

[31] ABA Report, *op. cit.*, p. xi. One of the most direct statements about altering human nature can be found in a January 2009 report by the New York State Bar Association Task Force on Wrongful Convictions: "Police officers should be trained to investigate alternate theories for a case at least until they are reasonably satisfied that they are without merit," p. 10.

[32] David Blumberg, "Habeas Leaps From the Pan and Into the Fire: Jacobs v. Scott and the Anti-Terrorism and Effective Death Penalty Act of 1996," *Albany Law Review*, 1997.

[33] The case citation is 295 F. 3d 839.

[34] Centurion Ministries newsletter, *op. cit.*

[35] Barry Scheck, Peter Neufeld and Jim Dwyer, *Actual Innocence: When Justice Goes Wrong and How to Make It Right* (2003), p. 282.

[36] Edwin M. Borchard, *Convicting the Innocent: Sixty-Five Actual Errors of Criminal Justice* (1932), p. v.

[37] Erle Stanley Gardner, *The Court of Last Resort* (1952); the quotation comes from a revised edition, published in 1954, p. 331. See Barbara Mantel, "Public Defenders," *CQ Researcher*, April 18, 2008, pp. 337-360.

[38] Michael L. Radelet, Hugo Adam Bedau and Constance E. Putnam, *In Spite of Innocence: Erroneous Convictions in Capital Cases* (1992). The U.S. Justice Department lawyers rebutting the Radelet-Bedau-Putnam research were Paul G. Cassell and Stephen J. Markman. The first version of their critique can be found at 41 *Stanford Law Review* 121 (1988).

[39] David Protess and Rob Warden, *Gone in the Night: The Dowaliby Family's Encounter With Murder and the Law* (1993), and *A Promise of Justice* (1998), p. 202.

[40] George (Woody) Clarke, *Justice and Science: Trials and Triumphs of DNA Evidence* (2007), p. 1.

[41] Ken Armstrong and Maurice Possley. "Trial and Error: How Prosecutors Sacrifice Justice to Win," *Chicago Tribune*, Jan. 10, 1999, p. A1.

[42] Among the most significant *Chicago Tribune* series after the January 1999 launch were by Steve Mills, Maurice Possley and Ken Armstrong, and appeared on Dec. 17-18, 2000, under the overall title "Executions in America." The primary headline reads "Shadows of Doubt Haunt Executions."

[43] The quotation was posted at www.illinois leader.com, Nov. 14, 2003.

[44] See Frederic N. Tulsky, "Tainted Trials, Stolen Justice," *San Jose Mercury-News*, Jan. 22-26, 2006.

[45] "Preliminary Report of the New York State Bar Association's Task Force on Wrongful Convictions for the Consideration of the House of Delegates," New York State Bar Association, Jan. 30, 2009.

[46] Jon B. Gould, *The Innocence Commission: Preventing Wrongful Convictions and Restoring the Criminal Justice System* (2008), p. 6.

[47] "A Vision for Justice: Report and Recommendations Regarding Wrongful Convictions in the Commonwealth of Virginia," Innocence Commission for Virginia March 2005, p. 73.

[48] Scott Turow, *Ultimate Punishment: A Lawyer's Reflections on Dealing With the Death Penalty* (2003), p. 28.

[49] See *Innocence Project Blog*, March 26, 2009, and Jim Siegel, "DNA Bill Hung Up on Side Issues/Law Enforcers Battle Provisions on Police Lineups, Recordings," *Columbus Dispatch*, March 26, 2009.

[50] For recent news reports on local proposals to enact judicial-system reforms designed to prevent wrongful convictions and to compensate those who have been wrongly convicted, see Shannon McCaffrey, "Police Officials Say No State Eyewitness Law Needed," The Associated Press, as published in the *Ledger-Enquirer* (Columbus, Ga.), Oct. 1, 2007, available at www.nacdl.org/sl_docs.nsf/freeform/Eyewitness ID041?OpenDocument; and Dave Montgomery, "Fort Worth family pushes for bills to aid the wrongfully convicted," *Star-Telegram* (Fort Worth, Texas), April 1, 2009.

[51] "DNA Exonerations: Transforming the Criminal Justice System," Innocence Project, Benjamin N. Cardozo School of Law, Yeshiva University, April 2009.

[52] See National Conference of State Legislatures, www.ncsl.org. The criminal justice information is located at www.ncsl.org/programs/cj.

[53] The case is *District Attorney's Office v. Osborne*, docket 08-6 in the Supreme Court

of the United States. For coverage, see Adam Liptak, "Convict Asks Justice to Find a Right to DNA Testing," *The New York Times*, March 3, 2009, p. A16.

[54] Michael Newsom, "Law Compensates Wrongfully Convicted," *Sun Herald* (Biloxi-Gulfport, Miss.), March 31, 2009; Keffie Sledge, "Josh White Closer to $709,000 Settlement," *Ledger-Enquirer* (Columbus, Ga.), March 22, 2009; www.innocenceproject.org.

[55] The Docket number is 07-591 in the Supreme Court of the United States. See *Innocence Project Blog*, June 24, 2008.

[56] Patricia R. Lykos, "Rachell Report," Office of District Attorney, Harris County, Texas, March 2009.

[57] Watkins' words and actions have been covered heavily locally, regionally and nationally. For one of the best accounts, see Zac Crain, "The Last Temptation of Craig Watkins," *D Magazine*, March 2009. The initiative receives prominent display at the district attorney's Web site, www.dallasda.com.

[58] Most innocence projects maintain Web sites, such as www.centurionministries.org and www.themip.org.

FOR MORE INFORMATION

American Bar Association, 321 N. Clark St., Chicago, IL 60654; (800) 285-2221; www.abanet.org. Professional association serving as the national representative of the legal profession.

American Society of Crime Laboratory Directors/Laboratory Accreditation Board, 139 J Technology Dr., Garner, NC 27529; (919) 773-2600; www.ascld-lab.org. Voluntary programs in which crime laboratories can demonstrate that their operations and facilities meet established standards.

Center for Public Integrity, 910 17th St., N.W., Suite 700, Washington, DC 20006; (202) 466-1300; www.publicintegrity.org. Produces original investigative journalism about public issues in order to make institutions more accountable.

Centurion Ministries, 221 Witherspoon St., Princeton, NJ 08542; www.centurion ministries.org. Nonprofit working to exonerate wrongly convicted individuals who have been sentenced to life or death.

The Innocence Network; www.innocencenetwork.org. Affiliation of organizations providing pro bono services to those seeking to prove their innocence.

Innocence Project, 100 Fifth Ave., 3rd Floor, New York, NY 10011; (212) 364-5340; www.innocenceproject.org. Litigation and public policy organization working to exonerate the wrongfully convicted through DNA testing and reforming the criminal justice system to prevent further injustice.

Midwestern Innocence Project, 6320 Brookside Plaza, Suite 1500, Kansas City, MO 64113; www.themip.org. Provides pro bono legal and investigative services to wrongfully convicted persons in prison.

National Academy of Sciences, 500 Fifth St., N.W., Washington, DC 20001; (202) 334-2000; www.nasonline.org. Honorific society dedicated to furthering science and technology for the benefit of general welfare.

National Association of Criminal Defense Lawyers, 1660 L St., N.W., 12th Floor, Washington, DC 20036; (202) 872-8600; www.nacdl.org. Works to ensure justice for persons accused of crimes or other misconduct.

National District Attorneys Association, 44 Canal Center Plaza, Suite 110, Alexandria, VA 22314; (703) 549-9222; www.ndaa.org. Professional organization working to maintain the honor and integrity of prosecuting attorneys in the United States.

Bibliography

Selected Sources

Books

Clarke, George "Woody," *Justice and Science: Trials and Triumphs of DNA Evidence*, **Rutgers University Press, 2007.**

Clarke, a San Diego County judge who spent 21 years as an assistant district attorney and played a significant role in understanding the use of DNA evidence, discusses its power to catch criminals and exonerate those wrongly charged.

Davis, Angela J., *Arbitrary Justice: The Power of the American Prosecutor*, **Oxford University Press, 2007.**

A public defender turned American University law professor explains how prosecutors gained untrammeled power, why they sometimes abuse their authority and what can be done to control those who overstep the law.

Gershman, Bennett, *Prosecutorial Misconduct*, **second edition, Thomson-West, updated 2009.**

A former prosecutor who teaches at Pace University Law School provides a comprehensive narrative — with case citations — demonstrating the long, repetitive history of questionable behavior by local, state and federal prosecutors.

Scheck, Barry, Peter Neufeld and Jim Dwyer, *Actual Innocence: When Justice Goes Wrong and How to Make It Right*, **New American Library, 2003 (expanded from the original edition, published by Doubleday in 2000).**

Two of the highest-profile criminal defense lawyers in the nation (Scheck and Neufeld) — who direct The Innocence Project — join a *New York Times* reporter to educate readers about the causes and impacts of wrongful convictions, with dramatic case studies peppering each chapter.

Articles

Armstrong, Ken, Steve Mills and Maurice Possley, *Chicago Tribune*, **1999-2008.**

A long-running investigatory series examines problems in the judicial system, including various issues involving crime laboratories (Oct. 11-21, 2004), in articles such as "From the Start, a Faulty Science" and "When Labs Falter, Defendants Pay; Bias Toward Prosecution Cited in Illinois Cases." Other reporters' bylines also appeared in the series, including Flynn McRoberts.

Berlow, Alan, "The Wrong Man," *Atlantic Monthly*, **November 1999.**

Freelance journalist Berlow was not the first investigator to survey the wrongful conviction phenomenon in a long magazine feature, and others have published magazine features since then. But nobody has done it more comprehensively or more compellingly.

Moushey, Bill, "Win at All Costs," *Pittsburgh Post-Gazette*, **Nov. 22-24 and 29-30, Dec. 1, 6-8 and 13, 1998.**

Most in-depth investigations have examined cases in the state courts, filed by local district attorneys. Moushey focuses on the cases filed by U.S. attorneys. No investigation of questionable filings by U.S. attorneys since Moushey's effort has attained the same breadth and depth.

Saks, Michael J., and David L. Faigman, "Failed Forensics: How Forensic Science Lost Its Way and How It Might Yet Find It," *Annual Review of Law and Social Science*, **December 2008.**

Law professors at Arizona State University (Saks) and the University of California-San Francisco debunk the stereotype of forensic examiners in police department laboratories as objective scientists.

Reports and Studies

"Achieving Justice: Freeing the Innocent, Convicting the Guilty," Criminal Justice Section, American Bar Association, 2006.

The 137-page booklet reaches a broad consensus regarding every major cause of wrongful convictions, then suggests reforms that it says both prosecutors and defense attorneys ought to support.

"Postconviction DNA Testing: Recommendations for Handling Requests," National Commission on the Future of DNA Evidence, Office of Justice Programs, U.S. Justice Department, September 1999.

The recommendations in this report by a blue-ribbon commission a decade ago have taken root in many states and are making a positive impact. Christopher H. Asplen, an assistant U.S. attorney, headed the staff, while Shirley S. Abrahamson, chief justice of the Wisconsin Supreme Court, served as chairwoman.

"Preliminary Report of the New York State Bar Association's Task Force on Wrongful Convictions, for the Consideration of the House of Delegates," New York State Bar Association, Jan. 30, 2009.

The report covers every major cause of wrongful convictions. It is especially powerful because the examples and the recommendations are based on authoritative in-depth studies of 53 wrongful convictions in New York state.

Strengthening Forensic Science in the United States: A Path Forward, **National Research Council of the National Academies, 2009.**

Several committees of experts in various arenas of forensics collaborated to write this book-length report. Unlike most reports emanating from committees, the language is unambiguous and the massive list of recommendations for reform demonstrates a desire to find common ground among warring parties while pushing ahead.

The Next Step:

Additional Articles from Current Periodicals

Causes

Fernandez, Manny, "Examining Human Error in Wrongful Convictions," *The New York Times*, Feb. 1, 2009, p. A25.

The root causes of wrongful convictions tend to be errors by prosecutors, judges and law enforcement officers.

Khanna, Roma, "Study: Witness Errors Cause Most Wrongful Convictions," *Houston Chronicle*, March 26, 2009, p. A1.

Mistaken witness identifications that are the cause of most wrongful convictions in Texas could be avoided with more sophistical lineup techniques, according to a justice reform group.

Liptak, Adam, "Study of Wrongful Convictions Raises Questions Beyond DNA," *The New York Times*, July 23, 2007, p. A1.

The leading cause of wrongful convictions has been erroneous identification by eyewitnesses, followed by faulty forensic evidence.

McGonigle, Steve, and Jennifer Emily, "A Blind Faith in Eyewitnesses," *Dallas Morning News*, Oct. 12, 2008, p. 1A.

Unreliable and false testimony factored heavily in 18 of 19 Texas cases overturned by DNA evidence.

Spano, John, "Forensic Science Errors Are Cited," *Los Angeles Times*, May 9, 2007, p. B7.

A California commission has said that forensic science errors are a major contributor to wrongful convictions.

Compensation

Fineout, Gary, "State House OK's $1.2M for Cleared Inmate," *Miami Herald*, March 27, 2008, p. B1.

The Florida House has unanimously voted to award $1.25 million to a man who spent 24 years in prison for two rapes he did not commit.

Hafenbrack, Josh, and Tonya Alanez, "Florida Sets Wrongful Imprisonment Compensation at $50,000 a Year," *South Florida Sun-Sentinel*, April 30, 2008.

The Florida Legislature has approved automatic compensation for individuals sentenced to prison for crimes they did not commit, but those with prior felony convictions are not eligible.

Hammel, Paul, "Should Wrongly Convicted Be Paid?" *Omaha World-Herald* (Nebraska), Nov. 4, 2008, p. 1A.

The release of a Nebraska inmate on DNA evidence has renewed talks of a compensation law in the state.

Paulson, Amanda, "What Do States Owe the Exonerated?" *The Christian Science Monitor*, May 30, 2007, p. 1.

As DNA exonerations become more plentiful, more and more states are moving on the compensation front.

Price, Stephen D., "Compensation Act Tricky," *Florida Today*, May 11, 2008, p. 12B.

Florida's Wrongful Incarceration Act — intended to compensate the exonerated — may be loaded with just as many complexities as the legislative process it's set to replace.

Santos, Fernanda, "Bill Would Give Tax Break to Exonerated Prisoners," *The New York Times*, Dec. 7, 2007, p. B4.

Sen. Charles E. Schumer, D-N.Y., has introduced a bill that would exempt exonerated prisoners from paying federal income taxes on compensation received for a wrongful conviction.

Santos, Fernanda, and Janet Roberts, "Putting a Price on a Wrongful Conviction," *The New York Times*, Dec. 2, 2007, p. D4.

Twenty-two states compensate exonerated prisoners using formulas ranging from lump sums to calculations of lost wages. [The number of states has since increased -ed.]

Warner, Gene, "Paying a Man Back for Decades of Injustice," *Buffalo News*, May 4, 2007, p. A1.

New York is one of several states with no cap on the maximum compensation for exonerated inmates.

Webster, Richard A., "State of Louisiana Offers the Wrongly Convicted Up to $150K in Compensation," *New Orleans City Business*, June 1, 2007.

Louisiana is offering a wrongly convicted prisoner $150,000 for being incarcerated 22 years for a rape he did not commit, but he must go on trial again and prove his innocence in court.

Weinstein, Henry, "State Fails Wrongly Convicted Prisoners," *Los Angeles Times*, Feb. 23, 2008, p. B3.

People wrongly convicted in California courts are offered fewer benefits than convicts released on parole, according to a state blue-ribbon commission.

DNA

"Court Clears Man Convicted in Gang Rape," The Associated Press, June 22, 2007.

A Texas court has exonerated a man who has spent 10 years in prison for a gang rape that DNA evidence proves he did not commit.

Dutton, Geoff, and Mike Wagner, "In 5 Ohio Cases, DNA Revealed a New Suspect," *Columbus Dispatch* (Ohio), May 4, 2008, p. 1G.

DNA tests that have cleared five Ohio inmates have pointed to new suspects who apparently committed other crimes before being exposed by DNA.

Eligon, John, "New Efforts Focus on Exonerating Prisoners in Cases Without DNA Evidence," *The New York Times*, Feb. 8, 2009, p. A26.

A growing number of DNA exonerations have made it difficult for prisoners trying to prove their innocence in cases that do not involve DNA evidence.

Floyd, Jacquielynn, "Dallas Willing, Able to Correct Injustices," *Dallas Morning News*, Aug. 8, 2008, p. 1B.

The only real debate left about DNA evidence is the numerical degree of its infallibility.

Messina, Lawrence, "DNA Champion Scheck Sees Progress in Court System," The Associated Press, June 12, 2008.

The Innocence Project counts 218 people nationwide who have been exonerated from alleged crimes by DNA results.

Moore, Solomon, "DNA Exoneration Leads to Change in Legal System," *The New York Times*, Oct. 1, 2007, p. A1.

State lawmakers nationwide are adopting broad changes to criminal justice procedures following the exoneration of 200 convicts via DNA evidence.

Villa, Judi, "DNA Exonerations Underline Mistakes," *Arizona Republic*, April 24, 2007, p. 12.

Policy makers and advocates for the wrongly convicted in Arizona are working to guarantee access to post-conviction DNA testing and the preservation of DNA evidence.

Willing, Richard, "DNA to Clear 200th Person," *USA Today*, April 23, 2007, p. 1A.

A former Army cook imprisoned for 25 years for a rape he did not commit is set to become the 200th person exonerated by DNA evidence.

Systematic Reform

Baker, Max B., "Exoneration Case May Lead to Criminal Justice System Reforms," *Fort Worth Star-Telegram* (Texas), Feb. 7, 2009.

The posthumous exoneration of a Texas inmate may lead to the passage of several criminal justice reforms by the state's legislature.

Baker, Max B., "Top Jurists Support Idea of Innocence Commission," *Fort Worth Star-Telegram* (Texas), May 18, 2008, p. B1.

Texas' top jurists are supporting a proposal that would create a statewide Innocence Commission to investigate wrongful convictions and recommend reforms.

Dutton, Geoff, and Mike Wagner, "Proposed Reforms Shown to Work," *Columbus Dispatch* (Ohio), Feb. 24, 2008, p. 1A.

A new bipartisan coalition in Ohio focused on preventing wrongful convictions is pushing for reforms on how crimes are investigated and prosecuted.

Jackson, Jesse, "System That Convicts Innocent Needs Reform," *Chicago Sun-Times*, July 22, 2008, p. A23.

Reform of the American criminal justice system has been ignored for too long, especially since many innocent individuals are being incarcerated.

McGonigle, Steve, "Police, DAs Resist Witness ID Reform," *Dallas Morning News*, March 31, 2009, p. 1A.

Police chiefs and prosecutors in Texas are blocking legislative attempts to provide more training for law enforcement officers on witness identification issues.

Moffeit, Miles, "Evidence Reform Advocated," *Denver Post*, Oct. 18, 2007, p. B3.

The Innocence Project is urging Colorado's DNA Task Force to develop a law requiring criminal-case items to be retained indefinitely.

Rankin, Bill, "Exonerations Urge Changes for Eyewitnesses," *Atlanta Journal-Constitution*, Dec. 25, 2008, p. 1C.

A spate of DNA exonerations is prompting Georgia lawmakers to improve the state's eyewitness identification procedures.

Rojas, Aurelio, "A Hard Look at Jail Snitches," *Sacramento Bee*, May 18, 2007, p. A3.

A new bill in the California Senate would require the testimony of jailhouse informants to be corroborated before being regarded as legitimate.

Virtanen, Michael, "Bar Task Force to Study Wrongful Convictions in NY," The Associated Press, June 4, 2008.

The New York State Bar Association is establishing a legal task force to identify rules, procedures and statutes contributing to the problem of wrongful convictions.

In-depth Reports on Issues in the News

Are you writing a paper?

Need backup for a debate?

Want to become an expert on an issue?

For 80 years, students have turned to *CQ Researcher* for in-depth reporting on issues in the news. Reports on a full range of political and social issues are now available. Following is a selection of recent reports:

Civil Liberties
Closing Guantánamo, 2/09
Limiting Lawsuits, 12/08
Affirmative Action, 10/08
Gay Marriage Showdowns, 9/08
America's Border Fence, 9/08
Immigration Debate, 2/08

Crime/Law
Mexico's Drug War, 12/08
Prostitution Debate, 5/08
Public Defenders, 4/08
Gun Violence, 5/07

Education
Reading Crisis? 2/08
Discipline in Schools, 2/08
Student Aid, 1/08
Racial Diversity in Public Schools, 9/07
Stress on Students, 7/07

Environment/Society
Future of Journalism, 3/09
Confronting Warming, 1/09
Reducing Carbon Footprint, 12/08
Protecting Wetlands, 10/08
Buying Green, 2/08

Health/Safety
Extreme Sports, 4/09
Regulating Toxic Chemicals, 1/09
Preventing Cancer, 1/09
Heart Health, 9/08
Global Food Crisis, 6/08

Politics/Economy
Business Bankruptcy, 4/09
Future of the GOP, 3/09
Middle-Class Squeeze, 3/09
Public-Works Projects, 2/09
The Obama Presidency, 1/09

Upcoming Reports

Judicial Elections, 4/24/09   High-Speed Trains, 5/1/09   Hate Groups, 5/8/09

ACCESS

CQ Researcher is available in print and online. For access, visit your library or www.cqresearcher.com.

STAY CURRENT

To receive notice of upcoming *CQ Researcher* reports, or learn more about *CQ Researcher* products, subscribe to the free e-mail newsletters, *CQ Researcher Alert!* and *CQ Researcher News*: http://cqpress.com/newsletters.

PURCHASE

To purchase a *CQ Researcher* report in print or electronic format (PDF), visit www.cqpress.com or call 866-427-7737. Single reports start at $15. Bulk purchase discounts and electronic-rights licensing are also available.

SUBSCRIBE

Annual full-service *CQ Researcher* subscriptions—including 44 reports a year, monthly index updates, and a bound volume—start at $803. Add $25 for domestic postage.

CQ Researcher Online offers a backfile from 1991 and a number of tools to simplify research. For pricing information, call 800-834-9020, ext. 1906, or e-mail librarysales@cqpress.com.

Published by CQ Press, a division of SAGE Publications

www.cqresearcher.com

Judicial Elections

Are races for judgeships bad for justice?

T he United States is the only country in the world that requires most judges to face popular elections to gain or hold office. Today, as in the past, most judicial elections attract little attention. Over the past three decades, however, political parties and interest groups have spent millions of dollars on targeted races for state supreme courts in order to change the tribunals' political or ideological composition. Business groups succeeded in recent elections in West Virginia and Wisconsin in backing candidates who defeated incumbent justices and tilted the courts toward business interests. Defenders of judicial elections say they help make sure courts are accountable and responsive to the public. Critics say the special-interest funding and misleading campaign tactics of many judicial campaigns threaten the integrity of the justice system. Proposals for change, however, are making little headway. Meanwhile, the U.S. Supreme Court is considering whether to require judges to bow out of cases involving major campaign supporters.

West Virginia Supreme Court Justice Brent Benjamin is part of a pending U.S. Supreme Court case focusing on whether judges must recuse themselves in cases involving campaign contributions or spending by someone with a stake in the outcome.

CQ Researcher • April 24, 2009 • www.cqresearcher.com
Volume 19, Number 16 • Pages 373-396

Cover: AP Photo/Bob Bird

CQ Researcher

April 24, 2009
Volume 19, Number 16

MANAGING EDITOR: Thomas J. Colin
tcolin@cqpress.com

ASSISTANT MANAGING EDITOR: Kathy Koch
kkoch@cqpress.com

ASSOCIATE EDITOR: Kenneth Jost

STAFF WRITERS: Thomas J. Billitteri, Marcia Clemmitt, Peter Katel

CONTRIBUTING WRITERS: Rachel Cox, Sarah Glazer, Alan Greenblatt, Barbara Mantel, Patrick Marshall, Tom Price, Jennifer Weeks

DESIGN/PRODUCTION EDITOR: Olu B. Davis

ASSISTANT EDITOR: Darrell Dela Rosa

FACT-CHECKING: Eugene J. Gabler, Michelle Harris

EDITORIAL INTERN: Vyomika Jairam

CQ PRESS

A Division of SAGE

PRESIDENT AND PUBLISHER:
John A. Jenkins

EXECUTIVE DIRECTOR,
REFERENCE INFORMATION GROUP:
Alix B. Vance

CQ Researcher (ISSN 1056-2036) is printed on acid-free paper. Published weekly, except; (Jan. wk. 1) (May wk. 4) (July wks. 1, 2) (Aug. wks. 3, 4) (Nov. wk. 4) and (Dec. wk. 4), by CQ Press, a division of SAGE Publications. Annual full-service subscriptions start at $803. For pricing, call 1-800-834-9020, ext. 1906. To purchase a CQ Researcher report in print or electronic format (PDF), visit www. cqpress.com or call 866-427-7737. Single reports start at $15. Bulk purchase discounts and electronic-rights licensing are also available. Periodicals postage paid at Washington, D.C., and additional mailing offices. POSTMASTER: Send address changes to CQ Researcher, 2300 N St., N.W., Suite 800, Washington, DC 20037.

Judicial Elections

BY KENNETH JOST

THE ISSUES

Chief Justice Shirley Abrahamson of the Wisconsin Supreme Court is well known not only at home but also across the country as an advocate for judicial independence. But when Abrahamson learned she would face an opponent for reelection to a fourth 10-year term, she pulled out all the political stops.

The 75-year-old Abrahamson hired a veteran political operative to head her campaign, collected endorsements from across the political spectrum and raised more than $1.3 million. "She came into the race prepared," says Charles Franklin, a political science professor at the University of Wisconsin in Madison.

Abrahamson had reason to take seriously the challenge by Randy Koschnick, an outspokenly conservative circuit court judge in Milwaukee. Just a year earlier, a conservative challenger had knocked off one of Abrahamson's fellow liberals on the bench with a hard-hitting, multimillion-dollar campaign financed in part by the state's business lobby. Michael J. Gableman's election as justice in April 2008 gave conservatives a 4-3 majority on the Wisconsin court.

One year later, however, Abrahamson's political efforts paid off on April 7 with a 59 percent to 41 percent victory over Koschnick. "I ran a good race and kept it clean," Abrahamson told Milwaukee's *Journal Sentinel* afterward. But she added that her financial advantage over Koschnick — who spent only $180,000 — was critical. "That makes a big difference in how you

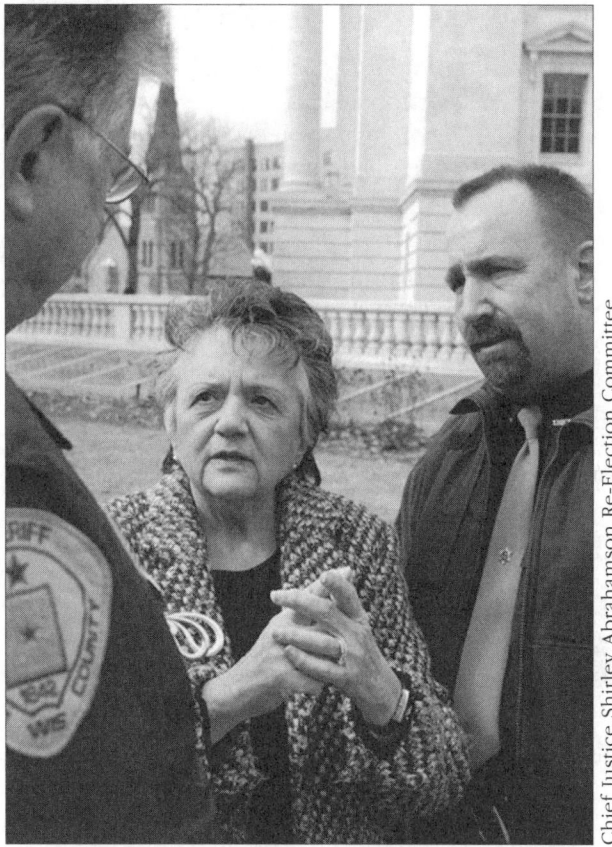

Chief Justice Shirley Abrahamson talks with police officers as she campaigns for reelection to a fourth term on the Wisconsin Supreme Court. Abrahamson raised $1.3 million for the campaign, which ended on April 7 with her 59 percent to 41 percent victory.

Chief Justice Shirley Abrahamson Re-Election Committee

can get your message out." [1] (*See sidebar, p. 384.*)

For most of the world, Abrahamson's victory would not be as remarkable as the fact of the election itself. Except for Japan and Switzerland, the United States is the only country that requires judges to face popular election to gain or hold office.* Even though federal judges serve life terms after nomination by the presi-

---

* In Japan supreme court justices are subject to retention elections shortly after appointment and at periodic intervals thereafter; none has ever been removed. In Switzerland's federal system, some of the 26 cantons have popular judicial elections, but judges are seldom defeated.

---

dent and confirmation by the Senate, 39 out of 50 states use some form of election for judgeships either at the trial or appellate level or both. The elections vary from traditional partisan contests to nonpartisan races to so-called retention elections in which incumbent judges run without an opponent and remain in office unless a majority votes to remove them. [2] (*See map, p. 376.*)

Today as in the past, most judicial elections attract little attention. Most vacancies are initially filled by gubernatorial appointment, and virtually all incumbents remain in office whether they face "contestable" or retention elections.

Over the past 30 years, however, judicial elections in a handful of states have become high-cost, bare-knuckle political battles. In particular, the U.S. Chamber of Commerce's decision in 2000 to dive into state judicial politics in a big way has led to multimillion-dollar campaigns like Wisconsin's 2008 contest that have succeeded — as in Wisconsin — in tilting some state supreme courts toward business interests on civil litigation and some other issues.

The Chamber — which now generally avoids direct comment on judicial election issues — said at the time it wanted to counteract political influence in the judicial selection process by trial lawyers' groups. Business groups like the Chamber, the National Association of Manufacturers and the American Tort Reform Association blame the plaintiffs' bar for a history of favorable rulings on personal injury suits only recently being cut back in some states.

The increasing cost and the deteriorating tone of judicial election campaigns worry many bar associations,

Most States Elect Judges for Highest Courts

Thirty-eight states select justices on their highest courts through popular elections. Seventeen use "merit selection and retention" systems, in which justices are appointed by the governor for their first term from a list submitted by a judicial selection commission and afterwards subject to a "yes-no" election. Justices in the other 21 states are picked in contested elections. Balloting in 13 of those states is nonpartisan; partisan affiliations are used in the eight others.

Among the 12 states with no popular election at the supreme court level, justices are appointed by the governor in 10 — subject to approval by the legislature or executive council — and elected by the legislature in the other two. Trial-level judgeships are subject to popular election in the 38 states with popular election for state supreme courts plus New York.

Selecting Judges for the States' Highest Courts

Method of Selection
- Merit/retention
- Partisan
- Nonpartisan
- No popular election

* Montana provides for a nonpartisan election; justices without opponents are subject to a retention election.

** Illinois and Pennsylvania use partisan elections for a justice's initial election, but retention elections thereafter.

Source: American Judicature Society, www.judicialselection.us/

traditional court reform organizations and liberal advocacy groups. "Over the last 20 years, and especially in the past seven years, we're seeing a race to the bottom with respect to financing and campaigning in judicial elections," says Seth Andersen, executive director of the American Judicature Society, a 95-year-old court reform organization that created the retention-election sys-

tems now used in 19 states.

"Judicial elections are now posing the single, greatest threat to fair and impartial courts," says Tommy Wells, a Birmingham, Ala., lawyer and president of the American Bar Association. The ABA along with state and local bar associations has been the major interest group supporting retention-election plans.

Wells and others fear that campaign contributions from businesses and from lawyers with cases before courts are undermining public confidence in judges' impartiality. "There's a real fear that money alone can be tipping scales of justice," says Bert Brandenburg, executive director of Justice at Stake, a Washington-based coalition of liberal-leaning legal advocacy groups. (*See graph, p. 380.*)

Judicial elections are strongly defended, however, by an assortment of Republican officials and leaders, business lobbies and conservative advocacy groups and experts. They emphasize that judges, especially state supreme court justices, have the power to make law in their respective jurisdictions — in some cases with no effective review by the federal judiciary.

"Judges are making law, and it's only appropriate for the people to choose judges," says James Bopp, a lawyer in Terre Haute, Ind., who has represented Republican and anti-abortion groups among others in campaign-speech cases at the U.S. Supreme Court and in lower federal courts. "The whole idea of popular sovereignty supports judicial elections."

Bopp and others profess little concern about the impact of increased campaign costs and spending by businesses and other interest groups. "If you are going to elect your judges, then you pretty much have to allow much of the same trappings that you do for any other election," says Sean Parnell, president of the Center for Competitive Politics, a Washington-based organization critical of campaign finance regulations.

Michael DeBow, a law professor at Samford University's Cumberland School of Law in Birmingham, Ala., and a member of the conservative-libertarian Federalist Society, says the public supports judicial elections despite concerns about the impact of contributions on judges' decisions. "They don't want to let go of judicial elections," DeBow says.

The debate over the impact of campaign contributions and spending is now pending at the U.S. Supreme Court. The justices are being asked to decide whether constitutional due process may require judges to step out of a case — in legal parlance, to recuse themselves — because of campaign contributions or spending by a party, lawyer or other individual with a stake in the outcome.

The issue reached the justices in a case brought by the president of a now defunct coal company in West Virginia who says state supreme court justice Brent Benjamin should have recused himself from ruling on the $50 million award the company won against a rival coal business. Benjamin refused to recuse himself even though the president of the rival company had spent more than $3 million to help Benjamin during his successful campaign for the supreme court seat in 2004. Benjamin eventually cast a critical vote in the 3-2 decision in March 2008 overturning the award. (*See sidebar, p. 386.*)

Stricter standards on recusal are among the reforms the ABA, Justice at Stake and other public-interest groups are urging to try to counteract what they see as the negative effects on public confidence in the judiciary due to judicial elections. They also express interest in public financing of judicial campaigns — a system now on the books in two states, North Carolina and New Mexico.

From the opposite perspective, judicial election supporters say stricter recusal standards may undermine elections by deterring campaign contributions or spending. They similarly argue that public campaign financing — accompanied by overall limits on candidates' spending — will reduce the amount of information for voters in judicial contests. (*See "At Issue," p. 389.*)

The arguments over judicial elections are drawing only limited at-

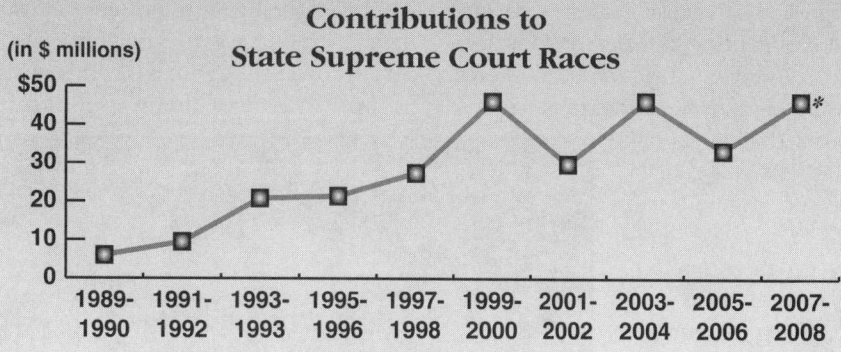

Contributions to Judges Topped $46 Million

Candidates for state supreme court judgeships in 2007-2008 received more than $46 million in contributions — a nearly sevenfold increase since 1989. Candidates received a total of more than a quarter of a billion dollars over the last 10 election cycles.

Contributions to State Supreme Court Races

(in $ millions)

Note: All contribution amounts in 2008 dollars.

* preliminary data

Source: National Institute on Money in State Politics (www.followthemoney.org)

tention from state legislators, who would have to be involved in making any changes in selection or election methods or campaign finance regulations. The general public also is largely unengaged on the issue. Indeed, despite public support for judicial elections in general, voter turnout is traditionally low in judgeship races. Wisconsin's relatively high-profile supreme court race in April 2008 drew 830,000 voters — fewer than one-third of the nearly 3 million state voters in the presidential election in November.

Still, legal advocacy groups on both sides are pressing their opposing views of what to do, if anything, about the current state of judicial campaigns. Here are some of the major questions being debated:

Should states take new steps to control campaign contributions or spending in judicial elections?

Republican Beverly Lake and Democratic incumbent Henry Frye spent $1.1 million between them in Lake's narrow victory in 2000 to become

North Carolina's first GOP chief justice. Some judicial contests in other states cost more that year, but the amounts were enough to jolt the state's General Assembly two years later to try to control the spending race by enacting a precedent-setting system of public financing for candidates for the state's appellate courts.

Three election cycles later, the head of a good-government group that lobbied for the change pronounces it a success. "It's removed any sort of notion or appearance of impropriety from judicial races," says Damon Zircosta, executive director of the North Carolina Center for Voter Education. "No longer is it solely attorneys who are bankrolling these elections. It's everyday voters who are making contributions to public financing."

National judicial election-reform groups view public financing schemes like North Carolina's and a similar system approved but not yet instituted in New Mexico as one step to reduce special-interest influence in contested races for judgeships. With public financing and the "voluntary" spending caps that go along with it, "judges don't have to dial for dollars," says Justice at Stake's Brandenburg. ABA President Wells agrees that public financing "takes away some of the more unseemly aspects of judicial elections."

Free speech-minded critics of campaign finance regulation question whether public financing actually protects judicial candidates from special-interest groups because candidates must first raise specified amounts on their own to qualify for the public subsidy. "Candidates simply get these interest groups to raise the qualifying amounts," says Parnell, at the Center for Competitive Politics. "I don't really see a public official being any less grateful to, say, the Teamsters Union because the Teamsters Union gave them a $5,000 PAC [political action committee] check and instead the Teamsters went out and raised [the qualifying amount] for them."

More broadly, ideologically conservative groups and advocates who are generally defending judicial elections these days minimize the dangers of special-interest influence. "People aren't being bought," says attorney Bopp. "They're being supported by people who think those candidates share those values."

Bopp and others also defend the increased spending in judicial contests as a means of getting information to voters so that they can hold judges accountable and influence the future shape of the judiciary. "They're costly because very often there are significant public-policy issues that separate the two candidates," says Cumberland

law professor DeBow. Airing the views, DeBow says, "is expensive, especially in TV ads."

The reform groups that criticize judicial elections counter by insisting that spiraling campaign costs heighten an all-but-inevitable potential for interest-group influence. "You have members of the bar and various industry groups and trade groups that are giving significant

Public financing of judicial campaigns is now on the books in two states, North Carolina and New Mexico. National judicial election-reform groups view public financing schemes as one step in reducing special-interest influence in contested races for judgeships. Above, the New Mexico capitol.

percentages to judicial candidates," says Adam Skaggs, counsel with the Brennan Center for Justice at New York University School of Law, which partners with Justice at Stake in publishing a series of critical reports on judicial elections. [3]

In addition, these groups and other critics of judicial elections say too many judicial campaigns — especially races against incumbent judges — are relying on simplistic slogans and messages that distort judicial decisions or legal issues. "The hot-button issue or cases likely to get attention in campaigns are a distortion — or almost entirely so — of what the judge or candidate has

done or can do," says Roy Schotland, a professor at Georgetown University Law Center who has studied judicial elections and campaign finance for more than three decades.

Public financing appeals as a possible reform in part because mandatory-spending limits on candidates are unconstitutional under the U.S. Supreme Court's landmark campaign-finance decision, *Buckley v. Valeo*. The 1976 ruling also bars spending caps for independent groups — an area of growing concern in judicial races, as in the West Virginia contest.

The court's ruling permits limits on campaign contributions by individuals, PACs or party committees. Most but not all states set some limits on contributions to candidates for state offices, including judgeships. In West Virginia, for example, an individual can contribute no more than $1,000 to a candidate for a judgeship. Bopp says he considers that figure too low.

The American Judicature Society has no position on public financing, but executive director Andersen notes that the schemes "do not solve the [independent-spending] problem." In fact, Andersen says, "it may even exacerbate the problem because 'legitimate money' can't go to the candidates themselves. It's an enticement for well-heeled groups to break the system."

While criticizing judicial campaigns, Schotland minimizes the concern about overall campaign costs. "It's not soaring out of sight," he says. From an opposite perspective, Ronald Rotunda, a well-known conservative now at Chapman University School of Law in Orange, Calif., somewhat similarly finds the overall spending unremarkable.

"The plaintiffs' tort bar has spent millions to elect judges favorable to their view, and the business side has spent millions to elect judges favorable to their view," Rotunda says. The spending race is "not surprising," he says, "given the stakes."

Should states adopt stricter rules for judges to recuse themselves?

West Virginia coal executive Don Blankenship donated $1,000 in 2004 to Brent Benjamin's campaign against incumbent state supreme court Justice Warren McGraw. Blankenship also spent another $3 million or so — either directly or through an independent group — to support Benjamin's candidacy.

Benjamin won the bitterly contested race, shifting the balance of power on the five-member court toward pro-business interests. Three years later, Benjamin cast a deciding vote in a 3-2 ruling to overturn a $50-million award against Blankenship's company for allegedly driving a rival coal company out of business. Benjamin rejected a motion by plaintiff Hugh Caperton that he recuse himself from the case because of the support Blankenship gave him in his campaign.

To critics of judicial campaign financing, Benjamin's election symbolizes the dangers of interest-group funding of judicial candidates, and the later appeal of a major suit involving his principal financial backer required him to step out of the case. "There may be cases where there's a lot of play around the edges, but there are other cases that are simply egregious," says the Brennan Center's Skaggs. Caperton's, he says, "is one of those cases."

Defenders of judicial campaign financing agree with Benjamin's decision to stay in the case — an action that he explained in a 66-page concurring opinion published in late July 2008, almost three months after the main decision. Attorney Bopp, for example, notes that Blankenship has

only a small stock holding in A.T. Massey Coal Co., the nation's fourth-biggest coal producer; that he gave only $1,000 directly to Benjamin's campaign; and that, apart from the Caperton case, Benjamin has voted against the Massey company in several other instances since becoming a justice.

Caperton's attorneys are now asking the Supreme Court to rule that the 14th Amendment's Due Process Clause requires state court judges to recuse themselves under some circumstances — and that his case meets whatever recusal standard the court lays down. Caperton gained the backing of an array of judicial reform groups for his appeal, including Justice at Stake and the Brennan Center, as well as the American Bar Association and the American Association for Justice, a trial lawyers' group.

"We're not talking just about impartiality, but also about the appearance of impartiality," says ABA President Wells. "Courts have to have the public support and belief that they are at least in the main fair and impartial."

Bopp and others counter that the Supreme Court has already established a standard requiring judges to recuse themselves only if they have a direct financial interest in the case or have demonstrated actual bias. The flexible, multiple-factor tests that Caperton and his supporters suggest would be difficult for judges to apply. "A rule that says appearance of impropriety is an awfully vague rule," says Chapman law professor Rotunda.

More broadly, supporters of judicial elections say critics are using the recusal issue to try to undermine elections altogether. "They're going to adopt rules that create such chaos in the administration of justice that it will force states to abandon judicial elections," says Bopp. "That's the goal."

The groups calling for tighter recusal standards counter that courts are routinely called on to apply flexible tests in other contexts. "If there were a bright-line test that could be applied

in every case, we'd hardly need a judge to decide it," says Wells. They also dispute warnings from the other side that tighter standards would invite a flood of recusal motions, including some strategically aimed not at an impartial court but a court favorable to one side or the other.

Above all, these groups say, a strong ethical standard for judges to step out of cases involving major campaign contributors is needed to maintain public confidence in the impartiality of the judiciary. "The public really wants a judge to step aside even if there's only a small amount of money involved," says Justice at Stake executive director Brandenburg.

Parnell of the Center for Competitive Politics argues, however, that a broader recusal rule would actually disenfranchise the voters in a judicial election. "Recusal essentially deprives voters of the justices that they voted for in a campaign," he says.

Besides asking for a broader rule, critics of current recusal practices also say procedural changes could help — for example, by requiring that a recusal motion be ruled on not by judges themselves but by another judge or some judicial panel. In Alabama and Texas, for example, the full state supreme court rules when a recusal motion is filed against an individual justice.

Like West Virginia and the majority of other states, the U.S. Supreme Court follows the practice of allowing the individual justice to decide whether to step out of a case. But, according to Georgetown professor Schotland, Justice Ruth Bader Ginsburg has said publicly that justices invariably confer with one or more of their colleagues before deciding whether to recuse themselves.

Should states with judicial elections modify their rules for selecting judges?

Wallace Jefferson has won three statewide elections in Texas since 2002, but he admits that most Texans "don't

Business Interests Gave Most to State Supreme Court Races

More than $15 million, or 44 percent of total contributions, was donated to the 88 candidates who raised funds for state supreme court races in 2005-06, the last year for which data are available. Lawyers contributed less than half as much.

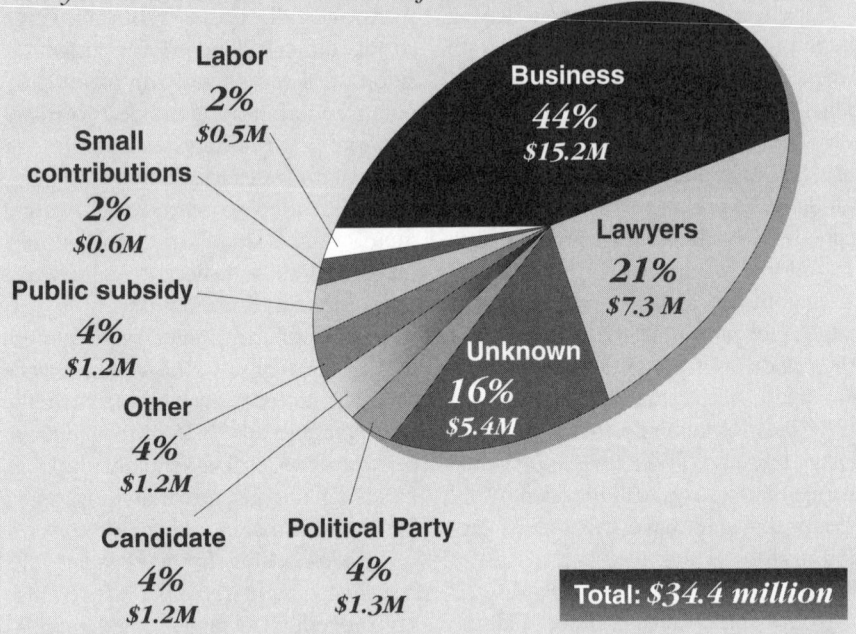

Labor
2%
$0.5M

Small contributions
2%
$0.6M

Public subsidy
4%
$1.2M

Other
4%
$1.2M

Candidate
4%
$1.2M

Political Party
4%
$1.3M

Business
44%
$15.2M

Lawyers
21%
$7.3 M

Unknown
16%
$5.4M

Total: $34.4 million

Note: Numbers do not add to 100 percent or to the funding total due to rounding.

Source: Rachel Weiss, et al., "New Politics of Judicial Elections," Brennan Center on Justice/ Justice at Stake, 2006, p. 18

know who I am." Instead, the first African-American to serve on and then head the Texas Supreme Court says he owes his three victories solely to his Republican Party label. "I won [in 2008] because Texans voted for Rick Perry, Kay Bailey Hutchison and John McCain," Jefferson says, referring to the state's GOP governor and U.S. senator and the party's unsuccessful presidential nominee. [4]

Jefferson — initially appointed by Perry as associate justice in 2001 and most recently elected to a full eight-year term as chief justice — has been going around the state calling for a change in what he calls an "irrational" system of contested, partisan elections used in only seven other states. He favors in- stead some form of "merit" selection followed by "retention" elections in which voters decide only to retain a judge in office or declare the position vacant to be filled by gubernatorial appointment.

Critics of contested judicial elections agree with Jefferson's diagnosis of the problems with such systems. "He's got it absolutely right," says Andersen at the American Judicature Society (AJS), "Voters don't pay much attention to judicial races."

The AJS has been pushing merit selection-retention ever since one of its founders, Northwestern University law professor Herbert Kales, first developed the idea in 1914. The system advanced after its first adoption in Missouri in 1940 to become the dominant judicial selection method by the 1970s, but it has stalled since the 1980s. The plan has been approved twice by the Texas state Senate but killed in the state House of Representatives.

An indication of the plan's dubious prospects is the decision by other critics of current judicial election practices to take a bye on the big question of changing the rules for election and reelection to the bench. "We're agnostic," says Justice at Stake's Brandenburg. In like vein, the Brennan Center's Skaggs says "there are arguments on both sides" for contested versus retention elections.

"I stay out of what mode of selection to use," says Georgetown's Schotland. "There's nothing new to say about it." Instead, Schotland says, "we should pay attention to what's going on in the various systems."

The conservative groups defending current campaign practices support contested elections, including the practice of partisan as opposed to nonpartisan balloting. Judicial elections "are one of the mechanisms that the people have chosen to keep judges within their proper bounds," says attorney Bopp. In addition, he says that it is "only appropriate" for the people to elect state judges because in all states except Louisiana judges have the power to make law through their common-law powers.

Andersen acknowledges the "strong, populist, democratic impulse" in favor of popular election of judges. But he says the difficulty of attracting voters' attention to low-profile races often brings out the worst in judicial campaigns.

"If you want to make an impression, especially in a statewide judicial election, you've got to use messages, themes that stir up emotions," Andersen says. "Every once in a while, you'll see a dignified election. But often that's just a matter of luck."

Parnell of the Center for Competitive Politics says the same criticism can be applied to political campaigns generally. "In terms of the language of political discourse," he says, "most campaigns are from annoying to loathsome. But that's the lifeblood of democracy."

Cumberland law professor DeBow also accepts the criticism, but only in part. He says campaigning by independent groups is often "pretty raw," and some candidates "don't run particularly helpful campaigns." Still, he insists, "some candidates do. You do get some discussion, and voters do get some information."

DeBow and others also defend partisan elections because party labels give voters useful information about a judicial candidate's likely legal philosophy. In his home state, DeBow says, the Alabama Supreme Court has been "transformed" through partisan election and now "reflects more nearly the conservative views of most Alabama voters."

By contrast, defenders of contested elections note that incumbent judges are rarely defeated in retention elections. Critics of contested elections, however, see turnover as a drawback, especially if tied to disapproval of specific decisions. "Judges are not supposed to be subject to the latest political winds," says Brandenburg.

For his part, Andersen acknowledges the difficulty of defeating an incumbent judge in a retention election but says incumbents also enjoy an advantage in contested races. In any event, he adds, "If you're choosing the right people in the first place and they're doing a good job, turnover for the sake of turnover in the judiciary is not necessarily a virtue."

Outspokenly liberal California Chief Justice Rose Elizabeth Bird and two other liberal colleagues were swept out of office in a retention election in the 1980s. At the time, the court was under fierce criticism for failing to uphold any death sentences from state courts. Business groups also criticized the court's pro-plaintiff rulings, while Republicans wanted to gain seats on the then all-Democratic seven-member court.

California Supreme Court Historical Society

Whatever the arguments, the prospects for change at the state level are clouded at best. "Changing selection systems has been like trench warfare," says Brandenburg.

In Texas, retired Supreme Court Justice Craig Enoch supports Jefferson's call for retention elections but doubts the legislature will go along. "It's something that ought to happen, but I don't see a major public outcry in Texas to change the system," he says. ∎

BACKGROUND

American Judges

Popular election of judges is an American invention of the early and mid-19th century and today remains — with the limited exceptions in Japan and Switzerland — a uniquely American phenomenon. The practice gained hold in the era of Jacksonian democracy, fueled by distrust of political and business elites and the other branches of state governments. The progressives of the early 20th century began efforts to counteract the political excesses of the practice with proposals later backed by bar and court-reform groups to institute merit selection and retention election systems. Those proposals advanced over several decades but stalled by the 1980s as judicial elections became pitched battles between opposing groups on criminal justice and civil justice issues. [5]

The Constitution — in Article III — provides for presidential appointment of federal judges with lifetime tenure subject to Senate confirmation. The 13 original states divided almost evenly between gubernatorial appointment (five) and legislative "election" of judges (seven), with one (Delaware) following the federal model of executive appointment and legislative confirmation. Up until 1845, every new state entered the Union with a constitution providing for legislative or executive appointment. By then, however, several states had begun experimenting with popular election: Mississippi in 1832 became the first to prescribe popular election; New York's decision to follow suit in 1845 helped confirm a trend toward popular election that continued through the 19th century.

Many reasons have been given for the movement toward popular elections, according to Matthew Streb, an associate professor of political science at Northern Illinois University in DeKalb. He lists, among others, resistance to English common law; the difficulty of impeachment; and a desire for responsiveness to local communities and for greater independence from other branches of government. Caleb Nelson, a University of Virginia law professor and Federalist Society member, sees safeguarding the independence of the judiciary from state legislatures as the dominant motivation and complains of the critical view of the movement among many scholars.

Whatever the motivation, the practice is widely regarded to have devolved by the end of the 19th century into elections dominated by political machines with little voter interest that produced — according to University of Michigan Law School professor Steven Croley — "judiciaries . . . plagued by incompetence and corruption." [6]

Nonpartisan election of judges emerged as an initial reform. The practice appeared first in Cook County (Chicago) in 1873 and had advanced to 12 states by 1927. But critics said voters still had little input into judicial selection and little information about the qualifications of judicial candidates. Three states abandoned the practice and returned to partisan elections.

A more far-reaching reform was first proposed in 1914 by Northwestern University's Kales, a cofounder of the American Judicature Society. In his book *Unpopular Government in the United States*, Kales depicted popular election as a sort of myth, with judges actually chosen by political and bar elites that he dubbed "politocrats." As a better selection method, Kales proposed judges be appointed by an elected chief justice. Then — with little elaboration — he proposed that a judge appointed in this manner be subject after an initial probationary period and again at periodic intervals to "a vote on whether the place which he holds shall be declared vacant." [7]

Over the next two decades, bar groups and others refashioned Kates' proposal by combining his distinctive contribution of noncompetitive retention elections with appointment by the governor from a list prepared by a special nominating commission. [8] The American Bar Association formally endorsed such a plan in 1937. Three years later, Missouri gave its name to the plan by becoming the first state to adopt, through a voter-approved constitutional amendment, a system of merit selection and retention elections. Two years later, Missouri voters rejected a proposal to scrap the plan.

The Missouri plan spread to other states in the 1960s, lifted by the growing support for a variety of legal reforms in Washington and in the states. By the end of the 1960s, eight states had adopted plans that combined merit selection systems with retention elections. Five other states used merit selection with traditional contested elections; two others used retention elections but not the nominating commission. Writing in 1970, Glenn Winters, the executive director of the American Judicature Society and editor of its magazine *Judicature*, confidently predicted that merit selection and tenure would become the dominant mechanism for choosing and retaining judges by the end of the next decade. The result, Winters wrote, would be to raise the level of the judiciary to the point that "problems of judicial personnel will have receded into the background and will have been supplanted by who knows what new crises that now lie below the horizon." [9]

Pitched Battles

Even as most judicial elections remained low-key and low-turnout contests, races in a handful of states became pitched battles in the 1980s and '90s. The battles took place against a generally conservative trend on law enforcement and government regulation. Law enforcement and so-called victims' rights groups targeted justices in some states for rulings deemed to be soft on crime or criminals. Business groups assailed justices who backed rulings favoring plaintiffs or striking down "tort reform" laws. In addition, Republicans built on gains in the once solidly Democratic South to gain a foothold in and later control of state high courts in Alabama, Mississippi and Texas. [10]

California witnessed the most convulsive single election of the period when three justices, including the outspokenly liberal Chief Justice Rose Elizabeth Bird, were swept out of office in a retention election. Long a leading liberal bench, the California Supreme Court was under fierce criticism in the 1980s for failing to uphold any death sentences from state courts. Business groups also criticized pro-plaintiff rulings, while Republicans wanted to gain seats on the then all-Democratic seven-member court. The combination of factors resulted in voter rejection not only of Bird — by a two-to-one margin — but also of two liberal colleagues. Appointments by Republican Gov. George Deukmejian lastingly turned the court into a predominantly Republican and conservative bench.

The transformation of the Texas Supreme Court began two years later, when voters elected three Republicans, including a newly appointed chief justice, to the nine-member bench. The court was in the national spotlight because of justices' ties to lawyers, particularly plaintiffs' attorneys, dramatized by a report by the CBS newsmagazine "60 Minutes" entitled "Justice for Sale." In the midst of the controversy, the Democratic chief justice, John Hill, retired in August 1988 with a blast at expensive partisan elections. Gov. Bill Clements named a veteran Republican judge, Thomas Phillips; he and two other Republicans won election in

Continued on p. 384

Chronology

Before 1960
Most states adopt popular elections for judges in 19th century; criticisms bring reforms in the 20th century.

1914
Northwestern law professor Herbert Kates proposes that judges, after initial appointment by chief justice, face voters in "yes/no" retention election.

1937
American Bar Association endorses plan combining screening of candidates for appointments with retention election.

1940
Missouri is first state to adopt combined merit selection/retention plan.

1960s-1970s
Missouri plan adopted in plurality of states.

1971
Tennessee adopts Missouri plan for appellate courts; restores partisan elections for supreme court in 1974.

1980s-1990s
Missouri plan stalls; supreme court races become more expensive, more contentious.

1984
Utah voters approve shift to merit selection — last state to do so through 2009.

1986
Liberal California Chief Justice Rose Bird, two colleagues defeated after campaign protesting death penalty

reversals; Republican appointees transform court to conservative.

1988
Three Republicans elected to Texas Supreme Court; combine with three Democrats to form conservative majority.

1994
Business-backed campaign criticizing Alabama Supreme Court for "jackpot justice" boosts Republican candidate over incumbent chief justice. . . . Justice reelected in Mississippi despite similar opposition from business-backed candidate.

1996
Tennessee Supreme Court Justice Penny White defeated in retention election by pro-death penalty campaign.

2000-Present
Business groups spend millions on high court races, shift balance of power in several states.

2000
U.S. Chamber of Commerce announces plan to spend $10 million on supreme court races to counter influence by trial lawyers. . . . Chamber-backed candidates sweep in Alabama and Michigan, win two of four races in Mississippi, lose to incumbent justice in Ohio.

2002
North Carolina is first state to approve public financing of campaigns for all state appellate courts; takes effect in 2004. . . . Business groups win two seats in Ohio, gaining majority on high court.

2004
Supreme Court Justice Antonin

Scalia rejects environmental group's motion to recuse himself in case involving Vice President Dick Cheney because of justice's hunting trip with Cheney. . . . Republican Lloyd Karmeier wins open seat on Illinois Supreme Court; candidates together spent record $9.3 million. . . . West Virginia Supreme Court Justice Warren MacGraw defeated by lawyer Brent Benjamin after coal executive Don Blankenship spends more than $3 million on race while preparing to appeal $50 million verdict against his company.

2006
Republicans gain seats on Michigan, Ohio courts; Alabama elects Democratic chief justice, Democratic incumbent holds on to seat in Georgia.

2007
New Mexico becomes second state to approve public financing for judicial campaigns. . . . Conservative Judge Annette Ziegler wins seat on liberal Wisconsin Supreme Court.

2008
Justice Benjamin refuses to step out of appeal by Blankenship's coal company; casts decisive vote in 3-2 ruling to overturn verdict. . . . Conservative judge ousts incumbent justice in Wisconsin, shifts court to conservative majority. . . . Missouri county adopts Missouri plan for local judges; first jurisdiction to shift from contested to retention election since 1984.

2009
Supreme Court hears argument on recusal issue in West Virginia case; decision due by end of June. . . . Wisconsin Chief Justice Shirley Abrahamson handily reelected. . . . Tennessee legislature to decide whether to revive Missouri plan after lapsing under general state sunset law.

Taking Care of Business on States' Top Courts

Big contributions help put friendly justices on the bench.

Wisconsin's business lobbies blasted the state's supreme court for its ruling in 2005 that paint manufacturers could be held liable for lead poisoning injuries even if a plaintiff could not identify an individual company at fault. Three years later, the state's biggest business group, Wisconsin Manufacturers and Commerce, spent nearly $1.8 million to defeat the author of the controversial decision, Justice Louis Butler.

The lead-paint ruling was hardly the focus, however, of Michael J. Gableman's successful effort in April 2008 to defeat a sitting justice for the first time in Wisconsin since 1967. Instead, Gableman, a white Republican and a former prosecutor, emphasized his law enforcement credentials and support in campaigning against Butler, an African-American Democrat and a former public defender.

In the campaign's most controversial episode, Gableman ran a television ad that showed Butler's picture alongside that of a black sex offender, Reuben Lee Mitchell, with this voiceover: "Butler found a loophole. Mitchell went on to molest another child." As noted in campaign coverage at the time, the ad did not explain that Butler had represented the defendant as public defender, that Mitchell's conviction was eventually upheld, and that his later offenses came after serving a full sentence for the earlier crime. [1]

The business group's independent expenditures gave Gableman a big edge over Butler even though the Butler campaign outspent Gableman's, $770,000 to $410,000. The race came one year after business groups had similarly spent $2.2 million to help Judge Annette Ziegler in her successful campaign in April 2007 for an open seat on the seven-member court. [2]

With Gableman's election, Wisconsin joined at least two other states — Ohio and West Virginia — where business groups' spending had recently helped elect business-friendly justices to create business-oriented majorities on the state's highest court. Business groups, including the U.S. Chamber of Commerce and American Tort Reform Association, have also contributed hundreds of thousands of dollars to successful pro-business supreme court candidates in other states, including Alabama, Illinois, Michigan, Mississippi and Texas.

The Chamber made a splash when it dived into judicial elections in 2000 but has lowered its profile since then. In 2002, business groups financed almost 50 percent of television advertising in supreme court races, but the Chamber's name appeared on none of them, according to a report by the Brennan Center for Justice at New York University School of Law. [3]

For this *CQ Researcher* report, both the Chamber and the tort reform group declined to grant on-the-record interviews about their participation in judicial elections. In a written statement, the Chamber said, "We believe it is important that those charged with seating state supreme court justices are fully aware of all relevant issues and positions that potential candidates have taken."

Continued from p. 382

November. Together with three conservative Democrats, the GOP justices helped form a reliable conservative majority.

The Alabama Supreme Court was the next southern bench to be flipped from Democratic to Republican. The transformation began with a GOP victory in 1994 engineered by a then little-known political consultant from Texas: Karl Rove, who later became President George W. Bush's deputy chief of staff. Recruited by a group called the Business Council of Alabama, Rove managed the campaign by retired judge Perry Hooper to unseat the incumbent chief justice, Ernest "Sonny" Hornsby. Rove stuck the Alabama court with the label "jackpot justice" by focusing on one high-profile case: a $4 million punitive damage award a plaintiff won

because of a defectively painted luxury automobile. Hornsby ended election night with a small lead, but Rove masterminded a yearlong recount battle that ended with hundreds of late absentee ballots excluded and Hooper declared the winner. Over the next decade, Republicans gained an 8-1 majority on what had been an all-Democratic court.

In neighboring Mississippi, Supreme Court Justice C.R. "Chuck" McRae drew business groups' fire before the 1994 election by writing a decision favorable to mass tort lawsuits. The American Tort Reform Association put McRae, a former president of the state trial lawyers' group, on the cover of its magazine, *Liability Week*, in an issue that urged members to focus on state judicial contests. Despite the attention, McRae was reelected to an eight-year term. But he

continued to face criticism from business groups and others, fueled by his no-contest plea to a drunken driving charge in 1995. The attacks eventually bore fruit with McRae's defeat in 2002. The victor in the race, Jess Dickinson, joined with two other business-backed winners in 2000 to shift the court toward business interests.

In Tennessee, partisan politics combined with anti-crime sentiment in 1996 to defeat a recently appointed supreme court justice in a retention election. Penny White had been named to the Tennessee Supreme Court in late 1994 by the outgoing Democratic governor after four years as a judge on lower courts. Two years later, with a Republican governor, the then little-known Tennessee Conservative Union targeted White, depicting her as soft on crime.

The plaintiffs' bar has been spending more on judicial races too, but has not matched the business groups. "The business community has participated in judicial elections in a big way," says Robert Peck, president of the Center for Constitutional Litigation, which is affiliated with the American Association for Justice, a group representing plaintiffs' attorneys. "The legal community has responded, but it doesn't come close to matching the amount of money that business spends."

Political scientists debate whether campaign contributions have an impact on a judge's later decisions. "Nobody has a real good answer on that," says Matthew J. Streb, an associate professor at Northern Illinois University who has studied judicial elections. But Adam Skaggs, counsel for the Brennan Center, thinks business groups are having an effect. "I don't think business would continue to pump millions and millions into judicial campaigns," he says, "if it didn't feel it was getting something."

In Wisconsin, business groups sat out the 2009 race between

Michael J. Gableman won a seat on the Wisconsin Supreme Court in 2008 with help from business groups. During his campaign, he ran a TV ad showing side-by-side photos of his opponent and a black sex offender.

Chief Justice Shirley Abrahamson, running for a fourth 10-year term, and her challenger, Randy Koschnick, a conservative circuit court judge in Milwaukee. Koschnick concentrated on Abrahamson's liberal record, especially criminal-law issues, and her age. She is 75. But he also cited the lead-paint ruling as an example of Abrahamson's "activist" record. Abrahamson responded by noting that a jury eventually ruled against the plaintiff in the case and that no paint manufacturer had yet been held liable under the decision. [4]

[1] The lead paint ruling is *Thomas v. Mallett*, 701 N.W.2d 523 (Wisc. 2005). See Gina Barton, "Justices allow lead-paint suit," *Milwaukee Journal Sentinel*, July 16, 2005, p. A1. For coverage of the Gableman television ad, see Stacy Forster, "Butler TV spot responds to allegations," *Milwaukee Journal Sentinel*, March 19, 2008, p. B3.

[2] Campaign spending information from Wisconsin Democracy Campaign (www.wisdc.org).

[3] Deborah Goldberg, "Interest Group Participation in Judicial Elections," in Matthew J. Streb (ed.), *Running for Judge: The Rising Political, Financial, and Legal Stakes of Judicial Elections* (2007), p. 50.

[4] See Steven Walters, "A high court race grows heated again," *Milwaukee Journal Sentinel*, Jan. 25, 2009, p. B1.

A Republican Party mailing before the Aug. 1 election criticized White's vote to reverse a death penalty conviction without noting that the five-member court was unanimous. Despite White's efforts to counter the campaign, she lost by a margin of 55,000 votes — 55 percent to 45 percent — in a race that drew fewer than 20 percent of eligible voters. Republicans did not repeat their success two years later, however, when a campaign to reject the Democratic-appointed chief justice fell short.

Stealth Campaigns

Judicial elections have become increasingly expensive over the past decade and the campaigns increasingly contentious — even "vicious," as one bipartisan group described the tone. The trend developed against the backdrop of a concerted, multimillion-dollar effort by the U.S. Chamber of Commerce and the National Association of Manufacturers to target state supreme court justices seen as favoring plaintiffs in personal injury cases and replace them with justices more favorable to business interests. Within two election cycles, the campaigns had paid off handsomely. The ensuing controversies caused business groups to lower their profiles, but they have continued to make gains by helping finance campaigns that highlight anti-crime instead of pro-business messages. [11]

The judicial campaigns also played out against the backdrop of a closely divided U.S. Supreme Court decision in 2002 that cast doubt on ethical rules on the books in nine states limiting campaign pronouncements by judges or their opponents in judicial races. The 5-4 ruling in *Republican Party v. White* struck down on free-speech grounds unenforced provisions in Minnesota's ethical codes for lawyers and judges prohibiting judicial candidates from "announcing" their positions on legal or political issues. The rule Justice Antonin Scalia wrote for the majority, amounted to "preventing candidates from discussing what the elections are about." In dissent, Justice Ruth Bader Ginsburg complained that judges should not "be treated as politicians simply because they are chosen by popular vote." [12]

The Chamber of Commerce began the decade by vowing in summer 2000 to spend $10 million on judicial elections in a handful of states. Jim Wootton, the

Following the Money in West Virginia

Coal executive's $3 million helped elect top judge.

Coal executive Don Blankenship is a man who knows what he wants and is accustomed to getting it. And in 2004 what he wanted was to see Brent Benjamin — an insurance lawyer with no prior judicial experience — sitting on the West Virginia Supreme Court of Appeals.

So Blankenship's decision to spend more than $3 million to help elect Benjamin struck one longtime political consultant in the state as perfectly in character. "When he's decided to go a specific route, he will do whatever it takes, including spending whatever it takes," Steve Canterbury told the *Charleston Gazette*. [1]

Canterbury, now the administrative director of the state's judiciary, was commenting a few days after Benjamin bested the incumbent justice, Warren McGraw. By ousting McGraw, a Democrat with a liberal, pro-plaintiff record, Benjamin became the first Republican elected to the five-member court without an initial appointment since 1924.

Now, as chief justice, Benjamin is getting passing marks from lawyers on both sides of the legal wars in the state over tort injury damages. "He's an interesting justice," says Thomas Hurney Jr., president of Defense Trial Counsel of West Virginia. From the opposite perspective, Allan Karlin, president of West Virginia Attorneys for Justice, the plaintiffs' group that opposed Benjamin in 2004, has a more favorable view today: "As the years pass, Justice Benjamin is going to surprise his critics."

The race that put Benjamin on the state high court, however, is viewed critically as an example of the dangers of high-cost, high-decibel judgeship races financed by special-interest groups. And Blankenship's role in financing Benjamin's election is at the center of a U.S. Supreme Court case challenging Benjamin's failure to recuse himself from ruling on a $50 million award against Blankenship's company, A.T. Massey Coal Co.

Before 2004, West Virginia's supreme court was widely regarded as very friendly terrain for plaintiffs, and McGraw was one of the justices responsible for that orientation. Massey was — and remains — one of the nation's biggest coal companies, and Blankenship is a no-nonsense chief executive responsible for the company's hard-nosed position on labor, environmental and financial issues.

Massey was also the losing defendant in legal battles fought in two states with the rival Harman Mining Co. Harman and its president, Hugh Caperton, sued Massey for breach of contract in a Virginia court and for broader fraud and misconduct claims in West Virginia. In brief, Harman charged that Massey had caused a company it owned to cancel a lucrative long-term contract with Harman as part of a plan to bankrupt its rival and take the contract for itself.

After losing the contract, Harman in fact was forced into bankruptcy in 1998. It won a $6 million breach of contract judgment in Virginia in 2001 and then pursued its broader suit in West Virginia. In August 2002, a jury found Massey guilty of tortious interference and fraud and awarded Harman a total of $50 million, including about $6 million in punitive damages.

West Virginia is one of eight states that elect justices to the state supreme court in partisan contests. Blankenship, a registered Republican, had contributed to political races in the past but only once to a state supreme court contest. Benjamin, a former state Republican treasurer, announced as a candidate in November 2003, saying that he wanted to restore "balance" to the state high court. [2]

Blankenship made a $1,000 contribution to Benjamin's campaign — the maximum permitted under state law. But he also contributed $2.5 million to an organization called And for the Sake of the Kids that opposed McGraw, contributed $500,000 to a second independent group and individually paid for other campaign solicitations. A researcher later found Blankenship's was the largest such individual contribution in any judicial contest in the United States in 2004. [3] In the meantime, Massey's legal efforts to undo the jury award were moving slowly. Judge Jay Hoke upheld the punitive damage award in July 2004. Hoke did not rule on Massey's motion for a new trial because of other legal issues, however, until March 2005 — after the supreme court election.

The McGraw-Benjamin campaign attracted national attention as an example of the injection of expensive, hard-hitting television advertising into judicial races. One ad criticized McGraw for voting to release "a child rapist" from prison. The ad did not detail the ruling: a 3-2 decision by the high court refusing to revoke probation for a juvenile offender recently turned 18 because of his use of alcohol and marijuana. And for the Sake of the Kids paid for the ad, but the Benjamin campaign defended it as accurate. [4]

McGraw also had an independent group supporting his candidacy: West Virginia Consumers for Justice, which received $1.9 million of its $2 million in contributions from the

executive director of the Chamber's then two-year-old Institute for Legal Reform, depicted the planned campaign as an effort to counteract "the new political influence" that trial lawyers had gained as a result of the $246 billion settlement with the tobacco industry in 1998. The campaign had substantial success. Republican-backed business candidates swept races for five supreme court seats in Alabama; three business-backed incumbents in Michigan beat candidates supported by trial lawyers, and two out of four business-backed candidates won in Mississippi. But the Chamber failed in a multimillion-dollar campaign to unseat Ohio Supreme Court Justice Alice Resnick, who had

trial lawyers' organization, then known as Consumer Attorneys of West Virginia. The group paid for four ads during the general election campaign — compared to 10 paid for by the Kids group.

Benjamin won the election with 53 percent of the vote. George Sprowls, a political science professor at Fairmont State University, pronounced the race "one of the dirtiest I've seen in my life." But Chris Hamilton, then the president of the West Virginia Coal Association, called the campaign "educational and enlightening." [5]

When Massey's appeal finally reached the state supreme court, Harman filed a motion asking Benjamin to recuse himself because of Blankenship's financial support during Benjamin's campaign. Benjamin refused. In November 2007, the court ruled that the suit in the West Virginia court was barred because it covered the same issues as the earlier Virginia case. Benjamin voted with the majority and filed a brief concurring opinion. While barring Harman's suit, the majority opinion characterized Massey's conduct as "outside the bounds of human decency and respectable business practices."

Two months later, however, Harman asked Justice Elliott Maynard to recuse himself because of photos showing him vacationing with Blankenship in Monaco in 2006. Maynard said he and Blankenship were longtime friends, denied any discussion of the case, but agreed to step aside anyway. The court withdrew the earlier ruling and agreed to rehear the case. Later, Justice Larry Stracher, one of the dissenters, recused himself because of critical statements he had made about Blankenship. But Benjamin still refused to bow out of the case.

With two judges sitting as substitutes, the high court issued a new ruling in April 2008. The 3-2 opinion was written by the same justice as the earlier decision and again barred Harman's suit in the West Virginia court. The new opinion, however, omitted any characterization of Massey's conduct. Benjamin, serving as acting chief justice, reserved the right to publish a concurring opinion later.

Benjamin's opinion, filed on July 28, reiterated his legal reasoning for barring Harman's suit, but then added an extraordinary 44-page explanation of his refusal to step out of the case. [6] Benjamin rejected "appearance" of impartiality as a criterion for recusal, defended West Virginia's use of partisan elections and attributed his victory over McGraw to a rambling and intemperate Labor Day speech by the incumbent justice.

Benjamin continued by saying he had no connection with the Kids group or Blankenship's contributions and rejected any due process requirement for judges to recuse themselves based on contributions from a litigant or lawyer before the court. "To surrender to such recusal temptations," Benjamin concluded, "would justly expose the judiciary to public contempt."

The U.S. Supreme Court's decision on Nov. 14 to hear Caperton's appeal on the recusal issue came 10 days after West Virginia voters elected Democrats Menis Ketchum, a lawyer, and Margaret Workman, a former circuit court judge and supreme court justice, to the state high court. They succeeded Maynard, who had been defeated in the May primary, and Stracher, who did not seek reelection. "Calmer, moderate court expected in '09," the *Charleston Gazette* said in a headline marking the opening of the new court's new term in January. [7]

While awaiting arguments before the U.S. Supreme Court, West Virginia legislators introduced two bills dealing with the issues raised by the case. One would have required that recusal motions be considered not by the challenged judge but by a panel of judges. Another would have established a system of public campaign financing for judicial races. Neither bill advanced, however.

[1] Quoted in Ken Ward Jr., "Blankenship used to controversy," *Charleston Gazette*, Nov. 7, 2004, p. 1A. Other background also drawn from the profile.

[2] Background on race drawn in part from Terry Juliet, "Benjamin hopes to shine light on justice," *The State Journal*, Nov. 5, 2004, p. 4.

[3] See Rachel Weiss, "Fringe Tactics: Special Interest Groups Target Judicial Races," National Institute on Money in State Politics, 2005, p. 5. The monograph was funded by the Open Society Institute.

[4] For stills of the ad, see Brennan Center/Justice at Stake, *The New Politics of Judicial Elections 2004*, pp. 4-5. For an account of the case, see Adam Liptak, "Judicial Races in Several States Become Partisan Battlegrounds," *The New York Times*, Oct. 24, 2004, sec. 1, p. 1.

[5] Quoted in Juliet, *op. cit.*

[6] Benjamin's opinion in *Caperton v. A.T. Massey Coal Co.*, No. 33350 (July 28, 2008), can be found on the court's Web site: www.state.wv.us/wvsca/docs/spring08/33350c4.htm. The U.S. Supreme Court case is *Caperton v. A.T. Massey Coal Co.*, 08-22.

[7] The story by The Associated Press' Lawrence Messina appeared in the *Gazette* on Jan. 14, 2009, p. 5A. A third new justice, Tom McHugh, was appointed on April 8 by Gov. Joe Manchin, a Democrat, to succeed Justice Joseph Albright, who died on March 23.

authored the 4-3 decision a year earlier striking down a business-backed tort reform law.

The Chamber enjoyed more success over the next two election cycles as campaigns became more expensive and more contentious. Through 2004, the Chamber was counting wins in all but four of 37 targeted races for state supreme court seats since wading into judicial elections in 2000. The most notable victories in 2002 came in Ohio, where an incumbent Republican was reelected and Republican Maureen O'Connor knocked off a Democratic incumbent. Republican legislators immediately predicted the "new" court would prove more receptive to tort

Financial Conflict Often Determines Judges' Recusal

Justice Scalia said hunting trip wouldn't bias his decision.

Supreme Court Justice Antonin Scalia faced an embarrassing torrent of publicity in 2004 for going on a hunting trip with Vice President Dick Cheney while the court was considering a case challenging Cheney's actions as head of a special energy task force. When the environmental group challenging Cheney's refusal to release the names of task force members asked Scalia to recuse himself, the justice refused.

Scalia acknowledged that he had flown to Louisiana for the Christmastime trip — at Cheney's invitation — on a government plane. But he tartly rejected the argument that the trip would bias his ruling in the case. "If it is reasonable to think that a Supreme Court Justice can be bought so cheap," Scalia wrote, "the Nation is in deeper trouble than I had imagined." [1]

The episode was unusual because of Scalia's public explanation for his decision, but completely in keeping with the justices' broad discretion in determining whether to recuse themselves from a pending case. Two months earlier, Chief Justice William H. Rehnquist had specifically reaffirmed the court's practice that recusal was completely up to each individual justice.

Financial conflicts are the most common cause for justices to recuse themselves, but court-watchers have to read justices' financial disclosure forms to deduce the reasons. Chief Justice John G. Roberts Jr. is one of several members of the court who have recently recused themselves apparently because of owning stock in one or more companies involved in a case. Immediately upon taking office in September 2005, Roberts also signed on to a policy joined by all but two of the justices calling for recusal when a case involves a family member's lawyer or the family member's firm. [2]

Supreme Court cases establish some recusal rules for judges in state or lower federal courts, including some governing potential financial conflicts. In 1927, the court effectively established a rule requiring judges to step out of a case if they had a "direct pecuniary interest" in a case. The ruling overturned a defendant's conviction because the municipal court judge received a portion of any fine imposed. Six decades later, the court ruled that an Alabama Supreme Court justice should have recused himself from reviewing a bad-faith insurance suit because he had a similar action pending against the company. [3]

---

[1] *Cheney v. U.S. District Court*, 541 U.S. 914 (March 18, 2004). For coverage, see David G. Savage, "Scalia Sees No Need to Sit Out Cheney Case," *Los Angeles Times*, March 19, 2004, p. A1.

[2] See Lyle Denniston, "Roberts' Recusal Policy," SCOTUSBlog, Sept. 30, 2005, www.scotusblog.com/wp/roberts-recusal-policy/.

[3] The cases are *Tumey v. Ohio*, 273 U.S. 510 (1927); *Aetna Life Ins. Co. v. Lavoie*, 475 U.S. 813 (1986).

---

reform — as it did five years later in upholding a new attempt to limit damage awards. Five Republicans swept to supreme court seats in Texas, including Chief Justice Phillips, who raised no money himself and denounced the spiraling campaign spending.

North Carolina passed its public-financing law the same year to try to stem the campaign spending race in judicial elections, but its example had little impact elsewhere. Instead, the 2004 elections brought the most expensive judicial campaign in the United States to date: $9.3 million spent by opposing candidates for an open seat on the Illinois Supreme Court representing the southern part of the state. Republican Judge Lloyd Karmeier narrowly beat a Democratic judge in a race fought mostly over medical malpractice reform. Benjamin's victory in ousting incumbent West Virginia

Justice McGraw the same year also underscored the salience of the medical malpractice issue for many voters. At the same time, Blankenship's multimillion-dollar spending in attacking McGraw showed the potent role that groups working independently from a judicial candidate could play in determining an election.

Over the next two election cycles, judicial contests became somewhat less volatile, and the campaign spending race somewhat less frantic, but with significant exceptions. Business interests consolidated gains in two Midwestern states: Michigan and Ohio. Two Republican incumbents won in Michigan, maintaining the GOP's 5-2 control of the state high court, while victories by a Republican incumbent and a Republican challenger gave the GOP all seven seats on the Ohio bench. Republican, business-backed candidates

suffered two high-profile defeats in southern states, however. In Alabama, Democrat Sue Bell Cobb, a veteran judge, defeated Chief Justice Roy Nabers, despite being outspent in a race that cost $8 million overall. In neighboring Georgia, Democratic Justice Carol Hunstein, facing an opponent for the first time in 12 years, survived a campaign that featured more than $1.5 million in independent spending by a group funded by Republicans and business interests.

Critics of judicial elections took heart from several referenda in 2006 that rejected what they saw as anti-court measures, such as a mandatory retirement proposal in Colorado. Over the next two years, however, Wisconsin voters showed that judicial elections remained a volatile area by electing two conservatives who outspent more

Continued on p. 390

At Issue:

Do judicial elections threaten the courts' impartiality?

BERT BRANDENBURG
EXECUTIVE DIRECTOR
JUSTICE AT STAKE CAMPAIGN

WRITTEN FOR *CQ RESEARCHER*, APRIL 2009

*f*or 15 years, the Supreme Court case of *Caperton v. Massey* has been a legal collision waiting to happen. In the 1990s, as competing interests realized that the tort wars meant billions to their bottom lines, spending on state supreme court judgeships began rising. Since 2000, it has exploded, more than doubling totals from a decade ago.

Now many Americans fear that justice is for sale. Polls show that large majorities doubt a judge can be fair and impartial when one side has paid heavily to elect that judge.

In *Caperton,* a coal executive spent $3 million to elect a new West Virginia Supreme Court justice, who voted to overturn a $50 million jury award against the executive's company.

The U.S. Supreme Court will soon decide whether this violated the losing litigant's constitutional right to a fair hearing. But the case brought together an unprecedented array of legal, business and civic leaders.

Those filing *amicus* briefs in *Caperton* included a group of 27 former state supreme court justices; a business coalition that included Wal-Mart, Pepsi, Intel and Lockheed Martin; the American Bar Association and civic-reform groups like the Brennan Center for Justice, Common Cause, the League of Women Voters and the American Judicature Society.

Their collective message: Runaway campaign spending is creating, to quote a *New York Times* editorial, "an unmistakable impression that justice is for sale." While some reformers, including former U.S. Supreme Court Justice Sandra Day O'Connor, prefer appointing judges, several reforms can preserve public trust in courts without eliminating elections:

• **Reduce special-interest money.** North Carolina and New Mexico have enacted public financing in state appellate court races. Except for small donations, candidates no longer "dial for dollars," and judges aren't indebted to those who appear before them.

• **End secret money in judicial races.** Growing amounts of money are spent behind a curtain by "independent" campaigns with innocuous, uninformative names. Given the compelling public interest in impartial courts, tougher campaign-disclosure laws must let the public know who is paying to put judges on the bench.

• **Update recusal rules.** Recent polls, including one by the Justice at Stake Campaign, show that 85 to 90 percent of the public believe judges should not hear cases involving major campaign supporters.

These reforms are based on one central fact: Courts are different from legislators and governors. Judges must make impartial decisions that are accountable to the law, not interest groups.

SEAN PARNELL
PRESIDENT
CENTER FOR COMPETITIVE POLITICS

WRITTEN FOR *CQ RESEARCHER*, APRIL 2009

*t*he majority of American judges — over 75 percent of trial judges and over 50 percent of appellate judges — are elected and have been for over 150 years. Those who argue that elections threaten judicial integrity bear a heavy burden of proof. To indict judicial elections is to indict American justice generally.

Appointment advocates claim that electing judges threatens impartiality because campaign contributions could sway rulings from the bench. But judges have accepted campaign contributions for years, and there is no evidence that elected judges have failed to uphold their oaths more than appointed judges.

Contributing to a campaign — for Congress or the state supreme court — is the exercise of a citizen's First Amendment right to associate with a candidate who supports his or her views. Indeed, numerous studies have found that elected officials vote based on their beliefs, party affiliation and constituent opinions, and most research shows no improper connection between campaign contributions and legislative action. There's no reason to believe that judges are any more susceptible to campaign corruption than legislators, who must face reelection far more frequently.

Moreover, appointing judges won't eliminate the perception problem some have with judicial elections. It will just shift the focus. In states that appoint judges, those selecting the judiciary have their own political interests and fundraising operations.

Appointment proponents point to a recently argued U.S. Supreme Court case, *Caperton v. A.T. Massey Coal Co.*, to assert that electing judges corrupts courts. A coal company CEO spent $3 million on independent advertisements in a state supreme court race. The winning justice then ruled in favor of the company in one case (after ruling against it in at least five others). The high court will decide whether such independent political speech somehow corrupts justice and requires recusal.

But appointments raise similar issues of undue influence. Independent groups seek to sway the nomination and confirmation processes for U.S. Supreme Court vacancies — speech that is protected by the First Amendment. To require recusal based on such advocacy would be unworkable. Justices don't have to recuse from every case brought or defended by the government headed by the president who appointed them, which is analogous to requiring recusal when an independent group speaks up in a judicial election.

Whether or not a state relies on appointments or elections to fill its bench, there's no corruption inherent in either method. Free speech is a necessity in democracy, not a barrier to good government.

Continued from p. 388

liberal opponents. Together with Judge Ziegler's victory for an open seat in 2007, Judge Gableman's ouster of incumbent Justice Butler in 2008 was seen as giving conservatives a 4-3 majority on some issues, including business-related disputes. ■

CURRENT SITUATION

Selection Methods

A dvocates of judicial retention elections are taking encouragement from one Missouri county's decision to switch to yes-no voting on local judges even as one state, Tennessee, is facing a switch to contested elections unless the retention system is renewed by June 30.

Voters in rapidly growing Greene County in southwestern Missouri (Springfield) gave 52 percent approval in November to a ballot measure to adopt the same merit selection/retention election system used for the state's appellate courts for local judgeships as well. Voter approval came even though the group fighting the initiative — organized by a leader of the conservative Federalist Society — appeared to have outspent supporters by roughly $100,000. [13]

In Tennessee, leaders of the Federalist Society are also arguing against the merit selection/retention system for the state's appellate courts that lapsed in 2008 because of a general state "sunset" law. The so-called Tennessee plan — a modified version of the plan first adopted in Missouri in 1940 — is currently in "wind-down" mode and will formally die if new legislation is not enacted by the June 30 deadline. [14]

The debates over merit selection and retention come after a nearly 25-year

period with virtually no action on a system that supporters say insulates the courts from politics. Opponents counter that the plan drives politics underground and shields judges from accountability.

In Missouri, the group Greene Countians for Fair and Impartial Judges qualified the measure for the ballot and raised about $150,000 to campaign for passage. The measure was endorsed by the *Springfield News-Leader*, the local bar association and chamber of commerce, and both the Republican and Democratic candidates for governor.

On the opposite side, Missourians for Open and Accountable Judicial Selection raised more than $250,000 to oppose the measure. State records listed William Placke, president of the St. Louis chapter of the Federalist Society, as the organizer. Without disclosing individual donors, spokesmen for the group said financing came from businesses, lawyers and the medical community. Two of the state's leading Republicans — outgoing Gov. Roy Blunt and former U.S. Attorney General John Ashcroft — also urged a no vote on the plan.

Greene became the first county in Missouri to opt into merit selection and retention since counties surrounding Kansas City did in 1973. The system is also used in counties around St. Louis.

In Tennessee, the legislature established a merit selection/retention system for the Tennessee Supreme Court and the two intermediate-level appellate courts in 1971. The five-justice state supreme court was removed from the system in 1974 but then brought back into it in 1994. Under the sunset law, however, the plan lapsed in 2008.

The Tennessee Bar Association and the Democratic governor, Phil Bredesen, are urging the legislature to reestablish the system before the June 30 deadline. "It's done an excellent job of procuring a knowledgeable, stable, predictable bench," says bar association executive director Alan Ramasaur. But the Republican lieutenant governor, Ron Ramsey, who serves as

speaker of the state Senate, is balking. Ramsey objects in particular to the composition of the judicial nominating commission, which screens candidates and submits a list of three possible nominees to the governor.

State law specifies that the commission include members chosen by various bar groups, including three from the state trial lawyers group but only one from the organization representing the insurance and civil defense bar. "It's problematic the way it's set up," says Ammon Smartt, a business lawyer in Nashville and a Federalist Society leader.

Vanderbilt University law professor Brian Fitzpatrick, another Federalist Society leader, also contends the system violates the Tennessee constitution's provision that judges be "elected." He notes that other states have adopted retention election systems through constitutional amendments. But he also opposes the plan on policy grounds. "Retention elections don't serve much of a purpose except to give judges life tenure," Fitzpatrick says. "A judge has to try to lose one of those things."

Despite the concerns, Ramsey has floated an interim proposal to reauthorize retention elections without a nominating commission and to put the issue before the voters as a constitutional amendment in 2014. The politics of the issue are complex: Republicans control the state Senate and have a one-vote edge in the state House. "It's up in the air," says veteran journalist Ed Cromer, editor of the *Tennessee Journal*, a political newsletter.

Apart from Tennessee's decision to bring Supreme Court justices into retention elections, the Greene County vote was the first extension of the Missouri plan since Utah adopted the system for the state's appellate courts in 1985. The conservative network now pushing judicial elections is resisting any further expansion of the yes-no balloting. "They are phony elections," says attorney Bopp. "They're the closest thing to a non-election election that the people who are trying to protect incumbent judges could come up with."

The American Judicature Society's Andersen disagrees. "We believe that they strike the right balance in providing the appropriate level of insulation from the most corrosive aspects of contestable elections while at the same time providing the same level of potential accountability to the voters through the retention mechanism," he says.

Recusal Debates

The U.S. Supreme Court is deliberating whether to establish a rule requiring state judges to step out of cases involving large campaign contributors following arguments that appeared to leave the justices divided along familiar ideological lines.

Liberal justices appeared sympathetic to arguments on March 3 by a lawyer representing a defunct West Virginia coal company that a state supreme court justice should have been required to recuse himself from ruling on its $50 million award against a rival company whose chief executive spent $3 million to help get the justice elected.

Conservative justices, however, appeared less troubled by the circumstances of the case and dissatisfied with the standards suggested to determine when due process requires a judge to step out of a case.

The decisive vote on the nine-member court appeared likely to lie with Justice Anthony M. Kennedy, a moderate conservative who often has the balance of power between the conservative and liberal blocs. Early in the hour-long session, Kennedy asked the lawyer for the now bankrupt Harman Coal Mining Co. and its former president, Caperton, for "more specific standards."

Later, however, Kennedy signaled interest in some constitutional standard to safeguard judicial impartiality. "Our whole system is designed to ensure confidence in our judgments," Kennedy told the attorney representing the rival A.T.

Massey Co. "It seems to me," Kennedy added, "litigants have an entitlement to that under the Due Process Clause."

Representing Caperton, Washington attorney and former U.S. solicitor general Theodore Olson opened by describing "a fair trial" and "a fair tribunal" as "a fundamental constitutional right." But he met skeptical questioning from Chief Justice John G. Roberts Jr. and a second conservative justice, Scalia. In his questions, Scalia minimized the ties between the West Virginia justice, Brent Benjamin, and Massey chief executive Blankenship.

Later, Scalia directly challenged Olson's proposal that judges be required to recuse themselves whenever there is "a probability of bias." "We can't run a system on such a vague standard," Scalia said.

Roberts pressed Olson on how far to extend the proposed recusal requirement. Would a judge have to step out of cases involving a trade association, a labor union or an advocacy group like Mothers Against Drunk Driving if the group supported his or her campaign? Roberts asked. "Probably not," Olson said initially, but then left open the possibility of mandatory recusal if the judge received a large campaign contribution from such a group.

For Massey, New York City lawyer Andrew Frey opened by saying the recusal issue should be left to state legislatures. "The Due Process Clause does not exist to protect the integrity or reputation of the state judicial systems," Frey said. He said the American Bar Association standard adopted by many states — impropriety or appearance of impropriety — was sufficient protection for the courts.

All four of the liberal justices — John Paul Stevens, David H. Souter, Ginsburg and Stephen G. Breyer — forcefully challenged Frey's stance. "We have never confronted a case as extreme as this one," Stevens said. Breyer agreed. "This is way outside the envelope," he said.

In his turn, Souter said he was not satisfied with leaving the ABA standard as advisory instead of constitutionally

required. The existing system, Souter said, "is not working very well."

But Frey countered by saying that an alternate standard — requiring recusal if an elected judge had a "debt of gratitude" to a litigant — would extend too far, even to newspaper endorsements or support from political officials.

The case drew friend of the court briefs from more than a dozen groups. Groups calling for tighter recusal standards included the ABA, the trial lawyers group American Association for Justice and the judicial reform organizations Justice at Stake and the Brennan Center. On the opposite side were two free-political-speech groups: the Center for Competitive Politics and the James Madison Center.

The Conference of Chief Justices, representing the chief judges in all 50 states and other jurisdictions, filed a brief supporting neither side but urging the Supreme Court to "articulate the circumstances and conditions" when due process "may prevent" a judge from ruling on a case "because of campaign support." The brief suggested seven criteria, including the size and timing of the support and the nature of the supporter's relationship with the judge and with the litigant.

Two other groups of current or former state justices took opposing sides. One group called for a due process standard for recusal, while the other warned that such an approach would undermine judicial elections by discouraging campaign contributions and advocacy.

After arguments, Bopp, who filed the James Madison Center brief, said he was encouraged by doubts voiced by some of the justices about establishing a due process standard. "They have to think long and hard about what kind of standard they're creating," he said.

From the opposite side, Justice at Stake executive director Brandenburg said the case will help focus attention on the issue no matter how the Supreme Court rules. "Regardless of how the case goes, we're going to see a surge of interest on the state side in stepping up their recusal codes," he said. ∎

OUTLOOK

'No Perfect System'

No method of selecting judges is perfect, and none completely free of politics. And no system of judicial tenure — popular election in some form, reappointment or lifetime tenure — ensures a perfect balance between judicial independence and judicial accountability.

Nearly universal agreement emerges on those two propositions from interest and advocacy groups on all sides, from experts and from judges themselves. But there is less agreement on what changes, if any, are needed — and seemingly little likelihood of major changes being adopted unless some broader consensus emerges.

Traditional court reform groups — chiefly, the American Judicature Society and the American Bar Association — succeeded in the 1960s and '70s in getting merit selection/retention systems adopted in a plurality of states. But despite resolute stands from leaders of the two groups, progress has stalled. "AJS and ABA have almost given up their fight," says political scientist Streb at Northern Illinois University.

For now, Streb says, much of the debate focuses on how to improve elections. Court reform groups say the need for change is urgent because of the increasing cost of judicial campaigns since the 1980s — and the role of special-interest groups in financing those campaigns. The problem, says ABA president Wells, is "uniquely American and fairly modern. We really didn't see this before the last 20 years."

Business interests are the new players in the contests, trial lawyers the perennial participants. "Both sides are trying to buy a judge in terms of electing a judge favorable to their view," says Chapman law professor Rotunda.

Judicial elections are "different from the kind of judicial elections we used to have," says Georgetown law professor Schotland. He discounts somewhat the concern about overall spending. Instead, Schotland focuses on what he calls the "corrosive" nature of the campaigns and the later influence on the winning candidate's decisions. The campaigns are "dangerous," he writes, because they try to "make judges answerable to special interests and political partisans rather than law and the Constitution." [15]

From a different perspective, Melinda Gann Hall, a professor of political science at Michigan State University in East Lansing, minimizes the unsavory aspects of judicial campaigns. "The proportion of races in which attack ads are used is actually declining," says Hall, coauthor of a new book defending judicial elections. In contrast to some other experts and advocates, Hall doubts that recent judicial campaigns have had any appreciable impact on public confidence in the courts. [16]

Critics of the recent trends in judicial elections, such as the Brennan Center and Justice at Stake, favor campaign-finance reforms as one way to counteract the influence of special-interest groups. Currently, 10 of the states with judicial elections — more than one-third of the total — have no general contribution limits for judicial elections. Besides favoring contribution limits, the groups also call for public financing for judicial elections, with candidates required to abide by overall spending limits as a condition of the public subsidy.

Public financing, however, is a hard sell for state legislatures. And even if contribution limits or public financing is enacted, neither would prevent nor limit the spending by independent groups such as those that outspent the candidates themselves in West Virginia's controversial 2004 supreme court election.

One lesser reform that has advanced is the creation of judicial campaign-oversight committees or commissions. At least 15 states currently have some monitoring body for judicial campaigns under the auspices of either the state judiciary or state bar, according to a compilation by the American Judicature Society. [17] Under the U.S. Supreme Court's decision in *Republican Party v. White*, however, the oversight bodies have limited power to sanction candidates for any campaign practices found to violate ethical restrictions.

Apart from the rules for judicial campaigns, the reform groups are also pushing for changes in recusal procedures as a way to limit the potential impact of special interests on judicial decisions. The Supreme Court's ruling in the West Virginia case — due by the end of June — will determine whether and under what circumstances a judge may be constitutionally required to step out of a case because of election support from a litigant or lawyer.

Whatever decision the justices make, court-reform advocates say one possible change is to follow the example of

---

About the Author

Associate Editor **Kenneth Jost** graduated from Harvard College and Georgetown University Law Center. He is the author of the *Supreme Court Yearbook* and editor of *The Supreme Court from A to Z* (both *CQ Press*). He was a member of the *CQ Researcher* team that won the American Bar Association's 2002 Silver Gavel Award. His previous reports include "Limiting Lawsuits" and "Medical Malpractice." He is also author of the blog *Jost on Justice* (http://jostonjustice blogspot.com).

the Alabama and Texas supreme courts and require a recusal motion to be ruled on by the full court instead of the individual judge. As a variant, Schotland calls for a state high court to create an advisory recusal panel to consult with the challenged judge before determining whether to step out of a case.

Among vocal advocates of judicial elections, the problem lies not with campaigns but with courts themselves. "To the extent that there are judicial activists, there will be vigorous campaigns," says attorney Bopp. "Judges can fix this: stay within their bounds, exercise restraint and there won't be any campaigns."

The critics, however, sense a growing recognition of problems created by the recent trends in judicial elections. "A growing number of the public sees that judges cannot be impartial if they're not independent — independent of partisan and special interests," says Justice at Stake executive director Brandenburg.

The Brennan Center's Skaggs agrees: "I would be surprised if there weren't efforts to address the problem." ■

Notes

[1] Quoted in Steven Walters, "Abrahamson solidly beats Koschnick," *Journal Sentinel* (Milwaukee), April 8, 2009. Some background also drawn from John Nichols, "What the big Abrahamson, Evers wins mean," *Capital Times*, April 8, 2009.

[2] For background on federal judges, see these *CQ Researcher* reports by Kenneth Jost: "Judges and Politics," July 27, 2001, pp. 577-600; "The Federal Judiciary," March 13, 1998, pp. 217-240.

[3] "The New Politics of Judicial Elections," Brennan Center/Justice at Stake, biennial series, 2000-2006, 2008 (forthcoming).

[4] Wallace B. Jefferson, "Select judges on merit, not party line," *San Antonio Express-News*, March 20, 2009, p. 6B. See also Martha Deller, "Texas Supreme Court chief justice criticizes how judges are selected," *Fort Worth Star-Telegram*, March 18, 2009, p. B4.

[5] Historical background can be found in Matthew J. Streb, "The Study of Judicial Elections," in Streb (ed.), *Running for Judge: The Rising Political, Financial, and Legal Stakes of Judicial Elections* (2007), pp. 8-11; Larry C. Berkson, updated by Rachel Caufeld, "Judicial selection in the United States: A Special Report," American Judicature Society, 2004, www.ajs.org/selection/docs/Berkson.pdf. See also Caleb Nelson, "A Re-evaluation of Scholarly Explanations for the Rise of the Elective Judiciary in Antebellum America," *American Journal of Legal History*, Vol. 37 (April 1993), pp. 190-224.

[6] Steven P. Croley, "The Majoritarian Difficulty: Elective Judiciaries and the Rule of Law," *University of Chicago Law Review*, vol. 62 (1995), p. 722, quoted in Streb, *op. cit.*, p. 10.

[7] Herbert M. Kales, *Unpopular Government in the United States* (1914), pp. 225-251.

[8] Historical narrative drawn from Glenn R. Winters, "The Merit Plan for Judicial Selection and Tenure: Its Historical Development," in Winters (ed.), *Judicial Selection and Tenure: Selected Readings* (1973), pp. 29-44.

[9] *Ibid.*, p. 44.

[10] Background drawn from Stephanie Mercimer, *Blocking the Courthouse Door: How the Republican Party and Its Corporate Allies Are Taking Away Your Right to Sue* (2006).

[11] Background drawn from Mercimer, *op. cit.*; Brennan Center/Justice at Stake, *op. cit.*

[12] The citation is 536 U.S. 765 (2002). For an account, see Kenneth Jost, "Court Strikes Down Limits on Judicial Candidates," in *Supreme Court Yearbook 2001-2002*, CQ Press.

[13] See Kelly Wiese, "Greene County joins court plan," *Missouri Lawyers Weekly*, Nov. 10, 2008; Dick VanderHart, "Court plan OK'd despite confusion," *Springfield News-Leader*, Nov. 7, 2008, p. 2A.

[14] See Richard Locker, "Tennessee lawmakers face a big decision this year: how to select or elect the interpreters of law," *The* (Memphis) *Commercial-Appeal*, March 15, 2009.

[15] Bert Brandenburg and Roy A. Schotland, "Keeping courts impartial amid changing judicial elections," *Daedalus*, fall 2008, pp. 102-109.

[16] Chris W. Bonneau and Melinda Gann Hall, *In Defense of Judicial Elections*, forthcoming (May 2009).

[17] See "Judicial Campaigns and Elections: Campaign Oversight," American Judicature Society, www.judicialselection.us/judicial_selection/campaigns_and_elections/campaign_oversight.cfm?state.

FOR MORE INFORMATION

American Association for Justice, 777 Sixth St., N.W., Suite 200, Washington, DC 20001; (202) 965-3500; www.justice.org. International coalition of legal professionals ensuring that victims of negligence can obtain courtroom justice.

American Bar Association, 321 N. Clark St., Chicago, IL 60654; (800) 285-2221; www.abanet.org. Serves as the national representative of the legal profession.

American Judicature Society, Opperman Center at Drake University, 2700 University Ave., Des Moines, IA 50311; (515) 271-2281; www.ajs.org. Nonpartisan organization of judges and attorneys seeking to improve the justice system.

American Tort Reform Association, 1101 Connecticut Ave., N.W., Suite 400, Washington, DC 20036; (202) 682-1163; www.atra.org. National organization dedicated to reforming the civil justice system.

Brennan Center for Justice, NYU School of Law, 161 Sixth Ave., 12th Floor, New York, NY 10013; (212) 998-6730; www.brennancenter.org. Public policy and law institute focusing on fundamental issues of democracy and justice.

Center for Competitive Politics, 124 West St. South, Suite 201, Alexandria, VA 22314; (703) 894-6800; www.campaignfreedom.org. Educates public on the effects of money on politics and promotes a more free and competitive electoral process.

Justice at Stake Campaign, 717 D St., N.W., Suite 203, Washington, DC 20004; (202) 588-9700; www.justiceatstake.org. Works for reforms to ensure that politics and special interests do not influence the courtroom.

National Center for State Courts, 300 Newport Ave., Williamsburg, VA 23185; (800) 616-6164; www.ncsconline.org. Seeks to improve the administration of justice through leadership and service to state courts.

U.S. Chamber of Commerce, 1615 H St., N.W., Washington, DC 20062; (202) 659-6000; www.uschamber.com. Represents 3 million U.S. businesses.

Bibliography

Selected Sources

Books

Bonneau, Chris W., and Melinda Gann Hall, *In Defense of Judicial Elections*, Routledge, forthcoming (May 2009).

Data from two decades of state supreme court elections are used to argue that the races enhance democracy and help create links between citizens and the judiciary. Bonneau is associate professor of political science at the University of Pittsburgh, Hall a professor of political science at Michigan State University. Includes notes, 10-page list of references.

Grisham, John, *The Appeal*, Doubleday, 2008.

The best-selling author tells the fictional story of a business executive's decision — following a big verdict against his company — to help select an unknown lawyer for an expensive and ultimately successful campaign for election to the state supreme court. The new justice then provides the decisive vote to overturn the award against the company. Grisham has said the novel was inspired by the 2004 race for a seat on the West Virginia Supreme Court of Appeals. In an afterword, Grisham writes, "there is a lot of truth in the story."

Sheldon, Charles H., and Linda S. Maule, *Choosing Justice: The Recruitment of State and Federal Judges*, Washington State University Press, 1997.

Although somewhat dated, the book provides a good overview of the history of judicial selection and elections in the United States along with informative accounts of judicial recruitment in states with different methods: partisan elections, merit selection and gubernatorial or legislative appointments. Sheldon was a professor at Washington State University until his death in 1999; Maule is a professor at Indiana State University.

Streb, Matthew J. (ed.), *Running for Judge: The Rising Political, Financial, and Legal Stakes of Judicial Elections*, New York University Press, 2007.

Eleven essays by experts representing a range of views cover such judicial election topics as campaign spending, interest group participation, voter responses and news media coverage. Streb, an associate professor of political science at Northern Illinois University, coauthors the final essay, which looks at the prospects for judicial election reforms. Includes notes, extensive statistical information and 19-page bibliography.

Articles

Brandenburg, Bert, and Roy A. Schotland, "Keeping Courts Impartial Amid Changing Judicial Elections," *Daedalus*, fall 2008.

The authors discuss the impact of the increasing cost of judicial campaigns and the increasing role of special interests, including business and plaintiffs' lawyers, in financing the campaigns. Brandenburg is executive director of Justice at Stake, Schotland a professor at Georgetown University Law Center. The article is one of 15 in a special issue devoted to judicial independence.

DeBow, Michael, "The Case for Partisan Judicial Elections," *Federalist Society*, 2003, www.fed-soc.org/publications/pub ID.90/pub_detail.asp.

A professor at Samford University's Cumberland School of Law in Birmingham, Ala., argues in favor of partisan judicial elections on the ground that they offer "an additional, significant measure of self-government to voters." DeBow chaired a six-member Federalist Society task force on the issue. The society's Web site also includes audio and video of the September 2006 program, "Are Judicial Elections a Threat to Judicial Independence?" featuring two state supreme court justices: Harold F. See Jr. of Alabama and Randall T. Shepard of Indiana.

Kritzer, Herbert, "Law Is the Mere Continuation of Politics by Different Means: American Judicial Politics in the Twenty-First Century," *DePaul Law Review*, Vol. 56 (April 2007), pp. 423-467.

A professor of political science and law at the University of Wisconsin-Madison traces Americans' ambivalence about judicial selection and retention to the "fundamentally conflicted" views about judicial accountability on one hand and judicial independence on the other.

Reports and Studies

"The New Politics of Judicial Elections," Brennan Center for Justice/Justice at Stake, biennial series, 2000-2006, 2008 (forthcoming).

The biennial series critically details the rising cost of judicial campaigns since 2000, the increasing role of business-group financing in those campaigns and the growing use of television advertising by candidates and independent special-interest groups.

On the Web

American Judicature Society (www.ajs.org).

The Des Moines, Iowa-based court-reform group, which is the author and principal advocate for merit selection and retention systems of judicial recruitment and tenure, maintains a comprehensive Web site with state-by-state information on judicial selection, appointment and election procedures.

The Next Step:

Additional Articles from Current Periodicals

Campaign Contributions

Jones, Barbara L., "Court to Judges: Don't Follow the Money," *Minnesota Lawyer*, **Dec. 29, 2008.**

The Minnesota Supreme Court has approved a new Code of Judicial Conduct that limits individual donations to judicial campaigns to $2,000 in an election year.

Liptak, Adam, "Looking Anew At Campaign Cash and Elected Judges," *The New York Times*, **Jan. 29, 2008, p. A14.**

Elected justices tend to decide cases in favor of their contributors 65 percent of the time, according to a new study.

Olsen, Lise, "The Pain of Probate Court," *Houston Chronicle*, **June 24, 2007, p. A12.**

Lawyers who got the most business in probate cases in a Texas county had contributed tens of thousands of dollars to the county's 2006 judicial races.

Slobodzian, Joseph A., "Traffic Court Judge Facing Campaign-Related Charges," *The Philadelphia Inquirer*, **June 21, 2008, p. B3.**

A Philadelphia traffic court judge told a state judicial panel he was unaware of campaign fundraising rules after he was caught on video soliciting funds from motorcyclists.

Federal Judges

Canham, Matt, "Chief Utah Federal Judge Apologizes for Rule-Violating Obama Donation," *Salt Lake Tribune*, **Oct. 24, 2008.**

Utah's chief federal judge apologized for campaign contributions to Barack Obama that appeared improper.

Hawpe, David, "Boggs Sees Nothing Wrong in FREE(bie) Trips, But Congress May," *Courier-Journal* **(Kentucky), Feb. 10, 2008, p. 2H.**

A Kentucky federal appeals court judge is under scrutiny after participating in junkets paid for by a special-interest group.

Rivkin Jr., David B., "Who Should Judge the Judges?" *Los Angeles Times*, **April 8, 2009, p. A25.**

The Supreme Court should resist the temptation to make federal judges the arbiters of state court ethics in order to maintain the sovereignty of states.

Recusal Standards

Barnes, Robert, "Case May Define When a Judge Must Recuse Self," *The Washington Post*, **March 2, 2009, p. A1.**

The case of a West Virginia justice who ruled in favor of a campaign contributor raises profound questions of when judges should recuse themselves.

Baxter, Christopher, "Northampton Judge to Rule on Request He Recuse Himself From Chrin Expansion," *Morning Call* **(Pennsylvania), Feb. 27, 2009, p. B6.**

A Pennsylvania judge filed a motion to hold a hearing over arguments requesting for his recusal in a case involving a defendant who gave him campaign contributions.

Egan, Paul, "Fieger Loses Lawsuit Over State Supreme Court Procedure," *Detroit News*, **Sept. 27, 2007.**

A Detroit attorney has lost a lawsuit in which he claimed it was unconstitutional for elected Michigan judges to decide for themselves when to recuse themselves from cases.

Hall, Dee J., "State's System of Electing Justices Called 'Troubling,' " *Wisconsin State Journal*, **Dec. 3, 2007, p. A1.**

Elected Wisconsin judges currently make their own decisions about when campaign ties and contributions create an appearance of impropriety.

Selection Process

Mitchell, Charlie, "How Can We Get the Best Judges?" *Biloxi Sun Herald* **(Mississippi), Feb. 6, 2008, p. C3.**

A hybrid system of electing and appointing judges may prove to be the best method for bringing the most-qualified judges to the bench.

Whitely, Joan, "Lawyers Support Appointing Judges," *Las Vegas Review-Journal*, **May 23, 2008, p. 1A.**

Two-thirds of lawyers in the Las Vegas area favor a system that appoints judges instead of electing them in order to diminish the influence of campaign contributions.

CITING CQ RESEARCHER

Sample formats for citing these reports in a bibliography include the ones listed below. Preferred styles and formats vary, so please check with your instructor or professor.

MLA STYLE
Jost, Kenneth. "Rethinking the Death Penalty." CQ Researcher 16 Nov. 2001: 945-68.

APA STYLE
Jost, K. (2001, November 16). Rethinking the death penalty. CQ Researcher, 11, 945-968.

CHICAGO STYLE
Jost, Kenneth. "Rethinking the Death Penalty." CQ Researcher, November 16, 2001, 945-968.

In-depth Reports on Issues in the News

Are you writing a paper?

Need backup for a debate?

Want to become an expert on an issue?

For 80 years, students have turned to *CQ Researcher* for in-depth reporting on issues in the news. Reports on a full range of political and social issues are now available. Following is a selection of recent reports:

Civil Liberties

Closing Guantánamo, 2/09
Limiting Lawsuits, 12/08
Affirmative Action, 10/08
Gay Marriage Showdowns, 9/08
America's Border Fence, 9/08
Immigration Debate, 2/08

Crime/Law

Mexico's Drug War, 12/08
Prostitution Debate, 5/08
Public Defenders, 4/08
Gun Violence, 5/07

Education

Reading Crisis? 2/08
Discipline in Schools, 2/08
Student Aid, 1/08
Racial Diversity in Public Schools, 9/07
Stress on Students, 7/07

Environment/Society

Future of Journalism, 3/09
Confronting Warming, 1/09
Reducing Carbon Footprint, 12/08
Protecting Wetlands, 10/08
Buying Green, 2/08

Health/Safety

Extreme Sports, 4/09
Regulating Toxic Chemicals, 1/09
Preventing Cancer, 1/09
Heart Health, 9/08
Global Food Crisis, 6/08

Politics/Economy

Business Bankruptcy, 4/09
Future of the GOP, 3/09
Middle-Class Squeeze, 3/09
Public-Works Projects, 2/09
The Obama Presidency, 1/09

Upcoming Reports

| High-Speed Trains, 5/1/09 | Hate Groups, 5/8/09 | Fertility Clinics, 5/15/09 |

ACCESS

CQ Researcher is available in print and online. For access, visit your library or www.cqresearcher.com.

STAY CURRENT

To receive notice of upcoming *CQ Researcher* reports, or learn more about *CQ Researcher* products, subscribe to the free e-mail newsletters, *CQ Researcher Alert!* and *CQ Researcher News*: http://cqpress.com/newsletters.

PURCHASE

To purchase a *CQ Researcher* report in print or electronic format (PDF), visit www.cqpress.com or call 866-427-7737. Single reports start at $15. Bulk purchase discounts and electronic-rights licensing are also available.

SUBSCRIBE

Annual full-service *CQ Researcher* subscriptions—including 44 reports a year, monthly index updates, and a bound volume—start at $803. Add $25 for domestic postage.

CQ Researcher Online offers a backfile from 1991 and a number of tools to simplify research. For pricing information, call 800-834-9020, ext. 1906, or e-mail librarysales@cqpress.com.

Published by CQ Press, a division of SAGE Publications

www.cqresearcher.com

High-Speed Trains

Does the United States need supertrains?

T he Obama administration has designated $8 billion in stimulus funds for high-speed passenger rail, buoying hopes that supertrains will operate throughout the American landscape as they do in Europe and Asia. The money, most likely to be divided among multiple corridors, won't buy a single fast-rail system. But supporters say it will help traditional trains run faster and pay for planning to make true high-speed rail networks a reality. Washington's support signals a transformation in federal policy that has long favored highway and air travel, experts say. Some argue that money should be focused first on building true high-speed service in the busy Northeast Corridor. But supporters in the Midwest, Florida, California and elsewhere are expected to vie for a portion of the rail funds. So far, California appears furthest ahead in planning for fast rail, aided by a $9.95 billion bond issue. But critics say the plan's benefits are exaggerated.

An artist's rendering envisions the future of high-speed rail travel in California. In November voters approved the sale of bonds to help pay for a 220-mph system between San Francisco and Los Angeles.

CQ Researcher • May 1, 2009 • www.cqresearcher.com
Volume 19, Number 17 • Pages 397–420

Cover: California High-Speed Rail Authority

CQ Researcher

May 1, 2009
Volume 19, Number 17

MANAGING EDITOR: Thomas J. Colin
tcolin@cqpress.com

ASSISTANT MANAGING EDITOR: Kathy Koch
kkoch@cqpress.com

ASSOCIATE EDITOR: Kenneth Jost

STAFF WRITERS: Thomas J. Billitteri, Marcia Clemmitt, Peter Katel

CONTRIBUTING WRITERS: Rachel Cox, Sarah Glazer, Alan Greenblatt, Barbara Mantel, Patrick Marshall, Tom Price, Jennifer Weeks

DESIGN/PRODUCTION EDITOR: Olu B. Davis

ASSISTANT EDITOR: Darrell Dela Rosa

FACT-CHECKING: Eugene J. Gabler, Michelle Harris

EDITORIAL INTERN: Vyomika Jairam

CQ PRESS

A Division of SAGE

PRESIDENT AND PUBLISHER:
John A. Jenkins

EXECUTIVE DIRECTOR,
REFERENCE INFORMATION GROUP:
Alix B. Vance

CQ Press is a registered trademark of Congressional Quarterly Inc.

CQ Researcher (ISSN 1056-2036) is printed on acid-free paper. Published weekly, except; (Jan. wk. 1) (May wk. 4) (July wks. 1, 2) (Aug. wks. 3, 4) (Nov. wk. 4) and (Dec. wk. 4), by CQ Press, a division of SAGE Publications. Annual full-service subscriptions start at $803. For pricing, call 1-800-834-9020, ext. 1906. To purchase a CQ Researcher report in print or electronic format (PDF), visit www. cqpress.com or call 866-427-7737. Single reports start at $15. Bulk purchase discounts and electronic-rights licensing are also available. Periodicals postage paid at Washington, D.C., and additional mailing offices. POSTMASTER: Send address changes to CQ Researcher, 2300 N St., N.W., Suite 800, Washington, DC 20037.

High-Speed Trains

BY THOMAS J. BILLITTERI

THE ISSUES

It's the dream of grounded airline passengers and aggravated drivers everywhere: Hop a sleek, futuristic train that whisks you in living-room comfort to your destination hundreds of miles away at speeds two, three or even four times that of an auto.

Outside the United States, the idea is hardly new. "Bullet trains" first appeared in Japan 45 years ago, and countries as diverse as France, Germany, Spain, Italy, China, Taiwan and South Korea have high-speed systems running or under construction. [1]

In America, supertrain development has long been stalled — but maybe not for long. President Barack Obama, seeking to make 21st-century train travel a signature issue of his administration, added $8 billion to this year's economic stimulus package for high-speed and other rail projects — the most ever allotted for rail at once. [2] In addition, Obama's 2010 budget proposes state grants for high-speed rail totaling $5 billion over five years. [3]

The money is aimed at two very different versions of what in the United States is defined as high-speed rail: conventional electric- or diesel-powered trains that can move at 110 miles an hour, or about 40 percent faster than most Amtrak trains travel today; and European-style high-speed trains that require special tracks and sophisticated locomotives to speed passengers at hundreds of miles an hour toward their destinations.

Right now, Amtrak's Washington-New York-Boston Acela Express counts as the closest thing to high-speed rail in the United States. It is capable of

Spain's sleek, new bullet train, the AVE, completes the 410-mile Barcelona to Madrid run in two-and-a-half hours at an average speed of 164 mph. Seven European and four Asian countries have high-speed rail. In the United States, however, the only high-speed train is Amtrak's Acela, which hits 150 mph for short stretches along the Northeast Corridor. Several more U.S. systems are under consideration.

AFP/Getty Images/Josep Lago

reaching 150 mph but averages roughly 80 mph on its Washington-New York route over tracks shared with freight and commuter trains. [4]

Experts say the $8 billion in stimulus money isn't enough to pay for even one high-speed system. Much of the money, they say, will be used to improve existing tracks shared by passenger and freight trains, to help traditional passenger trains run faster in key corridors, such as one linking Chicago with other Midwest cities. But some of the money will likely be used for real bullet trains proposed in California, Florida, Texas and elsewhere. The government has identified 10 intercity corridors, plus the Northeast Corridor linking Washington and Boston, as potential recipients of federal money.

Obama said the nation requires "a smart transportation system equal to the needs of the 21st century." [5] Transportation Secretary Ray LaHood calls high-speed rail a "transformational initiative" for the economy. [6] In April the president issued a strategic plan for high-speed rail, and by June the Transportation Department must explain how groups can seek grants. [7] The competition for money "is going to be pretty severe," said Democratic Gov. Jim Doyle of Wisconsin, which is part of the Midwest high-speed rail effort. [8]

However the stimulus money is used, rail advocates say it marks an historic shift in federal transportation policy, which for decades has favored highways and airports over trains.

"It is laying the groundwork for a high-speed rail system, and it's setting the tone that we're going to have one," says James P. RePass, founder and CEO of the National Corridors Initiative, a group that advocates transportation-infrastructure development, with an emphasis on rail. While both government and private money will be required to develop high-speed trains, RePass says, the federal stimulus money signals "a sea change in the attitude of the national administration about rail."

Ross B. Capon, president of the National Association of Railroad Passengers, calls the stimulus money "a serious beginning."

"Eight billion dollars is not going to fulfill the dreams of people who see a [French-style 200 mph] TGV going everywhere," he says, "but it can lay the groundwork for that if it's the first installment on a serious commitment."

But high-speed trains face huge obstacles in the United States. Beyond massive infrastructure outlays, experts say

High-Speed Rail Corridors Designated

The Federal Railroad Administration has designated 10 high-speed rail corridors as potential recipients of federal money, plus the Northeast Corridor. The 1,920-mile Midwest corridor based in Chicago is the longest, followed by the 1,022-mile Gulf Coast corridor.

Proposed High-speed Rail Corridors

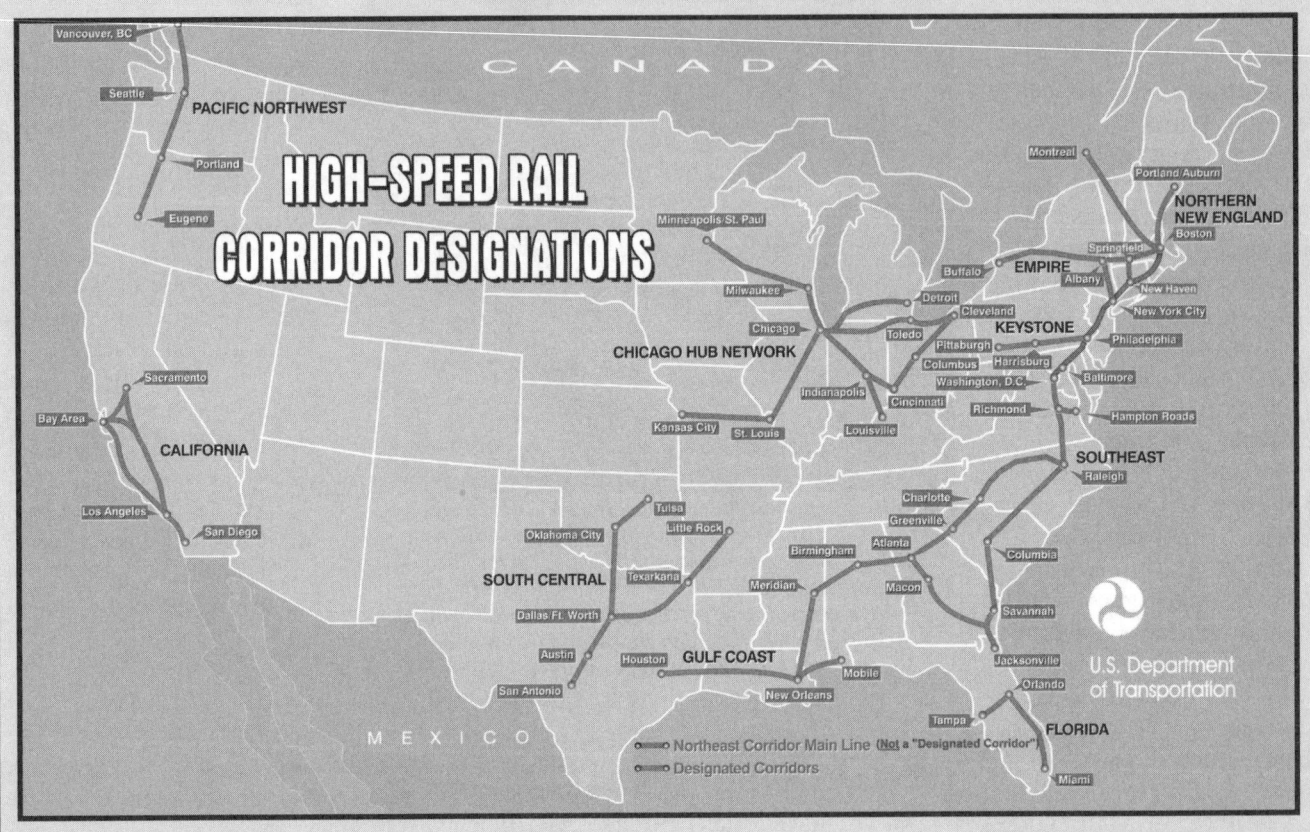

Source: Federal Railroad Administration

they require a distinct set of geographic and demographic circumstances to make them worthwhile. They must serve cities within a few hundred miles of each other — otherwise it's faster for passengers to fly. Population densities along the route must be high — otherwise trains can't generate adequate revenue. Passengers must have an easy, cheap way to get from a train station to their final destination — requiring integrated public-transit systems in urban areas. And with gasoline far cheaper in the United States than in Europe, consumers must have an incentive to ditch their cars in favor of trains.

"Unlike Europe, we've been wedded to the auto in so many ways," says Carlos Schwantes, a professor of transportation studies at the University of Missouri-St. Louis. "Our cities are very diffuse, very spread out. Urban sprawl goes on for hundreds of miles. If we put in high-speed trains, where would we site the stations that would benefit many Americans? People don't live downtown, and they would have to secure space to park their autos. We don't have a support network of trolleys, trams and so on."

Efforts to build true high-speed systems have faltered in the past. In Florida, where a Tampa-Orlando-Miami route has long been contemplated, voters passed a constitutional amendment in 2000 directing the legislature to develop a system capable of going faster than 120 mph. But Republican Gov. Jeb Bush helped quash the project. Efforts to build systems in Texas and California also failed in the past.

Today a renewed effort in California has come closest to achieving a true high-speed system. In November voters approved the sale of $9.95 billion in bonds to help pay for a 220-mph system between San Francisco and Los Angeles/Anaheim and eventually Sacramento and San Diego. However, the state — mired in a fiscal crisis — faces a challenge in raising the money.

The California High-Speed Rail Authority says the 800-mile system will cost $45 billion in government and private funds to build. Once in operation, the system will generate more than $1 billion in annual profits and need no operating subsidies, the authority claims. [9] It also says the system will create thousands of jobs, have huge environmental benefits and draw as many as 117 million riders a year by 2030.

"By building this system, California will retain its rightful place as America's premier economic, transportation and environmental leader," declared Quentin Kopp, chairman of the state rail authority. [10]

But critics say California's claims are grossly exaggerated. A study by the Reason Foundation, a free-market-oriented think tank, and two other groups — Citizens Against Government Waste and the Howard Jarvis Taxpayers Association — concluded that the system would cost tens of billions more than the authority's estimate and that ridership and greenhouse-gas reductions would be much lower. [11]

"My bottom line: It is a terrible financial loser," says Wendell Cox, a transportation consultant and coauthor of the study.

As rail backers begin vying for federal stimulus money, a fundamental question remains: How much funding should be allocated for true high-speed systems and how much for incremental improvements in existing rail systems to make traditional trains run faster.

Joseph Vranich, coauthor of the Reason Foundation study and former president of the High Speed Rail Association, said he would "focus all this money where it's needed": on a true high-speed rail system in the New York-Washington corridor, "by far the No. 1 market" for high-speed rail.

"Population density in the corridor is high, distances are short enough to make trains a viable alternative to air-

California System Would Cost $45 Billion

Three-fourths of the $45 billion cost of a statewide, 800-mile high-speed rail network in California would be spent on building the San Francisco-Los Angeles/Anaheim leg, with the estimated $33.6 billion cost mostly provided by government, according to the California High-Speed Rail Authority.

Expected Funding for High-Speed Rail Network Between San Francisco and Los Angeles

(in $ billions)

- Federal government: $12.0-16.0
- State government: $9.0
- Public-private partnerships: $6.5-7.5
- Local governments: $2.0-3.0

Source: California High-Speed Rail Authority

planes, rights-of-way for new track already exist and construction of a new airport in the New York area to accommodate future travel demand would be difficult," he says. "Once the country — public agencies and private companies — are smarter about how to build a high-speed system, then we can evaluate some other lines."

But Capon of the rail passengers group argues that concentrating stimulus money in a single rail market would simply discourage others from moving ahead with projects that he contends are vitally needed. "If we say to 49 states, this is not your money, states may just give up."

As government officials, private companies, taxpayers and rail experts ponder the future of high-speed rail, here are some of the questions they are debating:

Do high-speed trains make economic sense?

Rick Harnish, executive director of the Midwest High Speed Rail Association — a Chicago-based advocacy group representing 1,500 individuals, cities and corporations — sees huge economic benefits to high-speed rail.

It would cut travel costs, induce more people to go places and foster commercial ties between cities, he says.

The group's immediate goal is upgrading tracks, signals and crossings between Chicago and other Midwest cities so conventional diesel-powered trains could travel up to 110 mph. On the 289-mile St. Louis route, that would cut the travel time to less than four hours, from the current 5.5 hours.

The association's ultimate goal is a 220-mph system linking Chicago with metropolitan areas throughout the Midwest.

"Our current system doesn't make sense economically," Harnish says. "Our airline industry is dying. The auto industry is dying. The Highway Trust Fund required an $8 billion subsidy last year. Households are hurting because they're spending too much on transportation. The only way to make a significant difference in getting transportation costs down is by expanding the railroad network."

Howard A. Learner, executive director of the Chicago-based Environmental Law and Policy Center, an advocacy group that backs high-speed rail in the Midwest, says rail projects not only create jobs but also "pull together the regional economy," making it easier for people to move between cities "in a way that makes business work better."

But critics remain unconvinced that expensive high-speed and supertrain systems can ever pay off.

"Close scrutiny of these plans reveals that they do not live up to the hype," argues Randal O'Toole, a senior fellow at the Cato Institute, a conservative think tank in Washington. "As attractive as 110-to-220-mile-per-hour trains might sound, even the most optimistic forecasts predict they will take few cars off the road. At best, they will replace for-profit private commuter airlines with heavily subsidized public rail systems. Taxpayers and politicians should be wary of any transportation projects that cannot be paid for out of user fees." [12]

O'Toole says the average Japanese rides that country's *Shinkansen* bullet train only 400 miles a year. "If we're going to move the average American 400 miles a year, it's not worth it" to build high-speed rail systems, he says.

The debate over the economic impact of high-speed rail is bound to heat up as competition grows over the federal stimulus money, especially for multi-state corridors. "Economists like to say, let's allocate the costs and the benefits among the states by population, distance, density and so on," says Steven R. Ditmeyer, former di-

rector of research and development at the Federal Railroad Administration. "It's like the theological debates over angels on the heads of pins. There are no right answers, and the debates can go on endlessly."

President Barack Obama signs legislation creating the $787 billion economic stimulus package, in Denver on Feb. 17, 2009. The president added $8 billion for high-speed and other rail projects, making high-speed rail a signature project of his administration. Vice President Joseph Biden looks on.

A 2000 report prepared for Amtrak and state transportation agencies concluded that an improved and expanded passenger rail system in the Midwest would produce $1.70 in benefits for every dollar spent to build, finance, operate and maintain the system. [13] In Florida, a 2002 report said a 150-mph route between Tampa and Orlando would generate $1.27 in benefits for every dollar in costs. [14]

And in California, boosters say the high-speed train project will create near-

ly 160,000 construction-related jobs plus another 450,000 permanent jobs by 2035 resulting from economic growth spurred by the rail system. They also claim the system will generate more than $1 billion in surplus revenue annually and increase productivity by easing congestion. [15]

Likewise, a 2008 study by the Bay Area Council Economic Institute, a public-private partnership of business, labor, government and higher education, concluded that in the San Francisco Bay Area high-speed rail would generate a sustained 1.1 percent increase in employment by 2030 — 48,000 new jobs — and spur tourism, construction spending and business productivity, the latter by reducing commuting time. [16]

In addition, the study said an expandable statewide rail system offers "the potential to meet a significant part" of California's needs for new airport and freeway construction in coming decades. [17]

But critics say the California plan is all but a pipe dream. The Reason Foundation study concluded it was unlikely that enough private money and public subsidies could be found to finance the complete plan and that "claims of profitability could not conceivably be credible under even the most optimistic assumptions, unless some or all capital and debt costs are ignored." The San Francisco-Los Angeles portion alone would lose up to $4.17 billion annually by 2030, "with a small profit possible under only the most optimistic and improbable conditions." [18]

California officials defend their projections. "This has been extensively studied," says Dan Levitt, deputy director of the state's high-speed rail authority. The state's assumptions "are based on an analysis of other systems that have been operating for decades in other parts of the world and [that have been] extensively proved," Levitt says.

Moreover, rail advocates point out that for more than half a century the federal government has poured billions of dollars into the Interstate Highway System and other roadways, subsidized car travel by keeping gasoline taxes low, funded airport expansion and, after the 2001 terrorist attacks, bailed out the airline industry. [19]

"There are people who, when someone buys cars or gas, they say that is the free market at work — hurrah!" says Capon of the National Association of Railroad Passengers. "And when the government puts on a tax to build a railroad, they say that's socialism, that's bad. They usually don't talk about all the government taxes, direct and indirect, that support highways and aviation because those systems have been constructed to give the false sense of minimal public subsidy."

Skeptics of high-speed rail don't buy such arguments, though. In a 2001 report, the fiscally conservative National Taxpayers Union pointed out that airline passengers and auto users pay a broad range of federal taxes designated for such things as air traffic control and roads. On the other hand, it said, Amtrak is funded through an annual congressional appropriation from the general fund and has received billions of dollars in state and federal subsidies since its formation in 1971.

"Amtrak's dismal track record and constant need for subsidies suggests that rail, high-speed or not, may not be viable in the United States," the group said. [20]

Would high-speed trains relieve highway and airport congestion?

When Ditmeyer, the former Federal Railroad Administration official, thinks about places where high-speed rail systems might make the most sense, he refers to a Census Bureau map featuring the U.S. land area in black, with groupings of white dots indicating lights in populated areas. The so-called "Nighttime Map" shows a pattern of brightness that Ditmeyer calls "the string of pearls." The Northeast Corridor looks ablaze. So, too, do corridors in Florida, North Carolina and ones radiating from Chicago. Out West, bright dots gleam along corridors in California and Colorado.

"Looking at that map tells you where high-speed rail fits," Ditmeyer says. The key requirements, he says: population density, reasonable proximity — 250 miles or so — between cities, and economic ties between the cities that will generate passenger volume. And, Ditmeyer adds, "it also helps if other modes of transportation are congested. Otherwise, people won't have much of a reason for diverting" from cars and planes to the train.

Congestion relief is indeed a key selling point among high-speed rail advocates. Drivers "will switch because [a fast train] is a good option," argues Learner of the Environmental Law and Policy Center. He also points to Chicago's O'Hare International Airport and its legendary congestion and says rail "will enable people to have a third option for intercity travel around the Midwest."

"The primary modes of intercity passenger travel now are highway or air, and both our roads and our airspace are challenged by costly congestion," Transportation secretary LaHood noted. "And driving a car doesn't allow a driver to use the time for work or recreation the way train travel does. With train stations largely within cities, access is simpler. That direct access to our intercities is very much consistent with our focus on creating livable communities." [21]

But skeptics question whether trains can lure enough people away from highways and airports to make much of a dent in congestion. Because California is furthest along among the states in planning for high-speed rail, some of the most vigorous debates so far have occurred there.

The California High-Speed Rail Authority said supertrains would alleviate the need for some 3,000 miles of new freeway lanes, five airport runways and 90 departure gates over the next two decades, at a total cost of almost $100 billion. Intercity and local travelers would save more than $42 billion by 2050 in congestion relief and another $14 billion in accident and pollution reduction. Airline passengers would realize another $2 billion in delay-reduction benefits, and airlines would see $1.8 billion in such benefits. [22]

Philip J. Romero, dean of the College of Business and Economics at California State University, Los Angeles, found that high-speed rail service not only would cut travel time between Los Angeles and San Francisco by at least 50 percent compared with auto travel but also ease auto congestion within Los Angeles County. [23] At least 41 percent of high-speed train trips in California would be for business travel, with the largest number — more than 18 million — within the county, according to Romero. "While the system has been designed with intercity travel in mind, the most common passengers will be Los Angeles-area commuters." [24]

Romero also argued that high-speed rail would encourage denser development near stations, further reducing car traffic. "Nearly 35,000 fewer undeveloped acres will be consumed by development in L.A. County by 2035" if high-speed rail is built, he wrote. [25]

Others are similarly optimistic. Dan Tempelis, project manager of the Los Angeles-to-Palmdale segment of California's proposed system, argued in the Los Angeles Times that freeway and airport congestion costs the state's economy about $20 billion a year in lost time and wasted fuel. [26] And Kopp, chairman of the California effort, warned that airports in Los Angeles,

Nations From Spain to China Boast Bullet Trains

Japan set the trend in high-speed rail in 1964.

Ever since the introduction of Japan's bullet train system — the Shinkansen *— in 1964, 10 other nations overseas have offered high-speed train service to passengers. Seven Western European countries currently have such trains, with several countries working to link up their systems. The introduction of high-speed rail trains in Asian countries such as China, Taiwan and South Korea has been credited with helping to boost their economic growth.*

High-speed Rail in Operation, Planned or Under Construction

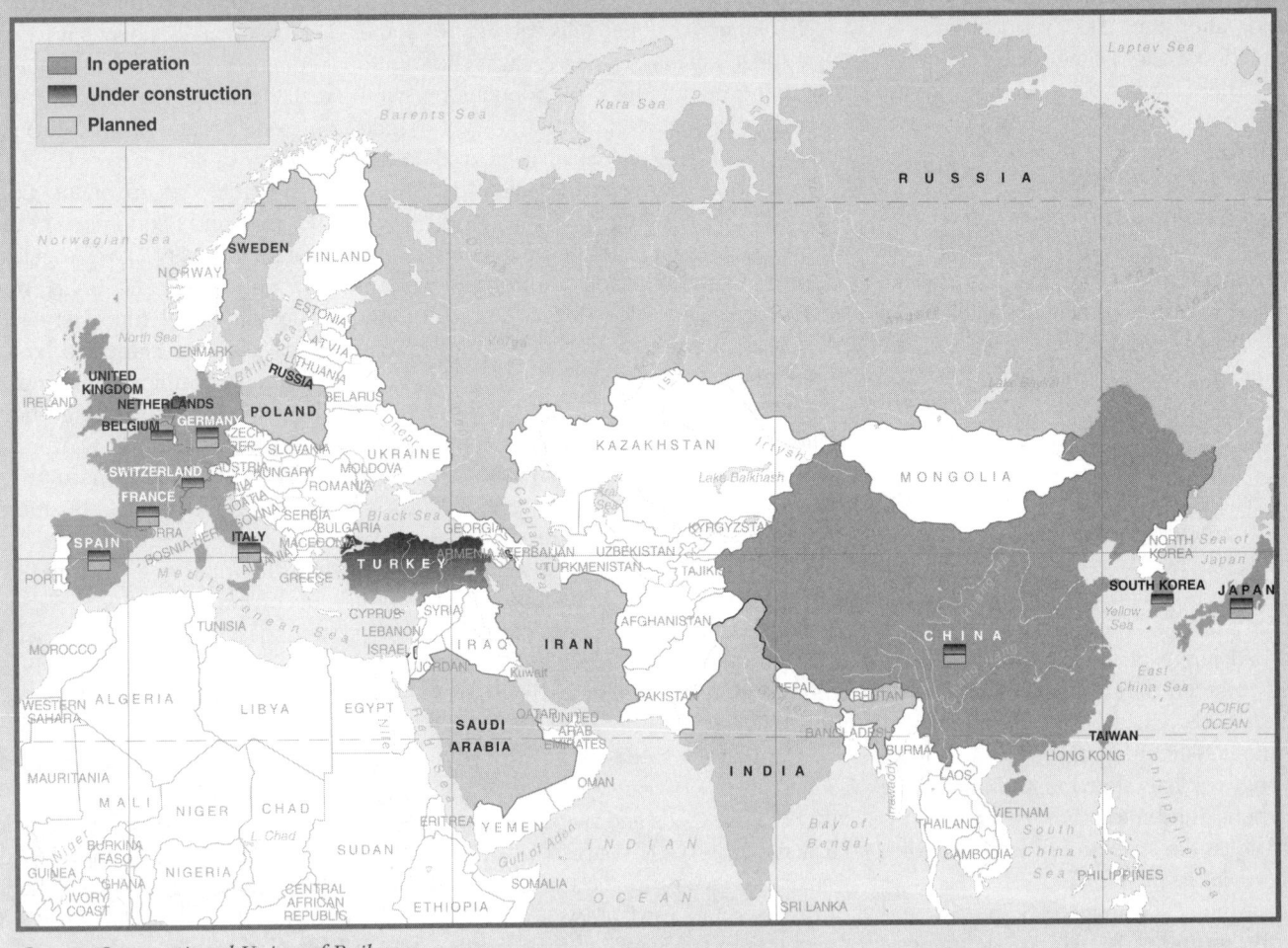

Source: *International Union of Railways*

San Diego and San Francisco will reach capacity in 20 years. "Building the 220-mph train system to solve this need for expanded capacity will require only one-third of the cost of pouring new concrete to add freeways and runways." [27]

But critics are highly skeptical of much of the data produced by the California planners. For one thing, they say, no matter how fast the train goes, local commuters heading to and from jobs are unlikely to abandon their cars in large numbers, especially if they don't have easy access to a rapid, convenient transit system that will whisk them from doorstep to train station.

Rail expert Vranich, coauthor of the Reason Foundation study, rejects the claim that high-speed rail will reduce auto traffic. "Most congestion occurs with commuters going to work" — not on long stretches of highways linking cities that might be served by rail.

Continued on p. 406

High-Speed Rail on Fast Track in Europe, Asia

Eleven nations have networks, with many more on the way.

Forty-five years after the first bullet train began operating in Japan, 10 other countries also have high-speed rail networks, and the United States just barely.*

High-speed rail has become one of the most practical solutions for land travel across Japan, where more than 70 percent of the land is unsuited for road travel due to mountainous and uninhabitable terrain. Construction of the world's first high-speed line — the *Shinkansen* ("Bullet Train") — was completed in 1964 from Tokyo to Osaka in the south, with a then-top speed of 130 mph; today it is 186 mph. In 1973 the transport minister, recognizing the interrelationship between land development and the high-speed rail network, approved construction plans to expand the *Shinkansen* nationwide with five additional lines.

Spurred by Japan's success, France in 1981 launched its *Train à Grande Vitesse* ("High-Speed Train") — better known as the TGV (pronounced tay jay vay) — between Paris and Lyon. Unlike Japan's *Shinkansen*, however, the TGV uses existing track in urban areas as well as high-speed rail infrastructure. The dual-route capability facilitated the creation of new lines in France in the 1980s and '90s.

Cross-border service into Germany eventually led to the construction of Germany's own ICE ("Inter City Express") lines in the late 1980s, also fitted for operation over older tracks and compatible with existing signaling systems.

Today seven European countries have high-speed rail services, with Spain becoming the latest newcomer. (*See map, p. 404.*) Launced in 2008, the sleek AVE (*Alta Velocidad Española*, or "Spanish High Speed") train completes the 410-mile journey from Barcelona to Madrid — a popular business route — in two-and-a-half hours at an average speed of 164 mph. Construction plans anticipate that all provincial cities will be no more than four hours from Madrid, the capital and largest city. And as in Japan, all routes are being assembled from scratch.

Ridership statistics indicate growing acceptance for the AVE. In early 2008 airlines accounted for 72 percent of the 4.8 million long-distance passengers in Spain who traveled by air or rail. Today that figure is down to 60 percent. High-speed rail travel in the country grew by 28 percent during the same period.

"The numbers will be equal within two years," says Josep Valls, a professor at the ESADE Business School in Barcelona.[1]

Moreover, high-speed rail tickets tend to be more affordable than air or road travel thanks largely to government subsidies, with one-way fares for the Madrid-Barcelona line as low as $50. Renfe, the state-owned company that operates the trains, claims a 99 percent on-time departure rate.

Doubts linger, however, over the profitability of such endeavors. Government-subsidized expansions to Japan's *Shinkansen*, along with the growth of air travel, had put the state-owned Japanese National Railways in the red by $200 billion by 1987, eventually leading to the privatization of high-speed rail in Japan. Further expansions, though, continue to receive government subsidies. A growing auto industry has also contributed to a steady decline in high-speed ridership, even during periods of rising fuel prices.

Similar subsidies abound in Europe, where motor fuel taxes of between 300 and 400 percent provide annual rail subsidies of about $100 billion. Furthermore, as in Japan, many countries are experiencing declining passenger levels at the expense of expanding automobile traffic.

The declining ridership has led TGV construction planners to reconsider the placement of intermediate stations in certain French localities, according to a report by the UK rail-research organization Greengauge21.[2]

But amid doubts over their viability, and even some questions over their usefulness, more and more high-speed lines are cropping up worldwide. Even China is getting on board. In April 2007 the country began operating several high-speed lines between major cities. Indeed, China's 3,800-mile network is longer than all European lines combined. China also boasts the Shanghai Maglev Train — the fastest commercial train in the world at 267 mph — although there have been criticisms over high ticket prices, limited operating hours and remote terminal locations.

A high-speed rail network also has emerged in nearby South Korea, with more planned in the Middle East and South Asia, in countries such as Iran, Saudi Arabia and India.

Despite the popularity of such trains, a lack of synergy between systems has historically complicated connections across national borders. Passengers on the TGV, for example, cannot easily make connecting reservations for high-speed trains on Germany's ICE system or take a train from southern France to Barcelona.

Last July seven European transportation representatives banded together to form Railteam, an alliance to create a seamless, high-speed network across Western Europe. Functioning much like an airline alliance, Railteam is coordinating a common reservation system that's scheduled to begin later this year.

"The idea of a European network of high-speed rail is at last being realized," said Guillaume Pépy, chairman of the high-speed London-Brussels-Paris Eurostar train service. "It will be a real alternative to air travel."[3]

— ***Darrell Dela Rosa***

---

* High-speed rail is usually defined as capable of 125 mph or more; the Amtrak Acela in the Northeast Corridor can hit 150 mph on short segments of the route.

[1] See Giles Tremlett, "Spain's High-Speed Trains Win Over Fed-Up Flyers," *The Guardian*, Jan. 13, 2009, www.guardian.co.uk/world/2009/jan/13/spain-trains.

[2] See "High Speed Trains and the Development and Regeneration of Cities," *Greengauge21*, June 2006.

[3] See Carol Matlack, "High-Speed Trains Erode Europe's Borders," *Spiegel Online*, Jan. 10, 2008, www.spiegel.de/international/business/0,1518,druck-527794,00.html.

Continued from p. 404

"[F]ew people live or work in downtowns anymore," wrote the Cato Institute's O'Toole. "As a result, even a 200-mph train won't take more than 3 or 4 percent of cars off the highways it parallels. Instead, the main effect of this heavily subsidized train will be to put struggling (and relatively unsubsidized) short-haul airlines out of business." [28]

Many also argue that U.S. policies that keep gas prices and road tolls low dampen demand for passenger rail — and its potential to reduce auto congestion. Without a change in U.S. oil policy, high-speed rail "is certainly less viable" here than in Europe or Asia, says Louis Thompson, who served as rail-policy adviser at the World Bank and associate administrator of the Federal Railroad Administration.

"In Europe and Japan, gas is $5 or $6 a gallon. That's what restricts auto travel. In the United States, we're pursuing what amounts to a conflicting policy."

Is high-speed rail good for the environment?

Besides high-speed rail's impact on infrastructure costs and congestion, a primary benefit of rail, proponents say, is its ability to reduce environmental damage. But skeptics say the environmental benefits of supertrains are often exaggerated.

Capon of the National Association of Railroad Passengers calls rail "green" transportation. "It is environmentally friendly, more energy efficient, supports energy-efficient real estate development as opposed to sprawl and it addresses quality-of-life issues and room-for-growth issues. In many cases the space doesn't exist to build the highways or airports that would be needed if you try to continue to be the only major industrialized nation that did it without a modern train system."

In California, the proposed train system would cut the state's carbon dioxide (CO_2) emissions — the main component of climate-warming greenhouse gases — by 12 billion pounds each year and reduce foreign-oil dependence by nearly 13 million barrels a year by 2030, the rail authority said. "Since it will use electric power, high-speed trains can be a key element in helping California meet . . . greenhouse-gas reduction goals" under a 2006 state act requiring emissions to drop to 1990 levels by 2020, "and will have far less environmental impact than expanding highways and airports." [29]

High-speed trains would reduce intercity car travel and provide Californians with more than $13.8 billion in highway-related benefits stemming from reduced traffic accidents and air pollution, the state rail authority says. That estimate likely understates environmental benefits, it says, because it includes only reductions in primary pollutants such as carbon monoxide and hydrocarbons.

In the Midwest, 110-mph trains running between Chicago and St. Louis would spew lower amounts of harmful gases, such as volatile organic compounds (VOCs) and carbon monoxide (CO), than cars and airplanes, and less nitrous oxides than cars per passenger mile, the Midwest High Speed Rail Association says. [30]

"High-speed trains draw power from the electrical grid, which is fueled primarily by domestically produced energy sources, such as coal," wrote Paul Weinstein Jr., chief operating officer of the Progressive Policy Institute, a liberal think tank in Washington. "Plus, trains require about one-third as much energy per passenger mile as automobiles and airplanes. Although nothing powered through the grid is entirely carbon-neutral, high-speed trains produce no direct emissions."

What's more, Weinstein said, high-speed rail produces half the carbon-dioxide emissions as airplanes and one-sixth that of cars. [31]

But critics are highly skeptical of the environmental benefits claimed by supporters.

"People trying to pass this off as green are almost bordering on the scary," says Alan E. Pisarski, author of a series of statistical reports on commuting trends published by the Transportation Research Board, part of the National Academy of Sciences. He points to the "embedded costs" and greenhouse-gas emissions inherent in building tracks and tunnels, leveling ground and doing other construction work for high-speed rail.

What's more, he says, the energy-saving potential of a rail system depends significantly on how electricity is generated to power the trains. If a train uses hydropower generated by the Hoover Dam, that's one thing, Pisarski says, "but if there are railcars bringing coal from Chicago" to run a bullet train, "it doesn't make a whole lot of sense."

Others are similarly skeptical. "[T]he environmental benefits will be minuscule," the Cato Institute's O'Toole argued. He labeled as "flawed," for example, an estimate that high-speed rail in California would save the amount of energy used to build the system in just five years.

"If autos and airplanes become, over the life of the high-speed rail project, an average of 20 percent more fuel efficient than they are today, then the payback period for high-speed rail rises to 25 years," he wrote. And that payback period "crucially depends" on the train system attracting the "high" ridership forecast by the rail authority.

"If ridership is lower, the payback period will be longer. And since rail lines require expensive and energy-intensive reconstruction and rehabilitation about every 30 years, it is quite possible that high-speed rail will save no energy at all." [32]

Continued on p. 408

Chronology

1869-1960
Train travel booms, but jet travel and interstate highways lead to a decline.

1869
Transcontinental Railroad completed.

1893
Train reaches record 112.5 mph in western New York.

1920
Passenger volumes on U.S. railroads peak, but then plunge during the Great Depression.

1941-1945
Wartime restrictions on autos spur ridership, but growing car ownership, the Interstate Highway System and jet travel soon lure people away from railroads.

1960
Trains carry about 327 million Americans, less than a third of the peak volumes of the 1920s.

1960s-1970s
Japan launches bullet train, but supertrains remain stalled in U.S.

1964
Japanese *Shinkansen* bullet-train links Tokyo and Osaka.

1965
High Speed Ground Transportation Act starts federal effort to develop high-speed rail technologies.

1968
Gordon T. Danby and James R. Powell of Brookhaven National Laboratory patent a magnetic levitation train.

1969
Metroliner begins service between Washington and New York.

1970
Rail Passenger Service Act leads to creation of Amtrak.

1974
Vehicle on rails sets speed record of 255.4 mph in Pueblo, Colo.

1978
U.S. airline industry is deregulated, helping to introduce low-cost fares and further suppress rail travel.

1980s-1990s
France and Germany make huge strides in high-speed rail, but plans stall in U.S.

1981
French TGV high-speed passenger rail line links Paris and Lyon.

1990
Department of Transportation commits $10 million for study of magnetic levitation rail technology; TGV hits record 320 mph.

1991
Germany introduces InterCity Express (ICE) high-speed rail service.

1992
Federal officials designate high-speed rail corridors in Midwest, Florida, California, Southeast and Pacific Northwest.

1998
German ICE train derails, killing 101 and injuring 88 in worst high-speed rail disaster. . . . Transportation Equity Act for the 21st Century authorizes six additional high-speed corridors.

2000-Present
High-speed rail gets financial boost from Washington.

2000
Amtrak's Acela Express begins service between Washington and Boston; Florida voters pass constitutional amendment requiring that a bullet train be built in the state, but the project is opposed by then-Gov. Jeb Bush; the amendment is repealed in 2004.

2001
Terrorist attacks in New York, Washington and Pennsylvania lead to shutdown of commercial airline system and surge in Amtrak ridership, notably in Northeast Corridor.

2007
Japan announces plan for privately financed magnetic levitation train in 2025.

2008
Gas prices surge to more than $4 a gallon before falling back, helping to revive support for passenger rail. . . . California voters approve $9.95 billion bond issue to help pay for proposed high-speed rail line between San Francisco and Los Angeles. . . . Plans for a German maglev train linking central Munich to city's airport are halted.

2009
Obama administration includes $8 billion for high-speed and other rail projects in $787 billion economic stimulus bill and seeks $5 billion over five years in 2010 budget; stimulus money boosts hopes of rail supporters but leads to Republican charges of wasteful spending; Obama administration issues strategic plan for high-speed rail, with grants to come as soon as late summer.

'Maglev' Proponents Push Projects in U.S.

But critics cite high cost and limited passenger demand.

The world's most advanced method of ground transport is attracting renewed attention in the United States. Magnetic levitation is as controversial as it is remarkable.

"Maglev" uses industrial-strength magnets to lift train cars a small distance above a special guideway and propel them at airplane speeds — 260 mph or even faster.

The theories behind magnetic levitation technology have been around for decades, but obstacles ranging from financing and logistics to questionable passenger demand and worries about the effects of electromagnetism on health have slowed maglev development, especially in the United States.

Now, however, proponents in Nevada, Pennsylvania and elsewhere are moving ahead with plans they hope will result someday in full-fledged maglev systems.

Critics say maglev systems are costly to build, require special infrastructure that regular trains can't utilize and consume such vast amounts of energy that they are harmful to the environment.

"You talk about an electricity hog," charges transportation consultant Wendell Cox, a former member of the Los Angeles County Transportation Commission, who is critical of high-speed rail projects generally. "Maglev is an environmental outlaw."

Moreover, some argue that maglev systems won't draw enough riders to justify their cost. While they can be super swift, such systems are not much faster than some less expensive high-speed trains that use conventional steel tracks. On the other hand, maglev systems don't move as rapidly as jet aircraft, making it hard for them to compete with planes on longer routes.

Proponents, however, have a far different view of maglev. They argue that the technology is more efficient than traditional steel-rail systems and less costly to maintain.

Magnetic levitation systems "represent a transportation revolution because several inherently undesirable characteristics of wheeled transport are eliminated or dramatically reduced, namely vibration, noise and wear and tear on parts from friction," according to Kevin C. Coates, a founder of the International Maglev Board. "Higher speeds are achievable without the penalty of increased maintenance costs. This translates into higher system reliability and increased sustainability due to the resulting longer service life and lower life-cycle costs."[1]

While maglev technology has been in development for decades in Japan and elsewhere, few systems are running or planned so far worldwide.

China, as one example, operates a system linking the Pudong commercial district in Shanghai to the city's airport. Speeds reach 268 miles per hour on the 19-mile route, cutting a 45-minute car trip to eight minutes.[2] But protests have arisen over extending the system, and residents have expressed concern over noise and potential effects of electromagnetic radiation.[3] In addition, 80 percent of the seats often are empty, and travelers have complained that the terminus station "is in the middle of nowhere, requiring a transfer to taxi or subway," according to *Wired*'s *Autopia* blog last year.[4]

In Japan, where maglev demonstrations have gone on for years, the country's central railway company announced plans

Continued from p. 406

Levitt, the California rail authority deputy director, defends the environmental benefits of a supertrain system in his state, however.

"Not only would it cost more" to expand highways and airports to meet future travel demand, he says, "but the environmental impacts would be considerably greater. It's not only in the fact that high-speed rail brings benefits for reduced CO_2 emissions and reduced energy consumption and dependence on fossil fuels. High-speed rail also is more compatible with California's goals for sustainable development. So it's not just the cost of building the roads, it's the environmental cost and the future-growth-of-the-state costs that need to be considered." ∎

BACKGROUND

The Golden Spike

Railroads have operated in the United States since the early 19th century, but it was a golden spike, driven into the barren soil of northern Utah in 1869, that trumpeted rail's promise to move people long distances at relatively fast speeds. There, at Promontory Summit, the Union Pacific and Central Pacific railroads were joined in the nation's first transcontinental system, spanning more than 1,500 miles from Omaha to Sacramento.

The project was marred by the Credit Mobilier scandal, in which Union Pacific officials enriched themselves in building the rail line. Nonetheless, the six-year endeavor stands as a watershed of technological achievement and personal mobility and a model of what high-speed rail enthusiasts hope to see repeated today.[33]

The transcontinental railroad was an example of "bold action and big ideas" accomplished during a time of "economic upheaval and transformation," President Obama reminded a joint session of Congress in February. "In the midst of civil war, we laid railroad tracks from one coast to another that spurred commerce and industry."[34]

in 2007 to build a maglev train linking Tokyo and Nagoya. The 180-mile route is supposed to open in 2025 and be financed entirely by the private sector. [5]

But in Germany, which also has had successful maglev demonstrations, plans for a maglev link from central Munich to the city's airport were halted last year. Construction costs had nearly doubled from $2.9 billion to $5.33 billion. [6]

No maglev systems operate in the United States, but proponents have been hoping that money set aside for high-speed rail in this year's $787 billion federal stimulus package will include maglev funding.

The federal government separately has made $45 million available to help finance preliminary work related to a proposed maglev link between Las Vegas and Anaheim, Calif., and it will soon make another $45 million available for projects east of the Mississippi River, according to Federal Railroad Administration (FRA) spokesman Warren Flatau. From fiscal 1999 to fiscal 2005, another $60 million was provided to maglev projects around the country, he said.

The East Coast region includes a proposed maglev system linking the Pittsburgh airport with the city and its eastern sub-

A maglev train links Shanghai's financial district with the city's airport. Speeds reach 268 miles per hour on the 19-mile route.

urbs. The FRA is close to issuing an environmental impact statement for the project, Flatau said. That could bring it a step closer to reality. Other projects that have been proposed in the eastern United States would link Baltimore and Washington, and Atlanta with Chattanooga.

The Las Vegas-Anaheim system has been in the planning stages for two decades. But funding and other obstacles so far have kept it from being built, and now it faces competition from a proposed, privately financed electric or diesel/electric wheel-on-steel train. [7]

[1] Kevin C. Coates, "Finally, Maglev Leadership," *Engineering News-Record*, March 2, 2009, http://enr.construction.com/opinions/viewPoint/2009/0225-MaglevLeadership.asp.

[2] "Maglev — the Great Debate," railway-technology.com, Feb. 11, 2008, www.railway-technology.com/features/feature1606/.

[3] *Ibid.*

[4] Alexander Lew, "Maglev Project in Munich: Cancelled," *Autopia* blog, March 28, 2008, http://blog.wired.com/cars/2008/03/maglev-project.html.

[5] "Maglev — The Great Debate," *op. cit.*

[6] Lew, *op. cit.*

[7] Abby Sewell, "City Council Votes to Support Anaheim to Vegas Train," *Desert Dispatch*, April 2, 2009.

As technology advanced in the late 19th and early 20th centuries, so too did train speeds. In 1893, the steam locomotive Empire State Express No. 999 reached a record 112.5 mph in western New York, becoming the first object on wheels to exceed 100 mph. [35] In the 1930s, the diesel-powered Zephyr matched that speed on a Denver-to-Chicago run. [36]

Still, ridership waxed and waned during the last century. The number of passengers carried by trains doubled between 1900 and the end of World War I but then dropped more than 60 percent during the Great Depression. Ridership regained some ground during World War II as government restricted the use of private autos. But after the

war, rising car ownership, construction of the Interstate Highway System and the advent of jet travel all helped to throw train travel into reverse. By 1960, passenger counts were only about half what they were in the opening years of the century. [37]

Meanwhile, the heavily regulated railroad industry was losing freight business to trucking, crimping the ability of the railroads to subsidize money-losing passenger routes.

In a review of high-speed rail issues in the mid-1990s, Thompson, the former World Bank adviser, wrote that "misguided government regulation of the railways — politically distorted rates and inability to adjust services — was one of the primary

reasons for the rail dilemma," along with government support of the highway and airline systems. [38]

Financial problems among the railroads led to a number of mergers and attempts by rail executives to close money-draining passenger routes. The federal government resisted many of those efforts, but as the 1960s came to a close passenger service in the United States was losing steam fast.

"The number of trains, which had reached 20,000 in 1920, was down to 500, and over 100 of these were the subject of discontinuance proceedings," economics professor George W. Hilton wrote in a 1980 study for the American Enterprise Institute. [39]

High-Speed Rail

Meanwhile, new high-speed rail technology was emerging on the global scene. In 1964 Japan began *Shinkansen* bullet-train service between Tokyo and Osaka, initially running at up to 125 mph. [40] In France, test runs of the electrified TGV (*Train à Grande Vitesse*) had begun in the early 1970s.

In the United States, bullet trains gained no traction. Still, federal officials remained interested in fast-rail travel. In 1965 Congress passed the High-Speed Ground Transportation Act, marking the start of an effort by the federal government to improve travel speeds. [41]

"In recent decades we have achieved technological miracles in our transportation," President Lyndon B. Johnson said in signing the act, "but there is one great exception. . . . We have the same tired and inadequate mass transportation between our towns and cities that we had 30 years ago." [42]

The Office of High-Speed Ground Transportation, then in the Department of Transportation, financed the development of new technology for use in the busy Northeast Corridor: electrically powered Metroliners for the Washington-New York segment, and gas-turbine-powered trains for the New York-Boston segment that would tilt around curves to help them travel faster. Metroliners and the jet-engine Turbotrains were capable of 160 and 170 mph, respectively, though track conditions and other problems forced considerably lower speeds. [43]

At the heart of the Metroliner's development was the late Robert Nelson, a professor of transportation economics who became head of the new Office of High-Speed Ground Transportation in 1965.

Nelson commissioned a study by Massachusetts Institute of Technology engineers to forecast transportation innovations over the next 15 years,

according to a *Washington Post* obituary on Nelson, who died last month. "In their report, the engineers envisioned jet-propelled, rail-less trains whisking through enclosed tubes on a cushion of air, [but] Dr. Nelson wanted more immediate results," the newspaper said.

"He prodded the Pennsylvania Railroad into signing a contract to demonstrate the viability of high-speed trains in the Washington-New York corridor" and won White House support and congressional and media attention. "To the surprise of almost everyone, the first Metroliner demonstration trains began running in 1968" — just a year after the Department of Transportation and the Federal Railroad Administration were created. [44]

While the Metroliner was a promising development, the American railroad industry was all but bankrupt by the early 1970s, and passenger rail needed rescuing if it was to survive at any speed.

Creation of Amtrak

In 1970 Congress passed legislation that led to the formation of Amtrak, which began operating the following year. It assumed from freight railroads the costly job of operating intercity rail service in most of the nation, including the busy Northeast Corridor. [45]

Today, The Congressional Research Service noted in a recent report, Amtrak operates some 44 routes over 22,000 miles of track, nearly all of it owned by freight-rail companies. (Exceptions are the 440-mile Northeast Corridor and a small section of track in Michigan.)

Although Amtrak was created as a for-profit enterprise, it has not made money — something it has in common with intercity passenger rail services in other nations, the report said. "During the last 35 years, federal assis-

tance to Amtrak has amounted to approximately \$30 billion." [46]

Under the \$787 billion stimulus bill passed this year by Congress, Amtrak will get \$1.3 billion for bridge and passenger-car repairs and other needs. "For too long," said Vice President Joseph Biden, a regular rider and strong supporter of the railway, "we haven't made the investments we needed to make Amtrak as safe, as reliable, as secure as it can be. That ends now." [47]

Over the years, though, some have been highly critical of Amtrak. "[T]he organization spends its capital subsidies on fruitless programs and remains insensitive to the travel marketplace," former High Speed Rail Association president Vranich wrote in a 2004 book, *End of the Line: The Failure of Amtrak Reform and the Future of America's Passenger Trains*. "[W]hile the United States needs passenger trains in selected heavily populated corridors, it does not need Amtrak's antiquated, far-flung route system, high operating costs, poor management practices that deflect innovation and capital program with abysmal rates of return." [48]

But supporters of Amtrak say government officials have stacked the deck against passenger rail, in part by subsidizing highways and air travel while withholding adequate money for infrastructure improvements to the rail network. Advocates such as National Corridors Initiative CEO RePass want to change that.

"Passenger trains do not pay for themselves anywhere in the world," he says. "They're too capital-intensive. But if you have a system to reinvest some revenue, then they can pay for themselves." RePass favors a system of Transportation Infrastructure Investment Zones, in which a portion of tax revenue collected within an area bordering a rail corridor is dedicated to infrastructure improvements along the rail line.

In Search of Supertrains

I n the early 1980s, partly in hopes of expanding Amtrak's political and funding support in Congress, Amtrak and the Department of Transportation began studying regions outside the Northeast Corridor that conceivably could support higher-speed systems. Grants totaling $4 million were allocated in 1984 for state studies on high-speed rail, and by 1986 at least a half-dozen states, including California, Florida and Texas, had created high-speed rail entities. [49]

Still, no supertrains emerged on the American landscape, but several states tried to move forward with private ventures, as Thompson noted in his mid-1990s review. [50]

• In California, Amtrak and Japanese investors proposed a Japanese bullet train-style system. The effort failed because of local opposition, doubts about ridership forecasts, questions about the ability of the private sector to bring the project to reality and the refusal of the federal and state governments to help finance the project.

• In Texas, a private consortium sought to link Dallas/Fort Worth, Houston and San Antonio using French TGV technology, but "the private sector alone simply was not capable of bringing the project to fruition," Thompson wrote. [51] In addition, it ran into opposition from Southwest Airlines, which saw the train as potential competition. [52]

• In Florida, a state commission offered a concession to private investors who would build and operate a system linking Tampa, Orlando and Miami, and a group headed by a real-estate development firm was named the winner. But projected profits were deemed insufficient, and state and federal officials declined to provide money.

Florida continued to try to develop a high-speed rail system, and in 2000 voters approved a constitutional amendment requiring that a bullet train

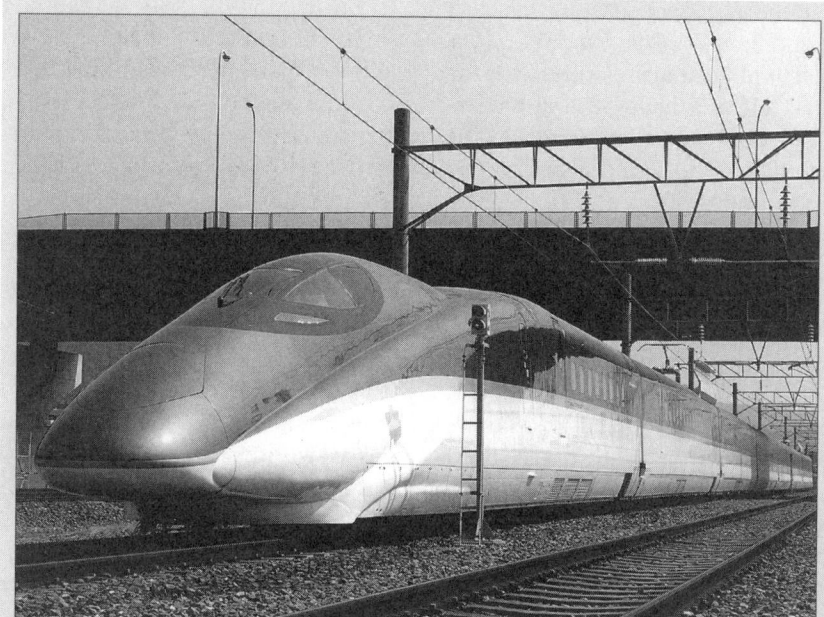

High-Speed, into the Future

The East Japan Railway's next-generation bullet train (top) is slated to hit 223 mph. Taiwan's bullet train (bottom) went into service in January 2007, linking the island's north and south at speeds up to 190 mph. Japan launched the high-speed era in 1964 with its Shinkansen *bullet train between Tokyo and Osaka. France, another high-speed pioneer, began test runs of the TGV in the early 1970s.*

be constructed in the state. But the project met heavy opposition from former Republican Gov. Jeb Bush, and voters subsequently repealed the amendment.

Ultimately, it was Amtrak that developed what has come to stand as the nation's most visible effort at high-speed train service: the Acela Express. Amtrak CEO Joe Boardman said the Acela has demonstrated that "we can do high-speed rail and reduce the trip time enough to make rail competitive with air." [53]

But the Acela also has drawn sharp criticism. In *End of the Line*, Vranich, a former public-affairs spokesman for Amtrak, offers a highly critical rendering of Acela's development, pointing to design flaws, neglected infrastructure and on-time performance problems. "The bottom line is that no other country in the world took so long to create a train as Amtrak did with Acela only to wind up with so technologically deficient a product," Vranich says.

While some rail proponents express disappointment that Amtrak hasn't done more to foster European-style high-speed rail in the United States, Thompson, in his mid-1990s review of the issue, noted the challenges Amtrak faces.

Amtrak's role is fragmented among providing high-density service in the Northeast Corridor, short intercity routes such as Los Angeles-San Diego and long-haul routes, he pointed out. Its "support comes from a political coalition requiring the agreement of supporters of all three types of service. Anything leading Amtrak too much in one direction comes at the potential cost of one of the others, and Amtrak's annual struggle for funding is usually too serious to permit offending any of its supporters." [54]

As individual states contemplate regional high-speed rail lines, some rail proponents advocate a nationwide web of supertrains — a 21st-century version of the transcontinental railroad that transformed the nation in the 19th century.

But others are deeply skeptical that a supertrain network spanning the entire continental United States makes sense. Schwantes, the University of Missouri transportation-studies professor, points out that distances from one end of the United States to another are far greater than in a country like France. "Chicago to Los Angeles would take, full bore, probably 10 hours" at the speed of a French TGV. "That," he says, "is still six hours longer than aviation."

Even without a nation-spanning system, the question remains why no true bullet trains have been built here, even on a regional or intercity basis, either by private investors or Amtrak, when they have been in existence elsewhere for more than 40 years.

"The key reasons are geography and demographics," says Thompson. "With some exceptions, we don't have the relatively short-haul, high-density markets that the Europeans have. That doesn't mean we won't develop them in the future, or that high-speed rail won't cause them to develop."

Low gas prices and massive investments in the Interstate Highway System also give Americans an incentive to drive rather than ride the rails, Thompson says.

And, he says, deregulation of the U.S. airline industry since 1978 also has lured travelers away from rail. In Europe and Japan, airlines were for many years run as state monopolies that kept air fares high, spurring rail travel, Thompson says. But, he says, passenger volume on some European trains has fallen as discount airlines have arisen to serve short routes such as Amsterdam-Paris. [55] ■

CURRENT SITUATION

Obama's Efforts

Before passage of the $787 billion stimulus bill — and its $8 billion for high-speed rail — White House Chief of Staff Rahm Emanuel asked House and Senate negotiators for an even bigger rail allocation: $10 billion, according to the online publication *Politico*.

"I put it in there for the president," Emanuel said. "The president wanted to have a signature issue in the bill, his commitment for the future." [56]

"This is not some fanciful, pie-in-the-sky vision of the future," Obama insisted in April as he announced the administration's strategic rail plan. "It's happening now. The problem is, it's happening elsewhere," the president said, citing countries that already have high-speed rail, such as Japan and France. [57]

But as the Obama administration presses ahead with spending on high-speed rail, Republican opponents are pushing back, underscoring the steep political terrain that proponents must climb if they are to see their dreams become reality.

Gov. Bobby Jindal of Louisiana, in the Republican response to Obama's address to Congress in February, said the stimulus package was "larded with wasteful spending," and he pointed to the $8 billion rail allocation as an example. [58]

Earlier, some Republicans tried to attribute the rail allocation in the federal stimulus bill to Senate Majority Leader Harry Reid, claiming he'd wanted it for a proposed high-speed line between Las Vegas in his home state of Nevada and Anaheim, Calif. But Reid told *Politico* he "didn't have much to do with" getting the rail outlay into the stimulus bill, and indeed the publication said, "there's little evidence that Reid had a decisive role." [59]

As the Department of Transportation figures out how to divide up the stimulus money among competing rail projects, fiscal reality is tempering the enthusiasm of those who hope to see European-style supertrains speeding through the American landscape.

For one thing, says former Federal Railroad Administration official Thompson, "$8 billion will not build very much. It may be good seed money, but if anybody thinks it's going to lead to a shiny, new high-speed rail system in a few years, no it isn't."

Continued on p. 414

At Issue:

Is high-speed rail a good investment?

WILLIAM W. MILLAR
PRESIDENT, AMERICAN PUBLIC TRANSPORTATION ASSOCIATION

WRITTEN FOR *CQ RESEARCHER*, APRIL 2009

*i*nvestment in high-speed rail now is essential for our country's future. It will not only provide greater mobility but also create economic prosperity, combat climate change and help to reduce our dependence on foreign oil. The vision of a connected America will not be complete without world-class high-speed rail.

It is time for an integrated transportation strategy that will increase mobility by maximizing the capacity and the efficiency of the nation's rail, road and aviation network. Congestion on our country's highways needs to be alleviated. The latest data from the Texas Transportation Institute state that highway congestion costs the United States more than $78 billion each year, and the average traveler is delayed in traffic almost 40 hours a year.

Intercity rail and high-speed rail that connect with airports and city core areas can also do a lot to mitigate air-traffic congestion. In much of Europe and in the Northeast Corridor of the United States, train travel is faster than airline travel, door-to-door. While air travel is the logical alternative for longer-distance trips, high-speed rail can efficiently accommodate many of the shorter-distance corridor services, connecting regional economic centers and providing a feeder service to airlines.

Beyond improving mobility and helping reduce congestion, the use of high-speed rail travel — instead of short-distance air travel and longer-distance highway trips — will significantly reduce energy consumption and greenhouse-gas emissions. Currently the use of public transportation in the United States saves 4.2 billion gallons of gasoline and reduces carbon emissions by 37 million metric tons. Imagine how much greater our energy savings and carbon reduction could be with the addition of high-speed rail service in corridors across the country.

The economic stimulus funds provided by the American Recovery and Reinvestment Act represent a down payment on what will become an ongoing high-speed and intercity rail program. This program will be the foundation of a new vision for American communities, while providing green jobs and helping create a sustainable future.

The bottom line is that a high-speed rail network can help America meet its national goals of economic growth, sustainability, energy independence and mobility. As a worthwhile investment for our future, high-speed rail is an idea that is right for the times and right for a new America.

RANDAL O'TOOLE
SENIOR FELLOW CATO INSTITUTE

WRITTEN FOR *CQ RESEARCHER*, APRIL 2009

i love trains, so at first the idea of high-speed rail sounded great. But when I examined it in detail, I found high-speed trains are an expensive form of travel that few people will use.

Throughout history, passenger trains served mainly a wealthy elite and have never given the average people of any nation even half as much mobility as our interstate highways. Moreover, the interstates paid for themselves out of gas taxes and other user fees, while high-speed rail requires huge subsidies from general taxpayers.

Adjusting for inflation, Japan has spent as much per capita, and France at least half as much, on high-speed rail as we spent on our Interstate Highway System. The average American travels 4,000 miles each year, and ships 2,000 ton-miles of freight, on the interstates. Meanwhile, the average residents of Japan and France ride only 400 miles per year on their bullet trains and TGVs, which carry no freight.

In developed nations, people of all income levels regularly travel by car, while only a small number regularly ride high-speed trains. For example, the average American drives for 85 percent of travel; the average resident of France 79 percent — not much difference.

Travelers pay at least $99 to ride Amtrak's subsidized Acela from New York to Washington. When unsubsidized bus fares start at $20, regular Acela riders are mainly bankers, bureaucrats and lobbyists whose expenses are covered by their employers.

High-speed rail's environmental benefits are also questionable. Autos and airplanes get more energy efficient every year. By the time high-speed trains are running, they are likely to use as much energy and emit as much greenhouse gas, per passenger mile, as the average car or jet plane. The moderate-speed, 110-mile-per-hour diesel trains that President Obama proposes in most regions will be especially polluting.

True high-speed trains are electrically powered, but electricity that comes from fossil fuels will produce as much greenhouse gas, per passenger mile, as autos or planes. As we develop more renewable electricity, we would do better to dedicate that power to plug-in hybrids or electric cars than to expensive but little-used trains.

We have a choice between a transportation system that everyone uses and that pays for itself, or one that everyone pays for through their taxes but is regularly used by only a small elite. Which is the better symbol for the America President Obama wants to build?

Continued from p. 412

What's more, the Transportation Department can use the $8 billion in any of three ways: to improve existing intercity passenger service, upgrade conventional trains to 110-mph service or help pay for high-speed rail development. It is not clear how the money will be divided among those options.

Nor is it clear whether outlays for high-speed rail will be concentrated in a few regions, such as California, the Northeast Corridor and the Midwest, or allocated more broadly among the federally designated high-speed corridors.

GOP Response

Beyond the stimulus money, Obama proposed an additional $5 billion in his budget for high-speed rail over five years. It is not clear how the proposal will fare in congressional budget battles. An alternate budget plan released by House Republicans in March makes no mention of rail projects and says the administration's budget "spends too much, taxes too much and borrows too much." [60]

Still, some Republicans have voiced strong support for high-speed rail projects. In addition to Transportation Secretary LaHood, they include Florida Rep. John L. Mica, the ranking Republican on the House Transportation and Infrastructure Committee. Mica has praised the $8 billion allocation for high-speed rail despite having voted against the overall $787 billion stimulus measure.

"If we could put a man on the moon, we should be able to move people from city to city quickly instead of wasting time on a congested highway," said Mica, whose home state is a prime high-speed rail contender. "I applaud President Obama's recognition that high-speed rail should be part of America's future." [61]

Mica has promoted the idea of a line between New York and Washington that would cut travel time to less than two hours, compared with the Acela's current 2 hours, 42 minutes, with stops. [62] "We think the

Germany's high-speed ICE ("Inter City Express") trains were launched in the late 1980s. Last July seven European nations formed an alliance to create a seamless, high-speed network across Western Europe. Railteam will operate a coordinated reservation system that's scheduled to begin in late 2009.

United States shouldn't become a Third World country when it comes to high-speed service," Mica said. [63]

On the Drawing Board

As federal officials prepare to begin allocating the rail-related stimulus money, a number of projects are likely contenders. Among them:

• **The Midwest network** — Covering some 3,000 miles in nine states — Illinois, Indiana, Iowa, Michigan, Minnesota, Missouri, Nebraska, Ohio and Wisconsin — it would use trains reaching 110 mph. A trip between Chicago and St. Paul, now eight hours, could be reduced to five hours, 30 minutes. [64]

"A network of states produces much better results than each individual state going its own way," said Randy Wade, passenger rail manager at the Wisconsin Department of Transportation, which is coordinating the Midwest effort. "We now have a political network, too, comprised of at least 18 U.S. senators." [65]

Learner, of the Environmental Law and Policy Center, points out that not only are Obama and chief of staff Emanuel from Illinois but so too are other key administration figures, including LaHood, Federal Railroad Administration chief Joseph Szabo and Amtrak board chairman Thomas Carper. Agriculture Secretary Tom Vilsack is a former governor of Iowa, another state in the Midwest network.

Learner also noted that Democratic Illinois Sen. Dick Durbin has been doggedly pushing for rail funding in his home state and has played a role in getting expanded funding for Amtrak.

"I don't want to pretend it's a done deal," Learner says of federal support for the Midwest rail network. "It's not right just to look at Illinois. On the other hand, the stars are very well-aligned for substantial federal support on the merits and because its advocates are well-positioned in the current administration and Congress."

AFP/Getty Images/John MacDougall

- **North Carolina** — A goal is 85-mph service linking Charlotte and Raleigh as part of building faster rail service along the 450-mile Southeast corridor between Washington and Charlotte. Officials say the passengers could go from Charlotte to Raleigh in two hours and 15 minutes, or about an hour less than is possible today. [66]

"You're not building a high-end, sexy bullet train, but you're building network capacity and reliability," Patrick Simmons, director of the North Carolina Department of Transportation rail division, told the *Charlotte Observer.* [67]

- **Florida** — Advocates are trying to revive plans for a high-speed route linking Tampa, Orlando and Miami after its derailment by former Gov. Bush. But the project depends on the support of current Republican Gov. Charlie Crist, who only recently endorsed the high-speed rail project. [68]

The Florida High Speed Rail Authority, which met in February for the first time in four years, wants to seek $2.5 billion in rail funds, according to the *Orlando Sentinel.* The newspaper said a 25-mile segment linking the Orange County Convention Center, Orlando International Airport and Celebration, a residential community developed by Walt Disney World, would run $1 billion. A line between the Orlando airport and Tampa would cost $2.5 billion, the *Sentinel* said. [69]

- **Texas** — Supporters want a train averaging 200 mph between Houston, San Antonio and Dallas by 2020, and after the state's failed attempt at high-speed rail 15 years ago, they are taking a new approach. [70]

"In the past, high-speed rail was not completed in Texas primarily because it was a top-down model driven by lobbyists out of Austin," the state capital, Robert Eckels, chairman of the nonprofit Texas High Speed Rail and Transportation Corp., told a state transportation briefing. [71]

But Eckels said a consortium that includes elected leaders, cities and counties and two airlines has now sought to address concerns of past opponents, according to the *Houston Chronicle.* A spokesman for Southwest Airlines told the *Chronicle* the company was neutral on the current proposal. [72]

Still, some landowners along the proposed route are troubled. "From a rural, agricultural standpoint, we're very concerned," Central Texas farmer Richard Cortese, a county commissioner and a leader in the Texas Farm Bureau, told the *San Antonio Express News.* "It just seems like every time we turn around, someone's got us in their crosshairs." [73]

- **Las Vegas-Anaheim** — The proposed route would feature revolutionary magnetic levitation technology, which uses powerful magnets to suspend trains on a cushion of air and propel them at rapid speeds along a special guideway. The Nevada project has been in the works for years but has struggled over money and other obstacles. It was unclear this spring whether the project will qualify for federal stimulus funds. [74] (*See sidebar, p. 408.*) ■

OUTLOOK

California Dreaming

Efforts to improve passenger rail in the United States face daunting twists and turns in the years ahead, whether the plan involves boosting the speed of conventional trains to 110 mph or building a true supertrain system like the one planned in California.

Because it would be the nation's most ambitious rail corridor and most like the bullet-train systems found overseas, the California project is generating some of the most attention.

Some are optimistic that it can attract sufficient money from private sources, in addition to government funds, to become reality. Development around stations will help make the project financially feasible, they contend.

But others are highly skeptical. "Unless they come up with a massive dose of federal money, I can't conceive of them going through with it," says Pisarski, the transportation consultant and author on commuting trends.

Less elaborate projects, such as raising the speed of conventional passenger trains in the Midwest, may not stir the same degree of excitement as do true bullet trains, but that doesn't bother supporters.

"Let's not let perfection get in the way of good," says Learner of the Environmental Law and Policy Center. Speeds of 110 mph "can be a huge jump-start. We ought to get that up and running."

Noting Obama's commitment to trains, Learner says, "We have a once-in-a-lifetime political and economic opportunity to achieve a breakthrough in higher-speed rail. At the same time, we ought to be thinking longer-term and planning for a future in which we can upgrade to European- or Japanese-style 200-mph high-speed rail. But one does not preclude the other."

Others, too, point to the Obama influence as a harbinger of growing government support for passenger rail.

"The fact that Mr. Obama seems to have stepped forward and said trains [are a priority] is important," says Ditmeyer, the former Federal Railroad Administration research and development director. "Some of us have waited our entire career for someone to say something like that."

But critics of high-speed rail worry that Washington's efforts to pour money into passenger rail will become something akin to adding steam to a runaway locomotive.

"We've got a little momentum, they're going to spend a bunch of money, it's not going to do much good, agencies are going to claim great success and the few people who ride [high-speed rail] are going to join coalitions to get more," says the Cato Institute's O'Toole.

Pisarski compares the push to finance new high-speed rail networks — especially expensive ones like the California supertrain — to "going to the moon" during the Kennedy administration.

"It suggests you're taking a new direction," he says. "But I would hope they do a rational analysis. I can't think of a situation where they could possibly justify it, other than on the grounds of greater glory." ∎

Notes

[1] For background see Richard L. Worsnop, "High-Speed Rail," *CQ Researcher*, April 16, 1993, pp. 313-336 and Peter Katel, "Emerging China," *CQ Researcher*, Nov. 11, 2005, pp. 957-980.

[2] Brian Naylor, "Stimulus Puts High-Speed Rail On The Fast Track," National Public Radio, Feb. 24, 2009, www.npr.org/templates/story/story.php?storyId=101073906. For background see Marcia Clemmitt, "Public-Works Projects," *CQ Researcher*, Feb. 20, 2009, pp. 153-176.

[3] For background see Kenneth Jost, *et al.*, "The Obama Presidency," *CQ Researcher*, Jan. 30, 2009, pp. 73-104.

[4] See Brian Hansen, "Future of Amtrak," *CQ Researcher*, Oct. 18, 2002, pp. 841-864.

[5] Brian Knowlton, "Obama Seeks High-Speed Rail System Across U.S.," *The New York Times*, April 16, 2009, www.nytimes.com/2009/04/17/us/politics/17train.html?ref=politics.

[6] "Is High-Speed Rail Worth It?" *National Journal Expert Blogs*, March 23, 2009, response of Ray LaHood, Secretary of Transportation, http://transportation.nationaljournal.com/2009/03/is-highspeed-rail-worth-it.php.

[7] Marilyn Adams, "$8 billion could help revive travel by train," *USA Today*, March 16, 2009.

[8] Quoted in *Ibid*.

[9] California High-Speed Rail Authority, "Questions & Answers: Financing/Costs," accessed March 18, 2009, www.cahighspeedrail.ca.gov/faqs/financing.htm.

[10] Quentin Kopp, "High-speed trains will power California forward," *Capitol Weekly*, April 17, 2008, www.capitolweekly.net/article.php?issueId=x1uh8zbb6q8afq&xid=x1uzt54ux6stf4&_adctlid=v%7Cjq2q43wvsl855o%7Cx1wzkesety80ym.

[11] Wendell Cox, Joseph Vranich and Adrian T. Moore, "The California High Speed Rail Proposal: A Due Diligence Report," Reason Foundation, Citizens Against Government Waste and Howard Jarvis Taxpayers Foundation, September 2008.

[12] Randal O'Toole, "High-Speed Rail: The Wrong Road for America," Cato Institute, "Policy Analysis No. 625," Oct. 31, 2008, www.cato.org/pubs/pas/pa-625.pdf.

[13] "Midwest Regional Rail System," Transportation Economics & Management Systems Inc., February 2000, p. 21, www.midwesthsr.org/pdfs/railmidwest.pdf.

[14] "Florida High Speed Rail Authority 2002 Report to the Legislature," HNTB Corp., January 2002, pp. 4-7 to 4-9, www.floridahighspeedrail.org/uploaddocuments/p25/January_2002_Report_to_the_Legislature.pdf.

[15] California High-Speed Rail Authority, "California's High-Speed Train System Will Boost California's Economy," www.cahighspeedrail.ca.gov/news/JOBS_lr.pdf.

[16] Sean Randolph, "California High-Speed Rail: Economic Benefits and Impacts in the San Francisco Bay Area," Bay Area Council Economic Institute, October 2008, p. 1, www.bayeconfor.org/media/files/pdf/CaliforniaHighSpeedRailOct2008Web.pdf.

[17] *Ibid.*, p. 5.

[18] Cox *et al.*, *op. cit.*

[19] Peter Katel, "Future of the Airlines," *CQ Researcher*, March 7, 2008, pp. 217-240.

[20] Paul Gessing, "High-Speed Rail: Making Tracks at Taxpayer Expense," National Taxpayers Union, *NTU Issue Brief 130*, Oct. 18, 2001, p. 3, www.ntu.org/main/press_issuebriefs.php?PressID=199&org_name=NTU.

[21] "Is High-Speed Rail Worth It?" *op. cit.*

[22] "California High-Speed Train Business Plan," November 2008, California High-Speed Rail Authority, pp. 6, 12, www.cahighspeedrail.ca.gov/images/chsr/20081107134320_CHSRABusinessPlan2008.pdf. Amounts are for 2010-2050 and are present value in 2008 dollars, discounted 4 percent through 2050.

[23] Philip J. Romero, "Unlocking the Gridlock in Los Angeles County's Transportation System: The Local Economic Benefits of High-Speed Rail," California High-Speed Rail Authority, www.cahighspeedrail.ca.gov/news/ReleaseLA.pdf, Oct. 8, 2008.

[24] *Ibid.*

[25] *Ibid.*

[26] Dan Tempelis, "A boost for our economy, infrastructure and environment," *Los Angeles Times*, Oct. 20, 2008.

[27] Kopp, *op. cit.*

[28] O'Toole, *op. cit.*, p. 2.

[29] "California High-Speed Train Business Plan," *op. cit.*, p. 13.

[30] Midwest High Speed Rail Association, "Why Railroads: A Cleaner Environment," www.midwesthsr.org/whyRail_cleaner.htm.

[31] Paul Weinstein Jr., "Putting America's Transportation System on Track," Progressive Policy Institute, September 2008, p. 4, www.ppionline.org/documents/High-Speed-Rail-0908.pdf.

[32] *Ibid.*, pp. 2, 8.

[33] Stephen E. Ambrose, *Nothing Like It In the World: The Men Who Built the Transcontinental Railroad 1863-1869* (2000).

[34] "Obama's Speech to Congress," transcript, CBS News, Feb. 24, 2009, www.cbsnews.com/stories/2009/02/24/politics/main4826494.shtml.

[35] "Historian's Note: Empire State Express No. 999," Genesee County, N.Y., www.co.genesee.ny.us/dpt/historian/ese999.html.

[36] PBS American Experience, "People & Events: The Burlington Zephyr's Dawn-to-Dusk Run," www.pbs.org/wgbh/amex/streamliners/peopleevents/e_dawn.html.

[37] "Seventy-Fourth Annual Report on Transport Statistics in the United States for the Year ended Dec. 31, 1960," Bureau of Transport Economics and Statistics, Table 155, p. 106.

[38] Louis S. Thompson, "High-Speed Rail (HSR) in the United States — Why Isn't There More?" *Japan Railway & Transport Review*, October 1994, p. 33.

About the Author

Thomas J. Billitteri is a *CQ Researcher* staff writer based in Fairfield, Pa., who has more than 30 years' experience covering business, nonprofit institutions and public policy for newspapers and other publications. His recent *CQ Researcher* reports include "Auto Industry's Future," "Middle-Class Squeeze" and "Financial Bailout." He holds a BA in English and an MA in journalism from Indiana University.

[39] Hilton is quoted in Joseph Vranich, "End of the Line: The Failure of Amtrak Reform and the Future of America's Passenger Trains," p. 9. Hilton's study is *Amtrak, The National Railroad Passenger Corporation* (1980). The quote is from p. 13 of the study.

[40] "Shinkansen High-Speed 'Bullet Train', Japan," railway-technology.com, www.railway-technology.com/projects/shinkansen/.

[41] U.S. Department of Transportation, Federal Railroad Administration, "High-Speed Ground Transportation for America," September 1997, p. 1-1, www.fra.dot.gov/Downloads/RRDev/cfs 0997all2.pdf.

[42] Lyndon B. Johnson, "Remarks at the Signing of the High-Speed Ground Transportation Act," Sept. 30, 1965, American Presidency Project, University of California, Santa Barbara, www.pres idency.ucsb.edu/ws/index.php?pid=27281.

[43] "Late Arrival of the Fast Trains," *Time*, Jan. 3, 1969.

[44] Joe Holley, "Transport Expert Called 'Father of the Metroliner," *The Washington Post*, March 20, 2009, p. 6B, www.washingtonpost.com/wp-dyn/content/article/2009/03/19/AR2009031903864 .html.

[45] U.S. Department of Transportation, *op. cit.*

[46] John Frittelli and David Randall Peterman, "Amtrak: Budget and Reauthorization," Congressional Research Service, Feb. 6, 2009.

[47] "Vice President Biden, Railroad Administrator, Members of Congress Announce Funding for Amtrak in Recovery Act," news release, White House, March 13, 2009.

[48] Vranich, *End of the Line*, *op. cit.*, p. 11.

[49] U.S. Department of Transportation, *op. cit.*, pp. 1-2.

[50] Thompson, *op. cit.*, p. 34.

[51] *Ibid.*

[52] Peggy Fikac, "High-speed rail idea re-embarking," *Houston Chronicle*, Jan. 29, 2009, p. 1A.

[53] Quoted in Marilyn Adams, "$8 billion could help revive travel by train," *USA Today*, March 16, 2009.

[54] Thompson, *op. cit.*, p. 36.

[55] See "Modern Rail, Modern Europe: Towards an Integrated European Railway Area," Directorate-General for Energy and Transport, European Commission, 2008, http://ec.europa.eu/trans port/publications/doc/modern_rail_en.pdf.

[56] David Rogers, "Obama plots huge railroad expansion," *Politico*, Feb. 17, 2009, www. politico.com/news/stories/0209/18924.html.

[57] "Obama: Better Trains Foster Energy Independence," The Associated Press, April 16, 2009, www.nytimnes.com.

[58] "The Republican Response by Gov. Bobby Jindal," transcript, *The New York Times*, Feb. 24, 2009.

[59] Rogers, *op. cit.*

[60] "The Republican Road to Recovery," March 2009, www.gop.gov/solutions/budget/road-to-recovery-final.

[61] Quoted in Michael Falcone, "Republicans Hail Parts of Bill That Few of Them Supported," *The New York Times*, Feb. 20, 2009, p. 18.

[62] Michael Dresser, "Bringing the Country Up to Speed With 21st Century Transportation," *Baltimore Sun*, Dec. 29, 2008, p. 3A.

[63] Quoted in *Ibid.*

[64] Jon Hilkevitch, "On the fast track — finally," *Chicago Tribune*, Oct. 6, 2008, p. 13.

[65] Quoted in *Ibid.*

[66] Steve Harrison and Bruce Siceloff, "Hoping for Fast Rail to Raleigh," *Charlotte Observer*, March 1, 2009, p. 1A.

[67] Quoted in *Ibid.*

[68] Dan Tracy, "Board: Bullet train rides on Crist's blessing," *Orlando Sentinel*, Feb. 27, 2009, p. 1B. See also, "Crist: Go For High Speed Rail Money," *Lakeland Ledger Blogs*, April 15, 2009, http://politics.theledger.com/default.asp?item=23 64360.

[69] *Ibid.*

[70] Fikac, *op. cit.*

[71] *Ibid.*

[72] *Ibid.*

[73] Peggy Fikac, "Landowners question high-speed rail," *San Antonio Express-News*, Feb. 8, 2009, p. 1B.

[74] Abby Sewell, "City Council Votes to Support Anaheim to Vegas Train," *Desert Dispatch*, April 2, 2009.

FOR MORE INFORMATION

American Public Transportation Association, 1666 K St., N.W., Suite 1100, Washington, DC 20006; (202) 496-4800; www.apta.com. Represents public bus and commuter rail systems and others involved in transit.

California High-Speed Rail Authority, 925 L St., Suite 1425, Sacramento, CA 95814; (916) 324-1541; www.cahighspeedrail.ca.gov. State agency promoting high-speed rail system linking major California cities.

Cato Institute, 1000 Massachusetts Ave., N.W., Washington, DC 20001-5403; (202) 842-0200; www.freetrade.org. Libertarian think tank that advocates global free markets and limited government.

Federal Railroad Administration, 1200 New Jersey Ave., S.E., Washington, DC 20590; www.fra.dot.gov. Enforces railroad safety and supports national railroad policy.

Midwest High Speed Rail Association, P.O. Box 805877, Chicago, IL 60680; (773) 334-6758; www.midwesthsr.org. Advocacy group promoting high-speed rail system linking Chicago hub with cities in the Midwest.

National Association of Railroad Passengers, 900 Second St., N.E., Suite 308, Washington, DC 20002; (202) 408-8362; www.narprail.org. Advocacy group for train and rail-transit passengers.

National Corridors Initiative, 59 Gates St., Boston, MA 02127; (617) 269-5478; www.nationalcorridors.org. Advocates transportation infrastructure development, with emphasis on rail.

Reason Foundation, 3415 S. Sepulveda Blvd., Suite 400, Los Angeles, CA 90034; (310) 391-2245; www.reason.org. Free-market public-policy research group that studies transportation and other issues.

Transportation Research Board, 500 Fifth St., N.W., Washington, DC 20001; www.trb.org. A division of the National Academies that studies innovation in transportation.

Bibliography

Selected Sources

Books

Ambrose, Stephen E., *Nothing Like It In the World: The Men Who Built the Transcontinental Railroad 1863-1869*, Simon & Schuster, 2000.

A prominent historian provides a sweeping look at "the greatest achievement of the American people in the 19th century."

Lynch, Thomas, ed., *High Speed Rail in the U.S.: Super Trains for the Millennium*, Gordon and Breach Science Publishers, 1998.

A collection of technically oriented articles covers land-use planning issues, financing of high-speed rail in Europe and noise abatement related to fast trains, among other topics.

Vranich, Joseph, *End of the Line: The Failure of Amtrak Reform and the Future of America's Passenger Trains*, American Enterprise Institute, 2004.

A former president of the High Speed Rail Association argues that "while fast rail can help on some short routes, there is no justification whatsoever for a national high-speed rail network."

Articles

Cooper, Michael, "Slice of Stimulus Package Will Go to Faster Trains," *The New York Times*, Feb. 20, 2009, www.nytimes.com/2009/02/20/us/20rail.html?scp=1&sq=%22slice%20of%20stimulus%20package%20will%20go%22&st=cse.

The $8 billion added to the economic stimulus package for high-speed rail won't likely do much, Cooper says.

Kopp, Quentin, "High-speed trains will power California forward," *Capitol Weekly*, April 17, 2008, www.capitolweekly.net/article.php?xid=x1uzt54ux6stf4.

The chairman of the California High-Speed Rail Authority argues that high-speed rail will combat global warming, create good jobs and alleviate freeway congestion.

Rogers, David, "Obama plots huge railroad expansion," *Politico*, Feb. 17, 2009, www.politico.com/news/stories/0209/18924.html.

White House chief of staff Rahm Emanuel says President Obama sees high-speed rail as a "signature issue" of his administration.

Thompson, Louis S., "High-Speed Rail (HSR) in the United States — Why Isn't There More?" *Japan Railway & Transport Review*, October 1994.

A former rail-policy adviser at the World Bank examines the myriad reasons — still pertinent 15 years after the article's publication — why the United States has lagged far behind Europe and Japan in rapid-train development.

Reports and Studies

"High-Speed Ground Transportation for America," U.S. Department of Transportation, Federal Railroad Administration, September 1997, www.fra.dot.gov/Downloads/RRDev/cfs0997all2.pdf.

Still highly useful more than a decade after its publication, the report delves into the historical background, financial assumptions, trends and other subjects related to high-speed rail.

"High Speed Rail and Greenhouse Gas Emissions in the U.S.," Center for Clean Air Policy and Center for Neighborhood Technology, January 2006, www.cnt.org/repository/HighSpeedRailEmissions.pdf.

The groups' analysis concludes that high-speed rail can bring about "substantial" greenhouse-gas emission savings.

"Vision for High-Speed Rail in America," U.S. Department of Transportation, Federal Railroad Administration, April 2009, www.fra.dot.gov/Downloads/RRdev/hsrstrategicplan.pdf.

The Obama administration offers its strategic plan for high-speed passenger rail service in intercity corridors.

Cox, Wendell, Joseph Vranich and Adrian T. Moore, "The California High Speed Rail Proposal: A Due Diligence Report," Reason Foundation, Citizens Against Government Waste and Howard Jarvis Taxpayers Foundation, www.reason.org/ps370.pdf.

The report questions a proposal for high-speed rail linking San Francisco, Sacramento, Los Angeles and San Diego.

Frittelli, John, and David Randall Peterman, "Amtrak: Budget and Reauthorization," Congressional Research Service, Feb. 6, 2009.

Last fall Congress passed an Amtrak reauthorization bill that included $1.5 billion in grants for 11 high-speed rail corridors.

O'Toole, Randal, "High-Speed Rail the Wrong Road for America," Cato Institute, *Policy Analysis No. 625*, Oct. 31, 2008, www.cato.org/pubs/pas/pa-625.pdf.

Proposals for high-speed rail are "high-cost, high-risk" projects that offer "little or no congestion relief, energy savings, or other environmental benefits," says a conservative analyst.

Weinstein, Paul Jr., "Putting America's Transportation System on Track," Progressive Policy Institute, September 2008, www.ppionline.org/documents/High-Speed-Rail-0908.pdf.

The chief operating officer of the liberal think tank and a visiting fellow at The Johns Hopkins University says that if the United States is serious about repairing the "mess" in air travel and alleviating congestion on highways, "there is a real, long-term solution: high-speed rail."

The Next Step:

Additional Articles from Current Periodicals

Environment

Nelson, Erik N., "Bullet Train Panel Seeks Eco-Friendly Power Source," *Inside Bay Area* **(California), Feb. 7, 2008.**

The California High-Speed Rail Authority is searching for ways to power a high-speed train via wind, solar energy and underground heat.

Oremus, Will, "Peninsula Could Be in For Years-Long Battle Over High-Speed Rail," *Contra Costa Times* **(California), April 1, 2009.**

Early supporters of California high-speed rail are now joining a lawsuit challenging the system's environmental approval.

Schultz, E.J., "Proposed High-Speed Rail Route Divisive," *Fresno Bee* **(California), Aug. 3, 2008, p. A1.**

Environmental groups have expressed opposition to proposed development sites for a potential California high-speed train.

Funding

Bishop, Shaun, "Funding For Rail Project Still Undecided," *San Jose Mercury News* **(California), April 2, 2009.**

The California High-Speed Rail Authority still needs to raise about $35 billion in order to complete funding for a route linking San Francisco and Los Angeles.

Wong, Nicole C., "Will Stimulus Funds Put Rail on the Fast Track?" *The Boston Globe*, **Feb. 25, 2009, p. B7.**

About $8 billion in stimulus funding likely won't move high-speed rail planners far enough to begin construction, but it serves as a down payment for an eventual system.

Zremski, Jerry, "Obama Includes Buffalo in High-Speed Train Match," *Buffalo News* **(New York), April 17, 2009, p. B1.**

The Obama administration is proceeding with plans to allow 10 rail corridors across the country to compete for up to $13 billion in federal funds.

Overseas Rails

Emling, Shelley, "High-Speed Rail Gains Popularity," *Atlanta Journal-Constitution*, **Oct. 28, 2007, p. 6K.**

Several European train companies have formed an alliance in order to facilitate cross-country travel within Europe.

Glionna, John M., "Japan Blurs the Line Between Bullets and Trains," *Los Angeles Times*, **March 24, 2009, p. A17.**

A planned network of bullet trains connecting major Japanese cities is set to feature magnetically levitated trains running in excess of 310 mph.

Pierson, David, "The Pursuit of Harmony, Now at Speeds of 125 MPH," *Los Angeles Times*, **May 6, 2007, p. A14.**

China has introduced a high-speed rail network despite a transportation system that has recently been overwhelmed by the country's economic growth.

Soriano, Cesar G., "European Trains Keep Getting Faster and Better," *Chicago Tribune*, **April 27, 2008, p. C6.**

High-speed rails in Europe are being updated and modernized in order to keep up with the recent boom in low-cost airlines.

Public Support and Opposition

Brown, Eliot, "Bloomberg Likes High(er)-Speed Rail to D.C.," *New York Observer*, **May 30, 2008.**

New York Mayor Michael Bloomberg has endorsed federal legislation that would create a faster train between New York and Washington, D.C., completing the route in two hours.

Cabanatuan, Michael, "New Way of Life Needed to Run High-Speed Rail," *The San Francisco Chronicle*, **Oct. 20, 2008, p. B1.**

Critics of a California high-speed rail system say the state lacks the appropriate population density needed for such a long-distance project to become successful.

Giles, Kevin, "All Aboard for Fast Trains?" *Star Tribune* **(Minnesota), Dec. 6, 2008, p. 1B.**

Amtrak's growing popularity in Minnesota has spurred interest in a high-speed rail line connecting St. Paul and Chicago.

Simon, Richard, "GOP Irked Over Stimulus Rail Project Funds," *Chicago Tribune*, **Feb. 15, 2009, p. A9.**

House Minority Leader John Boehner, R-Ohio, has called a proposed Anaheim-to-Las Vegas high-speed train a territorial pet project.

CITING *CQ RESEARCHER*

Sample formats for citing these reports in a bibliography include the ones listed below. Preferred styles and formats vary, so please check with your instructor or professor.

<u>MLA STYLE</u>

Jost, Kenneth. "Rethinking the Death Penalty." <u>CQ Researcher</u> 16 Nov. 2001: 945-68.

<u>APA STYLE</u>

Jost, K. (2001, November 16). Rethinking the death penalty. *CQ Researcher, 11*, 945-968.

<u>CHICAGO STYLE</u>

Jost, Kenneth. "Rethinking the Death Penalty." *CQ Researcher*, November 16, 2001, 945-968.

In-depth Reports on Issues in the News

Are you writing a paper?

Need backup for a debate?

Want to become an expert on an issue?

For 80 years, students have turned to *CQ Researcher* for in-depth reporting on issues in the news. Reports on a full range of political and social issues are now available. Following is a selection of recent reports:

Civil Liberties
Closing Guantánamo, 2/09
Affirmative Action, 10/08
Gay Marriage Showdowns, 9/08
America's Border Fence, 9/08
Immigration Debate, 2/08

Crime/Law
Judicial Elections, 4/09
Mexico's Drug War, 12/08
Prostitution Debate, 5/08
Public Defenders, 4/08
Gun Violence, 5/07

Education
Reading Crisis? 2/08
Discipline in Schools, 2/08
Student Aid, 1/08
Racial Diversity in Public Schools, 9/07
Stress on Students, 7/07

Environment/Society
Future of Journalism, 3/09
Confronting Warming, 1/09
Reducing Carbon Footprint, 12/08
Protecting Wetlands, 10/08
Buying Green, 2/08

Health/Safety
Extreme Sports, 4/09
Regulating Toxic Chemicals, 1/09
Preventing Cancer, 1/09
Heart Health, 9/08
Global Food Crisis, 6/08

Politics/Economy
Business Bankruptcy, 4/09
Future of the GOP, 3/09
Middle-Class Squeeze, 3/09
Public-Works Projects, 2/09
The Obama Presidency, 1/09

Upcoming Reports

Hate Groups, 5/8/09   Fertility Ethics, 5/15/09   Future of Books, 5/29/09

ACCESS

CQ Researcher is available in print and online. For access, visit your library or www.cqresearcher.com.

STAY CURRENT

To receive notice of upcoming *CQ Researcher* reports, or learn more about *CQ Researcher* products, subscribe to the free e-mail newsletters, *CQ Researcher Alert!* and *CQ Researcher News*: http://cqpress.com/newsletters.

PURCHASE

To purchase a *CQ Researcher* report in print or electronic format (PDF), visit www.cqpress.com or call 866-427-7737. Single reports start at $15. Bulk purchase discounts and electronic-rights licensing are also available.

SUBSCRIBE

Annual full-service *CQ Researcher* subscriptions—including 44 reports a year, monthly index updates, and a bound volume—start at $803. Add $25 for domestic postage.

CQ Researcher Online offers a backfile from 1991 and a number of tools to simplify research. For pricing information, call 800-834-9020, ext. 1906, or e-mail librarysales@cqpress.com.

CQResearcher

Published by CQ Press, a division of SAGE Publications

www.cqresearcher.com

Hate Groups

Is extremism on the rise in the United States?

N ational crises create opportunities for extremists. Today the global economic crisis now wreaking havoc on millions of American households is hitting while the first black president is in the White House and the national debate over illegal immigration remains unresolved. Already, some far-right extremists are proclaiming that their moment is arriving. Indeed, an annual tally by the Southern Poverty Law Center shows 926 hate groups operating in 2008, a 50 percent increase over the number in 2000. And the Department of Homeland Security concludes that conditions may favor far-right recruitment. But a mix of conservatives and liberal free-speech activists warn that despite concerns about extremism, the administration of Barack Obama should not be intruding on constitutionally protected political debate. Some extremism-monitoring groups say Obama's election showed far-right power is waning, not strengthening. But that equation may change if the economic crisis deepens, the experts caution.

Followers of the neo-Nazi National Socialist Movement demonstrate at the opening of the Illinois Holocaust Museum and Education Center in Skokie, Ill., on April 19, 2009.

CQ Researcher • May 8, 2009 • www.cqresearcher.com
Volume 19, Number 18 • Pages 421-448

Cover: Getty Images/Scott Olson

CQ Researcher

May 8, 2009
Volume 19, Number 18

MANAGING EDITOR: Thomas J. Colin
tcolin@cqpress.com

ASSISTANT MANAGING EDITOR: Kathy Koch
kkoch@cqpress.com

ASSOCIATE EDITOR: Kenneth Jost

STAFF WRITERS: Thomas J. Billitteri, Marcia Clemmitt, Peter Katel

CONTRIBUTING WRITERS: Rachel Cox, Sarah Glazer, Alan Greenblatt, Barbara Mantel, Patrick Marshall, Tom Price, Jennifer Weeks

DESIGN/PRODUCTION EDITOR: Olu B. Davis

ASSISTANT EDITOR: Darrell Dela Rosa

FACT-CHECKING: Eugene J. Gabler, Michelle Harris

EDITORIAL INTERN: Vyomika Jairam

CQ PRESS

A Division of SAGE

PRESIDENT AND PUBLISHER:
John A. Jenkins

**EXECUTIVE DIRECTOR,
REFERENCE INFORMATION GROUP:**
Alix B. Vance

CQ Researcher (ISSN 1056-2036) is printed on acid-free paper. Published weekly, except; (Jan. wk. 1) (May wk. 4) (July wks. 1, 2) (Aug. wks. 3, 4) (Nov. wk. 4) and (Dec. wk. 4), by CQ Press, a division of SAGE Publications. Annual full-service subscriptions start at $803. For pricing, call 1-800-834-9020, ext. 1906. To purchase a *CQ Researcher* report in print or electronic format (PDF), visit www. cqpress.com or call 866-427-7737. Single reports start at $15. Bulk purchase discounts and electronic-rights licensing are also available. Periodicals postage paid at Washington, D.C., and additional mailing offices. POSTMASTER: Send address changes to *CQ Researcher*, 2300 N St., N.W., Suite 800, Washington, DC 20037.

Hate Groups

BY PETER KATEL

THE ISSUES

Two police officers drove up to a brick house in the middle-class Pittsburgh neighborhood of Stanton Heights on April 4, responding to an emergency call from a woman about her 22-year-old son. "I want him gone," Margaret Poplawski told a 911 operator. [1]

She also said that he had weapons, but the operator failed to share that crucial information with the police, who apparently took no special precautions in responding. Seconds after officers Stephen J. Mayhle and Paul J. Sciullo walked into the house, Richard Poplawski opened fire, killing both men. He then shot and killed Eric Kelly, a policeman outside the house. After a four-hour standoff, Poplawski surrendered. [2] Hours after that, the Anti-Defamation League and a *Pittsburgh Post-Gazette* reporter traced a March 13 Web post by Poplawski to the neo-Nazi Web site Stormfront.

"The federal government, mainstream media and banking system in these United States are strongly under the influence of — if not completely controlled by — Zionist interest," the post said. "An economic collapse of the financial system is inevitable, bringing with it some degree of civil unrest if not outright balkanization of the continental U.S., civil/revolutionary/racial war. . . . This collapse is likely engineered by the elite Jewish powers that be in order to make for a power and asset grab." [3]

Obsessions with Jewish conspiracy, racial conflict and looming collapse of the political and social order

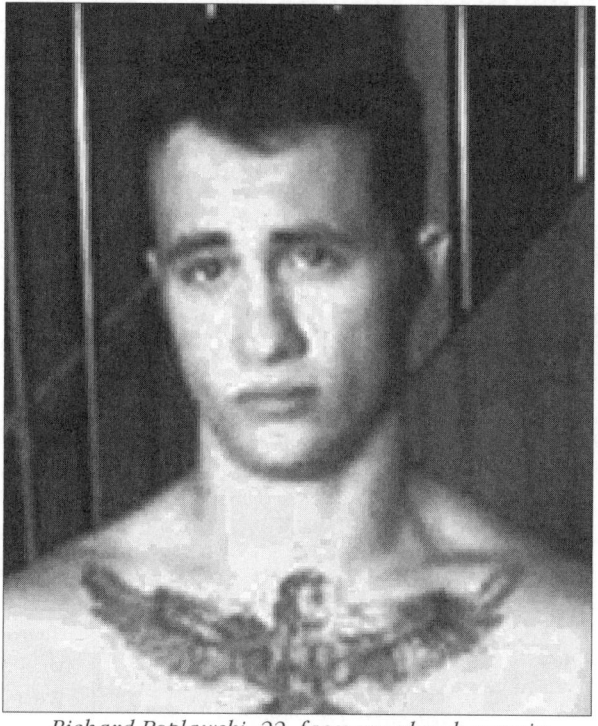

Richard Poplawski, 22, faces murder charges in Pittsburgh after allegedly shooting and killing three police officers on April 4, 2009. Three weeks earlier, Poplawski, who tatooed on his chest what he reportedly described as an "Americanized" Nazi eagle, apparently posted an anti-Semitic message on Stormfront, a neo-Nazi Web site. The number of active hate groups in the nation has jumped to 926 groups — a 50 percent increase — since 2000.

have long festered in the extreme outposts of U.S. political culture. While extremists typically become active in times of social and economic stress, Timothy McVeigh, the Oklahoma City bomber, struck in 1995 during a relatively tranquil, prosperous time. (*See "Background," p. 435.*)

Now, law enforcement officials warn, dire conditions throughout the country have created a perfect storm of provocations for right-wing extremists. In the midst of fighting two wars, the country is suffering an economic crisis in which more than 5 million people have lost their jobs, while the hypercharged debate over immigration — and the presence of about 12 million illegal immigrants — continues unresolved. [4]

"This is the formula — the formula for hate," says James Cavanaugh, special agent in charge of the Bureau of Alcohol, Tobacco, Firearms and Explosives (ATF) Nashville, Tenn., division and a veteran investigator of far-right extremists. "Everything's aligning for them for hate."

The Department of Homeland Security (DHS) drew a similar conclusion in early April, adding a concern over the apparent rekindling of extremist interest in recruiting disaffected military veterans.

"The consequences of a prolonged economic downturn . . . could create a fertile recruiting environment for right-wing extremists and even result in confrontations between such groups and government authorities," the DHS said. [5]

The election of Barack Obama as the nation's first African-American president also could prompt an extremist backlash. "Obama is going to be the spark that arouses the white movement," the Detroit-based National Socialist Movement * — considered a leading neo-Nazi organization — announced on its Web site. [6]

But the Obama effect will be negligible among hardcore, violent extremists, says an ex-FBI agent who worked undercover in right-wing terrorist cells in the early 1990s. "They're in an alternative universe," says Mike German, author of the 2007 book *Thinking Like a Terrorist*, and now a policy counselor to the American Civil Liberties Union on national-security issues. "When you believe the American

---

* "Nazi" is the German-language contraction of "National Socialist."

Hate Groups Active in All But Two States

Hate groups were active in all the states except Hawaii and Alaska in 2008, according to the Southern Poverty Law Center. Iowa, California, Texas and Mississippi had the largest concentrations of groups.

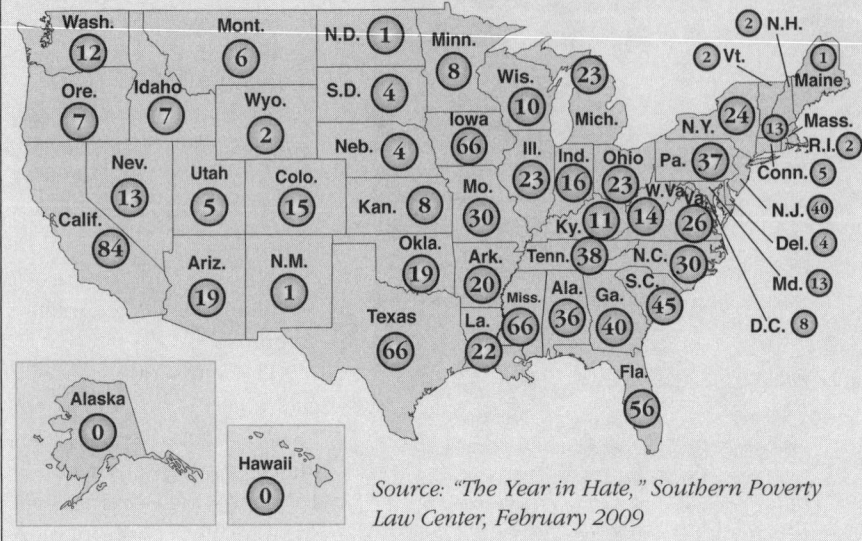

Wash. (12)
Mont. (6)
N.D. (1)
Minn. (8)
N.H. (2)
Vt. (2)
Maine (1)
Ore. (7)
Idaho (7)
Wyo. (2)
S.D. (4)
Wis. (23)
Mich. (10)
N.Y. (24)
Mass. (13)
R.I. (2)
Nev. (13)
Utah (5)
Colo. (15)
Neb. (4)
Iowa (66)
Ill. (23)
Ind. (16)
Ohio (23)
Pa. (37)
Conn. (5)
Calif. (84)
Kan. (8)
Mo. (30)
Ky. (11)
W.Va. (14)
N.J. (40)
Del. (4)
Ariz. (19)
N.M. (1)
Okla. (19)
Ark. (20)
Tenn. (38)
N.C. (30)
S.C. (26)
Md. (13)
Texas (66)
La. (66)
Miss. (36)
Ala. (40)
Ga. (45)
D.C. (8)
Fla. (56)
Alaska (0)
Hawaii (0)

Source: "The Year in Hate," Southern Poverty Law Center, February 2009

government is the puppet of Israel, whether Obama is the face of the government instead of George W. Bush makes little difference."

Indeed, says Columbia University historian Robert O. Paxton, the Obama victory demonstrated that the country's worrisome conditions haven't sparked widespread rejection of the political system — the classic catalyst for major upsurges of extremism. "Sure, we have a black president, but if the Right were really at the door, we wouldn't have elected him," says Paxton, a leading scholar of European fascism. (*See sidebar, p. 434.*)

Still, Paxton and others caution that the sociopolitical effects of the economic crisis may take a while to hit. The Montgomery, Ala.-based Southern Poverty Law Center (SPLC), which tracks the Ku Klux Klan and other "hate groups," reports activity by 926 such groups in 2008, a 50 percent increase over the number in 2000.[7] "That is a real and a significant rise," says Mark Potok, director of the cen-

ter's Intelligence Project. Despite the increased activity, the center says there's nothing approaching a mass movement. Moreover, drawing connections between extremist organizations and hate crimes can be complicated.

"Most hate crimes are not committed by members of organized hate groups," says Chip Berlet, senior analyst for Political Research Associates of Somerville, Mass., who has been writing about the far right for a quarter-century. "These groups help promote violence through their aggressive rhetoric. But you're more likely to be victim of hate crime from a neighbor."

For example, three young men from Staten Island, N.Y., charged with beating a 17-year-old Liberian immigrant into a coma on presidential election night last year were not accused of membership in anything more than a neighborhood gang. Their victim, who also lives on Staten Island, said his attackers, one of them Hispanic, yelled "Obama" as they set on him.[8]

Mental health problems also may play a role in such violence, not all of which is inspired by hate rhetoric. In the single deadliest attack on immigrants in memory, Jiverly Wong is charged with killing 13 people (and then himself) at an immigrants' service center in Binghamton, N.Y., one day before Poplawski's alleged killings in Pittsburgh. Eleven of Wong's victims were immigrants, like Wong, a native of Vietnam. Wong left a note in which he complained of his limited English-speaking ability and depicted himself as a victim of police persecution.[9]

But in other recent cases in which immigrants were targeted, the alleged shooters did invoke far-right views. Keith Luke, 22, who lived with his mother in the Boston suburb of Brockton, was charged in January with killing a young woman, shooting and raping her sister and killing a 72-year-old man — all immigrants from Cape Verde. His planned next stop, police said, was a synagogue. Luke, whom one law enforcement source described as a "recluse," allegedly told police he was "fighting extinction" of white people.[10]

A similar motive was expressed by a 60-year-old Destin, Fla., man charged with killing two Chilean students and wounding three others, all visiting Florida as part of a cultural-exchange program. Shortly before the killings, Dannie Roy Baker had asked a neighbor, "Are you ready for the revolution?" And last summer, he had sent e-mails to Walton County Republican Party officials — who forwarded them to the sheriff's office. One said, in part, "The Washington D.C. Dictators have already confessed to rigging elections in our States for their recruiting dictators to overthrow us with foreign illegals here."[11]

Some immigrant advocates say such comments indicate that extremists are exploiting resentment of immigrants in the hope of stirring up more attacks.

"It is the perfect vehicle, particularly with the decline of the economy," says Eric Ward, national field director of the Chicago-based Center for New Community, which works with immigrants. "With American anxiety building, they hope that they can use immigrants as scapegoats to build their movement."

"Illegals are turning America into a third-world slum," says one of a series of leaflets distributed in the New Haven, Conn., area in early March by North-East White Pride (NEWP). "They come for welfare, or to take our jobs and bring with them drugs, crime and disease."

The NEWP Web site carries the cryptic slogan, "Support your local 1488." In neo-Nazi code, "88" represents "Heil Hitler," words that begin with the eighth letter in the alphabet. And "14" stands for an infamous, 14-word racist dictum: "We must secure the existence of our people and a future for white children." Its author was the late David Lane, a member of the violent neo-Nazi organization, The Order, who died in prison in 2007. [12]

The Order, whose crimes included the murder of a Jewish radio talk-show host in Denver in 1984, sprang from the far-right milieu, as did Oklahoma City bomber McVeigh. And a source of inspiration in both cases was a novel glorifying genocide of Jews and blacks, *The Turner Diaries*, authored by the late William Pierce, founder of the neo-Nazi National Alliance, based in West Virginia. [13]

Pierce's death from cancer in 2002 was one of a series of developments that left a high-level leadership vacuum in the extremist movement. One of those trying to fill it is Billy Roper, 37, chairman of White Revolution, a group based in Russellville, Ark. Roper predicts that racial-ethnic tensions will explode when nonstop immigration from Latin America forces the violent breakup of the United States.

Dozens of Extremist Events Planned This Summer

More than two dozen gatherings of white extremists will be held around the nation this summer, according to the Anti-Defamation League. Many are being held in traditional Ku Klux Klan (KKK) strongholds in the South and Midwest by groups such as the KKK, National Socialist Movement and Christian Identity organizations.

Upcoming Extremist Events in the United States
(Partial list, May–October)

Location	Event
Russelville, Ala.	Courthouse rally organized by Church of the National Knights of the Ku Klux Klan.
Odessa, Mo.	Paramilitary training organized by the Missouri Militia.
Phoenix, Ariz.	Gathering organized by neo-Nazi Nationalist Coalition Arizona with invitations to members of Stormfront, a hate Web site.
York County, Pa.	Open meeting of the neo-Nazi National Socialist Movement for current and interested members.
Marshall, Texas	KKK cookout on private property organized by the United White Knights.
Las Vegas, Nev.	Workshop organized by Paper Advantage, a sovereign citizen group advocating right-wing anarchy.
Champaign County, Ohio	Paramilitary training with the Unorganized Militia of Champaign County.
Burlington, N.C.	Conference organized by the neo-Confederate North Carolina Chapter of League of the South.
New Albany, Miss.	KKK rally at county courthouse followed by a gathering and cross-burning on private property.
Dawson Springs, Ky.	Annual Nordic Fest white power rally organized by the Imperial Klans of America.
Oceana and Muskegon counties, Mich.	Camping trip organized by the white-supremacist forum White Pride Michigan.
Schell City, Mo.	National youth conference organized by Church of Israel, whose followers practice Christian Identity, a racist and anti-Semitic religion.
Jackson, Miss.	Annual national conference of racist group Council of Conservative Citizens.
Sandpoint, Idaho	Weekend conference organized by America's Promise Ministries, practitioners of Christian Identity.
Pulaski, Tenn.	Weekend gathering commemorating the birthday of Nathan Bedford Forrest — the first KKK leader — including a march, cross-burning and fellowship.

Source: Anti-Defamation League

"We're at a pre-revolutionary stage, where it's too late to seek recompense through the political process, and too early to start shooting," Roper says.

As police and scholars monitor extremist groups, here are some of the key questions they are asking:

Could the election of a black president and the nation's economic crisis spark a resurgence of far-right political activity or violence?

The precedent-shattering nature of Obama's presidency could provide enough of a spark for racist reaction, some extremism experts argue. Others question whether that's enough to propel significant numbers of people into outright rejection of the political system, even amid the nation's economic turbulence. They note that organized racist violence against African-Americans was already fading by the late 1960s, after civil rights had become the law of the land.

Nonetheless, at least some members of the far right are reacting. Shortly before the presidential election last year, federal agents charged an 18-year-old from Arkansas and a 20-year-old from Tennessee with plotting to kill Obama after first killing 88 black people, beheading 14 of them — apparent references to the "88" and "14" codes. The father of one of the young men said the alleged plans were no more than "a lot of talk." According to the SPLC, the 20-year-old, Daniel Cowart, had been a probationary member of a new and active skinhead organiza-

tion, Supreme White Alliance, though the organization said he'd been expelled before the alleged murder plot was conceived. [14]

Michael Barkun, a professor of political science at Syracuse University,

Members of the World Order of the Ku Klux Klan, one of scores of Klan groups in the United States, rally on Sept. 2, 2006, at Gettysburg National Military Park, site of a decisive Civil War battle.

AP Photo/Bradley C. Bower

says older extremists may see Obama's election as a big favor to their movement. "They tend to think of it as a great recruiting tool," says Barkun, who specializes in political and religious extremism. "My sense is that from their point of view, they would see it as a continuation of what they regard as the marginalization of the white population: 'See, we were right all along.' "

But extremists may be disappointed, Barkun adds, given how the election itself showed the extent to which racism has weakened.

Still, the economic crisis offers recruiting possibilities to extremists, because millions of people are suffering its effects. "I would be surprised if the economic crisis did not produce some very nasty side effects," he says, citing the pseudo-constitutional interpretations adopted by the "Posse Comitatus" movement that flourished in the 1980s. "Certainly some of the fringe legal doctrines on the far right lend themselves to exploitation here." *

Yet for a segment of U.S. society, Obama's election is already stoking the fires of rage, says another veteran observer of the far right. Michael Pitcavage, investigative research director for the Anti-Defamation League, says that immediately after the election, extremists with MySpace pages started including the slogan, "I have no president."

These are anecdotal signs, Pitcavage acknowledges. But he notes that at least one president in the recent past did prompt an extreme reaction on the far right. "The election of Bill Clinton, I would call one of the secondary causes of the resurgence of right-wing extremism in the 1990s," he says. Clinton's Vietnam War draft avoidance and his evasive acknowledgement of past drug use aroused enormous anger among extremists (as among mainstream conservatives), Pitcavage

---

* Posse Comitatus means "power of the county," a phrase that adherents used to denote the supposed illegitimacy of the federal government. The Posse Comitatus Act of 1878 was passed to remove the U.S. Army from domestic law enforcement activities.

says — sentiments that expanded into conspiracist views after a violent confrontation between federal law enforcement officers and a heavily armed religious group in Waco, Texas.

But at least one right-wing writer on racial issues says that in his circles Obama's presidency has had little effect. "We have always had sophisticated readers whose views of the world are not going to be knocked askew by some unforeseen political event," says Jared Taylor, editor of *American Renaissance*, a magazine based in Oakton, Va., a Washington suburb. "Though I don't wish to detract at all from the symbolic importance of a non-white American president, it's very much part of a predictable sequence. Readers of *American Renaissance* don't necessarily approve of the idea of a black president, but it's not something that wakes them up to something they weren't aware of before." Taylor greeted Obama's election with an article headlined, "Transition to Black Rule?" [15]

Taylor's magazine opposes all anti-discrimination and affirmative-action laws but doesn't espouse violence. However, attendees at the magazine's annual conference in 2006 included well-known extremists, including David Duke. When the former Louisiana Klan leader raised the issue of Jewish influence, a Jewish attendee walked out. Taylor later wrote that he would never exclude Jews, adding, "Some people in the [*American Renaissance*] community believe Jewish influence was decisive in destroying the traditional American consensus on race. Others disagree." [16]

As for the ailing economy, Taylor says it hasn't been helping his publication. "We haven't seen any sort of sudden leap in subscribers," he says. "If anything, the economic conditions are bad for us because we're a non-profit organization. We depend on contributions; people have less to contribute."

Still, the sociopolitical consequences of the economic crisis transcend financial problems at individual outposts of right-wing opinion.

Cavanaugh, the longtime ATF official, is one of many who sees the global economic meltdown as an echo of the crisis in Germany's Weimar Republic in the 1920s and early '30s, which enabled Hitler's National Socialist Party to come to power.

"This is how they recruited," says Cavanaugh. "Nazism was founded on blaming the Jewish people for the economic crisis." In today's United States, Cavanaugh hypothesizes, extremists could try to make immigrants the group responsible for the crisis.

But Cavanaugh doubts that Obama's presidency, per se, appeals to extremists. Many of them view the conventional political system as the "Zionist Occupation Government," or ZOG. "The president has done more to unite the country — you can feel it," he says. "That doesn't help hate groups get stronger. They can rail against any president, and they have. Any president to them is the head of ZOG."

Are immigrants in danger from extremist violence?

Black Americans have been far and away the major targets of 20th-century extremist violence.

But organized racist violence, from cross-burning to bombings, lynching and assassinations of black community leaders or white civil rights supporters, has faded from the scene, despite episodic hate crimes that sometimes target Jews as well as blacks.

Obama's election demonstrated the extent to which the black-white divide in American life has narrowed. Indeed, when it comes to arousing political passion, race has been replaced by illegal immigrants, who number an estimated 12 million in the United States. [17]

"Black people are here, and no one is talking about deporting them," says Taylor of *American Renaissance*. "Im-

migration is a current and constant flow that is, in my view, only building up problems and conflict for the future, and that's a process that could be stopped. That is why it is much more a subject of political interest."

Bipartisan congressional legislation to provide a "path to citizenship" — restrictionists prefer the term "amnesty" — for illegal immigrants" stalled during the George W. Bush administration.

Aside from mainstream political debate over the solution to illegal immigration, immigrant advocates say they're worried that violence against Latinos — or brown-skinned people thought to be immigrants — is on the rise. According to the most recent FBI statistics, there were 830 attacks of various kinds on Hispanics in 2007. By comparison, 1,087 attacks were made on homosexuals, who are also frequent targets of hate speech. [18] In 2000, there were 557 reported attacks on Hispanics compared to 1,075 attacks against homosexuals. [19]

But both conservatives and liberals take a dim view of those FBI statistics. Marcus Epstein, a conservative anti-immigration activist who draws a line between his views and those of extremists, criticizes the FBI categorization scheme for using the ethnic term "Hispanic" only for crime victims. Offenders, by contrast, are listed only by race, so "Hispanic" doesn't appear. The result, he argues, is that statistics are skewed so that any Hispanic hate-crime perpetrators are statistically invisible. (The FBI says that the agency "does not agree" that its categories "render the data invalid for statistical purposes.")

Epstein, executive director of The American Cause, a conservative organization founded by political commentator and immigration restrictionist Pat Buchanan, is particularly concerned about illegal immigrants with criminal records committing further crimes. He cites the case of Manuel Cazares, who turned himself in to police in Hannibal, Mo., in March, saying he'd killed an ex-girlfriend and a male friend of hers. Cazares, a Mexican citizen, was in the United States illegally, but police hadn't checked his status, although federal immigration authorities said his name wasn't in their database. [20] "Illegal immigrants kill American citizens — that greatly outweighs the number of crimes committed by right-wing white Americans against immigrants," Epstein says.

He cites a statistical analysis by Edwin S. Rubinstein, an economic consultant in Indianapolis and former senior fellow at the Hudson Institute, a conservative think tank. Writing on the VDare Web site, which opposes immigration except by white people, Rubinstein, while acknowledging that national data on crime and ethnicity are thin, extrapolated from California and national figures to estimate that in any given year illegal immigrants "could kill 2.6 persons per day across the U.S." [21]

The vast majority of violent crimes fall within city and state jurisdictions, not all of which collect data on ethnicity. Mark Hugo Lopez, associate director of the Pew Hispanic Center, and co-author of a recent report on Hispanics and federal crime, says. "The reason that we used federal statistics is that those are the cleanest data." The Pew study showed that 70 percent of Latino offenders were non-citizens, and that 3.1 percent of all Latino convicts were sentenced for crimes of violence, including murder. [22]

Others warn that hate crime statistics aren't reliable where immigrants are concerned. "One of the difficulties we have is getting certain communities to report hate crime," said Brian Levin, director of the Center for the Study of Hate and Extremism at California State University, San Bernardino. Illegal immigrants are especially reluctant, says Levin, in a widely shared observation. [23]

Hate Groups Increased by 50 Percent

The number of hate groups active in the United States — including skinheads, Ku Klux Klan and neo-Nazis — increased more than a 50 percent from 2000 to 2008.

Hate Groups in the U.S.

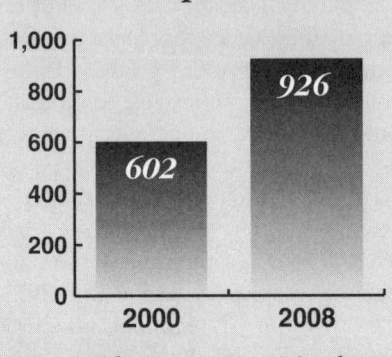

Source: "The Year in Hate," Southern Poverty Law Center, February 2009

In any event, supercharged rhetoric from extremists has ratcheted up fear among immigrants and their advocates. Ward of the Center for New Community says that recent episodes of violence targeting immigrants reflect a general hostility toward immigrants that he's sensing on the street. For example, he says, following an organizational meeting in Wilmer, Minn., a town in the meat-processing factory belt of the upper Midwest, "A woman pulls up behind a car of our field people and starts screaming racial epithets."

Though of little significance by itself, Ward says it reflects an atmosphere that reminds him of "things I saw in the 1980s and '90s during the rise of the neo-Nazi movement." He adds, "These kinds of incidents, I would call an early warning of what will be the backlash."

Immigration restrictionists argue that their political foes are whipping up passions in an effort to create the appearance that Latinos in general and immigrants in particular face growing danger.

"All hate crimes are abominable, and any decent person would oppose them no matter who the target is," says Ira Mehlman, national media director of the Federation for American Immigration Reform (FAIR), which advocates restricting immigration. "But they are hyping the statistics on hate crimes. Hate crimes against Hispanics are much fewer in actual number than attacks against gays or Jews, who represent much smaller percentages of the population."

Hard-core extremists still rank Jews as their No. 1 enemy, says Pitcavage at the Anti-Defamation League, which was formed in 1913 to combat anti-Semitism.

Some of the most horrific hate crimes are committed by "mission offenders," or mentally ill people who hear voices that command them to rid the world of a particular set of evildoers, Pitcavage says. [24] While they may target Jews — and those are often some of the most horrific crimes — "racial/ ethnic targets" — including Latinos and immigrants in general — do run a risk from hate crime because they're "more visually identifiable and thus better targets of opportunity," he says.

Is right-wing and extremist speech encouraging hate crimes?

The killings of three Pittsburgh police officers intensified the ongoing debate over free speech and its consequences. Some liberal and left-wing commentators saw Richard Poplawski's horrific crime as an outgrowth, at least in part, of the far-right conspiracy culture that had influenced him, judging by his Web posts. In addition, they say, his rage had been stoked by conservative commentators. Still, the Pittsburgh reporter who helped trace those posts argues in the online magazine *Slate* that the writings reveal more inner torment than ideology.

Journalist Dennis B. Roddy wrote that Poplawski also posted to a non-racist conspiracist site — Infowars, which describes its politics as libertarian. There, the alleged cop-killer "seemed to find . . . a bridge from the near-mainstream to a level of paranoid obsession in search of an explanation for his life's failures. For that, one does not need an ideology, just an inclination." [25]

Nevertheless, Roddy acknowledges that Poplawski complained on Infowars that the site neglected race. Other commentators insisted that Poplawski's posts follow a clear pattern. "Poplawski's black-helicopter and anti-Semitic ravings put him at the outer edge of the right," wrote Gary Kamiya, executive editor of *Salon*, a liberal online magazine. "But his paranoid fear that Obama was going to take away his AK-47 is mainstream among conservatives . . . fomented by the NRA and echoed by right-wing commentators from Lou Dobbs to Limbaugh." [26]

Kamiya doesn't propose limiting free-speech rights, but he does argue that extreme anti-Obama and gun-rights rhetoric is bound to produce more episodes like the Pittsburgh shootings.

The U.S. Supreme Court has ruled that even hate-filled racist speechmaking is protected by the First Amendment. In 1969, the court overturned the terrorism-advocacy conviction of an Ohio Ku Klux Klan leader who'd given a speech including a call to "send the Jews back to Israel," and to "bury the niggers." The court ruled unanimously that the government may not "forbid or proscribe advocacy of the use of force or of law violation except where such advocacy

is directed to inciting or producing imminent lawless action." [27]

Worries about the effects of vicious and hyperbolic speech haven't only come from the left. In 2005, Freedom House, a human-rights advocacy organization then headed by former CIA director James Woolsey, a neoconservative, issued a report accusing the government of Saudi Arabia of disseminating "hate propaganda" — targeting Christians, Jews and converts from Islam — in religious publications sent to mosques. [28]

Oklahoma City bomber Timothy McVeigh, a neo-Nazi Army veteran, was executed in 2001 for killing 168 people, including 19 children, at the Murrah Federal Building. While extremists typically become active in times of social and economic stress, McVeigh struck in 1995 during a period of relative tranquility.

In late March, an American writer of Arab descent wrote on a conservative Web site that American Muslims who get their news on satellite TV from the Middle East are, in effect, being brainwashed into a pro-jihadist outlook. "We must never underestimate the power of hate propaganda," Nonie Darwish wrote, "because, quite simply, it works. Believe it or not, if

you grow up hearing 'holy' cursing day in and day out, it can feel and sound normal, justified and even good." Darwish didn't call for banning the transmissions. [29]

But the more explosive recent disputes over speech arise from the immigration conflict. At the center of the controversy are radio and cable TV commentators like Glenn Beck, of Fox News. In June 2007 (before he had joined Fox), Beck read on his radio program a fake commercial for "Mexinol" — a fuel produced from the bodies of illegal immigrants from Mexico. [30]

"We have a butt load of illegal aliens in our country," said the fake ad, which was ascribed to Evil Conservative Industries. "With Mexinol, your raw materials come to you in a seemingly never-ending stream." Beck tried to put some distance between himself and the ad's authors, though in a lighthearted tone. "I don't even know if that's conservative," he said, chuckling. "That would be . . . psychotic, perhaps?" [31]

Last year, Janet Murguía, president of the National Council of La Raza, a leading Hispanic organization, cited the segment in calling for cable channels to "to clean up the rhetoric of their own commentators or take them out of their chairs." She argued that much of the commentary by the hosts and some of their guests spurred anti-immigrant violence. "When free speech transforms into hate speech, we've got to draw that line." [32]

Epstein of The American Cause argues that Murguía is trying to

AFP/Getty Images/Bob Daemmerich

"muzzle" free speech. The painful reality of the nation's economic crisis, not anti-immigrant rhetoric — explains more about anti-Hispanic violence, he says.

"People should not hold an individual Hispanic responsible for the fact that wages are being depressed, and they can't get a job, or that schools are overcrowded, that there's an increase in crime in the community," he says. "But that's the reason these people are lashing out. In the few cases of [violence], they're responding to the problems that immigration causes."

Epstein argues that mainstream anti-immigration groups like FAIR provide a legitimate channel for citizens who favor limiting immigration to express their views. "If there was no one actually speaking for Americans, they're going to turn to more radical groups," he says. Epstein posts his writings on the VDare Web site but says he doesn't agree with all the views expressed on the site, some of them virulently racist.

A recent post by one contributor argued that hiring people of South Asian Indian ancestry guaranteed "corruption and ethnocentric discrimination"; another opined that hiring better public school teachers and firing less competent ones means "on net, firing blacks and hiring whites." And another contributor attacked "the cultural pollution of our 'entertainment industry,' which promotes diversity, multiculturalism and white demoralization." [33]

Cavanaugh of the ATF says he's aware that a constellation of legal organizations provide moral backing even for violent actions. In the civil rights days, such groups were known as the "white-collar Klan," he says. "They support people who will go out and do those things."

But, he says, free speech is free speech. "Is it illegal?" he asks rhetorically. "It's awful, but I can't do much about awful, and I shouldn't be able to." ∎

BACKGROUND

Building Movements

Extreme-right political movements reached their peak in the 1930s in the United States and abroad. Adolf Hitler came to power in Germany in 1933. Benito Mussolini, originator of the term "fascism," who began his rule of Italy in 1922, soon forged an alliance with Hitler. Other far-right movements triumphed in Central Europe. The United States, of course, never succumbed to totalitarian rule. But the American extreme right did command a sizable sector of public opinion. [34]

As in Germany and elsewhere (though not to a major extent in Italy), hatred of Jews played a key role in the American right-wing mobilization, with communists and socialists close behind on the enemies list.

Henry Ford, founder of the Ford Motor Co., actively spread anti-Semitism in the 1920s, using a newspaper that he owned, the *Dearborn Independent*, to publish vast amounts of propaganda about a Jewish plot for world domination. [35]

After Ford withdrew from public anti-Semitic activity under pressure from Jewish organizations and the U.S. government, other leaders emerged. Gerald L. K. Smith, a minister and failed political candidate allied with hate-mongers, denounced President Franklin D. Roosevelt (FDR) and African-Americans as well as Jews. William Dudley Pelley led the fascist Silver Legion — the "Silver Shirts" — which dedicated itself mainly to marches and other publicity-seeking events expressing hatred of Jews, blacks and all minorities.

The Rev. Charles Coughlin, a Roman Catholic priest, known as "Father Coughlin," soared to national prominence and influence through radio broadcasts from his church outside Detroit.

At first a Roosevelt supporter, the "radio priest" by 1934 was raging against FDR and the Jews, on whom he blamed the Great Depression.

After the United States entered World War II, the Catholic Church and the federal government forced Coughlin off the air. Pelley was convicted in 1942 of sedition and intent to cause insurrection in the military and was sentenced to 15 years in prison. [36]

By war's end, American fascism as a mass movement had ended. But a core of committed activists kept the far right alive, spurred on by the Cold War against the Soviet Union and the first stirrings of the civil rights movement. [37]

As public opposition to communism grew, Smith preached that Jews and communists were one and the same and that the Holocaust never occurred.

The founding of the John Birch Society in 1958 marked the reemergence of conspiratorial, far-right views — minus the anti-Semitism — in respectable society. Birch Society doctrine viewed the United Nations as a communist organization. Founder Robert Welch, an executive in his brother's candy company, went further, calling President Dwight D. Eisenhower "a dedicated, conscious agent of the communist conspiracy." [38]

Welch's wild accusation stoked outrage in the political mainstream. President Harry S Truman reportedly called the Birch Society "the Ku Klux Klan, without nightshirts." [39]

By the mid-1960s, the Klan — established in 1866 in Pulaski, Tenn. — had become the center of extremist resistance to the civil rights movement. Members and ex-members of the secret organization carried out some of the most notorious crimes of the era, including the 1963 bombing of the 16th Street Baptist Church in Birmingham, Ala., in which four young girls were killed; the assassination of civil rights leader Medgar Evers in

Continued on p. 432

Chronology

1930s-1960s

Attempts to create U.S. versions of European fascism fail, but far-right activists build smaller organizations after World War II.

1934
The Rev. Charles Coughlin ("Father Coughlin") gains a nationwide following for denouncing President Franklin D. Roosevelt and Jews.

1941-1942
Coughlin is forced off the air and another far-right leader, William Dudley Pelley, is sent to prison for sedition.

1952
Anti-Semite Gerald L.K. Smith fails to persuade the Republican Party to link communism and Jews.

1958
John Birch Society is founded.

1963
Ku Klux Klan members bomb a black church in Birmingham, Ala., killing four young girls.

1967
American neo-Nazi leader George Lincoln Rockwell is killed by an embittered ex-aide.

1969
U.S. Supreme Court rules that a Ku Klux Klan leader's denunciations of blacks and Jews are constitutionally protected speech.

1970s-1980s

Anti-government and anti-Jewish organizations turn to violence, most often against police officers, who are seen as agents of the "Zionist Occupation Government."

1971
Anti-Semitic, Christian Identity activist William Potter Gale formulates the doctrine underlying the radically anti-government Posse Comitatus movement, which by 1976 has at least 12,000 members, according to the FBI.

1978
The Turner Diaries, a genocide fantasy by neo-Nazi William Pierce (pseudonym: Andrew Macdonald), is published.

1983
Posse Comitatus leader Gordon Kahl kills two federal marshals in North Dakota, later dies in a shootout with federal agents in Arkansas.

1984
The Order, a small extremist group inspired by *The Turner Diaries*, murders a Jewish talk-show host in Denver who had denounced racism. . . . The group's founder is killed later in a shootout in Washington state.

1988
A federal jury in Arkansas acquits 14 right-wing extremists, including five members of The Order, on sedition and other charges.

1990s

Extremist violence climaxes in armed confrontations with federal officers.

1992
An attempt to arrest survivalist and Christian Identity proponent Randy Weaver in Ruby Ridge, Idaho, ends with the deaths of a marshal and Weaver's wife and young son.

1993
Extremist leaders gather in Estes Park, Colo., to plan cooperation with less-threatening groups. . . . Federal siege of the Branch Davidian religious-cult compound in Waco, Texas, leads to deaths of more than 80 people. . . . Extremists depict Ruby Ridge and Waco as examples of government ruthlessness. . . . Outrage at government helps build "patriot militia" movement.

1995
Timothy McVeigh, an extremist military veteran inspired by *The Turner Diaries*, detonates truck bomb outside Alfred P. Murrah Federal Building in Oklahoma City, killing 168 people. . . . Militia membership declines.

2000s

Extremist movement erodes further following 9/11 attacks and the removal of major figures by death and imprisonment, but economic crisis ignites fears of a resurgence.

2001
McVeigh executed by lethal injection.

2004
Richard Butler, influential leader of Idaho-based "Aryan Nations," dies of natural causes.

2005
Up-and-coming extremist leader Matthew Hale, founder of World Church of the Creator, is sentenced to 40 years for conspiracy to commit murder.

2009
Homeland Security Department warns extremists could exploit economic crisis as a recruiting opportunity; critics blast department for focusing on ideology rather than criminal acts.

Concern About Extremism Rising in Europe

Czech Republic expels ex-Klan leader David Duke.

Memories of the horrific consequences of far-right extremism remain strong in Europe. Yet nearly 65 years after the Nazi Holocaust, the extreme right has been gaining ground in parts of the continent, prompting worries that ultranationalism is on the upswing.

"The possibilities for a rise of the far right in the light of the financial and economic crisis are there," Anton Pelinka, a professor of politics at Central European University in Budapest, Hungary, told *The Guardian*, a leading British newspaper. [1]

So far, the European far right is advancing further — at the polls and in the expansion of illegal neo-Nazi organizations — than in the United States. But the gains by European extremists give heart to their U.S. counterparts, who have long maintained ties to Europe, though some European governments do their best to disrupt the relationships. In April, the Czech Republic expelled ex-Ku Klux Klan leader David Duke, a neo-Nazi, who had been invited by an extremist Czech group to lecture in Prague and Brno.

And the British government announced in early May that it had barred — among others — Don Black, founder of the Stormfront Web site, from entering Britain.

Duke's aborted visit notwithstanding, transatlantic ties may have frayed somewhat following the 2002 death of William Pierce. The American neo-Nazi leader had been traveling regularly to Europe for meetings, says Mark Potok, Intelligence Project director at the Southern Poverty Law Center, in Birmingham, Ala. But even if Duke fails to take Pierce's place as emissary to the Old World, American far-right Web sites commonly post links to extremist Web sites and news from Europe. [2]

The news is plentiful. In Austria, the country's two far-right parties together won 29 percent of the vote in national parliamentary elections last year. One of the parties had been found-

ed by Jörg Haider, who died in a car crash shortly after the vote. Haider made his brand of politics a major force by combining salesmanship, xenophobic opposition to immigration and appeals to the Nazi heritage of Adolf Hitler's country of birth.

Haider had been forced to quit as a provincial governor in 1991 (he was reelected in 1999) after praising Hitler's "orderly employment program." And in 1995 he praised Waffen SS veterans as "decent men of character who remained faithful to their ideals." [3]

Indicators of the growing strength of extremism extend into Germany and Britain as well as parts of the former Soviet bloc. In Russia, where ultranationalist groups, including neo-Nazis, are part of the political landscape, there were at least 85 systematic killings of migrant workers from Central Asia, as well as others seen as ethnically non-Slavic, in 2008, according to the Sova Center, a Moscow-based hate crime-monitoring group. The victims included a migrant worker from Tajikistan who was beheaded. Human-rights advocates who denounce these killings have been threatened with death themselves. [4]

Violence isn't limited to Russia. In late 2008, the police chief of Passau, a Bavarian town with a strong neo-Nazi presence, was stabbed following his 2008 order to open the grave of a former Nazi who had been buried with an illegal Swastika flag. [5]

The attack took place against a backdrop of increasing violence by German neo-Nazi organizations. A German newspaper reported that violent crimes originating in the extremist right increased by 15 percent during the first 10 months of 2008. And a government research institute reported that a greater segment of male teenagers — 5 percent — were involved in neo-Nazi groups than in mainstream politics in 2007-2008. In formerly communist-ruled eastern Germany, nearly 10 percent of youths participated in far-right groups. [6]

Continued from p. 430

Jackson, Miss., that same year; the murder of three civil rights workers in 1964 in Neshoba County, Miss.; and the killing of another civil rights worker in Alabama in 1965. [40]

Anti-civil rights violence ebbed after enactment of the Voting Rights Act in 1965. From then on, the extremist right became steadily more influenced by neo-Nazism. George Lincoln Rockwell, founder of the American Nazi Party, pioneered the white-nationalist trend. The former Navy pilot and World War II veteran was shot and killed by a dismissed follower in 1967. [41]

Rockwell had been a mentor to William Pierce, a former university physics professor who in 1974 founded the National Alliance, which became a major influence in the extremist right. Pierce became nationally notorious in the 1990s as author of *The Turner Diaries*, which laid out a scenario for white genocide of blacks, Jews and "race traitors" — a process led by a secret brotherhood known as The Order, which sets events in motion by blowing up FBI headquarters with a truck bomb.

The first open sign of a Klan-Nazi nexus was the 1979 killing in broad day-

light of five Communist Workers Party members who were starting an anti-Klan march in Greensboro, N.C., in 1979.

Fighting and Killing

Less visibly, another trend was under way. An extreme anti-government and anti-Jewish movement founded in 1971 by William Potter Gale began growing, especially in the West and Midwest. Posse Comitatus ("Power of the County") held that the federal government was constitutionally illegitimate. For example, county justices of

Throughout Western Europe, the enormous growth of immigrant populations, especially from Muslim countries, has provided the biggest boost to right-wing parties — from traditional conservative groups to neo-Nazis — over the past two decades.

However, the European far right's growth isn't uniform. In France, Jean-Marie Le Pen, an apologist for Nazism who was one of the pioneers of the post-World War II extreme right, saw his National Front party win only 4.3 percent of the vote in parliamentary elections in 2007. [7] Analysts said that President Nicolas Sarkozy effectively co-opted Le Pen's anti-immigration politics, though without the ethnic and religious extremism. In 2002, Le Pen had finished second in the first round of the presidential race. [8]

Le Pen's counterparts across the English Channel are showing more success. The British National Party (BNP) is seen by some British politicians as likely to win the most votes in an election in June to choose European Parliament representatives. BNP leaders portray their party as defending the country against non-white immigrants. Pro-immigrant policies "have made white Britons second-class citizens," the party says. [9]

Meanwhile, the BNP is trying to play down its historic anti-Semitism. Party leader Nick Griffin wrote in 2007 that taking an "Islamophobic" stance "is going to produce on average much better media coverage than . . . banging on about 'Jewish power.'" [10]

That purely tactical shift notwithstanding, others in the European political world argue that old-school anti-Semitism is flourishing — on the left as well as the right — often disguised as opposition to Israeli policies.

"The extravagant rhetoric of the demagogic left and right is gaining ground, and the most obvious manifestation is the return of anti-Semitism as an organizing ideology," Dennis Mac-Shane, a Labor Party member of Parliament, wrote in late 2008.

"As jobs are lost and welfare becomes meaner and leaner, the politics of blaming the outsider can only grow." [11]

[1] Quoted in Kate Connolly, "Haider is our Lady Di," *The Guardian*, Oct. 18, 2008, p. A29. For background, see Sarah Glazer, "Anti-Semitism in Europe," *CQ Global Researcher*, June 2008, pp. 149-181.

[2] For example, see "Stormfront forum, international," www.stormfront.org/forum/forumdisplay.php?f=18; Kinism.net — Occidental Christianity, http://kinism.net/; The French Connection, http://iamthewitness.com/; League of American Patriots, http://leagueap.org/wordpress/?page_id=17.

[3] Quoted in Matt Schudel, "Jörg Haider; Politician Made Far-Right Party a Force in Austria," *The Washington Post*, Oct. 12, 2008, p. C8.

[4] Michael Schwirtz, "Migrant Worker Decapitated in Russia," *The New York Times*, Dec. 13, 2008; Luke Harding, "Putin's worst nightmare: Their mission is to cleanse Russia of its ethnic 'occupiers,'" *The Observer* magazine (U.K.), Feb. 8, 2009, p. 32; "Neo-Nazis threaten to murder journalists in Russia," Committee to Protect Journalists, Feb. 11, 2009, http://cpj.org/2009/02/neo-nazis-threaten-to-murder-journalists-in-russia.php.

[5] Nicholas Kulish, "Ancient City's Nazi Past Seeps Out After Stabbing," *The New York Times*, Feb. 12, 2009, p. A18; "Police Chief Long Reviled by NPD Leadership," *Spiegel Online International*, Dec. 19, 2008, www.spiegel.de/international/germany/0,1518,597645,00.html.

[6] *Ibid.*; and "German teens drawn to neo-Nazi groups — study," Reuters, March 17, 2009, http://in.reuters.com/article/worldNews/idINIndia-385546 20090317.

[7] In 2008, Le Pen was fined 10,000 Euros for having called the Nazi occupation of France "not especially inhumane, even if there were a number of blunders." Quoted in "Le Pen fined over war comments," *The Irish Times* (Reuters), Feb. 9, 2008, p. A10.

[8] Adam Sage, "Hard-up National Front sells office to immigrants," *The Times* (London), Aug. 13, 2008, p. A37.

[9] "Immigration — time to say ENOUGH!" British National Party, undated, http://bnp.org.uk/policies-2/immigration. Also see Andrew Grice, "The BNP are now a bigger threat than ever," *The Independent* (London), April 10, 2009, p. A12.

[10] Quoted in Matthew Taylor, "BNP seeks to bury antisemitism and gain Jewish votes in Islamophobic campaign," *The Guardian* (London), April 10, 2008, p. A17.

[11] Denis MacShane, "Europe's Jewish Problem," *Newsweek*, International Edition, Dec. 15, 2008, p. 0.

the peace held legal supremacy over the U.S. Supreme Court, according to Posse ideology, and federal currency was invalid. [42]

Posse alienation went far deeper. An anti-Semitic religious doctrine known as "Christian Identity" exerted deep influence on many Posse leaders and members, including Gale (despite his own definitively proved Jewish descent, which he denied). The doctrine — rejected by all mainstream Christian denominations — holds that white people are the genuine descendants of the Biblical Hebrews. That is, they're God's chosen people, and Jews and blacks are the devil's

spawn. By 1976, the FBI estimated Posse membership at 12,000 to 50,000, not including sympathizers.

Posse Comitatus played a major role in raising the level of far-right extremism to a fever pitch in the last two decades of the 20th century. In the early 1980s, economic crisis gripped the Farm Belt, bringing a wave of foreclosures. The Posse launched a major recruiting drive, preaching that Jewish bankers were to blame for the falling grain prices and land values that brought many farmers to ruin.

One Posse tactic was to flood the federal court system with amateur lawsuits to cancel farmers' loan obligations, on the grounds that the loans were illegal. When authorities enforced foreclosure orders, trouble sometimes erupted.

In 1983, Gordon Kahl, a Christian Identity Posse activist who had served a prison term for tax evasion, killed two federal marshals following a meeting to recruit members in North Dakota. Kahl fled and was killed three months later in a gunfight with federal agents in Arkansas. Kahl became a martyr in extremist circles.

An almost identical episode took place the next year near Cairo, Neb., when a Posse sympathizer, Arthur Kirk, was killed in a shootout with state police officers serving foreclosure papers. Before the shooting started, Kirk denounced Jews, bankers and the Israeli intelligence agency, Mossad, to officers trying to get him to surrender. [43]

Ideology aside, some farmers who accepted help from the Posse were trying to survive financial crisis. Another group formed in the 1980s dedicated itself purely to violence.

The Order (its name borrowed from *The Turner Diaries*) vowed to strike the "Zionist Occupation Government" in defense of "White America." Robert Mathews founded the small group with eight other men in the early 1980s. By 1983, The Order had begun committing armed robberies to raise money. In 1984, the group assassinated a Denver radio talk-show host, Alan Berg, who was Jewish, and had argued with racists on the air. Later that same year, the group robbed an armored car of $3.6 million.

Mathews died in a shootout with federal agents on Whidbey Island, near Seattle, in December 1984.

In 1985, 23 surviving members of the group went to trial or pleaded guilty to racketeering charges, with most receiving sentences of 40 to 100 years. David Lane later was sentenced to 150 years in a separate trial for participating in Berg's murder. [44]

Federal prosecutors in Fort Smith, Ark., failed, however to convict Lane and 13 other extremists of sedition in 1988. They'd been charged with plotting to overthrow the government and set up a separate white nation in the Pacific Northwest. [45]

That same year, in that very region, an upsurge of anti-minority violence by skinheads claimed the life of Ethiopian immigrant Mulugeta Seraw, who was bludgeoned to death with a baseball bat by the East Side White Pride gang. Three years later, Tom Metzger, an infamous San Diego extremist, was found responsible for the death, along with others, on the grounds that his

White Aryan Resistance group had incited the group who killed Seraw. The verdict, in a civil suit brought by the SPLC, required Metzger and his codefendants to pay $12.5 million to Seraw's family. [46]

Explosion and Aftermath

The violence that marked the 1980s intensified in the '90s, sparked by the botched 1992 arrest of survivalist and Christian Identity adherent Randy Weaver for failing to appear in court on a gun-law charge. (He'd been given the wrong court date.) Weaver had holed up with his family in remote Ruby Ridge, in northern Idaho, which had become a center for the extreme right and was home to Christian Identity leader Richard Butler. [47]

When federal marshals attempted to arrest Weaver, who had not been involved in previous violence, a gunfight broke out in which Weaver's son and a marshal were killed; later, during a siege of the family's cabin, an FBI sniper killed Weaver's wife. Weaver surrendered and was sentenced to 18 months in prison. [48]

FBI handling of the case was widely considered a fiasco, and worse. But on the far right, a more ominous view prevailed: Ruby Ridge seemed to validate conspiracist fears of government violence against gun owners and opponents of the "New World Order" — far-right code for U.N.-controlled global government.

Months after Ruby Ridge, Christian Identity preacher Peter Peters organized a meeting of about 150 extremists at Estes Park, Colo. In a keynote speech, Louis Beam, a former leader of the Texas Klan and one of those acquitted in the Arkansas sedition case, outlined a strategy of "leaderless resistance" — formation of small cells of committed activists without central direction. A Vietnam veteran, Beam also spoke of the need

for "camouflage" — the ability to blend in the public's eye the more committed groups of resistance "with mainstream 'kosher' associations that are generally seen as harmless." [49]

Similarly, others at the meeting advocated uniting with less extreme groups to form a broad anti-government movement. [50]

Meanwhile, a related development had just shocked the mainstream political establishment. David Duke, a former Klan leader who hadn't renounced his anti-black or anti-Jewish views, won the 1991 Republican primary for Louisiana governor. (He went on to lose the general election.) [51]

Following the Estes Park conclave, "militias" sprang up around the country, especially in the rural Midwest and West. Ideas animating the movement included survivalism, gun-rights defense and — among many members, but not all — far-right conspiracy theories. Among those who passed through militia circles was a U.S. Army veteran of the 1990-1991 Persian Gulf War, Timothy McVeigh.

But before McVeigh's name hit the headlines, a series of events near Waco, Texas, would seize national attention and electrify the far right. Members of the Branch Davidian religious cult, led by a fiery preacher named David Koresh, fired on ATF agents attempting to search for guns and ammunition believed to be stored at the Davidians' compound; four agents were killed. On April 19, 1993, after a 51-day siege, FBI agents moved on the compound with tanks. In the conflagration that resulted, Koresh and about 80 other Davidians died, including many children.

A widespread suspicion that FBI teargas canisters started the fire became a certainty on the far right. In those circles, Waco stood as evidence of government ruthlessness. Koresh, who had followed the Weaver case closely, probably wouldn't have been surprised. "Koresh spoke to me frequently on the phone about Ruby Ridge," says Special Agent Cavanaugh of the ATF, who negotiated with the Branch Davidian leader during the siege. Koresh and his top aide "were well-versed in everything that happened there and were spitting out 'New World Order' crackpot conspiracy theories."

In 2000, an outside counsel to the Justice Department concluded that the canisters hadn't started the fire but that Davidians themselves ignited it. [52]

But by then, April 19 had become notorious for another reason. On April 19, 1995, McVeigh detonated a bomb in a rented truck he parked in front of the Alfred P. Murrah Federal Building in Oklahoma City, killing 168 people, including 19 children. Arrested hours later after a traffic stop, McVeigh was later often described as a lone wolf. But, among other activities, he had sold *The Turner Diaries* at gun shows, which were popular with militia members and with extremists in general.

"McVeigh was not a lone extremist; instead, he was trained to make himself look like a lone extremist," wrote former FBI agent German. "It's a right-wing terrorism technique that comes complete with written instruction manuals." [53]

The bombing — for which McVeigh was executed in 2001 — made *Turner Diaries* author Pierce and his National Alliance notorious. But the bombing also saw a steep decline in militia membership, as those without a high level of commitment to extremist politics dropped away.

More blows followed. Pierce died of cancer in 2002. Two years later Butler died; earlier he had lost his Idaho compound after losing a civil lawsuit filed by the Southern Poverty Law Center. [54]

Then, in 2005, Matthew Hale, 33, considered an up-and-coming extremist leader as head of the World Church of the Creator, was sentenced to 40 years in federal prison for conspiring

to kill a federal judge. Since his imprisonment, extremist-watchers say, no charismatic leader has emerged from the extremist world. ■

CURRENT SITUATION

Hate in April

Hitler was born in April, which marks the beginning of the public rally season for right-wing extremists, and for opponents who mount counterdemonstrations. [55]

This year promises to be a busy one for haters. In April alone, 32 conferences, celebrations, militia training sessions and other events were planned by neo-Nazi, Klan, Christian Identity and related organizations in 22 states, according to the Anti-Defamation League; dozens more events are scheduled into October. [56]

The list includes Hitler birthday commemorations in Illinois and North Carolina and a march by robed Klan members in Pulaski, Tenn., where Confederate veterans founded the Klan.

Counterdemonstrators showed for an NSM rally of about 70 members the day before at the Gateway Arch in St. Louis, Mo. No one was arrested, but the two groups yelled at each other and traded "Heil Hitler" salutes and raised-middle-finger retorts. A second group of counterdemonstrators organized by the ADL held a "rally for respect" at a nearby site. [57]

Commenting on the NSM rally, Lewis Reed, president of the St. Louis Board of Aldermen, said, "It's sad that there are still people today, in 2009, that only want to divide the races and breed hate." [58]

Yet neo-Nazi rallies, at least in major metropolitan areas, typically don't draw big crowds of extremists. In Skokie, Ill., a Chicago suburb with a large Jewish population — including Holocaust survivors — the opening of a state holocaust museum in April drew a neo-Nazi demonstration — of seven people. Twelve thousand people attended the opening ceremony, where former President Bill Clinton spoke. [59]

This year's rally season began with a snag. "East Coast White Unity" and "Volksfront" ("Peoples' Front" in German) had planned to meet in Boston over the April 11 weekend. But after the Boston Anti-Racist Coalition told the Veterans of Foreign Wars (VFW) about the nature of the "Patriot's Day" rally, the VFW withdrew permission to use their hall. Instead, the event was held at an American Legion Hall in Loudon, N.H. [60]

"These racist speakers, bands and their supporters will always have to walk on egg shells and face the very real prospect of their events being exposed to the general public, wherever and whenever they rear their ugly heads," the coalition said in a post on an anarchist Web site. [61]

But Roper of White Revolution replied, "Because a venue, or two, or three, has cancelled on us due to the efforts of anti-white, communist and Jewish activists, the event has not been cancelled and will go on," he said. "We plan for such eventualities in depth." [62]

For its part, One People's Project, an anti-supremacist organization, says it infiltrates neo-Nazi and Klan groups to find out about planned events in time to organize countermobilizations. "We can't keep on allowing groups like the Klan, Aryan Nations, National Alliance, National Vanguard and the National Socialist Movement to hold society at-large hostage," Daryle Lamont Jenkins of One People's Project said. [63]

'Fascism' Label Comes in Handy for Critics

But respected writers say it's a legitimate — if unlikely — concern.

Accompanying today's worries about an extremist resurgence are fears that the United States could, if economic conditions worsen, embrace fascism — the totalitarian ideology that modern hate groups champion.

But the concern focuses on the federal government itself, not fringe, neo-Nazi organizations. Indeed, some of President Barack Obama's foes are calling him a fascist, the same label some had applied to President George W. Bush.

The labeling would seem to show once again that "fascist" is one of the most loosely applied — and handy — terms in the political lexicon. Nevertheless, fascism isn't foreign to the United States, even though the word comes from 1920s Italy. Italian dictator Benito Mussolini coined "fascismo" to name the violence-glorifying, socialist-hating and ultranationalist movement he formed after World War I, appropriating a term then used for militant political groups of all stripes. [1]

Notwithstanding those Italian roots, Robert Paxton, one of the leading historians of the European far right, wrote that the first fascist group in history may have been the Ku Klux Klan. "By adopting a uniform . . . as well as by their techniques of intimidation and their conviction that violence was justified in the cause of their group's destiny," wrote Paxton, a Virginia native, "the first version of the Klan in the defeated American South was arguably a remarkable preview of the way fascist movements were to function in interwar Europe." [2]

But Paxton, an emeritus professor of social science at Columbia University, dismisses the attempt to label Obama fascist as a desperation move. "When there's a popular figure and you can't get a grip on opposing him, you call him a fascist," he says. "As opposed to Hitler and Mussolini in uniform, shrieking into microphones and juicing up the nationalism of crowds, Obama is a calm, reasonable person whose basic drives have all been toward bolstering democracy and the rule of law."

Obama's extreme critics insist otherwise. Obama heads a "Gestapo government," conservative blogger David Limbaugh (brother of radio commentator Rush Limbaugh) told a radio interviewer. And *The American Spectator*, a conservative magazine, likened Obama's economic policies to those of Mussolini. [3]

The author of the *Spectator* piece, senior editor Quinn Hillyer, added that he wouldn't go so far as to compare Obama's administration to that of Adolf Hitler, whose version of fascism turned out far deadlier than the Italian original. Still, he wrote, "The comparison of today's situation to that of Italian fascism is no mere scare tactic but a serious concern." [4]

In calling Obama a fascist, critics may simply be hoping for better results than they got when they tried pinning the "socialist" label on him during and after the 2008 presidential campaign. "We've so overused the word 'socialism' that it no longer has the negative connotation it had 20 years ago, or even 10 years ago," Sal Anuzis, former chairman of the Michigan Republican Party, told *The New York Times*. "Fascism — everybody still thinks that's a bad thing." [5]

To be sure, only a small minority accepts "fascist" as a compliment. But aiming it at a politician after first denouncing him as a leftist seems an odd tactic, given fascists' historic hatred of socialists. [6]

But that seemed to bother Obama's foes as little as the fact that they were borrowing from the vocabulary that some critics of the Bush administration used in 2001-2008.

The liberal group MoveOn.org, for instance, created an ad in 2004 that tried to connect Bush to Hitler, intoning: "A nation warped by lies. Lies fuel fear. Fear fuels aggression. Invasion. Occupation. What were war crimes in 1945 is foreign policy in 2003." [7]

Liberal author Naomi Wolf made a similar case in her book *The End of America*, published toward the end of the Bush administration. [8]

On April 19, 2008, 30 to 40 members of the National Socialist Movement (NSM) rallied in Washington for an anti-immigration march from the National Mall to the U.S. Capitol. They were greeted by raucous counterdemonstrators, five of whom were arrested for allegedly assaulting police officers with pepper spray and a pole. [64]

White supremacist gatherings don't tend to be large affairs. Roper told a reporter by phone from the New Hampshire event that 200 people were participating, making it one of the bigger events of its type. But no independent confirmation was available.

In 2005, Roper organized a protest demonstration outside an event in Boston commemorating the 60th anniversary of the liberation of Nazi death camps. Police and counterprotesters far outnumbered Roper and his dozen or so demonstrators. [65]

However, on occasion, supremacists' crowds have been bigger, and violence has erupted. In 2002, about 60 supporters of the now-imprisoned

Matthew Hale's World Church of the Creator gathered in York, Pa., where a former mayor and eight others had been charged in the 1969 death of a black woman during a racially charged riot. Several hundred counterprotesters fought with Hale's supporters in the city streets, as police tried to separate the groups. Twenty-five people were arrested. [66]

However, in April of that year, only about 30 to 40 neo-Nazis showed up in York for a Hitler's birthday celebration. [67]

"The Nazis rose to power in a living, if battered, democracy," Wolf wrote. "Dictators can rise in a weakened democracy even with a minority of popular support." [9]

Drawing in part from Paxton's most recent book on fascism, Wolf argued that erosions of civil liberties under the Bush administration paralleled events in Italy and Germany as Mussolini and Hitler moved toward totalitarian rule.

But these arguments leave out the widespread loss of faith in democracy, and the state of near-civil war that served as the backdrop to the rise of fascism in Italy and Germany, Paxton says.

By contrast, Americans opposed to Bush expressed their discontent within the system, by voting in Obama, Paxton notes. And the political climate even before that, when Wolf was writing, didn't begin to approach the Italian and German precedents. "In the collection of pre-conditions, you need something worse," he says. "A lost war, big-time national humiliation — we might get there, but we're not quite there yet — and a sense that our existing way of doing politics isn't working. And then power moving to the streets, with paramilitary organizations. I don't see any of that."

Paxton does agree that the detention and intelligence-gathering policies adopted after the Sept. 11, 2001, terrorist attacks could be compared with early moves by Hitler upon

Followers of the neo-Nazi NPD party stand defiantly near a "Berlin against Nazis" poster during a demonstration in Berlin on May 1, 2009. Anti-immigration neo-Nazis and skinheads often clash with anti-fascists on May Day in Germany.

AFP/Getty Images/Axel Schmidt

winning election as chancellor in 1933. "You can draw some parallels — with care," he says. "The focus should be on steps away from the rule of law."

Still, Paxton discourages complacency. "In three years, if we're not out of this mess, we could see something that would call itself the patriotic party or the minutemen, a symbol that has a nice nationalistic resonance," he says. "It would sweep up all the discontented from the left and the right; it would be light on ideology. The immigration issue would be a very plausible gathering point for some sort of movement like this."

[1] Robert O. Paxton, *The Anatomy of Fascism* (2004), pp. 4-5.

[2] *Ibid.*, p. 49.

[3] Quinn Hillyer, "Il Duce, Redux?" *The American Spectator*, April 2, 2009, http://spectator.org/archives/2009/04/02/il-duce-redux. Limbaugh quoted in Carla Marinucci and Joe Garofoli, "Fascist? Socialist? Attacks on Obama take a shrill tone," *San Francisco Chronicle*, April 9, 2009, p. A1.

[4] Hillyer, *op. cit.*

[5] Quoted in John Harwood, "But Can Obama Make the Trains Run on Time?" *The New York Times*, April 20, 2009, www.nytimes.com/2009/04/20/us/politics/20caucus.html?scp=1&sq=fascism&st=cse.

[6] Paxton, *op. cit.*, pp. 60-67.

[7] Marinucci and Garofoli, *op. cit.*

[8] Naomi Wolf, *The End of America: Letters of Warning to a Young Patriot, A Citizen's Call to Action* (2007).

[9] *Ibid.*, pp. 39-40.

Free Speech, Hate Speech

Some conservatives are attacking the Department of Homeland Security (DHS) examination of far-right extremism as a barely disguised attack on political foes of the Obama administration.

"One of the most embarrassingly shoddy pieces of propaganda I'd ever read out of DHS," thundered conservative blogger Michelle Malkin. Others in the conservative blogosphere shared her view that the report tried to tie conservatives to extremists. [68] Homeland Security Secretary Janet Napolitano later responded that the agency is on "the lookout for criminal and terrorist activity but we do not — nor will we ever — monitor ideology or political beliefs." [69]

The report noted that extremists are especially interested in recruiting veterans, an observation that triggered angry criticism from some veterans' organizations (see below). In essence the 14-page assessment holds that economic turmoil, the election of a black president and a growing number of veterans — whom right-wing extremists have a documented interest in recruiting — are creating a climate in which far-right extremism could flourish again. Specifically, the report said the DHS "assesses that right-wing extremist groups' frustration over a perceived lack of government action on illegal immigration has the potential to incite individuals or small groups toward violence." But any such violence would likely be "isolated" and "small-scale." [70]

Though critics later said the DHS failed to distinguish between extremists and mainstream political advocates, the report did try to draw that line. Debates on gun rights and other constitutional issues are often intense — but perfectly legal, the report said. "Violent extremists," it added, "may attempt to co-opt the debate and use the controversy as a radicalization tool." [71]

But Berlet of Political Research Associates argues that the report itself crosses into the potentially unconstitutional territory of monitoring ideological trends.

"The government should not be in the business of undermining radical ideas," he says. "As citizens we have a responsibility to challenge rhetoric that demonizes and scapegoats, but I don't think the First Amendment allows the government to be in that battle."

Despite attacks from the left as well as right, some commentators defended the report against its critics. "This DHS assessment was begun more than a year ago, before Barack Obama was even nominated," blogger Charles Johnson — a political independent who had been popular with conservative critics of Islam — wrote on his influential "Little Green Footballs" site. "It was not done at the behest of the Obama administration. . . . The DHS report is not intended to target anyone but the most extreme elements of the far right, and it's depressing to see so many bloggers jumping to totally unwarranted conclusions." [72]

Reaction to the document may have been especially intense because it followed closely on an uproar that greeted disclosure of a report on the "Modern Militia Movement" in Missouri. It was produced by a "fusion center," one of 70 around the country that were set up by law enforcement agencies after Sept. 11 to ensure that intelligence is shared between federal, state and local officers. The report mostly summarized information on extremist activities in the 1990s and outlined some ideas said to be circulating now on the far right. [73]

But the report lumped together extremists and mainstream political activists with no violent inclinations. "Militia members most commonly associate with third-party political groups," the report said, going on to name supporters of 2008 libertarian presidential candidate Bob Barr, Constitution Party candidate Chuck Baldwin and Rep. Ron Paul, R-Texas, who ran for the Republican Party presidential nomination. [74]

"This smacks of totalitarian regimes of days gone by," said Baldwin, one of many to react furiously to the document. [75]

Within weeks, the Missouri State Highway Patrol had apologized to the three politicians and replaced the head of the fusion center. [76]

Not all critics came from the right. "This is part of a national trend where intelligence reports are turning attention away from people who are actually doing bad things to people who are thinking thoughts that the government, for whatever reason, doesn't like," former FBI agent German told The Associated Press. [77]

The ACLU, where German is now a policy counselor, noted that the North Central Texas Fusion System had produced a report in February that tied former Rep. Cynthia McKinney and former U.S. Attorney General Ramsey Clark to "far left groups" that allegedly sympathize with the Iranian-backed Hezbollah militia of Lebanon and other armed movements in the Middle East. [78]

Fusion centers, German said, are an "equal opportunity infringer" on civil rights of citizens on the right and the left. [79]

Indeed, DHS says that it produced a report earlier this year on left-wing extremists. That report soon leaked out as well. The document forecast a rise in cyber-attacks aimed at businesses, especially those deemed to be violators of animal rights. [80]

Extremism-watchers, for their part, greeted the DHS report as an echo of their own conclusions. "This Homeland Security report reinforces our view that the current political and economic climate in the United States is creating the right conditions for a rise in extremist activity," said Potok of the SPLC. [81]

But one of the center's most ferocious left-wing critics, writer Alexander Cockburn, ridiculed that reasoning, accusing the center of "fingering militiamen in a potato field in Idaho" instead of "attacking the roots of Southern poverty, and the system that sustains that poverty as expressed in the endless prisons and death rows across the South, disproportionately crammed with blacks and Hispanics." [82]

Fights are also continuing over broadcasters' commentaries. In Boston, radio station WTKK-FM suspended right-wing radio talk-show host Jay Severin after he responded to the influenza outbreak with comments including: "So now, in addition to venereal disease and the other leading exports of Mexico — women with mustaches and VD — now we have swine flu." Mexicans, he said, are "the world's lowest of primitives." [83]

Franklin Soults, a spokesman for Massachusetts Immigrant and Refugee Advocacy Coalition, called Severin's language "dehumanizing."

Severin himself referred questions to his lawyer, George Tobia, who told the *Boston Globe* that he expected the broadcaster to be back on the air soon. "But I don't know when." [84]

Recruiting Veterans

Discharged from the U.S. Marine Corps after being arrested for allegedly taking part in armed robberies at two hotels in Jacksonville, N.C., a former lance corporal now faces prosecution for allegedly threatening President Obama's life.

Continued on p. 440

At Issue:

Is anti-immigration rhetoric provoking hate crimes against Latinos?

MARK POTOK
DIRECTOR, INTELLIGENCE PROJECT, SOUTHERN POVERTY LAW CENTER

WRITTEN FOR *CQ RESEARCHER*, APRIL 2009

a cross the board, nativist organizations in America have angrily denounced those who suggest that demonizing rhetoric leads to hate violence. One of them even recently issued a press release criticizing the "outrageous behavior" of groups like the Southern Poverty Law Center that propose such a link and "provide no proof whatsoever."

Nativist organizations take the remarkable position that hate speech directed against Latino immigrants has no relationship at all to hate crime — not even the utterly false allegations that Latinos are secretly planning to hand the American Southwest over to Mexico, are far more criminal than others, are bringing dread diseases to the United States, and so on.

In addition to defying common sense, that head-in-the-sand approach completely ignores the statements that are typically made by hate criminals during their attacks.

Take the case of Marcelo Lucero, who was allegedly murdered by a gang of white teenagers in the Long Island town of Patchogue, N.Y., last November. Prosecutors say the suspects told detectives they regularly went "beaner jumping" — beating up Latinos — and that they used racial epithets during the attack. "Let's go find some Mexicans to [expletive] up," one said beforehand, according to *Newsday*.

Nativist groups use the fact that we don't know precisely where the teens' fury comes from to deny it was related to nativist demonization. But just because it's not possible to pinpoint the exact source of their racial anger — rhetoric from nativist groups, their parents, local anti-immigrant politicians, or pundits — does not mean it magically popped into the assailants' minds.

There is also hard evidence to back up the link between demonization and violence. According to FBI statistics, anti-Latino hate crimes went up 40 percent between 2003 and 2007 — the very same period that saw a remarkable proliferation of nativist rhetoric.

Experts agree that there is a link. "Racist rhetoric and dehumanizing images inspire violence perpetrated against innocent human beings," says Jack Levin, a nationally known hate crime expert at Northeastern University. "It's not just the most recent numbers. It's the trend over a number of years that lends credibility to the notion that we're seeing a very real and possibly dramatic rise in anti-Latino hate incidents."

Ignoring the role that demonization plays in such violence is a surefire way to generate more of it. Marcelo Lucero's murder is only the latest in a sad list of violent incidents inspired by ugly rhetoric that will certainly grow longer.

MARCUS EPSTEIN
EXECUTIVE DIRECTOR, THE AMERICAN CAUSE

WRITTEN FOR *CQ RESEARCHER*, APRIL 2009

l ast year, Barack Obama accused broadcasters Lou Dobbs and Rush Limbaugh of "feeding a kind of xenophobia." He added that their broadcasts were a "reason why hate crimes against Hispanic people doubled last year."

Obama's facts and logic are plain wrong. The FBI found only 745 anti-Latino hate crimes nationwide in 2007, down from 770 in 2006. In fact anti-Hispanic hate crimes per capita dropped 18 percent over the last decade.

Most of these hate crimes were for minor offenses, such as graffiti or name-calling, with only 145 aggravated assaults, two murders and no rapes in 2007. To put this in perspective, former Hudson Institute economist Ed Rubenstein estimates illegal aliens murder at least 949 people a year.

There is also no evidence that hate crimes are motivated by the immigration-control movement. Those who claim there's a connection cannot point to a single, significant commentator or politician who has advocated violence against Latinos. Nor can they find a single hate crime committed by their followers.

Although whites are the vast majority of listeners of conservative talk radio and television, they committed only 52 percent of hate crimes against Latinos — a percentage well below their proportion of 66 percent of the population. Moreover, Los Angeles County classified 42 percent of black-on-Hispanic hate crimes as "gang related." This is not to suggest that blacks cannot be racist, but that they are unlikely to be influenced by the purveyors of supposed anti-immigrant rhetoric.

The 2008 murder of José Osvaldo Sucuzhanay in Brooklyn by blacks who targeted him because they mistook him as gay was denounced as a significant anti-Hispanic, anti-immigrant hate crime by all New York politicians and by *The New York Times*. Even when they were at large, the race of the killers was rarely mentioned.

Groups like the Southern Poverty Law Center that perpetuate misconceptions about anti-Latino hate crimes make no secret of their goals. They want supporters of immigration control silenced because, in the words of La Raza president Janet Murguía, "We have to draw the line on freedom of speech, when freedom of speech becomes hate speech."

These organizations run relentless smear campaigns accusing virtually all opponents of illegal immigration — no matter how nuanced or tempered — of hate speech that must not be allowed on the airwaves, in print, or in front of Congress.

Before we abandon our core democratic principles of free speech and open debate in the name of stopping hate crimes, we should at least get our facts straight.

Continued from p. 438

Kody Brittingham, 20, who served in the 2nd Tank Battalion, 2nd Marine Division, was indicted in February for the alleged threat by a federal grand jury in Raleigh, N.C. An unnamed federal law enforcement official told the Jacksonville (N.C.) *Daily News* that the charge followed discovery of a journal in Brittingham's barracks at Camp Lejeune in which he laid out a plan to kill Obama, who at that point hadn't yet been inaugurated. Investigators reportedly also found white-supremacist literature among Brittingham's possessions. [85]

How plausible the alleged assassination plans were is not clear. But the arrest did reawaken concerns about white-supremacist and neo-Nazi recruitment of men with military training, especially those with combat experience (Brittingham, however, had never served overseas).

Those concerns aren't limited to extremist-watchers from advocacy organizations. An FBI report last year counted 203 individuals with "confirmed or claimed" military experience who had been spotted in extremist groups since the Sept. 11 attacks, which effectively marked the beginning of a period in which hundreds of thousands of military personnel began acquiring battlefield experience. [86]

Those 203 individuals represent a minuscule fraction of the country's 23.8 million veterans or 1.4 million active-duty personnel, the report acknowledged. [87]

The recent DHS assessment discussed extremist groups' interest in recruiting veterans, only to prompt outraged reaction from some veterans' organizations and some politicians. "To characterize men and women returning home after defending our country as potential terrorists is offensive and unacceptable," House Republican leader John Boehner of Ohio said in a press release. The Department of Homeland Security owes our veterans an apology." [88]

In discussing extremists' interest in veterans, the FBI said that neo-Nazis were not discouraged by the small number of vets who might be responsive to recruiting pitches.

Members of the National Socialist Movement demonstrate on the grounds of the U.S. Capitol on April 19, 2008. Fifteen years earlier, on another April 19, a fire during an FBI siege at the Branch Davidian compound outside Waco, Texas, killed David Koresh and about 80 followers, including many children.

"The prestige which the extremist movement bestows upon members with military experience grants them the potential for influence beyond their numbers," said the report, which is marked "unclassified/for official use only/law enforcement sensitive." The report, now available online, has circulated among journalists and nongovernmental specialists. [89]

Among a handful of specific cases, the FBI noted that two privates in the elite Army 82nd Airborne Division received six-year prison sentences for attempting to sell body armor and other equipment in 2007 to an undercover agent posing as a white-supremacist movement member. And in 2005, a former Army intelligence analyst who'd been convicted of a firearms violation founded a skinhead group that reportedly advocated training members in firearms, knife-fighting, close-quarters combat and "house sweeps." [90]

The FBI intelligence assessment followed an investigation by the SPLC. In 2006 the center published a detailed report that quoted neo-Nazi vets, a supremacist who had renounced the extremist cause, as well as a Defense Department investigator. Extremists "stretch across all branches of service, they are linking up across the branches once they're inside, and they are hardcore," investigator Scott Barfield told the SPLC. "We've got Aryan Nations graffiti in Baghdad." [91]

Worries about a neo-Nazi presence in the military had surfaced years before U.S. troops were deployed to Iraq and Afghanistan. The trigger was the random murder in 1995 of a black man and woman in Fayetteville, N.C., by two soldiers in the elite Army 82nd Airborne Division, whose home base is nearby Fort Bragg. In the uproar that followed, 22 members of the 82nd — including those arrested for the killing — were found by the Army to have extremist ties. [92]

But far-right efforts to penetrate the Armed Forces apparently continued. The SPLC published excerpts from a 1999 article in the *National Alliance* magazine by an Army Special

Forces veteran who urged young supremacists to sign up. "Light infantry is your branch of choice," he wrote, "because the coming race war, and the ethnic cleansing to follow, will be very much an infantryman's war. It will be house-to-house, neighborhood-by-neighborhood, until your town or city is cleared and the alien races are driven into the countryside where they can be hunted down and 'cleansed.' " [93]

Supremacists who enlisted were told to stay undercover: "Do not — I repeat, do not — seek out other skinheads. Do not listen to skinhead 'music.' Do not keep 'racist' or 'White-supremacist tracts' where you live. During your service you will be subjected to a constant barrage of equal opportunity drivel. . . . Keep your mouth shut." [94] ∎

OUTLOOK

Guns in Holsters

The possibility that far-right extremists will emerge from the margins is as uncertain as the course of today's economic crisis, veteran analysts say.

For their part, extremists including Roper of White Revolution harbor no doubt that the medium-term future will see the outbreak of major racial and ethnic violence accompanying the breakup of the United States. "A lot of people might think it's impossible, but if you had gone to those same people in 1980 and told them the Berlin Wall was going to fall and the Soviet Union was going to collapse without a single missile being launched, they would have thought that was impossible too," Roper says.

Others would argue that U.S. society and government have firmer foundations than the Soviet system, which came to power in 1917 and sustained itself first by mass terror and then by mass repression.

In any event, the consensus among monitors of the far right is that extremist intensity hasn't even reached the level of the 1990s — the point at which the extremist movement "goes from red-hot to white-hot," as Pitcavage of the ADL puts it.

A key indicator of the latter stage is the discovery of major conspiracies or actual large-scale attacks, such as the Oklahoma City bombing. "In the 1980s and mid-'90s, a variety of white-supremacist or anti-government extremist groups had huge plots — start a white revolution, break off part of the country, hit military targets," Pitcavage says. "What they shared was an elaborate large-scale conception, often far larger than actual capabilities. If we start seeing some more of these we will know that things are starting to go white-hot again."

The present crisis is too new to suddenly spawn a new wave of high-intensity extremism, Pitcavage adds. "Movements don't start overnight," he says. "It takes a while for people to experience these things and form a reaction to them."

But Barkun at Syracuse University says today's conditions are far more alarming than those of the "white-hot" years. War and global economic crisis alone open the possibility of a new extremism paradigm, he says.

"We're in an economic situation which is so dire and so long-lasting that it will have social and political effects," Barkun says. "Things may develop along entirely novel lines that don't necessarily arise out of pre-existing groups, or that can readily be placed along the right-wing continuum, where the extreme right and the extreme left come together."

He adds that he hasn't seen any evidence of this taking place. However, left-right extremes have met before, at least elsewhere. Mussolini's early fascist movement took in former socialists like him. The "socialist" in Germany's National Socialist (Nazi) Party did express some — short-lived — opposition to capitalism. Attempts by some European far-rightists to co-opt left-wing anarchists represent an attempt to revive that tradition.

Also up in the air, to Barkun and others, is whether America's tradition of racial conflict will reassert itself in a country whose demography has been transformed from the old, white majority-black minority pattern.

One effect of the growing Latino political presence likely will be an accommodation by the Republican Party, where most support for tougher immigration control has centered, says Potok of the Southern Poverty Law Center. The result would be that white, non-Hispanic voters alienated by demographic change fall away from the conventional political system. "When that happens, a lot of these people would just go home, but some percentage of them would go into that extremist world," he speculates. "For them, there's no way out of a multiracial system. So it's 'Let's go off and start our own country.' "

On the organizational side, Potok theorizes, the absence of major, controlling figures, such as Pierce of the National Alliance and Butler of Aryan Nations may be a danger sign. "I understand that a lot of really scary people, like The Order, came out of the Alliance," he says, adding that some extremist leaders have a history of depicting a need for violence only at some indefinite point in the future. "Leaders ultimately have the effect of holding people back: 'We're going to kill the Jews, but keep your guns in your holsters.' " ∎

Notes

[1] Quoted in Jonathan D. Silver, "911 Operator Failed to Warn About Weapons," *Pittsburgh Post-Gazette*, April 7, 2009, p. A1. Unless otherwise indicated, all details of this event are drawn from *Post-Gazette* articles published April 5-8, 2009.

[2] Quoted in Michael A. Fucco, "Deadly Ambush Claims the Lives of 3 City Police Officers," *Pittsburgh Post-Gazette*, April 5, 2009, p. A1.

[3] Quoted in Dennis B. Roddy, "On Web: Racism, Anti-Semitism, Warnings," *Pittsburgh Post-Gazette*, April 7, 2009, p. A1.

[4] "The Employment Situation: March 2009," U.S. Bureau of Labor Statistics, April 3, 2009, www.bls.gov/news.release/empsit.nr0.htm; Jeffrey Passel and D'Vera Cohn, "Trends in Unauthorized Immigration," Pew Hispanic Center, Oct. 2, 2008, http://pewhispanic.org/reports/report.php?ReportID=94. *CQ Researcher* has published reports on immigration going back to the early 1920s. Three of the most recent are: Reed Karaim, "America's Border Fence," Sept. 19, 2008, pp. 745-768; Alan Greenblatt, "Immigration Debate," Feb. 1, 2008, pp. 97-120, and Peter Katel, "Real ID," May 4, 2007, pp. 385-408.

[5] "Rightwing Extremism: Current Economic and Political Climate Fueling Resurgence in Radicalization and Recruitment," Homeland Security Department, April 7, 2009, http://images.logicsix.com/DHS_RWE.pdf.

[6] "Why Obama is Good for Our Movement," National Socialist Movement, undated, www.nsm88.org/activities/why obama is good for our movement.html. See also Alan Greenblatt, "Race in America," *CQ Researcher*, July 11, 2003, pp. 593-624.

[7] David Holthouse, "The Year in Hate," Intelligence Report, Southern Poverty Law Center, spring 2009, www.splcenter.org/intel/intelreport/article.jsp?aid=1027. For background, see Kenneth Jost, "Hate Crimes," *CQ Researcher*, Jan. 8, 1993, pp. 1-24.

[8] Tom Hays, "Feds charge 3 men in election bias attacks," The Associated Press, Jan. 7, 2009; Christine Hauser and Colin Moynihan, "Three Are Charged in Attacks on Election Night," *The New York Times*, Jan. 8, 2009, p. A25.

[9] Manny Fernandez and Javier C. Hernandez, "Binghamton Victims Shared a Dream of Living Better Lives," *The New York Times*, April 5, 2009, www.nytimes.com/2009/04/06/nyregion/06victims.html?scp=7&sq=Jiverly Binghamton&st=cse; Al Baker and Liz Robbins, "Police Had Few Contacts With Killer," *The New York Times*, April 7, 2009.

[10] Quoted in Jessica Fargen, "Sicko Kill Plot Emerges," *Boston Herald*, Jan. 23, 2009, p. 5; Milton J. Valencia, "Father of attacked Brockton sisters calls for justice," *Boston Herald*, Jan. 24, 2009, p. B3.

[11] Quoted in Melissa Nelson, "FL man acted oddly before Chilean students' deaths," The Associated Press, March 13, 2009.

[12] "Hate on Display: A Visual Database of Extremist Symbols, Logos and Tattoos," ADL, undated, www.adl.org/hate_symbols/numbers_14-88.asp. For a Web site filled with praise for Lane see www.freetheorder.org/dlrip.html.

[13] Jeffrey Gettleman, "William L. Pierce, 68; Ex-Rocket Scientist Became White Supremacist," *Los Angeles Times*, July 24, 2002, p. B10.

[14] Quoted in John Krupa, "Teen in plot lists drinking as his job," *Arkansas Democrat-Gazette*, Oct. 29, 2008; see also Holthouse, *op. cit.*

[15] Jared Taylor, "Transition to Black Rule," *American Renaissance*, Nov. 14, 2008, www.amren.com/mtnews/archives/2008/11/transition_to_b.php.

[16] Jared Taylor, "Jews and American Renaissance," *American Renaissance*, May 2006, www.amren.com/mtnews/archives/2006/04/jews_and_americ.php.

[17] Passel and Cohn, *op. cit.*

[18] "Hate Crime Statistics, Victims, 2007," FBI, www.fbi.gov/ucr/hc2007/table_07.htm.

[19] *Ibid.*

[20] Jim Salter, "Mo. town outraged over killings, illegal immigrant," The Associated Press, March 20, 2009; "Hannibal murder suspect is illegal alien," The Associated Press, March 4, 2009.

[21] Edwin S. Rubinstein, "Illegals kill a dozen a day?" *VDare*, Jan. 12, 2007, www.vdare.com/rubenstein/070112_nd.htm.

[22] Mark Hugo Lopez and Michael T. Light, "A Rising Share: Hispanics and Federal Crime," Pew Hispanic Center, Feb. 18, 2009, p. 4, http://pewhispanic.org/files/reports/104.pdf.

[23] Quoted in Sarah Burge, "Hate Crimes Continue Their Rise in Riverside County," *Press-Enterprise* (Riverside, Calif.), July 20, 2006, p. B1. See also Denes Husty III, "Crime vs. Hispanics up," *The News-Press* (Fort Myers, Fla.) Feb. 11, 2007, p. A1, and Troy Graham, "Hate Crime Statistics Belie Truth," *Daily Press* (Newport News, Va.), Jan. 30, 2000, p. A1.

[24] "A Local Prosecutor's Guide For Responding to Hate Crimes," American Prosecutors Research Institute, undated, www.ndaa.org/pdf/hate_crimes.pdf.

[25] Dennis B. Roddy, "An Accused Cop Killer's Politics," *Slate*, April 10, 2009, www.slate.com/id/2215826/.

[26] Gary Kamiya, "They're coming to take our guns away," *Salon.com*, April 7, 2009, www.salon.com/opinion/kamiya/2009/04/07/richard_poplowski.

[27] Quoted in Adam Liptak, "The Nation: Prisons to Mosques; Hate Speech and the American Way," *The New York Times*, Jan. 11, 2004. The Supreme Court decision is *Brandenburg v. Ohio*, 395, U.S. 444 (1969).

[28] Quoted in Katherin Clad, "Group cites Saudi 'hate' tracts," *The Washington Times*, Jan. 29, 2005, p. A1.

[29] Nonie Darwish, "Muslim Hate," *FrontPageMagazine.com*, March 25, 2009, www.frontpagemag.com/Articles/Read.aspx?GUID=A629F1F3-BBBA-420D-8C31-D340A577A083.

About the Author

Peter Katel is a *CQ Researcher* staff writer who previously reported on Haiti and Latin America for *Time* and *Newsweek* and covered the Southwest for newspapers in New Mexico. He has received several journalism awards, including the Bartolomé Mitre Award for coverage of drug trafficking, from the Inter-American Press Association. He holds an A.B. in university studies from the University of New Mexico. His recent reports include "Mexico's Drug War," "Homeland Security" and "Future of the Military."

[30] "Glen Beck joins Fox News," Reuters, Oct. 16, 2008, www.reuters.com/article/televisionNews/id USTRE49G0NW20081017.

[31] Eric Boehlert and Jamison Foser," On radio show, Beck read 'ad' for refinery that turns Mexicans into fuel," County Fair blog, Media Matters for America, June 29, 2007, (audio clip is posted), http://mediamatters.org/items/200706290010.

[32] Ariel Alexovich, "A Call to End Hate Speech," The New York Times, The Caucus blog, Feb. 1, 2008, http://thecaucus.blogs.nytimes.com/2008/02/01/a-call-to-end-hate-speech/?scp=1&sq=murguia%20hate%20speech&st=Search; "President and CEO Janet Murguia's Remarks at the Wave of Hope press briefing," National Council of La Raza, Jan. 31, 2008, www.nclr.org/content/viewpoints/detail/50389/.

[33] Steve Sailer, "What Obama hasn't figured out yet," Vdare, April 27, 2009, http://blog.vdare.com/archives/2009/04/27/what-obama-hasnt-figured-out-yet-better-teachers-means-___/; Patrick Cleburne, "More Indians means more . . .," Vdare, April 19, 2009, http://blog.vdare.com/archives/2009/04/19/more-indians-means-morefill-in-blank/; Cooper Sterling, "Tom Tancredo at American University: Maybe It Is About Race," Vdare, March 14, 2009, www.vdare.com/sterling/090314_tancredo.htm.

[34] Unless otherwise indicated this subsection draws on Robert O. Paxton, The Anatomy of Fascism (2004); William E. Leuchtenburg, Franklin D. Roosevelt and the New Deal (1963); and Chip Berlet and Matthew N. Lyons, Right-Wing Populism in America: Too Close for Comfort (2000); Daniel Levitas, The Terrorist Next Door: The Militia Movement and the Radical Right (2002).

[35] See Binjamin Segel, A Lie and a Libel: The History of the Protocols of the Elders of Zion (1996). For an article in the Dearborn Independent that takes the Protocols as fact, see Henry Ford and the editors of the Dearborn Independent, " 'Jewish Protocols' Claim Partial Fulfillment," www.churchoftrueisrael.com/Ford/original/ij12.html.

[36] Biographical sketch in "William Dudley Pelley Collection," University of North Carolina at Asheville, D. H. Ramsey Library, http://toto.lib.unca.edu/findingaids/mss/pelley/default_pelley_william_dudley.htm.

[37] Unless otherwise indicated, this subsection draws on Levitas, op. cit.; and Berlet and Lyons, op. cit.

[38] Quoted in ibid., p. 180.

[39] Quoted in Thomas M. Storke, "How Some Birchers Were Birched," The New York Times, Dec. 10, 1961.

[40] See Shaila Dewan, "Revisiting '64 Civil Rights Deaths, This Time in a Murder Trial," The New York Times, June 12, 2005, p. A26; Manuel Roig-Franzia, "Reopened Civil Rights Cases Evoke Painful Past," The New York Times, Jan. 10, 2005, p. A1. For background on the KKK, see the following Editorial Research Reports, predecessor to CQ Researcher: K. Lee, "Ku Klux Klan," July 10, 1946; W.R. McIntyre, "Spread of Terrorism and Hatemongering," Dec. 3, 1958; H.B. Shaffer, "Secret Societies and Political Action," May 10, 1961; R.L. Worsnop, "Extremist Movements in Race and Politics," March 31, 1965; S. Stencel, "The South: Continuity and Change," March 7, 1980, and M.H. Cooper, "The Growing Danger of Hate Groups," May 12, 1989.

[41] Fred P. Graham, "Rockwell, U.S. Nazi, Slain," The New York Times, Aug. 26, 1967.

[42] Except where otherwise indicated, this subsection is drawn from Levitas, op. cit., and James Ridgeway, Blood in the Face: The Ku Klux Klan, Aryan Nations, Nazi Skinheads, and the Rise of a New White Culture (1990).

[43] Wayne King, "Right-Wing Extremists Seek to Recruit Farmers," The New York Times, Sept. 20, 1985, p. A13. See also "Arthur Kirk: Kirk & Radical Farm Groups," nebraskastudies.org, undated, ww.nebraskastudies.org/1000/frameset_reset.html?www.nebraskastudies.org/1000/stories/1001_0112.html.

[44] "Supremacists Sentenced," The Washington Post, Dec. 4, 1987; "Five White Supremacists Get Long Prison Terms," Los Angeles Times, Feb. 7, 1986, p. A41; "40-Year Sentences Given to 5 in White-Supremacist Group," The New York Times (The Associated Press), Feb. 8, 1986, p. A17.

[45] "13 Supremacists Are Not Guilty of Conspiracies," The New York Times, April 8, 1988, p. A14.

[46] Richard A. Serrano, "Metzger Must Pay $5 Million in Rights Death," Los Angeles Times, Oct. 23, 1990, p. A1.

[47] Elaine Woo, "Richard Butler, 86; Supremacist Founded the Aryan Nations," Los Angeles Times, Sept. 9, 2004, p. B8.

[48] David Johnston with Stephen Labaton, "F.B.I. Shaken by Inquiry Into Idaho Siege," The New York Times, Nov. 25, 1993, p. A1.

[49] Louis Beam, "Leaderless Resistance," February 1992, www.louisbeam.com/leaderless.htm. See also "Militias," in Peter Knight, ed., Conspiracy Theories in American History: An Encyclopedia (2003), pp. 467-476.

[50] Leonard Zeskind, "Armed and Dangerous," Rolling Stone, Nov. 2, 1995.

[51] Megan K. Stack, "Duke Admits Bilking Backers," Los Angeles Times, Dec. 19, 200, p. A22.

[52] Susan Schmidt, "Investigation Clears Agents at Waco," The Washington Post, July 22, 2000, p. A1. See also "Final Report to the Deputy Attorney General Concerning the 1993 Confrontation at the Mt. Carmel Complex," John C. Danforth, Special Counsel, Nov. 8, 2000, www.apologeticsindex.org/pdf/finalreport.pdf.

[53] Mike German, Thinking Like a Terrorist: Insights of a Former FBI Undercover Agent (2007), p. 71.

[54] Woo, op. cit.; "William Pierce, 69, Neo-Nazi Leader, Dies," The New York Times, July 24, 2002, p. A16.

[55] "Hitler's birthday was April 20, 1889. Unwelcome distinction as Hitler's birthday burdens Austrian town," The Globe and Mail (Toronto), (Reuters), April 20, 1989.

[56] "Schedule of Upcoming Extremist Events: 2009," regularly updated, www.adl.org/learn/Events_2001/events_2003_flashmap.asp.

[57] Steve Giegerich, "Angry words fill air at neo-Nazi rally," St. Louis Post-Dispatch, April 19, 2009, p. A4.

[58] Quoted in ibid.

[59] Lisa Black, "Holocaust museum opens to 'fight capacity for evil,' " Chicago Tribune, April 20, 2009, p. A8.

[60] Padraig Shea," Spurned by Hub hall, supremacist group holds rally in N.H.," The Boston Globe, April 12, 2009, p. B3; "White supremacists' event shifted to N.H.," UPI, April 12, 2009.

[61] "We shut down the fascists!" Boston Anti-Racist Coalition, April 8, 2009, www.anarkismo.net/article/12633.

[62] Billy Roper, "One If By Land, Two If By Sea," White Revolution, April 8, 2009, http://whiterevolution.com.

[63] "Ku Klux Klan Coming to Your Town?" The Tennessee Tribune (Nashville), July 6, 2006, p. C8.

[64] "Arrests, fights break out at neo-Nazi march," wtop.com, April 19, 2009, www.wtop.com/?sid=1389944&nid=25. Video available at Albert Xavier Barnes, "The Arrests, Counter-Demo," undated, www.truveo.com/The-Arrests-Counter-Demo-NSM-March-on-DC-19/id/3760920024.

[65] Brooke Donald, "Two arrested outside Boston Holocaust gathering," The Associated Press, May 9, 2005.

[66] R. Scott Rappold, "Mobs clash in York," York Sunday News, Jan. 13, 2002 , p. A1.

67 Marc Levy, "White supremacist rally sparsely attended," The Associated Press, April 22, 2002.

68 Michelle Malkin, "Confirmed: The Obama DHS hit job on conservatives is real," michelle-malkin.com, April 14, 2009, http://michelle-malkin.com/2009/04/14/confirme-the-obama-dhs-hit-job-on-conservatives-is-real/. See also Stephen Gordon, "Homeland Security document targets most conservatives and libertarians in the country," The Liberty Papers (blog), April 12, 2009, www.theliberty papers.org/2009/04/12/homeland-security-document-targets-most-conservatives-and-libertarians-in-the-country.

69 Quoted in "Napolitano defends report on right-wing extremist groups," CNN, April 15, 2009, www.cnn.com/2009/POLITICS/04/15/extremism.report/.

70 "Rightwing Extremism. . . .," op. cit., p. 5.

71 Ibid., p. 6.

72 "About That DHS Report on Right-Wing Extremism," Little Green Footballs, April 14, 2009, http://littlegreenfootballs.com/article/33364_About_That_DHS_Report_on_Right-Wing_Extremism.

73 "The Modern Militia Movement," MIAC [Missouri Information Analysis Center] Strategic Report, Feb. 20, 2009, pp. 3-4, www.scribd.com/doc/13290698/The-Modern-Militia-MovementMissouri-MIAC-Strategic-Report-20Feb09-; David A. Lieb, "Analysis: Militia report unites ACLU, Republicans," The Associated Press, April 6, 2009.

74 "Modern Militia Movement," op. cit.

75 Chad Livengood, "Agency apologizes for militia report on candidates," Springfield (Mo.) News-Leader, p. A1.

76 Chris Blank, "Mo. Patrol names new leader for information center," The Associated Press, April 6, 2009.

77 Quoted in Lieb, op. cit.

78 Quoted in "Prevention Bulletin," North Central Texas Fusion System, Feb. 19, 2009, p. 4, www.privacylives.com/wp-content/uploads/2009/03/texasfusion_021909.pdf.

79 Quoted in Lieb, op. cit.

80 "Leftwing Extremists Likely to Increase Use of Cyber Attacks over the Coming Decade," Department of Homeland Security, Jan. 26, 2009, www.fas.org/irp/eprint/leftwing.pdf.

81 Quoted in "Homeland Security: Economic, Political Climate Fueling Extremism," Southern Poverty Law Center, April 15, 2009.

FOR MORE INFORMATION

The American Cause, 501 Church St., Suite 315, Vienna, VA 22180; (703) 255-2632. Educational organization founded in 1993 by conservative commentator Pat Buchanan that supports "conservative principles of national sovereignty, economic patriotism, limited government and individual freedom."

Anti-Defamation League, Law Enforcement Agency Research Network; http://adl.org/learn/default.asp. A monitoring and research program aimed mainly at keeping law enforcement agencies up to date on extremism.

Federal Bureau of Investigation, J. Edgar Hoover Building, 935 Pennsylvania Ave., N.W., Washington, DC 20535; www.fbi.gov/hq/cid/civilrights/hate.htm. Provides statistics, information on the agency's anti-hate crime program and links to other sites.

Political Research Associates, 1310 Broadway, Suite 201, Somerville, MA 02144; (617) 666-5300; www.publiceye.org. A left-oriented think tank that investigates the far right.

Southern Poverty Law Center, 400 Washington Ave., Montgomery, AL 36104; www.splcenter.org/intel/intpro. Specializes in suing extremist organizations; maintains a research arm that monitors the extreme right.

Stormfront, P.O. Box 6637, West Palm Beach, FL 33405; (561) 833-0030; www.stormfront.org/forum. A heavily trafficked far-right site.

White Aryan Resistance, Tom Metzger P.O. Box 401, Warsaw, IN 46581; www.resist.com. A Web site maintained by a longtime extremist leader.

82 Quoted in ibid. Alexander Cockburn, "King of the Hate Business," The Nation, May 18, 2009, www.thenation.com/doc/20090518/cockburn.

83 Quoted in David Abel, "WTKK-FM suspends Severin for derogatory comments about Mexicans," The Boston Globe, April 30, 2009, www.boston.com/news/local/breaking_news/2009/04/_jay_severin.html.

84 Quoted in ibid.

85 Lindell Kay, "U.S. charges former Marine with making a threat against Obama," Jacksonville Daily News, Feb. 27, 2009, www2.journalnow.com/content/2009/feb/27/us-charges-former-marine-with-making-a-threat-agai.

86 "White Supremacist Recruitment of Military Personnel since 9/11," FBI, Counterterrorism Division, July 7, 2008, http://wikileaks.org/wiki/FBI:_White_Supremacist_Recruitment_of_Military_Personnel_2008.

87 Ibid.

88 "Boehner: Homeland Security Report Characterizing Veterans as Potential Terrorists is 'Offensive and Unacceptable,' " press release, April 15, 2009, http://republicanleader.house.gov/News/DocumentSingle.aspx?DocumentID=122567.

89 "White Supremacist Recruitment . . . ," op. cit. See also Jim Popkin, "White-power groups recruiting from military," "Deep Background — NBC News Investigates," July 16, 2008, http://deepbackground.msnbc.msn.com/archive/2008/07/16/1202484.aspx.

90 "White Supremacist Recruitment," op. cit.

91 David Holthouse, "A Few Bad Men," Intelligence Report, Southern Poverty Law Center, July 7, 2006, www.splcenter.org/intel/news/item.jsp?pid=79.

92 Art Pine, "Ft. Bragg Troops Restricted After Swastikas Are Painted," Los Angeles Times, July 17, 1996, p. A9; William Branigin and Dana Priest, "3 White Soldiers Held in Slaying of Black Couple," The Washington Post, Dec. 9, 1995, p. A1.

93 "Planning a Skinhead Infantry," sidebar to "A Few Bad Men," op. cit., www.splcenter.org/intel/news/item.jsp?sid=21.

94 Ibid.

Bibliography

Selected Sources

Books

Berlet, Chip, and Matthew N. Lyons, *Right-Wing Populism in America: Too Close For Comfort*, Guilford Press, 2000.
Longtime analysts of the far right chronicle the long history of a movement that's larger than right-wing extremism.

German, Mike, *Thinking Like a Terrorist*, Potomac Books, 2007.
A former FBI agent recounts his undercover assignments in violent, far-right cells while arguing for government focus on law-breaking, not ideology.

Levitas, Daniel, *The Terrorist Next Door: The Militia Movement and the Radical Right*, St. Martin's Press, 2002.
The life of Posse Comitatus founder William Potter Gale provides the framework for an independent scholar's detailed history of domestic militias.

Paxton, Robert O., *The Anatomy of Fascism*, Alfred A. Knopf, 2004.
A leading scholar of the European extreme right distinguishes between its historic relics and the elements that survive.

Raspail, Jean, *The Camp of the Saints*, Charles Scribner's Sons, 1975.
Popular on the far right, this novel by a well-known French writer anticipates the fervent opposition to immigration from developing countries by depicting it as an invasion that will topple Western democratic societies.

Ridgeway, James, *Blood in the Face: Ku Klux Klan, Aryan Nations, Nazi Skinheads, and the Rise of a New White Culture*, Thunder's Mouth Press, 1990.
Journalist Ridgeway's prescient book includes documentary extremist material.

Articles

Blow, Charles M., "Pitchforks and Pistols," *The New York Times*, April 3, 2009, www.nytimes.com/2009/04/04/opinion/04blow.html.
A columnist argues that apocalyptic talk from conservative commentators preaching revolution and warning of gun-grabbing plans by the Obama administration may set off unstable minds.

Hedgecock, Roger, "Disagree with Obama? Gov't has eyes on you," WorldNetDaily, April 13, 2009, http://wnd.com/index.php?fa=PAGE.view&pageId=94799.
The conservative columnist who obtained the first leaked copy of the Department of Homeland Security's recent assessment of the far right attacks it as a justification for political surveillance of Obama administration critics.

Jenkins, Philip, "Home-grown terrorism," *Los Angeles Times*, March 10, 2008, p. A17.
During the presidential campaign, a prominent Penn State historian of religion forecast a new wave of right-wing extremism — and of repressive Democratic response.

Roddy, Dennis B., "An Accused Cop Killer's Politics," *Slate*, April 10, 2009, www.slate.com/id/2215826/.
A reporter who investigated the man charged in the recent Pittsburgh police killings finds his political ideas jumbled.

Serrano, Richard A., " '90s-style extremism withers," *Los Angeles Times*, March 11, 2008, p. A1.
Writing before the latest wave of concern about extremism, a veteran correspondent reported that the far right hadn't recovered from the blows it suffered early in the decade.

Shapiro, Walter, "Long Shadow," *The New Republic*, April 1, 2009, www.tnr.com/politics/story.html?id=9b2152b7-07fc-4503-9f33-4e2d222161d8.
A veteran political writer sees a likely surge in populist rage with violent undertones.

Reports and Studies

"The Modern Militia Movement," Missouri Information Analysis Center, Feb. 20, 2009, www.scribd.com/doc/13290698/The-Modern-Militia-MovementMissouri-MIAC-Strategic-Report-20Feb09.
The report, later repudiated by Missouri officials, triggered a nationwide controversy over government intrusion in political debate.

"Rightwing Extremism: Current Economic and Political Climate Fueling Resurgence in Radicalization and Recruitment," Department of Homeland Security, April 7, 2009, www.fas.org/irp/eprint/rightwing.pdf.
The controversial evaluation of the potential for a resurgence of the far right prompted a backlash against governmental monitoring of ideological trends.

"White Supremacist Recruitment of Military Personnel since 9/11," Federal Bureau of Investigation, July 7, 2008, http://wikileaks.org/wiki/FBI:_White_Supremacist_Recruitment_of_Military_Personnel_2008.
This recent and more focused FBI report on extremists' interest in recruiting veterans received little attention, except among specialists.

The Next Step:

Additional Articles from Current Periodicals

Europe

Baker, Andrew, "America Is Walking Away From Fighting Hate in Europe," *The Forward* **(New York), March 14, 2008, p. 11.**

The State Department is backing out of a proposed initiative to train European police how to effectively respond to hate crimes.

Besser, James D., "Jew Hatred Cited By European Rights Group," *Chicago Jewish Star*, **June 8, 2007, p. 1.**

Anti-Semitic hate crimes in Europe are occurring at a much higher frequency than in the 1990s, according to several international human rights groups.

Danilova, Maria, and Olga Bondaruk, "Ukraine Grapples With Alarming Rise in Hate Crimes," The Associated Press, July 11, 2008.

The alarming rise of hate crimes in the Ukraine may hinder its chances of securing a spot in the European Union and NATO.

Marquand, Robert, " 'Fitna': Dutch Leader's Anti-Islam Film Brings Strife," *The Christian Science Monitor*, **March 26, 2008, p. 1.**

An incendiary film against Muslims by a right-wing Dutch party leader has led to Islamic riots in the country and abroad.

Momigliano, Anna, " 'Xenophobic Climate' Fueling Policies, Violence in Italy," *The Christian Science Monitor*, **Oct. 1, 2008, p. 4.**

A recent wave of racially motivated attacks in Italy has caused a backlash from those who feel like they are being treated as second-class citizens.

Sonne, Paul, "Russians Sentenced for 19 Hate Killings," The Associated Press, Dec. 15, 2008.

Seven young Russians have been sentenced to prison amid a series of hate crimes involving racist assaults, xenophobia and neo-Nazism.

Immigrants

"Latinos' Deaths Prompt Calls for Hate Crimes Law," The Associated Press, Dec. 16, 2008.

Recent beatings of Latino immigrants have led Hispanic groups to lobby for a federal hate crimes law.

Bello, Marisol, "White Supremacists' New Angle," *USA Today*, **Oct. 21, 2008, p. 3A.**

Recent membership gains in supremacist groups have been fueled by the debates on illegal immigration and the struggling economy.

Collins, Kristin, "Hispanic Leaders Fear for Safety," *News & Observer* **(North Carolina), July 19, 2008, p. A1.**

Several of North Carolina's prominent Hispanic advocates have received an abundance of profanity-laced messages.

Constable, Pamela, "Neo-Nazis Clash With Protesters," *The Washington Post*, **April 20, 2008, p. C3.**

Violence erupted after the neo-Nazi National Socialist Movement marched in Washington, D.C., to denounce illegal immigration.

de la Isla, Jose, "Hispanics Victims of Hate Crimes," *San Angelo Standard-Times* **(Texas), Dec. 21, 2008.**

Many who commit crimes against immigrants in Texas claim that it is because immigrants pose a public-safety threat.

Jones, Bart, "Latino Group Seeks U.S. Probe," *Newsday* **(New York), Dec. 23, 2008, p. A22.**

A Latino rights group has asked the Department of Justice to investigate alleged lax attention to hate crimes by law enforcement officials in Suffolk County, N.Y.

Marquez, Myriam, "Innocent Chilean Students Paid Savage Price for Man's Hate," *Miami Herald*, **March 1, 2009, p. B1.**

Several Chilean college students were killed during an anti-immigration rampage by a Florida man.

Reddy, Sumathi, "Attacks Against Latinos Increasing, FBI Reports," *Seattle Times*, **Nov. 24, 2008, p. A4.**

Hate-related attacks on Hispanics grew 40 percent from 2003 to 2007, while the total number of hate-related incidents nationwide has remained steady over the same period.

Ross, Janell, "Hate Crimes Rise Against Hispanics and the Disabled," *The Tennessean*, **May 10, 2008.**

Hate crimes against Hispanics in Tennessee more than doubled from 2006 to 2007, while those against the disabled grew from 1 to 30.

Walker, Devona, "To Fringe, Border Debate Is a Boon," *The Oklahoman*, **June 6, 2008, p. 1A.**

Most members of the National Socialist Movement are concerned over the continued flow of undocumented immigrants.

Watanabe, Teresa, "Crimes Rooted in Hatred Increase," *Los Angeles Times*, **July 25, 2008, p. B3.**

Hate crimes in Los Angeles County have reached their highest point in five years largely due to increased attacks on Latinos and blacks, according to county officials.

Whaley, Monte, "Climbing Reports of Hate Crime Tell Bad-News/Good-News Story," *Denver Post*, **April 11, 2008, p. A1.**

Statistics suggest that hate crime in the Denver area is not due to any anti-immigration sentiments.

Obama

Asbury, John, "Attacks Linked to Election of Obama, Police Say," *Press Enterprise* **(California), Jan. 18, 2009, p. C1.**

Local police believe that a series of attacks in a California suburb stem from the election of Barack Obama as the first black president.

Curry, George E., "Obama Triumph Sparks Increase in Racist Behavior," *Wave West* **(California), Nov. 20, 2008, p. A6.**

A recent rise in racist incidents is a reminder that hate groups still flourish despite the election of Barack Obama as the nation's first black president.

Hauser, Christine, and Colin Moynihan, "Three Are Charged in Attacks on Election Night," *The New York Times,* **Jan. 8, 2009, p. A25.**

A group of Staten Island men have been charged with attacking black men on election night after it became clear that a black man would be elected president.

Jonsson, Patrik [cq], "After Obama's Win, White Backlash Festers in US," *The Christian Science Monitor,* **Nov. 17, 2008, p. 3.**

Obama's presidential victory and the political marginalization of certain Southern whites could produce a backlash against what some have called the dawn of a post-racial America.

Saslow, Eli, "Hate Groups' Newest Target," *The Washington Post,* **June 22, 2008, p. A6.**

Barack Obama's achievements as a symbol of racial progress and cultural unity have also sparked an increase in white-supremacist activity.

Toone, Stephanie, "Some Fear for Obama's Safety as Race Nears End," *Augusta Chronicle* **(Georgia), Nov. 3, 2008, p. A3.**

A foiled amateur plot to assassinate Barack Obama has raised concerns over his safety amid a growing number of hate groups.

Witt, Howard, "Hate Incidents in U.S. Surge," *Chicago Tribune,* **Nov. 23, 2008, p. A4.**

More than 200 hate-related incidents have been reported within three weeks after Barack Obama was elected president.

Speech

Gamboa, Suzanne, "Latino Group Claims 'Hate Speech' Emerging Over Immigration," The Associated Press, Jan. 31, 2008.

The National Council of La Raza has launched a web site to counter what it considers to be 'hate speech' that has emerged from immigration debates.

Goldberg, Daniel, "Term 'Hate Crime' Rejected for Free Speech Reasons," *Herald-Sun* **(North Carolina), Feb. 27, 2009, p. C5.**

The University of North Carolina refuses to use the term "hate crime" in its student codes of conduct because of the complexities and constitutional guarantees of free speech.

Liptak, Adam, "Freedom to Offend Outside U.S., Hate Speech Can Be Costly," *The New York Times,* **June 12, 2008, p. A1.**

Hate speech is more constitutionally protected in the United States than in other countries, including democracies.

Lowry, Rich, "Hate-Speech Complaint Battles Free-Speech Ideal," *Sun Journal* **(Maine), June 12, 2008, p. A8.**

A Canadian human rights group has accused a journalist of "hate speech" for publishing a scathing editorial against Muslims.

Miller, Matthew, "Free Speech Controversy Split Campus," *Lansing State Journal* **(Michigan), March 2, 2008, p. 1A.**

Debates over whether hate speech is free speech has created a rift between several student groups at Michigan State University.

Murse, Tom, "Pitts Opposes Expansion of Hate Crimes Law," *Lancaster New Era* **(Pennsylvania), April 30, 2009, p. B1.**

Rep. Joe Pitts, R-Pa., has opposed speech protections based on sexual orientation and gender identity over the belief that they would crimp free speech.

Torres, Joe, "FCC to Investigate Link Between Hate Speech and Hate Crimes," *La Prensa San Diego,* **Feb. 6, 2009, p. 1.**

The National Hispanic Media Coalition has called on the Federal Communications Commission to investigate the impact of hate speech over the airwaves on the Latino community.

Ziner, Karen Lee, "New Initiative Aims to Stop 'Hate Speech,' " *Providence Journal* **(Rhode Island), March 21, 2008, p. B1.**

A new initiative borne out of an altercation between a store owner and Spanish-speaking customers seeks to stop hate speech directed at immigrants and communities of color.

CITING CQ RESEARCHER

Sample formats for citing these reports in a bibliography include the ones listed below. Preferred styles and formats vary, so please check with your instructor or professor.

MLA STYLE
Jost, Kenneth. "Rethinking the Death Penalty." CQ Researcher 16 Nov. 2001: 945-68.

APA STYLE
Jost, K. (2001, November 16). Rethinking the death penalty. *CQ Researcher, 11,* 945-968.

CHICAGO STYLE
Jost, Kenneth. "Rethinking the Death Penalty." *CQ Researcher,* November 16, 2001, 945-968.

In-depth Reports on Issues in the News

Are you writing a paper?

Need backup for a debate?

Want to become an expert on an issue?

For 80 years, students have turned to *CQ Researcher* for in-depth reporting on issues in the news. Reports on a full range of political and social issues are now available. Following is a selection of recent reports:

Civil Liberties
Closing Guantánamo, 2/09
Affirmative Action, 10/08
Gay Marriage Showdowns, 9/08
America's Border Fence, 9/08
Immigration Debate, 2/08

Crime/Law
Judicial Elections, 4/09
Mexico's Drug War, 12/08
Prostitution Debate, 5/08
Public Defenders, 4/08
Gun Violence, 5/07

Education
Reading Crisis? 2/08
Discipline in Schools, 2/08
Student Aid, 1/08
Racial Diversity in Public Schools, 9/07
Stress on Students, 7/07

Environment/Society
Future of Journalism, 3/09
Confronting Warming, 1/09
Reducing Carbon Footprint, 12/08
Protecting Wetlands, 10/08
Buying Green, 2/08

Health/Safety
Extreme Sports, 4/09
Regulating Toxic Chemicals, 1/09
Preventing Cancer, 1/09
Heart Health, 9/08
Global Food Crisis, 6/08

Politics/Economy
Business Bankruptcy, 4/09
Future of the GOP, 3/09
Middle-Class Squeeze, 3/09
Public-Works Projects, 2/09
The Obama Presidency, 1/09

Upcoming Reports

Fertility Ethics, 5/15/09   Future of Books, 5/29/09   Children's Rights, 6/5/09

ACCESS

CQ Researcher is available in print and online. For access, visit your library or www.cqresearcher.com.

STAY CURRENT

To receive notice of upcoming *CQ Researcher* reports, or learn more about *CQ Researcher* products, subscribe to the free e-mail newsletters, *CQ Researcher Alert!* and *CQ Researcher News*: http://cqpress.com/newsletters.

PURCHASE

To purchase a *CQ Researcher* report in print or electronic format (PDF), visit www.cqpress.com or call 866-427-7737. Single reports start at $15. Bulk purchase discounts and electronic-rights licensing are also available.

SUBSCRIBE

Annual full-service *CQ Researcher* subscriptions—including 44 reports a year, monthly index updates, and a bound volume—start at $803. Add $25 for domestic postage.

CQ Researcher Online offers a backfile from 1991 and a number of tools to simplify research. For pricing information, call 800-834-9020, ext. 1906, or e-mail librarysales@cqpress.com.

Published by CQ Press, a division of SAGE Publications

www.cqresearcher.com

Reproductive Ethics

Should fertility medicine be regulated more tightly?

N adya Suleman, an unemployed, 33-year-old, single mother from Southern California, felt her six children weren't enough. Last January, after a fertility doctor implanted six embryos she had frozen earlier, Suleman gave birth to octuplets — and was quickly dubbed "Octomom." Many fertility experts were shocked that a doctor would depart so far from medical guidelines — which recommend implantation of only one, or at most two, embryos for a woman of Suleman's relatively young age. Although multiple births often do result from in vitro fertilization (IVF) and other assisted-reproduction technologies, the number of multiples has dropped over the past few years, they point out. Other analysts note, however, that government statistics show a large percentage of clinics frequently ignore the guidelines on embryo implantation. In response, lawmakers in several states have introduced proposals to increase regulation of fertility clinics.

Nadya Suleman, a single mother from Southern California, was quickly dubbed "Octomom" after giving birth to octuplets in January. In apparent violation of accepted medical practice, a physician implanted at least six embryos in Suleman during in vitro fertilization (IVF).

CQ Researcher • May 15, 2009 • www.cqresearcher.com
Volume 19, Number 19 • Pages 449-472

RECIPIENT OF SOCIETY OF PROFESSIONAL JOURNALISTS AWARD FOR
EXCELLENCE ◆ AMERICAN BAR ASSOCIATION SILVER GAVEL AWARD

Cover: AFP/Getty Images/Robyn Beck

CQ Researcher

May 15, 2009
Volume 19, Number 19

MANAGING EDITOR: Thomas J. Colin
tcolin@cqpress.com

ASSISTANT MANAGING EDITOR: Kathy Koch
kkoch@cqpress.com

ASSOCIATE EDITOR: Kenneth Jost

STAFF WRITERS: Thomas J. Billitteri, Marcia Clemmitt, Peter Katel

CONTRIBUTING WRITERS: Rachel Cox, Sarah Glazer, Alan Greenblatt, Barbara Mantel, Patrick Marshall, Tom Price, Jennifer Weeks

DESIGN/PRODUCTION EDITOR: Olu B. Davis

ASSISTANT EDITOR: Darrell Dela Rosa

FACT-CHECKING: Eugene J. Gabler, Michelle Harris

EDITORIAL INTERN: Vyomika Jairam

CQ PRESS

A Division of SAGE

PRESIDENT AND PUBLISHER:
John A. Jenkins

EXECUTIVE DIRECTOR,
REFERENCE INFORMATION GROUP:
Alix B. Vance

CQ Press is a registered trademark of Congressional Quarterly Inc.

CQ Researcher (ISSN 1056-2036) is printed on acid-free paper. Published weekly, except; (Jan. wk. 1) (May wk. 4) (July wks. 1, 2) (Aug. wks. 3, 4) (Nov. wk. 4) and (Dec. wk. 4), by CQ Press, a division of SAGE Publications. Annual full-service subscriptions start at $803. For pricing, call 1-800-834-9020, ext. 1906. To purchase a CQ Researcher report in print or electronic format (PDF), visit www.cqpress.com or call 866-427-7737. Single reports start at $15. Bulk purchase discounts and electronic-rights licensing are also available. Periodicals postage paid at Washington, D.C., and additional mailing offices. POSTMASTER: Send address changes to CQ Researcher, 2300 N St., N.W., Suite 800, Washington, DC 20037.

Reproductive Ethics

BY MARCIA CLEMMITT

THE ISSUES

After 33-year-old Nadya Suleman, a mother of six, gave birth to octuplets on Jan. 26, the California fertility specialist who treated her was summoned to appear before the Medical Board of California. The board — which can revoke physicians' licenses for egregious misconduct — is investigating whether Michael Kamrava, head of the West Coast IVF Clinic in Beverly Hills, violated accepted standards of medical practice when he implanted at least six embryos in Suleman during in vitro fertilization (IVF) treatment in 2008, leading to the multiple birth. [1]

Suleman has told reporters that all 14 of her children were conceived using IVF — a high-tech treatment in which eggs are fertilized in the laboratory, then implanted into a woman's uterus for gestation — and that six embryos were implanted in each of her six pregnancies, although she's had only two multiple births: the octuplets and a set of twins. But professional guidelines from the American Society for Reproductive Medicine recommend implanting only one or two embryos in younger women, such as Suleman, because of the high risk multiple births pose to children and mothers.

Multiple-birth babies, including twins, have a significantly higher risk for developing severe, debilitating disabilities such as chronic lung diseases or cerebral palsy, which occurs six times more often among twins and 20 times more often in triplets than it does in single babies. [2]

Wendy Kramer of Nederland, Colo., and her son Ryan — who was conceived through donor insemination — founded and run the Donor Sibling Registry to help donor-conceived children locate siblings and learn about their genetic lineage. Ryan has learned of six half-sisters to date. As of February, more than 6,200 siblings have been connected via the online registry, which was launched in 2000.

AP Photo/David Zalubowski

The cost to the health-care system of multiple births is enormous. "The cost of caring for the octuplets would probably cover more than a year of providing IVF for everyone in L.A. County who needed it," says David L. Keefe, professor of obstetrics and gynecology at the University of South Florida, in Tampa. "The likelihood that some of those kids will get cerebral palsy means they'll need a lifetime of care."

The high-profile Suleman case has spurred calls for government regulation of fertility medicine — sometimes called assisted reproductive technologies, or ART. (*See box, p. 464.*) Like U.S. medicine generally, ART is not regulated by the federal government and only lightly supervised by state agencies. Since 1978 — when the world's first IVF baby, Louise Brown,

was born in England — more than 3 million ART babies have been born worldwide, and some experts and ethicists fear the field's rapid expansion leaves too much room for abuses. [3]

Others argue that lack of insurance coverage for IVF is the biggest problem with ART in the United States. Fertility treatments can cost more than $12,000 per cycle, pushing cash-strapped would-be parents to opt for the higher-risk, multiple-embryo implantation to increase their chances of a pregnancy.

By contrast, in most European countries — where IVF procedures are paid for through universal health-care systems — doctors generally implant only one fertilized embryo at a time. In Sweden and Finland, for instance, where the procedure is covered by insurance, doctors perform single-embryo implantations 70 percent and 60 percent of the time, respectively, compared to only 3.3 percent of the time in the United States. [4] (*See graph, p. 457.*)

In fact, some European governments prohibit multiple-embryo transfers for women under 36 and limit older women to no more than two embryos per cycle. As a result, "Triplets have virtually disappeared in Europe," a Danish doctor told European colleagues at a 2006 fertility conference. [5]

Self-regulation of ART in the United States clearly isn't working, said Marcy Darnovsky, associate executive director of the Oakland, Calif.-based Center for Genetics and Society, which advocates for responsible use of genetic technologies. According to the federal Centers for Disease Control and Prevention (CDC), to which ART clinics

Most States Don't Require Infertility Coverage

Only 12 states require all state-regulated health insurance plans to cover infertility diagnosis and treatment. Two states — California and Texas — require only that every insurer offer at least one plan with fertility coverage.

States Mandating Infertility Insurance Coverage

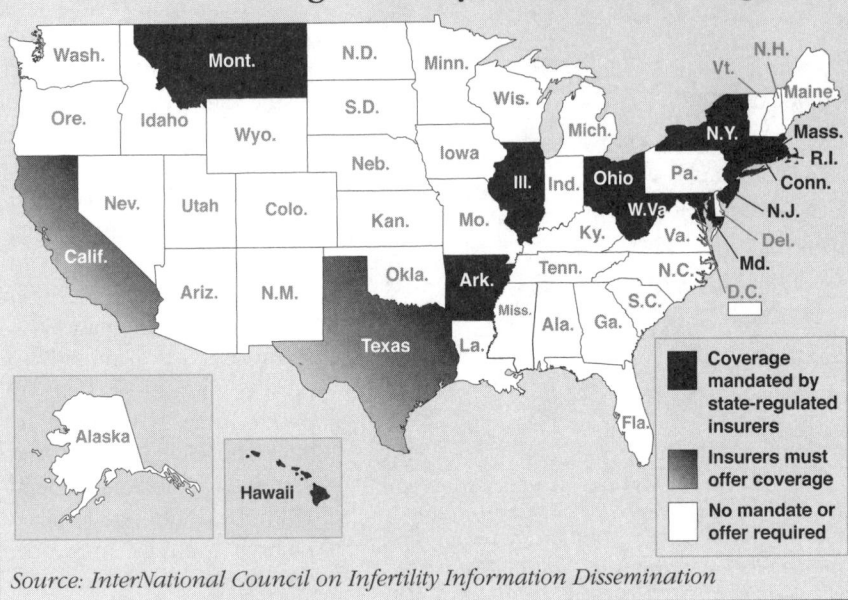

Source: InterNational Council on Infertility Information Dissemination

must report data, 80 percent of programs do not strictly follow American Society for Reproductive Medicine guidelines, making government regulation "long overdue," she said. [6]

"In reproductive matters, individuals are making decisions [that affect] not just themselves, but . . . others as well," which makes regulation appropriate, said Johns Hopkins University scholars Franco Furger and Francis Fukuyama. Reproductive medicine is headed toward giving prospective parents "a range of . . . techniques to make specific choices about a baby's health and sex and eventually about other attributes," said Furger, a research professor, and Fukuyama, a professor of international political economy, both at the Paul H. Nitze School of Advanced International Studies in Washington, D.C. "It would be misguided to take a wait-and-see attitude." [7]

Industrialized countries that pay for IVF through their universal health-care

systems strictly regulate which services may be provided, says Susannah Baruch, director for law and policy at the Genetics & Public Policy Center, a think tank at John Hopkins funded by the Pew Charitable Trusts. The services typically include pre-implantation genetic diagnosis (PGD) — genetic testing of embryos. While PGD to detect serious genetic illnesses is conducted routinely, many countries strictly limit other PGD uses, such as selecting a child's gender, because they aren't considered in the public interest, she says.

However, in the United States — even though U.S. reproductive-medicine experts roundly criticize Kamrava's implantation of multiple embryos in the Suleman case — many ART experts also argue that government regulation of the industry is not necessarily a solution.

Suleman's case is much more of an outlier today than it would have been 15 years ago, when it wasn't unusual

to have six embryos transferred, says Josephine Johnston, a research scholar at the Hastings Center for bioethics research in Garrison, N.Y. "I would have bet money that it was not IVF" that led to the octuplet birth, she says, but the use of ovary-stimulating drugs — a much cheaper, far less controllable method of assisted reproductive technology.

Multiple-embryo implantation is being phased out as ART technologies improve, Johnston says, and six-embryo implantation is "so far outside the guidelines it's amazing that a physician would do it."

Such hair-raising cases are virtually always outliers and shouldn't be used to hastily enact laws, some analysts say.

For example, ever since artificial insemination was introduced sperm banks have promised would-be parents a genetic lineage of intelligence, athleticism and good looks for babies born from donor sperm, says R. Alta Charo, a professor of law and bioethics at the University of Wisconsin Law School. But "it hasn't undermined Western culture as we know it," she says. "So why do we think that people are very likely to go through much more onerous PGD to choose traits?" Very few will try to use it to enhance their baby's intelligence or appearance, so there would be little point in prohibiting such behavior, she says.

A recent study by New York University's Langone Medical Center supports Charo's view somewhat. Of 999 patients who completed a survey on traits they thought warranted use of PGD screening, solid majorities named potential conditions such as mental retardation, blindness, deafness, heart disease and cancer. Only 10 percent said they might use PGD to choose a child with exceptional athletic ability and 12.6 percent, high intelligence. [8]

"People are after different things" in calling for ART regulation, making legislation difficult, Charo says. Some may want limits on the number of embryos implanted per cycle, but most are calling for rules to enforce "personal morality," such as whether gay couples should become parents or whether lower-income mothers should be allowed to have very large families, Charo says. "We must then ask why we would regulate these [reproductive] personal choices differently from other personal choices."

ART-related law would likely be based on the unusual cases that make headlines, "and bad cases make bad policy," she says.

Opposition to regulation might drop considerably if insurance covered IVF and other artificial reproduction procedures, but today only 12 states require such coverage. (*See map, p. 452.*)

For instance, limitations on multiple-embryo implantations might be acceptable if insurance covered several single-embryo implantations for all patients who have experienced six months of proven infertility, suggests Ronald M. Green, a professor of ethics and human values at Dartmouth College.

Because of the high cost of IVF treatments, the lack of insurance coverage has deprived "the vast majority of the middle class" in America, as well as the poor, from the modern ART "revolution," says Keefe at the University of South Florida. "Once you have the middle class covered, then I have no trouble saying, 'We're not going to pay' " for multiple-embryo implantation.

Furthermore, the procedure doesn't have to cost $12,000 per cycle, as evidenced by the lower amounts accepted by IVF clinics when insurance companies that are required to cover the procedure negotiate lower fees, he says. "It's a lot cheaper [for society] to pay for IVF at $3,000 or $4,000 per procedure and deliver only singletons," thus avoiding the harrowing medical problems and high costs associated with multiple births, he says.

Mandating coverage not only reduces the number of multiple births but also increases access for the middle class. "I practiced in Massachusetts and Rhode Island [which require coverage], where sheet-metal workers and

Majority of ART Pregnancies Result in a Live Birth

About 82 percent of the U.S. pregnancies resulting from assisted reproductive technology (ART) in 2006 resulted in live births. More than half were a single-child birth, and a quarter were multiple-infant births. Nearly three-quarters of U.S. ART procedures use fresh, non-donor sperm or eggs.

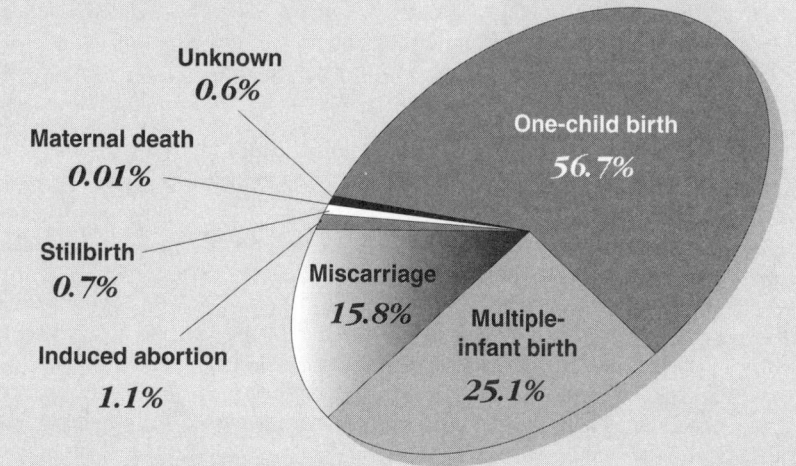

Outcomes of Pregnancies Resulting From ART Cycles Using Fresh, Non-donor Eggs or Embryos, 2006

Unknown **0.6%**

Maternal death **0.01%**

Stillbirth **0.7%**

Induced abortion **1.1%**

Miscarriage **15.8%**

Multiple-infant birth **25.1%**

One-child birth **56.7%**

* *Percentages do not total 100 due to rounding.*

Source: "Assisted Reproductive Technology Success Rates 2006," Centers for Disease Control and Prevention, 2008

heiresses from Newport" mingled at IVF clinics because insurance picked up the tab, Keefe says.

However, not all fertility doctors would opt into a fully insured system, says Dawn Gannon, director of professional outreach for RESOLVE, the National Infertility Association, which advocates that insurance companies treat infertility like any other medical condition. For example, when New Jersey mandated coverage, in 2001, "some clinics didn't take insurance at all, and some started taking it and then stopped," she says, because "they got less money per procedure."

If the United States enacts universal health-care coverage, advocates for the infertile hope ART will be covered as it is in other industrialized countries.

But universal coverage would still leave thorny issues unsettled, such as

whether taxpayer subsidies should support ART for unmarried women or women over 40. For older women, the debate centers on whether it is appropriate for health insurance to subsidize an infertility problem that is the result of natural aging and not the result of a medical condition. Also, pregnancy is riskier for both the older mother and the child.

Earlier in IVF's history, many clinicians routinely refused ART to single women, older women, lesbians and, in some cases, poor people. A 1993 survey of Finnish ART clinics found that many doctors "preferred not to treat either lesbian or single women," arguing that they "wanted to protect children from having inappropriate parents, primarily 'bad mothers,' " according to Maili Malin, a medical sociologist at Finland's

As Technology Advances, Questions Emerge

Multiple births threaten poor families.

Ghazala Khamis and her husband, a farmworker, had three daughters, but they longed for a son. Last year, the 27-year-old Egyptian woman gave birth to healthy septuplets, four boys and three girls, by Caesarian section near the end of her eighth month of pregnancy. Before the septuplets, she had not conceived for five years. [1]

Khamis conceived the septuplets using one of the oldest fertility technologies, introduced in the 1950s and '60s — fertility drugs that stimulate women's ovaries to produce multiple eggs. While effective for many, the drugs — which are becoming cheap and widely available around the world — are also among the most dangerous and unpredictable treatments, often leading to multiple births, and as they spread into poor communities the consequences can be dire.

"I'm really scared," Khamis said, soon after her delivery. "We live in a mud hut with only two rooms. I don't know how we're going to afford 10 children." [2]

The positive side of the medications' increased availability is that poor people have the greatest risk of infertility and, until recently, had literally no access to help. "The less money you have, the more likely you are to have difficulty conceiving," wrote Liza Mundy, author of a 2007 book on fertility medicine, *Everything Conceivable*. "Much infertility has always been caused by infections that can damage reproductive passageways," and "the lower your tax bracket, the less likely you are to have received the fairly simple medical treatment that can stave off these consequences." [3]

But the spread of the hard-to-control drugs, coupled with many families' desire for sons, can create tragedies in poor communities, especially in the developing world. Khamis' delivery ultimately went well, but because Egypt doesn't have enough respirators for newborns, doctors held back from performing the Caesarian section until long after Western doctors would have removed the children. "We were simply blessed by God that no complication happened," Khamis' physician, Mahmoud Meleis, said. "If there had been a complication, Ghazala would have died." [4]

As older fertility technologies spread, newer ones are being created, sometimes solving problems but sometimes creating new ones.

A fledgling technique — freezing women's eggs, rather than embryos, for later use — could eventually help solve two problems with fertility treatments, says John Jain, head of an IVF clinic in Santa Monica, Calif., and an early U.S. adopter of egg freezing, which began in 2005 in Italy. First, freezing eggs can offset the fertility problems often caused by the upward creep in the age at which people start families. Second, freezing eggs causes fewer moral and religious qualms than freezing embryos,

"I have patients flying in because I will freeze eggs rather than embryos," thus allowing women to bank their own eggs against future infertility, whatever its cause, such as cancer treatment or aging, he says. "The pregnancy rate from frozen eggs is as good as from frozen embryos."

But others warn that egg freezing hasn't been fully tested. "The biggest misconception coming down the pike is freezing eggs,'" says David L. Rosenfeld, director of the Center for Human

National Institute of Public Health. A single woman's marital status and "wish to have a child" were both "considered indications of . . . questionable mental health." [9]

Whatever the outcome, the coverage debate will generate intense emotion. "So much of your life feels out of control when you want a child but find that you can't have one," says Jan Elman Stout, a clinical psychologist in Chicago. "This is often the very first challenge that people encounter in their lives that, no matter how hard they work at it, it may not work out for them."

As ethicists, lawmakers and physicians debate how best to provide access and oversight for reproductive medicine, here are some of the questions being asked:

Should fertility medicine be regulated more vigorously?

Should a mother of six with limited income be allowed to give birth to eight additional children through IVF? If a man donates sperm that results in hundreds of babies — technically making them all half brothers and sisters — should the offspring be given the identity of their biological father so they won't end up dating or marrying a half-sibling? Is a father whose child was the product of donated egg and sperm liable for child support if the couple divorces?

These are just a handful of the sticky ethical questions that have emerged from the brave, new world of sperm and egg donation. [10]

Of course, outlier cases like that of the California octuplets quickly spur

vociferous calls for government limits on in vitro fertilization. And others say the well-being of patients demands at least some rules. Finally, since many ART-related questions wind up in court, judges say they need more legislative guidance than the current case-by-case approach being used to settle IVF cases.

"No matter what one thinks of artificial insemination, and — as now appears in the not-too-distant future, cloning and even gene splicing — courts are still going to be faced with the problem of determining legal parentage," declared a unanimous California Court of Appeals ruling in the 1998 case *Buzzanca v. Buzzanca*. "Courts can continue to make decisions on an ad hoc basis . . . or the legislature can act to improve a broader

Reproduction at the North Shore-Long Island Jewish Health System in Manhasset, N.Y. "It's experimental, and right now the public expectations are unreal." Currently it's unknown how long frozen eggs can be stored — whether they'll be like embryos and sperm, which can be stored long term without apparent harm, or more fragile. "The technology will improve, but expectations are running way ahead of that," he says.

Like all reproductive technology, egg freezing could still raise ethics issues. In April 2007, a Canadian woman triggered a bioethical debate when she froze some of her own eggs so that her 7-year-old daughter, who has a genetic disorder that causes infertility, could use them as an adult.

A daughter potentially giving birth to her mother's child is unusual enough so that "we have to look very carefully into what we're doing here," said Margaret Somerville, an ethicist at McGill University in Toronto.

But other ethicists aren't troubled a bit. "It's hard for me to see what difference it'd make to the child that one of her gametes came from her grandmother [rather] than her mother," said Wayne Summer, a University of Toronto philosophy professor. [5]

Meanwhile, a new sperm-donation technique is drastically changing fertility medicine. Intra-cytoplasmic sperm injection, or ICSI, allows even a single, weak sperm to fertilize an egg. ICSI is quickly displacing sperm donation, once widely used by heterosexual infertility patients but increasingly used only by single women and lesbian couples. ICSI now allows many men to become fathers who previously could not have conceived,

and it's spread like wildfire in the past decade. In Europe in 2005 — the most recent year for which data has been analyzed — the technique was used in 63.3 percent of all assisted-reproduction cases, up from 34.7 percent in 1997, when European data collection began. [6]

Using ICSI and other techniques, "you're probably helping people have a child that Mother Nature wouldn't have allowed for," and that has both risks and benefits, says Angeline Beltsos, medical director of the Chicago-based Fertility Centers of Illinois.

Indeed, evidence is growing that sons conceived through ICSI inherit their father's infertility, raising questions about consequences generations down the road.

"We may have tens of thousands of boys born with infertility," said Tommaso Falcone, head of obstetrics and gynecology at the Cleveland Clinic. [7]

[1] For background, see Hadeel Al-Shalchi, "Egypt Septuplets Stir Debate on Fertility Drugs," The Associated Press, ABC News Web site, Aug. 26, 2008, http://abcnews.go.com/print?id=5661108.

[2] Quoted in *ibid*.

[3] Liza Mundy, *Everything Conceivable* (2007), p. xiv.

[4] Quoted in Al-Shalchi, *op. cit*.

[5] Quoted in "Assisted Human Reproduction: Regulating and Treating Conception Problems," CBC News Web site, Feb. 5, 2009, www.cbc.ca.

[6] "Fertility Treatments: Researcher Says that ICSI May Be Over-used in Some Countries," *Science Daily* Web site, July 9, 2008, www.sciencedaily.com.

[7] Quoted in JoNel Aleccia, "Pass It On: Sons of Infertile Men May Be Next," MSNBC.com, Sept. 27, 2008, www.msnbc.msn.com.

order which . . . would bring some predictability to those who seek to make use of artificial reproductive techniques," said the justices in a case involving a divorcing husband who claimed no financial responsibility for his daughter, conceived from donor egg and sperm and borne by a surrogate mother. [11]

Creating a federal-government registry of information on egg and sperm donors would give adults born from donated gametes (sperms or eggs) access to their genetic history in order to prevent half-siblings from marrying each other. It would also allow limits on the numbers of children created through one person's donations, said Naomi Cahn, a research professor at the George Washington University Law School. In England, no more than

10 children can be created from a single donor's sperm. [12]

The federal government should exercise more aggressively the authority it already has to oversee the safety and efficacy of some ART technologies, say some experts.

For instance, inserting one woman's egg into another woman's body is arguably a type of tissue transplant — a procedure over which the Food and Drug Administration (FDA) has jurisdiction but has been lax in regulating, says the University of Wisconsin's Charo. "That's an appropriate place to step in to ask whether we have assurance of safety for the stuff that's being developed," she says.

The FDA has a role in determining whether genetic tests are safe and whether they work or are medically useful, says

Baruch of the Genetics & Public Policy Center. For instance, many labs manufacture genetic tests that they don't market to other companies — called "homebrew" tests — but the FDA "has chosen not to regulate them," she says. "We believe that they have the authority" and would like to see them do it.

Genetic testing of embryos — preimplantation genetic diagnosis or PGD, which requires permanent removal of one cell from an eight-cell embryo — is much more technically difficult than other forms of genetic testing but gets less government scrutiny, according to Baruch's organization. And, the center points out, even the general quality standards for laboratories under the federal Clinical Laboratory Improvement Amendments of 1988 are not being applied to PGD labs. [13]

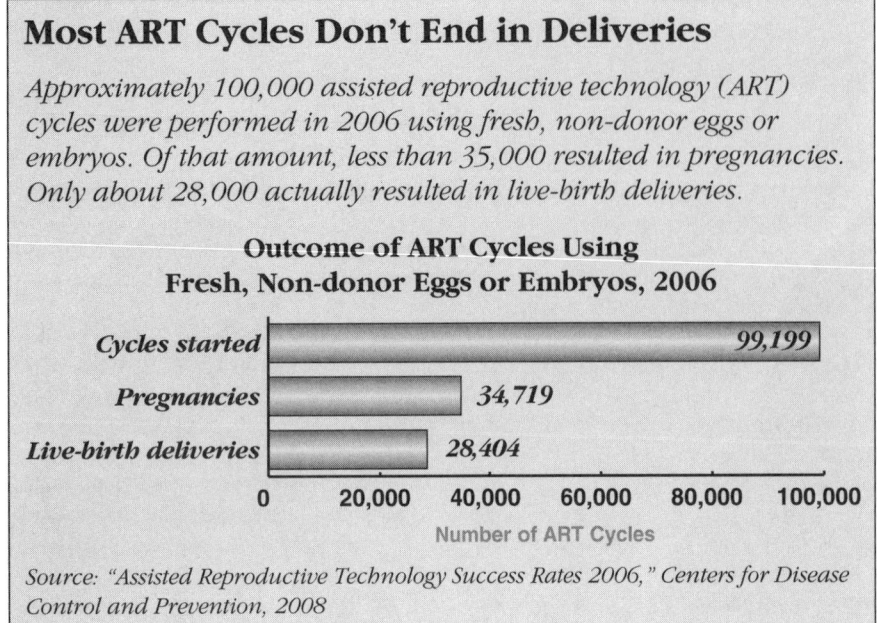

Most ART Cycles Don't End in Deliveries

Approximately 100,000 assisted reproductive technology (ART) cycles were performed in 2006 using fresh, non-donor eggs or embryos. Of that amount, less than 35,000 resulted in pregnancies. Only about 28,000 actually resulted in live-birth deliveries.

Outcome of ART Cycles Using Fresh, Non-donor Eggs or Embryos, 2006

Cycles started	99,199
Pregnancies	34,719
Live-birth deliveries	28,404

Number of ART Cycles

Source: "Assisted Reproductive Technology Success Rates 2006," Centers for Disease Control and Prevention, 2008

But aside from testing the safety and efficacy of medical products and drugs, the U.S. government does not, in general, regulate the practice of medicine, says Wisconsin's Charo. "That being the case, the issue of regulating fertility clinics actually becomes, 'Should they be regulated differently from the rest of medicine?' " she says. "It would be difficult to make that case."

"Muddling through" without regulation "is a respectable policy option, especially for a pragmatic people faced with irreconcilable moral quandaries" such as those often posed by ART, said John A. Robertson, a professor at the University of Texas College of Law in Austin. "This non-system 'system' has served well to date — even if not all the time and never perfectly — both in other contexts and for assisted reproduction." The current system can deal with even thorny issues, he adds, such as questions surrounding the "genetic screening of embryos . . . and the other edge technologies looming ahead." [14]

Furthermore, he pointed out, the President's Council on Bioethics appointed by George W. Bush examined the ART field for more than a year and found that the biggest problems were "on the margins, not at the core." The panel recommended only "tinker[ing] with ways to get more data" and making professional self-regulation more effective. [15]

National Infertility Association Executive Director Barbara L. Collura also advocates caution in regulating ART. While limiting the number of embryos implanted per cycle may seem like a no-brainer, she says, such a rule could be prohibitively difficult because of the wide variety of medical conditions that could occur. For example, she argues, while the American Society of Reproductive Medicine strongly recommends transferring only one — or at most two — embryos at a time, if a woman has already had three or four cycles of IVF and her embryo quality is poor, a doctor could easily justify implanting multiple embryos. "How do you put that into a law?" she asks.

And some fertility doctors argue that they're already more regulated than most other U.S. physicians. "FDA put in tons of rules a few years ago . . . [that] added hundreds of dollars to the cost," says John Jain, who heads a fertility clinic in Santa Monica, Calif. The guidelines, which mainly dealt with disease-testing of donated gametes, involved "viruses I've

never seen in my life." He fears that other regulations "will add to the already exorbitant cost."

David L. Rosenfeld, director of the Center for Human Reproduction at the North Shore-Long Island Jewish Health System in Manhasset, N.Y., makes the same point. "We're already highly scrutinized," he says. Thanks to the CDC's fertility-clinic database, he adds, reproductive-medicine specialists are "the only physicians in the country whose numbers are published nationally."

Sanctions for outlier physicians already exist at state licensing boards such as the one scrutinizing Suleman's doctor, says Jain. "As a physician, how far do I need to be policed? If there are poor outcomes, a level of public scrutiny" emerges — as it has in the octuplets' case — which helps rein in doctors inclined to go too far, he says.

Finally, some doctors contend that having light government oversight allows U.S. medicine to advance rapidly.

"We are probably leaders in the field of reproductive medicine because we can advance without government interference," says Angeline Beltsos, medical director of the Chicago-based Fertility Centers of Illinois. "Creating guidelines is critical, but legislating is dangerous."

Should parents be allowed to choose their babies' characteristics, such as gender?

When pre-implantation genetic diagnosis is used in combination with in vitro fertilization, parents can select specific embryos for their characteristics, raising a variety of ethical questions. [16]

Today, PGD — which removes one cell from an eight-cell embryo — can generally test for only one trait. But soon "we're going to be able to look for many markers at once," opening the door to choosing various characteristics, explains Baruch of the Genetics & Public Policy Center. For instance, eventually hair and eye color will be on the list, "and that'll give people pause."

Many analysts see no problem with allowing parents to opt for PGD, since it seems unlikely that many would go through the rigors of IVF just for the chance to choose a child's gender or appearance.

"We've exercised the ability to choose characteristics for a long time, by deciding who we'll marry or by carefully choosing" a sperm donor for artificial insemination, yet history shows that few people put much effort into choosing traits that might produce a "superior" human, the University of Wisconsin's Charo says. "I'm the only person sent by Congress on taxpayer money to see" the so-called Nobel Prize-winner sperm bank, the Repository for Germinal Excellence, in Southern California, and "I found that nobody ever used that sperm."

Some bioethics experts say there's nothing necessarily wrong with choosing a baby's gender. "I'm the mother of four boys and . . . my sons are marvelous, but at the same time, I certainly would have liked to have had a girl," said University of Chicago professor of medicine Janet D. Rowley during a 2003 deliberation by the President's Council on Bioethics. "This is an area we should leave alone . . . unregulated." [17]

Sex selection to achieve what some call "gender balance" in a family is probably acceptable, says Robertson of the University of Texas. "I have a hard time finding sexism or bias" in a family with three daughters using PGD to have a son, he says.

Meanwhile, Robertson says selecting out genes for non-medical conditions or attributes like looks, personality and abilities probably won't be possible anytime soon. "Most conditions aren't controlled by a single gene," he explains, and scientists don't know which genes make the difference for potentially desirable traits like athleticism or intelligence. Even for single-gene traits, like "fast-twitch muscles" that help some athletes, "the idea of going through IVF when your child won't necessarily become a top athlete anyway seems

Single-Embryo Use Is Rare in U.S.

In countries where insurance pays for IVF procedures, doctors generally implant single embryos in women. By contrast, single-embryo implantation is rare in the United States, where the procedure is not usually covered by insurance, which forces women to have multiple implantations.

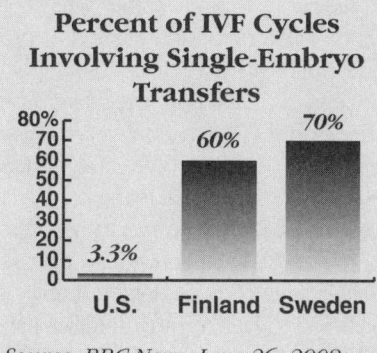

Percent of IVF Cycles Involving Single-Embryo Transfers

Source: BBC News, June 26, 2008, http://news.bbc.co.uk/2/hi/health/7475392.stm

outlandish," he says. "I think the fears of designer babies are overblown."

Likewise, Paul Miller, a former commissioner of the Equal Employment Opportunity Commission, thinks fears are probably unfounded that allowing parents to select against characteristics like shortness or baldness would increase stigmatization of those traits. "There have been opportunities to terminate fetuses with Down's syndrome . . . for a generation," Miller said, "and yet I don't believe that individuals . . . with Down's syndrome are any more or less excluded or that . . . society has the sense that [such] a child . . . should have been prevented." [18]

But others say there's more interest among the public in choosing traits like gender than had been expected and that it's worrisome.

"Looking to the future, some observers view PGD, or any technology that allows parents to choose the characteristics of their children, as having the potential to fundamentally alter the way we view human reproduction and our offspring," noted researchers from the Genetics & Public Policy Center think tank. Rather than viewing "reproduction as a mysterious process that results in the miraculous gift of a child," children may become viewed as a commodity, created by a "series of meticulous, technology-driven" parental choices, said a center report. [19]

Potentially, wealthier people could increase their social advantage because they could afford to create babies with "genes selected to increase their chances of having good looks, musical talent . . . or whatever," thus worsening social inequalities, said the report. In addition, if trait selection becomes common, children born with genetic traits such as hereditary deafness or small stature could face increased social stigma, and parents could face pressure to use PGD to avoid having such children, center analysts speculated. [20]

While Baruch finds it difficult to believe anybody would go through IVF and PGD just to choose their child's gender, recent data indicate that there has been an unexpected uptick in interest in sex selection. "I have heard directly from IVF clinics who were surprised to have people come in primarily for sex selection," she says. Nevertheless, "we need to see better numbers before we call for regulation."

Researchers are finding evidence that some Asian immigrant families, for instance, are using ART to have sons. In some Asian countries, boys are so highly valued over girls that many families have selectively aborted or even murdered girl babies, leading to whole generations in which boys greatly outnumber girls. [21]

Separate research from scholars at Columbia University and the University of Texas concludes that some Asian families in the United States have used and are using whatever technology is available to produce sons, especially for second, third and subsequent children. In the 1990s, the chosen technique was most likely gender-selective abortion, but today more families appear to be using PGD as well. [22]

The researchers found that during the 1990s Chinese, Indian and Korean families' first children mirrored the gender balance in non-Asian families, but their subsequent children included significantly higher proportions of sons. Among Indian families in Santa Clara County, Calif., for example, University of Texas economist Jason Abrevaya found a 58-percent likelihood that a third child would be a son — significantly higher than the natural 51-percent chance of having a boy. [23]

In 2004, at least 70 percent of the parents using the Fertility Institute of Los Angeles wanted to choose their child's gender — far more than those who wanted the clinic's services to test for genetic diseases, reported Deborah L. Spar, a professor of business administration at Harvard Business School. [24] The clinic's medical director, Jeffrey Steinberg, generated some controversy in February when *The Wall Street Journal* reported that his clinic would now offer not only gender selection but selection for physical traits like eye and hair color, which he dubbed "cosmetic medicine." [25]

From some religious perspectives, PGD is immoral for any purpose, including ensuring a child will be free of a deadly genetic disease, wrote Marilyn E. Coors, associate professor of bioethics and genetics at the University of Colorado at Denver. In Catholic teaching, she wrote, PGD is "intrinsically immoral, because it involves the creation and destruction of human lives, replaces the conjugal act and involves third-party intervention in conception." [26]

Some ethicists warn that trait selection of any kind "treats the children . . . as 'products' as we try to

mix the right characteristics," said Toby L. Schonfeld, assistant professor of medical ethics at the University of Nebraska Medical Center. "The increased pressure on these children to fulfill the goals of the parents . . . seems to minimize their autonomy and even exploit them." [27]

The proper use of PGD is for curing or averting disease, and "sex is not a disease," said PGD pioneer Mark Hughes, founder of the Genesis Genetics Institute in Detroit, Mich., explaining why he opposes gender selection. [28]

"I . . . fear . . . that clinics offering trait selection to satisfy the whims of parents will turn people against a procedure that can save lives," said Allen Goldberg, a marketing executive from Washington, D.C., whose 7-year-old son Henry died in 2002 of a rare genetic disease, Fanconi anemia. In the late 1990s, Goldberg and his wife tried unsuccessfully to use PGD to conceive a disease-free sibling who could donate umbilical-cord blood to Henry; other families have used the approach successfully.

However, some ethicists also condemn this use of PGD, arguing that the trait-selected newborn is being unfairly used as a tool to serve the medical needs of its sibling. [29]

Should doctors be able to refuse ART services to gay, older or single people?

The University of South Florida's Keefe says that a gay, male couple came into his clinic in Tampa and were at their wits' end. They had been to several assisted reproductive technology (ART) clinics seeking services, only to be turned away because center officials said they didn't want to be known as a clinic that welcomed gay families.

"These were taxpaying Americans who were very loving to each other, and they'd been bounced from one place to another," says Keefe, who helped the couple conceive a child using donor eggs and a surrogate.

Indeed, some doctors refuse to provide IVF to would-be parents because of their single, gay or elder status, usually citing religious or ethical reasons — or, in the case of older parents — concern about the long-term welfare of the child.

Some ethicists say clinics must first consider the welfare of the children in choosing whom to treat, and questions of religion and conscience figure strongly in such decisions.

In a 2007 report, the ethics committee of the American College of Obstetricians and Gynecologists described a California physician who refused to perform artificial insemination for a lesbian couple, "prompted by religious beliefs and disapproval of lesbians having children." In reproductive medicine, the report said, "health-care providers may find that providing indicated, even standard, care would present for them a personal moral problem — a conflict of conscience." The committee upheld doctors' right to refuse care on those grounds, but said doctors who refuse service must refer patients to other providers. [30]

Because the desire to raise children is not a medical need, physicians may ethically refuse to help people seeking IVF services, argued Julien S. Murphy, a professor of philosophy at the University of Southern Maine. In general, "it is assumed that physicians have a duty to treat 'medical conditions,' " she wrote, "but addressing the fulfillment of reproductive possibilities" opened up by new technology "is an optional matter." [31]

A 2005 survey of fertility doctors found that only 44 percent believed doctors do not have the right to decide who is fit to procreate, according to *Everything Conceivable* author Mundy. Nearly half the physicians surveyed said they'd refuse services to a gay couple, 40 percent said they'd refuse service to a couple on welfare who wanted to pay with Social Security disability checks and 20 percent said they would turn away a single woman. [32]

Continued on p. 461

Chronology

1980s-1990s
First U.S. in vitro fertilization (IVF) clinics open, with early success rates around 5 percent. Concerns grow about fate of frozen IVF embryos.

1981
Elizabeth Jordan Carr is first U.S. IVF baby, the 15th worldwide.

1982
The Sperm Bank of California opens in Berkeley to serve lesbians and single women; the next year it launches first U.S. program allowing donors to release their identities to offspring.

1984
Sweden is first nation to give grown offspring access to sperm donors' identities.

1985
Maryland requires all insurance plans to cover IVF.

1987
Massachusetts and Hawaii require all insurance plans to cover IVF. . . . Texas requires all insurers to offer a plan that covers IVF.

1989
Rhode Island requires all insurance plans to cover IVF. . . . Connecticut requires all insurers except HMOs to offer a plan covering IVF.

1991
Illinois requires all insurance plans to cover IVF.

1992
Congress requires all fertility clinics to report success rates annually.

1993
Richard Paulson, a University of Southern California fertility scientist, demonstrates that women in their 50s can become pregnant with donated eggs. . . . Canada's Royal Commission on New Reproductive Technologies says fertility doctors aren't following professional standards and that stronger laws are needed.

1995
Congress passes Dickey-Wicker amendment, banning government funding of research that may harm a human embryo. Subsequently, it is passed annually in spending bills for the Department of Health and Human Services.

1997
Californian Arceli Keh becomes a first-time mother at 63, after falsely telling IVF doctor Paulson she is in her 50s. . . . Denmark, widely considered a gay-friendly nation, limits government-provided artificial-insemination services to women in relationships with men, effectively shutting out lesbians and single women.

2000s
Fertility treatments become more widely available worldwide.

2001
American Society of Reproductive Medicine (ASRM) enrages some feminist groups with public-service announcements that list a woman's advancing age as among the top threats to fertility. . . . New Jersey requires all insurance plans to cover IVF.

2003
Norway revises its reproductive-medicine laws, ending anonymity for sperm donors but retaining a ban on egg donation.

2004
Canada bans sale of human eggs and sperm and sex selection of children. . . . ASRM recommends that parents inform IVF children they were born from donated eggs or sperm.

2005
Sperm donors in the United Kingdom must release identifying information to grown offspring. . . . Food and Drug Administration requires sperm banks to test for HIV and other communicable diseases.

2006
Canada establishes Assisted Human Reproduction Agency to regulate reproductive medicine.

2008
An impoverished 27-year-old Egyptian mother of three delivers septuplets after taking inexpensive fertility drugs now available worldwide, including in countries lacking health-care facilities to manage multiple births. . . . Colorado voters reject a referendum to amend the state constitution to consider a human embryo a legal "person."

2009
A 33-year-old California woman, Nadya Suleman, has octuplets after requesting that her doctor implant six frozen embryos created by IVF. . . . Reproductive tourism to Italy, one of the few European countries that don't regulate IVF, is up 75 percent since 2003. . . . England's reproductive-medicine regulatory agency says it will inform donor-conceived children at age 16 whether they're genetically related to a person they plan to be sexually intimate with. . . . Georgia legislature considers but doesn't enact law granting personhood to embryos. . . . California and Missouri legislatures consider legislation to regulate fertility clinics.

Searching the Web for Biological Parents

The era of anonymous egg and sperm donors may be ending.

The 15-year-old American boy had been conceived by his mother using an anonymous sperm donor. But the youth wanted to know the identity of his biological father, and in 2005 he made news and perhaps history by tracking down the donor online.

"This is the first time that I know of it being done," said Bryan Sykes, a geneticist at the University of Oxford in the United Kingdom. [1]

The case raises the question of whether the anonymity long promised to many egg and sperm donors is realistic in the 21st century.

Indeed, as happened over the past few decades with adoption, egg and sperm donation is gradually becoming an open process, analysts say.

"We're moving toward giving donors the opportunity to be contacted or identified," as more donation-organizations offer this option and online donor registries are established, says John A. Robertson, a professor at the University of Texas College of Law at Austin. "As a psychological matter, there's wide agreement that it's good to disclose, but you won't see anything in the United States as draconian as in England, where you can't be anonymous."

The American teenager sent his own DNA to an online genealogy Web site for testing and then was able to contact two men with closely matching DNA who were likely relatives. Using their surnames, plus information his mother had received about the donor's date and place of birth, he paid another online site for a list of everyone born in that place on that day. In less than two weeks, he had made contact with the donor. [2]

The incident reveals the "hunger for . . . connection and an understanding of this invisible part of themselves" that many donor offspring experience, according to Wendy Kramer, a Colorado mother who launched a voluntary Internet registry for donors, donor-conceived children and their families. [3]

"This boy did wonder why it was always assumed that the rights of a donor to remain anonymous trumped a child's right to know his genetic heritage" since he "had not entered into . . . anonymity agreements with anyone," wrote Kramer, who started the Donor Sibling Registry with her donor-conceived son Ryan about nine years ago. "Will every kid who swabs his cheek find his donor? Probably not. But we can expect this to happen with greater frequency as DNA data banks swell." [4]

The move away from anonymity and toward establishing a registry is spurred by more than young people's curiosity, says Jan Elman Stout, a clinical psychologist in Chicago. As the number of children born from donor sperm has increased, so has the likelihood that children from the same donor might unknowingly fall in love, have sexual relations or marry.

That possibility is particularly strong in smaller nations, which are acting to head off the problem. Beginning this October, for example, teens 16 and older in the United Kingdom who plan to become sexually intimate can contact the government's reproductive-medicine agency to find out whether they are genetically related to their partners. [5]

Statisticians say the United States is below the threshold where there's much chance sperm donors' children will meet and marry, "but I'm not sure the reporting of successful births is reliable enough" to be certain, says Stout. Some U.S. mental-health professionals are championing establishment of a centralized donor registry, but there's pushback both from patients and doctors, who worry that an end to anonymity will mean many fewer men will donate sperm, she says.

Laws in several countries ending donor anonymity are too new to draw firm conclusions.

When two Australian states abolished anonymity, donations fell off drastically. Western Australia, with a population of 1.4 million people, ended up with only 35 available sperm donors. Some Australian clinics offered all-expense-paid tours of their country — complete with free visits to dance clubs and other night spots — to Canadian college students, in return for sperm donations. [6]

But widespread concern that laws abolishing donor anonymity will cut the number of donors permanently may not be justified, according to Ken Daniels, a professor of social work at the University of Canterbury in Christchurch, New Zealand. For the most part, surveys showing that donors are super-leery of being identified have only polled people who had donated before disclosure laws had taken effect and could be expected to be biased against it, he said. [7]

Under new non-anonymity laws, a new and different group of potential donors — possibly older, married people with children — may come forward, inspired by their own parenthood to help others conceive, Daniels predicts. He recounts a conversation with a donor who said that, as a young man, he donated for the money, but "having his own children has made him aware of the child's perspective and the possible need for information." [8]

---

[1] Quoted in Alison Motluk, "Anonymous Sperm Donor Traced on Internet," *New Scientist online*, Nov. 5, 2005, www.newscientist.com.

[2] *Ibid.*

[3] Wendy Kramer, "DNA and the Exploding Myth of Donor Anonymity," Donor Sibling Registry Web site, www.donorsiblingregistry.com.

[4] *Ibid.*

[5] *The HFEA Register*, Human Fertilisation and Embryology Authority Web site, www.hfea.gov.uk/.

[6] Liza Mundy, *Everything Conceivable* (2007), p. 187.

[7] Ken Daniels, "Donor Gametes: Anonymous or Identified," *Best Practice & Research: Clinical Obstetrics and Gynecology*, February 2007, pp. 113-128.

[8] Quoted in *ibid.*, p. 119.

Continued from p. 458

Such ethical debates are not limited to the United States. Arguing for a ban on ART for single or lesbian women, a member of the Danish Parliament stated that such women have "completely, freely chosen to live" in a manner that "cannot naturally produce children," making providing ART to them "completely against nature, artificial and absurd." [33]

Many English fertility clinics will not serve single women, said Clare Murray, a psychologist at City University London. "Clinics treat lesbian couples at the drop of a hat, but still won't treat single women. They're the pariahs of the assisted-reproduction field." [34]

And University of Pennsylvania bioethicist Arthur L. Caplan argues that physicians have every right — and perhaps a moral duty — to refuse ART for people who are too old. He was commenting on the 2005 Caesarian-section birth of a daughter to 66-year-old Adriana Iliescu, an unmarried professor in Bucharest, Romania.

Such pregnancies are medically risky, Caplan noted. For instance, in Iliescu's IVF treatments, she initially had a miscarriage, then a stillbirth and, finally, a live child born prematurely from a "life-threatening emergency C-section." Furthermore, he pointed out, when the daughter enters high school, Iliescu will be 80, too old to raise a teenager to adulthood.

Caplan said he would refuse ART to single people over 65 or to a couple with one member who is 65 or older, making their total age higher than 130, and to any woman age 55 or older who could not pass "a rigorous physical examination." [35]

But other physicians say that — aside from screening out patients with severe mental disorders — deciding who may have children should not be up to the doctor. "How does that become my responsibility?" says Beltsos, of the Fertility Centers of Illinois. The case of octuplet-mother Suleman is "a tough one, but just because I might think it's inappropriate or irresponsible to have 14 kids, does

Sixty Percent of ART Users Are Over 35

About 60 percent of women who turned to assisted reproductive technology (ART) in 2006 were over age 35. Women's fertility begins to drop off around age 24 and declines steeply after 35.

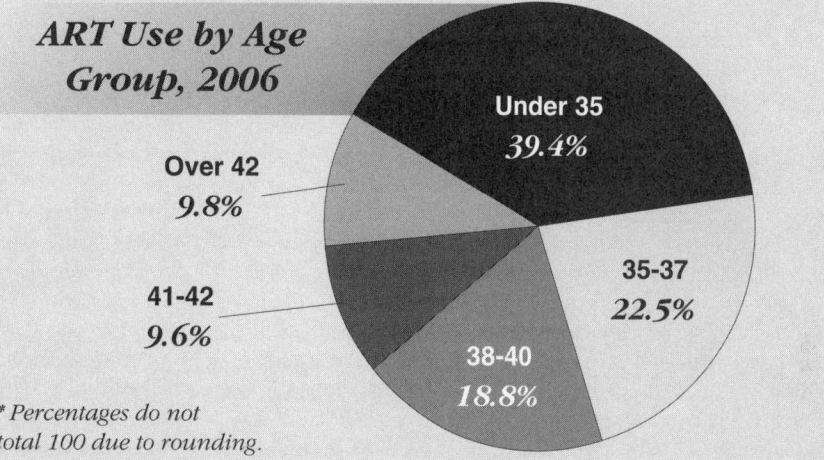

ART Use by Age Group, 2006

- Under 35 **39.4%**
- 35-37 **22.5%**
- 38-40 **18.8%**
- 41-42 **9.6%**
- Over 42 **9.8%**

* Percentages do not total 100 due to rounding.

Source: "Assisted Reproductive Technology Success Rates 2006," Centers for Disease Control and Prevention, 2008

that mean I can decide for someone else? Where does the line get drawn?"

As for worrying about the welfare of the child, the Hastings Center's Johnston says that IVF clinics deal with people who fervently want children. "This is not the population where the real child-welfare problem is," she says. "We take wanting a child as kind of placeholder for doing a pretty good job with the child," so she says she probably wouldn't support clinics adding child-welfare considerations to their protocols for accepting ART patients.

In August 2008, the California Supreme Court ruled that denying ART services to a lesbian constitutes unlawful discrimination under a law requiring businesses to guarantee all persons "full and equal accommodations." [36]

In *North Coast Women's Care Medical Group, Inc. v. Superior Court* the court ruled in favor of Guadalupe Benitez, a lesbian in a long-term relationship who sued the facility after two physicians refused to artificially inseminate her and referred her to another clinic. The doctors argued that their rights to religious liber-

ty would be violated if they were required to provide ART to all comers. But the court said the state's civil rights law trumps the religious-liberty claim and requires the clinic to either offer ART to no one or have at least one physician on staff who will provide it to all clients. [37]

An American Society of Reproductive Medicine ethics committee declared in 2006 that, "as a matter of ethics, we believe the ethical duty to treat persons with equal respect requires that fertility programs treat single persons and gay and lesbian couples equally with married couples in determining which services to provide." [38]   ∎

BACKGROUND

Stigma and Silence

T hroughout history, many childless couples have struggled to have a child to call their own. [39]

Insurance Coverage Affects Fertility Decisions

More people use IVF when insurance covers the procedure.

With more and more patients turning to alternative means of reproduction over the past two decades, 14 states have enacted legislation offering at least some insurance coverage to help people have the families they long for.

Most of these states require all insurers under state regulation to include at least some infertility coverage in all insurance plans they sell, while two states, California and Texas, only require all insurers to "offer" everyone coverage — that is, insurers must offer at least one plan that covers infertility treatments.

While the laws may be similar, the actual coverage provided is anything but. States run the gamut from covering only screening tests to ascertain whether a couple is infertile to full coverage of multiple in vitro fertilization (IVF) treatments. Each state also limits who can access infertility treatment. For example, a state might limit the medical condition of infertility to apply only to a married couple who have tried unsuccessfully for a specified amount of time to conceive. In that state, an unmarried woman would not be eligible for any treatment coverage.

Insurance mandates definitely improve access. In Europe, for example, where IVF often is funded by government-financed health coverage, up to 4 percent of children are born following some kind of fertility procedure, compared to only about 1 percent in the United States. [1]

Increasing access by helping people pay for infertility treatments matters because "the less money you have, the more likely you are to have difficulty conceiving," wrote reporter Liza Mundy, author of the 2007 book *Everything Conceivable*. "Much infertility has always been caused by infections that can damage reproductive passageways," and "the lower your tax bracket, the less likely you are to have received the fairly simple medical treatment that can stave off these consequences." [2]

Insurance coverage — or the lack of it — "greatly impacts the decisions that doctors and patients make," says Angeline Beltsos, medical director of the Chicago-based Fertility Centers of Illinois. Illinois will pay for four IVF tries for a first baby for an infertile woman, regardless of her age.

In a state without an insurance mandate, a couple with a one-in-five chance of conceiving through IVF is highly likely to look at the average $12,000 price tag for one IVF cycle and simply give up, trying donor eggs, adoption or cheaper drug or surgical interventions instead, Beltsos says. "But here in our state you get a very different approach. Here, people say, 'OK, let's try IVF before we try donor eggs.' " Even some "younger couples who probably could get pregnant without IVF" opt for it because it costs them little.

And few Illinois patients try lower-tech drug or surgical procedures — which also may not work — Beltsos says. "They just go into IVF" instead, and "don't waste years and years with things that may not work very well, ultimately ending up in IVF only when they're so old" that simple, age-related fertility decline may doom IVF to failure, she says.

Once IVF treatment begins, patients in insured states again behave differently, Beltsos says. For example, "no insurance covers the $200 to $1,000 cost of freezing extra embryos," so people with IVF coverage are more likely to say "go ahead and destroy" the extras, she says. "But if you had paid for that cycle, they'd be begging to have the embryos frozen" since doing so "would significantly reduce the cost" of subsequent cycles, she says.

— Additional reporting by Vyomika Jairam

---

[1] Liza Mundy, *Everything Conceivable* (2007), pp. 3-4.
[2] *Ibid.*, p. xiv.

The biblical book of *Genesis* describes how Sarah, the infertile wife of Israelite patriarch Abraham, was so distraught over the couple's childlessness that she offered her maid Hagar as a surrogate mother with whom Abraham conceived a child, his son Ishmael. [40]

In England, King Henry VIII married wife after wife, primarily in order to satisfy his desire for a male heir. That 16th-century saga not only demonstrates how fierce the desire for children can be but also how the concept of fertility is intertwined with male virility. "The wives of Henry VIII knew all too well how women tend to be blamed for male-

factor [fertility] issues," since several ended up divorced, with their marriages involuntarily annulled or even beheaded in Henry's quest for sons, observed *Everything Conceivable* author Mundy. [41]

Ironically, the "father of our country," U.S. President George Washington, was most likely infertile. But he blamed his wife Martha when he could not father children, "despite the rather glaring evidence of her fertility, provided by four children from a recent prior marriage," wrote Mundy. [42]

Bemoaning his childless state at age 54, Washington wrote that "if Mrs. Washington should survive me, there

is a moral certainty of my dying without issue." Furthermore, he wrote, "should I be longest lived, the matter . . . is hardly less certain for . . . I shall never marry a girl; and it is not probable that I should have children by a woman of an age suitable to my own." [43]

Despite clear evidence of Washington's infertility, it is hardly ever mentioned in historical accounts of his life, said John K. Amory, associate professor of medicine at the University of Washington School of Medicine in Seattle.

The silence probably results from a "frequent erroneous assumption that infertility is mostly female in origin," Amory wrote, and fear that discussion of Washington's infertility "would diminish him in some way," even though infertility has nothing to do with one's other characteristics and occurs "without regard to [one's] historical stature." [44]

Stigma and silence may also help keep fertility treatment out of the mainstream of American medicine, some analysts say. Unlike most medical specialties, except plastic surgery, fertility medicine is largely provided on a cash-pay basis because it is not covered by insurance.

By definition, "infertility is an illness" — an "impairment of normal biological functioning that causes great distress," says Dartmouth's Green. "Nevertheless, we don't think of it that way because it affects only a few people. I teach an ART course to undergraduates, and they often don't get it, because at their age the big problem for most is keeping their fertility in check. But when you are ready to have a child, it becomes a grave, grave matter." The "mental suffering is as bad as that for cancer."

Nevertheless, it's been difficult to assemble a strong advocacy community around expanding IVF insurance coverage because "there's still a lot of public stigma," says Collura of the National Infertility Association. "We're where breast cancer was 25 years ago."

Breast-cancer and AIDS patients eventually "came out" and forced the public to confront those diseases, but igniting such a movement may be even harder for infertility, she says. "It's such a personal, private thing, so emotionally painful; and because people are private about it, we don't realize the extent of it."

But even with public recognition of how many people infertility affects, some experts doubt the U.S. health-care system — in which more than 45 million people lack coverage entirely — can afford to add more services, especially one as costly as IVF. [45]

ART "can be quite expensive," notes the National Conference on State Legislatures (NCSL). "On average each cycle of IVF costs $8,158 plus an average of $4,000 for medications — and debate exists about whether insurance plans should be required to cover

The online Donor Sibling Registry makes a unique family reunion possible in Fresno, Calif., for three mothers and their children. The children were all conceived after their mothers were artificially inseminated by sperm from the same donor and thus are half-siblings. From left: Dawn Warthen and Allyson, Michelle Jorgenson and Cheyenne, and Jenafer Elin and Joshua.

them." Estimates of the monthly cost to mandate IVF coverage range from $.20 to $2.00 per insurance-plan member, according to the NCSL. [46]

"Not having these treatments covered is unfortunate, but it is not unfair," because, "in fact, people don't have the [legal] right to any health care in this country except emergency care," said George J. Annas, professor of health law and bioethics at the Boston University School of Public Health. "To mandate [ART coverage], given the growing numbers of uninsured people, makes no legal, economic or health-care sense." [47]

Moreover, notes the NCSL, the use of ART over the years has raised overall health-care costs by contributing to an increase in multiple births, which have a higher rate of prematurity than single births. By 2004, for example, the percentage of babies considered to have low birth weight had risen to 8.1 percent, the highest level since the early 1970s, driven largely by ART-caused multiple births. [48]

Advocates of insurance coverage argue that it might eventually lower health-system costs, because there would be fewer high-risk multiple births if parents-to-be could opt for several single-embryo procedures rather than one multiple-embryo implantation. "The rate of triplets in insurance-mandate states is much lower," says Keefe, of the University of South Florida.

"In states where infertility treatments are not paid for, physicians run up expensive tabs for services that aren't needed, like surgery to reconnect scarred fallopian tubes," argues Green. Fertility doctors in those states may also spend too much time trying to diagnose the condition — because the diagnostics are often paid for by insurance — when it would have been cheaper just to try IVF immediately, he adds.

Since the 1980s, 14 states — Arkansas, California, Connecticut, Hawaii, Illinois, Maryland, Massachusetts, Montana, New Jersey, New York, Ohio, Rhode Island, Texas and West Virginia — have required insurers to either cover or offer at least one plan that covers some ART, although not necessarily IVF, according to the NCSL. (*See map, p. 452, and sidebar, p. 462.*)

Using Assisted Reproductive Technology
The ART birth cycle from beginning to end

Here are the steps toward pregnancy and live birth using assisted reproductive technology (ART) and fresh, non-donor eggs or embryos:

1. Cycle starts: *Woman starts taking medication to stimulate the ovaries to develop eggs or, if no drugs are given, the woman begins having her ovaries monitored for natural egg production.*

2. Egg retrieval: *If eggs are produced, a surgical procedure is used to collect them from the ovaries.*

3. Egg and sperm combine: *In vitro fertilization combines egg and sperm in the laboratory. If fertilization is successful, one or more of the resulting embryos are transferred, most often into the uterus through the cervix.*

4. Pregnancy: *If one or more embryos implant within the uterus, the cycle may progress to pregnancy.*

5. Birth: *The pregnancy may progress to the delivery of one or more live-born infants.*

Two of the states, California and New York, explicitly exclude IVF from the coverage mandate while covering other services such as diagnosis of infertility problems. [49] However, in 2002, New York authorized a demonstration program — still ongoing — to test the effects of IVF coverage by picking up a share of the costs for some patients, with the subsidy prorated by income. [50]

Fertility Industry

Physicians see advantages and disadvantages in fertility medicine's "cash-only" status.

"There are very few fields" in medicine as lucrative, says Jain of the Santa Monica Fertility Specialists.

As a result, when it comes to technical innovation, "I don't think there's a field that's evolved as rapidly as ours in the last 20 years," says Rosenfeld of New York's North Shore-Long Island Jewish Health System. With no public insurers and few private insurers involved, "we don't have any oversight

— only our peers — so there's a lot more room for freelancing, for entrepreneurialism," Jain says.

Entrepreneurialism can lead to innovation but can also in many cases "be a euphemism for exploitation," Jain says. For example, "some will overrecommend IVF because it's so lucrative," rather than saving IVF as a last resort and taking patients through less-extreme procedures first, according to Jain.

The CDC keeps a database of fertility-clinic data as an oversight tool, in lieu of stronger policing, but when that information is combined with the highly competitive nature of the business, it can backfire, says Rosenfeld.

"How do people decide which clinic to choose?" he asks. They go online to the database, Rosenfeld says, and find that one clinic, for example, has a 46-percent success rate and another, 48 percent. But they don't realize that a clinic with a higher success rate might accept only patients with a higher probability of conceiving, so the data reporting process provides an incentive for physicians to "do things they might not

otherwise do," such as rejecting patients with a low likelihood of conception or using the data as a marketing tool, without including caveats about what it actually means, he says.

The University of South Florida's Keefe headed an American Society of Reproductive Medicine committee on the CDC registry and "wanted to put a "Click to see [patient] inclusion criteria' " button on each clinic's statistics to help patients understand them better, he recalls. "But everybody said, 'That would be too confusing,' " so it didn't happen.

The profit motive extends to egg donation, according to author Mundy. In the early days of IVF, many donors were women who'd finished childbearing and wanted to help others, and "women helping women" was the byword of the then-nonprofit organizations that arranged for donation, she said. Today, most donors are young women in need of cash and, because some donors "are paid a lot" — based on physical and intellectual characteristics, such as an Ivy League diploma — private commercial agencies have gotten more aggressive in procuring eggs, she said. [51]

The profit motive in egg donation may be dangerous both to donors and potential offspring, Tucson, Ariz.-based physician Jennifer Schneider told a congressional briefing in November 2007. Schneider's college-age daughter Jessica donated eggs to supplement her income and, six years later, at age 29, died of colon cancer, a condition that her mother suspects could have been related to the donation process, in which women take fertility drugs to stimulate multiple egg production. [52]

Unfortunately, "I'm here to tell you that hardly anything is known" about an egg-donation-colon-cancer link — also present in several other cases of unusual colon cancers in young women — "because once a young woman walks out of an IVF clinic, she is of no interest to anyone," Schneider told lawmakers.

Continued on p. 466

At Issue:

Should egg and sperm donors be paid?

JOSEPHINE JOHNSTON
DIRECTOR OF RESEARCH OPERATIONS
THE HASTINGS CENTER

WRITTEN FOR *CQ RESEARCHER*, MAY 2009

*m*odest payments for gametes are fair, necessary for some kinds of fertility treatment and show respect for the autonomy and dignity of donors. Egg donors should receive more than sperm donors given the invasive and sometimes painful procedures they endure.

Sperm donation isn't as quick or pleasurable as one might assume, but it isn't terribly arduous either. Eggs are another story. Egg donors are medically assessed before beginning the daily routine of mixing and injecting themselves in the stomach or thigh with hormones to suppress and then dramatically increase egg production. They visit the fertility clinic regularly over the month-long process for blood tests and ultrasounds to monitor egg development. They then undergo minor surgery to remove the eggs, followed by a day of bed rest. The hormones and the surgery carry physical risks and often result in discomfort or pain. The drugs can cause emotions to fluctuate, and some anxiety often accompanies the process (how will her body respond to the drugs, what does an unsuccessful attempt imply about her own fertility?).

In the United States, sperm donors are usually paid (not much, but they can donate every five days). Egg donors receive far more, from $2,000 to tens of thousands of dollars. Technically, the money is for time and effort, not the gametes produced. Whether or not you buy that distinction, egg donation in particular can provide significant income.

I share the concern that $10,000 or $50,000 could easily persuade someone to undergo procedures without proper consideration of the risks. But the average egg donor receives just over $4,000 for the weeks she spends in and out of physician's offices, the daily self-administered injections and surgical retrieval of her eggs. Not to mention the discomfort, pain and apprehension. Would you do this for free? Few do.

While money for sperm rarely raises concern, many remain uneasy about paying egg donors. Is it because eggs, even if plentiful, are more difficult to remove and (perhaps) limited in number? If it's the risks, isn't doing it for free just as dangerous? Or does the unease represent an unexamined desire to control women's bodies, particularly their reproductive capacity, and a mistrust of their ability to make medical and reproductive decisions?

This society allows young women to make the same life-changing choices as any other adult. If few will donate their eggs for free, we should trust that they can make an ethical decision to do so for pay.

SCOTT B. RAE
PROFESSOR OF CHRISTIAN ETHICS
TALBOT SCHOOL OF THEOLOGY
BIOLA UNIVERSITY

WRITTEN FOR *CQ RESEARCHER*, MAY 2009

*p*aying sperm and egg donors should be discouraged. Egg selling involves often unrecognized health risks to the donor. The egg-harvesting process is highly invasive. Women run a short-term risk of ovarian hyperstimulation syndrome (OHSS). OHSS can cause potentially serious long-term thrombosis, liver and renal problems and respiratory distress — and in rare instances, death. Over time, donors risk future infertility and, potentially, development of cancers related to the synthetic hormones used to hyperstimulate the ovaries. Bear in mind, the egg donor is an otherwise healthy woman, not an infertile "patient" who chooses to assume these risks for the benefit of a baby.

Granted, sperm "donors" are not paid that much, and sperm "donation" does not entail risks to donors, but other concerns still apply.

Paying "donors" may undermine a child's right to know his or her biological parents. Most donors do not want to be identified, and in countries where the law requires identification, not surprisingly, the number of donors has diminished quickly. The Donor Sibling Registry has thousands of children still looking for their other biological parent. And, while they may not find their fathers, they often connect with many (10 or more) half-siblings, with uncertain consequences. One site (donorsibling.com) has traced over 100 children back to a single donor.

An apparent interest in eugenics has moved society toward "designer children," another issue potentially exacerbated by donor payments. One advertisement for an egg donor offered $75,000 if the donor was 5'10" or above, blond, blue-eyed, athletic and scored above 1400 on her SAT exams. In a culture that values diversity, producing designer children risks reinforcing damaging stereotypes.

Another concern comes with new types of families that are being intentionally preplanned. "Single mothers by choice" are increasingly common, yet a growing body of empirical evidence shows the importance of fathers to children's well-being. That is not to say that single-parent families that result from widowhood or divorce can't adequately raise children. But those situations are different from preplanned single-parent families.

Increasing the number of gamete donors by offering payment could also lead to a decrease in traditional adoptions or adoptions of existing embryos. I often suggest adoption of embryos to couples contemplating using donor eggs, because it provides the experience of pregnancy and birth but avoids using a "procreative pinch-hitter."

Continued from p. 464

Egg brokers "make enormous sums" of money and want to maximize the number of eggs they have, giving them "every reason to avoid follow-up of egg donors and studies of their possible long-term risks," she said. When she called Jessica's broker to warn that children born of her eggs should be tested, since the cancer may be genetic, Schneider was told that the records had already been destroyed, and offspring could not be tracked. [53]

Research Stinted

Fertility research has not been funded through the traditional routes, such as the National Institutes of Health (NIH), says fertility specialist Jain. Although the NIH funds most medical research in America, fertility medicine gets little NIH attention because the field operates largely without public and private insurance and because legislators have religion- and morality-based qualms about research using human embryos.

"IVF has had a 30-year life span," says Jain. "It came out of Ph.Ds who worked in zoos," conducting embryo research on animals. "But there's an absence of NIH funding for the basic science in human embryology. The field has had to sponsor its own studies."

After 30 years of IVF, there have been no multi-center studies — large-scale research coordinated at several clinical sites — the gold standard of medicine, says Dartmouth's Green. In the early 1990s, the National Institute on Child Health and Development (NICHD) tried to get research going, he says, after an advisory panel that he served on recommended increased federal funding.

But in 1995, Congress not only rejected NICHD's pitch but banned federal funding of any "research in which a human embryo or embryos are destroyed, discarded or knowingly subjected to risk of injury or death." Congress has included the ban as a part

of annual appropriations legislation ever since then. [54]

While discussions of the ban usually focus on its effect on stem-cell research, it also significantly limits what scientists know about infertility and the early stages of human development. "We know very little about what is a good and what's a bad embryo," says Collura of the National Infertility Association. As a result, one of the top questions for any embryologist is which among a group of embryos are most likely to produce a full-term baby. "But if you have 10 different embryologists in a room, you'll get 10 different answers."

Knowing the answer would help reduce multiple births. "If you want singletons, it's important to know which embryos are the right ones to transfer," she says. ∎

CURRENT SITUATION

Regulating IVF

In the wake of the octuplets' birth, a California legislator introduced a proposal that the state regulate fertility clinics, [55] and the Georgia legislature considered limiting the number of eggs that may be fertilized and embryos implanted during IVF. [56]

In the past year, a spate of state proposals have addressed fertility medicine, many by granting legal "personhood" to embryos, about 500,000 of which now sit frozen in fertility clinics around the country, their ultimate fate undecided since many of the families who created them are now finished with childbearing. [57] No bill has yet gained much traction, however.

The California bill, which would bring fertility clinics under the juris-

diction of the Medical Board of California and set accreditation standards, is one of a handful that would increase government oversight of fertility clinics. Missouri's House Bill 810, for instance, would require doctors to follow American Society of Reproductive Medicine (ASRM) guidelines on embryo implantation or face sanctions. [58]

"The people of this state don't need to be paying millions of dollars for some woman who has eight babies at once," said the bill's sponsor, Republican Missouri state Rep. Bob Schaaf. [59]

ASRM supports Schaaf's proposal. "We are very supportive of the bill," said Sean Tipton, ASRM director of public affairs, "because it defers to medical knowledge and experience and protects both women and unborn children." [60]

Legislative efforts to grant "personhood" to embryos — such as Colorado's proposed constitutional Amendment 48 defeated by voters last November — are heavily criticized by the reproductive-medicine community but win plaudits from right-to-life groups.

After fierce legislative wrangling and numerous language changes, Georgia's Senate-passed personhood bill was not brought to the House floor before the 2009 legislative session ended in March. The Georgia Right to Life group praised the bill for its attempt to limit the number of embryos created.

"The human embryo is one of us, fully human with great potential," and "we do not . . . need to sacrifice human life for money and economic development or the remote possibility of a medical cure for someone else," said Daniel Becker, the group's president. [61]

But ASRM's Tipton said the measure would hurt infertile people by presuming "that politicians know what is best . . . and not physicians." [62]

"Some of the people writing legislation don't understand ART," says Collura of the National Infertility Association. For example, some Georgia lawmakers backed language allowing doctors to fertilize only two eggs per

IVF cycle. That's unworkable, she says, because currently IVF is a process in which as many eggs as possible are fertilized in order to improve the chances that some embryos will be viable.

Those who would ban processes like embryo freezing don't realize how many people would be hurt, including cancer patients who can bear children after their ovaries are surgically removed only if their embryos are frozen before the treatment, she says.

Social Changes

Powerful social trends make it likely that usage of advanced assisted reproductive technology will increase.

The delay in childbearing until women are older, for instance, has increased the incidence of infertility. Human biology "is not built for a society where [women] first go to medical school" before bearing children, says Dartmouth's Green, so "we are seeing increasing infertility."

In addition, some large-scale recent studies have suggested — though not proven — that men's sperm counts have been declining for a half-century or so, mainly in industrialized countries. For example, a large 2000 study by Shanna Swan, professor of obstetrics, gynecology and environmental medicine at the University of Rochester's School of Medicine and Dentistry in New York state, suggested that sperm counts were dropping by about 1.5 percent a year in the United States and 3 percent annually in Europe and Australia. Rural areas seemed to have the lower counts, perhaps due to agricultural chemicals. [63]

Increasing the pressure on those hoping to start a family, the number of infants available for adoption in the United States has dropped steadily for decades. Before 1973, for example, nearly 20 percent of never-married, white, pregnant women relinquished the babies to adoption. By the mid-1990s, the percentage had plummeted

to 1.7 percent — a "dramatic decline" that shows no signs of a turnaround, according to the Department of Health and Human Services. [64]

During the 1990s, international adoptions by Americans skyrocketed, partly compensating for the declining availability of U.S. infants, but recently some countries have clamped down on such adoptions out of fear of baby selling. [65]

Meanwhile, most people remain unaware of how quickly the average woman's fertility declines after age 30 and how many women and men have other medical issues that decrease fertility.

Celebrity births to women over age 40 and even over 50 — hyped in the media with no mention that virtually all resulted from IVF and, in many cases, donor eggs — contribute to a false public impression, said author Mundy. "A parade of high-profile women . . . have made 40-something motherhood seem almost natural," she wrote, citing actresses Jane Seymour, who had a baby at 44; Susan Sarandon, 46; Geena Davis, twins at 47; Holly Hunter, twins at 47; and the late playwright Wendy Wasserstein, who had a premature daughter at 48. [66]

"They're perpetuating a false impression" that fertility wanes less quickly than it does, says psychologist Stout. "They're also perpetuating a cultural notion that all of this is secret," thus helping maintain the social stigma that surrounds ART, she says. "The more we open up, the better." ∎

OUTLOOK

Health-care Reform

Congress and the Obama administration plan to propose massive health-care reform. If the United States moves to a health-care system with

guaranteed coverage for all, intense debate will surround the question of which services should be covered.

Coverage for a procedure can easily be nixed if enough people say, "I'm a taxpayer and I object to that," since everyone would be subsidizing the system, says Wisconsin's Charo. Although all other industrialized countries have universal health care, and most pay for a very broad range of ART services, including IVF, discussions in the United States would be difficult "because women's sexuality and childbirth resonate so strongly" with many religious groups here, she says.

Some countries, such as Australia, subsidize IVF partly to boost birthrates, a goal the government and much of the public support, says Washington-based health-care consultant Gleason, but even in such situations, payment for ART bumps up against the economic reality that there aren't enough dollars to go around.

Today "we use [services like IVF] only a tenth as much as France and Israel," for example, says Keefe of the University of South Florida. "There's a huge, unmet need."

Universal coverage would lead to more regulation, including holding clinics accountable for following medical guidelines, Keefe says. "You wouldn't give coverage for it just the way it's done now," he says.

Questions would be raised as to "whether you'd cover IVF generally and for what purposes you'd cover PGD," says Baruch at the Genetics & Public Policy Center. Another question, she says: Could people still pay privately for whatever additional services they want or would some procedures be banned altogether?

If universal coverage is provided, "we'll have to get used to drawing lines" regarding coverage, and not just for ART, says Dartmouth's Green. "In Great Britain, for example, nobody over age 65 gets dialysis," he says. When it comes to IVF, government might well say, "We won't pay after you've already had two children."

Whether universal coverage would help or hurt ART "would depend on how they restricted care," says Rosenfeld at the North Shore-Long Island Jewish Health System. "If they started restricting it like they do in Europe" — where some countries outlaw implantation of more than one or two embryos, for example — "it would be a problem."

Oregon and Massachusetts have both experimented with universal coverage — Oregon in the 1990s and Massachusetts currently — and ART fared differently in each of those states, Rosenfeld notes. In Massachusetts, a state law mandates IVF coverage, but when Oregon deliberated over which services to cut, given budget constraints, reproductive medicine "fell below the line and wasn't paid for," offering a sobering example of how universal coverage mandates can cut both ways, he says. ∎

Notes

[1] "Medical Society Probes Octuplets' Conception," The Associated Press, MSNBC.com, Feb. 10, 2009, www.msnbc.msn.com/id/29123731.

[2] Liza Mundy, *Everything Conceivable* (2007), p. 217.

[3] For background, see "Three Million Babies Born Using Assisted Reproductive Technologies," *Medical News Today*, June 25, 2006, www.medicalnewstoday.com.

[4] See Marcy Darnovsky, *Biopolitical Times blog*, Center for Genetics and Society, Feb. 27, 2009, www.biopoliticaltimes.org/article.php?id=4550.

[5] See " 'One Egg' IVF Strategy Launched," BBC News, June 26, 2008, www.news.bbc.

co.uk/2/hi/health/7475392.stm. Also see Mundy, *op. cit.*, p. 214.

[6] Marcy Darnovsky, "Voluntary Isn't Working," *Modern Healthcare*, April 13, 2009, www.modernhealthcare.com/apps/pbcs.dll/article?Date=20090413&Category=SUB&ArtNo=304139998&SectionCat=&Template=printpicart.

[7] Franco Furger and Francis Fukuyama, "A Proposal for Modernizing the Regulation of Human Biotechnologies," *Hastings Center Report*, July/August 2007, pp. 16-20.

[8] "Consumers Desire More Genetic Testing, But not Designer Babies," *ScienceDaily*, Jan. 26, 2009, www.sciencedaily.com/releases/2009/01/090126100642.htm.

[9] Maili Malin, "Good, Bad and Troublesome: Infertility Physicians' Perceptions of Women Patients," *European Journal of Women's Studies*, August 2003, pp. 301-319.

[10] For background, see Brian Hansen, "Cloning Debate," *CQ Researcher*, Oct. 22, 2004, pp. 877-900.

[11] *Buzzanca v. Buzzanca*, Cal. App. 4th 1410 (1998), quoted in Linda S. Maule and Karen Schmid, "Assisted Reproduction and the Courts: The Case of California," *Journal of Family Issues*, April 1, 2006, pp. 464-482.

[12] Naomi Cahn, Necessary Subjects: The Need for a Mandatory National Donor Gamete Registry, April 2008, *DePaul Journal of Healthcare Law*, http://papers.ssrn.com/sol3/papers.cfm?abstract_id=1120389.

[13] Audrey Huang and Susannah Baruch, "Oversight of PGD," issue brief, Genetics & Public Policy Center, July 2007, www.dnapolicy.org/policy.issue.php?action=detail&issuebrief_id=8.

[14] John A. Robertson, "The Virtues of Muddling Through," *Hastings Center Report*, July/August 2007, pp. 26-28.

[15] *Ibid.*

[16] For background, see David Masci, "Designer Humans," *CQ Researcher*, May 18, 2001, pp. 425-440.

[17] Transcript, discussion of staff working paper, "Ethical Aspects of Sex Control," President's Council on Bioethics, Jan. 16, 2003, http://bioethicsprint.bioethics.gov/transcripts/jan03/session4.html.

[18] Quoted in "Reproductive Genetic Testing: Issues and Options for Policymakers," Genetics & Public Policy Center, 2004.

[19] "Preimplantation Genetic Diagnosis: A Discussion of Challenges, Concerns, and Preliminary Policy Options Related to the Genetic Testing of Human Embryos," Genetics & Public Policy Center, January 2004, www.dnapolicy.org/pub.reports.php?action=detail&report_id=8.

[20] *Ibid.*, p. 7.

[21] For background, see Scott Baldauf, "India's 'Girl Deficit' Deepest Among Educated," *The Christian Science Monitor*, Jan. 13, 2006, www.csmonitor.com/2006/0113/p01s04-wosc.html, and "Female Deficit in Asia," conference proceedings, Committee for International Cooperation in National Research in Demography, December 2005, www.cicred.org/Eng/Seminars/Details/Seminars/FDA/FDdraftpapers.htm.

[22] Mike Swift, "It's a Boy! Asian Immigrants Use Medical Technology to Satisfy Age-old Desire: A Son," *San Jose* [California] *Mercury News*, Jan. 7, 2009.

[23] *Ibid.*

[24] Deborah L. Spar, *The Baby Business: How Money, Science, and Politics Drive the Commerce of Conception* (2006), p. 99.

[25] For background, see Gautam Naik, "A Baby, Please. Blond, Freckles — Hold the Colic," *The Wall Street Journal*, Feb. 12, 2009, p. A10.

[26] Marilyn E. Coors, "Genetic Enhancement: Custom Kids and Chimeras," United States Conference of Catholic Bishops, Secretariat for Pro-Life Activities, www.usccb.org/prolife/programs/rlp/coors05finaleng.pdf.

[27] Toby L. Schonfeld, "Smart Men, Beautiful Women: Social Values and Gamete Commodification," *Bulletin of Science, Technology and Society*, June 2003, p. 168.

[28] Quoted in Ronald M. Green, *Babies by Design* (2007), p. 45.

[29] Allen Goldberg, *Dear Henry blog*, March 8, 2009, http://henrystrongingoldberg.blogspot.com.

[30] "The Limits of Conscientious Refusal in Reproductive Medicine," American College of Obstetrics and Gynecology, Committee on Ethics, November 2007.

[31] Julien S. Murphy, "Should Lesbians Count as Infertile Couples? Antilesbian Discrimination in Assisted Reproduction," in Anne Donchin and Laura Martha Purdy, eds., *Embodying Bioethics* (1999), p. 107.

About the Author

Staff writer **Marcia Clemmitt** is a veteran social-policy reporter who previously served as editor in chief of *Medicine & Health* and staff writer for *The Scientist*. She has also been a high-school math and physics teacher. She holds a liberal arts and sciences degree from St. John's College, Annapolis, and a master's degree in English from Georgetown University. Her recent reports include "Preventing Cancer" and "Public-Works Projects."

[32] Mundy, *op. cit.*, p. 202.

[33] Quoted in Ingrid Lüttichau, " 'We Are Family': The Regulation of 'Female-Only' Reproduction," *Social and Legal Studies*, March 2004, pp. 81-101.

[34] Quoted in Mundy, *op. cit.*, p. 160.

[35] Arthur L. Caplan, "How Old Is Too Old to Have a Baby?" *The American Journal of Bioethics*, Bioethics.net, Jan. 24, 2005, www.bioethics.net.

[36] For background, see Joanna Grossman, "The California Supreme Court Rules that Fertility Doctors Must Make Their Services Available to Lesbians, Despite Religious Objections," *FindLaw.com*, Sept. 2, 2008, http://writ.lp.findlaw.com.

[37] *Ibid.*

[38] "Access to Fertility Treatment by Gays, Lesbians, and Unmarried Persons," Ethics Committee of the American Society for Reproductive Medicine, Fertility and Sterility, November 2006, p. 1333.

[39] For background, see Susan C. Phillips, "Reproductive Ethics," *CQ Researcher*, April 8, 1994, pp. 289-312; see also Mundy, *op. cit.*

[40] *Genesis*, ch. 16.

[41] Mundy, *op. cit.*, p. 72.

[42] *Ibid.*

[43] Quoted in John K. Amory, "George Washington's Infertility: Why Was the Father of Our Country Never a Father," *Fertility and Sterility*, March 2004, pp. 495-499.

[44] *Ibid.*

[45] For background, see Marcia Clemmitt, "Rising Health Costs," *CQ Researcher*, April 7, 2006, pp. 289-312; Marcia Clemmitt, "Universal Coverage," *CQ Researcher*, March 30, 2007, pp. 265-288.

[46] "State Laws Related to Insurance Coverage for Infertility Treatment," National Conference of State Legislatures, www.ncsl.org/programs/health/50infert.htm.

[47] Quoted in Esther B. Fein, "Calling Infertility a Disease, Couples Battle With Insurers," *The New York Times*, Feb. 22, 1998, www.nytimes.com/specials/women/warchive/980222_2181.html.

[48] "State Laws Related to Insurance Coverage for Infertility Treatment," *op. cit.*

[49] *Ibid.*

[50] "NYS Infertility Demonstration Program," New York State Department of Health, www.health.state.ny.us/community/reproductive_health/infertility.

[51] Mundy, *op. cit.*, p. 59.

[52] Jennifer Schneider, "It's Time for an Egg-Donor Registry and Long-term Follow-up," Nov. 14, 2007, www.geneticsandsociety.org.

[53] *Ibid.*

[54] For background, see Adriel Bettelheim,

FOR MORE INFORMATION

American Society of Reproductive Medicine, 1209 Montgomery Highway, Birmingham, AL 35216-2809; (205) 978-5000; www.asrm.org/. Publishes information on infertility medicine and legal and legislative developments related to assisted reproduction.

The Center for Bioethics and Human Dignity, Trinity International University, 2065 Half Day Road, Deerfield, IL 60015; (847) 317-8180; www.cbhd.org. Explores Christian viewpoints on assisted reproduction and other bioethics issues.

Center for Genetics and Society, 436 14th St., Suite 700, Oakland, CA 94612; (510) 625-0819; www.geneticsandsociety.org. Promotes responsible oversight of genetic technologies.

Centers for Disease Control and Prevention, Assisted Reproductive Technology, 1600 Clifton Rd., Atlanta, GA 30333; (404) 639-3311; www.cdc.gov/ART. Federal agency that provides information and data on assisted reproduction, including success rates for U.S. clinics.

Donor Sibling Registry, P.O. Box 1571, Nederland, CO 80466; www.donorsibling registry.com. Provides information on donor-gamete issues and a forum for donor-conceived children to locate genetic relatives.

Genetics & Public Policy Center, 1717 Massachusetts Ave., N.W., Suite 530, Washington, DC 20036; (202) 663-5971; www.dnapolicy.org. Research center connected to Johns Hopkins University that analyzes and proposes public policy on genetic technologies.

The Hastings Center, 21 Malcolm Gordon Rd., Garrison, NY 10524; (845) 424-4040; www.thehastingscenter.org. Researches and provides information on bioethics issues from various ethical perspectives.

Human Fertilisation and Embryology Authority, 21 Bloomsbury St., London, UK, WC1B 3HF; 020 7291 8200; www.hfea.gov.uk. The United Kingdom's oversight agency for assisted reproduction; sets standards of practice and provides information on assisted reproduction.

RESOLVE: The National Infertility Association, 1760 Old Meadow Rd., Suite 500, McLean, VA 22102; (703) 556-7172; www.resolve.org. Advocates for improved access to infertility services and provides support for patients.

"Embryo Research," *CQ Researcher*, Dec. 17, 1999, pp. 1065-1088; Marcia Clemmitt, "Stem Cell Research," *CQ Researcher*, Sept. 1, 2006, pp. 697-720.

[55] For background, Malcolm Maclachlan, " 'Octomom' Inspires Bill to Regulate Fertility Clinics," *Capitol Weekly*, March 5, 2009, www.capitolweekly.net/article.php?xid=xt1wfvpujdxifs.

[56] For background, see Betsy McKay, "In-Vitro Fertilization Limit Is Sought," *The Wall Street Journal online*, March 3, 2009, http://online.wsj.com/article/SB123603828823714509.html.

[57] For background, see Liza Mundy, "Souls on Ice: America's Embryo Glut and the Wasted Promise of Stem-Cell Research," *Mother Jones*, July/August 2006, p. 39, www.motherjones.com/politics/2006/07/souls-ice-americas-embryo-glut-and-wasted-promise-stem-cell-research.

[58] For background, see Michael Bushnell,

"Missouri House Bill Seeks Limits on Embryo Implants," *Columbia Missourian*, March 5, 2009, www.columbiamissourian.com.

[59] *Ibid.*

[60] *Ibid.*

[61] "Georgia Takes Action: SB 169 to Protect Human Embryos," press release, Georgia Right to Life, Christian NewsWire, March 9, 2009, www.christiannewswire.com/index.php?module=releases&task=view&releaseID=9682.

[62] Quoted in Bushnell, *op. cit.*

[63] Mundy, *Everything Conceivable*, *op. cit.*, p. 69.

[64] "Voluntary Relinquishment for Adoption," Child Welfare Information Gateway, 2005, www.childwelfare.gov/pubs/s_place.cfm.

[65] "International Adoption Facts," Adoption Institute, www.adoptioninstitute.org/FactOverview/international.html.

[66] Mundy, *Everything Conceivable*, *op. cit.*, p. 54.

Bibliography

Selected Sources

Books

Green, Ronald M., *Babies by Design*, Yale University Press, 2007.

A Dartmouth University ethicist lays out probable scenarios for the choices genetic technology will soon lay before parents and argues that such "directed human evolution" can operate for humanity's good.

Knowles, Lori P., and Gregory E. Kaebnick, eds., *Reprogenetics: Law, Policy, and Ethics*, The Johns Hopkins University Press, 2007.

Bioethicists from Canada's University of Alberta (Knowles) and the Hastings Center in New York assemble essays discussing international regulatory schemes for assisted reproductive technology (ART) and related issues.

Mundy, Liza, *Everything Conceivable: How the Science of Assisted Reproduction Is Changing Men, Women, and the World*, Anchor, 2008.

A science writer reports on the rapidly changing landscape of assisted reproduction, based on interviews with parents, gamete donors, doctors and scientists.

Spar, Debora L., *The Baby Business: How Money, Science, and Politics Drive the Commerce of Conception*, Harvard Business School Press, 2006.

A professor of business at Harvard describes the commercial workings of reproductive medicine and adoption in the United States, including gamete donation and fertility clinics, and discusses possibilities for regulating the field.

Articles

Al-Shalchi, Hadeel, "Egypt Septuplets Stir Debate on Fertility Drugs," The Associated Press, Aug. 26, 2008, www.msnbc.msn.com/id/26408452.

Cheap, unpredictable fertility drugs pose dilemmas in developing countries.

Hopkins, Jim, "Egg-Donor Business Booms on Campuses," *USA Today*, March 15, 2006, p. A1.

College women are the most sought-after donors in the growing market for human eggs.

Naik, Gautam, "A Baby, Please. Blond, Freckles — Hold the Colic," *The Wall Street Journal*, Feb. 12, 2009, p. A10.

Preimplantation genetic diagnosis (PGD) — the technique of testing three-day-old in vitro fertilization (IVF) embryos for genetic characteristics — is increasingly used for choosing children's traits, not just to screen for serious genetic diseases, as in the past.

Roan, Shari, "On the Cusp of Life, and of Law," *Los Angeles Times*, Oct. 6, 2008.

Some 500,000 embryos are preserved in freezers in the U.S., some destined for further IVF cycles but many belonging to mothers who've finished with childbearing and now struggle to decide whether to discard the leftover embryos.

Reports and Studies

"2006 Assisted Reproductive Technology Success Rates," *National Summary and Fertility Clinic Reports*, Centers for Disease Control and Prevention/American Society for Reproductive Medicine, November 2008, www.cdc.gov/ART/ART2006.

The report analyzes practices and outcomes in U.S. fertility medicine in 2006, based on mandatory reporting by fertility clinics nationwide.

The Hastings Center Report, July-August 2007, Hastings Center, July 2007, Vol. 37, No. 4, www.thehastingscenter.org/Publications/HCR/Default.aspx?id=752.

Scholars discuss the potential for regulating ART from various legal and ethical perspectives.

"Old Lessons for a New World; Applying Adoption Research and Experience to Assisted Reproductive Technology," Evan B. Donaldson Adoption Institute, February 2009, www.adoptioninstitute.org.

A nonprofit advocacy group for improved adoption practices argues that reproductive medicine would benefit from adopting state regulation and establishing a national database of adoptees' records.

"Reproductive Genetic Testing: Issues and Options for Policymakers," Genetics & Public Policy Center, 2004, www.dnapolicy.org/images/reportpdfs/ReproGenTestIssuesOptions.pdf.

A nonprofit think tank lays out the pros and cons for policy questions, such as, Should governments ban or establish strict rules for reproductive genetic testing, and Should doctors increase the amount of genetic counseling they provide to prospective parents?

"Reproductive Genetic Testing: What America Thinks," Genetics & Public Policy Center, 2004, www.dnapolicy.org/images/reportpdfs/ReproGenTestAmericaThinks.pdf.

Americans are divided over the morality of genetic testing of embryos, but many agree that it's probably acceptable to use the technology to avoid giving birth to a child with a life-threatening childhood illness or to try to conceive a child who could donate tissue to a sick sibling.

The Next Step:

Additional Articles from Current Periodicals

Insurance

Davidson, Terri, "State's Infertility Mandate Is Friendly Toward Family Values," *Telegram & Gazette* **(Massachusetts), June 28, 2007, p. A19.**

Massachusetts became the first state to provide mandated fertility insurance coverage in 1987.

Graham, Judith E., "Couples' Fertility Care Threatened," *Chicago Tribune***, Jan. 30, 2009, p. A27.**

A contract dispute between a chain of fertility centers in Illinois and the state's largest HMO threatens to disrupt the medical care of hundreds of couples trying to become pregnant.

Henry, Ray, "R.I. Governor Blocks Bill Requiring Infertility Treatment Coverage for the Unmarried," The Associated Press, July 20, 2007.

Rhode Island Gov. Don Carcieri has vetoed a bill requiring health insurers to cover infertility treatments for unmarried couples.

Yee, Chen May, "Miracles for Sale," *Star Tribune* **(Minnesota), Oct. 22, 2007, p. 1A.**

Infertile couples are finding their insurance coverage is the primary factor in making it possible to have a child.

Refusal

Moran, Greg, "High Court Hearing Pits Religious vs. Equal Rights," *San Diego Union-Tribune***, May 29, 2008, p. B1.**

A California lesbian is suing doctors at a fertility clinic for refusing to perform a fertility procedure.

Tarkan, Laurie, "Lowering the Odds of Multiple Births," *The New York Times***, Feb. 19, 2008, p. F1.**

Many fertility centers are trying to reduce multiple births by limiting the number of embryo transfers per patient.

Turner, Allan, "Time Running Out in Fight for Embryos," *Houston Chronicle***, April 10, 2008, p. B1.**

A Houston woman is trying to persuade the Supreme Court to give her control of three embryos doctors refused to inseminate after her husband changed his mind.

Registries

Campbell, Colleen Carroll, "Children's Rights Often Overlooked in Today's Brave New World," *St. Louis Post-Dispatch***, April 16, 2009, p. A15.**

Assisted reproductive technologies can make donor-conceived children's natural longing to understand their origins particularly confusing and painful.

Goldberg, Carey, "The Search for DGM 2598," *The Boston Globe***, Nov. 23, 2008, p. A1.**

More children of anonymous donors want to know who fathered them, but sperm banks say donor supplies would drop dramatically if anonymity is prohibited.

Montgomery, Rick, "Through the Web, Kids of Sperm-Donor Dads Connect With Siblings," *The Kansas City Star***, March 22, 2009, p. A1.**

Thousands of individuals conceived from sperm or egg donations have found relatives through the Donor Sibling Registry.

Regulation

Barlow, Rich, "In Baby Business, What Are the Rules?" *The Boston Globe***, March 15, 2008, p. B2.**

Proponents of fertility regulation say fertility clinics should disclose the health risks of any procedure as well as the relevant success rates.

LaFee, Scott, "Octuplet Case Sparks Calls for Fertility-Industry Curbs," *San Diego Union-Tribune***, Feb. 12, 2009, p. A1.**

Fertility doctors generally oppose government regulation, arguing that the industry has been good at policing itself.

Yoshino, Kimi, "Fertility Industry Oversight Is Urged," *Los Angeles Times***, March 5, 2009, p. A8.**

The Center for Genetics and Society wants Congress to examine the largely unregulated $3 billion fertility industry.

Zarembo, Alan, "Does In-Vitro Need Rules?" *Orlando Sentinel***, Feb. 16, 2009, p. A2.**

Fertility treatment is a private matter between doctors and patients that is insulated from outside influences and free from government regulation.

Citing *CQ Researcher*

Sample formats for citing these reports in a bibliography include the ones listed below. Preferred styles and formats vary, so please check with your instructor or professor.

MLA STYLE
Jost, Kenneth. "Rethinking the Death Penalty." CQ Researcher 16 Nov. 2001: 945-68.

APA STYLE
Jost, K. (2001, November 16). Rethinking the death penalty. *CQ Researcher, 11,* 945-968.

CHICAGO STYLE
Jost, Kenneth. "Rethinking the Death Penalty." *CQ Researcher,* November 16, 2001, 945-968.

In-depth Reports on Issues in the News

Are you writing a paper?

Need backup for a debate?

Want to become an expert on an issue?

For 80 years, students have turned to *CQ Researcher* for in-depth reporting on issues in the news. Reports on a full range of political and social issues are now available. Following is a selection of recent reports:

Civil Liberties
Closing Guantánamo, 2/09
Affirmative Action, 10/08
Gay Marriage Showdowns, 9/08
America's Border Fence, 9/08
Immigration Debate, 2/08

Crime/Law
Judicial Elections, 4/09
Mexico's Drug War, 12/08
Prostitution Debate, 5/08
Public Defenders, 4/08
Gun Violence, 5/07

Education
Reading Crisis? 2/08
Discipline in Schools, 2/08
Student Aid, 1/08
Racial Diversity in Public Schools, 9/07

Environment/Society
Hate Groups, 5/09
Future of Journalism, 3/09
Confronting Warming, 1/09
Reducing Carbon Footprint, 12/08
Protecting Wetlands, 10/08
Buying Green, 2/08

Health/Safety
Extreme Sports, 4/09
Regulating Toxic Chemicals, 1/09
Preventing Cancer, 1/09
Heart Health, 9/08
Global Food Crisis, 6/08

Politics/Economy
Business Bankruptcy, 4/09
Future of the GOP, 3/09
Middle-Class Squeeze, 3/09
Public-Works Projects, 2/09
The Obama Presidency, 1/09

Upcoming Reports

Future of Books, 5/29/09   Children's Rights, 6/5/09   Drug Decriminalization, 6/12/09

ACCESS
CQ Researcher is available in print and online. For access, visit your library or www.cqresearcher.com.

STAY CURRENT
To receive notice of upcoming *CQ Researcher* reports, or learn more about *CQ Researcher* products, subscribe to the free e-mail newsletters, *CQ Researcher Alert!* and *CQ Researcher News*: http://cqpress.com/newsletters.

PURCHASE
To purchase a *CQ Researcher* report in print or electronic format (PDF), visit www.cqpress.com or call 866-427-7737. Single reports start at $15. Bulk purchase discounts and electronic-rights licensing are also available.

SUBSCRIBE
Annual full-service *CQ Researcher* subscriptions—including 44 reports a year, monthly index updates, and a bound volume—start at $803. Add $25 for domestic postage.

CQ Researcher Online offers a backfile from 1991 and a number of tools to simplify research. For pricing information, call 800-834-9020, ext. 1906, or e-mail librarysales@cqpress.com.

Published by CQ Press, a division of SAGE Publications

www.cqresearcher.com

Future of Books

Will traditional print books disappear?

Amazon's Kindle 2 digital book reader can store
hundreds of books and read text aloud. Like the
electronic Sony Reader, the Kindle features glare-free
text easier on the eyes than a computer screen.

The migration of books to electronic screens has been accelerating with the introduction of mobile reading on Kindles, iPhones and Sony Readers and the growing power of Google's Book Search engine. Even the book's form is mutating as innovators experiment with adding video, sound and computer graphics to text. Some fear a loss of literary writing and reading, others of the world's storehouse of knowledge if it all goes digital. A recent settlement among Google, authors and publishers would make more out-of-print books accessible online, but some worry about putting such a vast trove of literature into the hands of a private company. So far, barely 1 percent of books sold in the United States are electronic. Still, the economically strapped publishing industry is under pressure to do more marketing and publishing online as younger, screen-oriented readers replace today's core buyers — middle-aged women.

CQ Researcher • May 29, 2009 • www.cqresearcher.com
Volume 19, Number 20 • Pages 473-500

CQ Researcher

May 29, 2009
Volume 19, Number 20

MANAGING EDITOR: Thomas J. Colin
tcolin@cqpress.com

ASSISTANT MANAGING EDITOR: Kathy Koch
kkoch@cqpress.com

ASSOCIATE EDITOR: Kenneth Jost

STAFF WRITERS: Thomas J. Billitteri, Marcia Clemmitt, Peter Katel

CONTRIBUTING WRITERS: Rachel Cox, Sarah Glazer, Alan Greenblatt, Barbara Mantel, Patrick Marshall, Tom Price, Jennifer Weeks

DESIGN/PRODUCTION EDITOR: Olu B. Davis

ASSISTANT EDITOR: Darrell Dela Rosa

FACT-CHECKING: Eugene J. Gabler, Michelle Harris

CQ PRESS

A Division of SAGE

PRESIDENT AND PUBLISHER:
John A. Jenkins

EXECUTIVE DIRECTOR,
REFERENCE INFORMATION GROUP:
Alix B. Vance

CQ Researcher (ISSN 1056-2036) is printed on acid-free paper. Published weekly, except; (Jan. wk. 1) (May wk. 4) (July wks. 1, 2) (Aug. wks. 3, 4) (Nov. wk. 4) and (Dec. wk. 4), by CQ Press, a division of SAGE Publications. Annual full-service subscriptions start at $803. For pricing, call 1-800-834-9020, ext. 1906. To purchase a CQ Researcher report in print or electronic format (PDF), visit www. cqpress.com or call 866-427-7737. Single reports start at $15. Bulk purchase discounts and electronic-rights licensing are also available. Periodicals postage paid at Washington, D.C., and additional mailing offices. POSTMASTER: Send address changes to CQ Researcher, 2300 N St., N.W., Suite 800, Washington, DC 20037.

Future of Books

THE ISSUES

The university bookstore ran out of the textbook assigned for your course? No problem. The young woman behind the counter can print one out in the time it takes to make an espresso.

Don't like the way the latest episode of the novel you're reading online has turned out? Write in a plot development of your own. (But be forewarned: Another reader may edit you out.)

Forgot to bring a book with you on the subway? You've got President Barack Obama's *Dreams from My Father* on your cell phone, right at the place you stopped reading last night on your Kindle. [1]

The world of reading is changing before our eyes. More books are becoming available than ever before, and in many more formats. It remains to be seen whether readers will flock to these or even more futuristic ways of reading. But already the innovations have caused anxiety in the troubled publishing industry because they suggest radical changes in how books are supplied to readers, much as technological changes are threatening the very existence of the newspaper industry.

"The publishing industry is in a difficult position," says Mike Shatzkin, CEO of the Idea Logical Co., a digital-publishing consulting firm. "We have all these new challenges to invest in, and meanwhile the old model for producing money is in trouble. So publishers are squeezed from both sides."

Amid troubling layoffs in publishing over the past year, cutbacks in

The recent Google Book Search settlement among Google, authors and publishers promises to make millions of out-of-print books available online that were once limited to the New York Public Library and great university collections. But many librarians worry that digital access to the world's great books will be in the hands of a private company.

new manuscript acceptances and tough times for bookstores, digital books have entered publishing's mainstream for the first time. In this pivotal year for e-books, Amazon.com introduced the Kindle 2.0 and the larger-format Kindle DX — which both permit the wireless download of a book in less than a minute — and Sony Reader acquired 500,000 titles from Google. Both companies' electronic readers employ a technology that does not require backlighting, making its glare-free text easier on the eyes than a computer screen. [2]

For years, e-book enthusiasts have said the product couldn't really take off until the equivalent of an iPod for books was developed. [3] It's not clear whether we're there yet, but the sud-

den popularity of reading on Apple's iPhone took many by surprise. Over 1.7 million users have downloaded Stanza software, which permits them to read a book on their cell phone from a selection of more than 100,000 titles. The announcements in February that both Amazon and Google were making their titles available on the iPhone only added to the buzz. [4]

"Suddenly there was a sense in 2008 that an e-book program was something a publisher couldn't be without," says Michael Bhaskar, digital editor at publisher Pan MacMillan in Britain. And if 2008 was about e-books, "this year is about smartphones," says Bhaskar. His company was one of the first major publishers to make its titles available on the iPhone and the BlackBerry and now plans to bring most new titles out in electronic as well as print format.

The fact that today's new books start out from the writer's desk as digital files has contributed to the growth of another way of producing books — print-on-demand. Theoretically, books can remain digital files until they're ordered by the customer, at which point they are printed on laser printers, order by order. Increasingly publishers are using this method for books about to go out of print and for scholarly or obscure books with low readership. For non-bestsellers, publishers can print out one book at a time, saving the expense of big print runs, storage and bookstore returns, while retailers can avoid holding inventory that doesn't sell.

Yet all these innovations still account for a small percentage of what passes for reading a book. Despite

www.cqresearcher.com   May 29, 2009   475

Wholesale E-Book Revenue Tops $50 Million

U.S. electronic book sales have risen steadily since 2002. Last year wholesale revenues exceeded $52 million, or nine times higher than in 2002. Digital books still make up less than 1 percent of books sold in the United States, however.

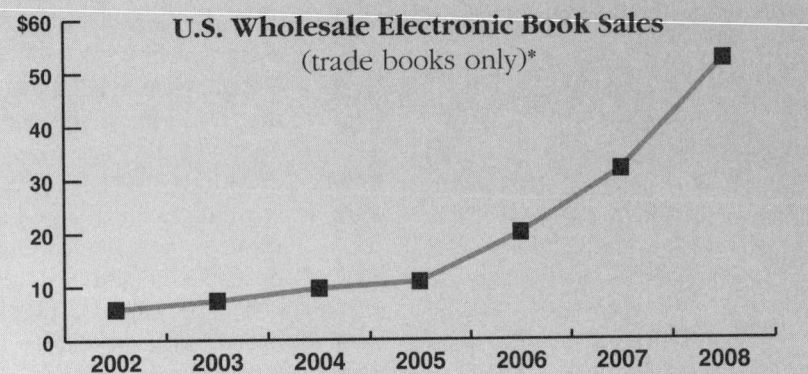

Wholesale Revenue (in $ millions)

U.S. Wholesale Electronic Book Sales
(trade books only)*

* Library, educational and professional electronic sales not included; retail figures may be as much as double the above wholesale figures.

Source: International Digital Publishing Forum

rapid growth, sales revenue generated by electronic books, whether read on a laptop, Kindle or cell phone, still accounts for only about 1 percent of the $11 billion adult trade book market in the United States, estimates Michael Smith, executive director of the International Digital Publishing Forum, a trade association.

Similarly, volumes produced through print-on-demand account for less than 1 percent of the more than 3 billion books printed each year in the United States, according to David Taylor, president of Lightning Source, the leading print-on-demand company. [5]

The Espresso Book Machine, which can deliver a bound paperback in less than five minutes, is currently installed in only a handful of bookstores in North America and England, but its manufacturers envision widespread use in college bookstores, on cruise ships and in remote areas of the world. (*See sidebar, p. 480.*)

Former Random House editorial director Jason Epstein, co-founder of On Demand Books, which markets the machine, says the publishing model of the last 500 years — in which publishers printed large runs and then had to warehouse and ship physical books at enormous costs — is headed for extinction.

Today, "you can go directly from the digital file to the end user with nothing in between," he points out. "That means you can store in theory every book ever written in whatever language at practically no cost. And deliver that file practically anywhere on Earth at no cost. This has a revolutionary effect on the way books are made and distributed."

Eventually, the traditional publishing industry would have collapsed anyway because of structural obsolescence, he says. "With this recession and the arrival of digitization, the process will be hastened."

Publishers are still trying to figure out how to appeal to young readers — who do most of their reading online — by offering free multimedia content digitally, while still making money for themselves and their authors.

"We're moving to a post-literate culture where YouTube is a search engine and video gaming is the main form of entertainment. How does that impact storytelling?" asks Pan MacMillan's Bhaskar.

This spring, Penguin Books won top awards at the hip SXSW (South by Southwest) interactive media festival in Austin, Texas, for its online storytelling experiment. Over a period of six weeks, readers clicking on a Penguin Web site could read a developing mystery being written by a novelist online, search for clues planted on the Internet and contribute plot suggestions to the author as the story was being written. Access to the site, "We Tell Stories," was free even though it drew on the skills of several published authors. [6]

Penguin's experiment "is fascinating, but I'm not sure how it ever makes money," comments Shatzkin of Idea Logical, expressing a widely shared worry in the industry. And he's puzzled by those who see it as the future of fiction: "Participatory content creation makes sense, but why are we calling it books?" he asks.

But those experimenting with online forms of literature suggest our definition of "book" itself needs to be more expansive. "A book is an experience, not a chunk of paper," Chris Meade, director of the London literary think tank if:book, recently told an audience of book club members in Oxford, England. "If you think of the experience of reading a great novel and take the novel away," you can still have a "fantastic" experience, he maintained.

An online book about William Blake recently launched by Meade's organization displays Blake's poems along with gorgeous graphics and videos of an interview with a Blake expert and an actor reading Blake's poem "London." Over the next few months, readers are invited to help it grow by contributing via Twitter and Blogger (a free blog-publishing tool from Google) and the Blake "netbook" itself. [7]

The ease of publishing a book from a digital file means many more actors can get into the act. Small presses can be formed in someone's living room or at a local bookstore. Authors who could never interest a big publisher with their family genealogy or purple-prose novel can be listed on Amazon or simply publish online.

With the cost down to a few hundred dollars to have your book published by one of the author-services companies (the new vanity presses), who needs publishers? On the defensive, publishers say they still play an aesthetic filtering role as the curators of good writing.

Yet more and more books and experimental writing are becoming available online for free without publishers' filters. And as publishers put out more digital books, it may be easier for hackers to convert copyrighted works into pirated editions. Some publishers are reporting that piracy has surged in recent months along with rising demand for e-books, raising concerns that piracy partly accounts for declining print book sales. Pirated editions of works by children's writer J.K. Rowling have been posted on Web sites like Scribd, and other copyrighted works are cropping up on file-sharing services like RapidShare. [8]

Still, some authors like *Wired* editor Chris Anderson and novelist Cory Doctorow claim that publishing for free online is actually the way to sell more print books because of the exposure it provides. [9]

Indeed, rather than chasing printed books into oblivion, some experts say digitization is making more books available than ever before, even if they're in a different format. A massive digitization project by the Library of Congress allows, for the first time, anyone with a computer at home to look at the first edition of Louisa May Alcott's *Little Women* and other 19th-century books too brittle to be handled.

The recent Google Book Search settlement among Google, authors and publishers — if approved by the court — promises to make millions of out-of-print books available online that were once limited to great university libraries. But the fact that this vast collection of 20th-century literature will be in the hands of a private company has many librarians worried as the world's treasure trove of books — past and future — becomes increasingly digital.

Here are some of the questions being debated by publishers, librarians and the ultimate consumers — readers:

Will the Google Book Search settlement restrict public access to digital books?

Last October, Google announced that it had reached a $125 million settlement with authors and publishers who had sued the company for scanning millions of books from university libraries without compensating them. [10]

The proposed settlement permits Google's Book Search engine to make entire copyrighted books available online for a fee and to show up to 20 percent of a copyrighted text at no charge. Google will keep 37 percent of the revenue from online book sales and advertisements that run next to previews of book pages; the remaining 63 percent will go to authors and publishers.

University and K-12 school libraries will be able to access the entire Google database, currently about 10 million books, by buying a subscription, while public libraries will be provided a terminal with free access to the digital collection. The biggest impact will be on books still under copyright but no longer in print — about 5 million of which have been scanned so far. Under the settle-

ment agreement, 51 percent of these out-of-print books scanned into the database will be priced initially at $5.99 and below. [11]

"For many of these books the only way you can get to them is if you're a student at Harvard," or some other major university, says Dan Clancy, engineering director at Google. "One of the things we found exciting was the fact that it broadened access not just to subscription holders but also to users at home, who get a free preview and the book for what looks to be an inexpensive price."

However, some librarians have harshly criticized the settlement because of fears that it puts too many restrictions on public access.

Harvard Library Director Robert Darnton has criticized the agreement for placing what could be the largest digital library in the world in the hands of a private company. In effect, he has written, the settlement hands Google a monopoly over the digitizing of "virtually all books covered by copyright in the United States." [12]

The settlement gives Google permission to continue scanning copyrighted books as long as they were published before Jan. 5, 2009.

"No new entrepreneurs will be able to digitize books within that fenced-off territory . . . because they would have to fight the copyright battles all over again," Darnton wrote in the *New York Review of Books*. "[O]nly Google will be protected from copyright liability." [13]

"What will happen if [Google's] current leaders sell the company or retire?" he asks. What will stop Google from charging exorbitant prices or favoring "profitability over access"?

"The settlement locks in a single player to offering access to the vast majority of the 20th-century's works," concurs Brewster Kahle, founder of the Internet Archive, a nonprofit organization that has scanned some 1.2 million works in the public domain (out of copyright), which it makes

Digital Era Arrives at London Book Fair

Publishers urged to confront "perfect storm" by maximizing digital content.

At the international London Book Fair this April, a stroll through the massive exhibition hall could have lulled a visitor into thinking the book business is alive and well: Publishers were busy striking deals over foreign rights for printed books, sipping white wine to celebrate.

But despite appearances, anxiety about the industry was palpable, as publishers and booksellers attended seminars on digital publishing with gloomy titles like "Where's the Money?"

At the fair's first-ever "Digital Zone," Janet Hawkins, an independent bookshop owner from Blessington, Ireland, was trying out a hand-held Sony Reader as she considered offering digital e-books downloadable from a computer terminal at her shop. Hawkins is "terrified" her business will be destroyed if Amazon's Kindle, a competitor of the Sony Reader now available only in the United States, is introduced in Britain. Unlike the Reader, which must download books from a separate computer, the wireless, hand-held Kindle downloads from Amazon's proprietary online bookstore and would eliminate any role for shops like hers. (Her window of opportunity may soon evaporate, however; the trade press has been reporting that Sony plans to join Amazon in producing a wireless reader. [1])

Last year's drop in American book sales, following years of little or no growth, led Michael Healy, executive director of the Book Industry Study Group, to ask if book publishing was "doomed to follow its dinosaur cousins, newspapers, to extinction." [2]

What little growth the industry has seen in recent years has been driven almost solely by increases in book prices, not the number of books sold, according to Healy, whose group tracks industry statistics. He bluntly told a roomful of publishers that theirs is "an industry in decline."

Publishing faces a "perfect storm" — more book titles every year but fewer people who want to read them, Healy warned, citing declining spending by households on books and independent bookshops struggling to survive.

The keys to survival, he told the publishers, are the proliferating channels of digital content able to reach the tens of millions of readers who look for information on the Web but don't frequent bookshops. Stop putting the physical book at the center of your thinking, he urged: "Experiment at all costs" by offering digital content — and make it free if necessary.

As further proof that the market is changing, the core audience of American book buyers — middle-aged women — will be dwindling in coming years, according to Bowker, a leading source of publishing industry data. By 2016, those baby boomers will be retiring, going onto fixed incomes, while the Gen X-ers stepping into their shoes will constitute a smaller, more screen-savvy generation of buyers. [3]

Despite all the attention to new mobile readers like the Kindle, desktop personal computers and laptops are still the devices used most frequently for reading e-books, and it may have something to do with all those female romance readers, who are leading purchasers of e-books. You're not likely to be detected reading a "bodice-ripper" at work if you do it on your PC, romance publisher Harlequin discovered from reader surveys.

Yet iPhones hold the greatest potential for growth among readers who don't have gray hair, Bowker Vice President for Publisher Services Kelly Gallagher predicted, even though a company survey found iPhones account for only 10 percent of e-book purchases, trailing behind PCs and Amazon's Kindle. Surprisingly, Kindle's largest ownership group is middle-aged, the survey found, countering its reputation as the reading device of future generations.

Over in the Digital Zone, fairgoers could see some of the reasons why 1.7 million (mainly young) people have downloaded the Stanza reading application onto their iPhones. Its latest features include 135 new background colors to pair with 21 crisp fonts as well as background "themes" like "bedroom" (red, satiny sheets) and links to a dictionary while reading.

available to the public for free via an online platform.

Kahle says he's particularly disturbed that the settlement gives Google legal immunity to scan potentially millions of books whose copyright holders can't be located easily — so-called "orphan" books. His organization would also like to scan those works but would risk being sued for copyright infringement. Kahle favors legislation to protect all scanners from copyright suits.

"Increasingly, people are gathering

that Google has been granted a release of liability to exploit that group of works that no one else has," Kahle says. Legislation could have made orphan works accessible to anyone. Google is in effect "legislating through settlement," he says.

Kahle also contends Google will feel no competitive pressure to do a good-quality job that ensures digital copies are as readable as possible. "Once you have a monopoly, the temptation is just to defend your monopoly

as opposed to working to make it better," he says. Moreover, the way Google structures its searches is not intended to help serious researchers do large-scale searches quickly but involves "speed bumps" aimed at maximizing the number of times a person views a search page with its accompanying ads, according to Kahle.

Google's Clancy responds that the settlement gives Google a "non-exclusive" arrangement to scan these works, meaning other groups could copy the

Worries About Piracy

Piracy discussions at the fair underscored a central anxiety — how to make money on digital publishing without being ripped off. One speaker pointed to a decision by a Swedish court as a sign that piracy is being stifled. On April 17 the court sentenced four founders of The Pirate Bay, a popular file-sharing site, to a year in jail for violating copyright. [4]

But skeptics at the fair predicted new piracy sites would pop up in its place. (As of May 27, Pirate Bay's Web site had not been shut down, and similar sites also were operating.)

The day after the digital seminar, *The Independent*, a British daily, reported substitute approaches already emerging. For example, searches for copyrighted material are being conducted by networks of individuals, avoiding the need for a legally vulnerable centralized Web site. [5]

Paradoxically, piracy has stimulated sales of some titles by giving them more publicity, according to a study cited by industry consultant Mike Shatzkin, CEO of Idea Logical Co. [6] He argued that publishers' encryption of e-books to prevent piracy — known as digital rights management — has been ineffective.

It would be more effective to price e-books cheaply enough so consumers don't feel they have to search for free versions on pirate sites, Shatzkin argued. Strong consumer demand for cheaper books is evident in the recent growth in used book purchases, which explain in part why fewer new books are being bought, he said.

Online books and hand-held digital readers were a big feature of this year's London Book Fair.

CQ Press/Sarah Glazer

Consumers expect e-books to be priced more cheaply than printed books, and they will be because publishers and booksellers have fewer expenses, Shatzkin predicted. That couldn't have been reassuring to the publishers in the room who wondered aloud why they should be investing in a sector that now commands barely 1 percent of U.S. book sales.

Indeed, British publishers at the packed "Where's the Money?" session argued heatedly against lower pricing for e-books. Such a move, Penguin Group Chairman and CEO John Makinson told the standing-room-only crowd, would be "short-changing authors." [7]

---

[1] Marion Maneker, "How the Next Kindle Could Save the Newspaper Business," *Wired*, May 6, 2009.

[2] The Book Industry Study Group (BISG) tracks publishing statistics. All statistics cited are for the U.S. market. According to the BISG, the number of books sold fell 1.5 percent from 2007 to 2008.

[3] Sixty-five percent of U.S. book buyers are women, according to Bowker, which publishes the authoritative *Books in Print*.

[4] "Court Jails Pirate Bay Founders," BBC News, April 17, 2009, http://news.bbc.co.uk/1/hi/technology/8003799.stm. The decision was expected to be appealed.

[5] Pat Pilcher, "Pirate Bay 'could soon be obsolete,'" *The Independent*, April 20, 2009, www.independent.co.uk.

[6] The study was conducted by Magellan Media Consulting Partners of New York City, www.magellanmediapartners.com/index.php/mmcp/Research/.

[7] See Lynn Andriani, "British Publishers Try to Find the Money in E-Books," *Publishers Weekly*, April 21, 2009, www.publishersweekly.com.

---

books as well. And Paul Aiken, executive director of the Authors Guild, one of the parties to the suit, says authors "want real competition in getting these books out to the world." At the same time, he cautions, these books "are out of print for a reason" — they're not commercially in demand. (*See "At Issue," p. 493.*)

Out-of-print books are vital to researchers, however, and Kahle contends the agreement is exclusive in practice: Libraries in the past have been unwilling to let his organization in to scan once Google has knocked on their door. Indeed, it's not clear why a library would let anyone in to scan except Google, since their legal protection for scanning copyrighted works appears to extend to the host library, according to Randall Picker, a professor of law at the University of Chicago.

Many libraries worry that Google is likely to abuse its monopoly by charging them exorbitant subscription prices, according to Jonathan Band, a lawyer representing the American Library Association and the Association of Research Libraries. His associations don't oppose the settlement. But in comments filed with the court responsible for approving the settlement, they are proposing "vigorous" court oversight to prevent artificially high pricing in the absence of competition. The libraries have also asked the judge to protect the privacy of users who read Google's books online. [14]

Continued on p. 481

Is This the Future of Book Publishing?

"Espresso" machine produces a book in five minutes.

About as big as a large photocopier, the machine is probably the last thing one would expect to see at the flagship store of Blackwell — Britain's leading academic bookseller. But tucked in an alcove at the store on Charing Cross Road in London, it offers a glimpse at a possible future for book publishing. As signs alluringly promise: "Become an author — Print your own book" and "Out of print, Out of stock books — Available Right Here Now."

The Espresso Book Machine, which its makers hope will one day become the ATM of books, can dispense a paper-bound book in under five minutes from a digital file, using ink-jet technology for the cover and high-end laser printing for the pages. To the average reader, the color cover and black-and-white pages are indistinguishable from the traditional published version.

"Suddenly, it's increased our stock by a million titles," says store manager Marcus Gipps, citing the number of digital files in the catalog offered by On Demand Books, the manufacturer. That's the equivalent of 23.6 miles of shelving, according to Blackwell. At least 250,000 of those titles are out of print, once inaccessible to most customers.

Previously, when customers asked for a book that wasn't on the shelf, the typical response was, "Can we order it for you?" Often the customer decided to look elsewhere."Now we say, 'Can we print it for you?'" says Gipps.

The Espresso was installed in the store in April as a test. If successful, it will be installed in more Blackwell shops, many located at universities, says Blackwell CEO Andrew Hutchings. He expects it to be particularly popular for self-publishing, publishing theses and printing course packs — selected chapters from textbooks assigned by professors.

As of mid-May, the Espresso had been installed in a dozen sites in North America, England and Australia, according to Dane Neller, CEO of On Demand Books. In the United States, an Espresso machine is in use at the University of Michigan Library, where it prints out-of-copyright and rare books from the library's digitized collections, and at Northshire Books, an independent bookstore in Manchester Center, Vt., among other sites.

Eventually, as On Demand Chairman Jason Epstein envisions it, customers will be able to order any book they want from a computer or cell phone and pick up a freshly printed copy in their neighborhood shop. (To accomplish that, publishers will have to digitize all of their titles, which some are

Customers can print their own books on the Espresso machine at the Blackwell bookstore in London.

AFP/Getty Images/Leon Neal

just starting to do.) In addition to bookstores, Epstein sees the Espresso being used in libraries, schools, hospitals, cruise ships and developing countries that lack book distribution networks.

Blackwell's machine cost about $100,000, according to a company spokesperson, but Gipps expects it to pay for itself in about six months. The machine can produce a book for about $3, with retail prices set by the publisher. The makers expect the Espresso's cost to decline significantly as more are marketed, and eventually hope to lease it out for about the same price as a photocopier.

That could make it attractive to libraries trying to save on purchasing and storing books, says Kari Paulsen, president of EBook Library, which markets e-books to more than 1,000 libraries worldwide. Increasingly, libraries trying to save on storage are telling her that if a book is not in e-book form they don't want it. With an Espresso, a librarian could tell a patron, "You can get it as an e-book or pick it up downstairs printed out in 15 minutes." A library might also make some revenue back by selling Espresso-printed books.

At the University of Alberta Bookstore in Edmonton, Canada, the Espresso has printed some 13,000 books since November 2007. "Edmonton is a long way from pretty much everything, so we have huge shipping bills and long delays," says Todd Anderson, director of the bookstore. The store has saved on shipping costs by acting as a local printer for publishers who would have to send a book thousands of miles; it saves inventory costs by printing only as many copies as students request. It's been able to save students money by printing assigned classics that are out of copyright, like *Frankenstein*, and selling them for less than the standard publisher's sticker price. The bookstore has also printed books of local interest like a 1908 visitors' guide to Edmonton, local self-published genealogical histories and original small-press books by local authors.

Because of the ease of printing digital files at outposts like Edmonton, the machine could make it possible to distribute "virtually every book ever published, in any language, anywhere on Earth as easily, quickly and cheaply as e-mail," claims On Demand's brochure.

Epstein, a former editorial director of Random House, thinks the effect on publishing could be revolutionary — and could even save precarious independent bookstores. "I think independent bookstores will flourish, and some will become publishers, as they were in the 18th century," he predicts.

Continued from p. 479

"I'm concerned that as Google seeks the market for this it could be so expensive for a public library that it will be out of our reach," says Sari Feldman, executive director of the Cuyahoga County Public Library in suburban Cleveland and executive president-elect of the Public Library Association.

Feldman is also concerned that the one terminal per building where Google will provide free access to its database "is not nearly going to satisfy the customer demand we have," especially since the agreement does not permit the database to be accessed remotely from library members' homes.

According to Clancy, the free terminal is intended to help libraries that can't afford the institutional subscription and could be expanded later. "It's a start," he says. University libraries that purchase subscriptions will be allowed to provide remote access to students and faculty. By contrast, K-12 school libraries will not have access to a free terminal; they will have to purchase a subscription. Nor will they be able to provide remote access to students and teachers; readers will have to use the database on school property to access full-length copyrighted works that are out of print. (In comments filed with the court, the American Library Association and Association of Research Libraries cite these differences as inequities between K-12 schools and higher education institutions that could deepen the "digital divide.") [15]

Google has discretion as to which books it copies, and under the agreement it does not have to make public its entire list of scanned books. [16] "A foreign government might put pressure on Google to exclude books about the Armenian genocide or [the 1989 protest at Beijing's] Tiananmen Square," library association attorney Band observes. And if Google has employees in those countries, Google might agree to leave those books out. "You could have a very important research base with holes dictated by foreign governments," he says.

Parties to the settlement — the American Association of Publishers and the Authors Guild — defend the agreement, maintaining that without Google such a vast digital library would never have existed.

"Wouldn't it be much better if the Library of Congress had done this? Yeah, probably it would have," said Patricia Schroeder, outgoing president of the publishers' association and a former Democratic congresswoman from Colorado. "But they didn't have the money to do it, and they didn't do it, and the libraries have copies of everything now. What do we do at this point as rights holders?" [17]

Before Google started scanning library books in 2004, even well-endowed libraries were digitizing less than 10,000 volumes per year — a rate Google ratcheted up to tens of thousands of volumes per week, observes University of Michigan librarian Paul Courant.

In his article, Darnton charged that the special status granted Google under the settlement dashes the Enlightenment philosophers' dream of establishing a Republic of Letters, in which anyone who could read would have access to the entire universe of knowledge. But Courant retorts: "In the absence of the settlement, we would not have the digitized infrastructure to support the 21st century Republic of Letters." [18]

Will traditional print books disappear from the marketplace?

The mother of a 10-year-old boy recently described the way her son reads a printed book: "He'll put the book down and go to the book's Web site. Then, he'll check what other readers are writing in the forums, and maybe leave a message himself, then return to the book. He'll put the book down again and Google a query that's occurred to him."

This description was recently posted on the Web by Bob Stein, founder and co-director of the Institute for the Future of the Book, a think tank based in New York and London. He suggested that "we change our description of reading to include the full range of these activities, not just time spent looking at the printed page." [19]

In Stein's view, as electronic books start to have links to yet more references and multimedia enrichment, the centrality of printed books in our culture will fade. "They'll stop being the principal way people exchange ideas," he predicts. "That role is shifting to things happening on screens on our desks or in our pockets. In all likelihood the future of the book is as an art object — beautiful objects that look like books — not what most of us will use as the way we take ideas from the culture."

Despite such futuristic scenarios, e-books — the main form in which digital books are sold — remain less than 1 percent of the entire U.S. book market, and some in the industry are skeptical that e-books will ever take over.

"When I first came to this job [more than eight years ago], people were predicting that e-books were here and any minute they would be taking over the world," says outgoing AAP president Schroeder. "The other thing people would tell me is, 'I don't know why you're going into books. Young people want whistles and bells and noise.' Then along came *Harry Potter*." As for e-books, "it's been a lot slower conversion than many people thought."

Publishing consultant Shatzkin agrees. "We're having a lot of conversation about something that doesn't have a lot of commercial heft right now," he says. "This is not a profit center for anybody in regular book publishing yet; this is still an experimental investment." As an example, he points to Amazon's policy of pricing most of its bestselling Kindle books at $9.99, significantly below publishers' retail prices, which means the company is taking a loss.

Some in the industry think 2009 will be the year that changes all that, with the introduction of the Kindle 2.0 and DX, the availability of Kindle books on the iPhone and Google Book Search's deal to provide millions of books to the Sony Reader. A new, lightweight, large-format reader, which feels like a plastic sheet of paper, Plastic Logic Reader, is due for commercial release next year. [20]

Yet skeptics note that electronic readers are expensive, and many find them annoying to use. On-demand publishers think digital will take over in another way — by making it possible to print out books on demand from digital files. For Taylor it means glorified printers at central plants; for Epstein it means ATMs for books widely distributed at bookstores, hotels, airports, cruise ships and remote locations in Africa and Asia.

If there's consensus, it's that nonfiction references like encyclopedias, atlases and dictionaries will continue to migrate online, where they can be updated continually, and where community efforts like Wikipedia have benefited from many contributors.

Whether read on screen or on paper, the classical book format has a much better chance of survival than newspapers and magazines, because books don't have advertisers to lose or subscribers they need to hold onto, according to Peter Osnos, founder of the independent publisher PublicAffairs. [21]

By the early 2000s, well over 30 percent of all books were publishers' excess inventory — largely the result of their policy that books shipped to retailers could be returned for full credit, Osnos observes. The costs in wasted paper, manufacturing, packing, shipping and the glut of remaindered books all depress profits.

That will begin to change after the current recession, Osnos predicts, now that digital technology for reading, listening and printing on demand is becoming easier to use. In the future, he predicts, bookstores will become mainly showrooms — places "to engage in the time-honored pleasures of browsing and conversation, with read-

ing and discussion groups, author visits and a renewed commitment to customer service."

An even more radical future is seen in China and India, countries without sophisticated publishing distribution. They may skip the traditional book stage entirely and move directly into electronic readers with purchasing enabled by their extensive cell phone network — much the way Kindle users buy books — to wirelessly download and purchase books; Amazon provides a free, perpetual cell phone subscription to Kindle users for this purpose.

In his 2008 book *Books as History*, David Pearson, director of the University of London Research Libraries, argues that books as owned objects have been important for historical research and may continue to be — at least if book owners still write in the margins. For example, by recording who the owners were and their margin notes on all surviving copies of the first two editions of Corpernicus' *De Revolutionibus*, scholar Owen Gingerich was able to show how quickly Copernicus' heliocentric ideas were accepted (or not) by 16th-century astronomers across Europe. [22]

Although many find the prospect of vast digital libraries that can be accessed on screens exciting, others see dire consequences if printed books are abandoned entirely in favor of digital storehouses.

Computers crash, they argue, and obsolescent digital information in the form of, say, old floppy disks sometimes can't be accessed with modern computers.

"Imagine if all the printed books disappeared," says Epstein. "If we blew a fuse, we'd all be savages again. Whoever we are is in these books."

Will literary reading and writing survive online?

The success of Wikipedia, written by thousands around the world, suggests that collaborative or "networked" books could be the wave of the fu-

ture — at least in nonfiction. But what about fiction?

In a recent post, Stein of the Institute for the Future of the Book suggests that novels will no longer be the dominant form of fiction in the future but will be replaced by something that looks more like the multiplayer online game "World of Warcraft." Its 10 million subscribers assemble into teams of 30 or more to accomplish specific goals.

"It's not a big leap to think of the person who developed the game as an author whose art is conceiving, designing and building a virtual world in which players (readers) don't merely watch or read the narrative" but actually contribute to it, Stein writes. In this vision, digital fiction would include video, sound and readers' comments. [23]

Many readers and publishers react in horror to the idea of communal creativity — what happens to the single, narrative voice that creates a world of the imagination into which the reader can plunge?

And what author would want to participate? As writer Cory Doctorow commented on Stein's post, "many authors lack the capacity to interact with their audiences. They are grumpy. To publish these authors successfully, publishers will either have to hire 'ghost-bloggers' or give them charm lessons." [24]

Already there have been several closely watched experiments online. In 2007 Penguin Books sponsored a wiki-novel writing experiment, *A Million Penguins*, written by hundreds of readers collaborating online. Penguin CEO John Makinson called it "not the most read, but possibly the most written novel in history."

Penguin kicked the novel off on a special Web site with the opening line from Charlotte Bronte's classic *Jane Eyre*: "There was no possibility of taking a walk that day."

"Within about five minutes it had completely changed. We had 1,500 edits the first couple of days," recalls Bruce Mason, a research fellow at the Uni-

The Long Tail Phenomenon

How "low-sellers" revolutionized bookselling.

In 2001 the first so-called digital natives came of age. Children who had started using the Internet in 1995 at age 12 turned 18, graduating into the 18-34-year-old demographic most sought after by advertisers. But they were fundamentally different from previous generations — TV viewership in their age bracket dropped for the first time in half a century. [1]

Instead they were occupying an online space where "niche economics rule," in the words of *Wired* magazine editor-in-chief Chris Anderson, using blogs and Web sites rather than mass-audience TV to explore interests and buy products.

In an October 2004 article in *Wired* (expanded into a 2006 book), Anderson introduced the term "The Long Tail," now widely used in the publishing and digital industries. He pointed out that the traditional marketing strategy of focusing on best-sellers at the top of the demand curve was missing the many low-sellers, which form the endlessly "long tail" of the same demand curve. [2] (*See graph, at right.*)

When aggregated, the low-sellers make up a big portion of the market, Anderson argued — a market that the new online sellers were uniquely positioned to take advantage of. For example, he pointed out that one-quarter of Amazon's book sales came outside their top 100,000 titles. [3]

Anderson credits Jeff Bezos with being the first to test this idea when he launched Amazon in 1995. Amazon uses online retail to aggregate a large inventory of low-sellers. At the time, even superstores carried only about 10 percent of the titles available in English.

Unlike brick-and-mortar retailers, Amazon didn't have to worry about filling up shelf space in valuable real estate. And with no shelf space to pay for, a niche product is just another sale with the same or better margins than a hit, Anderson points out.

The 1988 low-seller *Touching the Void* is an example of how specialist niches help unknown books. By 2004 it was outselling Jon Krakauer's best-seller *Into Thin Air* on the same subject of mountain climbing tragedies, because of word of mouth and Amazon reader reviews.

The long tail phenomenon affected other aspects of the book business, too. In 1997 Alibris was launched as an online retailer for used books. It aggregated the inventories of some 12,000 used-book stores and made the database available to Amazon and Barnes & Noble's bn.com, bringing millions of users to the used-book market. Even though used books are usually sold one at a time, Alibris was soon growing at double digits.

The long tail phenomenon has tapped into a growing community of people interested not only in consuming but also producing information about a huge range of topics, many of them obscure. In 2001, Jimmy Wales, a wealthy options trader, came up with the idea of getting millions of amateur experts to create an online encyclopedia, using a software application called wiki. Wikipedia was a far cry from the *Encyclopaedia Britannica*, which recruited experts to write its entries. Yet by 2005, Wikipedia had become the largest encyclopedia on the planet, with more than 1 million articles compared to the *Britannica*'s 80,000. [4]

The Impact of 'Low-Sellers'

Best-sellers sell the most copies and make the most money. While books far down on the sales charts sell fewer copies and make less money individually, they bring in a large portion of total publishing revenue because so many so-called low-sellers (the long tail of the graph) are sold overall.

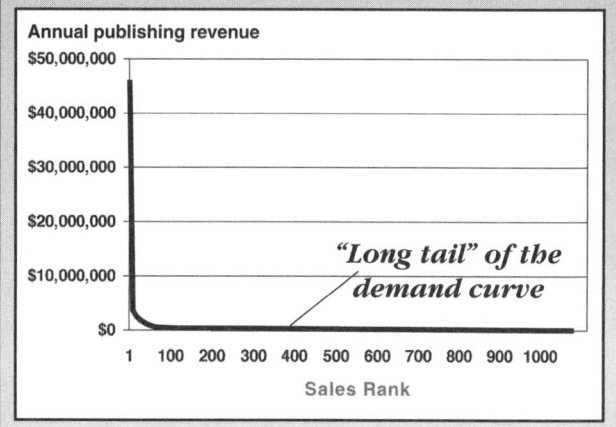

Annual publishing revenue

"Long tail" of the demand curve

Sales Rank

Source: Book Industry Study Group

---

[1] Chris Anderson, *The Long Tail* (2006), p. 95.

[2] *Ibid.* Also see Chris Anderson, "The Long Tail," *Wired*, October 2004, www.wired.com/wired/archive/12.10/tail.html.

[3] Anderson, *The Long Tail, op. cit.*, p. 23.

[4] *Ibid.*, p. 66.

versity of Edinburgh specializing in folklore who helped to run the experiment. So many people tried to get onto the site in the first few days that the server was overwhelmed, and the project had to be moved to another. At first, vandals tried to delete much of the novel, and along the way some contributors insisted on reshaping the plot continually according to their liking.

When the wiki-novel finally closed on March 7, 2007, at least 75,000 different people had viewed the site. Of those, 1,476 people had registered as users of the wiki. The ultimate, chaotic product, which involved 11,000 edits and 1,500 pages, wasn't really literature, most observers agreed, but it demonstrated the way that passionate, online literary communities can form. [25]

"The final product itself . . . is more akin to something produced by the wild, untrammeled creativity of the folk imagination," researchers Mason and Sue Thomas, professor of new media at Britain's De Montfort University, Leicester, wrote, describing it as "rude, chaotic, grotesque, sporadically brilliant, anti-authoritarian and, in places, devastatingly funny. As a cultural text it is unique, and it demonstrates the tremendous potential of this form to provide a stimulating social setting for writing, editing and publishing." [26]

Yet the narrative didn't really hold together as a single story line, and the writing varied from "exciting and talented to really bad clichés," according to Mason.

"I don't really think the wiki novel makes sense," says Thomas, who co-authored the research report and helped run the experiment. "A novel has to be quite controlled. We didn't produce a novel; we produced something fascinating."

In another Penguin-sponsored exercise, an award-winning novelist was asked to write a detective-story version of *Alice's Adventures in Wonderland*, to which readers were invited to contribute. Readers searched for clues hidden on Craigslist and other Internet sites, interacting in real time with the novelist/narrator to give her solutions to the mystery.

The result: a charming story, written with a sly slant. Unlike *A Million Penguins*, it succeeded as a coherent story — probably because the novelist had ultimate control over how the story was composed and which contributions to incorporate. (*See sidebar, p. 490.*)

Publishers are experimenting with these new formats because they think the younger generation reads in a fundamentally different way from older

generations, requiring more multimedia content and more participation, says Pan MacMillan digital publisher Bhaskar.

Networked books (like *A Million Penguins*) are "quite a nebulous concept in that nobody really knows exactly what one might look like. Almost by definition it's an experiment," says Bhaskar. And with the current recession, "I think right now the climate is less forgiving for these eye-catching, high-profile experiments that have no revenue stream attached."

And so far, even in networked book communities, barely 1 percent of those who sign on tend to be interested in actively contributing; the rest just read what's going on. [27]

University of Chicago sociologist Wendy Griswold thinks there will continue to be readers of print books, but they will be an elite reading class that is highly educated, older and predominantly female — much like today's core group of book buyers.

Surprisingly, though, a similar demographic group has been drawn to the Kindle. The largest group of Kindle owners is middle-aged (56-64 years old) and includes slightly more women than men, according to a survey of 120,000 book purchasers presented by Bowker at the London Book Fair on April 19. [28] (Men are more frequent adaptors of the iPhone, the survey found.)

And other traditional literature is migrating onto the new screens.

Narrative — an online literary magazine that publishes stories by celebrated veterans like Joyce Carol Oates as well as new talents — has become the first literary magazine available on Kindle.

If readers are going to be viewing literature on a screen no bigger than a beer coaster, the writing needs "to be sharper, smarter and more economically and elegantly expressed than ever," writes Philip Gwyn Jones, publisher of Granta and Portobello books. In his view, most of the debate so far

is about "transport methods" rather than the cargo being shipped. "Everyone wants to be captivated by a great story or a great argument." [29]

Mary Harrington, an associate at the Institute for the Future of the Book in London, is more skeptical that long-form fiction will migrate from print to digital. "The Internet is very good for conversation, but once the conversation's been had, it makes sense to finalize it in print," she says. She points to the new science fiction novel *Playing for Keeps*, by Mur Lafferty. [30] It started out as free digital content (in this case podcasts), built up an online community and then became a print book.

The physical nature of a book gives it qualities that are completely inverted when it comes to the Internet, Harrington points out. As a fixed entity between covers, a book must limit and choose its words carefully. Its authorial voice has made the book authoritative ever since the creation of sacred works like the Bible, and its message can be universal.

By contrast, Harrington says, the Internet is "boundless, never authoritative — there's always someone who has something to add," on a blog or a Web site. "And it's never universal," since writers online are writing for fragmented audiences. "Because the Internet is boundless, intangible and not edited, you can never publish the definitive anything online." ∎

BACKGROUND

In the Beginning

The Greek philosopher Socrates (469-399 B.C.) lamented the loss of knowledge because the media of transmission were changing. Before the

Continued on p. 486

Chronology

19th Century
Publishing becomes an established industry in Europe and the United States; modern presses speed printing and reduce the cost of books.

1810
Steam press invented.

1817
Harper Brothers, one of the nation's earliest publishers, begins as a New York printer.

1850
By mid-century, New York is shipping millions of books to the rest of the country.

1891
International Copyright Act passed by Congress extending protection to foreign copyright holders.

- • -

1920s-1930s
Readership expands during golden age of publishing.

1926
Book of the Month Club founded.

1928
Random House founded.

1939
Pocket Books launched, introducing paperbacks.

- • -

1960s-1980s
Mergers and takeovers by conglomerates combined with migration of Americans from cities to suburbs kill downtown bookstores and large inventories.

1965
RCA acquires Random House.

1975
Gulf & Western Industries acquires Simon & Schuster.

1980
German publisher Bertelsmann acquires Bantam, later Dell, Doubleday and Random House.

1989
Rupert Murdoch's News Corp. acquires HarperCollins.

- • -

1990s
Publishing industry becomes more concentrated; World Wide Web introduces digital reading, online bookstores.

1994
Viacom acquires Simon & Schuster.

1995
Amazon founded as online bookstore. . . . Germany's Holtzbrinck Group acquires St. Martin's Press.

1997
Alibris, an online retailer for used books, launched.

1998
Bertelsmann acquires Random House, making half of top 20 U.S. publishers foreign-owned.

- • -

2000s
New electronic readers like Kindle and iPhone boost e-book sales.

2000
Best-selling American author Stephen King publishes novella *Riding the Bullet* solely in electronic form.

2001
Wikipedia, an online encyclopedia written by readers, is launched; first "digital natives," who used computers at age 12, turn 18.

2004
Wired magazine editor Chris Anderson publishes seminal article about "The Long Tail" in publishing.

2007
Penguin sponsors online wiki-novel, *A Million Penguins*. Hundreds contribute, 75,000 view it.

2008
Google reaches landmark settlement over book scanning. . . . Troubled publishing industry hit with layoffs and pay freezes on "Black Wednesday" (Dec. 3). . . . Amazon's Kindle sells out in United States by Christmas.

2009
American Association of Publishers announces 2008 book revenue dropped 2.8 percent from 2007. . . . Book Industry Study Group reports 1.5 percent fewer books were sold in the U.S. in 2008 than in 2007, for a total of 3.1 billion books sold, including e-books and traditional trade, educational and professional books. . . . Amazon launches Kindle 2.0 (February) and large-screen Kindle DX. . . . Google announces deal to provide 500,000 e-books to Sony Reader. . . . University of Michigan announces its scholarly publications will be digital only. . . . More than 1.7 million people have downloaded Stanza reading applications onto an iPhone. . . . Scribd.com launches online vanity press (May 18). . . . On Oct. 7, 2009, the U.S. District Court for the Southern District of New York will hold a hearing to accept or reject the Google Book Search settlement with authors and publishers.

Print-on-Demand Flips Traditional Publishing Model

'Sell first, then print' is publisher's new motto.

When Sarah Palin was picked last August as Sen. John McCain's presidential running mate, the publisher of the only existing biography of the once-obscure Alaskan governor found itself in a quandary. Printing more copies on a traditional offset press would have taken weeks — and missed the sales window for the book.

Instead, Epicenter Press turned to a leading print-on-demand company. Within a few hours of receiving a digital file, Lightning Source was producing copies of *Sarah* on its giant, high-quality laser printers, and within days — not weeks — it had 30,000 copies. [1]

A sudden spike in demand is only one of the ways that traditional publishers are starting to use print-on-demand (POD). More than a decade ago, Ingram Book Group, the word's leading book wholesaler, was trying to cut down on the unsold books crowding its warehouse. Out of this need it created a company that would print books from digital files only when Ingram needed them.

Today that company, Lightning Source, makes a profit printing an average order of only 1.8 books — capitalizing on the "long tail" phenomenon, in which individual orders for unpopular books add up to a lot of sales.

Print-on-demand technology is best known for fueling the recent explosion in self-publishing. Authors who can't break into mainstream publishing get their book listed on Amazon or another database, usually expecting to sell only a few copies to their friends and families, each one printed in response to an order.

But increasingly, large publishing houses and retailers like Amazon are also using print-on-demand to fill orders when books are out of stock or out of print.

As David Taylor, president of Lightning Source, puts it, print-on-demand reverses the traditional sequence of printing, warehousing and then selling. Instead, his motto is "sell first, then print."

Now the world's leading POD printer, Lightning Source more than doubled its monthly printing volume from 600,000 books in 2005 to more than 1.4 million last year.

The company's plant in Milton Keynes, a sprawling "new town" 60 miles northwest of London, produces a stunningly eclectic variety of books. A single copy of an accounting dictionary in Spanish was pumped out right after eight copies of *E-business in Healthcare* and *Multivariate Density Estimation*.

"I've been amazed at the most obscure books that someone wants to read," says Taylor. Many of those titles would be dead without print-on-demand, he says, because "you would never print them speculatively" hoping for a sale.

Only about 40 percent of Lightning Source's production is for mainstream publishers; the remainder is for non-traditional publishers like self-publishers, micro-publishers with as few as one or two titles and content aggregators like bibliolife.com, which offers out-of-print books that are printed only in response to an order.

Despite the significant cost savings to be gained from avoiding storing, shipping and pulping unsold books, mainstream publishers have been slow to adopt print-on-demand, mainly because the printing cost per book is higher — especially for best-sellers. Many publishers also have sunk costs in warehousing or haven't realized that there are potential cost savings, according to industry analysts.

However, some publishers aiming for a small, professional readership in areas like medicine and accounting, as well as some academic presses, are going straight to print-on-demand, because it is economical for small printings.

POD has also stimulated some innovative new uses: Readers can assemble their favorite articles from Wikipedia or Wikitravel, for example, and have them bound in a customized book by the German company PediaPress. [2]

Digital printing now accounts for only about 1-3 percent of all the books printed in North America, but the business is projected to grow 15-20 percent over the next three years, according to Gilles Biscos, president of Interquest, a market research company in Charlottesville, Va.

Increasingly, Lightning Source's business is shifting toward traditional publishers as they rethink the way they do business, according to Taylor. He thinks this trend will continue, particularly in an economic climate where publishers are looking to cut costs wherever possible.

---

[1] "Gov. Sarah Palin Biography brought to market by Epicenter Press and Ingram Content Companies," Lightning Source press release, Sept. 2, 2008.
[2] http://pediapress.com.

Continued from p. 484

invention of the Greek alphabet 2,500 years ago, knowledge and stories were recited aloud, much like Homer's epic poem *The Odyssey*.

The new technology of writing meant stories no longer needed to be memorized, a development Socrates feared would weaken the Greeks' mental capacities for memorizing and retelling. (Paradoxically, we only know about Socrates' concerns because they were written down by his student Plato in his famous *Dialogues*.) [31]

The shape of contemporary books can be traced to the invention of the "codex" — parchment pages bound together between covers, initially made of wood or leather and later of cloth. The form proved usable and durable, and sometimes labor-intensive. The great texts of Greek learning, Christian theology and medieval literature were preserved through laborious hand copying by library scribes and monks.

The next revolution for books came with the 15th-century invention of printing with changeable type. The invention is attributed to German metalsmith Johannes Gutenberg, who cast type in molds using a melted metal alloy and constructed a wooden-screw printing press to transfer the image onto paper.

Gutenberg's first and only large-scale printing effort was the now iconic Gutenberg Bible in the 1450s — a Latin translation from the Hebrew Old Testament and the Greek New Testament, copies of which can be viewed on the British Library Web site. Gutenberg's invention made mass production of texts possible for the first time. Although the Gutenberg Bible itself was stratospherically expensive, printed books began to spread widely over European trade routes during the next 50 years, and by the 1500s printed books had become more widely accessible and less costly. [32]

By the 17th century, books were being printed by the thousands, instead of hundreds. By this time, too, America had its first printers — in Boston, Cambridge and Philadelphia.

By the 19th century, publishing was an established industry in both Europe and the United States, and publishing houses emerged that dealt in a general book list, which they sold to a growing mass market of readers.

Golden Age

From its origins more than two centuries ago, the American publishing industry has followed a historic pattern that has varied little: Copy is delivered to a printer who ships inventory to a publisher's warehouse from which it is sent to bookstores. [33]

The Lightning Source print-on-demand company prints some 1.4 million volumes a month. About 40 percent of the printing is for mainstream publishers, but President David Taylor, above, at the plant in Milton Keynes, outside London, expects the percentage to increase as publishers revamp the way they do business. Digital printing now accounts for only about 1-3 percent of all the books printed in North America, but the business is projected to grow 15-20 percent over the next three years.

Technological developments have made the process more efficient: Steam presses were invented in 1810, and stereotype plates developed in 1846 made it possible to produce longer runs at less cost per copy. The type produced printed sheets that were then folded, sewn together and bound, much as in Gutenberg's times.

Much as today's traditionalists fear the disappearance of print books, there were those who decried what they saw as the mediocrity of machine-made books. The private hand-press movement began in the 19th century as a reaction to the loss of this craft, led by Arts and Crafts artists like William Morris, and such works continue to be valued by collectors. [34]

Harper Brothers, one of the earliest American publishers, began as a New York printer in 1817. The firm was soon competing with other printers to ship books via the Erie Canal, which gave New York printers an advantage over competitors in Boston and Philadelphia, and helped turn New York into publishing's center.

American publishers made a brisk business of publishing pirated works by British authors like Charles Dickens, William Thackeray and the Bronte sisters throughout most of the 19th century, ignoring international copyright. By the 1840s, the American market had become big enough for Dickens to cross the ocean to protest the theft of his property, but his plea for copyright protection was ignored. [35]

Soon after, however, American authors asked for protection for their own works in foreign editions. By the end of the century Congress had passed the International Copyright Act, which allowed publishers to contract for exclusive rights to the works of British and other foreign writers and earn a profit from them.

By the 1850s, New York publishers were shipping millions of books to the rest of the country.

The 1920s have been called "the golden age" of American publishing. The firms that were launched in the '20s were still run by some of these distinctive personalities in the 1950s. Bennett Cerf founded Random House. Richard Simon, Max Schuster and Alfred A. Knopf all founded houses that bear their names. They introduced to American readers many

CQ Press/Sarah Glazer

of the great modernist writers of the time, from James Joyce to Gertrude Stein. Thousands of bookstores in towns and cities were the main distribution channel for these writers.

Publishers also saw a growing readership for their books as U.S. illiteracy declined from 7.7 percent in 1910 to 2.9 percent in 1940. School enrollments and libraries grew, and the increasingly urbanized nation created receptive homes for bookstores. Book readership also expanded through the Book of the Month Club, founded in 1926, and paperback books, launched by Pocket Books in 1939.

The explosion in recreational reading was an historical exception to a tradition in which reading had been limited to elites — and it didn't last, argues University of Chicago sociologist Griswold. "The period from the mid-19th to mid-20th century was unusual because you had high, universal literacy and a middle class, but you didn't have a lot of alternatives" for entertainment, she says. By the 1950s TV began to erode the primacy of reading as entertainment. "We're returning to a period where lots of reading is a minority pastime," she says, even though many people read for work and online.

Decline of the Backlist

By the mid 1970s, as American book customers migrated from the city to the suburbs, the great downtown bookstores with their large "backlists" — inventories of books other than new releases and current bestsellers — began to disappear.

Bookstores cropping up in shopping centers now had the same limited space and high rent as the clothing store next door and needed the same quick turnover — forcing them to focus on best-selling authors and books by celebrities. By the 1980s, backlists were in steep decline. Thou-

sands of titles disappeared into the "orphan" category — no longer in print but still in copyright.

In the 1950s, no publisher survived without its backlist, and best-sellers were viewed as lucky accidents, according to former Random House editorial director Epstein, who first worked for Doubleday in the 1950s. "Publishers depended on the existence of thousands of independent bookstores that knew how to sell backlist," he recalls. In Epstein's view, the steep decline in backlists turned the industry upside down, forcing publishers to shave their profits by vying for best-selling authors with unrealistically high advances and guarantees.

Such difficulties forced increasing consolidation of the industry. But the big entertainment conglomerates — CBS, ABC, RCA and MCA-Universal — that acquired publishing houses in the 1970s and '80s found them a burden on the balance sheets and sold them off. [36]

Between 1986 and 1996, 63 of the 100 best-selling titles were written by only six writers — Tom Clancy, John Grisham, Stephen King, Dean Koontz, Michael Crichton and Danielle Steel. Publishers often sacrificed much of their normal profit and incurred losses to keep these highly successful authors. [37]

"Publishing was never a profitable business," says Epstein. "You didn't do it to make money; you did it as a vocation."

By the beginning of the 21st century, U.S. publishing was dominated by five financial empires: the German conglomerates Bertelsmann, which had acquired the Random House group, and Holtzbrinck, which now owns St. Martin's and Farrar, Straus and Giroux; London-based Longmans, Pearson (owner of Viking, Penguin, Putnam and Dutton); Rupert Murdoch's News Corp., which owns HarperCollins and William Morrow, and Viacom, which had taken over Simon & Schuster and Pocket Books. [38]

Dawn of the Digital Revolution

In the 1990s as the World Wide Web's popularity grew, entrepreneurs began jockeying to use Web sites to reach millions of customers at little cost — driving the first dot.com bubble from the mid-1990s to its collapse in 2000. By the end of the '90s, the publishing world was filled with speculation about electronic books and Internet publishing.

At the time, industry analysts optimistically predicted the nascent e-book market would reach $2.5 billion by 2002. But the market remained remarkably sluggish until recent years. Even by 2006, it had increased to a total of only about $20 million, from $7 million in 2003. [39]

Publishers also hoped to make money selling CD-ROMs (acronym for "compact disc: read-only memory"). Although the CD encyclopedia *Encarta* proved popular at first, CD-ROMs failed to become significant sellers. After the CD-ROM bubble burst, "a widespread cynicism arose about digital publishing, which has continued among publishers into the networked era and has only begun to adjust," write Harrington and Meade in a recent report on digital possibilities for literature. [40] ■

CURRENT SITUATION

Publishing Woes

Some observers think the tough times for publishing signal the end of traditional ways of doing business, not just a temporary reaction to the recession.

Last November, Houghton Mifflin Harcourt — whose authors include literary giants such as Philip Roth, Gunter Grass and J.R.R. Tolkien — was awash in so much debt that it announced an unprecedented buying freeze on new manuscripts. [41] At the time, other houses had also frozen acquisitions unofficially. [42]

Then on Dec. 3 — dubbed Black Wednesday — Penguin and Harper-Collins announced pay freezes. The same day Random House announced it was dissolving Doubleday and Bantam Dell and distributing their remainders among the conglomerate's other three publishing groups, ultimately causing more layoffs. [43]

"To be a journalist or author these days in America is to be a lumberjack in Wisconsin in the 1930s or a steelworker in Pennsylvania in the 1980s or an auto worker in Michigan, well, right now. It is to be watching your industry, and indeed your way of life, collapsing around you," Samuel Freedman, an author and professor at the Columbia School of Journalism, recently wrote. [44]

In recent years the U.S. book market as a whole has remained relatively static at 3 billion books sold annually. At the end of last year, book revenues tracked by the American Association of Publishers were down 2.8 percent from 2007. [45]

The continuing trend towards conglomerates got some of the blame. In 2006 an Irish firm, Riverkeep, bought Houghton Mifflin and by July 2007 had taken over one of Mifflin's largest rivals, Harcourt, in a $4 billion acquisition that left the parent company billions of dollars in debt.

"There were hedge fund guys with no background in publishing buying up publishing houses," New Press Founder Andre Schiffrin told *Salon*. In his view, corporate owners expected unheard-of 15-20 percent profit margins in an industry with traditional margins of 3 to 4 percent. [46]

The practice at Barnes & Noble and Borders of requiring publishers to pay "co-op" fees to get their books placed prominently in a store also pinches publishers' profits. American

Reading Devices, Here and Now

More than 1.7 million users of the Apple iPhone (top) have downloaded Stanza software, which permits them to read a book on their cell phone from a selection of more than 100,000 titles. In March Google announced plans to offer its more than half a million digitized public-domain books on the Sony Reader (bottom).

publishers' practice of accepting returned books from stores for full credit has become another major expense; returns now represent nearly 40 percent of all hardbacks shipped. [47]

While the big book chains have been blamed for driving out small bookshops and squeezing publishers, they're now having their own problems. Borders hovers near bankruptcy, after investing

Writing a Tale With Help From Your Readers

Readers collaborate with novelist to create a modern take on Alice *in Wonderland.*

"I looked at the black mirror, and suddenly it was like I was falling into a dream." Alice Klein is a character in a novel who suffers from writer's block — until she finds a strange, black mirror in the second-hand bookshop where she's working. When she looks into the mirror, it sends her into a trance and seems to get her writing again. But the mirror also turns out to have evil powers.

That's the plot real British novelist Naomi Alderman cooked up when Penguin Books asked her to write an online tale based on Lewis Carroll's classic, *Alice's Adventures in Wonderland.* [1]

But she didn't write the story by herself.

Over six weeks, Alderman posted (almost) daily blogs written in the voice of her protagonist, Alice Klein. Readers were sent to six different locations on the Web to search for secret messages providing clues to the mystery of the mirror that Alice was trying to untangle. These ranged from answering an ad on Craigslist to showing up at a live event in London where readers could meet a character who had valuable information. Then they e-mailed helpful suggestions to the author.

At one point in the story, Alice decides to break into the offices of an evil doctor to steal the mirror. While Alice was attempting to break in, she asked readers — blogging live with her — to offer clues. "What buttons do you think I should press?" she asked when she reached a locked door with a mysterious design. Readers sent solutions. "You're all geniuses! It worked!" Alice responded.

Alderman calls this kind of writing a literary form that is in its infancy. But it has historical antecedents. The earliest English novels, Samuel Richardson's *Pamela* (1740) and *Clarissa* (1748), are told through characters writing letters in "real time." Dear reader, my pursuer is knocking at my door at this very moment!

"It was very exciting to be involved in something so new where you're making the rules as you're writing," Alderman says. "It's a different kind of writing; it's much more collaborative." Readers' suggestions about the direction of the plot ranged from great to "lousy," according to Alderman, who likened the activity to a chef choosing ingredients.

As the lead writer on the Alternate Reality Game "Perplex City," which has sent hundreds of players running around London searching for clues to a murder mystery, Alderman says the rewards in this kind of collaboration are different from writing novels. But she insists she enjoys both. Alderman won the distinguished Orange Prize for New Writers for her first novel, *Disobedience*, published in 2006, about growing up in an orthodox Jewish family in England.

"If I just sit in my house and write novels all day, eventually I go crazy because being alone with the imaginary people you've made up in your head does send you crazy," Alderman says. "But if I'm constantly working with other people, I begin to feel like I don't have any ownership over my own work, and that also sends me crazy."

---

heavily in music sections just as CDs were going out of style. By February, Barnes & Noble's stock price had fallen by more than half in the previous 18 months, triggering job cutbacks. [48]

Meanwhile the Internet has been invading newspapers' book reviewing territory, with a flourishing dialogue on literary blogs. Two years ago, bloggers were already reporting that they were being courted by publishers sending them pre-publication galleys in hopes of a mention. As of mid-May, only two newspapers still had separate book-review sections: *The New York Times* and *The San Francisco Chronicle.* [49]

Reference books also have been badly hit by Wikipedia and other free works on the Web. Estimates of online retailers' current share of the U.S.

market are as high as 30 percent. Their heavy discounting further squeezes publishers' profit margins and spells more difficulty for brick-and-mortar bookshops.

Revolutionary Changes

This past year, almost every month seemed to herald a revolutionary development in the still small but growing e-books market.

In February, Amazon launched a sleeker version of its $359 Kindle, with wireless access to more than 230,000 electronic books. The following month Google announced plans to offer its more than half a million digitized public domain books on the Sony Reader device. Industry analysts described the two deals

as jockeying by industry giants to make their device the iPod of books. [50]

But some were betting on another horse. At year's end, *Forbes* magazine declared Apple's iPhone the most popular e-reader, given that 395,000 users had downloaded the Stanza reading application, which enables the downloading of 100,000 book titles — half of them for free. [51]

Now more than 1.7 million unique users have downloaded Stanza — along with more than 7 million e-books — according to Lexcycle, Stanza's maker. On April 27, Amazon purchased Lexcycle, leading some industry observers to suggest that Amazon really seeks to dominate the entire electronic books market, not just Kindle devices. [52]

Is iPhone the most popular e-reader? It's hard to say because rival companies

What about the widely held view that art has to be the product of a single imagination?" I think we're a little too hung up on the idea of the artist as this magnificent individual with his or her magnificent genius that comes only from them and has nothing to do with the wider world," Alderman responds. "Actually, we're all products of the stories that we hear, of conversations and writers we've been exposed to."

She likens readers' real-time responses to the experience of a playwright, where the live audience responds to the words as they are spoken. Her "Alice in Storyland" had about 1,000 unique hits, with about 150 people actually contributing ideas, according to Alderman. In that sense, she says, it's similar to a magic show where only a few audience members will volunteer, "but it's quite fun to watch" everyone else.

"Alice in Storyland" is filled with sly references to the classic, starting with the character's names: Alice Klein (Klein means "little" in German/Yiddish) is a stand-in for Alice Liddell, the "little" girl for whom Carroll wrote the classic and who in-

With help from online readers, British novelist Naomi Alderman wrote a tale based on Lewis Carroll's classic, Alice's Adventures in Wonderland.

Getty Images/Chris Jackson

spired the Alice of his *Wonderland* tales. Another character, Mr. Marsh Ayre, is reminiscent of the March hare.

In the last episode, Alice is awakened by a phone call from her agent congratulating her on writing her second novel — something she has no memory of writing — much the way the original Alice wakes from her Wonderland dream.

"Apparently I've written my second novel," she writes in her final blog post. "At least according to Penguin I have."

The link takes readers to a real Penguin Web site that seems to be selling a book entitled *A Trickle of Ink*, described as a "rip-roaring" instant classic by Alice Klein, complete with a price and reader review. [2] Except that no matter how hard you click, you can't buy the novel. Like Alice Klein, it doesn't really exist.

---

[1] http://wetellstories.co.uk. For "Alice in Storyland," see http://treacleandink. wordpress.com/category/uncategorized/.

[2] www.penguin.co.uk/nf/Book/BookDisplay/0,,9780141885025,00.html.

---

like Amazon won't say how many Kindles they've sold. But industry analysts say up to 500,000 Kindles were sold last year, and up to a million of both versions have been sold so far. [53] As of mid-March, Sony had sold 400,000 of its $350 Readers. [54]

Stanza is only one of several reading applications accessible to iPhone users (owners can also download Kindle and Google books, among others), which suggests even more iPhone users are reading on their phones. But most e-book reading still occurs on laptops or desktops, according to the recent Bowker survey, which found 48 percent of all e-book purchases are for PCs. The survey found the Kindle came in second at 22 percent, followed by the iPhone at 10 percent.

But how many people want to

read a book on a tiny screen? When Lexcycle CEO Neelan Choksi is confronted with that question, he retorts, "Aren't you the same person who read 50 e-mails on your BlackBerry yesterday?" And some users say they find the crisp iPhone screen with its ability to choose 125 background colors easier to read than the gray and black Kindle.

Most people will go back home to get it if they've forgotten their cell phone, not so likely with a Kindle, Choksi points out. "If you're 30 or under, you're used to reading blogs and Facebook on your cell phone already."

The ultimate reader, Choksi thinks, will have to be "something with the convenience of the iPhone." (Unique uses reported in Stanza's customer survey included in the bathroom at work

and on a submarine.) "It has to have color and be multifunctional; it will have to have video." All the content you get on your PC, not just books, will have to be available through it, Choksi believes.

Mary Klement, a San Diego engineer who travels frequently, has 150 books loaded onto her iPod Touch, which she also uses to watch her favorite HBO series while flying and to check e-mail. She likes the convenience of always having a "book" with her that's easy to hold in her palm while waiting at the airport baggage claim. She can download books anywhere in the world where there's a wireless Internet connection — an advantage over the Kindle, which only works over Sprint's U.S. cell phone network.

With so much activity, e-books are "getting closer to a tipping point" for market success, says Smith at the International Digital Publishing Forum.

E-book retail sales last year increased 68 percent over 2007 to an estimated total of $107 million, according to the organization. (*See graph, p. 476.*) But that doesn't include some of the largest publishers that have been reporting triple-digit growth, according to Smith. Nor does it include library or higher-education sales, sectors that both boast twice the electronic sales of trade publishers. Meanwhile, Overdrive, a leading seller of e-books to libraries, logged 10 million downloads in 2008.

In addition, e-books' fourth-quarter sales doubled last year over the same period in 2007, Smith pointed out, and this January sales jumped 174 percent over the first month of last year. Penguin announced its e-book sales jumped 500 percent in 2008 over the previous year, although e-book sales are still less than 1 percent of total revenue. [55] Random House and Simon & Schuster also expected e-book revenue to at least double. [56]

"I don't think the traditional print book will be replaced, but I do expect reading habits of the younger generation will change," says Smith. "My 9-year-old gets in the car and wants the Sony Reader all the time; she reads her *Nancy Drew* titles on it."

Appealing to Youths

Publishers are enticing young readers using combinations of Web content and books. For instance, Scholastic's *The 39 Clues* — aimed at 9-12-year-olds — combines online game playing and card collecting with a series of traditional books; its first one, *Maze of Bones*, became a best-seller. [57]

Penguin's children's division ran a month-long giveaway of Johan Flana-

gan's *The Ruins of Gorlan*, which included posting downloadable e-books on Scribd.com (a YouTube for books); in the first two weeks, 20,000 people downloaded the book. [58]

Just this winter, HarperCollins started releasing e-book versions along with its new print titles for children in six e-book formats including Kindle and Sony Reader. [59] The top three novels downloaded from libraries last year were from Stephenie Meyer's popular teen vampire *Twilight* series, according to library distributor Overdrive. [60]

Aiming for the millions of Nintendo DS machines in British children's hands, HarperCollins launched its *100 Classic Book Collection* in December, making 100 classics from *Romeo and Juliet* to *Treasure Island* readable on the portable devices. The publisher has sold 200,000 copies of the collection, which can also play appropriate background music for about $23 extra. [61]

In February, Sourcebooks became the first major print publisher to release a digitally enhanced picture book. Readers of Laura Duksta's *I Love You More* can hear the voice of the mother and the son as they read along. [62]

The market position of e-books could be improved by the adoption last year of a uniform standard for e-books known as .epub, developed by Smith's organization. Usable on a variety of platforms, it saves publishers the cost of producing digital files in several different formats.

Some publishers see a big digital future. HarperCollins CEO Victoria Barnsley has estimated that "within 10 years more than half our sales will come from digital downloads." [63]

Last October, *Newsweek* announced it would publish four books about the presidential and vice presidential candidates, available only electronically on the Kindle. [64]

In March, the University of Michigan Press announced that it will shift its scholarly publishing from a primarily print operation to digital-only editions, although

readers will be able to produce printed versions with print-on-demand systems.

"Why try to remain in a territory you know is doomed? Scholarly presses will be primarily digital in a decade," said press director Phil Pochoda. Other university presses, including Penn State, are moving to digital-only for some books. [65]

Settlement Fallout

As a result of the Google Book Search settlement, up to 10 million out-of-print books where copyright holders can't be located could now be the exclusive province of Google to scan and commercially exploit, according to Internet Archive founder Kahle's estimate.

A variety of groups are planning to file comments in court raising concerns over the settlement, including the Internet Archive, the Institute of Information Law and Policy at New York Law School (which has financing from Microsoft), the American Library Association and the Association of Research Libraries. [66]

At the end of April, *The New York Times* reported that the Justice Department was launching an inquiry into the antitrust implications of Google's settlement and was talking with groups opposed to the settlement, including the Internet Archive and Consumer Watchdog. That same month, Judge Denny Chin of U.S. District Court in New York, who is overseeing the settlement, postponed until Sept. 4 the deadline for parties to file briefs opposing the settlement and for authors to opt out of it. The court's hearing to decide whether to accept the settlement and to consider objections was also postponed, to Oct. 7, 2009. [67]

Under the settlement, revenue generated from subscriptions and advertising on Google search pages will be split — with 37 percent going to Google

Continued on p. 494

At Issue:

Will the Google book settlement expand access to digital books?

DAN CLANCY
GOOGLE ENGINEERING DIRECTOR

WRITTEN FOR *CQ RESEARCHER*, MAY 26, 2009

six years ago, Google embarked on a massive project to digitize millions of books to make them as searchable as Web pages. Today, as a result, anyone in the U.S. can search across the entire texts of more than 10 million books for free, simply by visiting Google Book Search. People can read and download 1.5 million public-domain books in their entirety, from the works of William Shakespeare to Benjamin Franklin.

Until now, though, we've only been able to show our users a few snippets of text for millions of in-copyright books we've scanned. Since most of these books are out of print, to actually read them you have to hunt them down at a library or a used bookstore. And if the only known copy is on the other side of the country — you're out of luck.

If approved by the court, our groundbreaking agreement with a broad class of authors and publishers stands to open access to millions of such books in the U.S. By unlocking access to these books, anyone, any place in the country will be able to benefit from the wealth of knowledge contained in our nation's most renowned libraries.

Users will be able to preview millions of works online from anywhere in the U.S. If they want to read the whole thing, they'll be able to go down to the public library to use a computer station with access to the whole book for free. And if they want a copy for themselves, they'll be able to purchase access to an electronic copy of the book. Meanwhile, schools around the country can obtain an institutional subscription to give their students access to most books that we've scanned.

Our non-exclusive agreement requires that these new services be priced for "broad access," which means they must be affordable enough to allow universities and libraries across the country to take advantage of them. Partners like the University of Michigan will be able to review the prices of all institutional subscriptions and challenge them through arbitration if they believe they're too high.

What's more, the settlement creates an independent, not-for-profit Book Rights Registry run by authors and publishers that can work with others (including Google's competitors) to build alternative or even competing digitization services.

Just because the University of Michigan — one of Google's many partners — isn't down the road or around the corner doesn't mean people around the country should be denied access to its library. As the discussion continues, it's important to understand what readers stand to gain.

BREWSTER KAHLE
*FOUNDER AND DIGITAL LIBRARIAN,
INTERNET ARCHIVE*

WRITTEN FOR *CQ RESEARCHER*, MAY 26, 2009

in the short term, the settlement negotiated between Google, the Authors Guild and the Association of American Publishers will certainly expand access to digital books. Google's 7 million books (and counting) is an important addition to the recent flood of digitized books. In the medium and long terms, however, the settlement will stall and stifle the exciting future of digital books by granting a single entity too much power and control.

If the settlement is approved, the outcome will be not one but two court-sanctioned monopolies. First, Google will be the only organization with an explicit license to scan and sell access to in-copyright but out-of-print books, which make up the majority of books published in the 20th century. The settlement also creates a new entity, called the Book Rights Registry (essentially, a monopoly), which, in conjunction with Google, will set prices for all commercial terms associated with those digital books.

We need to learn from our experiences with other companies that have come to dominate different types of digital content: Lexis-Nexis and Westlaw in law publishing and Elsevier with academic journals. Each aggressively pursued acquisitions and digitization to gain a strong position, while enjoying enthusiastic support from libraries and universities. It was difficult for them to see the future effects of allowing companies to gain dominance in a market: Elsevier grabbed control of academic journal publishing by aggregating journals and selling them in bundles to libraries — progressively raising subscription prices. Similarly, Lexis-Nexis and Westlaw left no real alternatives for accessing law materials.

The publishing and distribution of digital books could face the same danger.

But there are alternatives to Google. Hundreds of libraries, publishers and technology firms are already digitizing millions of books, with the goal of creating an open, freely accessible system.

If Google is allowed to create a monopoly on access to a large segment of digitized books, the entire publishing environment will weaken. Publishers will see their opportunities for selling limited. Authors will suffer as one company's Web site increasingly dictates who an author's readers will be. And readers, who for generations have seen their lives enriched by a diverse world of book publishing and libraries, will also suffer.

As controlling entities turn from innovation and competition to defending their dominant positions, access to digital books will suffer. Google might get richer, but society will become much poorer.

Continued from p. 492

and 63 percent going to authors and publishers. Some of the settlement money will go to establish a Book Rights Registry to administer the system and ensure that authors and publishers get paid.

"The court needs to supervise the registry in its interactions with Google very carefully to make sure that the monopoly the settlement creates does not abuse its power," says attorney Band, who represents the library associations.

Legislation passed by the U.S. Senate last year (but not by the House) would have limited the copyright infringement liability for libraries or companies wishing to scan or otherwise use "orphan" books. [68] At press time, no new orphan-works bill had been introduced in this congressional session.

Google's Clancy notes that his company supports even stronger orphan-works legislation than the Senate measure and that Google's efforts to identify rights holders under the settlement could actually help clarify which books still have identifiable copyright holders. But most observers agree the settlement takes the wind out of the sails of new legislative efforts — at least for books covered by the settlement.

Bypassing Publishers

On May 18, Scribd, the popular Web site that bills itself the YouTube of writing, launched an on-line vanity press and bookstore that allows anyone to upload and sell their own work. Although other companies offer digital self-publishing, the announcement received a lot of

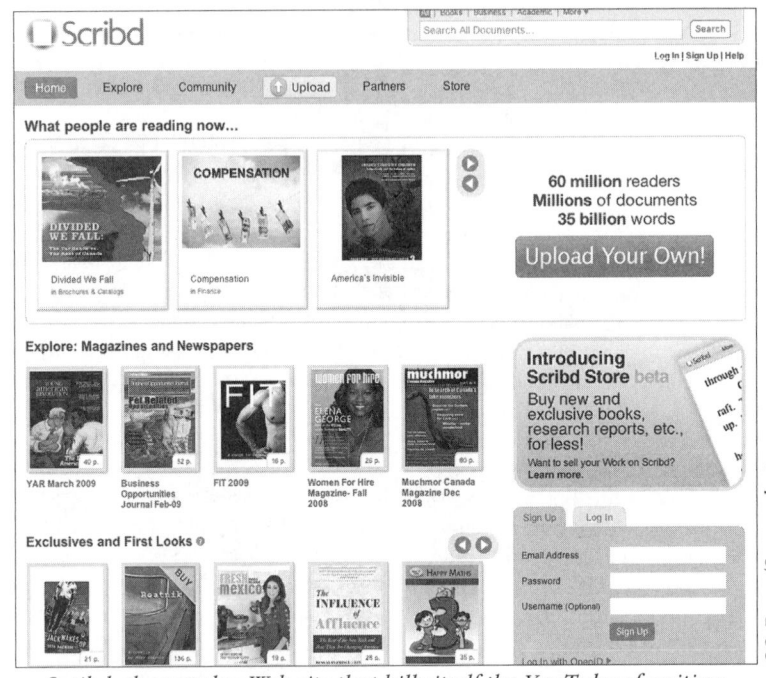

Scribd, the popular Web site that bills itself the YouTube of writing, launched an online vanity press and bookstore on May 18 that allows anyone to upload and sell their own work. The announcement received heavy media attention because Scribd claims 60 million users a month, and its audience has been doubling every six months.

media attention because Scribd claims 60 million users a month, and its audience has been doubling every six months. [69]

Several authors (none famous) announced they would be publishing their new books for the first time in digital form and selling them on the site for only $2 but would still make more money than going the conventional publishing route. Scribd allows authors or publishers to set the price and keep 80 percent of the revenue. (Mainstream publishers pay authors royalties of 15 percent or less.)

"As more and more authors become bloggers, individuals now can market their own books in a way they never could before," says Choksi of Lexcycle, which added a self-publishing company, Smashwords, to its Stanza iPhone application earlier this year. Admittedly, he notes, many of these books are amateurish affairs like family genealogies, which might only attract a few buyers who know the author personally.

However, one sure-fire big seller went the self-publishing route to get a bigger cut of the revenues. Amy Fisher's 2004 memoir about shooting her lover's wife when she was 17, *If I Knew Then . . .*, was published as a print-on-demand book by self-publisher iUniverse and appeared briefly on *The New York Times* best-seller list. [70]

Some publishers fear that kind of authorial entrepreneurship could cut into their business. But so far, successful writers have, for the most part, continued to seek out name-brand publishers.

In addition to its vanity press, Scribd is trying to position itself as a potential rival to Amazon by offering books for sale that can be read on any device, unlike Amazon's Kindle, and hopes to carry the full digital catalog of books from publishing partners like Random House. [71]

Scribd claims to offer publishers an advantage over Kindle, which sets the price and keeps the majority of revenue on some titles. Some publishers are worried that Amazon is gaining too much market power and may start squeezing publishers' revenue even more — especially if it continues to price bestsellers as low as $9.99. [72]

In a move reminiscent of iTunes, which sold one song at a time for $1, Scribd will now sell a chapter or two of a travel guide for as little as $3, under arrangements with publishers like Lonely Planet. [73]

Meanwhile, the National Endowment for the Arts (NEA) reported in January that for the first time since 1982, the number of adults who said they had read a novel, short story, poem or play in the past 12 months had risen — from 47 percent of the population in 2002 to more than 50 percent in 2008. [74]

While one expert called the rise "just a blip," others cited a 24-percent rise among young men ages 18-24. [75] The survey questions did not distinguish between online and print reading.

Former NEA chairman Dana Gioia called the rise at least partly a reaction to earlier reports of a reading crisis. "Reading has become a higher priority," he said. [76] Still, 22 percent of Americans did not read a book last year because they couldn't — one of the worst illiteracy rates among wealthy countries. ■

OUTLOOK

The iPod of Books?

Books may be changing, but in a direction that appeals to many different audiences — from the computer-linked to the print loyalists.

For years, publishers have said, "We're looking for the iPod for books" — the universal device that makes it easy to load and read books whenever and wherever you want.

Have we found it with the iPhone, Kindle or Sony Reader? Probably not yet. Some think the next generation will be a lightweight electronic reader — offering the advantages of a large-format screen, which can display the front page of a newspaper or a complicated nautical chart, with the convenience of a gadget that can be folded up.

The Plastic Logic Reader, which almost fits that description (it's bendable and is thinner than a pad of paper but can't be folded up and put in your pocket), is to be introduced in pilots later this year and will be widely available by early next year.

Amazon's new, large-format Kindle DX appears to be targeting the same market — business travelers — since it also permits wireless exchange of documents. It's not clear Amazon's other target audience, student textbook readers, will be enticed by a device costing close to $500. Major textbook publisher Pearson Education reports about 25 percent of its sales are digital — with most of them read on laptops. [77]

Amazon's April release of the DX seemed timed to beat not only Plastic Logic but also other devices whose announcement is expected imminently from Apple, Palm and possibly Murdoch's News Corp. Sony's expected release of a wireless version of its Reader will likely intensify competition. [78]

Some are skeptical of all the devices and think print is still the perfect technology. "I don't think there will ever be an iPod moment" with the book, says Lightning Source's Taylor. Instead, he sees print-on-demand exploding in the next few years as publishers try to cut costs in a tough economic climate. Marketing researcher Interquest projects annual growth of 15-20 percent over the next three years for the digital-printing market because of new ink-jet technology that will make somewhat longer press runs more economical.

Smaller on-site computer printers, like the Espresso, could make it possible to print out books almost anywhere — whether in bookstores, rural African outposts or on ships at sea.

It's still unclear how big an e-book audience will emerge. Ironically, if electronic devices come down in price, some think they could have a bigger market in the underdeveloped world, which has little publishing infrastructure

but is quickly installing cell phone networks, the method for purchasing and downloading books on the Kindle.

Publishers must also decide whether to continue to exercise so-called digital rights management (DRM) over e-books, aimed at preventing piracy and free sharing of files. (*See sidebar, p. 479.*)

Some see protective encoding as an impediment to further adoption of digital books because it locks in each e-book to a proprietary format and limits the variety of devices on which it can be read. "It's as if you had a DVD you can't play on your laptop or on a friend's DVD player," says Lexcyle's Choksi. "I think e-books as an industry would do so much better if DRM were used only for encryption and for managing the rights the publishers want managed."

Most authors and publishers can be expected to stand by DRM as the only bulwark protecting their copyright and income.

Eventually, piracy could become irrelevant if publishers turn to storing e-books "in the cloud" — i.e. in cyberspace like Google Mail, with a user password to gain access. "In the long run we won't need DRM," predicts Idea Logical CEO Shatzkin, because, "We'll stop having hard drives; everything will be on the Internet."

Research libraries are running to catch up with all the online activity. Already, some scholarly journals have been migrating to electronic-only versions, and many libraries are canceling their print-version subscriptions in favor of electronic versions. Some think books will follow suit.

Much like Wikipedia, the sciences are being revolutionized by the ability to share scholarly papers online without waiting for peer-reviewed publication. "We know scholars are depositing and sharing their work way outside the traditional scholarly framework" of publication, says Columbia University chief librarian James Neal. "Our challenge is how do we get in there, capture and preserve that stuff?"

Paradoxically, digitization is preserving many printed books that are now too brittle to be handled. The Library of Congress has digitized some 29,000 books, going back to the early 19th century, which can be viewed on the Internet Archive Web site. Some are so fragile they will be sent to a climate-controlled vault at Fort Meade, in Maryland.

"So for all intents and purposes they will never be handled again," says Mike Handy, who supervises the digitization effort at the library.

Amidst all this activity, the U.S. print-book market will probably continue to hover at about 3 billion sales per year.

"It's a flat market because there's a lot of competition from electronic media," says Gilles Biscos, president of Interquest, a market research company in Charlottesville, Va. "People have other things to do than read books, and they spend a great deal of time on the Internet reading screens."

That's where both the opportunity and the challenge lie for the future of books. ■

Notes

[1] Whispersync permits Kindle owners to access their library of previously purchased books at no additional cost and to pick up where they left off through automatic bookmarks.

[2] The screen displays ink particles electronically to create a reading experience much closer to printed paper than most computer displays.

[3] For background, see Kenneth Jost, "Future of Books," *CQ Researcher*, June 23, 2000, pp. 545-568.

[4] Miguel Helft, "Google and Amazon to Put More Books on Cellphones," *The New York Times*, Feb. 6, 2009, www.nytimes.com.

[5] If digital printing used by publishers for short runs of up to 1,200 books are counted, digitally printed books accounted for 3 percent of all books published in North America, according to Interquest, a market research firm.

[6] www.wetellstories.co.uk.

[7] www.songsofimaginationanddigitisation.net.

[8] Motoko Rich, "Print Book are Target of Pirates on the Web," *The New York Times*, May 12, 2009, www.nytimes.com.

[9] *Ibid.*

[10] Miguel Helft and Motoko Rich, "Google Settles Suit over Book-Scanning," *The New York Times*, Oct. 29, 2008.

[11] The formula only applies to books for which the rights holder has not set a price. The purchaser gets perpetual online access to the book.

[12] Robert Darnton, "Google & the Future of Books," *The New York Review of Books*, Feb. 12, 2009, www.nybooks.com.

[13] *Ibid.*

[14] Miguel Helft, "Libraries Ask Google to Monitor Google Books Settlement," *The New York Times*, May 4, 2009, www.googlebooksettlement.com.

[15] K-12 users will still be able to view up to 20 percent of a book's content, as part of the free search function, as will all other users in the United States. For background, see Kathy Koch, "The Digital Divide," *CQ Researcher*, Jan. 28, 2000, pp. 41-64.

[16] Google is obligated to reveal only 85 percent of the books it has scanned into the database, under the agreement.

[17] The association announced on Feb. 27 that Schroeder would step down as president on May 1, www.publishers.org.

[18] Paul Courant, "Google, Robert Darnton, and the Digital Republic of Letters," *Au Courant*, (Paul Courant's blog), http://paulcourant.net.

[19] See www.futureofthebook.org/blog/archives/2008/09/a_unified_field_theory_of_publ_1.html.

[20] Brad Stone and Motoko Rich, "Amazon Unveils a Large-Screen Kindle Aimed at Textbooks and Newspapers," May 7, 2009, *The New York Times*, www.nytimes.com. The three newspapers are *The New York Times*, *The Boston Globe* and *The Washington Post*.

[21] Peter Osnos, "Rise of the Reader," *Columbia Journalism Review*, March/April 2009, pp. 38-39.

[22] David Pearson, *Books as History* (2008), p. 25.

[23] Bob Stein, "A unified field theory of publishing in the networked era," if:book, www.futureofthebook.org/blog/archives/2008/09/a_unified_field_theory_of_publ_1.html.

[24] *Ibid.*

[25] Bruce Mason and Sue Thomas, "A Million Penguins Research Report," April 24, 2008, De Montfort University, Leicester, U.K., www.ioct.dmu.ac.uk/projects/amillionpenguins report.pdf.

[26] *Ibid.*

[27] *Ibid.*

[28] Presentation by Bowker Vice President for Publisher Services Kelly Gallagher, "Understanding tomorrow's digital consumer by knowing what they are up to today," London Book Fair, April 19, 2009, www.bowker.com.

[29] "Publishing's High Flyers," *newbooks*, March/April 2009, p. 30, www.newbooksmag.com.

[30] www.playingforkeepsnovel.com.

[31] Marcia Clemmitt, "Learning Online Literacy," in "Reading Crisis?" *CQ Researcher*, Feb. 22, 2008, pp. 169-192.

[32] British Library, "Treasures in Full: Gutenberg Bible," www.bl.uk/treasures/gutenberg/background.html.

[33] Jason Epstein, "An Autopsy of the Book Business," *Daily Beast*, Jan. 8, 2009, www.dailybeast.com.

[34] Pearson, *op. cit.*, p. 65.

[35] Jason Epstein, *Book Business* (2001), pp. 97-98.

[36] *Ibid.*, p. 33.

[37] *Ibid.*, p. 33.

[38] *Ibid.*, p. 11.

[39] "Interquest Report: High Growth Segments of Digital Book Printing — Market Analysis and Forecast 2007," Interquest, 2007.

[40] Mary Harrington and Chris Meade, "read:write Digital Possibilities for Literature," A Report for Arts Council England, July 2008, www.futureofthebook.org.uk.

About the Author

Sarah Glazer, a London-based freelancer, is a regular contributor to the *CQ Researcher*. Her articles on publishing, health and social-policy issues have appeared in *The New York Times*, *The Washington Post* and *Gender and Work*, a book of essays. Her most recent *CQ Researcher* report was "Declining Birthrates." She graduated from the University of Chicago with a B.A. in American history.

[41] Motoko Rich, "Book Publisher Suspends New Acquisitions," *The New York Times*, Nov. 25, 2008, www.nytimes.com.

[42] Colin Robinson, "Diary," *London Review of Books*, Feb. 26, 2009.

[43] Jason Boog, "Read it and Weep," *Salon.com*, Dec. 23, 2008.

[44] Samuel Freedman, "In the Diaspora: The ever-dying people of the ever-dying book," *Jerusalem Post*, March 5, 2009, www.jpost.com.

[45] American Association of Publishers, press release, "AAP Reports Book Sales Estimated at $24.3 Billion in 2008," March 31, 2009.

[46] Boog, *op. cit.*

[47] Robinson, *op. cit.*

[48] *Ibid.*

[49] Freedman, *op. cit.*

[50] Geoffrey A. Fowler and Jessica E. Vascellaro, "Sony and Google Team Up to Battle Amazon," *The Wall Street Journal*, March 19, 2009.

[51] Dave Caolo, "iPhone the most popular ebook reader," The Unofficial Apple Weblog, Oct. 3, 2008, www.tuaw.com.

[52] See Kassia Krozser, "Amazon Buys Lexcycle," April 28, 2009, booksquare.com and Andrew Ross Sorkin, "Dealbook: Amazon Buys Lexcycle," http://dealbook.blogs.nytimes.com.

[53] Peter Osnos, "Platform: The Kindle Surge and Beyond," *teleread.org*, May 19, 2009, www.teleread.org.

[54] Geoffrey A. Fowler and Jessica E. Vascellaro, "Sony and Google Team Up to Battle Amazon," *The Wall Street Journal*, March 19, 2009.

[55] Jim Milliot, "Penguin Posts Solid Gains Worldwide," *Publishers Weekly*, March 2, 2009.

[56] Dominic Rushe, "Market Warms to Electronic books," *Timesonline*, Aug. 31, 2008, http://business.timeonline.co.uk.

[57] www.the39clues.com.

[58] Judith Rosen, "Taking Steps into the Digital Future," *Publisher's Weekly*, Feb. 16, 2009, www.publishersweekly.com.

[59] *Ibid.*

[60] "OverDrive Announces 2008 Library Download Statistics and Milestones," Jan. 6, 2009, www.overdrive.com.

[61] Vicky Frost, "Waiting for the iPod Moment," *The Guardian*, April 20, 2009.

[62] Rosen, *op. cit.*

[63] Robinson, *op. cit.*

[64] Richard Perez-Pena, "Campaign Articles from Newsweek Become E-Books for Amazon Kindle," *The New York Times*, Oct. 13, 2008, www.nytimes.com.

[65] Scott Jaschik, "Farewell to the Printed Monograph," *Inside Higher Ed*, March 23, 2009, www.insidehighered.com.

FOR MORE INFORMATION

American Library Association, 50 E. Huron, Chicago, IL 60611; (800) 545-2433; www.ala.org. Represents librarians in the United States.

Association of American Publishers, 50 F St., NW, 4th Floor, Washington, DC 20001; (202) 347-3375; www.publishers.org. Principal trade association for the publishing industry.

The Authors Guild, 31 East 32nd St., 7th Floor, New York, NY 10016; (212) 563-5904; www.authorsguild.org. Represented authors in the Google Book Search settlement.

http://books.google.com. Google's Web site for searching books explains how the search engine would change under the out-of-court settlement with authors and publishers.

www.googlebooksettlement.com. Official Web site run by the administrator of the Google Book Search settlement.

Institute for the Future of the Book, 74 N. 7th St., #3, Brooklyn, NY 11211; www.futureofthebook.org. Think tank experimenting with future forms of the book in New York and London.

International Digital Publishing Forum; P.O. Box 215, Toronto, Ontario M3C 2S2 Canada; (905) 235-IDPF (4373); www.openebook.org. Trade association for the e-book industry.

Kernochan Center for Law, Media and the Arts, Columbia University School of Law, 435 W. 116th St., Box A-17, New York, NY 10027; (212) 854-7424; http://kernochancenter.org. Streaming video of the center's March 13, 2009, conference on the Google Book Search settlement.

Scribd; www.scribd.com. A Web site where users share and sell original writing, and mainstream publishers are starting to post free excerpts.

We Tell Stories; http://wetellstories.co.uk. This Penguin experiment with online storytelling won the "Best in Show" prize at the SXSW interactive festival in Austin, Texas.

[66] Miguel Helft, "Google's Plan for Out-of-Print Books is Challenged," *The New York Times*, April 4, 2009, www.nytimes.com.

[67] Miguel Helft, "Justice Dept. Opens Antitrust Inquiry into Google Books Deal," *The New York Times*, April 29, 2009, www.nytimes.com. Also see official Google Book Settlement Web site, www.googlebooksettlement.com.

[68] www.thomas.gov/.

[69] Kenneth Li, "Scribd launches online book market," *Financial Times*, May 18, 2009, www.ft.com.

[70] See Sarah Glazer, "The Book Business: How to Be Your Own Publisher," *The New York Times*, April 24, 2005, www.nytimes.com.

[71] Li, *op. cit.*

[72] Brad Stone, "Site Lets Writers Sell Digital Copies," *The New York Times*, May 17, 2009, www.nytimes.com.

[73] See www.scribd.com.

[74] "Reading on the rise," National Endowment for the Arts, www.arts.gov/research/ReadingonRise.pdf.

[75] *Ibid.*

[76] "Adult literacy: the readers," *The Economist*, Jan. 17, 2009. pp. 411-412.

[77] Brad Stone and Mokoto Rich, "Amazon Introduces Big-Screen Kindle," *The New York Times*, May 6, 2009, www.nytimes.com.

[78] Marion Maneker, "How the Next Kindle Could Save the Newspaper Business," *Wired*, May 6, 2009, www.wired.com.

Bibliography

Selected Sources

Books

Anderson, Chris, *Free: The Future of a Radical Price*, Hyperion, July 7, 2009.

"Every industry that becomes digital eventually becomes free," including books, *Wired* editor-in-chief Anderson argues. He has even promised there will be a way to get this book free.

Anderson, Chris, *The Long Tail*, Random House Business Books, 2006.

The editor-in-chief of *Wired* magazine introduced the term "long tail" into the business lexicon to argue that aggregating many low-selling items creates a lot of sales — in books (think Amazon and print-on-demand), music and other areas.

Epstein, Jason, *Book Business: Publishing Past Present and Future*, W.W. Norton, 2001.

The former editorial director of Random House sprinkles personal reminiscence about his 50 years in publishing throughout this discussion of publishing's history and where it's headed.

Pearson, David, *Books as History*, The British Library and Oak Knoll Press, 2008.

In this beautifully produced book, the director of University of London Research Library Services discusses the importance of physical books as artifacts in understanding history.

Articles

"Sony, Google Challenge Amazon," *The Wall Street Journal*, March 19, 2009, http://onlinwsj.com.

The Wall Street Journal describes Google's deal to provide 500,000 books to the Sony Reader as a challenge to Amazon's Kindle.

Courant, Paul, "Google, Robert Darnton and the Digital Republic of Letters," *Au Courant: Paul Courant's blog*, Feb. 4, 2009, ttp://paulcourant.net/2009/02/04/google-robert-darnton-and-the-digital-republic-of-letters.

The University of Michigan's dean of libraries counters Darnton's critique (below), arguing that such a vast digital library could never have been assembled without Google.

Darnton, Robert, "Google and the Future of Books," *New York Review of Books*, Feb. 12, 2009.

Harvard Library's director expresses concern that Google will abuse its "virtual monopoly" over what could be the biggest digital library in the world as a result of its recent out-of-court settlement with authors and publishers.

Osnos, Peter, "Rise of the Reader: How Books Got Wings," *Columbia Journalism Review*, March/April 2009, pp. 38-39.

The vice chairman of the *Columbia Journalism Review* and founder of PublicAffairs books imagines the future world of the book, digital and otherwise, in 2014.

Pullinger, Kate, "My Digital Evolution in Fiction," *Internet Evolution*, March 18, 2009, www.internetevolution.com.

A published novelist suggests that works of literature by a single author may be a "relic of a cultural moment" as literature becomes increasingly collaborative and multimedia — online and on our phones.

Reports and Studies

"Book Industry Trends 2008," Book Industry Study Group, www.bisg.org.

An industry trade association issues a comprehensive report each year on trends in publishing revenues and output. The 2009 report was to be released May 29.

Band, Jonathan, "A Guide for the Perplexed: Libraries and the Google Library Project Settlement," Nov. 23, 2008, www.arl.org/pp/ppcopyright/google.

An attorney for the Association of Research Libraries provides a detailed description of the Google Book Search settlement from the perspective of libraries.

Harrington, Mary, and Chris Meade, "Read: Write: Digital Possibilities for Literature," Arts Council of England, www.futureofthebook.org.uk, July 2008.

Two members of a London literary think tank, The Institute for the Future of the Book, report on online experiments with literature.

Mason, Bruce, and Sue Thomas, "A Million Penguins Research Report," De Montfort University, Leicester, U.K., April 24, 2008, www.ioct.dmu.ac.uk/projects/million-penguinsanalysis.html.

Two British academics analyze a wiki novel-writing experiment sponsored by Penguin that attracted hundreds of contributors to a developing plot online.

On the Web

***Songs of Imagination and Digitisation*, if: book, www.songsofimaginationanddigitisation.net.**

Click onto this book by and about the British poet William Blake to get an idea of the future multimedia "netbook," containing poems and essays along with videos, inventive computer graphics and an invitation to contribute online. Published by the London literary think tank if: book with support from the Arts Council of England.

The Next Step:

Additional Articles from Current Periodicals

Google Book Search

Gibson, James, "Google's New Monopoly?" *The Washington Post*, **Nov. 3, 2008, p. A21.**

Google is the only Internet company with enough funds and resources to compensate copyright owners in a project to digitize vast collections of books.

Harmanci, Reyhan, "Google, Trade Groups Settle," *The San Francisco Chronicle*, **Oct. 29, 2008, p. C1.**

Google has agreed to pay $125 million to start the Book Rights Registry to compensate authors for providing online access to their books.

Helft, Miguel, "Microsoft to Stop Scanning Books," *The New York Times*, **May 24, 2008, p. C8.**

Microsoft has decided to end a project to scan millions of books onto the Internet amid tough competition from Google.

Larson, Erik, "Authors to Consider Google Deal," *The Boston Globe*, **April 29, 2009, p. B11.**

A federal judge in New York has given thousands of authors a four-month extension to decide on whether to join a settlement with Google over its book-scanning project.

Print-on-Demand

Bonenti, Charles, "Publishing Your Novel in Minutes," *Berkshire Eagle* **(Massachusetts), March 8, 2008.**

The Espresso Book Machine automates virtually every aspect of book production.

Kitchen, Patricia, "Publish and Prosper?" *Orlando Sentinel*, **July 25, 2007, p. F1.**

An author writing a book about diabetes has decided to bypass traditional publishing routes and produce copies of her work via print-on-demand services.

Meyer, Ann, "Entrepreneurs Get Book Smart," *Chicago Tribune*, **June 9, 2008, p. C5.**

Self-publishing of books through print-on-demand services is an effective way for business owners to build credibility.

Reading Devices

Baig, Edward C., "iPod Touch, iPhone Join Kindle's Book Club," *USA Today*, **March 4, 2009, p. 3B.**

Apple's App Store is providing a free application that allows iPhone and iPod Touch users to read electronic books from Amazon that so far have only been compatible with the Amazon Kindle.

Nelson, Sara, "Sony Adds to Book Download Stockpile," *Los Angeles Times*, **March 19, 2009, p. B3.**

Sony has become the first major electronics company to offer a digital book device — the Sony Reader — telling customers half a million books optimized by Google will be available for download.

Stone, Brad, and Motoko Rich, "Amazon Unveils a Large-Screen Kindle Aimed at Textbooks and Newspapers," *The New York Times*, **May 7, 2009, p. B7.**

Amazon has introduced a larger version of its Kindle reading device, touting it as a new way to read traditionally large items such as school textbooks and newspapers.

Traditional Books

Burnett III, James H., "E-books Bringing New Power to the Printed Word," *Miami Herald*, **Nov. 15, 2008, p. A2.**

Traditional ink-on-paper books continue to dominate book fairs, but more and more readers are being tempted to read paperless electronic books on handheld devices.

Cuevas Jr., Andres, "Students Prefer Hard Copy," *State Hornet* **(California), Sept. 17, 2008.**

The majority of college students still prefer traditional hard-copy textbooks despite the growing popularity of electronic versions.

James, Andrea, "Books a Weighty Issue for Law Schools," *Seattle Post-Intelligencer*, **Sept. 11, 2008, p. E1.**

Representatives from law schools across the country are set to discuss the future of heavy bound textbooks in their courses.

Lekwa, Claire, "Books Not So 'E-easily' Accepted," *Daily Iowan*, **May 15, 2008.**

Traditional books are not likely to be eliminated despite the increasing popularity of electronic books.

CITING *CQ RESEARCHER*

Sample formats for citing these reports in a bibliography include the ones listed below. Preferred styles and formats vary, so please check with your instructor or professor.

MLA STYLE

Jost, Kenneth. "Rethinking the Death Penalty." CQ Researcher 16 Nov. 2001: 945-68.

APA STYLE

Jost, K. (2001, November 16). Rethinking the death penalty. *CQ Researcher, 11,* 945-968.

CHICAGO STYLE

Jost, Kenneth. "Rethinking the Death Penalty." *CQ Researcher,* November 16, 2001, 945-968.

In-depth Reports on Issues in the News

Are you writing a paper?

Need backup for a debate?

Want to become an expert on an issue?

For 80 years, students have turned to *CQ Researcher* for in-depth reporting on issues in the news. Reports on a full range of political and social issues are now available. Following is a selection of recent reports:

Civil Liberties
Closing Guantánamo, 2/09
Affirmative Action, 10/08
Gay Marriage Showdowns, 9/08
America's Border Fence, 9/08
Immigration Debate, 2/08

Crime/Law
Judicial Elections, 4/09
Mexico's Drug War, 12/08
Prostitution Debate, 5/08
Public Defenders, 4/08
Gun Violence, 5/07

Education
Reading Crisis? 2/08
Discipline in Schools, 2/08
Student Aid, 1/08
Racial Diversity in Public Schools, 9/07

Environment/Society
Hate Groups, 5/09
Future of Journalism, 3/09
Confronting Warming, 1/09
Reducing Carbon Footprint, 12/08
Protecting Wetlands, 10/08
Buying Green, 2/08

Health/Safety
Reproductive Ethics, 5/09
Extreme Sports, 4/09
Regulating Toxic Chemicals, 1/09
Preventing Cancer, 1/09
Heart Health, 9/08
Global Food Crisis, 6/08

Politics/Economy
Business Bankruptcy, 4/09
Future of the GOP, 3/09
Middle-Class Squeeze, 3/09
Public-Works Projects, 2/09

Upcoming Reports

Student Rights, 6/5/09   Drug Decriminalization, 6/12/09   Retirement Crisis, 6/19/09

ACCESS

CQ Researcher is available in print and online. For access, visit your library or www.cqresearcher.com.

STAY CURRENT

To receive notice of upcoming *CQ Researcher* reports, or learn more about *CQ Researcher* products, subscribe to the free e-mail newsletters, *CQ Researcher Alert!* and *CQ Researcher News*: http://cqpress.com/newsletters.

PURCHASE

To purchase a *CQ Researcher* report in print or electronic format (PDF), visit www.cqpress.com or call 866-427-7737. Single reports start at $15. Bulk purchase discounts and electronic-rights licensing are also available.

SUBSCRIBE

Annual full-service *CQ Researcher* subscriptions—including 44 reports a year, monthly index updates, and a bound volume—start at $803. Add $25 for domestic postage.

CQ Researcher Online offers a backfile from 1991 and a number of tools to simplify research. For pricing information, call 800-834-9020, ext. 1906, or e-mail librarysales@cqpress.com.

Published by CQ Press, a division of SAGE Publications

www.cqresearcher.com

Student Rights

Have courts gone too far or not far enough?

T he Supreme Court introduced a new era in public education in the United States in 1969 by declaring that students do not shed their constitutional rights at the schoolhouse gate. Four decades later, state and federal court dockets are dotted with suits by students or parents challenging disciplinary decisions and school policies and practices. The Supreme Court, which has upheld random drug testing of students, is currently considering whether an Arizona school district violated a teenaged girl's rights by strip-searching her because of what proved to be an unfounded accusation that she was carrying a prescription-strength pain reliever. Student-speech cases often pose difficult issues as administrators, principals and teachers seek to reconcile students' free-speech rights with the need to prevent disruption, maintain discipline and protect rights of teachers and other students. In recent years, judges appear to be giving more deference to schools — a trend applauded by many educators but criticized by student-rights advocates.

Savana Redding, 19, leaves the U.S. Supreme Court on April 21, 2009, after it considered whether Arizona school officials violated her constitutional rights when they strip-searched her for drugs when she was 13. A decision is expected at the end of June.

CQ Researcher • June 5, 2009 • www.cqresearcher.com
Volume 19, Number 21 • Pages 501-524

RECIPIENT OF SOCIETY OF PROFESSIONAL JOURNALISTS AWARD FOR
EXCELLENCE ◆ AMERICAN BAR ASSOCIATION SILVER GAVEL AWARD

Cover: Getty Images/Mark Wilson

CQ Researcher

June 5, 2009
Volume 19, Number 21

MANAGING EDITOR: Thomas J. Colin
tcolin@cqpress.com

ASSISTANT MANAGING EDITOR: Kathy Koch
kkoch@cqpress.com

ASSOCIATE EDITOR: Kenneth Jost

STAFF WRITERS: Thomas J. Billitteri,
Marcia Clemmitt, Peter Katel

CONTRIBUTING WRITERS: Rachel Cox,
Sarah Glazer, Alan Greenblatt,
Barbara Mantel, Patrick Marshall,
Tom Price, Jennifer Weeks

DESIGN/PRODUCTION EDITOR: Olu B. Davis

ASSISTANT EDITOR: Darrell Dela Rosa

FACT-CHECKING: Eugene J. Gabler,
Michelle Harris

CQ PRESS

A Division of SAGE

PRESIDENT AND PUBLISHER:
John A. Jenkins

EXECUTIVE DIRECTOR,
REFERENCE INFORMATION GROUP:
Alix B. Vance

CQ Press is a registered trademark of Congressional Quarterly Inc.

CQ Researcher (ISSN 1056-2036) is printed on acid-free paper. Published weekly, except; (Jan. wk. 1) (May wk. 4) (July wks. 1, 2) (Aug. wks. 3, 4) (Nov. wk. 4) and (Dec. wk. 4), by CQ Press, a division of SAGE Publications. Annual full-service subscriptions start at $803. For pricing, call 1-800-834-9020, ext. 1906. To purchase a *CQ Researcher* report in print or electronic format (PDF), visit www. cqpress.com or call 866-427-7737. Single reports start at $15. Bulk purchase discounts and electronic-rights licensing are also available. Periodicals postage paid at Washington, D.C., and additional mailing offices. POSTMASTER: Send address changes to *CQ Researcher*, 2300 N St., N.W., Suite 800, Washington, DC 20037.

Student Rights

BY KENNETH JOST

THE ISSUES

Savana Redding recalls it as "the most humiliating experience" of her life: the day she was forced to undress to her underwear at her school in Safford, Ariz., in what proved to be a fruitless strip-search for a prescription-strength pain reliever.

Authorities at Safford Middle School were on edge about drugs in fall 2003, partly because a year earlier a student had had a serious reaction to a prescription pill given to him by one of his schoolmates. So assistant principal Kerry Wilson reacted quickly on Oct. 8 when a student handed him what turned out to be a 400-mg ibuprofen tablet and told him the pills were being passed out for students to take at lunchtime.

The student's accusation led first to eighth-grader Marissa Glines, who was found to have several ibuprofen tablets in her wallet. Glines said she had gotten the pills from her classmate Redding. But when Wilson brought Redding to his office, she denied any knowledge of the pills.

A search of her backpack found nothing, but Wilson remained suspicious. He asked his administrative assistant Helen Romero to take Redding to the office of the school nurse, Peggy Schwallier, to look — as the school district's lawyers later put it — "for any pills that might be discreetly hidden in her clothes."

Redding, then 13, was directed first to remove her shoes and socks and then her shirt and pants. With nothing found, she was then told to shake the band on her bra and then the elastic on her underwear. Still nothing.

A supporter of the group Students for a Sensible Drug Policy demonstrates at the U.S. Supreme Court in March 2007 during arguments in the case of Alaska high-school student Joseph Frederick, who was suspended for displaying his "Bong Hits 4 Jesus" banner during a school-sponsored event off school grounds. In a 5-4 decision, the court upheld schools' power to punish students for advocating or promoting illegal drug use.

Redding was never touched, but, as she recalled later, she felt "violated" by the strip-search. Romero allowed her to get dressed and return to class, but the experience was so humiliating that Savana decided to transfer to another school. She says now she developed stomach ulcers as a result.

Nearly six years after the episode, Redding, now 19, sat before the nine justices of the U.S. Supreme Court on April 21 listening as they considered whether the strip-search violated her right under the Fourth Amendment to be free from "unreasonable" searches. [1]

In years past, Redding's grievance would have gone no further than the local school board — if she or her family had complained at all. But for the past 40 years, ever since a landmark Supreme Court decision, student-rights have been a staple on the dockets of state and federal courts up to and including the nation's highest tribunal.

The student-rights era began with a 1969 decision, *Tinker v. Des Moines*, that upheld the right of three middle- and high-school students to wear black armbands to signal their support for a Christmastime cease-fire in the Vietnam War. "It can hardly be argued," Justice Abe Fortas wrote, "that either students or teachers shed their constitutional rights to freedom of speech or expression at the schoolhouse gate." [2]

In the years since, "few realms of educational policy have escaped the courtroom," according to Frederick Hess, director of education policy studies at the American Enterprise Institute (AEI), a conservative think tank in Washington. The Supreme Court has established due process standards for student discipline and some limits on searches of students and their belongings. Today, lower courts are grappling with issues ranging from the free-speech rights of gay — and anti-gay — students and censorship of high-school newspapers to schools' efforts to police students' outside-school postings on the Internet. (*See sidebars, p. 506, p. 512, p. 516.*)

Four decades after *Tinker*, civil liberties advocates say the decision is one to celebrate. "The *Tinker* decision was a watershed moment," says Jamin Raskin, a professor at American University's Washington College of Law and editor of a book on student

'Students Are Entitled to Freedom of Expression'

The U.S. Supreme Court's landmark decision in Tinker v. Des Moines Independent Community School District *decision launched the student-rights era. The 7-2 ruling upheld the right of three middle- and high-school students to wear black armbands to signal their support for a Christmastime cease-fire in the Vietnam War.*

"School officials do not possess absolute authority over their students. . . . In the absence of a specific showing of constitutionally valid reasons to regulate their speech, students are entitled to freedom of expression of their views."

Justice Abe Fortas, Tinker v. Des Moines *(1969)*
(majority opinion)

"This case . . ., wholly without constitutional reasons in my judgment, subjects all the public schools in the country to the whims and caprices of their loudest-mouthed, but maybe not their brightest, students."

Justice Hugo L. Black, Tinker v. Des Moines *(1969)*
(dissenting opinion)

rights. "The Supreme Court essentially declared that education is about becoming a full-fledged citizen of democracy." [3]

"It seems a strange way to train children to be members of society to tell them that they have fewer rights than others," says Catherine Crump, a staff attorney in the First Amendment Working Group at the American Civil Liberties Union (ACLU). "That doesn't seem like a good way to turn kids into adults who are fully participating members of our democratic society."

Hess, who organized an AEI conference on education-related litigation in October 2008, agrees that recognition of student rights has had some benefits. "It's expected that adolescents will be more expressive," he says. "Bringing some of that into the school environment seems both inevitable and constructive."

On balance, however, Hess says the net impact of student rights has been "a substantial negative." The movement, he says, "has significantly curtailed the ability of educational leaders and classroom teachers to set expectations, enforce discipline or aggressively shape a school culture that is conducive to teaching and learning." [4]

Richard Arum, a professor of sociology at New York University, agrees. "The expansion of students' legal entitlements has not only had unintended consequences on the capacity of schools to socialize youth effectively," Arum writes, "but it has also increased the potential for student dissent in U.S. schools — whether of a political, religious or other ideological character." [5]

Without overruling *Tinker*, the Supreme Court has seemed more and more sympathetic to school administrators' concerns since the 1980s. In a

pair of rulings under Chief Justice William H. Rehnquist, the court approved random drug testing for many high school students. And under current Chief Justice John G. Roberts Jr., the court in 2007 ruled that public schools can punish students for advocating or promoting illegal drug use. [6]

Representing Redding before the Supreme Court, Adam Wolf, of the ACLU's Drug Law Reform Project, acknowledges public concern about drug use by students. "We all want our schools to be safe and to be drug-free, but that does not give schools carte blanche to do anything they want," Wolf says. "Some policies just clearly cross the line and unreasonably invade student privacy."

But Matthew Wright, the Phoenix lawyer representing the school district, urged the justices to give schools flexibility in dealing with students suspected of using or distributing drugs. Schools are "in the untenable position of either facing the threat of lawsuits for their attempts to enforce a drug-free policy or for their laxity in failing to interdict potentially harmful drugs," Wright said in a statement prior to argument. [7]

As the justices deliberate over the strip-search case, here are some of the broad questions about student rights being debated by educators, parents and students themselves:

Do schools' anti-drug enforcement policies violate students' rights?

Parents in the small north Texas town of Lockney raised alarms in fall 1998 when authorities indicted 11 people for cocaine dealing. Even though none of the suspects was a student, the Lockney school board responded by instituting a program of mandatory drug testing for students in grades six through 12.

Out of 400 families, Larry and Traci Tannahill were the only parents to object to the testing program. On behalf of their then 12-year-old son Bradley, they sued the school district in federal court in Lubbock and won a court ruling in March 2001 barring the program as an unconstitutional invasion of students' rights against unreasonable searches. Judge Sam Cummings ruled the district had shown no special need for what he called an "intrusive" policy. [8]

Drug testing is one of the flash points between public school educators on one hand and student-rights advocates on the other. In Lockney, school officials — on advice of counsel — decided not to appeal the ruling. Instead, they trimmed the testing policy to apply only to students engaged in extracurricular activities. A year later, the U.S. Supreme Court upheld a similar drug testing policy adopted by a school district in Oklahoma. [9]

School officials say random testing helps deter drug use among students and amounts to only a minimal invasion of students' privacy. Anne Proffitt Dupre, a professor at the University of Georgia School of Law in Athens, says the Supreme Court decision validates the argument. "The Supreme Court has said that we can take judicial notice that we have a serious drug problem in our schools and that we can test students in that regard," she says.

The Supreme Court has never ruled on the constitutionality of schoolwide drug testing, but ACLU lawyer Wolf thinks the justices would strike down an unlimited policy. "When a school district tries to analyze the bodily fluids of any and all students, that violates the Constitution," he says.

Opponents add that the limited drug testing program is counterproductive because it may discourage some students from participating in extracurricular activities. "The best way to keep a kid from having a substance abuse problem is to keep them occupied [after school]," says Kris Krane, executive director of Students for Sensible Drug Policy. "If they're unsupervised and unoccupied, they're

Student Speech Cannot Promote Illegal Drug Use

The Supreme Court's 5-4 decision in Morse v. Frederick *(2007) upheld schools' power to punish students for advocating or promoting illegal drug use. Joseph Frederick, a high school student in Alaska, had been suspended for displaying off school grounds a banner reading "Bong Hits 4 Jesus."*

"The question thus becomes whether a principal may, consistent with the First Amendment, restrict student speech at a school event, when that speech is reasonably viewed as promoting illegal drug use. We hold that she may."

Chief Justice John G. Roberts Jr., Morse v. Frederick
(majority opinion)

"[T]he Court's ham-handed, categorical approach is deaf to the constitutional imperative to permit unfettered debate, even among high-school students, about the wisdom of the war on drugs or of legalizing marijuana for medicinal use."

Justice John Paul Stevens, Morse v. Frederick
(dissenting opinion)

much more likely to get involved in substance abuse."

Krane also criticizes the zero-tolerance policies adopted in many school districts — policies that in some cases prescribe suspensions for seemingly minor drug-related violations. [10] "Zero-tolerance policies break down trust between students and their superiors at schools," says Krane, who joined the 10-year-old organization in 2006 after having previously worked with the National Organization for the Reform of Marijuana Laws (NORML). The policies, he says, "discourage students from talking with teachers, principals, guidance counselors."

"Some local communities prefer zero-tolerance policies, some do not," says Francisco Negron, general counsel of the National School Boards Association. "What is clear is that schools

need to have a tool to ensure the safety of their kids."

Many experts, however, think schools go too far with their anti-drug policies. "I can understand why schools would adopt some policies to try to prevent dangerous activities," says Joshua Dunn, an assistant professor of political science at the University of Colorado in Colorado Springs. "But when you hear about students being suspended for bringing in [some non-prescription medication], that sort of thing is excessive."

An official with the National Association of Secondary School Principals agrees. "Zero-tolerance policies need to be administered with good judgment," says Richard Flanary, senior director for leadership programs and services for the Reston, Va.-based association. "There are some documented cases where that has not been the case."

Are Students' Critical Blog Comments Protected?

Student-rights advocates and school administrators disagree.

Avery Doninger called Burlington, Conn., school administrators "douchebags" in a blog posting and urged readers to complain to the school superintendent. Katherine Evans created a Facebook page calling her English teacher in Pembroke Pines, Fla., "one of the worst teachers I've ever had" and invited other students to share their "hatred" of her on the page.

Both students ended up being punished for their Internet speech even though they wrote the postings off school campuses. Doninger was barred from serving on the student council, Evans suspended for three days and pulled out of honors classes. And both went to federal court, claiming that the disciplinary actions — even if relatively mild — violated their right to free speech.

The Internet had not been invented in 1969 when the Supreme Court issued its landmark decision in *Tinker v. Des Moines* protecting students' free-speech rights unless they disrupted the school or interfered with the rights of others. It was still in its infancy in the 1980s when the court narrowed students' rights by upholding educators' power to punish vulgar speech or to censor student newspapers that were part of the school curriculum.

Today, the Internet age has spawned social-networking sites such as Facebook and MySpace, which are especially popular among high-school students as forums for, among many other things, unfiltered news and comment about school life. And students' use of the sites has forced courts to reconsider the prior assumption that any power to punish student speech ended once students were past the schoolhouse gate.

School administrators say schools not only can but must punish disruptive Internet speech by students. "When there is an impact on the school environment, then I think the school has an obligation to act," says Francisco Negrón, general counsel of the National School Boards Association.

Student-rights advocates disagree. "Students cannot be punished for posting comments online from their home computers criticizing their teachers," says Maria Kayanan, associate legal director of the American Civil Liberties Union of Florida, which is representing Evans in her suit. "Absent a credible threat of harm, criticism is protected by the First Amendment."

Evans was a senior at Pembroke Pines Charter High School in November 2007 when she vented on Facebook about her English teacher, Sarah Phelps. The page drew favorable and unfavorable comments about Phelps until Evans removed it after three days. Evans, now a freshman at the University of Florida, sued to have the disciplinary record removed. She is seeking attorneys' fees but no damages.

City officials in Pembroke Pines have declined to comment on the pending litigation, but school officials in Broward County have generally defended the punishment. "When you start inviting people to say that they hate a teacher, that crosses the line," Pamela Brown, assistant director for the Broward County School District, told *The New York Times*. Pembroke Pines is in Broward County (Fort Lauderdale) and uses the Broward County disciplinary guidelines. [1]

Other experts, however, say that educators deserve more support because of the difficulties they face in dealing with student drug use. "We don't realize what an impossible situation we put teachers and principals in," says the AEI's Hess. "If there are drugs in school, the public is going to come down hard on the schools for not doing enough to prevent drugs in the schools."

Despite that view, Hess says he considers the strip-search in Redding's case to have been "inappropriate." Flanary is similarly critical. "I could never envision doing a strip-search of a student under those circumstances," says Flanary, who was a middle-school principal in Virginia for 12 years before assuming his current post.

School boards association counsel Negrón disagrees. "The principal acted in a way that was very measured," he says. "It was done in a way to protect the integrity of the student."

Do schools improperly limit students' free-speech rights?

The dress code at Waxahachie High School, in suburban Dallas, proscribed all-black outfits and T-shirts with any writing other than school- or college-related insignia. So Paul "Pete" Palmer knew on the morning of Sept. 21, 2007, that he was pushing the envelope when — after being admonished for wearing all black — he accepted his father's suggestion to wear an "Edwards '08" T-shirt instead.

But the Edwards T-shirt did not pass muster either, and Palmer, then 15, was kept out of class until his mother brought an acceptable shirt. A month later, Palmer's attorney father filed a federal court suit on his son's behalf, challenging the school's dress code as a violation of student-speech rights guaranteed by the Supreme Court's landmark 1969 *Tinker* decision.

In her ruling, however, U.S. District Judge Barbara Lynn upheld the dress code, applying a lesser standard from another Supreme Court decision that allows some restrictions on speech if they further a substantial government interest, such as maintaining discipline. Lawyers for Liberty Legal Institute, a pro-Christian public-interest law firm representing Palmer,

Doninger was a junior at Lewis S. Mills High School in Burlington in spring 2007 when she fumed online about school administrators' decision to cancel a planned student festival. The school responded by barring Doninger from running for reelection as class secretary.

Opposing lawyers in her case take different views of the legal import of the new medium. Thomas R. Gerarde, who represents school officials, says that the online posting amounts to "the student talking to a full audience of the student body because he or she can reach every one of those students." But Jon L. Schoenhorn, Doninger's attorney, counters that the Internet is nothing more than "a bigger soapbox." [2]

Two lower courts sided with the school district. In its decision in May 2008, the Second U.S. Circuit Court of Appeals held that Doninger's posting could be punished because it "created a foreseeable risk of substantial disruption" at her school.

That decision appears to conflict somewhat with a ruling by a federal judge in Pittsburgh in 2007 that nullified a school's punishment of a student for an online parody of the school's principal. "The mere fact that the Internet may be accessed at school

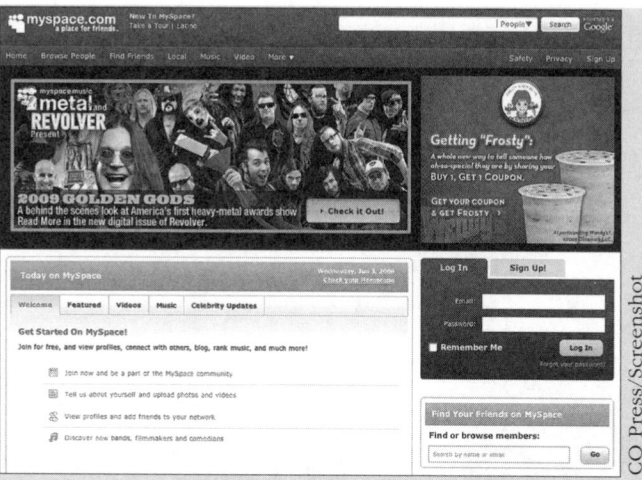

CQ Press/Screenshot

Students' use of social-networking sites such as MySpace has forced courts to reconsider the prior assumption that schools' power to punish student speech ended at the schoolhouse gate.

does not authorize school officials to become censors of the world-wide web," U.S. District Judge Terrence F. McVerry wrote. [3]

Experts appear to be as divided on the subject as judges. "If it affects what's going on in the school classroom, I think we would say that [schools] would be remiss if they didn't step in," says Anne Proffitt Dupre, a professor at the University of Georgia School of Law in Athens. But Jamin Raskin, a professor at American University's Washington College of Law, says school administrators are waging an impossible fight. "Censorship never works," Raskin says, "and it especially doesn't work in the age of the Internet."

[1] Quoted in Carmen Gentile, "Student Fights Record of 'Cyberbullying,' " *The New York Times*, Feb. 8, 2009, p. A20. See also Jennifer Moody Piedra, "Student, suspended for blog rant, sues," *The Miami Herald*, Dec. 10, 2008, p. A1. The case is *Evans v. Bayer*, 08-CV61952 (S.D. Fla.); the complaint is on the ACLU-Florida Web site: www.aclufl.org/news_events/?action=view Release&emailAlertID=3689.

[2] Quoted in Arielle Levin Becker, "Web Speech: When May Schools Act?" *The Hartford Courant*, Feb. 1, 2009, p. A1. Some other background also drawn from story. The decision is *Doninger v. Niehoff*, 527 F.3d 41 (2nd Cir. 2008).

[3] The decision is *Layshock v. Hermitage School Dist.*, 496 F.Supp 2d 587 (W.D. Pa. 2007).

are now preparing to challenge the decision before the federal appeals court in New Orleans. [11]

The case exemplifies the continuing disputes over student speech despite the *Tinker* decision. A range of student-speech advocacy groups, including both traditional civil liberties organizations and more recently established religious-rights groups, continue to pepper federal and state courts with suits challenging school administrators' restrictions on students' expression.

Lawyers with those groups say courts are increasingly inclined to side with educators and against students in those cases. "It's hard to feel optimistic about where student free-speech rights are going in this country," says the ACLU's Crump. David Cortman, a lawyer with the pro-Christian Alliance Defense Fund, agrees that free speech for students is in jeopardy. "It's our concern that that right is slowly, and I would say rather quickly, being eviscerated by the courts," he says.

Some educators and experts, however, applaud what they see as the courts' evolving recognition of schools' need to limit speech that distracts from students' learning. "Adults in school settings are operating *in loco parentis* [in the place of parents]," says the AEI's Hess. "They're responsible as stewards for students for seven to eight hours per day" throughout the school year.

In its most recent decision, the Supreme Court in 2007 upheld a high-school principal's decision in Juneau, Alaska, to suspend a student for displaying a banner — "Bong Hits for Jesus" — that she interpreted as promoting the use of illegal drugs. [12] In arguments before the court, lawyers for the school district argued for a broad standard to permit restrictions on any speech inconsistent with a school's "educational mission." In a pivotal concurring opinion in the case, however, Justice Samuel A. Alito Jr. said such a sweeping standard would have given school officials too much discretion to limit student speech.

Crump says the court's decision has eroded student rights, but some experts disagree. "I don't think the right of students to freedom of expression

To Bong or Not to Bong

Joseph Frederick (above), a student at Juneau-Douglas High School in Alaska, was given a 10-day suspension for displaying his "Bong Hits 4 Jesus" banner on Jan. 24, 2002 (top). In a 5-4 decision in 2007, the Supreme Court upheld schools' power to punish students for advocating or promoting illegal drug use.

www.juneauempire.com

has been fundamentally altered," says New York University's Arum. The most recent ruling, he says, "was not a fundamental change in the right of political expression."

Dupre, at the University of Georgia School of Law, says, however, that the decision has not resolved uncertainty about student-speech rights in the lower courts. "The courts are reeling from one side to another," says Dupre, author of a recent book on student-rights litigation. "There is no standard that seems to give guidance in many of these situations." [13]

Dress codes are one of the difficult-to-chart areas, even though the *Tinker* decision upheld students' right to wear a political symbol — specifically, black armbands to protest the Vietnam War. Among the recent court cases is one from the federal appeals court in St. Louis rejecting an Arkansas school's decision to discipline students for wearing black armbands to protest the school's uniform policy. [14]

"Most schools do have dress codes," says Flanary at the principals' group. As in Waxahachie, the codes are aimed in part at barring "pictures or slogans that are provocative, offensive, sexual or suggestive in nature, vulgar, lewd or obscene." A post-*Tinker* decision by the Supreme Court upholds school authorities' power to punish sexually suggestive speech. [15]

Flanary says students' actions testing the dress codes are "inevitable," but can be minimized by developing the codes in collaboration with students and with using "good judgment" in dealing with exceptions. And he says teaching about student rights is part of a school's responsibility. "We educate kids to thrive in the real world," he says. "We have to be mindful of the world in which they live, and that is a part of it."

Do schools improperly limit students' religious freedoms?

Fifth-grader Joel Curry made candy-cane-style Christmas ornaments for a classroom project at Handley Elementary School in Saginaw, Mich., in December 2003. At his father's suggestion, Joel attached a card to the ornaments linking the candy cane to the story of Jesus. After consulting with an assistant superintendent, however, the school's principal, Irene Hensinger, decided that Joel could not use religious items as part of the classroom exercise.

With the religious messages removed, Joel received an A for the assignment. Even so, his parents filed a federal court suit on his behalf, saying that the school's actions violated Joel's freedom of religious speech. In January 2008, the federal appeals court in Cincinnati rejected Paul and Melanie Curry's suit, saying the school had "legitimate pedagogical concerns" for barring the religious-themed messages from the classroom project. [16]

The episode illustrates what Alliance Defense Fund (ADF) attorney Cortman calls "an increasing hostility toward religious speech in public schools." (Other attorneys from the group represented the Currys in the case.) "It seems they have an allergic reaction any time that religious speech occurs in the public-school setting even if it's engaged in by the student," Cortman says.

Church-state separation advocates, on the other hand, worry that some schools run afoul of Supreme Court decisions that bar any officially sponsored religious activities. "There are schools where there are regular invitations to outside clergy to come to schools to talk to students or where there are what appear to be officially sanctioned prayers," says Barry Lynn, executive director of Americans United for Separation of Church and State. A primer from the American Jewish Congress criticizes schools that invite "para-church groups" [17]

For his part, school boards association counsel Negrón says schools generally respect student rights while steering clear of giving any official imprimatur

Avery Doninger was a high-school junior in Burlington, Conn., when she blogged that school administrators were "douchebags" for canceling a planned student festival. The school responded by barring Doninger from running for reelection as class secretary. In May 2008, the Second U.S. Circuit Court of Appeals said Doninger could be punished because her posting "created a foreseeable risk of substantial disruption" at her school.

http://granby01033.blogspot.com

to religious activities. "Schools are aware that students have the right to engage in religious expression as long as it's done in an appropriate way under the school's rules," he says.

The difficulties in the area stem from Supreme Court decisions dating from the early 1960s that prohibit school-sponsored religious exercises ranging from classroom prayers or Bible reading to officially organized prayers at graduation ceremonies or athletic contests. The schools' role in organizing or sponsoring the religious exercises runs

afoul of the First Amendment's Establishment Clause, which prohibits government action amounting to "establishment" of religion. [18]

A separate line of decisions, however, also limits school officials' discretion to exclude religious speech in situations where other forms of speech are allowed. Pro-Christian law firms such as ADF and Liberty Legal have aggressively used these free-speech rulings in support of students seeking to distribute religious materials at schools. But some school administrators fear religious solicitations can raise legal concerns, distract from classwork and offend or intimidate students of other faiths and non-believers.

The seemingly conflicting court decisions and the opposing points of view leave principals with "some uncertainty as to what they can and can't do," according to the University of Colorado's Dunn. "They legitimately live in legal fear of antagonizing one side or the other," he says.

Congress acted to strengthen religious rights in one area with the 1984 Equal Access Act, requiring any federally funded schools to allow student religious clubs to meet outside classroom time on the same basis as other extracurricular organizations. Cortman says the law is clear, but disputes continue. "We still to this day are getting cases denying equal access to religious groups, including pro-life groups," Cortman says. "We obviously win all of those cases, but it's extremely surprising that we have to bring them at all." [19]

Marc D. Stern, acting co-executive director of the American Jewish Congress, says the group had misgivings that the law would lead to active proselytizing of non-Christian pupils. But he says those fears have not come to pass. "The courts have reached a fairly good balance on what constitutes state-endorsed religious speech in schools and what's private speech," he says.

Stern says he has little concern about Christian messages attached to Christmas candy canes or Valentine's Day cards, but Lynn is "skeptical" of the practice, especially in elementary schools. He says teachers' involvement in holiday observances risks creating "an appearance of favoritism."

The AEI's Hess calls existing law "reasonably workable" but thinks religion has been unduly marginalized. "I worry that we try to enforce education and discipline while we divorce these from the Judeo-Christian traditions or Islamic tradition," he says. "I worry that it's destructive of the ability to develop really effective, culturally powerful schools."

"Tolerance and respect are sometimes hard to come by when these issues arise," says Flanary of the principals' association. "Trying to find that common ground is important." ∎

BACKGROUND

Schools' Missions

For much of U.S. history, public-school students were expected to be seen but not heard from. The schools' prescribed curricula and strict discipline left students only limited room to shape their educational experiences. Progressive reforms in education beginning in the early 20th century placed greater emphasis on students' self-expression. Around the same time, courts began to intervene in some educational policy disputes.

Only in the 1960s and '70s, however, did the Supreme Court recognize affirmative free-speech rights and due process protections for students in public schools. [20]

The public-school system that began to evolve in the early 19th century inherited from English common law the view that schools acted *in loco parentis* ("in the place of parents"), with all the authority over students in school that parents held over them outside the school. Courts gave teachers and principals a wide berth. In a Vermont case, for example, the court in 1859 found no fault with administering corporal punishment to a student who used a mocking nickname for his teacher. The teacher's power to punish disruptive speech, the court wrote, was "essential to the preservation of order, decency, decorum and good government in schools." Later 19th-century cases similarly upheld punishments for profane or disruptive comments and even a student's warning about unsafe conditions at the school. [21]

The progressive movement in education associated with the American philosopher John Dewey questioned schools' authoritarian approach to learning and discipline and gave students a more active role in their education. Overly rigid discipline, Dewey wrote in 1916, served "to cow the spirit, to subdue inclination" and to "increase indifference and aversion" to schools. [22] As the progressive movement advanced, public schools also found themselves embroiled in court cases challenging policies given to them under state laws. In 1923, for example, the Supreme Court invalidated a Nebraska law that forbade the teaching of foreign languages in public schools before the eighth grade. The law interfered with the rights of both teachers and parents, the court said. Two decades later, the court struck down on free-speech grounds a West Virginia law requiring teachers and students to salute the flag and recite the Pledge of Allegiance

each day. The law impinged on "intellectual individualism" and "cultural diversities," the court explained. [23]

In a more dramatic intervention, the Supreme Court in 1954 outlawed the then prevalent practice of racial segregation in public schools. The court's historic ruling in *Brown v. Board of Education* capped a decades-long campaign by African-American students and families coordinated nationwide by the NAACP and its legal arm, the NAACP Legal Defense and Educational Fund. The ruling marked the beginning of decades of still continuing judicial supervision of efforts to promote racial diversity and equality in public schools. It also served to validate a litigation model for other students, families and groups to use in challenging school policies or decisions. [24]

The court opened the door to student-speech lawsuits with its 1969 ruling in the *Tinker* case. Three teenaged students in Des Moines — Christopher Eckhardt and John and Mary Beth Tinker — had been suspended for wearing black armbands to their schools in December 1965 to protest the government's policy in Vietnam. The school board, which learned of the plans beforehand, had issued an edict prohibiting the symbolic protest. In a ruling in September 1966, U.S. District Judge Roy Stephenson said the school board's authority to maintain order outweighed any free-speech rights the students might enjoy. The Supreme Court, however, disagreed. In the majority opinion, Fortas said schools could censor student speech only to prevent "substantial disruption" or to protect the rights of other students. In an angry dissent, Justice Hugo L. Black said the ruling "ushers in . . . an entirely new era in which the power to control pupils . . . is . . . transferred to the Supreme Court." [25]

In a lesser known but arguably more important ruling, the court effectively

Continued on p. 512

Chronology

Before 1960
Student rights unrecognized in 19th century; Supreme Court enters field in 20th century.

1960s-1970s
Supreme Court recognizes students' rights to free speech, due process.

1969
Supreme Court overturns disciplinary actions against three students for wearing black armbands to protest Vietnam War; 7-2 ruling in *Tinker v. Des Moines* permits restrictions on speech only to prevent disruption or protect rights of others.

1972
Title IX prohibits discrimination based on sex in schools receiving federal funds.

1975
Supreme Court says schools must provide some procedural rights before disciplining students; 5-4 ruling in *Goss v. Lopez* requires notice of charge, explanation of evidence, opportunity to respond.

1977
California passes law protecting student journalists' freedom of expression; seven other states have similar laws by 2009, but California's remains broadest.

1980s-1990s
Supreme Court backs schools on anti-drug policies; drugs, violence in schools lead to "zero tolerance" policies.

1984
Equal Access Act requires schools to give equal access to facilities for extracurricular groups, including religious clubs; Supreme Court upholds law in 1990, expands reach in 2001.

1985
Schools can search student lockers, Supreme Court rules.

1986
Schools can punish "vulgar" speech, Supreme Court rules.

1988
Schools can censor student newspapers if part of the school's curriculum, Supreme Court rules; decision prompts more states to pass student-press rights statutes. . . . First gay-straight alliance established at private Concord Academy in Massachussetts; by 2009, more than 4,000 such clubs are in schools.

1994
Gun Free Schools Act requires one-year suspension of any student found with a firearm.

1995
Supreme Court rules, 6-3, that schools may require random, suspicionless drug testing of student athletes.

Late 1990s
Many school districts adopt zero-tolerance policies requiring discipline of students even for minor drug violations or other misconduct.

1999
Twelve students, one teacher killed in shooting at Columbine High School in Colorado; student shooters commit suicide at scene.

2000-Present
Bush administration pushes accountability, school choice; Supreme Court backs vouchers, limits racial diversity policies.

2001
President George W. Bush pushes No Child Left Behind Act through Congress; law requires schools to raise student performance, sets financial penalties for "failing" schools.

2002
Supreme Court permits schools to require random drug testing for all students engaged in extracurricular activities. . . . Justices uphold school vouchers; challengers said aid to parochial students violated separation of church and state.

2006
U.S. Department of Education modifies sex discrimination rules to permit school districts to establish single-sex classes, schools. . . . Federal appeals court upholds ban on student's anti-gay T-shirt; Supreme Court erases ruling in 2007.

2007
Supreme Court rules, 5-4, that schools can punish students for advocating or promoting illegal drug use. . . . Justices also vote 5-4 to limit school districts' racial diversity policies; race-based pupil assignments held to violate equal protection principles. . . . School districts in Connecticut, Florida punish students for postings on social networking sites; court rulings on issue in conflict.

2009
Supreme Court weighs drug enforcement, student rights in Arizona strip-search case; ruling due by end of June.

Student Articles on 'Hooking Up' Lead to Crackdown

Flap reflects tenuous state of students' free-press rights.

The Jan. 30 issue of *The Statesman*, the student newspaper at Adlai Stevenson High School in Lincolnshire, Ill., flew off the lunchroom and hallway tables.

The sudden interest among the school's 4,600 students was easy to explain. A two-page inside spread examined "hooking up," complete with first-person accounts and an hour-by-hour timeline for how to score in today's dating scene.

"A lot more kids were reading the paper," recalls Jamie Hausman, a graduating senior and the paper's design editor. "They were excited about it."

Parents and school administrators, on the other hand, were less than thrilled. Jim Conrey, director of public information at the suburban Chicago school, faults the articles for having no interviews with students in favor of abstinence or with any of the school's health-education teachers. As for the timeline, Conrey, a former journalist, calls it "a how-to guide for a sexual predator." [1]

Controversy about the issue flared at a packed school board meeting. *The Chicago Tribune* weighed in with a favorable editorial, while the Illinois Family Institute countered that sex should be off-limits for a school newspaper.

Now, the flap has resulted in a new policy requiring pre-publication review by the director of the communications arts program and other administrators and the resignation of the newspaper's longtime adviser, Barbara Thill. She will continue to teach English but not journalism at the school.

Conrey says the new policy brings the newspaper in line with the collaborative philosophy of the rest of the curriculum. But Evan Ribot, a copy editor, said the policy has resulted in more "trepidation" and less time for reporting, editing and layout. [2]

The episode illustrates the tenuous state of free-press rights for journalists in public high schools. In the governing decision, the Supreme Court in 1988 upheld the power of school administrators to censor student newspapers if they were part of the school's curriculum. "A school must be able to set high standards for the student speech that is disseminated under its auspices," Justice Byron R. White wrote for the 5-3 majority in *Hazelwood School District v. Kuhlmeier.* [3]

The impact of the ruling has been weakened somewhat by laws on the books in seven states that generally give newspaper editors at high schools and public colleges the final say on editorial content. In California — the first state to adopt such a law — a court has gone so far as to say that a principal improperly intimidated a student author by post-publication criticism of a column he had written opposing immigration. [4]

But Frank LoMonte, a lawyer and executive director of the Student Press Law Center, says school administrators "are taking full advantage of the latitude" they have under *Hazelwood* to control the content of student newspapers. "Any kind of content that might cause the principal's phone to ring with complaints is too disruptive to be published," he says.

At Stevenson, Conrey insists the school administration is merely trying to instill professional journalistic standards at the student newspaper. He notes, for example, that the newspaper sought to conceal the identity of students interviewed by using only their first names, but that some of them were easily identifiable anyway. He also says the administration had previously complained about a story concerning a student's later-disavowed claim to be selling drugs at the school.

"The writing was on the wall," Hausman acknowledges. She agrees that the date timeline may have gone too far, but generally defends the rest of the issue as informative for students and parents alike. "Our parents' generation was so different from ours," says Hausman, who plans to study journalism at the University of Missouri beginning in the fall. "We decided to explore that a little bit."

"There's no doubt that it raised the level of discussion about the topic," replies Conrey. "It's good in the aggregate, but just because you talk about something doesn't make it a valid discussion."

---

[1] For background, see Jane Friedman, "Teen Sex," *CQ Researcher*, Sept. 16, 2005, pp. 761-784; and Kathy Koch, "Encouraging Teen Abstinence," *CQ Researcher*, July 10, 1998, pp. 577-600.

[2] Quoted in "School paper loses adviser over sex edition," Chicago Breaking News Center, April 1, 2009. See also "Stevenson High School adviser resigns position after prior review policy enforced," Student Press Law Center, April 21, 2009.

[3] The citation is 484 U.S. 260 (1988). For background, see Susan Phillips, "Student Journalism," *CQ Researcher*, June 5, 1998.

[4] The decision is *Smith v. Novato Unified School Dist.*, 150 Cal.App.4th 1439 (Cal. Ct. App. 2007), cited in Frank D. LoMonte, "Student Journalism Confronts a New Generation of Legal Challenges," *Human Rights*, Vol. 35, No. 3 (summer 2008).

Continued from p. 510

established minimal procedural rights for students nationwide before any disciplinary suspension, even for as little as one day. The 5-4 decision in *Goss v. Lopez* (1975) invalidated an Ohio law permitting suspensions of up to 10 days without any hearing. Instead, Justice Byron R. White wrote, school authorities must give a student "oral or written notice of the charges," "an explanation of the evidence" and "an opportunity to present his side of the story." The "rudimentary precautions," White said, were "less than a fair-minded school principal" would adopt. In dissent, Justice Lewis F. Powell Jr., a former school board president, called the decision "an unprecedented intrusion into the process of elementary and secondary education." [26]

Continued from p. 510

Schools' Concerns

The Supreme Court's solicitude for student rights began with *Tinker* and peaked with *Goss*. Beginning in the 1980s, the justices evinced greater concerns for the difficulties that educators faced on such issues as drugs, sex and offensive or hate speech. Major Supreme Court decisions in the decade upheld schools' anti-drug policies and narrowed protections for student speech. The trend continued in the 1990s, even as many school districts adopted zero-tolerance policies that called for disciplining students even for minor infractions.

In the first of the rulings, the court in *New Jersey v. T.L.O.* (1985) extended Fourth Amendment protections to students with one hand but narrowed them with the other. [27] A teenaged student in Piscataway, N.J., who had been caught smoking cigarettes with a classmate, challenged the principal's subsequent search of her purse, which uncovered marijuana. The court upheld the search in a 6-3 decision. Instead of applying the traditional probable-cause requirement, Justice White said that accommodating "the substantial need of teachers and administrators for freedom to maintain order in the schools" called for permitting searches of students and their belongings based on "the reasonableness" of the search "under all the circumstances."

A year later, the court invoked *Tinker*'s exception for "disruptive" speech to significantly narrow protections for students. Matthew Fraser, a high school student in Washington state, had been suspended for three days and barred from election as commencement speaker after using what the court called "an explicit, graphic sexual metaphor" in a nominating speech for a student council candidate. The court's 7-2 decision in *Bethel School Dist. No. 403 v. Fraser* (1986) upheld the school's power to discipline students for comments "disruptive to the educational process."

As Chief Justice Warren E. Burger explained, "It is a highly appropriate function of public-school education to prohibit the use of vulgar and offensive terms in public discourse." [28]

Two years later, high-school journalists suffered a setback when the court upheld school administrators' power to censor student newspapers, at least when the newspapers were part of the school's curriculum. The 5-3 decision in *Hazelwood School District v. Kuhlmeier* (1988) upheld the decision by a principal in a suburban St. Louis high school to delete two pages of a student newspaper because of articles dealing with teenage pregnancy and divorce. [29] For the majority, White treated the school-financed newspaper as part of the school's curriculum and found no obligation to allow students to publish articles that conflicted with the school's "legitimate pedagogical goals." Citing *Tinker*, dissenting justices said the articles should have been allowed because they did not disrupt classwork or invade the rights of other students.

Meanwhile, however, Congress had strengthened the rights of student organizations to use school facilities outside class hours. Religious groups originally pushed what became the Equal Access Act of 1984 in response to actions by school administrators and rulings by some federal and state courts preventing student Bible clubs from meeting on campus. The final bill applied more broadly to require equal access for any voluntary extracurricular group. The Supreme Court in 1990 voted 8-1 to uphold the law as constitutional. [30] The immediate impact was to give a green light to Christian student groups, but over time the act was also used to force some reluctant school administrators to allow students to form gay-straight alliances — or, in some instances, to disband extracurricular clubs altogether to prevent them.

Student rights receded as an issue in the 1990s as educators and the public alike grew increasingly concerned about such behavioral issues

Mary Beth Tinker and her brother John were suspended from classes at North High School in Des Moines, Iowa, in 1965 along with three other students for wearing black armbands to mourn Vietnam War dead. In 1969 the Supreme Court upheld a suit filed by the Tinkers and a third student, Christopher Eckhardt, arguing they had a right to display such political symbols. "It can hardly be argued," Justice Abe Fortas wrote, "that either students or teachers shed their constitutional rights to freedom of speech or expression at the schoolhouse gate."

as violence, drugs, gang activity and bullying. [31] Zero-tolerance policies prescribed mandatory discipline for various offenses, often with little regard for the severity of the misconduct. A federal law passed in 1994 required a one-year suspension for any student found in possession of a firearm on campus. Security and discipline codes were tightened nationwide after the deadly shootings at Columbine High School in Colorado in 1999 when two heavily armed students killed 12 students and one teacher before committing suicide themselves.

The get-tough atmosphere also gave birth to drug-testing policies that a handful of school districts adopted to try to detect students using illegal drugs. Twice, the Supreme Court upheld the policies against claims that random, suspicionless testing violated students' Fourth Amendment rights against unreasonable searches. In the first ruling, the justices in 1995 voted 6-3 to uphold an Oregon school district's policy requiring random drug testing of all student athletes. For the majority, Justice Antonin Scalia said schools' interest in protecting athletes' safety and deterring drug use among perceived role models outweighed the "negligible" impact on privacy. Seven years later, the court in 2002 voted 5-4 in an Oklahoma case to extend the rationale to permit drug testing of students in any extracurricular activity. Despite the rulings, there appeared to be no rush by school districts across the nation to institute drug testing. [32]

Standards and Choice

Under President George W. Bush, the federal government put its weight behind a view of student rights embodied in standards-based accountability for schools and enrollment choices for students and families dissatisfied with individual schools. The No Child Left Behind Act required an-

High-school students Lindsay Earls and Daniel James of Tecumseh, Okla., sued in 1999 to overturn their school's policy of mandatory drug testing for students participating in extracurricular activities. Two Supreme Court rulings in 1995 and 2002 approved random drug testing for many high-school students.

Getty Images/Jerry Laizure

nual standardized testing of public school students and gave students the right to transfer out of "non-performing" schools. The administration joined school-choice advocates in winning a pivotal Supreme Court decision upholding the constitutionality of publicly funded vouchers for students to attend private, including religious, schools. Later, Bush's two appointees to the Supreme Court provided critical votes for a ruling somewhat limiting student-speech rights and a separate decision limiting school districts' ability to engineer racial diversity in enrollment.

Bush pushed No Child Left Behind through Congress in his first months in office in 2001. [33] The law — which came to be known in educational circles as the pronounceable acronym "nicklebee" — requires school districts receiving federal funds to raise performance levels for students, especially minority or other disadvantaged students. Schools that fail to meet the standards must provide students transfers, tutoring or other supplementary services and face the threat of "restructuring" or closure. Passed with wide bipartisan support, the law proved controversial in its implementation. Teachers, administrators and school board members criticized standards as inflexible and federal funding to meet the goals as inadequate. The administration made some changes over time but continued to defend the law throughout Bush's eight years in office.

A year after the law's passage, the Supreme Court in June 2002 gave the administration an important legal victory by ruling, 5-4, that state and local governments can provide vouchers to students to attend parochial schools without violating separation of church and state. [34] The decision upheld a voucher program in Cleveland, established pursuant to a state law, that provided up to $2,250 for students to use for tuition at private schools. The vast majority of students attended parochial schools. Despite the ruling and the Bush administration's continued support, voucher programs failed to advance as much as supporters hoped. Teachers' unions strongly opposed the programs, and courts in some states — notably Florida — ruled vouchers unconstitutional on state law grounds.

The Bush administration also gave its support to a different form of school choice by adopting rules to allow single-sex education in public schools. The rules, approved by the Department of Education in October 2006 after a two-year period of comment and deliberation, allowed voluntary single-sex classes or schools despite the federal law known as Title IX that generally prohibits sex discrimination in public schools. Single-sex education was touted by proponents as improving education for boys and girls alike and criticized by women's groups, among others, as ill suited to preparing students for the real world. By 2009, advocates were counting some 95 single-sex schools and 445 single-sex classes nationwide. [35]

In another clash with public school lobbies and traditional civil rights groups, the Bush administration sided with white families in a critical Supreme Court case challenging racial diversity policies in local school districts. The policies in Seattle and Louisville-Jefferson County, Ky., assigned some pupils to out-of-neighborhood schools in order to have some degree of racial balance at individual schools. White families in both districts challenged the policies as unconstitutional race-based discrimination. The court in June 2007 agreed, with Bush's two Supreme Court appointees — Chief Justice Roberts and Justice Alito — helping form the 5-4 majority. The ruling barred individual race-based assignments, but in a pivotal concurring opinion Justice Kennedy said school districts could use other policies, such as magnet schools or new school-site selection, to promote racial balance. [36]

Three days earlier, Roberts and Alito had also provided critical votes in the 5-4 decision upholding schools' power to punish students for advocating or promoting illegal drug use. Joseph Frederick, a student at Juneau-Douglas High School in Alaska, had been given a 10-day suspension for displaying his "Bong Hits 4 Jesus" banner off school grounds on Jan. 24, 2002. Principal Deborah Morse viewed the banner as pro-drug advocacy, while Frederick depicted it as nonsense. "The First Amendment does not require schools to tolerate at school events student expression that contributes to [the] dangers" of drug use, Roberts wrote for the majority. For the dissenters, Justice John Paul Stevens warned the ruling would limit student debate about drug policy.

Meanwhile, Savana Redding's strip-search case was moving toward the high court. Redding's mother April originally filed a civil rights damage suit on her daughter's behalf in Arizona state court against principal Wilson, his assistant Romero and nurse Schwallier. The Safford School District removed the case to federal court, where U.S. Magistrate Judge Nancy Fiora ruled that the strip-search satisfied the two requirements established under the Supreme Court's *T.L.O.* decision: justified at its inception and permissible in scope.

A three-judge panel of the Ninth U.S. Circuit Court of Appeals agreed in September 2007, but Redding won a hearing before a panel of 11 judges, who divided 6-5 in her favor on July 11, 2008. "Common sense informs us that directing a 13-year-old girl to remove her clothes, partially revealing her breasts and pelvic area, for allegedly possessing ibuprofen, an infraction that poses an imminent danger to no one, and which could have been handled by keeping her in the principal's office until a parent arrived or simply sending her home, was excessively intrusive," Judge Kim McLane Wardlaw wrote for the majority. The court said the principle was so well established that Wilson — though not Romero or Schwallier — could be ordered to pay damages for the search. Safford appealed both holdings to the Supreme Court, which agreed on Jan. 16 to hear the case. ∎

CURRENT SITUATION

Deferring to Educators

State legislatures and federal courts alike appear to be leaning away from expanding student rights and toward giving greater deference and stronger legal protections to school administrators and teachers alike.

The trend can be seen in the enactment of laws in at least eight states to strengthen teachers' legal protections against damage suits for disciplinary actions against students. It can also be seen in recent federal appeals court decisions that the Supreme Court left standing favoring teachers or administrators in student discipline incidents.

Indiana became the most recent state to enact a so-called teacher protection law when Republican Gov. Mitch Daniels signed a bill on May 11 to give teachers "qualified immunity" from suit if they act in good faith under school policy in disciplining students or breaking up fights. [37] Daniels endorsed the proposal in campaigning for re-election to a second four-year term in 2008 and included it in the legislative program he submitted to the GOP-controlled legislature.

The bill was sponsored in the legislature, however, by a Democrat: state Rep. Clyde Kersey of Terre Haute. Kersey, a former teacher, said the bill "will restore order and discipline in the classroom that we haven't had in a long time because of the courts." The head of a local teachers' union also said the measure was needed. "Teachers have to be reasonably certain that they're not going to be sued for every frivolous case that comes up," Al Wolting, president of the Indianapolis Education Association, told the *Indianapolis Star*.

Gay-Rights and Christian Groups Embrace *Tinker* Decision

Courts generally side with students, not school officials, on speech rights.

Eighth-grader Chris Quintanilla started wearing a rainbow-colored wristband with the inscription "Rainbows Are Gay" to Parkridge Elementary School in Peoria, Ariz., in February. Principal David Svorinic took a skeptical look at the wristband and two days later called Chris' mother, Natali, to either suggest or demand that Chris stop wearing it or at least turn it over to conceal the pro-gay message.

As Natali recalls the conversation, Svorinic said the wristband was offending some of the teachers at the suburban Phoenix school and causing a disruption. A spokeswoman for the school says Svorinic never forbade Chris from wearing the wristband, but she acknowledges the principal observed that Chris was "putting his sexuality out there" by wearing it.

Natali contacted the Arizona affiliate of the American Civil Liberties Union (ACLU), which sent a sternly worded letter in March to Superintendent Denton Santarelli accusing the school of violating Chris' free-speech rights under the Supreme Court's landmark decision *Tinker v. Des Moines.* A month later, the ACLU reported the incident closed, with an assurance from the school that it would not prevent Chris from wearing the wristband in the future.

"I'm very proud of my son for standing up for his rights," Natali was quoted as saying in an ACLU press release, "and we both hope this means that other gay students won't be silenced at his school in the future."

The modern gay rights movement was only beginning to emerge when the Supreme Court issued the *Tinker* decision in late February 1969. (The "Stonewall" riot in New York City occurred four months later.) But today the debate over homosexuality is one of the most frequently litigated topics in student free-speech cases.

Students on both sides of the debate run afoul of school administrators at times, but courts generally side with the students. In July 2008, the ACLU got a federal court to nullify a decision by a principal in northern Florida to ban students from displaying pro-gay slogans. A few months earlier, the Alliance Defense Fund, a Christian public interest law firm, won a ruling from the federal appeals court in Chicago guaranteeing a student's right to wear a "Be Happy, Not Gay" T-shirt. [1]

In one notable exception, the federal appeals court in California upheld a decision by a principal in San Diego County to

prohibit anti-gay students from wearing T-shirts proclaiming "Homosexuality Is Shameful" on the same day as the school's gay-straight alliance sponsored a day of silence. The 2-1 decision by the Ninth U.S. Circuit Court of Appeals in April 2006 held that the First Amendment does not protect "derogatory and injurious remarks directed at students' minority status such as race, religion and sexual orientation." [2]

The Supreme Court effectively erased the decision in March 2007 by vacating the ruling and directing the case be dismissed as moot because the plaintiff had graduated. The Alliance Defense Fund, which represented the student, applauds the end result. "What a person may be offended by is too fluid for constitutional purposes," says David Cortman, a senior legal counsel with the Alliance Defense Fund, which litigated the case.

The ACLU also favors students' right to wear anti-gay T-shirts despite what Catherine Crump, a staff attorney with its First Amendment Working Group, calls its "strong support" for equality for gay students. "The traditional answer to [offensive] speech," Crump says, "is more speech."

The ACLU and other gay-rights groups have also enjoyed general success in safeguarding the right — guaranteed under the federal Equal Access Act — to form gay-straight alliances in schools and in winning gay couples the right to attend school proms. In a recent dispute, the ACLU challenged the use in Tennessee schools of a computer software filter that blocked gay news sites but not Web sites maintained by anti-gay groups.

For its part, the Gay, Lesbian, and Straight Educational Network (GLSEN) says free-speech disputes detract from the more tangible problem that LGBT students face in school: name-calling, bullying and harassment. "The real core issue is that words like faggot and dyke are still ubiquitous in the hallways," says executive director Eliza Byard. "Before we work on the fine points, I would like to see everyone come together and deal with the bullying and harassment that is so clearly unacceptable."

In a case brought by a Christian public-interest law firm, a federal court in Chicago in 2008 said a student could wear an anti-gay shirt.

http://3.bp.blogspot.com

---

[1] The decisions are *Gillman v. School Bd. for Holmes County, Florida*, 567 F.Supp.2d 1359 (N.D.Fla.2008); *Nuxoll v. Indian Prairie School District*, 523 F.3d 668 (7th Cir.2008).

[2] The decision is *Harper v. Poway Unified School Dist.*, 445 F.3d 1166 (9th Cir. 2006). For later developments, see "Anti-gay challenge to dress code is rejected," The Associated Press, March 6, 2007.

Daniels' office said seven other states had enacted similar laws: Alabama, Arkansas, Georgia, Minnesota, Mississippi, Texas and Wyoming. Legislatures in at least two other states — Missouri and South Carolina — considered similar proposals this year. The proposals are modeled after provisions

Continued on p. 518

At Issue:

Do student rights interfere with teaching in public schools?

FREDERICK M. HESS
DIRECTOR, EDUCATION POLICY STUDIES
AMERICAN ENTERPRISE INSTITUTE

WRITTEN FOR *CQ RESEARCHER*, JUNE 1, 2009

*w*e have unwittingly transformed K-12 schools from places where educators are expected to shape character, set boundaries and foster respect to ones where they are hesitant and unsure of their authority.

The greatest effect has been what former San Diego superintendent and California Secretary of Education Alan Bersin has termed "the anaconda in the chandelier" — the looming fear that a misstep could lead to lawsuits or grave professional consequences. The survey firm Public Agenda has reported that 47 percent of superintendents would operate differently if "free from the constant threat of litigation" and that 85 percent of teachers indicate that "most students suffer because of a few persistent troublemakers."

Fully 77 percent of teachers report that "if it weren't for discipline problems, I could be teaching a lot more effectively."

The most effective schools have always been unapologetic about setting norms and disciplining misbehavior. Journalist David Whitman, in his acclaimed 2008 book *Sweating the Small Stuff*, argues that the key to the success of high-performing charter schools like the KIPP Academies is their willingness to tell students exactly how they are expected to behave, with rewards for compliance and penalties for breaking the rules. Whitman shows how teachers ceaselessly monitor conduct and character to ensure that students act respectfully, develop self-discipline, work hard and take responsibility for their actions.

Thanks to more than a generation of court rulings, lawsuits and learned timidity, most schools shy from such muscular norms. The result is that educators have less authority, schools less discipline and students less opportunity to learn. Ironically, this all matters most in schools serving at-risk students, who start with fewer advantages and are most likely to be stuck in chaotic school environments.

Scholars Scott Carrel and Mark Hoekstra have documented the ill-effects of lax discipline, reporting that adding a single disruptive student to a class has a statistically significant negative effect on their peers' reading and math achievement.

It is too easy, of course, to blame the current state of affairs on the judicial process. Nations wind up with the schools they desire and deserve. In an era of confessional television and helicopter parents lobbying college professors for paper extensions, it is little wonder that schools have been buffeted by an insistence that they understand rather than discipline. Putting educators in a position to educate is not just a matter of law, it is also a question of character.

JAMIN RASKIN
DIRECTOR, PROGRAM ON LAW AND GOVERNMENT, WASHINGTON COLLEGE OF LAW, AMERICAN UNIVERSITY

WRITTEN FOR *CQ RESEARCHER*, MAY 28, 2009

*e*ver since the Supreme Court struck down compulsory classroom prayer, group Bible readings and religiously inspired bans on teaching evolution, the defense of student rights has always meant improved teaching and learning in our schools. The deployment of the Establishment Clause in school cases has made it possible for science teachers to teach science and students not to be anxious all day because they pray differently or — God forbid — not at all.

The whole point of Justice Abe Fortas' landmark decision in *Tinker v. Des Moines* is that the free-speech rights of students are not an impediment to the learning process but a crucial ingredient of it. "In our system, state-operated schools may not be enclaves of totalitarianism," he wrote, and "students may not be regarded as close-circuited recipients of only that which the state chooses to communicate." Each student has something precious to offer the others, and "intercommunication among the students" is "an important part of the educational process."

It is the Supreme Court's determined retreat from this vision of student rights that has undermined learning. In *Hazelwood v. Kuhlmeier* (1988), the Court broke from *Tinker* and upheld a principal's censorship of two articles written by students for their school newspaper that had been enthusiastically approved by their journalism teacher. One concerned the impact of parental divorce on students, the other the problem of teen pregnancy as seen through the experiences of three students. The school thus squashed mature and thoughtful student expression about issues of profound importance to young people.

To be sure, the post-Columbine massacre era is a scary time to go to school. But that is because of the absurd availability of guns everywhere, which has nothing to do with student rights. (Why should students lose their First Amendment rights because adults refuse to face their Second Amendment responsibilities?) Students have lost every school drug-testing case that has gone to the Supreme Court, and no lawsuit has ever stopped a school from using a metal detector.

If students have been able to maintain a shred of privacy and personal liberty during this age of "zero tolerance" authoritarianism, then more power to them — they may get a taste of what it is like to live in a free society. More likely, they encounter random drug tests for extracurricular activities, humiliating strip searches for Midol, knee-jerk censorship of the school paper and yearbook and a relentless regime of testing.

Continued from p. 516

that Congress included in the No Child Left Behind Act in 2001.

The federal Teacher Protection Act protects a school employee from civil liability if a student is injured in an attempt to discipline or control a student. But the immunity does not apply if an employee violated federal, state or local law; committed a sexual offense; or was guilty of gross negligence, reckless conduct or conscious indifference to the student's rights or safety.

Even without such legislation, federal appeals courts have recently been ruling in favor of teachers or administrators in suits, according to cases compiled on The School Law Blog by *Education Week* reporter Mark Walsh. [38]

In one case, the federal appeals court in Cincinnati rejected a suit filed on behalf of a seventh-grade student charging the Grant County (Ky.) Board of Education and various officials with violating her constitutional rights by questioning her about her actions in giving a prescription medication to a fellow student. The student argued that the school principal's actions in summoning her to his office and requiring her to write out an explanation of the incident that he later turned over to the local sheriff's office violated her rights under the Fourth and Fifth Amendments.

In a unanimous decision, however, a three-judge panel of the Sixth U.S. Circuit Court of Appeals ordered the suit dismissed, saying the principal had not acted at the behest of law enforcement. The U.S. Supreme Court declined on April 27 to hear the student's appeal of the ruling.

In an earlier case, the federal appeals court in New Orleans rejected a suit against a San Antonio charter school in connection with the paddling of an 18-year-old high school senior in 2004. Jessica Serafin claimed she was restrained by two school employees while principal Brett Wilkinson paddled her for leaving the school campus to buy breakfast, in violation of school rules. She was treated at a hospital emergency room for injuries to her hand sustained while trying to block the blows.

In defending against the suit, the school noted that an enrollment form signed by Serafin's guardian included permission for corporal punishment. In a brief and unsigned ruling in October 2007, the Fifth U.S. Circuit Court of Appeals said it was "well settled" that corporal punishment violates a public-school student's rights only if it is "arbitrary, capricious, or wholly unrelated to the legitimate state goal of maintaining an atmosphere conducive to learning."

The Supreme Court declined to hear Serafin's appeal in June 2008. The high court has not revisited the issue of corporal punishment since a closely divided decision in 1977 that upheld the practice and rejected any need for school administrators or teachers to give a student procedural rights before administering such punishment. [39]

Experts on both sides of the student-rights issue agree on the trend toward greater deference to educators. "We're going to see a continuing deference to schools when it comes to questions of safety," says school boards association counsel Negrón.

American University law professor Raskin views the trend less positively. "We have just had a strong judicial tilt away from liberty and toward authority," he says.

Debating a Strip-Search

Supreme Court justices are weighing how to prevent drug use while protecting student rights as they consider whether administrators at an Arizona middle school went too far in strip-searching a teenaged girl while looking for a commonly used pain medication.

Liberal justices pressed the attorney for the Safford school district to justify the strip-search of Savana Redding during the opening half-hour of oral arguments on April 21. But some of them appeared to join conservative justices by the end of the hour in giving greater weight to the need to give school authorities considerable leeway in investigating reports of unauthorized drugs on campus, even commonly available pain pills.

"Better embarrassment than violent sickness or death," the generally liberal Justice David H. Souter remarked near the end of Redding's lawyer's time. "What's wrong with that reasoning under the Fourth Amendment?"

Representing the school district, Phoenix attorney Wright opened by stressing that principal Kelly Wilson had reason to suspect Redding of possessing unauthorized pills that constituted a health and safety risk. With an enrollment of 400, the school had rules prohibiting students from possessing any medication — over-the-counter or prescription — without approval from the school nurse.

School authorities have "custodial and tutelary responsibility" for students, Wright explained. The court, he argued, "should defer to their judgment when they believe that certain rules are important and not second-guess those rules."

Wright encountered skepticism from justices across the ideological spectrum. Chief Justice Roberts and fellow conservative Justice Scalia pressed Wright on how far authorities could go. What about body cavity searches? Scalia asked. Wright ruled them out.

Liberals Souter and Justice Ruth Bader Ginsburg followed by questioning the details of the investigation. Did administrators have any reason to suspect Redding other than the accusation from her classmate who herself was caught with the unauthorized extra-strength ibuprofen? Ginsburg asked.

In his turn, Souter suggested it was "silly" to lump all unauthorized medications together. "If your rule . . . would put aspirin in the contraband category and justify the kind of search that went on here, I think we've reached the questionable point," Souter said.

Representing the Bush administration, assistant solicitor general David O'Neil argued that what he called "intrusive body searches" required "greater justification" than the reasonableness standard applicable, for example, to a search of a student's locker. Searching a student's underwear, he said, required specific information that the student was hiding drugs there. And in Safford's case, O'Neil explained, the school had no information or experience that students were doing that.

For Redding, the ACLU's Wolf echoed O'Neil's argument that school officials should have "location-specific" information before strip-searching a student. "The Fourth Amendment . . . does not countenance rummaging on or around a 13-year-old girl's naked body," Wolf said.

Wolf met resistance, however, from Roberts and the moderate-conservative Justice Anthony M. Kennedy, who asked whether a strip-search would have been justified if Redding had been suspected of having a more dangerous drug, such as heroin or methamphetamine. When Wolf said it would not have made a difference, Kennedy appeared dubious. "You don't mind our deciding the case as if this were a search for meth that was going to be consumed at noon?" Kennedy asked pointedly.

Later, liberal Justice Stephen G. Breyer raised doubts whether the search was as intrusive as Wolf was depicting. "I'm trying to work out why is this a major thing to say strip

down to your underclothes, which children do when they change for gym, they do fairly frequently?" Breyer asked.

Ginsburg jumped in before Wolf could answer. "It wasn't just that they were stripped to their underwear," Ginsburg said, referring to the searches of both Redding and her accuser. "They were asked to shake their bra out, to shake, stretch the top of their pants and shake that out."

In a brief rebuttal, Wright acknowledged that some school districts have rules prohibiting strip-searches of students. But he used the concession to emphasize the argument for leaving the issue up to local officials' discretion. Administrators need "a bright-line rule," he said, permitting them to search any place where contraband might reasonably be hidden.

The justices are due to decide the case before they begin a summer recess at the end of June. The court could avert the main issue by dismissing Redding's suit on the ground that school officials had no reason to know the search was unconstitutional. But all three lawyers appeared to favor the justices ruling on the merits of the dispute. ∎

OUTLOOK

Changing Times

As she looked forward to the 40th anniversary of the Supreme Court's decision in her case, Mary Beth Tinker acknowledged that the ruling gives school administrators a lot of leeway to censor student speech. But she said she planned to celebrate "a Supreme Court that stood with young people to affirm their rights." And she

urged students themselves to celebrate "by becoming engaged in issues that are important to their lives." [40]

Tinker, her brother John and their friend Christopher Eckhardt decided on their act of defiance in an era when principals and teachers enjoyed largely unquestioned authority in their schools, and students had no recognized legal rights enforceable in courts. With the divisions over Vietnam beginning to emerge, Eckhardt worried that pro-war classmates might beat him up; but in fact no disruption or violence occurred at any of the three schools that he and the Tinkers attended.

More than 40 years later, public schools in the United States have been transformed — in many ways, for the better; in some ways, not. Legally enforced racial segregation has ended, though most students still attend racially identifiable schools. Students with disabilities have a federally guaranteed right to an "appropriate" public education. Teachers have been encouraged to adopt interactive, collaborative instructional methods. And students generally do not risk derision or discipline for questioning authority.

Yet school life is far more troubled in some ways today than it was in the supposedly tumultuous '60s. Bullying once confined to the classroom or playground now becomes far more hurtful when posted — often anonymously — on the Internet for all to read and see. Deadly school shootings have combined with the daily fear of weapon-carrying students to make metal detectors commonplace in inner-city, suburban and rural schools alike. The drug problem has grown from an occasional pot-smoker to more widespread use of marijuana, other illegal drugs and unauthorized prescription medications. And many principals and teachers say they live and work with the fear of physical violence from students and legal rebukes from the courts.

With the changing times, courts are changing too. "A pattern is developing that in terms of dangers that are serious and palpable, there is some duty and obligations [on the part of] the schools to do what they have to do to make the kids safe," says school boards association counsel Negrón. New York University's Arum sees "hints" of greater deference to educators in court rulings as well in public discussion of school policies.

In past rulings such as *Tinker*, the Supreme Court "imposed some liberty restraints on what schools can do," says American University law professor Raskin. "Now there are judges who essentially tell us that children should be seen and not heard."

The Supreme Court's role in creating the trend can be seen in its most recent decisions rejecting lower court rulings that backed student-rights pleas in the Oklahoma drug testing case in 2002 and the "Bong Hits 4 Jesus" case in 2007. "There are five votes on the court now for trying to pull back," says R. Shep Melnick, a professor of political science at Boston College.

Melnick says, however, that the changes are less than a complete reversal. "It will be around the edges," he says. In fact, the court shows no inclination to reconsider *Tinker* despite a strongly argued call by Justice Clarence Thomas in the 2007 decision to overrule it. No justice joined Thomas' opinion.

For now, educators and student-rights advocates alike are awaiting the court's latest pronouncement on the issue in Savana Redding's strip-search case, with a decision due by the end of June. Despite criticism of the Safford principal's actions in the incident, even from some educators, the justices' decision is hard to predict.

Redding, now 19 and a college freshman, attended the arguments and had mixed reaction to the proceedings. "It was pretty overwhelming," she told reporters assembled on the Supreme Court plaza after the session. "Some things made me mad, and other things I was glad to see that the judges could comprehend." [41] ∎

Notes

[1] The case is *Safford Unified School Dist. No. 1 v. Redding*, 08-479. For documents in the case, see SCOTUSWiki, www.scotuswiki.com/index.php?title=Safford_United_School_District.

[2] *Tinker v. Des Moines Independent Community School District*, 393 U.S. 503 (1969). For a full account of the case, see John W. Johnson, *The Struggle for Student Rights:* Tinker v. Des Moines *and the 1960s* (1997).

[3] See Jamin B. Raskin, *We the Students: Supreme Court Cases for and about Students* (3rd ed., 2008).

[4] See "From *Brown* to 'Bong Hits': Assessing a Half Century of Judicial Involvement in Education, American Enterprise Institute, Oct. 15, 2008, www.aei.org/event/1746. See Mark Walsh, "Scholars Weigh Court Influence Over School Practices, Climate," *Education Week*, Oct. 22, 2008, p. 9.

[5] Richard Arum and Doreet Preiss, "Still Judging School Discipline," in Joshua Dunn and Martin R. West (eds.), *From Schoolhouse to Courthouse: The Judiciary's Role in American Education* (2009, forthcoming).

[6] The drug testing decisions are *Vernonia School Dist. No. 47J v. Acton*, 515 U.S. 645 (1995), and *Board of Education v. Earls*, 536 U.S. 822 (2002). The more recent decision is *Morse v. Frederick*, 551 U.S. 393 (2007).

[7] Quoted in Arthur H. Rotstein, "Supreme Court to get Ariz. teen strip-search case," The Associated Press, April 19, 2009.

[8] The case is *Tannahill v. Lockney Independent School District*, 133 F.Supp. 2d. 919. (N.D.Tex. 2001). For coverage, see David Stevens, "Drug-testing policy is struck down," *Dallas Morning News*, March 3, 2001, p. 33A. A documentary on the case, "Larry v. Lockney," premiered on PBS in July 2003.

[9] The case is *Board of Education v. Earls*, 536 U.S. 822 (2002).

[10] For background, see Thomas J. Billitteri, "Discipline in Schools," *CQ Researcher*, Feb. 15, 2008, pp. 145-168; and Kathy Koch, "Zero Tolerance," *CQ Researcher*, March 10, 2000, pp. 185-208.

[11] The case is *Palmer v. Waxahachie Independent School District*, 08-10903. The earlier Supreme Court decision, *United States v. O'Brien*, 391 U.S. 367 (1968), upheld a conviction for burning a draft card. The court held that the government can restrict so-called expressive conduct if the restriction furthers an important or substantial government interest, is unrelated to suppression of speech and prohibits no more speech than necessary to further that interest.

[12] The case is *Morse v. Frederick*, 551 U.S. 393 (2007).

[13] Anne Proffitt Dupre, *Speaking Up: The Unintended Costs of Free Speech in Public Schools* (2009).

[14] The case is *Lowry v. Watson Chapel School District*, 540 F.3d 572 (8th Cir. 2008). The Supreme Court declined to review the decision. For coverage, see Alberto D. Morales, "Appellate court rules school district violated First Amendment rights of students who wore black armbands to schools," Student Press Law Center, Sept. 8, 2008, www.splc.org/newsflash_archives.asp?id=1803&year=2008.

[15] The case is *Bethel School Dist. No. 43 v. Fraser*, 478 U.S. 675 (1986).

[16] The case is *Curry v. Hensinger*, SB F.3d 570 (6th Cir. 2008). The U.S. Supreme Court declined to review the decision. For coverage, see LaNia Coleman, "Candy-cane case dies at high court's door," *The Saginaw* (Mich.)

About the Author

Associate Editor **Kenneth Jost** graduated from Harvard College and Georgetown University Law Center. He is the author of the *Supreme Court Yearbook* and editor of *The Supreme Court from A to Z* (both *CQ Press*). He was a member of the *CQ Researcher* team that won the American Bar Association's 2002 Silver Gavel Award. His previous reports include "Racial Diversity in Public Schools" and "Free-Press Disputes." He is also author of the blog *Jost on Justice* (http://jostonjusticeblogspot.com).

News, Dec. 10, 2008.

[17] See "Religion and the Public Schools: A Summary of the Law," *American Jewish Congress*, February 2009, www.ajcongress.org/site/DocServer/2009_RPS_-_February_09_Revision.pdf?docID=3421.

[18] For background, see Patrick Marshall, "Religion in Schools," *CQ Researcher*, Jan. 12, 2001, pp. 1-24.

[19] For background, see Kenneth Jost, "Religion in Schools," *CQ Researcher*, Feb. 18, 1994, pp. 145-168.

[20] Background drawn in part from Dupre, *op. cit.*; Raskin, *op. cit.* For an up-to-date, one-volume history, see William J. Reese, *America's Public Schools: From the Common School to "No Child Left Behind"* (2005).

[21] Justice Clarence Thomas collected the cases in his concurring opinion in *Morse v. Frederick*, 551 U.S. 393 (2008).

[22] John Dewey, *On Democracy and Education: An Introduction to the Philosophy of Education* (1916), p. 129, quoted in Richard Arum, *Judging School Discipline: The Crisis of Moral Authority* (2003), p. 32.

[23] The cases are *Meyer v. Nebraska*, 262 U.S. 390 (1923), and *West Virginia State Board of Education v. Barnette*, 319 U.S. 624 (1943).

[24] For background see Kenneth Jost, "Racial Diversity in Public Schools," *CQ Researcher*, Sept. 14, 2007, pp. 745-768.

[25] For background, see H. B. Shaffer, "Discipline in Public Schools," in *Editorial Research Reports*, Aug. 27, 1969, available online at CQ Press Electronic Library, http://library.cqpress.com/cqresearcher/cqresrre1969082700.

[26] The citation is 419 U.S. 565 (1975).

[27] The citation is 469 U.S. 325 (1985).

[28] The citation is 478 U.S. 675 (1986). The school is in Spanaway, 10 miles south of Tacoma.

[29] The citation is 484 U.S. 260 (1988).

[30] The decision is *Westside Community Schools v. Mergen*, 496 U.S. 226 (1990). See also *Good News Club v. Milford Central School*, 533 U.S. 98 (2001).

[31] For background, see these *CQ Researcher* reports: Thomas J. Billitteri, "Discipline in Schools," Feb. 15, 2008, pp. 145-168; John Greenya, "Bullying," Feb. 4, 2005, pp. 101-124.

[32] The decisions are *Vernonia School Dist. No. 47J v. Acton*, 515 U.S. 646 (1995), and *Board of Education v. Earls*, 536 U.S. 822 (2002). For coverage, see respective editions of *Supreme Court Yearbook* (CQ Press). Also see Kathy Koch, "Drug Testing," *CQ Researcher*, Nov. 20, 1998, pp. 1001-1024.

[33] For background, see Barbara Mantel, "No Child Left Behind," *CQ Researcher*, May 27,

2005, pp. 469-492. Also see Kenneth Jost, "Testing in Schools," April 20, 2001, *CQ Researcher*, pp. 321-344.

[34] The decision is *Zelman v. Simmons-Harris*, 536 U.S. 639 (2002). For coverage, see Jost, *Supreme Court Yearbook 2001-2002*, *op. cit.* Also see Kenneth Jost, "School Vouchers Showdown," *CQ Researcher*, Feb. 15, 2002, pp. 121-144; and Kathy Koch, "School Vouchers," *CQ Researcher*, April 9, 1999, pp. 281-304.

[35] See Jennifer Medina, "Boys and Girls Together, Taught Separately in Public Schools," *The New York Times*, March 11, 2009, p. A24. For background, see Kenneth Jost, "Single-Sex Education," *CQ Researcher*, July 12, 2002, pp. 569-592.

[36] The decision is *Parents Involved in Community Schools v. Seattle School District No. 1*, 551 U.S. — (2007). For coverage, see Kenneth Jost,

Supreme Court Yearbook 2006-2007, *op. cit.*

[37] Background from Andy Gammill, "Teachers shielded from suits," *The Indianapolis Star*, May 12, 2009, p. 15A.

[38] The cases discussed are *S.E. v. Grant County Board of Education*, 6th Cir., Oct. 10, 2008, and *Serafin v. School of Excellence in Education*, 5th Cir., Oct. 30, 2007. See The School Law Blog, http://blogs.edweek.org/edweek/school_law/.

[39] The Supreme Court decision is *Wright v. Ingraham*, 430 U.S. 651 (1977).

[40] See "A Conversation with Mary Beth Tinker," *Human Rights*, Vol. 35, No. 3 (summer 2008), p. 6.

[41] Quoted in Joan Biskupic and Greg Toppo, "Girl's strip search argued in court," *USA Today*, April 22, 2009, p. 3A. See also Jesse J. Holland, "Justices hear arguments over school strip search," The Associated Press, April 22, 2009.

Bibliography

Selected Sources

Books

Law of the Student Press (3d ed.), Student Press Law Center, 2008.

The 402-page compendium provides comprehensive coverage of general media-law topics such as libel, privacy and copyright as well as legal developments specifically relating to student print, broadcast and online media. Includes chapter notes, appendix materials.

Arum, Richard, *Judging School Discipline: The Crisis of Moral Authority*, Harvard University Press, 2003.

A professor of sociology at New York University and a former public-school teacher uses extensive empirical research to argue that U.S. public schools face "a crisis in the legitimacy of school discipline." Includes extensive research data, notes.

Dunn, Joshua, and Martin R. West (eds.), *From Schoolhouse to Courthouse: The Judiciary's Role in American Education*, Brookings Institution Press/Thomas F. Fordham Institute, forthcoming (August 2009).

Ten experts from law, education and political science examine school-related litigation in such areas as desegregation, high-stakes testing, school finance, discipline, special education, school choice, religious freedom and student speech. Dunn is an assistant professor of political science at Colorado State University; West is an assistant professor of education at Brown University.

Dupre, Anne Proffitt, *Speaking Up: The Unintended Costs of Free Speech in Public Schools*, Harvard University Press, 2009.

A professor at the University of Georgia School of Law critically examines the impact of free-speech rulings, which she says have "dramatically changed the way public schools operate." Includes notes.

Johnson, John W., *The Struggle for Student Rights: Tinker v. Des Moines and the 1960s*, University Press of Kansas, 1997.

A history professor at the University of Northern Iowa provides a detailed account of the landmark *Tinker* case from the Des Moines students' initial decision to wear black armbands to school protest the Vietnam War through the Supreme Court decision upholding their free-speech rights and the aftermath of the ruling. The ruling, Johnson says, "will be remembered as long as students demand the right to be heard as well as seen." Includes a five-page chronology of the case and a short bibliographical essay.

Olivas, Michael A., and Ronna Greff Schneider (eds.), *Education Law Stories*, Thomson/West, 2008.

The book recounts the stories of a dozen landmark education-related cases in such areas as religion, school finance, race, gender and disabilities. Olivas is a professor at the University of Houston Law Center, Schneider a professor at the University of Cincinnati College of Law.

Raskin, Jamin, *We the Students: Supreme Court Cases for and about Students* (3d ed.), CQ Press, 2008.

The high school text includes excerpts from and discussion of major decisions affecting students from the U.S. Supreme Court and other federal and state courts. Raskin is a professor at American University's Washington College of Law. Includes glossary, five-page bibliography.

Reichman, Henry, *Censorship and Selection: Issues and Answers for Schools*, American Library Association, 2001.

The longtime editor of the American Library Association's *Newsletter on Intellectual Freedom* gives practical guidance for school administrators, librarians and teachers on free-speech rights affecting school curricula, student newspapers and library acquisition policies. Includes notes, summary of major legal decisions and seven-page bibliography. Reichman is also professor of history at California State University, East Bay.

Valente, William D., with Christina M. Valente, *Law in the Schools* (6th ed.), Merrill Prentice Hall, 2005.

The textbook's nine chapters cover a full range of legal issues for public and private schools, including issues of student rights and discipline. Includes notes, select table of cases and glossary. William Valente is professor emeritus at Villanova University School of Law; his wife assisted on the book.

Articles

"Student Rights," *Human Rights*, Vol. 35, No. 3 (summer 2008), www.abanet.org/irr/hr/summer08/.

The nine articles in this issue of the quarterly journal of the American Bar Association's Section on Individual Rights and Responsibilities examine such topics as the impact of *Tinker*, student journalism and educational access for women and girls and for LGBT students.

On the Web

The School Law Blog, http://blogs.edweek.org/edweek/school_law/.

The blog provides news and analysis on legal developments affecting schools, educators, students and parents. Author Mark Walsh is a contributing writer to *Education Week* who has covered education-related issues in the courts for 17 years.

The Next Step:

Additional Articles from Current Periodicals

Blogs

Barrouquere, Brett, "Nursing Student Sues After Dismissal Over Blogging," The Associated Press, March 13, 2009.

A nursing student from the University of Louisville says her free-speech rights were violated because she was dismissed over posts about patient activities on her blog.

Becker, Arielle Levin, "Web Speech: When May Schools Act?" Hartford Courant, Feb. 1, 2009, p. A1.

Lawmakers in Connecticut are considering a bill to better clarify the rights of students, especially those relating to free speech.

Fermino, Jennifer, "Blog Teen's Supreme Ire," The New York Post, May 29, 2009, p. 15.

As a federal judge, Supreme Court nominee Sonia Sotomayor once ruled that a Connecticut teen could not pursue a student-government position after she posted a vulgar message about school administrators on her personal blog.

Drug Enforcement

Barnes, Robert, "Strip-Search Case Could Redefine Student Privacy," The Washington Post, April 11, 2009, p. A1.

An Arizona student was made to strip in the nurse's office to prove that she was not carrying prescription-strength ibuprofen.

Hong, Robert S., and Alfred Lee, "Pasadena Class Teaches How to Legally Dispense Marijuana," Pasadena Star-News, March 1, 2009.

Although medical marijuana dispensaries are illegal in Pasadena, Calif., teaching how to use them is protected.

Saunders, Debra J., "Freedom of Expression Takes a Bong Hit," The San Francisco Chronicle, June 26, 2007, p. B5.

The decision by the Supreme Court to allow schools to punish messages promoting drug use implies that the court can suppress ideas they simply don't like.

Savage, David G., "Schools Can Ban Pro-Drug Banners," Los Angeles Times, June 26, 2007, p. A11.

A decision by the U.S. Supreme Court allows schools to punish students for statements that could promote illegal drug use.

Gay Rights

Carroll, Elaine Cushman, "Picketers Are on the Way," The Boston Globe, March 19, 2009, p. Reg1.

A school play at a Massachusetts high school about prejudice and gay rights is creating a controversy.

Kirby, Cassondra, "Court Rules in School, Gay Case," Lexington Herald Leader, Oct. 27, 2007, p. A1.

A Kentucky high school student has been allowed to pursue

damages against his school district for what he claims is the suppression of his opposition to homosexuality.

Moran, Greg, "School Curbs Girl's Report on Gay Rights Activist Milk," San Diego Union-Tribune, May 21, 2009, p. A1.

A San Diego sixth-grader has been told that she can't present a report on slain gay-rights advocate Harvey Milk to fellow students unless their parents sign permission slips.

Religious Freedom

Harsanyi, David, "Student Spoke Up, School Let Her Down," The Denver Post, Sept. 9, 2007, p. C1.

A school principal in Colorado initially denied a diploma to a class valedictorian for proselytizing about Jesus Christ.

Haynes, Charles C., "Commencement Prayers Should Be Silent Ones," News-Press (Florida), May 28, 2009, p. 8B.

Public schools are wary of creating graduation free-speech forums in which students can engage in religious or anti-religious expression.

Perez, Erica, "Catholic Student Group Wins Suit," Milwaukee Journal Sentinel, Jan. 18, 2008, p. B3.

A U.S. district court judge has ordered University of Wisconsin officials to stop denying funds to student groups that use the money for prayer, worship or proselytizing.

Shimron, Yonat, "Ex-Enloe Teacher Fights on in Flap Over Anti-Islam Speaker," News & Observer (North Carolina), June 13, 2007, p. A1.

Students at a North Carolina high school are trying to get a social studies teacher reinstated after he invited a guest speaker who was accused of denigrating Islam.

CITING CQ RESEARCHER

Sample formats for citing these reports in a bibliography include the ones listed below. Preferred styles and formats vary, so please check with your instructor or professor.

MLA STYLE

Jost, Kenneth. "Rethinking the Death Penalty." CQ Researcher 16 Nov. 2001: 945-68.

APA STYLE

Jost, K. (2001, November 16). Rethinking the death penalty. CQ Researcher, 11, 945-968.

CHICAGO STYLE

Jost, Kenneth. "Rethinking the Death Penalty." CQ Researcher, November 16, 2001, 945-968.

In-depth Reports on Issues in the News

Are you writing a paper?

Need backup for a debate?

Want to become an expert on an issue?

For 80 years, students have turned to *CQ Researcher* for in-depth reporting on issues in the news. Reports on a full range of political and social issues are now available. Following is a selection of recent reports:

Civil Liberties
Closing Guantánamo, 2/09
Affirmative Action, 10/08
Gay Marriage Showdowns, 9/08
America's Border Fence, 9/08
Immigration Debate, 2/08

Crime/Law
Judicial Elections, 4/09
Mexico's Drug War, 12/08
Prostitution Debate, 5/08
Public Defenders, 4/08
Gun Violence, 5/07

Education
Reading Crisis? 2/08
Discipline in Schools, 2/08
Student Aid, 1/08
Racial Diversity in Public Schools, 9/07

Environment/Society
Future of Books, 5/09
Hate Groups, 5/09
Future of Journalism, 3/09
Confronting Warming, 1/09
Reducing Carbon Footprint, 12/08
Protecting Wetlands, 10/08

Health/Safety
Reproductive Ethics, 5/09
Extreme Sports, 4/09
Regulating Toxic Chemicals, 1/09
Preventing Cancer, 1/09
Heart Health, 9/08
Global Food Crisis, 6/08

Politics/Economy
Business Bankruptcy, 4/09
Future of the GOP, 3/09
Middle-Class Squeeze, 3/09
Public-Works Projects, 2/09

Upcoming Reports

Decriminalizing Marijuana, 6/12/09   Retirement Crisis, 6/19/09   Depression, 6/26/09

ACCESS

CQ Researcher is available in print and online. For access, visit your library or www.cqresearcher.com.

STAY CURRENT

To receive notice of upcoming *CQ Researcher* reports, or learn more about *CQ Researcher* products, subscribe to the free e-mail newsletters, *CQ Researcher Alert!* and *CQ Researcher News*: http://cqpress.com/newsletters.

PURCHASE

To purchase a *CQ Researcher* report in print or electronic format (PDF), visit www.cqpress.com or call 866-427-7737. Single reports start at $15. Bulk purchase discounts and electronic-rights licensing are also available.

SUBSCRIBE

Annual full-service *CQ Researcher* subscriptions—including 44 reports a year, monthly index updates, and a bound volume—start at $803. Add $25 for domestic postage.

CQ Researcher Online offers a backfile from 1991 and a number of tools to simplify research. For pricing information, call 800-834-9020, ext. 1906, or e-mail librarysales@cqpress.com.

CQ Researcher

Published by CQ Press, a division of SAGE Publications

www.cqresearcher.com

Legalizing Marijuana

Should pot be treated like alcohol and taxed?

From statehouses to the White House, attitudes toward marijuana laws are changing. California's top tax collector is endorsing proposed state legislation to legalize and tax pot, and Republican Gov. Arnold Schwarzenegger says he'd like the idea debated. More than a dozen other states have enacted or are considering laws to permit medical-marijuana use or remove criminal penalties for possession. In Congress, Democratic Sen. Jim Webb of Virginia — a hard-nosed Marine combat veteran — wants marijuana legalization considered in a top-to-bottom review of sentencing and drug laws. Full-scale, nationwide legalization still seems distant, but the Obama administration has declared a hands-off approach toward California's medical-marijuana outlets, unless the state-sanctioned sites are determined to be trafficking operations. Opponents of marijuana legalization object on moral and health grounds, but the opposition appears to be weakening, especially in a time when the economic crisis is cutting into police and prison budgets nationwide.

*Cheryl Aichele, a marijuana activist in Los Angeles who smokes pot to relieve chronic back pain, protests on Feb. 5 against the arrest of medical-marijuana dispensary operators in California.
In March the Obama administration said it would de-escalate the Bush campaign against state-authorized dispensaries in California and 13 other states.*

CQ Researcher • June 12, 2009 • www.cqresearcher.com
Volume 19, Number 22 • Pages 525-548

Cover: AP Photo/Reed Saxon

CQ Researcher

June 12, 2009
Volume 19, Number 22

MANAGING EDITOR: Thomas J. Colin
tcolin@cqpress.com

ASSISTANT MANAGING EDITOR: Kathy Koch
kkoch@cqpress.com

ASSOCIATE EDITOR: Kenneth Jost

STAFF WRITERS: Thomas J. Billitteri, Marcia Clemmitt, Peter Katel

CONTRIBUTING WRITERS: Rachel Cox, Sarah Glazer, Alan Greenblatt, Barbara Mantel, Patrick Marshall, Tom Price, Jennifer Weeks

DESIGN/PRODUCTION EDITOR: Olu B. Davis

ASSISTANT EDITOR: Darrell Dela Rosa

FACT-CHECKING: Eugene J. Gabler, Michelle Harris

CQ PRESS

A Division of SAGE

PRESIDENT AND PUBLISHER:
John A. Jenkins

EXECUTIVE DIRECTOR,
REFERENCE INFORMATION GROUP:
Alix B. Vance

CQ Press is a registered trademark of Congressional Quarterly Inc.

CQ Researcher (ISSN 1056-2036) is printed on acid-free paper. Published weekly, except; (Jan. wk. 1) (May wk. 4) (July wks. 1, 2) (Aug. wks. 3, 4) (Nov. wk. 4) and (Dec. wk. 4), by CQ Press, a division of SAGE Publications. Annual full-service subscriptions start at $803. For pricing, call 1-800-834-9020, ext. 1906. To purchase a CQ Researcher report in print or electronic format (PDF), visit www. cqpress.com or call 866-427-7737. Single reports start at $15. Bulk purchase discounts and electronic-rights licensing are also available. Periodicals postage paid at Washington, D.C., and additional mailing offices. POSTMASTER: Send address changes to CQ Researcher, 2300 N St., N.W., Suite 800, Washington, DC 20037.

Legalizing Marijuana

BY PETER KATEL

THE ISSUES

Cmdr. Marc Alcantara of the San Mateo County Narcotics Task Force has his priorities, and they don't include pot-smokers toking on a joint at home or growing a couple of cannabis plants in the backyard or under a basement grow light.

"If people are truly growing it for personal consumption," he says, "it's not an issue with us."

Instead, Alcantara and his 22-officer unit focus on commercial marijuana-growing. It's a booming industry in the affluent coastal county between Silicon Valley and San Francisco. From 2006 to 2008, task force seizures of marijuana grown indoors rose 265 percent, to more than 36,000 plants from 39 sites.

"Indoor grow operations are capable of turning out three crops a year," he says, "typically grossing $250,000 per crop."

That's $250,000 in untaxed revenue per crop — or a potential total of more than $25 million just for those 39 sites in San Mateo County. In a state where desperate politicians are wrestling with a bankruptcy-threatening $24 billion budget deficit, the prospect of adding any kind of business to the tax rolls can start to sound like a plan.

Enter Tom Ammiano, a freshman Democratic state assemblyman from San Francisco. With marijuana already a lucrative California crop, with the state's medical-marijuana system now 13 years old and with personal use effectively decriminalized, the 68-year-old Ammiano says California ought to go all the way: legalize the entire cannabis industry and tax the product.

Democratic Sen. Jim Webb of Virginia is proposing a national commission to study the nation's drug laws and prison policies. "We are not protecting our citizens from the increasing danger of criminals who perpetrate violence and intimidation as a way of life, and we are locking up too many people who do not belong in jail," he said.

"Our drug policies have failed; the state of California is in dire economic need," he says. "We're looking at a perfect storm."

Ammiano's proposal has major support. A legalize-and-tax plan is favored by 56 percent of Californians, according to the Field Poll. Tax boss Betty T. Yee, chairwoman of the State Board of Equalization, backs the plan and says it could produce annual tax revenues of $1.4 billion. "I think the tide is starting to turn in terms of marijuana being part of the mainstream," she said." [1]

Marijuana-reform advocates point to signs of a national climate change as well. In Massachusetts, a pot-decriminalization law took effect this year that calls for no jail time for the first-time possession of a small amount of pot. And though the Food and Drug Administration doesn't classify marijuana as medication, 14 states permit it to be used by cancer patients and others to control pain. Several other states are considering medical-pot bills as well, though some proposals have died. National polls register a trend in favor of decriminalization — though falling short of a majority.

"I do sense a change in the discussion, a willingness of mainstream politicians, Republican and Democrat, maybe not to come out in favor of ending prohibition, but at least to talk about it," says Bruce Mirken, national spokesman for the pro-legalization Marijuana Policy Project. "For a long time, it was only people on the relatively far left and libertarian right."

But moderate Republican Gov. Arnold Schwarzenegger, carefully avoiding condemning the idea, is more cautious. "I think it's not time for that, but it's time for debate," he said in response to Ammiano's proposal. [2]

Scott Burns, deputy drug czar during most of the vehemently anti-marijuana George W. Bush administration, argues that changes in rhetorical tone here and there shouldn't be confused with a genuine political trend, even on the less politically charged issue of medical marijuana.

"If they have that much support, either in science or the will of people, they should call their local senators or congressmen," says Burns, now executive director of the National District Attorneys Association. "But right now nobody can convince the U.S. Congress that smoking weed is medicine."

Still, the Obama administration is getting only token pushback after reversing many Bush administration policies.

Ten States Ease Penalties on Pot Possession

Possession of a small quantity of marijuana is a misdemeanor for the first offense in all the states, with penalties varying widely, including jail time. In 10 states, however, there is no jail time in such cases. So-called medical marijuana is permitted in 14 states.

State Marijuana Laws

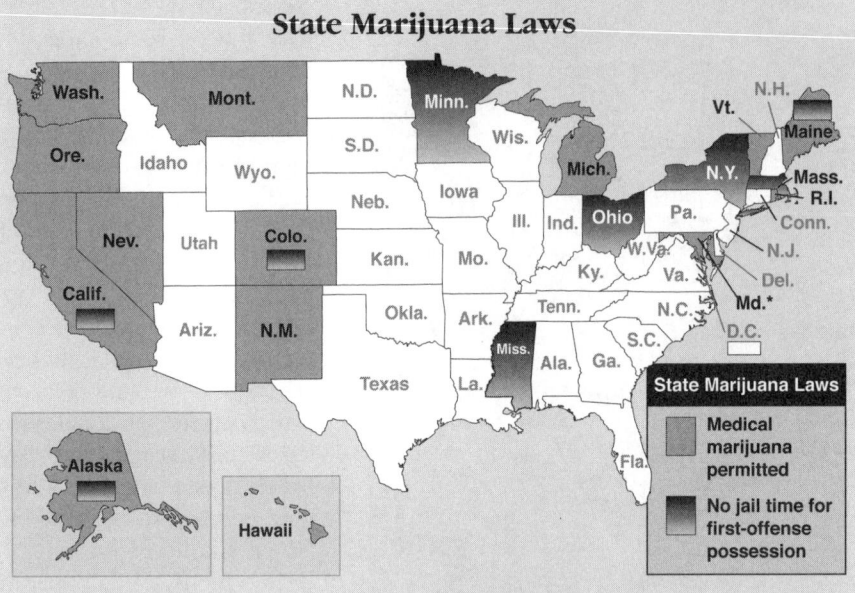

State Marijuana Laws

- Medical marijuana permitted
- No jail time for first-offense possession

* No program, but allows courts to consider marijuana for medical use as a mitigating factor in marijuana-related prosecution. If a defendant is successful in proving medical necessity, the maximum fine is $100.

Source: National Organization for the Reform of Marijuana Laws

In March, Attorney General Eric H. Holder Jr. announced that federal authorities would de-escalate the Bush campaign against California's state-authorized medical-marijuana dispensaries and, by extension, medical-pot distributors in the other 13 states that have legalized medical-marijuana, targeting only drug traffickers who "use medical-marijuana laws as a shield." [3]

The reversal of the Bush policy of declaring all the state's hundreds of pot outlets vulnerable to federal raids prompted only gentle criticism from Sen. Charles Grassley, R-Iowa, and Los Angeles Police Chief Howard Bratton, who called the new policy "unfortunate." [4]

Obama drug czar Gil Kerlikowske himself rejected the doctrine that most presidents have adopted — or at least not repudiated — ever since President Richard M. Nixon declared a "war on drugs" in the early 1970s.

"Regardless of how you try to explain to people [that] it's a war on drugs or a war on a product, people see a war as a war on them," Kerlikowske told *The Wall Street Journal.* "We're not at war with people in this country." [5]

But later, in a speech to law-enforcement officials in Nashville in May, Kerlikowske made clear that the Obama administration has placed a limit on its drug-policy objectives. "Legalization isn't in the president's vocabulary, and it certainly isn't in mine," he told a gathering of law-enforcement officials. [6]

Still, the drug czar also made clear that his top priority for now is prescription-drug abuse. [7] And in another sign of changing times, some of the toughest critics in the marijuana debates include drug policy experts, who also question the effectiveness of prohibition. "I deny that prohibiting drugs causes a drug-free America, and that not prohibiting drugs ends the drug problem," says Mark A. R. Kleiman, director of the drug policy analysis program at the University of California, Los Angeles (UCLA) and author of a forthcoming book on criminal-justice policy. [8]

Kleiman and others argue, however, that the solution to the nation's drug problem must inevitably include a law-enforcement dimension regardless of marijuana's legal status.

"The general public's view is that marijuana use is harmless, and in one's own home I think it is the case," says Rosalie Liccardo Pacula, co-director of the Drug Policy Center at the RAND Corp., a California think tank. "The problem is, it's not only used alone. Youths using it are also using alcohol, and alcohol used with cannabis increases risk more than alcohol alone."

Indeed, marijuana arrests figure prominently in the nation's overall crime statistics. Roughly 14 million people a year are arrested nationwide on all charges. In a 2007 study of 10 U.S. counties, 40 percent of the arrestees tested positive for marijuana. At that rate, when extrapolated for the nation as a whole, about 5.6 million of the 14 million would recently have smoked pot. Overall, the federal government's annual survey of drug, alcohol and tobacco use estimates that about 14.4 million people a year smoke marijuana monthly in the United States and about 25 million at least once a year. [9]

Americans hardly have a monopoly on cannabis use. But of 17 countries studied by the World Health Organization, the United States leads the list, with 42 percent of the entire U.S. population estimated to have used marijuana at some point in their lives.

"Drug use is not . . . simply related to drug policy," the study said, "since countries with stringent user-level illegal-drug policies did not have lower levels of use than countries with more liberal ones." [10]

The high level of marijuana use is even raising questions in Congress, which long has resisted following the states in softening marijuana laws. Conservative Democratic Sen. Jim Webb of Virginia is proposing a national commission to study the law-enforcement system, including marijuana policies. "I saw more drug use at Georgetown Law School than anywhere else I've been," the much-decorated Vietnam War veteran told columnist Neal Peirce. "A lot of those people went on to be judges." [11]

And in the House, veteran Rep. Charles Rangel, D-N.Y., powerful chairman of the tax-writing Ways and Means Committee, has endorsed ending federal marijuana prohibition.

"There's no question that with the limited resources . . . that we put on law enforcement, that we ought to decriminalize it," he told the House Judiciary Subcommittee on Crime, Terrorism and Homeland Security on May 21. [12]

Subcommittee member Dan Lungren, R-Calif., posed the only counterargument, noting that today's marijuana is more dangerous because of its higher content of THC (tetrahydrocannabinol, the main active compound in cannabis). And marijuana crops are "devastating wilderness areas, national parks . . . controlled by foreign nationals armed with assault weapons in some cases, a far more serious situation today than it was 10 years ago, 20 years ago." [13]

Last summer, the Bush administration launched a campaign against large-scale growing operations in California's Sequoia National Forest thought to be run by Mexican drug cartels; 420,000 plants were destroyed. [14]

And yet, across the border from Ciudad Juárez, which has been devastated by warring Mexican drug gangs, the El Paso City Council voted in January to open a debate on whether to end marijuana prohibition, as a way to

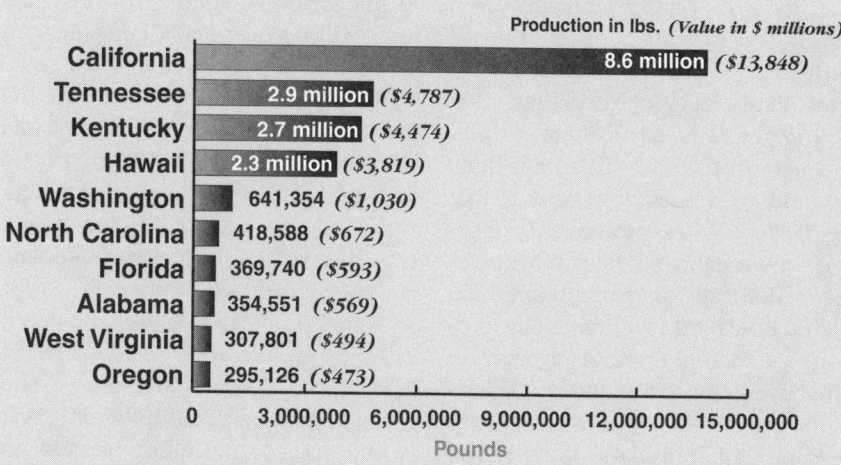

California Is Nation's Marijuana Heartland

According to one of many estimates, California growers produced nearly 9 million pounds of marijuana in 2006 worth nearly $14 billion — or more than the value of the next-three biggest producers.

Top Marijuana-Producing States, 2006

Production in lbs. *(Value in $ millions)*

State	Production in lbs. (Value in $ millions)
California	8.6 million ($13,848)
Tennessee	2.9 million ($4,787)
Kentucky	2.7 million ($4,474)
Hawaii	2.3 million ($3,819)
Washington	641,354 ($1,030)
North Carolina	418,588 ($672)
Florida	369,740 ($593)
Alabama	354,551 ($569)
West Virginia	307,801 ($494)
Oregon	295,126 ($473)

Source: Jon Gettman, "Marijuana Production in the United States (2006)," Bulletin of Cannabis Reform, December 2006

deprive cartels of at least some of their revenue. The resolution's author, council member Beto O'Rourke, said news coverage of the proposal "did confirm that we're part of much larger national and hemispheric conversation about the failure of our drug policies."

Mayor John Cook vetoed the resolution, however, and O'Rourke's colleagues backed off overturning Cook after Rep. Silvestre Reyes, D-Texas, and the county's delegation to the state House said the resolution would obstruct their efforts to secure aid for the city. [15]

Judging by public opinion on marijuana, those politicians are still on safe ground. Nationwide surveys show a majority still opposing legalization, though results vary sharply between surveys — from 46 percent opposed (the Rasmussen Poll) to 63 percent (CBS News). [16]

Still, Gallup reports a decades-long trend of growing support for legalization — from 12 percent in 1969 to 36 percent in 2005, the most recent Gallup survey data available. [17]

Decades of news reports crediting marijuana with relieving pain and suffering may have softened resistance to marijuana liberalization. But political analyst Nate Silver argues that the key to the outcome may be the nation's changing demographics.

"As members of the Silent Generation are replaced in the electorate by younger voters, who are more likely to have either smoked marijuana themselves or been around those that have, support for legalization is likely to continue to gain momentum," Silver wrote recently. [18]

As policy advocates, politicians and citizens debate decriminalization, here are some of the questions being asked:

Should marijuana be legalized and taxed?

California legislator Ammiano has put the big marijuana question squarely on the table.

The interest his bill has drawn owes as much to his taxation plan as to the legalization aspect. But evaluating marijuana as a revenue source requires solid estimates of the size of marijuana crops, and the figures vary widely.

California tax chief Yee's $1.4 billion tax revenue estimate was itself derived from an estimate of a California crop worth $14 billion, a figure that traces back to a nationwide cannabis crop estimate of 10 million metric tons — worth $35.8 billion — by the White House drug-policy office in 2003. [19]

Some experts dismiss the 10 million metric ton figure. "To accept [that], it would be necessary to assume that the United States produces 4 to 10 times more cannabis than it needs to cover domestic consumption," said Martin Bouchard, a criminology professor at Simon Fraser University in Vancouver, British Columbia. "This is highly implausible." He estimates U.S. consumption at probably only around 1,000-2,500 metric tons. [20]

"Discussing it in terms of the California budget crisis — that's a joke," says Kleiman of UCLA, arguing that California's cannabis crop is far smaller than the $14 billion wholesale price estimate. He notes that a nationwide estimate of drug prices in 2000 concluded that Americans paid about $11 billion a year for marijuana at the retail level. [21]

The costs of enforcing marijuana prohibition are difficult to calculate because there are many variables, such as determining how many arrested for marijuana possession are charged with other crimes. Jeffrey A. Miron, a senior economics lecturer at Harvard University, took that factor into account when he came up with the most recent prohibition cost estimate: about $13 billion in federal and state enforcement-related expenses. Miron estimated that 50 percent of possession arrests are for possession alone. But he did not include estimates of drug-treatment and other health system costs that some legalization opponents argue would increase if marijuana became a legal product. [22]

Estimates aside, legalizing and taxing marijuana wouldn't work fiscally, argues Kleiman, who opposes marijuana prohibition. "If you made it licit, and taxed it, the price would collapse," he says, arguing that marijuana's illegality accounts for its relatively high price.

"The commercial product I can think of that's closest to fancy pot is fancy tea. Really, really, really fancy tea can go for up to $100 a pound."

Narcotic News, a Web site for the law-enforcement community, cites wholesale prices of up to $3,500 a pound for high-grade cannabis — consistent with a price average of $3,572 a pound calculated by the pro-legalization online *Bulletin of Cannabis Reform.* [23]

Some prohibition critics, however, call the possible economic benefits of legalization a secondary issue. "The moral and human cost of the drug war is the most compelling reason to change the law," says El Paso City Council member O'Rourke. One of those costs, he says, is measured in bodies. "Because it's a black market that does not have access to our judicial system, any business conflict has to be resolved outside of it — often very violently."

O'Rourke now advocates marijuana decriminalization — not merely a debate. If pot consumption were legal, he says, the high drug prices created by prohibition would decline, taking economic support away from the violent Mexican cartels now ravaging Ciudád Juárez and other communities in Mexico.

"Our drug policy is directly responsible for the murder and violence that people are experiencing in our sister community," he says, arguing that legalization would create economic benefits as well. Decriminalization would "relieve a lot of the costs related to interdiction and imprisonment and enforcement and tap new revenues we're missing out on."

Meanwhile, law-enforcement experts say Mexican drug gangs have opened pot-growing and sales operations in the United States, including in national forests. [24]

But Burns at the National District Attorneys Association says taxation won't work. "I doubt that Mexican cartels are going to want to be regulated or taxed — that's a pipe dream," he said. [25]

Burns also opposes legalization in principle, citing the frequent comparisons of marijuana to alcohol — with its obvious links to drunken driving and alcoholism. "Should we legalize marijuana for the sake of the argument that alcohol is as bad or worse, that it's become the social norm?" he asks. "That amounts to — if you've smashed your thumb with a hammer, smash the other one."

Yet a comparison between marijuana and legally available — but unhealthy — substances can serve a pro-legalization argument as well. Bill Piper, national affairs director of the Drug Policy Alliance Network, notes that cigarette smoking has declined drastically in recent decades as publicity campaigns have driven home the message of its harmful effects. In 2005, for example, the 378 billion cigarettes sold in the United States was the lowest number since 1951, when the nation's population was about half its present size. [26]

"The number of people who smoke cigarettes has plummeted, and you didn't have to arrest a single person," Piper says. "That suggests that regulation is far superior to prohibition."

Would pot legalization spur a big increase in consumption?

The nature of marijuana's effects lie at the heart of the legalization debate. In fact, that is where the entire subject of marijuana and the law began. When politicians and law-enforcement officials began campaigning in the early-20th century for national marijuana prohibition, the effect of cannabis on the mind and body had been hotly debated, and exaggerated. The lurid hyping of marijuana as a catalyst for violent crime that was a popular mass-media storyline in the 1920s and '30s is now valued for its comic effect.

In an era in which millions of people are personally familiar with marijuana's effects, prohibition advocates have downplayed such descriptions. Instead, the debate centers on the dangers of chronic use and on whether more people will develop dependence on marijuana if the number of marijuana users booms as a result of legalization.

The National Institute on Drug Abuse (NIDA) now focuses almost entirely on chronic use in discussing marijuana's dangers.

"Long-term marijuana use can be addictive for some people," NIDA says. "A study of 129 college students found that among heavy users of marijuana — those who smoked the drug at least 27 of the preceding 30 days — critical skills related to attention, memory and learning were significantly impaired, even after they had not used the drug for at least 24 hours."

NIDA also cites scientific evidence that frequent marijuana use in early adolescence can increase the likelihood of drug problems later in life. [27]

For their part, those campaigning for legalization or decriminalization accept that heavy, long-term use — as well as use by the very young — can be problematic. But they emphasize the relatively small percentage of marijuana users who develop dependence.

"A small minority of Americans — less than 1 percent — smoke marijuana on a daily basis," the Drug Policy Alliance Network says. "An even smaller minority develop a dependence on marijuana." [28]

That conclusion is consistent with the judgment of the Institute of Medicine, which published a major study of marijuana in 1999. "Compared to most other drugs . . . dependence among marijuana users is relatively rare," the institute said, adding that daily use of marijuana is rare. "Dependence appears to be less severe among people who use only marijuana than those who abuse cocaine, or those who abuse marijuana with other drugs (including alcohol)." [29]

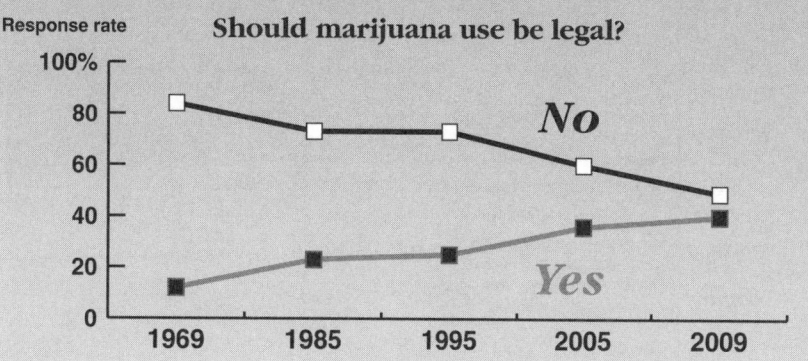

Support for Marijuana Legalization Growing

Forty percent of Americans polled in 2009 said marijuana use should be legalized — more than three times the percentage from 1969. Opposition to legalization dropped by 35 percentage points — from 84 percent to 49 — over the same period.

Should marijuana use be legal?

Response rate

Sources: Joseph Carroll, "Who Supports Marijuana Legalization?" Gallup, November 2005; "40 Percent Say Marijuana Should Be Legalized," Rasmussen Reports, February 2009.

The institute cited studies showing that marijuana is much less addictive, for instance, than alcohol. Marijuana dependence ranges from 4.4 percent to 9 percent of the adult population at one time or another, compared to 13.8 percent for alcohol. [30]

As varied as the survey data can be, all of it was gathered about a drug that remains largely illegal. Kleiman of UCLA argues that if marijuana were legalized under the same conditions as alcohol or cigarettes, the laws of the marketplace would push sellers into massive promotion in order to increase consumption. "If you set it up as a system where a number of peoples' wealth depends on creating pot addicts, they will do so," he says. "Selling cannabis or any other intoxicant to people who use it moderately gets you no money."

In a new book on reducing crime and punishment, Kleiman argues for permitting homegrown marijuana, as well as marijuana grown by consumer cooperatives, but prohibiting advertising and commercial production. That

policy, he says, would remove commercial incentives for cannabis producers and sellers to expand their market, thereby adding to the drug-dependent population. [31]

Drug-war advocates argue that the best policy is to continue prohibition. "When you push back [with tough laws], use gets reduced," says Burns of the district attorneys association, citing National Survey on Drug Use and Health data. They show a decline in adolescent marijuana use from 8.2 percent in 2002 to 7.6 percent in 2007 under the Bush administration's stringent anti-marijuana policies. [32]

"Fewer young people are smoking" marijuana today, Burns says. "But if you say that it's legal, you reduce the perception of risk — and clearly it would become much more available — that use is going to go up."

Among adults ages 50-59, however, rates of illicit drug use rose during the same period, from 2.7 percent to 5 percent. The pattern was similar for those even older. "This is the generation that used and abused drugs at

Pot Smoking in U.S. Tops the Charts

An estimated 42 percent of Americans and New Zealanders have smoked marijuana at least once, significantly more than most nations and more than twice the percentage of European countries.

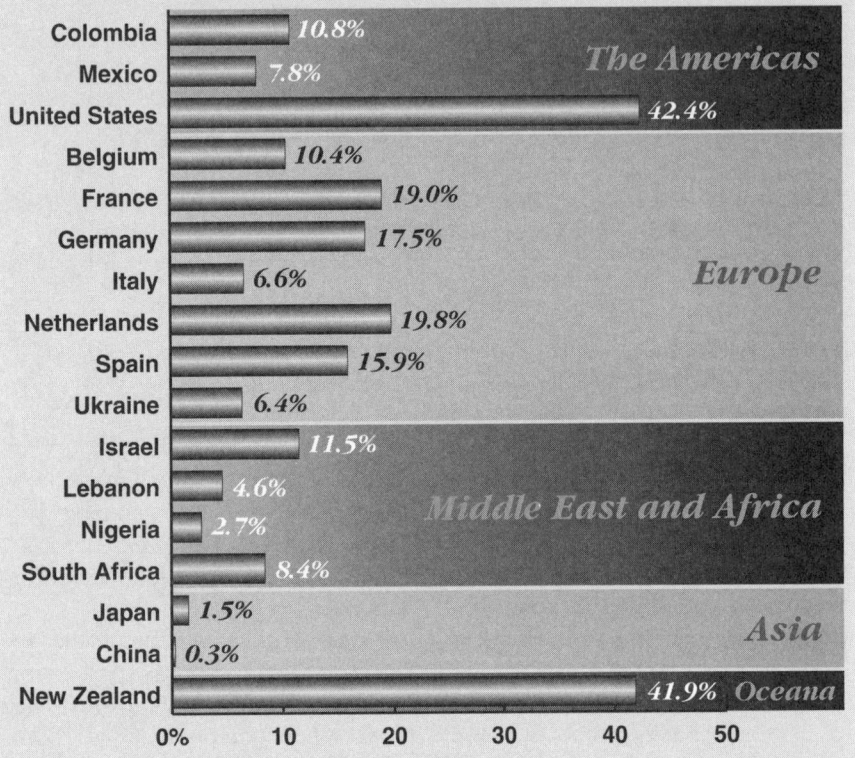

Estimated Cannabis Use Among Population
(at least one usage)

Region	Country	Percentage
The Americas	Colombia	10.8%
	Mexico	7.8%
	United States	42.4%
Europe	Belgium	10.4%
	France	19.0%
	Germany	17.5%
	Italy	6.6%
	Netherlands	19.8%
	Spain	15.9%
	Ukraine	6.4%
Middle East and Africa	Israel	11.5%
	Lebanon	4.6%
	Nigeria	2.7%
	South Africa	8.4%
Asia	Japan	1.5%
	China	0.3%
Oceana	New Zealand	41.9%

Source: Louisa Degenhardt, et al., "Toward a Global View of Alcohol, Tobacco, Cannabis, and Cocaine Use: Findings from the WHO World Mental Health Surveys," PloS Medicine, July 2008

a much higher level when they were younger," Burns says. "For many people, it's for life."

In El Paso, Councilman O'Rourke concedes that the possibility of a spike in use is a "very valid concern." But he argues that decriminalizing or legalizing marijuana is the first step toward creating an effective regulatory system.

"When it's criminalized and underground, the criminals decide what the market is," he says. "They're selling to 10-year-olds and 12-year-olds."

Would legalizing marijuana help the criminal-justice system?

Advocates of legalization or decriminalization argue that law-enforcement time and resources shouldn't be spent on arresting marijuana users. Those who want to keep marijuana illegal say that whatever negative effects may exist are negligible compared with the advantages of allowing police and prosecutors to keep a crime-control tool that proves useful.

The context of the debate is a law-enforcement climate in which marijuana use and small-quantity possession is a low priority, at least in much of the country.

With the vast majority of marijuana users — as opposed to dealers — spending no more than a night behind bars, the criminal-justice argument has shifted to the issue of whether police and courts should spend any time or resources on low-level pot busts.

Considerable — if anecdotal — evidence can be found of police tolerance of low-level drug use. A recent *Washington Post* review of a concert by The Dead (formerly the Grateful Dead) described seeing in the audience a "50-something with a tucked-in, button-down shirt and a BlackBerry holster on his hip slyly taking a hit off a joint." [33]

In commentator Andrew Sullivan's popular blog the Daily Dish, the "Cannabis Closet" series features reports from readers that provide further anecdotal indications of police tolerance. "I live in Boulder, CO and there is no closet here," a reader e-mailed. "People just assume that you smoke pot. And the police don't care about it unless you are a big-time grower. . . . We smoke joints openly in public, and the cops usually won't even ask us to put it out if they see us doing it. I've smoked pot with a cop. In public." [34]

New York City, however, appears to be an exception to no-bust policies. The New York Civil Liberties Union in a 2008 report documented a 10-fold increase in street marijuana arrests over the previous 10 years. According to city statistics, the report said, arrests began to soar during the 1994-2001 administration of Mayor Rudolph Giuliani and continued under Michael Bloomberg. The number rose from 3,200 in 1987 to 39,700 in 2007. [35]

In the New York system, arrestees spend no more than a night in jail on a first or second offense, and then serve a version of probation for six months to a year, when the case is dismissed if no other infractions have occurred. [36]

Elsewhere in the country as well, even marijuana-prohibition critics acknowledge that most people serving time for marijuana are dealers. "By and large, it's not the case that you're going to go to prison for smoking a joint these days," says Marc Mauer, executive director of the Sentencing Project, which advocates reduced use of incarceration.

Still, says Mauer, who co-authored a study on the subject, 40 percent of the country's annual 1.8 million drug arrests are for marijuana — mostly low-level dealers, with higher-level dealers being the ones who end up doing time. [37] Though most of those arrested don't go to prison, "Law-enforcement resources go into arresting, processing, the court system parceling out cases," he says. "Clearly we're talking about tens of millions of dollars in police processing time. And for every hour police spend on making and processing marijuana arrests, that's an hour not responding to domestic violence or conducting community policing."

Burns of the district attorneys association counters that the vast majority of pot cases soak up relatively little in law-enforcement resources. "Low-level possession cases are already diverted — citation, dismissal, maybe a day or two in jail after multiple offenses — and by the time a court invests time and money in an offender via drug court or an intense diversion program, the offender has engaged in felony activity on multiple occasions," he says.

Nor do pot busts divert police from other duties, argues Burns, once a prosecutor in Zion, Utah. "The citation usually occurs when someone is being stopped or investigated for something else — traffic offense, assault, petty theft — so an officer is going to be there anyway. And there is a fine associated with the marijuana violation that more than pays for the officer's time."

Some prohibition opponents downplay the issue of criminal-justice resources. "The budget issue is very important, but we should not lose sight of the moral component — 700,000 Americans are being arrested every year for nothing more than marijuana possession," says Piper of the Drug Policy Alliance.

He adds that those arrested face consequences even if they don't go to jail or prison. "Those arrested are separated from their loved ones, branded criminals, denied jobs and in many cases prohibited from accessing public assistance for life."

Pacula at the RAND Corp. argues that questions of morality aren't a government province and shouldn't play a part in the debate.

Pacula argues that data on prohibition's law-enforcement costs should be weighed against projected costs to the system of legalizing or decriminalizing. "All of the literature suggests to me that harms will go up," she says. "And the cost of those harms is not zero."

She points to a 2004 study she co-authored that found a statistical association between increased marijuana use — because of lower pot prices — and income-producing crimes such as robbery, burglary, vehicle theft, forgery and prostitution. [38]

But Pacula acknowledges that the study isn't absolutely definitive, because it's based on data from crime in general, and from marijuana arrests — that is, not from the entire population of marijuana users, but from those who get charged with crimes. The conclusion she draws would be familiar to anyone who has seen a "Cheech and Chong" film: "It may be that people are more likely to get caught if they're using marijuana." ∎

BACKGROUND

'The Poisonous Weed'

In the late 19th century, the use of opium and its derivatives — morphine and heroin — as well as cocaine, began emerging as an issue for state and federal governments. By the early 20th century, states were starting to regulate medical prescriptions more rigorously. And in 1914, the Harrison Narcotics Act strictly limited access to opiates, cocaine and other drugs. [39]

Meanwhile, marijuana — often incorrectly demonized as a narcotic — was making its way into the United States. Mexican immigrants and Caribbean sailors had introduced the drug, which soon became popular in big cities, especially in the black community, and, in the West and Southwest, among Mexican-Americans.

By 1930, 24 states had prohibited marijuana, though the public at large still had little awareness of it. That changed with the 1930 formation of the Federal Bureau of Narcotics within the Treasury Department. Its fabled director — Harry J. Anslinger, who held the job until 1962 — was widely considered the father of marijuana prohibition.

Many authors attribute to him the wildly sensationalized tales of marijuana-induced crimes that became staple fare in tabloids, true-crime magazines and movies in the 1930s. The blizzard of lurid tales made for entertaining reading and viewing decades later, including the 1936 film "Tell Your Children" — known as "Reefer Madness" — which became a cult classic among college students in the 1970s and went on to inspire an off-Broadway musical. [40]

However, David F. Musto, who teaches the history of medicine at Yale University and is considered the leading historian of U.S. drug use and drug policy, debunks the popular view of Anslinger as an anti-marijuana crusader. In the early and mid-1930s, he writes, Anslinger's main priority was heroin; he wanted to keep marijuana a state matter. [41]

But pressure for a federal law, especially from law enforcement agencies in the Southwest, proved irresistible. That pressure included breathless newspaper headlines, such as this one in a newspaper published by the then-powerful Hearst chain: "MARIJUANA MAKES FIENDS OF BOYS IN 30 DAYS; HASHISH GOADS USERS TO BLOOD LUST." [42]

Even the relatively staid *New York Times* joined the campaign to make marijuana illegal nationwide. "The poisonous weed . . . maddens the senses and emaciates the body of the user," said a 1934 story from Denver about marijuana's wide availability in the West. "Most crimes of violence in this section, especially in the country districts, are laid to users of the drug." [43]

The Times also noted that marijuana was "particularly popular with Latin Americans." Such scare stories aimed to drive home the point that no federal law against marijuana existed, and that state laws often weren't rigorously enforced.

In 1937, Congress passed the Marihuana Tax Act, which, despite its name, was effectively a prohibition measure. And by that year, all states had enacted marijuana prohibition laws of their own. [44]

In the wake of the new law, Anslinger promoted anti-marijuana campaigns, but Musto says he didn't push scare stories that gave the impression of an out-of-control problem.

Drug Culture

For about 20 years after the Marihuana Tax Act, marijuana remained in the cultural and legal shadows. Alcohol and tobacco were the only socially approved drugs, said a 1972 report from the National Commission on Marihuana and Drug Abuse, a panel appointed by President Nixon and headed by former Pennsylvania Gov. Raymond P. Shafer. [45]

But by the time the Shafer commission began its work, the tables had turned. "While marihuana is perceived as less harmful than before, alcohol and tobacco are regarded as more harmful," the panel reported. [46]

The commission also noted that Americans had been using alcohol and tobacco since colonial times (and, in the case of American Indians and tobacco, since before European settlers arrived). But marijuana, the opiates and cocaine had all arrived relatively recently. "And the users of these drugs were either aliens, like the Chinese opium smokers, or perceived to be marginal members of society," the commission noted. [47]

But the social revolution of the 1960s and '70s blurred the boundaries between mainstream and marginal. Sowers of the seeds of change included the poets and novelists who became known as "the Beats," notably poet Allen Ginsberg. He won respectful attention in some cultural institutions for his argument that marijuana and psychedelics had benign uses. "Marijuana is a useful catalyst for specific optical and aural aesthetic perceptions," he wrote in *The Atlantic* in 1966. [48]

Ginsberg had by then cofounded the New York chapter of the country's first anti-prohibition organization, LeMar (Legalize Marijuana), which had been formed in San Francisco in 1964. The poet's role drew law-enforcement attention. "From what I have read and heard, it would appear that the reported increased and widespread use of marihuana by college students could be attributed in part to the influence of Allen Ginsberg and persons of his ilk," a Federal Bureau of Narcotics agent reported in 1965. [49]

As the war in Vietnam escalated during the late 1960s, in turn strengthening the antiwar movement, pot smoking took on a political character, representing rejection of laws and social codes seen as unjust — like the war itself — and antiquated.

U.S. forces in Vietnam embraced the rebelliousness. In 1970, a *New York Times* correspondent reported how soldiers returning from a 10-day jungle mission shared a joint on the helicopter with the door gunner. Another soldier told the reporter he smoked marijuana constantly while on patrol. [50]

In fact, the *Times* said that in some areas 20-40 percent of soldiers used the drug. But a Vietnam vet, John Steinbeck IV, son of the Nobel Prize-winning novelist, told a Senate subcommittee in 1968 that 60 percent of the troops ages 19 to 27 smoked marijuana. [51]

On the home front, too, news media and popular culture began to acknowledge widespread marijuana use. In music, a number of songs depicted or praised drug use — the Jefferson Airplane's "White Rabbit," with its exhortation to "feed your head," heads the list. In films, the iconic "Easy Rider" (1969) and "Woodstock" (1970) started the trend. By the 1970s, any number of films contained matter-of-fact scenes or references to drug use.

The major annual national survey on drug use among young people confirmed the impression that use of marijuana and other drugs climbed during the 1970s. "Monitoring the Future," a federally funded project of the University of Michigan's Institute for Social Research, shows that marijuana use by 12th-graders climbed during the '70s in all regions and among all racial and ethnic groups, and social classes, peaking for most of them in 1979. By then an all-time high of 50.8 percent of all high-school seniors had used marijuana. [52]

Drug War

As drug use mounted, a succession of presidential administrations searched for ways to respond. The enduring "war on drugs" metaphor is attributed to President Nixon, who took office in 1969, though he favored emphasizing treatment for those addicted to drugs. [53]

Nixon's administration funded programs that treated heroin addicts with methadone, a policy that some hardliners opposed because it replaced one drug with another. And under Nixon, the federal government focused on narcotics addicts, not marijuana users.

Continued on p. 536

Chronology

1930s *Marijuana is prohibited nationwide.*

1930
Federal Bureau of Narcotics is established in the Treasury Department.

1937
Congress passes the Marihuana Tax Act, which effectively bans the drug.

— • —

1960s-1970s
During political upheavals, drug culture spreads from artists and writers to universities and broader society, prompting conflicting government responses.

1968
Novelist's son and Vietnam veteran John Steinbeck IV testifies in Congress that 60 percent of young troops in Southeast Asia are smoking pot.

1969
Film "Easy Rider" starts a cinematic trend of depicting pot smoking.

1970
Comprehensive Drug Abuse Treatment Act combines tough measures such as no-knock searches with low penalty for first-time marijuana offenders; classifies marijuana as a Schedule 1 drug with no medical uses and high abuse potential.

1975
Half of all high-school seniors have smoked marijuana — an all-time peak.

1977
President Jimmy Carter endorses decriminalization of marijuana possession of one ounce or less, but the plan dies after a scandal involving his drug-policy adviser.

1978
New Mexico lawmakers pass the nation's first medical-marijuana law.

— • —

1980s-1990s
Drug policy reverts to hard-line enforcement, partly in response to epidemic of crack cocaine use in inner cities; marijuana-liberalization forces gather strength.

1982
U.S. Food and Drug Administration (FDA) shuts down a tiny program that supplied medical marijuana.

1983
First lady Nancy Reagan launches "Just Say No" anti-drug campaign.

1985
Reagan administration adopts U.S. Navy's "zero tolerance" doctrine.

1986
Drug Abuse Act strengthens drug law, imposes heavy mandatory-minimum sentences.

1990
Opposition to mandatory sentences includes some federal judges, including a Reagan appointee who resigns from the bench in protest. . . . President George H. W. Bush says drug convicts deserve no sympathy.

1996
California voters pass a medical-marijuana law, opening a new era of medical-pot legislation. . . . Arizona voters also approve medical-pot law, but legislature kills it.

1999
In exhaustive scientific study of marijuana, Institute of Medicine recommends clinical trials of therapeutic uses of the drug.

2000s *Medical marijuana moves to center of debate as public opinion appears to shift toward legalization.*

2000
Hawaii's legislature creates first medical-marijuana law promoted by lawmakers rather than citizens.

2001
Drug Enforcement Administration refuses to remove marijuana from Schedule 1 classification, based on Department of Health and Human Services recommendation.

2005
Gallup Poll shows one-third of Americans support legalizing marijuana, up from 25 percent in 1995.

2006
FDA says marijuana has no medical use and that smoking it is harmful.

2007
Gov. M. Jodi Rell, R-Conn., vetoes medical-marijuana law.

2008
Sen. Jim Webb, D-Va., advocates creation of a commission to review the criminal-justice system, including drug laws.

2009
Attorney General Eric H. Holder Jr. says Obama administration will defer to state medical-marijuana laws. . . . U.S. Supreme Court declines to hear two California counties' challenge to state medical-marijuana law. . . . Minnesota medical-marijuana law and Massachusetts marijuana decriminalization take effect. . . . California Assemblyman Tom Ammiano proposes legalizing and taxing marijuana. . . . Senate Judiciary Crime and Drugs Subcommittee schedules June 11 hearing on Webb's commission bill.

California Pot Dispensaries Are Flourishing

"And the state hasn't gone to hell."

Some states are cautious about medical marijuana. They limit the number of marijuana "prescriptions" that one doctor can write, prohibit the opening of supply outlets, and permit only sufferers from certain specific illnesses to qualify. [1]

Seen from California, such precautions can look a little timid. In the Golden State, where the modern medical-marijuana era began with a law passed by voter initiative in 1996, medical marijuana is available from hundreds of storefront "dispensaries" and has spawned a large market in cannabis grown for these outlets.

At least 200,000 Californians are authorized medical-marijuana users, according to Americans for Safe Access, an Oakland-based medical-marijuana advocacy organization. [2] "Certainly in Northern California, well over 1 percent of the adult population are medical-marijuana users, in some places 2 percent," says Dale Gieringer, veteran state coordinator for California NORML (National Organization for the Reform of Marijuana Laws).

Law-enforcement officials concede that Californians on the whole support the system as it's developed. Yet that system and the state laws that underpin it fly in the face of federal law prohibiting sale, possession and use of cannabis, law-enforcement authorities argue. But the Obama administration's new policy of deferring to state medical-marijuana laws was followed by a California law-enforcement defeat on medical marijuana in the U.S. Supreme Court.

In May, the high court declined to consider a challenge to California's law that was based on its inconsistency with federal law. San Diego and San Bernardino counties had pursued that argument unsuccessfully through California state courts. The U.S. Supreme Court turned down without comment the counties' appeal of a California Supreme Court decision. [3]

But an attorney representing the California Police Chiefs Association maintains that city governments are still prohibited from violating federal law. "Since distribution of marijuana violates federal law," Martin J. Mayer wrote in a May memo to all police chiefs and sheriffs, "passing a zoning ordinance which, for ex-

ample, only allows such operations to be conducted in the industrial or commercial zone of a city, would still be in violation of the laws of the United States and, therefore, prohibited." [4]

So far, that argument hasn't carried much weight with California's cities and counties. "The limited legal protections afforded to pot growers and dispensary owners have turned marijuana cultivation and distribution in California into a classic 'gray area' business, like gambling or strip clubs, which are tolerated or not, to varying degrees, depending on where you live and on how aggressive your local sheriff is feeling that afternoon," David Samuels of *The New Yorker* reported last year in a long, from-the-inside look at the state's marijuana industry. [5]

Since then, the "gray area" has expanded. In June, the *Los Angeles Times* reported that at least 600 medical-marijuana "dispensaries" — many if not most of them storefronts — are operating in Los Angeles County alone. They've proliferated because of a loophole in a city moratorium on new dispensaries. A hardship exemption allows outlets that opened after the moratorium began to keep running while the City Council prepares a comprehensive ordinance. That project has been under way for more than a year. [6]

Some in law enforcement argue that dispensaries are illegal even under the state medical-marijuana law. Storefront outlets aren't mentioned either in the 1996 law that voters passed nor in the 2004 law designed to provide further specifications of how the medical-marijuana system would operate, medical-marijuana advocates acknowledge. [7]

The law does mention that nonprofit cooperatives can supply marijuana. California Attorney General Edmund G. Brown Jr. concluded in formal guidelines issued last year that dispensaries could meet legal requirements as long as they could prove they weren't making profits, nor allowing any pot to enter the non-medical market. [8]

The guidelines also said that cooperatives shouldn't buy cannabis from non-members. California NORML, which has played an active

Continued from p. 534

The Comprehensive Drug Abuse Treatment Act of 1970 — the Nixon administration's milestone in drug-law history — represented a compromise between the treatment and law-enforcement approaches to drug policy. For example, the penalty for a first offense for possessing a small amount of marijuana would be probation. But police also were authorized to mount surprise, "no-knock" searches. And the law created a drug-categorization scheme that defined marijuana as a Sched-

ule 1 drug — that is, a substance with "a high potential for abuse" and "no currently accepted medical use." [54]

The Watergate scandal coincided with growing acceptance of marijuana. President Gerald R. Ford, who became president when Nixon resigned in disgrace, had little effect on drug policy. But President Jimmy Carter attempted to revamp federal marijuana policy. In 1977, he endorsed legislation to remove criminal penalties for possession of an ounce or less of marijuana. [55]

Carter also advocated some hard-line steps, including an order to the Justice Department to consider removing restrictions on government access to personal financial information on known drug traffickers — in effect drawing a line between personal use and participation in the illegal trade in drugs. [56]

Moreover, the administration agreed to pay for the Mexican government to spray a herbicide, paraquat, on marijuana and opium-poppy plantations. That created a scandal that sank the

role in the evolution of the medical-marijuana system, challenges that conclusion. But, NORML adds, "In practice, this restriction can be easily avoided by simply enrolling all outside vendors as members of the collective." [9]

But that approach doesn't look so kosher to police.

"Too often 'medical marijuana' has been used as a smokescreen for those who want to legalize it and profit off it, and storefront dispensaries established as cover for selling an illegal substance for a lucrative return," the California Police Chiefs Association says in a 2009 "white paper" on dispensaries. [10]

The paper also concedes that protests haven't erupted, which in turn influences city and county officials. "Because the majority of their citizens have been sympathetic and projected a favorable attitude toward medical-marijuana patients, and have been tolerant of the cultivation and use of marijuana, public officials . . . have taken a hands-off attitude."

The public acceptance may reflect the fact that marijuana use hasn't exploded in the state's high schools — though, to be sure, the level is relatively high. The California attorney general's most recent annual survey of high-school students reported that since 2003, the share of students who have smoked pot in the previous six months has remained stable, at about 20 percent for ninth-graders and 31 percent for 11th-graders. [11]

"One of the most disturbing findings of the current survey is, among older students, recreational use of diverted (not prescribed by physicians) prescription painkillers ranks highest in illegal use behind marijuana," the report said.

Joshua Braun sells numerous varieties of marijuana at his HortiPharm Caregivers dispensary in Santa Barbara, Calif.

Getty Images/Rod Rolle

In short, says Ellen Komp, a spokeswoman for California NORML, the medical-marijuana system is providing cannabis to patients without causing social disruption.

"Dispensaries are operating in neighborhoods," she says, "and the state hasn't gone to hell."

[1] "Active State Medical Marijuana Programs," National Organization for the Reform of Marijuana Laws, http://norml.org/index.cfm?Group_ID= 3391#top.

[2] "Activist Newsletter," Americans for Safe Access, March 2009, p. 2, www.safeaccessnow.org/downloads/ASA_mar09_newsletter.pdf.

[3] David G. Savage, "Justices reject California appeals on medical pot," *Los Angeles Times*, May 19, 2009, p. 19.

[4] Martin J. Mayer, "Client Alert Memorandum," California Police Chiefs Association, May 19, 2009, www.californiapolicechiefs.org/nav_files/marijuana_files/vol_24_no_14_may_09.pdf.

[5] David Samuels, "Dr. Kush: How Medical Marijuana Is Transforming the Pot Industry," *The New Yorker*, July 28, 2008.

[6] John Hoeffel, "L.A.'s medical pot dispensary moratorium led to a boom instead," *Los Angeles Times*, June 3, 2009, www.latimes.com/news/local/la-me-medical-marijuana3-2009jun03,0,6866563,full.story.

[7] "California NORML Advice for Medical Marijuana Providers," California NORML, April 2009, www.canorml.org/prop/collectivetips.html.

[8] "Guidelines for the Security and Non-Diversion of Marijuana Grown for Medical Use," California Department of Justice, August 2008, http://ag.ca.gov/cms_attachments/press/pdfs/n1601_medicalmarijuanaguidelines.pdf.

[9] "New AG Guidelines Don't Substantially Conflict With Previous Guidelines," California NORML, Aug. 27, 2008, www.canorml.org/news/AGguides.html.

[10] "White Paper on Marijuana Dispensaries,' California Police Chiefs Association, April 2009, p. vi, www.californiapolicechiefs.org/nav_files/marijuana_files/MarijuanaDispensariesWhitePaper_042209.pdf.

[11] Gregory Austin and Rodney Skager, "Highlights, 12th Biennial California Student Survey, Drug, Alcohol and Tobacco Use, 2007-2008," California Attorney General's Office, winter 2008, pp. 10, 24, http://safestate.org/documents/CSS_12th_Highlights_Report.pdf.

marijuana-decriminalization proposal.

Keith Stroup, founder of the country's first Washington-based, pro-legalization lobbying group — the National Organization for the Reform of Marijuana Laws (NORML) — had been friendly with Peter Bourne, a physician who was Carter's drug-policy adviser. But after Bourne endorsed the spraying, a furious Stroup gave a reporter the names of witnesses to Bourne's presence at a party where some guests — possibly including Bourne — snorted cocaine. [57]

The ensuing scandal not only ended Bourne's government career but also the prospects of drug-decriminalization legislation, linked as it was to the disgraced ex-drug adviser. [58]

President Ronald W. Reagan, who succeeded Carter, came to embody the drug war more than any other president before or since. Politically, drug use and drug tolerance had become linked with Democrats and the left. Moreover, Reagan's two terms (1981-1989) coincided with a boom in cocaine trafficking from

South America and the beginnings of what became the crack cocaine boom.

Cocaine got most of the attention. But the Reagan administration made clear its hard-line approach applied to all drugs — a policy embodied in the "Zero Tolerance" and "Just Say No" slogans. First lady Nancy Reagan debuted the latter line in 1983. The administration apparently borrowed "zero tolerance" from the U.S. Navy. [59]

More substantively, the Reagan administration won passage of the tough

Would Legalizing Pot Hurt the Mexican Cartels?

Former President Vicente Fox: "It's time to open the debate."

The bloody war raging in Mexico among drug cartels is fueling arguments on both sides in the marijuana-decriminalization debate heating up in the United States. The gangs, which are fighting the government as well as each other, get most of their revenue from U.S. drug consumers, including marijuana smokers. [1]

"Legalizing drugs is the worst thing we could do for President Felipe Calderón and our Mexican allies." the George W. Bush administration's drug czar, John P. Walters, wrote in *The Wall Street Journal* in April. "It would weaken the moral authority of his fight, and the Mexicans would immediately realize that we have no intention of reducing consumption. Who do we think would take the profits from a legal drug trade? U.S. suppliers would certainly spring up, but that wouldn't preclude Mexican suppliers as well." [2] Walters is now executive vice president of the Hudson Institute, a nonpartisan think tank.

But how much the cartels make from marijuana alone is uncertain. The Justice Department's National Drug Intelligence Center (NDIC) says marijuana seizures on the U.S. side of the border increased in recent years, to about 1.4 million kilograms (about 3 million pounds) in 2007, but with a projected falloff for 2008 to 1.1 million kilos. U.S. domestic production was seen as increasing, but the center said no estimates were considered reliable enough to cite. [3]

Amid the uncertainty, Mark A. R. Kleiman, director of the drug policy analysis program at the University of California, Los Angeles, noted in a blog posting that marijuana couldn't account for most cartel revenues "since most of our cocaine still comes through Mexico, and the cocaine market is 250 percent the size of the pot market." [4]

Still, says the NDIC — reflecting a law-enforcement community consensus — Mexican gangs, known in Justice Department lingo as Drug-Trafficking Organizations (DTOs), also run large outdoor marijuana-growing operations in the West, which have been hit hard by drought and stepped-up police operations; drug agents eradicated a total of 6.6 million plants in 2007, some 2.6 million of them on public lands. [5]

In principle, legalizing marijuana would lower prices by removing the risk of arrest and by allowing more participants to enter the field. The extent to which Mexican gangs would be hit in the pocketbook, though, is as uncertain as crop estimates.

Scott Burns, executive director of the National District Attorneys Association, ridicules the idea that outlaw gangs would meekly join the legal business world, or give way to new competitors. It would be naïve to think, he says, "That cartels would file for tax status, that they'd somehow stop and say, 'We don't have a business license, so we won't grow those 20,000 plants in Yosemite this year.'"

Legalization advocates say law-enforcement agencies, unburdened by the duty to take on the entire drug industry, could focus their efforts on DTOs operating illegally.

"If we could take tens of millions of dollars away from the Mexican DTOs, are they still going to be making money?" asks Bill Piper, national affairs director of the Drug Policy Alliance. "Yes, but they may not still have $20 million a year for bribery and buying machine guns. It would be a crime issue but not a national security issue for Mexico and the United States."

Similar views are now being heard from Mexico and elsewhere in Latin America, where drug-producing countries have been a centerpiece of U.S. anti-drug policy for three decades.

Indeed, ex-drug czar Walters wrote his anti-legalization column in response to a call for decriminalization throughout the region from a commission headed by the former president of Mexico,

Anti-Drug Abuse Acts of 1986 and 1988. The laws' provisions included life sentences — and the death penalty in some circumstances — for top figures in major drug organizations. But the two statutes would become better known for a 100-to-1 disparity between mandatory-minimum sentences for crack cocaine and cocaine powder. The minimum for just five grams of crack (mainly used by blacks) was five years — the same penalty as for 500 grams of powder (used mainly by whites). [60]

Mandatory minimums also applied to marijuana. A conviction in a case involving at least 100 kilograms (220 pounds) of marijuana, or 100 plants, requires a five-year sentence. [61]

The sentencing scheme soon generated opposition — by judges, among others — who argued that low-level drug runners were getting longer terms than higher-ups with information to trade for lesser charges. "I can't continue to do it — I can't continue to give out sentences that I feel in some instances are unconscionable," U.S. District Judge J. Lawrence Irving of San Diego, a Reagan appointee, said in announcing he was quitting the bench. [62]

Prosecutors and other drug-war advocates told the critics to save their sympathies for victims of the drug trade, not traffickers, even low-level ones. Then President George H. W. Bush, asked about a 19-year-old sentenced to 10 years for selling crack within 1,000 feet of a school, said: "I can't feel sorry for this fellow." [63]

Decriminalization Push

Tough sentencing laws re-energized decriminalization campaigns. State legislatures didn't abolish marijuana laws, but most did reduce first-offense possession cases involving small

Ernesto Zedillo, together with the ex-presidents of Colombia, César Gaviria, and Brazil, Henrique Cardoso. "The available empirical evidence shows that the harm caused by this drug [marijuana] is similar to the harm caused by alcohol or tobacco," the Latin American Commission on Drugs and Democracy said in a policy proposal issued in April. "Most of the damage associated with cannabis use — from the indiscriminate arrest and incarceration of consumers to the violence and corruption that affect all of society — is the result of the current prohibitionist policies." [6]

Another former Mexican president, Vicente Fox, is largely in agreement. "I believe it's time to open the debate over legalizing drugs," he told CNN in May. "It must be done in conjunction with the United States, but it is time to open the debate." [7]

As president, Fox vetoed legislation from the Mexican Congress to decriminalize small quantities of cocaine and marijuana. [8] But he made that move under U.S. pressure, and before Mexico's drug violence skyrocketed after his successor, Calderón, mounted a major offensive against the drug gangs. An estimated 6,300 Mexicans were killed last year alone, though Mexican authorities reported in April that the toll had fallen by 25 percent during the first three months of this year, to about 1,600, compared to the final quarter of 2008. [9]

Most of the killing results from turf battles along the border between rival gangs, though police and journalists have also been targeted, and associated violence has also claimed the lives of

Former Mexican President Vicente Fox.

AFP/Getty Images/Luis Acosta

uninvolved civilians.

In El Paso, Texas, whose twin city of Ciudad Juárez, Mexico, is connected by a bridge over the Rio Grande, City Councilman Beto O'Rourke acknowledges that the marijuana decriminalization he favors likely wouldn't play a major role in reducing the violence. he says, "because until you get to a holistic solution that gets to the production and distribution supply chain, you're not going to end the situation with the cartels."

[1] For background, see Peter Katel, "Mexico's Drug War," *CQ Researcher*, Dec. 12, 2008, pp. 1009-1032.

[2] John P. Walters, "Drugs: To Legalize or Not," *The Wall Street Journal*, April 25, 2009, accessible at www.hudson.org/index.cfm?fuseaction=publication_details&id=6198.

[3] "National Drug Threat Assessment, 2009," National Drug Intelligence Center, December 2008, pp. 21-22, www.usdoj.gov/ndic/pubs31/31379/31379p.pdf.

[4] Mark A.R. Kleiman, "Joe Klein on drug legalization: same old, same old," The Reality-Based Community (blog), April 3, 2009, www.samefacts.com/archives/drug_policy_/2009/04/joe_klein_on_drug_legalization_same_old_same_old.php.

[5] "National Drug Threat Assessment," *op. cit.*, p. 20.

[6] "Drugs and Democracy: Toward a Paradigm Shift," Latin American Commission on Drugs and Democracy, April 2009, pp. 8-9, http://drugsanddemocracy.org/files/2009/02/declaracao_ingles_site.pdf.

[7] Arthur Brice, "Former Mexican president calls for legalizing marijuana," CNN, May 13, 2009, http://edition.cnn.com/2009/WORLD/americas/05/13/mexico.fox.marijuana/index.html.

[8] Marc Lacey, "In an Escalating Drug War, Mexico Fights the Cartels, and Itself," *The New York Times*, March 30, 2009, p. A1.

[9] Michael O'Boyle, "Mexico says death toll from drug war is falling," Reuters, April 3, 2009, http://uk.reuters.com/article/worldNews/idUKTRE5320CG20090403.

amounts to misdemeanors, in some cases eliminating the requirement that offenders serve jail time. [64]

Support for legalizing marijuana also drew strength from the growing "medical-marijuana" movement. Efforts to authorize use of the drug for medicinal purposes had begun in the 1970s among sufferers from chronic diseases such as glaucoma and multiple sclerosis, as well as cancer patients receiving chemotherapy. Speaking to state legislatures, journalists and anyone else who would listen, they said that smoking marijuana relieved their symptoms. A sizable number of doctors agreed. [65]

The first state to take action was New Mexico. In 1978, the legislature authorized medical marijuana in response to a campaign waged nearly single-handedly by a 26-year-old Vietnam veteran, Lynn Pierson, who'd been left painfully thin by testicular cancer and chemotherapy. Only marijuana (smoked on a doctor's recommendation) allowed him to endure the therapy, he said. [66]

But Pierson didn't live to see the result of his work. Only after he died, in August 1978, did the state medical-marijuana program receive any marijuana from its required supplier, the federal government. [67]

Following New Mexico's lead, other states passed similar laws, all permitting use of marijuana or THC, its psychoactive ingredient, supplied by the federal government. By 1980, 24 states had such laws, but only five or six had received either drug, according to the National Institute on Drug Abuse. [68]

The government's slowness in providing medical marijuana discouraged the activists, as did its preference for THC capsules, which many patients said did not provide the relief they received from smoking. The push for medical marijuana gained strength as the HIV/AIDS crisis worsened, and some sufferers said that only marijuana restored their appetites, enabling them to survive.

But the Food and Drug Administration didn't classify marijuana as medication, and in 1992 the U.S. Public Health Service stopped providing marijuana to certified medical users. [69]

In 1996, California voters approved a more radical approach authorizing anyone, including caregivers, to grow or possess marijuana if recommended by a physician for medical reasons. The referendum passed by a 56 percent-44 percent vote.

Other states began to follow California's lead, but with uneven results. Arizona voters in 1996 approved a medical-pot law by referendum, but the legislature overturned the measure, and another referendum failed in 2002. Hawaii in 2000 became the first state to act by legislative action rather than referendum. [70] Republican Connecticut Gov. M. Jodi Rell vetoed in 2007 a medical-marijuana bill that the legislature had passed. [71] By then, the Bush administration had been waging its own campaign against the "medical-marijuana" trend.

In 2001, the Drug Enforcement Administration refused a request to remove marijuana from the Schedule 1 category, citing a Health and Human Services Department assessment. In 2006, the U.S. Food and Drug Administration, in an apparent rebuttal of the 1999 Institute of Medicine report, issued an opinion that no scientific basis existed for use of marijuana as medicine. [72] ∎

CURRENT SITUATION

Action in the States

California may get the headlines on marijuana-law issues, but other states are grappling with a variety of marijuana-decriminalization measures.

Massachusetts cities and towns are coming to terms with a law approved by 65 percent of voters last year that defines possession of one ounce or less of pot as a civil offense. That law makes the state among the most liberal of even the other 10 states that have abolished jail time for first-offense, small-quantity possession. [73]

The Massachusetts law imposed a $100 fine for the offense — significantly less than the $300 fine for drinking in public — and didn't mention smoking in public. So, police argue, the new law effectively favors public pot-smokers.

"I just see this as a problem that wasn't addressed in the law that was passed," Lt. Joseph Aiello of the Gloucester Police Department said. "What does that say to kids? It says: Don't drink beer — smoke pot, because if you drink a beer you're going to get arrested; if you smoke pot you're only going to get a citation for $100." [74]

Aiello advocated a $300 fine for public pot-smoking — but the Gloucester City Council rejected the proposal, which had mixed results elsewhere in the state. Marijuana-legalization advocates say police are looking for problems with a new law that rubs them the wrong way. "This seems to be much more about people who never liked the law to begin with looking for an end run around the will of the voters," said Dan Bernath, a spokesman for the Marijuana Policy Project. [75]

In other states, the focus of marijuana-law debates remains medical pot. Michigan is making history this year, becoming the first — so far, the only — Midwestern state to put a medical-marijuana law into effect. In 2008, Michigan voters approved cannabis use for people with cancer, HIV/AIDS, glaucoma and other chronic diseases whose symptoms marijuana has long been said to ease.

The new Michigan law refrains from authorizing California-style dispensaries.

Medical users, or their caregivers, can grow their own. If they buy it on the black market, they won't be charged, but the sellers would be. And the law doesn't protect medical-pot users who are fired for failing job drug tests. [76] Majorie Russell, a professor at Thomas M. Cooley Law School in Lansing, said the voter initiative that passed the law succeeded because many citizens have experienced chemotherapy or chronic pain, or know people who've suffered those conditions. "That changed a lot of attitudes," she said. [77]

Elsewhere in the Midwest, though, the prospects for medical-marijuana laws are mixed. Republican Minnesota Gov. Tim Pawlenty vetoed legislation in May that would have authorized cannabis use solely for terminally ill patients. "While I am very sympathetic to those dealing with end-of-life illnesses and accompanying pain, I stand with law enforcement in opposition to this legislation," the governor said. Police and prosecutors had said that even the restricted approach would expand the general availability of marijuana. The bill had passed by votes of 36-28 in the Senate, and 70-64 in the House. [78]

Medical-marijuana backers immediately vowed to mount a ballot initiative next year to put the issue directly before voters. "Our basic approach is, we would spend what's needed," said Mirken at the Marijuana Policy Project. [79]

In Illinois, the state Senate passed a medical-marijuana bill on May 27 on a close 30-28 vote; the bill's House sponsor was considering delaying action until the fall in order to build more support. [80]

Political support for medical marijuana runs far stronger in other states. In New Mexico for example, a law that took effect in 2007 authorizes patients or caregivers — upon individual application — to cultivate cannabis to relieve symptoms of 15 specific conditions or illnesses, including cancer, Lou Gehrig's disease and HIV/AIDS. [81]

Continued on p. 542

At Issue:

Does permitting medical marijuana amount to "back-door legalization" of pot?

JOHN LOVELL
LEGISLATIVE COUNSEL, CALIFORNIA NARCOTIC OFFICERS ASSOCIATION

WRITTEN FOR *CQ RESEARCHER*, JUNE 8, 2009

*a*lthough presented to voters as providing relief to the terminally ill, medical-marijuana laws have become a subterfuge for recreational use of the drug. California is a pointed example of the evasion of the stated intent of the law.

Under California law, a physician is not required to issue a prescription for medical marijuana — that would invite professional inquiry into the appropriateness of that prescription. Instead, physicians are permitted to "recommend" marijuana to patients who think they require it. There are no medical standards governing that recommendation — as with prescription drugs — nor is there any serious medical oversight in determining whether a "recommendation" should be issued.

Thus, California has seen recommendations for the use of medical marijuana given to males for *their* menstrual cramps, to females for the discomfort high heels may cause them, to slackers to "ease the stress of life." Still another received "caregiver" status to provide marijuana for his dog! These are all specific examples of recommendations that have been given by compliant physicians. Such frivolous reasons should not be confused with the practice of medicine.

In other words, medical marijuana has virtually nothing to do with medicine and everything to do with attempting to evade controlled-substance laws. To allege that there are medical benefits to smoking marijuana is analogous to arguing for a medical benefit to the smoking of opium.

In addition to a law that permits easy evasion, medical-marijuana laws have spawned so-called medical-marijuana dispensaries. These large, retail outlets are not authorized under California law (which only permits co-ops for distribution where no profit is earned from distribution) and have become magnets for criminal activity. The fact that they are magnets for crime and have a corrosive impact on neighborhoods should not be a surprise — they have dope and large amounts of cash and have caused genuine alarm in the communities where the dispensaries are located. California crime reports are replete with incidences of violence in and around these locations.

California's medical-marijuana laws have been manipulated to evade California's controlled-substance laws. A true "medical" statute would have provided strict guidelines for prescribing the drug, would have fairly informed patients of the side-effects of the drug and would have imposed strict distribution controls.

The fact that the drafters of California's medical-marijuana law chose not to replicate standard medical practices speaks volumes about their true intent.

BRUCE MIRKEN
DIRECTOR OF COMMUNICATIONS MARIJUANA POLICY PROJECT

WRITTEN FOR *CQ RESEARCHER*, JUNE 6, 2009

*o*ne of the oldest and lamest arguments against laws allowing medical use of marijuana is that they somehow constitute "back-door legalization." The notion is absurd but continues to be stated with a straight face by those who oppose medical marijuana.

I say this as representative of an organization that believes marijuana should be treated like alcoholic beverages: Legal for adults but subject to sensible regulations and taxes.

But that's an entirely separate question. We can and do allow lots of drugs for medical use — morphine, OxyContin, even methamphetamine — that are not legal as toys. Personally, I got involved in this issue because I have friends with AIDS who are literally alive today because of medical marijuana.

The question here is not, "Might someone who isn't in legitimate medical need manage to possess marijuana under the guise of medicine?" Of course, a few manage to do so, just as about 7 million Americans illegally use prescription drugs in a given month, according to federal surveys. There has never been a system devised by humans that someone won't manage to cheat.

But even in California, whose loosely written medical-marijuana law has led to often-hysterical media reports of alleged abuse, marijuana arrests have increased — not declined — since the law went into effect in 1996. In 2007, 74,000 Californians were busted on marijuana charges, 80 percent of them for possession. If that's legalization, it's sure come in an odd form.

Other state medical-marijuana laws are much more tightly controlled than California's. Most require patients to register with the state, keep a copy of their doctor's recommendation on file and carry an ID card identifying them as a legal patient. Only specific conditions enumerated in the statute qualify for legal protection. These restrictions are not applied to any prescription drug, not even morphine or OxyContin.

That may surprise some, but it's true. A physician can legally prescribe any approved drug for any purpose, regardless of whether or not the FDA OK'd it for that use. About half of all prescriptions are written "off-label" — i.e. for uses not approved by the FDA. And you don't have to apply to the state or get an ID card to have your morphine prescription filled.

If anyone wants to talk about whether marijuana should be legal for adults, we're happy to have that discussion. But muddying the waters by claiming that limited, highly restricted laws aimed at protecting the sick and suffering are "back-door legalization" is simply dishonest.

Continued from p. 540

Rhode Island, however, may follow the California model in expanding its 2006 medical-marijuana law. Under the law, about 600 residents currently are authorized to use cannabis, but they and their political backers are arguing that without state-authorized dispensaries the only sources of supply are dope dealers. [82]

In early June the legislature passed a dispensary bill and sent it to Republican Gov. Donald L. Carcieri, who was expected to veto it. But members said they had the votes to override. [83]

Elsewhere in the Northeast, medical-cannabis bills are pending in New York, New Jersey and New Hampshire, where Democratic Gov. John Lynch is expected to veto the measure, which Attorney General Kelly Ayotte and county prosecutors have aggressively opposed.

Among other objections, Ayotte called marijuana a gateway to harder drugs, a traditional argument against any moves to soften marijuana laws. "Studies have shown that very few young people turn to illegal drugs such as cocaine or heroin without first experimenting with marijuana," Ayotte said in a letter to lawmakers.

But Sen. Kathy Sgambati, a Democrat, called Ayotte's point irrelevant to the medical-marijuana legislation and the patients who would benefit. "Ninety percent at least of the people who testified have medicine chests full of opiates," she said, adding that they weren't seeking "a stronger drug," but an effective one. [84]

In New York and New Jersey, medical-pot bills were given good chances in late May of reaching the floors of both houses, but the legislative sessions had only one month left to run. Both David A. Paterson, the New York governor, and New Jersey Gov. Jon Corzine, both Democrats, are expected to sign the bills if they pass. [85]

In New Jersey, where Attorney General Anne Milgram has also backed the bill, legislation has passed the Senate and is pending in the lower house. [86]

The Webb Approach

Freshman Sen. Jim Webb, D-Va. argues that the criminal-justice system demands urgent attention. "Justice statistics . . . show that 47.5 percent of all the drug arrests in our country in 2007 were for marijuana offenses," Webb wrote in *Parade* in March. "Additionally, nearly 60 percent of the people in state prisons serving time for a drug offense had no history of violence or of any significant selling activity." [87]

Yet mounting drug arrests in general, and marijuana arrests in particular, have simply flooded prisons with new convicts without making a dent in the market for drugs, including hard drugs, Webb insists. "We are not protecting our citizens from the increasing danger of criminals who perpetrate violence and intimidation as a way of life, and we are locking up too many people who do not belong in jail," Webb argued. [88]

Webb has introduced legislation calling for a National Criminal Justice Commission to examine all aspects of the system, including drug laws. Webb hasn't rejected pot legalization, but he hasn't advocated it either.

"It's true, we have way too many people in prison," Tom Riley, a spokesman for the Bush administration's drug czar, told *The Washington Post* in late 2008. "But it's not because the laws are unjust, but because there are too many people who are causing havoc and misery in the community." [89]

And J. Scott Leake, a Republican strategist in Virginia, told *The Post* that Webb was making a mistake in tackling laws that, Leake said, brought crime rates down. "If Sen. Webb were to try to roll some of that back, I think he would have a fight on his hands." [90]

The metaphor is apt. A decorated Marine and Vietnam veteran, Webb served as Navy secretary in the Reagan administration, long before he changed his party affiliation to Democrat. Webb has taught pistol marksmanship, and in his 2006 Senate campaign he displayed his concealed-weapon permit. [91]

In short, Webb is about as far from the stereotypical bleeding-heart liberal as one can get. "With Jim's personality, he's never going to strike somebody as being soft on crime or any other issue," said Virginia state Sen. J. Chapman Petersen, a Democrat. [92]

Toughness aside, Webb isn't proposing immediate changes to the system. But he minces no words in arguing that drug policy is a failed part of a failed system. "In 1980, we had 41,000 drug offenders in prison," he said on the Senate floor, when formally introducing his bill. "Today we have more than 500,000, an increase of 1,200 percent . . . and a significant percentage of those are incarcerated for possession or nonviolent offenses stemming from drug addiction." [93]

OUTLOOK

Congress' Move

Some newcomers to the long-running marijuana debate argue that the present state of affairs can't continue past another decade. "In 10 years, certainly, marijuana will be decriminalized," says El Paso City Council member O'Rourke, likening the present day to the last years of alcohol prohibition. "We're like we were in the early '30s. Our leaders are going to say, 'We can't afford to spend on this any more.' The country will come to that conclusion soon."

Veteran criminal-justice system analysts tend to make more nuanced forecasts. "I think we're likely to see a number of jurisdictions in effect decriminalizing marijuana," says Mauer at The Sentencing Project. "I don't know how many legislative bodies will take the step to do it in a formal way. I think there is still a reluctance to put their names on bottom lines."

Mainstream politicians approach marijuana prohibition in much the same way as they do the death penalty, Mauer says. "A couple of states have abolished capital punishment, but in practice prosecutors in many places have lost enthusiasm for it; it's a cost and a burden. That's a likely scenario for marijuana: 'Let's not get too worked up about it.' Enforcing it as a criminal-justice issue will decline in popularity."

Burns at the National District Attorneys Association is on the other side of the criminal-justice debate. But to some extent he shares Mauer's view on politicians' reluctance to dive into changing marijuana law. The Obama administration, Burns says, has no interest in turning up the heat on the debate, which would focus attention on its hands-off approach to state medical-marijuana laws.

In general, there's no reason to think that the marijuana-prohibition fight is anywhere near over, Burns says. "Debates go on in opinion pages of large and small papers; it's interesting for radio talk shows or late-night TV, in bars," he says. "But until the U.S. Congress says it's legal, or the FDA says it's a medicine, I don't know what the debate is about."

Still, further state actions to decriminalize cannabis are possible, says Pacula at the RAND Corp. think tank. But full-scale legalization — putting the entire cannabis business within the law — would require Congress to act. "The federal government doesn't have a strong reason to legalize marijuana right now," she says. "In 10 years, this issue will have been determined by the federal government, or we'll still be having this discussion."

Piper at the Drug Policy Alliance makes a similar forecast. A decade from now, he says, "I think we'll be at a point where several states have passed legalization, and we may very well be in a position on legalization that we are in medical marijuana right now. Federal law is still in the way, and the conflict will have to be resolved."

But another possibility is a continuing erosion of marijuana prohibition that leads to de facto legalization, says Kleiman of UCLA. The mechanism could easily be medical-marijuana authorization. "I don't think I know anybody who has a medical recommendation for cannabis; I can easily imagine that changing over the next five years," he says. "If it became non-weird to have that [authorization] card, you really have legalized pot. And without any sharp demarcation line, you could go from a situation where cannabis is illegal to where it's medical and it's sort of legal."

Kleiman adds, "I used to laugh at people who said medical marijuana is legalization. I don't laugh any more." ∎

Notes

[1] Quoted in Karl Vick, "In Calif., Medical Marijuana Laws Are Moving Pot Into the Mainstream," *The Washington Post*, April 12, 2009, p. A3, www.washingtonpost.com/wp-dyn/content/article/2009/04/11/AR2009041100767_pf.html. Schwarzenegger quoted in Jonathan Lloyd, "Schwarzenegger: High Time for Marijuana Debate," NBC Los Angeles, May 5, 2009, www.nbclosangeles.com/news/local/Arnold-Ready-to-Look-into-Legalization.html. See also "The Field Poll," April 30, 2009, http://field.com/fieldpollonline/subscribers/Rls2306.pdf.

[2] Quoted in Lloyd, *op. cit.*

[3] Quoted in David Johnston and Neil A. Lewis, "Ending Raids of Dispensers of Marijuana for Patients," *The New York Times*, March 19, 2009, p. A20.

[4] Quoted in "LA chief calls state marijuana laws 'Looney Tunes,' " MercuryNews.com (The Associated Press), April 2, 2009, www.mercurynews.com/news/ci_12056082?nclick_check=1.

[5] Quoted in Gary Fields, "White House Czar Calls For an End to 'War on Drugs,' " *The Wall Street Journal*, May 14, 2009, http://online.wsj.com/article/SB124225891527617397.html.

[6] Donna Leinwand, "U.S.' new drug czar targets prescription abuse as priority," Freep.com, May 21, 2009, http://content.usatoday.net/dist/custom/gci/InsidePage.aspx?cId=freep&sParam=35111116.story.

[7] *Ibid.*

[8] Mark A. R. Kleiman, *When Brute Force Fails: How to Have Less Crime and Less Punishment* (2009).

[9] "Estimated Number of Arrests, United States, 2005," FBI, September 2006, www.fbi.gov/ucr/05cius/data/table_29.html; "Results from the 2007 National Survey on Drug Use and Health: National Findings," Sept. 4, 2008, www.oas.samhsa.gov/NSDUH/2k7NSDUH/2k7results.cfm#Ch2.

[10] Louisa Degenhardt, *et al.*, "Toward a Global View of Alcohol, Tobacco, Cannabis, and Cocaine Use: Findings from the WHO World Mental Health Surveys," *PloS Medicine*, July 2008, www.plosmedicine.org/article/info:doi/10.1371/journal.pmed.0050141.

[11] Quoted in Neal Peirce, "Webb Leads the Charge in Much-Needed Drug, Prison Reform," *Richmond Times-Dispatch*, April 5, 2009, www.timesdispatch.com/rtd/news/opinion/commentary/article/webb_leads_the_charge_for_much-needed_drug_prison_reform/249095/.

[12] "House Judiciary Subcommittee on Crime, Terrorism and Homeland Security Holds Hearing on Unfairness in Federal Cocaine Sentencing," CQ Congressional Transcripts, May 21, 2009.

[13] *Ibid.* For background see Peter Katel, "Mexico's Drug War," *CQ Researcher*, Dec. 12, 2008, pp. 1009-1032.

[14] Dan Simon, "Mexican cartels running pot farms in U.S. national forest," CNN, Aug. 8, 2008, www.cnn.com/2008/CRIME/08/08/pot.eradication/.

[15] Letter, state Reps. Joe C. Pickett, Chente Quintanilla, Joseph E. Moody, Norma Chávez, Marisa Marquez, Jan. 12, 2009; letter, Rep. Silvestre Reyes, Jan. 13, 2009.

[16] "Washington Post-ABC News Poll," April 21-24, 2009, www.washingtonpost.com/wp-srv/politics/polls/postpoll_042609.html; "Possible Law Changes," CBS News Poll, March 19, 2009, www.cbsnews.com/htdocs/pdf/poll_031909_marijuana.pdf; "40 Percent Say Marijuana Should Be Legalized," Rasmussen Reports, Feb. 19, 2009, www.rasmussenreports.com/public_content/lifestyle/general_lifestyle/february_2009/40_say_marijuana_should_be_legalized.

[17] Joseph Carroll, "Who Supports Marijuana Legalization?" Gallup, Nov. 1, 2005, www.gallup.com/poll/19561/Who-Supports-Marijuana-Legalization.aspxLegalization.aspx.

[18] Nate Silver, "Why Marijuana Legalization is Gaining Momentum," FiveThirtyEight, April 5, 2009, www.fivethirtyeight.com/2009/04/why-marijuana-legalization-is-gaining.html.

[19] Jon Gettman, "Marijuana Production in the United States (2006)," *Bulletin of Cannabis Reform*, December 2006, www.drugscience.org/Archive/bcr2/MJCropReport_2006.pdf.

[20] Martin Bouchard, "A capture-recapture-derived method to estimate cannabis production in industrialized countries," School of Criminology, Simon Fraser University, 2007, www.issdp.org/conferences/oslo2007/Martin_Bouchard.pdf.

[21] "What America's Users Spend on Illegal Drugs," Abt Associates, December 2001, pp. 32-33, www.whitehousedrugpolicy.gov/publications/pdf/american_users_spend_2002.pdf. Abt is a Cambridge, Mass.-based consulting firm working under contract for the ONCDP.

[22] Jeffrey A. Miron, "The Budgetary Implications of Drug Prohibition," Department of Economics, Harvard University, December 2008, www.economics.harvard.edu/faculty/directory/faculty/M/O.

[23] "Wholesale Marijuana Prices," *Narcotic News*, undated, www.narcoticnews.com/Marijuana/Prices/USA/Marijuana_Prices_USA.html; "Price Index for the Years 2003 to 2006 Converted to 2007 Constant Dollars," DrugScience.org, 2007, www.drugscience.org/Archive/bcr4/Table11.html.

[24] Solomon Moore, "Tougher Border Can't Stop Mexican Marijuana Cartels," *The New York Times*, Feb. 1, 2009, www.nytimes.com/2009/02/02/us/02pot.html?sq=mexicancartelsmarijuanau.s.&st=cse&scp=1&pagewanted=all.

[25] *Ibid.*

[26] Marc Kaufman, "Smoking in U.S. Declines Sharply," *The Washington Post*, March 9, 2006, p. A1.

[27] "Marijuana Abuse," National Institute on Drug Abuse, July 22, 2008, www.nida.nih.gov/researchreports/marijuana/Marijuana3.html.

[28] "Marijuana: The Facts," Drug Policy Alliance, undated, www.drugpolicy.org/marijuana/factsmyths/.

[29] Janet E. Joy, *et al.*, *Marijuana and Medicine: Assessing the Science Base* (1999), Institute of Medicine, pp. 94-97, www.nap.edu/openbook.php?record_id=6376&page=94.

[30] *Ibid.*

[31] Kleiman, *op. cit.*

[32] "Results from the 2007 National Survey on Drug Use and Health: National Findings," *op. cit.*

[33] David Malitz, "One Night With the Dead Turns Into Eternal Jamnation," *The Washington Post*, April 16, 2009, p. C3.

[34] Chris Bodenner, "The Daily Dish," May 24, 2009, http://andrewsullivan.theatlantic.com/the_daily_dish/2009/05/the-cannabis-closet-safe-havens.html.

[35] Harry G. Levine and Deborah Peterson Small, "Marijuana Arrest Crusade: Racial Bias and Police Policy in New York City 1997-2007," New York Civil Liberties Union, April 2008, p. 7, www.nyclu.org/files/MARIJUANA-ARREST-CRUSADE_Final.pdf.

[36] *Ibid.*

[37] Ryan S. King and Marc Mauer, "The War on Marijuana: The Transformation of the War on Drugs in the 1990s," The Sentencing Project, May 2005, www.sentencingproject.org/Admin\Documents\publications\dp_waronmarijuana.pdf.

[38] Rosalie Liccardo Pacula and Beau Kilmer, "Marijuana and Crime: Is There a Connection Beyond Prohibition?" RAND, January 2004, www.rand.org/pubs/working_papers/2004/RAND_WR125.pdf.

[39] Except where otherwise noted, this subsection is drawn from Martin Booth, *Cannabis: A History* (2004); Rudolph J. Gerber, *Legalizing Marijuana: Drug policy Reform and Prohibition Politics* (2004); and David F. Musto, *The American Disease: Origins of Narcotic*

Control (1999).

[40] "Reefer Madness: The Movie Musical (2005)," Internet Movie Database, www.imdb.com/title/tt0404364/.

[41] Musto, *op. cit.*, pp. 221-225.

[42] Quoted in Gerber, *op. cit.*, p. 7.

[43] "Use of Marijuana Spreading in West," *The New York Times*, Sept. 16, 1934.

[44] "Marihuana: A Signal of Misunderstanding," The National Commission on Marihuana and Drug Abuse, 1972, www.druglibrary.org/Schaffer/Library/studies/nc/mis2_6.htm. For background, see Peter Katel, "War on Drugs," *CQ Researcher*, June 2, 2006, pp. 481-504.

[45] Unless otherwise noted, this subsection draws on "Marihuana: A Signal . . .," *op. cit.*; and Musto, *op. cit.*

[46] "Marihuana: A Signal . . .," *op. cit.*

[47] *Ibid.*

[48] Quoted in Booth, *op. cit.*, pp. 210-211.

[49] *Ibid.*, p. 210.

[50] Quoted in James P. Sterba, "G.I.'s Find Marijuana Is Plentiful," *The New York Times*, Sept. 2, 1970.

[51] "U.S. Troops in Vietnam Are Said to Get Pep Pills," *The New York Times*, March 6, 1968.

[52] Lloyd D. Johnston, *et al.*, "Demographic Subgroup Trends for Various Licit and Illicit Drugs, 1975-2007," *Monitoring the Future*, 2008, p. 274, www.monitoringthefuture.org/pubs/occpapers/occ69.pdf.

[53] Unless otherwise indicated, this subsection draws on Musto, *op. cit.* Also see Michael Massing, *The Fix* (2000). For additional background, see Mary H. Cooper, "Drug-Policy Debate," *CQ Researcher*, July 28, 2000, pp. 595-620.

[54] Mark Eddy, "Medical Marijuana: Review and Analysis of Federal and State Policies," Congressional Research Service, March 31 2009, p. 3, www.fas.org/sgp/crs/misc/RL33211.pdf.

[55] Edward Walsh, "Carter Endorses Decriminalization of Marijuana," *The Washington Post*, Aug. 3, 1977, p. A1.

[56] *Ibid.*

[57] Patrick Anderson, *High in America: The True Story Behind NORML and the Politics of Marijuana* (1981), pp. 274-284.

[58] Kenneth J. Meier, *The Politics of Sin: Drugs, Alcohol, and Public Policy* (1994), pp. 48-49.

[59] Paul Houston, "Bumper Stickers Would Brand Offenders," *Los Angeles Times*, May 28, 1988, A1; Peter Kerr, "Anatomy of the Drug Issue," *The New York Times*, Nov. 17, 1986, p. A1; Donnie Radcliffe, "Seafarer Nancy Reagan," *The Washington Post*, July 2, 1985, p. C2; Philip H. Dougherty, "Drug Drive Outlined to First Lady," *The New York Times*, Oct. 12, 1983, p. D22.

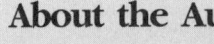

About the Author

Peter Katel is a *CQ Researcher* staff writer who previously reported on Haiti and Latin America for *Time* and *Newsweek* and covered the Southwest for newspapers in New Mexico. He has received several journalism awards, including the Bartolomé Mitre Award for coverage of drug trafficking, from the Inter-American Press Association. He holds an A.B. in university studies from the University of New Mexico. His recent reports include "Mexico's Drug War," "Hate Groups" and "Vanishing Jobs."

[60] Gerald M. Boyd, "Reagan Signs Anti-Drug Measure," *The New York Times*, Oct. 28, 1986; Deborah J. Vagins and Jesselyn McCurdy, "Cracks in the System: Twenty Years of the Unjust Federal Crack Cocaine Law," ACLU, October 2006, www.aclu.org/pdfs/drugpolicy/cracksinsystem_20061025.pdf.

[61] David Risley, "Mandatory Minimum Sentences: An Overview," Drug Watch International, May 2000, www.drugwatch.org/MandatoryMinimumSentences.htm.

[62] Quoted in Michael Isikoff and Tracy Thompson, "Getting Too Tough on Drugs," *The Washington Post*, Nov. 4, 1990, p. C1.

[63] Quoted in *ibid.*

[64] For a state-by-state list of marijuana penalties, see "State By State Laws," National Organization for Reform of Marijuana Laws, Aug. 5, 2006, www.norml.org/index.cfm?Group_ID=4516.

[65] For background, see Kathy Koch, "Medical Marijuana," *CQ Researcher*, Aug. 20, 1999, pp. 705-728.

[66] Anderson, *op. cit.*, pp. 245-248.

[67] Larry Calloway, "New Mexico's Been There, California," *Albuquerque Journal*, Dec. 1, 1996, p. B1. Eugene L. Meyer, "Uncle Sam's Aunt Mary," *The Washington Post*, Oct. 22, 1995, p. F1.

[68] Susan Okie, "Cancer Victims to Get Marijuana Ingredient," *The Washington Post*, Nov. 11, 1980, p. A1.

[69] Dianne Klein, "The Empty Pot," *Los Angeles Times*, April 1, 1992, p. A3.

[70] "Hawaii Becomes First State to Approve Medical Marijuana Bill," *The New York Times*, June 15, 2000, www.nytimes.com/2000/06/15/us/hawaii-becomes-first-state-to-approve-medical-marijuana-bill.html.

[71] Anjanette Riley and Amanda Crawford, "Arizona voters might get another shot at medical marijuana," *Arizona Capitol Times*, April 24, 2009; Matthew J. Malone, "Medical Marijuana Measure Falls With Connecticut Governor's Veto," *The New York Times*, June 20, 2007.

[72] Eddy, *op. cit.*, p. 11. For additional details on the 1999 IOM report, see Koch, *op. cit.*

[73] "State By State Laws," *op. cit.*

[74] Quoted in Steven Rosenberg, "Drug use in public targeted," *The Boston Globe*, April 9, 2009, p. B1.

[75] Quoted in Jonathan Saltzman, "Towns try to punish public marijuana use," *The Boston Globe*, March 25, 2009, p. B1. See also Patrick Anderson, "Council nixes hike in pot fines," *Gloucester Daily Times*, May 7, 2009, www.gloucestertimes.com/archivesearch/local_story_126224820.html.

[76] Tim Jones, "Legal pot debuts in Midwest," *Chicago Tribune*, March 20, 2009, p. A4.

[77] Quoted in *ibid.*

[78] Quoted in Jason Hoppin, "Pot fight on ballot? That's their plan," *St. Paul Pioneer Press*, May 27, 2009; Mark Brunswick, "Minnesota Senate approves medical marijuana," *StarTribune.com*, April 30, 2009, www.startribune.com/politics/state/44005777.html.

[79] *Ibid.*

[80] Kevin McDermott, "As deadline nears, Illinois House dawdles on tax hike," *St. Louis Post-Dispatch*, May 30, 2009, p. A1.

[81] "Severe chronic pain added to medical marijuana," The Associated Press, May 7, 2009; Sue Major Holmes, "First medical marijuana producer in NM approved," The Associated Press, March 19, 2009.

[82] Cynthia Needham, "House OKs plan to establish up to 3 marijuana dispensaries," *Providence Journal-Bulletin*, May 21, 2009, p. A6.

[83] *Ibid.*

[84] Quoted in Lauren R. Dorgan, "Marijuana debate sharpens," *Concord Monitor*, May 14, 2009.

[85] "Medical Marijuana: New York Bill Wins Senate Committee Vote," *Drug War Chronicle*, May 29, 2009, http://stopthedrugwar.org/chronicle/587/new_york_medical_marijuana_bill_wins_senate_committee_vote; Tom Precious, "Approval predicted for medical marijuana," *Buffalo News*, April 22, 2009, p. A1.

[86] Adrienne Lu, "Backers of medical marijuana hopeful in N.J.," *The Philadelphia Inquirer*, March 9, 2009, p. A1.

[87] Sen. Jim Webb, "Why We Must Fix Our Prisons," *Parade*, March 29, 2009, www.parade.com/news/2009/03/why-we-must-fix-our-prisons.html.

[88] *Ibid.*

[89] Quoted in Sandhya Somashekhar, "Webb Sets His Sights on Prison Reform," *The Washington Post*, Dec. 29, 2008, p. B1.

[90] Quoted in *ibid.*

[91] Allison Klein, "Webb Aide Tried to Take Gun Into Senate Building, Capitol Police Say," *The Washington Post*, March 27, 2007, www.washingtonpost.com/wp-dyn/content/article/2007/03/26/AR2007032602102.html.

[92] Quoted in Somashekhar, *op. cit.*

[93] "Sen. Jim Webb's Floor Speech to Introduce 'The National Criminal Justice Commission Act of 2009,'" March 26, 2009, http://webb.senate.gov/email/incardocs/FS_CrimJust_3-26-09.pdf.

FOR MORE INFORMATION

Drug Free America Foundation, 5999 Central Ave., Suite 301, St. Petersburg, FL 33710; (727) 828-0211; www.dfaf.org. Advocates drug prohibition and serves as a clearinghouse for information on marijuana's adverse effects.

Drug Policy Alliance Network, 70 West 36th St., 16th Floor, New York, NY 10018; (212) 613-8020; www.drugpolicy.org. Advocates an end to law-enforcement-oriented policies for substances including marijuana.

Marijuana Policy Project, P.O. Box 77492, Capitol Hill, Washington, DC 20013; (202) 462-5747; www.mpp.org. Seeks to liberalize laws on marijuana.

National Institute on Drug Abuse, 6001 Executive Blvd., Room 5213, Bethesda, MD 20892; (301) 443-1124; www.nida.nih.gov. The government's lead agency on addiction makes available data and studies on addiction and drug dependency.

National Organization for the Reform of Marijuana Laws, 1600 K St., N.W., Suite 501, Washington DC 20006; (202) 483-5500; http://norml.org. Spearheaded the marijuana-decriminalization campaign of the early 1970s.

Office of National Drug Control Policy/Drug Policy Information Clearinghouse, P.O. Box 6000, Rockville, MD 20849; (800) 666-3332; whitehousedrugpolicy.gov. Provides information on government strategy and priorities.

The Sentencing Project, 514 10th St., N.W., Suite 1000, Washington, DC 20004; (202) 628-0871; www.sentencingproject.org. Advocates less use of incarceration in criminal-justice drug policies.

Bibliography

Selected Sources

Books

Anderson, Patrick, *High in America: The True Story Behind NORML and the Politics of Marijuana*, Viking, 1981.
A veteran journalist tells the inside story of the rise and fall of decriminalization attempts during the Carter administration.

Booth, Martin, *Cannabis: A History*, St. Martin's Press, 2004.
The late British novelist and biographer entertainingly chronicles marijuana back to its earliest known use in China.

Gerber, Rudolph J., *Legalizing Marijuana*, Praeger, 2004.
A retired Arizona Court of Appeals judge attacks drug laws as an unjust exercise of government power backed by hyped scientific evidence.

Kleiman, Mark A. R., *When Brute Force Fails: How to Have Less Crime and Less Punishment*, Princeton University Press, 2009.
Proposed new approaches to drug use, including marijuana, form a major part of the plans advocated by a veteran criminal-justice policy expert, now at UCLA.

Musto, David F., *The American Disease*, Oxford University Press, 1999 (revised).
A Yale University medical historian and psychiatrist has written what many consider the definitive history of U.S. drug policy.

Articles

Dubner, Stephen J., "What Would Happen if Marijuana Were Legalized?" Freakonomics blog, *The New York Times*, May 22, 2009, http://freakonomics.blogs.nytimes.com/2009/05/22/pot-quorum/.
Several experts debate the question, including an ex-marijuana smuggler and a former Drug Enforcement Administration official.

Egelko, Bob, "Impact of pot proposal depends on federal law," *San Francisco Chronicle*, May 11, 2009, p. A1.
The hometown daily of California's major pro-legalization legislator examines his proposal.

Meeks, Torrey, "El Paso 'dialogue' on drugs leaves some speechless," *The Washington Times*, Feb. 2, 2009, p. A1.
Meeks reports on a controversial decriminalization proposal in a major Texas border city.

Padgett, Tim, "On the Bloody Border," *Time*, April 23, 2009, www.time.com/time/magazine/article/0,9171,1893512,00.html.
Mexico's vicious drug-cartel wars are pushing some Americans to reconsider drug decriminalization.

Rosenberg, Steven, "Drug use in public targeted," *The Boston Globe*, April 9, 2009, p. B1.
Massachusetts' major decriminalization law has some police chiefs worrying that it could encourage pot smoking in public.

Samuels, David, "Dr. Kush: How medical marijuana is transforming the pot industry," *The New Yorker*, July 28, 2008, www.newyorker.com/reporting/2008/07/28/080728fa_fact_samuels.
A journalist with an inside track to the California cannabis industry paints a detailed picture of its members.

Vick, Karl, "In Calif., Medical Marijuana Laws Are Moving Pot Into the Mainstream," *The Washington Post*, April 12, 2009, p. A3.
A veteran correspondent reports from ground zero of the medical-marijuana trend.

Reports

"White Paper on Marijuana Dispensaries," California Police Chiefs Association, April 2009, www.californiapolicechiefs.org/nav_files/marijuana_files/MarijuanaDispensariesWhitePaper_042209.pdf.
The association concludes that, as enforced in much of the state, the medical-marijuana law functions as legal cover for profit-making enterprises that provide cannabis to virtually anyone.

Eddy, Mark, "Medical Marijuana: Review and Analysis of Federal and State Policies," Congressional Research Service, March 31, 2009, www.fas.org/sgp/crs/misc/RL33211.pdf.
A criminal-justice policy expert for Congress' research arm provides an up-to-date assessment of state and national trends.

Gettman, Jon, "Marijuana Production in the United States," *Bulletin of Cannabis Reform*, 2006, www.drugscience.org/Archive/bcr2/MJCropReport_2006.pdf.
In a widely cited paper that some dispute, a marijuana-legalization advocate analyzes a variety of data to conclude that marijuana is the nation's No. 1 cash crop.

Joy, Janet E., *et al.*, "Marijuana and Medicine: Assessing the Science Base," Institute of Medicine, 1999, www.nap.edu/openbook.php?record_id=6376.
The institute attempts to present a balanced, academically sound examination of marijuana as intoxicant and potential medication.

Paluca, Rosalie Liccardo, and Beau Kilmer, "Marijuana and Crime: Is There a Connection Beyond Prohibition?," RAND Corp., January 2004, www.rand.org/pubs/working_papers/2004/RAND_WR125.pdf.
Researchers find data that point to marijuana-crime connections, though not necessarily to crime-causing effects of cannabis.

The Next Step:

Additional Articles from Current Periodicals

Consumption

Plumb, Taryn, "Changes Sought in Marijuana Laws," *The Boston Globe*, Feb. 10, 2008, p. Reg1.

An increase in marijuana use will also increase crime and various accidents stemming from the use of the drug.

Roetlin, J. J., "Legalizing Drugs Would Cause More Harm Than Good," *Iowa City Press-Citizen*, Feb. 15, 2008, p. 13A.

Drug use and drug-related deaths will inevitably increase if recreational use of marijuana is permitted.

Sabet, Kevin A., "California Can't Afford to Legalize Marijuana," *San Jose Mercury News*, March 8, 2009.

Legalizing marijuana in California would increase the drug's consumption and enormous social costs.

Medical Marijuana

"Critics Denounce Proposed Medical Marijuana Ban for Parolees," The Associated Press, March 6, 2008.

Critics in Montana have denounced a proposed rule that would bar anyone on parole or probation from obtaining marijuana as a prescription drug.

Bailey, Eric, "Doctors Urge Easing of Marijuana Ban," *Los Angeles Times*, Feb. 15, 2008, p. A14.

The American College of Physicians wants the United States to drop marijuana from the list of drugs that have no medicinal value.

Davis, Scott, "Acquiring Medical Marijuana Remains a Challenge," *Lansing State Journal*, April 20, 2009, p. 1A.

Michigan's medical-marijuana law makes no provisions for patients to obtain the drug at pharmacies or retail sources.

Ostrom, Carol M., "Medical Marijuana: How Much Is Enough?" *Seattle Times*, May 21, 2008, p. A1.

A Washington Health Department proposal that medical-marijuana patients be allowed more than two pounds of pot every month prompted Democratic Gov. Christine Gregoire to tell health officials to start over.

Schirripa, Nick, "Medicinal Marijuana OK, But the Critics Persist," *Battle Creek Enquirer*, Nov. 23, 2008, p. 1A.

Supporters say the medical value of pot justifies legalization, but opponents say it would only lead to more abuse.

Public Opinion

Saltzman, Jonathan, "Towns Try to Punish Public Marijuana Use," *The Boston Globe*, March 25, 2009, p. A1.

Dozens of Massachusetts cities and towns are taking steps to impose fines for smoking marijuana in public, but critics say such initiatives undermine the state ballot question that voters approved to decriminalize possession of small amounts of the drug.

Simerman, John, "Legalize Pot? Advocates Thrilled With Change in Polls, Governor's Call for Debate," *Contra Costa Times*, May 12, 2009.

A shift in California public opinion is apparently leaning toward the legalization, possession and taxation of marijuana.

Vitiello, Michael, "Should Marijuana Be Legal?" *Sacramento Bee*, April 5, 2009, p. E1.

Critics of decriminalization in California say it would not decrease prison overcrowding because not many prisoners are incarcerated for marijuana possession.

Taxation

Buchanan, Wyatt, "Effort to Ease Pot Laws Gets a Boost," *The San Francisco Chronicle*, May 6, 2009, p. A1.

California Gov. Arnold Schwarzenegger has called for a public debate regarding the legalization and taxation of marijuana.

Sanders, Jim, "Legal Pot: A Cash Harvest for State?" *Sacramento Bee*, Feb. 24, 2009, p. A1.

A proposed bill in California would allow recreational use of marijuana for adults 21 and older and would tax both users and distributors of the drug.

Woo, Stu, "Oakland Council Backs a Tax on Marijuana," *The Wall Street Journal*, April 30, 2009, p. A4.

The City Council of Oakland, Calif., has approved a 1.8-percent tax on medical marijuana in an effort to help close the city's budget shortfall.

CITING *CQ RESEARCHER*

Sample formats for citing these reports in a bibliography include the ones listed below. Preferred styles and formats vary, so please check with your instructor or professor.

MLA STYLE

Jost, Kenneth. "Rethinking the Death Penalty." CQ Researcher 16 Nov. 2001: 945-68.

APA STYLE

Jost, K. (2001, November 16). Rethinking the death penalty. *CQ Researcher, 11,* 945-968.

CHICAGO STYLE

Jost, Kenneth. "Rethinking the Death Penalty." *CQ Researcher,* November 16, 2001, 945-968.

In-depth Reports on Issues in the News

Are you writing a paper?

Need backup for a debate?

Want to become an expert on an issue?

For 80 years, students have turned to *CQ Researcher* for in-depth reporting on issues in the news. Reports on a full range of political and social issues are now available. Following is a selection of recent reports:

Civil Liberties
Closing Guantánamo, 2/09
Affirmative Action, 10/08
Gay Marriage Showdowns, 9/08
America's Border Fence, 9/08
Immigration Debate, 2/08

Crime/Law
Judicial Elections, 4/09
Mexico's Drug War, 12/08
Prostitution Debate, 5/08
Public Defenders, 4/08
Gun Violence, 5/07

Education
Reading Crisis? 2/08
Discipline in Schools, 2/08
Student Aid, 1/08
Racial Diversity in Public Schools, 9/07

Environment/Society
Future of Books, 5/09
Hate Groups, 5/09
Future of Journalism, 3/09
Confronting Warming, 1/09
Reducing Carbon Footprint, 12/08
Protecting Wetlands, 10/08

Health/Safety
Reproductive Ethics, 5/09
Extreme Sports, 4/09
Regulating Toxic Chemicals, 1/09
Preventing Cancer, 1/09
Heart Health, 9/08
Global Food Crisis, 6/08

Politics/Economy
Business Bankruptcy, 4/09
Future of the GOP, 3/09
Middle-Class Squeeze, 3/09
Public-Works Projects, 2/09

Upcoming Reports

Retirement Crisis, 6/19/09   Treating Depression, 6/26/09   Examining Forensic Science, 7/17/09

ACCESS

CQ Researcher is available in print and online. For access, visit your library or www.cqresearcher.com.

STAY CURRENT

To receive notice of upcoming *CQ Researcher* reports, or learn more about *CQ Researcher* products, subscribe to the free e-mail newsletters, *CQ Researcher Alert!* and *CQ Researcher News*: http://cqpress.com/newsletters.

PURCHASE

To purchase a *CQ Researcher* report in print or electronic format (PDF), visit www.cqpress.com or call 866-427-7737. Single reports start at $15. Bulk purchase discounts and electronic-rights licensing are also available.

SUBSCRIBE

Annual full-service *CQ Researcher* subscriptions—including 44 reports a year, monthly index updates, and a bound volume—start at $803. Add $25 for domestic postage.

CQ Researcher Online offers a backfile from 1991 and a number of tools to simplify research. For pricing information, call 800-834-9020, ext. 1906, or e-mail librarysales@cqpress.com.

CQ Researcher

Published by CQ Press, a division of SAGE Publications

www.cqresearcher.com

Rethinking Retirement

Can Americans afford to retire?

rospects for a secure retirement are more imperiled now than at any time since before the creation of the Social Security program in 1935. Low savings rates and credit abuse have contributed to the problem, but the recent economic crisis, which has led to massive layoffs and a collapse of the stock market, is forcing even those who have prepared and saved to rethink their retirement strategies. The entire retirement structure, including the shift away from traditional guaranteed pension plans toward 401(k) accounts, is under scrutiny, and Congress has called for greater transparency in the way such accounts are administered. Meanwhile, retirement experts are counseling workers to stay on the job longer to ensure their retirement security, and some economists are calling for reductions in Social Security benefits to shore up the entitlement system and accommodate the impending wave of retirements among the post-World War II baby-boom generation.

Eighty-three-year-old Irene Massey — the nation's oldest mail carrier — celebrates her retirement in Concord, Calif., in 2005. The ongoing economic crisis is forcing even those who have saved for retirement to continue working to recoup their losses.

CQ Researcher • June 19, 2009 • www.cqresearcher.com
Volume 19, Number 23 • Pages 549-572

CQ Researcher

June 19, 2009
Volume 19, Number 23

MANAGING EDITOR: Thomas J. Colin
tcolin@cqpress.com

ASSISTANT MANAGING EDITOR: Kathy Koch
kkoch@cqpress.com

ASSOCIATE EDITOR: Kenneth Jost

STAFF WRITERS: Thomas J. Billitteri,
Marcia Clemmitt, Peter Katel

CONTRIBUTING WRITERS: Rachel Cox,
Sarah Glazer, Alan Greenblatt, Reed Karaim
Barbara Mantel, Patrick Marshall,
Tom Price, Jennifer Weeks

DESIGN/PRODUCTION EDITOR: Olu B. Davis

ASSISTANT EDITOR: Darrell Dela Rosa

FACT-CHECKING: Eugene J. Gabler,
Michelle Harris

CQ PRESS

A Division of SAGE

PRESIDENT AND PUBLISHER:
John A. Jenkins

EXECUTIVE DIRECTOR,
REFERENCE INFORMATION GROUP:
Alix B. Vance

CQ Researcher (ISSN 1056-2036) is printed on acid-free paper. Published weekly, except; (Jan. wk. 1) (May wk. 4) (July wks. 1, 2) (Aug. wks. 3, 4) (Nov. wk. 4) and (Dec. wk. 4), by CQ Press, a division of SAGE Publications. Annual full-service subscriptions start at $803. For pricing, call 1-800-834-9020, ext. 1906. To purchase a CQ Researcher report in print or electronic format (PDF), visit www. cqpress.com or call 866-427-7737. Single reports start at $15. Bulk purchase discounts and electronic-rights licensing are also available. Periodicals postage paid at Washington, D.C., and additional mailing offices. POSTMASTER: Send address changes to CQ Researcher, 2300 N St., N.W., Suite 800, Washington, DC 20037.

Cover: Getty Images/David Paul Morris

Rethinking Retirement

BY THOMAS J. BILLITTERI

THE ISSUES

Roberta Tim Quan, a 74-year-old retired teacher in San Pablo, Calif., says she and her husband saved responsibly during their working years, but their hopes of a "reasonable retirement" of travel and family visits didn't come true.

As Quan recounted to a congressional hearing last fall, her husband needed expensive medical care for Alzheimer's disease. Meanwhile, utility and food bills were on the rise. And then the clincher: The financial crisis slammed Quan's retirement account.

"My situation is in shambles with expenses exceeding income," Quan said. "A lifetime of savings in catastrophic decline is demoralizing. . . . The word 'fear' looms on the horizon." [1]

Such woe is all too common these days among retirees and those approaching the end of their working lives. Millions of Americans are watching their retirement dreams evaporate amid steep investment losses, rising health-care costs, late-career layoffs and fears of outliving their savings. For many, working longer and saving more could mean the difference between an old age of plenty and one of poverty.

Only 13 percent of workers responding to an Employee Benefit Research Institute survey this year were very confident about having enough money to retire comfortably, the lowest proportion since the survey began asking the question in 1993. Among retirees, only one in five said they were very confident about their financial security. [2]

Retired nurse Barb Blume, 75, at right, helps a customer at the Mosaic Yarn Studio in Des Plaines, Ill. Blume turned her knitting hobby into a second career at the shop, where she is the assistant manager and knitting instructor. Retirement experts counsel workers to stay on the job longer to ensure their retirement security.

Getty Images/Tim Boyle

"Even before the current financial crisis, retirement was a very scary proposition, and now it's really frightening," says David Madland, director of the American Worker Project at the Center for American Progress, a liberal Washington think tank.

The retirement picture is not universally dim. Americans are living longer, healthier lives than ever before. Many older Americans choose to work well into their 60s and 70s, some in so-called encore careers at nonprofit organizations or in "phased retirement" arrangements that allow for reduced hours or less demanding duties. (*See sidebar, p. 562.*)

But for many Americans, the golden years have lost their gleam. Stock-market losses gutted trillions of dollars from retirement accounts, and the exploding housing bubble blew away many older Americans' biggest financial asset: the equity in their homes.

The Center for Economic and Policy Research, a liberal think tank in Washington, projected that median net worth among households headed by people 55 to 64 years old fell between 47 and 55 percent from 2004 to 2009, to as little as $143,200, because of the busts in housing and stocks. [3]

"The crash of the housing bubble and the subsequent collapse in the stock market has left [baby boomers] very poorly prepared for retirement," Dean Baker, the center's co-director, told a Senate panel. [4] Many will have only Social Security and Medicare to rely on in retirement, he said. [5]

And relying on those entitlement programs, which serve more than 50 million Americans, is becoming increasingly worrisome. Hammered by the recession, the Medicare fund is expected to be insolvent in 2017, two years earlier than projected, and the Social Security trust fund in 2037, four years earlier, the Obama administration warned in May. [6]

Medicare, which covers hospital care for the elderly, and Social Security, which distributes monthly checks to retirees, face mushrooming demand from the aging baby-boom generation. And lately, with job losses mounting, the government is taking in less money in payroll taxes from current workers to support the programs.

The Congressional Budget Office forecast this spring that because of low inflation stemming from the economic

Most Americans Lack Retirement Plans

More than half of American workers lacked retirement plan coverage at their jobs in 2007, the same percentage as in 1992. During the same period, the percentage of workers with defined-contribution plans, such as 401(k)s, increased by 11 percentage points while those with traditional-style defined-benefit pensions decreased by more than half.

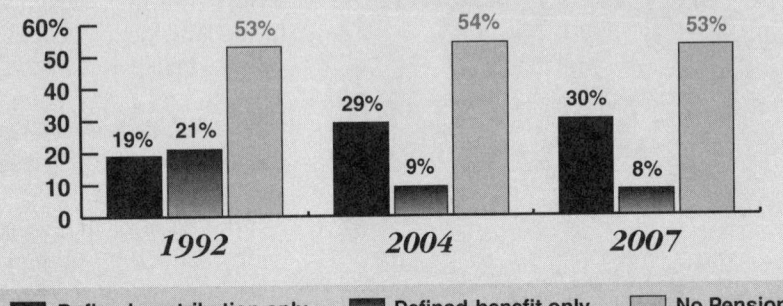

Retirement Plan Coverage of Workers on Current Job

■ Defined-contribution only   ■ Defined-benefit only   ☐ No Pension

Source: Center for Retirment Research at Boston College, based on "Survey of Consumer Finances," U.S. Board of Governors of the Federal Reserve System

downturn, Social Security will pay no cost-of-living increase in 2010 or 2011, the first such freeze in more than three decades. [7] The recently enacted stimulus bill did provide a one-time additional payment of $250. [8]

The pressures on Social Security and Medicare are just part of the strains facing older workers. A 2009 survey by Chicago consulting company Spectrem Group found that since January 2008 a third of U.S. employers had reduced or dropped matching contributions into employee 401(k)-style retirement accounts, and 29 percent aimed to do so in the coming year. [9]

Many workers are cutting their own contributions to their retirement accounts, too. A fifth of workers age 45 or older who responded last September to an AARP survey said they had stopped putting money into a retirement account during the previous year. Sixty-five percent said they expected to delay retirement unless the economy improved significantly. [10]

Even big earners are salting away less in company-sponsored deferred-compensation plans — tax-friendly accounts designed for people making $250,000 or more a year. Voluntary deposits have shrunk as companies chopped executive bonuses, corporate losses mounted and employers tightened account-withdrawal policies, *The Wall Street Journal* noted. [11]

If and when the economy recovers, the retirement outlook may improve for many Americans, particularly younger ones still working. But huge obstacles loom on both the near and distant horizons, and policy fights are expected over the best way to overcome them.

One such obstacle is the long-term health of Social Security. Many liberals argue that the system is basically sound and that only modest changes, such as requiring high earners to pay more into the system, will ensure its fiscal viability well into the future. Many conservatives are pushing for more

fundamental changes, such as benefit cuts that include raising the age at which retirees are eligible for full Social Security payments.

Controversy also has been brewing over the viability of employer-sponsored 401(k) and other "defined-contribution" retirement plans, which have largely supplanted traditional guaranteed pensions — known as defined-benefit plans — in recent years.

The plans have strong defenders, including the American Benefits Council, a Washington advocacy group for employer-sponsored benefit programs. It calls 401(k)-style plans "a successful cornerstone" of the nation's retirement system, one that reaches "tens of millions of workers" and provides "an important source of retirement savings." [12]

But critics argue that the growth of 401(k) plans has shifted inordinate financial risk onto the shoulders of workers who may be ill-prepared to manage their investment assets or who, for whatever reason, may decide not to contribute money to a plan if one is available.

To many, the recent stock-market crash has underscored the need for changes in national retirement policy. "We have been saying even before the economic downturn that 401(k)s cannot be the sole retirement savings plan for workers, and if anything the current economic situation has proven us right," says Nancy Hwa, communications director for the Pension Rights Center, a consumer-advocacy group in Washington. Such accounts "are just not secure enough. They're too subject to the volatility of the stock market."

Some advocate new policies to increase private retirement savings, such as requiring employers that don't have a pension or 401(k) plan to offer to enroll workers in an Individual Retirement Account (IRA), a private, tax-deferred savings plan.

Others want to make retirement savings mandatory, an idea that seems to have support from some workers themselves. A survey by HSBC, a London-based international financial-services institution, found that 32 percent of working Americans and 34 percent of retirees believe the first step government should take to support the aging population is to enforce additional private savings. [13]

But others reject the idea of mandatory savings. "I think you should give people tax incentives, and the default should be that you're enrolled [in a retirement plan] and you have to actively opt out if that's what you want to do," says David Blau, an Ohio State University economist who studies retirement decisions. "But I don't think you should force people to save. In a sense, we do that through Social Security," which is funded by a payroll tax, "and that's probably enough forced savings."

As the economy continues to take a toll on older Americans, here are some of the questions policy makers and workers are asking:

Will most Americans be able to afford a secure retirement?

Generalizing about the financial readiness of Americans who are retired or close to it is difficult. Some are well prepared to live their golden years in comfort and security. Others face penury.

"There is no single story," says Sara Rix, strategic policy adviser with AARP's Public Policy Institute. "We're talking about a really diverse population, buffeted by a lot of headwinds. People are in different situations, and they're going to respond differently."

Studies by the University of Michigan Retirement Research Center show that older Americans who moved into retirement in the 1990s are, on average, well prepared. "I'm surprised at the number who have quite substantial financial resources," says John Laitner, the center's director. "When you put together their house, pension rights, Social Security and so on, I've seen

Retirement Delays Blamed on Economy

The poor economy and losses in the stock market are the reasons most often cited by workers for postponing retirement. Only 3 percent said they wanted to continue to work.

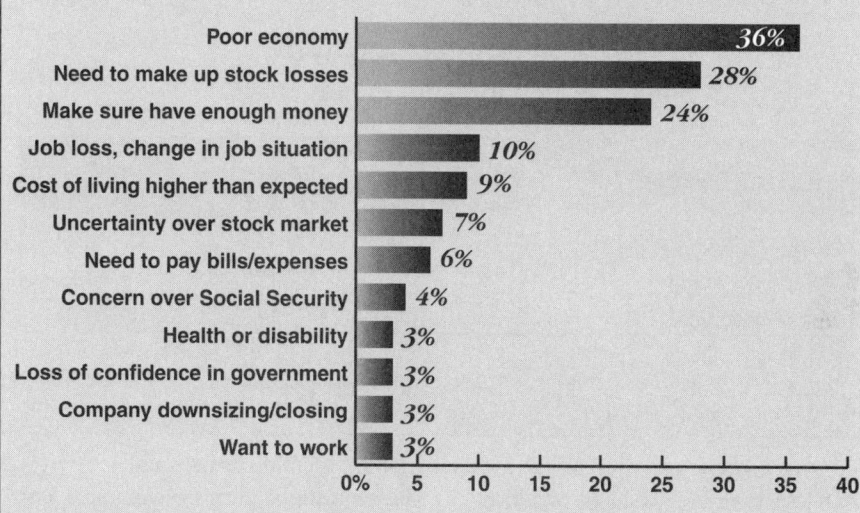

Reasons for Changing Expected Retirement Age

Reason	Percent
Poor economy	36%
Need to make up stock losses	28%
Make sure have enough money	24%
Job loss, change in job situation	10%
Cost of living higher than expected	9%
Uncertainty over stock market	7%
Need to pay bills/expenses	6%
Concern over Social Security	4%
Health or disability	3%
Loss of confidence in government	3%
Company downsizing/closing	3%
Want to work	3%

Source: "2009 Retirement Confidence Survey," Employee Benefit Research Institute

figures showing the average would be a half-million dollars."

But the future may not be as bright for people who have just left the workforce or are five or 10 years away from retirement. Not only do many of them lack adequate assets in a pension or 401(k) account, but the implosion of the stock and housing markets has left them little time to recover from steep financial losses. "The closer to retirement they are, the worse shape they're in," says Hwa of the Pension Rights Center.

Public angst over retirement finances is reflected in this year's Employee Benefit Research Institute (EBRI) "retirement confidence" survey. Only one in five retirees was "very confident" of having a financially secure retirement, half the rate of two years earlier. What's more, 28 percent of workers said the age at which they expected to retire changed in the past year, with the overwhelming majority saying they postponed retirement to improve their finances. [14]

One big obstacle facing those seeking a secure retirement is a lack of preparation. "Many workers still do not have a good idea of how much they need to save for retirement," EBRI noted in a summary of this year's survey results. "Only 44 percent of workers report they and/or their spouse have tried to calculate how much money they will need to have saved by the time they retire — and an equal proportion . . . simply guess at how much they will need for a comfortable retirement." [15]

Many people fail to factor into their planning the possibility that they could outlive their assets — an increasingly worrisome possibility as people live longer than ever. On average, a 65-year-old can expect to live to nearly 84, almost five more years than in 1950. [16]

Over the decades, people have been retiring earlier even as they have been living longer, a trend that has proven costly to many older Americans. Monthly Social Security benefits are

Confidence About Retirement at Record Low

A record-low 13 percent of American workers are "very confident" of having enough money to live comfortably in retirement — a 50 percent decline since 2007. At the same time, more than twice as many workers are "not at all confident" they will have enough, compared with two years ago.

Worker Confidence in Having Enough Money for Retirement, 1993-2009

Confidence Level	1993	1994	1999	2004	2005	2006	2007	2008	2009
Very confident	18%	20%	22%	24%	25%	24%	27%	18%	13%
Somewhat confident	55	45	47	44	40	44	43	43	41
Not too confident	19	17	21	18	17	17	19	21	22
Not at all confident	6	17	9	13	17	14	10	16	22

Source: "2009 Annual Retirement Confidence Survey," Employee Benefit Research Institute

lower for those retiring at 62 rather than at, say, 66. And by working a few years longer people can save more for retirement and shorten the number of years they will need to rely on their nest egg.

In the 2008 book *Working Longer: The Solution to the Retirement Income Challenge*, Alicia H. Munnell, director of the Center for Retirement Research at Boston College, and colleague Steven Sass argued that if people work full-time until at least age 66, their retirement incomes can be a third higher than if they stop working at age 62. [17]

"The most powerful thing people who have taken a financial hit can do is to keep working," Munnell says. "If you can extend your work life, you have a really good chance of offsetting this decline."

Even before the economic crisis, people born between 1948 and 1974 have been at a growing risk of not having enough money in retirement, according to data from the Boston College research center. Rising life expectancy, growing medical costs, modest savings in 401(k) plans and the fact that Social Security has been re-

placing a smaller and smaller share of pre-retirement earnings all have contributed to the risk, researchers say.

Without accounting for health-care costs, the center calculates that 44 percent of baby boomers and those in so-called Generation X — people born between 1965 and 1974 — are at risk of being unable to maintain their living standard in retirement.

When health-care costs are added to the mix, the proportion rises to 61 percent. And when the cost of long-term care is factored in, it shoots to 65 percent. [18]

"People are going to live a long time in retirement, and the decisions they make are really important," Munnell says. "They're hard decisions, not just about savings, but about figuring out how to spread [one's assets] over a lifetime, especially if you are going to need long-term care."

Should Social Security benefits be cut to strengthen the system?

When *USA Today* argued in an editorial this spring that "Social Security is in trouble" and should be fixed, the response from Baker at the Center for

Economic and Policy Research was sharp and swift. [19]

At a time when "elites" are doling out trillions of dollars to "bankers who wrecked the economy," he wrote, "they are proposing to cut Social Security in the name of fiscal responsibility." [20]

The exchange underscored the deep divide about the perceived seriousness of Social Security's fiscal problems and what should be done about them.

Often called the "third rail" of politics, Social Security has zapped even the most determined reformists. President George W. Bush failed in his controversial attempt to let younger workers invest part of their Social Security payroll taxes in private investment accounts — an idea that conservative Sen. Lindsey Graham, R-S.C., now says is "off the table" in the wake of the Wall Street bust. [21]

Meanwhile, President Barack Obama has run into opposition from congressional Democrats in his attempt to form a task force to study ways to ensure the long-term solvency of Social Security. Many Democrats want him to tackle health-care reform and other issues first. [22]

Hopes remain alive in Congress for a bipartisan effort to address the problems facing Social Security and the far more serious ones confronting Medicare. Together, spending on the programs totaled more than $1 trillion in 2008 — more than a third of the federal budget. [23]

In its editorial, *USA Today* argued that "preserving Social Security for the long term isn't that complicated." Gradually raise the retirement age for able-bodied workers, rein in benefit growth and levy more in payroll taxes on well-paid workers, it advised.

Yet, any revision in the Social Security system is sure to stir deep passions. Some argue, for example, that raising the eligibility age for benefits could hurt low-income workers toiling in backbreaking blue-collar jobs that are hard to sustain physically into the mid-to-late 60s.

Liberals have often sought to protect the system from benefit cuts, and many deny that the program is in crisis. "It's not in a crisis at all," says Madland of the Center for American Progress. Social Security faces "challenges," but they are "long term," he says. "It has more than enough to meet obligations for many, many years. Even way down the line, it just won't be able to pay out all the benefits unless there are changes, but it will still be able to pay out the vast majority."

Madland says it would take only "minor, small scale" changes to restore Social Security's long-term solvency. The center has said the fairest way to strengthen the program is to eliminate the wage cap on payroll taxes and force high earners to pay more into the system.

The wage cap is indexed for inflation, and this year applies to a worker's first $106,800 of annual gross income. The tax rate is 12.4 percent, split equally between workers and employers.

But conservatives have long argued that raising the wage cap would hike taxes for many middle-class workers, hurt small business and slow the economy.

Harvard economist Jeffrey Miron, a libertarian who was among 166 academic economists who signed a letter opposing the Bush administration's financial bailout plan last fall, said this spring that Social Security is "in serious trouble" and that he wants to see the eligibility age for benefits rise gradually to as high as 75.

"Life expectancy and health for the elderly have expanded substantially since we created the program in 1935," he told PBS' "Nightly Business Report." "So 65 was the right age then. Something like 70 to 75 is probably about the right age now. Phasing in over a period of 10, 20 years that higher age and eligibility would put the system back into balance to a substantial degree and still be completely consistent with the spirit of the original program." [24]

Workers 'Not Too' Confident in Social Security

Two-thirds of workers are "not too" or "not at all confident" that Social Security will continue to provide benefits at least equal to those retirees receive today. Skepticism about Social Security has remained at roughly the same level for the past five years. It is below the 77 percent skepticism level in 1994.

Worker Confidence That Social Security Will Continue to Provide Benefits of at Least Equal Value to Today's Benefits, 1992-2009

Confidence Level	1992	1994	1999	2004	2005	2006	2007	2008	2009
Very confident	3%	4%	7%	7%	8%	6%	7%	5%	6%
Somewhat confident	27	18	21	28	23	27	24	21	26
Not too confident	44	38	38	31	33	33	34	34	28
Not at all confident	24	39	33	32	35	34	34	37	39

Source: "2009 Annual Retirement Confidence Survey," Employee Benefit Research Institute

In Congress, members in both parties have been advocating reforms to put Social Security on a stronger foundation.

Republican Sen. Graham calls Social Security "a math problem" that can be solved with bipartisan cooperation. "You can do a combination of things, give a little here and give a little there, and get it done," said Graham, whose ideas include reduced benefits for the wealthy, more revenue for the system and a higher retirement age. [25]

House Majority Leader Steny Hoyer, D-Md., put forth a similar plan in a speech in May to the Bipartisan Policy Center, and he blamed both political parties for foot-dragging on the issue.

The options for overhauling Social Security "are well and widely understood," Hoyer said. "We can bring in more revenues. We can restrain the growth of benefits, particularly for higher-income workers, while we strengthen the safety net for lower-income workers. And/or we can raise the retirement age, recognizing that our life expectancy is significantly higher today."

What's missing, Hoyer continued, is "political will," not ideas. "The bipartisan trust we need for compromise has been sorely damaged. And both sides are guilty — Democrats for using Social Security as the 'third rail' for political advantage, and Republicans for walking away from the table at the first mention of raising revenues." [26]

Munnell, of Boston College, agrees that Social Security "is an easy fix if we have the political will." But she adds that "there is no free lunch" and says that rather than raise the eligibility age for full benefits or otherwise cut benefits, the best way to ensure the system's solvency for decades to come is to require a small increase in payroll taxes paid by workers and employers and to invest a portion of the Social Security trust fund in stocks to boost the system's earnings.

By raising the payroll tax rate by about 2 percentage points — one point each for workers and employers — the government could pay the current menu of benefits for all who reach retirement age at least through 2083, Munnell says. For a worker earning $50,000 a year, that would cost an extra $500 annually each for the worker and employer.

Most Workers Haven't Saved Much

Among American workers ages 55 and up, nearly one-third have less than $10,000 in total savings and investments, and 49 percent have less than $50,000.

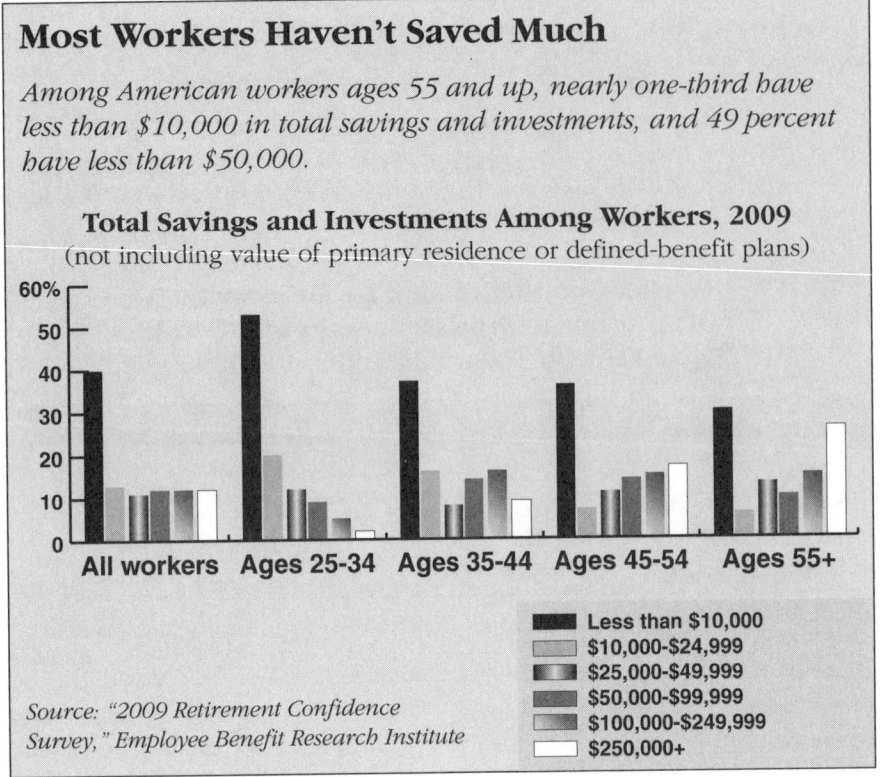

Total Savings and Investments Among Workers, 2009
(not including value of primary residence or defined-benefit plans)

Legend:
- Less than $10,000
- $10,000-$24,999
- $25,000-$49,999
- $50,000-$99,999
- $100,000-$249,999
- $250,000+

Source: "2009 Retirement Confidence Survey," Employee Benefit Research Institute

Are new rules needed to foster greater private retirement savings?

As daunting as the financial challenges of old age may be, many Americans are unable or unwilling to make adequate preparations for retirement. In the aftermath of the Wall Street collapse, some policy analysts are asking whether new strategies are needed to ensure that workers save for the future.

Much of the debate has focused on whether 401(k) accounts, which rely largely on voluntary contributions from workers, have succeeded or failed as a pillar of retirement planning. (*See "At Issue," p. 565.*)

The average 401(k) balance sank 28 percent — to $57,200 — at the end of 2008, according to a report by Hewitt Associates. [27]

Some defend the 401(k) system. "Retirement-saving assets are down — in all forms of accounts — because the stock market is down, not because of any fundamental flaw in 401(k)s," the Investment Company Institute, a trade group for mutual funds

and other investment companies, said in February. [28]

But others are critical of 401(k) plans. "The 401(k) is not the right vehicle as the only supplement to Social Security," argues Boston College's Munnell. Madland of the Center for American Progress says the plans can be improved but that under their current structure "the experiment in 401(k)s hasn't worked out very well" for most people.

The 401(k) system has drawn fire for a variety of reasons. Some argue, for example, that many workers are ill-prepared to manage their retirement accounts wisely, leaving them vulnerable to the kind of steep market declines that occurred in recent months.

Critics also say that too many workers, including many in low-wage jobs, don't have access to a 401(k) plan. In a report this year, the nonpartisan Congressional Research Service presented data showing that workers below age 35, those who didn't attend college, those with incomes in the lowest quartile and those who worked at small

companies all were less likely than other workers to have worked for an employer that sponsored a 401(k)-style plan. [29]

Others say that too many workers choose not to participate in a 401(k) plan even when one is available. One approach, however, has helped boost participation in retirement-savings plans: automatic enrollment of employees, with an opt-out feature.

Companies already have the right — though not the duty — to automatically enroll employees in a 401(k) plan, thanks to a policy change adopted during the Clinton administration and strengthened by the Pension Protection Act of 2006. David C. John, a senior research fellow and retirement expert at the conservative Heritage Foundation, says 401(k) auto-enrollment has already helped increase participation rates dramatically, especially among low-income, female, young and minority workers.

A study by the University of Pennsylvania's Wharton School found that 401(k) participation soared from 13 percent to 80 percent by making enrollment automatic with an opt-out feature. [30]

"As far as we can tell, auto-enrollment basically solves the problem of under-participation," John says.

Now the Obama administration has proposed building on the auto-enrollment idea. It wants to require companies that don't offer a 401(k) or other retirement plan to automatically enroll workers in an Individual Retirement Account, allowing workers who wish not to participate to opt out. Alternately, companies could ask employees ahead of time if they want to participate in an IRA program, requiring each worker to respond yes or no.

The plan, which is contained in the president's 2010 budget, would apply to companies with more than 10 employees that have been in business at least two years. They would deduct a small percentage of a participating worker's pay and deposit it into the employee's

IRA account. Employers would receive a tax credit to help them set up the auto-deduction program.

Under a separate proposal, a tax benefit known as the Saver's Credit would be expanded to give households earning less than $65,000 a year a tax credit for contributing to a retirement-savings plan, whether an auto-IRA, other IRA or 401(k). [31]

Nearly 75 million people work for companies that don't offer a retirement plan of any kind, and John says automatic IRAs could result in tens of millions of additional American workers saving for retirement. "This would be the largest increase in retirement savings in one chunk that we've had in this country," he says.

John and J. Mark Iwry, until recently a senior fellow at the liberal-leaning Brookings Institution and now a Treasury Department adviser in the Obama administration, have worked across ideological lines to spearhead the auto-IRA effort.

John also is working with Brookings scholars to advocate a program in which workers could use a portion of their tax-deferred retirement savings to purchase an annuity on a trial basis. For two years they would receive payments from the annuity, which is an insurance contract that pays an income for life. After two years, they could decide to keep the annuity or take back their money and manage it themselves.

The idea, John says, is to encourage people to plan in a way that they are "most likely to have their money last the rest of their life."

Emily Burton, 25, earns $22,000 as a cook in the deli at a grocery store in Parkville, Mo. "I could save for retirement," she said, "but that would mean scrimping for the next 10 years, and scrimping isn't fun."

AP Photo/Charlie Riedel

Some retirement experts believe the best approach to ensuring retirement security is to make saving mandatory. For example, Teresa Ghilarducci, a professor at the New School for Social Research in New York, advocates a plan called Guaranteed Retirement Accounts. All workers not enrolled in an equal or better traditional pension plan would be required to participate. A contribution equal to 5 percent of their earnings would go into an account each year, with the cost split between employer and worker.

A $600 annual federal tax credit would offset employees' contributions. The money would earn a guaranteed 3 percent return above the inflation rate under government management, and upon a worker's retirement the account would convert to an annuity that provides income until death.

"After 30 years of experience with voluntary participation in the 401(k)

system, in my opinion, it has failed," Ghilarducci told *U.S. News & World Report.* "The only retirement system that all people have is Social Security, and Social Security isn't enough. We need a universal supplement to Social Security so that everyone can retire." [32]

But others resist the idea of mandatory retirement savings. "On the one hand, it's obviously better for an individual to have savings," says John. But he argues that people need to retain the option of stopping their retirement savings if a medical crisis or some other urgent problem makes it hard for them to set money aside.

"The individual is the best judge of what his or her circumstances are at any particular time," he says. ∎

BACKGROUND

Rise of 401(k) Plans

Many early Americans did not — indeed, could not — indulge in the dream of a long, financially secure retirement. In fact, people typically kept working until their health began to fail.

"The concept of leaving the labor force simply because one reaches an arbitrary age is a fairly recent phenomenon," the Social Security Advisory Board noted. "Historically, it was quite common for people to remain in the labor force as long as they were physically able to do so because they simply did not have enough income to retire. Even as recently as the late 1940s nearly half of the men age 65 and over were still in the labor force, compared to only about one in five today." [33]

The first U.S. employer to offer a private retirement plan was American Express, in 1875, but the program had severe limitations: Only disabled, elderly workers at least 60 years old with 20 years of service were eligible. Moreover, an employee needed the recommendation of the company's general manager and approval of the Board of Directors' Executive Committee. [34]

By 1900 only a dozen private pension plans existed in the United States. [35] But the number increased as manufacturing companies rose to prominence, tax rules on the deductibility of employer contributions were clarified and group annuity contracts came on the scene, allowing plan expenses to be spread among multiple people. [36]

Still, pensions did not always guarantee financial security in old age. "Typically, in the first half-century of significant [pension] plan growth (1880-1930), during which more than 400 private plans were established, almost all plans were discretionary," Labor Department economist Patrick W. Seburn wrote. "This meant that employers could modify, suspend or annul the pension program at any time. Additionally, it was also understood that the company could withhold or terminate the pension of any employee for any reason, at any time." [37]

During the Great Depression of the 1930s, financial pressures and the advent of Social Security led some companies to cut pension benefits, terminate plans or require workers to contribute toward them. [38]

After World War II, as the U.S. economy flourished and big corporations rose on the employment scene, many more workers came under the umbrella of private pension plans. Yet, perhaps contrary to popular perception, pension coverage was far from universal during the postwar boom years. At the end of 1960, for example, roughly half of the private-sector workforce was not covered by a pension. [39]

Moreover, to become eligible for pension benefits, workers often had to stay with a single employer for years or even decades, discouraging the kind of job mobility that — for better or worse — has become common today.

Starting in the early 1980s, 401(k) plans began to emerge. Munnell of Boston College points out that they were intended as supplements to employer-financed pension plans, not the retirement mainstays they have become.

Labor Department data indicate that the number of 401(k)-style plans rose sharply in the 1980s and '90s, from about 17,300 in 1984 to more than 465,000 in 2006. [40]

With the advent of 401(k) plans, the responsibility for building a retirement nest-egg became more complicated for many workers. Some observers argue that the rise of 401(k) plans shifted huge amounts of risk onto the shoulders of individual workers. Not only must they contribute to the plans from their own pockets, but they also must figure out how to invest their retirement money in a way that will produce sufficient income in retirement.

"As recently as 25 years ago, more than 80 percent of large- and medium-sized firms offered a [traditional] defined-benefit [pension] plan; today, less than a third do, and the share continues to fall," Jacob Hacker, a political scientist and co-director of the Center for Health, Economic and Family Security at the University of California at Berkeley, told a House panel last fall. "Companies are rapidly . . . preventing new workers from joining the [plans] and shifting them over to alternative forms . . . that are more like 401(k)s," Hacker stated. But, he added, 401(k) plans are not pensions in the traditional sense of providing a fixed benefit in retirement, but rather private employer-sponsored investment accounts. "As a result, they greatly increase the degree of risk and responsibility placed on individual workers in retirement planning." [41]

Munnell says that while the pension system that prevailed before the 1980s wasn't perfect, it made retirement far more "simple and predictable" than it is today. Retirees covered by a pension "had to make no decisions — just pick up two checks: one from Social Security and one from your company," she says. What's more, because pensions provide a predictable income flow, "You knew when you were going to retire. Now people really don't know when they should stop working."

But 401(k) plans have many defenders, among them the financial-services industry.

"Critics say that because Americans' retirement accounts are down, 401(k) plans should be scrapped or shoved aside," John V. Murphy, chairman of the Investment Company Institute, said in remarks prepared for delivery in May to the group's general membership meeting. "We reject that idea, and so do Americans."

In a survey of 3,000 households last fall — "during the darkest days of the market decline" — the institute found "overwhelming" support for 401(k) plans, said Murphy, who also is chairman of Oppenheimer Funds Inc., a major investment company.

Almost three out of four rejected the idea of reducing tax breaks for 401(k)-style plans and Individual Retirement Accounts, and nearly nine in 10 "rejected the idea of barring individuals from making their own investment decisions in these plans," Murphy said. [42]

Continued on p. 560

Chronology

1875-1930s
Number of companies offering pensions increases during the industrial era, but many older workers remain unprotected.

1875
American Express is first U.S. firm to offer a private retirement plan.

1900
Only a dozen private pension plans exist nationwide.

1930
More than 400 pension plans have been started; about 10 percent of non-government workers have plans.

1929
Great Depression begins, forces many companies to pare retirement benefits or ask workers to contribute.

1935
President Franklin D. Roosevelt signs Social Security Act into law. . . . First Social Security check, for $22.54, sent to Ida May Fuller, of Ludlow, Vt., in January 1940.

1940s-1970s
Postwar population explosion presages financial problems for Social Security, Medicare.

1946
Baby boom begins, extends to 1964.

1950
Congress enacts first cost-of-living adjustment for Social Security.

1956
Early-retirement Social Security benefits made available to women at age 62; benefits at age 62 for men made available in 1961.

1965
Medicare provides health insurance for people 65 and older; Medicaid provides health care for low-income people.

1975
Automatic, annual cost-of-living adjustments linked to inflation rate instituted for Social Security recipients.

1974
Employee Retirement Income Security Act (ERISA) sets standards for employer-sponsored plans and insures benefits against pension-plan termination if a company goes bankrupt.

1978
Revenue Act lets employers offer defined-contribution, or 401(k), plans.

1980s-2000s
New 401(k) plans begin eclipsing traditional pensions; concern grows over Social Security's solvency as baby boomers age.

1983
Congress taxes Social Security benefits, includes federal employees in the system and proposes raising the eligibility age for full benefits.

1990
Proportion of working men 65 and older continues to decline; 17.5 percent of married males in that age category are in the labor force, compared with nearly 30 percent in 1970; among married women 65 and older, however, 8.5 percent were in the labor force in 1990, up from 7.3 percent in 1970.

1997
Tax law changes expand eligibility for deductible contributions to in-dividual retirement accounts (IRAs) and create Roth IRAs, which allow tax-free withdrawal of assets at retirement.

2001-Present
Economic crisis spurs concerns about older workers' ability to have a secure retirement.

2001
Commission to Strengthen Social Security, appointed by President George W. Bush, recommends allowing workers to use part of their Social Security payroll taxes for private investment accounts, but many consider the proposal dead following the 2008 stock market crash.

2006
Pension Protection Act makes it easier for companies to automatically enroll employees in 401(k) plans.

2008
The first baby boomers turn 62 and become eligible for reduced Social Security benefits; economic crisis decimates retirement accounts, leads to millions of job losses and forces many older workers to delay retirement.

2009
Congressional Budget Office forecasts Social Security won't pay cost-of-living increase in 2010 and 2011 because of low inflation stemming from the recession. . . . Government warns Medicare fund is expected to be insolvent in 2017, two years earlier than projected, and the Social Security trust fund in 2037, four years earlier. . . . Pension Benefit Guaranty Corp. reports that its deficit tripled in last six months, to $33.5 billion, but says assets are adequate to protect workers' pensions for years.

Social Security Is a Thin Lifeline

High living isn't an option.

For the working poor, the golden years may be the lean years. With low incomes and meager savings, millions of Americans face a retirement with little but Social Security and Medicare to depend on, even as they struggle to stay ahead of rising medical and energy bills.

"Low-income people are unlikely to have savings and any kind of pension," says Deborah Weinstein, executive director of the Coalition on Human Needs, a Washington advocacy group. "Some may have owned a home, [but] the equity in those homes in many instances may have diminished, so that's less of a help to them. Many never owned a home. So really, what it comes down to is Social Security."

The average monthly Social Security old-age insurance benefit for retired workers was $1,158.10 in May, or $13,897 annually. [1]

The poorest households headed by people nearing retirement have been among the hardest hit, according to a study this year by the Center for Economic and Policy Research, a liberal Washington think tank. Using data from the Federal Reserve Board's Consumer Finance Survey as its basis, the center projected that average net worth among the bottom 20 percent of households headed by a person 55 to 64 years old fell from $8,300 in 2004 to between $1,200 and a negative $2,600 (with debt exceeding assets) this year.

The center also found that the recent economic collapse cost the poor a far bigger chunk of their wealth, in percentage terms, than it did the rich. In what economist David Rosnick, co-author of the study, noted in an interview was the most optimistic projection, net wealth fell 85 percent from 2004 among the poorest Americans, but only 25 percent among the wealthiest. [2]

For the poor, Social Security is often a lifeline in retirement, if only a thin one.

Gary V. Engelhardt, an economics professor at Syracuse University who studies Social Security and the elderly, says that Social Security has kept a growing proportion of people 65 and older out of poverty in recent decades. The percentage of elderly people below the federal poverty threshold has fallen from about 40 percent in the 1940s and '50s to about 9 percent today, he says.

Social Security replaces a bigger proportion of a low-income worker's pre-retirement income than a high earner's and thus is fairly effective at smoothing the transition from work to retirement for those on the lower rungs of the wage scale, Engelhardt says. Still, he cautions, "We should not confuse that with these people living high on the hog."

Wider Opportunities for Women, an advocacy group in Washington, points out that women are more likely than men to rely solely on Social Security in retirement. Citing Social Security Administration figures, the group said more than 43 percent of elderly, unmarried women receiving Social Security benefits relied on Society Security for 90 percent or more of their income in 2004.

And, it said, because of "pay-equity issues, the occupational segregation of women in low-wage jobs and their cycling in and out of the workforce due to care-giving responsibilities, women often find themselves with a Social Security record that provides inadequate income." [3]

For low-income people generally, Weinstein says Social Security may not respond adequately to rising costs for health care, prescription drugs, electricity and other necessities.

Some elderly people may be eligible for other government aid, such as state Medicaid payments for health care or federal Supplemental Security Income (SSI) payments for the needy. But to gain such benefits, recipients typically must exhaust nearly all their savings. In general, a person can retain a mere $2,000 in assets to qualify for SSI, or $3,000 for a couple.

The low thresholds discourage many poor, elderly people from seeking Medicaid or SSI, for fear of having no cash cushion left to fix a broken furnace or handle some other emergency, Weinstein says. "It could mean the difference between a real catastrophe and affording the catastrophe," she says.

[1] "Monthly Statistical Snapshot," U.S. Social Security Administration, May 2009, www.ssa.gov/policy/docs/quickfacts/stat_snapshot/.

[2] David Rosnick and Dean Baker, "The Wealth of the Baby Boom Cohorts After the Collapse of the Housing Bubble," Center for Economic and Policy Research, February 2009, p. 14, www.cepr.net/documents/publications/baby-boomer-wealth-2009-02.pdf.

[3] "Single Women's Retirement Income Falls Short of the Elder Economic Security Standard Index," Wider Opportunities for Women, www.wowonline.org/pdf/NationalEESIfactsheet_single.pdf.

Continued from p. 558

Delaying Retirement

Whatever the arguments for or against 401(k) plans, retirement experts uniformly agree that many older workers will need to stay in the workforce longer — even a year or two, if not more — to recoup savings lost in the recent economic collapse and to account for the fact that they may need to live off their retirement savings and Social Security for three decades or more.

"There is only one realistic way to prevent aging boomers from experiencing a significant decline in their living standards and becoming a multi-decade drag on U.S. and world economic growth," the McKinsey Global Institute said in a report last fall. "Boomers will have to continue working beyond the traditional retirement age, and that will require important changes in public policy, business practices and personal behavior."

McKinsey estimated that a two-year increase in the median retirement age over the next decade would add nearly $13 trillion to the inflation-adjusted U.S. gross domestic product during the next 30 years and roughly halve the number of baby boomers who would be financially unprepared for retirement. [43]

A long-term study sponsored by the National Institute on Aging (NIA) shows that although retirement rates shoot up when workers become eligible for Social Security benefits, many older people remain in either full- or part-time jobs. Comparing data from 1992 and 2004, researchers said "a substantially larger proportion" of baby boomers in their early to mid-50s expected to work after age 65. "The differences between 1992 and 2004 are striking, and the highest levels are generally seen among those who have attended or graduated from college," they said. [44]

NIA researchers said that the decline of traditional pensions and expansion of 401(k)-style accounts over the past two decades "may be playing a role in ending the trend toward earlier retirement." People with traditional pensions, usually including retirement incentives, lifelong benefits and "reduced pension investment risk," leave the work world an average of 1.3 years earlier than those with 401(k)-style plans, researchers said. [45]

A Congressional Research Service analysis last year found that nearly 33 percent of men ages 65 to 69 were

A demonstrator at the Social Security Administration office in Chicago protests proposals to privatize Social Security in April 2005. President George W. Bush failed in his controversial attempt to let workers invest part of their Social Security payroll taxes in private investment accounts. In the wake of the Wall Street bust, the idea is now considered "off the table."

Getty Images/Tim Boyle

employed in full- or part-time jobs in 2008, compared with 26 percent in 1990. The rate for women was nearly 27 percent in 2008, compared with 17 percent in 1990. [46]

Older workers want to remain on the job for a variety of reasons, ranging from a desire to remain active to a need for income or company-sponsored health insurance until Medicare kicks in at age 65.

An important influence generally is that people, on average, are living longer than previous generations. That has raised the number of years that a person may spend in retirement. By working longer, a person has more time to accumulate savings while also

reducing the time spent in retirement when money may be needed.

Yet older workers wanting to stay in the workforce often run into legal, cultural and institutional barriers. Social Security rules are an example. The program imposes an earnings penalty that withholds $1 in benefits for every $2 earned above a certain limit — $14,160 this year — for those receiving benefits between age 62 and their full retirement age. [47]

Tough Economy

The difficult economy is yet another obstacle. "The deteriorating job market is a tough place for older people," the New School's Ghilarducci wrote recently on a *New York Times* blog focusing on older workers. "The good news is that workers over age 45 are still less likely to be laid off than newly hired workers. However, older workers face heavy pressure to retire early and take buyouts when firms are cutting costs. But the early pension and buyout are usually not enough to live on." And, Ghilarducci added, "when displaced older workers do find new jobs, they tend to earn much lower wages." [48]

One way older workers can stay on the job longer is through so-called phased retirement arrangements, in which, for example, they work part time. The downside, though, is that such arrangements — when they are available — often come with conditions that workers find unpalatable, such as the loss of health-care benefits or change in job title.

'Encore' Careers Beckon Many After Retirement

Midlife changes combine personal interest and social purpose.

When Microsoft co-founder Bill Gates announced he would step aside in mid-2008 from his day-to-day management role at the technology giant, a golf course fairway wasn't on his mind.

"It's not a retirement, it's a reordering of my priorities," said Gates, who now works part time for Microsoft and full time for the Bill and Melinda Gates Foundation, the $30 billion philanthropy he founded with his wife that focuses on world health and education issues. [1]

Gates' shift is perhaps the most visible example of what retirement experts, social-service advocates and demographers call the "encore" career — the midlife transition into a paid or volunteer position that combines personal interest and a social purpose.

No one knows exactly how many Americans have moved into encore careers, but surveys suggest the trend is gaining momentum among the approximately 77-million-member post-World War II baby-boom generation. Some boomers have chosen to leave established careers in search of meaningful positions in education, social services, nonprofit health care and other realms. Others have gotten a nudge into an encore career by the recession, which is forcing millions of older Americans to seek jobs in new fields — or become volunteers sooner than expected.

Experts define encore careers in different ways. For some, it might simply mean a less stressful or more flexible job in a new field of personal interest for someone nearing retirement. For others, it might mean volunteer work at a food bank or inner-city school.

At Civic Ventures, a San Francisco-based nonprofit group that is a major champion of the encore concept, the idea has a very specific meaning. John Gomperts, the group's 53-year-old president, says encore careers lie "at the intersection of social impact, personal meaning and continued income."

Those pursuing an encore career are "people who finish a midlife career, who make a large commitment to doing public-purpose work in their post-midlife careers. We think most often that will happen in the form of paid work."

Based on survey data gathered last year by the MetLife Foundation and Civic Ventures, researchers estimated that between 5.3 and 8.4 million Americans ages 44 through 70 —

most from managerial, professional and other white-collar backgrounds — have begun "encore careers." [2]

What's more, nearly 45 percent of respondents not already in an encore career expressed interest in one. More than a third said they wanted to be an advocate for a group or issue they care about. Other desired jobs included work with children and youth, environmental preservation and teaching.

"If people do the thing they love and it has real impact and provides real income, it's not absurd to think people would spend five to 10 years in their encore careers," Gumperts says.

Laura Gassner Otting, president of the Nonprofit Professionals Advisory Group, a Massachusetts-based executive-search and leadership-development firm, sees vast new encore opportunities in the nonprofit world opening up. Gassner Otting, author of *Change Your Career: Transitioning to the Nonprofit Sector*, says a "leadership vacuum" exists in the philanthropic world because of huge numbers of retirements at charities and foundations.

"We've got baby boomers that are retiring at almost 8,000 per day, and there are huge opportunities at every level of every organization in the for-profit and nonprofit sector because of this," she says. Even in the poor economy, she adds, "we're still seeing people retire at huge rates, and so it's really allowing opportunities for people to step into careers that they might not have trained their entire lives for but for which they are passionate and actually skilled."

In her book, Gassner Otting notes that "the baby boomer generation is responsible for creating and leading many of the nation's nonprofits, and as this group retires over the next decade, the rate of nonprofit executive transition is expected to climb 10 to 15 percent, meaning that three to four out of every five executive director jobs will be vacated between now and 2010. This will produce a leadership vacuum unparalleled in the history of the nonprofit sector, leaving nonprofits scrambling for experienced managers. More than just causing change at the top, leadership vacuums create ripple effects, sending waves of turnover throughout every level of the organizational chart." [3]

Gomperts expects the newly enacted Edward M. Kennedy Serve America Act, which authorizes as much as $6 billion in new spend-

In 2002 Robert Hutchens, a professor of labor economics at Cornell University, studied phased-retirement opportunities for white-collar workers age 55 and older. Nearly three-quarters of the employers he surveyed said some form of phased retirement could be arranged. [49] Yet phased retirement remains relatively rare, though not for

the reason Hutchens said he assumed.

"I went into it expecting the reason we don't see very much phased retirement was that employers were resistant to it. The surprise was that there wasn't strong evidence of that. The employers seemed to be open to the possibility of phased retirement. But the major hypothesis [of the study] is that the terms in which they're willing to do phased retirement were terms that workers often find not acceptable."

In the future, shortages of younger workers and demand for older ones could make employers more flexible in accommodating the wishes of older employees, and employees themselves

ing over five years to increase volunteerism and community service, to broaden the appeal of encore careers. The measure features an array of programs that expand opportunities for paid and volunteer community service, including for people 55 and older.

Included in the act, for example, are programs under which people 55 and older who perform volunteer service can receive an education stipend that is transferable to a child or grandchild. The law also established a limited number of fellowships — similar to internships and including modest stipends — designed to help older Americans transition into nonprofit leadership positions. [4]

Civic Ventures was deeply involved in advocating for the measure and its expansion of opportunities for older Americans, Gomperts says. "This bill has the potential to be a tremendous breakthrough in engaging people in midlife careers doing high-impact service," he says.

Still, those looking for meaningful work in the nonprofit field may also face barriers, including what some see as outdated human-resource practices at many charities and foundations.

A 2007 report by The Conference Board noted that while the nonprofit world faces a "talent" shortage as many nonprofit workers retire, "nonprofits are seriously lagging behind the government and private sectors in efforts to both retain highly skilled potential retirees within their organizations and actively recruit older hires from other industry sectors." [5]

The Conference Board noted, for example, that "few nonprofit organizations have developed flexible work options to meet baby-boomer preferences." [6]

Gomperts concedes that human-resource issues can be a "significant barrier" to people seeking midlife encore careers with nonprofit organizations. But he also points to survey data gathered by the MetLife Foundation and Civic Ventures showing that nonprofit employers are interested in hiring encore workers.

After losing her job several years ago, Anne Nolan found her life's work running a service organization for the homeless in Rhode Island.

© Civic Ventures/Ilene Perlman

Half of those surveyed said they saw encore workers as highly appealing, and most said they offer flexible work arrangements, though only 40 percent allowed employees to work from a mobile office or home. [7]

The recession could both hurt and help the movement of older workers into nonprofit jobs, Gomperts says. "The tightening in the job market makes it a little more difficult to move from aspiration to action," he says. On the other hand, he says, because of the recession many more older workers will be staying in the job market — and possibly looking for new opportunities in encore careers.

"It's not a question of 'will you work longer,' it's a question of 'what will you do?' " says Gomperts. "Many people are attracted to the kind of opportunities encore careers hold, so that's a huge advantage."

[1] Amanda Cantrell, "Gates to leave day-to-day role at Microsoft," CNN-Money.com, June 16, 2006, http://money.cnn.com/2006/06/15/technology/microsoft_news/index.htm.

[2] Metlife Foundation/Civic Ventures, "Encore Career Survey," June 2008.

[3] Laura Gassner Otting, *Change Your Career: Transitioning to the Nonprofit Sector* (2007), p. 5.

[4] For details of the legislation, see "Highlights of the Edward M. Kennedy Serve America Act," Corporation for National & Community Service, March 30, 2009, www.nationalservice.gov/about/newsroom/releases_detail.asp?tbl_pr_id=1283. See also Elizabeth Pope, "A Move to Expand Volunteer Ranks," *The New York Times*, April 2, 2009, www.nytimes.com/2009/04/02/business/retirementspecial/02program.html?scp=1&sq=a%20move%20to%20expand%20volunteer%20ranks&st=cse.

[5] "Non-Profit Firms Face Challenges and Some Opportunities With Advent of Retirement of Baby-Boomers," press release, The Conference Board, May 31, 2007, www.conference-board.org/utilities/pressDetail.cfm?press_ID=3142. The full report is Jill Casner-Lotto, "Boomers Are Ready for Nonprofits — But Are Nonprofits Ready for Them?" The Conference Board, 2007, www.conference-board.org/publications/describe.cfm?id=1319.

[6] Press release, *ibid.*

[7] Metlife Foundation/Civic Ventures, "Tapping Encore Talent," October 2008, pp. 8-9.

may be more willing to bend when it comes to accepting tradeoffs.

Census data show that by 2025 the number of people between 55 and 64 is projected to rise more than 36 percent, while those 25 to 54 — the prime working ages — will rise only 3.8 percent, noted the Congressional Research Service, which pointed to "a

substantial shift toward a greater number of older individuals and a relative scarcity of young people entering the labor force." [50]

Rix, the AARP policy expert, says that once the current economic downturn ends, demand for older workers could rise sharply. "If those worker shortages materialize, employers will

make available all sorts of options to workers to attract and retain them. Look at the demographics. It's pretty clear those workers are going to be at the upper end of the age span, not at the lower, because [adequate numbers of younger workers] are just not there."

Still, Rix counsels caution right now for older people wanting to remain in the workforce, especially those hoping to transition into a new career field or into a part-time job that offers both flexibility and satisfaction.

"As much as many workers say they want to retire to another job and do something new in retirement, they should recognize how difficult it is, certainly right now, to find anything new," she says. ∎

CURRENT SITUATION

Financial Challenges

As the nation struggles to extricate itself from one of the worst recessions in decades, policy makers worry about the financial condition of Social Security and Medicare, whose already precarious status has deteriorated further because of the steep economic downturn.

In May, Treasury Secretary Timothy F. Geithner called Medicare's financial challenges "larger and more imminent" than those facing Social Security.

"Medicare faces demographic challenges [and] rapidly growing health-care costs," he said, "and the short-term outlook has been hurt by the recession." The program's annual costs totaled 3.2 percent of gross domestic product (GDP) last year, nearly three-fourths the level of Social Security's costs, he said. But Medicare's annual bill is projected to reach 11.4 percent of GDP in 2083, compared with 5.9 percent for Social Security.

That is not to say that Social Security lacks significant challenges, Geithner indicated. Because of the recession and other pressures, he said, the Social Security trust fund is expected to be exhausted in 2037,

four years sooner than earlier projections.

Geithner said the Obama administration is attacking the problems of Medicare and Social Security in three ways: by working to end the recession; overhauling the health-care system to control costs and improve quality in order to strengthen Medicare; and, after passing health-care legislation, building "a bipartisan consensus to ensure the long-term solvency of Social Security." Obama, he said, "explicitly rejects the notion that Social Security is . . . untouchable politically." [51]

But fixing Social Security is a daunting task whose obstacles are not just political but demographic.

"The cause of the rising cost of Social Security is straightforward: Our population is steadily growing older," the Social Security Advisory Board said last fall.

Birth rates dropped in the 1960s and remained at roughly those lower levels, while, at the same time, people are living longer, the group noted. "In 1960, only 9 percent of the population was age 65 or over. By 2000, that had risen to 12 percent. By 2030, 19 percent of the population will be age 65 or over. As the very large baby-boom generation enters its retirement years, the share of the population that is no longer in the workforce rises dramatically."

And because Social Security is a pay-as-you-go system, with payroll taxes of current workers covering benefits for retirees, the system will come under increasing stress as the population ages and more people become eligible for benefits. Over the next quarter-century, the Social Security Advisory Board said, "our society will shift from having about one retiree for every three workers to having about one retiree for every two workers. As a result, the cost of our Social Security system will increase by 25 percent." [52]

Strengthening 401(k) Plans

As policy makers look hard at future challenges to retirement, they also are looking for ways to strengthen the existing retirement-savings system. A major center of debate is the 401(k) plan.

U.S. Reps. George Miller, D-Calif., chairman of the House Committee on Education and Labor, and Rob Andrews, D-N.J., chairman of the Health, Employment, Labor and Pensions Subcommittee, have introduced legislation requiring the financial-services industry to disclose all 401(k) costs and fees associated with each investment option. The bill would also require 401(k)-style plans seeking limited liability against investment losses to offer at least one low-cost index fund — a mutual fund that tracks a specific stock index, such as the S&P 500. [53]

"Current law does not require all fees workers pay to be disclosed, and even for information that is available, it can be difficult for workers to find," Miller's committee said. Citing Government Accountability Office data, it said only a single percentage point in excessive fees can cut a 401(k) account balance by 20 percent or more over a worker's career. [54]

Rep. Richard E. Neal, D-Mass., introduced a separate bill in June that is aimed at providing transparency on fees and expenses charged to 401(k)-style plans and improving other kinds of plan-related communication.

The Investment Company Institute said in a statement that it and the fund industry "strongly support 401(k) disclosure that's clear, concise and complete for all 401(k) investment options" and that they would continue to work with Miller, Neal and others "on achieving better disclosure for 401(k) investors."

Still, the investment industry has defended its fee structure. "The critics talk a lot about the fees that 401(k)

Continued on p. 566

At Issue:

Do 401(k) plans ensure a secure retirement?

IANTHE ZABEL
SENIOR DIRECTOR,
PUBLIC COMMUNICATIONS
INVESTMENT COMPANY INSTITUTE

WRITTEN FOR *CQ RESEARCHER*, JUNE 8, 2009

*t*he track record of 401(k) plans shows how vital they are in helping Americans enjoy a secure retirement. They are well-suited to our flexible workforce and have had remarkable success in encouraging Americans to save and invest.

Consider the numbers. Even though 401(k)s have been around for less than 30 years — not even a full working career — Americans have accumulated $2.4 trillion in these plans. And that doesn't count hundreds of billions of dollars saved in 401(k)s and rolled over into IRAs.

Assessing the significance of that accumulation, economists James Poterba of MIT, Steven Venti of Dartmouth and David Wise of Harvard conducted a detailed study of 401(k)s in 2007. They concluded: "Our projections suggest that the advent of personal account saving will increase wealth at retirement for future retirees across the lifetime earnings spectrum." In another paper, Poterba, Venti, Wise and Joshua Rauh of the University of Chicago found that the average wealth accrued under private-sector defined-contribution (DC) plans like 401(k)s would generally exceed the wealth accrued under traditional pensions.

The Employee Benefit Research Institute and the Investment Company Institute got similar results in 2002, when they projected what 401(k)s could accumulate across a full career. That study found that 401(k) assets could replace at least half of pre-retirement income for more than 60 percent of 401(k) participants reaching age 65 between 2030 and 2039. Add in Social Security, and median replacement rates range from 106 percent of pre-retirement income for the lowest income group to 84 percent for the highest.

Americans recognize the value of their 401(k)s. Last year, despite tumultuous markets, only 3.7 percent of participants stopped contributing to their DC plans. In a fall 2008 survey of 3,000 households, Americans with DC plans said that payroll deduction makes it easier to save and that immediate tax deductions offer a big incentive to contribute.

Like all forms of retirement savings, 401(k) plans suffered in the market downturn. And 401(k)s, despite their remarkable track record, aren't perfect. We should improve disclosure, encourage more employers to offer plans and make financial literacy a national priority.

We should also preserve the best attributes of 401(k)s: portable benefits, fiduciary standards for plan decisionmakers, diversification opportunities and the ability to take advantage of catch-up contributions and employer matches. Preserving and strengthening 401(k)s is a vital goal. They are an integral part of America's retirement system.

TERESA GHILARDUCCI
BERNARD L. AND IRENE SCHWARTZ CHAIR
OF ECONOMIC POLICY ANALYSIS,
THE NEW SCHOOL FOR SOCIAL RESEARCH

WRITTEN FOR *CQ RESEARCHER*, JUNE 8, 2009

*s*ecure retirements are not guaranteed by 401(k)s, but it's a surprise they aren't; after all, 401(k) plans look great on paper. Advocates for 401(k) plans — lobbyists for the mutual fund industry, the Investment Company Institute and 401(k) consultants — produce spreadsheets showing that ideal human beings and their employers — those who contribute consistently over a lifetime of work and invest prudently in balanced portfolios — can amass $400,000 or more at retirement. Yet after nearly three decades, the average 401(k) account balance for people nearing retirement is approximately $60,000 — far below what we would have expected and far less than a middle-class earner needs.

Why aren't 401(k) plans ensuring a secure retirement?

It's because real human beings don't live spreadsheet lives. And neither do employers. Employers need not provide 401(k) plans — half of the workforce has no 401(k) plan or any other pension plan. When employers actually do sponsor 401(k) plans, their contributions are voluntary.

Since November 2008, for example, name-brand employers — including Motorola and FedEx — have led the way for employers to drop their matching contributions. And when employers and employees contribute, the amount is usually 3-5 percent of pay; experts recommend 5-10 percent.

Even if people have accumulated 401(k) funds, they may withdraw them before retirement, especially in the face of an income shock: being laid off, changing jobs, divorcing, paying for education, buying houses or coping with illness or injury. And as is often underappreciated, there is a large public cost to a voluntary feature — "voluntary" is expensive.

Congress considers saving a public good, but not enough to mandate it. Instead, lawmakers incentivize savers by giving them tax breaks for their pension contributions and earnings. The U.S. Treasury spends over $100 billion per year providing these "bribes," which go to the earners in the highest tax bracket — the group that saves anyway. The tax breaks are, at best, ineffective.

Americans manage their 401(k) plans through for-profit financial-service providers who have conflicted relationships with employers and few reasons to disclose fees. Moreover, the individual account structure disadvantages the worker by preventing the commingling of funds, the spreading of risk and the bargaining for lower fees. These factors lead to worse 401(k) net-of-fee returns than for traditional plans. The 401(k) system fails because it is voluntary, commercial and based on poorly prepared individuals making financial decisions.

Continued from p. 564
service providers charge," Murphy of the Investment Company Institute said in his remarks in May. "What they don't mention is the long list of services that 401(k) plans provide — not just investment management and recordkeeping but legal services, audits, Web sites and call centers and participant education."

Murphy said critics have tended to inflate the amount of fees that are charged and have "taken advantage of the fact that there isn't comprehensive data on fees across a range of 401(k) plans." To address that data gap, Murphy said, the institute engaged Deloitte Consulting, which surveyed 130 plans of "all sizes and types" and calculated what he called an "all-in fee" that covered all the services — both investment and administrative — for each plan.

"The bottom line?" Murphy said. "The median all-in fee for these plans was . . . less than three-quarters of 1 percent — quite a bargain compared to the 3 percent that some critics cite." [55]

Helping Savers

As congressional Democrats are pressing for more regulation of investment companies, House Republicans have sought to allow higher contribution limits for retirement accounts and reduce investment taxes.

The Savings Recovery Act, introduced in April by Minority Leader John Boehner, R-Ohio, and other House Republicans, would raise both the con-

Treasury Secretary Timothy F. Geithner discusses Social Security and Medicare funding at a press conference on May 12. Geithner called Medicare's financial challenges "larger and more imminent" than those facing Social Security. Secretary of Health and Human Services Kathleen Sebelius is at right.

tribution limits on retirement accounts and the higher "catch-up" amount that people over age 50 can contribute to such accounts. It also would double the amount people can earn without penalty while receiving Social Security benefits. The bill's tax breaks include suspension of the capital-gains tax on newly acquired assets for the next two years and a suspension of taxes on dividend income through 2011.

In addition, the measure would suspend through 2012 a mandate that people withdraw money from their Individual Retirement Accounts when they turn 70 1/2. [56] The requirement was suspended this year in the wake of the stock-market crash. Many retirees complained they were being forced to sell assets at rock-bottom prices to meet the withdrawal requirement even if the money wasn't needed at the time.

In expressing support for the Republican bill, the American Benefits Council noted a longstanding concern about the minimum-withdrawal requirement.

"Retirement security often would be better served by keeping the savings

in the plans to ensure there are sufficient assets to meet retirees' greater longevity," said council president James A. Klein. "Those concerns about forced withdrawals have been exacerbated by the economic downturn and the decline in retirement savings. Now is not the time to force individuals to deplete their savings."

As older workers struggle to shore up their 401(k) accounts and Congress mulls potential policy changes, advocates in some states have been urging legislatures to create "universal voluntary retirement accounts" that would allow employees of companies that don't offer a retirement plan to have a tax-deferred savings account. The accounts would be portable, allowing workers to move them from job to job. A state agency would manage the plans or contract the management to an outside firm.

Baker at the Center for Economic and Policy Research, a major proponent of the idea, has written that it "would provide a huge step towards increasing workers' retirement security. First, and most obviously, it gives every worker in the country a convenient mechanism for saving," he wrote. "They could contribute regardless of where they worked, or even if they are self-employed. They also could keep a single account through their entire working career, regardless of how many times they switched employers."

Helping Small Employers, Too

The idea also would benefit small employers, Baker said. "The reason most often cited by small employers for not providing pensions is the administrative hassle it involves," he wrote.

Getty Images/Win McNamee

Employers could contribute to workers' voluntary accounts without having to assume the costs and risk of managing their own pension plan. [57]

To date, no state has adopted such a plan, but legislators or officials in more than a half-dozen states have advocated the approach, according to Gary Burris, senior policy associate at the Economic Opportunity Institute, a public-policy research group in Washington state that has been backing voluntary accounts there since 2001. This spring bills reflecting the approach were pending in California and Connecticut.

"What we see happening in our state and across the country is that about half of the workforce doesn't have a way to invest at their place of work, and it's more typical among smaller-sized businesses," Burris says. In addition, "folks at the lower-to-middle-earnings level have much less access" to a retirement plan at work.

Many small businesses are "stymied by the complexity" of setting up a plan, wary of the costs of setting up a plan or concerned that hidden fees could wind up hurting their employees, Burris says. State governments already have the expertise and infrastructure to set up and manage a voluntary-account system, though he says such a system would incur additional costs, at least initially, that would have to be covered by state or federal funding or other sources.

Ron Snell, director of the state services division of the National Conference of State Legislatures, says some legislators and retirement-fund administrators have opposed voluntary accounts because of the potential for administrative problems in collecting employee contributions from small employers, similar to the problems states sometimes face in collecting unemployment-compensation payments from small businesses.

And some investment and insurance companies oppose voluntary accounts because they view them as competition, Burris says. But he says voluntary accounts would create a new generation of investors who could wind up doing business with financial-services companies.

"Hundreds of thousands of workers aren't investing now," he says. "I think it would be creating business for them." ■

OUTLOOK

Focus on Savings

In the near future, at least, the fortunes of people in or near retirement will depend in no small way on how quickly the recession ends, the stock market recovers and the economy begins to grow.

The Employee Benefit Research Institute calculated how long it might take workers to recoup investment losses from last year's Wall Street crash and found that under some scenarios recovery could take years.

For example, if stocks earn a 5 percent rate of return, workers with the longest tenure with their current employer would need a median of two years to recover their losses, but most would need longer — as much as five years. If stock returns drop to zero for the next several years, employees with the longest tenure would need up to a decade to recover. [58]

Meanwhile, the future course of the overall economy will influence the Social Security trust fund. If unemployment remains high — it stood at 9.4 percent in May — fewer workers will be paying into the system, slowing the flow of revenue into an already weak system.

Some have argued that increased immigration could relieve some of Social Security's shortfall. But analysts say the impact of immigration at best would be modest.

"Immigration keeps the population from aging as rapidly as it otherwise would," but "is that enough to save [Social Security's] solvency? No," says the University of Michigan's Laitner.

Likewise, Paul N. Van de Water, a senior fellow at the Center on Budget and Policy Priorities, concluded last fall that increases in immigration tend to make Social Security's financial condition better, and decreases tend to make it worse, but higher immigration "would likely eliminate only a small portion of Social Security's long-term shortfall." He found that "the impact of immigration on Social Security's finances is modest and should not be a major factor in setting either immigration or Social Security policy." [59]

Beyond the challenges facing Social Security and the stock-market turmoil roiling retirement accounts, policy makers are weighing what, if anything, should be done to reshape the way workers save for retirement.

"A lot should be done in the short term to improve 401(k) and defined-benefit [pension] plans," says Hwa of the Pension Rights Center. But she says "further down the road" a strategy is needed "that takes the patchwork we have right now and the system that doesn't cover everyone and come up with something that does provide universal coverage and retirement security for everyone."

An effort called Retirement USA — developed by the Economic Policy Institute, National Committee to Preserve Social Security and Medicare, the Pension Rights Center and the Service Employees International Union — is exploring the subject. A working paper released in March argues that the nation's retirement system has provided adequately for many people but failed many others. It said "a comprehensive approach to retirement security" is needed "that can provide universal coverage and benefits that are adequate and secure." [60]

The group said it remains committed to keeping and improving pension and 401(k) plans that are providing adequate and secure benefits. But, it added, "we cannot ignore the fact that the current system — regardless of how many changes are made — will remain inaccessible, inadequate and/or insecure for millions of workers. Therefore, we must begin a dialogue now about the type of retirement system we need for the future." [61] ∎

Notes

[1] Statement of Roberta Tim Quan before House Committee on Education and Labor, "The Impact of the Financial Crisis on Workers' Retirement Security," Oct. 22, 2008, http://edlabor.house.gov/testimony/2008-10-22-RobertaQuan.pdf.

[2] "The 2009 Retirement Confidence Survey: Economy Drives Confidence to Record Lows; Many Looking to Work Longer," Employee Benefit Research Institute, *EBRI Issue Brief No. 328*, April 2009, www.ebri.org/publications/ib/index.cfm?fa=ibDisp&content_id=4226. For background, see the following *CQ Researchers* by Mary H. Cooper: "Retirement Security," May 31, 2002, pp. 481-504; "Employee Benefits," Feb. 4, 2000, pp. 65-88; and "Social Security Reform," Sept. 24, 2004, pp. 781-804; and by Alan Greenblatt: "Pension Crisis," Feb. 17, 2006, pp. 145-168, and "Aging Baby Boomers," Oct. 19. 2007, pp. 865-888.

[3] David Rosnick and Dean Baker, "The Wealth of the Baby Boom Cohorts After the Collapse of the Housing Bubble," Center for Economic and Policy Research, February 2009, www.cepr.net/documents/publications/baby-boomer-wealth-2009-02.pdf. The figures are projections based on the Federal Reserve Board's 2004 "Survey of Consumer Finances."

[4] Testimony of Dean Baker before Senate Special Committee on Aging, Feb. 25, 2009, http://aging.senate.gov/events/hr204db.pdf.

[5] "Housing Market Meltdown and Stock Market Collapse Threaten Retirement Wealth of Millions of Baby Boomers," press release, Center for Economic and Policy Research, Feb. 25, 2009, www.cepr.net/index.php/press-releases/press-releases/housing-market-meltdown-and-stock-market-collapse-threaten-retirement-wealth-of-millions-of-baby-boo/.

[6] Robert Pear, "Recession Drains Social Security and Medicare," *The New York Times*, May 13, 2009, www.nytimes.com/2009/05/13/us/politics/13health.html?scp=1&sq=recession%20drains%20social%20security%20and%20medicare&st=cse.

[7] Robert Pear, "Social Security Benefits Not Expected to Rise in '10," *The New York Times*, May 2, 2009, www.nytimes.com/2009/05/03/us/politics/03benefits.html.

[8] Karoun Demirjian, "The News Gets Worse for Social Security Recipients," *CQ Today*, April 22, 2009.

[9] "One-Third of U.S. Employers Have Reduced or Eliminated Retirement Plan Matches in Economic Crisis," press release, Spectrem Group, March 25, 2009, www.spectrem.com/custom.aspx?id=96. Spectrem said the online survey in February 2009 of more than 150 plan sponsors has a margin of error of plus or minus 8 percentage points.

[10] Colette Thayer, "Retirement Security or Insecurity? The Experience of Workers Aged 45 and Older," *AARP*, October 2008, www.aarp.org/research/work/retirement/retirement_survey_08.html.

[11] Jilian Mincer, "Higher-Paid Putting Less Aside," *The Wall Street Journal*, April 30, 2009, p. 4D.

[12] American Benefits Council, "Defined Contribution Plans: A Successful Cornerstone of Our Nation's Retirement System," Feb. 5, 2009, www.appwp.org/documents/dc_success_paper021709.pdf.

[13] HSBC, "The Future of Retirement," fact sheet, 2008, www.hsbc.com/1/PA_1_1_S5/content/assets/retirement/2008_for_factsheet_usa.pdf.

[14] Employee Benefit Research Institute, *op. cit.*

[15] *Ibid.*

[16] "Health, United States, 2008, With Chartbook," Table 26, National Center for Health Statistics, 2009, p. 203, www.cdc.gov/nchs/data/hus/hus08.pdf#026.

[17] See Alicia H. Munnell and Steven Sass, *Working Longer: The Solution to the Retirement Income Challenge* (2008).

[18] Alicia H. Munnell, Anthony Webb, Francesca Golub-Sass and Dan Muldoon, "Long-Term Care Costs and the National Retirement Risk Index," Center for Retirement Research at Boston College, March 2009, http://crr.bc.edu/images/stories/Briefs/ib_9-7.pdf.

[19] "Our view on retirement: Recession adds urgency to Social Security fix," *USA Today*, April 7, 2009, http://blogs.usatoday.com/oped/2009/04/our-view-on-retirement-recession-adds-urgency-to-social-security-fix.html.

[20] Dean Baker, "Opposing View: Hands Off Social Security," *USA Today*, April 7, 2009, http://blogs.usatoday.com/oped/2009/04/hands-off-social-security.html.

[21] Quoted in Lori Montgomery, "Lawmakers Seeking Consensus On Social Security Overhaul," *The Washington Post*, May 6, 2009, www.washingtonpost.com/wp-dyn/content/article/2009/05/05/AR2009050503850.html.

[22] See Jackie Calmes, "Democrats Resisting Obama on Social Security," *The New York Times*, Feb. 23, 2009, www.nytimes.com/2009/02/23/us/politics/23social.html?scp=1&sq=obama%20and%20social%20security%20and%20democrats&st=cse.

[23] Pear, "Recession Drains Social Security and Medicare," *op. cit.*

[24] "Nightly Business Report," Public Broadcasting Corp., "Harvard Economist Jeff Miron's Social Security Solution," May 12, 2009, www.pbs.org/nbr/site/onair/transcripts/harvard_economist_jeff_miron_says_retire_at_75_090512/.

[25] Montgomery, *op. cit.*

[26] Steny Hoyer, "Hoyer Delivers Keynote Address on Entitlement and Health Care Reform," May 6, 2009, www.hoyer.house.gov/newsroom/index.asp?ID=1383.

[27] Hewitt Associates, "Despite Historical Losses, Few U.S. Employees Changed Their 401(k) Saving and Investing Habits in 2008, According to Annual Hewitt Study," May 13, 2009, www.hewittassociates.com/Intl/NA/en-US/AboutHewitt/Newsroom/PressReleaseDetail.aspx?cid=6808.

[28] Investment Company Institute, "10 Myths About 401(k)s — And the Facts," February 2009, www.ici.org/home/faq_myths_about_401k.pdf.

[29] Patrick Purcell, "Retirement Plan Participation and Contributions: Trends from 1998 to 2006," Congressional Research Service, Jan. 30, 2009, p. 5.

[30] Carole Fleck, "White House Budget Touts Auto-IRAs," *AARP Bulletin Today*, March 23,

About the Author

Thomas J. Billitteri is a *CQ Researcher* staff writer based in Fairfield, Pa., who has more than 30 years' experience covering business, nonprofit institutions and public policy for newspapers and other publications. His recent *CQ Researcher* reports include "Auto Industry's Future," "Middle-Class Squeeze" and "Financial Bailout." He holds a BA in English and an MA in journalism from Indiana University.

2009, http://bulletin.aarp.org/yourmoney/personalfinance/articles/white_house_budget_touts_auto_iras_.html.

[31] Contributions to Roth IRAs would not be included in the credit.

[32] Emily Brandon, "Teresa Ghilarducci: The 401(k) Retirement System Has Failed," *U.S. News & World Report*, Jan. 30, 2009, www.usnews.com/blogs/planning-to-retire/2009/01/30/teresa-ghilarducci-the-401k-retirement-system-has-failed.html.

[33] Social Security Advisory Board, "Working for Retirement Security," September 2008, p. 17.

[34] Patrick W. Seburn, "Evolution of employer-provided defined benefit pensions," *Monthly Labor Review*, December 1991, p. 16, www.bls.gov/opub/mlr/1991/12/art3full.pdf.

[35] Dora L. Costa, *The Evolution of Retirement* (1998), p. 16.

[36] Seburn, *op. cit.*, p. 18.

[37] *Ibid.*

[38] *Ibid.*, p. 19.

[39] *Ibid.*, p. 20.

[40] U.S. Department of Labor, *Private Pension Plan Bulletin*, December 2008.

[41] Testimony of Jacob S. Hacker before the House Committee on Education and Labor, Oct. 22, 2008.

[42] Remarks of John V. Murphy as prepared for delivery, "ICI Chairman's Address, 2009 General Membership Meeting," Investment Company Institute, May 6, 2009, www.ici.org/new/09_gmm_murphy_spch.html.

[43] Eric D. Beinhocker, Diana Farrell and Ezra Greenberg, "Why baby boomers will need to work longer," *The McKinsey Quarterly*, McKinsey Global Institute, November 2008.

[44] National Institute on Aging, "Growing Older in America: The Health & Retirement Study," March 2007, pp. 40 and 49-50, www.nia.nih.gov/NR/rdonlyres/D164FE6C-C6E0-4E78-B27F-7E8D8C0FFEE5/0/HRS_Text_WEB.pdf.

[45] *Ibid.*, p. 40.

[46] Patrick Purcell, "Older Workers: Employment and Retirement Trends," Congressional Research Service, Tables 3 and 4, Sept. 15, 2008.

[47] Carole Fleck, "Ask the Experts," *AARP Bulletin*, May 2009. In the year a person reaches full retirement age, Social Security withholds $1 for every $3 earned above a limit, which is $37,680 in 2009, according to the *Bulletin*. It adds: "The penalty ends in the month you reach full retirement age. After that, you can earn as much as you want without penalty."

[48] "Older Workers Need Not Apply," Room for Debate blog, *The New York Times*, April 12, 2009, http://roomfordebate.blogs.ny-
times.com/2009/04/12/older-workers-need-not-apply/?scp=1&sq=older%20workers%20need%20not%20apply&st=cse.

[49] Robert Hutchens, "The Cornell Study of Employer Phased Retirement Policies: A Report on Key Findings," Cornell University School of Industrial and Labor Relations, October 2003, http://digitalcommons.ilr.cornell.edu/lepubs/1/. See also, "Phased Retirement: Opportunities for Some but Not for All," *Impact Brief No. 3*, Cornell University ILR School, March 2006, http://digitalcommons.ilr.cornell.edu/cgi/viewcontent.cgi?article=1002&context=impactbrief.

[50] Purcell, "Older Workers," *op. cit.*, p. 2.

[51] "Statement by Secretary Geithner on the Releases of Social Security and Medicare Trustees Reports," May 12, 2009, www.ustreas.gov/press/releases/tg126.htm.

[52] Social Security Advisory Board, *op. cit.*, p. 5.

[53] H.R. 1984, the 401(k) Fair Disclosure for Retirement Security Act.

[54] Committee on Education and Labor, "Legislation Needed Now to Expose Hidden 401(k) Fees, Witnesses Tell House Ed & Labor
Subcommittee," April 22, 2009, http://edlabor.house.gov/newsroom/2009/04/legislation-needed-now-to-expo.shtml.

[55] Murphy, *op. cit.*

[56] The legislation is HR 2021.

[57] Dean Baker, "Universal Voluntary Accounts: A Compromise Retirement Solution," Center for American Progress, March 19, 2004, www.americanprogress.org/issues/2004/03/b38731.html/index.html.

[58] Jack VanDerhei, "The Impact of the Recent Financial Crisis on 401(k) Account Balances," Employee Benefit Research Institute, *Issue Brief No. 326*, February 2009, www.ebri.org/pdf/briefspdf/EBRI_IB_2-2009_Crisis-Impct.pdf.

[59] Paul N. Van de Water, "Immigration and Social Security," Center on Budget and Policy Priorities, Nov. 20, 2008, www.cbpp.org/cms/index.cfm?fa=view&id=1272.

[60] Robert Stowe England, "Principles For A New Retirement System," Retirement USA, *Working Paper*, March 10, 2009, www.retirement-usa.org, p. 14.

[61] *Ibid.*, p. 16.

FOR MORE INFORMATION

AARP, 601 E St., N.W., Washington, DC 20049; (888) 687-2277; www.aarp.org. Membership organization representing the interests of people age 50 and over.

American Benefits Council, 1501 M St., N.W., Suite 600, Washington, DC 20005; (202) 289-6700; www.appwp.org. Advocates for employer-sponsored benefit programs.

Center for Retirement Research, Boston College, Hovey House, 140 Commonwealth, Chestnut Hill, MA 02467-3808; (617) 552-1762; http://crr.bc.edu. Promotes research on retirement issues, trains new scholars on the subject and broadens access to retirement data.

Employee Benefit Research Institute, 1100 13th St., N.W., Suite 878, Washington, DC 20005; (202) 659-0670; www.ebri.org. Provides research and data on employee benefit programs and policy.

Investment Company Institute, 1401 H St., N.W., Washington, DC 20005; (202) 326-5800; www.ici.org. Trade association for investment companies, including mutual funds.

National Institute on Aging, 31 Center Dr., MSC 2292, Bethesda, MD 20892; (302) 496-1752; www.nia.nih.gov. Federal agency that conducts research on aging and related health issues, such as Alzheimer's disease.

Social Security Advisory Board, 400 Virginia Ave., S.W., Suite 625, Washington, DC 20024; (202) 475-7700; www.ssab.gov. Independent, bipartisan board that advises government officials on Social Security and Supplemental Security Income programs.

University of Michigan Retirement Research Center, P.O. Box 1248, Ann Arbor, MI 48104; (734) 615-0422; www.mrrc.isr.umich.edu. Promotes research on retirement and Social Security policy.

U.S. Department of Labor, Frances Perkins Building, 200 Constitution Ave., N.W., Washington, DC 20210; (866) 487-2365; www.dol.gov. Federal agency that oversees employment issues and collects data on labor and employment trends.

Bibliography
Selected Sources

Books

Béland, Daniel, *Social Security: History and Politics from the New Deal to the Privatization Debate*, University Press of Kansas, 2005.

A sociologist presents a sweeping look at the political and policy debates that have shaped Social Security from its inception, including the Bush administration's failed effort to reshape the program.

Costa, Dora L., *The Evolution of Retirement: An American Economic History, 1880-1990*, University of Chicago Press, 1998.

In this data-filled analysis, a Massachusetts Institute of Technology economics professor traces retirement trends over the past century, including the rise of a leisure class and forces shaping pension and Social Security policy.

Kotlikoff, Laurence J., and Scott Burns, *The Coming Generational Storm*, MIT Press, 2004.

A Boston University economics professor (Kotlikoff) and a financial journalist offer a stark view of the nation's economic future and prospects for retirement security, arguing that "we are heading into one God-awful fiscal storm, the full dimensions of which are hard to fathom."

Articles

Colin, Chris, "To Your Left, a Better Way of Life," *The New York Times*, June 11, 2009, p. 1D.

Co-housing communities around the country address the increasingly common feeling in these tough economic times that one pays too much for one's home.

Greene, Kelly, "Law Opens Up 'Encore' Careers," *The Wall Street Journal*, April 2, 2009.

The Edward M. Kennedy National Service Act encourages "encore" careers for older Americans as part of an effort to expand national community service.

Greenhouse, Steven, "Working Longer as Jobs Contract," *The New York Times*, Oct. 23, 2008, www.nytimes.com/ 2008/10/23/business/retirement/23SQUEEZE.html.

The economic downturn has forced many older workers to stay in the job market longer than they planned, and some are losing their jobs just when they need them the most.

Pear, Robert, "Recession Drains Social Security and Medicare," *The New York Times*, May 13, 2009, www.ny times.com/2009/05/13/us/politics/13health.html?scp=1&sq= recession%20drains%20social%20security&st=cse.

Medicare is expected to run out of money in 2017, and the Social Security Trust Fund will be depleted in 2037, according to a new Obama administration report.

Reports and Studies

Beinhocker, Eric D., Diana Farrell and Ezra Greenberg, "Why Baby Boomers Will Need to Work Longer," McKinsey Global Institute, November 2008, www.mckinseyquarterly.com/ Why_baby_boomers_will_need_to_work_longer_2234.

To avoid a sharp drop in their living standards and keep from dragging down U.S. and global economic growth, aging baby boomers should continue to work past the traditional retirement age, the researchers conclude.

England, Robert Stowe, "Principles for a New Retirement System," Retirement USA, Working Paper, March 10, 2009, www.retirement-usa.org.

A group composed of the Economic Policy Institute, National Committee to Preserve Social Security and Medicare, the Pension Rights Center and the Service Employees International Union argues that the nation's retirement system has failed too many Americans.

"Growing Older in America: The Health & Retirement Study," National Institute on Aging, March 2007, www. nia.nih.gov/NR/rdonlyres/D164FE6C-C6E0-4E78-B27F-7E8 D8C0FFEE5/0/HRS_Text_WEB.pdf.

This massive longitudinal study covers a broad range of topics, including labor-force participation, the nature of work among older people, income, wealth and health issues.

Purcell, Patrick, "Older Workers: Employment and Retirement Trends," Congressional Research Service, Sept. 15, 2008.

The report provides useful data and analysis on the aging of the labor force, trends in workforce participation among older workers, phased retirement and other topics.

Schieber, Sylvester J., "Beyond the Golden Age of Retirement," University of Michigan Retirement Research Center, *Policy Brief No. 6*, May 2008, www.mrrc.isr.umich.edu/pub lications/policy/pdf/Schieber.pdf.

The chairman of the Social Security Advisory Board argues that "continuing down our current path in regard to retirement policy has the potential to reduce standards of living for large segments of our population."

"Working for Retirement Security," Social Security Advisory Board, September 2008, www.ssab.gov/documents/ ssab_report2008_508.pdf.

Policy makers should examine ways to make it easier for older workers to remain in the labor force as a way of improving the retirement security of American workers.

The Next Step:

Additional Articles from Current Periodicals

Affordability

Armour, Stephanie, "Mortgage Crisis Robbing Seniors of Golden Years," *USA Today*, **June 5, 2009, p. 1A.**

Declining home prices in retirement-rich states undermine the use of home equity as a retirement nest egg.

Cruz, Humberto, "Americans Face Reality of Needs for Retirement," *Chicago Tribune*, **May 4, 2008, p. C7.**

Americans are increasingly worried over the affordability of retirement amid a troubled economy, rising health-care costs and declining home values.

Moos, Bob, "When Retirement Has to Wait," *Dallas Morning News*, **Aug. 12, 2008, p. 1D.**

One in five workers between the ages of 55 and 64 intend to delay retirement due to the economic downturn.

Encore Careers

Kornblum, Janet, "Baby Boomers in the Mood to Give Back," *Miami Times*, **June 25, 2008, p. 5A.**

Millions of baby boomers are coming out of retirement to pursue new careers that contribute to society.

Morrison, Jacqueline, "AARP: Older Workers Bring Great Value to Michigan's Economy, Workplace," *Michigan Chronicle*, **March 12, 2008, p. B10.**

Many of Michigan's workers who have not yet retired plan to pursue encore careers, according to AARP.

Powell, Robert, "Evaluate Goals for Post-Retirement Work," *Myrtle Beach Sun-News* **(South Carolina), July 15, 2007, p. D2.**

When seeking encore careers, retired Americans need to stress their life experiences and evidence of maturity.

Satullo, Chris, "Do-Good Boomers Out to Rework Retirement," *The Philadelphia Inquirer*, **Aug. 3, 2008, p. A3.**

The nation's finances — as well as those of individuals — will require many baby boomers to work past traditional retirement age in encore careers.

Savings

Boselovic, Len, "Government Should Lead By Example on Retirement Savings," *Pittsburgh Post-Gazette*, **Sept. 30, 2007, p. C1.**

Early results indicate that 401(k) legislation has encouraged workers to save more money for retirement.

Dugas, Christine, "For Boomers, recession is redefining retirement," *USA Today*, **June 17, 2009, p. A1.**

In the face of the current recession, the Baby Boom genera-

tion is realigning its retirement expectations, planning to work more and spend less.

Wilkins, Jimmie, "Saving for Retirement Needs to Be a Priority," *Statesman Journal* **(Oregon), Aug. 26, 2008, p. 7.**

Thirty-six percent of working adults have not begun to save for retirement, while 16 percent have only saved $10,000 or less.

Social Security

Biggs, Andrew G., "Good News on Social Security?" *The Christian Science Monitor*, **April 15, 2008, p. 9.**

The complexity of calculating Social Security benefits leads to complications over underestimating what is actually going to be provided for retirees, but it could urge more Americans to save for retirement.

Block, Sandra, "Boomers' Eagerness to Retire Could Cost Them," *USA Today*, **Jan. 14, 2008, p. 1A.**

Filing for Social Security at age 62 raises the risk that retirees will outlive whatever money they have.

Smith, Jack Z., "The Question Isn't Whether Social Security Will Be Around But How We'll Pay for It," *Fort Worth Star-Telegram*, **May 25, 2009, p. C1.**

Social Security's trust funds are expected to be exhausted by 2037, leaving the program with only enough revenues to pay about 75 percent of benefits.

Stewart, Kirsten, and Christopher Smart, "New Utah School District May Opt Out of Social Security," *Salt Lake Tribune* **(Utah), May 31, 2009.**

The Canyons School District in Utah may opt out of Social Security due to concerns over the program's future solvency.

CITING CQ RESEARCHER

Sample formats for citing these reports in a bibliography include the ones listed below. Preferred styles and formats vary, so please check with your instructor or professor.

<u>MLA STYLE</u>

Jost, Kenneth. "Rethinking the Death Penalty." <u>CQ Researcher</u> 16 Nov. 2001: 945-68.

<u>APA STYLE</u>

Jost, K. (2001, November 16). Rethinking the death penalty. *CQ Researcher, 11,* 945-968.

<u>CHICAGO STYLE</u>

Jost, Kenneth. "Rethinking the Death Penalty." *CQ Researcher,* November 16, 2001, 945-968.

In-depth Reports on Issues in the News

Are you writing a paper?

Need backup for a debate?

Want to become an expert on an issue?

For 80 years, students have turned to *CQ Researcher* for in-depth reporting on issues in the news. Reports on a full range of political and social issues are now available. Following is a selection of recent reports:

Civil Liberties
Closing Guantánamo, 2/09
Affirmative Action, 10/08
Gay Marriage Showdowns, 9/08
America's Border Fence, 9/08
Immigration Debate, 2/08

Crime/Law
Legalizing Marijuana, 6/09
Judicial Elections, 4/09
Mexico's Drug War, 12/08
Prostitution Debate, 5/08
Public Defenders, 4/08

Education
Reading Crisis? 2/08
Discipline in Schools, 2/08
Student Aid, 1/08
Racial Diversity in Public Schools, 9/07

Environment/Society
Future of Books, 5/09
Hate Groups, 5/09
Future of Journalism, 3/09
Confronting Warming, 1/09
Reducing Carbon Footprint, 12/08
Protecting Wetlands, 10/08

Health/Safety
Reproductive Ethics, 5/09
Extreme Sports, 4/09
Regulating Toxic Chemicals, 1/09
Preventing Cancer, 1/09
Heart Health, 9/08
Global Food Crisis, 6/08

Politics/Economy
Business Bankruptcy, 4/09
Future of the GOP, 3/09
Middle-Class Squeeze, 3/09
Public-Works Projects, 2/09

Upcoming Reports

Treating Depression, 6/26/09   Examining Forensic Science, 7/17/09   Energy Policy, 7/24/09

ACCESS

CQ Researcher is available in print and online. For access, visit your library or www.cqresearcher.com.

STAY CURRENT

To receive notice of upcoming *CQ Researcher* reports, or learn more about *CQ Researcher* products, subscribe to the free e-mail newsletters, *CQ Researcher Alert!* and *CQ Researcher News*: http://cqpress.com/newsletters.

PURCHASE

To purchase a *CQ Researcher* report in print or electronic format (PDF), visit www.cqpress.com or call 866-427-7737. Single reports start at $15. Bulk purchase discounts and electronic-rights licensing are also available.

SUBSCRIBE

Annual full-service *CQ Researcher* subscriptions—including 44 reports a year, monthly index updates, and a bound volume—start at $803. Add $25 for domestic postage.

CQ Researcher Online offers a backfile from 1991 and a number of tools to simplify research. For pricing information, call 800-834-9020, ext. 1906, or e-mail librarysales@cqpress.com.

CQ Researcher

Published by CQ Press, a division of SAGE Publications

www.cqresearcher.com

Treating Depression

Is effective treatment available?

Depression and suicide always increase in tough economic times, as indicated by a rash of suicides by men despondent over their families' financial troubles. Meanwhile, a wave of suicides and mental disorders — mainly post-traumatic stress disorder (PTSD) and depression — has hit military personnel returning from repeated deployments in Afghanistan and Iraq, swamping military health-care systems. Depression, the most common serious mental illness, is sometimes caused by genetics, but it also can be triggered by stress or trauma. Access to treatment has expanded in recent years, as more and more primary-care doctors screen for the disease. And a new mental-health-care "parity" law passed by Congress in 2008 is expected to increase insurance coverage as well as access to mental-health services. But many people with severe depression remain uninsured and dependent on public health-care programs, which recession-plagued states are cutting back as revenues dwindle.

Movie actor Owen Wilson, 40 — known as a happy-go-lucky "slacker" on screen — shocked fans in August 2007 when he reportedly slit his wrists and took a drug overdose in a suicide attempt. It was later revealed that he has fought a longtime battle with depression.

CQ Researcher • June 26, 2009 • www.cqresearcher.com
Volume 19, Number 24 • Pages 573-596

Cover: AFP/Getty Images/Robyn Beck

CQ Researcher

June 26, 2009
Volume 19, Number 24

MANAGING EDITOR: Thomas J. Colin
tcolin@cqpress.com

ASSISTANT MANAGING EDITOR: Kathy Koch
kkoch@cqpress.com

ASSOCIATE EDITOR: Kenneth Jost

STAFF WRITERS: Thomas J. Billitteri, Marcia Clemmitt, Peter Katel

CONTRIBUTING WRITERS: Rachel Cox, Sarah Glazer, Alan Greenblatt, Reed Karaim Barbara Mantel, Patrick Marshall, Tom Price, Jennifer Weeks

DESIGN/PRODUCTION EDITOR: Olu B. Davis

ASSISTANT EDITOR: Darrell Dela Rosa

FACT-CHECKING: Eugene J. Gabler, Michelle Harris

CQ PRESS

A Division of SAGE

PRESIDENT AND PUBLISHER:
John A. Jenkins

EXECUTIVE DIRECTOR,
REFERENCE INFORMATION GROUP:
Alix B. Vance

CQ Press is a registered trademark of Congressional Quarterly Inc.

CQ Researcher (ISSN 1056-2036) is printed on acid-free paper. Published weekly, except; (Jan. wk. 1) (May wk. 4) (July wks. 1, 2) (Aug. wks. 3, 4) (Nov. wk. 4) and (Dec. wk. 4), by CQ Press, a division of SAGE Publications. Annual full-service subscriptions start at $803. For pricing, call 1-800-834-9020, ext. 1906. To purchase a CQ Researcher report in print or electronic format (PDF), visit www. cqpress.com or call 866-427-7737. Single reports start at $15. Bulk purchase discounts and electronic-rights licensing are also available. Periodicals postage paid at Washington, D.C., and additional mailing offices. POSTMASTER: Send address changes to CQ Researcher, 2300 N St., N.W., Suite 800, Washington, DC 20037.

Treating Depression

BY MARCIA CLEMMITT

THE ISSUES

At Fort Campbell, the Kentucky Army base that is home to the 101st Airborne Division — the famed Screaming Eagles — three soldiers committed suicide during a recent two-week period.

The deaths brought the number of suicides at the base this year to at least 11 and prompted base commander Brig. Gen. Stephen Townsend to order a temporary suspension of regular duties on May 27 for what he called a "suicide stand-down."

"It will be better tomorrow," Townsend consoled his troops, urging them not to become discouraged. "Don't take away your tomorrow." [1]

A wave of suicides and mental disorders — mainly post-traumatic stress disorder (PTSD) and depression — has swept over the U.S. military in the past few years, likely triggered by the stress of repeated deployments to Iraq and Afghanistan. By 2007, suicide attempts among soldiers in the Army were occurring six times more often than in 2002, before combat began in Iraq. [2]

Meanwhile, the economic recession may be triggering another spike in depression and suicide among Americans overall. In one of several family murder-suicides making news around the country this year, a 34-year-old Maryland man was found dead in his home alongside his wife and three children in April — victims of a murder-suicide. Police said that Christopher Alan Wood, a salesman for CSX railroad, faced household debts of nearly half a million dollars and had struggled with anxiety and depression. [3]

Author Marya Hornbacher's memoir Madness: A Bipolar Life *chronicles her bouts of mania and depression — the result of her lifelong struggle with bipolar disorder. Of the 16 percent of Americans who have some form of depressive illness, about 2 percent have bipolar disorder.*

AP Photo/Dawn Villella

"The suicide rate, like the incidence of depression, rises when the economy falls," said M. Harvey Brenner, a professor emeritus at the Johns Hopkins Bloomberg School of Public Health. "It is so regular a pattern among most of the industrialized countries of the world that it is virtually an economic indicator." [4]

Depression is loosely defined as a mental and emotional disorder with symptoms of constant sadness, lethargy, irritability and a loss of interest and pleasure; it's sometimes triggered by trauma or stress, but its symptoms are out of proportion to the cause and last longer than would normally be expected. Depression, including severe depression, also can occur without being triggered by stressors, and scientists believe that some people are simply biologically more vulnerable to the illness.

Some depression is "reactive" and clearly triggered by events, says Ronald C. Kessler, a professor of health-care policy at Harvard University. "There's more depression now in Michigan," for example, as the bad economy and collapsing automobile industry take a toll, he says. Such "reactive depressions" are less likely to have a genetic basis than other forms of depression.

Kessler says epidemiologists estimate that about 16 percent of Americans will experience some type of depression sometime during their lives, with 6 or 7 percent suffering at least one bout of major depression and 2 percent bipolar disorder — a mood disorder in which patients cycle between extreme emotional highs, called mania, and deep depression. [5]

Many mental-health experts are leery about linking murder-suicides like the Wood case with depression. Associating violence with mental illness is "a misconception," said Ken Duckworth, medical director for the National Alliance on Mental Illness (NAMI). "While it is true that a subset of persons with psychiatric illnesses are violent, the percentage is very small." And untreated substance abuse, not the mental disorder, often drives the violence, he said. [6]

But others argue that unacknowledged and untreated depression may be behind many such cases, especially when the perpetrators are men.

"Hidden depression drives several of the problems we think of as typically male," including domestic violence, according to Terrence Real, a

South Dakota Has Best Mental Health

The least depressed Americans in 2007 lived in South Dakota, Hawaii and New Jersey. The rankings were based on the percentage of residents who reported having at least one major depressive episode or serious psychological distress that year and the average number of days in the past month when their mental health was "not good." States with the highest rates of depression were in Appalachia and the mountain West.

State Rankings by Depression Level

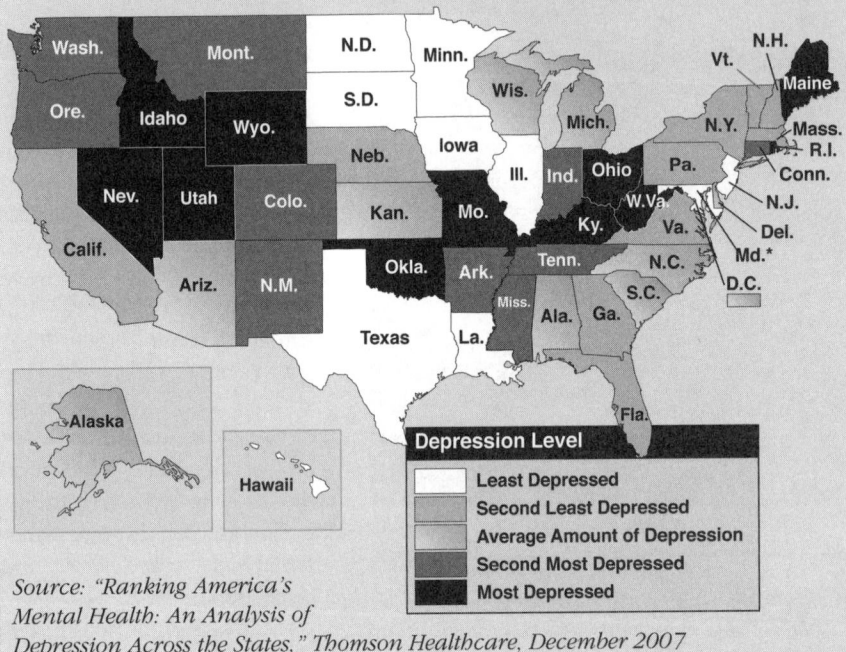

Depression Level

- Least Depressed
- Second Least Depressed
- Average Amount of Depression
- Second Most Depressed
- Most Depressed

Source: "Ranking America's Mental Health: An Analysis of Depression Across the States," Thomson Healthcare, December 2007

psychotherapist in Cambridge, Mass., and author of *I Don't Want to Talk About It: Overcoming the Secret Legacy of Male Depression.* Because signs of depression are widely considered "unmanly" in our society, many men don't acknowledge depression but attempt to mask it with other feelings and activities, including violent ones, Real wrote. To succeed in warding off feelings of depression, an activity must "transform one's . . . feelings of [depression-fueled] worthlessness to feelings of extraordinary worth and well-being," and "the rush of physical violence" is one form of "intoxication" that can accomplish this, he argues. [7]

Regardless of whether depression is linked to violence, the disease

takes a severe toll on its sufferers, their friends and families and society as a whole.

Depression's ability to cause suffering — judged by the number of depressed people who take their own lives, for example — places it among the top three most painful diseases, says Dennis S. Charney, professor of psychiatry of the Mount Sinai School of Medicine in New York City. "When you see people with the clinical disease, they tell you it's as painful as any other medical disease," he says.

Among people with two or more medical conditions, depression is the most common co-occurring illness, diagnosed in up to a third of people who suffer from any medical condition at all. [8]

People with severe mental illness — including major depression and bipolar disorder, along with schizophrenia — die, on average, 25 years earlier than the general population, according to a study by the National Association of State Mental Health Program Directors. The younger death rates are caused by higher rates of suicide, injuries, substance abuse and chronic conditions like diabetes and heart disease, which worsen more quickly because mentally ill patients go untreated or don't adhere to medical regimens. [9]

Major depression — which, together with bipolar disease afflicts about three-quarters of the 5 to 7 percent of people with a severe mental illness that compromises their ability to function — takes its toll in every area of life. Between 15 and 25 percent of severely mentally ill people are unemployed and less educated, and those who attend college have an 85 percent chance of withdrawing before graduation, says Marc Salzer, an associate professor of psychology at the University of Pennsylvania School of Medicine.

But not all depression is categorized as "major" or "clinical," and drawing a line between cases that qualify as medical disorders and those that are more or less ordinary sadness can be tricky.

In the early 1980s, doctors began diagnosing more and more people with depressive disorders, a trend known as "diagnosis creep." Ironically, it grew out of psychiatry's attempt to make diagnoses less subjective by defining each via a list of symptoms in the American Psychiatric Association's *Diagnostic and Statistical Manual of Mental Disorders* (*DSM*), says New York University Professor of Social Work Jerome C. Wakefield. But the current symptom list makes it too easy for diagnosticians to confuse cases of "normal sadness" with actual depressive disorders, in which people become deeply depressed absent a significant triggering event and remain depressed far longer than a healthy person would, Wakefield argues.

Today, most diagnoses of major depression are made by general practitioners rather than specialists, leading to overdiagnosis, he contends. A requirement to examine the context in which a person's sad mood arose — to determine whether the mood is proportionate to the triggering event — "is not built into the screening instrument," says Wakefield. As a result, he worries that calling sadness an illness could lead to overtreatment and stigmatization of ordinary emotions.

"There is some controversy over the cutoff point" between depression that is a disordered medical condition and what critics call "normal sadness," and "some in the field may have been overly inclusive," terming as depression some normal variations in mood, acknowledges David Shern, president of the mental-health advocacy group Mental Health America (MHA).

Nevertheless, depression is "a reliably diagnosable medical condition," Shern says. Overdiagnosis is unlikely to occur because "it's only when people are impaired by depression that they're motivated to get treatment."

Researchers continue to seek reliable biomarkers for depression and to define the threshold for the condition as a disorder, but "my guess is that setting an absolute threshold point will remain very difficult," Shern says. "People have different tolerance for pain," emotional as well as physical.

Meanwhile, with primary-care doctors now able to diagnose and treat depression with medications, access to depression care is better than in the past.

"Even compared to 10 years ago, depression is very treatable, and as chronic diseases go, it's not even terribly costly," says Trevor Hadley, a professor of psychiatry at the University of Pennsylvania. Treatment includes talk therapies proven to work for depression — mainly cognitive behavioral therapy (CBT), he notes. [10] Fifteen sessions of CBT only cost around $1,500, total, and even if that's combined with

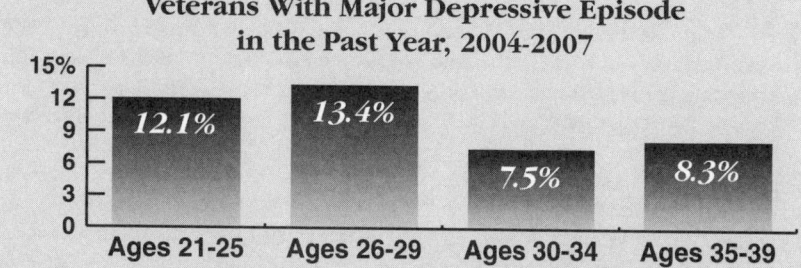

Depression Afflicts Younger Veterans More

More than 12 percent of veterans in their 20s experienced a major depressive episode between 2004 and 2007 compared to about 8 percent of older vets.

Veterans With Major Depressive Episode in the Past Year, 2004-2007

Ages 21-25	Ages 26-29	Ages 30-34	Ages 35-39
12.1%	13.4%	7.5%	8.3%

Source: "Major Depressive Episode and Treatment for Depression Among Veterans Aged 21 to 39," The NSDUH Report, National Survey on Drug Use and Health, November 2008

a generic antidepressant, the total cost of treatment doesn't exceed $4,000, "and you get a three-to-four-year remission," he says. "I had a CT scan the other day, and it was probably $3,000 to $4,000 at least."

Nevertheless, a lot more is known about treating and diagnosing depression than is implemented in medical practice, Hadley says, such as making proper use of cognitive behavioral therapy.

Access to care remains dicey for the most severely ill people. Insurance coverage — and access to the care it provides — matters greatly, says Shern. "Where uninsurance rates are high, suicide rates are high."

Unfortunately, a high proportion of people with major mental illness are uninsured, says Angela Kimball, director of state policy for NAMI. Among the 10 million people with a major mental disorder in 2005 (the latest year for which data have been analyzed), 20 percent were uninsured and 16.2 percent were on Medicaid, she says. Furthermore, 32 percent of seriously mentally ill people have incomes below the poverty level, which increases their stress and makes paying for care more difficult, she notes.

Well-intentioned efforts to increase services haven't gone far

enough, says Salzer. For example, employee-assistance programs that offer services such as referral to mental-health counselors can be very helpful, "but they're underutilized and probably being underfunded by many companies."

As mental-health clinicians and patients confront a potential wave of depressive illness, here are some of the questions being asked:

Does depression lead some people to violence?

The tough economic times have brought several horrifying acts of family violence into the headlines. Newspapers in California, Maryland, Ohio and Washington have carried front-page stories of families murdered by husbands and fathers, presumably in despair over collapsing finances.

Depression plays a role in some of these cases, say psychologists. "They become very depressed as the breadwinner," and "with their distorted, depressive perceptions they feel that rather than allow their children to go hungry, they . . . take their family with them as they end their own life," Philip Resnick, director of forensic psychiatry at Case Western Reserve University in Cleveland, told CNN. [11]

Stigma Prevents Sufferers From Seeking Help

Some colleges bar depressed students.

When Joel Gurin, gives speeches about depression, "at least half the time somebody will come up to me and say, 'I need to talk to you later.' " Invariably the discussion will be about a loved one with serious mental illness.

Gurin, acting president of the National Alliance for Research on Schizophrenia and Depression (NARSAD), is pleased that people are willing to talk about mental-health concerns, but "having these conversations a little more openly will be better," he says, adding, "That will happen over the next five years or so."

Depression may be gradually losing its long-entrenched social stigma, but it's "still pervasive" enough to keep sufferers — especially older adults — from seeking treatment, says Jo Anne Sirey, an associate professor of clinical psychology at Cornell University's Weill Medical College in New York City. Elderly patients worry they will be put on an addictive medication or lose the community support they had, she says.

If she could find an older woman who would come out and say publicly that she suffers from the illness, "it would make my day," says Sirey. "We have this old, kind of puritanical culture" that "shuns feelings, that values a stiff upper lip and we have a hard time realizing the influence of mind over body and body over mind" — that overcoming a mental disorder may not simply be a matter of will power. To many, she adds, depression "looks like laziness."

Moreover, recent shootings on school and college campuses by mentally disturbed individuals have clouded public perceptions about depression. In several cases, students who voluntarily sought treatment for depression have been barred from campus and suspended, according to the Bazelon Center for Mental Health Law, a legal advocacy group in Washington.

Following incidents like the 2007 shootings at Virginia Tech University by a mentally ill student, "people often look for quick solutions to reestablish a sense of safety," said Bazelon senior staff attorney Karen Bower. [1]

"Virginia Tech has led to a backlash against students" with mental disorders, says Marc Salzer, an associate professor of psychology at the University of Pennsylvania School of Medicine. Colleges today "are more inclined to throw the students out." That's especially troubling because in most major mental illnesses, including depression, the first breakdown may come at age 18 or 19, he points out.

"Often, when people step forward seeking help for their depression, they're asked to take a leave of absence," Salzer says, because most colleges and universities have codes of conduct stating that a student must not be a danger to himself or others. "I've heard of students who are then discouraged from or actively prevented from getting back in," perhaps due to liability fears.

While some students with mental illnesses take advantage of special accommodations available for them — such as extra time to take a test or permission to drink water in class to combat the "dry mouth" caused by psychotropic drugs, Salzer says, most are "less engaged" in their college environments so they don't use the accommodations.

As the U.S. military faces repeated deployments in Iraq and Afghanistan, the stigma connected to depression and post-traumatic stress disorder (PTSD) has become a huge issue for service members, says M. Audrey Burnam, a senior behavioral scientist at the RAND Corp., a think tank in Santa Monica, Calif. Military culture demands that people "shake off ailments and get on with the job," so those wanting mental-health treatment are justifiably concerned about damaging their careers or being seen by colleagues as "unreliable", she says.

At the Army's Fort Carson in Colorado, a rash of "preventable" suicides, prescription overdoses and murders has called attention to the "unaddressed madness and despair" — often in the form of severe depression — that veterans returning from multiple deployments are bringing home with them, write Mark

But other mental-health experts say existing research shows virtually no link between depression and violence.

"Depression does not make a person dangerous to anybody but themselves," says Nada Stotland, president of the American Psychiatric Association (APA). Depression is "basically immobility," making it unlikely that a depressed person would have the wherewithal to commit violence.

The mentally ill are more likely to be crime victims than perpetrators, a fact that's obscured by "TV shows connecting mental health and crime," says

the University of Pennsylvania's Hadley.

Even in family murders, which popular accounts often link to untreated depression, "the killer may or may not have been depressed," says Hadley. "There's plenty of evidence that these kinds of acts do not come from mental illness."

Research on the link between depression and violent acts is sparse and inconclusive. "The relationship between depression and violence is relatively poorly studied," Charles Nemeroff, a professor of psychiatry and behavioral sciences at Emory University, in At-

lanta, acknowledged to ABC News. Long considered one of the country's top depression experts, Nemeroff was stripped of his department chairmanship by Emory last year after he failed to disclose large speaking fees he'd received from drug manufacturer GlaxoSmithKline while conducting clinical trials on an antidepressant the company marketed. (*See sidebar, p. 584.*)

An Australian analysis of murder-suicides found little or no link between violence and depression. It found that in murder-suicide cases references to a perpetrator's mental illness came

Benjamin, a national correspondent for the online magazine *Salon*, and Michael de Yoanna, a Colorado-based freelance journalist. Even though soldiers' mental-health symptoms are "predictable," in light of combat stress, the Army has responded "for the most part with disciplinary action rather than treatment." [2]

The military's own statistics indicate there may indeed be a great deal of untreated depression among veterans. In 2007, the U.S. Army reports, suicide attempts among active-duty soldiers occurred six times more often than in 2002, before combat began in Iraq. [3] (*See graph, p. 588.*)

In November 2007 at Congress' urging the Department of Defense established a "centers of excellence" program for psychological and brain injuries, which includes suicide and mental-illness prevention efforts. In May, the program launched an anti-stigma campaign to educate service members about the availability of mental-health treatment. [4]

A leader in the effort is Major General Mark Graham, commander of the Army's Fort Collins, Colo., installation, whose 21-year-old son Kevin, a ROTC cadet at the University of Kentucky, hung himself in 2003 after trying to battle depression largely on his own because he feared being stigmatized if he sought treatment. As part of Graham's anti-stigma efforts, Fort Carson soldiers who commit suicide receive full military fu-

After returning from duty in Iraq, Spec. Timothy Bowman, 23, of the Illinois National Guard endured eight months of nightmares, night sweats and sleeping in a closet with a 9-mm handgun. Then on Thanksgiving Day, 2005, the former Humvee turret gunner from Forreston, Ill., shot himself in the head. Since their son's suicide, Mike and Kim Bowman, have been urging the military to help eliminate the stigma felt by veterans seeking help for post-traumatic stress disorder and depression.

Wounded Times Blog

nerals and memorial services, a mark of respect. [5]

Stigma also helps to cloud access-to-care issues, said David Shern, president of the mental-health advocacy group Mental Health America. Mental-health clinics and assistance programs are often among the first targets of state budget cuts in recessionary times. While "we wouldn't tolerate people with infectious disease not getting access to . . . antibiotics" or being turned away from emergency rooms, "we routinely tolerate it when it's behavioral health conditions," he said. [6]

Society continues to stigmatize mental illness as "moral weakness," with sometimes disastrous consequences, said Shern.

[1] Karen Bower, "How Not to Respond to Virginia Tech," *Inside Higher Ed*, May 1, 2007, http://insidehighered.com/views/2007/05/01/bower.

[2] Mark Benjamin and Michael de Yoanna, "Death in the USA: The Army's Fatal Neglect," *Salon*, Feb. 9, 2009, www.salon.com.

[3] Concern Mounts Over Rising Troop Suicides," CNN.com, Feb. 3, 2008, www.cnn.com/2008/US/02/01/military.suicides/index.html.

[4] For background, see Loree K. Sutton, testimony before the Senate Armed Services Subcommittee on Personnel, March 18, 2009, http://armed-services.senate.gov/statemnt/2009/March/Sutton%2003-18-09.pdf; see also "FAQ," Real Warriors Web site, www.realwarriors.net/faq.

[5] "The Impact of War: Reducing Suicide Rates in the Military," National Public Radio, May 13, 2009, www.npr.org/templates/story/story.php?storyId=104008228.

[6] Quoted in Steve Bogira, "Starvation Diet: Coping With Shrinking Budgets in Publicly Funded Mental Health Services," *Health Affairs*, May/June 2009, pp. 667-675.

up only 25 percent of the time, and only 13 percent of the perpetrators had been treated for mental illness. [12] A study of 693 Finnish murders found evidence of a link between violence and diagnoses of schizophrenia and antisocial personality disorder but no link with depression. [13]

Other research has found a somewhat stronger link. "Mental illness alone does not increase the risk of violence," but a mental illness such as depression combined with substance abuse does, said Eric Elbogen, assistant professor of psychiatry at the University

of North Carolina School of Medicine. In a study with nearly 35,000 participants, Elbogen found that only 2.4 percent of those reporting a serious mental illness said they'd committed a violent act, such as sexual assault, fighting or arson. However, among those who had both major depression and a substance-abuse problem, 6.5 percent had been violent. "There is a relationship" between mental illness and violence, but "it's much weaker than most people think," Elbogen said. [14]

Some studies suggest that people who commit suicide after murdering a

close associate are somewhat likely to suffer depression, while murderers who do not kill themselves are not. One analysis found that depression was "the most convincing, unifying diagnosis" common to all subtypes of murder-suicide; another found that 75 percent of the homicide-suicide perpetrators in one database were clinically depressed, according to researchers from the University of New Mexico Health Sciences Center. [15]

Untreated depression among men may lie behind some violent acts, some psychologists argue.

Deeper Cuts Expected in Mental-Health Budgets

State mental-health agencies (SMHAs) in 32 states received budget cuts averaging 5 percent this fiscal year. In fiscal 2011, 13 agencies anticipate nearly double the level of cuts.

Reductions in SMHA Budgets, fiscal 2009-fiscal 2011

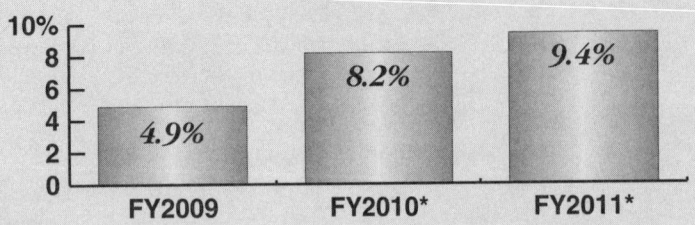

* Estimated

Source: "SMHA Budget Shortfalls: FY 2009, 2010, & 2011," NASMHPD Research Institute, National Association of State Mental Health Program Directors, December 2008

While many women "internalize" depression — focusing on "how poorly I feel and what a bad person I am" — men are more likely to externalize depressed feelings, "to cast them out on the world, focusing on how 'They shouldn't have treated me that way!' " says Sam V. Cochran, a clinical professor of counseling psychology at the University of Iowa, in Iowa City, and author of *Men and Depression: Clinical and Empirical Perspectives.* Such "externalizing" can lead to violence, especially murder-suicide and "suicide by cop," in which a person makes armed threats or takes other actions to get police to shoot him. "The message surely is, 'Those guys need help, but they aren't getting it.' "

Statistics show that many fewer men than women suffer from depressive disorder, based on who seeks treatment or reports depressive symptoms. But Cochran suspects that men's higher rates of alcohol abuse and violence mask untreated depression. "Men are not coming in and saying, 'I'm sad.' Instead, they're fighting," he says.

Among adolescents, "depression is a major factor" in suicides and other violence, according to M. Allan Cooperstein, a psychologist in Pennsylvania.

"Adolescents often 'act out,' obscuring depression with aggression . . . or anti-social acts." [16]

Having a severe mental illness such as depression does make it more likely that a person will commit suicide.

"Untreated depression is the No. 1 cause for suicide" and "can also lead to murder-suicide," declares Suicide.org, a Web-based education and assistance group run by family members of suicide victims. [17] Studies also show that between 25 and 50 percent of all people with bipolar disorder attempt suicide, according to Suicide.org founder Kevin Caruso. [18]

Between 60 and 90 percent of suicide victims have a major psychiatric illness at the time of their deaths, with depression and bipolar disorder perhaps the most common, says the federal Substance Abuse and Mental Health Services Administration (SAMHSA). [19]

Nearly a third of veterans treated in Veterans Affairs facilities suffer from depression, greatly increasing their risk of suicide, according to Marcia Valenstein, an associate professor of psychiatry at the University of Michigan Health System. [20]

All severe mental disorders — including major depression and bipolar disease — increase suicide risk, says Thomas Joiner, a professor of psychology at Florida State University, in Tallahassee, and author of *Why People Die by Suicide.* Nevertheless, "by themselves the illnesses are not very explanatory" of what happens in suicide, since millions of Americans have these disorders but don't die by their own hands, he says.

Certain people are more likely to turn to the violence of suicide because they've "developed fearlessness over their life spans" that arms them to face the pain and violence suicide entails, says Joiner.

Other evidence indicates that some antidepressive drugs — notably, selective serotonin reuptake inhibitors (SSRIs), such as the Eli Lilly drug fluoxetine, brand-name Prozac — increase the risk of suicide or violent behavior for some patients. Beginning in August 2004, the U.S. Food and Drug Administration (FDA) required antidepressants to carry a label warning that "anxiety, agitation . . . irritability, hostility, [and] aggressiveness . . . have been reported in adult and pediatric patients" using the drug. [21]

Do depression sufferers have adequate access to effective treatments?

The number of available treatments for depression has vastly increased in recent decades, and insurance coverage and state public-health programs have improved access. Nevertheless, many mental-health authorities say it's still difficult to find skilled psychotherapists and that the most severely depressed people still face serious barriers to obtaining care.

Different drugs work for different people, so not everyone will find help on the first try, but studies now show that if even severely ill patients keep on "trying new medicines . . . you are likely to hit one over time that works," said NAMI's Duckworth. "Is it arduous? Of course," but help is available, he said. [22]

Some evidence indicates that access to specialty mental-health care is increasing in the general population, says Sherry Glied, professor of health policy and management at the Columbia University Mailman School of Public Health. For one thing, she says, "more psychiatrists take insurance" now than in the past.

Access to treatment is better today mainly because most primary-care physicians screen for depression and prescribe medications.

While the quality of primary-care physicians' skills at treating depression ranges from "terrific" to "not good at all," says the University of Pennsylvania's Hadley, the odds are now "around 70-30 that you'll get good care" from a primary-care doctor, up from 50-50 odds just 10 years ago. Fifteen years ago most primary-care physicians were uncomfortable prescribing antidepressants, he said.

Nevertheless, there's much room for improvement, especially among some vulnerable populations. When seeking depression treatment in primary care especially, if a patient's depression doesn't improve on the first course of antidepressant treatment, "then it's a crap shoot," says Hadley. If patients don't respond well to the first try, sometimes they don't come back to get a prescription for a different medication, "and primary-care doctors generally won't chase you around."

"It's very hard to get high-quality cognitive behavioral therapy," the main therapy proven to work against depression, says Joiner of Florida State. "People will say they provide it," but "in fact many mental-health types don't want to do" CBT, because some regard it as overtechnical, cookbook medicine. (*For details on CBT, see Background, pp. 588, 590.*)

Doing proper CBT therapy is essentially a very demanding teaching job, "and it's beyond a lot of people," although younger therapists "are getting better and better" at it, he says, adding that 10 years ago only 10 percent of

Women More Prone to Depression

More than one-fifth of U.S. women are expected to develop a major depressive disorder sometime in their lifetime compared to fewer than 13 percent of men.

Lifetime Prevalence of Major Depressive Disorder

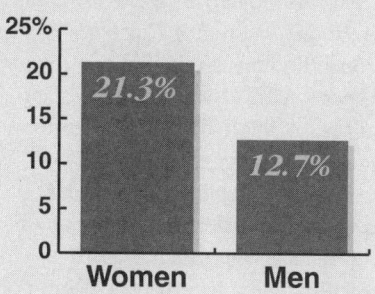

Source: Ronald C. Kessler, et al., "The Epidemiology of Major Depressive Disorder," Journal of the American Medical Association, *2003.*

therapists did proper CBT. Now about 20 percent do.

There's growing evidence that therapists must perform CBT well — not just in a minimally competent manner — in order to be effective, and "it's surprisingly difficult to measure what competence is in a therapist," says Dan Strunk an assistant professor of psychology at Ohio State University.

"It's harder to learn to be a really successful therapist than it is to prescribe a drug," says Joel Gurin, acting president of the National Alliance for Research on Schizophrenia and Depression (NARSAD), a private group that funds research on severe mental illness.

Military veterans may face particularly difficult access issues, says M. Audrey Burnam, a senior behavioral scientist at the RAND Corp., a think tank in Santa Monica, Calif. Among the more than 18 percent of Iraq/Afghanistan war veterans with mental-health problems —

mostly depression and PTSD — half have had no treatment at all in the last year, and for those who were treated, just over half the treatment was rated as "minimally adequate" or better, she says.

The Department of Veterans Affairs (VA) has been beefing up its mental-health capabilities, but not all vets are willing or able to make the often-long trip to a VA facility and instead seek care in their own communities, where it may either be unavailable or inadequate, Burnam says. The country has only a limited pool of specialty mental-health providers, and they are especially rare in rural areas.

Active-duty military members have another hurdle: Commanders must be notified when service members seek mental-health care, and many in the military fear their careers will be harmed if their illnesses are revealed.

And that can be dangerous, says Matthew Friedman, executive director of the Department of Veterans Affairs' National Center for Posttraumatic Stress Disorder, because the longer treatment is delayed the more likely a patient is to develop chronic disorders. Friedman, who is also a professor of psychiatry at Dartmouth Medical School, speaks on his own behalf and not for the VA.

In the 1950s and early '60s, outrage among some psychologists and mental-health advocates about horrifying conditions in state mental hospitals — where patients were frequently chained and shackled — led Congress to pass and President John F. Kennedy to sign the Community Mental Health Act of 1963, funding community mental-health centers to replace asylums.

"These centers will . . . provide better community facilities for all aspects of mental-health care," Kennedy said in a February 1963 message to Congress. "Located in the patient's own environment and community, the center would make possible a better understanding of his needs, a more cordial atmosphere for his recovery and a continuum of treatment [for] all but a small portion" of those who were then confined in state hospitals. [23]

In the ensuing years, however, funding and support for locally based mental-health care has sputtered, and many people have ended up on the street without the needed care. Worse, as the economy stumbles, more people need care, but states have less money to provide it.

"Mental-health needs are counter-cyclical" — i.e., bad financial times increase the need for services, says NAMI's Kimball. "I don't know if you could legislate this, but you need reserves" to tide state mental-health agencies over in tight times.

Access problems are worst for those with the most severe depression, says Columbia's Glied. Less than half of the severely mentally ill are getting care, "and access may be declining," she says. Furthermore, although the amount patients must pay out-of-pocket for mental-health care has been dropping overall, "costs aren't dropping for the most seriously ill."

Severely mentally ill people must meet income criteria and qualify as disabled in order to receive subsidized health care under Medicaid. Disability certification takes a long time and is "only available to those who have already been severely impaired by their illness," says Kimball. So, in effect, one doesn't qualify unless he or she has gone untreated for a long time or has had treatment that hasn't really been effective, she says.

In the past two or three years, rising awareness of new evidence-based practices that improve care has led many states to begin significantly expanding mental-health programs. But with the new recession, "now they're cutting back," Kimball says.

Do doctors and researchers overestimate the number of people with depression?

Most epidemiological studies find that 10 to 20 percent of people suffer depression at some point over a life-time. However, several major studies — notably polls that question people repeatedly and often about their past mood problems — find a prevalence closer to 50 percent, says Kenneth S. Kendler, a professor of psychiatry at Virginia Commonwealth University in Richmond.

Depressive illness may not be restricted to a minority but actually may be "waiting for most of us," with close to half the population experiencing one or more bouts over a lifetime, an international trio of scholars opined in a 2005 analysis in the *British Journal of Psychiatry*. [24]

Such findings are highly controversial. "If you want to make psychiatrists squirm, mention the 50 percent" number, says Kendler.

Psychiatry skeptics warn that attributing depressive disorder to large numbers of people risks stigmatizing normal emotions and giving too many people poorly understood drugs. They also say it draws attention away from the serious plight of the severely mentally ill and the social and interpersonal problems that may lie behind depressed feelings.

Over the past three decades, our culture has shifted its focus from social conditions that may make healthy people depressed to the idea that all depressed people suffer from a mental disorder, New York University's Wakefield and Rutgers University sociology professor Allan V. Horwitz write in their 2007 book, *The Loss of Sadness: How Psychiatry Transformed Normal Sorrow Into Depressive Disorder.* [25]

For example, American playwright Arthur Miller's 1949 play, "Death of a Salesman," is the story of middle-aged salesman Willy Loman, whose largely unsuccessful struggle to attain the American dream of prosperity leads to a suicidal car crash. During the play's successful 1949 Broadway run, audiences were moved by Willy's "embodiment of the Everyman in American life who embraced the goal of achieving great wealth but found himself destroyed by it," Horwitz and Wakefield write. [26]

But when a New York theater mounted a 1999 revival, "the director . . . sent the script to two psychiatrists, who diagnosed Loman as having a depressive disorder," Horwitz and Wakefield note. "The transformation of Willy Loman from a social to a psychiatric casualty represents a fundamental change in the way we view the nature of sadness," they conclude. [27] Playwright Miller weighed in against the psychiatric diagnosis of his character, writing that "Willy Loman is not a depressive. . . . He is weighed down by life. There are social reasons for why he is where he is." [28]

The *DSM* cautions clinicians that people suffering intense sadness due to the death of a loved one should not be confused with depressed people. But Horwitz and Wakefield argue that other losses can also trigger intense sadness. For instance, they said, studies show that 30 to 50 percent of people in a disintegrating marriage "experience symptoms comparable in intensity to those of depressive disorders." Yet those feelings are generally considered "normal sadness." [29]

Increasingly, physicians are making preliminary assessments of imminent depression risk based on "subthresholds" — having three of the *DSM*'s nine depression symptoms rather than five, as the manual requires for a full-fledged diagnosis, says Horwitz. But such determinations too easily slip into a full-blown diagnosis of depression, he says.

Diagnosing clinical depression based on such a low threshold "risks normal human emotional states being treated as illness," which can lead to inappropriate management of people's emotional states — such as prescribing unneeded drugs — and can threaten the credibility of psychiatric diagnosis altogether, said Gordon Parker, a professor of psychiatry at the University of South Wales in Sydney, Australia. [30]

The medicalization of depressed states may blind clinicians to the

Continued on p. 584

Chronology

1940s-1970s
First modern antidepressant drugs come on the market. Electroshock therapy for depression grows in popularity, then wanes, because of its sometimes severe side effects.

1949
The naturally occurring chemical element lithium is found to relieve symptoms of bipolar disease.

1956
American psychiatrist Nathan Kline discovers that a tuberculosis drug relieves depression symptoms, launching a new class of antidepressants — the monoamine oxidase inhibitors.

1957
Swiss psychiatrist Roland Kuhn discovers the first in another new class of antidepressant drugs — tricyclics.

1967
University of Pennsylvania psychiatrist Aaron T. Beck publishes *Depression: Causes and Treatment*, outlining his "cognitive therapy" approach to treatment; clinical trials eventually prove its effectiveness.

1970
Food and Drug Administration (FDA) approves lithium as a treatment for bipolar illness.

1972
Eli Lilly & Co. scientists discover fluoxetine, later marketed as the antidepressant Prozac. . . . Democratic vice presidential nominee Thomas F. Eagleton resigns from the ticket after confirming media reports that he was treated with electroshock treatments for severe depression.

1980s
New depression drugs, mostly selective serotonin reuptake inhibitors (SSRIs) like fluoxetine, enter the market. Mental-health advocates strive to end depression's stigma.

1987
FDA approves Prozac for depression.

1990s
Primary-care doctors take over primary diagnosis and treatment for depression, as new screening instruments and safer, easier-to-dispense antidepressants flood the market. Depression treatment expands as a result, but reports surface that the drugs may trigger suicide and violence.

1991
FDA panel concludes that evidence doesn't show a link between antidepressants like Prozac and suicide or violent behavior.

1992
FDA approves the SSRI drug Paxil — paroxetine — to treat depression.

2000s
Growing body of research shows some specific psychotherapies are effective depression treatments. Antidepressants become the most widely prescribed medication in the United States, but some studies question whether the drugs work any better than placebos.

2004
FDA orders antidepressants to carry a "black box" warning — the strongest the agency issues — that the drugs may increase suicide risk in children and teenagers.

2005
A report in the *British Journal of Psychiatry* estimates that nearly half the populations of developed nations experience one or more episodes of depression during a lifetime.

2006
United Kingdom's National Health Service recommends that doctors use cognitive behavioral therapy for patients with mild to moderate depression before prescribing an antidepressant.

2007
FDA expands warnings on antidepressants to include young adults up to age 24, whose risk of suicide may be increased by the drugs. . . . Pentagon reports that an average of five members of the military attempt suicide each day, more than six times the rate in 2002, before the Iraq war.

2008
Federal mental-health parity law is enacted requiring insurance plans that cover mental-health care to do so on an equal basis with medical/surgical coverage. . . . Sen. Charles Grassley, R-Iowa, launches an investigation into financial ties between pharmaceutical companies and some prominent university depression researchers.

2009
Federal government begins finalizing rules to implement parity for mental-health coverage in insurance plans. . . . Recession forces closures and cutbacks in Medicaid and state mental-health programs that provide care to many of the most severely depressed patients.

Brain Imaging Links Depression and Stress

Brains of those suffering from depression are different.

Scientists studying the basic biology of depression are marking progress "inch by inch," says Dennis S. Charney, a professor of psychiatry at the Mount Sinai School of Medicine in New York City. But as brain imagery improves and the genes connected to depression are identified, the science should move faster, he predicts.

The link between depression and stress is getting a lot of scientific attention, says Joel Gurin, acting president of the National Alliance for Research on Schizophrenia and Depression (NARSAD). Although scientists have been working for decades on how stress affects the body, he says, now they are seeing "how experience and environmental effects translate into biomedical effects."

Many studies have shown that "stress is a major predictor" of depression, says Andrew Miller, a professor of psychiatry and behavioral sciences at Emory University School of Medicine in Atlanta. But recent findings show that "psychosocial stressors" known to trigger depression — such as divorce, illness or loss of a loved one — can activate the body's immune response, causing inflammation, he notes.

Because of the inflammation connection, stress and depression may be "the worst of both worlds" in terms of their effect on overall health, says Miller. Previously, the immune system was thought to be less active in depressed patients — potentially making them more susceptible to disease, Miller explains. But the inflammation finding complicates that picture, because while depression is triggering the inflammatory response other defenses — such as T-cells, which help fight off infection — are being suppressed.

And while inflammation is vital for fending off infection in a wounded person, he says, "when the body goes overboard" by running the inflammatory system too long and too strongly, it can destroy human tissue. Excessive inflammation can also worsen other illnesses, such as cardiovascular disease and diabetes, which often occur in tandem with depression.

Brain imaging is also revealing new aspects about depression. For instance, a recent study found that the cortex — the large outer layer of the brain responsible for higher mental functions, such as thinking — is thinner in depressed persons and in those at higher risk for depression based on family history, says Bradley Peterson, a lead author of the study and director of child and adolescent psychiatry at Columbia University Medical Center in New York City. [1]

Many imaging studies have looked for signs of depression in other regions of the brain more closely tied to emotion — such as the hippocampus — so finding a strong relationship between depression and the cortex was a surprise, says Peterson. The thin cortex found in depressed and at-risk people may be devoted to paying attention to and remembering social and emotional events, a supposition buttressed by the fact that those with thin cortex regions demonstrated a poor memory for social interactions, he says.

Such cognitive problems may serve "to isolate people from the interpersonal world," which could set up a vicious cycle of worsening depression, Peterson suggests.

While research continues, mental-health practitioners are frustrated by the lack of new effective treatments and prevention strategies and severe depression's intractability to treatment.

The stress-depression connection may indicate a possible prevention strategy, says Miller. A study headed by Charles Raison, clinical director of Emory's Mind-Body Program, found that college students trained in "compassion meditation," based on Tibetan Buddhist practices, had less severe inflammatory responses to psychological stress than those not trained in the practice, raising the question of whether meditation might help ward off stress-related illnesses like depression. [2]

Continued from p. 582

fact that sadness often arises from troubled social bonds — and may be eased or eradicated by helping people rebuild bonds, says Thomas J. Scheff, a professor emeritus of sociology at the University of California, Santa Barbara.

"When you feel accepted, you feel like somebody," he says. "When you're rejected, you feel like nobody." Therapists predisposed to making a medical diagnosis rather than examining the context of the emotions are too likely to dispense a pill rather than addressing the cause of the disordered emotion, he argues.

Overestimating depression's prevalence drives the proliferation of screening programs designed to locate previously undiagnosed people who haven't presented themselves for treatment, says Wakefield. That could lead to a troubling increase in "social control" — in which society exerts more top-down control over individuals' feelings and presentation of self, he says.

"If every kid is being screened for depression in junior high and high school and at the doctor's office — and if positive screening leads you to treatment, even if you're pre-symptomatic — then this same process could also be applied to other" traits that society might eventually deem undesirable, such as being "antisocial."

"In a pluralistic society, you want to have an acceptance of a broad range of things as normal," Wakefield argues. Otherwise, "it could be a world where, if you're feeling out of sorts, you have to go to your [doctor] and get medicated" or face disapproval or even forced treatment for a presumed illness, he says.

In addition, chemical pathways involved in the inflammatory response have suggested new avenues for drug research, Miller says. He warned, however, that previous attempts to develop drugs based on depression's link to stress usually haven't panned out.

Electroconvulsive therapy, or "electroshock," was widely used through the 1960s but was abandoned as drug treatments became available, out of concern for side effects, including memory loss. But today physicians are using new types of electrical or magnetic brain stimulation on severely depressed patients when drugs and psychotherapy are unsuccessful.

A recent study found that electrical "cortical brain stimulation" relieved symptoms in patients who had remained depressed for an average of 27 years and after trying, on average, 10 different medications, said Emad N. Eskandar, associate professor of neurosurgery at Harvard Medical School and a study author. "These were very, very sick people who were out of options." [3]

Research on treatments for depression sometimes stirs controversy. For example, some fear that depression's prevalence — and the potential for overdiagnosis — tempts drug companies to buy off researchers to skew research findings and oversell drugs' virtues to physicians. The controversy is partly being driven by studies casting doubt on how well existing antidepressants — which are among the most commonly prescribed drugs in the United States — actually work. [4]

A 2008 analysis of clinical data submitted to the Food and Drug Administration found that antidepressants known as selective serotonin reuptake inhibitors, or SSRIs, "do not produce clinically significant improvements" for patients with moderate or very severe depression and show "significant effects" only for the most severely depressed patients. And, the researchers said, the severely ill patients may only be benefiting from the so-called placebo effect — patients' tendency to say their symptoms have lessened even when given sugar pills because they believe the treatment will work. [5]

Last fall, Sen. Charles E. Grassley, R-Iowa, launched an inquiry into whether financial ties between drug companies and scientists skew research and prescribing habits. After questioning about 20 doctors and research institutions, Grassley said it appeared that some researchers were receiving hundreds of thousands of dollars from drug companies without reporting those potential conflicts of interest to their universities. "It looks like problems of transparency are everywhere," he said. [6]

One prominent depression researcher, Charles B. Nemeroff of Emory University, for instance, was found to have received more funds from GlaxoSmithKline, manufacturer of the antidepressants Wellbutrin and Zyban, than he had reported. But Nemeroff, who has been stripped of his departmental chairmanship, told his university administrators that "to the best of my knowledge, I have followed the appropriate university regulations concerning financial disclosures" concerning drug-company income. [7]

---

[1] Bradley S. Peterson, et al., "Cortical Thinning in Persons at Increased Familial Risk for Major Depression," Proceedings of the National Academy of Sciences, Feb. 11, 2009, www.pnas.org/content/106/15/6273.abstract.

[2] "Meditation Linked to Health Benefits, Again," Science & Religion Today blog, Oct. 13, 2008, http://scienceandreligiontoday.blogspot.com.

[3] "Brain Stimulation Therapy Eases Tough-to-Treat Depression," HealthDay online, May 7, 2009, www.nlm.nih.gov/medlineplus/news/fullstory_83965.html.

[4] See Table 97, in Health: United States 2008, Centers for Disease Control and Prevention (2009), p. 366, www.cdc.gov/nchs/data/hus/hus08.pdf#097.

[5] Irving Kirsch, et al., "Initial Severity and Antidepressant Benefits: A Meta-Analysis of Data Submitted to the Food and Drug Administration," PLos Hub for Clinical Trials, Feb. 26, 2008, www.plosmedicine.org.

[6] Quoted in Gardiner Harris, "Top Psychiatrist Didn't Report Drug Makers' Pay," The New York Times, Oct. 4, 2008, p. A1.

[7] Ibid.

But other experts say depression's incidence is not overestimated and that, if anything, the disease is underdiagnosed and undertreated.

Today's diagnostic criteria are effective in "making it very clear" that the disease of depression is different from a 10-minute mood, says APA president Stotland. Far from being overdiagnosed, the data clearly show that depression is, in fact, "very undertreated."

Massive overtreatment will not result from broad screening, says Mount Sinai's Charney, because "making the diagnosis doesn't tell you what to do about it," and clinicians don't treat everyone who shows up as depressed on a screening test.

Furthermore, it's not surprising that modern stresses plunge many vulnerable people into depression. "We live in remarkably stressful times, filled with information overload, demands to perform at high speed and pressure to multitask," wrote Charney and colleagues in the 2004 book The Peace of Mind Prescription: An Authoritative Guide to Finding the Most Effective Treatment for Anxiety and Depression. However, "our brains, our moods, and our emotional responses evolved over millions of years to deal with the challenges of a hunter-gatherer lifestyle, in which new information came at a trickle and the pace of life was, literally, at a walk." [31]

Peter D. Kramer, a psychiatrist in Providence, R.I., and author of the 2005 book Against Depression, argues that patients and society would, in fact, benefit from expanding the diagnosis of depression to less severe disorders. "Most people who complain of hopelessness and low energy fall short of the diagnosis, even when their discomfort is substantial," he said. But "these despairing-but-not-depressed patients are the ones

Family History and Stress Predict Depression Risk

"Genetic effects are important, but not overwhelming."

As epidemiologists unravel the risk factors for depression, family history and stress are topping the list of culprits.

A person's risk of developing depression is "elevated about threefold" if he is a parent, child or sibling of a depression sufferer, says Kenneth S. Kendler, a professor of psychiatry at Virginia Commonwealth University in Richmond.

Depression can be inherited, although not to the degree of some other traits, says Kendler. Based on studies of twins, scientists have determined that inheritance accounts for about 38 percent of depression cases, compared to 80 percent for schizophrenia and 90 percent for height and weight tendencies. "That makes genetic effects important but not overwhelming," he says.

Environment and personal experiences — such as trauma and stress — can alter risk, Kendler says. A woman who has suffered a severe trauma, such as rape, in the past month will have an eight- or tenfold increase in her risk of developing depression.

Half of all those with major depression suffer their first bout by their mid-20s, and about half have suffered from another mental disorder — such as anxiety, impulsivity or substance abuse — earlier in life, says Ronald C. Kessler, a professor of health-care policy at Harvard University.

"If depression starts young, the likelihood of its recurring in adulthood is very high," says Judy Garber, a professor of psychology at Vanderbilt University. Nevertheless, "you can also get depressed as an adult, never having been depressed before."

Furthermore, each depressive episode "makes you more vulnerable to having additional episodes," says Nada Stotland, president of the American Psychiatric Association. After one episode, there's a 50 percent chance of another, and after two episodes a 70 percent chance of a third, she explains.

Current statistics show that depression strikes about twice as many women as men — 21 percent, compared to 13 percent — over a lifetime. [1] (*See graph, p. 581.*) "There are many, many factors," both social and biological, that lead to that result, says Susan Nolen-Hoeksema, a professor of psychology at Yale University.

For instance, hormonal factors and higher rates of violence, such as domestic-partner abuse, experienced by women can contribute to depression, Nolen-Hoeksema says. And depression is closely linked to individuals' sensitivity to disrupted social relationships. In general, women tend to be "more reactive to rejection," she says.

In addition, many more women than men engage in an activity she calls "ruminating — going over and over memories, trying to figure out what incidents "mean" but without "going on to problem solving." Women who "are unable to pull themselves out of" such bouts of rumination are especially susceptible to depression, she says.

But Sam V. Cochran, a clinical professor of counseling psychology at the University of Iowa is not convinced that women's depression rates are much higher than men's.

"Boys are socialized to avoid sad feelings, avoid crying, avoid any emotional states that are associated with depression," and depression screenings ask questions like, "'Have you felt sad' recently?' Men may deny these things," Cochran says. As a result, "we have this paradox of men committing suicide" more often than women, even though statistics show that many fewer men are depressed.

In an ongoing study of a group of Massachusetts children who were kindergarteners in 1977, "There's no question we have more girls" with depression than boys, says Helen Reinherz, a professor

---

who cost the medical system the most. They show up in doctors' offices with physical complaints that are expensive to work up — and that turn out to arise from a minor mood disorder." [32]

Harvard's Kessler says mistaking bipolar illness for depression is a valid overdiagnosis issue. Screening instruments don't pick up bipolar disease, and if a doctor notices and tries to treat depression alone in a bipolar patient, it can have "some dangerous consequences," he says. Among other things, a bipolar patient must take a mood stabilizer before taking an antidepressant to avoid spiraling into very intense mania, Kessler explains. ∎

BACKGROUND

Romantic Melancholia

As far back as ancient Greece, physicians have distinguished severe depression — a lengthy and severe mood disorder that the Greeks called "melancholia" and blamed on too much "black bile" in the body — from "melancholy," or deep sadness arising from tragic events. [33]

But behind the distinction lies a hard-to-answer question. When treating a patient suffering from melancholia today, should doctors strive to eradicate all the signs and symptoms associated with depression? Or are some depressive traits — like self-doubt, quick perception of the darker sides of life and intense sensitivity to personal setbacks and rejections — valuable attributes to the melancholic individual and to society?

For many mental-health practitioners, the goal is healing and curing depression, which can destroy individuals and families, writes psychiatrist Kramer. But

at Massachusetts' Simmons School of Social Work and head of the Simmons Longitudinal Study.

Among the study's subjects, now 37 years old, men who've become depressed showed a previously unnoticed risk factor, she says. They had health problems neonatally and up to the age of about 5. And "while an early history of anxiety is a sign of risk for anyone, anxious boys seem to be especially at risk," Reinherz says.

Rep. Patrick Kennedy (D-R.I.), who suffers from depression, speaks during a rally at the U.S. Capitol on March 5, 2008, in support of mental-health legislation. The bill, which has since been signed into law, requires insurers who provide mental-health benefits to offer the same coverage for mental disorders as for other illnesses.

Children can show clear signs of depression, even though they often go unnoticed by adults, says Tanya West, a 72-year-old retiree and mental-health volunteer in south-central Pennsylvania who's had several bouts with major depression. "I, for example, was a very sad child. You could see it in pictures, in the eyes, after I was about 6 or 7," she says. "The markers are often there" but unnoticed by adults.

As the baby boom generation turns elderly in the coming decades, "we'll have a very high percentage of people with at least moderate depression" since "the elderly are more at risk, even if they haven't had it earlier," says Trevor Hadley, a professor of psychiatry at the University of Pennsylvania. For example, "people who have been drinking all their lives but not to excess may get depression in their 60s and onward."

Scientists are learning more about how depressed minds operate.

Among depressive traits is a "tendency to overgeneralize things — insisting that things are either black or white," says Cochran. Psychologists believe that, to some extent, people "learn themselves into depression" as such thinking habits take firmer root in their minds over time.

In a study in which depressed and non-depressed people played a game for points using beans that were labeled "good" or "bad," depressed people had a much harder time remembering which beans were the "good," point-earning ones, says Dan Strunk, an assistant professor of psychology at Ohio State University. The finding may reveal a "processing bias" in which depressed people have difficulty remembering positive aspects of experience but easily remember the negatives.

Reinherz's study is turning up some protective factors. If an at-risk child — such as a child with a depressed mother — can find mentors to provide "a sense of being of value, a sense that 'I'm an important person in my family, in my world,' " it can help protect against future emotional difficulties, she says.

[1] Ronald C. Kessler, *et al.*, "The Epidemiology of Major Depressive Disorder," *Journal of the American Medical Association*, 2003.

that intention is complicated by the fact that our society as a whole embraces the idea that deep sadness, one of the symptoms of depression, helps to create "depth" in art and life. [34]

The idea that depression imparts depth is also common among patients, says Kramer, citing the case of "Emily," a depressed woman who disparaged a "neighbor's good humor" as "illogical, as if he did not appreciate a truth about his own existence." She also called her non-depressed husband "dear and lovable, but a bit superficial," and, like other non-depressives she knew, "emotionally obtuse." [35]

Western culture appears to agree with Emily's view that melancholia imparts a special wisdom, Kramer argues, because it generally considers depressed and pessimistic people "intellectual" or "great artists," seldom attributing such characteristics to happy or optimistic figures.

Art like Pablo Picasso's works painted during his "blue period" — sad-themed pieces completed after a friend's suicide — is generally lauded above cheerful works reflecting the human capacity for resilience and joy, said Kramer. "We stand within the tradition of heroic melancholy," the idea, which surfaced

even among the ancient Greeks, that melancholic people are "exceptional — brave and imaginative," he wrote. [36]

Kramer says it's time to get past romanticizing melancholia. "See enough depression, and you cast a jaundiced eye on extremes of otherwise arguably attractive traits," like languor and "dark" moods, he writes. [37]

Depression President

Perhaps no one figure captures the paradox of "heroic melancholy" existing alongside the ravages of severe depression better than President Abraham Lincoln, who shepherded the nation through the Civil War.

Lincoln had at least two suicidal breakdowns as a young man and was plagued by severe depression throughout his life, facts well known not only to his friends and family but also to political allies and opponents, wrote Joshua Wolf Shenk, author of the 2005 book *Lincoln's Melancholy*. [38] In 1836, a fellow candidate for the Illinois state legislature, Robert L. Wilson, wrote of Lincoln that "he was the victim of terrible melancholy." To relieve those feelings, Lincoln "sought company, and indulged in fun and hilarity without restraint," Wilson wrote. "Still, when by himself, he told me that he was so overcome with mental depression, that he never dare carry a knife in his pocket." [39]

As a young state legislator in 1841, Lincoln sank into an acute mental collapse, perhaps triggered by romantic troubles. He missed legislative sessions and votes and eventually sought medical treatment, which left him "reduced and emaciated," according to Shenk. Standard treatments for melancholia, which aimed to "stimulate and invigorate" depressed patients and cleanse their systems, were grueling, painful and dangerous. "Mustard rubs produced terrific pain. Black pepper drinks were like a bomb in the stomach," and mercury, arsenic and strychnine used to purge the stomach and bowels are actual poisons, Shenk writes. [40]

"Doctors approved of the green stools that resulted" from taking mercury because they believed that "black bile was being cleared out." But "we now know that mercury was killing the healthy intestinal bacteria that make stools brown" and also damaged the central nervous system. [41]

"If Lincoln were alive today, his depression would be considered a 'character issue' — a political liability," as was the case when 1972 Democratic vice presidential candidate Tom Eagle-

Army Suicide Attempts at Record Level

More than 2,000 soldiers attempted suicide in 2007, the highest annual total for the Army and six times higher than five years earlier.

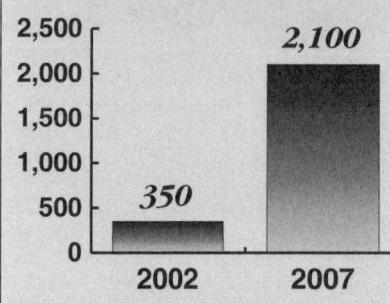

Attempted Suicides in U.S. Army, 2002 and 2007

Source: Dana Priest, "Soldier Suicides at Record Level," The Washington Post, January 2008, citing an unpublished "U.S. Army Medical Command Suicide Prevention Action Plan"

ton withdrew from the race after reporters learned he'd been treated for severe depression, noted Shenk. [42] But contemporaries' knowledge of Lincoln's melancholia may actually have helped him, he noted, with the number of people finding his moods "odd and curious" outnumbered by those who sympathized with him. [43]

In the 19th century "people understood the obvious point that . . . each cognitive style has assets and defects that change according to circumstances," and Lincoln's melancholic view may have been valuable in pre-Civil War America, Shenk suggests. [44]

Recent research shows that depression sufferers perceive negative information more quickly, while non-depressed people quickly grasp positive information. And while depressed people often are blind to the positive aspects of a situation, Lincoln's difficulties — a son

died and he ruled a country split by bitter divisions — may have turned his personal pain into an advantage, Shenk hypothesizes. "It is no coincidence that Lincoln found his power at a time when the skies turned dark in the United States." [45]

Lincoln's ability to devote himself intensely to leading the country through and out of war — and thus his political greatness — stemmed from a decision he made when he pulled himself back from the brink of suicide as a young man, said Shenk. "Having flirted with a desire to die, he asked himself what he needed to live for" and found that he had an "irrepressible desire" to "link his name with something that would redound to the interest of his fellow man." [46]

This hard-won resolve along with a carefully cultivated sense of humor that he used daily to ward off melancholia "underlay his every move as president," Shenk theorizes. [47]

Treatment Watershed

D epression treatments didn't advance much beyond the primitive methods of Lincoln's time until the mid-20th century. The first medications to lessen depression symptoms like sadness and lack of energy — the so-called tricyclic antidepressants — were introduced in the 1950s. [48] A similar treatment revolution occurred for bipolar disorder when lithium was introduced in the United States in 1960, says Charney of Mt. Sinai.

Tricyclics — and another early class of drugs, monoamine oxidase inhibitors — change the chemical balance in the brain so that some depressed people feel better. Since the drugs for the first time allowed many depressed patients to be successfully treated outside the hospital, psychiatrists and patients embraced them as a vast improvement over older treatments, Charney says.

Continued on p. 590

At Issue:

Will the mental-health parity law help patients?

JAMES E. PURCELL
CEO, BLUE CROSS & BLUE SHIELD OF RHODE ISLAND

FROM TESTIMONY BEFORE HOUSE ENERGY AND COMMERCE SUBCOMMITTEE ON HEALTH, JUNE 15, 2007

*b*lue Cross & Blue Shield of Rhode Island (BCBSRI) [is] an independent, local, nonprofit insurer. Our vision is to improve the lives of our members and all Rhode Islanders by improving their health.

I am of the passionate view that without full integration of physical and behavioral health care, we cannot fully realize our vision. And without meaningful behavioral health parity, that will not happen on a national level.

Like most insurers, BCBSRI is not generally supportive of coverage mandates, as they intend to increase premiums. This [proposed legislation] is different. Since the initial passage of Rhode Island's partial mental-health parity state mandate in 1994, we have continued to modify our coverage to reflect additional changes in state and federal law. But more than that, in a number of instances we voluntarily went beyond the letter of the law, instituting policies that achieve de facto parity.

Why on Earth would we do this when we weren't forced to do it by law? It's good care and good business. It was definitely in the best interest of our members to do this. Where is the line separating behavioral health and physical health for an obese diabetic suffering from depression and eating disorders? Treating just the physical symptoms without treating the behavioral issues is less than adequate care.

It is also cost-effective. We've seen the results. Yes, it adds some up-front costs, but it provides better care to people who desperately need it. And the price tag is not that big.

For BCBSRI's commercial business, non-drug behavioral health-care benefits are 3.6 percent of premium expenses. These costs are distributed about 32 percent for inpatient care, 12 percent for facility outpatient care and 56 percent for professional services (mostly office visits).

About one out of 10 of our members received professional behavioral health-care services in 2006. Of those members, 71 percent had 10 or fewer office visits, and 90 percent had 20 or fewer office visits. The impact on claims costs of limiting annual coverage to 15 visits would have been about 0.3 percent of total claims.

The big problem is to get people to see their behavioral-health provider. Very few need more than 30 visits a year, but those who do really, really need them. Otherwise, where do they end up? Right — the emergency room, for a much bigger bill. This is more humane care, at a lower cost.

JOHN C. GOODMAN
PRESIDENT, NATIONAL CENTER FOR POLICY ANALYSIS

FROM GOODMAN'S HEALTH POLICY BLOG, WWW.JOHN-GOODMAN-BLOG.COM, NOV. 14, 2008

*i*t was easy to overlook in the midst of a historic financial crisis, but buried in the middle of the bailout bill was a mental-health parity law. Ostensibly, employers of more than 50 people must apply the same co-payments, deductibles, etc. to mental-health services as they have for medical services. But the employer doesn't have to cover mental health at all. And if there is coverage, employers can pick and choose which disorder they will cover.

It is an example of a very bad law. It does the opposite of what good public policy should be all about.

There may be a legitimate social interest in whether people insure for catastrophic mental-health-care costs, just as there may be a legitimate interest in insurance for other catastrophic costs. But given some level of catastrophic coverage, there is rarely any good reason to substitute the judgment of legislators for the judgment of the marketplace with respect to the division between self-insurance and third-party insurance.

And there is no conceivable reason to dictate how private insurance contracts allocate coverage between third-party insurance and individual self-insurance, while leaving the private sector completely free to answer "no" to the question whether they cover the treatment costs at all.

Further, the legislation gets the allocation of coverage all wrong. There is no conceivable circumstance in which rational people would freely choose to be in plans in which deductibles and co-payments are the same for all services. To the contrary, people should self-insure for those services where it is appropriate and desirable for patients to exercise discretion. They should rely on third-party insurance for services where it is inappropriate and undesirable for patients to exercise discretion.

Mental-health services frequently have the very characteristics that make patient discretion highly desirable. Patients should pay more of their bill when they exercise discretion. In mental health, this principle applies in spades because the illness is often experienced subjectively; there are no objective standards for diagnosis or treatment; doctors often exercise enormous discretion; patients also exercise a lot of discretion; and patient cooperation is often crucial to any cure. Unlike fixing a broken leg, these are precisely the conditions that make patient cost-sharing highly desirable.

Therefore, it is far more efficient to put funds for mental-health care in Health Savings Accounts and let patients make more of their own decisions about spending them.

Continued from p. 588

But they also have many side effects, including increased heart rate, blurred vision and weight gain. And tricyclics "can be fatal in overdoses," said Madhukar H. Trivedi, director of the Depression and Anxiety Disorders Program at the University of Texas' Southwestern Medical School in Dallas. "Since suicide and suicidal thoughts are symptoms of depression, it is not good to provide a medication that could be used to achieve it." [49]

As a result, antidepressant medications didn't reach the mainstream until the 1980s, when the first SSRIs — selective serotonin reuptake inhibitors — came on the market. "Earlier drugs could kill you," and it was difficult to adjust the dosage to fit the patient, says Shern of Mental Health America.

When the safer SSRIs became available, primary-care physicians began screening and treating patients for depression, greatly expanding the number of people treated, he says. Then, in recent decades, psychotherapy for depression made great strides, as research provided evidence that some "talk" therapies are effective — especially cognitive behavioral therapy.

A CBT therapist elicits a patient's thoughts in response to an event and then gets the patient to examine what impact those thoughts have on the patient's mood and future actions, says Ohio State's Strunk. In this, the "cognitive" part of the treatment, the therapist and patient also consider "whether the thought is true or not," he says.

Evidence shows that patients who best internalize the skills they've been

Mourners gather at Loyola College in Baltimore, Md., for a memorial mass for sophomore Stephanie Parente, 19, and her family — the victims of an apparent murder-suicide on April 21, 2009. Police said William Parente, 59, apparently distraught over financial troubles, killed Stephanie, his wife Betty and his younger daughter Catherine, all of Garden City, N.Y. Experts say when the economy falters, depression and suicide rise — a pattern among the industrialized countries that is so regular it is virtually an economic indicator.

AP Photo/*The Baltimore Sun*/Kenneth K. Lam

taught — such as "being very skeptical about their own thoughts" and "being able to look at their thoughts from different points of view" — stay well longer without a relapse, Strunk says.

The therapy is not about "telling people not to have an emotion," but to examine one's thoughts regarding a situation to figure out whether the thoughts accompanying the emotion are accurate, explains Judy Garber, a professor of psychology at Vanderbilt University, in Nashville, Tenn. "If what you believe is actually true," then a strong emotion is appropriate, "and the next step is to figure out what to do about the situation."

The "behavioral" part of the treatment involves the patient keeping track of his moods and how those moods relate to daily activities, says Strunk. "Maybe the patient is spending time in front of the TV, and they may think that they're avoiding pain, but the strategy may not be working well."

Some concrete skills also may come into play, says Garber, in which the therapist helps the patient develop

strategies to deal with his situation. For instance, if the depression was triggered by job loss, the therapist may help the patient get his résumé in order.

CBT has some downsides, too. When the basic job is to help someone be skeptical about fairly personal beliefs, "there are lots of ways for a therapist to do that wrong and to rub people the wrong way," says Strunk.

It may take longer to see the positive effects of therapy compared to medication, but the benefits may last longer if the patient continues to work on it, Garber says. "There are skills you can learn, but you've got to keep doing them," she says. ∎

CURRENT SITUATION

Preparing for Parity

The Department of Health and Human Services is reviewing recommendations for rules implementing a new federal law requiring health insurers who cover mental-health care to maintain "parity" — or the same level of coverage — for mental-health care as they provide for medical and surgical care. [50]

The recommendations were submitted in late May by mental-health practitioners, patient advocates, insurers and others. The new rules will implement the Paul Wellstone and Pete Domenici Mental Health Parity and Addiction Equity Act of 2008, passed after years of debate last fall as part of the $700 billion financial bailout bill. [51]

The law was created in part because it was realized that better mental-health coverage "may bring down costs" overall, says Shern of Mental Health America (MHA).

Since the 1990s, nearly every state has mandated that insurers reduce disparities in mental-health and medical/surgical coverage. Many states require insurers to provide equivalent coverage in both areas, although the laws apply only to about 20 percent of privately insured people. A 1996 federal law had already required insurance plans offering mental-health coverage to offer the same annual and lifetime coverage limits for mental-health care that they set on other care. [52]

The new law will greatly expand the number of people whose health plans have equivalent coverage by applying an overall parity requirement to so-called ERISA health plans — multistate employer-sponsored health plans not governed by state laws. [53]

The regulations will determine how far the new law extends parity beyond the 1996 requirements for equal dollar limits on care.

The law specifies only one requirement: Insurers cannot impose stricter limits on hospital stays or outpatient visits for mental-health care than they have for medical and surgical care, says Kristen Beronio, MHA's senior director of government affairs. "But we think a more expansive view should be taken" of what parity includes, she says. "We don't want to get back into the position we were in after the 1996 law," which addressed only spending limits. After that law was enacted, insurance plans "found other ways to limit coverage," effectively evading Congress' intention.

MHA wants parity rules to bar health plans from imposing higher evidentiary standards for determining the "medical necessity" or effectiveness of mental-health treatments compared to evidence

standards they apply to medical/surgical treatments, she says.

Setting the rules will be difficult because "you can't just [treat] mental health as if it is entirely like everything else," says Glied, the Columbia University health policy professor. For instance, those with severe mental illness need "psychosocial elements," such as social workers and residential care, and medical insurance doesn't pay for those for other conditions.

Surprisingly, some patients will have to pay more out-of-pocket for mental-health services — the result of an "unintended consequence" of soon-to-be-finalized parity regulations, says Douglas A. Nemecek, national medical director at CIGNA Behavioral Health, a national provider of mental-health insurance based in Eden Prairie, Minn. That's because mental-health services now are generally managed by specialty insurers with lower co-pays and deductibles than most people get for medical/surgical benefits, he explains.

Opponents of parity predicted many people would use an open-ended mental-health benefit to embark on years of pricey psychotherapy. But Nemecek points out that when CIGNA eliminated preauthorization requirements for mental-health outpatient treatment several years ago spending didn't skyrocket.

"Runaway utilization is simply not going to be the issue," he says.

Care Cutbacks

Many severely depressed Americans get care from public programs funded by Medicaid, Social Security disability assistance and state-funded community mental-health programs. The severely mentally ill make up 5 to 7 percent of the population, with about 1 percent of those suffering from schizophrenia, 1 percent with bipolar disorder and 3 to 5 percent with major depression, says the University of Pennsylvania's Salzer.

But many states squeezed by the economic recession have already cut — or are planning to cut — Medicaid funding and community mental-health programs, says Kimball of the National Alliance on Mental Illness. California has recently made major cuts in its mental-health programs, and Texas, where the programs weren't very well funded to begin with, has also made cuts, says Hadley of the University of Pennsylvania. Michigan has tried to beef up Medicaid but has cut community mental-health services as the economy has struggled, says Kimball. Nevada has cut a third of its state mental-health programs — shutting down medication and walk-in clinics, she says.

As job losses continue to eat into state tax revenues, many states also are considering cutting provider reimbursement rates, which will further reduce access to care, Kimball says.

"States are looking at cutting the pharmacy budget, which will . . . make it hard to get access to a full array of antidepressants," she says. That's troubling, she says, because any given antidepressant works only for a subset of people, and many people cycle through several drugs before they find one that's effective.

Funds for hospitalization also will be cut, raising suicide risks for many, she says. State-government hiring freezes and layoffs mean "there will be fewer people available to help you get access" to services.

Meanwhile, the recession plus the return of veterans from Iraq and Afghanistan increases demand for care, Kimball says. She cites the Michigan family in which the father of a bipolar son lost his job and subsequently plunged into depression. The boy's mother lamented that "we can only get help if one attempts suicide and we go to the hospital," Kimball reports.

And access to publicly funded programs will only get worse in the next two years, says Hadley, because the recession will continue to affect state tax revenues for many months after it ends. ∎

OUTLOOK

Health-Care Reform

As Congress tackles health reform, advocates hope mental health gets more than lip service.

It would have been preferable to nail down the parity benefits before the health-reform debate began, says Shern of Mental Health America, but it's still good to have parity established as a principle as the larger debate ensues.

Past attempts to increase mental-health coverage repeatedly foundered on fears that it would raise health-care costs too much. But in fact, "forgoing substance-abuse and mental-health benefits can raise medical costs by 25 to 50 percent," says Nemecek of CIGNA, because mental illnesses can worsen co-occurring conditions like diabetes and heart disease, making it harder and more expensive for patients to comply with treatment.

Mental Health America would like to have more patient input into reform discussions so that "patient-centered care" and patient preferences are valued, MHA's Beronio says. For instance, some severely mentally ill patients might prefer a community mental-health clinic, rather than a general-practice physician, as their "medical home" — the coordinating point for all their care, she says.

Prevention is another priority. "There's lots of research on protective factors [against depression] and how to strengthen them," says Shern. In today's system, though, "the illnesses show up in adolescents but aren't treated for 10 years," making them eventually harder and more expensive to treat.

Furthermore, because chronic or traumatic stress can lead to depression, as well as to other mental illnesses, "stress education should be taught alongside sex education to school kids," says Friedman at the VA's National Center for Posttraumatic Stress Disorder.

"There's some evidence that we can teach kids skills — similar to what we teach in therapy — that could reduce or prevent depression by helping teens learn to look at what they're thinking" to see if it matches reality, says Garber of Vanderbilt. That is easier to do if the tactic has been internalized as a more automatic skill, she says.

"The average age of onset of a mental-health condition is 14," and "there's a window of two to four years between when a symptom first arises and a full-blown diagnosis," so there's time to act, says Beronio.

Some interventions could be handled in the health-care system while others would be school- or community-based, and "Congress is open to funding some of those," she says. Nevertheless, "it's hard to get people to understand that mental health is a prevention issue." ∎

About the Author

Staff writer **Marcia Clemmitt** is a veteran social-policy reporter who previously served as editor in chief of *Medicine & Health* and staff writer for *The Scientist*. She has also been a high-school math and physics teacher. She holds a liberal arts and sciences degree from St. John's College, Annapolis, and a master's degree in English from Georgetown University. Her recent reports include "Preventing Cancer" and "Public-Works Projects."

Notes

[1] For background, see Dan De Luce, "U.S. Army Base Shuts Down After Rise in Suicides," Agence France-Presse, May 28, 2009, www.google.com/hostednews/afp/article/ALeqM5gOEDhkP9VVYuG0sPh4b3QJTRCNHA, and Troy Langenburg, "Townsend Leads Response to Suicides," U.S. Army, May 29, 2009, www.army.mil/-news/2009/05/29/21895-townsend-leads-response-to-suicides.

[2] "Concern Mounts Over Rising Troop Suicides," CNN.com, Feb. 3, 2008, www.cnn.com/2008/US/02/01/military.suicides/index.html.

[3] "Debt and Depression Cause Murder-Suicide in Maryland," NowPublic.com, April 18, 2009, www.nowpublic.com/world/money-troubles-blamed-tragic-murder-suicide-maryland-christopher-wood-video-4-18-09.

[4] Quoted in Stephani Desmon and Scott Calvert, "As Economic Crisis Goes on, Financial Fears Can Push Some Over the Edge," *The Baltimore Sun*, April 23, 2009, www.baltimoresun.com/news/local/bal-te.md.strain23apr23,0,453118.story.

[5] For the definition of major depression, see "DSM IV: Major Depressive Episode," *Depression Today*, www.mental-health-today.com/dep/dsm.htm.

[6] Quoted in Therese J. Borchard, "Ken Duckworth, MD: How Do You Move Beyond Blue?" *Beyond Blue* blog, BeliefNet.com, Sept. 21, 2007, http://blog.beliefnet.com/beyondblue.

[7] Terrence Real, *I Don't Want to Talk About It: Overcoming the Secret Legacy of Male Depression* (1998), p. 63.

[8] "The Unrecognized Link: Depression Co-occurring With Other Medical Conditions," Health Place: America's Mental Health Channel, Dec. 19, 2008, www.healthyplace.com/depression/nimh/the-unrecognized-link-depression-co-occurring-with-medical-conditions/menu-id-1419/.

[9] "Morbidity and Mortality in People with Serious Mental Illness," Medical Directors Council, National Association of State Mental Health Program Directors, October 2006, www.nasmhpd.org/general_files/publications/med_directors_pubs/Technical%20Report%20on%20Morbidity%20and%20Mortaility%20-%20Final%2011-06.pdf.

[10] For background, see Sarah Glazer, "Treating Anxiety," CQ Researcher, Feb. 8, 2002, pp. 97-120.

[11] Madison Park, "Despondent Dads Driven to Kill Loved Ones," CNN.com, May 19, 2009.

[12] Jo Barnes, "Murder Followed by Suicide in Australia: 1973-1993, a Research Note," *Journal of Sociology*, March 2000, pp. 1-11.

[13] Elizabeth Kandel Englander, *Understanding Violence* (2002), p. 75.

[14] Quoted in Kathleen Doheny, "Mental Illness and Violence: A Link," *WebMD*, Feb. 2, 2009, www.webmd.com.

[15] Laura Banks, *et al.*, "A Comparison of Intimate Partner Homicide to Intimate Partner Homicide-Suicide," *Violence Against Women*, September 2008, p. 1065.

[16] M. Allan Cooperstein, "The Storms of Youth: Violence and Depression in Adolescents," athealth.com Web site, http://athealth.com/practitioner/particles/Guest_Cooperstein2.html.

[17] "Murder-Suicide: Grandfather Kills Grandson, then Himself," *Suicide.org*, Aug. 15, 2004, www.suicide.org.

[18] Kevin Caruso, "Bipolar Disorder and Suicide," *Suicide.org*, www.suicide.org.

[19] "Picture This: Depression and Suicide Prevention," Substance Abuse and Mental Health Services Administration/Entertainment Industries Council, www.eiconline.org/resources/publications/z_picturethis/Desorder.pdf.

[20] Steven Reinberg, "With Depression, Vets Face Higher Suicide Risk," *HealthDay*, Jan. 12, 2009, www.healthday.com/Article.asp?AID=622964.

[21] For background, see David Healy, Andrew Herxheimer and David B. Menkes, "Antidepressants and Violence: Problems at the Interface of Medicine and Law," *PLoS Medicine*, Sept. 12, 2006, www.plosmedicine.org/article/info:doi/10.1371/journal.pmed.0030372.

[22] Quoted in Borchard, *op. cit.*

[23] John F. Kennedy, "Special Message to the Congress on Mental Illness and Mental Retardation," The American Presidency Project, www.presidency.ucsb.edu/ws/index.php?pid=9546.

[24] Gavin Andrews, Richie Poulton and Ingmar Skoog, "Lifetime Risk of Depression: Restricted to a Minority or Waiting for Most?" *British Journal of Psychiatry*, December 2005, pp.495-496, http://bjp.rcpsych.org/cgi/content/full/187/6/495.

[25] Allan V. Horwitz and Jerome C. Wakefield, *The Loss of Sadness: How Psychiatry Transformed Normal Sorrow Into Depressive Disorder* (2007), p. 3.

[26] *Ibid.*

[27] Quoted in *ibid.*

[28] *Ibid.*, p. 4.

[29] Horwitz and Wakefield, *op. cit.*, p. 34.

[30] Gordon Parker, "Is Depression Overdiagnosed? Yes," *British Medical Journal*, Aug. 18, 2007, p.328, www.bmj.com/cgi/content/full/335/

7615/328.

[31] Dennis S. Charney and Charles B. Nemeroff, with Stephen Braun, *The Peace of Mind Prescription: An Authoritative Guide to Finding the Most Effective Treatment for Anxiety and Depression* (2004), p. 2.

[32] Peter D. Kramer, *Against Depression* (2005), p. 166.

[33] See Joshua Wolf Shenk, *Lincoln's Melancholy: How Depression Challenged a President and Fueled His Greatness* (2005).

[34] Kramer, *op. cit.*, p. 44.

[35] *Ibid.*

[36] *Ibid.*, p. 212.

[37] *Ibid.*, p. 273.

[38] Shenk, *op. cit.*, p. 5.

[39] *Ibid.*, p. 23.

[40] *Ibid.*, p. 58.

[41] *Ibid.*, p. 59.

[42] For background, see Francis Wilkinson, "The Running Mate Who Wasn't," *The New York Times Magazine*, Dec. 30, 2007, www.nytimes.com/2007/12/30/magazine/30wwln-eagleton-t.html, p. 14.

[43] Shenk, *op. cit.*, p. 167.

[44] *Ibid.*, p. 135.

[45] *Ibid.*, p. 136.

[46] Quoted in *ibid.*, p. 65.

[47] *Ibid.*, p. 178.

[48] For background, see Mary H. Cooper, "Prozac," *CQ Researcher*, Aug. 19, 1994, pp. 721-744, and Jane Tanner, "Mental Illness Medication Debate," *CQ Researcher*, Feb. 6, 2004, pp. 101-124.

[49] Quoted in John Morgan, "Terry Bradshaw's Winning Drive Against Depression," *USA Today*, www.usatoday.com/news/health/spotlighthealth/2004-01-30-bradshaw_x.htm.

[50] For background, see Jane Tanner, "Mental Health Insurance," *CQ Researcher*, March 29, 2002, pp. 256-288.

[51] For background, see Thomas J. Billitteri, "Financial Bailout," *CQ Researcher*, Oct. 24, 2008, pp. 865-888.

[52] For background, see "110th Congress Brings Victories for People with Mental Disabilities," Bazelon Center Mental Health Policy Reporter, Bazelon Center for Mental Health law, Oct. 16, 2008, www.bazelon.org.

[53] For background, see Samuel H. Zuvekas and Chad D. Meyerhoefer, "State Variations in the Out-of-Pocket Spending Burden for Outpatient Mental Health Treatment," *Health Affairs*, May/June 2009, p. 713.

FOR MORE INFORMATION

American Psychiatric Association, 1000 Wilson Blvd., Suite 1825, Arlington, VA 22209-3901; (702) 907-7300; www.psych.org. Membership organization of psychiatrists; produces the Diagnostic and Statistical Manual of Mental Disorders (DSM).

Bazelon Center for Mental Health Law, 1101 15th St., N.W., Suite 1212, Washington, DC 20005; (202) 467-5730; www.bazelon.org. Public-interest law firm specializing in rights of people with mental disabilities.

Depression and Bipolar Support Alliance, 730 N. Franklin St., Suite 501, Chicago, IL 60654-7225; (800) 826-3632; www.dbsalliance.org. Supports research and provides information and patient support through peer-led groups around the country.

Mental Health America (formerly National Mental Health Association), 2001 N. Beauregard St., 12th Floor, Alexandria, VA 22311; (703) 684-7722; www.nmha.org. Advocacy group working to increase access to appropriate mental-health care.

National Alliance for the Mentally Ill, 2107 Wilson Blvd., Suite 300, Arlington, VA 22201-3042; (703) 524-7600; www.nami.org. Advocacy group works to increase access to appropriate care for seriously mentally ill people.

National Alliance for Research on Schizophrenia and Depression (NARSAD), 60 Cutter Mill Rd., Suite 404, Great Neck, NY 11021; (800) 829-8289; www.narsad.org. Nonprofit group that funds research on severe mental illness.

National Institute of Mental Health, 6001 Executive Blvd., Rockville, MD, 20852; (301) 443-3673; www.nimh.nih.gov/health/topics/depression/index.shtml. The federal research agency for mental health.

Bibliography

Selected Sources

Books

Beck, Aaron T., and Brad A. Alford, *Depression: Causes and Treatment*, 2nd Edition, University of Pennsylvania Press, 2008.

Beck, a University of Pennsylvania professor emeritus in psychiatry, and Alford, a professor of psychology at the University of Scranton, update Beck's classic 1960s text on depression and cognitive therapy, the first psychotherapy proven effective as a depression treatment and originated by Beck.

Frank, Richard G., and Sherry A. Glied, *Better But Not Well: Mental Health Policy in the United States*, The Johns Hopkins University Press, 2006.

Based on epidemiological data, professors of health policy at Harvard (Frank) and Columbia universities conclude that more private-insurance coverage and expanded public programs have improved the lot of the average person suffering from a disorder like depression but that the most severely ill people still face an uphill struggle to get effective care.

Horwitz, Allan V., and Jerome C. Wakefield, *The Loss of Sadness: How Psychiatry Transformed Normal Sorrow into Depressive Disorder*, Oxford University Press, 2007.

Horwitz, a Rutgers University professor of sociology, and Wakefield, a New York University professor of social work, argue that today's depression diagnoses often extend beyond those with a mental disorder to include people suffering from "normal sadness."

Kramer, Peter D., *Against Depression*, Viking Penguin, 2005.

A psychotherapist and author of the controversial 1993 book *Listening to Prozac* discusses the history of melancholia and depression in Western society. He argues against what he calls our culture's misplaced veneration of "heroic melancholy" and calls for heightened respect for an often overlooked human capability — resilience in the face of trouble.

Articles

Bogira, Steve, "Starvation Diet: Coping With Shrinking Budgets in Publicly Funded Mental Health Services," *Health Affairs*, May/June 2009, p. 667.

State facilities offering care to severely mentally ill people are threatened with cutbacks, and advocates in several states are uniting to oppose the cuts.

Vedantam, Shankar, "The Depression Test," *The Washington Post*, May 26, 2009, p. E1.

Depression screening for children and teenagers is intended to head off mental illness before it takes hold, but critics argue that screening too often leads to an antidepressant prescription rather than counseling or psychotherapy to help the young person cope with problems.

Reports and Studies

Depression in Parents, Parenting, and Children: Opportunities in Improved Identification, Treatment, and Prevention, Committee on Depression, Parenting Practices, and the Healthy Development of Children, Institute of Medicine, 2009.

Parents with depression need much more extensive assistance to offset the severe consequences parental depressive illness can have on children.

Morbidity and Mortality in People with Serious Mental Illness, National Association of States Mental Health Program Directors, Oct. 2006, www.nasmhpd.org/general_files/pub lications/med_directors_pubs/Technical%20Report%20on% 20Morbidity%20and%20Mortaility%20-%20Final%2011-06. pdf.

On average, people with severe mental illness die 25 years earlier than the general population.

Preventing Mental, Emotional, and Behavioral Disorders Among Young People: Progress and Possibilities, Committee on the Prevention of Mental Disorders and Substance Abuse Among Children, Youth, and Young Adults, Institute of Medicine, 2009.

Research has uncovered early interventions that could effectively decrease the number of people who develop depression and other mental illnesses, according to an expert panel. The group recommends that mental-health prevention receive government and private-sector funding and attention equivalent to what's now provided for treatment of mental illness.

Ranking America's Mental Health: An Analysis of Depression Across the States, Thomson Healthcare/Mental Health America, Dec. 11, 2007, www.nmha.org/files/Ranking_Americas_ Mental_Health.pdf.

States with more mental-health workers, better health-insurance coverage, better access to insurance coverage for mental health and a better educated population have significantly lower rates of depression and suicide, according to a mental-health advocacy group.

Burnam, M. Audrey, Lisa S. Meredith, Terri Taniellan and Lisa H. Jaycox, "Mental Health Care for Iraq and Afghanistan War Veterans," *Health Affairs*, May/June 2009, p. 771.

Analysts from the RAND Corp. think tank find that 18.5 percent of returning troops suffer from either post-traumatic stress syndrome or depression and that increases in and additional targeted training of the mental-health workforce are required to treat these illnesses successfully.

The Next Step:

Additional Articles from Current Periodicals

Causes

Carey, Benedict, "Report on Gene for Depression, Widely Hailed in '03, Is Now Found to Be Flawed," *The New York Times*, June 17, 2009, p. A15.

The discovery, in 2003, of a gene that was supposedly responsible for causing depression has apparently not held up to scientific scrutiny.

Katz, Abram, "Brain Structure Examined in Mood Disorder?" *New Haven Register* (Connecticut), Aug. 21, 2008, p. A5.

Yale researchers are suggesting new ways to understand depression by examining the genetics of brain structure.

McDonough, Pat, "Teens Have Reason to Be Depressed," *Newsday* (New York), May 7, 2009, p. A31.

Family stress due to the economic downturn can aggravate depression among teenagers, especially for those already suffering.

Health Effects

"Depression May Up COPD Flare-Ups and Hospitalizations," Reuters Health Medical News, Oct. 24, 2008.

Depression and possibly anxiety appear to risk hospitalizations for chronic obstructive pulmonary disease.

"Depression May Up Risk of Alzheimer's Disease," Reuters Health Medical News, April 7, 2008.

People with a history of depression, especially if it began early in life, are apparently more vulnerable to Alzheimer's disease.

Elias, Marilyn, "Depression Can Break the Heart," *USA Today*, March 4, 2009, p. 7D.

Mounting scientific evidence indicates that depression makes individuals more vulnerable to heart disease.

Mental-Health Funding

Brooks, Matt, "Falling Short in Mental Health Care," *Indianapolis Star*, Dec. 9, 2007, p. 3.

A lack of mental-health care funding at the federal and state levels affects the ability of providers to deliver needed services to their communities.

Hogstrom, Erik, "Mental health care report: Poor grades for tri-states," *Telegraph Herald* (Dubuque, IA), March 24, 2009, p. A1.

Iowa and Illinois both received "Ds" from the National Alliance on Mental Illness (NAMI) on its latest report card assessing the nation's public mental-health care system for adults. Oklahoma showed the greatest improvement, rising from a D to a B. The assessment is based on criteria such as access to medicine, housing, family education and support for National Guard members.

Liebman, Glenn, "Safeguard N.Y.'s Mental Health Care," *Times-Union* (New York), Nov. 24, 2008, p. A9.

An economic recession should not preclude the New York state government from beefing up mental-health care funding.

Salzer, James, and Andy Miller, "Mental Care Funds at Risk," *Atlanta Journal-Constitution*, June 12, 2008, p. 1A.

Georgia Gov. Sonny Perdue is expected to shift $8.4 million in mental-care funding to other state programs.

Suicide

Grubbs, Miranda, "Teenagers fight depression, suicide; Colorado ranks high in troubling statistics," *Daily Camera* (Boulder, Colorado), July 27, 2008.

Colorado tops the nation in teen depression and ranks eighth in teen suicide.

McCall, William, "Study: Many asking suicide help may be depressed," The Associated Press, Oct. 7, 2008.

A new study suggests that one out of four terminally ill patients who request a prescription for a lethal overdose under Oregon's assisted suicide law may suffer from depression.

McCrimmon, Katie Kerwin, "Army Steps Up Battle Against Suicide," *Rocky Mountain News* (Colorado), Jan. 30, 2009, p. 30.

Depression among troops is largely attributed to repeated and long tours of duty in Iraq and Afghanistan.

Simon, Greg, "Childhood Depression and Suicide," *Seattle Post-Intelligencer*, July 5, 2007, p. B7.

About one in 20 adolescents suffers from clinical depression, with suicide being the third-ranking cause of deaths among teens.

CITING *CQ RESEARCHER*

Sample formats for citing these reports in a bibliography include the ones listed below. Preferred styles and formats vary, so please check with your instructor or professor.

MLA STYLE

Jost, Kenneth. "Rethinking the Death Penalty." CQ Researcher 16 Nov. 2001: 945-68.

APA STYLE

Jost, K. (2001, November 16). Rethinking the death penalty. *CQ Researcher, 11*, 945-968.

CHICAGO STYLE

Jost, Kenneth. "Rethinking the Death Penalty." *CQ Researcher*, November 16, 2001, 945-968.

In-depth Reports on Issues in the News

Are you writing a paper?

Need backup for a debate?

Want to become an expert on an issue?

For 80 years, students have turned to *CQ Researcher* for in-depth reporting on issues in the news. Reports on a full range of political and social issues are now available. Following is a selection of recent reports:

Civil Liberties
Closing Guantánamo, 2/09
Affirmative Action, 10/08
Gay Marriage Showdowns, 9/08
America's Border Fence, 9/08
Immigration Debate, 2/08

Crime/Law
Legalizing Marijuana, 6/09
Judicial Elections, 4/09
Mexico's Drug War, 12/08
Prostitution Debate, 5/08
Public Defenders, 4/08

Education
Reading Crisis? 2/08
Discipline in Schools, 2/08
Student Aid, 1/08
Racial Diversity in Public Schools, 9/07

Environment/Society
Future of Books, 5/09
Hate Groups, 5/09
Future of Journalism, 3/09
Confronting Warming, 1/09
Reducing Carbon Footprint, 12/08
Protecting Wetlands, 10/08

Health/Safety
Reproductive Ethics, 5/09
Extreme Sports, 4/09
Regulating Toxic Chemicals, 1/09
Preventing Cancer, 1/09
Heart Health, 9/08
Global Food Crisis, 6/08

Politics/Economy
Business Bankruptcy, 4/09
Future of the GOP, 3/09
Middle-Class Squeeze, 3/09
Public-Works Projects, 2/09

Upcoming Reports

Examining Forensic Science, 7/17/09   Energy Policy, 7/24/09   Fraying Safety Nets, 7/31/09

ACCESS

CQ Researcher is available in print and online. For access, visit your library or www.cqresearcher.com.

STAY CURRENT

To receive notice of upcoming *CQ Researcher* reports, or learn more about *CQ Researcher* products, subscribe to the free e-mail newsletters, *CQ Researcher Alert!* and *CQ Researcher News*: http://cqpress.com/newsletters.

PURCHASE

To purchase a *CQ Researcher* report in print or electronic format (PDF), visit www.cqpress.com or call 866-427-7737. Single reports start at $15. Bulk purchase discounts and electronic-rights licensing are also available.

SUBSCRIBE

Annual full-service *CQ Researcher* subscriptions—including 44 reports a year, monthly index updates, and a bound volume—start at $803. Add $25 for domestic postage.

CQ Researcher Online offers a backfile from 1991 and a number of tools to simplify research. For pricing information, call 800-834-9020, ext. 1906, or e-mail librarysales@cqpress.com.

Published by CQ Press, a Division of SAGE

www.cqresearcher.com

Examining Forensics

Are new research and oversight needed?

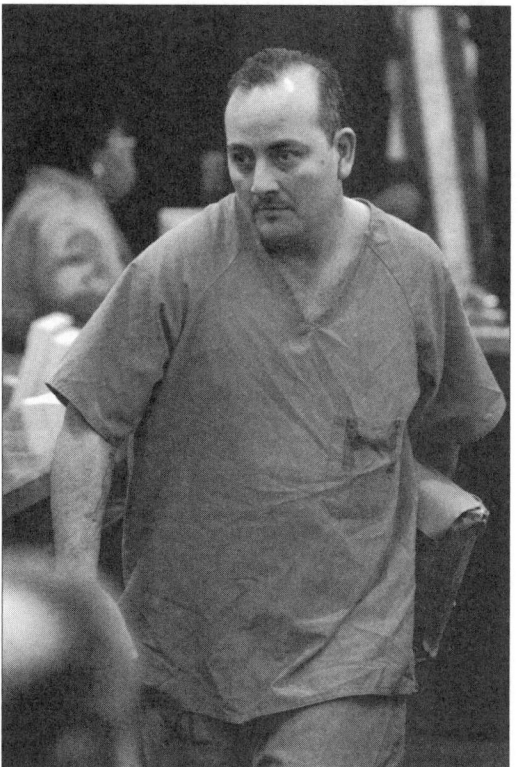

George Rodriguez is free after spending 17 years in a Texas prison for a rape he did not commit. Rodriguez, who was awarded $5 million, is one of four men released from prison in recent years because of errors in trial testimony by Houston crime lab examiners.

C rime-scene investigations play an important role in gathering evidence for criminal trials — from finger-prints and blood samples to DNA and digital data. But expert witnesses known collectively as forensic scientists or criminalists must analyze the evidence to help the judge and jury determine a defendant's guilt or innocence. A con-gressionally mandated study, however, says major changes are needed to strengthen forensic science. The reliability of some iden-tification techniques used in court is unproven, the report says, and even established techniques such as fingerprint analysis are less certain than commonly believed. In addition, crime laboratories are underregulated, underfunded and understaffed — and may have a conflict of interest because they are tied to law enforce-ment agencies. Criminal-defense lawyers are applauding the report, as are some forensics experts. But resistance from law enforcement agencies and crime labs themselves may slow or block reforms.

CQ Researcher • July 17, 2009 • www.cqresearcher.com
Volume 19, Number 25 • Pages 597-620

RECIPIENT OF SOCIETY OF PROFESSIONAL JOURNALISTS AWARD FOR
EXCELLENCE ◆ AMERICAN BAR ASSOCIATION SILVER GAVEL AWARD

Cover: AP Photo/David J. Phillip

CQ Researcher

July 17, 2009
Volume 19, Number 25

MANAGING EDITOR: Thomas J. Colin
tcolin@cqpress.com

ASSISTANT MANAGING EDITOR: Kathy Koch
kkoch@cqpress.com

ASSOCIATE EDITOR: Kenneth Jost

STAFF WRITERS: Thomas J. Billitteri, Marcia Clemmitt, Peter Katel

CONTRIBUTING WRITERS: Rachel Cox, Sarah Glazer, Alan Greenblatt, Reed Karaim Barbara Mantel, Patrick Marshall, Tom Price, Jennifer Weeks

DESIGN/PRODUCTION EDITOR: Olu B. Davis

ASSISTANT EDITOR: Darrell Dela Rosa

FACT-CHECKING: Eugene J. Gabler, Michelle Harris

CQ PRESS

A Division of SAGE

PRESIDENT AND PUBLISHER:
John A. Jenkins

EXECUTIVE DIRECTOR,
REFERENCE INFORMATION GROUP:
Alix B. Vance

CQ Press is a registered trademark of Congressional Quarterly Inc.

CQ Researcher (ISSN 1056-2036) is printed on acid-free paper. Published weekly, except; (Jan. wk. 1) (May wk. 4) (July wks. 1, 2) (Aug. wks. 3, 4) (Nov. wk. 4) and (Dec. wk. 4), by CQ Press, a division of SAGE Publications. Annual full-service subscriptions start at $803. For pricing, call 1-800-834-9020, ext. 1906. To purchase a CQ Researcher report in print or electronic format (PDF), visit www.cqpress.com or call 866-427-7737. Single reports start at $15. Bulk purchase discounts and electronic-rights licensing are also available. Periodicals postage paid at Washington, D.C., and additional mailing offices. POSTMASTER: Send address changes to CQ Researcher, 2300 N St., N.W., Suite 800, Washington, DC 20037.

Examining Forensics

BY KENNETH JOST

THE ISSUES

George Rodriguez spent 17 years in a Texas prison for a rape he did not commit. Scientific evidence helped put him behind bars. Scientific evidence got him out.

Now, Houston is being ordered to pay Rodriguez $5 million for a wrongful conviction that a federal court jury blamed on "deliberate indifference" to systemic problems at the city's crime laboratory. It was erroneous testimony from the director of the crime lab's biology unit, James Bolding, that helped convict Rodriguez in 1987 of the kidnap-rape of a teenage girl. And it was DNA testing years later that helped prove Rodriguez was innocent and another suspect — wrongly cleared by Bolding's evidence — possibly the perpetrator. [1]

The June 25 verdict and seven-figure damage award in Rodriguez's civil trial came after years of controversy over mismanagement and alleged misconduct at the Houston crime laboratory. "They had a policy of inadequate supervision and training," says Mark Wawro, one of Rodriguez's attorneys in the eight-day civil trial. "It was an absolute mess."

The trial also played out against the backdrop of a larger national debate not only about crime labs but also about the role that scientific evidence plays in criminal trials. Crime labs around the country, understaffed and overworked, are facing criticism for being too closely tied to law enforcement. At the same time, many of their techniques — including seemingly well-established methods such as fingerprinting and ballistics analysis — are

Mistakes by FBI fingerprint examiners led to the arrest of Oregon lawyer Brandon Mayfield after the deadly terrorist train bombings in Madrid, Spain, in 2004. He was released 18 days later. Crime labs around the country are facing criticism for being too closely tied to law enforcement. And many well-established forensic techniques — including fingerprinting — are routinely presented to juries as more precise than they actually are.

Getty Images/Greg Wahl-Stephens

being critically examined as inadequately grounded in true science and routinely presented to juries and courts as more precise and more reliable than they actually are. (*See sidebar, p. 602.*)

In a 255-page report released in February, the National Academy of Sciences' National Research Council (NRC) called for major changes in the way that forensic science is practiced, studied and governed in the United States. The report calls for:

• Mandatory accreditation of forensic science laboratories;

• Removal of public forensic laboratories from administrative control of police or prosecutors' offices;

• Individual certification of forensic

science professionals;

• New standards and quality control procedures; and

• Creation of an independent National Institute of Forensic Science to help fund research and oversee the profession. [2]

Forensic science — derived from the Latin word for "forum" to refer to the use of scientific evidence in court — is receiving increased attention in the United States these days thanks to the highly rated "CSI" family of television shows focusing on crime-scene investigations in Las Vegas, Miami and New York City. The mastery of forensic techniques used by TV crime lab examiners to unravel the most puzzling of crimes has led prosecutors and defense lawyers alike to talk of the "CSI effect" in criminal trials. The supposed effect is said either to help prosecutors if they present convincing forensic evidence as part of their case or to help the defense if the prosecution's case is short of the kind of compelling evidence found on the fictitious TV shows.

The NRC's report notes that advances in forensic science — especially DNA technology — have helped law enforcement identify and convict many criminal offenders. But it also says that in some cases "faulty forensic analyses may have contributed to wrongful convictions of innocent people." [3]

Rodriguez is one of four men released from prison in recent years because of belatedly found errors in trial testimony by Bolding or other Houston crime lab examiners. In 1987, Rodriguez was one of two suspects Houston police were investigating for the abduction and rape of a teenage girl after one of the assailants confessed but re-

From Bite Marks to DNA

Twelve distinct forensic science disciplines have been identified by the National Institute of Justice. Some are laboratory-based, such as DNA analysis, toxicology and drug analysis; some are based on expert interpretation of observed patterns, such as fingerprints, writing samples and bite marks; and some require training in law enforcement, such as crime-scene investigation, blood spatter analysis and crime reconstruction.

Forensic Science Disciplines

1. General toxicology
2. Firearms/toolmarks
3. Document verification
4. Trace evidence
5. Controlled substances
6. Biological/serology screening (including DNA analysis)
7. Fire debris/arson analysis
8. Impression evidence
9. Blood pattern analysis
10. Crime scene investigation
11. Medico-legal death investigation
12. Digital evidence

Source: National Institute of Justice, 2006

fused to identify his accomplice.

Police charged Rodriguez after Bolding said an analysis of pubic hair found on the victim excluded the other suspect, Isidro Yanez, but not Rodriguez. Bolding later testified to the same effect in Rodriguez's trial.

That testimony, Bolding conceded during Rodriguez's civil trial for damages, was wrong, but he claimed he thought it was right at the time. Rodriguez's lawyers argued that it was more than wrong. They contended there was no scientific basis for excluding the other suspect — blood-typing analysis is not that precise — and that Bolding had to have known

that at the time.

Fifteen years later, the Innocence Project took up Rodriguez's case. The New York City-based legal center has led the efforts to apply DNA testing to exonerate death-row inmates and other prisoners wrongfully convicted in the years before the more sophisticated identification technique became widely available. Tests showed the DNA evidence in the case did not come from Rodriguez but could have come from Yanez. Based on that evidence, Rodriguez was freed from prison in 2004 and his conviction set aside by the Texas Court of Criminal Appeals the next year. [4]

Representing Rodriguez in the civil

trial, Wawro and Innocence Project co-founder Barry Scheck argued the city was blind to the risk of constitutional violations from shoddy work by the crime lab. Lawyers for the city blamed the wrongful conviction on Bolding, who resigned his post in 2003, as well as on bad lawyering by both the prosecutor and Rodriguez's attorney in his criminal trial.

After initially reporting a deadlock, the eight-person jury agreed that the city had been "deliberately indifferent" to the risk of constitutional violations from problems at the crime lab. The $5 million award to Rodriguez, 48, who is now working in construction in Houston, represented compensation for lost earnings and pain and suffering. The city's lawyers say they will review the trial transcript before deciding whether to appeal.

William C. Thompson, a professor of law and criminology at the University of California-Irvine who investigated problems at the Houston crime lab for the local television station KHOU, calls the verdict "a costly but important lesson" for the city and for other crime labs. "Verdicts of this type show government officials that failure to maintain oversight and quality control can be expensive," he says.

Like Thompson, many other legal experts on forensic science are praising the National Research Council's (NRC) report for focusing attention on problems in the field that many practitioners have either minimized or denied. "There's quite a lot of problematic forensic science," says Jennifer Mnookin, a professor at the University of California-Los Angeles (UCLA) Law School and coauthor of a recently published legal treatise on expert evidence. "We need a significantly more substantial research basis for all this science." [5]

The president of the American Association of Forensic Sciences agrees. "A number of very important forensic theories and methods that have been sending people to prison have never been scientifically validated," says Thomas Bohan, a forensic science consultant in Peaks Island, Maine. But Bohan is also quick to note that forensic science practitioners were among those who called on Congress in 2005 to ask for the National Research Council study.

Bohan agrees with many of the recommendations in the report, including the removal of forensic science laboratories from control by law enforcement or prosecutorial agencies. The controversy in Houston has led to proposals, unacted on so far, to create an independent, regional crime laboratory. "It would be a good thing to get them out of police departments," Bohan says, "but I don't think it's going to happen."

Criminal defense lawyers are also praising the NRC report. "It's a great report," says Betty Layne DesPortes, a lawyer in Richmond, Va., and vice chair of the National Association of Criminal Defense Lawyers' forensic evidence committee. "It's a strong call for reforms."

Crime lab directors and prosecutors, however, temper any praise for the report with sharp criticism of many of its recommendations. "Overall, the community really embraces the report," says Dean Gialamas, director of forensic science services for the Orange County (Calif.) Sheriff-Coroner's Office and president of the American Society of Crime Laboratory Directors. But he disagrees with the report's call for more scientific validation of forensic techniques now used in courtrooms. "The community feels that there's enough science in what we do," he says.

"There are many, many good and positive things that can come from the report," says Scott Burns, executive director of the National District Attorneys Association. But Burns says some of the proposals would be "crippling to the criminal justice system." And he strongly defends the integrity of crime labs. "I very much disagree with the conclusion that they are not inde-

Backlogged Cases on the Rise

Backlogs* in the nation's 389 crime laboratories jumped 25 percent from 2002 to 2005. Overall, an estimated 2.7 million new cases were received by local, state and federal crime labs in 2005.

Case Backlogs at U.S. Crime Laboratories

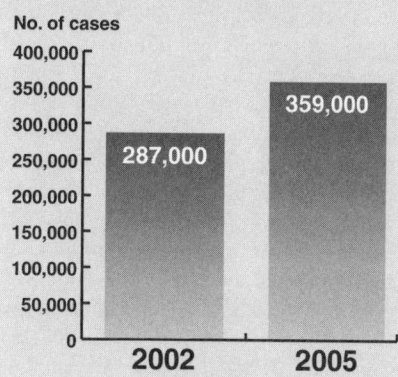

* *Cases not completed within 30 days*

Source: "Strengthening Forensic Science in the United States," National Research Council, 2009

pendent, not efficient, not professional or well-regulated," Burns says. "I would say they are all of these things."

The two opposing criminal-law groups differ on the role forensic science has played in the wrongful convictions that have been uncovered in the past — more than 200 of them as a result of DNA testing. They also differ on the need for judges to be more assertive in policing the use of forensic evidence in criminal trials. The report faults judges for allowing the use of forensic evidence without "fully understanding" the limitations of some forensic science disciplines. But it also concludes, "Judicial review, by itself, cannot cure the infirmities of the forensic science community."

As the debate over the report and

its recommendations continues within and outside the forensic science community, here are some of the major questions being considered:

Does misuse of forensic evidence contribute to wrongful convictions?

More than any other evidentiary method, DNA testing represents the gold standard of forensic science: a technique developed and tested in the laboratory and rigorously debated in courts before gaining widespread acceptance. And it has had a huge impact in the criminal justice system, helping to identify suspects, convict defendants, and, most dramatically, exonerate more than 200 people through post-conviction challenges in the United States since 1989.

Forensic science may have helped correct injustices in those cases, but a closer examination of the cases tells a disturbing story about the typical use of forensic science in criminal justice, according to Brandon Garrett, an associate professor at the University of Virginia Law School. In an article coauthored with Peter Neufeld, codirector of the Innocence Project, Garrett found that forensic evidence was misstated at trial in 60 percent of the cases available for study. That is, Garrett explains, the testimony given by forensic experts was "invalid" — either "unscientific" or "contrary to empirical data." [6]

Garrett and Neufeld stop short in the article of blaming any of the wrongful convictions on the overstated forensic evidence. But Innocence Project cofounder Scheck did make the connection as the National Research Council report was being released in February. "Judges and juries hear this evidence and rely on it to come up with convictions that have later proven to be wrong," Scheck told National Public Radio on Feb. 19. [7]

A prominent crime lab director, however, says the study gives a misleading picture of the role forensic science plays

Accuracy of Fingerprint Identification Is Questioned

National Research Council report calls for more research.

For more than a century, fingerprint analysis has been accepted, first in British and then in American courts, as evidence to help convict criminal defendants. No forensic technique is better known nor — until the advent of DNA profiling — was more widely accepted.

But fingerprint identification is not infallible. Just ask Brandon Mayfield, the Oregon civil rights lawyer who was wrongly implicated in the March 2004 terrorist train bombing in Madrid, Spain, on the basis of a fingerprint misidentification by two FBI examiners.

The FBI entered the case after Spanish police asked for help identifying a "latent print" — an accidental impression typically invisible to the naked eye — found on a piece of evidence in the investigation. Using the FBI's database containing millions of fingerprint records, an examiner identified the print as Mayfield's. Informed of the identification, a second examiner agreed.

Mayfield, a Muslim who had once represented a convicted terrorist in a child-custody dispute, was placed under surveillance and in May arrested as a material witness. By mid-April, however, Spanish police had concluded that the print was not Mayfield's; on May 19 they positively identified the fingerprint as that of an Algerian national.

Mayfield was released and given an apology and later $2 million in compensation. Meanwhile, the Justice Department's inspector general in March 2006 concluded that the examiners had failed to follow standard rules in their analysis. The misidentification could have been avoided, the inspector general's report concluded, by "a more rigorous application of several principles of latent fingerprint identification." [1]

At first telling, the episode may seem to contradict the accepted wisdom that an individual's fingerprints are unique. But the case actually teaches a different lesson, according to Simon Cole, an associate professor of criminology, law and society at the University of California-Irvine and author of a book on fingerprinting, *Suspect Identities.* [2]

"The uniqueness of fingerprints doesn't really tell you anything about the accuracy of fingerprint identification," Cole explains. "You and I don't need to have identical fingerprints. All we need is to have fingerprint patterns similar enough so that a fingerprint left by me might be attributed to you."

In short, Cole says, misidentifications are inevitable, but their frequency is unknown. "We really know almost nothing," he says. When mistakes come to light, the disclosures are often fortuitous, Cole adds. In Mayfield's case, for example, the misidentification would never have become known if the FBI had bowed to the doubts raised by the Spanish police and refrained from arresting him before the real suspect was found.

Despite wide agreement among experts on the risk of error, FBI examiners have routinely testified in court that fingerprint identification is always accurate. Cole says he appeared as a defense witness in a federal court hearing in Pennsylvania in 1999, where two of the FBI's leading examiners helped persuade a judge to reject a defense motion to limit fingerprint testimony.

Three years later, a different federal judge in Pennsylvania stunned the legal and forensic science communities in January 2002 with a ruling in a major murder case to prevent fingerprint examiners from declaring a latent print to be a "match" of a defendant's print. Two months later, however, Judge Louis

in criminal trials generally and the role it played in the wrongful convictions. The article "painted forensic sciences as being much more influential and powerful in the courtroom than they actually are," says John M. Collins, director of the DuPage County (Ill.) crime lab and chief managing editor of *Crime Lab Report.*

In a lengthy critique of an early version of Garrett's study, Collins and co-editor Jay Jarvis analyzed the same cases and found eyewitness misidentifications and false confessions a more frequent problem in the case than forensic science issues. [8] "When you look at the whole package, forensic science has been the leading preven-

ter of wrongful convictions," Collins says. "The chance of having a bad forensic result in a wrongful conviction . . . is so minuscule that it is not worth any public resource going into finding any remedies beyond what any crime laboratory is doing right now."

Prosecutors call the Innocence Project statistics misleading because they count as "exonerations" cases where convictions were reversed without a finding of actual innocence. "A lot of these people are not guilty, and a lot of them are not innocent," says Burns, with the district attorneys' group.

In any event, Burns stresses that the number represents cases over more than a decade, only four of them

since 2000. "A lot of the problems with professional standards have been corrected," he says.

For his part, crime lab director Gialamas blames misuse of forensic testimony not so much on crime lab examiners themselves as on the lawyers and judges. "We don't know as forensic scientists what happens to our testimony after we leave the courtroom," he says. "We don't know what's left in the minds of the court or the jury."

The National Research Council report, however, says "some" forensic science examiners are too reluctant to acknowledge potential errors and too likely to claim definitive conclusions from lab tests. "Assertions of a '100 percent

Pollak reversed himself. "In short, I have changed my mind," Pollak wrote in the 59-page opinion. [3]

Pollak's short-lived decision stood as the only ruling to limit fingerprint testimony in the United States until October 2007, when a Baltimore County, Md., judge barred fingerprint testimony altogether in a state murder case. Citing the Mayfield case, Judge Susan Souder said the prosecution had failed to prove that fingerprinting is an infallible methodology. Under Maryland rules, the pretrial ruling could not be appealed. Prosecutors responded by getting the U.S. attorney's office to indict the defendant on federal charges. The case is pending. [4]

Judge Louis Pollak blocked fingerprint examiners from declaring a latent print a "match" of a defendant's print in a murder case. He later reversed himself.

was given to DNA profiling before its acceptance. The report calls for more research but makes no recommendation about admitting or excluding fingerprint evidence until then. [5]

Cole is not calling for excluding fingerprint evidence, but he says courts have long allowed examiners to give "scientifically unsupportable" testimony that a latent print matches the defendant's. "That individualization testimony is too strong," he says. "That should not be permitted."

— *Kenneth Jost*

Law enforcement groups defend fingerprinting. "It's certainly a valid process," says Dean Gialamas, forensic services chief for the Orange County (Calif.) Sheriff-Coroner's Office.

Scott Burns, executive director of the National District Attorneys' Association, calls fingerprint identification "the gold standard" of forensic techniques, but adds, "There are always going to be some misidentifications."

The National Research Council report on forensic sciences published in February 2009 noted critically that courts have accepted fingerprint evidence "without the scientific scrutiny" that

[1] "A Review of the FBI's Handling of the Brandon Mayfield Case," Office of Inspector General, Department of Justice, March 2006, www.usdoj.gov/oig/special/s0601/final.pdf. For coverage of a summary of the report released earlier, see Tomas Alex Tizon, "Report Says Mistaken Arrest Was Due to FBI's Sloppy Work," *Los Angeles Times*, Jan. 7, 2006, p. A10.

[2] Simon A. Cole, *Suspect Identities: A History of Fingerprinting and Criminal Identification* (2001).

[3] The decision is *United States v. Llera Plaza*, 118 F.Supp.2d 549 (E.D. Pa. 2002). For coverage, see Joseph A. Slobodzian, "Judge to allow fingerprint evidence," *The Philadelphia Inquirer*, March 14, 2002.

[4] The decision is *Maryland v. Rose*, Case No. K06-0545 (Balt. County Cir. Court Oct. 19, 2007). For coverage, see Jennifer McMeniman, "Judge Bars Use of Fingerprints in Murder Trial," *The Baltimore Sun*, Oct. 23, 2007, p. A1.

[5] "Strengthening Forensic Science in the United States: A Path Forward," National Research Council, February 2009, pp. 3-14—3-16.

match' contradict the findings of proficiency tests that find substantial rates of erroneous results in some disciplines," such as voice identification and bite analysis, the report states. [9]

Bohan, president of the forensic science association, concedes that practitioners have been reluctant to concede weaknesses in the disciplines. "They say, 'Forensics has been validated by 100 years of jury trials,' " Bohan says. "This report is going to put the lie to that."

But Bohan also says the National Research Council report "spread the brush too widely" in suggesting that forensic science practitioners are generally guilty of exaggerating the certainty of their

testimony in court, "by which they mean the FBI," Bohan says. "It's the FBI people that go in there and say our techniques have no error at all."

Prosecutors say that even if dubious forensic testimony is presented in court, defense lawyers have more than sufficient opportunity under the adversary system to challenge or refute it. But defense lawyers say they often lack the time, resources or expertise to successfully challenge forensic testimony.

Bohan as well as many academic experts agree with the defense lawyers. "The adversarial system isn't up to" weeding out misleading testimony, Bohan says.

"The Houston Police Department

crime lab was miscomputing the statistics in DNA testing for well over a decade," the University of California's Thompson says. "If the criminal justice system is so good at uncovering the problem, why did it take journalists to uncover it?"

Should judges adopt stricter standards on the use of forensic science?

An FBI toolmark examiner was one of the government's witnesses in Timothy McVeigh's trial for the 1995 bombing of the federal office building in Oklahoma City. U.S. District Judge Richard Matsch allowed the examiner to testify that a drill bit found in the home of codefendant Terry Nichols "produced marks" found on a padlock from the quarry from which the explosives used in the bombing were stolen.

When the examiner appeared in Nichols' separate trial a few months later, however, U.S. District Court Judge Steven Taylor prevented him from testifying to an actual match. Instead, the judge allowed the examiner to testify only about "what he saw through the microscope" and then to point out "the similarities" that he observed. [10]

The judges' different approaches illustrate one of the issues emphasized by forensic science critics. The University of California's Thompson labels the problem "overclaiming — the tendency of forensic scientists to make extremely strong claims, such as the ability to identify a particular fingerprint or a particular gun as unique in the world, without having done studies to back that up."

Thompson views the National Research Council's report as "an indictment of the judiciary for not adequately policing and screening scientific evidence, notwithstanding the fact that courts under their own rules of evidence only allow that evidence to go to the jury if it has scientific validity." Despite those rules, he says, "they've been allowing all sorts of forensic evidence to go to the jury without there being a scientific foundation for it."

In federal courts, the admissibility of scientific evidence is governed by a 1993 Supreme Court decision, *Daubert v. Merrill Dow Pharmaceuticals.* The ruling requires expert testimony to have a "reliable foundation" but gives judges broad discretion in carrying out what the opinion calls the "gatekeeper" function on admitting or excluding such evidence. [11] States set their own rules on admissibility of expert evidence, and they vary widely.

The forensic science association's Bohan believes the National Research Council report will prompt judges to

look harder before admitting scientific testimony. "Some judges excluded things that should not have been excluded, and some judges let in things that should not have been let in, because they didn't understand it," he says. "Many of the judges would be the first to admit they're not scientists."

The report faults judges, saying that courts "have been utterly ineffective" in addressing the problem of inadequately validated scientific testimony. But it cites judges' "lack of scientific expertise" in explaining that the solution to the problem lies with the forensic science community, not the courts. "The legal system is ill-equipped to correct the problems of the forensic science community," the report states. [12]

"I would have liked them to have confronted more directly the admissibility question for courts," says UCLA's professor Mnookin. "They don't come out and give a judge who is trying to think through these things any clear advice about what to do."

In its report, the National Research Council questions the basis of many types of forensic evidence introduced in court, especially in criminal cases. The report finds no scientific support for use of hair comparisons as individual identification, no scientific studies to support bite-mark matches and only limited knowledge for bullet-match reviews. Even fingerprint science, the report says, "does not guarantee that two analysts following it will obtain the same results." [13]

Prosecutors generally defend the use of forensic testimony, even in some of the disputed areas, according to Burns, who was a trial prosecutor in Utah for 16 years and deputy drug czar in the Bush administration before assuming his post with the district attorneys' group. For example, he says toolmark evidence "has proven to be a legitimate forensic science and helpful as one aspect or one piece of evidence." He also says he has introduced bite-mark evidence in cases himself but

was careful to present the evidence as "consistent" with identification rather than proof of an absolute match.

Interestingly, crime lab director Collins in Illinois wants judges to be more cautious in controlling forensic science testimony. "Many of us in forensic science feel it would be better if we go in and make presentations and then answer questions," he says. He blames "overzealous prosecutors" for exaggerating the results in many instances.

For their part, criminal defense lawyers agree that judges need more education about scientific issues and should be stricter in deciding whether and how to admit forensic evidence. But DesPortes of the criminal defense lawyers' group says a greater need is for judges to provide funds for the defense to hire their own experts in indigent cases. "A lot of times you don't get an expert because you can't tell why you need an expert," she says. "You can't show a court why the conclusion is wrong until you have your own expert."

Should crime laboratories be independent of law enforcement agencies?

When the Michigan State Police completed an audit of the Detroit Police Department crime lab in September 2008, examiners reported finding a nearly 10 percent error rate out of 200 ballistics analyses studied, along with a host of other procedural and quality-control lapses. The problems were so widespread that Mayor Ken Cockrel Jr. and Police Chief James Barren responded on Sept. 25 by closing the facility altogether.

Six months later, Wayne County prosecutor Kym Worthy reported that her office had identified 147 cases of convicted defendants requiring re-examination of evidence in the light of the crime lab's problems. Those cases were just "the tip of the iceberg," Worthy told the *Detroit Free Press.* Meanwhile, the state police crime lab is facing a six-to-eight-month backlog because of a near tripling of its caseload with the addition of about 20,000 cases taken over from Detroit. [14]

Like Detroit's, most crime labs in the United States are administered by law enforcement agencies, including, most conspicuously, the 500-employee FBI laboratory in Quantico, Va., outside Washington. Such arrangements lead to "significant concerns related to the independence of the laboratory and its budget," the National Research Council report says.

To resolve the concerns, the report says that public forensic science laboratories should be "independent of or autonomous within law enforcement agencies." Under such a structure, the report says the laboratory would set its own priorities and not have to compete with the parent law enforcement agencies for funds. In addition, independence or autonomy would resolve the "cultural pressures" created by different missions between the laboratory and the parent agency. [15]

The report also calls for creation of a new National Institute of Forensic Science as an independent federal entity charged with establishing standards for laboratories, promoting peer-reviewed research and funding state and local forensic science agencies. The report acknowledges that "budgetary constraints" would have to be overcome, but says, "Congress must take aggressive action if the worst ills of the forensic science community are to

be cured." [16]

The various groups and experts differ on the merits of those two proposals but generally agree that both remedies are somewhere between improbable and impossible. The national institute is "a good idea," says Bohan of the forensic science association. But he quickly adds, "Everybody thinks that Congress is not going to do that."

"I agree with the report that in order for us to have the kind of revolutionary change that the report is calling for, we're going to need a new federal agency of some sort," says the University of California's Thompson. "Whether there will be political support for that, I don't know."

Burns of the district attorneys' group flatly opposes the idea. "It's too expensive, and frankly, I don't see there being a need," he says. The Department of Justice went on record questioning the proposal as unnecessary at a Senate Judiciary Committee hearing in March. From the other side,

DesPortes of the defense lawyers group says the proposal could help increase funding for forensic science, but adds, "I think the reforms can be done without it."

Independence or autonomy for forensic laboratories at the state or local level may be more achievable. Virginia, for example, moved its Division of Forensic Science from the Department of Criminal Justice Services into a new Department of Forensic Science in 2005 under the governor's secretary of public safety.

But Burns disputes the need for any change. "As for independence, I think it is absurd for those of us in the criminal justice system to say that we're not impartial," he says.

Gialamas, head of the crime laboratory association, says the group favors autonomy, but not separation from law enforcement agencies. "We don't feel the physical removal of the labs from the agencies is necessary," he says.

Crime lab director Collins says a structural change would not necessarily improve the quality of work. "There are many, many police agencies out there that do a good job," he says. But Collins says the competition for funds between labs and the parent law enforcement agency is a problem. "If crime labs are ever pulled out of police agencies, it will be because they are not advocating for them, they are not making sure that they're providing the funding, the management support that the labs need," he says.

From the opposite side, DesPortes calls removing laboratories from law enforcement agencies "a good first

The ability of TV crime scene investigators to solve the most puzzling cases has created the so-called "CSI" effect in criminal courtrooms. It supposedly either helps prosecutors if they present convincing forensic evidence or aids the defense if the prosecution's case lacks the kind of dramatic evidence typically uncovered on the fictitious TV shows.

www.sidereel.com

step." But, she adds, "I don't think it solves the problem."

"Pressure on examiners can exist even having the lab out of law enforcement," DesPortes says. "You can have that even when law enforcement isn't the oversight agency. I don't know that it's who is your boss. It's which expert are you talking to." ∎

BACKGROUND

'Silent Evidence'

The use of science and medicine to detect crime and identify wrongdoers dates from ancient times in Egypt, Greece, Rome and China. Forensic science and forensic medicine began to emerge as systematic disciplines in Europe in the 16th and 17th centuries, and the use of forensic techniques in civil and criminal trials spread throughout Western Europe by the end of the 19th century. The 20th century brought the establishment of the first crime laboratories and the widespread use of such well-known techniques as fingerprinting and blood typing. With the increasing use of forensic evidence, however, came formal debates in court about its limits and potential risks. [17]

Some evidence of medico-legal associations can be found in Egyptian codes of law dating from 1700 to 1400 B.C., according to a historical survey in a book examining the current controversies about forensic science by forensic nurse Kelly M. Pyrek. [18] Evidence about medical issues was presented in courts in Greece by the physician Hippocrates (ca. 460 B.C.-370 B.C.) and by experts identified as *amici curiae* (friends of the court) in Roman times. The Roman physician Antistius conducted a post-mortem on the body of Julius Caesar (44 B.C.) and of the 23 stab wounds identified one to the

chest as the cause of death. A Chinese handbook published in 150 A.D. outlined general autopsy techniques and included comments on determining, for example, whether a person found in water was dead or alive before submersion.

Forensic medicine started to become a more systematic discipline by the late Renaissance period (16th and 17th centuries). A major figure was the Roman physician Paolo Zacchia (1584-1659), whose nine-volume work *Quaestiones Medico-Legales* covered a full range of forensic medicine topics and earned him the title of father of legal medicine. Zacchia testified frequently in court, where one scholar has written he respected the judge's role but also recognized the judge's need for expert assistance in deciding matters outside the judge's competence. [19] By the mid-17th century, physicians were also being called on to testify in trials throughout Europe.

Forensic sciences advanced more rapidly in the 19th and early 20th centuries. Mathieu Orfila (1787-1853) is credited as the father of forensic toxicology for his treatise on the detection of poisons. The French police officer Alphonse Bertillon (1853-1914) pioneered the study of anthropometry — the use of human body measurements for criminal identification. The son of a statistician, Bertillon devised a system of measuring the head and body and recording tattoos or other markings as a more reliable method of identification than eyewitness testimony. The English scientist Francis Galton (1822-1911), a half-cousin to Charles Darwin, built on earlier work by two other Britons to develop the first scientific study of fingerprinting. The classification system he devised remains in use today. Also still in use today is the technique of blood typing, first demonstrated in 1915 by the Italian scientist Leone Lattes (1887-1954).

A unifying construct for these various advances was provided early in the 20th century by Edmond Locard

(1877-1966), a French academic trained in law and medicine. Locard's "exchange principle" holds that every criminal leaves traces at the scene of a crime and takes traces of the crime scene away. This "silent" evidence "cannot be wrong," Locard postulated, and its value can be diminished only by "human failure to find it, study and understand it." Along with this theoretical advance, Locard is also credited with establishing the first police crime laboratory when he persuaded the Lyons police department to provide him two attic rooms and two assistants for practical application of his work.

From early times on, courts had generally welcomed the evidence developed from these advancing forensic techniques. In the United States, however, a federal court in 1923 drew the line at admitting evidence from a primitive "lie detector." The ruling in *Frye v. United States* established what stood for 70 years as the prevailing standard for allowing forensic evidence in court. In *Frye*, a murder defendant's lawyer sought to introduce testimony from an examiner who had administered a "systolic blood pressure deception test" to the defendant. The evidence was disallowed, the defendant convicted and the issue raised on appeal. In a terse, 644-word opinion, the appeals court recognized that experts could testify in court about specialized subjects, but said the discipline or method "must be sufficiently established to have gained general acceptance in the particular field in which it belongs." The "deception test," the judges concluded, had not passed that test, and the results were properly disallowed. [20]

'Deficient Practices'

Forensic science appeared to be advancing through the 20th century with the seeming professionalization of police crime laboratories and the development of new identification tech-

Continued on p. 608

Chronology

Before 1900
Science and medicine are used in criminal investigations and trials since ancient times; forensic disciplines develop rapidly in 19th century.

17th Century
Roman physician Paolo Zacchia (1584-1659) authors nine-volume work on forensic medicine.

1900-1970s
Forensic techniques gain widespread acceptance in U.S.

1910-1911
Fingerprints introduced as evidence in murder trial in Illinois (1910); Illinois Supreme Court rules evidence admissible (1911).

1915
First demonstration of blood typing.

1923
Federal appeals court disallows evidence from early lie detector.

1932
FBI crime laboratory established.

1963
FBI develops bullet-lead analysis; method is later discarded but not repudiated.

1978
Law Enforcement Assistance Administration finds significant error rates in nation's crime laboratories.

1979
FBI begins automating fingerprint records. . . . Bite-mark evidence helps convict American serial killer Theodore Bundy.

1980s-1990s
DNA analysis is introduced in police work; Supreme Court sets "reliability" standard for scientific evidence.

1987
DNA typing first used as evidence in criminal cases in U.S.

1990
FBI launches DNA databank; expanded in 1998 to include profiles from state, local law enforcement agencies.

1992
Innocence Project founded at New York University School of Law to use DNA testing to reexamine evidence in suspected wrongful convictions.

1993
Supreme Court says federal judges must ensure scientific evidence is "reliable" before admitting it in court. . . . West Virginia Supreme Court of Appeals faults "willful false testimony" by former state serologist Fred Zain in dozens of cases.

Mid-1990s
Backlogged cases mount at crime labs nationwide.

1997
Inspector general finds FBI guilty of "deficient practices."

1999
FBI establishes integrated fingerprint identification system.

2000-Present
Forensic science gains in popularity with "CSI" TV series; controversies grow.

2000
"CSI: Crime Scene Investigation" premieres on CBS-TV. . . . Congress authorizes financial assistance for crime labs, but over next six years appropriates only a small fraction of total amount.

2002
Federal judge, in high-profile murder case, initially bars fingerprint examiners from testifying to a "match," but reverses decision two months later.

2003
Houston crime lab's DNA unit is closed after state audit finds widespread errors.

2004
Oregon lawyer Brandon Mayfield is wrongly implicated in terrorist bombings in Madrid because of fingerprint misidentification by FBI.

2007
Innocence Project study finds forensic evidence misused in many wrongful convictions. . . . State judge in Maryland bars fingerprint testimony in murder case.

2008
Detroit crime lab closed after audit discloses error in ballistics analysis, procedural irregularities.

2009
National Research Council report on forensic science calls for more funding, better research, stronger oversight and new federal agency; report is well-received, but major changes are resisted by law enforcement, crime labs. . . . Supreme Court says lab examiners must testify in court; written "certificates of analysis" not sufficient. . . . Houston man awarded $5 million for wrongful conviction attributed to "deliberate indifference" to crime lab problems.

Digital Detectives Are Just a Click Away

Criminals who use electronics invariably leave a trail.

Criminals who surf the Web and use cellphones leave digital trails that investigators often can easily follow. The virtual impossibility of erasing their electronic tracks has made digital forensics a key tool for criminal investigators, along with fingerprint identification and DNA analysis.

Dennis Rader, the infamous BTK ("Bind, Torture and Kill") serial killer who plagued Wichita, Kan., for years, was caught because of a message on a floppy disk he sent to police to taunt investigators. Although Rader had erased the disk's contents before sending his message, data on the disk still contained the name "Dennis" and linked him to a local Lutheran church. Standard police work did the rest.

"As I understand it, [the disk] had a number or [electronic] thumbprint on it that showed it had been used in the church computer," recalled the Rev. Michael Clark of Christ Lutheran Church. [1]

In 2008, in Burlington, Vt., a couple of weeks after police found the body of 12-year-old Brooke Bennett, investigators uncovered online correspondence on her estranged stepfather's computer linking her 42-year-old uncle to sexually assaulting and murdering his niece. [2]

And in a trial now in progress in Perugia, Italy, investigators used data on a notebook computer to discredit the alibi of Raffaele Sollecito, the former boyfriend of American exchange student Amanda Knox. She is charged along with Sollecito with the sexual assault and murder of Knox's British roommate, Meredith Kercher. Sollecito and Knox claimed to have been watching a movie on Sollecito's computer in his apartment on the night of Kercher's murder, but no streaming or downloads occurred on the laptop during that period, police said. [3]

Responding to the growing use of digital forensics, the U.S. Secret Service in June 2008 launched the National Computer Forensics Institute (NCFI) near Birmingham, Ala., to train law enforcement personnel from across the country. The FBI's Regional Computer Forensics Laboratory network provides 14 digital forensics laboratories — with two more in Southern California and New Mexico currently in development — accessible by 4,750 law enforcement agencies across 17 states. More are planned for the future in order to accommodate other states.

NCFI deputy director and former prosecutor Barry Page said that until fairly recently digital evidence uncovered by investigators almost always involved child pornography cases. Now digital evidence is used in a wide range of cases. Drug dealers arrange drug buys via text messaging. Murderers often search the Internet to learn about poisons or how to dispose of a body. E-mails provide clues to timelines and motives. [4]

The viral nature of digital information almost always ensures retrieval by investigating authorities. "When you look at a simple text message that you and I exchange, yeah, it might be on my phone and it might be on your phone, but it could also be somewhere on the phone company's logs," said Gavin Manes, president of Digital Forensics Professionals, in Tulsa, Okla. "It's very

---

Continued from p. 606

niques. By the end of the 20th century, however, many of the techniques, including bite-mark analysis and bullet-lead analysis, were being questioned as lacking in scientific validity. In addition, high-profile scandals involving false or erroneous testimony by forensic examiners highlighted the risk of institutional bias in the close connection between law enforcement and forensics. Despite those problems, however, one powerful forensic technique emerged in the 1980s and, after some controversy, gained acceptance by the 1990s: DNA analysis.

From the 1920s on, the FBI has led the way in the United States in applying forensic techniques to solving and prosecuting crimes. The bureau's legendary director, J. Edgar Hoover, began hiring experts on a case-by-case basis

after taking office in 1924 and then backed agent Charles Apfel in establishing an in-house laboratory in 1932. In an official history, the FBI credits the laboratory with helping convict the Lindbergh baby kidnaper Bruno Richard Hauptmann, cracking enemy codes during World War II and pioneering the detection of computer crimes by the end of the century. [21] From the start, the bureau also shared its work with state and local law enforcement agencies. By the 1970s, it was also spurring the creation of counterpart crime labs in local police departments.

The growing interest in forensic science in the United States and elsewhere was reflected in the establishment of the American Association of Forensic Sciences in 1950 and the publication the next year of one of the

first comprehensive criminalistics textbooks, *Crime Investigations*, by University of California criminologist Paul Kirk. Meanwhile, criminalists were continuing to refine existing methods of identification, such as fingerprinting and blood typing, and to explore new methods. In the United States, the FBI began developing bullet-lead analysis in the 1960s, based on the theory that each bullet has a unique chemical composition. Bite-mark analysis began to be introduced as evidence in the 1950s and gained currency when it helped to convict American serial killer Theodore Bundy in 1979.

Law enforcement put these techniques into practice, however, faster than academic scientists could test the methods or professional associations could police forensic examiners. [22] A three-year

hard to get rid of information once it is created, especially if you release it to the Internet or the phone company. Once you give it to someone else, it is very difficult to pull it back." [5]

When criminals cannot get rid of shared material, they may try to manipulate potentially damaging digital information. Such evidence, by its very nature, has become easy to change. The science of steganography allows digital files and messages to be rendered invisible via data concealment and encryption techniques.

Photos have been doctored via Photoshop to eliminate possibly incriminating evidence. Even the al Qaeda terrorist group is thought to have concealed messages in photos posted on the online auction site eBay. [6] But digital forensic experts have devised software programs that reveal messages and flaws in altered photos by examining factors such as lighting, color, geometric differences and incongruent patterns.

Similarly, forensic detectives use special software programs to detect non-Internet-related and unshared activity on a hard drive, even after the "delete" button has been hit. Most people "aren't savvy enough to cover their tracks," said digital detective Chris Kitto of Beaverton, Ore. "For the most part, they're not rocket scientists."

"Somebody might have written an embezzlement letter from home, printed it out, but didn't save it. There are three or four places on the hard drive where we can recover it," Kitto explained. [7]

Can electronic evidence ever be totally erased? Breaking a hard drive apart and burning it will completely destroy files. And supposedly foolproof data-deletion programs, such as FINALeRASER and Active Kill Disk, will do the trick less messily, but they require a high degree of technical prowess to employ.

For the most part, however, the difficulty in eliminating information that has already been created tends to give investigators the upper hand.

"Digital information never goes away," says Manes. "It is very difficult to delete or remove something that is digital." [8]

— *Darrell Dela Rosa*

[1] Quoted in Dion Lefler and Tim Potter, "Pastor: Disk Gave Police Key Clue," *Wichita* [Kan.] *Eagle*, March 2, 2005, p. A1.

[2] Joel Banner Baird, "Digital Sleuths Play a Key Role in Brooke's Case," *Burlington* [Vt.] *Free Press*, July 13, 2008, p. A1.

[3] Marta Falconi, "Witness: No Proof for Slay Suspect Alibi," The Associated Press, March 14, 2009.

[4] Val Walton, "Computer Forensics Institute Trains Hundreds," *Birmingham* [Ala.] *News*, July 2, 2009, p. B1.

[5] Quoted in Jim Stafford, "Sender Beware!" *The Oklahoman*, Jan. 29, 2008, p. 2B.

[6] Jack Kelley, "Militants Wire Web With Links to Jihad," *USA Today*, July 10, 2002, p. A1.

[7] Quoted in Tom Vogt, "FBI Lab Clues Police In," *The* [Wash.] *Columbian*, Feb. 12, 2009, p. A1.

[8] Quoted in Stafford, *op. cit.*

investigation of crime labs by the federal Law Enforcement Assistance Administration in the late 1970s found what a scholar later described as a "surprisingly large number" of erroneous reports. The crime lab group responded with a voluntary accreditation program, which went into operation in 1989. But by the mid-1990s only one-third of the nation's 400 crime labs had complied. Mandatory accreditation proposals went unacted on through the 1990s, as did proposals for certification of individual examiners. [23]

High-profile scandals failed to overcome resistance to regulation and oversight. In one of the most dramatic instances, West Virginia's highest court found in 1993 that Fred Zain, a former state police serologist, had falsified evidence in dozens of cases; by

that time, Zain had gone on to work in Bexar County, Texas (San Antonio), where he was fired amidst similar accusations. [24] The FBI lab itself was rocked by disclosures in 1997 of shoddy work and overstated testimony by 13 employees. In a massive report, the Justice Department's inspector general found instances of "deficient practices" in many cases, including the trial of the 1993 World Trade Center bombing conspirators. FBI Director Louis Freeh acknowledged the failings and promised to institute changes. [25]

Courts also posed few obstacles to use of forensic evidence in criminal trials. A broad revision of the *Federal Rules of Evidence* in 1975 established a lax standard for admitting "probative" evidence unless it might be prejudicial, confusing or misleading. De-

fense lawyers in civil cases criticized the rule for allowing plaintiffs to use "junk science" to link disease or injuries to corporate conduct. The Supreme Court gave them a partial victory in 1993 with a ruling, *Daubert v. Merrill Dow Pharmaceuticals*, which stressed federal judges' responsibilities to make sure that any scientific evidence was "reliable." [26] The ruling appeared to have some modest impact in civil cases, but hardly any in criminal trials. Indeed, bullet-lead and bite-mark analyses continued to be introduced through the 1990s despite emerging doubts about the validity of both techniques. [27]

The success of DNA analysis — labeled "DNA fingerprinting" in its early years — gave forensic science enhanced prestige even though it emerged not

Gathering Evidence on the Battlefield

Forensic scientists are tracking terrorists in Iraq and Afghanistan.

Forensic technology is leaving the streets of the United States for the deserts of Iraq and the mountains and valleys of Afghanistan. "Battlefield forensics" is the Pentagon term for a major, new initiative to equip combat personnel with tools and training to gather evidence. Fingerprints can be used, for instance, to hunt down bomb-makers.

According to the Army, its database of more than 3 million biometric files has led to nearly 700 detentions in Iraq, and to 18 convictions in Baghdad's Central Criminal Court. In addition, about 60 potential terrorists were blocked from entering the United States. [1]

"Just as traditional law enforcement investigations utilize forensic science, so can the military to support counterinsurgency efforts," Lt. Col. Lee M. Packnett, a U.S. Army spokesman, says in an e-mail interview.

Counterinsurgency warfare puts U.S. personnel in areas where enemy fighters often blend in with ordinary civilians. Hence the rising military interest in biometrics and other forensic tools with which troops can zero in on enemies. "When a crime or terrorist activity is committed, materials are collected from the scene and upon appropriate analysis can yield information regarding who, what, when, where and how an incident occurred," Packnett wrote. "As terrorist activity has grown in recent years, there has been greater focus on forensic evidence collection and necessary training at the tactical level."

Until recently, the only armed forces units that did forensics work were the military police, Packnett says. Now, the Army is teaching evidence-collection techniques to members of front-line units such as the 82nd Airborne Division, as well as all other units that will pass through the Joint Readiness Training Center at Fort Polk, La., this year. Two counterpart installations, the National Training Center in Fort Irwin, Calif.; and the Joint Multinational Readiness Center in Hohenfels, Germany, are also hosting forensics sessions. [2]

In Iraq, a so-called weapons intelligence team composed of Air Force, Army and Navy personnel trained in explosives detonation, photography, intelligence and other specialties runs "crime-scene investigations" at sites hit by improvised explosive devices (IEDs) in order to trace bombs back to those who built and installed them. "Our adversaries are out there using modified explosives and trying to find unique ways to use those weapons against Iraqis and coalition forces," Air Force Chief Master Sgt. Kevin Touhey, the team's superintendent, told the Defense Department's American Forces Press Service. "So our role is to go out there and provide battlefield forensics to better defeat them, and beyond that, try to stop them from ever being on the streets." [3]

The Defense Department (DoD) isn't limiting itself to training troops in forensics skills such as dusting surfaces for fingerprints. On its Web site for prospective contractors, the Pentagon invites proposals for battlefield adaptations of several forensic tools, including: a device or kit that a "warfighter in the field" can use to test for explosives ingredients and gunshot residue, as well as the presence of opium, marijuana, tranquilizers and other drugs; a "documentation device," part camera with date- and location-identifiers built in, along with a printer for an adhesive coded tag for each piece of evidence and a tool to capture digital images of latent fingerprints on paper documents of all sizes. [4]

In addition to specific requests, the Pentagon is casting a wide net. "DoD seeks novel, rugged approaches to any forensic task expected to be carried out in field conditions," the department's Web site for technical proposals tells prospective inventors. "You may submit any idea, innovation, concept or research topic." [5]

---

from crime labs but from true scientific laboratories. But it also added to the day-to-day problems that crime labs faced. By the mid-1990s, the FBI was estimating that only one-fifth of the nearly 300,000 DNA samples collected had actually been analyzed. A comprehensive survey by *USA Today* in 1996 found increasing case backlogs at more than three-fourths of the labs responding. "Justice isn't being served," Michele Kestler, director of the Los Angeles Police Department's crime lab, told the newspaper, "and that's true all over." [28]

'Room for Improvement'?

Two forensic identification techniques — fingerprinting and DNA typing — were helping to fill nationwide databanks as the 20th century ended and the 21st began. DNA analyses were used to exonerate wrongfully convicted defendants even as police were using DNA samples from offenders to solve cold cases. Alongside those successes, however, missteps or worse were found at crime labs around the country, including the FBI's. Congress tried to help in 2000 by authorizing

grants to crime labs, but lawmakers appropriated only a fraction of the promised sums. The decision in 2005 to commission the National Research Council study then set the stage for a broad look not only at funding and staffing levels but also at basic questions about the organization and governance of forensic science.

The FBI had begun automating fingerprint records in 1979 and marked a milestone two decades later with the establishment of the Integrated Automated Fingerprint Identification System (IAFIS) in 1999. With 55 million fingerprint and criminal history records collected from

One group of scientists is proposing to develop for combat conditions a portable X-ray fluorescence device designed to analyze small pieces of material for important evidence. "If you're looking at an explosive and want to know where it came from, the metal in the container might tell you," says one of the developers, Jeff Schweitzer, a professor of physics at the University of Connecticut in Storrs.

Originally, Schweitzer and his colleagues had civilian police uses in mind, but they found the National Institute of Justice — where they were seeking a grant to produce a final prototype — focused almost entirely on projects related to DNA evidence.

To a great extent, the Pentagon has no choice but to push for new high-tech tools. The enemy is taking the same approach. A draft report last year by the Army's 304th Military Intelligence Battalion disclosed that Islamist militants in Iraq and Afghanistan were actively researching, training in and using a variety of smartphone capabilities, including cameras. A member of the Mujahedeen Army of Iraq — which ran its own online discussion group on mobile technology — "recommended using the phone/video camera for monitoring enemy activities and operations," said the report, classified "For Official Use Only," and disclosed on the Federation of American Scientists Web site. [6]

Perhaps not coincidentally, the Pentagon's request-list of proposals for specific technology includes a "small, rugged" device that would determine the source of images in a cellphone camera — that is, were they snapped "live" or downloaded? [7]

U.S. and Canadian soldiers remove a body from an al Qaeda mass grave in Afghanistan's Tora Bora region in 2001 for examination by forensic experts.

Getty Images/Joe Raedle

Despite jihadists' growing technological sophistication, American forensics experts argue the military's forensics initiative plays to U.S. strength. "This fits with America's MO," says Brian Gestring, one of Schweitzer's colleagues on the X-ray project and a former criminal investigator for the New York medical examiner, now with the forensic sciences department at Cedar Crest College in Allentown, Pa. "We have always looked for smart technology. I don't think battlefield forensics will replace feet on the ground but will make those feet on the ground smarter."

— *Peter Katel*

[1] Spc. Michael J. MacLeod, "Paratroopers learn battlefield forensics," *Army.mil*, June 3, 2009, www.army.mil/-news/2009/06/03/22040-paratroopers-learn-battlefield-forensics/.

[2] *Ibid.*

[3] Quoted in Staff Sgt. Tim Beckham, "Troops Prevent Attacks With Battlefield Forensics," American Forces Press Service, March 24, 2009, www.defenselink.mil/news/newsarticle.aspx?id=53616. See also James Dao, "Afghan War's Buried Bombs Put Risk in Any Step," *The New York Times*, July 15, 2009, p. A1.

[4] "DoD Needs in Battlefield Forensics," DefenseSolutions.gov, undated, www.defensesolutions.gov/needs_BF.html.

[5] *Ibid.*

[6] "Supplemental to the 304th MI Bn Periodic Newsletter — Sample Overview: al-Qaida-Like Mobile Discussions & Potential Creative Uses," Federation of American Scientists, Oct. 16, 2008, p. 4, www.fas.org/irp/eprint/mobile.pdf. For additional reporting, Noah Schactman, "Spy Fears: Twitter Terrorists, Cell Phone Jihadists," Danger Room blog, *Wired*, Oct. 24, 2008, www.wired.com/dangerroom/2008/10/terrorist-cell.

[7] "DoD Needs," *op. cit.*

law enforcement agencies around the country, IAFIS promised to complete a standard fingerprint check in criminal cases within two hours — and with around-the-clock accessibility. Meanwhile, the FBI in 1990 had launched the Combined DNA Indexing System (CODIS) and expanded it in 1998 to include DNA profiles submitted by state and local law enforcement. Today, the FBI's database includes more than 7 million offender DNA profiles; the bureau claims to have recorded more than 90,000 hits in about 89,000 investigations.

Congress recognized crime labs' funding needs in 2000 by passing a law —

named after the late Georgia senator, Paul Coverdell — authorizing $500 million in grants to crime labs over a six-year period. Over the next six years, however, Congress only appropriated $53.5 million — barely one-tenth of the promised amount. Meanwhile, forensic science research funding from the National Institute of Justice was declining from $78 million in fiscal 2002 to only $33 million in fiscal 2009, according to the National Research Council's report. Congress did provide $300 million of the $1 billion that President George W. Bush requested to improve DNA use in the criminal justice system, but the NRC

says most of those funds have been used to try to reduce the backlog of unanalyzed DNA samples. [29]

Funding needs and case backlogs alone did not account for the series of high-profile scandals that befell crime labs beginning with Houston's in 2003. When *The New York Times* reported in March 2003 on a rape conviction overturned because of a faulty DNA analysis used at trial, the newspaper quoted unnamed legal experts as describing Houston's as "the worst crime lab" in the country. As noted in the National Research Council report, the State Police Department's audit of the

Houston crime lab completed late in 2002 had found "routine" failures to run scientific controls, prevent contamination of samples or accurately compute statistical frequencies. [30]

Virginia's central forensic laboratory came under similar scrutiny but with different results in 2005. Gov. Mark Warner ordered a review of the lab's procedures because of criticism of the handling of DNA evidence in a case involving a death row inmate, Earl Washington Jr., who had been convicted in 1984 of a rape-murder two years earlier. Washington's death sentence had been commuted in 1994, but a DNA analysis then still left him implicated for the offense. A new review in 2000, however, implicated another man, already in prison for a separate rape conviction. The review ordered by Warner — conducted by five DNA examiners from outside the state — ended in September 2005 with a finding of no systemic deficiencies but "room for improvement." Innocence Project lawyers, however, called the report a whitewash. [31]

Meanwhile, the FBI had suffered a black eye in 2004 because of the fingerprint misidentification of an Oregon lawyer, Brandon Mayfield, as a "material witness" in the deadly March 2004 terrorist train bombings in Madrid, Spain. Mayfield was arrested on May 6 after FBI examiners said his fingerprints matched a partial print forwarded by Spanish police. Only 18 days later, the FBI acknowledged that it had made a mistake and released Mayfield. Two years later, a review by the Justice Department's inspector general blamed the mistake on multiple "errors" and said it could have been avoided by "rigorous application" of fingerprint analysis principles. [32]

The shutdown of the Detroit crime lab in September 2008 renewed attention to the mishandling of forensic evidence as the National Research Council (NRC) report was nearing completion. "I cannot have anybody convicted based

on this kind of evidence that's inaccurate," Wayne County prosecutor Worthy told the Detroit City Council on Oct. 29 after receiving the state police's final audit of the lab's work. [33]

The NRC underscored the impact of crime labs' problems as it released its report in January 2009. Forensic laboratories are "underresourced and understaffed," the report stated, "which contributes to case backlogs and likely makes it difficult for laboratories to do as much as they could to (1) inform investigations, (2) provide strong evidence for prosecutions and (3) avoid errors that could lead to imperfect justice." [34] ∎

CURRENT SITUATION

More Resources Needed

The forensic science community is uniting in calls for more money and more staff to deal with growing case backlogs, even as disagreements persist on the structural changes recommended by the NRC report.

Forensic laboratory directors are citing lack of resources as their biggest problem in coping with increased work due, in particular, to stepped-up drug prosecutions. "The biggest things that have plagued crime labs is a real lack of resources," says Orange County lab director Gialamas, president of the lab directors' association. "Our capacity is increasing, yet our backlogs are increasing at the same time."

The lab directors' group and the Consortium of Forensic Science Organizations, which also represents medical examiners, among others, have emphasized funding needs in their responses to the NRC report since its release in February. "The state and local

crime labs, as well as the medical-examiner community, have not been receiving the support they need, but the caseloads have been increasing exponentially," Peter Marone, chair of the consortium and director of the Virginia Department of Forensic Science, told a House subcommittee in May. [35]

Marone was one of the 17 members of the committee that prepared the NRC report. The report describes forensic sciences as "under resourced," but the two co-chairs of the committee are emphasizing the need for institutional changes to ensure that additional funds are used most effectively.

"Simply increasing the number of staff within existing crime laboratories and medical examiners' offices will not solve the problems of the forensic science community," Judge Harry Edwards of the District of Columbia Circuit Court of Appeals, one of the cochairs, told the Senate Judiciary Committee in March. [36]

What's needed are "more resources, but also more of an institutional development that will be able to absorb these resources," says Constantine Gatsonis, the other cochair and a professor of medical science at Brown University in Providence, R.I.

Both Edwards and Gatsonis emphasize the creation of the proposed National Institute of Forensic Science (NIFS) as a key to sponsoring and funding research on the validity of forensic techniques. "There is no entity out there that can summarize and guide the development of research in the forensic sciences," Gatsonis says.

Edwards said the proposed institute needs to be "a new, strong, independent entity." "If we had a director of NIFS" comparable to the White House science adviser, he told the Senate committee, "we'd be in really good shape."

Even apart from the difficulty of creating a new federal agency at a time of rising budget deficits, however, the proposed forensic science institute is

Continued on p. 614

At Issue:

Should forensic labs be separated from law enforcement agencies?

WILLIAM C. THOMPSON
PROFESSOR OF CRIMINOLOGY, LAW AND SOCIETY, UNIVERSITY OF CALIFORNIA, IRVINE

WRITTEN FOR *CQ RESEARCHER*, JULY 13, 2009

*t*he National Research Council's scathing report found that entire disciplines of forensic science rest on deficient scientific foundations, that procedures routinely used for interpretation are lacking in rigor, that analysts routinely take inadequate measures to avoid error and bias and that they testify with unwarranted certainty. When considering proposals for reform, we must first ask how forensic science came to be in such a sorry state.

According to the NRC report, these problems are systemic — rooted in the institutional structure of forensic science. Forensic science has not been an independent realm of academic inquiry; it has been, and is, a technical field in which procedures are designed and performed specifically to play a role in criminal prosecutions. The great majority of forensic scientists are employed either directly or indirectly by law enforcement agencies. By controlling the purse strings, law enforcement officials have had the final say in what research gets done, what programs are expanded or cut and who gets hired and promoted — and these decisions have shaped the field.

For example, law enforcement officials have seen no need to fund research into the accuracy of methods such as latent print analysis or firearm and toolmark examination. From their perspective, research on the accuracy of these methods is not only unnecessary but might be harmful as it could potentially undermine (or be used to challenge) some of the helpful testimony that analysts have been presenting.

The problem with the current structure, as the NRC report recognized, is that the interests of law enforcement sometimes diverge from the imperatives of good science. The report noted that forensic scientists "sometimes face pressure to sacrifice appropriate methodology for the sake of expediency." But the problem is less about direct pressure and personal integrity than it is about institutional incentives and priorities. For law enforcement agencies, the serious deficiencies the NRC report documented are simply not high-priority problems.

The NRC's proposal to separate crime labs from law enforcement agencies is one element of an ambitious agenda of structural reform. Other key elements are the creation of a National Institute of Forensic Science to establish best-practice standards and promote research, and the development of new graduate-education programs to link forensic science more closely to the academic community. These are sound proposals. They deserve serious consideration.

JOHN M. COLLINS
CHIEF MANAGING EDITOR, CRIME LAB REPORT *(WWW.CRIMELABREPORT.COM)*

WRITTEN FOR *CQ RESEARCHER*, JULY 8, 2009

*i*ndependence is a cultural phenomenon, not an organizational arrangement. It can't be sketched in an organizational chart or promised by managers simply because they don't wear badges. It is a mindset nourished by training, education and conscientious leadership. Any organization is capable of preserving it. Any organization is capable of destroying it.

Since early in the 20th century, the forensic sciences have been cultivated by the law enforcement community mainly because no one else was interested. There were no grants to fund private laboratories and no "CSI" shows on television to fuel public fascination. As crime rates began to skyrocket in the early 1960s, it was law enforcement that needed the means to more objectively solve crime. No one else was going to do it.

We can concede that many police organizations are ill-suited to run their own crime laboratories; therefore, most do not, and some should not. They don't have the expertise, the money or the willingness to invest the time and resources needed to operate a reputable laboratory. But for those that clearly demonstrate a commitment to good science and the betterment of the profession, the arbitrary separation of their crime laboratories simply to push a semi-fashionable policy position would be an intolerable failure of leadership. Each agency must be evaluated on its own merits.

It is a myth that forensic scientists in the United States are being bullied away from their scientific foundations by imposing police commanders. Those of us who make our living in the profession of forensic science often find that the opposite is true. Highly competent police executives frequently admit to being awestruck and sometimes intimidated by the complexity of forensic evidence. As a result, they avoid the open sharing of their personal theories and expectations, knowing that scientific results could wind up embarrassing them in front of their peers and subordinates.

While private laboratories are sometimes showcased as being inherently independent and immune from undue influence, they are not. A defense attorney who frequents a private laboratory for DNA testing is every bit as capable of exercising undue influence over testing results as a commander who runs a police crime laboratory. The hand that writes the check is always attached to a person who has hopes, interests, fears and goals.

Thankfully, the overwhelming majority of forensic scientists employ a special strategy to combat this kind of nonsense. It is called professionalism.

Continued from p. 612

drawing opposition from the Justice Department and the forensic lab community.

"It is not clear that a new organization is necessary to achieve implementation of most of the report's recommendations," Kenneth Melson, acting director of the Justice Department's Bureau of Alcohol, Tobacco, and Firearms, told the House subcommittee. "In fact, it could detract from this effort by refocusing energies and resources toward bureaucracy-building rather than substantive improvement in the field."

The crime lab directors' group signaled its opposition to a new institute in a letter to the Senate Judiciary Committee in March, citing "the current fiscal realities" as one factor. "Creating a new federal bureaucracy at this point in time and in this particular financial climate is not the way to go," Gialamas says. Instead, the group says Congress should identify "an existing government body" to be charged with establishing "enforceable standards" for forensic science.

Gatsonis says, however, that other government agencies considered are ill-suited for the task. The National Institute of Justice is part of the Justice Department, a law enforcement agency, she notes, while the National Institute of Standards and Technology and the National Science Foundation have incompatible missions.

In his testimony, Melson said the Justice Department endorses many of the NRC's recommendations, including the calls for research on the reliability of and sources of error in forensic techniques. The department also supports mandatory accreditation of laboratories and certification of examiners. In its March position paper, the crime lab group also backed mandatory accreditation, saying the move would have "immediate, substantial, and positive impacts" on forensic practices.

Both Justice and the crime lab group, however, opposed the NRC's call to separate forensic labs from law enforcement agencies. The crime lab group said Congress "should not remove" crime laboratories from law enforcement agencies as long as the parent agency gave the lab "scientific autonomy" and "freedom to conduct testing and report results without pressure." In his testimony, Melson said labs need to be autonomous, but said that "full independence" was not "advisable or feasible."

In its report, the NRC called either for autonomy or separation, saying that forensic science practices are currently suffering because labs are under the administrative control of prosecutors or police. The labs should not be beholden to the law enforcement side," Edwards said in the Senate hearing.

More Work Ahead?

Forensic examiners are bracing for more time-consuming court appearances in the wake of a Supreme Court decision guaranteeing criminal defendants the right to question technicians and scientists about laboratory reports in drug and other kinds of cases.

The high court jolted the forensic science community with a 5-4 decision on June 25 striking down a procedure in Massachusetts that allowed lab reports on drug samples to be introduced as "certificates of analysis" without the examiners testifying in court.

Writing for the majority in *Melendez-Diaz v. Massachusetts*, Justice Antonin Scalia said the procedure violated the Sixth Amendment's Confrontation Clause, which guarantees a defendant "the right . . . to be confronted with the witnesses against him." [37]

Leaders of crime lab and prosecutors' groups are warning of likely increased work for forensic examiners in the estimated 30 states that do not now require live testimony from lab analysts in criminal trials. "It will have an impact on crime labs, and it will be felt," says Gialamas, president of the crime lab directors association.

The ruling will have "a doubly detrimental effect," Gialamas told *Forensic Magazine*. "Crime labs are losing positions, and those existing will have an increased workload." [38]

Burns of the district attorneys' association acknowledges some uncertainty about how the ruling will be put into effect, but he says the decision could result either in increased backlogs in crime labs or more dismissals or plea bargains in court. "District attorneys think it's going to be a train wreck," he says.

As one example, Burns cites North Dakota, which he says has one crime lab with two analysts to serve the entire state. Without counting time in court, a lab examiner can spend as much as 10 hours on the round-trip from the state capital of Bismarck to a court appearance in remote parts of the state. It's going to be physically impossible" to cover all the cases, Burns says.

From the opposite side, defense lawyers are praising the ruling but also playing down the likelihood of significant changes in most criminal trials. "It's the only ruling that makes sense," says Richmond lawyer DesPortes. "You can't have forensic science experts being treated differently than other witnesses."

DesPortes predicts, however, that analysts will not be called to testify in many run-of-the-mill cases. "When there is no question, an expert will not be called," she says. Many defense lawyers will continue to agree with the prosecution to stipulate to the findings in lab reports, she adds. "Defense lawyers often don't know what they should be looking for."

The Supreme Court case stemmed from the cocaine-trafficking conviction of Luis Melendez-Diaz in a Massachusetts state court after his arrest in a drug investigation in Boston in 2001. The evidence included a lab report identifying as cocaine the 22 grams of white powder found in 19 plastic bags recovered from the police car used to transport him and a codefendant to the police station.

Melendez-Diaz's lawyers unsuccessfully challenged the admission of the lab report by citing a 2004 Supreme Court decision, *Crawford v. Washington*, which generally barred the use of affidavits instead of live witnesses for any "testimonial" statements. The trial judge and the Massachusetts Appeals Court both said the ruling did not apply to the state's procedure allowing introduction of "certificates of analysis" by laboratory examiners.

In explaining the decision to apply the Confrontation Clause to lab reports, Justice Scalia cited the NRC report to show the need to subject forensic evidence to cross-examination in court. "Serious deficiencies have been found in the forensic evidence used in criminal trials," Scalia wrote. Confrontation, he said, could "weed out not only the fraudulent analyst but the incompetent one as well."

Speaking for the four dissenters, Justice Anthony M. Kennedy said the Confrontation Clause applied only to "conventional witnesses" and "does not serve to detect errors in scientific tests." Citing a brief filed by 35 states and the District of Columbia, Kennedy said the ruling would impose "enormous costs on the administration of justice." He called the decision "a windfall for defendants."

Massachusetts Attorney General Martha Coakley made a similar prediction after the decision was issued. "There will be drug dealers who will not be punished," she said. "They will walk out of court." The state's forensic science chief had previously told *The Boston Globe* that the state would need to hire 100 chemists at a cost of $5 million per year if analysts were routinely forced to testify. [39]

Some prosecutors noted, however, that many states — estimated at 15 to 20 — already followed the rule requiring live testimony from lab analysts upon a defendant's request. "Perhaps the best indication the sky will not fall after today's decision is that it has not done so already," Harris County (Houston) District Attorney Pat Lykos told the *Houston Chronicle*. [40]

For his part, Innocence Project codirector Neufeld said the ruling validated defense lawyers' criticism of the reliability of scientific evidence. "The Supreme Court rejected the notion that forensic science is always neutral and based on solid science," Neufeld told the magazine *Lawyers USA*. "The court said our criminal justice system can't rely blindly on forensic analysts' reports because they may distort results to favor the prosecution." [41]

The court is set to return to the issue in its new term, which begins in October. The justices on June 29 agreed to hear a case challenging Virginia's procedure allowing the use of written lab findings but guaranteeing the defendant the right to call the lab analyst as a witness. Some experts say a ruling to allow the procedure would blunt the ruling in the Massachusetts case. The new case, *Briscoe v. Virginia*, is likely to be argued in January 2010. [42] ■

OUTLOOK

Fiction and Reality

Despite more than 25 years on the federal bench, District of Columbia Circuit Judge Edwards was taken aback by what he learned as cochair of the National Research Council's forensic science committee. Edwards says he was "surprisingly mistaken" in his assumptions about the reliability and validity of forensic techniques routinely used in courtrooms in the United States today.

The quality of practice in forensic disciplines "varies greatly," Edwards told the Senate Judiciary Committee on March 18. The work also suffers from a "paucity of research," lack of autonomy for forensic laboratories, absence of mandatory accreditation and certification and lack of effective oversight. The need for an overhaul, he concluded, is "obvious and compelling." [43]

As an expert in statistics, however, cochair Gatsonis says he already knew that forensic science is less reliable than commonly believed. "There is a picture out there in the world that's being propagated by television and others that forensics is accurate, that they pull a rabbit out of a hat," Gatsonis says. "Anybody in science knows that is not true. That's just fiction."

Many in the forensic science community acknowledge the limitations of the discipline. Indeed, the community helped push for creation of the NRC committee tasked with strengthening both the research and the practice in the field. When he testified to the House subcommittee in May, Virginia forensics chief Marone said that forensic scientists had been calling for years for more research to determine the validity of such disciplines of fingerprints, firearms and toolmarks.

"It's not that toolmark examiners are highly inaccurate," says Stephen Fienberg, a professor of statistics and social science at Carnegie-Mellon University in Pittsburgh. "We just don't know. There are no standards."

Some crime lab examiners, however, appear reluctant to acknowledge limits on some forensic techniques in use. For example, Orange County lab chief Gialamas defends the use of comparative bullet-lead analysis, a technique that the FBI developed in the 1960s but abandoned a few years ago. "There are some who say it is junk science," says Gialamas. "I absolutely disagree with that."

The NRC report drew a spike of generally favorable attention when released in February and supportive reactions at the two, poorly attended congressional hearings in March and May. At the Senate hearing, Judiciary Committee Chairman Patrick Leahy, D-Vt., called the report "rather chilling."

Many academics are also praising the report. "The view from the academic community is it's a pretty solid effort," says UCLA professor Mnookin. "I've heard some people say it's far better than expected."

Mnookin voices some "quibbles," however. She says the committee should have dealt more directly with the issue of admissibility of forensic evidence.

More broadly, Mnookin says the committee failed to confront the likelihood the proposed national institute will not be created. "If [the National Institute of Forensic Science] doesn't come into being, the report doesn't give much guidance for alternative policy solutions," she says.

Gatsonis says the committee made a deliberate decision to avoid specific recommendations on admissibility issues. "The report was not about what the courts ought to do," he says. "It was not about making new law."

As for the politics of implementing the report, Gatsonis says that job falls to others. "It's in the public domain," he says, "and things take their course." He notes that a National Academy of Sciences committee in 1928 recommended that elective coroner offices be abolished and replaced by scientifically trained medical examiners. Eighty years later — with county coroners still being used in more than half the states — the new committee repeated that recommendation.

Gialamas expects the report will help put some "some low-hanging fruit" into effect, including mandatory accreditation of forensic labs. He also expects judges to "get more involved in admissibility issues."

But University of California professor Thompson notes that judges have no power to improve the scientific basis of forensic evidence. "Courts can exclude evidence, but they can't do the research to make it better," he says.

Increased funding and structural changes depend on action by Congress, which has many more urgent issues on its agenda. Even if Congress acts, however, Fienberg says more is needed.

"It's not going to change dramatically in the short term without an enormous amount of education from the top to the bottom of the system," says Fienberg. "We need Congress to do something, but then we need for the system to respond, and respond in a positive fashion." ■

Notes

[1] For coverage, see Roma Khanna, "Jurors: 17 years worth millions," *The Houston Chronicle*, June 26, 2009, p. A1. Some background drawn from daily trial coverage by Khanna or Mary Flood. For background on the Houston crime lab, see Jim McKay, "Houston PD Crime Lab Upgrades After Critical Investigation," *Texas Technology*, April 28, 2008, www.govtech.com/tt/articles/301675?printall.

[2] "Strengthening Forensic Science in the United States: A Path Forward," National Research Council, National Academies Press, February 2009, www8.nationalacademies.org/onpinews/newsite m.aspx?RecordID=12589. For coverage of the report, see Jason Felch and Maura Dolan, "Report urges overhaul of crime lab system," *Los Angeles Times*, Feb. 19, 2009, p. A9.

[3] *Ibid.*, p. S-3. For background, see these *CQ Researcher* reports: Steve Weinberg, "Wrongful Convictions," April 17, 2009, pp. 345-372 and Kenneth Jost, "DNA Databases," May 28, 1999, pp. 449-472.

[4] The Innocence Project's account is at www.innocenceproject.org/Content/246.php.

[5] David H. Kaye, David E. Bernstein and Jennifer L. Mnookin, *The New Wigmore: A Treatise on Evidence: Expert Evidence* (2004).

[6] Brandon L. Garrett and Peter J. Neufeld, "Invalid Forensic Science Testimony and Wrongful Convictions," *Virginia Law Review*, Vol. 95, No. 1 (March 2009), pp. 1-97. For an earlier version, see Brandon L. Garrett, "Judging Innocence," *Columbia Law Review*, Vol. 100, No. 2 (2007).

[7] Dina Temple-Raston, "Call for Forensics Overhaul Linked to 'CSI' Effect," "Morning Edition," National Public Radio, Feb. 19, 2009.

[8] John M. Collins and Jay Jarvis, "The Wrongful Conviction of Forensic Science," *Crime Lab Report*, July 16, 2008, www.crimelab report.com/library/pdf/wrongful_conviction.pdf.

[9] "Strengthening Forensic Science," *op. cit.*, pp. 1-9 — 1-10.

[10] The cases are noted in Kaye, *et al.*, *op. cit.*, pp. 496-498.

[11] The citation is 509 U.S. 579 (1993). For an account, see Kenneth Jost, *The Supreme Court Yearbook, 1992-1993*.

[12] "Strengthening Forensic Science," *op. cit.*, pp. 1-14.

[13] Summary drawn from Dan Vergano, "Real-life police forensics don't resemble 'CSI,'" *USA Today*, Feb. 19, 2009, p. 4D.

[14] See Amber Hunt and Ben Schmitt, "147 Cases in Police Lab Mess Are 'Tip of Iceberg,'" *Detroit Free Press*, March 15, 2009, p. 1; Ben Schmitt and Joe Swickard, "Troubled Crime Lab Shuttered," *Detroit Free Press*, Sept. 26, 2009, p. 1.

[15] "Strengthening Forensic Science," *op. cit.*, p. 6-1.

[16] *Ibid.*, pp. S-14 — S-15.

[17] Background drawn in part from Kelly M. Pyrek, *Forensic Science Under Siege: The Challenges of Forensic Laboratories and the Medico-Legal Investigation System* (2007), chap. 1. For legal developments in the United States, see Kaye, *et al.* Some biographical information drawn from Wikipedia entries.

[18] Pyrek, *op. cit.*, p. 7. As source, Pyrek cites

About the Author

Associate Editor **Kenneth Jost** graduated from Harvard College and Georgetown University Law Center. He is the author of the *Supreme Court Yearbook* and editor of *The Supreme Court from A to Z* (both *CQ Press*). He was a member of the *CQ Researcher* team that won the American Bar Association's 2002 Silver Gavel Award. His previous reports include "DNA Databases" and "Prosecutors and the Law." He is also author of the blog *Jost on Justice* (http://joston justiceblogspot.com).

D.J. Spitz, "History and development of forensic medicine and pathology," in Werner U. Spitz, *Medico-Legal Investigation of Death: Guidelines for the Application of Pathology to Crime Investigations* (4th ed.), 2006.

[19] Joseph Bajada, *Sexual Impotence: The Contribution of Paolo Zacchia* (1988), p. 24. Spitz spells the name "Paulo Zacchias." Lie detector tests remain inadmissible today.

[20] The citation is 293 F. 1013 (D.C. Cir. 1923). The text can be found on a site, Daubertontheweb.com, maintained by a Philadelphia lawyer, Peter Nordberg: www.daubertontheweb.com/frye_opinion.htm.

[21] *The FBI: A Centennial History, 1908-2008*, www.fbi.gov/book.htm.

[22] Some background drawn from John F. Kelly and Phillip K. Wearne, *Tainting Evidence: Inside the Scandals at the FBI Crime Lab* (1998), pp. 9-35.

[23] See Randolph N. Jonakait, "Forensic Science: The Need for Regulation," *Harvard Journal of Law and Technology*, Vol. 4, spring 1991, pp. 109-191, http://jolt.law.harvard.edu/articles/pdf/v04/04HarvJLTech109.pdf.

[24] See *In the Matter of an Investigation of the West Virginia State Police Crime Laboratory*, 438 S.E.2d 501 (W. Va. 1993) (*Zain I*) and 445 S.E.2d 165 (*Zain II*). At least 10 convictions were overturned.

[25] "The FBI Laboratory: An Investigation into Laboratory Practices and Alleged Misconduct in Explosive-Related and Other Cases," U.S. Department of Justice, Office of Inspector General, April 1997, www.usdoj.gov/oig/special/9704a/index.htm.

[26] For background, see Kenneth Jost, "Science in the Courtroom," *CQ Researcher*, Oct. 22, 1993, pp. 913-936.

[27] The citation is 509 U.S. 579 (1993). For the impact of the ruling, see "Strengthening Forensic Science," *op. cit.*, pp. 3-8 - 3-11.

[28] See Becky Beaupre, "Crime lab crisis: staff, funding haven't kept up with caseload," *USA Today*, Aug. 20, 1996, p. 1A.

[29] "Strengthening Forensic Science," *op. cit.*, pp. 2-6 - 2-7, 2-13.

[30] See Adam Liptak, "Houston DNA Review Clears Convicted Rapist, and Ripples in Texas Could Be Vast," *The New York Times*, March 11, 2003, p. A14; "Strengthening Forensic Science," *op. cit.*, pp. 1-8.

[31] See Michael D. Shear and Maria Glod, "Va. DNA Review Finds No Pattern of Problems," *The Washington Post*, Sept. 16, 2005, p. B1. See also Pyrek, *op. cit.*, pp. 97-102.

[32] "A Review of the FBI's Handling of the Bran-

don Mayfield Case," Office of the Inspector General, U.S. Department of Justice, March 2006, www.usdoj.gov/oig/special/s0601/final.pdf. For coverage of the earlier summary of the report, see Tomas Alex Tizon, "Report Says Mistaken Arrest Was Due to FBI's Sloppy Work," *Los Angeles Times*, Jan. 7, 2006, p. A10.

[33] Quoted in Naomi R. Patton, "Worthy Blasts Detroit Police," *Detroit Free Press*, Oct. 30, 2008, p. 1.

[34] "Strengthening Forensic Science," *op. cit.*, p. S-10.

[35] "Strengthening Forensic Science in the United States: A Path Forward: Hearing on the National Research Council's Publication," House Judiciary Subcommittee on Crime, Terrorism and Homeland Security, May 13, 2009, http://judiciary.house.gov/hearings/hear_090513.html.

[36] "The Need to Strengthen Forensic Science in the United States: The National Academy of Sciences' Report as a Path Forward," Senate Judiciary Committee, March 18, 2009, http://judiciary.senate.gov/hearings/hearing.cfm?id=3714.

[37] The citation is 557 U.S. — — (2009). The opinion is available on the Supreme Court's Web site: www.supremecourtus.gov/opinions/08pdf/07-591.pdf. For coverage, see Adam

Liptak, "Justices Rule Crime Analysts Must Testify on Lab Results," *The New York Times*, June 26, 2009, p. A1, and Tom Jackman, "Lab Analyst Decision Complicates Prosecutions," *The Washington Post*, July 15, 2009, p. A1.

[38] See Rebecca Waters, "Supreme Court Ruling Requires Lab Analysts to Testify," *Forensic Magazine*, July 1, 2009, www.forensicmag.com/News_Articles.asp?pid=595.

[39] Coakley and John A. Grossman, undersecretary of forensic science and technology in the state public safety office, were both quoted in Jonathan Saltzman and John Ellement, "Accused win right to query forensics," *The Boston Globe*, June 26, 2009, p. 1.

[40] Quoted in "Supreme Court's welcome ruling supports defendants' right to confront witnesses" (editorial), *The Houston Chronicle*, July 1, 2009, p. 8.

[41] Kimberly Atkins, "Supreme Confrontation: Impact of the Court's lab report decision," *Lawyers USA*, June 26, 2009.

[42] See Lyle Denniston, "Is Melendez-Diaz Already Endangered?" SCOTUSBlog, June 29, 2009, www.scotusblog.com/wp/new-lab-report-case-granted/.

[43] Senate Judiciary Committee, *op. cit.*

Bibliography

Selected Sources

Books

Cole, Simon A., *Suspect Identities: A History of Fingerprinting and Criminal Identification*, Harvard University Press, 2001.

The book traces the history of fingerprinting from its origins in the 19th century as a device of social control through its acceptance as a primary technique of criminal identification and its current status alongside the more scientific method of identification: DNA typing. Cole is an associate professor of criminology, law and society at the University of California-Irvine. Includes notes.

Kaye, David H., David E. Bernstein and Jennifer L. Mnookin, *The New Wigmore: A Treatise on Evidence: Expert Evidence*, Aspen, 2004.

The treatise comprehensively covers the background and current case law on expert evidence, including a chapter specifically on forensic science. Includes page notes, 29-page list of authorities. Kaye is Regents' Professor at Arizona State University with appointments at the Sandra Day O'Connor College of Law and the Center for Law, Science and Technology; he is also the author of *The Double Helix and the Law of Evidence* (Harvard University Press, January 2010). Bernstein is a professor at George Mason University School of Law; Mnookin is vice dean and professor at UCLA Law School.

Kelly, John F., and Phillip K. Wearne, *Tainting Evidence: Inside the Scandals at the FBI Crime Lab*, Free Press, 1998.

Two journalists deliver a strong indictment of practices at the FBI Laboratory based on the disclosures by whistle-blowing crime lab scientist Frederick Whitehurst and the ensuing congressional and internal investigations. Includes notes.

Pyrek, Kelly M., *Forensic Science Under Siege: The Challenges of Forensic Laboratories and the Medico-Legal Investigation System*, Academic Press, 2007.

At more than 500 pages, the book is both comprehensive and up-to-date in detailing the forensic science system in the United States for lay readers. Pyrek, a forensic nurse, is supportive but not uncritical; she closes with suggestions for reform that the forensic system be "built up, not torn down." Includes suggested references chapter by chapter.

Ramsland, Katherine, *Beating the Devil's Game: A History of Forensic Science and Criminal Investigation*, Berkeley Books, 2007.

A well-known forensic expert and author provides a popularized account of the history of forensic science from ancient times through the late-20th-century development of DNA profiling.

Articles

Fountain, Henry, "Plugging Holes in the Science," *The New York Times*, May 12, 2009, p. D1.

The "Science Times" article provides a good overview of the National Research Council report on forensic science and the scientific community's reaction to the report.

Holden, Constance, "Forensic Science Needs a Major Overhaul, Panel Says," *Science*, Vol. 323, Feb. 27, 2009, p. 1155.

The article highlights the National Research Council's call for providing a sounder scientific basis for forensic techniques used in investigating crimes and suspicious deaths.

Mnookin, Jennifer L., "Clueless 'science,'" *Los Angeles Times*, Feb. 19, 2009, p. A21.

The op-ed by a forensic science expert at UCLA School of Law praises the National Research Council's report and criticizes the forensic science community for being "wary of and often downright hostile to" inquiry into the validity of forensic techniques.

Reports and Studies

National Research Council, "Strengthening Forensic Science in the United States: A Path Forward," National Research Council, National Academies Press, February 2009, www8.nationalacademies.org/onpinews/newsitem.aspx?RecordID=12589.

The congressionally mandated report, prepared under the direction of a 17-member committee broadly representative of legal and forensic disciplines, found serious deficiencies in the structure and practice of forensic science in the United States today. The 255-page report provides extensive background information on the development of forensic sciences and the use of forensic evidence in court along with a total of 13 recommendations, many of them with multiple components. Includes notes.

On the Web

"Forensic Science for the 21st Century: The National Academy of Science Report and Beyond," Sandra Day O'Connor College of Law, Arizona State University, April 3-4, http://lst.law.asu.edu/FS09/index.html.

The two-day conference featured a keynote address by Judge Harry T. Edwards, cochair of the National Academy's committee on forensic science, and presentations by more than three dozen judicial, legal and forensic experts. Major presentations are available in pdf form on the school's Web site. The papers are to be published later in the American Bar Association's journal, *Jurimetrics: The Journal of Law, Science, and Technology*, and in the Oxford University Press journal, *Law, Probability & Risk*.

The Next Step:

Additional Articles from Current Periodicals

Battlefield Forensics

Eisler, Peter, "Pentagon Database Swells to 80,000 DNA Profiles," USA Today, Dec. 12, 2008, p. 5A.

The Pentagon has catalogued 80,000 DNA profiles on foreign terrorism suspects and detainees in Iraq and Afghanistan.

Thompson, Estes, "Green Beret Faces Jury on Charge of Killing Afghan," The Associated Press, Feb. 19, 2009.

A lack of forensic evidence may exonerate a Green Beret accused of fatally shooting an Afghan man he mistakenly suspected to be a Taliban fighter.

Willing, Richard, "Overhaul of Military Labs Urged," USA Today, Nov. 12, 2007, p. 1A.

The Defense Department needs to spend $195 million to improve how it gathers forensic evidence in Iraq and Afghanistan, according to a Pentagon report.

Digital Forensics

Bernstein, Maxine, "Computer Detectives Dig Up Digital Clues," The Oregonian, June 16, 2008, p. A1.

The Northwest Regional Computer Forensics Laboratory has helped police solve many homicide and fraud cases.

Gaylord, Chris, "Digital Detectives Discern Photoshop Fakery," The Christian Science Monitor, Aug. 29, 2007, p. 13.

As image-manipulation programs become easier to use and harder to detect, researchers are working to find solutions to combat digital fraud.

Gregory, Kathryn, "Hidden Digital Files May Be Going Unnoticed By Law Enforcement," Charleston (W. Va.) Gazette, Jan. 26, 2009.

Steganography allows criminals to conceal and manipulate digital images to evade discovery by authorities.

Walton, Val, "Computer Forensics Institute Trains Hundreds," Birmingham (Ala.) News, July 2, 2009, p. 1B.

The National Computer Forensics Institute — established by the Secret Service — provides training to law enforcement officials on how to recover and analyze digital evidence.

Standards

Green, Frank, "New Study Questions Forensic Sciences," Richmond Times Dispatch (Virginia), Feb. 19, 2009, p. A5.

Inconsistent standards and a lack of funding have created a system of crime labs in disarray, according to a study by the National Academy of Sciences.

Mills, Steve, "Some Techniques Long Suspect," Chicago Tribune, Feb. 19, 2009, p. A6.

A number of forensic disciplines — including some used in police stations and courtrooms — have relied on flawed science.

Mnookin, Jennifer L., "Judges Should Monitor Use of Forensic Evidence," Fort Wayne Journal Gazette (Indiana), Feb. 22, 2009, p. 14A.

Judges need higher standards for forensic evidence to protect the criminal justice system.

Wrongful Convictions

Dutton, Geoff, "DNA May Reveal Case's Real Rapist," Columbus (Ohio) Dispatch, Oct. 5, 2008, p. 1B.

DNA forensics offers hope in solving a 1990 rape case in Columbus, Ohio, in which DNA has already exonerated an innocent man.

Estes, Andrea, "Crime Lab Neglected 16,000 Cases," The Boston Globe, July 15, 2007, p. A1.

Forensic evidence samples from thousands of crime scenes across Massachusetts were never analyzed by the State Police crime lab, according to a state investigation.

McGonigle, Steve, and Jennifer Emily, "A Blind Faith in Eyewitnesses," Dallas Morning News, Oct. 12, 2008, p. 1A.

Nineteen cases in Dallas County, Texas, have been overturned by DNA evidence, 18 of which initially relied heavily on unreliable testimony.

Santos, Fernanda, "State Urged to Do More to Halt False Convictions," The New York Times, Oct. 18, 2007, p. B3.

The loss, destruction and misplacement of forensic evidence has delayed and defeated attempts by wrongfully convicted individuals to prove their innocence.

CITING CQ RESEARCHER

Sample formats for citing these reports in a bibliography include the ones listed below. Preferred styles and formats vary, so please check with your instructor or professor.

MLA STYLE

Jost, Kenneth. "Rethinking the Death Penalty." CQ Researcher 16 Nov. 2001: 945-68.

APA STYLE

Jost, K. (2001, November 16). Rethinking the death penalty. CQ Researcher, 11, 945-968.

CHICAGO STYLE

Jost, Kenneth. "Rethinking the Death Penalty." CQ Researcher, November 16, 2001, 945-968.

Published by CQ Press, a Division of SAGE

www.cqresearcher.com

Energy and Climate

Should carbon-based fuels be phased out?

C ongress and the Obama administration are advancing policies directly aimed — for the first time — at cutting emissions from burning carbon fuels. The Environmental Protection Agency plans to regulate greenhouse-gas emissions, which scientists link to global warming. The House recently passed a comprehensive energy bill that would institute a "cap-and-trade" system imposing an increasingly tight cap on carbon emissions by requiring polluters such as electric-power companies to buy emission permits or switch to cleaner energy sources. The legislation is backed by most major energy and environmental groups. Some critics say the bill is fatally flawed, however, partly because the trading market in which big carbon-emitting companies may buy unused pollution permits will make carbon-fuel prices too unpredictable and open to manipulation. It's also unclear whether public support for regulating carbon will continue if the effort significantly raises prices for electric power and manufactured goods.

Smoke and steam pour from a coal-fired power plant in western Pennsylvania. A measure recently passed in the House would impose increasingly tight caps on emissions from burning carbon-based fuels.

CQ Researcher • July 24, 2009 • www.cqresearcher.com
Volume 19, Number 26 • Pages 621-644

ENERGY AND CLIMATE

Cover: Getty Images/Robert Nickelsberg

CQ Researcher

July 24, 2009
Volume 19, Number 26

MANAGING EDITOR: Thomas J. Colin
tcolin@cqpress.com

ASSISTANT MANAGING EDITOR: Kathy Koch
kkoch@cqpress.com

ASSOCIATE EDITOR: Kenneth Jost

STAFF WRITERS: Thomas J. Billitteri, Marcia Clemmitt, Peter Katel

CONTRIBUTING WRITERS: Rachel Cox, Sarah Glazer, Alan Greenblatt, Reed Karaim Barbara Mantel, Patrick Marshall, Tom Price, Jennifer Weeks

DESIGN/PRODUCTION EDITOR: Olu B. Davis

ASSISTANT EDITOR: Darrell Dela Rosa

FACT-CHECKING: Eugene J. Gabler, Michelle Harris

CQ PRESS

A Division of SAGE

PRESIDENT AND PUBLISHER:
John A. Jenkins

EXECUTIVE DIRECTOR,
REFERENCE INFORMATION GROUP:
Alix B. Vance

CQ Press is a registered trademark of Congressional Quarterly Inc.

CQ Researcher (ISSN 1056-2036) is printed on acid-free paper. Published weekly, except; (Jan. wk. 1) (May wk. 4) (July wks. 1, 2) (Aug. wks. 3, 4) (Nov. wk. 4) and (Dec. wk. 4), by CQ Press, a division of SAGE Publications. Annual full-service subscriptions start at $803. For pricing, call 1-800-834-9020, ext. 1906. To purchase a *CQ Researcher* report in print or electronic format (PDF), visit www. cqpress.com or call 866-427-7737. Single reports start at $15. Bulk purchase discounts and electronic-rights licensing are also available. Periodicals postage paid at Washington, D.C., and additional mailing offices. POSTMASTER: Send address changes to *CQ Researcher*, 2300 N St., N.W., Suite 800, Washington, DC 20037.

Energy and Climate

BY MARCIA CLEMMITT

THE ISSUES

When the House Energy and Commerce Committee approved the first-ever House energy bill focusing on climate change on May 21, the historic vote did not come without controversy.

Environmental groups have long called for phasing out carbon-based fuels like oil and coal — which, when burned, emit "greenhouse gases" (GHGs) that scientists believe contribute to rapid, potentially devastating climate change. But some environmentalists say the proposed American Clean Energy and Security Act of 2009 — known as Waxman-Markey after its chief authors, Reps. Henry A. Waxman, D-Calif., and Edward J. Markey, D-Mass. — is less a boon for the environment than a giveaway to GHG-emitting industries.

"This is a climate mugging of the American people" and "a coal industry welfare bill," said Mike Tidwell, director of the advocacy group Chesapeake Climate Action Network (CCAN). Tidwell was arrested along with 14 other CCAN members in a protest outside the Capitol Hill office of Rep. Rick Boucher, D-Va., who had successfully fought to get assistance in the bill for the coal industry, an important economic player in his rural district. [1]

"We will inevitably have controls on greenhouse gases," said Boucher. But "I've been working extensively to fashion a . . . program that . . . will preserve coal jobs, create the opportunity for increasing coal production and keep electricity rates in regions like Southwest Virginia affordable." [2]

Members of the Chesapeake Climate Action Network protest outside the Capitol Hill office of Rep. Rick Boucher, D-Va., who got aid for the coal industry included in the recently passed House energy bill. President Obama and many congressional Democrats want to make climate change a key focus of U.S. energy policy, but critics say the proposed legislation will hurt the economy and destroy jobs.

Chesapeake Climate Action Network/Chris Eichler

The dispute between Boucher and CCAN protesters epitomizes the struggle being waged in Washington this summer as President Barack Obama and many congressional Democrats try to make climate change a key focus of U.S. energy policy.

Both Obama and Waxman had originally proposed strict phaseout plans for carbon-based fuels, with rapidly tightening "caps" on the amount of GHG emissions allowed to be spewed into the Earth's atmosphere. Obama also advocated creating "permits" to emit carbon and then selling the permits to pollution-emitting companies, with the proceeds returned to the U.S. government. But in order to line up votes for the bill, the sponsors struck compromises with business and regional interests, including an agreement to give away most of the emissions permits free.

As a result, many environmentalists say the measure (HR 2454), which passed the full House by a slim 219-212 vote on June 26, compromises too much.

"Obama in February said he wanted a 100 percent auction of carbon-emission permits and to give a significant amount of the money back to the public, but we've gone from that to an 85 percent giveaway," which translates to much less pressure on emitting industries to change their ways, says Tidwell.

But others are skeptical of the bill on other grounds. In Europe, says Peter Dorman, an economics and environmental policy professor at Evergreen State University in Olympia, Wash., a similar cap-and-trade system "has been an abject failure," and has not significantly cut emissions at all. [3] "I see no evidence that Waxman-Markey will lead to a reduction of carbon emissions in the next few years."

Tidwell attributes the current legislation to a widespread belief "that the U.S. has been so bad on climate change for so long that we simply need a bill, any bill, as soon as possible, and that anything is better than nothing. But many scientists say that just any bill won't do" and what's needed are much bigger cuts in GHG emissions.

Proponents of the measure argue that compromise is the only way to take an all-important first step.

If we cap greenhouse-gas emissions, "we're essentially going to put [fossil-fuel-based industries] out of business as they know it," says Victor Flatt, a professor of

Most States Have Renewable Portfolio Standards

Thirty states and the District of Columbia have mandatory renewable portfolio standards (RPS) that require electric utilities to generate a certain amount of electricity from renewable energy sources like wind. An additional five states have voluntarily renewable goals.

Renewable Portfolio Standards (RPS) in the States

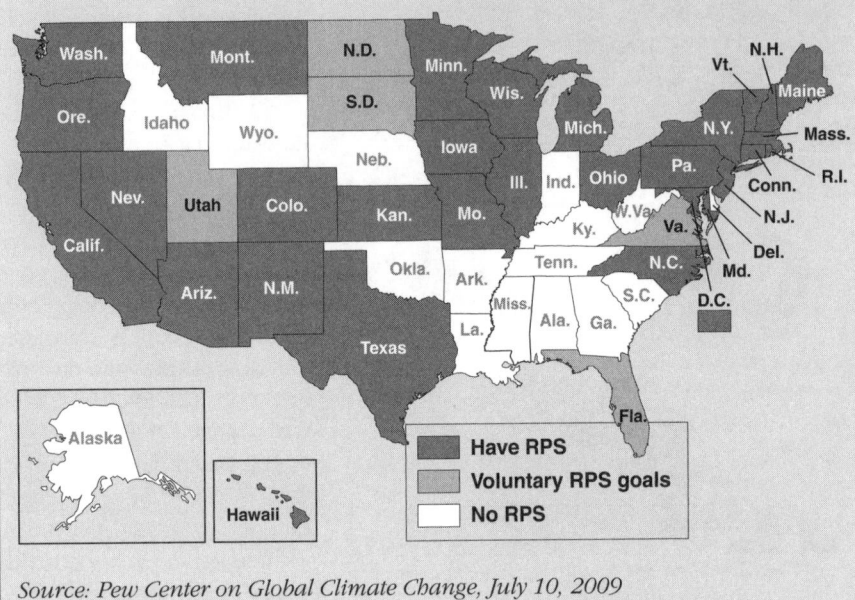

Have RPS
Voluntary RPS goals
No RPS

Source: Pew Center on Global Climate Change, July 10, 2009

environmental law at the University of North Carolina in Chapel Hill. "So until we give them incentives, why would they do anything?"

Severin Borenstein, a professor of business administration and public policy at the University of California at Berkeley's Haas School of Business, says although the bill would give away most of the emission permits, it will cut emissions over the lifetime of the measure and is not just a giveaway to industry. "I'm all for it, as opposed to doing nothing."

To support efforts to combat climate change, it's crucial to pass the climate bill by December, when the U.N. Climate Conference meets in Copenhagen, Denmark, to discuss new agreements on cutting global emissions, says Elizabeth Perera, Washington representative of the Union of Concerned Scientists (UCS), an envi-

ronmental research and advocacy group. Waxman-Markey "is the best thing anybody in the world is currently looking at," she says, so if it's enacted, the United States "will have the moral authority to lead the negotiations there, and most countries will follow what we do."

Legislation supporters say retooling the nation's energy system will provide both jobs and a cleaner environment. The House energy bill "will spur the development of low-carbon sources of energy — everything from wind, solar and geothermal power to safer nuclear energy and cleaner coal," said Obama in his weekly radio address on June 17. "Most importantly, it will make possible the creation of millions of new jobs. Make no mistake: This is a jobs bill." [4]

Other bill supporters give more cautious assessments of the bill's economic effects.

"Environmentalists say it will create jobs," and there is some truth to that, says Bryan K. Mignone, a fellow at the centrist Brookings Institution think tank in Washington. "There will be winners and losers," with jobs lost in some industries and gained in others. Some studies suggest there may be a net gain, but the energy bill shouldn't be expected to be a huge job creator, he says. "The rhetoric can get a little out of control," says Mignone. "Many industries will fare poorly, and many of them are in parts of the country that are already struggling.

"There's a real price in the economy — a carbon price — that wasn't there before," and that will have consequences, Mignone says. Industries like coal mining will obviously suffer, as well as manufacturing industries that compete globally, although some green industries might expand their international markets, he says.

Conservative commentators, however, say the bill would destroy both the economy and jobs. "Entire regions of coal-producing states will see their local economies tank and thousands of jobs lost" as carbon-fuel prices rise, and "manufacturers . . . relocate to countries that don't adopt business-busting, draconian schemes," said Rep. Darrell Issa, R-Calif. [5]

"Waxman-Markey would be the biggest tax increase in the history of the world and the biggest government intervention in people's lives since the Second World War," said Myron Ebell, director of Energy and Global Warming Policy at the Competitive Enterprise Institute, a free-market think tank that has argued the evidence on human-caused climate change is weak. [6]

But supporters of climate-focused energy policy say the costs of doing nothing would be far worse. Climate change is already affecting the United States and will increase its economic and environmental toll if left unchecked, said a U.S. Global Change Research Program report released at a June 16 White House press conference.

The report cites falling catches from Alaskan fisheries; destruction of Pacific, Atlantic and Gulf Coast communities as sea levels rise; a drier, warmer climate that may leave the Northwest, Southwest and Great Plains with inadequate water supplies; and a hotter Midwest, plagued by heavier spring rains that could stress livestock and increase insect and weed infestations on farms. [7]

"We are subsidizing current energy prices at the expense of our progeny," the *St. Louis Post-Dispatch* editorialized May 28. "It's as if we are financing our lifestyle with an interest-only mortgage," and "there's a big balloon payment looming in our future. If we do not start reducing our global warming liabilities now, we will be overwhelmed with the debt later." [8]

Convincing other nations to cut emissions — including developing countries like China and India — will greatly affect climate-change progress, says Borenstein, and the bill is needed to do that. "To get international cooperation we have to overcome the reputation of a decade of not doing anything."

Nevertheless, Borenstein and other proponents of the measure worry that the bill includes too little research-and-development funding for alternative energy sources, which are crucial to achieving worldwide emissions cuts.

Other analysts worry that, even as the climate bill advances, policy makers have not clearly outlined a new overall energy policy, which could compromise public support for tough measures down the line. "There's a huge amount of confusion about why we need an energy policy," says Flatt. "A major reason is climate change, and the other major reason people talk about is energy security, by which some mean, 'Stop giving money to hostile nations' " by buying their oil. But the two goals often conflict, and hammering out a set of overarching policy priorities could help move past such conflicts, he says.

If energy security were the sole concern, he says, "You would just make a

How Emission Permits Would Be Allocated

The proposed American Clean Energy and Security Act of 2009 — known as Waxman-Markey — would allocate emission permits, or carbon credits, both to regulated industries and those not covered by the bill. If a company cuts its emissions so much that it has surplus permits, it can sell them to other companies or bank them for future use. If a company needs permits, it can buy more. Non-regulated entities, such as banks and individual investors, can also buy and sell permits. This is the "trade" part of the cap-and-trade program. Companies that emit more than their permits allow would be fined twice the value of the permits they should have purchased.

Some of the permits would be given away to industries regulated under the bill, including:

- 15% to energy-intensive industries such as iron, steel and cement
- 5% to producers of coal-generated electricity
- 2% to oil refineries
- 2% to electricity utilities

Some permits would be given to industries not covered under the bill, which would sell them and use the proceeds, including:

- 30% to local electricity distribution companies, which would use the proceeds to keep consumer electricity prices low
- 10% to state governments, for renewable-energy and transportation projects
- 9% to local natural-gas companies, for developing renewable energy and to keep consumer prices low (natural gas emits less carbon than oil and coal)
- 3% to the automobile industry from 2012 to 2017, to develop clean-car technologies

Source: Kate Sheppard, "Everything You Always Wanted to Know About the Waxman-Markey Energy/Climate Bill," Grist.org, June 2009

huge investment in coal," which America has in abundance. But if the goal is to fight climate change, switching to coal or even ethanol, which U.S. farmers have long pushed as a solution to energy independence, "actually becomes a disastrous thing to do."

As lawmakers, environmentalists and businesses debate proposals for a "clean" energy policy, here are some of the questions being asked:

Are climate-focused energy proposals too costly?

As President Obama and many con-

gressional Democrats try to craft a U.S. energy policy that limits GHG emissions, critics say the proposals would damage the economy. [9]

Since Jan. 1, 2005, when the European Union launched a carbon cap-and-trade mechanism similar to the one proposed in Waxman-Markey, "power prices in EU countries have increased significantly," wrote researchers from the Energy Center of the Netherlands in a December 2008 report. [10]

The legislation will raise prices across the economy for several decades and cost some jobs, on net, says an analy-

Many States Enacted Climate Initiatives

But new federal policy may disrupt regional schemes.

In 1998 and 1999, at least 16 states passed legislative resolutions criticizing international calls for mandatory greenhouse gas (GHG) emissions. Since then, however, growing concern about climate change has prompted many more states to control emissions. [1]

By 2006, 21 states had enacted mandatory "renewable portfolio standards" requiring a portion of electrical power to be generated from renewable sources. And by this year, 30 states plus the District of Columbia had adopted mandatory standards and another five states had set "goals" for renewable use. [2]

"Up to now, the biggest push for energy efficiency and renewable energy has come from states," says Victor Flatt, a professor of environmental law at the University of North Carolina School of Law in Chapel Hill.

The most visible state efforts involve groups of states, along with some Canadian provinces, which have launched regional cap-and-trade groups. Such alliances "attempt to level the playing field," explains Ron Ezekiel, an energy lawyer in Vancouver. Otherwise, a state or province acting on its own to cap emissions could drive businesses into neighboring states without such restrictions. States and provinces in cap-and-trade alliances agree that the region as a whole will reduce its GHG emissions by a certain percentage over time. Emitting industries must either cut their carbon emissions by that amount or buy emissions "credits" or "offsets" from others whose emissions are below the agreed-upon targets.

Established in 2005, the Regional Greenhouse Gas Initiative (RGGI) in the Northeast was the first group. RGGI's cap-and-trade market was launched last September, when six of the states auctioned the first emission permits issued under the trading system. Electrical utility companies bought the permits for about $40 million, which the states will spend mainly on developing renewable energy and electricity demand-reduction programs. [3]

The Western Climate Initiative (WCI), the second group to form, includes Arizona, California, Montana, New Mexico, Oregon, Utah, Washington and the Canadian provinces of British Columbia, Manitoba, Ontario and Quebec. Now nine Midwestern states — Wisconsin, Minnesota, Illinois, Indiana, Iowa, Michigan, Kansas, Ohio and South Dakota — and Manitoba have agreed to develop a third cap-and-trade market. [4]

Within the groups, states are moving at different rates, wrote Ezekiel and Ivan Gold, an energy attorney in Portland, Ore. In the WCI, for example, California and British Columbia have already enacted legislation authorizing cap and trade, while Washington and Oregon have not. [5]

The state groups "plugged along until Obama got elected, but then, with the strong possibility of a federal cap-and-trade scheme on the horizon, everything ground to a halt," says Ezekiel. States "were worried that the federal program would preempt" regionally set targets and trading rules, he says.

Some expect that U.S. climate legislation would preempt state standards initially but then allow states to pursue more

sis prepared for the National Black Chamber of Commerce by CRA International, a Washington, D.C.-based consultancy. Gasoline prices would rise about 12 cents per gallon in 2015 — the first year emissions are expected to decline — and more in succeeding years as caps tighten. And despite "substantial gains in 'green jobs,'" the authors predict that shifting resources to pay higher energy costs would cost 2.3 million to 2.7 million jobs annually between about 2015 and 2030. [11]

Electric-utility costs would decline by about 0.5 percent through 2015, as energy-efficiency measures came into use, but then rise by 4 percent to 5 percent between 2020 and 2025 and "more dramatically" in ensuing years, the group projects. [12]

The CRA report "is very blunt that it's

going to cost, and it has to cost," says William H. Babcock, director for energy and environment in the Cambridge, Mass., office of LECG, an Emeryville, Calif.-based international business consultancy. "Go back to Economics 101. There's something we haven't valued before — CO_2 emissions. Now we value it, so we'll have to buy it. Any time we're buying stuff we didn't have to buy before, that's going to hurt."

Critics say the costs would be too high. "This cap-and-trade legislation is . . . an economic declaration of war on the Midwest by liberals in Washington, D.C., and it must be opposed," says Rep. Mike Pence, R-Ind., chairman of the House Republican Conference. [13]

The Midwest would be heaviest hit if carbon prices rise because coal — the heaviest carbon emitter — provides

up to 90 percent of the electrical power in the Midwest, explains former Sen. J. Bennett Johnston, D-La., longtime chairman of the Senate Energy Committee and now a lobbyist and policy consultant in Washington. On the nation's coasts coal only provides about 10 percent of the electrical power.

Furthermore, when President Obama recently declared that new U.S. automobiles must average 42 miles per gallon by the year 2016, analysts estimated the move would cost $1,300 per car, noted Ronald Bailey, science correspondent for libertarian *Reason* magazine. "When prices go up, people buy less," leading to job loss across the economy, he wrote. [14]

But supporters of action on climate change insist the financial pinch must be weighed against the consequences

aggressive goals on their own, if they chose. If a federal law is enacted requiring preemption of state standards, the states in the WCI and the Midwestern group "would spend their effort on the national plan," says Ezekiel.

If the states pull out of regional schemes, efforts to set significant emissions cuts in Canada could be adversely affected. Several provinces are taking "strong climate measures," wrote Liz Barrett-Brown, a senior attorney for the environmental advocacy group Natural Resources Defense Council. However, in Alberta carbon-based fuel extracted from tar sands — sand or clay saturated with dense petroleum — has become a valuable economic commodity.

Canada's federal government and Alberta have made it clear that protecting tar sands development "is more important than stemming global warming pollution," Barrett-Brown said. Indeed, "It's so important that Canada has repeatedly meddled in U.S. efforts to reduce" its own carbon emissions, such as by opposing California's low carbon-fuel standard regulations." [6]

While regional carbon-trading schemes may be the highest-profile initiatives, some states and localities have undertaken many other energy-use programs. Some states and cities have hired "sustainability managers" to make government power use more efficient, for example. In 2007, the Supreme Court ruled, 5-4, in favor of 12 states that had jointly sued the federal Environmental Protection Agency to get the agency to regulate GHG emissions. The court ordered the EPA to review whether greenhouse gases threaten public health and therefore fall under its regulatory purview. [7] California has also sought a waiver from the EPA to regulate tailpipe emissions on its own, which the Obama administration granted on June 30.

Not all states have advanced equally, however, says Suzanne Watson, policy director of the American Council for an Energy-Efficient Economy. In general, the Northeast, the Northwest and California have taken the lead, and the Southeast has been slowest to adopt energy-efficiency measures.

---

[1] For background, see Alan Greenblatt, "Confronting Warming," *CQ Researcher*, Jan. 9, 2009, pp. 1-24.

[2] "Renewable Portfolio Standards," Pew Center on Global Climate Change Web site, www.pewclimate.org/what_s_being_done/in_the_states/rps.cfm.

[3] Anne Polansky, "Regional CO_2 Cap-and-Trade Program (RGGI) Is Launched: How Will Auction Revenues Be Spent?" ClimateScienceWatch blog, Oct. 2, 2008, www.climatesciencewatch.org. Members are Connecticut, Delaware, Maine, Maryland, Massachusetts, New Hampshire, New Jersey, New York, Rhode Island and Vermont.

[4] "Governors Sign Energy Security and Climate Stewardship Platform and Greenhouse Gas Accord," press release, Midwestern Governors Association.

[5] Ron Ezekiel and Ivan Gold, "Greenhouse Gas Cap-and-Trade Legislation and the Western Climate Initiative: Issues at Hand," bulletin, Fasken Martineau, May 2009.

[6] Liz Barrett-Brown, "Waxman-Markey Bill Ups the Ante on Tar Sands and Other Dirty Energy," Switchboard blog, Natural Resources Defense Council, May 15, 2009, http://switchboard.nrdc.org.

[7] *Massachusetts v. Environmental Protection Agency*, 549 U.S. 497 (2007).

---

of inaction. To find the arguments for an emissions cap convincing, you calculate "what's going to happen if you don't do it," suggests UNC's Flatt.

"Unless aggressive measures are taken to halt global warming, the consequences of human . . . displacement" — in the form of "climate refugees" — "could . . . vastly exceed anything that has occurred before," according to the international charity CARE. The Waxman-Markey bill "is vital to efforts to begin to mitigate these negative impacts," such as heat, drought and rising sea levels that may deprive millions of their homes and agricultural livelihoods, says the group. [15]

"Some may ask, 'What's the difference between raising the price of energy with carbon permits and having OPEC jack up oil prices? They're both bad!' " says Dorman of Evergreen State, referring to the Organization of Petroleum Exporting Countries, a global oil producers' cartel. But with a permit system "we pay ourselves" rather than paying OPEC, because emitters eventually will have to buy permits from the U.S. government to burn carbon fuels, he explains. So while utilities and other companies will charge consumers more to cover the cost of permits, "the money comes right back to Americans," making the key question for lawmakers "how to get that money back in the hands of the public as soon as possible," he says.

Some analysts say the costs will be much less severe than critics contend. The average American will only pay an additional $30.89 per year in energy-related spending in 2015 under a Waxman-Markey-style program, according to the Massachusetts Institute of Technology (MIT) Joint Program on the Science and Policy of Global Change. [16] That cost level was verified by John Reilly, senior lecturer at MIT's Sloan School of Management and a report author, when he was queried by PolitiFact, the political fact-checking Web site run by the *St. Petersburg Times*, after the House Republican Conference began citing the MIT report as estimating the annual cost per U.S. household at $3,128. [17]

Reilly said the GOP conference's analysis of his findings is "wrong in so many ways it's hard to begin" to explain what is wrong with their analysis. While a cap-and-trade program is designed to push up prices for carbon-based fuels, other provisions — such as greater energy efficiency and competition from

Wealthier Americans Would Pay the Most

Critics have charged that the national cap-and-trade system proposed by House Democrats will cost American taxpayers thousands of dollars per year, while proponents say the cost to each household will be negligible. The nonpartisan Congressional Budget Office estimates the annual economy-wide cost of the program in 2020 will be $22 billion, or about $175 per household. The lowest income group would see an average net benefit of $40; the highest cost would be $340.

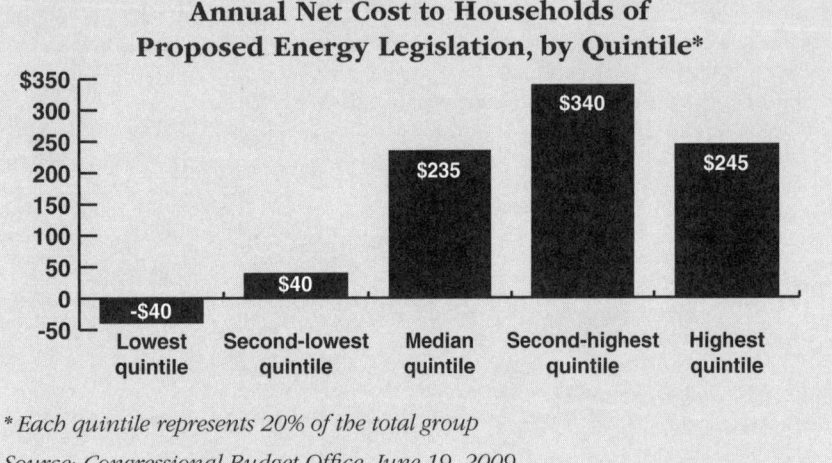

Annual Net Cost to Households of Proposed Energy Legislation, by Quintile*

* Each quintile represents 20% of the total group

Source: Congressional Budget Office, June 19, 2009

alternative fuels — would moderate the cost, he explained, and the government would give rebates to help consumers offset price increases. [18]

After 2015, as the carbon-emission cap is lowered, cost to individual consumers would increase, but the average annual cost over time in today's dollars comes out to $85 per person, according to Reilly. [19]

The nonpartisan Congressional Budget Office (CBO) estimates that "the net annual economy-wide cost of the cap-and-trade program in 2020 would be $22 billion — or about $175 per household." [20]

Under Waxman-Markey about 15 percent of revenues from auctioning emission permits would be used to reimburse low-income households for higher prices on energy and manufactured goods, using rebates and tax credits, says the liberal Center on Budget and Policy Priorities. [21] As a result, the cost of the bill would vary among house-

holds, says the CBO. In 2020, for example, households in the lowest fifth of the income scale might see an annual net benefit of about $40; households in the second lowest fifth in income would spend $40 more; and households in the top three-fifths in income would spend between $235 and $340, due to increased energy costs, the CBO estimates. [22]

The prospect of losing jobs to international competitors is real for energy-intensive industries such as aluminum, cement, fossil fuels, glass, iron and steel, and paper, said Robert Stavins, director of the Harvard University Environmental Economics Program. And while that issue must be addressed by policy makers, he said, "the actual competitiveness impacts . . . would not . . . constitute a major economy-wide economic issue," because international differences in business environments, such as labor costs, "swamp differences in costs due

to environmental policies," including climate-change policies. [23]

A shift in energy use will cause upheaval, but "jobs get created and destroyed all the time" in response to technological and cultural changes, says Jim Fulton, a new-technology lawyer in Palo Alto, Calif. "There is a case to be made that the shift to renewable energy will have benefits for our economy as a whole longer term because the old model is not sustainable."

Similar initiatives like the Clean Air Act and a GHG cap-and-trade system formed in the past few years by a group of Northeastern states "stirred up huge amounts of controversy before they were passed," but once they became law, "the market adjusted," and now "you don't hear a peep," says Perera of the Union of Concerned Scientists.

Will the Waxman-Markey bill help reduce climate change?

While conservatives blast climate-change policy as an economy killer, some environmentalists say the House-passed Waxman-Markey bill isn't strong enough.

The current legislation is "a nightmare, and very little carbon reduction will come from it," says Dorman of Evergreen State. "I would urge environmentalists to oppose Waxman-Markey."

"It's great that Congress is looking at an actual cap," but the bill needs a stronger emissions-cuts target, says the Chesapeake Climate Action Network's Tidwell. "If we don't reduce coal use, we will lose the ability to stabilize the climate." Under the current bill, "if everything went perfectly, you might get an emissions level in the U.S. 20 percent below 1990 levels by 2020," which is completely inadequate, he says.

"Probably the biggest disappointment for environmentalists is the pace and target of reduction," wrote the University of North Carolina's Flatt. "The original Waxman-Markey discussion draft called for a 20 percent reduction (from 2005 levels) in greenhouse gases from capped sources by 2020, and the new bill only calls for a 17 percent reduction (though it still estimates that by using other policies besides cap and trade, the overall reduction might still approach 20 percent). . . . Most scientists estimate that we need larger reductions earlier to . . . avoid catastrophic changes to the environment." [24]

Under the current bill, during the early years of cap and trade emitters can avoid cutting emissions altogether by buying "offset credits" from sources that reduce GHGs, such as a forest-planting project in the Midwest or a new renewable-energy project like a hydropower dam in a developing country. A company "buys" the offset and the government accepts the offset's effect in reducing global GHG emissions as a substitute for emission cuts by the business.

Offsets are supposed to be new initiatives launched as a result of the new program. But skeptics aren't sure it will be possible to ascertain whether that's the case. "If as little as 15 percent of the offsets are bogus — or are [projects] that actually would have been done anyway — then the whole thing is wasted," says Washington lawyer N. Hunter Johnston, a son of former Sen. Johnston.

The bill allows a billion tons of emissions to be offset by projects on U.S. soil and another billion abroad. But "where would a billion tons of domestic offsets come from?" asks William Bumpers, head of the global climate change group in the Washington office of the international law firm Baker Botts. He doubts there are enough agricultural projects in this country, such as low-till farming or reforestation efforts, to offset a billion tons of carbon emissions.

And overseas, it's difficult to even verify who owns a plot of land in a country such as Brazil, says former Sen. Johnston. "What if somebody sells the offsets? Who's going to follow up to see that they don't cut the trees down?"

Some business people say more offsets could be available more quickly than skeptics believe. For example, chlorofluorocarbons (CFCs) — chemicals

Energy Plan Targets Carbon Emitters

Current environmental laws permit industrial polluters to emit carbon dioxide (CO_2) without charge. The proposed American Clean Energy and Security Act of 2009 initially would raise the price to about $16 per ton of CO_2 emitted but increase fourfold by 2050.

Estimated Cost of Emitting a Ton of CO_2

(in constant 2009 dollars)

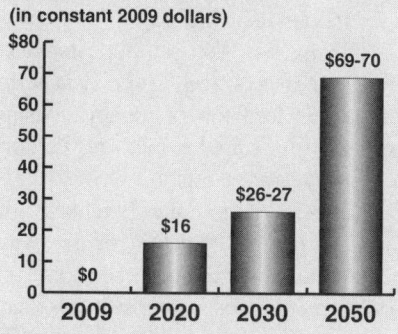

Source: Pew Center on Global Climate Change

once used for refrigeration and other industrial purposes that were banned after they were found to deplete the Earth's ozone layer — are believed to also have a major role in climate change. In Waxman-Markey, projects to properly dispose of CFCs are considered offsets but are available only to a specific group of emitters.

"We're suggesting they be made available to the market at large," says Joe Madden — CEO of EOS Climate, a Silicon Valley-based company developing emission-reduction programs — to increase the number of quickly available offsets and to create green jobs such as refrigerator take-back programs.

But every proposed offset raises its own questions, which often involve the issue of "additionality" — verifying that an offset actually is a new program, an

"addition" to emissions-cutting activities that would have occurred without the cap-and-trade program. "Additionality is always a huge question," and CFC disposal is a case in point, says Catherine Wolfram, associate professor of economics at the University of California at Berkeley's Haas School of Business.

For instance, the Indian government wanted to establish a national standardized CFC-disposal program, Wolfram says. "But they didn't do it because, if they had, people couldn't have gotten credit for doing [CFC disposal] as an offset" because the climate-friendly program would already have been in progress. That failure to establish a program amounts to an unfortunate gaming of the offset idea, she explains, because it means projects may be counted as "additional" when, in fact, they would have been done anyway.

But many analysts say the bill is necessary and that its many perceived flaws are provisions that were necessary to win support. For example, "a gradual but inexorable ramp-up [to strict emission caps] is the right way to proceed," says Tufts University professor of economics Gilbert Metcalf. "If we can provide a very strong signal that this will grow more stringent over time, that will make things more predictable for business and will help get international agreements." Metcalf prefers a tax on emissions over cap and trade but says a phase-in would be required for either.

"Instead of a utility starting out with efficiency measures — which have a big cost to consumers — they can plant a forest, which costs the consumers less and still gets the environmental benefit," says Eron Bloomgarden, president for environmental markets at Equator, a New York City-based company that manages offsets.

"The emission targets are ambitious but reasonable," says Mignone at the Brookings Institution. "The trajectory to an 80 percent reduction from today's levels by 2050 fits with what is known scientifically about what it takes to accomplish climate targets."

And getting a U.S. policy in place before the U.N. Climate Conference tries to reach new agreements on cutting carbon emissions in Copenhagen in December "is the absolutely critical thing," says UNC's Flatt. "Ultimately China will go with a target" for lower emissions once they see that the United States has declared one. "But if the U.S. hasn't signaled, China will do nothing."

Moreover, he says, Europe's cap-and-trade scheme is beginning to work. The most recent data show "a real drop" in Western Europe's emissions.

Verifying whether offsets actually reduce emissions is "not as squishy as you might think, though there are uncertainties," says energy lawyer Bumpers of Baker Botts. For example, "There's lots of information about how much carbon is sequestered in low- and no-till farming," and data about how forests and farms at particular longitudes and latitudes affect emissions, he says.

The EPA has been running offset programs for sulfur dioxide and nitrous oxide, which cause acid rain, since the '70s, says Perera at the Union of Concerned Scientists, giving the government a lot of experience with offset validation. Non-governmental organizations will keep a close eye on offset validity, "and I'm sure there will be organizations willing to sue if the EPA and the [Department of Agriculture] don't do the job correctly," she says.

In addition, the science on offsets "will really begin to move," once cap and trade becomes established policy, says Equator's Bloomgarden.

Will Democrats' alternative-energy policies produce enough energy?

As carbon-intensive fuels are phased out, new energy sources will be needed, both in the United States and abroad. White House and congressional proposals, including Waxman-Markey, have provisions intended to build a new system, but critics call them inadequate.

"We like the Waxman-Markey bill — for the fundamental reason that it's a

step in the right direction," says Matt Cheney, CEO of the San Francisco-based renewable-energy firm MMA Renewable Ventures. "I think a better deal could be cut" for renewable-energy producers, "but who can blame people for at least trying to do something?"

"Waxman and Markey deserve credit . . . for reserving some 16 percent of the cap-and-trade revenue for clean-energy development and deployment," wrote Mark Muro, director of the metropolitan policy program at the Brookings Institution. He also applauds the bill's allocation of 1 percent of cap-and-trade permit revenues to establish eight Clean Energy Innovation Centers — regional R&D hubs. [25]

"Obama has also set out alternative energy as a goal and, in the near term, has put aside a ton of money" to support it in the stimulus bill, says Califorina energy lawyer Fulton.

Bumpers of the Baker-Botts law firm says he is "kind of a fan" of the Waxman-Markey bill's establishment of a national standard for how much electricity must come from renewable sources, called the "renewable energy standard." Currently, many states have their own individual standards, which makes it difficult for renewable-energy producers to operate, he says.

Others praise the bill's "smart grid" provisions, which would help modernize the nation's electrical transmission system to accommodate the fluctuating nature of alternative-energy sources, such as wind and solar power, and allow consumers to monitor their own household energy use.

Califorina energy lawyer Michael Hindus said the bill's push for "inter-operability standards" is vital because as alternative-energy sources come on line, the grid must operate like the Internet, with all kinds of power-generating and power-using devices hooked up to it in an interactive way.

Hindus also likes the fact that the bill would allow energy efficiency to count toward the renewable standard.

"Time and time again, studies show that increasing energy efficiency is the cheapest way" to convert to a cleaner system, he says. "In California, we got into efficiency in the '70s, and as a result our electrical usage has not increased despite our incredible growth and the enormous growth in appliance use," making it easier for renewable sources — which tend to be smaller than traditional coal-powered plants — to meet demand, he says.

Suzanne Watson, policy director of the American Council for an Energy-Efficient Economy (ACEEE), agrees. "If you get enough efficiency in the mix, it makes renewables affordable," she says, because overall energy demand will be lower. Efficiency should be first on the agenda — before a major switch-over to renewable power — because the efficiency technologies are already available, she says.

Nevertheless, Watson complains, the bill could have a much more aggressive efficiency target. It's been shown that improving national energy efficiency by 15 percent is doable by 2020, she says, but the bill proposes only 8 percent. And the Senate looks likely to propose an even lower goal, she says.

Some say energy-conservation goals are unlikely to be met because Waxman-Markey would not raise costs enough to spur customers to opt for them. The legislation will raise electricity costs by between 10 and 20 percent over a decade or so, estimates Babcock of the LECG consultancy. "That's not enough to spur big behavior changes." Legislative provisions to protect consumers "by mitigating the cost increases end up cutting the incentive for people to change their behavior," he says.

"Renewable energy is a bit orphaned" in the bill, says Cheney. A carbon tax, with revenues directed to supporting renewable energy, would have worked better, he argues. "I think the electric-utility industry could do more and would do more [on renewables] if they were asked to, and

Continued on p. 632

Chronology

1970s-1980s
Two major oil "shocks" and fluctuating oil prices put focus on energy security and conservation.

1973
Arab oil producers embargo exports to U.S. for five months.

1977
President Jimmy Carter declares a national energy crisis and calls for measures to promote conservation and reduce demand.

1979
Reactor leak at Three Mile Island nuclear plant near Harrisburg, Pa., raises safety concerns that eventually end new U.S. nuclear-plant construction. . . . Hostage-taking at U.S. Embassy in Iran causes prices to skyrocket; Carter redoubles his conservation policies.

1986
Catastrophic explosion at a nuclear plant in Chernobyl, Ukraine, increases fears about nuclear power, eventually causes thousands of deaths.

1988
United Nations and World Meteorological Organization create the International Panel on Climate Change to assess scientific data on global warming.

1990s
Concern that human activity is causing climate change begins to shift energy policies worldwide.

1992
World Environmental Summit in Rio de Janeiro establishes U.N. Framework Convention on Climate Change, calling on industrialized nations to voluntarily reduce greenhouse gas (GHG) emissions to 1990 levels by 2000. . . . Energy Policy Act of 1992 increases investment in energy efficiency, renewable energy and alternative fuels.

1996
U.S. delegates to United Nations Framework Convention on Climate Change in Geneva agree to press for mandatory emissions cuts.

1997
Kyoto Protocol is adopted, calling for GHG emissions cuts averaging 5.2 percent below 1990 levels by 2009; Clinton administration signs the agreement, but the Senate refuses to ratify it because developing nations are not required to make cuts.

2000s
United States turns away from climate-change concerns after George W. Bush repudiates the Kyoto Protocol.

2005
President Bush signs Energy Policy Act of 2005, but critics say the bill does too little to promote energy efficiency and renewable energy in favor of oil drilling offshore and on public lands. . . . Kyoto Protocol takes effect when Russia provides the last needed signature. . . . Seven Northeastern states form Regional Greenhouse Gas Initiative (RGGI) to limit emissions. . . . Fifty-three U.S. senators support non-binding resolution stating that human-caused climate change is occurring and will require mandatory emissions cuts. . . . European Union activates its cap-and-trade system for controlling GHGs.

2006
California Global Warming Solutions Act of 2006 establishes statewide GHG emissions cap for 2020. . . . California promises to cut emissions 25 percent by 2020 and start trading emissions in 2012. . . . Boulder, Colo., enacts carbon tax.

2007
Seven Western states — Arizona, California, Montana, New Mexico, Oregon, Utah and Washington — and four Canadian provinces — British Columbia, Manitoba, Ontario and Quebec — form Western Climate Initiative to establish a regional cap-and-trade system. . . . U.S. Supreme Court rules, 5-4, that the Environmental Protection Agency (EPA) can regulate carbon dioxide as a pollutant.

2008
A bipartisan bill to impose mandatory carbon-emissions cuts, sponsored by Sens. Joseph I. Lieberman, I-Conn., and John Warner, R-Va., is pulled after Senate leaders fail to garner 60 votes to override a filibuster. . . . Democratic presidential hopeful Barack Obama makes combating climate change a major campaign theme. . . . British Columbia enacts a carbon tax.

2009
Limits on carbon emissions take effect in Northeast. . . . Obama administration allows California to regulate tailpipe emissions. . . . EPA says it will regulate carbon dioxide as a threat to the environment. . . . The first House energy legislation to focus on climate change passes, 219-212, on May 21; the American Clean Energy and Security Act of 2009 (HR 2454) is sponsored by Reps. Henry A. Waxman, D-Calif., and Edward J. Markey, D-Mass. . . . Senate scheduled to take up climate legislation in the fall. . . . In December, the U.N. Climate Conference meets in Copenhagen, Denmark, to sign new agreements for worldwide emissions cuts.

Can Current Technology Support a Low-Carbon Future?

Putting a man on the moon skewed the debate.

Slowing climate change will take more than phasing out carbon-based fuels. It will also require technology to replace them.

"Public opinion about the possibility of technology solving a problem is shaped by the shot to the moon," says former Sen. J. Bennett Johnston, D-La., now a lobbyist in Washington. The historic space flight took a mere eight years from President John F. Kennedy's announcement of the Apollo program to the first moon landing. But, Johnston cautions, "technological breakthroughs are always more expensive and take a lot longer than people think."

Meanwhile, the Obama administration is trying to jump-start more federal energy research. "We don't have a National Energy Institute [comparable to the National Institutes of Health], and the Department of Energy is trying to become one on very short notice," says Severin Borenstein, a professor of business administration and public policy at the University of California-Berkeley's Haas School of Business. "It's not within their current capabilities, but to their credit they're trying."

The technologies being debated include:

Carbon capture and sequestration — Advocates of continued reliance on America's large coal reserves put their faith in carbon capture and sequestration (CCS) — which traps CO_2 from burning fossil fuels and stores it under the Earth or ocean or chemically transforms it into a stable mineral form. CCS has had small-scale demonstrations, and debate remains heated.

The barriers to large-scale CCS are "huge" and could "increase the cost of electricity generation by 81 percent" if added to existing power plants, said Michael Brune, executive director of the environmental group Rainforest Action Network. [1]

Others say carbon-free coal can quickly become a viable technology. "CCS technology is ready to begin deployment at large, commercial scale today," and would be in use already except that "it makes no sense to invest in such a plant if there are no limits" on carbon emissions, wrote George Peridas, a science fellow at the Natural Resources Defense Council, an environmental advocacy group. [2]

Nuclear power — For the first time since safety worries shelved its development in the 1980s, nuclear power is gener-ating interest. "The safest and most efficient way for utility companies to control carbon emissions is to increase their supply of nuclear energy," said Rep. Mike Pence, R-Ind., who advocates building new nuclear plants. [3]

A key barrier to developing nuclear power has been concern over disposal of used reactor fuel rods. The rods contain radioactive elements, including uranium-235 and plutonium — used in nuclear bombs. Critics argue that stored waste would tempt terrorists and endanger nearby populations by leaking into water supplies.

"Estimates for new nuclear power place these facilities among the costliest private projects ever undertaken," and "independent studies have concluded new nuclear power is not economically competitive," compared to wind, biomass and landfill gas, wrote Craig A. Severance in an analysis published by the liberal group Center for American Progress. [4]

But advocates say reprocessing solves the waste problem. France, for example, has generated 75 percent of its power from nuclear plants for three decades, said William Tucker, author of the 2008 book *Terrestrial Energy: How Nuclear Power Will Lead the Green Revolution and End America's Long Energy Odyssey*. France, he wrote recently in *The Wall Street Journal*, "completely reprocesses all of its nuclear material" and "stores all the unused remains . . . beneath the floor of a single room at La Hague," a nuclear-processing facility in the Normandy region of France. [5]

Hydrogen, Solar, Wind — Virtually all technologies that might replace carbon fuels have their skeptics.

"I don't think hydrogen fuel will ever work," says Johnston. "Wind is a good technology, but its potential cannot be realized unless Congress solves the difficult problem of transmission, since wind does not blow steadily close to where people live."

Solar power also has drawbacks, wrote Robert Glennon, a professor of law and public policy at the University of Arizona's James E. Rogers College of Law. Small-scale solar installations, like rooftop solar panels, have limited use because the sun doesn't shine consistently, and good storage options for the power haven't been developed. [6]

Continued from p. 630

if we had a plan to redirect money toward alternative-energy investment."

The current Waxman-Markey renewable energy standard (RES) will not "deploy significant amounts of solar," wrote Annie Carmichael, director of federal solar policy, and Jim Baak, director of utility-scale solar policy at the advocacy group Vote Solar Initiative. A Department of Energy analysis found that even a somewhat more aggressive RES would lead only "to a 35 percent increase in solar by 2025, and "when you're starting at 0.001 percent, 35 percent growth doesn't amount to much." [26]

The industry group American Wind Energy Association (AWEA) says it's unfortunate that the current House bill sets such a low RES — less than half the level originally proposed by President Obama and in the original discussion draft of the Waxman-Markey bill. The low RES "could severely blunt the signal to the private sector to invest billions of dollars and expand production, manufacturing and job creation," says the AWEA. [27]

Bumpers explains that Waxman-Markey sets up two different trading systems — one to trade carbon-emission

Meanwhile, large-scale solar power — usually produced by a system called "concentrating solar power" (CSP) — "uses four times as much water as a natural gas plant and twice as much as a coal or nuclear plant," said Glennon. If CSP remains the dominant solar technology, a coming water shortage in the West could doom it, he said. [7]

The "Smart" Electrical Grid — The nation's aging electrical-transmission grid needs a major upgrade to make it more efficient — thus decreasing total power needs — and to accommodate renewable sources like wind and solar power.

Who will pay for new transmission lines is one dilemma. "If a wind farm in North Dakota is to send power to Chicago, you want to make sure that the customers who benefit are the ones who pay," a principle that raises practical difficulties since electricity is mainly sold regionally, says San Francisco-based energy lawyer Michael Hindus.

Wind-power producers themselves can't be expected to pick up the transmission tab, a point driven home earlier this month by Texas oilman and wind power enthusiast T. Boone Pickens, who scuttled highly touted plans for a massive wind-power facility in the Texas Panhandle after he couldn't raise the cash to build transmission lines to big cities. [8]

Incorporating many small, widely distributed energy sources into the grid also requires upgrades.

"If we had a million plug-in hybrid cars, they could push power back into the grid" and solve some energy-shortage problems, but today "utilities wouldn't know what to do with" such "micro-power production," nor could current transmission mechanisms handle it, says Victor Flatt, a professor of environmental law at the University of North Carolina School of Law in Chapel Hill.

"We're 15 years behind other countries in this transformation" to a "smart" grid with digital — rather than mechanical — switches that can adapt to fluctuating power supply and demand in an instant, says Kurt Yeager, executive director of the Galvin Electricity Initiative, a nonprofit that researches and advocates for modernizing the grid.

"Because we live in a digital society," even a fraction of a second's power outage "results in lost productivity as data is lost and assembly lines may shut down," he says. U.S. households average four hours a year without power, while Western Europe averages an hour or two, Japan seven minutes, and Singapore under one minute; the "unreliability costs our nation $150 billion a year."

A complete transformation of the nation's electrical grid into a so-called smart grid would cost $250 billion and allow incorporation of more renewable power sources, including small-scale sources, such as consumers selling back power to utilities from rooftop photovoltaics, Yeager says. Moreover, smart-grid technology would enable utilities to send minute-by-minute power prices to every home, and consumers could opt to have air-conditioning or other systems automatically shut off when energy prices were high.

In the United States, various localities worried about power reliability are incorporating smart-grid technology, "but the best solution would have federal leadership," such as a federal power-reliability standard all states would have to meet, Yeager suggests.

[1] Mike Brune, "There Is No Such Thing as Clean Coal," SolveClimate.com, Oct. 17, 2008, http://solveclimate.com.

[2] George Peridas, "Waxman-Markey: Breaking the Deadlock on CCS," Switchboard blog, Natural Resources Defense Council, April 3, 2009, http://switchboard.nrdc.org.

[3] Mike Pence, "American Energy Solutions Group Introduces Comprehensive Energy Plan Without Raising Taxes," statement, www.mikepence.house.gov.

[4] Craig A. Severance, "Business Risks and Costs of New Nuclear Power," Climate Progress Web site, http://climateprogress.org/wp-content/uploads/2009/01/nuclear-costs-2009.pdf.

[5] William Tucker, "There Is No Such Thing as Nuclear Waste," *The Wall Street Journal*, March 13, 2009, http://online.wsj.com/article/SB123690627522614525.html.

[6] Robert Glennon, "Is Solar Power Dead in the Water?" *The Washington Post*, June 7, 2009, p. B2.

[7] *Ibid.*

[8] Andy Stone, "What the Pickens Fiasco Means to Green," *Forbes.com*, July 8, 2009, www.forbes.com/2009/07/08/boone-pickens-wind-power-business-energy-pickens.html.

permits and the other to trade "renewable energy credits" (RECs) that companies can use to meet the RES standards. The idea is for renewable-energy producers to be rewarded for producing non-carbon-emitting power with RECs that they can sell to others who can't meet the RES on their own, he explains.

However, "they should allow a renewable-energy person to decide whether they get a carbon credit or an REC," energy lawyer Bumpers says. Ironically, "if we go beyond the RES" — generating more power from renewable sources than the law requires — "the REC prices will actually plummet," which would end up punishing renewables producers because with so many RECs available, their value will decrease, he says. ∎

BACKGROUND

Energy Security

G overnment efforts to ensure the United States has an adequate supply of affordable energy have intensified over the past 30 years, as global politics has threatened oil supplies and scientists have recognized that oil will eventually run out. [28]

More recently, however, a competing environmental concern has complicated energy policy debates: the conviction among scientists that burning carbon-based fuels — coal, oil, natural gas and ethanol — is a prime culprit in potentially drastic climate change. [29]

The tension between these competing concerns has turned debates over energy policy into fractious brawls and stalemates. Liberal Democrats have pushed for energy conservation and a switch to renewable energy like wind power to offset climate change, while some conservative Democrats and most Republicans have championed aggressive development of carbon-based fuels available in the United States, such as coal, offshore oil and ethanol, to make the country less dependent on foreign suppliers. [30]

There is "massive tension" between the goals of energy security and climate-change action, says the University of California's Borenstein. If energy security "were all you cared about, the important thing would be to make a massive investment in coal." But if climate change is the top worry, increasing coal use would be "the worst thing" to do because "clean coal simply doesn't exist" today, he says.

In the 1970s, two energy "shocks" made energy security a U.S. government priority. The first came in 1973, when Arab oil producers embargoed exports to the United States for five months in retaliation for U.S. support of Israel during the Yom Kippur War. President Richard M. Nixon responded by imposing price controls on oil and gas, and his successor, Gerald R. Ford, established the Strategic Petroleum Reserve — an emergency stockpile of oil stored underground in states along the Gulf of Mexico.

By 1977, newly elected President Jimmy Carter was warning Americans that energy security was "the greatest challenge our country will face dur-

ing our lifetimes." Carter created the Cabinet-level Department of Energy (DOE), which undertook conservation measures like nationwide home weatherization and efficiency standards for large appliances.

The second oil shock hit in 1979 after Iranian revolutionaries seized the U.S. Embassy in Tehran on Nov. 4 and held 52 employees hostage for 444 days. World oil prices skyrocketed to record highs, and Carter redoubled his efforts to promote conservation and efficiency and began dismantling some of Nixon's price controls to increase domestic supplies and lower prices.

In 1980, Carter signed the Energy Security Act, which funded research on biomass, solar, geothermal and ocean-thermal energy.

Soon after President Ronald Reagan took office in 1981 the world was awash in oil, thanks to huge, new non-OPEC supplies opening up in the North Sea and Alaska's Prudhoe Bay. World oil prices plummeted to record lows. New auto-efficiency standards also kicked in, helping to slow the growth of U.S. oil demand. Reagan chose to reduce funding for efficiency and renewable-energy programs, favoring instead encouraging greater use of plentiful U.S. coal supplies and nuclear power.

However, two frightening accidents at nuclear-power plants — in 1979 at the Three Mile Island plant near Harrisburg, Pa., and in 1986 in Chernobyl, Ukraine — turned Americans against nuclear power, and the drive to develop it as a homegrown energy source largely fizzled.

Climate Concerns

Economic boom times in the 1990s left Americans relatively unfazed by fluctuating oil prices, and for a time energy security faded from the national agenda. At the same time, however, worries about climate change were growing, setting up the policy struggle that continues today between

those who deem energy security the top concern and those who see climate change as the larger threat.

Largely due to that ideological divide, U.S. energy policy remained stalemated after enactment of the 1992 Energy Policy Act, which deregulated electrical utilities and increased investment in alternative energy. Throughout the 1990s, many in the United States resisted acting on climate change, since capping GHG emissions would raise energy prices and likely force changes in Americans' energy-dependent lifestyles, with gas-guzzling cars and aggressively air-conditioned and heated buildings. Many in both political parties argued it would be unfair to force Americans to cut emissions when emissions were expected to rise dramatically in rapidly industrializing and urbanizing countries like China and India.

Nevertheless, in 1993, in the wake of international meetings declaring human-caused climate change a catastrophic threat, the Bill Clinton administration unveiled its Climate Change Action Plan, recommending that U.S businesses take voluntary measures to stabilize emissions. Clinton also limited oil and gas exploration in U.S. wilderness areas, despite pressure from energy-security advocates to expand exploration on public lands.

The Clinton White House supported international efforts on emissions caps and even signed the U.N. climate-change treaty, called the Kyoto Protocol. But Clinton never sent the treaty to the Senate for ratification, because the Republican-led Senate had voted 95-0 for a resolution opposing it.

In 2000, Texas Gov. George W. Bush pledged to continue U.S. participation in the Kyoto discussions when he campaigned for president. But shortly after taking office in 2001, he repudiated the agreement. Gasoline was hovering at near $2 a gallon — a record level — and energy security once again became the public's top concern. Acting on the advice of an energy task force led by

Continued on p. 636

Taxes vs. Cap and Trade: Which Works Best?

Both systems have advantages and problems.

Economists agree that raising the price of carbon-based fuels is the key to phasing them out. But they disagree over the best way to hike prices — a tax or a so-called cap-and-trade system like the one in the Waxman-Markey energy bill currently moving through Congress.

A tax is a time-honored way to brake unwanted behavior, such as the heavy federal tax on cigarettes to reduce smoking. Several countries and localities around the world — including Sweden, the Canadian province of British Columbia and Boulder, Colo. — use taxes to limit the use of some carbon-emitting fuels.

In June the City Council in Boulder, which generates electrical power with a coal-fired plant, increased the carbon tax city voters first enacted in 2006. The city adds a charge to residents' utility bills and uses the revenue to fund aggressive energy-efficiency measures, such as home visits by technicians to install programmable thermostats. The tax increase — from about $11 per year to $21 per household, and from an average $43 per year to $94 for businesses — is expected to provide an additional $810,000 annually to help the city reduce its greenhouse gas (GHG) emissions below 1990 levels within four years.[1] GHGs are thought to cause climate change.

Many residents urged the council to raise the tax. "I think that the more carbon tax we have, the better. This city has the opportunity to lead the nation" in carbon reduction, said a resident at the June meeting.[2]

"The major argument for taxes is that they're simpler — they build on existing [revenue-collecting] structures," says Gilbert Metcalf, a professor of economics at Tufts University, near Boston. In addition, unlike a cap-and-trade market, a tax clearly sets the price of emissions, "and from a business point of view, that would protect against the risk of changing carbon prices," he says.

Under cap and trade, such as the system the European Union launched in 2005, lawmakers issue permits to businesses for a certain level of emissions that is deemed allowable — under an emissions "cap" that gets increasingly restrictive over time. At the same time, a trading market is established enabling businesses with extra permits to sell them to businesses whose own emissions would otherwise exceed the cap.

While a tax sets a price to drive emissions to the desired level, a cap-and-trade scheme sets an emissions limit and lets the resulting trading market set prices. Europe's cap-and-trade scheme has produced short-term volatility in energy prices, Metcalf says. If the United States enacts cap and trade, "if the prices go too high, Congress may just bypass the market and lower the prices," he says. That might be a boon to consumers but would be a misfortune for companies who had bought emissions permits under an earlier, higher price, he notes.

Some economists argue that emissions caps should be applied to fuel-producing industries like coal mines and oil importers rather than to fuel-using industries, like electrical utilities and manufacturing plants, as both the European Union's cap-and-trade scheme and Waxman-Markey do.

Capping importation and production of carbon fuels "is much easier to monetize and enforce" than capping fuel-user emissions, partly because many fewer businesses would be directly involved, says Peter Dorman, a professor of economics and environmental policy at Evergreen State University in Olympia, Wash. Furthermore, "it would apply to both large and small emitters because both use the fuel, and you would eliminate the unintended consequence of everybody currying favor with everybody" to get special breaks for their industry, he says. In the Waxman-Markey bill, for example, only big-business emitters have their emissions capped, and even some big businesses, notably large agribusinesses, have successfully argued that their emissions should not be capped.

Other analysts say emissions caps are better applied to fuel users. "I prefer [capping] the utilities because that's where the change must come" to switch the country off carbon fuels, says William Bumpers, an energy lawyer in Washington. "The coal mine can't do anything about the fact that coal is a carbon-based fuel," while electrical utilities, manufacturers and other fuel users can launch energy-efficiency programs and search for alternative fuel sources to cut emissions, Bumpers explains.

"There's been a very strong political constituency for cap and trade rather than a tax," says Bryan K. Mignone, a fellow at the centrist Brookings Institution think tank in Washington. For example, many environmental groups back cap and trade "because you don't get the same emissions certainty" with a tax, since, under a tax, the government specifies the price of emitting but not how much emission will be allowed, he explains.

The affected industries also prefer cap and trade because those who make investments to cut emissions can get an immediate reward as they sell their unneeded emissions permits to others and thus "recoup their investments" in emission-limiting technologies, Mignone explains.

Furthermore, once carbon-emission permits become a financial asset that companies can sell, buy and hold, "they only have value as long as the system remains in place, so you're creating a constituency for the system," Mignone says.

But others wonder whether strong support for cap and trade will continue when emissions caps really begin to lower, about a decade from now. "The evidence is pretty thin" that having a market creates a constituency, says Severin Borenstein, a professor of business administration and public policy at the University of California-Berkeley's Haas School of Business.

---

[1] Heath Urie, "Falling Short of Kyoto Goals, Boulder Raises Carbon Tax," [Boulder] *Daily Camera* online, June 4, 2009, www.dailycamera.com/news/2009/jun/04/kyoto-boulder-raises-carbon-tax/.

[2] Quoted in *ibid*.

Continued from p. 634

Vice President Dick Cheney, Bush launched an energy policy centered on increasing domestic supply, including reversing Clinton's ban on oil and gas exploration on public lands.

The Bush administration eventually acknowledged that human activity played a role in climate change but argued that taxing or capping emissions would cripple the economy. The Republican-dominated Congress approved Bush's budget, which called for increased money to develop so-called "clean coal" technology but severe cuts in energy-conservation programs and research on renewable-energy sources.

With the United States focusing on energy security, the Kyoto treaty went into effect in 2005 after being ratified by a majority of U.N. member countries. The European Union immediately launched its mandatory cap-and-trade system to try to limit emissions. [31]

By then, a growing number of U.S. senators, including some Republicans, became convinced that human activities drive climate change and that government action might be warranted. The Senate, though not the House, has debated several measures to address climate change. In 2008, a bill that would impose mandatory emissions cuts — sponsored by Sens. Joseph I. Lieberman, I-Conn., and John Warner, R-Va. — gained support of a bipartisan majority. Ultimately, however, the bill was pulled from consideration after supporters failed to gain the 60 votes needed to override a filibuster. ∎

CURRENT SITUATION

Seismic Change

If Congress passes climate-focused energy legislation in 2009, the event will constitute a seismic shift in U.S. energy policy.

Signs of change began in 2008, as then Democratic presidential hopeful Barack Obama's candidacy began picking up steam. During his campaign, Obama pledged to promote a national cap-and-trade system and to be a strong partner to states and companies pursuing energy efficiency and non-carbon energy sources.

The new administration quickly put climate change on its agenda. The economic-stimulus package that Obama called for upon inauguration and signed into law Feb. 17 had provisions aimed at developing a low-carbon energy system. It called for doubling U.S. production of renewable energy over three years, making federal buildings and millions of homes more energy efficient and putting a million plug-in hybrid cars on the road by 2015. [32]

The provisions were an "important down payment" on tackling climate change and "long overdue," climate-change advocate and former Vice President Al Gore told the Senate Foreign Relations Committee. [33]

The administration took a bigger step toward limiting GHG emissions when the EPA announced on April 17 that a scientific review ordered by a 2007 Supreme Court decision found GHGs "contribute to air pollution that may endanger public health or welfare." [34] Based on that finding the EPA has begun the process of issuing federal rules to limit emissions.

Nevertheless, it's unclear how much the agency can do on emissions caps, given the scope of its legal authority. "I believe that EPA can do a trading regime for carbon under the Clean Air Act," says UNC's Flatt. "But can it set the level of allowable carbon? Not so much." Nevertheless, the agency could effectively set a temporary limit because "it would take four or five years [for cases challenging the move] to percolate up through the courts."

Perhaps more important, the EPA's promise to regulate emissions spurred the utility industry to support a legislatively based cap-and-trade system, hoping that lawmakers would be more sensitive to their concerns than the agency rulemaking process, Flatt says.

The Obama administration's energy-policy staff is clearly focused on climate change, observers note.

"The impacts of climate change are not just life and death, but they are economic costs that are hard to extrapolate into the future," EPA Administrator Lisa Jackson told ABC News. [35]

But some industry observers say the energy team lacks technological expertise.

"In the previous administration, as much as they were all about putting politics over policy, they did employ a lot of people from the private sector," says Cheney of MMA Renewable Ventures. "The new administration is just the other way, and we need more ideas from the private sector," because while the staff "is great in many ways, they're somewhat out of touch with where environmental technology is.

"I think the Obama administration is listening" to concerns from the renewable-energy sector, for example, "but they have an in-box that's eight-years deep," Cheney says.

Waxman-Markey Bill

Last November's election was a game changer in Congress as well as in the White House. Democrats strengthened their majorities in the House and Senate, and climate-legislation proponent Waxman challenged longtime Chairman Rep. John Dingell, D-Mich., for leadership of the Committee on Energy and Commerce.

Waxman ultimately won the member vote, defeating Dingell, a champion of his home state's carbon-emitting auto industry. The switch left many analysts predicting that Waxman would take a tough stance on global warming. Waxman is

Continued on p. 638

At Issue:

Will the Waxman-Markey bill harm the economy?

REP. FRED UPTON, R-MICH.
RANKING MEMBER, ENERGY AND COMMERCE SUBCOMMITTEE ON ENERGY AND ENVIRONMENT

WRITTEN FOR *CQ RESEARCHER*, JULY 2009

Our economy continues to struggle. We shed 467,000 jobs in June and have hemorrhaged 3.2 million since Jan. 1. In Michigan, unemployment has soared to 15.2 percent. Yet, despite our economic maladies, Democratic leaders are pursuing a reckless climate bill that would bankrupt America's working families with no guarantee of helping the environment.

The carbon mandates under cap and tax would mean the United States could not emit more in 2050 than we emitted in 1910, essentially requiring us to scale back emissions to a per capita level equivalent to those of the tiny coastal nation of Belize.

Study after study has predicted cap-and-tax will result in skyrocketing energy bills and massive job losses. The Congressional Budget Office conservatively estimated that meeting the mandated reductions would cost $864 billion, while some anticipate closer to $1.5 trillion. CBO predicted gasoline costs would increase by 77 cents per gallon and diesel by 88 cents.

It is not just inside-the-Beltway analysts forecasting exorbitant costs to families. In Michigan, Consumers Energy predicts hefty rate increases — in excess of 38 percent over the next 15 years — just to comply with cap and tax. The increases will surely be higher as Consumers did not take into account inflation or rising fuel and construction costs. Some Michigan manufacturers say they will solely operate at night, when electric rates are cheaper.

Efforts to improve the legislation with constructive amendments were blocked every step of the way. We sought to add consumer protections to safeguard working families, but were rebuffed. Efforts to include the world's leading emitters in the legislation were also thwarted.

Meaningful climate legislation requires global participation, especially by India and China. According to the July 16 edition of *The New York Times*, Energy Secretary Steven Chu said that if China's emissions of global warming gases keep growing at the pace of the last 30 years, the country will emit more such gases in the next three decades than the United States has in its entire history.

Without international participation, jobs and emissions will simply shift overseas to countries that require few, if any, environmental protections, harming the global environment as well as the U.S. economy.

We should take an "all of the above" approach to reducing emissions, with an emphasis on renewable sources of energy like wind and solar, as well as nuclear power. We can simultaneously preserve our environment and create jobs.

DANIEL A. FARBER
PROFESSOR OF LAW, UNIVERSITY OF CALIFORNIA BERKELEY SCHOOL OF LAW

WRITTEN FOR *CQ RESEARCHER*, JULY 2009

In the short term, climate-change legislation will cause modest increases in energy costs but will help cut the federal deficit a bit. In the long run, it will safeguard us against dangerous changes in climate and help Americans become leaders in the emerging clean-tech industry.

One reason for the modest cost is that the legislation will create a cap-and-trade system rather than directly telling companies how much to reduce their emissions. Cap and trade is the brainchild of economists who believe conventional environmental regulation is too expensive. The whole purpose is to cut industries' costs. Companies will get "allowances" for each ton of carbon dioxide they emit. The total number of allowances is the "cap." Companies can use the allowances themselves or sell them to other companies. That's the "trade" part of cap and trade, and it makes the program more cost-effective.

Under the bill that passed the House of Representatives, most allowances would be given away, but some would be auctioned. Auction proceeds would pay for government programs like vouchers for buying fuel-efficient vehicles and energy rebates for low-income consumers.

How much would this cost? The most reliable cost estimates come from the nonpartisan Congressional Budget Office rather than ideological advocates like the American Enterprise Institute.

A few weeks before the House passed the climate-change bill, the CBO estimated utilities would pay $15-$26 per allowance from 2010-2019. The impact on consumers would be small — a $20 charge per ton of emissions amounts to 1.4 cents per kilowatt-hour of electricity. CBO later admitted that its cost estimate had been on the high side, because it ignored other ways that companies could reduce their compliance costs.

When CBO's original report was released, opponents of the legislation squawked that the legislation would "cost" the government over hundreds of billions of dollars. It turns out that what the CBO meant was simply that the government was losing out on potential revenue by giving most of the allowances away instead of auctioning them. According to economists, auctioning permits is better.

And what about the deficit? CBO estimates that climate legislation would decrease the national debt by $24 billion over the next decade by allowing the federal government to earn income from auctioning allowances.

In short, climate-change legislation is not the huge economic burden claimed by opponents. It's a cost-effective way of combating a serious threat to our long-term well-being.

Continued from p. 636

"an avid environmentalist" with a "combative stance on climate change" that could alienate Republicans and moderate Democrats, wrote Associated Press reporter Andrew Taylor. [36]

Ironically, however, the bill that emerged from Waxman's committee not only has drawn criticism from congressional Republicans but is strongly opposed by some environmentalists as a giveaway to GHG-emitting industries. In the House, eight Republicans voted for the measure and 44 Democrats voted against, with a handful of the Democrats — Reps. Pete Stark, Calif., Peter DeFazio, Ore., and Dennis Kucinich, Ohio — demurring on the grounds that the bill is an insufficient response to climate change.

The bill "sets [emission] targets that are too weak, especially in the short term, and sets about meeting those targets through Enron-style accounting methods" such as allowing emitters to purchase "offsets," said Kucinich. "It gives new life to one of the primary sources of the problem that should be on its way out — coal — by giving it record subsidies." [37]

Republican critics, meanwhile, call the bill a liberal economy killer.

"The cost of this policy will be certain, massive and immediate," said Gov. Mitch Daniels, R-Ind. "The benefits . . . will be dubious, minuscule and decades in the distance." [38]

Among HR 2454's provisions are these: [39]

• A national requirement for major GHG emitters to reduce emissions by 17 percent from 2005 levels by 2020 and by 80 percent by 2050;

• Development of a cap-and-trade market in which heavy emitters can meet emission-cut targets by buying credits from businesses whose emissions already meet target levels as well as emission offsets, such as a newly planted forest. In the market's early years, the government would give permits free to businesses, but later permits would be auctioned and the government would get the proceeds;

• A national requirement for electric utilities to produce 20 percent of their demand using energy-efficiency improvements and renewable-energy sources like biomass, wind and landfill gas by 2020;

• Federal investments in technology development including for energy efficiency; renewable-energy sources; carbon capture and sequestration to cut GHG emissions from burning coal; an electrical-transmission "smart grid" to accommodate new, variable sources like wind and solar and new users like hybrid cars; and electric and other advanced vehicles;

• National energy-saving standards for buildings and appliances;

• Monetary rebates to help protect industries hit hardest by the shift from carbon fuels;

• Training to prepare workers for jobs in a low-carbon economy, such as "green" building construction, water and energy conservation and agriculture techniques like low- and no-till farming that offset GHG emissions; and

• Monetary rebates to consumers to help offset energy price increases.

Something for Everyone?

Environmentalists' pent-up desire for climate action and businesses' trepidation about a major change in the energy system have attracted floods of Washington lobbyists eager to shape the new policies.

If enacted, the bill will be a major departure from all previous energy legislation, "moving from an incentive-based energy policy to one that actually creates penalties" over time for GHG emissions, says Washington energy lawyer Hunter Johnston.

"Every line of the text has billions and billions of dollars riding on it," and "people will do and say anything" to get a share of the money, including environmentalists who hope federal revenues from eventual auction of emissions permits will help their cause, says Evergreen State's Dorman.

In the first quarter of 2009 alone, 140 additional businesses and organizations joined the crowd lobbying on energy and climate change, a 14 percent increase over a year ago, according to a Washington-based nonprofit investigative group, the Center for Public Integrity. [40]

Large food producers, represented by the American Beverage Association and the American Meat Institute, for example, want some of the free emission permits the Waxman-Markey bill is handing out to other industries, such as electrical utilities. Companies with energy-saving products to sell, such as the Santa Clara, Calif.-based computer company Sun Microsystems, which has developed more energy-efficient computer servers, have lined up to lobby for stringent national energy-efficiency standards to give businesses incentive to buy their products. [41]

Members of Congress have also sought provisions favoring their home regions.

Waxman and Markey won the undecided vote of Rep. Marcy Kaptur, D-Ohio, when they added a loan program for renewable-energy and economic-development projects in the Midwest. [42]

The bill owes its momentum to many groups who sought and got provisions they wanted, says Johnston. For example, he says, feeling that "it was inevitable that there would be some kind of carbon policy, utilities had the foresight to work out agreements that would put them in a strong position in the bill."

The "bill is complicated," in large part to "ensure that the burden is shared in such a way that it can pass," says Metcalf of Tufts. "You could lop out about 400 pages" by setting a comprehensive cap on GHG emissions and charging emitters — via a tax — for emissions beyond the cap, a plan many economists, including Metcalf, favor.

Waxman-Markey's complications come "partly because the Energy and Commerce Committee is full of people from coal states," who sought and won many provisions to help industries in their home districts, says Metcalf.

Then other industries lined up for assistance, too. "The wind people say that wind power is more expensive today, so they need a [renewable-energy] credit" to incentivize development of more wind power. "But wind is only a little more expensive than [natural] gas, and once we put in the carbon price, it'll raise the price of gas and make it comparable with wind," so wind power probably doesn't need extra help, Metcalf says. "Nevertheless, once the wind developers are in there, the biomass people want in too," and so on.

In the end, "we're picking winners and losers, which is always more expensive" than simply imposing a tax on carbon and letting more expensive, less-effective technologies fall by the wayside as the market sorts things out, Metcalf says.

Waxman and Markey steered a course between the bill they wanted and a bill that can realistically pass, supporters say.

"There's simply nobody else in Congress whose record of progressive legislative accomplishments can hold a candle to Waxman's," wrote Matthew Yglesias, a blogger at the liberal Center for American Progress. "When you draw intersecting curves of "what needs to be done" and "what can realistically be done," Waxman has time and again put himself at the intersection, and I think it involves a fair amount of hubris to think that you know better than [he] what the best feasible legislative outcome is." [43]

Cosponsor Markey also "has been a passionate champion of environmental and clean energy," wrote David Corn, Washington bureau chief for the liberal magazine *Mother Jones*. "Like Waxman, he gives a damn about this and truly wants to pass the toughest bill possible." [44]

More to Come

As Waxman-Markey continues its journey through Congress — eventually to be taken up by the Senate — lawmakers continue to push for amendments.

After committee passage and before the bill came to the House floor, Chairman Waxman reached an agreement with House Agriculture Committee Chairman Collin Peterson, D-Minn., to explicitly exempt the agriculture and forestry industries from emissions caps. Earlier drafts had left open the possibility that large factory farms might be subject to caps.

The revised bill also removes jurisdiction over "offsets" — projects like forest planting and no-till farming that carbon-heavy industries can buy to "offset" their GHG emissions — from EPA and gives it to the U.S. Department of Agriculture (USDA), a move that makes environmentalists wary because, unlike the EPA, the USDA's mission is promoting agriculture, not protecting health and the environment. [45]

Among Senate proposals on the table is an energy bill approved June 17 by the Senate Energy and Natural Resources Committee that would set much less stringent national energy-efficiency and renewable-energy requirements than the House bill. [46]

House Republicans are promoting a plan to revamp nuclear-power regulation to encourage licensing of 100 new reactors over the next 20 years. The plan also calls for exploration for offshore oil and for oil shale — sedimentary rock from which organic chemicals can be extracted and turned into synthetic crude oil — in the mountain West, said GOP House Conference Chairman Rep. Pence. [47]

Some Democrats continue to oppose giving away emissions permits free. Under a plan advanced by Rep. Christopher Van Hollen, D-Md., all permits would be auctioned with proceeds returned to the public in the form of a monthly dividend to every legal U.S. resident. To succeed, a climate bill "must attract and retain . . . popular support," and a dividend "offers the best chance to get the job done," Van Hollen said. [48]

Despite the wheeling and dealing, however, "I still don't see any real coalescence around an energy policy for the country," says UNC's Flatt. "We haven't really decided what we want — less GHG emission? Energy security? Lower cost? We want all three, and we assume we can get there, but they sometimes conflict." ■

OUTLOOK

On to Copenhagen

The fate of climate-change legislation in the 111th Congress is undecided, but what happens has huge implications for struggling international efforts to halt climate change.

"It will be a challenge to get to 60 [veto-proof] votes in the Senate," largely because regional interests play such a large role, says former Sen. Johnston. Midwestern states, for example, rely heavily on coal, while Southeastern states have little access to renewable-energy sources.

But the Union of Concerned Scientists' Perera thinks Senate passage is likely. Numerous Senate committees have jurisdiction over parts of the legislation, and "so many people will have a hand in the bill that they'll feel as if they have a stake in it, as if they're part of the final product," she says.

In addition, the Senate has regularly debated climate bills and resolutions for several years and is much more educated and concerned about the issue than the House, Perera says. She attributes the House's narrow margin of passage to the shorter time the House has had to assimilate climate-change issues. "The House is at the high-school level, and the Senate is at the college level" in understanding climate change, she says.

If passed, the bill will make possible an international deal in Copenhagen on global emissions cuts "as well as a bilateral deal with China, hopefully sooner," said Joseph Romm, a senior fellow at the liberal Center for American Progress. [49]

Rising emissions from developing countries, especially China and India, are often cited as an argument for the United States to hold off on passing a carbon ban, on the grounds that an emission ban here and the resultant higher energy costs would give those countries unfair competitive advantage in manufacturing. And not everyone is convinced that passing Waxman-Markey would get China to make its own cuts.

"It's going to be difficult to get to China. They understand the problem, but they've got tens of millions of peasants" the government hopes to urbanize, and "employing them depends on cheap energy," says Johnston.

Farther down the line, it's not clear the United States will have the will to continue the strict phase-out of carbon fuels, some analysts warn. "For Americans, right after the right to buy a gun comes the right to buy gas at cheap prices, so I'm worried that we won't stick with" the gasoline, coal and natural-gas price increases that the Waxman-Markey bill will impose "a decade or so from now, when carbon prices really begin to bite," the University of California's Borenstein says. ∎

Notes

[1] Quoted in Alex Pasternack, "Waxman-Markey Bill Moves Forward, After Arrests and a Speed Reading," *Huffington Post*, May 21, 2009, www.huffingtonpost.com.

[2] Quoted in Charles Owens, "Boucher: Cap and Trade Deal Preserves Coal Jobs," *Bluefield* [W. Va.] *Daily Telegraph*, May 16, 2009, www.bdtonline.com/local/local_story_136191739.html.

[3] For background, see Jennifer Weeks, "Carbon Trading," *CQ Global Researcher*, Nov. 1, 2008, pp. 295-320.

[4] "Prepared Remarks of President Barack Obama," weekly address, The White House, June 27, 2009, www.whitehouse.gov/the_press_office/UPDATED-and-FINAL-WEEKLY-ADDRESS-President-Obama-Calls-Energy-Bill-Passage-Critical-to-Stronger-American-Economy/.

[5] Darrell Issa, "Climate Bill a Pain in the Gas," *Politico*, June 5, 2009, www.politico.com/news/stories/0609/23356.html.

[6] Myron Ebell, "Waxman-Markey Energy-Rationing Bill," press release, Competitive Enterprise Institute, June 23, 2009, http://cei.org/pubsbytype/news_release.

[7] "Global Climate Change Impacts in the United States," U.S. Global Change Research Program, May 2009, www.globalchange.gov/publications/reports/scientific-assessments/us-impacts/download-the-report.

[8] "Wallowing in Denial: Inaction Is No Option on Global Warming," *St. Louis Post-Dispatch*, May 29, 2009, p. A16.

[9] For background, see Marcia Clemmitt, "Climate Change," *CQ Researcher*, Jan. 27, 2005, pp. 73-96.

[10] J.P.M. Sijm, *et al.*, "The Impact of the EU ETS on Electricity Prices: Final Report to the DG Environment of the European Commission," ECN Policy Studies, Dec. 19, 2008, www.ecn.nl/docs/library/report/2008/e08007.pdf.

[11] David Montgomery, *et al.*, "Impact on the Economy of the American Clean Energy and Security Act of 2009 (H.R. 2454)," CRA International/National Black Chamber of Commerce, May 2009, p. 4, www.nationalbcc.org/images/stories/documents/CRA_Waxman-Markey_%205-20-09_v8.pdf.

[12] *Ibid.*

[13] "Pence Says Democrats Need to 'Come Clean' About the Cost of Cap and Trade," press release, GOP.gov, April 23, 2009, www.gop.gov/press-release/09/04/23/pence-says-democrats-need-to.

[14] *Ibid.*

[15] "Climate Change Bill — House to Vote Friday," press release, CARE, June 24, 2009, www.care.org/newsroom/articles/index.asp?articletype=pressrelease&s_src=170920500000&s_subsrc=.

[16] For background, see Sergey Paltsev, *et al.*, "Assessment of U.S. Cap and Trade Proposals," MIT Joint Program on the Science and Policy of Global Change, April 2007, web.mit.edu/globalchange/www/MITJPSPGC_Rpt146.pdf.

[17] Quoted in "GOP Full of Hot Air About Obama's 'Light Switch Tax,' " PolitiFact.com, March 24, 2009, www.politifact.com.

[18] *Ibid.*

[19] *Ibid.*

[20] "The Estimated Costs to Households of the Cap-and-Trade Provisions of H.R. 2454," Congressional Budget Office, June 19, 2009, www.cbo.gov/ftpdocs/103xx/doc10327/06-19-CapAndTradeCosts.pdf.

[21] Chad Stone, Sharon Parrott and Dottie Rosenbaum, "Waxman-Markey Climate Change Bill Fully Offsets Average Purchasing Power Loss for Low-Income Consumers," Center on Budget and Policy Priorities, May 20, 2009, www.cbpp.org.

[22] "The Estimated Costs to Households of the Cap-and-Trade Provisions of H.R. 2454," *op. cit.*, p. 2.

[23] Robert Stavins, "Worried About International Competitiveness? Another Look at the Waxman-Markey Cap-and-Trade Proposal," *Huffington Post*, June 19, 2009, www.huffingtonpost.com.

[24] Victor Flatt, "Waxman-Markey Climate Change Bill Not a Disaster for the Environment," University of Houston Law Center Faculty blog, May 26, 2009, www.uhlawblog.com.

[25] Mark Muro, "Waxman-Markey: What About Innovation?" Brookings Institution, June 8, 2009, www.brookings.edu.

[26] Annie Carmichael and Jim Baak, "Solar Takes a Backseat in National Climate and Energy Bill," Thinking Green, Speaking Green blog, June 10, 2009, www.votespisak.org.

[27] "Wind Industry Praises Chairmen Waxman

About the Author

Staff writer **Marcia Clemmitt** is a veteran social-policy reporter who previously served as editor in chief of *Medicine & Health* and staff writer for *The Scientist*. She has also been a high-school math and physics teacher. She holds a liberal arts and sciences degree from St. John's College, Annapolis, and a master's degree in English from Georgetown University. Her recent reports include "Preventing Cancer" and "Public-Works Projects."

and Markey for Upholding Renewable Electricity Standard in House Climate and Energy Bill," press release, American Wind Energy Association Web site, May 22, 2009, www.awea.org.

[28] For background, see Mary H. Cooper, "Energy Security," *CQ Researcher*, Feb. 1, 2002, pp. 73-96.

[29] For background, see Peter Katel, "Oil Jitters," *CQ Researcher*, Jan. 4, 2008, pp. 1-24.

[30] For background, see the following *CQ Researcher* reports: Barbara Mantel, "Energy Efficiency," May 19, 2006, pp. 433-456; Mary H. Cooper, "Alternative Energy," Feb. 25, 2005, pp. 173-196; Mary H. Cooper, "Energy Policy," May 5, 2001, pp. 441-464; and Mary H. Cooper, "The Politics of Energy," *CQ Researcher*, March 5, 1999, pp. 185-208.

[31] For background, see Jennifer Weeks, "Carbon Trading," *CQ Global Researcher*, November 2008, and Colin Woodard, "Curbing Climate Change," *CQ Global Researcher*, February 2007.

[32] For background, see Recovery.gov, www.recovery.gov.

[33] Quoted in Eoin O'Carooll, "Gore: Stimulus Package Will Help Curb Climate Change," Bright Green Blog, *The Christian Science Monitor*, Jan. 28, 2009, http://features.csmonitor.com.

[34] "EPA Finds Greenhouse Gases Pose Threat to Public Health, Welfare/Proposed Finding Comes in Response to 2007 Supreme Court Ruling," press release, Environmental Protection Agency, April 17, 2009, http://yosemite.epa.gov.

[35] David Kerley and Huma Khan, "EPA's Greenhouse Gas Mandate Causes Both Joy and Concern," ABC News, April 17, 2008, http://abcnews.go.com.

[36] Andrew Taylor, "Waxman Ousts Dingell from Energy Chair in Bruising Dem Fight," The Associated Press, Nov. 20, 2008, www.huffingtonpost.com/2008/11/20/waxman-beats-dingell-in-d_n_145178.html.

[37] Quoted in Muriel Kane, "Dennis Kucinich Votes Against Climate Change Bill," Raw Story blog, June 26, 2009, http://rawstory.com/08/news/2009/06/26/dennis-kucinich-votes-against-climate-change-bill/.

[38] Quoted in Brian A. Howey, "Hoosier GOP Sound Alarm Over Cap & Trade," Howey Politics Indiana blog, May 27, 2009, www.howeypolitics.com.

[39] For background, see "The American Clean Energy and Security Act (HR 2454)," summary, House Committee on Energy and Commerce Web site, June 23, 2009, http://energycommerce.house.gov/Press_111/20090623/hr2454_rulessummary.pdf.

[40] Marianne Lavell, "The Climate Lobby's Non-

stop Growth," Center for Public Integrity Web site, May 19, 2009, www.publicintegrity.org.

[41] *Ibid.*

[42] Edward Felker, "Rep. Kaptur Gets $3.5 Billion Sweetener in Climate Bill," *The Washington Times*, July 1, 2009, www.washingtontimes.com/news/2009/jul/01/sweetener-helped-sway-vote-on-house-climate-bill/.

[43] Matthew Yglesias, "Waxman, Peterson Reach Deal; Climate/Energy Bill Set to Move Forward," Yglesias blog, Center for American Progress Web site, June 24, 2009, http://yglesias.thinkprogress.org/archives/2009/06/waxman-peterson-reach-deal-climateenergy-bill-set-to-move-forward.php.

[44] David Corn, "Mick Jagger and the Climate Change Bill," Kevin Drum blog, *Mother Jones* Web site, June 24, 2009, www.motherjones.com/kevin-drum/2009/06/mick-jagger-and-climate-change-bill.

[45] Meredith Niles, "Peterson's Waxman-Markey Amendment: The Nity Gritty and What It Means," Grist online, June 25, 2009, www.grist.org.

[46] Kate Sheppard, "Enviros Cringe as Senate Committee Approves Energy Bill," *Grist* online, June 17, 2009, www.grist.org.

[47] Mike Pence, "American Energy Solutions Group Introduces Comprehensive Energy Plan Without Raising Taxes," statement, www.mikepence.house.gov.

[48] "Van Hollen Introduces the Cap and Dividend Act of 2009," press release, April 1, 2009, http://vanhollen.house.gov.

[49] Joseph Romm, "The U.S. House of Representatives Approves Landmark (Bipartisan!) Climate Bill, 219-212," Climate Progress blog, June 26, 2009, http://climateprogress.org/2009/06/26/house-approves-landmark-bipartisan-clean-energy-and-climate-bill-final-vote-waxman-markey/.

Bibliography
Selected Sources

Books

Bryce, Robert, *Gusher of Lies: The Dangerous Delusions of Energy Independence*, PublicAffairs Books, 2008.

A Texas energy reporter argues that U.S. "energy-independence" is an unrealistic and dangerous dream.

Giddens, Anthony, *Politics of Climate Change*, Polity Press, 2009.

A professor emeritus of sociology at the London School of Economics and House of Lords member argues that climate change demands a rethinking of how we make political decisions and engage the public in policy dialogue.

Randolph, John, and Gilbert M. Masters, *Energy for Sustainability: Technology, Planning, Policy*, Island Press, 2008.

A professor of environmental planning at Virginia Polytechnic Institute (Randolph) and a Stanford University professor emeritus of civil and environmental engineering trace the historical development of energy use and describe technologies available for creating a sustainable energy future.

Shaffer, Brenda, *Energy Politics*, University of Pennsylvania Press, 2009.

A professor of political science at Israel's University of Haifa examines how the need to obtain energy, along with concerns about national security and climate change, shape national politics and international alliances.

Articles

Kane, Paul, "Push and Pull in Senate May Recast Climate Bill," *The Washington Post*, July 7, 2009, p. A3.

Senators bring their own regional and economic concerns to energy policy.

Lavelle, Marianne, "The Climate Lobby's Nonstop Growth," Center for Public Integrity, May 19, 2009, www.public integrity.org.

A writer for a nonprofit investigative group examines the industries with a stake in energy legislation.

Reports and Studies

"Bad Deal for the Planet: Why Carbon Offsets Aren't Working and How to Create a Fair Global Climate Accord," International Rivers, 2008, www.internationalrivers.org/node/2826.

A river advocacy group argues the World Bank's carbon-emissions offset program is not reducing emissions.

"Climate 2030: A National Blueprint for a Clean Energy Economy," Union of Concerned Scientists, May 2009, www.ucsusa.org/global_warming/solutions/big_picture_solutions/climate-2030-blueprint.html.

An environmental group argues that investments in energy efficiency can cut GHG emissions while largely offsetting increased carbon-fuel prices.

"The Estimated Costs to Households from the Cap-and-Trade Provisions of H.R. 2454," Congressional Budget Office, June 19, 2009, www.cbo.gov/ftpdocs/103xx/doc 10327/06-19-CapAndTradeCosts.pdf.

Congress' budget agency estimates overall net costs per household of the Waxman-Markey bill would average 0.2 percent of after-tax income.

"Impact on the Economy of the American Clean Energy and Security Act of 2009," National Black Chamber of Commerce/CRA International, May 2009, http://epw.sen ate.gov/public/index.cfm?FuseAction=Files.View&FileStore_id=8230a041-2d13-4812-b5ed-ea9b2965faa0.

An international economics consultancy argues the cost of switching to renewable energy should be weighed against the possible benefits.

"Potential Impacts of Climate Change in the United States," Congressional Budget Office, May 2009, www.cbo.gov/ftp docs/101xx/doc10107/05-04-ClimateChange_forWeb.pdf.

Congress' nonpartisan budget agency finds human activities are potentially leading to serious and expensive changes in regional climates and ocean and shore conditions.

Eldridge, Maggie, *et al.*, "The 2008 State Energy Efficiency Scorecard," American Council for an Energy-Efficient Economy, Report Number E086, October 2008, http://aceee.org.

Analysts for a nonprofit advocating energy efficiency report on state efficiency programs.

Orszag, Peter R., "Containing the Cost of a Cap-and-Trade Program for Carbon Dioxide Emissions," Congressional Budget Office, May 20, 2008, www.cbo.gov/ftpdocs/92xx/doc9276/05-20-Cap_Trade_Testimony.1.1.shtml.

The former chief of the Congressional Budget Office — now director of the White House Office of Management and Budget — says cap-and-trade programs to lower GHG emissions have costs for consumers, as do other such mechanisms.

Pollin, Robert, *et al.*, "Green Recovery: A Program to Create Good Jobs and Start Building a Low-Carbon Economy," Center for American Progress/University of Massachusetts (Amherst) Political Economy Research Institute, September 2008, www.peri.umass.edu/green_recovery/.

Liberal analysts argue that "green" policies can bolster the economy through job creation.

The Next Step:

Additional Articles from Current Periodicals

Alternative Energy

Gillentine, Amy, "Alternative Energy Might Save Economy in Colorado," *Colorado Springs Business Journal*, Jan. 9, 2009.

Developing a new energy work force in Colorado is part of Gov. Bill Ritter's economic policy for the state.

Herszenhorn, David M., "House Passes Renewable Energy Credits," *The New York Times*, Feb. 28, 2008, p. A20.

The House of Representatives has approved a bill to extend $17 billion in tax credits for renewable resources.

Simon, Richard, "Cloud Over Corn's Moment in Sun," *Los Angeles Times*, Nov. 28, 2007, p. A18.

An ethanol mandate is seen as crucial to passing an energy bill, but many Democrats oppose it over fear that it could raise the price of corn used for food.

Cap-and-Trade

Asbell, O. David, "Cap and Trade System Will Solve Water Woes," *Atlanta Journal-Constitution*, Nov. 27, 2007, p. 11A.

A cap-and-trade system would allow the nation to better manage water demand without rigid regulation from the government.

Lange, Mark, "Cap and Trade Is Still the Right Call," *The Christian Science Monitor*, April 13, 2009, p. 9.

Cap-and-trade effectively acts as a market that allows companies to invest in efficiency.

Samuelson, Robert J., "Just Call It 'Cap-and-Tax,' " *The Washington Post*, June 2, 2008, p. A13.

A cap-and-trade system would practically act as a taxing mechanism due to its ability to regulate economic activity.

Steffy, Loren, "Cap-and-Trade System Has Too Much Room for Abuse," *Houston Chronicle*, May 4, 2008, p. B1.

A cap-and-trade system creates incentives — as opposed to mandates — that will not effectively curb global warming.

Drilling

Shadegg, John, "Dems' Energy Policy Holding Back Economy," *Arizona Republic*, Oct. 8, 2008, p. A47.

The decision by Democrats to keep known resources in the outer continental shelf off limits and their refusal to open up the Arctic National Wildlife Refuge for development have jeopardized the nation's economy.

Wang, Herman, "Corker: More Drilling an Interim Solution to Oil Woes," *Chattanooga Times Free Press* (Tennessee), June 17, 2008, p. A1.

Sen. Bob Corker, R-Tenn., does not believe that drilling for more oil will immediately satisfy the country's energy needs and bring gas prices down.

Witt, Howard, "Drilling to Core of Oil Debate," *Chicago Tribune*, Oct. 23, 2008, p. A5.

Waters off the East and West coasts have remained largely off-limits to oil and gas exploration due to moratoriums relating to environmental concerns.

Waxman-Markey Bill

Broder, John M., "Energy Bill Unfinished, But Vote Nears," *The New York Times*, June 24, 2009, p. A17.

President Obama has dispatched Cabinet officials to six states to drum up support for the Waxman-Markey bill.

Dlouhy, Jennifer A., "Some Fear Energy Bill Will Cost Jobs," *Houston Chronicle*, April 24, 2009, p. B3.

Leaders from major U.S. manufacturers have joined labor unions in pleading with Congress to insulate American jobs when analyzing the merits of the Waxman-Markey bill.

Mufson, Steven, "Climate Bill to Cost Average Consumer $175 a Year: CBO," *The Washington Post*, June 23, 2009, p. A13.

The current Waxman-Markey bill would cost the average household $175 annually by 2020, according to the Congressional Budget Office.

Tankersley, Jim, "Climate Bill Built of D.C. Deals," *Chicago Tribune*, June 28, 2009, p. A6.

Support for the Waxman-Markey bill has been garnered by making key concessions to crucial groups such as farmers and coal producers.

CITING *CQ RESEARCHER*

Sample formats for citing these reports in a bibliography include the ones listed below. Preferred styles and formats vary, so please check with your instructor or professor.

MLA STYLE
Jost, Kenneth. "Rethinking the Death Penalty." CQ Researcher 16 Nov. 2001: 945-68.

APA STYLE
Jost, K. (2001, November 16). Rethinking the death penalty. *CQ Researcher, 11*, 945-968.

CHICAGO STYLE
Jost, Kenneth. "Rethinking the Death Penalty." *CQ Researcher*, November 16, 2001, 945-968.

In-depth Reports on Issues in the News

Are you writing a paper?

Need backup for a debate?

Want to become an expert on an issue?

For 80 years, students have turned to *CQ Researcher* for in-depth reporting on issues in the news. Reports on a full range of political and social issues are now available. Following is a selection of recent reports:

Civil Liberties
Closing Guantánamo, 2/09
Affirmative Action, 10/08
Gay Marriage Showdowns, 9/08
America's Border Fence, 9/08
Immigration Debate, 2/08

Crime/Law
Examining Forensics, 7/09
Legalizing Marijuana, 6/09
Mexico's Drug War, 12/08
Prostitution Debate, 5/08
Public Defenders, 4/08

Education
Reading Crisis? 2/08
Discipline in Schools, 2/08
Student Aid, 1/08
Racial Diversity in Public Schools, 9/07

Environment/Society
Future of Books, 5/09
Hate Groups, 5/09
Future of Journalism, 3/09
Confronting Warming, 1/09
Reducing Carbon Footprint, 12/08
Protecting Wetlands, 10/08

Health/Safety
Treating Depression, 6/09
Reproductive Ethics, 5/09
Extreme Sports, 4/09
Regulating Toxic Chemicals, 1/09
Preventing Cancer, 1/09
Heart Health, 9/08
Global Food Crisis, 6/08

Politics/Economy
Business Bankruptcy, 4/09
Future of the GOP, 3/09
Middle-Class Squeeze, 3/09

Upcoming Reports

Fraying Safety Nets, 7/31/09	The Afghanistan Dilemma, 8/7/09	Health Reform, 8/28/09

ACCESS

CQ Researcher is available in print and online. For access, visit your library or www.cqresearcher.com.

STAY CURRENT

To receive notice of upcoming *CQ Researcher* reports, or learn more about *CQ Researcher* products, subscribe to the free e-mail newsletters, *CQ Researcher Alert!* and *CQ Researcher News*: http://cqpress.com/newsletters.

PURCHASE

To purchase a *CQ Researcher* report in print or electronic format (PDF), visit www.cqpress.com or call 866-427-7737. Single reports start at $15. Bulk purchase discounts and electronic-rights licensing are also available.

SUBSCRIBE

Annual full-service *CQ Researcher* subscriptions—including 44 reports a year, monthly index updates, and a bound volume—start at $803. Add $25 for domestic postage.

CQ Researcher Online offers a backfile from 1991 and a number of tools to simplify research. For pricing information, call 800-834-9020, ext. 1906, or e-mail librarysales@cqpress.com.

CQ Researcher

Published by CQ Press, a Division of SAGE

www.cqresearcher.com

Straining the Safety Net

Is joblessness overwhelming aid programs?

A
s unemployment keeps mounting, millions more Americans are being forced to rely on a network of federal and state programs to meet their basic needs. The added pressure on the so-called safety net has prompted increases in unemployment insurance payments and expanded food-stamp and welfare caseloads, authorized under this year's $787 billion stimulus package. Budget crises, however, are forcing some states to cut back on safety-net programs, including health care and meals for disadvantaged children. At the same time critics say welfare reforms enacted in 1996 requiring aid recipients to work don't mesh with the reality of today's job shortage. But supporters of the reforms say the extra spending on benefits shows the system is working. With employment growth unlikely any time soon, a renewed debate on government responsibility to the disadvantaged is gathering force.

Julie Morris, with daughter Hailey, moved to the Family Gateway homeless shelter in Dallas in May with her three daughters and husband after he was laid off from his construction job.

CQ Researcher • July 31, 2009 • www.cqresearcher.com
Volume 19, Number 27 • Pages 645-668

CQ Researcher

July 31, 2009
Volume 19, Number 27

MANAGING EDITOR: Thomas J. Colin
tcolin@cqpress.com

ASSISTANT MANAGING EDITOR: Kathy Koch
kkoch@cqpress.com

ASSOCIATE EDITOR: Kenneth Jost

STAFF WRITERS: Thomas J. Billitteri,
Marcia Clemmitt, Peter Katel

CONTRIBUTING WRITERS: Rachel Cox,
Sarah Glazer, Alan Greenblatt, Reed Karaim
Barbara Mantel, Patrick Marshall,
Tom Price, Jennifer Weeks

DESIGN/PRODUCTION EDITOR: Olu B. Davis

ASSISTANT EDITOR: Darrell Dela Rosa

FACT-CHECKING: Eugene J. Gabler,
Michelle Harris

CQ PRESS

A Division of SAGE

PRESIDENT AND PUBLISHER:
John A. Jenkins

EXECUTIVE DIRECTOR,
REFERENCE INFORMATION GROUP:
Alix B. Vance

CQ Researcher (ISSN 1056-2036) is printed on acid-free paper. Published weekly, except; (Jan. wk. 1) (May wk. 4) (July wks. 1, 2) (Aug. wks. 3, 4) (Nov. wk. 4) and (Dec. wk. 4), by CQ Press, a division of SAGE Publications. Annual full-service subscriptions start at $803. For pricing, call 1-800-834-9020, ext. 1906. To purchase a CQ Researcher report in print or electronic format (PDF), visit www. cqpress.com or call 866-427-7737. Single reports start at $15. Bulk purchase discounts and electronic-rights licensing are also available. Periodicals postage paid at Washington, D.C., and additional mailing offices. POSTMASTER: Send address changes to CQ Researcher, 2300 N St., N.W., Suite 800, Washington, DC 20037.

Cover: Getty Images/John Moore

Straining the Safety Net

By Peter Katel

THE ISSUES

Tanya Gray used to earn a decent living doing office work in Washington, D.C. When computers and other desktop technology made her skills superfluous, however, she turned to home care for elderly people.

"I'm very good, and I love my job, so people refer me," she says. "I try to work with clients that can't really afford to pay me what I'm worth."

But as the recession cuts into the limited earnings of the working people she serves, Gray is having trouble again. Unable to afford her own apartment, she is staying at her mother's place while waiting for a federal Section 8 rent subsidy. Gray receives food stamps and is covered by Medicaid, the federal health program for the poor.

Even so, food sometimes runs short. That's when Gray depends on a monthly bag of groceries from Bread for the City, a private, nonprofit social-services organization in the working-class Shaw neighborhood, about 1.5 miles from the White House. Without the government and private aid, she says, "I'd be destitute."

The 54-year-old Gray has plenty of company. Low-wage workers making about $20,000 a year or less account for between a quarter and a third of the country's 140 million labor force.[1] Gray is in large and growing company in her reliance on the package of government programs known collectively as the "safety net."

A product of New Deal social policies launched in the 1930s, the safety net was expanded during the War on Poverty that began in 1964. Now, with

The economic recession has increased the demand for services at Bread for the City, a nonprofit social-services organization in Washington, D.C. Such private aid programs are reinforcing state and federal "safety-net" programs — many hit by budget cutbacks.

Bread for the City/Steve Goldenberg

a recession wreaking havoc on employment nationwide, social-protection programs are undergoing their toughest test since sweeping welfare reforms were instituted in 1996.

During decades of debate leading to the reforms, people at the bottom of the socioeconomic ladder were seen as dependent on welfare checks and often portrayed as lazy and unwilling to work. The law was designed to discourage long-term assistance. Instead, states are required to push aid recipients into the workplace. Some 1.7 million families with 3 million children are enrolled in Temporary Assistance for Needy Families (TANF), which the 1996 law created in place of the previous Aid to Families with Dependent Children (AFDC). In 1995,

the year before the reforms were implemented, twice as many people were receiving AFDC benefits: 4.5 million families and 8.4 million children.[2]

"Our safety net was redesigned to focus on working families," says Sheila Zedlewski, director of the Income and Benefits Policy Center at the liberal Urban Institute think tank. "And some of the policies and procedures that states have in place don't serve well in this time, when there are no jobs."

But Robert Rector, a senior research fellow at the conservative Heritage Foundation and ardent defender of the welfare law overhaul, says critics of the reforms are arguing that joblessness caused by the recession is a reason to return to the old welfare system. Unemployment effects are "overblown," he says. "People are being hired all the time."

Some job-seekers have indeed been finding work since the recession began in December 2007. In 2008, about 56 million people were hired in non-agricultural jobs, but hiring was down about 7 million from 2007, and 8 million from 2006. On the other side of the equation, 24 million people were laid off last year, but that was 2 million more than the year before, and 3 million more than in 2006.[3]

A 58-year-old Staples cashier in Alexandria, Va., says many part-time workers are seeing their hours cut back from 30 to 20 hours a week. "Pamela" said she earns $16,000 a year working full time, with crucial financial help from Section 8 housing allowances, Medicaid and Bread for the City. "I'm not saying it would be impossible without them, but it would be real difficult," she said.

One in Eight Americans Live in Poverty

More than 38 million Americans were living at or below the poverty level in 2007, or about 13 percent of the entire population. Moreover, 15 percent were determined to be "food insecure" or worse.

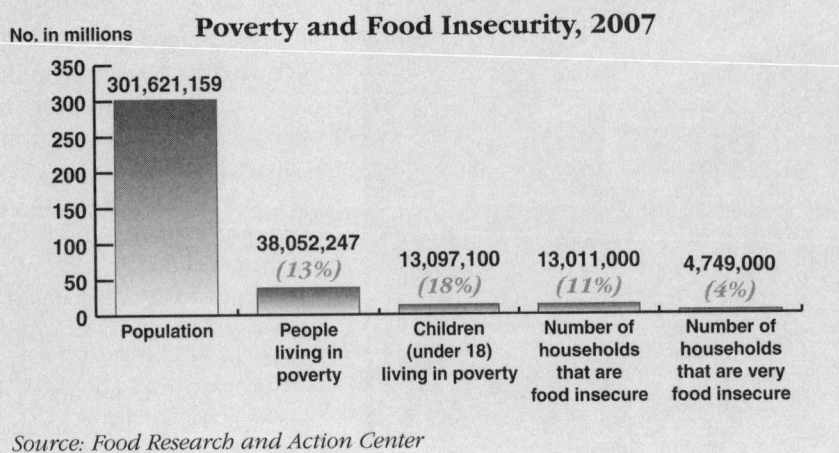

Poverty and Food Insecurity, 2007

No. in millions

- Population: 301,621,159
- People living in poverty: 38,052,247 (13%)
- Children (under 18) living in poverty: 13,097,100 (18%)
- Number of households that are food insecure: 13,011,000 (11%)
- Number of households that are very food insecure: 4,749,000 (4%)

Source: Food Research and Action Center

Meanwhile, an economic revival — when and if it occurs — isn't expected to spark big jumps in employment. "Businesses are likely to be cautious about hiring, implying that the unemployment rate could remain high for a time, even after economic growth resumes," Federal Reserve Chairman Ben S. Bernanke told Congress' Joint Economic Committee in May. [4]

The bleak climate prompted the White House and Congress earlier this year to temporarily strengthen the safety-net system, including TANF and unemployment insurance, as part of the $787 billion economic stimulus law enacted in February.

Also in February, Congress passed a measure proposed by President Barack Obama that stepped up funding for the Children's Health Insurance Program and encouraged states to loosen eligibility so that more children could be covered. Financially strapped California and Michigan, as well as Texas, didn't act, but at least 13 states have enrolled about 250,000 more children, *The New York Times* reported. "In a downturn, the number of people who need the safety net increases," said Democratic Gov.

Bill Ritter Jr. of Colorado, where an additional 21,000 children are now covered. [5]

Similarly, enactment of the stimulus was followed by increases in TANF enrollments in 23 of the 30 biggest states, according to a *Wall Street Journal/ National Conference of State Legislatures* survey. [6]

California is among the states showing an increase in TANF enrollments — 10.4 percent, for the 12 months ending in March. But that increase seems unlikely to be sustained. The new California budget will cut $528 million from the state's TANF program, known as CalWorks, and $178.6 million from the program that provides medical coverage for low-income children. [7]

Even with California excluded, the increases are uneven. Michigan, devastated by the near-collapse of its auto industry, suffered the nation's highest unemployment rate in May — 14.1 percent. Yet during the 12 preceding months, Michigan's TANF caseload dropped 4.8 percent. [8] And from April 2008 to April 2009, food stamp rolls climbed 14.5 percent. [9]

The discrepancy between soaring

food stamp enrollment and declining TANF caseload has caught the eye of one of the key players in the 1996 congressional passage of the new welfare law. "It sure does make you suspicious," says Ron Haskins, co-director of the Center on Children and Families at the Brookings Institution think tank. "I really wonder what's going on in Michigan." Haskins, was staff director of the Republican-controlled House Ways and Means Human Resources Subcommittee during the welfare battle of 1996.

More generally, Haskins acknowledges that the employment emphasis of the 1996 law hurt single mothers who were pushed off TANF for failure to find work.

"These are generally mothers who have more than one problem — more than three kids, and bad transportation access, for instance." These people are "slipping through the cracks," Haskins says.

Meanwhile, Michigan may be only at the beginning of a trend toward increased demand for cash assistance. Laid-off factory workers have been getting unemployment insurance (UI), says Rick McHugh, Midwest coordinator of the National Employment Law Project, an advocacy organization, but benefits will start phasing out in August. By year's end, 100,000 laid-off workers will have used up their UI eligibility.

"Many of those people will not get TANF initially because they still have equity in their homes, they may still own more than one car, they even have bank accounts that have money in them," says McHugh. "In three to five years they may get to the point where they're looking at TANF."

Former industrial workers who do find new jobs are likely also to find that they pay far less. Lawrence M. Mead, a New York University political scientist and advocate of the 1996 welfare law, acknowledges that employment opportunities today largely are to be found in "jobs that don't pay very well."

On the other side of the coin, "ease of employment has replaced the safety net as the main substitute for serious employment," Mead says. "You may not get the job you want, you may get thrown out of a job on Wall Street, but you can get a job at Waldbaum's," a popular New York area supermarket chain.

But relying on low-wage employment for a major part of the workforce carries its own dangers, argues Peter Edelman, director of the Center on Poverty, Inequality, and Public Policy at Georgetown University Law Center and a longtime anti-poverty activist.

"The real question is: What is our standard of living, going forward?" he says. "And if a continuing, very large number of people are not being paid a living wage, are we going to use public policy to add appropriately to their income?"

To aid working families who earn too little, Edelman advocates strengthening the Earned-Income Tax Credit — which reduces low-wage workers' taxes — and providing expanded health-care and child-care coverage.

Back at the Bread for the City office in Washington, Tanya Gray is pinning her hopes for the future on her herself, as well as a power stronger than that wielded by politicians. "If I take the first step," she says, "God will carry me the rest of the way."

As the recession brings more Americans into contact with the nation's safety net, here are key questions being debated:

Are safety nets working?

Many experts gauge safety-net effectiveness in hard times by the level of Temporary Assistance to Needy Families payments. The population TANF serves — low-income households almost always headed by a single parent — is especially vulnerable to economic reversals.

Others view food stamps (officially, the Supplemental Nutrition Assistance Program) as a more sensitive indicator. Enrollment in SNAP is relatively sim-

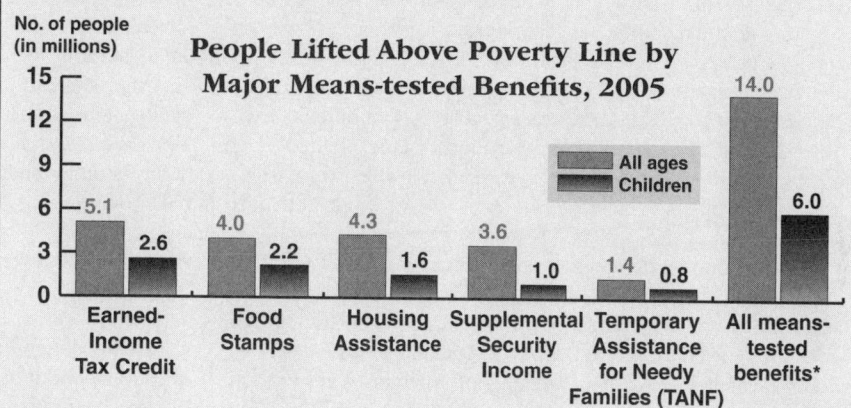

Programs Lift 14 Million Out of Poverty

Major means-tested benefit programs — available to only those with limited incomes and assets — lifted 14 million Americans out of poverty in 2005. The Earned-Income Tax Credit was responsible for more than one-third of that amount. Temporary Assistance for Needy Families only accounted for one-tenth.

People Lifted Above Poverty Line by Major Means-tested Benefits, 2005

No. of people (in millions)

	All ages	Children
Earned-Income Tax Credit	5.1	2.6
Food Stamps	4.0	2.2
Housing Assistance	4.3	1.6
Supplemental Security Income	3.6	1.0
Temporary Assistance for Needy Families (TANF)	1.4	0.8
All means-tested benefits*	14.0	6.0

* Some individuals counted more than once if enrolled in more than one program.

Source: Arloc Sherman, "Safety Net Effective at Fighting Poverty But Has Weakened for the Very Poorest," Center on Budget and Policy Priorities, July 2009

ple, and statistics show the program is responding effectively to growing hardship. Nationwide, food stamp enrollment rose 20 percent, to 5 million recipients, during the 12 months ending in April 2009. [10]

Meanwhile, as President Obama put it recently, the recession is clobbering many people traditionally considered outside the target populations for SNAP and TANF. This group includes employees laid off from well-paid jobs that once offered considerable stability — autoworkers are the classic case. As of July, 1.9 million manufacturing jobs had vanished since the recession began in December 2007 — including 335,000 in car and auto-parts factories. [11]

Still another group of laid-off workers includes ex-TANF recipients, or future ones. The low-wage jobs they held provided paycheck-to-paycheck living but little or no cushion to fall back on when the jobs disappeared.

In other ways as well, low-wage workers enjoy less of a safety net than those

laid off from better-paying, more stable jobs. A Congressional Research Service expert reported in February that low-wage workers are less likely to receive UI benefits. Some states, for example, bar UI participation by those who earned below a set amount. In any event, as of November 2008, 55 percent of unemployed people weren't receiving unemployment benefits. [12]

The huge economic stimulus bill the Obama administration pushed through Congress in February included a series of measures designed to expand the safety net's coverage.

TANF got an extra $5 billion to be distributed to states according to their needs for cash welfare and work subsidies. [13] The food stamp program received $20 billion to be spent over five years in boosting allotments, for example by $80 a month for a family of four. [14]

And the stimulus bill included a series of provisions to increase unemployment insurance benefits, in-

Food Pantries and Other Groups Struggle to Keep Up

Demand at free clinics has skyrocketed.

In normal times, millions of Americans depend on nonprofit service organizations such as food pantries, medical clinics and storefront legal-services offices. But judging from rising demand stemming from the recession, at least some of the nation's thousands of private providers are struggling to keep up.

"Over the last year, free clinics have seen patient load increase by 40 to 50 percent," said Nicole D. Lamoureux, executive director of the National Association of Free Clinics, which represents more than 1,200 clinics nationwide. "People who just last year had health coverage are now out of work and need to have their health-care needs met." [1]

No one knows how many private organizations aid low-income people. A database maintained by the Urban Institute's National Center for Charitable Statistics lists 3,858 "human services" nonprofits registered with the Internal Revenue Service. But that category excludes providers of emergency aid in food, clothing, cash and child care. [2]

Among President Barack Obama's proposals for fiscal 2010 is a $50 million appropriation to the Social Innovation Fund, which Congress created last year to fund successful private social-service providers that want to expand. [3]

If any provider were to discover a way to expand services without requiring additional funding, that organization would become a nonprofit sector star. Like conventional, profit-oriented businesses, nonprofits are struggling to cope with declining revenues, as contributors cut back on donations.

"Our spending is down by 15-20 percent since last year," said Gloria Verrone, spokeswoman for the CIGNA Foundation, which funds free medical clinics in Philadelphia and Con-

necticut. "We've decided not to eliminate working with organizations that need our help, but we have had to decrease funding amounts in order to keep those relationships. We also haven't been able to accept any new groups this year, but we're hopeful to start doing so again by next year." [4]

Other organizations also are doing more with less. "Our donations have gone down, particularly from law firms, because they themselves are laying people off," says Luan Huynh, supervising attorney at East Bay Community Law Center in Berkeley, Calif. But among clients, she says, "We're now seeing an increase in people who were never getting public benefits because they've always been gainfully employed but now need help because they can't get a job."

The law center receives some government funding, but other nonprofits depend entirely on public funds, and they face tough questions about performance and results when government revenues plummet. "The real challenge in those conversations is that they often become political," said Sandra Hernandez, CEO of the San Francisco Foundation and former director of public health for the city and county. "If they are really underperforming but have been there a long time, it may be very hard to get de-funding to stick in the political process." [5]

In Washington, D.C., controversy has erupted over $21 million in proposed cuts in city funding of nonprofits. "The word that comes to mind is 'devastating,' " Ed Orzechowski, CEO of Catholic Charities, said in a July 20 statement released by the Coalition for Community Investment, a group of business, nonprofit and other organizations in the city. "We all recognize that the budget gap needs to be closed, but we must do so pro-

cluding a 33-week extension in high-unemployment states, and $7 billion worth of incentives to states that expand UI eligibility to part-time employees and others; by mid-June, half the states had done so. [15]

"Food stamps and TANF have responded as they were intended to do, with the government spending more money," says Haskins at the Brookings Institution.

He adds that he — unlike some Republicans — supports expansion of TANF caseloads as long as states maintain pressure on recipients to find work. "If you don't have state programs that emphasize work and penalize people who don't look for work, then

people stay on the rolls much longer. A lot of people do find jobs, especially in services, during a recession."

Liberals who opposed the 1996 welfare law argue that the recession has shown the safety net in general, and TANF in particular, to be inadequate, especially by dropping recipients if they're not working or looking for work.

"In general, TANF is too hard to get on, and too many people are being kicked off," says Georgetown University's Edelman, who resigned as assistant secretary of Health and Human Services when President Bill Clinton signed the 1996 welfare reform law.

Moreover, the entire safety net system is strained far beyond its capacity. Even before the recession, the country was engulfed in a slow-motion socioeconomic disaster created by the expansion of the low-wage economy, Edelman argues. "You have to figure out how you're going to get a decent income to people who are being failed by the labor market," he says. "The labor market functioning as a 'free market' is injuring millions and millions of people who are just playing by the rules."

But the Heritage Foundation's Rector, a longtime critic of anti-poverty programs, argues that the safety net actually is working in ways that liberals

tecting those who simply cannot shoulder the impact." [6]

The affected organizations include arts programs as well as groups such as Capital Area Asset Builders, which was formed to help low-income families with taxes and other financial issues. A planned $250,000 city grant was slated to be cut to $100,000. [7]

Meanwhile, Washington nonprofits that don't depend on government grants also face tough times. "We've seen a 10-20 percent increase in demand for all of our programs over the past four years," says Jeannine Sanford, deputy director of Bread for the City, which provides food and medical and legal services, as well as guidance in navigating the government social-services bureaucracy. Demand for the latter kind of aid has increased 75 percent.

For example, in largely black and poor Ward 8, the jobless rate stood at 23.8 percent in April while affluent and mainly white Ward 3 registered 2.5 percent unemployment. [8]

To make matters worse, the city's already high cost of living means that many gainfully employed residents can't survive without assistance, says Sanford. "You can work full time in this economy, taking no vacation, and be well below the poverty line," she says.

Bread for the City, meanwhile, cut staff and management salaries 10 and 12 percent, respectively, while closing on Fridays.

President Obama wants to spend $50 million to enlarge successful nonprofits.

Getty Images/Ron Sachs

"We struggle with the rising costs of operation: essentials like health care and food prices are placing great strains on our budget," the organization said. "These changes . . . are necessary if we are to avoid substantial cuts to client services and staff." [9]

[1] Quoted in Everton Bailey Jr., "Free clinics hit with more patients, less funding," The Associated Press, July 20, 2009, http://news.yahoo.com/s/ap/20090720/ap_on_re_us/us_free_health_clinics.

[2] "NCCS All Registered Nonprofits Table Wizard," National Center for Charitable Statistics, Urban Institute, http://nccsdataweb.urban.org/tablewiz/tw_bmf.php.

[3] Suzanne Perry, "Administration Provides 'Fact Sheet' on Social Innovation Fund," *The Chronicle of Philanthropy*, July 22, 2009, http://philanthropy.com/news/government/8941/administration-provides-fact-sheet-on-social-innovation-fund.

[4] Quoted in Bailey, *op. cit.*

[5] C. W. Nevius, "Time for a hard look at funding nonprofits," *San Francisco Chronicle*, July 27, 2009, p. B1.

[6] Quoted in Susan Kinzie, "Nonprofits Revisit Budgets as Earmark Cuts Loom," *The Washington Post*, July 21, 2009, www.washingtonpost.com/wp-dyn/content/article/2009/07/20/AR2009072002994.html.

[7] *Ibid.*

[8] V. Dion Haynes and Emma L. Carew, "In D.C., More Jobs and More Jobless," *The Washington Post*, June 20, 2009, www.washingtonpost.com/wp-dyn/content/article/2009/06/19/AR2009061901600.html; "Unemployment rates by state, seasonally adjusted, June 2009," U.S. Bureau of Labor Statistics, http://data.bls.gov/map/servlet/map.servlet.MapToolServlet?survey=la.

[9] "A Message to the Community," Bread for the City, March 6, 2009, www.breadforthecity.org/Page.aspx?pid=434.

support and that he opposes. Government programs provide "a permanent subsidy to people in the lowest one-third of income distribution." In a paper in February, he listed some 50 programs aiding people below a certain income threshold, including Pell grants for low-income college students. [16]

As for TANF, Rector argues that the stimulus funds effectively return the welfare system to pre-1996 days, when states got more money as their caseloads expanded. "We are now in the business of paying states to put more people on welfare," he says, predicting that that provision will be transformed from a one-time measure into a permanent feature of the system.

Zedlewski at the Urban Institute argues that a far bigger issue confronts the entire safety net system. "The great recession shines a light on the somewhat misguided notion that you could just focus on work supports" in revamping the welfare system. "You now have a much larger group of low-income parents who don't have work, and are not getting the Earned-Income Tax Credit because they don't have a job and don't qualify for unemployment insurance. What do you do there?"

Furthermore, Zedlewski argues, the rebuilt welfare system, with its focus on pushing recipients into jobs, has never served people with disabilities

that keep them from working but don't qualify them for disability benefits. "I don't think anybody's really come up with a great solution for that group, who account for a large share of our poverty population."

Are fundamental changes needed in the federal welfare program?

The creation of TANF marked a major change in social policy. Supporters argue that the law was built to withstand the pressures that a recession would create. A $2 billion contingency fund (expanded to $5 billion by the stimulus law) for larger state caseloads in times of high unemployment was part of TANF from the beginning.

TANF is under the microscope both because of the recession and because the law creating it is up for reauthorization next year. With the legislative calendar and economic hard times coinciding, critics will have a perfect moment to push for changes in the much-debated law.

Advocates of the law remain deeply committed to its underlying doctrine: To impart the value of work to people who, so the thesis goes, have never been taught the value of honest toil. Blogger Mickey Kaus, who campaigned for TANF while writing for the liberal *New Republic*, remains a fervent partisan. "An able-bodied person who fails to work and relies instead on the dole can't have full respect in our society, and shouldn't," Kaus wrote in February. "The attempt to confer equal respect by spreading around cash — as opposed to guaranteeing work and making work pay — is doomed." [17]

The moral value of work aside, the structure of TANF — which Congress created during economic boom times — is bringing the new welfare system face-to-face with practical issues arising from the recession.

For one thing, the welfare-to-work law can't create jobs. For another, its block-grant financing, designed to prevent caseloads from expanding automatically as more people apply for assistance, may hinder efforts to help participants find or keep jobs — the overhauled welfare system's entire purpose.

"TANF's fixed funding poses this policy dilemma: curtail increases in cash welfare caseloads and not expand other forms of recession-related aid, or cut TANF funding for initiatives launched in better economic times," the Congressional Research Service reported in February. The kinds of non-cash aid include child care for parents looking for work or already working. [18]

And most states aren't in a position to fund such programs entirely

Social Security Lifts 22 Million Out of Poverty

About 22 million Americans were boosted out of poverty in 2005 by Social Security, the most effective "universal," or non-means-tested, safety-net program.

People Lifted Out of Poverty by "Universal" Safety-Net Programs, 2005

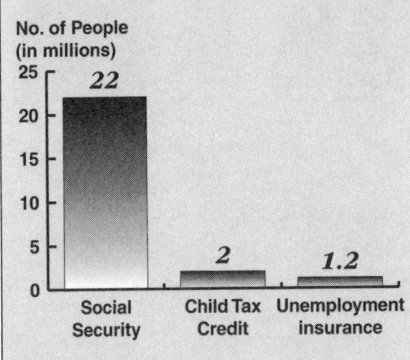

Source: Arloc Sherman, "Safety Net Effective at Fighting Poverty But Has Weakened for the Very Poorest," Center on Budget and Policy Priorities, July 2009

on their own, says Heather Boushey, a senior economist at the Center for American Progress, a think tank with close ties to the Obama administration. "State budgets are slammed," she says. "So you find that your child-care subsidy has been cut, and you can't afford child care for your kid, and you end up going to work late a couple of days, because your neighbor couldn't watch your child, and then you lose your job."

The bottom line, Boushey argues, is that TANF cannot cope with the effects of the severe recession. She's uncertain whether ending the block-grant system, or changing some TANF requirements, would help. But, she says,

"I do not think the system as it is, is working."

Such arguments overlook a considerable elasticity built into the TANF law, argues New York University's Mead, whose writing on welfare and work helped set the stage for the 1996 law. "The TANF system has more ways of adjusting to unemployment than people realize," he says, pointing to a provision that allows a higher number of recipients to be looking for work — as opposed to already working — if a state is classified as "needy" due to high joblessness.

Mead isn't troubled if caseloads expand. And — unlike the Heritage Foundation's Rector — he doesn't see the extra contingency money added in the stimulus law as undercutting the 1996 law. But he is ready to oppose proposals next year for bigger changes, such as an end to block grants. "There might be attempts by liberals to go back to an entitlement," he says. "That would be a big mistake. I don't see any need for major change."

But the variety of state approaches that TANF authorizes can conceal systemic problems, argues Sharon Parrott, director of the welfare reform and income support division at the Center on Budget and Policy Priorities. "Some states have policies in place that can make it difficult for families to apply for assistance, and some are quick to terminate families from assistance — there are a variety of ways that states can keep caseloads down."

States' differing approaches to TANF raise a question that goes deeper than the block-grant versus open-ended funding argument, Parrott says. She cites federal data showing that the share of eligible families receiving cash assistance dropped from about 80 percent during the 1980s and early '90s to 40 percent in 2005. "Is this the way we want our safety net for the very poorest families with children to operate?" she asks. "If it isn't, what different set of requirements are there for states to keep a focus on work, but also have programs to protect kids against deep poverty?" [19]

Haskins of Brookings argues that the recession doesn't call for any major retooling of the 1996 law. Working within the law as it exists, he says, the Obama administration and Congress were able to make more money available to states to allow them to take on new TANF recipients. And the recession is not a Great Depression-scale event. "Americans are still getting jobs, especially in the service sector," he says.

Indeed, the Bureau of Labor Statistics jobs report shows that in the service sector — where women workers are concentrated — 5.4 million Americans found jobs from September 2007 to September 2008, the most recent figures available. More jobs were lost — but some of those hired stayed employed. [20] "A lot of people do find jobs, especially in services during a recession," Haskins says. "States just need to keep this balance of emphasizing work, with a safety net if they can't find jobs."

Is more job training needed?

In a year when the bankruptcy of two industrial giants — Chrysler and General Motors — marked the further erosion U.S. manufacturing, the time-honored practice of offering retraining to laid-off factory workers is encountering skepticism.

That response is especially marked in Michigan, home of the Big Three U.S. car companies, which has become the nation's unemployment capital. "I know that for a long time there have been politicians who have spoken of training as a silver bullet and college as a cure-all," President Obama acknowledged at Macomb Community College in Warren, Mich., on July 14. "I can't tell you how many workers who've been laid off, you talk to them about training and they say, 'Training for what?' So I understand the frus-

trations that a lot of people have, especially if the training is not well-designed for the specific jobs that are being created out there." [21]

Obama was announcing the availability of federal grants for community colleges that offer programs to train students in job skills that are in demand, and to connect them with actual jobs. In a related move in May, the president urged states to discard rules that barred laid-off workers from receiving unemployment insurance if they enrolled in school or training courses. Generally, states have required UI beneficiaries to be actively looking for work. [22]

In addition to Obama's retraining initiatives for laid off, longtime workers — "dislocated workers" in economists' jargon — there is also training for people with little experience in the workaday world, and few of the skills it demands.

Job training for the unskilled has represented a great hope of safety-net creators and advocates at least since President Lyndon B. Johnson's War on Poverty of the 1960s. "He didn't want the people on welfare getting a dole, he wanted them getting skills," LBJ biographer Robert Dallek told National Public Radio on the 40th anniversary of Johnson's best-known anti-poverty speech in 1964. [23]

Johnson didn't see his vision fulfilled. Among the poor, welfare rolls expanded more than the ranks of employees, Dallek said. As a result, job-training as a way out of poverty gets a cool reception from conservatives.

"I don't think job training is the solution for the lower-skilled," says Mead of NYU, an advocate of the 1996 TANF law. "It shouldn't be a substitute for work. We used to say to people on welfare, 'You go to school first, and then work.' It turns out they never went to work, or continued schooling either."

Mead does see a place for training people who already have started jobs. "Under TANF rules you can satisfy the

work requirement if you work a certain number of hours and then get training." Overall, though, he sees a more realistic, big-scale approach in low-wage work, accompanied by subsidies that stretch out paychecks, or political or labor union campaigns to raise wages. "In general, fundamental skill limitations and family problems prevent job progression for many low-income people," he says. We can't expect that education is going to solve the problem."

But Georgetown's Edelman argues that younger people who've never been in the labor market do benefit from training geared to their backgrounds. "The models I'm talking about combine learning and working at the same time," Edelman says, essentially agreeing with Mead. "That's the key — so that you don't say to somebody, 'You have to go through this thing and then you can go to work.' "

As for training dislocated workers, Edelman echoes the widespread skepticism spawned by the shrinking manufacturing sector. "We've perpetuated mythologies that we can train somebody up and get them a new working suit and it'll be fine," he says. "We really haven't been honest with them. If they're in Michigan, they either have to get income support for the rest of their lives or move where there are jobs."

Labor Secretary Hilda Solis has been peppered with questions about the extent to which retraining can help dislocated workers find new jobs. She echoes the Obama administration line that "green jobs" in a renewable-energy industry that government officials are trying to propel will provide part of the solution. But she hedged that response at a House Appropriations subcommittee hearing in May, noting, "I think that green jobs are not a silver bullet, by any means." [24]

The previous month Solis had cited an administration forecast of 3.5 million available jobs in the nascent renewable-energy industry (including an unstated number that already exist). But with more than 5 million jobs already lost since the recession began (as of mid-July, after she testified, the number had reached 7.2 million), she conceded, there were more job seekers than jobs. Still, some slots are unfilled for lack of trained personnel. "We do have a shortage of skilled individuals to go into these jobs," she said. "If we had done more homework, we wouldn't be in such a bad position . . . where we have to work really hard to get people trained in a rapid manner." [25]

Nevertheless, in the heart of the Rust Belt, even training-program supporters argue that expectations of what training can deliver may be exaggerated.

"My sense is that we're going to have a lower level of consumption for a number of years," says McHugh, a former United Auto Workers lawyer, "and that means the service economy and those kinds of jobs that in the past 15 years have been pointed to as places where manufacturing workers will go are not really a viable answer.

"In Michigan, they were saying, 'Go into health care.' All autoworkers now have lost eye care and dental care. That means every kid training to be a dental hygienist has a problem." ∎

BACKGROUND

Safety Net Created

Before the New Deal and the advent of federal social programs, aid the jobless, for single mothers and for others needing a helping hand varied widely among the states and cities — when aid existed at all. Historian Arthur Schlesinger Jr., a specialist on President Franklin D. Roosevelt's New Deal, created the doctrine of "federal

responsibility for Americans who found themselves, through no fault of their own, in economic or social distress." Social Security and unemployment Insurance were two of the specific results. [26]

However, Roosevelt harbored grave doubts about the federal government providing cash assistance — "relief," it was then called — for the jobless. He first signaled his concern following establishment of the Civil Works Administration (CWA), which created thousands of public-works jobs from a half-billion-dollar emergency appropriation by Congress in 1933. Half the workers came from the rolls of relief programs; the other half was unemployed men who hadn't received relief.

Roosevelt worried about the cost as well as the danger of creating a permanent class of workers dependent on government-subsidized jobs and insisted that the CWA end soon. These kinds of jobs could "become a habit with the country," he told his aides. In 1935, after the CWA was replaced by an even bigger program to put 3.5 million jobless men to work, Roosevelt ordered that another 1.5 million recipients of federal relief be transferred to local charities. [27]

This time, Roosevelt went public with his opposition to relief payments. In a January 1935 address to Congress, he called them "a narcotic, a subtle destroyer of the human spirit." And, he said, "The federal government must and shall quit this business of relief." [28]

The new labor laws and safety-net measures all sprang from the same political doctrine, that government had an obligation to ensure the minimum conditions of a decent life. And government growth was seen as a positive development — needed to rein in business power, which expanded enormously.

Roosevelt and the New Deal prevailed against big-business opponents, but not before a ferocious battle. In 1936, Clinton L. Bardo, president of

the National Association of Manufacturers, called for "liquidation" of the New Deal. And the association's chairman of the board, Robert L. Lund, condemned "the deliberate firing of class hatred by the New Dealers in their effort to hold political power." [29]

Some Democrats, especially in the deep South, were even more strident. Gov. Eugene Talmadge of Georgia declared in 1936 that the New Deal law banning child labor had been "copied from Russia." As for Roosevelt, Talmadge vowed that his state would "start the punch that will go all over America and put the Communist out of the White House and never let him return." [30]

War on Poverty

New Deal programs gained widespread acceptance after World War II. Democrat Harry S Truman and President Dwight D. Eisenhower, the first Republican to win the presidency following Roosevelt's unprecedented four terms, saw acknowledging the consensus as political common sense. "Should any political party attempt to abolish Social Security, unemployment insurance and eliminate labor laws and farm programs, you would not hear of that party again in our political history," Eisenhower told his brother, Edgar. [31]

By the end of Eisenhower's second term, liberal and left-wing intellectuals began to argue that New Deal programs represented only a first step toward eliminating deep poverty. In his 1962 classic, *The Other America: Poverty in the United States*, Michael Harrington, a moderate socialist, best summed up this view. The best-seller persuaded millions of Americans, including President John F. Kennedy, that a major, new government initiative was required. [32]

Continued on p. 656

Chronology

1930s First national safety-net programs created during Depression by President Franklin D. Roosevelt's New Deal.

1933
Emergency program created to provide cash payments — known as "relief" — to jobless.

1935
Social Security pension system created. . . . Aid to Dependent Children (welfare system) created. . . . Unemployment insurance created. . . . Roosevelt warns of Americans' dependence on relief payments.

1936
National Association of Manufacturers accuses Roosevelt of stoking "class hatred."

1960s President Lyndon B. Johnson declares War on Poverty, expands safety net.

1962
Author/activist Michael Harrington's *The Other America: Poverty in the United States* leads to politicians' growing awareness of poverty, including Democratic President John F. Kennedy, who is assassinated the following year.

1964
President Lyndon B. Johnson launches War on Poverty to create new poverty-fighting agencies and programs, emphasizing job training.

1968
Poverty rate falls to 12.8 percent in last year of Johnson administration, down from 19 percent when "war" began, largely as result of growth in welfare rolls.

1969
President Richard M. Nixon's proposed Family Assistance Plan, featuring a guaranteed minimum income, dies in Congress.

1970s-1990s Opposition to welfare system leads to work requirements.

1971
Gov. Ronald Reagan, R-Calif., champions "workfare," requiring welfare recipients to get jobs.

1976
Echoing a common, racially tinged criticism of welfare, Reagan refers to a "strapping young buck" buying steaks with food stamps, during campaigning for the Republican presidential nomination.

1983
Harvard social scientists conclude 65 percent of welfare recipients at any time would be on welfare rolls for at least eight years.

1988
Congress passes compromise welfare bill, the Family Support Act of 1988, which includes work requirements that conservatives call too weak.

1992
Democratic presidential candidate Bill Clinton vows to "end welfare as we know it."

1994
Republicans vow major overhaul of welfare system after taking control of both houses of Congress.

1996
Aid to Families with Dependent Children (AFDC) program is replaced by Republican-authored Temporary Assistance to Needy Families (TANF), which limits welfare benefits to five years; Clinton signs it into law. . . . Three top administration officials, including Assistant Health and Human Services Secretary Peter Edelman, quit in protest.

1997
Welfare system critic Sen. Daniel Patrick Moynihan, D-N.Y., says new TANF program breaks the New Deal "social contract" with America's poor.

2000s Welfare policy debate gathers force as recession hits middle-class Americans.

2001
Critics note on the five-year anniversary of welfare reform that while the law's tough requirements did not add to poor peoples' misery, 40 percent of the recipients who were forced off the rolls for failure to find work remained unemployed.

2008
As recession takes hold, family homelessness rises from previous year by 43,000 people, to 516,000 family members. . . . Fifty-five percent of unemployed people are ineligible or fail to apply for unemployment insurance. . . . Unemployment rate rises during the year from 4.9 percent to 7.2 percent.

2009
Congress enacts anti-recession stimulus bill containing emergency funds for TANF, food stamps and unemployment insurance. . . . TANF caseloads begin to rise in some states, but increase in food stamp use is more widespread. . . . TANF critics and supporters start preparing for reauthorization fight in 2010.

Do Safety Nets Undermine European Economies?

Some blame rigid labor policies, not generous welfare.

Even though he lost his job for an auto-parts maker this year, German worker Alfred Butt still took his weeklong Mediterranean vacation. Since state benefits will replace most of his lost salary for a full year, and since he keeps his full medical insurance under Germany's universal system, being out of work "hasn't changed my life that much," he told *The Wall Street Journal.* [1]

Contrast his situation to the familiar pain of an unemployed Illinois auto worker, Dylan DeRoberts. He lost his health insurance along with his job and can't afford the premiums to replace it. And he will receive only about a quarter of his former salary in jobless benefits for 59 weeks. [2]

Western Europeans receive far more generous assistance than Americans when they fall on hard times. In most countries in the region, the government replaces 60-90 percent of a jobless person's wages, compared to just over 50 percent in the United States, on average. [3] The length of compensation is also longer — for example, two years in Norway and unlimited in Belgium — compared to the normal maximum of six months in the United States. [4]

But experts have long debated whether Europe's level of assistance is ultimately a drag on the economy, as conservatives argue, or a built-in stimulus that enables the unemployed to continue spending. Can Europe's far lower poverty rates be attributed to its welfare benefits, they ask, and if so, are they worth the continent's much bigger share of welfare spending?

From the 1990s until the present economic crisis, the United States enjoyed significantly lower unemployment than such major European economies as France, Germany, Italy and Spain. The high cost to European employers of creating jobs has come in for much of the blame, especially from conservatives. In Germany, over half the cost of employing a worker consists of income tax and mandatory contributions to programs like unemployment insurance and pensions. [5]

"In Europe there are more protections [for workers], but that makes the economy less flexible," says Vincent R. Reinhart, res-

ident scholar at the American Enterprise Institute, a conservative think tank in Washington. "They grow a little slower and have a higher unemployment rate. We've chosen a different point along the trade-off — less safe and faster."

The current recession may be shifting that debate. When the U.S. unemployment rate hit 8.5 percent in March, it surpassed the rate in 16 members of the Organization for Economic Co-operation and Development — including Sweden, Italy, Britain and Norway. To the Center for Economic and Policy Research, a liberal Washington think tank, the rising U.S. jobless rate turned the case for America's superior flexibility "almost entirely on its head." [6]

But to others, it's a sign the United States can turn on a dime. "That just shows the economy is more responsive: You're laying off people more easily, and you also hire more easily" than in Europe, counters Justin Vaisse, a senior fellow at the Brookings Institution, a centrist Washington think tank. Employers in his native France who want to lay off workers have to prove the economic case for downsizing or else pay sizable severance packages — all of which makes businesses reluctant to hire in the first place, he says.

Yet some experts say it's those rigid labor policies, rather than the cost of welfare benefits, that slow European economies down. The Nordic welfare states of Denmark, Finland, Norway and Sweden offer generous family-assistance programs, including free child care and a year of paid parental leave. But all four economies have grown faster than the United States over the last 15 years, and Finland and Sweden have been pioneers in knowledge-based, high-technology industrial sectors like telecommunications. [7]

"If you compare continental European countries with the U.S. and Britain, you can say that in exchange for more social protection and poverty reduction, they've had to pay a price in employment and growth. But once you throw Nordic countries into the mix, you don't see that trade-off at all," says Jonas Pontusson, a professor of politics at Princeton University.

Continued from p. 654

Kennedy was assassinated, in 1963, before he could follow through. His successor, Lyndon B. Johnson — who had begun his own congressional career as a Roosevelt Democrat — determined that his legacy would be "an unconditional War on Poverty." Eventually, it embraced programs such as Head Start, Medicaid, job training and free legal assistance, proving enormously popular with its

target population as well as with liberal Democrats.

Some scholars say that the War on Poverty came to be mischaracterized as a series of giant programs to pay poor people for not working. In fact, the guiding doctrine of Office of Economic Opportunity (OEO), the agency that administered the anti-poverty initiative, was to provide the means for poor people to climb the socioeconomic ladder.

Johnson launched his "war" simultaneously with another major initiative, the "Great Society." The two are often confused, but "Great Society" programs were aimed largely at the middle class and included highway beautification, public broadcasting and federal aid to education.

Johnson, like Roosevelt, wanted to give people the tools to enter the work force, or to rise within it. "Johnson's fundamental conception was that this

The key, he says, is that the Scandinavian countries don't try to guarantee job security with rigid rules against firing, like the French, but offer serious job retraining in new skills along with unemployment insurance to ease the transition to new jobs.

When it comes to poverty, the United States leads wealthy countries with more than twice as big a share of

Then-French Prime Minister Dominique de Villepin visits a company child-care center near Paris in December 2006. France spends twice as much of its gross domestic product on social programs as the United States.

its population as continental Europe in poverty and almost triple the Nordic countries' share. [8] The most important factor in preventing poverty, research finds, is mothers who contribute to the family income, assisted by good-quality, free child care, as in Sweden, according to Gosta Esping-Andersen, a sociologist at Pompeu Fabra University in Barcelona, Spain. And because so many fewer children in Sweden are in poverty than most countries, Pontusson says, they're more capable of taking advantage of Sweden's free, high-quality education system, which in turn is an engine of high-wage economic growth.

France spends twice as big a share of its gross domestic product on social programs as the United States. [9] How do they afford it? "Health care imposes less of a burden on the economy for Europeans, and their family-benefit system doesn't have the perverse incentives of the U.S. welfare system," since child benefits go to all families, not just to single, impoverished mothers who don't work, says Princeton sociologist Paul Starr.

American observers have heard surprisingly little talk from European politicians about cutting back welfare benefits in dealing with the economic crisis. [10] "It's precisely when there's a crisis that you don't want to reduce payments to people spend-

ing on consumption," Vaisse observes. "It's very bad economics." Europeans tend to see benefits like unemployment compensation as a well-earned right, not charity, he adds.

"They wouldn't find it normal that someone laid off — for which they're not responsible — should be miserable without the collective system making up for at least part of it."

— Sarah Glazer

[1] Marcus Walker and Roger Thurow, "U.S., Europe Are an Ocean Apart on Human Toll of Joblessness," *The Wall Street Journal*, May 7, 2009, http://on line.wsj.com.

[2] *Ibid.* The 59 weeks is an extension in Illinois of the usual 26 weeks as part of stimulus measures.

[3] "Unemployment Insurance Benefits, 2005," from "Benefits and Wages, 2007," Organization for Economic Co-operation and Development, Table 1.1 www.oecd.org.

[4] *Ibid.*

[5] Walker and Thurow, *op. cit.*

[6] John Schmitt, *et al.*, "U.S. Unemployment Now as High as Europe," Center for Economic Policy Research, May 2009, www.cepr.net.

[7] Jonas Pontusson, "Once Again a Model: Nordic Social Democracy in a Globalized World," January 2009, forthcoming in James Cronin, *et al.*, eds., *Futures of the Left.* Average annual growth of real gross domestic product (GDP) per capita 1995-2007 was 2.8 percent for the United States and averaged 3.2 percent for Denmark, Finland, Norway and Sweden.

[8] *Ibid.*

[9] Total public social expenditure was 16 percent of GDP in the U.S. and 28.7 percent of GDP in France in 2003. "Society at a Glance: OECD Social Indicators," 2006 Edition. Organization for Economic Co-operation and Development (2007), ww.oecd.org/els/social/indicators/SAG.

[10] An exception is President Nicolas Sarkozy's recent proposal to increase the retirement age in France, aimed at France's long-term problem of a dwindling population of young workers to support retirees.

should not be a handout but what he called a hand up," historian Dallek, a Johnson biographer, told National Public Radio in 2004. [33]

Johnson's programs failed to completely meet that standard. While the share of the population living in poverty fell from 19 percent in 1964 to 12.8 percent in 1968, "this was done . . . by getting them on to expanding welfare rolls," Dallek said. [34]

The most dramatic increase came in the Aid to Families with Dependent Children (AFDC) program — typically referred to simply as "welfare" — which saw its caseload soar 230 percent from 1963 to 1973. [35]

Much of the growth occurred under Johnson's Republican successor, Richard M. Nixon. In fact, Nixon also proposed a Family Assistance Plan that would have revolutionized the welfare system by granting a mini-

mum income to every family through a small payment of $1,600 a year. To Haskins the proposal evidences Nixon's "proto-liberal" tendency on domestic policy.

But liberal journalist Elizabeth Drew says the diary of Nixon aide H. R. Haldeman indicates Nixon never had any intention of pushing the bill through Congress, where it died in 1970. [36]

Workfare

The traditional system of providing cash to single mothers who had no official income had prompted skepticism even while Johnson was still in office. The key figure urging a retooling of welfare was Daniel Patrick Moynihan, who as a member of the Labor Department's Office of Policy Planning and Research had written a 1965 report that aroused a storm of controversy. "The Negro Family: The Case for National Action" concluded that family structures among African-Americans were eroding. High unemployment for males and welfare payments acted as both cause and effect of family disintegration, wrote Moynihan (later a longtime Democratic U.S. senator from New York).

"We have shown a clear relation between male employment," the so-called "Moynihan Report" said, "and the number of welfare-dependent children. Employment in turn reflects educational achievement, which depends in large part on family stability, which reflects employment." [37]

The majority of black children received welfare assistance at one point or another, Moynihan reported. In at least one city, Chicago, recipients of nearly 90 percent of Aid to Families with Dependent Children were black. And the share of welfare families in which the father had deserted the home had climbed from one-third when AFDC began in 1935, to two-thirds. [38]

The report reverberated not only because it emphasized the importance of work over welfare but also because it connected welfare policy and race — a connection that still resounds in debates over poverty and safety nets.

The policy effects of the "Moynihan Report" began in California in the 1970s, when Gov. Ronald W. Reagan championed a "workfare" program in his state's 1971 Welfare Reform Act.

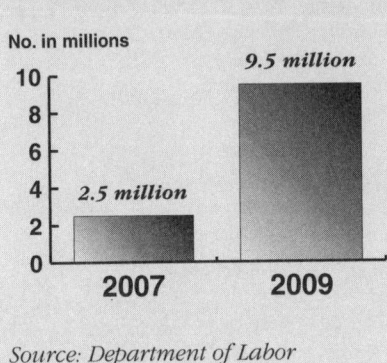

Unemployment Claims Rose Fourfold

About 9.5 million Americans have claimed unemployment benefits in 2009, nearly a fourfold increase from 2007.

Number of Americans Claiming Unemployment Benefits, 2007 and 2009

No. in millions

2007: 2.5 million
2009: 9.5 million

Source: Department of Labor

The three-year pilot program — formally the Community Work Experience Program — required welfare recipients to get jobs.

Popular politically, the program failed to make headway on the ground. William Bagley, the former Republican legislator who helped fashion the legislation, told the *Los Angeles Times* that counties essentially ignored the program. "There are only so many people who can rake leaves," he said. A 1976 study by the state Employment Development Department, concluded that workfare "did not prove to be administratively feasible and practical." [39]

Reagan's successor as governor, Democrat Edmund G. Brown Jr., allowed the program to die. But once in the White House, Reagan touted California's experiment as a rousing success.

And as a candidate in the 1976 presidential primary, Reagan made opposition to welfare one of his selling points. He didn't shy away from lump-

ing various safety-net programs together as objectionable — nor did he avoid racial stereotypes. Reagan told a Fort Lauderdale rally of working peoples' outrage when standing in supermarket checkout lines and seeing a "strapping young buck" buying T-bone steaks with food stamps. In those days, the term was an unmistakable, and racially charged, reference. [40]

Reagan lost that primary. But when he finally won the presidency in 1980, his California law became a template for changes in welfare that he demanded from Congress. A competing bill in the Democrat-controlled House proposed expanding access to benefits. Moynihan, who had been elected to the Senate in 1976, worked out a compromise. He summed up his legislation to the *Los Angeles Times*: "Welfare mothers need work. Fathers have to support their families. Children need care. Our purpose is to free these women and children from the stigma of dependency." [41]

Congress passed the Family Support Act in 1988. But even at the time, experts said that the reshaping of welfare would require years. Moynihan himself said that work requirements would be phased in so gradually that significant results wouldn't appear until 2000. [42]

At the heart of the Family Support Act of 1988 was the Jobs Opportunities and Basic Skills Training Program, known as JOBS. Each state was required to establish its own JOBS program by 1990, with education, vocational training and placement, along with support services such as child care. [43]

As soon as it was enacted, some liberals called the changes minor. Conservatives, for their part, argued that the law was too benefits-oriented. And the nonpartisan Congressional Budget Office forecast in 1989 that the law would reduce welfare rolls by only 50,000 people over five years — far from the major decrease that conservatives had been demanding.

In fact, as the economy went into recession in 1989, state welfare caseloads increased. As of December 1991, the nation's welfare population had grown more than 20 percent, to more than 4.5 million families — a bigger uptick than the increases registered during the three other recessions that had occurred since 1970.

Welfare Reform

The 1988 law whetted political appetites for a much tougher approach to rewriting welfare law. While Reagan and other politicians had been denouncing the welfare system for encouraging long-term dependency, a pool of generally conservative policy experts had been busy gathering the intellectual ammunition for a comprehensive overhaul of the system. [44]

A key source of data for conservatives was a study by two Harvard social scientists, which showed that 65 percent of welfare recipients at any given moment would be on the rolls for at least eight years. Charles Murray, a fellow of the American Enterprise Institute, wrote extensively about illegitimate births as a major cause of poverty. He said that births outside marriage were also a consequence of safety-net programs that provided extra support for each additional child born to an unwed mother.

The Brookings Institution's Haskins, who was staff director of the House Ways and Means Human Resources Subcommittee when it was under Republican control in 1995-1996, wrote later that Murray's claim of a welfare-illegitimacy link was "weak and somewhat inconsistent." But Haskins conceded that the claim rang true to the public at large, and conservatives used it to fire up anti-welfare sentiment.

Some Democrats recognized the political appeal of attacking the welfare system. Running for president in 1992,

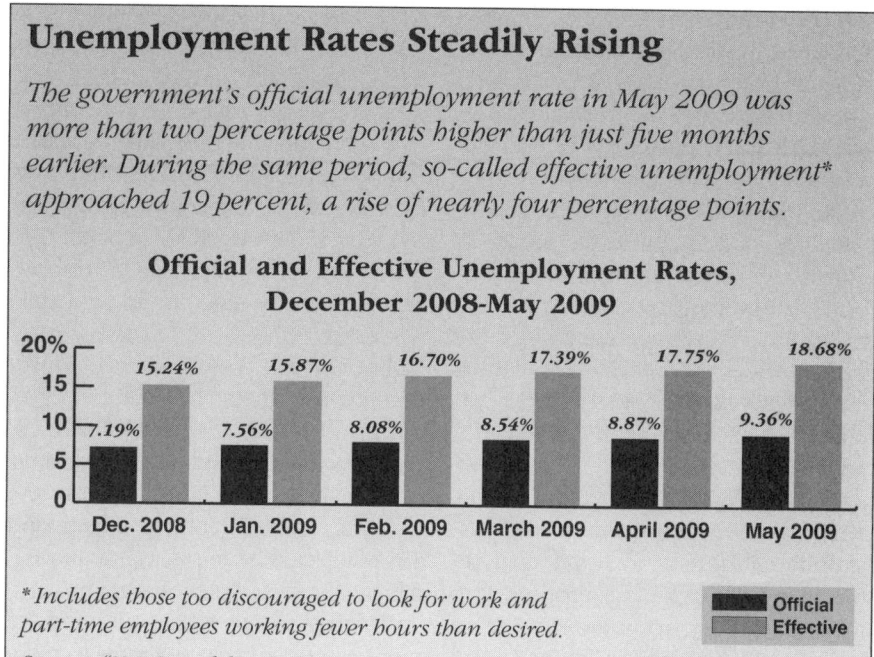

Unemployment Rates Steadily Rising

The government's official unemployment rate in May 2009 was more than two percentage points higher than just five months earlier. During the same period, so-called effective unemployment* approached 19 percent, a rise of nearly four percentage points.

Official and Effective Unemployment Rates, December 2008-May 2009

	Dec. 2008	Jan. 2009	Feb. 2009	March 2009	April 2009	May 2009
Official	7.19%	7.56%	8.08%	8.54%	8.87%	9.36%
Effective	15.24%	15.87%	16.70%	17.39%	17.75%	18.68%

* Includes those too discouraged to look for work and part-time employees working fewer hours than desired.

Source: "Not Out of the Woods," New America Foundation, June 2009

Democrat Bill Clinton vowed to "end welfare as we know it."

But for the first two years after Clinton took office, his administration treated welfare-law changes with little urgency, in the view of those pushing for major overhaul. A White House proposal did emerge in 1994. The Clinton plan would have given welfare recipients two years from enrollment to find work. Federally subsidized jobs would be open to those who failed to get work. As a money-saving measure, Clinton proposed covering only welfare recipients born after 1971.

The proposal found little support among liberals, who opposed the two-year limit. Republicans responded harshly. They pointed to the failure to cover the entire caseload, and to what they called too much flexibility in enforcing time limits. Republicans also objected to what they called ineffective measures to discourage illegitimate births.

A Republican sweep in the 1994 congressional elections changed the entire political climate on welfare. Now in control of both houses of Congress, the GOP set itself the goal of producing the kind of welfare law for which it had been pushing for the better part of three decades.

The key elements of what became known as "welfare reform" — fundamentally a Republican product — included: the end of AFDC, which was replaced by TANF; a five-year time limit on assistance, which would only be granted in the first place to a parent who prepares for employment and gets a job; and a limit on federal assistance to state welfare programs — effectively preventing them from simply growing as caseload demand increases.

Moreover, thanks to provisions allowing states flexibility in designing their own welfare programs, about half the states prohibited increasing benefits to recipient mothers who had additional children while in TANF — a measure designed to discourage illegitimate births.

The Senate passed the legislation 78-21; the House vote, on July 31, was 328-101. Clinton signed it into law on Aug. 22, 1996.

That didn't end debate, however. In August, Wendell E. Primus, a deputy assistant secretary of Health and Human Services, resigned in opposition to Clinton's enactment of the law, which Primus' office had predicted would add 1 million children to the poverty population. He was followed out the door by assistant secretaries of Health and Human Services Edelman and Mary Jo Bane. [45]

And Sen. Moynihan opposed the law, which he had fought in the Senate as punitive and risky. Attacking a later proposal to overhaul Social Security, he called that effort a consequence of the welfare law and its abolition of "the social contract of the 1930s, in which we undertook the care of the elderly, the unemployed, the children." [46]

Nevertheless, the first five years of TANF didn't produce the social catastrophe critics had predicted, even as the national caseload dropped by more than 50 percent from its peak in 1994. The economic boom of the late 1990s certainly played a role by producing millions of service-sector jobs that former recipients could fill.

But, at the five-year mark, critics noted that 40 percent of former recipients who were forced off the rolls still weren't working. And the potential effects of a major recession on the TANF system and its participants remained a source of concern. ∎

CURRENT SITUATION

State Nets Fraying

Reeling from declining revenues as home prices drop and jobs disappear, state governments are having a harder time keeping up their safety-net programs. Budget crises in statehouses across the country are showing the extent to which programs created by the federal government depend on state money and administration.

In California, where the budget crisis had forced the state to issue IOUs to some contractors and vendors, a new state budget has shut off enrollments to new applicants in the state's Healthy Families program for children from low-income families. Some advocates say the move could deny medical care to 400,000-570,000 children, according to competing estimates by state officials and child advocates. [47]

Elsewhere, Louisiana and North Carolina said they'd run out of money to finance previously authorized expansions in their child-health programs. And lawmakers in Alaska, Delaware, Georgia, Missouri, Rhode Island and Texas rejected attempts to expand eligibility for their states' programs. [48]

To be sure, other states did find the money to open their programs to more children, including Alabama, Arkansas, Indiana, Iowa, Montana, Nebraska, North Dakota, Oklahoma, Oregon and West Virginia. Ohio may do likewise.

"Our economy is tough here," Democratic Alabama state Sen. Roger H. Bedford Jr. said. "But our decision was to fund the health-care needs of our children because a healthy child learns better, and they don't show up at the emergency room needing acute care." [49]

Arguments over children's health care aside, the budget shortfalls in all but two states are revealing the vast differences in how states administer safety-net programs. Much of the safety net is partly funded by the federal and state governments but run by states, to which most programs give great latitude in making rules and setting eligibility standards.

According to a survey by The New York Times, the differences run deep. In California, 50 percent of those eligible for food stamps receive them, versus 98 percent in Missouri. Unemployment Insurance goes to 67 percent of laid-off workers in Idaho but only 19 percent in South Dakota. [50]

The only rule among state programs is inconsistency, The Times concluded. "You've got this kind of jigsaw puzzle that doesn't really fit together," conservative social-policy expert Stewart Butler, vice president for domestic and economic policy studies at the Heritage Foundation, told The Times. [51]

As often happens with major national issues, California provides the most dramatic examples of the collision between safety-net programs and hard-pressed state government.

For decades, California has enjoyed a high national ranking in providing for its least well-off citizens. In 2002 (the most recent data available), the state spent 70 percent more per capita on social services than the rest of the country. [52]

But the budget crisis seems certain to slash safety-net programs. In Oakland, an economically struggling city in the San Francisco Bay Area, advocates for low-income residents say many of their clients are nearing the point of desperation.

Recipients of "general assistance" — available to single people who can't work but don't qualify for other programs — were expecting to see their aid cut from year-round to three months. "What are they going to do for the remaining nine?" asks Ed Barnes, director of income practice at the East Bay Community Law Center. "When you're telling people on General Assistance that for nine months they're going to have nothing, some are going to get sick, some are going to die, some are going to break into your house and mine and steal your plumbing."

Funding for CalWorks, California's TANF program, was slashed under the new budget. Republican Gov. Arnold Schwarzenegger said that applying eligibility rules more strictly would save $753 million this year, and $1.5 billion starting in 2010. The new standards, he said, would end "waste, fraud and abuse of your hard-earned tax dollars." [53]

Continued on p. 662

At Issue:

Does Europe have a better safety-net system than the U.S.?

PETER EDELMAN
DIRECTOR, CENTER ON POVERTY, INEQUALITY AND PUBLIC POLICY GEORGETOWN LAW CENTER

WRITTEN FOR *CQ RESEARCHER*, JULY 13, 2009

*i*n some ways it's a really easy question. Every European country has universal health coverage. Most have far better systems of child care than we have. And so on.

Some say the European systems are "too good," especially with regard to income support — too generous and consequently too expensive, requiring unacceptably high taxes, etc.

But you don't see the kind of extreme poverty in Europe that we have in the United States. More than 15 million people in the U.S. — over 5 percent of our population — have incomes more than halfway below the poverty line — below $8,500 for a family of three. That's pretty shocking. European countries typically have a family allowance or a child allowance that creates a floor of income that prevents the rather unbelievable situation we have.

A critique of the European systems is that they make it too easy for people to stay out of the labor market. Of course the other side of that coin is that the Europeans can live with higher unemployment rates than was the norm for the U.S. in recent years because they have a more adequate safety net than we do.

Nonetheless, there is an issue. The United Kingdom and the United States both came to the conclusion in the mid-1990s that they had people receiving cash assistance who could be working. But they responded in basically opposite ways, and I think the U.K. got it right.

The American solution was to shrink the welfare rolls by getting tough. Each state was largely allowed to decide for itself, but the basic idea was to make it harder for people to get help, unpleasant for those who manage to receive help and easier to push people off who fail to cooperate in some way.

The Brits said, let's make it more remunerative for people to work than to be on the dole, and let's do that not by cutting benefits or pushing people away, but by beefing up the income supplementation that we make available to low-wage workers so they can have a living income. It's like what we've done with the Earned-Income Tax Credit, but much more so.

The United States would do well to emulate the Europeans' approach to health care and child care. But in the area of income support for non-disabled people of working age, or at least those with children, the most important lesson is the one that comes from the United Kingdom.

LAWRENCE M. MEAD
PROFESSOR OF POLITICS AND PUBLIC POLICY, NEW YORK UNIVERSITY

WRITTEN FOR *CQ RESEARCHER*, JULY 15, 2009

*t*he chief difference between the American and European safety nets is that the United States typically provides less assistance to those of working age. Our unemployment insurance is relatively restrictive, and benefits are time-limited. In Europe, unemployment coverage is wider and open-ended, at least for the low-income. In America, cash welfare is confined largely to the disabled and needy single mothers. Other low-income people get only wage subsidies or food stamps (now called the Supplemental Nutrition Assistance Program) for buying groceries. In contrast, Europe typically provides some form of guaranteed income to all needy people, in cash.

The European system assures broad security but fosters long-term dependency. Single mothers and the jobless can live on the government indefinitely without taking serious steps to support themselves. There is widespread fraud, with many people claiming benefits who could work. America minimizes dependency because unemployment and welfare claimants face more pressure to move into jobs. Thus, a higher share of the population works in America than in many European countries. That promotes social integration and limits poverty, since few of the steadily employed are poor.

Critics demand that a minimum income be guaranteed to everyone, regardless of work effort, but Congress has repeatedly refused to enact it. This reflects public opinion. Americans want government to help the poor, but they also demand that adult recipients work alongside taxpayers. In the 1990s welfare reform strengthened work tests for welfare mothers, causing most of them to leave welfare for jobs. Recently, Europe has also begun to demand work of people on unemployment and welfare benefits. There, as here, the main motivation is not to save money but to promote social integration and curb non-work and poverty, especially for children.

The very image of a "safety net" implies that the employable actively seek work, needing help only if they fail. With its emphasis on short-term aid, America's system is truer to that image than Europe's, where people have been supported apart from employment. On both continents, low-paid jobs are widely available. Immigrants, often illegal, are doing many of them. The message of welfare reform is that those who need income should first take available jobs, and only then look to government.

In hard times like now, jobs will be less available, so public aid is needed. But assistance should not become, as in Europe, a right that people claim without any serious effort to work.

Continued from p. 660

Homelessness

Big-city Americans may have gotten used to congregations of homeless individuals in downtowns across the country. But a growth in families with kids without shelter may not be so easy to overlook, or accept.

The most recent Housing and Urban Development Department (HUD) annual survey of homelessness reported a "considerable rise" in families without shelter. The estimated number increased by 43,000 people, to more than 516,000 from 2007 to 2008, accounting for nearly one-third of populations in shelters. [54]

The rise in homeless families is another indication of how the recession — which is closely linked to falling home prices and foreclosures — is hurting families. "In addition to fewer people coming from situations in which they already were homeless, more came from situations that previously had been relatively stable," the report said.

One advocate says the new homeless are coming from the low-wage workforce. "It's poor people who are becoming homeless," says Nan Roman, president of the National Alliance to End Homelessness. "They had no cushion. Work for them is a paycheck-to-paycheck deal."

Nevertheless, Roman hopes an additional $1.5 billion provided in the stimulus law will benefit at least 300,000 families. The money will be disbursed over two years to the federal Homelessness Prevention and Rapid Rehousing Program, which provides rent assistance to prevent evictions or help renters acquire new housing before they become homeless.

Housing instability frequently is ignored as a safety-net matter, Roman says. But the causes and effects of homelessness place it squarely in the same cluster of socioeconomic issues as layoffs and hunger. "It's hard to think about getting a job or staying employed, or keeping the kids in school, without stable housing," she says.

Rental rates increased more than take-home pay in most parts of the country, Roman and others argue, pointing

California teachers and supporters in Los Angeles protest state and local budget cuts on Jan. 29, 2009.

to homelessness as a problem that's surged only over the past 30 years.

In an innovative approach, Robert Lerman, a professor of economics at American University in Washington, proposes that the federal government buy homes at their present low prices and subsidize part of the mortgage payments for people otherwise eligible for rent assistance.

"We would expand demand for owner-occupied dwellings, and lower the share of eligible low-income people on the waiting list for housing," Lerman argues. "We'd kill two birds with one stone."

Reauthorization

The longstanding conflict over the government's social responsibility could reignite next year, when the 1996 welfare law comes back before Congress. Scheduled reauthorization of the law would provide an opportunity for critics and supporters to fight their battle in the new context provided by the recession.

Reauthorization — a congressional device for taking a new look at a law — doesn't always occur, even when a reauthorization date is built into a statute. Some laws simply remain in effect. That happened with a scheduled TANF reauthorization in 2002. But those on both sides of the safety-net debates are operating on the assumption that the 2010 TANF reauthorization debate will take place.

"Legal Momentum," a liberal women's-rights advocacy organization, has already started organizing to use reauthorization as a vehicle to make major changes in the law.

"Reauthorization offers a fresh opportunity for advocates to press Congress for measures to make TANF responsive to the mothers and children the program is intended to serve," the organization says on its Web site. [55]

Zedlewski of the Center on Budget and Policy Priorities, says she expects "a lot of conversation about how we should be serving low-income

Getty Images/David McNew

families with a tentative attachment to the labor market that falls apart during periods of high unemployment."

Brookings' Haskins, one of the top strategists behind the TANF law, sees a chance at raising a closely related issue — mothers who have lost their eligibility for cash assistance but who also have failed to find work. Typically, these former TANF participants face a series of obstacles to employment, such as finding reliable and affordable child care and being able to afford transportation to and from work. "Generally, research shows that if she just has one barrier, she can overcome it," Haskins says. "Not if there are more."

Whatever attempts are made at changing TANF in 2010, they won't be the first efforts undertaken via reauthorization. In 2002-2005, fights over whether and how to change welfare-to-work requirements in the law stalled reauthorization, which stayed in force under temporary arrangements. Another of these arrangements was made in 2005. [56]

The Heritage Foundation's Rector argues that the reauthorization fights of the early 2000s "seriously weakened" the 1996 welfare reforms by effectively loosening work requirements. During next year's reauthorization process, he says, "Every indication is that, far from strengthening those work requirements, they will make them weaker." ∎

OUTLOOK

New Approach?

Forecasts concerning government safety-net programs often diverge sharply, depending on experts' view of today's picture.

Mead of NYU rejects talk of the recession as a world-shaking event. In the slowdown of the early 1980s, he says, "There was much more of a sense that the world was coming apart. Ten percent was the highest unemployment we'd seen" since the Great Depression. "And we were losing factory jobs much more rapidly than we are now. What I sense now is the lack of acute distress of the kind we saw then."

And the upshot was that the country soared out of trouble and became wealthier in the 1990s, Mead argues.

Ten years from now, Mead says the present recession will also have blown over. "I think we're going to go on as we are. We're likely to see continuing reliance on low-wage employment as the main safety net."

Those on the other side of the ideological divide are less optimistic. "Welfare reform has been basically an effort of moving people from very low levels of public benefits to very low levels of wages," says McHugh, of the National Employment Law Project. "That doesn't really address poverty."

McHugh sees a possibility that future developments may weaken one of the central doctrines of the 1996 welfare law — and perhaps prompt a different approach. "The TANF model is based on the idea that attitudinal or cultural reasons get in the way of people going to work. But at this point in Michigan we've got a lot of families where the parents actually have skills, they have degrees, and now they're 45 or 50 and they don't have the prospect of getting reemployment in fields in which they've got experience."

The growth in population of laid-off industrial workers may lead to programs to develop meaningful employment for factory hands and white-collar workers laid off from the auto industry and its offshoots, McHugh says.

Economist Lerman of American University cautions that progress on that front may be slow, given the difficulties of designing such programs. "I think we'll probably do a bit better over time," he says. "I would like to see constructive efforts to improve peoples' earning outcomes."

As one of the architects of the 1996 law, Haskins of Brookings sees a need to move to social engineering that promotes social mobility — not just employment. "That is a very tough one. Education is going to be very important — a more technical kind of education, as opposed to a four-year degree." [57]

But plans for educational expansion depend on government funding, which is highly uncertain, Haskins acknowledges. "The thing that would really precipitate a crisis would be a failure to sell our [U.S. Treasury] bonds," he says, arguing that the danger is real.

Whatever the next step may be, Haskins maintains that the 1996 law laid a good foundation. "We are going to have millions of low-wage workers, and many of them are going to be parents, especially single moms," he says. "It is much better to have them working than wasting away on welfare. We've built a pretty good system."

Georgetown's Edelman, who opposed the 1996 law to the point of quitting the Clinton administration in protest, argues that it reflected disdain for single mothers who for a variety of reasons weren't able to work. "We have this national attitude that there is something wrong if they're receiving cash assistance on any kind of continuing basis," he says. "We really need to talk about that again. We had that debate and it came out the other way. That shouldn't be the end."

The best solution for them is a guaranteed minimum income of the kind proposed during the Nixon administration, Edelman says, noting that it could be designed to encourage work.

Edelman agrees with some of his adversaries, however, that another big challenge of the future will center on low-wage workers. "We have to be aware of the possibility that in the 21st century in a globalized world we may have full employment, but the median wage may not improve all that much." ∎

Notes

[1] Heather Boushey, *et al.*, "Understanding Low-Wage Work in the United States," *The Mobility Agenda*, March 2007, www.mobility agenda.org/lowwagework.pdf; "May 2008 National Occupational Employment and Wage Estimates," U.S. Bureau of Labor Statistics, www.bls.gov/oes/2008/may/oes_nat.htm#b00-0000.

[2] "Combined TANF and SSP-MOE, Total Number of Child Recipients, Total Number of Families," Administration for Children and Families, updated May 19, 2009, www.acf.hhs.gov/programs/ofa/data-reports/caseload/caseload_recent.html.

[3] "Job Openings and Labor Turnover Summary," U.S. Bureau of Labor Statistics, July 7, 2009, www.bls.gov/news.release/jolts.nr0.htm; "Employment Situation Summary," U.S. Bureau of Labor Statistics, July 2, 2009, www.bls.gov/news.release/empsit.nr0.htm; Databases, hires, http://data.bls.gov/PDQ/servlet/SurveyOutputServlet;jsessionid=a230513c648019747a85; Databases, layoffs and discharges, http://data.bls.gov/PDQ/servlet/SurveyOutputServlet;jsessionid=a2302412b9b6645207b7.

[4] Ben S. Bernanke, "The Economic Outlook," testimony before Joint Economic Committee, May 5, 2009, www.federalreserve.gov/newsevents/testimony/bernanke20090505a.htm.

[5] Quoted in Kevin Sack, "Defying Slump, 13 States Insure More Children," *The New York Times*, July 18, 2009, www.nytimes.com/2009/07/19/us/19chip.html?%2334;Kevin Sack=&_r=1&sq=&st=cse&%2334;=&scp=2&pagewanted=all.

[6] Sara Murray, "Numbers on Welfare See Sharp Increase," *The Wall Street Journal*, June 22, 2009, http://online.wsj.com/article/SB124562449457235503.html. "TANF Caseloads Increase in Most Big States," National Conference of State Legislatures, undated, www.ncsl.org/default.aspx?TabId=17772.

[7] Evan Halper and Shane Goldmacher, "Governor, legislative leaders start building support for their budget pact," *Los Angeles Times*, July 21, 2009, www.latimes.com/news/local/la-me-california-budget22-2009jul22,0,1856950.story.

[8] "Climbing Caseloads," *The Wall Street Journal*, June 22, 2009, http://s.wsj.net/public/resources/documents/st_WELFAREINCREASE0906_20090619.html.

[9] "Supplemental Nutritional Assistance Program: Number of Persons Participating," U.S. Food and Nutrition Service, updated June 30, 2009, www.fns.usda.gov/pd/29SNAPcurrPP.htm.

[10] *Ibid.*

[11] "Employment Situation Summary," *op. cit.*

[12] Gene Falk, "The Potential Role of the Temporary Assistance for Needy Families (TANF) Block Grant in the Recession," Congressional Research Service, pp. 16-18, http://assets.opencrs.com/rpts/R40157_20090224.pdf.

[13] *Ibid.*, pp. 1,4.

[14] "American Recovery and Reinvestment Act of 2009," U.S. Food and Nutrition Service, undated, www.fns.usda.gov/fns/recovery/recovery-snap.htm.

[15] Alison M. Shelton, *et al.*, "Unemployment Insurance Provisions in the American Recovery and Reinvestment Act of 2009," Congressional Research Service, March 4, 2009, http://assets.opencrs.com/rpts/R40368_20090304.pdf; "Federal Stimulus Funding Produces Unprecedented Wave of Unemployment Insurance Reforms," National Employment Law Project, June 16, 2009, www.nelp.org/page/-/UI/UIMA.Roundup.June.09.pdf?nocdn=.

[16] Robert E. Rector and Katherine Bradley, "Welfare Spendathon: House Stimulus Bill Will Cost Taxpayers $787 Billion in New Welfare Spending," Heritage Foundation, Feb. 6, 2009, www.heritage.org/research/economy/upload/wm_2276.pdf.

[17] Mickey Kaus, "The Money Liberal Conspiracy At Work," *Slate*, Feb. 10, 2009, www.slate.com/blogs/blogs/kausfiles/default.aspx.

[18] Falk, *op. cit.*

[19] "Indicator 4, Rates of Participation in Means-Tested Assistance Programs — table IND 4a," in *2008 Indicators of Welfare Dependence*, Health and Human Services Department, Chapter II, http://aspe.hhs.gov/hsp/indicators08/ch2.shtml.

[20] "Business Employment Dynamics," U.S. Bureau of Labor Statistics, May 19, 2009, p. 3, www.bls.gov/news.release/pdf/cewbd.pdf.

[21] "Remarks by the President on the American Graduation Initiative," The White House, July 14, 2009, www.whitehouse.gov/the_press_office/Remarks-by-the-President-on-the-American-Graduation-Initiative-in-Warren-MI/.

[22] "Remarks by the President on Job Creation and Job Training," The White House, May 8, 2009, www.whitehouse.gov/the_press_office/Remarks-by-the-President-on-Job-Creation-and-Job-Training-5/8/09.

[23] Madeleine Brand, "40th Anniversary of LBJ's 'War on Poverty,'" National Public Radio, Jan. 8, 2004, www.npr.org/templates/story/story.php?storyId=1589416.

[24] "House Appropriations Subcommittee on Labor, Health and Human Services, Education and Related Agencies," CQ Congressional Transcripts, May 12, 2009.

[25] "Senate Health, Education, Labor and Pensions Committee Holds Hearing on Green Skills Training for Workers," CQ Congressional Transcripts, April 21, 2009; "Employment Situation Summary," *op. cit.*

[26] Arthur Schlesinger Jr., "The 'Hundred Days' of FDR," *The New York Times*, April 10, 1983, Sect. 3, p. 1. Unless otherwise indicated, this subsection also draws on William E. Leuchtenburg, *Franklin D. Roosevelt and the New Deal*

About the Author

Peter Katel is a *CQ Researcher* staff writer who previously reported on Haiti and Latin America for *Time* and *Newsweek* and covered the Southwest for newspapers in New Mexico. He has received several journalism awards, including the Bartolomé Mitre Award for coverage of drug trafficking, from the Inter-American Press Association. He holds an A.B. in university studies from the University of New Mexico. His recent reports include "Mexico's Drug War," "Homeland Security" and "Legalizing Marijuana."

(1963). For background, see Peter Katel, "Vanishing Jobs," *CQ Researcher*, March 13, 2009, pp. 225-248.

[27] Quoted in Leuchtenburg, *op. cit.*, p. 122.

[28] Quoted in *ibid.*, p. 124.

[29] B. Putney, "Politics and Business in 1936," *Editorial Research Reports*, Jan. 4, 1936, available at *CQ Researcher* Plus Archives.

[30] Quoted in "Presidential Candidates, 1936," *Editorial Research Reports*, Feb. 18, 1936.

[31] Quoted in Louis Galambos and Daun van Ee, "A President's First Term: Eisenhower's Pursuit of 'The Middle Way,'" *Humanities*, January-February, 2001, www.neh.gov/news/humanities/2001-01/eisenhower.html.

[32] Brendon O'Connor, *A Political History of the American Welfare System: Where Ideas Have Consequences* (2004), pp. 22, 55-57.

[33] Brand, *op. cit.*

[34] *Ibid.* Also see "Historical Poverty Tables," U.S. Census Bureau, www.census.gov/hhes/www/poverty/histpov/hstpov2.html.

[35] For background, see Sarah Glazer, "Welfare Reform," *CQ Researcher*, Aug. 3, 2001, pp. 601-632.

[36] Ron Haskins, *Work Over Welfare: The Inside Story of the 1996 Welfare Reform Law* (2006), pp. 1, 5; Elizabeth Drew, *Richard M. Nixon* (2007), pp. 53-54.

[37] "The Negro Family: The Case for National Action," U.S. Department of Labor, March, 1965, Chapt. V, www.dol.gov/oasam/programs/history/webid-meynihan.htm. For attribution of the report to Moynihan, see "History at the Department, Documents," www.dol.gov/oasam/programs/history/webidrpage.htm.

[38] *Ibid.*, Chapt. II.

[39] Quoted in Richard Padock, "Gov. Reagan's Workfare: No 'Gang Busters' In a Short Life," *Los Angeles Times*, Feb. 10, 1986, p. A3. For background, see Kenneth Jost, "Welfare Reform," *CQ Researcher*, April 10, 1992, pp. 313-336.

[40] Quoted in Robert G. Kaiser, "On Welfare: Democrat Bullish, Republican Bearish (but Less Now)," Oct. 23, 1980, p. A2. See also Jason DeParle, "The 'W' Word, Re-Engaged," *The New York Times*, Feb. 8, 2009, "Week in Review," p. 1.

[41] Quoted in William J. Eaton, "New Welfare Plan Stresses Work, Family Responsibility," *Los Angeles Times*, May 15, 1988, p. A14.

[42] William K. Stevens, "Welfare Bill's Radical Goals Would Take Years," *The New York Times*, Oct. 2, 1988, p. A20.

[43] *Ibid.*

[44] Except where otherwise indicated, this subsection draws from Haskins, *op. cit.* For background, see Chris Conte, "Welfare, Work and the States," *CQ Researcher*, Dec. 6, 1996, pp. 1057-1080; and Glazer, *op. cit.*

[45] Alison Mitchell, "Two Clinton Aides Resign to Protest New Welfare Law," *The New York Times*, Sept. 12, 1996, p. A1.

[46] Daniel Patrick Moynihan, "Social Security, As We Knew It," *The New York Times*, Jan. 5, 1997, p. A13.

[47] Sack, *op. cit.*; Judy Lin, "Schwarzenegger, lawmakers restart budget talks," The Associated Press, July 17, 2009, http://news.yahoo.com/s/ap/20090717/ap_on_re_us/us_california_budget.

[48] Sack, *op. cit.*

[49] Quoted in *ibid.*

[50] Jason DeParle, "For Victims of Recession, Patchwork State Aid," *The New York Times*, May 9, 2009, www.nytimes.com/2009/05/10/us/10safetynet.html?pagewanted=all.

[51] Quoted in *ibid.*

[52] Steve Gorman, "California's needy may bear brunt of budget crisis," Reuters, July 15, 2009, http://news.yahoo.com/s/nm/20090715/us_nm/us_usa_states_budget_california.

[53] Quoted in *ibid.*

[54] "The 2008 Annual Homeless Assessment Report to Congress," Department of Housing and Urban Development, July 2009, pp. 18-19, www.hudhre.info/documents/4thHomelessAssessmentReport.pdf.

[55] "TANF Reauthorization," Legal Momentum, undated, www.legalmomentum.org/our-work/social-safety-net/tanf-reauthorization-2010.html.

[56] Vee Burke and Gene Falk, "TANF Reauthorization: Side-by-Side Comparison of Current Law and Two Versions of H.R. 4 (108th Congress)," Congressional Research Service, March 1, 2005, www.nationalaglawcenter.org/assets/crs/RL32210.pdf; Gene Falk, "TANF, Child Care, Marriage Promotion, and Responsible Fatherhood Provisions in the Deficit Reduction Act of 2005," Congressional Research Service, March 1, 2007, http://wikileaks.org/leak/crs/RS22369.pdf.

[57] For background, see the following *CQ Researchers*: Alan Greenblatt, "Upward Mobility," April 29, 2005, pp. 369-392; Kenneth Jost, "Downward Mobility," July 23, 1993, pp. 625-648; and Thomas J. Billitteri, "Middle-Class Squeeze," March 6, 2009, pp. 201-224.

Bibliography

Selected Sources

Books

Edelman, Peter, *Searching for America's Heart: RFK and the Renewal of Hope*, Houghton Mifflin, 2001.
The director of the Center on Poverty, Inequality, and Public Policy at Georgetown Law Center contrasts the poverty-fighting record of one former boss, Sen. Robert F. Kennedy, with a more recent one, President Bill Clinton; Clinton comes in second.

Haskins, Ron, *Work Over Welfare: The Inside Story of the 1996 Welfare Reform Law*, Brookings Institution Press, 2006.
A former top congressional staffer who was an architect of the 1996 welfare law recounts the story of its passage.

O'Connor, Brendon, *A Political History of the American Welfare System: When Ideas Have Consequences*, Rowman & Littlefield, 2004.
An Australian specialist in U.S. politics examines the doctrines and legislation that created and changed the safety net.

Wilson, William Julius, *When Work Disappears: The World of the New Urban Poor*, Vintage Books, 1997.
A Harvard sociologist who is a leading scholar of African-American society examines the early results of the deindustrialization of the American economy.

Articles

Bosman, Julie, "As More Apply for Welfare, Concern for Those Denied," *The New York Times*, April 29, 2009, p. A19.
New York state welfare enrollment had been decreasing even though applications were on the rise, leaving advocates concerned about overly restrictive eligibility standards.

Cauchon, Dennis, "Benefit spending soars to new high," *USA Today*, June 4, 2009, p. A1.
The percentage of Americans relying on government assistance has increased to a record level.

DeParle, Jason, "As Ranks of Unemployed Swell, Wait for Benefits Worsens Pain," *The New York Times*, July 24, 2009, p. A1.
Inefficiencies and revenue shortfalls in the unemployment insurance system hurt recipients.

Eckholm, Erik, "States Slashing Social Programs For Vulnerable," *The New York Times*, April 12, 2009, p. A1.
Budget shortfalls are leading to major cutbacks in state funding of safety-net programs.

Goldmacher, Shane, and Evan Halper, "Budget accord reached," *Los Angeles Times*, July 21, 2009, www.latimes.com/news/local/la-me-budget21-2009jul21,0,5521044.story.
California politicians cut safety-net programs to balance the budget.

Pugh, Tony, "America's humming economy leaves more and more behind as poverty deepens to record levels," *The Miami Herald*, Feb. 25, 2007, p. A1.
This detailed report on growing poverty came out before the recession began.

Strom, Stephanie, "Financial Safety Net of Nonprofit Organizations is Fraying, Survey Finds," *The New York Times*, March 26, 2009, p. A17.
Nonprofit social-service providers are facing budget shortfalls even as demand rises.

Reports and Studies

"The 2008 Annual Homeless Assessment Report to Congress," Department of Housing and Urban Development, July 2009, www.hudhre.info/documents/4thHomeless AssessmentReport.pdf.
The annual report on homelessness highlights the possibility that the recession is forcing people into shelters who never before had faced eviction.

"Can We Put Poor Men to Work?" conference transcript, American Enterprise Institute, May 27, 2009, www.aei.org/docLib/CanWePutPoorMentoWork-EventTranscript.pdf.
Experts of varying views discuss solutions to employment problems involving low-income men.

Bradley, Katherine, and Robert Rector, "Stronger Welfare Work Requirements Can Help Ailing State Budgets," Heritage Foundation, June 19, 2009, www.heritage.org/Research/welfare/wm2496.cfm.
The authors call for toughening work requirements they say have been weakened in recent years.

Falk, Gene, "The Potential Role of the Temporary Assistance for Needy Families (TANF) Block Grant in the Recession," Congressional Research Service, Feb. 24, 2009, http://assets.opencrs.com/rpts/R40157_20090224.pdf.
A social-policy specialist examines the effectiveness of a major safety-net program in the face of the economic crisis.

Sherman, Arloc, "Safety Net Effective at Fighting Poverty but Has Weakened for the Very Poorest," Center on Budget and Policy Priorities, July 6, 2009, www.cbpp.org/files/7-6-09pov.pdf.
A welfare system expert concludes the safety net doesn't extend to people in deep poverty.

The Next Step:

Additional Articles from Current Periodicals

Europe

"Economic Crisis Squeezes Europe," *Grand Rapids Press* **(Michigan), April 5, 2009, p. A6.**

Europeans heavily rely on the state to provide middle-class lifestyles and take care of the poor.

King, Llewellyn, "Euro-Socialism's Pluses, Minuses," *Chattanooga* **(Tennessee)** *Times Free Press,* **June 21, 2009, p. F2.**

Most Europeans like their system of social contracts, while Americans view it as a threat to free-market principles.

Kulish, Nicholas, "Europe, Aided By Safety Nets, Resists U.S. Push on Stimulus," *The New York Times,* **March 27, 2009, p. A1.**

Europeans have no further need for stimulus incentives because their social safety nets automatically provide help.

Job Training

Evangelista, Benny, "Catching Up on Computers," *The San Francisco Chronicle,* **Oct. 20, 2008, p. D1.**

A San Francisco employment program is offering free computer training to individuals with no access to a computer.

Graham, Chad, and Betty Beard, "The Stimulus Job-Training Quandary," *Arizona Republic,* **April 12, 2009, p. 1.**

Arizona's job placement agencies are set to receive $7.87 million from the federal government, but officials are unsure as to how to implement the most effective job training programs.

Haynes, V. Dion, "Region's Jobless Turning to Training Programs," *The Washington Post,* **May 4, 2009, p. A11.**

Many of Washington, D.C.'s unemployed are opting for job training, some of which use government funds.

O'Brien, James, "There's Help Retooling for a New Career," *The Boston Globe,* **May 10, 2009, p. B5.**

Massachusetts' unemployed are turning to the Department of Workforce Development for job training and career development.

Nonprofits

Barnett, Howard, "New Alliance Creates a Unified Voice for Oklahoma's Nonprofits," *Tulsa World* **(Oklahoma), Nov. 26, 2008, p. A21.**

The Oklahoma Alliance of Nonprofits is seeking to protect the state's nonprofit organizations that provide safety nets amid declining financial donations.

Eder, Steve, "2 Nonprofits Unite to Weave Safety Net for Needy," *Toledo Blade* **(Ohio), Feb. 11, 2009, p. B1.**

Two nonprofits in Toledo, Ohio, have teamed up to create the Safety Net Fund to aid groups that provide food, clothing and shelter to the needy.

Hersh, Kathy, "Don't Poke Holes in Social Safety Net," *The Miami Herald,* **Jan. 31, 2009, p. A23.**

Many Florida social service nonprofits, which rely heavily on funding from the state, have ceased operations amid falling tax revenues.

Program Spending

Cauchon, Dennis, "Benefit Spending Soars to New High," *USA Today,* **June 4, 2009, p. 1A.**

The value of the safety net of government benefits will top $2 trillion in 2009, an average of $17,000 provided to each household.

DePledge, Derrick, "Welfare Funding Disputed," *Honolulu Advertiser,* **April 7, 2008, p. 1A.**

State lawmakers in Hawaii are trying to stop Gov. Lingle from spending more than $20 million in federal welfare money in order to build up a reserve amid a slowing economy.

Karlin, Rick, "Life on Welfare Gets Tougher Amid Cutbacks," *Times Union* **(Albany, N.Y.), Sept. 17, 2008, p. A3.**

Most states started cutting their social welfare spending in 2002 after federal grants were curtailed, according to the Rockefeller Institute.

Larrabee, Brandon, "Welfare Could Soon Face Deficit," *Florida Times-Union,* **June 5, 2008, p. B1.**

Georgia's welfare program could soon be facing a $33-million deficit largely due to previous spending of surplus funds.

In-depth Reports on Issues in the News

Are you writing a paper?

Need backup for a debate?

Want to become an expert on an issue?

For 80 years, students have turned to *CQ Researcher* for in-depth reporting on issues in the news. Reports on a full range of political and social issues are now available. Following is a selection of recent reports:

Civil Liberties
Closing Guantánamo, 2/09
Affirmative Action, 10/08
Gay Marriage Showdowns, 9/08
America's Border Fence, 9/08
Immigration Debate, 2/08

Crime/Law
Examining Forensics, 7/09
Legalizing Marijuana, 6/09
Mexico's Drug War, 12/08
Prostitution Debate, 5/08
Public Defenders, 4/08

Education
Reading Crisis? 2/08
Discipline in Schools, 2/08
Student Aid, 1/08
Racial Diversity in Public Schools, 9/07

Environment/Society
Energy and Climate, 7/09
Future of Books, 5/09
Hate Groups, 5/09
Future of Journalism, 3/09
Confronting Warming, 1/09
Reducing Carbon Footprint, 12/08

Health/Safety
Treating Depression, 6/09
Reproductive Ethics, 5/09
Extreme Sports, 4/09
Regulating Toxic Chemicals, 1/09
Preventing Cancer, 1/09
Heart Health, 9/08
Global Food Crisis, 6/08

Politics/Economy
Business Bankruptcy, 4/09
Future of the GOP, 3/09
Middle-Class Squeeze, 3/09

Upcoming Reports

| The Afghanistan Dilemma, 8/7/09 | Health Reforms, 8/28/09 | Financial Literacy, 9/4/09 |

ACCESS

CQ Researcher is available in print and online. For access, visit your library or www.cqresearcher.com.

STAY CURRENT

To receive notice of upcoming *CQ Researcher* reports, or learn more about *CQ Researcher* products, subscribe to the free e-mail newsletters, *CQ Researcher Alert!* and *CQ Researcher News*: http://cqpress.com/newsletters.

PURCHASE

To purchase a *CQ Researcher* report in print or electronic format (PDF), visit www.cqpress.com or call 866-427-7737. Single reports start at $15. Bulk purchase discounts and electronic-rights licensing are also available.

SUBSCRIBE

Annual full-service *CQ Researcher* subscriptions—including 44 reports a year, monthly index updates, and a bound volume—start at $803. Add $25 for domestic postage.

CQ Researcher Online offers a backfile from 1991 and a number of tools to simplify research. For pricing information, call 800-834-9020, ext. 1906, or e-mail librarysales@cqpress.com.

Published by CQ Press, a Division of SAGE

www.cqresearcher.com

Afghanistan Dilemma

Is President Obama pursuing the right course?

N early eight years ago, U.S. forces first entered Afghanistan to pursue the al Qaeda terrorists who plotted the Sept. 11 terror attacks. American troops are still there today, along with thousands of NATO forces. Under a new strategy crafted by the Obama administration, military leaders are trying to deny terrorists a permanent foothold in the impoverished Central Asian country and in neighboring, nuclear-armed Pakistan, whose western border region has become a sanctuary for Taliban and al Qaeda forces. The Afghanistan-Pakistan conflict — "Af-Pak" in diplomatic parlance — poses huge challenges ranging from rampant corruption within Afghanistan's police forces to a multibillion-dollar opium economy that funds the insurgency. But those problems pale in comparison with the ultimate nightmare scenario: Pakistan's nuclear weapons falling into the hands of terrorists, which foreign-policy experts say has become a real possibility.

A U.S. Marine frisks an Afghan man in southern Helmand Province on July 5. Marines began a massive assault in the area in July to quash insurgent violence and strengthen Afghanistan's legal and security institutions.

CQ Researcher • Aug. 7, 2009 • www.cqresearcher.com
Volume 19, Number 28 • Pages 669-692

AFGHANISTAN DILEMMA

Cover: Getty Images/Joe Raedle

CQ Researcher

Aug. 7, 2009
Volume 19, Number 28

MANAGING EDITOR: Thomas J. Colin
tcolin@cqpress.com

ASSISTANT MANAGING EDITOR: Kathy Koch
kkoch@cqpress.com

ASSOCIATE EDITOR: Kenneth Jost

STAFF WRITERS: Thomas J. Billitteri, Marcia Clemmitt, Peter Katel

CONTRIBUTING WRITERS: Rachel Cox, Sarah Glazer, Alan Greenblatt, Reed Karaim Barbara Mantel, Patrick Marshall, Tom Price, Jennifer Weeks

DESIGN/PRODUCTION EDITOR: Olu B. Davis

ASSISTANT EDITOR: Darrell Dela Rosa

FACT-CHECKING: Eugene J. Gabler, Michelle Harris

CQ PRESS

A Division of SAGE

PRESIDENT AND PUBLISHER:
John A. Jenkins

**EXECUTIVE DIRECTOR,
REFERENCE INFORMATION GROUP:**
Alix B. Vance

CQ Researcher (ISSN 1056-2036) is printed on acid-free paper. Published weekly, except; (Jan. wk. 1) (May wk. 4) (July wks. 1, 2) (Aug. wks. 3, 4) (Nov. wk. 4) and (Dec. wk. 4), by CQ Press, a division of SAGE Publications. Annual full-service subscriptions start at $803. For pricing, call 1-800-834-9020, ext. 1906. To purchase a CQ Researcher report in print or electronic format (PDF), visit www. cqpress.com or call 866-427-7737. Single reports start at $15. Bulk purchase discounts and electronic-rights licensing are also available. Periodicals postage paid at Washington, D.C., and additional mailing offices. POSTMASTER: Send address changes to CQ Researcher, 2300 N St., N.W., Suite 800, Washington, DC 20037.

Afghanistan Dilemma

BY THOMAS J. BILLITTERI

THE ISSUES

On the outskirts of Now Zad, a Taliban stronghold in southern Afghanistan's violent Helmand Province, the past, present and future of the war in Afghanistan came together this summer.

The past: After the U.S.-led invasion of Afghanistan in 2001, Now Zad and its surrounding poppy fields and stout compounds were largely tranquil, thanks in part to the clinics and wells that Western money helped to build in the area. But three years ago, when the war in Iraq intensified and the Bush administration shifted attention from Afghanistan to Iraq, insurgents moved in, driving out most of Now Zad's 35,000 residents and foreign aid workers.

The present: This summer U.S. Marines engaged in withering firefights with Taliban militants dug in on the northern fringes of the town and in nearby fields and orchards.

The future: The situation in Now Zad and the surrounding war-torn region of southern Afghanistan is a microcosm of what confronts the Obama administration as it tries to smash the Taliban, defang al Qaeda and stabilize governance in Afghanistan. "In many ways," wrote an Associated Press reporter following the fighting, Now Zad "symbolizes what went wrong in Afghanistan and the enormous challenges facing the United States." [1]

Nearly eight years after U.S.-led forces first entered Afghanistan to pursue al Qaeda and its Taliban allies in the wake of the Sept. 11, 2001, terrorist attacks, the country remains in chaos, and President Barack Obama

An Afghan security officer guards two tons of burning heroin, opium and hashish near Kabul, Afghanistan's capital, on March 18, 2009. Nearly eight years after U.S.-led forces first entered Afghanistan, many challenges still confront the U.S., Afghan and coalition forces seeking to stabilize the country: fanatical Taliban and al Qaeda fighters, rampant police corruption, shortages of Afghan troops and a multibillion-dollar opium economy that supports the insurgents.

AP Photo/Fraidoon Pooyaa

faces what many consider his biggest foreign-policy challenge: bringing stability and security to Afghanistan and denying Islamist militants a permanent foothold there and in neighboring nuclear-armed Pakistan.

The challenge is heightened by the war's growing casualty figures. July was the deadliest month in Afghanistan for U.S. soldiers since the 2001 invasion began, with 43 killed. [2] Twenty-two British troops also died last month, including eight in a 24-hour period. In nearly eight years of war in Afghanistan, 767 U.S. troops have died there, along with 520 coalition forces, according to the Web site iCasualties.org. Thousands of Afghan civilians also have died.

The Afghanistan-Pakistan conflict — "Af-Pak" in diplomatic parlance —

poses a witch's brew of challenges: fanatical Taliban and al Qaeda fighters, rampant corruption within Afghanistan's homegrown police force and other institutions, not enough Afghan National Army forces to help with the fighting and a multibillion-dollar opium economy that supplies revenue to the insurgents.

But those problems pale in comparison with what foreign-policy experts call the ultimate nightmare: Pakistan's nuclear weapons falling into the hands of jihadists and terrorists, a scenario that has become more credible this summer as suicide bombers and Taliban fighters have stepped up attacks in Pakistani cities and rural areas, using Pakistan's lawless western border region as a sanctuary. [3]

"The fact that Pakistan has nuclear weapons and the question of the security of those weapons presses very hard on the minds of American defense planners and on the mind of the president," says Bruce Riedel, who led a 60-day strategic policy review of Afghanistan and Pakistan for the Obama administration. "If you didn't have that angle," adds Riedel, who has since returned to his post as a Brookings Institution senior fellow, "I think this would all be notched down one level of concern."

Pakistan is important to the Afghan conflict for reasons that go beyond its nuclear arsenal. Pakistan has been a breeding ground for much of the radical ideology that has taken root in Afghanistan. A failure of governance in Afghanistan would leave a void that Islamist militants on either side of the border could wind up filling, further destabilizing the entire region.

An Unstable Nation in a Volatile Neighborhood

Almost as large as Texas, Afghanistan faces Texas-size problems, including desperate poverty, an economy dominated by illicit drugs and an unstable central government beset by Taliban militants. Afghanistan's instability is compounded by longstanding tensions between neighboring Pakistan and India, both armed with nuclear weapons. Many Western experts also say Pakistan has failed, despite promises, to rein in Taliban and other Islamist extremists.

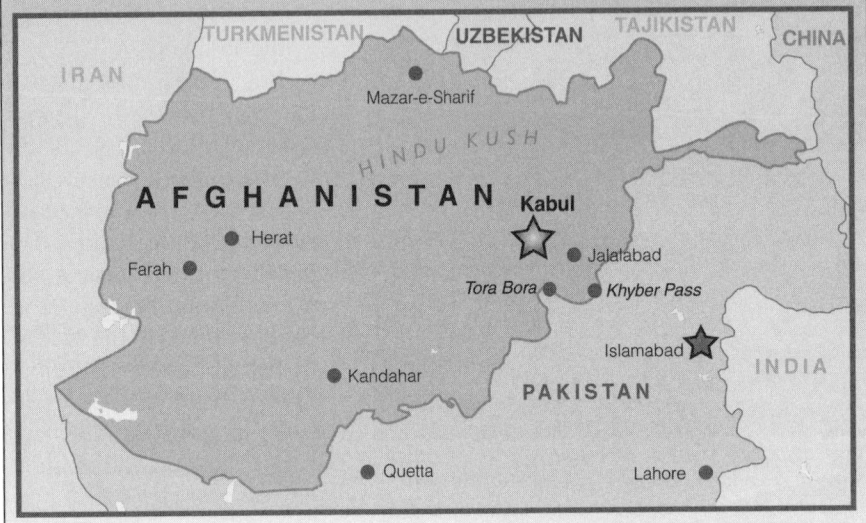

In March Obama announced what he called a "comprehensive, new strategy" for Afghanistan and Pakistan that rests on a "clear and focused goal" for the region: "to disrupt, dismantle and defeat al Qaeda in Pakistan and Afghanistan, and to prevent their return to either country in the future." [4]

Key to the strategy is winning over the local Afghan population by protecting it from insurgent violence and improving governance, security and economic development. [5]

The effort includes new troop deployments — a total of 21,000 additional U.S. soldiers to fight the insurgency in Afghanistan and train Afghan security forces, plus other strategic resources. By year's end, U.S. troop levels are expected to reach about 68,000. NATO countries and other allies currently are supplying another 32,000 or so, though many are engaged in development and relief work but not offensive combat operations. [6]

An immediate goal is to heighten security in Afghanistan in the run-up to a high-profile presidential election on Aug. 20. None of Afghan President Hamid Karzai's main challengers are expected to beat him flat out, *The Washington Post* noted, but some observers said other candidates could "do well enough as a group to force a second round of polling, partly because of recent blunders by Karzai and partly because many Afghans are looking for alternative leadership at a time of sustained insurgent violence, economic stagnation and political drift." [7]

Observers say Obama's approach to the Af-Pak conflict represents a middle path between counterterrorism and counterinsurgency — protecting civilians, relying on them for information on the enemy and providing aid to build up a country's social and physical infrastructure and democratic institutions. [8]

Among the most notable features of the new approach is a vow among military officials — beginning with Gen. Stanley A. McChrystal, the newly appointed commander of U.S. and NATO forces in Afghanistan — to avoid civilian casualties. McChrystal pledged to follow a "holistic" approach in which protecting civilians takes precedence over killing militants. [9]

"I expect stiff fighting ahead," McChrystal told the Senate Armed Services Committee at his confirmation hearing. But "the measure of effectiveness will not be the number of enemy killed," he added, "it will be the number of Afghans shielded from violence." [10]

The United Nations said that 1,013 civilians died in the first six months of 2009, up from 818 during the same period last year. The U.N. said 310 deaths were attributed to pro-government forces, with about two-thirds caused by U.S. air strikes. [11]

As part of his strategy, Obama called for a "dramatic" increase in the number of agricultural specialists, educators, engineers and lawyers dispatched to "help the Afghan government serve its people and develop an economy that isn't dominated by illicit drugs." He also supports economic-development aid to Pakistan, including legislation to provide $1.5 billion annually over the next five years. But Obama's approach on Pakistan also reflects long-held Western concerns that the Pakistani government has been at best negligent — and perhaps downright obstructionist — in bringing Taliban and other Islamist extremists to heel. Pakistan, whose situation is complicated by longstanding tensions with nearby India, will get no free pass in exchange for the aid, Obama vowed. "We will not, and cannot, provide a blank check," he said, because Pakistan had shown "years of mixed results" in rooting out terrorism. [12]

As Obama goes after the insurgency, his Af-Pak policy is under the microscope here at home.

Some have demanded that the administration describe its plans for ending military operations in Afghanistan. A measure proposed by Rep. Jim McGovern, D-Mass., requiring a report from the Obama administration by the end of the year on its exit strategy, drew significant support from Democrats but was defeated in the House this summer amid heavy Republican opposition.

And some critics question the validity of Obama's rationale for the fighting in Afghanistan, particularly the assumption that if the Taliban were victorious they would invite al Qaeda to return to Afghanistan and use it as a base for its global jihad. John Mueller, a political science professor at Ohio State University and author of *Overblown: How Politicians and the Terrorism Industry Inflate National Security Threats, and Why We Believe Them*, contends that al Qaeda does not need Afghanistan as a base. The 2001 terrorist attacks were orchestrated mostly from Hamburg, Germany, he points out.

What's more, he argues, "distinct tensions" exist between al Qaeda and the Taliban. Even if the Taliban were to prevail in Afghanistan, he says, "they would not particularly want al Qaeda back." Nor, he says, is it clear that al Qaeda would again view Afghanistan as a safe haven. [13]

But administration officials disagree. The Taliban are "the frontrunners for al Qaeda," said Richard Holbrooke, Obama's special envoy to Pakistan and Afghanistan. "If they succeed in Afghanistan, without any shadow of a doubt al Qaeda would move back into Afghanistan, set up a larger presence, recruit more people and pursue its objectives against the United States even more aggressively." [14]

As the war in Afghanistan continues, here are some of the questions people are asking:

Gates Warns About Civilian Deaths

The number of civilians killed in Afghanistan more than doubled from 2006 to 2008, but based on the toll for the first six months of 2009, the rate may be somewhat lower in 2009 (graph at left). In 2008 nearly half of the civilian deaths were caused by executions or suicide and IED (improvised explosive device) attacks by the Taliban and other anti-government groups (graph at right). Concern over civilian deaths prompted Defense Secretary Robert Gates to call such casualties "one of our greatest strategic vulnerabilities."

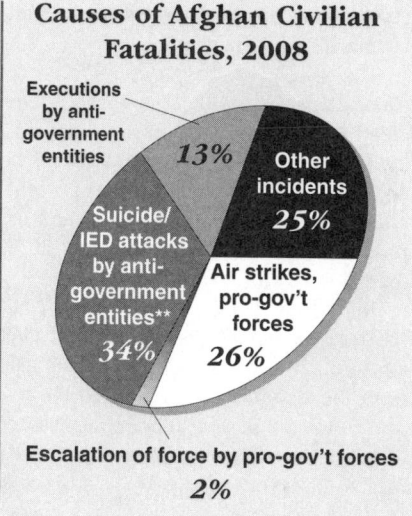

Estimated Afghan Civilian Fatalities, 2006-2009*
(from fighting between pro-government forces and opposition groups)

- 2006: 929
- 2007: 1,523
- 2008: 2,118
- 2009*: 893

Legend:
- Non-attributable
- Armed opposition groups
- Government and pro-government forces

Causes of Afghan Civilian Fatalities, 2008

- Executions by anti-government entities: 13%
- Other incidents: 25%
- Air strikes, pro-gov't forces: 26%
- Suicide/IED attacks by anti-government entities**: 34%
- Escalation of force by pro-gov't forces: 2%

* Through June; the total is 1,013, according to the U.N.

** Includes Taliban and other insurgents

Source: "Afghan Index: Tracking Variables of Reconstruction and Security in Post-9/11 Afghanistan," Brookings Institution, July 15, 2009

Is the Obama administration pursuing the right course in Afghanistan?

Early in July, thousands of U.S. Marines began a massive assault in Afghanistan's Helmand River valley, the biggest American offensive of the Obama presidency and a key test of his new strategy in the region.

The operation included 4,000 troops from the 2nd Marine Expeditionary Brigade, who poured into the area in helicopters and armored vehicles. The Marines have run into stiff opposition, but the ultimate goal remains intact: protect local Afghans from insurgent violence and strengthen Afghanistan's legal, judicial and security institutions.

"Our focus must be on getting this [Afghan] government back up on its feet," Brig. Gen. Lawrence D. Nicholson, commander of the brigade, told his officers. [15]

But the mission is fraught with huge risks and challenges, and skepticism about it runs deep, even among some of Obama's fellow Democrats.

In May, House Appropriations Chairman David Obey, D-Wis., suggested that if the White House doesn't demonstrate progress by next year, funding for the war could slow. Asked if he could see Congress halting funding completely, Obey said, "If it becomes a fool's errand, I would hope so," according to *The Hill* newspaper. The

Opium Trade Funds Taliban, Official Corruption

"It's clear that drug money is paying for the Taliban's operational costs."

In the crowded Afghan capital of Kabul, opulent marble homes sit behind guard houses and razor wire. "Most are owned by Afghan officials or people connected to them, men who make a few hundred dollars a month as government employees but are driven around in small convoys of armored SUVs that cost tens of thousands of dollars," reporter Tom Lasseter noted recently. "[M]any of the houses were built with profits harvested from opium poppy fields in the southern provinces of Helmand and Kandahar." [1]

The so-called "poppy palaces" are outward signs of a cancer eating Afghanistan to its core: illicit drugs and narcoterrorism, aided by official corruption.

According to the United Nations Office on Drugs and Crime, Afghanistan grows more than 90 percent of the world's opium, which is used to produce heroin and morphine. [2] Total opium production for 2008 was estimated at 7,700 metric tons, more than double the 2002 level. [3]

In her new book, *Seeds of Terror: How Heroin Is Bankrolling the Taliban and Al Qaeda*, journalist Gretchen Peters says militant groups are raising hundreds of millions of dollars a year from the opium trade.

"It's clear that drug money is paying for the Taliban's operational costs within Afghanistan," she told *Time* magazine. "That means that every time a U.S. soldier is killed in an IED attack or a shootout with militants, drug money helped pay for that bomb or paid the militants who placed it. . . . The Taliban have now thrown off their old masters and are a full-fledged criminal force on both sides of the [Afghan-Pakistan] border." [4]

The biggest challenge to curbing the drug trade, Peters said, is corruption. "As much money as the insurgents are earning off the drug trade, corrupt officials in Afghanistan and Pakistan are earning even more," she said. "It's going to be very complex for the U.S. and for the international community, for NATO, to find reliable and trustworthy partners to work with. I don't think that it is widely understood how high up the corruption goes within the Pakistani government, particularly within their military and intelligence forces."

In recent weeks, the Obama administration has shifted U.S. drug policy in Afghanistan from trying to eradicate poppy fields to seizing drugs and related supplies and helping farmers grow alternative crops. [5]

"The Western policies against the opium crop, the poppy crop, have been a failure," Richard C. Holbrooke, the administration's special representative for Afghanistan and Pakistan, said. "They did not result in any damage to the Taliban, but they put farmers out of work and they alienated people and drove people into the arms of the Taliban." [6]

The Bush administration had advocated intense efforts to eradicate poppy fields, but some experts have said the approach is counterproductive.

"The United States should de-emphasize opium eradication efforts," Air Force Lt. Col. John A. Glaze wrote in a 2007 report for the U.S. Army War College. It recommended a multi-pronged strategy including higher troop levels, more economic aid for Afghanistan, pursuit of drug lords and corrupt officials and development of alternative livelihoods for Afghans, plus exploration of the possibility of participating in the market for legal opiates used for morphine and other medicines.

success or failure of the Afghan policy is not in the hands of the president or Congress, Obey said, but "in the hands of the practicing politicians in Pakistan and Afghanistan. And I'm dubious about those hands." [16]

Much of the American public is similarly dubious. A June *New York Times*-CBS News poll found that 55 percent of respondents believed the war in Afghanistan was going somewhat or very badly for the United States, an increase of two points since April. Only 2 percent said the war was going "very well." [17]

Critics question the prospect of success in a country long divided by ethnic rivalries, a resistance to central governance and rampant graft that ranges from demands for petty bribes to drug corruption in high levels of government. [18]

"To pacify the place in the absence of reconciliation of the main tribes, * you'd need a very large national army" — one that would have to be financially subsidized by outside powers, says Stephen Walt, a professor of international affairs at Harvard University's Kennedy School of Government. Such an army "would have to be drawn from all these groups and imbued with cen-

tral loyalty to the state. And there's never been a strong central state. Politics [in Afghanistan is defined by] factional alignments." And, he adds, the challenge is "compounded by levels of corruption and lack of institutions."

"We're sort of trying to impart a Western model of how the Afghan state should be created — with a central government, ministries, defense and so on. That's not the way Afghanistan has been run for centuries. The idea that we know how to do that, especially in the short term," Walt says, is "far-fetched."

Malou Innocent, a foreign-policy analyst at the conservative Cato Institute think tank, says America faces the

---

* The main ethnic groups are the Pashtun (42%); Tajik (27%), Hazara (9%), Uzbek (9%), Aimak (4%), Turkmen (3%) and Baloch (2%).

"U.S.-backed eradication efforts have been ineffective and have resulted in turning Afghans against U.S. and NATO forces . . . ," Glaze wrote. "While the process of eradication lends itself well to the use of flashy metrics such as 'acres eradicated,' eradication without provision for long-term alternative livelihoods is devastating Afghan's poor farmers without addressing root causes." [7]

Brookings Institution scholar Vanda Felbab-Brown, an expert on Afghanistan's opium-poppy economy, says rural development, not poppy eradication, is the best way to attack the drug economy. "Any massive eradication right now . . . , we would lose Afghanistan," she says. "In the absence of resources available to farmers, any eradication would just prompt massive destabilization and invite the Taliban in."

Felbab-Brown says the development of new crops is key, but that such crops must be "high-labor-intensive, high-value crops" that offer more than subsistence income.

"People don't have to become rich, but they cannot continue existing in excruciating poverty. Many people will be willing and motivated to switch to a legal crop," she says, but "it needs to offer some chance of advancement."

Vegetable, fruit and horticultural crops are better options, Felbab-Brown says. Wheat, on the other hand, "has no traction" because the prices are low, people in vast parts of the country don't have enough land to make the crop pay, and wheat is much less labor-intensive than poppy growing, affording fewer opportunities for employment, she says.

For rural development to offer an alternative to illicit poppy production, it must include not only access to land, legal mi-

crocredit and other features, but security for Afghan farmers, Felbab-Brown stresses.

"The lack of security in many ways is the key structural driver of illicit crop cultivation, because the risks of cultivating legal crops in insecure settings are just tremendous," she says.

Rural development, for example, "needs to involve roads, and not just their physical presence but also security on the roads," Felbab-Brown says. Roads are now insecure due to both the insurgents and the Afghan National Police.

"In much of the south, travel on the road is three times as expensive as travel in the north because of the number of bribes that one needs to pay at check stops. For many people, simply to take crops from Laskar Gah to Kandahar, by the time they pay the bribes that they need to pay, they will have lost all profit."

---

[1] Tom Lasseter, "Western Military Looked Other Way as the Afghan Drug Trade Boomed," *Charlotte Observer*, May 10, 2009, p. 13A.

[2] "World Drug Report 2009 Highlights Links Between Drugs and Crime," United Nations Office on Drugs and Crime, June 2009, www.unodc.org/unodc/en/press/releases/2009/june/world-drug-report-2009-highlights-links-between-drugs-and-crime.html.

[3] "World Drug Report 2009," United Nations Office on Drugs and Crime, www.unodc.org/documents/wdr/WDR_2009/WDR2009_eng_web.pdf.

[4] Bobby Ghosh, "Q&A: Fighting the New Narcoterrorism Syndicates," *Time*, July 17, 2009, www.time.com/time/nation/article/0,8599,1910935,00.html.

[5] Rachel Donadio, "New Course for Antidrug Efforts in Afghanistan," *The New York Times*, June 28, 2009, www.nytimes.com/2009/06/28/world/asia/28holbrooke.html?scp=1&sq=holbrooke+drug%20policy+afghanistan+rome&st=cse.

[6] Quoted in *ibid.*

[7] John A. Glaze, "Opium and Afghanistan: Reassessing U.S. Counternarcotics Strategy," U.S. Army War College, www.strategicstudiesinstitute.army.mil/Pubs/Display.Cfm?pubID=804.

prospect of an "ambiguous victory" because it is caught amid long-simmering tensions between Pakistan and India, a dynamic, she argues, that the Obama administration has failed to adequately take into account.

Pakistan has long feared an alliance between Afghanistan and India. To hedge its bets, Pakistan aids the insurgency in Afghanistan by providing shelter to the Taliban and other militants, Innocent says. At the same time, she says, Pakistan has accused India of funneling weapons through Afghanistan to separatists in Pakistan's unstable Balochistan province. [19] The ongoing India-Pakistan dispute over Kashmir also remains a cause of friction in the region.

"The regional dynamics are too intractable," Innocent says. "The countries in the region have an incentive to foment and maintain Afghanistan's instability. So we should be looking to get out of Afghanistan within a reasonable time frame — say at least in the next five years."

Innocent sees a U.S. role in training Afghanistan's own security forces and says covert operations against specific insurgent targets could make sense. But the Taliban threat centered along the Afghanistan-Pakistan border cannot be definitively eradicated, she argues. "We can contain the militancy" and weaken it, she says, "but we can't believe we can have a victory with a capital V."

But Peter Bergen, a counterterrorism analyst and senior fellow at the New America Foundation, is more sanguine about the war's prospects in Afghanistan. In a *Washington Monthly* article, he challenged those who say Afghanistan is an unconquerable and ungovernable "graveyard of empires" where foreign armies have come to ignominious ends.

One telling fact, in Bergen's view, is that "the Afghan people themselves, the center of gravity in a counterinsurgency, are rooting for us to win." He cited BBC/ABC polling data indicating that 58 percent of Afghans named the Taliban — viewed favorably by only 7 percent of Afghans

Social Conditions Worsened in Many Areas

Living conditions deteriorated between 2007 and 2008 in areas such as education, water quality and availability of electricity, according to surveys of Afghan citizens.

Condition of Infrastructure in Localities, 2007 and 2008

	Very/Quite Good (%)		Quite/Very Bad (%)	
	2007	2008	2007	2008
Availability of clean drinking water	63%	62%	36%	38%
Availability of water for irrigation	59	47	40	49
Availability of jobs	30	21	69	78
Supply of electricity	31	25	68	74
Security situation	66	No data	33	No data
Availability of medical care	56	49	44	50
Availability of education for children	72	70	28	29
Freedom of movement	72	No data	28	No data

Source: "Afghan Index: Tracking Variables of Reconstruction and Security in Post-9/11 Afghanistan," Brookings Institution, July 15, 2009

— as the biggest threat to their country, while only 8 percent named the United States.

"[T]he growing skepticism about Obama's chances for success in Afghanistan is largely based on deep misreadings of both the country's history and the views of its people, which are often compounded by facile comparisons to the United States' misadventures of past decades in Southeast Asia and the Middle East," wrote Bergen. "Afghanistan will not be Obama's Vietnam, nor will it be his Iraq. Rather, the renewed and better-resourced American effort in Afghanistan will, in time, produce a relatively stable and prosperous Central Asian state." [20]

Stephen Biddle, a senior fellow at the Council on Foreign Relations, a think tank in New York City, said victory in Afghanistan is possible but only if steps are taken to strengthen Afghanistan's governance. "I do think it's possible to succeed," Biddle said in late July after spending a month as part of a group helping McChrystal formulate a strategic assessment report on the war, due this month. But, he added,

"there are two very different requirements for success.

"One is providing security, [and] the other is providing enough of an improvement in Afghan governance to enable the country to function without us. We can keep the patient on life support by providing security assistance indefinitely, but if you don't get an improvement in governance, you'll never be able to take the patient off the ventilator. Of those two challenges, providing security we know how to do. It's expensive, it's hard, it takes a long time, but if we invest the resources there's a substantial probability that we can provide security through our assistance. Governance improvement is a more uncertain undertaking. There are a lot of things we can do that we have not yet done to improve governance, but ultimately the more uncertain of the two requirements is the governance part." [21]

Another member of McChrystal's strategic assessment group, Anthony Cordesman, a scholar with the Center for Strategic and International Studies, also believes the war is winnable, but that the United States and its allies

must "act quickly and decisively" in a number of ways, including "giving the Afghan government the necessary legitimacy and capacity" at national, regional and local levels, reducing official corruption and "creating a level of actual governance that can ensure security and stability." [22]

Are troop levels in Afghanistan adequate?

When the Marine assault in Helmand Province got under way this summer, only about 400 effective Afghan fighters had joined the American force of nearly 4,000, according to *The New York Times*, citing information from Gen. Nicholson. [23]

Commanders expressed concern that not enough homegrown forces were available to fight the insurgency and build ties with the local population. Gen. Nicholson said, "I'm not going to sugarcoat it. The fact of the matter is, we don't have enough Afghan forces. And I'd like more." [24] Capt. Brian Huysman, a Marine company commander, said the lack of Afghan forces "is absolutely our Achilles' heel." [25]

"We've seen a shift over the past few years to put a lot more resources, including money and attention, toward building Afghan national security forces, army and police forces," Seth Jones, a political scientist at the RAND Corporation, told the "NewsHour" on PBS. "I think the problem that we're running into on the ground in Afghanistan, though: There are not enough Afghan national security forces and coalition forces to do what Gen. McChrystal and others want, and that is to protect the local population." [26]

Worries about the size of the Afghan force have been accompanied by concerns over whether U.S. forces are adequate to overcome the Taliban threat and secure local areas long enough to ensure security and build governance capabilities.

According to a report this summer by veteran *Washington Post* reporter Bob

Woodward, National Security Adviser James L. Jones told U.S. commanders in Afghanistan the Obama administration wants to keep troop levels steady for now. Gen. Nicholson, though, told Jones that he was "a little light," suggesting he could use more troops, and that "we don't have enough force to go everywhere," Woodward reported. [27]

"The question of the force level for Afghanistan . . . is not settled and will probably be hotly debated over the next year," Woodward wrote. "One senior military officer said privately that the United States would have to deploy a force of more than 100,000 to execute the counterinsurgency strategy of holding areas and towns after clearing out the Taliban insurgents. That is at least 32,000 more than the 68,000 currently authorized." [28]

Adm. Mike Mullen, chairman of the Joint Chiefs of Staff, said on CBS News' "Face the Nation" on July 5 that in southern Afghanistan, where the toughest fighting is expected, "we have enough forces now not just to clear an area but to hold it so we can build after. And that's really the strategy." He noted that Gen. McChrystal was due to produce his 60-day assessment of the war this summer, adding "we're all committed to getting this right and resourcing it properly." [29]

But senior military officials told *The Washington Post* later that week that McChrystal had concluded Afghan security forces must be greatly expanded if the war is to be won. According to officials, the *Post* said, "such an expansion would require spending billions more than the $7.5 billion the administration has budgeted annually to build up the Afghan army and police over the next several years, and the likely deployment of thousands more U.S. troops as trainers and advisers." [30]

As combat has intensified this spring and summer and more troops entered the war zone, commanders focused on one of the most pernicious threats to the U.S.-led counterinsurgency strategy:

Afghanistan Ranks Low in Developing World

Afghanistan ranked as the second-weakest state in the developing world, after Somalia, in 2008, according to the Brookings Institution* (left). It consistently ranks near the bottom among countries rated for corruption by Transparency International (right).

Afghanistan's Rank

Index of State Weakness in Developing World, 2008			Corruption Perceptions Index		
Rank	Country	Overall Score	Year	Rank	No. of Countries Surveyed
1	Somalia	0.52	2008	176	180
2	Afghanistan	1.65	2007	172	180
3	Dem. Rep. Congo	1.67	2006	No data	163
4	Iraq	3.11	2005	117	159
5	Burundi	3.21			

* *Brookings surveyed 141 nations, allocating a score of 0-10 points for each of four categories: economic, political, security and social welfare. Benin had the median score, 6.36; the Slovak Republic was the least weak, with a score of 9.41.*

Source: "Afghan Index: Tracking Variables of Reconstruction and Security in Post-9/11 Afghanistan," Brookings Institution, July 15, 2009

the potential for civilian casualties, which can undermine efforts to build trust and cooperation with the local population. Concern over civilian deaths rose sharply in May, when a high-profile U.S. air strike in western Farah province killed at least 26 civilians, according to American investigators. [31] This spring commanders instituted strict new combat rules aimed at minimizing civilian deaths, and Defense Secretary Robert M. Gates has called such casualties "one of our greatest strategic vulnerabilities." [32]

While some fear that the deployment of more troops to Afghanistan could heighten civilian casualties, others say the opposite is true.

"In fact, the presence of more boots on the ground is likely to *reduce* civilian casualties, because historically it has been the over-reliance on American air strikes — as a result of too few ground forces — which has been the key cause of civilian deaths," wrote Bergen of the New America Foundation. [33]

Should the United States negotiate with the Taliban?

In early March, shortly before announcing his new strategy for Afghanistan and Pakistan, *The New York Times* reported that Obama, in an interview aboard Air Force One, "opened the door to a reconciliation process in which the American military would reach out to moderate elements of the Taliban." [34]

In broaching the idea of negotiating with the Taliban, the president cited successes in Iraq in separating moderate insurgents from the more extreme factions of al Qaeda. Still, he was cautious about reconciliation prospects in Afghanistan.

"The situation in Afghanistan is, if anything, more complex" than the one in Iraq, he said. "You have a less governed region, a history of fierce independence among tribes. Those tribes are multiple and sometimes operate at cross-purposes, and so figuring all that out is going to be much more of a challenge." [35]

Nevertheless, the notion of seeking some sort of reconciliation with elements of the Afghan Taliban has received fresh attention recently.

Opponents of the idea argue that it could project an image of weakness and embolden the insurgency and that Taliban leaders cannot be trusted to uphold any deals they may make.

But proponents argue the Taliban is not a unified bloc, but rather an amalgam that includes those who joined the insurgency out of frustration at the lack of security in their villages or because they were forcibly drafted, among other reasons. (*See sidebar, p. 680.*)

"If you look at a security map of Afghanistan between, say, 2003 and today, you have this creep of the insurgency sort of moving up from the south and east into other parts of the country," J. Alexander Thier, senior rule of law adviser with the United States Institute of Peace. That trend, he says, suggests many local communities and commanders that may have once supported the Afghan government have turned neutral or are actively supporting the Taliban. "There's real room in there to deal with their grievances and concerns about security and justice and the rule of law so as to change that tide."

Thier says he's not talking about seeking a "grand bargain" with the Taliban leadership now ensconced in Pakistan. "If what you're envisioning is [Afghan President] Karzai and [Taliban leader] Mullah Omar sitting on the deck of an aircraft carrier signing an armistice, I don't think that's feasible or realistic," he says. What is feasible are "micro level" negotiations.

"There is an enormous opportunity to work on what I would call mid- and low-level insurgents who, for a variety of reasons, were likely not engaged in the insurgency just a few years ago and were either pro-government or at least neutral. And I think they can and should be brought back to that position."

In an article this summer in *Foreign Affairs*, Fotini Christia, an assistant professor of political science at MIT, and Michael Semple, former deputy to the European Union special representative to Afghanistan, wrote that while "sending more troops is necessary to tip the balance of power against the insurgents, the move will have a lasting impact only if it is accompanied by a political 'surge,' a committed effort to persuade large groups of Taliban fighters to put down their arms and give up the fight." [36]

For reconciliation to work, say Fotini and Semple, Afghans first must feel secure. "The situation on the ground will need to be stabilized, and the Taliban must be reminded that they have no prospect of winning their current military campaign," they wrote. "If the Afghan government offers reconciliation as its carrot, it must also present force as its stick — hence the importance of sending more U.S. troops to Afghanistan, but also, in the long term, the importance of building up Afghanistan's own security forces. Reconciliation needs to be viewed as part of a larger military-political strategy to defeat the insurgency."

Some favor waiting to begin negotiation efforts, while others say they should occur simultaneously with the military campaign. Riedel of Brookings says he sees reason to believe that "a fair number" of Taliban foot soldiers and local commanders are not deeply dedicated to the core extremist cause as espoused by leaders such as Omar. Many rank and file Taliban may be "in this for one reason or another" — perhaps because "their tribe is aligned with the Taliban for local reasons, they're getting paid by the Taliban to do this better than they could be paid by anyone else, or simply because if you're a 17-year-old Pashtun male in Kandahar, fighting is kind of how you get your right of passage," Riedel says.

If the momentum changes on the battlefield "and it's a lot more dangerous to support the Taliban," Riedel continues, "my sense . . . is that these people will either defect or simply go home — they just won't fight."

Still, he says, it's not yet time to begin negotiations. First must come intelligence networks and greater political savvy in each district and province to capitalize on any Taliban inclinations to bend, he argues. "That is primarily an Afghan job, because they're the only people who are going to know the ins and outs of this. That's one of the things the new [U.S.] command arrangement needs to focus on the most. I don't think we're there. This requires really intense local information."

Yet, while the hour for negotiating may not be ripe, "the time is now to do the homework to do that," Riedel says, in order to develop "fine-grained knowledge of what's going on."

But Rajan Menon, a professor of international relations at Lehigh University, says "not coupling" the military campaign against the Taliban "with an olive branch is probably not effective."

Because huge challenges face the military operation — from the threat of civilian casualties to the weakness of the country's central government — the prospect of a long and costly war looms, he says. To avoid that, Menon says, the military effort should be occurring simultaneously with one aimed at encouraging "pragmatic" elements of the Taliban to buy into a process in which they "have to sell [their] ideas in the political marketplace."

The Taliban pragmatists, he says, would be offered a choice: either a long, open-ended war with heavy insurgent casualties or the opportunity to enter the political process as a group seeking victory through the ballot box.

"The question is, can you fracture the [insurgency] movement by laying down terms that are pretty stringent and test their will," Menon says. Nobody knows if the arms-and-olive branch approach would work, he says, but "you lose nothing by trying." ∎

Continued on p. 680

Chronology

1838-1930s
Afghanistan gains independence, but ethnic and religious conflicts persist.

1838-42; 1878
Afghan forces defeat Britain in two wars, but Britain retains control of Afghanistan's foreign affairs under 1879 treaty.

1893
British draw Afghan-Pakistan border, split Pashtun ethnic group.

1919
Afghanistan gains independence after Third Anglo-Afghan War.

1934
Diplomatic relations between United States and Afghanistan established.

1950s-1980s
Political chaos wracks Afghanistan during Cold War.

1950s-1960s
Soviets and Americans funnel aid to Afghanistan.

1953
Gen. Mohammed Daoud becomes prime minister, seeks aid from Soviets, institutes reforms.

1964
New constitution establishes constitutional monarchy.

1973
Daoud overthrows king, is killed in Marxist coup in 1978.

1979-1989
Civil war rages between communist-backed government and U.S.-backed Mujahedeen. Soviets withdraw in 1989, 10 years after they invaded.

1990-2001
Taliban emerges amid postwar chaos; al Qaeda forges ties with Afghan militants.

1992
Burhanuddin Rabbani, an ethnic Tajik, rises to power, declares Afghanistan an Islamic state.

1994
Taliban emerges; the militant Islamist group is mainly Pashtun.

1996
Taliban gains control of Kabul.

1996
Taliban leader Mullah Omar invites al Qaeda leader Osama bin Laden to live with him in Kandahar.

1997
Osama bin Laden declares war on U.S. in interview with CNN.

2001
U.S. and coalition forces invade Afghanistan on Oct. 7 after Sept. 11 terrorist attacks; Taliban retreats.

2002-Present
U.S.-led invasion of Iraq shifts focus off Afghanistan; Taliban resurges.

2002
Hamid Karzai elected head of Afghan Transitional Authority; International Security Assistance Force deployed in Kabul; international donors pledge $4.5 billion for reconstruction.

2003
U.S.-led invasion of Iraq begins, leading to charges Bush administration shifted focus and resources away from Afghanistan; commission drafts new Afghan constitution.

2004
Draft constitution approved; Karzai elected president; Pakistani nuclear scientist A. Q. Khan admits international nuclear-weapons trading; President Pervez Musharraf pardons him.

2005
Afghanistan holds its first parliamentary elections in some three decades.

2006
NATO takes over Afghan security; donors pledge $10.5 billion more.

2007
Musharraf and Karzai agree to coordinate efforts to fight Taliban, al Qaeda; allied troops kill Taliban leader Mullah Dadullah.

2008
More than 50 die in suicide bombing of Indian Embassy in Kabul in July. . . . More than 160 die in November terror attacks in Mumbai, India; India accuses Pakistani militants of carrying out the attacks; in July 2009 a young Pakistani admits to taking part in the attacks as a soldier for Lashkar-e-Taiba, a Pakistan-based Islamic group.

2009
Obama announces new strategy "to disrupt, dismantle and defeat al Qaeda in Pakistan and Afghanistan"; Gen. Stanley McChrystal replaces Gen. David McKiernan as top U.S. commander in Afghanistan; Marines attack Taliban in southern Helmand Province; July is bloodiest month for U.S. and foreign troops in Afghanistan, with 43 Americans killed. . . . Concern grows over security surrounding Aug. 20 presidential election.

The Many Faces of the Taliban

Adherents include violent warlords and Islamist extremists.

When President Barack Obama announced his administration's new Afghanistan strategy in March, he declared that if the Afghan government were to fall to the Taliban, the country would "again be a base for terrorists who want to kill as many of our people as they possibly can." [1]

But defining "the Taliban" is tricky. Far from a monolithic organization, the Taliban is a many-headed hydra, and a shadowy one at that. It is a mélange of insurgents and militants, ranging from high-profile Islamist extremists and violent warlords to local villagers fighting for cash or glory. Western military strategists hope to kill or capture the most fanatical elements of the Taliban while persuading others to abandon their arms and work within Afghanistan's political system.

"You have a whole spectrum of bad guys that sort of get lumped into this catch-all term of Taliban . . . because they're launching bullets at us," a senior Defense official told *The Boston Globe*. "There are many of the groups that can probably be peeled off."

The Defense official quoted by *The Globe* was among "hundreds of intelligence operatives and analysts" in the United States and abroad involved in a broad study of tribes tied to the Taliban, the newspaper said. The aim is to figure out whether diplomatic or economic efforts can persuade some to break away, according to the paper. The examination "is expected to culminate later this year in a detailed, highly classified analysis of the different factions of the Taliban and other groups," *The Globe* said. [2]

Many experts break down the Taliban into four main groups:

• **The Early Taliban** — Insurgents emerged under Mullah Omar and other leaders during the civil war that wracked Afghanistan in the mid-1990s, following the end of the Soviet occupation of the country. Early members were a mix of fighters who battled the Soviets in the 1980s and Pashtuns who attended religious schools in Pakistan, where they were aided by the Pakistani Inter-Services Intelligence agency. [3]

• **The Pakistani Taliban** emerged under a separate organizational structure in 2002, when Pakistani forces entered the country's tribal region in the northwest to pursue Islamist militants. [4]

"At the time of the U.S.-led military campaign in Afghanistan in late 2001, allies and sympathizers of the Taliban in Pakistan were not identified as 'Taliban' themselves," wrote Hassan Abbas, a research fellow at Harvard's Belfer Center for Science and International Affairs. "That reality is now a distant memory. Today, Pakistan's indigenous Taliban are an effective fighting force and are engaging the Pakistani military on one side and NATO forces on the other." [5]

• **Hizb-e-Islami** — Formed by the brutal warlord Gulbuddin Hekmatyar, the group is "a prominent ally under the Taliban umbrella," says *Christian Science Monitor* journalist Anand Gopal. [6]

Hizb-e-Islami ("Islamic Party") was allied with the United States and Pakistan during the decade-long Soviet war, Gopal wrote, but after the 2001 U.S. invasion of Afghanistan a segment led by Hekmatyar joined the insurgency. *The New York Times* has described Hekmatyar as having "a record of extreme brutality." [7]

Hizb-e-Islami fighters have for years "had a reputation for being more educated and worldly than their Taliban counterparts, who are often illiterate farmers," Gopal wrote last year. In the 1970s, Hekmatyar studied engineering at Kabul University, "where he made a name for himself by hurling acid in the faces of unveiled women." [8]

Continued from p. 678

BACKGROUND

'Graveyard of Empires'

Afghanistan has long been known as the "crossroads of Central Asia," an apt name given the long list of outsiders who have ventured across its borders. It also is known as the "graveyard of empires," reflecting the difficulty faced by would-be conquerors of its remote terrain and disparate peoples.

The list is long. It includes the Persian king Darius I in the 6th century B.C. and the Macedonian conqueror Alexander the Great in 328 B.C., followed by the Scythians, White Huns, Turks, Arabs (who brought Islam in the 7th century A.D.), and the Mongol warrior Genghis Khan in 1219 A.D. [37]

Afghanistan's more recent history is a story of struggle against foreign domination, internal wrangling between reformists and traditionalists, coups, assassinations and war.

Modern Afghanistan began to take shape in the late 19th century, after a bitter fight for influence in Central Asia between the burgeoning British Empire and czarist Russia in what is known as "the Great Game." The contest led to Anglo-Afghan wars in 1839 and 1878. In the first, Afghan warriors forced the British into a deadly retreat from Kabul. The Afghans also had the upper hand over the British in the second war, which resulted in a treaty guaranteeing internal autonomy to Afghanistan while the British had control of its foreign affairs.

In 1880 Amir Abdur Rahman rose to the throne, reigning until 1901. Known as the "Iron Amir," he sought to institute reforms and weaken Pashtun resistance to centralized power but used methods, later emulated by the Taliban, to bring Uzbeks, Hazaras and Tajiks under Kabul's authority. [38] During his reign, Britain drew the so-called Durand Line separating

Today the group has a "strong presence in the provinces near Kabul and in Pashtun pockets in the country's north and northeast," Gopal wrote. In 2008 Hizb-e-Islami participated in an assassination attempt on President Hamid Karzai and was behind a 2008 ambush that killed 10 NATO soldiers, according to Gopal.

"Its guerrillas fight under the Taliban banner, although independently and with a separate command structure," Gopal wrote. "Like the Taliban, its leaders see their task as restoring Afghan sovereignty as well as establishing an Islamic state in Afghanistan."

• **The Haqqani network** — Some of the most notorious terrorist actions in recent months have been linked to the network, including the kidnapping of a *New York Times* reporter and the abduction of a U.S. soldier. Haqqani is "not traditional Taliban, they're more strongly associated with al Qaeda," said Haroun Mir, director of Afghanistan's Center for Research and Policy Studies in Kabul. [9]

Thought to control major parts of eastern Afghanistan, the network in recent years "has emerged . . . as a powerful antagonist to U.S. efforts to stabilize that country and root out insurgent havens in the lawless tribal areas of Pakistan," according to *The Washington Post*. [10]

The network is controlled by Jalaluddin Haqqani and his son, Sirajuddin, the *Post* said. Analysts call the son a "terrorist mastermind," according to *The Christian Science Monitor*. [11]

New York Times reporter David Rohde, who was abducted in Logar Province in Afghanistan and taken across the Pakistani border to North Waziristan, was held by the Haqqani network until he escaped in June after seven months in captivity. [12]

The network also is suspected of the suicide bombing of the Indian Embassy in Kabul in July 2008 that left more than 50 dead, *The Post* said. [13]

According to Gopal, "The Haqqanis command the lion's share of foreign fighters operating in [Afghanistan] and tend to be even more extreme than their Taliban counterparts. Unlike most of the Taliban and Hizb-e-Islami, elements of the Haqqani network cooperate closely with al Qaeda." [14]

[1] "Remarks by the President on a New Strategy for Afghanistan and Pakistan," The White House, March 27, 2009, www.whitehouse.gov.

[2] Bryan Bender, "U.S. probes divisions within Taliban," *The Boston Globe*, May 24, 2009, p. 1.

[3] See Eben Kaplan and Greg Bruno, "The Taliban in Afghanistan," Council on Foreign Relations, July 2, 2008, www.cfr.org/publication/10551/taliban_in_afghanistan.html.

[4] *Ibid.*

[5] Hassan Abbas, "A Profile of Tehrik-i-Taliban Pakistan," *CTC Sentinel*, Vol. 1, Issue 2, pp. 1-4, www.ctc.usma.edu/sentinel/CTCSentinel-Vol1Iss2.pdf.

[6] Anand Gopal, "Briefing: Who Are the Taliban?" *The Christian Science Monitor*, April 16, 2009, http://anandgopal.com/briefing-who-are-the-taliban/.

[7] Dexter Filkins, "Taliban said to be in talks with intermediaries about peace; U.S. withdrawal is called a focus," *The New York Times*, May 21, 2009, p. 4.

[8] Anand Gopal, "Who Are the Taliban?" *The Nation*, Dec. 22, 2008, www.thenation.com/doc/20081222/gopal.

[9] Quoted in Issam Ahmed, "Captured U.S. soldier in Taliban video: Held by Haqqani network?" *The Christian Science Monitor*, Global News blog, July 19, 2009, http://features.csmonitor.com/globalnews/2009/07/19/captured-us-soldier-in-taliban-video-held-by-haqqani-network/.

[10] Keith B. Richburg, "Reporters Escape Taliban Captors," *The Washington Post*, June 21, 2009, p. A1.

[11] Ahmed, *op. cit.*

[12] *Ibid.*

[13] Richburg, *op. cit.*

[14] Gopal, *The Nation, op. cit.*

Afghanistan from what was then India and later became Pakistan.

Rahman's son succeeded him but was assassinated in 1919. Under his successor, Amanullah — Rahman's grandson — Afghanistan gained full independence as a result of the Third Anglo War. Amanullah brought reforms that included ties with other countries and coeducational schools. But the moves alienated traditionalists, and Amanullah was forced to abdicate in 1929. His successor and cousin, Nadir Shah, was assassinated in 1933.

His death led to the 40-year reign of Crown Prince Mohammad Zahir Shah, Nadir Shah's son, who assumed power at 19.

Chaos and War

Under Zahir, Afghanistan sought to liberalize its political system. But the effort collapsed in the 1970s, and the country became a battleground between communist-backed leftists and a U.S.-backed Islamist resistance movement.

Afghanistan had tilted toward the Soviets in the Cold War era of the 1950s, partly because of U.S. ties to Pakistan, a country created by the partition of India in 1947. Afghan leaders wanted independence or at least autonomy for the Pashtun-dominated areas beyond the Durand Line.

Border tensions led Kabul to seek help from the Soviets, who responded with development loans and other aid in 1950. The United States sought to counter the Soviet Union's influence, and in the 1960s both countries were helping to build up Afghanistan's infrastructure.

Between 1956 and 1978, according to Pakistani journalist Ahmed Rashid, Afghanistan received some $533 million in economic aid from the United States and $2.5 billion in both economic and military aid from the Soviets. [39]

In the 1960s Zahir introduced a constitutional monarchy and pressed for political freedoms that included new rights for women in voting, schooling and

U.S. Troop Deaths Rose Steadily

U.S. troop fatalities have risen steadily since the United States entered Afghanistan in 2001 (graph at left). So far this year, IEDs (improvised explosive devices) caused slightly more than half the deaths (right).

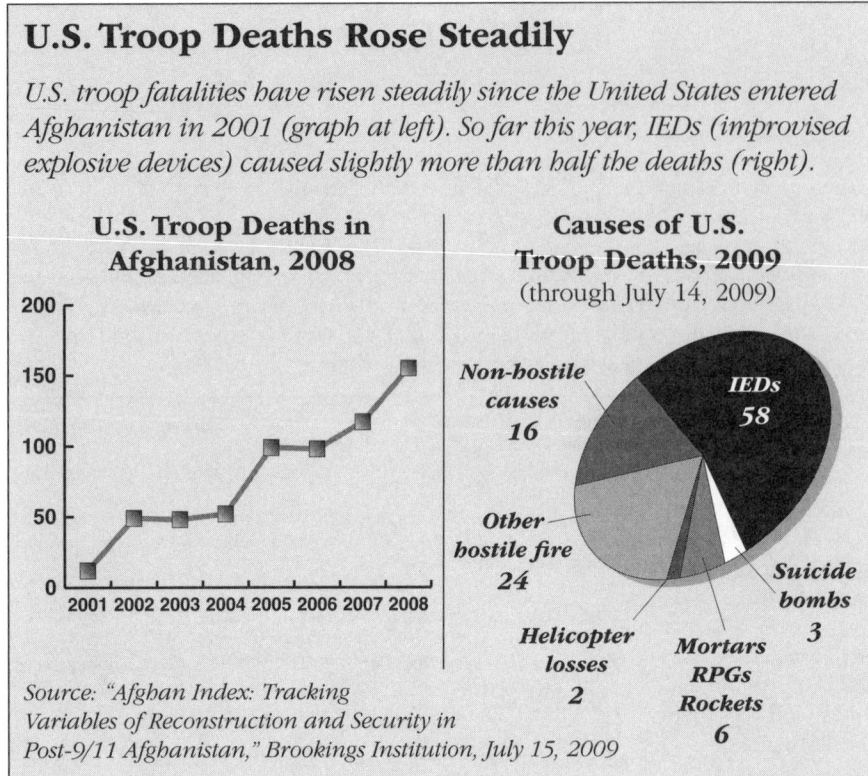

U.S. Troop Deaths in Afghanistan, 2008

Causes of U.S. Troop Deaths, 2009
(through July 14, 2009)

Non-hostile causes 16

IEDs 58

Other hostile fire 24

Suicide bombs 3

Helicopter losses 2

Mortars RPGs Rockets 6

Source: "Afghan Index: Tracking Variables of Reconstruction and Security in Post-9/11 Afghanistan," Brookings Institution, July 15, 2009

employment. "These changes, in a deeply traditional Islamic society, were not popular with everyone," the *Times* noted in a 2007 obituary of Zahir. "But his years were characterized by a rare long period of peace. This tranquility is recalled now with immense nostalgia. On the other hand, peace was not accompanied by prosperity, and the king was faulted for not developing the economy." [40]

Zahir's "experiment in democracy" did not lead to many lasting reforms, but "it permitted the growth of unofficial extremist parties on both the left and the right," including the communist People's Democratic Party of Afghanistan that was ideologically aligned with the Soviets, the U.S. State Department noted. The party split into rival groups in 1967 in a rift that "reflected ethnic, class and ideological divisions within Afghan society." [41]

In 1973 Zahir was ousted while in Europe for medical treatment. His cousin, former Prime Minister Sardar Mohammad Daoud Khan, whom Zahir had forced out in the 1960s, seized power in a bloodless coup. Daoud tried to institute reforms,

but political unrest persisted. He aligned closely with the Soviets, but his efforts to build his own political party and forge some links with the United States alienated communist radicals. In 1978, the People's Democratic Party overthrew Daoud, killing him and most of his family.

Soviet Invasion

More upheaval followed. The new leader, Nur Mohammad Taraki, imposed Marxist reforms that angered Islamic traditionalists and ethnic leaders, sparking revolts. Taraki was ousted and killed, and his successor, Hafizullah Amin, who resisted Soviet pressure to moderate his policies, was himself executed in 1979 by the Soviets.

Shortly before Amin's killing, the Soviets mounted a massive invasion of Afghanistan, starting a decade-long war that would permanently alter Afghanistan's profile in world affairs. In Amin's place, the Soviets installed Babrak Karmal. With Soviet military aid, he

tried to impose authority throughout Afghanistan but ran into stiff opposition, especially in rural regions. An Islamist resistance movement called the Mujahedeen began receiving weapons and training from the United States and other countries in 1984, and soon the Soviet invasion was on the ropes.

In 1986 Karmal was replaced by Muhammad Najibullah, former head of the Afghan secret police, but the war continued to sour for the Soviets, who also were dealing with powerful political opposition at home. In 1988 Moscow signed agreements, along with the United States, Pakistan and Afghanistan, calling for an end to foreign intervention in Afghanistan. The Soviets withdrew early the following year, and in 1991 the USSR collapsed.

The Soviet invasion affirmed the idea of Afghanistan as a "graveyard" for invaders. Between 1979 and the Soviet withdrawal in 1989, some 14,500 Soviets died. [42] For the Afghan people, however, the war was a bloodbath that all but destroyed the economy and educational system and uprooted much of the population. The U.S. State Department estimates a million died. [43] Some estimates are higher.

Yet the end of the Soviet invasion brought no peace, but rather more chaos. After the Soviets departed, President George H. W. Bush withdrew support from Afghanistan, setting the stage for the conflict engulfing Afghanistan today. "Having won the Cold War," journalist Rashid wrote, "Washington had no further interest in Afghanistan or the region. This left a critical power vacuum for which the United States would pay an enormously high price a decade later." [44]

When the Soviet Union collapsed and the United States disengaged from Afghanistan, they left a country "that had become a cockpit for regional competition, a shattered state with no functioning security forces or civilian political process, a highly mobilized and armed population increasingly dependent on international organizations and cash for livelihood (including through the drug trade), and a multiplicity of armed groups linked transnationally to both state and non-state patrons," wrote Barnett Rubin, director of studies at the Center on International Cooperation at New York University, where he directs a program on Afghan reconstruction. [45]

The Mujahedeen were not a party to the accord leading to Soviet withdrawal, and through the early 1990s they continued fighting the Najibullah regime. In 1992 his government fell, and Burhanuddin Rabbani, an ethnic Tajik, became president. He declared Afghanistan an "Islamic state" but failed to ensure order.

By 1994 Afghanistan "was fast disintegrating," Rashid wrote. "Warlord fiefdoms ruled vast swathes of countryside. President Rabbani . . . governed only Kabul and the northeast of the country, while the west, centered on Herat, was under the control of warlord Ismael Khan. Six provinces in the north were ruled by the Uzbek general Rashid Dostum, and central Afghanistan was in the hands of the Hazaras. In the Pashtun south and east there was even greater fragmentation. . . . Warlords seized people's homes and farms for no reason, raped their daughters, abused and robbed the population and taxed travelers at will. Instead of refugees returning to Afghanistan, more began to leave the south for Pakistan." [46]

In 1994 a militant Islamist group — known as the Taliban and made up mainly of Pashtuns — sprang up in the south to oppose Rabbani. Their rise stemmed directly from the chaos wracking Afghanistan, Rashid wrote. "Frustrated young men who had fought

Afghan President Hamid Karzai may face a runoff after the presidential election on Aug. 20, partly because many Afghans are looking for alternative leadership in the face of sustained insurgent violence, economic stagnation and political drift.

AFP/Getty Images/Massoud Hossaini

against the Soviets and then returned to madrassas in Pakistan to resume their religious studies or to their villages in Afghanistan gathered around their elders demanding action." [47]

The Taliban took over Kabul in 1996, and by the early 2000s Rabbani's anti-Taliban Northern Alliance was limited to a slice of northern territory. "The Taliban instituted a repressive version of sharia law that outlawed music, banned women from working or going to school and prohibited freedom of the press," wrote Jones, the RAND political scientist. "While it was a detestable regime that committed gross human rights violations, the Taliban succeeded in establishing law and order throughout most of the country." [48]

At the same time, the Taliban was forging links to al Qaeda. In 1996 Taliban leader Mullah Omar invited Osama bin Laden to stay with him in Kandahar, and even though "the CIA already considered bin Laden a threat . . ., he was left alone to ingratiate himself with Omar by providing money, fighters and ideological advice to the Taliban," Rashid wrote. "Bin Laden gathered the Arabs left behind in Afghanistan and Pakistan from the war against the Soviets, enlisted more militants from Arab countries, and es-

tablished a new global terrorist infrastructure." [49]

The al Qaeda threat reached full force with the Sept. 11, 2001, attacks on the United States. In October President George W. Bush responded with a military assault called Operation Enduring Freedom. The Taliban promptly collapsed, and its leadership, along with that of al Qaeda, fled, in the view of many analysts, to Pakistan.

Yet still more trouble was to follow.

A Weakening Government

"The collapse of the Taliban government . . . created a condition of emerging anarchy," Jones wrote. In late 2001 a United Nations-sponsored conference in Bonn, Germany, laid down a process to rebuild Afghanistan's political system. With the Bonn agreement, "on paper, Afghanistan looked like it had a central government," Jones wrote. But "in practice . . ., Afghanistan had a fragile government that became weaker over time." [50]

The new government couldn't provide essential services, especially in rural areas, and a 2005 World Bank study found that "the urban elite" were the main beneficiaries of help, Jones wrote. [51] Meanwhile, the Afghan government had various problems, including the inability to provide security outside of Kabul, in large measure due to "the inability of the U.S. government to build competent Afghan security forces, especially the police." [52]

American force levels were low, too, with "the number of U.S. troops per capita in Afghanistan . . . significantly less than in almost every state-building effort since World War II," Jones wrote. [53] Moreover, the United States gave "significant assistance to local warlords, further undermining governance and weakening the ability of the Afghan state to establish law and order." [54]

The Taliban rebounded, aided by what critics have called a lack of focus by the Bush administration after its decision to invade Iraq in 2003. In Afghanistan, reconstruction and security issues were left unattended, critics say, leaving an opening for the Taliban — along with criminals, warlords, drug traffickers and others — to assert brutal control. Afghan opium production soared, al Qaeda sanctuaries in the border region of Pakistan festered and once again the region threatened to unleash a new wave of global terrorism.

The threat came not only from Afghanistan, but Pakistan, too.

In an article last year on the emboldened Taliban and al Qaeda forces in the Pakistani border region, celebrated *New York Times* war correspondent Dexter Filkins noted that Islamist militants continued to be backed by Pakistani military and intelligence services. Then, in 1994, came Pakistan's "most fateful move," he wrote. Concerned about the mayhem that swept through Afghanistan after the Soviet withdrawal, Pakistani Prime Minister Benazir Bhutto and her administration intervened on behalf of the Taliban, Filkins wrote.

"We created the Taliban," Bhutto's interior minister, Nasrullah Babar, told Filkins. "Mrs. Bhutto had a vision: that through a peaceful Afghanistan, Pakistan could extend its influence into the resource-rich territories of Central Asia." Her dream didn't materialize — the Taliban's conquest of Afghanistan fell short, and Bhutto was assassinated in late 2007. But as Filkins noted, the Taliban training camps, sometimes supported by Pakistani intelligence officials, "were beacons to Islamic militants from around the world." [55]

Concerns persist about Pakistan's intentions and security capabilities. In recent weeks, as militants threatened Islamabad and other Pakistani cities,

Pakistan has gone after insurgents in the Swat Valley and elsewhere. But Pakistani officials also have criticized U.S. attacks on insurgent strongholds using unmanned drone planes.

The big question, as posed by Filkins and others, is whether Pakistan is willing — or able — to control the radical forces within its border region. "This was not supposed to be a major worry," Filkins wrote, noting that after the Sept. 11 attacks Pakistani President Pervez Musharraf backed the United States, helped find al Qaeda suspects, attacked militants in Pakistan's remote tribal areas and vowed to fight terrorism — all in return for $10 billion in U.S. aid since 2001.

But Pakistani military and civilian leaders have survived by playing a "double game," Filkins wrote, promising the United States they were cracking down on militants, and sometimes doing so, while also allowing, and even helping, the same militants.

One reason for the "double game" is Pakistan's longstanding tension with India, especially over the disputed border region of Kashmir. "You can't address Pakistan without dealing with India," says Riedel, the Brookings scholar.

Some experts say Pakistan views its support of the Taliban as a hedge against an India-friendly government coming to power in Afghanistan.

"The Pakistanis have convinced themselves that India's objective is a friendly Afghanistan that can pose a second front against Pakistan," says Riedel. "They see the Afghan Taliban, in particular, as a very useful asset. It keeps Afghanistan from becoming an Indian client state, and their conviction is that . . . it's only a matter of time" until the United States leaves Afghanistan. The Pakistanis believe that "if they wait it out, their client will be the dominant power at least in southern and eastern Afghanistan."

The Cato Institute's Innocent says the Obama administration has made a "profound strategic miscalculation" by not recognizing how much Pakistani leaders fear

a non-Pashtun, India-leaning government assuming power in Kabul.

India has used its influence in Afghanistan, she says, to funnel weapons to a separatist movement in southwest Pakistan's sprawling Baluchistan region — a movement that some say could pose an existential threat to Pakistan. That, in turn, has given Pakistan an incentive to keep Afghanistan from growing closer to India.

Says Innocent, "This rivalry between [Pakistan and India] is the biggest impediment to stabilizing Afghanistan." ■

CURRENT SITUATION

Measurable Metrics

In the weeks leading up to this summer's Helmand River operation, Defense Secretary Gates expressed optimism about the war in Afghanistan, but acknowledged that the American public's patience with its progress could be limited.

"I think what the people in the United States want to see is the momentum shifting to see that the strategies that we're following are working," he said on CBS' "60 Minutes." "And that's why I've said in nine months to a year, we need to evaluate how we're doing." [56]

Part of that evaluation will be done through "metrics," statistical measurements on everything from civilian casualties to the strength of the Afghan National Army. The approach is part of the Obama strategy.

"Going forward, we will not blindly stay the course," Obama said, but rather "we will set clear metrics to measure progress and hold ourselves accountable. We'll consistently assess our efforts to train Afghan security forces

Continued on p. 686

At Issue:

Should the president announce an Afghanistan exit strategy?

MALOU INNOCENT
FOREIGN POLICY ANALYST
CATO INSTITUTE

WRITTEN FOR *CQ RESEARCHER*, JULY 2009

*n*o strategic, political or economic gains could outweigh the costs of America maintaining an indefinite military presence in Afghanistan. Washington can continue to disrupt terrorist havens by monitoring the region with unmanned aerial vehicles, retaining advisers for training Afghan forces and using covert operatives against specific targets.

Many policy makers and prominent opinion leaders are pushing for a large-scale, long-term military presence in Afghanistan. But none of their rationales for such a heavy presence withstands close scrutiny.

Al Qaeda poses a manageable security problem, not an existential threat to America. Washington's response, with an open-ended mission in Afghanistan, is both unnecessary and unsustainable.

Policy makers also tend to conflate al Qaeda with indigenous Pashtun-dominated militias, such as the Taliban. America's security, however, will not necessarily be at risk even if an oppressive regime takes over a contiguous fraction of Afghan territory.

Additionally, the argument that America has a moral obligation to prevent the reemergence of reprehensible groups like the Taliban seems instead a justification for the perpetuation of American empire. After all, America never made a substantive policy shift toward or against the Taliban's misogynistic, oppressive and militant Islamic regime when it controlled Afghanistan in the 1990s. Thus, the present moral outrage against the group can be interpreted as opportunistic.

Some policy makers claim the war is worth waging because terrorists flourish in failed states. But that cannot account for terrorists who thrive in states with the sovereignty to reject external interference. That is one reason why militants find sanctuary in Pakistan. In fact, attempts to stabilize Afghanistan *destabilize* Pakistan. Amassing troops in Afghanistan feeds the perception of a foreign occupation, spawning more terrorist recruits for Pakistani militias and thus placing undue stress on an already-weakened, nuclear-armed nation.

It's also important to recognize that Afghanistan's landlocked position in Central Asia will forever render it vulnerable to meddling from surrounding states. This factor will make sealing the country's borders from terrorists impossible.

Finally, Americans should not fear appearing "weak" after withdrawal. The United States accounts for almost half of the world's military spending, wields one of the planet's largest nuclear arsenals and can project its power around the globe. Remaining in Afghanistan is more likely to weaken the United States militarily and economically than would withdrawal.

ILAN BERMAN
VICE PRESIDENT FOR POLICY
AMERICAN FOREIGN POLICY COUNCIL

WRITTEN FOR *CQ RESEARCHER*, JULY 2009

*i*t has been called the "graveyard of empires," a place that for thousands of years has stymied invading armies. Today, Afghanistan remains one of the West's most vexing international security conundrums — and a pressing foreign policy challenge for the Obama administration.

Indeed, for almost as long as Obama has been in office, critics have counseled the new U.S. president to set a date certain for an American exit from Afghanistan. To his credit, Mr. Obama has done no such thing. To the contrary, through the "Af-Pak" strategy unveiled in March, the White House has effectively doubled down on the American investment in Afghanistan's security. It has done so for two principal reasons.

The first has to do with Afghanistan's importance to the overall struggle against radical Islam. In the years before Sept. 11, Afghanistan became an incubator of international terrorism. And the sinister synergy created there between al Qaeda and the ruling Taliban movement was directly responsible for the most devastating terrorist attack in American history. Preventing a repeat occurrence remains an overriding priority, which is why Washington has committed to propping up the fragile government of Afghan President Hamid Karzai with the troops and training necessary to hold its ground.

The second is an understanding that Afghanistan is essentially a derivative problem. Much of the instability that exists there today is a function of radicalism nurtured next door, in Pakistan. The Taliban, after all, was an invention of Pakistan's Inter-Services Intelligence back in the mid-1990s, and Islamabad's intelligence czars (as well as their military counterparts) remain heavily invested in its future. Today, the Taliban poses perhaps a greater threat to Pakistan's own stability than to that of Afghanistan. But a retraction of U.S. and allied forces from the latter is sure to create a political vacuum that Islamic radicals will be all too eager to exploit.

These realities have defined the Obama administration's approach. Unlike previous foreign powers that have gotten involved in Afghanistan, the United States today is interested simply in what the military calls "area denial." The goal is not to conquer and claim, but to deny the Taliban the necessary breathing room to regroup and re-entrench.

Setting a firm date for an American withdrawal would fundamentally undermine that objective. It would also serve to provide regional radicals with far greater certainty that the U.S. investment in Afghanistan's stability is both limited and reversible.

Continued from p. 684

and our progress in combating insurgents. We will measure the growth of Afghanistan's economy and its illicit narcotics production. And we will review whether we are using the right tools and tactics to make progress towards accomplishing our goals." [57]

One measure attracting rising attention in recent weeks is that of troop levels. Michael E. O'Hanlon, a senior fellow at Brookings, wrote this summer in the *Washington Examiner* that "for all its virtues," the Obama administration's Afghan strategy "may still lowball requirements for the Afghanistan mission to succeed."

"The administration's decisions in March to increase U.S. troop numbers to 68,000 (making for about 100,000 foreign troops in all), and Afghan army and police to about 215,000 will leave combined coalition forces at only half the levels in Iraq during the surge," O'Hanlon wrote, "and Afghanistan is slightly larger and more populous."

O'Hanlon cautioned against closing the door on adding more troops and pointed to "troubling signs that the Obama administration may be digging in against any future troop requirements." While "we may or may not have enough forces in Afghanistan" to accomplish the mission's full range of goals, he concluded, "let's not close off the conversation until we learn a little bit more." [58]

NATO's Cold Shoulder

Among the thorniest of the troop-level issues is the role of NATO forces in Afghanistan. As of June, countries participating in the NATO-led International Security Assistance Forces (ISAF), a mission mandated by the U.N. under the 2001 Bonn agreement, have committed about 32,000 troops to Afghanistan, not counting those from the United States, according to the Brookings Institution. The top three were the United Kingdom, which had committed 8,300 troops, Ger-

many (3,380) and Canada (2,830). Several countries, including the U.K. and Germany, were expected to send a small number of additional troops to provide security for the Aug. 20 election.

The Obama administration has been largely unsuccessful in prodding European nations to send more troops to Afghanistan. In April, in what the online edition of the *Times* of London billed as a "charm offensive" by Obama on his "debut international tour," leaders on the European continent "turned their backs" on the president, with British Prime Minister Gordon Brown "the only one to offer substantial help." Brown offered to send several hundred extra troops to provide election security, the *Times* noted, "but even that fell short of the thousands of combat troops that the U.S. was hoping to [gain] from the prime minister." [59]

Nonetheless, Obama has mustered some recent support for his Afghan policy. In late July Spain's prime minister, José Luís Rodríguez Zapatero, said his country was willing to increase its force on long-term deployment to Afghanistan, *The New York Times* reported. [60]

Early this month, NATO approved a reorganized command structure for Afghanistan, agreeing to set up a New Intermediate Joint Headquarters in Kabul under U.S. Lt. General David M. Rodriquez, who will manage the war on a day-to-day basis and report to McChrystal. NATO made the move at the first meeting of its governing body, the North Atlantic Council, under new NATO Secretary General Anders Fogh Rasmussen, former Danish prime minister. [61] Rasmussen, in his first comments as secretary general, called on the United Nations and European Union to help defeat the Taliban. "NATO will do its part, but it cannot do it alone," he said. "This needs to be an international effort, both military and civilian." [62]

The effectiveness of having more NATO troops in Afghanistan has been a matter of debate. At a forum in June, Brookings scholar Jeremy Shapiro, re-

cently back from a visit to southern Afghanistan, suggested U.S. commanders have had little faith in the NATO command structure.

"Each of the main countries there is really running its own provincial war," Shapiro said. "The overall problem is that there really is no unity of command in Afghanistan so we're unable . . . to prioritize and to shift resources to deal with the most important problems. . . . It's related to the fact that for every NATO force in Afghanistan including the Americans, there are two chains of command, one up through the NATO commander who is an American, and one to the national capital, and in case of conflict, the national capital command always takes priority.

"The result is that each of the lead countries in the south, the Canadians in Kandahar, the British in Helmand, the Dutch in Uruzgan, are focused on their own priorities, on improving specific indicators in their piece of the war in their own province or district without a great deal of attention to the impact of that measure on the overall fight."

In impoverished Uruzgan Province, for example, the Dutch are doing "impressive things" with development efforts, but Uruzgan "is to a large degree serving as a sanctuary for insurgents to rest and refit and plan and to engage in the struggle in Kandahar and Helmand" province, Shapiro said.

The Canadians and British "would argue . . . that the priority for Afghanistan is not Uruzgan, it is Kandahar and Helmand and [if] the development of Uruzgan comes at the cost of strengthening the insurgency in other provinces, it's perhaps not the best use of resources."

Shapiro said he believes that as the number of U.S. troops has increased, especially in southern Afghanistan, "the focus for the U.S. military command is on . . . assigning roles to coalition partners that don't require intense coordination. . . . What that presages is an Americanization of the war, including in the south." By next year, Shapiro said, NATO will remain in command, "but I would be very dubious that we'll be truly fighting a NATO war at that point." [63]

Americanizing the War

Such predictions of an Americanized war are at odds with the administration's perception of the Afghan mission. Obama told *Sky News*, a British news outlet, that British contributions to the war effort are "critical" and that "this is not an American mission. The mission in Afghanistan is one that the Europeans have as much if not more of a stake in what we do. . . . The likelihood of a terrorist attack in London is at least as high, if not higher, than it is in the United States." [64]

Any further Americanization of the war will doubtlessly fuel scrutiny of the Afghan strategy in Congress and bolster demands for the Obama administration to set forth an exit strategy.

This summer, the U.S. House of Representatives strongly rejected an amendment calling on the defense secretary to submit a report no later than Dec. 31 outlining an exit strategy for U.S. forces in Afghanistan.

"Every military mission has a beginning, a middle, a time of transition and an end," said Rep. McGovern, the Massachusetts Democrat who sponsored the measure. "But I have yet to see that vision articulated in any document, speech or briefing. We're not asking for an immediate withdrawal. We're sure not talking about cutting or running or retreating, just a plan. If there is no military solution for Afghanistan, then please just tell us how we will know when our military contribution to the political solution has ended." [65]

But "focusing on an exit versus a strategy is irresponsible and fails to recognize that our efforts in Afghanistan are vital to preventing future terrorist attacks on the American people and our allies," argued Rep. Howard McKeon, R-Calif. [66]

The amendment's defeat did nothing to allay scrutiny of the war. Sen. John F. Kerry, D-Mass., chairman of the Senate Foreign Relations Committee, told *GlobalPost*, an online international-news site, that he planned to hold oversight hearings on U.S. involvement in Afghanistan. [67]

"End of summer, early fall," Kerry said, "we are going to take a hard look at Afghanistan." ■

OUTLOOK

More Violence

Military strategists say the Afghan war is likely to get more violent in coming months as U.S. and NATO forces battle the insurgency.

One immediate concern is whether the Taliban will make good on threats to disrupt this month's presidential election. While additional troops are being deployed to guard against attacks, officials have said ensuring the security of all 28,000 polling places is impossible. [68]

Meanwhile, tensions are likely to remain between those calling for a strict timetable for de-escalating the war and those arguing in favor of staying the course.

"I certainly do not think it would be a wise idea to impose a timeline on ourselves," says Riedel of Brookings, although he points to "political realities" that include the idea "that some measure of improvement in the security situation on the ground needs to be apparent over the course of the next 18 to 24 months."

Riedel expresses confidence that will occur. Once all scheduled troop deployments are in place, he says, "it's reasonable to expect that you can see some impact from [those deployments] in 18 to 24 months. Not victory, not

the surrender of [Taliban leader] Mullah Omar, but some measurable decline in the pace of Taliban activity, some increase in the number of districts and provinces which are regarded as safe enough for [non-governmental organizations] to work in."

Beyond demands for on-the-ground progress in Afghanistan, the Obama administration faces other pressures as it struggles to get a grip on the Afghanistan and Pakistan region. One is helping U.S. allies maintain support for the war. In Britain, Prime Minister Brown has faced an uproar over growing British casualties that critics say stem from an underfunded defense budget that led to inadequate troop levels and equipment. [69] At home, as the financial crisis, health-care reform and other issues put pressure on the federal budget, Obama is likely to face opposition in Congress over additional war funding.

And Obama also is under pressure to address incendiary issues left over from the Bush administration. In July, a *New York Times* report detailed how the Bush administration repeatedly sought to discourage an investigation of charges that forces under U.S.-backed warlord Gen. Abdul Rashid Dostum massacred hundreds or even thousands of Taliban prisoners of war during the 2001 invasion of Afghanistan. [70]

In an editorial, the *Times* said Obama has directed aides to study the issue and that the administration is pressing Afghan President Karzai not to return Dostum to power. But, it added, Obama "needs to order a full investigation into the massacre." [71]

In the long run, one of the biggest challenges facing the Obama administration is its effort to instill sound governance in a country saturated with graft.

Afghanistan's corruption "reveals the magnitude of the task," says Walt, the Harvard international affairs professor. "Fixing corrupt public institutions is really hard once a pattern of behavior has been established, where money is flowing in non-regular ways. It's very difficult for outsiders to re-engineer those social and political practices, even if we were committed to staying five or 10 years."

Walt says he hopes he's wrong — "that the injection of the right kind of American power will create space for some kind of political reconciliation." But he's not optimistic. "I believe several years from now, [Afghanistan] will look like a sinkhole." ∎

Notes

[1] Chris Brummitt, "Afghan firefight shows challenge for U.S. troops," The Associated Press, June 21, 2009, http://news.yahoo.com/s/ap/20090621/ap_on_re_as/as_afghan_taking_on_the_taliban.

[2] Laura King, "6 U.S. troops killed in Afghanistan," Los Angeles Times, Aug. 3, 2009, www.latimes.com/news/nationworld/world/la-fg-afghan-deaths3-2009aug03,0,3594308.story.

[3] For background, see Robert Kiener, "Crisis in Pakistan," CQ Global Researcher, December 2008, pp. 321-348, and Roland Flamini, "Afghanistan on the Brink," CQ Global Researcher, June 2007, pp. 125-150.

[4] "Remarks by the President on a New Strategy for Afghanistan and Pakistan," White House, March 27, 2009, www.whitehouse.gov.

[5] See www.boston.com/news/nation/washington/articles/2009/07/23/obama_victory_not_right_word_for_afghanistan/.

[6] For background, see Roland Flamini, "Future of NATO," CQ Global Researcher, January 2009, pp. 1-26.

[7] Pamela Constable, "For Karzai, Stumbles On Road To Election," The Washington Post,

July 13, 2009, www.washingtonpost.com/wp-dyn/content/article/2009/07/12/AR2009071202426.html.

[8] See, for example, Fred Kaplan, "Counterinsurgenterrorism," Slate, March 27, 2009, www.slate.com/id/2214726/.

[9] Ann Scott Tyson, "New Approach to Afghanistan Likely," The Washington Post, June 3, 2009, www.washingtonpost.com/wp-dyn/content/article/2009/06/02/AR2009060203828.html.

[10] Ibid.

[11] Sharon Otterman, "Civilian death toll rises in Afghanistan," The New York Times, Aug. 1, 2009, www.nytimes.com/2009/08/01/world/asia/01afghan.html?scp=1&sq=civilian%20death%20toll%20rises&st=cse.

[12] White House, op. cit.

[13] See also John Mueller, "How Dangerous Are the Taliban?" foreignaffairs.com, April 15, 2009, www.foreignaffairs.com/articles/64932/john-mueller/how-dangerous-are-the-taliban.

[14] Matthew Kaminski, "Holbrooke of South Asia," The Wall Street Journal, April 11, 2009.

[15] Quoted in Rajiv Chandrasekaran, "Marines Deploy on Major Mission," The Washington Post, July 2, 2009, www.washingtonpost.com/wp-dyn/content/article/2009/07/01/AR2009070103202.html.

[16] Jared Allen and Roxana Tiron, "Obey warns Afghanistan funding may slow unless significant progress made," The Hill, May 4, 2009, http://thehill.com/leading-the-news/obey-warns-afghanistan-funding-may-slow-unless-significant-progress-made-2009-05-04.html.

[17] The New York Times/CBS News Poll, June 12-16, 2009, http://graphics8.nytimes.com/packages/images/nytint/docs/latest-new-york-times-cbs-news-poll/original.pdf.

[18] See Dexter Filkins, "Afghan corruption: Everything for Sale," The New York Times, Jan. 2, 2009, www.nytimes.com/2009/01/02/world/asia/02iht-corrupt.1.19050534.html?scp=2&sq=everything%20for%20sale&st=cse.

[19] See Malou Innocent, "Obama's Mumbai problem," The Guardian, Jan. 27, 2009, www.guardian.co.uk/commentisfree/cifamerica/2009/jan/27/obama-india-pakistan-relations.

[20] Peter Bergen, "Winning the Good War," Washington Monthly, July/August 2009, www.washingtonmonthly.com/features/2009/0907.bergen.html#Byline.

[21] Greg Bruno, "U.S. Needs a Stronger Commitment to Improving Afghan Governance," Council on Foreign Relations, July 30, 2009, www.cfr.org/publication/19936/us_needs_a_stronger_commitment_to_improving_afghan_governance.html?breadcrumb=%2Fpublication%2Fpublication_list%3Ftype%3Dinterview.

[22] Anthony H. Cordesman, "The Afghanistan Campaign: Can We Win?" Center for Strategic and International Studies, July 22, 2009. Cordesman expands on his ideas in a paper available at http://csis.org/files/publication/090722_CanWeAchieveMission.pdf.

[23] Richard A. Oppel Jr., "Allied Officers Concerned by Lack of Afghan Forces," The New York Times, July 8, 2009, www.nytimes.com/2009/07/08/world/asia/08afghan.html?ref=world.

[24] Quoted in Associated Press, "Marines: More Afghan Soldiers Needed in Helmand," CBS News, July 8, 2009, www.cbsnews.com/stories/2009/07/08/ap/politics/main5145174.shtml.

[25] Quoted in Oppel, op. cit.

[26] Transcript, "Death Toll Mounts as Coalition Forces Confront Taliban," "The NewsHour with Jim Lehrer," PBS, July 15, 2009, www.pbs.org/newshour/bb/military/july-dec09/afghancas_07-15.html.

[27] Bob Woodward, "Key in Afghanistan: Economy, Not Military," The Washington Post, July 1, 2009, www.washingtonpost.com/wp-dyn/content/article/2009/06/30/AR2009063002811.html.

[28] Ibid.

[29] "Face the Nation," CBS News, July 5, 2009.

[30] Greg Jaffe and Karen De Young, "U.S. General Sees Afghan Army, Police Insufficient," The Washington Post, July 11, 2009, www.washingtonpost.com/wp-dyn/content/article/2009/07/10/AR2009071002975.html.

[31] Greg Jaffe, "U.S. Troops Erred in Airstrikes on Civilians," The Washington Post, June 20, 2009, www.washingtonpost.com/wp-dyn/content/article/2009/06/19/AR2009061903359.html.

[32] Quoted in Robert Burns, "Analysis: reducing Afghan civilian deaths key goal," The Associated Press, June 13, 2009, www.google.com/hostednews/ap/article/ALeqM5hyNJNBigtMGe2M12B2s3w6OCoAbQD98Q2VP80.

[33] Bergen, op. cit.

[34] Helene Cooper and Sheryl Gay Stolberg,

About the Author

Thomas J. Billitteri is a *CQ Researcher* staff writer based in Fairfield, Pa., who has more than 30 years' experience covering business, nonprofit institutions and public policy for newspapers and other publications. His recent *CQ Researcher* reports include "Auto Industry's Future," "Middle-Class Squeeze" and "Financial Bailout." He holds a BA in English and an MA in journalism from Indiana University.

"Obama Ponders Outreach to Elements of Taliban," *The New York Times*, March 8, 2009, www.nytimes.com/2009/03/08/us/politics/08obama.html?scp=1&sq=obama%20ponders%20outreach%20to%20elements%20of%20taliban&st=cse.

[35] Quoted in *ibid*.

[36] Fotini Christia and Michael Semple, "Flipping the Taliban: How to Win in Afghanistan," *Foreign Affairs*, July/August 2009, p. 34, www.foreignaffairs.com/articles/65151/fotini-christia-and-michael-semple/flipping-the-taliban. Co-author Semple, who has significant background in holding dialogues with the Taliban, was expelled from Afghanistan in 2007 by the Karzai government amid accusations he and another diplomat held unauthorized talks with the Taliban.

[37] See, "Background Note: Afghanistan," U.S. Department of State November 2008, www.state.gov/r/pa/ei/bgn/5380.htm; also, *Grolier Encyclopedia of Knowledge*, Vol. 1, 1991. See also Kenneth Jost, "Rebuilding Afghanistan," *CQ Researcher*, Dec. 21, 2001, pp. 1041-1064.

[38] Ahmed Rashid, *Descent into Chaos* (2008), p. 8.

[39] *Ibid*.

[40] Barry Bearak, "Mohammad Zahir Shah, Last Afghan King, Dies at 92," *The New York Times*, July 24, 2007, www.nytimes.com/2007/07/24/world/asia/24shah.html.

[41] U.S. State Department, *op. cit.*

[42] *Ibid*.

[43] *Ibid*.

[44] Rashid, *op. cit.*, p. 11.

[45] Barnett R. Rubin, "The Transformation of the Afghan State," in J. Alexander Thier, ed., *The Future of Afghanistan* (2009), p. 15.

[46] Rashid, *op. cit.*, pp. 12-13.

[47] *Ibid.*, p. 13.

[48] Seth G. Jones, "The Rise of Afghanistan's Insurgency," *International Security*, Vol. 32, No. 4, spring 2008, p. 19.

[49] Rashid, *op. cit.*, p. 15.

[50] Jones, *op. cit.*, p. 20.

[51] *Ibid*. The reference to "the urban elite" comes from "Afghanistan: State Building, Sustaining Growth, and Reducing Poverty," World Bank Report No. 29551-AF, 2005, p. xxvi.

[52] *Ibid.*, pp. 20, 22.

[53] *Ibid.*, p. 24.

[54] *Ibid.*, p. 25.

[55] Dexter Filkins, "Right at the Edge," *The New York Times*, Sept. 7, 2008, www.nytimes.com/2008/09/07/magazine/07pakistan-t.html.

[56] "Bob Gates, America's Secretary of War," "60 Minutes," May 17, 2009, www.cbsnews.com/stories/2009/05/14/60minutes/main5014588.shtml.

[57] White House, *op. cit.*

[58] Michael O'Hanlon, "We Might still Need More Troops In Afghanistan," *Washington Examiner*, July 7, 2009, www.washingtonexaminer.com/politics/50044002.html.

[59] Michael Evans and David Charter, "Barack Obama fails to win NATO troops he wants for Afghanistan," *Timesonline*, April 4, 2009, www.timesonline.co.uk/tol/news/world/us_and_americas/article6032342.ece.

[60] Victoria Burnett and Rachel Donadio, "Spain Is Open to Bolstering Forces in Afghanistan," *The New York Times*, July 30, 2009, www.nytimes.com/2009/07/30/world/europe/30zapatero.html?ref=world.

[61] Steven Erlanger, "NATO Reorganizes Afghan Command Structure," *The New York Times*, Aug. 4, 2009, www.nytimes.com/2009/08/05/world/05nato.html.

[62] Thomas Harding, "New NATO head calls for 'international effort' in Afghanistan," *Telegraph*, Aug. 3, 2009, www.telegraph.co.uk/news/worldnews/asia/afghanistan/5967377/New-Nato-head-calls-for-international-effort-in-Afghanistan.html.

[63] "Afghanistan and Pakistan: A Status Report," Brookings Institution, June 8, 2009, www.brookings.edu/~/media/Files/events/2009/0608_afghanistan_pakistan/20090608_afghanistan_pakistan.pdf.

[64] "Taliban pushed back, long way to go: Obama," Reuters, July 12, 2009, www.reuters.com/article/topNews/idUSTRE56A2Q420090712?feedType=RSS&feedName=topNews&rpc=22&sp=true.

[65] Quoted in Dan Robinson, "U.S. Lawmakers Reject Amendment Calling for an Exit Strategy from Afghanistan," VOA News, June 26, 2009, www.voanews.com/english/2009-06-26-voa1.cfm.

[66] Quoted in *ibid*.

[67] John Aloysius Farrell, "Kerry: 'We are going to take a hard look at Afghanistan,'" *GlobalPost*, updated July 10, 2009, www.globalpost.com.

[68] Pamela Constable, "Karzai's Challengers Face Daunting Odds," *The Washington Post*, July 6, 2009, p. 7A.

[69] John F. Burns, "Criticism of Afghan War Is on the Rise in Britain," *The New York Times*, July 12, 2009, www.nytimes.com/2009/07/12/world/europe/12britain.html?scp=1&sq=criticism%20of%20afghan%20war%20is%20on%20the%20rise&st=cse.

[70] James Risen, "U.S. Inaction Seen After Taliban P.O.W.'s Died," *The New York Times*, July 11, 2009, www.nytimes.com/2009/07/11/world/asia/11afghan.html?scp=1&sq=U.S.%20Inaction%20Seen%20After%20Taliban&st=cse.

[71] "The Truth About Dasht-i-Leili," *The New York Times*, July 14, 2009, www.nytimes.com/2009/07/14/opinion/14tue2.html?scp=5&sq=U.S.%20Inaction%20Seen%20After%20Taliban&st=cse.

FOR MORE INFORMATION

American Foreign Policy Council, 509 C St., N.E., Washington, DC 20002; (202) 543-1006; www.afpc.org. Provides analysis on foreign-policy issues.

Brookings Institution, 1775 Massachusetts Ave., N.W., Washington, DC 20036; (202) 797-6000; www.brookings.edu. Liberal-oriented think tank that provides research, data and other resources on security and political conditions in Afghanistan and Pakistan and global counterterrorism.

Cato Institute, 1000 Massachusetts Ave., N.W., Washington, DC 20001; (202) 842-0200; www.cato.org. Libertarian-oriented think tank that provides analysis on U.S. policy toward Afghanistan and Pakistan.

RAND Corp., 1776 Main St., Santa Monica, CA 90401; (310) 393-0411; www.rand.org. Research organization that studies domestic and international policy issues.

United Nations Office on Drugs and Crime, U.N. Headquarters, DC1 Building, Room 613, One United Nations Plaza, New York, NY 10017; (212) 963-5698; www.unodc.org. Helps member states fight illicit drugs, crime and terrorism; compiles data on opium poppy production.

United States Institute of Peace, 1200 17th St., N.W., Washington, DC 20036; (202) 457-1700; www.usip.org. Provides analysis, training and other resources to prevent and end conflicts.

Bibliography

Selected Sources

Books

Coll, Steve, *Ghost Wars*, Penguin Press, 2004.
The former *Washington Post* managing editor, now president of the New America Foundation think tank, traces the CIA's involvement in Afghanistan since the Soviet invasion in the 1970s.

Kilcullen, David, *The Accidental Guerrilla*, Oxford University Press, 2009.
A former Australian Army officer and counterterrorism adviser argues that strategists have tended to conflate small insurgencies and broader terror movements.

Peters, Gretchen, *Seeds of Terror*, Thomas Dunne Books, 2009.
A journalist examines the role of Afghanistan's illegal narcotics industry in fueling the activities of the Taliban and al Qaeda.

Rashid, Ahmed, *Descent into Chaos*, Viking, 2008.
A Pakistani journalist argues that "the U.S.-led war on terrorism has left in its wake a far more unstable world than existed on" Sept. 11, 2001.

Wright, Lawrence, *The Looming Tower*, Knopf, 2006.
In a Pulitzer Prize-winning volume that remains a must-read for students of the wars in Afghanistan and Iraq, a *New Yorker* staff writer charts the spread of Islamic fundamentalism and emergence of al Qaeda that gave rise to the Sept. 11 attacks.

Articles

Bergen, Peter, "Winning the Good War," *Washington Monthly*, July/August 2009, www.washingtonmonthly.com/ features/2009/0907.bergen.html.
A senior fellow at the New America Foundation argues that skepticism about the Obama administration's chances of victory in Afghanistan are based on a misreading of that nation's history and people.

Christia, Fotini, and Michael Semple, "Flipping the Taliban," *Foreign Affairs*, July/August 2009.
A political scientist (Christia) and a specialist on Afghanistan and Pakistan who has talked with the Taliban argue that while more troops are necessary, "the move will have a lasting impact only if it is accompanied by a political 'surge' " aimed at persuading large groups of Taliban fighters to lay down arms.

Hogan, Michael, "Milt Bearden: Afghanistan Is 'Obama's War,' " *Vanityfair.com*, Feb. 5, 2009, www.vanityfair.com/ online/politics/2009/02/milt-bearden-afghanistan-is-obamas-war.html.
Bearden, the former CIA field officer in Afghanistan when U.S. covert action helped expel the Soviet Union, says in this

Q&A that "the only thing that is absolutely certain about this war is that it's going to be Obama's war, just as Iraq will be Bush's war."

Jones, Seth G., "The Rise of Afghanistan's Insurgency," *International Security*, Vol. 32, No. 4, spring 2008, http:// belfercenter.ksg.harvard.edu/files/IS3204_pp007-040_ Jones.pdf.
A RAND Corporation political scientist analyzes the reasons a violent insurgency began to develop in Afghanistan earlier this decade.

Mueller, John, "How Dangerous Are the Taliban?" *Foreign affairs.com*, April 15, 2009, www.foreignaffairs.com/ articles/64932/john-mueller/how-dangerous-are-the-taliban.
An Ohio State University political science professor questions whether the Taliban and al Qaeda are a big enough menace to the United States to make a long war in Afghanistan worth the cost.

Riedel, Bruce, "Comparing the U.S. and Soviet Experiences in Afghanistan," *CTC Sentinel*, Combating Terrorism Center, May 2009, www.brookings.edu/~/media/Files/rc/articles/ 2009/05_afghanistan_riedel/05_afghanistan_riedel.pdf.
A Brookings Institution scholar and former senior adviser to President Barack Obama examines the "fundamental differences" between the Soviet and U.S. experiences in the region.

Rosenberg, Matthew, and Zahid Hussain, "Pakistan Taps Tribes' Anger with Taliban," *The Wall Street Journal*, June 6-7, 2009, p. A14.
Pakistani anger at the Taliban in tribal regions bordering Afghanistan is growing, and Pakistan's military leaders hope to capitalize on that anger as they mount a grueling campaign against insurgents in North and South Waziristan.

Reports and Studies

Campbell, Jason, Michael O'Hanlon and Jeremy Shapiro, "Assessing Counterinsurgency and Stabilization Missions," Brookings Institution, Policy Paper No. 14, May 2009, www.brookings.edu/~/media/Files/rc/papers/2009/05_coun terinsurgency_ohanlon/05_counterinsurgency_ohanlon.pdf.
Brookings scholars examine the status of change in Afghanistan and Iraq and explain why "2009 is expected by many to be a pivotal year in Afghanistan."

Tellis, Ashley J., "Reconciling With the Taliban?" Carnegie Endowment for International Peace, 2009, www.carnegie endowment.org/files/reconciling_with_taliban.pdf.
Efforts at reconciliation today would undermine American credibility and jeopardize the success of the U.S.-led mission in Afghanistan, argues a senior associate at the endowment.

The Next Step:

Additional Articles from Current Periodicals

Drug Trade

Barker, Kim, "NATO-led Force Engages in Poppy Eradication in Afghanistan," *Chicago Tribune*, **Feb. 8, 2009, p. A1.**

NATO's International Security Assistance Force is working to destroy Afghan poppy fields that fund the Taliban.

Dilanian, Ken, "Poppy Farms Pose Dilemma," *USA Today*, **March 31, 2009, p. 6A.**

Profits from poppy farming fields have fueled the insurgency in Afghanistan, but destroying the fields is likely to be just as helpful to the insurgents.

Gearan, Anne, "U.S. Eradication of Afghan Poppy Wanes," *Newsday* **(New York), July 11, 2009, p. A20.**

U.S. authorities are abandoning Bush-era policies of destroying Afghan cash crops as a waste of money.

Lasseter, Tom, "Drug Trade Permeates Afghanistan," *Wichita* **[Kansas]** *Eagle*, **May 10, 2009, p. A1.**

Afghanistan produces about 90 percent of the world's opium — worth $3.4 billion in 2008 — which has led Afghan officials to open highways to opium and heroin trafficking.

Obama Administration

DeYoung, Karen, "Obama Outlines Afghan Strategy," *The Washington Post*, **March 28, 2009, p. A1.**

President Obama's strategy assumes the terrorists who planned the Sept. 11 attacks are devising more plots.

Landler, Mark, "U.S. to Pledge $40 Million for Afghanistan Elections," *The New York Times*, **March 31, 2009, p. A13.**

The United States has committed $40 million to underwrite the cost of elections in Afghanistan.

Lubold, Gordon, "US Troop Buildup in Afghanistan Could Be a Defining Moment," *The Christian Science Monitor*, **Feb. 19, 2009, p. 1.**

President Obama's decision to deploy an additional 17,000 troops to Afghanistan will either reverse the deteriorating situation or burden the administration with a war with no foreseeable end.

Tyson, Ann Scott, "Top General in Afghan Conflict Forced Out," *The Boston Globe*, **May 12, 2009, p. A5.**

The top American general in Afghanistan, David McKiernan, has been replaced amid calls for more counterinsurgency tactics.

Pakistan

Magnier, Mark, "Taliban in Pakistan Is Not Easily Defined," *Chicago Tribune*, **May 11, 2009, p. A11.**

Turmoil in Pakistan has made it seem as though a unified Taliban is gathering in the northwest areas of the country, but Pakistanis don't see the group as much of a threat.

Qazi, Raza, and Sara A. Carter, "3 Taliban Leaders Unite Against U.S. in Pakistan," *The Washington Times*, **Feb. 24, 2009, p. A1.**

An alliance among three Taliban leaders in Pakistan could hamper U.S. efforts to flush out al Qaeda in the country's lawless borderlands.

Rashid, Ahmed, "Pakistan Seems Ready to Crack Down on Taliban," *The Miami Herald*, **July 2, 2009, p. A1.**

Pakistan has begun a military offensive to drive the Taliban out of South Waziristan.

Taliban

Barnes, Julian E., and Greg Miller, "U.S. Strategy Aims to Stop Taliban Push," *Los Angeles Times*, **March 27, 2009, p. A1.**

Senior defense officials have called for more training of Afghan forces in order to thwart an attempt by the country's former Taliban leader from reclaiming power.

Cooper, Helene, "Dreaming of Splitting the Taliban," *The New York Times*, **March 8, 2009, p. WK1.**

European governments have pressed the United States for some time over negotiating with the Taliban.

Filkins, Dexter, "Taliban Said to Be in Talks With Intermediaries About Peace," *The Boston Globe*, **May 21, 2009, p. A4.**

Taliban leaders are said to be considering peace agreements, with initial demands focused on U.S. troop withdrawal.

CITING CQ RESEARCHER

Sample formats for citing these reports in a bibliography include the ones listed below. Preferred styles and formats vary, so please check with your instructor or professor.

MLA STYLE

Jost, Kenneth. "Rethinking the Death Penalty." CQ Researcher 16 Nov. 2001: 945-68.

APA STYLE

Jost, K. (2001, November 16). Rethinking the death penalty. *CQ Researcher, 11,* 945-968.

CHICAGO STYLE

Jost, Kenneth. "Rethinking the Death Penalty." CQ Researcher, November 16, 2001, 945-968.

In-depth Reports on Issues in the News

Are you writing a paper?

Need backup for a debate?

Want to become an expert on an issue?

For 80 years, students have turned to *CQ Researcher* for in-depth reporting on issues in the news. Reports on a full range of political and social issues are now available. Following is a selection of recent reports:

Civil Liberties
Closing Guantánamo, 2/09
Affirmative Action, 10/08
Gay Marriage Showdowns, 9/08
America's Border Fence, 9/08
Immigration Debate, 2/08

Crime/Law
Examining Forensics, 7/09
Legalizing Marijuana, 6/09
Mexico's Drug War, 12/08
Prostitution Debate, 5/08
Public Defenders, 4/08

Education
Reading Crisis? 2/08
Discipline in Schools, 2/08
Student Aid, 1/08
Racial Diversity in Public Schools, 9/07

Environment/Society
Energy and Climate, 7/09
Future of Books, 5/09
Hate Groups, 5/09
Future of Journalism, 3/09
Confronting Warming, 1/09
Reducing Carbon Footprint, 12/08

Health/Safety
Straining the Safety Net, 7/09
Treating Depression, 6/09
Reproductive Ethics, 5/09
Extreme Sports, 4/09
Regulating Toxic Chemicals, 1/09
Preventing Cancer, 1/09
Heart Health, 9/08

Politics/Economy
Business Bankruptcy, 4/09
Future of the GOP, 3/09
Middle-Class Squeeze, 3/09

Upcoming Reports

Health Reforms, 8/28/09　　　Financial Literacy, 9/4/09　　　U.S. Nuclear Arsenal, 9/11/09

ACCESS

CQ Researcher is available in print and online. For access, visit your library or www.cqresearcher.com.

STAY CURRENT

To receive notice of upcoming *CQ Researcher* reports, or learn more about *CQ Researcher* products, subscribe to the free e-mail newsletters, *CQ Researcher Alert!* and *CQ Researcher News*: http://cqpress.com/newsletters.

PURCHASE

To purchase a *CQ Researcher* report in print or electronic format (PDF), visit www.cqpress.com or call 866-427-7737. Single reports start at $15. Bulk purchase discounts and electronic-rights licensing are also available.

SUBSCRIBE

Annual full-service *CQ Researcher* subscriptions—including 44 reports a year, monthly index updates, and a bound volume—start at $803. Add $25 for domestic postage.

CQ Researcher Online offers a backfile from 1991 and a number of tools to simplify research. For pricing information, call 800-834-9020, ext. 1906, or e-mail librarysales@cqpress.com.

Published by CQ Press, a Division of SAGE

www.cqresearcher.com

Health-Care Reform

Is universal coverage too expensive?

F
or the first time in 15 years, health-care reform has moved to the top of Washington's agenda. A new Democratic president and Democratic majorities in the House and Senate have declared two major goals: increase coverage to near-universal levels and stop the huge, annual cost increases that are gradually putting health care out of reach for small businesses and low-income families. Most proposals would subsidize insurance for low-income Americans and create new, government-regulated insurance markets for those without employer-provided coverage. One controversial scheme would create a publicly run insurance plan and require individuals to buy coverage. Congressional Republicans and some Democrats argue, however, that the plan would be too expensive and would allow government to meddle too much in health care. And at angry town hall meetings in August, some even charged, incorrectly, that the arrangement would establish "death panels" that would deny treatment to elderly and disabled patients.

A citizen sounds off during a town hall meeting on health-care reform in Lebanon, Pa., held by Sen. Arlen Specter, D-Pa., on Aug. 11, 2009.

CQ Researcher • Aug. 28, 2009 • www.cqresearcher.com
Volume 19, Number 29 • Pages 693-716

CQ Researcher

Aug. 28, 2009
Volume 19, Number 29

MANAGING EDITOR: Thomas J. Colin
tcolin@cqpress.com

ASSISTANT MANAGING EDITOR: Kathy Koch
kkoch@cqpress.com

ASSOCIATE EDITOR: Kenneth Jost

STAFF WRITERS: Thomas J. Billitteri,
Marcia Clemmitt, Peter Katel

CONTRIBUTING WRITERS: Rachel Cox,
Sarah Glazer, Alan Greenblatt, Reed Karaim
Barbara Mantel, Patrick Marshall,
Tom Price, Jennifer Weeks

DESIGN/PRODUCTION EDITOR: Olu B. Davis

ASSISTANT EDITOR: Darrell Dela Rosa

FACT-CHECKING: Eugene J. Gabler,
Michelle Harris

CQ PRESS

A Division of SAGE

PRESIDENT AND PUBLISHER:
John A. Jenkins

**EXECUTIVE DIRECTOR,
REFERENCE INFORMATION GROUP:**
Alix B. Vance

CQ Press is a registered trademark of Congressional Quarterly Inc.

CQ Researcher (ISSN 1056-2036) is printed on acid-free paper. Published weekly, except; (Jan. wk. 1) (May wk. 4) (July wks. 1, 2) (Aug. wks. 3, 4) (Nov. wk. 4) and (Dec. wk. 4), by CQ Press, a division of SAGE Publications. Annual full-service subscriptions start at $803. For pricing, call 1-800-834-9020, ext. 1906. To purchase a CQ Researcher report in print or electronic format (PDF), visit www.cqpress.com or call 866-427-7737. Single reports start at $15. Bulk purchase discounts and electronic-rights licensing are also available. Periodicals postage paid at Washington, D.C., and additional mailing offices. POSTMASTER: Send address changes to CQ Researcher, 2300 N St., N.W., Suite 800, Washington, DC 20037.

Cover: Getty Images/Chris Gardner

Health-Care Reform

BY MARCIA CLEMMITT

THE ISSUES

As a public-relations executive for CIGNA, the giant, Philadelphia-based health insurer, Wendell Potter lived large. Indeed, when he flew to meetings on the company's jet, he dined on gold-rimmed china using gold-plated flatware, he recently told Amy Goodman, host of Pacifica radio's "Democracy Now!" [1]

But his view of the corporate good life radically changed one rainy day in the coal country of southwest Virginia. Despite the downpour, hundreds of uninsured area residents waited at the local fairgrounds for free medical treatment from Remote Area Medical, a volunteer group that once brought doctors to impoverished countries such as Guyana, on the northern coast of South America.[2]

"When I walked through the fairground gates, it was just absolutely overwhelming," Potter recalled. People were lined up by the hundreds. "It looked like . . . a war-torn country . . . and it just drove home to me, maybe for the first time, that we were talking about real human beings" — casualties of "the things [insurers] do to maximize their profit, which really boils down to dumping the sick" by, among other tactics, jacking up the rates for small businesses whose workers have had serious illnesses. [3]

The experience spurred Potter to resign from CIGNA and begin speaking out about problems in America's profit-focused health-care system.

And the problems are daunting: More than 45 million Americans are uninsured, millions more face losing their insurance if they lose their jobs and U.S.

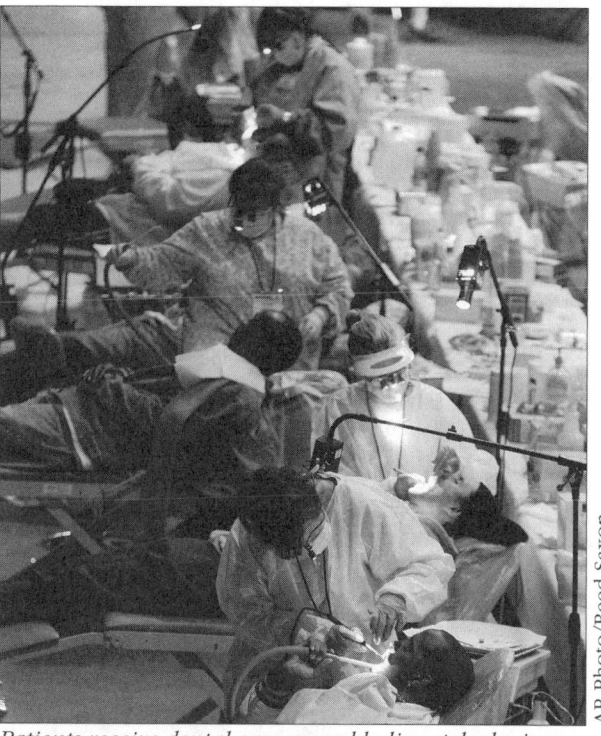

Patients receive dental care assembly-line style during an eight-day free clinic this month at the Forum arena in Inglewood, Calif. The nonprofit group Remote Area Medical provided medical and dental treatment for about 10,000 people, most without health or dental insurance. Many waited all night for admission. President Obama and House and Senate Democrats have introduced proposals to cover the nation's 45 million uninsured and slow the rising cost of health care.

AP Photo/Reed Saxon

health costs are at least 40 percent higher than in any other country.

Although Democrats such as the late Sen. Edward M. Kennedy, D-Mass., who died on Aug. 26, have never given up the goal of universal coverage, major health-care changes are being debated this year for the first time since 1993. President Barack Obama and Democrats in both the House and Senate have introduced so-called universal coverage proposals to cover the uninsured and begin slowing the budget-busting growth in health-care costs that's expected to price millions of Americans out of coverage in the coming years.

Opponents, however — who include Republicans and some conservative Democrats — argue that universal coverage is far too expensive.

"Every health-care proposal Democrats . . . have offered would only hurt the economy," said Senate Minority Leader Mitch McConnell, R-Ky. [7]

Critics also warn that increasing government influence over health care could threaten Americans' freedoms — and even their very lives.

Former Alaska governor Sarah Palin, 2008 Republican candidate for vice president, warned on her Facebook page that increased government influence in health care would lead to creation of "death panels" to "decide, based on a subjective judgment of their 'level of productivity in society,' " whether Americans like her aging parents or her baby with Down Syndrome "are worthy of health care." [4]

The accusation, which other conservative leaders have repeated since, apparently stemmed from two concerns: that government-financed health care means severe rationing of services and that proposed House legislation would enable Medicare to pay for end-of-life counseling by physicians if patients choose it.

In fact, such counseling does the opposite of what Palin claimed, putting end-of-life decisions into people's own hands, said Republican Sen. Johnny Isakson, of Georgia, who proposed a similar provision in the Senate. Many patients get huge amounts of painful, expensive — usually completely useless — treatment in the last 60 days of life because medical personnel and administrators decide what to do if patients are "not in a capacity to make decisions for themselves," he said. Rather than getting into such a situation "if everyone had an end-of-life directive . . . you could instruct at

High Premiums Stymie Poor and Employers

Health insurance costs represent such a significant percentage of poor people's earnings that employers are less likely to buy them coverage, and few families can afford the premiums on their own. Premiums cost nearly 40 percent of the total income of a family earning $36,620 a year — twice the current federal poverty threshold — compared to 12 percent for a family earning $109,860.

Family Health Insurance Premiums for Various Income Levels, 2009

%Federal Poverty Level	Annual income	Annual premium	Premium as % of income	Examples of occupations in which two breadwinners can earn that income
100%	$18,310	$13,446	73%	....
200%	$36,620	$13,446	37%	Cafeteria attendant and shampooer
300%	$54,930	$13,446	24%	Receptionist and secretary
400%	$73,240	$13,446	18%	Police officer and child care worker
500%	$91,550	$13,446	15%	Legal secretary and electrician
600%	$109,860	$13,446	12%	Real estate agent and librarian
950%	$174,000	$13,446	8%	Administrative law judge and aerospace engineer

Source: Health Policy Institute, Georgetown University

a time of sound mind and body what you want to happen." [5]

Comparing the provision to euthanasia "is nuts," Isakson said. [6]

To those who say reform would cost too much, advocates counter that universal coverage offers incalculable savings and benefits, including making low-cost preventive care available to all so the uninsured don't wait until their illness reaches the critical stage and then end up in an emergency room, where treatement costs more and is subsidized by higher premiums for insured consumers.

In addition, many uninsured young people who are in good health think the rising cost of insurance is too expensive and not worth the cost. But swine flu, for example, often strike s just this population. "So, if there is any kind of pandemic, we are far more at risk because so many people are walking around" without coverage, says pediatrician Margaret Flowers, a member of the group

Physicians for a National Health Program (PNHP).

Advocates like Flowers are pressing for enactment of a so-called single-payer coverage plan, in which the government would act as the insurer in a tax-based system for all, similar to Medicare, the public, single-payer program for the elderly.

But Obama and many analysts say single payer is not feasible in this country because too many people — and business interests — have a stake in maintaining the current system.

"I don't believe the votes are there for single payer, and I don't believe the politics are right for single payer, but single payer has some good things to recommend it," especially that "it is just incredibly cost-effective relative to any other system," said Howard Dean, a medical doctor, former Democratic National Committee chief and author of the 2009 book *Howard Dean's Prescription for Real Healthcare Reform.* [8]

The main proposals on the table all leave the current employer-based coverage system intact for those who want it, while adding a new, more tightly regulated insurance-purchasing option for others, explained *New York Times* columnist and Princeton University economics professor Paul Krugman, winner of the 2008 Nobel Prize in economics. "The essence is really quite simple: regulation of insurers, so that they can't cherry-pick only the healthy, and subsidies, so that all Americans can afford insurance," he said. "Everything else is about making that core work." [9]

To safeguard the financial stability of the new coverage, he noted, individuals would be required to buy coverage "to prevent gaming of the system by people who don't sign up until they're sick," and mandated employer coverage would hold down government costs "by preventing a rush by employers to drop insurance." [10]

Most proposals also would establish a government-run insurance plan as an additional choice for insurance buyers — and to keep for-profit insurers honest — but conservatives and insurers are fighting hard against that provision, claiming it would run private insurance companies out of business.

To believe "that a public and private plan will compete on a true, level playing field . . . you have got to believe . . . that [liberal congressmen like longtime single-payer proponent] Pete Stark, [D-Calif.] and Henry A. Waxman, [D-Calif.], . . . will do nothing to stack the deck in favor of this public plan," said Stuart Butler, vice president for domestic and economic policy studies at the conservative Heritage Foundation think tank. [11]

Dean argued that a public option would push private insurance plans to operate more efficiently. "If the companies don't do their job in the employer-based system, there will be a lot of public clamor to change their insurance over to the public option."

Having that happen is "what the Republicans are terrified of," Dean acknowledged. "But . . . that's what competition is all about — it's giving people choices to do what's in their best interest." [12]

As lawmakers and citizens debate reforming the health-insurance system, here are some of the questions that are being asked:

Could a single-payer health-care system work for America?

In a single-payer health insurance system, the government collects taxes and insurance premiums and pays doctors, hospitals and other health-care providers directly. In most countries, such as in Canada, the providers are private. In the United States, the elderly have a single-payer system — Medicare — and the doctors and hospitals who serve Medicare are private. Only a handful of countries, notably the United Kingdom, have nationalized, or "socialized," health care, in which the government actually owns most health facilities and employs the doctors and other providers.

Although single-payer systems are common, a proposal to switch to single payer was absent from the 2009 health-reform debate until some advocates — mainly Physicians for a National Health Program — staged protests in Washington. "We had to threaten to protest at the White House" just to get Rep. John Conyers, D-Mich., a longtime single-payer advocate, invited to legislative roundtables on reform, says pediatrician Flowers.

The resistance to single payer reflects what even many supporters argue: That it's not politically feasible for the United States to shift to such a system today.

The history of U.S. health care unfortunately makes single payer unrealistic, said former Democratic National Committee chief Dean. Europeans, most of whom use some form of single payer, "have much more comprehen-

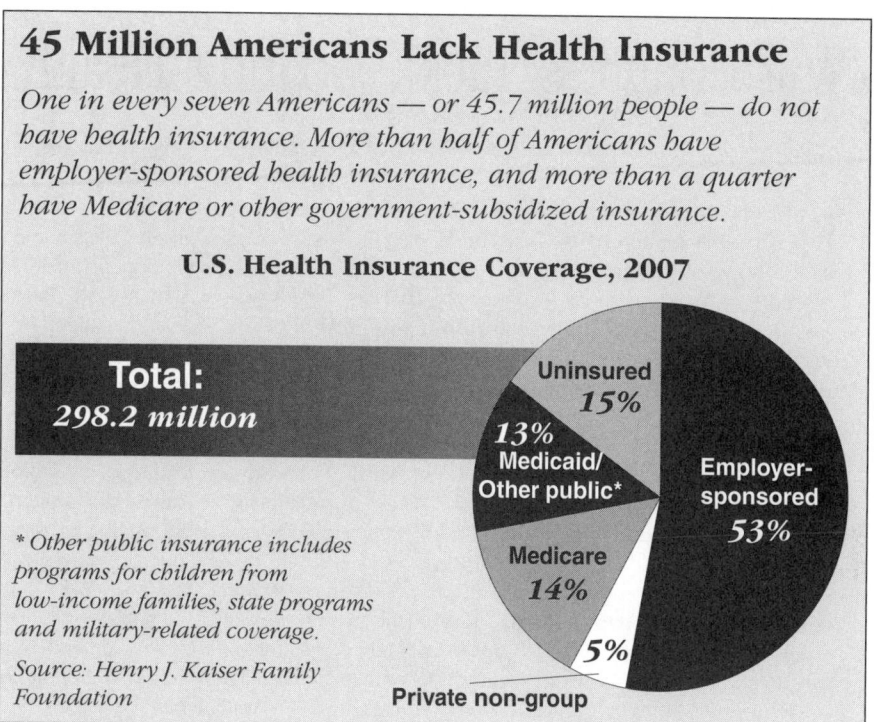

45 Million Americans Lack Health Insurance

One in every seven Americans — or 45.7 million people — do not have health insurance. More than half of Americans have employer-sponsored health insurance, and more than a quarter have Medicare or other government-subsidized insurance.

U.S. Health Insurance Coverage, 2007

Total: 298.2 million

Uninsured 15%

13% Medicaid/Other public*

Employer-sponsored 53%

Medicare 14%

5% Private non-group

* Other public insurance includes programs for children from low-income families, state programs and military-related coverage.

Source: Henry J. Kaiser Family Foundation

sive and cheaper health-care plans than we have, but they got there because their health-care systems were essentially destroyed during World War II," leaving them free to rebuild from scratch, he said.

The United States, by contrast "grew our private [multiple-payer] health-care system" around the same time, when "the only way that American employers could give their employees a raise was to enhance health-insurance benefits," said Dean. "You've got to start from where you are, not from where you wish you were." [13]

Conservatives, contend that government financing and regulation cripple innovation and drive up costs.

"Let individuals control their health-care dollars, and free them to choose from a wide variety of health plans and providers," says Michael F. Cannon, director of health-policy studies at the libertarian Cato Institute. "Experts suggest that one-third of U.S. health-care spending, or about 6 percent of gross domestic product, is pure waste," and that's mainly because government already "controls half of our

nation's health-care dollars and lets employers control an additional quarter," Cannon says. "Nobody spends other people's money as carefully as they spend their own."

And, while some comparisons show that single-payer plans have significantly lower administrative costs, conservatives say such studies are simply wrong. Such comparisons fail to include "what it costs employers and government to collect . . . taxes" and "the salaries of politicians and their staff members who set government health-care policy," argues David Hogberg, a conservative, Washington-based writer. [14]

Most tax-supported single-payer systems control costs by determining the efficacy and cost-effectiveness of medical interventions — a component that is included in the pending measure. But conservatives say the cost-containing provision amounts to dangerous government "rationing" of health care.

The Obama administration is "proposing a new federal health board to decide whether health-care services

Will Congress Tackle Soaring Health Costs?

Expanding coverage may force belt-tightening.

If Congress guarantees health coverage for all, the nation, at last, will be forced to focus on reining in costs. That's the hope of reformers, anyway.

According to virtually all health-policy analysts, health-care price inflation has significantly outstripped the growth of the rest of the economy and could soon put health care out of the reach of many more Americans.

"Health-insurance premiums have more than doubled in a decade, rising four times faster than wages," said Princeton University Professor of Bioethics Peter Singer. "Health care now absorbs about one dollar in every six the nation spends, a figure that far exceeds the share spent by any other nation" and is on track to double in cost by 2035. [1]

So far, "every innovation that's been promised to hold down costs has failed," says Jacob Hacker, a Yale University professor of political science. In the 1970s, "health planning" — limiting the number of hospitals in an area to discourage them from providing excessive or redundant services, for example — was the dominant mode, while in the 1990s policy makers pinned their hopes on managed care. Neither succeeded, for various reasons, including strong pushback from providers who didn't want anyone interfering with their practice patterns or business decisions. Although previous efforts have stalled, some methods for controlling cost growth have been shown to work, economists say.

At the top of most cost-cutting lists is the current "fee-for-service" payment scheme, says Stuart Altman, a professor of national health policy at Brandeis University. Paying doctors and hospitals for every service performed encourages them to offer unnecessary services to boost income, especially if fees are cut to control costs, he says.

On the other hand, having physicians work in coordinated groups, then reimbursing the group with a "bundled" prepayment would encourage coordinated, effective and cost-efficient care, Altman says. Payments could cover a six-month period for a healthy patient or an entire episode of acute illness or injury, with penalties if an ill patient relapses or has to be readmitted to the hospital.

However, implementing ideas like bundling payments can be politically unpopular, so Sen. Jay Rockefeller, D-W. Va., introduced legislation earlier this year to create an independent executive agency to recommend such changes for public programs like Medicare. "It's a wonderful idea," says Stan Dorn, a senior research associate at the nonpartisan Urban Institute think tank. "It's like the military base closings. Everybody [in Congress] knew they had to take the medicine," but nobody was willing to recommend closing a base in their own district. Instead of Congress having to recommend specific cost-cutting measures, "Let the expert agency make proposals to Congress for an up or down vote."

Because no U.S. insurers cover the same patients for life, they have no incentive to prevent long-term, costly illness, says Katherine Baicker, a professor of health economics at the Harvard School of Public Health. A private insurer, for example, ultimately hands off its enrollees to Medicare, and businesses change insurers frequently, she says.

Insurance regulations could be devised to "make sure everybody has a long-term horizon," Baicker says. For example, insurers could be penalized for handing over sicker patients to Medicare when they retire.

But all potential cost-control measures are "painful and politically difficult," and "win-win solutions don't really exist," says

are 'effective' or 'appropriate,' " said John C. Goodman, president of the free-market-oriented National Center for Policy Analysis in Dallas. In the United Kingdom, he warns, the National Institute for Health and Clinical Excellence "has adopted a rule of thumb that health expenditures are inappropriate if they involve spending more than $22,000 to save six months of life." Under that standard, "British cancer patients do not have access to drugs that are routinely available in the United States." [15]

While both private insurers and governments refuse to cover some procedures, one's doctor has more in-fluence with a private insurer than he would with a federal bureaucracy, says Scott Gottlieb, a resident fellow at the free-market think tank American Enterprise Institute (AEI).

Single-payer, universal coverage also would require all taxpayers to subsidize care for irresponsible people, including "heroin addicts, meth heads and others who brought their health problems on themselves through poor individual decisions," argued the conservative blog The Next Right. "Who likes the idea of their tax dollars being spent on the health of junkies?" [16]

But advocates say that only a single-payer system can extend coverage to all as well as provide incentives to cut costs.

The single-payer systems that Canada has in each province hold down costs while covering everyone, argued Sen. Hugh Segal, a Conservative Party member of the Canadian Senate. In 2006, "The U.S. spent $6,714 per capita" without covering all its citizens, "while Canada . . . spent $3,678" with universal coverage, he said. [17]

A single-payer plan is more accountable to patients because "when you have something publicly administered,

Michael Chernew, a professor of health-care policy at Harvard Medical School. Implementing a "medical home" model, which gives every patient a source of preventive care and a gatekeeper for specialist interventions, sounds more benign than other potential cost-savers, for example, and "there are people who are optimistic that this could be a win-win approach," says Chernew. But "we simply don't know to what extent, if any, that would control spending growth."

The backlash in the 1990s against health maintenance organizations, or HMOs — which bundled payments — partly explains why some Washington lawmakers are loath to propose similar solutions today, says Altman. "You have some key legislators in the House . . . the old guard, who killed managed care, and they are still philosophically opposed" to anything that smacks of it.

Some providers say that basing their pay partly on patient outcomes sounds like an incentive to provide good, efficient care. But it overlooks the fact that patients often fail to take their medication or follow the doctor's orders to get more exercise. "Providers say, 'Oh, my gosh, I can't control this because I can't control my patients!' " says Crystal Haynes, chief executive at St. Louis University Hospital.

Another often-heard suggestion — smoothing out huge geographical variations in how much health care people use — is also more problematic than it seems, says Haynes. In many parts of Florida, for example, Medicare costs are high because the elderly visit doctors more frequently than people in other states. But those doctors' visits play an important role because most of Florida's elderly have retired there, far from families and old friends.

"A lot of times those visits are their social life," and are valu-able to health and well-being, she says. "The elephant in the room is always that these are cultural and societal issues," not just matters of cost-efficiency.

Squeezing out excess cost growth would inevitably mean some pain for the many people with a financial stake in the current system, says Pamela Farley Short, a professor of health policy and administration at Yale University. Some cities, such as Pittsburgh, for example, have partly replaced a sagging manufacturing economy with health-care services, "and many of us hold pharmaceutical stocks in our retirement accounts."

Behind closed doors this summer President Barack Obama controversially conceded some cost savings to win drugmakers' support for reform. In return for pledges to cut some prices and refrain from opposing reform, Obama vowed not to allow the government to negotiate lower drug prices.

"When an industry gets secret concessions out of the White House in return for a promise to . . . support . . . legislation . . . that's called extortion," said former Labor Secretary Robert Reich, a professor of public policy at the University of California, Berkeley. [2]

But the government often sweetens the pill for financial stakeholders when making big changes, says Yale's Hacker. When Aneurin Bevan, the Welsh politician who oversaw the United Kingdom's transition to its National Health Service (NHS), was asked how he quelled doctors' objections, he famously replied that he had "stuffed their mouths with gold," Hacker notes.

---

[1] Peter Singer, "Why We Must Ration Health Care," *The New York Times Magazine*, July 19, 2009, p. MM38.
[2] Robert Reich, "How the White House's Deal with Big Pharma Undermines Democracy," Talking Points Memo blog, Aug. 9, 2009, http://tpmcafe.talk ingpointsmemo.com.

you have much more transparency" than you have with private insurers, who can shield virtually all their decision-making as proprietary business information, says pediatrician Flowers of Physicians for a National Health Program.

Sticking with a mostly employer-based system rather than a single payer also is a drag on the economy, she says. "We're squandering our potential as a people" because an employer-sponsored system often "keeps people in jobs they don't want."

In a single-payer system, "you find your actuarial cost for the whole population, and then you set a tax of some kind to match that," says Norman Daniels, a professor of population ethics and population health at the Harvard School of Public Health. Without such a tax-based system, "I don't think we can get the hardest-to-cover covered," because the market will always price some low-income and chronically ill consumers out of insurance, he says.

Daniels says effective cost control depends on having some form of single payer. "Unless the premise is that we must cover everybody," the will to rein in costs simply doesn't exist.

Furthermore, most private insurers simply aren't big enough and "don't have the leverage" to successfully bargain with hospitals and drug companies for better prices, Daniels says.

The United States "did not start becoming an extreme outlier [on the high cost side] until the 1980s," when government attempts at controlling costs were dropped in favor of a free-market approach, says Stan Dorn, a senior research associate at the nonpartisan Urban Institute think tank. "From then on our costs began growing at a much faster rate than in other countries. . . . Our motto is, 'Let's make as much money as possible on health care, whether it helps health care or not.' "

"There is more market competition in U.S. health care than in any other country [most of which have single payer systems], so if market competition is the answer [to cost control, as conservatives argue], why are our prices twice as high?" Daniels asks.

Should reform include a publicly run health insurance plan?

In the past, efforts to expand health-insurance coverage have focused on either improving the private insurance market — such as by making it easier for people to buy into a former employer's coverage temporarily during a job change — or launching a stand-alone public program like SCHIP (State Children's Health Insurance Program) to cover a particular population.

In 2009, however, many Democrats back a new and unusual amalgam of the two approaches — implementation of regulated markets where people can shop for coverage offered by both private insurers and a new public insurance program.

The public-plan option is "neither single payer nor private, and it's come out of the woodwork to quickly become a rallying cry for the left and a hate symbol for the right," says Stuart Altman, a professor of national health policy at Brandeis University and a former deputy assistant secretary for health planning under President Richard M. Nixon.

"The need for greater competition is why I proposed" a public-plan option, says Jacob Hacker, the Yale University professor of political science who is the chief architect of the idea. "The health-insurance market has become so consolidated that we need competition, and a public plan could supply that and be one of the game changers to bring down costs."

In our market-based system, "effective competition requires many competitors on both sides of the market, and that just simply is fading away" as health insurers consolidate, said John Holahan, director of the Health Policy Research Center at the Urban Institute. Adding a public plan to the mix could help create competition, he says. Many insurers have little incentive to be tough negotiators because they themselves have few or no competitors to whom dissatisfied enrollees could switch, he explains. "Without effective competition . . . we just have . . . growth in costs . . . that we all know we can't sustain." [18]

A public plan could join with Medicare to implement reimbursement rules encouraging more cost-efficient care, Hacker suggests. Because of the combined size of the programs, cost-saving measures would quickly spread through the system. Both Medicare and private insurers reimburse the same doctors and hospitals.

To those who argue that a public plan might have unfair competitive advantages, Hacker responds that no market requires "competitors to be equal but [only] that they have an equal chance to succeed if they are equally good at doing what consumers want." [19]

A public plan is a scary option only for those who don't like Medicare, said Dean: "It's what . . . your grandparents and your parents have had for years," and are generally happy with. [20]

A public plan would have lower administrative costs than private plans, although not as low as some advocates believe, said Holahan. The best estimates put Medicare administrative costs at 6 to 11 percent lower than private insurers' costs, he said. [21]

Holahan argues that checks and balances would prevent a public plan from trimming providers' pay too much. The federal Medicare Payment Advisory Commission (MedPAC) would likely oversee quality in a new public plan, as it does now for Medicare. Furthermore, "providers do and will lobby the Congress if rates are unfairly reduced," he said. Finally, since there would be public-private competition, consumers could switch to a private plan if they don't have access to the providers they want, which would impose "a real constraint" on any attempts to ride roughshod over providers. [22]

But many conservatives argue that the public option would not improve care or cut costs and could put private insurers out of business.

Under a public plan, "we could arbitrarily reduce costs by paying less for things," but until much better ways are developed to monitor the quality of care, paying less would simply lead to lower quality, says Tom Miller, a resident fellow at the conservative American Enterprise Institute.

"Under a new government-run plan, Americans will find it more and more difficult to make appointments with physicians" because "lower payments will make it increasingly unaffordable for providers to see" them, said the Senate Republican Policy Committee. [23]

"Government health care creates a great deal of misperception about who's responsible for paying the bill," and "resource consumption increases when people think somebody else is shouldering the cost," said Donald P. Condit, an orthopedic surgeon and blogger for the Grand Rapids, Mich.-based Acton Institute think tank, which supports conservative political and religious principles. As a result, patients would visit doctors more often and costs would rise. [24]

With a public plan in the mix, "there's no way to run a side-by-side competition" that would be fair to private insurers, said Karen Ignagni, chief executive of the health-insurance lobby America's Health Insurance Plans (AHIP). [25] With public payers able to negotiate more aggressively for low costs, more and more people would end up in the public-option plan because it would be cheaper, and eventually "there would be very little left of the private system." [26]

Private insurers often end up being charged higher rates by doctors and hospitals who "shift those costs" to private insurers by charging them more than the government pays for the same services, explained Ignagni. With another public plan for working-age people, providers could shift fewer costs to the private sector, so they would have much less money coming in, she said. "The major flagship hospitals would be losing a very significant amount of money, and there is a great deal of doubt about whether they [could] survive." [27]

"A new public insurance plan to compete with private health plans . . . is a Trojan horse for government control and the progressive destruction of Americans' private . . . coverage," as more people shifted into what would almost certainly be a lower-cost option, said Robert E. Moffitt, director of health-policy studies at the Heritage Foundation. That would lead to a "highly regulated and painfully sluggish centrally controlled system of health care." [28]

Some conservatives argue that today's health-system deficiencies are rooted in the government's first forays into providing health coverage with Medicare and Medicaid. In 1965 it created government-subsidized insurance for the poor (Medicaid) and the elderly and disabled (Medicare) because private insurers were not offering them affordable coverage.

"You could certainly argue that government should have never gotten in the health-care business," said Rep. Roy Blunt, R-Mo. "Government already distorts the marketplace," and government programs have kept the nation from creating "the competitive marketplace that I'd like to see put in place." [29]

Would universal coverage be too expensive?

A top goal of Democrats' health-care plans is to get everyone covered by health insurance. Despite the existence of Medicare and Medicaid, more than 45 million Americans today lack health insurance. Meanwhile, health costs that

Sen. Edward M. Kennedy, D-Mass., shown in January at the Capitol, died of brain cancer on Aug. 26. During his 46 years in the Senate, he was an unrelenting champion of health-care reform that would provide all Americans with reliable, affordable health insurance.

rise far more steeply than the gross domestic product (GDP) threaten to price even more people out of coverage.

Critics of the plans, however, say that the federal budget deficit is already too high and the economy too weak to justify additional taxes or raising the deficit further.

"This is about the woman in Colorado who paid $700 a month to her insurance company only to find out that they wouldn't pay a dime for her cancer treatment," said Obama in a July 22 press conference. "This is about the middle-class college graduate from Maryland whose health insurance expired when he changed jobs and who woke up from emergency surgery that" saddled him "with $10,000 worth of debt." [30]

When it comes to potential ways to pay for universal coverage, "the fundamental issue is, 'Will those of us who are doing OK continue to take what we get now while others suffer, or will we be willing to give something up?' " says Pamela Farley Short, a professor of health policy and administration at Yale University. "It's basically a moral and a political issue" since the money to expand coverage exists, but it's currently being put to different purposes, she says.

"If Canada, England, France and every other developed nation in the world can afford it, it's . . . laughable to suggest that it's too expensive for America," wrote Gerald E. Scorse, a New York-based member of Responsible Wealth, an advocacy group for corporate responsibility and progressive taxes whose members include only people with personal wealth in the top 5 percent nationally. [31]

Earlier this summer, when the nonpartisan Congressional Budget Office (CBO) estimated the cost to the government of a pending bill at $1.6 trillion over 10 years, many conservative commentators declared the effort was just too expensive. But proponents say that, taken in context, the number isn't as extreme as it appears.

While the price seems daunting on the surface, it amounts to "less than 1 percent" of our gross domestic product (GDP) over that period, said Urban Institute analysts Linda J. Blumberg and John Holahan. Furthermore, other government costs would be significantly reduced if coverage were expanded, they said. "For example, multiple threads of federal and state spending currently devoted to financing uncompensated care" — services hospitals provide free to uninsured people

Getty Images/Chip Somodevilla

— "could be reduced substantially, if not eliminated," cutting the bill's total 10-year cost to about $1.2 trillion, a 3.5 percent increase in overall projected government health spending. [32]

Higher government spending would also be offset by "private savings to employers and individuals resulting from reform," Blumberg and Holahan argued. Some small businesses and individuals, especially people with chronic or pre-existing illnesses, would get their insurance much cheaper under a reformed system, for example. [33]

Proponents say universal coverage could be financed using a variety of methods, including various taxes and cost reductions in programs like Medicare.

"Changing the tax treatment of health insurance could be one of the best ways to raise revenue," says Katherine Baicker, a professor of health economics at the Harvard School of Public Health. Because the tax break for employer-provided health insurance benefits is not capped, "We subsidize an unlimited benefit," she says. The tax break therefore goes mainly to high-income people, for whom companies are willing to provide extremely generous health-insurance packages.

One House proposal — raising taxes for households earning more than $350,000 a year — is not nearly as onerous as critics claim because it would amount to only a partial reversal of major tax cuts those households received during the Bush administration, proponents say. The 2001 and 2003 tax cuts gave these families $715 billion in tax breaks over 10 years. The proposed surtax would raise about $544 billion over the same period, said Patrick Garofalo, an economics researcher for the liberal Center for American Progress. [34]

Current proposals would also implement reimbursement and medical-practice changes that will save money for the whole system down the line, says David Cutler, a professor of applied economics at Harvard University. "Evidence is increasing that the amount . . . we can save" by such means "is enormous."

Not all advocates of coverage expansion endorse every potential tax proposal to pay for it, however.

Taxing "Cadillac" employer-based health coverage, in particular, could do serious unintentional harm, said Merrill Goozner, a journalist and author of the 2004 book *The $800 Million Pill: The Truth Behind the Cost of New Drugs*. While some employer insurance plans are expensive because they offer overly generous benefits, most plans that would be taxed have high premiums because the firm s are located in high health-care-cost regions or because they employ older or unhealthier people, said Goozner. Taxing those plans would be unfair, he argued. [35]

Many conservatives argue that lack of health-insurance coverage is not a big enough problem to warrant the expense involved.

"Of all the people who are uninsured today, less than half will be uninsured a year from now," and "less than one in 10 will be uninsured two years from now," said Goodman of the National Center for Policy Analysis. [36]

"Although the president claims he can finance" universal coverage "by raising taxes only on high-income individuals . . . tax experts know that this won't work," said Harvard University professor of economics Martin Feldstein. "Raising the top income-tax rate from 35 percent today to more than 45 percent — the effect of adding the proposed health [tax] to the increase resulting from letting the Bush tax cuts expire for high-income taxpayers — would change the behavior of high-income individuals in ways that would shrink their taxable incomes and therefore produce less revenue," he said That would lead to larger deficits and, eventually, "higher taxes on the middle class." [37]

Countries with universal health care generally have much higher taxes than the United States, which harms them economically, said Shikha Dalmia, an analyst at the libertarian Reason Foundation. "America's 2007 [income] taxation rate was 28.3 percent of GDP; Canada's was 33.3 percent; Germany's 36.2 percent; England's 36.6 percent and France's 43.6 percent," Dalmia said. Meanwhile, since "there is no major industrialized economy with universal coverage that has performed as well as — let alone better than — the United States in the last decade . . . there is zero evidence that [universal coverage] has put them on a more solid footing." [38]

The proposed taxes would be "onerous during a recession," said Rep. Dave Camp, R-Mich. "They're going to fall on families, small businesses, manufacturers — and they're going to cost us millions of jobs." [39]

"This bill is so expensive it will literally bankrupt states," said Sen. Lamar Alexander, R-Tenn., referring to legislation proposed by the late Sen. Kennedy's Senate Health, Education, Labor and Pensions Committee. "Just the expansion of Medicaid in the bill could cost Tennessee $1.2 billion a year by 2015." [40]

"I don't like the idea of raising taxes in the worst economic crisis since World War II," said Arkansas Rep. Mike Ross, one of the conservative "Blue Dog" Democrats who oppose many reform proposals. [42]   ∎

BACKGROUND

Private America

Only in the late 19th century did medical treatment become developed enough — and thus expensive enough — to require special financing to help people pay for it. Germany

Continued on p. 704

Chronology

1880s-1930s

As health care grows more expensive, nations around the world consider national insurance systems, and some large U.S. industries begin contracting with insurance companies to cover their workers.

1883
Germany creates the first universal health-care system.

1920
Expert panels in California, New Jersey, Ohio and New York recommend universal and state-sponsored health insurance.

———— • ————

1940s-1950s

Industrialized countries begin adopting universal-coverage systems. Congress rejects President Harry S Truman's single-payer proposal.

1943
National War Labor Board declares employer contributions for health insurance as tax free, allowing companies to offer health-insurance packages instead of higher wages to attract workers.

1946
United Kingdom launches National Health Service, a fully nationalized universal coverage system.

1948
President Truman's National Health Insurance initiative fails after the American Medical Association criticizes it, and some Republicans compare it to communism.

1960s-1990s

As costs rise, millions of Americans remain uninsured, spurring several presidents to propose expanding coverage. Newly industrializing nations begin adopting universal coverage.

1965
President Lyndon B. Johnson signs Medicare and Medicaid bills into law.

1971
President Richard M. Nixon places wage and price controls on medical services and proposes a universal-coverage plan.

1988
Brazil adopts universal health coverage.

1993
President Bill Clinton proposes health-system reforms based on recommendations from a committee headed by his wife, Hillary, now the secretary of State. The plan features a compromise between government price controls and private-sector competition among insurers, but it is quickly defeated by opposition from the health-care industry and employers who fear new costs. . . . Colombia launches incremental efforts to provide universal health coverage.

1995
Israel enacts compulsory universal health coverage. . . . Taiwan enacts compulsory single-payer plan.

1997
Congress enacts State Children's Health Insurance Program (SCHIP) to help states provide public insurance for low-income kids.

2000s
Health-care reform gets little attention from Washington for most of the decade, even as costs rise steeply and the ranks of uninsured Americans grow.

2001
Thailand implements universal coverage.

2006
Vermont enacts voluntary coverage with subsidized insurance and cost trimming. . . . Federal court strikes down Maryland plan to force large employers to supply coverage or pay into a state pool.

2007
Massachusetts requires all residents to purchase health insurance beginning on July 1.

2009
Mexico implements universal coverage for all pregnant women. Peru enacts universal health-care program. . . . Connecticut legislators override Republican Gov. Jodi Rell's veto of a bill to make health coverage available to all state residents regardless of age, health status or employment. . . . Massachusetts officials consider "payment bundling" — paying doctors and hospitals a flat fee upfront to cover patients — in order to control cost growth in their universal coverage plan. . . . President Obama and congressional Democrats try to push coverage-expansion legislation through Congress in the face of growing opposition from conservative commentators and law makers, as well as angry citizens at town hall meetings across the country. . . . Health-care reform advocate Sen. Edward M. Kennedy, D-Mass., dies at 77 of brain cancer on Aug. 26.

Low-Income Workers and the Young Still Not Covered

Last hurdle to universal coverage is hardest to overcome.

Perhaps the biggest hurdle the country faces in reforming health care is the fact that the easy-to-cover populations are already covered.

Lawmakers decided in the 1960s that the disabled, the very poor and many of the elderly were being priced out of the private insurance market, so those groups were offered special government-run programs — Medicare and Medicaid. Since then, Congress has added coverage for some children of low-income parents — the State Children's Health Insurance Program (SCHIP) — and has attempted some other reforms, such as making health insurance more "portable" for job changers.

However, a significant coverage gap persists: specifically young adults and low-income working-age people. "The gap that's left is the hardest to cover," says Norman Daniels, a professor of population ethics at Harvard's School of Public Health.

Companies with low-wage workers often don't offer health coverage because current premium prices are huge relative to wages. The typical family health-insurance premium costs $13,446 — a whopping 37 percent of the total annual income of a family earning $36,630 a year, which is double the federal poverty level. And many young people don't buy insurance because they would rather spend their limited funds on other priorities.

Lower-wage earners could buy a "catastrophic" or "high-deductible" insurance, which covers a large share of the tab if a serious accident or illness strikes. Those plans have lower premiums but higher deductibles — typically $1,000 — so the consumer must make sure they have money in the bank to pay the deductible, which can be a stretch for new graduates or other low-income people, said Cheryl Fish-Parcham, deputy director for health policy at the advocacy group Families USA. [1]

The most important goal for reform legislation is to "subsidize low-income people's access to insurance," says Stan Dorn, a senior research associate at the nonpartisan Urban Institute. By 2008, a family health insurance policy costs as much as a minimum-wage worker earns in a year, and "the situation becomes increasingly unsustainable" as costs continue to rise.

Low-income families also face fluctuating income, says Dorn. Typical proposals in today's health-market reform plans would open Medicaid only to the lowest-income people and then subsidize employer-provided coverage for those at a slightly higher level. That risks "ping-ponging people back and forth between programs," creating gaps in their care, he says.

For years, many conservative commentators recommended handling coverage expansion through special regulated health-insurance markets known as exchanges, like the Federal Employee Health Benefit (FEHB) program. Although most Democratic plans feature various types of exchanges, some conservatives now caution against them.

Unlike the typical uninsured person, federal employees "are typically well paid," healthy enough to hold down steady jobs

Continued from p. 702

created the first national health-care financing system in 1883, when it added health care to an existing "social insurance" system — in which citizens contribute to a common fund that offers population-wide benefits. [43]

Over the past century, most industrialized countries have launched health coverage for all by "pooling" risk — i.e., requiring residents to make regular payments into a national insurance system. By means of such a "risk pool," the cost of illness or injury, which for most people is both temporary and highly unpredictable, is spread across the entire population — only a few of whom are ill at one time — and across one's lifetime. Such "risk spreading" protects the sick and injured from the added hardship of high medical bills when they are suffering.

Today, every wealthy industrialized nation except the United States mandates universal health coverage paid wholly or in part by taxes. In the past two decades, several newly industrialized, middle-income countries, such as Thailand and South Korea, also have launched universal insurance. Only the United Kingdom and a few other countries, however, have "socialized medicine," in which the government owns hospitals and employs physicians. Often, including in the U.K., private insurers supplement the public coverage. (*See sidebar, above.*)

Most Americans buy coverage from private, for-profit companies, usually through their employers, and health risk and payments are pooled on an employer-by-employer basis rather than nationally or regionally. The U.S. system reflects the nation's strong belief in the virtues of private-sector markets.

But the system is not without flaws — mainly the failure to offer affordable coverage for poorer or sicker patients. A succession of presidents have attempted to fix that flaw.

Since World War II, however, only President Harry S Truman (1945-53) has proposed an all-public plan for universal coverage, says Robert Blendon, a professor of health policy and political analysis at the Harvard School of Public Health.

In the late 1940s, Truman pushed for adoption of mandatory, tax-supported national universal coverage. At the time, "the need and probably public support for reform was greater than at any other time" in history, with about half of all Americans uninsured, Blendon says.

But despite apparently favorable circumstances, "extreme wariness about socialism and communism" doomed

and "believe in insurance," notes Joseph Antos, a scholar at the American Enterprise Institute. By contrast, uninsured people often have low incomes, some level of disability or chronic illness or may prefer to spend their limited money on things other than health care. "So, short of subsidizing people to 100 percent," it would be hard to get the uninsured to buy into a FEHB-like system, he says.

The private insurance market is also reluctant to cover children with disabilities, says Dorn. Private insurers often refuse speech therapy, for example, on the grounds that it is not healing an illness when it's provided for a child who has never spoken, he says. Yet Medicaid and SCHIP do pay for such care, because they cover high numbers of disabled children.

Self-employed people and employees of small businesses face extremely high premiums because each individual or small group must shoulder its own health risk. Companies charge each group based on the worst-case illness or injury scenario in a given year. Larger employers, can "pool" each year's risks across the workforce. Since only a few people are likely to be ill in any given year, the group's healthy members subsidize care for the sick, keeping premiums lower in large companies.

But "any health-care reform provision that relies exclusively on maintaining the current employer-sponsored health-insurance system will not be as relevant for rural areas," because those areas have many very small businesses and self-employed people,

said Jon M. Bailey, director for research and analysis at the Center for Rural Affairs in Lyons, Neb.[2]

People with a chronic illness or previous serious illness also have difficulty finding insurance.

"The top priority of for-profit companies is to drive up the value of their stock," primarily by controlling medical costs, former insurance executive Wendell Potter told the Senate Committee on Commerce, Science, and Transportation in June. "Even very profitable companies can see sharp declines in stock prices moments after admitting they've failed to trim medical costs." [3]

Consequently, Potter said, insurers "routinely dump" policyholders who get sick or small businesses with high medical claims. When executives of three of the nation's largest health insurance companies were asked about this practice by the House Energy and Commerce Committee, they refused to end the practice of canceling policies for sick enrollees . . . because dumping a small number . . . can have a big effect on the bottom line," said Potter.[4]

---

[1] Quoted in Michelle Walbaum, "Congratulations on Graduating. Now Go Get Health Insurance," *USA Today,* July 16, 2009, http://usatoday.com.

[2] Jon M. Bailey, "The Top 10 Rural Issues for Health Care Reform," Center for Rural Affairs, March 2009, www.cfra.org.

[3] Testimony before Senate Committee on Commerce, Science and Transportation, June 24, 2009, http://voices.washingtonpost.com/ezra-klein/Potter%20Commerce%20Committee%20written%20testimony%20-%2020090624-%20FINAL.pdf.

[4] *Ibid.*

Truman's effort, says Blendon. Employers and unions were generally happy with the developing private insurance system, and the powerful American Medical Association (AMA), fearing government constraints on physicians under a public plan, strongly — though inaccurately — condemned Truman's proposal as "socialized medicine." Ultimately, Congress let the plan die in committee.

Closing the Gaps

Convinced by Truman's failure that universal public coverage wouldn't fly, subsequent administrations have proposed "public-private" initiatives, reserving public programs for particular populations difficult to cover by private means, Blendon says. "Presidents have too many memories of Truman getting beaten up"

to propose public universal coverage again, he says.

Nevertheless, as early as the 1950s it became clear that private insurance was not reaching many elderly people, ironically the very population that needs it most. Some insurers sold individual health-insurance policies, but the individual market generally does not "pool" risks, so policies for sicker people were prohibitively expensive.

In 1950, two-thirds of Americans over age 65 had incomes of less than $1,000 a year, and only one in eight had health insurance, according to an official history posted on the Social Security Administration Web site. "Old people were long considered 'bad risks' by commercial insurers, and unions had not made much headway in obtaining coverage for retired workers through employer-sponsored plans." [44]

As a result, the idea of offering public coverage to Social Security beneficiaries began brewing in Washington in the late 1940s — about the same time that proposals for universal public coverage were abandoned. By 1956, Congress had appointed a Special Committee on Aging to investigate problems of the elderly, including health coverage, and lawmakers were hotly debating whether to add permanently disabled people over age 50 to the list of those eligible for Social Security benefits. [45]

The proposal to extend Social Security to the disabled was enacted in 1956 over the strenuous objections of the AMA, which feared public payments to the disabled would open the door to government interference with medical practice. Enactment encouraged advocates to renew the push for

Other Countries Spend Less, Get Better Results

U.S. lags far behind other nations with universal health care.

The United States is the only industrialized country without some form of government-financed universal health coverage. But while some analysts say it's astonishing that U.S leaders don't pay more attention to international experience, free-market advocates say increased government involvement would greatly hinder Americans' freedom of choice.

"Among the industrialized countries, it wouldn't matter whom we imitated, because they're all doing better than we are," declares Pauline Rosenau, a professor of management, policy and community health at the University of Texas School of Public Health in Houston.

"Countries do fairly diverse things" to control costs, but the two things they all have in common are "having everybody in the system and making some attempt to budget," says Jacob Hacker, a Yale University professor of political science. The U.S. failure to do the former is "a moral disaster," while failure in the latter is "an economic disaster" that has allowed health costs to spiral far higher than in other nations, he says.

Even middle-income and emerging economies are adopting universal health coverage, note David Hughes, a professor of health research at Swansea University in Wales, and Songkramchai Leethongdee, an assistant professor of public health at Mahasarakham University in Thailand. "The income threshold at which countries are achieving universal coverage is getting lower," they pointed out. Countries like South Korea, Peru and Brazil all have some form of universal care, and Thailand has universal coverage with a "relatively comprehensive benefit package."[1]

Not only do other countries cover all their citizens, but they do it while spend significantly less money than the United States spends to provide only partial coverage. The Organisation for Economic Co-operation and Development (OECD) reports that the United States spent $7,290 per person on health care in 2007, while the next biggest spenders — Norway and Switzerland — spent about 40 percent less while providing universal coverage.[2]

And for all its higher spending, the United States lags far behind France, Canada, Germany and the United Kingdom in overall life expectancy and health status.[3] A recent survey found "far more Americans [with serious chronic illnesses] . . . forgoing health care because of cost" than patients in Australia,

Canada, France, Germany, the Netherlands, New Zealand and the United Kingdom, points out Peter Singer, a Princeton University professor of bioethics. Fifty-four percent of the respondents said they hadn't filled a prescription, visited a doctor when sick or followed recommended care, compared to just 13 percent in the U.K. and 7 percent in the Netherlands.[4]

Health insurance systems around the world vary enormously, but they all embrace an explicit national commitment to insure all, or nearly all, residents and endorse a health-care budget process centered on that commitment.

In some countries, government is the "single payer," functioning like a U.S. private insurer. In others, the government collects revenues and sets rules, but private insurers do the health-care purchasing. The U.K. is the only Western European government that owns hospitals and employs doctors directly.

International experience demonstrates that under the right conditions, private insurers can provide universal coverage and control costs, according to Uwe E. Reinhardt, a Princeton professor of political economy. Germany, the Netherlands and Switzerland "all rely on purely private, nonprofit or for-profit insurers that are guided by tight regulations to work toward socially desired ends. And they do so at average per-capita health costs far below those of the United States" — less than half as high in Germany and the Netherlands, Reinhardt says.

To make such a system work, however, insurers must accept much stricter regulation; the nation must make an explicit commitment to insuring its entire population and insurers must share risk with each other, rather than competing to get lower-risk patients as the U.S. system encourages today, Reinhardt said.[5]

In Germany, everyone must buy health insurance; taxes subsidize premiums based on families' income level and the government collects all premiums in a national pool. The government then divvies the money out to insurers based on the relative health risks of their enrollees, Reinhardt explained. Enacting such a plan would be difficult in the United States, however, because many Americans object to mandated coverage, and the country's insurers might object to "acting as purchasing agents on behalf of the central fund and patients."[6]

Switzerland and the Netherlands have multiple insurers in their

---

coverage for the elderly, and in 1957 Rep. Aime J. Forand, D-R.I., introduced legislation.[46]

Thus began the battle for Medicare — tax-supported health coverage for the elderly. Among those lobbying hard for it was the newly merged AFL-CIO, the country's largest labor union coalition, with 14 million members.[47]

The AMA strongly opposed enactment, as did the U.S. Chamber of Commerce, the National Association of Manufacturers, the Pharmaceutical Manufacturers Association and a new health-insurance lobby — the Health Insurance Association of America. The American Hospital Association (AHA), was torn, partly fearing increased gov-

ernment interference but worried that elderly, uninsured patients showing up in emergency rooms could bankrupt hospitals.[48]

Conservative lawmakers fought hard against Medicare, arguing that private markets were far superior. "I was there, fighting the fight, voting against Medicare . . . because we knew it

universal programs, including publicly traded, for-profit insurers, says Rosenau. But while U.S. insurers earn their profits by competing to avoid sick enrollees, "both countries have large risk pools" that extend to all the insurers, she explains. If one insurer ends up with more sick people than others, "they get compensated" more from the overall budget. In other words, insurers have a financial incentive to enroll and procure good care for sicker people, rather than a financial incentive to avoid them. "I wonder why U.S. insurers aren't screaming for this," she says.

Many Americans also fear universal coverage because they think it would mean health-care rationing — especially targeting the elderly. That's simply not true, said John Bruton, the European Union's ambassador to the United States. "I know of no European country where people would be denied a hip replacement," for example, "simply because they were too old," Bruton said. "My late mother had a hip replacement in her 80s. It all depends on one's capacity to withstand the trauma of the anesthetic and the surgery, not on age or the expense of the operation." [7]

Such contentions are hotly debated among U.S. conservatives and some in the health-care industry, who say universal-coverage programs would impinge on personal freedoms to an intolerable extent.

In France, for example, "the government recently began imposing restrictions on access to physicians," urging patients to choose a "preferred doctor as a care 'gatekeeper' who limits access to spe-

cialists, tests and some advanced treatment options," wrote Michael Tanner, director of Health and Welfare Studies at the libertarian Cato Institute. In Norway, as well, "citizens must choose a general practitioner (GP)" who "acts as a gatekeeper for other services" and can switch GPs no more than twice a year. [8]

"If U.S. policy makers can take one lesson from national health-care systems around the world, it is not to follow the road to government-run national health care but to increase consumer incentives and control," Tanner says. [9]

[1] David Hughes and Songkramchai Leethongdee, "Universal Coverage from The Land of Smiles: Lessons from Thailand's 30 Baht Health Reforms," *Health Affairs*, July/August 2007, pp. 999-1008.

[2] "OECD Health Data 2009," Organisation for Economic Co-operation and Development, June 2009, www.oecd. org/document/30/0,3343,en_2649_346 31_12968734_1_1_1_37407,00.html.

[3] Gerard F. Anderson and Patrician Markovich, "Multinational Comparisons of Health Systems Data," The Commonwealth Fund, November 2008.

[4] Peter Singer, "Why We Must Ration Health Care," *The New York Times Magazine*, July 19, 2009, p. MM38.

[5] Uwe E. Reinhardt, "Health Reform Without a Public Plan: The German Model," Economix blogs, *The New York Times*, April 17, 2009, http://economix. blogs.nytimes.com.

[6] *Ibid.*

[7] John Bruton, "The Healthcare Debate," Weekly Message, European American Chamber of Commerce New York, July 14, 2009, www.eaccny.com/index. php?id=867.

[8] Michael Tanner, "The Grass Is Not Always Greener: A Look at National Health Care Systems Around the World," Policy Analysis No. 613, Cato Institute, March 18, 2008.

[9] *Ibid.*

wouldn't work in 1965," said Sen. Robert Dole, R-Kan., during his 1996 presidential campaign. He was one of 12 House members who voted against Medicare's creation. [49]

After eight years of debate, on July 30, 1965, President Lyndon B. Johnson, a longtime proponent, signed the program into law, giving public

coverage to 19 million elderly Americans. Seated next to Johnson at the signing was 81-year-old former President Truman. After the signing, Johnson presented Truman with the first Medicare card ever issued. Medicaid, the tax-supported public coverage program for some poor families, was created in the same legislation. [50]

Coverage Gaps Persist

A significant percentage of Americans received health coverage under the 1965 law, but rising costs and, for some, a decision not to buy insurance, left many without coverage.

The gap prompted President Nixon, a Republican, to try to expand coverage. His Comprehensive Health Insurance Act of 1974 would have required most employers to offer private coverage and provided a public plan for low-income families, with premiums subsidized according to income level. Universal public coverage "is not the way we do things here in America," Nixon declared. [51]

Nixon also backed establishment of health maintenance organizations, or HMOs, in hope that reimbursing doctors and hospitals on an annual basis for all care, rather than paying them for each treatment, could hold down costs.

When the Watergate scandal threatened a quick end to Nixon's presidency, however, liberal groups, along with unions, pressed congressional Democrats to abandon the proposal in hopes of getting public universal coverage under the next — presumably Democratic — administration. [52]

Vice President Gerald R. Ford, who finished Nixon's term after his resignation, proposed universal coverage and price controls for health care, as did Democratic President Jimmy Carter, elected in 1976. But Carter's single term was plagued by too many competing problems for health-care reform to rise on the agenda, and starting in 1981 Republicans who were uninterested in a health-care overhaul held the White House for 12 years.

When Democratic President Bill Clinton took office in 1993, health costs had been rising much faster than GDP for decades, and nearly 40 million people — more than 15 percent of the population — were uninsured. Another 69 million had subsidized government coverage through Medicare, Medicaid and the military. [53]

In the beginning of Clinton's term, Democrats held both houses of Congress, a rare occurrence that seemed to bode well for coverage expansion, says Blendon. However, Washington was well aware that Clinton had won election

with only 43 percent of the vote — third-party candidate Ross Perot had garnered 19 percent — undercutting Clinton's political power.

Nevertheless, Clinton proposed a plan for near-universal coverage through improved regulation of private insurance. The complicated plan was developed by a panel headed by then f irst lady Hillary Rodham Clinton. It required individuals to buy insurance and employers to cover their workers, while regulated regional "insurance exchanges" would facilitate the marketing of health plans with standardized benefit packages to make comparison shopping easy. But despite the plan's focus on market forces, insurers, pharmaceutical companies, the AMA and others quickly criticized it as overregulation of medicine, and Congress never voted on it. [54]

The ranks of the uninsured continued to grow, however, and in 1997 Clinton and a bipartisan congressional coalition enacted SCHIP to cover children in low-income families. [55]

When George W. Bush campaigned for the presidency in 2000, he said he would focus on increasing access to care rather than on broadening insurance coverage, beefing up funding for public clinics to provide primary — but not specialty — care. Bush ultimately doubled funding for community health centers but vetoed several attempts to expand SCHIP.

Frustrated by the continued rise in the ranks of the uninsured, several states — and San Francisco — launched universal-coverage systems. For example Maryland, North Carolina, Pennsylvania, Ohio and West Virginia have implemented subsidies, tax credits and other programs to help small-business owners offer coverage to their workers. [56]

In the highest-profile effort, Massachusetts in 2005 enacted a universal-coverage plan requiring residents to buy state-subsidized insurance and regulating the market to help people find affordable coverage. [57]

"The experience of Massachusetts has really changed the nature of the political debate," says Yale's Short. "We can look at them and say, 'They pulled it off.' There are issues of cost now, of course, but, still, they made it happen." And, with the state in 2009 taking a hard look at major reimbursement-system changes, "it may be that once you've got universal coverage, it becomes a little easier to see what to do" about costs, she says. ∎

CURRENT SITUATION

Democratic Majority

Congress and the White House are undertaking the first significant health-insurance overhaul since the Clinton plan failed in the early 1990s. And for the first time in 60 years, this year's debate involves a public-coverage option for most Americans, says Harvard's Blendon.

Nevertheless, with Democrats controlling both the White House and Congress, advocates of single-payer coverage had hoped for more. Market tinkering and the creation of small, specialized government-coverage programs, such as SCHIP, have been repeatedly tried and failed to cover all the uninsured or hold down costs, says pediatrician Flowers of Physicians for a National Health Program. "Why do we think it's going to be any different now?"

But many policy analysts say a single-payer system is simply a non-starter today because the current system is too entrenched.

"If we were starting from scratch, it would be completely different," says Yale's Short. Many of the changes required to create a single-

Continued on p. 710

At Issue:

Should government ration health care?

DANIEL CALLAHAN
PRESIDENT EMERITUS,
THE HASTINGS CENTER

WRITTEN FOR *CQ RESEARCHER*, AUGUST 2009

*f*or at least 40 years — since the Nixon administration — our country has wrestled with the problem of rising health costs. Nothing has worked for long to control these expenses, now rising at an annual rate of 6 percent. At that pace, Medicare will be insolvent in eight years, and overall health-care costs will double in a decade. More than a few analysts have concluded that nothing less than sharp cuts in physician fees, hospital reimbursements, drug prices and insurance premiums, as well as a reduction in patient benefits, will seriously deal with rising costs.

Rationing will be necessary. We are near the end of the road on evasions and magic bullets to dodge that issue. Of course, the notion of rationing brings out the hives in most ' Americans. Liberals prefer to focus on eliminating inefficiency, and President Obama has asserted there will be no Medicare benefit cuts. Conservatives recommend more consumer choice and enhanced provider competition. Each set of proposals could help but likely is insufficient.

Neither side is willing to grasp a simple historical fact about modern scientific medicine, with medical progress and technological innovation as its core values. Those values produce better health and longer lives — great prizes. Yet the cost always rises, in great part because the war against disease and bodily decay enables partial victories only, notably the ability to keep chronically ill people alive longer than in the past, supported by costly technologies. Cancer is not being cured, but its victims live longer, not inexpensively, and the same is true of most other chronic diseases.

We will have to learn better how to live with that reality, to understand that limits to health care are necessary. We can not afford endlessly expensive progress. Concretely, that means we will have to accept rationing. Any other possibility is a delusion.

How might rationing be best and most fairly pursued? No present, politically acceptable pathway is discernible, but it is not hard to imagine what might work, acceptable or not. A strong government regulatory and price-control role is imperative, but no less so than a change in our personal aspirations for ever more health care. The latter goal is understandable. Who wants to get sick? Yet ever-rising aspirations are not compatible in the long run with affordable and sustainable health care. A good way to destroy our future health care is to avert our eyes from that unpleasant likelihood.

DEVON HERRICK
SENIOR FELLOW, NATIONAL CENTER FOR
POLICY ANALYSIS

WRITTEN FOR *CQ RESEARCHER*, AUGUST 2009

*a*ll scarce resources must be rationed. Health care is no exception. In most markets, goods and services are rationed using prices. Buyers are free to make trade-offs in terms of cost, quality and other amenities. Producers are always looking to repackage or reprise goods in ways that will entice a purchase.

However, health care is rationed using other means. Long before a patient enters a doctor's office, third parties have decided what they will pay for and how much they will pay. This is because patients do not control most of the dollars that pay for their care. If patients don't make the decisions about which medical services hold value, someone else will. That someone else is insurers, employers and, increasingly, government. As government expands its reach further into health care, it will increasingly make rationing decisions for patients.

For instance, the stimulus bill appropriated $1.1 billion to create a council charged with comparing the effectiveness of treatments, drugs and therapies. Never mind the fact that what works well for one patient may not work as well for another. Few people would object to better understanding the effectiveness of common treatments. But it's only a small step from comparing "effectiveness" to comparing "cost-effectiveness."

Instead of researching whether the red pill works better than the blue pill, bureaucrats will be tempted to compare how many more of the (cheaper) blue pills could be purchased if the red pill is eliminated. If this fails to control costs sufficiently, the temptation will be to emulate a policy used by the National Institute for Clinical Excellence (NICE) in Britain. NICE sets a value on a year of life, and those therapies that exceed that cost per life-year saved are not funded.

Another form of rationing, used by Canada, involves price controls where the government dictates an artificially low price on drug therapies. It declines to approve some therapies it deems redundant or not cost-effective. The prices paid for newer, more advanced drugs, are often closely tied to the older, less advanced drugs they replace. This leaves drug makers little incentive to develop newer therapies since the rewards are less lucrative.

When patients themselves control more of their own health-care dollars, they have more control over the medical services they receive. If consumers abdicate this responsibility to government, they also lose the rights that accompany it.

Continued from p. 708

payer system could arouse enormous public pushback, partly because few people understand how today's system actually works, Short says. For example, although economists say rising health-insurance premiums are mostly taken out of what would otherwise be workers' wage increases, many people believe their employers — not they — actually pay the insurance premiums, she says. That means many would fear a shift from the employer-based system would hurt them financially while "letting employers off the hook," she says.

Public Plan vs. Co-ops

The ultimate aim of all current proposals is both to extend insurance coverage to all Americans and begin reining in rampant cost growth that threatens to price health care out of the reach of all but the wealthiest.

Health costs have grown faster than the rest of the economy for decades, an unsustainable trend for any economic sector, says Michael Chernew, a professor of health-care policy at Harvard Medical School. "A higher percentage of our raises every year goes to health care," he explains.

A few decades from now, even as national income would continue to rise, "spending on everything but health care would actually have to begin dropping" year to year as ballooning health costs entirely outstripped the size of each year's total national income growth, he says.

By 2018, health-care spending will equal 20.3 percent of the national income, if it continues at the current pace. [58] A recent study by the Santa Monica, Calif.-based RAND Corporation found that due to skyrocketing costs, companies that provide health insurance cannot hire as many new workers or contribute as much to the nation's GDP as other comparable companies. [59]

In 2009, most pending reform plans have this general outline: Employer-based coverage would remain, but for Americans who don't have it, a new, regulated insurance market — often called an "exchange" — would facilitate competition under tightened federal rules between one government-run health plan and numerous private insurers. Leading House Democrats and the late Sen. Kennedy's Senate Health, Education, Labor and Pensions Committee favor adding an optional government-run plan. And the Democrats' control of Congress means legislation should pass even without Republican backing.

However, many conservative Democrats, including Senate Budget Committee Chairman Kent Conrad of North Dakota and Finance Committee Chairman Max Baucus of Montana, have serious reservations about the government-run option because its inclusion might drive private insurers out of business and would mean the bills could not garner bipartisan support.

As an alternative, Conrad suggests that nonprofit "consumer co-operative" insurance plans — which are owned by their members — could substitute for a government-run insurer.

Substituting co-ops for a public plan might win "broad bipartisan support," said Conrad. "Because these plans will be owned by their members, they will focus on getting the best value for consumers, rather than maximizing plan revenues or profits." [60]

The insurance industry, except for health insurance, has several longstanding co-operatives — the "mutual" insurers such as Mutual of Omaha and Northwestern Mutual — that prove co-ops can work in the marketplace, said a group of Heritage Foundation analysts led by senior research fellow Edmund F. Haislmaier. However, for co-ops to gain conservative backing the government would have to take a totally hands-off approach, he wrote. The co-ops must be regional, not national — as many Democrats propose

— and they must "not receive anti-competitive government support in any form," including start-up capital, subsidies or "access to government pricing." [61]

But co-op critics say regional health-insurance co-ops historically have been unable to compete with huge national insurers. To avoid financial catastrophe, they would need "a very large insurance pool" to spread costs, and that wouldn't be possible for regional plans with a slew of competitors, said former Democratic National Committee chairman Dean. [62]

"The co-operative landscape is . . . littered with failures," said Karen Davis, president of the New York-based Commonwealth Fund, which supports research on health access. "Group Health Association in Washington, D. C., for example, failed in the early 1990s after intense conflicts between consumer-led management and the medical group." [63]

The success of co-ops in other sectors, such as rural electricity distribution, isn't a good predictor of whether health-care co-ops could succeed because they can "leverage purchasing power to obtain lower rates," but health-care co-ops couldn't do that in an industry dominated by large companies, Davis suggested. [64]

If the aim is gaining bipartisan support, even introducing co-ops into the new insurance market exchanges might not help.

Although conservatives had long recommended insurance exchanges, they've now backed away from them. The new insurance exchange "sounds like a very wonderful, positive, benign thing, but in these bills it's used as a regulatory mechanism," and regulation itself destroys markets' ability to hold down costs and spur innovation, argues the American Enterprise Institute's Miller. The exchanges would simply be a way for the government to "rent the private system's infrastructure to get the benefit of public control."

Money Money Money

Many congressional critics of Democratic proposals focus on potential out-of-control costs.

The concern speaks directly to voters' anxieties, says Harvard's Blendon. Today, as in 1993, when the Clinton reforms failed, health care was the No. 2 public concern, after the economy. "If anything, the economy is a much bigger worry today," potentially making voters hyper-leery of tax hikes.

Much of the debate has focused on "scores" — 10-year estimates of various bills' effects on the federal budget — prepared by the CBO. Earlier this summer, the CBO estimated the cost to the government of one bill at $1.6 trillion over 10 years. Meanwhile, a proposal to trim government health spending by authorizing an expert panel to implement reimbursement changes and other cost-effectiveness measures would save only $2 billion over a decade. [65]

Conservatives are using those numbers to bolster their case.

"Your wallet will take a big hit" under any Democratic plan, said Bernadine Healy, health editor of *U.S. News & World Report* and a former director of the National Institutes of Health. "By law, you and your family will be required to have health insurance," and "taxpayers will also shell out whatever it takes to help those who can't afford coverage." [66]

But others say the estimates should be taken with more than a grain of salt.

Even a bill that included solid long-run cost-cutting provisions might get a CBO "score" that would dub it as high-cost, says Harvard's Baicker. "The types of things that are likely to control costs in the long run often won't cut costs in the short run" — thus, any savings they'd produce would be outside the five- or 10-year "budget window," she explains.

Even conservative analysts agree that cost-cutting measures are hard to estimate. Few have "been done widescale" so there's no way analysts can estimate how well they'd work if implemented nationally, says AEI resident fellow Gottlieb.

"The CBO's track record in predicting the effects of health legislation is abysmal," said Bruce Vladeck, a former chief of the Medicare and Medicaid agency and a senior adviser to the Greater New York Hospital Association's Nexera Consulting group. It overestimated the five-year cost of Medicare's prescription-drug benefit "by more than 35 percent. Even more dramatically, the CBO estimates of Medicare's savings from [cost-cutting measures in] the Balanced Budget Act of 1997 underestimated the impact, on average, by a full 100 percent. That's right; In the BBA's first three years, Medicare spending fell fully twice as fast as the CBO had projected." [67]

Some liberals are outraged that many members of Congress have focused so strongly on costs. "Recall that there was no discussion — zero — when the last administration asserted without any debate that we were engaged in a war without end, for which costs could not be measured nor should they be," fumed the prominent Santa Monica, Calif., author of the liberal blog Hullabaloo. "But when it comes to directly benefiting Americans with a life and death threat of another sort, that's all [they] talk about." [68]

"The real problem is politics. We don't have a lot of people lined up pushing for" coverage expansion, says Harvard's Daniels. Meanwhile, with providers and insurers in the approximately $2.5-trillion industry knowing that a commitment to covering everyone eventually will mean cutting costs, "just plain greed stands in the way." ■

OUTLOOK

Prognosis Uncertain

As Congress headed into its August recess without a vote on health reform in either chamber, opposition grew heated, with conservative protesters — some apparently backed by industry-funded groups and local Republican leaders — shouting down Democratic lawmakers at "town hall" meetings around the country.

Crowds chanting "Just say no" drowned out Rep. Lloyd Doggett, D-Texas, for example, as he spoke at a meeting in Austin on Aug. 1. [69] Rosemary Edwards, local GOP chairman, had urged in her blog that "all Patriot friends . . . SHOW UP, STAND UP and SPEAK UP!" and "BE LOUD!" [70]

"Tyranny! Tyranny! Tyranny!" shouted a crowd in Tampa, Fla., on Aug. 6 as Rep. Kathy Castor, tried to explain the Democrats' plans. [71]

However, it's unclear how widespread the protestors' views are. A national poll this summer found that, while public confusion over Democrats' reform plans persists, 76 percent of respondents still deemed it "extremely" or "quite" important to give people the choice of a private health insurer or a government-run plan. [72] Even a poll prepared for the Republic National Committee found that 58 percent of respondents favored "creating a government-run health insurance agency that will compete with private insurance companies." [73]

The legislative outcome is uncertain.

Some say the clock has already run out on a strong public-plan option, partly because of well organized industry opposition. The insurance industry "has already accomplished its main goal of at least curbing, and maybe blocking altogether, any new publicly administered insurance program that could grab market share from the corporations that dominate the business," concluded two *Business Week* reporters in an analysis of the industry's 2009 lobbying efforts. [74]

"The political calendar is now working against the president and Congress," since 2010 is an election year, when Congress is unlikely to enact major initiatives, says Miller of AEI. "This package will go down."

But Harvard's Blendon says it is unthinkable "that Congress will go home at the end of the year" without passing a bill, because Democrats know failure would seriously harm the party. "At the end of the day, there will be something." Democrats "will not give up the public plan until they take the vote and find out they're seven short" of Senate passage. Nevertheless, speed is of the essence, Blendon acknowledges. "The longer you debate it, the more Americans you lose, because whatever you do always has some pain for somebody." ■

Notes

[1] Quoted in Amy Goodman, "'They Dump the Sick to Satisfy Investors': Insurance Exec Turned Whistleblower Wendell Potter Speaks Out Against Healthcare Industry," "Democracy Now!" Pacifica Radio, July 16, 2009, www.democracynow.org.

[2] *Ibid.*

[3] *Ibid.*

[4] Quoted in "Death panel," "Schott's Vocab: A Miscellany of Modern Words and Phrases," *The New York Times,* Aug. 10, 2009, http://schott. blogs.nytimes.com/2009/08/10/death-panel.

[5] See Ezra Klein, "Is the Government Going to Euthanize Your Grandmother? An Interview with Sen. Johnny Isakson," Ezra Klein blog, *The Washington Post,* Aug. 10, 2009, http://voices.washingtonpost.com/ezra-klein/2009/08/is_the_government_going_to_eut.html.

[6] *Ibid.*

[7] "Health-Care Plan," MarketWatch Web site, June 20, 2009, www.marketwatch.com.

[8] Quoted in Joshua Holland, "Howard Dean: 'This Is Ridiculous, We're 60 Years Behind the Times' on Fixing Health Care," truthout/AlterNet blog, July 8, 2009, www.truthout.org.

[9] Paul Krugman, "Health Reform Made Simple," The Conscience of a Liberal blog, *The New York Times,* Aug. 1, 2009, http://krugman.blogs.nytimes.com/2009/08/01/health-reform-made-simple.

[10] *Ibid.*

[11] "Public Plan Option: Fair Competition or a Recipe for Crowd Out?" Briefing transcript, Alliance for Health Reform, April 27, 2009, www.allhealth.org/briefingmaterials/Transcript4-27Final-1455.pdf.

[12] Holland, *op. cit.*

[13] Deborah Solomon, "Questions for Howard Dean," *The New York Times,* July 12, 2009.

[14] David Hogberg, "The Myths of Single-Payer Health Care," www.freemarketcure.com.

[15] John Goodman, "Rationing Health Care," John Goodman's blog, National Center for Policy Analysis, July 22, 2009, www.johngoodman-blog.com.

[16] "The Fallacy of 'Rationing' — and Some Better Arguments Against Socialized Medicine," The Next Right, My 12, 2009, www.thenextright.com.

[17] Gloria Galloway, "Tory Senator Goes to Bat for Health Care," [Toronto] *Globe and Mail,* July 8, 2009, www.theglobeandmail.com.

[18] "Public Plan Option," *op. cit.*

[19] Igor Volsky, "Jacob Hacker: Stripping Away 'Inherent Advantages' From a Public Plan 'Is at Odds With True Competition,' " The Wonk Room

blog, Center for American Progress, April 9, 2009, http://wonkroom.thinkprogress.org.

[20] Holland, *op. cit.*

[21] "Public Plan Option," *op. cit.*

[22] *Ibid.*

[23] "A Government-Run 'Public' Health Insurance Plan: Why Doctors, Hospitals, and Patients Will Lose," U.S. Senate Republican Policy Committee, March 24, 2009, http://rpc.senate.gov.

[24] Donald P. Condit, "What's the Matter With Socialized Medicine?" Acton Commentary, Jan. 9, 2008, www.acton.org.

[25] Quoted in Reed Abelson, "A Health Plan for All and the Concerns It Raises," *The New York Times,* March 25, 2009, www.nytimes.com, p. B1.

[26] "Public Plan Option," *op. cit.*

[27] *Ibid.*

[28] Robert E. Moffitt, "How a Public Health Plan Will Erode Private Care," Backgrounder No. 2224, Heritage Foundation, Dec. 22, 2008, www.heritage.org.

[29] Quoted in "Roy Blunt: It Would Have Been 'Best' if Medicare and Medicaid Never Existed," Fired Up! Missouri blog, July 9, 2009, www.firedupmissouri.com.

[30] Rachel Slajda, "Transcript of Obama's Press Conference, July 22, 2009," Talking Points Memo, July 23, 2009, www.talkingpointsmemo.com.

[31] Gerald E. Scorse, "The GOP on Health Care: Double 'No'." Talking Points Memo blog, July 14, 2009, http://tpmcafe.talkingpointsmemo.com.

[32] Linda J. Blumberg and John Holahan, "Beyond the $1.6 Trillion Sticker Shock," Urban Institute/Robert Wood Johnson Foundation, July 2009, www.urban.org/UploadedPDF/411923_beyond_sticker_shock.pdf.

[33] *Ibid.*

[34] Pat Garofalo, "Blue Dogs Threatening to Quash Health Bill Over Surtax Voted for Bush Tax Cuts," Think Progress blog, Center for American Progress, July 15, 2009, http://thinkprogress.org.

[35] Merrill Goozner, "Taxing Benefits — A Lose-Lose Proposition," Gooznews blog, July 6, 2009, www.gooznews.com.

[36] John Goodman, "The 2-percent Solution," John Goodman's blog, National Center for Policy Analysis, July 20, 2009, www.john-goodman-blog.com.

[37] Martin Feldstein, "Obama's Plan Isn't the Answer," *The Washington Post,* July 28, 2009, www.washingtonpost.com.

[38] Shikha Dalmia, "Obama's Health Care Quackery," Reason online, Reason Foundation, May 7, 2009, www.reason.com.

[39] John Fritze, "House Dems' Health Bill

About the Author

Staff writer **Marcia Clemmitt** is a veteran social-policy reporter who previously served as editor in chief of *Medicine & Health* and staff writer for *The Scientist.* She has also been a high-school math and physics teacher. She holds a liberal arts and sciences degree from St. John's College, Annapolis, and a master's degree in English from Georgetown University. Her recent reports include "Preventing Cancer" and "Public-Works Projects."

Would Tax Rich," *USA Today*, July 15, 2009, www.usatoday.com.

40 Greg Johnson, "A Mountain View," *Knoxville* [Tennessee] *News*, http://blogs.knoxnews.com.

41 Ted Roelofs, "Obama's Health Care Plan Will Be 'Incredibly Expensive,' Ron Paul Tells East Grand Rapids Conservative Luncheon," Mlive.com blog, July 24, 3009, http://blog.mlive.com.

42 Garofalo, *op. cit.*

43 For background, see Marcia Clemmitt, "Universal Coverage," *CQ Researcher*, March 30, 2007, pp. 265-288, and Marcia Clemmitt, "Rising Health Costs," *CQ Researcher*, April 7, 2006, pp. 289-312.

44 Peter A. Corning, "The Evolution of Medicare: From Idea to Law," Social Security Administration, www.ssa.gov/history/corningchap4.html.

45 *Ibid.*

46 *Ibid.*

47 *Ibid.*

48 *Ibid.*

49 Igor Volsky, Wonk Room blog, Center for American Progress, July 29, 2009, http://wonkroom.thinkprogress.org/2009/07/29/medicare-44.

50 "Medicare Is Signed into Law," Social Security Online, www.ssa.gov/history/lbjsm.html.

51 Tim Foley, "The President Who Took Us the Closest to Universal Health Care, Part 2," Change.org, Feb. 16, 2009, http://healthcare.change.org.

52 *Ibid.*

53 "Historical Health Insurance Tables," U.S. Census Bureau, www.census.gov/hhes/www/hlthins/historic/hlthin05/hihistt1.html.

54 Foley, *op. cit.*

55 *Ibid.*

56 Meredith Hughes, "In the States: Yearly Checkup for State Reform Efforts," New Health Dialogue blog, New America Foundation, Feb. 6, 2009, www.newamerica.net.

57 Daniel C. Vock, "For Universal Health Care, Two States Push Big Plans," Stateline.org, Jan. 11, 2008, www.stateline.org.

58 "Trends in Health Care Costs and Spending," Kaiser Family Foundation, www.kff.org/insurance/upload/7692_02.pdf.

59 Neeraj Sood, Arkadipta Ghosh and José J. Escarce, "Health Care Cost Growth and the Economic Performance of U.S. Industries," RAND Corporation, June 3, 2009, www.randcompare.org/publications/summary/health_care_cost_growth_and_the_economic_performance_of_us_industries.

60 Kent Conrad, "Bridging the Divide with a Co-operative Health Care Proposal," press statement, June 30, 2009, http://conrad.senate.gov.

FOR MORE INFORMATION

Alliance for Health Reform, 1444 I St., N.W., Suite 910, Washington, DC 20005; (202) 789-2300; www.allhealth.org. Nonpartisan, nonprofit group disseminating information about policy options for expanded coverage.

Center for American Progress, 1333 H St., N.W., 10th Floor, Washington, DC 20005; (202) 682-1611; www.americanprogress.org. Progressive think tank analyzing health insurance coverage and cost-cutting proposals.

Commonwealth Fund, One East 75th St., New York, NY 10021; (212) 606-3800; www.cmwf.org. A private foundation funding independent research on health care.

Council for Affordable Health Insurance, 127 S. Peyton St., Suite 210, Alexandria, VA 22314; (703) 836-6200; www.cahi.org. Organization of insurers that sells individual and small-group health plans and supports market-oriented coverage.

Health Care Policy and Marketplace Review; http://healthpolicyandmarket.blogspot.com. Blog by former health-insurance executive Robert Laszewski that examines insurance proposals from a business standpoint.

Heritage Foundation, 214 Massachusetts Ave., N.E., Washington, DC 20002-4999; (202) 546-4400; www.heritage.org. Conservative think tank advocating market-based health reform.

Physicians for a National Health Program, 29 E. Madison St., Suite 602, Chicago, IL 60602; (312) 782-6006; www.pnhp.org. Nonprofit group advocating for single-payer national health insurance.

Sick Around the World, Frontline, PBS; www.pbs.org/wgbh/pages/frontline/sickaroundtheworld/etc/links.html. Web site of a PBS documentary on international health systems; includes expert interviews.

61 Edmund F. Haislmaier, Dennis G. Smith and Nina Owcharenko, "Health Care Co-operatives: Doing It the Right Way," WebMemo #2493, The Heritage Foundation, June 18, 2009, www.heritage.org.

62 Holland, *op. cit.*

63 Karen Davis, "Co-operative Health Care: The Way Forward?" The Commonwealth Fund blog, June 22, 2009, www.commonwealthfund.org.

64 *Ibid.*

65 Brian Beutler, "Battle of the Math Nerds: Two Number Crunchers Square Off Over Health Care," Talking Points Memo, July 27, 2009, http://tpmdc.talkingpointsmemo.com.

66 Bernadine Healy, "Seven Ways Health Reform Is Going to Affect You," *US News & World Report*, Aug. 3, 2009, http://health.usnews.com/blogs/heart-to-heart.

67 Bruce Vladeck, "Paralysis by Analysis," *Roll Call*, July 28, 2009, www.rollcall.com.

68 "The Deficit Club," Digby's blog, July 28, 2009, http://digbysblog.blogspot.com.

69 Jackie Frank, "Debate over Obama Healthcare Plan Turns Rancorous," Reuters, Aug. 6, 2009, www.reuters.com.

70 Christina Vara, "Local Protest Gains National Notoriety," *The Oak Hill* [Texas] *Gazette*, Aug. 5, 2009, http://oakhillgazette.com.

71 Adam Smith, "Is This a Near Riot or a Health Care Forum?" *St. Petersburg Times*, Aug. 6, 2009, www.tampabay.com.

72 "NBC News/Wall Street Journal Survey," Study #6095, Hart/McInturff, June 2009, http://msnbcmedia.msn.com/i/msnbc/sections/news/090617_NBC-WSJ_poll_Full.pdf.

73 Sam Stein, "Internal RNC Poll Called for Health Care Slowdown, Found Public Plan Support," *Huffington Post*, July 24, 2009, www.huffingtonpost.com.

74 Chad Terhune and Keith Epstein, "The Health Insurers Have Already Won," *Business Week*, Aug. 6, 2009.

Bibliography

Selected Sources

Books

Geyman, John, *Do Not Resuscitate: Why the Health Insurance Industry Is Dying, and How We Must Replace It*, Common Courage Press, 2009.

A professor emeritus of family medicine at the University of Washington argues that government's repeated failure to successfully prevent health insurers from cherry-picking healthy patients means that, without drastic system change, prices will continue to skyrocket and more Americans will be left underinsured.

Halvorson, George C., *Health Care Reform Now! A Prescription for Change*, Jossey-Bass, 2007.

The Kaiser Foundation Health Plan CEO argues that lowering costs and driving down workplace error rates can help make health care more efficient and error-free.

Herzlinger, Regina E., *Who Killed Health Care? America's $2 Trillion Medical Problem — and the Consumer-Driven Cure*, McGraw-Hill, 2007.

A Harvard Business School professor of business administration argues that having third parties pay for health care has warped our system and alternatives would make doctors and hospitals more accountable for results.

Relman, Arnold, *A Second Opinion: Rescuing America's Health Care*, PublicAffairs, 2007.

A professor emeritus at Harvard Medical School proposes the United States adopt a single-payer health-care system, supported by an earmarked, progressive tax.

Articles

Galloway, Gloria, "In a Pandemic, Where's the Moral Ground?" *The Globe and Mail* (Toronto), July 27, 2009, www.theglobeandmail.com.

Canada's single-payer health system considers how to allocate medical services if the swine flu pandemic threatens to overwhelm the system's resources.

Gawande, Atul, "Getting There from Here," *The New Yorker*, Jan. 26, 2009, p. 26, www.newyorker.com/reporting/2009/01/26/090126fa_fact_gawande.

Every industrialized nation except the United States has government-funded universal health coverage, but their systems developed in different ways.

Klein, Ezra, "Health Reform for Beginners: The Difference Between Socialized Medicine, Single-Payer Health Care and What We'll Be Getting," blog, *The Washington Post*, June 9, 2009, http://washingtonpost.com.

Democratic health bills don't propose a single-payer program or socialized medicine.

Reinhardt, Uwe E., "Health Reform Without a Public Plan: The German Model," Economix blog, *The New York Times*, April 17, 2009, http://economix.blogs.nytimes.com.

A Princeton economics professor describes the German health system, which has no public-plan option but uses tightly regulated private insurers and a global budget to provide cheaper coverage than the United States.

Reports and Studies

"Public Plan Option: Fair Competition or a Recipe for Crowd-Out," briefing transcript, Alliance for Health Reform, April 27, 2009, www.allhealth.org/briefingmaterials/Transcript4-27Final-1455.pdf.

Analysts representing a broad range of perspectives discuss what a public insurance plan for non-poor and non-elderly enrollees might look like and the potential consequences of creating such a plan.

"Uncle Sam, M.D.: AEI Scholars on Health Care and Pharmaceutical Reform," American Enterprise Institute, 2009, www.aei.org/docLib/Uncle%20Sam%20MD%20-2.pdf.

Scholars from a free-market-oriented think tank discuss health-care reform proposals and the potential impact on the uninsured and Medicare and Medicaid.

Person, Chris L., and Rachel Burton, "U.S. Health Care Spending: Comparison with Other OECD Countries," Congressional Research Service Report for Congress, Sept. 17, 2007, http://assets.opencrs.com/rpts/RL34175_20070917.pdf.

Congress' nonpartisan research arm describes international health-spending patterns.

Tanner, Michael, "The Grass Is Not Always Greener: A Look at National Health Care Systems Around the World," Policy Analysis No. 613, Cato Institute, March 18, 2008, www.cato.org/pub_display.php?pub_id=9272.

A libertarian analyst argues that international universal health-care systems ration care, have long waiting lists and don't control costs any better than the U.S. system.

Whelan, Ellen-Marie, and Judy Feder, *Payment Reform to Improve Health Care: Ways to Move Forward*, Center for American Progress, June 2009, www.americanprogress.org/issues/2009/06/pdf/healthpaymentreform.pdf.

An expert panel assembled by the liberal think tank discusses proposed cost-saving methods for health-care reform legislation.

The Next Step:

Additional Articles from Current Periodicals

International Programs

Cheng, Maria, "Europe's Health Care System Has Critics, Fans," *Lewiston* (Idaho) *Morning Tribune*, July 5, 2009.
Costs have skyrocketed for several European public health systems, and some patients have needlessly suffered and died.

Darzi, Ara, and Tom Kibasi, "In Defense of Britain's Health System," *The Washington Post*, Aug. 17, 2009, p. A13.
Although Great Britain's health system is cost-effective, a similar approach may not be the best prescription for the U.S.

Ruse, Michael, "Canadians Face Less Health Care Paperwork," *Tallahassee* (Florida) *Democrat*, July 10, 2009.
Health care in Canada — unlike in the United States — is open and available to everyone without direct cost.

Public Plans

Edelman, Marian Wright, "A Public Health Insurance Plan Can Cover Our Children," *Michigan Chronicle*, April 29, 2009, p. A6.
A public health insurance plan would encourage competition based on quality and cost, not by denying care.

Mankiw, N. Gregory, "The Pitfalls of the Public Option," *The New York Times*, June 28, 2009, p. BU5.
A public plan without any taxpayer support essentially becomes a nonprofit company offering health insurance.

Webb, Susan, "Public Option Is 'Core Fight' in Health Reform Battle," *People's Weekly World* (Illinois), May 23, 2009, p. 1.
Securing a public option is the top priority, according to former Democratic National Committee Chairman Howard Dean.

Single-Payer Plans

Adams, John S., "Baucus Regrets Not Including Single-Payer Advocates," *Great Falls* (Montana) *Tribune*, June 4, 2009, p. 1A.
Sen. Max Baucus, D-Mont., regrets not including single-payer advocates in earlier Senate discussions over health care.

Eggen, Dan, "Backers of 'Single-Payer' Insurance Challenge Democrats," *The Washington Post*, June 7, 2009, p. A1.
President Obama is facing complaints that a single-payer program has been left out of the health-care debate.

Heid, Kermit, "Single-Payer Health Care Has Better Record," *Salt Lake Tribune*, July 11, 2009.
Administrative costs for single-payer systems in the United States are about one-third of the costs for private insurers.

Holan, Angie Drobnic, "Obama Has Praised Single-Payer Plans in the Past," *St. Petersburg* (Florida) *Times*, Aug. 12, 2009.
President Obama contradicted himself during a town hall meeting in New Hampshire when he said he has never supported single-payer health-care plans.

Uninsured

Coley, Jill, "Brink of Ruin," *Post and Courier* (South Carolina), March 20, 2009, p. B1.
A serious injury or illness can lead to financial catastrophe for the uninsured because no one negotiates on their behalf.

Gosselin, Kenneth R., "Cost of Treating Uninsured Keeps Going Up," *Hartford* (Connecticut) *Courant*, June 10, 2009, p. A11.
The cost of hospital stays in Connecticut for uninsured patients has increased by more than 40 percent since 2005, even though the number of such patients has declined.

Hutson, Wendell, "New State Law Lowers Hospital Costs for Under- and Uninsured Patients," *Chicago Defender*, April 8, 2009, p. 3.
A new Illinois law affords the uninsured and working poor the same discounts on medical bills as those with insurance.

Lee, Renee C., "Uninsured Patients Visit ER Less Often," *Houston Chronicle*, April 18, 2009, p. B3.
Uninsured residents in Harris County (Houston) are visiting emergency rooms for minor illnesses less often because of improved access to primary-care programs, according to the University of Texas School of Public Health.

CITING CQ RESEARCHER

Sample formats for citing these reports in a bibliography include the ones listed below. Preferred styles and formats vary, so please check with your instructor or professor.

MLA STYLE
Jost, Kenneth. "Rethinking the Death Penalty." CQ Researcher 16 Nov. 2001: 945-68.

APA STYLE
Jost, K. (2001, November 16). Rethinking the death penalty. *CQ Researcher, 11*, 945-968.

CHICAGO STYLE
Jost, Kenneth. "Rethinking the Death Penalty." *CQ Researcher*, November 16, 2001, 945-968.

In-depth Reports on Issues in the News

Are you writing a paper?

Need backup for a debate?

Want to become an expert on an issue?

For 80 years, students have turned to *CQ Researcher* for in-depth reporting on issues in the news. Reports on a full range of political and social issues are now available. Following is a selection of recent reports:

Civil Liberties
Closing Guantánamo, 2/09
Affirmative Action, 10/08
Gay Marriage Showdowns, 9/08
America's Border Fence, 9/08
Immigration Debate, 2/08

Crime/Law
Examining Forensics, 7/09
Legalizing Marijuana, 6/09
Mexico's Drug War, 12/08
Prostitution Debate, 5/08
Public Defenders, 4/08

Education
Reading Crisis? 2/08
Discipline in Schools, 2/08
Student Aid, 1/08

Environment/Society
Afghanistan Dilemma, 8/09
Energy and Climate, 7/09
Future of Books, 5/09
Hate Groups, 5/09
Future of Journalism, 3/09
Confronting Warming, 1/09
Reducing Carbon Footprint, 12/08

Health/Safety
Straining the Safety Net, 7/09
Treating Depression, 6/09
Reproductive Ethics, 5/09
Extreme Sports, 4/09
Regulating Toxic Chemicals, 1/09
Preventing Cancer, 1/09
Heart Health, 9/08

Politics/Economy
Business Bankruptcy, 4/09
Future of the GOP, 3/09
Middle-Class Squeeze, 3/09

Upcoming Reports

Financial Literacy, 9/4/09   State Budget Cuts, 9/11/09   Gays in the Military, 9/18/09

ACCESS

CQ Researcher is available in print and online. For access, visit your library or www.cqresearcher.com.

STAY CURRENT

To receive notice of upcoming *CQ Researcher* reports, or learn more about *CQ Researcher* products, subscribe to the free e-mail newsletters, *CQ Researcher Alert!* and *CQ Researcher News*: http://cqpress.com/newsletters.

PURCHASE

To purchase a *CQ Researcher* report in print or electronic format (PDF), visit www.cqpress.com or call 866-427-7737. Single reports start at $15. Bulk purchase discounts and electronic-rights licensing are also available.

SUBSCRIBE

Annual full-service *CQ Researcher* subscriptions—including 44 reports a year, monthly index updates, and a bound volume—start at $803. Add $25 for domestic postage.

CQ Researcher Online offers a backfile from 1991 and a number of tools to simplify research. For pricing information, call 800-834-9020, ext. 1906, or e-mail librarysales@cqpress.com.

Published by CQ Press, a Division of SAGE

www.cqresearcher.com

Financial Literacy

Should courses be mandatory in schools?

P oor understanding of basic personal-finance and economic issues has left millions of students and adults mired in credit-card debt, prey to unscrupulous mortgage brokers and prone to making risky bets with their retirement money. High-school seniors correctly answer only about half the questions on personal-finance surveys, and those who take personal-finance courses tend to score no better than those who don't. Studies show similar deficits among adults. Yet experts disagree on a solution. Only a handful of states require at least a semester course on personal finance, and some advocates want Congress or state legislatures to mandate financial education for all K-12 students. Others question the effectiveness of financial-literacy programs in schools, and some worry that corporations may have too much influence on curriculum and instruction. A better approach to improving financial literacy, some argue, is to tighten government regulation to make credit cards, mortgages and other products easier to understand.

A volunteer for Operation Hope's Banking on Our Future program drills elementary school students in Los Angeles on the ABC's of financial literacy.

CQ Researcher • Sept. 4, 2009 • www.cqresearcher.com
Volume 19, Number 30 • Pages 717-740

I N S I D E

THIS REPORT

CQ Researcher

Sept. 4, 2009
Volume 19, Number 30

MANAGING EDITOR: Thomas J. Colin
tcolin@cqpress.com

ASSISTANT MANAGING EDITOR: Kathy Koch
kkoch@cqpress.com

ASSOCIATE EDITOR: Kenneth Jost

STAFF WRITERS: Thomas J. Billitteri,
Marcia Clemmitt, Peter Katel

CONTRIBUTING WRITERS: Rachel Cox,
Sarah Glazer, Alan Greenblatt, Reed Karaim
Barbara Mantel, Patrick Marshall,
Tom Price, Jennifer Weeks

DESIGN/PRODUCTION EDITOR: Olu B. Davis

ASSISTANT EDITOR: Darrell Dela Rosa

FACT-CHECKING: Eugene J. Gabler,
Michelle Harris

CQ PRESS

A Division of SAGE

PRESIDENT AND PUBLISHER:
John A. Jenkins

EXECUTIVE DIRECTOR,
REFERENCE INFORMATION GROUP:
Alix B. Vance

CQ Press is a registered trademark of Congressional Quarterly Inc.

CQ Researcher (ISSN 1056-2036) is printed on acid-free paper. Published weekly, except; (Jan. wk. 1) (May wk. 4) (July wks. 1, 2) (Aug. wks. 3, 4) (Nov. wk. 4) and (Dec. wk. 4), by CQ Press, a division of SAGE Publications. Annual full-service subscriptions start at $803. For pricing, call 1-800-834-9020, ext. 1906. To purchase a CQ Researcher report in print or electronic format (PDF), visit www. cqpress.com or call 866-427-7737. Single reports start at $15. Bulk purchase discounts and electronic-rights licensing are also available. Periodicals postage paid at Washington, D.C., and additional mailing offices. POSTMASTER: Send address changes to CQ Researcher, 2300 N St., N.W., Suite 800, Washington, DC 20037.

Cover: Operation Hope, Inc.

Financial Literacy

BY THOMAS J. BILLITTERI

THE ISSUES

At East Middle School in Farmington Hills, Mich., an upscale Detroit suburb, seventh-grade teacher Dena Shammami says pupils find her elective class in personal finance "really cool."

"Students want to sign up," she says, "and when they don't get in, they're bummed out."

Taught in partnership with a local federal credit union, the class features lessons in saving, spending, credit, management and work ethics, plus real-life experience working in a branch of the credit union set up at the school.

Shammami says part of her goal is to make her students savvier consumers. But she also hopes to help prepare some of them for professional careers in which they can seek solutions to the kind of financial turmoil that has shaken the American economy to the core in recent months. "I want them to be smart and responsible," she says, "and also critical thinkers."

Creating savvy consumers is a long-held but elusive dream of "financial literacy" advocates, not only for American schoolchildren but for adults, too. Millions of Americans lack a basic understanding of personal-finance and economic issues, which has left many mired in credit-card debt, prey to unscrupulous mortgage brokers and prone to making risky bets with their retirement money. [1]

The "lack of financial literacy and poor financial management have profound implications for individual consumers and the U.S. as a whole," said Rep. Ruben Hinojosa, D-Texas, a member of the House Subcommittee

Students at Bay Meadows Elementary School in Orlando, Fla., get a financial-literacy lesson from U.S. Rep. Alan Grayson, D-Fla., as part of the American Bar Association's Teach Children to Save program. Financial-literacy advocates want states to mandate programs in schools, but critics question their effectiveness, or worry that corporate sponsors have too much influence on content and instruction.

ABA Education Foundation

on Financial Institutions and Consumer Credit, which held hearings on the subject this summer. [2]

Studies and surveys have helped to document the financial-literacy problem and its potential consequences. A 2007 survey of teens by the Charles Schwab Corp., the financial-services giant, found "significant gaps" in awareness about finances. Only 26 percent said they were knowledgeable about how credit-card interest and fees work, and only 14 percent about how income taxes work. [3]

Likewise, high-school seniors taking a biennial 31-question financial-literacy survey given by the Washington-based Jump$tart Coalition for Personal Financial Literacy could correctly answer an average of only 48 percent of ques-

tions in 2008, down from 57 percent in 1997. College students taking the same survey last year scored an average of 62 percent, and seniors scored about 65 percent.

College graduates "are close to being financially literate and probably will be so with more life experience," the coalition said. Even so, experts point to the Jump$tart results — especially the high-school scores — as strong evidence for concern.

For one thing, those scores not only have been falling, but students who have taken a course in personal finance have tended to do no better on the survey than those who haven't.

What's more, whites have tended to do better than blacks and Hispanics, and students from wealthy families have tended to score better than those from low-income backgrounds. The gaps have reinforced concerns that disparities in financial literacy have significantly contributed to inequality between rich and poor. [4]

And while college scores were somewhat better than those of high-school students, "the bad news is that just 25 percent of our young adults are graduating from college," the Jump$tart Coalition noted. "This means that 75 percent of young American adults are likely to lack the skills needed to make beneficial financial decisions." [5]

Indeed, many adults remain clueless about the basics of personal finance and the market economy, researchers say.

Annamaria Lusardi, a Dartmouth College economist, found "an alarmingly low level of financial literacy" among adults in a recent study. Only half of respondents age 50 or older knew enough to

Most States Don't Require Finance Instruction

Fewer than half the states require personal-finance instruction as a requirement for graduation. Only three states — Utah, Missouri and Tennessee — require at least a one-semester personal-finance course.

State Financial-Education Requirements

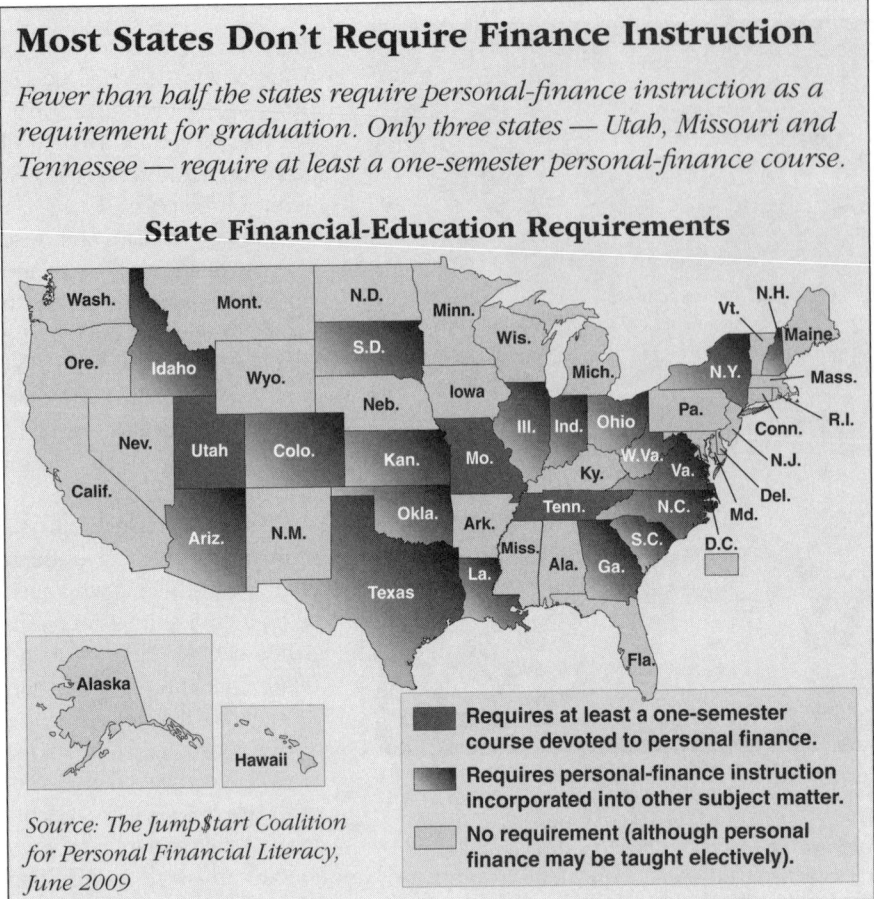

Requires at least a one-semester course devoted to personal finance.

Requires personal-finance instruction incorporated into other subject matter.

No requirement (although personal finance may be taught electively).

Source: The Jump$tart Coalition for Personal Financial Literacy, June 2009

correctly answer a pair of basic questions on interest rates and inflation, and only half knew that buying stock in a single company was usually riskier than investing in a stock mutual fund. [6]

"Knowledge matters, and it matters a lot in the current world," Lusardi says. "The surprise of our research was how little people know. This is what we should be worried about. We are asking people to make complex decisions," she says, and yet "very few people know the difference between bonds and stocks."

With many adults unable to navigate a world of subprime mortgages and credit-card default penalties, they are often ill-equipped to offer sound advice about money to their children. More than two-thirds of parents responding to a 2008 Charles Schwab survey said they felt less prepared to guide their teens on investing than on the "birds

and bees," and a majority said they could be doing a better job of teaching their children about budgeting and saving. In fact, 70 percent of parents said they'd shown their teens how to do laundry, but only 29 percent had taught them how credit-card interest and fees work, and a mere 14 percent had explained what a 401(k) plan is. [7]

That the nation's level of financial literacy is, in Lusardi's words, "bad . . . to very bad" is of little dispute among researchers and advocates. But how to improve the picture is a matter of debate.

Many agree with a recommendation by the President's Advisory Council on Financial Literacy, appointed by former President George W. Bush in January 2008, that Congress or state legislatures should mandate financial education in all schools in grades kindergarten through 12. [8]

But such a mandate would take money. The Financial and Economic Literacy Improvement Act of 2009, introduced in the Senate by Sens. Patty Murray, D-Wash., and Thad Cochran, R-Miss., and in the House by Rep. Carolyn McCarthy, D-N.Y., would provide $250 million in state grants annually over five years to support financial-literacy education in schools and colleges. "If we are going to avoid many of the mistakes" that led to the economic crisis, "we need to focus on giving Americans the skills to understand the fine print and avoid mounting debt," Murray said. [9]

Others argue that classroom training has done little or nothing to improve financial literacy among young people, though they differ on how best to address that problem.

One approach is to start the training in the earliest grades and integrate it with math, social studies and other classes throughout elementary and high school, rather than try to teach personal finance in a one-shot high-school course.

Even so, the question remains of what educators should be teaching. Some advocate practical lessons — how to make a budget, write a check and apply for credit. Others argue that because financial products are constantly changing, it is more valuable to teach universal economic principles — supply and demand and the working of the market economy, for instance.

Considerable debate also exists over the widespread use of resources supplied by the for-profit world — especially banks, brokerages and other financial-service corporations — in school-based financial-literacy training. Some argue that companies providing materials and instruction have a vested interest in promoting their products to easily swayed students. Others defend the use of corporate resources, saying cash-strapped school systems would not be able to afford financial-literacy classes without the corporate help.

Lauren Willis, a professor at Loyola Law School in Los Angeles, says the best way to improve financial literacy is not with more classes, but by rewriting financial regulations in ways that "respond to the realistic abilities of consumers" to understand financial products like mortgages and credit-card agreements. (*See "At Issue," p. 733.*) "A society that believes that financial-literacy education will solve consumer financial problems," she argues in an academic paper on the subject, "has an all-too-convenient excuse not to engage in the difficult task of finding better consumer-finance public policies." [10]

As experts grapple with how best to raise the public's level of financial literacy, here are some of the questions being debated:

Is financial-literacy education effective?

As the national economy nosedived in the spring of 2008, Federal Reserve Chairman Ben S. Bernanke trumpeted the importance of financial-literacy training.

"In light of the problems that have arisen in the subprime mortgage market," he said at a briefing on the Jump$tart Coalition's biennial survey of high-school seniors, "we are reminded of how critically important it is for individuals to become financially literate at an early age so that they are better prepared to make decisions and navigate an increasingly complex financial marketplace." [11]

But whether financial-literacy programs aimed at students and other consumers are the answer remains a matter of debate among educators and researchers. Some argue that financial-literacy programs are effective and even vital for protecting consumers. Others argue that it's most important to improve government regulation to make financial products more transparent and fair.

William B. Walstad, an economics professor at the University of Nebraska-

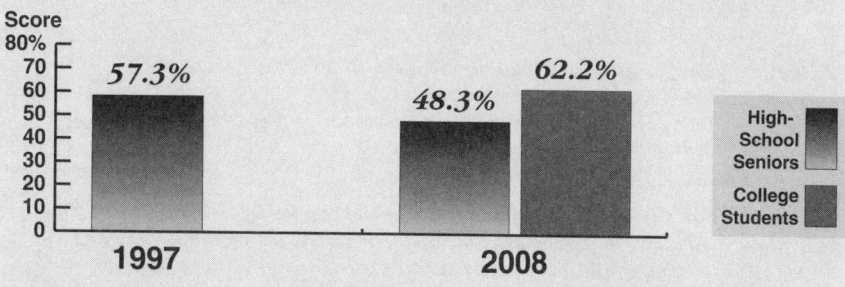

High School Financial Literacy Hits New Low

High-school seniors scored an average of 48.3 percent on a financial-literacy test in 2008, the lowest on record and 9 percentage points lower than a decade earlier. College students, however, achieved an average score of 62.2 percent, or slightly above the passing grade of 60. "The good news is that most college graduates are financially literate," said the Jump$tart Coalition. "The bad news is that only 25 percent of Americans graduate from college, leaving three-quarters ill-equipped to make critical financial decisions."

Source: "The Financial Literacy of Young American Adults," Jump$tart Coalition for Personal Financial Literacy, 2008

Lincoln and an expert on financial-literacy education, sees financial-literacy training for youths as valuable. "The only other source [of information] may be parents, who we know may be as [financially] illiterate as their students," he says.

Low scores on national financial-literacy tests — even among students who have taken financial-literacy classes — aren't a good indicator of the merits of financial-training programs in schools, he says. "A course taught in one state or school or district may be quite different than in another district — the emphasis might be different," he says. And, "we don't know how well-trained the teachers are."

Walstad points to a study he did involving a personal-finance program for high-school students called "Financing Your Future." "We put in the strongest possible controls we could. We had a standardized curriculum, a standardized amount of time, some training for teachers and we collected data in classes in four states. There, you see a rather significant increase" in financial literacy, he says.

Laura Levine, executive director of the Jump$tart Coalition, also maintains that financial-literacy education works, even though scores on the Jump$tart survey remain low and youngsters who have taken a financial-literacy course have tended to do no better than those who haven't. (*See "At Issue," p. 733.*)

For one thing, she says, the Jump$tart survey is not designed to find out how effective these courses have been. And Levine says Jump$tart is still trying to learn what educational approaches are most effective for teaching students about finances.

"We're just too new at this," she says. "Our guess is we're not getting [the training to students] early enough and not repeating it often enough. How much are we expecting from a one-semester course?

"As proud as I am of our research," she adds, "it's a 31-question test. I don't think we can draw the conclusion that we shouldn't be putting money into financial education" based on the test.

Ted Beck, president and CEO of the National Endowment for Financial Education, a Colorado-based nonprofit group

Test Your Financial Literacy

The questions below are from a test given to 7,000 high school and college students in 2008. The average score among high-school seniors was 48.3 percent. The college students averaged 62.2 percent. The passing score is 60.

1. Inflation can cause difficulty in many ways. Which group would have the greatest problem during periods of high inflation that last several years?
a) Older, working couples saving for retirement
b) Older people living on fixed retirement income
c) Young couples with no children who both work
d) Young working couples with children

2. Which of the following is true about sales taxes?
a) The national sales tax percentage rate is 6 percent
b) The federal government will deduct it from your paycheck
c) You don't have to pay the tax if your income is very low
d) It makes things more expensive for you to buy

3. Rebecca has saved $12,000 for her college expenses by working part time. Her plan is to start college next year, and she needs all of the money she saved. Which of the following is the safest place for her college money?
a) Locked in her closet at home
b) Stocks
c) Corporate bonds
d) A bank savings account

4. Which of the following types of investment would best protect the purchasing power of a family's savings in the event of a sudden increase in inflation?
a) A 10-year bond issued by a corporation
b) A certificate of deposit at a bank
c) A twenty-five year corporate bond
d) A house financed with a fixed-rate mortgage

5. Under which of the following circumstances would it be financially beneficial to borrow money to buy something now and repay it with future income?
a) When you need to buy a car to get a much-better-paying job
b) When you really need a week's vacation
c) When some clothes you like go on sale
d) When the interest on the loan is greater than the interest you get on your savings

6. Which of the following statements best describes your right to check your credit history for accuracy?
a) Your credit record can be checked once a year for free
b) You cannot see your credit record
c) All credit records are the property of the U.S. Government and access is only available to the FBI and lenders
d) You can only check your record for free if you are turned down for credit based on a credit report

7. Your take-home pay from your job is less than the total amount you earn. Which of the following best describes what is taken out of your total pay?
a) Social Security and Medicare contributions
b) Federal income tax, property tax, and Medicare and Social Security contributions
c) Federal income tax, Social Security and Medicare contributions
d) Federal income tax, sales tax and Social Security contribution

8. Retirement income paid by a company is called:
a) 401(k)
b) Pension
c) Rents and profits
d) Social Security

that provides free financial-literacy curricula and resources to students and adults, including low-income people and those hit by financial hardships, says "financial education is a very key and effective tool" for improving financial behavior. As a private foundation that funds its own programs, he says, "we're our own toughest critic."

One piece of evidence Beck offers: An independent evaluation by the University of Minnesota of the endowment's curriculum, which he says is used annually by about 600,000 students nationwide, found that the programs had improved students' financial behavior not only immediately but at least three months after they'd taken a course.

He also says a study funded by the endowment of 2,000 University of Arizona freshmen found that three factors reduce risky financial behavior: strong positive family influence; whether students had taken a financial-literacy class; and whether they had a part-time job. "The Arizona study shows that [financial-literacy training] is a piece of the whole solution," Beck says.

But others are skeptical about financial-literacy education, including Lewis Mandell, the scholar who has conducted Jump$tart's student surveys since they began in 1997. "By and large, the value of specific education in this field seems to be almost negligible," says Mandell, a professor of finance and business economics at the University of Washington and senior fellow in the Aspen Institute's Initiative on Financial Security. "I haven't seen any impact on literacy of having taken courses in high school or college. It's also true [of financial training] in the workplace."

In Jump$tart's 2008 survey of college students, Mandell says, those "who had a full semester course in high school were no more financially literate than those who didn't." Still, Mandell says he has seen evidence that young people who had received financial training in high school tended to save more and avoid debt a few years into adulthood, suggesting financial-literacy courses had some effect on future behavior.

Mandell says he is not ready to close the door on financial-literacy training in the schools. But he contends that for it to work it must begin in elementary school, and teaching methods must change. He says his research suggests that the best way to train young minds to be financially responsible is to bring in other young people — and not stuffy bankers or other adults — to tell personal tales of woe about going through bankruptcy or having their credit revoked.

"These are the kinds of things that are likely to stick," he says. "The single most important thing you can do is kind of scare the crap out of students — tell them stories and reach them emotionally." Emotional content seems to carry through to youngsters much more effectively than pedagogical content, he says.

Mandell says his findings also suggest that school-based bank accounts, through which students can learn the fundamentals of saving and investing, should be far more prevalent than they are. "They use the child's ownership of assets to personalize financial education," says Mandell, who is actively researching the issue. "It's hands-on, real-time and involves something that belongs to the student."

Willis of Loyola Law School says she supports the teaching of basic financial information, such as how interest compounding works, but that financial-literacy courses aren't needed to impart that kind of knowledge. "The truth is, we have math classes now," she says. "The issue is not, 'Let's teach a new class,' it's, 'Let's teach current math class better.' "

In some cases financial-literacy programs can give people a false sense of knowing more than they actually do, leading them to make risky bets in the financial marketplace that come

9. Many people put aside money to take care of unexpected expenses. If Juan and Elva have money put aside for emergencies, in which of the following forms would it be of LEAST benefit to them if they needed it right away?
a) Invested in a down payment on the house
b) Checking account
c) Stocks
d) Savings account

10. David just found a job with a take-home pay of $2,000 per month. He must pay $900 for rent and $150 for groceries each month. He also spends $250 per month on transportation. If he budgets $100 each month for clothing, $200 for restaurants and $250 for everything else, how long will it take him to accumulate savings of $600?
a) 3 months
b) 4 months
c) 1 month
d) 2 months

11. Sara and Joshua just had a baby. They received money as baby gifts and want to put it away for the baby's education. Which of the following tends to have the highest growth over periods of time as long as 18 years?
a) A checking account
b) Stocks
c) A U.S. government savings bond
d) A savings account

12. Barbara has just applied for a credit card. She is an 18-year-old high-school graduate with few valuable possessions and no credit history. If Barbara is granted a credit card, which of the following is the most likely way that the credit-card company will reduce its risk?
a) It will make Barbara's parents pledge their home to repay her credit-card debt
b) It will require Barbara to have both parents co-sign for the card
c) It will charge Barbara twice the interest rate it charges older cardholders
d) It will start Barbara with a small line of credit to see how she handles the account

13. Chelsea worked her way through college earning $15,000 per year. After graduation, her first job pays $30,000. The total dollar amount Chelsea will have to pay in federal income taxes in her new job will:
a) Double, at least, from when she was in college
b) Go up a little from when she was in college
c) Stay the same as when she was in college
d) Be lower than when she was in college

14. Which of the following best describes the primary sources of income for most people ages 20-35?
a) Dividends and interest
b) Salaries, wages, tips
c) Profits from business
d) Rents

15. If you are behind on your debt payments and go to a responsible credit-counseling service such as the Consumer Credit Counseling Services, what help can they give you?
a) They can cancel and cut up all of your credit cards without your permission
b) They can get the federal government to apply your income taxes to pay off your debts
c) They can work with those who loaned you money to set up a payment schedule that you can meet
d) They can force those who loaned you money to forgive all your debts

Answers: 1b; 2d; 3d; 4d; 5a; 6a; 7c; 8b; 9a; 10b; 11b; 12d; 13a; 14b; 15c

Source: Jump$tart Coalition for Personal Financial Literacy, 2008

back to haunt them, Willis argues. What's more, she says, financial products are so complex, and change so fast, that educators and consumers can have a hard time keeping up.

Should financial-literacy courses be mandatory in elementary and high schools?

The news on high-school students' knowledge of personal-finance and economic issues isn't entirely bad.

The National Assessment Governing Board, whose members include governors, legislators, school officials and business representatives, said a 2006 test of 11,500 12th-graders in 590 public and private schools found that about four in 10 had reached the "proficient" level: They could "identify and apply key economic concepts and relationships dealing with national and international economic issues and important aspects of personal finance." Seventy-nine percent scored at or above the "basic" level.

"While there is clear room for improvement, the results are not discouraging," Darvin M. Winick, governing board chairman, said in a 2007 news release. "Given the number of students who finish high school with a limited vocabulary, not reading well and weak in math, the results may be as good as or better than we should expect."

Still, the assessment showed significant disparities in race and gender. For example, about half of white students scored at or above the proficient level, compared with 16 percent of black and 21 percent of Hispanic students. At the basic level or higher, whites (87 percent) outscored blacks (57 percent) and Hispanics (64 percent). Males outperformed females on average and at the proficient level, though they were even at the basic level. [12]

Only a handful of states require at least a one-semester course devoted to personal finance. According to the Jump$tart Coalition's most recent count, three do so: Missouri, Tennessee, Utah.

Parents' Income Affects Test Scores

College students' scores on financial-literacy tests rise with the income and education of parents, and females do better than males. White college students have an average score of 63.3 percent in contrast to just 56.3 percent for African-Americans. "A very disturbing finding," according to the Jump$tart Coalition, is that the difference between the financial literacy of white and black college students perseveres through college.

Test Results of College Students
(by background)

Parents' Income	Avg. Score
Less than $20,000	51.9
$20,000-$39,999	62.2
$40,000 to $79,999	63.8
$80,000 or more	64.6
Highest Level of Parents' Education	
Neither finished H.S.	54.3
Completed H.S.	62.5
Some college	58.2
College grad or more	64.0
Sex	
Female	62.6
Male	59.7
Race	
White	63.3
African-American	56.3
Hispanic-American	59.8
Asian-American	57.1

Source: "The Financial Literacy of Young American Adults," Jump$tart Coalition for Personal Financial Literacy, June 2009

And 18 states require that personal-finance information be incorporated into other subject matter, the group says. The remaining states have no requirement, though personal finance may be taught as an elective.

A different measure, by the Council for Economic Education, a 60-year-old New York group, found in 2007 that 17 states required a course in economics for high-school graduation, and that seven states required a course in personal finance for graduation from high school.

Making financial education mandatory for all elementary and high-school students has considerable support, including that of the President's Advisory Council on Financial Literacy. Its 2008 annual report, issued early this year as the Obama administration prepared to take office, included 15 recommendations for improving the financial literacy of students and adults. First on the list was a recommendation that Congress or state legislatures mandate financial education in all schools for students in kindergarten through 12th grade. [13]

Mandatory financial training has broad support in some education circles, too, though supporters warn that the idea falls flat without the proper level of government funding for materials, curricula and teacher training. "You can't have a federal mandate [that says] you have to do this, and you figure out how to pay for it," says Levine of Jump$tart.

Still, the idea of a federal mandate could face opposition from local educators accustomed to shaping curricula themselves. "In our system, state and local control over education is in many ways sacrosanct," says Joseph Peri, acting president and CEO of the Council for Economic Education, which advocates for economic and financial-literacy programs, provides classroom materials for teachers and K-12 students and offers professional development for teachers. "We certainly don't count on any of that being changed" in the foreseeable future, Peri says. "So realistically, what we want to focus on is affecting policy at the state level."

Yet some advocates say federal legislation makes sense despite differences in local education standards.

Dan Hebert, state president of the New Hampshire Jump$tart Coalition and its northeast regional director, supports a federal mandate. "I get the argument [against federal legislation] because in many of our states we just love this idea of local control," Hebert says. "There's sort of a bad taste in everyone's mouth with No Child Left Behind," a controversial law proposed by former President George W. Bush and passed in 2002 that sets standards for public schools.

But Hebert says failure to create a national policy on financial education in the schools will simply make the problem worse. With financial-literacy training, "you end up in a debate over whether it's an unfunded mandate, whether it's funded, and before long the debate takes away from what's needed: teachers teaching children in a classroom about balancing your budget and all the basics. Sometimes the discussion just delays what's necessary."

Yet some critics argue that financial-literacy programs can steal time from important lessons in other academic areas and also may serve the interests of financial-services companies involved in providing course materials or instruction.

In her 2009 book, *The Death of 'Why?': The Decline of Questioning and the Future of Democracy*, Andrea Batista Schlesinger, on leave as executive director of the Drum Major Institute for Public Policy, a liberal think tank in New York, raises a variety of concerns about corporate influence on financial-literacy training, including what she sees as loaded questions extolling a conservative, anti-tax agenda on financial-literacy surveys.

Students from Fairfax High School in Los Angeles do the math as part of the Operation Hope Banking on Our Future program. A survey of teens by Charles Schwab & Co. found "significant gaps" in awareness about finances. Only 26 percent said they were knowledgeable about how credit-card interest and fees work, and only 14 percent about how income taxes work.

"Everybody has to make decisions about the best use of school time," she says in an interview. "My view is that one day a week to teach fourth-graders about checking and savings accounts is not the best use of time. Obviously, I want children to grow up to be financially literate adults. But this web of relationships between institutions that have an agenda down to financial-literacy executives that have no practice in teaching — that forces us to ask questions about whether the classroom is an appropriate place to be

experiencing financial education in this way."

Should college students receiving government loans have to pass a financial-literacy exam or course?

Concern is widespread that college students lack solid academic training in financial matters, whether personal finance or more traditional economics. When the American Council of Trustees and Alumni surveyed 100 leading colleges and universities for a report this year on general education requirements, it found that only the University of Alaska in Fairbanks and the U.S. Military Academy at West Point required students to take at least one introductory economics class. [14]

Among the recommendations of the President's Advisory Council on Financial Literacy, chaired by investment-company founder Charles R. Schwab, was one sure to get the attention of college students: To qualify for a federally funded or federally guaranteed student loan, the council suggested, students should have to take a financial-literacy course that is more comprehensive than the current entrance and exit counseling requirements for student borrowers, or they should have to pass a competency test.

"By connecting the acceptance of a government-backed student loan with mandatory financial education, the council believes college students can be reached at one of their most 'teachable' moments, and that the lessons can have a real-world application," the group said. [15]

Separately, a bill (HR 1325) sponsored this year by Rep. Sheila Jackson-Lee, D-Texas, would require colleges and universities to provide at least four hours of financial-literacy counseling to student borrowers and include information on such matters as banking, budgeting, credit cards, investing, loans and housing.

Many college students borrow heavily to pay for their education. Median student loan debt among borrowers in 2007-2008 rose 11 percent from 2003-2004, to $15,123, according to the College Board, and the rise in debt was far steeper among students enrolled in for-profit colleges and students seeking two-year degrees. [16]

"We are asking people to bear more and more of the cost of higher education through borrowing, since neither state spending, need-based aid or family incomes have kept up with the costs," Lauren Asher, president of the Project on Student Debt, a nonprofit research organization, told *The New York Times*. [17]

Many experts agree with the President's Council that students receiving federal loans should have to demonstrate financial competence. "I certainly think something that would require students to have some education is a wise thing to do," says Peri of the Council for Economic Education.

"Absolutely, it's a good idea" to require student borrowers to take a course or pass a test as a condition of financial aid," says the Jump$tart Coalition's Levine. She even favors the approach for students receiving privately backed student loans, which typically have come with even more rigorous payment conditions than government-backed loans.

Many students get loans at the beginning of their college years, and while they "do it with the very best intention," they often overestimate how much they will earn when they finish their degrees or how much their salaries will stretch, Levine says. "Then we hear

about students getting into credit-card challenges, and students who have taken on other debt."

Requiring a financial-literacy course or test "might help to lower the default rate" on student borrowing, and also reduce the cost to taxpayers left holding the bag for unpaid loans, she says.

Lusardi of Dartmouth College says the President's Council's recommendation is an "interesting suggestion" that might also apply to people receiving mortgages. "In other areas, we ask people to show some competency," she says. "Before we put you out on the road, you have to show you can drive."

Still, requiring students or other borrowers to take a comprehensive course or a test without providing adequate training isn't wise, Lusardi says. "We have to do it carefully and be smart about it." Otherwise, she says, "such a program becomes a tax on people."

Other experts are resistant to the idea. "That can be problematic," says the University of Nebraska's Walstad. "I would prefer that if you take out a student loan, maybe you ought to attend a seminar on it." He compares such an approach not to the licensing of new drivers but to marriage counseling for troubled couples. "It doesn't guarantee the marriage will make it," he says, "but maybe it focuses your attention more."

Mandell of the University of Washington also is skeptical of mandatory financial-literacy coursework or testing for student-loan recipients. He fears that for-profit tutoring institutions would offer $1,000 cram courses that merely teach students seeking loans how to answer the questions on a financial-literacy exam correctly, without giving them a deeper understanding of the economy or personal finance. "The real problem is that bright kids can study for anything and pass it," he says. "How much have we really gained in that situation?"

And, he says, whether students take

a cram course or an entire semester course in financial literacy, the content isn't likely to be "sticky" — to sink in and change long-term behavior. "When we're dealing with life-skills issues, it's really the 'stickiness' that's most important," says Mandell. ∎

BACKGROUND

Early Education Efforts

The term "financial literacy" has come into vogue only in the past decade or two, but the roots of formal training in matters related to "home economics," "consumer science" and personal finance stretch back to the emerging women's movement of the 19th century.

In the mid-1800s, Catharine Esther Beecher's *A Treatise on Domestic Economy, For the Use of Young Ladies at Home and at School* advised that "care be taken to know the amount of income and of current expenses, so that the proper relative proportion be preserved, and the expenditures never exceed the means." [18]

In the early 20th century, "home economics" programs, tailored to female students, often focused on such matters as nutrition, clothing, child care and hygiene. And books and magazine articles on budgeting and saving proliferated as the U.S. economy grew more urbanized, a middle class took root and Americans lived through the post-World War I boom and then the Great Depression.

"[I]f prosperity, with individuals as with nations, is to endure, it is not the *making* of money so much as the wise, intelligent *using* of it, that should command attention and interest," Florence Barnard declared in the forward of her 1919 work, *The Prosperity Book*.

Continued on p. 728

Chronology

1840s-1945
Home-economics movement emphasizes efficiency in household management; economic crises plague U.S. consumers.

1841
Catharine Beecher's *A Treatise on Domestic Economy, For the Use of Young Ladies at Home and at School* is published.

1862
Morrill Act leads to increase in land-grant colleges, which include "domestic science" courses.

1907
Panic of 1907, sparked by copper speculators, marks first major financial crisis of 20th century.

1918
World War I ends; recession begins.

1919
Junior Achievement is organized to teach students about entrepreneurship and financial literacy.

1929
Stock market crash precedes deep depression, which spawns growth of consumer safety net.

1935
Social Security signed into law.

1939
Food Stamp program started.

1945
U.S. emerges from World War II as industrial power, presaging rise of middle-class consumerism.

1946-1980
American classrooms emphasize economic literacy amid

Cold War struggle between capitalism and communism.

1949
Forerunner of current Council for Economic Education is formed to promote economic education.

1960
National Task Force on Economic Education formed to help guide the teaching of economics.

1970
High-school enrollment in economics courses grows as nation faces industrial globalization, inflation and other pressures.

1973-1975
Spiraling oil prices and stagnant economic growth force consumers to watch their personal finances.

1978
Supreme Court allows credit-card issuers to bypass state usury laws.

1980-2000
Financial deregulation, cuts in pensions and credit cards add pressure on consumers.

1980-1982
Steep recession forces surge in prices and unemployment.

1982
Seven states require high-school students to take economics; number rises to 13 by 1987 and 16 in 1990.

1993
Credit-card companies send 1.5 billion offers to American households.

1995
Jump$tart Coalition for Personal Financial Literacy formed; American Savings Education Council organized.

1996
Supreme Court removes dollar limit on credit-card penalties.

1997
High-school seniors taking Jump$tart Coalition's first financial-literacy survey answer an average of only 57 percent of the questions correctly; average score drops to 50 percent in 2002.

2001-Present
Economic crisis slams millions of consumers holding risky mortgages and high credit-card debt.

2001-2006
Home prices surge, and home-equity loans spur consumer spending, debt.

2003
Financial Literacy and Education Commission formed to educate consumers.

2005
New federal law makes bankruptcy filing more expensive and restrictive; personal-savings rate turns negative for first time since Great Depression.

2008
High-school seniors taking Jump$tart's financial-literacy survey score an average of only 48 percent, down from 52 percent in 2006; college students score 62 percent.

2009
Congress passes stiff law regulating credit cards, and President Barack Obama proposes new Consumer Financial Protection Agency to regulate financial-services industry. . . . U.S. unemployment rate climbs toward 10 percent as recession destroys trillions of dollars in consumer wealth.

Using Video Games to Teach Financial Literacy

"We teach driver's ed and sex education, but not financial education."

When Tom Davidson graduated from Bowdoin College in Brunswick, Maine, he was saddled with heavy student loans and two maxed-out credit cards. Now, 15 years later, he says he had no clue about credit scores, loan interest rates and repayment plans.

"I was ground zero for this problem of financial literacy," he says.

Elected to the Maine House of Representatives at age 23, Davidson says his six years in the state legislature shed further light on the problem. "Serving in politics, it became clear that we turn out hundreds of thousands of kids that have no idea about their financial lives," he says.

In 2007, after dabbling with a few tech start-ups following his departure from politics, Davidson and two fellow Bowdoin alums founded EverFi, an online financial-literacy program that uses video games to turn young adults into savvy consumers by teaching them what high schools and universities do not.

"There is hardly any conversation at schools about issues relating to financial health," Davidson argues. "It's crazy that we teach things such as driver's ed and sex education, but we don't teach financial education."

"EverFi could have stumbled into the next $100 billion industry," said Ntiedo Etuk, CEO of New York-based educational gaming company Tabula Digita. [1]

Video games guide users through a five-hour series of real-world experiences — from the New York Stock Exchange to examinations of credit-card statements — and encourages them to control the spending habits of the characters in dramatic situations, much like the popular Sim City games. In the process, rewards are given for good choices — such as picking a low-cost mortgage — and consequences are suffered for bad ones, such as making a late payment on a credit card.

"After I took this program, I'm like, No, I've got to wait [to get a credit card]," said high-school student Shanetta Francis of Trenton, N.J. "I am not trying to get into debt at such a young age in my life; I'll wait." [2]

Users who satisfactorily pass all the levels and show enough of an understanding of personal finance become "EverFi Certified," a proof-of-completion that can be presented on college applications, job résumés and to potential lenders.

Since launching EverFi in February, Davidson and his team have pitched the program to high schools, universities, community organizations and nonprofits across the country.

EverFi has also targeted large organizations with a national reach, including PayPal, the United Negro College Fund and the National Black Chamber of Commerce. African-Americans have been targeted because they score lower on financial-literacy tests than other groups.

The company has encouraged customers to promote the software under their own brands, allowing them to take ownership and serve as local ambassadors for youth financial literacy. Several

Continued from p. 726

"The spending of money implies living in the present; the saving and giving of money looks beyond into the future. In the well-balanced life all three are necessary." [19]

In the 1930s and '40s, library shelves groaned with works warning consumers and students of questionable advertising practices (*Your Money's Worth: A Study in the Waste of the Consumer's Dollar*, 1927), advised them on the availability of credit (*Do You Need Some Money? Consumer Credit as a Means to Economic Stability*, 1941) and offered guidance on finances (*Using Dollars and Sense*, 1942).

New Economic Gospel

As World War II drew to a close and the Cold War began, the United States emerged as the foremost world power, and the curriculum in American schools reflected the capitalist gospel of industrial might and economic supremacy.

"During the twenty to twenty-five years after World War II, children in the United States were increasingly taught to understand their nation, its history and its economic greatness — as an 'economy' — rather than in social, moral, philosophical or political terms (i.e., as a society, a community, a republic, etc.)," wrote Andrew Yarrow, vice president and Washington director of Public Agenda, a nonprofit, public-opinion research group. [20]

"Equally powerful," Yarrow added, "was its message that the U.S. economy was an unprecedented marvel of productivity and a facet of Americanness of which to be proud and to defend."

During this period, he wrote, "not only did an economics-education movement emerge, but economics increasingly was taught as part of social studies, history or other classes, and a huge amount of curricular material was developed and disseminated for classroom use." [21]

As the postwar academic focus on economics grew, new groups emerged to promote it. They included the Joint Council on Economic Education, founded in 1949 and the forerunner of the current Council for Economic Education.

Peri, the council's acting CEO, says that after World War II a broad group of business and corporate leaders, educators in social studies and other disciplines and people from organized labor "came together and saw there was a dearth of basic education in the

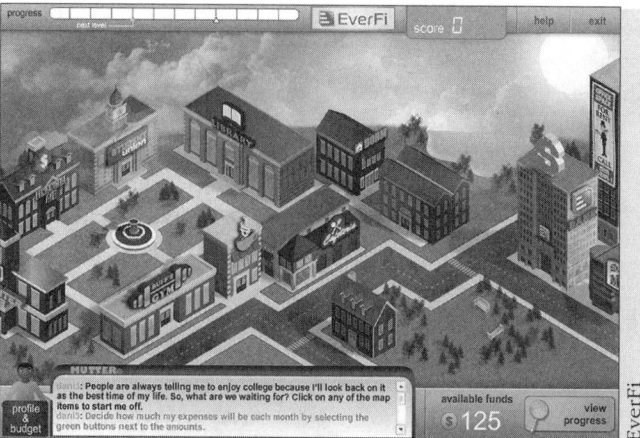

The EverFi online financial-literacy program uses video games and real-life problems to teach young adults.

EverFi licenses have been donated to promote the proprietary platform, and sales have followed. EverFi says it is currently being used in 600 outlets across 35 states as well as the District of Columbia.

PayPal has purchased licenses for 500 students in San Jose, Calif., and Timonium, Md., where the company conducts operations. The Chamber of Commerce in Washington, D.C., bought 1,250 licenses to launch its Financial Scholars Program for students.

EverFi hopes to enroll 20,000 students by the end of 2009, generating $4 million in sales, and 100,000 students by 2011. [3]

Although the dismal economic climate has adversely affected EverFi's sales, Davidson nonetheless regards the recession as a selling point as well as an obstacle.

"A lack of financial responsibility is one of the reasons we've been in this financial mess," he says. "While the economic meltdown has made it tough, it's provided an opportunity to tell people why they should use our product."

Fifteen years have passed since Davidson trashed his own financial record as an undergraduate. Today he hopes that EverFi will prevent today's adolescents from making the same mistakes, affecting struggling communities for the better in the process.

He points out that Selma and Tuskegee, Ala., each has about 400 students who are Ever-Fi Certified. As many of these students sign their first lease, secure their first credit card and fill out their first W-2 form after getting their first job, he says they will be prepared to make sound financial decisions.

In turn, he hopes that creditors, investors and corporations will look at the two communities — and their financially savvy consumers — more favorably.

"Tuskegee and Selma, five years later, may be good places to lend," he says.

— *Darrell Dela Rosa*

[1] Jessica Bruder, "Financial Literacy Through Video Games," CNNMoney.com, May 13, 2009, http://money.cnn.com/2009/05/12/smallbusiness/young_adult_financial_literacy.fsb/.

[2] Kelly Wallace, "Virtual Finance 101," Couric & Co. Blog, CBS News, July 16, 2009, www.cbsnews.com/blogs/2009/07/16/couricandco/entry5166751.shtml.

[3] Bruder, *op. cit.*

schools on how the economy worked. There was very little at the time in the curriculum on either how the market economy works, or the individual household economy.

"It was a sense in the postwar period that we had enormous growth in the economy, all of these returning veterans were coming back to work, there was an explosion in families being formed and our economy was getting more complex," Peri says. "There was really a sense that to be successful participants in the economy, people had to understand it more than in the past."

Still, little time was devoted to formal instruction in economics for high-school pupils before 1960, and courses in "consumer economics" or "consumer education" reached only a small fraction of students, Walstad of the University of Nebraska concluded in a 1992 research article on the subject. [22] In the early 1960s, only about 2 percent of high-school graduates had taken consumer economics and consumer-education courses, he noted. [23]

New Trend

The trend began to change in the 1970s and '80s. By 1987, 14 percent of high-school graduates had taken consumer-type courses, according to Walstad's research. [24]

Meanwhile, a growing number of states were requiring economics training of some sort for graduation, he noted. In 1982, seven states, covering 11 percent of public high-school graduates, required an economics course. By 1987, 13 states, accounting for about a fourth of high-school graduates, had mandates. In 1990 California, Indiana and New York adopted mandates, raising the coverage to 45 percent of public high-school graduates. [25]

Most of the classes were akin to traditional economics courses, Walstad wrote, but some state legislation reflected "a special emphasis." Seven states called for courses that featured the characteristics and preached the benefits of the "free-enterprise system," he noted, while four stressed coverage of consumer-education topics. North Carolina called for combining economics training with civics or government instruction, and New Hampshire mandated "basic business and economic education." [26]

More and more attention shifted toward "financial literacy" during the 1980s and early '90s, as the financial-

Getting an Early Start on Life Lessons

The Junior Board of Directors at the Ariel Community Academy in Chicago meets to discuss the class' investments (top). The one-of-a-kind public elementary school, established in 1996 by the money-management firm Ariel Capital Management, promotes financial literacy and gives kids money to invest. An 11-year-old student works on a financial-literacy course offered during "Kids Kollege," a summer-enrichment program at San Juan College in Farmington, N.M.

services industry was deregulated, many employers replaced guaranteed pensions with 401(k) plans and a consumer culture of easy credit and declining savings arose.

Jump$tart's genesis, as traced by the University of Washington's Mandell, reflected that evolutionary movement. He and a co-author wrote that a group of people who formed Jump$tart ini-

tially got together in the mid-1990s "to try to understand two powerful but seemingly opposite trends. On one hand, it was the best of economic times with increasing affluence for people of every income. On the other hand, it was the worst of times, with personal bankruptcies threatening to wipe out the assets of a million families in a single year. How could so many people be doing so poorly at a time when the general economy was doing so well?

"We concluded that much of the problem was due to a newly deregulated but very innovative financial system that demanded of its users a high level of financial sophistication. Our suspicion was that many Americans lacked the basic financial literacy necessary to make decisions in their own best interest." [27]

Dire Consequences

That lack of basic financial knowledge has had dire consequences for millions of American consumers slammed by the recent economic crisis. Some people borrowed beyond their means to buy homes, betting wrongly real estate values would keep rising. Some piled up credit-card debt. Some gambled foolishly on Wall Street with their savings. And countless consumers, critics say, were hoodwinked by everything from slick credit-card come-ons to mortgage terms that were too good to be true.

"Over the past few months, it has become apparent that the lack of education among consumers about financial systems and products is one of the key elements of our nation's current economic crisis," Rep. McCarthy said in introducing the Financial and Economic Literacy Improvement Act. "In many cases, consumers were preyed on by financial institutions and sold into debts that they were not capable of fulfilling. At its root, this has been a defining factor of the current economic crisis." [28]

Hebert of the New Hampshire Jump$tart Coalition says his long professional background in consumer banking gave him insight into the effects of poor financial training.

"I was seeing trends in lending and collections related to young people that were really troubling to me," he says. "I know in my heart of hearts kids don't want to make mistakes with money. They just haven't been given direction. We've taught them that $5,000 flat-screen TVs are no big deal. And the world out there is so consumer-driven. I worry about the 20-somethings — how they're going to make it."

Hebert blames both the financial world and consumers for the recent economic crisis. "In the lending world from the '90s on, we no longer said 'no' — we just found a way to say 'yes,' " he says. "If a borrower went to a bank and wanted a mortgage and the answer was no, the response was, 'I'll just go next door to your competitor.' " But at the same time, he says, "a whole generation of folks only has known the good times."

If Americans' financial security has been eroded by a combination of market excesses and unreasonable consumer expectations, it also has been hurt by what scholars call innumeracy — mathematical illiteracy, or the inability to understand and perform basic numerical calculations.

In an unpublished study, researchers Kris Gerardi of the Federal Reserve Bank of Atlanta, Lorenz Goette of the Université de Lausanne and Stephan Meier of Columbia University found a strong correlation between poor numerical skills and mortgage delinquencies and defaults. People who are bad at basic math are far more likely to have mortgage problems than people who are good with arithmetic, they concluded. [29]

In fact, foreclosures are two-thirds lower among people with the strongest numerical ability compared with those with the weakest, the researchers found. What's more, financial-literacy training, general intelligence or the number of years of formal education are far less important than numerical ability in determining whether a person stays current on a mortgage, they found.

While the study stopped short of trying to determine why poor math skills are related to mortgage delinquency, Meier said in an interview he believes innumeracy may lead "to an accumulation of small mistakes" that cause big financial headaches. People weak in numerical ability might save too little and get hit by an unexpected financial emergency, he says, or they might run their credit card up and get caught in a cycle of ever-expanding monthly balances.

Schools Lead the Way

As concerns about financial literacy have grown in recent years, a huge array of groups, programs and personal-finance Web sites have sprung up to guide consumers.

The efforts include such groups as the American Savings Education Council, which promotes saving and retirement planning, among other resources. Likewise, the National Financial Education Network aims to promote financial education at the state and local levels. In addition, the federal government offers resources, including the Treasury's Office of Financial Education and the U.S. Financial Literacy and Education Commission, which offers a MyMoney.gov Web site and a toll-free hotline.

Still, schools in many ways are on the front lines of training youngsters about personal finance. Yet resources to carry out such training are in short supply, especially as the economic

crisis has eroded government budgets. That has led many schools, along with financial-literacy advocacy groups, to form partnerships with for-profit financial-services companies — a trend that some see as necessary and even useful but others as troublesome.

The Council for Economic Education derives about a fourth of its funding from the financial-services industry, according to Peri, who adds that the proportion "will vary from year to year." On its Web site, the council lists a wide variety of supporters from the business world, including Allstate and State Farm insurance companies, Bank of America Charitable Foundation and Wells Fargo.

Peri says that as a developer of educational material, the council has "very rigid and strict guidelines. When we have relationships with financial institutions that support some of our work, we will accept their support but will clearly create the materials ourselves using rigorous academic benchmarks."

Jump$tart receives "a lot" of its budget from financial-services companies in the form of dues, project sponsorships and donations made at a fundraising dinner, says Levine, the group's executive director. Corporate supporters include American Express, Capital One, HSBC-North America, Wells Fargo and Visa. Money also comes from nonprofit groups that themselves receive corporate donations, Levine points out.

The Merrill Lynch Foundation provided money for the Jump$tart financial-literacy surveys of high-school and college students between 2004 and 2008, Levine says. But Merrill Lynch disappeared last fall when the brokerage giant — crippled by bad mortgage investments amid what critics call a massive demonstration of corporate financial illiteracy on Wall Street — was swallowed up by Bank of America.

Levine defends the role of corporate sponsors and says Jump$tart reviews materials "to make sure the information is correct and relevant, that it adheres to national standards and that it's not marketing material in disguise." Materials that come from the financial-services industry "often are the most timely" and therefore useful in understanding an economic landscape that changes with the blink of an eye, she says. What's more, she says, the potential for problems arising from corporate influence has decreased in recent years "because teachers and schools have gotten more sophisticated about where the money flows from."

But others express concern about corporate influence in financial-literacy training.

"The financial industry should not be devising curriculum for the schools and what to teach," says Dartmouth's Lusardi. "It's critically important in the financial-education arena that there is complete independence from the financial industry and the suppliers of financial products."

In *The Death of 'Why?'* Schlesinger wrote, "I don't oppose financial-literacy education. Young people should be prepared to make good financial choices. Those working in the trenches to improve students' financial-management skills are motivated by real concern that young people are accruing debt from which they will never recover."

But, she added, "What does it say that we have opened up America's public school classrooms for banks to hock their wares — supposedly in the name of our children's advancement? What does it say about us that we are embracing financial literacy in the schools — and what does it say about the members of corporate America that are underwriting it?" [30]

In an interview, Schlesinger criticized the practice employed by some schools of using people from the financial-services industry to give lessons to stu-

dents. "They're not teachers, not trained to be teachers — their ability to effectively educate is limited," Schlesinger said. "I think the curriculum is designed less to engage students and more to offer lessons and to plug products, and I don't think that translates to true learning." ∎

CURRENT SITUATION

New Efforts

Although the current financial crisis has focused unprecedented attention on financial-literacy training, critics say the efforts are fragmented. As *Business Week* noted this summer, "When it comes to financial literacy, a lot is happening, but there is not one national agenda — yet." [31]

The movement is "at that state where we're just getting organized," said Beck of the National Endowment for Financial Education. "We're getting a lot of well-meaning people to work together." [32]

In Washington, a number of federal agencies, such as the Federal Trade Commission and Federal Deposit Insurance Corp., have long offered consumer-oriented educational resources, and new efforts are under way.

For example, the Securities and Exchange Commission this year formed the Investor Advisory Committee to give investors a greater voice in the SEC's work, and one topic identified at its first meeting in July was how the agency can promote early financial-literacy and investor education. [33] The Social Security Administration announced plans for a Financial Literacy Research Consortium aimed at creating tools "to better inform the public about key fi-

nancial-literacy topics related to retirement savings and planning." [34]

Yet, some worry that federal efforts to promote financial literacy are becoming redundant or fragmented. Others are concerned about the effectiveness of existing programs.

A U.S. Government Accountability Office (GAO) study this year pointed to shortcomings within the Financial Literacy and Education Commission, which was established in 2003 to coordinate financial-education efforts throughout the federal government and encourage partnerships between pubic and private sectors, among other things.

The GAO said the commission, which is coordinated by the Treasury and composed of 20 federal agencies, had made progress in fostering partnerships at the federal, state and local levels. But its national strategy remains "largely descriptive rather than strategic," and it does not have an independent budget, the GAO said. [35]

Many consumer activists see promise for financial literacy in a newly enacted law regulating credit cards. Among other things, the measure requires card companies to warn customers 45 days before raising interest rates or otherwise making major changes to a contract. In addition, card companies must send bills at least three weeks before the payment due date, and they must let consumers decline a rate increase, allowing them to pay off their balance at the existing rate instead. [36]

What's more, the law requires the departments of Education and Treasury to work with the President's Advisory Council on Financial Literacy to inventory existing federal financial- and economic-literacy education programs and develop a plan to expand such education. [37]

Consumer advocates hail the bill as a boon to financial literacy.

"[G]reater transparency and fairness in the system is critical, and I think this

Continued on p. 734

At Issue:

Does financial-literacy education work?

LAURA LEVINE
*EXECUTIVE DIRECTOR, JUMP$TART
COALITION FOR PERSONAL FINANCIAL
LITERACY*

WRITTEN FOR *CQ RESEARCHER*, SEPT. 1, 2009

*r*esearch shows that financial education increases knowledge
as well as students' ability and inclination to make smart financial choices. Some examples of key research include:

• Students who played The Stock Market Game scored significantly higher than their peers in math and financial literacy,
according to a recent FINRA Foundation study.

• Students showed significant improvement in financial
knowledge, behavior and confidence after participating in the
NEFE High School Financial Planning Program, according to
University of Minnesota evaluations.

• Students who completed the full semester Family Economics and Financial Education program showed a 12 percent
increase in post-test scores, an independent study found.

• Both financial knowledge and appropriate behavior increased among students who took the Cooperative Extension's
"Money Talks: Should I Be Listening?" program.

Some critics have cited Jump$tart's biennial survey as evi-
dence that financial education does not work, because it indicates low levels of financial knowledge, and those students who
had taken a course in personal finance did not perform substantially better than their peers. While the results are disappointing,
the survey was not designed to assess the effectiveness of financial education and, therefore, does not.

As it was intended, however, Jump$tart's survey does show
a clear lack of financial knowledge among young people. And
while we continue to learn about and develop how and
when best to provide financial education — *my personal belief is earlier and more often* — it would be a mistake to try
to remedy these low levels of financial literacy by decreasing
or stopping financial education in the meantime, in favor of
regulatory solutions alone.

Perhaps we should be asking whether financial education is
worthwhile — and the answer is even more emphatically, yes.
While education alone won't guarantee financial well-being, it
must be part of the equation — along with adequate information, consumer protection, access to fair and convenient services
and a better understanding of social and emotional influences.

As the director of a coalition representing hundreds of organizations that conduct and support standards-based financial
education, and as the mother of a young son, I believe that
financial education is crucial to providing future generations
with the knowledge and skills they'll need not only to make
smart financial decisions for themselves, but to know when
and how to seek help.

LAUREN E. WILLIS
*PROFESSOR OF LAW, LOYOLA LAW
SCHOOL, LOS ANGELES*

WRITTEN FOR *CQ RESEARCHER*, SEPT. 1, 2009

*f*inancial-literacy education does not work, nor should
we expect it to. In tests of high-school seniors, those
who had taken a personal-finance course performed
worse than those who had not. After financial training,
soldiers were less likely to pay off credit-card bills in full and
were less likely to use a formal budget than soldiers who did
not receive the training. Longitudinal data reveal that financial-
education requirements in public schools have had no effect on
financial outcomes in adulthood.

The quality of personal-finance courses is suspect. Industry
develops and sponsors many programs and has a profit incentive to encourage consumers to spend money on financial services. Yet would well-intentioned classes designed by a neutral
source likely be effective? No.

Lessons about personal finance are quickly obsolete. What
is called a graduated-payment mortgage one day might be
called a buydown the next. Those taught that usury laws
would protect them can be blindsided by 29 percent interest
rates today. Retirement-planning classes uniformly advised that
real estate was a safe investment, until it was not.

Consumers have no time for classes. Instead, at the very
moment they want to learn about the products available arrives
a broker to convince them to select the product that produces
the highest commission. Salespeople can talk circles around
vaguely remembered school lessons.

What might be helpful is not teaching financial literacy but
basic consumer education. Consumers need to know how little
they know, how quickly things change and where to get unbiased, accurate information.

But knowledge alone will not be enough. Knowing how
difficult the financial marketplace is to navigate could even be
paralyzing. We need to redesign the marketplace to comport
with realistic expectations about consumers.

Reducing the variety of financial products available to a few
options, each containing standardized features with just a few
moving parts, could enable consumers to discern costs and benefits and meaningfully shop among the options. Consumers could
safely rely on their brokers if we banned compensation schemes
that create a conflict of interest between sellers and consumers.
For some inevitably complex decisions, we should provide pro
bono financial advice, possibly through computerized systems.

Current laws requiring reams of unintelligible disclosures
are make-work for industry and do not benefit consumers.
Financial-literacy education feeds the disclosure machine. The
goal should be regulation that is responsive to real people.

Continued from p. 732

bill addresses that," Adam Levin, chairman and founder of Credit.com, a consumer education and advocacy group, said on PBS' "NewsHour with Jim Lehrer." "It's not the silver bullet, but it's a start. . . .

"We've been woefully shortsighted in the way we've treated financial literacy in this country. And part of the problem that's happened in the financial-services industry is the fact that many of these documents, many of the notices, many of the contracts that involve credit cards have been very confusing. In some congressional hearings, they've talked about being written in 27th-grade English.

"So that's part of what this law is designed to address: to give consumers more time, to give consumers more disclosure and to give consumers an opportunity to develop strategies in the event that something goes horribly wrong relative to their rate or relative to the fees they face." [38]

New Consumer Agency

Besides the credit-card law, financial-literacy advocates are also watching an administration proposal to overhaul the financial-regulatory system. President Obama wants to create a controversial Consumer Financial Protection Agency that would have broad power to oversee financial products and services.

The president has said the government must step in to thwart a "culture of irresponsibility" among both banks and borrowers. [39] The agency "should give consumer protection an

Elementary school students in Atlanta participate in Operation Hope's youth financial-literacy program. More than two-thirds of parents responding to a 2008 Charles Schwab & Co. survey said they felt less prepared to guide their teens on investing than on the "birds and bees."

Operation Hope, Inc.

independent seat at the table," the administration argues. [40] According to legislative proposals in Congress, the proposed agency would coordinate efforts with member agencies of the Financial Literacy and Education Commission to enhance their financial-literacy education efforts and make them consistent.

But trade groups such as the American Bankers Association and other business organizations are heavily opposed to the plan to create a new oversight agency, and Congress has yet to approve it. [41]

Elizabeth Warren, a Harvard Law School professor who chairs a congressional oversight panel on the Troubled Asset Relief Program — the $700 billion "TARP" bank-bailout plan — is a key advocate of the proposed agency. [42] An expert on consumer law and credit, she argues that "the market for consumer financial products is broken."

"It is broken because incomprehensible legalese prevents consumers from being able to understand the basic features of financial products and from comparing those products," she told *Consumer Reports* in a four-part interview.

Warren added: "The market has remained broken in large part because our regulatory system is fragmented, cumbersome and complex. While various regulators — including the Federal Reserve and the chief banking supervisors — have long had the legal authority to protect consumers, they have refused to do so."

Warren said the proposed agency would approve templates for "plain vanilla" contracts such as 30-year fixed mortgages that would be "designed to be read in a few minutes. . . . Consumers would be able to lay out a half-dozen simple-to-read contracts on the kitchen table and see which product best fits their needs." Lenders could still offer complex or risky products but would have to disclose the risks "clearly enough that customers can understand them without a lawyer nearby," she said.

Warren said that although the agency could help consumers become savvier, transparency and fairness in financial transactions are key elements for improving financial literacy.

"Financial education is important, and the administration and others are examining how the current education models can be improved and expanded," she said. "One advantage of the [agency] is that it can be a home for policy innovation in this area and also a platform for advancing financial literacy." Still, "no amount of education will empower consumers to compare reams of mortgage disclosures or dozens of pages of credit-card fine print that are designed to be incomprehensible. Consumer-protection regulations need to be streamlined and simplified so that consumer education can work." [43]

More Requirements

Aside from Obama's plan for an independent financial regulator, some are calling for Congress to make more money available for consumer-training programs. "I was very disappointed when the TARP money came out," says Hebert, the New Hampshire Jump$tart official, referring to last fall's bank-bailout plan. "I didn't see early on any money spent toward financial education."

The Financial and Economic Literacy Improvement Act of 2009, introduced by Sens. Murray and Cochran and Rep. McCarthy, would provide $250 million in state grants annually over five years to support financial-literacy training for kindergarten, elementary and high-school students and students attending two- and four-year colleges. [44] Murray's office said the measure would "for the first time . . . make the federal government a major supporter in teaching financial literacy to students and adults." [45] Congress has not yet voted on the proposal.

Separately, some states have been moving to strengthen financial education in the classrooms. For example, a Michigan law enacted in December allows school districts to offer a one-semester course in personal finance to fulfill a student math credit. [46] The New Jersey Board of Education in June revised its high-school graduation standard by adding a half-year of economics and financial literacy to the state's core curriculum. [47]

And in Kansas, a 2009 law requires education officials, when selecting textbooks for math, economics, consumer science or certain other courses, to choose ones that contain substantive provisions about personal finance. The law also directs officials to develop curriculum standards for personal financial literacy and to include questions on personal financial literacy in the statewide assessments for math and social studies when those are reviewed or rewritten. [48]

As lawmakers and other government officials examine ways to improve financial literacy, academic researchers are asking more fundamental questions: Which approaches work, which don't and what are the best ways to structure financial-education efforts in the future?

In a working paper published early this year, Shawn Cole of the Harvard Business School and Gauri Kartini Shastry of the University of Virginia found that higher levels of education and cognitive ability caused increased participation in financial markets but that financial-literacy education did not affect individual savings decisions. [49]

Meier, the Columbia University professor studying the link between numerical skills and financial literacy, also has examined why more adults — especially those who can benefit the most from financial-literacy training — don't go looking for it more often. In a study done with a colleague from the University of California, San Diego, Meier found that patient people — those willing to wait for a larger amount of money in the future rather than receiving a smaller amount quickly — were more likely to sign up for financial counseling than impatient people. [50]

"We know very little about whether financial literacy actually works," Meier said in a Columbia University summary of the study. "That's because most of the studies done so far don't account for the fact that people who self-select into these programs are more patient and future-oriented than those who don't." ∎

OUTLOOK

Race and Income Level

While some researchers debate the value of financial-education programs, others say demand has nowhere to go but up as credit cards and mortgages grow more complex and consumers bear increasing responsibility for their financial and retirement security.

"Twenty-five years ago, you didn't have things like variable-rate mortgages, and most people didn't jump around in jobs — they had the old defined-benefit-type pension plans," says Peri of the Council for Economic Education.

"They may not have understood it, but they knew it was going to be there. And health care was a much easier issue to deal with. When you put all these things together, it may have been that at one time being economically or financially illiterate wasn't as a big a deal." But now, Peri says, "it's all the more important that people understand things."

A major concern of financial-literacy advocates — one that is likely to get more attention in coming years — is how to help poor and minority populations gain a better understanding of economic and personal-finance issues. On the 2008 Jump$tart survey of high-school seniors, students from the highest-income category — those whose parents made at least $80,000 — had average scores of 52.3 percent, while those from the lowest-income category — with parents' income of less than $20,000 — averaged only 43.4 percent. And white students, with average scores of 52.5 percent, did considerably better than black (41.3 percent), Hispanic (45.1 percent) and Native-American (37.7 percent) students.

The University of Washington's Mandell noted the implications of the disparities during a presentation of survey results last year at the Federal Reserve Board of Governors.

"These dramatic differences understate the true magnitude of the problem since we surveyed only high-school seniors in the middle of their last year and know that many students of color never made it this far in school and were therefore not included in the survey," he said. "In many urban areas . . . , fewer than half of African-American males graduate from high school, and it is not unreasonable to assume that those who left school before their senior years are less financially literate than those who are completing high school. Therefore, the financial literacy of all African-Americans who are 17-19 years old is probably even lower than 41.3 percent. . . .

"The relationship between financial literacy, race and income combine to further exacerbate differences in standards of living which are the product of financial resources and financial literacy." [51]

Meanwhile, proponents of stronger, more consumer-friendly regulation say improvements in financial literacy will depend heavily on how aggressively the government acts.

Willis of Loyola Law School says creation of a federal Consumer Financial Protection Agency is an important step because it would harmonize financial-services regulations among various federal agencies and make consumer transactions easier to understand.

Willis also says that if financial education is to be made part of school curricula, it is important for states to put adequate money into teacher training, curriculum development and materials for financial-literacy programs. Otherwise, she says, too many schools may depend on help from financial-services companies that may not teach students

that borrowers and lenders, or investors and brokers, have different incentives.

"If schools are not getting support from the state," she says, "they're going to take whatever program is free." ■

Notes

[1] For background see the following *CQ Researcher* reports: Marcia Clemmitt, "Regulating Credit Cards," Oct. 10, 2008, pp. 817-840; Barbara Mantel, "Consumer Debt," March 2, 2007, pp. 193-216, and Pamela M. Prah, "Teen Spending," May 26, 2006, pp. 457-480.

[2] Remarks of Rep. Ruben Hinojosa, hearing on "Improving Consumer Financial Literacy Under the New Regulatory System," House Financial Services Subcommittee on Financial Institutions and Consumer Credit, June 25, 2009, www.house.gov/apps/list/hearing/financialsvcs_dem/june_25th_mc_remarks_at_financial_institutions_hearing_on_financial_literacy.pdf.

[3] Charles Schwab, "2007 Teens and Money Survey," www.schwabmoneywise.com/views/survey/teensAndMoney.php. The survey polled 1,000 teens ages 13-18 and was conducted on behalf of Schwab and Boys & Girls Clubs of America.

[4] For background see Thomas J. Billitteri, "Middle-Class Squeeze," *CQ Researcher*, March 6, 2009, pp. 201-224, and Alan Greenblatt, "Upward Mobility," *CQ Researcher*, April 29, 2005, pp. 369-392.

[5] Lewis Mandell, The Financial Literacy of Young American Adults," Jump$tart Coalition for Personal Financial Literacy, 2008, p. 5. www.jumpstart.org/upload/2009_FinLit-Mandell.pdf.

[6] Annamaria Lusardi, "Financial Literacy: An Essential Tool for Informed Consumer Choice?" *NBER Working Paper No. 14084*, www.dart

mouth.edu/~alusardi/Papers/Lusardi_Informed_Consumer.pdf.

[7] Charles Schwab, "2008 Parents and Money Survey Findings," www.schwabmoneywise.com/downloads/Parents_Money_Survey_Fact sheet.

[8] "2008 Annual Report to the President," President's Advisory Council on Financial Literacy, U.S. Treasury, 2009, p. 3, www.treas.gov/offices/domestic-finance/financial-institution/fin-education/docs/PACFL_ANNUAL_REPORT_1-16-09.pdf.

[9] News release, office of Sen. Patty Murray, March 19, 2009, http://murray.senate.gov/news.cfm?id=310067. For background on the economic crisis, see Kenneth Jost, "Financial Crisis," *CQ Researcher*, May 9, 2008, pp. 409-432.

[10] Lauren Willis, "Against Financial-Literacy Education," *Iowa Law Review*, Vol. 94, 2008, p. 272, www.law.uiowa.edu/documents/ilr/willis.pdf.

[11] Remarks of Ben S. Bernanke, "The Importance of Financial Education and the National Jump$tart Coalition Survey," Federal Reserve System Board of Governors, April 9, 2008, www.federalreserve.gov/newsevents/speech/bernanke20080409a.htm.

[12] "The Nation's Report Card: Economics 2006," National Assessment Governing Board, http://nces.ed.gov/nationsreportcard/pdf/main2006/2007475.pdf. The assessment was administered by the National Center for Education Statistics, U.S. Department of Education.

[13] "2008 Annual Report to the President," *op. cit.*

[14] "What Will They Learn?" American Council of Trustees and Alumni, 2009, www.goacta.org/publications/downloads/WhatWillTheyLearn Final.pdf.

[15] "2008 Annual Report to the President," *op. cit.*, pp. 18-19.

[16] Tamar Lewin, "Study Shows Rise in Average Borrowing by Students," *The New York Times*, Aug. 12, 2009, www.nytimes.com/2009/08/12/education/12college.html?ref=us.

[17] Quoted in *ibid.*

[18] Catharine Esther Beecher, *A Treatise on Domestic Economy, For the Use of Young Ladies at Home and at School*, rev. ed. (1856). Beecher was a sister of abolitionist Harriet Beecher Stowe.

[19] Florence Barnard, *The Prosperity Book* (1919).

[20] Andrew L. Yarrow, "Beyond Civics and the 3 R's: Teaching Economics in the Schools," *History of Education Quarterly*, Vol. 48, No. 3, August 2008, p. 397.

About the Author

Thomas J. Billitteri is a *CQ Researcher* staff writer based in Fairfield, Pa., who has more than 30 years' experience covering business, nonprofit institutions and public policy for newspapers and other publications. His recent *CQ Researcher* reports include "Auto Industry's Future," "Middle-Class Squeeze" and "Financial Bailout." He holds a BA in English and an MA in journalism from Indiana University.

[21] *Ibid.*

[22] William B. Walstad, "Economics Instruction in High Schools," *Journal of Economic Literature*, Vol. XXX, December 1992, pp. 2019-2051.

[23] *Ibid.*, p. 2024.

[24] *Ibid.* Six percent of high-school graduates had taken courses in consumer economics and 8 percent in consumer education, according to Walstad.

[25] *Ibid.*, pp. 2024-2025.

[26] *Ibid.*, p. 2025.

[27] Lewis Mandell and Maykala Hariharan, "A Dream of Financial Literacy," *Credit Union Magazine*, January 2004, pp. 21-22A.

[28] News release from the office of Sen. Murray, *op. cit.*

[29] Kris Gerardi, Lorenz Goette and Stephan Meier, "Sustainable Homeownership and Numerical Ability," 2009, unpublished.

[30] Andrea Batista Schlesinger, *The Death of 'Why?': The Decline of Questioning and the Future of Democracy* (2009).

[31] Ben Steverman, "Financial Literacy: The Time Is Now," *Business Week*, July 22, 2009.

[32] Quoted in *ibid.*

[33] "Announcement From the SEC Investor Advisory Committee," Securities and Exchange Commission, July 29, 2009, www.sec.gov/news/press/2009/2009-175.htm.

[34] "Special Initiative to Encourage Saving," Social Security Administration, May 6, 2009, www.ssa.gov/retirementpolicy/financial_literacy.htm.

[35] Statement of Richard J. Hillman, managing director, Financial Markets and Community Investment, Government Accountability Office, before Senate Homeland Security and Government Affairs Subcommittee on Oversight of Government Management, the Federal Workforce, and the District of Columbia, April 29, 2009, www.gao.gov/new.items/d09638t.pdf.

[36] "Tougher Credit Card Rules Offer New Consumer Guards," "The NewsHour With Jim Lehrer," Aug. 20, 2009, www.pbs.org/newshour/bb/business/july-dec09/credit_08-20.html.

[37] The requirement is spelled out in Section 510 of HR 627.

[38] Transcript, "NewsHour," *op. cit.*

[39] Binyamin Appelbaum, "Obama Defends Financial Overhaul," *The Washington Post*, June 18, 2009, www.washingtonpost.com/wp-dyn/content/article/2009/06/17/AR2009061701834.html.

[40] U.S. Treasury, "Financial Refulatory Reform: A New Foundation," 2009, p. 56, www.financialstability.gov/docs/regs/FinalReport_web.pdf.

[41] Appelbaum, *op. cit.*

[42] For background, see Thomas J. Billitteri, "Financial Bailout," *CQ Researcher*, Oct. 24, 2008, pp. 865-888.

[43] ConsumerReports.org, "Prof. Elizabeth Warren on why we need the CFPA," in four parts, Aug. 12-21, 2009, http://blogs.consumerreports.org/money/elizabeth-warren/index.html.

[44] S. 638 and H.R. 1645.

[45] News release from office of Sen. Patty Murray, *op. cit.*

[46] Michigan Senate Bill 834.

[47] Megan DeMarco, "N.J. makes financial literacy a graduation requirement," *Philadelphia Inquirer*, July 1, 2009, www.philly.com/inquirer/local/nj/20090701_N_J__makes_financial_literacy_a_graduation_requirement.html.

[48] Kansas Senate Bill 41. See Kansas Office of the Governor, "Governor Parkinson signs Omnibus Crime Bill," May 21, 2009, www.governor.ks.gov/News/NewsRelease/2009/nr-09-0521a.htm.

[49] Shawn Cole and Gauri Kartini Shastry, "Smart Money: The Effect of Education, Cognitive Ability, and Financial Literacy on Financial Market Participation," Harvard Business School, Working Paper 09-071, February 2009, www.hbs.edu/research/pdf/09-071.pdf.

[50] "Discounting financial literacy," Columbia Ideas At Work, Columbia University, Oct. 31, 2008, http://www4.gsb.columbia.edu/ideasatwork/feature/34369/Discounting+financial+literacy.

[51] Lewis Mandell, "2008 Jump$tart Financial Literacy Surveys of High School Seniors and College Students," narrated PowerPoint Presentation from Press Conference at the Board of Governors of the Federal Reserve, April 9, 2008, http://74.125.95.132/search?q=cache:H8QxDUkOR7MJ:www.clevelandfed.org/Our_Region/Community_Development/Events/Seminars/20080425_Fin_Lit/Mandell_paper_slides.doc+financial+literacy%2Bsample+exam&cd=10&hl=en&ct=clnk&gl=us.

FOR MORE INFORMATION

American Savings Education Council, 1100 13th St., N.W., Suite 878, Washington, DC 20005; (202) 659-0670; www.choosetosave.org/asec/. National coalition of public and private groups promoting savings and retirement planning.

Council for Economic Education, 122 E. 42nd St., Suite 2600, New York, NY 10168; (212) 730-7007; www.councilforeconed.org/. Advocates for school-based economic and personal financial education offering related programs for teachers and students.

Initiative on Financial Security, Aspen Institute, One Dupont Circle, N.W., Suite 700, Washington, DC 20036; (202) 736-5800; www.aspeninstitute.org/policy-work/financial-security. Policy program focused on helping Americans save and invest.

Jump$tart Coalition for Personal Financial Literacy, 919 18th St., N.W., Suite 300, Washington, DC 20006; (202) 466-8604; www.jumpstart.org. National coalition of organizations seeking to improve the financial literacy of students in kindergarten through college.

National Endowment for Financial Education, 5299 DTC Blvd., Suite 1300, Greenwood Village, CO 80111; (303) 741-6333; www.nefe.org. Provides free financial-literacy curriculum and resources to students and adults.

U.S. Financial Literacy and Education Commission; www.mymoney.gov. Web site and toll-free hotline (888-MYMONEY) providing basic financial information and resources.

Women's Institute for Financial Education, P.O. Box 910014, San Diego, CA 92191; (760) 736-1660; www.wife.org. Nonprofit group providing financial information to women seeking financial independence.

Bibliography

Selected Sources

Books

Gosselin, Peter, *High Wire*, Basic Books, 2008.

The national economics correspondent for the *Los Angeles Times* argues that more and more Americans "are in danger of taking steep financial falls."

Manning, Robert D., *Credit Card Nation*, Basic Books, 2000.

How, an economic sociologist asks, "can postindustrial society maintain social order if its citizens are conditioned to prefer short-term pleasure (consumption) over pain (production) or spending over saving?"

Quinn, Jane Bryant, *Smart and Simple Financial Strategies for Busy People*, Simon & Schuster, 2006.

A veteran personal-finance writer argues that "managing money ought to be simple — and can be, as long as you get the principles right."

Schlesinger, Andrea Batista, *The Death of "Why?": The Decline of Questioning and the Future of Democracy*, Berrett-Koehler, 2009.

The executive director of the liberal Drum Major Institute for Public Policy uses parts of her book to cast a critical eye on financial-literacy programs in the schools.

Articles

Burns, Greg, "Financial education leaving Americans behind," *Chicago Tribune*, Feb. 15, 2009, http://archives.chicagotribune.com/2009/feb/15/business/chi-mon-burns-financial-literacyfeb16.

Several academic researchers argue that financial-literacy courses are ineffective.

Mandell, Lewis, "Two Cheers for School-Based Financial Education," Initiative on Financial Security, The Aspen Institute, June 2009, www.aspeninstitute.org/publications/two-cheer-school-based-financial-education.

This critique concludes that financial education might be more useful when introduced to younger children.

Marte, Jonnelle, "Credit Card Rules for Under-21s: Wise Idea or Ticket To Financial Hardship?" *The Wall Street Journal*, Aug. 10, 2009.

Experts have differing views about a new federal law that makes it harder for people under 21 to get a credit card.

Moltz, David, "Dollars and Sense," *Inside Higher Ed*, Oct. 22, 2008, www.insidehighered.com/news/2008/10/22/finance.

Colleges and universities are seeing heightened interest in financial-literacy programs in the wake of the economic crisis.

Shiller, Robert J., "How About a Stimulus for Financial Advice?" *The New York Times*, Jan. 18, 2009, www.nytimes.com/2009/01/18/business/economy/18view.html?scp=1&sq=how%20about%20a%20stimulus%20for%20financial%20advice?&st=cse.

A Yale economics and finance professor argues in favor of a "major [government] program to subsidize personal financial advice for everyone."

Steverman, Ben, "Financial Literacy: The Time Is Now," *Business Week*, July 22, 2009, www.businessweek.com/investor/content/jul2009/pi20090722_420432.htm.

The economic crisis is spurring new interest in financial-literacy programs in schools and workplaces, say several articles on the subject.

Willis, Lauren E., "Against Financial Literacy Education," *94 Iowa Law Review*, 2008, www.law.uiowa.edu/documents/ilr/willis.pdf.

"The search for effective financial-literacy education should be replaced by a search for policies more conducive to good consumer financial outcomes," argues an associate professor at Loyola Law School in Los Angeles.

Reports and Studies

Mandell, Lewis, "The Financial Literacy of Young American Adults," 2009, Jump$tart Coalition for Personal Financial Literacy, www.jumpstart.org/upload/2009_FinLit-Mandell.pdf.

The sixth biennial survey for the Jump$tart Coalition for Personal Financial Literacy finds that financial literacy among high-school students fell to its lowest level ever in 2008.

"President's Advisory Council on Financial Literacy: 2008 Annual Report to the President," U.S. Department of the Treasury, January 2009, www.treas.gov/offices/domestic-finance/financial-institution/fin-education/docs/PACFL_ANNUAL_REPORT_1-16-09.pdf.

Created by former President George W. Bush in early 2008 to improve financial literacy, the council offers 15 recommendations, including that Congress or state legislatures "mandate financial education in all schools for students in grades kindergarten through 12."

Vitt, Lois A., *et al.*, "Goodbye to Complacency: Financial Literacy Education in the U.S. 2000-2005," AARP and Institute for Socio Financial Studies, 2005, www.isfs.org/GoodbyetoComplacency.pdf.

Researchers provide a broad overview of efforts by public and private groups to improve personal financial education.

The Next Step:

Additional Articles from Current Periodicals

Bankruptcy

Aucoin, Don, "A Crash Course in Credit," *The Boston Globe,* **May 6, 2008, p. E1.**

Boston-area high-school students watched a mock bankruptcy hearing to help them become more financially savvy.

Brodeur, Nicole, "Give Judge Credit for Debt Smarts," *Seattle Times,* **May 15, 2009, p. B1.**

A bankruptcy judge in Washington state is fighting to bring financial literacy into schools amid a rise in bankruptcy filings.

Stull, Elizabeth, "Western District of New York Bankruptcy Judge Seizes a Teachable Moment," *Daily Record of Rochester* **(New York), March 24, 2009.**

A bankruptcy judge in New York state has blamed an increase in bankruptcy filings on a lack of financial literacy.

Economic Crisis

Garrison-Sprenger, Nicole, "As Our Financial System Crumbles, Financial Advocates Say We Need to Learn to Do the Math," *St. Paul* **(Minnesota)** *Pioneer Press,* **April 11, 2009.**

Consensus has been building for Americans to get a firmer grip on financial fundamentals.

Hansard, Sara, "Lack of Financial Know-How Wreaks Havoc," *Investment News,* **April 21, 2008, p. 14.**

Poor financial literacy among Americans is partly to blame for the country's economic woes, according to Rep. Barney Frank, D-Mass., chairman of the House Financial Services Committee.

Losey, Bill, "The Real Economic Crisis: Financial Illiteracy," *Press & Sun-Bulletin* **(New York), July 28, 2008, p. 2B.**

Americans will continue to rack up debts and fall behind on bills unless financial literacy becomes more mainstream.

Summey, Mike, "Lack of Education Has Contributed to Economic Woes," *Asheville* **(North Carolina)** *Citizen-Times,* **Oct. 3, 2008, p. 6D.**

Many critics say today's economic crisis might have been averted if basic money management was taught more in schools.

Mandates

Forster, Dave, "Lawmaker Calls for More Teaching on Money — Again," *Virginian-Pilot,* **Jan. 28, 2009, p. A9.**

Virginia high schools are required to teach financial literacy but are not required to report whether they are in compliance.

Gootee, Richard, "Bill Would Help Youths Boost Financial Smarts," *Indianapolis Star,* **March 24, 2009, p. 22A.**

A state lawmaker in Indiana is suggesting adding a financial-literacy section to a series of mandatory school exams.

Millard, Sarah, "Financial Literacy Now Mandatory for Graduation," *Herald Times Reporter* **(Wisconsin), Nov. 12, 2008, p. 3A.**

The school district of Manitowoc, Wis., is mandating high-school students to pass a financial-literacy course in order to graduate.

Rosen, Steve, "Use Bailout Bucks for Financial Literacy," *Orlando Sentinel,* **June 29, 2008, p. G5.**

Money used to bail out banks from the subprime mortgage mess should be redirected toward mandatory financial-education courses for high-school students.

Nonprofits

Cortez, Ashley, "Bank Awards $400,000 in Grants to Area Nonprofit Organizations," *Houston Chronicle,* **Dec. 18, 2008, p. 3.**

Capital One Bank has awarded $400,000 in grants to 12 Houston nonprofit organizations to support local financial-education initiatives.

Riley, Sheila, "Financial Literacy Web Sites Target Those As Young As 8," *Investor's Business Daily,* **Aug. 14, 2009, p. A4.**

The American Institute of Certified Public Accountants has teamed up with the nonprofit Advertising Council to do public-service announcements for financial-literacy courses.

Tatum, Cheryl, "Nonprofit Offers Help for Those in Debt," *The Tennessean,* **June 12, 2009.**

Dominion Financial Services, a nonprofit serving consumers in Tennessee, has helped people become more financially secure by teaching financial literacy.

CITING CQ RESEARCHER

Sample formats for citing these reports in a bibliography include the ones listed below. Preferred styles and formats vary, so please check with your instructor or professor.

<u>MLA STYLE</u>

Jost, Kenneth. "Rethinking the Death Penalty." CQ Researcher 16 Nov. 2001: 945-68.

<u>APA STYLE</u>

Jost, K. (2001, November 16). Rethinking the death penalty. *CQ Researcher, 11,* 945-968.

<u>CHICAGO STYLE</u>

Jost, Kenneth. "Rethinking the Death Penalty." CQ Researcher, November 16, 2001, 945-968.

In-depth Reports on Issues in the News

Are you writing a paper?

Need backup for a debate?

Want to become an expert on an issue?

For more than 80 years, students have turned to *CQ Researcher* for in-depth reporting on issues in the news. Reports on a full range of political and social issues are now available. Following is a selection of recent reports:

Civil Liberties
Closing Guantánamo, 2/09
Affirmative Action, 10/08
Gay Marriage Showdowns, 9/08
America's Border Fence, 9/08
Immigration Debate, 2/08

Crime/Law
Examining Forensics, 7/09
Legalizing Marijuana, 6/09
Mexico's Drug War, 12/08
Prostitution Debate, 5/08
Public Defenders, 4/08

Education
Reading Crisis? 2/08
Discipline in Schools, 2/08
Student Aid, 1/08
Racial Diversity in Public Schools, 9/07

Environment/Society
Energy and Climate, 7/09
Future of Books, 5/09
Hate Groups, 5/09
Future of Journalism, 3/09
Confronting Warming, 1/09
Reducing Carbon Footprint, 12/08

Health/Safety
Health-Care Reform, 8/09
Straining the Safety Net, 7/09
Treating Depression, 6/09
Reproductive Ethics, 5/09
Extreme Sports, 4/09
Regulating Toxic Chemicals, 1/09
Preventing Cancer, 1/09

Politics/Economy
Business Bankruptcy, 4/09
Future of the GOP, 3/09
Middle-Class Squeeze, 3/09

Upcoming Reports

State Budget Crisis, 9/11/09   Gays in the Military, 9/18/09   CIA Interrogations, 9/25/09

ACCESS

CQ Researcher is available in print and online. For access, visit your library or www.cqresearcher.com.

STAY CURRENT

To receive notice of upcoming *CQ Researcher* reports, or learn more about *CQ Researcher* products, subscribe to the free e-mail newsletters, *CQ Researcher Alert!* and *CQ Researcher News*: http://cqpress.com/newsletters.

PURCHASE

To purchase a *CQ Researcher* report in print or electronic format (PDF), visit www.cqpress.com or call 866-427-7737. Single reports start at $15. Bulk purchase discounts and electronic-rights licensing are also available.

SUBSCRIBE

Annual full-service *CQ Researcher* subscriptions—including 44 reports a year, monthly index updates, and a bound volume—start at $803. Add $25 for domestic postage.

CQ Researcher Online offers a backfile from 1991 and a number of tools to simplify research. For pricing information, call 800-834-9020, ext. 1906, or e-mail librarysales@cqpress.com.

Published by CQ Press, a Division of SAGE

www.cqresearcher.com

State Budget Crisis

Are permanent changes in spending needed?

S tate budgets always fall out of balance during recessions, but in the current downturn states are facing the worst budget crunch since the Great Depression. Over the past two years, states have had to close budget gaps exceeding $300 billion. Many have raised taxes, but they've mainly dealt with the challenge by cutting spending. State workers are facing layoffs and unpaid furloughs. Social services, including health insurance for children, are being cut dramatically. Even normally sacrosanct areas such as K-12 education and public safety are taking hits. The federal stimulus package included fiscal relief for states, but that money will soon run out. And states expect to face continuing problems. Their revenues will grow more slowly than they've come to expect over the past 30 years, leading some observers to wonder whether states have to make fundamental changes in the scope and scale of the services they provide.

High-school librarian Melissa Payne, of Morrow, Ga., is starting the school year with $1,000 less in her paycheck. Across the country, once-secure state workers are facing layoffs, pay cuts and furloughs as states confront crushing budget shortfalls.

CQ Researcher • Sept. 11, 2009 • www.cqresearcher.com
Volume 19, Number 31 • Pages 741-764

CQ PRESS

RECIPIENT OF SOCIETY OF PROFESSIONAL JOURNALISTS AWARD FOR
EXCELLENCE ◆ AMERICAN BAR ASSOCIATION SILVER GAVEL AWARD

Cover: AP Photo/Joe Sebo

CQ Researcher

Sept. 11, 2009
Volume 19, Number 31

MANAGING EDITOR: Thomas J. Colin
tcolin@cqpress.com

ASSISTANT MANAGING EDITOR: Kathy Koch
kkoch@cqpress.com

ASSOCIATE EDITOR: Kenneth Jost

STAFF WRITERS: Thomas J. Billitteri, Marcia Clemmitt, Peter Katel

CONTRIBUTING WRITERS: Rachel Cox, Sarah Glazer, Alan Greenblatt, Reed Karaim Barbara Mantel, Patrick Marshall, Tom Price, Jennifer Weeks

DESIGN/PRODUCTION EDITOR: Olu B. Davis

ASSISTANT EDITOR: Darrell Dela Rosa

FACT-CHECKING: Eugene J. Gabler, Michelle Harris

CQ PRESS

A Division of SAGE

PRESIDENT AND PUBLISHER:
John A. Jenkins

EXECUTIVE DIRECTOR,
REFERENCE INFORMATION GROUP:
Alix B. Vance

CQ Press is a registered trademark of Congressional Quarterly Inc.

CQ Researcher (ISSN 1056-2036) is printed on acid-free paper. Published weekly, except; (Jan. wk. 1) (May wk. 4) (July wks. 1, 2) (Aug. wks. 3, 4) (Nov. wk. 4) and (Dec. wk. 4), by CQ Press, a division of SAGE Publications. Annual full-service subscriptions start at $803. For pricing, call 1-800-834-9020, ext. 1906. To purchase a CQ Researcher report in print or electronic format (PDF), visit www. cqpress.com or call 866-427-7737. Single reports start at $15. Bulk purchase discounts and electronic-rights licensing are also available. Periodicals postage paid at Washington, D.C., and additional mailing offices. POSTMASTER: Send address changes to CQ Researcher, 2300 N St., N.W., Suite 800, Washington, DC 20037.

State Budget Crisis

BY ALAN GREENBLATT

THE ISSUES

Arnold Schwarzenegger just hosted an enormous garage sale. On Aug. 28, California's Republican governor appeared at a Sacramento-area warehouse sale of prison uniforms, office furniture, computers and pianos, along with a surfboard and an Xbox 360 gaming system.

The two-day sale included unclaimed property from state parks and items confiscated by law enforcement, along with 600 state-owned vehicles — 15 of them sporting visors autographed by the governor. All told, the state collected $1.6 million for the surplus stuff. "This is a win-win for the state and for shoppers," Schwarzenegger said. "Together, we are eliminating waste and providing great deals in this tough economy." [1]

States have long sold off their surplus goods, but the size of Schwarzenegger's sale and the personal appeals he made both online and in person were a testament to California's desperate financial situation. If anything, Schwarzenegger has curbed his ambitions as a salesman. Earlier this year, he unsuccessfully proposed selling some of the state's best-known landmarks, including the Los Angeles Coliseum, San Quentin prison and the state fairgrounds.

After all, $1.6 million doesn't go far in a state that was staring at a $26.3 billion budget shortfall before Schwarzenegger signed off on a budget deal in July. The state is still drowning in red ink, even after California legislators in February and July cut spending for fiscal years 2009 and 2010 by $31 billion.

"Tea partiers" on Staten Island, N.Y., protest tax increases on April 15, 2009. Faced with falling revenues and gaping budget deficits, many states — including those with Republican governors — are raising taxes, bucking the decades-old, GOP-led anti-tax movement and sparking TEA (Taxed Enough Already) party demonstrations.

AFP/Getty Images/Emmanuel Dunand

Even normally sacrosanct areas such as education took hits, with class sizes spiking upward. But the biggest cuts were in social services. Cost of living adjustments for the disabled were canceled, state workers' paychecks were cut by double-digit percentages and more than 1 million children from working families are expected to lose their health coverage.

California's problems may be outsized, but struggling budget writers in Sacramento have plenty of company in capitals elsewhere. All states except Vermont are constitutionally required to maintain balanced budgets — yet every state except Montana and North Dakota found itself short of funds as the 2009 fiscal year drew near its close. (State fiscal years typically run from July 1 until June 30 of the following year, meaning states are now in the third month of fiscal 2010.)

Battered by the recession and collapse of the housing market, state tax collections have fallen by the highest percentage on record — down 11.7 percent in the first quarter of the year, according to the State University of New York's Nelson A. Rockefeller Institute of Government.[2] Things grew even worse in April, the most important month for personal income tax collections. The 45 states that have reported tax receipts for April and May saw collective declines of about 20 percent compared with the same months in 2008. [3]

As a result, legislators and governors had to close $113 billion worth of budget shortfalls in fiscal 2009 and faced more than $143 billion worth of unexpected shortfalls in the fiscal 2010 budgets they adopted in the spring and early summer. [4] Now, less than three months into the new fiscal year, at least 15 states already are projecting budget gaps totaling more than $28 billion. [5]

The federal stimulus package enacted in February will provide $787 billion, mostly through state and local government governments. But the bulk of that money is targeted to specific programs, meaning states can only count on about $135 billion for settling their accounts. States used stimulus dollars to fill about 40 percent of their shortfalls this year.

Budget Shortfalls Top 25% in 10 States

At least 48 states and Washington, D.C., have addressed or still face shortfalls in their budgets for fiscal year 2010 totaling $168 billion, or 24 percent of state budgets. Ten states had gaps exceeding 25 percent, and 21 had gaps of from 15-25 percent.

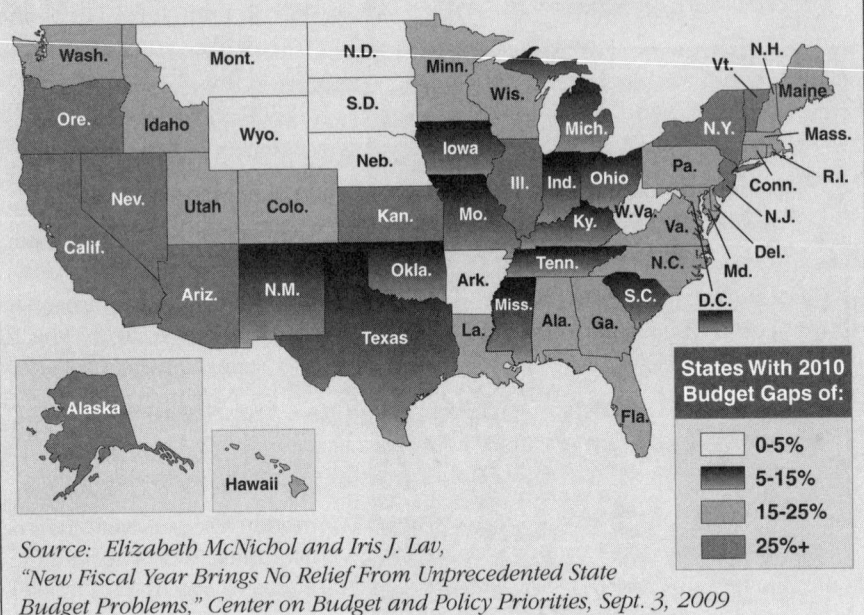

States With 2010 Budget Gaps of:

- 0-5%
- 5-15%
- 15-25%
- 25%+

Source: Elizabeth McNichol and Iris J. Lav, "New Fiscal Year Brings No Relief From Unprecedented State Budget Problems," Center on Budget and Policy Priorities, Sept. 3, 2009

To fill the remaining gaps, at least 30 states have raised taxes this year, according to the Center on Budget and Policy Priorities, a think tank based in Washington. Maine is now taxing candy and ski tickets, while Kentucky is taxing cell phone ring tones. [6] A bill introduced in the California Assembly would legalize marijuana for recreational use in hopes of taxing it to the tune of more than $1.2 billion — an idea Schwarzenegger said was worthy of serious study. [7]

But, in terms of sheer dollars, the overall size of tax increases has been dwarfed by spending cuts. Utah hasn't suffered as much fallout from the housing boom and bust as some of its Southwestern neighbors, but state officials nonetheless began their budget process this year staring at a 12 percent hole in their general-fund budget.

At ground level, this meant, for example, a funding reduction of nearly 40 percent for a program that pro-

vides disabled adults with stipends of $261 per month. The program helps many adults who can't work keep body and soul together while waiting out the often years-long process of applying for federal disability assistance.

Matt Minkevitch, executive director of The Road Home, which operates Utah's largest homeless shelter, predicts the disability cutbacks will result in 500 to 600 more people showing up at his shelter — where demand has already increased 52 percent over the past two years. "We don't know that there are any other stopgaps from other organizations that can work with this population," says Melissa Smith, an analyst with the Community Action Partnership of Utah. "They will be in homeless shelters without any financial help at all."

Countless other state programs are being cut. Illinois has stopped paying funeral costs for indigents. Arizona, which has been wrestling with a $3.4 billion shortfall, is considering selling off its

legislative buildings with the intent of leasing them back, in hopes of raising $735 million. Ohio's rainy-day fund — the reserves meant to patch budgets during bad times — has dwindled from $1 billion to 89 cents. [8]

State workers, who typically have enjoyed greater job security than their private-sector counterparts, find themselves on the receiving end of hiring freezes, layoffs, pay cuts and furloughs — days they must take off without pay. Many state and local governments are also rethinking generous pensions and retirement health coverage that have generated multibillion-dollar deficits of their own.

As bad as things are now, they are likely only to grow worse. Even if the recession — which officially started in December 2007 — ends soon, states will be in bad shape for a long time, because tax collections take at least several months to recover. Deficits will continue at least into next year, if not into 2011 — well after the federal stimulus money will run out. (Stimulus dollars must be spent or "obligated" by the end of 2010.) "By and large, there's very little planning for what will happen when the money runs out," says Donald J. Boyd, a senior fellow at the Rockefeller Institute.

States should be preparing for a more austere future, suggests Scott Pattison, executive director of the National Association of State Budget Officers.

"Our data show that at the state level, [revenue] growth over the next five to 10 years will be roughly half what we've seen over the last 30," he says. "We'll be surprised if we go back to this high growth rate. That's the new normal for states."

Given the amount of pain states are in — and the amount of time they're likely to remain in trouble — some people are suggesting a fundamental restructuring of state budgets and operations. Either state tax codes must be updated to better reflect the contemporary economy, or states must rethink the amount and types of programs they can afford to offer.

As states continue to struggle with record shortfalls, here are some of the questions policy makers are debating:

Should states raise taxes?

Faced with a budget shortfall in excess of $15 billion, New York Gov. David A. Paterson, a Democrat, decided to tax just about everything but the proverbial kitchen sink. At the end of 2008 he proposed raising or imposing taxes on 137 separate items and activities, including haircuts, beer, movie tickets, taxi rides, yachts, private jets and massages. He even sought an 18 percent "obesity tax" on sugary sodas and an "iPod tax" on Internet downloads. [9]

After months of negotiations with legislators — as the budget gap grew to $17 billion — Paterson signed a budget in April that included millions in fee increases, raised taxes on high-income individuals and ended a property tax rebate program. The iPod tax, however, was withdrawn.[10]

Thirty-six states answering a survey from the National Conference of State Legislatures in July had raised net taxes a total of $24 billion for fiscal 2010. Sixteen states had raised taxes by more than 1 percent, 19 made no significant tax policy changes and one state — North Dakota — cut individual and business taxes by $50 million. [11]

"If you're going to do a cuts-only approach, then it's actually hard to find the dollars without looking at education, without looking at health care," says Nicholas Johnson, director of the State Fiscal Project at the Center on Budget and Policy Priorities. "That is a reason tax increases are on the table in a lot of places."

The net increase in taxes represented a hike of 3.1 percent above the previous year's rates. That's roughly double the size of the tax increases imposed in 2002 and 2003, when states

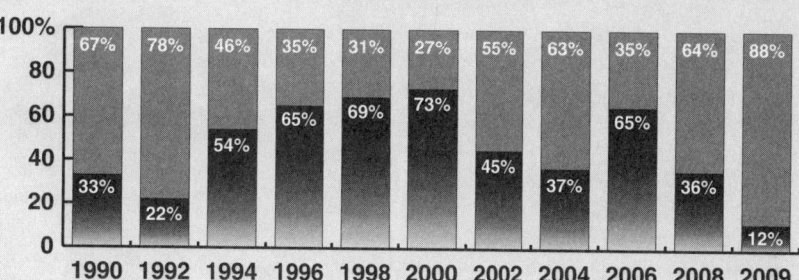

Most Cities 'Less Able' to Meet Needs

City finance officers in nearly 90 percent of U.S. cities said their cities were "less able" to meet their fiscal needs in 2009 than in 2008, when the figure was 64 percent. Pessimism about cities' abilities to meet their needs is at the lowest level in the history of the National League of Cities' 24-year survey.

Ability of Cities to Meet Financial Needs, FY 1990—FY 2009

Source: Christopher W. Hoene and Michael A. Pagano, "Research Brief on America's Cities: City Fiscal Conditions in 2009," National League of Cities, September 2009

- Better able
- Less able

last faced widespread shortfalls. The National Governors' Association claimed then that states were facing the worst budget climate since World War II. Yet, during those two years, states mainly patched their budget holes by cutting spending. They raised taxes 1.6 percent, or roughly $9 billion, each of those years. But those increases were largely on things like cigarettes and didn't represent broader changes in sales or income tax rates.

Those relatively modest tax increases stood in stark contrast to states' approaches during the recessions of the 1980s and '90s, when major tax increases were very much part of the mix. Given the severity of the current downturn, states are again showing some willingness to consider tax increases. "When you have Republicans in the Utah legislature floating ideas for tax increases, that tells you some of the dynamics must have changed," says Pattison, of the state budget officers association.

As in New York, other states are looking long and hard at taxing the

wealthy. Connecticut Gov. M. Jodi Rell, a Republican, on Aug. 26 proposed raising state income tax for individuals making more than $500,000 a year, in exchange for a sales tax cut. [12] Oregon, Hawaii, New Jersey and Washington have already raised top income tax rates this year.

Sales taxes are down more sharply than a few years ago, the Rockefeller Institute's Boyd notes, adding to states' revenue woes. And, in contrast to recent recessions, after which state revenues recovered quickly and sharply, few expect tax collections to rebound as smartly in the next couple of years. "The budget gaps that they had to fill were significant enough that it would have been difficult to fill them through cuts alone," says Susan K. Urahn, managing director of the Pew Center on the States, a foundation-supported think tank.

However, there's some evidence that the anti-tax message that has been a central Republican tenet for 30 years has lost some of its power. In contrast to the 2002-03 recession,

Education Receives One-Third of State Spending

Funding for education in fiscal 2007 comprised nearly one-third of all state spending — more than for any other function; the least went to public aid, or welfare. General funds covered about 45 percent of all state expenditures, and federal funds about a quarter. Personal and sales taxes provided nearly three-quarters of the general funds.

Total State Expenditures by Function, FY 2007

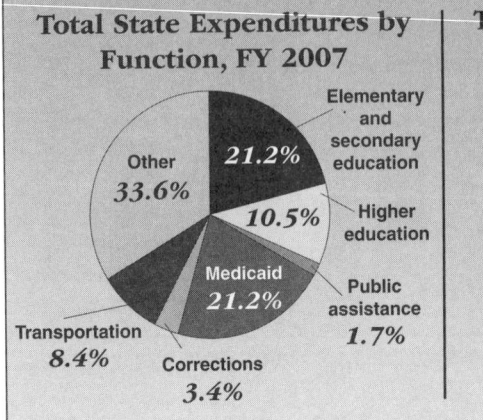

- Other 33.6%
- Elementary and secondary education 21.2%
- Higher education 10.5%
- Medicaid 21.2%
- Public assistance 1.7%
- Corrections 3.4%
- Transportation 8.4%

Total State Expenditures by Funding Source, FY 2007

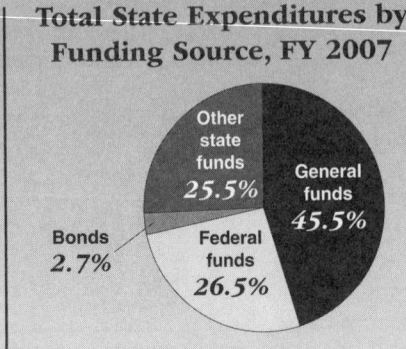

- Other state funds 25.5%
- General funds 45.5%
- Federal funds 26.5%
- Bonds 2.7%

Revenue Sources in the General Fund, FY 2007

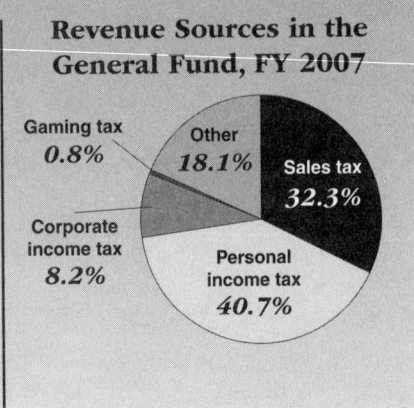

- Gaming tax 0.8%
- Other 18.1%
- Sales tax 32.3%
- Corporate income tax 8.2%
- Personal income tax 40.7%

* Figures may not total 100 due to rounding.

Source: "State Expenditure Report: Fiscal Year 2007," National Association of State Budget Officers, 2008

when even Democratic governors kept to "no-tax" pledges, now even Republicans such as Rell and Jan Brewer of Arizona are saying tax increases are a painful necessity. In May, the Nevada legislature overrode Gov. Jim Gibbons' veto of a $781 million two-year tax-increase package.[13]

But California voters in May rejected a $16 billion, two-year tax increase that would have simultaneously capped state spending. When Illinois Gov. Pat Quinn, a Democrat, proposed a hefty tax increase this year, the legislature was quick to table the matter until next January, at the earliest.

Particularly in states such as Illinois, where state spending has grown at a pace well above the rate of inflation for the last two decades, many people are wondering whether government shouldn't be forced to slim down rather than raise taxes on a populace reeling from the recession.

"The government shouldn't be as expansive as it is," says Chris Edwards, director of tax policy studies at the Cato Institute, which leans libertarian.

The average state tax burden has risen 42 percent since 1999 — about 50 percent more than would have been needed to keep up with inflation. By 2008, state spending had risen 77 percent above 1998 levels.[14]

"Medicaid, for example, has had a big expansion of coverage and shouldn't cover as many things and people, in my view," Edwards says.

Joseph Henchman, director of state projects at the Tax Foundation, a Washington-based public education group, says states like California that have increased spending above sustainable levels need to expenditures rather than raise taxes. And income tax hikes aimed at big earners are "bad public policy," he argues. "Higher taxes mean less incentive for productive activity, and you need to have incentives whether or not you're in a recession."

But Henchman favors extending sales taxes to cover services —an idea that has long been a holy grail among state tax officials. State tax codes are still locked in an era when manufacturing was far more dominant than it

is today, taxing tangible goods but not most services. "The evolution from manufacturing to a service-based economy, and the whole area of online transactions, most of that activity is not captured by the sales tax," says Sujit CanagaRetna, a senior fiscal analyst with the Council of State Governments.

States such as North Carolina and Kentucky, prodded by the current crisis, have begun considering overhauling their tax codes in order to capture more of today's economic activity. Should they proceed, they'll find, as have other states that tried to go down that road, that taxing services is a difficult political argument to win.

Maryland officials in 2007 explored taxing a long list of services. One by one, lobbyists for the various targeted industries blocked them. In the end, the legislature only imposed a tax on computer services. But like tattoo parlors and dry cleaners elsewhere, Maryland techies complained that they'd been unfairly singled out, so the computer tax was soon repealed.

Are public-sector workers' benefits too generous?

State and local workers have long enjoyed more generous benefits and greater job security than their counterparts at private companies. Public retirement benefits, however, are suddenly receiving much greater scrutiny due to the current budget environment.

A 2007 study by the Pew Center on the States found that state pension plans nationwide were about 85 percent funded — meaning that the funds had sufficient assets to cover 85 percent of the expected future obligations. To make up the 15 percent short fall, states would need $361 billion. [15]

Even then, 20 of the 50 states were underfunded by more than 20 percent. And that was before the stock market began its nosedive last year. State and local pension funds lost an estimated $1 trillion in value since October 2007. [16] Two University of Chicago economists last year estimated that state and local pension funds are underfunded by $3.12 trillion — triple the states' estimates. [17] Alicia Munnell, director of the Boston College Center for Retirement Research, says because of market losses state pensions are now only 65 percent funded.

In addition to escalating pension costs, states are also facing billions of dollars in unfunded liabilities for retiree health costs — as well as the growing cost of providing coverage for current workers. With private-sector companies cutting back on health insurance benefits and fewer private employers offering guaranteed pension payments, state and local officials are under pressure to consider cuts in workers' benefits.

"Public opinion is just very different than it was three years ago," says Jay Williams, the mayor of Youngstown, Ohio. "Those who hold onto the notion that we have to preserve our benefits, that this is how it's always been, that's not going to be tenable to the general public."

Downsizing — California-Style

Facing an unprecedented multibillion-dollar budget shortfall, California's Gov. Arnold Schwarzenegger has proposed a variety of innovative ways to cut state spending and raise revenues, ranging from an unsuccessful effort to sell off prime state real estate like the state prison at San Quentin (top) to holding a gigantic "garage" sale of unclaimed or surplus goods. More than 5,000 items were sold in the two-day event in August, including office furniture, prison uniforms, computers, pianos, a surfboard, an Xbox 360 gaming system and 600 state-owned vehicles, such as a BMW motorcycle autographed by the governor (bottom).

State Budget Shortfalls Expected to Worsen

All states except Montana and North Dakota face budget shortfalls totaling $168 billion in fiscal 2010. If the economy does not begin to significantly recover in 2010 the deficits in fiscal 2010 and 2011 are likely to exceed $350 billion. Budget shortfalls are more serious in the current recession than earlier in the decade because state fiscal problems are more severe and unemployment has already hit 9.7 percent, vs. 6.3 percent in the previous recession.

State Budget Shortfalls in Each Fiscal Year
(in $ billions)

Source: Elizabeth McNichol and Iris J. Lav, "New Fiscal Year Brings No Relief From Unprecedented State Budget Problems," Center on Budget and Policy Priorities, September 2009

Under federal law, promised pension benefits usually can't be rescinded. But states such as Alaska and North Dakota have experimented with moving new employees into 401(k)-type plans — essentially, investment accounts that do not guarantee a set income upon retirement. Numerous states, including Georgia, Nevada, New Mexico and Rhode Island, this year have significantly reduced benefit packages offered to new workers. Texas and Nebraska have required all employees to contribute more themselves to their pension plans, while states like Maine, Louisiana and Connecticut are reducing pension benefits offered to workers.

"What you're seeing is this reevaluation of the kind of benefits you offer your employees," says CanagaRetna, at the Council of State Governments.

Not only are generous benefits costly but they're increasingly hard to defend when states are borrowing billions to pay for liberal pensions while cutting essential services.

An initiative meant to rein in state worker pensions failed to make the California ballot last year, but there continues to be a campaign to direct unflattering attention their way. A group called the California Foundation for Fiscal Responsibility has posted on the Web a list of the 5,100 California state and local government workers who receive pensions in excess of $100,000, including retired firefighters, police and former university presidents and city managers. The Sacramento Fire Department — with 50 former employees pulling down $100,000-plus pensions — took the distinction as the local entity with the wealthiest public retirees. [18]

"I expect pensions to hit us even more than the real estate decline," says Marcia Fritz, the foundation's vice president. "It's a ticking time bomb. Actu-

ally, it's going off — it's not a ticking time bomb any more."

Public-employee unions argue that employment costs, including benefits, make up a fairly small proportion of state budgets, which are dominated by prisons, health care and education. According to the American Federation of State, County and Municipal Employees (AFSCME), the average annual payment to a retired public worker is about $20,000.

"It doesn't seem like anybody is getting rich from that," says Kerri Korpi, AFSCME's director of research and collective bargaining. "They have paid for that and in some cases traded off that benefit for wage increases."

Korpi notes that most public employees contribute to their own pension plans. Where state pensions are underfunded, she says, it's often the state's fault. Many states neglect to make needed pension payments, skipping some years entirely because pension funds have increased due to market advances.

In that sense, guaranteed pensions can sometimes be cheaper than private retirement accounts modeled on 401(k) plans. "On average, taxpayers fund only 25 percent of the pension benefit," AFSCME President Gerald W. McEntee wrote in *USA Today.* "Employee contributions and investments make up the rest." [19]

The point of pensions and benefits such as retiree health coverage is to attract and retain good workers — which is especially important when "food stamps and unemployment programs are swamped with demand," Korpi says.

"People still want services to be provided by highly qualified individuals," says Johnson of the Center on Budget Policies and Priorities. "Most of the jobs in state and local government [are] teachers, firefighters, police officers. It's not clear anyone wants less-qualified people in those jobs."

"The private sector and governments both do a lousy job of paying for their promised pension benefits," says John D. Donahue, a lecturer in public policy at Harvard University's Kennedy School of Government, "but this looks like a bigger problem in government, because unlike the private sector governments haven't stopped offering pensions."

Will the recession force states to make fundamental changes?

No state has been cutting spending longer than Michigan, the one-time auto-manufacturing giant that was suffering a "one-state recession" for years before bad times hit the rest of the country. Michigan faced a $1.8 billion shortfall as legislators struggled this summer to finish drafting their budget. That's on top of $7 billion worth of cuts, accounting shifts and tax increases made over the past eight years.

The state's revenues are now down to 1988 levels. "The big difference here is that we have very little to fall back on," said Robert L. Emerson, the state budget director. "Michigan has already done a lot of the things other states are only thinking about doing now." [20]

Because state revenues are not likely to rebound to robust levels, given the sorry state of the domestic auto industry, Michigan officials are now thinking along more radical lines. Under a charge from Democratic Gov. Jennifer Granholm, Lt. Gov. John Cherry has been touring the state this summer, looking for ideas about how to streamline government. Granholm wants him to come up with a plan by Dec. 1 on how to

Sacramento firefighters hose down hot spots at a home destroyed by fire in 2007 in Meyers, Calif. It was revealed this year that Sacramento firefighters have the largest number of retirees receiving more than $100,000 a year in state pensions. California now is considering cutbacks to generous pensions for state workers, which have helped to create massive state deficits.

Getty Images/Justin Sullivan

reduce the number of Michigan cabinet departments from 18 to no more than eight.

Cherry's goal is to figure out which functions state government simply must perform — maintaining public safety, quality education and a healthy environment, for instance — but chucking the rest. "Those things that don't fit probably become ripe for elimination," he said. [21]

Whether other states will take similarly bold steps in the face of deep and long-standing deficits is "the $64,000 question," says Urahn of the Pew Center on the States.

"If there is going to be fundamental change, the necessary preconditions are a sufficient pressure over an extended period of time — that states can't hold their fingers in the dike long enough," Urahn says. "This recession is more severe than anything we've seen in 40 or 50 years, and I think it's going to have a long tail for states."

States this year, despite huge shortfalls, were pretty much able to muddle

through, using federal stimulus dollars to cover roughly 40 percent of their budget gaps. They drained their rainy-day accounts and raised taxes, but for the most part they made program cuts.

In most states, the pain was spread pretty much across the board, with all or most agencies ordered to find savings of 5 to 10 percent, or more. It's difficult work, but, as happened after the 2002-03 downturn, programs that aren't eliminated can always see their spending levels rise again with a recovery.

But the prospect of diminishing revenues continuing into next year and quite possibly 2011 — by which time the stimulus dollars will have run out — has many policy makers thinking about restructuring state government to make it permanently leaner.

"There are some really tough decisions to be made," says Jay Emler, who chairs the Ways and Means Committee in the Kansas Senate. "All the stimulus did was delay the decision-making for one year on the hope and a prayer that the economy is going to turn around enough to get us where we need to be, and I don't think it's going to happen."

Citing a small example, CanagaRetna of the Council of State Governments noted that Virginia closed 18 highway rest areas in July in an effort to help close a $2.6 billion transportation funding shortfall. Officials noted that the state could stop providing facilities for travelers that can now be found in fast food restaurants and gas stations.

"States seem to be moving away from the model where they seem to do everything, to a very core set of functions," CanagaRetna says. Looking for areas where functions can be taken over by the private sector "will be part of the whole big-picture discussion state officials will engage in."

Pattison, of the state budget officers' association, says even if states maintain a presence in certain sectors, they may not maintain funding. In other words, more programs will move toward a model akin to higher education, in which states provide less and less funding and expect institutions to find their own financing.

Pattison notes that numerous states raised fees for parks this year. "The general fund subsidy to the department of parks and recreation, that gradually goes down all the time. Eventually, the park service finds other ways to get revenues, maybe through an advertising initiative. Eventually, the amount of state money to the park service shrinks to a small percentage."

But Michael S. Greve, director of the Federalism Project at the conservative American Enterprise Institute (AEI) in Washington, D.C., is skeptical that states will grapple with deep questions about their core missions anytime soon. "At all three levels of government you have potent reasons to do something fairly drastic, but I just don't see the political will," he says. "It's amazing how short-term the calculations have turned out to be."

Although it would clearly be better for states to think in terms of longer time frames and look down the road

several years in order to game out the consequences of their present actions, legislators and other officials usually grasp onto any solution that will help them get through their current-year troubles, even if they know it means mortgaging the future. Because of one- and two-year budget cycles, lawmakers often put off dealing with future problems created by pension obligations or bonds issued against future tobacco or lottery revenues. "It's just so difficult for these institutions — legislatures in particular, governors maybe a little less so — to look very

During the Great Depression — when many jobless people were forced to get handouts from soup kitchens like this one in Los Angeles in 1930 — states expanded their budgets, operations and tax codes to handle new responsibilities, which included doling out federal funds for new social programs.

far ahead, or to act very far ahead no matter how far they look," says Alan Rosenthal, a political scientist and expert on legislatures at Rutgers University's Eagleton Institute of Politics in New Brunswick, N.J.

"They have enough trouble today putting together each budget without anticipating the long-term or the medium-term future," he says. "They have to muddle through year to year, election to election, all the while praying for an economic recovery and higher revenues coming into the treasury." ∎

BACKGROUND

Modernizing and Growing

In the early 20th century, states were little more than glorified highway departments. Most government spending was done not in state capitals or in Washington but on the local level. The federal government didn't tax income until the 1913 adoption of the 16th Amendment but even then didn't have a formal budgeting process. Instead, the federal government passed bills stipulating how much money it needed at any given time, and then raised it. States tended to operate similarly. [22]

The big shift occurred during the Great Depression of the 1930s. Under President Franklin D. Roosevelt's New Deal, the federal government became the dominant fiscal force in the country. Federal spending composed just 1.6 percent of gross domestic product in 1929, compared with more than 19 percent in 2008. State and local government spending was several times larger than federal expenditures until 1941. [23]

"Thinking back to the Depression, it really altered intergovernmental relations," says William Pound, executive director of the National Conference of State Legislatures. "It forced everybody to raise more revenue, for instance from sales taxes, because states had to meet the federal match requirements as the federal government created these programs."

Continued on p. 752

Chronology

1930s-1970s
State governments expand rapidly and modernize their tax systems in response to economic and federal pressures.

1930
Mississippi enacts first modern general sales tax.

1933
President Franklin D. Roosevelt launches New Deal, rapidly turning federal government into the states' dominant fiscal partner as they receive large transfers for federally sponsored social and economic programs.

1940
State government spending has grown by more than 250 percent since 1927.

1965
President Lyndon B. Johnson signs into law Medicaid, the federal-state health insurance program for the needy and disabled.

1978
California voters approve Proposition 13, severely limiting state property tax rates and sparking nationwide anti-tax revolt that continues today.

1980s-1990s
States enter cycle of recession-driven busts — but mainly booms, as economic activity and stock market rallies fill their coffers.

1992
Colorado voters approve Taxpayer Bill of Rights, limiting increases in state spending.

1999
Throughout the 1990s, most states enact permanent tax cuts, lowering revenues by 8.2 percent.

2000s
State budgets are hit by collapse of dot-com and housing bubbles.

2002
With state revenues dropping, states defer maintenance and infrastructure spending.

2003
Most states cut funding for higher education and social services; 27 propose Medicaid reductions; Congress sends states $10 billion in extra Medicaid money and $10 billion for general funds. . . . By a 2-to-1 margin, Alabama voters reject a proposed $1.2 billion tax hike. . . . Electricity brownouts and a $38 billion shortfall prompt California voters to recall Gov. Gray Davis, select actor Arnold Schwarzenegger.

2004
Government Accounting Standards Board requires all states, beginning in 2007, to publish the cost of state workers' retirement health benefits over the next 20 years.

2005
San Diego Mayor Richard Murphy resigns in the face of a $1.4 billion pension shortfall. . . . Schwarzenegger presents a politics and budget "reform" package to voters, who reject all of it.

2007
No state ends the fiscal year with a budget deficit. . . . Foreclosure filings increase by 75 percent over the previous year — with the rate almost doubling in December, when the nation slips officially into recession.

2008
Vallejo, Calif., seeks bankruptcy protection, citing declines in sales taxes and home values. . . . State and local government jobs peak in August, with 55,000 cut over the following year.

2009
Feb 17: President Obama signs $787 billion stimulus package. Most of the money will be spent through states and localities, but only about $135 billion is available for states to balance their budgets. . . . May 19: California voters turn down ballot propositions that would have tweaked spending requirements from earlier ballot measures and raised taxes by $16 billion in exchange for a spending cap. . . . June 4: South Carolina Supreme Court orders Gov. Mark Sanford to apply for $700 million in federal stimulus funds. Like several other Republican governors, Sanford had balked at accepting federal dollars he felt would create future financial liabilities for the state. . . . July 1: As the fiscal year begins, every state but North Dakota and Montana has had to cut spending or raise taxes to grapple with budget shortfalls for fiscal 2010 that total $168 billion, or one-fourth of total state budgets. . . . July 2: Facing a $26.3 billion shortfall, California starts issuing IOUs to its vendors. . . . Sept. 4: Unemployment hits a 26-year high at 9.7 percent, with the U.S. economy having lost 7.4 million jobs since the recession began at the end of 2007. . . . Dec. 1: A government-streamlining commission will recommend ways to reduce the size of Michigan's government from 18 cabinet departments to no more than eight.

Local Governments Face Tough Times

Collapse of municipal bond market was added blow.

For the past 18 months, Jefferson County, Ala. — home to 660,000 residents and the city of Birmingham — has teetered on the edge of bankruptcy. Since April 2008, the county has failed to make payments to creditors holding bonds that paid for its sewer system.

With $3 billion in bonds for a system that serves only 150,000 customers, the county simply built more sewers than it could afford. "It's a terrible situation," said Bettye Fine Collins, president of the Jefferson County Commission. "I don't think there's another situation in this country that would compare." [1]

The roots of Jefferson County's financial problems may be unusual, but they're not unique. The county's sewer debt has been around for years, but the problem only spun out of control after Jefferson refinanced its bonds using securities for which the market collapsed, along with much of the rest of the financial system, last year.

Local governments haven't been hit quite as hard as states by the economic downturn, but they aren't exactly flush. Sales taxes are down, while property taxes — the main source of revenue for localities — are being adjusted slowly downward to reflect plummeting housing values. (Most properties are not reassessed on an annual basis.) "Sales taxes, property taxes, building permit fees — they're all down," says Jim Phillips, a spokesman for the National Association of Counties. "It's an 'all of the above' type of suffering."

A survey released Sept. 1 by the National League of Cities found that 88 percent of local finance officers find that's it harder to cover the costs of running their governments than it was a year ago, with a similar number predicting still worse fortunes in 2010. That's the most pessimistic assessment since the survey began in 1986. [2]

Detroit Mayor Dave Bing recently laid off 200 city employees, but that wasn't enough to plug a cash shortfall approaching $80 million. The Motor City is watching property and income taxes go down at the same time Michigan is cutting aid to localities — a cost-saving move being pursued by many states. "I don't see the city getting out of this financial mess short of a bankruptcy," said Joe Harris, a former chief financial officer for Detroit. [3]

The collapse of the municipal bond insurance market, sparked by last year's financial meltdown, has affected local governments all over the country. Such insurance enabled state and local governments to borrow money more cheaply because they had the backing of private guaranty companies. Dallas, for example, used to pay about 4 percent for construction bonds that had the backing of private insurers. However, since that kind of insurance is now almost impossible to find, the city would have to now pay 6.5 percent. That difference in cost has put, among other things, a $700 million hotel project on hold.[4]

Rep. Barney Frank, D-Mass., who chairs the House Financial Services Committee, intends to push legislation this fall that would allow the U.S. Treasury to insure municipal bonds, making it cheaper for states and localities to issue debt.

"I know that a lot of people are looking for ways for the federal government to help out state and local governments that aren't based on spending," says Tracy Gordon, a public-finance expert at the University of Maryland. "Some people think perhaps there will be another stimulus involving more payments to states and localities, but others say that's not politically viable."

Municipal bonds have been nearly as safe an investment as Treasury bonds. According to Moody's, a bond-rating agency, the 10-year default rates for all investment-grade municipals is 0.1 percent, compared with 2.1 percent for investment-grade corporate bonds.

Continued from p. 750

Under Roosevelt, economic and social spending increased vastly with the creation of programs such as Social Security. States expanded their budgets and operations to handle new responsibilities, including doling out federal funds to the unemployed. And, because states were either in or near default because of the Depression, they adopted income taxes and sales taxes, which had originated among local authorities. The modern state budget was born in the 1930s. "States as a group revolutionized their tax systems in the 1930s, laying the foundation of the system of state and local government finance that exists in the 21st century," writes Ronald Snell, director of state services for the National Conference of State Legislatures. "Revenue raised from state sources increased 250 percent from 1927 to 1940 because of the widespread adoption of taxes that had been insignificant or nonexistent before 1930." [24]

The next great increase in state budgets came in the 1960s, mainly as a result of President Lyndon B. Johnson's Great Society program, which created, among other entitlements, Medicaid, the federal-state health insurance program for the poor and the disabled. Throughout the 20th century, states also received federal dollars apart from money needed to run New Deal or Great Society programs. Typically, these cash transfers were the result of either states seeking federal money for specific projects or of Washington giving states money to implement specific programs it wanted carried out. By the early 1970s, concerned about financial pressure on cities losing

Cities Favor Layoffs, Project Cuts

More than 60 percent of U.S. cities sought to offset budget shortfalls in 2009 by hiring freezes or layoffs and cutbacks on capital projects. A quarter of the cities modified workers' health benefits and 11 percent cut human-services budgets. Nine in 10 finance officers reported their cities are making spending cuts in 2009, and 82 percent predicted further cuts in 2010.

How Cities Respond to Budget Shortfalls, 2009

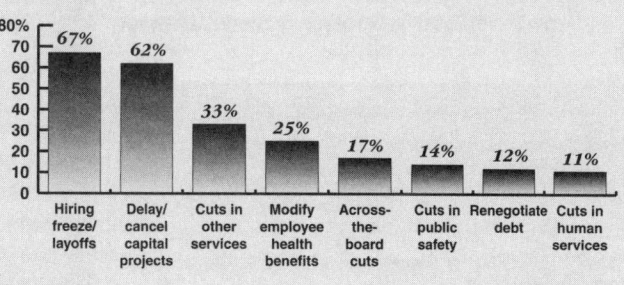

Source: "Research Brief on America's Cities," National League of Cities, September 2009

But although municipal bankruptcies are extremely rare, defaults on municipal bonds are becoming more common. There were only 29 municipal defaults in 2007, totaling $300 million worth of bonds. In 2008, those numbers leapt to record highs: 150 defaults, totaling $7.8 billion, according to Richard Lehmann, publisher of *Forbes/Lehmann Income Securities Investor.*

And cities and counties that go bankrupt don't act the same as bankrupt companies. They can't be forced to liquidate the way bankrupt chains such as Circuit City or Linens 'n Things have been. This gives local governments nearing default a tremendous amount of leverage in demanding that creditors make allowances. Jefferson County's creditors have offered $1.3 billion in concessions, but county commissioners haven't felt sufficiently pressured to take the deal.

The fear of taking on responsibility for debt issued by city, county and state governments may make Frank's proposal a hard sell. "If you were in debt, would you be more or less likely to increase your liabilities if you knew someone else would pay them off?" asks Richard W. Rahn, a senior fellow at the Cato Institute, a libertarian think tank. "Many children can quickly figure out the answer to this question, but it seems to be a real stumper for members of the House Financial Services Committee." [5]

The political wind Frank's bill faces may be one reason why the National League of Cities is pushing a separate proposal to create a mutual insurance company that would be owned by states and localities seeking muni bond insurance. But that plan calls for federal assistance, too — at least initially. The league figures it needs $5 billion from the U.S. Treasury to jump-start the effort but that the money could be paid back from profits.

[1] Josh Goodman, "Drained," *Governing,* August 2009, p. 38, www.governing.com/article/drained.

[2] Christopher A. Hoene and Michael W. Pagano, "City Fiscal Conditions in 2009," National League of Cities, September 2009, www.nlc.org/ASSETS/E0A769A03B46496 3A81410F40A0529BF/CityFiscalConditions_09%20%282%29.pdf.

[3] Suzette Hackney and John Wisely, "Ex-Auditor Foresees Detroit Bankruptcy," *Detroit Free-Press,* Aug. 30, 2009, p. 1A, www.freep.com/article/20090830/NEWS05/908300547/1319/Detroit-nearing-financial-ruin-city-s-ex-auditor-says.

[4] Robert Barkin, "Financial Lockdown," *American City & County,* Aug. 1, 2009, p. 32, http://americancityandcounty.com/admin/finance/bond-insurance-delays-200908/index1.html.

[5] Richard W. Rahn, "Insuring Bankruptcy," *The Washington Times,* June 10, 2009, p. A21, www.washingtontimes.com/news/2009/jun/10/insuring-bankruptcy/.

residents to suburban development and a slowing economy as the Vietnam War wound down, President Richard M. Nixon created general-revenue sharing (GRS) as a way to distribute some $6 billion a year to states with only one restriction — that it be used for governmental purposes.

The Reagan administration ended GRS in 1986, after it had distributed a total of about $85 billion. Since the early 1980s, when double-digit inflation pushed the country into a severe recession and created many state budget gaps, federal assistance has not been readily available to close state deficits. As a result, "Every recession has produced deficits in the states," notes Alice M. Rivlin, former director of the Office of Management and Budget under President Bill Clinton and a senior fellow at the Brookings Institution.

Recent Recessions

Since the late 1970s, states have had to weigh their need to make up for revenue lost during recessions with political pressures not to raise taxes. An anti-tax revolt was kicked off by passage of Proposition 13 in California in 1978, which put strict limits on property tax rates and imposed a requirement that any tax increase be passed by a two-thirds supermajority.

Other states also became constricted by tax and expenditure limit laws, or TELs, which typically limit the amount of growth from one budget year to the next. The most famous example is in Colorado, where voters

Teetering on the Brink, California Issues IOUs

Some want the state to start over again from scratch.

California has become the poster child for state budget woes, its political system barely able to cope with chronic budget shortfalls that at one point this year exceeded $25 billion. Many are convinced that California has become such a mess that the state needs to start over again from scratch.

A group of leading Bay Area businessmen is sponsoring a pair of initiatives for next June's ballot that would allow the entire state constitution to be rewritten. "We're in such terrible shape that anything would be better than what we have now," says Robert M. Stern, president of the Center for Governmental Studies in Los Angeles.

No one would deny that the Golden State is in terrible shape. After voters rejected a set of tax hikes and spending cuts on a special May ballot, the state was forced to issue IOUs to pay some of its bills while Gov. Arnold Schwarzenegger and legislators argued about how to fill a $26.3 billion hole, well past the June 30 deadline for approving a new budget. In July, Fitch, a credit-rating agency, downgraded California's bond rating — already the lowest in the nation — to BBB, just above "junk" status." [1]

Enacted on July 29, the tight budget will force California's student-teacher ratio, already a third higher than the national average, to rise even higher. In addition, some welfare benefits will be cut by as much as half, and the University of California system lost 20 percent of its state funding. Tuition for UC students is going up 9.3 percent this term — and 32 percent in the separate California state university system. About half the children covered under the state's Healthy Families medical insurance program for the working poor are expected to be dropped from the rolls. [2]

Despite these real cuts, much of the budget hole was filled through gimmicks, such as deferring expenses into the next fiscal year beginning next July, including $6.3 billion in education expenses. The state pushed back a payday for state workers, hiding $900 million in costs. The state also "borrowed" $2 billion from local governments, some of which are now suing. In July, Schwarzenegger announced that state workers — who were already being kept home without pay two days a month — would be furloughed the first three Fridays every month.

The constant bickering over the budget has meant state officials have been unable to deal with other pressing problems, including water distribution, infrastructure and prisons. On Aug. 4, a panel of federal judges ordered the state to come up with a plan by mid-September to reduce its overcrowded prison population by nearly 43,000 inmates — more than 25 percent — over the next two years. [3] Schwarzenegger had proposed releasing 27,000 inmates as a cost-saving move but was opposed by law enforcement and victims'-rights groups.

Unemployment reached 12.1 percent in August — among the highest rates in the country. And, like other states in the Southwest, California has suffered disproportionately from the foreclosure crisis.

But Schwarzenegger has long felt that California's budget and governance problems are rooted in the dysfunctional culture of Sacramento, the capital. In 2005, he put before voters a package of so-called reform measures that would have capped state spending, given more power to the governor to cut spending, tightened teacher work rules and changed the political role public employee unions could play. All were rejected. But Schwarzenegger, undaunted, succeeded last year in convincing voters to change the

in 1992 approved TABOR — the Taxpayer Bill of Rights — which limits spending increases to no more than is warranted by inflation and population growth.

That type of limit ignores the fact that costs for the main spending items in states — education and health care — typically rise faster than the rate of inflation. It also puts severe constraints on a state after a recession. If states have to cut spending by 10 percent, for example, during a recession, it could take several years to rebuild programs if they're only allowed to raise spending in subsequent years by, say, 3 percent.

TABOR laws have been rejected by voters in some states in recent years, including Maine, Nebraska and Oregon, which all turned down versions of the law in 2006. Nonetheless, the anti-tax message has remained resonant in states for 25 years — and perhaps up until the present day. States were notably reluctant to raise taxes in 2002 and 2003 — compared with previous downturns — during widespread budget shortfalls after the post-Sept. 11 recession.

This was despite the fact that states cut taxes by 8.2 percent overall during the boom years of the 1990s, according to the Center on Budget and Policy Priorities. [25] States were not willing to raise

taxes back to where they had been before flush times had allowed them to cut rates. On the other hand, they were also often guilty of increasing spending even as revenues had begun to fall. "You drive fast on the freeway, when you pull off, it's hard to slow down," says the Cato Institute's Edwards.

From Boom to Bust

During the economic boom of the late 1990s, states enjoyed huge windfalls as the high-tech market powered the economy to dizzying heights. With more money than expected coming in, states expanded

way legislative districts are drawn. On Aug. 19, he met with a group pushing the idea of making the legislature a part-time institution.

But the Bay Area Council's proposal for a constitutional convention — which Schwarzenegger supports — is drawing the most attention. In a sense, hoping voters will call a convention is an ironic solution to a set of problems many believe has been caused in large measure by California's robust culture of ballot initiatives. (Three of the rejected ballot measures in May were designed to tweak earlier voter-approved propositions.)

Amended more than 500 times, California's constitution is the second-longest of any state, after Alabama. Many voter-approved amendments affect the budget directly, such as the requirement that the state spend at least 40 percent of its general fund on education. Proposition 13, approved by voters in 1978, not only lowered property tax rates but also required that any tax increases be approved by a two-thirds vote in the legislature.

California is the only state that requires two-thirds "supermajority" votes to pass both its annual budget and any tax increases. That's given a relatively small minority in the legislature — in recent years, Republicans — an effective veto over the budget-making process. "They just have lots of constitutional provisions

California State University students, faculty and others protest budget cuts during a CSU trustees meeting in Long Beach, on July 21, 2009. California's financial crisis has prompted the CSU system to raise tuition 32 percent.

AP Photo/Reed Saxon

that hinder them in their ability to be flexible in responding to these budget problems," says Corina Eckl, director of the fiscal affairs program at the National Conference of State Legislatures.

Rewriting constitutions is being considered in other troubled states as well, such as New York. If California moves ahead, it would signal the end of a long period of relative quiet in constitutional revisions.

But Bruce Cain, a political science professor at UC Berkeley who has worked on a constitutional revision commission, doubts a convention will succeed, even if voters call for one. It's too easy for opponents of particular changes to form coalitions against a package that tries to take on all the state's major issues at once, he says. "The danger of the whole process being captured by the same interests that are already stalemating the state are really, really high."

[1] "Meltdown on the Ocean," *The Economist*, July 11, 2009, p. 29, www.economist.com/world/unitedstates/displaystory.cfm?story_id=13998608.

[2] Mitchell Landsberg, "In the Details, a Far Less Golden State," *Los Angeles Times*, July 22, 2009, p. A1.

[3] Carol J. Williams, "State Gets Two Years to Cut 43,000 From Prisons," *Los Angeles Times*, Aug. 4, 2009, p. A1, www.latimes.com/news/local/la-me-prisons5-2009aug05,0,1866042.story. For background, see Peter Katel, "Prison Reform," *CQ Researcher*, April 6, 2007, pp. 289-312.

services and programs, including loosening Medicaid eligibility requirements — with the approval of the federal government — offering Medicaid to people with incomes 200 percent or even 300 percent of the official poverty line (vs. the previous ceiling of 150 percent). States also instituted health-insurance coverage for children.

However, diminished revenues and increased spending created deficits in 2002 and 2003 that were considered the worst fiscal crisis for states in decades. In 2003, states filled their budget gaps by cutting spending by $14.5 billion and raising taxes by $17.5 billion — record totals for cuts and hikes in a single year. As a per-

centage of overall budgets, however, the tax increases were meager compared to hikes that had been enacted in the early 1980s and '90s. States also received $20 billion in assistance from the federal government — $10 billion each for general revenues and Medicaid.

States seemed out of the woods by 2004, given a period of growth in the economy. They also benefited from a housing boom that drove up property values — and thus property-tax collections. States also collected sales taxes when Americans spent billions on home improvement and furnishings — as well as when they bought other goodies, often using equity lines

of credit. People were able to borrow enough money against the increased value of their homes that economists talked about how folks were using homes as ATMs.

By fiscal 2007, no state reported a deficit. But, as it turned out, of course, the housing market had become a bubble. As housing foreclosures rapidly increased the economy slipped into recession. In September 2008, an already battered stock market was brought down rapidly by the collapse of the brokerage firm Lehman Brothers. Soon, state revenues were in freefall, with collections of sales and income taxes plummeting faster than at any time in decades. ■

New Taxes

Cigars, beer, soda, massages and shoes (top) are among the products and services that New York Gov. David Paterson wants to tax to offset the state's budget crisis. In Maine taxes have even been levied on the use of ski lifts. Seth Wescott, a member of the USA Olympic Snowboard team, rides the lift at Sugarloaf in Carrabassett Valley, Maine. (bottom).

CURRENT SITUATION

Fiscal Federalism

M ost of the $787 billion federal stimulus package enacted in Feb- ruary is being spent through transfers to state and local governments. As a result, in the first quarter of this year Washington became for the first time the largest, single source of revenue for the lower levels of government, supplanting sales taxes. [26]

Today's situation stands in stark contrast to 2007, when California Gov. Schwarzenegger and New York City Mayor Michael Bloomberg appeared together embracing one another on the cover of *Time* under the headline "Who Needs Washington?" The accompanying package of stories touted their initiatives in policy areas where Congress was stymied, such as the environment and health care. [27]

Just two years later, that cover looks like an artifact from an entirely different era. The reason, of course, is the economic downturn. "Now Washington is everything," says Jennifer A. Bradley, a senior research associate with the Metropolitan Policy Program at the Brookings Institution, a Washington think tank. "Everyone is looking to Washington to save the day and prime the pump."

"The action is here in Washington because the money is here in Washington," says Donald J. Borut, executive director of the National League of Cities. "This is a unique moment in terms of the scale of expenditures, because we have an economic crisis."

But the federal largesse comes with some strings. Only about 17 percent of the stimulus dollars are available for states to spend as they see fit. The bulk must be spent on federal priorities such as high-speed rail and energy-efficiency programs — a total of 140 different categorical grant programs in all.

President Barack Obama and Vice President Joseph R. Biden have warned state and local officials that they would "call you out" if the money is wasted or spent on programs that don't meet federal goals. [28] Much of the money comes with new requirements that states and localities provide more public information about exactly how federal dollars are being spent — an echo of the general revenue-sharing program of the 1970s, which required local governments to audit their books, which many did for the first time. [29]

In addition to demanding more information, state and local officials expect to face further policy demands from Washington. The Obama administration

Continued on p. 758

At Issue:

Do budget shortfalls mean states must raise taxes?

NICHOLAS JOHNSON
DIRECTOR, STATE FISCAL PROJECT CENTER ON BUDGET AND POLICY PRIORITIES

WRITTEN FOR *CQ RESEARCHER*, SEPTEMBER 2009

*i*t's the cruel irony of a recession: Struggling families need crucial services more than ever, but states have much less money to pay for those services. Wisely, most states are taking a balanced approach in their response to this conundrum, putting tax increases in the mix rather than attempting the impossible by closing their large budget shortfalls only with cuts in spending.

Make no mistake: All 30 of the states that have raised taxes since January have also reduced spending sharply. But in the face of plummeting revenues — down an unprecedented 12 percent since last year — a cuts-only approach would not only decimate vital services like health care and education but also further damage the economy, making the recession even worse.

That's because, as more than 100 economists advised in a letter to policy makers during New York state's budget debate, "Almost every dollar that states and localities spend on aid for the needy, salaries of public employees and other vital services enters the local economy immediately. So if states cut their spending in these areas, overall demand suffers at a time when demand is already too low and support services are most needed."

Tax increases take less money out of the economy and reduce demand less than spending cuts, because some of the additional taxes collected come from money that would have been saved rather than spent. This is particularly true of tax increases on households with high incomes and greater savings.

Budget cuts and tax increases are simply not an "either-or" choice in difficult times. Indeed, in the last two recessions as well as the current one, most states raised taxes to help balance their budgets — states in every part of the country, some governed by Democrats and others by Republicans.

It didn't make them less competitive. Data show that the states that raised taxes enjoyed the same post-recession economic growth as those that didn't.

Balancing budgets through measures like eliminating medical treatment for kids and putting college out of the reach of talented moderate-income students is no way to build a prosperous future. States can avoid the worst of these cuts by including tax increases, preferably focused on those best able to pay, in their budget-balancing plans.

When the economy recovers, the states in the best shape will be those that didn't act like a farmer eating his seed corn.

CHRIS EDWARDS
DIRECTOR, TAX POLICY CATO INSTITUTE

WRITTEN FOR *CQ RESEARCHER*, SEPTEMBER 2009

*m*edia stories are highlighting the supposedly draconian cuts that state and local governments are making to their budgets. And it is true that state policy makers need to make tough choices to balance their budgets during recessions. But for the states overall, the data do not reveal draconian cuts, just a lull in spending growth after years of substantial increases.

According to the Bureau of Economic Analysis (BEA), total state and local spending surged 30 percent in the five-year period 2003 to 2008. Data for the first half of calendar 2009 show that spending has leveled off since the first half of 2008. Spending in 2009 will probably end up being about the same as it was in 2008. On the revenue side, a drop in state and local tax receipts of 6.5 percent so far in 2009 has been made up by an increase in federal grants of 18 percent.

Now compare this flat government spending to the drop in private-sector economic activity during this recession. Private-sector wages are down 5 percent in the first half of 2009 compared to the same period last year, while U.S. business investment is down a stunning 25 percent, according to BEA data.

Families and businesses are tightening their belts and restructuring their finances, and there is no reason why governments shouldn't be doing the same. Just as recessions weed out the least successful businesses in the economy, policy makers should use the recession as an opportunity to weed out their least successful programs.

Looking ahead, state and local revenues will likely be stagnant for some time, so additional restraint will be needed. One place to look for savings is in the compensation packages of the nation's 16 million state and local workers. Half of all state and local spending — $1.1 trillion out of $2.2 trillion in 2008 — goes toward employee wages and benefits.

Thus, policy makers should look at trimming government labor forces, freezing worker wages until the economy recovers and restructuring the generous benefit packages that many state and local workers receive.

Some policy makers are trying to balance their budgets by increasing taxes, but that will cause long-term problems for budgets by suppressing economic activity. Instead, by focusing on restructuring programs and worker-compensation packages, policy makers will make their own jobs easier down the road by creating lasting budget savings.

Continued from p. 756

presents a paradox when it comes to federalism. This president appears to care more about intergovernmental relations than his recent predecessors — he has created a White House Office of Urban Affairs, and the administration consults more often with state officials and certainly local leaders than presidents George W. Bush or Bill Clinton did.

At the same time, though, Obama is presiding over a massive centralization of both power and policy making in Washington, of which the stimulus package may just be the first example. It's not clear what final form, if any, congressional health-care legislation will take, but any new law is bound to have an impact on states. There are proposals to expand Medicaid, for example, which would cost states.

States already complain that they now have less flexibility under Medicaid than they used to, because of audits and other measures taken by the Bush administration. They wonder whether, like Bush, Obama will also impinge on the traditionally largely state and local responsibility of providing K-12 public education.

The stimulus package contains nearly $100 billion for education, including an unprecedented $5 billion in discretionary funds with which Education Secretary Arne Duncan can reward innovative states. Duncan has made it clear the money will go to states that follow administration priorities, such as lifting limits on the number of charter schools. The Education Department recently published a proposal to require states and local school districts to provide much more data on student achievement, without regard to the large amount of money that will cost them.

By potentially making big policy changes in health and education alone, Washington is impinging on areas where states spend half their money. "When the feds have the money and the states don't have the money, then of course the feds are going to be better able to dictate the rules of the game," Bradley says.

The kinds of initiatives states and localities have been able to pursue in recent years — the programs that landed Schwarzenegger and Bloomberg on

Many cash-strapped states are cutting back on assistance for the homeless, like this man sleeping in his tent in Las Vegas, Nev., where unemployment and home foreclosures have added to the homeless population.

Time's cover — are awfully hard to pull off when they're barely able to pay their bills. Experiments in recent years in providing universal health insurance in Massachusetts, Vermont and Maine, for example, "wouldn't have been done if we were in the condition we're in right now," says Pound, of the National Conference of State Legislatures.

Greve, of AEI, predicts that the era when "states experimented on the federal dime" — citing the Massachusetts health-care experiment and welfare rule changes in Wisconsin in the 1990s

— is over. It's possible that the federal government will perform more services directly, rather than relying on states to carry out its plans. The federal dollars that continue to flow are going to come with more strings and, Greve says, "it may well be about the question of whether this model of handing money over to the states works at all well any more."

More Cuts to Come

Putting aside the question of how much federal, state and local relationships are likely to change under Obama, the fact is that the federal tap will soon flow less freely. States must spend (or "obligate," to use the budget term) all of the funds from the stimulus — officially the American Recovery and Reinvestment Act or ARRA — by the end of 2011. Most observers predict that states will still be financially weak at that time, but few believe that Washington — which is facing a $1.6 trillion deficit this year — will enact a second stimulus.

"Fiscal year 2012 is going to be the first one where there's really not going to be much ARRA money left," says Marcia Howard of Federal Funds Information for States, which tracks federal grants available to states. "It's reasonable to expect that state revenues won't really have recovered to their pre-recession levels yet. But state officials don't spend a lot of time thinking about that; they're busy thinking about what they're going to do next week."

State budget writers are having a hard time trying to stay in the black. After he took office in 2007, Maryland

Gov. Martin O'Malley, a Democrat, realized that his state faced an ongoing structural deficit — a situation in which revenues aren't keeping pace with spending growth — due to tax cuts and education spending increases enacted under prior administrations. So O'Malley decided he had to change the tax code.

Although his attempts to tax a long list of services came to nothing, O'Malley did create a new, top personal income tax rate and increased the sales tax by a cent. Despite a total of $1.4 billion in tax increases passed at the end of his first year in office, O'Malley has done practically nothing since then except cut spending. "We've gone now six times in the middle of the fiscal year to amend the budget because of this unprecedented erosion and contraction in the global and national economy," O'Malley says.

On Aug. 26, the state Board of Public Works approved O'Malley's latest package of cuts — $454 million worth — which came on top of $280 million in cuts approved a month earlier. The latest round included layoffs and furloughs for state workers, with the heaviest share borne by the state Department of Health and Mental Hygiene. [30]

As O'Malley points out, other states have it worse. The hardest-hit states remain those in the Sun Belt, where the collapse of the housing market has been deepest, and in the Rust Belt, which is suffering massive unemployment. Republican Gov. Don Carcieri of Rhode Island, which has the nation's second-highest unemployment rate after Michigan, announced on Aug. 24 that 81 percent of state workers would have to take 12 furlough days by the end of the fiscal year, in order to save the state $22 million.

Even the energy-producing states that had been skating through unscathed are now facing serious problems. Texas has seen its revenue from gas-production taxes drop by 43 per-

cent from last year, costing the state $1 billion. Oklahoma, which relies on natural gas production for up to 20 percent of its revenues, saw those taxes drop 75 percent in July compared with the same month last year. The Sooner State recently ordered all government divisions to cut budgets by 5 percent, with more to come. [31]

Such stories are endemic. This spring, the total two-year state budget in Maine shrank by $500 million, from the previous biennium's $6.3 billion. That means spending went down in actual dollars for the first time in 35 years. State employees are getting hit on both wages and benefits, with 20 unpaid furlough days over the next two years, plus an increase in health insurance costs and a freeze on raises. Public hospitals and universities will be looking at smaller payrolls and smaller workforces.

In fact, says Christopher St. John, executive director of the Maine Center for Economic Policy, "There is no function of state government, whether inland fisheries and wildlife or environmental protection or transportation," that won't be facing serious challenges just to continue the work it's been doing.

Georgia is another state that managed to muddle through a bad situation this year. It closed a $3.3 billion shortfall but left itself open to further difficulties down the road. The stimulus filled $1.4 billion of the fiscal hole, while the state depleted its rainy-day accounts to come up with another $300 million. That left $1.6 billion to cut, because proposed tax increases on tobacco and a plan to impose new fees on hospitals and medical providers went nowhere in the legislature.

Nearly every department in Georgia ended up with cuts this year ranging from 6 to 10 percent, with some losing as much as 14 percent. Gov. Sonny Perdue, a Republican, sought to limit reductions in education and health care, but the only program that was spared any cuts at all was Medicaid.

Looking ahead, Georgia can count on only $1.1 billion in stimulus dollars to shore up its budget next year. That's assuming the state doesn't have to dip deeper into stimulus funds to fill fresh holes this year. Georgia also has appreciably less money in its reserve funds. The state will therefore have fewer resources with which to fill gaps that were papered over this year using one-time funds.

In July — just one month into the new fiscal year — Perdue ordered state agencies to cut spending by 5 percent to address Georgia's brand new $900 million shortfall. ∎

OUTLOOK

Slow Recovery?

Economists are predicting that the recession will end this fall, but that any recovery will be shallow — "a recovery only a statistician could love," as Wells Fargo senior economist Mark Vitner put it, with continuing high unemployment. [32] Although housing prices have begun to pick up, and the "cash for clunkers" program helped dealers sell nearly 700,000 cars, both the housing and auto markets remained glutted. And, with households trying to rebuild their own balance sheets following market losses, increased savings will continue to put a damper on spending.

Even as the economy begins to rebound, it's going to take some time for state budgets to catch up. State tax collections tend to lag even after a recession ends. "We know that it takes 12, 14 or even 18 months for state revenues to recover after a recession," says Corina Eckl, director of the fiscal affairs program at the National Conference of State Legislatures.

"The problem is our tomorrow looks no different from today," said Robert Emerson, budget director in Michigan, where revenues have dropped to levels last seen more than 20 years ago. [33]

"It's going to be 2012ish before states get back to 2008 levels in nominal dollars," says Pattison, at the National Association of State Budget Officers. By that time, he notes, "the stimulus money stops. For a lot of reasons, unless we have some really unexpected economic boom, it's going to be really tough for the next five to 10 years for states and localities."

With states having relied so far on spending cuts much more than tax increases to shore up their budgets, Korpi, the director of research and collective bargaining at AFSCME, hopes that "people are going to start realizing the value of public services and understand that parks and libraries and the social safety net and clean air are things that we as a society need. Hopefully, we'll get beyond the rhetoric about taxes and realize that we're paying for things in other ways. At some point, it seems like we need to have an adult conversation about what is it we expect states to deliver, and how do we pay for it."

Howard, of Federal Funds Information for States, says that for "all the doom and gloom" and "real pain" states are now facing, they somehow will manage. "Over the long term, states take it on the chin when times are tough and rise back up. They do raise taxes when they need them, and then cut them."

Although more states have been willing to raise taxes this year than during the downturn of 2002-03, there appears to be little political will or appetite to raise taxes significantly enough to make up the shortfalls in budgets. "There's no indication that the public wants to pay higher taxes if that's what it will take to right these structural deficits," says Rutgers political scientist Rosenthal, "and there's no indication that they can get away with really diminishing the services people really rely on."

Faced with that paradox, few states have shown a desire so far to make lasting changes either to their tax code or to the programs they offer. All the incentives in state budgeting, it seems, still point toward finding short-term fixes.

"The more desperate people get, the more they look for one-time lifelines — as opposed to saying, 'Even if we have to take a hit now, it's better than a sustained disaster,' " says Greve, the AEI federalism scholar.

"That's the paradox of the situation," he says. "If this is not a crisis, then what is? And still the system just motors along." ∎

Notes

[1] Judy Lin, "Everything Must Go! Calif. Holds Giant Garage Sale," The Associated Press, Aug. 28, 2009, http://tech.yahoo.com/news/ap/20090828/ap_on_hi_te/us_california_garage_sale.

[2] Donald J. Boyd and Lucy Dadayan, "State Tax Decline in Early 2009 Was the Sharpest on Record," State Revenue Report No. 76, Rockefeller Institute of Government, July 2009, www.rockinst.org/pdf/government_finance/state_revenue_report/2009-07-17-SRR_76.pdf.

[3] Amy Merrick and Conor Dougherty, "Plunging Revenue Squeezes State Budgets Further," The Wall Street Journal, July 17, 2009, p. A3, http://online.wsj.com/article/SB124776520979752661.html.

[4] "State Budget Update: July 2009," National Conference of State Legislatures, July 2009, www.ncsl.org/documents/fiscal/StateBudgetUpdateJulyFinal.pdf.

[5] "Elizabeth McNichol and Iris J. Lav, "New Fiscal Year Brings No Relief From Unprecedented State Budget Problems," Center on Budget and Policy Priorities, Sept. 3, 2009, p. 1, www.cbpp.org/files/9-8-08sfp.pdf.

[6] Abby Goodnough, "States Turning to Last Resorts in Budget Crisis," The New York Times, June 22, 2009, p. A1, www.nytimes.com/2009/06/22/us/22states.html.

[7] Rebecca Cathcart, "Schwarzenegger Urges a Study on Legalizing Marijuana Use," The New York Times, May 7, 2009, p. A21, www.nytimes.com/2009/05/07/us/07arnold.html. For background see Peter Katel, "Legalizing Marijuana," CQ Researcher, June 12, 2009, pp. 525-548.

[8] Peter Slevin, "States Straining to Repair Budgets," The Washington Post, July 7, 2009, p. A4, www.washingtonpost.com/wp-dyn/content/article/2009/07/06/AR2009070603515.html.

[9] James Bone, "Gov David Paterson calls for 'iPod tax' to close state's budget deficit," Times Online, Dec. 18, 2008, www.timesonline.co.uk/tol/news/world/us_and_americas/article5361269.ece.

[10] Ross Goldberg, "From Albany, Taxes Raised Enough to Hurt," The New York Times, April 5, 2009, p. WE5, www.nytimes.com/2009/04/05/nyregion/westchester/05budgetwe.html.

[11] "State Tax Update: July 2009," National Conference of State Legislatures," July 2009, www.ncsl.org/documents/fiscal/StateTaxUpdateJuly2009.pdf.

[12] Christopher Keating, "Rell Tax Shift Breaks Impasse," Hartford Courant, Aug. 27, 2009, p. A1, www.courant.com/news/politics/hc-rell-budget-0827.artaug27,0,4156621.story.

[13] Molly Ball, "Tax Increases Saved," Las Vegas Review-Journal, May 30, 2009, p. 1A, www.lvrj.com/news/46539447.html.

[14] Steve Chapman, "States in a Fiscal Hole They Dug," Chicago Tribune, July 30, 2009, p. 19.

[15] Katherine Barrett and Richard Green,

About the Author

Alan Greenblatt is a staff writer at *Governing* magazine. He previously covered elections, agriculture and military spending for *CQ Weekly*, where he won the National Press Club's Sandy Hume Award for political journalism. He graduated from San Francisco State University in 1986 and received a master's degree in English literature from the University of Virginia in 1988. His recent *CQ Researcher* reports include "Confronting Warming," "Future of the GOP" and "Immigration Debate."

"Promises With a Price," Pew Center on the States, December 2007, p. 4, www.pewtrusts. org/uploadedFiles/wwwpewtrustsorg/Reports/ State_policy/pension_report.pdf.

[16] "Unsatisfactory State," *The Economist*, July 11, 2009, www.economist.com/displaystory.cfm?story_ id=13983688.

[17] Robert Novy-Marx and Joshua Rauh, "The Intergenerational Transfer of Public Pension Promises," National Bureau of Economic Research Working Paper No. 14343, September 2008, www.nber.org/papers/w14343.

[18] "$100k Pension Club Is Growing," *The Sacramento Bee*, May 6, 2009, p. 14A, www.sacbee.com/ editorials/story/1836917.html.

[19] Gerald W. McEntee, "Pensions Benefit Taxpayers," *USA Today*, July 13, 2009, p. 9A, http://blogs.usatoday.com/oped/2009/07/op posing-view-pensions-benefit-taxpayers.html.

[20] Monica Davey, "In Michigan, Deficits Defy Years of Cutting," *The New York Times*, July 12, 2009, p. A14, www.nytimes.com/2009/07/12/us/ 12michigan.html.

[21] Kathy Barks Hoffman, "Michigan LG Starts Work to Restructure Government," The Associated Press, May 26, 2009, www.cnbc.com/ id/30949447.

[22] For background, see William Triplett, "State Budget Crises," *CQ Researcher*, Oct. 13, 2003, pp. 821-844.

[23] Ronald Snell, "State Finance in the Great Depression," National Conference of State Legislatures, March 2009, p. 2, www.ncsl.org/ print/fiscal/statefinancegreatdepression.pdf.

[24] *Ibid.*, p. 5.

[25] Thomas A. Garrett and Gary A. Wagner, "State Government Finances: World War II to the Current Crises," *Federal Reserve Bank of St. Louis Review*, March/April 2004, p. 21, https:// research.stlouisfed.org/publications/review/04/ 03/Garrett.pdf.

[26] Dennis Cauchon, "Federal Aid Is Top Revenue for States," *USA Today*, May 5, 2009, p. 1A, www.usatoday.com/news/nation/2009-05-04-fed states-revenue_N.htm.

[27] Michael Grunwald, "The New Action Heroes," *Time*, June 25, 2007, p. 32, www.time.com/time/ nation/article/0,8599,1632736,00.html.

[28] Peter Nicholas, "Cities Are Shortchanged by Stimulus, Mayors Say," *Chicago Tribune*, June 22, 2009, p. 28, www.chicagotribune.com/news/ nationworld/chi-tc-nw-stimulus-0621-0622jun22,0, 6951508.story.

[29] Donald F. Kettl, "Imbalance of Powers," *Governing*, June 2009, p. 18, www.governing. com/column/imbalance-powers/.

FOR MORE INFORMATION

Brookings Institution, 1775 Massachusetts Ave., N.W., Washington, DC 20036; (202) 797-6000; www.brookings.edu. Think tank whose Metropolitan Policy Program studies and promotes efforts to build stronger regions and is releasing a series of reports on how they are spending and being affected by federal stimulus dollars.

Cato Institute, 1000 Massachusetts Ave, N.W., Washington, DC 20001; (202) 842-0200; www.cato.org. Libertarian-leaning think tank promoting policies of limited government and free enterprise.

Center on Budget and Policy Priorities, 820 First St., N.E., Suite 510, Washington, DC 20002; (202) 408-1080; www.cbpp.org. Liberal-leaning think tank that issues regular reports on state expenditures and tax policy.

Federal Funds Information for States, 444 N. Capitol St., N.W., Suite 642, Washington, DC 20001; (202) 624-5849; www.ffis.org. Monitors federal grant money available to states.

Government Finance Officers Association, 203 N. LaSalle St., Suite 2700, Chicago, IL 60601; (312) 977-9700; www.gfoa.org. Provides training and education to state and local finance officers and keeps them abreast of developments in their field and in Washington.

National Association of Counties, 25 Massachusetts Ave., N.W., Suite 500, Washington, DC 20001; (202) 393-6226; www.naco.org. Regularly surveys its members about their finances, making the results public to policy makers, the media and the public.

National Association of State Budget Officers, 444 N. Capitol St., N.W., Suite 642, Washington, DC 20001; (202) 624-5849; www.nasbo.org. Issues regular comprehensive surveys of state fiscal conditions and state expenditures.

National Conference of State Legislatures, 7700 E. First Place, Denver, CO 80230; (303) 364-7700; www.ncsl.org. Issues reports based on surveys of state budget and tax conditions.

National League of Cities, 1301 Pennsylvania Ave., N.W., Suite 550, Washington, DC 20004; (202) 626-3000; www.nlc.org. Association of municipal governments that issues occasional reports on financial conditions, including an annual survey of local fiscal officers.

Nelson A. Rockefeller Institute of Government, State University of New York, 411 State St., Albany, NY 12203; (518) 443-5522; www.rockinst.org. Public-policy research arm that publishes regular reports surveying state and local finances.

Pew Center on the States, 901 E St., N.W., 10th Floor, Washington, DC 20004; (202) 552-2000; www.pewcenteronthestates.org. Foundation-supported think tank that produces comprehensive reports on state policy matters such as pensions and corrections.

[30] Aaron C. Davis, "Md. Approves $454 Million Cut to Fill Latest Gap," *The Washington Post*, Aug. 27, 2009, p. B1, www.washingtonpost. com/wp-dyn/content/article/2009/08/26/AR2009 082603612.html.

[31] Ben Casselman, "Budget Pain Spreads to Energy Rich States," *The Wall Street Journal*, Aug. 24, 2009, p. A3, http://online.wsj.com/ article/SB125106951994952269.html.

[32] Annys Shin, " 'A Recovery Only a Statistician Could Love,' " *The Washington Post*, Aug. 12, 2009, p. A1, www.washingtonpost.com/wp-dyn/ content/article/2009/08/11/AR2009081100988.html.

[33] Davey, *op. cit.*

Bibliography
Selected Sources

Books

Donahue, John D., *The Warping of Government Work*, Harvard University Press, 2008.

A Harvard public policy lecturer examines how benefits and financial incentives have changed in the private sector but much less so for public employees, complicating workforce management for governments.

Lowenstein, Roger, *While America Aged*, Penguin Press, 2008.

The financial journalist looks at how pension debts "ruined" San Diego, the New York City subway system and General Motors.

Articles

Cauchon, Dennis, "Federal Aid Is Top Revenue for States," *USA Today*, May 5, 2009, p. 1A, www.usatoday.com/news/nation/2009-05-04-fed-states-revenue_N.htm.

Federal grants to states and localities grew by 15 percent in the first quarter of this year, making Washington for the first time the single largest source of revenue for local governments.

Chapman, Steve, "States in a Fiscal Hole They Dug," *Chicago Tribune*, July 30, 2009, p. 19, www.chicagotribune.com/news/columnists/chi-oped0730chapmanjul30,0,1207567.column.

An editorial writer says unsustainable state spending and tax burdens made the present shortfalls inevitable.

Davey, Monica, "In Michigan, Deficits Defy Years of Cutting," *The New York Times*, July 12, 2009, p. A14, www.nytimes.com/2009/07/12/us/12michigan.html.

Declining revenues in Michigan have forced state officials to consider jettisoning or consolidating more than half the cabinet departments.

Eaton, Leslie, "Pinched States Wrestle With More Cuts," *The Wall Street Journal*, July 30, 2009, p. A3, http://online.wsj.com/article/SB124891089628491887.html.

With budget shortfalls continuing, states are ordering across-the-board cuts among their agencies, reducing payments to state workers and cutting back on maintenance efforts.

Landsberg, Mitchell, "In the Details, a Far Less Golden State," *Los Angeles Times*, July 22, 2009, p. A1, www.latimes.com/news/local/la-me-impact22-2009jul22,0,6954970,full.story.

California's latest budget will deny medical coverage to children, release thousands of prison inmates, shorten the school year and take money from local governments.

Silverblatt, Rob, "States Draw Down Rainy Day Funds," *Stateline.org*, Aug. 27, 2009, www.stateline.org/live/details/story?contentId=421718.

In dealing with fiscal 2009 and 2010 budget shortfalls, many states are depleting their reserve accounts.

Reports and Studies

"State Tax Update: July 2009," National Conference of State Legislatures, July 2009, www.ncsl.org/documents/fiscal/StateTaxUpdateJuly2009.pdf.

Thirty-six states raised taxes by a net total of $24 billion for fiscal 2010, a 3 percent increase.

Boyd, Donald J., and Lucy Dadayan, "State Tax Decline in Early 2009 Was the Sharpest on Record," Rockefeller Institute of Government, State Revenue Report No. 76, July 2009, www.rockinst.org/pdf/government_finance/state_revenue_report/2009-07-17-SRR_76.pdf.

State tax collections dropped a record 11.7 percent during the first quarter of 2009 compared to the same period in 2008.

Garrett, Thomas A., and Gary A. Wagner, "State Government Finances: World War II to the Current Crises," *Federal Reserve Bank of St. Louis Review*, March/April 2004, p. 21, https://research.stlouisfed.org/publications/review/04/03/Garrett.pdf.

The economists survey state budgets from the 1940s through 2004, detailing changes such as rainy-day funds, tax and expenditure limits and new sources of revenue such as lotteries.

McNichol, Elizabeth, and Iris J. Lav, "New Fiscal Year Brings No Relief From Unprecedented State Budget Problems," Center on Budget and Policy Priorities, Sept. 3, 2009, www.cbpp.org/files/9-8-08sfp.pdf.

The states closed budget gaps totaling $168 billion, but they are continuing to bleed red ink as fiscal year 2010 begins.

Novy-Marx, Robert, and Joshua Rauh, "The Intergenerational Transfer of Public Pension Promises," National Bureau of Economic Research Working Paper No. 14343, September 2008, www.nber.org/papers/w14343.

The 116 largest state and local public pension plans are underfunded by $3.12 trillion — triple the states' estimates.

Snell, Ronald, "State Finance in the Great Depression," National Conference of State Legislatures, March 2009, p. 2, www.ncsl.org/print/fiscal/statefinancegreatdepression.pdf.

The Great Depression brought about an unprecedented response from government, including sales and personal income taxes in states.

The Next Step:

Additional Articles from Current Periodicals

Benefits

Cauchon, Dennis, "Public, Private Pay Gap Grows," *USA Today*, April 10, 2009, p. 1A.

Public employees are enjoying sizable growth in their benefits packages even during a distressed economy.

Horstman, Barry M., "Generous Pensions in Deep Hole," *Cincinnati Enquirer*, April 3, 2009.

Generous pensions allow Cincinnati public employees to look forward to secure and comfortable retirements.

Ryan, Lisa G., "Corzine Signs Benefits Bill," *Courier-Post* (New Jersey), Sept. 30, 2008.

New Jersey Gov. Jon S. Corzine signed a bill designed to reduce pension and health-care costs, hopefully plugging a budget shortfall.

Smith, Ron, "Baltimore Pension Dispute Illuminates Public/ Private Divide," *Baltimore Sun*, May 22, 2009, p. 21A.

Baltimore faces a growing gap between pension obligations to retired workers and the city's ability to pay for them.

California

Wetzel, Kimberly S., "State Budget Delay Could Affect Stimulus Funds for California Education," *Contra Costa* (California) *Times*, Feb. 18, 2009.

An ongoing state budget rift in California could delay the amount of money the state's schools receive under the federal stimulus package, according to state education officials.

Yamamura, Kevin, "How Federal Aid Request Plays Into Budget Battle," *Sacramento Bee*, Dec. 4, 2008, p. A1.

California Gov. Arnold Schwarzenegger considers potential federal aid an "investment" in the state as opposed to a bailout.

Zapler, Mike, and Edwin Garcia, "Schwarzenegger Signs Budget Deal," *San Jose Mercury News*, Feb. 20, 2009.

California Gov. Arnold Schwarzenegger has signed a $41 billion budget package full of steep tax hikes and spending cuts.

Layoffs

Christensen, Rob, and Mark Johnson, "Perdue Wants Layoff Plans — In Case," *News & Observer* (Raleigh, N.C.), Feb. 4, 2009, p. B1.

The governor of North Carolina wants state agencies to prepare for layoffs, but she hopes they won't be necessary.

Ludwig, Mike, "Trustees Give McDavis Authority to Offer More Workers Buyouts," *Athens* (Ohio) *News*, Jan. 26, 2009.

Ohio University is scheduled to offer employees more buyout packages amid a severe shortfall in funding from the state.

Menchaca, Charles, "Possible Layoffs of 21 Merrill Teachers Could Increase Class Sizes," *Wausau* (Wisconsin) *Daily Herald*, Feb. 11, 2009.

A school district in Wisconsin has issued 21 layoff notices because of a lack of funding, with the move likely to increase classroom sizes.

Taxes

Arnold, Elias C., "Goodyear Will Raise Sales Tax," *Arizona Republic*, June 6, 2009, p. 6.

Residents of Goodyear, Ariz., will start paying higher sales taxes to help balance the city's declining budget amid faltering development revenues.

Helderman, Rosalind S., "Johnson Backs Off Request That Assembly Raise Taxes," *The Washington Post*, Feb. 20, 2009, p. B6.

An official from Prince George's County, Md., has opposed a measure that would raise property taxes in order to close a potential shortfall in the county's budget.

Klas, Mary Ellen, "Florida Senate Pushes Tax Increases to Fund Education Budget," *Miami Herald*, March 26, 2009, p. B1.

Florida Senate budget writers are recommending increases in cigarette and sales taxes to help pay for funding shortfalls in education.

Niolet, Benjamin, and Lynn Bonner, "House Weighs Higher Taxes," *Charlotte Observer*, June 9, 2009, p. 1A.

The N.C. state House is considering raising income taxes for the wealthiest residents to offset education and social services cuts.

CITING *CQ RESEARCHER*

Sample formats for citing these reports in a bibliography include the ones listed below. Preferred styles and formats vary, so please check with your instructor or professor.

MLA STYLE

Jost, Kenneth. "Rethinking the Death Penalty." CQ Researcher 16 Nov. 2001: 945-68.

APA STYLE

Jost, K. (2001, November 16). Rethinking the death penalty. CQ Researcher, 11, 945-968.

CHICAGO STYLE

Jost, Kenneth. "Rethinking the Death Penalty." CQ Researcher, November 16, 2001, 945-968.

In-depth Reports on Issues in the News

Are you writing a paper?

Need backup for a debate?

Want to become an expert on an issue?

For more than 80 years, students have turned to *CQ Researcher* for in-depth reporting on issues in the news. Reports on a full range of political and social issues are now available. Following is a selection of recent reports:

Civil Liberties
Closing Guantánamo, 2/09
Affirmative Action, 10/08
Gay Marriage Showdowns, 9/08
America's Border Fence, 9/08
Immigration Debate, 2/08

Crime/Law
Examining Forensics, 7/09
Legalizing Marijuana, 6/09
Mexico's Drug War, 12/08
Prostitution Debate, 5/08
Public Defenders, 4/08

Education
Reading Crisis? 2/08
Discipline in Schools, 2/08
Student Aid, 1/08
Racial Diversity in Public Schools, 9/07

Environment/Society
Energy and Climate, 7/09
Future of Books, 5/09
Hate Groups, 5/09
Future of Journalism, 3/09
Confronting Warming, 1/09
Reducing Carbon Footprint, 12/08

Health/Safety
Health-Care Reform, 8/09
Straining the Safety Net, 7/09
Treating Depression, 6/09
Reproductive Ethics, 5/09
Extreme Sports, 4/09
Regulating Toxic Chemicals, 1/09
Preventing Cancer, 1/09

Politics/Economy
Business Bankruptcy, 4/09
Future of the GOP, 3/09
Middle-Class Squeeze, 3/09

Upcoming Reports

Gays in the Military, 9/18/09   Interrogating the CIA, 9/25/09   Nuclear Armaments, 10/2/09

ACCESS

CQ Researcher is available in print and online. For access, visit your library or www.cqresearcher.com.

STAY CURRENT

To receive notice of upcoming *CQ Researcher* reports, or learn more about *CQ Researcher* products, subscribe to the free e-mail newsletters, *CQ Researcher Alert!* and *CQ Researcher News*: http://cqpress.com/newsletters.

PURCHASE

To purchase a *CQ Researcher* report in print or electronic format (PDF), visit www.cqpress.com or call 866-427-7737. Single reports start at $15. Bulk purchase discounts and electronic-rights licensing are also available.

SUBSCRIBE

Annual full-service *CQ Researcher* subscriptions—including 44 reports a year, monthly index updates, and a bound volume—start at $803. Add $25 for domestic postage.

CQ Researcher Online offers a backfile from 1991 and a number of tools to simplify research. For pricing information, call 800-834-9020, ext. 1906, or e-mail librarysales@cqpress.com.

Published by CQ Press, a Division of SAGE

www.cqresearcher.com

Gays in the Military

Should the ban on homosexuals be lifted?

P
olitical passions over the ban on open homosexuality in the U.S. military are stirring again. A new legislative fight on the issue may be headed for House and Senate hearings as early as this fall. Iraq War veteran Rep. Patrick J. Murphy, D-Pa., is proposing legislation to end sexuality-based discrimination in the armed forces. Under the "don't ask, don't tell" policy, gays and lesbians are barred from military service unless their orientation stays hidden. The policy was designed as a compromise to a 1993 call to lift the ban. Supporters of the policy say dropping it would degrade the "unit cohesion" that is critical to battlefield effectiveness. But Murphy and some other recent vets argue that most of today's warriors don't care about their comrades' sexuality. In another element of political drama, some gay political activists are questioning President Barack Obama's level of commitment to pushing for repeal, as he has promised to do.

Army National Guard Lt. Daniel Choi symbolizes the debate over whether gays should be allowed to serve openly in the military. The West Point graduate and Arabic language specialist faces discharge because he revealed he is gay, in violation of the "don't ask, don't tell" policy.

CQ Researcher • Sept. 18, 2009 • www.cqresearcher.com
Volume 19, Number 32 • Pages 765-788

Cover: AP Photo/Damian Dovarganes

CQ Researcher

Sept. 18, 2009
Volume 19, Number 32

MANAGING EDITOR: Thomas J. Colin
tcolin@cqpress.com

ASSISTANT MANAGING EDITOR: Kathy Koch
kkoch@cqpress.com

ASSOCIATE EDITOR: Kenneth Jost

STAFF WRITERS: Thomas J. Billitteri,
Marcia Clemmitt, Peter Katel

CONTRIBUTING WRITERS: Rachel Cox,
Sarah Glazer, Alan Greenblatt, Reed Karaim
Barbara Mantel, Patrick Marshall,
Tom Price, Jennifer Weeks

DESIGN/PRODUCTION EDITOR: Olu B. Davis

ASSISTANT EDITOR: Darrell Dela Rosa

FACT-CHECKING: Eugene J. Gabler,
Michelle Harris

CQ PRESS

A Division of SAGE

PRESIDENT AND PUBLISHER:
John A. Jenkins

EXECUTIVE DIRECTOR,
REFERENCE INFORMATION GROUP:
Alix B. Vance

CQ Press is a registered trademark of Congressional Quarterly Inc.

CQ Researcher (ISSN 1056-2036) is printed on acid-free paper. Published weekly, except; (Jan. wk. 1) (May wk. 4) (July wks. 1, 2) (Aug. wks. 3, 4) (Nov. wk. 4) and (Dec. wk. 4), by CQ Press, a division of SAGE Publications. Annual full-service subscriptions start at $803. For pricing, call 1-800-834-9020, ext. 1906. To purchase a *CQ Researcher* report in print or electronic format (PDF), visit www. cqpress.com or call 866-427-7737. Single reports start at $15. Bulk purchase discounts and electronic-rights licensing are also available. Periodicals postage paid at Washington, D.C., and additional mailing offices. POSTMASTER: Send address changes to *CQ Researcher*, 2300 N St., N.W., Suite 800, Washington, DC 20037.

Gays in the Military

BY PETER KATEL

THE ISSUES

Lt. Col. Victor Fehrenbach, an Air Force weapons control officer decorated for heroism in Iraq, was expecting to be deployed back to a war zone last year when his military career suddenly blew up.

A male civilian with whom Fehrenbach had had a sexual encounter at his Boise, Idaho, home falsely accused him of rape. Fehrenbach successfully rebutted the accusation, but to do so he had to acknowledge to police and Air Force investigators that he is gay. In the end, Fehrenbach was not charged with a crime, but his superiors at Mountain Home Air Force Base in Idaho began proceedings to honorably discharge the 18-year veteran. [1] Air Force Secretary Michael Donley is expected to make a final decision within a month.

The proposed discharge is based on Fehrenbach's alleged violation of the "don't ask, don't tell" regulations adopted by the Defense Department in 1993. They require anyone identified as gay or lesbian or who has engaged in homosexual activities to be expelled from the military. However, the rules do not require dismissal of homosexuals whose orientation remains secret.

"I kept my private life private for 18 years," Fehrenbach, the son of two Air Force officers, says in a telephone interview. "I didn't even tell my family; none of my coworkers knew. My dream for my whole life was to serve my country and be in the Air Force."

Air Force Lt. Col. Victor Fehrenbach, a decorated Iraq War veteran with more than 80 combat missions, could be discharged over his homosexuality. Nearly 12,800 gay or lesbian service members were discharged from 1994-2008. The debate over gays in the military has intensified this year because President Barack Obama opposes the military's "don't ask, don't tell" policy and because gay service members are fighting and dying in Afghanistan and Iraq.

The "don't ask, don't tell" policy and a related law banning homosexual conduct by service members grew out of a 1993 political firestorm, sparked by newly elected President Bill Clinton's attempt to keep a campaign promise and lift the military's longtime ban on homosexuals. Instead, the Clinton administration crafted regulations that drew a line between sexual "orientation" and behavior and prohibited questioning service members and potential enlistees about their sexuality. The president also signed into law a bill that Congress passed in 1993 that doesn't mention orientation at all. Instead, it reinforces the military's ban on gays serving in the armed services:

"The presence in the armed forces of persons who demonstrate a propensity or intent to engage in homosexual acts, would create an unacceptable risk to the high standards of morale, good order and discipline, and unit cohesion that are the essence of military capability," the law says. [2]

Both sides dislike the "don't ask, don't tell" regulations, but they disagree over whether the law banning homosexuals from serving openly in the military should be repealed. Opponents of the law say current policies have made little change in the military's practice of weeding out gays and lesbians. Supporters of the ban say prohibiting homosexual conduct is impossible without asking service members or potential members if they are gay or lesbian.

In any case, the 1993 compromise didn't tamp down the controversy. Nearly 12,800 men and women have been discharged from the military on the basis of homosexuality between fiscal 1994 and 2008. [3] And the controversy has intensified this year, because President Barack Obama opposes the policy and because gay service members are fighting in Afghanistan and Iraq.

The Senate Armed Services Committee is expected to hold hearings on the policy this fall for the first time since 1993, and a House panel is tentatively planning its own hearing. Rep. Patrick J. Murphy, D-Pa., an Iraq combat veteran who served with the 82nd Airborne Division, has introduced a bill to repeal the 1993 law and prohibit sexuality-based discrimination in the military.

AP Photo/Charlie Litchfield

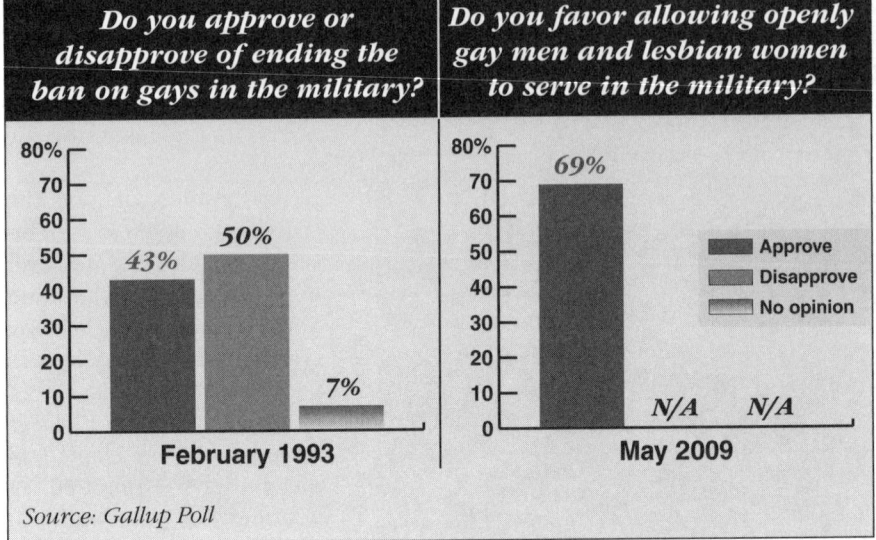

Views Shift on Gays in the Military

About seven in 10 Americans favor allowing gays to openly serve in the military, an increase of 26 percentage points since 1993, when the "don't ask, don't tell" policy was created.

Do you approve or disapprove of ending the ban on gays in the military?

Do you favor allowing openly gay men and lesbian women to serve in the military?

February 1993: 43%, 50%, 7%

May 2009: 69%, N/A, N/A

Approve / Disapprove / No opinion

Source: Gallup Poll

"It hurts our national security when we let go of 13,000 honorable troops, not for any misconduct but just because they happen to be gay," Murphy says.

For instance, opponents like Murphy note, at least 20 gay and lesbian Arabic and Farsi linguists were discharged between 1998 and 2004. [4] Army National Guard Lt. Daniel Choi, an Arabic specialist facing discharge after "coming out," has become the public face of that trend. The ban's supporters, however, say the dismissals prove the law prohibiting homosexuality should be better enforced so gays and lesbians don't enter the military in the first place.

Murphy's supporters say public opinion has changed dramatically since 1993, when opposition ran high. A Gallup Poll in June showed 69 percent of adults favor allowing open homosexuals in the military, up from 43 percent in 1993. Strikingly, 58 percent of self-identified conservatives support gays serving in the military — up from 46 percent four years ago. [5]

But Congress, not Gallup, must decide the fate of the bill. And Murphy and his cosponsors would have to overcome opposition from a phalanx of retired senior commanders.

"Team cohesion and concentration on missions would suffer if our troops had to live in close quarters with others who could be sexually attracted to them," four former high-level commanders said in a *Washington Post* op-ed last April. * "There is no compelling national security reason for running these risks to our armed forces." They and more than 1,000 other retired general and flag officers had signed a letter advocating retaining the ban, they said. [6]

The retired brass and their allies disdain the example of 25 other coun-

---

* The four are retired Army Gen. James J. Linday, first commander of U.S. Special Operations Command; retired Adm. Jerome Johnson, former vice chief of naval operations; retired Lt. Gen. E. G. "Buck" Shuler, former commander of the Strategic Air Command's 8th Air Force; and retired Gen. Joseph J. Went, former assistant commandant of the Marine Corps.

tries, including some key U.S. allies, which allow openly gay troops in their armed forces. "This is hardly convincing, to say, 'The others are doing it, so we should too,' " said Brian E. A. Maue, a professor of policy analysis at the U.S. Air Force Academy in Colorado Springs, speaking only for himself. [7]

Obama promised gay political activists who supported his presidential campaign that he will move to lift the prohibition — though he didn't say when. Some activists want Obama simply to halt homosexuality discharges by executive order.

Those favoring that approach argue that prospects for immediate congressional action are dim. Still, simply prohibiting discharges by presidential order would allow a successor president to restart discharges and would leave the homosexuality law on the books. A president can't repeal a law.

In any case, Obama has opted to toss the hot potato to Congress, asking lawmakers to discard the 1993 law, entitled, "Policy concerning homosexuality in the armed forces."

"My administration is already working with the Pentagon and members of the House and the Senate on . . . ending this policy, which will require an act of Congress," the president told gay and lesbian activists gathered at the White House on June 29 to mark the 40th anniversary of the "Stonewall Riots" in New York City, which launched the gay-rights movement. [8]

The U.S. Supreme Court could also strike down the policy as unconstitutional. In 2003 the court held that civilian laws prohibiting homosexual sex were unconstitutional. But in June, the court declined to hear a challenge to the military's "don't ask, don't tell" policy. [9]

The justices didn't explain their action. But it underlined a distinction between civilian and military codes of conduct. Indeed, advocates on both sides cite the importance of attitudes within the military. Those favoring a ban cite the most recent annual survey by the nongovernmental *Military Times* newspaper, which found that 58 percent of 1,900 active-duty respondents opposed lifting the ban. [10]

"In the field environment, you're in very close proximity to one another," Army Capt. Steven J. Lacy of the 71st Transportation Battalion at Fort Eustis, in Newport News, Va., told the paper. "The fact that someone could be openly gay could exacerbate stress on teams and small units when you're already at a high stress level." [11]

Ten percent of the respondents warned that they wouldn't re-enlist if the prohibition ended. [12] Elaine Donnelly, a key figure in efforts to retain the prohibition, cites that finding as evidence of disruptions that would occur if the ban were lifted. "With even just a few thousand departures in mid-level ranks you have crippled our all-volunteer force," she says. Donnelly is president of the Center on Military Readiness (CMR), an advocacy organization, in Livonia, Mich.

Some high-level military retirees discount the threat of departures. "I don't believe a large number would do that," says retired Brig. Gen. John Adams. "People who are unwilling to accommodate equal opportunity in the matter of open service — I would say the military is not for them."

Military Times says the survey results "are not representative of the military as a whole," because the Army is over-represented and minorities, women and junior enlisted personnel are underrepresented. The newspaper's subscribers are generally older and more conservative. [13]

However, older personnel and retirees don't uniformly support the ban. "Within the military, the climate has changed dramatically since 1993," retired Gen. John M. Shalikashvili, chairman of the Joint Chiefs of Staff in the Clinton administration, wrote in a *Washington Post* op-ed in June. "Conversations I've held with service

Discharges Number of Homosexuals Declined

The U.S. military discharged 634 homosexual personnel in 2008 — less than half the number discharged in 1980. Some say the decline reflects the effectiveness of the policy; others say the military knowingly retains homosexual personnel during times of crisis and conflict. Overall, 32,050 homosexuals have been discharged from the military during the 28-year period.

Fiscal year	Homosexual discharges	Percentage of total active force
1980	1,754	0.086
1985	1,660	0.077
1990	941	0.046
1995	757	0.050
2000	1,212	0.088
2005	726	0.052
2008	634	0.045

Source: David F. Burrelli, "Don't Ask, Don't Tell:" The Law and Military Policy on Same-Sex Behavior, Congressional Research Service, August 2009

members make clear that, while the military remains a traditional culture, that tradition no longer requires banning open service by gays." Last year, 104 retired generals and admirals signed a letter calling for an end to "don't ask, don't tell." [14]

Some outside experts share Shalikashvili's view. "There is a much clearer generation gap" on the issue than in the past, says David R. Segal, a professor of sociology at the University of Maryland and director of its Center for Research on Military Organization. "There are still senior people in the Army — the Army in particular — who do not want it to happen, but more junior people who, unlike their seniors, had gone to high school and college with people who were gay and 'out' were not as threatened."

Segal sees changed attitudes firsthand. "Talking to soldiers and sailors I'm finding more people who are gay and out than ever before," he says. "A lot of people are officially not out, but they're out to somebody, and usually

the somebodies are buddies in their units, sometimes their platoon leaders or company commanders — more likely than to their first sergeants, because the first sergeants are from a different generation."

Fehrenbach, meanwhile, says he's suffered no problems with the men he serves with since he came out as gay, despite the macho culture of combat aviation. "From guys I've flown with in combat, I hear, 'I would go to war with you tomorrow.' "

As the conflict over allowing open homosexuals to serve in the military continues, these are among the key issues:

Can military units function effectively with openly homosexual members?

The debate over whether homosexuals belong in the military centers predominantly on the effect openly gay and lesbian service members would have on their units.

In the past, no doubts existed about the effect. As the United States

Fierce Defender of the 'Culture of the Military'

Gays and lesbians don't belong, says Elaine Donnelly.

Among supporters of the military's ban on homosexuals, all roads lead to Elaine Donnelly, founder and president of the Center on Military Readiness in Livonia, Mich. Donnelly's steadfast defense of the ban runs through the nearly two decades that the issue has been on the public agenda.

"We defend the culture of the military," she says, a characterization that she prefers to "social conservative," though she doesn't reject the term. She does reject any suggestion that military culture is becoming any more open to its gay and lesbian members.

Donnelly says her omnipresence results from military strictures against senior active-duty personnel speaking out on political issues. "As a civilian woman, I am more free to address these controversial issues."

She's been doing so, under one organizational umbrella or another for decades. Her story began, she says, in the 1970s when she was a "young mother concerned about my family and the defense of this country." Feminist organizations were pushing for passage of an Equal Rights Amendment (ERA), with some supporters arguing that gender equality meant that women should be eligible for the draft. Donnelly, the mother of two young daughters, opposed the idea — which aroused considerable opposition among social conservatives, who blocked the measure by lobbying in state legislatures to prevent ratification by the required three-quarters of the states.

During the Reagan administration, involvement in Republican politics led to Donnelly's 1984 appointment to the Defense Advisory Committee on Women in the Services.

In 1992, President George H. W. Bush named her to the Presidential Commission on the Assignment of Women in the Services, where she helped engineer a narrow, 8-7 majority in favor of continuing to bar women from direct combat assignments.

"Equal opportunity is not the primary goal of the military. Defending the country is," she said during earlier deliberations. [1]

The following year, as the fledgling Bill Clinton administration was attempting to overturn the military's ban on homosexuals, Donnelly founded the Center on Military Readiness, based in her hometown, to oppose Clinton's attempt.

Days before Christmas, when Defense Secretary Les Aspin issued the 1993 "don't ask, don't tell" regulations that represented the administration's compromise, Donnelly called them a "crowning insult in what has been a painful year for the military. President Clinton is playing Santa to homosexuals and liberals, while dropping lumps of coal into the stockings of the military." [2]

Since then, Donnelly seems to have lost nothing of her take-no-prisoners manner. Speaking at a House Armed Services Subcommittee on Military Personnel hearing last year, she painted a bleak picture of the military's future if the ban were repealed: "Inappropriate passive/aggressive actions common in the homosexual community, short of physical touching and assault, will be permitted in all military communities, to include Army and Marine infantry battalions, Special Operations Forces. Navy SEALS and cramped submarines that patrol the seas for months at a time." [3]

Rep. Vic Snyder, D-Ark., called the remark "just bonkers."

Donnelly offered an explanation: "What do I mean by passive/aggressive behavior? It means something of a sexualized [action] short of assault. It means the kind of thing like a woman who is stared at — her breasts are stared at. She is made to feel uncomfortable. She feels she has no recourse. She feels she cannot say anything, can't complain about it, because that would hurt her career. That's the kind of thing I'm talking about."

---

geared up for the mass mobilization of World War II psychiatric consultants to the military developed a thesis based on the medical conclusion that homosexuality was a psychological disorder. "The reason for excluding them as psychopaths was that . . . they were considered to be irresponsible troublemakers who were unable to control their desires or learn from their mistakes and thus threatened the other men," wrote historian Allan Bérubé in a groundbreaking account of gays and lesbians in the Second World War. [15]

The psychiatrists were also concerned about what would later be called "unit cohesion." Homosexuals would be unable to cope with regimentation and lack of privacy, so they would become magnets for aggression by their heterosexual comrades.

When the conflict over homosexuals in the military first became a nationwide issue in 1993, medical professionals no longer defined homosexuality as a malady, and stereotypes of all gays as effeminate and all lesbians as "mannish" were fading. Even so, debate still centered on the effect that openly declared

homosexuals would have on the morale and performance of the units to which they'd be assigned.

"At the very least, the lifting of the ban will create a controversy over the issue of privacy," Charles Moskos Jr., a leading sociologist of the military, wrote in 1993. "Just as most men and women dislike being stripped of all privacy before the opposite sex, so most heterosexual men and women dislike being exposed to homosexuals of their own sex." [16]

Moskos, who died in 2008 and frequently advised military leaders,

Rep. Ellen Tauscher, D-Calif. (now under secretary of state for arms control and disarmament), asked another witness, retired U.S. Navy Capt. Joan Darrah, who came out as a lesbian after leaving the military, "Do you think that because there are gay or lesbians in a work environment, that the work environment becomes sexualized, as Ms. Donnelly wants us to believe?"

"No," Darrah said. "When I was the deputy and chief of staff at the Naval Intelligence Command, I had about 400 military and about 1,100 civilians and contractors. I had several openly gay civilians. We all worked together. Everybody was judged on their performance and their ability, and there was no problem at all."

The answer didn't sway Donnelly. Nor did testimony from a gay Iraq War veteran, retired U.S. Marine Staff Sgt. Eric Alva, who lost his right leg to a land mine in Iraq. "I have proudly served a country that was not proud of me," Alva told the subcommittee.

Donnelly later said she respected the service of Alva, Darrah and "everybody who serves in the military."

Rep. Chris Shays, R-Conn., shot back, "How do you respect their service? You want them out."

"I'm standing for sound policy, congressman," Donnelly answered. "In the military we don't make policy based on individuals."

Donnelly laid out her views in some detail in 2007. In a 138-page article in the *Duke Journal of Gender Law and Policy*, she

"Equal opportunity is not the primary goal of the military," says Elaine Donnelly, president of the Center for Military Readiness.

Center for Military Readiness

made a detailed legal argument for maintaining the combat elements of the military as heterosexual male preserves. She also made clear that her technical arguments spring from a social doctrine.

"Many institutions in civilian life have been affected negatively by unsuccessful social experimentation," she wrote. "The baby boomer and 'Gen-X' generations, for example, have been subjected to 'look-say' reading, 'new math' and 'civics' courses that fail to teach students fundamentals. . . . In matters of urban policy, whole cities have been threatened by unrestrained crimes, ruinous taxes and crumbling neighborhoods." [4]

The military, by contrast, can't be subjected to social tinkering, Donnelly argued. "Americans have every right to question the flawed assumptions of social engineers who demand radical change in the culture of the military." [5]

---

[1] Quoted in Matt Yancey, "Panel Recommends Women Be Assigned Combat Positions Under Some Circumstances," The Associated Press, Nov. 3, 1992.

[2] Quoted in Bill Gertz, "Policy on gays detailed," *The Washington Times*, Dec. 23, 1993, p. A1.

[3] Unless otherwise noted, the following testimony comes from "House Armed Services Subcommittee on Military Personnel Holds Hearing on a Review of Don't Ask Don't Tell Policy," CQ Congressional Transcripts, July 23, 2008.

[4] Elaine Donnelly, "Constructing the Co-Ed Military," *Duke Journal of Gender Law & Policy*, June 18, 2007, p. 948, www.law.duke.edu/journals/cite.php?14+Duke+J.+Gender+L.+&+Pol%2527y+815.

[5] *Ibid.*, p. 818.

---

lawmakers and executive branch officials, is credited with originating the "don't ask, don't tell" policy. [17] At the time, his views reflected majority sentiment from senior military leadership to the rank and file. Today, gay and straight opponents of the ban argue that military opinion has shifted.

"We knew of [gay] men in our unit, or kind of had suspicions," says Iraq veteran Rep. Murphy, who is sponsoring a bill to lift the ban on gays serving in the military. "But as long as they could do the job, fire their M-4 rifle, stand guard at 4 in the morning,

lead a convoy at 2 in the afternoon in high heat and bring the guys home alive — that's what we cared about."

Murphy dismisses concerns about privacy in close quarters, in the presence of known homosexuals. "I happen to be heterosexual, but every woman that I come across, whether on a beach or in a supermarket, I'm not attacking her every time there's no one around," he says. "When people bring up these false arguments they're really questioning the professionalism of the best fighting force this Earth has ever seen."

But Maue of the Air Force Academy said in a recent debate at the McCormick Freedom Museum in Chicago that military life is filled with rules designed to minimize the risks associated with interactions between men and women thrown together in crowded facilities.

"We know that all human beings do not behave all of the time," said Maue. "This holds for both straight as well as homosexual people. . . . I'm 10 years married, faithful to my wife, no reason to stray. But the military is still not going to let me go into the female showers." [18]

Repealing the ban, Maue argues, would expand the kinds of interpersonal problems that arise. "The risk of demoralizing misconduct will escalate to include male-male and female-female issues in addition to those that already occur."

The gay ban generates its own problems, says Jon Soltz, chairman of VoteVets, which is campaigning to end the prohibition. For instance, while gay linguists were being discharged during the Iraq War, recruiting standards were being relaxed so that recruits like Steven D. Green — who was sentenced to life in prison earlier this year for raping and murdering a 14-year-old Iraqi girl and killing her family — were allowed to enlist. Green, who had a record of drug and alcohol abuse, had received a "morals waiver" to enter the Army. [19]

"The drama we have comes from a bunch of policies that are bad for unit cohesion — like allowing in Steven Green," says Soltz, who served as an Army captain in Iraq in 2003. "What's worse for unit cohesion, the interpreters you kicked out who helped me as a young officer, or someone who kills civilians?"

Yet Brian Jones, who retired from the Army as a master sergeant after a 21-year career in special operations, including Delta Force, testified that units working in rugged, dangerous conditions would be subjected to hazardous stresses if the ban were lifted. "As a U.S. Army Ranger, I performed long-range patrols in severe cold weather conditions — teams of 10 — with only mission-essential items in our backpacks — no comfort items," Jones told the House Armed Services Subcommittee on Personnel in 2008. "The only way to keep from freezing at night was to get as close as possible for body heat, which means skin to skin." [20]

In these circumstances, Jones testified, "Any attraction to the same-sex teammates, real or perceived, would be known and would be a problem. The presence of openly gay men in these situations would elevate tensions and disrupt unit cohesion and morale."

Is the "don't ask, don't tell" approach to differentiating sexual "orientation" from conduct a viable compromise?

"Don't ask, don't tell" grew out of political compromise, but it's under constant attack both from those who want to strengthen restrictions on homosexuals in the military and from those who advocate allowing gays and lesbians to serve openly.

The 1993 law on homosexuality in the military prohibits homosexual "behavior" and/or declarations of homosexuality or bisexuality.

The "don't ask, don't tell" regulations — which are distinct from the law — attempt to draw a more visible line between sexuality and conduct. "Applicants for enlistment, appointment, or induction shall not be asked or required to reveal their sexual orientation," the regulations say. Nevertheless, "Homosexual conduct is grounds for separation from the Military Services." [21]

Despite those differences the law and the regulations reflect a similar approach, a legal analyst at the nonpartisan Congressional Research Service (CRS) wrote recently. 'Both the law and the regulations . . . are structured entirely around the concept of homosexual conduct as opposed to orientation." [22]

However, the regulations say conduct can include speech. "A statement by a member that demonstrates a propensity or intent to engage in homosexual acts" would be grounds for discharge. While the regulations acknowledge that speech isn't generally considered conduct, a discharge that resulted from a statement wouldn't be based on "orientation," the regulations say, but on an understanding that the "statement indicates a likelihood that the member engages in or will engage in homosexual acts." [23]

The legal arguments surrounding orientation, speech and conduct would seem to show that the practice of separating sexuality from sexual behavior is inherently complicated. "Attempts to implement the statute, or analyze and evaluate it, in terms of sexual orientation, have resulted in confusion and ambiguity, and are likely to continue to do so," the CRS analysis said. [24]

The Pentagon also worries about the ban as a tool of vengeance. Defense Secretary Robert M. Gates bemoaned to reporters on June 30 that the 1993 law "doesn't leave . . . a lot of flexibility" and he is seeking a "more humane" way to apply it. "Do we need to . . . take action . . . if we get information from somebody who may have vengeance in mind or blackmail or somebody who has been jilted?" Gates asked. "I don't know the answer to that, and I don't . . . pretend to." [25]

Donnelly responds: "If the secretary of Defense wants a more humane way to enforce the law, we wrote to him and said, 'The best thing you can do is explain what the law actually says, that everybody can serve the country in some way, but not everyone is eligible to serve in the armed forces.' "

Donnelly's group also cites Pentagon figures showing that homosexuality discharges account for far fewer expulsions than other violations of regulations. In fiscal 2008, drug violations accounted for nearly 29 percent and failure to meet weight standards, 23 percent. Only 3.2 percent of discharges were for homosexuality. [26]

Opponents of allowing homosexuals to serve in the military want to retain the law but scrap the "don't ask, don't tell" regulations. The Air Force Academy's Maue says that in his opinion, "It's a bad policy. People think, 'Oh, I can serve if I'm homosexual and it won't create any problems,' but it certainly has not been completely intelligible to the [service] members."

The main confusion, Maue argues, derives from the conflict between the law and the regulations. As he reads the law, "Congress directly and intelligibly . . . reaffirms the longstanding military judgment that homosexuality is incompatible with military service." But the regulations effectively allow homosexuals to serve if they keep their sexuality secret.

Those seeking to lift the ban on gays also attack the "don't ask, don't tell" regulations — though they also want the law authorizing discrimination based on sexual conduct discarded. "That policy says, 'Even though we know there are gays in the military, we're going to institute a policy where no one talks about it,' as though soldiers are like children who, if they close their eyes, believe the problem will go away," argues Nathaniel Frank, who was Maue's opponent in the Chicago debate earlier this year. Frank, author of a book criticizing the prohibition, is a senior research fellow at Palm Center, a think tank at the University of California, Santa Barbara, that specializes in critical analysis of the military ban on homosexuality. [27]

As for the law under which the regulations exist, Frank and others question the basis for the statute. "The language of the law says openly gay service members would be an unacceptable risk," Frank says. "That was

never rooted in anything. . . . It relied on this old stereotype that gays are somehow nonconformists, who are incapable of disciplined behavior and who are always engaging in something unusual or sexual." [28]

Donnelly of the Center for Military Readiness says the "don't ask, don't tell" regulations are "indefensible in court."

The regulations supposedly enforce a law that bars military service to people likely to engage in homosexual acts, Donnelly says, but the regulations effectively prohibit finding out

Members of ACT UP (AIDS Coalition to Unleash Power) at the military recruitment center in Times Square, New York City, protest on March 15, 2007, after then-chairman of the Joint Chiefs of Staff Peter Pace described homosexual acts as "immoral" and likened homosexuality to adultery.

who those people are. " 'Don't ask, don't tell,' if it applied to laws regarding use of alcohol, would say that you must be 21 to purchase or use alcohol, however the bartender is forbidden to ask about age and is not allowed to post a sign saying, 'We check ID.' "

David Hall, an Air Force staff sergeant who was honorably discharged after he was "outed," says "don't ask, don't

tell" created more confusion than it resolved. "I believe the intent . . . was that the military was not going to ask, and you were not going to tell the military. That means, I'm not going to tell my commander, but the way it's been implemented, it means, 'Don't tell anybody ever.' "

Hall says young service members, raised in the increasingly open civilian culture, are especially vulnerable to that misreading. "There are 18- and 20-year-olds putting it on Facebook. If the military comes across that, that's [the same as] telling."

Should the United States follow other countries' examples and allow gays to serve openly in the military?

Countries that allow military service by openly gay service members have reported no difficulties because of the policy, according to the Government Accountability Office (GAO), which in 1993 studied foreign militaries that both banned and allowed homosexuals to serve.

"Military officials . . . [said] the presence of homosexuals in the military is not an issue and has not created problems in the functioning of military units,' " the GAO said of four countries it studied in depth — Canada, Israel, Germany and Sweden. [29]

But the report pointed out that homosexuals in foreign militaries are "reluctant to openly admit their sexual orientation for a variety of reasons" — creating a kind of informal version of "don't ask, don't tell." "Homosexuals fear discrimination or negative reactions from their peers or superiors if they reveal their sexual orientation, and homosexuals do not see any advantage to openly identifying their homosexuality," the report said. [30]

The GAO's findings closely tracked the conclusions of a similar but separate massive study for the Pentagon that same year by the RAND Corp., a Santa Monica, Calif., think tank. "Service members who acknowledged their homosexuality were appropriately circumspect in their behavior while in military situations," the RAND researchers reported. "Problems that did arise were generally resolved satisfactorily on a case-by-case basis." [31]

Since 1993, more than a dozen additional foreign militaries have lifted restrictions on service by homosexuals, bringing the total number to 25. [32] Of these, the most important, symbolically, is Great Britain, which has deep cultural and military ties to the United States. Britain's military began admitting openly homosexual recruits in 2000, and saw gay and lesbian service members march as a unit in the annual Pride London parade last July 4. [33]

Israel, an important ally whose military is among the world's most battle-hardened, has a longtime policy of open service. An Israeli military magazine this year featured a cover photo of two gay soldiers hugging each other. Editor Maj. Yoni Schonfeld, who was open about his homosexuality while commanding a paratrooper company, told The Associated Press, "If you're gay and live in the 'manly' world, there are no problems." He added, "Those who are more feminine in their speech and appearance have a harder time fitting in." [34]

Those who oppose the U.S. ban on gays in the military often cite the strength of Britain's and Israel's U.S. ties, the growth in the number of countries allowing gays to serve and the reportedly trouble-free result. But advocates of maintaining the ban counter that the United States has no real counterparts, either in size, in the worldwide scope of its responsibilities

nor in the intensity of its present commitments in Afghanistan and Iraq.

Donnelly of the Center on Military Readiness notes that Israel's small size and its defensive military mission mean its troops don't spend months and years overseas. "There are no long deployments," she says. "The defense perimeter is a few miles away, so people can live on bases close to home, or at home." Hence, in her view, the problem of living in close quarters — often cited by opponents of gays in the military — are minimal in the Israeli forces. [35]

She also points out that Israel is a socially conservative society. "There is a cultural prohibition that is very real," she says. "You don't have people walking around flaunting their homosexuality, which is the cultural demand for what is being asked in this country — the celebration of homosexuality as a normal alternative lifestyle."

But Segal of the University of Maryland's Center for Research on Military Organization says the differences in military culture between U.S., Israeli and British armed forces matter less than the similarities. "We have one of the few armies that expects to fight wars," he says. "The Brits are a warfighting army; the Israelis are a warfighting army. They don't deploy over the ocean, but they're highly cohesive."

These experiences are relevant to the United States, he says. The record shows that "there may be some resistance to gays in units at first, but once they show they can do the job there are few problems," he says.

Opponents of lifting the ban argue that those who cite other nations as examples have the U.S.-foreign military relationship backwards. "I've worked alongside a lot of them — Britain, France, Poland, the Italians," retired Master Sgt. Jones told the House Armed Services Subcommittee on Military Personnel last year. "The common thread between all of them is they want to be like us."

The feature of U.S. forces that inspires the most admiration from foreign militaries, Jones said, is the creation of highly disciplined and mutually supportive small units. "It's the way we train and mold teams," he said. "When you talk about cohesion, we have the best cohesive armed forces across the board of anybody in this world."

Rep. Murphy, the Iraq veteran pushing to lift the ban, counters that American forces have a long tradition of engaging in joint exercises and competitions with foreign militaries — including those of countries that allow open service by gays — and learning from them. "We always send our elite forces versus their elite forces," he says. "To make it sound like we have to ignore what they do — and I'm not saying we have to do exactly how they do — is frankly laughable."

When he served in the 1st Armored Division in Germany, he says, "I went through the requirements for the German Armed Forces proficiency badge. We do activities of that kind because it makes us more well-rounded; it's a staple of our training. That German proficiency badge is one that I proudly wore." ∎

BACKGROUND

Practical Realities

The U.S. military explicitly prohibited homosexuality in 1916 through an anti-sodomy provision in the Articles of War. But homosexuality didn't emerge as a major military issue until decades later, as the military launched the largest mobilization in U.S. history for World War II. By the end of the war, 12 million people were serving. [36] Wartime eligibility standards

Continued on p. 776

Chronology

1940s *A World War II attempt to screen out homosexuals from the military faces practical complications, which resurface decades later in a legal challenge during the Vietnam War.*

1941
The Army, Navy and Selective Service System develop procedures for spotting and excluding homosexual draftees from military service.

1945
As World War II ended, only 4,000-5,000 men have been rejected from military service for being gay. Thousands of lesbians enlisted, largely because asking women about their sexuality violated the era's standards of behavior.

1960s-1980s
Modern gay-rights movement begins, encouraging gays and lesbians to stop hiding their sexuality — a development eventually leading to service members demanding to serve openly.

1968
Perry J. Watkins is drafted as nation mobilizes for Vietnam War, despite his declaration that he's gay.

1969
Gay-rights movement is launched after police raid gay bar (Stonewall Inn) in New York, leading to days of street protests.

1981
Watkins, now a sergeant, is discharged from the Army. He files a lawsuit challenging the move.

1982
New Defense Department rule formalizes ban on gays in the military. . . . Demonstrators at Bolling Air Force Base near Washington, D.C., protest what they call efforts to discharge gay service members.

1990s
As gay-rights movement grows, military service becomes a major issue, leading Democratic presidential candidate Bill Clinton to promise to lift the ban.

1990
Watkins wins his lawsuit because the Army had allowed him to serve for years with full knowledge of his homosexuality.

1992
Candidate Clinton calls for repealing the ban on gays in the military. . . . After the election, senior military and political figures protest the idea.

1993
President Clinton backs a compromise that allows homosexuals to serve if they don't disclose their sexuality. . . . Congress prohibits military service by anyone with a "propensity or intent to engage in homosexual acts." . . . Defense Department "don't ask, don't tell" regulations call sexual orientation "personal and private" but require discharge for "homosexual conduct."

1998
Pentagon acknowledges that gay discharges have risen since the new rules took effect.

2000s
With the military stretched thin by two wars, excluding homosexuals takes on new prominence. Barack Obama is elected president after vowing to push for lifting the ban.

2003
Military discharges nine homosexual service members training as linguists, most of them in Arabic, leading opponents of the gay ban to argue that the prohibition endangers national security.

2005
Palm Center think tank says 20 gay Arabic and Farsi linguists have been discharged.

2008
In first congressional hearing on the issue since 1993, a gay Marine veteran who lost a leg in Iraq says his sexuality wasn't an issue in combat and a special operations veteran says unit cohesion would suffer if open homosexuals serve. . . . Subscriber survey by *Military Times* newspaper reports that strong support exists for maintaining the ban, but acknowledges that subscribers tend to be from the older, more conservative sector of the military and retiree population.

2009
Rep. Patrick J. Murphy, D-Pa., introduces bill to repeal ban on gays in the military. . . . More than 1,000 retired high-ranking officers call for retaining the ban. . . . Some gay-rights activists ask Obama to repeal the "don't ask, don't tell" rules, but he asks Congress to repeal the policy. . . . Obama acknowledges impatience of gay and lesbian supporters who perceive lack of White House urgency but vows continued support for lifting the ban. . . . Chairmen of House and Senate Armed Services committees say hearings on the issue may be held as early as the fall. . . . Air Force Lt. Col. Victor Fehrenbach and Army National Guard Lt. Daniel Choi challenge their discharges, publicizing opposition to ban.

President Obama Tries to Reassure LGBT Community

'This will buy him some time, but he'll have to deliver.'

President Barack Obama knew his star was fading a bit among a community with which he'd enjoyed the closest of ties. So, when he invited gay and lesbian political activists to the White House, he did so with great attention to positive symbolism.

For starters, the gathering was held on June 29, the official anniversary of the "Stonewall Riots" — the New York street protests that are considered the founding event of the modern lesbian, gay, bisexual and transgender (LGBT) movement.

And Obama made a point of connecting its struggles to those of the civil rights movement. "I know that many in this room don't believe that progress has come fast enough, and I understand that," the president told a crowd of about 250 gathered in the East Room. "It's not for me to tell you to be patient, any more than it was for others to counsel patience to African-Americans who were petitioning for equal rights a half-century ago." [1]

The president also acknowledged that the gay community's impatience wasn't a general sentiment, but one directed at him. "I want you to know that I expect and hope to be judged not by words, not by promises I've made, but by the promises that my administration keeps," the president said, to applause. "We've been in office six months now. I suspect that by the time this administration is over, I think you guys will have pretty good feelings about the Obama administration." [2]

For some of the invitees, Obama's message hit home. "He reminded us to continue to hold him accountable," Joe Solomonese, president of the Washington-based Human Rights Campaign, told *The Washington Post*. "There certainly was the appropriate and inspiring acknowledgment that he made of what this community has been through. It's important for people to be reassured by the president." [3]

Others in homosexual political circles were more skeptical. Alan van Capelle, executive director of the Empire State Pride Agenda in New York, who said he hadn't gotten an invitation, likened the gathering to fashionable restaurant food — skimpy on the portions but expensive. "It costs a whole lot to get into the White House, but somehow, the meal feels unfulfilling," he said. "There are a lot of us who believe in change but do not believe it is a passive word. It is an active word. There is a level of disappointment that exists." [4]

Disillusionment had been building during the weeks leading up to the event. Some time before the gathering, Steve Hildebrand, a high-ranking Obama campaign operative who is gay, met privately with Obama to tell him that the president's gay supporters were feeling "hurt, anxiety and anger" over White House handling of matters on the gay-rights agenda. [5]

President Bill Clinton's adviser on gay issues, Richard Socarides, said the Obama team was "paralyzed" on gay-community issues. [6]

One of three big disappointments was the administration's legal defense of the federal anti-gay-marriage law, the Defense of Marriage Act (DOMA). [7] Obama told the Stonewall Day crowd that his administration was following longtime federal policy of defending statutes on the books. But he has called for repealing the law. (A bill to repeal DOMA, sponsored by Rep. Jerrold Nadler, D-N.Y., is expected to be introduced in mid-September). [8]

The administration's perceived foot-dragging in pushing for a federal hate-crimes bill also has stirred criticism, along with its perceived slowness in tackling the ban on homosexuals in the armed forces. "Although candidate Obama had suggested that efforts to repeal the ban would begin when he became president, rhetoric shifted immediately after the in-

Continued from p. 774

excluded gay men, given what were considered their physical and moral weaknesses. [37]

But practical realities intervened. The military's immense manpower needs influenced draft board officials to accept as many men as possible. Most gay draftees were eager to do their duty — and in many cases to prove their bravery, then seen as synonymous with heterosexuality. Another powerful incentive to keep homosexual orientation secret: Potential civilian employers had access to draft records. Some military examiners preferred admitting homo-

sexuals to burdening them with the stigma of being rejected because they were homosexual.

Enforcing a ban on lesbians proved even more difficult, as nearly 400,000 women enlisted in female military formations. [38] "Masculine" women were seen as potentially valuable to military performance, and questioning women about their sexuality violated the era's standards of decency.

For all the pragmatic realities that complicated the ban on homosexuals, the idea that gays and lesbians might demand the right to join the military without hiding their sexual orientation would

have been unimaginable in the 1940s.

That trend didn't arise until after the gay liberation movement got started, following the 1969 "Stonewall Riots" in New York's Greenwich Village. New York City police raided a gay bar, the Stonewall Inn, provoking an explosion of outrage from homosexuals. The episode came to stand for the end of gay shame and the rise of gay pride.

But campaigning on behalf of gay soldiers wasn't a high priority in the early years of post-Stonewall activism. Homosexual militancy was politically on the left, which at that time was defined

auguration," wrote Aaron Belkin, director of the Palm Center at the University of California, Santa Barbara, a think tank focusing on the military's ban on homosexuals. [9]

Belkin and his colleagues advocate presidential action to suspend discharges of gay and lesbian personnel as a way to jar Congress into repealing the military law on homosexuality. Gay activists and journalists share the blame with Obama, Belkin argued, for choosing to ask Congress to repeal the law rather than having Obama act by executive order.

"We had momentum, and then the gay community took its foot off the gas pedal," Belkin says. "The bottom line is that we're at the bottom of a very, very long list of crises and emergencies."

He adds, "Maybe I'll be wrong, and the White House will smile on our issue in the next three-and-a-half years."

At the White House, Obama reiterated his choice of the congressional repeal strategy, even while acknowledging that gays and lesbians are still being expelled from the military under his administration. "I know that every day that passes without a resolution is a deep disappointment to those men and women who continue to be discharged under this policy — patriots who often possess critical language skills and years of training and who've served this country well," he said. "But what I hope is that these cases underscore the urgency of re-

President Barack Obama told gay activists he wants Congress to overturn the ban on gays and lesbians serving openly in the military.

Getty Images/Olivier Douliery

versing this policy not just because it's the right thing to do, but because it is essential for our national security." [10]

Socarides remained skeptical after the event, which he didn't attend. But he credited Obama with explaining the reasons for his decisions. "This will buy him some time," Socarides said, "but he'll have to deliver." [11]

[1] "Remarks by the President at LGBT Pride Month Reception," White House, June 29, 2009, www.white-house.gov/the_press_office/Remarks-by-the-President-at-LGBT-Pride-Month-Reception/.

[2] *Ibid.*

[3] Michael D. Shear, "At White House, Obama Aims to Reassure Gays," *The Washington Post*, June 30, 2009, p. A1.

[4] Quoted in *ibid.*

[5] Quoted in Adam Nagourney, "Political Shifts on Gay Rights Are Lagging Behind Culture," *The New York Times*, June 28, 2009, p. A1.

[6] Quoted in *ibid.*

[7] Linda Deutsch and Lisa Leff, "Obama Admin Moves to Dismiss Defense of Marriage Act Challenge," The Associated Press, June 12, 2009, ww.huffington post.com/2009/06/12/obama-defends-antigay-def_n_214764.html.

[8] Kerry Eleveld, "DOMA Repeal Bill Coming Next Week," *The Advocate*, Sept. 10, 2009, www.advocate.com/News/Daily_News/2009/10/DOMA_Repeal_Bill_Coming_Next_Week/.

[9] Aaron Belkin, "Self-Inflicted Wound: How and Why Gays Give the White House a Free Pass on 'Don't Ask, Don't Tell,' " Palm Center, July 27, 2009, p.1, www.palmcenter.org/files/active/0/SelfInflictedWound.pdf.

[10] "Remarks by the President. . . ," *op. cit.*

[11] Quoted in Sheryl Gay Stolberg, "On Gay Issues, Obama Asks to Be Judged on Vows Kept," *The New York Times*, June 30, 2009, p. A14.

by opposition to the Vietnam War and, by extension, to the armed forces themselves. "Many liberal gay organizers still saw their struggle . . . as a movement to allow every gay person the right to be a homosexual leftist," wrote Randy Shilts, a gay journalist and author. [39]

After the Vietnam War ended (in 1975), and the gay movement abandoned revolution for reform, an openly gay soldier took to the courts in the early 1980s to challenge attempts to throw him out of the military. Sgt. Perry J. Watkins had remained in the Army after he was drafted in 1968, at the height of the Vietnam War. Inducted even though he said

he was gay, he openly moonlighted as a drag artist under the name Simone.

In 1975, Watkins' commanding officer concluded that Army regulations didn't allow an openly gay soldier to remain in the ranks. The commander began discharge proceedings — despite his high regard for Watkins' military performance. But an Army discharge board found no evidence of misconduct.

A subsequent attempt to deny Watkins a new security clearance on the grounds of his homosexuality led him in 1981 to sue the Army. The military initiated another discharge proceeding, this one successful.

Other legal challenges to the military on homosexuality were becoming troublesome as well. In 1982, the Defense Department enacted a new regulation designed to eliminate all ambiguities. "Homosexuality is incompatible with military service," the regulation said. No one who practiced homosexuality or demonstrated "a propensity to engage in homosexual conduct" would be allowed to enter or remain in the service. But an expulsion for homosexuality would not by itself be grounds for a less-than-honorable discharge. [40]

Another early sign of discontent over military policy on homosexuality came in the form of a small demonstration in 1983 at Bolling Air Force Base in Washington, D.C. About 50 people protested what one called "witchhunt investigations of gay servicemen" at the base and other installations in the Washington area. [41]

Meanwhile, Watkins had continued his legal battle even after he was discharged. Eventually, the 9th U.S. Circuit Court of Appeals ruled in 1989 that he should be reinstated, in part because the Army had failed to justify its ban on homosexuals.

Then, in November, 1990, the U.S. Supreme Court refused to consider the Army's challenge to the appeals court ruling — effectively approving the reinstatement order. After his victory, Watkins reached a settlement with the Army that included an honorable discharge, full retirement benefits and retroactive promotion from staff sergeant to sergeant first class.

Transition

Watkins' unexpected legal victory boosted the morale of gay and lesbian service members and their allies. But the outcome reflected his unusual unbroken record of sexual candor. There seemed to be no other cases of service members who had openly declared their homosexuality from the moment they were examined for fitness to serve in the military.

Underlining that difference, the Watkins ruling followed a U.S. Supreme Court decision earlier that year to let stand the expulsions of Army Reservist Miriam Ben-Shalom and former Navy Ensign James Woodward. Ben-Shalom had "come out" to her commander after graduating from an Army Reserve drill instructor's school. Woodward also acknowledged his homosexuality after joining the Navy.

Moreover, a 1986 Supreme Court decision had upheld state anti-sodomy laws against homosexuals — prohibitions then in effect in 24 states and in

Washington, D.C. Sanctions against gay sex had "ancient roots" in English common law, the high court's majority opinion said. A concurring opinion by Chief Justice Warren E. Burger cited prohibitions on homosexuality "throughout the history of Western civilization." [42]

The decision didn't directly touch on the issue of gays in the military. But, taken together with the Ben-Shalom/Woodward ruling, the anti-sodomy ruling confirmed the wisdom of staying at least part-way in the closet while serving in the military. Meanwhile, the services' investigative agencies actively pursued cases of suspected homosexuals. In 1983, for instance, 1,815 service members were discharged for violating the gay ban. The following year, 1,822 were discharged. [43] Still, many more homosexuals remained, sometimes because they were valued by commanders who shielded them from discharge investigations.

In that uneasy and inconsistent state of affairs, the HIV-AIDS epidemic hit in the early 1980s. In the civilian world, the rapid advance of the disease, its inevitably fatal outcome and its predominant connection with gay sexual practices, focused new attention on the homosexual population. But the military still didn't see itself in the picture.

That response seemed to be confirmed by an early study by a military doctor, who found that about one-third of a small sample of AIDS sufferers in the armed forces reported contracting the infection from heterosexual sex. Later, those results were shown to be a result of the gay ban. Service members afraid of being thrown out of the military had refused to admit homosexual sexual contacts.

As the infection continued to spread, results of servicewide HIV tests that began in 1985 exploded like a bombshell. By late 1987, more than 3,300 military personnel tested positive. The infection rate was highest in the Navy at 2.4 per 1,000 members; in the Army the rate was 1.4 per 1,000, and the

Air Force and Marine Corps were each at 1 per 1,000 members. By 1988, 6,000 personnel and recruits had tested positive.

To the shock of some in the military community, the infected included not only members of elite combat units, including the 82nd Airborne Division, but also high-ranking officers, including active-duty colonels and senior Pentagon staff officers.

Meanwhile, the armed forces continued to investigate suspected gays and lesbians. At Parris Island, S.C., the Marines' recruit training camp for the Eastern United States, 18 female drill instructors and other personnel were discharged by 1988. Three women were convicted at courts-martial of sodomy, obstruction of justice and other offenses and were sentenced to prison. Most officers caught up in the probe were allowed to resign, and other female Marines at the base quit rather than face investigators and discharges — as many as 65 women in all.

The Parris Island cases, taking place as the gay-rights movement grew in strength and as the AIDS epidemic gave new prominence to all issues involving homosexuals, helped build opposition to the military ban.

In late 1988, the National Gay and Lesbian Task Force, the National Organization for Women, Women's Equity Action League, the Lesbian-Gay Rights Project of the American Civil Liberties Union and the Military Law Project of the National Lawyers Guild joined forces to create the Gay and Lesbian Military Freedom Project. The organization was designed to stand behind gays in the military and to press for an end to the ban and associated rules.

'Don't Ask, Don't Tell'

Homosexual-rights organizations were also expanding their national political presence. During the 1992 presidential campaign, Democrat Clinton bid for gay support against incumbent President George H. W. Bush by promising repeatedly to lift the ban on gays and lesbians in the military. [44]

Following his victory, Clinton restated his commitment. "I don't think [sexual] status alone, in the absence of some destructive behavior, should disqualify people," he told reporters following a Veterans Day speech to active-duty and retired officers. [45]

Within days, military opposition began building. Gen. Colin Powell, chairman of the Joint Chiefs of Staff, told reporters: "The military leaders in the armed forces of the United States — the Joint Chiefs of Staff and the senior commanders — continue to believe strongly that the presence of homosexuals within the armed forces would be prejudicial to good order and discipline." [46]

Similar attitudes were heard lower in the ranks and in veterans' organizations. Politicians weighed in against using the military for what they termed social experimentation. Clinton — whose record of having avoided service in Vietnam was enough by itself to chill relations with the military and veterans' groups — showed himself open to compromise. In January 1993, he gave his newly appointed defense secretary, Les Aspin, until July 15 to draft an executive order ending "discrimination on the basis of sexual orientation in determining who may serve in the armed forces." [47]

As part of the same compromise, the Joint Chiefs agreed to stop asking about sexual orientation during the enlistment process. And Congress abstained from immediately passing legislation to retain the ban on enlisting homosexuals.

The Senate and House then launched four months of hearings. Midway through the process, Senate Armed Services Committee Chairman Sam Nunn, D-Ga., disclosed that lawmakers were leaning toward what he described as a "don't ask, don't tell" policy — an approach at which Clinton had hinted in his emphasis on ending discrimination based on "sexual orientation."

Essentially, the emerging congressional consensus would halt the questioning of potential enlistees about their sexual orientation. Gay and lesbian recruits could keep their homosexuality private. Those who didn't would be barred from service or discharged if already serving. The measure also would continue the ban on homosexual activity by anyone actively serving in the military, which covered behavior at any time, regardless of whether the service member was on base or on leave.

President Clinton accepted that approach. In a July 19, 1993, announcement he added that a declaration of homosexuality by a service member would create a presumption that he or she planned to "engage in prohibited conduct." [48] But the presumption would be "rebuttable." That is, the service member could present evidence that he or she had no intention of having sex. [49]

The power of sexual desire aside, the drawing of a line between orientation and conduct was more complicated than might have seemed at first. Under some definitions, "sexual orientation" includes behavior.

Regulations on discharge specify what a service member could show to fight a proposed discharge for homosexual conduct. He or she could try to prove that the acts broke with customary behavior and are unlikely to recur; that no force or coercion was involved; that other circumstances make retaining the service member important to the military; or that the member doesn't have the "propensity or intent" to engage in homosexual acts. [50]

Wartime Controversies

Lulls in the debate over gays serving in the U.S. military have been only temporary. Confusion and complications have abounded within the military. On the one hand, regulations require respecting sexual privacy while homosexual conduct and declarations of homosexuality are grounds for discharge.

"The balance that the policy strikes . . . has posed a challenge to the Services," a Pentagon report said in 1998, using a classic bureaucratic code word ("challenge") for "major problem." [51]

The report also acknowledged that the number of discharges rose after the new law and policy took effect. After dropping sharply in the early 1980s, discharges of homosexuals rose from 597 in 1994 to 997 in 1997. [52]

Examining discharges closely, military researchers found that more than 80 percent followed declarations of homosexuality, rather than the discovery of sexual acts. Questions could still be raised about the circumstances in which service members declared their sexuality. But the report said the military services "believe" the statements were given voluntarily. Most of the declarations were given during the first years of service. [53]

In 1999, the murder of a gay soldier at Ft. Campbell, Ky., the home base of the 101st Airborne Division, raised questions about whether soldiers were being harassed due to sexual orientation. After the bludgeoning death of Pfc. Barry L. Winchell by a fellow soldier, investigators found that commanders had ignored reports that Winchell was being harassed over his presumed sexuality. [54]

Apparently prompted in part by Winchell's killing, discharges continued to increase. In June 2001, Pentagon figures showed the highest number of discharges since "don't ask, don't tell" took effect — 1,212 during the previous year. [55]

Three months later, when the military went on a war footing after the Sept. 11 terrorist attacks, the issue of gays and lesbians in the armed forces might have been expected to fade.

Instead, a new element was added to the controversy. Opponents of the ban asked whether the armed forces could afford to shed personnel qualified in all respects except for sexual orientation. But supporters of prohibition said wartime was the worst time to tinker with social changes in the ranks.

Even before the war in Iraq began in 2003, the dismissal of nine service members training mostly as Arabic linguists — a language skill in short supply in the military — focused attention on whether the ban is practical in wartime. [56]

In 2005, the Center for the Study of Sexual Minorities in the Military (the Palm Center's earlier name) found that 20 Arabic and Farsi linguists or linguists in training had been discharged between 1998 and 2004. [57]

Supporters of the gay ban said the discharges showed the weakness of the "don't ask, don't tell" policy and its prohibition of any questions concerning a military volunteer's sexuality. "Resources unfortunately were used to train young people who were not eligible to be in the military," Donnelly, of the Center on Military Readiness, told The Associated Press. [58] ∎

CURRENT SITUATION

Strategic Differences

Advocates of allowing gays to serve in the military may agree on the ultimate goal — but not on how to reach it. President Obama, for instance, wants Congress to repeal the 1993 law banning homosexuality in the armed forces. Congress passed the law, so Congress must undo it, he reasons.

But gay-ban opponents at the University of California's Palm Center say the congressional route is a dead end, at least for now.

"We don't think there is any chance of getting legislation through Congress any time soon," says Aaron Belkin, the center's director. "The issue in Congress is completely stalled."

Instead, he and five colleagues argued in a paper last May, the president should use authority granted him by the so-called "stop loss" law to halt sexuality-based discharges of military personnel. As the Palm Center team analyzes the law and related statutes, the president is authorized to prevent discharges during periods of national emergency if it is found that keeping personnel from leaving is essential to national security. [59] The liberal Center for American Progress advocates the same strategy.

Such a move, Belkin says, would show opponents that allowing gays and lesbians to remain in the ranks does no harm. With that result established, he says, "Politically and operationally, it would be extremely difficult to get this toothpaste back in the tube."

Remaking military policy by executive fiat would eventually make congressional action easier, not harder, he argues, although repealing the law would be necessary eventually. "It doesn't take any political capital to sign an order because the issue is polling at 75 percent in favor," he says, citing recent surveys. [60]

Ban supporter Donnelly at the Center on Military Readiness says bypassing the political process would be "outrageous," and an admission of desperation. "I don't think the president is politically unwise enough to do something like that."

The Palm Center also sees the proposed move as a way of short-circuiting Pentagon opposition, she notes. Indeed, a follow-up paper by the center said: "The legislative process would open a can of worms by allowing military leaders to testify at hearings and

forge alliances with opponents on the Hill. A swift executive order would eliminate opportunities for them to resist." [61]

The Washington-based Service-members Legal Defense Network, however, views congressional action as the only practical approach — and one with excellent prospects. "We're looking at the next 12 months for repeal," says Kevin Nix, the network's communications director. That time frame would put the matter before the Democratic-controlled 111th Congress, which runs through 2010.

Congressional-strategy advocates say hearings expected later this year will create new legislative momentum by providing a national forum for evidence of the practical and moral benefits of opening the armed forces to gays.

By early September, however, no dates had been set for the hearings. On the House side, an aide to Armed Services Committee Chairman Ike Skelton, D-Mo., said the panel is unlikely to take up the issue until a new under secretary for personnel and readiness has been allowed to settle into the position. The Senate Armed Services Committee hasn't set a date either. Chairman Carl Levin, D-Mich., has said he would hold a hearing in the fall.

"We firmly believe that repeal can get done in this Congress," Nix says.

Fehrenbach's Case

Meanwhile, the case of Lt. Col. Fehrenbach is serving a strategic purpose for those on both sides of the conflict over gays in the military. His exemplary record and his ease in front of TV cameras made him a natural spokesman for gays and lesbians in the military facing exclusion.

"My initial reaction was, I just wanted . . . a quick, quiet, fair, honorable discharge," the officer told liberal TV commentator Rachel Maddow on

Continued on p. 782

At Issue:

Should the U.S. follow the example of nations that allow gays to openly serve in the military?

REP. PATRICK J. MURPHY, D-PA.
VETERAN OF IRAQ WAR AND SPONSOR OF A BILL TO PROHIBIT SEXUALITY-BASED DISCRIMINATION IN THE MILITARY

WRITTEN FOR *CQ RESEARCHER*, SEPTEMBER 2009

O ur troops are currently fighting in two wars in Iraq and Afghanistan. These men and women in our military are stretched dangerously thin. Yet since "don't ask, don't tell" (DADT) took effect in 1993, more than 13,000 honorable men and women — the equivalent of over three and a half combat brigades — have been discharged from our armed forces.

They were removed not for any misconduct, but simply because they are gay.

I frequently hear the criticism about whether we should be using other countries' armed forces as an example for our military, but it rings false. Our heroes in uniform are the best fighting force in the world, plain and simple. Overturning DADT is about making decisions that allow our military to perform at its peak and keep our country safe.

Opponents of lifting the ban argue that allowing gays and lesbians to serve openly would be detrimental to unit cohesion and morale. As a former Army officer, that is an insult to me, and, more importantly, to my fellow soldiers still serving. In Iraq, my men and I didn't care whether a soldier was gay or straight or about their race, creed or color. We cared about completing our mission with honor and getting every member of our unit home alive.

More than 20 nations, including Great Britain and Israel, allow gays and lesbians to openly serve without any detrimental impact on unit cohesion. Believe me, our heroes in uniform are the best fighting force in the world, and just as professional as those of our strongest allies. What's more, we serve alongside these allies in numerous missions throughout the world every day.

The policy isn't working for our armed forces, it hurts our military readiness and it is making us less safe. Among the 13,000 service members who have been discharged are 800 "mission critical" individuals, including fighter pilots, battlefield medics and even Arabic and Farsi translators who are key to the success of our missions in Iraq and Afghanistan. Former senior military leaders agree that this policy is hurting our national security.

To remove honorable, talented and committed Americans from serving our country is contrary to the values that our military fights for and our nation holds dear. My time in Bosnia and Iraq taught me that our military needs and deserves the best and the brightest that are willing to serve. Overturning this wrongful policy is a long-overdue step toward this goal.

ELAINE DONNELLY
PRESIDENT, CENTER ON MILITARY READINESS

WRITTEN FOR *CQ RESEARCHER*, SEPTEMBER 2009

t he experiences of 25 countries without official restrictions on professed homosexuals in their militaries — out of 200 nations around the globe — do not justify repeal of the 1993 law that is usually mislabeled "don't ask, don't tell." With all due respect to Austria, Belgium, Czech Republic, Denmark, Estonia, Finland, France (excepting the elite Foreign Legion), Ireland, Italy, Lithuania, Luxembourg, New Zealand, Norway, Slovenia, South Africa, Spain, Sweden, Switzerland and Uruguay — none of these 19 nations' small militaries bear burdens and responsibilities comparable to ours. The U.S. Army, Navy, Air Force and Marines accept far-away, months-long deployments, and our direct ground combat battalions, special operations forces and submarines require living in conditions with little or no privacy.

Service in the Israeli Defense Force is mandatory, but deployments and housing conditions are not comparable to that of America's military. Germany has conscription for both civilian and military duties, but homosexuals serve primarily in civilian capacities. The Dutch, Australian and Canadian forces represent countries with social cultures far more liberal than ours. These forces primarily deploy for support or peacekeeping missions that depend on the nearby presence of U.S. forces. Most homosexuals are discrete, but American gay activists are demanding special status, mandatory "diversity" training and "zero tolerance" of dissent in order to enforce full acceptance.

That leaves the U.K., which demonstrated fundamental differences with American culture when it capitulated to a 1999 European Court of Human Rights order to accommodate homosexuals in the military. Not surprisingly, British activists claim success, since same-sex partners get to live in military family housing and march in gay pride parades. The Ministry of Defence meets regularly with lesbian, gay, bisexual and transgender (LGBT) activists to discuss further advances. Imagine the reaction of American military families — and our Muslim allies in Iraq and Afghanistan — if Pentagon leaders followed Britain's example in promoting the LGBT agenda.

Conspicuously missing from the list of 25 gay-friendly militaries are potential adversaries China, North Korea and Iran. Their 3.8 million combined forces (not counting reserves) represent more than twice as many active-duty personnel as the 25 foreign countries with gays in their militaries (1.7 million).

Congress is being asked to impose a risky military social experiment that has not been duplicated anywhere else in the world. Instead, Congress should focus on national security, putting the needs of our military first.

Continued from p. 780

May 19. "But the more I thought about it, about how wrong this policy is, I thought that I had to fight it and, perhaps with my unique perspective, I could speak out and help other people." [62]

Advocates of the ban don't challenge Fehrenbach's record, which includes an Air Medal for heroism during the invasion of Iraq in 2003. But the circumstances of his involuntary outing, they say, show that gays want better-than-equal treatment.

A heterosexual male in equivalent circumstances would have been discharged, argues gay-prohibition advocate Donnelly. "It [would have been] the end of his career," she said, based on her reading of the *Idaho Statesman* account of the circumstances that led to Fehrenbach's recommended discharge.

But Fehrenbach's lawyer, Emily Hecht of the Servicemembers Legal Defense Network, says, "If the same, exact allegation had been made against an Air Force officer by a woman and had been investigated in exactly the same manner with exactly the same findings and outcome — that officer would have gone back to work."

An expert with no connection to the case agrees. "A male officer, meeting a woman online, a meeting leading to non-adulterous, non-commercial fornication, would not be discharged," says Eugene R. Fidell, president of the National Institute of Military Justice and a senior research scholar and lecturer at Yale Law School. But that might not be the case, he adds, if nude pictures were an element of the case. The *Statesman* said Fehrenbach's one-time partner had seen nude photos of the officer, though the circumstances are unclear.

Fehrenbach's lawyer declines to discuss that issue. But the formal discharge notification cites only one justification for discharge: "I am taking this action because you did . . . en-gage in homosexual acts with another man," wrote U.S. Air Force Lt. Gen. Norman R. Seip, commander of the 12th Air Force. [63]

As Fehrenbach waits for Air Force Secretary Donley to decide his case, the Servicemembers Legal Defense Network notes that the Air Force discharge board found no "aggravating circumstances" that would trigger a less-than-honorable discharge.

Following Orders

On one point, everyone agrees: The U.S. military isn't a debating society. "The president has made his strategic intent very clear," Adm. Mike Mullen, chairman of the Joint Chiefs of Staff, said in August. "He wants to see this law changed. . . . When the law changes, if we get to that point, we'll carry out the law." [64]

"The units aren't going to collapse, and the mission will still get done," Maue said at the Chicago debate in June. "People can suck up an awful lot in the military and make sure the mission still gets done." [65] But, he adds, "That doesn't mean it's a good policy."

"The military is a culture of discipline, of obedience, of professional service members," said Nathaniel Frank, a senior research fellow at the Palm Center and Maue's debate opponent. "It is a real vote of no confidence in them to suggest that telling the truth, that allowing our law, our policy and our rhetoric to catch up with the reality on the ground is somehow going to . . . undermine cohesion." [66]

Throughout the debate, some advocates and experts have cited racial desegregation as a precedent for abolishing long-held traditions that seemed inviolable. Desegregation began with an executive order by President Harry S Truman in 1948, according to the Army, though racially integrated units weren't formed until the Korean War in the early 1950s. [67]

"That experience shows that it is possible to change how troops behave toward previously excluded (and despised) minority groups, even if underlying attitudes toward those groups change very little," the RAND Corp. think tank said in a 2000 summary of a massive 1993 study that it performed for the Pentagon on the question of open homosexuals in the military. "When integration was mandated in the late 1940s, it was said to be inconsistent with prevailing societal norms and likely to create tensions and disruptions in military units and to impair combat effectiveness." [68]

RAND acknowledged that race and sexuality weren't directly analogous. That point was driven home in 1993 by then chairman of the Joint Chiefs of Staff Powell, who had experienced the gradual desegregation of the armed forces and was the highest-ranking African-American in the history of the American military.

"Open homosexuality in units is not to the benefit of our military force, and it is something quite different than the acceptance of benign characteristics such as color or race or background," Powell told the House Armed Services Committee in 1993, in remarks that were widely reported and influential. [69]

By 2008, Powell and former Georgia Sen. Nunn, who helped to devise the "don't ask, don't tell" system, had moderated their views. "I think it's appropriate to review it now," Nunn said at a conference in Aspen, Colo. "We certainly are having a lot of people who are getting out because of it. But on the other hand, there are an awful lot of people that may be affected the other way." [70]

"It's been 15 years, and attitudes have changed," Powell said during a television interview. "Let's review it, but I'm not going to make a judgment as to whether it should be overturned until I hear from the chairman of the Joint Chiefs of Staff . . . the commanders who are responsible for our armed forces in a time of war." [71]

Powell explained that the military has special characteristics. "It is not like any other institution in our system," Powell said. "You are told who you will live with. You are told who you will share your most intimate accommodations with. You are told whether you will live or die."

The Center on Military Readiness' Donnelly acknowledges that obedience is part of that culture. "Could we do it?" she asks. "Sure. Should we? Absolutely not. It would absolutely harm good order and morale. Military culture has to be taught, reinforced. Anybody who doesn't support a new policy — they're the ones who'd be out of bounds."

Opponents of the ban acknowledge that service members who oppose lifting the prohibition would have to adjust. "People come into the Army with values they learned in their own homes and communities, and we hope they hold onto those values," says retired Army Lt. Gen. Claudia Kennedy, who advocates training that would explain a new policy as a matter of extending anti-discrimination regulations. "But there are Army values we teach them in the first eight weeks, and you are not allowed to ignore the lawful orders of those above you." ■

OUTLOOK

Question of Timing

Throughout American society — in the workplace, in movies, in television and in many families — homosexuality is being accepted to an extent that would have been hard to imagine when the Stonewall Riots exploded 40 years ago. But whether those societal changes make a similar trans-

formation in the armed forces inevitable is by no means a decided issue.

Former Senate Armed Services Committee Chairman Nunn predicted last year that the prohibition would be lifted. "If you're going to have open service by gays and lesbians — and I think we will eventually have that — the question's timing." [72] What that timing might be, he didn't say.

Donnelly of the Center for Military Readiness argues that the demands of military life and combat weigh more heavily than social changes among civilians. "The claim that younger generations see this differently only applies to the civilian world," she says. "As long as we have need for a strong, cohesive military, as long as we have a need to engage an enemy in land combat, and as long as human beings remain the flawed beings that they are, I believe the law will indeed still be there."

The present campaign to lift the ban is "very intense," she acknowledges. But if it fails to succeed within the next two years, she predicts the ban is likely to remain in place for the foreseeable future.

Some critics of the ban agree. "Unless there's a major change of mood among our legislative leaders, or a president who is willing to make a big ruckus — a ruckus that likely would be extremely unpopular in parts of the country — how is it going to get changed?" asks Fidell, the military law expert at Yale.

Barring an intense campaign by a high-ranking former military figure, he says, only one other scenario would offer the possibility of change — but it wouldn't be a happy scenario. "If, God forbid, we had a substantially increased need for personnel, and everything was on the table other than conscription, that could be a galvanizing event. But I hope we don't face something like that, and I think our leaders are intelligent enough not to get us into that position."

Organizations leading the charge for allowing open gays and lesbians

to serve argue that the combination of societal change, public support for opening the ranks and growing realization that homosexuals are already serving make change inevitable.

But immediate change is unlikely, say some critics of prohibition. "It's not the end of the game," says retired Lt. Gen. Kennedy. "Don't anyone come out of the closet right now. I don't think the individual sacrifice of careers is necessary to make it happen."

A loosening of restrictions — by executive order as the Palm Center advocates — would make plain that no catastrophe would ensue, says the center's Frank. "A few months down the road, [the president] could go to Congress and say, 'We have an official reality of officially gay service, and the sky hasn't fallen' — which is my prediction — 'and now, Congress, let's act to get this off the books.' "

So far Obama has rejected that approach. But even if he takes what some see as a slower approach, one expert says the ban's days are numbered.

"I cannot see it lasting 10 years," says Segal, the University of Maryland military sociologist, "because of the rate of social change. Society is becoming more tolerant at a rapid rate. The military reflects society, and the generational shift takes place more rapidly in the military than outside, because careers are shorter."

Change would have to come from Congress, whose members often enjoy long careers. But, Segal argues, citing what he calls growing public support for gays in the military, "If Congress sees its constituents moving in that direction, they're not likely to lead by example, but they are likely to follow public opinion." ■

Notes

[1] Dan Popkey, "Gay Boise Air Force Pilot 'outed' by false accusation," *Idaho Statesman*, Aug. 23, 2009, www.idahostatesman.com/273/story/874410.html.

2 10 U.S. Code Sect. 654, http://law.justia.com/us/codes/title10/10usc654.html.

3 David Burrelli, " 'Don't Ask, Don't Tell:' The Law and Military Policy on Same-Sex Behavior," Congressional Research Service, Aug. 14, 2009, p. 10, www.fas.org/sgp/crs/misc/R40782.pdf.

4 "Report: More gay linguists discharged than first thought," The Associated Press, Jan. 13, 2005, www.msnbc.msn.com/id/6824206. Carol J. Williams, "No rush to end 'don't ask, don't tell,' " Los Angeles Times, May 20, 2009, p. A18.

5 Lymari Morales, "Conservatives Shift in Favor of Openly Gay Service Members," Gallup, June 4, 2009, www.gallup.com/poll/120764/conservatives-shift-favor-openly-gay-service-members.aspx. "More favor keeping gay ban in place," USA Today, Feb. 3, 1993, p. A8.

6 James J. Linday, et al., "Gays and The Military: A Bad Fit," The Washington Post, April 14, 2009, www.washingtonpost.com/wp-dyn/content/article/2009/04/14/AR2009041402704.html.

7 " 'Don't Ask, Don't Tell': The Struggle Continues," McCormick Freedom Museum, Chicago, June 20, 2009. Recordings of the debate are not available from open sources, but a summary by an unnamed museum staffer is accessible at www.facebook.com/note.php?note_id=128287001752.

8 "Remarks by the President at LGBT Pride Month Reception," White House, June 29, 2009, www.whitehouse.gov/the_press_office/Remarks-by-the-President-at-LGBT-Pride-Month-Reception/.

9 William Branigin, "Supreme Court Turns Down 'Don't Ask' Challenge," The Washington Post, June 8, 2009, www.washingtonpost.com/wp-dyn/content/article/2009/06/08/AR2009060801368.html.

10 Brendan McGarry, "Troops oppose repeal of 'don't ask,' " Army Times, Dec. 29, 2008, www.armytimes.com/news/2008/12/military_poll_main_122908; Brendan McGarry, "2008 Military Times Poll: Wary about Obama," Army Times, Jan. 7, 2009, www.armytimes.com/news/2008/12/military_poll_main_122908.

11 Quoted McGarry, in "Troops oppose. . . ," ibid.

12 Ibid.

13 Ibid.

14 "104 Generals and Admirals: Gay Ban Must End," Palm Center, Nov. 17, 2008, www.palm-center.org/files/active/0/104Generals11-17-08.pdf; John M. Shalikashvili, "Gays in the Military: Let the Evidence Speak," The Washington Post, June 19, 2009, p. A25.

15 Allan Bérubé, Coming out Under Fire: The History of Gay Men and Women in World War Two (1990), p. 15.

16 Charles Moskos Jr., "From Citizens' Army to Social Laboratory," in Wilbur J. Scott and Sandra Carson, Stanley, eds., Gays and Lesbians in the Military: Issues, Concerns, and Contrasts (1994), p. 53.

17 Douglas Martin, "Charles Moskos, Policy Adviser, Dies at 74," The New York Times, June 5, 2008, p. B7.

18 " 'Don't Ask, Don't Tell': The Struggle Continues," op. cit.

19 James Dao, "Ex-Soldier Gets Life Sentence for Iraq Murders," The New York Times, May 21, 2009, www.nytimes.com/2009/05/22/us/22soldier.html.

20 "House Armed Services Subcommittee on Military Personnel Holds Hearing on a Review of Don't Ask Don't Tell Policy," CQ Congressional Transcripts, July 23, 2008.

21 "Qualification Standards for Enlistment, Appointment, and Induction," Department of Defense, July 11, 2007, www.dtic.mil/whs/directives/corres/pdf/130426p.pdf; "Enlisted Administrative Separations," Department of Defense, Aug. 28, 2008, www.dtic.mil/whs/directives/corres/pdf/133214p.pdf; "Separation of Regular and Reserve Commissioned Officers," Dec. 11, 2008, www.dtic.mil/whs/directives/corres/pdf/133601p.pdf.

22 Jody Feder, "'Don't Ask, Don't Tell': A Legal Analysis," Congressional Research Service, Sept. 2, 2009, p. 2, www.fas.org/sgp/crs/misc/R40795.pdf.

23 "Enlisted Administrative Separations," and "Separation of Regular and Reserve. . . ," op. cit.

24 Feder, op. cit., p. 2.

25 "Press Conference with Secretary Gates En Route From Germany," U.S. Department of Defense, News Transcript, June 30, 2009, www.defenselink.mil/transcripts/transcript.aspx?transcriptid=4441.

26 "False 'National Security' Argument for Gays in the Military," Center for Military Readiness, September 2009, http://cmrlink.org/CMRDocuments/DoDDischarges-090809.pdf.

27 Nathaniel Frank, Unfriendly Fire: How the Gay Ban Undermines the Military and Weakens America (2009).

28 " 'Don't Ask, Don't Tell': The Struggle Continues. . . ," op. cit.

29 "Homosexuals in the Military: Policies and Practices of Foreign Countries," General Accounting Office [later renamed Government Accountability Office], June, 1993, p. 3, http://archive.gao.gov/t2pbat5/149440.pdf.

30 Ibid., pp. 3-4.

31 "Sexual Orientation and U.S. Military Personnel Policy: Options and Assessment," RAND (prepared for the office of the Secretary of Defense), 1993, p. xix, www.rand.org/pubs/monograph_reports/MR323/index.html.

32 "Countries That Allow Military Service by Openly Gay People," Palm Center, June, 2009, www.palmcenter.org/files/active/0/CountriesWithoutBan.pdf.

33 Quoted in David Crary, "U.S. Allies Embrace Gay Military Personnel," The Associated Press, www.huffingtonpost.com/2009/07/13/us-allies-embrace-gay-mil_n_231075.html.

34 Ibid.

35 Reuven Gal, "Gays in the Military: Policies and Practices in the Israeli Defense Forces," in Scott and Carson, op. cit., p. 181.

36 Moskos, op. cit.

37 Except where otherwise indicated, material on World War II in this subsection is drawn from Bérubé, op. cit., and "Sexual Orientation and U.S. Military Personnel Policy. . . ," op. cit.

38 "World War II: Women and the War," Women in Military Service for America Memorial Foundation Inc., undated, www.womensmemorial.org/H&C/History/wwii.html.

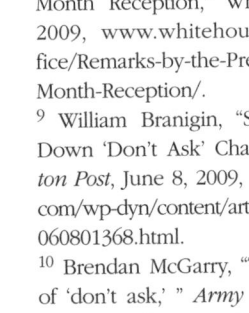

About the Author

Peter Katel is a *CQ Researcher* staff writer who previously reported on Haiti and Latin America for *Time* and *Newsweek* and covered the Southwest for newspapers in New Mexico. He has received several journalism awards, including the Bartolomé Mitre Award for coverage of drug trafficking, from the Inter-American Press Association. He holds an A.B. in university studies from the University of New Mexico. His recent reports include "Mexico's Drug War," "Hate Groups" and "Vanishing Jobs."

[39] Randy Shilts, *Conduct Unbecoming: Gays & Lesbians in the U.S. Military* (2005), p. 425.

[40] *Ibid.*

[41] Quoted in Edward D. Sargent, "Homosexuals Protest At Bolling Over Probe," *The Washington Post*, Dec. 4, 1983, p. B3.

[42] *Bowers v. Hardwick*, 478 U.S. 186 (1986). The Supreme Court overturned *Bowers* in its 2003 decision in *Lawrence v. Texas*. See www.law.cornell.edu/supct/html/historics/USSC_CR_0478_0186_ZS.html. Majority opinion quoted in Stuart Taylor Jr., "High Court, 5-4, Says States Have the Right to Outlaw Private Homosexual Acts," *The New York Times*, July 1, 1986, p. A1. Burger opinion quoted in Shilts, *op. cit.*, p. 540.

[43] Burrelli, *op. cit.*

[44] Curtis Wilkie, "Harvard tosses warmup queries to Clinton on eve of N.H. debate," *Boston Globe*, Oct. 31, 1991, p. A22; Gwen Ifill, "Clinton's Platform Gets Tryouts Before Friends," *The New York Times*, May 20, 1992, p. A21. Except where otherwise indicated, this subsection draws on Burrelli, *op. cit.*

[45] Quoted in Michael Weisskopf, "Clinton Backs Early Military Retirement," *The Washington Post*, Nov. 12, 1992, p. A9.

[46] John H. Cushman Jr., "Top Military Leaders Object to Lifting Homosexual Ban," *The New York Times*, Nov. 14, 1992, p. A9.

[47] "Sexual Orientation and U.S. Military Personnel Policy," *op. cit.*, p. xvii.

[48] Burrelli, *op. cit.*, p. 1.

[49] *Ibid.*

[50] "Enlisted Administrative Separations," and "Separation of Regular and Reserve Commissioned Officers," *op. cit.*

[51] Quoted in "Review of the Effectiveness of the Application and Enforcement of the Department's Policy on Homosexual Conduct in the Military," Office of the Under Secretary of Defense (Personnel and Readiness), April, 1998, p. 2, www.dtic.mil/cgi-bin/GetTRDoc?AD=ADA353107&Location=U2&doc=GetTRDoc.pdf.

[52] *Ibid.*

[53] *Ibid.*

[54] Elaine Sciolino, "Army Exonerates Officers in Slaying of Gay Private," *The New York Times*, July 19, 2000, p. A16.

[55] Paul Richter, "Dismissal of Gays Rises in the Military," *The New York Times*, June 2, 2001, p. A12.

[56] John Johnson, "9 Gay Linguists Discharged From the Army," *Los Angeles Times*, Nov. 16, 2002, p. B10.

[57] "Report: More gay linguists discharged than first thought," *op. cit.*

FOR MORE INFORMATION

Center for Military Readiness, P.O. Box 51600, Livonia, MI 48151; (202) 347-5333; http://cmrlink.org. An advocacy organization providing material supporting maintenance of the ban on gays in the military.

Federation of American Scientists, 1725 DeSales St., N.W., Washington, DC 20036; (202) 546-3300; www.fas.org/sgp/crs/index.html. Posts Congressional Research Service (CRS) studies, which are not provided to the public.

Flag & General Officers For the Military, http://flagandgeneralofficersforthemilitary.com. Represents senior military retirees, who maintain close ties to the Center for Military Readiness.

Palm Center, University of California, Santa Barbara, CA 93106; (805) 893-5664; www.palmcenter.org. Leading think tank for studies seeking to show the ban is militarily ineffective and unjust.

Servicemembers Legal Defense Network, P.O. Box 65301, Washington, DC 20035; (202) 328-3244; www.sldn.org. Represents gay and lesbian military personnel facing discharge and other actions based on their sexuality.

VoteVets.org, 303 Park Ave. So., New York, NY 10010; (646) 415-8429; www.votevets.org. Iraq and Afghanistan veterans who advocate repealing the prohibition on gays and lesbians in the military.

[58] *Ibid.*

[59] Aaron Belkin, *et al.*, "How to End 'Don't Ask, Don't Tell': A Roadmap of Political, Legal, Regulatory, and Organizational Steps to Equal Treatment," Palm Center, May, 2009, www.palmcenter.org/files/active/0/Executive-Order-on-Gay-Troops-final.pdf. For background on stop-loss, see Pamela M. Prah, "Draft Debates," *CQ Researcher*, Aug. 19, 2005, pp. 661-684. Lawrence J. Korb, *et al.*, "Ending 'Don't Ask, Don't Tell': Practical Steps to Repeal the Ban on Openly Gay Men and Women in the U.S. Military," Center for American Progress, June 2009, www.americanprogress.org/issues/2009/06/dont_ask_dont_tell.html.

[60] Morales, *op. cit.*

[61] Aaron Belkin, "Self-Inflicted Wound: How and Why Gays Give the White House a Free Pass on 'Don't Ask, Don't Tell,' " Palm Center, July 27, 2009, www.palmcenter.org/files/active/0/SelfInflictedWound.pdf.

[62] "Lt. Col. Victor Fehrenbach Discusses His Discharge Notice With Rachel Maddow," msnbc.com, May 19, 2009.

[63] "Memorandum for Lt. Col. Victor J. Fehrenbach," Department of the Air Force, Headquarters of the 12th Air Force, Sept. 12, 2008, made available by Servicemembers Legal Defense Network.

[64] Chairman's podcast, http://dodvclips.mil/index.jsp?auto_band=x&rf=sv&fr_story=FRdamp359676Ch.

[65] " 'Don't Ask, Don't Tell:' The Struggle Continues," *op. cit.*

[66] *Ibid.*

[67] Gerry J. Gilmore, "Truman's Military Desegregation Order Reflects American Values, Gates Says," American Forces Press Service, July 23, 2008, www.defenselink.mil/news/newsarticle.aspx?id=50583. "Sexual Orientation and U.S. Military Personnel Policy. . . ," *op. cit.*, p. 20.

[68] "Changing the Policy Toward Homosexuals in the U.S. Military," RAND Research Brief, 2000, www.rand.org/pubs/research_briefs/RB7537/index1.html.

[69] "Statement by Secretary of Defense Les Aspin [and Powell] Before the House Armed Services Committee," July 21, 1993, http://dont.stanford.edu/regulations/aspin.pdf.

[70] Jim Galloway, "Nunn: Open service for gays to come 'eventually,' " *Atlanta Journal-Constitution*, July 9, 2008.

[71] "Colin Powell Interview," Global Public Square [TV], Dec. 14, 2008.

[72] Galloway, *op. cit.*

Bibliography

Selected Sources

Books

Bérubé, Allan, *Coming Out Under Fire: The History of Gay Men and Women in World War Two*, Free Press, 1990.

This meticulously documented, groundbreaking classic was written by a founder of the San Francisco Lesbian and Gay History Project, who died in 2007.

Scott, Wilbur J., and Sandra Carson Stanley, *Gays and Lesbians in the Military: Issues, Concerns, and Contrasts*, Aldine de Gruyter, 1994.

The issues explored in this compilation — which emphasizes work by academics, including Charles Moskos, originator of "don't ask, don't tell" — remain current.

Shilts, Randy, *Conduct Unbecoming: Gays & Lesbians in the U.S. Military*, St. Martin's Press, 2005 edition.

Based on hundreds of interviews and documents, this lengthy but highly readable narrative focuses on the period during and after the Vietnam War; written by a journalist and author (now deceased) acclaimed for coverage of the onset of the AIDS crisis.

Articles

Brachear, Manya A., "Evangelicals fear new president," *Chicago Tribune*, Dec. 19, 2008, p. A6.

Fear that Obama might lift the military ban on open homosexuals adds to concerns about the incoming administration among socially conservative Christians.

Bumiller, Elisabeth, "In Military, New Debate Over Policy Toward Gays," *The New York Times*, May 1, 2009, p. A14.

A *Times* correspondent reports from the U.S. Military Academy at West Point on nuanced opinions about the possible end of the ban on open gays and lesbians.

Scarborough, Rowan, "Obama to delay repeal of 'don't ask, don't tell,'" *The Washington Times*, Nov. 21, 2008, p. A1.

An early and prescient report predicts that the Obama administration would not be pushing early to repeal the ban on gays in the military.

Stolberg, Sheryl Gay, "Gay Issues in View, Obama Is Pressed to Engage," *The New York Times*, May 7, 2009, p. A1.

Five months into the new administration, gay and lesbian political activists were sensing a lack of urgency by the new administration concerning homosexuals in the military and other matters of concern to them.

Vuoto, Grace, "Is Obama administration listening to the troops?" *The Washington Times*, July 30, 2009, p. B2.

An online survey by the Military Officers Association showed majority support for maintaining the ban, but the association removed the results from its Web site without explanation.

Reports and Studies

"Changing the Policy Toward Homosexuals in the U.S. Military," RAND, 2000, www.rand.org/pubs/research_briefs/ RB7537/index1.html.

A Defense research think tank summarized a massive 1993 report that concluded that lifting the ban on gays serving openly in the military would not degrade military effectiveness.

"Homosexuals in the Military: Policies and Practices of Foreign Countries," General Accounting Office (now the Government Accountability Office), June 1993, http:// archive.gao.gov/t2pbat5/149440.pdf.

Congress' investigative arm studied an issue that remains hotly debated, concluding that countries that allowed homosexuals in their militaries reported no problems — a conclusion that prohibition supporters argue is irrelevant to the U.S. armed forces.

Burrelli, David F., " 'Don't Ask, Don't Tell': The Law and Military Policy on Same-Sex Behavior," Congressional Research Service, Aug. 14, 2009, www.fas.org/sgp/crs/ misc/R40782.pdf.

The nonpartisan agency examines the legislative history and practical effects of the 1993 law and regulations on open homosexuals serving in the military.

Donnelly, Elaine, "Constructing the Co-Ed Military," *Duke Journal of Gender Law & Policy*, June 18, 2007, www.law.duke.edu/journals/cite.php?14+Duke+J.+Gender+ L.+&+Pol%2527y+815.

A leading advocate of maintaining the ban on gays in the military provides a detailed explanation of her position.

Feder, Jody, " 'Don't Ask, Don't Tell': A Legal Analysis," Congressional Research Service, Sept. 2, 2009, www.fas. org/sgp/crs/misc/R40795.pdf.

The report focuses on the meaning, interpretation and legal support for the 1993 law and regulations.

Moradi, Bonnie, and Laura Miller, "Attitudes of Iraq and Afghanistan War Veterans Toward Gay and Lesbian Service Members," Palm Center, July 2009, www.palmcenter.org/files/ active/0/MoradiMillerAttitudesofIraqandAfghanistanWar Veterans.pdf.

Researchers find declining support in military ranks for the ban on homosexuals serving in the military. Data is based on an online survey — which ban supporters call an inadequate source.

The Next Step:

Additional Articles from Current Periodicals

Discharges

Garcia, Malcolm, "Kansan's Discharge Heightens Debate on 'Don't Ask, Don't Tell' Policy," *Kansas City Star*, Feb. 16, 2009, p. A1.

A National Guard specialist was discharged after she was seen kissing another woman at a Wal-Mart checkout line.

Rutledge, Margo, "Gay Officer With Local Ties Faces Discharge," *Dayton Daily News*, May 28, 2009, p. A10.

A lieutenant colonel is facing an honorable discharge from the military after deciding to go public with his homosexuality.

Wisckol, Martin, "Discharge Advised for Gay Officer," *Orange County* (Calif.) *Register*, July 1, 2009.

A New York military panel has decided to discharge an Arabic linguist after announcing he was gay on national television.

"Don't Ask, Don't Tell"

Bender, Bryan, "Obama Seeks Assessment on Gays in Military," *The Boston Globe*, Feb. 1, 2009, p. A1.

Obama wants the Pentagon to study the implications on national security of overturning "don't ask, don't tell."

Drobnyk, Josh, "Iraq Vet Will Lead Effort to Scrap 'Don't Ask, Don't Tell,' " *Los Angeles Times*, July 2, 2009, p. A18.

Rep. Patrick J. Murphy, D-Pa., is an Iraq War veteran spearheading a Democratic effort to overturn "don't ask, don't tell."

Frank, Nathaniel, " 'Don't Ask, Don't Tell' Was Always on Shaky Grounds," *USA Today*, March 12, 2009, p. 9A.

"Don't ask, don't tell" was never grounded in research over what was good for the military, but was based on fear and ignorance, according to this opinion piece by the author of *Unfriendly Fire: How the Gay Ban Undermines the Military and Weakens America*.

LaPlante, Matthew D., "Supreme Court Won't Tackle 'Don't Ask, Don't Tell,' " *Salt Lake Tribune*, June 8, 2009.

The Supreme Court has declined to hear arguments challenging the constitutionality of the "don't ask, don't tell" policy.

Public Approval

Lewis, Gregory, "Survey: Most in U.S. Back Gay Rights," *Sun-Sentinel* (South Florida), Dec. 3, 2008, p. 3B.

About six in 10 Americans favor allowing openly gay individuals to serve in the military.

Reed, Bill, "Survey Suggests State is Warming to Gay Issues," *The Gazette* (Colorado Springs), Dec. 5, 2008, p. ME2.

More Colorado residents appear to be embracing ideas such as civil unions, gay marriage and gays serving in the military.

Rutledge, Margo, "Will Policy on Gays Be Overturned?" *Dayton Daily News*, May 29, 2009, p. A5.

Significantly more Americans favor allowing gays to openly serve in the military than when "don't ask, don't tell" was first enacted.

Serving Openly

Bumiller, Elisabeth, "In Military, New Debate Over Policy Toward Gays," *The New York Times*, May 1, 2009, p. A14.

Evidence suggests that most West Point cadets oppose allowing gays to openly serve in the military.

Cohen, Richard, "Open the Military Closet," *The Washington Post*, June 30, 2009.

In this op-ed, the columnist says the military's "don't ask, don't tell" policy recognizes and enforces bigotry and ignorance, and he calls on President Obama to scrap the policy, despite the reluctance of many present and former military officers.

Shalikashvili, John M., "Gays in the Military: Let the Evidence Speak," *The Miami Herald*, June 19, 2009.

Although the military remains a traditional culture, that tradition no longer requires banning open service by gays, says the former chairman of the Joint Chiefs of Staff. "There will undoubtedly be some teething pains, but I have no doubt our leadership can handle it," he said.

Williams, Carol J., "No Fast Answers on 'Don't Ask,' " *Chicago Tribune*, May 25, 2009, p. A14.

Proponents of allowing gays to openly serve in the military say that continuing the current ban leads to a loss of skills that homosexuals have to offer.

Citing *CQ Researcher*

Sample formats for citing these reports in a bibliography include the ones listed below. Preferred styles and formats vary, so please check with your instructor or professor.

<u>MLA Style</u>

Jost, Kenneth. "Rethinking the Death Penalty." CQ Researcher 16 Nov. 2001: 945-68.

<u>APA Style</u>

Jost, K. (2001, November 16). Rethinking the death penalty. *CQ Researcher, 11*, 945-968.

<u>Chicago Style</u>

Jost, Kenneth. "Rethinking the Death Penalty." *CQ Researcher*, November 16, 2001, 945-968.

In-depth Reports on Issues in the News

Are you writing a paper?
Need backup for a debate?
Want to become an expert on an issue?

For more than 80 years, students have turned to *CQ Researcher* for in-depth reporting on issues in the news. Reports on a full range of political and social issues are now available. Following is a selection of recent reports:

Civil Liberties
Closing Guantánamo, 2/09
Affirmative Action, 10/08
Gay Marriage Showdowns, 9/08
America's Border Fence, 9/08
Immigration Debate, 2/08

Crime/Law
Examining Forensics, 7/09
Legalizing Marijuana, 6/09
Mexico's Drug War, 12/08
Prostitution Debate, 5/08
Public Defenders, 4/08

Education
Reading Crisis? 2/08
Discipline in Schools, 2/08
Student Aid, 1/08
Racial Diversity in Public Schools, 9/07

Environment/Society
Energy and Climate, 7/09
Future of Books, 5/09
Hate Groups, 5/09
Future of Journalism, 3/09
Confronting Warming, 1/09
Reducing Carbon Footprint, 12/08

Health/Safety
Health-Care Reform, 8/09
Straining the Safety Net, 7/09
Treating Depression, 6/09
Reproductive Ethics, 5/09
Extreme Sports, 4/09
Regulating Toxic Chemicals, 1/09

Politics/Economy
State Budget Crisis, 9/09
Business Bankruptcy, 4/09
Future of the GOP, 3/09
Middle-Class Squeeze, 3/09

Upcoming Reports

Interrogating the CIA, 9/25/09   Nuclear Armaments, 10/2/09   Future of NASA, 10/9/09

ACCESS

CQ Researcher is available in print and online. For access, visit your library or www.cqresearcher.com.

STAY CURRENT

To receive notice of upcoming *CQ Researcher* reports, or learn more about *CQ Researcher* products, subscribe to the free e-mail newsletters, *CQ Researcher Alert!* and *CQ Researcher News*: http://cqpress.com/newsletters.

PURCHASE

To purchase a *CQ Researcher* report in print or electronic format (PDF), visit www.cqpress.com or call 866-427-7737. Single reports start at $15. Bulk purchase discounts and electronic-rights licensing are also available.

SUBSCRIBE

Annual full-service *CQ Researcher* subscriptions—including 44 reports a year, monthly index updates, and a bound volume—start at $803. Add $25 for domestic postage.

CQ Researcher Online offers a backfile from 1991 and a number of tools to simplify research. For pricing information, call 800-834-9020, ext. 1906, or e-mail librarysales@cqpress.com.

CQ Researcher

Published by CQ Press, a Division of SAGE

www.cqresearcher.com

Interrogating the CIA

Should its role in terrorism cases be reexamined?

Attorney General Eric H. Holder Jr. wants cases reopened in which CIA agents may have used unauthorized interrogation techniques, including a mock execution. The decision drew criticism from the intelligence community and former Vice President Dick Cheney but praise from human-rights and civil liberties advocates.

A ttorney General Eric H. Holder Jr. has asked a career federal prosecutor to reexamine evidence of possible abuses by Central Intelligence Agency operatives years ago in the questioning of "high-value" terrorism suspects. The CIA's role in interrogating detainees has been controversial because the agency used so-called "enhanced" techniques, including waterboarding. Under President George W. Bush, the Justice Department approved the harsh measures even though many critics said some amount to torture. President Obama has now barred the use of the techniques, but former Vice President Dick Cheney is among those who say the practices yielded valuable intelligence that helped keep the country safe after the Sept. 11 terrorist attacks in 2001. A newly released internal CIA report documents several apparent abuses during the interrogation program. The release of the report is said to be hurting morale at the CIA even as it prompts renewed calls for a broad investigation of the Bush administration's policies in the war on terror.

CQ Researcher • Sept. 25, 2009 • www.cqresearcher.com
Volume 19, Number 33 • Pages 789-812

INSIDE THIS REPORT

Cover: AFP/Getty Photo/Mandel Ngan

CQ Researcher

Sept. 25, 2009
Volume 19, Number 33

MANAGING EDITOR: Thomas J. Colin
tcolin@cqpress.com

ASSISTANT MANAGING EDITOR: Kathy Koch
kkoch@cqpress.com

ASSOCIATE EDITOR: Kenneth Jost

STAFF WRITERS: Thomas J. Billitteri,
Marcia Clemmitt, Peter Katel

CONTRIBUTING WRITERS: Rachel Cox,
Sarah Glazer, Alan Greenblatt, Reed Karaim
Barbara Mantel, Patrick Marshall,
Tom Price, Jennifer Weeks

DESIGN/PRODUCTION EDITOR: Olu B. Davis

ASSISTANT EDITOR: Darrell Dela Rosa

FACT-CHECKING: Eugene J. Gabler,
Michelle Harris

CQ PRESS

A Division of SAGE

PRESIDENT AND PUBLISHER:
John A. Jenkins

**EXECUTIVE DIRECTOR,
REFERENCE INFORMATION GROUP:**
Alix B. Vance

CQ Press is a registered trademark of Congressional Quarterly Inc.

CQ Researcher (ISSN 1056-2036) is printed on acid-free paper. Published weekly, except; (Jan. wk. 1) (May wk. 4) (July wks. 1, 2) (Aug. wks. 3, 4) (Nov. wk. 4) and (Dec. wk. 4), by CQ Press, a division of SAGE Publications. Annual full-service subscriptions start at $803. For pricing, call 1-800-834-9020, ext. 1906. To purchase a CQ Researcher report in print or electronic format (PDF), visit www. cqpress.com or call 866-427-7737. Single reports start at $15. Bulk purchase discounts and electronic-rights licensing are also available. Periodicals postage paid at Washington, D.C., and additional mailing offices. POSTMASTER: Send address changes to CQ Researcher, 2300 N St., N.W., Suite 800, Washington, DC 20037.

Interrogating the CIA

By Kenneth Jost

THE ISSUES

Abd al-Rahim al-Nashiri, the accused mastermind of the bombing of the *USS Cole* in October 2000, was captured by Central Intelligence Agency (CIA) operatives in the United Arab Emirates in November 2002 and taken to a secret CIA prison in Thailand. Immediately upon arrival, around Nov. 15, al-Nashiri — identified as the chief of operations in the Persian Gulf for the terrorist group al Qaeda — was subjected to one or more of the harsh measures that the CIA calls "enhanced interrogation techniques" and that human-rights advocates say can amount to torture.

Al-Nashiri continued to be harshly interrogated until Dec. 4 — including two instances of waterboarding, or simulated drowning, on his 12th day in custody —

and then for another two weeks later in the month. By then, the agents deemed al-Nashiri to be "compliant" and turned him over to a "debriefer" from CIA headquarters.

By the end of the month, however, the debriefer — untrained in interrogation and not authorized to use any of the 10 enhanced techniques sanctioned by the CIA and the Justice Department under President George W. Bush — determined that al-Nashiri was "withholding" information. He decided, after consultation with an unnamed individual, to go beyond the approved interrogation methods. With al-Nashiri shackled, the debriefer entered the cell with an unloaded pistol and racked the weapon "once or twice" next to al-Nashiri's head. "Probably" on the same

The CIA's questioning of accused al Qaeda terrorist Abd al-Rahim al-Nashiri may be among the cases ordered reexamined by Attorney General Eric H. Holder Jr. to see whether CIA operatives exceeded official interrogation guidelines. With al-Nashiri shackled, a CIA debriefer racked an unloaded pistol next to al-Nashiri's head. Later, he revved a power drill near a naked and hooded al-Nashiri.

day, the debriefer entered the cell again and, with al-Nashiri naked and hooded, revved a power drill.

The debriefer made no report of the episode to CIA headquarters in Langley, Va., outside Washington. But CIA officers who arrived in January heard of the incident and reported it to Langley, prompting an investigation by the CIA's inspector general (IG), John Helgerson, and a referral to the Justice Department for possible prosecution. After review by prosecutors in the U.S. attorney's office in Alexandria, Va., however, the government in September 2003 formally decided not to bring criminal charges and left any discipline up to the CIA.

Now, six years later, the case may be one of those that Attorney General

Eric H. Holder Jr. has asked a respected career prosecutor to reexamine. On Aug. 24 Holder announced his decision to reopen cases in which CIA agents may have gone beyond official guidelines, just as the agency was itself releasing under court order a 158-page report documenting more than a dozen instances of possible abuse over the first two years of the CIA's controversial interrogation program. The other "unauthorized" techniques described in the report included a staged mock execution, a threat to sexually abuse a detainee's mother, a threat to kill another's children and the choking of another prisoner to the point of losing consciousness. [1]

The IG's report — first released in May 2008 but with much heavier redactions than in the new version — was part of the latest batch of documents on the Bush administration's treatment of suspected terrorists unearthed by two Freedom of Information Act (FOIA) lawsuits filed by the American Civil Liberties Union (ACLU) beginning in 2004. ACLU officials are praising Holder's decision to reopen the cases against CIA agents but say more needs to be done. The latest information "further underscores the need for a comprehensive investigation into the torture of detainees and those who authorized it," says Jameel Jaffer, director of the ACLU's National Security Project. [2]

President Obama decided on Jan. 22 — his second full day in office — to bar the use of waterboarding or any of the other enhanced techniques by CIA or military interrogators. "We believe we can abide by a rule that says, we don't torture, but we can effectively obtain the intelligence we need," Obama said

Interrogation Techniques Included Waterboarding

Ten "enhanced interrogation techniques" were approved by the Department of Justice for use by Central Intelligence Agency (CIA) interrogators. The legal memorandum approving the techniques, dated Aug. 1, 2002, was signed by Jay Bybee, assistant attorney general for the Office of Legal Counsel, and prepared by his deputy, John Yoo.

Attention grasp — Detainee is grasped with both hands, one hand on each side of collar opening, in "a controlled and quick motion," and in the same motion drawn toward interrogator.

Walling — Detainee is pulled forward and then "quickly and firmly" pushed into flexible false wall so that shoulder blades hit wall. Head and neck are supported with rolled towel to prevent whiplash.

Facial hold — Detainee's head is immobilized by interrogator placing open palm on either side of detainee's face; interrogator's fingertips "are kept well away from" detainee's eyes.

Facial or insult slap — With fingers "slightly spread apart," the interrogator's hand "makes contact with" area between tip of detainee's chin and bottom of corresponding earlobe.

Cramped confinement — Detainee is placed in confined space, typically a small or large box, usually dark; confinement can last up to two hours in small space, up to 18 hours in larger space.

Insects — "Harmless" insect is placed in confinement box with detainee.

Wall standing — Detainee stands about 4 to 5 feet from wall with feet spread to shoulder width, arms stretched out in front of him, and fingers resting on wall to support body weight. Not allowed to reposition hands or feet.

Stress positions — Detainee sits on floor with legs extended straight out in front of him with arms raised above head or kneels on floor while leaning back at 45-degree angle.

Sleep deprivation — "Will not exceed 11 days at a time."

Waterboarding — Detainee is bound to bench with feet elevated above head; head is immobilized and interrogator places cloth over detainee's mouth and nose while pouring water onto cloth in controlled manner. "Airflow is restricted for 20 to 40 seconds, and the technique produces the sensation of drowning and suffocation."

Source: CIA, Inspector General, "Special Review: Counterterrorism Detention and Interrogation Activities (September 2001-October 2003)," May 7, 2004.

in a White House ceremony on Jan. 22 attended by a group of former military officers assembled by human-rights groups. He also promised to close the prison camp at the Guantánamo Bay Naval Base in Cuba within one year. [3]

Republicans and national security-minded conservatives immediately began attacking the Obama policies, with former Vice President Dick Cheney assuming the highest-profile role among the critics. Cheney is continu-ing his attacks on the president since Holder's decision to reopen the CIA cases. He calls Holder's action "po-litical" and credits use of the harsh methods with preventing any attacks on the United States following the Sept. 11, 2001, attacks.

"My sort of overwhelming view is that the enhanced interrogation tech-niques were absolutely essential in saving thousands of American lives and preventing further attacks against the United States," Cheney said on "Fox News Sunday" on Aug. 30. "I think they were directly responsible for the fact that for eight years we had no further mass casualty attacks against the United States." [4]

Seven former CIA directors raised the stakes in the controversy with a letter on Sept. 18 asking Obama to reverse Holder's decision to reopen the investi-gations. The group, including CIA di-rectors in Republican and Democratic administrations, said the investigation of previously closed cases was unfair to the officers involved, would "seriously dam-age" other officers' willingness to "take risks to protect the country" and would damage the ability to obtain coopera-tion from foreign intelligence agencies.

Obama rebuffed the suggestion in an appearance on one of several Sun-day talk shows on Sept. 20. "I appre-ciate the former CIA directors wanting to look after an institution that they helped to build," he told host Bob Schieffer on the CBS program "Face the Nation." "But I continue to believe that nobody's above the law. And I want to make sure that, as president of the United States, I'm not asserting in some way that my decisions over-rule the decisions of prosecutors who are there to uphold the law."

At the same time, *The Washington Post* reported that the investigation may be narrower than once thought, with perhaps only two or three cases being seriously considered for possi-ble indictments. *The Post* based the story on two unnamed sources who

CIA Report Evaluates Interrogation Techniques

Here are major conclusions from a May 2004 report by the Central Intelligence Agency's inspector general on counterterrorism and interrogation activities from September 2001 through October 2003:

- Program provided intelligence that helped identify and apprehend terrorists and warned of planned terrorist attacks on U.S., other countries.
- Office of General Counsel "worked closely" with Justice Department to determine legality of "enhanced interrogation techniques" (EITs) and also "consulted" with White House and National Security Council regarding techniques.
- Justice Department legal opinion "consists of finely detailed analysis" to support conclusion that EITs, "properly" carried out, would not constitute torture; opinion did not address whether practices were consistent with U.S. voluntary undertaking to prevent "cruel, inhuman or degrading" treatment.
- A number of agency officers are concerned that they "may be vulnerable" to legal action in the United States or abroad and that the U.S. government "will not stand behind them."
- Officers are concerned that future public revelation of the program is "inevitable" and "will seriously damage" reputations of personnel, agency.
- Agency "generally" provided "good guidance and support" to officers using EITs, in particular at "these [redacted] foreign locations."
- Agency in early months of program "failed to provide adequate guidance, staffing, guidance and support" to agents involved in interrogation at [redacted location(s)].

- "Unauthorized, improvised, inhumane, and undocumented detention and interrogation techniques were used [redacted] referred to the Department of Justice (DoJ) for potential prosecution."
- Agency "failed to issue in a timely manner comprehensive written guidelines for detention and interrogation activities."
- "Such written guidance as does exist . . . is inadequate."
- Waterboarding was used during interrogation of two detainees "in a manner inconsistent with" the Justice Department's legal opinion; one key al Qaeda terrorist [Khalid Shaikh Mohammed] was subjected to waterboarding 183 times and denied sleep for 180 hours. In this and another instance, "the technique of application and volume of water used differed from the DoJ opinion."
- CIA's Office of Medical Services provided "comprehensive medical attention," but did not issue formal medical guidelines until April 2003.
- EITs may have been applied "without justification" in some instances based not on analytical assessments but on agents' "presumptions" about individual's knowledge.
- Agency faces "potentially serious long-term political and legal challenges" because of use of EITs and government's inability to decide what it will ultimately do with detainees.

Source: "Counterterrorism Detention and Interrogation Activities," Office of Inspector General, Central Intelligence Agency, May 7, 2004

---

were described as having been briefed on the investigation. [5]

In the Jan. 22 session, Obama appointed an interagency task force to be headed by Holder to recommend new policies on interrogation and detainee transfers. The task force's recommendations announced by Holder on Aug. 24 reaffirmed Obama's decision to bar any interrogation techniques other than those outlined in the latest version of the *U.S. Army Field Manual*. The manual — revised in 2006 by the Bush administration after the disclosure of abuses of Iraqi prisoners by U.S. military personnel at the Abu Ghraib prison outside Baghdad — details 17 different techniques of interrogation and bars any use of physical force or degrading treatment against prisoners. (*See story, p. 796.*)

Holder said the task force, including members of the intelligence community, was unanimous in concluding that the manual provides "adequate and effective means of conducting interrogations." Obama accepted the task force's further recommendation to take interrogation of so-called high-value detainees away from the CIA and assign the responsibility to a new group comprising specially trained experts from several agencies that will be housed at the FBI and overseen by the National Security Council. [6]

Obama also drew sharp criticism earlier for revoking and then directing the Justice Department to release controversial legal opinions from its Office of Legal Counsel (OLC) that concluded the CIA's enhanced interrogation techniques were legal and

did not constitute torture under U.S. or international law. The release of the memos in the ACLU's FOIA suit — with the most graphic description until then of the CIA's harsh techniques — came after a strong plea by CIA Director Leon Panetta to withhold or heavily edit the documents. Instead, the memos were released on April 16 with few redactions.

In releasing the memos, however, Obama appeared to rule out prosecutions of CIA operatives who conducted interrogations according to the techniques he was ordering discarded. "It is our intention," Obama said in the April 16 statement, "to assure those who carried out their duties relying in good faith upon legal advice from the Department of Justice that they will not be subject to prosecution." [7]

At the same time, Obama reiterated his opposition to a broad reexamination of the Bush administration's counterterrorism policies. Obama described the events as "a dark and painful chapter in our history," but added, "Nothing will be gained by spending our time and energy laying blame for the past."

Nevertheless, some lawmakers and many civil liberties and human-rights groups continue to press for a full investigation of the Bush policies either by a special congressional committee or a bipartisan, independent commission comparable to the commission that reexamined events leading up to the 9/11 terrorist attacks. "An independent commission would take a broader look at the policies that have troubled so many people and look at how we can avoid going in that direction again," says Virginia Sloan, president and founder of the bipartisan Constitution Project.

Meanwhile, Obama is making only slow progress toward meeting his goal of closing the Guantánamo prison camp by Jan. 20, 2010. The review of individual cases is moving slowly, other countries are reluctant to accept transferred detainees and Republican politicians are opposing relocating any of the detainees to U.S. soil.

The national security issues complicate Obama's political standing as he tries to move the country out of the economic doldrums and push an ambitious domestic agenda through Congress.

Here are some of the questions being debated:

Should CIA agents be prosecuted for exceeding interrogation guidelines?

Abdul Wali, an Afghan farmer, turned himself in to U.S. authorities in June 2003 after learning he had been implicated in rocket attacks on the U.S. military base at Asadabad, near the Pakistani border. But David Passaro, a former Special Forces medic working on contract as a CIA interrogator, got angry when Wali was unable to answer his questions.

Former Vice President Dick Cheney harshly criticizes President Obama's decision to bar waterboarding and other enhanced techniques used by CIA and military interrogators. Cheney labels Attorney General Eric Holder's decision to reopen the CIA interrogation cases "political" and credits the harsh methods with preventing any attacks on the United States following the Sept. 11, 2001, attacks.

Witnesses said the enraged Passaro repeatedly struck Wali with a foot-long flashlight and his fists and kicked him in the groin while wearing combat boots. Wali died two days later. Today, Passaro is serving time in a federal prison after a federal jury in North Carolina convicted him in August 2006 of assault. [8]

The CIA itself referred Passaro's case to the Justice Department for possible prosecution, and then CIA Director Michael Hayden stressed after the verdict that Passaro's conduct was "neither authorized nor condoned" by the agency. The agency also referred other cases to Justice, but career prosecutors in the U.S. attorney's office in Alexandria decided not to bring criminal charges in any of the others.

Attorney General Holder's Aug. 24 decision to designate John Durham, a career federal prosecutor from Connecticut, to take a second look at those cases is drawing heavy criticism from the intelligence community, including high-ranking CIA officials from Democratic and Republican administrations.

Jeffrey Smith, the CIA's general counsel for two years under President Bill Clinton, warns that prosecutions could set a "dangerous precedent" of using criminal law to settle policy differences at the expense of career officials. And former CIA Inspector General Helgerson says a successful prosecution would be "very difficult" because of the Justice Department's approval of the interrogation program. "I do not believe there was any criminal intent among those involved," Helgerson told *The Washington Post* after the release of his 2004 report on interrogation practices. [9]

In his television interview, Cheney cited the previous investigations, including the prosecution of Passaro, as evidence of a political motivation in Holder's action. Robert Alt, a senior legal fellow with the conservative Heritage Foundation, also notes that any prosecution would face substantial legal hurdles, including the five-year statute of limitations for most federal offenses. "When you put all that together and you hear the howl from the political left about the need for more action, it begins to look political," says Alt, deputy director of Heritage's Center for Legal and Judicial Studies.

Civil liberties and human-rights advocates defend Holder's action in part by criticizing what they describe as the Bush administration's politicization of the Justice Department. "I'm not convinced that those prosecutors had access to all the facts," says Elisa Massimino, chief executive officer and executive director of Human Rights First. "I'm not convinced that they were operating in the appropriate legal framework to make those decisions."

ACLU lawyer Alex Abdo notes that Holder has only asked for a review of the cases and would have to decide later whether to bring any prosecutions. A legal fellow with the ACLU's National Security Project, Adabo dismisses accusations of political motivations. "The question of whether the law was broken is strictly a legal question, not a political one," he says.

Cheney also warned of the effect the decision is having on the morale of CIA officers. "We ask those people to do some very difficult things. Sometimes, they put their own lives at risk," Cheney said in the Fox News interview. "And if they are now going to be subject to being investigated and prosecuted by the next administration, nobody's going to sign up for those kinds of missions."

Massimino counters that CIA morale suffered because the agency was given the assignment to interrogate the high-value detainees using legally questionable tactics that Cheney famously characterized shortly after the 9/11 attacks as "the dark side."

"There were a lot of people at the CIA who were devastated by the idea that they were the agency that would go to what Vice President Cheney called the dark side, that they were the agency that would violate the law," Massimino says. "People who are concerned about the morale, where were those people when there was pressure on people at the agency to go beyond the law? Why

didn't they stand up then for the morale of the intelligence officers who are trying to serve their country honorably?"

Cheney and other critics also warn that the review of the CIA cases is merely a first step toward possible criminal investigations against others in the Bush administration involved in the interrogation policies, including Justice Department lawyers who sanctioned the enhanced interrogation techniques. Many critics "will not be satisfied until they see former Bush administration officials paraded in orange jump suits," says Alt.

In fact, the ACLU and Human Rights First are among the groups pressing for broader inquiries. "Given what's on the public record, we should be investigating attorneys in the Department of Justice and other senior officials who were the architects of the CIA's enhanced interrogation program," says Abdo.

Should the CIA be allowed to use "enhanced interrogation techniques" when questioning "high-value" detainees?

With Democratic majorities in both chambers, Congress in 2008 moved to prohibit any of the "enhanced interrogation techniques" that CIA operatives had been using against selected "high-value" detainees. But President Bush vetoed the measure, saying the harsh measures were needed to overcome resistance techniques learned by al Qaeda members during training.

"It is vitally important," Bush said in the March 8, 2008, veto message, "that the Central Intelligence Agency be allowed to maintain a separate and classified interrogation program." [10]

In his Jan. 22 executive order, President Obama accomplished what Congress had sought by limiting all interrogations to those practices authorized in the *U.S. Army Field Manual*. [11] Seven months later, Holder announced that the task force Obama had appointed to review the policy reaf-

firmed the president's decision. "The task force concluded that the *Army Field Manual* provides appropriate guidance on interrogation for military interrogators and that no additional or different guidance was necessary for other agencies," Holder said.

Despite Obama's decision, the debate over the legality and effectiveness of the CIA interrogation program is continuing. Cheney and other defenders of the practices say the CIA interrogations produced valuable intelligence after proper review and approval by the Justice Department. As evidence, they point to the CIA inspector general's bottom-line conclusion that the agency's interrogations provided "actionable intelligence" that helped identify and apprehend terrorists and warned of planned terrorist attacks against the United States or other countries.

In his interview, Cheney said that two of the most valuable al Qaeda detainees — Khalid Shaikh Mohammed and Abu Zubaydah — provided information only after being subjected to some of the enhanced interrogation techniques (EITs). "The evidence is overwhelming that the EITs were crucial in getting them to cooperate," he said.

Critics of the practices reject the now-repudiated Justice Department advisories that said the techniques did not constitute torture as defined by U.S. law. They also question whether the enhanced techniques were necessary to obtain information from detainees. As evidence, they point to the caveat in the CIA inspector general's report that the effectiveness of the techniques in eliciting information that would not have been obtained otherwise "cannot be so easily measured." [12]

"What the report doesn't say and doesn't conclude is that torture was responsible for the information that was obtained or that the intelligence could not have been obtained without torture," says ACLU lawyer Abdo.

After years of secrecy, the operational details of the CIA interrogation program

Army Prohibits Force in Questioning Prisoners

The U.S. Army's 384-page field manual on "human intelligence (HUMINT) collection" details more than a dozen "approaches" to questioning an enemy prisoner of war (EPW) or detainee, none entailing physical force, coercion or threat of violence. The manual, as revised in September 2006, included specific prohibitions against abusive practices documented at the Abu Ghraib prison in Iraq, including forced nudity and use of military dogs to harass or intimidate prisoners. Here are the approaches listed in the manual:

Direct approach: HUMINT collector "asks direct questions." Effective 90 percent of time during World War II, 95 percent of time in Operation Desert Storm in Iraq (1991); preliminary studies indicate "dramatically less successful" in Afghanistan (2001-2002) and Iraq (2003).

Incentive approach: HUMINT collector "may use incentives to enhance rapport and to reward the source for cooperation and truthfulness." May not state or imply that basic rights under international, national law are contingent on cooperation.

Emotional approaches: HUMINT collector "can often identify dominant emotions that motivate the EPW/detainee." These approaches are:

Emotional love approach: HUMINT collector "focuses on the anxiety felt by the source . . . , his isolation from those he loves, and his feelings of helplessness." Has "a chance of success" if source can be shown what he can do to improve the situation of the object of his emotion: family, homeland, comrades.

Emotional hate approach: HUMINT collector must "build on [source's hate] so the emotion overrides the source's rational side." Hate may be directed to his country's regime, immediate superiors, officers in general or fellow soldiers.

Emotional fear-up approach: HUMINT collector "identifies a preexisting fear or creates a fear" within source and "links" elimination or reduction of fear to source's cooperation. Must be "extremely careful" not to threaten or coerce source.

Emotional fear-down approach: HUMINT collector "mitigates existing fear in exchange for" source's cooperation.

Emotional-pride and ego-up approach: HUMINT collector "exploits a source's low self-esteem" by flattery. "This should produce positive feelings on the part of the source," who "will eventually reveal pertinent information to solicit more favorable comments. . . ."

Emotional-pride and ego-down approach: HUMINT collector attacks ego or self-image of source, who in defense "reveals information to justify or rationalize his actions."

Emotional-futility: HUMINT collector convinces source that resistance is futile.

Other approaches: Most "require considerable time and resources." They are:

We Know All: HUMINT collector "subtly" convinces source that questioning is perfunctory because information is already known.

File and Dossier: HUMINT collector prepares dossier with all known information about source and uses the file to convey impression that source is only confirming information already known.

Establish Your Identity: HUMINT collector accuses source of being "infamous individual" wanted on more serious charges; source then attempts to establish his true identity in an effort to clear himself.

Repetition: HUMINT collector repeats question and answer several times; source then answers "fully and truthfully . . . to gain relief from the monotony. . . ."

Rapid Fire: HUMINT collector asks rapid-fire questions to confuse source, who "will tend to contradict himself" and then be caught in inconsistencies.

Silent: HUMINT collector says nothing, looks squarely at source and waits for source to break eye contact.

Change of Scenery: Source is removed from "intimidating" atmosphere to "setting where he feels more comfortable speaking."

Mutt and Jeff: Requires two HUMINT collectors, both "convincing actors." One adopts formal, unsympathetic stance ("bad cop"); the second gains source's confidence by scolding colleague's stance ("good cop"). No violence or threats may be used.

False Flag: Goal is to trick detainee into cooperating by convincing him he is being interrogated by non-U.S. forces; use must be approved by superiors; no "implied or explicit threats" that non-cooperation will result in harsh treatment by non-U.S. entities.

Source: U.S. Department of the Army, *Human Intelligence Collection Operations*, September 2006, www.army.mil/institution/armypublicaffairs/pdf/fm2-22-3.pdf.

are now coming to light with the release of the inspector general's report and a second document: a Dec. 30, 2004, description of the program for the Justice Department written by an unidentified lawyer. The 19-page background paper — written after the Bush administration's decision in 2003 to discontinue use of waterboarding — groups the techniques then in use into three categories: "conditioning techniques," including nudity, sleep deprivation and "dietary manipulation"; "corrective techniques," including facial slap, abdominal slap, facial hold and attention grasp; and "coercive techniques," including "walling," water dousing, stress positions, wall standing and cramped confinement.

The paper describes the use of the techniques sequentially from less to more severe. The objective, the paper says, is to place the detainee in "a state of learned helplessness and dependence conducive to the collection of intelligence in a predictable, reliable, and sustainable manner."

The Justice Department memos in August 2002 concluded the techniques did not constitute torture under applicable federal law, which prohibits actions "under the color of law intended to inflict severe physical or mental pain or suffering." In his Fox News interview, Cheney stressed the Justice Department's approval of the enhanced techniques, but also agreed to a question from host Chris Wallace that he was "comfortable" with the program even when interrogators went beyond the authorized practices. Cheney has also been reported to be planning to write in his forthcoming memoir that he disagreed with Bush's decision to discontinue use of waterboarding. [13]

Today, waterboarding has few vocal defenders, but the legal status of the other harsh interrogation techniques remains a subject of dispute. "Most of the techniques fall pretty clearly on the legal side of the torture line," says Alt at the Heritage Foundation. "Most fall into the category of mind games, which is what interrogation is."

But the ACLU's Abdo says the techniques "in combination" amounted "either to torture or cruel, inhuman and degrading treatment, both of which are prohibited by international law as well as our own laws." The prohibition against inhuman treatment was added by the Detainee Treatment Act of 2005, enacted after the Justice Department memo and the period covered by the CIA inspector general's report.

For now, the legal debate is moot, since the Obama administration decided to limit interrogation to the non-coercive techniques permitted under the *Army Field Manual*. The White House asked that the interrogation issue be kept out of a pending bill to reauthorize intelligence activities.

As for the debate on the need for the techniques or their effectiveness, Benjamin Wittes, a Brookings Institution senior fellow who has studied the interrogation of post-9/11 detainees, says the answer may be unknowable.

"It's very hard to do a controlled experiment," Wittes says. "The CIA wasn't trying to do a controlled experiment. They were trying to get actionable intelligence and save lives."

Should Congress authorize an in-depth investigation of past detention and interrogation practices?

A little more than a year after the Sept. 11 terrorist attacks, Congress in November 2002 passed legislation to create an independent, bipartisan commission to examine why the government had failed to prevent the attacks and what could be done to guard against future attacks. President Bush reluctantly agreed to the measure, which Democrats in Congress had pushed with strong backing from many of the families of the nearly 3,000 people killed in the attacks.

The commission's report, issued in July 2004, identified a host of intelligence failures under Bush as well as President Clinton that underestimated the threat posed by al Qaeda and missed clues to the group's plan to hijack airplanes and crash them into landmark buildings in the United States. The commission recommended a number of steps to guard against future attacks, including the creation of a new national intelligence director with authority over both the CIA and FBI. That step was one of several that were eventually adopted. [14]

A coalition of 18 civil liberties and human-rights advocates is pressing for a similar investigation of the Bush administration's detention and interrogation policies. "We can't entirely move forward unless we look back and find out what happened," says Sloan of the Constitution Project. "The American people don't know what was done in their name, and we're entitled to know." [15]

Sloan approves of Obama's decision to change detention and interrogation policies but says a broad inquiry is needed for Congress to consider legislative changes. "That's an executive branch decision that the president

has made, but another president could change that," she says.

Proposals for an independent commission have support among some Democratic lawmakers, including House Speaker Nancy Pelosi, D-Calif. But Pelosi's counterpart, Senate Majority Leader Harry Reid, D-Nev., prefers investigations by individual congressional committees. Republican lawmakers generally oppose any look back as unnecessary and politically motivated. "I don't see what we're going to learn that congressional leaders didn't already know," House Minority Leader John Boehner of Ohio remarked in April. [16]

For his part, President Obama has generally opposed any broad inquiry into the Bush administration policies. "We should be looking forward, not backwards," Obama said in an April 21 news conference, five days after release of the Justice Department memo. But he went on to indicate a preference for an independent commission over congressional committees as a forum for any investigation. "I think it's very important for the American people to feel as if this is not being dealt with to provide one side or another political advantage but rather is being done in order to learn some lessons so that we move forward in an effective way," he said.

Conservatives echo the concerns about political recriminations from any broad investigation. "Part of the question is whether it's needed to get at the truth or whether it becomes a political rehashing," says the Heritage Foundation's Alt. "Given the time that has elapsed, one wonders whether it's not simply an attempt to criminalize or vilify differences with the past administration."

ACLU lawyer Abdo counters that a broad investigation is needed to compile "an accurate historical record of what took place during the last eight years." The ACLU favors a select congressional committee for that purpose. "It's unlikely that anybody could compile as accurate and comprehensive a record as Congress," he says.

Sloan says the coalition has a "slight preference" for an independent commission over congressional inquiries. "So much in Congress gets politicized and bogged down," she says. "We thought a commission that would be independent of that kind of politics would be better."

Whatever forum might be used for an investigation, Sloan says Congress should use the results to draft legislation. "If you don't have laws, then you're leaving things to the discretion of the executive branch," she says, "and that seems to be what got us into trouble in the first place." ∎

BACKGROUND

Eliciting the Truth

The use of coercive interrogation techniques dates to ancient times, and so too the debate over their value in eliciting the truth. In the Western world, pain has been wielded as an instrument of judicial interrogation by the ancient Greeks and Romans, European monarchs and 20th-century dictators. For several centuries, the Roman Catholic Church inflicted pain on presumed heretics to educe confessions. Throughout, some have argued that — apart from moral considerations — coercion is an inefficient technique that often produces unreliable information from subjects willing to say anything to stop the pain. [17]

CIA Director Leon Panetta warns that "exceptionally grave damage" to national security could result — including exposing individual CIA officers to "grave risk" — if additional documents about the CIA detention and interrogation program are released under a Freedom of Information Act request by the American Civil Liberties Union and other groups. President Obama opposes a broad reexamination of the Bush administration's counterterrorism policies.

AFP/Getty Images/Paul J. Richards

As University of Wisconsin history professor Alfred W. McCoy notes, torture was practiced by the ancient Greeks on slaves and by the Romans on slaves and freemen alike. The third-century Roman jurist Ulpian defined *quaestio* (torture) as "the torment and suffering of the body in order to elicit the truth," but recognized its limitations. Some people have "such strength of body and soul" that there is "no means of obtaining the truth from them," he wrote, while others "are so susceptible to pain that they will tell any lie rather than suffer it." [18]

Torture fell out of use in Christian Europe during the first millennium, but resurfaced among civil and ecclesiastical authorities by the 12th and 13th centuries. The Catholic Church's "inquisitions" aimed at suppressing heretical movements took on torture as an instrument of interrogation under a papal bull issued by Pope Innocent IV in 1252. One of the techniques used by the Italian Inquisition was to suspend the subject by rope in five degrees of escalating severity — hence,

the modern term "third degree." Church manuals prescribed techniques of interrogation. In one, Nicholas Eymerich, 14th-century inquisitor general of Aragon, cataloged 10 techniques of "evasion and deception" by heretics; he went on to specify methods for interrogators to counter them that entailed physical intimidation as well as psychological manipulation.

Civil authorities in Europe also used torture from medieval times into the 18th and 19th centuries both as coercive interrogation and public punishment. England's King Henry VIII and Queen Elizabeth I both used torture against their opponents; the Tower of London housed a rack and other instruments of torture. In Paris, the Bourbon kings confined prisoners in the Bastille under torture-like conditions.

Legal acceptance of torture began to recede with its abolition by Prussia in 1754. Ten years later, the Italian penal reformer Cesare Beccaria denounced torture as "a sure route for the acquittal of robust ruffians and the conviction of weak innocents." By the late 19th century, the French author Victor Hugo felt justified in declaring that torture "has ceased to exist." The widespread use of torture by such 20th-century dictatorial regimes as the Soviet Union and Nazi Germany, however, proved the reports of its demise to be exaggerated.

The United States has no acknowledged experience with legally sanctioned torture, but coercive interrogation was a widespread if unacknowledged law enforcement practice as late as the mid-20th century. "Our

Continued on p. 800

Chronology

Cold War

Central Intelligence Agency established, given covert roles in propaganda, subversion; disclosures of CIA operations often bring controversy.

1947
National Security Act of 1947 establishes CIA to collect and analyze intelligence; mandate expanded next year to include covert propaganda, support for anti-communist movements.

1950s
CIA's MKUltra program experiments with interrogation techniques using hypnosis, drugs and physical coercion; terminated in late 1960s, records destroyed in 1973.

1963
Secret CIA manual — *Kubark counterintelligence interrogation-July 1963* — details "coercive" interrogation techniques.

Mid-to-late 1960s
Widespread torture carried out by South Vietnamese forces in Operation Phoenix, CIA-designed counterinsurgency program.

1960s-1970s
CIA-trained and funded police forces in Latin America are accused of abuse, torture.

1983
Secret CIA "Human Resource Exploitation Training Manual" details non-physical methods for coercive interrogation: "debility, disorientation and dread."

1997
CIA declassifies interrogation manuals in response to threatened Freedom of Information Act suit by *Baltimore Sun*.

2001-Present

CIA given lead role in interrogating "high-value" terrorism suspects after Sept. 11 attacks; gains permission for "enhanced" techniques that critics say amount to torture.

September 2001
Vice President Dick Cheney says U.S. will have to "work the dark side" to combat al Qaeda (Sept. 16); President George W. Bush signs order directing CIA to interrogate "high-value" detainees (Sept. 17).

Fall-winter 2001-2002
CIA arranges to hold future detainees in secret prisons overseas.

March 2002
Abu Zubaydah, purported adviser to Osama bin Laden, captured in Pakistan; CIA proposes using "enhanced interrogation techniques."

2002
Justice Department approves use of 10 "enhanced" CIA interrogation techniques." . . . Abd al-Rahim al-Nashiri, accused mastermind of *USS Cole* bombing, captured, taken to secret prison in Thailand, subjected to waterboarding; later threatened with pistol, power drill.

2003
CIA inspector general opens investigation of interrogation practices (January), later refers some cases to Justice Department for prosecution. . . . Khalid Shaikh Mohammed (KSM), alleged architect of 9/11 attacks, captured in Pakistan (March), waterboarded 183 times; dispute continues about value of information elicited by enhanced techniques.

April-May 2004
Photos of abuse of Iraqi prisoners in U.S. military prison outside Baghdad provoke outcry in U.S., around world. . . . CIA report questions implementation of interrogation program; notes agents' concern about potential backlash if disclosed.

November-December 2005
Washington Post publishes first detailed story on CIA secret prisons. . . . CIA destroys 92 videotapes of interrogation of KSM, others. . . . Detainee Treatment Act prohibits "cruel, inhuman or degrading" treatment by military, but not CIA, interrogators.

August 2006
CIA contractor David Passaro convicted of assault in death of Afghan farmer Abdul Wali after interrogation in June 2003; later given prison term. . . . Bush orders 14 remaining "high-value" detainees in CIA prisons transferred to Guantánamo Bay Naval Base, Cuba.

March 2008
Bush vetoes bill passed by Congress barring enhanced interrogation techniques by CIA; says techniques vital to war on terror.

2009
President Obama bars enhanced-interrogation techniques, orders CIA prisons closed; promises closure of Guantánamo within one year. . . . Obama declassifies Justice Department memos approving use of enhanced interrogation techniques; rules out prosecution of agents who followed guidelines. . . . CIA inspector general's report declassified in August, yields detailed picture of CIA interrogation program. . . . Attorney General Eric H. Holder Jr. asks career prosecutor to review CIA interrogation cases where agents exceeded guidelines; move brings strong criticism from Republicans, conservatives and former CIA officials.

'Extraordinary Rendition' of Terrorists Challenged

Detainees say they were abducted and tortured.

The Obama administration continues to invoke a "state secrets" privilege to block a federal lawsuit seeking damages from a CIA-contractor airline for transporting prisoners to foreign countries where they were allegedly tortured.

The two-year-old lawsuit in a federal appeals court in California is one of several American Civil Liberties Union (ACLU) efforts to challenge the practice known as "extraordinary rendition." Under President George W. Bush, the Central Intelligence Agency (CIA) was accused of transferring suspected terrorists, often apprehended in foreign countries under questionable circumstances, to countries known to abuse or torture prisoners.

The Obama administration has continued to hand over suspected terrorists to other countries but is vowing to prevent abuses against U.S.-captured detainees by more frequent inspection of foreign prison facilities. ACLU lawyers say those efforts are inadequate because prisoners held in other countries are unlikely to report abuse to visiting U.S. monitors. [1]

Meanwhile, Justice Department lawyers are asking the federal appeals court in San Francisco to reconsider its April 28 decision to allow five former or current detainees to pursue a lawsuit charging Jeppesen Dataplans, a Bay-area airline, with knowingly assisting the CIA in forcibly transporting them to other countries to be tortured. A federal judge in San Jose had granted the government's motion to dismiss the suit on "state secrets" grounds, a privilege the government can use to limit evidence or even throw out a suit altogether if state secrets might be disclosed. However, the 9th U.S. Circuit Court of Appeals overturned that decision.

In rejecting the privilege for now, the three-judge panel said the subject of the suit — the agreement between the government and the airline, a Boeing subsidiary — was not secret. The ruling, which the government now wants the full appeals court to hear, left the question open as to whether the government can invoke the privilege in regard to specific evidence as the case proceeds. [2]

Khaled el-Masri, a German citizen, says he was abducted and tortured by the CIA.

Getty Images/Suedwest Presse/Volkmar Koenneke

The lead plaintiff in the case, Ethiopian-born British citizen Binyam Mohamed, was arrested by Pakistani authorities in 2002, turned over to U.S. authorities and transferred to Morocco. He claims he was tortured during 18 months of captivity there before being transferred to U.S. facilities in Afghanistan and then in Guantánamo Bay, Cuba. He was finally released in February 2009. Of the other four plaintiffs, two remain in prison, one in Egypt, one in Italy; two others have been released.

The ACLU filed a similar suit in 2005 on behalf of Khaled el-Masri, a German citizen who said he was abducted in Macedonia and taken to a secret CIA prison in Afghanistan where he was tortured. El-Masri was eventually released without charges; he was apparently confused with a suspected terrorist with a similar name.

The federal appeals court in Richmond, Va., cited the state secrets privilege in dismissing el-Masri's earlier suit against former CIA Director George Tenet and three CIA-contractor airlines; the Supreme Court declined to hear el-Masri's appeal in October 2007. The ACLU is now asking the Inter-American Commission on Human Rights to hear the case; the government has two months from the Aug. 27 filing to respond.

Attorney General Eric Holder announced on Sept. 23 new limits on the use of the state secrets privilege. It will be invoked only to prevent "genuine and significant harm" to national security or foreign policy, Holder said, and not to conceal violations of law or prevent embarrassment to the government. The policy was described as applying to cases after Oct. 1 — apparently ruling out any direct effect on the *Jeppesen* case. [3]

---

[1] See David Johnston, "Renditions to Continue, but With Better Oversight, U.S. Says," *The New York Times,* Aug. 25, 2009, p. A8.

[2] The decision is *Mohamed v. Jeppesen Dataplan, Inc.,* 08-15693 (9th Cir. 2009), as amended Aug. 31, 2009, www.ca9.uscourts.gov/datastore/opinions/2009/08/31/08-15693.pdf. See Bob Egelko, "U.S. fights rendition suit against Bay Area firm," *San Francisco Chronicle,* Aug. 10, 2009, p. C1.

[3] See Department of Justice, "Attorney General Establishes New State Secrets Policies and Procedures," Sept. 23, 2009, www.usdoj.gov/opa/pr/2009/September/09-ag-1013.html. For advance coverage, see Carrie Johnson, "Obama to Set Higher Bar for Keeping State Secrets," *The Washington Post,* Sept. 23, 2009, p. A1.

Continued from p. 798

police, with no legal sanction, employ duress, threat, bullying, a vast amount of moderate physical abuse and a certain degree of outright torture," the author and social critic Ernest Jerome Hopkins wrote in 1931. [19] In a succession of cases beginning in 1936 and continuing through the 1950s, the Supreme Court began throwing out convictions based on confessions that police secured either by physical or psychological coercion. Frustrated with the case-by-case adjudications, the court in 1966 laid down the famous

Miranda rule requiring police to notify suspects of their rights. Chief Justice Earl Warren, a former district attorney, stressed that the rule was aimed at preventing the use of physical beatings or incommunicado interrogation to coerce confessions from suspects in custody. [20]

World War II gave the United States its first sustained experience with interrogating wartime captives. Far removed from the battlefield, the government built two special detention centers in the United States to interrogate German and Japanese prisoners. The two facilities — Fort Hunt, in Northern Virginia near Washington, D.C., and Camp Tracy, near Stockton, Calif. — were kept secret during and for decades after the war. During the war, the military even delayed or avoided telling the International Committee of the Red Cross about the camps — a violation of the Geneva Conventions. Interrogators emphasized rapport-building instead of coercion. "I never laid hands on anyone," one of the Fort Hunt veterans told a *Washington Post* reporter in 2007. But the interrogators also gathered intelligence by secretly monitoring and recording the prisoners' cellblock conversations. [21]

Mind Control

The Cold War between the United States and two communist states — the Soviet Union and China — featured the use of interrogation on both sides for multiple purposes. The principals used interrogation to gather intelligence and to create propaganda. They also fostered the use of interrogation by proxy states to suppress or intimidate domestic opposition. The CIA was a prime player in secretly developing techniques of interrogation in the 1950s and '60s that became intensely controversial when publicly disclosed in later decades. [22]

Terrorism Suspects Transferred from Secret Sites

Fourteen "high-value" terrorism suspects were transferred from secret CIA sites to the prison camp at the Guantánamo Bay Naval Base in Cuba in September 2006. Five have been charged with helping plan the Sept. 11 terrorist attacks on the United States; the government is deciding whether to continue prosecuting them in special military tribunals or move the trials to a regular federal court. Formal charges have not been brought against the other nine detainees. The now disbanded combatant status review tribunals at Guantánamo confirmed their status as "enemy combatants."

Here are the 14 "high-value" detainees and the role the government alleges they played in terrorism:

The five 9/11 detainees — *Each defendant is charged with conspiracy and a number of separate offenses including murder in violation of the law of war, attacking civilians, destruction of property in violation of the law of war and terrorism.*

Khalid Shaykh Muhammad: principal al Qaeda operative directing 9/11 attacks.

Walid Bin Attash: linked indirectly to the 1998 U.S. Embassy bombings in Tanzania and Kenya and the *USS Cole* bombing in 2000.

Ramzi Bin al-Shibh: coordinator of 9/11 attacks.

Mustafa al-Hawsawi: linked to detailed computer records of al Qaeda members, finances.

Ammar al-Baluchi: linked to arrangements for 9/11 attacks.

The other nine high-value detainees yet to be charged are:

Ahmed Khalfan Ghailani: linked to bombing of U.S. Embassy in Tanzania.

Mohd Farik bin Amin ("Zubair"): arranged financing for bombing of J. W. Marriott Hotel in Jakarta, Indonesia, in 2003.

Al Nashiri, Abd Al Rahim Hussein Mohammed: linked to *Cole* bombing.

Bashir bin Lap ("Lillie"): linked to planning of bombing of J. W. Marriott Hotel.

Rjduan bin Isomuddiiu ("Hambali"): linked to bombings in Indonesia, efforts to topple Malaysian government.

Zayn al Abidin Muhammad Husayn ("Abu Zubaydah"): Head of al Qaeda training camps in Afghanistan; diary entries include unacted-on plans for attacks within United States.

Guleed Hassan Ahmed: al Qaeda cell leader in Djibouti.

Majid Khan: linked to alleged al Qaeda money-laundering plot.

Abu Faraj al-Libi: deputy to al Qaeda's 3rd in command.

Source: Combatant Status Review Tribunals/Administrative Review Boards, U.S. Department of Defense, Oct. 17, 2007; accessed online on Sept. 21, 2009. Note: The DOD's name spellings are used; variations are often used in the news media.

The CIA was created in 1947, and the next year given a broad congressional charter to collect and analyze intelligence and carry out covert operations overseas without disclosing its budget, staffing or other information. As the new agency was taking shape, the nations of the world were also laying the foundations of a new framework of international law, including the Universal Declaration of Human Rights in 1948 and the rewritten and expanded Geneva Conventions in 1949. Included in the fourth Geneva Convention regarding treatment of civilians was a new provision that barred the use of "physical or mental coercion" for any purpose, including "to obtain information from them or third parties." The official commentators described the provision, Article 31, as "an important step forward in international law."

Despite this international law prohibition, the CIA worked over the course of two decades to develop new interrogation techniques using hypnosis, drugs and various forms of physical discomfort. The initiatives stemmed in part from information about the use of hypnosis, drugs and electroshock by Nazi interrogators during World War II. They gained urgency from the belief that the Soviet and Chinese regimes had developed mind-control techniques that — whether applied to Soviet citizens in the Stalinist-era "show trials" or to U.S. prisoners in the Korean War — could induce the subjects to say almost anything the interrogators wanted them to say. Edward Hunter, a journalist secretly on the CIA's payroll, gave a frightening name to the techniques with his 1951 book *Brainwashing in Red China.* [23]

In his critical account, University of Wisconsin history professor McCoy chronicles a secret program code named MKUltra, whose findings and techniques were later codified in a 1963 manual called *Kubark.* The program used human subjects in experiments with the newly discovered hallucinogen LSD and with such sensory-deprivation techniques as isolation in a cramped box or water tank. Drug-induced interrogation proved to be a blind alley, but sensory deprivation proved more efficacious in inducing a state of helplessness in the subjects. McCoy describes the CIA's discovery of "no-touch torture" as "the first real revolution in the cruel science of pain in centuries."

The official directing the program was Richard Helms, assistant deputy director of operations in the 1950s and later the director of the CIA from 1966 to 1973. In one of his final acts in office, Helms directed the destruction of all documents pertaining to the program — in advance of imminent journalistic and congressional investigations of the agency.

By then, however, the CIA had come under intense criticism for its role in a counterinsurgency program in the Vietnam War known as Operation Phoenix. The CIA-designed program as carried out by the South Vietnamese entailed the use of outright torture, including beatings and electric shocks; the South Vietnamese attributed nearly 41,000 deaths to the program. In hearings on his nomination to succeed Helms as CIA director in 1973, William Colby, who had served as the CIA's chief of pacification in Vietnam, told the Senate Foreign Relations Committee he was aware of reports of abuse but had instructed CIA personnel not to participate. [24]

McCoy depicts the CIA as guilty of "propagating torture" also through a program in the 1960s and '70s that funneled aid to police forces in pro-American governments. The program was housed in the Office of Public Safety in the Agency for International Development (U.S. AID), but was headed by a former CIA official and operated in what McCoy describes as "close coordination with the agency's intelligence mission." Latin American countries sent police recruits to a clandestine academy in Washington for training. A report by what was then the General Accounting Office (GAO) in 1976 acknowledged allegations that the academy "taught or encouraged the use of torture," but made no formal finding on the claims. Amnesty International, however, claimed to have documented widespread torture by police in at least two dozen countries that had received aid under the program.

Allegations of CIA complicity in torture were renewed in the 1980s — notably, in Latin America. A *New York Times* report on the CIA's role in counterinsurgency in Honduras in 1988 prompted a closed-door hearing by the Senate Intelligence Committee that disclosed to lawmakers — but not the public — a CIA instructional manual on interrogation used in at least seven Latin American countries in the 1980s. *The Human Resource Exploitation Training Manual,* adapting methods outlined in *Kubark* two decades earlier, cautioned against physical torture in favor of non-physical coercive techniques: "debility, disorientation, and dread." The 1983 manual suggests, among other techniques, "persistent manipulation of time," "disrupting sleep schedules" and "serving meals at odd times." The CIA declassified and released both manuals in 1997 in response to the threat of a Freedom of Information Act suit by *The Baltimore Sun.* [25]

'Using Any Means'

Within weeks of the 9/11 attacks, the CIA was tasked with helping capture and then interrogate high-ranking officials in the al Qaeda terrorist network despite the agency's lack of recent experience in questioning adversaries. Some "high-value" detainees were kept in secret prisons and questioned using the "enhanced" techniques approved by the Justice Department despite concerns among some operatives about the reaction to their eventual disclosure. With information leaking out, the Bush administration eventually discarded the harsh measures and in September 2006 transferred the remaining 14 detainees from CIA prisons to Guantánamo. Even with the Obama administration's change in policy, however, some Bush officials and supporters of the former administration continue to defend both the legality and effectiveness of the interrogations. [26]

Vice President Cheney set the mood for the administration's war on terror with his statement on NBC's "Meet the Press" on Sept. 16, 2001, that the government would "have to work through sort of the dark side if you will. . . . It's going to be vital for us to use any means at our disposal, basically, to achieve our objective," Cheney said. [27] Against that backdrop, the CIA seemed the logical choice for any off-the-books counterterrorism work. And the agency had an interest in restoring its reputation after a major pre-9/11 failure: The CIA had failed to notify domestic law enforcement of the entry into the United States of two known al Qaeda operatives who later became two of the 9/11 hijackers.

As journalist Jane Mayer relates in her sharply critical book, *The Dark Side*, the agency had focused on where to house high-value detainees in late 2001 and early 2002, before it even had anyone in custody. Guantánamo, chosen to hold those captured by the military in Afghanistan, was rejected as too visible; a suggestion to use perpetually circumnavigating aircraft was rejected as impractical. Eventually, friendly governments were asked and agreed to provide secret sites for the detainees transported under the so-called "extraordinary rendition" program. Thailand, Lithuania, Poland and Romania were later identified, but none acknowledged their role.

Meanwhile, the agency had turned to a retired military psychologist, John Mitchell, to prepare a paper on al Qaeda's resistance techniques. Mitchell and his partner and fellow psychologist John Bruce Jessen had served in the Air Force in a program called Survival, Evasion, Resistance, Escape (SERE) that trained U.S. service members in countering coercive techniques that an adversary might employ. As the CIA inspector general's report notes, the pair "developed a list of new and more

aggressive EITs that they recommended for use in interrogations." [28]

The capture of the senior al Qaeda operative Abu Zubaydah in Pakistan in late March 2002 provided the template for the CIA's enhanced interrogations. Zubaydah, an al Qaeda veteran believed to be personally close to Osama bin Laden, was captured in a joint raid by FBI, CIA and Pakistani law-enforcement and intelligence officers outside Faisalabad. With the badly wounded Zubaydah in custody, the FBI team was pushed aside by a CIA team headed by Mitchell. The measures used on Zubaydah, including being confined in a coffin-like box and waterboarded, formed the basis of the Aug. 2, 2002, Office of Legal Counsel opinion sanctioning a total of 10 enhanced techniques. The memo carried the signature of Jay Bybee, who had the rank of assistant attorney general as head of the office, but was actually written by his deputy, John Yoo, a soft-spoken but hard-edged proponent of expansive presidential power on leave from the University of California's Berkeley Law School.

According to later information, Nashiri became the second detainee to be waterboarded following his capture in November 2002. The inspector general's investigation of the program began in January 2003; the report is ambiguous as to whether the account of Nashiri's treatment was the catalyst. Even with the internal probe going on, however, CIA interrogators conducted the most extensive use of coercive measures two months later after the capture of the highest-value detainee: Khalid Shaikh Mohammed.

The self-described mastermind of the 9/11 hijackings, KSM, as he came to be known, was captured on March 1, 2003, in Rawalpindi, Pakistan, thanks to a $25 million reward paid to an informant. The inspector general's report states that he was waterboarded 183 times, but the remainder of the account of his treatment is redacted in the version released in August. Mohammed himself later described being kept naked for more than

a month, chained to a wall in a painful crouch, subjected alternately to extreme heat or cold and doused with water. Mohammed's interrogation is the focal point of the dispute over the need or effectiveness of these coercive measures. Supporters say KSM provided invaluable information but only after use of the enhanced techniques. Opponents say he was glad to boast of his role in al Qaeda but also deliberately fed false information to his interrogators.

As some in the agency had feared, the details of the CIA interrogations slowly leaked out, but only after pictures of abuses of Iraqi prisoners by U.S. military personnel at Abu Ghraib prison gained worldwide attention in April and May 2004. It also was revealed that leaders of the congressional intelligence oversight committees, who had been secretly briefed on the CIA's activities, had raised no public objections.

By 2005, CIA and military interrogators were being publicly implicated in deaths of detainees in Afghanistan and Iraq. In the most notorious case, Manadel al-Jamadi, an Iraqi suspected in the bombing of a Red Cross office in Baghdad, died in November 2003 during interrogation by Navy SEALS and a CIA interrogator. An image of Jamadi's ice-packed corpse with a smiling U.S. service member standing over it was among the Abu Ghraib photos published in 2004. In February 2005, The Associated Press reported that Jamadi died while hung from his wrists — a technique dubbed "Palestinian hanging." In October, the ACLU reported that documents obtained in Freedom of Information Act litigation showed at least 44 detainees' deaths during interrogation, with 21 of those classified in official autopsies as homicides. A report by the group Human Rights First published in February 2006 raised the number of deaths to 100, with 34 classified as homicides. [29]

The controversies spawned by the Abu Ghraib photographs and detainees' deaths helped drive Congress to pass the Detainee Treatment Act of 2005, with a ban on "cruel, inhuman or degrading treatment" of detainees. The provision was written by Sen. John McCain, the Arizona Republican who was held by North Vietnam as a prisoner of war for five years, and reluctantly accepted by President Bush. But the ban applied only to military interrogators, not to the CIA.

Meanwhile, *The Washington Post* had published in November 2005 a well-informed story on the CIA's secret prisons and its program of "extraordinary renditions." [30] Unbeknownst to the public at the time, the International Committee for the Red Cross (ICRC), officially designated under the Geneva Conventions to monitor wartime captives, was denied any access to the detainees despite repeatedly expressing concerns about their whereabouts. ICRC monitors were first allowed to visit the detainees in October 2006, after their transfers to Guantánamo. In a confidential report written in February 2007 and disclosed by author-journalist Mark Danner in March 2009, the ICRC described the prisoners' allegations of their treatment as amounting to "torture and/or cruel, inhuman or degrading treatment." [31]

Bush's decision in September 2006 to transfer the high-value detainees to Guantánamo symbolized the retreat on the issue. But the prisoners were still kept separate from other detainees. And through the end of the administration, both Bush and Cheney continued to defend the interrogation program as the key to having prevented al Qaeda from any subsequent attacks on U.S. soil. ∎

CURRENT SITUATION

Fighting Over Disclosure

The Obama administration is continuing to resist disclosure of some details of the CIA's interrogation program, even after disavowing the harsh measures used on some "high-value" detainees and shutting down the secret prisons once used to hold them.

The administration is invoking national security and other grounds in federal court filings to block release of hundreds of documents that the ACLU and other civil liberties and veterans' groups are seeking from the CIA through Freedom of Information Act (FOIA) litigation. *

The documents withheld include President George W. Bush's original Sept. 17, 2001, order authorizing the CIA's detention and interrogation program and scores of messages between CIA headquarters and field operatives on implementation of the program. Also being withheld are some documents pertaining to the CIA's destruction of 92 videotapes of the interrogations in November 2005 and the contents of the tapes. [32]

John Durham, a career federal prosecutor in Connecticut, was designated in 2008 by Attorney General Michael Mukasey to conduct an independent investigation of the destruction of the tapes; Durham was then chosen by Attorney General Holder to review the cases involving CIA interrogation of detainees.

President Obama has declassified and ordered the release of some of the documents sought in the litigation, including the CIA inspector general's critical May 2004 report on the program. In court filings, however, CIA Director Panetta and an agency FOIA officer are warning that further releases could do "exceptionally grave damage" to national security, endanger cooperation with foreign intelligence services and expose individual CIA officers to "grave risk."

The legal scrapping on the CIA issues is playing out in front of a federal judge in New York City, Alvin

---

* Other plaintiffs in the litigation are the Center for Constitutional Rights, Physicians for Human Rights, Veterans for Common Sense and Veterans for Peace.

Hellerstein, who previously chastised the Bush administration for its "glacial pace" in responding to the ACLU litigation. Hellerstein is scheduled to hear arguments on Sept. 30 on the ACLU's objections to some redactions in three Justice Department memos released on April 16 and to the withholding of the documents pertaining to the destruction of the videotapes. [33]

Meanwhile, in a separate part of the FOIA litigation, the government is asking the Supreme Court to block the release of photographs of abuse of prisoners held by the military in seven facilities in Afghanistan and Iraq. The New York-based 2nd U.S. Circuit Court of Appeals ruled in September 2008 in favor of the ACLU's FOIA request for the photographs, which are in addition to photographs already released of prisoners at Abu Ghraib being abused.

The Justice Department originally decided not to appeal, but in May Obama said that release of the photos could harm U.S. service members abroad by inflaming anti-American sentiment. The government is arguing the photographs fall within the Freedom of Information Act's exemption for "information compiled for law enforcement purposes" that "could reasonably be expected to endanger the life or physical safety of any individual." In its ruling, the appeals court said the government's use of the exemption was too broad. [34]

In the CIA case, the government's legal arguments are based on four other exemptions from the information act, which protect classified information, information specifically exempted by other statutes, attorney-client communications and personnel and medical files. In broader terms, the CIA's most recent court filing, on Aug. 31, warns that further disclosures regarding the interrogation program are "reasonably likely to degrade the [U.S. government's] ability to effectively question terrorist detainees." In addition, the agency says that disclosure of cooperation from

Continued on p. 806

At Issue:

Did harsh CIA interrogations amount to torture?

DAVID KAYE
*EXECUTIVE DIRECTOR, UCLA SCHOOL OF
LAW INTERNATIONAL HUMAN RIGHTS
PROGRAM*

WRITTEN FOR *CQ RESEARCHER*, SEPTEMBER 2009

Senior officials in the Bush administration initiated and authorized a policy of harsh treatment of terrorism suspects held by the United States. Recent documents released by the Obama administration — some only released under court orders — demonstrate that CIA interrogation techniques included waterboarding, extensive sleep deprivation, forced confinement in extremely small spaces, threats with handguns and power drills, threats against the lives and well-being of detainees' family members, severe stress positions, "walling" detainees by slamming them against fixed spaces during interrogations, forced standing and shackling, exposure to cold and other forms of torture or cruel, inhuman or degrading treatment.

In my opinion, these techniques constituted torture or, at a minimum, cruel or inhuman treatment prohibited by U.S. law.

Since the United States had long been at the forefront of objecting to torture under any circumstance, it should not be a surprise that the U.S. government, prior to 2001, had joined many treaties that prohibit torture — including the 1949 Geneva Conventions, the 1966 International Covenant on Civil and Political Rights and the 1984 Convention Against Torture — and enacted domestic laws criminalizing it. The anti-torture statute in the U.S. Code prohibits acts "specifically intended to inflict severe physical or mental pain or suffering," defining such mental pain or suffering as, among other things, "the threat of imminent death." The War Crimes Act similarly prohibits torture and cruel or inhuman treatment (such as "serious physical abuse"). Neither permits any sort of exceptional circumstance to justify torture.

As a bipartisan report of the Senate Armed Services Committee underscored last year, the Justice Department under President Bush distorted the meaning of these criminal laws beyond recognition, approving harsh techniques that the United States has condemned in other contexts. Many of the abuses noted above are prohibited under any good-faith reading of U.S. law, some plainly constituting torture. Take waterboarding, which creates a profound sensation of drowning and imminent death: Even one application amounts to the kind of physical and mental abuse prohibited by U.S. law, but interrogators applied it 83 times to one detainee and 183 times to another, according to the CIA inspector general.

While the argument against prosecuting CIA agents for these acts may be understandable, the argument that these techniques are permitted by U.S. law is simply wrong. As we consider the kind of detention policy our country deserves, defining our past conduct in the proper terms — that is to say, recognizing it as torture, cruel and inhumane — is an important step forward.

JEFFREY F. ADDICOTT
*DIRECTOR, CENTER FOR TERRORISM LAW,
ST. MARY'S UNIVERSITY SCHOOL OF LAW*

FROM TESTIMONY SUBMITTED TO SENATE JUDICIARY
SUBCOMMITTEE ON ADMINISTRATIVE OVERSIGHT
AND THE COURTS, MAY 13, 2009.

In the context of the Department of Justice legal memorandums that approved certain CIA enhanced interrogation techniques, the issue is whether they amounted to "torture" — especially the use of "waterboarding" on high-value al-Qaeda detainees.

Since the detainees are not entitled to prisoner of war status, international law does not forbid interrogation. By its very nature, even the most reasonable interrogation process places the detainee in emotional duress and causes stress to his being — both physical and mental. Allegations of "torture" roll off the tongue with ease. Recognizing that not every alleged incident of interrogation or mistreatment necessarily satisfies the legal definition of torture, it is imperative that one view such allegations with a clear understanding of the applicable legal standards set out in law and judicial precedent.

In this manner, allegations or claims of illegal interrogation practices can be properly measured as falling above or below a particular legal threshold. In my legal opinion, the so-called CIA enhanced interrogation practices approved by the Department of Justice in several detailed legal memorandums did not constitute torture under international law or U.S. domestic law.

The 1984 U.N. Convention Against Torture and Other Cruel, Inhuman or Degrading Treatment or Punishment is the primary international agreement governing torture. It defines torture as:

"[A]ny act by which severe pain or suffering, whether physical or mental, is intentionally inflicted on a person for such purposes as obtaining . . . information or a confession."

Even the worst of the CIA techniques — waterboarding — would not constitute torture under the Torture Convention. (CIA waterboarding lasted no more than 40 seconds and appears similar to what we have done hundreds of times to our own military special-operations soldiers in training courses.)

As foreboding as the term enhanced interrogation techniques may sound, responsible debate must revolve around legal case law associated with interpreting the Torture Convention and not simply cases that use the word torture.

For example, in *Ireland v. United Kingdom*, the European Court of Human Rights ruled by a sweeping vote of 13-3 that certain British interrogation techniques used against suspected Irish terrorists — which included wall-standing for up to 30 hours and subjection to loud noises — were not torture. If the British techniques were deemed not to constitute torture by this leading court, then even the worst of the American interrogation techniques fell far below what the British interrogators practiced.

Continued from p. 804

other countries "would damage the CIA's relations with these foreign governments and could cause them to cease cooperating with the CIA on such matters."

ACLU lawyers call the administration's stance in the litigation inconsistent with President Obama's past criticisms of the Bush administration's policies. "It's disappointing that the government continues to withhold these vital documents that would fill in the remaining gaps in the public record," says ACLU legal fellow Abdo.

From the opposite side, the administration has faced pressure from within the CIA and from past CIA directors to limit disclosures. Former CIA Director Hayden was one of four past heads of the agency who contacted the White House in April to urge the president not to release the Justice Department memos approving use of the enhanced interrogation techniques. Appearing on "Fox News Sunday" at the time, Hayden said the disclosures were making it "more difficult for CIA officers to defend the nation." [35]

Human-rights advocates, however, say the public needs still more information about the detention and interrogation programs. "We've learned a lot," says John Sifton, a human-rights investigator and attorney in New York City. But, he adds, "there's still a lot of things that are unclear." [36]

Meanwhile, the ACLU filed a new FOIA suit in federal court in New York City on Sept. 22 seeking records from the Pentagon and the CIA on prisoners held at Bagram Air Force Base in Afghanistan. In announcing the suit, ACLU staff attorney Melissa Goodman described Bagram as "the new Guantánamo," but complained that the public "is still in the dark" about basic facts about the facility, including the number of prisoners and rules and conditions of confinement. The ACLU said that the Defense Department had identified a list of prisoners, but declined to release it on national security and privacy grounds. [37]

Getting to Trial?

The government is weighing its next move in the trial of the five CIA "high-value" detainees charged with helping plan the Sept. 11 attacks. In question is whether to continue prosecuting them in special military tribunals or move the trial to a regular federal court.

Justice Department attorneys disclosed the pending decision in court filings on Sept. 16 that opposed a motion by one of the detainees, Ramzi bin al-Shibh, seeking to bar all proceedings before the military commission already convened at Guantánamo to try the five. While opposing the motion, the lawyers also filed a new motion asking the military judges to temporarily stay the proceedings in order for the government to decide by mid-November whether to shift the trial to a civilian federal court.

The lawyers noted that Congress is currently considering changes to the Military Commissions Act, the 2006 law that added new procedural safeguards to the military commissions set up by the Bush administration in order to comply with a Supreme Court decision. [38] In addition, the lawyers pointed to "upcoming decisions" on the forum for the trial that would be made within 60 days by Attorney General Holder in consultation with Defense Secretary Robert Gates. [39]

The requested continuance — which the military judge granted on Sept. 21 — is the third delay since January in the government's highest-profile proceeding against detainees rounded up in other countries by the Bush administration. The lead defendant is Khalid Shaikh Mohammed, the accused chief planner of the 9/11 attacks and one of three CIA detainees known to have been waterboarded.

The trial was thrown into disarray on Dec. 8 when all five defendants said they wanted to plead guilty to the broad conspiracy charges filed against them in February 2008. The proceedings were put on hold, however, to allow the tribunal time to determine whether bin al-Sibh and a second defendant, Mustafa Ahmed al-Hawsawi, were mentally competent to decide to proceed without an attorney. Mohammed and two others had already been granted permission to represent themselves.

President Obama moved to put all the military commissions on hold after taking office in January as part of his promise to close Guantánamo within a year. He tasked Holder with deciding how to proceed against what were then the camp's remaining 241 prisoners. Since then, 14 inmates have been transferred to other countries and about 80 others approved for resettlement.

Bin al-Shibh has been described as the coordinator of the 9/11 attacks. Al-Hawsawi is alleged to have assisted, another of the defendants, Ali Abd al-Aziz Ali, in handling financial arrangements for the hijackers. Aziz Ali, also known as Ammar al-Baluchi, is a nephew of Mohammed and allegedly acted as his lieutenant for the operation. The fifth defendant, Waleed bin Attash, also known as Khallad, is alleged to have helped select and train some of the hijackers.

A sixth defendant, Mohammed al-Qahtani, was originally charged, but his case was dismissed in May 2008 without explanation. Al-Qahtani has been identified as the "twentieth hijacker" in the attacks because he tried to enter the United States before Sept. 11 but was denied entry. In January 2009, the presiding military judge, Susan Crawford, said she dismissed charges against al-Qahtani because she concluded he had been tortured at Guantánamo. [40]

The five remaining defendants are among 14 detainees from CIA sites who were transferred to Guantánamo in September 2006. The government has not brought formal charges against the other nine, who are challenging their detentions in federal habeas corpus proceedings. All nine were given hearings before the now disbanded combatant status review tribunals at

Guantánamo, which confirmed their status as "enemy combatants."

As part of its Freedom of Information Act litigation, the ACLU obtained redacted transcripts in June of some of those proceedings, including testimony by Mohammed and three others that they had been tortured or abused while in U.S. custody. Transcripts released during the Bush administration had deleted all references to abuse, the ACLU said. The transcripts quote Mohammed as saying he used to "make up stories" for CIA interrogators after being tortured. Al Nashiri, one of the waterboarded detainees, said that interrogators would "drown me in water." [41]

ACLU lawyers favor shutting down the military commissions altogether. "We have said from the beginning that these are illegitimate proceedings," says Denny LeBoeuf, head of the John Adams Project, a joint venture with the National Association of Criminal Defense Lawyers that is providing attorneys for detainees in the 9/11 and other capital cases.

LeBoeuf says that any evidence obtained by torture will not be allowed in either the military commissions or in federal courts, but that other evidence will be admissible. "There'll be civilian lawyers, there'll be military lawyers and they'll argue about what evidence should be admitted." In the end, she adds, "some people will get convicted." ∎

OUTLOOK

Change and Continuity

Four days after releasing details of the harsh interrogation measures used by the CIA against suspected terrorists, President Obama visited the agency's headquarters on a politically sensitive morale-boosting mission.

"Don't be discouraged by what's happened in the last few weeks,"

Obama told the assembled employees on April 20. The government's willingness to acknowledge "serious mistakes" and "move forward," Obama said, "is precisely why I am proud to be president of the United States, and that's why you should be proud to be members of the CIA." [42]

Four months later, Obama's attorney general undercut the president's efforts to reassure CIA employees by asking a federal prosecutor to investigate agency operatives who may have gone beyond the "enhanced interrogation techniques" that the Justice Department authorized. "Morale at the agency is down to minus 50," said A. B. "Buzzy" Krongard, the third-ranking CIA official at the time of the use of harsh interrogation practices. [43]

"The agency feared this day would come," says Amy Zegart, a professor of public policy at UCLA who has studied intelligence agencies' role in counterterrorism. "They did everything that was legally authorized by the Department of Justice and politically sanctioned by the White House. And now they feel they're being hung out to dry."

Some human-rights advocates are applauding Holder's decision to refer the CIA interrogation cases for further investigation. "It's important for the United States to be able to return to a system of operating under law," says Human Rights First executive director Massimino.

Many want Holder to go further. Human-rights investigator Sifton calls for an investigation of "any and all violations of law that took place in connection with the detention and interrogation program," including possible obstruction of justice by officials at the Justice Department and White House up to and including Vice President Cheney and President Bush. "No one wants to go after low-level CIA officers," Sifton says. "That's not accountability. That's scapegoating."

Others, however, disagree with Holder's decision. "I'm opposed to prosecutions," says Joseph Marguiles, a veteran human-rights advocate who is

representing Abu Zabaydah. Like other human-rights advocates, however, Marguiles strongly favors a full investigation by a congressional committee or independent commission.

Among the new proposals to emerge in that regard is a suggestion by Fred Hiatt, editorial page editor of the *Post*, for a "truth commission" to be chaired by two retired Supreme Court justices: Sandra Day O'Connor and David H. Souter. "A fair-minded commission," Hiatt wrote on Aug. 30, "could help the nation come to grips with its past and show the world that America is serious about doing so." [44]

The prospects for a full-blown investigation of that sort, however, appear to be dim. "I don't get any sense that the Obama administration is willing to see this full discussion take place," says Marguiles. "In fact, there's every indication they don't want it to take place." For her part, Zegart doubts that an investigation could produce a "sober" assessment in what she calls "this partisan, poisonous atmosphere."

National-security law expert Robert Chesney at the University of Texas Law School in Austin says Obama has tried to navigate the political shoals with measured steps in revising the Bush administration's counterterrorism policies. Obama has scrapped the "enhanced interrogation techniques" but continues to defend the power to detain enemy combatants with limited judicial review. He has changed review procedures at the prison camp at Bagram Air Force base in Afghanistan, but continues to oppose habeas corpus rights for the detainees there. The government is also continuing to invoke the state-secrets privilege in such cases as one in federal court in California seeking to hold CIA-contractor airlines liable for their role in transporting detainees to other countries.

"People are going to find what they want to find," says Chesney, who served this summer with the task force that Obama created on detention policy. "If they want to see continuity [with the Bush policies], they are going to see continuity. If they want to see change, they're going to see change."

The CIA's role in future interrogations remains to be worked out with the new high-value detainee information group that Obama created and placed under the FBI instead of the CIA. The plans call for interagency cooperation, but Zegart calls the plan a "terrible idea." "Since when did interagency processes work well in intelligence?" she asks.

In his visit to Langley, however, Obama tried his best to reassure the agency that it is still needed in dealing with terrorist threats. "We're going to have to operate smarter and more effectively than ever," Obama said in closing. "So I'm going to be relying on you, and the American people are going to rely on you." ■

Notes

[1] "Special Review: Counterterrorism Detention and Interrogation Activities (September 2001-October 2003)," Inspector General, Central Intelligence Agency, May 7, 2004, http://luxmedia.vo.llnwd.net/o10/clients/aclu/IG_Report.pdf. For coverage, see these stories by Peter Finn, Jory Warrick and Julie Tate in *The Washington Post*: "CIA Report Calls Oversight of Early Interrogations Poor," Aug. 25, 2009, p. A1; "CIA Releases Its Instructions on Breaking a Detainee's Will," Aug. 26, 2009, p. A1.

[2] For background on the ACLU litigation, see Scott Shane, "A.C.L.U. Lawyers Mine Documents for Truth," *The New York Times*, Aug. 30, 2009, sec. 1, p. 4. The ACLU maintains a comprehensive archive of documents in the litigation: www.aclu.org/safefree/torture/index.html. For a compilation of some of the documents and a narrative overview, see Jameel Jeffer and Amrit Singh, *Administration of Torture: A Documentary Record from Washington to Abu Ghraib and Beyond* (2007).

[3] For background, see these *CQ Researcher* reports: Kenneth Jost, "Closing Guantánamo," Feb. 27, 2009, pp. 177-200; Kenneth Jost and the *CQ Researcher* Staff, "The Obama Presidency," Jan. 30, 2009, pp. 73-104; Peter Katel and Kenneth Jost, "Treatment of Detainees," Aug. 25, 2006, pp. 673-696. See also Seth Stern, "Torture Debate," *CQ Global Researcher*, September 2007, pp. 211-236.

[4] For transcript, see www.foxnews.com/story/0,2933,544522,00.html. For coverage of comments from others, see Rachel L. Swarns, "Cheney Offers Sharp Defense of C.I.A. Tactics," *The New York Times*, Aug. 31, 2009, p. A1.

[5] See Carrie Johnson, Jerry Markon and Julie Tate, "Inquiry Into CIA Practices Narrow," *The Washington Post*, Sept. 19, 2009, p. A1. The full text of the letter can be found on RealPolitics.com: www.realclearpolitics.com/politics_nation/cialetter0918.pdf. For Obama's reply, see CBS "Face the Nation," Sept. 20, 2009, www.cbsnews.com/stories/2009/09/20/ftn/main5324077.shtml?tag=cbsnewsTwoColUpperPromoArea.

[6] "Special Task Force on Interrogations and Transfer Policies Issues Its Recommendations to the President," Department of Justice, Aug. 24, 2009, www.usdoj.gov/opa/pr/2009/August/09-ag-835.html. For coverage, see Anne E. Kornblut, "New Unit to Question Key Terror Suspects," *The Washington Post*, Aug. 24, 2009, p. A1.

[7] See "Statement of President Barack Obama on Release of OLC Memos," April 16, 2009, www.whitehouse.gov/the_press_office/Statement-of-President-Barack-Obama-on-Release-of-OLC-Memos/. For coverage, see Mark Mazzetti and Scott Shane, "Memos Spell Out Brutal Mode of C.I.A. Interrogation," *The New York Times*, April 17, 2009, p. A1.

[8] Estes Thompson, "Ex-CIA Contractor Guilty in Afghan Death," The Associated Press, Aug. 18, 2006. Passaro was convicted of assault with a dangerous weapon and assault with intent to inflict serious injury. He was sentenced in 2007 to eight-and-a-half-years in prison, but the 4th U.S. Circuit Court of Appeals on Aug. 10, 2009, ordered resentencing on the ground that Judge Terence Boyle had not justified a sentence longer than recommended under the federal sentencing guidelines.

[9] See Jeffrey H. Smith, "CIA Accountability," *The Washington Post*, Aug. 24, 2009, p. A15; Walter Pincus and Jory Warrick, "Ex-Intelligence Officials Cite Low Spirits at CIA," *ibid.*, Aug. 30, 2009, p. A2.

[10] The veto message appears in the *Congressional Record* on March 10, 2008: http://fas.org/irp/congress/2008_cr/veto.html. For coverage, see Steven Lee Myers, "Bush Vetoes Bill on C.I.A. Tactics, Affirming Legacy," *The New York Times*, March 9, 2008, p. A1.

[11] "Executive Order — Ensuring Lawful Interrogations," Jan. 22, 2009, www.whitehouse.gov/the_press_office/EnsuringLawfulInterrogations/.

[12] "Special Review," *op. cit.*, p. 100.

[13] Barton Gellman, "Cheney Uncloaks His Frustration With Bush," *The Washington Post*, Aug. 13, 2009, p. A1.

[14] *The 9/11 Commission Report: Final Report of the National Commission on Terrorist Attacks Upon the United States*, 2004. For background, see Kenneth Jost, "Re-examining 9/11," *CQ Researcher*, June 4, 2004, pp. 493-516.

[15] Other groups include Amnesty International USA, Human Rights First, Human Rights Watch, Open Society Institute, Physicians for Human Rights and Rutherford Institute. For a complete list, see www.commissiononaccountability.org/.

[16] Quoted in Bennett Roth, "Democrats Split on Interrogation Inquiry," *CQ Weekly*, April 27, 2009, p. 978.

[17] Background drawn from Alfred W. McCoy, *A Question of Torture: CIA Interrogation, from the Cold War to the War on Terror* (2006), pp. 16-20; Pauletta Otis, "Educing Information: The Right Initiative at the Right Time by the Right People," in Intelligence Science Board, "Educing Information: Interrogation: Science and Art; Foundations for the Future: Phase 1 Report," December 2006, pp. xv-xx. See also Stern, *op. cit.*; David Masci, "Torture," *CQ Researcher*, April 18, 2003, pp. 345-368.

About the Author

Associate Editor **Kenneth Jost** graduated from Harvard College and Georgetown University Law Center. He is the author of the *Supreme Court Yearbook* and editor of *The Supreme Court from A to Z* (both *CQ Press*). He was a member of the *CQ Researcher* team that won the American Bar Association's 2002 Silver Gavel Award. His previous reports include "Closing Guantánamo" and "The Obama Presidency" (with *CQ Researcher* staff). He is also author of the blog *Jost on Justice* (http://jostonjusticeblogspot.com).

[18] McCoy, *op. cit.*, p. 16.

[19] Ernest Jerome Hopkins, *Our Lawless Police* (1931), quoted in Richard A. Leo, "From Coercion To Deception: The Changing Nature of Police Interrogation in America," *Crime, Law and Social Change*, Vol. 18 (1992), p. 35.

[20] The decision is *Miranda v. Arizona*, 384 U.S. 436 (1966).

[21] Petula Dvorak, "Fort Hunt's Quiet Men Break Silence on WWII," *The Washington Post*, Oct. 6, 2007, p. A1; Roni Gehlke, "New book out about Byron's Camp Tracy," *Contra Costa* (Calif.) *Times*, July 8, 2009. The referenced book is Alexander Corbin, *The History of Camp Tracy: Japanese WWII POWs and the Future of Strategic Interrogation* (2009).

[22] For background, see McCoy, *op. cit.*, chs. 2 & 3; Laura L. Finley, "The Central Intelligence Agency and Torture," in *The Torture and Prisoner Abuse Debate* (2008).

[23] McCoy, *op. cit.*, pp. 24-25.

[24] *Ibid.*, pp. 68-69.

[25] See Gary Cohn, Ginger Thompson and Mark Matthews, "Torture was taught by CIA," *The Baltimore Sun*, Jan. 27, 1997.

[26] Background drawn from Jane Mayer, *The Dark Side: How the War on Terror Turned Into a War on American Ideals* (2008). See also "Special Review," *op. cit.* Approximately 100 prisoners were held at the secret CIA sites at one time or another.

[27] Quoted in Mayer, *op. cit.*, pp. 9-10.

[28] "Special Review," p. 13; the report does not identify Mitchell and Jessen by name. See also Mayer, *op. cit.*, pp. 157-158.

[29] See Seth Hettena, "Iraqi Died While Hung From Wrists," The Associated Press, Feb. 17, 2005; "U.S. Operatives Killed Detainees During Interrogations in Afghanistan and Iraq, CIA, Navy Seals and Military Intelligence Personnel Implicated," American Civil Liberties Union, Oct. 24, 2005, www.aclu.org/intlhumanrights/gen/21236prs20051024.html; Human Rights First, "Command's Responsibility: Detainee Deaths in U.S. Custody in Iraq and Afghanistan," February 2006, www.humanrightsfirst.org/us_law/etn/dic/exec-sum.aspx. For an account of Jamadi's interrogation and death, see Mayer, *op. cit.*, pp. 238-258. Mark Swanner, the CIA interrogator, has denied any wrongdoing; Mayer said the agency's inspector general referred the case to the Justice Department "for possible criminality," but no charges were brought.

[30] Dana Priest, "CIA Holds Terror Suspects in Secret Prisons," *The Washington Post*, Nov. 2, 2005, p. A1. Priest won a Pulitzer Prize for her reporting on the sites.

[31] Mark Danner, "U.S. Torture: Voices from the Black Sites," *New York Review of Books*, April 9, 2009. The ICRC keeps its reports confidential to preserve its impartiality with individual governments. After Danner obtained the report, the *New York Review* posted the complete document on its Web site: www.nybooks.com/icrc-report.pdf.

[32] See Mark Mazzetti, "U.S. Says CIA Destroyed 92 Tapes of Interrogations," *The New York Times*, March 3, 2009, p. A16.

[33] The consolidated cases are *American Civil Liberties Union v. Dep't of Defense*, 04 Civ. 4151, and *American Civil Liberties Union v. Dep't of Justice*, 05-9620. For coverage of Panetta's declaration, see R. Jeffrey Smith, "CIA Urges Judge to Keep Bush-Era Documents Sealed," *The Washington Post*, June 9, 2009, p. A1.

[34] The Supreme Court case is *U.S. Defense Dep't v. American Civil Liberties Union*, 09-160. For coverage, including links to the government's petition and the lower court ruling, see Lyle Denniston, "Transparency in wartime at issue," SCOTUSBlog, Aug. 24, 2009, www.scotusblog.com/wp/transparency-in-wartime-at-issue/. See also Adam Liptak, "Obama's About-Face on Detainee Photos Leads to Supreme Court," *The New York Times*, Sept. 15, 2009, p. A13.

[35] "Fox News Sunday," April 19, 2009, www.foxnews.com/story/0,2933,517158,00.html.

[36] See John Sifton, "What's Missing from the CIA Docs," *The Daily Beast*, Aug. 25, 2009, www.thedailybeast.com/blogs-and-stories/2009-08-25/whats-missing-from-the-cia-docs/.

[37] The case is *ACLU v. Dep't of Defense*, 09 CV 8071 (S.D.N.Y.) For background, see Bagram FOIA (8/13/2009), www.aclu.org/safefree/detention/40715res20090813.html.

[38] The decision is *Hamdan v. Rumsfeld*, 548 U.S. 557 (2006). For an account, see Kenneth Jost, *The Supreme Court Yearbook 2005-2006*.

[39] For coverage, including a link to the government's filing, see Lyle Denniston, "Decision soon on 9/11 trials," SCOTUSBlog, Sept. 16, 2009, www.scotusblog.com/wp/decision-soon-on-911-trials/. See also David Johnston, "U.S. Seeking 3rd Delay on Guantánamo Cases," *The New York Times*, Sept. 17, 2009, p. A17, from which some background has been drawn.

[40] Bob Woodward, "Detainee Tortured, U.S. Official," *The Washington Post*, Jan. 14, 2009, p. A1.

[41] See "Newly Released Detainee Statements Provide More Evidence of CIA Torture Program," June 15, 2009, www.aclu.org/safefree/torture/39868prs20090615.html. For coverage, see Julian E. Barnes and Greg Miller, "Detainee says he lied to the CIA," *Los Angeles Times*, June 16, 2009, p. A1.

[42] The text of the speech is on the CIA's Web site: www.cia.gov/news-information/speeches-testimony/president-obama-at-cia.html. For coverage, see Peter Baker and Scott Shane, "Pressure Grows to Investigate Interrogations," *The New York Times*, April 21, 2009, p. A1.

[43] See Pincus and Warrick, *op. cit.*, p. A2.

[44] Fred Hiatt, "Time for a Souter-O'Connor Commission," *The Washington Post*, Aug. 30, 2009, p. A21.

Bibliography

Selected Sources

Books

Finley, Laura L., *The Torture and Prisoner Abuse Debate*, Greenwood Press, 2008.

The book, part of Greenwood's "Historical Guides to Controversial Issues in America," includes chapters on the origins of torture, the CIA and torture and abusive interrogations and detentions in Afghanistan and Iraq and at Guantánamo. Finley teaches in the women's studies department at Florida Atlantic University. Includes chapter notes, seven-page bibliography.

Mayer, Jane, *The Dark Side: How the War on Terror Turned Into a War on American Ideals*, Doubleday, 2008.

The book details the origins and implementation of harsh interrogation practices by military and CIA interrogators after Sept. 11 and strongly criticizes the practices on legal, moral and pragmatic grounds. Mayer is an author and staff writer for *The New Yorker*. Includes notes, bibliography.

McCoy, Alfred W., *A Question of Torture: CIA Interrogation, from the Cold War to the War on Terror*, Metropolitan Books, 2006.

A professor of history at the University of Wisconsin traces the history of the CIA's controversial interrogation practices. Includes notes, 23-page bibliography.

Wittes, Benjamin, *Law and the Long War: The Future of Justice in the Age of Terror*, Penguin, 2008.

A leading researcher on national security argues for legislation to authorize administrative detention of suspected enemy combatants and some methods of interrogation at least for the CIA beyond those authorized in the *U.S. Army Field Manual*. Wittes is a research fellow at the Brookings Institution and a member of the Hoover Institution's National Security Task Force. His paper co-authored with Stuart Taylor Jr., "Looking Forward, Not Backward: Refining American Interrogation Law," is being published in *Legislating the War on Terror: An Agenda for Reform* (Brookings, 2009).

Articles

Herman, Arthur, "The Gitmo Myth and the Torture Canard," *Commentary*, June 2009, www.commentarymagazine.com/viewarticle.cfm/the-gitmo-myth-and-the-torture-canard-15154?search=1.

The historian and longtime *Commentary* contributor argues that reports of abusive interrogation by the military and CIA have been exaggerated, part of a "Gitmo myth" created to "ruin the Bush administration" and "blacken" the United States' reputation.

Sullivan, Andrew, "Dear President Bush," *The Atlantic*, October 2009, p. 78, www.theatlantic.com/doc/200910/bush-torture.

The well-known author-journalist lays out a searing critique of detention and interrogation practices by the military and the CIA and asks former President George W. Bush to support "a full accounting and report from an independent body."

Reports and Studies

"Educing Information: Interrogation: Science and Art; Foundations for the Future: Phase 1 Report," Intelligence Science Board NDIC Press, December 2006, www1.umn.edu/humanrts/OathBetrayed/Intelligence%20Science%20Board%202006.pdf.

The official advisory body at the National Defense Intelligence College laments the limited knowledge about the efficacy of specific interrogation techniques and recommends scientific studies on the questions. Includes introductory essays, 10 scientific papers and annotated bibliography.

"Inquiry Into the Treatment of Detainees in U.S. Custody," Senate Armed Services Committee, Nov. 20, 2008, as declassified April 20, 2009, http://graphics8.nytimes.com/packages/images/nytint/docs/report-by-the-senate-armed-services-committee-on-detainee-treatment/original.pdf.

The report provides the most thorough accounting to date of the harsh interrogation practices approved at the highest levels of the Bush administration.

Bibliographic Note

The Bush administration's "war on terror" has already produced a number of accounts, some from participants, others from journalists. In his memoir, *At the Center of the Storm: My Years at the CIA* (HarperCollins, 2007), former CIA Director George Tenet writes boastfully of the agency's interrogation of "high-value" detainees. In *The Terror Presidency: Law and Judgment Inside the Bush Administration* (W.W. Norton, 2007), Jack L. Goldsmith, former head of the Justice Department's Office of Legal Counsel, writes of his role in rescinding OLC memos approving "enhanced-interrogation techniques."

Two journalist authors published books in 2006 detailing what was then known about CIA interrogations: Ron Suskind, *The One Percent Doctrine: Deep Inside America's Pursuit of Its Enemies Since 9/11* (Simon & Schuster), and James Risen, *State of War: The Secret History of the CIA and the Bush Administration*. (Thorndike Press).

The Next Step:

Additional Articles from Current Periodicals

Enhanced Interrogation Techniques

Cillizza, Chris, "Some Call It Torture. In One Poll, Most Call It Justified," *The Washington Post*, May 18, 2009, p. A2.

Most Americans believe that enhanced interrogation techniques amount to torture, but a majority also think such techniques have made the country safer.

Meyer, Josh, "Eric Holder: Waterboarding Is Torture," *Chicago Tribune*, Jan. 16, 2009.

Attorney General Eric Holder told the Senate Judiciary Committee during his nomination hearing that waterboarding constitutes torture.

Miller, Greg, "Cheney Defends Harsh Tactics," *Chicago Tribune*, Aug. 26, 2009, p. A14.

Former Vice President Dick Cheney has defended the Bush administration's enhanced interrogation techniques despite criticism from President Barack Obama.

Thiessen, Marc A., "The CIA's Questioning Worked," *The Washington Post*, April 21, 2009, p. A23.

Memos made public by the Obama administration indicate that enhanced interrogation techniques have been effective.

Extraordinary Rendition

Egelko, Bob, "Obama Justice Dept. Keeps Bush Stance on Rendition Lawsuits," *The San Francisco Chronicle*, Feb. 10, 2009, p. A9.

Although Obama has issued bans on torture and closures for secret prisons, he has sent mixed signals on the practice of extraordinary rendition.

Eisler, Peter, "Panetta Outlines New U.S. Rendition Policy," *USA Today*, Feb. 6, 2009, p. 4A.

CIA Director Leon Panetta said the United States will stop sending terrorism suspects to nations in which they are likely to be tortured.

Sell, Julie, "U.N. Report Says U.S. Led 'Black Site' Renditions in War on Terrorism," *The Miami Herald*, March 11, 2009, p. A9.

The United States has violated international law in carrying out extraordinary renditions and torture of terror suspects, according to a report by the U.N. Human Rights Council.

Prosecutions

Nicholas, Peter, and Greg Miller, "Obama Open to Inquiry on CIA Tactics," *Los Angeles Times*, April 22, 2009, p. A1.

President Obama has said that CIA agents suspected of torture won't face prosecution, but that those who created the legal framework might.

Rotella, Sebastian, and Maria De Cristofaro, "Italian Court Rules Against Prosecution in CIA Case," *Los Angeles Times*, March 13, 2009, p. A26.

Italian prosecutors are pursuing a case against U.S. intelligence agents accused of abducting an Egyptian extremist in Milan.

Sisk, Richard, "Prosecutor to Review CIA Agents," *Daily News*, Aug. 25, 2009, p. 22.

Attorney General Eric Holder named a special prosecutor to investigate the alleged torture of suspected terrorists.

Secret Prisons

DeYoung, Karen, "CIA Has Quit Operating Secret Jails, Chief Says," *The Washington Post*, April 10, 2009, p. A3.

The Central Intelligence Agency no longer operates any secret prisons overseas, according to new Director Leon Panetta.

Hess, Pamela, "Red Cross Accuses CIA of Torture," The Associated Press, March 17, 2009.

The Red Cross has accused the CIA of torturing 14 "high-value detainees" in secret prisons overseas.

Johnston, David, and Mark Mazzetti, "A Window Into C.I.A.'s Embrace of Secret Jails," *The New York Times*, Aug. 13, 2009, p. A1.

Overseas CIA secret prisons were built to house about six detainees each, according to a former agency official.

Miller, Greg, "CIA's Black Sites, Illuminated," *Los Angeles Times*, Aug. 31, 2009.

The CIA's secret overseas "black sites" have been dismantled, eluding inspection by congressional committees and the International Red Cross.

In-depth Reports on Issues in the News

Are you writing a paper?

Need backup for a debate?

Want to become an expert on an issue?

For more than 80 years, students have turned to *CQ Researcher* for in-depth reporting on issues in the news. Reports on a full range of political and social issues are now available. Following is a selection of recent reports:

Civil Liberties
Closing Guantánamo, 2/09
Affirmative Action, 10/08
Gay Marriage Showdowns, 9/08
America's Border Fence, 9/08
Immigration Debate, 2/08

Crime/Law
Examining Forensics, 7/09
Legalizing Marijuana, 6/09
Mexico's Drug War, 12/08
Prostitution Debate, 5/08
Public Defenders, 4/08

Education
Reading Crisis? 2/08
Discipline in Schools, 2/08
Student Aid, 1/08

Environment/Society
Gays in the Military, 9/09
Energy and Climate, 7/09
Future of Books, 5/09
Hate Groups, 5/09
Future of Journalism, 3/09
Confronting Warming, 1/09
Reducing Carbon Footprint, 12/08

Health/Safety
Health-Care Reform, 8/09
Straining the Safety Net, 7/09
Treating Depression, 6/09
Reproductive Ethics, 5/09
Extreme Sports, 4/09
Regulating Toxic Chemicals, 1/09

Politics/Economy
State Budget Crisis, 9/09
Business Bankruptcy, 4/09
Future of the GOP, 3/09
Middle-Class Squeeze, 3/09

Upcoming Reports

Nuclear Armaments, 10/2/09	Manned Spaceflight, 10/9/09	Prescription Drug Abuse, 10/16/09

ACCESS

CQ Researcher is available in print and online. For access, visit your library or www.cqresearcher.com.

STAY CURRENT

To receive notice of upcoming *CQ Researcher* reports, or learn more about *CQ Researcher* products, subscribe to the free e-mail newsletters, *CQ Researcher Alert!* and *CQ Researcher News*: http://cqpress.com/newsletters.

PURCHASE

To purchase a *CQ Researcher* report in print or electronic format (PDF), visit www.cqpress.com or call 866-427-7737. Single reports start at $15. Bulk purchase discounts and electronic-rights licensing are also available.

SUBSCRIBE

Annual full-service *CQ Researcher* subscriptions—including 44 reports a year, monthly index updates, and a bound volume—start at $803. Add $25 for domestic postage.

CQ Researcher Online offers a backfile from 1991 and a number of tools to simplify research. For pricing information, call 800-834-9020, ext. 1906, or e-mail librarysales@cqpress.com.

Published by CQ Press, a Division of SAGE

www.cqresearcher.com

Nuclear Disarmament

Will President Obama's efforts make the U.S. safer?

P eace activists have sought to eliminate nuclear weapons for decades, but now they have a new ally. President Barack Obama has pledged to negotiate new U.S.-Russian arms reductions, end U.S. nuclear testing and reduce the role of nuclear weapons in national defense policy. Obama argues that these steps, plus new measures to combat nuclear smuggling and theft, will make the United States safer. But critics say further nuclear cuts will embolden rogue countries like North Korea and Iran, which are widely thought to be seeking nuclear capabilities. Although the U.S. and Russia have drastically shrunk their Cold War arsenals, the United States still spends at least $52 billion annually on nuclear-related programs. Liberals and conservatives sharply disagree about addressing post-Cold War security threats with nuclear arms. But some experts warn that new, regional nuclear arms races could break out if the U.S. fails to rebuild global support for nuclear reductions.

A submarine-launched Trident missile — capable of carrying multiple nuclear warheads — lifts off during a test.

CQ Researcher • Oct. 2, 2009 • www.cqresearcher.com
Volume 19, Number 34 • Pages 813-836

Cover: AP Photo/Lockheed Martin Corp.

Oct. 2, 2009
Volume 19, Number 34

MANAGING EDITOR: Thomas J. Colin
tcolin@cqpress.com

ASSISTANT MANAGING EDITOR: Kathy Koch
kkoch@cqpress.com

ASSOCIATE EDITOR: Kenneth Jost

STAFF WRITERS: Thomas J. Billitteri,
Marcia Clemmitt, Peter Katel

CONTRIBUTING WRITERS: Rachel Cox,
Sarah Glazer, Alan Greenblatt, Reed Karaim
Barbara Mantel, Patrick Marshall,
Tom Price, Jennifer Weeks

DESIGN/PRODUCTION EDITOR: Olu B. Davis

ASSISTANT EDITOR: Darrell Dela Rosa

FACT-CHECKING: Eugene J. Gabler,
Michelle Harris

CQ PRESS

A Division of SAGE

PRESIDENT AND PUBLISHER:
John A. Jenkins

EXECUTIVE DIRECTOR,
REFERENCE INFORMATION GROUP:
Alix B. Vance

CQ Press is a registered trademark of Congressional Quarterly Inc.

CQ Researcher (ISSN 1056-2036) is printed on acid-free paper. Published weekly, except; (Jan. wk. 1) (May wk. 4) (July wks. 1, 2) (Aug. wks. 3, 4) (Nov. wk. 4) and (Dec. wk. 4), by CQ Press, a division of SAGE Publications. Annual full-service subscriptions start at $803. For pricing, call 1-800-834-9020, ext. 1906. To purchase a CQ Researcher report in print or electronic format (PDF), visit www. cqpress.com or call 866-427-7737. Single reports start at $15. Bulk purchase discounts and electronic-rights licensing are also available. Periodicals postage paid at Washington, D.C., and additional mailing offices. POSTMASTER: Send address changes to CQ Researcher, 2300 N St., N.W., Suite 800, Washington, DC 20037.

Nuclear Disarmament

BY JENNIFER WEEKS

THE ISSUES

Speaking to the United Nations General Assembly on Sept. 23, President Barack Obama pledged his administration would work with other nations to strengthen world peace and prosperity.

"First, we must stop the spread of nuclear weapons, and seek the goal of a world without them," Obama said. "If we fail to act, we will invite nuclear arms races in every region, and the prospect of wars and acts of terror on a scale that we can hardly imagine." [1]

It is an ambitious goal, especially for the United States. Nuclear weapons have been integral to U.S. defense policy since the end of World War II. Even today, nearly 20 years after the Cold War ended, the United States still spends more than $50 billion every year on nuclear armaments and related programs, including weapons systems, missile defenses and environmental and health costs from past nuclear weapons production. [2]

Many civilian and military experts say abolishing nuclear weapons is impossible. Moreover, they argue, doing so would make the world less safe, because rogue states and terrorists would feel freer to threaten other countries.

But in 2007, four men who had shaped U.S. national security policy for decades — both Democrats and Republicans — warned that relying on nuclear weapons to keep the peace was "becoming increasingly hazardous and decreasingly effective." The problem, said former secretaries of state Henry Kissinger and George Shultz, former Defense Secretary William Perry

President Barack Obama called for new efforts to stop the spread of nuclear weapons during an address before the U.N. General Assembly on Sept. 23. The next day the Security Council called for nuclear reductions and disarmament and tighter controls on nuclear technology. Many experts warn that abolishing nuclear weapons would make the world less safe, in part by enabling terrorists and rogue states to threaten other nations.

AFP/Getty Images/Stan Honda

and former Senate Armed Services Committee Chairman Sam Nunn, was that countries like India, Pakistan, North Korea and Iran were seeking the bomb, and a global black market in nuclear materials was expanding. Instead, they argued, the best way to reduce nuclear dangers was to work toward completely eliminating nuclear weapons. [3]

President Obama agrees. His proposed fiscal 2010 budget eliminates funds for designing new nuclear warheads, which his predecessor, George W. Bush, had argued were needed to replace older weapons in the U.S. arsenal. On April 5, in Prague, Czechoslovakia, Obama laid out a broad agenda for moving toward nuclear abolition. First, he said, the U.S. would reduce the role of nuclear

weapons in its own security strategy by:

- Negotiating new strategic (long-range) arms reductions with Russia;
- Ratifying a treaty ending nuclear weapons testing; and
- Seeking a new international treaty to end production of fissile materials for nuclear weapons. [4]

Obama also proposed strengthening the Nuclear Non-Proliferation Treaty (NPT), under which 188 nations have pledged not to seek nuclear weapons, by:

- Giving international inspectors more authority;
- Agreeing on consequences when nations break the rules; and
- Creating an international nuclear-fuel bank so countries with nuclear power reactors would not need nuclear technology to produce their own fuel.

Finally, Obama announced new actions to keep nuclear weapons away from terrorists, including measures to secure vulnerable nuclear materials worldwide and stronger programs to detect nuclear smuggling.

"I'm not naïve. This goal will not be reached quickly — perhaps not in my lifetime," Obama said. "But now we, too, must ignore the voices who tell us that the world cannot change." [5]

Obama took another important step in mid-September, canceling Bush administration plans to deploy antimissile defense systems in Poland and the Czech Republic. The installations were intended to defend Europe against missile strikes from Iran. But Russian leaders saw them as a provocative intrusion into Eastern Europe and argued that the system might be expanded and reconfigured to threaten Russia. Instead, the

Nuclear Weapons Network Spans Seven States

Eight nuclear facilities in seven states make up the U.S. nuclear weapons complex. Responsibilities at each site range from the design and production of the nation's nuclear arsenal to testing and improving bomb yield.

The U.S. Nuclear Weapons Network

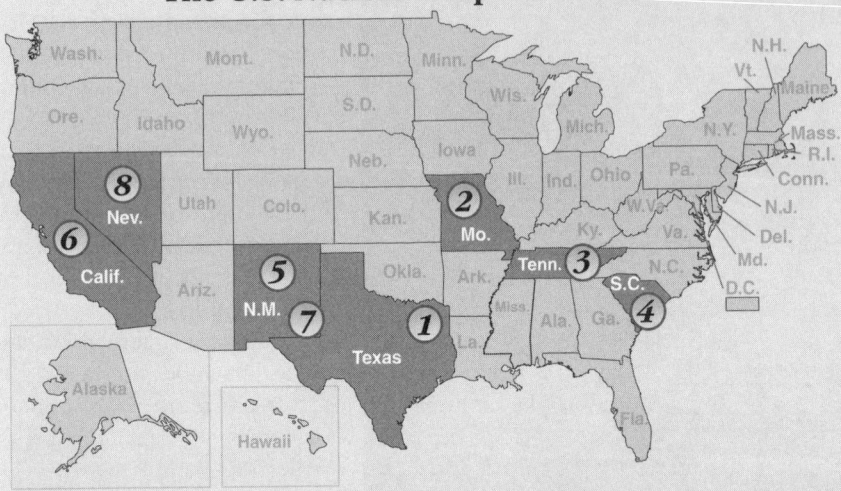

1 Pantex: Tests, retrofits and repairs weapons in the stockpile and dismantles surplus nuclear weapons.

2 Kansas City Plant: Produces non-nuclear components for nuclear weapons.

3 Y-12: Produces and reworks nuclear weapon components and stores enriched uranium and plutonium.

4 Savannah River: Produces radioactive tritium to boost the yield of nuclear weapons.

5 Los Alamos National Laboratory: Designs and certifies the safety and reliability of the explosive cores of nuclear weapons; oversees refurbishment of all weapons in the stockpile.

6 Lawrence Livermore National Laboratory: Designs and certifies safety and reliability of nuclear weapons; conducts research on weapons physics.

7 Sandia National Laboratory: Designs the non-nuclear components of nuclear weapons.

8 Nevada Test Site: Performed nuclear tests until 1992; conducts underground sub-critical tests and maintains the capability to resume testing if so directed.

Source: "Nuclear Matters: A Practical Guide," Office of the Under Secretary of Defense for Acquisition, Technology and Logistics, 2008

Obama administration said it would field shorter-range interceptors, initially based on ships, which could be targeted more easily against Iranian threats. [6]

Russian Prime Minister Vladimir Putin called Obama's move a "correct and brave decision." [7] But conservatives said Obama was undermining U.S.

security commitments to European allies. "Given the serious and growing threats posed by Iran's nuclear and missile programs, now is the time when we should look to strengthen our defenses, and those of our allies," said Republican senator and former presidential candidate John McCain of Arizona. "I believe the decision to abandon [the land-based system] unilaterally is seriously misguided." [8]

On Sept. 24 the Security Council unanimously passed a resolution urging all countries to work toward nuclear reductions and disarmament and to put tighter controls on nuclear technologies and materials. [9] U.N. Secretary-General Ban Ki-Moon welcomed the council's new resolve and urged states to follow through on the resolution. "Together we have dreamed about a nuclear-weapon-free world. Now we must act to achieve it," he said.

Other heads of state who had long supported faster nuclear reductions echoed the secretary-general. "While we sleep, death is awake. Death keeps watch from the warehouses that store more than 23,000 nuclear warheads, like 23,000 eyes open and waiting for a moment of carelessness," said Oscar Arias Sanchez, president of Costa Rica. [10]

The world has lived with nuclear threats for more than 60 years, but today's challenges differ dramatically from those during the Cold War, when the greatest global security risk was war between the United States and the Soviet Union. Under the doctrine of "mutual assured destruction," each country fielded tens of thousands of nuclear weapons to ensure that it could survive a first strike and still inflict catastrophic damage on its enemy. The policy kept the peace, advocates argued, by making each side afraid to start a war.

But accidents and misread signals nearly caused nuclear explosions more than once, when nations came close to nuclear exchanges or troops mishandled their own nuclear weapons. (*See sidebar, p. 824.*) Many experts still worry that too many nuclear weapons are on high alert, and that U.S. or Russian leaders might misinterpret an accidental launch as a planned strike and respond by launching more missiles and killing millions of people.

Now the threat of terrorism has compounded the danger. "The greatest threat to our security is that al Qaeda will acquire a nuclear weapon from Pakistan's or Russia's arsenal, or the material to build one from any of a dozen countries that don't guard their material adequately," says Joseph Cirincione, president of the Ploughshares Fund, which supports efforts to prevent the spread of nuclear weapons. "Another risk is that nuclear weapons could be used in a regional war — for example, between India and Pakistan."

The United States and Soviet Union (succeeded by Russia) have always possessed nearly all the nuclear weapons in the world. Together they have about 24,500 nuclear weapons today, down from a peak of roughly 64,000 in 1986. [11] (*See graph, p. 820.*) More than half of these weapons are held as spares, in reserve, or are awaiting dismantlement. But advocates say the U.S. and Russia should make further cuts, both to reduce the risk of a nuclear exchange and to build support for strong, global nonproliferation policies.

"The NPT requires the nuclear powers to move toward disarmament," says Daryl Kimball, executive director of the nonprofit Arms Control Association. "If we don't, other countries will be less willing to support tough controls on nuclear bomb material and sanctions on countries that try to develop nuclear weapons. Treading water is not a feasible option. And nuclear weapons aren't practical tools to deal with terrorist threats or conventional conflicts. Their only defensible purpose is to deter use of nuclear weapons by another country, and only Russia has an arsenal as big as ours."

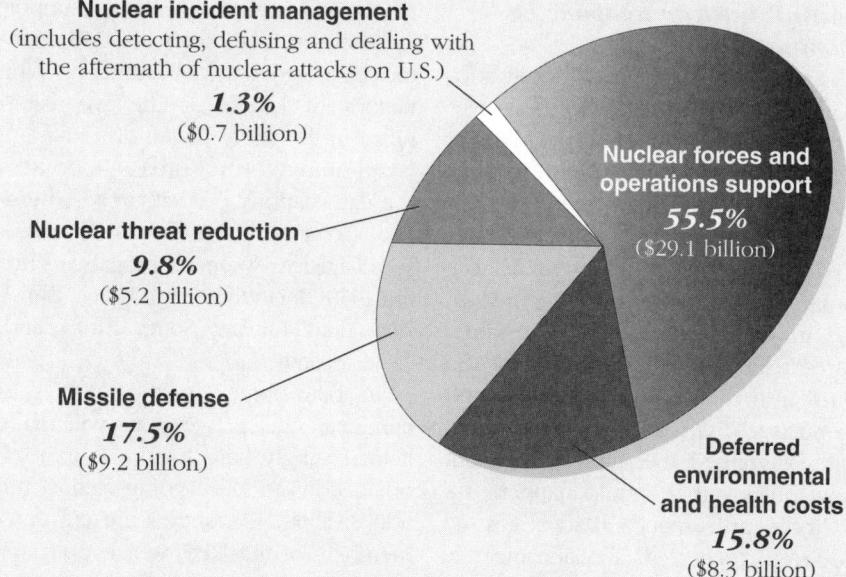

Budget on Nuclear Weapons Exceeds $52 Billion

At least $52 billion was appropriated for nuclear weapons and related expenses in fiscal 2008.* Most of the money was allocated for nuclear forces and operations support.

U.S. Nuclear Weapons-Related Appropriations, FY 2008
(includes nuclear delivery systems, warheads and bombs)

Nuclear incident management
(includes detecting, defusing and dealing with the aftermath of nuclear attacks on U.S.)
1.3%
($0.7 billion)

Nuclear forces and operations support
55.5%
($29.1 billion)

Nuclear threat reduction
9.8%
($5.2 billion)

Missile defense
17.5%
($9.2 billion)

Deferred environmental and health costs
15.8%
($8.3 billion)

* The total does not include costs for air defense, antisubmarine warfare, classified programs and most nuclear-weapons-related intelligence programs.

Note: Figures do not total 100 due to rounding.

Source: Stephen I. Schwartz and Deepti Choubey, "Nuclear Security Spending: Assessing Costs, Examining Priorities," Carnegie Endowment for International Peace, 2009

Most advocates agree the U.S. should maintain a strong deterrent force as long as other countries have nuclear weapons. Earlier this year, a congressionally appointed bipartisan commission concluded the United States could make more nuclear reductions jointly with Russia, but it recommended retaining bombers, land-based missiles and submarines to deliver them. The report also left open an option for developing new warheads, and commission members disagreed over ending U.S. nuclear testing. [12]

Defense hawks argue that treaties constrain the U.S. but do nothing to reduce threats from countries determined to acquire nuclear weapons. One of their prime examples, Iran, made headlines less than 24 hours after the Security Council's disarmament resolution, when it was revealed that Iran was building a secret underground plant to enrich uranium. [13]

Obama and his British and French counterparts accused Iran — a member of the NPT — of flouting its non-nuclear pledges. Obama warned that if Iran did not disclose all of its nuclear activities immediately, it would face "sanctions that bite." But critics said negotiations would not curb Iran's alleged bomb program.

"In the bitter decades of the Cold War, we learned the hard way that the only countries that abide by disarmament treaties are those that want to be disarmed," *The Wall Street Journal* argued in an editorial. [14]

In the debate over U.S. nuclear policies, here are some issues under consideration:

Can all nuclear weapons be eliminated?

The United States has officially supported abolishing nuclear weapons ever since President Lyndon B. Johnson signed the Non-Proliferation Treaty in 1968. Article VI requires the five countries that then possessed nuclear weapons (United States, Soviet Union, Britain, France and China) to "negotiate in good faith on effective measures relating to the cessation of the nuclear arms race at an early date and to nuclear disarmament." [15] But advocates disagreed then and now about how quickly that should happen.

Today, arms reduction advocates say key steps to nuclear abolition include:

• Ending nuclear testing so that nations cannot develop new weapons;

• Ceasing production of fissile material for military use;

• Setting up a global civilian nuclear fuel bank so nations won't need to build plants that can produce bomb-usable material; and

• Drastically reducing U.S. and Russian nuclear arsenals.

Disarmament advocates argue that once the superpowers have made major cuts, perhaps below 1,000 warheads each, other nations with nuclear weapons would join the disarmament process. As arsenals shrink toward zero, they say, all countries then would have to accept intrusive inspections and monitoring to show that they were keeping their pledges.

Some supporters envision such a scenario within several decades. For example, Global Zero, an international coalition led by more than 100 former political and military leaders from the United States, Russia, China, Britain, and other countries, issued a plan last June to eliminate nuclear weapons by 2030. [16] "It's in the national interest of every country to live in a world free of nuclear weapons," says former U.S. Air Force nuclear weapons launch officer Bruce Blair, president of the World Security Institute in Washington and a Global Zero coordinator.

As evidence of worldwide support for abolition, Blair notes that 188 countries have signed the NPT, and only nine nations worldwide — the five recognized in the treaty plus India, Pakistan, Israel and North Korea — possess nuclear weapons. [17] What's more, a number of countries have abandoned once-secret nuclear weapons programs since the 1970s, including South Korea, Brazil, Argentina, Taiwan, South Africa and, most recently, Libya. [18]

In Blair's view, serious efforts to eliminate nuclear weapons will make it increasingly hard for the four holdout nations to keep going against the tide. "All other countries are currently members of the NPT, which obligates them to remain nuclear weapons-free. So they would have no reason not to sign a Global Zero accord, and strong reason to support the trend toward zero," Blair says.

Others believe disarmament will take more than political pressure. "You would have to believe that there will be a time when Russia doesn't feel beleaguered and dependent on nuclear weapons, that Israel feels at peace with its neighbors and that India isn't at war with Pakistan," says Linton Brooks, who headed the National Nuclear Security Administration during George W. Bush's administration. "Then you have to ask how we'll know that people have given up nuclear weapons. Then you have to figure out what to do if you discover somebody is cheating."

In Brooks' view, the solution will take many decades and should not divert attention from current nuclear challenges. "Abolition has focused a lot of intellectual energy in the think-tank community on something that will happen in 40 and 50 years, instead of current problems like what we'll do if we can't keep Iran from producing nuclear weapons," he warns. "I think we're not spending enough intellectual time on near-term problems."

Another argument often raised against going to zero points out that the basics of how nuclear weapons work are widely known. "Proliferating states, even if they abandoned these devices under resolute international pressure, would still be able to clandestinely retain a few of their existing weapons — or maintain a standby, break-out capability to acquire a few weapons quickly, if needed," wrote former Defense Secretary Harold Brown and former Energy Secretary and CIA Director John Deutch in 2007. [19]

But others say a breakout nation could not achieve very much with a handful of nuclear bombs. "Nuclear weapons make it harder for other people to threaten you and conquer you, but they're not good for blackmailing or getting your way in many international political situations," says Stephen Walt, a professor of international affairs at Harvard University.

Going nuclear actually may be counterproductive for would-be regional powers like Iran, Walt contends, because their neighbors will arm in response. "Iran will have more influence in the Persian Gulf if no one has nuclear weapons, so I think it's in their interest not to develop nuclear weapons," he says. "The way we make that point is to stop holding a gun to their heads and try to persuade them that they're better off not weaponizing their technology. They should know that if they produce weapons they'll go to the top of our potential terrorist source list. Our goal should be persuading them to be more like Japan and less like Pakistan."

Making disarmament viable for countries like Pakistan with enemies next door will require creative strategies for taming regional conflicts. "Pakistani leaders are worried about an attack from India, so giving them enough political will to abandon nuclear deterrence may mean creating a demilitarized zone between Pakistan and India," says Sharon Squassoni, a senior associate at the Carnegie Endowment for International Peace. "The weakest nation with nuclear weapons will have to feel comfortable letting go of that safety net and believe that it will be better off without it."

Should the United States end nuclear testing?

From 1945 through 1992 the United States detonated more than 1,000 nuclear weapons. Most other nuclear nations, including Russia, Britain, France, China, India, Pakistan and North Korea, are known to have also carried out nuclear tests.

Arms control advocates have long sought a global ban on nuclear testing to keep nations from developing and validating new warhead designs. Since 1996 148 countries have signed and ratified the Comprehensive Test-Ban Treaty (CTBT), which bars members from carrying out or helping with nuclear explosions and sets up an international monitoring system to detect clandestine tests. If a member country is suspected of conducting a test, other countries can request on-site inspections of its facilities. [20] But for the CTBT to enter into force, it must be ratified by nine more states: the U.S., China, North Korea, Egypt, India, Indonesia, Iran, Israel and Pakistan. [21]

President Bill Clinton signed the CTBT in 1996, but the Republican-controlled Senate delayed action on ratifying the treaty. Although the United States had adopted a moratorium on nuclear tests five years earlier (initiated by a Democratic Congress), many conservative critics argued the treaty was not verifiable because cheaters could easily hide low-level nuclear tests. They also contended tests were essential to assure that U.S. nuclear weapons remained safe

and reliable over time, and that ending U.S. tests would have little impact on proliferator countries. [22]

In 1999 Senate Republicans forced a quick debate and rejected the CTBT on a 51-48 vote. Support fell far short of the 67 votes required under the Constitution to ratify a treaty, even though the Energy and Defense departments and Joint Chiefs of Staff urged approval. In his Prague speech earlier this year, President Obama promised to try again.

"After more than five decades of talks, it is time for the testing of nuclear weapons to finally be banned," Obama said.

But critics argued that without testing the nation's nuclear deterrent would be weakened. Sen. Jon Kyl, R-Ariz., and former Assistant Secretary of Defense Richard Perle asserted that ending nuclear testing, together with Obama's decision not to fund new nuclear warhead designs, amounted to "unilateral disarmament by unilateral obsolescence." [23]

CTBT supporters predict that all Senate Democrats will support ratification and that some Republicans who voted no in 1999 will reconsider their positions, including Sens. Richard Lugar of Indiana and Arizona's McCain. (As a presidential candidate in 2008, McCain promised to keep an open mind on the issue.) But others still believe the treaty undercuts U.S. security interests.

"I know of no information that suggests that the matters that led the Senate to reject the treaty have changed for the better," said Sen. Kyl earlier this year. "CTBT, a bad idea shrouded in good intentions, would not even be capable of detecting political tantrums like the North Korean test [in May], even when the international monitoring system is told where and when to look." [24]

In fact, the CTBT's international monitoring system — with 130 seismic monitoring stations worldwide — detected North Korea's first test in 2006 as well as last May's test, which registered as far away as Texas. On the day of the test, CTBT officials said the system could pinpoint the location of the explosion

to an area the size of Berlin, and would be able to make that estimate much more precise with further analysis. [25]

Such findings indicate the CTBT can detect cheaters, advocates say. "The design objective for the monitoring system was to be able to detect explosions measuring one kiloton or less in any medium anywhere in the world, and it looks as though we're doing better than that," says Princeton University physicist Frank von Hippel, a former arms control adviser during the Clinton administration. "North Korea's test was a fraction of a kiloton. Seismologists have become very sophisticated at discriminating between explosions and other signals like earthquakes. A nuclear test is a sudden expansion of a gas in all directions, and that creates a very different signal from two sides of a fault shifting against each other." (See "At Issue," p. 829.)

Advocates of continued testing question whether the Department of Energy can maintain a robust nuclear weapons stockpile without conducting tests, in part because some of the precisely engineered materials in nuclear weapons change over time, including plutonium cores and the chemical explosives that compress bomb cores to critical mass. A 2002 National Academy of Sciences study acknowledged that aging would make stewardship of the U.S. stockpile increasingly challenging, but said, "[W]e see no reason that the capabilities of those mechanisms . . . cannot grow at least as fast as the challenge they must meet." [26]

The directors of the three DOE laboratories that design and build nuclear weapons (Los Alamos and Sandia in New Mexico and Lawrence Livermore in California) must certify annually to Congress that U.S. nuclear weapons are safe and reliable. (See map, p. 816.) So far they have made that certification each year, but questions persist. "[A]s the weapons age, a thing that is referred to as margins begins to decrease," said Gen. Kevin Chilton, head of the U.S. Strategic Command, early last year.

Global Stockpiles on the Decline

The United States has a little more than 5,200 nuclear weapons stockpiled this year, about one-sixth of the amount it had in the mid-1960s when stockpiles were at their highest. Similarly, stockpiles have steadily declined for Russia since the collapse of the Soviet Union.

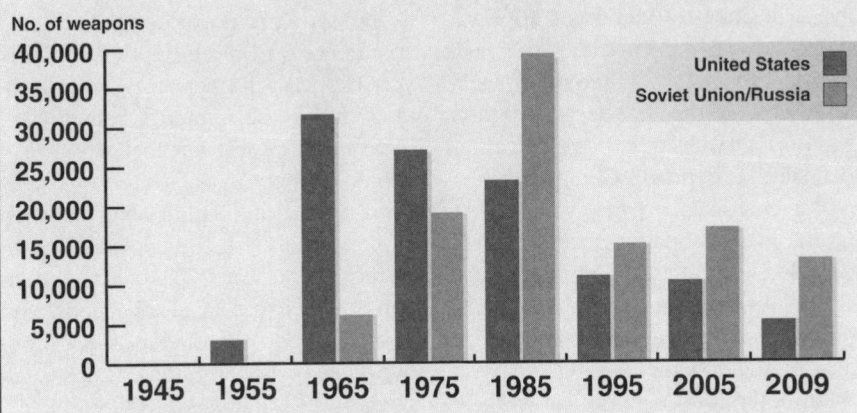

U.S., Russian Nuclear Stockpiles, 1945-2009

No. of weapons

Legend: United States, Soviet Union/Russia

Note: France, China and the United Kingdom have a few hundred nuclear weapons each.

Source: Natural Resources Defense Council

"A simple way to think of [margin] is the likelihood it's going to work the way you want it to work the day you need it. . . . And margin, because of shelf life and chemistry, is decreasing." [27]

Siegfried Hecker, a professor of management science and engineering at Stanford University and former director of Los Alamos National Laboratory, argues that stockpile stewardship creates some uncertainty and is a slower and more expensive way to resolve certain questions than testing. But Hecker nonetheless supports ratifying the CTBT because, in his view, other nations need nuclear tests more than the U.S. does.

"The single most important reason to ratify the CTBT is to stop other countries from improving their arsenals — China, India, Pakistan, North Korea, and Iran if it ever progresses that far," says Hecker. "We gain substantially more from limiting other countries than we lose by giving up testing — even with a gradual loss of confidence, which stockpile stewardship has held to an

acceptable level. The U.S. has carried out more than 1,000 nuclear tests, and the Chinese have done about 45. You can see the difference in the sophistication of our arsenals."

Does the United States need new nuclear weapons?

The United States built its last nuclear weapon in 1992 — nearly 20 years ago — and today experts sharply disagree over whether new weapons are needed. New-construction advocates say the thousands of weapons in the current stockpile were not designed for shelf lives longer than about 20-30 years, and that simply refurbishing them would leave uncertainty about how they will perform. Opponents say the stockpile is reliable and can be kept that way through regular maintenance, and that producing new models would signal an expanding role for nuclear weapons in U.S. security policy.

After the Persian Gulf War in 1991, when air strikes failed to destroy many

of Iraq's underground military facilities, some defense planners proposed developing low-yield nuclear weapons that could destroy buried targets. Congress rejected the idea in 1993, barring work on "mini-nukes" with explosive yields of five kilotons or less. But conservative legislators and weapon designers continued to press the issue of usable nuclear weapons to destroy "very hard targets." [28]

Spurred by its search for al Qaeda leader Osama bin Laden in the caves of Afghanistan, the Bush administration sought funding from Congress starting in 2003 for a Robust Nuclear Earth Penetrator (RNEP), But critics, led by Rep. David Hobson, R-Ohio, argued the so-called "bunker buster" would cause too much damage in the area surrounding a target, and that building it would undermine U.S. nonproliferation policy. "It gave people a lot of reason to build their own weapons," Hobson later said. [29]

After Congress zeroed out bunker buster funding in 2004 and 2005, Hobson urged the Bush administration instead to develop what became known as the Reliable Replacement Warhead (RRW) program to design safer, more durable replacements for the most problematic weapons in the stockpile. But when DOE responded by proposing an entire new generation of nuclear warheads, Hobson and other critics zeroed funding for RRW, arguing that first the U.S. needed to develop post-Cold War deterrence strategies and decide how many weapons it needed to carry them out. [30]

Although Obama did not include RRW in his fiscal 2010 budget request, some senior administration officials are on record supporting new nuclear weapons. In October 2008, Defense Secretary Robert Gates described the long-term outlook for the U.S. nuclear stockpile as "bleak," thanks to aging weapons and an aging nuclear work force. RRW, said Gates, "is not about new capabilities — suitcase bombs or bunker busters or tactical nukes. It is about safety, security and reliability. It is about the future credibility of our strategic deterrent, and it deserves urgent attention." [31]

At a congressional hearing last March, the Strategic Command's Gen. Chilton said, "We do not need a new weapon with new capabilities. But I do believe we have a great opportunity here to develop modern nuclear weapons . . . that have 21st-century requirements put into their designs," such as higher reliability and better security features in case a weapon is stolen by terrorists.

Then-Rep. Ellen Tauscher, D-Calif., who is now Under Secretary of State for Arms Control and International Security, agreed, "as long as the [constraints] include no testing; no new capabilities for the weapons in the sense that we're not increasing yield . . . and that it is all done in a context of ratifying [the CTBT] and taking down weapons and dismantling them." [32]

Opponents counter that warheads in the stockpile are safe and reliable. The 2002 National Academy of Sciences study on technical issues associated with the CTBT concluded that thanks to investments in nuclear weapons science that do not involve testing, "confidence in the reliability of the stockpile is better justified technically today than it was [in 1992 when the U.S. stopped testing]." [33]

More recently, studies released in 2006 by the JASON group, a panel of high-level experts that provides independent scientific advice to the U.S government, and by the Livermore and Los Alamos national laboratories, concluded that plutonium "pits," or cores, for most U.S. nuclear weapons would be reliable for at least 85 years — about twice as long as scientists had previously estimated. The JASON report concluded that the weapons laboratories "have also made significant progress in prioritizing the unresolved questions regarding the aging of stockpile weapons" and have "identified key metrics to assess the effects of aging." [34]

In addition to studying scientific problems like plutonium aging, the DOE is carrying out "life extension" programs on each of the major weapon types in the U.S. stockpile. Designed to extend the lives of warheads by 20 to 30 years, the programs involve refurbishing some components and replacing others that have degraded or pose technical problems. As of mid-2009, DOE had completed a life extension on the B61, an air-delivered bomb, and was working on the W76 warhead, which is carried on submarine-launched ballistic missiles. [35]

Debate over building new nuclear weapons is part of a larger discussion about the future of the aging DOE nuclear complex and the increasing challenge of recruiting talented scientists to maintain the U.S. nuclear stockpile and develop new weapons if they ever are needed (a stated U.S. policy goal). [36] "The U.S. is experiencing a serious brain drain in the loss of veteran nuclear weapons designers and technicians," Gates said last October. "Half of our nuclear lab scientists are over 50 years old, and many of those under 50 have had limited or no involvement in the design and development of a nuclear weapon." [37]

But it is less obvious that U.S. military leaders want new nuclear weapons. In a 2008 poll of more than 3,400 senior active-duty and retired military officers, only about 2 percent of respondents thought the U.S. needed to develop a new generation of nuclear weapons. [38] "Nuclear weapons don't factor into the kinds of missions that most military officers perform day to day, and it's civilian leaders who make the decision about pressing the button," says Carnegie Endowment analyst Squassoni. "Military leaders are much more focused on issues like getting their forces to the theater and communicating with them."

Many observers predict that to win votes for CTBT ratification, Obama may strike a deal that increases funding and activities related to nuclear weapon de-

sign (but not production). "There are a lot of things you can do to ensure the safety and reliability of the arsenal in between nothing and developing new warheads, and that's where the discussion is happening now," says the Ploughshares Fund's Cirincione. "You can already see the outlines of a compromise around robust research and development at the labs. We need to find a balance between making sure that our nuclear weapons work as intended and avoiding activities that make other countries think we're improving our capabilities while we tell them to reduce theirs." ∎

BACKGROUND

Dawn of Arms Race

The United States made the world's first nuclear weapons, drawing on work by researchers in England, Italy, France and Germany. Through the 1930s and early '40s these scientists solved pieces of the central challenge — splitting the atom and releasing huge quantities of energy. But only the United States, its research ranks swelled by top European physicists fleeing the Nazi government, undertook a full-scale effort to build the bomb.

In October 1941, with the nation on the brink of war, President Franklin D. Roosevelt ordered advisers to find out whether an atomic bomb could be built and what it would cost. Three months later, after Japan's surprise attack on Pearl Harbor, Roosevelt approved the Manhattan Project — a crash program to develop nuclear weapons. Working in secret, the Army Corps of Engineers built a nuclear production complex by 1945 that was as large as the U.S. auto industry. At its peak the Manhattan Project employed some 130,000 people from Washington state to South Carolina. [39]

On July 16, 1945, the world's first nuclear test lit up the desert at Alamogordo, New Mexico. Describing it, J. Robert Oppenheimer, the Manhattan Project's scientific director, recalled a statement in Hindu scripture by the god Vishnu: "Now I am become Death, the destroyer of worlds." A month later U.S. bombers dropped two atomic bombs in three days on the Japanese cities of Hiroshima and Nagasaki, killing more than 100,000 people immediately, and perhaps twice that number within weeks from radiation poisoning. [40]

Although scientists urged Roosevelt and his successor, President Harry S Truman, to tell the Soviet Union about the bomb program, Truman only told Premier Josef Stalin that the U.S. was working on "a new weapon of great force" 12 days before the Hiroshima bombing. [41] In 1946 U.S. negotiator Barnard Baruch presented a plan to the United Nations to destroy all existing atomic bombs and put atomic energy technology under international control. But the Soviet Union, which by then had launched its own atomic bomb program, rejected the plan.

In 1949 the Soviets tested their first atomic bomb. Truman then approved development of even more powerful thermonuclear, or hydrogen, bombs. By 1953 both superpowers had tested H-bombs and were expanding their nuclear stockpiles rapidly, each seeking the ability to respond instantly and massively to a sudden nuclear attack.

President Dwight D. Eisenhower renewed the idea of international control in his 1953 "Atoms for Peace" speech, which urged the United Nations to promote peaceful uses of atomic energy. The proposal led to establishment of the International Atomic Energy Agency in 1957 but did not slow the growth of nuclear arsenals. Emulating the United States and Soviet Union, Britain had tested a nuclear weapon in 1952. France and China would follow in the 1960s.

The arms race intensified in 1957,

when the Soviet Union launched its *Sputnik* satellite into orbit, demonstrating that it could build a long-range ballistic missile. [42] *Sputnik* raised U.S. fears of falling behind and becoming vulnerable to nuclear blackmail. Concerns about a "missile gap" persisted until 1961, when satellite photographs showed that the U.S.S.R. had deployed only four long-range ballistic missiles. [43] The United States had more than 24,000 nuclear weapons — roughly 10 times as many as the Soviets. [44]

Early Agreements

Democratic President John F. Kennedy (1961-63) came to office supporting limits on nuclear testing, but friction with the Soviet Union obstructed progress. In 1962 the superpowers came to the brink of nuclear war when U.S. satellite photographs revealed that Russians were installing nuclear missiles in Cuba that could reach U.S. territory. [45]

Some advisors recommended conventional air strikes on the Cuban missile sites, but instead Kennedy imposed a naval quarantine on Cuba and insisted that the weapons be removed. After a 13-day standoff, Soviet Premier Nikita Khrushchev agreed to remove the missiles. In return the U.S. promised not to invade Cuba (a fear that had spurred the Soviets to install the missiles), and also agreed confidentially to remove its own nuclear missiles from Turkey.

After the Cuban Missile Crisis, Kennedy renewed efforts to limit nuclear testing, hoping to make it harder for other countries to develop nuclear weapons. In March 1963 Kennedy said, "I see the possibility in the 1970s of the president of the United States having to face a world in which 15 or 20 or 25 nations may have these weapons. I regard that as the greatest possible danger and hazard." And he argued that even if a test ban constrained the U.S., it would still make the nation safer. [46]

The Limited Test Ban Treaty, signed later that year, banned nuclear tests in the atmosphere, outer space and under water, but allowed underground tests to continue. [47]

Under Kennedy's successor, Lyndon B. Johnson, the U.S. and Russia joined with other countries to negotiate the Nuclear Non-Proliferation Treaty, which barred members other than the current nuclear powers (the U.S., Soviet Union, Britain, France, and China) from acquiring nuclear weapons. In return signatories were guaranteed access to peaceful nuclear energy technologies, and the five nuclear states agreed to negotiate toward disarmament, although without any time frame. [48] Ninety-eight countries signed the NPT when it was completed in 1968, and many more joined later.

By this time the United States had more than 28,000 nuclear weapons, down from a peak of 31,700 in 1966, and the Soviet Union had nearly 10,000. [49] Both sides were developing weapons that could deliver multiple warheads to different targets, known as MIRVs (multiple independently targetable reentry vehicles), and anti-ballistic missile defense systems that could shoot down attacking missiles.

Unable to agree on a broad nuclear disarmament plan, the superpowers shifted to a more modest goal in the late 1960s: setting some upper limits on their arms race. In 1972 U.S. and Soviet leaders signed an interim agreement (referred to as SALT I because it was negotiated during the Strategic Arms Limitation Talks) freezing the number of each side's long-range ballistic missiles, bombers and submarines, and also the Anti-Ballistic Missile (ABM) Treaty, which limited each country to a single defensive system around its capital and another at a missile launch area. [50] By preventing either country from developing a nationwide missile defense system, the ABM Treaty sought to maintain the so-called "balance of terror" that kept the superpowers from attacking each other.

Continued on p. 824

Chronology

1940s-1960s
Atomic Age begins.

August 1945
U.S. drops atomic bombs on Hiroshima and Nagasaki, Japan, killing 250,000 people.

1949
Soviet Union tests atomic bomb.

1952
Britain tests first nuclear bomb; U.S. tests hydrogen bomb.

1957
International Atomic Energy Agency (IAEA) is created to promote peaceful uses of nuclear energy.

1960
France tests nuclear bomb.

1962
Cuban Missile Crisis brings U.S., Soviet Union to brink of nuclear war.

1963
Limited Test Ban Treaty bars tests in atmosphere, space, underwater.

1964
China tests its first nuclear bomb.

1968
Nearly 100 countries sign Nuclear Non-Proliferation Treaty (NPT).

1970s-1980s
Developing countries start acquiring nuclear arms.

1972
U.S. and U.S.S.R. conclude Strategic Arms Limitation Talks (SALT I).

1974
India carries out "peaceful" underground nuclear explosion.

1979
U.S. and U.S.S.R. sign SALT II, cutting long-range missiles.

1983
U.S. deploys nuclear missiles in Western Europe, triggering widespread protests.

1986
President Ronald Reagan and Soviet Premier Mikhail Gorbachev discuss eliminating nuclear weapons at summit in Reykjavik, Iceland. Talks collapse but lay base for 1987 Intermediate-Range Nuclear Forces Treaty.

1989
Pakistan is revealed to be developing "nuclear capability."

1990s-2000s
U.S., Russia reduce Cold War arsenals; other proliferation threats increase.

July 31, 1991
President George H. W. Bush and Gorbachev sign Strategic Arms Reduction Treaty (START I). . . . Inspectors begin destroying Iraq's nuclear weapons research sites. . . . Soviet Union collapses; U.S. provides aid to safeguard nuclear weapons.

1993
U.S., Russia sign START II treaty, reducing number of deployed strategic warheads by end of 2007. Russia conditions ratification on preservation of ABM Treaty's limits on development of missile defense systems.

1994
North Korea agrees to stop producing plutonium in return for food and energy aid. . . . START I enters into force for 15 years.

1996
Comprehensive Test Ban Treaty (CTBT) signed by 71 nations.

1998
India, Pakistan test nuclear weapons.

1999
U.S. Senate votes 51-48 against CTBT.

2002
U.S. withdraws from ABM Treaty, which President George W. Bush says prevents protection of Americans from rogue or terrorist attacks. Russia repudiates START II. The two countries conclude Strategic Offensive Reduction Treaty (SORT).

2003
U.S. invades Iraq, claiming it is developing weapons of mass destruction; no nuclear weapons program is found. . . . North Korea withdraws from NPT. . . . Libya agrees to dismantle clandestine nuclear weapons program.

2006
North Korea conducts nuclear test. . . . U.N. Security Council learns Iran has uranium enrichment program.

2008
Poland, Czech Republic agree to host U.S. missile defense systems; Russia says it will deploy missiles near Poland.

2009
President Barack Obama pledges steps toward nuclear-free world, including new nuclear reduction agreements with Russia and CTBT ratification and cancels missile defense deployment in Eastern Europe. . . . North Korea conducts second nuclear test. . . . Obama and Russian President Dmitry Medvedev sign joint understanding on treaty to reduce nuclear forces.

What If an Armed Nuclear Bomber Crashed?

Potentially catastrophic accidents have occurred.

The terms are vaguely military, but innocent-sounding: "bent spears" and "broken arrows." But they refer to a dreadful reality: potentially catastrophic incidents involving nuclear weapons.

"Broken arrows" are the most serious, such as the accidental or unauthorized launch of a nuclear weapon that could lead to nuclear war, an explosion of nuclear or non-nuclear weapon components, radioactive contamination or loss or seizure of a nuclear weapon. To date, the U.S. military has logged 32 such incidents — all before 1983 and none resulting in a nuclear detonation. [1]

But some came close. In 1966 an American B-52 bomber carrying four hydrogen bombs collided with a tanker plane during mid-air refueling off the coast of Spain. The bomber broke apart, and three of the bombs fell on land near a small fishing village; the bombs didn't detonate, but non-nuclear explosives in two of the bombs did go off, contaminating a square mile with radioactive material. The fourth bomb landed in the Mediterranean Sea and was recovered intact two months later. [2]

"Bent spears" involve the mishandling of nuclear weapons or incidents that pose a risk of explosion, radioactive contamination or damage to the weapon. [3] The most recent bent spear occurred in 2007, when crewmen loaded what they thought were 12 unarmed cruise missiles onto a bomber at Minot Air Force Base in North Dakota. The airmen and the officer in charge didn't realize that six of the missiles carried nuclear warheads. The loaded plane stood unguarded on the runway for 15 hours before flying to a base in Louisiana, where the nuclear missiles were discovered nine hours later. [4]

Afterwards, seven officers at Minot were reassigned, and 90 service members temporarily lost authority to handle nuclear weapons. [5] In 2008, after it was disclosed that another Air Force unit had mislabeled fuses for nuclear missiles and accidentally shipped them to Taiwan, Defense Secretary Robert Gates ordered an investigation of the Air Force's problems handling nuclear weapons. In June, the Air Force's military chief of staff and civilian secretary were forced to resign. [6]

Many security experts say the risk of accidental nuclear war has grown since the end of the Cold War, largely because the United States and Russia still maintain hundreds of nuclear weapons at a high stage of alert. In addition, Russia's computer systems degraded after the Soviet Union disintegrated, raising concerns that leaders might misinterpret a malfunction or false signal as an attack and launch weapons in response. Indeed, false alarms indicating a Soviet attack occurred in the United States in 1979 and 1980, and in 1995 Russian leaders almost launched a nuclear attack on the U.S. in response to what turned out to be a Norwegian research rocket. [7]

"About 800 to 900 U.S. warheads, and a comparable number of Russian warheads, are launch ready — fuelled, armed, targeted and will instantly fire if they receive a very short stream of computer launch signals," says Bruce Blair, president of the World Security Institute and a former Air Force nuclear missile launch officer. "Nothing has been done to change these legacy postures, except for a cosmetic detargeting agreement between [President Bill] Clinton and [Soviet President Boris] Yeltsin in 1994." The U.S. and Russia agreed not to target each other, but nuclear weapons can be retargeted in seconds.

Military leaders maintain that launch-ready warheads are under rigorous controls, including design features, safety rules and procedures, accident prevention or mitigation measures, physical security and coded control systems. [8] U.S. Strategic Command head Gen. Kevin Chilton said in 2008 that nuclear weapons are "in the holster" with two combination locks, which must be opened by two people who can only act under authenticated orders from the president. [9]

Nonetheless, former Senate Armed Services Committee Chairman Sam Nunn, D-Ga., has urged the United States and Russia

Continued from p. 822

Negotiations during the Ford and Carter administrations produced the SALT II treaty in 1979, which set permanent limits on many types of nuclear weapons but did not require any existing weapons to be destroyed. After the Soviet Union invaded Afghanistan in 1980, President Jimmy Carter asked the Senate to put SALT II ratification on hold and signed a directive that stated, "To continue to deter in an era of strategic nuclear equivalence . . . we must be capable of fighting [a nuclear war] successfully," so that the enemy would recognize that it could not possibly benefit from attacking. [51]

New Directions

President Ronald Reagan (1981-1989) ran on a platform that called for rebuilding U.S. military power, and some of his senior advisers alarmed the public with statements about planning for nuclear war. For example, in 1981 Deputy Under Secretary of Defense T. K. Jones argued that with a robust civil defense program, most Americans could survive a nuclear attack. "Dig a hole, cover it with a couple of doors and then throw three feet of dirt on top," Jones said. [52]

Many Americans rejected such views and supported proposals to freeze and reduce nuclear arsenals. One of the biggest anti-nuclear rallies, in New York's Central Park in 1982, drew 700,000 people. [53] When the U.S.

to remove all nuclear weapons from high-alert status. "We are running the irrational risk of an Armageddon of our own making," Nunn said in 2004. [10]

During the 2008 presidential campaign, President Barack Obama pledged to "work with Russia to take U.S. and Russian ballistic missiles off hair-trigger alert." That issue will be addressed during the congressionally mandated Nuclear Posture Review, a study of U.S. nuclear forces and policies scheduled for completion by the end of this year.

Cyber-intrusion by computer hackers could also pose a risk. [11] "If outside actors, perhaps with insider collusion that provides passwords and other access information, manage to break into 'closed' nuclear communications and computer networks, then this risk could become high as long as nuclear missiles remain on launch-ready alert," Blair warns.

In fact, since 2006 hackers have breached the networks at the Defense, Commerce and State departments, the Federal Aviation Administration and the military's U.S. Central Command, according to the Center for Strategic and International Studies, a Washington think tank. [12] The Defense Department is creating a new military command to manage offensive and defensive computer warfare, in coordination with a new civilian cybersecurity initiative announced by President Obama last May. [13]

No other countries keep their forces on launch-ready alert, according to Blair, and other nations usually keep warheads separated from delivery vehicles. However, he worries that India, Pakistan and China may start mating warheads with missiles and adopting quick-launch postures.

"If there's a crisis, they will be more likely to assemble weapons and bombs, mate them to delivery vehicles and prime them for use," Blair says. "That's the context in which mistaken or unauthorized launch becomes a concern."

To avoid that scenario, Blair recommends that all countries with nuclear weapons agree to prohibit launch-ready postures except in extreme circumstances and require pre-notification and information exchange about steps governments take to alert their forces.

"A joint warning center with multinational crews from all of the nuclear weapons countries (except North Korea) and links to all their national early-warning centers would also help to minimize misinterpretation of missile launches," he says.

— Jennifer Weeks

[1] Office of the Deputy Assistant to the Secretary of Defense (Nuclear Matters), *Nuclear Matters: A Practice Guide* (2008), p. 183, www.acq.osd.mil/ncbdp/nm/nm book/index.htm.

[2] For details see Barbara Moran, *The Day We Lost the H-Bomb: Cold War, Hot Nukes, and the Worst Nuclear Weapons Disaster in History* (2009).

[3] Office of the Assistant to the Secretary of Defense for Nuclear and Chemical and Biological Defense Programs, Nuclear Weapons Accident Response Procedures, Feb. 22, 2005, pp. 28-29, www.dtic.mil/whs/directives/corres/pdf/315008m.pdf.

[4] Joby Warrick and Walter Pincus, "Missteps in the Bunker," *The Washington Post*, Sept. 23, 2007.

[5] Marc V. Schanz and Suzann Chapman, "No More Bent Spears," *Air Force Magazine.com*, Feb. 15, 2008.

[6] Kristin Roberts, "U.S. Mistakenly Sent Nuclear Missile Fuses to Taiwan," Reuters, March 25, 2008; "Moseley and Wynne Forced Out," *Air Force Times*, June 9, 2008.

[7] Lachlan Forrow, *et al.*, "Accidental Nuclear War — A Post-Cold War Assessment," *New England Journal of Medicine*, vol. 338, no. 18 (April 30, 1998), pp. 1326-32; Geoffrey Forden, "False Alarms on the Nuclear Front," NOVA, updated December 2001, www.pbs.org/wgbh/nova/missileers/falsealarms.html.

[8] E-mail from U.S. Strategic Command to Arms Control Association, Nov. 28, 2007, www.armscontrol.org/interviews/20071204_STRATCOM.

[9] Elaine M. Grossman, "Top U.S. General Spurns Obama Pledge to Reduce Nuclear Alert Posture," Global Security Newswire, Feb. 27, 2009.

[10] "Nunn Urges U.S. and Russia to Remove All Nuclear Weapons from Hair-Trigger," Nuclear Threat Initiative, June 21, 2004.

[11] See Peter Katel, "Homeland Security," *CQ Researcher*, Feb. 13, 2009, pp. 129-152.

[12] James Andrew Lewis, "Cyber Events Since 2006," Center for Strategic and International Studies, June 11, 2009, http://csis.org/publication/cyber-events-2006.

[13] David E. Sanger and Thom Shanker, "Pentagon Plans New Arm to Wage Cyberspace Wars," *The New York Times*, May 29, 2009.

started deploying medium-range nuclear missiles in Western Europe in 1983 (a step approved during the Carter administration to balance new Soviet missiles), protests spread to European capitals. The U.S. Conference of Catholic Bishops weighed in with a pastoral letter that argued, "The arms race is one of the great curses on the human race; it is to be condemned as a danger, an act of aggression against the poor, and a folly which does not provide the security it promises." [54]

Reagan opposed a nuclear freeze and argued that increasing U.S. military power was the best way to preserve peace. But he also believed that once Soviet leaders saw that they could never win an arms race, nuclear weapons could be eliminated. In 1983 Reagan further complicated arms control discussions when he called for "rendering nuclear weapons impotent and obsolete" by developing a national missile defense system.

Reagan envisioned sharing missile defense technology with the Soviet Union, but Soviet leaders and U.S. critics argued that the Strategic Defense Initiative (SDI), popularly known as "Star Wars," would escalate the nuclear arms race and make cuts in offensive weapons impossible. Many scientists also argued that it was technically impossible to build effective defenses against a large-scale nuclear attack. [55] In a 1986 summit meeting at Reykjavik, Iceland, Reagan and Soviet General Secretary Mikhail Gorbachev nearly agreed on a proposal to eliminate nuclear weapons but deadlocked

U.S. Seeks New Roles for Bomb Builders

Nation's science leadership faces "precipitous decline."

As the United States downsizes its nuclear arsenal and makes cutbacks at its nuclear weapons laboratories, managers are finding it harder and harder to recruit and retain top-level nuclear scientists and engineers.

"We've slowly but steadily lost the capabilities that have made these places incredibly good scientific institutions," says former Los Alamos Director Siegfried Hecker.

More broadly, "Our nation is witnessing a precipitous decline in global science and technology leadership," warned a task force last spring convened by the Henry L. Stimson Center think tank in Washington, D.C. To start reversing that decline, members called for diversifying the labs' core mission so they can "address an array of 21st-century national security challenges." [1]

The nation's three nuclear weapons laboratories — Los Alamos and Sandia in New Mexico and Livermore in California — face both budget challenges and bureaucratic red tape, says Hecker. While other agencies use the labs' world-class facilities and technology in joint non-nuclear projects — such as developing advanced conventional munitions — those initiatives have not provided steady funding for the labs. "Other agencies have typically come into the labs as users of the technologies, not builders of it," he says, "so they've never supported the underlying science and technology base." Furthermore, he adds, "It's hard to do anything experimentally because the labs have been driven toward a zero-risk environment."

Still, the labs have made important contributions to non-weapons initiatives. In the 1980s, for instance, Los Alamos created the human DNA libraries that laid the groundwork for the Human Genome Project, which identified all of the genes in human DNA. And both Los Alamos and Livermore have developed strong climate-modeling programs.

To expand the labs' core mission, the task force recommended moving them from the Energy Department's National Nuclear Security Administration (NNSA) to a new, independent Agency for National Security Applications. The agency's mission would still be nuclear-related but also would include verifying compliance with arms control treaties; nuclear forensics (analyzing recovered nuclear materials to identify their sources); counter-terrorism research; and analysis of intelligence information on foreign nuclear weapons programs.

"Almost everyone understands the labs' role poorly," says Stimson Center senior fellow and study director Elizabeth Turpen. "They have been servicing broader national security needs beyond the nuclear stockpile since before the end of the Cold War, and they're huge in the nuclear nonproliferation arena. But they should be bigger."

The challenge is most urgent for Los Alamos and Livermore, which were created to design nuclear weapons and today are primarily focused on ensuring the safety and reliability of those weapons. Sandia, which designs and produces non-nuclear components of nuclear weapons, "has already turned the corner," says Turpen. "Only about 42 percent of their current budget comes from defense programs, so they already think of themselves as a national security laboratory."

---

over missile defense. Gorbachev insisted that the U.S. should adhere to the ABM Treaty, but Reagan refused, saying that would constrain SDI. [56]

A year later, however, Reagan and Gorbachev signed the Intermediate Nuclear Forces (INF) Treaty, the first agreement to eliminate an entire class of nuclear weapons (ground-launched missiles with ranges of 500 to 5,500 kilometers). [57] Negotiations continued, and in 1991 Gorbachev and President George H. W. Bush signed the Strategic Arms Reduction Treaty (START I) — the first agreement to require each side to make major cuts in long-range nuclear weapons. START I limited each side to 6,000 "accountable" (deployed) warheads and set up an intrusive verification system.

Opportunities and Threats

In December 1991, a few months after START I was signed, the Soviet Union dissolved. Now Russia posed a new kind of nuclear threat: with its economy in crisis and its borders no longer secured, many leaders worried that nuclear weapons and materials from former Soviet republics might be stolen or sold on the black market.

In response the U.S. started providing aid for so-called Cooperative Threat Reduction (CTR) — joint work by the superpowers to secure weapon-usable nuclear materials and destroy the Soviet Union's surplus nuclear weapons. Starting at $400 million in 1991, the initiative (pop-

ularly known as Nunn-Lugar after its lead Senate sponsors, Sens. Sam Nunn, D-Ga., and Indiana Republican Richard Lugar), grew into a multi-agency, multi-year program. Through fiscal 2008 the U.S. had provided about $15 billion to help other countries destroy or improve controls over nuclear, chemical, biological and missile technologies, weapons and materials. [58]

The end of the Cold War and Russia's economic collapse undercut many of the assumptions underlying U.S. nuclear policies. Just before leaving office, President Bush and Russian President Boris Yeltsin took another big step by signing the START II treaty, which called for each side to reduce its deployed strategic warheads to between 3,000 and 3,500 by 2007. START II also set

In 2000 the NNSA was split off as an autonomous agency within the Department of Energy (DOE) after security lapses and alleged Chinese spying at the labs raised congressional concerns that DOE was not overseeing the weapons complex effectively. [2] But that made it harder to broaden their portfolios, partner with other agencies and attract talented young scientists, the Stimson task force concluded.

"NNSA has never achieved the autonomy that Congress intended, just an overlay of bureaucracy," says Turpen. "And DOE's bureaucratic culture is very risk-averse in all of its decisions about the labs. There are lots of stovepipes, and anyone can stop a decision."

Early this year the Office of Management and Budget (OMB) asked for a cost-benefit analysis of putting the labs under the control of the Pentagon or another agency. Housing them within DOE "hasn't been a good marriage," said former Sandia Director C. Paul Robinson. [3] But others point out that the United States has had a longstanding policy of civilian control.

"For the past 63 years non-military control over the development of nuclear weapons technology has ensured independence of technical judgment over issues associated with our nuclear arsenal, has attracted the best scientific and technical talent to these important programs and has served to underline the crucial differences between nuclear weapons and conventional military munitions," a bipartisan group of U.S. senators wrote to OMB in March. [4]

The future of the labs is part of a larger debate over what kind of nuclear weapons complex the U.S. needs to support a post-Cold War arsenal. Some former production sites have been closed for cleanup, but the DOE still conducts weapons-related activities at eight sites. (*See map, p. 816.*) A Bush administration plan — originally called Complex 2030 and later renamed Complex Transformation — would have modernized many facilities and equipped them to produce a new stockpile of Reliable Replacement Warheads and maintain sizeable nuclear reserves. [5]

Now, however, the replacement warhead is off the table, and President Obama has called for further nuclear reductions. Many observers say the United States should complete its ongoing Nuclear Posture Review before deciding what goals nuclear weapons will serve. Then the size and scope of the nation's nuclear weapons infrastructure can be shaped accordingly.

— Jennifer Weeks

[1] "Leveraging Science for Security: A Strategy for the Nuclear Weapons Laboratories in the 21st Century," Henry L. Stimson Center, March 2009, p. 9, www.stimson.org/cnp/pdf/Leveraging_Science_for_Security_FINAL.pdf.

[2] "Congress Approves DOE Reorganization; Clinton Leaves Control with Energy Secretary," *Arms Control Today,* September/October 1999.

[3] Sue Vorenberg, "Feds Ponder Switching Labs to Military Agency," *Santa Fe New Mexican,* Feb. 4, 2009.

[4] "Senators Ask Obama Administration to End Study of Proposal to Move DOE Weapons Labs to Defense Department," Senate Energy and Natural Resources Committee, March 18, 2009. The senators were Sens. Jeff Bingaman (D-NM), Lisa Murkowski (R-AK), Byron Dorgan (D-ND), Robert Bennett (R-UT), and Bill Nelson (D-FL).

[5] For details see National Nuclear Security Administration, "Complex Transformation SPEIS," www.complextransformationspeis.com/index.html, and Philip Coyle III, "The Future of the DOE Complex Transformation Program," testimony before the House Committee on Appropriations, Subcommittee on Energy and Water, March 17, 2009, www.cdi.org/pdfs/CoyleHouseDOE3.09.pdf.

other limits, such as barring multiple warheads on land-based missiles.

To assess what these changes meant for U.S. security policy, Congress ordered the Clinton administration to carry out an assessment of U.S. nuclear forces and policies in a post-Cold War world. The first Nuclear Posture Review, completed in 1994, stuck to the status quo in many ways. It endorsed continued reliance on a triad of nuclear delivery systems (bombers, land-based missiles and submarine-launched missiles). And it recommended that the U.S. should "lead but hedge" on arms control by supporting nuclear reductions but keeping warheads removed from service in storage, where they could be reloaded quickly onto missiles and bombers if U.S.-Russian relations deteriorated. [59]

Clinton was the first world leader to sign the Comprehensive Test Ban Treaty (CTBT) when it was completed in 1996. But a Republican-led Senate rejected the treaty in 1999, with opponents arguing it would not keep other countries from going nuclear (India and Pakistan had each tested nuclear weapons a year earlier), and that ending U.S. nuclear testing would make it harder to ensure that U.S. nuclear weapons were safe and reliable.

President George W. Bush's administration (2001-2009) was cooler toward nuclear arms control and argued that the U.S. needed many options to deter rogue countries or terrorist groups with nuclear weapons. In 2002 a second Nuclear Posture Review by Bush's Defense Department argued that the ABM Treaty and the CTBT were not applicable to current security conditions. [60]

A leaked version of the study named countries against which the U.S. should be ready to use nuclear weapons — including Russia, China, Iran, Iraq, Libya, North Korea, and Serbia — and proposed developing new warheads, spurring charges that Bush was expanding U.S. reliance on nuclear weapons. [61] But the administration rejected that view. "We were trying to make nuclear weapons less usable, not more usable," says Brooks, the former National Nuclear Security Administration director under Bush.

In 2002 Bush traveled to Moscow and with Russian President Vladimir Putin signed the Strategic Offensive Reduction Treaty (SORT), a pact to reduce U.S. and Russian deployed strategic warheads to between 1,700 and 2,200 each by 2012. The agreement superseded START II, which had never been enacted because Russia's legislature conditioned its approval of that agreement on the U.S. adhering to the ABM Treaty. Unlike START II, the Moscow treaty did not specify how each side's pledges would be verified or dictate what would be done with warheads removed from service. [62] A few weeks later the U.S. withdrew from the ABM Treaty and pledged to deploy missile defenses against growing threats from countries like North Korea and Iran.

Russia's response was subdued at first, but the issue heated up in 2007 when the Bush administration started negotiating to put missile interceptors and radar in Poland and the Czech Republic. U.S. officials said they were needed to counter Iranian attacks on European and American targets, but Russian leaders argued the new sites could become part of a defensive network against Russian missiles. Putin said the U.S. defense system would lead to "an inevitable arms race" and suggested Russia might target its own weapons on Poland and the Czech Republic. [63] ■

CURRENT SITUATION

Reshaping U.S. Forces

The Obama administration is currently carrying out the third U.S. Nuclear Posture Review (NPR) since the end of the Cold War. This study, due in December, will establish policies for the next five to 10 years governing U.S. nuclear deterrence doctrine,

strategies, and the makeup of U.S. nuclear forces. Congress, executive branch officials, and many advocacy groups expect the NPR to define how nuclear weapons fit into President Obama's foreign and military agendas.

"The most important measure of whether President Obama is serious about pursuing a nuclear-free world will be how the NPR defines the future role of U.S. nuclear weapons," says Kimball of the Arms Control Association. "The president ought to articulate that nuclear weapons no longer play a useful role in deterring or fighting wars that start as conventional conflicts. They're not useful to deter or counter chemical and biological warfare threats. Mission statements dictate targets and requirements, so if the Obama administration crafts that kind of nuclear vision, the U.S. and Russia will be able to reduce their stockpiles to 1,000 warheads or fewer apiece. That will let us engage other countries in a discussion about multilateral nuclear disarmament."

To conservatives, however, nuclear weapons serve many important security functions, including reassuring U.S. allies that they are protected under a strong nuclear umbrella. "The key elements of a robust deterrent are under extreme stress today and will be imperiled further by a presidential determination to pursue a 'world without nuclear weapons' and the attendant policy of not investing in modernization of the stockpile," a group of former U.S. security officials warned in July. [64] The authors, with years of service in mainly Republican administrations, argued that modernizing U.S. nuclear weapons and delivery systems and developing national missile defenses should take priority over negotiating any new nuclear reduction agreements with Russia.

In that same month, however, Obama and Russian President Medvedev agreed on new warhead reduction targets for a follow-on treaty to START I, which expires in December. Under the new targets the United States and Rus-

sia pledge to reduce their deployed strategic nuclear warheads from the current limit of 2,200 each by 2012 to between 1,500 and 1,675 each by 2016. Both sides would also make some cuts in nuclear bombers and missiles. [65]

Alarmed over these new proposed reductions, Senate conservatives attached several non-binding resolutions to a defense spending bill stating that the new treaty should not limit missile defenses, space capabilities or advanced conventional weapons, and endorsing the Bush administration's proposed missile defense system based in Poland and the Czech Republic. "I have yet to hear a convincing strategic rationale that would justify going this low [on warheads and delivery vehicles]," said Sen. Jeff Sessions, R-Ala., who warned that he would condition his support for any START follow-on agreement on "a serious commitment by the administration to modernize our nuclear deterrent." [66]

Some observers predict that with hawks pushing back, President Obama may have trouble making radical policy changes in the Nuclear Posture Review. "There are a lot of Bush administration holdovers in the nuclear bureaucracy, so the NPR may not end up being all that path-breaking," says Carnegie Endowment analyst Squassoni. "The real question is whether the president will step in and make a difference."

North Korea and Iran

As the U.S. reexamines its own nuclear weapons policies, it is also working to limit options for proliferators, especially North Korea and Iran. North Korea expelled international inspectors and withdrew from six-nation denuclearization talks in April, then conducted its second nuclear test in May. Although security experts estimate North Korea has produced enough plutonium for perhaps four to eight bombs, they mainly fear Pyongyang will sell

Continued on p. 830

At Issue:

Can we detect Nuclear Test Ban cheaters?

RICHARD L. GARWIN
FELLOW EMERITUS, THOMAS J. WATSON RESEARCH CENTER, IBM

WRITTEN FOR *CQ RESEARCHER*, SEPTEMBER 2009

i have been involved in detecting clandestine nuclear explosions since before December 1958, when I had a role in the U.N. Conference of Experts in Geneva devoted to seismic detection. The weapons that destroyed Hiroshima and Nagasaki were in the 10-kiloton range, but stockpile nuclear weapons today range to considerably more than a megaton yield (1 million tons of TNT equivalent).

Now 247 of the 337 facilities planned for the International Monitoring System (IMS) have been certified. These include primary and auxiliary seismic stations, infrasound sensors, hydroacoustic detectors and radionuclide laboratories.

The seismic sensors in particular are augmented by thousands of university seismometers in cooperative networks, with advancing capabilities to detect earthquakes. These networks can be focused even after the fact on nuclear test sites or suspect locations. The technology of detection has continuously improved, as well as the ability to distinguish underground explosions from background earthquakes. There has been no such evolution in means of hiding nuclear explosions.

According to a 2002 National Academy of Sciences study that analyzed the planned capability for Comprehensive Test Ban Treaty (CTBT) verification and possible military advances by any foreign testing that might evade detection, "[T]he only evasion scenarios that need to be taken seriously at this time are cavity decoupling and mine masking." The IMS network readily meets its goal of confident detection of a one-kiloton explosion non-evasively tested anywhere in the world, and has sensitivity a thousand times greater to explosions in the oceans.

In general, advanced nuclear weapon states that could hide a one-kiloton explosion would have little to gain from successfully doing so, and much to lose if concealment failed. Emerging nuclear powers are unlikely to be successful in such concealment and would also have little benefit, because the test explosive would have to be so modified to limit its yield as to bear little resemblance to an actual weapon.

The CTBT provides for on-site inspections (OSI) following a questionable seismic detection, allowing the search of 1,000 square kilometers of terrain. An OSI exercise of similar size was practiced in Kazakhstan in August 2008, with good results.

Former U.S. arms control negotiator Paul Nitze wrote in 1999 that the CTBT can be verified "with great confidence," more than meeting his prior general requirement that an arms control agreement be "adequately verifiable." I am now involved in a reassessment of this question.

THOMAS SCHEBER
VICE PRESIDENT, NATIONAL INSTITUTE FOR PUBLIC POLICY

WRITTEN FOR *CQ RESEARCHER*, SEPTEMBER 2009

t o be effective, a CTBT detection and verification regime would need to be highly intrusive and guarantee timely on-site inspections to resolve indications of cheating. The planned treaty regime is incapable of doing that.

First, there cannot be confidence in verification if major parties to the treaty don't agree on what is banned and permitted. The treaty is not clear. The CTBT prohibits all nuclear explosions. The U.S. interprets this prohibition strictly as zero-yield. Apparently Russia and possibly China do not accept the U.S. criterion and conduct low-yield nuclear tests.

Second, a zero-yield treaty poses an unattainable verification challenge. Evasion techniques can reduce the signature of a nuclear explosion by factors of 50 to 100; evidence can be obscured by natural geologic activity or man-made explosions. A National Academy of Sciences report on the CTBT addressed testing techniques to evade detection or attribution and concluded that, with evasive techniques, verification of testing below a kiloton could be problematic. These techniques include cavity decoupling, masking, or testing in an environment that makes attribution difficult. A CIA assessment concluded: "an evader could successfully contain a decoupled test in hard rock, using a cautious experimental approach, and thereby avoid detection by sensors external to its country."

Third, nuclear tests below a kiloton can provide valuable data — perhaps more valuable for the Russians than for the U.S. Russia has extensive experience with low-yield nuclear testing and a system to fully contain very low-yield tests. When U.S. personnel helped clean up a former Soviet test site in Kazakhstan, they discovered that 20 percent of the tests conducted there had escaped detection. These tests were low-yield and designed for special weapon effects. Recently, Russia has gone to great expense to restore its nuclear testing infrastructure.

Fourth, even the planned, inadequate verification provisions won't be fully implemented because CTBT cannot enter into force until it is ratified by North Korea, Iran, China, India, Pakistan, Israel, and Egypt.

Finally, verifying compliance would require timely on-site challenge inspections to investigate evidence of cheating. The CTBT requires that 30 of 51 members of an Executive Council consider the evidence and vote for inspection. Only 10 of the 51 member-states would be from North America or Western Europe; the U.S. is not even guaranteed a vote. This is a prescription for inaction.

Bottom line: A "zero-yield" nuclear test ban treaty is not verifiable.

Continued from p. 828

nuclear materials and technology to other countries or groups. [67]

Because North Korea is diplomatically isolated, the U.S. has little direct leverage over its behavior. In the short term, U.S. leaders want to keep the North from spreading nuclear technology abroad. "You can't do anything about North Korea until it wants to have a different kind of relationship with the world, so the problem is to contain its impact," says Harvard's Walt.

Other nations also support containment of North Korea. In June the U.N. Security Council unanimously condemned its May nuclear test, tightening trade sanctions and calling on member countries to inspect and destroy all banned cargo coming to or from North Korea. China and Russia, both former allies of North Korea, both condemned the test. [68]

"We still want North Korea to come back to the negotiating table, to be part of an international effort that will lead to denuclearization," said Secretary of State Hillary Rodham Clinton in July. "But we're not going to reward them for doing what they said they would do in 2005 and 2006." [69]

Defense Secretary Gates said after the May test that the U.S. "will not accept North Korea as a nuclear state." [70] However, many observers believe North Korea hopes the U.S. will ultimately do just that — much as it opposed but ultimately recognized India's and Pakistan's nuclear programs. [71]

The challenge is different with Iran, which still belongs to the Nuclear Non-Proliferation Treaty and maintains that its nuclear research activities are strictly for peaceful purposes. But that position rings hollower than ever after last month's disclosure that Iran had built a second secret uranium enrichment plant. [72] President Obama's emphasis on diplomatic engagement and enforcing international treaties will be tested as the United States works to rally a strong international response.

The United States wants Iran to suspend enrichment activities, declare all of its nuclear activities, and open its nuclear facilities to international inspections.

"[I]f the U.S. extends a defense umbrella over the region, if we do even more to support the military capacity of those in the [Persian] Gulf, it's unlikely that Iran will be any stronger or safer, because they won't be able to intimidate and dominate, as they apparently believe they can, once they have a nuclear weapon," Secretary Clinton said in July. Officials in Washington said this was the first time the U.S. had publicly discussed offering defensive support to other Middle Eastern countries like Saudi Arabia and Egypt if Iran continued to pursue a nuclear capability. [73]

One of Obama's major diplomatic goals will be persuading Russia and China to support strong international sanctions on Iran if its leaders refuse to disclose their nuclear activities. Both countries have trade relationships with Iran and have resisted sanctions in the past. However, they also supported the Security Council resolution, which reaffirms the need to strengthen the NPT.

"It's all very well and good for the U.N. to condemn proliferator countries, but state actions supporting those measures determine whether they'll work or not," says Squassoni. "We can't be the global nuclear weapons policemen on our own. We need collaboration from our allies and Russia and China and a lot of other states."

New START with Russia

President Obama's administration came into office determined to "press the reset button with Russia," in Vice President Joseph Biden's words, and restore cooperation with Moscow on many issues — particularly arms control — where cooperation had deteriorated under President Bush. [74]

"We can and should cooperate to secure loose nuclear weapons and ma-

terials to prevent their spread, to renew the verification procedures in the START Treaty, and then go beyond existing treaties to negotiate deeper cuts in both our arsenals," Biden said in February. "The United States and Russia have a special obligation to lead the international effort to reduce the number of nuclear weapons in the world." [75]

Obama and Russian President Medvedev issued a joint statement in April affirming that they had committed both nations to "achieving a nuclear free world" through steps including a follow-on agreement to the START Treaty and efforts to strengthen international nuclear non-proliferation policies, bring the Comprehensive Test Ban Treaty into force and negotiate a fissile production cutoff treaty. They also noted the possibility of U.S.-Russian cooperation on missile defense issues — no longer a far-fetched prospect in the wake of Obama's decision not to base mid-range defenses in Eastern Europe. [76]

But putting these agreements into action will require much more work. For example, the July agreement on post-START reductions identified ranges, not final numbers. Nuclear warheads would be limited to between 1,500 and 1,650 on each side, while delivery vehicles (bombers and missiles) would be reduced to between 500 and 1,100 each. Russia reportedly favors the lower numbers, while U.S. negotiators pushed for the higher figures. Nonetheless, observers saw the targets as a good first step.

"Russia is eager to do a START follow-on because its nuclear forces are coming down anyway," says former NNSA administrator Brooks. "And the transparency measures in the new treaty will be important, because we're still deeply suspicious of Russia's technology efforts, and they're suspicious of ours."

Since 1992 the United States and Russia have worked together under the Cooperative Threat Reduction (CTR) partnership, popularly known as the Nunn-Lugar initiative, to deactivate more than 7,000 warheads and destroy hundreds of bombers and long-range ballistic missiles. [77] CTR has also greatly improved security at many sites that store warheads and nuclear materials, although much remains to be done to consolidate the former Soviet Union's sprawling nuclear complex. [78]

"This work is essential in preventing nuclear terrorism and deserves greater support and government resources," said Nunn last May after the United States, Russia and the International Atomic Energy Agency helped remove 162 pounds of weapon-grade uranium (enough for about three bombs) from Kazakhstan. [79]

But even the popular Nunn-Lugar program faces constant budget pressures. Indeed, while Obama announced a new international effort in his Prague speech to "secure all vulnerable nuclear material around the world within four years," his 2010 budget request for nuclear threat reduction and related programs totals about $2.8 billion, about $150 million below the current level. [80] ∎

OUTLOOK

Tipping Point?

In April 2010, members of the Nuclear Non-Proliferation Treaty (NPT) will hold their next five-year review conference to assess how well the pact is working. Most observers see the meeting as a critical decision point. If governments agree that progress is being made toward international arms control goals, they will be likely to make new commitments to support it. Conversely, if nations cannot agree on how to achieve key nonproliferation goals — as happened at the 2005 review conference — some experts worry that more proliferation, not less, could be the result.

"The 2005 review conference was a total disaster," says the Arms Control Association's Kimball. "The nonproliferation

regime was in crisis: North Korea was withdrawing from the NPT and producing plutonium, Iran had been discovered to be developing a nuclear capability and the Bush administration had rejected the Comprehensive Test Ban Treaty as counter to U.S. interests. It was an important time for the world to come together and strengthen the treaty, and it didn't, partly because the United States didn't lead."

The tone has been more optimistic in preparatory meetings for the 2010 conference, and progress toward new U.S. and Russian reductions will help to demonstrate that the nuclear superpowers are serious about their disarmament commitments. "Obama's new approach is already producing some results," says Kimball, "but the U.S. and other countries will have to work hard to build consensus for an action plan that sets new limits on nuclear weapon development."

Many steps could be taken to strengthen the NPT regime. For example, says the Carnegie Endowment's Squassoni, states could endorse limits on reprocessing plutonium and enriching uranium. In addition, supporting the creation of an international nuclear fuel bank to replace national facilities would take the moral high ground away from countries like Iran that use civilian nuclear programs as cover for military activities.

"In 2005 countries like Iran talked about their rights to enrichment, reprocessing and peaceful use of nuclear energy under the NPT, and a lot of nonaligned states bought it," she says. "The debates were very polemical, not constructive."

Other helpful steps could include agreement on how NPT members should react if another state emulates North Korea and withdraws from the treaty, or more states adopt so-called additional protocols (intrusive inspections and monitoring) to their basic nuclear safeguard agreements with the International Atomic Energy Agency. As of mid-2009, 42 countries had not brought additional protocols into force, including Iran. [81]

Either as part of the review conference or separately, many experts would like to see cooperative threat reduction (CTR) programs expanded globally, as President Obama pledged in Prague. "I'd like to see it extended to all countries that have fissile materials," says Stanford University's Hecker, who has discussed protection, control and accounting for nuclear materials with officials in countries including Russia, India and North Korea. "There's very little uniformity across the world in how countries handle these materials or what they think needs to be done to provide a comprehensive safeguards system."

Some observers say that CTR programs could be much more effective. Rens Lee, an independent security consultant and author of a book on nuclear smuggling, argues that Obama needs a more proactive strategy that includes sharing intelligence with Russia about nuclear trafficking. "[A]ctual sharing remains woefully inadequate, both bilaterally and with international organizations such as the International Atomic Energy Agency," Lee wrote in July. [82]

But the basic concept of CTR has broad support. A congressionally mandated National Academy of Sciences study, released earlier this year, called for dramatically scaling up CTR programs to reduce threats from weapons of mass destruction in regions including the Middle East and Asia.

"The world is smaller than it was in 1992," the study said. "Ignoring globalization is not an option, whether in economics, public health, combating terrorism, or reducing the threat of WMD [weapons of mass destruction]. While our technological and military capabilities will continue to play an essential role, engagement is also one of the most important tools in the national security arsenal." [83] ∎

Notes

[1] "Text of Obama's speech to the United Nations General Assembly," *The New York Times*, Sept. 23, 2009.

[2] Stephen I. Schwartz with Deepti Choubey, *Nuclear Security Spending: Assessing Costs, Examining Priorities* (2009), p. 7, www.carnegie endowment.org/files/nuclear_security_spending_low.pdf.

[3] George P. Shultz, *et al.*, "A World Free of Nuclear Weapons," *The Wall Street Journal*, Jan. 4, 2007.

[4] Nuclear weapons get their explosive power from materials that are fissile, meaning that their atoms can be split by certain types of sub-atomic particles (neutrons). The main fissile materials are uranium-233, uranium-235, and plutonium-239.

[5] Remarks by President Barack Obama, Prague, Czech Republic, April 5, 2009, www.white house.gov/the_press_office/Remarks-By-President-Barack-Obama-In-Prague-As-Delivered/.

[6] "U.S. Scraps Missile Defense Shield Plans," CNN.com, Sept. 17, 2009.

[7] Clifford J. Levy and Peter Baker, "Putin Applauds Brave U.S. Decision on Missile Defense," *The New York Times*, Sept. 19, 2009.

[8] "Statement of Senator John McCain," Sept. 17, 2009, http://mccain.senate.gov/public/.

[9] "Historic Summit of Security Council Pledges Support for Progress on Stalled Efforts to End Nuclear Weapons Proliferation," United Nations, Sept. 24, 2009.

[10] *Ibid.*

[11] Natural Resources Defense Council, "Archive of Nuclear Data: Table of Global Nuclear Weapons Stockpiles, 1945-2002," www.nrdc.org/nuclear/nudb/datab19.asp.

[12] America's Strategic Posture: Final Report of the Congressional Commission on the Strategic Posture of the United States (2009), chapters 2, 5 and 9, www.usip.org/files/file/strat_posture_report_adv_copy.pdf.

[13] David E. Sanger and Helene Cooper, "Iran is Warned Over Nuclear Deception," *The New York Times*, Sept. 26, 2009.

[14] "The Disarmament Illusion," editorial, *The Wall Street Journal*, Sept. 26, 2009.

[15] For the treaty's history and full text, see www.state.gov/www/global/arms/treaties/npt.html.

[16] www.globalzero.org/files/pdf/gzap_3.0.pdf.

[17] For background see Mary H. Cooper, "Nuclear Proliferation and Terrorism," *CQ Researcher*, April 2, 2004, pp. 297-320.

[18] Joseph Cirincione, *Bomb Scare: The History & Future of Nuclear Weapons* (2007), pp. 126-127.

[19] Harold Brown and John Deutch, "The Nuclear Disarmament Fantasy," *The Wall Street Journal*, Nov. 19, 2007.

[20] Treaty text is at www.state.gov/www/global/arms/treaties/ctb.html.

[21] Annex 2 of the treaty lists 44 countries that must sign and ratify the treaty for it to enter into force. As of mid-2009, 35 of these countries had done so.

[22] Damien J. LaVera, "Looking Back: The U.S. Senate Vote on the Comprehensive Test Ban Treaty," Arms Control Today, October 2004.

[23] Jon Kyl and Richard Perle, "Our Decaying Nuclear Deterrent," *The Wall Street Journal*, June 30, 2009.

[24] Congressional Record, June 8, 2009, p. S6238.

[25] Comprehensive Nuclear Test Ban Treaty Organization, "CTBTO's Initial Findings on the DPRK's 2009 Announced Nuclear Test," May 25, 2009, www.ctbto.org/press-centre/press-releases/2009/ctbtos-initial-findings-on-the-dprks-2009-announced-nuclear-test/.

[26] National Academy of Sciences, Technical Issues Related to the Comprehensive Nuclear Test Ban Treaty (National Academy Press, 2009), p. 5.

[27] Speech at Strategic Weapons in the 21st Century Conference, Washington, D.C., Jan. 31, 2008, pp. 2-3, www.lanl.gov/conferences/sw/docs/chilton-speech-SW21-31Jan08.pdf.

[28] Charles D. Ferguson, "Mini-Nuclear Weapons and the U.S. Nuclear Posture Review," Monterey Institute of International Studies, April 8, 2002, http://cns.miis.edu/stories/020408.htm.

[29] James Sterngold, "Failure to Launch," *Mother Jones*, January 2008.

[30] Jonathan Medalia, "The Reliable Replacement Warhead Program: Background and Current Developments," Congressional Research Service, Sept. 12, 2008, pp. 45-46, www.fas.org/sgp/crs/nuke/RL32929.pdf.

[31] Robert Gates, "Nuclear Weapons and Deterrence in the 21st Century," speech at Carnegie Endowment for International Peace, Oct. 28, 2008, p. 5, www.carnegieendowment.org/files/1028_transcrip_gates_checked.pdf.

[32] Hearing before House Armed Services Committee, March 17, 2009, www.stratcom.mil/speeches/21/.

[33] *Technical Issues Related to the Comprehensive Nuclear Test Ban Treaty*, National Academy of Sciences (2002), p. 5.

[34] "Pit Lifetime," MITRE Corporation, Nov. 20, 2006, p. 16, www.nukewatch.org/facts/nwd/JASON_ReportPuAging.pdf; National Nuclear Security Administration, "Studies Show Plutonium Degradation in U.S. Nuclear Weapons Will Not Affect Reliability Soon," Nov. 29, 2006.

[35] National Nuclear Security Administration, "Life Extension Programs," http://nnsa.energy.gov/defense_programs/life_extension_programs.htm.

[36] For details see U.S. Government Accountability Office, "Nuclear Weapons: Annual Assessment of the Safety, Performance, and Reliability of the Nation's Stockpile," Feb. 2, 2007, p. 14.

[37] Gates, *op. cit.*, p. 5.

[38] "The U.S. Military Index," *Foreign Policy*, March/April 2008, p. 77.

[39] U.S. Department of Energy, Office of History and Heritage Resources, "The Manhattan Project: An Interactive History," www.cfo.doe.gov/me70/manhattan/retrospect.htm.

[40] *Ibid.*

[41] McGeorge Bundy, *Danger and Survival: Choices About the Bomb in the First Fifty Years* (1988), p. 113.

[42] A ballistic missile is powered during the launch phase of its flight and then falls freely toward its target.

[43] Bundy, *op. cit.*, p. 350.

[44] Natural Resources Defense Council, "Table of Global Nuclear Weapons Stockpiles, 1945-2002," www.nrdc.org/nuclear/nudb/datab19.asp.

[45] For an account and analysis of the crisis, see Bundy, *op cit.*, pp. 391-452. Bundy was President Kennedy's national security advisor during the missile crisis.

[46] News conference 52, March 21, 1963, www.jfklibrary.org/Historical+Resources/Archives/Reference+Desk/Press+Conferences/.

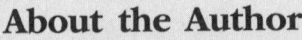

About the Author

Jennifer Weeks is a *CQ Researcher* contributing writer in Watertown, Mass., who specializes in energy and environmental issues. She has written for *The Washington Post, The Boston Globe Magazine* and other publications, and has 15 years' experience as a public-policy analyst, lobbyist and congressional staffer. She has an A.B. degree from Williams College and master's degrees from the University of North Carolina and Harvard.

[47] Text and background at www.state.gov/www/global/arms/treaties/ltbt1.html.

[48] *Ibid.*

[49] Natural Resources Defense Council, *op. cit.*

[50] Text and background at www.state.gov/www/global/arms/treaties/salt1.html and www.state.gov/www/global/arms/treaties/abm/abm2.html.

[51] Presidential Directive 59, July 25, 1980, www.fas.org/irp/offdocs/pd/pd59.pdf.

[52] Robert Scheer, *With Enough Shovels: Reagan, Bush and Nuclear War* (1983), p. 20.

[53] Michael Goodwin, "Antinuclear Protest Cost the City $1.8 Million," *The New York Times*, July 25, 1982.

[54] U.S. Catholic Bishops' Pastoral Letter on War and Peace, May 3, 1983, www.nuclearfiles.org/menu/key-issues/ethics/issues/religious/us-catholic-bishops-pastoral-letter.htm.

[55] For background see Mary H. Cooper, "Missile Defense," *CQ Researcher*, Sept. 8, 2000.

[56] Nikolai Sokov, "Reykjavik Summit: the Legacy and a Lesson for the Future," Nuclear Threat Initiative, December 2007.

[57] Text and background at www.state.gov/www/global/arms/treaties/inf1.html.

[58] Compiled from Nuclear Threat Initiative, "Threat Reduction Budgets," www.nti.org/e_research/cnwm/overview/cnwm_home.asp.

[59] Nuclear Threat Initiative, "U.S. Nuclear Posture Reviews," www.nti.org/f_wmd411/f2c.html.

[60] *Ibid.*

[61] Philipp C. Bleek, "Nuclear Posture Review Leaks: Outlines Targets, Contingencies," *Arms Control Today*, April 2002.

[62] Arms Control Association, "START II and Its Extension Protocol at a Glance," January 2003, www.armscontrl.org/print/2562; Nuclear Threat Initiative, "The SORT Treaty," updated July 2009www.nti.org/f_wmd411/f2b2_1.html.

[63] Steven A. Hildreth and Carl Ek, "Long-Range Ballistic Missile Defense in Europe," Congressional Research Service, June 22, 2009, p. 17, www.fas.org/sgp/crs/weapons/RL34051.pdf.

[64] New Deterrent Working Group, "U.S. Nuclear Deterrence in the 21st Century: Getting It Right," Center for Security Policy, July 2009, p. 12, http://204.96.138.161/upload/wysiwyg/center%20publication%20pdfs/NDWG-%20Getting%20It%20Right.pdf.

[65] Clifford J. Levy and Peter Baker, "U.S.-Russia Nuclear Agreement is first Step in Broad Effort," *The New York Times*, July 7, 2009.

[66] Congressional Record, July 22, 2009, p. S7850.

[67] Siegfried S. Hecker, "The Risks of North Korea's Restart," Bulletin of the Atomic Scientists, May 12, 2009; David E. Sanger, "Tested Early by North Korea, Obama Has Few Options," *The New York*

Times, May 26, 2009. For background see Mary H. Cooper, "North Korean Crisis," *CQ Researcher*, April 11, 2003, pp. 321-344.

[68] United Nations Department of Public Information, "Security Council, Acting Unanimously, condemns in Strongest Terms Democratic People's Republic of Korea Nuclear Test, Toughens Sanctions," June 12, 2009.

[69] Interviewed on Meet the Press, July 26, 2009, www.msnbc.msn.com/id/32142102/ns/meet_the_press/.

[70] Neil Chatterjee, "U.S. Says Will Not Accept N. Korea as Nuclear State," Reuters, May 30, 2009.

[71] See Martin Fackler, "Test Delivers a Message for Domestic Audience," *The New York Times*, May 26, 2009,

[72] David E. Sanger and Helene Cooper, "Iran Is Warned Over Nuclear Deception," *The New York Times*, Sept. 26, 2009.

[73] Mark Landler and David E. Sanger, "Clinton Speaks of Shielding Mideast from Iran," *The New York Times*, July 23, 2009.

[74] For background see Roland Flamini, "Dealing with the 'New' Russia," *CQ Researcher*, June 6, 2008, pp. 481-504.

[75] "Biden's full remarks at the Munich conference," *Politico.com*, Feb. 7, 2009, www.politico.com/news/stories/0209/18535.html.

[76] "Joint Statement by President Obama and President Medvedev," The White House, April 1, 2009.

[77] Office of Sen. Richard G. Lugar, "The Nunn-Lugar Scorecard," http://lugar.senate.gov/nunnlugar/scorecard.html.

[78] Matthew Bunn, "Securing the Bomb 2008," Harvard University, November 2008, pp. vi-xi, www.nti.org/e_research/STB08_Executive_Summary.pdf.

[79] "NTI Co-chairman Sam Nunn Commends Successful Removal of Dangerous Nuclear Material from Kazakhstan," Nuclear Threat Initiative, May 19, 2009.

[80] Kingston Reif and Cuyler O'Brien, "Obama Nuclear Nonproliferation Budget Disappointing," Center for Arms Control and Non-Proliferation, June 2, 2009.

[81] International Atomic Energy Agency, "Strengthened Safeguards System: Status of Additional Protocols," July 9, 2009, www.iaea.org/OurWord/SV/Safeguards/sg_protocol.html.

[82] Rens Lee, "Toward an Intelligence-Based Nuclear Cooperations Regime," Foreign Policy Research Institute, July 2009.

[83] Committee on International Security and Arms Control, National Academy of Sciences, *Global Security Engagement: A New Model for Cooperative Threat Reduction* (2009), p. 9.

FOR MORE INFORMATION

Alliance for Nuclear Accountability, 903 West Alameda St., #505, Santa Fe, NM 87501; (505) 473-1670; www.ananuclear.org. A network of local, regional and national organizations working to control pollution from nuclear weapons production.

Arms Control Association, 1313 L St., N.W., Suite 130, Washington, DC 20036; (202) 463-8270; www.armscontrol.org. A nonprofit, nonpartisan organization that promotes public understanding of and support for effective arms control policies.

Atomic Heritage Foundation, 910 17th St., N.W., Suite 408, Washington, DC 20006; (202) 293-0045; www.atomicheritage.org. A nonprofit organization working to preserve and interpret the Manhattan Project and its legacy.

Center for International Security and Cooperation, 616 Serra St., E200, Stanford University, Stanford, CA 94305-6055; (650) 723-9265; http://cisac.stanford.edu. Studies nuclear weapons strategy and proliferation.

National Institute for Public Policy, 9302 Lee Hwy., Suite 750, Fairfax, VA 22301-1214; (703) 293-9181; www.nipp.org. A nonprofit education organization focusing on foreign and defense policy from a conservative perspective.

National Nuclear Security Administration, U.S. Department of Energy, 1000 Independence Ave., S.W., Washington, DC 20585; (800) 342-5363; http://nnsa.energy.gov. Manages the nation's nuclear stockpile and related laboratories and production plants.

Nuclear Threat Initiative, 1747 Pennsylvania Ave., N.W., 7th Floor, Washington, DC 20006; (202) 296-4810; www.nti.org. Works to strengthen global security by preventing the spread of weapons of mass destruction.

Ploughshares Fund, Fort Mason Center B-330, San Francisco, CA 94123; (415) 775-2244; www.ploughshares.org. Opposes the spread of nuclear weapons.

Bibliography

Selected Sources

Books

Allison, Graham, *Nuclear Terrorism: The Ultimate Preventable Catastrophe*, Times Books, 2004.
A Harvard professor and former Defense Department official explores the risk of terrorist nuclear attacks on the U.S.

Bundy, McGeorge, *Danger and Survival: Choices About the Bomb in the First 50 Years*, Vintage, 1990.
A national security adviser to presidents Kennedy and Johnson examines factors that led nations to pursue or forswear nuclear weapons during World War II and the Cold War.

Moran, Barbara, *The Day We Lost the H-Bomb: Cold War, Hot Nukes, and the Worst Nuclear Weapons Disaster in History*, Presidio Press, 2009.
Journalist Moran revisits the 1966 collision of a U.S. B-52 bomber carrying four hydrogen bombs with a refueling plane over Spain.

Shultz, George P., *et al.*, eds., *Reykjavik Revisited: Steps Toward a World Free of Nuclear Weapons*, Hoover Institution Press, 2008.
National security experts examine the steps required to reduce threats from nuclear weapons and move toward their elimination.

Articles

Bender, Bryan, "Obama Seeks Global Uranium Fuel Bank," *The Boston Globe*, June 8, 2009.
Bender outlines an idea advocated by many arms control specialists: creating an international nuclear fuel supply so that countries would not need to build fuel production systems that could produce weapon-grade nuclear material.

Broad, William J., and David E. Sanger, "Obama's Youth Shaped His Nuclear-Free Vision," *The New York Times*, July 5, 2009.
President Obama's support for nuclear abolition dates back to his college years.

DeSutter, Paula A., "The Test Ban Treaty Would Help North Korea," *The Wall Street Journal*, June 1, 2009.
A former Bush administration official argues that ending nuclear testing would erode U.S. nuclear credibility.

Kimball, Daryl, "Change Nuclear Weapons Policy? Yes, We Can," *Foreign Policy in Focus*, Nov. 25, 2008.
The director of the Arms Control Association contends that without action by the Obama administration to shrink nuclear arsenals and transform U.S. nuclear policy, global risks of nuclear proliferation and terrorism will increase.

Suri, Jeremi, "The Nukes of October: Richard Nixon's Secret Plan to Bring Peace to Vietnam," *Wired*, Feb. 25, 2008.
A professor details how in 1969 President Richard M. Nixon sent nuclear-armed bombers to the edge of Soviet airspace to convince Soviet leaders and their North Vietnamese allies that unless they joined talks to end the Vietnam War, the United States might end it with nuclear weapons.

Reports and Studies

"Leveraging Science for Security: A Strategy for the Nuclear Weapons Laboratories in the 21st Century," Henry L. Stimson Center, March 2009, www.stimson.org/cnp/pdf/Leveraging_Science_for_Security_FINAL.pdf.
A task force co-chaired by former senior officials from the Clinton and Bush administrations recommends moving nuclear weapons laboratories in the United States into a new agency that would maintain the nuclear arsenal and analyze national security problems.

"U.S. Nuclear Weapons Policy," Council on Foreign Relations, Independent Task Force Report No. 62, 2009, www.cfr.org/content/publications/attachments/Nuclear_Weapons_TFR62.pdf.
Nuclear security experts recommend how to reshape U.S. nuclear forces and policies to address nuclear proliferation and other post-Cold War security threats.

"White Paper on the Necessity of the U.S. Nuclear Deterrent," National Institute for Public Policy, Aug. 15, 2007, www.nipp.org/Publication/Downloads/Publication%20Archive%20PDF/Deterrence%20Paper%20-%20version%202.pdf.
Conservative security scholars and former government officials contend the United States still needs nuclear weapons for deterring attacks, destroying strategic military targets and stemming nuclear proliferation.

Perkovich, George, *et al.*, "Abolishing Nuclear Weapons: A Debate," Carnegie Endowment for International Peace, February 2009, www.carnegieendowment.org/files/abolishing_nuclear_weapons_debate.pdf.
Security experts in 13 countries examine what would be required to achieve nuclear disarmament.

Schwartz, Stephen I., with Deepti Choubey, *Nuclear Security Spending: Assessing Costs, Examining Priorities* (2009), p. 7, www.carnegieendowment.org/files/nuclear_security_spending_low.pdf.
A review of U.S. funding for programs related to nuclear weapons finds that the nation is still spending more than $50 billion annually in this area nearly two decades after the Cold War.

The Next Step:

Additional Articles from Current Periodicals

Disarmament

Cirincione, Joseph, "A Critical Mass for Disarmament; Change, Failure, and Fear are Propelling Us Toward a World Without Nuclear Weapons," *Los Angeles Times*, June 4, 2008, p. A23.

Nuclear disarmament is supported by Cold War-era politicians who argue that nuclear weapons in politically unstable countries could promote nuclear terrorism.

Gearan, Anne, "Obama Envisions a Nuke-Free World," *Star-Ledger* **(New Jersey), April 4, 2009, p. 4.**

President Obama has called for a world without nuclear weapons by increasing diplomatic efforts with nuclear starter states such as Iran.

Kristol, William, "Nuclear Fantasy; Disarmament Requires a World Without War," *The Washington Post*, **April 7, 2009, p. A23.**

Regulation of the deployment of nuclear weapons and limits on nuclear production and the export of nuclear materials are feasible solutions to nuclear proliferation.

Monroe, Robert R., "Decision Time on Deterrence; Only a Strongly Armed America Can Prevent Proliferation," *The Washington Times*, **May 7, 2009, p. A23.**

The United States has decreased its nuclear weaponry in recent years, which has not deterred other countries from developing their own arsenals.

Pincus, Walter, "Elements of 1960 CIA Report Hold True Today," *The Washington Post*, **June 16, 2009, p. A19.**

A newly declassified CIA report says North Korea and Iran are unlikely to abandon their nuclear ambitions without complete trust in other nations doing the same.

New Weapons

Bowden, Mark, "Best New Foreign Policy? Ban Nukes," *The Philadelphia Enquirer*, **Jan. 13, 2009.**

While North Korea and Iran are trying to develop new nuclear weapons, it is in the best interest of the United States not to do the same.

Dyer, Gwynne, "Nuclear Weapons: Putting the Cart Before the Horse," *Salt Lake Tribune*, **July 8, 2009.**

None of the countries engaged in the Nuclear Non-Proliferation Treaty have taken steps to get rid of their existing weapons.

Krieger, David, "U.S. Leadership Is Needed for a Nuclear Weapons-Free World," *Santa Barbara Independent* **(California), Oct. 18, 2007, p. 15.**

Congress is divided on whether or not the United States should develop any new nuclear weapons.

Testing

DeTar, Carleton, and Farrell Edwards, "U.S. Should Ratify Comprehensive Nuclear Test Ban Treaty," *Salt Lake Tribune*, **March 7, 2009.**

The United States should ratify the Comprehensive Nuclear Test Ban Treaty to show its commitment to halting the spread of nuclear weapons and weapons testing.

Gaffney Jr., Frank, "Peace Through Weakness?" *The Washington Times*, **Feb. 17, 2009, p. A14.**

President Obama's plan to end nuclear testing opens the door for other countries to increase their nuclear capabilities.

Lederer, Edith M., "UN Council Condemns North Korea's Nuclear Testing; Threatens New Sanctions for Violation," *The Boston Globe*, **May 26, 2009, p. A6.**

The U.N. Security Council has condemned North Korea's recent nuclear testing and is considering imposing sanctions.

Lobsenz, George, "NNSA: RRW Makes Return to Nuke Testing Less Likely," *Defense Daily*, **March 6, 2008.**

The National Nuclear Security Administration is encouraging the development of the "reliable replacement warhead" in order to eliminate the necessity of nuclear testing.

Parsons, Christi, and Tom Hamburger, "A Pledge to Curb the Nuclear Threat; Obama Says the U.S. is Ready to Lead the Effort to Reduce, and One Day Eliminate, the World's Atomic Stockpile," *Los Angeles Times*, **April 6, 2009, p. A1.**

President Obama told a crowd in Prague about his intent to ban the testing of nuclear weapons and outlined a plan to secure loose fissile material from terrorists.

In-depth Reports on Issues in the News

Are you writing a paper?

Need backup for a debate?

Want to become an expert on an issue?

For more than 80 years, students have turned to *CQ Researcher* for in-depth reporting on issues in the news. Reports on a full range of political and social issues are now available. Following is a selection of recent reports:

Civil Liberties
Closing Guantánamo, 2/09
Affirmative Action, 10/08
Gay Marriage Showdowns, 9/08
America's Border Fence, 9/08
Immigration Debate, 2/08

Crime/Law
Interrogating the CIA, 9/09
Examining Forensics, 7/09
Legalizing Marijuana, 6/09
Wrongful Convictions, 4/09
Prostitution Debate, 5/08

Education
Reading Crisis? 2/08
Discipline in Schools, 2/08
Student Aid, 1/08

Environment/Society
Gays in the Military, 9/09
Energy and Climate, 7/09
Future of Books, 5/09
Hate Groups, 5/09
Future of Journalism, 3/09
Confronting Warming, 1/09
Reducing Carbon Footprint, 12/08

Health/Safety
Health-Care Reform, 8/09
Straining the Safety Net, 7/09
Treating Depression, 6/09
Reproductive Ethics, 5/09
Extreme Sports, 4/09
Regulating Toxic Chemicals, 1/09

Politics/Economy
State Budget Crisis, 9/09
Business Bankruptcy, 4/09
Future of the GOP, 3/09
Middle-Class Squeeze, 3/09

Upcoming Reports

Prescription Drug Abuse, 10/9/09   Manned Spaceflight, 10/16/09   Conspiracy Theories, 10/23/09

ACCESS

CQ Researcher is available in print and online. For access, visit your library or www.cqresearcher.com.

STAY CURRENT

To receive notice of upcoming *CQ Researcher* reports, or learn more about *CQ Researcher* products, subscribe to the free e-mail newsletters, *CQ Researcher Alert!* and *CQ Researcher News*: http://cqpress.com/newsletters.

PURCHASE

To purchase a *CQ Researcher* report in print or electronic format (PDF), visit www.cqpress.com or call 866-427-7737. Single reports start at $15. Bulk purchase discounts and electronic-rights licensing are also available.

SUBSCRIBE

Annual full-service *CQ Researcher* subscriptions—including 44 reports a year, monthly index updates, and a bound volume—start at $803. Add $25 for domestic postage.

CQ Researcher Online offers a backfile from 1991 and a number of tools to simplify research. For pricing information, call 800-834-9020, ext. 1906, or e-mail librarysales@cqpress.com.

Published by CQ Press, a Division of SAGE

www.cqresearcher.com

Medication Abuse

Is tighter regulation of prescription drugs needed?

M ichael Jackson's shocking accidental death in June was only the latest in a string of high-profile fatalities from multiple prescription medications. Actor Heath Ledger and the model and sex symbol Anna Nicole Smith died recently in comparable circumstances. But celebrities aren't the only abusers of painkillers, sedatives and stimulants. Prescription drug abuse has become a growing problem in the United States, even as illegal drug use has gradually declined. In 2005, for example, more people ages 45 to 54 died from drug overdoses — mostly prescription painkillers — than in car crashes. Many people believe prescription drugs are safer than illegal drugs, so changing public attitudes is a challenge. Also, many prescription narcotics are being diverted to dangerous, recreational use, but doctors, dentists and nurses are poorly informed about the potential for abuse. Meanwhile, government drug-education programs focus on illegal drugs while largely ignoring the risks of prescription abuse.

The sudden death of pop superstar Michael Jackson in June from an accidental overdose of sedatives and other drugs is seen as a wake-up call about the danger of prescription drugs.

CQ Researcher • Oct. 9, 2009 • www.cqresearcher.com
Volume 19, Number 35 • Pages 837-860

CQ Researcher

Oct. 9, 2009
Volume 19, Number 35

MANAGING EDITOR: Thomas J. Colin
tcolin@cqpress.com

ASSISTANT MANAGING EDITOR: Kathy Koch
kkoch@cqpress.com

ASSOCIATE EDITOR: Kenneth Jost

STAFF WRITERS: Thomas J. Billitteri,
Marcia Clemmitt, Peter Katel

CONTRIBUTING WRITERS: Rachel Cox,
Sarah Glazer, Alan Greenblatt, Reed Karaim
Barbara Mantel, Patrick Marshall,
Tom Price, Jennifer Weeks

DESIGN/PRODUCTION EDITOR: Olu B. Davis

ASSISTANT EDITOR: Darrell Dela Rosa

FACT-CHECKING: Eugene J. Gabler,
Michelle Harris

CQ PRESS

A Division of SAGE

PRESIDENT AND PUBLISHER:
John A. Jenkins

EXECUTIVE DIRECTOR,
REFERENCE INFORMATION GROUP:
Alix B. Vance

CQ Researcher (ISSN 1056-2036) is printed on acid-free paper. Published weekly, except; (Jan. wk. 1) (May wk. 4) (July wks. 1, 2) (Aug. wks. 3, 4) (Nov. wk. 4) and (Dec. wk. 4), by CQ Press, a division of SAGE Publications. Annual full-service subscriptions start at $803. For pricing, call 1-800-834-9020, ext. 1906. To purchase a CQ Researcher report in print or electronic format (PDF), visit www. cqpress.com or call 866-427-7737. Single reports start at $15. Bulk purchase discounts and electronic-rights licensing are also available. Periodicals postage paid at Washington, D.C., and additional mailing offices. POSTMASTER: Send address changes to CQ Researcher, 2300 N St., N.W., Suite 800, Washington, DC 20037.

Cover: Getty Images/Joshua Gates Weisberg-Pool

Medication Abuse

BY MARCIA CLEMMITT

THE ISSUES

Michael Jackson's sudden death in June from an overdose of prescription sedatives and other drugs focused worldwide attention on prescription-drug abuse. Ultimately, manslaughter charges may be filed against the physician who injected the legendary entertainer with propofol, a hospital anesthetic given to Jackson as a sleep aid. [1]

Jackson's tragic story, while lurid, is far from unique. Prescription-drug abuse has become an increasingly large part of America's drug-abuse problem in recent decades, even as use of illegal narcotics has dropped. The most recent wave of increases began in the early 1990s, and abuse rates currently mirror the high levels reached in the early-to-mid 2000s.

Furthermore, with the introduction over the past few decades of new opiate painkillers chemically related to heroin, prescription-drug abuse may be more dangerous today than in the past.

Deaths from unintentional drug overdoses have increased steadily since the early 1970s, and "over the past 10 years they have reached historic highs," led by prescription opioids, * Leonard J. Paulozzi, a medical epidemiologist at the federal Centers for Disease Control and Prevention (CDC), told a Senate subcommittee last year. Rates of death from drug overdoses "are currently four to five times

---

* Opioids are chemical compounds that have narcotic properties similar to opium-based drugs like heroin.

Former Playboy *model Anna Nicole Smith died in 2007 from a lethal combination of drugs prescribed by her physicians. Deaths from unintentional drug overdoses have increased steadily since the early 1970s, with medications outpacing illegal drugs like heroin and cocaine as the cause. Often easier to obtain than illegal drugs, prescription drugs have become a powerful gateway to addiction and other drug-abuse problems.*

Getty Images/Patrick Riviere

higher than . . . during the 'black tar' heroin epidemic in the mid-1970s and more than twice what they were during the peak years of crack cocaine in the early 1990s," said Paulozzi. "For the first time, more people in the 45-54 age group now die of drug overdoses than from traffic crashes." [2]

Celebrity entertainers have been prominent among the victims. In late September, the New York City medical examiner announced that the August death of 36-year-old club disc jockey and musician DJ AM — Adam Goldstein — resulted from an accidental overdose of cocaine and a large

number of different prescription drugs, including anti-anxiety drugs that he reportedly was taking after surviving a plane crash in 2008. [3]

In February 2007, the death of Anna Nicole Smith dominated the gossip media for months after the model and sex symbol died from a lethal combination of drugs prescribed by her physicians. Last month, court documents revealed that at least one pharmacist refused to sell prescribed drugs to Smith, telling her doctor that the prescriptions amounted to "pharmaceutical suicide." [4]

"The stars — the problem is they have money," says Doug Thorburn, the author of *Drunks, Drugs & Debits: How to Recognize Addicts and Avoid Financial Abuse.* "Those who depend on a star for their livelihood have position, power and money at stake" if they refuse to give celebrities drugs or urge them to go into rehab. Michael Jackson's nanny "tried to do the right thing and lost her job several times because she said, 'Go to rehab,' " he adds.

Celebrity prescription-drug abuse might be expected to alert the public and the medical profession to the dangers of prescription-drug misuse, but it hasn't really had that effect, analysts say.

"We have a tendency to minimize" substance-abuse problems, says Kitty Harris-Wilkes, director of the Center for the Study of Addiction and Recovery at Texas Tech University in Lubbock. "If people really knew how much prescription-drug abuse happens, they'd freak out. There's a lot more going on than statistics show."

With many people finding prescription medications easier to procure

Monitoring Programs Target Abuse

Thirty-four states require the posting of patient prescription information online through prescription-drug monitoring programs (PDMPs), to allow investigators to obtain pharmacy data from multiple locations at once. Ten states and the District of Columbia have no legislation or programs.

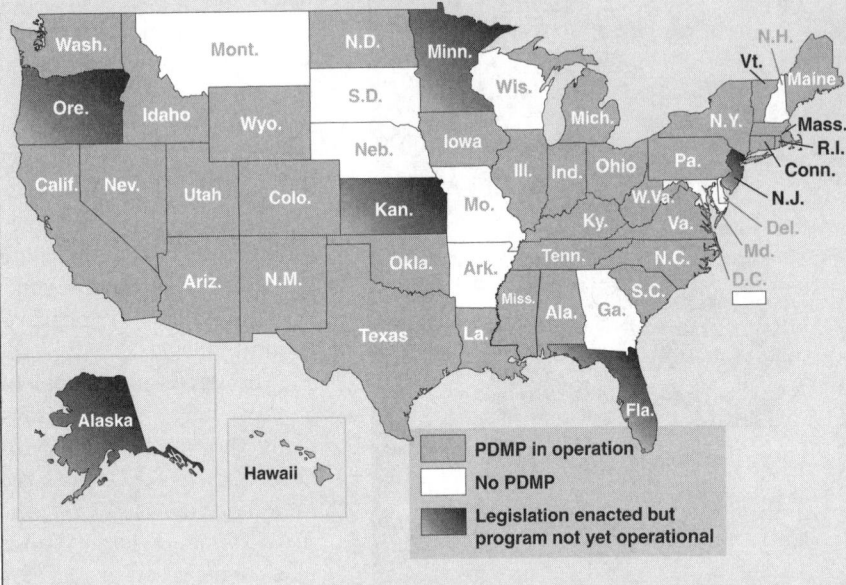

PDMP in operation
No PDMP
Legislation enacted but program not yet operational

Source: "Status of State Prescription Drug Monitoring Programs (PDMPs)," National Alliance for Model State Drug Laws, July 2009

than illegal drugs, prescription drugs have become a powerful gateway to addiction and other drug-abuse problems, says Harris-Wilkes. "Drug availability often drives use. It's 'What am I willing to risk to buy dope off the street?' versus 'What am I willing to risk looking into somebody's medicine cabinet and nicking some Vicodin or other pills when I visit their house?' "

Nevertheless, since pharmaceutical companies, pharmacies and physicians are all regulated by the government, "you have many more places to intervene" to head off abuse of legal drugs compared to illegal ones, says Thomas R. Kosten, a professor of psychiatry and neuroscience at Baylor College of Medicine in Houston. For example, pharmaceutical companies can find ways to make potentially addictive products more tamper-resistant or less abusable by

means such as "putting an opiate blocker into the drug," a tactic that's proven to "stop abuse very quickly."

Efforts are also under way to combat prescription abuse. For example, "Washington state and a number of others use information about the drug use of their Medicaid populations to identify high-volume users," sometimes " 'locking in' such users to a single physician and a single pharmacy to reduce the likelihood of 'doctor shopping' " to get multiple prescriptions, said Paulozzi. [5]

As of summer 2009, at least 40 state legislatures had authorized some kind of prescription-monitoring program, according to the National Alliance for Model State Drug Laws. (*See map, above.*) [6] Nevertheless, many analysts say current initiatives fall short.

"Doctors and nurses just turn off information" about the dangers of

prescription-drug abuse, charges Bryan Liang, a professor of law at the California Western School of Law in San Diego. For example, when patients overdose, "doctors just treat them, give them the antidote for the acute problem" and "think they've done their job."

Not surprisingly, drug manufacturers haven't been proactive about developing drugs that are less easily abusable, says Marvin P. Seppala, chief medical officer of the Hazelden Foundation, an addiction treatment facility in Center City, Minn. "If I'm a pharmaceutical manufacturer, making remarkable sales partly because people are misusing the drugs, I don't have much motivation to change that."

Some patients and physicians argue that campaigns to limit prescription-drug abuse have severely hampered medical pain treatment.

The Drug Enforcement Administration (DEA) and the Justice Department consistently overreach on prescription-narcotics control, John P. Flannery, a federal drug prosecutor turned private-practice attorney, told a House subcommittee in 2007. The Supreme Court declared in 1975 that a "physician had to act 'outside the course of professional medical practice' and with the 'intent' to act as a drug pusher" to warrant prosecution under the Controlled Substances Act, he said. But "the Justice Department recently has been allowing these prosecutions to modify and restrict pain medicine in this nation to a dangerous degree." [7]

But while "there's been a lot of talk over the years about fear of DEA damaging pain prescriptions, only 40 percent of doctors say it's a problem, so it's not as big an issue as people think," says Susan Foster, director of policy research and analysis for the National Center on Addiction and Substance Abuse (CASA) at Columbia University in New York City.

As public health workers, addiction specialists and law-enforcement agencies seek ways to combat prescription-drug abuse, here are some of the questions being asked:

Is prescription-drug abuse as serious as illegal drug abuse?

The use of legitimate prescription drugs like opioid painkillers and stimulants to treat attention deficit hyperactivity disorder (ADHD) has soared in the United States over the past two decades. But along with increased legitimate use of opioids like Vicodin and OxyContin and stimulants like Ritalin and Adderall has come extensive abuse.

In recent years, prescription drugs have outpaced illegal drugs like heroin and cocaine as the cause of overdose deaths, according to both federal statistics and data from many states. "The number of deaths . . . that involved prescription opioid analgesics increased from 2,900 in 1999 to at least 7,500 in 2004," up "150 percent in just five years," with painkiller deaths more numerous than heroin- and cocaine-related deaths put together, said the CDC's Paulozzi. [8]

While the CDC has not analyzed data beyond 2004, the trend is likely to continue, said Paulozzi. The Substance Abuse and Mental Health Services Administration (SAMHSA), has found that "the number of emergency department visits for opioid overdoses increased steadily through 2007," so that "the mortality statistics through 2005 probably underestimate the present magnitude of the problem." [9]

Considering the high rate at which Americans consume prescription drugs, there should be little surprise in such numbers, some analysts say.

Indeed, frequently abused Vicodin is the most-prescribed drug in the United States, with 117 million prescriptions written in 2008, says David S. Kloth, a Danbury, Conn., anesthesiologist and past president of the American Society of Interventional Pain Physicians (ASIPP). By comparison, another heavily used drug, the cholesterol-lowering medicine Lipitor, was prescribed 61 million times last year, Kloth says.

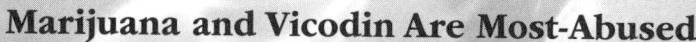

Marijuana and Vicodin Are Most-Abused

Prescription and over-the-counter drugs account for seven out of 11 of the most frequently abused drugs among high-school seniors. The powerful painkiller Vicodin, used by 10 percent of seniors, is the most abused prescription drug. Marijuana is used by nearly one-third of 12th-graders.

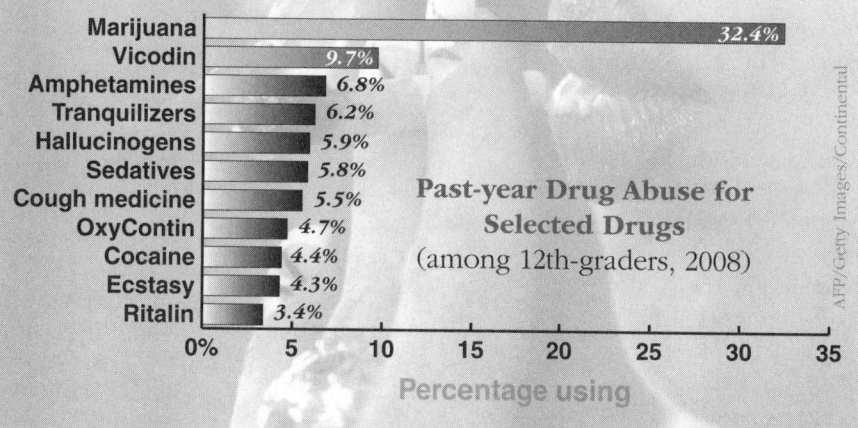

Past-year Drug Abuse for Selected Drugs (among 12th-graders, 2008)

Drug	Percentage using
Marijuana	32.4%
Vicodin	9.7%
Amphetamines	6.8%
Tranquilizers	6.2%
Hallucinogens	5.9%
Sedatives	5.8%
Cough medicine	5.5%
OxyContin	4.7%
Cocaine	4.4%
Ecstasy	4.3%
Ritalin	3.4%

Source: "Monitoring the Future," University of Michigan, Dec. 11, 2008

Ninety-nine percent of the world's hydrocodone — Vicodin's opioid component — and 80 percent of the world's supply of narcotics, generally, are consumed in the United States, he says. "The actual, indirect societal costs [of prescription-drug abuse] are so huge that the problem can no longer be ignored," says Kloth. "We have doctors assisting patients in abuse."

There also has been a dramatic increase in deaths from methadone — in the wafer form prescribed as a pain medication, not the liquid form used as maintenance for former heroin addicts, says Hazelden's Seppala. "The pill is a lethal drug because it's so slow going out of one's system," he says. But unwary people "take a whole bunch because it acts so slowly that they don't realize they're getting high," and they end up dying from the drug's toxicity, he explains.

Today there is more abuse of prescription opiates than marijuana, says Kosten of Baylor College of Medicine. "The average first-time user is 15 years old," and, unlike with most drug epidemics, females are as likely as males to abuse prescription medications. With illegal drugs, "boys are more likely to go out to find a dealer and get them," but boys and girls can get prescription opiates on their own, for free, from their families' medicine chests, he says.

"Illicit drugs come and go," but abuse of prescription drugs is likely to keep on expanding because of their availability, says Western Law School's Liang. "It's a growth industry for our kids, and addicted children become addicted adults."

Among his students, "it's a normal thing to buy on the Internet," Liang says. "This is the health-care system for kids today. And when you hear the justifications of college students — like, 'I'm using [Adderall] because I'm trying to get into med school,' followed by the admission that 'I couldn't really cope with the test because I was so buzzed from the drug' — you understand how serious substance-abuse-related problems can quickly grow," he says.

Furthermore, "there's a real synergy between opioids diverted to illegal use and heroin, since many people get hooked on the diverted opioids" and then shift to illegal drugs or add them to the mix, says Robert G. Carlson, director of the Center for Interventions, Treatment and Addictions Research at Wright State University's Boonshoft School of Medicine in Dayton, Ohio. Abuse of prescription drugs also likely brings sellers of illegal drugs like heroin into areas where illegal-drug pushers haven't previously operated. "Sellers follow the drugs," Carlson says.

Nevertheless, some observers say that facts on the ground may not warrant the alarms some substance-abuse specialists are sounding. "I haven't seen any communication from anyone indicating we're near a crisis mode or things have gotten a lot worse . . . in the recent past," said Ron Petrin, vice president of the Board of Pharmacy in New Hampshire, a state in which some analyses find a surging epidemic of prescription-drug addiction. [10]

Just as with illegal drugs, the number of people who initially abuse prescription drugs is far higher than those who actually become dependent, says Kosten. For both kinds of drugs, "eight people try opiates and one becomes dependent," he says. For that reason, "it's a good bet that a substantial proportion [of prescription-drug abusers] will outgrow" the habit. Nevertheless, Kosten adds, "a lot of damage can happen in the meantime,"

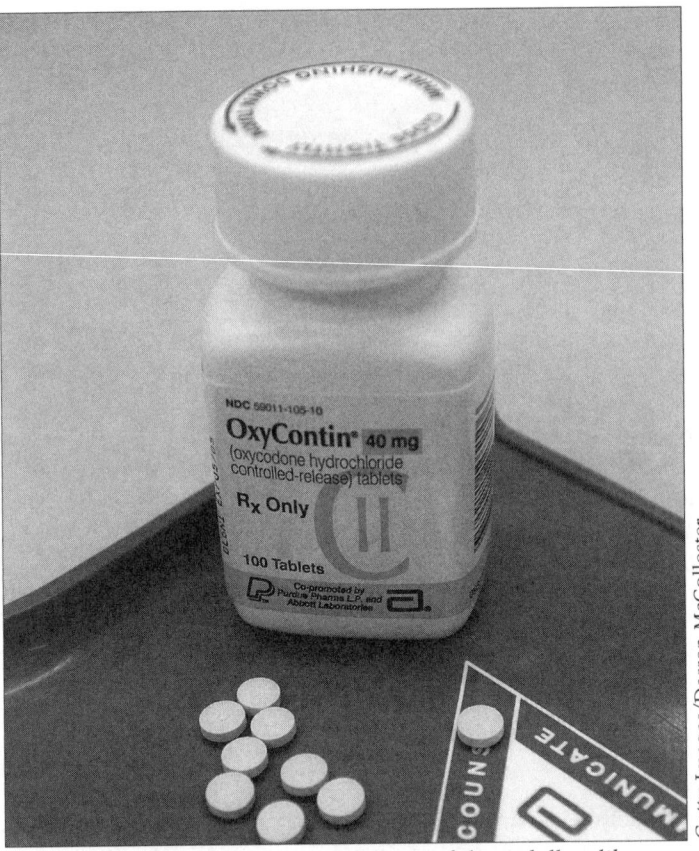

The increased legitimate use of powerful painkillers like OxyContin has been accompanied by extensive abuse. Heavy and somewhat deceptive marketing of OxyContin in the 1990s, when the drug was sold in a highly abusable form, has led to a backlash against it by some physicians and even some addicts. Nonetheless, OxyContin and the popular painkiller Vicodin remain at or near the peak levels of abuse they hit in the mid-2000s.

including education setbacks, such as poor grades, that take years to overcome, he says.

Abuse of prescription "opioids hit a peak in 2006, and it's still staying there, not really on the rise, but not dropping either," says Michael H. Lowenstein, co-director of the Waismann Institute, a detoxification center in Beverly Hills, Calif.

Still, an alarming story making the media rounds may be more legend than fact, says Hazelden's Seppala. Beginning in the early 2000s, some news reports described "pharm parties," in which teenagers scrounge up all the prescription drugs they can find, get together, toss all the drugs into a bowl, and grab and consume random hand-

fuls of the medications. The story reached the mainstream with a *USA Today* account on June 13, 2006. [11] But while some "pharm parties" probably do occur, "I don't think it's a common phenomenon," says Seppala, who has researched them.

Similarly, while prescription sleeping pills are addictive, "the vast, vast majority of people never have a problem with them," says Leslie Lundt, a psychiatrist in Boise, Idaho, who is the author of *Think Like a Psychiatrist: Understanding Psychiatric Medicines.* "Nearly 100 percent of the people who have issues with the 'sleepers' have had another substance-abuse or gambling issue."

Some aspects of prescription drugs may ultimately make them easier for society to control than illegal drugs. As compared to alcoholics and heroin addicts, for example, "We see opioid pill addicts a lot earlier" in their substance-abusing lives, says Seppala. For all opioids, including heroin, "the addiction starts more quickly" than with most other substances, but pill addicts often find it harder to get a daily supply of their drug than street-drug addicts, and so fall into the pain of withdrawal sooner, which brings them to treatment, he says.

Unlike with illegal drugs, if abuse becomes a problem with a legal medication, "we can just make less of it, or make it a lot harder to get" by limiting the places at which the drug can be dispensed, requiring buyers to fill out certain forms, or the like, says Kosten.

Is enough being done to combat medication abuse?

Government and private efforts are under way to head off prescription-drug abuse and shut down enterprises — such as Internet pharmacies — that facilitate abuse, but some analysts say the problem dwarfs the programs that combat it.

The National Institute on Drug Abuse launched a prescription-drug-abuse program in 2001 and continuously monitors trends, said NIDA Director Nora Volkow. NIDA is "helping to develop a protocol doctors and others can use to screen patients for prescription abuse and conduct brief but effective interventions," she said. [12]

The institute also is developing new pain-treatment methods to sidestep addiction potential. For example, Volkow said, "compounds are being developed that act on a combination of two distinct opioid receptors," potentially giving them the ability "to induce strong analgesia without producing tolerance or dependence." [13]

The Food and Drug Administration is addressing the issue, too. For example, the FDA now orders pharmaceutical manufacturers to conduct post-marketing surveillance of drugs, including collecting data to answer the question, "Is our drug being abused?" says Baylor College's Kosten.

For its part, the federal Drug Enforcement Administration is making prescription-drug abuse a top priority, says Western Law School's Liang. "The DEA is going crazy over this," he says.

"Drug companies have become more responsible" about trying to quell abuse, says detox physician Lowenstein. For example, Vicodin maker Abbott Laboratories, in Abbott Park, Ill., is working with the Partnership for a Drug-Free America to develop an online educational program, "Not in My House," aimed at helping parents discourage prescription-drug abuse by teenagers.

Some Internet- and pharmacy-oversight groups say they've made significant efforts to control illicit prescriptions. The Go Daddy Group — a coalition of companies that host Web sites and register Internet domain names — "routinely investigates sites involving online drug sales" and works with law enforcement "in their attempts to remove such Web sites from our network," General Counsel Christine N. Jones told a House subcommittee last year. [14]

But many analysts say the response has not been up to the problem. "We in the U.S. are just naïve" about the seriousness of prescription-drug abuse, although "the rest of the world recognizes it," says Liang. The International Council of Nurses, for example, which represents some 12 million nurses worldwide, sponsored a "Counterfeits Kill" campaign to warn against the dangers of medication abuse. "The only country where they didn't get the nurses involved in this was the United States," Liang says.

After over a decade of rising abuse, "the states still aren't spending any money on prevention," says Liang. At the federal level, the CDC "is not really on it" either, he says.

Good information and education campaigns make a difference, as evidenced by the success of the Partnership for a Drug-Free America's anti-inhalant campaign, says Lloyd D. Johnston, a distinguished senior research scientist at the University of Michigan. Currently, though, the federal government is doing too little, says Johnston, who is the principal investigator for the ongoing Monitoring the Future study of teenagers' substance abuse. The Bush administration focused its anti-drug efforts on marijuana, "a very

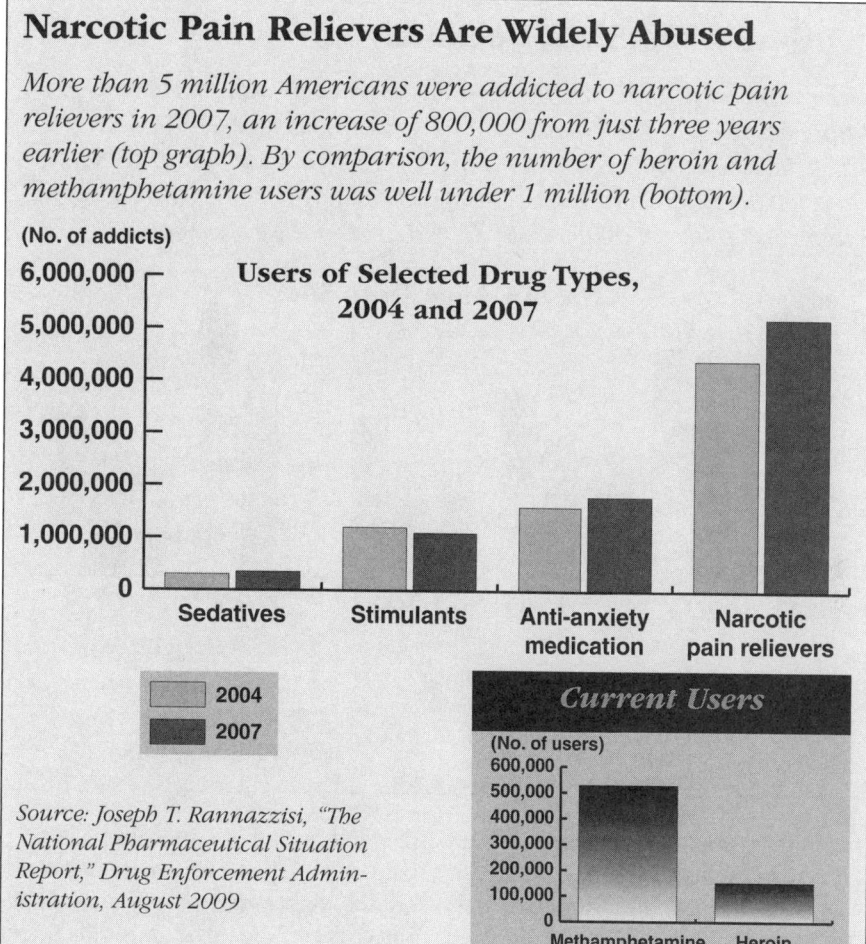

Narcotic Pain Relievers Are Widely Abused

More than 5 million Americans were addicted to narcotic pain relievers in 2007, an increase of 800,000 from just three years earlier (top graph). By comparison, the number of heroin and methamphetamine users was well under 1 million (bottom).

Users of Selected Drug Types, 2004 and 2007

(No. of addicts)

2004 / 2007

Sedatives / Stimulants / Anti-anxiety medication / Narcotic pain relievers

Current Users

(No. of users)

Methamphetamine / Heroin

Source: Joseph T. Rannazzisi, "The National Pharmaceutical Situation Report," Drug Enforcement Administration, August 2009

Online Drug Sites Declined

The number of Internet sites that illegally sell or advertise prescription drugs decreased in 2008 to its second-lowest level in five years. The decline reflects efforts by law enforcement agencies, Internet service providers, package delivery services and credit card companies to stop illegal activities by "rogue" pharmacy operators.

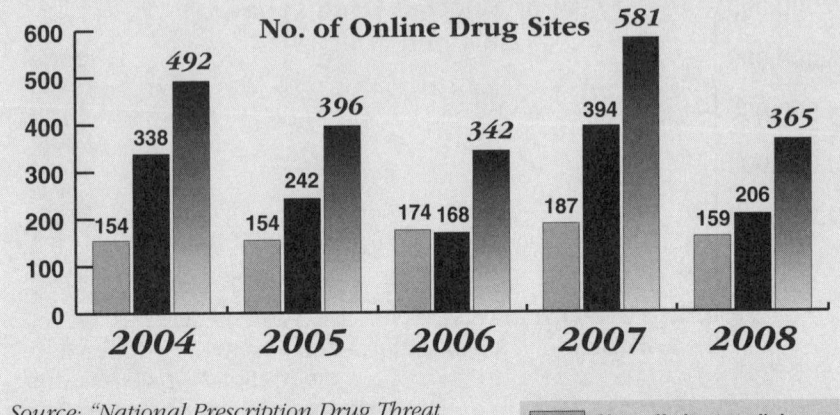

No. of Online Drug Sites

2004: 154, 338, 492
2005: 154, 242, 396
2006: 174, 168, 342
2007: 187, 394, 581
2008: 159, 206, 365

- Sites offering to sell drugs
- Sites advertising drugs
- Total sites

Source: "National Prescription Drug Threat Assessment," National Drug Intelligence Center, Drug Enforcement Administration, U.S. Department of Justice, April 2009

hard target," and the campaign showed "no effect or may even have caused a rebound" in use, Johnston explains. "Congress got mad about" the poor targeting and bad results and cut funding for federal anti-drug programs across the board, he says. "They threw the baby out with the bathwater."

When it comes to Internet pharmacies that operate illegally, the number and clout of other businesses — such as search engines — that profit from the stores' existence greatly limits the extent to which companies help rein them in, some analysts report. Microsoft's Bing.com search engine, for example, "enables 'rogue' Internet pharmacies that violate U.S. federal and state laws as well as Microsoft's stated policies," according to the Internet pharmacy-verification group LegitScript and the Internet-compliance company KnujOn. [15]

Search engines like Bing can't really control which Web pages show up in actual search results, but they earn ad

revenue from the "sponsored links" — paid ads — that are generally posted on the right side of a search page. Since these are paid ads, Microsoft "has the ability to require that they meet certain criteria" and should decline ad dollars from companies that break laws, say the groups. However, "of the prescription drug and online pharmacy advertisements . . . that we reviewed, 89.7 percent led to 'rogue' Internet pharmacies that do not require a [written] prescription for prescription drugs, or are otherwise acting unlawfully or fraudulently," such as by selling counterfeit drugs manufactured outside the U.S. or Canada, LegitScript and KnujOn say. [16]

"About 40 percent of doctors have had some training on substance abuse and about 19 percent on diversion" of legal drugs to illicit purposes, says anesthesiologist Kloth. "But the real truth is that this amounts to one lecture in medical school, with most doctors having virtually no training" in

these areas. Government agencies should work with professional groups to institute physician-certification programs for doctors authorized to prescribe abusable drugs, he says.

When it comes to blame for allowing prescription-drug abuse to worsen, "there's enormous responsibility to go around," says Foster, at the National Center on Addiction and Substance Abuse. For example, drug companies have known that they were producing addictive drugs in easy-to-abuse forms but produced and promoted the drugs anyway, such as when Purdue Pharma did "really extreme marketing of OxyContin," which was packaged in a very easy-to-abuse form in the early 2000s.

Are patients in pain suffering because doctors fear prosecution for medication abuse?

Pain drugs are the most likely to result in addiction when they are taken to get high rather than to ease pain — and some pain patients argue that anti-abuse efforts have gravely hampered pain treatments.

In the 19th century, narcotics like opium and the morphine-containing medicine laudanum, legally prescribed to treat pain and other medical conditions, got far out of hand in the United States, creating many addicts. By the 1940s the government had restricted legal use of opioids to medicines "prescribed by physicians according to strict regulatory controls," wrote Jane C. Ballantyne, professor of anesthesiology and critical care at the Hospital of the University of Pennsylvania, and Jianren Mao, director of the Massachusetts General Hospital Center for Translational Pain Research. "The immediate result of such strict regulatory control was that physicians became reluctant to prescribe opioids," fearing the loss of medical licenses and criminal prosecutions, and "as a result pain was woefully undertreated," Ballantyne and Mao explain. [17]

Similarly, the backlash against the painkiller OxyContin in the early 2000s "has caused physicians to treat pain less aggressively in many cases, to the detriment of their seriously ill patients," said John Shuster, a psychiatrist and palliative care specialist in Alabama. "The emphasis on managing pain is fairly new [in medicine], and I fear many patients will suffer needlessly as physicians rethink using any powerful painkillers in the wake of the adverse publicity" surrounding OxyContin. [18]

In 2002 alone, the DEA prosecuted 410 physicians "for recklessly prescribing opioids — an 800 percent increase in . . . prosecutions from 1999," wrote Steven P. Cohen, director of medical education in the pain management division at Johns Hopkins School of Medicine in Baltimore, and Srinivasa N. Raja, director of the division of pain medicine in the Department of Anesthesiology and Critical Care Medicine. [19]

Undertreatment of pain "is still a serious problem," said Brietta Clark, a professor of law at Loyola Law School in Los Angeles. Despite new state laws and professional guidelines stating that doctors must make pain treatment a priority and promising immunity from punishment if they follow treatment guidelines, "physicians report a continuing fear of scrutiny if they prescribe certain kinds of medications," said Clark. [20]

That's largely because doctors believe, correctly, that "liability for undertreatment" of pain is "difficult to prove, in part because there is no objective, verifiable measure of pain," Clark explained. Meanwhile, "physician overprescribing remains easier to identify and punish."

Insurance plans also are adopting "fail first" medication policies, said Clark. "Plans make patients try cheaper, weaker pain medications to prove they do not work, before they will pay for stronger medication prescribed by the physician. They justify this ostensibly on safety and cost grounds," but pain treatment suffers as a result, she argued. [21]

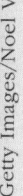

Victims of Addiction

The death in August of 36-year-old New York City club disc jockey DJ AM — Adam Goldstein (top) — resulted from an accidental overdose of cocaine and a number of prescription drugs. Conservative radio host Rush Limbaugh (bottom) has admitted he became addicted to painkillers when suffering from back pain. In 2006 he pleaded "not guilty" to "doctor shopping" to obtain prescriptions and agreed to undergo random drug testing.

Siobhan Reynolds, founder of the advocacy group Pain Relief Network, said that "all the available evidence shows us that we are . . . living in an ongoing and worsening medical crisis as concerns the undertreatment of pain." The DEA made an agreement in the 1990s with the FDA and medical professional societies clearing the way for aggressive pain treatment and giving doctors and DEA agents clear, consistent guidelines on what was and was not allowable, Reynolds said. [22]

Since then, however DEA has "reneged on this agreement," Reynolds charged. As a result, "general searches of private patient records began to take place all over the country, physician's assets were seized prior to trial and physician after physician went down on drug trafficking convictions." In the end, Reynolds said, only a few tiny pain clinics were left around the country, while doctors were left in fear and patients in pain. [23]

But some pain experts note that advocacy by pain patients and physicians over the past two decades has convinced state governments and medical-oversight organizations, such as the Joint Commission on the Accreditation of Healthcare Organizations, to urge physicians to treat pain aggressively.

"The alleged undertreatment of pain as a major health problem in the United States has led to development of initiatives to address the multiple alleged barriers responsible," said Laxmaiah Manchikanti, founder and CEO of the American Society of Interventional Pain Physicians and an associate clinical professor of anesthesiology and perioperative medicine at the University of Louisville. [24]

"Patient advocacy groups and professional organizations have been formed with a focus on improving the management of pain, and numerous clinical guidelines also have been developed," although none have been "developed using evidence-based medicine," Manchikanti said. In addition, "over one-third of the state legislatures have instituted intractable-pain treatment acts that provide immunity from discipline" for doctors who follow the rules when prescribing opioids. [25]

In 1999, the U.S. Veteran's Health Administration announced that it would begin considering pain as a "fifth vital sign" — alongside temperature, pulse, respiratory rate and blood pressure —

to encourage aggressive treatment. In 2000, the health care accrediting commission followed suit, says the Hazelden Foundation's Seppala.

Meanwhile, some analysts suggest that the best way out of the pain/addiction dilemma lies in a different direction: backing off the heavy reliance on opioids, which are proving to have some unsuspected downsides, while broadening the medical tools used to combat pain.

"Chronic non-cancer pain is undertreated in the United States for a variety of reasons," but fear of prosecution for overprescription isn't the key one, says Michael Ashburn, a professor of anesthesiology and director of the pain medicine and palliative care center at the University of Pennsylvania in Philadelphia. "Doctors are not well trained to diagnose and treat" pain, and pain specialists are scarce. In addition, interdisciplinary pain management teams were becoming the norm a few decades ago, but "few exist any more" because insurers were skeptical about their worth and stopped paying for them.

"I would argue that the most common error in pain treatment is the overreliance on a single drug class" — opioids — which can too easily slip into overuse and abuse, says Ashburn. In fact, "the scientific literature supporting opioids for non-cancer pain" is "pretty minimal," he says.

Furthermore, addiction doctors are now learning that, after a certain time, opiate painkillers may actually increase patients' sensitivity to pain, says Seppala. A young veterinarian he treated developed addiction to opioids after back surgery and, while her life had not yet spiraled out of control — as many addicts' lives do — she entered substance-abuse treatment because her drug habit had left her with no energy to work or live her life, says Seppala. "She was at unbelievably high doses of opioids, but after we got her off she was able to return

to work basically pain free — a dramatic case but one that we're now finding is not that unusual," he says. "In at least some folks, these medications backfire, and they become more sensitive to pain." ■

BACKGROUND

Historic Highs

In the late 19th century, the average narcotics addict was a middle-class white woman addicted to medicinal drugs like morphine and laudanum, widely prescribed for depression, menopausal symptoms, menstrual cramps and other ills. [26]

An 1885 Iowa survey reported that repeat opiate users in the state were 63.8 percent female, and that opium addicts generally were middle-aged and middle-class, with the average user 46.5 years old and better educated than the average citizen. "The merchant, lawyer and physician are to be found among the host who sacrifice the choicest treasures of life at the shrine of Opium," said *Catholic World* magazine in 1881. [27]

Opiate medications — narcotic drugs extracted from seed capsules of the opium poppy or made from synthetic opium — may have provided a path to addiction for many who might not otherwise have encountered addictive drugs. "The extent to which alcohol-drinking by women was frowned upon may . . . have contributed to the excess of women among opiate users," observed a history of American drug use published by *Consumer Reports*. "Husbands drank alcohol in the saloon; wives took opium at home." [28]

Medications containing opiates were sold legally, at low, affordable prices, by groceries and general stores as

Continued on p. 849

Chronology

1800s–1909
Addiction to opium and cocaine-based medications swells across social classes.

1840
Less than one American in 1,000 is addicted to drugs.

1887
Oregon bans selling cocaine without a prescription.

1890
Five Americans in 1,000 are addicts.

1909
First International Opium Conference is held in Shanghai, China, amid growing worldwide concern.

1910s–1980s
Illegal drug use overtakes prescription-drug abuse as a cause of addiction.

1914
Congress passes Harrison Narcotics Tax Act, requiring all prescribers, sellers and handlers of opium and cocaine-based drugs to register and pay a tax.

1919
Supreme Court bans physicians from prescribing narcotics as "maintenance" drugs to help addicts avoid withdrawal pain.

1937
Prescription amphetamines in tablet form are sold to treat narcolepsy and attention problems.

1960
Doctors begin prescribing stimulant Ritalin for attention deficit disorder.

1970
Congress passes Controlled Substances Act, categorizing all drugs deemed dangerous and addictive into five "schedules" subject to various levels of regulation.

1990s
Substance abuse begins rising after a long decline. By decade's end, "no-prescription" Web sites selling controlled substances emerge.

1995
Prescription of stimulants like Ritalin soar, with 2 million American children taking the drug for attention deficit hyperactivity disorder (ADHD).

1996
Use of OxyContin, a time-release form of the opiate painkiller oxycodone that is easily abused, spreads among substance abusers, especially in rural areas.

1999
Veterans' Affairs health facilities begin monitoring patients for excessive pain following reports physicians aren't treating pain aggressively for fear of prosecution.

2000s
More overdose deaths involve prescription drugs than illegal drugs. Anti-drug programs focus on prescription abuse.

2001
National Institute on Drug Abuse launches research program on prescription drugs.

2003
Conservative radio host Rush Limbaugh admits he became addicted to painkillers when suffering from back pain and enters treatment.

2005
Congress passes National All Schedules Prescription Reporting Act (NASPER) to establish or improve prescription monitoring programs in all states but doesn't fund the effort until 2009.

2006
Limbaugh pleads "not guilty" to "doctor shopping" to obtain painkiller prescriptions and agrees to undergo random drug testing. . . . Up to 20 percent of college students may use ADHD stimulant drugs to get high or to stay awake while studying.

2007
Model and sex symbol Anna Nicole Smith, 39, dies of an overdose of multiple prescription drugs she obtained from her personal physicians.

2008
Australian actor Heath Ledger, 28, dies in New York after accidentally overdosing on prescription drugs, including sleeping pills. . . . Congress passes Ryan Haight Act, requiring online pharmacies to comply with state prescribing rules and post contact information online.

2009
Pop singer Michael Jackson, 50, dies from prescription-drug overdose. Officials label his death a homicide and begin investigating his personal physician. . . . Ryan Haight Act goes into effect. . . . Musician and disc jockey DJ AM (Adam Goldstein) dies of an overdose of multiple prescription drugs. . . . Washington state suspends its prescription-monitoring program due to budget cuts. . . . Court papers reveal a pharmacist refused to fill prescriptions for model Smith, dubbing it "pharmaceutical suicide."

Fickle Finger of Fate Can Make Painkillers Addictive

Biological factors cause some people to get "high."

Painkillers, when used responsibly, usually don't make the user "high" or lead to substance abuse. "People who take opiates because they're getting their teeth pulled generally don't" develop substance-abuse problems, says Thomas R. Kosten, a professor of psychiatry and neuroscience at Baylor College of Medicine in Houston. For most people, "if you're in significant pain, the drug takes the pain away," and "you feel a little sedated, a little nauseous."

"I've taken two Vicodin in my life, for dental procedures, and it just made me feel bad. I got nauseated," says Michael H. Lowenstein, co-director of the Waismann Institute, a detoxification center in Beverly Hills, Calif.

But about one-in-eight people "get high" from prescription painkillers, which can lead to drug abuse and addiction. Many prescription-drug abusers "start with a legitimate medical complaint," says Marvin P. Seppala, chief medical officer of the Hazelden Foundation, an addiction treatment facility in Center City, Minn.

Biological factors strongly influence who gets a rush from drugs and therefore has high risk of substance abuse, Kosten says.

For example, a person's genetic makeup may cause them to be both ultrasensitive to chemicals like opiates and to release more of the body's own stimulating chemicals in response to ingesting alcohol or an opiate drug. When people with that physical makeup take a powerful drug like Vicodin, their already supersensitive bodies actually receive an additional shot of chemicals, which creates an intense high, Kosten explains. "They're having an experience that's very, very different," and far more compelling, than what other people taking the same drug experience.

About 30 percent of Europeans and 50 percent of Chinese have a physical makeup that puts them at risk when they take prescription drugs with addiction potential, but most people at risk don't realize it, Kosten says.

Other factors also probably raise addiction risks, says Lowenstein. For example, "the majority of people we see" in detox "have some underlying issue" that's helped drive the drug abuse, "such as depression or anxiety."

Alcohol and drug abuse "are nothing but a desired altered state of consciousness," says Kitty Harris-Wilkes, director of the Center for the Study of Addiction and Recovery at Texas Tech University in Lubbock. "If I don't like the way I feel, I'll do something to change it." Such a desire can exist in anyone, "whether you're 13 or 83."

The urge to escape society's pressures and stress is at the root of much substance abuse today, she says. At schools like Texas Tech, for example, there is often a "higher level of chemicals" used in the Honors College, where more students feel they're under intense pressure, she says.

Nevertheless, people should not be afraid to take a drug for pain relief, especially if they keep their doctor informed and follow instructions, says Leslie Lundt, a Boise, Idaho, psychiatrist and author of *Think Like a Psychiatrist: Understanding Psychiatric Medicines*. If a patient is suffering from insomnia and has had no personal or family substance-abuse problems, "I say, 'So all of a sudden you're going to become a prostitute on a street corner just to get your sleeping pills?' "

Doctors, especially anesthesiologists, are at high risk for prescription-drug abuse. "The best estimate is that 20 percent of doctors are addicted" to some substance, says Doug Thorburn, author of *Drunks, Drugs & Debits: How to Recognize Addicts and Avoid Financial Abuse*.

Anesthesiologists' high rate of substance abuse shows the frightening power of addiction, says Seppala. "In spite of having the knowledge and awareness of addiction risks that they do, many anesthesiologists still get into it," he says. Anesthesiology residents are the most likely doctors to be addicted. "Some people who are already experimenting with substance abuse actually go into the field to get the drugs." Others apparently get involved out of "curiosity," Seppala says. Some anesthesia patients report that "it feels so good," and the doctors "start to wonder," he says.

Women may be at higher risk for abusing prescription drugs than illegal drugs, mainly because of ease of access. If one has both health insurance and a middle-class or higher income, it can be easy to get a legitimate prescription for an addictive drug and fill it at multiple pharmacies.

Seppala describes a 52-year-old stay-at-home mom who kept up an addiction for years because she had five doctors prescribing her the same amount of opioids repeatedly.

"She never showed up to get more pills before her prescription was scheduled to run out, and she never complained," so no doctor or pharmacist ever flagged her as a potential abuser, he says. The woman had a history of migraines and "knew what they were like, so she could give a good description" of her pain to justify her prescriptions, he says.

Because she was able to pay out of her own pocket for so many drugs, "she was kind of an exception" to the norm, he says. She only entered treatment when, finally, facing a divorce and foreclosure on her house, she was unable to pay for the drugs, he says.

"A group we're seeing more of is teens and young adults," often getting started on "their mothers' or grandmothers' medicine," says Christy Valentine, an internal-medicine and pediatrics physician in New Orleans. "The number of teens who've tried one of these narcotic medications or say they know someone who has is rampant," she says.

How do you know you're in trouble with a prescription drug? One strong indication is "that the drug becomes a central organizing pattern of your life" — you always know where it is, how much you have and where you can get more, says Harris-Wilkes.

Continued from p. 846

well as pharmacies and dispensed directly by physicians. For example, in 1885 in Iowa — a state with a population of under 2 million — 3,000 stores sold opiate drugs. Mail-order opiates were also sold. [29]

The pharmaceutical use of opiates — as well as stimulants like cocaine — went far beyond pain medication. Numerous "patent medicines" were advertised as treatment for ills ranging from consumption (tuberculosis) to coughs and diarrhea, and some narcotic medicines were even sold in the form of "soothing syrups," intended for teething babies, along with cocaine toothache drops for children and cocaine-containing lozenges for sore throats. [30]

"Careless prescription, incessant dispensation and hidden distribution of harmful drugs — the addictive effects of which were unknown until too late — fostered a large addict population which continued to increase in the early 20th century," wrote Richard J. Bonnie, a professor of law and medicine at the University of Virginia School of Law, and the late Charles H. Whitebread, II, a law professor at the University of Southern California's Gould School of Law. [31]

The rate of opiate addiction in the United States swelled from fewer than one addict per 1,000 people around 1840 to 4.59 per thousand in the 1890s, according to David T. Courtwright, a professor of history at the University of North Florida in Jacksonville. [32]

While many people disapproved of opium use, the earliest laws against the drugs were probably intended mainly to control the activities of Chinese immigrants — widely resented, especially on the West Coast, because they were perceived as taking jobs from Americans. In the 1870s and '80s, California and San Francisco prohibited opium smoking in commercial "opium dens," for example.

Soon, however, laws were enacted to tighten medical control of opiate drugs. For example, an 1887 Oregon

Few Doctors Receive Addiction Training

More than half of American physicians say they are primarily responsible for preventing prescription-drug abuse, but few received medical school training in its prevention and identification or the proper prescription methods for controlled drugs.

According to the National Center on Addiction and Substance Abuse, physicians say they . . .

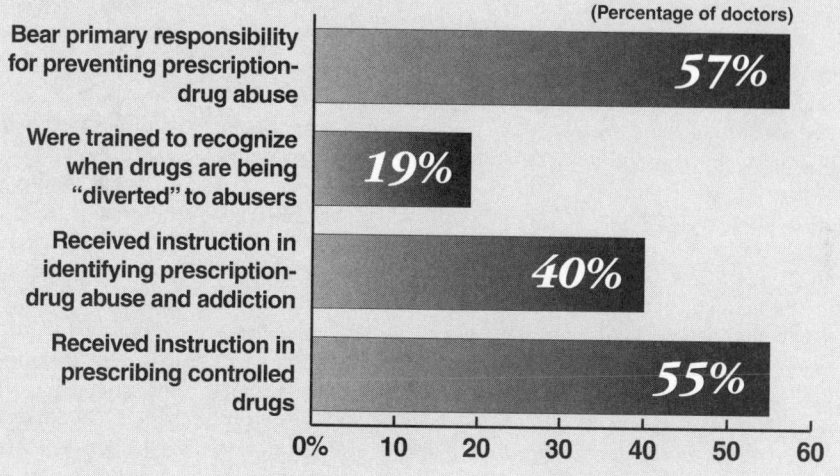

(Percentage of doctors)

- Bear primary responsibility for preventing prescription-drug abuse — **57%**
- Were trained to recognize when drugs are being "diverted" to abusers — **19%**
- Received instruction in identifying prescription-drug abuse and addiction — **40%**
- Received instruction in prescribing controlled drugs — **55%**

Source: "Under the Counter: The Diversion and Abuse of Controlled Prescription Drugs in the U.S.," National Center on Addiction and Substance Abuse, Columbia University, July 2005

statute barred the sale of cocaine without a doctor's prescription. By 1914, 46 states had similar cocaine bans, and 29 states had included non-prescription opiates in their sales bans. Only about six states had outlawed simple possession of restricted drugs, however. [33]

Federal Action

With many states as well as foreign governments attempting crackdowns on non-medicinal drug use, and increased awareness that some drugs were highly addictive, pressure built for the U.S. to act. In 1909, the first federal legislation regulating narcotics distribution limited opium to a few entry ports and only for medicinal uses.

Major legislation soon followed that focused federal regulation of addictive drugs on pharmacies and prescribing physicians. The Harrison Narcotics Tax Act of 1914 required anyone who imported, produced, sold or otherwise dispensed opium, cocaine or drugs derived from them to register with the federal government and pay a special tax. In effect, the new law established a registered class of people authorized to possess the drugs and by extension outlawed their possession by unregistered sellers or users with no drug prescription.

"During the period of little or no regulation . . . innocent addicts were regarded as victims of an unfortunate sickness in need of treatment," and "usually they could find a friendly physician or druggist willing to sustain their habits," observed Bonnie and Whitebread. [34]

How to Avoid Problems With Medications

Don't underestimate drugs' addictive power, experts warn.

Prescription drugs play a major and positive role in the lives of millions of Americans, but the public's generally positive attitude about them may lead some people to underestimate medications' risks and treat them too casually. Here are some of the ways drug experts say medication users can stay out of trouble:

Don't share prescriptions. "Your specific attributes," such as weight, gender, age and medical history, "make it just Russian roulette" to assume that a drug prescribed for someone else would help you, too, says Jack E. Fincham, a professor of pharmacy practice and administration at the University of Missouri, Kansas City.

Sharing medications is rife in our society, says Richard Goldsworthy, CEO and director of research and development for The Academic Edge, a research firm in Bloomington, Ind. In studies with both adults and teenagers, Goldsworthy found that many people had extremely casual attitudes about sharing prescription drugs. Much of the activity is "altruistic sharing" — handing a drug to a friend because you think it might help them — and around 30 percent of adults and 20 percent of teenagers report they've been on one end or the other of such a transaction, often involving antibiotics, antihistamines and even birth-control pills.

The high numbers suggest there's very little understanding of drug side effects and rules for usage, such as the importance of taking the full course of some drugs, such as antibi-

otics, to make them work properly, he says. This also "indicates that our society is very laissez-faire about prescription drugs in general," which could increase comfort with taking dangerous drugs, he says.

ADHD drugs are more dangerous than you think. "If you look at Ritalin structurally, it's the closest relative to cocaine," but since the drug's been widely prescribed for youngsters with ADHD — Attention Deficit Hyperactivity Disorder — many people believe that it's quite safe, said Scott Teitelbaum, medical director of the Florida Recovery Center at the University of Florida, Gainesville.

Ritalin is also cheap and easy to procure. A friend with a prescription may sell it to you for just the price of their insurance co-pay, and "the modern student is . . . smart enough to go to a doctor and . . . tell them exactly what the [ADHD] symptoms are . . . to get stimulants," Teitelbaum said. [1]

But then the trouble begins. "Somebody might think if 10 milligrams keeps most people up, I need 20 or 30 or 40 to stay awake longer. I need more because I need to study, and I'm way behind." But that's not the way drug doses work, Teitelbaum said. "A higher dose might make them more likely to have an irregular heartbeat or get hyperthermia, or there could be another medicine that the person is on that could interact." [2]

Addicts are not who you think. If relatives and friends wait until someone actually shows signs of losing control over the abused substance, they'll be able to identify only very late-

---

In 1919, however, the Supreme Court cracked down on such "maintenance" prescriptions. [35] Although Memphis doctor W. S. Webb and pharmacist Jacob Goldbaum were registered as legitimate providers under the Harrison Act, they were convicted in Tennessee of "prescribing and selling narcotics not to cure but to keep the addicts comfortable," wrote historian R. Alton Lee. [36]

The pair appealed on the grounds that, since the Harrison Act was a revenue measure, the law could not rightly stipulate to whom drugs might be prescribed and sold. The Supreme Court upheld the conviction, effectively establishing the principle that maintenance of an addiction was not a legitimate medical reason to dispense drugs. As a result, doctors largely stopped

prescribing drugs to people they believed were addicts, helping drive trade in opium, cocaine and similar drugs underground. [37]

As laws made addictive drugs harder to get, addiction rates waned. In 1970 Congress consolidated regulation of all federally restricted drugs under the Controlled Substances Act. The law classifies drugs as belonging to one of five "schedules" with decreasing levels of control and scrutiny applied to each successive category. Schedule I drugs, including marijuana and heroin, are deemed to have high abuse potential and no currently accepted medical use, and are essentially banned. Schedule V drugs, such as cough medicines that contain the low-level opiate codeine, which have accepted medical uses

and a relatively low potential for physical or psychological dependence, are regulated but don't require a doctor's prescription. [38]

Nevertheless, prohibitions haven't stopped some addicts from getting their hands on addictive substances, including pharmaceuticals, over the years.

"Passing forged prescriptions was standard operating procedure" for obtaining drugs in small-town Arkansas in the 1960s and '70s, wrote addiction psychiatrist Martha A. Morrison, who became an addict as a teenager. "I could rip off prescription pads in a heartbeat; I'd just walk into a doctor's office, ask for an appointment, grab one of the pads that were always lying around, and slip it into my purse or down my pants." Later, Morrison would "write five or six prescriptions" and stage addicts, says Doug Thorburn, author of *Drunks, Drugs & Debits: How to Recognize Addicts and Avoid Financial Abuse*. "Behavioral disorders" are a strong sign of addiction. "Whenever we shake our heads and say, 'What was he thinking?' about someone's behavior, the thought that 'This might be addiction' " should quickly follow, he argues.

So, intervene early, says Thorburn. "What are we waiting for? Just for more stuff to happen that they'll need to make amends for down the road?"

"Intervening early is one of the best things you can do," says Kitty Harris-Wilkes, director of the Center for the Study of Addiction and Recovery at Texas Tech University in Lubbock. For example, "you can hit young people with pretty specific consequences," like kicking them out of school on a second offense. It's vital to send signals loud enough for addicts to actually hear, she says.

Lock up or discard prescription meds. "If I pay for a prescription painkiller but don't use it all, I'm liable to wonder why I can't just save it in case I sprain my ankle a year from now," says Seppala. Use your judgment about that, but at the very least "you have to limit access to it — put it in a

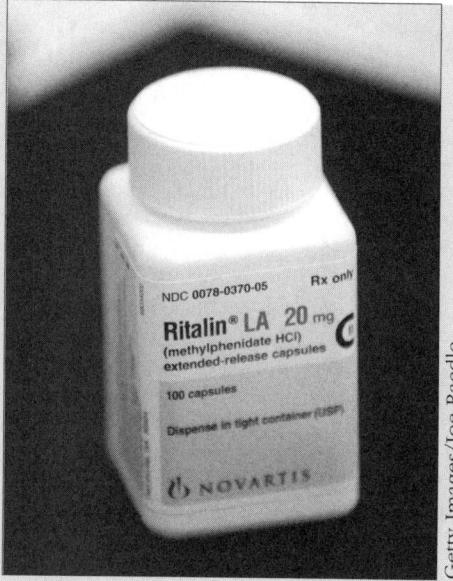

Ritalin® LA 20 mg
(methylphenidate HCl)
extended-release capsules
NDC 0078-0370-05
Rx only
100 capsules
Dispense in tight container (USP)
NOVARTIS

The ADHD drug Ritalin is easy to obtain and deceptively easy to misuse.

Getty Images/Joe Raedle

locked place," to avoid tempting others, especially teens looking to experiment.

"I know plenty of adult addicts who go on open house tours and look in the medicine cabinets, too," he says.

Mixing meds can be substance abuse, too. So many medications are floating around today that it's easy to misuse them dangerously without even knowing it, says Fincham. For example, "many well-intentioned people take over-the-counter medications and herbal products," mixing them with prescription drugs without consulting a doctor or pharmacist.

"Every drug, prescription or not, can have a good effect, a bad effect and a null effect and if it's a null effect," the reaction of many people is to simply take more of the drug or take another drug on top of the first — both huge mistakes, Fincham says. The resulting overdoses and drug interactions are "a big and very understated problem in the United States."

---

[1] "Ritalin Abuse Poses Risks During College Exam Week," press release, University of Florida, May 10, 2007.

[2] *Ibid.*

"spend a day driving all over Arkansas" filling them at different stores. [39]

"The only time I was questioned was in a little drugstore in a city about 120 miles south of Fayetteville," where a pharmacist objected, saying, "I don't recognize this doctor's handwriting." After an "indignant" response from Morrison that she lived 120 miles away and was staying in town with relatives, "he filled it."

Internet and Beyond

Over the past two decades, several trends have converged to drive prescription-drug abuse upwards. Beginning in the 1940s so-called integrated pain-treatment teams, including

physical therapists and psychologists, proliferated around the country, successfully treating severe chronic pain by a variety of means including drugs, says the University of Pennsylvania's Ashburn. But beginning in the early 1980s, insurers stopped paying for "integrated" treatment and the concept withered, leaving physicians and patients with "very few options" for pain management, he says. The decline of pain management, combined with the aggressive marketing of some pain medications in recent years, and an explosion in the use of opiates for chronic non-cancer pain, had dire consequences for increased drug abuse, Ashburn says.

On college campuses, meanwhile, stimulants are being used the most, notably drugs like Adderall that have

been prescribed for attention deficit hyperactivity disorder (ADHD), says Harris-Wilkes of Texas Tech. Students believe, "If you don't have ADHD or a similar condition, these drugs will give you a huge buzz and you can stay up for days," she says.

Stimulant abuse has increased partly because the drugs are so widely available and well accepted, but societal stress also is a driver, Harris-Wilkes believes. "If you stand back and look at it, it's just an extension of the same thing we see with energy drinks like Red Bull and Rock Star. Hello, it's 10 o'clock in the morning, should you really be drinking this?" Nevertheless, she says, many teens are driven to stimulant abuse because they worry, "If I don't do well on my SAT, I'm not going to college."

Doctors Faulted for Prescribing Addictive Painkillers

Pain experts call for more awareness, holistic approaches.

"As a profession, we're not adequately treating pain," says Marvin P. Seppala, chief medical officer of the Hazelden Foundation, an addiction treatment organization in Center City, Minn. "At the same time, doctors have people coming in every day trying to scam them" to get addictive drugs for non-medical uses.

Both patients and doctors should be more aware of the abuse potential of pain medications, however, Seppala says. "These are really important medications, but if you're going to use them for an extended period you need to know that they can lead to addiction."

Addictive painkillers often are prescribed without much or any discussion, and even when they may not be necessary. "I went in with a broken foot and wasn't allowed to leave without a prescription for an addictive painkiller," even though "my foot didn't hurt unless I walked on it," says Susan Foster, director of policy research and analysis for the National Center on Addiction and Substance Abuse (CASA) at Columbia University in New York City.

All doctors who prescribe narcotic painkillers should query patients about any history of substance abuse, one of the biggest risk factors for running into trouble with the drugs, says Seppala.

Scheduled for a surgery of his own, Seppala, a recovering addict, told his physician about his substance-abuse history and asked for pain treatment that wouldn't trigger the addiction. "But as soon as I heard the surgeon say, 'Don't worry!' I knew he didn't get it," he says. After a relatively minor operation, he found himself in possession of 180 tablets of the opiate painkiller Vicodin. "I used only two the first night," he says.

Knowing the dangers, Seppala lined up his wife and an anesthesiologist friend to carefully oversee his painkiller use to keep him out of danger, but other at-risk people may not realize they should do this, he says.

Pain specialists are finding more downsides with pain treatment that relies heavily on opiates, says Michael Ashburn, a professor of anesthesiology and director of the pain medicine and palliative care center at the University of Pennsylvania. For example, "A fair amount of patients on very high opioids are seeing unforeseen problems," ranging from mental and other errors to criminal behavior. The university's pain center cares for about 75 patients at a time who have extremely serious chronic pain, "and every day I have to address drug-related behavior with a patient or two," he says.

"I have a love-hate relationship with opioids," he says. "In many people they can make a world of difference, but in some other patients the side effects" are extreme and very disturbing, he says.

As a result, more physicians are realizing that good pain treatment requires a more complex approach, Ashburn and others say. "We need to do more with cognitive behavioral therapy, acupuncture" and other non-opioid treatments for pain, says Michael H. Lowenstein, co-director of the Waismann Institute, a detoxification center in Beverly Hills, Calif.

But it's not always easy for patients to understand that the best way to treat pain often involves a pain specialist and other professionals like physical therapists, says Christy Valentine, an internal-medicine and pediatrics physician in New Orleans. That's where education and communication come in, she says.

"It's important to help patients recognize that there is a special process going on" to assemble the right multifaceted treatment for their pain, and that it's a different and more effective thing than "what they're used to, which is just going to the doctor and getting medications."

Changing the pain paradigm to a less opiate-focused, more holistic venture "is often easier when you get patients who haven't had a lot of pain before," says Valentine, because "the patient has to do the real work," engaging in exercise or cognitive behavioral therapy rather than just taking a pill.

But good pain treatment often is hard to find, many doctors say. "There are a lot of pain management doctors around the country and also a lot of wannabe" pain doctors who specialize in handing out pills, "and that's where the problem lies," says David S. Kloth, an anesthesiologist in Danbury, Conn., and past president of the American Society of Interventional Pain Physicians. Some so-called pain doctors in Miami, for example, are actually "pill mills" that "see hundreds of people a day," actually diagnosing and treating nothing but contributing hugely to the flow of prescription narcotics into society, he says.

The Internet also facilitates prescription abuse. Many Internet pharmacies dispense drugs without a prescription or even sell bogus prescriptions of their own that buyers can use at other drugstores. In 2006, for example, 34 Internet pharmacies known or suspected to be illicit operations dispensed 98.5 million doses of medicine containing the opiate hydrocodone, according to the DEA. The doses accounted for 95 percent of the stores' business and were enough to supply 410,000 patients with a month's dosage each. By contrast, controlled substances account for just 11 percent of the sales at "brick and mortar" pharmacies, according to the agency. [40]

Illegal Internet pharmacies are extremely difficult to stamp out, says Jack E. Fincham, a professor of pharmacy practice and administration at the University of Missouri, Kansas City. "One can be shut down by authorities and be back in business immediately" because enforcement agencies can't find its physical location.

Continued on p. 854

At Issue:

Can the Ryan Haight Act curb prescription-drug abuse?

JOSEPH T. RANNAZZISI
DEPUTY ASSISTANT ADMINISTRATOR,
DRUG ENFORCEMENT ADMINISTRATION

TESTIMONY BEFORE HOUSE JUDICIARY SUBCOMMITTEE ON CRIME, TERRORISM AND HOMELAND SECURITY, JUNE 24, 2008

prescription drugs can be illegally acquired through a variety of means. While the Drug Enforcement Administration and other law enforcement investigations have shown that OxyContin and other Schedule II drugs are most commonly obtained illegally through "doctor shopping" or other, more traditional methods of illegally acquiring controlled pharmaceutical substances, this has not been the case for Schedule III or Schedule IV substances (e.g., anti-anxiety medications, hydrocodone combination products and anabolic steroids). [They] are often illegally purchased through the Internet. Unlike someone stealing a few pills out of the medicine cabinet . . . illicit Internet sales commonly involve 100 or more high-potency pills; these sales occur hundreds of times every day.

The Internet has become one of the fastest-growing methods of diverting controlled pharmaceuticals. Certainly there are benefits to allowing individuals with a valid prescription to fill their prescriptions over the Internet, ranging from simple convenience to providing individuals in remote areas or with limited mobility with greater access to needed medications. Legitimate pharmacies operate every day providing services over the Internet and operate well within the bounds of the law and sound medical practice.

Unfortunately, other so-called "pharmacy" sites on the Internet illegally sell controlled pharmaceuticals. These rogue Internet sites are not there to benefit the public but to generate millions in illegal sales.

The controlled-substance laws and regulations were written before the advent of fax machines, let alone high-speed Internet service and the complexities associated with the advent of this technology. It should be noted that inter-agency engagement on how best to bring the laws that protect the American people from drug traffickers up to speed with the methods these traffickers now routinely employ has been ongoing for years. These discussions culminated with the Bush administration's formal endorsement of the Ryan Haight Online Pharmacy Consumer Protection Act.

The act updates the Controlled Substances Act to set forth both permissible and impermissible conduct for Internet Web site operators, medical practitioners and pharmacists involved in the distribution of controlled substances by means of the Internet. This legislation balances the legitimate benefits derived from using the Internet to provide consumers with controlled substances obtained through valid prescriptions with the need to combat the illegal online distribution of these same drugs.

PATRICK J. EGAN
PARTNER, FOX ROTHSCHILD LLP,
PHILADELPHIA

TESTIMONY BEFORE HOUSE JUDICIARY SUBCOMMITTEE ON CRIME TERRORISM AND HOMELAND SECURITY, JUNE 24, 2008

by criminalizing the sale of controlled substances without a valid prescription by online pharmacies, the Ryan Haight Online Pharmacy Consumer Protection Act fails to attack the source of addiction to prescription medication. Drug users have multiple, superior sources to acquire medication. Under the assumption that controlled substances used for medical purposes improve the lives of patients, the benefits of prescription medicine sold by online pharmacies without the need for a valid prescription significantly outweigh the risks of abuse of the drugs for non-medical purposes, especially in teens.

The benefit to low-income Americans and elderly Americans of having the ability to purchase prescription medicine from online pharmacies without a valid prescription grossly outweighs the risk to adults and teens purchasing pain medication from online pharmacies. For example, if the uninsured were forced to go to doctors to get a valid prescription, they would not go at all because these individuals cannot afford medical care. Thus, online pharmacies give uninsured Americans a unique benefit not offered elsewhere.

In 2006, 17.4 percent of the 17-year-old population had used pain relievers for non-medical use. In addition to pain medication, diet pills are commonly purchased through online pharmacies. But . . . the majority of these drugs are obtained from friends and relatives, not online pharmacies.

The Office of National Drug Control Policy reports that 70 percent of teens get the products from friends and relatives. More than three in five teens say they got prescription pain relievers from parents' medicine cabinets. The Ohio Prescription Monitoring Program attributes "doctor shopping" as a predominant factor and means of getting prescription medication for non-medical use. Additionally, the attorney general of Maryland cites stealing pills from the pharmacy as a means of obtaining prescription meds. Lastly, doctors individually contribute to the distribution of pain medication for non-medical purposes.

Therefore, the minor impact of requiring online pharmacies to only distribute controlled substances with a valid prescription would not be attacking the true and majority source of non-medical use of pain relievers. The most efficient means of attack are through parenting education and supervision. Moreover, those adolescents who are inclined to purchase controlled substances through online pharmacies will continue to do so. Only now the drugs they are purchasing will be from offshore pharmacies that the Ryan Haight Act cannot reach and will be more likely to be adulterated or counterfeit.

Continued from p. 852

Meanwhile, Internet "search engines are profiting off ads" from bogus pharmacies, giving them every reason to avoid cracking down on the stores, says Liang of Western Law School. "All the search engines" — such as Microsoft, Yahoo and Google — "say they use pharmacychecker.com, but that's a joke, because when you go to the sites they've ranked, many are not requiring prescriptions."

E-mailed "spam" can also bring controlled substances right to your door. "Most people who use e-mail have experienced sifting through unsolicited e-mails that offer controlled substances online," wrote Robert F. Forman, director of clinical resources and education for the biotech firm Alkermes, a maker of addiction treatments in Cambridge, Mass. "For individuals addicted to prescription drugs . . . those e-mails are equivalent to getting a phone call from a drug dealer." [41]

Researchers also find that many prescription drugs pass to abusers through informal networks of family and friends, networks that for young people, in particular, may be much larger than in the past because of Internet social networking, says Richard Goldsworthy, CEO and director of research and development for The Academic Edge, a research firm in Bloomington, Ind.

With so many people holding legitimate prescriptions to abusable drugs — young athletes who are prescribed opiates after injuries, for example — "access to these things is incredible through a clandestine network based on cellphones and texting," says Wright State's Carlson.

The increasingly positive view Americans generally have of prescriptions is also helping to drive abuse, analysts say, along with the proliferation of drug advertising.

"As a society, we have the idea that we shouldn't feel any discomfort," says the Waismann Institute's Lowenstein.

"It got to the point where, if you had any ache or pain, you took Vicodin. . . . Sixty percent of Vicodin-using teens tried it before age 15, and most took it from grandparents' and parents' medicine cabinets."

For a health problem like insomnia, for example, "almost always there's a solution" that is not a pill, but pills are what doctors and patients usually opt for first, says psychiatrist Lundt. "People want to get the simplest solution, rather than putting money, time and energy into seeking out causes like sleep apnea," or prostate or hormonal problems, or making lifestyle changes like "getting the dog or the TV out of the bedroom," she says. As a result, many physicians "just throw Ambien at people."

Today's physicians "were basically trained by drug companies," making doctors less likely to suggest non-drug treatments when drugs are available, says Lowenstein.

Direct-to-consumer (DTC) advertising of prescription medicines was first permitted in the late 1990s, and it's contributed to a cultural attitude that "Hey, it's acceptable to take drugs," says Western Law School's Liang.

"I don't know why DTC is accepted," says Fincham. "The U.S. stands alone in allowing it. It's not done in Canada, the U.K., or Western Europe." But Americans, bombarded by drug ads "with attractive people feeling absolutely great, are lulled into complacency" about potential risks of prescription drugs, he says.

States and the federal government have noted the prescription-abuse problem and devoted some attention to it, but with many competing priorities funding has lagged.

In 2005, for example, the American Society of Interventional Pain Physicians successfully advocated for the National All Schedules Prescription Electronic Reporting Act, says anesthesiologist Kloth, the society's immediate

past president. The bill "was supposed to implement and improve prescription-monitoring programs" in all states but "was never funded," although Congress has provided $2 million in start-up funds in 2009.

That's especially ironic as Congress frets over how to pay for health-coverage expansion, says Kloth. About 15 percent of Medicare drugs — and about 38 percent of Medicaid drugs — are diverted to abusive purposes, along with hefty but unknown amounts of drugs for which privately insured people get prescriptions they fill at multiple pharmacies. The state of Missouri, for example, found that five drug-abusing patients alone ran up $400,000 in pharmacy bills. "We could potentially save millions of dollars" by beefing up monitoring efforts, he says. ■

CURRENT SITUATION

High, Not Rising

Prescription-drug abuse is no longer rising rapidly, as it was in the early 2000s, though levels are still high. "Among the general population, non-medical use of controlled prescription drugs was stable from 2003 to 2007, with 7 million Americans, age 12 and older, reporting past-month non-medical use," the White House Office of National Drug Control Policy (ONDCP) reported in May. [42]

As abuse of illegal drugs has declined, prescription-drug abuse has become a larger part of the nation's drug epidemic than it was in the past, even while it remains a relatively unrecognized issue, says University of Michigan research scientist Johnston.

"Prescription drugs have always been part of the problem" of drug abuse, with teenage abuse of amphetamines, tranquilizers, sedatives and other drugs reaching peaks in the 1970s and early '80s that have not been seen since, Johnston says. Beginning in the late 1970s, abuse of all drugs, including prescription drugs, dropped off for a decade or so, but began rising again in the early 1990s, he says.

Abuse of prescription drugs has generally leveled off after rising since about 1992, says Foster at the National Center on Addiction and Substance Abuse. But she says abuse still is rising for one group — 50- to 59-year-olds. "Baby boomers had higher drug use anyway, and they can get more prescriptions" than teenagers, she says. Boomers also may risk worse consequences from the drugs — a quicker path to addiction and health problems — than younger users, Foster says. "Older women don't realize that their bodies are more sensitive" to drugs as they age, for example.

Among teens, the Monitoring the Future survey reveals that use of the prescription amphetamine Ritalin — often prescribed for ADHD — continued to fall in 2008, having declined by about a third since 2001. Abuse of many other prescription medications, such as sedatives and tranquilizers, also has been modestly dropping among teens, says Johnston, the survey's principal investigator.

Some prescription narcotics, however, such as OxyContin and Vicodin, remain at or near the peak levels of abuse they hit in the mid-2000s. Unlike for most other prescription medications, the high abuse rates the two powerful drugs attained this decade were "new highs, at levels we hadn't seen before," says Johnston. "New drugs within that class [of prescription opioids] have helped to stimulate use."

Abuse of over-the-counter cough and cold medications also remains prevalent, Johnston says.

When abuse of any drug rises, it's mainly due to a decreased "perception of harm" connected with it in the public's mind, says Foster. For example, some prescription-drug abusers "won't touch OxyContin" because of the intense attention it received as a dangerous substance, says Carlson of Wright State. "They fear what they've heard," even though those fears don't translate into equivalent caution about other very similar opiate painkillers.

Thus, Johnston warns, even though prescription-drug abuse has generally plateaued or is currently dropping for most populations, it's no time to back off anti-abuse messages.

Ryan Haight Act

The nation "is in a period like the early 1990s," when policy makers and others let drug abuse slide from a public agenda crowded with other issues, raising the likelihood that drug abuse will rise again, Johnston says.

"This is the kind of problem that will recur and recur because all kids are susceptible to the same issues of curiosity" that draws people to try out substances, he says.

To counter that curiosity, education about the risks of drug addiction must be ongoing to reach each new cohort, Johnston says.

On Oct. 15, 2008, President Bush signed into law the federal government's most recent initiative to thwart prescription-drug abuse — the Ryan Haight Act. The Justice Department issued rules implementing the law in April 2009.

The law memorializes an 18-year-old high-school varsity tennis player and A student from La Mesa, Calif.,

who died in 2001 from an overdose of the painkiller Vicodin that he obtained over the Internet. The law officially prohibits anyone from selling or shipping "controlled substances" ordered over the Internet unless the customer has a "valid prescription" issued by a doctor during a live, in-person visit. [43] Haight had obtained his drugs after "consulting" with a physician online, a ploy that many online drug sellers use to get around state prescribing laws. [44]

The law also requires online pharmacies to comply with state laws for pharmacy licensure in all states in which they operate; post their address and telephone number, along with the qualifications of their lead pharmacist, on the Internet homepage; and notify states' attorneys general and pharmacy boards at least 30 days before offering to dispense any controlled drugs. The act also increases penalties for violations of prescribing laws. [45]

DEA Acting Administrator Michele M. Leonhart called it "landmark" legislation that "will bring rogue pharmacy operators out of the shadows by establishing a clear standard for legitimate online pharmaceutical sales." [46]

Other analysts say, however, that the law won't even touch the real culprits — actual "rogue" Internet pharmacies that already operate completely outside of the extensive state rules for pharmacy operation.

"It's an important thing, but they're just targeting legitimate Internet pharmacies" and totally missing the many rogue enterprises, says Liang of Western Law School. "Every state already requires a prescription anyway, so the legitimate sellers already do" what the Ryan Haight Act requires.

Meanwhile, many if not most of the bogus online pharmacies are operated by Chinese and Indian nationals, "Russian mafia guys," or others at mainly offshore sites, Liang says. "None of these people care" what U.S. law says.

■

OUTLOOK

'Unmet Needs'

With illegal drug use waning somewhat and legal prescriptions of addictive drugs rising, prescription-medication abuse has become a more important issue for substance-abuse and addiction treatment. Substance-abuse treatment capacity continues to lag behind need, however, and the medical profession is only beginning to recognize its potential role in heading off and treating prescription-drug abuse.

Currently, there are "enormous unmet needs" for better substance-abuse treatment as well as for education and prescription monitoring to prevent abuse, says Foster at the National Center on Addiction and Substance Abuse.

"The number of people needing care is overwhelming the treatment centers" in Ohio, for example, says Wright State University's Carlson.

Treatment efforts have lagged partly because of the blame long attached to drug abuse, but growing medical evidence that addiction is an illness may be gradually changing that, Foster says. "There have been a lot of examples of disease blamed on the patient," including tuberculosis and depression, and over time those views have shifted, as they are gradually shifting now for addiction, she says. "We still have a long way to go," however.

For one thing, the medical profession must recognize prescription-drug abuse and addiction generally as medical problems it must confront, and there are "signs of movement" in that direction, says Foster. For example, the Joint Commission on the Accreditation of Healthcare Organizations is proposing that all hospitals be required to screen for substance abuse, make treatment referrals and perform brief, evidence-based interventions for patients who show signs of abuse. [47]

Historically, however, addiction has not been viewed as a medical problem, Foster points out, even though the American Medical Association labeled it a disease as early as the 1950s. Consequently, she says, addicts of all kinds are "generally treated outside of medicine," in self-help groups like Narcotics Anonymous and at treatment centers run by non-physicians.

Despite studies demonstrating that addiction is a medical disease that "can become chronic" if untreated, "doctors are still uncomfortable" even talking about addiction with patients, let alone treating them, Foster says. In surveys, 47 percent of doctors "said they are uncomfortable discussing prescription-drug abuse" with patients.

Those barriers are gradually giving way, however, and "we're actually getting close to considering it malpractice" to prescribe addictive drugs without counseling about abuse risks and screening patients for any history of substance abuse in them or their families, she says.

It's also important to eliminate the easy availability of abusable prescription drugs, says University of Michigan research scientist Johnston. "Can we get physicians and dentists to give smaller prescriptions" of pain relievers, for example? "That would reduce the number of people who have leftover stuff in their medicine cabinets."

The Center on Addiction and Substance Abuse has "also petitioned the FDA to require abusable drugs to be made in less abusable forms," says Foster.

Nonetheless, drug-abuse battles will have to be refought in each new generation, says Carlson. "If we were able to solve the drug problem, we would have done so a long time ago." ∎

Notes

[1] For background, see "Coroner Rules Jackson's Death a Homicide," MSNBC.com, Aug. 24, 2009, www.msnbc.msn.com.

[2] Leonard J. Paulozzi, "Trends in Unintentional Drug Overdose Deaths," testimony before Senate Judiciary Subcommittee on Crime and Drugs, March 12, 2008.

[3] Gil Kaufman, "DJ AM's Death Caused by Accidental Overdose," Mtv.com, Sept. 29, 2009, www.mtv.com.

[4] Quoted in Harriet Ryan, "Pharmacist Refused to Fill Anna Nicole Smith's Prescription," Los Angeles Times, Sept. 22, 2009.

[5] Paulozzi, op. cit.

[6] "Prevention of Prescription Drug/Pharmaceutical Overdose and Abuse," National Conference of State Legislatures, June 2009, www.ncsl.org.

[7] Testimony before House Judiciary Subcommittee on Crime, Terrorism and Homeland Security, July 12, 2007.

[8] Ibid.

[9] Ibid.

[10] Quoted in Elaine Grant, "Pharmacy Board Stalls Drug Abuse Prevention Efforts, Advocates Say," New Hampshire Public Radio, July 27, 2009, www.Nhpr.org.

[11] Donna Leinwand, "Prescription Drugs Find Place in Teen Culture," USA Today, June 13, 2006, p. 1A. David Emery, "Are Pharm Parties for Real?" David Emery's Urban Legends Blog, About.com, March 24, 2009, http://urbanlegends.about.com/b/2009/03/24/are-pharm-parties-for-real.htm.

About the Author

Staff writer **Marcia Clemmitt** is a veteran social-policy reporter who previously served as editor in chief of *Medicine & Health* and staff writer for *The Scientist*. She has also been a high-school math and physics teacher. She holds a liberal arts and sciences degree from St. John's College, Annapolis, and a master's degree in English from Georgetown University. Her recent reports include "Preventing Cancer" and "Treating Depression."

[12] Testimony before Senate Committee on the Judiciary, March 12, 2008, http://judiciary.authoring.senate.gove/hearings/testimony.cfm.

[13] Ibid.

[14] Testimony before House Judiciary Subcommittee on Crime, Terrorism, and Homeland Security, June 24, 2008.

[15] "No Prescription Required: Bing.com Prescription Drug Ads," LegitScript and KnujOn, Aug 3, 2009, www.legitscript.com/BingRxReport.pdf.

[16] Ibid., p. 3.

[17] Jane C. Ballantyne and Jianren Mao, "Opioid Therapy for Chronic Pain," *New England Journal of Medicine*, Nov. 13, 2003, p. 1943, www.nejm.org.

[18] "OxyContin Backlash," press release, University of Alabama at Birmingham, About.com: Mental Health, http://mentalhealth.about.com/library/sci/0301/bloxycontin301.htm.

[19] Steven P. Cohen and Srinivasa N. Raja, "The Middle Way: A Practical Approach to Prescribing Opioids for Chronic Pain," Nature Clinical Practice, *Neurology*, Nov. 16, 2006, www.medscape.com.

[20] Brietta Clark, "A Painful Lesson," *Daily Journal*, Loyola Law School, July 22, 2009, http://media.lls.edu/DJclark072209.html.

[21] Ibid.

[22] Testimony before House Judiciary Subcommittee on Crime, Terrorism and Homeland Security, July 12, 2007.

[23] Ibid.

[24] Lakmaiah Manchikanti, "Prescription Drug Abuse: What Is Being Done to Address this New Drug Epidemic?" *Pain Physician*, October 2006, pp. 287-321, www.painphysicianjournal.com/2006/october/2006;9;287-321.pdf.

[25] Ibid.

[26] For background, see David T. Courtwright, *Dark Paradise: A History of Opiate Addiction in America* (2001).

[27] Quoted in Edward M. Brecher and editors of *Consumer Reports*, "The Consumers Union Report on Licit and Illicit Drugs," 1972, www.druglibrary.org/schaffer/Library/studies/cu/cu3.html.

[28] Ibid.

[29] Ibid.

[30] "Before Prohibition, Addiction Science Network," http://addictionscience.net/ASNpreprohibition.htm.

[31] Richard J. Bonnie and Charles H. Whitebread, "The Forbidden Fruit and the Tree of Knowledge: An Inquiry Into the Legal History of American Marijuana Prohibition," *Virginia Law Review*, October 1970, www.drugtext.org/index.php/en/reports/229-the-forbidden-fruit-and-the-tree-of-knowledge-an-inquiry-into-the-legal-history-of-american-marijuana-prohibition.

[32] Courtwright, *op. cit.*, p. 9.

[33] Bonnie and Whitebread, *op. cit.*

[34] Ibid.

[35] R. Alton Lee, *A History of Regulatory Taxation* (1973), p. 122.

[36] Ibid.

[37] Ibid.

[38] "The Controlled Substances Act," U.S. Drug Enforcement Administration Web site, www.usdoj.gov/dea/pubs/abuse/1-csa.htm.

[39] Martha A. Morrison, *White Rabbit: A Doctor's Own Story of Addiction* (1991), p. 70.

[40] Testimony before Senate Committee on the Judiciary, May 16, 2007.

[41] Robert F. Forman, "Narcotics on the Net: The Availability of Web Sites Selling Controlled Substances," *Psychiatric Services*, January 2006, p. 24.

[42] "Prescription Opioid-related Deaths Increased 114 Percent from 2001 to 2005, Treatment Administration Up 74 Percent in Similar Period; Young Adults Hardest Hit," press release, Office of National Drug Control Policy, May 20, 2009, www.whitehousedrugpolicy.gov.

[43] Rhiannon Coppin, "What Is the Ryan Haight Act?" Behind Online Pharma Web site, Jan. 14, 2009, http://behindonlinepharma.com/2009011452/faqs/what-is-the-ryan-haight-act.

[44] Francine Haight, "Ryan Haight's Story," Get Smart About Drugs Web site, Drug Enforcement Administration, www.getsmartaboutdrugs.com/stories/ryan_haights_story.html.

[45] Coppin, *op. cit.*

[46] "Congress Passes Ryan Haight Online Pharmacy Consumer Protection Act," press release, Drug Enforcement Administration, Oct. 1, 2008, www.usdoj.gov/dea/pubs/pressrel/pr100108.html.

[47] Bob Curley, "Proposed Accreditation Standards Could Compel U.S. Hospitals to Screen Patients for Addictions," Join Together Web site, National Center on Addiction and Substance Abuse, Sept. 11, 2009, www.jointogether.org/news/features/2009/proposed-accreditation.html.

FOR MORE INFORMATION

Community Anti-Drug Coalitions of America (CADCA), 625 Slaters Ln., Suite 300, Alexandria, VA 22314; (800) 542-2322; www.cadca.org. National coalition of community-based groups that conducts anti-drug programs, including for medication abuse.

Drug Enforcement Administration, Mailstop: AES, 8701 Morrissette Dr., Springfield, VA 22152; (202) 307-1000; www.usdoj.gov/dea. Monitors and prosecutes unlawful prescribing and diversion of medications to illegal use.

LegitScript, (877) 534-4879; www.legitscript.com. A private company that disseminates information about online pharmacies and has formulated standards for recognizing legitimate pharmacies.

Monitoring the Future, www.monitoringthefuture.org. An annual National Institutes of Health-sponsored study that has surveyed teen substance use since 1975.

National Alliance for Model State Drug Laws, 1414 Prince St., Suite 312, Alexandria, VA 22314; (703) 836-6100; www.namsdl.org. A congressionally funded group that assists states in monitoring medication abuse.

National Center on Addiction and Substance Abuse at Columbia University (CASA), 633 Third Ave., 19th Floor, New York, NY 10017-6706; (212) 841-5200; www.casacolumbia.org. Conducts research and oversees information campaigns.

National Institute on Drug Abuse, 6001 Executive Blvd., Room 5213, Bethesda, MD 20892-9561; (301) 443-1124; www.nida.nih.gov. A branch of the National Institutes of Health that sponsors research on addiction-related health issues, including strategies for manufacturing medications like painkillers that are less susceptible to abuse.

White House Office of National Drug Control Policy, Drug Policy Information Clearinghouse, P.O. Box 6000, Rockville, MD 20849-6000; (800) 666-3332; www.whitehousedrugpolicy.gov. Establishes national drug-control policy and has declared prescription-drug abuse a priority.

Bibliography

Selected Sources

Books

Colvin, Rod, *Overcoming Prescription Drug Addiction: A Guide to Coping and Understanding*, 3rd edition, 2008.

The author, whose brother died at age 35 from abusing painkillers and tranquilizers, relates accounts of recovery from other prescription-drug abusers and describes in layman's terms the range of treatment options available.

Courtwright, David T., *Dark Paradise: A History of Opiate Addiction in America*, Harvard University Press, 2001.

A professor of history at the University of North Florida chronicles how opiate addiction shifted from a mostly middle-class problem in the 19th century to poor, urban communities in the 20th century and outlines the roles law and medicine may have played in the shift.

Hodgson, Barbara, *In the Arms of Morpheus: The Tragic History of Laudanum, Morphine and Patent Medicines*, Firefly Books, 2001.

A British novelist describes the widespread use of opiate medications in the 18th and 19th centuries, when physicians prescribed opium-containing drugs for conditions including tuberculosis and cholera, and habitual opium users included such cultural icons as Louisa May Alcott, George Washington and Florence Nightingale.

Musto, David F., *The American Disease: Origins of Narcotic Control*, 3rd edition, Oxford University Press, 1999.

A Yale University professor of child psychiatry and social historian describes how U.S. narcotics laws developed amid American society's repeatedly shifting, love-hate relationship with alcohol and drugs.

Articles

Grant, Elaine, "Prescription Drug Abuse a Serious, Growing Problem," New Hampshire Public Radio, June 9, 2009, www.nhpr.org/special/prescriptiondrugs.

The first story in a series on prescription-drug abuse in New Hampshire reports that state legislators have repeatedly failed to create a prescription-drug monitoring program to stem abuse, although overdose deaths quadrupled from 1995 to 2007, with much of the rise likely connected to prescription medications.

Tisch, Chris, and Abbie Vansickle, "Deadly Combinations," *St. Petersburg Times*, Feb. 17, 2008, www.tampabay.com/specials/2008/reports/drug-deaths.

The first article in a series on Florida's severe prescription-drug abuse problem reports that overdoses have increased rapidly and now kill about 500 people each year just in the Tampa Bay area — three times the number of deaths associated with illegal drugs such as cocaine and heroin.

Reports and Studies

"Children of the Mountains," ABC News Special Report, Feb. 13, 2009, http://abcnews.go.com/Video/playerIndex?id=6885766.

ABC News anchor Diane Sawyer spent two years researching this disturbing special report on the grim conditions faced by children growing up in the mountains of Eastern Kentucky, where poverty and prescription drug abuse are rampant.

"Monitoring the Future: National Survey Results on Drug Use, 1975-2008," National Institute on Drug Abuse, December 2008, http://monitoringthefuture.org/pubs/monographs/vol1_2008.pdf.

Prescription-drug abuse among teens is generally holding steady at or near the relatively high levels seen in the early-to-mid-2000s following a decade-long rise.

"National Prescription Drug Threat Assessment 2009," Drug Enforcement Administration, April 2009, www.usdoj.gov/ndic/pubs33/33775/index.htm.

In 2007 approximately 6.9 million Americans ages 12 or older reported they currently were non-medical users of prescription drugs.

"No Prescription Required: Bing.com Prescription Drug Ads," Legitscript and Knujon, August 2009, www.legitscript.com/BingRxReport.pdf.

Ninety percent of prescription drug and online pharmacy ads on the Bing.com search engine lead to "rogue" pharmacies, many of which don't require prescriptions to dispense controlled drugs, according to groups that accredit Internet pharmacies and monitor regulatory compliance of Web-based companies.

"Prescription Drug Overdose: State Health Agencies Respond," Centers for Disease Control and Prevention/Association of State and Territorial Health Officials, 2008, www.cdc.gov/HomeAndRecreationalSafety/Poisoning/prescription_overdose.html.

State public-health officials describe efforts to stem the rise in mortality from prescription drugs that has occurred since 1999, focusing on nine states, including several with the highest death rates.

"Under the Counter: The Diversion and Abuse of Controlled Prescription Drugs in the U.S.," National Center on Addiction and Substance Abuse at Columbia University, July 2005, www.casacolumbia.org.

Prescription-drug abuse has crept upward over the past two decades, even as abuse of other substances has dropped. Only 19 percent of physicians, however, say they've been educated about how to prevent diversion of prescription drugs to illegal use.

The Next Step:

Additional Articles from Current Periodicals

Abusers

Al-Husaini, Mudhafer, and Erica Goode, "Increasingly, Iraqi Soldiers Are Abusing Prescription Drugs to Endure Stress of War," *The New York Times*, Dec. 21, 2008, p. A28.

The stresses of war and lack of strict government regulation have led more Iraqi soldiers to abuse prescription drugs.

Mariano, Willoughby, "Prescription-Drug Overdoses on the Rise," *Orlando Sentinel*, July 2, 2009, p. B2.

Florida deaths caused by anti-anxiety drugs and painkillers surpassed those from cocaine in 2008, according to a commission of state medical examiners.

Newhouse, Eric, "Prescription Drugs 'Newest Monster' in Indian Country," *Great Falls Tribune*, July 10, 2009, p. 1A.

Prescription-drug abuse is continually increasing among American Indians across northern Montana.

Waters, TaMaryn, "Prescription Drug Abuse Among Teens Stays Steady," *Tallahassee Democrat*, Nov. 18, 2008, p. 10A.

About 5 percent of Florida high-school seniors have reported abusing prescription drugs, more or less the same percentage as in 2002.

Law Enforcement

Bush, Rudolph, "Doctor Faces Federal Charges in 14 Fatal Overdoses," *Chicago Tribune*, May 23, 2007, p. 7.

A Chicago doctor allegedly dispensed narcotic pain medication illegally, resulting in 14 overdose deaths.

Fausset, Richard, "The Nation; Sunshine State has Become a Magnet for Pain Pill Buyers; Florida's Regulation Void is Causing Drug Troubles in Appalachia," *Los Angeles Times*, April 25, 2009, p. 17.

Appalachian prescription-drug addicts take advantage of poorly regulated "pain clinics" in Florida, the largest state without a prescription-monitoring program.

"Painkiller Prescriptions Highest in Eastern Kentucky, Report Says," *Los Angeles Times*, Jan. 20, 2003, p. 18.

From 1998 to 2001, legal drug outlets in eastern Kentucky received the most prescription painkillers per capita in the nation, resulting in skyrocketing possession and trafficking charges and many more addicts in treatment.

Pain Treatment

Haskell, Meg, "Proposed Law Seeks to Limit Painkiller Abuse," *Bangor Daily News* (Maine), July 22, 2009, p. B1.

Doctors propose formal patient-physician contracts, random pill counts and urine tests to detect the abuse or diversion of prescription drugs.

Jamison, Michael, "Treating Pain Can be a Tricky Business," *Ventura County Star* (California), July 9, 2009.

Doctors call for a national narcotic data bank to prevent patients from "doctor shopping" to obtain multiple prescriptions.

Klein, Jeffrey S., "Chronic Pain Sufferers Deserve Treatment with Dignity," *Battle Creek Enquirer* (Michigan), June 22, 2008, p. 7A.

The Drug Enforcement Administration (DEA) has too much power to limit the amount and types of drugs, particularly narcotic drugs, that physicians prescribe, causing doctors to under-prescribe painkillers to avoid investigation.

Regulations

Boutselis, Kirk, "Lowell Unites to Combat Drug Abuse," *Lowell Sun*, April 16, 2009.

A Massachusetts state legislator is calling for increased regulation of prescription drugs to end fake prescriptions.

Del Marcus, Jonathan, "Resolution Takes Aim at Prescription Drug Abuse," *Sun-Sentinel*, April 30, 2009, p. 9.

The city of Oakland Park, Fla., has unanimously approved a resolution urging the state legislature to pass a bill curtailing the abuse of prescription drugs.

Pramik, Mike, "Pending Law Will Regulate Online Prescription-Drug Sales," *Columbus* (Ohio) *Dispatch*, Oct. 12, 2008, p. 14A.

Congress recently approved the Ryan Haight Online Pharmacy Consumer Protection Act, which curbs the illegal sale of prescription drugs over the Internet.

In-depth Reports on Issues in the News

Are you writing a paper?

Need backup for a debate?

Want to become an expert on an issue?

For more than 80 years, students have turned to *CQ Researcher* for in-depth reporting on issues in the news. Reports on a full range of political and social issues are now available. Following is a selection of recent reports:

Civil Liberties
Closing Guantánamo, 2/09
Affirmative Action, 10/08
Gay Marriage Showdowns, 9/08
America's Border Fence, 9/08
Immigration Debate, 2/08

Crime/Law
Interrogating the CIA, 9/09
Examining Forensics, 7/09
Legalizing Marijuana, 6/09
Wrongful Convictions, 4/09
Prostitution Debate, 5/08

Education
Reading Crisis? 2/08
Discipline in Schools, 2/08
Student Aid, 1/08

Environment/Society
Gays in the Military, 9/09
Energy and Climate, 7/09
Future of Books, 5/09
Hate Groups, 5/09
Future of Journalism, 3/09
Confronting Warming, 1/09
Reducing Carbon Footprint, 12/08

Health/Safety
Nuclear Disarmament, 10/09
Health-Care Reform, 8/09
Straining the Safety Net, 7/09
Treating Depression, 6/09
Reproductive Ethics, 5/09
Extreme Sports, 4/09

Politics/Economy
State Budget Crisis, 9/09
Business Bankruptcy, 4/09
Future of the GOP, 3/09
Middle-Class Squeeze, 3/09

Upcoming Reports

Manned Spaceflight, 10/16/09   Conspiracy Theories, 10/23/09   Human Rights, 10/30/09

ACCESS

CQ Researcher is available in print and online. For access, visit your library or www.cqresearcher.com.

STAY CURRENT

To receive notice of upcoming *CQ Researcher* reports, or learn more about *CQ Researcher* products, subscribe to the free e-mail newsletters, *CQ Researcher Alert!* and *CQ Researcher News*: http://cqpress.com/newsletters.

PURCHASE

To purchase a *CQ Researcher* report in print or electronic format (PDF), visit www.cqpress.com or call 866-427-7737. Single reports start at $15. Bulk purchase discounts and electronic-rights licensing are also available.

SUBSCRIBE

Annual full-service *CQ Researcher* subscriptions—including 44 reports a year, monthly index updates, and a bound volume—start at $803. Add $25 for domestic postage.

CQ Researcher Online offers a backfile from 1991 and a number of tools to simplify research. For pricing information, call 800-834-9020, ext. 1906, or e-mail librarysales@cqpress.com.

Human Spaceflight

Are missions to the Moon and Mars feasible?

Published by CQ Press, a Division of SAGE

www.cqresearcher.com

N ASA's human spaceflight program is stuck in low orbit, held back by budget constraints, political bickering, competing visions and daunting technical challenges. A White House-commissioned panel has warned that the program is on an "unsustainable trajectory" because of funding limitations, and plans to build a new generation of rockets, return to the Moon and eventually go to Mars are under intense scrutiny. Meanwhile, the impending termination of the Space Shuttle could leave a seven-year gap during which the United States could have to rely on Russia to ferry astronauts to space. The future of NASA's human spaceflight program — including whether to build a lunar settlement — rests heavily on whether the Obama administration presses for more space funding. Meanwhile, private companies are working to build rockets of their own. Entrepreneurs hope to transport not only cargo into space but astronauts too. At the same time, private operators are gearing up for an emerging business taking wealthy space tourists into orbit.

An artist's rendering shows an Ares I rocket, part of the $80 billion Constellation space exploration program designed to eventually travel to Mars. The program is under review by the Obama administration

CQ Researcher • Oct. 16, 2009 • www.cqresearcher.com
Volume 19, Number 36 • Pages 861-884

Cover: NASA/Marshall Space Flight Center

CQ Researcher

Oct. 16, 2009
Volume 19, Number 36

MANAGING EDITOR: Thomas J. Colin
tcolin@cqpress.com

ASSISTANT MANAGING EDITOR: Kathy Koch
kkoch@cqpress.com

ASSOCIATE EDITOR: Kenneth Jost

STAFF WRITERS: Thomas J. Billitteri,
Marcia Clemmitt, Peter Katel

CONTRIBUTING WRITERS: Rachel Cox,
Sarah Glazer, Alan Greenblatt, Reed Karaim
Barbara Mantel, Patrick Marshall,
Tom Price, Jennifer Weeks

DESIGN/PRODUCTION EDITOR: Olu B. Davis

ASSISTANT EDITOR: Darrell Dela Rosa

FACT-CHECKING: Eugene J. Gabler,
Michelle Harris

CQ PRESS

A Division of SAGE

PRESIDENT AND PUBLISHER:
John A. Jenkins

**EXECUTIVE DIRECTOR,
REFERENCE INFORMATION GROUP:**
Alix B. Vance

CQ Researcher (ISSN 1056-2036) is printed on acid-free paper. Published weekly, except; (Jan. wk. 1) (May wk. 4) (July wks. 1, 2) (Aug. wks. 3, 4) (Nov. wk. 4) and (Dec. wk. 4), by CQ Press, a division of SAGE Publications. Annual full-service subscriptions start at $803. For pricing, call 1-800-834-9020, ext. 1906. To purchase a *CQ Researcher* report in print or electronic format (PDF), visit www. cqpress.com or call 866-427-7737. Single reports start at $15. Bulk purchase discounts and electronic-rights licensing are also available. Periodicals postage paid at Washington, D.C., and additional mailing offices. POSTMASTER: Send address changes to *CQ Researcher*, 2300 N St., N.W., Suite 800, Washington, DC 20037.

Human Spaceflight

BY THOMAS J. BILLITTERI

THE ISSUES

When *Apollo 11* astronaut Neil Armstrong stepped onto the moon 40 years ago in his iconic "giant leap for mankind," America's space program stood at a technological and geopolitical zenith.

Today, NASA's human spaceflight program is stuck in low orbit, held back by budget constraints, political bickering, competing visions and daunting technological challenges. Astronauts have not ventured beyond about 400 miles from Earth since the last mission to the Moon in 1972, and space experts say that unless President Barack Obama fights for more money for space, the International Space Station may mark the boundary of U.S. exploration of the cosmos by American astronauts for decades.

In September, a White House-commissioned advisory committee warned that NASA's current annual budget of about $18 billion would need to rise by an additional $3 billion per year through fiscal 2014 for any "meaningful" human exploration beyond the Space Station. * "The U.S. human spaceflight program appears to be on an unsustainable trajectory," declared the panel, chaired by former Lockheed Martin Corp. CEO Norman Augustine. [1]

---

* Some space experts have construed the Augustine panel's conclusions to mean that NASA's budget would need to rise gradually over the next five years to an additional $3 billion in 2014, rather than $3 billion per year through fiscal 2014.

The Space Shuttle Discovery *delivers new crew quarters and other equipment to the International Space Station in late August. The Shuttle is scheduled for retirement next year, but a new craft, the* Ares I *rocket, won't be ready for years. In September a White House-commissioned study warned that the U.S. human spaceflight program is on an "unsustainable trajectory" and needs more money for "meaningful" human exploration beyond the Space Station.*

The Augustine panel, which was asked to present options for human space exploration rather than recommendations, nonetheless raised doubts about a goal announced by former President George W. Bush to return astronauts to the Moon by 2020 and then send humans to Mars and beyond.

Bush's vision has evolved into a massive program called Constellation that includes plans for new *Ares I* and heavy-lift *Ares V* rockets, an *Orion* crew capsule and *Altair* lunar landing craft. NASA's current budget isn't big enough to make the Constellation plan viable under its current schedule, the panel said. *Ares I* and *Orion* are intended in part to transport astronauts to the Space Station. That function is now performed by the Space Shuttle, which is scheduled for retirement next year. But the new craft won't be ready for years, leaving the United States dependent on Russian rockets and spacecraft to get Americans to and from the station.

For a return to the Moon by 2020, Constellation is budgeted to spend more than $80 billion, but the Augustine committee determined that it would take $50 billion more — not including the cost of flying the rockets — to meet that schedule, according to the *Orlando Sentinel*. [2]

One option the panel presented calls for the government to rely on commercial companies to take astronauts to the Space Station, potentially freeing up money for NASA to focus on more ambitious trips into space. The idea is controversial. While commercial rockets routinely place satellites into orbit, one has never carried humans beyond suborbital range.

The Augustine panel also said that assuming NASA's budget grows enough to send humans beyond low-Earth orbit, a "flexible path" toward an ultimate Mars landing could be a viable alternative to going directly to the Moon or Mars. A flexible approach would entail sending astronauts on missions of increasing complexity to such destinations as lunar orbit, near-Earth asteroids or one of Mars' two moons.

"Mars is the ultimate destination for human exploration," the panel said, "but it is not the best first destination."

The panel's work has sparked pushback from Constellation's supporters on

Space Station Serves as Orbiting Laboratory

The $100 billion International Space Station (ISS) has served as a research laboratory in space since 2000. The United States, Canada, Japan, Russia, Brazil and 18 nations of the European Space Agency contribute scientific and technological resources and personnel to the station. Orbiting about 250 miles above Earth, it allows extended studies of the effects of decreased gravity and low atmospheric pressure on plants, animals and crew members, which will aid scientists in determining whether sustained weightlessness is possible. The station typically carries a crew of six, with personnel arriving and departing in pairs or small groups. In 2016, the Space Station is scheduled to be taken out of orbit, which will cause it to reenter the atmosphere, turn into a fireball and crash into the Pacific Ocean.

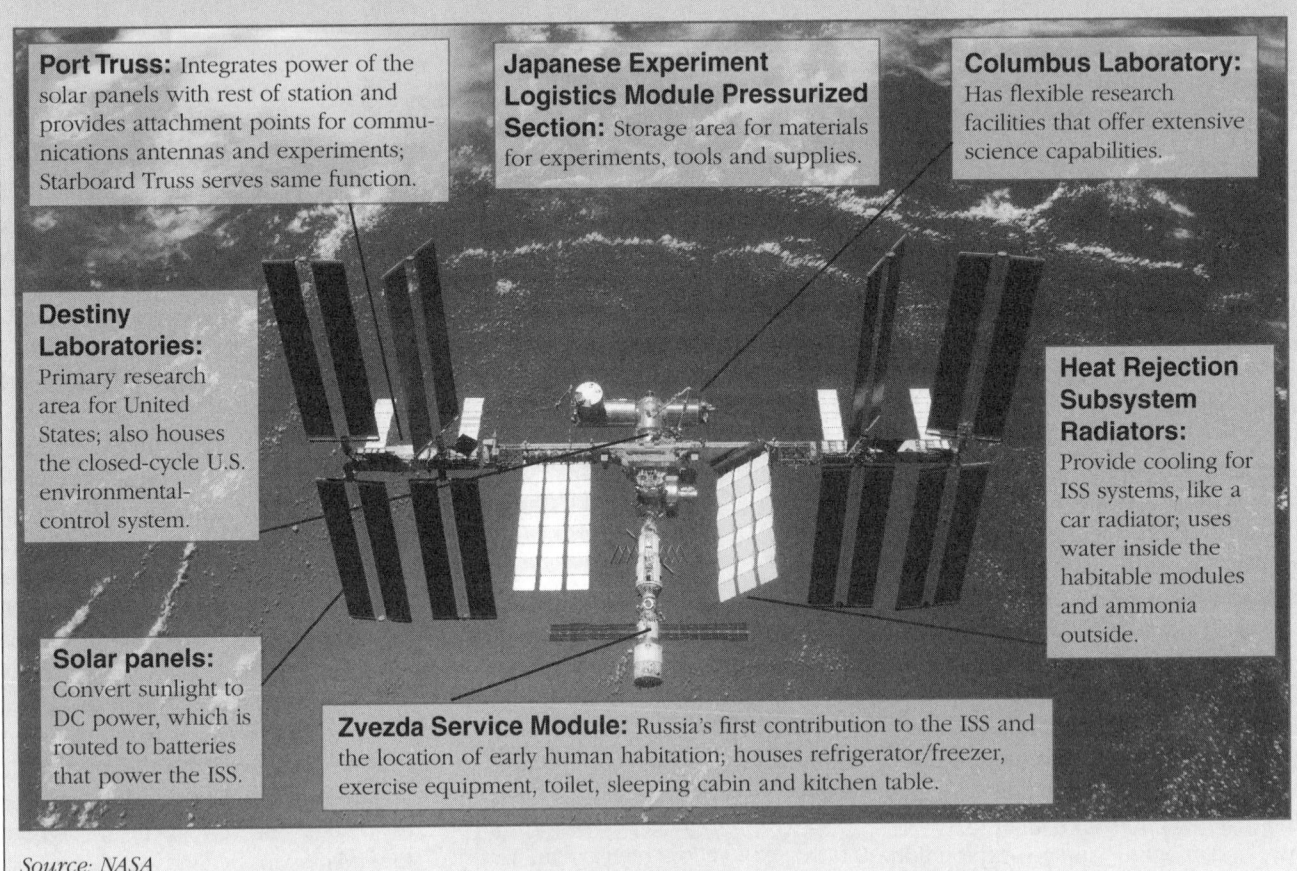

Port Truss: Integrates power of the solar panels with rest of station and provides attachment points for communications antennas and experiments; Starboard Truss serves same function.

Japanese Experiment Logistics Module Pressurized Section: Storage area for materials for experiments, tools and supplies.

Columbus Laboratory: Has flexible research facilities that offer extensive science capabilities.

Destiny Laboratories: Primary research area for United States; also houses the closed-cycle U.S. environmental-control system.

Heat Rejection Subsystem Radiators: Provide cooling for ISS systems, like a car radiator; uses water inside the habitable modules and ammonia outside.

Solar panels: Convert sunlight to DC power, which is routed to batteries that power the ISS.

Zvezda Service Module: Russia's first contribution to the ISS and the location of early human habitation; houses refrigerator/freezer, exercise equipment, toilet, sleeping cabin and kitchen table.

Source: NASA

Capitol Hill. In recent years Republican- and Democrat-controlled Congresses have passed laws supporting the program, which provides thousands of jobs in states such as Texas, California, Alabama and Colorado.

"It's hard for me to understand why the president is seeking new options at all when there has been an agreed-upon plan for several years," Rep. Ralph M. Hall, R-Texas, declared at a hearing on the Augustine panel's findings. "Why

don't we just fund the [Constellation] program we've all agreed to?" [3]

Yet Constellation also has critics. *Ares I* has encountered cost overruns and technical problems, and detractors view Constellation as ill-conceived.

Review of the human spaceflight program comes amid rising international interest in space and new discoveries. In 2003 China became the third nation, along with the United States and Russia, to launch humans

into space, and China's military-run space program has plans for lunar exploration. Meanwhile, Japan last month launched an unmanned cargo ship on a maiden rendezvous with the Space Station. [4] And an Indian lunar probe using a NASA instrument detected signs of water on the Moon. [5] The finding could spur new interest in a lunar settlement.

In October, another probe — part of a NASA satellite named the *Lunar*

Crater Observation and Sensing Satellite — or *LCROSS* — slammed into the Moon in a search for signs of ice. If significant amounts are found, the discovery could make human settlements on the Moon more feasible because the ice could provide water and oxygen. [6]

How the public might view a contraction or expansion of spending on human spaceflight is unclear. Forty-four percent of respondents to a Rasmussen poll in July said the United States should reduce space exploration because of economic conditions, and about half said current space goals should not include a human Mars mission. Only 29 percent were in favor. [7]

Yet a Gallup Poll found that 58 percent believe the space program has produced enough benefits to justify its costs, and 60 percent thought spending on space should remain at current levels (46 percent) or rise (14 percent). [8]

The White House has said little about its space objectives, and it could be months before it lays out its plans for NASA. It "would be premature for anyone to draw conclusions from the [Augustine] committee's work," a White House spokesman said. Obama is committed to a "vigorous and sustainable path" for human spaceflight. [9]

Clearly, though, the administration faces hard choices. Among them: whether to maintain U.S. financial support of the International Space Station beyond fiscal 2016, a deadline set under the Bush plan to free up money for a Moon and Mars program.

American money accounts for the bulk of the Space Station's funding, and the orbiting lab's supporters want to keep it open until at least 2020. They argue that it is just reaching completion and a full crew after years of delays, and they point out that its work includes research on prolonged human spaceflight needed for a Mars mission. Plus, they say, closing the station would alienate Japan, Canada, Russia and the European Space Agency — partners likely needed for human exploration of the Moon or Mars.

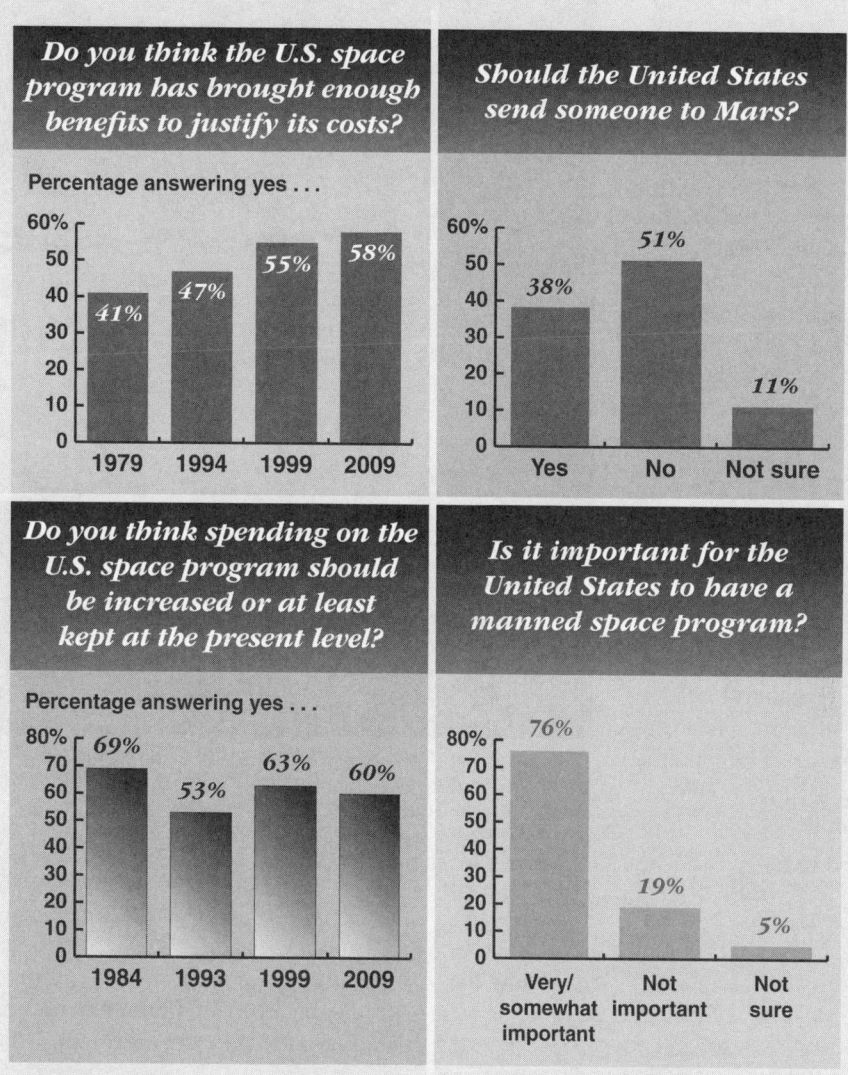

Majority of Public Reject Mars Mission

Three-fourths of the American public think the U.S. should have a human spaceflight program, but less than 40 percent think the country should send someone to Mars. Overall, nearly six in 10 Americans think the country's space program has yielded enough benefits to justify its costs — the highest percentage in at least 30 years.

Do you think the U.S. space program has brought enough benefits to justify its costs?

Percentage answering yes ...

1979: 41%
1994: 47%
1999: 55%
2009: 58%

Should the United States send someone to Mars?

Yes: 38%
No: 51%
Not sure: 11%

Do you think spending on the U.S. space program should be increased or at least kept at the present level?

Percentage answering yes ...

1984: 69%
1993: 53%
1999: 63%
2009: 60%

Is it important for the United States to have a manned space program?

Very/somewhat important: 76%
Not important: 19%
Not sure: 5%

Sources: Jeffrey M. Jones, "Majority of Americans Say Space Program Costs Justified," Gallup Poll, June 2009; "51% Oppose U.S. Manned Mission to Mars," Rasmussen Reports, July 2009

But critics argue that the station is of minimal scientific value and that its funding can be put to better use.

If the Space Shuttle ends next year as scheduled and the Space Station remains, it could be years until the *Ares I* or a commercial rocket is available to take American astronauts to the orbiting lab. Meanwhile, the United States could have to rely on Russia for transportation during that time gap. "The only way to significantly close the gap is to extend the life of the Shuttle program," the Augustine panel said.

Yet extending the Shuttle poses different problems. One is money. The Shuttle's budget of around $3 billion a year accounts for roughly a sixth of NASA's annual funding. Another is safety. Joseph W. Dyer, chairman of NASA's Aerospace Safety Advisory Panel, told a House committee that the panel strongly opposes extending the Shuttle beyond its six remaining flights. [10]

Against the backdrop of budget pressures and decisions over space hardware loom questions about the role of humans in space. Some argue that it is more cost-effective to rely on robotic spacecraft for exploration. "There is this persistent view — it's almost religion — that man needs to move on beyond the Earth and explore the universe," says John Gibbons, former director of the White House Office of Science and Technology Policy in the Clinton administration. "We're doing that now, but with instrumentation, which is the way to go."

But others say that while robots are useful, they can't replace astronauts. "The interest that humans have in human spaceflight won't go away just because we have really good rovers up there," argues Louis Friedman, executive director of the Planetary Society, which advocates a human expedition to Mars.

Ultimately, the direction of the space program rests with the White House. Marcia S. Smith, president of

the Space and Technology Policy Group, a consulting company, and former director of the Space Studies Board at the National Research Council, says the future of the space program "will be on Mr. Obama's desk."

Mars comes within 36 million miles of Earth during its revolution around the Sun and moves as far away as 250 million miles. A flight to Mars would take from six to nine months. Once on the "Red Planet," astronauts would have to remain up to 18 months before Mars was close enough to Earth again to make a return trip possible.

As policy makers and space experts weigh the prospects for NASA's human spaceflight program, here are some of the questions they are debating:

Should the Obama administration push for higher spending on NASA?

A key question facing the Obama administration is whether, amid an avalanche of budget pressures, funding for human space exploration should grow.

Under the president's fiscal 2010 budget request, the space agency would get about $18.7 billion. Human spaceflight

would receive about $10 billion of the total, with $3.2 billion for the Shuttle, $2.3 billion for the Space Station and the rest for the Constellation program. Robotic scientific exploration, including planetary probes, space telescopes (such as the Hubble), helio-physics (study of the sun and its effects) and earth science would get about $4.5 billion.

Overall, NASA's 2010 budget is about 5 percent more than in fiscal 2009, and Obama has proposed keeping future NASA funding basically flat through 2014.

In early October, 28 Republican and Democratic members of Texas' 34-member congressional delegation urged Obama to divert $3 billion from last year's economic stimulus package to NASA's human spaceflight program. [11]

Smith favors a bigger budget for both human and robotic space exploration for what she calls "all the tangible and intangible reasons," including inspiring young people to study math and science and promoting American leadership in the world.

But Alex Roland, a Duke University history professor and a former NASA historian, says "NASA can work with the current budget or less. NASA spends more than all the rest of the world combined on space."

Roland, a prominent NASA critic, says the space agency's human spaceflight program is based on the use of liquid-fueled rockets that are "too expensive" and "very inefficient." Human spaceflight to the Moon and Mars requires the heaviest payloads, for which current launch technology is ill-suited,

It's a Long Way to Mars

Human spaceflight has traveled a long way since Soviet cosmonaut Yuri Gagarin became the first person to orbit the Earth in 1961, reaching an altitude of about 187 miles. The International Space Station orbits at an altitude of about 250 miles. The Moon is an average distance from Earth of about 235,000 miles — a mere hop compared to Mars, which comes within 36 million miles of Earth on its closest pass.

Distances From Earth (in miles)

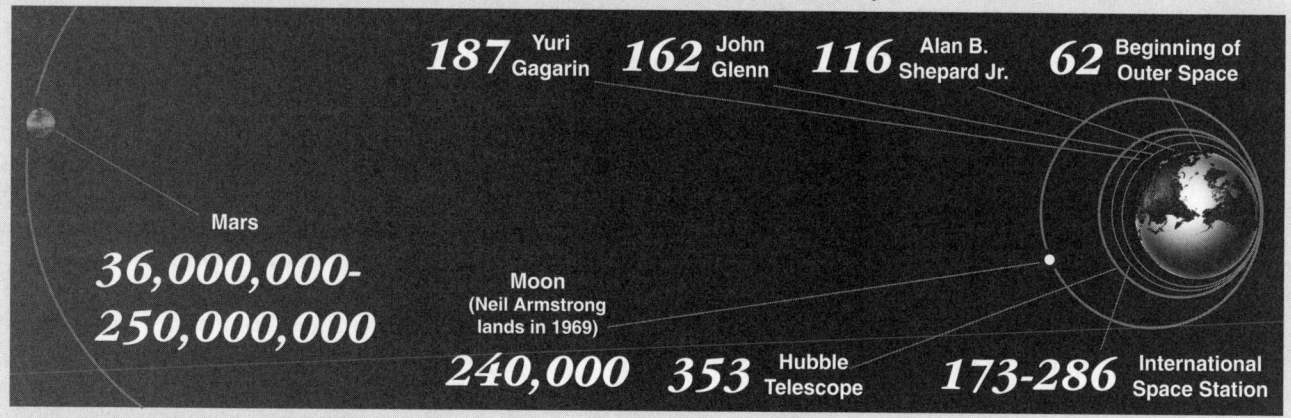

187 Yuri Gagarin **162** John Glenn **116** Alan B. Shepard Jr. **62** Beginning of Outer Space

Mars
36,000,000- 250,000,000

Moon (Neil Armstrong lands in 1969)
240,000 **353** Hubble Telescope **173-286** International Space Station

---

he argues. Until NASA finds an alternative way to transport astronauts, the agency should confine its exploration activities to robotic spacecraft — an approach that is within the agency's current budget, Roland says.

Some advocates of a bigger space-exploration budget are optimistic more money will come. "I believe there's a willingness and recognition of the necessity of increasing [NASA's budget] by some meaningful amount," says John M. Logsdon, professor emeritus in the Space Policy Institute at George Washington University.

Edward Ellegood, a space policy analyst at Embry-Riddle Aeronautical University, in Daytona Beach, Fla., also favors expanding NASA's budget. He calls for at least a sustained $3 billion addition to the NASA budget to fund a "meaningful" exploration program to destinations beyond low-Earth orbit. "It's not a big expenditure in comparison with what we spend on military projects," Ellegood contends, "and in fact the military has a bigger budget for space projects than NASA's entire budget."

In fiscal 2007 the Defense Department and the U.S. intelligence community spent

$22.4 billion on classified and unclassified "national security" space activities, compared to NASA's $16.3 billion budget that year. Defense and national security space programs include satellite systems for reconnaissance, navigation, communications, weather tracking and early warning of missile launches and nuclear detonations. Many have civil and commercial applications, blurring the line between military and civilian space systems. For instance, the Global Positioning System (GPS) navigation satellites operated by the Defense Department enable civilian and commercial applications ranging from precision farming to automobile navigation systems. [12]

For years, Ellegood argues, "NASA has been asked to do things on the cheap, and again and again they've found they have to go back to Congress and ask for more money. And if they don't get that money the program they're trying to conduct ends up in turmoil. It's not smart program management to continue to underfund projects they've been asked to do."

Scott Pace, director of George Washington University's Space Policy Institute and former NASA associate administrator

for program analysis and evaluation in the Bush administration, says his "gut sense" is that Obama will press for additional money but that it's uncertain whether the money would only be enough to extend the Space Station program or rather to keep the station flying plus continue human exploration beyond low-Earth orbit.

In any case, Pace looks for Obama to push for more funds "because of the positive feedback he'll get" internationally and from the science and technology community and because of the importance of local politics in space-job states, such as Florida, Texas and Alabama, as NASA transitions from the Shuttle. While human spaceflight might not be Obama's top priority for NASA, Pace says, he doesn't think "this president will be the one who chose to stop" human space exploration by holding back on spending.

For some scientists and space enthusiasts, the biggest problem isn't NASA's budget but rather what they see as a lack of clear goals for exploration beyond low-Earth orbit.

"The first thing needed is focus," says aerospace engineer Robert Zubrin, president of the Mars Society and author

Handful of Countries Have Launched Satellites

Iran this year became the first country in two decades to begin launching satellites. Seven individual countries and a European consortium have launched satellites for weather, navigation, communications and other purposes. The former Soviet Union launched the world's first satellite — Sputnik — 42 years ago.

Countries with satellite-launching capabilitiy	Year of First Launch
Russia *	1957
United States	1958
Japan	1970
China	1970
European Space Agency **	1979
India	1980
Israel	1988
Iran	2009

* *Formerly the Soviet Union*

** *The agency's 18 members include France and Great Britain, which launched satellites in 1965 and 1971, respectively, as part of their national space programs before joining the agency. Launches of the agency's* Ariane *space vehicle are conducted by France's Arianespace.*

Source: Marcia Smith, "International Space Activities," Space Policy Online

of *The Case for Mars.* NASA is "dissipating its money in all kinds of directions," he argues.

Zubrin says that for $9 billion per year — roughly the portion of NASA's budget assigned to human spaceflight — astronauts could be walking on Mars in eight years if NASA focuses on that goal alone, ends U.S. involvement in the Space Station and funding for the Shuttle, converts some Shuttle-rocket technology for heavy-lift cargo-launch capability and contracts with a private company to build a Mars vehicle and living quarters. Zubrin says NASA's current $18 billion budget, after adjusting for inflation, is the same as what the space agency received on average per year from 1961 to 1973 during the *Apollo* era.

Gibbons, the former White House science official, argues that keeping NASA's funding in check during the Clinton

years helped to balance the federal budget without hurting space exploration. "We made progress by using more and more productivity," says Gibbons, a former director of the Congressional Office of Technology Assessment. It's better, he says, to focus NASA's spending on instrument- and robotic-based scientific exploration, rather than pouring billions more into rockets for human spaceflight.

Robert L. Park, a University of Maryland physicist, agrees. "I would love to see more money put into NASA," he says. "I would just like to see it put into the right places." And that would mean that only a "few percent" of the NASA budget would be used for human spaceflight — just enough to be able to launch an astronaut "if something shows up where you really want to put a human being out there," he says. Otherwise, the money should go

for robotic exploration, Park argues. (*See "At Issue," p. 877.*)

"The big argument usually is made that . . . the public won't support space exploration without human spaceflight: 'No Buck Rogers, no bucks,' " Park says. But, he adds, "this is the cyber generation. Young people today empathize as much with robotic as with human exploration. As usual, the public, I think, is ahead of the science and ahead of the government."

Should NASA rely on private companies to take astronauts to low-Earth orbit destinations such as the Space Station?

In a letter to White House advisory committee Chairman Augustine in July, former NASA Administrator Michael D. Griffin noted the "strategic" importance of "independent and assured human access to space," and suggested it would be wrong to depend wholly on the commercial sector to accomplish that objective.

"It cannot be left solely to the discretion and ability of private entities, whose interests can never, and should never, be wholly aligned with those of government, to provide such capability," he wrote. "It is one thing to say, as I have on many occasions, that we should purchase commercial service in lieu of utilizing government systems when the former becomes available. It is another thing entirely for the very existence of a strategic capability to be held hostage to the vagaries of the marketplace." [13]

Smith, of the Space and Technology Policy Group, also worries about relying solely on commercial companies to ferry astronauts. "It's a tempting proposition, but I just don't see the market for this to be a truly commercial enterprise," she says.

But others say that commercial companies are on track to becoming viable alternatives to NASA for delivering astronauts to low-Earth orbit — meaning the Space Station. "The Defense Department believes its satellites are of strategic national importance, yet you don't see the Air Force operating its own rockets anymore — they rely on private companies," says Ellegood of Embry-Riddle Aeronautical University.

He compares the current era to the early days of aviation, when barnstormers gave people rides at county fairs and then the government — recognizing the potential of private operators — began contracting with nascent airlines to ferry mail among cities. "We're kind of in an analogous situation, where governments are more likely to get more economical service for something that's been proven," Ellegood says. "This isn't an R&D program anymore."

In fact, the prospect of private companies taking people and goods into space isn't as far-fetched as it might have seemed only a few years ago.

The Augustine commission said commercial services to ferry crews to low-Earth orbit are "within reach." It is time to consider handing that job over to the commercial sector, the panel said, suggesting that a new competition should be established among small and large companies to carry out such missions.

Last year NASA awarded $3.5 billion in contracts to two companies to bring cargo to the Space Station once the Shuttle stops flying: an eight-flight, $1.9 billion contract to Orbital Sciences, a Virginia company that makes rockets, satellites and other space hardware for commercial, military and government customers; and a 12-flight, $1.6 billion contract to Space Exploration Technologies, or SpaceX, a company established by American physicist and entrepreneur Elon Musk, who also co-founded the PayPal electronic payment system and Tesla Motors, an electric-car company. [14]

Musk has galaxy-sized plans for space. After several early failures, SpaceX launched a Malaysian satellite into orbit this summer atop its *Falcon 1* rocket, its second successful launch. The satellite

has a high-resolution camera used to monitor natural resources. [15] Next year Musk, who has put about $100 million into SpaceX, aims to send the first cargo flight to the Space Station. [16]

He also talks about transporting astronauts to the orbiting lab. "At SpaceX we feel pretty confident in being able to do it for about $20 million per seat," roughly 40 percent of the cost on a Russian spaceship, he said. [17] Musk even talks about putting a human on Mars by 2020. [18]

Meanwhile, Virgin Galactic, a company established by British entrepreneur Richard Branson, is among those developing a space-tourism business. (*See sidebar, p. 872.*)

But relying solely on private companies to transport astronauts to low-Earth orbit poses challenges, not the least of which is political.

A salient example is the *Ares I*. Responding to Constellation's critics who want to stop the *Ares I*, the rocket's backers — including government contractors such as Boeing, Lockheed Martin and Pratt & Whitney — started a public relations campaign to save the rocket, the *Orlando Sentinel* noted. Over the past four years, NASA has spent more than $3 billion on the rocket and $3 billion more on the *Orion* crew capsule, according to the paper. A video on the online site YouTube even encourages people to tell Washington to keep the spacecraft and not "take a chance" on others. [19]

In May, Sen. Richard Shelby, R-Ala. — whose state is home to NASA's Marshall Space Flight Center, the project manager for the *Ares I* and *Ares V* rockets — challenged supporters of private space companies, especially SpaceX, labeling the claims of commercial-launch supporters as "grandiose." [20]

Shelby also criticized the Obama administration's decision to undertake the Augustine review, arguing that it would slow the Constellation program despite the bipartisan support in Congress it already has garnered. [21]

But George Washington University's Logsdon says commercial companies ought to have the chance to prove they can compete with government for space business. He argues that Shelby is trying to throw roadblocks in front of an emerging private spaceflight industry. "I would hope," Logsdon says, "that the parochial interest of one senator would not sway the decision on a capability that is central to the United States for the next generation."

Should a lunar base and mission to Mars be the next big human spaceflight goals?

In 1989, on the 20th anniversary of the *Apollo 11* moon landing, President George H. W. Bush called for a return to the Moon as a step toward a human mission to Mars. Fifteen years later his son, President George W. Bush, did the same.

"We'll build new ships to carry man forward into the universe, to gain a new foothold on the Moon and to prepare for new journeys to the worlds beyond our own," the younger Bush proclaimed. [22]

Yet critics say neither Bush pushed for adequate funds for those plans. And even if government dollars were as numerous as stars, the question remains of whether it makes sense — especially in an era when robotic spacecraft are growing in sophistication and capability — to build an expensive lunar base and then aim for a human settlement on Mars.

Some Mars enthusiasts see the Moon as an important steppingstone to the Red Planet, while for others a stop on the lunar surface 40 years after *Apollo 11* landed there holds little if any appeal.

One thing is certain, though: Reaching Mars presents daunting challenges.

Astronauts would have to survive brutal cosmic radiation and prolonged weightlessness on the perhaps nine-month trip. They also would have to live for roughly 18 months on Mars, which has a third the gravity of Earth, until Earth and Mars aligned for the trip home. What's more,

NASA would need a spacecraft powerful enough to get to Mars and back. The powerful *Ares V*, which remains on the drawing board, is contemplated for that task as well as for carrying cargo on a lunar expedition.

The Planetary Society's Friedman isn't necessarily opposed to a brief lunar landing as a steppingstone to Mars — "that would be second-guessing the engineering teams," he says. But he argues that putting astronauts back on the Moon would delay the ultimate goal of a human expedition to Mars.

A lunar settlement "creates a giant infrastructure that doesn't have a lot of purpose — not for national security or science," Friedman contends. "It's enormously expensive" to develop the technology to support people on the lunar surface, and "all that time you're not making progress toward exploration beyond the Moon." What's more, he argues, "the focus on the Moon has led to uninspiring response from the public."

But others strongly defend the idea of a lunar landing, including George Washington University's Pace. He supports the Constellation plan, noting that he helped shape it when he served at NASA during the Bush administration, although he suggests the plan's 2020 target date for a Moon landing is looking less realistic. "If we could do it by 2025, I'd be thrilled," he says.

Pace says a lunar landing makes sense because "going directly to Mars is not technically feasible. We don't know how to land humans on the Martian surface, build systems two years away from Earth, deal with the biological hazards and so on. It's frankly irresponsible to gear up and go directly to Mars. It's not just developing technology. You're actually trying to train an organization" for prolonged deep-space human flight.

Pace says his idea of lunar settlement is a "fairly austere international outpost" comparable to the Antarctic research base. "It's not '2001: A Space Odyssey.' That may happen, but that's up to the private sector to build."

Logsdon, too, supports a lunar base and says international partners could make such a venture far more feasible than if the United States tries to go it alone. He points out that other countries are strong in some relevant technology — Japan with robotics, Russia with rocket propulsion and European nations with sensors.

"One option is making this a global undertaking with significant cost sharing," he says. "That may enable building the equipment to land on the Moon."

Under some scenarios, astronauts would create a permanent lunar settlement, mine the lunar soil to make rocket energy and use the Moon as a Mars launch pad. But critics of such a plan argue that breaking away from the moon's gravity would require more fuel and other weight, adding to the cost and technical challenge of a Mars trip. Why, they ask, blast off from two large bodies — the Earth and Moon — to get to Mars?

"It's an outright stupid idea," says Duke University's Roland. He opposes not only a lunar settlement but also a human expedition to Mars. Until NASA finds cost-effective rocket technology, the expense of sending astronauts to the Red Planet will remain "prohibitive," he contends. Robots could do a better job than humans at exploring Mars within NASA's budget constraint, he adds, and far more safely. "There's no rationale for why we're going, except for the sake of going." ■

BACKGROUND

Early Efforts

NASA's roots go back to the heady days of early airplane flight, when courageous pilots experienced triumph and tragedy in what sometimes seemed equal measure.

In 1915 — only a dozen years after Wilbur and Orville Wright's first successful airplane flight at Kitty Hawk — Congress created the National Advisory Committee for Aeronautics "to supervise and direct the scientific study of the problems of flight, with a view to their practical solutions." [23]

The time was ripe. European engineers were making big strides in aeronautics, World War I was underscoring the strategic importance of military aircraft and demand was growing in the scientific community for aviation research. [24]

At this early stage, of course, most attention was focused on airplanes — not rockets. Even so, rocket experimentation was already under way. In 1907, student Robert Goddard, who came to be known as the father of modern rocketry, was experimenting on a gunpowder-fueled rocket in the basement of the physics building at Worcester Polytechnic Institute in Massachusetts. Seven years later he held patents for liquid- and solid-fuel rockets. [25]

In 1920 Goddard advanced the notion of using rockets to get to the Moon — an idea that promptly drew derision from *The New York Times*. The newspaper opined that without an atmosphere to provide resistance, rockets couldn't travel in space. Goddard didn't even possess "the knowledge ladled out daily in high schools." [26] But Goddard stood fast. "Every vision is a joke until the first man accomplishes it," he said. "Once realized, it becomes commonplace." [27]

In 1969, after *Apollo 11* began its epic trip to the Moon, *The Times* looked back on its 1920 comments and wrote, "Further investigation and experimentation have confirmed the findings of Isaac Newton in the 17th century, and it is now definitely established that a rocket can function in a vacuum as well as in an atmosphere. *The Times* regrets the error." [28]

Continued on p. 872

Chronology

1900-1940s
Beginning of military use of rockets and development of long-range spacecraft technology.

1915
Congress creates National Advisory Committee for Aeronautics.

1920
Robert Goddard advances notion of using rockets to reach the Moon.

1939
World War II begins; Germany develops V-2 rockets to attack England.

1945
German rocket scientists taken to U.S., Soviet Union after war.

* * *

1957-1969
Cold War space race spurs advances in human spaceflight.

1957
Soviet Union launches two *Sputnik* satellites, causing concern in U.S.

1958
National Aeronautics and Space Administration is born. . . . U.S. successfully launches *Explorer* rocket; onboard experiment finds evidence of radiation belt around Earth.

1960
NASA launches *Pioneer 5* space probe.

1961
Soviet cosmonaut Yuri Gagarin becomes first human in space; the following month U.S. astronaut Alan B. Shepard Jr. is launched on 15-minute, 300-mile suborbital flight. . . . President John F. Kennedy sets Moon goal.

1962
John Glenn becomes first American to orbit Earth.

1967
Three *Apollo* astronauts die in pre-launch training exercise.

1969
Apollo spacecraft lands astronaut Neil Armstrong on Moon.

* * *

1970s-1980s
Budget woes, Vietnam War and other pressures lead to new directions for space program.

1970
NASA cancels three *Apollo* missions.

1972
Last U.S. moon landing occurs. . . . President Richard M. Nixon agrees to reusable "Space Shuttle" system.

1973
Orbiting *Skylab* space station is launched, visited by three crews over the next year or so.

1976
Robotic *Viking 1* and *2* spacecraft orbit and land on Mars.

1981
Space Shuttle begins flying.

1984
President Ronald Reagan calls for "permanently manned space station . . . within a decade."

1986
Shuttle *Challenger* blows up during liftoff, killing all seven astronauts.

1988
Shuttle flies for first time since *Challenger* disaster.

1989
President George H. W. Bush calls for return to Moon and then flight to Mars.

* * *

1990s-Present
Disaster again hits Shuttle; U.S. eyes return to Moon, human exploration of Mars.

1993
President Bill Clinton adds Russia to International Space Station (ISS) partnership.

1998
Assembly of ISS begins.

2000
First crew occupies Space Station.

2003
Second Space Shuttle disaster kills all seven astronauts on board.

2004
President George W. Bush proposes venture to Mars.

2005
NASA establishes Constellation program, which includes *Ares I* and *V* rockets, *Orion* crew capsule and *Altair* lunar lander.

2009
White House panel headed by former Lockheed Martin CEO Norman Augustine says additional money is needed for "meaningful" human space exploration. . . . NASA satellite slams into Moon seeking signs of water ice. . . . Cirque du Soleil founder Guy Laliberté returns to Earth on Oct. 11 after spending two weeks on the International Space Station.

Entrepreneurs Say Space Tourism Ready for Takeoff

So far 250 adventurers have signed up at $200,000 per flight.

The payoff dangled before spacecraft entrepreneurs by the Ansari X Prize was a tidy $10 million. The challenge: Fly a privately financed rocket 62 miles (100 kilometers) into space twice within two weeks — proving that commercial space exploration is both reliable and financially viable.

In 2004, the *SpaceShipOne*, a craft sponsored by the Scaled Composites aerospace company, claimed the prize after a second successful flight over California.

Many people were watching with interest, including British mogul Richard Branson and American venture capitalist Alan Walton. Branson, founder of Virgin Airways, immediately signed an agreement to use the technology in a planned second-generation design — *SpaceShipTwo* — to fly commercial passengers into space via his newly formed Virgin Galactic enterprise by 2007. And Walton promptly forked over $200,000 for the chance to someday ride into space himself. [1]

"For most of us, escaping the constraints of gravity is only something we've been able to achieve in our dreams, until now," said Branson. [2]

But turning the dream into reality has taken longer than many have expected. Regulatory roadblocks and mounting concerns over passenger safety have so far limited private spaceflight to a select few wealthy individuals, who have dished out millions for rides on Russian *Soyuz* launches to the International Space Station.

In 2001, American investor Dennis Tito paid a reported $20 million to become the first space tourist aboard the sta-

tion, orbiting Earth for nine days along with its crew of astronauts. Six others have followed, the latest being Cirque du Soleil founder and CEO Guy Laliberté this month.

"Very few people can afford to travel into space as I did," Tito told a congressional committee in 2003, but "audiences seem genuinely inspired by the plausibility that one day they or their children could fly into space themselves." [3]

To date, around 250 would-be astronauts have committed to Virgin Galactic's more affordable $200,000 fare — with $20,000 deposits — which includes a three-day preflight training session.

If all goes according to plan, said President Will Whitehorn, the inaugural flight could occur by mid-2011, carrying Branson, his family and *SpaceShipTwo* designer Burt Rutan into space for a two-hour sightseeing jaunt just beyond Earth's atmosphere. [4]

But Walton intends to ask for his deposit back if there's no fixed launch date by April 2010, when he'll turn 74. "This was going to be the highlight of my old age," he said. [5]

X Prize founder Peter Diamandis, CEO of Zero Gravity Corp., insists that despite current obstacles, the industry is moving forward. "The personal spaceflight industry has had over $1 billion invested in it" since the X Prize was awarded, he said. [6]

In addition to Virgin Galactic, several other companies are planning space ventures. Blue Origins, set up by Amazon.com founder Jeff Bezos, anticipates having weekly manned spaceflights by 2012. Germany's Project Enterprise plans to test unmanned flights by 2010.

Continued from p. 870

Goddard continued his rocket work in the 1930s and, as World War II loomed, he grew concerned that German engineers were developing missile technology for military use. Goddard failed to persuade the U.S. Army of the military potential of rockets, and, to his later chagrin, learned that some of his technological wizardry had fallen into the hands of the Nazis, who used it to build V-2 missiles that rained terror on London. Before he died in August 1945, Goddard got his hands on a V-2 and recognized his own work. [29]

"Goddard accepted paternity of his bastard V-2, and that, as it turned out, was the last rocket he fathered while alive," wrote *Time* senior writer Jeffrey Kluger. Goddard's "technological spawn, however, did not stop," Kluger added.

"American scientists worked alongside émigré German scientists to [turn] the killer missile into the Redstone [rocket], which put the first Americans into space. The Redstone led directly to the *Saturn* moon rockets [used by the *Apollo* astronauts] and indirectly to virtually every other rocket the U.S. has ever flown." [30]

Modern Era

The modern era of human spaceflight had its birth in the Cold War atmosphere of the 1950s, when the post-World War II superpowers — the United States and the Soviet Union — reached for the cosmos.

The U.S.S.R. got there first, in 1957, with the launch of *Sputnik 1*, a beach ball-sized satellite that emitted a

"beep, beep" heard round the world — including in the United States, where the Soviets' bold accomplishment caused a frenzy of fear, recrimination and concern that America's education system had failed to keep up with the communists. [31]

"It is downright terrifying with [*Sputnik*] staring down at us," the *Portland Oregonian* declared. *Time* said: "The U.S. takes deep pride in its technical skills and technological prowess, in its ability to get things done — first. Now, despite all the rational explanations, there was a sudden, sharp national disappointment that Americans had been outshone by the Red moon." [32]

The Soviets added to the disappointment by launching *Sputnik 2* later in 1957 with a small dog aboard. ("Laika" did not survive.)

Confident in the potential scientific benefits that could arise from commercial space exploration, the state of New Mexico has committed $200 million to the construction of Spaceport America, which will serve as the base for Virgin Galactic and other commercial space operations.

The federal government has released a set of proposed rules for space tourism, including passenger-screening procedures and training for emergency situations.

And the nonprofit Space Tourism Society has been formed to educate the public and promote the industry.

Enough will be accomplished logistically, technologically and legally to allow flights within 24 months, insists Diamandis. He promises that like the hoopla that accompanied the X Prize, there will be "another large injection of excitement in public interest once those vehicles begin operating and the public starts getting flown." [7]

Diamandis says the *SpaceShipOne* flight has spawned a new space industry, just as Charles Lindbergh's 1927 flight across the Atlantic Ocean helped spur today's $300 billion aviation industry.

Cirque du Soleil founder Guy Laliberté clowns around before his trip via a Russian Soyuz TMA-16 rocket to the International Space Station. He returned on Oct. 11 after a two-week stay.

"Not only did these historic flights culminate in a beautiful exhibition . . . in the National Air and Space Museum," Diamandis said. "The most important legacy and meaning of the Ansari X Prize on its five-year anniversary lies in the fact that the event kicked off a new industry." [8]

— *Darrell Dela Rosa*

[1] John Antczak and Alicia Chang, "Space Tourism Yet to Fly, 5 Years Since 1st Flight," The Associated Press, Oct. 3, 2009.

[2] Virgin Galactic, www.virgingalactic.com.

[3] Dennis Tito, testimony before Senate Committee on Commerce, Science and Transportation and House Committee on Science, July 2003, www.globalsecurity.org/space/library/congress/2003_h/030724-tito.pdf.

[4] Simon Hancock and Alan Moloney, "Work Starts on New Mexico Spaceport," BBC News, June 20, 2009, http://news.bbc.co.uk/2/hi/science/nature/8111243.stm.

[5] Antczak and Chang, *op. cit.*

[6] Peter Diamandis, "Reflections on the Five Year Anniversary of the Ansari X Prize," *The Huffington Post*, Oct. 4, 2009, www.huffingtonpost.com/peter-diamandis/personal-spaceflight-indu_b_308444.html.

[7] *Ibid.*

[8] *Ibid.*

The space race was on, but the United States would taste failure before it savored success. In December 1957, in the wake of the *Sputnik* flights, a Vanguard test rocket carrying a three-pound payload crashed on the launch pad, stirring new doubts and fears. Finally, in January 1958, a two-pound payload atop an *Explorer* rocket made it into space, and an onboard experiment turned up evidence that a belt of radiation encircles the Earth. [33] Scientists — and the public — breathed a sigh of relief over the mission's success.

Meanwhile, policy makers were engaged in a spirited debate about whether America's emerging space program should come under military or civilian control. President Dwight D. Eisenhower favored separate military and civilian space programs, and his view prevailed.

On Oct. 1, 1958, the civilian National Aeronautics and Space Administration was born. The law that created NASA also assigned military space activities to the Defense Department.

The race for space supremacy accelerated, presaging the robust scientific exploration and human spaceflight achievements that would follow in the coming decades. Rockets remained unpredictable — in 1959 seven of 17 launches failed. [34] But both the United States and Soviet Union made huge strides in a short time toward space exploration.

In March 1960 NASA launched *Pioneer 5* into interplanetary space, and the spacecraft communicated at a record distance of 22 million miles. [35] *Tiros 1*, a satellite that produced more than 22,000 weather photos, and *Echo 1*, a communications satellite, followed. [36]

But America still lagged behind the Soviets. In the spring of 1961 Soviet cosmonaut Yuri Gagarin circled the globe and landed in the history books as the first human in space. Gagarin traveled 25,000 miles around Earth and spent 89 minutes in weightlessness. The following month, NASA launched astronaut Alan B. Shepard Jr. and his *Freedom 7* Mercury capsule on a 15-minute, 300-mile suborbital flight that included five minutes of weightlessness. While successful, Shepard's flight didn't match Gagarin's in technological prowess. [37]

The tide soon began to turn, however. In May 1961, President John F. Kennedy, in a speech to a joint congressional session, called space a "new frontier of human adventure" and famously proclaimed a goal "of landing a man on the moon and returning

Monitoring the Cosmos for Killer Asteroids

"You could have millions dead and trillions in property damage."

Last March, an asteroid zipping through space came within about 41,000 miles of Earth — too far away to cause a problem but near enough to be troublesome.

The asteroid measured perhaps 60 or 70 feet across, or a little smaller than the space rock that exploded over Siberia in 1908, destroying hundreds of square miles of forest.

"It's pretty unusual to see one this close," said Timothy Spahr, director of the minor-planet center at the Harvard-Smithsonian Center for Astrophysics. "If an object of this size were to impact the Earth, it would be equivalent to a small nuclear explosion." [1]

It's a scenario that, while considered remote, keeps scientists and global security officials on the lookout — not just for the next asteroid but for ways to deal with one should it threaten Earth.

Lindley Johnson, program executive for NASA's Near-Earth Object Observation Program, said asteroids pose "a rare but worrisome threat." A strike "doesn't happen very often, but when it does occur, it can do significant damage, probably more than any other natural disaster that we know of." Even so, Johnson added, "this is something we could easily predict if we had the systems to detect these things."

So far, though, efforts to monitor the cosmos for so-called near-Earth objects and to come up with ways to deflect them remain less than reassuring.

"[T]o date there has been relatively little effort by the U.S. government to survey, discover, characterize and mitigate the threat," the National Academy of Sciences concluded this year. Congress has ordered NASA to detect and track space objects, the academy noted, but adequate funds have not been provided. What's more, the United States is the only nation with an operating program to survey and detect space objects, the National Academy said. Canada and Germany are building space-

craft that could contribute to the discovery of near-Earth objects, but "neither mission will detect fainter or smaller objects [better] than ground-based telescopes," the academy said. [2]

In 1998 Congress directed NASA to detect and track 90 percent of big, globe-threatening near-Earth objects — those with a diameter of 1 kilometer (about two-thirds of a mile) or more. Then, four years ago, Congress told NASA to find and track 90 percent of smaller objects by 2020 — those with a diameter of 140 meters — about 153 yards — or larger.

Johnson said that as of the end of September, 6,482 near-Earth objects of all sizes had been found; an estimated 874 of the objects are bigger than 1 kilometer, and perhaps 20 percent are smaller than 140 meters, he said.

NASA is using space- and ground-based telescopes originally developed for other purposes to look for near-Earth objects, and while those have helped the agency detect some objects, they are not adequate to reach the congressionally mandated goal of finding 90 percent of the smaller objects by 2020, Johnson said. "It will take systems more designed to address this problem," he said.

The National Academy report said meeting the 2020 goal may require one or more additional observatories, possibly including one based in space, but that "[t]he administration has not requested and Congress has not appropriated new funds to meet this objective." It added that "only limited facilities are currently involved in this survey/discovery effort, funded by NASA's existing budget."

Smaller space objects are more prevalent than massive ones, and they strike Earth more frequently. Johnson said an object about 50 meters across hits Earth every few hundred years, while one 100 meters across strikes perhaps every few thousand years. "A 50-foot (15-meter) object hits about once a decade, and we've seen these occur — bright fireballs but no effects at ground level," Johnson said.

him safely to Earth" before the end of the decade. [38]

The U.S. space program moved into high gear. In early 1962, astronaut John Glenn piloted his *Friendship 7* spacecraft on a nearly five-hour, three-orbit mission that reached an altitude of 162 miles, becoming the first American to orbit Earth. [39] (Glenn would fly in space again, in 1998 at the age of 77, aboard the Space Shuttle.)

Over the next seven years leading to the *Apollo 11* moon landing, Americans ventured into space on 17 progressively more challenging missions that included the first rendezvous be-

tween spacecraft with astronauts aboard, the first U.S. spacewalks, the first ventures into lunar orbit and a rehearsal flight in May 1969 that brought astronauts within about 10 miles of the Moon. By the time Neil Armstrong planted his shoe in moon dust on July 20, NASA had expended billions of dollars toward the singular goal articulated by President Kennedy a mere eight years earlier.

And why did the astronauts go? Armstrong answered this way: "I think we're going to the Moon because it's in the nature of the human being to face challenges. It's by the nature of

his deep inner soul. Yes, we're required to do these things, just as salmon swim upstream." [40]

Many view the *Apollo* lunar landings as the apogee of the American space program. The Soviet space threat had been vanquished — Russian cosmonauts never made it to the Moon, and instead the Soviets focused on space-station construction. But thick clouds had begun to obscure NASA's lunar program almost as soon as it began, says Smith of the Space and Technology Policy Group. "It was not nearly as popular with the public and politicians as our memories recall," she says.

An object of, say, 140 meters falling onto an urban area could wreak havoc, experts say. "If that happens over a city, you could have millions dead and trillions in property damage over a widespread area," says Louis Friedman, executive director of the Planetary Society, a space advocacy group.

Whether NASA or some other federal agency, such as the Department of Defense, should be in charge of the space-rock hazard is a matter of debate within the scientific community, and a larger issue is whether a global effort needs to be mounted to coordinate an international response.

Last year the Houston-based Association of Space Explorers, an international professional association of astronauts and cosmonauts who have orbited the Earth, issued a lengthy report on the asteroid threat urging the United Nations to oversee a global, coordinated response to the problem. The report did not recommend that the U.N. take it upon itself to deflect asteroids, but rather to play the lead role in setting up a framework for nations to evaluate threats and decide on a course of action.

"[I]f the international community fails to adopt an effective, internationally mandated program, society will likely suffer the effects of some future cosmic disaster — intensified by the knowledge that loss of life, economic devastation and long-lasting societal disruption could have been prevented," the report said. [3]

Scientists have considered a variety of methods to deal with Earth-threatening space rocks. One approach, known as kinetic impact, envisions using a small spacecraft to slam into a space object, nudging it off course.

Another potential approach would use a "gravity tractor" — a spacecraft that hovers over an asteroid and over time uses the gravitational pull between the asteroid and spacecraft to divert the object's course. [4] Other, perhaps less likely approaches include:

• Using a nuclear weapon or some other explosive device to break up an asteroid, though that could cause the object to fragment, threatening multiple spots on Earth.

• Detonating nuclear explosions close enough to an asteroid to alter its course.

• Landing a spacecraft on an asteroid and using the engines to steer it away from Earth;

• Using a "mass driver" to eject material from the object and thus alter its direction, and

• Focusing solar energy on the object, using the resulting vaporization of material to provide thrust to divert its course.

However scientists ultimately deal with a giant space rock heading for Earth, vigilance and international will are widely viewed as essential.

"For the first time in our planet's 4.5-billion-year history, the technical capacities exist to prevent such cosmic collisions with Earth," the Association of Space Explorers said in its report. "The keys to a successful outcome in all cases are preparation, planning and timely decision-making." [5]

— *Thomas J. Billitteri*

[1] Stewart Bishop, "Phew! Asteroid's passing was a cosmic near-miss," *The Boston Globe*, March 4, 2009, www.boston.com/news/local/breaking_news/2009/03/phew_asteroids.html.

[2] "Near-Earth Object Surveys and Hazard Mitigation Strategies," National Academy of Sciences, Interim Report, 2009, www.nap.edu/catalog.php?record_id=12738.

[3] "Asteroid Threats: A Call For Global Response," Association of Space Explorers, 2008, p. 5, www.space-explorers.org/ATACGR.pdf.

[4] Stefan Lovgren, " 'Gravity Tractor' Could Deflect Earth-Bound Asteroids," National Geographic News, Nov. 9, 2005, http://news.nationalgeographic.com/news/2005/11/1109_051109_asteroid_tug.html.

[5] Association of Space Explorers, *op. cit.*, p. 3.

In 1966 NASA's budget peaked, and then cuts to *Apollo* began. By the time *Apollo 8* orbited the moon in December 1968, NASA "was trying to staunch the bleeding, but without success," Smith says.

Right after the *Apollo 11* landing in 1969, a task force headed by Vice President Spiro Agnew, in an exercise similar to today's Augustine panel, made a series of recommendations for the space program, including a long-range goal of sending humans to Mars.

But the Agnew panel had little effect. In 1970 NASA cancelled three *Apollo* missions and plans for several Earth-orbiting space stations. Those plans were reduced to a single station, *Skylab*, which was launched in 1973, visited by three crews over the next year or so and then left to re-enter the atmosphere in an uncontrolled fashion in 1979.

Nixon OKs Space Shuttle

In 1972 President Richard M. Nixon, under whose watch the NASA budget had further and sharply declined, agreed to a reusable system — the Space Shuttle — for transporting astronauts to and from low-Earth orbit. That same year, the last *Apollo* lunar mission occurred.

"The worldwide euphoria over mankind's greatest voyage of exploration did not rescue the NASA budget," historian Roger E. Bilstein noted in a NASA review of the space program. "At its moment of greatest triumph, the space program was being drastically cut back from the $5 billion budgets that had characterized the mid-1960s." [41]

While some reductions were expected because *Apollo*'s biggest expenses had already been met, Bilstein continued, "the depth of the cut stemmed from emotional changes in the political climate, mostly centering on the unpopular Vietnam War — its sapping expenses in lives and money, the debilitating protests at home. As Congress read the public pulse, the cosmos could wait; the Soviet threat had for the moment been put to rest; the new political reality lay in domestic problems."

Still, the *Apollo* program "created a model of government-driven technology . . . that became embedded in NASA culture," wrote W. Henry Lambright, a professor of political science and public administration at Syracuse University and director of its Center for Environmental Policy and Administration. What's more, he wrote, *Apollo* helped generate huge sums used in space science and activities such as satellite communication. [42]

As *Apollo* drew to a close, officials debated what should come next. A permanent space station with rotating crews, serviced by a reusable shuttle-type spacecraft, was a key goal of NASA, but budget pressures led the agency to build the Space Shuttle first. [43]

At the same time, scientific exploration of the cosmos and the use of technology in space were proceeding apace. *Landsat*, the first Earth-observing satellite, was launched in 1972. The robotic *Viking 1* and *2* spacecraft orbited and landed on Mars in 1976.

The Space Shuttle began flying in 1981, and in his 1984 State of the Union address President Ronald Reagan directed NASA to take what he saw as the next step: to develop "a permanently manned space station . . . within a decade." [44]

The words echoed Kennedy's Moon challenge. But Reagan's plan didn't turn out as hoped. As Shuttle flights became more and more routine during the first half of the 1980s, space enthusiasts began to see promising vistas ahead. As Lambright noted, "In theory, the nation would phase down spending on the Shuttle and phase up funding of the Space Station." In fact, he noted, some even talked of privatizing the Space Shuttle. [45]

But in 1986 disaster struck. The Space Shuttle *Challenger* blew up during liftoff, killing all seven astronauts, including New Hampshire schoolteacher Christa McAuliffe, chosen to become the first teacher in space.

"*Challenger* shattered a key misconception about the Space Shuttle," wrote Pat Duggins, a public-radio journalist who covers NASA. "While its critics and supporters debated its usefulness and its lack of a central mission, the orbiter wasn't considered particularly hazardous to fly. Now, it was." [46]

The *Challenger* crash cast a pall over the entire space program. Not since three astronauts died in 1967 during an *Apollo* pre-launch test had a U.S. astronaut been killed on duty. The Shuttle program slowed to a crawl as investigators worked to find out what had gone wrong. They determined that the failure of an "O ring" seal between segments of one of the Shuttle's solid-fuel rocket boosters was the direct cause, but a dysfunctional management culture at NASA was viewed as the root of the problem.

Not until September 1988 did a Shuttle fly again. But arguments persisted that the Shuttle program lacked a clear mission, and many wanted a more ambitious goal for human spaceflight. A congressionally directed National Commission on Space study, published in 1986, and a NASA study led by astronaut Sally Ride in 1987 advanced bold objectives.

In 1989 the first President Bush called for a return to the Moon and then flight to Mars. But the price tag was steep. One NASA estimate put it at more than $450 billion. [47] Congress had sticker shock, and the venture went nowhere.

Meanwhile, the Space Station's costs skyrocketed and its schedule slipped. In 1993 President Bill Clinton added Russia to the international partnership that included Canada, Japan and the Europeans, in part as a budgetary move, but more importantly, as a geopolitical one. [48]

The Clinton decision "made the station part of the U.S. foreign policy agenda to encourage Russia to abide by agreements to stop the proliferation of ballistic missile technology, and to support Russia economically and politically as it transitioned from the Soviet era," the Congressional Research Service noted. [49]

Still, assembly of the Space Station did not begin until 1998, and the first crew didn't occupy the lab until 2000.

The Shuttle continued to fly throughout the 1990s and into the 21st century, but its costs were high, its usefulness a constant matter of debate and its safety and reliability in question. In 2003 another disaster struck when the shuttle *Columbia* disintegrated during re-entry, killing seven astronauts. Foam insulation that had broken off during launch had damaged a wing.

Following the *Columbia* disaster, the younger President Bush repeated his father's bid for a return to the Moon and eventual venture to Mars, and he called for termination of the Shuttle to help pay for the plan. But without the Shuttle, the Space Station will be accessible only by Russian *Soyuz* spacecraft until the United States develops a new low-Earth-orbit vehicle or a commercial one becomes available — leaving the time gap the Augustine panel warned about. ■

CURRENT SITUATION

Budget Battle

In mid-September, as Augustine testified before Congress on the future of the human spaceflight program, NASA's No. 2 official was talking about a major barrier to outer space: NASA's budget.

Continued on p. 878

At Issue:

Should the United States aim to send humans to Mars?

LOUIS FRIEDMAN
EXECUTIVE DIRECTOR
PLANETARY SOCIETY

WRITTEN FOR *CQ RESEARCHER*, OCTOBER 2009

*t*he United States, together with other spacefaring nations, should indeed "aim" to send humans to Mars. We should not say "rush" or "immediately," but we should make Mars the explicit goal for human space exploration.

Mars is the world on which humanity's destiny as a multi-planet and spacefaring species will be determined. It is the only world beyond Earth accessible to humans that has an atmosphere and water — not just their presence, but in a form that can be used to sustain life.

Mars is more like Earth than any other body in our solar system. It has mountains and valleys, polar ice caps and dry riverbeds. It has seasons, an atmosphere with clouds, winds and dust storms, and a solid, rocky surface.

Mars is also the only accessible world that may indeed have life or once had life. Indeed, searching for life is what compels us to explore space — and to risk lives and spend billions doing so. Any lesser goal may not be worth the risk or cost of human exploration, and might be better served by robots.

But sending humans to Mars is not easy. NASA has said it is not ready to make that leap now. We don't have to achieve Mars in one giant leap. It can be done in steps that first go beyond the Moon and enter interplanetary space, and then progress through new milestones of flight, traveling ever farther from Earth and ever closer to Mars. On the way we can reach, touch and explore near-Earth asteroids — the objects we need to learn so much more about before another one eventually impacts the Earth.

Just as we reached the Moon in 1969 after a series of milestones of flight via *Mercury*, *Gemini* and *Apollo*, so too can we go step by step to Mars. We can use the steps to build the international team that will be necessary for a Mars endeavor, as well as to build the physiological and life-support infrastructure that our astronauts will need for the multiyear missions. Robotic exploration missions — returning with multiple Mars samples — should be milestones, too. They assure that scientific progress will support the human explorers.

We can't set our sights beyond Mars — at least not for humans in this century. But if we set our sights below Mars, we can't expect great public or fiscal support, nor will we have a program that sustains itself for very long.

And if we give up on human exploration altogether, then we are doomed to be dropouts in human achievement. Mars beckons — let's aim for it.

ROBERT L. PARK,
RESEARCH PROFESSOR, DEPARTMENT OF
PHYSICS, UNIVERSITY OF MARYLAND

WRITTEN FOR *CQ RESEARCHER*, OCTOBER 2009

*t*he century-old obsession of earthlings with the planet Mars was born of mingled hope and dread. Finding life to which we are not related is the most compelling quest in space, but if Mars becomes contaminated with life from Earth, the experiment could never be repeated.

To prevent that, the *Viking 1* lander in 1976 was thoroughly autoclaved prior to launch. Twenty-five seconds after touching down on the *Chryse Planitia* — the "golden plain" — *Viking 1* began transmitting a panoramic image of its surroundings. The entire world was transfixed as the barren, rock-strewn plain stretched out beneath a cloudless, faintly pink sky. In the four minutes it took to transmit the image, every speculation about Mars, both scientific and fictional, was reduced to mere historical footnotes. No hint of life was visible on the surface.

With no magnetosphere to screen out solar and galactic radiation, Martian life could likely exist only beneath the surface. *Viking 1* sought to answer the life question by putting a scoop of Martian soil into a nutrient solution. The gas that evolved was initially interpreted as an indication of life, but there were other possibilities and the experiment was later described as "inconclusive."

That was 33 years ago. Suppose we now send human astronauts to Mars to search for life. The first challenge would be to get them there alive. Shielding could be added to the spacecraft to protect them from solar and galactic radiation during the nine-month trip. Once there, the planet itself would shield them from half the radiation, but they must wait 18 months for the right planetary conjunction to return to Earth.

Some of the time could be used to explore in the vicinity of the spaceship, but they would need to wear spacesuits in the thin Martian atmosphere when they emerge. They would also need to limit their exposure to radiation. In effect, they would have only the sense of sight. In other words, they would be far less capable as explorers than the telerobotic Mars rovers, *Spirit* and *Opportunity*, that preceded them.

In the 18 months waiting for the planet to come close enough to Earth to make a return trip possible — 36 million miles — each member of the crew would generate more than a ton of feces, swarming with single-celled life. Any life they find might look very familiar. Contamination of Mars by the myriad of life forms that dwell in every human gut would be almost inevitable.

Are we alone in the universe? We long to know. The search for alien life is what draws humans to Mars — and it is the reason they must not go there.

Continued from p. 876

Deputy Administrator Lori Garver, a NASA official during the Clinton administration, suggested the agency's funding is unlikely to grow.

"Budgets were tight when I was here in the '90s, but they're even tighter today," she told the American Institute of Aeronautics and Astronautics. "Our budget has to compete with not only other scientif-

to the Constellation plan. "I thought that we were going to take a hard, cold, sobering look at the Constellation program and tell us exactly what we needed to do here in Congress with our budget in order to maximize the chances of success," said Rep. Gabrielle Giffords, D-Ariz., wife of Shuttle astronaut Mark E. Kelly. She added: "I don't see the logic of scrapping

get is known. The budget "is the key to all of this," she says. "If there's not going to be any more money, this is all pretty moot. To the extent there's going to be a fight between two ends of Pennsylvania Avenue, it's going to depend first and foremost on whether the president antes up more money for human spaceflight. Once that decision is made, you can argue about details."

Democratic Rep. Bart Gordon of Tennessee, chairman of the Science and Technology Committee, has voiced support for more funding for NASA. Noting that his committee will be working on a multiyear budget authorization for NASA this fall, Gordon said in early September that the space agency "has not been given resources matched to the tasks it has been asked to undertake. That has to change." [54]

Still, Gordon, too, suggested the best path for human space exploration might be to stick with Constellation. "NASA has been working for more than four years on the Constellation program, a development program in support of which Congress has invested billions of dollars over that same period," he said. "I think that good public policy argues for setting the bar pretty high against making significant changes in direction at this point." [55]

Griffin, the former NASA administrator, staunchly defended the Constellation plan at the House hearing and criticized the Augustine panel for failing to give "clear-eyed" assessments not only of Constellation's progress and status but also of "what would be required to get and keep that program on track."

Still, Griffin said it is "not possible to recover fully" from past funding cuts, and he suggested a middle path for the future:

• Marriage of some elements of the Constellation plan, including completion of the *Ares I* rocket and *Orion* capsule, to travel to the Space Station;

• Delay in development of the *Altair* lunar landing craft until money is available, and

> "If there's not going to be any more money, this is all pretty moot. To the extent there's going to be a fight between two ends of Pennsylvania Avenue, it's going to depend first and foremost on whether the president antes up more money for human spaceflight."
>
> — *Marcia S. Smith,*
> *President, Space and Technology Policy Group*

ic programs but all government service. To earn our trust from taxpayers we have to help create a better future through programs aligned with both the short-term and long-term national interest." [50]

Another NASA official, Dave Radzanowski, went even further. "I really don't expect there to be significant increases in NASA's budgets over the next 10 years," he said. "A sustained increase, I think, will be difficult. . . . We need to think about . . . operating under a flat budget." [51]

But Augustine told the House Science and Technology Committee that unless more money is forthcoming, the Constellation program, with its "Moon first, then Mars" approach, is "fatally flawed," and that the same is true for the other options the panel presented for human flight beyond low-Earth orbit. [52]

Still, several lawmakers expressed anger at the Augustine panel's options

what the nation has spent years and billions of dollars to develop." [53]

The Space and Technology Policy Group's Smith says the point House members were trying to make is that they see "no point starting in a different direction if there's no compelling reason to stop the Constellation program." She notes that two separate Congresses — in 2005 under Republican control, and in 2008 under the Democrats — voted to support Constellation and that "the White House is going to have to [offer] a compelling reason to change" it.

Even so, Smith says, the first bridge to cross in deciding the future of human spaceflight "is whether there's going to be more money." Smith says that any discussion in Congress, or between Congress and the Obama administration, about specific space missions and rockets will be only that — discussion — until NASA's human spaceflight bud-

• Development and use of the bigger *Ares V* rocket and *Orion* capsule to take astronauts to other destinations before putting them on the Moon or Mars — the Augustine panel's "flexible path" option. [56]

On Oct. 27 a prototype of the *Ares I* is scheduled to undergo a two-minute test launch that is expected to produce valuable information on the rocket's design progress. Earlier tests showed problems with shaking during flight.

What Will Obama Do?

How the Obama administration ultimately proceeds with NASA's human spaceflight program remains an open question. Some observers are frustrated that the White House has not said more about its vision for a comprehensive space policy. PolitiFact, a project of the *St. Petersburg Times* that checks the accuracy of statements by politicians, found that Obama so far has taken no action on six of 18 promises he has made about space, including one to "support a robust research and technology development program that addresses the long-term needs for future human and robotic missions." [57]

Yet, some in Congress are optimistic the White House will advance a vigorous human spaceflight policy. "It's a tough, tough time, because of what we're facing with the budget deficit," said Sen. Bill Nelson, D-Fla., who traveled aboard the Space Shuttle in 1986. "I believe the president is a visionary, and I believe that the president is going to make a bold stroke, not unlike President Kennedy." [58]

Impetus for such a bold stroke could come from the ambition that other nations have for space. In September, for example, Japan launched a powerful rocket on a $680 million International Space Station resupply mission. [59] In August South Korea launched its first space rocket, developed with Russian help, though a scientific satellite did not

reach its intended orbit. South Korea hopes to build a rocket on its own by 2018 and launch a lunar probe by 2025, in addition to developing a commercial service to put satellites into space. [60]

Meanwhile, India last October launched the probe that found evidence of water on the Moon. India lost contact with the probe in August, but officials are undeterred. They hope to land a robotic Moon rover by 2012, according to Bloomberg News. [61]

While a number of countries' space programs are maturing quickly, none is being more closely watched than China's. Since 1970, the communist nation has launched more than 100 orbital missions, and in 2003 it joined the United States and Russia as the only countries to put humans into space. [62]

Over the past six years China has launched three human missions, including one last year that included the country's first spacewalk. China's ambitions include construction of its own orbiting space station and eventual human exploration of the Moon. [63] The country already has a probe in lunar orbit and plans robotic rovers on the Moon's surface over the next decade. [64]

Some advocate greater cooperation between the United States and China on space, but assessing China's intentions are tricky. In 2007 Beijing destroyed one of its own satellites in an anti-satellite weapons test, spewing debris into the path of other countries' orbiters and sparking anger worldwide.

In a report to Congress last year, the U.S.-China Economic and Security Review Commission said, "China continues to make significant progress in developing space capabilities, many of which easily translate to enhanced military capacity. In China, the military runs the space program, and there is no separate, distinguishable civilian program. Although some Chinese space programs have no explicit military intent, many space systems — such as communications, navigation, meteorological and imagery systems — are dual use in nature." [65] ∎

OUTLOOK

The Great Beyond

For many advocates of space exploration — especially those who want to reach for Mars and beyond — the heavens remain the ultimate human destiny.

"The Earth is not the only world," Mars Society president Zubrin told the Augustine commission. "There are numerous other planetary objects in our own solar system, millions in nearby interstellar space and hundreds of billions in the galaxy at large. The challenges involved in reaching and settling these new worlds are large, but not beyond humanity's ultimate capacity. Were we to become spacefarers, we would open up a prospect for a human future that is vast in time and space, and rich in experience and potential to an extent that exceeds the imagination of anyone alive today." [66]

Yet, concerns about money, mission priorities and other obstacles are likely to keep such ideals in check. For one thing, Obama already faces a $1.4 trillion federal deficit and could decide not to press for more money for NASA. Or, if he does, the money still might not be enough to get astronauts beyond the boundaries reached by the *Apollo* crews decades ago.

Also, the limits of human endurance for space travel, along with the threat of damaging cosmic radiation and other obstacles, could discourage astronauts from going to distant places like Mars and returning to Earth. A controversial solution posed by Lawrence M. Krauss, director of the Origins Initiative at Arizona State University, calls for sending astronauts on a one-way trip to the Red Planet. "To boldly go where no one has gone before does not require coming home again," he argued recently in *The New York Times*. [67]

In the more immediate future, NASA faces the question of how to transport astronauts to low-Earth orbit if the Space Station remains open and the Shuttle ends. While relying on Russia's *Soyuz* is considered an option, the Center for Strategic and International Studies noted in a study early this year that the craft are severely limited in their ability to bring back cargo to Earth from the Space Station, which could curtail the ability of international partners to use the orbiting lab for research. "Without that research capability, many in [Space Station] partner countries would see the station as a failure, including those politicians and policy makers that have a say in funding future manned space exploration," said the center, whose study presented options and recommendations to address space goals. [68]

And if European and Japanese partners can't demonstrate success with the Space Station, the center added, they would find it difficult to get the money needed for further projects, "making their participation in a human lunar program quite unlikely."

"Given that the United States is already relying on international cooperation on the lunar surface, an inability to attract partners in lunar exploration would severely limit the likelihood of achieving current U.S. plans . . . of resuming human space exploration beyond Low Earth Orbit," said the center. ∎

Notes

1 "Summary Report of the Review of U.S. Human Space Flight Plans Committee," Sept. 8, 2009, www.nasa.gov/pdf/384767main_SUMMARY%20REPORT%20-%20FINAL.pdf.

2 Robert Block and Mark K. Matthews, "Ares may look dead but keeps kicking," *Orlando Sentinel*, Sept. 6, 2009, www.orlandosentinel.com/news/space/orl-ares-rocket-not-dead-090609,0,1246493.story.

3 "House Science and Technology Holds Hearing on NASA's Human space Flight Program," CQ Congressional Transcripts, Sept. 15, 2009, www.cq.com/display.do?dockey=/cqonline/prod/data/docs/html/transcripts/congressional/111/congressionaltranscripts111000003203429.html@committees&metapub=CQ-CONGTRANSCRIPTS&searchIndex=0&seqNum=15.

4 William Harwood, "Shuttle Landing Delayed," *The New York Times*, Sept. 11, 2009, www.nytimes.com/2009/09/11/science/space/11shuttle.html?hpw.

5 Kenneth Chang, "In Surprise, Moon Shows Signs of Water," *The New York Times*, Sept. 24, 2009, www.nytimes.com/2009/09/24/science/space/24moon.html?hpw.

6 Kenneth Chang, "In Test of Water on Moon, Craft Hits Bull's Eye," *The New York Times*, Oct. 10, 2009, www.nytimes.com/2009/10/10/science/space/10moon.html?hp.

7 "51% Oppose U.S. Manned Mission to Mars," Rasmussen Reports, July 21, 2009, www.rasmussenreports.com/public_content/lifestyle/general_lifestyle/july_2009/51_oppose_u_s_manned_mission_to_mars.

8 Jeffrey M. Jones, "Majority of Americans Say Space Program Costs Justified," Gallup Poll, July 17, 2009, www.gallup.com/poll/121736/Majority-Americans-Say-Space-Program-Costs-Justified.aspx.

9 Quoted in Jeff Bliss, "NASA Needs $3 Billion More a Year, Panel Tells Obama," Bloomberg, Sept. 8, 2009, www.bloomberg.com/apps/news?pid=20601103&sid=arN6HfgXtPPM.

10 Testimony before House Committee on Science and Technology, Sept. 15, 2009, http://democrats.science.house.gov/Media/file/Commdocs/hearings/2009/Full/15sep/Dyer_Testimony.pdf. Dyer is a retired Navy vice admiral.

See also "Aerospace Safety Advisory Panel Annual Report for 2008," www.hq.nasa.gov/office/oer/asap/documents/2008_ASAP_Annual_Report.pdf.

11 Stewart M. Powell, "Texas delegation wants stimulus money for NASA," *Houston Chronicle*, Oct. 5, 2009, www.chron.com/disp/story.mpl/space/6653790.html.

12 For more information, see "Military/National Security Space Activities," *SpacePolicyOnline.com*, www.spacepolicyonline.com/pages/index.php?option=com_content&view=article&id=61&Itemid=18#brief.

13 Accessed at www.spacepolicyonline.com/pages/images/stories/Letter_to_Augustine_Panel_26_Jul_09.pdf.

14 "NASA Awards Space Station Commercial Resupply Services Contracts," NASA, Dec. 23, 2008, www.nasa.gov/home/hqnews/2008/dec/HQ_C08-069_ISS_Resupply.html.

15 Aaron Rowe, "SpaceX Launch Successfully Delivers Satellite Into Orbit," *Wired*, July 14, 2009, www.wired.com/wiredscience/2009/07/spacexlaunch.

16 Ronald Grover, "To the Moon: Elon Musk's High-Powered Visions," *Business Week*, Sept. 11, 2009, www.businessweek.com/bwdaily/dnflash/content/sep2009/db20090910_452749.htm.

17 Musk's comments in a conference call with reporters were quoted in Jason Paur, "NASA's Loss Is Space Tourism's Gain," *Wired.com*, Sept. 11, 2009, www.wired.com/autopia/2009/09/space-tourism-2/. Paur wrote that the figures are based on a minimum contract of four flights a year carrying seven passengers on SpaceX's *Dragon* capsule.

18 In a video interview, Musk said, "We'll try" to put a man on Mars by 2020. See "Uber Entrepreneur: An Evening with Elon Musk," FORA.TV, http://fora.tv/2009/04/07/Uber_Entrepreneur_An_Evening_with_Elon_Musk#Elon_Musk_Bets_Manned_Mission_to_Mars_by_2020.

19 Block and Matthews, *op. cit.*

20 Mark Matthews, "Shelby knocks Constellation study; orbiting astronauts talk to Senate," The Write Stuff blog, *Orlando Sentinel*, May 21, 2009, http://blogs.orlandosentinel.com/news_space_thewritestuff/2009/05/shelby-knocks-constellation-study-orbiting-astronauts-talk-to-senate.html.

21 *Ibid.*

22 David E. Sanger and Richard W. Stevenson, "Bush Backs Goal of Flight to Moon to Establish Base," *The New York Times*, Jan. 15, 2004, www.nytimes.com/2004/01/15/us/bush-backs-

About the Author

Thomas J. Billitteri is a *CQ Researcher* staff writer based in Fairfield, Pa., who has more than 30 years' experience covering business, nonprofit institutions and public policy for newspapers and other publications. His recent *CQ Researcher* reports include "Auto Industry's Future," "Afghanistan's Future" and "Financial Literacy." He holds a BA in English and an MA in journalism from Indiana University.

goal-of-flight-to-moon-to-establish-base.html?scp=
1&sq=bush%20backs%20goal%20of%20flight%20
to%20moon&st=cse.

23 Roger E. Bilstein, "Orders of Magnitude: A
History of the NACA and NASA, 1915-1990,"
NASA, 1989, http://history.nasa.gov/SP-4406/
contents.html.

24 *Ibid.*

25 "Robert Goddard: A Man and His Rocket,"
NASA, March 9, 2004, www.nasa.gov/missions/
research/f_goddard.html.

26 Jeffrey Kluger, "Robert Goddard: He
launched the space age with a 10-ft. rocket in
a New England cabbage field," *The Time 100:
Scientists & Thinkers*, *Time*, March 29, 1999,
www.time.com/time/time100/scientist/profile/
goddard.html.

27 "Goddard," NASA, *op. cit.*

28 Kluger, *op. cit.*

29 *Ibid.*

30 *Ibid.*

31 William Manchester, *The Glory and the
Dream*, Vol. 2 (1974), p. 963.

32 *Oregonian* and *Time* quotes from *ibid.*, p.
965.

33 Bilstein, *op. cit.*

34 *Ibid.*

35 *Ibid.*

36 *Ibid.*

37 *Ibid.*

38 John F. Kennedy, excerpts from "Urgent
National Needs" speech to a Joint Session of
Congress, May 25, 1961, accessed at
http://history.nasa.gov/Apollomon/apollo5.pdf.

39 NASA biographical data on John Glenn Jr.,
January 1999, www.jsc.nasa.gov/Bios/htmlbios/
glenn-j.html.

40 Craig Nelson, *Rocket Men* (2009), p. 27.

41 Bilstein, *op. cit.*

42 W. Henry Lambright, ed., *Space Policy in
the 21st Century* (2003), pp. 2-3.

43 Carl E. Behrens, "The International Space
Station and the Space Shuttle," Congressional
Research Service, March 18, 2009, p. 1.

44 Ronald Reagan, State of the Union address,
Jan. 25, 1984, available at www.presidency.ucsb.
edu/ws/index.php?pid=40205.

45 Lambright, *op. cit.*, p. 4.

46 Pat Duggins, *Final Countdown* (2007), p. 81.

47 Lambright, *op. cit.*, p. 5. Lambright cites
Robert Zubrin, *The Case for Mars* (1996), p. 47.

48 Behrens, *op. cit.*

49 *Ibid.*

50 Amy Klamper, "NASA Officials Warn of Tight
Budgets Ahead," *Space News*, Sept. 17, 2009,
www.spacenews.com/policy/nasa-officials-warn-
tight-budgets-ahead.html.

51 Quoted in *ibid.*

52 CQ Congressional Transcripts, *op. cit.*

53 *Ibid.*

54 "Chairman Gordon's Statement on Augustine Committee Summary Report on Human
Spaceflight," press release, House Science and
Technology Committee, Sept. 8, 2009, www.
science.house.gov/press/PRArticle.aspx?NewsID
=2592.

55 "Funding Will be Key Determinant of America's Human Space Flight Future, Committee and
Witnesses Agree," press release, House Committee on Science and Technology, Sept. 15, 2009,
www.science.house.gov/press/PRArticle.aspx?
NewsID=2606.

56 Testimony of Michael D. Griffin, "Options and
Issues for NASA's Human Space Flight Program:
Report of the 'Review of U.S. Human Space
Flight Plans' Committee," House Committee on
Science and Technology, Sept. 15, 2009, http://
democrats.science.house.gov/Media/file/Comm
docs/hearings/2009/Full/15sep/Griffin_Testimo
ny.pdf.

57 See www.politifact.com/truth-o-meter/prom
ises/subjects/space.

58 CQ Congressional Transcripts, "Senate Commerce, Science and Transportation Subcommittee on Science and Space Holds Hearing on
NASA Human Space Flight Plans," Sept. 16, 2009,
www.cq.com/display.do?dockey=/cqonline/prod/
data/docs/html/transcripts/congressional/111/
congressionaltranscripts111-000003204990.html@
committees&metapub=CQ-CONGTRANSCRIPTS
&searchIndex=0&seqNum=7. Nelson is chairman
of the subcommittee.

59 William Harwood, "Japan launches new
cargo craft to space station," Sept. 10, 2009,
http://news.cnet.com/8301-19514_3-10350052-
239.html.

60 Lee Jae-won, "South Korea launches first
rocket," Reuters, Aug. 25, 2009, www.reuters.
com/article/topNews/idUSTRE57O1KJ20090825.

61 Jay Shankar and Ed Johnson, "India Ends
Lunar Mission After Losing Probe Signal,"
Bloomberg, Aug. 31, 2009, www.bloomberg.
com/apps/news?pid=20601087&sid=anHW54Ny
N9Y4#.

62 Jeffrey Logan, "China's Space Program: Options for U.S.-China Cooperation," Congressional
Research Service, updated Sept. 29, 2008.

63 Christopher Bodeen, "China breaks ground
on space launch center," The Associated Press,
Sept. 14, 2009, www.google.com/hosted
news/ap/article/ALeqM5jszhZZpw8KvbElAp
GPkWEikezcBAD9AN1KRO0.

64 Logan, *op. cit.*

65 "2008 Report to Congress," U.S. China Economic and Security Review Commission, November 2008, p. 167, www.uscc.gov/annual_
report/2008/annual_report_full_08.pdf.

66 Testimony before Augustine Committee for
Review of U.S. Human Space Flight, Aug. 5,
2009, www.nasa.gov/pdf/376695main_13%20-%
20Robert_Zubrin-Testimony-5_August_2009.pdf.

67 Lawrence M. Krauss, "A One-Way Ticket to
Mars," *The New York Times*, Sept. 1, 2009, www.ny-
times.com/2009/09/01/opinion/01krauss.html?scp
=1&sq=one-way%20ticket%20to%20mars&st=cse.

68 Vincent Sabathier, G. Ryan Faith and Ashley Bander, "Mid- and Long-Term Prospects
for Human Spaceflight: Mitigating the Gaps,"
Center for Strategic and International Studies,
February 2009, http://csis.org/files/media/csis/
pubs/090223_sabathier_midlongtermprospects_
web.pdf.

FOR MORE INFORMATION

Association of Space Explorers, 1150 Gemini Ave., Houston, TX 77058; (281)
280-8172; www.space-explorers.org. Supports space science and education and
encourages international cooperation in human space exploration.

Embry-Riddle Aeronautical University, 600 S. Clyde Morris Blvd., Daytona Beach, FL
321143900; (386) 226-6000; www.erau.edu. Trains students in aeronautics and aviation.

NASA, Public Communications Office, NASA Headquarters, Suite 5K39, Washington,
DC 205460001; (202) 358-0001; www.nasa.gov. Conducts human and scientific exploration and aeronautical research.

The Planetary Society, 65 N. Catalina Ave., Pasadena, CA 911062301; (626) 793-5100;
www.planetary.org. Advocacy group for space exploration.

Space and Technology Policy Group, LLC, 2503D N. Harrison St., Arlington, VA
22207; (571) 286-9168; www.spacepolicyonline.com. Provides news, information and
analysis about space-program policy, international space activities and space law.

Bibliography

Selected Sources

Books

Bilstein, Roger E., *Orders of Magnitude: A History of the NACA and NASA, 1915-1990*, NASA, 1989, http://history.nasa.gov/SP-4406/contents.html.

A historian provides a useful overview of American aeronautical development and the rise of the space program.

Duggins, Pat, *Final Countdown*, University Press of Florida, 2007.

A senior public-radio news analyst well-known for his NASA coverage tells the story of the Space Shuttle program, its scheduled termination and what may come next for human spaceflight.

Lambright, W. Henry, ed., *Space Policy in the 21st Century*, Johns Hopkins University Press, 2003.

Space experts offer useful overviews of such issues as space commerce, asteroid avoidance, the International Space Station and NASA's role in the search for extraterrestrial life.

Nelson, Craig, *Rocket Men*, Viking, 2009.

On the 40th anniversary of *Apollo 11*, a veteran writer offers a detailed account of the epic lunar landing.

Zubrin, Robert, with Richard Wagner, *The Case for Mars*, Simon & Schuster, 1996.

The Mars Society president argues that humans could travel to Mars within a decade using current technology.

Articles

Block, Robert, and Mark K. Matthews, "Ares May Look Dead but Keeps Ticking," *The Orlando Sentinel*, Sept. 6, 2009, www.orlandosentinel.com/news/space/orl-ares-rocket-not-dead-090609,0,1246493.story.

Critics of the *Ares 1* rocket, designed to replace the Space Shuttle, have all but pronounced it dead, but the project's builders are fighting to keep it alive.

Krauss, Lawrence M., "A One-Way Ticket to Mars," *The New York Times*, Sept. 1, 2009, www.nytimes.com/2009/09/01/opinion/01krauss.html?scp=1&sq=a%20one-way%20ticket%20to%20mars&st=cse.

"Why are we so interested in bringing the Mars astronauts home again?" asks the director of the Origins Initiative at Arizona State University in a provocative opinion piece.

Griffin, Michael D., "Let's Reach for The Stars Again," *The Washington Post*, July 19, 2009, www.washingtonpost.com/wp-dyn/content/article/2009/07/17/AR2009071702019.html.

On the 40th anniversary of the *Apollo* moon landing, a former NASA administrator asks, "Do we want to have a real space program, or do we just want to talk about what we used to be able to do?"

Overbye, Dennis, "One Giant Leap, Followed by Decades of Baby Steps," *The New York Times*, Sept. 25, 2007, www.nytimes.com/2007/09/25/science/space/25cosm.html.

A science writer looks back on the *Apollo* moon landing and expresses mixed feelings about the space program, lamenting that new vistas such as Mars remain to be visited by humans but celebrating the scientific achievements of NASA's unmanned spacecraft.

Reports and Studies

"Near-Earth Object Surveys and Hazard Mitigation Strategies: Interim Report," National Research Council, 2009, www.nap.edu/catalog.php?record_id=12738.

"There has been relatively little effort by the U.S. government to survey, discover, characterize and mitigate the threat" posed by asteroids and other near-Earth objects, the study concludes.

"Summary Report of the Review of U.S. Human Space Flight Plans Committee," Sept. 8, 2009, www.nasa.gov/pdf/384767main_SUMMARY%20REPORT%20-%20FINAL.pdf.

Chaired by former Lockheed Martin CEO Norman Augustine, a panel of experts reviewed the manned space program and came to a sobering conclusion: "The U.S. human spaceflight program appears to be on an unsustainable trajectory."

Behrens, Carl E., "The International Space Station and the Space Shuttle," Congressional Research Service, March 18, 2009, www.fas.org/sgp/crs/space/RL33568.pdf.

The report gives a detailed overview of funding and policy issues surrounding the orbiting laboratory and shuttle.

Eveker, Kevin, "An Analysis of NASA's Plans for Continuing Human Spaceflight After Retiring the Space Shuttle," Congressional Budget Office, Nov. 3, 2008, www.cbo.gov/ftpdocs/98xx/doc9886/NASA_Letter.3.1.shtml.

The budget office examines the consequences of the Space Shuttle's termination and NASA's plans for the *Ares 1* rocket and *Orion* capsule that are part of the Constellation Program.

Sabathier, Vincent, G. Ryan Faith and Ashley Bander, "Mid- and Long-Term Prospects for Human Spaceflight: Mitigating the Gaps," Center for Strategic & International Studies, February 2009, http://csis.org/files/media/csis/pubs/090223_sabathier_midlongtermprospects_web.pdf.

The authors offer recommendations for dealing with challenges stemming from the termination of the Space Shuttle and a lunar return.

The Next Step:

Additional Articles from Current Periodicals

Government Funding

Borenstein, Seth, "Over Budget $1B, NASA Gets $1B More From Stimulus," The Associated Press, March 4, 2009.

NASA has received $1 billion from the new economic stimulus package to make up for $1.1 billion in cost overruns.

Matthews, Mark K., ' "Pony Up' for Spaceflight, Nelson Tells White House," Orlando Sentinel, Sept. 17, 2009, p. A9.

Sen. Bill Nelson, D-Fla., is urging the Obama administration to invest an additional $3 billion in the space program, especially for human spaceflight.

Powell, Stewart M., "Hutchison May Be Key to Extra NASA Funds," Houston Chronicle, May 14, 2008, p. A7.

Houston's congressional delegation is relying on Sen. Kay Bailey Hutchison, R-Texas, to convince the Senate Appropriations Committee to provide $2 billion in aid for NASA's Space Center.

Spotts, Peter N., "Congress in Hot Seat Over Human Spaceflight," The Christian Science Monitor, Sept. 16, 2009, p. 2.

A report requested by the Obama administration offers several financial suggestions to ensure the continuation of American manned spaceflight.

Mars

Chang, Alicia, "US, Europe May Team Up for Mars Missions," Record Searchlight (California), June 12, 2009, p. D4.

A NASA chief says that a partnership between the United States and the European Space Agency is the best way to pursue the shared ambitions of sending astronauts to Mars.

Halvorson, Todd, "NASA Celebrates Landmark Mars Find," Times Union (New York), Aug. 1, 2008, p. A4.

A robotic NASA rover in the Martian Arctic has confirmed the presence of water ice beneath the planet's surface.

Vergano, Dan, "Imagination Takes a Flight to Mars," USA Today, July 21, 2008, p. 1D.

Economic and budget uncertainties could potentially undermine any human spaceflight to Mars.

Private Companies

Ellegood, Edward, "Commercial Launch Options," Florida Today, Sept. 26, 2009.

Pointing to the Air Force's successful use of commercially produced rockets, a space-policy analyst says turning to private companies might ensure the continuation of manned spaceflight.

Kaufman, Marc, "Aiming for Stars, Entrepreneurs May Also Fill Gaps," The Washington Post, Sept. 25, 2008, p. G2.

PayPal's founder wants to be the first entrepreneur to compete with other nations in the business of flying cargo to the International Space Station.

Schwartz, John, "With U.S. Help, Private Space Companies Press Their Case: Why Not Us?" The New York Times, Dec. 30, 2008, p. D4.

More and more private companies are engineering new spacecraft and rockets to help NASA better fulfill its goals.

Space Tourism

Birch, Douglas, "Russian Spacecraft With Circus Tycoon Lands Safely," The Associated Press, Oct. 11, 2009.

The Russian *Soyuz* capsule carrying Cirque du Soleil CEO Guy Laliberté landed safely in Kazakhstan, ending the entertainment tycoon's $35 million visit to space.

Foreman, Chris, "Vacation in Space No Flight of Fancy," Tribune-Review (Pennsylvania), April 16, 2008.

A former chief historian for NASA says the space industry needs a breakthrough in chemical propulsion to make space tourism relatively affordable for the masses.

Hao, Sean, "Hawaii May Apply for Spaceport License to Alleviate Tourism Slump," Honolulu Advertiser, July 14, 2009.

Hawaii is looking to provide a jolt to the state's tourism business through commercial space exploration.

Richmond, Todd, "A Trip That's Out of This World," Los Angeles Times, Aug. 2, 2009, p. A6.

Virgin Galactic has conducted a test flight of *WhiteKnightTwo*, an aircraft designed to propel spaceships for commercial voyages into space.

CITING CQ RESEARCHER

Sample formats for citing these reports in a bibliography include the ones listed below. Preferred styles and formats vary, so please check with your instructor or professor.

MLA STYLE

Jost, Kenneth. "Rethinking the Death Penalty." CQ Researcher 16 Nov. 2001: 945-68.

APA STYLE

Jost, K. (2001, November 16). Rethinking the death penalty. CQ Researcher, 11, 945-968.

CHICAGO STYLE

Jost, Kenneth. "Rethinking the Death Penalty." CQ Researcher, November 16, 2001, 945-968.

In-depth Reports on Issues in the News

Are you writing a paper?

Need backup for a debate?

Want to become an expert on an issue?

For more than 80 years, students have turned to *CQ Researcher* for in-depth reporting on issues in the news. Reports on a full range of political and social issues are now available. Following is a selection of recent reports:

Civil Liberties
Closing Guantánamo, 2/09
Affirmative Action, 10/08
Gay Marriage Showdowns, 9/08
America's Border Fence, 9/08
Immigration Debate, 2/08

Crime/Law
Interrogating the CIA, 9/09
Examining Forensics, 7/09
Legalizing Marijuana, 6/09
Wrongful Convictions, 4/09
Prostitution Debate, 5/08

Education
Reading Crisis? 2/08
Discipline in Schools, 2/08
Student Aid, 1/08

Environment/Society
Gays in the Military, 9/09
Energy and Climate, 7/09
Future of Books, 5/09
Hate Groups, 5/09
Future of Journalism, 3/09
Confronting Warming, 1/09
Reducing Carbon Footprint, 12/08

Health/Safety
Medication Abuse, 10/09
Nuclear Disarmament, 10/09
Health-Care Reform, 8/09
Straining the Safety Net, 7/09
Treating Depression, 6/09
Reproductive Ethics, 5/09

Politics/Economy
State Budget Crisis, 9/09
Business Bankruptcy, 4/09
Future of the GOP, 3/09
Middle-Class Squeeze, 3/09

Upcoming Reports

Conspiracy Theories, 10/23/09   Human Rights, 10/30/09   Vocational Education, 11/6/09

ACCESS
CQ Researcher is available in print and online. For access, visit your library or www.cqresearcher.com.

STAY CURRENT
To receive notice of upcoming *CQ Researcher* reports, or learn more about *CQ Researcher* products, subscribe to the free e-mail newsletters, *CQ Researcher Alert!* and *CQ Researcher News*: http://cqpress.com/newsletters.

PURCHASE
To purchase a *CQ Researcher* report in print or electronic format (PDF), visit www.cqpress.com or call 866-427-7737. Single reports start at $15. Bulk purchase discounts and electronic-rights licensing are also available.

SUBSCRIBE
Annual full-service *CQ Researcher* subscriptions—including 44 reports a year, monthly index updates, and a bound volume—start at $803. Add $25 for domestic postage.

CQ Researcher Online offers a backfile from 1991 and a number of tools to simplify research. For pricing information, call 800-834-9020, ext. 1906, or e-mail librarysales@cqpress.com.

CQ Researcher

Published by CQ Press, a Division of SAGE

www.cqresearcher.com

Conspiracy Theories

Do they threaten democracy?

P
resident Barack Obama is a foreign-born radical
plotting to establish a dictatorship. His predecessor,
George W. Bush, allowed the Sept. 11 attacks to
occur in order to justify sending U.S. troops to Iraq.
The federal government has plans to imprison political dissenters
in detention camps in the United States. Welcome to the world of
conspiracy theories. Since colonial times, conspiracies both far-
fetched and plausible have been used to explain trends and events
ranging from slavery to why U.S. forces were surprised at Pearl
Harbor. In today's world, the communications revolution allows
conspiracy theories to be spread more widely and quickly than
ever before. But facts that undermine conspiracy theories move
less rapidly through the Web, some experts worry. As a result,
there may be growing acceptance of the notion that hidden forces
control events, leading to eroding confidence in democracy, with
repercussions that could lead Americans to large-scale withdrawal
from civic life, or even to violence.

*A demonstrator questions President Barack Obama's
U.S. citizenship — a popular conspiracists' issue — at
the recent "9-12 March on Washington" sponsored by
the Tea Party Patriots and other conservatives
opposed to tax hikes.*

CQ Researcher • Oct. 23, 2009 • www.cqresearcher.com
Volume 19, Number 37 • Pages 885-908

CQ Researcher

Oct. 23, 2009
Volume 19, Number 37

MANAGING EDITOR: Thomas J. Colin
tcolin@cqpress.com

ASSISTANT MANAGING EDITOR: Kathy Koch
kkoch@cqpress.com

ASSOCIATE EDITOR: Kenneth Jost

STAFF WRITERS: Thomas J. Billitteri,
Marcia Clemmitt, Peter Katel

CONTRIBUTING WRITERS: Rachel Cox,
Sarah Glazer, Alan Greenblatt, Reed Karaim
Barbara Mantel, Patrick Marshall,
Tom Price, Jennifer Weeks

DESIGN/PRODUCTION EDITOR: Olu B. Davis

ASSISTANT EDITOR: Darrell Dela Rosa

FACT-CHECKING: Eugene J. Gabler,
Michelle Harris

CQ PRESS

A Division of SAGE

PRESIDENT AND PUBLISHER:
John A. Jenkins

CQ Press is a registered trademark of Congressional Quarterly Inc.

CQ Researcher (ISSN 1056-2036) is printed on acid-free paper. Published weekly, except; (Jan. wk. 1) (May wk. 4) (July wks. 1, 2) (Aug. wks. 3, 4) (Nov. wk. 4) and (Dec. wk. 4), by CQ Press, a division of SAGE Publications. Annual full-service subscriptions start at $803. For pricing, call 1-800-834-9020, ext. 1906. To purchase a CQ Researcher report in print or electronic format (PDF), visit www. cqpress.com or call 866-427-7737. Single reports start at $15. Bulk purchase discounts and electronic-rights licensing are also available. Periodicals postage paid at Washington, D.C., and additional mailing offices. POSTMASTER: Send address changes to CQ Researcher, 2300 N St., N.W., Suite 800, Washington, DC 20037.

Cover: Jeff Malet

Conspiracy Theories

BY PETER KATEL

THE ISSUES

Radio-show host Alex Jones says Americans should be scared — really scared. Pretty soon, he warned listeners earlier this year, trucks will be pulling up in front of their houses to take them to Federal Emergency Management Agency (FEMA) detention camps.

Televised government propaganda will assure people the camps are for their safety, says Jones, and to outward appearances everything will be fine —"except for those being . . . put in an acid bath or killed or flown to a black site. You've got to ask [yourself] when the truck pulls up, 'Are you going to go to the camp? . . . That's the point where it's lock-and-load time. I'm not going to a camp where some piece of filth guard is going to break my family up and take me off for interrogation where they can torture me for two years." [1]

Until recently, Jones was largely unknown outside the circle of conspiracy-theory fans of his Austin, Texas-based show. Over the past several months, however, his over-the-top claims have landed him on Fox News and brought celebrity guests to his own program, such as actor Charlie Sheen, a supporter of the so-called "truther" movement, which claims that airborne terrorists couldn't have inflicted the damage done by the Sept. 11 attacks and that, consequently, there must have been some degree of government involvement. "The official 9/11 story is an absolute fairy tale, a work of fiction," he said. [2]

Jones' own views about the Sept. 11, 2001, terror attacks run along the same lines. "I see this whole cover-up collapsing," he told Sheen.

Radio-show host Alex Jones warns listeners that Americans could be taken to detention camps by the government and tortured and murdered. Actor Charlie Sheen, a so-called "truther," recently declared on Jones' show, "The official 9/11 story is an absolute fairy tale, a work of fiction." Jones' popularity reflects the enduring appeal of conspiracy theories throughout U.S. history.

http://mesikammen.wordpress.com

Jones maintains a Web site that gets roughly as much traffic as those of either conservative talk-show host Rush Limbaugh or the liberal news site Talking Points Memo. [3]

The popularity of Jones' Web site points to the widespread appeal today of conspiracy theories and the corresponding emergence of hundreds of conspiracy-oriented Web sites, videos and books. Among their recent claims: President Barack Obama isn't a U.S. citizen, and the "truth" about 9/11 remains hidden from most Americans.

Such theories represent only the latest variations on a conspiracy theme that traces its origin to the nation's earliest days. The early conspiracists believed that American presidents headed criminal or treasonous conspiracies, some of them linked to longtime "villains," such as international bankers and Jews. Indeed, presidential conspiracy theories run in an unbroken chain since President George H. W. Bush proposed a New World Order

and, conspiracists believed, plotted the takeover of the United States.

The 2007 documentary-style movie "Zeitgeist," for example, links 9/11 to an alleged plot that drew the United States into both world wars as well as the Vietnam War. An earlier, Web-distributed movie, "Loose Change," played a key role in fostering the conspiracist view of the Sept. 11 attacks. More recently, best-selling author Dan Brown draws on conspiracy notions about the Freemasons in his new novel, *The Lost Symbol*, much as his phenomenally popular *Da Vinci Code* involved an ancient conspiracy within the Roman Catholic Church.

Oliver Stone's 1991 film "JFK" presented one of the most persistent conspiracy subjects — President John F. Kennedy's assassination — including the purported involvement of U.S. intelligence and military agencies. "The X-Files," a hit TV series in the '90s, merged Kennedy assassination and space-alien theories.

The view of events as stage-managed affairs designed to fool the public runs deep enough that an estimated 6 percent of the American people believe that the 1969 moon landing was a hoax. "A model of the moon is used for the *Apollo 11* descent footage," wrote Bart Sibrel, a Nashville filmmaker who made a movie to argue his theory. "Anyone with basic knowledge of motion pictures can see it's a fake moon." The National Aeronautics and Space Administration is concerned enough about the doubters to post detailed rebuttals on its Web site. [4]

Underlying many conspiracy theories is distrust of government, says John E. Moser, a history professor at Ohio's Ashland University. "We don't trust leaders anymore," says Moser, a specialist in

From UFOs to Secret Societies

The popular conspiracy theory Web sites below are among hundreds of sites that present alternative theories on everything from 9/11 to environmental policies. They use the Internet to question mainstream ideas and have acquired a large following in recent years.

1 Above Top Secret www.abovetopsecret.com/
With nearly 176,000 members, the site is the Internet's largest and most popular community dedicated to a wide range of conspiracy topics, including UFOs, paranormal activity, secret societies, political scandals, "new world order" and terrorism.

2 Prison Planet www.prisonplanet.com/
Affiliated with radio host Alex Jones, the site features forums where members can discuss alternative theories on everything from 9/11 to swine flu vaccinations.

3 Infowars www.infowars.com
Radio broadcaster Alex Jones examines numerous topics and presents interviews with fellow "9/11 Truthers," such as country singer Willie Nelson.

4 911Truth www.911truth.org
Calls into question the U.S. government's account of the events of 9/11/2001 and discusses alternative theories. The site wtc7.net features similar content.

5 Centre for Research on Globalization http://globalresearch.ca/
Based in Canada, the site promotes the "unspoken truth" on issues ranging from the U.S. invasion of Iraq to environmental policies.

6 What Really Happened www.whatreallyhappened.com
Presents alternative theories focusing on the War on Terror and accuses the U.S. government of hiding information.

7 The Zeitgeist Movement www.thezeitgeistmovement.com
Promotes the idea that nations, governments, races, religions, creeds and social classes are false distinctions. Seeks to achieve unity among people through a common conception of nature.

8 The Jeff Rense Program www.rense.com
Radio broadcaster Rense positions himself as an opponent to mainstream news coverage. His Web site and radio broadcasts cover the daily news from an alternative perspective.

9 YouTube www.youtube.com
Most conspiracy theorists are putting their content here now in order to gain a wide audience.

10 David Icke www.davidicke.com/index.php/
Icke is popular with people who want to ridicule conspiracy theorists because he presents radical conspiracy theories, but he does not have a significant following among conspiracy theorists themselves.

Source: Edward L. Winston, conspiracyscience.com, Oct. 15, 2009

20th-century conspiracism. "Maybe that's a good thing, but it certainly leaves the door open to kookery. At various points in history, conspiracy theories captured a great part of the population, but they fizzled out as the sense of crisis passed. Now, conspiracy theories tend to stick around. I'm wondering if we're not in a permanent crisis mode."

Some experts even worry that the cynicism reflected in conspiracy theories today endangers U.S. democracy, not to mention Americans' health: Conspiracy theorists even have stoked the widespread opposition to swine flu vaccine. (*See "Current Situation," p. 900.*)

One thing is certain: Thanks to the ever-expanding Internet, disclosures of genuine government misdeeds have intensified the public's suspicions. (*See sidebar, p. 898.*) Moreover, today's unsettled climate — dominated by scandal, economic turmoil, war and intense partisan conflict — stimulates a search for explanations that often reach extremes.

A Public Policy Polling survey in September showed that 41 percent of Americans — and 64 percent of Republicans — didn't believe or weren't sure President Obama was born in the United States. Indeed, many "birthers" believe Obama has engaged in a decades-long deception about his place of birth. And 22 percent of all voters — and 37 percent of Democrats — either believed or questioned whether former President George W. Bush purposely allowed the 9/11 attacks to occur to provide a pretext for war in the Middle East. [5]

Although the sample size was a relatively small 621 respondents, the results were consistent with a broader 2007 poll showing 22 percent of respondents thought Bush knew of the 9/11 attacks in advance. [6]

The "birther" movement is raising enough jitters in the political mainstream that the Senate and House passed resolutions last July stating that Obama was born in Hawaii. [7]

The resolutions followed the introduction of "birther"-influenced legislation proposed by Rep. Bill Posey, R-Fla., that would require presidential candidates to provide birth certificates; 11 House Republicans signed the bill. Limbaugh and Michael Savage, another conservative commentator, last year joined the chorus of those deriding Obama's citizenship credentials. [8]

Administration officials, however, touch conspiracy matters at their peril. In September, Van Jones, an Obama environmental adviser, resigned after disclosure that he had signed a 2004 petition, popular with some on the left, calling for "immediate inquiry into evidence that suggests high-level government officials may have deliberately allowed the Sept. 11 attacks to occur." [9]

Those who've tried arguing with "truthers" often find themselves accused of being in on the plot — a classic feature of conspiracy theories. For example, after an exhaustive investigation by *Popular Mechanics* debunked 9/11 conspiracy theories, the magazine was accused of being a CIA front and a friend of Israeli intelligence. [10]

"A common refrain in conspiracy circles is the claim that, 'We're just asking questions,' " wrote editor-in-chief James B. Meigs. "One would think that at least some quarters of the conspiracy movement might welcome a mainstream publication's serious, nonideological attempt to answer those questions. One would be wrong."

Conspiracists such as the late W. Cleon Skousen insist that major public figures can generate smoke screens that obscure conspiracies in action. A former Brigham Young University professor and FBI agent, Skousen heavily influenced Fox TV talk-show host Glenn Beck, whose introduction to one of Skousen's books describes his writing as "divinely inspired." [11]

Skousen envisioned a plot by banker David Rockefeller and others in the financial elite to establish "ruler's law" — as opposed to God's law — in the U.S. "Rockefeller . . . has a plan,"

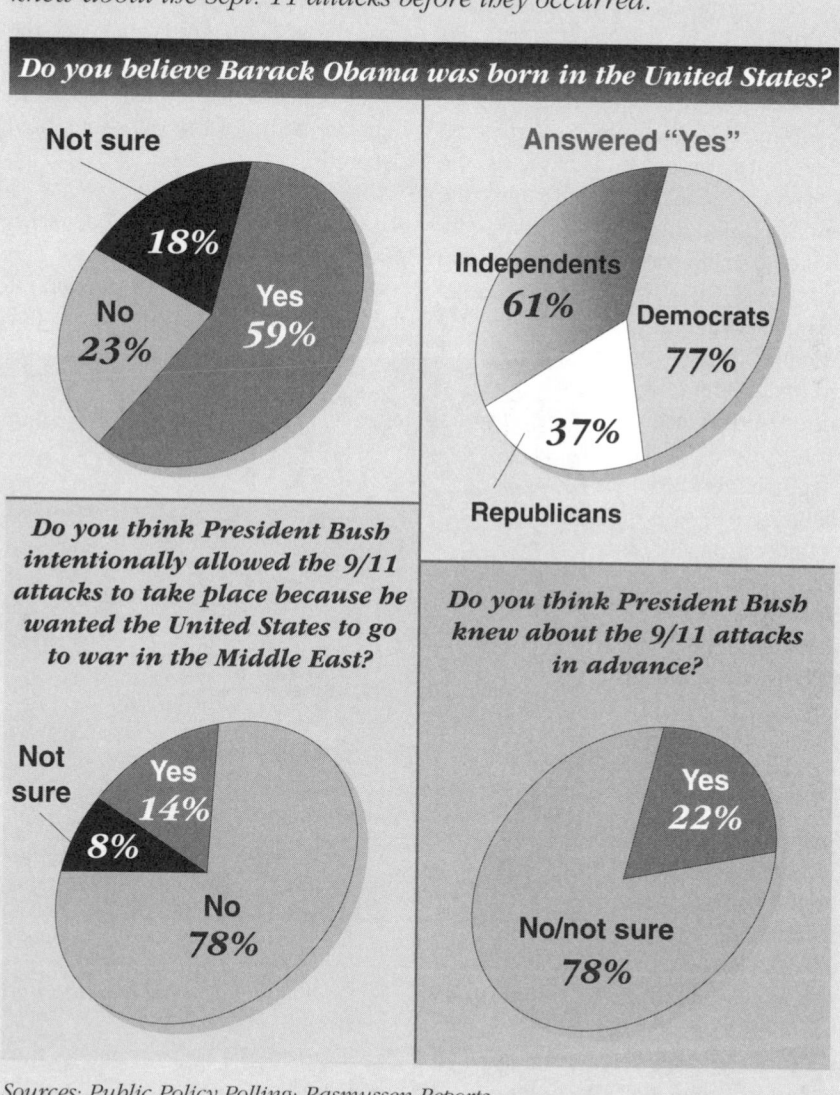

Most Regard Obama as American-Born

More than half of Americans believe that President Obama was born in the United States, not Kenya, including more than three-fourths of Democrats. But more than 60 percent of Republicans are skeptical. Nearly a quarter of Americans believe President George W. Bush knew about the Sept. 11 attacks before they occurred.

Do you believe Barack Obama was born in the United States?

Not sure 18%
Yes 59%
No 23%

Answered "Yes"
Independents 61%
Democrats 77%
37%
Republicans

Do you think President Bush intentionally allowed the 9/11 attacks to take place because he wanted the United States to go to war in the Middle East?

Not sure 8%
Yes 14%
No 78%

Do you think President Bush knew about the 9/11 attacks in advance?

Yes 22%
No/not sure 78%

Sources: Public Policy Polling; Rasmussen Reports

Skousen once said. "He wants to restore ruler's law and force the stupid masses — those are Lenin's words — to do what's good for them." [12]

Beck hasn't explicitly endorsed that view. But in September he hinted at a connection between the Rockefeller family, radical politics and Obama appointee Van Jones. The takeoff point was Beck's interpretations of the artwork at Rockefeller Center by early-20th-century fascist- and communist-inspired artists. "It makes sense that you feel a little uneasy, and everything seems to be a little hidden," Beck said. "Progressives, fascists, communists — now what do they all have in common today? That's something you're going to have to figure out." But

Oct. 23, 2009

he added, "The Rockefeller Foundation, they gave a big award and an awful lot of credibility to — oh, Van Jones, our new green jobs czar." [13]

Beck had flirted with the idea that FEMA was setting up detention camps, but he eventually said evidence was lacking, telling CBS News anchor Katie Couric that the camps theory was "easy to debunk." He also told her he is not a conspiracy theorist. [14]

Jerome R. Corsi, a frequent guest on Alex Jones' program, also rejects the conspiracist label. [15] "I don't think the term has any meaning," he says. "It's an intentionally politically charged term that's used to demonize work somebody doesn't agree with politically." He describes himself as an investigative reporter and is active in the network of Obama-citizenship challengers.

But conspiracist or not, Corsi readily evokes the specter of Nazi Germany in describing a House bill introduced in January by Rep. Alcee Hastings, D-Fla. The bill would create six National Emergency Centers on military bases for use by communities hit by natural disasters. [16]

Corsi wrote that the legislation "appears designed to create the type of detention center that those concerned about use of the military in domestic affairs fear could be used as concentration camps for political dissidents, as in Nazi Germany." [17]

Jones also depicts those he sees as the country's enemies in the most sinister terms, along with the mainstream media that he accuses of serving the conspiracy. Jones' Web site said the H1N1 flu originated with "powerful industrialists operating a crime ring [who] are behind the pandemic's creation, media persuasions, vaccination preparations and health official promotions." [18]

The "globalists" who run the conspiracy have to be fought, Jones preaches. "I just want to get my hands around their throats. . . . And you know they feel the same about us." [19]

As conspiracy theories proliferate, here are some of the questions being debated:

Are conspiracy theories becoming part of mainstream politics?

Conspiracy theories are woven into the fabric of U.S. history. Some have

Apollo 11 astronaut Buzz Aldrin walks on the Moon on July 20, 1969. Six percent of Americans think the historic landing was a government hoax, prompting NASA to post detailed rebuttals on its Web site.

become national issues, such as those involving a real secret society — but one that never left Europe — known as the Illuminati, whose supposed goal was subverting the nation.

The Illuminati theory was transplanted to the newly founded United States by defenders of the old European order that was overthrown by the French Revolution. Anti-Masonic theories, also transplanted from Europe, typically were adopted by conspiracists who argued that the Masons were out to destroy Christianity.

Past generations of conspiracists, however, didn't enjoy the global electronic megaphone — the Internet — that their political descendants now command. Radio and cable TV talk shows also have helped conspiracists reach wider audiences.

One of the day's hottest issues concerns Obama's birthplace. "Where's the birth certificate?" asked a placard-carrying demonstrator at the "09.12.09 March on Washington." [20] Other signs at the rally depicted the president as, variously, a Nazi, a socialist and a communist.

While the embrace of the "birthers" by some radio and cable-TV talk-show hosts demonstrates the reach of conspiracy theories, experts disagree whether their appeal imbues them with political relevance. (Some conservative Obama foes vigorously reject the birthers.)

Political analyst Chip Berlet, a longtime chronicler of conspiracy movements, argues that conspiracy theories are on the upswing both in volume and influence. [21] "The government lacks transparency, which encourages a sense of delegitimization," says Berlet, of Political Research Associates, a liberal consultancy in Cambridge, Mass. "And for a lot of conservative people, to have a black boss whom they see as a bully is quite unsettling. Proxies for that attitude are seen in claims Obama is a Muslim, or was not born in the United States or plans to socialize the economy through health-care reform."

Berlet argues that conspiracy theories can help knit together groups that fundamentally have little use for each other — the Christian right, economic libertarians and white nationalists, to name a few. "All these sectors are pushing the idea that Obama is conspiring against the well-being of America."

Not all conspiracy experts see an immediate danger. The fact that conspiracy theories are widely disseminated doesn't in itself constitute a threat, says Daniel Pipes, director of the Philadelphia-based Middle East Forum, which advocates for U.S. interests in the Middle East. "Ultimately, it's the impact that's more important than volume," says Pipes, who has written about conspiracy theories in U.S., Middle Eastern and European settings. "I see them more than I did 15 years ago, but their impact is still limited. You don't see them really having an impact on the policies of government and the actions of Americans."

Pipes cites the long-lived constellation of conspiracy theories about JFK's death that has spread throughout popular culture to little political effect. "Kennedy assassination theories are voluminous, but irrelevant," he says.

Other scholars argue that conspiracy theories challenging Obama's legitimacy as president have the potential to be influential. "It seems that the election of an African-American president has triggered the anxieties of a big segment of the white population," says Kathryn S. Olmsted, a professor of history at the University of California, Davis, and author of the new book *Real Enemies: Conspiracy Theories and American Democracy, World War I to 9/11*. [22]

The racial factor, she says, adds a dimension that was absent in the conspiracy theories centering on President Bill Clinton. They reflected the fear and suspicion of growing federal power — as seen in violent confrontations between federal agents and armed government opponents. Whether the anti-Obama theories reach that level of intensity remains to be seen, Olmsted acknowledges. But, she says, "I think we're in new territory."

The communications revolution alone ensures that conspiracy theorists

can reach millions more people, says Ashland University's Moser. "Back in the 1930s, what we call today the mainstream media was pretty much *the* source of information," says Moser, author of a biography of Pearl Harbor conspiracy theorist John T. Flynn. [23] "In the archives, you find conspiracy theories back then were expressed in very amateurish-looking newsletters, created on typewriter and circulated by mimeograph. Today they're in very slick online formats."

Still, presentation and audience don't automatically confer influence, Moser adds. In fact, the easy accessibility of platforms may encourage some media figures to latch on to conspiracy theories — the more attention-grabbing the better — simply to get or keep audiences. For instance, "If you have a radio show, and you're going to be on for three or four hours a day," he says, "you have to say things that are going to get peoples' attention. There's no place for wonkishness in the talk-radio format."

Do conspiracy theories appeal more to the right than the left?

A long tradition among historians and political scientists links conspiracy theories with the far right. Historian Richard Hofstadter's classic 1963 essay, "The Paranoid Style in American Politics," focused exclusively on right-wing conspiracism. "The modern right wing . . . feels dispossessed: America has been largely taken away from them and their kind," he wrote. "The old national security and independence have been destroyed by treasonous plots, having as their most powerful agents not merely outsiders and foreigners but major statesmen seated at the very centers of American power." [24]

Increasingly, however, conspiracy theory-watchers are concluding that conspiracism's appeal goes beyond ideology. For instance, the "truther" theories about the 9/11 attacks have attracted both left- and right-wingers. Indeed, some scholars have argued in recent years that theories once closely associated with the

right have been attracting followers from the left. Anti-Semitism is the classic case, in the form of left-wing attacks on Israel that challenge its right to exist.

Shortly before the war in Iraq began in 2003, a conflict erupted in the anti-war left after Rabbi Michael Lerner of Berkeley, Calif., was blocked from speaking at a peace rally in San Francisco. Lerner had criticized one of the organizations sponsoring the event for planning to use it for anti-Israel propaganda purposes. "Fellow progressive Jews, some anxious to speak at these rallies, have urged me to keep quiet about anti-Semitism on the left," Lerner wrote in *The Wall Street Journal*. [25]

Since then, however, the furor over anti-Jewish prejudice on the left has quieted along with the anti-war movement. And some conspiracy theory opponents view the major conspiracist current of the moment as a right-wing trend. "Of all the conspiracy theorists, 90 percent are on the far right," says Edward L. Winston, a St. Louis software engineer who runs a conspiracy-debunking Web site (conspiracyscience.com).

But Winston adds that the widespread and growing skepticism about government favors the expansion of conspiracism beyond what he considers its natural right-wing constituency. Media productions such as the first "Zeitgeist" movie — which mixes classical conspiracy theories about "international bankers" and new ones about Sept. 11 — may be broadening the ranks of conspiracy believers, he says. "I was surprised how popular 'Zeitgeist' was and how many people believed it," he says.

Conspiracy scholar Pipes argues that linking conspiracy theories exclusively to the right is a long-standing and erroneous response. "It's as much a left phenomenon as it is right," he says. "I would argue that the whole premise of communist ideology is a conspiracy theory — that the bosses are stealing your money."

Vladimir I. Lenin — founder of the Soviet state — in effect confirmed the vision of those who denounced communist conspiracies, Pipes has argued. Lenin had concluded the countries that embraced capitalism took that path because the big-business class had covertly seized government power. Communists should follow that example, Lenin argued, and greet charges of conspiratorial methods as "flattering." [26]

The University of California's Olmsted argues that right-wing conspiracy theories tend to gain more traction, though she acknowledges that conspiracy theories appeal to the extremes on both right and left. "They feel they know the truth, yet the majority of the country votes against them," she says. "Most people don't share their beliefs — or they think evil people in power are manipulating things."

Still, conspiracy theories that appeal to those on the right usually become more prominent, Olmsted says, "because they're backed generally by people with more power." Contrasting the attention that Limbaugh and other radio and TV talk-show hosts have given the "birther" theories, Olmsted notes that comparably popular supporters can't be found for the "truther" conspiracists. "Is there anyone really significant out there" among the 9/11 conspiracists "who has a real platform?" The "truther" movement generated no congressional legislation along the lines of the recent bill on birth certificates for presidential candidates.

Even so, the economic crisis may favor a resurgence of conspiracy theories that appeal to the left, says Michael Barkun, a professor of political science at Syracuse University who has studied conspiracies throughout his career. But that holds true for right-oriented theories as well, he adds. "Going well back into the 19th century, American conspiracists had almost a stylistic preference for conspiracy theories that emphasize financial power or financial manipulation," he says. That preference applies on the left and right.

In general, conspiracy theories draw their strength from deep-seated needs

and emotions, not from ideology, Barkun says. "Conspiracy theories have the psychological benefit of taking a complex reality and simplifying it. Whatever these things that bother you, they all are the result of some single cause."

Do conspiracy theories threaten democracy?

The American system of government has survived more than 250 years of conspiracy theories, but the global picture is far grimmer.

In the 20th century alone, Nazi leader Adolf Hitler convinced millions of Germans that Jews were an evil force that had to be exterminated. Josef Stalin persuaded communists and sympathizers around the world that the millions of revolutionaries — and ordinary citizens — executed in the "Great Terror" of 1937-1938 had been plotting the destruction of the Soviet state.

But conspiracy theories cooked up abroad also have proved dangerous to Americans. The 19 men who carried out the Sept. 11 attacks on the United States had been deeply influenced by a conspiratorial ideology that saw Muslims in general and Arabs in particular as the objects of manipulation by Western powers and Jews. [27]

Mohammed Atta, the terrorists' on-scene commander, believed the Jews were behind wars against Muslims in the former Yugoslavia and Chechnya (now a Russian province). Even the White House sex scandal involving President Clinton fit into Atta's conspiratorial worldview, writes Lawrence Wright in his Pulitzer Prize-winning chronicle of the roots of the 2001 attacks. "He believed that Monica Lewinsky was a Jewish agent sent to undermine Clinton, who had become too sympathetic to the Palestinian cause." [28]

Made-in-the-U.S.A. conspiracy theories generally have generated passion and activism — and violence — without producing major alterations in the course of events, even when

believers have tried to exert influence. Timothy McVeigh, who detonated the powerful fertilizer bomb that destroyed the federal building in Oklahoma City in 1995, apparently believed he would spark a revolution against the Jewish-dominated system he perceived. [29]

McVeigh killed 168 people, including 19 children, but no revolution occurred. Other conspiracists also were involved in conflicts that ended in multiple deaths, notably the 1993 showdown near Waco, Texas, at the Branch Davidian compound, in which about 80 sect members and four federal agents died. Church leader David Koresh had expounded "new world order" conspiracy theories in the 1990s. And earlier this year, a man in Pittsburgh, Richard Poplawski, was charged with killing three police officers in a confrontation apparently sparked by his beliefs in a coming social collapse engineered by "elite Jewish powers." [30]

Those deaths, and others, bolster the argument by some conspiracy scholars that conspiracism represents a danger not to be taken lightly. "They can be a threat to democracy in the sense that conspiracy theories are premised on the idea that nothing is as it seems, that appearances can never be trusted," says Barkun of Syracuse University." If you take that seriously, as many conspiracy believers do, then the work of democratic institutions is deemed fraudulent or a charade."

If large numbers of people believe the real work of government is carried out by people pulling strings behind the scenes, Barkun says, "that delegitimizes the political process."

The Middle East Forum's Pipes agrees, in principle, that conspiracy theories could threaten democracy. In practice, though, he thinks their appeal to Americans is limited. "I don't see a surge" in conspiracy believers, he says. For example, Pipes notes, the fringe views of Obama's former minister in Chicago, the Rev.

Jeremiah Wright — who believed HIV was a government-invented tool of genocide — proved unacceptable in mainstream politics. [31]

"He was marginalized and repudiated," Pipes says.

Conspiracy-watchers who have direct contact with conspiracy theory believers tend to be more likely to sense danger. "They don't care about the republic," debunker Winston says of people who post comments on his Facebook page. "Anyone who disagrees is an enemy. Conspiracy theorists claim that I really work for the government, that I'm getting paid to do this. Since I mounted a Web site, the consensus is that if I'm smart enough to do that, I must be getting paid."

Winston has heard worse. "When I had my e-mail address posted, probably 50 percent of the e-mails I got were death threats or threats in general," he says. "So I didn't have it up for long."

Even John Hawkins, who edits the "Right Wing News" Web site — slogan: "kneecapping Barack Obama at every opportunity" — has attracted hate mail for his scornful treatment of Obama-birthplace challenges, which he calls groundless. But that response hasn't persuaded him that conspiracism represents a threat. "It would have to cross into the mainstream, and so many people who knew better would have to say nothing."

Conspiracy theories do exert a strong appeal, given the natural urge to find explanations for events and trends, Hawkins says. But the theories, he argues, tend to be so intricate and dependent on leaps of faith that they're easily punctured. "Everybody wants to believe that everything is not random and that somebody has control," he says. "But I'm a conservative, I believe that government is too dumb to carry out these conspiracies. If you had enough people addressing a lot of these conspiracy theories, they would die down." ▪

BACKGROUND

Witch Hysteria

In 1692, nearly a century before American independence, 20 men and women were executed in Salem, Mass. Their crime: They were thought to be witches plotting evil in the service of the devil. Historian Jeffrey L. Pasley of the University of Missouri calls the witch hysteria that briefly swept New England "the very first American conspiracy theories." [32]

As Americans were fighting for independence in 1776, a law professor in Bavaria (now a German state) founded Illuminism, a political philosophy that sought to create a world ruled by reason, not clerics — a blasphemous notion in a Roman Catholic state. [33]

In 1784, the Society of the Illuminati, which had joined forces with the anti-clerical Freemasons, was outlawed in Bavaria amid a series of lurid confessions and supposed instructions on poisoning and counterfeiting. Defenders of the old order that was being shaken by the winds of change said the evidence proved the Illuminati had survived repression and were behind the French Revolution and ensuing Jacobin Reign of Terror and ultimately sought world domination.

Two books, one by a University of Glasgow scientist and the other by a French Jesuit priest, soon brought the Illuminati conspiracy theory to the United States. They claimed to have proved that the Illuminists aimed at world domination and the destruction of religion and morality. The Federalists, headed by President John Adams, feared that American acolytes of the radical Jacobin wing of the French revolutionaries were planning a wave of anti-religious destruction. However, after Thomas Jefferson — a French Revolution supporter whom some Federalists considered an Illuminist —

became president in 1801, Illuminist conspiracy fears faded.

But a wave of accusations against the Freemasons followed. Masonry, a conspiracy theorist claimed, was "an engine of Satan . . . blasphemous, murderous, anti-republican and anti-Christian." [34]

Denunciations of Masonry were followed by a more influential conspiracy theory centered on the Catholic Church. "A conspiracy exists . . . its plans are already in operation," wrote Samuel Morse, inventor of the telegraph, in the 1830s. Its agents, he said, included "Jesuit missionaries traveling through the land." [35]

As in other countries, U.S. conspiracy theories flourished during conflicts leading to war. Before the Civil War, abolitionists feared that Southern conspiracists were plotting to take over the federal government to ensure slavery's survival. [36]

Southerners and others indeed wanted to ensure slavery's future, and its extension to newly created states, such as Kansas and California. While no proof of a federal takeover conspiracy surfaced, the so-called "slave power" plot set the stage for 20th-century conspiracy theories that built on established fact.

Conspiracy American-Style

Americans in the 19th century began shaping their own conspiracy theories. But unlike their Old World models, which reflected threats to an ethnic homogeneity unknown in the U.S. melting pot, American conspiracy theories tended to focus on powerful and evil men acting in secret.

"A small, unelected minority representing un-American interests . . . takes over the federal government and uses it against the people," writes conspiracy scholar Pipes at the Middle East Forum. [37] Even U.S. conspiracism focusing on Jews and Catholics typically centered on alleged manipulation rather than on threats to racial purity. Europe's Rothschild banking family typically was cited to signify alleged Jewish control of world finances. As for Catholics in the late 19th century, they were "suspect as the pawns of a foreign power." [38]

By the mid-20th century, fear of foreign powers had morphed into fear that U.S. leaders were selling out the country's interests to foreigners. Following the devastating Japanese surprise attack on Pearl Harbor on Dec. 7, 1941, some U.S. isolationists claimed President Franklin D. Roosevelt had known about — and allowed — the attack because it would plunge the United States into the war in Europe.

In a 1944 article —"The Truth About Pearl Harbor" — *The Chicago Tribune* argued that Roosevelt had deliberately incited Japanese hostility, learned of the impending attack, failed to warn commanders at Pearl Harbor — and then blamed them for the absence of preparation. [39]

In fact, Roosevelt and his aides did believe that U.S. entry into the war was inevitable and did conclude — days before Pearl Harbor — that American attempts to mitigate hostilities with Japan had failed. No one, however, expected Pearl Harbor to be a target.

A postwar disclosure during congressional hearings (1945-1946) added fuel to the conspiracists' fire: Before the war began, the United States had broken the Japanese diplomatic code, which provided major evidence of U.S. awareness of pre-war Japanese intentions. The majority report said no evidence supported the claim that the FDR administration had schemed to get America into the war. But two Republicans signed a minority report claiming the administration withheld warnings from Pearl Harbor commanders in furtherance of "some long-range plan which was never disclosed to Congress or the American people." [40]

However, the conspiracists didn't produce what would later be called a "smoking gun." The decrypted Japanese cables — code named "Magic" — did reveal the Japanese saw war as imminent — but no cables mentioned an attack on Pearl Harbor.

Cold War Conspiracies

Threats of communist subversion dominated the conspiracy landscape following the war. The era's rabid anti-communism — known as McCarthyism — was spawned by Sen. Joseph McCarthy, R-Wis., who depicted himself as a crusader against communist infiltration of the government.

In 1951, McCarthy accused Secretary of State Dean Acheson and Defense Secretary George C. Marshall of being Soviet agents. The false accusations were followed by news that Americans spying for the Soviet Union — Julius and Ethel Rosenberg, executed in 1953 — had been charged with stealing U.S. atomic bomb secrets. At the same time, American troops were fighting Soviet- and Chinese communist-backed forces in Korea. In this atmosphere, McCarthy's sensational allegations of a "vast conspiracy . . . on a scale so immense as to dwarf any previous venture in the history of man" polarized the country.

Notwithstanding McCarthy's demagoguery and disregard for fact, Soviet spies had, in fact, penetrated the U.S. government and defense contractors — but in the 1930s and '40s. By the time McCarthy launched his campaign, the spies who had transmitted nuclear, high-tech and diplomatic information had been arrested, fled the country or gone to ground. [41]

Even before McCarthy surged to prominence, investigators and loyalty boards in federal and state governments had begun probing thousands of public employees who might have participated in communist political activities in the 1930s and '40s; some lost their jobs. When McCarthy's Permanent Investigations Subcommittee took up the cause, alleged — and in a few cases actual — communists or ex-communists in government, entertainment and higher education were interrogated, sometimes in highly theatrical, televised public hearings. [42]

While the injustice of the McCarthy "witch hunts" is widely acknowledged, some on the communist-influenced left hyped the McCarthy era into the equivalent of early Nazi Germany. "It seemed to us that America was veering toward fascism, a fascism that would be much the same as that of Nazi Germany," Morton Sobell, an associate of the Rosenbergs who served 19 years for espionage, wrote in a 2001 memoir, recounting what he and his comrades had forecast as imminent in the early 1950s. "We saw mass roundups, concentration camps and death ovens." Sobell confessed in 2008 that he had been a Soviet spy. [43]

McCarthy himself ended in political disgrace. After Republican President Dwight D. Eisenhower was elected in 1952, McCarthy stayed on the attack, and his Republican allies abandoned him.

Despite his political collapse, McCarthy helped spur an important development in conspiracism. His targeting of Acheson, an esteemed member of the East Coast foreign policy establishment, led other conspiracists to scrutinize the liberal Council on Foreign Relations (CFR), an influential think tank in New York whose members are high-profile scholars and former and future diplomats. [44] For the new generation of right-wing conspiracists, the CFR figured prominently — along with the Rockefeller family — in alleged takeover plots. David Rockefeller, the senior member of the oil-and-banking dynasty, is now the council's honorary chairman.

"The ultimate aim of the Council on Foreign Relations (however well-intentioned its prominent and powerful members may be) is the same as the ultimate aim of international communism: to create a one-world socialist system and make the United States an official part of it," Dan Smoot, a former FBI agent and far-right activist and author, wrote in his influential 1962 book, *The Invisible Government*. [45]

But scholars scoff at such efforts to link the CFR to conspiracy. "Finding a

Continued on p. 896

Chronology

1700s-1850s
European-inspired conspiracy theories evolve into American-style conspiracism.

1776
Bavarian law professor founds "Illuminism" movement, a secret society devoted to creating a world ruled by reason instead of clerics.

1798
Anti-"Illuminati" propaganda reaches U.S., sparking fear that Thomas Jefferson seeks to destroy religion.

1830s
Anti-Catholic conspiracy theory flourishes.

1840s-1850s
"Slave Power" conspiracists see a federal takeover by slaveholding interests.

1940s-1950s
World War II and Cold War prompt fear of takeover of U.S.

1944
Chicago Tribune alleges President Franklin D. Roosevelt provoked 1941 Pearl Harbor attack.

1945-46
Congressional hearings conclude Roosevelt didn't purposely prompt Pearl Harbor attack.

1951
Sen. Joseph McCarthy, R-Wis., falsely accuses secretaries of state and defense of being Soviet agents.

1958
John Birch Society founded to promote theory that Illuminati conspirators have penetrated government.

1960s-1970s
Kennedy assassination opens era of disbelief in government explanations.

1962
Joint Chiefs of Staff chairman secretly proposes faked Cuban attacks to create pretext for U.S. military intervention in Cuba.

1963
Assassination of President John F. Kennedy provokes conspiracy theories still in circulation today.

1972
Revelations that government doctors injected black farmers with syphilis — the "Tuskegee Experiment" — fuel later suspicion that government invented AIDS.

1975
Church Committee produces evidence of secret drug tests on U.S. citizens.

1980s-1990s
Conspiracy theories based on actual and imagined government misdeeds build a following.

1982
CIA ignores reports that Nicaraguan guerrillas are trafficking drugs — sparking conspiracy theory on the origin of crack cocaine epidemic.

1986
"Iran-Contra" scandal reveals secret U.S. plan to sell arms to Iran.

1987
Soviet-bloc scientists spread rumor that U.S. military created AIDS.

1991
Televangelist Pat Robertson warns of global takeover plot.

1993
Suicide of White House aide Vincent Foster prompts theories that President Bill Clinton and/or his wife, Hillary, had Foster killed. . . . Branch Davidian confrontation near Waco, Texas, spurs growth of conspiracist-influenced militia movement.

1997
Militia movement leader Linda Thompson calls "black helicopters" — a frequent element of conspiracy theories — part of a CIA-sponsored government takeover plot.

2000s
Sept. 11 attacks involve President George W. Bush in conspiracy theories; later theories target President Barack Obama.

2004
"Truther" conspiracy theorists demand investigation of government's "deliberate" failure to prevent 9/11 attacks.

2005
Popular Mechanics debunks conspiracy theories of the attacks.

2007
Poll shows 22 percent of respondents believe Bush knew about attack.

2008
Presidential campaign spurs theories that Obama is Muslim. . . . Rev. Jeremiah Wright, Obama's former minister, endorses conspiracy theory on AIDS origin.

2009
"Birther" activists take their arguments to federal court. . . . Obama appointee Van Jones resigns after disclosure he signed "truther" petition. . . . Conspiracists help spur resistance to flu shots.

Critics Skewer Conspiracy Theories

"They have no clue what they're talking about."

Noam Chomsky, intellectual superstar of the international left, has been harshly analyzing U.S policies since the Vietnam War. As *The New Yorker*'s Larissa MacFarquahar wrote, his works are a "catalogue of crimes committed by America, terrible crimes, and many of them . . . but it is not they that produce the sensation of blows: it is Chomsky's rage as he describes them." [1]

No wonder, then, that people certain the George W. Bush administration connived in the Sept. 11 attacks have been trying to recruit Chomsky, an emeritus professor of linguistics at the Massachusetts Institute of Technology (MIT). "I am bombarded with letters about this subject," he said in a 2007 interview.

Many commentators shy away from tackling conspiracy theories, given the passion or fanaticism they inspire. But Chomsky subjected the 9/11 conspiracy theories to the same unsparing scrutiny that he focuses on government. "With regard to the physical evidence, can you become a highly qualified civil and mechanical engineer and expert in the structure of buildings by spending a couple of hours on the Internet?" he asked in 2007. "If you can, we can get rid of the civil and mechanical engineering departments at MIT." [2]

Another critic is Edward L. Winston, a 31-year-old software engineer in St. Louis who runs a Web site, "ConspiracyScience.com," devoted to his merciless analyses of popular conspiracy themes.

In one of his responses to the most common Obama-birthplace theories, Winston took on the notion advanced by some "birthers" that a "natural born citizen" of the United States — an eligibility standard for the presidency — must be the child of two U.S. citizens. (Obama's Kenya-born father was a British subject.) [3]

"They have no clue what they're talking about," Winston writes. "Anyone born within the borders of the United States or within the territories of the United States is a natural born citizen. That even includes individuals born to two illegal immigrants on U.S. soil." [4]

Winston's site also includes some of the messages he receives on his Facebook page from conspiracy believers. "With a last name like Winston, I'm sorry but you've got Jew in your blood," one e-mailer wrote him. "So don't say you're not Jewish just because you don't practice it. Jew is blood. Jew is usury." [5]

"Little Green Footballs," an influential blog by Web designer Charles Johnson — once known for attacking radical Islamists and defending Israel — has in recent years been ridiculing far-right conspiracists. "Unbelievable," Johnson wrote in September. "Now the Christian far right is promoting the mind-bogglingly dim 'birther' conspiracy theory, with an IQ-destroying infomercial. . . . (The site pictures President Obama with the caption 'God's Enemy.')" [6]

Conservative blogger John Hawkins combined mockery with textual analysis in a 2006 debate with the author of a theory that President George W. Bush was planning to erode U.S. sovereignty. Jerome R. Corsi had written: "President Bush is pursuing a globalist agenda to create a North American Union, effectively erasing our borders with both Mexico and Canada. This was the hidden agenda behind the Bush ad-

Continued from p. 894

hierarchy where none exists, reading discipline into a voluntary organization, the Right fingers the CFR as the 'invisible government' that really runs the United States," writes conspiracism scholar Pipes. [46] The Trilateral Commission, a similar group founded in 1973, also prompts conspiracist suspicions.

Members of the far right have gone even farther back in time in tracing the roots of plotting against the United States. "The John Birch Society has long held that the conspiracy of the Illuminati . . . is the predecessor of a modern-day conspiracy warring against our country and civilization," John F. McManus, president of the right-wing organization, wrote in 2007. Long centered in Massachusetts, it is now based in Appleton, Wis., McCarthy's hometown.

JFK and Beyond

The assassination of President Kennedy in 1963 launched the modern era of conspiracism. Ordinary citizens by the thousands embraced conspiracy theories about "what really happened," and terms such as "grassy knoll" and "lone gunman" became staples of popular culture." [47]

Citizen interest in the assassination got a major boost when the murder of Kennedy's assassin, Lee Harvey Oswald, was broadcast live to millions of homes. Similarly, an 8 mm movie of the assas-

sination — shot by Abraham Zapruder, a bystander along Kennedy's limousine route — became a staple piece of evidence for assassination buffs, historians and conspiracists. [48]

The conclusion of the government commission headed by Chief Justice of the United States Earl Warren — that Oswald conceived and carried out the assassination by himself — was greeted skeptically by many. The most widely circulated theories said that U.S. military and business interests had had Kennedy killed because he opposed their plans to escalate the Vietnam War; or that the Cuban government and/or its Soviet patron were responsible, in retaliation for U.S. plans to have Cuban leader Fidel Castro killed.

ministration's true open-borders policy. . . . President Bush intends to abrogate U.S. sovereignty to the North American Union, a new economic and political entity which the President is quietly forming." [7]

Debating Corsi, Hawkins, editor of the "Right Wing News" Web site, wrote, "There's no real evidence . . . anywhere except in Jerome's fevered imagination. . . . The misleading trash you're cranking out on a weekly basis is duping people who would normally know better." [8]

Of course, the U.S.-Mexico-Canada borders remained intact after Bush's term ended. But Corsi, who rejects the conspiracy theorist label, maintains that North American integration plans remain in place. "Certainly the writing that I and others did brought the agenda to light," he says. "Largely, that was my goal."

Whatever the precise goals of those who embrace theories about Sept. 11 and other events, anti-conspiracists from the left argue that the theories do serious damage to the left-liberal side even when presented under its banner. Chomsky, in fact, argued that the "power centers" preferred to see activists obsessing about conspiracy theories. "It's a terrible drain of energy away from much more serious problems," he said. [9]

David Corn, Washington bureau chief for the leftist magazine *Mother Jones* and a harsh critic both of the Bush administration and the "truthers," pointed to the latter as largely responsible for the resignation under pressure of Obama administration environmental appointee Van Jones, who had signed a 2004 "truther" petition.

"The American taxpayers have lost a public servant who was uniquely qualified to help move the country in the right direction," Corn wrote in September. "Jones is responsible for his own actions, but the 9/11 truthers are also responsible for concocting and spreading the poison that he drank." [10]

— *Peter Katel*

[1] Larissa MacFarquhar, "The Devil's Accountant," *The New Yorker*, March 31, 2003.
[2] Noam Chomsky, *What We Say Goes: Conversations on U.S. Power in a Changing World*, interviews with David Barsamian (2007), pp. 35-37; excerpted in: "Noam Chomsky on the 9/11 Conspiracy Kooks," harmonicminor (blog), Sept. 21, 2009, http://harmonicminor.com/2009/09/21/noam-chomsky-on-the-911-conspiracy-kooks/.
[3] "Does Barack Obama have Kenyan citizenship?" Factcheck.org, Aug. 29, 2008, www.factcheck.org/askfactcheck/does_barack_obama_have_kenyan_citizenship.html.
[4] "Barack Obama — Obama was not born in the United States," *Conspiracy Science*, undated, http://conspiracyscience.com/articles/obama/obama-was-not-born-in-the-united-states/#obama_cannot_be_president_because_both_parents_must_be_citizens_for_one_to_be_eligible.
[5] "Anti-Semite Comedy Goldmine," *Conspiracy Science* blog, Sept. 27, 2009, http://conspiracyscience.com/blog/2009/09/27/anti-semite-comedy-goldmine.
[6] "Nirthers on Television," Little Green Footballs, Sept. 26, 2009, http://littlegreenfootballs.com/article/34760_Nirthers_on_Television.
[7] Jerome R. Corsi, "North American Union to Replace USA?" Human Events.com, May 19, 2006, www.humanevents.com/article.php?id=14965.
[8] "John Hawkins vs. Jery Corsi: Round 4," July 6, 2009, www.humanevents.com/rightangle/index.php?1=1&title=john_hawkins_vs_jerry_corsi_round_1.
[9] Chomsky, *op. cit.*
[10] David Corn, "How 9/11 Conspiracy Poison Did In Van Jones," *Inside Politics Daily*, Sept. 7, 2009, www.politicsdaily.com/2009/09/07/how-9-11-conspiracy-poison-did-in-van-jones/.

Mistrust of government in general grew even more in the late 1960s and early 1970s, as the Vietnam War ended in U.S. defeat in 1975, after years of optimistic official reports that the war was being won. Two years earlier, the Watergate scandal began coming to light, with its revelations of systematic official deceit and law-breaking and, ultimately, President Richard M. Nixon's resignation.

Reports of questionable government activities continued during the Gerald R. Ford administration. In 1975, a commission headed by Vice President Nelson Rockefeller reported on a massive pattern of illegal CIA activities within the United States during the 1960s. And the Senate conducted

a larger investigation headed by Sen. Frank Church, D-Idaho, that revealed the attempted FBI blackmail of the Rev. Martin Luther King Jr., the CIA's attempt to use Mafia members to assassinate Castro, assassination plots against other foreign leaders and a host of other actions that might once have been dubbed the ravings of conspiracy theorists.

During President Ronald Reagan's two-terms (1981-1989), White House officials were revealed to have been involved in a scheme to sell arms to the Islamic revolutionary government of Iran — a hostile power — in an effort to secretly raise money for weapons for U.S.-supported guerrillas fighting the Soviet-backed Nicaraguan government.

The chain of scandals contributed to a sense that the real actions of government were so secretive they were only rarely revealed.

Against that backdrop, President George H. W. Bush described the geopolitical scene as the Soviet Union neared collapse — and as a U.S.-assembled alliance was preparing to oust Iraqi dictator Saddam Hussein's army from Kuwait in 1990 — as the hoped-for beginning of a "new world order." Conspiracists seized on the term as a kind of admission that the global elite — an updated version of the Illuminati — were bent on submitting the United States to internationalist rule.

In 1991, TV evangelist and one-time Republican presidential primary

Secret Files Shed Light on Real Conspiracies

"Operation Northwoods" fed suspicions about government plots.

Some conspiracy theories sound unbelievable, and they are. Others sound just as wild, but the paper trails they have left erase any doubts.

In 1962, soon after the Cuban Missile Crisis, Gen. Lyman L. Lemnitzer, chairman of the Joint Chiefs of Staff, proposed a series of fake Cuban attacks on the United States or its allies designed to provide a pretext for U.S. military intervention in Cuba.

"Operation Northwoods," which was never approved, is one of a series of secret plans that, once revealed, provided supporting evidence for conspiracists who believe in secret plots by government agents.

The government's penchant for keeping secrets confers some value on conspiracy theories, says historian Kathryn Olmsted of the University of California, Davis. "They get people skeptical and demanding answers," she says. "And you get big investigations that, at times, produce a lot of information."

For example, Olmsted writes, a controversial *San Jose Mercury-News* investigation of an alleged CIA partnership with Central American drug dealers prompted a CIA internal investigation. That probe effectively confirmed that agency officials had worked closely with traffickers because they were part of a campaign to destabilize the communist-supported Nicaraguan government.[1] However, the newspaper's probe veered into conspiracism when it blamed the CIA, through its trafficker allies, of playing a key role in sparking the crack cocaine boom of the 1980s and '90s

"Operation Northwoods" took far longer to come to light. The scheme included a shootdown — elaborately engineered to look like Cuban action — of a pilotless drone aircraft designed as an exact replica of a plane carrying passengers; shootings of Cuban exiles in Miami and the blowing up of a ship off the U.S. Naval Base at Guantánamo.[2]

Kennedy administration Defense Secretary Robert McNamara threw out the entire proposal, wrote author James L. Bamford, who discovered the "Northwoods" memo in 2001, months before the Sept. 11 attacks.[3]

In the years that followed, the "Northwoods" documents took on new life as support material for 9/11 "truther" theories.

"Some of the ideas, such as the proposal to 'blow up a U.S. ship in Guantánamo Bay and blame Cuba,' would have required killing Americans," wrote James Ray Griffin, a retired professor of philosophy and religion at Claremont School of Theology and a "truther" activist, suggesting that the government wasn't beyond manufacturing the 9/11 attack.[4]

Ten years after the "Northwoods" proposal, The Associated Press reported that the U.S. Public Health Service had for decades been injecting syphilis germs into illiterate black sharecroppers in Alabama without telling them what they were receiving. The justification was that the disease's effects could be studied. The so-called "Tuskegee Experiment" was named after Tuskegee Institute (now Tuskegee University) Hospital, where the project was carried out.[5]

The experiment helped sustain a strong belief today among black Americans — hit hard by HIV — that AIDS was produced in a government laboratory. About 50 percent of African-Americans share that view, according to a 2002-2003 survey by the RAND Corp. think tank and Oregon State University.[6]

"The government lied about inventing the HIV virus as a means of genocide against people of color," the Rev. Jeremiah Wright of Chicago said during one of the sermons that caused then-presidential candidate Barack Obama to back away from his ex-pastor.[7]

Wright later cited the Tuskegee experiment in defending his statement. "I believe our government is capable of doing anything," Wright said at the National Press Club.[8]

No credible scientific evidence exists to support the notion that the government developed AIDS. But an AIDS-origin conspiracy did exist in the Soviet intelligence establishment. In the mid-1980s, when the AIDS epidemic was generating global alarm, the Soviet Union heavily promoted the notion that the U.S. military invented AIDS. "The AIDS virus is the unfortunate

candidate Pat Robertson promoted this conspiratorial vision in a best-selling book, *New World Order.* He wrote of "a single thread (that) runs from the White House to the State Department to the Council on Foreign Relations to the Trilateral Commission to secret societies to extreme New Agers." Robertson also invoked the specter of the Illuminati, the purported villains in the oldest conspiracy theory in U.S. history: "The New Age religions, the beliefs of the Illuminati, and Illumi-

nated Freemasonry all seem to move along parallel tracks with world communism and world finance."[49]

The flames of conspiracism that Robertson helped fan reached new heights during Bill Clinton's two terms (1993-2001). Clinton and his wife, Hillary, were targeted by a series of allegations about their real estate dealings and commodities trades that grew progressively more conspiratorial, especially after the 1993 suicide of lawyer Vincent Foster, a senior White House aide.

Hardcore anti-Clinton activists developed a wealth of evidence that showed, they said, that Foster had been murdered, possibly on the Clintons' orders — contrary to what police and an independent counsel reported.[50]

In addition to Foster's death, Clinton conspiracists also zeroed in on Clinton's supposed involvement in drug-smuggling and the training of Nicaraguan guerrillas while he had been Arkansas governor.[51]

product of work in preparation for waging bacteriological war," a Soviet-bloc scientist, Jakob Segal of East Germany, wrote in the English-language *Moscow News* in 1987. [9]

Distributed by a Soviet press agency, versions of the conspiracy theory appeared in newspapers in 50 countries, a Reagan administration official wrote in 1987. "Obviously the United States is technically capable of almost anything," a government official in Africa told Deputy Assistant Secretary of State Kathleen Bailey. "Also, why would such a story be in so many newspapers if it's not true?" [10]

Further instigating suspicion about U.S. government activities, an American spy agency waited until 1995 to release documentary evidence of spying by hundreds of Americans for the Soviet Union before and during World War II.

The "Venona Papers" were a series of decryptions by American and British decoding experts of messages between spy-handlers in the United States and their bosses in Moscow.

Venona was so secret that even President Harry S Truman was kept in the dark — though Moscow knew about the project by 1949. "The president thus saw little proof of a real espionage conspiracy but heard many tales told by self-interested and alarmist conspiracists," historian Olmsted writes. As a result, Truman remained highly skeptical of reports of Soviet spying. [11]

A few years later, Sen. Joseph McCarthy, R-Wis., made his wild accusations of a government completely penetrated by Soviet spies. The charge flourished because only a handful of people were aware about how much the government actually knew. "Had we learned about the Venona Project in the late 1940s, had the FBI revealed it was following Soviet spies, that would have shut up McCarthy," argues historian John E. Moser of Ohio's Ashland University,

In the end, Moser says, excessive government secrecy can provide fertile soil for conspiracy theories. "So many theories from the 18th and 19th centuries focused on monasteries and convents, because they were closed institutions. A fevered imagi-

nation can come up with all kinds of ideas."

Indeed, some Kennedy assassination experts say that the CIA — to this day — is giving conspiracists plenty of grounds for suspicion. The spy agency is still fighting releasing documents concerning a CIA officer's ties to an anti-Castro group that clashed with Lee Harvey Oswald, who later killed Kennedy, *The New York Times* reported on Oct. 16. [12]

Gerald Posner, author of a book rebutting conspiracy theories of the assassination, says of the CIA's conduct: "It feeds the conspiracy theorists who say, 'You're hiding something.' " [13]

— Peter Katel

[1] Kathryn Olmsted, *Real Enemies: Conspiracy Theories and American Democracy, World I to 9/11* (2009), pp. 188-192.

[2] "Pentagon Proposed Pretexts for Cuba Invasion in 1962," National Security Archive, April 30, 2001, www.gwu.edu/~nsarchiv/news/20010430.

[3] James L. Bamford, "Bush wrong to use pretext as excuse to invade Iraq," *USA Today*, Aug. 29, 2002, p. A13.

[4] David Ray Griffin, "The American Empire and 9/11," 2007, www.journalof911studies.com/volume/200704/DavidRayGriffin911Empire.pdf.

[5] Borgna Brunner, "The Tuskegee Syphilis Experiment," undated, Tuskegee University, www.tuskegee.edu/global/story.asp?s=1207586

[6] Jeffrey Weiss, "Obama pastor Jeremiah Wright's incendiary quotes illuminate chasm between races," Dallasnews.com, April 8, 2008, www.dallasnews.com/sharedcontent/dws/dn/religion/stories/040808dnmetwrightchasm.442a11fb.html.

[7] "Best of Jeremiah Wright's Sermons Pt. 1," YouTube, March 15, 2008 (posting date), www.youtube.com/watch?v=617eK2XIaLk.

[8] "The Full Wright Transcript," Marc Ambinder blog, April 28, 2008, http://marcambinder.theatlantic.com/archives/2008/04/the_full_wright_transcript.php.

[9] "AIDS Virus Product of Genetic Manipulation," BBC Summary of World Broadcasts, April 29, 1987.

[10] Kathleen Bailey, "Soviets Sponsor Spread of AIDS Disinformation," *Los Angeles Times* (op-ed), April 19, 1987, Part 5, p. 2.

[11] Olmsted, *ibid.*, pp. 91-92; Steven T. Usdin, *Engineering Communism: How Two Americans Spied for Stalin and Founded the Soviet Silicon Valley* (2005), pp. 122-125.

[12] Scott Shane, "C.I.A. Is Still Cagey About Oswald Mystery," *The New York Times*, Oct. 16, 2009, www.nytimes.com/2009/10/17/us/17inquire.html?hpw.

[13] Quoted in *ibid.*

Meanwhile, two deadly events sparked a wave of far-right conspiratorial thinking. In 1992, a mother and son were killed by federal agents during the siege of a right-wing survivalist family at Ruby Ridge, in northern Idaho. A year later came the botched confrontation and lethal fire at the Branch Davidian compound near Waco, Texas. [52]

In far-right circles, the deaths were interpreted in light of a conspiracist belief that black helicopters were constantly sweeping through the U.S.-

Canadian border area in preparation for military occupation by U.N. troops that would rule the United States as part of the "New World Order." [53]

However, another leading conspiracist, Linda Thompson, who headed the Indianapolis-based America Justice Federation, took a more limited view of the black helicopters. Holding that the government murdered the Waco cult members, she claimed the choppers were part of a CIA-sponsored "private mafia" aiming at "a military

takeover of the United States through a combination of drug running, gun running, lobbying, blackmailing congressmen and terrorism." [54]

Thompson's was a prominent voice of the militia movement, a loosely organized group that included far-right extremists and apolitical survivalists, many given to conspiracism. The movement virtually disappeared after the 1995 bombing of the federal building in Oklahoma City by Army veteran McVeigh, who had traveled in militia circles. ∎

CURRENT SITUATION

Swine Flu Plot?

Medical professionals are battling a host of conspiracy theories and other scares about the swine flu pandemic and the vaccine against it.

"We have the right vaccine for this virus," Health and Human Services Secretary Kathleen Sebelius told ABC News in early October. "We also have years of clinical data on seasonal flu vaccine and a great safety record." [55]

Yet 41 percent of adults told pollsters for the Harvard School of Public Health they won't get vaccinated. And only 51 percent said they definitely would vaccinate their children. [56]

Forty-eight percent of those not getting vaccinated said lack of trust in public officials' information on the vaccine played a role in their decision. [57] The survey didn't ask about the sources of that mistrust, but flu-related conspiracy theories have been flying around the Web since news of the new flu strain broke last spring.

Dr. Paul A. Offitt, chief of infectious diseases at the Children's Hospital of Philadelphia, sees two major schools of conspiracism — the belief the U.S. Centers for Disease Control and Prevention is misrepresenting or falsifying data, and that profit-obsessed pharmaceutical companies are indifferent to vaccine quality.

"As far as the most extreme theories — that they're making products to kill us — that is so outlandish that I have trouble commenting on it," Offitt says.

Yet such over-the-top theories are plentiful. Mike Adams, editor of a "natural health" Web site, asked readers in April: "Could world governments, spooked by the prospect of radical climate change

caused by overpopulation of the planet, have assembled a super-secret task force to engineer and distribute a super-virulent strain of influenza designed to 'correct' the human population (and institute global Martial Law)?" [58]

A writer for the respected British magazine *New Scientist* dismissed such speculation. "Deliberately engineering a virus of this kind would be a huge challenge," wrote Michael Le Page, though he conceded a laboratory mistake could conceivably have a played a role. [59]

Extreme conspiracism that sees the H1N1 flu and/or the vaccine as deliberately fatal coexists with generalized suspicion. Right-wing radio and TV hosts Glenn Beck and Rush Limbaugh have been skeptical and belligerently suspicious, respectively. "Screw you, Mrs. Sebelius! I'm not going to take it precisely because you're telling me I must," Limbaugh shouted on his show. [60]

But Limbaugh's response was mild compared with some of the flu conspiracies taking shape on the Web. "In the next few months, we are about to face our own American soldiers who have killed and maimed indiscriminately in Iraq and Afghanistan," wrote Ilya Sandra Perlingieri, who writes frequently on health matters from an anti-medical establishment viewpoint. "These soldiers will now probably be deployed to accompany FEMA to come door-to-door into our homes to force us to take these poisonous injections. . . . We are at the brink of even the loss of our very own lives all under the guise of protecting us from a non-existent 'pandemic.' [They will] genetically engineer the flu in some bioweapons lab, and then create debilitating and deathly vaccines that will do further harm to everyone." [61]

Perlingieri's denunciation was posted on rense.com, a site with a heavy interest in Holocaust denial and so-called anti-Zionism. One graphic on the site shows a baby about to be stabbed to death on an altar bearing a Star of David overlaid with a "Z" as Obama and other world leaders,

dressed in black robes, look on.

Outside that wing of the conspiracist community, the focus is on pharmaceutical companies. Paul Joseph Watson, a writer on Alex Jones' "Prison Planet" site blames a "mammoth level of fearmongering" on drug firms' appetite for profits during a recession. The high level of public resistance to the vaccine is anti-corporate victory in the face "of such a huge effort on behalf of the pharmaceutical industry and their soapbox, the mass media." [62]

"Birthers" Challenged

U.S. District Judge David O. Carter of Orange County, Calif., is weighing dismissal of a lawsuit challenging President Obama's citizenship and, consequently, his eligibility for office. If the recent actions of other federal judges in similar suits are any guide, the suit's chances are slender.

All of the legal action has centered on what the "birther" movement insists is lack of definitive official proof that Obama was born in the United States — evidence to the contrary notwithstanding. Orly Taitz, the Southern California lawyer who has filed the most recent of these cases, takes that claim of a non-U.S. birthplace several steps further.

Taitz told *The Washington Post* she thought Obama had been born in Kenya — his father's native country — then brought to Hawaii by his mother, who persuaded state workers to falsify his birth record. She also entertained the idea — a common one among "birthers" — that Obama was also a citizen of Indonesia, where he lived for several years as a child while his mother was married to her second husband, who was Indonesian. "He is lying about his identity, he is hiding his whole identity, this is dangerous!" Taitz told the newspaper. [63]

Weeks earlier, U.S. District Judge Clay D. Land of Columbus, Ga., had

Continued on p. 902

At Issue:

Are conspiracy theories now a threat to democracy?

CHIP BERLET
SENIOR ANALYST
POLITICAL RESEARCH ASSOCIATES

WRITTEN FOR *CQ RESEARCHER*, OCT. 15, 2009

JOHN E. MOSER
PROFESSOR OF HISTORY
ASHLAND UNIVERSITY

WRITTEN FOR *CQ RESEARCHER*, OCT. 15, 2009

conspiracy theories are not harmless. They are exaggerated stories falsely portraying a scapegoated group as plotting against the common good. Throughout the history of our country, mass movements have been built around conspiracy theories targeting witches, Freemasons, Catholics, Jews, immigrants and "Reds."

In the 1800s, an angry mob near Boston was so enraged by conspiracy stories about Catholic priests and nuns that it burned a convent school to the ground. Between 1919 and 1921, thousands of Italian and Russian immigrants were rounded up and deported by our government based on conspiracy fearmongering falsely targeting them as subversives and terrorists. The McCarthy period illustrated the damage conspiracy theories can do to a society.

The administration of President Bill Clinton was sidetracked by waves of conspiracy theories claiming he had ordered the assassination of a key aide or was plotting a U.N. takeover of America with jackbooted troops arriving in black helicopters.

Now the "birthers" and other conspiracy theorists circulate false allegations that President Obama is not really a U.S. citizen; is planning to merge the U.S., Canada and Mexico into a North American Union or that he is a secret Muslim plotting more terror attacks. The xenophobic and racist subtext here is clear. Some people have acted on these base and baseless claims. Since Obama's inauguration there have been nine murders where the alleged killers have been entangled in white supremacist or anti-Semitic conspiracy theories.

James W. von Brunn, accused of killing a guard at the U.S. Holocaust Memorial Museum in Washington, D.C., feared a conspiracy of Jews and Freemasons to control the world and keep white Christians subjugated while at the same time elevating blacks to undeserved positions of power. Other conspiracists blame Muslims, immigrants, Mexicans, feminists and gay people.

The recent "Tea Party" protests and town hall disruptions are awash in conspiracy claims and false and misleading information. Democracy is based on informed consent — not myths and lies woven into conspiracy theories.

It is unlikely that conspiracy theorists will overthrow the government. They can, however, poison the body politic; distort and derail public policy debates; spread bigotry and paranoia and wind up some people so tightly that they commit acts of violence against targeted scapegoats. Conspiracy theories are toxic to democracy.

angry right-wing talk radio hosts suggest that financier/philanthropist George Soros is secretly pulling the strings of the Obama White House, while equally angry "birthers" deny that the president was born in the United States. A few years ago, we heard from the left that the election of 2000 had been "stolen," that 9/11 was an "inside job" and that Halliburton, the global oil field services company once headed by Dick Cheney, was secretly behind the war in Iraq.

Conspiracy theories do seem to be everywhere in today's society, although, like body odor, they are generally things that other people have. Are they a threat to our democracy? One might be tempted to say so, until one recognizes that conspiracy theories have an old and distinguished place in American political history. It is hard to imagine that the War of Independence would have been fought had Britain's American colonists in 1775 not been convinced that George III was actively plotting to enslave them. New Englanders were convinced in the late 1790s that the country had been infiltrated by members of a secret organization known as the Bavarian Illuminati, and Thomas Jefferson, it was claimed, was one of their agents.

Nor is it likely that there would have been a Civil War — or the subsequent destruction of slavery — had it not been for Northern claims of a "slave power conspiracy," matched only by the Southern notion that their neighbors to the North were intent on destroying their way of life. Fears of communist subversion shaped the 1950s as surely as theories over who shot President Kennedy influenced the 1960s.

Some may claim, however, that conspiracy theories pose a greater danger today because they seem to circulate so quickly. This is certainly the case, thanks largely to so-called "new media" such as talk radio, the Internet and 24-hour news networks. Moreover, thanks to the Watergate scandal, Americans today understand that major conspiracies can, and do, exist.

Yet what is striking about so many of the conspiracy theories that have found adherents throughout American history is that they all purport to identify threats to our form of government. In addition, they represent a deep distrust of traditional authority, whether it be the government, corporations, the mainstream media or "the experts." In other words, far from being a danger, the presence of such theories — as silly as most of them are — might actually be seen as a sign of a healthy democracy.

Continued from p. 900

dismissed a similar case, ruling that it was based on "sheer conjecture and speculation." The judge also remarked that Taitz "is a self-proclaimed leader in what has become known as 'the birther movement.' " [64]

Taitz fired back with a motion to remove Land from the case. In it, she called "birther" a "pejorative appellation (often coupled with even more colorful epithets such as 'batshit crazy')." [65]

The preferred designation among Obama birth-certificate challengers is "eligibility movement." [66]

Even before Obama was elected, some of them questioned why his original birth certificate wasn't on file in the Hawaii public records system. Hawaii had stored all original birth certificates, making them available only to people with "a tangible interest" in the documents. The state does make available a "certification of live birth" — as opposed to a "certificate" — which states that Obama was born in Hawaii. [67]

Then, in early August, *WorldNet Daily*, a Web site that has made the theme a specialty, posted a story reporting that Taitz's discovery of an alleged Kenyan birth certificate for Obama could be "the smoking gun" of the entire subject. [68]

But *Politifact*, a fact-checking arm of the *St. Petersburg Times*, reported persuasive evidence that the "Kenyan" certificate was a digitally altered Australian birth certificate that its owner had posted on a genealogy Web site. "Same format," *Politifact* said. "Same book and page number in the birth registry. Some of the officials' last names were even the same." Factcheck.org, owned by the University of Pennsylvania's Annenberg Public Policy Center, has also concluded that challenges to Obama's citizenship are groundless. [69]

By the time *Politifact* posted its report, *WorldNet Daily*'s editor and CEO, Joseph Farah, had backed away from the story. "No one here has made a judgment that it is real," he wrote. [70]

Farah went on to question the "Certification of Live Birth" that *Politifact* posted. "Anyone could march into a Hawaii Public Health Department office and say he or she had a baby, fill out a form with the pertinent details, sign it and there would be no questions asked," he wrote. [71]

But even before the election, Chiyome Fukino, Hawaii Health Department director, said that she and the registrar of vital statistics "have personally seen and verified that the Hawaii State Department of Health has Sen. Obama's original birth certificate on record." [72]

Robert Farley of *Politifact* acknowledged that Obama hasn't posted his original birth certificate. "Maybe the original would identify the hospital where Obama was born, but that's irrelevant," he wrote. "The issue is in what city, and therefore country, was he born. The document posted by the campaign proves Obama was born in Honolulu, according to Health Department officials. And that's really the central issue here." [73]

Even outside the *WorldNet Daily* orbit, not everyone agrees Obama has resolved the issue satisfactorily. "There are legitimate questions about the documentation of Obama's birth certificate," Camille Paglia, a political iconoclast who largely supports Obama, said on National Public Radio's "Fresh Air" in September. "I'm sorry, I've been following this closely from the start." [74]

Others argue that those challenging Obama's eligibility are operating outside the world of fact and evidence. "If the long-form birth certificate were released, with its unequivocal identification of Hawaii as Obama's place of birth, the cycle would almost certainly continue," Alex Koppleman, a staff writer for the online magazine *Salon*, wrote before Obama was sworn in. He noted that talk-show hosts Limbaugh and Savage, as well as author Corsi, had questioned Obama's mid-campaign trip to Hawaii to see his dying grandmother. "It's got to do with his birth certificate," Savage said of the trip. [75]

Obama may well have concluded

that releasing his original birth certificate would never quiet the attackers. "As long as he doesn't, the 'birthers' are going to keep going, and as long as they do, they're going to look ridiculous," suggests Ashland University historian Moser. "The people who believe in the theory, they're never going to go for him. So why not keep it alive?" ∎

OUTLOOK

Looking for Answers

Conspiracy theories will be part of the national conversation over the next decade, Moser says. "This is a side effect of America losing its unquestioned position of dominance in the world that it has enjoyed since World War II," he explains. "We're not going to become a Third World country, but we're not going to be on top, as many Americans are used to seeing the United States. People are going to look for conspiracy theories to explain that."

At the same time, he's skeptical that conspiracism will come to dominate the political landscape. "You can be a listener to talk radio and enjoy it, but that doesn't mean you're going to buy into the whole master theory," he says, likening talk radio to pro wrestling.

But the political system may be vulnerable in ways that an entertainment spectacle is not, argues Berlet of Political Research Associates. "Conspiracism is a threat because democracy is not a stable system," he says. "It's constantly being buffeted by people who want to subdue subversives or an external threat. Constant waves of scapegoating and bigotry have to be pushed back."

Moreover, Berlet says, the so-called mainstream media have effectively relinquished their monitoring role — "watchdogs on Valium," he calls them. "There are no stories about maybe something is wrong in society if people are this unhappy. There is almost no analytical presence in the media that most people consume — no coverage of ideas."

However, conservative blogger John Hawkins says fact-based Web media can react more quickly when conspiracy theories appear. "In the old world, media didn't have to address these," he says. "In the new world, people will address them and kill them in their cradle."

Speed is important, Hawkins says, because of the Web's oft-noted role in propagating conspiracy theories. "I think it's very important to turn these things around before people get them in their heads," he says. "If you do a Google search on a conspiracy theory, you'll find 50 articles all borrowing from each other, each saying there's a conspiracy. Joe Average will say, 'Maybe it's true; I don't see anything going in the other direction.'"

Historian Olmsted at the University of California is uncertain if conspiracism will gather strength over the next decade, noting that the "truther" theories lost momentum once Bush left office. For now, "There is always a surge in conspiracy theories when there's an economic crisis," she says. "Also, it seems that the election of an African-American president has triggered the anxieties of a significant segment of the white population."

Along the same lines, anti-conspiracist Web writer Winston of St. Louis also notes an Obama effect. "If he's reelected, I would say that conspiracy theories definitely will not die down."

Winston adds, "A minority of them are dangerous enough to warrant people being a little worried about them."

Still, conspiracy expert Pipes hasn't seen present-day theories rise to the level they sometimes reached in the early and middle 19th century.

Further, some well-known conspiracy theories center on the facts of past events, Pipes notes. So, by definition, these theories look backward instead of forward. As a result, "Something like the 'truther' phenomenon looks pretty impactless," he says.

But radio host Jones is looking to the future. And it's a grim one. "You're in locked-down prison cities," he said, in a message that he says is aimed at people living 20 or 30 years from now. "Your mother, your father, your children are dying from the bioweapons, you're dying from the engineered cancers."[76]

The only positive feature of this horrific universe, Jones said, is that people would know who their enemies are. "If you're listening to me 20-30 years in the future," he said, "just please fight against the new world order." As for present-day listeners who laugh at Jones' forecast, he called them "buffoons."[77]

Clearly, Jones has a perspective on the future. But even conspiracy theories that don't focus on what's ahead may build constituencies for forward-looking theories. "My guess is that people who believe in the 'birther' theory have probably folded it into other conspiracy theories," says Syracuse University's Barkun.

Whether conspiracy theories maintain their present momentum or not, Barkun says one facet of conspiracist thinking seems unlikely to change: adherents' resistance to argument. "Some months ago I got an e-mail from someone teaching at a university in Montana," he says. "All her neighbors were listening to Alex Jones. What could she do about it? How could she convince them they were mistaken? I told her, I don't think you can do anything."

Statement of Ownership Management, Circulation

Act of Aug. 12, 1970: Section 3685, Title 39, United States Code

Title of Publication: CQ Researcher. Date of filing: October 1, 2009. Frequency of issue: Weekly (Except for 1/2, 5/22, 7/3, 7/10, 8/14, 8/21, 11/27, 12/25/09). No. of issues published annually: 44. Annual subscription price for libraries, businesses and government: $803. Location of known office of publication: CQ Press, 2300 N Street, N.W., Suite 800, Washington, D.C. 20037. Names and addresses of publisher, editor and managing editor: Publisher, John A. Jenkins, CQ Press, 2300 N Street, N.W., Suite 800, Washington, D.C. 20037; Managing Editor, Thomas J. Colin, CQ Press, 2300 N Street, N.W., Suite 800, Washington, D.C. 20037. Owner: SAGE Publications, Inc., McCune Inter-Vivos Trust, David F. McCune, 2455 Teller Road, Thousand Oaks, CA 91320. Known bondholders, mortgagees and other security holders owning or holding 1 percent or more of total amount of bonds, mortgages or other securities: None.

Extent and Nature of Circulation	Average Number of Copies of Each Issue During Preceding 12 months	Actual Number of Copies of Single Issue Published Nearest to Filing Date
A. Total number of copies printed (Net press run)	1,597	1,501
B. Paid and/or requested circulation		
(1) Paid/requested outside-county mail subscriptions stated on Form 3541	1,283	1,237
(2) Paid in-county subscriptions stated on Form 3541	25	25
(3) Sales through dealers and carriers, street vendors, counter sales, and other non-USPS paid distribution	25	25
(4) Other classes mailed through the USPS	—	—
C. Total paid and/or requested circulation	1,333	1,287
D. Free distribution by mail (Samples, complimentary, and other free copies)		
(1) Outside-county as stated on Form 3541	—	—.
(2) In-county as stated on Form 3541	—	—
(3) Other classes mailed through the USPS	75	75
E. Free distribution outside the mail (Carriers or other means)	—	—
F. Total free distribution	75	75
G. Total distribution	1,408	1,362
H. Copies not distributed	158	100
I. Total	1,566	1,462
J. Percent paid and/or requested circulation	95%	94%

Notes

[1] "FEMA Concentration Camps, Rant (Part 1)," "Alex Jones Show," Feb. 9, 2009, www.youtube.com/watch?v=qecd5d-fySc&feature=related.

[2] "Alex Jones Interviews Charlie Sheen," Infowars.com, Sept. 8, 2009, www.infowars.com/

twenty-minutes-with-the-president/; Lee Fang, "Gohmert Trades Ideas With Conspiracy Theorist," ThinkProgress, July 27, 2009 (audio clip), http://thinkprogress.org/2009/07/27/gohmert.conspiracies.alexjones.

[3] Alexa, the Web Information Company, Oct. 7, 2009, www.alexa.com/siteinfo/infowars.com.

[4] "Top 10 Reasons Why No Man Has Ever Set Foot on the Moon," Moonmovie.com, undated, www.moonmovie.com/moonmovie/default.asp; Christina Caron, "Refuting the Most Popular Apollo Moon Landing Hoax Theories," ABC News, July 19, 2009, http://abcnews.go.com/Technology/Apollo11MoonLanding/story?id=8104410&page=1&page=1; "The Great Moon Hoax," NASA, Feb. 23, 2001, http://science.nasa.gov/headlines/y2001/ast23Feb_2.htm.

[5] "Obama's approval steady," Public Policy Polling, Sept. 23, 2009, www.publicpolicypolling.com/pdf/PPP_Release_National_819513.pdf.

[6] "22% Believe Bush Knew About 9/11 Attacks in Advance," Rasmussen Reports, May 4, 2007, www.rasmussenreports.com/public_content/politics/current_events/bush_administration/22_believe_bush_knew_about_9_11_attacks_in_advance.

[7] Kathleen Hunter and Jonathan Allen, "Senate Affirms Obama's U.S. Citizenship," CQ Today, July 28, 2009.

[8] Ibid., and "Conservative media figures alleged Obama's Hawaii trip is about discredited birth-certificate rumors, not his ailing grandmother," Media Matters for America, Oct. 23, 2008, http://mediamatters.org/research/200810230020.

[9] "Respected Leaders and Families Launch 9/11 Truth Statement Demanding Deeper Investigation Into Events of 9/11," 911Truth.org, Oct. 26, 2004, www.911truth.org/article.php?story=20041026093059633.

[10] David Dunbar and Brad Reagan, eds., Debunking 9/11 Myths: Why Conspiracy Theories Can't Stand Up to the Facts (2006).

[11] Quoted in Sharon Haddock, "Beck's backing bumps Skousen book to top," Deseret News, March 20, 2009, www.deseretnews.com/article/1,5143,705292222,00.html?pg=1.

[12] "The History of Secret Combinations, Part 3," W. Cleon Skousen, 1976, YouTube, www.youtube.com/watch?v=I8fo6bdudVI&feature=related.

[13] "Glenn Beck analyzes fascist and communist symbolism in artwork at Rockefeller Center," YouTube, Sept. 2, 2009, /www.youtube.com/watch?v=xWL-pfCao-U.

[14] Glenn Beck interview, @katiecouric, CBS News, Sept. 22, 2009, www.cbsnews.com/video/watch/?id=5330485n&tag=cbsnewsSectionsArea.0.

[15] "Alex Jones — Corsi Pt2," "Alex Jones Show," May 4, 2009, www.youtube.com/watch?v=j2qKUhdjHj8&feature=related.

[16] "Hastings Reintroduces National Emergency Centers Establishment Act," Hastings Web site, Jan. 22, 2009, http://alceehastings.house.gov/index.php?option=com_content&task=view&id=243&Itemid=98; H.R. 645, http://thomas.loc.gov/cgi-bin/query/z?c111:H.R.645.

[17] Jerome R. Corsi, "Bill creates detention camps in U.S. for 'emergencies,' " WorldNet Daily, Feb. 1, 2009, www.wnd.com/index.php?pageId=87757.

[18] "The Drug Cartel and Pandemic H1N1 Swine Flu Viruses and Vaccines," Infowars, Sept. 21, 2009, www.infowars.com/the-drug-cartel-and-pandemic-h1n1-swine-flu-viruses-and-vaccines/; Leonard G. Horowitz, "Introgenocide: The Biotechnology, Politics, and Economics of Emerging Pandemics," Tetrahedron Publishing Group, undated, www.tetrahedron.org.

[19] "Alex Jones TV," July 21, 2009, www.youtube.com/watch?v=KkoHZ4DylH4.

[20] "09.12.09 March on Washington: The Tea Party Movement Goes to Capitol Hill," http://912dc.org; Talking Points Memo, www.talkingpointsmemo.com/gallery/2009/09/hearses-nazi-dogs-and-crucified-liberty-scenes-from-the-912-march.php?img=24.

[21] Chip Berlet, "Toxic to Democracy: Conspiracy Theories, Demonization & Scapegoating," Political Research Associates, 2009, www.publiceye.org/conspire/toxic2democracy/Toxic-2D-all-rev-04.pdf.

[22] Kathryn S. Olmsted, Real Enemies: Conspiracy Theories and American Democracy, World War I to 9/11 (2009).

[23] John E. Moser, Right Turn: John T. Flynn and the Transformation of American Liberalism (2005).

[24] Richard Hofstadter, The Paranoid Style in American Politics (2008 edition), pp. 23-24. For a view of Hofstadter as ahead of his time, see Thomas Frank, "From John Birchers to Birthers," The Wall Street Journal, Oct. 21, 2009, p. A21.

[25] Michael Lerner, "The Antiwar Anti-Semites," The Wall Street Journal, Feb. 12, 2003, www.opinionjournal.com/editorial/feature.html?id=110003061.

[26] Quoted in Daniel Pipes, Conspiracy: How the Paranoid Style Flourishes and Where It Comes From (1997), p. 175.

[27] Among numerous books on the subject, see Lawrence Wright, The Looming Tower: Al-Qaeda and the Road to 9/11 (2006).

[28] Ibid., p. 346.

[29] For background, see Peter Katel, "Hate Groups," CQ Researcher, May 8, 2009, pp. 421-448.

[30] Ibid.

[31] Juliet Lapidos, "The AIDS Conspiracy Handbook," Slate, March 19, 2008, www.slate.com/id/2186860/

[32] Jeffrey L. Pasley, "Conspiracy Theory and American Exceptionalism from the Revolution to Roswell," paper for symposium, May 13, 2000, http://pasleybrothers.com/conspiracy/CT_and_American_Exceptionalism_web_version.htm.

[33] Unless otherwise indicated, this subsection is drawn from Jeffrey L. Pasley, "Illuminati," chapter in Peter Knight, ed. Conspiracy Theories in American History: An Encyclopedia (2003); chapter published separately online at http://pasleybrothers.com/conspiracy/readings/Pasley_CTAHE_articles.pdf; and Hofstadter, op. cit.

[34] Quoted in ibid., p. 17.

[35] Ibid., pp. 19-20.

[36] James C. Foley, "Slave Power," in Knight, op. cit., pp. 658-662.

[37] Pipes, op. cit., p. 91.

[38] Michael Barkun, A Culture of Conspiracy: Apocalyptic Visions in Contemporary America (2003), pp. 51, 128.

[39] Except where otherwise noted, material on Pearl Harbor and subsequent events are drawn from Kathryn S. Olmsted, Real Enemies: Con-

About the Author

Peter Katel is a *CQ Researcher* staff writer who previously reported on Haiti and Latin America for *Time* and *Newsweek* and covered the Southwest for newspapers in New Mexico. He has received several journalism awards, including the Bartolomé Mitre Award for coverage of drug trafficking, from the Inter-American Press Association. He holds an A.B. in university studies from the University of New Mexico. His recent reports include "Mexico's Drug War," "Hate Groups" and "Vanishing Jobs."

spiracy Theories and American Democracy, World War I to 9/11 (2009).

[40] Quoted in *ibid.*, p. 79.

[41] Quoted in Steven T. Usdin, *Engineering Communism: How Two Americans Spied for Stalin and Founded the Soviet Silicon Valley* (2005); Sam Tanenhaus, *Whittaker Chambers: A Biography* (1998).

[42] Pipes, *op. cit.*, p. 116; the subcommittee's closed sessions are now online, "Historic Senate Hearings Published," United States Senate, www.senate.gov/artandhistory/history/common/generic/McCarthy_Transcripts.htm.

[43] Quoted in Usdin, *op. cit.*, p. 151. See also Sam Roberts, "57 Years Later, Figure in Rosenberg Case Says He Spied for Soviets," *The New York Times*, Sept. 12, 2008, p. A1.

[44] Peter Grose, "Continuing the Inquiry: The Council on Foreign Relations From 1921 to 1996," Council on Foreign Relations, undated, www.cfr.org/about/history/cfr/.

[45] Dan Smoot, *The Invisible Government* (1962), available online, www.gutenberg.org/files/20224/20224-h/20224-h.htm.

[46] Pipes, *op. cit.*, p. 116.

[47] Except where otherwise indicated, material for this subsection is drawn from Olmsted, *op. cit.*

[48] The film is now viewable on the Web; "The Zapruder Film," www.youtube.com/watch?v=E66__vymfPA.

[49] Quoted in Paul Feldman, "Conspiracy Talk a U.S. Tradition," *Los Angeles Times*, May 29, 1995, p. A3.

[50] Philip Weiss, "The Clinton Haters," *The New York Times Magazine*, Feb. 23, 1997, p. 35.

[51] *Ibid.*, Micah Morrison, "Mysterious Mena," *News & Record* (Greensboro, N.C.), July 31, 1994, p. F1.

[52] Katel, *op. cit.*

[53] Barkun, *op. cit.*, pp. 69-71.

[54] Quoted in *ibid.*

[55] "Fear of Swine Flu Vaccine? Why Are Parents Saying No?" "Good Morning America," ABC News, Oct. 7, 2009.

[56] "Survey Finds Just 40% of Adults 'Absolutely Certain' They Will Get H1N1 Vaccine," Harvard School of Public Health, Oct. 2, 2009, www.hsph.harvard.edu/news/press-releases/2009-releases/survey-40-adults-absolutely-certain-h1n1-vaccine.html.

[57] *Ibid.*

[58] Mike Adams, "As Swine Flu Spreads, Conspiracy Theories of Laboratory Origins Abound," Natural News.com, April 27, 2009, www.naturalnews.com/026141.html.

[59] Michael Le Page, "Is swine flue a bioterrorist virus?" *Short Sharp Science* (blog), April 27,

2009, www.newscientist.com/blogs/short sharpscience/2009/04/is-swine-flu-a-bioterrorist-vi.html.

[60] "PMSNBC Doctor Rips Rush for Refusing to Take Sebelius Flu Shot," "Rush Limbaugh Show," Oct. 8, 2009, www.rushlimbaugh.com/home/daily/site_100809/content/01125108.guest.html. Also, Christopher Beam, "Pig Pile: the bizarre alliance of the far left and far right against swine flu vaccinations," *Slate*, Oct. 12, 2009, www.slate.com/id/2232187/.

[61] Ilya Sandra Perlingieri, "Dangers In The Shots," *rense.com*, Aug. 4, 2009, www.rense.com/general86/dngers.htm.

[62] Paul Joseph Watson, "Swine Flu Shot Propaganda Goes Into Overdrive," *PrisonPlanet*, Oct. 14, 2009, www.prisonplanet.com/swine-flu-shot-propaganda-goes-into-overdrive.html.

[63] Quoted in Liza Mundy, "Burden of Proof on Obama's Origins," *The Washington Post*, Oct. 6, 2009, www.washingtonpost.com/wp-dyn/content/article/2009/10/05/AR2009100503819_pf.html.

[64] *Rhodes v. MacDonald*, Case No. 4:09-CV-106 (CDL), U.S. District Court for the Middle District of Georgia, Columbus Division, 9/16/09, pp. 1, 12, http://ftpcontent.worldnow.com/wtvm/ConnieRhodesvsArmy.pdf.

[65] Motion to Recuse the Honorable Clay D. Land," Civil Action No: 09-106, Document 24, Oct. 2, 2009, p. 10, www.the-peoples-forum.com/cgi-bin/readart.cgi?ArtNum=14733.

[66] Spencer Kornhaber, "Meet Orly Taitz, Queen Bee of People Obsessed With Barack Obama's Birth Certificate," *OC Weekly*, June 18, 2009.

[67] Robert Farley, "Obama's birth certificate: Final chapter," *Politifact.com*, July 1, 2009, www.poli

tifact.com/truth-o-meter/article/2009/jul/01/obamas-birth-certificate-final-chapter-time-we-mea/.

[68] "Is this really smoking gun of Obama's Kenyan birth?" *WorldNet Daily*, Aug. 2, 2009, www.wnd.com/index.php?fa=PAGE.view&pageId=105764.

[69] "Alleged Obama birth certificate is a hoax," *Politifact.com*, Aug. 21, 2009, www.politifact.com/truth-o-meter/statements/2009/aug/21/orly-taitz/alleged-obama-birth-certificate-kenya-hoax/; Jess Henig, "Born in the U.S.A.," Jess Henig, Factcheck.org, Aug. 21, 2008, http://factcheck.org/elections-2008/born_in_the_usa.html. *The St. Petersburg Times* is the former owner of CQ Press.

[70] Joseph Farah, "Why I doubt Kenyan birth document," *WorldNet Daily*, Aug. 4, 2009, www.wnd.com/index.php?fa=PAGE.view&pageId=105902.

[71] *Ibid.*

[72] Quoted in Farley, *op. cit.*

[73] *Ibid.*

[74] Quoted in David Weigel, "Paglia: 'Birthers' Aren't Racist, and They Have a Point," *Washington Independent*, Sept. 17, 2009, http://washingtonindependent.com/59655/paglia-birthers-arent-racist-and-they-have-a-point.

[75] Quoted in "Conservative media figures . . .," *op. cit.*; Alex Koppleman, "Why the stories about Obama's birth certificate will never die," *Salon*, Oct. 13, 2009, /www.salon.com/news/feature/2008/12/05/birth_certificate/.

[76] "Alex Jones — A Message to the Future," YouTube, Jan. 12, 2008, www.youtube.com/watch?v=I_6nz1Dhxn4.

[77] *Ibid.*

FOR MORE INFORMATION

Defend Our Freedoms Foundation, 29839 Santa Margarita Pkwy., Rancho Santa Margarita, CA 92688; (949) 683-5411; www.orlytaitzesq.com. The Web site of Orly Taitz, a leader among those claiming that President Obama wasn't born in the U.S.

Conspiracy Science; http://conspiracyscience.com. Rebuts the leading conspiracy theories, in extensive detail.

911truth.org; (785) 597-5729; www.911truth.org. Assembles key "truther" documents to raise questions about the origin of the Sept. 11 attacks.

Alex Jones' Infowars.com. Offers access to conspiracy theorists' daily broadcasts, as well as interpretations of current events from the conspiracist perspective.

Political Research Associates, 1310 Broadway, Suite 201, Somerville, MA 02144; (617) 666-5300; www.publiceye.org. A liberal think tank that monitors conspiracism on the right but also reports critically on theories that attract left-wing followers.

Snopes.com; www.snopes.com. A nonpartisan Web site that investigates the veracity of rumors, "urban legends" and conspiracy theories.

Bibliography
Selected Sources

Books

Barkun, Michael, *A Culture of Conspiracy: Apocalyptic Visions in Contemporary America*, University of California Press, 2003.
A leading conspiracy scholar at Syracuse University explores the links between conspiracism and "new age" beliefs.

Hofstadter, Richard, *The Paranoid Style in American Politics*, Vintage Books Edition, 2008.
The late Columbia University historian authored a key work in the study of American conspiracism.

Olmsted, Kathryn S., *Real Enemies: Conspiracy Theories and American Democracy, World War I to 9/11*, Oxford University Press, 2009.
A University of California, Davis, historian explores how conspiracism grows out of real events and trends.

Marrs, Jim, *Rule by Secrecy: The Hidden History That Connects the Trilateral Commission, the Freemasons, and the Great Pyramids*, Perennial-HarperCollins, 2001.
A former newspaper reporter lays out world history as one big conspiracy theory.

Pipes, Daniel, *Conspiracy: How the Paranoid Style Flourishes and Where It Comes From*, Free Press, 1997.
The director of a Middle East-related think tank analyzes the roots and consequences of U.S. and Western conspiracy theories.

Articles

Farley, Robert, "Obama's birth certificate: Final chapter. This time we mean it!" *Politifact.com*, July 1, 2009, www.politifact.com/truth-o-meter/article/2009/jul/01/obamas-birth-certificate-final-chapter-time-we-mea/.
A respected fact-checking organization says President Barack Obama's birthplace and nationality are definitively established.

Goldberg, Michelle, "Truther Consequences," *The New Republic*, Oct. 7, 2009, www.tnr.com/article/politics/truther-consequences.
An influential liberal profiles radio host Alex Jones, judging his influence to be growing.

Kornhaber, Spencer, "Anti-Obama 'Eligibility' Movement Members Are Breaking Ties With Laguna Niguel Attorney/Birther Orly Taitz," *OC Weekly*, Sept. 24, 2009.
Fights within the Obama-birthplace movement are becoming more intense, a Southern California weekly newspaper reports.

McManus, John F., "Speaker Pelosi Pushes 'New Order of the Centuries,' " John Birch Society, Jan. 8, 2007, www.jbs.org/jbs-news-feed/795-speaker-pelosi-pushes-qnew-order-of-the-centuriesq.
The president of the far-right John Birch Society links a Democratic Party leader and a globalist conspiracy.

Mosk, Matthew, "An Attack That Came Out of the Ether," *The Washington Post*, June 28, 2008, p. C1.
A *Washington Post* report chronicles an academic's exploration of the origins of a conspiracist notion of candidate Obama as a radical Muslim.

Shane, Scott, "C.I.A. Is Still Cagey About Oswald Mystery," *The New York Times*, Oct. 16, 2009, www.nytimes.com/2009/10/17/us/17inquire.html?hp=&pagewanted=all.
Even today, the intelligence agency is resisting disclosing some Kennedy assassination-related files.

Thomma, Steven, "Secret camps and guillotines? Groups make birthers look sane," McClatchy Newspapers, Aug. 28, 2009, www.mcclatchydc.com/336/story/74549.html.
A news organization with a track record of skepticism toward government takes an equally skeptical look at conspiracy theories.

Zaitchick, Alexander, "Meet the man who changed Glenn Beck's life," *Salon*, Sept. 16, 2009, www.salon.com/news/feature/2009/09/16/beck_skousen/print.html.
Zaitchick reports on the intellectual influence of the late W. Cleon Skousen on radio host Glenn Beck.

Reports and Studies

Berlet, Chip, "Toxic to Democracy: Conspiracy Theories, Demonization & Scapegoating," Political Research Associates, 2009, www.publiceye.org/conspire/toxic2democracy/Toxic-2D-all-rev-04.pdf.
A conspiracy expert concludes that the trend is on the rise and dangerous.

"Final Report on the Collapse of World Trade Center Building 7," National Institute of Standards and Technology, November 2008, http://wtc.nist.gov/NCSTAR1/PDF/NC-STAR%201A.pdf; and "Answers to Frequently Asked Questions — National Institute of Standards and Technology Federal Building and Fire Safety Investigation of the World Trade Center Disaster," National Institute of Standards and Technology, Aug. 30, 2006, http://wtc.nist.gov/pubs/fact sheets/faqs_8_2006.htm.
Two lengthy and technically detailed analyses of the Sept. 11 attacks attempt to answer questions raised by the "truther" movement.

The Next Step:

Additional Articles from Current Periodicals

Alex Jones

Bauknecht, Sara, "Film's Goal: Candid Look at Conspiracy Theorists," Pittsburgh Post-Gazette, Oct. 19, 2009, p. B5.

A new film documents the conspiracy theories of Alex Jones and challenges viewers to question the politics around them.

Lloyd, Robert, "Perceived Threats to World Order," Los Angeles Times, May 26, 2009, p. D3.

Alex Jones and his followers believe that many of the government's actions are designed to bring about a "new world order" that puts a select few in control.

Starr, Michael, "Who's Zoomin' Who?" The New York Post, May 25, 2009, p. 57.

Alex Jones believes Wall Street is trying to create a "one-world government" in which it has the upper hand.

"Birthers"

Farley, Robert, "Alleged Obama Birth Certificate From Kenya Is a Hoax," St. Petersburg Times, Aug. 21, 2009.

An Obama birth certificate supposedly certifying the president's birth in Kenya was manufactured using the template of a real birth certificate in Australia.

Louis, Errol, "The Birth of a Nutty Nation," Daily News (New York), July 23, 2009, p. 25.

At least a dozen lawsuits were filed trying to block Barack Obama from being sworn in as president on the grounds that he was not a naturally born citizen of the United States.

Shea, Jim, "Birthers Make Wacky Conspiracy Theories Trendy Again," Hartford (Connecticut) Courant, July 25, 2009, p. C1.

"Birthers" believe Barack Obama is not eligible to be president of the United States because he was born overseas, and no amount of evidence can convince them otherwise.

Smith, Sylvia A., "Conspiracy Birthing a Rift in the GOP," Fort Wayne (Indiana) Journal Gazette, Aug. 2, 2009, p. 11A.

Many constituents are demanding that Republican legislators resolve the argument over whether Barack Obama was born in the United States.

Sept. 11, 2001, Attacks

Brown, Marian Gail, "9/11 Fiction Often Confused With Reality," Connecticut Post, Sept. 6, 2008.

Conspiracies began almost immediately after the attacks in order to make sense of the disaster.

Christianson, J. Scott, "9/11 Conspiracy Theories Twist Logic," Columbia (Missouri) Daily Tribune, Oct. 30, 2007.

An entire American subculture has emerged that suggests the government was behind the 9/11 attacks.

Doll, Julie, "It's Not the Truth that Conspiracy Theorists Seek," Journal and Courier (Indiana), Feb. 17, 2008, p. 8A.

The conspiracy claims about 9/11 are so outrageous and the evidence so flawed that supporters must ignore logic in order to believe.

Soltis, Andy, " 'Blame U.S. for 9/11' Idiots in Majority," The New York Post, Nov. 24, 2007, p. 8.

About two-thirds of Americans believe the federal government had warnings about 9/11 but chose to ignore them, according to a national survey.

Validity

Campos, Paul, "The Never-Ending Nonstory," Rocky Mountain News (Colorado), Feb. 25, 2009, p. 31.

The rise of independent media has spawned conspiracy theories that many regard as legitimate subjects of journalistic inquiry.

Rodriguez, Gregory, "Truth Is in the Ear of the Beholder," Los Angeles Times, Sept. 28, 2009, p. A19.

Political rumors and conspiracy theories thrive only in the minds of people who are predisposed to believe them.

Rubin, Trudy, "Internet Fueling Rise in False Theories," Deseret Morning News (Utah), Sept. 13, 2009.

The Internet has popularized many conspiracy theories in which facts are largely absent or buried under mounds of fiction.

CITING CQ RESEARCHER

Sample formats for citing these reports in a bibliography include the ones listed below. Preferred styles and formats vary, so please check with your instructor or professor.

MLA STYLE

Jost, Kenneth. "Rethinking the Death Penalty." CQ Researcher 16 Nov. 2001: 945-68.

APA STYLE

Jost, K. (2001, November 16). Rethinking the death penalty. CQ Researcher, 11, 945-968.

CHICAGO STYLE

Jost, Kenneth. "Rethinking the Death Penalty." CQ Researcher, November 16, 2001, 945-968.

In-depth Reports on Issues in the News

Are you writing a paper?

Need backup for a debate?

Want to become an expert on an issue?

For more than 80 years, students have turned to *CQ Researcher* for in-depth reporting on issues in the news. Reports on a full range of political and social issues are now available. Following is a selection of recent reports:

Civil Liberties
Closing Guantánamo, 2/09
Affirmative Action, 10/08
Gay Marriage Showdowns, 9/08
America's Border Fence, 9/08
Immigration Debate, 2/08

Crime/Law
Interrogating the CIA, 9/09
Examining Forensics, 7/09
Legalizing Marijuana, 6/09
Wrongful Convictions, 4/09
Prostitution Debate, 5/08

Education
Reading Crisis? 2/08
Discipline in Schools, 2/08
Student Aid, 1/08

Environment/Society
Human Spaceflight, 10/09
Gays in the Military, 9/09
Energy and Climate, 7/09
Future of Books, 5/09
Hate Groups, 5/09
Future of Journalism, 3/09
Confronting Warming, 1/09

Health/Safety
Medication Abuse, 10/09
Nuclear Disarmament, 10/09
Health-Care Reform, 8/09
Straining the Safety Net, 7/09
Treating Depression, 6/09
Reproductive Ethics, 5/09

Politics/Economy
State Budget Crisis, 9/09
Business Bankruptcy, 4/09
Future of the GOP, 3/09
Middle-Class Squeeze, 3/09

Upcoming Reports

Human Rights, 10/30/09   Value of a College Education, 11/6/09   Women in the Military, 11/13/09

ACCESS

CQ Researcher is available in print and online. For access, visit your library or www.cqresearcher.com.

STAY CURRENT

To receive notice of upcoming *CQ Researcher* reports, or learn more about *CQ Researcher* products, subscribe to the free e-mail newsletters, *CQ Researcher Alert!* and *CQ Researcher News*: http://cqpress.com/newsletters.

PURCHASE

To purchase a *CQ Researcher* report in print or electronic format (PDF), visit www.cqpress.com or call 866-427-7737. Single reports start at $15. Bulk purchase discounts and electronic-rights licensing are also available.

SUBSCRIBE

Annual full-service *CQ Researcher* subscriptions—including 44 reports a year, monthly index updates, and a bound volume—start at $803. Add $25 for domestic postage.

CQ Researcher Online offers a backfile from 1991 and a number of tools to simplify research. For pricing information, call 800-834-9020, ext. 1906, or e-mail librarysales@cqpress.com.

Published by CQ Press, a Division of SAGE

www.cqresearcher.com

Human Rights Issues

Are they a low priority under President Obama?

uman rights advocates are voicing disappointment with what they have seen so far of President Obama's approach to human rights issues in forming U.S. foreign policy. They applaud Obama for working to restore U.S. influence on human rights by changing President George W. Bush's policies on interrogating and detaining terrorism suspects. But they also see evidence that the Obama administration is reluctant to challenge authoritarian governments for clamping down on political dissidents or rigging elections. As one example, these critics complain that Obama should not have tried to curry favor with the Chinese government by postponing a meeting with the Dalai Lama until after the president visits China in November. Administration officials insist Obama is devoted to human rights and democratization and cite among other moves the decision to join the United Nations Human Rights Council. Conservative critics, however, say the council is a flawed institution and the United States should have stayed out.

President Barack Obama reaffirmed U.S. support for human rights during an address to the United Nations General Assembly on Sept. 23. Two weeks later he was awarded the Nobel Peace Prize "for his extraordinary efforts to strengthen international diplomacy and cooperation between peoples."

CQ Researcher • Oct. 30, 2009 • www.cqresearcher.com
Volume 19, Number 38 • Pages 909-932

CQ Researcher

Oct. 30, 2009
Volume 19, Number 38

MANAGING EDITOR: Thomas J. Colin
tcolin@cqpress.com

ASSISTANT MANAGING EDITOR: Kathy Koch
kkoch@cqpress.com

ASSOCIATE EDITOR: Kenneth Jost

STAFF WRITERS: Thomas J. Billitteri, Marcia Clemmitt, Peter Katel

CONTRIBUTING WRITERS: Rachel Cox, Sarah Glazer, Alan Greenblatt, Reed Karaim Barbara Mantel, Patrick Marshall, Tom Price, Jennifer Weeks

DESIGN/PRODUCTION EDITOR: Olu B. Davis

ASSISTANT EDITOR: Darrell Dela Rosa

EDITORIAL INTERN: Emily DeRuy

FACT-CHECKING: Eugene J. Gabler, Michelle Harris

CQ PRESS

A Division of SAGE

PRESIDENT AND PUBLISHER:
John A. Jenkins

CQ Researcher (ISSN 1056-2036) is printed on acid-free paper. Published weekly, except; (Jan. wk. 1) (May wk. 4) (July wks. 1, 2) (Aug. wks. 3, 4) (Nov. wk. 4) and (Dec. wk. 4), by CQ Press, a division of SAGE Publications. Annual full-service subscriptions start at $803. For pricing, call 1-800-834-9020, ext. 1906. To purchase a CQ Researcher report in print or electronic format (PDF), visit www. cqpress.com or call 866-427-7737. Single reports start at $15. Bulk purchase discounts and electronic-rights licensing are also available. Periodicals postage paid at Washington, D.C., and additional mailing offices. POSTMASTER: Send address changes to CQ Researcher, 2300 N St., N.W., Suite 800, Washington, DC 20037.

Cover: AFP/Getty Images/Stan Honda

Human Rights Issues

THE ISSUES

As a young boy, Tenzin Gyatso, the 14th Dalai Lama, received a gift in his Tibetan homeland from President Franklin D. Roosevelt: a gold watch showing the phases of the moon and the days of the week.

Nearly seven decades later, the leader of the Tibetan government in exile as well as the spiritual leader of Tibetan Buddhists had the watch with him in 2007 as another U.S. president, George W. Bush, bestowed on him the Congressional Medal of Freedom.

When he visited Washington in early October, however, the 74-year-old Buddhist monk was less warmly received by the current president, Barack Obama. To avoid offending the Chinese government over its political and cultural struggles with Tibetan dissidents, Obama decided to postpone a personal meeting with the Dalai Lama until after the president's visit to China in November.

Administration officials insisted that deferring what has been since 1991 a regular drop-in at the White House was no slight. They noted that the postponement had been agreed to in meetings between the Dalai Lama's advisers and one of Obama's closest aides, Valerie Jarrett, in advance of the monk's weeklong visit to Washington in early October.

The Dalai Lama himself brushed off any hint of hurt feelings from the postponement. In an Oct. 7 interview, he told CNN's Wolf Blitzer that he considered Obama "sympathetic" to the

The Dalai Lama says he is not upset about not meeting with President Obama during his visit to Washington in early October. Obama postponed meeting with the Tibetan leader to avoid offending the Chinese government over its treatment of Tibetan dissidents; the meeting will occur after Obama visits China in November. Human rights advocates see the postponement as a sign of weakness in the administration's support for human rights and democratization.

Getty Images/Ralph Orlowski

Tibetan cause and expected the president to raise the issue with Chinese leaders during his mid-November visit. "More serious discussion is better than just a picture, so I have no disappointment," he said. [1]

Human rights advocates, however, see the postponement as a mistake in itself and a troubling sign of weakness in the Obama administration's approach in promoting human rights and democratization in other countries. "It plays into the narrative that the administration will defer to power rather than principle," says Tom Malinowski, Washington director for Human Rights Watch.

"That obviously sends a message," says Elisa Massamino, chief executive officer of Human Rights First. "Decisions like that can be very powerfully damaging to the solidarity with the people who we claim to be standing with."

Obama cheered human rights advocates with the steps he took in his first days in office to scrap some of the controversial detention and interrogation policies that his predecessor, Bush, had adopted to deal with suspected terrorists following al Qaeda's Sept. 11, 2001, attacks on the United States. "You can't overstate the importance of that in terms of sending a signal to our own people and to the rest of the world that the United States is going to return to taking those commitments to fundamental human rights seriously," says Massamino.

In the months since then, however, human rights advocates on the political left and political right have been finding more to fault than to praise in Obama's dealings with countries viewed as human rights violators.

"They haven't yet come up with a consistent approach to human rights as to what they're trying to get in human rights as opposed to what they're trying to get country by country," says Jennifer Windsor, executive director of Freedom House, an older group generally seen as more conservative than such newer organizations as Human Rights First and Human Rights Watch. "I sort of wonder why it's taking them so long," Windsor says. "They keep on apologizing."

"So far, his administration has been characterized by a marked turning away

www.cqresearcher.com   Oct. 30, 2009   911

Global Freedom Declines for Third Year

Global freedom suffered its third consecutive year of decline in 2008, according to the annual survey by Freedom House. Overall, the human rights monitoring and advocacy organization rated 89 countries with a total population of 3.1 billion as free, 62 countries with 1.4 billion people as partly free and 42 countries with 2.3 billion people as not free.

Notable developments during the year, according to the report, included declines in Russia and in the non-Baltic countries of the former Soviet Union; stagnation in the Middle East and North Africa and substantial reversals for democracy in sub-Saharan Africa. The group also voiced disappointment with China's failure to improve its human rights situation during the year it hosted the Summer Olympic Games.

Among countries of particular importance to the United States, Iraq was credited with registering a small gain because of ebbing violence and reduced political terror, while Afghanistan was moved from partly free to not free because of "rising insecurity and increasing corruption and inefficiency in government institutions."

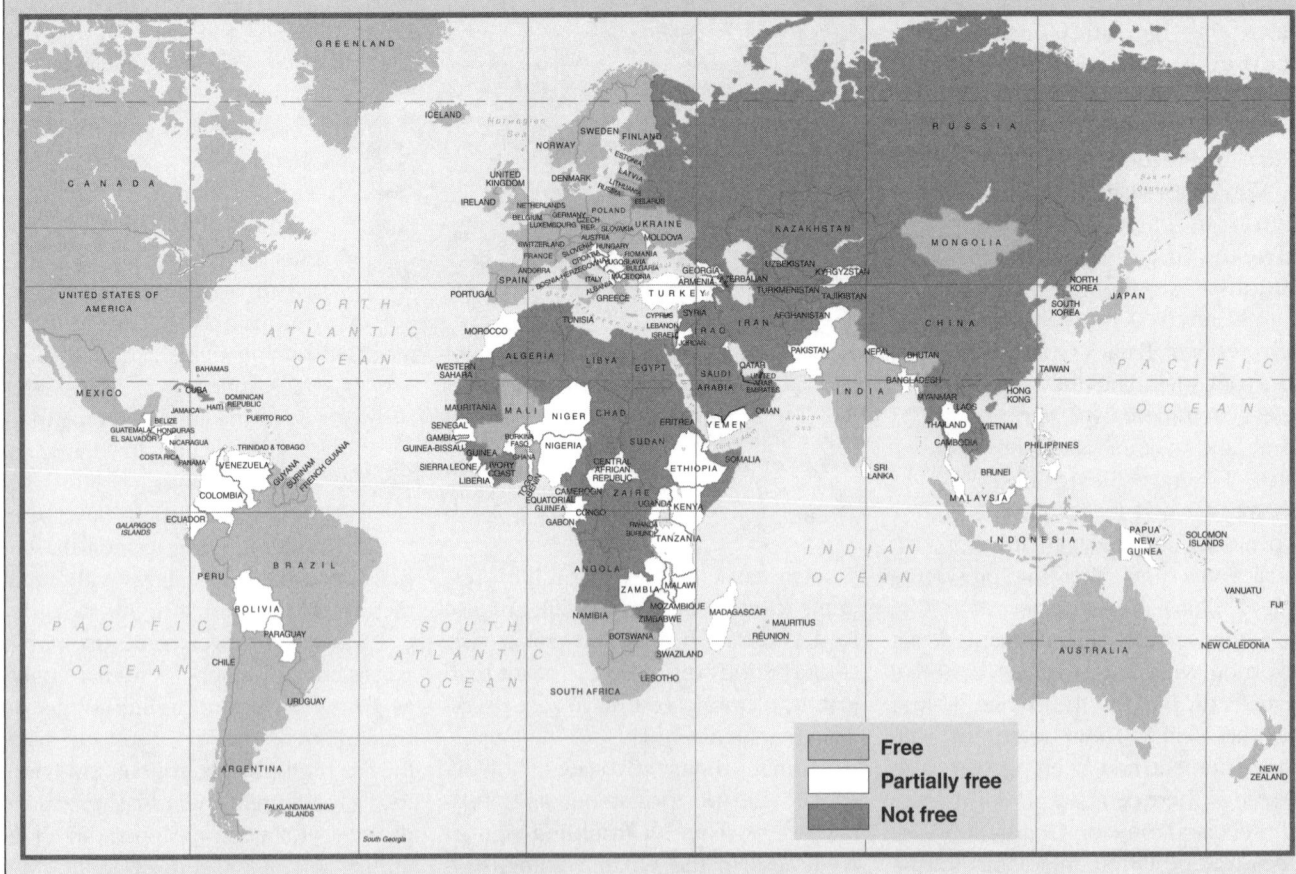

Source: "Freedom in the World 2009," Freedom House, www.freedomhouse.org/template.cfm?page=363&year=2009

from interest in human rights and democracy that has been a feature of United States foreign policy since the presidency of Jimmy Carter," says Joshua Muravchik, a fellow at the Foreign Policy Institute at Johns Hopkins University's School of Advanced and International Studies in Washington and a leading neoconservative expert on human rights.

Grumbling about the president's human rights record was already widespread before Obama became the unanticipated recipient on Oct. 9 of this year's Nobel Peace Prize. In selecting

Obama, the Norwegian Nobel Committee said he had created "a new atmosphere of international politics," adding, "Democracy and human rights are to be strengthened." [2]

A few hours later, Obama said he was "surprised" and "humbled" by the award. "I do not feel that I deserve to be in the company of so many transformative figures that have been honored by this prize," he said. But Obama said he would accept the award as "a call to action to confront the common challenges of the 21st century."

The reaction to the award in the United States and around the world was decidedly mixed. "Too early," said Lech Walesa, the Polish labor leader and later prime minister who was the 1983 Nobel laureate. But other previous winners applauded the selection. In a congratulatory letter, the Dalai Lama, the 1989 laureate, told Obama that the Nobel committee "has rightly noted your efforts towards a world without nuclear weapons and your constructive role in environmental protection."

Within the United States, Democrats and some Republicans voiced approval of the selection, but many GOP politicians were unenthusiastic to negative. Much of the reaction among mainstream media commentators and bloggers was skeptical, even from some liberals. (*See "At Issue," p. 925.*)

The divisions over the peace prize mirror experts' evaluations of Obama's contributions on human rights issues after nine months in office. "The jury is still out, but I think the Obama administration is headed in the right direction," says David Kaye, head of the International Human Rights Clinic at UCLA Law School and a former State Department official under Presidents Bill Clinton and George W. Bush.

But Michael Mandelbaum, director of the foreign policy program at Johns Hopkins, says the administration has downplayed human rights. "They very conspicuously backed away from the strong advocacy of rights, from putting

Obama: Democracy Is a Human Right

President Obama has stressed the importance of democracy and human rights in four recent speeches to international audiences, beginning with a widely hailed address at Cairo University in June. Human rights groups say they are encouraged by Obama's remarks but are looking for more concrete actions from the administration to support democratization and civil society movements.

"America does not presume to know what is best for everyone, just as we would not presume to pick the outcome of a peaceful election. But I do have an unyielding belief that all people yearn for certain things: the ability to speak your mind and have a say in how you are governed; confidence in the rule of law and the equal administration of justice; government that is transparent and doesn't steal from the people; the freedom to live as you choose. These are not just American ideas; they are human rights. And that is why we will support them everywhere."
— remarks at Cairo University, Cairo, Egypt, June 4, 2009

"The arc of history shows us that governments which serve their own people survive and thrive; governments which serve only their own power do not. Governments that represent the will of their people are far less likely to descend into failed states, to terrorize their citizens, or to wage war on others. Governments that promote the rule of law, subject their actions to oversight, and allow for independent institutions are more dependable trading partners. And in our own history, democracies have been America's most enduring allies, including those we once waged war with in Europe and Asia — nations that today live with great security and prosperity."
— remarks at the New Economic School graduation, Moscow, July 7, 2009

"America will not seek to impose any system of government on any other nation — the essential truth of democracy is that each nation determines its own destiny. What we will do is increase assistance for responsible individuals and institutions, with a focus on supporting good governance — on parliaments, which check abuses of power and ensure that opposition voices are heard; on the rule of law, which ensures the equal administration of justice; on civic participation, so that young people get involved; and on concrete solutions to corruption like forensic accounting, automating services, strengthening hotlines, and protecting whistle-blowers to advance transparency and accountability."
— remarks to the Ghanaian Parliament, Accra, July 11, 2009

"Democracy cannot be imposed on any nation from the outside. Each society must search for its own path, and no path is perfect. Each country will pursue a path rooted in the culture of its people and in its past traditions. And I admit that in the past America has too often been selective in its promotion of democracy. But that does not weaken our commitment, it only reinforces it. There are basic principles that are universal; there are certain truths which are self-evident — and the United States of America will never waver in our efforts to stand up for the right of people everywhere to determine their own destiny."
— remarks to United Nations General Assembly, New York, Sept. 23, 2009

Source: The White House, www.whitehouse.gov/the_press_office

that at the center of their policies and putting that at the center of their rhetoric," he says.

The United States took the lead after World War II in the adoption of international human rights agreements, but human rights took a back seat to global power politics during the tensest years of the Cold War. In the late 1970s, however, President Jimmy Carter made human rights an explicit centerpiece of U.S. foreign policy. Every president since then has continued the stated commitment to human rights, though in markedly different ways. [3]

President George W. Bush continued to voice support for human rights and used his second inaugural address in 2005 to put promoting democracy at the center of his foreign policy goals. The results of Bush's policies — in Iraq, the Mideast and the rest of the world — are disputed. Whatever Bush's final legacy may be, many experts and advocates say Obama is shaping his approach to the issues in conscious distinction with Bush's more aggressive approach. "They are almost afraid to speak out against human rights abuses in any country because it's going to be like Bush," says Freedom House's Windsor.

Admirers note that Obama has given four major foreign policy speeches reaffirming U.S. support for human rights, most recently at the United Nations General Assembly. (See box, p. 913.) They also point out that Obama appointed two longtime human rights advocates to pivotal posts at the State Department. Harold Hongju Koh, a former Yale Law School dean, is serving as the department's legal adviser; Michael Posner, the longtime head of Human Rights First, was confirmed in late September as assistant secretary of state for human rights, democracy and labor. "These two guys are really, really committed to a value-driven, human rights-oriented U.S. foreign policy," UCLA's Kaye says.

The admirers acknowledge, however, and critics emphasize that Obama has also sought to "engage" with several countries with deplorable human rights records, including Egypt, Syria, Iran and Myanmar (formerly Burma). Muravchik accuses Obama of "a rush to have new and friendly relations with a whole series of the most cruel and dictatorial regimes."

The debate over Obama's policies takes place against what Freedom House describes in its most recent annual report as the third consecutive year of decline in global freedom. The report credits Bush — and his two predecessors, Clinton and his father George H. W. Bush — with helping promote positive developments for democracy since the end of the Cold War. But it also points to "a turnaround in democracy's fortunes" in Bush's second term and points to "the lack of . . . durable gains" in the Middle East and North Africa as "a major disappointment for American policy." [4] (See map, p. 912.)

Apart from the changes in the post-9/11 interrogation and detention policies, Obama's most concrete action to date is the decision to join the United Nations Human Rights Council, a U.N. forum reconstituted in 2006 that the Bush administration pointedly boycotted. As with Obama's moves on anti-terrorism policies, reactions to the decision divide along ideological lines: Liberals support the move; conservatives do not. (See sidebar, p. 916.)

Obama's trip to China will be closely watched for new clues on how human rights fits in with other U.S. interests — economic, diplomatic, strategic — in dealing with countries with less than exemplary human rights records.

As the president prepares for the trip, here are some of the major questions that human rights watchers are debating:

Is the Obama administration deemphasizing human rights in U.S. foreign policy?

In a visit to China and other Asian countries in February, Secretary of State Hillary Rodham Clinton raised eyebrows among human rights advocates by appearing to put rights issues below other U.S. concerns. In comments to the traveling press corps, Clinton said the United States would continue pressing China on Tibet, Taiwan and free-speech issues, but added, "Our pressing on those issues can't interfere with the global economic crisis, the global climate change crisis and the security crisis."

Human rights groups complained in advance about signals that human rights issues were to be downgraded on the trip. "Extremely disappointed," said Amnesty International USA. Today, many human rights advocates continue to question Clinton's statement. "We're not going to talk about human rights until we solve global warming and the economic crisis?" asks Muravchik, the Johns Hopkins fellow. "That gives them a pretty large margin of impunity." [5]

Beyond U.S.-China relations, the administration appears to be basing its human rights policies on a view that private diplomacy is more effective than public rhetoric in encouraging authoritarian governments to turn away from repressive policies. Human rights advocates on the left and right disagree.

"They're saying they want to achieve real gains and to engage in order to get something accomplished," says Freedom House's Windsor. "In the past, we have not seen quiet diplomacy work."

"It's not enough to say we're going to talk with people," says Massamino of Human Rights First. "It's not an end in itself."

A former Bush administration official goes further. "It seems clear to me that the Obama administration has no human rights policy," Elliott Abrams, deputy national security director for democracy in Bush's second term and now a senior fellow with the Council on Foreign Relations, tells the conservative FrontPageMagazine.com. "That is, while in some inchoate sense they would like respect for human rights to grow around the world, as all Americans would, they have no actual policy to achieve that goal — and they subordinate it to all their other policy goals." [6]

Other human rights advocates, however, say the criticism is overblown. "The administration understandably wanted to distinguish itself from what it saw as the [Bush administration's] overly messianic and at times aggressive and hectoring approach toward these issues," says Human Rights Watch's Malinowski. "The narrative of Bush cared and Obama doesn't," he adds, "is extraordinarily simplistic and misguided."

Thomas Carothers, vice president for studies at the Carnegie Endowment for International Peace in Washington, also says the criticism of Obama's policies is exaggerated. "The idea that we've suddenly gone soft on Russia, on China and so forth tends to be a bit of an overstatement," he says.

Still, Malinowski says human right advocates have cause for concern. Obama's apparent approach, he says, "can easily be interpreted and to some extent is being interpreted by the permanent foreign policy bureaucracy at the State Department as an argument for engaging [repressive] governments without pressure, without sanctions, without a significant emphasis on what [bureaucrats] dismiss as moral issues."

Muravchik, the Johns Hopkins fellow, says the administration's approach reflects a wrongheaded effort to differentiate Obama's policies from Bush's. "There was an obvious opening in keeping with his desire to be critical of Bush's legacy to say that in this area Bush pronounced good ideas but didn't deliver," Muravchik says. "Instead, he's said that Bush was on the wrong track in essence by telling other governments how to behave."

Obama's engagement strategy, Muravchik concludes, "necessarily involves a downgrading if not betrayal of human rights." Other human rights watchers, however, are prepared to suspend judgment to see what results are achieved by the approach reflected, for example, in Clinton's comments on China.

"A charitable reading of that is that we need to find new tactics; we're not going to engage in a Kabuki dance; that's not getting results," says Massamino of Human Rights First.

"There's a lot to be said for the idea that in pushing a human rights agenda,

Secretary of State Hillary Rodham Clinton visits with South African soldiers assigned to U.N. peacekeeping duties in the Democratic Republic of the Congo during her weeklong visit to war-torn Africa in August. Earlier in the year she was criticized for saying human rights should not "interfere" with U.S.-China relations.

sometimes and in some places and with some countries it's better to push it quietly," says UCLA professor Kaye. "Over time, it may be that the Obama administration will either see that working or will see it not working. In those situations where they see it not working, they may move the disagreements from the private channels to the more public ones.

"It's too early to conclude that they are sacrificing the human rights agenda for some Kissingerian realpolitik," he concludes, referring to Henry Kissinger, who served as secretary of state under Presidents Richard M. Nixon and Gerald R. Ford. "I don't think that's what's happening."

Is the Obama administration reducing U.S. support for democratization in other countries?

President Obama used one of his first major foreign policy speeches abroad to reaffirm to his Egyptian audience and the broader Muslim world the United States' support for promoting democracy. Democratic principles such as freedom, equality and rule of law "are not just American ideas," Obama said in the June 4 address in Cairo. "They are human rights. And that is why we will support them everywhere."

Obama made no reference in the speech, however, to the repressive policies of his host, Egyptian President Hosni Mubarak. In advance, he even rejected a reporter's suggestion to describe Mubarak as "authoritarian." And when Obama hosted the Egyptian leader at the White House on Aug. 18, the subject of democracy was unmentioned in public comments. [7]

The on-again, off-again invocation of the democracy message leaves human rights advocates less than satisfied. "President Obama could have been more explicit," says Malinowski, the Human Rights Watch director in Washington. "It's important that the president's private messages to leaders like Mubarak be emphasized with public messages. I agree that was a missed opportunity."

Former Bush administration official Abrams bluntly criticized Obama for selecting Cairo as the site of the earlier address and then omitting any mention of human rights in the joint press availability with Mubarak at the White House. "Democracy activists in Egypt have been abandoned," he said in the *FrontPageMagazine.com* interview.

Muravchik, the Johns Hopkins fellow, is similarly critical of Obama's delayed

Report on Abuses in Gaza Sparks Concern

Critics see anti-Israel tilt by U.N. Human Rights Council.

Israel launched a three-week air and ground assault on Gaza in December 2008 aimed at stopping Palestinian militants from firing missiles at civilian targets across the border. During and after the invasion, the ruling Hamas government in Gaza charged that Israeli forces had committed war crimes by wantonly attacking Palestinian civilians. [1]

Now, a respected South African jurist has found both sides responsible for endangering civilians during the conflict. In a report commissioned by the United Nations Human Rights Council, Judge Richard Goldstone recommends that Israel and Gaza conduct their own investigations of human rights abuses by their side during the fighting. If no investigations are forthcoming within six months, Goldstone wants the U.N. Security Council to turn the dispute over to the International Criminal Court. [2]

Goldstone's report has drawn critical reactions from both sides. Israel has condemned Goldstone, who is Jewish, for furthering what they perceive to be the council's constant berating of the Jewish state. [3] Many Israelis complain that complying with the investigation would be fruitless because the council is already biased against them.

While Hamas has lauded Goldstone for denouncing Israeli military tactics and agreed to investigate some portions of the report, the rival Palestinian Authority originally decided to defer action, citing an inadequate number of people needed to support an investigation. However, after facing criticism for their decision, the authority requested that the U.N. conduct a special session on the conflict.

Several prominent human rights organizations, specifically Amnesty International and Human Rights Watch, have defended the report for calling attention to rights abuses. The U.N.'s top human rights official, Navi Pillay, has offered her endorsement, as well.

The report has focused worldwide attention on the Human Rights Council, a 47-nation body created in 2006 to replace a larger U.N. human rights forum widely denounced as ineffective. Critics said the earlier U.N. Commission on Human Rights was unsuccessful at prosecuting nations that violated human rights and showed poor judgment in allowing countries with questionable human rights records, including China and Russia, to be members. Under President George W. Bush, the United States criticized the commission and refused to join the council.

President Obama changed the policy, however, and the United States joined the council in May 2009. Critics say the council is still fundamentally flawed and inordinately critical of Israel. But human rights groups are applauding the shift. They say that U.S. involvement and an altered structure will help bring human rights abusers to justice.

The council has enacted a new, periodic review of all 192 U.N. member states in order to monitor human rights conditions in every state. Council members are chosen by the U.N. General Assembly instead of by the Economic and Social Council, which was previously in charge of elections. Additionally, a complaints procedure allows individuals and organizations to bring potential violations to the attention of the council. [4]

Proponents of the council say the changes signal a vast improvement over the commission, but many claim that a disproportionate amount of time continues to be spent on Israel's alleged human rights violations while others, such as Sudan, face little investigation. The council has appointed an independent expert to monitor Sudan and asked the country to remedy human rights violations but has taken no disciplinary action against the government. [5]

During its three-year existence, the council has passed a resolution on freedom of expression that prohibits limiting expression

response to evidence of irregularities in the Iranian presidential election in June. "Obama was so devoted to this course of making friends with the dictators that he refused for the first week to say or do anything to encourage the Iranian people," Muravchik says. "After a week went by, it was clear that his stand was untenable in terms of the views of the Iranian people, the American people and the stands of some other Western leaders. So he spoke out, which was all to the good but quite belated."

To democratization expert Carothers, Obama's speech represents a recasting

of the Bush administration's approach to promoting democracy. "He set out an alternative rhetorical framework that emphasizes that we will not impose democracy on others, that we recognize that different kinds of democracy exist and that we will be sure not to equate elections with democracy," Carothers says.

Carothers says Obama's approach will be "more appealing to people in many parts of the world." But he adds, "It is clear that this administration is not going to make democracy promotion a major emphasis of its policy."

In Egypt, the administration seems to be trying to heal the rift in U.S.-Egyptian relations, which were seen to have suffered in the Bush years because of his administration's criticisms of Egypt's record on human rights. The Bush policies were widely credited, however, with encouraging some liberalization by the Mubarak government.

Today, human rights advocates say repressive policies are returning in Egypt just as U.S. support for democratization efforts is lagging. "Despite the president's speech, there's been little indication that the Egyptian government's

in order to protect religion. It has examined the continuing conflict in Gaza and passed resolutions aimed at remedying rights violations in Myanmar (formerly Burma) and the Democratic Republic of the Congo (DRC), particularly those involving women and children.

Many cite the ability of the United States to broker the freedom of expression resolution with Egypt as a sign that the council is enacting positive change. However, critics still claim that the council shows favoritism towards some countries, with bloc voting by region significantly furthering that bias. Specifically, the Arab countries and many of the African countries vote together on resolutions, making it difficult to pass those that allow the examination of rights violations in places like the DRC.

The Goldstone report has again brought these criticisms to the surface. In the special session requested by the Palestinian Authority, the council endorsed the report, a move that allows the investigation to be taken before the U.N. Security Council. This is the seventh of 12 sessions in the past year involving Israel — another indication many say, of the rights council's bias against Israel. The United States voted against the report and has veto power over the Security Council's agenda, making it unlikely the investigation will travel that far. China and Russia voted for the report but have since indicated their opposition to involving the Security Council. [6]

Last month, speaking in Geneva, U.S. Assistant Secretary for Democracy, Human Rights and Labor Michael Posner and State Department legal adviser Harold Hongju Koh expressed hope that U.S. involvement in the council would help to create a nonpolitical U.N. body able to support victims and prosecute rights violators. [7] But the United States and Israel have expressed concern that the Goldstone report and proceedings within the rights council demonstrate a political bias against Israel and do not focus enough on human rights violations by the Palestinians.

In a 24-page assessment, Freedom House gives the council mixed ratings, with a passing grade only on the use of so-called special rapporteurs and failing grades on adoption of resolutions on urgent human rights crises. The organization specifically criticizes the council for a "disproportionate" number of resolutions critical of Israel. More broadly, the report concludes that democratic countries on the council have failed to counter the "considerable resources" devoted by a "small but active group" of non-democratic countries to limiting the council's effectiveness in protecting human rights. [8]

— *Emily DeRuy*

[1] For background, see Irwin Arieff, "Middle East Peace Prospects," *CQ Global Researcher*, May 2009, pp. 119-148.

[2] See "Human Rights in Palestine and Other Occupied Arab Territories: Report of the United Nations Fact-Finding Mission on the Gaza Conflict," Sept. 25, 2009, www2.ohchr.org/english/bodies/hrcouncil/docs/12session/A-HRC-12-48.pdf. See Christiane Amanpour, "A Look at the Allegations of Israeli and Hamas War Crimes," CNN International, Sept. 30, 2009, for interviews with Judge Goldstone and former U.S. Secretary of State Madeleine Albright.

[3] See Amir Mizroch, "Grappling with Goldstone," *The Jerusalem Post*, Sept. 18, 2009, p. 9.

[4] See "The Human Rights Council," The U.N. Human Rights Council, www2.ohchr.org /english/bodies/hrcouncil/ for full description of council structure.

[5] "Human Rights Council Establishes Mandate of Independent Expert on Sudan for One Year," U.N. Human Rights Council, June 18, 2009, www.unhchr.ch/huricane/huricane.nsf/view01/91B0E40B4256A0C3C12575D900712245?opendocument. For background, see Karen Foerstel, "Crisis in Darfur," *CQ Global Researcher*, September 2008, pp. 248-270.

[6] See Neil MacFarquhar, "U.N. Council Endorses Gaza Report," *The New York Times*, Oct. 16, 2009, www.nytimes.com/2009/10/17/world/middleeast/17nations.html ?_r=1&scp=1&sq=Goldstone%20report%20&st=cse.

[7] "Geneva Press Briefing by Harold Hongju Koh and Michael Posner," United States Mission, Sept. 28, 2009, http://geneva.usmission.gov/2009/09/28/koh-posner/.

[8] See "The U.N. Human Rights Council Report Card: 2007-2009," Freedom House, Sept. 27, 2009, www.freedomhouse.org/uploads/special_report/84.pdf.

human rights record is at all a concern to this administration or that they're willing to put any material support or diplomatic heft in order to get a reversal of the deteriorating situation in Egypt," says Freedom House's Windsor.

U.S. aid to democratization programs in Egypt, including funding for civil society groups, fell from $55 million in fiscal 2008 to $20 million in the current fiscal year. The Obama administration is proposing a modest increase to $25 million for the current year.

Overall, the administration is requesting $2.81 billion for democratization programs for fiscal 2010, an increase of $234 million, according to an analysis by Freedom House. "To their credit, they actually kept democracy and human rights levels up," says Windsor. [8]

Windsor says U.S. support for pro-democracy groups is important because of the resistance by authoritarian countries to outside aid. "Over the last three to four years, there's been a backlash by governments to make sure that no 'color revolution' occurs in their own country," she says, referring to the pro-democracy "Orange Revolution" in Ukraine and "Rose Revolution" in Georgia.

"We think neither the Bush administration nor the Obama administration has fully stood up for the right to cross-border help to fulfill human rights," Windsor continues.

In Egypt, a U.S. embassy official insisted in response to criticism from Egyptian activists that U.S. support continues. "We may have changed tactics, but our commitment to democracy and human rights promotion in Egypt is steadfast," an embassy official said in an e-mailed response to a reporter's questions. [9] But Carothers says human rights issues generally are getting only limited attention as the administration deals with other major foreign policy problems in Iraq, Iran and Afghanistan.

"They have been very busy with the major crises on their hands and have neither articulated nor begun to implement any kind of broad approach on human rights," Carothers says. "These are really pressing, and human rights seems to be of secondary concern."

Was President Obama right to have the United States join the United Nations Human Rights Council?

When a Danish newspaper published a full page of satirical depictions of the Prophet Muhammad in 2005, Muslim leaders around the world denounced the publication as a defamation of Islam. Many called on the Danish government to take legal action against the newspaper. A Danish prosecutor found no basis for proceeding against the newspaper, however. And many leaders and commentators in Europe and the United States criticized the Muslim response as a threat to freedom of expression.

The dispute exemplified the tension between many Muslims and much of the rest of the world over how to reconcile free speech with freedom of religion. Now, the United States and predominantly Muslim Egypt have joined in sponsoring a broad U.N. reaffirmation of freedom of expression that condemns religious intolerance but significantly omits any legal sanctions for criticizing religion or specific faiths.

The freedom of expression resolution, adopted Oct. 2 by consensus by the United Nations Human Rights Council, marked the first significant accomplishment by the United States since the Obama administration's decision to join the still-new U.N. forum. The Bush administration had refused to join the council after it was created in 2006 to replace the U.N. Commission on Human Rights, which was widely criticized as weak and ideologically polarized. [10]

Many human rights advocates say the passage of the freedom of expression resolution demonstrates the Obama administration was right to join the council. "The United States was successful in reaching out to Egypt," says Neil Hicks, senior adviser on U.N. issues for Human Rights First. By omitting any reference to defamation of religion, the resolution means that "there will no longer be an effort to weaken protection of freedom of expression in the name of protecting religion," Hicks says.

Other human rights advocates, however, are troubled by passages in the resolution critical of the rising incidence of religious intolerance and stereotyping. The resolution has "some very good language and some problematic language," says Paula Schriefer, director of advocacy at Freedom House, who follows U.N. issues. "There's some question whether this foray has been completely successful."

Hicks acknowledges the resolution is only "a step in the right direction" and may not end the dispute. Like most human rights advocates, however, including Freedom House, Hicks applauds the U.S. decision to participate in the council. "Our hope is that with U.S. membership there will be a concerted effort to stand up for democratic values in the council," Hicks says. "We're waiting for that to happen."

Some conservative human rights watchers, however, say the United States should have stayed out. "It was a token of the Bush administration's devotion to human rights that it would refuse to wade into this cesspool," says Johns Hopkins fellow Muravchik. "It is a great pity that the Obama administration has reversed that."

To join the council, the United States won election by 167 of the 192 members of the U.N. General Assembly in balloting in May. Among the 14 other countries elected were five with checkered human rights records, including two major powers, China and Russia; the regional power Saudi Arabia; and two smaller countries, Cameroon and Cuba. [11]

The U.N. Commission on Human Rights, the predecessor forum, had drawn criticism for being open to membership by — and domination by — human rights violators. In an effort to remedy the problem, membership in the new council requires an absolute majority of votes from the General Assembly rather than election from a regional bloc.

Proponents say the council is also stronger because all U.N. members will be subject to a "universal periodic review" of their records on rights issues, with council members up for review first. The commission had no procedure for reviewing human rights conditions in every country, Hicks says.

Supporters say membership by human rights violators is inevitable, but U.S. membership will strengthen the democratic bloc within the council. "Without United States leadership, other democratic countries rarely stand up effectively for human rights," says Human Rights Watch's Malinowski. "And repressive countries tend to band together quite effectively."

Mandelbaum at Johns Hopkins faults both the council and its predecessor for an anti-Israel bias. "They spend all their time persecuting the only country in the Middle East that takes human rights seriously: Israel," he says. Israel, which is not a member of the council, strongly criticized a report commissioned by the council that accused Israeli forces of human rights abuses during the invasion of Gaza launched in December 2008. (*See sidebar, p. 916.*)

Hicks agrees that the U.N. rights bodies have been guilty of "overconcentration on the Israeli-Palestinian situation," but he says that council actions adopting country-specific resolutions on Myanmar and Congo this year have shown some signs of reduced geographic-bloc voting.

In any event, most human rights experts applaud the Obama administration's decision to join the council. "The United States goes into these

Continued on p. 920

Chronology

1945-1990s

U.S. takes lead in establishing United Nations, writing international human rights law; U.S. support for democracy tempered by Cold War rivalry with communist bloc.

1945
United Nations established.

1948
Universal Declaration of Human Rights adopted by the U.N.

1950s
U.S. supports coups to oust leftist regimes in Guatemala, Iran; blocks unified election in Vietnam; sends no aid to anti-communist revolt in Hungary.

1960s
U.S. role in Vietnam War escalates; U.S. takes no action as Soviet Union crushes reform movement in Czechoslovakia.

1975
Vietnam War ends with fall of Saigon government, reunification under communist regime. . . . Helsinki Accords signed; Soviet bloc agrees to respect human rights.

1977-1981
President Jimmy Carter puts human rights at center of U.S. foreign policy.

1980s
U.S. support for right-wing regimes in Central America, contras in Nicaragua widely criticized in U.S., elsewhere; U.S. aid helps oust authoritarian leaders in Philippines, Haiti.

1989
Berlin Wall falls; Eastern European countries throw off communist governments; Cold War ends.

1990s
Human rights machinery institutionalized at United Nations: U.N. high commissioner for human rights created; war crimes tribunals established in former Yugoslavia, Rwanda.

———— • ————

2001-Present

Bush administration war on terror policies criticized, democracy promotion legacy questioned; Obama administration criticized for downplaying human rights.

2001
President George W. Bush launches invasion of Afghanistan for harboring al Qaeda after Sept. 11, 2001, attacks on U.S.; prepares aggressive policies to detain, interrogate "enemy combatants."

2002
U.S. opens prison camp for suspected terrorists at Guantánamo Bay Naval Base in Cuba; move widely criticized in Muslim world and by some European allies. . . . International Criminal Court established; U.S. declines to participate.

2003
U.S.-led invasion of Iraq topples Saddam Hussein; with U.S. support, parliamentary elections, referendum on new constitution held in 2005.

2004
U.S. labels killings of civilians in Sudan's Darfur province "genocide." . . . With U.S. backing, Hamid Karzai elected president of Afghanistan; parliamentary elections follow in 2005.

2005
Bush, in second inaugural address, promises U.S. support for democracy "in every nation and culture."

2006
U.S. declines to participate in newly created United Nations Human Rights Council.

2008
Bush prepares to leave office with democracy, human rights legacy sharply debated.

January-March 2009
Barack Obama inaugurated; repudiates Bush policies on detention and interrogation; promises to close Guantánamo within year (January). . . . Secretary of State Hillary Rodham Clinton draws fire for saying human rights should not "interfere" with U.S.-China relations (February). . . . U.S. signs U.N. petition favoring decriminalization of homosexual conduct (March). . . .

April-June 2009
U.S. wins election to U.N. Human Rights Council; administration signals support for U.N. convention to eliminate discrimination against women (May). . . . Obama says U.S. will support human rights "everywhere"; U.N. Ambassador Susan Rice indicates administration support for U.N. pact on children's rights (June).

July-September 2009
Clinton visits war-torn Congo during Africa visit (August). . . . Obama tells U.N. General Assembly U.S. has "too often been selective" in promoting democracy (September).

October 2009
Human Rights Council adopts freedom of expression resolution; endorses report opposed by U.S. that accuses Israel of targeting civilians in Gaza; U.S. critics say stance shows need to pull out of council. . . . Clinton, others unveil new policy on Sudan/Darfur; "carrots and sticks" approach criticized by some.

Clinton Vows Opposition to Violence Against Gays

'Killing campaign' in Iraq goes unpunished, rights group says.

The victim was taken from his parents' Baghdad home late one evening in April by four armed, masked men, who shouted insults as they dragged him away. His body was found in a garbage dump in the neighborhood the next day, his genitals cut off and a piece of his throat ripped out.

The victim's offense: He was gay. Three weeks later, when Human Rights Watch investigators spoke with the victim's 35-year-old partner, he struggled to speak. "In Iraq, murderers and thieves are respected more than gay people," he said. [1]

The incident was part of the group's report, published in August, which describes a "killing campaign" by "death squads" that swept through Iraq in the early months of 2009. The campaign was concentrated in Baghdad's Sadr City, the stronghold of supporters of the anti-American Shiite cleric Moktada al-Sadr, but killings also were reported in other cities.

The killings were done "with impunity," according to the report, based on three weeks of on-site interviews by Scott Long, director of Human Rights Watch's LGBT Rights Project, and a second investigator. Iraqi police and security forces did little to investigate or try to halt the killings, the report said. No arrests or prosecutions had been announced when the report was published.

Iraq is one of many countries where violence against lesbian, gay, bisexual or transgender persons occurs and goes unpunished or is even abetted by authorities. In many others, LGBT persons are subject to harassment, intimidation and even prosecution because of their sexual orientation or gender identity. In Senegal, nine people, including the head of an AIDS service organization, were arrested in December 2008 and given long prison sentences the next month, purportedly for engaging in homosexual conduct. [2]

Now, Secretary of State Hillary Rodham Clinton is promising that the United States will do more to track and oppose violence in other countries against LGBT persons. "Where it happens anywhere in the world, the United States must speak out against it and work for its end," Clinton said in a Sept. 11 speech to the Roosevelt Institute in New York City, where she was receiving the institute's Four Freedoms Medal. [3]

Despite widespread criticism of President Obama for allegedly downplaying human rights, LGBT rights advocates are giving the administration positive marks for increased attention to those issues after eight years of general neglect under President George W. Bush. "They've been very open to the dialogue," says Michael Guest, senior counselor at the Council for Global Equality, a coalition founded in 2008 to work for LGBT rights around the world.

Guest notes that the Obama administration decided in March to support a United Nations petition sponsored by France and the Netherlands calling for decriminalization of homosexual conduct. The Bush administration had taken no position on the resolution, now supported by 67 countries. Guest served as ambassador to Romania in the second Bush administration until his resignation in 2007 over the lack of spousal benefits and privileges for his partner.

In her speech, Clinton promised to give increased attention to violence against the LGBT community in the State Department's annual country-by-country reports on human rights. The most recent report, published in February and compiled during the Bush administration, includes what Guest calls the most detailed listing of LGBT rights violations to date. Among the incidents in 2008 noted were the murder of a transgender activist in Honduras, imprisonment in Egypt of men suspected

Continued from p. 918

things recognizing that the council is not a perfect body," says UCLA's Kaye. "Rather than sitting outside and complaining, it's now inside the tent." ∎

BACKGROUND

'Unalienable' Rights

As the first of the United States' founding documents, the Declaration of Independence affirmed a belief in the "unalienable" human rights of "life, liberty, and the pursuit of happiness" and the democratic principle of "consent of the governed." Those beliefs have remained central American ideals ever since. In the 20th century, the United States put its military and diplomatic might behind efforts to promote democracy and human rights — with limited success after World War I, somewhat more after World War II. Human rights remained a talking point during the Cold War but often took a back seat to geopolitics in the conflicts with two communist powers: the Soviet Union and China. [12]

The American Revolution succeeded in part because of aid from France. The young Republic turned a deaf ear in the 1820s, however, to pleas for help in the Greek war of independence. Then-Secretary of State John Quincy Adams said the United States was a "well-wisher to the freedom and independence of others," but "champion and vindicator only of her own." In the century's two major external wars — with Mexico (1846-1848) and Spain (1898) — the United States claimed to be spreading democracy, but the conflicts were aimed, in fact, at continental expansion and imperial conquest, respectively. [13]

of being HIV-positive and extensive discrimination in India against gays and lesbians in education and employment. [4]

The United States raised the issue of violence and rights violations against LGBT persons on Oct. 8 at a meeting of the Organization for Security and Co-operation in Europe, a regionwide human rights forum. Earlier, a U.S. representative had noted concern about the refusal in some countries to grant permits for pro-LGBT "pride" parades. Guest says increased U.S. attention to documenting LGBT issues is important because problems often go unreported. "LGBT communities in many countries are extremely marginalized, and social and cultural norms are such that nobody complains," he says.

Long also applauds the administration's statements on LGBT rights but says more concrete actions are needed. "What we're still looking for is action at the embassy level in countries where egregious things are going on," he says.

As one example, Long points to Uganda, where legislation was introduced in parliament in early October to tighten an existing prohibition on homosexual conduct by making any advocacy of or information about homosexuality a crime. [5] Long notes that Uganda received substantial funding under the Bush administration's AIDS initiative. "It will be a test of the Obama administration to see if it uses its leverage to oppose this bill,

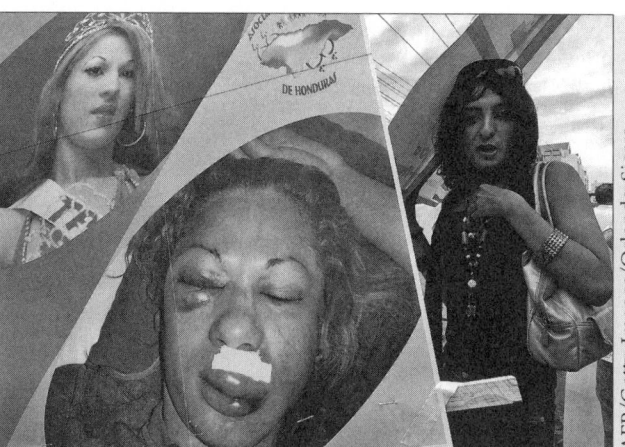

LGBT activists in Tegucigalpa, Honduras, protest the murder of a transgender activist on May 15, 2009. Secretary of State Hillary Clinton has promised to give increased attention to violence against the LGBT community.

which would be devastating to gays and lesbians," he says.

In its report on the Iraq killings, Human Rights Watch calls on the United States and U.S.-led multinational forces in Iraq to assist Iraqi authorities in investigating the killings and vetting and training Iraqi police on human rights issues with "no exceptions for sexual orientation and gender expression or identity." Long sees no action thus far on either of the recommendations. "It's not clear the embassy has done anything," he says.

— *Kenneth Jost*

[1] "They Want Us Exterminated," Human Rights Watch, August 2009, www.hrw.org/en/reports/2009/08/16/they-want-us-exterminated. The report does not identify the victim and uses a pseudonym for his partner.

[2] See Donald G. McNeil Jr., "Senegal: Where AIDS Efforts Are Often Praised, Prison for Counselors Is a Surprise," *The New York Times*, Jan. 20, 2009, p. D6.

[3] The full text is on the State Department's Web site: www.state.gov/secretary/rm/2009a/09/129164.htm. The one-paragraph reference drew coverage only in LGBT media. See Rex Wockner, "Clinton Says U.S. Will Fight Anti-Gay Violence Worldwide," *Windy City Times* (Chicago), Sept. 23, 2009.

[4] "2008 Country Reports on Human Rights Practices," U.S. State Department, Feb. 25, 2009, www.state.gov/g/drl/rls/hrrpt/2008/index.htm. See also "U.S. Government Documents Trend of Severe Human Rights Abuse Against LGBT People," Council for Global Equality, February 2009, www.globalequality.org/storage/cfge/documents/dos_human_rights_report_2008_analysis.pdf.

[5] See "Rights Groups Challenge Uganda's New Same-Sex Proposal," Voice of America English Service, Oct. 16, 2009.

As an emergent global power, the United States entered World War I with an explicit goal to "make the world safe for democracy." President Woodrow Wilson envisioned a postwar order founded on national self-determination with peace maintained by the League of Nations. With the United States out after the Senate's refusal to ratify the Versailles Treaty, the League was weakened from birth. The newly independent nations of Central and Eastern Europe mutated into dictatorships in the 1920s and '30s. And an isolationist-minded United States did nothing during the Spanish Civil War to prevent Francisco Franco's fascists from ousting a democratic government.

World War II brought a renewed commitment to human rights and democracy from the United States. Before the U.S. entry into the war, President Franklin D. Roosevelt in January 1941 identified four freedoms — freedom of speech and expression, freedom of religion, freedom from want and freedom from fear — as fundamental to people "everywhere in the world." Roosevelt's major wartime partner, British Prime Minister Winston Churchill, vowed in October 1942 that the war would end with "the enthronement of human rights." Like Wilson before him, Roosevelt envisioned a postwar order of national self-determination, including decolonization by wartime al-

lies Britain and France. Decolonization proceeded only slowly over the next two decades, however. And the postwar settlement with the Soviet Union, an ally in the war, left Moscow in effective control of Eastern Europe.

As the war ended, the United States took the lead role in establishing an institutional and legal infrastructure intended to preserve the peace while promoting human rights. The charter of the newly created United Nations declared the goal of promoting "human rights and fundamental freedoms for all." As a member of the U.S. delegation, Eleanor Roosevelt, the late president's widow, helped create and became the first head of the U.N. Commission on Human Rights. And the commission organized the drafting of the Universal Declaration of Human Rights, adopted by the U.N. General Assembly on Dec. 10, 1948. The treaty's 30 articles detail individual rights that are to serve "as a common standard of achievement for all peoples and all nations."

Hopes for a worldwide flourishing of human rights fell victim to the Cold War. As UCLA's Kaye points out, the ideological conflict with the Soviet Union forced the United States to struggle between devotion to human rights and pursuit of other geopolitical interests. Republican and Democratic presidents alike often resolved the conflict by supporting U.S. allies despite poor records on human rights and democracy. During the Chinese civil war, U.S. support for the Nationalist leader Chiang Kai-shek failed to prevent the communist takeover in 1949, which made Asia — like Europe — a major locus of ideological conflict with the United States and its allies.

A combination of ideological and economic interests led the United States during this period to organize coups that replaced leftist, democratically elected governments with right-wing U.S. allies in such countries as Iran (1953), Guatemala (1954) and Chile (1973). After the French defeat in Vietnam in 1954, the United States divided the nation rather than allow an election likely to have been won by the communist leader Ho Chi Minh. The United States did nothing, however, when Hungarians revolted against

the communist government in 1956 or when Czechoslovakians rose up against their communist rulers in 1968. By then, the United States was bogged down in the Vietnam War, which ended in 1975 with the country unified under communist rule.

Rights Commitments

The end of the Vietnam War coincided with other developments that helped give human rights new prominence both domestically and internationally. The Soviet Union and its Eastern European satellites joined with the United States and Western Europe in 1975 in the historic Helsinki

Palestinian youths throw stones at Israeli soldiers near the West Bank town of Hebron on Oct. 12, 2009. The United States has opposed a U.N. Human Rights Council report that accuses Israel of targeting Palestinian civilians in Gaza.

AFP/Getty Images/Hazem Bader

Accords, which committed all signatories to respect for human rights. In the United States, President Carter's election and four years in office left a lasting legacy of human rights as a central theme in U.S. foreign policy for future presidents, Republicans and Democrats alike. Then in the 1990s the fall of the Soviet Union and the end of the Cold War allowed

human rights to be given greater priority in comparison to other national interests in the formation of U.S. foreign policy.

The Helsinki Accords — technically, the Final Act of the Conference on Security and Co-operation in Europe — were signed by the United States, Canada, the Soviet Union and all European countries but two (Albania and Andorra). They committed all of the countries to "respect for human rights and fundamental freedoms, including the freedom of thought, conscience, religion or belief." In signing the agreement, the Soviet Union won the West's recognition of postwar borders, but with the proviso that they could be changed by peaceful means. The Soviet Union and the West remained at odds over how to define rights, but the accords spawned the creation of "Helsinki watch" monitoring groups that helped focus attention on alleged abuses.

Democrat Carter won election over Republican Gerald R. Ford in 1976 largely because of Ford's pardon of former President Richard M. Nixon for the Watergate scandal. In keeping with his moralistic approach to domestic and foreign issues alike, Carter promised in his campaign to make human rights a centerpiece of U.S. foreign policy. He institutionalized that commitment in his first year in office by creating in the State Department the Bureau of Human Rights and Humanitarian Affairs (now, the Bureau of Human Rights, Democracy and Labor). With the 30th anniversary of the Universal Declaration of Human Rights in 1978, Carter vowed again to make human rights central to U.S. policy as long as he was president. In the next year,

Secretary of State Warren Christopher told a congressional committee that the United States had contributed to the atmosphere that enabled civilian regimes to replace military rulers in several countries and release political prisoners in some others.

With the election of the conservative Republican Ronald Reagan in 1980, rights issues became a sharp partisan divide in the United States. Democrats criticized Reagan for a renewed hard line in relations with the Soviet Union and for support of right-wing, rights-abusing regimes in El Salvador and Guatemala and rightwing rebels in Nicaragua. Under Reagan, however, U.S. aid to democratic movements abroad was institutionalized with the establishment of the National Endowment for Democracy as a publicly funded, privately operated entity. And by his second term Reagan was being credited with a turnaround on human rights exemplified by the U.S. backing of the successful ouster of two authoritarian U.S. allies: Ferdinand Marcos in the Philippines and Jean-Claude Duvalier in Haiti.

The dissolution of the Soviet Union and the ouster of communist regimes throughout Eastern Europe came with stunning suddenness during the presidency of George H. W. Bush. Reagan's admirers credit the downfall to his hard-line stance, but they and lesspartisan observers also say the communist regimes failed because of the failure of communism itself. Whatever the causes, the events opened the door to opportunities for democratization and liberalization. Two decades later, Russia remains under critical scrutiny on rights issues, but many of the Eastern European countries are credited with successful transitions to democratic, rights-respecting governments.

Despite the easing of East-West tensions and a professed commitment to human rights, President Clinton was seen by rights advocates as falling short in some actions — for example, in delinking rights and trade with China and moving slowly to confront the humanitarian crises in the Rwanda conflict and in the wars in the former Yugoslavia. UCLA professor Kaye notes, however, that Democrat Clinton had to contend with a Republican-controlled House for six of his eight years in office and a GOP-controlled Senate for four.

The 1990s saw great progress, however, in the institutionalization of rights machinery at the United Nations, beginning in 1993 with the creation of the position of High Commissioner for Human Rights. Despite continuing controversy for its alleged anti-Israel bias, the Commission on Human Rights became an invaluable source of information by increase the use of so-called special rapporteurs to investigate and report on conditions in individual countries and in broad areas such as arbitrary detention, child prostitution and violence against women. The U.N. Security Council also approved the creation of war crimes tribunals for the Balkan and Rwandan conflicts, even as a U.N.-sponsored conference was drafting a treaty to create a permanent International Criminal Court (ICC). Concerned with possible prosecution of U.S. service members, however, the United States was one of seven countries to vote against approval of the treaty in the U.N. General Assembly in 1998.

Rights Dichotomies

President Bush's record on human rights was sharply disputed during his eight years in the White House and remains sharply disputed today. Bush's admirers say the wars in Afghanistan and Iraq brought human rights improvements in both countries; critics say rights conditions in both countries continue to be unsatisfactory. The opposing camps similarly disagree on the detention and interrogation policies that Bush adopted in his "war on terror." Even Bush's critics concede, however, that his administration took positive steps on some human right fronts unconnected with the post-9/11 events.

Bush adopted an aggressive legal strategy after the Sept. 11, 2001, attacks on the United States to apprehend, detain and interrogate suspected al Qaeda members and sympathizers. Most notably, he claimed that the Geneva Conventions did not apply to the "enemy combatants" rounded up in Afghanistan and elsewhere and that they could be held at the Guantánamo Bay Naval Base in Cuba outside jurisdiction of federal courts. Both claims stirred strong opposition from European allies and from human rights groups within and outside the United States. Both claims were also rejected by the Supreme Court, which held in a series of cases that the Guantánamo detainees were protected by the Geneva Conventions' so-called Common Article 3 and that they could use federal habeas corpus petitions to challenge the legality of their imprisonment.

Bush mixed national security objectives with human rights goals in the wars both in Afghanistan and in Iraq. Admirers see human rights gains. "There are free elections in Iraq," says Johns Hopkins professor Mandelbaum. "Women go to school in Afghanistan."

In its most recent annual report issued in February 2009, however, Human Rights Watch is sharply critical of rights conditions in each. In Iraq, the government — described as resting on a narrow ethnic and sectarian base — is blamed for widespread torture and abuse of detainees. The report says girls and women are subject to gender-based violence; gays and lesbians are also subject to violence "by state and non-state actors." In Afghanistan, the government — described as weak and riddled with corruption — is faulted for taking no action on a justice-and-reconciliation plan adopted in 2006. Education for girls continues to lag, the report says, because of violence in some regions and social pressures elsewhere.

While criticizing Bush for taking "backward" steps on the war on terror, UCLA's Kaye says his presidency should not be viewed "as purely a dark period" on human rights issues. As one example, he notes the administration's decision in 2004 to accuse the Sudanese government of genocide in the rebellious province of Darfur. The administration also contributed to an international peace-keeping force and opposed a suspension of the ICC warrant against Sudan's president, Omar Hassan al-Bashir, for allegedly overseeing genocide in Darfur. Kaye also praises Bush for expanding U.S. programs to combat HIV/AIDS abroad. Bush won congressional approval for a $15 billion anti-AIDS initiative in 2003; as it was set to expire in 2008 he signed a five-year, $48 billion expansion. Kaye also gives Bush credit for tackling other global issues, such as human trafficking.

The Bush administration had less interest, however, in international human rights treaties. Most notably, the administration strongly opposed ratification of the treaty creating the ICC. Clinton had signed the treaty in 2000 but deferred asking the Senate to ratify it until after the court was in operation. Once the court began operations in 2002, however, Bush said he would not ask for ratification unless U.S. service members were exempted from possible prosecutions. Kaye notes that Bush also did not push for U.S. action on other international human rights covenants, including the Convention on the Rights of the Child and the Convention on the Elimination of All Forms of Discrimination Against Women. In its report, Human Rights Watch also cites the U.S. opposition to the U.N. Human Rights Council as an example of the Bush administration's "arrogant approach to multilateral institutions."

During his campaign, Obama strongly criticized the Bush administration's anti-terrorism policies as having lowered respect for the United States around the world. In his acceptance speech at the Democratic National Convention on Aug. 27, 2008, he promised to "restore our moral standing." He also vowed to "build new partnerships to defeat the threats of the 21st century: terrorism and nuclear proliferation, poverty and genocide, climate change and disease."

As president, Obama moved quickly to redeem one of his promises by reversing some of Bush's anti-terror policies in his first week in office. He scrapped legal opinions that had questioned the applicability of the Geneva Conventions to suspected terrorists, shuttered the Central Intelligence Agency's secret prisons and set a one-year deadline for closing the Guantánamo prison camp.

In a series of foreign policy addresses from June through September, Obama also sought to reengage with the international community on a wide range of issues, including democracy and human rights. In his June 4 speech in Cairo, Obama pointedly underlined for the Muslim world the importance of religious tolerance and women's rights. In Ghana on July 11, he faulted post-colonial Africa for too much corruption and too little good governance. A few days earlier in Moscow, however, Obama steered clear of any direct criticism of Russia's restrictions on political freedoms. And his Sept. 23 speech to the U.N. General Assembly included only a single paragraph on democracy — but with the significant admission that the United States "has too often been selective in its promotion of democracy." ∎

CURRENT SITUATION

Rights Policies in Flux

The Obama administration shows signs of becoming more active on international human rights issues, but it continues to draw mixed reactions from human rights groups and experts.

In the weeks since Obama's address to the U.N. General Assembly, the administration has unveiled a new strategy aimed at easing the humanitarian crisis in the Sudanese province of Darfur and implementing the 2005 peace accord between the country's predominantly Arab North and Christian and animist South. The administration has also strongly protested the Sept. 28 massacre and mass rapes of political protesters in the West African nation of Guinea, called for investigation of possible abuses during Sri Lanka's now-ended civil war and protested the arrest of a prominent human rights lawyer in Syria.

UCLA professor Kaye applauds the new Sudan policy for use of "benchmarks" to judge the government's compliance with the requested actions, but he adds, "The jury's still out." He says the statements on Guinea, Sri Lanka and Syria are "important signals" of the administration's human rights policy, but more action is needed. "One should hope that the statements of opposition and outrage are followed up by diplomatic moves," he says.

Johns Hopkins fellow Muravchik questions what he calls "the softer line" toward the Sudan government. Like Kaye, he views the U.S. stances on Guinea, Sri Lanka and Syria as unexceptional. The United States has "nothing at stake in Guinea or Sri Lanka," Muravchik says, "and issuing a protest about the arrest of a human rights lawyer is a fairly routine and mild thing to do."

The Sudan policy, announced by Clinton on Oct. 19, represents a conscious effort to find a balance between a hard-line approach emphasizing punitive sanctions and a refusal to deal with Sudanese President Bashir and a more conciliatory stance combining positive incentives and engagement with Bashir's government. [14]

Continued on p. 926

At Issue:

Does President Obama deserve the Nobel Peace Prize for 2009?

BEN COHEN
EDITOR, THEDAILYBANTER.COM

WRITTEN FOR *CQ RESEARCHER*, OCT. 25, 2009

*a*lthough Obama has governed as a centrist, one can't help but think that he is turning a very heavy ship ever so slowly leftwards, and that deep down, his heart lies far further to the left than he would like to let on. There is little doubt that Obama would, if he could, enact the extension of equal rights to gays, end the war in Iraq and Afghanistan, reconcile the Israelis and Palestinians and seriously reform the financial system.

The truth is, however, that a country taken over by special interests cannot be turned around quickly.

It is true that Obama has largely failed to deliver on all the above. But then again, he has only been in power for 11 months. And there has been progress — the engagement with the Middle East, multilateralism as the first option rather than the last, substantially increased unemployment benefits, cheaper student loans, a commitment (on paper at least) to reducing carbon dioxide emissions and a rebranding of America abroad.

Does this warrant a Nobel Peace Prize? Yes, and here's why.

The United States became a feared and despised state under the rule of the George W. Bush administration. The brazen disregard for global opinion, the trampling of international law and the overt environmental destruction were hallmarks of a presidency determined to project American power at all costs. With one election, the world forgave — and almost forgot — the tragic Bush years as a young, black president who spoke of hope rather than hatred, and cooperation rather than force, swept into power.

This monumental shift cannot and must not be underestimated.

Obama's Peace Prize was not necessarily given to him for what he has accomplished. It was given to him for what he can accomplish. As South African Archbishop Desmond Tutu put it:

"It is an award that speaks to the promise of President Obama's message of hope."

Hope will not fix the environment, stop the wars in Afghanistan and Iraq or prevent bankers from stealing all of our money.

Obama can certainly do better, much better than he is doing now. But it is too early to cast judgment, and he deserves time to make the changes he promised.

Obama has won the most prestigious prize for contributions to humanity in the world.

Now he must earn it.

ERICK ERICKSON
EDITOR-IN-CHIEF, REDSTATE.COM

WRITTEN FOR *CQ RESEARCHER*, OCT. 26, 2009

*i*n July 2006, speaking to schoolchildren, Betty Williams, the Nobel Peace Prize winner from Northern Ireland, said she would "love to kill George W. Bush." This year's recipient, Barack Obama, has yet to encounter a problem for which blaming Bush is not a solution. He fits the Nobel Peace Prize mold, which by and large is determined by a committee that runs an affirmative-action program giving preference to those people who view world peace as an absence of American influence — extra points to Americans who hate the American ideal.

Like Al Gore and Jimmy Carter before him, Barack Obama has done nothing to further peace in our time but has repudiated strong American leadership. The Nobel committee, possessed by the spirit of former British Prime Minister Neville Chamberlain, has descended to farcically awarding prizes for prospective peace that will never come and global warming fixes that will never work, but will make Al Gore a very rich man.

The Peace Prize long ago ceased to have any relevance to anyone outside the left. Awarding the prize to Yasser Arafat, who had the blood of thousands on his hands, was akin to awarding a safe-driving certificate to Ted Kennedy. The only thing the prize now stands for is approval from the anti-American European left. We should hope the president of the United States would pause to consider that, but as he did not, we can be sure he agrees.

In fact, in Barack Obama's short tenure as president he has done his best to apologize for perceived American abuses of power and arrogance, backpedaled on key issues of national security and flirted with some of the most kleptocratic, tyrannical regimes in modern history. Siding with tyrants over the democracy-loving people of Honduras, giving lip service to freedom as Iranians were gunned down in the streets of Tehran and coddling up to our Chinese bankers have ingratiated the man with those who have always been offended by the last 10 words of "The Star Spangled Banner." If that merits a peace prize, most Americans would probably prefer war.

The prospective peace the Nobel committee hopes for will not come. It is as illusory as the pot of gold at the end of the rainbow. Barack Obama's vanity will, however, compel him to pursue it. We can be sure his peace will be America's loss.

Continued from p. 924

The six-year-long crisis in Darfur — part of the turmoil in Africa's largest country spanning more than two decades — has defied peacekeeping and mediation efforts by the international community. Government-aided militias are blamed for killing at least 350,000 people; more than 2.4 million people have been displaced, most of them living in refugee camps that depend on international humanitarian groups for food and other supplies. In his campaign, Obama had called for strong sanctions against Bashir's government.

Darfur advocacy groups are voicing guarded optimism about the new approach. Jerry Fowler, president of the Washington-based Save Darfur Coalition, said the policy was similar to the "balance of incentives and pressures" that the group had been calling for. But he said the policy would not succeed without "substantial presidential leadership."

From a critical perspective, however, Bret Stephens, a *Wall Street Journal* columnist, mocked the administration's "menu of incentives and disincentives" in the policy. "It's the kind of menu Mr. Bashir will languidly pick his way through till he dies comfortably in his bed," Stephens wrote. [15]

On Guinea, Clinton registered a strong protest over the killing of more than 150 demonstrators in the capital of Conakry opposing the military government of Capt. Moussa "Dadis" Camara. There were also reports of dozens of rapes — including mass rapes and sexual mutilation of the victims — by government soldiers. Clinton on Oct. 7 denounced the brutality and violence as "criminality of the greatest degree" and called on Camara to step down. She also dispatched William Fitzgerald, deputy assistant secretary of state for African affairs, to Guinea to deliver the protest. [16]

The State Department's report on Sri Lanka, issued on Oct. 22, detailed alleged atrocities by both sides in the now-ended insurgency by a militant Tamil group seeking to create a separate homeland on the South Asian island nation. The report, requested by Congress, described as credible allegations that the government had targeted civilians and that the Tamil United Liberation Front had recruited children for the fighting. The report called for a full investigation by the government. "A very important part of any reconciliation process is accountability," State Department spokesman Ian Kelly said. [17]

On Syria, the administration joined Britain, France and international human rights groups in calling for the release of the prominent lawyer and former judge Haitham Maleh, who has been jailed since his Oct. 14 arrest. Maleh, 78, has opposed Syria's Baathist government and called for lifting the state of emergency it imposed after taking power in 1963. The arrest is "the latest Syrian action in a two-year crackdown on lawyers and civil society activists," the State Department said. [18]

The flurry of new statements "doesn't change the picture much," says Muravchik. "It's always true that any U.S. administration will be on the side of human rights if there is no cost to it in the coin of other U.S. foreign policy goals," he explains. "The problem that every administration faces is that insofar as we use some of our political influence and capital to press for human rights, we necessarily create frictions with governments that abuse human rights that make it harder for us to do other kinds of business with them."

Rights Treaties in Limbo

The Obama administration is signaling support for ratifying two long-pending United Nations-sponsored treaties on women's rights and children's rights, but Senate action is in doubt because of continued opposition from social conservatives and others.

The United States is all but alone in failing to join the two treaties: the Convention on the Elimination of All Discrimination Against Women and the Convention on the Rights of the Child. Besides the United States, only six other countries have failed to ratify the treaty on sex discrimination: Iran, Nauru, Palau, Somalia, Sudan and Tonga. Somalia is the only other country not to have approved the children's rights charter. [19]

The United States signed both treaties during Democratic administrations, but Republican opposition in Congress — fueled by opposition from social conservatives — has prevented the Senate ratification needed to give the treaties force of law. Now, the Obama administration says it wants both treaties ratified, but it has not set a timetable for moving on either one.

Social conservatives say both treaties pose threats to traditional family roles in the United States and to states' prerogatives on social issues. Some critics also question the treaties' practical effect since the signatories include any number of countries with poor human rights records. But human rights groups and other social welfare advocates say U.S. support for the treaties is important both symbolically and in practice. But they reject warnings that the treaties would impinge on private family arrangements.

The treaty on women's rights — sometimes known by the acronym CEDAW — was completed in 1979 and signed by the United States the next year while Carter was president. The Senate Foreign Relations Committee held hearings on the treaty in 1988, 1990, 1994 and 2002.

President Clinton submitted the treaty for ratification in 1994 with reservations on some issues including paid maternity leave and combat assignments for women. In the face of GOP opposition, Clinton never pressed for a Senate floor vote. Under

Democratic control, the Foreign Relations Committee again recommended ratification in 2002, but the Bush administration opposed the treaty, and no floor vote was held.

In her confirmation hearing, U.N. Ambassador Rice said the administration considered the women's rights treaty "a priority." The treaty was included in May on a list of those recommended for action, but no action has been taken. Conservative groups continue to denounce the treaty. "It's the Equal Rights Amendment on steroids," says Wendy Wright, head of Concerned Women for America. Among other provisions, opponents complain of one that calls for nations to work to eliminate "stereotyped roles for men and women." [20]

The Reagan and George H. W. Bush administrations played a part in negotiating the children's rights pact but never signed it because of concern about its impact on U.S. law. The Clinton administration signed the treaty in 1995, but did not seek Senate ratification. The George W. Bush administration actively opposed the treaty.

Obama voiced concern during his campaign about the U.S. failure, along with Somalia, to approve the treaty. In a classroom session with schoolchildren in New York City in June, Rice said officials are actively discussing "when and how it might be possible to join." Again, no concrete action has been taken.

Conservative groups strongly oppose the pact. Stephen Groves, a fellow at the Heritage Foundation, a conservative think tank in Washington, says the treaty would give a U.N. body "a say over how children in American should be raised, educated or disciplined." [21]

The Obama administration's receptiveness to multilateral rights accords is viewed as a positive by human rights groups, but Human Rights Watch's Washington director Mali-nowski says political considerations still shape the ratification strategies. "They're rightly starting with the ones on which there's the most consensus," he says. Johns Hopkins fellow Muravchik questions the value of the charters. "I wouldn't say they are empty exercises, but their importance is quite secondary," he says.

On a more contentious issue, Human Rights Watch is urging the administration to move away from Bush's strong opposition to the ICC and instead "develop a constructive relationship" with the tribunal. Without joining the court, the group says the United States can lend assistance to investigations and prosecutions. It also wants the administration to oppose provisions passed by Congress in 2002 that, among other things, prohibited U.S. participation in peacekeeping missions unless U.S. service members were granted immunity from possible war crime prosecutions before the tribunal. So far, the administration has backed the ICC's prosecution of Sudan's President Bashir but has not outlined a general policy toward the court. ∎

OUTLOOK

Waiting for Results

When President Obama arrives in Beijing in mid-November, he will be seeking to enlist China's help in dealing with some of the United States' most pressing issues, including nuclear proliferation, climate change and the global economic slowdown. Despite a newly published report by the joint Congressional-Executive Commission criticizing China for increased repression in some areas, however, U.S. experts expect human rights to be low on the agenda for Obama's visit.

"Elevating human rights . . . is not going to serve U.S. interests at this point," says Elizabeth Economy, director of Asia studies for the Council on Foreign Relations, a New York-based think tank.

The administration's critics, particularly partisan conservatives, accuse Obama of an across-the-board downgrading of human rights. Administration officials, however, depict the president as fully committed to promoting human rights abroad.

"The president's policy on these issues is clear," State Department legal adviser Koh told reporters at a Sept. 29 briefing in Geneva during a U.N. Human Rights Council session. "He promotes human rights through engagement. He promotes human rights through diplomacy. He promotes human rights through efforts to find common ground. And he's prepared to do this in both bilateral and multilateral settings."

Some experts see logic in the administration's apparent preference for engagement over confrontation but still warn about the risks of a perceived weakening of U.S. opposition to abusive practices. Obama "believes that solving foreign policy problems requires engaging with America's adversaries and ending the lecturing (and hectoring) tone of his predecessor," writes James Goldgeier, a senior fellow with the Council on Foreign Relations and a professor of political science and international affairs at George Washington University.

The strategy "might seem to make sense," Goldgeier continues. "Unfortunately, it sends a signal to repressive regimes that no one is going to call them to account for their human rights violations. And those fighting for freedom in their home countries may soon worry that the United States is no longer their champion." [22]

Johns Hopkins professor Mandelbaum is less convinced that the administration has merely shifted tactics on human rights issues without reducing their priority as a foreign policy goal. "No administration wants to say that it is downgrading human rights, so of course that's what they would say," Mandelbaum remarks. "Maybe they'll turn out to be correct."

Some of the administration's tactical choices are evidently open to debate, such as the decision to defer Obama's meeting with the Dalai Lama until after the China trip. Economy calls it a mistake. "The Dalai Lama is a global leader," she says. "Deciding to meet with him is unrelated to the China issue."

But Douglas Paal, a China expert at the Carnegie Endowment for International Peace who was on the National Security Council staff under Presidents Reagan and George H. W. Bush, calls the decision "a reasonable choice." "Tibet is at the head of China's core interests," he says. "Taking note of that, the administration doesn't want to have a debate about meeting with the Dalai Lama."

In a detailed report published on Oct. 16, the Congressional-Executive Commission on China finds increased repression in Tibet and the predominantly Uighur Xinjiang province along with increased harassment of human rights lawyers and advocates throughout the country. On Tibet, the report recommends that the United States urge China to open a dialogue with the Dalai Lama. It also calls on the government to increase aid to non-governmental organizations (NGOs) for programs to aid Tibetans. [23]

In other sections, the report similarly urges a mix of government-to-government pressure along with concrete steps by the U.S. government and NGOs. The commission, created in 2000, includes nine senators, nine House members and five executive branch appointees. The Obama administration's seats on the commission are vacant; the administration has been slow in filling many executive branch slots.

With a full plate of major international crises and a challenging domestic agenda, the Obama administration is understandably hard-pressed to find time and resources to devote to human rights issues that — as in Sudan — present difficult and complex policy choices. Clinton, however, took time in August for a weeklong trip to Africa that included meetings with rape victims and visiting a refugee camp in the war-torn Democratic Republic of the Congo. [24] And in a visit to Russia in October, the secretary of state used a speech to university students to urge Moscow to open the political system. As *The New York Times*' reporter noted, "Mrs. Clinton spoke far more forcefully about human rights and the rule of law than she did on a trip to China earlier this year." [25]

With U.S. influence on other nations' internal policies necessarily limited, the likely impact of Clinton's Africa tour or Moscow speech is easily doubted. Human rights groups, however, believe the United States has made a difference in the past. Now, they are waiting with some impatience and skepticism to see whether the Obama administration will devote enough time, attention and resources to make a difference again.

"I keep hearing from the administration an interest in focusing on results," says Human Rights First Executive Director Massamino. "That's how I think they ought to be judged." ■

Notes

[1] Quoted in "Dalai Lama Shrugs Off Apparent Snub by Obama," Reuters, Oct. 8, 2009. For earlier coverage, see John Pomfret, "Obama's Meeting With the Dalai Lama Is Delayed," *The Washington Post*, Oct. 5, 2009, p. A1. The story notes that since 1991 three U.S. presidents — George H. W. Bush, Bill Clinton, and George W. Bush — have had a total of 10 meetings with the Dalai Lama at the White House; all were private photo opportunities except the Congressional Medal of Freedom ceremony in 2007. For background on China and Tibet, see Thomas J. Billitteri, "Human Rights in China," *CQ Researcher*, July 25, 2008, pp. 601-624; Brian Beary, "Separatist Movements," *CQ Global Researcher*, April 2008, pp. 85-114.

[2] The official press release is at http://nobel prize.org/nobel_prizes/peace/laureates/2009/press.html.

[3] For previous coverage, see Peter Katel, "Exporting Democracy," *CQ Researcher*, April 1, 2005, pp. 269-292; and in *Editorial Research Reports*: Kenneth Jost, "Human Rights," Nov. 13, 1998, pp. 977-1000; Mary H. Cooper, "Human Rights in the 1980s," July 19, 1985, pp. 537-556; and Richard C. Schroeder, "Human Rights Policy," May 18, 1979, pp. 361-380.

[4] See Arch Puddington, "Freedom in the World 2009: Setbacks and Resilience," Freedom House, July 2009, www.freedomhouse.org/template.cfm?page=130&year=2009. Puddington is Freedom House's director of research.

[5] Clinton is quoted in "Clinton: human rights

About the Author

Associate Editor **Kenneth Jost** graduated from Harvard College and Georgetown University Law Center. He is the author of the *Supreme Court Yearbook* and editor of *The Supreme Court from A to Z* (both *CQ Press*). He was a member of the *CQ Researcher* team that won the American Bar Association's 2002 Silver Gavel Award. His previous reports include "Closing Guantánamo" and "The Obama Presidency" (with *CQ Researcher* staff). He is also author of the blog *Jost on Justice* (http://jostonjusticeblogspot.com).

can't interfere with other crises," CNN, Feb. 22, 2009; Amnesty International's statement can be found at www.amnestyusa.org/document.php?id=ENGUSA20090220001&rss=iar#. For coverage, see Mark Landler, "Clinton Paints China Policy With a Green Hue," *The New York Times*, Feb. 22, 2009, p. A8.

[6] Jamie Glazov, "Obama's Human Rights Disaster," *FrontPageMagazine.com*, Aug. 25, 2009, http://frontpagemag.com/readArticle.aspx?ART ID=36042.

[7] The text of the president's address in Cairo can be found on the White House Web site: www.whitehouse.gov/the_press_office/Remarks-by-the-President-at-Cairo-University-6-04-09/. For analysis, see Peter Baker, "Following a Different Map to a Similar Destination," *The New York Times*, June 9, 2009, p. A10. The text of Obama's and Mubarak's Aug. 18 remarks to reporters is on the White House Web site: www.whitehouse.gov/the_press_office/Remarks-by-President-Obama-and-President-Mubarak-of-Egypt-during-press-availability/.

[8] "Making Its Mark: An Analysis of the Obama Administration FY2010 Budget for Democracy and Human Rights," Freedom House, July 2009, www.freedomhouse.org/uploads/FY2010Budget Analysis.pdf. For figures on Egypt, see Sudarsan Raghavan, "Egyptian Reform Activists Say U.S. Commitment Is Waning," *The Washington Post*, Oct. 9, 2009, p. A14.

[9] Quoted in *ibid*.

[10] The text of the resolution can be found on the U.N. Council on Human Rights' Web site: www2.ohchr.org/english/bodies/hrcouncil/12session/docs/A_HRC_RES_12_16_AEV.pdf. For coverage of the council's action, see Frank Jordans, "UN rights body approves US-Egypt free speech text," The Associated Press, Oct. 2, 2009. For background, see Warren Hoge, "As U.S. Dissents, U.N. Approves a New Council on Rights Abuse," *The New York Times*, March 16, 2006, p. A3.

[11] See Neil MacFarquhar, "U.S. Joins Rights Panel After Vote in the U.N.," *The New York Times*, May 13, 2009, p. A5. The other countries elected to the council were Bangladesh, Djibouti, Jordan, Kyrgyzstan, Mauritius, Mexico, Nigeria, Senegal and Uruguay.

[12] Background drawn from previous *CQ Researcher* reports, footnote 3. See also Robert L. Maddex (ed.), *International Encyclopedia of Human Rights: Freedoms, Abuses, and Remedies* (2000).

[13] Adams quoted in Joshua Muravchik, *Exporting Democracy: Fulfilling America's Destiny* (1991), p. 19.

---

[14] For the State Department's background paper, see www.state.gov/r/pa/prs/ps/2009/oct/130676.htm. For background, see Karen Foerstel, "Crisis in Darfur," *CQ Global Researcher*, September 2008, pp. 243-270.

[15] Bret Stephens, "Does Obama Believe in Human Rights?" *The Wall Street Journal*, Oct. 20, 32009, p. A19.

[16] "Clinton: Violence in Guinea 'Criminal,' " The Associated Press, Oct. 7, 2009.

[17] "Report to Congress on Incidents During the Recent Conflict in Sri Lanka," U.S. Department of State, Oct. 22, 2009, www.state.gov/documents/organization/131025.pdf. For coverage, see "U.S. Details Possible Sri Lanka Civil War Abuses," Reuters, Oct. 7, 2009.

[18] "U.S. Says Syria Should Release 78-Year-Old Dissident," Reuters, Oct. 24, 2009.

[19] Background drawn from two Congressional Research Service reports, both by Luisa Blanchfield: "The United Nations Convention on the Elimination of All Forms of Discrimination Against Women," Aug. 7, 2009, http://assets.opencrs.com/rpts/R40750_20090807.pdf; "The United Nations Convention on the Rights of the Child: Background and Policy Issues," Aug. 5, 2009, http://assets.opencrs.com/rpts/R40484_20090805.pdf.

[20] Wright quoted in David Crary, "Discord likely over ratifying women's rights pact," The Associated Press, March 7, 2009.

[21] Quoted in Robert Kiener, "Rescuing Children," *CQ Global Researcher*, October 2009, p. 265.

[22] See "Critics say Obama is punting on human rights. Agree or disagree," *The Arena*, www.politico.com/arena/archive/obama-human-rights.html. The online forum hosted by *Politico* included comments from eight other experts and political activists.

[23] "Congressional-Executive Commission on China," Annual Report 2009, Oct. 10, 2009, www.cecc.gov/pages/annualRpt/annualRpt09/CECCannRpt2009.pdf.

[24] See Jeffrey Gettleman, "A Flash of Pique After a Long Week in a Continent Full of Troubles," *The New York Times*, Aug. 13, 2009, p. A8.

[25] Mark Landler, "In Russia, Clinton Urges Russia to Open Its Political System," *The New York Times*, Oct. 15, 2009, p. A6.

Bibliography
Selected Sources

Books

Muravchik, Joshua, *Exporting Democracy: Fulfilling America's Destiny*, AEI (American Enterprise Institute) Press, 1991.

With the Cold War ending, a leading neoconservative author laid out the case for an active U.S. role in promoting democracy in other countries. Includes notes.

Traub, James, *The Freedom Agenda: Why America Must Spread Democracy (Just Not the Way George Bush Did)*, Farrar Straus and Giroux, 2008.

As George W. Bush's presidency was ending, journalist Traub argued that aid to civil-society organizations focused on political liberalization, economic modernization and social welfare is the best way for the United States to promote democracy abroad. Includes six-page note on sources.

Articles

Bolton, John, "Israel, the U.S., and the Goldstone Report," *The Wall Street Journal*, Oct. 19, 2009, p. A19.

The former U.S. ambassador to the United Nations argues that the U.N. Human Rights Council's approval of the report by South African jurist Richard Goldstone critical of Israel's conduct during the Gaza war shows that the Obama administration made a mistake in joining the body and should now withdraw.

Carothers, Thomas, "The Democracy Crusade Myth," *The National Interest online*, July 1, 2007, www.national interest.org/PrinterFriendly.aspx?id=14826.

A leading democratization expert at the Carnegie Endowment for International Peace says that despite pro-democracy rhetoric, the Bush administration actually gave traditional security and economic interests priority over promoting democracy abroad.

Krauthammer, Charles, "Three Cheers for the Bush Doctrine," *Time*, March 14, 2005, p. 28.

The conservative columnist argues that President Bush's plan for democratization has sparked free elections in numerous countries.

Kristof, Nicholas D., "What to Do About Darfur," *The New York Review of Books*, July 2, 2009, www.ny-books.com/articles/22771.

The New York Times foreign affairs columnist, in reviewing several books on the crisis in Sudan's Darfur province, calls the Obama administration's approach to the crisis inadequate but only a start. The article was written before the administration's announcement in October of a new "carrots and sticks" policy toward Sudan aimed at easing the Darfur crisis and fully implementing the 2006 accord that ended the Sudanese civil war.

Risen, Clay, "Does Human Rights Talk Matter?" *The New Republic*, Feb. 24, 2009, www.tnr.com/blog/the-plank/does-human-rights-talk-matter.

The article argues that Secretary of State Hillary Rodham Clinton gave a green light to rights abusers throughout the world with her statement that China's human rights violations would not interfere with U.S.-China relations. Risen is a free-lance writer and managing editor of *Democracy: A Journal of Ideas*.

Reports and Studies

"Annual Report 2009," Congressional-Executive Commission on China, Oct. 10, 2009, www.cecc.gov/pages/annual Rpt/annualRpt09/CECCannRpt2009.pdf.

A commission established to monitor human rights and the rule of law in China finds that the country's continued use of repression undermines its stated international commitments to create a more open society. The 468-page report calls on the U.S. government to monitor Chinese progress in turning the principles outlined in the National Human Rights Action Plan of 2009 into tangible results.

"2008 Country Reports on Human Rights Practices," U.S. Department of State, Feb. 25, 2009, www.state.gov/g/drl/rls/hrrpt/2008/index.htm.

The State Department's congressionally mandated country reports on human rights practices points to three overarching trends during 2008: "a growing worldwide demand for greater personal and political freedom; governmental efforts to push back on those freedoms, and further confirmation that human rights flourish best in participatory democracies with vibrant civil societies."

"Freedom in the World 2009," Freedom House, July 2009, www.freedomhouse.org/template.cfm?page=363&year=2009.

The organization's annual survey, covering 193 countries and 16 territories, finds a third consecutive yearly decline in global freedom. In an overview, the group's research director says the United States and other democracies face "serious challenges" in confronting "a forceful reaction" by authoritarian governments against democratic reformers and outside assistance for democratization.

"World Report 2009," Human Rights Watch, www.hrw.ort/world-report-2009.

The group's 19th annual review, covering human rights practices in more than 90 countries, opens with an essay by Executive Director Kenneth Roth arguing that intergovernmental discussions of human rights have recently been dominated by "human rights spoilers" — countries and leaders opposed to enforcement of human rights.

The Next Step:

Additional Articles from Current Periodicals

Gays

Londo, Ernesto, "Gay Men Targeted in Iraq, Report Says," *The Washington Post*, **Aug. 17, 2009, p. A6.**

The Iraqi government must do more to protect gay men who are being targeted by militias, says Human Rights Watch.

Riley, Michael, "Polis Takes Iraq to Task Over Attacks on Gays," *Denver Post*, **April 9, 2009, p. A1.**

Rep. Jared Polis, D-Colo., is an openly gay member of Congress who toured Iraq to investigate the treatment of gays.

Sly, Liz, "Gays Being Targeted and Killed in Iraq, Groups Say," *Los Angeles Times*, **Aug. 18, 2009, p. A19.**

A London-based group supporting gays in Iraq says 87 killings have occurred so far in 2009 related to anti-gay sentiments.

Global Crises

Burns, Robert, "Obama Sets New Policy to Nudge Sudan Toward Peace," The Associated Press, Oct. 19, 2009.

The Obama administration has outlined a new policy that provides incentives for the Sudanese government to end violence in Darfur.

Klug, Foster, "Obama Postpones Meeting With Dalai Lama," *News Journal* **(Delaware), Oct. 6, 2009.**

President Obama has decided not to meet with the Dalai Lama to discuss human rights in China until first meeting with President Hu Jintao in Beijing.

Mann, William C., "Obama's Policy on Darfur Lacks Clarity, Advocates Say," *The Boston Globe*, **June 20, 2009, p. 4.**

Human rights groups fear for the survival of 2.5 million Darfurians in refugee camps if the Obama administration doesn't commit to plans to ensure their security.

Nuechterlein, Donald, "Human Rights Take Back Seat to Realpolitik," *Saginaw* **(Michigan)** *News*, **March 8, 2009.**

Human rights are not as important to U.S. interests as vital economic and strategic considerations in dealing with China.

Goldstone Report

Boudreaux, Richard, "War Crimes in Gaza Reported," *Los Angeles Times*, **Sept. 16, 2009, p. A19.**

The deaths of nearly 1,400 Palestinians in Gaza during the 22-day Israeli offensive amounted to war crimes — and possible crimes against humanity — according to U.N. investigator Judge Richard Goldstone.

Cumming-Bruce, Nick, "U.N. Investigator Presents Report on Gaza War," *The New York Times*, **Sept. 30, 2009, p. A3.**

The lead U.N. investigator for the Gaza conflict says the lack of accountability for war crimes in the region has reached a crisis point.

Sanders, Edmund, "Fact-Finding Mission in Gaza Faces Skeptics," *Los Angeles Times*, **June 29, 2009, p. A14.**

A United Nations panel investigating war crimes in Gaza has been labeled as biased by Israelis, while Palestinians believe any inquiries won't amount to much.

U.N. Human Rights Council

Guest, Iain, "Obama's Moment on Human Rights," *The Christian Science Monitor*, **Dec. 10, 2008, p. 9.**

U.S. membership in the Human Rights Council would give hope to moderate governments yearning for a stronger U.N. human rights program.

Higgins, Alexander G., "U.N. Chief Urges U.S. to Join Human Rights Body," *Lewiston* **(Idaho)** *Morning Tribune*, **Dec. 13, 2008.**

U.N. Secretary-General Ban Ki-moon has urged the United States to play a more active role in the United Nations' protection of human rights by joining the Human Rights Council.

Holmes, Kim R., "Liberty Forum Better Than U.N. Rights Council," *The Washington Times*, **Dec. 25, 2008, p. A4.**

The Human Rights Council has become a protection racket for the world's worst human rights abusers.

Lynch, Colum, "U.S. to Seek Seat on U.N. Human Rights Council," *The Washington Post*, **April 1, 2009, p. A2.**

The Obama administration is seeking to enter a new era of engagement in American foreign policy by seeking a seat on the U.N. Human Rights Council.

CITING *CQ RESEARCHER*

Sample formats for citing these reports in a bibliography include the ones listed below. Preferred styles and formats vary, so please check with your instructor or professor.

<u>MLA STYLE</u>

Jost, Kenneth. "Rethinking the Death Penalty." CQ Researcher 16 Nov. 2001: 945-68.

<u>APA STYLE</u>

Jost, K. (2001, November 16). Rethinking the death penalty. *CQ Researcher, 11*, 945-968.

<u>CHICAGO STYLE</u>

Jost, Kenneth. "Rethinking the Death Penalty." *CQ Researcher*, November 16, 2001, 945-968.

In-depth Reports on Issues in the News

Are you writing a paper?

Need backup for a debate?

Want to become an expert on an issue?

For more than 80 years, students have turned to *CQ Researcher* for in-depth reporting on issues in the news. Reports on a full range of political and social issues are now available. Following is a selection of recent reports:

Civil Liberties
Closing Guantánamo, 2/09
Affirmative Action, 10/08
Gay Marriage Showdowns, 9/08
America's Border Fence, 9/08
Immigration Debate, 2/08

Crime/Law
Interrogating the CIA, 9/09
Examining Forensics, 7/09
Legalizing Marijuana, 6/09
Wrongful Convictions, 4/09
Prostitution Debate, 5/08

Education
Reading Crisis? 2/08
Discipline in Schools, 2/08
Student Aid, 1/08

Environment/Society
Conspiracy Theories, 10/09
Human Spaceflight, 10/09
Gays in the Military, 9/09
Energy and Climate, 7/09
Future of Books, 5/09
Hate Groups, 5/09
Future of Journalism, 3/09

Health/Safety
Medication Abuse, 10/09
Nuclear Disarmament, 10/09
Health-Care Reform, 8/09
Straining the Safety Net, 7/09
Treating Depression, 6/09
Reproductive Ethics, 5/09

Politics/Economy
State Budget Crisis, 9/09
Business Bankruptcy, 4/09
Future of the GOP, 3/09
Middle-Class Squeeze, 3/09

Upcoming Reports

Online Privacy, 11/6/09   Women in the Military, 11/13/09   Prisoner Reentry, 11/20/09

ACCESS

CQ Researcher is available in print and online. For access, visit your library or www.cqresearcher.com.

STAY CURRENT

To receive notice of upcoming *CQ Researcher* reports, or learn more about *CQ Researcher* products, subscribe to the free e-mail newsletters, *CQ Researcher Alert!* and *CQ Researcher News*: http://cqpress.com/newsletters.

PURCHASE

To purchase a *CQ Researcher* report in print or electronic format (PDF), visit www.cqpress.com or call 866-427-7737. Single reports start at $15. Bulk purchase discounts and electronic-rights licensing are also available.

SUBSCRIBE

Annual full-service *CQ Researcher* subscriptions—including 44 reports a year, monthly index updates, and a bound volume—start at $803. Add $25 for domestic postage.

CQ Researcher Online offers a backfile from 1991 and a number of tools to simplify research. For pricing information, call 800-834-9020, ext. 1906, or e-mail librarysales@cqpress.com.

CQ Researcher

Published by CQ Press, a Division of SAGE

www.cqresearcher.com

Online Privacy

Do Americans need better protection?

Consumers' visits to online shopping sites — as well as other sites — now can be tracked with new electronic tools by advertisers, Internet service providers and hackers.

he Internet has become not only a primary means of communication but a place where millions of Americans store important personal data, from credit-card numbers and bank account information to family photos and histories of their online purchases. But that data does not have the same legal protection as data that Americans store in their homes. What's more, powerful new technologies are creating unexpected challenges to privacy online. Advertisers, for example, can now track the Web sites you visit, and actions you take on those sites, to analyze how to more effectively sell products to you. And they may sell the information they collect to others. Privacy advocates, and some lawmakers in Congress, say the growing threats to online privacy point to the need for stronger laws to protect users' data. But Republicans in Congress warn that overregulation may cripple the economic foundation of the Internet.

CQ Researcher • Nov. 6, 2009 • www.cqresearcher.com
Volume 19, Number 39 • Pages 933-956

CQ Researcher

Nov. 6, 2009
Volume 19, Number 39

MANAGING EDITOR: Thomas J. Colin
tcolin@cqpress.com

ASSISTANT MANAGING EDITOR: Kathy Koch
kkoch@cqpress.com

ASSOCIATE EDITOR: Kenneth Jost

STAFF WRITERS: Thomas J. Billitteri,
Marcia Clemmitt, Peter Katel

CONTRIBUTING WRITERS: Rachel Cox,
Sarah Glazer, Alan Greenblatt, Reed Karaim
Barbara Mantel, Patrick Marshall,
Tom Price, Jennifer Weeks

DESIGN/PRODUCTION EDITOR: Olu B. Davis

ASSISTANT EDITOR: Darrell Dela Rosa

EDITORIAL INTERN: Emily DeRuy

FACT-CHECKING: Eugene J. Gabler,
Michelle Harris

CQ PRESS

A Division of SAGE

PRESIDENT AND PUBLISHER:
John A. Jenkins

CQ Researcher (ISSN 1056-2036) is printed on acid-
free paper. Published weekly, except; (Jan. wk. 1)
(May wk. 4) (July wks. 1, 2) (Aug. wks. 3, 4) (Nov.
wk. 4) and (Dec. wk. 4), by CQ Press, a division of
SAGE Publications. Annual full-service subscriptions
start at $803. For pricing, call 1-800-834-9020, ext. 1906.
To purchase a CQ Researcher report in print or electronic format (PDF), visit www. cqpress.com or call
866-427-7737. Single reports start at $15. Bulk pur-
chase discounts and electronic-rights licensing are also
available. Periodicals postage paid at Washington, D.C.,
and additional mailing offices. POSTMASTER: Send address changes to CQ Researcher, 2300 N St., N.W.,
Suite 800, Washington, DC 20037.

Cover: CQ Press/Screenshot

Online Privacy

BY PATRICK MARSHALL

THE ISSUES

C ould this happen to you? You return home from vacation to find your apartment has been burglarized. In your snail mail is a notice from your health insurer canceling your policy. And when you check your e-mail your minister is asking why you recently purchased a book about devil worship.

Privacy experts say such things happen countless times a day because of new electronic tools that allow Internet service providers, advertisers, hackers and others to track consumers' Web searches, site visits, e-mails and social networking sites.

For instance, burglars reading your Facebook page could easily find out when you are going on vacation. Even if you don't include your home address, a criminal may easily be able to find the information on your profile page. Your health insurer may have canceled your insurance after receiving information from a marketing firm whose online survey you just completed in hopes of winning a new iPod. And when you bought the devil worship book out of curiosity online, the information about the purchase was automatically posted to your Facebook friends, including your minister.

"With social networking, people are leaving trails of digital DNA sprinkled about everywhere in the world," says Tim Sparapani, director of public policy at Facebook.

But the danger isn't just limited to social networking sites like Facebook, say privacy advocates; for example:

• A Dartmouth University professor said he retrieved tens of thousands

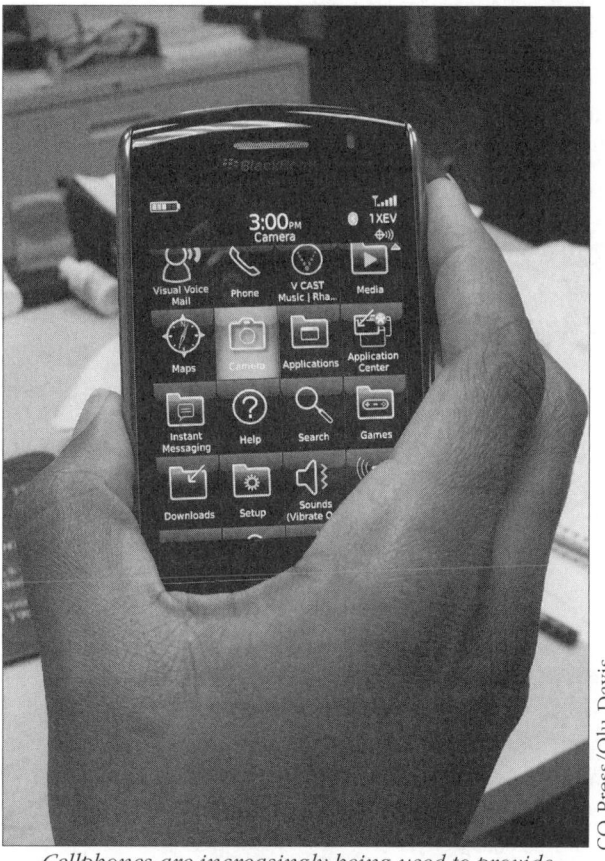

Cellphones are increasingly being used to provide location information, such as where to find the nearest pizza or the cheapest gasoline. Law enforcement agencies are also turning to service providers to obtain location information on subjects of investigation, raising concern among privacy advocates that Americans' privacy rights could be violated.

CQ Press/Olu Davis

of medical files — including names, addresses and Social Security numbers — from a peer-to-peer network, or system of linked computers. [1]

• The wife of a senior British intelligence official inadvertently revealed sensitive information in postings to her Facebook site. [2]

• An investment firm employee inadvertently exposed information about clients, including Social Security numbers, when he logged into a peer-to-peer network to share music and movie files. [3]

• A graphic designer in Seattle used Craigslist to pose as a woman seeking sexual encounters and then post-

ed all 178 responses he got to an open Web site, including photographs and personal contact details. [4]

But most online privacy intrusions never receive public attention, despite the growing number of incursions that have come to light in recent years.

"With the advent of personal Web sites, blogs, social networks and Twitter, people are sharing information about themselves that would certainly make their grandparents blush," Richard Bennett, publisher of *BroadbandPolitics.com*, told lawmakers on Capitol Hill in April. "Stories abound about young people who've posted drunken party pictures of themselves while they were in college finding the embarrassment often costly when they apply for jobs and have to explain their antics to Google-savvy recruiters. The Internet is a harsh mistress, and much of what happens there stays there, seemingly forever." [5]

Avoiding social networking sites is not, however, a guarantee of privacy. Internet service providers (ISPs) and search engine providers can learn a good deal about customers by tracking the searches they make.

Search engines, indeed, offer a deep mine of data. In fact, according to one count, Americans performed more than 13 billion searches in September alone. [6] The search engines typically record not only the terms searched for but also the date, time and location of the computer performing the search. While search engine companies generally "anonymize" records of searches, that is no guarantee of complete anonymity.

In addition, advertisers and their agents are able to track the Web activities of

Internet Users Welcome Privacy Polices

Most Internet users — especialy older people — are uncomfortable when Web sites use data about their online activities, but when privacy and security measures are put in place, a majority of users feel comfortable.

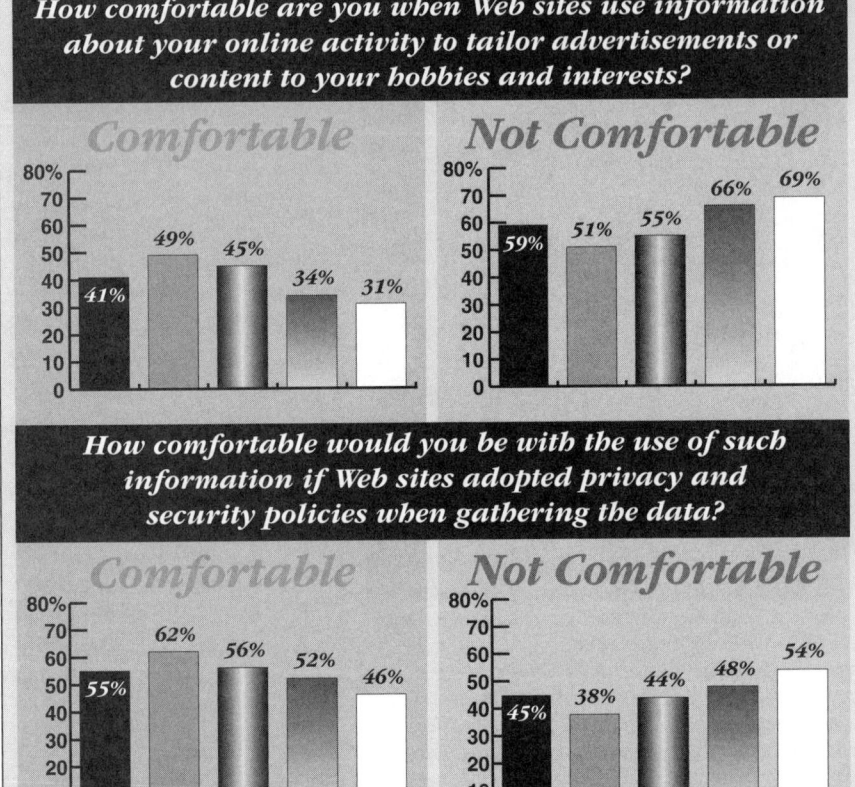

How comfortable are you when Web sites use information about your online activity to tailor advertisements or content to your hobbies and interests?

Comfortable — 41%, 49%, 45%, 34%, 31%

Not Comfortable — 59%, 51%, 55%, 66%, 69%

How comfortable would you be with the use of such information if Web sites adopted privacy and security policies when gathering the data?

Comfortable — 55%, 62%, 56%, 52%, 46%

Not Comfortable — 45%, 38%, 44%, 48%, 54%

All | 18-31 year-olds | 32-43 | 44-62 | 63+

Source: The Harris Poll, April 2008

users by the use of "cookies" — small text files that are deposited on users' computers when they visit a site.

Finally, service providers — as well as hackers, government agencies and anyone else who can tap into the flow of Internet traffic — can also employ "packet analysis" to examine the content of users' unencrypted communications across the Internet.

It's no surprise that these technologies are extremely popular with Internet advertisers. In fact, the highest-profile current threat to online privacy, according to most privacy advocates, is a new practice called "behavioral targeting" of advertising. By tracking users' actions on specific Web sites and their movements across many sites, advertisers develop user profiles and then target advertising to individual users based on their profiles.

A user might, for example, visit an airline site looking for flights to New York City, then might search for opera CDs. An advertising service following that user's movements might then deliver ads to the user's browser offering tickets to the Metropolitan Opera.

While some users might find such targeted ads helpful, others may feel that having their Web activities tracked and recorded is intrusive. Even those who don't mind the targeted advertising may not like the idea that their Internet activities could potentially be reported to other parties. For example, would users about to apply for health insurance want the insurer to know that they had recently been searching for "symptoms of colon cancer"?

Indeed, when Charter Communications, the nation's fourth-largest cable company, announced in the spring of 2008 that it was preparing to deliver just such advertising services in conjunction with a company called NebuAd, complaints from consumers and privacy advocates prompted congressional hearings. Apparently as a result of fallout from the hearings, NebuAd lost so many clients that it went out of business.

While Charter dropped its plan, others are picking up the idea. A recent study by Datran Media, an advertising consulting group, found that 65 percent of marketers currently use or plan to use behavioral targeting. [7]

"The private sector as a whole has tremendous technical means and tremendous economic incentives to collect as much granular data as they can about as many customers as possible," says Jay Stanley, director of public education at the American Civil Liberties Union. "That kind of information about people is money. And in a capitalist system people don't leave money lying around unpicked."

Of course, advertisers aren't the only ones interested in users' online activities. Users' privacy is under even more significant threat from the federal government, according to Stanley. "The National Security Agency is monitoring our telecommunications," he says, including Internet communications.

In addition, he notes, the government has easy access to a broad swath of the data being collected by service providers. "While the private sector is collecting all this information because of its own incentives," says Stanley, "the legal protections against the government swooping in and getting it are precisely what have been loosened over the past decade." Stanley cites in particular provisions of the USA Patriot Act regarding warrantless searches of electronic data. [8]

Recent polls show that advocacy groups aren't the only ones concerned about Internet privacy. According to the *Consumer Reports* National Research Center, 72 percent of American adults polled in July 2008 were concerned that their online behaviors are being tracked and profiled by companies. [9] In addition, 93 percent of respondents believe Internet companies should ask for permission before using personal information.

"I do think users are starting to feel a little bit out of control," says Ari Schwartz, vice president of the nonprofit Center for Democracy and Technology.

There have been several unsuccessful attempts in recent years to legislate stronger protections for online users' data. In the current Congress, the highest-profile effort is being led by Rep. Rick Boucher, D-Va., who has promised to introduce legislation aimed at regulating data collection by advertisers and service providers.

As privacy advocates, advertisers and consumers debate the privacy issue, here are some of the questions being asked:

Should advertisers' collection of data on Web users be regulated?

Advertisers — working with ISPs, search engine providers and individual Web sites — are turning to ever more powerful tools to gather information about users so that they can more accurately target their ads. There

---

Ten Ways to Protect Your Facebook Privacy

Facebook users cannot control all the photos and videos of themselves that show up on other people's Facebook pages, but they can adjust the privacy and invisibility settings on their own profiles. If you are a Facebook user, here are ways to protect your privacy:

1. *Use Friend Lists*   You can create groups of friends by type and send messages to each group. Friends can be in more than one group, and different groups can have different privacy settings applied to them.

2. *Remove Self from Facebook Search Results*   By default, Facebook makes your presence visible to people in your network. You can change your privacy settings, however, so that only certain groups, such as your social friends, can see your information.

3. *Remove Self from Google*   Facebook displays your profile picture, a list of your friends, a link to add you as a friend, a link to send you a message and a list of your fan pages in search engines. By changing your privacy settings, you can control the visibility of your public search listing.

4. *Avoid Photo, Video Tag Mistakes*   You can be fired at work for incriminating photos and videos, or even suffer damage to relationships. You can, however, keep tagged photos private or make them visible only to some friends.

5. *Protect Your Photo Albums*   People often turn off tagged photo visibility to certain friend lists, yet keep their photo albums public. If you want your photos to be invisible, you must adjust your privacy settings for each album.

6. *Prevent Stories From Appearing in Friends' News Feeds*   You can hide your relationship status completely, or you can avoid making things uncomfortable if your status does change by preventing friend notification. You can prevent friend notification for other stories, as well.

7. *Protect Against Unpublished Application Stories*   When you add an application, a news feed item is often immediately published in your profile. You should check your profile to ensure that no embarrassing notification has been posted, or avoid using applications entirely.

8. *Make Contact Information Private*   Many people make contact information public, such as phone numbers and e-mail addresses. If you want that information kept private, or you start receiving messages from strangers, you can create custom privacy settings for each contact listed. Again, you can allow certain friend lists to see certain contact information.

9. *Avoid Embarrassing Wall Posts*   You may use Facebook for business, but not all of your friends will. You can customize the visibility of your wall postings and control which friends post to prevent work colleagues from seeing embarrassing recaps of the weekend.

10. *Keep Friendships Private*   You may like to show off that you have lots of friends, but your friends may not want to live public lives. It is often a good idea to turn off your friends' visibility to others so that others do not visit your profile and selectively pick off your friends, such as those relevant to them for marketing purposes or other reasons.

Source: Nick O'Neill, "10 Privacy Settings Every Facebook User Should Know," All Facebook, Feb. 2, 2009, www.allfacebook.com/2009/02/facebook-privacy/

are, however, very few checks on what advertisers and service providers can do with the data.

"Users have little idea how much information is gathered, who has access to it or how it is used," Marc Rotenberg, executive director of the Electronic Privacy Information Center (EPIC) and a professor at Georgetown University Law Center, told Congress last spring. [10] "This last point is critical because in the absence of legal rules, companies that are gathering this data will be free to use it for whatever purpose they wish — the data for a targeted ad today could become a detailed personal profile sold to a prospective employer or a government agency tomorrow."

In fact, in most cases the only constraints on service providers in their collection and use of personal data are their own privacy policy statements. According to Peder Magee, senior staff attorney in the Federal Trade Commission's Division of Privacy and Identity Protection, if a company's practices violate its published promises, "that would be a deceptive claim and something we could take some action against."

Privacy advocates warn, however, that some service providers don't offer promises about privacy at all. "As long as you don't actually promise anybody any privacy — and companies have gotten very good at writing privacy policies that contain all kinds of warm, ringing tones about how they care for your privacy without actually making any legal commitments — then they don't have to deliver any," says Stanley at the American Civil Liberties Union.

As Stanley notes, even sites and service providers that do offer privacy statements generally do so in the form of rarely read, long and difficult-to-understand documents buried under an obscure link on a Web site. As a result, many if not most users are unaware of the extent of data being gathered about them and the uses to which it may be put.

With or without their knowledge, "people are giving information to a Web site in order for that site to provide them with a service," says Stanley. "They don't expect that Web site will then turn around and share the information with six other sites, combine the information to create a profile and give it to an advertiser who will decide whether you're rich or poor and give you different opportunities as a result."

Most users are also unaware that their Internet searches are recorded and can be used for profiling. "Internet search records are very, very intrusive records," says Stanley. "The things that you do searches for indicate your hopes and fears, what you're thinking about, what you may be reading, diseases that you have and diseases you fear you might have, things you believe about other people."

Advertisers justify collection of user data on two grounds. First, they argue that advertising is critical to keeping the Web vibrant. "The great majority of . . . Web sites and services are currently provided to consumers free of charge," Charles Curran, executive director of the Network Advertising Initiative, an industry group, told a congressional hearing last June. [11] "Instead of requiring visitors to register and pay a subscription fee, the operators of Web content and services subsidize their offerings with various types of advertising. These advertising revenues provide the creators of free Web content and services — site publishers, bloggers and software developers — with the income they need to pay their staffs and build and expand their online offerings."

Second, advertisers argue the collection of user data helps advertisers better serve consumers. "Targeted advertising is extraordinarily important for everybody," says Dan Jaffe, vice president of government relations for the Association of National Advertisers. That, he says, is because the more

information advertisers have about users the fewer irrelevant ads will be delivered to those users.

Conversely, Jaffe says, restrictions on behavioral targeting won't cut down on advertising. "A lot of people seem to think that if they can stop behavioral advertising that they will somehow stop advertising," he says. "Quite the contrary. Instead, you'll see an explosion of untargeted ads. You'll essentially increase the amount of spam because spam is, in effect, untargeted advertising."

Rather than legislated restrictions on advertising practices, the advertising industry argues that self-regulation — including full disclosure through clear privacy statements and procedures for users to opt out of selected data-collection programs — should be sufficient to protect users' privacy interests.

Berin Szoka, director of the Center for Internet Freedom, a project of the Progress & Freedom Foundation, a "market-oriented" think tank in Washington, agrees. "I think industry can do this on its own," says Szoka. "We should want companies to really make disclosures robust so that people really understand what they're doing." Then, he says, leave it up to the Federal Trade Commission to deal with companies that violate their privacy agreements. "They should be going out and finding the truly bad actors in industry and bringing enforcement actions against them," Szoka urges. "If they need more resources, we can talk about that."

Szoka adds that user education is another important part of the solution. "What we should be doing here is trying to educate users about what is going on online and empowering them to make decisions for themselves," he says. "If you really are very concerned about your privacy online, you have a very simple tool. You can go into your browser and use the basic cookie controls to opt out of browsing altogether, or site by site. You can create your own white lists or black lists. I would like to see those tools become much more powerful."

Privacy advocates, however, are very skeptical of self-regulation. "While we remain hopeful that advertising models based on non-personally identifiable information can be made, there are still too many instances where companies, particularly where there is no regulation, fail to fulfill their responsibilities," Rotenberg of the Electronic Privacy Information Center (EPIC) told lawmakers last spring.

"Second, even if these privacy techniques are shown to be reliable, it will still be necessary to enact legislation to place the burden on the advertising company to prevent the reconstruction of user identity," he added. "Without this statutory obligation, there would be no practical consequence if a company inadvertently disclosed personal information or simply changed its business model to true user-based profiling."

Are social networking sites doing enough to protect users' privacy?

Privacy advocates maintain that social networking sites present special challenges for privacy protection because the sites by design encourage users to offer and share personal information.

According to Facebook's Sparapani, the information-sharing nature of social networking sites is actually a plus for privacy awareness, in the sense that when people post data they know it is being shared. "Rather than having information randomly collected about you," says Sparapani, "you know what is being collected about you because we're telling you forthrightly. You can then go claim that data and put your own stamp on it."

Critics note, however, that users may not be aware that the data they provide is available not only to their designated friends but also to advertisers, albeit with personal identifiers removed. And many are not aware

A Glossary of Common Internet Terms

Behavioral Targeting — *A type of targeted advertising in which advertisers glean information from user data to tailor ads to user interests, limiting irrelevant ads.*

Cloud — *A metaphor for the Internet, based on how the Internet is depicted in computer network diagrams. Cloud computing services provide business applications online that are accessed from a browser, while the software and data are stored on servers.*

Cookie — *A message given to a browser by a server, which is then sent back to the server each time the browser requests a page. Identifies users and prepares customized Web pages for them.*

Cookie controls — *Some kinds of cookies facilitate tracking of Internet users or store identifying information. Cookie controls let users decide which cookies can be stored on their computers or transmitted to Web sites.*

Deep-packet inspection — *The examination of contents of Internet transmissions using "packet analysis" software. In addition to content transmitted by users, such as passwords or e-mails, each packet in a transmission contains the address of its origin and destination and information that connects it to the related packets being sent.*

GPS — *The Global Positioning System is a network of satellites and software that provides positioning, navigation and timing services to worldwide users. Many cellphones now include GPS receivers and software that allow the delivery of location-based services to users.*

Location-based services — *software programs that employ GPS to deliver a variety of information related to users' current location, such as routing or information about nearby points of interest, such as stores or restaurants.*

Privacy mode — *Browsers typically retain visited Web sites, downloaded files, terms searched, data — including passwords — typed into online forms, and cached versions of files locally on users' computers. Privacy mode reduces local storage of this information, providing increased privacy on shared computers.*

Web browser — *A software application used to locate and display Web pages, such as Internet Explorer and Mozilla Firefox.*

Web server — *A computer program, such as Apache, that delivers Web pages to browsers as well as other data to Web-based applications.*

Source: "Browser Privacy Features: A Work in Progress," Center for Democracy and Technology, August 2009, www.cdt.org/privacy/20090804_browser_rpt_update.pdf; "Definitions," Webopedia, Oct. 29, 2009, www.webopedia.com/.

Many Internet Users Ill-Informed About Privacy

More than 60 percent of Internet users are confident that their online activities are private and cannot be shared without their permission. A similar percentage, though, incorrectly thinks Internet companies are mandated to disclose their intentions for collecting data. And about half incorrectly believe that consent is required for companies to use personal information collected from users.

What Internet Users Think About Priviacy

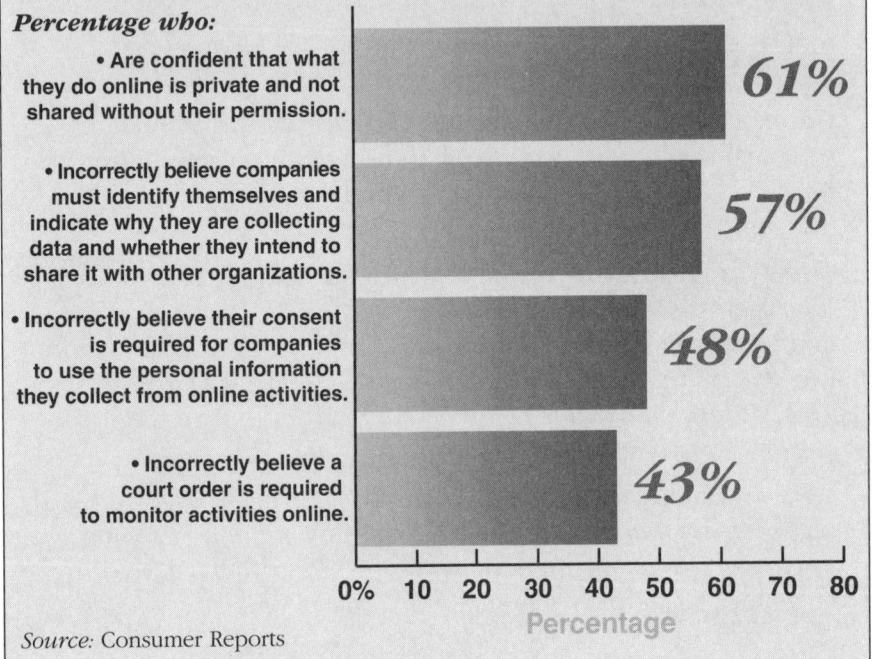

Percentage who:

- Are confident that what they do online is private and not shared without their permission. **61%**

- Incorrectly believe companies must identify themselves and indicate why they are collecting data and whether they intend to share it with other organizations. **57%**

- Incorrectly believe their consent is required for companies to use the personal information they collect from online activities. **48%**

- Incorrectly believe a court order is required to monitor activities online. **43%**

0% 10 20 30 40 50 60 70 80

Percentage

Source: Consumer Reports

---

that when they access any of the applications made available on Facebook — from quizzes and games to movie guides — by default the application developers have access not only to the users' data but also to that of friends of the users.

"Consciously or unconsciously you're in a marketing environment," says Lillie Coney, EPIC's associate director. "If you have a pet, you might be more inclined to give to an animal rescue group. Is that fair to use a consumer? Did you know that what you are seeing is being influenced by the communications you share with others who are your intimate friends in a social networking context? Should that be used in a way to sell you something?"

Coney also worries that the collection of data on social networking sites could lead to "differential marketing," in which not only the products but also the prices offered to users vary depending upon their characteristics. "Are you being presented items at prices that are based on your ability to pay rather than the quality of the item?" she wonders. "They can change the price depending on your profile."

In response to concerns voiced by users and privacy advocates, many social networks — including MySpace and Facebook — have recently introduced extensive enhancements to user privacy controls protecting what information on a user's site is made available to different parties. Users can,

for example, prevent applications from having access to personal data.

"Some people want to share everything about themselves at all times with everybody," says Sparapani. "Other people don't want to share much with anybody at all. And everyone else falls in between. What Facebook has done is not just provide privacy controls, it is actually for the first time giving people at every level of the spectrum abilities to do exactly what they want or don't want with their data."

What's more, Sparapani emphasizes that when Facebook does share users' data with third parties, it is always stripped of personally identifiable data.

"We sell ad space, and we agree to serve ads to demographics that you tell us to target," says Sparapani. "But we never turn around and give you data other than to say, yes, your ads were served to these following groups of people with these demographic characteristics. It's a really important distinction."

Facebook also has taken steps to protect users from application developers who might abuse user data. Users can now block applications entirely or block them from accessing personal data.

Also, says Sparapani, "We do spot-checks of applications." Facebook staff review applications to see what data they are gathering and whether it is relevant to their apparent purpose. "We also have built the platform such that no application can access the most sensitive information that you have on your profile, such as contact information."

Coney acknowledges that Facebook has made significant strides in improving privacy controls and statements. "It is very important that companies are making an effort," she says. "It is important that they recognize that privacy is a major issue with their consumers."

At the same time, Coney says the efforts aren't enough. "A lot of these sites give an impression that they are private," she says. "But the privacy notices are so complicated. I know they're written with concern about liability exposure, but they have to be simpler."

Sparapani contends that the best protection is an educated user base. And he praises the capabilities of the majority of Facebook users. "Our users are really quite savvy as a group," he says. "Our users are the best police force out there. They know when an application doesn't do what it says it does, or when it does more than it should, and they feel free to report us, and then we initiate a review of that specific application."

Many users, however, are not so savvy, says Coney, noting, "That's why we have regulatory agencies that stand up for the consumers."

While agreeing that educating users is a crucial step, Coney argues that broader protections for personal information are needed. "We also need to see a uniform foundation for privacy protection established," she says. "This requires the regulatory agencies such as the Federal Trade Commission to establish a regulatory framework that companies have to operate in, and it requires Congress to establish laws that are not technology centric but that are based on collection and use of personally identifiable information."

Do federal privacy policies regarding the Internet need to be updated?

Calls for changes in federal policies regarding privacy on the Internet come primarily on two fronts: use of cookies on federal Web sites and revision of the Electronic Communications Privacy Act of 1986 (ECPA), the primary federal legislation regulating non-commercial aspects of Internet activity.

Issued in 2000, current federal cookie policy prohibits federal agencies from using cookies and other tracking technologies on federal Web sites. "There is an exception to that, which is used quite rarely: If the department or agency head makes a finding that there's a compelling need to use a cookie, the agency or department can do so," says a senior Office of Management and Budget (OMB) official, who agreed to be interviewed without being named. For example, the official said, Web sites operated by the National Aeronautics and Space Administration and the National Institutes of Health have received such exemptions.

Last June, however, the OMB began seeking comments to the following proposed changes in this policy: Federal Web sites would be allowed to employ Web tracking technologies as long as they post clear and conspicuous notice on the Web site, provide a clear and understandable means for users to opt-out of such tracking and do not limit users' access to information if they opt-out of the tracking. [12]

The suggestion has alarmed privacy advocates. "This is a sea change in government privacy policy," Michael Macleod-Ball, acting director of the Washington legislative office of the American Civil Liberties Union (ACLU), said in a press release in August. "Without explaining this reversal of policy, the OMB is seeking to allow the mass collection of personal information of every user of a federal government Web site. Until the OMB answers the multitude of questions surrounding this policy shift, we will continue to raise our strenuous objections."

According to the OMB official, the policy change is not a done deal. "There are no actual proposed changes in the sense that anything is hardwired to be changed," he says. While he acknowledges that cookies carry potential privacy concerns, he says "making certain that people's privacy is protected in an extremely robust way is going to be a paramount concern of this administration, should any changes be proposed."

At the same time, he said, "it may be the case that there are ways in which judicious use of cookies on government Web sites can enable the Web sites to be more interactive, more robust, richer in terms of content and features and capabilities, so that they can really enable government to work better for people. That is the animating goal here."

While most privacy advocates oppose changes to existing cookie policies on federal Web sites, most advocacy groups are calling for major changes to ECPA on the grounds that the 1986 legislation is seriously out of date and no longer adequately protects sensitive data.

"This very important law, which I think in many ways does effectively protect people's privacy online, has understandably become outdated as the pace of technological change has increased," says Kevin Bankston, a senior attorney at the Electronic Frontier Foundation. "There are at this point fundamental questions about what ECPA protects that are unanswered and maybe are unanswerable without additional congressional guidance."

According to Bankston, nothing more pointedly demonstrates how out of date ECPA is than its provisions regarding e-mail. "E-mail is a technology that actually existed in 1986, and ECPA was drafted with that in mind," he says. "And yet there still critical questions about how ECPA applies to e-mail."

Under ECPA, for example, an electronic communication that has been in electronic storage with an electronic storage provider for 180 days or fewer requires a warrant if the government wants to access it. "The reason 180 days is required is because of differences in the past technology," says Bankston. "Back in 1986, when you dialed into your e-mail service and you downloaded your e-mail, it was erased off the server. So if you had left your e-mail there for six months, the fair assumption was that you had abandoned it and therefore it was not deserving of special protection."

What's more, says Bankston, a number of emerging technologies aren't specifically treated under ECPA. The issue of how ECPA applies to the government getting data from Internet search logs is, he says, "completely unsettled."

While Bankston and other privacy advocates call for reforms in ECPA, no party is actively opposing such reform. Many privacy advocates, however, believe that the Department of Justice would prefer to see the current law remain as it is. "I think it is fair to say that they may be resistant," says Jim Dempsey, vice president for public policy at the Center for Democracy and Technology. "To some extent, the Justice Department is doing a good job of manipulating the ambiguities and the loopholes in the statute now."

While he did not directly respond to Dempsey's charge of manipulating ambiguities and loopholes in ECPA, a Department of Justice official says, "We've been looking for places where there are gaps and trying to resolve issues. We've also been working within the structure created by Congress, which tried to be technology neutral to some extent in passing the statute. Where there are interpretive gaps, we are presenting that to the courts. And there is opportunity, of course, to have the courts interpret the statute.

"I wouldn't say ECPA is out of date," added the official, who asked that his name not be used. "I would say there are concepts in it where Congress might have had a technology in mind when it was legislating and that technology is no longer in place. The courts have then tried to

adapt to newer technologies that replaced it."

Nor has Congress actively taken up the issue of ECPA reform in recent years. According to Dempsey, "Up until now the issues have been discussed and debated only among the true ECPA nerds. It is a relatively small community of people who know about the statute, who understand the statute and who see how it works, so up until now the issue has not received a lot of public prominence." ■

Rep. Rick Boucher, D-Va., (left), chairman of the House Subcommittee on Communications, Technology and the Internet, says he will introduce legislation this fall to protect online privacy. Rep. Cliff Stearns, R-Fla., favors consumer education efforts and industry self-regulation and warns against overregulation.

BACKGROUND

Tracking Technologies

From 1967, when the Internet was born, until the mid-1990s, privacy was a non-issue. There was no advertising, no security measures apart from log ins, no spam and, until 1989, no graphic interfaces — no icons, images, windows, etc.

It was not until 1994 that the first tracking tool — the "cookie" — was introduced by Netscape Communications to check on whether visitors to the Netscape Web site had been there before. Early advertisers also found uses for cookies. When users downloaded pages from a Web site that included an advertisement or other content from the advertiser's server, a "third-party cookie" could also be included. That enabled advertisers not only to determine when their ads were viewed but also to detect what other sites the user visited where that cookie was also present.

Initially, cookies attracted little public notice. Users were not informed when cookies were deposited on their computers, and Web browsers did not have tools for blocking cookies. It wasn't until the *Financial Times* of London published an article about cookies in February 1996 that the general public knew about cookies. By that time, a working group of the Internet Engineering Task Force, an international standards group, identified cookies — and especially third-party cookies — as a potential threat to user privacy.

While the task force recommended that third-party cookies not be allowed, or at least be blocked by browsers by default, both Netscape and Microsoft Corp. — makers of the two dominant browsers — declined to follow the recommendation.

But, while cookies may present risks for user privacy, they also offer convenience and a richer Web experience. For example, cookies can be used to allow automated logins to Web sites or

Continued on p. 944

Consumer Electronics Association (Boucher) Getty Images/Johnathan Ernst (Stearns)

Chronology

1980s-1990s
Internet service providers (ISPs) and advertisers develop tools for tracking user visits and online behaviors.

1986
Electronic Communications and Privacy Act (ECPA) protects transmissions of electronic data by computers.

1994
First Internet tracking tool — the "cookie" — is introduced by Netscape Communications to check users' visits to its Web site.

1995
DoubleClick Web advertising company begins using cookies to track Internet users' Web visits.

1996
Internet Engineering Task Force identifies cookies as a potential threat to privacy. The next year the group calls for third-party cookies — those that feed data to a party other than the visited Web site — to be disabled in Web browsers. Microsoft and Netscape — the two major browser makers — reject the recommendation.

1998
Children's Online Privacy Protection Act of 1998 restricts the collection for commercial purposes of personal information about children under age 13.

1999
Network Advertising Initiative, launched by 12 advertising companies, begins developing standards for Internet advertising. . . . Federal Trade Commission holds its first workshop on behavioral targeting in Internet advertising.

2000s
Federal government begins to look more closely at legislation and regulation to protect Web users as Internet service providers, advertisers and federal agencies get more sophisticated in user tracking.

2000
Clinton administration sets strict rules on the use of cookies on federal Web sites. . . . FBI introduces Carnivore program for monitoring Internet users' activities.

2001
USA Patriot Act amends ECPA to allow the FBI to access data by simply issuing "National Security Letters" to ISPs, rather than obtaining a warrant.

2005
A disgruntled employee reveals on her blog that Kaiser Permanente had inadvertently posted private patient information on its Web site. The healthcare provider is ultimately fined $200,000 by the state of California.

2006
Department of Justice asks federal judge to force Google to turn over user-search queries as part of an investigation of violations of online pornography laws; Google successfully resists the subpoena. . . . America Online makes the records of 20 million subscriber searches available to Internet researchers; some users are identified, underscoring the potential for privacy incursions.

2007
Facebook's Beacon advertising campaign uses information gathered from users' activities on other Web sites that are partnering with Facebook. After public criticism, Facebook changes the program to track users' activities only if they specifically opt-in to the program. . . . Sen. Patrick Leahy, D-Vt., introduces Personal Data Privacy and Security Act of 2007, aimed at enhancing criminal penalties and increasing reporting requirements. The bill does not come to a vote in the full Senate. . . . Ask.com announces that it will allow users to control whether their search terms are saved by the search service, a move applauded by privacy advocates. . . . *The Washington Post* reveals that federal officials are routinely asking courts to order cellphone companies to furnish real-time tracking data so they can pinpoint the whereabouts of drug traffickers and other suspects.

2008
Charter Communications, an ISP, and NebuAd, an advertising company, announce plans to analyze subscribers' Internet traffic and then tailor ads to users whose profiles indicate a match of interests; congressional lawmakers hold hearings and pressure the companies to abandon the project. . . . A federal judge in Pittsburgh declines prosecutors' attempts to obtain people's cellphone tracking information without a warrant.

2009
House Subcommittee on Communications, Technology and the Internet holds hearing on behavioral targeting by Internet advertisers. . . . Office of Management and Budget proposes loosening federal restrictions on use of cookies on federal Web sites. . . . National Archives and Records Administration concedes it sent a defective hard drive back to a vendor before erasing the health records of as many as 70 million veterans. . . . Canada's privacy commission reports that Facebook violates Canadian privacy laws in four areas and gives the site 30 days to change its policies.

Is Data Storage 'in the Cloud' Safe?

Privacy advocates warn there is no legal protection.

Back in the early days of the Internet, users stored their personal information on floppy discs and the hard drives of their computers.

That's all changed now. Increasing numbers of users are storing data on the Internet — or "in the cloud" — and using cloud applications, such as Google Apps, or cloud data storage like Microsoft LiveMesh. The convenience is obvious: Once data is stored online, it can be accessed from any Internet-connected computer.

But privacy advocates warn that the legislation protecting the privacy of users' data hasn't changed to keep up. As a recent story on National Public Radio noted, while the checkbook sitting in your desk at home is protected by the Fourth Amendment from being accessed by government agents without a warrant, that protection may not apply to data you keep in an online checking account. [1]

And since the data is stored remotely it may be difficult for users to even know how vulnerable it is. Is the third-party server holding the data reliable? Is the data encrypted, or is it susceptible to theft by hackers? Are there assurances the storage company will not share the data with others? What if the company shuts down the service, or the government asks the company for access to a customer's stored data or a party to a lawsuit demands the data?

Privacy advocates warn, for example, that some cloud service providers claim to "support" various security technologies — such as data encryption — when those technologies may not be enabled by default (automatically) and may require the user to request them.

Indeed, in June 38 researchers and academics in computer science, information security and privacy law signed a letter to Google asking the company to follow through on protecting the data of users of its cloud applications by turning on the supported HTTPS Web-encryption technology. [2] Google engineer Alma Whitten replied, "We're currently looking into whether it would make sense to turn on HTTPS as the default for all G-mail users," as well as for users of other Google cloud applications. [3]

While no major problems have occurred thus far with cloud storage, privacy advocates say clear, legal protections for stored data don't exist. In fact, according to a recent report by the World Privacy Foundation, data stored in the cloud may have more than one legal location, with differing legal consequences depending upon the location.

"A cloud provider may, without notice to a user, move the user's information from jurisdiction to jurisdiction, from provider to provider or from machine to machine," the report notes. "The legal location of information placed in a cloud could be one or more places of business of the cloud provider, the location of the computer on which the information is stored, the location of a communication that transmits the information from user to provider and from provider to user, a location where the user has communicated or could communicate with the provider, and possibly other locations." [4]

The foundation cautions users that the application of current privacy law to the data stored in the cloud is "unpredictable," in that the courts, without clear direction from Congress, are applying the laws inconsistently. What's more, it warns, "The government is not the only entity that might seek to obtain a user's record from a cloud provider. A private litigant or other party might seek records from a cloud provider rather than directly from a user because the cloud provider would not have the same motivation as the user to resist a subpoena or other demand."

— Patrick Marshall

---

[1] Martin Kaste, "Online Data Present A Privacy Minefield," "All Things Considered," National Public Radio, Nov. 4, 2009, www.npr.org/templates/story/story.php?storyId=114163862.

[2] http://files.cloudprivacy.net/google-letter-final.pdf.

[3] http://googleonlinesecurity.blogspot.com/2009/06/https-security-for-web-applications.html.

[4] Robert Gelman, "Privacy in the Clouds: Risks to Privacy and Confidentiality from Cloud Computing," World Privacy Forum, Feb. 23, 2009, p. 7.

Continued from p. 942

to deliver content that is customized according to user preferences. And Web site managers can use the information in cookies to improve the design and navigation of sites by seeing how users traverse pages.

While there is no federal law governing the use of cookies on non-governmental Web sites, the Clinton administration in 2000 set strict rules on cookie use at federal Web sites fol-

lowing disclosures that the White House Office of National Drug Control Policy had used cookies to track users visiting its site.

Search engine logs represent another rich source of user data. The search engine technologies that concern privacy advocates, however, were developed relatively late in the game to enhance security and the user experience.

The first software tool for searching the Internet was a program called

Archie. Created in 1990, it simply sought out and downloaded directory listings of files on public FTP (file transfer protocol) sites. Archie did not index or display the contents of the files.

The Web's first actual search engine — Aliweb — debuted in November 1993. Unlike today's search engines, which send out "robots" to visit Web sites and generate an index of contents, Aliweb relied on Web site administrators to submit links to index files.

The first program developed to "crawl" the Web to find sites and index them for searching was Jump-Station, which appeared in December 1993, but it indexed only titles and headings rather than the entire contents of pages.

Beginning in 1994, several search engines appeared that performed full-text indexing of Web sites. It wasn't until 2000, however, that a clear winner — Google — emerged in the race to become the dominant search engine. Google introduced page ranking, which allowed users to more quickly and reliably retrieve Web sites of interest, using search terms. By 2008, Google accounted for more than 82 percent of search engine traffic worldwide.

The key concern privacy advocates have about search engines is the electronic logs that they keep of users' searches. According to Google, the logs are primarily generated to help in improving the service. By examining search activity coming from a specific Internet Protocol (IP) address — and each computer on the Internet is assigned a unique IP address — the company can detect problems developing on the network.

"The ability on Google's side to look at what is happening from a particular IP address over time is the kind of thing that we often look at to prevent abuse or to do certain kinds of machine learning on," says Alma Whitten, a Google software engineer. More specifically, says Whitten, Google engineers will monitor the logs to look for patterns that may tip off the presence of "denial of service" attacks. And engineers use the logs in an effort to improve the algorithms that make searches possible.

Advertisers Self-regulate

As early as 1995, the pioneering Web advertising firm DoubleClick began using cookies to track users on the Web.

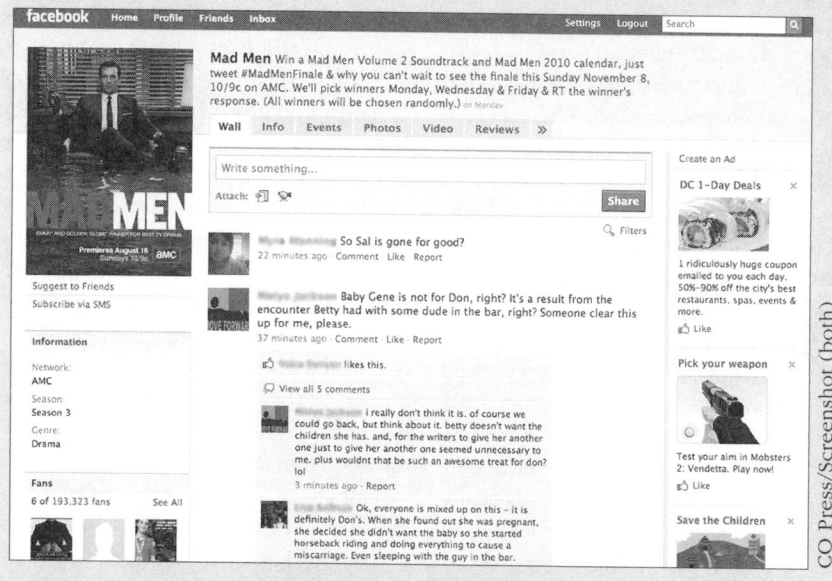

CQ Press/Screenshot (both)

Government and Private Industry Sites

Federal agencies are prohibited by federal policies from using "cookies" and other tracking technologies on their Web sites. However, some sites, including those operated by the National Institutes of Health (top), have received exemptions. Proposed changes in federal policies regarding the Web have alarmed privacy advocates, who say the changes would "allow the mass collection of personal information of every user of a federal government Web site." In response to concerns voiced by users and privacy advocate, many social networks — including Facebook (bottom) — have recently introduced extensive enhancements to user privacy controls protecting what information on a user's site is made available to different parties.

At the same time, some in the advertising industry also realized that while tracking technology offered opportunities for marketing, it also represented a challenge to consumer confidence.

"Back in the early 1990s, the few people trying to use [the Internet for marketing] were being flamed [criticized] because a lot of people on the Internet claimed that it should be a marketing-free zone," recalls Jaffe, at the Association of National Advertisers. "We said back then that if this was going to be an effective medium, adequate concern about consumer privacy issues had to be one of the pillars it was built on."

In fact, most efforts to ensure privacy protections with respect to marketing on the Internet have been accomplished through self-regulation with the assistance and oversight of the Federal Trade Commission (FTC). The one legislative exception to this is the Children's Online Privacy Protection Act of 1998, which placed restrictions and requirements on the collection for commercial purposes of personal information of children under the age of 13. [13]

The Network Advertising Initiative (NAI), a nonprofit industry group formed by 12 companies, was created in 1999 to work with the FTC to develop a set of principles to govern Internet advertising efforts. The principles basically required NAI member companies to post a notice on all Web sites served by their networks informing users the advertiser may place a third-party cookie on their computers. In addition, members were required to offer an opt-out tool for users who didn't want targeted ads from NAI members, and to refrain from merging personally identifiable information with Web browsing data without users' opt-in.

The FTC convened a town hall forum with industry representatives in 2007 to discuss the need for further regulation of online adverting activities. After the forum, the NAI issued revised guidelines in December 2008 that expanded members' commitment to provide security for data and also required:

• Consumer opt-in for "sensitive" information used with behavioral targeting, such as health conditions or treatments, and location information;

• Parental consent to use non-personally identifiable data to target behavioral advertising to children under age 13, and

• An annual in-house compliance review.

Similar standards were adopted by another industry group, the Interactive Advertising Bureau, in 2008.

While efforts at self-regulation may have provided some assurances to the public, they have not slowed the use of tracking cookies or newer tracking technologies, such as deep-packet inspection, by advertising firms and service providers. (*See glossary, p. 939.*)

The limitations on self-regulation became clear to the public and to Congress in 2008, when Charter Communications, an Internet service provider, and NebuAd, an advertising company, announced plans to perform deep-packet inspection on subscribers' Internet traffic. By examining users' activities on the Web, the companies planned to tailor ads and target them to users whose profiles indicated a match of interests.

Congressional hearings resulted in the plans being dropped. But while some legislators argued that the proposed practice violated existing wiretap and privacy laws, no legislation resulted that might clarify the legality of deep-packet inspection.

Some analysts on Capitol Hill tie the prospect for privacy legislation to growing public awareness and concern. "It's clear that the technology exists to monitor where consumers go and what they do on the Internet. It's also clear that a lot of companies are looking to monetize it," Jessica Rosenworcel, senior communications counsel for the Senate Commerce panel, said after the hearings last spring. "What is less clear is what consumers are aware of and what they're comfortable with." [14]

Federal Tracking

Congress has generally taken a hands-off approach to Internet privacy issues, except for the Electronic Communications Privacy Act of 1986. ECPA basically extended federal restrictions on wiretaps of telephone calls to protect transmissions of electronic data by computers. Title II of the act, the Stored Communications Act, protects communication held in storage, specifically e-mails, though with less stringent protections than are accorded under Title I, which protects transmissions. Under Title II, if an unopened e-mail has been in storage for 180 days or less, the government must obtain a search warrant to access it.

ECPA's protections were weakened by the USA Patriot Act of 2001, which allowed the FBI to access data by simply issuing so-called National Security Letters to ISPs, which allow FBI investigators to obtain information without a warrant.

"So once the private companies gather and store the information, it is there to be plucked by the government with very little judicial oversight," says the ACLU's Stanley. "Basically, the Patriot Act took judges out of the equation."

While Congress has shown reluctance since 1986 to weigh in on online privacy issues — even to bring the provisions of ECPA up to date with respect to changes in Internet technologies — the executive branch has made repeated efforts to expand its capabilities to monitor Internet activity.

The FBI introduced its Carnivore program in 2000 to conduct Internet surveillance — purportedly under the guidance of ECPA. The software, which was apparently a tool for deep-packet analysis, attracted such negative coverage in the media that the name was changed to DCS1000. The bureau apparently abandoned Carnivore in 2005 in favor of other commercially available monitoring tools.

In 2002, the U.S. Defense Advanced Research Projects Agency proposed developing an Internet surveillance system — "Total Information Awareness" — that would monitor content across the Internet. The project apparently was dropped after the U.S. Senate voted for restrictions on its development in 2003.

That same year, the Bush administration announced plans to build an Internet monitoring center to detect and respond to attacks on key systems. The Global Early Warning Information System was to be developed under the National Communications System, a Defense Department agency.

The Department of Justice has repeatedly taken Google to court in an effort to gain access to search records. In 2005, for example, the DoJ filed a motion in federal court to force Google to comply with a subpoena for the text of search "strings" entered into the search engine over a one-week period. The court granted part of the request, but denied the government access to users' specific search strings. [15]

The next year the Department of Justice again asked a federal judge to force Google to turn over user search queries as part of an investigation of violations of online pornography laws. Google successfully fought the subpoena. [16]

In April 2008 the FBI called for legislation that would allow federal law enforcement agencies to monitor Internet traffic for "illegal activity." [17] ∎

CURRENT SITUATION

Action in Congress

Internet privacy for consumers is attracting some attention in Congress.

In April the House Energy and Commerce Subcommittee on Communications, Technology and the Internet, chaired by Virginia Rep. Boucher, held hearings on consumer privacy. And in June the House Energy and Commerce Subcommittee on Commerce, Trade and Consumer Protection, chaired by Rep. Bobby Rush, D-Ill., held hearings specifically on behavioral targeting of online advertising.

Boucher and Rush have made clear that the two subcommittees are working closely together in conducting hearings. "There are currently no federal laws specifically governing behavioral advertising nor do we have a comprehensive general privacy law," Rush noted in opening the June hearings. "As members of Congress, we have anticipated for some time that this hearing would be highly informative and very valuable in helping us answer the question that everyone seems to ask: Is federal privacy legislation necessary, or should companies be trusted to discipline and regulate themselves?"

Boucher has been more assertive in his view that legislation is necessary. "I think that as far as they go the voluntary codes that have been adopted within the industry are constructive," Boucher told *CQ Researcher*. "They represent a step forward. The problem is that not every Web site will be a part of that voluntary commitment." As a result, Boucher has promised to introduce legislation during the current Congress, promising that it will be bipartisan.

While Democrats on both subcommittees seem generally more inclined toward regulating online advertisers, Republicans seem to prefer self-regulation. Nevertheless, comments by committee members during the hearings suggest there is room for bipartisanship. "It is still a little bit of a Wild West out there [on the Internet], and I think it is time that Congress begins to look at and try to bring some law and order to that

particular Wild West area," Rep. Joe Barton, R-Texas, said. [18]

Rep. Cliff Stearns, R-Fla., said he favored consumer education efforts and warned the hearing against overregulation. "Consumers' online activities provide advertisers with valuable information upon which to market their products and their services," Stearns said. "Collecting this type of information for targeted advertising is very important because it simply allows many of these products and services to remain free to consumers. Without this information, Web sites would either have to cut back on their free information and services or would have to start charging a fee. Neither result is good for the consumers." [19]

Stearns added that "Overreaching privacy regulation could have a significant negative economic impact at a time when many businesses in our economy are struggling, so let us be very careful on these issues before we leap to legislative regulatory proposals."

While the privacy of consumer data is receiving increasing attention, government access to users' online data is drawing relatively little attention, although many privacy advocates say government access is potentially the greater threat.

Federal monitoring programs tend to have a lower profile because they generally take place behind the scenes, say privacy advocates. Internet monitoring by the super-secret National Security Agency and other intelligence organizations, of course, is classified information and rarely subjected to public scrutiny. And even cases involving the Department of Justice are rarely in the spotlight.

"At some level the Justice Department retains control over the cases that emerge into the public light," says the Center for Democracy and Technology's Dempsey. "A lot of recipients of government orders are generally prohibited from disclosing their existence. And they don't necessarily want to disclose the order because they don't want to scare their customers.

Is Your Smartphone Keeping Tabs on You?

Advertisers and police tune in, but civil libertarians worry.

Global positioning system (GPS) chips in cellphones and mobile navigation devices have turned location-based services into a booming industry. Already some cellphone applications and auto GPS devices tell you where to find pizza close by, or the cheapest gasoline.

Indeed, according to *The Wall Street Journal*, location-based services will be a $13-billion-a-year business by 2013, compared to $515 million last year. [1]

But it's not just advertisers who are interested in accessing cellphone and vehicle location information. Law enforcement agencies are increasingly turning to service providers to obtain location information on subjects of investigation.

The laws applying to such actions, however, are not clear. "Federal officials are routinely asking courts to order cellphone companies to furnish real-time tracking data so they can pinpoint the whereabouts of drug traffickers, fugitives and other criminal suspects, according to judges and industry lawyers," noted *Washington Post* reporter Ellen Nakashima. "In some cases, judges have granted the requests without requiring the government to demonstrate that there is probable cause to believe that a crime is taking place or that the inquiry will yield evidence of a crime." [2]

"The question of what legal process the government needs to follow to track your cell phone is hotly disputed in front of magistrate judges across the country," says Kevin Bankston, an attorney with the Electronic Frontier Foundation.

Bankston says his group only became aware of the issue in 2005, mainly because such government actions generally are kept secret. "Typically, we don't know what is going on at that level," he explains. "It all occurs under seal. Unless something comes out at a criminal trial, we don't know what they're doing."

Under the circumstances, says Bankston, "The only solution is Congress — it could step in and provide clear rules for cellphone tracking."

Some privacy advocates also point to the potential for abuse of location information from "other" parties, such as stalkers and domestic abusers.

In recent congressional testimony, Leslie Harris, president of the Center for Democracy and Technology, called for three measures, the first two of which would require congressional action:

• The disclosure of precise location information in a commercial context must only be made with specific, informed, opt-in consent in which a user has the ability to selectively disclose locations only to trusted parties. As Congress contemplates enacting baseline consumer privacy legislation, such a requirement could easily be part of a broader framework governing sensitive consumer data.

• The standards for government and law enforcement access to location information must be amended to make clear that a probable-cause warrant is required for the government to obtain location information.

• Location-based services and applications should follow technical standards that give users clear control over the use of their location information and that require the transmittal of privacy rules with the location information itself. [3]

— *Patrick Marshall*

[1] Amol Sharma and Jessica E. Vascellaro, "Companies Eye Location-Services Market," *The Wall Street Journal*, Nov. 21, 2008, http://online.wsj.com/article/SB122722971742046469.html.

[2] Ellen Nakashima, "Cellphone Tracking Powers on Request, Secret Warrants Granted Without Probable Cause," *The Washington Post*, Nov. 23, 2007, www.washingtonpost.com/wp-dyn/content/article/2007/11/22/AR2007112201444.html.

[3] Statement before House Energy and Commerce Subcommittee on Communications, Technology and the Internet, April 23, 2009.

"The companies grapple with these issues quietly behind the scenes, in negotiations with the Justice Department," Dempsey continues. What's more, privacy advocates note, the Justice Department has near complete control over the cases it chooses to litigate. "The Justice Department will drop charges or decide not to use the evidence against anybody in a case that might be going against them," says Dempsey. "So the Justice Department gets to go public with the issues only in the context of drug trafficking, child abuse and terrorism — those cases the deptartment prefers to talk about."

Accordingly, some privacy advocates believe that one of the most important reforms needed in the Electronic Communications Privacy Act is requirements for reporting. "Right now the government can bend the rules and make really outrageous arguments," says Bankston of the Electronic Frontier Foundation. "Because the proceedings are sealed, and there's no adversary there to point out when the government is over-reaching, they can in fact get powers that were not given to them by Congress for years at a stretch before they are found out. This problem could be addressed if Congress were to require reporting."

Privacy advocates note that privacy threats occur in part because legislative and regulatory policies generally seem to trail behind the capabilities of emerging technologies.

"Our courts have not kept up with technology and have not kept up with

Continued on p. 950

At Issue:

Should Congress regulate online behavioral advertising?

JEFF CHESTER
EXECUTIVE DIRECTOR,
CENTER FOR DIGITAL DEMOCRACY

**FROM TESTIMONY BEFORE HOUSE SUBCOMMITTEE
ON COMMUNICATIONS, TECHNOLOGY AND THE
INTERNET, JUNE 18, 2009**

Some in the online ad industry appear to suggest that any legislative attempt to place consumers in charge of their online data would undermine the economic role of the Internet media. But I believe that by legislatively creating a system where consumers can be assured that their data are protected and transactions are structured to further empower them, trust and confidence in our online marketplace will grow and thrive. I firmly believe that we can protect privacy and also see the online marketplace and medium prosper.

Behavioral targeting and related technologies may provide "marketing nirvana," as one company explained, but it leaves consumers unaware and vulnerable to an array of marketing communications that are increasingly tied to our financial and health activities.

[Advertisers'] privacy policies are an inadequate mechanism that fail to protect the public. As documented in a recent University of California-Berkeley School of Information study on online privacy, privacy policies are difficult to read; the amount of time required to read them is too great; they lead consumers to falsely believe their privacy is protected; there [aren't] meaningful differences between policies, leaving consumers with no alternatives; and consumers aren't really aware of the "potential dangers."

The FTC [Federal Trade Commission] has been largely incapable of ensuring American privacy is protected online. Staff has been reined in from more aggressively pursuing the issue, primarily to ensure that industry self-regulation remains as the agency's principal approach.

The FTC needs to have additional resources, especially so it can better protect consumers from digital marketing transactions involving their financial and health data. Congress should press the FTC to be more proactive in this arena.

The failure to adequately regulate the financial sector greatly contributed to the worst economic crisis since the Great Depression. Regulation isn't a dirty word. It's essential so consumers and businesses can conduct their transactions with assurance that the system is as honest and accountable as possible.

The uncertainty over the loss of privacy and other consumer harms will continue to undermine confidence in the online advertising business. That's why the online ad industry will actually greatly benefit from privacy regulation. Given a new regulatory regime protecting privacy, industry leaders and entrepreneurs will develop new forms of marketing services where data collection and profiling are done in an above-board, consumer-friendly fashion.

BERIN SZOKA (LEFT)
*DIRECTOR, CENTER FOR
INTERNET FREEDOM*
ADAM THIERER
*DIRECTOR, CENTER FOR
DIGITAL MEDIA FREEDOM
PROGRESS & FREEDOM
FOUNDATION*

**FROM "ONLINE ADVERTISING AND USER PRIVACY: PRINCIPLES
TO GUIDE THE DEBATE," SEPTEMBER 2008**

To the extent that effective, self-help privacy tools exist, they provide a means of solving policy problems that is not only "less restrictive" than government regulation but generally more effective and customizable as well. Why settle for one-size-fits-all solutions of incomplete effectiveness when users can quite easily and effectively manage their own privacy?

Fortunately, a wide variety of self-help tools and "technologies of evasion" are readily available to all users and can easily thwart traditional cookie-based tracking, as well as more sophisticated tracking technologies, such as packet inspection.

The "free" Internet economy is based on a simple value exchange: Users get access to an ever-expanding collection of content and services at no cost from Web sites that are able to generate revenue from "eyeballs" on their pages by selling space on their sites to advertisers, usually through ad networks. The smarter that advertising, the more free content and services it can support.

As users face an increasingly clear choice between (1) getting content and services for free supported by behavioral advertising and (2) paying to receive those same services and content without tracking or even without ads altogether, policy makers will finally see whether users are really as bothered by profiling as the advocates of [online behavioral advertising] regulation insist. Given the ongoing and widespread replacement of fee- or subscription-supported Web business models with ad-supported models, it seems likely that the vast majority of consumers will continue to choose ad-supported models, including profiling.

Indeed, if smarter online advertising will not fund the Internet's future, what will? As both the desire for "free" services and content and the need for bandwidth expand, [online behavioral advertising] has the potential to offer important new revenue sources that can help support the entire ecosystem of online content creation and service innovation, while also providing a new source of funding for Internet infrastructure and making ads less annoying and more informative.

But looming legislative and regulatory action could stop all of that by replacing the current regime — in which the FTC merely enforces industry self-regulatory policies — with one in which the government preemptively dictates how data may be collected and used.

Continued from p. 948

the needs of privacy," says the ACLU's Stanley. "When the Fourth Amendment was written, most of people's lives took place in the home. Your medical life, your correspondence, your financial records were in the home. And the founding fathers recognized the need for privacy and put in strong protections for privacy in the home. But much of our lives are now stored on the servers of international corporations. And yet we have not extended privacy to cover that."

One solution to that problem suggested by some privacy advocates is adoption of an information-centric approach to privacy, rather than the current technology-centric approach.

"We're interested in getting a comprehensive privacy law," says Schwartz of the Center for Democracy and Technology. "Right now, we have laws protecting medical privacy and video rental records. But we don't have the general overarching privacy law that some other countries do."

Advertisers Press Ahead

While Internet service providers have apparently acceded to pressure from Congress to refrain from monitoring users' Internet activity, search engine companies and advertisers are moving ahead. Most notably, Google last March launched its own behavioral targeting program, "AdSense." The program tracks Web visits and search terms in order to build a profile of users' interests. Google is then able to display targeted ads when a user visits a participating Web site.

To avoid the complaints that ultimately sank NebuAd, Google allows users to opt out of the program and to view and edit the categories they are assigned to by Google based on their Web site visits.

"Because we're very aware that people might have privacy concerns about this, we've put a great deal of effort into being very transparent about how this will work," says Google software engineer Whitten.

"On any of those ads where we're doing this there is a link across the bottom, and if the user clicks on that they get taken to a page where Google explains how this works and gives them the opportunity to view the interest categories that Google has associated with their cookie and offers to let them opt out of the whole thing," explains Whitten. "We've made sure that all of the categories involved are very innocuous." According to Whitten, the categories include such interests as cooking, travel and sports. More personal and intrusive topics, such as cancer and political affiliations, are not included.

Schwartz at the Center for Democracy and Technology praises Google's decision. "We're targeted in so many ways and in so many categories" by advertisers, he says. "There's discussion about what kind of information is sensitive. You hear less concern about that when Google makes the categories they are targeting available. It doesn't solve every problem to make them available and let you change them, but it helps."

Microsoft is reportedly also working hard on developing behavioral targeting tools, though the company declined comment.

And some social networking sites have moved into providing behavioral targeting services for advertisers. In 2007 Facebook introduced its Beacon advertising campaign, which uses information gathered from a user's activities on other Web sites that are partnering with Facebook. If, for example, consumers purchase books at Amazon.com, an item about those purchases might appear on their page. Facebook did offer an opt-out to users, but the service nevertheless attracted so much criticism that the company scaled back Beacon in several important ways. First, and most significantly, Beacon now only works with users who choose to opt in to the program.

At the same time that major advertising companies and service providers are refining and developing behavioral targeting programs, they are working closely with each other and with the Federal Trade Commission to develop self-regulation standards for the rapidly emerging capabilities. And not coincidentally, both the FTC and a coalition of advertisers this year released reports on self-regulation of behavioral-targeted advertising programs.

On Feb. 12, the FTC issued its report, citing as one of the primary reasons the fact that "staff recognized that existing self-regulatory efforts had not provided comprehensive and accessible protections to consumers. Accordingly, in issuing the proposed principles, staff intended to guide industry in developing more meaningful and effective self-regulatory models than had been developed to date." [20]

About the Author

Patrick Marshall is a freelance writer in Seattle, Wash., and contributing writer for *CQ Researcher* who writes about public policy and technology issues. He is a computer columnist for *The Seattle Times* and holds a BA in anthropology from the University of California at Santa Cruz and a master's in international studies from the Fletcher School of Law & Diplomacy at Tufts University.

The four broad principles are:

- **Transparency and control:** Companies should provide "meaningful disclosures" about the practice and choice about whether to allow it.

- **Security and data retention:** Companies should provide reasonable data security measures and should retain data "only as long as necessary for legitimate business or law enforcement needs."

- **Material changes:** Before a company uses data in a manner that is "materially different" from promises made when the company collected the data, it should obtain "affirmative express consent" from the consumer.

- **Sensitive data:** Before using data about children, health or finances, companies should obtain affirmative express consent.

The report noted that the FTC had received many objections from industry representatives about proposals requiring companies to receive affirmative, express consent before using data in a materially different manner and before collecting sensitive data.

Nevertheless, the commission vote to approve the report was unanimous. However, in a concurring statement included in the report, Commissioner Jon Leibowitz warned advertisers, "Industry needs to do a better job of meaningful, rigorous self-regulation, or it will certainly invite legislation by Congress and a more regulatory approach by our commission. Put simply, this could be the last, clear chance to show that self-regulation can — and will — effectively protect consumers' privacy in a dynamic, online marketplace."

Several months after the FTC issued its report the coalition of advertisers released its own, identically titled report. [21] Moreover, the industry principles are nearly identical with the FTC's, except regarding consent required for collecting sensitive data or making material changes in the use of data. While the FTC calls for requirements that users must actively "opt-in," the industry group would see an individual's refraining from opting out of the system as sufficient. [22]

For now, the FTC is taking a wait-and-see approach to attempts at self-regulation. "We felt when we released the principles that companies need to do a much better job," says senior staff attorney Magee. "Since our principles came out, we have seen some positive steps by business. But we probably haven't had enough time to see the full impact of them and how some of these self-regulatory programs are going to be operationalized and what it is going to mean to consumers.

"It's a good start. But how long we support that approach and how long Congress holds off on legislating remains to be seen." ■

OUTLOOK

'A Number of Issues'

Chairman Boucher of the House Subcommittee on Communications, Technology and the Internet intends to introduce legislation this fall to regulate behavioral targeting in online advertising.

"There are a number of issues that we will seek to address," says Boucher. "Fundamental to all the protections we're proposing will be a requirement that any Web site that collects information from Internet users have a clear statement on the Web site of what information is collected and provide to the Internet user the opportunity to opt out of having any information collected."

Boucher adds that there would be further requirements for more sensitive data, such as financial and medical data as well as any information about children.

But Boucher also intends to offer advertisers a "safe harbor." If advertisers follow a specified set of "best practices," their data collection would be subject only to opt-outs by consumers. Opt-ins, which advertisers argue are much more difficult to obtain from consumers, would not be required.

"We're looking at a growing list of possible practices that would fit within that category and trying to make some determination at this point as to where the line is drawn," says Boucher. "That is a work in progress. We've not drafted a bill yet. We're still at the information-collection stage on this question . . . and we may ultimately decide to leave that determination to the Federal Trade Commission."

For its part, the advertising industry continues to warn against relying on legislation for regulating online advertisers. "A lot of people ask, 'Why not have legislation to solve the problem?' " says Jaffe at the Association of National Advertisers. "Because locking in policy in an area that is changing as rapidly as this is risky. Where technology is changing rapidly, almost inevitably legislation stands in the way of innovation and misses the target and is overly rigid."

Some members of Boucher's subcommittee during the April hearing also expressed hesitation about regulating the online advertising industry. "As we move forward towards privacy legislation, we must empower consumers to make their own privacy-related decisions," said Florida Rep. Stearns, the subcommittee's ranking Republican. "Only the consumer knows how he or she feels about the information that is being collected, the parties doing the collecting and the actual purpose for which the information will ultimately be used. Congress cannot and should not make that decision for them." [23]

Privacy advocates, for their part, would like to see something even broader than what Boucher has in mind. While some interest groups are calling for a comprehensive privacy law that focuses on people's data rather than the technology used to collect it, others argue the law should give citizens an advocate when it comes to privacy.

"This is an area where you need privacy guardians who have some power and who are dedicated to privacy issues to monitor and regulate," says the ACLU's Stanley. "The European Union and most every industrialized country have privacy commissioners who have the power to do that."

As for providing protections from government monitoring of online data, privacy advocates concede that progress will be slow. "On the Electronic Communications Privacy Act front, I do believe that the civil liberties organizations and industry are coming close to reaching a consensus position to put before Congress," says Bankston of the Electronic Frontier Foundation.

But that's only the beginning of the process, says Dempsey at the Center for Democracy and Technology. "It will be a long effort, and actually achieving legislation will require "a long and cautious process," he says. "We have to educate the members of Congress. We have to, to a certain extent, educate the public." ■

FOR MORE INFORMATION

American Civil Liberties Union, 125 Broad St., 18th Floor, New York, NY 10004; www.aclu.org. Provides education and legal support for civil liberties issues.

Association of National Advertisers, 708 Third Ave., 33rd Floor, New York, NY 10017; (202) 296-1883; www.ana.net. Provides information, advocacy and lobbying efforts for the advertising industry.

Center for Democracy and Technology, 1634 Eye St., N.W., #1100, Washington, DC 20006; (202) 637-9800; www.cdt.org. Advocates and informs on privacy, copyright and openness to keep the Internet "open, innovative and free."

Center for Digital Democracy, www.democraticmedia.org. "Works to promote an electronic media system that fosters democratic expression and human rights."

Electronic Frontier Foundation, 454 Shotwell St., San Francisco, CA 94110-1914; (415) 436-9333; www.eff.org. EFF defines itself as "the leading civil liberties group defending your rights in the digital world."

Electronic Privacy Information Center, 1718 Connecticut Ave., N.W., Washington, DC 20009; (202) 483-1140; www.epic.org. Provides information as well as lobbying and advocacy efforts on a wide range of privacy issues.

Network Advertising Initiative, 62 Portland Road, Suite 44, Kennebunk, ME 04043; (207) 467-3500; www.networkadvertising.org. An industry organization formed to develop standards for online advertising.

Privacy Rights Clearinghouse, 3100-5th Ave., Suite B, San Diego, CA 92103; (619) 298-3396; www.privacyrights.org. An advocacy group and clearinghouse that assembles a great deal of information from varied sources on privacy issues.

Progress and Freedom Foundation, 1444 I St., N.W., Suite 500, Washington, DC 20005; (202) 289-8928; www.pff.org. Describes itself as "a market-oriented think tank that studies the digital revolution and its implications for public policy."

Notes

[1] See www.tuck.dartmouth.edu/faculty/publications/forum/johnson.html.

[2] Sarah Lyall, "On Facebook, a Spy Revealed (Pale Legs, Too)," *The New York Times*, July 6, 2009, p. A1.

[3] Brian Krebs, "Justice Breyer Is Among Victims in Data Breach Caused by File Sharing," *The Washington Post*, July 9, 2008, p. A1.

[4] Matthias Schwartz, "Malwebolence," *The New York Times*, Aug. 3, 2008, p. MM24.

[5] Testimony before House Energy and Commerce Subcommittee on Communications, Technology and the Internet, April 23, 2009.

[6] www.comscore.com/Press_Events/Press_releases/2009/10/comScore_Releases_September_2009_U.S._Search_Engine_Rankings.

[7] See www.reuters.com/article/pressRelease/idUS148003+27-Jan-2009+MW20090127.

[8] For background, see the following *CQ Researcher* reports: Kenneth Jost, "Civil Liberties Debate," Oct. 24, 2003, pp. 893-916; Kenneth Jost, "Government Secrecy," Dec. 2, 2005, pp. 1005-1028; Marcia Clemmitt, "Privacy in Peril," Nov. 17, 2006, pp. 961-984.

[9] See www.consumersunion.org/pub/core_telecom_and_utilities/006189.html.

[10] Statement of Marc Rotenberg, executive director, EPIC, and adjunct professor, Georgetown University Law Center, before House Energy and Commerce Subcommittee on Communications, Technology and the Internet, April 24, 2009.

[11] Statement of Charles Curran, executive director, Network Advertising Initiative, before House Energy and Commerce Subcommittee on Commerce, Trade, and Consumer Protection and Subcommittee on Communications, Technology and the Internet, June 18, 2009.

[12] http://blog.ostp.gov/category/cookie-policy/.

[13] For background, see Marcia Clemmitt, "Cyber Socializing," *CQ Researcher*, July 28, 2006, pp. 625-648.

[14] Adrianne Kroepsch, "Deeper Ad Probes Sound Web Alarm," *CQ Weekly*, May 11, 2009, p. 1076.

[15] See http://epic.org/privacy/gmail/doj_court_order.pdf.

[16] See www.google.com/press/images/ruling_20060317.pdf.

[17] See http://news.cnet.com/8301-10784_3-9926899-7.html.

[18] Preliminary transcript of the hearing available at: http://energycommerce.house.gov/Press_111/20090618/transcript_20090618_ct.pdf.

[19] *Ibid.*

[20] "Self-regulatory Principles for Online Behavioral Advertising," Federal Trade Commission, February 2009, p. 11.

[21] "Self-regulatory Principles for Online Behavioral Advertising," American Association of Advertising Agencies, Association of National Advertisers, Council of Better Business Bureaus, Direct Marketing Association, Interactive Advertising Bureau, July 2, 2009.

[22] *Ibid.*, p. 10.

[23] "House Energy and Commerce Subcommittee on Communications, Technology and the Internet Holds Hearing on Communications Networks and Consumer Privacy: Recent Developments," CQ Congressional Transcripts, Congressional Hearings, April 23, 2009.

Bibliography
Selected Sources

Books

Bahadur, Gary, *et al.*, *Privacy Defended: Protecting Yourself Online*, Que, 2002.
A user-friendly book by network security experts explains why Internet users should care about online privacy and security.

Chander, Anupam, *et al.*, eds., *Securing Privacy in the Internet Age*, Stanford University Press, 2008.
Essays by experts in the field focus primarily on legal standards and litigation of Internet-related privacy issues.

Holtzman, David H., *Privacy Lost: How Technology is Endangering Your Privacy*, Jossey-Bass, 2006.
A former chief scientist at IBM's Internet Information Technology group covers virtually every aspect of online privacy, from the technologies that enable incursions to legal standards to the impact on personal life.

Solove, Daniel J., and Marc Rotenberg, *Information Privacy Law*, Aspen, 2003.
Coauthor Rotenberg, president of the Electronic Privacy Information Center, surveys the full range of privacy issues, not just online privacy. Includes extensive discussion of key statutes and regulations.

Articles

Burstein, Aaron J., "Amending the ECPA to Enable a Culture of Cybersecurity Research," *Harvard Journal of Law & Technology*, Vol. 22, No. 1, fall 2008.
Burstein argues there is a need to provide an exemption in the Electronic Communications Protection Act (ECPA) to allow researchers to perform cybersecurity studies and programs.

Clifford, Stephanie, "Fresh Views at Agency Overseeing Online Ads," *The New York Times*, Aug. 5, 2009, p. B1.
The article examines the pros and cons of Federal Trade Commission efforts to strengthen its oversight of online advertisers.

Griffith, Eric, "How to Reclaim Your Online Privacy," *PC World*, Feb. 1, 2009.
Griffith offers a wealth of practical tips on how to configure your computer to protect your privacy while you're on the Internet.

Kopytoff, Verne, "Paying Attention to Online Privacy: Google lawyer says the entire concept is changing as technology marches forward," *The San Francisco Chronicle*, Dec. 30, 2007, p. D1.
A lawyer for Google discusses how technology is changing peoples' views on privacy.

Studies and Reports

"FTC Staff Report: Self-Regulatory Principles For Online Behavioral Advertising," Federal Trade Commission, February 2009.
The Federal Trade Commission examines behavioral targeting of online advertising as well as the advertising industry's efforts at self-regulation.

"Privacy Online: Fair Information Practices in the Electronic Marketplace, A Report to Congress," Federal Trade Commission, May 2000.
The FTC called for legislation ensuring consumer online privacy, a call Congress has not yet answered.

"Self-regulatory Principles for Online Behavioral Advertising," American Association of Advertising Agencies, Association of National Advertisers, Council of Better Business Bureaus, Direct Marketing Association, Interactive Advertising Bureau, July 2, 2009.
While this report carries the same title as an FTC staff report that preceded it by six months, it reaches somewhat different conclusions. Specifically, the advertisers call for opt-out protections for consumers' sensitive data, while the FTC staff calls for opt-in to be required for advertisers to access sensitive data.

Dixon, Pam, "The Network Advertising Initiative: Failing at Consumer Protection and at Self-Regulation," World Privacy Forum, fall 2007.
This report looks in detail at online advertisers' efforts at self-regulation and finds them wanting.

Gellman, Robert, "Privacy in the Clouds: Risks to Privacy and Confidentiality from Cloud Computing," World Privacy Forum, Feb. 23, 2009.
Gellman provides a detailed discussion of the legal questions surrounding user data stored by third parties.

Landesberg, Martha K., *et al.*, "Privacy Online: A Report to Congress," Federal Trade Commission, June 1998.
The FTC's first in-depth look at online marketing and its impact on consumer privacy explores whether the advertising industry is capable of self-regulation.

Szoka, Berin, and Adam Thierer, "Online Advertising & User Privacy: Principles to Guide the Debate," Progress & Freedom Foundation, September 2008.
The authors argue in favor of behavioral targeting and recommend regulation only as a last resort.

The Next Step:

Additional Articles from Current Periodicals

Advertising

"New Tool Will Help Online Advertisers Develop Stronger Privacy Practices," States News Service, Jan. 28, 2009.

The Center for Democracy and Technology has unveiled an assessment tool to help online advertising companies develop appropriate privacy protections for users.

Cauley, Leslie, "Feel Like Someone's Watching You?" USA Today, Feb. 9, 2009, p. 1B.

Google and Yahoo — the two biggest players in online search advertising — say their self-imposed privacy policies provide sufficient protection for users.

Helft, Miguel, "Google to Offer Ads Based on Interests, With Privacy Rights," The New York Times, March 11, 2009, p. B3.

Google will begin showing ads based on users' previous online activities, but the move has drawn criticism from privacy advocates.

Puzzanghera, Jim, "Tough Cookies for Web Surfers Seeking Privacy," Los Angeles Times, April 19, 2008, p. B1.

Internet users can adjust browser settings to block advertisers that track user activities, but anti-Spyware programs can often negate such settings.

Puzzanghera, Jim, and Jessica Guynn, "Google, Obama May Be Clicking," Los Angeles Times, Jan. 24, 2009, p. A1.

Newfound political ties between Google and the Obama administration heighten concerns over data-privacy issues and its grip on the online advertising market.

Steel, Emily, "FCC Backs Web-Ad Self-Regulation," The Wall Street Journal, Feb. 13, 2009, p. B7.

The Federal Communications Commission (FTC) has endorsed industry self-regulation as a means of protecting consumer privacy in the online advertising market.

Federal Regulations

Ackerman, Elise, "Google Gets OK to Buy Ad Firm," San Jose (California) Mercury News, Dec. 21, 2007.

Google has won FTC approval to buy the online advertising agency DoubleClick, but such a merger could compound dilemmas over online privacy.

Ackerman, Elise, "FTC Revises Guidelines for Online Behavioral Targeting," San Jose (California) Mercury News, Feb. 12, 2009.

The FTC has introduced guidelines that would require sites to disclose the data they are collecting from users and give them the chance to opt out.

Clifford, Stephanie, "Web Privacy on the Radar in Congress," The New York Times, Aug. 11, 2008, p. C1.

Issues relating to data collection and Internet privacy policies are beginning to attract the attention of Congress.

Gage, Deborah, "Privacy Laws Need Better Controls, Panelists Say," The San Francisco Chronicle, Dec. 16, 2007, p. E1.

An advocacy group says clearer laws and better technological controls are needed over what online information can be made public.

Glass, Kat, "FTC Opts to Stay Out of Regulating Web Privacy," Wichita (Kansas) Eagle, July 10, 2008, p. A1.

The FTC has indicated it will leave it to Internet companies to decide how best to protect users' privacy.

Hansell, Saul, "Agency Skeptical of Internet Privacy Policies," The New York Times, Feb. 13, 2009, p. B5.

The FTC says Internet companies are not clearly explaining to users what data they collect and what it is used for.

Hart, Kim, "A New Voice in Online Privacy," The Washington Post, Nov. 17, 2008, p. A6.

A group of privacy lawyers, scholars and corporate officials has launched an advocacy organization calling for tougher regulations on the collection and storage of online user data.

Hsu, Spencer S., and Cecilia Kang, "U.S. Web-Tracking Plan Stirs Privacy Fears," The Washington Post, Aug. 11, 2009, p. A2.

The Obama administration is proposing to scale back a ban on tracking how people use government Web sites.

Kopytoff, Verne, "Rules Suggested for Tracking Internet Use," The San Francisco Chronicle, Feb. 13, 2009, p. C1.

Federal regulators have issued new guidelines for Internet companies that track user behavior online and use such data to tailor advertisements accordingly.

Newell, Ben, "Senate Looks at Privacy Options," The Washington Times, July 10, 2008, p. A9.

Sen. Byron L. Dorgan, D-N.D., is proposing a "do not track" list to prevent Internet companies from collecting personal information.

Steel, Emily, "Web Privacy Efforts Targeted," The Wall Street Journal, June 25, 2009, p. B10.

The possibility of new Internet privacy regulations has prompted online advertisers to give online users more control over how their information is collected and used.

Tessler, Joelle, "Microsoft, Google Back Broad Privacy Legislation," The Associated Press, July 10, 2008.

Both Microsoft and Google told Congress to pass basic privacy legislation to protect information regarding consumers' Web-surfing habits.

Smartphones

Cauley, Leslie, "FCC Taking 3-Part Look at Wireless," *USA Today*, **Aug. 24, 2009, p. 4B.**

The Federal Communications Commission is examining the state of the wireless communications industry in order to better address consumer privacy concerns.

Hettich, Colter, "Where's Waldo?" *Abilene* **(Texas)** *Reporter-News*, **Feb. 9, 2009.**

A new Google software program makes it possible for individuals to locate one another by using their cellphones.

Markoff, John, "You're Leaving a Digital Trail. Should You Care?" *The New York Times*, **Nov. 30, 2008, p. BU1.**

New technologies, such as smartphones, have become so powerful that they threaten the protection of individual privacy.

Nakashima, Ellen, "When the Phone Goes With You, Everyone Else Can Tag Along," *The Washington Post*, **July 12, 2008, p. A1.**

The launch of the iPhone 3G signals the augmentation of precise-location technology and online advertising.

Nathanson, Rick, "They Are Watching You," *Albuquerque* **(New Mexico)** *Journal*, **June 15, 2008, p. E1.**

As smartphones and other technologies become more complex, privacy becomes more and more of an illusion.

Stone, Brad, "The High Security Risk Attached to Obama's Belt," *The New York Times*, **Jan. 12, 2009, p. B1.**

Barack Obama has been denied the use of his BlackBerry upon taking office because of concerns over security and privacy.

Weddle, Eric, "Smile, You May Be on Someone's iPhone," *Journal and Courier* **(Indiana), Sept. 3, 2009.**

A student at Purdue University in Indiana has developed a smartphone application that makes it possible to view 29 Web cameras on campus.

Social Networking

Baig, Edward C., "Users: Facebook's Getting 'Grabby' With Our Data," *USA Today*, **Feb. 18, 2009, p. 3B.**

Facebook has introduced a clause that gives itself rights to user data even after it's been deleted.

Boudreau, John, "Facebook Adding Safeguards Against Cyber-Bullying, Porn," *San Jose* **(California)** *Mercury News*, **May 8, 2008.**

Social networking site Facebook is adding 40 safeguards to protect youths from sexual predators and cyber-bullies.

Huang, Lily, "Protect the Willfully Ignorant," *Newsweek*, **March 24, 2008, p. 54.**

Internet users can't make decisions about privacy in online networks if they don't know what the trade-offs are.

Kopytoff, Verne, "Facebook Tidies Up Privacy Settings," *The San Francisco Chronicle*, **July 2, 2009, p. C3.**

Facebook is trying to simplify methods for users to adjust their privacy settings on its site, acknowledging that the current process has become complicated.

Leber, Holly, "Facebook Users Urged to Be Cautious With Content They Post," *Chattanooga* **(Tennessee)** *Times Free Press*, **March 3, 2009, p. E1.**

Critics warn that content posted on social networking sites can fall into the wrong hands, regardless of whether people have been classified as "friends" on such sites.

Regan, Tom, "Facebook Faces Up to Privacy Concerns — Again," *The Christian Science Monitor*, **Dec. 12, 2007, p. 16.**

A new Facebook application allows users to be informed about the Web-surfing habits of their "friends."

Stone, Brad, and Robbie Brown, "Web of Risks," *Newsweek*, **Aug. 21, 2006, p. 76.**

Students adore social networking sites such as MySpace, but indiscreet postings and a lack of privacy can cause trouble.

Wong, Wailin, "Web Footprints Leave Easy Trail," *Chicago Tribune*, **Dec. 25, 2008, p. A35.**

Social networking sites are allowing users to take their profile data to other places on the Internet, putting at stake their private data and reputations.

CITING *CQ RESEARCHER*

Sample formats for citing these reports in a bibliography include the ones listed below. Preferred styles and formats vary, so please check with your instructor or professor.

<u>MLA STYLE</u>

Jost, Kenneth. "Rethinking the Death Penalty." <u>CQ Researcher</u> 16 Nov. 2001: 945-68.

<u>APA STYLE</u>

Jost, K. (2001, November 16). Rethinking the death penalty. *CQ Researcher, 11,* 945-968.

<u>CHICAGO STYLE</u>

Jost, Kenneth. "Rethinking the Death Penalty." *CQ Researcher,* November 16, 2001, 945-968.

In-depth Reports on Issues in the News

Are you writing a paper?

Need backup for a debate?

Want to become an expert on an issue?

For more than 80 years, students have turned to *CQ Researcher* for in-depth reporting on issues in the news. Reports on a full range of political and social issues are now available. Following is a selection of recent reports:

Civil Liberties
Human Rights Issues, 10/09
Closing Guantánamo, 2/09
Affirmative Action, 10/08
Gay Marriage Showdowns, 9/08
America's Border Fence, 9/08
Immigration Debate, 2/08

Crime/Law
Interrogating the CIA, 9/09
Examining Forensics, 7/09
Legalizing Marijuana, 6/09
Wrongful Convictions, 4/09

Education
Reading Crisis? 2/08
Discipline in Schools, 2/08
Student Aid, 1/08

Environment/Society
Conspiracy Theories, 10/09
Human Spaceflight, 10/09
Gays in the Military, 9/09
Energy and Climate, 7/09
Future of Books, 5/09
Hate Groups, 5/09
Future of Journalism, 3/09

Health/Safety
Medication Abuse, 10/09
Nuclear Disarmament, 10/09
Health-Care Reform, 8/09
Straining the Safety Net, 7/09
Treating Depression, 6/09
Reproductive Ethics, 5/09

Politics/Economy
State Budget Crisis, 9/09
Business Bankruptcy, 4/09
Future of the GOP, 3/09
Middle-Class Squeeze, 3/09

Upcoming Reports

Women in the Military, 11/13/09   Value of a College Education, 11/20/09   Prisoner Reentry, 12/4/09

ACCESS

CQ Researcher is available in print and online. For access, visit your library or www.cqresearcher.com.

STAY CURRENT

To receive notice of upcoming *CQ Researcher* reports, or learn more about *CQ Researcher* products, subscribe to the free e-mail newsletters, *CQ Researcher Alert!* and *CQ Researcher News*: http://cqpress.com/newsletters.

PURCHASE

To purchase a *CQ Researcher* report in print or electronic format (PDF), visit www.cqpress.com or call 866-427-7737. Single reports start at $15. Bulk purchase discounts and electronic-rights licensing are also available.

SUBSCRIBE

Annual full-service *CQ Researcher* subscriptions—including 44 reports a year, monthly index updates, and a bound volume—start at $803. Add $25 for domestic postage.

CQ Researcher Online offers a backfile from 1991 and a number of tools to simplify research. For pricing information, call 800-834-9020, ext. 1906, or e-mail librarysales@cqpress.com.

Published by CQ Press, a Division of SAGE

www.cqresearcher.com

Women in the Military

Should combat roles be fully opened to women?

T
he number of women serving in the military has reached historic highs in the past decade, with women now representing more than 14 percent of the total force. In 2008, Ann E. Dunwoody, the Army's top supply officer, became the first female four-star general. This fall the Army tapped Sgt. Maj. Teresa L. King to head its ultra-tough drill-sergeant training program, the first woman to hold the post. At the same time, controversy swirls around the under-the-table recruitment of Army and Marine women into some ground-combat missions in Iraq and Afghanistan — which is contrary to official military policy — as well as the Navy's plans to add women to submarine crews. Advocates of continuing to bar women from those jobs argue that sexual tensions and mis-trust harmful to the military mission inevitably accompany gender-integration of combat teams. Meanwhile, women vets are suffering high levels of post-traumatic stress disorder and homelessness.

Gen. Ann E. Dunwoody, a master parachutist and supply specialist, broke through the so-called brass ceiling in 2008, when she became the nation's first female four-star general. Women, who comprise 14 percent of the U.S. military, make up 15 percent of the officer corps.

CQ Researcher • Nov. 13, 2009 • www.cqresearcher.com
Volume 19, Number 40 • Pages 957-980

CQ Researcher

Nov. 13, 2009
Volume 19, Number 40

MANAGING EDITOR: Thomas J. Colin
tcolin@cqpress.com

ASSISTANT MANAGING EDITOR: Kathy Koch
kkoch@cqpress.com

ASSOCIATE EDITOR: Kenneth Jost

STAFF WRITERS: Thomas J. Billitteri, Marcia Clemmitt, Peter Katel

CONTRIBUTING WRITERS: Rachel Cox, Sarah Glazer, Alan Greenblatt, Reed Karaim Barbara Mantel, Patrick Marshall, Tom Price, Jennifer Weeks

DESIGN/PRODUCTION EDITOR: Olu B. Davis

ASSISTANT EDITOR: Darrell Dela Rosa

EDITORIAL INTERN: Emily DeRuy

FACT-CHECKING: Eugene J. Gabler, Michelle Harris

CQ PRESS

A Division of SAGE

PRESIDENT AND PUBLISHER:
John A. Jenkins

CQ Press is a registered trademark of Congressional Quarterly Inc.

CQ Researcher (ISSN 1056-2036) is printed on acid-free paper. Published weekly, except; (Jan. wk. 1) (May wk. 4) (July wks. 1, 2) (Aug. wks. 3, 4) (Nov. wk. 4) and (Dec. wk. 4), by CQ Press, a division of SAGE Publications. Annual full-service subscriptions start at $803. For pricing, call 1-800-834-9020, ext. 1906. To purchase a CQ Researcher report in print or electronic format (PDF), visit www. cqpress.com or call 866-427-7737. Single reports start at $15. Bulk purchase discounts and electronic-rights licensing are also available. Periodicals postage paid at Washington, D.C., and additional mailing offices. POSTMASTER: Send address changes to CQ Researcher, 2300 N St., N.W., Suite 800, Washington, DC 20037.

Cover: AFP/Getty Images/Kris Connor

Women in the Military

BY MARCIA CLEMMITT

THE ISSUES

Army Spec. Shannon Morgan came home from Iraq changed by war. When she enlisted at age 20 and left rural Arkansas, shortly after Sept. 11, 2001, she hoped to help defend her country against more terrorist attacks while earning money for college. Eight years later, she's back home, hoping for a nursing career but diagnosed with post-traumatic stress disorder. [1]

Morgan enlisted as a vehicle mechanic and never expected to kill anyone in Iraq. Instead, she became one of the first women in U.S. history to take part in direct ground combat and killed at least one Iraqi. Even though military policy bars women from participating in such missions, Morgan was recruited into the first Lioness team — an ad hoc group of Army women who supported male front-line troops in both the Army and the Marines by dealing with women and children in houses where soldiers were pursuing potential insurgents.

In April 2004 she accompanied a Marine unit searching for insurgents in the central Iraqi city of Ramadi. Unfamiliar with Marine signals and commands, she suddenly found herself alone on a street — and being fired at — when the squad abruptly withdrew from a neighborhood after walking into an ambush.

Morgan hesitated at first and then began returning fire with her light machine gun.

"For that second, I was like, 'God, is this right?' . . . I don't want to go to hell someday because I killed some-

Then-President-elect Barack Obama and former U.S. Army helicopter pilot Tammy Duckworth, who lost both legs in combat in Iraq, prepare to place a wreath at The Bronze Soldiers Memorial in Chicago on Veterans' Day in 2008. Duckworth now serves as an assistant secretary of the Department of Veterans Affairs.

body," she recalls. "Then I realized, 'I betcha he's not caring over there, or he wouldn't be shooting at me.'" Today, she says she doesn't regret what she did but wishes it had never happened. [2]

The quiet use of women in ground-combat roles from which they are officially barred is not the only evidence that women's role in the U.S. military is growing more prominent. In September, Command Sgt. Maj. Teresa L. King, the 48-year-old daughter of a sharecropper near Fort Bragg, N.C., became the Army's top drill sergeant, the first woman to be named commandant of the Fort Jackson, S.C., school that trains all of the Army's drill instructors.

"When I look in the mirror, I don't see a female. I see a soldier," said Sgt. Maj. King. Recruiting more women into the school is one of her top priorities. [3]

In 2008, another so-called brass ceiling was broken when Gen. Ann E. Dunwoody, a master parachutist and logistics and supply specialist, became the first female four-star general. "Her issue is, when are people going to stop being surprised?" said a friend, retired Maj. Gen. Jeanette Edmunds. [4]

Still, some military analysts are not only surprised but chagrined at the pace of women's integration into the armed forces and particularly at the Army's surreptitious moves to place women in frontline ground-combat areas.

Elaine Donnelly, president of the Center for Military Readiness, a Michigan-based think tank opposed to both ground-combat roles for women and gays serving openly in the military, says that as women have moved into more and more military jobs over the years, double standards for women's and men's physical performance have weakened overall military standards and sown seeds of discord among the ranks. [5]

Furthermore, the Army has "defied logic in retaining co-ed basic training" and setting different standards of physical achievement for men and women, Donnelly wrote. Such "gender-normed standards emasculate" the military's "warrior training" when they "[assure] 'success' for average female trainees" by setting the bar lower. "Soldiers know that there is no gender-norming on the battlefield." [6]

For example, for a 1.5-mile run, the Navy awards a "satisfactory" physical-readiness rating to a man who runs

Women Are 14 Percent of U.S. Military

Women make up 14.3 percent of the 1.3-million-member U.S. military and 15.1 percent of the officer corps. The Air Force has the highest percentage of women overall as well as the highest percentage of female officers. The Marine Corps has the lowest percentages.

Active Duty by Branch of Service, September 2007

Branch of Service and Status*	Number of Women	Number of Men	Total	Women as Percentage of Total
**Department of Defense ** **				
Officer	33,567	187,952	221,519	15.1%
Enlisted	162,424	981,628	1,144,052	14.2%
Total	**195,991**	**1,169,580**	**1,365,571**	**14.3%**
Army				
Officer	12,983	71,699	84,682	15.3%
Enlisted	58,117	374,984	433,101	13.4%
Total	**71,100**	**446,683**	**517,683**	**13.7%**
Air Force				
Officer	11,835	53,887	65,722	18.0%
Enlisted	52,595	210,777	263,372	20.0%
Total	**64,430**	**264,664**	**329,094**	**19.6%**
Navy				
Officer	7,611	43,820	51,431	14.8%
Enlisted	41,144	239,694	280,838	14.6%
Total	**48,755**	**283,514**	**332,269**	**14.7%**
Marine Corps				
Officer	1,138	18,546	19,684	5.8%
Enlisted	10,568	156,173	166,741	6.3%
Total	**11,706**	**174,719**	**186,425**	**6.3%**
Coast Guard				
Officer	1,160	6,891	8,051	14.4%
Enlisted	3,790	28,809	32,599	11.6%
Total	**4,950**	**35,700**	**40,650**	**12.2%**

* Officers include warrant officers

** Does not include the Coast Guard, which in peacetime is part of the Department of Homeland Security

Source: U.S. Department of Defense, Defense Manpower Data Center, unpublished data. Compiled by the Women Research & Education Institute, January 2008

the distance in 13 minutes and 15 seconds, while a woman gets the same rating — and earns the same number of points toward boot-camp graduation — for a 15-minute, 15-second time, she said. [7]

A sure path to a weaker military is favoring women's interest in total workplace equality over military-readiness concerns, Donnelly said, and, "Right now we're favoring women's desire for careers over everything else."

But Melissa Sheridan Embser-Herbert, a professor of sociology at Hamline University in St. Paul, Minn., and a former captain in the Army Reserve, says "the argument over combat is ridiculous." Women, who comprise 14 percent of the overall military workforce, make up about 11 percent of those who have served in Iraq and Afghanistan, where combat is all around, she says. Yet the high number of women has not harmed the mission.

More than 120 female soldiers have been killed in those conflicts — 66 of them killed in combat. "Regardless of whether we label a job as a combat job, people are in harm's way" because of how wars are fought today, she says. Women should be recognized — and trained — for the combat roles they occupy today, she says.

As philosophical struggles persist over how aggressively full gender-integration of the military should be pursued, so do practical difficulties with creating a harmonious gender-integrated force.

For example, early this year the Department of Defense (DoD) released 2008 data on sexual assaults involving military victims or military perpetrators, showing that reported assaults increased by 8 percent overall from the previous year — and by a whopping 26 percent in Iraq. Sexual-assault rates generally run much higher in combat zones than in non-combat areas or in peacetime.

"I had one woman tell me, 'You just expect it. That's why we go to the latrine in pairs,' " or "create a brother/sister relationship with a male soldier," says Francine D'Amico, an associate professor of international relations at Syracuse University, who's studied female military officers. "I heard that from at least six different women."

However, the military is working much harder to crack down on sexual violence and harassment and will continue to do so, partly because it has become a "resource issue," says Darlene M. Iskra, program coordinator for the University of Maryland's Leadership Education and Development Center and a retired Navy commander who in May 1990 became the first woman to command a Navy ship. With an all-volunteer force, the military must compete with the civilian economy for good, skilled workers and spend significant resources to train enlistees, "so they can't allow them to leave" because of fear of a hostile environment, something that could be corrected, she says.

"The Pentagon has made some efforts to manage this epidemic — most notably in 2005, after the media received anonymous e-mails about the high rate of sexual assaults at the U.S. Air Force Academy," said Rep. Jane Harman, D-Calif. "The press scrutiny and congressional attention that followed led DoD to create the Sexual Assault Prevention and Response Office (SAPRO)," which initiated training and improved reporting of assaults. [8]

As Congress, military leaders and an interested public debate the issue of integrating women into military service, here are some questions being debated:

Are efforts to fully integrate women into the armed services harming military readiness?

Over the past 40 years, the number of women in the U.S. armed forces has grown from under 2 percent to more than 14 percent today. The range of military jobs women may hold and the number of females who become

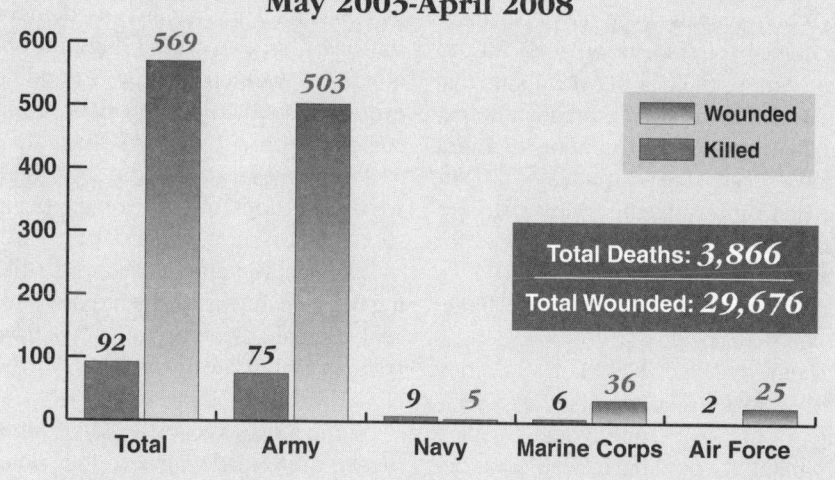

Women Suffered 2 Percent of Iraq War Casualties

More than 650 military women were killed or wounded in the Iraq War between May 2003 and April 2008, most of them in the Army. The 92 female deaths represent 2 percent of the 3,866 U.S. service members killed in the war.

Female Military Personnel Killed and Wounded May 2003-April 2008

Wounded / Killed

Total Deaths: **3,866**
Total Wounded: **29,676**

	Total	Army	Navy	Marine Corps	Air Force
Wounded	569	503	5	36	25
Killed	92	75	9	6	2

Source: Hannah Fischer, et al., "American War and Military Operations Casualties: Lists and Statistics," Congressional Research Service, May 2008

high-ranking officers also have grown substantially. Supporters of these trends say there's no evidence that military readiness has suffered, but critics say they have resulted in lower standards and morale problems that have been swept under the rug.

Setting unequal standards to allow women to succeed despite their physical differences from men damages unit cohesion by creating a backlash against the women, says Donnelly of the Center for Military Readiness. "Women say, 'I get resentment because my high scores aren't as high as the men's,' " she says.

In order to gender-integrate training, the military has had to reduce standards for physical performance because experiments in the early 1980s "found that women got injured trying to keep up with the men," said Stephanie Gutmann, author of *The Kinder Gentler*

Military: Can America's Gender Neutral Fighting Force Still Win Wars? [9]

"I'm not sure people are aware of how little similarity there is between men and women" when it comes to physical characteristics such as upper-body strength. "Ninety-nine percent of the time a man is stronger," says Kingsley Browne, a law professor at Wayne State University in Detroit and author of *Co-Ed Combat: The New Evidence that Women Shouldn't Fight the Nation's Wars*. These strength differences matter greatly in many situations, such as when a ship suffers damage from a missile or other weapon and all sailors — including the cooking staff, for example — must seal off compartments and carry injured people to safety.

Moreover, "what happens when you take a cohesive group of men and introduce women into the group? The men begin to compete for the women," to the detriment of their bonds of trust with one another, says Browne. In addition, a "ready" military depends on having all workforce positions filled so the force can immediately respond when it's needed. But with women making up a larger portion of the forces, pregnancy may get in the way, say many analysts.

When she was doing pre-deployment processing of soldiers on their way to Iraq, Army Sgt. Erica Crawley found that "many women became pregnant to get out of deploying," according to Laura Browder, an English professor at Virginia Commonwealth University in Richmond, who interviewed Crawley for a forthcoming book, *When Janey Comes Marching Home: Portraits of Women Combat Veterans.* [10]

Retired Army Maj. Lori Sweeney told Browder that when she was serving in Iraq she saw women getting pregnant. It could have been done deliberately in order to cut their deployments short, said Sweeney, or accidentally, since military doctors are not allowed to prescribe birth control because sex is prohibited. [11]

Deliberate or not, pregnancies that allow women to escape difficult jobs cause a "major morale problem" for the troops who remain on duty, says Browne. "Other people have to pick up the slack, and that can cause a lot of resentment."

Women typically join the military for career purposes rather than a desire to go to war, says Browne. Evidence of that appeared in the early 2000s, when previously rising numbers of new female recruits began dropping off. That was "probably because prior to that they weren't subjected to the possibility of being blown up," Browne says.

Men are much more likely to enlist because they wish to fight, Browne says. "The eagerness of many men to go to war" is well-known, he wrote. In the early stages of World War I —

before the United States went to war — "Americans crossed the border into Canada to join the Canadian army before the 'fun' was over," he wrote. [12]

However, James Martin, a retired Army colonel and professor of social work at Bryn Mawr College near Philadelphia, says that, critics notwithstanding, "The question has been answered about whether women will ruin the military. They haven't, as demonstrated by, among other things, the senior roles women occupy, extending even to commanding troops in combat operations."

Twenty years ago, Martin says, there were "questions about women being successful on ships, and today they are" — an achievement made more striking because the first women didn't have senior female mentors. Today "we have women integrated throughout the Navy, becoming captains."

Martin says exactly the same arguments were made against fully integrating black soldiers into all-white units. "Just substitute the word 'women' for the word 'black,' " he says.

"The conspicuous 'femaleness' of women presents some challenges to group cohesion in the military, especially insofar as sexual friction . . . result[s] from their presence," acknowledged Regina M. Titunik, a professor of political science at the University of Hawaii in Hilo. However, these factors "do not seem to preclude the type of bonding that is such an essential part of military service." A major 1997 analysis from the RAND Corporation think tank, for example, found that, among members of the military, "gender integration is perceived to have a relatively small effect on readiness, cohesion and morale," Titunik wrote. [13]

Many military women point out that once their male colleagues see them in action, they quickly gain respect, says Browder. One convoy gunner she interviewed said that she could not win the respect of older men in her unit until she ended up in charge dur-

ing a tense situation and "was the one who had to radio for help and decide who to kill," says Browder. "After that she had no difficulty getting respect."

Browder says she was surprised by "how many women talk about being soldiers and Marines first, not about being mothers and wives." Women "are in the military for all the same reasons as men," including a desire to blow things up, she says. "I heard over and over again that bonds in the [military] unit became stronger than family bonds," shedding doubt on the idea that gender-integrated units lack cohesion.

Furthermore, many women Browder spoke with "were really looking forward to going to war," including one young Marine who was excited to learn that the post she was headed to "had been blown up the night before." And a B-52 bomber pilot she interviewed "wished she could have dropped more bombs." Like many male soldiers, many women thought of this as "the ultimate existential challenge," Browder says.

For some observers, there remains little doubt that some women can be as aggressive and persistent as men in the face of violence. For example, Army Lt. Gen. Bob Cone singled out two women as performing with special heroism in the Nov. 5 mass shooting at Fort Hood, in Texas. Civilian Fort Hood police officer Kimberly Munley sought out and shot the gunman four times despite being shot herself, in "an amazing and an aggressive performance," said Cone. Another "amazing young lady," 19-year-old Pfc. Amber Bahr, a nutritionist, put a tourniquet on a wounded fellow soldier and carried him to get medical care before realizing that she, too, had been shot, Cone said. [14]

"Look at the facts. There have been an increasing number of women in our military" over the past two decades, "and our military is not weak. Women have not diluted our readiness," says

Iskra of the University of Maryland.

"Our young people today are used to seeing women in authority, in and out of the military," she says. "They are working with women and going to school with women," so "this selective segregation doesn't make sense to the new generation. They see differences, but they don't see them as negative."

Should combat roles be fully opened to women?

More than 90 percent of armed-services jobs are open to women. The largest remaining all-male job category is ground-combat units — infantry troops that directly seek out and engage the enemy in fire.

In interviews with military officers and analysts, "we were told repeatedly that, if relevant and realistic tests existed so that only qualified women (and men) were assigned to these positions, gender integration would not be an issue," said analysts from the RAND Corporation think tank in an influential 1997 analysis. [15]

"Women are already engaged in combat" because under today's conditions, "combat is everywhere," says Martin of Bryn Mawr. So the old distinctions between front-line positions that are barred to women versus more secure rear areas — where women are allowed — are no longer relevant and should be scrapped, he says.

Command Sgt. Maj. Teresa L. King became the Army's top drill sergeant in September when she was named commandant of the Fort Jackson, S.C., school that trains all of the Army's drill instructors. "When I look in the mirror, I don't see a female" she says. "I see a soldier." Recruiting more women into the school is one of her top priorities.

AP Photo/Mary Ann Chastain

"Units comprised of women and men have bonded . . . and maintained good order for centuries — or did they have separate-sex wagon trains pioneering the West?" wrote blogger and retired Air Force Capt. Barbara A. Wilson. "I have known some pretty weak men who wouldn't protect the back of their own mother in a crisis or combat situation and some strong women who would go to the wall for a total stranger in the trenches — and vice versa." [16]

Arguments against women in combat sometimes rest on "the military's mission to make professional killers" of its combat soldiers and women's sup-

posed unsuitability for that role, says Iskra of the University of Maryland. But, in fact, "everybody recognizes that women can kill," she says. "It's just not the cultural norm," so it's easy to ignore.

Furthermore, there's now proof that "women in the combat area tend to defuse explosive situations just by their presence," says Iskra. The evidence comes from the Lioness groups of women soldiers who accompany male Army and Marine Corps units on counterinsurgency missions, she says. With the women there, gaining control of explosive situations in hostile territory becomes mainly a matter of separating women and children out and "talking rather than shooting," she says. "Imagine if somebody broke into your home. Of course the Iraqi men are shouting, panicking." But "with the women there they know that their wives won't be raped," and that confidence helps defuse the danger, she says.

Nevertheless, "the type of ground combat that involves directly attacking the enemy, actively rooting out enemy forces — not simply being in harm's way," still exists, and there's no guarantee such aggressive missions won't be needed in the future, says Donnelly.

That being the case, "the strongest argument and the one that research backs up is that female soldiers do not have an equal opportunity to survive or help others survive" in situations requiring them to "go out and seek out the enemy," Donnelly says. "Nobody questions the bravery of our

Women Hit Hardest by Divorce

Female soldiers and Marines divorce at nearly three times the men's rate and experience nearly four times as much unwanted sexual contact.*

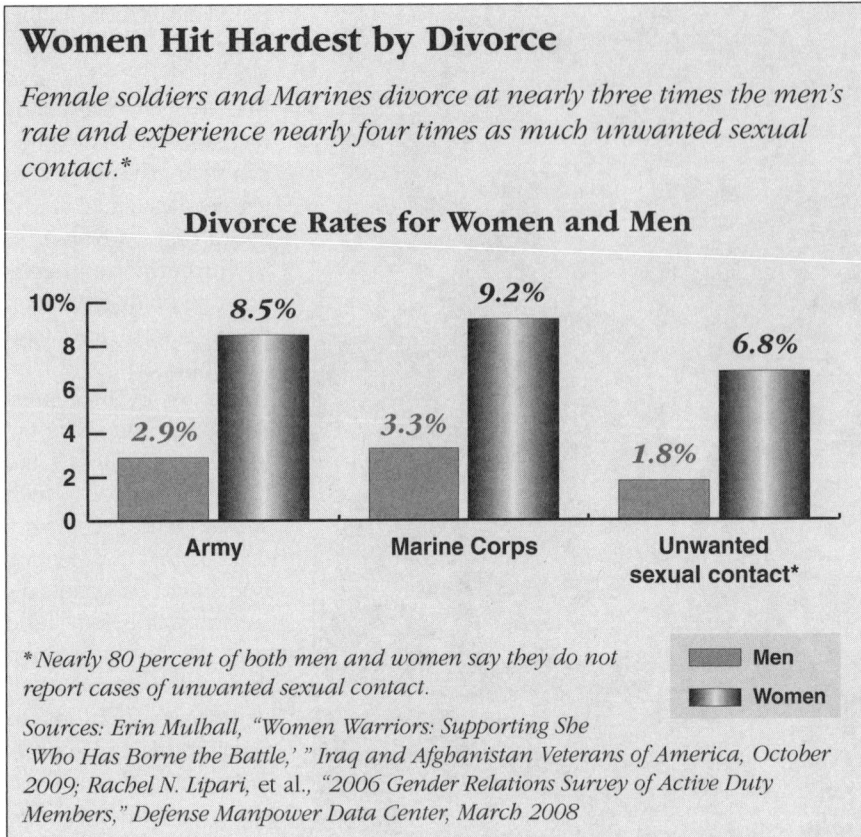

Divorce Rates for Women and Men

* Nearly 80 percent of both men and women say they do not report cases of unwanted sexual contact.

Sources: Erin Mulhall, "Women Warriors: Supporting She 'Who Has Borne the Battle,' " Iraq and Afghanistan Veterans of America, October 2009; Rachel N. Lipari, et al., "2006 Gender Relations Survey of Active Duty Members," Defense Manpower Data Center, March 2008

women soldiers," she continues, but "it's not fair to the women and not fair to the men" to put women in jobs serving directly with ground-combat troops because most women can't carry out required duties, such as carrying a wounded soldier from the front.

In combat areas toilet and washing facilities are rudimentary at best and, often, nonexistent, and some studies have found that, for women soldiers, "unmet basic hygiene needs affect morale" and their ability to cope in combat circumstances, says Browne of Wayne State. In such situations, some women "retained urine and stool and limited their water intake to reduce the number of times they would have to go to the bathroom," which both increased their risk of urinary-tract infections and dehydration and decreased their ability to work at top efficiency. [17]

Though the military is not willing to discuss the topic, sexual attraction would be inevitable in a mixed-gen-

der combat unit and would quickly damage the required atmosphere of life-or-death trust, says a former infantry officer and West Point graduate who did three tours of duty in Iraq, including as a ground-combat officer in the August 2004 battle to control the city of Najaf in southern Iraq.

Women served in one supply company for his unit, and "when you'd go back there, you'd start looking at those girls and thinking, 'My goodness,' " says the officer. If the women had served alongside the men in combat, "you would be distracted. A woman there would just get prettier and prettier every day," he says. "I wouldn't do anything inappropriate, but I would worry because I know there'd be guys in my platoon who would act on their feelings, whether the woman wanted them to or not" — an extra concern for an officer already bearing the burden of leading troops in battle.

Is enough being done to reduce sexual violence in the military?

Allegations of sexual assault of women service members have been a feature of military life as long as the military has been gender integrated. But many factors complicate efforts to stamp out such problems.

For one thing, because most military personnel are 18-to-20-somethings, many away from home for the first time, the armed forces must struggle with "all the issues of any college-age population, including binge drinking and reckless behavior," including assault and date rape, "which are normative in that age group," says Martin of Bryn Mawr.

"Research shows that there's a much lower incidence [of sexual assault] in non-combat zones, and higher rates in combat areas," says D'Amico of Syracuse.

When men and women in the same unit "are counting on each other to watch their backs" in potentially deadly situations, there are many opportunities for miscommunication, says Embser-Herbert of Hamline University. "You're having to create a situation of trust, but you're also hoping that everyone understands boundaries" and that cues meant to signify "we trust each other" aren't misread as invitations to make unwanted sexual moves, she says.

In previous military occupations, sex industries quickly grew up around U.S. military bases, but in the Middle East that's happened much less, "so you have a lot of displaced sexual energy" in young people "who are also frustrated because they're being told they're going to go home, and then they don't get to go home," says D'Amico. The military had not been doing a good job of managing those tensions, including sexual tensions, she says.

But over the past five years, the military has stepped up its efforts to combat sexual assault.

High-ranking defense leaders, including Defense Secretary Robert Gates and Joint Chiefs of Staff Chairman

Adm. Mike Mullen, now express "real concern" about the issue, and the Army, in particular, "is making strides," said Rep. Harman. [18]

The Department of Defense also has required every major defense installation to appoint a Sexual Assault Response Coordinator to monitor care for victims and organize prevention, education and outreach campaigns, said Rep. Louise Slaughter, D-N.Y. [19]

Mullen "has come out with a new strategy for preventing harassment," focusing on men's responsibility, says the University of Maryland's Iskra. "Before it was, 'Don't dress provocatively,' directed at women, but now the focus is on the men, where it should be. People need to be held accountable." A similar approach worked for stopping racial harassment, she notes. "You don't hear racist statements anymore." [20]

The DoD also is working to develop a database for complaints about abusive or harassing behavior, Iskra says. "So if you see patterns of complaints about a person," even if the separate reports are of a slightly different character or occur at different posts, commanders can become aware of a potential problem, she says.

Nevertheless, sexual violence against military women persists, despite numerous congressional hearings on the subject and recent DoD attempts at reform, said Helen Benedict, a journalism professor at Columbia University and author of a 2009 book on women soldiers serving in Iraq. [21] At least 41 percent of female veterans treated at the West Los Angeles Veterans Affairs Health Center said they had experienced sexual assault in the military, and 29 percent say they were raped, said Harman. [22]

"At the heart of this crisis is an apparent inability or unwillingness to prosecute rapists in the ranks," Harman said. Only 181 out of 2,212 subjects — or 8 percent — investigated for sexual assault in 2007 were referred to courts martial, she said, and

they generally only received "slaps on the wrist . . . even for convicted offenders." By contrast, in the civil justice system, 40 percent of those arrested for rape are prosecuted, she pointed out. [23]

Military language, charged Benedict, reveals an "unabashed hatred of women," which creates a rape-friendly culture. Drill instructors "routinely denigrate recruits by calling them pussy, girl, bitch, lady and dyke," and military men still sing misogynist rhymes that have been around for decades. So the message sent from the top is "that women are second-class soldiers," fit mainly to serve as "sexual prey." [24] ∎

BACKGROUND

Forgotten Amazons?

Throughout history women have participated in wars, frequently as victims but often by supporting troops with farm or industrial labor on the home front. And in smaller numbers but persistently through time women have served as spies, saboteurs and armed combatants, especially when military manpower was in short supply. When wars end, however, women's involvement often is written out of the history books as too minimal to matter. [25]

"Women have not engaged in warfare at all times and in all places, but they have fought bravely and well in many times and in many places," wrote Robert B. Edgerton, a professor of anthropology at the University of California, Los Angeles.

Throughout time, some cultures have claimed to have had warrior women — ranging from the Amazons of Greek mythology and France's legendary Joan of Arc to the Scythian women of southern Russia. But histo-

rians today disagree on whether these women played as big a role in physical combat as their legends portray.

However, one culture in which the role of warrior women has not been disputed was the West African Kingdom of Dahomey, which existed in the 18th and 19th centuries in the area where modern-day Benin is located. "Full-time professional women soldiers fought so ferociously and successfully for so many years that they eventually became the elite force of Dahomey's professional, highly successful standing army," according to Edgerton. [26]

In one 1864 battle, Dahomean male and female troops, led by the king's corps of elite fighting woman, attacked the stronghold of a neighboring people — the Egba, who possessed much better, more modern weaponry. As the Egba opened fire with cannon and muskets, the poorly armed Dahomeans "led by Amazons screaming, 'Conquer or die,' sprinted toward the city," wrote Edgerton. "One woman lost her arm in the attack but shot an Egba with her other hand before being killed with a sword. . . . One woman sat on the wall for some time smoking her pipe and contemptuously staring at the Egba before she was shot down." [27]

Virtually every war has had some female combatants. At least 400 women are known to have fought in the American Civil War, for example, many dressed as men. Some women whose gender was discovered while they were on active duty were jailed or assigned to traditional female jobs, such as laundress or seamstress, wrote Lisa Tendrich Frank, author of *Women in the Civil War*. Others were discharged and sent home, but "some determined female combatants reenlisted in other units and continued to fight until they were discovered again," according to Frank. [28]

In 1901, the U.S. Army established an official nurse corps for women, and the Navy established a nurse corps in 1908. In World War I, about 34,000

American women worked for the U.S. military. Most were nurses, but others filled noncombat jobs such as clerk, translator, telephone operator, radio electrician and camouflage designer. The War Department resisted calls to establish specific women's corps in the armed services, except for the nurses' corps, and even the nurses did not have full military status. After the war the non-nurses were demobilized, and while some military analysts argued that a women's corps would be needed if another war occurred, the War Department and Congress resisted making any plans for that.

Women and Manpower

In World War II, European and American armed forces saw the greatest influx of women ever. When the war began, most governments were reluctant to enlist women even into auxiliary, home-front roles in the armed forces. As manpower shortages appeared, however, attitudes changed.

Initially, "many negative stereotypical images of women" existed among top military leaders and in written policies, said Patricia M. Shields, a professor of political science at Texas State University in San Marcos. "Prior to World War II women were considered more costly" for the military, regardless of the job. For example, "two women typists were calculated to be needed to replace one male typist" when, "in fact, the reverse was true," said Shields. [29]

Early in the war, British Prime Minister Winston Churchill was reluctant to bring women into auxiliary military roles, such as support and technical jobs in air defense units, says Bernard Cook, a professor of European history at Loyola University in New Orleans. "But when someone told [Churchill] that doing it would save 40,000 men who could then be deployed over-

seas," he quickly changed his mind, says Cook.

The hard-pressed Soviet army employed the most women in the widest range of jobs, says Cook. Between 800,000 and 1 million Soviet women fought — about 8 percent of the total force — filling roles from tank driver to pilot. About 400,000 women were drafted, and the rest volunteered. Some were awarded medals for heroism, and many served in front-line areas, including during the fall of Berlin in spring 1945, the last great battle of the war, says Cook.

Meanwhile, because Hitler held an ultra-traditional view of women as embodying an idealized femininity, Germany held out as long as it could against allowing women to help the war effort, says Cook. Unlike in other nations, Hitler even insisted that German factories continue producing consumer goods like cosmetics during the war, rather than turning out war goods. Eventually, however, women took air-defense posts — looking out for and providing technical help to soldiers trying to shoot down or deflect incoming enemy airborne attacks — and finally, as Germany grew more desperate, some received weapons training.

In the United States, the nation's first peacetime draft for men was implemented in 1940, with war already raging in Europe. Even so, military workforce shortages reached crisis proportions shortly after the country's December 1941 entry into the war.

At that point, many argued that women should be officially brought into the armed services. "Men who would have filled positions in combat units were being siphoned out . . . to fill jobs in non-combat units" that many believed could be performed by women, observed retired Air Force Maj. Gen. Jeanne Holm. [30]

Women also ate less than men — and thus would cost the government a bit less money to feed — increasing the government's interest in re-

cruiting them, said Titunik of the University of Hawaii. [31]

But some military analysts maintain deep skepticism, even today, about whether the armed forces should have opened their doors to women in the 1940s.

"The duties women performed for the War and Navy departments in Washington, D.C., where most military women were stationed, could just as easily have been performed by the men who were not drafted or by civilian men and women," said Brian P. Mitchell, author of *Women in the Military: Flirting With Disaster.* "Their other uses hardly justified the trouble of establishing and maintaining separate women's components of the Army, Navy, Coast Guard and Marines." [32]

Seeing women performing war work around the world changed many minds, however. "Until my experience in London I had been opposed to the use of women in uniform," said President Dwight D. Eisenhower, a five-star general who served as Supreme Commander of the Allied Forces in Europe during the war. "But in Great Britain I had seen them perform so magnificently in various positions, including service in active anti-aircraft batteries, that I had been converted."

In fact, said Eisenhower, women proved so effective that by the end of the war even the "most stubborn diehards" were convinced that they could be useful to the war effort "and demanded them in increasing numbers." [33]

A bill to establish a Woman's Army Auxiliary Corps was introduced in Congress in May 1941, but it languished until manpower shortages in 1942 finally compelled its passage. Congress also established a Navy Women's Reserve in 1942, and in June 1943 lawmakers established the Women's Army Corps, in which the enlistees enjoyed full military status, unlike those who had enlisted in the auxiliary corps.

Continued on p. 968

Chronology

1800s-1930s
Some American women serve in military support roles, such as nurses, cooks, clerks, telephone operators and translators (World War I), but during the Civil War, some sneaked into combat, most dressed as men.

1940s-1960s
Wartime personnel shortages lead to recruitment of women for support roles.

1942
First official female Navy and Army units are established; women fill labor shortages in support jobs like control-tower operators, parachute riggers and navigation instructors.

1943
American Medical Association drops objection to recruiting female physicians.

1948
Women officially become eligible for membership in all military branches, with their numbers capped at 2 percent.

1967
Two percent cap on female enlisted personnel is dropped; all but top officer ranks open to women.

1970s-1980s
Armed forces recruit more women, but not for combat jobs.

1973
Draft ends; recruitment of women increases.

1976
Service academies open to women.

1978
Navy assigns women to non-combatant ships for first time.

1980
Congress rejects President Jimmy Carter's proposal to register women for future drafts.

1981
Supreme Court rules in *Rostker v. Goldberg* that a male-only draft does not violate Constitution's "equal protection" clause.

1989
All Coast Guard and Air Force jobs open to women, along with 59 percent of Navy jobs, 52 percent of Army jobs and 20 percent of Marine jobs. . . . For first time, female officers command Marine Corps units: a recruiting station and a reserve support unit.

1990s
Women take on more military roles, but sexual-assault scandals cast doubt on whether gender integration works.

1990
Cmdr. Darlene Iskra is first woman to command a Navy ship, the rescue and salvage vessel *USS Opportune.*

1991
Congress lifts ban on women flying combat missions.

1994
Army women join men at boot camps. . . . Jobs on combat ships and aircraft are opened to women. . . . Lt. Kara Hultgreen, the Navy's first female fighter pilot, dies when her F-14 crashes on approach to a carrier landing.

1995
Air Force Lt. Kelly Flinn becomes the first female B-52 bomber pilot. She later resigns to avoid a court martial stemming from an affair with a married civilian.

1996
Female recruits at Aberdeen Proving Grounds in Maryland charge male drill sergeants with harassment, rape. A company commander and three drill sergeants are sent to prison.

2000s
Iraq and Afghanistan wars see record numbers of women in wartime service.

2003
Manpower shortages in Iraq lead Army to send women on counterinsurgency missions, against regulations.

2005
Bill to ban women in land combat fails to advance in Congress.

2008
Ann E. Dunwoody, commander of the Army Materiel Command, becomes first female four-star general, the highest rank attained by a woman.

2009
Navy announces plans to put women on submarines. . . . Sgt. Maj. Teresa L. King becomes first female chief of Army drill-sergeant training. . . . Uptick in sexual-assault reports seen as evidence that more women are reporting crimes. . . . Navy inspector general reports ships face serious labor shortages as more pregnant women leave their deployments.

Can Women Handle Combat?

"Most guys discover women are just like everybody else."

Critics of opening military combat roles to women often argue that while men tend to be enthusiastic warriors by temperament, women generally are not, which makes combat an unsuitable and unhealthy place for women.

Proponents of women in combat, however, say that while women respond to some situations differently from men, they, too, have a great capacity for aggression, loyalty to comrades and other traits traditionally associated with warriors.

Citizens who try to stop crimes provide a concrete measure of the difference between men and women, such as physical aggressiveness and risk-taking, according to Kingsley Browne, a law professor at Wayne State University in Detroit. For example, "a study of individuals intervening to thwart violent crimes, such as muggings, armed robberies and bank holdups, found that only one of 32 individuals in the sample was a woman," Browne wrote. [1]

The importance of mothers to children's survival means that women have likely "evolved to rate the costs of physical danger higher than men do," which explains women's lower levels of aggression and risk-taking, Browne said. [2]

Moreover, Browne says some female officers' zeal for career advancement has led to myth-making about women's zest for war. "When Demi Moore's character in [the 1997 movie] 'G.I. Jane' claimed that wanting to 'blow shit up' was her motivation for joining the [Navy] SEALs, we already knew enough about her character to realize that she was not telling the truth," Browne wrote. "She wanted a combat assignment to further her career, which . . . is the principal motivation of women seeking to serve in combat units." [3]

In recent years, largely due to workforce shortages, the Army has circumvented official military policy to put women into ground-combat situations in Iraq and Afghanistan. Predictably, the experience has proved difficult for many women, who generally don't desire such roles, says Elaine Donnelly, president of the Center for Military Readiness, the Michigan think tank she founded that advocates for military personnel policies such as barring women from ground combat.

Donnelly cites the case of Spec. Stephanie Filus, who attempted suicide when she realized she faced deployment in a unit required to be all-male — due to its combat-related

mission — even though her recruiter had assured her that she would not see close combat. "I certainly do not approve of her choice of action, but it is regrettable that she felt that she had no recourse," says Donnelly. "Our young women should not be kept in the dark about the obligations they will face if they enlist, mistakenly believing that they will not be assigned or placed in a direct ground-combat unit that used to be all-male."

Awareness that women are serving in combat roles today hasn't hit home with the public or even with military institutions, such as the Veterans Affairs health-care system. Unlike with men, women's combat-related post-traumatic stress disorder (PTSD) is often overlooked and underestimated by their families and others, including health workers, because, unlike men, "they're not supposed to punch a wall, they're not supposed to get aggressive with their spouse," said Carri-Ann Gibson, director of the Trauma Recovery Program at the James A. Haley Veterans' Hospital in Tampa, Fla. [4]

Other analysts argue that, while many women do respond differently to their wartime experiences than men, their responses in no way make them liabilities.

Women have the same level of devotion to their military mission as men, not less, says Erin Solaro, author of the 2006 book *Women in the Line of Fire*. "Some women volunteered for Lioness* missions, others didn't, but I never met a woman who felt free to decline one, because that meant someone else would have to go in her place, and if no women went, the mission was more dangerous than it otherwise would have been." [5]

Capt. Anastasia Breslow, a member of one of the original Lioness teams, recalled, "I still can't believe that I was in a firefight. Me, a female signal officer, someone expected to support from a desk was out there. . . . They needed a Lioness team so badly . . . that even as a support officer I was pulled in. I hope I don't have to do them very often, but I will never try to get out of it." [6]

---

* Lioness teams are ad hoc groups of Army and Marine women who support male ground combat troops by dealing with the women and children in Iraqi and Afghan homes where soldiers are pursuing potential insurgents.

Continued from p. 966

More than 1,000 female pilots also served, primarily ferrying planes from manufacturing facilities to military bases. However, despite several legislative attempts to extend military status to the pilots, the Women Airforce Service Pilots organization — WASP

— was never militarized. Its members were considered civil servants and denied military benefits.

All told, more than 350,000 American women served in military roles in World War II.

At war's end, most who'd seen military service — men and women

— returned to civilian life. In most countries, the late 1940s saw a nearly complete exodus of women from the armed forces, says Cook. In the Soviet Union, for example, where women had made up a full 8 percent of the wartime service, "the women were decommissioned and

"I don't think my experiences [in combat] were any different than my male counterparts," said another Lioness member, Maj. Kate Guttormsen. "I think some of my coping mechanisms were different. For example, I'm sure I cried more . . . behind closed doors."[7]

In fact, some women do enter the military with a desire to "blow things up," just like men, says Laura Browder, a professor of English at Virginia Commonwealth University in Richmond, who has interviewed many women who've served in Iraq.

"I grew up in New Jersey in the ghetto. I was always getting in trouble, getting into fights," Marine Sgt. Jocelyn Proano told Browder. "I did Army boot camp. And I loved it so much. . . . It was just awesome, marching and all that . . . And then I started hearing about the Marines. . . . They're the most hard core. . . . I chased the recruiter down. . . . I just wanted to go out, get some adventure, travel, go out to war, do the whole nine [yards]."[8]

Her first night in Al-Asad, Iraq, she was awakened by a mortar strike on a fuel storage area, said Proano. "It exploded. Smoke everywhere," she recalls. "And I wasn't even scared — I was pretty excited. I was like 'holy crap — we're at war. This is going to be good.'"[9]

"Most guys I know discover, once they have worked with women, that women are just like everybody else," said Brig. Gen. Rhonda Cornum, who was taken prisoner during the first Gulf War, in 1991, and is now director of Comprehensive Soldier Fitness for the Army. "There are some [women] that are just awesome, some that are absolutely worthless, and most of them are just in between. And I think the percentage of males who are that way is the same."[10]

"In reality, women have always been capable of killing,"

A female Italian paratrooper is one of 2,800 Italian soldiers serving in the North Atlantic Treaty Organization's (NATO) peacekeeping mission in Afghanistan. Italy is one of 12 NATO countries — out of the 28 — that allow females to serve in combat. Most began allowing it in the late 1980s and early '90s.

Getty Images/Laura Lezza

wrote Linda Grant De Pauw, a historian and founder of the Maryland-based Minerva Center, an education foundation on women and warfare. "Even a small woman catching a man unaware or able to add poison when she prepared his food could end his life." But most cultures, including our own, have "profound, complex and emotionally charged" reasons — involving human psychology and societies' mythical images of themselves — for drawing a veil over this reality, she argued. For one thing, "when combat serves as a puberty ritual for boys, girls cannot participate without destroying its meaning. If girls could qualify as both mothers and warriors, there would be no unique identity for boys."[11]

— *Marcia Clemmitt*

[1] Kingsley Browne, *Co-Ed Combat: The New Evidence that Women Shouldn't Fight the Nation's Wars* (2007), p. 35.

[2] *Ibid.*, p. 52.

[3] *Ibid.*, p. 119.

[4] Quoted in Damien Cave, "Women at Arms: A Combat Role, and Anguish, Too," *The New York Times*, Oct. 31, 2009, p. A1.

[5] Erin Solaro, *Women in the Line of Fire: What You Should Know About Women in the Military* (2006), p. 77.

[6] "Interview with Capt. Anastasia Breslow, Team Lioness," Public Broadcasting System, www.pbs.org.

[7] "Interview with Maj. Kate Guttormsen, Team Lioness," Public Broadcasting System, www.pbs.org.

[8] Quoted in Laura Browder, *When Janey Comes Marching Home: Portraits of Women Combat Veterans* (forthcoming), p. 23.

[9] *Ibid.*, p. 30.

[10] "War Story: Rhonda Cornum," "PBS Frontline: The Gulf War," Public Broadcasting System, www.pbs.org., January 1996.

[11] Linda Grant De Pauw, *Battle Cries and Lullabies: Women in War from Prehistory to the Present* (2000), p. 12.

got veterans' benefits. But very few stayed on," Cook says. By 1959, out of a Soviet army of more than 4 million, only 659 were women, he says.

In the United States, however, a 1948 law established a legitimate place for women in the military, but also strictly limited their participation. The Women's Armed Services Integration Act, signed into law by President Harry S Truman on June 12, 1948, gave permanent status to women in the regular and reserve branches of all the services. It capped women's participation at 2 percent in each service branch and set a 10-percent limit on female officers, who could advance in rank no further than lieutenant colonel or Navy commander. Women could enlist at age 18 but needed parental permission until age 21, while men could enlist at 17 and only needed parental permission until age 18.[34]

Services for Military Women Lagging Behind

Many don't seek health care, even when eligible.

With thousands of women now serving in the military, including in combat roles, and the number of female veterans poised to double over the next decade, military policy makers are struggling to develop appropriate responses to issues ranging from child care to post-traumatic stress disorder (PTSD). [1]

For example, while around 22 percent of male veterans use Veterans Affairs (VA) health-care facilities in a given year, "utilization rates" for female veterans range from 11 to 19 percent. Research shows that many women veterans don't even think of themselves as bona fide veterans whose service makes them eligible for benefits like health care, even when they've served in combat zones, so many don't apply for benefits, said Joy J. Ilem, deputy national legislative director of Disabled American Veterans. To make matters worse, said Ilem, nearly 19 percent of women veterans who reported they had no access to health care actually have service-connected disabilities that would fully qualify them for VA health services. [2]

Because many women who do use VA health facilities suffer from PTSD connected to sexual assaults in the military, the VA is promising to make its facilities more woman-friendly. But progress is slow. For example, the Government Accountability Office found earlier this year that women's exam-room tables in some VA facilities still faced doors rather than walls, raising privacy concerns, and that women sometimes had to walk through waiting rooms to get to restrooms. [3]

Another concern is the growing number of homeless women vets.

"I had a young woman Air Force veteran come in initially asking for help finding a job, but at the end of our conversation it became evident she was homeless," Tia Christopher, women veterans coordinator for Swords to Plowshares, told a Senate Committee in July. "It broke my heart that this sister veteran" who "honorably served her country . . . was now selling her body just to get by." The story makes clear that "services are insufficient for women veterans," but when a veterans' assistance organization connected the woman with another woman veteran, "she felt comfortable asking for help," and relieved not to have to confront the VA's notorious bureaucracy, Christopher said. [4]

As of September, the VA estimated there were 13,100 homeless female veterans, many with serious mental-health problems and about 40 percent of whom say they were sexually assaulted by a fellow service member. Moreover, many homeless women vets are parents of young children, complicating the situation. Among women vets who participate in one of the VA's homelessness programs, 23 percent have children under age 18, according to Iraq and Afghanistan Veterans of America. And since the VA is legally barred from providing "direct care to children or spouses of veterans, this becomes a huge unmet need," says the group. [5]

"Motherhood complicates everything" for service members, says Laura Browder, a professor of English at Virginia Commonwealth University in Richmond, who has conducted extensive interviews with active-duty female soldiers. For example, "while many, many soldiers have talked to me about PTSD, no mothers have," says Browder. She surmises that mothers' silence may stem from the fact that "being a bad mother is the ultimate taboo" in our society, which may intensify pressures on military women.

"I feel that the Army should have something like a sabbatical for dual military couples, when it comes . . . to deployments,"

The law barred women from combat aircraft and from all Navy ships except hospital ships and transports. From the outset, different services had different levels of gender integration, with Air Force women generally governed by the same organization structure as men but the Army maintaining a separate Women's Army Corps for training, promotions and other management functions. [35]

Over time, the military jobs that had been open to women during the war were trimmed back, and the services went out of their way to emphasize a traditionally feminine image for women in uniform, said Maj. Gen. Holm. In the Air Force, for example, "beginning in 1958 . . . enlisted women were phased out of fields where their representation had been small," such as intelligence, control-tower operation and some equipment-maintenance jobs, and were moved into desk jobs. [36]

Furthermore, "all basic training programs were heavily sprinkled with courses to enhance feminine appearance," said Holm. Female Marines, for example, "were told their lipstick and nail polish had to match the braid on their uniform hats, which was Marine Corps scarlet," while Air Force women were told to use lipstick and nail polish in a "natural shade." [37]

Volunteers All

In 1973, women accounted for 1.6 percent of military personnel. And, after years of growing public distaste for the Vietnam War, the United States ended the draft, opting to move forward with an all-volunteer military. Then, as public opposition to the war limited the number of men who enlisted, recruitment of women was stepped up to help fill the gap. [38]

But, points out Titunik, of the University of Hawaii, the increased use of women in the military between 1973

Army Spec. Rebecca Nava told a PBS television interviewer. Currently, military couples, as well as single parents, must present detailed plans for how their children will be cared for if they're deployed overseas, but in families where both parents are military, that difficulty could be overcome if spouses' deployments were timed so that "one parent goes . . . and then when that one gets back the other one goes," Nava said. "If one parent is with the child at all times, they don't have to worry" so much about the family's well-being. [6]

"Twenty years ago, when I was a young lieutenant, I felt I was committed to a career and could not have a family," says Darlene M. Iskra, program coordinator for the University of Maryland's Leadership Education and Development Center and a retired Navy commander who was the first woman to command a U.S. Navy ship. "Now women think they can have it all, and many are managing it, although the attrition rate is higher for women."

And the armed forces are looking at some family-friendly policies, says Iskra. For example, "The Navy has started a pilot program of sabbaticals offering up to three years off for men and women" to care for children or elderly parents, go to grad school or other purposes. People on sabbatical would remain on Navy rolls so they could have health insurance, and they would retain their rank when they returned. Currently, the program is open to 40 people, she says. Such programs — utterly unheard of in the past — are becoming important today, says Iskra. "Both women and men are becoming more family oriented. That's a sea change."

Unintended pregnancies also are a problem for military women, in part because of strict federal policies on abortion and emergency contraception. The so-called Hyde Amendment, attached to government spending bills each year, has barred federal funding for abortions since 1976. The Department of Defense currently allows women to pay for their own abortions at military facilities overseas — but only if their pregnancies endanger their lives or resulted from rape or incest. In addition, under current rules military facilities are not required to stock emergency contraception. [7]

As a result, women stationed overseas "face two unpalatable choices: Fly elsewhere for a safe, legal abortion, or seek a risky abortion off-base in the country where they are stationed," wrote Caitlin Borgmann, a professor of law at the City University of New York, in an August letter to *The New York Times.* [8]

— *Marcia Clemmitt*

[1] Genevieve Chase, testimony before Senate Committee on Veterans Affairs, July 14, 2009, http://veterans.senate.gov.

[2] Testimony before Senate Committee on Veterans Affairs, July 14, 2009, http://veterans.senate.gov.

[3] Erin Mulhall, "Women Warriors: Supporting She Who Has Borne the Battle," Iraq and Afghanistan Veterans of America, October 2009, http://media.iava.org/IAVA_WomensReport_2009.pdf.

[4] Testimony before Senate Committee on Veterans Affairs, July 14, 2009, http://veterans.senate.gov.

[5] Mulhall, *op. cit.*

[6] "Interview with Spec. Rebecca Nava, Team Lioness," Public Broadcasting System, www.pbs.org.

[7] "Military Women Should Have Full Access to Reproductive Health Care," National Women's Law Center, Women's Research & Education Institute, and Alliance for National Defense, December 2008.

[8] Caitlin Borgmann, letter to the editor, *The New York Times,* Aug. 17, 2009.

and the early 1990s "was connected primarily with military necessity, not direct feminist pressure." [39]

Economics also played a role in increasing the number of female recruits, says Linda Grant De Pauw, a historian and founder of the Maryland-based Minerva Center, an education foundation on women and warfare. "The economy declined so much that one man could no longer support a family," leaving more women seeking careers, including new ones provided by the volunteer military.

Women joined the armed forces rapidly during the 1970s. In 1975, President Gerald Ford signed legislation officially admitting women to the Army's military academy (West Point) and the Naval and Air Force academies at Annapolis and Colorado Springs. The first women matriculated in the fall of 1976, and the first co-ed classes graduated in 1980.

With an aggressive push by President Jimmy Carter, the percentage of women recruited swelled from under 2 percent to 8.9 percent by September 1981, for a total of 184,651 women across all service branches. The Carter administration announced a recruitment goal of 254,300 women — 12.5 percent of the force — by 1985. [40]

In early 1981, however, "military leaders asked the incoming Reagan administration to hold down the number of women enlistees until their impact on force readiness could be determined. In August 1982, the administration announced it would lower goals for female recruitment, make 23 additional job categories male-only, and establish new strength tests for other jobs that would close or nearly close them to women. [41]

Recruitment of women slowed somewhat but continued, and by 1985, women made up 10 percent of the military and, by 1990, 11 percent. In the 2000s, the percentage has hovered at about 14 percent. [42]

In the past two decades, more military jobs have opened to women, with more than 90 percent of jobs now open to women, including as ship commanders and bomber pilots.

In 1993, after the successful performance of women in the first Persian Gulf War, Congress repealed its previous ban on women serving on combat aircraft and on permanent duty on combat ships, noted scholars from the University of Maryland's Center for Research on Military Organization. (However, military policies continued to exclude women from serving in ground-combat positions, Special Operations forces, submarines and some other positions.) [43]

By now, more than 120 women have been killed in the Iraq and Afghanistan wars, but the expected public recoil from the death of women soldiers has not materialized, says Browder of Virginia Commonwealth University. "The American public is able to handle mothers getting killed."

During the last eight years of war, women have proven their value to the military mission. "They're attaining Silver Stars for valor," says Iskra of the University of Maryland.

But other analysts argue that women's desire for equal opportunity has swamped considerations about military missions.

"The overwhelming focus of integrationists has been the argument for equal rights rather than national security," wrote Wayne State's Browne. Putting women into ground combat roles risks potential loss of public support for a war if civilians at home react badly to seeing women — whom they may view as being like their mothers, daughters and sisters — taken captive in combat zones. It also risks requiring men in gender-integrated combat units to pick up some of the slack for women when it comes to heavy lifting, since the overwhelming majority of women have less upper-body strength than men, he says. [44]

For those reasons, "the exclusion of women from combat aviation should also be reinstated," said Browne. "Combat aviation crews may end up fighting for survival on the ground," and physical strength can also become "a critical factor in maintaining control" of aircraft hit by enemy fire. Pilots flying over enemy territory risk being shot down, "and it is in the national interest not to have women taken prisoner, even if individual women are willing to take the risk." [45]

Nevertheless, military workforce needs have opened more positions to women, including real — though ostensibly unofficial — roles in units serving with ground-combat forces. Beginning around 2003, U.S. military commanders began adding women to units engaged in direct ground combat, skirting the rule that women cannot be "assigned" to such units by having records state that they are only "attached" to the units.

For example, in 2004 and 2005, retired Lt. Col. Michael A. Baumann commanded 30 enlisted women and six female officers in a unit patrolling Baghdad's Rashid district, a hotbed of violence at the time and officially off-limits to female soldiers. But "we had to take everybody," said Baumann. "Nobody could be spared to do something like support." Moreover, he added, "I saw them with my own eyes. I had full trust and confidence in their abilities." [46]

"When they need boots on the ground, they'll put women where they need them," says D'Amico of Syracuse University.

But that is exactly the problem, says Donnelly of the Center for Military Readiness. The Army has assigned women to new roles in combat areas surreptitiously and without consulting Congress or the public about what amounts to a major — and, in her view, ill-advised — change in policy, she says.

Back in 1994, then-Secretary of Defense Les Aspin announced the "col-location rule" — declaring that women could be barred not only from ground-combat units but also from other units, such as supply units, that are "required to physically collocate and remain with direct ground combat units." [47]

Aspin's statement is valid and should stand, says Donnelly. "If the Army wants to change that, they're supposed to notify Congress 30 days earlier — come in and talk about it," so Congress can weigh in with legislation if they object, she says. "Instead, the Army has tried to redefine this, without going to Congress."

In 2005, congressional Republicans, led by Rep. Duncan Hunter, Calif., Chairman of the House Armed Services Committee, sponsored a bill to codify women's exclusion from ground combat. The provision was approved by committees in both the House and Senate, but lawmakers ultimately abandoned it. President Bush's Defense Secretary, Donald Rumsfeld, also expressed opposition to the legislation. [48]

"President George W. Bush immediately after [September 11, 2001] should have issued a call for young men, especially, to volunteer for the combat Army," says Donnelly. "He never did that, so instead we've got single mothers out there" because of heavy recruiting of young women to make up the workforce slack, she says. "I think the president missed the big picture here." ∎

CURRENT SITUATION

Woman Submariners?

I n 2009, arguments over what military jobs should be open to women have heated up, following

Continued on p. 974

At Issue:

Should military combat roles be fully opened to women?

MELISSA SHERIDAN EMBSER-HERBERT
PROFESSOR OF SOCIOLOGY, HAMLINE UNIVERSITY, AND ARMY VETERAN

WRITTEN FOR *CQ RESEARCHER*, NOVEMBER 2009

Combat positions should be open to those who are qualified, regardless of sex. Note that the question is not whether women should be permitted to *serve* in combat. That's because people are finally realizing that women already *are* in combat. Their job may not be "coded for combat," but improvised explosive devices (IEDs) don't know that. Snipers don't know that. The question is whether, acknowledging that women play vital roles in today's military and do serve in combat, the country will make more occupational categories and assignments available to women.

Those opposed to such a move claim, among other things, that women complain of being lied to by recruiters when they end up in combat-support units, and that men instinctively try to protect women. But while those entering the military do receive training in a particular occupation, in the Army everyone is a soldier first. There's a reason that even truck drivers complete Basic Combat Training, the "nine-week journey from civilian to soldier." No matter the career field or assignment coding, everyone knows — including women — that they may end up taking, and returning, fire. As for chivalry, the Army, as one example, would not have had to establish a Sexual Harassment/Assault Response & Prevention (SHARP) program if male military personnel were "predisposed to protect" female colleagues.

The military needs qualified personnel. If a woman demonstrates that she meets the requirements to perform a job, she should be allowed to do it. The requirements should include physical ability, and if this means that few women make the cut, so be it. Physical-fitness tests should be tied to the demands of one's military occupation, not one's sex. An infantry soldier *should* have higher physical-fitness standards than a cook. If the military is serious about wanting the strongest military possible — truly ready to defend the nation — it needs to start thinking about *people*, not reproductive organs and archaic ideas regarding the ability of women and men to work together.

Since 2001, more than 200,000 women have served in Iraq and Afghanistan. More than 100 have died, thousands have sustained serious physical injuries and an untold number suffer from post-traumatic stress disorder. To continue to deny women the right to serve honorably — and in combat — is insulting and disingenuous. Moreover, refusing the service of women who are willing and capable of serving in an expanded combat role is detrimental to the military mission.

ELAINE DONNELLY
PRESIDENT, CENTER FOR MILITARY READINESS

WRITTEN FOR *CQ RESEARCHER*, NOVEMBER 2009

In March 2003 an aggressive ground assault by infantry, armor, Special Operations Forces and Marines liberated Baghdad. In November 2004 the same forces cleaned out Fallujah, an enemy stronghold. Both battles involved brutal street-to-street, door-to-door fighting — the very definition of "direct ground combat." Despite assurances that today's wars "have no front lines," missions of close combat troops remain unchanged. All deployed personnel serve "in harm's way," but that is not the same as direct ground combat: closing with and destroying the enemy with deliberate *offensive action* under fire.

For many reasons, under current regulations battalion-level units in or near direct ground-combat battalions must be all-male. Infantrymen routinely must carry weapons, ammunition, electronic equipment and protective/survival gear weighing more than 100 pounds. All are prepared to lift and evacuate an injured fellow soldier in order to save his life. Female soldiers and Marines face hazardous duty inspecting female civilians in war zones, but in direct ground combat women do not have an "equal opportunity" to survive or to help fellow soldiers survive.

Current law requires the Defense Department to notify Congress well in advance of proposed changes in regulations affecting women. Instead, Army officials have redefined regulations unilaterally, without authorization. The result has been "anything goes" policies, combined with misguided recruiting priorities that attract single mothers and create problems for families left behind.

Navy officials now are pushing for women on submarines, despite irresolvable health risks identified by experts in undersea medicine. Elevated trace elements in the constantly recycled atmosphere, such as carbon monoxide and carbon dioxide, are safe for adults but not for a developing embryo in the earliest weeks before a sailor knows she is pregnant. Life-threatening ectopic pregnancies, which are not statistically rare, would require immediate, extremely hazardous mid-ocean evacuations that compromise undersea missions. Submarine habitability standards are difficult enough, and 100 percent manning requirements are incompatible with enlisted pregnancy rates that jumped from 12 to 19 percent in only two years.

Pride in our courageous military women and their impressive accomplishments should not deter questions about flawed policies that encourage social problems affecting discipline, deployability, morale and readiness. Congress should provide responsible oversight, holding Pentagon officials accountable. Equal opportunity is important, but if there is a conflict, the needs of the military must come first.

Continued from p. 972

statements by Joint Chiefs Chairman Mullen and other Navy leaders that they hope to begin integrating women into submarine crews. [49]

Mullen, formerly chief of naval operations, wrote to the Senate Armed Services Committee that, "as an advocate for improving the diversity of our force . . . one policy I would like to see changed is the one barring their service aboard submarines." [50]

In interviews with the *Navy Times* newspaper, the heads of the Navy Submarine Force and Fleet Forces Command — the organization in charge of the Atlantic fleet — described near-term plans for integrating women into the submarine fleet. Top Navy and Pentagon leaders still must sign off on the plan, and Congress must be given 30 days' notice of the Navy's intentions before money can be spent implementing the change. The process of seeking those approvals is just beginning, Vice Adm. Jay Donnelly of the Submarine Force recently told the *Navy Times*. [51]

Female junior officers — ensigns and lieutenants — will be the first women onboard because their smaller numbers mean that modifications to accommodate them will be cheaper, Vice Adm. Donnelly said. Sub officers share three-person or two-person staterooms, some of which would be reserved for the women. Female officers would share a bathroom — each of which has just a single shower, sink and toilet — with male officers, using a sign to indicate whether men or women are using the facility. Initially, the Navy would add women only to the crews of 18 large

U.S. Navy Lt. Kara S. Hultgreen — the nation's first woman combat pilot — was killed off the coast of San Diego when her F-14 crashed on approach to the aircraft carrier USS Abraham Lincoln *in 1994.*

Reuters/STR New

subs, the so-called *Ohio*-class subs, which launch ballistic and guided missiles, not to the smaller, "fast-attack" subs, like the *Seawolf* class. [52]

The women would require 15 to 16 months of training, putting the earliest possible date for the integration in 2011 or 2012, Donnelly said. [53]

For proponents of fully integrating women into the military, the news is welcome.

Sub duty is a traditional path to career advancement, says Hillman of the University of California. Top officers are generally chosen from among infantry and submarine officer pools — not from the military police or other job categories where most women serve today.

Many of the arguments against women serving on submarines are similar to those expressed against integrating women onto surface ships, said the University of Maryland's Iskra, who in 1990 became the first woman to command a Navy vessel. "Issues such as fraternization and sexual harassment" can be "dealt with as disciplinary issues," and "shipboard pregnancy is related to negative com-

mand climate and leadership," she argued. Moreover, she pointed out, "Since women serve on submarines in Australia, Canada, Norway and Sweden, it may be assumed that necessary privacy can be achieved." [54]

But other analysts argue that life on a submarine is different enough from shipboard conditions to make including women on subs dangerous both to the sub's mission and to some of the women. "The biggest mistake the Navy could make would be to gender-integrate the submarine force," says Donnelly of the Center for Military Readiness.

If a woman became pregnant, both she and her fetus would face serious medical risks by staying aboard a submarine, according to retired Rear Adm. Hugh P. Scott. "One of the more serious problems . . . in the sealed environment of a submarine is the off-gassing of several thousand organic trace contaminants" that escape from construction and maintenance operations, as well as "exposures to increased levels of carbon monoxide and carbon dioxide" arising from cigarette smoking, overheated insulation and other sources in a closed atmosphere, Scott said. [55]

Although the pollution poses no more danger to non-pregnant women than to men, it would be very dangerous to a fetus during the first trimester of pregnancy, Scott wrote. It could interfere with fetal oxygen supply during critical stages of development and could cause ectopic pregnancies — pregnancies that occur outside the uterus and are not survivable by an embryo, he argued. [56]

"If a woman discovers she's pregnant, the captain has only two choices," says

Donnelly. One would be to "surface and evacuate her," a very complicated and potentially dangerous process in some conditions, such as if the sub is under the polar ice cap. Alternatively, she says, the captain could "keep the woman there and risk birth defects. Women are not being told about these risks."

Sexual Assault

Whether one favors or opposes it, no one argues that harmonious gender integration of the armed forces comes without problems.

Early this year the Defense Department released 2008 data on sexual assaults involving military personnel, showing that reported assaults increased by 8 percent overall from the previous year and by 26 percent in Iraq, a combat zone. But while that may strike some as bad news, the Pentagon said the rise is just what it wanted to see. [57]

Increased reports mean "the department's policy of encouraging victims to come forward is making a difference," said Kaye Whitley, director of SAPRO, the Pentagon's Sexual Assault and Prevention Office. "We're getting the victims in to get care." In both civilian and military life, sexual assault is the least-reported crime, and what's not reported can't be remedied, she pointed out. [58]

Of the 2,908 reports, 643 were made as "restricted" reports — an option the Pentagon began offering in 2005 in order to allow victims to report an assault to get care without reporting the incident to law enforcement or military commanders. Of the 2,265 "unrestricted" reports, 1,594 victims were armed-forces members, while the other 671 were civilians. [59]

Some members of Congress called the data alarming. "While the report shows modest improvement, we're far from 'Mission Accomplished,' " said Rep. Harman. "Military women are more likely to be raped by a fellow soldier than killed by enemy fire in Iraq. [60]

In February, Rep. Slaughter introduced the Military Domestic and Sexual Violence Response Act, which would establish an Office of Victims' Advocate in the DoD to help those reporting assaults get care, establish a sexual-assault care team at each military medical facility, require commanders who receive reports of violence to investigate and report them and establish a Director of Special Investigations to refer cases for prosecution. No action has occurred on the bill, however. [61]

Meanwhile, advocates of limiting gender integration argue that maintaining some gender-segregated units is the best way to cut down on all kinds of sexual misconduct, including sexual assault. "Sexual misconduct is a problem in a gender-mixed force even though we've tried everything," says Donnelly. The best approach is probably to "separate genders as much as possible," she says. "The Marines have separate-gender training, and the Army should return to it."

But others say the future does not lie in gender segregation. Policy makers are moving forward to integrate women into roles such as the submarine service despite problems and significant dissent from both inside and outside the military, says Bryn Mawr's Martin. "Policies drive public understanding and perception," not the other way around, he says. "If you waited to get everybody on board, it would never happen."

Moreover, with the Army bringing women into ground-combat positions in Iraq and Afghanistan — even in advance of official policy changes — "we might be up for more action on the policy level" once the current wars have ended, says Rosemarie Skaine, author of the 1998 book *Women at War.* That would open positions that have been opened de facto already.

"The reality is that the women are already there," she says. ■

OUTLOOK

Gender Roles

For those who believe women should participate fully in the armed services, recent events like the Navy's push to open submarine duty to women suggest that it's mainly a matter of time before all military roles are gender-neutral.

But skeptics say focusing on the armed services as a necessary step in achieving equal workplace opportunity is likely to backfire, potentially opening the door to abuse of some valuable female soldiers by forcing them into combat roles they have no wish to enter and for which they are unsuited.

Time alone may work much of the change, says D'Amico of Syracuse. "The new generations — generations X, Y and the ones that follow — look really differently at every sort of institution. My students tend to ask, 'Why should women not be in the military? What's the problem?' " and that sentiment includes many politically conservative students, she says.

"We aren't going to go back," and "the barriers will fall," including the barrier to serving in ground combat, says Virginia Commonwealth's Browder.

Furthermore, social expectations outside the military play a major role in holding women back from military advancement, and, while gender expectations are shifting throughout society, such change occurs slowly, says Bryn Mawr's Martin. "For example, we still define women as having significant responsibility for caring for elderly parents," a cultural norm that keeps military women — like women in some other professions, notably academic science — from "reaching certain benchmarks required for promotion."

But "the campaign to force young women into or near the violence of close combat" flies in the face of some traditional — and important — American values, requiring "psychological acceptance of the idea that men can and should place women in physical or mortal danger," said Donnelly of the Center for Military Readiness. [62]

There's a deep disconnect between efforts to protect military women believed to be victims of sexual violence or harassment and the simultaneous movement to push them into super-dangerous combat roles, said Donnelly. "Many officials in Congress, the Pentagon and the service academies are eager to establish ubiquitous 'victim advocate' offices, staffed by professionals who vow to protect military women from the slightest form of harassment, real or imagined." Meanwhile, "the same officials simultaneously promote the deliberate exposure of military women to extreme abuse and violence in close, lethal combat, where females do not have an equal opportunity to survive." [63]

Furthermore, "indications are . . . that many female recruits are not being informed, prior to enlistment, that regulations no longer exempt women from assignments known to involve a 'substantial risk of capture,' " Donnelly said. "Nor are the female recruits being told that their 'job description' might involve involuntary placement in ground-combat-collocated units, despite regulations requiring those units to be coded for men only." [64]

Rather than trying to establish a completely equal career playing field for women within the armed services, a fairer regime for the many women who currently enter the military as a career move might be to expand government benefits like health insurance and education currently available only to armed-forces members to a much wider range of public-service jobs, says Marie De Young, a former Army chaplain and operations officer and co-author of *Women in Combat: Civic Duty or Military Liability?*

"We predicted in the early 1990s that we'll be short 10 million teachers," and other public-service roles also need filling, such as emergency first-responders, she says. "So why are we valorizing only the military? The people who are really going in for the benefits — why not let them do civil service and community service in other ways?" ∎

Notes

[1] For background, see David Koon, "A New Soldier Story," *Arkansas Times*, May 15, 2008, www.arktimes.com.

[2] Quoted in "Lioness: There for the Action, Missing from History," a documentary film by Meg McLagan and Daria Sommers, 2008, www.lionessthefilm.com.

[3] Quoted in James Dao, "First Woman Ascends to Top Drill Sergeant Spot," *The New York Times*, Sept. 22, 2009, p. A1.

[4] Rachel L. Swarns, "Commanding a Role for Women in the Military," *The New York Times*, June 30, 2008, p. A17.

[5] See Peter Katel, "Gays in the Military," *CQ Researcher*, Sept. 18, 2009, pp. 765-788.

[6] Elaine Donnelly, "The Army's Gender War," *National Review Online*, Jan. 7, 2005, www.nationalreview.com.

[7] Elaine Donnelly, "Constructing the Co-Ed Military," *Duke Journal of Law and Gender Policy*, June 18, 2007, p. 881.

[8] Jane Harman, testimony to the House Oversight and Government Reform Subcommittee on National Security and Foreign Affairs, July 31, 2008.

[9] Transcript, "Ben Wattenberg's Think Tank," PBS, Sept. 16, 2000, www.pbs.org/thinktank/transcript895.html.

[10] Laura Browder, *When Janey Comes Marching Home: Portraits of Women Combat Veterans*, forthcoming, p. 4.

[11] *Ibid.*

[12] Kingsley Browne, *Co-Ed Combat: The New Evidence that Women Shouldn't Fight the Nation's Wars* (2007), p. 115.

[13] Regina F. Titunik, "The First Wave: Gender Integration and Military Culture," *Armed Forces & Society*, winter 2000, p. 248.

[14] "Military Hails Two Heroes from Ft. Hood Rampage," MSNBC.com, Nov. 6, 2009, www.msnbc.msn.com.

[15] Margaret C. Harrell and Laura L. Miller, "New Opportunities for Military Women; Effects Upon Readiness, Cohesion, Morale," RAND, 1997, p. xvii.

[16] Barbara W. Wilson, "Women in Combat: Why Not," Military Women Veterans blog, http://userpages.aug.com/captbarb/combat.html.

[17] Browne, *op. cit.*, p. 259.

[18] Harman, *op. cit.*

[19] Louise Slaughter, testimony to the House Oversight and Government Reform Subcommittee on National Security and Foreign Affairs, July 31, 2008.

[20] For background, see Craig Donegan, "New Military Culture," *CQ Researcher*, April 26, 1996, pp. 361-384.

[21] Helen Benedict, testimony before the House Oversight and Government Reform Subcommittee on National Security and Foreign Affairs, June 25, 2009, http://nationalsecurity.oversight.house.gov.

[22] Harman, *op. cit.*

[23] *Ibid.*

[24] Benedict, *op. cit.*

[25] For background see, Bernard Cook, ed., *Women in War: A Historical Encyclopedia*

About the Author

Staff writer **Marcia Clemmitt** is a veteran social-policy reporter who previously served as editor in chief of *Medicine & Health* and staff writer for *The Scientist*. She has also been a high-school math and physics teacher. She holds a liberal arts and sciences degree from St. John's College, Annapolis, and a master's degree in English from Georgetown University. Her recent reports include "Preventing Cancer" and "Treating Depression."

from Antiquity to the Present (2006).

[26] Robert B. Edgerton, *Warrior Women: the Amazons of Dahomey* (2000), p. 3.

[27] *Ibid.*, p. 100.

[28] Lisa Tendrich Frank, "American Women Combatants During the Civil War," in Cook, *op. cit.*, p. 118.

[29] Patricia M. Shields, "Women as Military Leaders: Promises and Pitfalls," Faculty Publications — Political Science, eCommons@Texas State University, http://ecommons.txstate.edu/polsfacp/42.

[30] Jeanne Holm, *Women in the Military: An Unfinished History* (1993), p. 23.

[31] Titunik, *op. cit.*, p. 229.

[32] Brian P. Mitchell, *Women in the Military: Flirting With Disaster* (1998), p. 4.

[33] Quoted in Titunik, *op. cit.*, p. 229.

[34] Holm, *op. cit.*, p. 120.

[35] *Ibid.*, p. 120.

[36] *Ibid.*, p. 184.

[37] *Ibid.*, p. 181.

[38] For background, see Marc Leepson, "Women in the Military," *Editorial Research Reports*, July 10, 1981, and Rodman D. Griffin, "Women in the Military," *CQ Researcher*, Sept. 25, 1992, pp. 833-856.

[39] Regina F. Titunik, "The Myth of the Macho Military," *Polity*, April 2008, p. 140.

[40] Ellen C. Collier, "Women in the Armed Forces," Issue Brief No. IB79045, Congressional Research Service, 1982, http://digital.library.unt.edu/govdocs/crs/permalink/meta-crs-8513:1.

[41] *Ibid.*

[42] Jake Willens and Daniel Smith, "Women in the Military: Combat Roles Considered," Center for Defense Information, 1998, www.cdi.org/issues/women/combat.html.

[43] Michelle Sandhoff, Mady Wechsler Segal and David R. Segal, "Gender Issues in the Transformation to an All-Volunteer Force: A Transnational Perspective," http://papers.ccpr.ucla.edu/papers/PWP-MPRC-2008-027/PWP-MPRC-2008-027.pdf.

[44] Browne, *op. cit.*, p. 295.

[45] *Ibid.*, p. 296.

[46] Quoted in Lizette Alvarez, "G.I. Jane Breaks the Combat Barrier," *The New York Times*, Aug. 16, 2009, p. A1.

[47] Les Aspin, "Memorandum from the Office of the Secretary of Defense," Jan. 13, 1994, Center for Military Readiness Web site, http://cmrlink.org/CMRNotes/LesAspin%20DGC%20DefAssign%20Rule%20011394.pdf.

[48] For background, see "Hunter Admonishes Army on Women in Land Combat," Center for Military Readiness Web site, June 1, 2005,

FOR MORE INFORMATION

Center for Military Readiness, P.O. Box 51600, Livonia, MI 48151; (202) 347-5333; www.cmrlink.org. Think tank and advocacy organization concerned with how personnel policies, such as assigning women to ground-combat units, could adversely affect military readiness.

Center for Women Veterans, Department of Veterans Affairs, 810 Vermont Ave., N.W., Washington, DC 20420; (800) 827-1000; www1.va.gov/WOMENVET. Provides services for and information about female veterans.

Defense Department Advisory Committee on Women in the Services, OUSD (P&R) DACOWITS, Room 2C548A, 4000 Defense Pentagon, Washington, DC 20301-4000; (703) 697-2122; http://dacowits.defense.gov. Civilian panel appointed by the Secretary of Defense to conduct research and provide recommendations on recruitment and retention of women in the military.

Defense Equal Opportunity Management Institute, 66 Tuskegee Airmen Dr., Patrick Air Force Base, FL 32925-3399; www.deomi.org. Department of Defense office that educates military leadership about diversity issues, including gender relations.

MilitaryWoman.org, 6574 N State Rd. 7, Suite 110, Coconut Creek, FL 33073; (877) 282-6620; www.militarywoman.org. Web site providing information, assistance and a gathering place to communicate on all issues affecting women who are in the military or are considering enlistment.

Service Women's Action Network, 123 William St., 16th Floor, New York, NY 10038; (646) 602-5621; www.servicewomen.org. Nonprofit providing assistance and advocacy for women veterans.

Sexual Assault Prevention and Response, Department of Defense; (703) 696-9422; www.sapr.mil. Provides information and coordinates the armed forces' response to sexual-assault reports in the military.

Women in Military Service for America Memorial Foundation, Dept. 560, Washington, DC 20042-0560; (703) 533-1155; www.womensmemorial.org. Web site associated with the Women's Memorial at Arlington National Cemetery; provides historical information on women's roles in the U.S. military.

http://cmrlink.org, and "House Drops Limitation on Women in Combat Bill," News Insider Web site, May 25, 2005, www.newsinsider.org.

[49] For background, see Andrew Scutro and Mark D. Faram, "Female Sailors Could Join Sub Crews by 2011," *Navy Times*, Oct. 12, 2009, www.navytimes.com, and "Mullen Wants Females on Subs," *Defense Tech*, Sept. 24, 2009, www.defensetech.org.

[50] Quoted in *ibid.*

[51] Scutro and Faram, *op. cit.*

[52] *Ibid.*

[53] *Ibid.*

[54] Darlene M. Iskra, "Attitudes Toward Expanding Roles for Navy Women at Sea: Results of a Content Analysis," *Armed Forces & Society*, January 2007, p. 203.

[55] Hugh P. Scott, letter to Rep. Floyd D. Spence, June 12, 2000, http://cmrlink.org/CMRNotes/HPScott%20061200.pdf.

[56] *Ibid.*

[57] William H. McMichael, "DoD: Sexual Assault Reports Increased in 2008," *Army Times*, March 17, 2009, www.armytimes.com.

[58] Quoted in *ibid.*

[59] *Ibid.*

[60] Quoted in *ibid.*

[61] For text and status of legislation, see http://thomas.loc.gov.

[62] Donnelly, "Constructing the Co-Ed Military," *op. cit.*, p. 930.

[63] *Ibid.*, p. 931.

[64] *Ibid.*

Bibliography

Selected Sources

Books

Browne, Kingsley, *Co-Ed Combat: The New Evidence that Women Shouldn't Fight the Nation's Wars*, Penguin, 2007.

A law professor at Wayne State University in Detroit lays out the arguments against integrating women fully into the military and into combat roles.

Cook, Bernard A., ed., *Women and War: A Historical Encyclopedia from Antiquity to the Present*, ABC-CLIO, 2006.

A professor of European history at Loyola University in New Orleans assembles expert-written articles on the extent and nature of women's participation as both victims and combatants in wars around the world, including guerrilla warfare, terrorism and the current wars in the Middle East.

Holm, Jeanne M., *Women in the Military: An Unfinished Revolution*, Presidio, 1993.

A retired Air Force major general who became the first female two-star general in the armed services and who championed women's full integration into the military describes women's changing military roles from the American Revolution through the Persian Gulf War.

Articles

Alvarez, Lizette, "G.I. Jane Breaks the Combat Barrier," *The New York Times*, Aug. 16, 2009, p. A1.

Due to personnel shortages, women regularly have been seeing combat in Iraq and Afghanistan, in defiance of official policy.

Cave, Damien, "A Combat Role, and Anguish, Too," *The New York Times*, Nov. 1, 2009, p. A1.

Female soldiers suffer from post-traumatic stress disorder and other combat-related mental and physical problems just like men, but they get less sensitive treatment at Veterans' Affairs hospitals, which sometimes treat them as if they don't believe they have combat-related conditions.

Donnelly, Elaine, "The Army's Gender War," *National Review Online*, Jan. 7, 2005, www.nationalreview.com.

Some women soldiers feel betrayed by the Army when they're assigned — counter to military policy — to accompany front-line ground-combat troops, according to a leading opponent of women's participation in ground combat.

Koon, David, "A New Soldier Story: 'Lioness' Tracks an All-Woman Combat Unit," *Arkansas Times*, May 15, 2008, www.arktimes.com.

A soldier who was profiled in the documentary film "Lioness," about women soldiers serving on offensive missions in combat zones in Iraq, has struggled to come to terms with taking an enemy life.

Lubold, Gordon, "Army 'Lionesses' Hit Streets with Marines on Combat Ops," *Marine Corps Times*, Aug. 4, 2004, www.militaryphotos.net/forums/showthread.php?t=18513.

Team Lioness, staffed by women from the Army's 1st Engineer Battalion, has accompanied Marines on offensive operations in Iraq's hottest combat zones, provoking both admiration and skepticism.

McMichael, William H., and Andrew Scutro, "SecNavy, CNO: Women Should Serve on Subs," *Navy Times*, Sept. 27, 2009, www.navytimes.com/news/2009/09/navy_roughead_subs_092409w.

The Navy plans to open submarine duty to women.

Tilghman, Andrew, "Report Outlines Pregnancy Policy Concerns," *Navy Times*, Oct. 19, 2009, www.navytimes.com.

In 2007, the Navy extended shore leave for new mothers from four months to 12 months, thus expanding the entire limited-duty period for pregnant women to 21 months. Apparently as a result, pregnancies in the Navy have increased, leaving many units deployed at sea with manpower shortages.

Yeager, Holly, "Soldiering Ahead," *The Wilson Quarterly*, summer 2007, www.wilsoncenter.org.

More women are gaining acceptance on the battlefield and as military leaders, but the jury is still out about how their growing numbers will alter traditional military culture.

Reports and Studies

"Military Personnel: DoD's and the Coast Guard's Sexual Assault Prevention and Response Programs Face Implementation and Oversight Challenges," Government Accountability Office, Aug. 29, 2008, www.gao.gov/products/GAO-08-924.

Congress' nonpartisan auditing agency finds that Department of Defense programs to prevent and respond to sexual-assault problems apparently undercount the number of assaults that occur and may not have enough resources to fulfill their responsibilities.

Burrelli, David F., "Women in the Armed Forces," Congressional Research Service, Sept. 29, 1998, www.fas.org/man/crs/92-008.htm.

Congress' nonpartisan research arm provides a history of the U.S. military's recruitment and job-assignment policies for women from the end of the draft in 1973 through the late 1990s.

The Next Step:

Additional Articles from Current Periodicals

Combat

"A Surge of Women in Combat," *The Oregonian*, Aug. 18, 2009.

About 6 percent of the nation's top military personnel are now women, including 57 generals and admirals.

Davis, Sandy, "Women at War," *The Advocate* (Louisiana), Oct. 19, 2008, p. A1.

Louisiana has contributed a high percentage of women to U.S. forces in Afghanistan and Iraq.

Hart, Betsy, "Women 'Attached' to Combat Units," *Times Record News* (Texas), Aug. 22, 2009, p. A19.

American women may be as courageous as Hollywood's "G.I. Jane," but that doesn't give the military the right to un-necessarily put women in combat.

Military Readiness

Donnelly, Elaine, "Gays and the Military; Democrats Prefer San Francisco-Style," *The Washington Times*, Jan. 3, 2008, p. A15.

Unauthorized and incremental repeal of women's exemptions from land combat will eventually affect the Marine Corps and Special Operations Forces.

Maze, Rick, " 'Caucus' Agenda Puts Military Women at Center Stage; Lawmakers Explore Issues Such as Maternity Leave, Sexual Assault," *Army Times*, March 24, 2008, p. 26.

Post-traumatic stress disorder (PTSD) from combat situations or sexual assault can require special counseling and treatment, especially for women.

Nargele, Dominik, "Sex and Combat Readiness," *The Washington Times*, Jan. 14, 2008, p. A16.

A disabled combat veteran argues that sexual relationships between men and women have no place in the armed forces when its members are trying to achieve optimum military readiness and performance.

Physical Differences

"Pulling for Change; Make Male, Female Marines Perform the Same PFT Exercises," *Marine Corps Times*, Oct. 13, 2008, p. 62.

If female Marines were held to the same physical standards as men, more equality would exist between the sexes.

Blumenthal, Les, "VA Struggles to Care for Female Veterans," *Chicago Tribune*, June 18, 2008, p. A5.

Female veterans have faced a number of problems, from clinics that don't have full-time obstetricians and gynecologists to uncomfortable group-therapy sessions where men

outnumber women and topics can include sexual assault and harassment.

Cutright, Courtney, "VMI Makes Changes to Fitness Tests," *The Roanoke Times*, April 18, 2009, p. A1.

Virginia Military Institute has revised fitness standards for women, but some female cadets oppose those changes, preferring instead to maintain traditional minimum fitness requirements.

Sexual Violence

"Rep. Slaughter Introduces Military Domestic and Sexual Violence Response Act," States News Service, Feb. 3, 2009.

While the Department of Defense has made numerous efforts to improve its prevention and response to domestic and sexual violence, health care and other services remain incomplete and inconsistent among the various branches, experts say.

McMichael, William H., "Program to Help Sex-Assault Victims Said to Be Working," *Marine Corps Times*, Feb. 9, 2009, p. 24.

The military's program to advocate for and support victims of sexual assault is working very well, according to three service members testifying before the House Armed Services Military Personnel Subcommittee.

Ream, Anne K., "When Death With Honor Shames The Military," *The Star-Ledger* (New Jersey), Jan. 25, 2008, p. 19.

The military policy of allowing honor burials for veterans convicted of rape sends the wrong message to victims.

CITING *CQ* RESEARCHER

Sample formats for citing these reports in a bibliography include the ones listed below. Preferred styles and formats vary, so please check with your instructor or professor.

MLA STYLE

Jost, Kenneth. "Rethinking the Death Penalty." CQ Researcher 16 Nov. 2001: 945-68.

APA STYLE

Jost, K. (2001, November 16). Rethinking the death penalty. *CQ Researcher, 11*, 945-968.

CHICAGO STYLE

Jost, Kenneth. "Rethinking the Death Penalty." *CQ Researcher*, November 16, 2001, 945-968.

In-depth Reports on Issues in the News

Are you writing a paper?

Need backup for a debate?

Want to become an expert on an issue?

For more than 80 years, students have turned to *CQ Researcher* for in-depth reporting on issues in the news. Reports on a full range of political and social issues are now available. Following is a selection of recent reports:

Civil Liberties
Closing Guantánamo, 2/09
Affirmative Action, 10/08
Gay Marriage Showdowns, 9/08
America's Border Fence, 9/08
Immigration Debate, 2/08

Crime/Law
Interrogating the CIA, 9/09
Examining Forensics, 7/09
Legalizing Marijuana, 6/09
Wrongful Convictions, 4/09
Prostitution Debate, 5/08

Education
Reading Crisis? 2/08
Discipline in Schools, 2/08
Student Aid, 1/08

Environment/Society
Conspiracy Theories, 10/09
Human Spaceflight, 10/09
Gays in the Military, 9/09
Energy and Climate, 7/09
Future of Books, 5/09
Hate Groups, 5/09
Future of Journalism, 3/09

Health/Safety
Medication Abuse, 10/09
Nuclear Disarmament, 10/09
Health-Care Reform, 8/09
Straining the Safety Net, 7/09
Treating Depression, 6/09
Reproductive Ethics, 5/09

Politics/Economy
State Budget Crisis, 9/09
Business Bankruptcy, 4/09
Future of the GOP, 3/09
Middle-Class Squeeze, 3/09

Upcoming Reports

Value of a College Education, 11/20/09   Prisoner Re-entry, 12/4/09   Bilingual Education, 12/11/09

ACCESS

CQ Researcher is available in print and online. For access, visit your library or www.cqresearcher.com.

STAY CURRENT

To receive notice of upcoming *CQ Researcher* reports, or learn more about *CQ Researcher* products, subscribe to the free e-mail newsletters, *CQ Researcher Alert!* and *CQ Researcher News*: http://cqpress.com/newsletters.

PURCHASE

To purchase a *CQ Researcher* report in print or electronic format (PDF), visit www.cqpress.com or call 866-427-7737. Single reports start at $15. Bulk purchase discounts and electronic-rights licensing are also available.

SUBSCRIBE

Annual full-service *CQ Researcher* subscriptions—including 44 reports a year, monthly index updates, and a bound volume—start at $803. Add $25 for domestic postage.

CQ Researcher Online offers a backfile from 1991 and a number of tools to simplify research. For pricing information, call 800-834-9020, ext. 1906, or e-mail librarysales@cqpress.com.

Published by CQ Press, a Division of SAGE

www.cqresearcher.com

The Value of a College Education

Is a four-year degree the only path to a secure future?

P resident Obama's $12 billion American Graduation Initiative — announced in July — aims to help millions more Americans earn degrees and certificates from community colleges. The president wants the United States to have, once again, the highest proportion of college graduates in the world. Along with the administration, economists and many students and parents embrace the notion that higher education offers the most promising ticket to financial security and upward mobility. However, some argue that many young people are ill-prepared or unmotivated to get a four-year degree and should pursue apprenticeships or job-related technical training instead. The debate is casting a spotlight on trends in high-school career and technical education — long known as vocational education — and raising questions about the ability of the nation's 1,200 community colleges to meet exploding enrollment demand.

CQ Researcher • Nov. 20, 2009 • www.cqresearcher.com
Volume 19, Number 41 • Pages 981-1004

A student learns welding at Central Piedmont Community College in Charlotte, N.C. Students in the fast-track program can earn career-readiness certificates in six months or less.

THE VALUE OF A COLLEGE EDUCATION

Cover: Central Piedmont Community College

Nov. 20, 2009
Volume 19, Number 41

MANAGING EDITOR: Thomas J. Colin
tcolin@cqpress.com

ASSISTANT MANAGING EDITOR: Kathy Koch
kkoch@cqpress.com

ASSOCIATE EDITOR: Kenneth Jost

STAFF WRITERS: Thomas J. Billitteri, Marcia Clemmitt, Peter Katel

CONTRIBUTING WRITERS: Rachel Cox, Sarah Glazer, Alan Greenblatt, Reed Karaim Barbara Mantel, Patrick Marshall, Tom Price, Jennifer Weeks

DESIGN/PRODUCTION EDITOR: Olu B. Davis

ASSISTANT EDITOR: Darrell Dela Rosa

EDITORIAL INTERN: Emily DeRuy

FACT-CHECKING: Eugene J. Gabler, Michelle Harris

CQ PRESS

A Division of SAGE

PRESIDENT AND PUBLISHER:
John A. Jenkins

CQ Press is a registered trademark of Congressional Quarterly Inc.

CQ Researcher (ISSN 1056-2036) is printed on acid-free paper. Published weekly, except; (Jan. wk. 1) (May wk. 4) (July wks. 1, 2) (Aug. wks. 3, 4) (Nov. wk. 4) and (Dec. wk. 4), by CQ Press, a division of SAGE Publications. Annual full-service subscriptions start at $803. For pricing, call 1-800-834-9020, ext. 1906. To purchase a *CQ Researcher* report in print or electronic format (PDF), visit www. cqpress.com or call 866-427-7737. Single reports start at $15. Bulk purchase discounts and electronic-rights licensing are also available. Periodicals postage paid at Washington, D.C., and additional mailing offices. POSTMASTER: Send address changes to *CQ Researcher*, 2300 N St., N.W., Suite 800, Washington, DC 20037.

The Value of a College Education

By Thomas J. Billitteri

THE ISSUES

Mike Rowe, host of the cable-TV show "Dirty Jobs," has a thing or two to say about work and education.

For 30 years, writes Rowe, whose show profiles some of the more challenging sides of blue-collar work, "we've convinced ourselves that 'good jobs' are the result of a four-year degree. That's bunk. Not all knowledge comes from college." [1]

Rowe's plainspoken view contradicts the lofty advice routinely dispensed to young people, that a bachelor's degree is a fundamental requirement for achieving the American Dream.

But with college costs soaring, skilled jobs such as welders and medical technicians in demand and millions of young adults ill-prepared for the rigors of a university education, some policy experts argue that while post-high-school education is vital in today's global economy, a four-year degree may be unnecessary for economic security — and perhaps even ill-advised.

"In many cases, young people think they are going to make substantial income just by having a college degree," says Edwin L. Herr, a professor emeritus of education at Pennsylvania State University and co-author of *Other Ways to Win*, a book that analyzes alternatives to the traditional bachelor's degree. "There are a lot of people destined for unhappiness if we simply say that everybody ought to go to college. I don't think society in general requires everybody to go to college. It certainly requires people who have skills, and there certainly are ways to

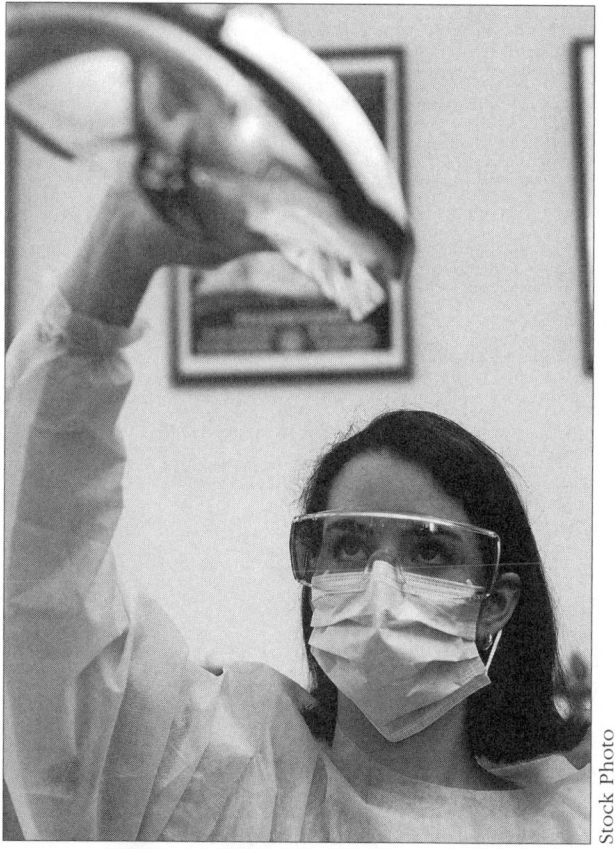

Courses in dental hygiene are popular at many of the nation's 1,200 community colleges. Today's "career and technical education" (CTE) programs integrate core academic training into job-specific courses like computer programming, medical technology, restaurant and hotel management and construction.

Stock Photo

obtain those skills other than a four-year college."

The Obama administration seems to agree. Under his American Graduation Initiative, announced in July, President Barack Obama is calling for an additional 5 million community college graduates by 2020, including those who earn associate degrees or certificates or who go on to graduate from four-year institutions. Beyond that, he wants every American to commit to at least a year of higher education or career training, whether at a community college or a four-year school, or through a vocational program or apprenticeship. [2]

The United States had the highest percentages of college graduates in the world for most of the post-World War II era, but now the rates remain stagnant, according to the Indianapolis-based Lumina Foundation for Education. About 39 percent of U.S. adults hold a two- or four-year degree, but in some countries, including Japan and South Korea, more than half of young adults ages 25 to 34 hold degrees, a foundation report said. "Even more disturbing for the U.S.," it added, "rates in these other countries continue to climb while ours remain stagnant."

Lumina estimated that at current college-graduation rates, "there will be a shortage of 16 million college-educated adults in the American workforce by 2025." [3]

Obama proposes to spend a record $12 billion over the next decade to strengthen the nation's system of 1,200 community colleges, part of a larger goal to restore the United States as the leader in college graduates by 2020.

"[F]or a long time there have been politicians who have spoken of training as a silver bullet and college as a cure-all," Obama said. "It's not, and we know that." But, he added, "We know that in the coming years, jobs requiring at least an associate degree are projected to grow twice as fast as jobs requiring no college experience. We will not fill those jobs — or even keep those jobs here in America — without the training offered by community colleges." [4]

To be sure, a bachelor's degree is a laudable goal for many young adults, one that can pay big dividends in personal satisfaction, career opportunities and earnings. In 2007 people with a bachelor's degree earned an average $57,181, or 63 percent more than those

Community Colleges at a Glance

More than 80 percent of the nation's approximately 1,200 community colleges are publicly supported. Of the 11.5 million students they serve, nearly 60 percent are enrolled part time, and 40 percent are among the first generation of their families to attend college.

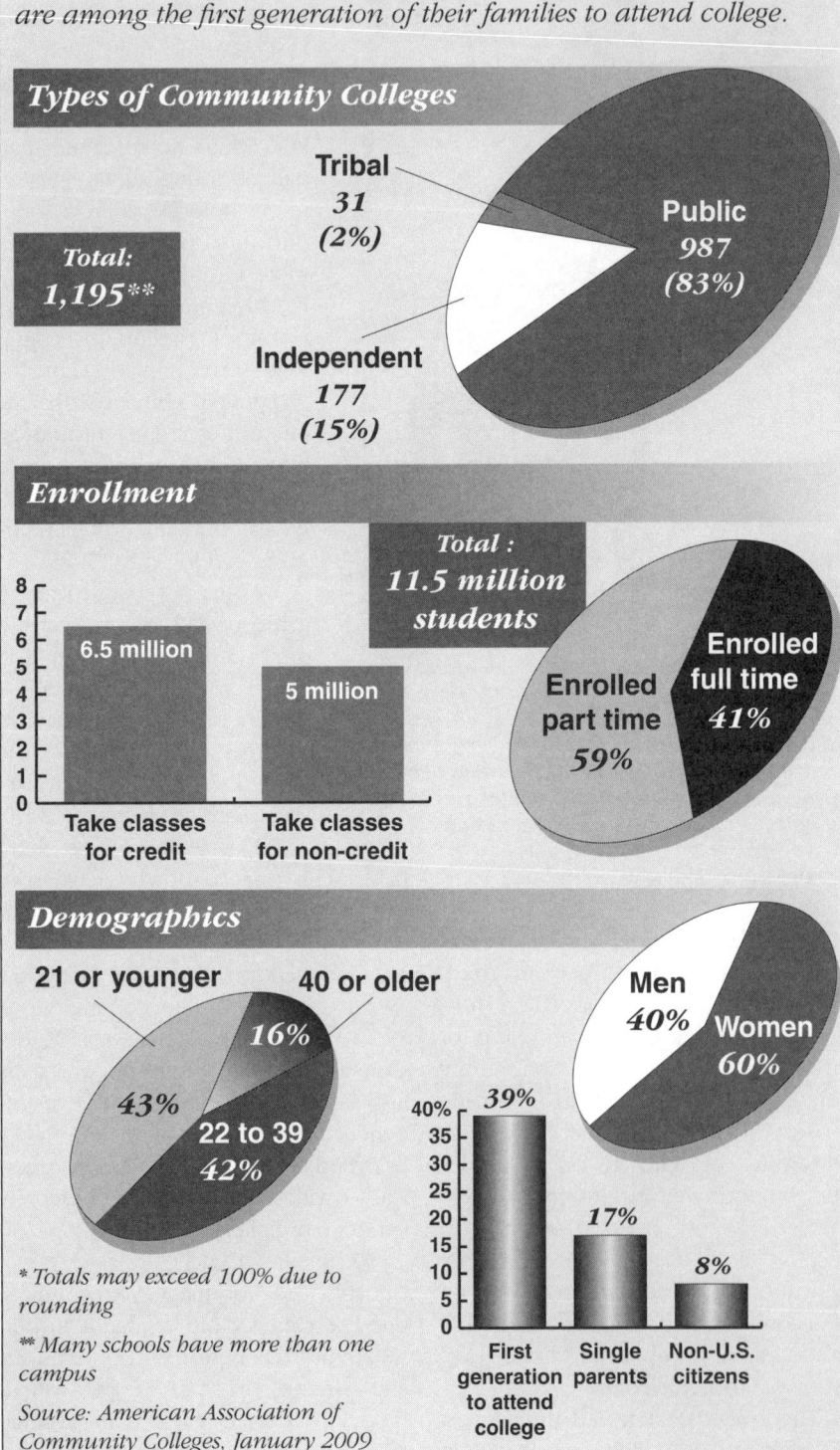

Types of Community Colleges

Tribal
31
(2%)

Public
987
(83%)

Total:
1,195**

Independent
177
(15%)

Enrollment

Total :
11.5 million
students

6.5 million

5 million

Take classes
for credit

Take classes
for non-credit

Enrolled
full time
41%

Enrolled
part time
59%

Demographics

21 or younger   40 or older

16%

43%

22 to 39
42%

Men
40%

Women
60%

39%

17%

8%

First
generation
to attend
college

Single
parents

Non-U.S.
citizens

* Totals may exceed 100% due to rounding

** Many schools have more than one campus

Source: American Association of Community Colleges, January 2009

with some college or an associate's degree and 83 percent more than those with only a high-school diploma. [5] (*See graph, p. 988.*) And the seasonally adjusted unemployment rate was 4.9 percent in September for adults 25 and older with a bachelor's degree or higher, compared with 8.5 percent for those with less college and 10.8 percent for those with only a high-school education. [6]

Still, a four-year degree is not always the best option, workforce and public-policy experts argue.

For one thing, many students simply aren't cut out for college. "No one wants to really talk about this, but a lot of [teens] come out of high school unprepared to do legitimate college-level work," says Kenneth C. Gray, a Pennsylvania State emeritus professor of education and coauthor with Herr of *Other Ways to Win.*

At the same time, four years of college demands a steep investment that may take years to recoup. In-state tuition, fees and room and board at a public four-year college now average $15,213 per year, up 5.9 percent in a year, though student aid often lowers the tab. At private schools, the bill — not counting any aid — runs $35,636 per year, up 4.3 percent in a year. [7] (*See graph, p. 987.*)

And a bachelor's degree is no guarantee of career success or upward mobility. Much may depend on the field of study. For instance, degrees in health care, computer science or engineering may offer far better prospects than those in the humanities.

Meanwhile, many good jobs simply don't require a bachelor's degree. About half of all employment is in so-called middle-skill occupations — jobs that require more than a high-school diploma but less than a four-year degree, according to a 2007 study by Robert Lerman, an economics professor at American University, and Harry J. Holzer, a professor at Georgetown University's Public Policy Institute. Demand for such workers will likely remain strong compared to the supply, they said. [8]

"Real pay for radiological technicians increased 23 percent between 1997 and 2005, speech/respiratory therapists saw real increases of 10 to 14 percent and real pay for electricians rose by 18 percent," they found. "These increases compare very favorably with the overall 5 percent increase for the average American worker." [9]

In June, in the depths of the current economic downturn, *The New York Times* noted that "employers are begging for qualified applicants for certain occupations, even in hard times." [10] Most of the jobs take years of experience, the newspaper noted. But some jobs in high demand, such as those in welding, don't require four years of college.

"Not everyone needs a degree, and not every job requires a four-year degree," says Tony Zeiss, president of Central Piedmont Community College, a six-campus institution in and around Charlotte, N.C., with more than 70,000 part- and full-time students. "For decades, only about 22 percent of jobs have required a baccalaureate degree or higher, and yet 75 percent of the jobs consistently require training beyond high school but below a baccalaureate. That's community college."

Still, whether community colleges, which get most of their money from recession-battered state and local governments, can keep up with demand remains an open question, especially as the Obama administration puts them at the center of his postsecondary education policy. [11]

Nearly 40 percent of 18- to 24-year-olds were enrolled in college last year, a record number that was propelled by swelling community college attendance, according to Pew Research Center data reported by *The New York Times*. [12]

"At the same time that we have tremendous increases in enrollment, states are cutting budgets like crazy," says Norma G. Kent, vice president for communications at the American

Canada Leads World in Young College Graduates

Canada has the highest percentage in the world of young adults with two- and four-year college degrees. The United States is tied for sixth place, with Australia, Spain and Sweden.

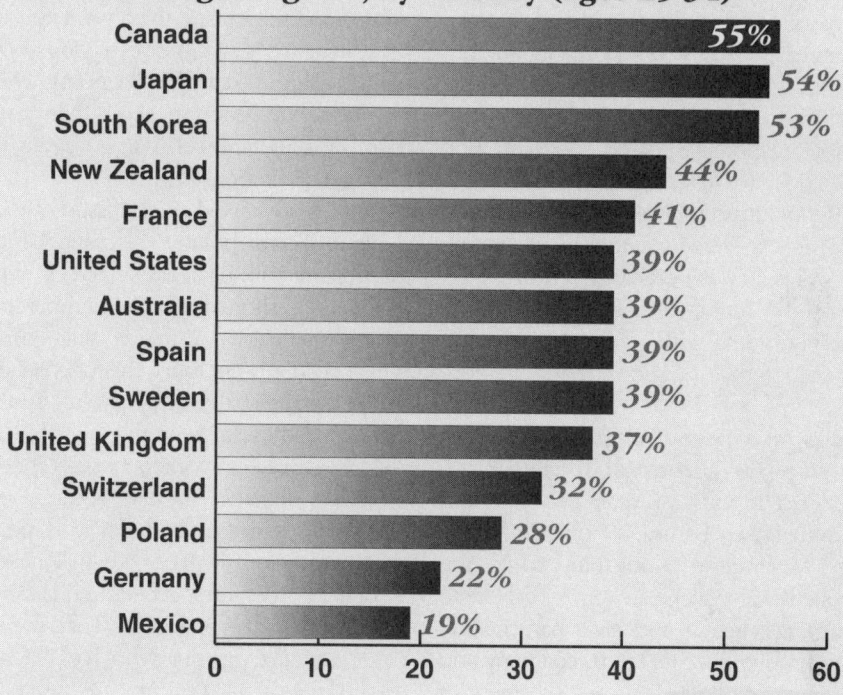

Percentage of Young Adults With Two- or Four-Year College Degrees, by Country (ages 25-34)

Country	Percentage
Canada	55%
Japan	54%
South Korea	53%
New Zealand	44%
France	41%
United States	39%
Australia	39%
Spain	39%
Sweden	39%
United Kingdom	37%
Switzerland	32%
Poland	28%
Germany	22%
Mexico	19%

Source: "A Stronger Nation Through Higher Education," Lumina Foundation for Education, February 2009

Association of Community Colleges. "Our tradition has been to do more with less, but there gets to be a stretching point beyond which you cannot go. Our credo is open access and open doors, and whether consciously or de facto, we are turning away students."

In California, community colleges lost $840 million in state funding in the combined fiscal 2008-2009 and 2009-2010 budgets, according to Scott Lay, president and CEO of the Community College League of California. Institutions face eliminating course offerings and turning away students, he says. "We believe when this all shakes out, total enrollment will drop by about

250,000 students," or 8.6 percent, by the 2010-2011 academic year, Lay says.

High-school vocational education programs have long offered the potential for non-college-bound students to learn the fundamentals of a marketable trade or craft, and then move directly into the job market or on to further training at a community college, technical school or even a four-year institution. Yet for decades "vo-ed" programs — typically wood shop or auto repair — carried a stigma, often unfairly, as a dumping ground for low achievers. In recent years, however, many vocational education programs have been transformed into progressive "career and technical education" (CTE) programs that integrate core academic training in math, reading and other essentials into job-specific courses like computer programming, medical technology, restaurant and hotel management and construction.

"Historically, there's been a real divide between the academic and vocational side," says Julian Alssid, executive director of the Workforce Strategy Center in New York, a national nonprofit group that focuses on making education and workforce development more responsive to the economy. But, he adds, "we're seeing much more melding" of academic and technical training in career and technical programs.

As policy experts and educators debate the merits of a four-year college degree versus other options, here are some of the questions being raised:

Is a four-year college degree necessary for financial security?

In a report last year, the American Youth Policy Forum, a nonprofit group in Washington, said that "while the benefits of college in terms of lifetime earnings, health and civic participation are known, success in our economy and society isn't limited to the attainment of a four-year college degree." [13]

Many well-paying fields don't require a bachelor's degree, the group noted. "All you have to do," says Betsy Brand, the report's author and the policy forum's executive director, "is look at [Labor Department] numbers to realize that yes, indeed, we need people with associate degrees and industry certificates in order to keep our economy running."

That is not to say that postsecondary education is unimportant or that a four-year degree isn't a worthy objective for many students. "I spent 40 years teaching in graduate schools and colleges," points out Herr, the Pennsylvania State emeritus professor and *Other Ways to Win* coauthor. "That's not the issue." The issue, he says, is having realistic expectations about a college degree and a clear-eyed understanding of the options.

In their book, Gray and Herr argue that "the current enthusiasm for a four-year college degree is excessive and unreasonable." Not all teenagers "are blessed with the academic talent to do college-level work or mature enough to pursue college at age 18," they write, and "many just plain do not like school." What's more, they assert, while most teens say they want to go to college to get a good-paying job, few consider "that the economy will not generate enough jobs that pay them a college-level wage" even if they get a degree. [14]

Studies are mixed on the issue of job demand. Some point to a rising need for workers with bachelor's degrees, and others to a shortfall in the number of people qualified for "middle-skill" jobs, which don't require four years of college.

For example, the Public Policy Institute of California said the supply of college-educated workers won't meet projected demand, in part because of impending retirements. In 2025, 41 percent of workers in the state will need a bachelor's degree if recent trends persist, the institute projected. That compares with 34 percent who had bachelor's degrees in 2006 and 28 percent in 1990. During that 16-year period, the institute noted, "The wages of college-educated workers grew substantially, whereas the wages of less-educated workers were relatively stagnant." [15]

But a separate study by the Workforce Alliance and two other groups that advocate for workforce-training education projected more than 2.7 million middle-skill job openings by 2016 in California. Such jobs would account for 43 percent of all openings in the state between 2006 and 2016, it said. [16] Studies in Rhode Island, Connecticut and elsewhere came to similar conclusions. [17]

Meanwhile, middle-class jobs requiring no college-level knowledge or skills are quickly vanishing, primarily because of global competition, the Lumina foundation said. And Americans who hold lower-skills jobs that do exist "are less

likely to have access to quality health care, save for retirement or assure their children access to higher education." Getting a middle-class job these days "is now mostly dependent on completing some form of postsecondary education." [18]

Still, experts in labor-force trends say the value of a degree depends in significant part on what academic field the degree is in, the quality of instruction and what job opportunities await the graduate.

"On average, people do better getting a four-year degree," says Lerman of American University, "but some [degrees] are better to begin with. . . . There is a lot of variability, and also a considerable amount of frustration" because many students aren't finding good jobs after graduation. "You're hearing that a fair number of them are going to community college later" to obtain a marketable skill, he says.

Alssid, of the Workforce Strategy Center, says that to achieve economic self-sufficiency "one really does need to have some form of postsecondary credentialing," but "the paper really has to have some value." And that, he argues, means that colleges and other training institutions should have a "much closer alignment" and a "strong partnership" with workforce and economic-development officials and industry.

Asked on the National Public Radio show "Tell Me More" whether a high-school graduate heading to a four-year college amid today's economic downturn is making an investment or a mistake, Syracuse University finance professor Boyce Watkins answered that "it's certainly an investment," but added: "The question is whether or not you get your return on that investment in actual financial capital or some sort of human capital or emotional capital or social capital.

"This blanket notion that going to college will guarantee you a better economic future is not always true," he continued. "When you have students who are going to college for economic advancement, and they choose majors that don't fit that particular objective and then take a lot of debt on in the process, then . . . you have to ask them, well, did you plan it all the way through when you ended up with an outcome that you didn't quite expect?"

Going to college is important, Watkins said, but "we have to be very intelligent about what we expect to get out of our education."

Another guest on the show, Ohio University economics professor Richard Vedder, said 45 percent of people who go to four-year colleges don't get a bachelor's degree within six years. Another group of people, he said, graduate but have trouble finding work and wind up taking jobs for which a college education isn't required. [19]

At the U.S. Chamber of Commerce, Arthur Rothkopf, a senior vice president in charge of the business group's Education and Workforce Initiative, says the Chamber "comes down very strongly" in favor of those "for whom a four-year degree is important and useful and is part of what they want to do with their lives," professionally or otherwise. But, he adds, "there needs to be far more emphasis on middle-skill jobs," whose requirements, he says, include both a rigorous high-school education and some form of postsecondary schooling such as a two-year degree or certificate.

"A lot of these middle-skill jobs are not going to get outsourced," whether the jobs entail working in factories, being welders, physician's assistants, technicians at nuclear power plants, or working for Intel, Cisco or Microsoft, Rothkopf says. "There are lots of jobs that don't require a four-year degree."

Are high-school career and technical-education programs adequately preparing students for upward mobility?

At Sussex Technical High School in Georgetown, Del., mathematics and English are incorporated into lessons in

---

Two-Year Colleges Cost the Least

Publicly supported community colleges have the lowest average tuition rates and usually no room and board fees, while private not-for-profit four-year colleges have the highest average tuition and room and board fees.

Type	Average Tuition and Fees, 2009-10	Average Room and Board, 2009-10	Average Total Charges 2009-10
Public two-year	$2,544	N/A	N/A
Public four-year in-state	$7,020	$8,193	$15,213
Public four-year out-of-state	$18,548	$8,193	$26,741
Private not-for-profit four-year	$26,273	$9,363	$35,636
Private, for-profit*	$14,174	N/A	N/A

* Subsidiaries of larger parent companies, such as DeVry or the Apollo Group, that offer degree and non-degree programs and compete with community colleges to teach students specific workforce skills.

Sources: "Tuition and Fee and Room and Board Charges, 2009-10," The College Board, Annual Survey of Colleges, 2009, www.trends-collegeboard.com/college_ pricing/pdf/2009_Trends_College_Pricing.pdf; Francesca Levy, "For-Profit Colleges Improve Their Financial Grades," BusinessWeek, August 12, 2008, www.business week.com/bschools/content/aug2008/bs20080812_253727.htm?chan=bschools_ bschool+index+page_top+stories

---

auto-body repair, cosmetology and computers, an approach that Patrick Savini, superintendent of the Sussex Technical School District, calls "techademics."

Technical instructors must know math and grammar, and academic teachers must be able to demonstrate how algebra and English apply to reading repair manuals and programming computers. "It's a dual expectation," Savini says. "It's the technical teacher understanding state standards [for] teaching math, science" and other core subjects, "and it's the academic teachers checking their ego at the door."

Sussex Technical has won recognition from the U.S. Department of Education and others, and not just for its integrated classroom approach. Ninth-graders get to explore six career majors

for about a month each before choosing one for the rest of the year — and perhaps their entire time at the school. Classes last 90 minutes, allowing for deeper engagement with lessons and minimizing discipline problems. And Sussex offers extracurricular activities common at traditional high schools: athletic teams, a band program and a prom.

"It's about options," says Savini. "If you do career tech right, you prepare [students] for immediate employment but also take their aspirations and have them reach beyond."

Such an approach defies the negative images that have long dogged high-school career-training programs, which over the decades have been accused of "tracking" minorities and others into academic dead-ends.

College Graduates Earn the Most

Workers with bachelor's degrees earned an average of $57,181 in 2007 — or 63 percent more than those with some college or an associate's degree and 83 percent more than those with only a high-school diploma.

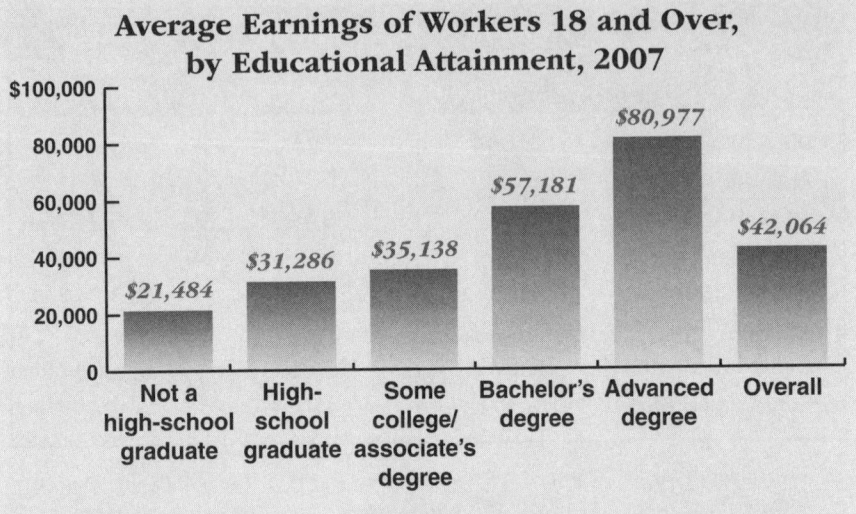

Average Earnings of Workers 18 and Over, by Educational Attainment, 2007

- Not a high-school graduate: $21,484
- High-school graduate: $31,286
- Some college/associate's degree: $35,138
- Bachelor's degree: $57,181
- Advanced degree: $80,977
- Overall: $42,064

Source: U.S. Census Bureau, www.census.gov/population/socdemo/education/cps 2008/tabA-3.xls, Table A-3.

"The public and many policy makers tend to have a negative and/or outdated image of CTE, believing that CTE lacks academic rigor, leads to antiquated, undesirable or low-paying jobs, limits access to college and serves only low-performing students," Brand noted in the American Youth Policy Forum report. [20] "But this is not today's reality," she added. CTE can increase student engagement, improve attendance and graduation, enhance academic learning and allow students to earn college credit while in high school, among other things, Brand wrote.

Still, CTE programs remain in flux. "High-quality CTE programs are not accessible to every student that wants to pursue such studies, and there are still outdated CTE programs that lack academic rigor and relevance to the labor market," Brand wrote.

Lerman of American University questions whether the types of course requirements being pushed for high-school diplomas "crowd out types of

learning that could be more directly linked to careers." Lerman, who supports "work-based" learning or "apprentice-type" activities," says that while "many [CTE] programs are pretty good," he would like to see more that link "much more directly" to careers and allow "people a chance to try things out. There's a lot about careers that you can only learn by doing," he says.

Measuring the success of CTE programs can be difficult. The Carl D. Perkins Career and Technical Education Act of 2006, or "Perkins IV" — the main federal law governing CTE programs — mandates that core academic subjects be integrated into career and technical programs and that schools assess results.

But a U.S. Government Accountability Office report this year said states say their biggest challenge is gathering data on students' attainment of technical skills and student placement in jobs or further education after completion of CTE programs. [21]

"There's a real debate about what constitutes an accurate assessment of student performance," says Richard Walter, a Penn State education professor who directs the university's Workforce Education and Development Program. "Are we talking industry credential? Test assessment?"

A related problem, he and others say, is that CTE students seeking to gain industry certification sometimes have to pay for their own qualification tests, which may discourage low-income students from receiving credentials for skilled jobs.

Still, CTE programs are making strides. "States have been working to increase the rigor and effectiveness" of CTE education, noted a September report by the Education Commission of the States that highlights noteworthy state policy efforts at accountability, dropout prevention, preparation for high-demand occupations and other categories. [22]

In an interview, Brand says high-performing CTE programs work closely with employers and have employer advisory boards that guide administrators on economic and employment trends and industry needs. Such programs "really see themselves as contributing to the economic-development and labor-market needs of the community or the state or region," she said. At the same time, she said, many high schools link their CTE programs with local community colleges, enabling high-school students to become certified for jobs in health care, computer programming and other fields.

"This is what career and tech education should look like," Brand says. "If it's not connected to business and industry and postsecondary education, if it doesn't lead to some of these skill certificates, it shouldn't be here." Still, while many CTE programs are putting all the pieces together, some are behind. "It's hard to get educators to change rapidly."

James Kemple, executive director of the Research Alliance for New York City Schools at New York University, led a study of one kind of CTE program —

Ph.D. Mechanic Celebrates Challenge of Manual Labor

Matthew B. Crawford straddles two worlds: He has a Ph.D. in political philosophy from the University of Chicago and is a fellow at the Institute for Advanced Studies in Culture at the University of Virginia. He also operates a motorcycle repair shop in Richmond and is author of the best-selling 2009 book *Shop Class as Soulcraft: An Inquiry into the Value of Work*, in which he argues that too often students are forced into a college track when manual trades offer a viable and rewarding alternative. Here are excerpts from the book:

"Today, in our schools, the manual trades are given little honor. The egalitarian worry that has always attended tracking students into 'college prep' and 'vocational ed' is overlaid with another: the fear that acquiring a specific skill set means that one's life is determined. In college, by contrast, many students don't learn anything of particular application; college is the ticket to an open future."

"The trades are then a natural home for anyone who would live by his own powers, free not only of deadening abstraction but also of the insidious hopes and rising insecurities that seem to be endemic in our current economic life."

Matthew B. Crawford, motorcycle mechanic and philosopher.

www.matthewbcrawford.com/Robert Adamo

"Piston slap may indeed sound like loose tappets, so to be a good mechanic you have to be constantly attentive to the possibility that you may be mistaken. This is an ethical virtue."

"I landed the job at the think tank because I had a prestigious education in the liberal arts, yet the job itself felt illiberal: coming up with the best arguments money could buy. This wasn't work befitting a free man, and the tie I wore started to feel like the mark of the slave."

"At issue in the contrast between office work and the manual trades is the idea of individual responsibility, tied to the presence or absence of objective standards."

"career academies" — which are schools within high schools that combine rigorous academics and training in such fields as travel and tourism, video technology, health care and finance. The academies establish close ties with local employers, raising students' familiarity with career options and providing opportunities for on-the-job experience.

Kemple says his study found that such programs produced a "substantial impact" on the long-term earnings and employment of participating students without decreasing the likelihood that the students would go on to college. [23]

Can community colleges meet rising demand for their programs?

At North Carolina's Central Piedmont Community College, Zeiss says he's never had to turn away students in the 42 years he's been in the higher education field — until last year.

"We turned away 5,000 students [who applied for at least one class] because we didn't have the money," he says. "We're up 35 percent in college-credit enrollment in the past two and half years, and we're down about 9 percent in budgets. You can increase your class sizes and number of students you counsel [only] so much, and we're bending at the limit. I've been spending my time raising private money so we can hire part-time teachers."

Central Piedmont's instructors each have 28 students per class on average this year, instead of the traditional 20, Zeiss says, and the counselor-to-student ratio is one-to-1,900. Meanwhile, applications for financial aid have doubled over the past year.

"We can't keep this up," Zeiss says. "Everybody loves us, and they're starting to put grants out there — Obama now and Bush before him. But we've got to shore up the revenue base of these colleges."

It's a message echoing throughout the nation's community college system, which educates nearly 12 million students, or 44 percent of the nation's undergraduates. Public community colleges depend on state and local revenues for about 60 percent of their funding — a source hit hard by the economic crisis.

What's more, community colleges typically lag four-year institutions in government support. "The country spends about three times more to educate students at four-year universities than to educate community college students," *USA Today* stated last year, citing Education Department data. [24]

In a survey this year, state directors of community college systems predicted that despite surging enrollment, state operating budgets for community colleges would decline an average of 1 percent while tuition is expected to rise at twice the inflation rate. Among 43 responding states, nine predicted cuts next year in their state student aid programs, and 21 forecast no increase. Many respondents expressed concern about what will happen as federal stimulus money — used by states to support education budgets — runs out. [25]

As states slash education budgets, the economic downturn has propelled huge numbers of unemployed adults into community colleges. "We've got a lot of adult learners who are out of a job or in a field that's going extinct, and they're coming back to community college for a lifeline," says Kent of the American Association of Community Colleges.

While Obama's proposed $12 billion community college plan would give the institutions a major boost, the money may not go as far as some would hope. It would be spread over a decade among 1,200 institutions, and $9 billion would be in the form of competitive grants requiring community colleges to improve student educational and employment outcomes.

Meeting such benchmarks could be a challenge for community colleges.

Typically, they not only grant two-year degrees but also do workforce training in areas such as health and computer science, provide English-as-a-second-language classes for non-native students, prepare some students for transfer to four-year schools and perhaps offer on-site training tailored to the specific needs of employers. Community colleges also often work with small businesses to provide training for entrepreneurs.

"Community colleges mean many different things," says Alssid of the Workforce Strategy Center. "A big part of the challenge for community colleges is that almost all of them are being called upon to fulfill this multiplicity of missions."

What's more, community colleges must provide remedial classes to a significant portion of incoming students — a problem that four-year institutions also face but is most pronounced at community colleges.

A study on college readiness by Strong American Schools, a project of Rockefeller Philanthropy Advisors, concluded that well over a third of all college students need remedial coursework to acquire basic academic skills and that 43 percent of students at public two-year institutions have enrolled in a remedial course.

"In many ways, the problem is the American high school," the study concluded. It noted that nearly 80 percent of students needing remedial work had a high-school grade-point average of 3.0 or higher, suggesting that many teens finish high school ill-prepared for college-level study. [26]

"Community colleges have huge amounts of energy siphoned away by providing remediation to students who aren't yet ready to do college-level work," says Alssid. "The country is going to have to figure out how to fix that problem."

Meanwhile, enrollment continues to grow at community colleges, fueled by people looking to acquire marketable skills. And many of those people are ones who already have four-year degrees. Gray, the Pennsylvania State

University emeritus professor, sees something of an irony in the trend.

"Community college enrollment is way up," he says, while most "noncompetitive" four-year colleges — those with easy admission standards — "are looking for students."

The noncompetitive colleges "attribute this to the fact that there's less money for financial aid, and therefore students are seeking less-expensive alternatives," Gray says, but "I'm not convinced of that. I suspect people are starting to sense that maybe they should go" to a community college to gain an industry credential "and get a four-year degree later." ∎

BACKGROUND

Rise of Community Colleges

From the Republic's earliest days, leaders stressed that education is important for the well-being of the nation and its citizens. "Knowledge, being necessary to good government and the happiness of mankind, schools and the means of education shall forever be encouraged," the Continental Congress wrote in the Northwest Ordinance in 1787. [27]

Yet questions arose in the new nation over how widespread higher education should be. In 1862 Congress passed the Morrill Act, also known as the Land Grant Act, which called for public land to be donated for colleges emphasizing agricultural and mechanical-arts training. The law was the cornerstone for a system of state colleges and universities that made higher education available to millions of students. [28] Still, not all Americans benefited. A second Morrill Act, in 1890, sought to expand college opportunities for African-Americans.

As the economy evolved from rural

Continued on p. 992

Chronology

1860s-1930s

As U.S. economy industrializes, country focuses more on higher education and vocational training for potential workforce.

1862
Congress passes Morrill Act, known as the Land Grant Act, which calls for public land to be donated for colleges that emphasize agricultural and mechanical-arts training.

1890
Second Morrill Act seeks to expand college opportunities for African-Americans.

1901
Nation's first public community college, Joliet (Illinois) Junior College, opens with six students.

1917
Congress passes landmark Smith-Hughes Act, which provides money to states for high-school vocational education.

1920
Only 3 percent of Americans 25 and older hold bachelor's degrees.

1940s-1970s

World War II baby boom and GI Bill trigger huge wave of college enrollment.

1944
GI Bill of Rights provides financial help for World War II veterans seeking to attend college.

1947
Truman Commission on Higher Education calls for a network of public community colleges. . . . College enrollment stands at 2.3 million.

1952
Veterans Readjustment Assistance Act of 1952 — the Korean War GI Bill — is passed, eventually helping 2.4 million vets attend college or receive on-the-job or other training.

1965
Congress passes Higher Education Act to provide financial aid to students pursuing higher education; college enrollment climbs to 5.6 million.

1975
Community colleges number more than 1,200; college enrollment nationwide grows to 10.9 million.

1980s-1990s

Vocational-education enrollment begins to decline sharply as more and more students pursue four-year college degrees.

1983
In "A Nation at Risk," U.S. Education Department warns of a "rising tide of mediocrity" in education and says the United States is falling behind in global economic competition.

1984
Congress passes Carl D. Perkins Vocational Education Act to help improve labor-force skills and provide broader job training for adults, disabled people and others.

1990
Tech-Prep program helps students begin learning a technical field in high school, then a certificate or two-year degree in that field at a community college. . . . Twenty percent of Americans 25 and older have at least a bachelor's degree, up from 7.7 percent in 1960 and 16.2 percent in 1980.

1991
College enrollment continues to climb; 63 percent of high-school graduates go directly to college, compared with 46 percent in 1973.

2000-Present

President Obama calls for higher graduation rates and more money for community colleges.

2000
Republican-dominated Congress does not renew School to Work Opportunities Act, passed during the Bill Clinton administration, which allows some students to earn academic credit for work experience.

2002
President George W. Bush signs No Child Left Behind Act, which holds schools accountable for student achievement.

2006
Perkins Act amendments mandate closer integration of skills training and core academic subjects in high-school vocational courses; the law replaces the term "vocational education" with "career and technical education," or "CTE." . . . Bush seeks to eliminate funding for vocational education, but funding is retained after protests.

2009
President Obama proposes to spend $12 billion over the next decade to strengthen the community college system and calls on every American to commit to at least a year of higher education or career training. . . . Obama eases Pell Grant restrictions for unemployed adults. . . . Unemployment rate exceeds 10 percent, sending many laid-off adults to community colleges in search of new skills.

Community Colleges Welcome Night Owls

But please take the bus, busy schools ask students.

Community colleges are getting so many applicants that sometimes they can't admit everybody, as they once did. Or they are turning to unorthodox approaches.

When a flood of new students descended on Bunker Hill Community College in Boston, the school inaugurated what has been dubbed the "Burning the Midnight Oil" schedule. It offers several popular introductory courses from 11:45 p.m. until 2:30 a.m. And the school pushed the first class of the day up to 7 a.m. Makeshift parking lots were created to accommodate the overload.

At Holyoke Community College, also in Massachusetts, parking was so strained by rising enrollment that the school sent postcards to all 7,500 students urging them to take public transportation.

Clackamas Community College in Oregon City, Ore., has been offering a late-night welding course since last spring.

Northern Virginia Community College (NVCC) added 20 popular lower-level classes, such as English, biology, psychology and accounting, this semester that begin before 7 a.m.; other classes run late into the evening.

"Over the last two years, our annual student enrollment has jumped over 8,000 students while our physical capacity has grown only modestly," says NVCC President Robert G. Templin, Jr. "To respond to the dramatic increase in student demand, we've stretched our class schedule by offering classes as early as 6 a.m., and pushed night classes past 10 p.m. Nearly everything we've offered has been snapped up regardless of the time or format."

But some schools control the overflow by closing their doors when they fill up. The six community colleges that are part of the City University of New York (CUNY) traditionally have accepted applications up to a week before classes start — enough time for students to apply for financial aid and receive the required immunizations. This fall, however, all but one of the campuses had to stop accepting applications a month before the semester began because it didn't have enough teachers and other resources to support the flood of new students.

"Enrollment has been growing steadily, but this was a tidal wave for us this fall," said Gail O. Mellow, president of LaGuardia Community College, in Long Island City. The school's student body has risen by almost 50 percent over the past decade. [1]

Virtually every state has had to deal with rising enrollments at public community colleges, according to the American Association of Community Colleges. Some in California have reported increases of 35 percent just since 2008. [2]

At Sinclair Community College in economically suffering Dayton, Ohio, enrollment has jumped 25 percent over the past year alone as laid-off General Motors employees and other auto industry workers seek new skills in the evolving labor market. Recent high-school graduates are also finding two-year institutions more preferable to pricier four-year colleges, as many parents struggle to make ends meet. School officials say they are trying to keep Sinclair affordable as many Dayton residents become financially challenged.

Sinclair currently offers high-school students in the area who take technical courses and maintain a C-plus average in their

Continued from p. 990

and agricultural to urban and industrial, education evolved, too. In 1901, Joliet Junior College, in Illinois, became the nation's first public community college, formed as an experimental program for high-school graduates.

College enrollment was still a rarity among young people in the early 20th century — Joliet Junior College started with just six students — and educational and political leaders debated how best to prepare for what they saw as increasingly competitive global economy.

"[T]he great battles of the world in the future are to be commercial rather than military," the educational historian Ellwood P. Cubberley wrote in 1909. He added: "Whether we like it or not, we are beginning to see that we are pitted against the world in a gigantic

battle of brains and skill, with the markets of the world, work for our people and internal peace and contentment as the prizes at stake." [29]

A key way to win those prizes, it was widely viewed, was to promote job-specific vocational education.

Educational theorist Charles Prosser, a steelworker's son, was critical of a single-minded focus on academics and scholarship. He argued that high schools should offer separate skills training to meet the interests, capabilities and job prospects of a significant portion of students. Traditionalists such as the philosopher and educational reformer John Dewey vehemently disagreed. In the end, Prosser's theories prevailed.

"World economic competition was viewed as the best strategy for national economic growth," Gray, the co-

author of *Other Ways to Win*, wrote in a 1996 journal article, and "the schools were accused of doing little to help the cause, particularly with regard to the education of children from working-class families who were beginning to go to high school in large numbers." The solution, he added, was to develop a separate curriculum in high schools tailored to training students for jobs in commerce, industry, agriculture and home economics. [30]

In 1914, a commission appointed by President Woodrow Wilson cited census data showing that more than 12 million Americans worked in agriculture and 14 million in manufacturing, mechanical and allied pursuits. But the commission concluded that probably fewer than 1 percent were adequately prepared for their jobs. [31]

junior and senior years an automatic $3,000 scholarship, enough to cover tuition for three semesters. Courses range from radiology to traditional information technology disciplines.

The community college also has helped 53 area high schools upgrade their technical courses and make it easier for students to transition to college. It recently made a $4 million grant to a local school district to create a "career technology" high school that offers advanced science courses and will serve as a feeder school for the college.

Such initiatives support President Obama's American Graduation Initiative — a 10-year, $12 billion plan to invest in community colleges and add 5 million new graduates by 2020. Obama has embraced the nation's community colleges, calling them "vital bulwarks" against the decline of the American middle class and, hence, the nation's competitiveness.

"Jobs requiring at least an associate degree are projected to grow twice as fast as jobs requiring no college experience," he said during a speech about vanishing jobs this July in Warren, Mich., among the recession's hardest-hit areas. "We will not fill those jobs — or even keep those jobs here in America — with-

The first session of Kathleen O'Neill's evening class in psychology draws a crowd at Bunker Hill Community College in Boston.

AP Photo/Josh Reynolds

out the training offered by community colleges." [3]

Meanwhile, some educators worry that community colleges may not have enough resources to meet the growing current demand.

"The community college is a second-chance institution for the country," said Patrick M. Callan, president of the National Center for Public Policy and Higher Education. "Most people would agree that this is not a good time in terms of the economic competitiveness of the country to be turning people away." [4]

— Darrell Dela Rosa

[1] Lisa W. Foderaro, "Two-Year Colleges, Swamped, No Longer Welcome All," *The New York Times*, Nov. 12, 2009, www.nytimes.com/2009/11/12/education/12community.html.

[2] Abby Goodnough, "New Meaning for Night Class at 2-Year Colleges," *The New York Times*, Oct. 28, 2009, www.nytimes.com/2009/10/28/education/28community.html.

[3] "Remarks by the President on the American Graduation Initiative," Office of the Press Secretary, The White House, July 14, 2009, www.whitehouse.gov/the_press_office/Remarks-by-the-President-on-the-American-Graduation-Initiative-in-Warren-MI.

[4] Foderaro, *op. cit.*

Three years later, Congress passed the landmark Smith-Hughes Act, which became known as the Magna Carta of vocational education. [32] Under Smith-Hughes, federal money was distributed to the states for vocational education in high schools, but unlike today's integrated approach for blending academics and skills training, the 1917 act drew a clear distinction. The law stipulated that vocational-education money could not be used to pay salaries of academic teachers, and it limited the amount of academic instruction a vocational student could receive. [33]

"By explicitly defining vocational education as preparation for occupations that did not require a bachelor's or advanced degree, the Smith-Hughes Act affirmed that vocational education

was not intended to prepare high-school students for college," wrote David Stern, an education professor at the University of California-Berkeley.

Still, college was less of an issue back then than it is today. As Stern noted, in 1920 a mere 3 percent of Americans age 25 and older held bachelor's degrees. [34]

Over the decades, vocational education served a variety of purposes — to strengthen national defense in the 1920s, ease unemployment in the 1930s, address wartime industrial needs in the 1940s and smooth the transition to peacetime after World War II. [35] But vocational education sometimes faced accusations that it provided an inferior education and was used to channel students into economic blind alleys.

James Fraser, former dean of the School of Education at Northeastern University in Boston, told *The Christian Science Monitor* that in the 1940s and '50s some groups began to see vocational education as problematic. "It was popular in working-class white communities," Fraser said, "but among immigrants and in communities of color it was mistrusted. They feared that [vocational education] was being used to steer their kids into second-class citizenship." [36]

College Degree Beckons

Meanwhile, a college degree beckoned more and more young people. Policy changes spurred the trend. The 1944 GI Bill of Rights provided financial help for World War II veterans seeking to attend college. After the war, a report by the President's Commission on Higher Education, known as the Truman Commission Report, called for a network of public community colleges that would charge little if anything in tuition, offer a comprehensive program emphasizing civic responsibility and serve their local areas. [37] The report also called for a doubling of college attendance by 1960. [38]

"[W]e shall aim at making higher education equally available to all young people . . . to the extent that their capacity warrants a further social investment in their training," the commission wrote. [39]

Later, Congress passed various financial-aid bills, notably the Higher Education Act of 1965.

Meanwhile, demographic, economic and geopolitical developments were fueling college enrollment. The postwar baby boom created a huge bubble of college-age young adults. The Cold War space race sparked enrollment in university science and technology programs. And in the 1960s and early '70s, the Vietnam War led millions of young men to seek college deferments from the military draft.

College enrollment exploded from about 2.3 million students in 1947 to 10.9 million in 1975, according to the U.S. Census Bureau. [40] It kept climbing as recession and global competition for manufactured goods fueled a perception in the 1980s that blue-collar work was no longer secure and a college education — preferably a four-year degree — was a ticket to economic success.

By 1990, 20 percent of the American population age 25 and older had at least a bachelor's degree, up from 7.7 percent in 1960 and 16.2 percent in 1980. By 2000, the figure stood at more than 24 percent. [41]

As four-year-college enrollments rose, community colleges also were booming. The number of institutions and their branch campuses exploded

from roughly 600 in 1955 to more than 1,200 in 1975 and about 1,600 (including multiple campuses) by the end of the 1990s. [42]

During this period, enrollment in high-school vocational programs fell sharply, beginning in the early 1980s, Gray wrote. Spurring the decline was not only a worry that secure, well-paid industry jobs were disappearing but also the notion that "in the eyes of the public the only thing that seemed to be at all certain was the increasingly publicized idea that college graduates made more money than high-school graduates," he wrote. [43]

"Faced with uncertainty about economic opportunities in the future and misinformation about career opportunities for future college graduates, and aided by an oversupply of college seats and thus open admissions at many colleges, students . . . [rejected] traditional vocational education offerings and [enrolled] in college preparatory programs. The nation concluded that there is only 'one way to win' . . . — to get a four-year baccalaureate degree." [44]

As a result, Gray argued, many "academically average" students who in the past would have taken vocational-education courses were instead on the college track and finished high school "prepared neither for college nor work."

In 1973, 46 percent of high-school graduates went directly on to college, Gray noted, citing Education Department data. By 1991, the proportion had risen to 63 percent. And the proportion continues to grow. [45]

"A new vocationalism" had emerged, Gray wrote, "manifested in the form of growing percentages of academically average students enrolling in traditional college preparatory programs." Motivating their enrollment, he wrote, was not "some newly found thirst for knowledge" but rather "vocational reasons."

Meanwhile, as economic and social conditions changed in the 1980s and '90s, American education came under severe scrutiny. In 1983, the Education

Department's "A Nation at Risk" report warned of a "rising tide of mediocrity" in schools and colleges and said the United States was falling behind in global economic competition. The report spurred deep soul-searching among reformers and government officials about how to improve the educational system — introspection that continues today as high-school and college dropout rates soar, and even elite universities have high numbers of students who need remedial coursework. [46]

Education Reforms

In the wake of the report, policy officials began to look for ways to reform the educational system, and some of those efforts centered on vocational education. In 1984 Congress passed the Carl D. Perkins Vocational Education Act with a goal of improving the nation's labor-force skills and providing broader job-training opportunities for adults, disabled people and so-called at-risk populations. Since then, the Perkins Act has gone through a series of reauthorizations and reforms aimed at strengthening the link between academic and vocational training.

In 1990, for example, more emphasis was placed on developing career prospects for all students, rather than just those who were not college-bound. Under a program called Tech-Prep, students could begin learning a technical field in high school and then earn a certificate or two-year degree in that field at a community college.

In a 2006 revision of the Perkins law, the term "career and technical education," or CTE, was officially adopted in place of "vocational education," and schools were required to more closely integrate core academic coursework into job-skills training.

At the same time, Washington was placing more and more emphasis on the ability of schools to meet academic benchmarks. That approach became enshrined in 2002 in the George W. Bush administration's No Child Left Behind Act, which holds schools accepting federal funds accountable for student achievement. [47]

By then, however, vocational education was under fire. In 2000 the Republican-dominated Congress did not renew the School to Work Opportunities Act, a Clinton-era law that in some cases allowed students to earn academic credit for job internships or other work experience. Conservatives argued that School to Work shifted the educational focus away from core academics. Others said it sought to replicate the German apprenticeship model and steered students too early onto a career path.

Then, in 2006, Bush sought to completely eliminate federal funding for vocational education, arguing that it had "produced little or no evidence of improved outcomes for students despite decades of federal investment."

"Bush wasn't impressed with CTE," says Walter of Pennsylvania State University. "He tried to zero out Perkins — tried to remove every cent, [in part because] that [was] the largest chunk of money that would have been available to him to work on high-school reforms" under No Child Left Behind.

Bush didn't succeed. Advocates, including community colleges, argued that vocational education enhanced student achievement and increased postsecondary enrollment. Still, while vocational funding survived, the federal outlay devoted to career and technical education has declined in recent years. Obama proposed keeping it flat at $1.3 billion in fiscal 2010, but CTE and community college advocates want it raised to at least $1.4 billion. [48]

At the same time, Obama has proposed expanding the overall 2010 education budget by $1.3 billion, including increasing spending on postsecondary education by 6 percent — or $200 million — to $3.6 billion. His budget would

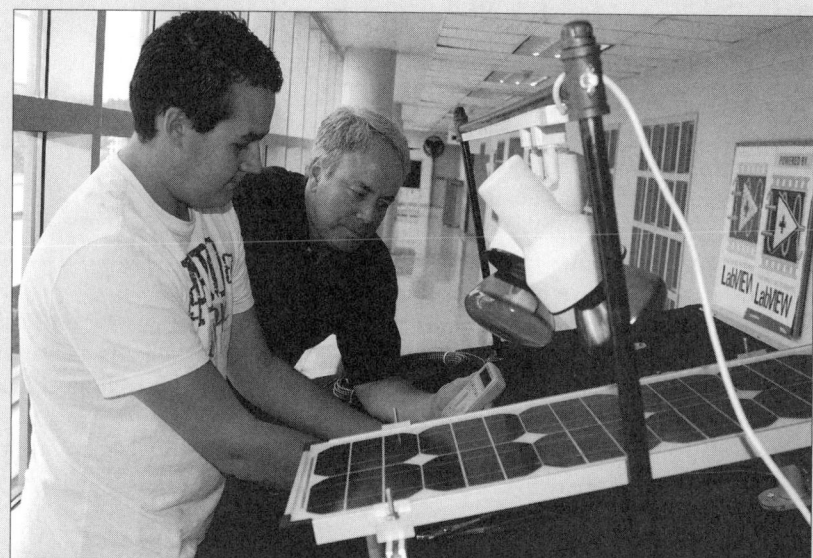

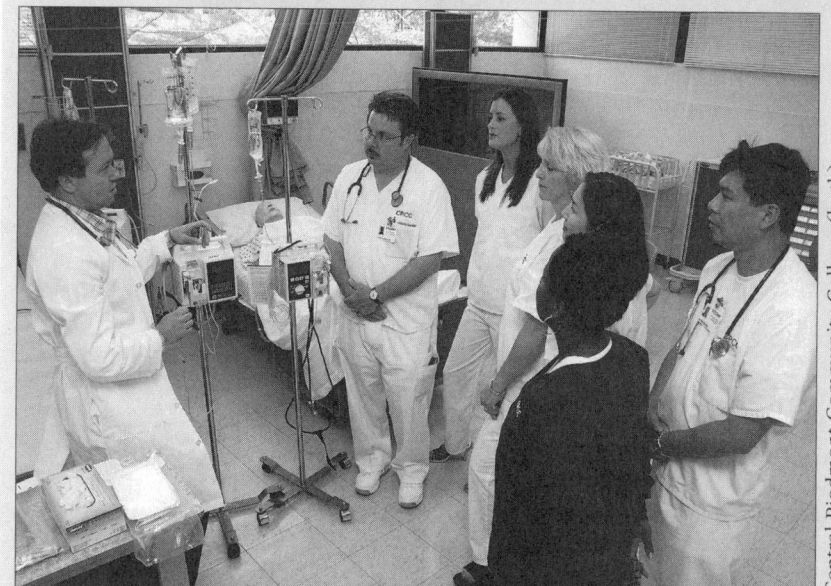

Central Piedmont Community College (both)

Training for the Workforce

A student (top left) in the sustainability technology program at Central Piedmont Community College in Charlotte, N.C., reviews a rooftop photovoltaic installation with his instructor. Two-year degrees offered at the school prepare students to work in the alternative energy, green construction and sustainable manufacturing fields. Nursing students (bottom) at the school can earn a two-year associate's degree and take the national test for licensing as a registered nurse.

expand student financial aid, elevate the role of community colleges and support innovative state efforts to help low-income students complete their college education. [49]

Even so, students face skyrocketing college costs at a time when family incomes remain stagnant and state education budgets are getting pounded. In a *Newsweek* article in October, Sen. Lamar

Alexander, R-Tenn., former education secretary in the George H. W. Bush administration, said state higher-education funding rose 17.6 percent from 2000 to 2006 but that average tuition at public four-year institutions shot up 63 percent, with state support for education hit hardest by "runaway" Medicaid costs. [50]

A big worry for many state officials is the looming termination of federal stimulus spending. Alexander cited a comment made by Tennessee Gov. Phil Bredesen in March, that "when this money ends 21 months from now, our campuses will suddenly need to begin operating with about $180 million less in state funding than they had this year."

Among the possible ways to cut college costs, Alexander advocates having students finish a bachelor's degree in three years. Schools could make year-round use of academic facilities, and students could reduce their college expenses, he argued.

But speeding up graduation is no small feat. A study this year by the American Enterprise Institute, a conservative Washington think tank, found that on average, four-year colleges graduate fewer than 60 percent of their freshmen within six years." [51] Another study, published in the new book *Crossing the Finish Line*, found that only 65 percent of students at highly selective flagship public universities graduated in four years. At several less selective state systems, only about 26 percent finished in four years. [52]

Coauthor William G. Bowen, president emeritus of both the Andrew W. Mellon Foundation and Princeton University, told the online publication *Inside Higher Ed* of an atmosphere at many schools that suggests it is normal to take six years to graduate.

"At a very highly regarded flagship university," Bowen said, "when you talk there to students about graduation rates, you can be told, as we were told by one person, 'graduating in four years is like leaving the party at 10 o'clock.' " [53] ■

CURRENT SITUATION

Obama's Initiative

In a speech to a joint congressional session in February, Obama declared that "a good education is no longer just a pathway to opportunity — it is a prerequisite." But he noted that while three-quarters of the fastest-growing occupations require education beyond high school, just over half of Americans have that much schooling.

What's more, Obama said, the United States has "one of the highest high-school dropout rates of any industrialized nation," and "half of the students who begin college never finish," which he called "a prescription for economic decline."

The centerpiece of Obama's effort to boost postsecondary education and college completion is the American Graduation Initiative, which he announced at Macomb Community College in Warren, Mich., the state's largest grantor of associate degrees. The aim of the record $12-billion, 10-year plan, Obama said, is to help an additional 5 million Americans earn degrees and certificates in the next decade. The money would be used to improve community college programs, buildings and classrooms and academic courses. [54]

"Community colleges are an undervalued asset in our country," Obama said. "Not only is that not right, it's not smart."

The administration's plan for community colleges makes up part of a much broader bill, called the Student Aid and Fiscal Responsibility Act, introduced in July in the House Education and Labor Committee and passed in the House in September. [55] The House bill would invest $10 billion in community colleges, $7 billion of it through competitive grants, according

to the committee. The measure includes $40 billion to incrementally raise the maximum annual Pell Grant scholarship over the next decade, $3 billion to help improve college access and completion and $2.55 billion for historically black colleges and other institutions that serve minorities.

Notably, the bill would replace guaranteed student loans administered by private lenders with direct government loans, a controversial idea that the administration says would save billions of dollars but that opponents argue would lead to inefficiencies. [56]

Separately, the $787 billion economic-stimulus bill passed this year expanded the Pell Grant student-aid program and raised the maximum annual award by $500 in the first year — to $5,350 — and more in the second.

And in May the administration made it easier for some unemployed adults to receive Pell Grants, a move advocates hail as an important step in linking jobs and education. Pell Grants cover tuition at most community colleges.

"The Pell move is pivotal because it shows that the president understands that postsecondary education is the workforce development system and a key piece of the workforce adjustment system in response to trade and technology change," wrote Anthony Carnevale, director of the Georgetown University Center on Education and the Workforce. Obama's remarks on education and jobs and his action on Pell Grants "is clearly more than another love note to community colleges, gushing over how they do so much with so little, or another boutique program funded with departmental transfers," he added. [57]

Not that Pell Grants are immune to criticism. Florida's *St. Petersburg Times* reported in October that more than $2.3 million in Pell Grants funded by the economic stimulus had gone to Tampa-area cosmetology and massage schools "to pay tuition for the hairdressers, masseuses and nail technicians

Continued on p. 998

At Issue:

Should college-preparatory and career-training programs get equal priority?

SEN. RODERICK D. WRIGHT (D-LOS ANGELES)
CALIFORNIA STATE SENATE

WRITTEN FOR *CQ RESEARCHER*, NOVEMBER 2009

*r*ecently, I attended a Senate committee hearing where someone quoted from a new report that stated 35 percent of all jobs would require a four-year college degree by 2020. The members of the committee responded by drafting legislation to increase college-preparatory requirements in California schools.

I looked at that same report, from The Workforce Alliance, and thought: What about the other 65 percent that won't require a bachelor's degree?

College was never intended for everyone. It used to be assumed that some kids would become plumbers and some would become doctors. Some would become police officers and some would become accountants.

But today's high-school students are told if they don't go to college they are failures who will never amount to anything. So kids with an aptitude for auto mechanics instead try to become lawyers or financial managers and end up with no job and no marketable skills.

This quest to send everyone to college has had disastrous consequences: High-school dropout rates are at all-time highs. The percentage of kids entering and not finishing college is at an all-time high. The percentage of kids with four-year degrees enrolled at vocational programs at community colleges, or dubious private postsecondary institutions, is at an all-time high. The number of high-school graduates with no job skills is at an all-time high. Here in California, the number of prison inmates is at an all-time high.

If we are going to rebuild our economy, we will need skilled workers more than ever. It is estimated that openings for middle-skill jobs such as electrical linemen, respiratory therapists and computer technicians will surge by 20 percent in the next decade.

As baby boomers retire, this lack of trained workers could stall our nation's economic recovery. Meanwhile, kids are being pushed into college, becoming disillusioned and dropping out of both high school and college. So society loses all the way around.

Clearly, we need to maintain our development of professional careers for kids with that aptitude. There will always be a need for engineers and doctors. I believe our educational system can and must prepare for both career and college tracks. One without the other is a complete failure.

ARUN RAMANATHAN
EXECUTIVE DIRECTOR
THE EDUCATION TRUST-WEST

WRITTEN FOR *CQ RESEARCHER*, NOVEMBER 2009

*w*e are long past the time when young people could graduate from high school and go directly into careers that guaranteed lifetime employment and a living wage. Now, the annual wage difference between a four-year college degree and a high-school diploma is $25,895. And, for African-Americans and Latinos, wage differences between high-school and college completion are striking.

An African-American woman with a college degree earns $16,836 more than an African-American woman without one. And a Latino male with some college earns almost $5,000 more than a Latino male with a high-school diploma. Times have changed, and there is no debating the link between educational opportunity and economic success.

What has not changed is the lack of educational opportunities for many low-income students and students of color. While it is true that not all students will go to college, far too often our most vulnerable students are tracked into low-level career-tech classes and end up prepared for neither college nor career. These students, if they graduate from high school, do so with the empty promise of a bright future in a trade, only to find they are missing the critical skills necessary for success. This matters, because even skilled trades — plumbing, auto technicians and manufacturing — all require intensive academic preparation.

Rigorous career technical education (CTE) classes integrated into a college-prep curriculum can enhance the students' academic experience and allow them to explore real-world applications in areas such as mathematics or physics. In some districts, innovative high schools, like Kearny Construction Tech School in San Diego, are doing just that.

Construction Tech aligns its classes with the graduation requirements of the University of California and California State University systems. As a result, its graduates have a true choice between college and career, and the skills to succeed in either.

The question is not whether school districts should give equal priority to college-prep and career-training programs. High schools must provide all students with a rigorous curriculum that prepares them for the challenges of college, career and civic participation so that young people can explore a wide range of options for work and higher education. If not, they may suffer crippling limitations that do a tragic disservice to them, their communities and our nation.

Continued from p. 996

of tomorrow" despite limited job opportunities. [58]

"It would raise the eyebrows of many Americans to know that is where their Pell Grant and stimulus money is going," Steve Ellis, vice president of Taxpayers for Common Sense, a watchdog group in Washington, told the newspaper. [59]

Overall, the president's education plans have been viewed with a mix of praise and skepticism.

"He is the first president I have ever heard . . . actually address" the need for postsecondary education without simply prescribing a four-year degree, says Walter, the Penn State workforce-education director.

Likewise, Nancy Cauthen, director of the Economic Opportunity Program at Demos, a liberal think tank in New York, said the proposed increase in community college funding "will increase postsecondary success and improve economic opportunity and mobility for young adults." It recognizes that "low graduation rates at these institutions will not increase if community colleges are forced to cut back their spending" and if students, particularly low-income and first-generation college students, can't afford to stay enrolled, she said. [60]

But Neal McCluskey, associate director of the Center for Educational Freedom at the Cato Institute, a libertarian think tank, termed Obama's call for a year of postsecondary education for everyone "essentially a 'consume-more-education' policy. We're encouraging people to consume education that they're either not prepared for or aren't really interested in by subsidiz-

The Institute of Culinary Education in New York City offers six- to 11-month career-training programs in culinary arts, pastry and baking and culinary management. The school holds night classes because of the increasing demand for cooking classes from both amateurs and aspiring professionals.

ing it and having our leaders tell us it's the ticket to the middle class and the American dream." [61]

Evolving Labor Market

The full Congress has yet to digest the Obama plan — a companion Senate bill hadn't been filed as of mid-November. Meanwhile, some education experts are focusing on the 2010 budget and their concerns about career and technical-education funding under the Perkins Act.

"It is refreshing that this administration recognizes the need for an investment in career technical education," said Kimberly A. Green, executive director of the National Association of State Directors of Career Technical Education Consortium. "However, I am disappointed that the president's budget proposes flat funding for Perkins. Level-funding this program is like putting a temporary patch on a hole in a dam that is ready to burst. Demand for these programs is up. The pace of technological change is increasing. Equipment needs are grow-

ing. To be able to support our country properly, CTE needs a significant new infusion of funding." [62]

Still, observers are hopeful that Obama will put more money into CTE after the nation's current budget woes ease. A positive sign, they say, is the appointment of Brenda Dann-Messier as assistant secretary for vocational and adult education. A former Clinton-era Education Department official, Dann-Messier most recently was president of Dorcas Place Adult and Family Learning Center, an educational facility for low-income residents in Providence, R.I.

"We're waiting to see how things play out with the new assistant secretary," Walter says. "She has a real background in adult education."

However things play out for CTE and the administration's broader education policy, the labor market will continue to evolve in ways that make some form of postsecondary education necessary for economic security, many experts say — but not without challenges for both employers and students.

For employers, one of the biggest challenges is finding workers with adequate skills. Nearly half of respondents to a 2008 survey of more than 200 employers said they provide remedial-training programs for newly hired graduates at three educational levels: high school, two-year college and four-year college. The programs are designed to remove deficiencies among new hires in skills the employers expected them to have when hired. But most companies said their training programs were only moderately or somewhat successful at best. [63]

"U.S. business is increasingly outspoken about the competitiveness threat posed by an ill-prepared workforce — but employers must do a better job of quantifying this threat and communicating it to key stakeholders," said Mary Wright, program director of the Workforce Readiness Initiative at The Conference Board, a business membership organization that participated in the survey. [64]

For students, figuring out a career path can pose daunting challenges. A 2008 study by researchers at MPR Associates, a research and consulting firm specializing in education, and the National Center for Education Statistics compared employment experiences of 1992-1993 bachelor's degree recipients 10 years after college. The study found that compared with graduates with academic undergraduate majors — such as social sciences, arts and math — those with career-oriented majors such as business, health and engineering "appeared to establish themselves in the labor force earlier, and relatively fewer obtained additional education." [65]

Some adults who already hold four-year degrees are finding themselves without the necessary skills to find work. In growing numbers, white-collar college graduates are turning to community colleges to upgrade their skills or learn new ones that might land them a second career. [66]

"Continuing education used to be personal enrichment, primarily, but it has moved steadily toward workforce development," James B. Jacobs, president of Macomb Community College, told *The New York Times*. "People would go to classes to learn to cook Chinese food to impress their friends and relatives or to learn interior decorating.

"Those courses have been transformed and have become areas for a lot of people coming out of white-collar jobs," he continued. "They now take culinary programs to help open a restaurant. They learn not just how to cook, but how to buy and how to run a restaurant." [67] ∎

OUTLOOK

Many Challenges

The issues surrounding educational pathways for young adults will no doubt become more complex in coming years.

Career and technical-education programs will have to satisfy the needs of college- and career-bound students seeking training in fields such as computers and health care while also making the vocational-education programs worthwhile for students who may not be cut out for postsecondary education or middle-skill jobs.

"A huge issue" for schools offering a CTE program is "who is it serving?" says Walter of Penn State. "There are two sides of the argument. How does CTE fulfill its mission?"

CTE programs also must figure out how to measure success as high-school career training, postsecondary education and industry certification become more integrated, Walter says. In the past, programs "were assessed by how many students graduated [from high-school CTE classes] and were placed in employment." Now, he says, success is often measured by whether students complete a CTE program in high school, advance to other training and then gain a good job.

Community colleges must absorb a growing enrollment load despite severe budget limitations. Zeiss, of Central Piedmont Community College, points out that money designated in the House education bill for improving community college facilities is in the form of loans for shovel-ready projects. Zeiss says he doesn't know of many states that allow community colleges to borrow money. He says he hopes the Senate version of the bill will call for grants — at least matching grants — instead of loans.

For students, perhaps the biggest hurdle to overcome is the rising cost of education. Many students receive financial aid, of course. Full-time students at private not-for-profit four-year institutions get an estimated average of $14,400 in grant aid and federal tax benefits, according to the College Board, cutting tuition and fees to about $11,900 on average. At public four-year institutions, the aid and benefits average about $5,400, reducing the tab to $1,600. [68]

Still, many students finish college in debt — a problem made worse when no job is waiting after graduation. In 2007-2008, 38 percent of bachelor's degree recipients from public four-year institutions had no school debts, but 6 percent owed at least $40,000, according to the College Board.

The debt load was lighter for community college students. Sixty-two percent of those graduating with associate degrees from two-year public institutions had no debt, and less than 1 percent owed $40,000 or more. [69] ∎

Notes

[1] Mike Rowe, "Work Is Not the Enemy," www.mikeroweworks.com.

[2] "Remarks of President Barack Obama, Address to Joint Session of Congress," The White House, Feb. 24, 2009, www.whitehouse.gov/the_press_office/Remarks-of-President-Barack-Obama-Address-to-Joint-Session-of-Congress.

[3] "A Stronger Nation through Higher Education," Lumina Foundation for Education, February 2009, www.luminafoundation.org/publications/A_stronger_nation_through_higher_education.pdf. The Lumina Foundation said its data source is the Organisation for Economic Co-operation and Development, "Education at a Glance 2008."

[4] "Remarks of President Barack Obama," *op. cit.* For background, see Scott W. Wright, "Community Colleges," *CQ Researcher*, April 21, 2000, pp. 329-352.

[5] U.S. Census Bureau, www.census.gov/population/socdemo/education/cps2008/tabA-3.xls.

[6] Bureau of Labor Statistics, Oct. 2, 2009, www.bls.gov/news.release/empsit.t04.htm.

[7] "Trends in College Pricing 2009," College Board, www.trends-collegeboard.com/college_pricing/pdf/2009_Trends_College_Pricing.pdf.

8 Harry J. Holzer and Robert Lerman, "America's Forgotten Middle-Skill Jobs," Workforce Alliance, November 2007, www.urban.org/UploadedPDF/411633_forgottenjobs.pdf. Holzer and Lerman are both scholars at the Urban Institute.

9 Ibid.

10 Louis Uchitelle, "Despite Recession, High Demand for Skilled Labor," The New York Times, June 24, 2009, www.nytimes.com/2009/06/24/business/24jobs.html?scp=1&sq=despite%20recession,%20high%20demand%20for%20skilled%20labor&st=cse.

11 For background on jobs and the economy, see the following CQ Researcher reports: Alan Greenblatt, "State Budget Crisis," Sept. 11, 2009, pp. 741-764; Peter Katel, "Vanishing Jobs," March 13, 2009, pp. 225-248; Marcia Clemmitt, "Public-Works Projects," Feb. 20, 2009, pp. 153-176; Kenneth Jost, et al., "The Obama Presidency," Jan. 30, 2009, pp. 73-104; Peter Katel, "Straining the Safety Net," July 31, 2009, pp. 645-668.

12 Tamar Lewin, "College Enrollment Set Record in 2008," The New York Times, Oct. 30, 2009, www.nytimes.com/2009/10/30/education/30college.html?scp=1&sq=college%20enrollment%20set%20record%20in%202008&st=cse.

13 Betsy Brand, "Supporting High Quality Career and Technical Education through Federal and State Policy," American Youth Policy Forum, May 2008, www.aypf.org/documents/SupportingHighQualityCTE.pdf.

14 Kenneth C. Gray and Edwin L. Herr, Other Ways to Win (2006), p. 8.

15 Deborah Reed, "California's Future Workforce: Will There Be Enough College Graduates?" Public Policy Institute of California, December 2008, www.ppic.org/content/pubs/report/R_1208DRR.pdf.

16 "New Report: More than 2.7 Million 'Middle-Skill' Job Openings Projected for California by 2016," press release, The Workforce Alliance, Skills2Compete and California EDGE Campaign, Oct. 19, 2009, accessed at www.reuters.com/article/pressRelease/idUS86731+19-Oct-2009+PRN20091019.

17 Press releases accessed at www.skills2compete.org/site/c.fhLIKYPLLuF/b.3356267/k.89B1/Media_Center.htm.

18 Lumina Foundation, op. cit.

19 "Is a College Education Worth the Debt?" "Tell Me More," National Public Radio, Sept. 1, 2009, www.npr.org/templates/story/story.php?storyId=112432364.

20 Brand, op. cit.

21 "Career and Technical Education: States Have Broad Flexibility in Implementing Perkins IV," U.S. Government Accountability Office, July 2009, www.gao.gov/new.items/d09683.pdf. For a discussion of this issue, see Demenic Giandomenico, "Career Technical Education Success Difficult to Measure," The Chamber Post, July 31, 2009, www.chamberpost.com/2009/07/career-technical-education-success-difficult-to-measure.html.

22 "Noteworthy State Legislation for Improving Career and Technical Education," Education Commission of the States, September 2009, www.ecs.org/clearinghouse/82/07/8207.pdf.

23 See James J. Kemple with Cynthia J. Willner, "Career Academies: Long-Term Impacts on Labor Market Outcomes, Educational Attainment and Transitions to Adulthood," MDRC, June 2008, www.mdrc.org/publications/482/overview.html.

24 Mary Beth Marklein, "Four-year schools get bigger share of revenue pie," USA Today, July 22, 2008, www.usatoday.com/news/education/2008-07-22-comcol-funding_N.htm.

25 Stephen G. Katsinas and Terrence A. Tollefson, "Funding and Access Issues in Public Higher Education: A Community College Perspective," University of Alabama Education Policy Center, 2009, http://education.ua.edu/edpolicycenter/documents/fundingandaccess2009.pdf.

26 "Diploma to Nowhere," Strong American Schools, 2008, www.deltacostproject.org/resources/pdf/DiplomaToNowhere.pdf. The group analyzed 2004 data.

27 "The People's Vote: 100 Documents that Shaped America, Morrill Act (1862)," U.S. News & World Report, www.usnews.com/usnews/documents/docpages/document_page33.htm.

28 Ibid.

29 Ellwood P. Cubberley, Changing Conceptions of Education (1909), pp. 49-50, accessed at http://books.google.com.

30 Kenneth Gray, "Vocationalism and the American High School: Past, Present and Future?" Journal of Industrial Teacher Education, vol. 33, no. 2, winter 1996, http://scholar.lib.vt.edu/ejournals/JITE/v33n2/gray.html.

31 Neville B. Smith, "A Tribute to the Visionaries, Prime Movers and Pioneers of Vocational Education, 1892 to 1917," Journal of Vocational and Technical Education, vol. 16, no. 1, fall 1999, http://scholar.lib.vt.edu/ejournals/JVTE/v16n1/smith.html.

32 Ibid.

33 "Smith-Hughes Act of 1917," Prentice Hall Documents Library, http://cwx.prenhall.com/bookbind/pubbooks/dye4/medialib/docs/smith917.htm.

34 David Stern, "Expanding Policy Options for Educating Teenagers," The Future of Children, vol. 19, no. 1, spring 2009, pp. 211-239, http://futureofchildren.org/futureofchildren/publications/docs/19_01_10.pdf. The journal is a collaboration of the Woodrow Wilson School of Public and International Affairs at Princeton University and The Brookings Institution.

35 Prentice Hall Documents Library, op. cit.

36 Marjorie Coeyman, "Practical skills vs. three R's: A debate revives," The Christian Science Monitor, July 8, 2003, www.csmonitor.com/2003/0708/p13s02-lepr.html.

37 "Significant Events," American Association of Community Colleges, www.aacc.nche.edu/AboutCC/history/Pages/significantevents.aspx.

38 "Statement by the President Making Public a Report of the Commission on Higher Education," Public Papers, No. 235, Harry S. Truman Library and Museum, Dec. 15, 1947, http://trumanlibrary.org/publicpapers/index.php?pid=1852.

39 Ibid.

40 U.S. Census Bureau, www.census.gov/population/socdemo/school/TableA-6.xls.

41 U.S. Census Bureau, "Decennial Census of Population," 1940 to 2000, www.census.gov/population/socdemo/education/phct41/table2.xls.

42 American Association of Community Colleges, www.aacc.nche.edu/AboutCC/history/Documents/np10.pdf.

43 Gray, op. cit.

44 Ibid.

45 Of the 3.2 million young people who graduated from high school from October 2007 to October 2008, 2.2 million — about 69 percent — were attending college in October 2008, according to the U.S. Labor Department.

About the Author

Thomas J. Billitteri is a CQ Researcher staff writer based in Fairfield, Pa., who has more than 30 years' experience covering business, nonprofit institutions and public policy for newspapers and other publications. His recent CQ Researcher reports include "Auto Industry's Future," "Afghanistan's Future" and "Financial Literacy." He holds a BA in English and an MA in journalism from Indiana University.

About 60 percent of those who enrolled in college attended four-year institutions. See "College Enrollment and Work Activity of 2008 High-school Graduates," April 28, 2009, www.bls.gov/news.release/pdf/hsgec.pdf.

[46] For background, see R. Thompson, "Teachers: The Push for Excellence," *Editorial Research Reports*, April 20, 1984, available at *CQ Researcher Plus Archive.*

[47] For background, see Barbara Mantel, "No Child Left Behind," *CQ Researcher*, May 27, 2005, pp. 469-492.

[48] An April 3, 2009, letter to Obama from officials of the Association for Career and Technical Education, the National Association of State Directors of Career Technical Education Consortium and the American Association of Community Colleges sought at least $1.4 billion in funding under the Perkins Career and Technical Education Act and said federal investment in the act had decreased by $42 million since fiscal 2002 while enrollments have soared to record highs. See www.acteonline.org/uploaded Files/Issues_and_Advocacy/files/FY10_President_Signon.doc.

[49] Office of Management and Budget, www. whitehouse.gov/omb/fy2010_department_education.

[50] Lamar Alexander, "The Three-Year Solution," *Newsweek*, Oct. 26, 2009, www.newsweek.com/id/218183.

[51] Frederick M. Hess, Mark Schneider, Kevin Carey and Andrew P. Kelly, "Diplomas and Dropouts," American Enterprise Institute, June 2009, www.aei.org/docLib/Diplomas%20and%20Dropouts%20final.pdf.

[52] William G. Bowen, Matthew M. Chingos and Michael S. McPherson, *Crossing the Finish Line* (2009).

[53] Quoted in Scott Jaschik, "(Not) Crossing the Finish Line," *Inside Higher Ed*, Sept. 9, 2009, www.insidehighered.com/news/2009/09/09/finish.

[54] "Remarks by the President on the American Graduation Initiative," The White House, July 14, 2009, www.whitehouse.gov/the_press_office/Remarks-by-the-President-on-the-American-Graduation-Initiative-in-Warren-MI/.

[55] The bill is HR 3221.

[56] See Michael A. Fletcher, "Obama Spotlights Student Loan Reform," *The Washington Post*, April 24, 2009, http://voices.washingtonpost.com/44/2009/04/24/obama_spotlights_student_loan.html. For an analysis of the bill, see "Congressional Budget Office Cost Estimate," July 24, 2009, www.cbo.gov/ftpdocs/104xx/doc10479/hr3221.pdf.

[57] Anthony Carnevale, "Postsecondary Educa-

tion Goes to Work," *Inside Higher Ed*, May 15, 2009, www.insidehighered.com/views/2009/05/15/carnevale. Obama spoke on "job creation and job training" on May 9, 2009; see www.white house.gov/the_press_office/Remarks-by-the-President-on-Job-Creation-and-Job-Training-5/8/09/.

[58] Will Van Sant, "$2.3 million in federal stimulus money is going to pay for Tampa Bay area beauty school tuition," *St. Petersburg Times*, Oct. 17, 2009, www.tampabay.com/news/education/23-million-in-federal-stimulus-money-is-going-to-pay-for-tampa-bay-area/1044637.

[59] Quoted in *ibid.*

[60] "President Obama's Plan to Invest in Community Colleges Could Vastly Improve Young People's Ability to Achieve Economic Security," *Demos*, July 22, 2009, http://demos.org/press.cfm?currentarticleID=BE413099%2D3FF4%2D6C82%2D5592F9B4EF236F90.

[61] Quoted in Kelly Field, "A Year of College for All: What the President's Plan Would Mean for the Country," *Chronicle of Higher Education*, May 22, 2009, accessed at http://cew.georgetown.edu/media/news/. McCluskey made his comments at a forum, according to the *Chronicle* article.

[62] "Obama Budget Level Funds Career Technical Education," press release, National Association of State Directors of Career Technical Education Consortium, May 7, 2009,

www.careertech.org/press_releases/show/28.

[63] Jill Casner-Lotto, Elyse Rosenblum and Mary Wright, "The Ill-Prepared U.S. Workforce," Corporate Voices for Working Families, American Society for Training & Development, Conference Board and Society for Human Resource Management, July 2009, www.astd.org/NR/rdonlyres/A7A0ECFF-333E-445C-BAA5-99486742F7F0/22788/Workforcekeyfindings0709final.pdf.

[64] "New Report Shows Employers Struggle with Ill-Prepared Workforce," The Conference Board, press release, July 14, 2009, www.conference-board.org/utilities/pressDetail.cfm?press_id=3693.

[65] Susan P. Choy, Ellen M. Bradburn and C. Dennis Carroll, "Ten Years After College: Comparing the Employment Experiences of 1992-93 Bachelor's Degree Recipients With Academic and Career-Oriented Majors," National Center for Education Statistics, February 2008, http://nces.ed.gov/pubs2008/2008155.pdf.

[66] Steven Greenhouse, "More White-Collar Workers Turn to Community Colleges," *The New York Times*, Aug. 19, 2009, www.nytimes.com/2009/08/20/education/20COMMUN.html.

[67] Quoted in *ibid.*

[68] College Board, "Trends in College Pricing," *op. cit.*

[69] "Trends in Student Aid 2009," College Board, p. 10, www.trends-collegeboard.com/student_aid/pdf/2009_Trends_Student_Aid.pdf.

Bibliography

Selected Sources

Books

Bowen, William G., Matthew M. Chingos and Michael S. McPherson, *Crossing the Finish Line*, Princeton University Press, 2009.

Public universities are crucial to the nation's future, yet fewer than 60 percent of students entering four-year colleges graduate, according to this scholarly examination of graduation rates at 21 flagship public universities and four statewide public higher-education systems.

Crawford, Matthew B., *Shop Class as Soulcraft: An Inquiry Into the Value of Work*, Penguin Press, 2009.

A think tank scholar turned motorcycle repair shop owner waxes philosophically about the satisfaction of working with one's hands and analyzes the unwillingness of American culture to recognize the merits of tradecraft and manual labor.

Gray, Kenneth C., and Edwin L. Herr, *Other Ways to Win*, Corwin Press, 2006.

Two Pennsylvania State University scholars focus on teens in the academic middle — those in the second and third quartiles of their high-school class — and question the premise that the only way to achieve economic security is by pursuing a four-year college degree.

Articles

Epstein, Jennifer, "Should Everyone Go to College?" *Inside Higher Ed*, Sept. 18, 2009, www.insidehighered.com/news/2009/09/18/college#.

In a panel discussion, four policy experts examine the question of whether everyone needs college — and how that postsecondary education should be defined.

Greenhouse, Steven, "At Sinclair Community College, Focus Is Jobs," *The New York Times*, Aug. 15, 2009, www.nytimes.com/2009/08/15/business/15college.html?scp=1&sq=sinclair%20community%20college&st=cse.

The Dayton, Ohio, community college is in the forefront of efforts to create a higher-skilled workforce — retraining thousands of laid-off autoworkers and helping local leaders foster growth industries and train workers for them.

Greenhouse, Steven, "More White-Collar Workers Turn to Community Colleges," *The New York Times*, Aug. 20, 2009, www.nytimes.com/2009/08/20/education/20COMMUN.html?scp=1&sq=more%20white-collar%20workers%20turn%20to%20community%20colleges&st=cse.

Many community college students are employed but want to increase their skills, while others have lost their jobs and are returning to school to obtain new skills.

Jan, Tracy, "These Bunker Hill Classes Make Late Arrival Mandatory," *The Boston Globe*, Sept. 11, 2009, www.boston.com/news/education/higher/articles/2009/09/11/these_bunker_hill_classes_make_late_arrival_mandatory/.

Several community colleges are working to accommodate the needs of their students by offering midnight courses in psychology, writing and "graveyard" welding classes.

Lewin, Tamar, "College Costs Keep Rising, Report Says," *The New York Times*, Oct. 21, 2009, www.nytimes.com/2009/10/21/education/21costs.html?ref=us.

While overall consumer prices fell last year, the cost of a college education rose significantly, with tuition and fees at four-year public colleges up an average of 6.5 percent and those at private colleges up 4.4 percent, the College Board reported.

Uchitelle, Louis, "Despite Recession, High Demand for Skilled Labor," *The New York Times*, June 24, 2009, www.nytimes.com/2009/06/24/business/24jobs.html?scp=1&sq=despite%20recession,%20high%20demand%20for%20skilled%20labor&st=cse.

Despite a national unemployment rate near 10 percent, some employers are seeking qualified applicants for skilled jobs in welding, critical-care nursing and other specialties.

Reports and Studies

"A Stronger Nation Through Higher Education," Lumina Foundation for Education, February 2009, www.luminafoundation.org/publications/A_stronger_nation_through_higher_education.pdf.

College-attainment rates are climbing in nearly every industrialized or post-industrial country except the United States, where about 39 percent of adults hold a two- or four-year degree, according to this examination.

Casner-Lotto, Jill, Elyse Rosenblum and Mary Wright, "The Ill-Prepared U.S. Workforce," The Conference Board, Corporate Voices for Working Families, American Society for Training & Development and Society for Human Resource Management, July 2009, www.cvworkingfamilies.org/system/files/Ill_Prepared_Workforce_KF.pdf.

Employers are finding that many new hires lack important basic and applied skills, but company training programs often are not correcting those deficiencies, the study concludes.

Holzer, Harry J., and Robert I. Lerman, "America's Forgotten Middle-Skill Jobs," Workforce Alliance, November 2007, www.urban.org/UploadedPDF/411633_forgottenjobs.pdf.

Researchers conclude that demand for workers to fill jobs that require more than a high-school diploma but less than a four-year degree will likely remain strong relative to supply.

The Next Step:

Additional Articles from Current Periodicals

Community Colleges

Calvan, Bobby Caina, "Programs at Colleges Grow to Help Meet Rising Demand," *Sacramento Bee* (California), April 26, 2009, p. B1.

Community colleges have added programs in health care, where the number of jobs continues to grow, with the help of companies that sponsor students to develop skills in various health occupations, including radiology.

Cawvey, Matthew, "Virtual Classrooms Fill; Community Colleges Lead Online Demand," *The Washington Times*, April 15, 2008, p. A2.

Many community colleges have turned to online course offerings in an effort to meet rising demands for courses through distance learning.

Giordano, Maria, "Columbia State Hopes Obama's Proposal Helps," *The Tennessean*, July 20, 2009.

Community colleges in Tennessee have been on wait lists for state funding for years, but many hope President Obama's emphasis on the importance of a college education will shake loose the federal funding needed to meet the goal of expansion.

Wilson, Matt, "De Anza May Turn Away Eligible Students as More Apply for Fewer Classroom Seats," *San Jose Mercury News*, Aug. 14, 2009.

Due to tight budgets, many community colleges have to turn away increasing numbers of eligible students while also cutting course offerings.

Financial Security

"Largest Investment in Higher Education in History Passes House," States News Service, Sept. 24, 2009.

U.S. Rep. Niki Tsongas, D-Mass., says everyone should go to college, not just for personal financial security but for the security of the United States in the global economy, as well.

Asimov, Nanette, "Survey Finds Many Troubled by College Cost; California," *San Francisco Chronicle*, Nov. 13, 2009, p. B1.

A California survey found that people think college is more necessary today than ever before for financial security, but many are worried about affording it.

Maddaluna, Michael, and Michael J. Herrera, "Guest Commentary: Technical Schools a Ticket to Success," *Courier News* (Bridgewater, N.J.), Sept. 23, 2009.

Technical training allows people to develop skills for important jobs, such as construction and nursing, which offer high wages and contribute to the health of the overall economy.

Rossi, Lisa, "Candidates Divided on Need to Cut College Cost," *Des Moines Register*, Dec. 11, 2007, p. 1A.

An Iowa State University associate professor argues that not everyone should go to college, but people feel pressured into attending, which may not be the best use of their skills.

Technical Training Programs

"College Plan Fine, but Don't Forget High School Problem," *The News-Messenger* (Fremont, Ohio), April 9, 2008, p. 4.

High-school programs in Ohio are not preparing students for college, or even retaining students long enough for them to graduate, leaving many people without the skills needed to succeed in the workforce.

"Peterson Garners National Recognition for Leadership on Technical Education," States News Service, April 1, 2008.

U.S. Rep. John Peterson, R-Pa., emphasizes the importance of transforming technical education as technology changes, in order to remain competitive in the global economy.

"Wave of the Future," *News & Record* (Greensboro, N.C.), May 25, 2008, p. H2.

Guilford County community colleges have successfully implemented technical-training programs to retrain displaced textile, tobacco and furniture employees for jobs in high-growth fields such as nursing and aviation.

Burk, Jennifer, "Tech Colleges Provide Training for New Companies," *The Macon Telegraph*, Feb. 1, 2008.

Quick Start, a technical-training and adult-education program in Georgia, provides training to new or expanding businesses free of charge, which has brought many companies to the state, including Kia and Boeing.

In-depth Reports on Issues in the News

Are you writing a paper?

Need backup for a debate?

Want to become an expert on an issue?

For more than 80 years, students have turned to *CQ Researcher* for in-depth reporting on issues in the news. Reports on a full range of political and social issues are now available. Following is a selection of recent reports:

Civil Liberties
Closing Guantánamo, 2/09
Affirmative Action, 10/08
Gay Marriage Showdowns, 9/08
America's Border Fence, 9/08
Immigration Debate, 2/08

Crime/Law
Interrogating the CIA, 9/09
Examining Forensics, 7/09
Legalizing Marijuana, 6/09
Wrongful Convictions, 4/09
Prostitution Debate, 5/08

Education
Financial Literacy, 9/09
Reading Crisis? 2/08
Discipline in Schools, 2/08

Environment/Society
Women in the Military, 11/09
Conspiracy Theories, 10/09
Human Spaceflight, 10/09
Gays in the Military, 9/09
Energy and Climate, 7/09
Future of Books, 5/09
Hate Groups, 5/09

Health/Safety
Medication Abuse, 10/09
Nuclear Disarmament, 10/09
Health-Care Reform, 8/09
Straining the Safety Net, 7/09
Treating Depression, 6/09
Reproductive Ethics, 5/09

Politics/Economy
State Budget Crisis, 9/09
Business Bankruptcy, 4/09
Future of the GOP, 3/09
Middle-Class Squeeze, 3/09

Upcoming Reports

Prisoner Reentry, 12/4/09   Bilingual Education, 12/11/09   Homelessness, 12/18/09

ACCESS

CQ Researcher is available in print and online. For access, visit your library or www.cqresearcher.com.

STAY CURRENT

To receive notice of upcoming *CQ Researcher* reports, or learn more about *CQ Researcher* products, subscribe to the free e-mail newsletters, *CQ Researcher Alert!* and *CQ Researcher News*: http://cqpress.com/newsletters.

PURCHASE

To purchase a *CQ Researcher* report in print or electronic format (PDF), visit www.cqpress.com or call 866-427-7737. Single reports start at $15. Bulk purchase discounts and electronic-rights licensing are also available.

SUBSCRIBE

Annual full-service *CQ Researcher* subscriptions—including 44 reports a year, monthly index updates, and a bound volume—start at $803. Add $25 for domestic postage.

CQ Researcher Online offers a backfile from 1991 and a number of tools to simplify research. For pricing information, call 800-834-9020, ext. 1906, or e-mail librarysales@cqpress.com.

Published by CQ Press, a Division of SAGE

www.cqresearcher.com

Prisoner Reentry

Can aid to ex-inmates significantly reduce recidivism?

N early three-quarters of a million prisoners will be released from state and federal prisons this year — an unprecedented number — and about half of them will be returned to prison over the next three years after committing new crimes or violating parole. As the recession makes it harder for ex-prisoners to find jobs and limits states' ability to house rising numbers of inmates, worries about revolving-door incarceration are escalating. Many experts see an answer to the problem in so-called reentry programs, which are designed to lower recidivism by helping soon-to-be-released or newly released prisoners land on their feet, sometimes assisting them in getting jobs before leaving prison. But even after enactment of former President George W. Bush's Second Chance Act, which supports reentry programs, they remain relatively scarce. In fact, in many states, funding for prison needs has overtaken proposals to pay for reentry.

Ex-inmate Ronald Birkmire Jr. found work with a Philadelphia construction firm despite his assault record. To reduce recidivism, a new city program offers $10,000 tax credits to businesses that hire ex-offenders and provide them tuition help or vocational training.

CQ Researcher • Dec. 4, 2009 • www.cqresearcher.com
Volume 19, Number 42 • Pages 1005-1028

RECIPIENT OF SOCIETY OF PROFESSIONAL JOURNALISTS AWARD FOR EXCELLENCE ◆ AMERICAN BAR ASSOCIATION SILVER GAVEL AWARD

CQ PRESS

THE ISSUES

SIDEBARS AND GRAPHICS

FOR FURTHER RESEARCH

Cover: AP Photo/Matt Rourke

CQ Researcher

Dec. 4, 2009
Volume 19, Number 42

MANAGING EDITOR: Thomas J. Colin
tcolin@cqpress.com

ASSISTANT MANAGING EDITOR: Kathy Koch
kkoch@cqpress.com

ASSOCIATE EDITOR: Kenneth Jost

STAFF WRITERS: Thomas J. Billitteri, Marcia Clemmitt, Peter Katel

CONTRIBUTING WRITERS: Rachel Cox, Sarah Glazer, Alan Greenblatt, Reed Karaim Barbara Mantel, Patrick Marshall, Tom Price, Jennifer Weeks

DESIGN/PRODUCTION EDITOR: Olu B. Davis

ASSISTANT EDITOR: Darrell Dela Rosa

EDITORIAL INTERN: Emily DeRuy

FACT-CHECKING: Eugene J. Gabler, Michelle Harris

CQ PRESS

A Division of SAGE

PRESIDENT AND PUBLISHER:
John A. Jenkins

CQ Press is a registered trademark of Congressional Quarterly Inc.

CQ Researcher (ISSN 1056-2036) is printed on acid-free paper. Published weekly, except; (Jan. wk. 1) (May wk. 4) (July wks. 1, 2) (Aug. wks. 3, 4) (Nov. wk. 4) and (Dec. wk. 4), by CQ Press, a division of SAGE Publications. Annual full-service subscriptions start at $803. For pricing, call 1-800-834-9020, ext. 1906. To purchase a CQ Researcher report in print or electronic format (PDF), visit www. cqpress.com or call 866-427-7737. Single reports start at $15. Bulk purchase discounts and electronic-rights licensing are also available. Periodicals postage paid at Washington, D.C., and additional mailing offices. POSTMASTER: Send address changes to CQ Researcher, 2300 N St., N.W., Suite 800, Washington, DC 20037.

Prisoner Reentry

BY PETER KATEL

THE ISSUES

When the big question comes — and it will — don't slouch in your chair, look down and mumble that you were in the wrong place at the wrong time. "That doesn't work," Hillel Raskas tells a quiet group of new residents at a pre-release center in the Washington suburb of Rockville, Md.

Instead, when the job interviewer asks if you've been convicted of a crime, Work-Release Coordinator Raskas advises the nine men and two women to sit up straight, look him in the eye and say: "Here's something I need to tell you. I have a conviction; I sold a few drugs, I made a mistake. I'm in a work-release program. I've been approved to work. I'm ready to work. I know what I need to do. I'm the right man, I'm the right woman. I'll be here every day."

With that approach, Raskas says, you'll have a real shot at the job.

If the newcomers at the Montgomery County corrections department's Pre-Release Center manage to get employed, put their pasts behind them and never enter another prison or jail, they will be among the fortunate 48 percent of America's growing army of ex-prisoners — 725,000-strong in 2007 — who are not re-incarcerated. [1]

The revolving-door nature of crime and punishment is plaguing lawmakers and policy experts nationwide. Caught up in the Great Recession, they're trying to dig their way out of budget disasters, and only Medicaid soaks up more state general fund money than prison systems — an estimated $47 billion in fiscal 2008. [2]

Inmate William Gray learns work skills at the Department of Corrections reentry facility in Plainfield, Ind. Many experts say reentry programs designed to help ex-prisoners land on their feet are an answer to the nation's rising prison population and high recidivism rate. But with states battered by the recession, relatively few reentry programs have been started.

In this atmosphere, calls to improve ex-prisoners' "reentry" chances are ringing more loudly than ever. With or without help, 95 percent of all prisoners in the United States are released. Reentry programs are designed to help them navigate the range of demands and needs they face — from finding a job and a place to live to dealing with drug or alcohol habits or psychological problems connected with past crimes. The emphasis on practical solutions largely distinguishes "reentry" from "rehabilitation" — a term mostly used in connection with attempts to help prisoners learn new skills and attitudes while they're incarcerated.

"We've got an unprecedented volume of people coming out of prison and jail,"

says Michael Thompson, director of the Council of State Governments' Justice Center, which has been working with state governments on the issue since 2001. At the same time, "Policy makers are looking at very high failure rates of people coming out of prison. That's obviously a public-safety problem. And states don't have the money to keep growing the prison and jail population. Suddenly you've got more momentum for improving reentry success rates than ever before."

It's no secret why so many prisoners are being released. As crime rates began rising in the 1970s, politicians began passing tough-on-crime laws that sent prison and jail populations soaring. At the same time, rehabilitation programs came to be seen as ineffective in curbing crime and fell out of favor. Prisons' main mission became punishment and removal from society. Even as prison populations soared, remedial education programs served fewer and fewer prisoners, the nonprofit Urban Institute reported in 2004. [3]

Although crime rates had begun falling by the early '90s, the effects of toughened sentencing laws still resonate: U.S. prisons and jails held more than 2 million prisoners by 2003 — the world's largest prison population, both per capita and in absolute terms. By 2007, America's prison population had grown to nearly 2.3 million.

In this climate, reentry programs are gaining ground. "As few as 10 years ago, very few state departments of corrections had divisions devoted to reentry," Thompson says. "But today every department of corrections in the country will identify for you a person in charge of administering reentry programs."

Prisoner Releases Almost Equal Admissions

More than 750,000 prisoners were admitted to federal and state prisons in 2007, quadruple the number in 1980. In 1980, the number of released prisoners was 87 percent of the total number admitted that year. By 2007, releases had reached 96 percent of admissions.

Admitted and Released Prisoners, Federal and State, 1980-2007

No. of inmates

800,000
700,000
600,000
500,000
400,000
300,000
200,000
100,000
0

1980   1990   2000   2007

Admitted
Released

Source: "Prisoners in 2007," Bureau of Justice Statistics, U.S. Department of Justice

"In order to reduce recidivism you can't hand them 100 bucks, a new suit and a bus ticket," says Florida state Sen. Victor D. Crist, a Tampa Republican (no relation to Gov. Charlie Crist) who helped toughen sentencing laws in the 1990s, but who argues that Florida doesn't do enough to get soon-to-be-released prisoners ready for their new lives. "You've got to help them establish a work ethic, cultivate meaningful skills and transition from life in the big house."

All reentry programs share those broad objectives, but the scale and scope vary widely. Michigan, for example, launched in 2005 what has grown into the statewide Michigan Prison ReEntry Initiative (MPRI), designed to provide each released prisoner with a "transition plan" as well as services designed to help with employment, housing and other matters. Coupled with early releases of some prisoners, MPRI is allowing the state to close up to three state prisons and five prison camps. [4]

Some observers are holding the applause, however. "We're suspicious," says Mel Grieshaber, executive direc-tor of the Michigan Corrections Organization, the prison employees' union. "We support the objective of keeping bad people from committing other crimes, and it seems to us that more objective data should be available to prove that it's working."

Some liberals are also raising questions. "I'm very supportive of reentry, but it leaves out the question of sentencing policy, which is driving prison numbers in the first place," says Marc Mauer, executive director of the Sentencing Project, which advocates alternatives to incarceration. "As long as we continue to send so many people to prison and increasingly keep them there for long periods of time, reentry is just trying to bail out the problem."

Still, reentry has risen to the top of the agenda in nearly all states. Kansas, New York and other states are also reducing their prison populations and recidivism rates by, among other things, expanding reentry services. Even Texas — long known for a hard-line approach to crime and punishment — rejected a prison expansion plan in 2007, creating instead the $241 million Justice Rein-vestment Initiative designed in part to lower recidivism. [5]

At the other extreme is California, which took no steps to lower an ever-expanding prison population — now the nation's highest at about 150,000 inmates, many of them parole violators — until federal judges in August ordered the state to do so. (*See "Current Situation," p. 1022.*) The state's latest plan to reduce its prison population by 40,000 over two years does include some reentry assistance. [6]

But even where reentry programs are being expanded, most newly released prisoners — and the neighborhoods to which nearly all of them return — still face enormous obstacles. "These communities — already struggling with poor schools, poor health care and weak labor markets — are now shouldering the burden of reintegrating record numbers of returning prisoners," says Jeremy Travis, president of John Jay College of Criminal Justice in New York. [7]

Though states make their own laws and build their own prisons, the federal government plays an influential role, in part via the grant-making process. The Justice Department has disbursed $28 million in grants this year to reentry programs.

"Even a modest reduction in recidivism rates would prevent thousands of crimes and save hundreds of millions of taxpayer dollars," U.S. Attorney General Eric Holder told the Vera Institute of Justice, last July. [8]

In promoting reentry, the Obama administration is following in the footsteps of its two predecessors. In 1999, President Bill Clinton's Attorney General Janet Reno formally launched what her then-adviser Travis calls the "reentry movement." And to the surprise of many, President George W. Bush — a classic tough-on-crime politician — took up the cause in his 2004 State of the Union address. "America is the land of second chances, and when the gates of the prison open, the path ahead should lead to a better life." [9]

Inescapable socioeconomic realities pose a major obstacle. Only 46 percent of all prison and jail inmates have high-school diplomas or GEDs. [10]

"Eighty percent of the people who come to CEO [Center for Employment Opportunities] have reading and math scores below eighth grade," says Mindy S. Tarlow, executive director of the New York-based non-governmental job placement program for ex-prisoners.

But while reentry programs and prison downsizing may appeal to cash-strapped state lawmakers, economic conditions are hindering reentering prisoners' job hunts. That's especially true for people like a man in his early 40s who was among Raskas' trainees at the Montgomery County Pre-Release Center. (See sidebar, p. 1016.) The former career drug dealer is finishing a three-year sentence for possession of cocaine with intent to distribute. His record shows four other drug charges and a few relatively minor offenses.

"I wasted a lot of time in life," he tells staff members. But he says he has turned a page and wants to support himself legally. "I actually don't have a problem working."

Center staff will help him refine that sales pitch. Recession or not, they say, someone somewhere is always hiring. Raskas, a former businessman and congressional staffer, tells his class that he's helped 1,400 people with backgrounds similar to theirs find work. "Eighty-five percent of people leave here with a job."

As criminal justice officials and reentry advocates struggle with how to help prisoners reestablish themselves in their communities, here are some of the questions being debated:

Are state governments doing enough to help prisoners reenter society?

The basic argument for expanding reentry programs is simple: Virtually all

Many Inmates Didn't Finish High School

More than 40 percent of inmates in the nation's prisons and jails in 1997 had not completed high school or its equivalent, according to the most recent data available from the U.S. Justice Department. By comparison, only 18 percent of the general population over age 18 had not finished 12th grade.

Educational Attainment of Inmates

Education level	Total incarcerated	State	Federal	Local jail inmates	Probationers	General population
High school or less	41.3%	39.7%	26.5%	46.5%	30.6%	18.4%
GED	23.4	28.5	22.7	14.1	11.0	n/a
High-school diploma	22.6	20.5	27.0	25.9	34.8	33.2
Postsecondary	12.7	11.4	23.9	13.5	23.6	48.4

Source: Caroline Wolf Harlow, "Educational and Correctional Populations," Bureau of Justice Statistics, U.S. Department of Justice, January 2003

prisoners will be released except those serving life sentences without the possibility of parole or facing execution. But if at least half of them will be returning to prison or jail, reducing that number by helping ex-prisoners gain a foothold in the outside world would be good for them — and for society.

Supporters of expanded reentry programs point out that even as state governments face budgetary strains ranging from serious to catastrophic, they can cut long-term prison costs by spending on reentry instead of on prison space, which is more expensive. States spend an average of $22,650 yearly to maintain one prisoner. [11]

However, to make that case to state legislatures, advocates must show hard data on which kinds of reentry programs lower recidivism most effectively. But solid numbers only now are being assembled and reported. Recidivism among New York's CEO program participants, for instance, was 5.7 percent lower over a three-year period than in a control group of ex-prisoners not in the program. (See sidebar, p. 1018.)

But even without precise statistics on which kinds of programs are most effective, plenty of evidence shows approaches that don't work, say reentry program advocates.

For example, California imposes parole supervision on virtually all released prisoners — but doesn't have money for intensive supervision. The result: 66 percent of ex-prisoners returned to prison in 2003-2004 — compared with a national rate of 40 percent at that time. Two-thirds of those sent back to prison had violated parole conditions, according to a recent Justice Department study, which showed a dearth of reentry services.

"It is estimated that two-thirds or more of all California parolees have substance-abuse problems, and nearly all of them are required to be drug tested," the study's authors reported. "Yet few of them will participate in appropriate treatment while in prison or on parole." [12]

Former prison inmate and California Republican state legislator Pat Nolan, now vice president of Prison Fellowship, a Christian rehabilitation group,

Jobs Program Reduced Recidivism Slightly

About 6 percent fewer ex-prisoners who participated in a jobs program were arrested, convicted or incarcerated within three years, compared with ex-prisoners who did not participate (left). The program provided coaching in life and jobs skills and assistance in finding a job. Among nearly 300,000 prisoners released in 15 states in 1994, more than two-thirds were rearrested within three years (right).* The recidivism rate was slightly lower in 1983.

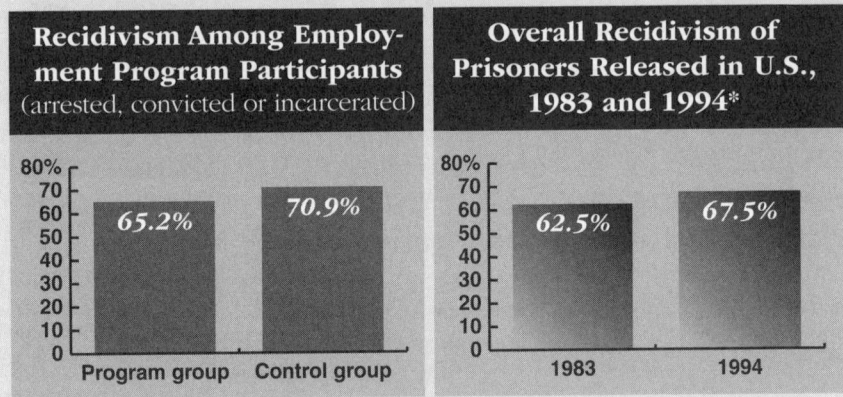

Recidivism Among Employment Program Participants (arrested, convicted or incarcerated)

Program group 65.2%
Control group 70.9%

Overall Recidivism of Prisoners Released in U.S., 1983 and 1994*

1983 62.5%
1994 67.5%

* The recidivism results are based on a 2002 study of 1994 data, which are the most recent available. The 272,111 former inmates released in 1994 represented two-thirds of all prisoners released in the United States that year.

Sources: Patrick A. Langan and David J. Levin, "Recidivism of Prisoners Released in 1994," Bureau of Justice Statistics, June 2002; Cindy Redcross, "Transitional Jobs for Ex-Prisoners," Association for Public Policy Analysis and Management, November 2009.

calls the combination of newly released prisoners with drug problems and a near-absence of treatment programs "one of the great scandals of our current California prison system." [13]

Nolan argues that the rigid enforcement of parole conditions such as no drug use means that ex-prisoners get sent back for relatively minor offenses. "Drug possession — bam, you take them [back] to prison," he says. "This guy can have a job, be supporting his family; he shouldn't use drugs, but do you want to disrupt his life, send him back to prison, for a first [parole] offense?"

But some prison system veterans say more reentry programs won't necessarily produce ex-prisoners better prepared to reenter society. "You can't make someone rehabilitate himself," says Gary B. King, a 19-year veteran of the Florida Corrections Department, one of the country's biggest prison agencies. "Over the years, what I have seen as the most rehabilitative thing we do is when we hold people accountable for their actions; when an inmate commits an infraction we apply administrative sanctions. The more we make them follow the rules while they're in prison, and do that across the board, the more we prepare them for going back into society."

King is now a classification officer who supervises individual prisoners' disciplinary records, progress reports and participation in educational or other programs at Columbia Correctional Institute, a medium-security institution near Lake City, Fla. He doubts a stronger emphasis on rehabilitation and reentry would make a big dent in Florida's recidivism rate. Nevertheless, he acknowledges that work-release programs do make sense for some prisoners nearing the end of their sentences, so they can experience the very different world outside prison. "Some inmates inside an institutional setting can do very well because their daily schedule is regimented, and they are quarantined from bad behavior and substance abuse," he says. "Once at liberty to do as they please and associate with whomever they please, they do not do well. Some inmates do not seem to handle well the responsibility that comes with freedom."

Yet even Crist, the conservative Republican Florida state senator, argues that the slim chances some prisoners have of staying out of trouble after release shouldn't block the state from expanding reentry programs for inmates who could benefit. "About one-third of the inmate population are hardened; you're going to have very little impact on them," he says. "Another two-thirds [deserve] a running chance."

Moreover, some prisoners with violent pasts may do well on the outside. "Somebody can go to prison with a first-degree felony and serve time and have an excellent track record and go through psychological testing and work release and have an excellent chance in the community," he says.

But some conservative experts who support reentry expansion on principle question how well helping hardcore prisoners reenter can be carried out in practice. "We don't know a lot about what works," says David B. Mulhausen, a senior policy analyst at the conservative Heritage Foundation's Center for Data Analysis. "Usually, the impact is rather small, and other communities haven't always been successful in replicating it."

Moreover, Mulhausen is skeptical about what he views as the political leanings of reentry advocates. "A lot of people [favoring] reentry programs really don't like prison," he says.

"They don't give credit to the fact that the drop in crime we've had in the past several years is partly due to incarceration."

But the Sentencing Project, the leading alternatives-to-incarceration organization, says that while imprisonment plays a role in the drop in crime, that role may be smaller than Mulhausen and others assert. Crime dropped by about 12 percent in 1998-2003 in states with high imprisonment — and declined by the same rate in states in which incarceration diminished or stayed the same.

"There was no discernible pattern of states with higher rates of incarceration experiencing more significant declines in crime," project staffers wrote. [14]

Should government or private organizations provide subsidized jobs for ex-prisoners?

Jobs are a major focus of virtually all reentry programs, and the No. 1 objective of most newly released prisoners. Their prospects are bleak, however, since their résumés indicate that they are former jail or prison inmates, and many have been outside the conventional workforce for most, if not all, of their lives and often have little education.

"Compared with the general population, those in prison were approximately twice as likely not to have completed high school or attained a GED," the Urban Institute reported in 2004. "And four times the number of young males in the general population had attended some college or postsecondary courses, compared with incarcerated males." [15]

Moreover, the vast expansion of the prison population far outpaced programs designed to help prisoners improve their prospects upon release, the institute concluded. "Only about half of the total inmate population receives educational or vocational training, a proportion that has been decreasing over time." [16]

But even where programs do exist, training and coaching can't improve

the grim employment environment that ex-prisoners enter upon leaving jails and prisons.

However, researchers find that former prisoners who land jobs do a better job of staying out of trouble. "Respondents who were employed and earning higher wages after release were less likely to return to prison the first year out," another group of Urban Institute researchers reported last year. [17]

For some reentry advocates, the best way to keep recidivism down — even in a dismal job climate — is to subsidize temporary jobs for ex-inmates in order to get them on the employment track. The nonprofit Joyce Foundation of Chicago created experimen-

tal "transitional jobs" programs in 2006 in Chicago, Detroit, Milwaukee and St. Paul in order to acquire data on whether the strategy — based on providing jobs for about four months to a total of about 1,800 ex-prisoners — helped participants avoid returning to prison. Results are expected in 2010. [18]

Director Tarlow of New York's CEO program argues that subsidizing jobs can attract public and political support, even when workers without prison records are having a hard time landing a job. "The cost of putting somebody in prison is five to six times greater than the cost of serving someone at CEO," Tarlow says. "You can't talk about the cost of CEO outside the context of not having CEO."

Parole Violations in Calif. Boost Recidivism

Two-thirds of California's offenders return to prison within three years, with nearly a third sent back for parole violations — a much higher rate than in other large states. A big reason for the higher violation rate is that virtually all offenders released in California go on parole supervision, while most large states do not have that policy. In addition, California has a large population of young offenders with criminal records, who tend to have higher recidivism rates.

Three-Year Recidivism Rates in California vs. Selected Big States

State	Returned to Jail or Prison		
	New Crime	Technical Violation	Total
	(by percentage)		
California	37%	32%	69%
Florida	32	8	40
Illinois	40	4	44
New York	49	14	63
North Carolina	45	8	53
Texas	31	7	38

Source: Ryan G. Fischer, "Are California's Recidivism Rates Really the Highest in the Nation? It Depends on What Measure of Recidivism You Use," Center for Evidence-Based Corrections, University of California-Irvine, September 2005

Prison Population Tops 2.2 Million Inmates

Nearly 2.3 million inmates were in custody in state and federal prisons and local jails in 2007. Slightly more than half were in state prisons, and about a third were in local jails.

Number of U.S. Inmates, December 2007

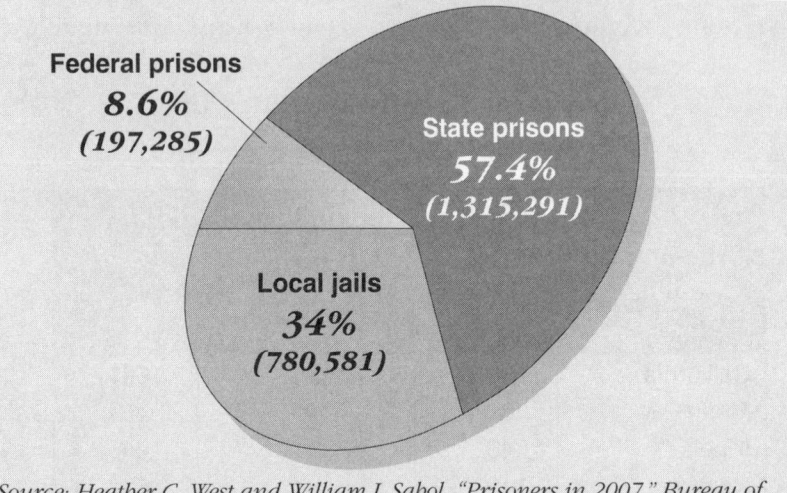

Federal prisons
8.6%
(197,285)

State prisons
57.4%
(1,315,291)

Local jails
34%
(780,581)

Source: Heather C. West and William J. Sabol, "Prisoners in 2007," Bureau of Justice Statistics, Dec. 31, 2008

Moreover, she adds, "The more dire the fiscal situation is, the more likely it is that [a state] government will take risks. In extremely difficult economic times, when prisons are overcrowded and incredibly expensive to run, so many people get incarcerated when they come out. Why? Because they don't have a job."

But Grieshaber, at the Michigan union for prison system employees, cites the state's 15.3 percent unemployment rate as a definitive obstacle to providing subsidized jobs. [19] "With this kind of unemployment, it's just impossible," he says.

Michigan's wide-ranging reentry program includes job-search assistance, Grieshaber notes. "But if anybody brought up subsidizing jobs — my goodness," he says. "You've already got people complaining about prisoners getting paid for working in the prisons."

Others also warn that the present bleak employment climate isn't the right political environment for a subsidized-jobs strategy. "There are people out of work who have never broken any law and aren't being offered that kind of job," Nolan of Prison Fellowship says.

But when the jobs picture improves, "I can see the advantage of a subsidized job," he says, especially for ex-prisoners with no formal employment experience who must learn to function in a workplace before they enter the labor market. "A lot of people have never had a job. A job teaches them discipline, showing up on time, to call if they're going to be late."

Others argue against subsidizing jobs. Montgomery County, Md., Corrections and Rehabilitation Director Art Wallenstein, an ardent reentry advocate, says a subsidized-jobs program would entangle his agency in political complications. "I don't want reentry to get bogged down on the issue of whether our unemployed are more valuable than your unem-

ployed," he says. "I can live without subsidized jobs."

Wallenstein isn't philosophically opposed to the subsidized-jobs strategy but argues that they're not essential. "I believe there are jobs out there," he says. "We can get offenders workforce-ready if we don't rely on magic but on tested, workforce-development programs that prepare people to engage in the job market. We don't need a leg up for offenders."

Do reentry programs significantly reduce recidivism?

Reentry programs have a major selling point: reducing recidivism. "The high recidivism rates that translate into thousands of new crimes each year could easily be averted through improved reentry efforts," New York City Mayor Michael Bloomberg told a Summit on Reentry and Employment held by the U.S. Conference of Mayors last year in New York.

"To keep inmates on the right path once they leave, we will link them to the benefits they need immediately upon release. They've paid their debt — but with no prospects, sadly, too many of them will return to jail. Let's help them build their future — which will help keep all of us safe." [20]

Experts readily acknowledge, however, that data is not yet available on which reentry strategies produce the best results. In Michigan, for instance, reentry program participants haven't been free long enough "to draw anything other than preliminary conclusions about recidivism findings," Dennis Schrantz, deputy director of the Michigan corrections department, told the House Appropriations Subcommittee on Commerce, Justice, Science and Related Agencies last March. [21]

But, in a sign of how the pendulum has swung from the days in which longer sentences were seen as the best approach to fighting crime, Schrantz also told lawmakers that the model of widespread and lengthy incarceration clearly was ineffective. "Prisoners who serve longer terms do not recidivate less frequently," he said. "Rearrest rates for former prisoners who serve one, two, three, four or five years in prison are nearly the same." [22]

However, so many politicians and policy experts are singing the praises of reentry that even some of those advocates worry that the concept could be dismissed as a fad, especially by prison system personnel.

"One of the problems we face with the corrections folks is that reentry has become the flavor of the month," says Nolan of Prison Fellowship. "They're basically tired of being guinea pigs. Frankly, reentry can mean all things to all people, so I can understand the jaundiced response."

"We want programs that work," says Grieshaber of the Michigan correction employees' union. "We're just suspicious that you don't get an honest evaluation when there are these massive budget pressures. We're kind of — 'Proceed with caution' on the whole thing."

More pointedly, Grieshaber questions whether politicians' recent call for greater emphasis on reentry is purely budget-driven. "If we didn't have these dramatic budget pressures, would we be letting all these prisoners out?" he asks. "A lot of us think the answer would be 'no.' "

But in Colorado, Attorney General John Suthers, a conservative Republican, argues that saving money by cutting recidivism is a worthwhile objective. "The vast majority of inmates going into prison every year are recidivists," he says. "If you can significantly reduce that, you can make tremendous savings."

Suthers acknowledges that recidivism declines are measured in small quantities. "Don't kid yourself — you're not going to reduce recidivism by 10 percent to 50 percent," he says. "But I do think 5 percent to 10 percent is possible, and well worth the effort."

AP Photo/*The Herald-Palladium*/John Madill

AP Photo/Steven Senne

Second Chances

Former inmate Tony Monk (top, foreground) landed a job at Regal Finishing in Coloma, Mich., after completing the state's Prisoner Reentry Initiative Program. He holds tractor headlight reflectors coated at the Regal plant. His boss, Jim Kodis, left, says Regal co-workers' support of Monk was critical to his success. Joshua Gomes (bottom) is a free man thanks to a new Rhode Island law that allows certain prisoners to get out early if they commit to rehabilitation programs. Gomes, 24, of Central Falls, R.I., went to prison after stealing a man's wallet and robbing a convenience store to feed his cocaine habit. He served about half of his two-year sentence.

Ordinary citizens might not consider that much of a drop. James M. Byrne, a professor of criminology at the University of Massachusetts, noted that although drug treatment, educational and other programs could cut "criminal behavior" by about 10 percent, bigger reductions would require social programs in "high-crime/poverty pocket" areas. [23]

"I suspect that the general public — already wary of the prospects for individual offender change — will be expecting a bit more for their investment in rehabilitation than marginal reductions in offender recidivism," Byrne told the House Appropriations subcommittee's March hearing on reentry programs.

Some optimists say the widespread emphasis on reentry programs could evolve into an approach with enormous potential. "The next frontier," says John Jay College president Travis, "is community-level intervention.

"People return to settings that are governed by institutions like family and peer groups and social interactions," he says. "Are they welcomed back home or shunned? Do we pay attention to the availability of positive peer group networks as opposed to the old gang on the corner?" ■

BACKGROUND

Crime Boom

Starting in the early 1970s, and fueled in the '80s by growing drug-related violence, the nation's crime rate skyrocketed, and fear of crime grew into a leading issue in cities and states — and eventually in Congress. [24]

After growing steadily throughout the 1960s, crime shot up in the '70s and '80s. By 1990, the violent crime rate had more than quadrupled —

from 160.9 per 100,000 population in 1960 to 731.8. [25]

During this period, harsh new anti-drug laws played a key role in boosting prison populations. In 1980, just 19,000 drug offenders were in state prisons and 4,900 in federal institutions. By 2003, state prisons held 250,900 drug offenders — 20 percent of the prisoner population, up from 6 percent in 1980. And drug offenders made up 55 percent of federal prisoners — up from 25 percent in 1980. [26]

Starting in the mid-1980s, a crack epidemic and the resulting massive government response played a role in filling the prisons. But the groundwork had been laid years before crack appeared on the scene. A new attitude about incarceration had replaced the old doctrine of rehabilitation, which held that psychological counseling and other prison programs could transform convicts into law-abiding citizens.

Academic research seemed to support the new view that rehabilitation didn't work and that prisons should punish rather than rehabilitate. Robert Martinson, an influential sociologist at City University of New York, wrote in 1974 that "with few and isolated exceptions, the rehabilitative efforts that have been reported so far have had no appreciable effect on recidivism." [27]

However, Martinson revised his sweeping conclusion four years later. In many cases psychological counseling in prison did keep recipients from returning to crime, he wrote in 1978. But by then Martinson's initial assessment had been embraced. And the idea that trying to rehabilitate lawbreakers was a waste of time fit in well with an increasingly popular view that criminals didn't need counseling — they needed to be locked up, and locked up longer.

In the 1970s, politicians of all ideological stripes were blaming the steady rise in crime on what they called a breakdown in the criminal justice system. One of Congress' leading liberals, Sen. Edward M. Kennedy, D-Mass., lent

his voice to the chorus — which also included Republican President Gerald R. Ford — demanding lengthier sentences.

" 'Revolving door' justice convinces the criminal that his chances of actually being caught, tried, convicted and jailed are too slim to be taken seriously," Kennedy wrote in an op-ed piece in *The New York Times* in 1975. "Our existing criminal justice system is no deterrent at all to violent crime in our society." [28]

Mandatory Minimums

Kennedy and many others pointed to laws throughout the country that mandated "indeterminate" sentences for specific crimes, such as prison terms of five to 15 years. Prison and parole authorities would decide when and if an inmate was rehabilitated enough to be released. [29]

But the approach was conditioned on the results of rehabilitative programs that were often shoddy and poorly financed. Conservatives viewed parole boards as irresponsible or naïve — falling for convicts' tales of reformation and letting hardened criminals back on the street.

Liberals, for their part, decried a system in which authorities had virtually total power to decide when a prisoner could be freed. The system lent itself to abuse, these critics said, especially since evaluating whether a prisoner had been rehabilitated was a highly subjective exercise.

By the time Kennedy called for a new system of "mandatory minimum" sentences, some states already had begun using that method, including New York. The state's so-called Rockefeller Drug Laws of 1973 had been championed by liberal-leaning Republican Gov. Nelson A. Rockefeller, who touted the harsh measures as a weapon against growing use of heroin.

The laws applied to all illegal drugs

Continued on p. 1016

Chronology

1970s-1980s
Escalating crime prompts many states and Congress to set harsh minimum sentences.

1970
Nation's violent crime rate more than doubles, jumping from 160.9 incidents per 100,000 population in 1960 to 363.5 per 100,000.

1973
New York state's "Rockefeller Drug Laws" establish long, fixed sentences for drug offenses.

1974
Influential study by sociologist Robert Martinson concludes that prison rehabilitation programs have "no appreciable effect on recidivism;" four years later, he reverses his conclusion.

1977
Liberal Sen. Edward M. Kennedy, D-Mass., introduces legislation mandating minimum sentences.

1983
All but two states have enacted mandatory minimum sentences.

1984
Congress passes Sentencing Reform Act, setting minimum sentences for a range of federal crimes.

1986
Crack cocaine epidemic coupled with intense media coverage prompts Congress to establish longer sentences for sales of crack than of powder cocaine.

1990s
Prison population booms, even as crime rates start falling.

1990
Federal and state prison population soars to more than 739,000 inmates, more than double the 1980 population of about 315,000.

1991
Sister of a man imprisoned for five years for growing marijuana starts Families Against Mandatory Minimums, which helps lead campaign to change sentencing laws. . . . Federal Judge J. Lawrence Irving of San Diego resigns to protest mandatory minimums.

1993
Violent-crime rate begins falling after years of steady increase.

1999
U.S. Attorney General Janet Reno calls for the criminal justice system to help ex-inmates reenter society.

2000s
Prison system costs and high recidivism rates prompt some states to expand reentry programs; President George W. Bush prods Congress to pass Second Chance Act with funding for reentry projects.

2002
Major Justice Department recidivism study finds that 67 percent of ex-prisoners in 15 biggest states are rearrested within three years, and 47 percent are convicted of new crimes and sent back to prison. . . . National Institute of Drug Abuse official says there is no physiological difference between the effects of crack cocaine and cocaine powder.

2003
Justice Department keeps focus on recidivism and soaring prison population with announcement that federal and state prisons and local jails hold more than 2 million people.

2004
Violent crime rate drops to 463 incidents per 100,000 population, from 747 per 100,000 in 1993. . . . President Bush calls America "the land of the second chance" and advocates federal support for reentry programs.

2005
New York legislature authorizes (but doesn't require) judges to lower some Rockefeller Drug Law sentences — to 12 to 24 years for selling 3 oz. of crack cocaine, for instance, from the former mandatory 25 years to life.

2007
Number of prisoners released from federal and state prisons reaches more than 725,000. . . . Texas legislature rejects prison-construction plan in favor of spending on parole supervision and alternatives to incarceration.

2008
Bush signs Second Chance Act. . . . Total state spending to operate prisons rises to $47 billion, even as some states cut prison costs.

2009
Justice Department awards $28 million in Second Chance Act grants to programs across the country. . . . Senate and House committees hold hearings on strengthening reentry programs. . . . Two-thirds of ex-prisoners in California are reincarcerated for parole violations, according to new recidivism study. . . . Plan to cut California's prison population proposes new parole standards to avoid reincarceration. . . . Michigan expands statewide reentry program, pursues plans to close eight prisons.

Halfway House Puts Focus on Jobs

"If you want to change your life, this is where you can do it at."

Making pizzas for slightly more than minimum wage — it's not a job that puts a spring in the step of a middle-aged man who has lived the life of a drug dealer.

"It's a humbling experience, to say the least," says the man, a resident at the Montgomery County Pre-Release Center (PRC), a halfway house in the Washington suburb of Rockville, Md. "The money I make in a week, I used to make that in a couple of hours."

The man, who asks to be called Mr. Nolton, tends to think carefully before he speaks. A couple of decades cycling in and out of jail and prison make you cautious, he explains. "Most of my adult life has been drug sales and incarceration," he says. "Pretty much, I'm at the end of my rope, in the sense that I would like to have something wholesome in my life as well as make my family proud, and try to make the best of whatever 'normal' life is."

Mr. Nolton is fairly typical of the older residents at PRC, who are accepted in the final four to six months of their sentences. Although Maryland state prison inmates and some federal prisoners are allowed to apply, Montgomery County jail inmates make up the majority of the approximately 170 residents at the center, most of whom have been incarcerated previously. The center sits

A sculpture captures the mission of the Montgomery County Pre-Release Center: Lunchbox in hand, a former prisoner kisses his wife good-bye as he goes to work.

CQ Press/Peter Katel

just a block from the shopping centers and restaurants of bustling Rockville Pike. The nicely landscaped building looks like a small office and bears no identification as an outpost of the Montgomery County Correction and Rehabilitation Department.

"The population here is exactly representative of the population of the jail," says Director Stefan LoBuglio. PRC staff evaluate applicants for potential danger to the community, but the center is willing to accept people with long criminal records if there is evidence they can be trusted to stay out of trouble.

Founded in 1969 and well-known to advocates of prisoner reentry programs, the center emphasizes the practical in getting its residents — don't call them inmates — ready for the outside world. They start off living in two-person rooms, not cells or dormitories, and residents can earn their way up a waiting list for a single room with private bathroom by following rules, which include looking for a job every day until finding one.

To be sure, staff members wear badges on their belts, unauthorized departure is classified as escape and residents are tested for alcohol three times a day and for drugs three times a week. But such restrictions come off as fairly mild to people whose days were filled until recently with the sounds of cell doors clanking, and with outdoor views of fences and barbed wire.

Continued from p. 1014

— cocaine as well as heroin (marijuana was removed from the list in 1977). Judges were required to impose sentences of 15 years to life for anyone convicted of selling two ounces of a drug, or possessing four ounces (amounts were later changed). The laws triggered a sixfold increase in the state prison population, from about 10,000 inmates in 1973 to more than 61,000 in 1992. By 1997, about a third of New York prisoners had been sentenced on drug charges — up from 9 percent in 1980. [30]

As criticism of "indeterminate" laws mounted, Congress spent years devising ways to assure standardized sentences in federal court, so that two people convicted for the same crime before different judges would receive equal punishment. A 1977 measure sponsored by Kennedy also would have restricted parole. Congress took no action on the bill. [31]

The 1980 election of conservative Republican President Ronald W. Reagan reenergized the movement to toughen federal sentencing. In 1984, Congress passed the Sentencing Re-

form Act (SRA), which ordered judges to follow a series of "mandatory minimum" sentences for some crimes involving drugs and firearms. Additional minimum sentences were added later for other crimes. And the law abolished parole for all offenders serving time in federal prisons who had been convicted of federal crimes committed after Nov. 1, 1987.

"The SRA and the guidelines make rehabilitation a lower priority than other sentencing goals," said a history published by the U.S. Sentencing Commission, which the law established. [32]

Above all, while prisons and jails are designed mainly to keep their populations locked up, the PRC's main mission is to help residents get out of jail and stay out — by helping them find jobs. Because today's job-application process has become virtually totally Web-centric, all residents have access to computers — restricted to job searches — and are required to obtain free Hotmail e-mail addresses — to make monitoring easier.

Residents at the Montgomery County center can use computers only for job searches. Computer training and help with résumé writing are also available.

Residents who need computer training get instructions in Web navigation and associated skills. Those who need help in regaining their driver's licenses can call on PRC staff for that as well.

And the center offers guidance in résumé-writing. "We have a lady who comes in on Wednesday," Work Release Coordinator Hillel Raskas tells a class of new arrivals. "She can make a résumé for anybody."

Raskas hands out a sample résumé that lists a "Career Exploration Certificate" from the Maryland Education Department at Jessup, Md. That's the location of a state prison, but leaving out that bit of information is all right, he says. He adds, though, that when an application asks about a criminal record, fill in the correct information. "Write, 'Will explain in interview.' Do not lie, do not leave it blank."

Some lucky residents have former jobs to go back to. One young man is expecting to return to a catering business. Another,

also barely out of his teens, said a cousin had arranged a supermarket job.

On a recent afternoon, a resident in his 20s walks into Unit Manager Chris Johnson's office and tells her with a big smile that he's landed a job after six weeks of looking — a $10-an-hour gig in a call center. "I probably could have gotten a job quicker if I didn't set my sights so high," he says. His ambition was understandable. Before he was sentenced to about five years on a drug conviction, he had been a computer engineering student.

Was his criminal record a problem in landing the job? "No, they're understaffed and overloaded," he tells Johnson. Still, she calls to verify the job offer and to make sure the employer knows of the young man's conviction. Everything checks out, and within days the man starts working.

While Mr. Nolton admits he does get a bit weary of the rules, he acknowledges that he owes a lot to the PRC. For one thing, the center banks his earnings, so he expects to have about $500 saved up by the time his sentence is up in five months. So he'll be able to rent a studio apartment.

"This place is really based on the individual," he says. "If you want to change your life and you want a good way back into the community, this is where you can do it at."

— Peter Katel

The law-and-order trend was reinforced in the mid- and late-1980s after crack cocaine arrived on the scene. The cheap, smokable form of cocaine spawned a crime wave in the nation's inner cities as dealers fought for turf and addicts committed crimes. But mass-media reports supported the then widely accepted notion that crack's chemical properties triggered greater violence than other drugs.

Acting on that belief, Congress passed a 1986 law imposing a mandatory sentence of five years for selling five grams of crack (the weight of two pennies) — the same penalty imposed

for selling 500 grams (about a pound) of powder cocaine. And someone convicted of selling 11 lbs. of powder cocaine got the same sentence as a person convicted of selling less than 2 oz. of crack — 10 years. [33]

Nearly two decades later, the view of crack as especially associated with violence still held sway in some law-enforcement circles. In 2002, Deputy Attorney General Larry D. Thompson told the U.S. Sentencing Commission that crack was more addictive than powder cocaine. [34] But Glenn Hanson, the acting director of the National

Institute on Drug Abuse, testified that crack and powered cocaine's had precisely the same physiological effects. [35]

Incarceration Boom

The Sentencing Reform Act ensured that more federal offenders were serving time and for longer sentences. By 2002, 86 percent of federal offenders were sent to prison — up from 69 percent in 1987 — and time served doubled from about 25 to 50 months. [36]

Reentry Experts Try to Answer '$64,000 Question'

"We still have much to learn about what works."

Advocates of reentry programs don't promise miracles — they know that reentry is a game of inches. In New York, an unspectacular-sounding 5.7 percent fewer ex-prisoners who participated in a reentry program sponsored by the Center for Employment Opportunities (CEO) were rearrested than ex-prisoners who didn't participate. [1]

That might strike a layman as a small-bore result. But Dan Bloom, who directed the CEO evaluation for MDRC, a social-policy research organization, and is running a bigger analysis of job-focused reentry programs in four Midwestern cities, calls the statistic "promising," noting that, "A 5 percent difference is what you tend to see in social programs."

In addition, he says, because the cost of keeping a prisoner incarcerated is quite high, "You don't need a big difference in recidivism to potentially save a lot of money." A cost-benefit analysis of the CEO results is under way.

The data Bloom is collecting ultimately may help answer questions about the most effective ways to help ex-prisoners. "There is so little [data] out there," Amy L. Solomon, a senior research associate at the Urban Institute's Justice Policy Center, recently told the Senate Subcommittee on Crime and Drugs. "We still have much to learn about what works." [2]

Criminal-justice specialists have been acknowledging as much for some time. "The $64,000 question still remains: Which programs should government agencies, nonprofit organizations and faith-based communities invest in?" wrote Joan Petersilia, a professor at Stanford University Law School and a noted expert on probation and parole systems. [3]

Criminal-justice system veterans, however, have learned to temper expectations. "Programs can't replace good parenting," says Colorado Attorney General John Suthers, former director of the state's prison system. He argues that recidivism reductions of 5 to 10 percent — though a worthwhile achievement — represent the limit of what reentry programs can achieve.

"If you want to look at a profile of America's prison population," Suthers says, "you can talk about minorities, drug problems, but the single defining characteristic is that two-thirds of them grew up in a home where they lived with their natural father." But for those who came from broken homes and didn't get solid early education, "It's too late for those guys," he says.

Suthers is a conservative Republican, but his conclusion is widely shared across the ideological spectrum.

But some still argue that more than modest results can be expected from reentry programs. "If we could implement effective programs for all returning prisoners, with all the resources needed, we could expect recidivism reductions of about 15-20 percent," said Jeremy Travis, president of John Jay College of Criminal Justice in New York City and a leading advocate of expanding reentry services. [4]

Whether the expectations are high or low, lawmakers — who control most program funding — demand statistics. In Michigan, which has one of the country's most comprehensive programs — the Michigan Prisoner ReEntry Initiative (MPRI) — administrators know better data is needed. "We cannot yet establish an empirical link between observed outcomes and MPRI processes, activities and spending," Dennis Schrantz, the state's deputy director of corrections, told a House subcommittee in March. [5]

On a more positive note, Schrantz said results thus far suggest MPRI is "contributing significantly to observed differences in outcomes, even though we cannot yet establish the causal links." [6]

State lawmakers were moving to the same beat: By 1983 48 states had enacted mandatory-minimum sentencing laws, and at least five had eliminated parole. By 1994, 11 states had enacted "three strikes" laws imposing life sentences with no parole for people convicted of a third felony (in some cases, a third violent felony). [37]

As the wave of get-tough laws washed over the country, the handful of critics decrying the social and economic effects of driving up imprisonment got little support. "Many states realize corrections costs are out of control, and they're looking for ways to save money," Alvin J. Bronstein, director of the American Civil Liberties Union's National Prison Project, said in 1994. "But at the same time they're talking about 'three strikes and you're out,' treating juveniles as adults and jamming through other laws that will jack up [prison] costs." [38]

In fact, an unprecedented expansion of prison systems was occurring across the country. In the 1980s, the federal and state prison population more than doubled, from 315,974 to 739,980; by 2000 it was more than 1 million. For the entire 20-year period, the nation saw a 318 percent increase in the number of people incarcerated. [39] To keep up, the number of state prisons rose from 592 in 1974 to 1,023 — a 73 percent increase. [40]

As the size of the incarcerated population kept expanding, critics tried repeatedly to mobilize opposition to the trend. "While there is surprising agreement within the criminal justice community that we lock up too many people and that we keep them in prison far too long, the United States seems to be on the verge of embarking on the most extensive prison construction program in the history

For example, Schrantz noted, the number of parolees sent back to prison for new crimes dropped to 98 per 1,000, the lowest rate in four years; the number of prisoners returned to prison for "technical" parole violations dropped to 89 per 1,000, the lowest level since 1992; and increases in the overall prison population fell to an average of 150 new prisoners a year from 2003-2007, in contrast to annual average growth of 1,925 prisoners from 1984-2002. [7]

Statistics also are important for ferreting out the approaches that actually may do more harm than good. Counterintuitively, programs that deal exclusively with nonviolent, first-time offenders are especially risky, says Michael Thompson, director of the Council of State Governments' Justice Center.

"Take a 40-year-old guy busted for writing bad checks, who has a fairly stable home life and a job — and a drinking problem," Thompson says. "The reentry program says, 'I'm going to put you in intensive alcohol treatment and make sure your parole officer visits you often. So the guy's got to leave his job to go to the parole office, and the parole officer visits his job site, and the guy gets fired. So he's back in the bar drinking. If we'd left him alone, he probably would have been fine."

Even as politicians and policy makers hunger for data, some experts have been urging researchers to expand their research

Stanford University Law School Professor Joan Petersilia calls for more evaluations of reentry programs.

goals beyond recidivism. Statistics should try to measure the extent of social reintegration, argued Petersilia. "For example, evaluations should measure whether clients are working, whether that work is full- or part time and whether the income derived is supporting families," she wrote. "We should measure whether programs increase client sobriety and attendance at treatment programs. We should track whether programs help convicts become involved in community activities, in a church, or in ex-convict support groups or victim sensitivity sessions." [8]

— Peter Katel

[1] Data furnished by MDRC.

[2] Testimony before hearing on "The First Line of Defense: Reducing Recidivism at the Local Level," Senate Judiciary Subcommittee on Crime and Drugs, Nov. 5, 2009, Webcast available at http://judiciary.senate.gov/about/sub committees/crime.cfm.

[3] Joan Petersilia, "What Works in Prisoner Reentry? Reviewing and Questioning the Evidence," *Federal Probation*, September 2004, www.uscourts.gov/fedprob/September_2004/whatworks.html.

[4] Testimony before hearing on "Successful Prisoner Reentry," House Appropriations Subcommittee on Commerce, Justice, Science, and Related Agencies," March 12, 2009.

[5] Testimony before hearing on "Innovative Prisoner Reentry Programs," House Appropriations Subcommittee on Commerce, Justice, Science, and Related Agencies, March 11, 2009.

[6] *Ibid.*

[7] *Ibid.*

[8] Petersilia, *op. cit.*

of the world," journalist Michael Specter wrote in 1982 in *The Nation*, a left-liberal magazine. [41]

In 1986, a group of lawyers founded The Sentencing Project, a Washington-based advocacy and research organization, which lobbied to eliminate mandatory-minimum sentences as well as the disparity between crack and powder cocaine sentences.

Eventually, a few members of the law-enforcement community began speaking out against the toughened sentencing laws, especially those applying to drug offenses. "You've got murderers who get out sooner than

some kid who did some stupid thing with drugs," said U.S. District Judge J. Lawrence Irving of San Diego, who was appointed to the bench by President Ronald Reagan in 1982 and resigned in 1991 rather than continue to hand down mandatory sentences. "These sentences are Draconian. It's a tragedy." [42]

But the prevailing law-enforcement view in the 1990s was summed up by Paul McNulty, then a spokesman for the First Freedom Coalition, which advocated tough drug laws, and later a deputy attorney general in the George W. Bush administration. "You can't get convicted [under] a drug law

unless you knew what you were doing," McNulty said in 1993. "After everything this country has been through with drug trafficking, it's very hard for people to look at these supposedly sympathetic cases and say, 'Gee, we feel sorry for you.'" [43]

Reentry Reality

As the debate over sentencing and incarceration policies sharpened during the 1990s, little attention was paid to the fact that eventually nearly all prisoners are released. Only when

U.S. Attorney General Reno raised the issue in 1999 did the question of how to reduce recidivism begin getting sustained attention.

"Too often, offenders leave prison and return to the community without supervision, without jobs, without housing," Reno said. "They quickly fall back into their old patterns of drug usage, gang activities and other crimes." [44]

Borrowing from the "drug court" model that began in Miami when she was chief prosecutor there, Reno proposed that state and local governments set up "reentry courts." She envisioned judges approving reentry plans for individual ex-prisoners and monitoring progress along the lines of a parole system." [45]

The court idea didn't spread widely. But Reno's proposal helped intensify the growing concern over the massive incarceration expansion that had been under way for more than two decades.

The fact that crime was going down perhaps helped to shift attitudes. The violent crime rate plummeted from 747 crimes per 100,000 in 1993 to 454 in 2008. [46]

Amid the crime downturn came the startling news in 2003 that the nation's prison and jail population had passed the 2 million mark — the world's highest. "When violent crime rates were higher, many politicians were afraid to be seen as soft on crime," *The New York Times* said in an editorial. "But now that crime has receded and the public is more worried about taxes and budget deficits, it would not require extraordinary courage for elected officials to do the right thing and scale back our overuse of jails and prison cells." [47]

In the following years, nearly half the states softened sentencing laws or probation-parole policies, mostly by diverting nonviolent drug offenders to non-prison treatment programs, expanding alternatives to incarceration for nonviolent offenders and reducing time

served behind bars while expanding probation and parole supervision. [48]

Meanwhile, matters took an unexpected turn at the federal level. Activists who had been advocating federal support for state reentry programs had concluded that the George W. Bush administration, out of an ideological distrust for alternatives to incarceration and preoccupation with war and terrorism, would not support reentry programs. But in his 2004 State of the Union address, Bush said, referring to the 600,000 prisoners expected to be released that year: "If they can't find work or a home or help, they are much more likely to commit crime and return to prison." [49]

Bush proposed a $300 million "reentry initiative" to expand job training and placement, provide temporary housing and connect newly released prisoners to mentors to help guide them after incarceration. Support from the president and other conservative Republicans was critical to the passage of the Second Chance Act of 2007. The bipartisan alliance that pushed the bill through Congress included prison-reform advocates such as former National Institute of Justice director Travis and the Prison Fellowship's Nolan. Many religious conservatives, who counted Bush as an ally, saw a spiritual reason to give offenders a second chance.

House and Senate versions were sponsored by bipartisan groups that included Sens. Sam Brownback, R-Kan., and Patrick Leahy, D-Vt., and Reps. Danny Davis, D-Ill., and Chris Cannon, R-Utah. Nevertheless, the bill didn't make its way to Bush's desk until 2008, among other reasons because Sen. Tom Coburn, R-Okla., put a "hold" on it in 2006, stopping its progress in the Senate for a time. He said he supported the legislation but argued that other federal programs served the same purpose. In fiscal 2008-2009, Congress appropriated $25 million for Second Chance Act grants and pilot projects across the country. [50] ■

CURRENT SITUATION

Upgrading Skills

Even as reentry advocates fight to spread basic programs around the country, some in the movement are starting to expand their goals.

In New York, a program is trying to take ex-prisoners beyond the world of low-paid, entry-level jobs. "I don't think anybody knows more than we do at the CEO how hard it is to get folks that first full-time job when they get out of prison, but it's not enough," says Center for Employment Opportunities executive director Tarlow. "People need to develop real careers and career pathways."

The CEO is in the second year of a fledgling program designed to open doors to high-paid, skilled trades, such as electrical work, plumbing and refrigeration. Criminal records aren't a bar to employment in those industries, as a rule. But trade school graduation is a prerequisite. Getting into trade school means passing tests, which can be an obstacle for people whose reading and math skills typically top out at middle-school levels.

That's where the CEO Academy comes in. Open to CEO participants working at entry-level jobs, the academy holds weeknight and Saturday classes in reading and math — geared toward helping participants pass trade-school entrance exams.

But it's a tough slog. The first 12-week class began with 35 participants. By the end of the session only 13 students remained. Eventually, 11 students entered trade school, and nine finished.

"Nothing is a slam dunk," says Marta Nelson, CEO's director of policy

Continued on p. 1022

At Issue:

Can reentry and rehabilitation programs reduce recidivism?

JEREMY TRAVIS
PRESIDENT, JOHN JAY COLLEGE OF CRIMINAL JUSTICE

FROM TESTIMONY BEFORE HOUSE APPROPRIATIONS SUBCOMMITTEE ON COMMERCE, JUSTICE, SCIENCE AND RELATED AGENCIES, MARCH 12, 2009

*t*he challenge we face is daunting: to make significant reductions in [the] very high rate of rearrest. The rate of failure — as defined by rearrest — is significantly higher in the initial months following release. If the risk of failure is highest in the first six months, then we should devote our efforts and resources to reducing the rate of failure in those months. It's a very simple but revolutionary concept: We align our resources to match the risk.

We know far more than we did a few decades ago about program effectiveness. Research allows us to see the potential for measurable reductions in recidivism. In fact, according to the best estimates of researchers in this field, if we could implement effective programs for all returning prisoners, with all the resources needed, we could expect recidivism reductions of about 15-20 percent. And, we can also state with great confidence that these investments would be cost-effective: They would pay for themselves by reducing future criminal justice and corrections costs.

We should not be satisfied with these results. In my opinion, we can only achieve results that match the magnitude of the reentry phenomenon if we recognize that our approach has been too timid. We have been constrained by a medical model that focuses on individual-level interventions, rather than also embracing an ecological model that focuses simultaneously on the community context within which individuals are struggling to thrive after prison. The next chapter of innovation in this area should test ideas that attempt to change the environment to which individuals return home.

Around the country, there are a number of demonstration projects that are testing a very new reentry model — a community-based approach to reentry. Recognizing that some communities are experiencing very high rates of incarceration and reentry, these projects approach reentry as a community phenomenon. These programs create coalitions of community organizations to interact with every person returning home from prison. They attempt to create a different climate in the neighborhood, one promoting successful reintegration.

These demonstration efforts represent a new frontier in reentry innovation. They do not focus exclusively on individual-level interventions. Rather, they create a coalition of support for individuals returning from prisons and jails, bring together law enforcement and community leaders, communicate clearly about the consequences of illegal behavior and provide a clear pathway out of a life of antisocial conduct.

JAMES M. BYRNE
PROFESSOR, DEPARTMENT OF CRIMINAL JUSTICE AND CRIMINOLOGY, UNIVERSITY OF MASSACHUSETTS

FROM TESTIMONY BEFORE HOUSE APPROPRIATIONS SUBCOMMITTEE ON COMMERCE, JUSTICE, SCIENCE AND RELATED AGENCIES, MARCH 12, 2009

*r*ehabilitation is back in vogue in the United States. Individual-offender rehabilitation is being presented to the public at large — and to federal and state policy makers — as the single-most-effective crime-control strategy. The argument is simple, seductive and not all that offender-friendly: Don't provide convicted offenders with treatment because it will help them as individuals. We need to provide rehabilitation because the provision of rehabilitation has been demonstrated to significantly reduce the likelihood of re-offending, which makes us — and our communities — safer. We are doing it for ourselves and our communities.

Some would argue that this represents one of the big lies of individual-offender rehabilitation, because even significant reductions in the recidivism [rate] in this country will not likely change the crime rates of most communities, because [ex-] offenders do not live — in large numbers — in most communities. They live in a small number of high crime/poverty pocket neighborhoods in a handful of states. Since residents of these communities do not have the social capital to adequately address the long-standing problems found in high-risk, poverty pocket areas, the prospects for community change are bleak.

We do know that traditional probation and parole programs are not as effective today as they were 30 years ago; we just don't know why. Any serious discussion of new strategies for addressing the prison reentry problem must begin with an examination of the reasons why these programs are ineffective.

Although the reported [results] for prison treatment and programs are modest (a 10 percent reduction in recidivism upon release using standard follow-up measures), there is reason to anticipate improvements in these effects in prison systems designed to focus on offender change rather than short-term offender control.

I suspect that the general public — already wary of the prospects for individual-offender change — will be expecting a bit more for their investment in rehabilitation than marginal reductions in offender recidivism. If we cannot demonstrate the link between participation in the next generation of individual-offender rehabilitation programs and community protection, then support for rehabilitation, tenuous at best, will quickly dissipate. While the general public appears to believe in the possibility of individual-offender change, I think you will find that most of us are skeptical about the probability of individual-offender change, particularly among individuals with serious substance-abuse and/or mental health problems.

Continued from p. 1020

and planning, who directs the program. Setbacks that have forced students out of the program, she says, include the shock of doing classroom work after many years out of school, health problems and rearrests — sometimes for something as simple as "leaving the state to visit a son and violating parole."

However, the second academy class of 62 had 42 graduates, and 31 were expected to graduate from trade school in late November. The program is now recruiting for a third class of 100.

So far, two trade-school graduates have landed skilled jobs with contractors. But CEO expects that number to go up now that a full-time employment counselor has been hired for the program.

CEO may be in a better position than most reentry programs to move ex-prisoners beyond the low-wage job scene. Established in the late 1970s as a project of the Washington-based Vera Institute of Justice, the organization has been on its own since 1996, funded by foundation grants and government contracts.

As participants work in their subsidized jobs, CEO helps them find work in the open economy. "We focus on small- to medium-size businesses that don't have human-resources departments, and act as their HR department," Tarlow says. "Say they want to hire a person off the street who doesn't have a felony conviction. They'd have to do a background check; it costs them to advertise. With

Inmates are stacked three-high in a gymnasium at Mule Creek State Prison in Ione, Calif. A panel of federal judges recently ordered California to reduce its prison population over two years from 150,000 to about 115,000. All California prisoners must be released on parole, so parole officers have little time to supervise or assist prisoners. Thousands of parolees a year are sent back to prison for parole violations.

Getty Images/Justin Sullivan

us, I'm saying right up front that my client has a felony conviction, but I'm telling you this person is working right now; I've got his attendance record right in front of me. And in the worst-case scenario, if it doesn't work out, I'll send you another person the next day."

California Meltdown

The country's biggest prison system has become the national example for what not to do when a state runs out of money to keep expanding incarceration.

The situation in California shows states "what will happen if they ignore the problem or say, 'There's not much we can do,' " says Michael Thompson, director of the Council of State Governments' National Justice Center, which advises states on reentry.

In mid-November, in the latest installment of a long-running crisis and legal battle, Gov. Arnold Schwarzenegger's administration finally came up with a plan to reduce the state's prison population over two years from 150,000 to about 115,000 — or 137 percent of the prisons' 84,000 capacity. [51] The reduction was ordered by a panel of federal judges. [52]

The bulging population partly reflects the state's overwhelmed parole system. California is one of a handful of states that require all prisoners to be released on parole, effectively swamping parole officers who have little time to supervise or assist prisoners. Consequently, thousands of parolees a year are sent back to prison for violating the terms of their release. But with reentry services facing severe budgetary pressures, even more released prisoners may end up back behind bars. (*See chart, p. 1011.*)

California's Division of Adult Probation Operations, which runs reentry services, expects to lose $41 million in funding, which director Robert Ambroselli said will be accomplished by delaying the activation of new reentry program sites, but no closures of current programs. "However . . . the implementation of other new programs is not being considered at this time," he pointed out. [53]

Existing programs — which help with housing, drug counseling and job searches — served about 18,449 parolees in California during the first nine months of 2009.

Though those services won't be expanded, a new state plan will exempt "low-level, lower-risk offenders" from being placed on active parole, which will reduce the number of offenders returning to prison for parole violations, according to the state Corrections and Rehabilitation Department. [54]

But the new plan apparently didn't resolve the political conflict over criminal-justice policy that accompanied the steady expansion of the prison population. Schwarzenegger will propose legislation next year that lawmakers rejected in 2009, which would — among other things — raise the threshold for grand theft from $400 to $950, allowing people convicted of stealing less to be sent to jail instead of prison. Those proposals prompted Republican Assemblyman Jim Nielsen to call the plan an "egregious compromise of justice." He wants the state to build more prisons. [55]

Meanwhile, a Democratic lawmaker has proposed changing the sentencing guidelines. And state Sen. Mark Leno, a Democrat from the San Francisco Bay Area, complained that the plan calls for 2,400 new prison beds and transferring 5,000 inmates to privately owned prisons.

"Building new beds doesn't address the problem that caused the symptom," he said. [56] ∎

OUTLOOK

Change in Tone

T he growing emphasis on reentry is changing the tone and substance of the long-polarized criminal-justice policy debate. Conservatives typically have insisted on locking up criminals for longer sentences, while liberals generally oppose mass incarceration and focus on social inequities that influence most offenders' backgrounds.

Traces of that debate certainly remain, but the focus has shifted to questions on how to boost reentry programs by, among other things, improving prisoners' and ex-prisoners' skills and expanding parole supervision to include reentry assistance.

"I won't say that reentry will be a well-oiled machine, but it will be a significant part of the rehabilitation process," says Florida state Sen. Crist, a Republican. For one thing, he predicts, the economy will need more of the kinds of labor ex-prisoners can provide.

"[With] the United States getting tougher on immigration, there's going to be a significant reduction of entry-level workers for jobs that most Americans don't want to do," Crist says. "And with technology advancing and more people in the educational system and moving toward higher-paying opportunities, there's going to be a need for construction, lawn care and restaurant workers — all these things have to be done by somebody."

At the policy end, however, officials must decide which reentry methods work best. "Right now is the crossroads," says Thompson, of the Council of State Governments' Justice Center. "The federal government is making a significant investment in testing and promoting certain reentry strategies, and states are deciding whether to scale back or build in some of these areas."

Meanwhile, he adds, "Corrections professionals recognize that if they don't generate the gains that leaders in the field said were possible, they'll have missed the key window of opportunity. And if they close the window, they'll exacerbate the prison-population problem."

Nolan of Prison Fellowship acknowledges that when ex-prisoners commit crimes it poses setbacks for reentry programs. "Things like that hurt the movement," he says.

Overall, however, Nolan is confident the reentry movement will lower recidivism. "Jesus wouldn't call us to something ineffective," he says.

However, an advocate of lowering the reliance on prison warns that reentry programs probably won't make a major dent in the national prison population. "It's slowly starting to shift," says Marc Mauer, executive director of the Sentencing Project, "but the scale is so enormous that it will take a much more substantial policy shift to turn things around. There's no reason to expect a change in the next five years."

And prison staffers are still skeptical about reentry programs. "Our guys are saying lots of bad characters are getting released," says Grieshaber of the Michigan corrections workers' union. "That's our bias. But we're holding our breath hoping we don't have a lot of bad things happening out there. I'm not talking about one dramatic thing — that can happen. I'm talking about an aggregation of events, where after a year or two you say, 'Oh, my God.' "

Skeptics are still to be found in the policy world as well. "I would suspect that the number of people released from prison will continue to be high," says Mulhausen of the Heritage Foundation. "Reentry is now the buzzword. In 10 years we'll probably be talking about a whole new thing."

But, in a sign of how the reentry movement has created a change in tone, Mulhausen adds, "I'm willing to admit that some things work, but they often don't work spectacularly well. We should do these programs, but they're not the magic bullet."

Still, some veterans of the prisoner reentry world are confident that prospects for improvement are excellent.

Tarlow of the Center for Employment Opportunities draws a connection between the reentry movement and the welfare reform law of 1996. The act forced mothers on public assistance into the workforce, in theory setting a better role model for their children. [57] The next step, she says, is to examine the effects on children of having their fathers incarcerated.

"People have come to realize that children have two parents, and that the father often has a connection to the criminal justice system," Tarlow says. "I believe that 10 years from now, this burgeoning movement about the importance of young men, who are fathers, coming home from jail and prison and needing work will really take hold," she says. "I think you're going to see an easier path from prison to work." [58] ∎

Notes

[1] Heather C. West and William J. Sabol, "Prisoners in 2007," Bureau of Justice Statistics, Department of Justice, updated May 12, 2009, www.ojp.usdoj.gov/bjs/pub/pdf/p07.pdf. Pre-2000 statistics furnished by Bureau of Justice Statistics (not available online).

[2] Christine S. Scott-Hayward, "The Fiscal Crisis in Corrections: Rethinking Policies and Practices," Vera Institute of Justice, July 2009, p. 3, www.vera.org/files/The-fiscal-crisis-in-corrections_July-2009.pdf.

[3] Amy L. Solomon, et al., "From Prison to Work: The Employment Dimensions of Prisoner Reentry," Urban Institute, Justice Policy Center, 2004, p. 8, www.urban.org/Uploaded PDF/411097_From_Prison_to_Work.pdf.

[4] Jim Suhr, "States target prisons for cuts, raising worries," The Associated Press, July 28, 2009; "The Michigan Prisoner ReEntry Initiative Progress Snapshot," March 2009, www.fce.msu.edu/Family_Impact_Seminars/pdf/FIS-Spring2009/Family_Impact_Seminar_MPRI_Snapshot_030809.pdf.

[5] Jamal Thalji, "Legislators Look West for Prison Solution," St. Petersburg Times, Nov. 18, 2009, p. B1; "Justice Reinvestment in Texas," Council of State Governments Justice Center, April 2009, http://justicereinvestment.org/states/texas/pub maps-tx.

[6] Bob Egelko, "State submits plan to reduce prison population," San Francisco Chronicle, Nov. 13, 2009, www.sfgate.com/cgi-bin/article. cgi?f=/c/a/2009/11/12/MNMV1AJNHV.DTL; "Defendants' Response to Three-Judge Court's Oct. 21, 2009 Order," Case3:01-cv-01351-TEH Document2274, Nov. 12, 2009, www.cdcr.ca.gov/News/2009_Press_Releases/docs/11-12_Filed-Stamped_Filing.pdf.

[7] "Successful Prisoner Reentry," House Appropriations Committee, Subcommittee on Commerce, Justice, Science and Related Agencies, March 12, 2009.

[8] "Remarks as Prepared for Delivery by Attorney General Eric Holder," July 9, 2009, www.justice.gov/ag/speeches/2009/ag-speech-0907 09.html.

[9] "State of the Union Address," Miller Center of Public Affairs, University of Virginia, Jan. 20, 2004, http://millercenter.org/scripps/archive/speeches/detail/4542.

[10] Caroline Wolf Harlow, "Education and Correctional Populations," Bureau of Justice Statistics, U.S. Justice Department, January 2003, www.ojp.usdoj.gov/bjs/pub/pdf/ecp.pdf.

[11] James J. Stephan, "State Prison Expenditures, 2001," Bureau of Justice Statistics, U.S. Justice Department, June 2004, www.ojp.gov/bjs/pub/pdf/spe01.pdf.

[12] Ryken Grattet, et al., "Parole Violations and Revocations in California: Analysis and Suggestions for Action," Federal Probation, June 2009, pp. 2-4, http://ucicorrections.seweb.uci.edu/sites/ucicorrections.seweb.uci.edu/files/Parole%20Violations%20and%20Revocations%20in%20CA.pdf.

[13] Jennifer Warren, "He found a calling in prison," Los Angeles Times, July 5, 2007, p. A1.

[14] Ryan S. King, et al., "Incarceration and Crime: A Complex Relationship," Sentencing Project, 2005, pp. 3-4, www.sentencingproject.org/doc/publications/inc_iandc_complex.pdf.

[15] Solomon, et al., op. cit.

[16] Ibid.

[17] Christy Visher, et al., "Employment After Prison: A Longitudinal Study of Releasees in Three States," Urban Institute, Justice Policy Center, October 2008, www.urban.org/Uploaded PDF/411778_employment_after_prison.pdf.

[18] "Transitional Jobs Reentry Demonstration," The Joyce Foundation, July 2009, www.mdrc.org/publications/522/policybrief.pdf.

[19] "Michigan Unemployment Rate (Seasonally Adjusted)," September 2009, Michigan.gov, www.milmi.org.

[20] Kathy Amoroso, "Mayors Highlight Innovative Strategies for Aiding Prisoner Reentry at National Summit," United States Conference of Mayors, March 10, 2008, http://usmayors.org/usmayornewspaper/documents/03_10_08/pg14_prisoner_reentry.asp.

[21] "Successful Prisoner Reentry," op. cit.

[22] Ibid.

[23] Ibid.

[24] Except where otherwise indicated, this subsection draws on Doris Layton MacKenzie, What Works in Corrections: Reducing the Criminal Activities of Offenders and Delinquents (2006).

[25] "Reported Crime in the United States," Bureau of Justice Statistics, updated Jan. 12, 2009, http://bjsdata.ojp.usdoj.gov/dataonline/Search/Crime/State/statebystaterun.cfm?stateid=52. For background, see Peter Katel, "Prison Reform," CQ Researcher, April 6, 2007, pp. 289-312.

[26] Marc Mauer and Ryan S. King, "A 25-year Quagmire: The War on Drugs and its Impact on American Society," The Sentencing Project, September 2007, pp. 9-10, www.sentencingpro

About the Author

Peter Katel is a *CQ Researcher* staff writer who previously reported on Haiti and Latin America for *Time* and *Newsweek* and covered the Southwest for newspapers in New Mexico. He has received several journalism awards, including the Bartolomé Mitre Award for coverage of drug trafficking, from the Inter-American Press Association. He holds an A.B. in university studies from the University of New Mexico. His recent reports include "Mexico's Drug War," "Hate Groups" and "Legalizing Marijuana."

ject.org/doc/publications/dp_25yearquagmire.pdf. For background see Peter Katel, "War on Drugs," *CQ Researcher*, June 2, 2006, pp. 481-504.

[27] Quoted in MacKenzie, *op. cit.*

[28] Edward M. Kennedy, "Punishing the Offenders," *The New York Times*, Dec. 6, 1975.

[29] Except where otherwise indicated, this subsection draws on MacKenzie, *op. cit.*

[30] Aaron D. Wilson, "Rockefeller Drug Laws Information Sheet," Partnership for Responsible Drug Information, Aug. 7, 2000, www.prdi.org/rocklawfact.html.

[31] Paul J. Hofer, *et al.*, "Fifteen Years of Guidelines Sentencing: An Assessment of How Well the Federal Criminal Justice System is Achieving the Goals of Sentencing Reform," U.S. Sentencing Commission, November 2004, pp. 1-35, www.ussc.gov/15_year/15_year_study_full.pdf.

[32] *Ibid.*, p. 13.

[33] Mauer and King, *op. cit.*, pp. 9, 22. Laura Murphy, "Testimony to U.S. Sentencing Commission," March 19, 2002, www.aclu.org/racial-justice_drug-law-reform_immigrants-rights_womens-rights/testimony-washington-national-office-.

[34] "Summary of Public Hearings on Cocaine Sentencing Policy," U.S. Sentencing Commission, 2002, pp. E-1-E-2, www.ussc.gov/r_congress/02crack/AppE.pdf.

[35] *Ibid.*, p. E-3.

[36] *Ibid.*, pp. 138-139.

[37] Larry Rohter, "In Wave of Anticrime Fervor, States Rush to Adopt Laws," *The New York Times*, May 10, 1994, p. A1; Stuart Taylor Jr., "Strict Penalties for Criminals: Pendulum of Feeling Swings," *The New York Times*, Dec. 13, 1983, p. A1.

[38] Quoted in William Claiborne, "Making Sentences Fit the Prisons," *The Washington Post*, July 16, 1994, p. A1.

[39] Sarah Lawrence and Jeremy Travis, "The New Landscape of Imprisonment: Mapping America's Prison Expansion," Urban Institute, April 2004, p. 7, www.urban.org/UploadedPDF/410994_mapping_prisons.pdf.

[40] *Ibid.*, p. 8.

[41] Michael Specter, "The Untried Alternative to Prisons," *The Nation*, March 13, 1982, p. 300.

[42] Alexandra Marks, "Rolling back stiff drug sentences," *The Christian Science Monitor*, Dec. 8, 1998, p. 1.

[43] Dirk Johnson, "As Mandatory Terms Pack Prisons, Experts Ask, Is Tougher Too Tough?" *The New York Times*, Nov. 8, 1993, p. A16.

FOR MORE INFORMATION

Center for Employment Opportunities, 32 Broadway, 15th Floor, New York, NY 10004; (212) 422-4430; www.ceoworks.org/index.php. Helps connect ex-prisoners with the job market.

Heritage Foundation, 214 Massachusetts Ave., N.E., Washington, DC 20002-4999; (202) 546-4400. A research and educational institute that formulates and promotes conservative public policies.

Michigan Prisoner ReEntry Initiative, Michigan Department of Corrections (MDOC), 206 E. Michigan Ave., Grandview Plaza, Lansing, MI 48933; (517) 373-3653; www.michigan.gov/reentry. Offers detailed information on reentry operations and goals.

National Institute of Justice, 810 7th St., N.W., Washington, DC 20531; (202) 307-2942; www.ojp.usdoj.gov/nij/topics/corrections/reentry/welcome.htm. Provides a variety of studies and other information on reentry.

National Reentry Resource Center, 100 Wall St., 20th Floor, New York, NY 10005; (646) 383-5721; info@nationalreentryresourcecenter.org. Offers all kinds of technical assistance to local governments.

Prisoner Reentry Institute, John Jay College of Criminal Justice, 555 W. 57th St., 6th Floor, New York, NY 10019; (212) 484-1399; www.jjay.cuny.edu/centers/prisoner_reentry_institute/2705.htm. Publishes research and holds conferences, all aimed at a specialist audience.

Urban Institute, 2100 M St., N.W., Washington, DC 20037; (202) 833-7200; www.urban.org/Pressroom/prisonerreentry.cfm. A nonpartisan social-policy organization that sponsors extensive research on reentry.

[44] Quoted in Michael J. Sniffen, "Reno Wants Prisoner Release Help," The Associated Press, Oct. 14, 1999.

[45] Quoted in *ibid.* For background, see Mary H. Cooper, "Drug-Policy Debate," *CQ Researcher*, July 28, 2000, pp. 593-624.

[46] "Crime in the United States by Volume and Rate per 100,000 Inhabitants, 1989-2008," FBI Uniform Crime Report, September 2009, www.fbi.gov/ucr/cius2008/data/table_01.html.

[47] "Two Million Inmates, And Counting," *The New York Times*, April 9, 2003, p. A18.

[48] Ryan S. King, "Changing Direction? State Sentencing Reforms 2004-2006," The Sentencing Project, March 2007, www.sentencingproject.org/doc/publications/sentencingreformforweb.pdf.

[49] "State of the Union Address," *op. cit.*

[50] "President Bush to Sign Unprecedented Prisoner Reentry Legislation," Reentry Policy Council, Council of State Governments, April 8, 2008, http://reentrypolicy.org/announcements/bush_sign_SCA; "Appropriations Update," Reentry Policy Council, undated, www.reentrypolicy.org/government_affairs/second_chance_act#OVERVIEW; Chris Suelleontrop, "The Right Has a Jailhouse Conversion," *The New York Times Magazine*, Dec. 24, 2006, p. 47.

[51] Egelko, *op. cit.*

[52] Carol J. Williams, "State gets two years to cut 43,000 from prisons," *Los Angeles Times*, Aug. 5, 2009, p. A1.

[53] "Defendants' Response to Three-Judge Court's October 21, 2009 Order," *op. cit.*

[54] "CDCR Files Response to Federal Three Judge Panel on Prison Management Plan," California Department of Corrections and Rehabilitation, Nov. 12, 2009, www.cdcr.ca.gov/News/2009_Press_Releases/Nov_12.html.

[55] Quoted in Egelko, *op. cit.*

[56] Quoted in *ibid.*

[57] For background, see Sarah Glazer, "Welfare Reform," *CQ Researcher*, Aug. 3, 2001, pp. 601-632.

[58] For background, see Kathy Koch, "Fatherhood Movement," *CQ Researcher*, June 2, 2000, pp. 473-496.

Bibliography

Selected Sources

Books

Kleiman, Mark A.R., *When Brute Force Fails: How to Have Less Crime and Less Punishment*, Princeton University Press, 2009.

A leading criminal justice policy expert, now at the University of California, Los Angeles, examines measures designed to lessen reliance on incarceration, including recidivism reduction.

MacKenzie, Doris Layton, *What Works in Corrections: Reducing the Criminal Activities of Offenders and Delinquents*, Cambridge University Press, 2006.

A University of Maryland criminologist examines the literature on reentry programs to find and analyze effective approaches.

Petersilia, Joan, *When Prisoners Come Home: Parole and Prisoner Reentry*, Oxford University Press, 2009.

A national expert on prisons examines reentry systems as they now exist and how to improve them.

Travis, Jeremy, *But They All Come Back: Facing the Challenges of Prisoner Reentry*, Urban Institute Press, 2005.

The leading advocate of reentry, now president of John Jay College of Criminal Justice in New York City, makes a case for expanding reentry programs.

Articles

Barnett, Ron, "Incarcerated getting educated," *USA Today*, Sept. 25, 2009, p. A3.

State prisons across the country are stepping up education programs to better inmates' reentry chances.

Bell, Dawson, "Prisons — 2nd Chance: 2 Succeed, 2 Struggle," *Detroit Free Press*, May 25, 2009, p. A7.

In part of a package of stories about Michigan's reentry system, a reporter chronicles the experiences of four newly released prisoners.

Buntin, John, "Job Freedom: Can the lessons of welfare reform be applied to the prison system?" *Governing*, August 2009, www.governing.com/article/job-freedom.

A reporter for a magazine for government administrators examines the single-minded dedication to finding jobs that characterizes a county-run pre-release center in Maryland.

Freedman, Samuel G., "Unlikely Allies on a Former Wedge Issue," *The New York Times*, June 28, 2008, p. B5.

A religion columnist reports on Christian conservatives joining forces with liberal advocates of alternatives to incarceration.

Gramlich, John, "At least 26 states spend less on prisons," *Stateline.org*, Aug. 11, 2009, www.stateline.org/live/details/story?contentId=418338.

A news service covering state governments reports on a trend of cutting back spending on prisons.

Miller, Carol Marbin, "Prison system change sought," *The Miami Herald*, June 24, 2009, p. B1.

Support builds in Florida for reducing incarceration by methods that include expanding reentry programs.

Rothfeld, Michael, "Gov. says prisons 'collapsing,' " *Los Angeles Times*, Aug. 20, 2009, p. A4.

California's governor paints a grim picture in the wake of a riot at a severely overcrowded state prison.

Reports and Studies

Brazzell, Diana, and Nancy G. La Vigne, "Prisoner Reentry in Houston: Community Perspectives," The Urban Institute, May 2009, www.urban.org/UploadedPDF/411901_prisoner_reentry_houston.pdf.

The high-crime communities to which most ex-prisoners return reflect the tensions of reentry.

"Criminal Justice Primer: Policy Priorities for the 111th Congress," The Sentencing Project, 2009, www.sentencing project.org/doc/publications/cjprimer2009.pdf.

A leading think tank advocating alternatives to prison presents a case for increased reentry funding, among other issues.

Harlow, Caroline Wolf, "Education and Correctional Populations," Bureau of Justice Statistics, U.S. Justice Department, April 15, 2003, www.ojp.usdoj.gov/bjs/pub/pdf/ecp.pdf.

A federal statistician details an issue widely discussed in policy circles — the educational shortcomings of most prison inmates.

"The Power of Work: The Center for Employment Opportunities Comprehensive Prisoner Reentry Program," Center for Employment Opportunities and MDRC, March 2006, www.mdrc.org/publications/426/full.pdf.

A New York-based nonprofit describes its strategy for helping ex-prisoners find work.

Visher, Christy, *et al.*, "Employment After Prison: A Longitudinal Study of Releasees in Three States," Urban Institute, Justice Policy Center, October 2008, www.urban.org/UploadedPDF/411778_employment_after_prison.pdf.

Reentry researchers present results on the importance of prison jobs and job-training to post-prison employment success.

The Next Step:

Additional Articles from Current Periodicals

Job Training

Essley, Liz, "Ex-Offenders Can't Find Jobs," *The Washington Times*, July 1, 2009, p. A15.

A proposed bill in the District of Columbia would help released prisoners avoid hiring bias during employment searches.

Owen, Mary, "Work Awaits After Prison," *Chicago Tribune*, May 8, 2009, p. C4.

A Chicago program trains and mentors former prisoners for jobs in a neighborhood that has the highest concentration of former prisoners in the city.

Saltzman, Jonathan, and Andrea Estes, "Senate to Take Up Crime Records," *The Boston Globe*, Nov. 18, 2009, p. B1.

The Massachusetts state Senate is considering a bill that would make it easier for inmates to find jobs after they are released from prison.

Varnon, Rob, "Bridgeport Gives Ex-Cons Shot at Jobs," *Connecticut Post*, April 28, 2009.

A program in Bridgeport, Conn., is teaching basic reading and math skills and providing job training to non-violent offenders who have gotten out of prison within the past 180 days.

Overcrowding

Boone, Rebecca, "Idaho Not in Contempt for Crowding at State Prison," *Lewiston* (Idaho) *Morning Tribune*, June 4, 2009.

A federal judge has decided not to hold Idaho in contempt for temporarily overcrowding a correctional institution after a housing unit was destroyed during a riot.

Rothfeld, Michael, "Judges Reject State Bid to Cut Prison Crowding," *Los Angeles Times*, Oct. 22, 2009, p. A3.

Three federal judges have rejected Gov. Schwarzenegger's proposal to reduce overcrowding in California prisons.

Rushton, Bruce, "Illinois, Other States Mull Early Release for Prison Inmates," *Springfield* (Missouri) *News-Leader*, July 13, 2009, p. 1.

Illinois may release some of its inmates early in order to ease the burden on the state's prison system.

Saltzman, Jonathan, "Prisoner Crowding Is Cited After Riot," *The Boston Globe*, July 7, 2009, p. B1.

A riot at a prison in Cambridge, Mass., has put the spotlight on overcrowding in the state's jails.

Recidivism Rates

Echegaray, Chris, "Tennessee Has High Rate of Repeat DUI Arrests," *The Tennessean*, Aug. 4, 2009.

More than 20 percent of people arrested for drunken driving in Tennessee were arrested again on the same charge.

Vogel, Ed, "Prisons Expert Says Nevada Among Lowest in Recidivism," *Las Vegas Review-Journal*, Oct. 21, 2009, p. 8B.

Nevada has one of the lowest recidivism rates in the country, but that may be due to prisoners who eventually end up in California prisons.

Reentry Programs

Bell, Dawson, "Released Prisoners Get Training, Support," *Detroit Free Press*, May 25, 2009, p. 7A.

The Michigan Prisoner Re-Entry Initiative has significantly reduced the number of parolees who return to prison.

Hamilton, Matthew, "Program Aimed At Dropping Recidivism," *News-Star* (Louisiana), March 15, 2009, p. 1A.

A proposed $750,000 grant for a correctional center in Louisiana would reduce recidivism rates in the area by 10 percent, according to law enforcement officials.

Madden, Charles, "Taking a One-Step Approach to Solving Re-Entry Problems," *News Journal* (Delaware), May 17, 2009, p. 23A.

The widespread belief that recidivism is a public safety and health issue has prompted the governor of Delaware to prioritize reentry programs.

Smith, Bruce C., "State to Expand Re-Entry Facility Model," *Indianapolis Star*, Feb. 21, 2009, p. 4X.

Indiana wants to implement more reentry facilities in minimum-security prisons across the state.

In-depth Reports on Issues in the News

Are you writing a paper?

Need backup for a debate?

Want to become an expert on an issue?

For more than 80 years, students have turned to *CQ Researcher* for in-depth reporting on issues in the news. Reports on a full range of political and social issues are now available. Following is a selection of recent reports:

Civil Liberties
Closing Guantánamo, 2/09
Affirmative Action, 10/08
Gay Marriage Showdowns, 9/08
America's Border Fence, 9/08
Immigration Debate, 2/08

Crime/Law
Interrogating the CIA, 9/09
Examining Forensics, 7/09
Legalizing Marijuana, 6/09
Wrongful Convictions, 4/09
Prostitution Debate, 5/08

Education
Value of a College Education, 11/09
Financial Literacy, 9/09
Reading Crisis? 2/08
Discipline in Schools, 2/08

Environment/Society
Women in the Military, 11/09
Conspiracy Theories, 10/09
Human Spaceflight, 10/09
Gays in the Military, 9/09
Energy and Climate, 7/09
Future of Books, 5/09

Health/Safety
Medication Abuse, 10/09
Nuclear Disarmament, 10/09
Health-Care Reform, 8/09
Straining the Safety Net, 7/09
Treating Depression, 6/09
Reproductive Ethics, 5/09

Politics/Economy
State Budget Crisis, 9/09
Business Bankruptcy, 4/09
Future of the GOP, 3/09
Middle-Class Squeeze, 3/09

Upcoming Reports

Bilingual Education, 12/11/09   Homelessness, 12/18/09   Animal Rights, 1/8/10

ACCESS

CQ Researcher is available in print and online. For access, visit your library or www.cqresearcher.com.

STAY CURRENT

To receive notice of upcoming *CQ Researcher* reports, or learn more about *CQ Researcher* products, subscribe to the free e-mail newsletters, *CQ Researcher Alert!* and *CQ Researcher News*: http://cqpress.com/newsletters.

PURCHASE

To purchase a *CQ Researcher* report in print or electronic format (PDF), visit www.cqpress.com or call 866-427-7737. Single reports start at $15. Bulk purchase discounts and electronic-rights licensing are also available.

SUBSCRIBE

Annual full-service *CQ Researcher* subscriptions—including 44 reports a year, monthly index updates, and a bound volume—start at $803. Add $25 for domestic postage.

CQ Researcher Online offers a backfile from 1991 and a number of tools to simplify research. For pricing information, call 800-834-9020, ext. 1906, or e-mail librarysales@cqpress.com.

Published by CQ Press, a Division of SAGE

www.cqresearcher.com

Bilingual Education vs. English Immersion

Which is better for students with limited English?

M ore than 5 million public school students have limited English proficiency, and the number is growing. Most English learners enter school behind fluent English speakers, and many never catch up either in language or other academic areas. In the 1960s and '70s, the federal government supported bilingual education: teaching English learners in both their native language and in English. A backlash developed in the 1980s and '90s among critics who attacked bilingual education as academically ineffective and politically divisive. They favored instead some form of "English immersion." Educators and policy makers continue to wage bitter debates on the issue, with each of the opposing camps claiming that research studies support its position. Some experts say the debate should focus instead on providing more resources, including more and better-trained teachers.

CQ Researcher • Dec. 11, 2009 • www.cqresearcher.com
Volume 19, Number 43 • Pages 1029-1052

First-grader Kasandra Herrera reads a book in Spanish in her dual-language classroom in Dodge City, Kan., where the Hispanic population has increased dramatically in recent years.

BILINGUAL EDUCATION VS. ENGLISH IMMERSION

Cover: AP Photo/Charlie Riedel

CQ Researcher

Dec. 11, 2009
Volume 19, Number 43

MANAGING EDITOR: Thomas J. Colin
tcolin@cqpress.com

ASSISTANT MANAGING EDITOR: Kathy Koch
kkoch@cqpress.com

ASSOCIATE EDITOR: Kenneth Jost

STAFF WRITERS: Thomas J. Billitteri, Marcia Clemmitt, Peter Katel

CONTRIBUTING WRITERS: Rachel Cox, Sarah Glazer, Alan Greenblatt, Reed Karaim Barbara Mantel, Patrick Marshall, Tom Price, Jennifer Weeks

DESIGN/PRODUCTION EDITOR: Olu B. Davis

ASSISTANT EDITOR: Darrell Dela Rosa

EDITORIAL INTERN: Emily DeRuy

FACT-CHECKING: Eugene J. Gabler, Michelle Harris

CQ PRESS

A Division of SAGE

PRESIDENT AND PUBLISHER:
John A. Jenkins

CQ Press is a registered trademark of Congressional Quarterly Inc.

CQ Researcher (ISSN 1056-2036) is printed on acid-free paper. Published weekly, except; (Jan. wk. 1) (May wk. 4) (July wks. 1, 2) (Aug. wks. 3, 4) (Nov. wk. 4) and (Dec. wk. 4), by CQ Press, a division of SAGE Publications. Annual full-service subscriptions start at $803. For pricing, call 1-800-834-9020, ext. 1906. To purchase a *CQ Researcher* report in print or electronic format (PDF), visit www. cqpress.com or call 866-427-7737. Single reports start at $15. Bulk purchase discounts and electronic-rights licensing are also available. Periodicals postage paid at Washington, D.C., and additional mailing offices. POSTMASTER: Send address changes to *CQ Researcher*, 2300 N St., N.W., Suite 800, Washington, DC 20037.

Bilingual Education vs. English Immersion

BY KENNETH JOST

THE ISSUES

Miriam Flores remembers that her daughter Miriam was doing well in her first two years in school in the border town of Nogales, Ariz.

"She knew how to read and write in Spanish," Flores says of her daughter, now a college student. "She would even correct the teacher on accents and spelling."

In the third grade, however, Miriam began having difficulties. Her grades went down, and she began having nightmares.

Miriam's mother has a simple explanation for the change. In the early 1990s, Nogales provided bilingual education — teaching English learners in both their native language and English — but only through the first two grades. "It was the language," Flores says.

Miriam's new teacher did not speak Spanish, taught only in English and seemed uninterested in Miriam's language difficulties, Flores says. "Miriam is a very quiet child, and I thought it was strange that the teacher would say that she talked a lot," Flores recalls today. "Then Miriam told me, 'I ask the other kids what the teacher is saying.' She didn't understand." [1]

Flores' frustrations with her daughter's schooling led her to join with other Spanish-speaking Nogales families in 1992 in filing a federal suit aimed at improving educational opportunities for non-English-speaking students in the overwhelmingly Hispanic town. The class action suit claimed the school district was failing to comply with a federal law — the Equal Educational Opportunities Act of 1974 — which requires

Protesters at Arizona's capitol in Phoenix oppose Proposition 203 on Nov. 6, 2000. The next day voters decisively approved the ballot measure ending bilingual education in the state in favor of so-called sheltered English immersion. Similar measures in California and Massachusetts at about the same time reflected a popular backlash against bilingual education since the 1980s.

AP Photo/Paul Connors

each state to take "appropriate action" to ensure that English-language learners (ELLs) enjoy "equal participation in its instructional programs."

Seventeen years later, the case is still in federal court. The plaintiffs won a pivotal decision in 2001 requiring Arizona to boost funding for English-language learning in Nogales and the rest of the state. In a narrowly divided decision in June, however, the Supreme Court gave state officials an opportunity to set aside the lower court ruling.

Writing for the 5-4 majority, Justice Samuel A. Alito Jr. said the federal district judge had failed to adequately consider changed circumstances since 2001. Among other changes, Alito

cited the state's decision to drop bilingual education in favor of so-called "sheltered English immersion" as the officially prescribed method of instruction for students with limited English proficiency. [2]

Arizona's voters had decisively rejected bilingual education in a 2000 ballot measure. Along with similar measures passed in California in 1998 and Massachusetts in 2002, Arizona's Proposition 203 embodied a popular backlash against bilingual education that had grown since the 1980s. Critics of bilingual teaching viewed it as a politically correct relic of the 1960s and '70s that had proven academically ineffective and politically divisive.

The debate between English-only instruction and bilingual education has been fierce for decades. "People get very hot under the collar," says Christine Rossell, a professor of political science at Boston University and critic of bilingual education.

Those who support a bilingual approach, says Arizona Superintendent of Instruction Thomas Horne, "aren't interested in teaching the kids English," but want to maintain "a separatist nationalism that they can take advantage of." Horne, a Republican, intervened with the state's GOP legislative leaders to try to undo the federal court injunction.

"When I tell people that the best way to learn English is to be taught in Spanish, they think I'm joking," says Rossell.

Supporters insist that bilingual education is the best way to ensure long-term educational achievement for English-language learners. "We have gone backwards on educating non-English speakers," says José Ruiz-Escalante, a professor of bilingual education at the

www.cqresearcher.com

Dec. 11, 2009 1031

English Learners Doing Poorly in Big States

More than 30 percent of the English-language learners are not making progress in 18 states, including those with big Hispanic populations, such as California, Florida, New York and Texas. Smaller states such as Connecticut, Delaware and Rhode Island have some of the best progress rates.

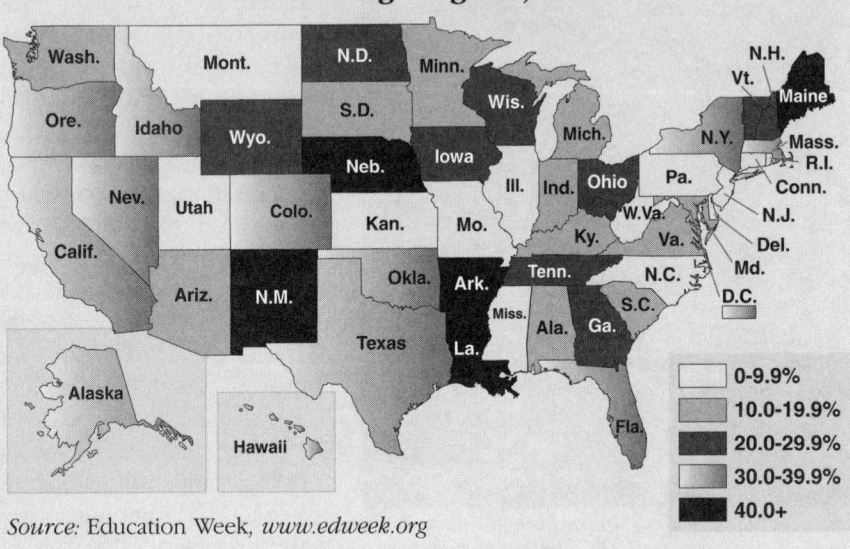

Percentage of English-Language Learners Not Making Progress, 2007

☐	0-9.9%
▨	10.0-19.9%
▨	20.0-29.9%
▨	30.0-39.9%
■	40.0+

Source: Education Week, *www.edweek.org*

University of Texas-Pan American in Edinburg and president of the National Association for Bilingual Education. English-only proponents, he says, are "in such a hurry for students to speak English that we're not paying attention to their cognitive development."

"The important thing that students need to learn is how to think," Ruiz-Escalante continues. "It doesn't matter whether you learn to think in Spanish or in English. Kids will learn to speak English, but they will be limited" in their academic learning. [3]

Out of nearly 50 million pupils in U.S. public elementary and secondary schools, about 5.1 million — more than one-tenth — are classified as having limited English proficiency. The number is growing because of increased immigration, both legal and illegal. The vast majority of English-language learners — nearly 80 percent — speak Spanish as their first language. But schools are also coping with rising numbers of students who speak a variety of other languages, almost all of which have far less similarity to English than Spanish has. *(See chart, p. 1036.)*

"It's a growing challenge," says Patte Barth, director of the Center for Public Education at the National School Boards Association (NSBA). "We have many more children coming into our schools for whom their first language is not English. At the same time, the need to educate every child to a high level is much more important than it was even 20 years ago."

The imperative for results stems in part from enactment early in 2002 of the No Child Left Behind Act, the centerpiece of President George W. Bush's educational-accountability initiative. The act mandated annual testing of students in grades 3-8 and required that schools demonstrate "adequate yearly progress," including closing the achievement gap for English-language learners, at the risk of financial penalties for noncompliance. [4]

The act also withdrew the federal preference for bilingual education over English-only instruction. Even so, Latino advocacy groups that have long complained of inadequate attention to Spanish-speaking students applaud the law's emphasis on accountability. The act "changed the debate from what kind of education and curriculum to one of how do you best educate these kids," says Raul Gonzalez, director of legislative affairs for NCLR, formerly the National Council of La Raza. "That's where we think the debate should be."

The federal government has no official count on the number of English learners in each instructional method, but the most recent survey by researchers indicates that the majority — about 60 percent — are in all-English curricula. Of that number, 12 percent receive no special services at all to aid English proficiency. The remaining English learners — about 40 percent — receive some form of bilingual instruction using their native language and English. The length of time in the bilingual programs varies from as little as one year to several. And, as Stanford University education professor Claude Goldenberg notes, there is no way to know the amount of support the students receive or the quality of the instruction. [5]

In Arizona, state policy calls for English-language learners to receive four hours a day of intensive English instruction apart from their mainstream, English-only classes. Since the so-called "pullout" policy was implemented in 2008, the rate of reclassifying students from English-language learners to English-proficient has increased, Horne says. "Students need to learn English quickly to compete," he says.

Tim Hogan, executive director of the Arizona Center for Law in the Public Interest and the lead attorney in the *Flores* case, says it is "too early to tell" whether the four-hour pullout approach will be more effective than past policies that he describes as ineffective. But Hogan alleges that the policy segregates Spanish speakers from other students and risks delaying graduation by taking class time away from academic subjects.

Hogan stresses, however, that the lawsuit is aimed at ensuring adequate funding for English-language instruction, not at imposing a specific educational method. "We proved that the state funding [for English-language instruction] was totally arbitrary," he says.

Horne counters that the Supreme Court decision leaves funding decisions up to the state. "The district court judges are being told not to micromanage the finances of the state education system," he says.

Voluminous, statistics-heavy studies are cited by opposing advocacy groups as evidence to support their respective positions on the bilingual versus English-only debate. But Barth says language politics, not research, often determines school districts' choice of instructional method. "A lot of it is political," she says. "A lot of decisions about language instruction aren't really informed by the research about what works for children."

Whatever approach is used, many researchers say English-language learners' needs are not being met. In their new book, *Educating English Learners for a Transformed World*, former George Mason University professors Virginia Collier and Wayne Thomas — who strongly advocate bilingual education — cite statistics showing a big achievement gap at the high-school level between native English speakers and students who entered school as English learners. Native English speakers have average scores on standardized tests around the 50th percentile, Collier and Thomas say, while English learners average around the 10th to 12th percentile. [6]

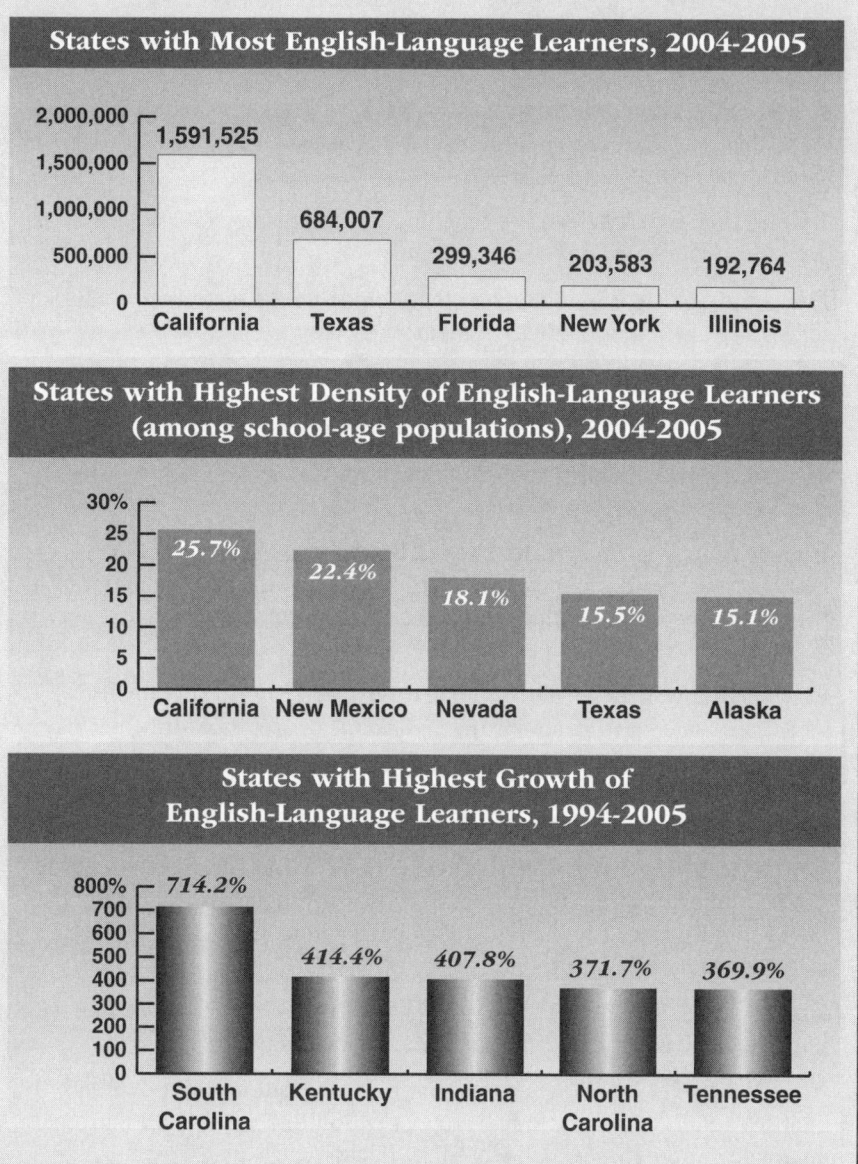

California Has Most English-Language Learners

More than 1.5 million English-language learners (ELLs) reside in California — one-quarter of the state's school-age population and by far the most in the nation (top graph). ELLs, however, are becoming more populous in Southern states such as South Carolina, Kentucky and Tennessee (middle graph). More than one in five students in California and New Mexico are ELL students (bottom graph).

States with Most English-Language Learners, 2004-2005

- California: 1,591,525
- Texas: 684,007
- Florida: 299,346
- New York: 203,583
- Illinois: 192,764

States with Highest Density of English-Language Learners (among school-age populations), 2004-2005

- California: 25.7%
- New Mexico: 22.4%
- Nevada: 18.1%
- Texas: 15.5%
- Alaska: 15.1%

States with Highest Growth of English-Language Learners, 1994-2005

- South Carolina: 714.2%
- Kentucky: 414.4%
- Indiana: 407.8%
- North Carolina: 371.7%
- Tennessee: 369.9%

Source: National Clearinghouse for English Language Acquisition

Despite decades of attention and debate on the issue, "not much has happened," says Kenji Hakuta, a professor at Stanford University's School of Education in Palo Alto, Calif. "The problems of English-language learners persist whether it's English-only or bilingual education."

A Bilingual/Immersion Glossary

The dizzying number of terms and acronyms in the teaching-English field reflects the intensity and complexity of the debate over which method works best. Here are some of the key terms:

Annual Measurable Achievement Objective (AMAO) — These are the criteria for the reports mandated by the No Child Left Behind Act (NCLB) on the progress of limited English proficiency (LEP) students in English-language acquisition and academic achievement.

Adequate Yearly Progress (AYP) — The accountability system mandated by NCLB requires each state to ensure all schools and districts meet set standards.

Bilingual Education — Teaching non-English-speaking people in both their native language and in English.

Dual Language — Programs that help students develop full literacy skills in English and another language.

Early Exit Transitional — Programs that help students develop English skills as quickly as possible, without delaying learning of academic core content. Instruction begins in native language and then moves rapidly to English, with students transitioning to mainstream classrooms as soon as possible.

Elementary and Secondary Education Act (ESEA) — Funds primary and secondary education, and forbids establishment of a national curriculum. Originally enacted in 1965, the act was reauthorized as the No Child Left Behind Act.

English Language Development (ELD) — Programs in which students leave mainstream classrooms to spend part of their day receiving ESL instruction focusing on grammar, vocabulary and communication skills, not academic content. Typically there is no support for students' native languages. Also known as ESL Pull-Out

English Language Proficiency (ELP) Standards — Assist teachers in evaluating LEP students' progress in their acquisition of English and facilitate the alignment of curriculum between ESL services and general education programs.

English as a Second Language (ESL) — Refers to non-English speakers and programs designed to teach them English.

ESL Push-In — These are programs for ESL students who attend mainstream classrooms and receive instruction in English with native-language support as needed from ESL teachers.

Heritage Language Programs — These target non-English-speaking students or those who have weak literary skills in their native language, frequently American Indians. Also known as Indigenous Language Programs.

As educators look for ways to best teach students with limited English skills, here are some of the major questions being debated:

Is bilingual education effective for English-language learners?

Todd Butler teaches social studies and language arts to fourth-grade English learners in Mansfield, Texas, a rapidly growing exurb south of Fort Worth. Butler, an Anglo who began studying Spanish in fourth grade himself, uses only Spanish for social studies but alternates day by day between English and Spanish for language arts.

Butler, recipient of the National Association for Bilingual Education's teacher of the year award in 2009, is firmly convinced of the merits of bilingual education, especially in the so-called dual-language model now used in Mansfield and advancing in other school districts. By contrast, the older model — known as "transitional bilingual education" — focuses on using bilingual education only for a limited period.

"We don't do kids any favor by shoving them into English as fast as we can," says Butler, a teacher with more than a quarter-century of experience. "The research shows very clearly that the longer we can give them support in their language, the better they're going to do not just in elementary school but in secondary school as well."

The strongest supporting evidence comes from long-term research by George Mason scholars Collier and Thomas. The veteran researchers examined achievement levels through high school among English learners in 35 school districts who were taught using different instructional models. "Our research shows what works in the long term is different from what works in the short term," Thomas explains.

There is little difference in achievement levels between English learners in the elementary grades, the researchers found, regardless of whether the students were taught in dual-language, transitional-bilingual or English-as-a-Second-Language (ESL) models. (*See glossary, p. 1034.*) By high school, however, the dual-language students come closer to narrowing the gap between them and the English-proficient students than those using the ESL approach. Students from transitional bilingual programs are in-between.

Students in English-only programs "look as though they're doing really well in early grades," Thomas explains, "but they've experienced a cognitive slowdown as they're learning English." As the two authors conclude in their book: "The more children develop their first language . . ., the more successful they will be in academic achievement in English by the end of their school years." [7]

The national school boards group agrees on the advantages of "first-language" instruction for English learners. "ELL students with formal schooling in their first language tend to acquire English proficiency faster than their peers without it," the NSBA's Center for Public Education concluded after reviewing the research. The center added that it takes four to seven years to become proficient in "academic English — the language needed to succeed in the classroom." [8]

Opponents of bilingual education say it fails because it does not completely close the gap between English learners and English-proficient students. "There is very little research to say that these programs are having good results," says Rosalie Pedalino Porter, a longtime critic of bilingual education who was ESL coordinator in Newton, Mass., in the 1980s. "It never proved itself effective, and all sorts of excuses are still being made." Porter now serves on the board of the pro-English advocacy group Center for Equal Opportunity.

To critics, bilingual education simply delays students' mastery of the new language: English. "If you don't pull them out [for English instruction], they're not

Immersion — Learning a language by spending all or part of the time speaking solely in the target language.

Late Exit Transitional — Instruction designed to help students develop some skills and proficiency in their native language, as well as strong skills and proficiency in English. Instruction in lower grades is in the native language, and in English in upper grades. Also known as Developmental Bilingual or Maintenance Education.

Limited English Proficiency (LEP) — Denotes individuals who cannot communicate effectively in English, such as those not born in the United States or whose native language is not English.

Local Education Agency (LEA) — A board of education or other public authority that has administrative control of, or performs a service for, publicly funded schools.

National Assessment of Educational Process (NAEP) — The continuing assessment of American students in targeted grades and various subject areas — known as the "Nation's Report Card" — is carried out by the U.S. Department of Education's National Center for Education Statistics.

National Clearinghouse for English Language Acquisition and Language Instruction Educational Programs (NCELA) — Supports the U.S. Department of Education's Office of English Language Acquisition in its mission to implement NCLB as it applies to English-language learners.

No Child Left Behind Act of 2001 (NCLB) — The most recent reauthorization of the ESEA calls for standards-based education reform and requires assessments of all students in certain grades before states can receive federal funding for schools.

Office of English Language Acquisition, Language Enhancement, and Academic Achievement for Limited English Proficient Students (OELA) — A U.S. Department of Education office that helps ensure English-language learners and immigrant students attain English proficiency and achieve academically.

Sheltered English Immersion — Classes specifically for ESL students aimed at improving their English-speaking, reading and writing skills. Prepares students for entry into mainstream classrooms.

Structured English Immersion (SEI) — Classes for LEP students only where the goal is fluency in English. All instruction is in English, adjusted to the proficiency of students so the subject matter is comprehensible.

Two-Way Immersion — Programs designed to develop proficiency in both native language and English through instruction in both languages. Also known as Two-Way Bilingual.

Source: "The Biennial Report to Congress on the Implementation of the Title III State Formula Grant Program," U.S. Department of Education, School Years 2004-2006, June 2008, www.ed.gov/about/offices/list/oela/title3biennial0406.pdf.

Most Student Native Speakers Are Hispanic

More than three-quarters of U.S. students with limited English proficiency (LEP) are native Spanish speakers. About 7 percent of LEPs are native speakers of Asian languages.

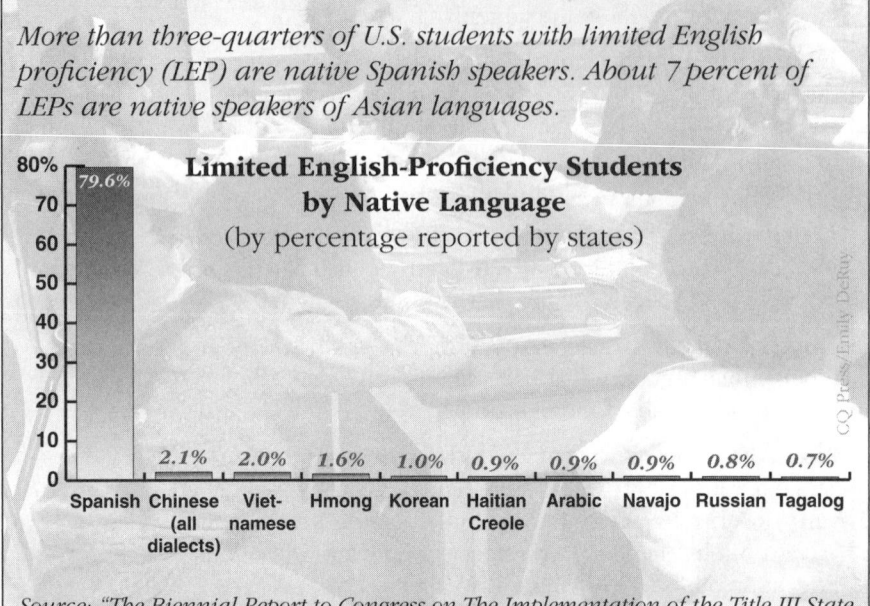

Limited English-Proficiency Students by Native Language
(by percentage reported by states)

Language	Percentage
Spanish	79.6%
Chinese (all dialects)	2.1%
Vietnamese	2.0%
Hmong	1.6%
Korean	1.0%
Haitian Creole	0.9%
Arabic	0.9%
Navajo	0.9%
Russian	0.8%
Tagalog	0.7%

Source: "The Biennial Report to Congress on The Implementation of the Title III State Formula Grant Program: School Years 2004-06," U.S. Department of Education, June 2008

going to learn English fast enough," says Arizona education chief Horne.

Supporters of bilingual education counter that the short-term perspective is ultimately detrimental for English learners. "Most districts are still in a hurry for them to learn English," says NABE president Ruiz-Escalante. They end up "learning English at the expense of an education."

"Schools are in a difficult position," says James Crawford, a bilingual-education advocate and author of a textbook on English learners now in its fifth edition. "Short-term pressures have determined how children are being taught." Crawford first developed an expertise in bilingual education as a writer and editor for *Education Week;* he also served as NABE's executive director until 2006. [9]

Some experts say the lines in the perennial and heated debate are beginning to blur. "The argument of bilingual education versus English immersion sounds like a fairly old way of characterizing the problem," says Stanford professor Hakuta.

Is "English immersion" effective for English learners?

As chief executive officer of the United Neighborhood Organization, Juan Rangel superintends a network of eight charter schools serving predominantly Hispanic communities in Chicago. UNO schools follow a philosophy of strong discipline, high expectations and English immersion — or teaching only using English — instead of bilingual education.

According to a study by the pro-English Lexington Institute, English learners from UNO schools score higher than their counterparts from other Chicago schools, who are subject to statewide bilingual-education requirements. [10] But Rangel says English immersion also promotes assimilation for Hispanic students. "What it means is having our families and children have an understanding of belonging," Rangel told *Education Week* reporter Mary Ann Zehr. "They have a role in developing this country." [11]

Rangel says bilingual education has not worked as intended. Some parents interviewed agreed. Guadalupe Garcia,

an immigrant from Mexico with a fourth-grade education, told Zehr that the bilingual education one of her daughters received in a regular Chicago school was "pura español" — pure Spanish. Another of her daughters entered a UNO school in second grade speaking no English but could speak English well within a year and a half.

Advocates of English immersion emphasize assimilation as one of their reasons for favoring it over bilingual instruction. "I believe in the beauty of bilingualism," says Porter, of the pro-English advocacy group Center for Equal Opportunity, "but I have a very, very strong commitment to children like me who don't speak English at all." Porter was born in Italy and spoke no English when she immigrated with her family at age 6.

But the advocates of English immersion also claim that studies in two states that changed from bilingual to English instruction — Arizona and California — show that the change improved academic performance. Justice Alito pointed to both studies in the Supreme Court's decision in the *Flores* case as evidence of "documented, academic support for the view that SEI [structured English immersion] is significantly more effective than bilingual education." [12] Critics, however, say both studies are flawed.

In one of the studies, Kelly Torrance, identified as an adjunct scholar with the Lexington Institute, a pro-English think tank based in Washington, D.C., cited statistics from California showing that the number of English learners who scored in the top two categories of proficiency on the state's English-language development test increased from 25 percent in 2001 to 47 percent in 2005. "This striking improvement is big news," wrote Torrance. [13]

Bilingual-education advocates dismiss the studies. Stephen Krashen, a linguistics professor at the University of Southern California in Los Angeles, says the state introduced the English test in 2001 and that improved scores are typical for the first few years after introduction of a new test. He points to several other studies by university academics that conclude dropping bilingual education did not accelerate English learners' development. [14]

The Arizona Department of Education similarly concluded in a report prepared in July 2004 that English learners in the state had benefited from the switch from bilingual education to English immersion following voters' decisive rejection of bilingual education in the 2000 ballot measure, Proposition 203. "Students in English immersion outperformed students in bilingual in all areas," Superintendent Horne says in describing the report. [15]

Jeff MacSwan, a professor of linguistics at Arizona State University in Tempe, says the state's report "has been completely discredited." In letters to the editor at the time and in comments since, MacSwan notes that the comparisons found in the study failed to control for other potential causes of the differences, including poverty, length of time in the United States or initial language proficiency. "That's a huge thing," he says.

In a more recent study he coauthored, MacSwan says it is impossible to determine whether English learners are doing better or worse since passage of Proposition 203, but that they continue to suffer "a persistent and dramatic achievement gap" in comparison to English-proficient students. [16]

Porter insists that English learners need only a little concentrated language instruction to become proficient. "They need two to three hours a day of intensive language instruction," she says. "These children within a year of this intensive instruction can make the transition from their native language to English."

Some supporters of bilingual education stop short of flatly dismissing English-only approaches. "You could find an elementary program that was English-only, and they did well," says Barth with the school boards' group. "But on average, that's an outlier."

"Any well-implemented program can work," says Stanford's Hakuta. "The issue is giving kids access to academic content that sparks their curiosity. The fundamental piece is that education isn't pouring knowledge into empty vessels. You have to get kids interested and excited in the content of what you're teaching."

Should funding for English-language learning be increased?

Twice in the past decade, federal district judges in Arizona have found that the state was not spending enough money to help English-language learners become proficient in English. State officials welcomed the first of the rulings, by Judge Alfred Marquez, in January 2000 as a useful spur to increase funding for English instruction.

In 2006, however, the state's Republican-controlled legislature approved only part of the funding increase proposed by then-Gov. Janet Napolitano, a Democrat, to satisfy the federal court. The new plan increased the special funding for English-language learners to $432 per student from the previous $358. Judge Raner Collins, who had taken over the *Flores* case after Marquez's retirement, found the new spending levels still inadequate.

In its ruling in June, the Supreme Court said that both Collins and the 9th U.S. Circuit Court of Appeals placed too much emphasis on funding levels in refusing the plea by the state's legislative leaders and Superintendent of Instruction Horne to reopen the case. Dissenting justices countered that the adequacy of the state's resources devoted to English-language instruction "has always been the basic contested issue" in the case.

Today, plaintiffs' attorney Hogan acknowledges that the Supreme Court's decision shifts the focus of the case away from funding and toward the effectiveness of the state's prescribed model of structured English immersion with English learners taken out of their mainstream English-only classes for four-hour "pull-out" sessions for intensive English instruction.

Nationwide, the question of funding for English-language instruction continues to be a point of discussion, but the lines are not as sharply drawn as they are on the instructional model used. "It's not about resources; it's about the quality of the program," says NABE president Ruiz-Escalante. "Whatever resources are available need to be devoted to appropriate programs that meet the educational needs of the students. Money alone is not the solution."

"The amount of money spent on a program is not a guarantee that a good education is produced," says English-immersion advocate Porter. "Certainly, there's a floor level. But to equate the amount of dollars with wonderful educational outcomes simply cannot be done. The real proof is not the amount of money but the evidence of student success."

Some bilingual-education advocates, in fact, minimize the need for additional resources for English-language learners. In their book, Collier and Thomas contend that bilingual (dual-language) instruction — that is, using a bilingual teacher to teach English learners in the same grade-level, mainstream curriculum as other students — is "the most cost-effective" educational model. The only additional cost, they say, is for materials. By contrast, they call ESL pull-out "the least cost-effective model," because extra resource teachers are needed.

For her part, Barth, with the school boards' Center for Public Education, also says educational costs for English learners are not necessarily higher than for English-proficient students. But she does point to some needed additional resources that "could use funding," such as "more ESL teachers" and "broader access to good pre-K programs."

"We also know that students who come into school without English tend to be in communities that are poorer, and they tend to go to schools that have fewer resources," Barth says. But she adds, "That's not the same as saying it costs more to educate an ESL child."

In Arizona, Superintendent Horne says the state is meeting federal requirements for teaching English learners. "The law requires appropriate action to teach kids English," he says. "We're clearly doing that. I think we're one of the leaders in the nation."

Gonzalez of NCLR (La Raza), however, says Arizona is misusing funds provided under Title III of the No Child Left Behind Act, the language-acquisition section. "The federal law says you cannot use Title III to supplant your state funds or your Title I funds," Gonzalez says, referring to the major federal aid program for disadvantaged school districts. "Title III is complementary. Arizona was supplanting funds and using Title III funds for those purposes."

Veronica Rivera, a legislative staff attorney with the Mexican American Legal Defense and Education Fund (MALDEF) in Washington, says funding is partly to blame for "inadequate" programs for Spanish-speaking students in some states and school districts. But she also points to a need for consistent standards for bilingual teachers. "Some states and local education agencies require some type of bilingual certification," Rivera says. "Most of them do, but not all of them."

Whatever federal funding is provided, Gonzalez says No Child Left Behind helps English learners by holding school districts accountable for measurable results. "Everyone knew that these kids weren't doing well in school for decades, but there was no accountability," he says. "No one suffered except the kids."

Julie Maxwell-Jolly, director of the Center for Applied Policy in Education at the University of California-Davis, agrees. "We have seen from No Child Left Behind that [English learners] are not achieving," she says. "That's been good. It's really shined a light." ■

BACKGROUND

American Languages

The American melting pot has always included many languages in addition to English — the dominant tongue since colonial times. Through much of the 19th century, non-English speakers commonly received some instruction in their native languages, whether in public or private schools. From the late 19th century on, however, opposition to rising immigration — along with anti-German sentiment during and after World War I — drove native-language instruction out of most public schools. The rise of bilingual education beginning in the 1960s was premised on a need to use native languages in some form for non-English speakers, but a backlash developed among critics who viewed the policy as failing either to educate or to assimilate youngsters with limited English proficiency. [17]

The European colonists encountered Native Americans who spoke a variety of mostly unwritten languages. Besides the British colonists, the early Americans included many Dutch and a lesser number of French, Germans and Swedes, who brought their native languages with them. African slaves, with limited if any formal schooling, learned English through their work, but not necessarily standard English. New waves of non-English speakers were added through the 19th and early 20th centuries with the conquests of the Mexican-American War (Spanish), the import of Chinese labor (Mandarin and Cantonese) and the immigration from southern and eastern Europe (Italian, Greek, Portuguese, Russian and Polish among many other European languages, along with Hebrew and Yiddish).

At first, the use of non-English languages was "supported, tolerated or sanctioned" by public and parochial schools, according to historian Guadalupe San Miguel Jr., a professor at the University of Houston. Language-policy decisions were made at the state and local level. By mid-century, however, the federal government began discouraging the use of languages other than English in newly acquired territories. States followed. California prescribed English in schools in 1855, five years after statehood. As immigration increased, many other states passed similar laws in the late 19th century. World War I fueled anti-German sentiment that led to English-only laws in the Midwest in states with large German populations.

By the 1920s, most states had English-only laws for public school instruction. Teachers and administrators supported the policies, sometimes even with corporal punishment. President Lyndon B. Johnson's biographer Robert Caro writes that as a teacher in southwest Texas, Johnson sometimes spanked Mexican-American students if he heard them using Spanish on the playground. Three decades later, however, Johnson's fellow Texan and Democrat, Sen. Ralph Yarbrough, came to see the English-only policy as "the cruelest form of discrimination" against the state's large Mexican-American population and others with limited English proficiency. With Johnson in the White House, Yarbrough authored the Bilingual Education Act to encourage and provide financial assistance for programs to recognize the special needs of limited-English-speaking children. The act, attached as Title VII to the omnibus Elementary and Secondary Education Act, cleared Congress in December 1967; Johnson signed it into law the next month.

The new law authorized up to $85 million in federal aid for bilingual education, but only $7.5 million was appropriated the first year. The law did not specify any instructional method for English-language learners. In 1970,

Continued on p. 1040

Chronology

1960s-1970s
Civil rights era sparks moves to improve language instruction for non-English-speaking students.

1967
Bilingual Education Act is passed by Congress and signed by President Lyndon B. Johnson; law provides financial aid to school districts to help students with limited English.

1970
Regulations issued by Department of Health, Education and Welfare (HEW) instruct federally financed school districts to "rectify" language deficiencies of non-English-speaking students.

1971
Massachusetts law requires "transitional bilingual education" in all public schools.

1974
Supreme Court in *Lau v. Nichols* requires public school systems to provide non-English-speaking students with "basic English skills" needed to profit from attendance. . . . Congress codifies requirement later in year in Equal Educational Opportunities Act.

1975
HEW's Office of Civil Rights issues *Lau* regulations requiring use of non-English languages for language-minority students.

1978
Study by private research institute questions the benefits of bilingual education.

1980s-1990s
Opposition to bilingual education forms, grows.

1980
Carter administration proposes regulations requiring bilingual education.

1981
Reagan administration cancels proposed bilingual-education regulation; begins reducing federal aid to English-language instruction. . . . Study by Education Department questions benefits of bilingual education. . . . Federal appeals court, in Texas case, says English-language instruction must be based on "sound educational theory," adequately resourced and proven to be effective (*Castañeda v. Pickard*).

1982
Federal appeals court lifts statewide injunction requiring Texas to improve English-language instruction after state legislature passes bilingual-education law.

1983
U.S. English organization founded to lobby for official English laws; many states pass such laws in 1980s, '90s.

1990
Veteran teacher Rosalie Pedalino Porter's book *Forked Tongue* sharply attacks bilingual education.

1991
Report prepared for U.S. Department of Education finds English-immersion and bilingual education both effective methods but says non-English-speaking students benefit from longer instruction in native language.

1992
Spanish-speaking families in Nogales, Ariz., file federal court suit saying school district fails to provide adequate language instruction.

1998
California voters approve Proposition 227 requiring English immersion for non-English-speaking students, with provision for parents to request waiver.

2000-Present
Support for bilingual education recedes further; plaintiffs in Arizona, Texas cases suffer setbacks.

2000
Arizona held in contempt of court by federal judge for not providing adequate funding for language instruction. . . . State's voters approve Proposition 203, prescribing English-only for language instruction.

2002
President George W. Bush signs No Child Left Behind Act, repealing Bilingual Education Act but holding school districts accountable for non-English-speaking students to meet proficiency standards; English-language acquisition aid is revamped, reducing assistance to districts with large numbers of language-minority students. . . . Massachusetts voters approve English-only instruction.

2006
Arizona legislature approves modest increase in state aid for language instruction; federal judge deems funding inadequate, reaffirms statewide injunction; state education chief intervenes to undo injunction.

2008-2009
Federal judge in Texas says state not satisfying federal standards for English learners in secondary schools; federal appeals court issues stay in February 2009. . . . Supreme Court in June 2009 orders judge in Arizona case to reconsider effort to undo injunction; new hearing set for Dec. 14.

Native Americans Fight Language Extinction

"It is about losing history and identity."

Leaders from three Cherokee nations came together in October to mark the opening of the Eastern Band of Cherokee Indians' Kituwah Academy, a language-immersion school for kindergarteners to fifth-graders in Cherokee, N.C.

"It is a wonderful initiative for the Cherokee," says Ellen L. Lutz, executive director for Cultural Survival, a nonprofit advocacy group in Cambridge, Mass., which promotes the rights of indigenous communities. "Young, self-confident Cherokee kids will not forget who they are because of the education they receive at this school."

In 1838 members of the Ketoowah and Cherokee nations in Oklahoma were relocated from their homes by military force in direct violation of an 1832 Supreme Court ruling affirming their right to remain on their traditional territory. Some evaded relocation while others returned to tribal lands in North Carolina. In recent years, profits from several enterprises have encouraged the tribes to take on the multigenerational challenge of preserving their own language. The Cherokee Nation of Oklahoma opened its own immersion school in 2003, and its curriculum serves as the basis for the Eastern Band's.

Many such Indian schools have opened throughout the nation, but some Indian communities have opted for informal language instruction outside the classroom. The Hualapai Tribe in Arizona, for example, holds summer camps for younger generations.

Of the nation's 175 surviving Native American dialects, only 20 are expected to remain in 2050, according to the Indigenous Language Institute (ILI), a nonprofit advocacy group in Santa Fe, N.M. Fifty currently surviving languages have five or fewer speakers — all older than 70 — and face imminent extinction, according to Cultural Survival.

"This is a linguistic emergency," says Ineé Yang Slaughter, executive director of ILI. "It is about losing history and identity."

More than a century ago, during attempts to assimilate Native Americans into mainstream society, the federal government targeted Native American languages in a campaign termed by some linguists as "linguistic genocide."

In an 1887 report, Commissioner of Indian Affairs J.D.C. Atkins wrote, "In the difference of language today lies two-thirds of our trouble. . . . Schools should be established, which children should be required to attend; their barbarous dialects should be blotted out and the English language substituted." [1]

During the same period, boarding schools established by the Bureau of Indian Affairs tried to stamp out native languages. Under English-only rules students were punished and humiliated for speaking their native language.

The coercive assimilation policy met with limited success in eradicating Indian languages, but over time the policies took a toll on the identity of many Indians, alienating them from their cultural roots. Moreover, the policies left a legacy of opposition toward bilingual and immersion education among Indians who remembered the pain they suffered in school and wanted to shield their children from similar experiences.

"The boarding schools turned to indoctrination. Native languages were burned out of their mouths," says Lutz. "Over time, the experience led grandparents to refuse to speak the native tongues to younger generations."

Continued from p. 1038

regulations issued by the old Department of Health, Education and Welfare (HEW) directed school districts receiving federal aid to "rectify" language deficiencies among non-English speakers but again did not specify a curriculum or instructional method. Meanwhile, however, states were beginning to enact their own initiatives. Massachusetts enacted a law in 1971 establishing what it called "transitional bilingual education." Texas followed suit two years later. Some other states passed laws authorizing but not mandating bilingual education.

The Supreme Court took on the issue in a case from San Francisco brought by Chinese-American students under Title VI of the Civil Rights Act of 1964, which prohibits discrimination in federally assisted services by state or local governments. The plaintiffs in *Lau v. Nichols* claimed that out of 2,856 Chinese-speaking students in the school system, only 1,000 received any supplemental instruction in English. Unanimously, the high court agreed that the school district was violating the Civil Rights Act.

"It seems obvious," Justice William O. Douglas wrote in the main opinion, "that the Chinese-speaking minority receive fewer benefits than the English-speaking majority from respondents' school system." Once again, the decision did not instruct local school systems on how to carry out the federal requirement. In a concurring opinion, Justice Harry A. Blackmun suggested that a school district with fewer non-English speakers might not be subject to the same requirement. [18]

Language Debates

With federal support, bilingualism advanced in the 1970s in schools as well as in society at large. With the election of Republican President Ronald Reagan, however, the federal government set itself against bilingual education and in support of "English-only" instruction. Opposition to bilingual education grew in the 1990s. Supporters of bilingual education succeeded in

The eventual economic and social mobility of Native Americans aided in the beginning of several grassroots movements in the 1970s to bring back mother tongues.

"The next generation would say, 'It's my language. It's my people. America took it from me. I want it back,' " explains Lutz.

Prodded by language activists, Congress passed the Native American Languages Acts in 1990 and 1992 to facilitate efforts to preserve Native American languages. Among other things, the laws concluded that academic performance was directly tied to a respect for the first language of students.

While the U.S. Department of Education and the National Science Foundation already provided federal help for cultural preservation, the acts made tribes eligible for funding to carry out language conservation and renewal.

Despite the recent surge in teaching Native Americans their native languages, several challenges still remain. Indian-language speakers often lack the academic credentials to teach, while outside teachers are not well-versed in the cultural and lin-

Eastern Band of the Cherokee Nation

Eastern Band Cherokee Indians attend the opening of Kituwah Academy, in Cherokee, N.C., in October. Housed in the renovated Boundary Tree Lodge, a historic visitors' lodge, the school teaches academic subjects and the Cherokee language (Kituwah).

guistic nuances of Native Americans.

"The key is teaching the language to communicate as opposed to more traditional textbook education," says Slaughter. Classroom teaching isn't always the best way to teach students to actually use the language in their communities."

But perhaps the biggest problem is the need to compete with other more pressing priorities such as health care, economic development, housing and general academic learning.

"These other issues are critical," Slaughter says. "But this is not just a language issue, it is an issue of cultural identity being lost. Once a language is gone, it is gone forever. We know that learning our languages strengthens us both as individuals and as a nation."

— Darrell Dela Rosa

[1] James Crawford, "Loose Ends in a Tattered Fabric," American Immigration Lawyers Association, www.ailadownloads.org/advo/Crawford-Language Rights.pdf.

getting Congress to reauthorize the federal law, but California in 1998 became the first of three states to approve voter initiatives to limit the use of languages other than English in public schools.

Congress responded to the Supreme Court's decision later in 1974 with a law, the Equal Educational Opportunities Act, which codified the requirement that school districts take affirmative steps to deal with the needs of language-minority children. The next year, Congress recognized language minorities in a different context by amending the Voting Rights Act to require bilingual registration and voting materials in electoral districts with at least 5 percent language-minority population. For schools, HEW's

Office of Civil Rights in 1975 issued the so-called *Lau* guidelines, which — for the first time — specifically required the use of non-English languages and cultures for language-minority students. The guidelines, however, stressed the goal of helping language-minority children gain proficiency in English.

The growing bilingual-education movement was challenged by several studies — including a major report published in 1978 under the auspices of the American Institutes for Research — that showed no achievement gains from the use of native-language instruction for non-English speakers. Despite the controversies, the Department of Education — carved out of HEW under President Jimmy Carter —

proposed regulations in August 1980 that tightened the requirement for bilingual education. The proposed guidelines, viewed by some as an appeal by Carter for Hispanic votes in the November election, called for bilingual education in any school with at least 25 limited-English-proficiency students in two consecutive grades.

The Reagan administration instituted what historian San Miguel calls a period of "retrenchment and redefinition" for bilingual education. On Feb. 2, 1981 — just two weeks after Reagan took office — Education Secretary Terrel Bell withdrew the proposed bilingual-education regulations from the Carter administration. Reagan himself told reporters he was opposed to bilingual education. He called it "absolutely wrong" to have a bilingual-education program "that is now openly, admittedly dedicated to preserving their native language and never getting them adequate in English." [19] Reagan's views helped encourage a growing English-only movement, which succeeded over the course of the decade in enacting official-English measures in more than a dozen states.

For schools, the administration began cutting funding for bilingual education; from a high of $158 million in fiscal 1979, federal support fell to $133 million by 1984. A study by two Education Department researchers published in 1981 again questioned the effects of bilingual education. The department's inspector general published a harsh audit of bilingual programs in seven school districts in Texas, which required them to refund federal grants because of failing to meet stated goals. Enforcement actions by the department's Office of Civil Rights to require bilingual programs, however, declined sharply.

The decline began and continued in the face of an influential ruling in 1981 by the federal appeals court for Texas that reinforced the federal requirement for bilingual instruction under the Equal Educational Opportunities Act. The ruling in *Castañeda v. Pickard* specified that bilingual-education programs must be "based on sound educational theory"; "implemented effectively with resources for personnel, instructional materials, and space"; and proven effective in overcoming language barriers and handicaps. [20]

As Reagan's Republican successor, President George H. W. Bush proved to be sympathetic to bilingual education. In a critical step, Bush allowed the publication in 1991 of an in-depth study of bilingual education commissioned under Reagan but withheld from publication. The Ramirez report — so-called after its principal investigator, J. David Ramirez — was summarized in a press release as affirming the ef-

fectiveness of the three most common language-instruction programs: immersion, early-exit bilingual or late-exit bilingual. As bilingual-education advocate Crawford notes, however, on closer examination the study supports longer bilingual instruction. The study found that students in late-exit programs had accelerated progress over time and that, regardless of instructional method, students generally needed five years or longer to achieve proficiency in English. [21]

The opposition to bilingual education continued to grow in the 1990s. After a decade of teaching English-language learners in bilingual Massachusetts, Porter harshly criticized the policy in her book, *Forked Tongue*, in 1990. Like other critics, Porter depicted bilingual instruction as ineffective educationally and politically and culturally divisive. Despite the criticism, the federal bilingual-education law was reenacted in 1994 under a Democratic-controlled Congress and a Democratic president, Bill Clinton.

Four years later, however, bilingual-education opponents won a major state-level victory with California's adoption of Proposition 227, a voter initiative that made so-called sheltered English-immersion the standard instructional method throughout the state for English-language learners. The initiative was bankrolled by Ron Unz, a millionaire businessman-turned-politician and political activist. Passed in 1998 with about 61 percent of the vote, the initiative requires sheltered English immersion for limited English proficiency (LEP) students during a transition not expected to last more than one year with transfer to mainstream classrooms after attaining "a good working knowledge" of English. Parents can waive the English-only rule if they show that native-language instruction would benefit their child. Two states followed California with stricter English-only initiatives: Arizona in 2000, Massachusetts in 2002.

Language Tests

Bilingual education had fallen so out of favor by the start of the 21st century that President George W. Bush and Congress combined to repeal the federal Bilingual Education Act and expunge the term from federal law. Bush successfully pushed for a new federal law, the No Child Left Behind Act, which required standardized testing of all schools with penalties for those found to be "underperforming." Supporters said the law would hold schools accountable for teaching English learners, but bilingual-education advocates feared misleading results from testing English learners only in English. Meanwhile, the Arizona bilingual education suit moved up to an eventual Supreme Court decision that tilted in favor of English immersion and appeared to limit federal courts' authority to order extra funding for English-language learners.

Bush made the education reform bill his major social policy initiative, securing bipartisan support by appealing to Republicans with test-based standards to hold schools accountable and to Democrats with increased funding to help schools meet the standards. Largely unnoticed in the main debates, the act's Title III replaced the Bilingual Education Act with the English Acquisition Act. As Crawford explains in his historical account, the act increased the authorized funding for English-language instruction but allocated the moneys according to a population-based formula instead of through competitive grants. As a result, funding was no longer concentrated on proven programs, but spread widely. Average grants the first year amounted to only $150 per student, far less than the average grant under the old law. [22]

The act — passed by Congress in December 2001 and signed by Bush on Jan. 8, 2002 — pointedly makes no recommendation as to a particular method of instruction for English learners. As part of the change, the Office of Bilingual Education was renamed the Office of English Language Acquisition, Language Enhancement, and Academic Achievement for Limited English Proficient Students — OELA for short. As the Department of Education explained, the act required state and local education agencies to establish English-proficiency standards; provide quality language instruction based on scientific research; and place highly qualified teachers in English-language classes. All English-language learners were to be tested annually "so that their parents will know how they are progressing." [23]

Nearly five years later, guidebooks issued by the Education Department late in 2006 designed to provide scientifically based recommendations on teaching methods continued to give school districts no guidance on the bilingual versus English-only debate. "We intentionally avoided that," Russell Gersten, a bilingual-education critic who headed the panel of experts that reviewed the guidebooks, told *Education Week*. David Francis, a University of Houston professor and bilingual-education supporter who led the writing of the guidebooks, concurred with the decision. But bilingual-education supporter Krashen at the University of Southern California complained that the guidebooks were "omitting something that is important." [24]

The debate that policy makers tried to duck continued among researchers.

A study of California schools published in March 2006 examining the impact of Proposition 227 concluded that no single instructional method for English learners was significantly better than another.

Unz, the English-only activist who had funded the initiative, criticized the study, insisting his analysis showed that the switch from bilingual to predominantly English-only had raised achievement levels. In any event, the study confirmed the drop in bilingual instruction from about 60 percent of English learners to only 8 percent. It also showed that only 40 percent of English learn-

First lady Michelle Obama attends a Cinco de Mayo celebration at the Latin American Montessori Bilingual (LAMB) Public Charter School in Washington, on May 4, 2009. Bilingual-education advocates are hoping for support from the Obama administration, which backs "transitional bilingual education" and promises to help English learners by "holding schools accountable for making sure these students complete school."

ers were reclassified as proficient after 10 years of public schooling. [25]

Two years later, two University of California research centers found no gains in English proficiency in California or the two other states with similar measures, Arizona and Massachusetts. "There's no visual evidence that these three states are doing better than the national average or other states" in educating English learners, Russell Rumberger, director of the Linguistic Minority Research Institute at UC-Santa

Barbara, told *Education Week*. The institute partnered with UCLA's Civil Rights Project on the study, which found a greater achievement gap for English learners in the three states than in two states, New Mexico and Texas, which continued to use native-language instruction for English learners. Gersten minimized the findings. He told the publication Proposition 227 had helped English learners by raising expectations and giving them the same curriculum as other students. [26]

Meanwhile, the Arizona suit had reached a critical stage with Judge Raner Collins' ruling in December 2005 that the state was in civil contempt for failing to "appropriately and constitutionally" fund English-language instruction. Collins' decision four months later to reject the legislature's funding increase and impose civil fines was set aside in August 2006 by the 9th U.S. Circuit Court of Appeals, which ordered a full hearing. After an eight-day hearing in January 2007, Collins reaffirmed his ruling, which the 9th Circuit upheld a year later.

On appeal by Superintendent Horne and the Republican legislative leaders, however, the Supreme Court in June 2009 ordered Collins to reconsider the motion to modify the injunction issued nine years earlier. For the majority, Justice Alito pointed to four changed circumstances warranting reconsideration, starting with the state's switch to English immersion. Research on English-language learning instruction, Alito wrote, "indicates there is documented, academic support for the view that SEI [sheltered English immersion] is significantly more effective than bilingual education." The other three factors cited were the federal No Child Left Behind Act; "structural and management reforms" in Nogales itself and the state's increased education funding.

Writing for the four dissenters, Justice Stephen G. Breyer said he would have upheld Judge Collins' order. The high court ruling, Breyer wrote, "will make it more difficult for federal courts to enforce . . . those federal standards." ■

CURRENT SITUATION

Lagging Indications

E nglish-language learners (ELLs) are lagging behind other students on math and reading achievement tests, and one-fourth are failing to make progress toward language proficiency, according to state data collected by the federal Department of Education.

Opposing camps in the bilingual versus English-immersion debate predictably blame the achievement and language-proficiency gaps on school districts' failure to adopt their differing prescriptions on the best instructional model to use for English learners. Some experts with less partisan views, however, point to other factors, including the concentration of English learners in high-poverty, lower-resourced schools. English learners score far below the national average for fourth-graders in both reading and math on the National Assessment of Educational Progress (NAEP), often called the nation's report card. The gap widens in test scores for eighth-graders, according to a recent analysis by the Pew Hispanic Center. [27]

The center's analysis of the 2005 NAEP showed, for example, that nearly three-fourths of fourth-grade English learners (73 percent) scored below "basic" on reading — double the national average of 36 percent. For eighth-graders, the national average of below-

basic scores fell to 27 percent, but the percentage of English learners scoring below basic remained almost unchanged at 71 percent.

A similar pattern was seen on math scores. Among English learners, 46 percent of fourth-graders scored below basic, compared to the national average of 20 percent. For eighth-graders, the gap widened markedly: 71 percent of English learners below basic compared to a national average of 31 percent.

On all four tests, only small fractions of English learners were rated as proficient or advanced, scores attained by roughly one-third of the students nationwide. The center's analysis, by senior researcher Richard Fry, found that English learners' scores were far below the average of white students and measurably below the averages for blacks and Hispanics.

Language-proficiency testing required of the states by the No Child Left Behind Act shows more directly the achievement gap for English learners. The federal law requires all public school students, including English learners, to meet reading and math proficiency standards by 2014. In tests administered in 2006 and 2007, however, only one-sixth of English learners nationwide were listed as having attained proficiency. One-fourth of the English learners were shown as not making progress. [28]

Both Fry and Barth at the school boards' Center for Public Education point to some precautions in interpreting the statistics. They both note, for example, that — in contrast to ethnic and racial groupings — students classified as English learners at one point can be reclassified as language-proficient later and no longer be included in the group.

Barth also stresses that English-language learners "are not a monolithic group." The vast majority are Spanish speakers, she says, but the others represent more than 400 different languages. Family backgrounds vary greatly as well: Some come from homes with

well-educated parents, while others have parents with limited education and literacy. As a result, Barth says, "the range of performance between the high- and low-performing ELL students is greater than the gap between ELLs and their English-speaking peers."

Despite those precautions, bilingual-education advocates decry what they see as the lagging achievement scores for English learners. "Most U.S. schools are dramatically under-educating" English learners, Collier and Thomas write. [29] Both they and journalist-author Crawford blame in part the popularity of English-immersion programs. English-only programs "continue to spread," and enrollment in bilingual programs declines, Crawford says, despite what he calls "increasing" evidence that bilingual programs are more effective.

From the opposite perspective, author Porter of the Center for Equal Opportunity says English-immersion programs are best-suited to the English learners who present the biggest challenges for schools: students from immigrant families typically poor and often headed by parents with limited education. "These children have to be given a priority education," Porter says. "What is important? First, give them English-language skills."

The Pew Center's Fry suggests, however, that English-learners' gaps may be related to the characteristics of the schools that most attend. In a second, recent report, Fry found that in the states with the largest concentration of English learners, the ELL students were concentrated in central city schools with higher average enrollment and higher student-to-teacher ratios than other public schools in the state. The schools with concentrated ELL populations also had a "substantially greater proportion" of students who qualified for free or reduced-price school lunches. [30]

Significantly, Fry found that the English learners' achievement gap was narrower in schools that had "at least a minimum threshold number of white

Continued on p. 1046

At Issue:

Is bilingual education best for English-language learners?

JAMES CRAWFORD
PRESIDENT, INSTITUTE FOR LANGUAGE AND EDUCATION POLICY; COAUTHOR, ENGLISH LEARNERS IN AMERICAN CLASSROOMS: 101 QUESTIONS, 101 ANSWERS

WRITTEN FOR *CQ RESEARCHER*, NOVEMBER 2009

bilingual education, perhaps the least understood program in our public schools, also turns out to be among the most beneficial. Its effectiveness — both in teaching English and in fostering academic learning in English — has been validated in study after study.

Yet U.S. media rarely report such findings. All too often, bilingualism is portrayed as a political controversy rather than a set of pedagogical challenges, a conflict over immigration instead of an effort to turn language "problems" into classroom resources.

In education, of course, there is no one-size-fits-all. What works for one student or group of students will not necessarily work for others. All things being equal, however, a large and consistent body of research shows that bilingual education is a superior way to teach English-language learners. Building on — rather than discarding — students' native-language skills creates a stronger foundation for success in English and academics.

This is a counterintuitive finding for many Americans, so it needs some explaining. Why does bilingual education work? Three reasons:

- When students receive some lessons in their native language, the teacher does not need to "dumb down" instruction in simplified English. So they have access to the same challenging curriculum as their English-speaking peers, rather than falling behind.
- The more these students progress in academic subjects, the more contextual knowledge they acquire to make sense of lessons in English. And the more "comprehensible input" they receive in English, the faster they acquire the language.
- Reading provides a foundation for all learning. It is much more efficiently mastered in a language that children understand. As they acquire English, these literacy skills are easily transferred to the new language. Once you can read, you can read!

Finally, let's consider the alternative: all-English "immersion." Independent studies have shown that after several years of such programs in California and Arizona, there has been no benefit for children learning English. In fact, the "achievement gap" between these students and fluent English speakers seems to be increasing.

Unfortunately, so is the gap between research and policy. Bilingual education has fallen out of favor politically for reasons that have nothing to do with its academic effectiveness. If we seriously hope to integrate immigrants as productive members of our society, that will have to change.

ROSALIE PEDALINO PORTER
BOARD MEMBER, CENTER FOR EQUAL OPPORTUNITY

WRITTEN FOR *CQ RESEARCHER*, DECEMBER 2009

bilingual education is the least effective method for teaching English-language learners. To meet the stated goals of federal and state laws of the past 40 years — that students would learn the English language rapidly and master school subjects taught in English — the experimental, theoretical model called bilingual education is a demonstrable, documented failure.

As a Spanish-English bilingual teacher in Massachusetts — the first state to mandate bilingual education — I saw firsthand the model's inadequacies. Our students were taught all subjects in Spanish most of the school day and provided brief English lessons. They were segregated by language and ethnicity in substantially separate classrooms for three to six years. The costs to school districts for this separate program are not as damaging as "the negative effect on English-language learner achievement," as documented in the 2009 study by the Texas Public Policy Foundation.

Reliable research was never the strong point in reporting on bilingual education in its first two decades. Valid studies of student achievement both in learning English and school subjects began to be published in the 1980s. Reliable studies must include two similar groups of students (socioeconomic status, level of English fluency), one enrolled in a bilingual program, one enrolled in an English-immersion program. At the end of two, three or four years, an objective assessment of which group of students showed measurable success in English language and academic learning can be determined.

From Dade County, Fla., in 1988, El Paso, Texas, in 1992, New York City in 1995, and numerous reports from California and Arizona over the past 10 years, English-immersion students outscored their counterparts in bilingual programs both in rapid acquisition of English language and literacy and on state tests of reading and math. The evidence for the superiority of English immersion surely influenced public opinion in the initiative referenda that legally threw out bilingual teaching by citizen vote in California (1998), Arizona (2000) and Massachusetts (2002). Of the 10 states that originally mandated native-language instruction bilingual programs, only four remain: Illinois, New Jersey, New York and Texas.

The debate is effectively over. A high accolade comes from the U. S. Supreme Court's recent ruling in the *Flores* case, which found "documented academic support for the view that structured English immersion is significantly more effective than bilingual education."

Continued from p. 1044

students." Barth similarly sees what she calls "linguistically isolated" schools as a substantial cause of the achievement gap.

"We sometimes give the least to the kids and the schools that have the least to begin with," Barth says. "Those schools have greater challenges and aren't being given much to work with in terms of resources."

Fighting in Court

Civil rights lawyers in two states with substantial Latino populations are waging legal battles begun decades ago to improve English-language instruction for Spanish-speaking students.

Lower federal court judges issued broad rulings in both cases telling state officials in Arizona to increase spending on English learners and in Texas to improve services and monitoring for English learners in secondary schools. But plaintiffs in both cases suffered setbacks earlier this year.

The 5th U.S. Circuit Court of Appeals issued a stay of the lower court judge's January 2008 order in the Texas case in February pending its own review of the decision. A three-judge panel is currently deliberating on the case following oral arguments on June 2. [31]

The Supreme Court's June 26 decision in the Arizona case (*Horne v. Flores*) sent that 17-year-old lawsuit back to federal district court in Phoenix. The ruling requires Judge Collins to reconsider the effort by Superintendent of Instruction Horne either to modify or dissolve the injunction re-

quiring more funding first issued by Judge Marquez in 2000 and reaffirmed by Collins in 2006.

Today, plaintiffs' lawyers in both cases say the state education systems are failing the public schools' English learners, who number more than 600,000 in Texas and nearly 170,000 in Arizona.

Roger Rice, an attorney who has worked on the Texas case since the early 1970s, blames poor performance and high dropout rates for English learners in secondary schools in part on lack of monitoring by state officials. "The Texas language program, particularly at the secondary level, is failing," says Rice, founder of the Massachusetts-based advocacy group META (Multicultural Education Training

Lourdes Carmona teaches Spanish pronunciation to first-graders at Birdwell Elementary School in Tyler, Texas. She was recruited from Spain, along with her husband, to teach Spanish-speaking youngsters in their native language.

and Advocacy). "And Texas has not evaluated the program to know why it's failing and has not made the changes to make it succeed."

In Arizona, plaintiffs' attorney Hogan says the state's model of four-hour pull-outs for language instruction for English learners segregates them unnecessarily and unlawfully. "This is classic segregation," Hogan says. "Kids in these classes are regarded by others as dumb, as second-class citizens."

State officials are defending their programs in both cases. Lawyers for the Texas Education Agency told the appeals court in June that a computerized tracking system adequately monitors performance of English learners. They also urged the appeals court to dismiss the entire case, originally filed by the Justice Department as a desegregation suit in 1970 and expanded by Latino advocacy groups in 1975 to specifically address English-learners' rights under the federal Equal Educational Opportunities Act.

Lawyers representing Horne and state legislative leaders told Supreme Court justices that the mandate for increased funding originally issued in 2000 had been superseded by the voter-approved decision to shift from bilingual to English immersion and by the passage of the federal No Child Left Behind Act. Since the ruling, Horne has continued to defend the new system. "Kids who come to this country need to learn English quickly," he says.

The Texas case lay dormant for a quarter-century after the 5th Circuit appeals court in 1982 reversed a ruling by U.S. District Judge Wayne Justice two years earlier that the state was not providing equal opportunities to English learners as the federal law required. The appeals court noted that the Texas legislature had passed a bilingual-education law and held that the state was entitled to time to bring schools into compliance.

With assistance from MALDEF, Rice moved to reopen the Texas case in 2006 after education officials decided to drop active monitoring of classes and materials for English learners. Justice initially ruled in 2007 that state officials were complying with the ruling, but he reversed himself in 2008 in an 88-page decision sharply critical of poor performance and high dropout rates for English learners in secondary schools.

In the Arizona case, Collins ruled in 2007 that the changes in educational policy and the additional funding approved by the legislature in 2006 did not solve what he termed the "resource" problem. The 9th U.S. Circuit Court of Appeals upheld his decision to leave the injunction in place, but the Supreme Court's conservative majority said Collins had given inadequate consideration to the various changes.

Significantly for the plaintiffs in Arizona and in other cases, however, the justices rejected the state's argument that compliance with the No Child Left Behind Act was sufficient to establish compliance with the earlier law requiring equal opportunities for English learners. The act's funding and its reporting and assessment schemes could be relevant, Alito explained, but not necessarily determinative under the 1974 act.

Appeals court judges closed the hearing in the Texas case in June by cautioning lawyers not to expect a quick ruling. In Arizona, opposing lawyers submitted new filings to Collins earlier in the fall; Collins is to hold a hearing on Dec. 14 to determine whether to limit further proceedings to Nogales schools or to apply any ruling statewide. ∎

OUTLOOK

Getting Results?

Two well-regarded school districts in the Washington, D.C., suburbs take different approaches to teaching English learners. Administrators in Montgomery County, Md., and Arlington, Va., both say they practice "immersion" as the best way to teach English to Latino students who enter their school systems more familiar with Spanish than with the nation's dominant tongue. But immersion has different meanings for the two systems. [32]

In Montgomery County, Spanish-speaking students at Sargent Shriver Elementary School — about half the student body — are immersed in English. ESL teachers "plug in" to mainstream classrooms to help English learners along or "pull out" students for individualized or group tutoring. Karen Woodson, the school district's head of ESL programs, says flexibility is important but stresses that the system strongly opposes use of native-language instruction to help students acquire English-language proficiency.

Across the Potomac River in Arlington, some Latino students are immersed in two languages: Spanish and English. At Francis Scott Key Elementary School ("Escuela Key"), each class is divided between Spanish and English speakers, and instruction is equally divided between the two languages. Principal Marjorie Myers says she favors dual-language immersion as the best long-term strategy for English learners even at the expense of short-term gains on language-proficiency tests.

In its influential *Castañeda* decision on the rights of English learners almost three decades ago, the federal appeals court in New Orleans said that courts ruling on such cases should examine three factors: whether a school system was using a program based on "sound educational theory," whether adequate resources were being provided and whether the program was proving to be effective.

In the intervening decades, many school systems picked one educational theory — bilingual education — or another — English immersion. The issue of adequate resources is muddy, with bilingual-education advocates claiming their approach is both better and cheaper. But the question of results appears less ambiguous. English learners lag in academic performance and in graduation rates, and the gaps do not appear to be narrowing.

With the number of English learners in public schools rapidly increasing — projected to be one-fourth of the school population by 2025 — the need to close that gap will only increase. [33] "It's going to be a long-term persistent problem," says Stanford professor Hakuta. "The number of English learners has increased to the point where it's no longer an issue like special education, a small subset. In many districts, it's a majority of the students."

Since the 1980s, teaching English learners has been an intensely political issue. English-immersion advocate Porter notes that former Boston University president John Silber, a critic of bilingualism and multiculturalism, once called English-language learning a "third-rail" issue — dangerous for politicians to touch.

In recent years, however, the politicization of the issue appears to be ebbing somewhat. "The black and white distinctions that existed before 1998 are no longer there," says Don Soifer, education analyst with the pro-English Lexington Institute.

In California, for example, the state's English-only initiative — Proposition 227 — remains on the books but has not stopped the Ventura County Unified School District from creating dual-language immersion programs at eight elementary- and middle-school campuses. "I think parents throughout the state recognize the value of having their kids be bilingual and biliterate," says associate superintendent Roger Rice. [34]

Bilingual-education advocates are hoping for support for their view from the Obama administration. The administration's stated agenda supports "transitional bilingual education" and promises to help English learners by "holding schools accountable for making sure these students complete school." The administration's education initiatives since January have given no emphasis to the issue, however, and the Education Department's Office of English Language Acquisition is operating with an interim director.

For educators, the next big event in Washington is the anticipated fight in Congress over reauthorizing the No Child Left Behind Act. Experts and advocates on both sides of the language-instruction issue applaud the act's goal — and 2014 deadline — of requiring language proficiency for English learners. But the National Education Association, the powerful teachers' union, wants more testing to be done in students' native language. Testing English learners in English "may be setting these students up for more failure," the NEA says in a policy brief. [35]

Despite the political controversies, some experts are predicting progress for English learners. "What we have now is good methodology about what works," says Barth with the school boards' Center for Public Education. "As we're collecting more data, we're seeing gains among English-language learners, and we're finding out more and more about what propels those gains. The more that information gets out, the politics will quiet down." ∎

Notes

[1] Flores was interviewed in Spanish by *CQ Researcher* staff writer Peter Katel. See also Eddi Trevizo and Pat Kossan, "Mom at Head of Suit Still Worried About English Learners," *The Arizona Republic*, June 26, 2009, p. 15.
[2] The decision is *Horne v. Flores*, 557 U.S. — (June 25, 2009). For coverage, see Pat Kossan, "A Win for State on English Learners," *The Arizona Republic*, June 26, 2009, p. 1.

[3] For previous coverage, see these *CQ Researcher* reports: Craig Donegan, "Debate Over Bilingualism," Jan. 19, 1996, pp. 49-72; and Richard L. Worsnop, "Bilingual Education," Aug. 13, 1993, pp. 697-720; and these in *Editorial Research Reports*: Sarah Glazer, "Bilingual Education: Does It Work?," March 11, 1988; pp. 125-140, and Sandra Stencel, "Bilingual Education," Aug. 19, 1977, pp. 617-636.
[4] For background, see Barbara Mantel, "No Child Left Behind," *CQ Researcher*, May 27, 2005, pp. 469-492.
[5] Claude Goldenberg, "Teaching English Language Learners: What the Research Does — and Does Not — Show," *American Educator*, summer 2008, www.aft.org/pubs-reports/american_educator/issues/summer08/goldenberg.pdf. Goldenberg cited A. M. Zehler, *et al.*, "Descriptive Study of Services to LEP0 Students and LEP Students with Disabilities, Vol. 1, Research Report," Development Associates, Inc., 2003.
[6] Virginia P. Collier and Wayne P. Thomas, *Educating English Learners for a Transformed World* (2009), pp. 3-4. The authors, professors emeriti at George Mason University, in Fairfax, Va., identify themselves as educational consultants on their Web site, www.thomasandcollier.com.
[7] *Ibid.*, p. 48. Statistical chart appears at p. 55.
[8] "What research shows about English language learners: At a glance," Center for Public Education undated, www.centerforpubliceducation.org/site/apps/nlnet/content3.aspx?c=lvIXIiN0JwE&b=5127871&content_id={DE9F2763-8DA4-4C2A-B3D1-9AEF8B3AEDA1}&notoc=1.
[9] James Crawford, *Educating English Learners: Language Diversity in the Classroom* (5th ed.), 2004.
[10] Collin Hitt, "Charter Schools and Changing Neighborhoods: Hispanic Students and English Learners in Chicago," Lexington Institute/Illinois Policy Institute, Sept. 29, 2009, www.lexingtoninstitute.org/library/resources/documents/Education/FinalProof9.29.09.pdf.
[11] See Mary Ann Zehr, "Nurturing 'School Minds': Through order and English immersion, a network of charter schools strives to turn Latino students into informed citizens and leaders inside and outside the community," *Education Week*, Oct. 7, 2009, p. 24.
[12] *Horne v. Flores, op. cit.*, p. 24 of slip opinion and footnote 10.
[13] Kelly Torrance, "Immersion Not Submersion: Converting English Learner Programs from Bilingual Education to Structured English Immersion in California and Elsewhere," October 2005; and "Immersion Not Submersion: Volume II: Lessons from Three California School Districts' Switch from Bilingual Education to Structured Immersion," March 2006, www.lexingtoninstitute.org/library/resources/documents/Education/immersion-not-submersion-converting-english.pdf.
[14] Stephen Krashen, "Proposition 227 and Skyrocketing Test Scores in California: An Urban Legend," *Educational Leadership*, December 2004/January 2005, www.sdkrashen.com/articles/prop227/index.html.
[15] See Arizona Department of Education, "The Effects of Bilingual Education Programs and Structured English Immersion Programs on Student Achievement: A Large-Scale Comparison," July 2004, http://epsl.asu.edu/epru/articles/EPRU-0408-66-OWI.pdf. The report is identified as a draft, but no later version was prepared.
[16] Kate Mahoney, Jeff MacSwan, Tom Haladyna and David Garcia, "*Castañeda*'s Third Prong: Evaluating the Achievement of Arizona's English Learners Under Restrictive Language Policy," in Patricia Gandara and Megan Hopkins, *Forbidden Language: English Learners and Restrictive Language Policies* (forthcoming January 2010).
[17] Background drawn from Guadalupe San Miguel Jr., *Contested Policy: The Rise and Fall of Federal Bilingual Education in the United States, 1960-2001* (2004). See also James Crawford, *Educating English Learners: Language Diversity in the Classroom* (5th ed.,), 2004; Rosalie Pedalino Porter, *Forked Tongue: The Politics of Bilingual Education* (2d ed.), 1996.
[18] The decision is *Lau v. Nichols*, 414 U.S. 563 (1974). San Miguel writes erroneously at one point that the court decided the case on constitutional grounds.
[19] Quoted in Crawford, *op. cit.*, p. 120.
[20] The citation is 648 F.2d 989 (5th Cir. 1981). Despite the favorable legal standard, the de-

About the Author

Associate Editor **Kenneth Jost** graduated from Harvard College and Georgetown University Law Center. He is the author of the *Supreme Court Yearbook* and editor of *The Supreme Court from A to Z* (both *CQ Press*). He was a member of the *CQ Researcher* team that won the American Bar Association's 2002 Silver Gavel Award. His previous reports include "Racial Diversity in Public Schools" and "Testing in Schools." He is also author of the blog *Jost on Justice* (http://jostonjusticeblogspot.com).

fendant Raymondville Independent School District, in south Texas near the Mexican border, ultimately won a ruling that it was providing adequate bilingual education to the Mexican-American students in the system. See Richard R. Valencia, *Chicano Students and the Courts: The Mexican American Struggle for Educational Equality* (2008), pp. 187-191.

[21] Crawford, *op. cit.*, pp. 148-152 in 4th ed.

[22] Crawford, *op. cit.*, pp. 356-357.

[23] Quoted in *ibid.*, p. 355.

[24] All three quoted in Mary Ann Zehr, "Guides Avoid Bilingual versus English-Only Issue," *Education Week*, Nov. 8, 2006, p. 20.

[25] Linda Jacobson, "Prop. 227 Seen as Focusing on 'Wrong Issue,'" *Education Week*, March 1, 2006, p. 18.

[26] Mary Ann Zehr, "NAEP Scores in States That Cut Bilingual Ed Fuel Concerns on ELLs," *Education Week*. May 14, 2008, p. 14. NAEP — commonly called the nation's report card — stands for National Assessment of Educational Progress.

[27] Richard Fry, "How Far Behind in Math and Reading are English Language Learners?," Pew Hispanic Center, June 6, 2007, http://pewhispanic.org/files/reports/76.pdf. The report does not include national averages, which were supplied from the National Assessment of Educational Progress Web site: http://nationsreportcard.gov/reading_math_2005/.

[28] Data from edweek.org, the Web site of *Education Week* and *Teachers Magazine*. See "English Language Learners" page on www.edcounts.org/createtable/viewtable.php.

[29] Collier and Thomas, *op. cit.*, p. 3.

[30] Richard Fry, "The Role of Schools in the English Language Learner Achievement Gap," Pew Hispanic Center, June 26, 2008, http://pewhispanic.org/reports/report.php?ReportID=89.

[31] The case is *United States v. Texas*, 08-40858. The Latino advocacy groups GI Forum and League of United Latin American Citizens (LULAC) intervened in 1975 in what was originally a school desegregation case to raise English-language learning issues under the Equal Educational Opportunities Act of 1974.

[32] Reporting by editorial intern Emily DeRuy, University of California, San Diego.

[33] See Goldenberg, *op. cit.*, p. 10.

[34] Quoted in Cheri Carlson, "Three more schools add bilingual immersion programs," *Ventura County Star*, July 15, 2009.

[35] "English Language Learners Face Unique Challenges," National Education Association, fall 2008, www.nea.org/assets/docs/mf_PB05_ELL.pdf.

FOR MORE INFORMATION

American Unity Legal Defense Fund, P.O. Box 420, Warrenton, VA 20187; www.americanunity.org. An educational organization that promotes conservative immigration reform in the legal arena.

Asian American Justice Center, 1140 Connecticut Ave., N.W., Suite 1200, Washington, DC 20036; (202) 296-2300; www.advancingequality.org. Works to advance human and civil rights for Asian Americans by providing them the tools and support needed to participate in the democratic process.

Asian American Legal Defense and Education Fund, 99 Hudson St., 12th Floor, New York, NY 10013; (212) 966-5932; www.aaldef.org. Promotes the civil rights of Asian Americans through litigation, advocacy, education and community organizing.

Center for Equal Opportunity, 7700 Leesburg Pike, Suite 231, Falls Church, VA 22043; (703) 442-0066; www.ceousa.org. Promotes color-blind public policies and seeks to block the expansion and use of racial preferences in employment, education and voting by promoting the assimilation of immigrants and opposing teaching in students' native languages.

Congressional Hispanic Caucus Institute, 911 2nd St., N.E., Washington, DC 20002; (202) 543-1771; www.chci.org. Helps increase opportunities for Hispanics to participate in the American policy-making process by offering educational and leadership-development programs.

English First, 666 Fu Zhou Rd., Shanghai, China 200001; +86 21 6133 6262; www.englishfirst.com. The world's largest private education company, specializing in language training, educational tours and cultural exchange.

Institute for Language and Education Policy, P.O. Box 5960, Takoma Park, MD 20913; www.elladvocates.org. Promoting research-based policies in serving English and heritage language learners to ensure that policies for serving children reflect the latest research about language and education.

Mexican American Legal Defense and Education Fund, 1016 16th St., N.W., Suite 100, Washington, DC 20036; (202) 293-2828; www.maldef.org. Promotes equality and justice through advocacy, litigation, public policy and education in the areas of employment, immigrants' rights, political access, voting rights and language rights.

National Association for Bilingual Education, 1313 L St., N.W., Suite 210, Washington, DC 20005; (202) 898-1829; www.nabe.org. Represents both English-language learners and bilingual education professionals through affiliate organizations in 23 states.

National Clearinghouse for English Language Acquisition, 2011 I St., N.W., Suite 300, Washington, DC 20036; (202) 467-0867; www.ncela.gwu.edu. Supports the U.S. Department of Education's Office of English Language Acquisition.

NCLR (National Council of La Raza), 1126 16th St., N.W., Washington, DC 20036; (202) 785-1670; www.nclr.org. The largest national Hispanic civil rights and advocacy organization in the U.S. works to improve opportunities for Hispanic Americans through applied research, policy analysis and advocacy.

National Education Association, 1201 16th St., N.W., Washington, DC 20036; (202) 833-4000; www.nea.org. An organization of 3.2 million members aimed at promoting the right of every child to quality public education, as well as advocating for education professionals.

National School Boards Association, 1680 Duke Street, Alexandria, VA 22314; (703) 838-6722; www.nsba.org. Seeks excellence and equity in public education through school board leadership in all communities.

Office of English Language Acquisition, Language Enhancement, and Academic Achievement for Limited English Proficient Students, 400 Maryland Ave., S.W., Washington, DC 20202; (202) 401-1423; www.ed.gov/about/offices/list/oela/index.html. Provides national leadership to help English-language learners and immigrant students attain English proficiency.

Bibliography

Selected Sources

Books

Collier, Virginia P., and Wayne P. Thomas, *Educating English Learners for a Transformed World*, Fuente Press, 2009.

Two former George Mason University professors specializing in research for "at-risk" students examine different methods for teaching English-language learners and repeat their research findings that English learners benefit from additional time in native-language instruction. The book closes with 11 recommendations for educators to follow in designing programs for English learners. Includes nine-page list of references.

Crawford, James, *Educating English Learners: Language Diversity in the Classroom* (5th ed.), Bilingual Education Services, 2004.

The longtime advocate for bilingual education provides a comprehensive history of language-education policies against the backdrop of growing language diversity due to increased immigration. Crawford, a former education reporter, served as executive director of the National Association for Bilingual Education and now writes and advocates on bilingual education as head of the Institute for Language Education and Policy. Includes chapter notes, 24-page compilation of sources and suggested readings.

Gandara, Patricia, and Megan Hopkins (eds.), *Forbidden Language: English Learners and Restrictive Language Policies*, Teachers College Press, forthcoming (January 2010).

The book examines the most up-to-date research on the impact of "restrictive language policies" adopted in three states by ballot measures: Arizona, California and Massachusetts. Gandara is professor of education at the University of California-Los Angeles; Hopkins is a doctoral student at UCLA's Graduate School of Education and Information Studies.

Porter, Rosalie Pedalino, *Forked Tongue: The Politics of Bilingual Education* (2d ed.), Transaction, 1996.

A prominent critic of bilingual education argues in favor of early and intensive instruction in English with no separation of language-minority children from fellow students. Porter served as director of language-instruction programs in Newton, Mass., in the 1980s and later as director of the READ Institute (Research in English Acquisition and Development), which has now been folded into the Center for Equal Opportunity. Includes chapter notes, four-page list of references. Porter is author most recently of the autobiographical *American Immigrant: My Life in Three Languages* (iUniverse, 2009).

San Miguel, Guadalupe Jr., *Contested Policy: The Rise and Fall of Federal Bilingual Education in the United States, 1960-2001*, University of North Texas Press, 2004.

The compact history traces the history of federal policy on education for English-language learners from the genesis of the Bilingual Education Act in the 1960s through its repeal with the No Child Left Behind Act in 2001. San Miguel is a professor of history at the University of Houston. Includes chapter notes, 45-page bibliographical essay organized by time period.

Schmid, Ronald Sr., *Language Policy and Identity in the United States*, Temple University Press, 2000.

A professor of political science at California State University-Long Beach examines the debate over bilingual education in the United States in the broader context of language policy with comparisons to policies in other multilingual countries. Includes chapter notes, 18-page list of references.

Valencia, Richard R., *Chicano Students and the Courts*, New York University Press, 2008.

A 46-page chapter sketches the history of bilingual education for Mexican-Americans since the Mexican-American War, discusses major bilingual-education suits in the 1970s and '80s and briefly treats the passage of state "English-only" initiatives and the repeal of the federal Bilingual Education Act. Valencia is a professor with the Center for Mexican American Studies at the University of Texas in Austin.

Articles

Goldenberg, Claude, "Teaching English Language Learners: What the Research Does — and Does Not — Show," *American Educator*, summer 2008, www.aft.org/pubs-reports/american_educator/issues/summer08/goldenberg.pdf.

A professor of education at Stanford University delineates three conclusions from the research on English learners, including the key finding that teaching students in their first language promotes higher levels of reading achievement in English. Adapted from "Improving Achievement for English Language Learners, in Susan B. Neuman (ed.), *Educating the Other America: Top Experts Tackle Poverty, Literacy, and Achievement in Our Schools* (Paul H. Brooke Publishing Co., 2008).

Reports and Studies

Rossell, Christine H., "Dismantling Bilingual Education, Implementing English Immersion: The California Initiative," Public Policy Institute of California, 2002, www.eric.ed.gov/ERICWebPortal/custom/portlets/record Details/detailmini.jsp?_nfpb=true&_&ERICExtSearch_Search Value_0=ED467043&ERICExtSearch_SearchType_0=no& accno=ED467043.

The detailed report by the Boston University political scientist concludes that Proposition 227, the California initiative that restricted bilingual education in public schools, may have benefited English learners but cautions that English learners continued to suffer achievement gaps because of immigration status and family backgrounds.

The Next Step:

Additional Articles from Current Periodicals

Dual Immersion

Burgarino, Paul, "In Any Language, Program Shows Moderate Results," *Contra Costa* **(California)** *Times*, **June 13, 2009.**

The school district in Pittsburg, Calif., has shown favorable results for its dual-immersion program.

Derby, Samara Kalk, "Spanish Spoken Here," *Capital Times* **(Wisconsin), April 15, 2009, p. 20.**

A dual-immersion program in Madison, Wis., has been gaining popularity despite low initial test scores.

Dollar, Heath, "Two Languages, One Future," *Dallas Morning News*, **Oct. 23, 2008, p. 14B.**

A dual-immersion system should be incorporated into America's schools to help immigrant and native students.

Stewart, Kirsten, "Chinese Coming to a School Near You," *Salt Lake Tribune*, **June 12, 2009.**

Dual-immersion programs in Mandarin are coming to 21 elementary schools in Salt Lake City, Utah, by 2010.

English Immersion

Benjamin, Marc, "Immersed in English," *Fresno* **(California)** *Bee*, **Sept. 4, 2009, p. A1.**

Many school districts are reporting success with an immersion program that focuses on teaching English instead of teaching the language as part of instruction in other subjects.

Guerra, Carlos, "What's the Goal? Learning English, or Learning?" *San Antonio Express-News*, **July 18, 2009, p. 1B.**

The U.S. Supreme Court has concluded that structured English immersion is significantly more effective than bilingual education.

Haver, Johanna, "Nogales' English Immersion Program Blazed Ariz. Trail," *Arizona Republic*, **July 3, 2009, p. 26.**

Students in Nogales, Ariz., have shown remarkable progress ever since school officials scrapped bilingual education in favor of more English-immersion techniques.

Kocian, Lisa, "English Period," *The Boston Globe*, **Sept. 25, 2008, p. Reg1.**

Some educators say a state law pushing immersion ahead of bilingual classes for immigrant students may be counterproductive.

Foreign-Language Instruction

Chandler, Michael Alison, "Budget Woes Frustrate Foreign Language Goals," *The Washington Post*, **Nov. 17, 2009, p. B1.**

Lack of funding has forced many school boards to scale back foreign-language instruction.

Jeter, Amy, "City Aims to Expand Foreign Language to Elementary Schools," *Virginian-Pilot*, **June 9, 2008, p. B1.**

The Virginia Board of Education encourages foreign-language instruction for elementary school students.

Salzer, James, "Foreign Language: A New Push to Restart Classes," *Atlanta Journal-Constitution*, **March 3, 2008, p. 1A.**

Georgia's Senate majority leader wants to restore foreign-language instruction in the state's elementary schools after it was cut by Republican Gov. Sonny Perdue.

Native Americans

Coldwell, Linda, "Lecture Examines Question of Official English," *Native American Times* **(Oklahoma), Sept. 18, 2009, p. 2.**

The movement to have English declared the official language of the United States has drawn criticism from educators advocating for Native American languages.

Moulton, Kristen, "Tribal Educators Told More Cultural, Native Language Learning Needed," *Salt Lake* **(Utah)** *Tribune*, **Sept. 25, 2008.**

Achievement among Native American students can be raised by teaching them more about their cultures and languages.

Wagner, Dennis, "Tribes Aren't Quiet About Language Loss," *Los Angeles Times*, **Aug. 3, 2008, p. B7.**

American Indians are using summer camps to encourage and teach youths about their native languages.

CITING *CQ RESEARCHER*

Sample formats for citing these reports in a bibliography include the ones listed below. Preferred styles and formats vary, so please check with your instructor or professor.

MLA STYLE

Jost, Kenneth. "Rethinking the Death Penalty." CQ Researcher 16 Nov. 2001: 945-68.

APA STYLE

Jost, K. (2001, November 16). Rethinking the death penalty. *CQ Researcher, 11*, 945-968.

CHICAGO STYLE

Jost, Kenneth. "Rethinking the Death Penalty." *CQ Researcher*, November 16, 2001, 945-968.

In-depth Reports on Issues in the News

Are you writing a paper?

Need backup for a debate?

Want to become an expert on an issue?

For more than 80 years, students have turned to *CQ Researcher* for in-depth reporting on issues in the news. Reports on a full range of political and social issues are now available. Following is a selection of recent reports:

Civil Liberties
Closing Guantánamo, 2/09
Affirmative Action, 10/08
Gay Marriage Showdowns, 9/08
America's Border Fence, 9/08
Immigration Debate, 2/08

Crime/Law
Prisoner Reentry, 12/09
Interrogating the CIA, 9/09
Examining Forensics, 7/09
Legalizing Marijuana, 6/09
Wrongful Convictions, 4/09

Education
Value of a College Education, 11/09
Financial Literacy, 9/09
Reading Crisis? 2/08
Discipline in Schools, 2/08

Environment/Society
Women in the Military, 11/09
Conspiracy Theories, 10/09
Human Spaceflight, 10/09
Gays in the Military, 9/09
Energy and Climate, 7/09
Future of Books, 5/09

Health/Safety
Medication Abuse, 10/09
Nuclear Disarmament, 10/09
Health-Care Reform, 8/09
Straining the Safety Net, 7/09
Treating Depression, 6/09
Reproductive Ethics, 5/09

Politics/Economy
State Budget Crisis, 9/09
Business Bankruptcy, 4/09
Future of the GOP, 3/09
Middle-Class Squeeze, 3/09

Upcoming Reports

Homelessness, 12/18/09   Animal Rights, 1/8/10   Government and Religion, 1/15/10

ACCESS

CQ Researcher is available in print and online. For access, visit your library or www.cqresearcher.com.

STAY CURRENT

To receive notice of upcoming *CQ Researcher* reports, or learn more about *CQ Researcher* products, subscribe to the free e-mail newsletters, *CQ Researcher Alert!* and *CQ Researcher News*: http://cqpress.com/newsletters.

PURCHASE

To purchase a *CQ Researcher* report in print or electronic format (PDF), visit www.cqpress.com or call 866-427-7737. Single reports start at $15. Bulk purchase discounts and electronic-rights licensing are also available.

SUBSCRIBE

Annual full-service *CQ Researcher* subscriptions—including 44 reports a year, monthly index updates, and a bound volume—start at $803. Add $25 for domestic postage.

CQ Researcher Online offers a backfile from 1991 and a number of tools to simplify research. For pricing information, call 800-834-9020, ext. 1906, or e-mail librarysales@cqpress.com.

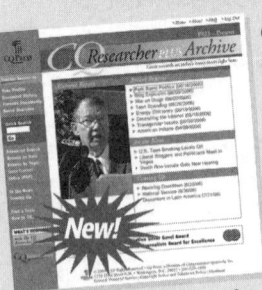

Published by CQ Press, a Division of SAGE

www.cqresearcher.com

Housing the Homeless

Is the solution more shelters or affordable housing?

T he face of homelessness is changing in the United States. In the past, the homeless typically were single men and women who lived on the street or in shelters; many were mentally ill or drug addicts, or both. But today's homeless may well be a suburban couple with children who lost their home to foreclosure and are staying with relatives or living at a shelter. As the recession continues to ravage the middle class and the working poor, job losses and medical emergencies add to the number of homeless Americans. Advocates for the homeless also cite a shortage of affordable housing. A 2008 federal government survey showed a one-year 9 percent increase in families relying on homeless shelters. In recent months, local governments and school districts have been reporting homelessness cases more than doubling this year. But funding shortages may force agencies that help the homeless to curtail services.

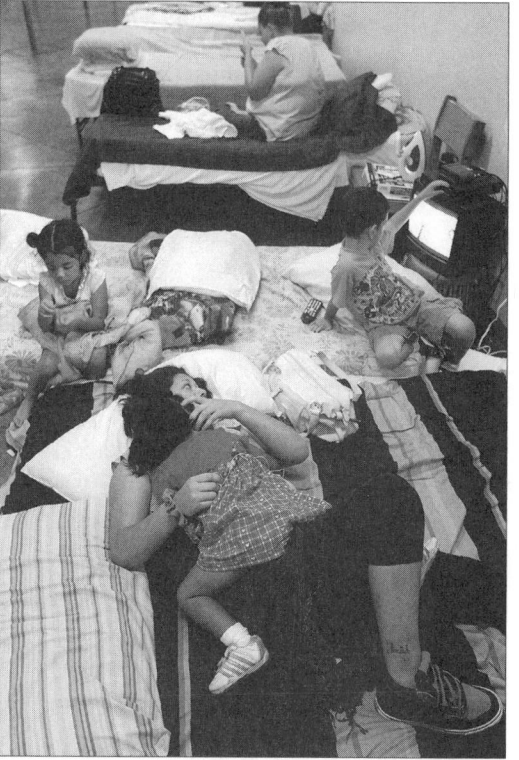

Unable to pay her rent or find a job, a mother rests with her three children at the Presbyterian Night Shelter in Fort Worth, Texas, on June 19. In the wake of the recession, growing numbers of families around the nation are living in shelters.

CQ Researcher • Dec. 18, 2009 • www.cqresearcher.com
Volume 19, Number 44 • Pages 1053-1076

CQ Researcher

Dec. 18, 2009
Volume 19, Number 44

MANAGING EDITOR: Thomas J. Colin
tcolin@cqpress.com

ASSISTANT MANAGING EDITOR: Kathy Koch
kkoch@cqpress.com

ASSOCIATE EDITOR: Kenneth Jost

STAFF WRITERS: Thomas J. Billitteri, Marcia Clemmitt, Peter Katel

CONTRIBUTING WRITERS: Rachel Cox, Sarah Glazer, Alan Greenblatt, Reed Karaim Barbara Mantel, Patrick Marshall, Tom Price, Jennifer Weeks

DESIGN/PRODUCTION EDITOR: Olu B. Davis

ASSISTANT EDITOR: Darrell Dela Rosa

FACT-CHECKING: Eugene J. Gabler, Michelle Harris

CQ PRESS

A Division of SAGE

PRESIDENT AND PUBLISHER:
John A. Jenkins

CQ Researcher (ISSN 1056-2036) is printed on acid-free paper. Published weekly, except; (Jan. wk. 1) (May wk. 4) (July wks. 1, 2) (Aug. wks. 3, 4) (Nov. wk. 4) and (Dec. wk. 4), by CQ Press, a division of SAGE Publications. Annual full-service subscriptions start at $803. For pricing, call 1-800-834-9020, ext. 1906. To purchase a CQ Researcher report in print or electronic format (PDF), visit www. cqpress.com or call 866-427-7737. Single reports start at $15. Bulk purchase discounts and electronic-rights licensing are also available. Periodicals postage paid at Washington, D.C., and additional mailing offices. POSTMASTER: Send address changes to CQ Researcher, 2300 N St., N.W., Suite 800, Washington, DC 20037.

Cover: Getty Images/John Moore

Housing the Homeless

BY PETER KATEL

THE ISSUES

Leida Ortiz was getting by. She lived with her sister and both of their children in an apartment in Worcester, Mass. Then, in the spring of 2007, her factory-worker father was diagnosed with stomach cancer, so Ortiz moved back into the home her parents owned to help her mother care for her father.

After he died, in December of that year, Ortiz and her mother couldn't afford the mortgage payments on the house. A move back to her sister's didn't work out, so Ortiz and her two children began sharing an apartment with a roommate. But she wasn't making enough from her part-time job as a nursing assistant to kick in her $400 share of the rent.

The roommate asked her and her 11-year-old son, Joseph, and 5-year-old daughter, Angelina, to leave.

"I became homeless in July," Ortiz said. "I cried every night, wondering if my kids were going to end up in different schools somewhere else. We were living out of our bags. We didn't know where we were going to end up next. The kids, they see that you're stressed, they get stressed. They see you putting yourself to sleep every night crying."

Speaking at a Capitol Hill briefing held by an advocacy group in early December, Ortiz recounted a happy ending to her family's two-week stay at a motel. She urged the assembled housing advocates and congressional staffers to work to expand the "prevention and rapid rehousing" program that she credited for her family's rescue.

Now working three part-time jobs, the 30-year-old Ortiz hardly fits the

Nursing assistant Leida Ortiz is working three part-time jobs and getting back on her feet after becoming homeless in July and living with her two children in a motel room for two weeks. At a recent briefing on Capitol Hill, she urged housing advocates to work to expand the emergency housing program that helped her family.

picture of "homeless" that hit the national consciousness in the early 1980s — seemingly unemployable people suffering mental illness or addiction or both. But in an economic climate shadowed by massive unemployment, some experts see working families facing threats to their housing stability that easily can escalate into homelessness, as in Ortiz's case. "When you're going into a recession starting with a limited supply of affordable housing, with families who are precariously housed and at risk, it's the perfect storm for families," says Mary K. Cunningham, a housing specialist at the nonpartisan Urban Institute think tank.

In 2008, homelessness among people in families rose by 9 percent over the number from the previous year, the U.S. Department of Housing and Urban Development (HUD) reported in an annual survey on homelessness. [1]

Overall, about 1.6 million people slept in homeless shelters or other temporary housing in the United States in 2008, the report said. [2] Whether that rough estimate shows an increase or decrease from the 1980s can't be determined, Cunningham says, given the vast differences in methodology from then until now.

Whatever the case, housing advocates are united in the belief that government action can eliminate homelessness once and for all. Conservatives tend to be more skeptical, though ideology isn't a reliable guide to views on homelessness.

"It is immoral," Cheh Kim, a staff member for Sen. Christopher Bond, R-Mo., told the Capitol Hill briefing. "People need to understand that anybody can slip into homelessness. Just go into shelters and talk to people and realize that a lot of them were middle-income, or owned small businesses, and because of one little thing in their life, they just fell down."

To be sure, Kim's overall view was that Congress has been responding effectively to the persistence of homelessness. A major piece of evidence: a $1.5 billion appropriation in mid-2009 for a new Homelessness Prevention and Rapid Re-Housing Program (HPRP).

But Joel Segal, a staffer for Rep. John Conyers, D-Mich., argued at the briefing that congressional attitudes remain an obstacle to a definitive solution to homelessness. "A majority of people in Congress do think that homeless people want to be homeless," Segal

California Has Largest Homeless Population

Nearly 160,000 people in California are homeless, more than twice as many as New York, the state with the next-largest homeless population. Seventeen states have more than 10,000 homeless people, while 11 states have fewer than 2,000.

Homeless Population by State
(on a single night in January 2008)

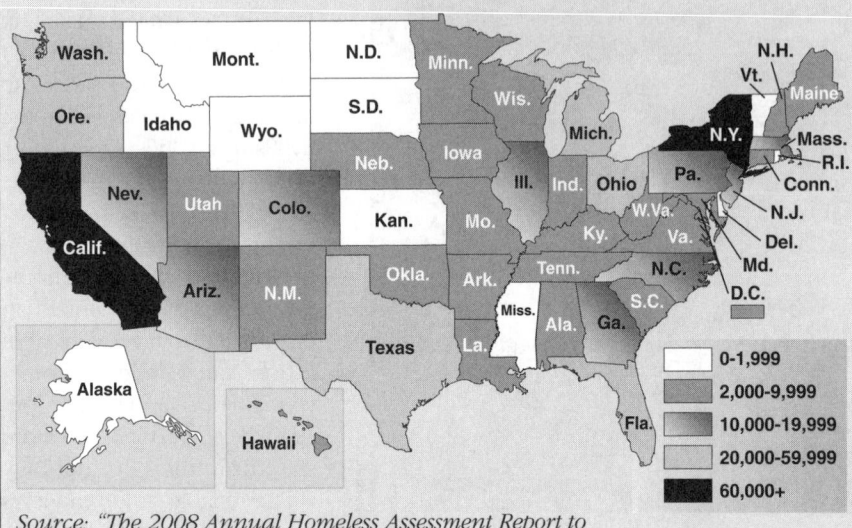

□	0-1,999
▨	2,000-9,999
▦	10,000-19,999
▩	20,000-59,999
■	60,000+

Source: "The 2008 Annual Homeless Assessment Report to Congress," U.S. Department of Housing and Urban Development, July 2009

told Kim and the rest of those present. "That's who they see in the streets pushing the baskets. Trust me on this — they do not know who's in those shelters, because most members of Congress are raising money from very wealthy donors.' "

Notwithstanding the staffers' emphasis on shelters, the growing consensus among advocates for the homeless is that a danger exists of policy makers focusing too heavily on shelters. That approach, they say, would effectively mean continuing to channel mentally unstable and chronically homeless people into shelters instead of expanding a newer strategy of building permanent facilities designed to meet their needs. And families in unstable housing situations — perhaps "doubled up" in relatives' homes — should be kept out of shelters in the first place.

"What we've learned over the past 10 years is that building up a bigger shelter system is a sort of self-fulfilling prophecy," says Nan Roman, president of the National Alliance to End Homelessness.

A number of sources report rising housing instability among families. HUD experts studying present-day trends see a link between the economic crisis and the growing number of families in shelters.[3] The National School Boards Association said in January 2009 that 724 of the country's nearly 14,000 school districts had already served 75 percent or more of the number of homeless students they'd served during the 2007-2008 school year.[4]

Districts track the trend because the Education for Homeless Children and Youth Act requires schools to provide the same level of education to students without fixed addresses as to all other children and youth. Schools can also use grants made under the law to provide homeless students with medical and dental care and other services.

A constellation of other laws authorizes programs designed for the "chronically" homeless, for households who can't afford decent housing and for veterans without homes.

This year, Congress added new forms of assistance, including the Homeless Emergency Assistance and Rapid Transition to Housing (HEARTH) Act for families facing imminent loss of housing or recently made homeless. The law also promotes the construction of so-called "supportive housing" for the long-term homeless, who need mental health services and similar services along with roofs over their heads.

Meanwhile, about 2 million families nationwide receive substantial help in paying their rents under the Section 8 Housing Choice Voucher Program, in place since 1974 and revamped in 1998. For many housing advocates, Section 8 vouchers represent a speedy way to expand the supply of affordable housing, the lack of which they view as a major contributor to homelessness.

Some conservative policy experts say the problem isn't a shortage of affordable housing but deeply rooted poverty — a condition they call ill-suited for resolution by housing subsidies. "The idea that housing is unaffordable and that we've done nothing about it — give me a break," says Howard Husock, vice president of the Manhattan Institute for Policy Research, a New York think tank. "What we've done to make housing more affordable over the past 30 years is so extensive that I would inquire of advocates what more they would have government do."

Even so, HUD, which administers three of those programs, calculates that a family with one full-time, minimum-wage worker can't afford a two-bedroom apartment anywhere in the country.[5]

As a practical matter, a one-earner family means a household headed by a single mother — the population segment that by all accounts is the most economically and socially vulnerable to deep poverty. The HUD annual report says that families in shelters are typically headed by a single mother. [6]

Ortiz, the once-homeless single mother in Worcester, Mass., says that she was able to start turning her life around only after her city's housing program helped her find an $850-a-month apartment, which she pays for with the help of a $700 monthly subsidy from the "rapid rehousing" program.

Before that, she says. "I couldn't get more work hours because of my kids getting out of school at 4:10. I didn't have anybody reliable enough to drop them off for me or pick them up if I did get a full-time job, and after-school programs cost so much."

Once she and her family got a place of their own, she found a friend who could pick up the children twice a week, allowing Ortiz to work two part-time jobs as a nursing assistant, and one in a party-supply store. In addition, she's studying for the GED, planning to then enroll in medical-technology training.

"Things are slowly falling into place for me," she says. "A shelter would have been no way for my kids to live. It's not the same as having your house."

As homeless advocates and public officials struggle with rising numbers of homeless families, here are questions being debated:

Can government end homelessness?

Homelessness has remained a social and political issue since it surfaced in the late 1970s and exploded in the early '80s.

The fact that more than a million and a half people every year experience homelessness makes plain that all the attention focused on the problem over the past three decades hasn't

Total No. of Homeless

About 1.6 million persons used a shelter or transition housing, including half a million individuals in families.

Over the Course of a Year
(Oct. 2007-Sept. 2008)

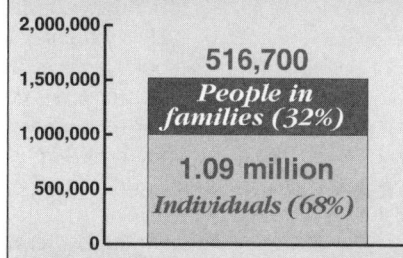

516,700
People in families (32%)

1.09 million
Individuals (68%)

At a Single Point in Time
(one night in January 2008)

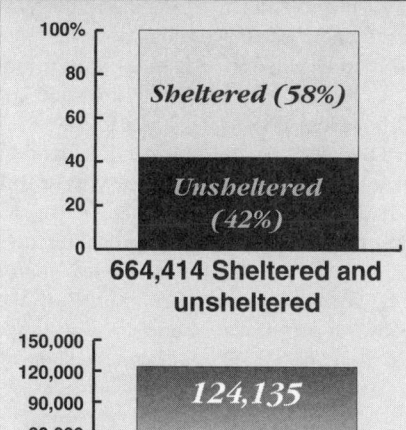

Sheltered (58%)

Unsheltered (42%)

664,414 Sheltered and unsheltered

124,135

Chronically homeless

Source: Department of Housing and Urban Development, July 2009

eliminated it. To some conservatives, the persistence of homelessness despite myriad government programs suggests they may be doing more to perpetuate the problem than to solve it — if a solution is possible at all, which some conservatives doubt.

Nevertheless, conservatives don't automatically reject government pro-

grams, especially those aimed directly at people shuttling between the street and shelters. In fact, the government committed itself to ending "chronic" homelessness in 10 years when Republican George W. Bush was in office (*see p. 1068*).

Housing advocates on the liberal side argue for expanding that goal to ensure that no families suffer loss of their homes, or, in the worst-case scenario, get help in acquiring new housing. That strategy is embodied in the expansion of the McKinney-Vento Homeless Assistance Act that President Obama signed into law in May. It provides "homelessness prevention" aid to families living in unstable housing conditions — moving in with relatives, for example.

Now, the housing advocates are pushing for more funding, arguing that as more families benefit, builders will respond. "The government can stimulate the housing market in a way to allow homeless people to become housed," says Linda Couch, deputy director of the National Low Income Housing Coalition. She advocates expanding government subsidies designed to make housing affordable for low-wage workers.

Responses that go beyond helping individuals cope with financial emergencies are also well within government's capability, Couch argues. "We know how to build housing," she says. "It's not rocket science, it's just too expensive for people earning the minimum wage, or even two times the minimum wage. Work doesn't pay enough."

Conservative analysts don't necessarily reject strategies designed to boost the purchasing power of low-wage workers. But they argue that such measures shouldn't be lumped in with responses to homelessness.

"Government should strive to end homelessness of single individuals — people who live on the street, who have mental illness and substance abuse problems," says Husock, at the Manhattan Institute. People who aren't on the street but who face housing crises,

Homeless in Nation's Capital Face Cold Winter

Funding cuts may reduce number of beds in shelters.

Mark Raymond is worried. He says funding cuts will prevent his organization's huge 1,350-bed shelter in Washington — among America's largest — from adequately serving homeless men and women in the nation's capital.

"Lots of programs that were started last year and this year are not to be funded next year," says Raymond, director of administrative offices at the Community for Creative Non-Violence.

In late September, Clarence Carter, director of the city's Department of Human Services, announced a $12 million cut in homeless-services funding for fiscal 2010. D.C. Council member Tommy Wells, D-Ward 6, contended the cut could be as large as $20 million. [1] Either way, homeless shelters say they will have to scramble to find enough beds for the lethally cold hypothermia season.

The current economy has forced more people onto the streets, including more families in which jobs have been lost and no savings exist. The slow housing market means an increasing number of electricians and construction workers are unemployed. [2] Half the homeless adults in Washington don't receive regular income, including Social Security and disability checks. The 20 percent who are employed have a median monthly income of $524.

According to a January 2009 survey, 6,228 homeless people live in shelters or transitional housing in the District, a 3 percent increase over 2008. [3] In July the total included 703 homeless families and more than 1,400 homeless children. Last year, homelessness among families across the nation rose 9 percent but 25 percent in the District. [4]

The number of teenagers without a place to live is also rising. But so is awareness of their plight. Recently, rappers Flava Flav, once homeless himself, and Chuck D., of the band Public

Enemy, shared a Thanksgiving meal with the young residents at the Sasha Bruce House in Washington, which features programs for children ages 11-17. Typically, youths are reunited with their families or transitioned into more permanent care. Counseling services are provided, particularly as children without families transition into adulthood.

The two entertainers encouraged the youngsters to stay in school. "It takes three times as much to get your education later as now, so do it now," Chuck D told the teens crowded around him. Later, Public Enemy performed, and Flava Flav stressed the importance of volunteerism. "If you're successful and can't talk to younger people in need, you got a problem," he said.

During his term, former Mayor Anthony A. Williams called for an end to homelessness by 2014. [5] A major component of his "Homeless No More" plan, now being implemented by current Mayor Adrian M. Fenty, is providing housing and financial support to those most at risk of becoming homeless. In early December, the District distributed $7.5 million in federal stimulus money to house homeless families and help struggling families remain in their homes. The money, from federal Homeless Prevention and Rapid Re-Housing funds awarded to the District in July, will help 680-800 households. [6] Those who have been homeless the longest and those with the most severe disabilities will be housed first. Proponents of the plan say programs in Denver, San Francisco, and Portland, Ore., have proven that providing housing and counseling is more humane and cost-effective than putting people in shelters.

Martha Burt and Sam Hall — researchers at the Urban Institute, a Washington think tank — endorse Fenty's focus on permanent supportive housing, but they caution he needs to

he argues, can be helped more effectively by programs that don't limit assistance to housing subsidies. "Let's say a blue-collar, two-parent family has been hurt by this recession," Husock says. "Why would we want to say, 'Here's a chit for housing?' All you can use that for is to rent an apartment from a landlord who is willing to take you. Why wouldn't we say we are increasing unemployment insurance, or the value of the earned-income tax credit, and you can use that money as you see fit? If you want to live with his parents for a year while you save, why wouldn't you have that choice?"

But the line isn't hard and fast between policy experts who are skeptical of government's capacity to end all homelessness, and those who argue that government programs can prevent homelessness as well as rescue the homeless from the street.

Roman has no preference for housing-only assistance over other kinds of aid. "Housing affordability has an income dimension and a supply dimension," she says. "You could make housing cheaper or figure out some way to supplement people's income through vouchers or tax credits — however you want to do it."

The bottom line, Roman says, is that the government can rescue long-term homeless people from the streets, even while ensuring that people who have homes don't lose them. "Do I think homelessness can be ended? Yes," she says. "People will always have housing crises, but I don't think there's any particular reason we can't end homelessness. I remember a time when we didn't really have homelessness."

Policy experts who advocate reducing government's efforts at social engineering doubt that politicians and bureaucrats can achieve anything close to a definitive result. "I don't think

keep the momentum going if homelessness is to be ended in the next four years. [7] However, Michael Ferrell, executive director of the District of Columbia Coalition for the Homeless, says ending homelessness by 2014 is "very highly unlikely" and calls for a multi-pronged approach.

"The first prong has to be prevention strategies, and quite frankly, that's preferable to addressing the problem on the back end," he says. Homeless individuals and families should be rehoused as soon as possible, he explains, but the long-term goal should be to provide enough rental assistance or subsidies for up to 12 months to prevent homelessness from occurring in the first place.

But Raymond cautions against shifting the focus away from shelters. "So many people need subsidized housing," he says, "that there is a year-and-a-half, two-year waiting list. Shelters are absolutely still necessary."

The shift towards permanent supportive housing instead of shelters, however, is a national trend. Philip F. Mangano, until recently executive director of the U.S. Interagency Council on Homelessness, had focused on getting people out of shelters and into homes. "When you ask the consumer what they want, they don't simply say a bed, blanket and a bowl of soup," he

A homeless man settles in at a Metro station in Washington, D.C., in May 2009. More than 6,000 homeless people live in shelters or transitional housing in the District.

AFP/Getty Images/Paul J. Richards

said. "They say they want a place to live. We have resources being provided to us at record levels. If you look at the numbers for chronic homelessness, we're winning." [8]

— Emily DeRuy

[1] Darryl Fears, "Officials Squabble, Service Providers Scramble; No Matter How You Do the Math, Advocates Say, Less Money Means More People on Streets," *The Washington Post*, Oct. 6, 2009, p. B2.

[2] Mary Otto, "A Growing Desperation; Housing, Economic Slumps May Portend Rise in Ranks of Region's Homeless, Survey Shows," *The Washington Post*, Jan. 25, 2008, p. B1.

[3] "A Summary of the 2009 Point in Time Enumeration for the District of Columbia," The Community Partnership for the Prevention of Homelessness, www.community-partnership.org/docs/TCP%20Fact%20Sheet%20Point%20in%20Time%202009.pdf.

[4] "In the News," Washington Legal Clinic for the Homeless, www.legalclinic.org/about/inthenews.asp.

[5] Anthony A. Williams, "Homeless No More: A Strategy for Ending Homelessness in Washington, D.C. by 2014," U.S. Department of Health and Human Services, www.hrsa.gov/homeless/statefiles/dcap.pdf.

[6] Darryl Fears, "District to Disburse $7.5M in Stimulus Money to Help Homeless," *The Washington Post*, Nov. 30, 2009.

[7] Martha Burt and Sam Hall, "What It Will Take to End Homelessness in D.C.," The Urban Institute, July 13, 2008, www.urban.org/publications/901185.html.

[8] Derek Kravitz, "Homelessness Official Wins Praise with Focus on Permanent Housing; Detractors Cite Mangano's Frequent Travel, Including Trips Abroad," *The Washington Post*, Dec. 30, 2008, p. A13.

government can end homelessness," says Michael D. Tanner, a senior fellow at the Cato Institute, a libertarian think tank.

But government could protect more people from homelessness by making affordable housing more available, argues Tanner, who specializes in domestic policy. County and city governments could modify zoning restrictions that, for instance, prohibit apartment building construction in some localities.

Should the definition of homeless include people in unstable housing situations?

The ways in which laws and poli-

cies define a condition also specify who will — and who won't — benefit from programs designed as remedies.

"Homeless" might seem to be an easily defined term. But some argue for expanding its definition to those with housing, albeit in unstable situations. Skeptics question whether that would blunt the effectiveness of programs designed to get unsheltered people off the streets.

The activists who first drew attention in the late 1970s to the homeless were advocating on behalf of the lost souls on skid rows in virtually every city, the looked-down-upon people

often described as hoboes, vagrants and bums. They slept in parks, bus stations or cardboard boxes in alleys or — at best — ultra-cheap hotels known as "flop houses" or "cage hotels" (featuring cubicles with wire-mesh roofs to prevent stealing).

At about the same time, concerns were also raised about veterans of the recently ended Vietnam War. Then came the recession of 1981-1982, and worries about homelessness began to focus on people who'd never been homeless before but were losing their houses after losing their jobs. (The unemployment rate rose to 10.8 percent in

Most Sheltered Homeless People Are Men

Nearly two-thirds of the people living in shelters in 2008 were men. One-fifth were under age 18, and 43 percent were disabled.

Percentage of All Sheltered Homeless Persons, 2008

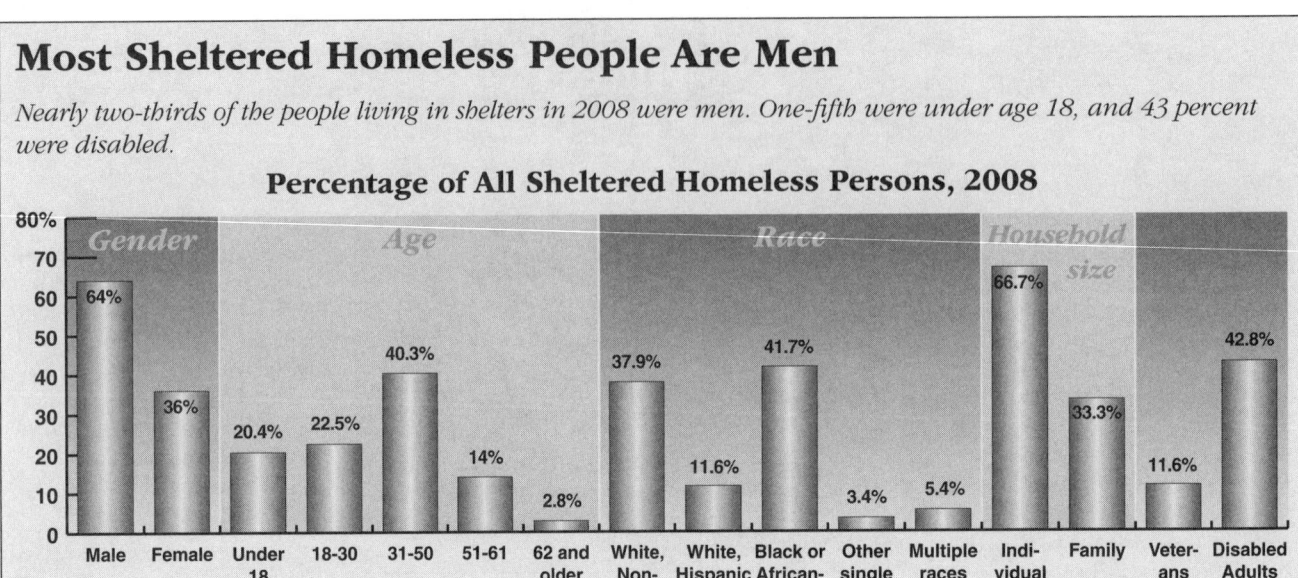

Source: "The 2008 Annual Homeless Assessment Report," U.S. Department of Housing and Urban Development, July 2009

December 1982, compared to 10.0 percent this November.) [7]

Citing an apparent connection between economic trends and threats to the housing stability of working Americans, some housing program advocates began arguing for a more expansive definition of homelessness.

But HUD, the federal agency most directly involved in the issue today, defines the term literally: A homeless person is someone who "lacks a fixed, regular and adequate nighttime residence," and who spends nights in a shelter of some kind, including places not designed for that use. [8]

That definition, however, doesn't control all federal law on homelessness. When it comes to public school students, the 2000 McKinney-Vento Homeless Assistance Act, which created most homelessness-related programs, effectively defines homelessness more expansively. Children who can enroll in programs for helping homeless children and youth include those who are sharing housing with others because of economic hardship; who are living in hotels, trailer parks or campgrounds out of necessity; who are awaiting foster care placement or those whose parents are migrant workers. [9]

The Runaway and Homeless Youth Act uses a still-broader definition. It makes young people eligible for transitional housing if they're 16-21 years of age, or for short-term shelter if under 18 and not living with relatives. [10]

As these interpretations of the word show, defining the term is the critical step in deciding who can benefit from government programs. "It's a waste of breath to argue with people who want an expansive definition that makes it look like we should do more, and with the others who want a restricted agenda so it makes it look like we should do less," says Christopher Jencks, a professor of social policy at Harvard University's Kennedy School of Government. "Both sides have agendas."

At the same time, Jencks favors the approach of housing advocates who want government to issue more housing subsidies. "I'm not sure that making the number bigger is the way to go," he says. "Do we want to say that 4 million people are homeless?"

Some housing advocates argue that a broader definition of homelessness applied to all government programs would, in fact, reflect reality. "We believe that everyone has a right to a home," says Couch of the National Low-Income Housing Coalition. "In my mind that doesn't include a van, or a garage or couch-surfing. It would be a real shame, after all we've learned about the importance of stable housing if, in response to the spike in family homelessness, we started building shelters."

Couch adds that HUD officials, along with lawmakers who specialize in housing issues, understand that building more facilities designed for the street-dwelling homeless population wouldn't respond adequately to the housing instability that threatens families who may have roofs over their heads but may also have to change lodgings frequently. "I think reason will prevail," Couch says. "People in housing know that homelessness is solved by housing."

Some of those who favor narrowing the scope of anti-homelessness programs argue that defining homelessness beyond the plain meaning of the word opens the door to unfocused strategies.

"In Hong Kong they talk about 'street sleepers,' " says Husock of the Manhattan Institute. "It's a very accurate description, and a useful one to distinguish them from people who are sharing accommodations with other family members."

People who are doubled-up clearly experience stress, Husock acknowledges. But it doesn't resemble the perils faced by people in the streets. "We should not confuse that issue with the problems faced by very-low-income people," he says. "Two or three generations under one household roof — it's not a common-sense definition of homelessness."

But even some who agree that the definition of homeless should be kept narrow also advocate that people at risk of becoming homeless — and currently bedding down at a relative's or friend's house where they're "doubled up" — should get assistance under homelessness prevention programs. That approach wouldn't require expanding the definition of "homeless."

"There are lots of people who are literally homeless," says Roman of the National Alliance to End Homelessness. "A substantial percentage of them are not sheltered at all. That's who is homeless. People who are doubled up and at risk of homelessness, we would not be in favor of calling homeless."

Are housing subsidies the best way to help families facing homelessness?

Since 1974, the Section 8 Housing Choice Voucher program has been the major federal provider of housing for low-wage workers. Its rental subsidy means recipients don't have to pay more than 30 percent of their income for housing. Through the voucher, the government pays the difference between that 30 percent and the monthly rent.

About 2 million U.S. households currently receive subsidies, which go to poor families who can document their inability to rent decent housing. But most cities also maintain waiting lists, some of them years long, because demand for vouchers outstrips supply. Overwhelmingly, housing experts say, the biggest share of vouchers go to households headed by single mothers, who make up the greatest

Housing Issues Central to Homelessness

Lack of affordable housing is seen as the biggest cause of homelessness — and the main solution — by officials from a majority of 27 U.S. cities surveyed. Most of the officials also called for permanent housing for the disabled and better-paying jobs.

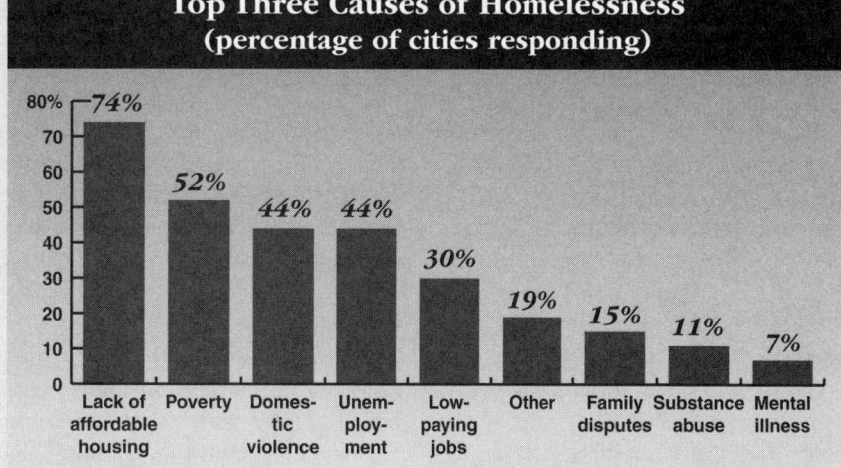

Top Three Causes of Homelessness
(percentage of cities responding)

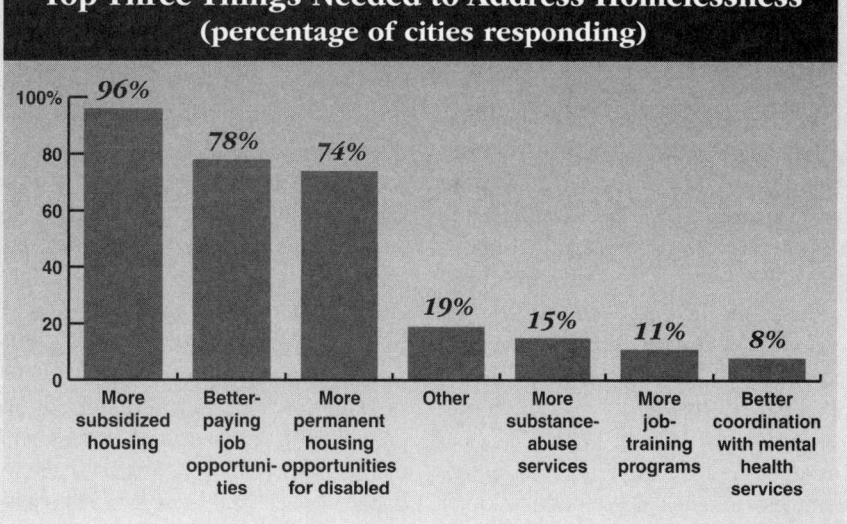

Top Three Things Needed to Address Homelessness
(percentage of cities responding)

Source: "Hunger and Homelessness Survey," United States Conference of Mayors, December 2009

share of low-income families threatened by housing instability. Vouchers may be simple in concept, but Section 8 isn't simple in operation. "The system is governed by hundreds of pages of regulations and guidance that make the program, some argue . . .

difficult to administer," the Congressional Research Service (CRS) reported last year. [11]

The program owes its complexity to its dual mission. Section 8 was designed to provide decent housing to poor people, with the longer-range aim of helping them climb out of poverty. But affordable housing alone may not be enough for some people to make that climb. Recognizing the key role of education in giving young people a chance at a better future, the so-called "portability" feature of Section 8 allows voucher recipients to live wherever a landlord will accept them (the feature also allows families to move to another state for a job).

"Portability offers the possibility for families with vouchers to move from areas of high concentrations of poverty, poor schools, and little opportunity to areas with low concentrations of poverty, good schools and more opportunity," the CRS report said. It added, "Researchers and advocates for low-income families have argued that the mobility potential of portability has not been fully reached. They argue for more funding for mobility counseling and performance standards that encourage mobility efforts." [12]

Some housing advocates argue that expanding the long-established program offers the fastest way to open affordable housing to more families. Rep. Maxine Waters, D-Calif., is sponsoring a bill to add 150,000 more vouchers next year. The National Low-Income Housing Coalition, which is backing the legislation, sees the legislation as the first step toward a larger goal of doubling the number of vouchers to 4 million by 2020.

"We know that vouchers solve homelessness," says Couch, at the National Low-Income Housing Coalition. "Often, homeless families need nothing other than a voucher. They don't need transportation or job training. Vouchers are a surefire way not only to prevent homelessness but also to get people out of that situation as quickly as possible."

An expansion is especially needed now, Couch argues, because the recession is hitting low-wage households so hard. "Typically, about 10 percent of people cycle off the program every year," she says. "But in the re-

cession, what we've seen is that, because people's incomes aren't going up, they're staying in the program longer than normal. The waiting lists in a lot of places are frozen."

Not all those who object to the proposed expansion oppose vouchers on principle. Rep. Barbara Capito, R-W. Va., the ranking Republican on the House Financial Services' Housing and Community Opportunity Subcommittee, voted against the Waters bill in the House Financial Services Committee. "It's a critical program, particularly at a time of economic challenge," Capito says. "I'd like to see the vouchers work better for people, but I'm concerned the Section 8 could swallow up the HUD budget."

Capito says adding 150,000 vouchers would lessen the housing agency's ability to deal with other issues, including substandard housing, which she calls a serious problem in her district. But the cost of the proposed voucher expansion is "way out of control," she says.

Deeper objections to Section 8 focus on what critics call the program's tendency to make beneficiaries dependent on the vouchers. "It makes much more sense to supplement the earnings of those at the low end of the income scale," says the Manhattan Institute's Husock. "It's much more efficient. If people have cash in their pocket, they can find something to rent."

Built into Husock's preferred approach is that recipients of income supplements would, by definition, have incomes — that is, they would have jobs. People suffering unstable housing who don't have jobs have other problems that aren't best solved by simply subsidizing apartments for them, he argues. Job training or help in job-seeking would be of more help. "Housing as a solution to the problem of poverty — it's not self-evident to me why that would be the best solution."

People who deal with individuals' housing problems agree to some ex-

tent with Husock's categorizations. "There are families who have substance-abuse problems, domestic violence, extreme disability issues such as a child with cerebral palsy," says Marta Beresin, a staff attorney with the Washington Legal Clinic for the Homeless. But she adds that a number of families in these circumstances couldn't be helped by income supplements tied to employment. "There are families where the head of household may not qualify for disability benefits but may have a lot of issues that make it difficult to hold down a steady job — domestic violence, mental health, kids with lot of health issues."

Those conditions, Beresin agrees, spring from deeply rooted poverty. But she differs with Husock on how to give families afflicted with these woes a toehold on a better existence. For these households, "The only way they're ever going to get out of a shelter is with a housing subsidy." ∎

BACKGROUND

The Right to Shelter

The sight of homeless people in big cities began to arouse public concern in the late 1960s and post-Vietnam War era when social activism was at its peak. At the end of the decade, a New York lawsuit played a key role in the emergence of homelessness as a national issue with legal and political dimensions.

Robert M. Hayes, a lawyer with the white-shoe Wall Street law firm Sullivan & Cromwell, filed a class action lawsuit against the city and state in 1979 on behalf of homeless men — represented by six homeless plaintiffs — demanding a right to shelter. Some

Continued on p. 1064

Chronology

1978-1980s

As homelessness grows into a major social and political-legal problem, advocates win important legal rights for those lacking permanent housing.

1978
Washington, D.C., activist Mitch Snyder leads a takeover of the National Visitors' Center by the homeless, forcing the city to open more shelter space.

1979
Wall Street lawyer Robert M. Hayes sues New York City and state, demanding a right to shelter for homeless men; initial ruling in case named for homeless plaintiff Robert Callahan is favorable to the homeless.

1981
Callahan dies while sleeping on the street. . . . In a landmark agreement, New York settles the case by agreeing to provide shelter for everyone who is homeless.

1982
Philadelphia law guarantees the homeless a right to shelter. . . . As deep recession brings unemployment, homelessness surges.

1983
Callahan agreement is amended to apply to women.

1984
After more attention-getting protests organized by Snyder and fellow activists, Washington voters pass the nation's first referendum guaranteeing overnight shelter to homeless people.

1987
President Ronald W. Reagan signs into law the McKinney (later re-named McKinney-Vento) Homeless Assistance Act, which becomes the major source of federal funds to help the homeless.

1990s
Persistent homelessness leads academics and think-tank analysts to crunch data in an effort to understand causes and possible cures and leads the Bill Clinton administration to step up its rhetoric on the issue.

1993
Martha R. Burt of the Urban Institute concludes that a shortage of affordable housing for working Americans clearly is one cause of the long-running homelessness crisis. . . . Homeless 43-year-old Yetta M. Adams freezes to death outside Washington, D.C., headquarters of the U.S. Department of Housing and Urban Development (HUD).

1994
Partly in response to Adams' death, the Clinton administration unveils a plan to reduce homelessness by one-third.

1998
Congress revamps Section 8 housing voucher program to require that vouchers for rental assistance go to very poor families.

2000s
Idea that government can eliminate homelessness gains strength, but the economic crisis at the end of the decade threatens to deepen the problem.

2002
George W. Bush administration vows to end chronic homelessness in 10 years.

2003
Administration hands out $48 million in grants to programs designed to get chronically homeless people off the streets.

2007
HUD count shows number of chronically homeless dropped since 2006 by about 30,000 to approximately 124,000. . . . Service providers begin warning of the potential for massive homelessness among Iraq-Afghanistan veterans.

2008
As recession grips the nation, progress on reducing the ranks of the chronically homeless halts; number remains essentially flat from previous year. . . . Bush creates National Housing Trust Fund, designed to finance affordable housing.

2009
Family homelessness is up 9 percent, apparently due to recession, with veterans slightly overrepresented among the homeless. . . . National School Boards Association reports growth in student homelessness in more than 700 school districts. . . . President Barack Obama signs law creating new Homelessness Prevention and Rapid Re-Housing program, funded with $1.5 billion. . . . U.S. Conference of Mayors says about three-quarters of a group of cities show rise in family homelessness and decline or leveling off of homelessness among individuals. . . . Advocacy groups launch drive to push Congress to appropriate another $1 billion to the program for fiscal 2010-2011.

Scotland's Homeless and the Right to Housing

Long-term housing soon will be available to almost everyone.

Scotland probably comes closer than any other country to implementing a right to housing for the homeless, according to American homeless advocates. [1] Since 1977, legally enforceable rights to housing have been on the books in Scotland, as well as England and Wales. But until recently the right was limited to "priority" categories of the most vulnerable people — families with children, the elderly, disabled and those displaced in natural disasters, among others. [2]

In 2003, Scotland forged ahead of the rest of Britain and greatly expanded the kinds of homeless individuals for whom the government has a duty to provide accommodation, including single adults. Scotland's uniquely expansive definition of homelessness "has no equivalent anywhere in Europe," according to Tom Mullen, a professor of law at the University of Glasgow. [3]

By 2012 the right to long-term permanent housing will extend to virtually all homeless people in Scotland under the revised law. In the interim, local authorities have a legal duty to provide immediate temporary shelter for all homeless persons and long-term permanent housing for a greatly expanded class of priority groups.

In 2004, the priority-need category was expanded to include homeless youth ages 16-17; 18-20-year-olds in danger of sexual or financial exploitation or drug abuse; adults discharged from prison, the armed forces or a hospital; adults with personality disorder, and those at risk from domestic abuse, violence or harassment.

"On paper we have the most progressive homelessness legislation in Europe, if not, possibly, the world," concedes Chris Campbell, deputy chief executive of the Scottish Council for Single Homeless, an umbrella group for homeless-service organizations.

But the challenge of making it work on the ground, he says, includes "changing public attitudes about the deserving vs. the undeserving: Someone's been on the waiting list paying their rent on time: Should they come before or second to someone who in their eyes is going to squander that tenancy with a drug issue?"

Homeless advocates say the tension comes essentially over allocating a scarce, desirable resource — public housing, which doesn't carry the same stigma as in the United States — and finding enough government money to increase the supply of affordable housing.

In 2005, a government-appointed monitoring group found that a shortage of affordable housing was a major obstacle to implementing the new law. [4] Towns short of housing have resorted to sending families to bed and breakfasts or towns up to 200 miles away, according to homeless advocates.

The shortage has produced one of the most commonly heard criticisms of the law. "Imagine a small town in Scotland with a family which has been there quite a long time and has made an application to move into social [public] housing. They see someone who is not from that area getting housing in front of them — quite legitimately because they're homeless. That can cause a problem," says Graeme Brown, director of Shelter Scotland, a homeless advocacy and advice organization.

Reluctance among some local government officials to shift toward the statute's more inclusive definition of those eligible for help has also been cited by government monitors as impeding the law's goals. [5]

Before passage of the 2003 act, those who did not fit into priority categories were entitled only to advice and assistance — not housing — which some observers viewed as a way of rationing scarce housing. [6]

Another rationing device was the lower-priority status the law gave to "intentional homelessness." The category was developed in response to local authorities' fears that large numbers of people would give up their existing accommodation to secure a better house under the legislation. After 2012, those deemed "intentionally homeless" are the only remaining group entitled only to temporary, not permanent, housing. [7]

Immediately after passage of the act, the number of homeless applications surged — a 34 percent increase in 2005-06 over the beginning of the decade. Some experts attribute the rise to more people becoming aware they were now eligible for help.

Homelessness figures in 2008-09 show a slight increase, but the steep rise seen earlier in the decade has now leveled off, coinciding with policy changes making housing rights available to more single adults, according to the Scottish government. [8]

"To be fair, local government has gotten better at preventing homelessness," Brown says. "The highly visible homeless sleeping on the streets that we saw 10 years ago in Edinburgh and Glasgow has declined."

Continued from p. 1062

shelter space was available, but government policy at the time was to deny shelter in order to pressure homeless people to find temporary housing on their own. [13]

In 1979, Judge Andrew R. Tyler of the New York Supreme Court (equivalent to district courts in other states) ruled that the U.S. and New York constitutions required that shelter space be available for every homeless man.

Technically, the ruling applied only to homeless men in the skid row area of New York known as the Bowery. But after the judge made his initial ruling to the case, Hayes and government lawyers settled the suit by

Two innovative Scottish programs hold out hope of keeping people in their homes in these times of rising foreclosures — which hit 6,500 households last year. Under the 2003 law, a lender who is about to foreclose on a homeowner or a landlord about to evict a tenant must inform the local government authority immediately. The idea is to give officials time to prevent eviction or find alternative housing.

Homeless people live under a bridge along the River Clyde in Glasgow, Scotland. Scotland has greatly expanded the government's obligation to house the homeless.

phone from Edinburgh, where it was raining, he added, "This is a northern European country; you need a roof over your head."

The law's ultimate success hinges on whether local governments manage to house the expanded universe of citizens who will qualify for help by the law's target date of 2012 — still an open question, homeless advocates say. [10]

— *Sarah Glazer*

Scotland has also pioneered an innovative mortgage-to-rent scheme, since imitated by England and Wales. Local nonprofit groups funded by government purchase a house that is about to be foreclosed upon and rent the house back to the residents. With funding limited, however, it will help only 250-300 of the 4,500 households that may be repossessed this year, according to the Scottish government.

In a recent law journal article on the 2003 legislation, attorney Eric S. Tars of the National Law Center on Homelessness and Poverty, in Washington, D.C., applauded a Scottish applicant's ability to sue if local government has not met its statutory duty to provide him housing — a right denied to Americans. [9]

But in Scotland's far less litigious society, suits are rare. If someone comes to Shelter Scotland for help after their local authority has wrongly denied them housing, "we find that almost always the [local] council will back down" after they are contacted, Gavin Corbett, Shelter Scotland's head of policy, said in an e-mail. Shelter could threaten the council with a judicial review of its decision in a higher court, but it rarely comes to that.

The lack of litigiousness may reflect greater social consensus around the issue of homelessness in Scotland than even in the rest of Great Britain, says Brown. "Culturally and politically, even in these post-industrial days, Scotland is still more of a nation concerned about their fellow citizens," he says in his lilting Scottish brogue. Speaking by

[1] Eric S. Tars and Caitlin Egleson, "Great Scot!" *Georgetown Journal on Poverty Law & Policy*, winter 2009, pp. 187-216, www.nlchp.org/view_report.cfm?id=314.

[2] The 1977 act, enacted under a Labor government, applied to all of Great Britain. Homeless rights under the act were reduced later under Conservative governments in 1979-1997 in England and Wales, but not Scotland, and largely restored under Labor in 2002.

[3] Tom Mullen, "The Right to Housing in Scotland," Homeless in Europe, European Federation of National Organizations Working with the Homeless, autumn, 2008. The law is the Homelessness, Etc. (Scotland) Act of 2003, www.feantsa.org/files/Month%20Publications/EN/Magazine_Homeless_in_Europe_EN/Homeless%20in%20Europe_Autumn08_EN.pdf.

[4] *Ibid*.

[5] *Ibid*., and Tars and Egleson, *op. cit*., p. 203.

[6] Mullen, *op. cit*.

[7] *Ibid*., p. 197. However, temporary housing can last up to one year, with further help after that.

[8] E-mail from Scottish Housing and Support Division.

[9] Tars and Egleson, *op. cit*., p. 215. The law provides a legally enforceable duty on the local government to meet the housing needs of its residents. Applicants unhappy with a decision may seek judicial review. However, in a judicial review a court cannot substitute its own opinion for that of the decision makers. It can strike down a decision on the grounds that the decision maker has exceeded or abused powers or failed to perform the duty delegated or entrusted or exhibited bias. (E-mail from Scottish Housing and Support Division.)

[10] Local authorities have targets to increase their numbers of priority-need assessments until all of those assessed as homeless have the same rights. Statistics published by the Scottish government in September indicate local authorities have increased their priority assessments to 83 percent of homeless households across Scotland.

agreeing that government was obliged to provide shelter for all men with no homes (women were included later). Underscoring the urgency of the homelessness issue, Robert Callahan, who led the list of named plaintiffs,

died on the street before the settlement was reached.

The August 1981, court-approved agreement led to a vast expansion of shelter space in New York. When Hayes had gone to court, shelter space was

scattered around the cheap, dormitory-style hotels known as "flophouses." By 1988, when demand for shelter reached a peak, city refuges could house as many as 10,000 people in 24 shelters. The accommodations went far beyond a place to sleep, meals and bathing facilities. The shelters also offered health care, mental health counseling, drug rehabilitation and job-training programs.

By 1981, homeless men and women were fixtures in cities across the country, often camping out in downtown areas and parks. Many were former residents of mental institutions who were turned out and left on their own after a wave of "deinstitutionalizations" prompted by horror stories about conditions in institutions. Some scholars say that President Ronald W. Reagan's administration further added to the ranks of the homeless by drastically cutting back on the number of recipients of federal disability payments, among them people too mentally ill to work. The administration also cut federal funds for public housing. [14]

New York's growing homeless population inspired activists and lawyers elsewhere. Pinning down the numbers proved difficult. Jencks, at Harvard University's Kennedy School, estimated that the nation's homeless population grew from 100,000 in 1980 to 200,000 in 1984 to 400,000 in 1987-1988. [15]

Mitch Snyder, a Washington-based advocate for the homeless, had put the number of homeless at 2 million to 3 million, but he later acknowledged the estimate had "no meaning, no value." [16]

Snyder dedicated himself to awakening the national conscience and challenging the political system. Starting in the late 1970s, he had begun organizing demonstrations designed to call attention to the unmet needs of homeless men and women in the streets of the nation's capital, often sleeping on steam-heat exhaust grates located near federal buildings.

Headline-grabbing protests that Snyder sparked — as a leader of a onetime anti-Vietnam War organization, the Community for Creative Nonviolence — included a December 1978 takeover of the National Visitors Center, near Union Station, by homeless

people. The action forced the city to provide more shelter space. [17]

In November 1981 — three months after the New York settlement — Snyder led a group of about 150 activists and homeless people in building and occupying a tent camp they called "Reaganville" in Lafayette Park, across from the White House. In naming the camp after President Reagan, the activists were trying to evoke the Great Depression, when the jobless and homeless built camps they called "Hoovervilles," after President Herbert Hoover.

The next year, Philadelphia enacted an ordinance that also guaranteed the right to shelter, and in 1984 Washington finally acted. Partly in response to Snyder's and other protests, Washington voters in 1984 passed the nation's first referendum measure guaranteeing "adequate overnight shelter" to homeless people — a statutory equivalent of the New York legal agreement. [18]

Beyond Shelter

The major federal response to rising homelessness came in the form of the Stewart B. McKinney Homeless Assistance Act, which Reagan signed in 1987. (It was retitled in 2000 as the McKinney-Vento Homeless Assistance Act.) [19]

The law authorized programs designed to expand or upgrade shelters and created a series of initiatives aimed at meeting other needs of the homeless population, including: HUD homeless assistance grants for emergency shelters; supportive housing for disabled people and SRO (single-room occupancy) rehabilitation; Veterans Administration and Department of Labor programs for homeless veterans who needed medical care and job-seeking help; Health and Human Services grants and medical care; and Education Department programs for homeless children and youth. [20]

The 1987 law made up the biggest part of the federal attempt to cope with homelessness, but some separate programs had already existed, and others were created later. These included services to homeless youth, provided under a 1974 law; grants to homelessness-prevention projects in local communities, authorized by a 1983 law; a series of programs aimed at homeless veterans, created over several years; and a Social Security Administration program begun in fiscal 2003 designed to help chronically homeless people apply for disability payments.

As Congress legislated, policy experts at universities and think tanks were trying to determine the size of the homeless population and its subgroups and whether socioeconomic changes played a part in the growth of homelessness. They zeroed in on changes in the housing market, the job market and care of the mentally ill.

By the early 1990s, a consensus had formed among liberals and centrists that the decreasing availability of affordable housing was the root cause of non-chronic homelessness among families and others.

"There is an absolute shortage of appropriate rental units to accommodate poorly housed families," wrote Martha R. Burt, a scholar at the Urban Institute think tank, in a 1993 book that analyzed voluminous data on housing availability, cost and other factors. She found, however, that families made up perhaps as little as 12 percent, of the homeless population. [21]

The bulk of the homeless were single men, almost all weighed down by mental illness, addiction or both — disabilities that had led to long periods of reliance on shelters or the streets. It was these chronically homeless who had been largely responsible for drawing attention to the issue.

They continued to do so, even in death. On Nov. 29, 1993, a homeless woman named Yetta M. Adams, 43, died of exposure on a bench outside the Washington headquarters of HUD Secretary Henry G. Cisneros, prompting new government attention.

In response, the Clinton administration launched a wave of spending — grants totaling $11 million to 187 homeless-assistance programs in 44 states. And in May 1994, the administration unveiled a plan aimed at reducing chronic homelessness by one-third.

Ending Homelessness

The Clinton plan didn't fulfill the expectations created by its announcement. Some programs took effect, said Donald Whitehead, executive director of the National Coalition for the Homeless, but "many other initiatives were never implemented, [and] HUD ended up with no real, substantial increase in new funding."[22]

Nonetheless, the idea took hold that the government could do more than simply respond to homelessness. In 2000, the National Alliance to End Homelessness released a 10-year plan to eliminate homelessness. "Housing has become scarcer for those with little money," the organization said. "Earnings from employment and from benefits have not kept pace with the cost of housing for low income and poor people. Services that every family needs for support and stability have become harder for very poor people to afford or find."[23]

The plan centered on mobilizing government and private organizations to provide housing and related services designed to reverse the conditions that the alliance saw as the core of the problem.

But the new Bush administration took a narrower approach. In 2002 it set a goal of ending chronic homelessness in 10 years. To carry it out, the administration revived the Interagency Council on Homelessness, which had been formed in 1987 but fell into inactivity in the 1990s.[24]

In a series of other actions designed to meet the 10-year goal, the administration in 2003 made grants totaling $48 million to programs designed to help chronically homeless

Tracy Munch (above) and her fiancé were evicted last February from the house they were renting in Adams County, Colo., after the owner stopped paying his mortgage. They managed to borrow enough money to rent another house for themselves and their four children, but not in time to avoid eviction.

people get jobs, permanent housing, substance-abuse treatment and mental health services.[25]

Over the following years, the Bush administration maintained its focus on the chronically homeless. For example, in evaluating grant applications for building housing for the chronically homeless, HUD gave preference to state and local agency applicants that had developed 10-year plans of their own.

Six years after the Bush administration launched its 10-year campaign, chronic homelessness seemed to be diminishing. From 2006 to 2008, for instance, the national one-night count of homeless people that HUD conducts every January showed a decrease from 155,623 to 124,135 chronically homeless people both in shelters and in other locations, such as streets and bus stations. (Despite the seeming precision of those numbers, HUD'S "point-in-time" count is an estimate, given the difficulty of locating every single homeless person on a single night.)[26]

From 2007 to 2008, however, HUD's count of the chronically homeless was virtually unchanged.[27]

"Ending chronic homelessness has been a national policy objective that has been supported by significant investments in developing permanent supportive housing," HUD said in its report, which was released this year. "For several years communities have reported declines in the number of persons experiencing chronic homelessness."[28]

Meanwhile, some organizations advocating a push to eliminate homelessness in all its forms were working to expand the definition of "homelessness." The goal was to enlarge the community of people who would benefit from programs aimed at the people who weren't included in the "chronic" segment of the homeless population.

In 2008, Rep. Gwen Moore, D-Wis., introduced a bill to expand the McKinney-Vento law's definition of "homeless" to include individuals or families who would "imminently lose" their housing and couldn't afford a new house or apartment, plus anyone fleeing domestic violence or another threat to life.

Moore's bill would also have authorized community programs to serve families with children, or children on their own, who were defined as homeless in other laws. The effect would have been to include people who had experienced prolonged periods without stable housing, and could be expected to remain in that condition because of chronic disabilities, chronic physical or mental health problems, addiction, histories of domestic violence, or multiple barriers to employment.

The legislation passed the House, but the Senate took no action on the measure. [29]

War and Recession

In the last two years of the Bush administration the economic and political climate in which politicians and advocates debated and crafted anti-homelessness measures was changing fast.

The foreclosure crisis that started in 2007, with millions of homeowners beginning to default on mortgages, led to the Wall Street meltdown and what economists began calling the Great Recession. [30]

The same HUD report that showed a decline in the number of chronically homeless people also seemed to contain an early warning about families. The report showed that the number of homeless people in families increased from 2007 to 2008 by 43,000, to 516,724, a 9 percent jump. And the number of families in shelters with children rose from 130,968 in 2007 to 159,142. "The most common demographic features of sheltered family members are that adults are women, children are young, the family identifies itself as belonging to a minority group, and the family has two or three members," the report said. [31]

The statistics confirmed anecdotal reports that had been circulating among advocates for low-income families. As a result, the advocacy organizations were able to bolster the argument they'd been making for increasing homelessness assistance and prevention funds to individuals and families who fell outside the "chronically homeless" category. Until then, says Roman of the National Alliance to End Homelessness, "We didn't have the data."

Economic conditions alone would have been enough to suggest that the ranks of the homeless would include growing numbers of low-income households hit by job loss or cutbacks in working hours. But another factor was present as well — the appearance of a new cohort of combat veterans. As men and women began returning from Iraq and Afghanistan, many in the veterans' and housing policy communities began warning against a repetition of what many believed to be a plague of homelessness among Vietnam vets.

Researchers in the 1990s had concluded that homeless veterans of the Southeast Asia war were not as numerous as many had thought. [32] Still, the reality of any veterans from the new century's wars wandering streets or sleeping in shelters was widely considered a reflection of failure by government's veteran-care and social services agencies. "We're beginning to see, across the country, the first trickle of this generation of warriors in homeless shelters," Phil Landis, chairman of Veterans Village of San Diego, a residence and counseling center, told *The New York Times* in 2007. "But we anticipate that it's going to be a tsunami." [33]

So far, no tidal wave has hit. But the HUD annual report does show that veterans account for 11.6 percent of the adult population that uses shelters, but a lesser share — 10.5 percent — of the national adult population. "The estimated number of homeless veterans should be watched closely," the report adds, "as the number of veterans returning from recent combat increases during the next few years." [34] ■

CURRENT SITUATION

Fund Drive

Housing advocacy groups are campaigning for increased federally funding for homelessness programs. But many are pessimistic due to the state of the economy, the growing government deficit and the Obama administration's growing list of priorities, including the newly announced Afghanistan troop surge.

At the same time, the gravity of the economic crisis may persuade politicians that homelessness has become more than a niche issue. "I can count on one hand the number of staffers who are actually invested, passionate, care about housing," Kim, the aide to Missouri Republican Sen. Bond, told a Capitol Hill briefing in early December organized by the National Alliance to End Homelessness. He added, "Now with the foreclosure crisis, there are probably people who are a little more sensitive to it."

Alliance president Roman went even further. Enactment earlier in the year of the Homelessness Prevention and Rapid Rehousing Program (HPRP) — designed to help families avoid losing their housing — marked a major shift in government strategy, she said. "We may actually come out of this difficult period with a better homelessness system than we went into it with, if we're

Continued on p. 1070

At Issue:

Should homelessness be redefined by HUD to include more youths and families?

PHILLIP LOVELL
VICE PRESIDENT FOR EDUCATION, HOUSING, AND YOUTH POLICY
FIRST FOCUS

WRITTEN FOR *CQ RESEARCHER*, DEC. 15, 2009

"*n***ot homeless enough."** That's the message sent to over 550,000 children who are considered homeless by the Department of Education and other agencies but are not homeless enough for the Department of Housing and Urban Development (HUD). Yes, you read that correctly. A child can be homeless enough for one federal agency, but not for another.

Increasingly, the homeless are families who lose their homes and temporarily "double up" with others or stay in motels, often because shelters are full. They do not live in "unstable housing situations." They have lost their homes, cannot afford another apartment and do not know where or when their next move will take place. No one staying in this type of temporary, often unsafe, situation can be said to have a home. Denying this fact is disastrous.

In 2007, a youth whom I will call John became homeless. Desperate, he accepted an offer to stay with an adult for two months. John was raped repeatedly and, as a result, contracted HIV.

When I met John, he looked like a normal kid. He was receiving a scholarship to help him go to college and was bright, articulate and smiling. He did not look homeless. But he was no less homeless, vulnerable or deserving of federal support.

The president recently signed legislation making modest improvements to the HUD definition. Now, a family in a doubled up or motel situation is considered homeless if they can only stay in their housing for 14 days. Additionally, families can be considered homeless if they are fleeing situations where the health and safety of children are jeopardized.

Neither provision would have helped John. He stayed in his doubled up situation until another temporary situation became available — well above the 14-day maximum. And the only way he would qualify for assistance under the health and safety clause is by being raped. This is unacceptable.

In the end, this is about our children. This is about keeping them safe and making sure they have the basic necessities of life. Congress must change HUD's definition of homelessness to reflect reality. A narrow definition masks the real problems facing our communities. Homelessness cannot be defined away.

It will be some time before Congress considers this issue again. In the meantime, HUD is required to issue regulations on the newly passed definition of homelessness. For all those who may follow in John's footsteps, let us hope HUD does so in a way that protects as many children, youth and families as possible.

HOWARD HUSOCK
VICE PRESIDENT FOR POLICY RESEARCH MANHATTAN INSTITUTE FOR POLICY RESEARCH AND AUTHOR, AMERICA'S TRILLION-DOLLAR HOUSING MISTAKE: THE FAILURE OF AMERICAN HOUSING POLICY

WRITTEN FOR *CQ RESEARCHER*, DEC. 15, 2009

W*ithout doubt*, the collapse of the U.S. housing market has caused hardship. Owners are stuck with homes worth less than the price they paid. Others have moved in with parents and extended families. We cannot, however, address our housing situation clearly by using emotional descriptions as arguments for a vast expansion of subsidized housing — which would be both difficult to afford and, just as significantly, ill-advised social policy.

The term "homelessness" dates to the early Reagan administration, when two trends overlapped. The deinstitutionalization of those suffering from mental illness or alcohol and substance abuse problems — begun as a liberal policy in the 1960s — utterly failed. Many people wound up living on the streets, becoming the public image of "homelessness." At the same time, reductions in public assistance forced some very low-income (primarily single-parent) households to double-up with relatives or live in more crowded conditions. Such households never fit the common-sense definition of homeless — known in Britain as "street-sleeping." But advocates of subsidized housing began to include them in estimates of homelessness — and, in some cities, they began to be admitted in large numbers to public group-living quarters (the very term "shelters" perpetuated the image that such households were living on the street). Those households also received priority for a rapidly expanding housing-voucher program, which allowed them to pay public housing rents for private apartments. This, in turn, ballooned the Section 8 voucher program — to the point that its budget now surpasses that for cash welfare assistance.

Now those who want to further expand such housing assistance are using the foreclosure and delinquency spike as a rationale for expanding that same housing-voucher program — by using the image of the recession-strapped working family as the new face of homelessness. Such problems are being addressed through federal efforts to modify loans and other methods. Doubling the size of the housing-voucher program is not likely even to reach such families.

Far better to continue to take steps to help the truly homeless — the mentally ill who should be assisted through housing combined with social services — and to adjust the voucher program by converting it to a cash payment expansion of the Earned Income Tax Credit. Let's help those of low income but not by costly, ineffective and inaccurately labeled remedies.

Continued from p. 1068

able to take advantage of the opportunity presented by HPRP."

Accordingly, Roman and her allies are urging Congress to add another $1 billion to the HPRP, on top of the $1.5 billion appropriated earlier this year.

They also want lawmakers to allocate $1 billion to the National Housing Trust Fund (NHTF), created by a 2008 law to provide funds to build or rehabilitate rental housing for households with very low incomes. The request is in line with a plan endorsed by the Obama administration for fiscal 2010-2011. "We will work with Congress to identify a financing source for the Housing Trust Fund, which will help provide decent housing for families hardest hit by the current economic downturn," HUD Secretary Shaun Donovan said in October. [35]

Rep. Barney Frank, D-Mass., chairman of the House Banking Committee, and Sen. Jack Reed, D-R.I., a member of the Housing, Transportation, and Community Development Subcommittee, have introduced bills to make the $1 billion allocation.

In the last month of 2009, the National Low-Income Housing Coalition was drumming up a grassroots campaign to pressure lawmakers into committing themselves to the trust fund legislation. "Our goal is to create an early-December blizzard of phone calls from all over in a compressed period of time to demonstrate strong and urgent support for an initial infusion of money for the NHTF," the coalition told its members. [36]

Advocacy groups are also pressing for the appropriation of $2.4 billion under the Homeless Emergency Assistance and Rapid Transition to Housing (HEARTH) Act. Enacted in 2009, but without funding for 2009-2010, HEARTH authorizes homeless-assistance

Homeless people pitch camp beside a Las Vegas street last April. Across the nation, another group of people is joining the growing number of low-income households hit by job loss and homelessness: men and women returning from the wars in Iraq and Afghanistan.

grants and supportive housing for homeless people with disabilities.

In addition, with the Temporary Assistance to Needy Families (TANF) system up for reauthorization in 2010, housing advocates are asking Congress to add funding for states with effective strategies against family homelessness. TANF was created under the Clinton administration as a new version of welfare aid to families with children.

Metropolitan Trends

Several big and medium-size cities are showing the same trend in homelessness that HUD reported in mid-2009. Homelessness among single individuals is declining or remaining flat, but more families are losing their homes, the U.S. Conference of Mayors reported in early December. [37]

"The recession and a lack of affordable housing were cited as the top causes of family homelessness in the surveyed cities," the organization said. [38]

The survey covered 27 cities from October 2008 to Sept. 30, 2009, including Boston, Chicago, Dallas and Los Angeles, as well as Gastonia, N.C., Louisville and St. Paul, Minn., among the smaller cities. About three-fourths of the cities reported an uptick in family homelessness — ranging from 1 percent in Salt Lake City to 41 percent in Charleston, S.C. Seventy-four percent of the municipal governments reported a lack of affordable housing as the top cause of homelessness.

Developments among families stood in sharp contrast to the trend for individuals. In 64 percent of the responding cities (16 cities), individual homelessness was reported decreased or at the same level as the previous year. Norfolk, Va., reported the highest increase, of 18 percent.

However, the survey isn't a precision instrument, as the Conference acknowledged. For instance, Los Angeles reported a 68 percent decline in family homelessness, basing that result on censuses it conducted in 2007 and 2009. "The steep decline . . . conflicts with anecdotal evidence from Los Angeles homeless service providers, who say the number of families seeking shelter has swelled recently because of the recession."

AFP/Getty Images/Jewel Samad

And the reported national drop in individual homelessness has at least one major exception. In New York, which didn't participate in the survey, lawyers representing homeless men and women took city government to court in early December, charging failure to live up to the landmark Callahan agreement of 1981. The city isn't keeping up with demand for shelter space, lawyers for the Legal Aid Society and the Coalition for the Homeless charged.

"The extreme situation now is reminiscent of problems that we haven't seen in years," Steven Banks, attorney in chief for Legal Aid, told *The New York Times*. "It's a failure to plan, and it's having dire consequences for vulnerable women and vulnerable men." [39]

A motion by the lawyers cited reports by monitors for the coalition. For example, they said two shelters in late September hadn't provided beds for 15 men. At another shelter in late October, 52 men slept in chairs or on the floor; 14 men were bused to shelters with beds, but 38 were left bedless for the night. At yet another shelter, two women slept on a dining room table.

Robert V. Hess, the city's commissioner of homeless services, called the motion "alarmist." He told *The Times:* "We've seen an uptick in demand, so our system, as you might expect, is a little tight. We're confident that we'll continue to be able to meet demand and meet our obligations throughout the winter." [40]

Capacity in the adult shelter system was at 99.6 percent on Dec. 8, Hess told *The Times*. The shelters held 4,934 men and 2,041 women that day. Not included were military veterans in short-term housing; chronically homeless people who've entered a program designed for them; and 30,698 people in families who were in short-term housing set aside for them.

Concerning the monitors' reports, Hess said that some of those without beds had refused them, or had arrived at shelters after 2 a.m. Of a report that some women were taken by bus to a shelter where they had less than five hours to sleep, Hess called the account "potentially correct."

Small-Town Woes

Homelessness is often considered a big-city phenomenon, but it's hitting rural communities and small towns as well.

"More companies are downsizing or closing," says Kay Moshier McDivitt, adviser to the Lancaster County Coalition to End Homelessness, in the heart of Pennsylvania's Amish country. "Now our demand has increased beyond our ability to respond."

Employment prospects in the area, a major tourist destination, are dominated by low-wage service jobs, which leave little cushion against job loss. Some service workers spend up to 75 percent of their incomes for housing, McDivitt says.

Speaking at the December Capitol Hill briefing organized by the National Alliance to End Homelessness, McDivitt said that in October and November of 2009 the coalition had received 1,500 requests for help paying rent or mortgages — a 400 percent increase over 2008. "Most of our families when they first become homeless spend a year or more moving among family and friends. By the time we see our families, they have often been homeless for a year or more, with lots of instability. They are ready for permanence and stability."

Demand for help has risen so sharply the coalition is setting up its first family shelters. Until now, McDivitt said, HPRP funds have enabled the county to help families pay rent so they never become homeless. But, she adds, "We expect family homelessness is going to increase."

A slightly less pessimistic assessment came from Kathy Wahto, executive director of Serenity House of Clallam County, Wash., which helps the homeless in Port Angeles, northeast of Seattle.

There, despite persistent poverty, a state-funded homelessness-prevention program had helped lower homelessness by about 40 percent over the past three years. But the recession has cut a major source of revenue for that program — document recording fees on real estate transactions. "That's $200,000 in revenue we're not going to have," Wahto said.

HPRP partly made up for the loss with an $89,000 infusion. "The ending of homelessness in our county was in sight," Wahto said. "We don't want to go backwards." ∎

OUTLOOK

'Modestly Positive' Trends

Housing advocates who've been pushing for years to expand homelessness services tend toward optimism about the medium-term future.

"If you had asked me last year if we would have $1.5 billion for HPRP, I would have said no," says the Urban Institute's Cunningham. "A lot of positive things are coming out of the present administration."

She concedes that homelessness programs are competing for money and attention in a time of crisis on several fronts. But it's within the administration's reach to go a long way toward eliminating homelessness, she says. "If you look at the research, the bottom line is, we know how to end homelessness. We just need the political will to do it."

Husock of the Manhattan Institute takes a somewhat more skeptical view, though not an entirely bleak one. "I would guess we would be closer to the status quo than any kind of big change," he says. But he says he's encouraged by the openness of HUD Secretary Donovan to programs in Atlanta and elsewhere that combine housing assistance with work requirements of the kind that transformed the welfare system.

"To me, Atlanta is pointing the way to the future," Husock says. Overall, he says, "The trend has been modestly positive."

The Cato Institute's Tanner takes a dimmer view, based on what he calls continuing attachment to regulatory controls that he argues slows construction of affordable housing. "I don't see any policy to expand the availability of low-income housing through eliminating rent control or zoning regulations."

That aside, he argues that the extent of homelessness over the next decade will largely be determined by the state of the economy. "If you get long-term economic growth, you'll get a lower number of people homeless because they lost their jobs."

On that point at least, virtually everyone agrees.

"How about you give me a prediction about where we'll be on the unemployment rate in 10 years," says Jencks of Harvard's Kennedy School of Government. "I would love to believe we won't be in this fix."

One nuance to the question, though, is that providing more services to homeless people may not result in an immediate reduction in their numbers. "Conservatives tend to argue, and they're not completely off-base, that when you do more, you're going to get more homeless people," Jencks says. "I don't take that as defeat. A lot of people are living in terrible circumstances, and if you give them the opportunity not to live with a belligerent brother-in-law, they will. Is that a waste? I don't think so."

Among those who deal daily with the heartaches and complexities of individual and family housing crises, the depth of the economic crisis leads to caution in forecasting when a homelessness turnaround might occur.

"A number of people are falling into poverty, and a number of governments are being hit by the recession and having to cut programs," says Beresin of the Washington Legal Clinic for the Homeless. "It takes a long time to bounce back from all that — not to mention that we've decided to send 30,000 more troops into Afghanistan."

In Washington, Beresin notes, some construction projects for affordable housing have been stopped in their tracks because a city government program that provides funding is itself short of revenue, which comes from a real-estate transaction tax. "D.C. definitely can't do it alone," she says. "It needs federal dollars, and if those aren't going to be there because the government is prioritizing other things, we don't have much control over that."

Still and all, among advocates who deal with Congress, the prevailing mood tends toward optimism. "In 10 years, I think there will be fewer homeless people," says Roman of the National Alliance to End Homelessness. "We've learned a lot about how to run a much better homeless system. We could probably get about half the way to ending homelessness with that."

The other half may be harder to solve. "The affordable housing crisis is the driver," she says. "When we didn't have that gap, we didn't have homeless people. People have lots of problems, but they used to be able to afford a place to live, and now they can't." ■

Notes

[1] "The 2008 Annual Homeless Assessment Report to Congress," U.S. Department of Housing and Urban Development, July 2009, p. v, www.hudhre.info/documents/4thHomeless AssessmentReport.pdf. HUD reported on 2008 in mid-2009; the 2009 report is scheduled for release in 2010.

[2] *Ibid.*

[3] "Affordable Housing," U.S. Department of Housing and Urban Development, Dec. 3, 2009, www.hud.gov/offices/cpd/affordablehousing/.

[4] Ellie Ashford, "Districts Cope With Rising Numbers of Homeless Students," School Board News, National School Boards Association, January 2009, www.nsba.org/HPC/Features/About SBN/SbnArchive/2009/January-2009/Districts-cope-with-rising-numbers-of-homeless-students. aspx.

[5] "Affordable Housing," *op. cit.*

[6] "The 2008 Annual Homeless Assessment," *op. cit.*, p. 31.

[7] "Labor Force Statistics from the Current Population Survey," U.S. Bureau of Labor Statistics, updated monthly, http://data.bls.gov/PDQ/servlet/SurveyOutputServlet.

[8] "Federal Definition of Homeless," U.S. Department of Housing and Urban Development, March 3, 2009, www.hud.gov/homeless/definition.cfm.

[9] Libby Perl, *et al.*, "Homelessness: Targeted Federal Programs and Recent Legislation," Congressional Research Service, Jan. 15, 2009, p. 2,

About the Author

Peter Katel is a *CQ Researcher* staff writer who previously reported on Haiti and Latin America for *Time* and *Newsweek* and covered the Southwest for newspapers in New Mexico. He has received several journalism awards, including the Bartolomé Mitre Award for coverage of drug trafficking, from the Inter-American Press Association. He holds an A.B. in university studies from the University of New Mexico. His recent reports include "Prisoner Reentry," "Hate Groups" and "Legalizing Marijuana."

http://web.mit.edu/lugao/MacData/afs.lugao/MacData/afs/sipb/contrib/wikileaks-crs/wikileaks-crs-reports/RL30442.pdf.

[10] *Ibid.*

[11] Maggie McCarty, "Section 8 Housing Choice Voucher Program: Issues and Reform Proposals in the 110th Congress," Congressional Research Service, p. 3, http://wikileaks.org/leak/crs/RL34002.pdf.

[12] *Ibid.*, p. 10.

[13] Details of the lawsuit and its effects are drawn from Kim Hopper, *Reckoning With Homelessness* (2003), pp. 186-191; Lyn Stolarwski, "Right To Shelter: History of the Mobilization of the Homeless as a Model of Voluntary Action," *Nonprofit and Voluntary Sector Quarterly*, 1988, http://nvs.sagepub.com/cgi/reprint/17/1/36.pdf; Robin Herman, "Pact Requires City to Shelter Homeless Men," *The New York Times*, Aug. 27, 1981, p. A1; Charles Kaiser, "A State Justice Orders Creation of 750 Beds for Bowery Homeless," *The New York Times*, Dec. 9, 1979.

[14] For background, see Charles S. Clark, "Mental Illness," *CQ Researcher*, Aug. 6, 1993, pp. 673-696. Chris Koyanagi, "Learning From History: Deinstitutionalization of People With Mental Illness as Precursor to Longterm Care Reform," Kaiser Commission on Medicaid and the Uninsured, August 2007, p. 8, www.kff.org/medicaid/upload/7684.pdf.

[15] Christopher Jencks, *The Homeless* (1994), pp. 16-17. For background, see William Triplett, "Ending Homelessness," *CQ Researcher*, June 18, 2004, pp. 541-564.

[16] *Ibid.*, pp. 1-2.

[17] Paul W. Valentine, "Street People in Visitor Center Vex U.S.," *The Washington Post*, Dec. 7, 1978, p. B1; Paul W. Valentine, "City Agrees to Provide More Homeless Shelters," *The Washington Post*, Dec. 16, 1978, p. D1.

[18] Sandra G. Boodman, "City Softens Opposition to Shelter Initiative," *The Washington Post*, Nov. 8, 1984, p. A58.

[19] Except where otherwise indicated, this subsection is drawn from Perl, *et al.*, *op. cit.*

[20] *Ibid.*

[21] Burt, *op. cit.*, pp. 16-17.

[22] Quoted in Triplett, *op. cit.*

[23] "A Plan, Not a Dream: How to End Homelessness in Ten Years," National Alliance to End Homelessness, June 1, 2000, www.endhomelessness.org/content/article/detail/585.

[24] Maggie McCarty, *et al.*, "Homelessness: Recent Statistics, Targeted Federal Programs, and Recent Legislation," Congressional Research Service, May 31, 2005, pp. 17-18,

www.fas.org/sgp/crs/misc/RL30442.pdf.

[25] *Ibid.*, pp. 17-18.

[26] "The 2008 Annual Homeless Assessment Report to Congress," *op. cit.*

[27] *Ibid.*

[28] *Ibid.*, p. 5.

[29] HR 7221, *CQ Billtrack*, Nov. 17, 2008.

[30] For background, see Marcia Clemmitt, "Mortgage Crisis," *CQ Researcher*, Nov. 2, 2007, pp. 913-936; Peter Katel, "Straining the Safety Net," *CQ Researcher*, July 31, 2009, pp. 645-668.

[31] "The 2008 Annual Homeless Assessment Report to Congress," *op. cit.*, pp. 31, 42.

[32] For background, see Peter Katel, "Wounded Veterans," *CQ Researcher*, Aug. 31, 2007, pp. 697-720.

[33] Quoted in Erik Eckholm, "Surge Seen in Number of Homeless Veterans," *The New York Times*, Nov. 8, 2007, www.nytimes.com/2007/11/08/us/08vets.html.

[34] "The 2008 Annual Homeless Assessment Report to Congress," *op. cit.*, p. 28.

[35] "Administration Calls on Congress to Approve Key Housing Measures," U.S. Department

FOR MORE INFORMATION

Manhattan Institute for Policy Research, 52 Vanderbilt Ave., New York, NY 10017; (212) 599-7000; www.manhattan-institute.org. A conservative leaning think tank on urban issues that tends to be skeptical about federal housing and homelessness policies.

National Alliance to End Homelessness, 1518 K St., N.W., Washington, DC 20005; (202) 638-1526; naeh@naeh.org. Works on legislation and program design and publishes research on causes and effects of homelessness.

National Center on Homelessness Among Veterans, U.S. Department of Veterans Affairs, 810 Vermont Ave., N.W., Washington, DC 20420; (800) 827-1000; www1.va.gov/Homeless/. Publishes information on federal homeless programs as well as research on veterans and homelessness.

National Coalition for the Homeless, 2201 P St., N.W., Washington, DC 20037; (202) 462-4822; www.nationalhomeless.org/index.html. Helps organize voter-registration drives for the homeless and other national campaigns.

National Law Center on Homelessness & Poverty; 1411 K St., N.W., Washington, DC 20005; (202) 638-2535; www.nlchp.org. Pursues judicial and legislative remedies to problems tied to homelessness.

U.S. Department of Housing and Urban Development, 451 7th St., S.W., Washington, DC 20410; (202) 708-1112; http://portal.hud.gov/portal/page/portal/HUD/topics/homelessness. Publishes detailed data on homelessness and government programs.

Urban Institute, 2100 M St., N.W., Washington, DC 20037; (202) 833-7200; www.urban.org/housing/index.cfm. A nonpartisan think tank that studies homelessness and policies designed to reduce or end it.

of Housing and Urban Development, press release, Oct. 29, 2009, http://treas.gov/press/releases/tg336.htm.

[36] "Please Call Congress December 1 or 2 for NHTF Money," National Low Income Housing Coalition, undated, http://capwiz.com/nlihc/issues/alert/?alertid=14407651.

[37] "Hunger and Homelessness Survey: A Status Report on Hunger and Homelessness in America's Cities, a 27-City Survey," United States Conference of Mayors, December 2009, www.usmayors.org/pressreleases/uploads/USCMHungercompleteWEB2009.pdf.

[38] "U.S. Cities See Sharp Increases in the Need for Food Assistance; Decreases in Individual Homelessness," United States Conference of Mayors, Dec. 8, 2009, www.usmayors.org/pressreleases/uploads/RELEASEHUNGERHOMELESSNESS2009FINALRevised.pdf.

[39] Quoted in Julie Bosman, "Advocates Say City is Running Out of Beds for the Homeless," *The New York Times*, Dec. 10, 2009, www.nytimes.com/2009/12/10/nyregion/10homeless.html?_r=1&ref=nyregion.

[40] Quoted in *ibid.*

Bibliography

Selected Sources

Books

Burt, Martha R., *Over the Edge: The Growth of Homelessness in the 1980s*, Russell Sage Foundation, 1993.
One of the leading scholars of homelessness wrote an early and influential analysis of its causes and extent.

Hopper, Kim, *Reckoning With Homelessness*, Cornell University Press, 2003.
Homelessness can be approached historically, through first-hand observation or anthropologically; one anthropologist blended all three approaches.

Husock, Howard, *America's Trillion-Dollar Housing Mistake: The Failure of American Housing Policy*, Ivan R. Dee, 2003.
A policy expert for the conservative-leaning Manhattan Institute critically analyzes federal subsidized-housing programs as a strategy that has promoted dependency instead of independence and social advancement.

Jencks, Christopher, *The Homeless*, Harvard University Press, 1994.
Writing from a perspective that remains relevant today, an influential policy scholar examines the causes and possible remedies for homelessness.

Articles

Bazar, Emily, "Tent cities filling up with casualties of the economy," *USA Today*, May 5, 2009, p. A1.
Money troubles are driving thousands of homeless people into tent encampments around the country, a national newspaper reports.

Chong, Jia-Rui, "Some vets of recent wars find homelessness at home," *Los Angeles Times*, June 29, 2009, p. A4.
A growing number of Iraq-Afghanistan combat veterans are winding up homeless, often because of the psychological effects of their battlefield experiences.

Eckholm, Erik, "More Homeless Pupils, More Strained Schools," *The New York Times*, Sept. 6, 2009, p. A1.
School systems are scrambling to meet the needs of children and youth living in various types of temporary housing, ranging from trailers in campgrounds to friends' and relatives' homes.

Fears, Darryl, "15 Homeless People Get Apartments Next Month," *The Washington Post*, Sept. 29, 2009, p. B4.
As part of a nationwide policy to provide "supportive housing" to chronically homeless people, Washington is moving forward with a plan to provide permanent housing for mentally ill people who had been living on the street.

Patterson, Thom, "U.S. seeing more female homeless veterans," CNN, Sept. 25, 2009, www.cnn.com/2009/LIVING/09/25/homeless.veterans.
As growing numbers of women return from the front lines, some are joining the ranks of homeless male veterans.

Rubin, Bonnie Miller, "Homeless, unless you count storage space," *Los Angeles Times*, Nov. 15, 2009, p. A12.
A reporter finds a Chicago-area family fallen on hard times whose illegal home is a storage locker, except on rare occasions when they can rent a motel room for a night.

Urbina, Ian, "Recession Drives Surge in Youth Runaways," *The New York Times*, Oct. 26, 2009, p. A1.
The number of teenagers living on their own — usually in perilous circumstances — is growing because of family stresses aggravated by the economic crisis.

Reports

"The 2008 Annual Homeless Assessment Report to Congress," U.S. Department of Housing and Urban Development, July 2009, www.hudhre.info/documents/4thHomelessAssessmentReport.pdf.
The federal government's annual study provides a wealth of statistics and analysis.

Cunningham, Mary K., "Preventing and Ending Homelessness — Next Steps," Urban Institute, February 2009, www.urban.org/publications/411837.html.
A longtime specialist provides a detailed summary of programs and recommends further measures.

DeHaven, Tad, "Three Decades of Politics and Failed Policies at HUD," Cato Institute, Nov. 23, 2009, www.cato.org/pub_display.php?pub_id=10981.
A budget analyst for the libertarian think tank recounts the history of scandals at the main federal agency in charge of program to alleviate homelessness.

Duffield, Barbara and Phillip Lovell, "The Economic Crisis Hits Home: The Unfolding Increase in Child and Youth Homelessness," National Association for the Education of Homeless Children and Youth, First Focus, December 2008, www.naehcy.org/dl/TheEconomicCrisisHitsHome.pdf.
Children's rights organizations examine the growth in homelessness and unstable housing among young people.

Perl, Libby, *et al.*, "Homelessness: Targeted Federal Programs and Recent Legislation," Congressional Research Service, Jan. 15, 2009, http://wikileaks.org/leak/crs/RL30442.pdf.
Specialists for Congress' research arm provide a wealth of detail about legislation designed to reduce homelessness.

The Next Step:

Additional Articles from Current Periodicals

Funding

Hoppin, Jason, "Minnesota's Bid to End Long-Term Homelessness Is Faltering," *St. Paul* **(Minnesota)** *Pioneer Press*, **April 19, 2009.**

A battered economy and a decrease in state funding have hampered Minnesota's ambitions to combat long-term homelessness.

Koch, Wendy, "Cutbacks Pinch Homeless Programs," *USA Today*, **Aug. 25, 2009, p. 3A.**

A reduction in state funds has led many states to curb service programs that help rehabilitate the homeless.

Lee, Renée C., "$17 Million Stimulus to Help Offset Drop in Private Charitable Giving," *Houston Chronicle*, **Oct. 8, 2009, p. B1.**

About $17 million in federal stimulus money is being allocated to Houston-area homeless-service agencies.

Marquez, Liset, "Ontario to Seek $997,000 to Prevent Homelessness," *Inland Valley Daily Bulletin* **(California), March 8, 2009.**

The city of Ontario, Calif., has qualified for nearly $1 million in funding to prevent homelessness.

Housing

Bosman, Julie, "Bloomberg Policy Blamed for Homelessness," *The New York Times*, **April 23, 2009, p. A23.**

Mayor Michael Bloomberg's policy of denying federal housing vouchers to the homeless has increased the number of families entering shelters in New York City.

Fagan, Kevin, "No Letup in Fight to House Homeless," *The San Francisco Chronicle*, **Dec. 1, 2009, p. A1.**

President Obama has received praise from homeless advocates for his initiatives to house homeless veterans.

Fernandez, Libby, and Joan Burke, "Affordable Housing Is Long-Term Solution," *Sacramento Bee*, **March 22, 2009, p. E5.**

The best solution to homelessness is to increase the availability of apartments at rents that the poor can afford.

Legere, Christine, "Homeless Residence Draws Some Objections," *The Boston Globe*, **March 29, 2009, p. B5.**

Residents of a neighborhood in Boston object to plans to build a house for the homeless.

Mental Illness

Corwin, Tom, "Grants Will Offer Aid to Homeless," *Augusta* **(Georgia)** *Chronicle*, **Oct. 13, 2009, p. C1.**

Several students at the Medical College of Georgia have been given $5,000 each from the American Psychiatric Foundation to perform mental health screening of the homeless.

Kelley, Debbie, "Grant to Assist Mentally Ill Homeless," *The Gazette* **(Colorado), Nov. 13, 2009, p. A3.**

A behavioral health group in Colorado is receiving a $1.5 million federal grant to provide job training and education to mentally ill homeless people.

Nett, Veronica, "State Mental Health System Is in Crisis, Advocates Warn," *Charleston* **(West Virginia)** *Gazette*, **Feb. 6, 2009.**

A decline in West Virginia support services has led to a dramatic increase in the homeless who are mentally ill.

Washington, D.C.

Dickson, Akeya, "A Note of Hope From Voices of Experience," *The Washington Post*, **Nov. 26, 2009, p. DZ22.**

Members of the hip-hop group Public Enemy visited a house for homeless youth in Southeast Washington and shared their own personal struggles with homelessness.

Fadel, Leila, "Homeless Numbers Grow in Nation's Capital," *Star-Ledger* **(New Jersey), Aug. 23, 2009, p. A21.**

The recession has helped reverse earlier progress toward reducing homelessness in Washington, D.C.

Labbé-DeBose, Theola, and Tim Craig, "Hate-Crimes Coverage Sought for the Homeless," *The Washington Post*, **June 4, 2009, p. DZ1.**

A member of the Washington, D.C., City Council wants to add the homeless to the city's hate-crimes statute.

In-depth Reports on Issues in the News

Are you writing a paper?

Need backup for a debate?

Want to become an expert on an issue?

For more than 80 years, students have turned to *CQ Researcher* for in-depth reporting on issues in the news. Reports on a full range of political and social issues are now available. Following is a selection of recent reports:

Civil Liberties
Closing Guantánamo, 2/09
Affirmative Action, 10/08
Gay Marriage Showdowns, 9/08
America's Border Fence, 9/08
Immigration Debate, 2/08

Crime/Law
Prisoner Reentry, 12/09
Interrogating the CIA, 9/09
Examining Forensics, 7/09
Legalizing Marijuana, 6/09
Wrongful Convictions, 4/09

Education
Bilingual Education, 12/09
Value of a College Education, 11/09
Financial Literacy, 9/09
Reading Crisis? 2/08
Discipline in Schools, 2/08

Environment/Society
Women in the Military, 11/09
Conspiracy Theories, 10/09
Human Spaceflight, 10/09
Gays in the Military, 9/09
Energy and Climate, 7/09

Health/Safety
Medication Abuse, 10/09
Nuclear Disarmament, 10/09
Health-Care Reform, 8/09
Straining the Safety Net, 7/09
Treating Depression, 6/09
Reproductive Ethics, 5/09

Politics/Economy
State Budget Crisis, 9/09
Business Bankruptcy, 4/09
Future of the GOP, 3/09
Middle-Class Squeeze, 3/09

Upcoming Reports

Animal Rights, 1/8/10   Government and Religion, 1/15/10   First Amendment Issues, 1/22/10

ACCESS

CQ Researcher is available in print and online. For access, visit your library or www.cqresearcher.com.

STAY CURRENT

To receive notice of upcoming *CQ Researcher* reports, or learn more about *CQ Researcher* products, subscribe to the free e-mail newsletters, *CQ Researcher Alert!* and *CQ Researcher News*: http://cqpress.com/newsletters.

PURCHASE

To purchase a *CQ Researcher* report in print or electronic format (PDF), visit www.cqpress.com or call 866-427-7737. Single reports start at $15. Bulk purchase discounts and electronic-rights licensing are also available.

SUBSCRIBE

Annual full-service *CQ Researcher* subscriptions—including 44 reports a year, monthly index updates, and a bound volume—start at $803. Add $25 for domestic postage.

CQ Researcher Online offers a backfile from 1991 and a number of tools to simplify research. For pricing information, call 800-834-9020, ext. 1906, or e-mail librarysales@cqpress.com.

Index

January 1991–December 2009

❖ *CQ Researcher* reports are indexed by title under boldface topic headings.

- Titles are followed by the date the report appeared and the first page number of its print version.

- Page numbers followed by an asterisk refer to a sidebar or the "At Issue" (Pro/Con) feature.

❖ This index is updated monthly and available at: http://www.cqpress.com/docs/cqrindex.pdf

❖ *CQ Researcher* can be accessed online at: www.cqresearcher.com

CQ PRESS

Published by CQ Press, a Division of SAGE

CQ Press is a registered trademark of Congressional Quarterly Inc.

Conservation. *See also Endangered species;*
Environmental Protection

	Date	Page		Date	Page